Advances in Consumer Research
volume XX

Leigh McAlister
Michael L. Rothschild
Editors

1993 Copyright © ASSOCIATION FOR CONSUMER RESEARCH

All rights reserved. No part of this publication may be reproduced, stored in a retrieval system or transmitted, in any form or by any means, electronic, mechanical, photocopying, recording, or otherwise, without prior written permission of the publisher.

International Standard Book Number (ISBN): 0-915552-30-2

International Standard Serial Number (ISSN): 0098-9258

Leigh McAlister and Michael L. Rothschild, Editors

Advances in Consumer Research, Volume 20

(Provo, UT: Association for Consumer Research, 1992)

Preface

The twentieth Annual Conference of the Association for Consumer Research was held at the Four Seasons Hotel in Vancouver, British Columbia, Canada on October 8-11, 1992. This volume contains the papers which were presented at these meetings.

Thirty-eight members of the Association were on the Conference Planning Committee; these members contributed many ideas to improve the conference and served as the review board for special sessions. In addition, 192 members served as reviewers for the competitive papers. In almost every case, the reviewers were diligent and thoughtful in executing their tasks. We thank these reviewers and committee members; without their contributions the conference would not have had the level of quality that it achieved.

Our colleagues submitted 152 competitive papers and 78 special sessions for review; 75 and 38 of these, respectively, were accepted for presentation and for inclusion in this volume. Four hundred and eighty-five consumer researchers attended the conference and 501 were on the program in some way. We thank all those who submitted and presented materials; without their contributions there would not be a conference or a proceedings. We also appreciate the care with which the authors responded to the reviewers comments; this responsiveness also contributed to the quality of the conference.

Thanks also to all of our colleagues for meeting all the deadlines that were imposed along the way to making the conference a reality. Special notice goes to two of our members who missed deadlines but were especially creative in their excuses. Lucette Comer, Florida International University, missed a deadline because of a hurricane, and Francis Piron, University of Alaska-Anchorage, blamed his missed deadline on a volcano eruption. Members who miss deadlines in future years will need to rise to this level of excuse in order to be accepted. The gauntlet has been laid down.

The Arrangements Committee was chaired by Jim Forbes and Therese Louie. They worked diligently to make sure that our events would occur on time and with a minimum of hassle; their precision rivaled that of any military operation, and culminated with the wonderful reception at the University of British Columbia Museum of Anthropology and the salmon barbecue at the University of British Columbia Faculty Club. For almost a year, we wondered if it would be possible to get several hundred academics to follow directions and walk in a straight line to the buses, and if these buses would show up and deliver their cargo across a large city during rush hour. Mostly we wondered if anyone would care enough to show up. Jim and Therese did a great job and everything worked just as they promised.

Special thanks goes to Jeff Inman who wrote software which would allow papers and reviewers to be matched more efficiently. This had always been the biggest hassle for past conference chairs. This year we matched 152 papers and 192 reviewers across over 100 content and method areas with ease.

Finally we thank Alan Andreasen for giving us the proper balance of guidance and freedom in planning, Keith Hunt for being a ready source of information and advice at every step of the way, Jim Muncy for his diligent work in creating the physical product which is in your hands, Jennifer Rothschild for the cover design, and Rona Velte for keeping all the threads from coming undone. There are many other people to thank; we have tried to list them in the conference program which is reproduced on the following pages. If we missed you, we apologize.

Creating the conference and proceedings was a great experience. We both feel that we owe a lot to ACR and were glad to have had the opportunity to give something back to the organization and its members. Thanks for that opportunity.

Leigh McAlister
University of Texas

Michael L. Rothschild
University of Wisconsin
Editors

Conference Committee

PRESIDENT
Alan R. Andreasen
University of Connecticut

CONFERENCE CHAIRS
Leigh McAlister, University of Texas
Michael L. Rothschild, University of Wisconsin

PROGRAM COMMITTEE

Mark Alpert, University of Texas
Eric Arnould, California State University-Long Beach
Rajeev Batra, University of Michigan
William Bearden, University of South Carolina
Mary Jo Bitner, Arizona State University
Paul Bloom, University of North Carolina
Ray Burke, Harvard Business School
Dipanker Chakravarti, University of Arizona
Cathy Cole, University of Iowa
Kim Corfman, New York University
Julie Edell, Duke University
Gary Ford, American University
Marian Friestad, University of Oregon
Meryl Gardner, University of Delaware
Deb Heisley, University of California-Los Angeles
Ron Hill, Villanova University
Donna Hoffman, University of Texas-Dallas
Wes Hutchinson, University of Florida
Jeff Inman, University of Southern California

Eric Johnson, University of Pennsylvania
Annamma Joy, Concordia University
Barbara Kahn, University of Pennsylvania
Kevin Keller, Stanford University
Don Lehmann, Columbia University
Debbie MacInnis, University of Arizona
Michael Mazis, American University
Grant McCracken, Institute of Contemporary Culture
David Mick, University of Florida
Pat Murphy, University of Notre Dame
John Murry, University of Wisconsin-Madison
Julie Ozanne, Virginia Polytechnic Institute & State University
C. W. Park, University of Pittsburgh
Dennis Rook, University of Southern California
Jay Russo, Cornell University
Linda Scott, University of Colorado-Boulder
Allan Shocker, University of Minnesota
Surrendra Singh, University of Kansas
Mita Sujan, Pennsylvania State University

ARRANGEMENTS COMMITTEE

Jim Forbes, University of British Columbia
Bob Krider, University of British Columbia

Anne Lavack, University of British Columbia
Therese Louie, University of British Columbia

AND SPECIAL THANKS TO

Rosalinda Castaneda, University of Texas
Susan Dillard, University of Texas
Colleen Gardner, University of Texas
H. Keith Hunt, Brigham Young University
Jeff Inman, University of Southern California

Jim Muncy, Clemson University
Tim Roloff, University of Wisconsin
Tracy Schilling, University of Wisconsin
Rona Velte, University of Wisconsin

REVIEWERS

Joseph W. Alba
Dana Alden
Chris Allen
Patricia Alvey
Helen H. Anderson
Laurel Anderson
Paul F. Anderson
Nancy Artz
Hans Baumgartner
Sharon E. Beatty
George Belch
Mickey Belch
James R. Bettman
Barbara Bickart
Gabriel J. Biehal
Peter Bloch
David Boush
Sheri Bridges
David Brinberg
Julia M. Bristor
George Brooker
Steven P. Brown
Merrie Brucks
Claus Buhl
Robert E. Burnkrant
Meg Campbell
Joel B. Cohen
Larry D. Compeau
T. Bettina Cornwell
Janeen Arnold Costa
Carolyn Costley
Joseph A. Cote
Eloise Coupey
Betsy Creyer
Ayn Crowley
Peter Dacin
Rita Denny
Rohit Deshpande
Steve Everett
Ronald Faber
Marla Felcher
Ed Fern
Eileen Fischer
Valerie S. Folkes
Susan Fournier
Jonathon Frenzen
Sharon Galbraith
Hubert Gatignon

Jim Gentry
Rashi Glazer
Linda L. Golden
Ronnie Goodstein
Cathy Goodwin
Jill Grace
Paul E. Green
Eric Greenleaf
Tom Gruca
Hari Hariharan
Bari Harlam
Curtis P. Haugtvedt
Bill Havlena
Scott A. Hawkins
Timothy B. Heath
Susan Heckler
Jan B. Heide
Pamela W. Henderson
Elizabeth C. Hirschman
Jacqueline Hitchon
Morris B. Holbrook
Douglas B. Holt
Martin I. Horn
Wayne Hoyer
Cynthia Huffman
H. Keith Hunt
Dawn Iacobucci
Chris Janiszewski
Bernard J. Jaworski
Deborah Roedder John
Marilyn Jones
Frank R. Kardes
Robert F. Kelly
Jerome B. Kernan
Tina Kiesler
Amna Kirmani
Rob Kleine
Susan Kleine
Lakshman Krishnamurthi
Michel Laroche
France Leclerc
James H. Leigh
Joan Meyers-Levy
Sid Levy
William B. Locander
Barbara Loken
Therese Louie
Richard J. Lutz

John Lynch
Scott B. Mackenzie
Carole Macklin
Durairaj Maheswaran
Prashant Malaviya
Gayathri Mani
Haim Mano
Howard Marmorstein
James McAlexander
John A. McCarty
Ann L. McGill
Mary Ann McGrath
Edward F. McQuarrie
Geeta Menon
Paul W. Miniard
Sanjay Mishra
Andrew A. Mitchell
Lois Mohr
Reza Moinpour
Marian Chapman Moore
Christine Moorman
John C. Mowen
James A. Muncy
J. Michael Munson
John Murry
Kent Nakamoto
Sunder Narayanan
Prakash Nedungadi
Rick Netemeyer
Tom Novak
Thomas O'Guinn
Carl Obermiller
Jerry C. Olson
Thomas J. Page
Pallab Paul
Mark Pavelchak
Cornelia Pechmann
James Peltier
Laura Peracchio
J. Paul Peter
Carol Pluzinski
Ved Prakash
Ivan L. Preston
Robert Prus
Christopher P. Puto
S. Ratnshwar
Peter H. Reingen
Marsha Richins

Scott D. Roberts
Randy Rose
Ivan Ross
Julie Ruth
Joel Saegert
Alan G. Sawyer
John A. Schibrowsky
John Schouten
Richard Semenik
Murphy Sewall
Stewart Shapiro
John F. Sherry
Terence A. Shimp
Carolyn J. Simmons
Itamar Simonson
Dan Smith
Robert E. Smith
Stephen M. Smith
Michael R. Solomon
Robert E. Spekman
Susan Spiggle
Narasimhan Srinivasan
Raj Srivastava
Douglas M. Stayman
Debra L. Stephens
Barbara Stern
Brian Sternthal
David W. Stewart
Harish Sujan
Mita Sujan
Jack Swasy
David M. Szymanski
Craig Thompson
Esther Thorson
David K. Tse
Alice Tybout
H. Rao Unnava
Joel Urbany
Meera Venkatraman
Beth Walker
Wanda Wallace
Brian Wansink
William L. Wilkie
Russell S. Winer
Newell Wright
Richard Yalch
Youjae Yi
George Zinkhan

Table of Contents and Conference Program

Preface iii

ACR Conference Committee and Reviewers iv

Table of Contents and Conference Program vi

Presidential Address
A Social Marketing Research Agenda for Consumer Behavior Researchers 1
    Alan R. Andreasen, University of Connecticut

ACR Fellow Awards
Presentation of the Award: Fellow in Consumer Behavior to James R. Bettman 6
    Harold H. Kassarjian, UCLA

Fellow's Award Speech: The Decision Maker Who Came In from the Cold 7
    James R. Bettman, Duke University

Special Contribution for ACR Contributors
The ACR Match Game–1992 12
    J. Jeffrey Inman, University of Southern California

ASSOCIATION FOR CONSUMER RESEARCH ANNUAL CONFERENCE

OCTOBER 8-11, 1992
FOUR SEASONS HOTEL
VANCOUVER, BRITISH COLUMBIA, CANADA

THURSDAY, OCTOBER 8

ACR EXECUTIVE BOARD MEETING
12:00 - 7:00

REGISTRATION
4:00 - 8:00

RECEPTION
6:00 - 8:00

FRIDAY, OCTOBER 9

REGISTRATION
8:00 - 11:50 and 2:10 - 5:30

SESSION 1
8:30 - 10:00

1.1 Special Session: The Transition from Communism to Capitalism, Part I: Asia and the Commonwealth of Independent States

Organizer: Melissa Martin Young, University of Utah
Chair: Clifford J. Shultz, Columbia University
Discussant: Eric J. Arnould, California State University, Long Beach

The Polish Consumer in Transition: Shopping Warsaw's Street Vendors and Open Air Markets 13
    Terrence H. Witkowski, California State University, Long Beach

Consumers in Rapid Transition: The Polish Experience 18
    Brian Lofman, Central Connecticut State University

Consumer Search and Decision Problems When Almost Everything Changes: A View from Budapest, Hungary
    Lawrence F. Feick, University of Pittsburgh
    Robin A. Higie, University of Connecticut
    Linda L. Price, University of Colorado, Boulder

Discussant Comments: The Transition from Communism to Capitalism 23
    Eric J. Arnould, California State University, Long Beach

1.2 Special Session: A New Perspective on the Effects of Advertising Repetition: The Mediating Role of Memory Structure

Organizer: Karen Finlay, University of Guelph
           Ida Berger, University of Toronto
Chair: Rebecca Holman, D'Arcy Masius Benton & Bowles, Inc.
Discussant: Rajeev Batra, University of Michigan, Ann Arbor

Summary of Special Session: A New Perspective on the Effects of Advertising Repetition: The Mediating Role of Memory Structure 26
    Karen Finlay, University of Guelph

Single Versus Dual-Process Models of Elaboration: The Moderation of Repetition Effects by the Advertising Context
    Prashant Malaviya, Northwestern University

The Role of Advertising Information and Repetition in Memory Structure and Attitude-Behavior Consistency
    Ida E. Berger, University of Toronto

Inducing Memory Structure: The Effect of Repetition of Incongruent Information
    Karen Finlay, University of Guelph

1.3 Special Session: The Effects of Corporate Branding Strategies on Brand Equity

Organizer: Kevin Lane Keller, Stanford University
Chair: Bill Ross, University of Pennsylvania
Discussant: Susan Broniarczyk, University of Texas, Austin

The Effects of Corporate Images and Branding Strategies on New Product Evaluations 27
    Kevin Lane Keller, Stanford University
    David A. Aaker, University of California, Berkeley

The Effects of Direct and Associative Brand Extension Strategies on Consumer Response to Brand Extensions 28
    C. Whan Park, University of Pittsburgh
    Michael S. McCarthy, University of Pittsburgh
    Sandra J. Milberg, Georgetown University

The Effects of Branding Strategy on Consumer Response to Brand-Line Stretches
    Sheri Bridges, Wake Forest University
    Amna Kirmani, Duke University

1.4   Special Session: Atmospheric Factors in the Retail Environment: Sights, Sounds and Smells

Organizers: Sevgin A. Eroglu, Georgia State University
                 Karen A. Machleit, University of Cincinnati
Chair: Elnora Stuart, Winthrop College
Discussant: Meryl P. Gardner, University of Delaware

Summary of Special Session: Atmospheric Factors in the Retail Environment: Sights, Sounds and Smells 34
    Sevgin A. Eroglu, Georgia State University
    Karen A. Machleit, University of Cincinnati

Theater of Retailing: Selling Through the Senses
    Randall E. Gebhardt, Retail Planning Associates

Olfaction and the Retailing Environment
    Terence A. Shimp, University of South Carolina
    Pam Scholder Ellen, Georgia State University
    Paula Fitzgerald Bone, West Virginia University

The Impact of Atmospheric Music and Retail Density on Retail Crowding Perceptions and Their Consequences.
Does Song Augment the Throng?
    Karen A. Machleit, University of Cincinnati
    James J. Kellaris, University of Cincinnati
    Sevgin A. Eroglu, Georgia State University

1.5   Special Session: The Feminine Imagination and Social Change: Four Feminist Approaches to Social Problems

Organizer: Julie L. Ozanne, Virginia Polytechnic Institute and State University
Chair: Barbara Stern, Rutgers, The State University of New Jersey, Newark
Discussant: Julie L. Ozanne, Virginia Polytechnic Institute and State University

Summary of Special Session: The Feminine Imagination and Social Change: Four Feminist Approaches to
Social Problems 35
    Julie L. Ozanne, Virginia Polytechnic Institute and State University
    Barbara B. Stern, Rutgers University

Women and the Environment: Applying Ecofeminism to Environmentally-Related Consumption 36
    Susan Dobscha, Virginia Polytechnic Institute and State University

Applications of Postmodernist Feminism: A Deconstruction of the Marketing Concept
    Julia M. Bristor, University of Houston
    Eileen Fischer, York University

Consumer Behavior Meets the Nouvelle Femme: Feminist Consumption in the Movies 41
    Elizabeth C. Hirschman, Rutgers University, New Brunswick

A Sociolinguistic Approach to Gender and Personal Selling 48
    William Val Larsen, Virginia Polytechnic Institute and State University

1.6 Competitive Paper Session: Ethnography

Chair: Rohit Deshpande, Dartmouth College
Discussant: John Schouten, University of Portland

An Investigation of Ethnicity and Sex-Role Attitude as Factors Influencing Household Financial Task Sharing Behavior 52
    Chankon Kim, Concordia University
    Michel Laroche, Concordia University
    Lianxi Zhou, Concordia University

A Primer for Ethnographic Research with a Focus on Social Policy Issues Involving Consumer Behavior 59
    Ronald Paul Hill, Villanova University

Ethno: A Methodology for Studying Process Information 63
    James H. Barnes, University of Mississippi

1.7 Competitive Paper Session: Acquisition of Values

Chair: Ruth Smith, Virginia Polytechnic Institute and State University
Discussant: Rao Unnava, Ohio State

Linking Emotions and Values in Consumption Experiences: An Exploratory Study 70
    Debra A. Laverie, Arizona State University
    Robert E. Kleine III, Arizona State University
    Susan Schultz Kleine, Arizona State University

Modes of Consumer Acculturation 76
    Sunkyu Jun, University of Nebraska, Lincoln
    A. Dwayne Ball, University of Nebraska, Lincoln
    James W. Gentry, University of Nebraska, Lincoln

Telling Stories: A Sociolinguistic Analysis of Language Use in a Marketplace 83
    Elisabeth Gilster, University of Arizona

FRIDAY, OCTOBER 9
SESSION 2
10:20 - 11:50

2.1 Special Session: The Transition from Communism to Capitalism, Part II: Eastern Europe

Organizer: Melissa Martin Young, University of Utah
Chair: Bernd Schmitt, Columbia University
Discussant: Gary Bamossy, Vrije Universiteit, The Netherlands

Social Control Versus Social Stability: A Conceptualization of Contradictory Goals and Hybrid Outcomes on Ethnic Relations, Consumer Satisfaction, and Entrepreneurship in the Former USSR 89
    Oleg I. Gubin, Moscow State University, Russia
    Melissa Martin Young, University of Utah
    Alexander G. Osipov, University of Utah
    Natasha Kostioutchenko, University of Utah

Complaints and Compliments About Service Encounters: A Comparison of American and Bulgarian Consumers 97
    Lalita A. Manrai, University of Delaware
    Ajay K. Manrai, University of Delaware

*The Development of Consumer Desire in Marketizing and Developing Economies: The Cases of
Romania and Turkey* 102
      Guliz Ger, Bilkent University, Turkey
      Russell W. Belk, University of Utah
      Dana-Nicoleta Lascu, University of Richmond

2.2   Special Session: "Yes, I remember it well...": The Role of Autobiographical Memory in Consumer Information Processing

Organizers: Geeta Menon, New York University
                 Gita Johar, Columbia University
Chair: Carolyn Simmons, University of Illinois, Urbana-Champaign
Discussant: Julie Edell, Duke University

*Summary of Special Session: "Yes, I remember it well...": The Role of Autobiographical Memory in
Consumer Information Processing* 108
      Geeta Menon, New York University
      Gita Johar, Columbia University

The Role of Autobiographical Memory in Consumer Memory, Judgment, and (Let Us Not Forget!) Behavior
      Thomas K. Srull, University of Illinois, Urbana-Champaign

Autobiographical Memories and Product Judgments
      Mita Sujan, Pennsylvania State University
      Hans Baumgartner, Pennsylvania State University
      James R. Bettman, Duke University

Valence of Autobiographical versus Reported Memory for Products and its Impact on Ad Processing
      Gita Johar, Columbia University
      Geeta Menon, New York University

2.3   Special Session: Ethical Decision-Making and Purchase Behavior

Organizer: N. Craig Smith, Georgetown University
Chair: Anusree Mitra, American University
Discussant: William L. Wilkie, University of Notre Dame

Unethical Seller Practices: A Neglected Issue in Consumer Satisfaction and Dissatisfaction Research 109
      Alan R. Andreasen, University of Connecticut

Ethical Segmentation: An Exploratory Study
      Doron Goldman, New York University
      Bruce Buchanan, New York University

Ethical Consumption Products and Ethical Space 113
      Elizabeth Cooper-Martin, Georgetown University
      Morris Holbrook, Columbia University

The Role of Ethical Concerns in Consumer Purchase Behavior: Understanding Alternative Processes 119
      Sandra J. Burke, Georgetown University
      Sandra J. Milberg, Georgetown University
      N. Craig Smith, Georgetown University

2.4 *Special Session*: Conceptualizing Consumer Resistance in the Marketplace: The Consumer Movement and Beyond

Organizers: Lisa Penaloza, University of Colorado, Boulder
Linda Price, University of Colorado, Boulder
Chair: Ven Venkatesan, University of Rhode Island
Discussant: Tom O'Guinn, University of Illinois, Urbana-Champaign

Consumer Resistance: To What and By Whom?
Mark Poster, University of California, Irvine

Consumer Resistance: A Conceptual Overview 123
Lisa Penaloza, University of Colorado, Boulder
Linda Price, University of Colorado, Boulder

Media Resistance to Consumer Resistance: On the Stonewalling of 'Adbusters' and Advocates 129
Richard W. Pollay, University of British Columbia

The Tactics of Consumer Resistance: Group Action and Marketplace Exit 130
Robert O. Herrmann, Pennsylvania State University

2.5 *Competitive Paper Session*: Multiattribute Models

Chair: Sanjay Mishra, University of Kansas
Discussant: Jill Klein, Northwestern University

A Comparison of Three Behavioral Intention Models: The Case of Valentine's Day Gift-Giving 135
Richard G. Netemeyer, Louisiana State University
J. Craig Andrews, Marquette University
Srinivas Durvasula, Marquette University

A Strategy for A Priori Segmentation in Conjoint Analysis 142
James B. Wiley, University of Alberta

A Hybrid Conjoint Model with Individual-Level Interaction Estimation 149
Paul E. Green, University of Pennsylvania
Abba M. Krieger, University of Pennsylvania
Catherine M. Schaffer, University of Denver

2.6 *Competitive Paper Session*: Advertising Issues

Chair: Margaret C. Campbell, UCLA
Discussant: Surendra N. Singh, University of Kansas

Does Humor in Advertising Enhance Systematic Processing? 155
Stephen M. Smith, Ohio State University

Physical Attractiveness and Personality in Advertising: More than Just a Pretty Face? 159
Anne M. Brumbaugh, Duke University

Effects of Advertising and Experience on Brand Judgments: A Rose by Any Other Frame 165
Alice A. Wright, California State University, Long Beach
Richard J. Lutz, University of Florida

Discussant Comments on "Advertising Issues" 170
Surendra N. Singh, University of Kansas

FRIDAY, OCTOBER 9

LUNCH
12:00 - 2:00

BUSINESS MEETING

PRESIDENTIAL ADDRESS
Alan R. Andreasen
"A Social Marketing Consumer Research Agenda For The 1990s"

FRIDAY, OCTOBER 9

SESSION 3
2:10 - 3:40

3.1 PRESIDENTIAL SESSION: Opportunities for Consumer Researchers in Third World Food and Nutrition Development Efforts

Chair: Melanie Wallendorf, University of Arizona
Discussants: Melanie Wallendorf, University of Arizona
Tim Frankenberger, University of Arizona
Eric Arnould, California State University, Long Beach

Food consumption is a life-threatening concern for many people. Much of the world's population faces either the distinct possibility of starvation or the daily challenge of meeting their food needs. In Africa in fiscal year 1990, more than 10 million people's lives were at risk due to famine; that number represents more people than the combined populations of the cities of New York and San Francisco. Worldwide 34.8% (188 million) of the children under age 4 are presently underweight, a commonly-used indicator of food deprivation in a society. Consumers in Third World countries face consumption problems that are seemingly different from the brand choice consumption problems confronting First World consumers. While the skills of consumer researchers have produced a published body of knowledge regarding the latter, consumer researchers have been less involved in generating knowledge regarding the food consumption problems of Third World citizens.

Agency Presenters: Frances Davidson, Office of Nutrition, U.S. Agency for International Development
Richard Caldwell, Office of Arid Land Studies, University of Arizona
Robert Haggerty, Post Harvest Institute for Perishables, University of Idaho

Academic Facilitators: Tim Frankenberger, University of Arizona
Eric Arnould, California State University, Long Beach

Opportunities for Consumer Researchers in Third World Food and Nutrition Development Efforts 172
Eric Arnould, California State University, Long Beach

3.2 Special Session: Adolescent Participation in Hazardous Activities: Identifying High Risk Groups and Implications for Intervention Policies

Organizer: William J. Burns, University of Iowa
Chair: Esther Thorson, University of Wisconsin, Madison
Discussant: Alice Tenderella, Anheuser-Busch

Summary of Special Session: Adolescent Participation in Hazardous Activities: Identifying High Risk Groups and Implications for Intervention Policies 176
William J. Burns, University of Iowa

Adolescents' Perception of Risk: Understanding and Preventing High Risk Behavior 177
    Herbert H. Severson, Oregon Research Institute
    Paul Slovic, Decision Research
    Sarah Hampson, Oregon Research Institute

Personality-Attitude-Behavior Models of Young Male Alcohol Consumption
    John P. Murry, Jr., University of Wisconsin, Madison
    John L. Lastovicka, Arizona State University
    Jon R. Austin, University of Wisconsin, Madison

Alcohol-Related Risk Taking Among Teenagers: An Investigation of Contributing Factors and a
Discussion of How Marketing Principles Can Help 183
    William J. Burns, University of Iowa
    Sarah E. Hampson, Oregon Research Institute
    Herbert H. Severson, Oregon Research institute
    Paul Slovic, Decision Research

3.3   *Special Session*: Consumer Behavior Processes as Bases to Segment the 'Green' Marketplace: Applications to Solid Waste Disposal

Organizers: Linda F. Alwitt, DePaul University
                Ida E. Berger, University of Toronto
Chair: Jonathan Schroeder, University of Rhode Island
Discussant: Debra L. Scammon, University of Utah

Summary of Special Session: Consumer Behavior Processes as Bases to Segment the 'Green' Marketplace:
Applications to Solid Waste Disposal 188
    Linda F. Alwitt, DePaul University
    Ida E. Berger, University of Toronto

Segmenting Target Markets in the New 'Green' Marketplace
    Robert E. Pitts, Depaul University
    Linda F. Alwitt, Depaul University

Encouraging Recycling in a Demographically Diverse City: Segmenting the Market in Chicago
    George I. Balch, University of Illinois, Chicago

Understanding the Link Between Environmental Attitudes and Consumer Product Choice: Measuring the
Moderating Role of Attitude Strength 189
    Linda F. Alwitt, Depaul University
    Ida E. Berger, University of Toronto

3.4   *Special Session*: Behavioral Decision Research: Theory and Applications

Organizer: Ravi Dhar, Yale University
Chair and
 Discussant: Rashi Glazer, University of California, Berkeley

Summary of Special Session: Behavioral Decision Research: Theory and Applications 195
    Ravi Dhar, Yale University

Modeling Loss Aversion and Reference Dependence Effects on Brand Choice
    Bruce G. S. Hardie, University of Pennsylvania
    Eric J. Johnson, University of Pennsylvania
    Peter S. Fader, University of Pennsylvania

Strategy Compatibility, Scale Compatibility, and the Prominence Effect
    Gregory W. Fischer, Duke University
    Scott A. Hawkins, University of Chicago

An Extended Paradigm of Consumer Satisfaction Based on Generalized Utility Theory
J. Jefferey Inman, University of Southern California
James S. Dyer, University of Texas

Choice Among Attractive Alternatives: Are Consumers Indifferent to Indifference?
Ravi Dhar, Yale University

3.5 Competitive Paper Session: Information Transfer and Information Acquisition

Chair: Tina Kiesler, New York University
Discussant: Merrie Brucks, University of Arizona

How Do Consumers Acquire a New Food Consumption System. When It Is Vegetarian 196
Susan Schultz Kleine, Arizona State University
Amy R. Hubbert, Arizona State University

Do Market Mavens Categorize Brands Differently? 202
Michael T. Elliott, University of Missouri, St. Louis
Anne E. Warfield, University of Missouri, St. Louis

The Effect of Familiarity on Consumers' Choice Agendas 209
Judy A. Wagner, Virginia Polytechnic Institute and State University
Noreen M. Klein, Virginia Polytechnic Institute and State University

3.6 Competitive Paper Session: Product Perceptions, Preferences, and Knowledge

Chair: Murphy Sewall, University of Connecticut
Discussant: George Brooker, Central Washington University

Consumers Reaction to Product Failure: Impact of Product Involvement and Knowledge 215
T. N. Somasundaram, University of San Diego

The Moderating Influence of Depth of Processing on Order of Entry Framing Effects 219
Karen H. Smith, University of Texas, Austin

Aesthetic Response and the Influence of Design Principles on Product Preferences 224
Robert W. Veryzer, Jr., University of Florida

Discussant Comments: Products, Perceptions, Preferences, and Knowledge: Decisions in Conducting Research 229
George Brooker, Central Washington University

FRIDAY, OCTOBER 9

SESSION 4
4:00 - 5:30

4.1 Special Session: **Vesting Objects and Experiences with Symbolic Meaning**

Note: This session will be held at the Museum of Anthropology, University of British Columbia. Buses will leave the hotel at 4:00. The session will be held using the museum collection and will last for 90 minutes. Buses will be available to return to the hotel at the conclusion of the session, however, a reception will be held at the museum immediately following the session (approximately 6 pm).

Organizer:	Robert F. Kelly, University of British Columbia
Chair:	Therese Louie, University of British Columbia
Discussant:	Robert F. Kelly, University of British Columbia

Summary of Special Session (with Discussant's Remarks): Vesting Objects and Experiences with Symbolic Meaning 232
       Robert F. Kelly, University of British Columbia

Museum as a Meaning Maker/Meaning Taker: A Study of the Reciprocal Exchange of Symbolic Properties Between the Museum, Its Objects, and Its Publics
       Grant McCracken, Royal Ontario Museum

The Role of Nostalgia in the Appreciation of the Dear Departed Past: Update on a Program of Research
       Morris Holbrook, Columbia University
       Robert Schindler, Rutgers University, Camden

Text and Image in Works of Art: Implications for Consumer Research
       Annamma Joy, Concordia University

4.2 Special Session: **Broadening the Concept of Consumer Judgment and Choice**

Organizer:	Christopher P. Puto, University of Arizona
Chair:	Williams J. Qualls, MIT
Discussant:	Jay E. Russo, Cornell University

Image Theory: An Alternative to Normative Decision Theory 235
       Lee Roy Beach, University of Arizona

Implications of a Recognitional Decision Model for Consumer Behavior 239
       Caroline E. Zsambok, Klein Associates, Inc.

Screening Versus Framing: Complements or Competitors?
       Christopher P. Puto, University of Arizona
       Carol Bruneau, University of Arizona

4.3 Competitive Paper Session: **Demographic Issues in Consumer Research**

Chair:	Haim Mano, Washington University
Discussant:	Marilyn Jones, University of Houston, Clear Lake

The Vulnerable Consumer in the High Blood Pressure Drug Market: Bother but Satisfied? 245
       Dev S. Pathak, Ohio State University
       Suzan Kucukarsalan, Ohio State University
       Deepak Sirdeshmukh, Ohio State University
       Richard Segal, University of Florida

A Preliminary Examination of the Effects of Context-Induced Felt Ethnicity on Advertising Effectiveness 253
    David B. Wooten, Columbia University
    Tiffany Galvin, Northwestern University

Age and Social Activity As Correlates of Television Orientation: A Replication and Extension 257
    Rose L. Johnson, Temple University

Discussant Comments: Emerging Issues in Demographics Research 262
    Marilyn Young Jones, University of Houston, Clear Lake

4.4 Special Session: What Causes Youths to Start Smoking? Converging Quantitative and Qualitative Evidence on the Role of Smoking-Related Advertising

Organizer:	Connie Pechmann, University of California, Irvine
	Tom Novak, Southern Methodist University
Chair:	Gerald J. Gorn, University of British Columbia
Discussant:	Elizabeth S. Moore-Shay, Boston College

Summary of Special Session: What Causes Youths to Start Smoking? Converging Quantitative and Qualitative Evidence on the Role of Smoking-Related Advertising 265
    Tom Novak, Southern Methodist University
    Connie Pechmann, University of California, Irvine

Diffusion Models for Smoking Onset and Cessation: A Segment-Level Historical Analysis
    Thomas P. Novak, Southern Methodist University
    Frank M. Bass, University of Texas, Dallas
    Wagner A. Kamakura, Vanderbilt University
    Clyde Dent, University of Southern California

Smoking-Related Advertising and Its Effects on Preteens: A Social Cognitive Perspective
    Cornelia (Connie) Pechmann, University of California, Irvine
    S. Ratneshwar, University of Florida

The Targeting of Youths by Cigarette Marketers: Archival Evidence on Trial 266
    Richard W. Pollay, University of British Columbia
    Anne Lavack, University of British Columbia

4.5 Special Session: Visual/Verbal Processing Issues in Advertising Research: Some New Topics and Perspectives

Organizers & Discussants:	Siva K. Balasubramanian, Southern Illinois University
	Susan Heckler, University of Arizona
Chair:	Francoise Jaffe, University of Michigan, Ann Arbor

Summary of Special Session: Visual/Verbal Processing Issues in Advertising Research: Some New Topics and Perspectives 272
    Siva K. Balasubramanian, Southern Illinois University
    Susan Heckler, University of Arizona

The Role of Ability and Motivation to Process Visual/Verbal Information on Ad-Related Effects
    Siva K. Balasubramanian, Southern Illinois University

Cross-Cultural Differences in the Use of Visual and Verbal Cues in Television Advertising: A Comparison Between Britain and the U.S.
    Esther Thorson, University of Wisconsin, Madison
    Jacqueline Hitchon, University of Wisconsin, Madison

Impact of TV Ad Processing on Print Ad Processing
   Julie A. Edell, Duke University
   Kevin Lane Keller, Stanford University

Examining the Importance of Aesthetic Appearance in the Processing of Print Advertisements: The Impact of Consumer Expectations
   Susan E. Heckler, University of Arizona
   Laura A. Peracchio, University of Wisconsin, Milwaukee

4.6 *Competitive Paper Session*: Consumer Judgements, Decisions, and Framing Dynamics

Chair: Tom O'Guinn, University of Illinois, Urbana-Champaign
Discussant: Narasimhan Srinivasan, University of Connecticut

Framing Dynamics: Measurement Issues and Perspectives 273
   Donald J. Hempel, University of Connecticut
   Harold Daniel, University of Connecticut

Effects of Multiple Measurement Operations on Consumer Judgment: Measurement Reliability or Reactivity? 280
   Frank R. Kardes, University of Cincinnati
   Chris T. Allen, University of Cincinnati
   Manuel J. Pontes, University of Florida

The Impact of Direction-of-Comparison on the Formation of Preference 284
   Gita V. Johar, Columbia University
   Elizabeth H. Creyer, New York University

Discussant Comments: Consumer Judgements, Decisions, and Framing Dynamics: An Informational Viewpoint 288
   Narasimhan Srinivasan, University of Connecticut

4.7 *Meeting of the 1993 ACR Conference Committee*

Chairs: Chris Allen, University of Cincinnati
          Deborah Roedder-John, University of Minnesota

FRIDAY, OCTOBER 9

RECEPTION
6:00 - 8:00
Museum of Anthropology
University of British Columbia

SALMON BARBECUE
8:00 - 10:00
Faculty Club
University of British Columbia

SATURDAY, OCTOBER 10

SESSION 5
8:30 - 10:00

5.1 PRESIDENTIAL SESSION: Designing Interventions to Prevent HIV/AIDS: Applications of Consumer Research Theory and Methods

Organizer: Susan E. Middlestadt, Academy for Educational Development
Chair: Gerald J. Gorn, University of British Columbia
Discussant: William Smith

Presidential Session Overview: Designing Interventions to Prevent HIV/AIDS: Applications of Consumer Research Theory and Methods 291
    Susan E. Middlestadt, Academy for Educational Development

Social Norms for Condom Use: Implications for HIV Prevention Interventions of a KABP Survey with Heterosexuals in the Eastern Caribbean 292
    Martin Fishbein, University of Illinois, Urbana-Champaign
    Susan E. Middlestadt, Academy for Educational Development
    David Trafimow, Virginia Polytechnic Institute

Encouraging Discussion with Partners and Building Negotiation Skills: HIV Prevention Strategies for Women in Relationships in Brazil, Tanzania and Indonesia 297
    Susan E. Middlestadt, Academy for Educational Development

Media Magic: The Use of Media Monitoring Methodology to Develop AIDS Education Interventions 302
    Carol Schechter, Academy for Educational Development
    Susan E. Middlestadt, Academy for Educational Development
    Lynne D. Doner, Porter/Novelli

5.2 *Special Session*: The New Advertising Rhetoric

Organizer &
Chair: Edward F. McQuarrie, Santa Clara University
Discussant: William D. Wells, University of Minnesota

Summary of Special Session: The New Advertising Rhetoric 308
    Edward F. McQuarrie, Santa Clara University

Reflections on Classical Rhetoric and the Incidence of Figures of Speech in Contemporary Magazine Advertisements 309
    Edward F. McQuarrie, Santa Clara University
    David Glen Mick, University of Florida

Advertising and Contemporary Rhetoric: Adapting Reader-Response Theory
    Linda M. Scott, University of Illinois, Urbana-Champaign

Getting Under the Hood: How the Advertisement Makes Meaning for the Product
    Grant McCracken, Royal Ontario Museum

5.3 *Special Session*: Putting More Emotion into Consumer Research: Integrating Emotional/Hedonic Experience with Traditional Attitude Models

Organizer: Chris T. Allen, University of Cincinnati
Chair: Chris Janiszewski, University of Florida
Discussant: Joel B. Cohen, University of Florida

Summary of Special Session: Putting More Emotion into Consumer Research: Integrating Emotional/Hedonic Experience with Traditional Attitude Models 314
    Chris T. Allen, University of Cincinnati

Predicting Prejudicial Attitudes: The Importance of Affect, Cognition, and the Feeling-Belief Dimension 315
    Geoffrey Haddock, University of Waterloo
    Mark P. Zanna, University of Waterloo

On the Value of Explicitly Incorporating Emotional Experience into the Fishbein Attitude Model: An Empirical Assessment
    Chirs T. Allen, University of Cincinnati
    Karen A. Machleit, University of Cincinnati
    Arti Sahni, University of Cincinnati

On the Dimensionality of 'Overall' Attitudes
    Rajeev Batra, University of Michigan, Ann Arbor

5.4 *Special Session*: Women, Consumption and the Management of Rites of Passage

Organizer: Cele Otnes, University of Illinois, Urbana-Champaign
Chair: Margaret Rucker, University of California, Davis
Discussant: Elizabeth C. Hirschman, Rutgers University, New Brunswick

Summary of Special Session: Women, Consumption and the Management of Rites of Passage 319
    Cele Otnes, University of Illinois, Urbana-Champaign

Baby Showers: A Rite of Passage in Transition 320
    Eileen Fischer, York University
    Brenda Gainer, York University

Til Debt Do Us Part: The Selection and Meaning of Artifacts in the American Wedding 325
    Cele Otnes, University of Illinois, Urbana-Champaign
    Tina M. Lowrey, Rider College

An Examination of Gift Exchange at Funerals
    Kina Mallard, Union University

5.5 *Special Session*: The Effects of Ambiguity on Consumer Information Processing: What, When, Why, and How

Organizers: Durairaj Maheswaran, New York University
              S. Ratneshwar, University of Florida
Chair: Paul M. Herr, University of Colorado, Boulder
Discussant: Stephen J. Hoch, University of Chicago

Summary of Special Session: The Effects of Ambiguity on Consumer Information Processing: What, When, Why, and How 330
    S. Ratneshwar, University of Florida

The Omission Detection Hypothesis: Implications for Judgment and Inference
    Frank R. Kardes, University of Cincinnati

Argument Ambiguity Can Bias Systematic Processing: Effects of Task Importance and Source Credibility on Persuasion
    Shelly Chaiken, New York University
    Durairaj Maheswaran, New York University

Consumer Covariation Judgments: Diagnosticity and the Effects of Prior Beliefs
    Cornelia (Connie) Pechmann, University of California, Irvine
    S. Ratneshwar, University of Florida

5.6   Competitive Paper Session: Shopping Experiences

Chair: Barbara Bickart, University of Florida
Discussant: Elizabeth Wilson, Louisiana State University

How Many Shopping Days Until Christmas?: A Preliminary Investigation of Time Pressures, Deadlines, and Planning Levels on Holiday Gift Purchases 331
    Anthony D. Miyazaki, University of South Carolina

The Influence of Background Music on Shopping Behavior: Classical Versus Top-Forty Music in a Wine Store 336
    Charles S. Areni, Texas Tech University
    David Kim, Texas Tech University

A Comparison of Emotional Reactions Experienced by Planned, Unplanned and Impulse Purchasers 341
    Francis Piron, University of Alaska Anchorage

5.7   Competitive Paper Session: Hedonism and Materialism

Chair: Helen H. Anderson, University of Arizona
Discussant: Michael R. Solomon, Rutgers University, New Brunswick

Beauty and the Beast (Of Advertising) 345
    Barry Vacker, University of Texas, Austin

An Emerald Green Jaguar, a House on Nantucket, and an African Safari: Wish Lists and Consumption Dreams in Materialist Society 352
    Susan Fournier, University of Florida
    Michael Guiry, University of Florida

Self-Gifts and the Manifestation of Material Values 359
    Kim K. R. McKeage, University of Massachusetts, Amherst
    Marsha L. Richins, University of Missouri
    Kathleen Debevec, University of Massachusetts, Amherst

SATURDAY, OCTOBER 10

SESSION 6
10:20 - 11:50

6.1 *PRESIDENTIAL SESSION*: Persuading Women to Have Mammograms: Practical and Theoretical Perspectives

Organizer &
Chair: Paul N. Bloom, University of North Carolina, Chapel Hill
Discussant: Christopher P. Puto, University of Arizona
Sharyn Sutton, National Cancer Institute

Summary of Presidential Session: Persuading Women to Have Mammograms: Practical and Theoretical Perspectives 365
  Paul N. Bloom, University of North Carolina, Chapel Hill

Using Qualitative Research to Develop Strategies to Reach Women with Cancer Screening Messages 366
  Cathy Coyne, AMC Cancer Research Center
  Diane L. Bloom, Bloom Research
  Julie M. Andresen, Bloom Research

Demographic and Lifestyle Data–A Practical Application To Stimulating Compliance With Mammography Guidelines Among Poor Women 371
  Cynthia Currence, American Cancer Society

Examining the Power of Numbers
  Radhika Puri, University of Chicago
  Joan Meyers-Levy, University of Chicago

When to Accentuate the Negative: The Effects of Perceived Efficacy and Message Framing on Intentions to Perform Cancer Detection/Prevention Techniques
  Lauren Goldberg Block, New York University
  Punam Anand, Columbia University

6.2 *Special Session*: Children as Consumers: Are They "Marketing" Literate?

Organizer: Deborah Roedder John, University of Minnesota
  Laura Peracchio, University of Wisconsin, Milwaukee
Chair: Kenneth Bahn, University of Texas, Arlington
Discussant: Marvin Goldberg, Pennsylvania State University

Summary of Special Session: Children as Consumers: Are They 'Marketing Literate? 373
  Deborah Roedder John, University of Minnesota
  Laura Peracchio, University of Wisconsin, Milwaukee

Effects of Channel One: Adolescent Knowledge of and Attitudes Toward Advertising
  Marian Friestad, University of Oregon
  David M. Boush, University of Oregon

Young Children's Understanding of Visual and Aural Televised Messages
  Laura A. Peracchio, University of Wisconsin, Milwaukee

How Capable are Children as Decision Makers? An Exploratory Study of Information Search Behavior
  Jennifer Gregan-Paxton, University of Minnesota
  Deborah Roedder John, University of Minnesota

6.3 *Special Session*: Temporal Dimensions of Decision-Making: How Long, and When, to Decide

Organizer: Deborah Mitchell, Temple University
Chair: Tina Kiesler, New York University
Discussant: Drazen Prelec, MIT

Summary of Special Session: Temporal Dimensions of Decision-Making: How Long, and When, to Decide 374
    Deborah Mitchell, Temple University

Introspection and Decision-Making: It's Not How Much, but What Kind of Thinking That Matters
    Deborah J. Mitchell, Temple University

Effects of Salience and Time Pressure on the Choice Process and Outcomes
    France LeClerc, Massachusetts Institute of Technology

Why Consumers Stop Delaying Purchase Decisions
    Eric A. Greenleaf, New York University
    Donald R. Lehmann, Columbia University

Accuracy in Predicting Time of Purchase: When Will I Buy My Next Car?
    Vicki G. Morwitz, New York University

6.4 *Special Session*: Context Effects on Consumer Goals, Brand Awareness, and Decision-Making

Organizer: Allan D. Shocker, University of Minnesota
Chair: Cynthia Huffman, University of Pennsylvania
Discussant: C. Whan Park, University of Pittsburgh

Special Session Overview: Context Effects on Consumer Goals, Brand Awareness, and Decision-Making 375
    Cynthia Huffman, University of Pennsylvania

The Role of Usage Context in Consumer Choice: A Problem Solving Perspective 377
    Luk Warlop, University of Florida
    S. Ratneshwar, University of Florida

Understanding Brand Awareness: Let Me Give You a C(l)ue! 383
    Stephen J. Holden, ESSEC, France

On the Transferability of Feature/Level Preferences Across Competing Products Serving the Same Purposes 389
    Milos D. Graonic, University of Minnesota
    Allan D. Shocker, University of Minnesota

Disscussant Comments: Context Effects on Consumer Goals, Brand Awareness, and Decision-Making 395
    C. Whan Park, University of Pittsburgh

6.5 *Competitive Paper Session*: Social Issues: A Review and Two Studies

Chair: M. Elizabeth Blair, Ohio University, Athens
Discussant: Howard Marmorstein, University of Miami

*Progress and Limitations of Social Marketing: A Review of Empirical Literature on the Consumption of
Social Ideas* 397
    Katryna Malafarina, University of Minnesota
    Barbara Loken, University of Minnesota

*A Longitudinal Examination of Addictive Consumption: Its Behavioral and Psychological Pattern
and Consequences* 405
    Keiko I. Powers, University of California, Los Angeles

Social Marketing and Consumer Behavior: Influencing the Decision to Reduce Alcohol Consumption 413
    Jean C. Darian, Rider College

6.6 Competitive Paper Session: Perceptions of Self

Chair: Beth Walker, Arizona State University
Discussant: J. Michael Munson, Santa Clara University

Assessing Self-Concept Discrepancy in Consumer Behavior: The Joint Effect of Private Self-Consciousness and Self-Monitoring 419
    Stephen J. Gould, Fairleigh Dickinson University

Dispossession and Perceptions of Self in Late Stage HIV Infection 425
    Teresa Pavia, University of Utah

The Evolving Self in Consumer Behavior: Exploring Possible Selves 429
    Amy J. Morgan, Memphis State University

Discussant Comments: Perceptions of Self: The Effects of Self-concept Discrepancy, Possible Selves and Dispossession 433
    J. Michael Munson, Santa Clara University

SATURDAY, OCTOBER 10

LUNCH
12:00 - 2:00

PRESENTATION OF AWARDS

ACR FELLOW ADDRESS
James R. Bettman
"The Decision Maker Who Came In From The Cold"

SATURDAY, OCTOBER 10

SESSION 7
2:10 - 3:40

7.1 Special Session: Differential Effects of Sales Promotions

Organizer: Ziv Carmon, University of California, Berkeley
Chair: Radhlka Puri, University of Chicago
Discussant: John Totten, A. C. Neilsen

Flyers and Filers: Modeling Differential Coupon Redemption Behavior Effects on Coupon Redemption Patterns
    J. Jeffrey Inman, University of Southern California

The Effect of Unneeded Features and Premiums on Purchase Decisions
    Itamar Simonson, University of California, Berkeley
    Ziv Carmon, University of California, Berkeley
    Suzanne O'Curry, University of California, Berkeley

Invivo Pricing Experiments
    Stephen J. Hoch, University of Chicago

7.2   Special Session: Consumer Research Priorities for the MSI Research Competition on "Using Marketing to Serve Society"

Organizer &
Chair: Paul N. Bloom, University of North Carolina, Chapel Hill

Panelists: William L. Wilkie, University of Notre Dame
               Michael B. Mazis, The American University
               Richard Staelin, Marketing Science Institute and Duke University

Summary of Special Session: Consumer Research Priorities for the MSI Research Competition on "Using Marketing to Serve Society" 436
    Paul N. Bloom, University of North Carolina, Chapel Hill

7.3   Special Session: Understanding Donation Behavior: Strategic Implications from Consumer Research

Organizer: James W. Peltier, University of Wisconsin, Whitewater
Chair: Michal Ann Strahilevitz, University of California, Berkeley
Discussant: Lynora Baylass, United Way of Las Vegas

Special Session Summary: Understanding Donation Behavior: Strategic Implications from Consumer Research 437
    James W. Peltier University of Wisconsin Whitewater
    April Atwood, University of Washington
    Lynora Bayless, United Way of Southern Nevada
    Tracy Bier, Puget Sound Blood Center
    William Carter, School of Business, University of Washington
    Catherine Cole, University of Iowa
    Mary Huneke, University of Iowa
    Patrick Murphy, University of Notre Dame
    Dee Myer, Puget Sound Blood Center
    John A. Schibrowsky, University of Nevada-Las Vegas
    Sandra Tausend, Puget Sound Blood Center

Modeling the Donation Process: Why People Give and How Much
    James W. Peltier, University of Wisconsin, Whitewater
    John A. Schibrowsky, University of Nevada, Las Vegas

The Decision to Donate Blood Again: Investigating Donor Retention
    April Atwood, University of Washington
    Tracy Bier, Puget Sound Blood Center
    William Carter, University of Washington
    Sandra Tausend, Puget Sound Blood Center
    Dee Myer, Puget Sound Blood Center

The Effect of Emotional and Informational Direct Mail Appeals on Consumers' Intentions to Donate
    Catherine Cole, University of Iowa
    Mary Huneke, University of Iowa
    Patrick Murphy, University of Notre Dame

7.4   Special Session: The Two Sides of the Accessibility Coin: Factors that Enhance and Impede Information Accessibility

Organizer: Prakash Nedungadi, Indiana University
Chair: John Lynch, University of Florida
Discussant: J. Wesley Hutchinson, University of Florida

*Summary of Special Session: The Two Sides of the Accessibility Coin: Factors that Enhance and Impede
Information Accessibility* 438
        Prakash Nedungadi, Indiana University

Retrieval Difficulty and Subsequent Recall in an Advertising Setting
        Kevin Lane Keller, Stanford University

Facilitating and Inhibiting Effects of Brand Cues on Recall, Consideration Sets, and Choice
        Manoj Hastak, American University
        Anusree Mitra, American University

Information Accessibility as a Mediator of AAd Effects
        Amitava Chattopadhyay, McGill University
        Prakash Nedungadi, University of Toronto

7.5 *Robert Ferber ACR/JCR Award for Consumer Research*

Chair: Kent B. Monroe, University of Illinois, Champaign-Urbana

Winner:
Contextual Influences on the Meanings Ascribed to Ordinary Consumption Objects
        Robert E. Kleine, III, Arizona State University

Honorable Mentions:
*Levels of Subjective Comprehension in Advertising Processing and Their Relations to Ad Perceptions,
Attitudes, and Memory*
        David Glen Mick, University of Florida

How Do Young Children Learn to Be Consumers? A Script-Processing Approach
        Laura A. Peracchio, University of Wisconsin, Milwaukee

7.6 *Competitive Paper Session*: **Post-Positivist Methods**

Chair: James H. McAlexander, Iowa State University
Discussant: Craig Thompson, University of Wisconsin, Madison

A Critique of Critical Theory: Response to Murray and Ozanne's "The Critical Imagination" 439
        William Val Larsen, Virginia Polytechnic Institute and State University
        Newell D. Wright, Virginia Polytechnic Institute and State University

Using Qualitative Techniques to Explore Consumer Attitudes: Insights from Group Process Theories 444
        Terry Bristol, Oklahoma State University
        Edward F. Fern, Virginia Polytechnic Institute and State University

Action Identification Theory: An Examination of Consumers' Behavioral Representations 449
        George W. Hunt, University of Texas, Austin
        Wayne D. Hoyer, University of Texas, Austin

*Discussant Comments: Interpretation Strikes Again, Again, and Again: A Postpositivist Reflection on Papers
by Bristol and Fern, Hunt and Hoyer, and Larsen and Wright* 455
        Craig J. Thompson, University of Wisconsin, Madison

7.7 Competitive Paper Session: **Families and Children**

Chair: Richard D. Johnson, University of Alberta
Discussant: Kim P. Corfman, New York University

Kinship Exchange Networks and Family Consumption 458
    Ritha Fellerman, University of Massachusetts
    Kathleen Debevec, University of Massachusetts

Children's Susceptibility to Peer Group Purchase Influence: An Exploratory Investigation 463
    Gwen Rae Bachman, University of Minnesota
    Deborah Roedder John, University of Minnesota
    Akshay R. Rao, University of Minnesota

Female-Headed Single Parent Families: An Exploratory Study of Children's Influence in Family Decision Making 469
    Roshan D. Ahuja, Xavier University
    Kandi M. Stinson, Xavier University

SATURDAY, OCTOBER 10

SESSION 8
4:00 - 5:30

8.1 Special Session: **Attraction and Compromise Effects in Choice: Moderating Influences and Differential Loss Aversion to Quality and Nonquality Attributes**

Organizers: Timothy B. Heath, University of Pittsburgh
             Subimal Chatterjee, University of Pittsburgh
Chair: Patricia West, University of Texas
Discussant: Jennifer Aaker, Stanford University

Summary of Special Session: Attraction and Compromise Effects in Choice: Moderating Influences and Differential Loss Aversion to Quality and Nonquality Attributes 475
    Timothy B. Heath, University of Pittsburgh
    Subimal Chatterjee, University of Pittsburgh

Reference Dependence and Loss Aversion in Consumer Choice Processes
    Shankar Sen, The University of Pennsylvania
    Eric J. Johnson, The University of Pennsylvania

The Impact of Time Pressure and Information Consistency on the Choice of Brands Spanning a Price-Quality Continuum
    Barbara Kahn, University of Pennsylvania
    Joel Huber, Duke University
    Morris Holbrook, Columbia University

Quality-Based Limitations of Attraction Effects on Consumer Choice: A Meta-Analysis
    Subimal Chatterjee, University of Pittsburgh
    Timothy B. Heath, University of Pittsburgh

The Effect of Paired Comparisons and Product Display Format on Choices Between Lower Price and Higher Quality
    Itamar Simonson, University of California, Berkeley
    Stephen Nowlis, University of California, Berkeley
    Katherine Lemon, University of California, Berkeley

8.2 *Special Session*: Imagery in Marketing Communications: Beyond Pictures and Visual Processing

Organizer: Gayathri Mani, University of Arizona
Chair: Brian Wansink, Dartmouth College
Discussant: Deborah J. MacInnis, University of Arizona

Summary of Special Session: Imagery in Marketing Communications: Beyond Pictures and Visual Processing 476
    Gayathri Mani, University of Arizona

Differing Effects of Imagery and Self-Referencing on the Persuasiveness of Fear and Nonfear Appeals
    Lauren Goldberg Block, New York University
    Punam Anand, Columbia University

Modality Specific Interference in the Processing of Advertising Information
    H. Rao Unnava, Ohio State University
    Sanjeev Agarwal, Iowa State University

Olfaction and Mental Representations: Memory Effects of Imagery Processes in Multiple Sensory Modalities
    Dipankar Chakravarti, University of Arizona
    Deborah J. MacInnis, University of Arizona
    Gayathri Mani, University of Arizona

8.3 *Special Session*: Societal and Public Policy Issues with Retail Pricing

Organizers: Dhruv Grewal, University of Miami
             Ronald Goodstein, UCLA
Chair: Howard Marmorstein, University of Miami
Discussant: Michael Mazis, American University

Summary of Special Session: Societal and Public Policy Issues with Retail Pricing 477
    Dhruv Grewal, University of Miami
    Ronald Goodstein, UCLA

UPC Scanner Pricing Systems: Is the Consumer Really Better Off? 478
    Ronald C. Goodstein, University of California, Los Angeles
    Jennifer Edson Escalas, Duke University
    Harold H. Kassarjian, University of California, Los Angeles

The Role of Price Premiums in Assuring Product Quality: Public Policy Implications
    Akshay Rao, University of Minnesota
    Kent B. Monroe, University of Illinois, Urbana-Champaign
    Mark E. Bergen, University of Chicago

Interpretations of Semantic Phrases in Comparative Price Advertisements: Some Preliminary Evidence on a Public Policy Issue 479
    Dhruv Grewal, University of Miami
    Larry Compeau, Clarkson University

8.4 *Competitive Paper Session*: The Greening of ACR

Chair: Lucette Comer, Florida International University
Discussant: Debra Stephens, Villanova University

An Investigation of Determinants of Recycling Consumer Behavior 481
    Anita L. Jackson, Louisiana State University
    Janeen E. Olsen, Louisiana State University
    Kent L. Granzin, University of Utah
    Alvin C. Burns, Louisiana State University

Exploring Green Consumers In An Oriental Culture: Role of Personal and Marketing Mix Factors 488
    Prem Shamdasani, National University of Singapore
    Gloria Ong Chon-Lin, National University of Singapore
    Daleen Richmond, National University of Singapore

Anatomy of Green Advertising 494
    Easwar Iyer, University of Massachusetts, Amherst
    Bobby Banerjee, University of Massachusetts, Amherst

8.5 Special Session: A New Look at the Determinants of Consumer Satisfaction

Organizers:	Michael D. Johnson, University of Michigan, Ann Arbor
	Youjae Yi, University of Michigan, Ann Arbor
Chair:	Madhu Viswanathan, University of Illinois, Urbana-Champaign
Discussant:	Robert A. Westbrook, Rice University

The Determinants of Satisfaction: The Moderating Role of Ambiguity
    Michael D. Johnson, University of Michigan, Ann Arbor

The Determinants of Consumer Satisfaction: The Moderating Role of Ambiguity 502
    Youjae Yi, University of Michigan, Ann Arbor

Hindsight Bias and Consumer Satisfaction: Foresight Versus Hindsight Expectations
    Rami Zwick, Pennsylvania State University
    Rik Pieters, Erasmus University, The Netherlands
    Hans Baumgartner, Pennsylvania State University

Expectations Versus Desires: A Direct Test of Two Comparison Standards Assessing Consumer Satisfaction 507
    Richard A. Spreng, Michigan State University
    Scott B. MacKenzie, Indiana University
    Richard W. Olshavsky, Indiana University

8.6 Competitive Paper Session: Gifts, Charity, and Giving

Chair:	Pallab Paul, University of Denver
Discussant:	Carole Macklin, University of Cincinnati

Hey You, Can Ya Spare Some Change? The Case of Empathy and Personal Distress As Reactions to Charitable Appeals 508
    Mitch Griffin, Bradley University
    Barry J. Babin, University of Southern Mississippi
    Jill S. Attaway, Illinois State University
    William R. Darden, Louisiana State University

Extrahousehold Giving in Popular Gift Categories: A Socioeconomic and Demographic Analysis 515
    Janet Wagner, University of Maryland
    Thesia I. Garner, Bureau of Labor Statistics

Three Motivations for Interpersonal Gift Giving: Experiential, Obligated and Practical Motivations 520
    Mary Finley Wolfinbarger, California State University
    Laura J. Yale, Fort Lewis College

8.7 Competitive Paper Session: **Men and Women**

Chair: Royce Anderson, Clark University
Discussants: Marla Felcher, Northwestern University

Measuring Cohort Role on Husband-Wife Differences in Temporal Behavior 527
    Jacob Hornik, University of Chicago

Gender Differences in the Perception of Leisure: A Conceptual Model 534
    Suzana de M. Fontenelle, University of Houston
    George M. Zinkhan, University of Houston

What's Mine is Mine and What's Yours is Ours: Challenging the Income Pooling Assumption 541
    Judith J. Marshall, Carleton University
    Frances Woolley, Carleton University

SATURDAY, OCTOBER 10

JCR EDITORIAL REVIEW BOARD MEETING
5:30 - 7:00
Aspen Room

RECEPTION AT HOTEL
6:00 - 8:00
In commemoration of the 25th Anniversary of its Consumer Behavior text, Dryden Press will honor James Engel, David Kollat, Roger Blackwell and Paul Miniard with champagne and hors d'oeuvres from 6:00 until 7:00.

SATURDAY, OCTOBER 10

SESSION 9
7:30 - 9:00

9.1 Special Session: **Self-Gifts: An Emerging Category of Consumer Behavior from Multiple Perspectives**

Organizer: David Mick, University of Florida
Chair: Ed Petkus, University of Tennessee
Discussant: Dennis Rook, University of Southern California

Summary of Special Session: Self-Gifts: An Emerging Category of Consumer Behavior from Multiple Perspectives 546
    David Mick, University of Florida

Fantasies and Realities of the Self-Gift
    Mary Ann McGrath, Loyola University
    John F. Sherry, Jr., Northwestern University
    Sidney J. Levy, Northwestern University

Self-Gifts: A Metacognition Perspective 547
    Richard W. Olshavsky, Indiana University
    Dong Hwan Lee, State University of New York, Albany

Self-Gifts Through the Lens of Attribution Theory 553
    Corinne Faure, University of Florida
    David Mick, University of Florida

Compulsive Buying and Self-Gifts: A Motivational Perspective 557
      Jon M. Shapiro, Virginia Polytechnic Institute and State University

9.2   Special Session: Music in Ads, Stores and Homes

Organizers &
Co-Chairs: Liz Blair, Ohio University
                  James Kellaris, University of Cincinnati
Discussant: Liz Blair, Ohio University

Summary of Special Session: Music in Ads, Stores and Homes 558
      Liz Blair, Ohio University
      James Kellaris, University of Cincinnati

The Role of Background Music: A Reexamination and Extension
      Terence A. Shimp, University of South Carolina
      Randall L. Rose, University of South Carolina

One Man's Beat, Another Man's Noise: Subjective Stimulus Properties as Mediators of Music's Influence on Affect
      James Kellaris, University of Cincinnati
      Robert J. Kent, University of Cincinnati

Music, Marketing and Multivocality: Popular Song and Emergent Discourse
      Linda M. Scott, University of Illinois, Urbana-Champaign

9.3   Competitive Paper Session: Love, Lust, and Other Misbehaviors

Chair: Gabriel J. Biehal, University of Maryland, College Park
Discussant: George Belch, San Diego State University

The Visible Hand in Marriage: An Exploratory Assessment of the Marriage Promotion Campaign in Singapore 559
      Siew Meng Leong, National University of Singapore
      Swee Hoon Ang, National University of Singapore

Segmenting Prostitutes' Need for Information About AIDS: A Field Study 565
      Per Østergaard, Odense University, Denmark

Choosing to Misbehave: A Structural Model of Aberrant Consumer Behavior 570
      Ronald A. Fullerton, Providence College
      Girish N. Punj, University of Connecticut

9.4 Competitive Paper Session: Brand Loyalty and Pricing Issues

Chair: Sunder Narayanan, University of Illinois, Urbana-Champaign
Discussant: Ved Prakash, Morgan State University

Brand Loyalty and Lineage: Exploring New Dimensions for Research 575
      Barbara Olsen, State University of New York-Old Westbury

Testing for Perceptual Underestimation of 9-Ending Prices 580
      Robert M. Schindler, Rutgers University, Camden
      Thomas Kibarian, Innovation and Information Consultants, Inc.

Effects of Prior Belief on Feature-Based Price Estimates 586
      Tridib Mazumdar, Syracuse University
      Cheoul Ryon Kim, Syracuse University

Some Brand Loyalty and Pricing Issues in Consumer Research 591
    Ved Prakash, Baltimore, Maryland

9.5 *Competitive Paper Session*: **Extensions of Brand Extension**

Chair: Jill Grace, University of Southern California
Discussant: Mary T. Curren, California State University, Northridge

The Effects of Adding Products to a Brand on Consumers' Evaluations of New Brand Extensions 594
    Peter A. Dacin, University of Wisconsin, Madison
    Daniel C. Smith, University of Pittsburgh

Line Extensions: A Categorization and an Information Processing Perspective 599
    Kalpesh Kaushik Desai, University of Texas, Austin
    Wayne D. Hoyer, University of Texas, Austin

An Examination of the Effects of Multiple Brand Extensions on the Brand Concept 607
    Sandy D. Jap, University of Florida

9.6 *Competitive Paper Session*: **Perceptions and Attitudes**

Chair: Patricia Anderson, Quinnipiac College
Discussant: Curtis P. Haugtvedt, Ohio State University

Candidates as Engendered Products: Prototypes in Political Person Perception 612
    Basil G. Englis, Rutgers University, New Brunswick
    Greta Pennell, Rutgers University, New Brunswick

A Framework for Explaining Multiple Request Effectiveness: The Role of Attitude Towards the Request 620
    Rohini Ahluwalia, Ohio State University
    Robert E. Burnkrant, Ohio State University

Attitudes Toward 'Buy America First' and Preferences for American and Japanese Cars: A Different Role for Country-of-Origin Information 625
    Irwin P. Levin, University of Iowa
    J. D. Jasper, University of Iowa
    John D. Mittelstaedt, University of Iowa
    Gary J. Gaeth, University of Iowa

SUNDAY, OCTOBER 11

SESSION 10
9:10 - 10:40

10.1 *Special Session*: **The Influence of Environmental Factors on Consumer Behavior: A Decade Later**

Organizer: Richard F. Yalch, University of Washington
Chair: Julie Ruth, University of Washington
Discussant: James Russell, University of British Columbia

Summary of Special Session: The Influence of Environmental Factors on Consumer Behavior: A Decade Later 630
    Richard F. Yalch, University of Washington

Store Atmosphere and Unplanned Purchasing
    Robert J. Donovan, University of Western Australia
    John R. Rossiter, Australian Graduate School of Management
    Andrew R. Nesdale, University of Western Australia

Effects of Store Image and Mood on Consumer Behavior: A Theoretical and Empirical Analysis 631
    Ruth Belk Smith, University of Baltimore
    Elaine Sherman, Hofstra University

Using Store Music for Retail Zoning: A Field Experiment 632
    Richard F. Yalch, University of Washington
    Eric Spangenberg, Washington State University

10.2 Competitive Paper Session: Issues in Structural Models

Chair: Steven P. Brown, University of Georgia
Discussant: Thomas J. Page, Michigan State University

Using Moderator Variables in Structural Equation Models 637
    Paul L. Sauer, Canisius College
    Alan Dick, State University of New York, Buffalo

A Structural Equation Analysis of the Relationships of Personal Values, Attitudes and Beliefs About Recycling, and the Recycling of Solid Waste Products 641
    John A. McCarty, University of Illinois, Urbana-Champaign
    L. J. Shrum, Rutgers University, New Brunswick

Testing Consumer Behavior Theories: LISREL Is Not a Panacea 647
    Banwari Mittal, Northern Kentucky University

Discussant Comments on "Issues in Structural Models" 654
    Thomas J. Page, Michigan State University

10.3 Special Session: Brand Name Memory Following Ad Exposure: Inhibition, Interference, and Attenuation Processes as Revealed by Direct and Indirect Tests of Memory

Organizers: Carol Pluzinski, New York University
                Shanker Krishnan, Indiana University
Chair: Elizabeth Creyer, New York University
Discussant: Dipankar Chakravarti, University of Arizona

Summary of Special Session: Brand Name Memory Following Ad Exposure: Inhibition, Interference, and Attenuation Processes as Revealed by Direct and Indirect Tests of Memory 655
    Shankar Krishnan, Indiana University
    Carol Pluzinski, New York University

The Determinants of Brand Name Accessibility as Measured by Direct and Indirect Tests of Memory
    Carol Pluzinski, New York University
    Gita V. Johar, Columbia University

Inhibition Effects Between Competitive Brand Advertisements
    Wanda Wallace, Duke University
    Lynn Hasher, Duke University

Word Frequency, Elaboration, and Repetition Effects on Direct and Indirect Tests of Brand Name Memory
    Stewart Shapiro, University of Arizona
    Shankar Krishnan, Indiana University

10.4 Competitive Paper Session: Satisfaction, Loyalty, and Beliefs

Chair: Eloise Coupey, University of Illinois, Urbana-Champaign
Discussant: Therese A. Louie, University of British Columbia

Leaving It All Behind: Service Loyalties in Transition 656
    Robin A. Higie, University of Connecticut
    Linda L. Price, University of Colorado, Boulder
    Julie Fitzmaurice, University of Connecticut

Attitudes, Advertising, and Automobiles: A Functional Approach 662
    Richard Ennis, University of Waterloo
    Mark Zanna, University of Waterloo

Valenced Emotions in Satisfaction: A Look at Affect in Shopping 667
    Mai Neo, University of Pittsburgh
    Audrey J. Murrell, University of Pittsburgh

10.5 Competitive Paper Session: Perceptions, Evaluations and Risk

Chair: Carolyn L. Costley, Texas A&M University
Discussant: Carl Obermiller, Seattle University

An Exploratory Investigation of Holistic and Analytic Modes of Product Perception 673
    Hans Baumgartner, Pennsylvania State University

Country-of-Origin, Perceived Risk and Evaluation Strategy 678
    Dana L. Alden, University of Hawaii
    Wayne D. Hoyer, University of Texas, Austin
    Ayn E. Crowley, Washington State University

The Roles of Country of Origin Information on Buyers' Product Evaluations: Signal or Attribute? 684
    Wai-kwan Li, University of Illinois, Urbana-Champaign
    Kwok Leung, Chinese University of Hong Kong
    Robert S. Wyer, Jr., University of Illinois, Urbana-Champaign

Discussant Comments: Comments of Evolving Country of Origin Research 690
    Carl Obermiller, Seattle University

10.6 Competitive Paper Session: Issues in Advertising and Involvement

Chair: Reza Moinpour, University of Washington
Discussant: Mickey Belch, San Diego State University

An Extended Perspective on the Role of Emotion in Advertising Processing 692
    Hyongoh Cho, University of Texas, Austin
    Patricia A. Stout, University of Texas, Austin

Poisoning the Well: Do Environmental Claims Strain Consumer Credulity? 698
    Robert N. Mayer, University of Utah
    Debra L. Scammon, University of Utah
    Cathleen D. Zick, University of Utah

Spokesperson Effects in High Involvement Markets 704
    Timothy B. Heath, University of Pittsburgh
    David L. Mothersbaugh, University of Pittsburgh
    Michael S. McCarthy, University of Pittsburgh

CONTRIBUTION FROM 1991 ACR CONFERENCE

The Consumption of Insignificant Rituals: A Look at Debutante Balls 709
    Jennifer Edson Escalas, Duke University

AUTHOR INDEX 717

PRESIDENTIAL ADDRESS
A Social Marketing Research Agenda for Consumer Behavior Researchers
Alan R. Andreasen, University of Connecticut

It was seventeen years ago that I had my first exposure to social marketing. I was asked by Bill Novelli, then head of Porter/Novelli, to become a marketing consultant to the National High Blood Pressure Education Program in Washington, D.C. High blood pressure was then — and is now — a leading cause of cardiovascular disease which kills more Americans than cancer, AIDS, drug addiction, and accidents combined. At the time, perhaps 32 million American were determined to be hypertensives (a figure since revised upward) and only 51% of them were aware of their problem. The remainder were individuals we thought of as walking time bombs unaware of their risk. Only a quarter of the population knew of the link between high blood pressure and heart disease.

It was fascinating to watch and learn from Bill and his colleagues as they developed a communications program using marketing concepts and techniques I was teaching in my classroom. The experience changed my career. I was an academic product of the social revolution of the late sixties and early seventies and frustrated with what I was doing. My friends in Sociology and Political Science were worrying about issues like poverty, the Viet Nam war, and military recruiting on campus, and so on, while I was busy teaching my students how to market Chevrolets and Clairol Shampoo.

Matters began to change when the Ghetto riots in the late 60s revealed intense frustration with the marketing system. For the first time, I could see that, by trying to understand and ameliorate these problems, I could match my academic skills to something that really mattered to me. And, as many of you know, over the years I have continued to have concern for the problems of disadvantaged consumers and others inhabiting what Beth Hirschman two years ago called the "dark side of the marketplace."

My 1975 encounter with Porter/Novelli and the NHBPEP opened my eyes to the potential for marketing to work *positively* for the good of society beyond merely (to use a classroom cliché of the time) "delivering a better standard of living." Since 1975, I have had the good fortune to continue to work with Porter/Novelli and to meet and learn from a wide range of individuals who now would call themselves social marketers at places like the American Cancer Society, the National Cancer Institute, the United Way, and the Academy for Educational Development. I have had the chance to work in such challenging environments as Colombia, Pakistan, Bangladesh, Mexico, and (to show it was not all hard duty) Barbados and Jamaica.

This fascinating and personally rewarding work has led me to this conference and to this podium. This ACR conference means a great deal to me in terms of my own ambitions and what I want to leave as a legacy to the society and my chosen academic discipline. I very much want this conference to be a watershed event after which there is a deluge of involvement on the part of consumer researchers in solving the myriad social problems for which consumer behavior holds the key. With the leadership of program chairs Leigh McAlister and Mike Rothschild, we have put together a program full of social marketing experiences and insights, peopled with many of the social marketers with whom I have worked over the years.

It is a time to jump start social marketing. But, I am not näive. I have been disillusioned before. In 1975, I published an overview of the work on what was then called "Ghetto Marketing" in which I pointed out that, after barely five years, this extremely important topic was in its decline phase (Andreasen 1978). Faddish researchers had moved on to new "hot" topics leaving behind crucial questions that were important not only to the social issues themselves but also to the marketing and consumer research discipline itself. I do not want this to happen again. But, I know it might. For this reason, the primary objective of my address today is to provide you with some additional motivational spark — if you still need some — to get involved.

However, you may be surprised at the approach I have chosen to take. Contrary to the expectations of many, I am not going to describe the very real, positive emotions that you would experience from working on important issues like getting people to control their high blood pressure or to stop smoking, getting parents in developing countries to have their kids immunized or promoting oral rehydration therapy to save the lives of the four million children who now die of diarrheal diseases. I will not point to the fascinating people you will meet and from whom you will learn. Nor will I dwell on the intense satisfaction you can have when you learn about the success of a program on which you have worked. (By 1980, NHBPEP could report that three-quarters of hypertensives were aware of their problem and by 1985 that 91% of the general public knew that high blood pressure increases one's chance of getting heart disease.)

Rather, I am going to talk about some things that are much more immediately relevant to most of us. Academic life, of which most of us are a part, revolves around scholarship, intellectual pursuit, and the joys of teaching. It is what we are rewarded for doing. But, it is also what we *like* to do. It is what got us into the profession in the first place. Thus, the case I want to make to you here today is that immersion in the real world of social marketing is not only good for the soul but good for the mind and the resumé as well. It is food for both the right and left sides of the brain. What I wish to argue is that by involving yourself in social marketing you can help *stretch the disciplines of consumer behavior and marketing*. I am convinced that involvement in these social marketing issues has already led to some important developments in our field. More importantly, however, the field of social marketing lays before us a set of research challenges that can help keep us productive, intellectually growing, and *highly relevant* for at least the next decade. Let me suggest some of the possibilities that can constitute a social marketing research agenda for the 1990s.

SOME DEFINING TERMS

Just so we are clear, let me start off with my own definition of social marketing and clear up some misconceptions people seem to have.

Social marketing is the adaptation of commercial marketing technologies to the analysis, planning, execution and evaluation of programs designed to influence the behavior of target audiences in order to improve their physical and mental well-being and/or that of the society of which they are a part.

As this definition should make clear, social marketing is not to be confused with what should be called "societal marketing" or, more generally, "marketing and public policy." The latter deals with the other, darker face of marketing about which I and others are also interested. Whereas *societal* marketing is protective: *social* marketing is proactive.

The definition also makes clear that the bottom line of social marketing is influencing *behavior*. I believe that what makes marketing different from many other social change approaches is its focus on the behavior of target consumers. Too many in social marketing confuse marketing with communication. While marketers communicate information, we are not in the *education* business. While we attempt to convince people of the rightness of certain beliefs, we are also not in the *propaganda* business. Many of the health programs I have observed or worked with around the world are, in fact, largely education and propaganda programs. Contrary to what Kotler and Zaltman said in 1971, social marketing *is not* an attempt "to influence the acceptability of social *ideas*" (Kotler and Zaltman 1971, emphasis added). Education and propaganda are only *useful* if they *lead to behavior change*. It is this behavioral mindset and its concommitant emphasis on customers that turns out to have massive appeal to social change practitioners and partially explains why many of them are here with us today.

THE CONSUMER FOCUS

While social marketing practitioners have much to learn from us, I would argue that we have much to learn from trying to think about how our approaches to consumer behavior might apply to their issues. Indeed, in my view, we have already benefitted significantly. I would claim that a major paradigm shift in our conceptualization of consumer behavior itself emerged from our thinking about social marketing issues. I am speaking of the shift from a view of marketing as a one-way attempt by a marketer to influence consumers through the four Ps to a view of the process as one of *creating exchanges*.

The rise of exchange theory, I believe, was given a major stimulus by marketing scholars trying to expand the concept of "consumer behavior" and "marketing" to encompass something as nontraditional as going to college, wearing seat belts, or giving blood. For example, promoting blood donations seemed to be an opportunity for "marketing," yet there were no products or services offered and no monetary payment made by the consumer. In fact, the consumer often *voluntarily* suffered when making the "purchase." Traditional unidirectional views of consumer behavior could not encompass such a strange case. We *needed* a new paradigm. The old way, like earth-centered astronomy before Copernicus, was simply not elastic enough to contain these new transactions. Thus, we slowly embraced exchange theory.

However, my work in social marketing presented several problems with the current paradigm. For example, for a time I was bothered by our use of the term *consumer* behavior to describe the behaviors I was trying to influence. In social marketing situations, it was hard to imagine *what is being consumed*. When a teenager gives up smoking marijuana as the result of a Centers for Disease Control campaign, a behavior has been influenced. But what is *consumed*? When someone gives blood, what is consumed? I shortly realized that my work and teaching in the commercial sector had seduced me into associating consumption with things but that, as we need to keep reminding ourselves, what is really consumed are *benefits*. Products and services are benefit-generating entities. Similarly, giving blood or abandoning drugs are benefit-generating activities.

But this logic leads to another intriguing conceptual and research problem. It turns out that many of the behaviors social marketers are trying to influence comprise benefits that *the consumer* generates with virtually no involvement of the marketer. In conventional transactions, there is a clear marketer who wants to influence the consumer by manipulating costs or benefits that the marketer controls, the price, the quality of the product or service, and so on. But, what of safe sex? One might argue that marketers control the benefits that follow from the behavior when they promote the *safety* of safe sex. But, suppose research has shown that the best way to get people, especially young people, to practice safe sex is to get them to learn that it can be sexy. Yet, the sexiness of the experience is something that the "consumer" controls. He or she can increase the benefits and provide rewards. If this is the case, then who is the marketer here?

What I believe is now needed is a conceptual framework for understanding how consumers benefit themselves in the consumption process and how we can make them *better* generators of their own benefits. This would have a number of interesting payoffs in the areas of health and nutrition where athletes and dieters have to convince themselves that, for the costs they are expending, the behaviors are worth it. If marketers encounter them in clinics or offices, they can praise them with positive feedback. But much exercise and dieting is a lonely process. The consumer must learn self-reward. If they cease to believe the behavior works (whatever that means for them), they will stop.

As I will argue throughout this presentation, the implications of research along these lines are not limited to social marketing. It is often pointed out that consumers are active participants in the production of services in the private sector. If one sees this service production process as one of generating benefits, then shouldn't service marketers learn how to help consumers generate more of their own benefits? Shouldn't an accomplished chef-restaurateur teach her patrons to appreciate a fine meal? Shouldn't a record company educate classical music buyers about what they are hearing?

COSTS AND BENEFITS

Consider again exchange theory. Although our terminology will differ, most of us teach and write about the exchange process as one in which the consumer pays some costs and gets some benefits in return. We then suggest — in very naive terms — that "all" a marketer has to do to be more successful is to improve the benefit/cost ratio relative to alternative behaviors, including inaction. Many of us then go on to propose some form of the expectancy-value framework to analyze customer perceptions about the consequences of the behavior being recommended.

But I have always been struck by something inconsistent in our use of this model. On the one hand, in exchange theory, we conceptualize the consumer decision making process as one where the consumer compares a bundle of benefits to a bundle of costs. Yet, when researchers develop expectancy-value models, they rarely model cost and benefit consequences *separately*. It would seem to me to be a very useful line of research to explore the potential of the latter. One could ask:

1. Are better predictions of intentions and/or behavior achieved through the use of separate cost-bundle and benefit-bundle constructs, each with its own weighting coefficient?

2. If this makes sense, are the weighting coefficients useful bases for segmentation?

3. Are weighting coefficients linked to other constructs we use? For example, are cost-bundle coefficients associated with such traits such as risk aversion, self-efficacy, and so on?

4. Does the relative importance of the cost and benefit bundles change over the decision process?

The last-mentioned hypothesis stems, in part, from my experience in social marketing projects involving long term high involvement behaviors. I have come to the tentative conclusion that, in many such cases, the relative importance of costs versus benefits changes over the life of the decision process. In the early stages of the process, benefits are extremely important. If consumers cannot be convinced that there are personal benefits to be derived from a particular behavior, such as getting their child immunized for measles, then cost considerations are irrelevant — he or she is not even going to contemplate action. However, once benefits are perceived, then costs become paramount. Indeed, I have argued that in many campaigns it is foolish to continue promoting benefits to most target audiences. Most people already know the benefits of quitting smoking, detecting breast cancer early, or wearing a seat belt. What *keeps them from behaving* is the perception that the costs are too high. I would argue that this accounts for some of the findings in Rick Bagozzi's pioneering attitude modeling research on blood donation behavior. In recent months, I have been arguing to many social marketing campaign planners that perhaps late-stage marketing should focus on *cost-reduction*, not benefit enhancement. I would, however, like to see a more scientific basis for this argument.

STAGE MODELS OF BEHAVIOR

As the preceding comment suggests, my work in social marketing has significantly increased my interest in what we have called hierarchical models of consumer decision making and other social scientists call stage models. The behaviors we deal with are very highly involving. We are trying to influence behavior related to sexuality, motherhood, one's own body, one's children, and potentially fatal diseases. Because these issues are so central to the target audience's self-image, they are frequently very slow to change.

Through an advisory panel at the American Cancer Society on which I sit, I have become aware of a number of so-called staged approaches to behavior change. Among the more interesting is the work of Jim Prochaska at the University of Rhode Island (Prochaska 1991). Jim proposes six stages:

1. *Precontemplation* where the individual has no intention of changing, possibly through ignorance of the problem;

2. *Contemplation* where the individual is seriously thinking of changing in some reasonably short time horizon;

3. *Preparation* where the individual has formed an intention and is planning to actually take the behavior;

4. *Action* where the individual is clearly changing;

5. *Maintenance* where the individual is attempting to hold to the new pattern;

6. *Termination* where the individual is not tempted to re-engage in the old undesirable behavior.

Prochaska develops specific measurable markers to identify each stage and then develops marketing actions that will move the individual to the next stage. The goal is not to change a person from not doing to doing a behavior but to moving them along a process. This approach has been highly effective with smokers. It raises a number of interesting questions for those of us in consumer research:

1. In cases where processes appear to take place in stages, is it still appropriate to use the concept of "intention" as a dependent variable in behavioral studies? Is it not just appropriate to the contemplation stage?

2. Are Prochaska's six stages the appropriate ones for the commercial sector? Should, for example, the contemplation stage be divided further? In the action stage, is it useful, as Bagozzi and Warshaw (1989) would suggest, to distinguish between trying to act and acting?

3. Are the appropriate sets of predictor variables different for different transitions?

READINESS TO CHANGE

One of the realities of social marketing is that program managers must address enormous problems with limited funds. For this reason, I spend a great deal of my time urging program managers to focus much of their budgets very tightly each planning period on target markets they feel they can immediately influence. I have also tried to find ways to help them locate those who are in some sense "ready to change." This line of thinking has led me to hypothesize that an individual's readiness to change at any point may be a function of three, possibly additive, factors:

1. *Basic readiness*, a personality trait undoubtedly related to innovativeness, sensation-seeking, preference for stasis, risk proneness, and so on. It is what we mean when we say: Sally will try more new things than Fred will.

2. *Category-specific readiness*, a recognition that each individual will have a range around their "basic readiness" reflecting the many types of decisions they have to make. It is what we mean when we say that, while Sally will, in general, try more new behaviors, she is less willing to vacation in foreign countries than Fred is.

3. *Situation-specific readiness*, a recognition that circumstances may alter category-specific readiness. It is what we mean when we say that, when Sally got divorced, she was much more willing to undertake foreign travel than "normal" while Fred, after his divorce, was *less* likely to want to travel.

As you may know, situational factors have interested me for some time (Andreasen 1984). The work I have done linking status change to change in preferences is of particular interest to social marketers. They would be delighted to learn that it is generally true that individuals undergoing status change are much more likely than others to be "ready to change." Then they could concentrate their efforts on target markets undergoing status change. Immunization programs could be concentrated in geographical areas where immigrants have recently moved, contraception programs could target new mothers in hospitals, and Vitamin A programs could target workers just hired on at a factory.

I have also thought that we need to learn much more about what I have come to call *behavioral triggers*. In many situations in both social and commercial marketing, we find that consumers will become quite favorably disposed towards some action, yet delay a long time in carrying it out. All too often, some new situational factor emerges to deflect them against it. If we knew more about the critical stimuli that finally gets action, we could close more transactions, and diminish the influence of situational deterrents.

WHAT IS CHANGE?

Given that social marketing's bottom line typically involves change, I have begun to think more carefully about the concept of change itself and whether it would be useful to develop a new taxonomy of change. The innovation adoption researchers, of course, have visited this issue before and their distinctions may continue to be useful in a social marketing context. However, I have tended to look at the issue somewhat differently. In my view, social marketers are seeking to influence behaviors that involve: (a) *starting* a behavior, such as giving blood for the first time or beginning contraception; (b) *stopping* a behavior, such as giving up drugs or shoplifting; and (c) *switching* a behavior, such as driving 55 instead of 65-plus or eating a low cholesterol diet instead of a high cholesterol diet. This distinction raises some interesting questions:

1. Are the concepts we use to predict behavior change the same for all three types of change? Do they work the same way? For example, are the effects of perceived self-efficacy the same if one is trying to acquire a new skill where the self-efficacy issue is one of "can I learn this thing or do it the right way" than if one is trying to stop a behavior where the self-efficacy issue may be one of willpower?

2. If we are trying to get people to switch behaviors, should we really work with *dual* models, one that predicts the elimination of the old behavior and one that predicts the adoption of the new behavior?

Two other change dimensions are important in social marketing, both involving the social context of the change. One dimension is public-private. Many changes, such as stopping smoking, are *very public* and, in such cases, social norms can play a big role in bringing about the change. Other changes, such as getting an anti-contraception injection of Depo-Provera, are or can be *very private* and must come about with very personalized persuasion. The second dimension is whether the change comes about by *individual* action or must be made by *collectivities*, whether a whole community or a couple as in the case of AIDS prevention. This taxonomy suggests twelve types of behavior change. I believe we should ask whether standard behavior change models are equally appropriate to all 12 cases. It is, again, clearly an area in which we very much need your help.

METHODOLOGICAL OPPORTUNITIES AND CHALLENGES

There are numerous challenges in social marketing for those whose interest is primarily in methodology. And there are also some interesting incentives. First of all, for those who prefer to work with traditional survey methodologies, there will be the distinct pleasure of once again doing personal interviews and having very large samples. Much social marketing work is in developing countries. Personal interviewing costs for research can range from $6 in Turkey to $12 to $13 in the Philippines.

Second, for those who like to work with secondary datasets, a number of opportunities for large scale reanalyses will be emerging in the next few years. Social marketing has been around long enough in the family planning and child survival areas that major databases are now being put in place and I am hopeful that at some future time soon many of them will become available to researchers in ACR.

Those involved in post-modern field methodologies will also find much to interest them in social marketing. To cite one instance, social marketers have a major need for what they have come to call "rapid ethnography." They need a quick, valid, and reliable technology for understanding the diverse cultural traditions, group norms, tribal hierarchies, and values in developing countries where they work.

Finally, those interested in psychometrics might find intriguing the problems social marketers have in developing valid and reliable measures of complex cognitive and behavioral phenomena that can be applied to nonliterate populations. How does one develop an expectancy-value model without having a potentially biasing field interviewer read questions? Can pictorial scales be effective? What are the effects on validity of alternative methods of pictorial representation? Are these effects similar across Latin American, African, and Asian cultures? More generally, are *any* measurement techniques we would like to use in social marketing valid and reliable across cultures?

OTHER ADVANTAGES FOR SCHOLARS

Before concluding, I want to mention two other career advantages I see from carrying out research in social marketing. First, conducting research on social marketing can be expected to increase the number of publication outlets for your research. Whereas many journals in the traditional social sciences might minimize the value of articles researching choices of automobiles or coffee, they are less likely to be biased against studies of mothers' use of oral rehydration solution or Vitamin A.

I would also argue that work in social marketing can help enrich our classrooms. There is ample evidence that students in general and business school students in particular are turning away from the self-centered pursuits common in the 1980s and developing a growing interest in social issues. Our students care about the homeless and AIDS and drug addiction. Bringing knowledge and applications from social marketing into the classroom can have two important effects: (a) it can make discussions more animated and can capture the attention of marginal students; and (b) it can show business school students that the technology and concepts they are learning can have uses beyond business confines. While not ready to join the Peace Corps or sign up with HEALTHCOM in Mali, they are delighted to learn that many of the things we consumer behaviorists teach them can help them if they choose to work in their own communities with unwed teenage mothers, smokers, drug addicts or people with AIDS.

CONCLUSION

I have tried to argue here that involvement in social marketing is not just good for the soul. It can provide rich intellectual challenges to ACR members of widely varying interests. It can lead to new ways of thinking and teaching about the field. It can lead to new ideas and new publications. The insights we can derive will stretch our basic discipline of consumer behavior in ways that will benefit *all* of our target audiences. And it will increase our real-world relevance, an objective Bill Wells, for one, argues we have too often forsaken.

We have before us the opportunity to make the work we do relevant to making our society and the world a healthier and happier place. I ask you to join me. It can make a difference, personally, professionally and societally.

You will not regret it.

REFERENCES

Andreasen, Alan R. (1978), "The Ghetto Marketing Life Cycle: A Case of Underachievement," *Journal of Marketing Research*, 15 (February), 20-28.

_____, (1984), "Life Status Changes and Changes in Consumer Preferences and Satisfaction," *Journal of Consumer Research,* 11 (December), 784-794.

Bagozzi, Richard P. (1981) "Attitudes, Intentions, and Behavior: A Test of Some Key Hypotheses," *Journal of Personality and Social Psychology* 41, 607-627.

_____, and Paul Warshaw (1989), "Trying to Consume" *Journal of Consumer Research,*

Kotler, Philip and Gerald Zaltman (1971), "Social Marketing: An Approach to Planned Social Change," *Journal of Marketing*, 3-12.

Prochaska, James O., W.F. Velicer, C.C. DiClemente, E. Guadagnoli and J.S. Rossi (1991), "Patterns of Change: Dynamic Typology Applied to Smoking Cessation," *Multivariate Behavioral Research*, 83-107.

PRESENTATION OF THE FELLOW AWARD
Fellow in Consumer Behavior to James R. Bettman
Harold H. Kassarjian, UCLA

The Fellow in Consumer Research award - the highest honor that ACR can bestow on any individual - has been given to only eleven recipients in the past. Those individuals had emerged from marketing and statistics and psychology - scholars who crossed over and became consumer researchers, migrating from other disciplines.

This year, the award, goes to a recipient who is somewhat unlike the others that have stood here before. He is first and foremost a researcher in consumer behavior. Although he may not have realized it at the time, for his entire academic and scholarly career he has always been a consumer researcher. His undergraduate work touched upon consumer choice. His dissertation, albeit in Operations Research, was a consumer behavior dissertation.

But, before discussing the man, perhaps it is appropriate to reiterate the intent of the award. The Fellow in Consumer Behavior Award was designed to recognize that individual who has made a long term, major scholarly impact in consumer research. It was not to be an entitlement that one earns by writing enough articles or collecting enough cites. It was not for a single work or book or monograph. It was not to be a routine event. The status, *Fellow in Consumer Behavior*, was to be reserved as recognition for scholarly contributions spanning not just a few years but rather a sustained distinguished long term commitment to consumer research.

The recipient this year - James R. Bettman, breezed through the tortous nomination, selection, and confirmation process. The decision was not only received enthusiastically, but the phrase often heard was an exasperated, "It's about time!" For we all know that Bettman, without any doubt, is an intellectual giant - many of us think the very best our field has to offer.

Jim started his academic career at Yale University as a freshman, and stayed on for his doctorate. For his dissertation, he followed two consumers around a grocery store for a two month period asking them to verbalize their thoughts. Bettman was attempting to record and model the behavior of real consumers in real grocery stores long before any of us had heard the term *naturalistic inquiry*.

At UCLA we had heard rumors that there was a brilliant young doctoral student at Yale. We believed that very smart people think very powerful thoughts. If nothing else, Jim Bettman was very smart and we wanted him. Within a few years we were proven correct. This man had become the best reviewer the *Journal of Consumer Research* had on its team. In time he was on the editorial board for the *Journal of Marketing*, the *Journal of Marketing Research*, and several other major journals. He was to become the co-editor of the *Journal of Consumer Research* for seven years. During those years that medium was transformed into one of the major scholarly journals in the world.

Bettman is a Fellow of the American Psychological Association, a Fellow of the American Psychological Society, and he was elected president of ACR in 1987. Few may realize that he is also a superb administrator.

But the *Fellow in Consumer Behavior Award* is meant to recognize life-long contributions to consumer research and I have not yet said much about his research. That is because his research is well known to every person sitting in this audience. His monograph, *An Information Processing Theory of Consumer Choice,* has been required reading for all of us for more than a decade. It is arguably the most cited piece in our field. That book incited and abetted a revolution in the direction consumer research would take in the following decades and made the term *information processing* a common word in all our lives. It won the 1992 Converse Award.

So too, we have all read his *Journal of Marketing* paper on "Memory Factors in Consumer Choice," for which he won the 1979 Maynard Award. His wonderful piece with Capon and Lutz on Cognitive Algebra in Multi-attribute Attitude Models in the *Journal of Marketing Research* was a finalist for the 1980 O'Dell Award.

Yes, we all know and have marveled at his work - for example, consider his brilliantly conceived concept of constructive processing - and we all know the impact his work has had on all of us as researchers. And yet, only a few may know the full extent of his scholarship - a dozen papers in the *Journal of Consumer Research* - his first being in Volume 1, No. 1 of the Journal. Some dozen chapters in books, and a powerful new book about to be published by Cambridge University Press. He has some 50 other papers published in such places as the *Journal of Marketing Research, Journal of Business, Journal of Experimental Psychology, Management Science,* and on and on. He is the only person I know who has been asked to write two chapters in the *Annual Review of Psychology*, in two different fields. And there is a much more... .

But, let us not ignore teaching, for Jim is a professor's professor - inspiring, intellectually powerful, creative, and most of all he displays a charming sense of humor. He has served on more than 50 doctoral committees and as chair for 15 dissertations. Four of those, Mita Sujan, Chris Puto, Kevin Keller, and Itamar Simonson have won ten dissertation awards of various sorts among them. As might be expected, teaching awards were to come - the George Robbins award at UCLA and, at Duke, the highly prestigious campus wide recognition as *Scholar-Teacher of the Year*.

Eric Johnson commented not long ago, "It is, in fact, impossible to imagine what consumer behavior would be like today without Jim Bettman." We agree. A friend and award winning teacher, a gentleman, a powerful intellect, a brilliant researcher, an editor extroardinaire, a legendary reviewer, and a professor's professor. In addition, a party animal well known for his comedy routines.

It is with deeply felt humility and a feeling of great honor that I stand here and make the *Fellow in Consumer Behavior Award* to James R. Bettman ...

In recognition of his singular contribution to understanding of consumer information processing and choice making, as researcher, teacher, mentor, and editor.

FELLOW'S AWARD SPEECH
The Decision Maker Who Came In from the Cold
James R. Bettman, Duke University

I feel deeply privileged to have been elected a Fellow of the Association for Consumer Research. I would first like to express my profound thanks and gratitude to all those who have helped me over the years, especially my colleagues at UCLA and Duke, my extended set of colleagues from ACR, and my wife Joan and son David. Hal Kassarjian should be singled out for special recognition as an early mentor and source of encouragement. Finally, I would like to publicly thank a particularly important group to me, my doctoral students: Debbie Scammon, Jack Swasy, Hubert Gatignon, Mita Sujan, Chris Puto, Kevin Keller, Betsy Creyer, Itamar Simonson, Helen Anderson, Ron Goodstein, Pete Nye, Eloise Coupey, Carolyn Yoon, Ellen Garbarino, and Mary Frances Luce. Over the years, they have provided a constant source of new ideas and excitement.

In this paper, I will first provide a very brief historical perspective on my work in consumer information processing, then outline my current perspectives on consumer choice, and close by considering ways to raise the temperature of typically cold information processing models of consumer decision making.

HISTORICAL PERSPECTIVE

My path to an information processing viewpoint on consumer choice was quite convoluted and marked by many episodes of serendipity. The first bit of good fortune was my introduction as an undergraduate to the work of Herbert Simon. The piece which affected me the most was his paper "A Behavioral Model of Rational Choice" (Simon, 1955). Simon's pioneering idea of bounded rationality, that individuals have limited capabilities and must simplify the world in order to deal with it, played a major role in all of my later thinking on consumer choice.

A second piece of luck was my exposure as a graduate student to the edited book *Computers and Thought* (Feigenbaum and Feldman, 1963), which provided examples of research using the idea of bounded rationality to model the actual strategies used by problem solvers. The specific paper in the book which gave me the idea for my dissertation was Clarkson's model of the choice processes of a trust investor (Clarkson, 1963). His work gave me a method for *implementing* the ideas I was generating about consumer choice; I saw that I could use verbal protocols from actual consumer choice episodes to build models of those consumers' choice processes. In my dissertation research, I followed two consumers around the grocery store as they shopped over a six to eight week period. I asked them to think aloud while they were shopping, tape recorded these verbalizations, and then interpreted these data in developing decision net models of their choice processes.

After finishing my dissertation and going to UCLA in 1969, I continued my work on consumer information processing and published an article in the *Journal of Marketing Research* in 1971 which proposed a general model of decision and choice (Bettman, 1971). By the time I was due for my first sabbatical in 1975, I decided that I would try to write a book that would flesh out that model in more detail and review research relevant to consumer choice processes. While doing the research for the book I fortunately encountered three major ideas which provided the foundation for my future work and necessitated radically changing the simple 1971 framework: 1) the particular strategies people use depend upon the nature of the task (Payne, 1976); 2) a detailed task analysis of the choice environment can provide a great deal of insight into the nature of the strategies and heuristics which are likely to be used in that environment (Newell and Simon, 1972); and 3) decision strategies may be constructed or made up on the spot instead of being available in memory and simply implemented (Nakanishi, 1974).

At the time I began writing my book, it was becoming increasingly clear that the answer to the question "How do people make decisions?" should be "It depends." In 1975 I happened to see a manuscript version of John Payne's 1976 paper, which was clearly a tour de force. This paper began the transition from demonstrating that decision behavior was contingent to understanding why decision processes were contingent; it also provided a methodological blueprint for carrying out and analyzing process-tracing research on contingent processing (I had also been independently exposed to one aspect of that blueprint, monitoring information acquisitions, by Jack Jacoby (e.g., Jacoby, 1975; Jacoby, Chestnut, Weigl, and Fisher, 1976)).

Newell and Simon's (1972) concept of a task analysis was also a major factor in changing my thinking about choice processes. They argued that the structure of the task imposed constraints on the types of strategies that could be used; hence, understanding that structure provided insights into how individuals were likely to behave if they wished to be successful at that task. As I wrote the chapter on consumer decision processes for my book in the fall of 1975, I tried to do analyses of typical tasks faced by consumers. It quickly became apparent to me (and to others at about that time) that memory processes should play a major role in thinking about consumer decision making. Newell and Simon's task analysis idea, therefore, indirectly led to the focus on memory evident in my book.

The final idea, and one whose consequences I am still working out, was the notion that decision strategies may be constructed on the spot, made up on the fly, so to speak. Masao Nakanishi was the main instigator when, in typical fashion, he asked me a deceptively simple question one day. He asked me if I *really* believed that consumers had these complex decision nets that I pictured in my articles stored in memory. The implication, of course, was that he did not believe that. In thinking about it, I decided that I did not believe it either. This led me to develop ideas about constructive processing that played a major role in the chapter on decision processes in my book.

These ideas were central to the transformation in my thinking from the simple 1971 flowchart to the theory embodied in the 1979 book (Bettman, 1979). In the next section, I briefly discuss my current perspectives on consumer choice and then consider how to heat up consumer information processing research.

CURRENT PERSPECTIVES ON CONSUMER CHOICE

My current perspectives on choice processes in general and on consumer choice are described in detail elsewhere (Payne, Bettman, and Johnson, in press; Bettman, Johnson, and Payne, 1991), so I will outline these ideas only briefly here. Most of these ideas have been developed jointly with John Payne, Eric Johnson, and our graduate students, so I will usually say "we" in the following. Many of these perspectives represent further development of the three main ideas discussed in the previous section.

The focus of my current work is on strategy selection in decision making. One of the major empirical observations regarding decision behavior is that individuals use different strategies in different situations. We argue that this use of multiple strategies is generally an adaptive response by a limited capacity information processor. Two major goals of decision makers which help us to understand which strategy an individual will use in any given situation are the desire to make a good decision and the desire to conserve cognitive effort. We argue that individuals select strategies based upon tradeoffs between the accuracy a given strategy might attain in a particular choice environment and the cognitive effort required to execute that same strategy in that choice environment.

For any given choice environment, different strategies provide different levels of accuracy and require different amounts of cognitive effort. In addition, the same strategy may be characterized by differing accuracy and effort levels across different environments. By modeling various strategies as sequences of elementary information processes (e.g., comparisons, additions, eliminations), measuring cognitive effort using counts of such operations, and running computer simulations of these strategies, we are able to estimate accuracy and effort levels for each strategy and then make predictions about which strategies will be used in a particular choice task (e.g., Payne, Bettman, and Johnson, 1988). In general, this approach has been very successful in predicting the patterns of adaptive strategy selection individuals exhibit in a variety of situations (Payne, Bettman, and Johnson, in press). Hence, we believe that this accuracy/effort tradeoff approach provides a useful conceptual framework for understanding contingent decision processes.

Much of this work has assumed that the decison maker possesses a repertoire of strategies, evaluates the accuracy and effort levels characterizing those strategies for a particular choice, and chooses a strategy which represents a reasonable accuracy/ effort tradeoff for that task. However, we have extended that view to take account of the fact that individuals often learn about the structure of a choice task as they go along and use information they have already extracted from the task to decide what to do next. As noted above, this is a constructive view of choice, where individuals can be opportunistic and change their processing to exploit what they have learned. For example, a consumer may start to compare alternatives on what is a priori the most important attribute and discover that there is little variation on that attribute across alternatives. He or she might then try to consider another attribute but find it too difficult to understand the information, and so on. Individuals sometimes make spur of the moment shifts in processing direction instead of merely executing some strategy determined beforehand. This constructive view implies that the resulting heuristics will be very sensitive to specific salient features of the choice situation.

Constructive processing is consistent with our accuracy/effort viewpoint in the sense that we postulate that the on the spot shifts in direction are based upon local, momentary accuracy/effort assessments. For example, if an individual notes that all values on an attribute are similar across alternatives and shifts to another attribute, that shift reflects a tradeoff of the low benefits from continued processing of that attribute versus the effort required to process it. This leads to a dynamic view of contingent processing, where the nature of the choice task changes as the individual progresses.

We have focused above on the notion that individuals build strategies on the fly. However, another possible approach to constructive processing was proposed by Eloise Coupey (1990). She argued that an individual can restructure the available data by transformation, elimination, reordering, and so on. Then the individual can make a choice by applying an existing heuristic to the restructured data. Whether individuals take the data as given and construct a heuristic, take heuristics as given and restructure the data, or use a combination of these two methods, however, it is clear that at least in some instances people make things up as the choice progresses. This viewpoint is becoming more widespread. As we have emphasized (Payne, Bettman, and Johnson, 1992), an underlying theme of much recent behavioral decision research is that preferences and beliefs regarding objects and events of any complexity are often constructed in generating a response to a judgment or choice task (e.g., Slovic, Griffin, and Tversky, 1990; Tversky, Sattath, and Slovic, 1988).

COMING IN FROM THE COLD

Much research on consumer information processing, including my 1979 book, is "cold" cognition. That is, such "hot" constructs as feelings and emotion are given little emphasis. The models are overbearingly cognitive; like the tin man in the Wizard of Oz, these models have no heart. Hal Kassarjian's initial reaction to draft chapters of my 1979 book was that no one could think that much about consumer choices (actually, he would often glance over at me and say that maybe *one* consumer thought that much). I believe that the time has come to begin to redress this imbalance, lest we, to paraphrase my favorite fictional private eye, Kinsey Millhone, come perilously close to boring ourselves insensible with mental processes (Grafton, 1987, p. 64). Some very nice work has already been done in some areas, such as the work of Edell and Burke (1987) on the role of feelings in the processing of advertisements. I would like to propose two additional areas for making consumer information processing "hot" rather than "cold": 1) considering the effects of invoking autobiographical memories via marketing stimuli and 2) examining decision making under stress.

Invoking Autobiographical Memories

Consumer information processing researchers have generally focussed on the more obvious attributes or benefits of products. However, one major critique from postmodern scholars is that we cannot understand consumer behavior without taking a much more global view about what consumers are trying to accomplish (Belk, 1987). If we take a functional perspective and ask what role consumer behavior plays in people's lives, we may need to consider a broader or deeper set of concerns that individuals have when they make their consumer choices. That is, we will have to consider not only what products *do*, but what they *mean* to consumers.

For example, Belk (1988) argues compellingly that possessions play a major role in shaping and reflecting our identities. In particular, one important set of meanings that possessions have for individuals is the events, people, or past experiences that they symbolize (e.g., Belk, 1991; however, see Wallendorf and Arnould (1988) for evidence that such meanings vary across cultures). The study of autobiographical memories considers similar phenomena (Brewer, 1986). An autobiographical memory is a recollection of a particular episode from one's past, and one of the general properties of such memories is that they are affectively charged. That is, feelings and emotions are often associated with such memories.

Hans Baumgartner, Mita Sujan, and I have proposed that one way that advertisements can evoke emotions and feelings is to cue the retrieval of product-related autobiographical memories. In a series of three studies, we demonstrated that cuing autobiographical memories led to reduced analysis of and memory for product information, led to stronger reported feelings, and influenced ad evaluations (Baumgartner, Sujan, and Bettman, 1992). In current research (Sujan, Bettman, and Baumgartner, 1992), we argue that the extent of transfer of autobiographical affect to brand evaluations depends upon the degree to which the ad forges a link between the brand and the autobiographical memory.

Autobiographical memory is also an intriguing approach for studying attachment to possessions, products, or even brand names. In particular, the centrality of the people and events in the autobiographical memories associated with a possession, product, or brand name should be related to the degree of felt attachment. Autobiographical memories involving important events and people significant to the individual should lead to greater attachment.

These ideas about autobiographical memory can be extended in several directions. First, consumers often *anticipate* how products might play a role in future events (e.g., a consumer may imagine the effect of wearing a particular outfit at a major social event). Thus, consumers may generate *autobiographical anticipations* when they envision possible outcomes for specific future events in which they themselves play a role. Again, the centrality of the events and individuals in these autobiographical anticipations may greatly influence how a consumer thinks about the product; if the anticipations include very important events/individuals, the consumer may become *pre-attached* to the product. That is, the product comes to have meaning to the individual prior to its use or perhaps even prior to its purchase. Such anticipations may also constrain the set of options an individual is willing to consider; for example, once the consumer has pictured him/herself in a particular type of outfit, he or she may find it difficult to consider other styles (I thank Julie Edell for this idea).

A second idea for generalizing these ideas about autobiographical memory involves emotional reactions to aesthetic events (Walters, 1989; Frijda, 1989). That is, a novel or a movie or an ad may make us teary-eyed even if no particular event from our past is evoked. How does this occur? As the papers by Walters and Frijda point out, it is very difficult to develop a theoretical framework for understanding such responses. However, I believe that they represent both an important category of emotional responses and an intriguing area for future research.

Decision Making Under Stress

In my dissertation and several studies following from it (e.g., Bettman, 1973), I attempted to examine the idea of perceived risk. My interest was sparked to a large extent by introspection; sometimes choosing involved feelings of great uncertainty and perhaps even worry or anxiety. In retrospect, my work at that time missed the point, since I tried to characterize risk cognitively rather than at a more visceral level. I have recently begun to consider the more general topic of individuals' reactions to decision making under stress.

In our first work involving stress, John Payne, Eric Johnson, and I examined how individuals respond to time pressure (Payne, Bettman, and Johnson, 1988). We found that individuals accelerated their processing, focussed on a subset of the available information, and changed processing strategies. In particular, under high time pressure individuals adapted by examining at least some information about all alternatives quickly rather than attempting to examine a limited number of options in more depth (see Eisenhardt (1989) for similar results from a case study of the computer industry).

Such externally-imposed stress is not the only possible source of stress, however. As in the case of perceived risk, individuals can generate stress and emotion *while* making a decision. In fact, there is evidence that generated stress has different effects than externally-imposed stress (Christianson, 1992). How might stress be generated during a decision? At least in part, stress and emotions are generated by autobiographical anticipations regarding the outcomes of a decision, the reactions of others, and so on (see Simonson, 1992 for an example of research considering anticipations of regret and responsibility). We hypothesize that the degree of stress/emotional response generated by such anticipations will be, as before, a function of the importance or centrality of the events and people involved. In addition, the degree of emotional response may be a function of the extent to which the anticipations contain the specific core relational themes characterizing different emotions (Lazarus, 1991). For example, anticipations of experiencing irrevocable loss would lead to sadness, anticipations of transgressing a moral imperative would lead to guilt, or anticipations of being slighted or demeaned to anger.

How might stress and emotion affect decision making? John Payne, Mary Frances Luce, and I have hypothesized in recent work in progress that stress generated during a decision makes any given decision process both more effortful and more error-prone. Given our accuracy/effort framework, that would imply greater use of simpler strategies. In addition, recent work on the effects of emotional stress on memory suggests that the level of emotion generated during a choice task will affect the type and amount of information recalled about the alternatives (i.e., higher emotion might lead to better recall of information central to the choice but less accurate memory for more peripheral items (Christianson, 1992)). Finally, we feel that introducing a broader range of dependent measures (e.g., feelings of conflict or the desire to procrastinate or avoid the choice) will provide more insights into some of the affective consequences of stress and emotion for decision making.

Autobiographical anticipations have emerged as a potentially important construct both in examining product meanings and in considering decision making under stress. Hence, in the next section I briefly consider the nature of autobiographical anticipations.

The Nature of Autobiographical Anticipations

How can we characterize autobiographical anticipations? We can probably say without much controversy that such anticipations, like autobiographical memories, are often affectively charged. However, what principles govern the elicitation and effects of these anticipations? For example, is their elicitation subject to principles similar to those of memory retrieval? The work of Marcia Johnson may be very relevant in answering such questions (e.g., Johnson and Raye, 1981; Johnson, Raye, Wang, and Taylor, 1979). Johnson has carefully studied the differences between and interactions among memory for real and imagined events. For example, she and her colleagues have shown that estimates of the frequency of actual events can be influenced by the degree to which similar events have been imagined (Johnson et al., 1979). In our context, if a consumer imagines certain sorts of uses involving a product before purchase (the notion of pre-attachment discussed above), this may later influence the consumer's recall of the frequency of that sort of product usage after purchase. Thus, pre-attachment can potentially influence both actual future usage patterns and the consumer's memory for those patterns.

However, actual events and autobiographical anticipations need not agree. As Kahneman and Snell (1990; 1992) have pointed out, individuals often may not have good insight into their future tastes and preferences. In addition, others involved in the event may not react to an individual's product choices as he or she had anticipated. It would be fascinating to study how such conflicts affect the resulting autobiographical memory for the event and anticipations for future events. In general, I believe that research on autobiographical anticipations represents a very fertile opportunity for consumer researchers.

CONCLUSIONS

The ideas above reflect my feeling that we should "come in from the cold" and thaw consumer information processing research by making it more "hot." Note that in several of the cases described above, insights from interpretive studies of consumer behavior have been used to generate ideas for studying consumer information processing in a different light, albeit still experimentally. In my view, such complementarity between research approaches, rather than competition, is both extremely desirable and potentially quite productive (see also McQuarrie and Mick, 1992).

Finally, as Stephen Jay Gould (1989) has emphasized, history is highly contingent. If we started the clock again and allowed evolution to unfold, the chances we would end up with humans and the other creatures we see today are probably vanishingly small. The same could be said for my journeys in consumer information processing, which have been subject to enormous serendipity. I am certainly glad they turned out the way they did and that I have had the great honor of being with you today.

REFERENCES

Baumgartner, Hans, Mita Sujan, and James R. Bettman (1992). Autobiographical Memories, Affect, and Consumer Information Processing. *Journal of Consumer Psychology, 1* (1), 53-82.

Belk, Russell W. (1987). ACR Presidential Address: Happy Thought. In Melanie Wallendorf & Paul F. Anderson (Eds.), *Advances in Consumer Research, Volume 14* (pp. 1-4). Provo, UT: Association for Consumer Research.

Belk, Russell W. (1988). Possessions and the Extended Self. *Journal of Consumer Research, 15* (September), 139-168.

Belk, Russell W. (1991). Possessions and the Sense of Past. In Russell W. Belk (Ed.), *Highways and Buyways: Naturalistic Research from the Consumer Behavior Odyssey* (pp. 114-130). Provo, UT: Association for Consumer Research.

Bettman, James R. (1971). The Structure of Consumer Choice Processes. *Journal of Marketing Research, 8* (November), 465-471.

Bettman, James R. (1973). Perceived Risk and Its Components: A Model and Empirical Test. *Journal of Marketing Research, 10* (May), 184-190.

Bettman, James R. (1979). *An Information Processing Theory of Consumer Choice*. Reading, MA: Addison-Wesley.

Bettman, James R., Eric J. Johnson, and John W. Payne (1991). Consumer Decision Making. In Thomas S. Robertson & Harold H. Kassarjian (Eds.), *Handbook of Consumer Behavior* (pp. 50-84). Englewood Cliffs, NJ: Prentice-Hall.

Brewer, William F. (1986). What Is Autobiographical Memory? In David C. Rubin (Ed.), *Autobiographical Memory* (pp. 25-49). Cambridge, England: Cambridge University Press.

Christianson, Sven-Åke (1992). Emotional Stress and Eyewitness Memory: A Critical Review. *Psychological Bulletin, 112* (September), 284-309.

Clarkson, Geoffrey P. E. (1963). A Model of the Trust Investment Process. In Edward A. Feigenbaum & Julian Feldman (Eds.), *Computers and Thought* (pp. 347-371). New York: McGraw-Hill.

Coupey, Eloise (1990). Decision Restructuring in Consumer Choice. Doctoral dissertation, Fuqua School of Business, Duke University.

Edell, Julie A. and Marian Chapman Burke (1987). The Power of Feelings in Understanding Advertising Effects. *Journal of Consumer Research, 14* (December), 421-433.

Eisenhardt, Kathleen M. (1989). Making Fast Strategic Decisions in High Velocity Environments. *Academy of Management Journal, 32* (September), 543-575.

Feigenbaum, Edward A. and Julian Feldman (Eds.). (1963). *Computers and Thought*. New York: McGraw-Hill.

Frijda, Nico H. (1989). Aesthetic Emotions and Reality. *American Psychologist, 44* (December), 1546-1547.

Gould, Stephen Jay (1989). *Wonderful Life*. New York: W. W. Norton.

Grafton, Sue (1987). *'D' Is for Deadbeat*. New York: Bantam Books.

Jacoby, Jacob (1975). Perspectives on a Consumer Information Processing Research Program. *Communication Research, 2* (July), 203-215.

Jacoby, Jacob, Robert W. Chestnut, Karl C. Weigl, and William Fisher (1976). Pre-purchase Information Acquisition: Description of a Process Methodology, Research Paradigm, and Pilot Investigation. In Beverlee B. Anderson (Ed.), *Advances in Consumer Research, Volume 3* (pp. 306-314). Chicago: Association for Consumer Research.

Johnson, Marcia K. and Carol L. Raye (1981). Reality Monitoring. *Psychological Review, 88* (January), 67-85.

Johnson, Marcia K., Carol L. Raye, Alvin Y. Wang, and Thomas H. Taylor (1979). Fact and Fantasy: The Roles of Accuracy and Variability in Confusing Imaginations with Perceptual Experiences. *Journal of Experimental Psychology: Human Learning and Memory, 5* (May), 229-240.

Kahneman, Daniel and Jackie Snell (1990). Predicting Utility. In Robin M. Hogarth (Ed.), *Insights in Decision Making: A Tribute to Hillel J. Einhorn* (pp. 295-310). Chicago: University of Chicago Press.

Kahneman, Daniel and Jackie Snell (1992). Predicting a Changing Taste: Do People Know What They Will Like? *Journal of Behavioral Decision Making, 5* (July-September), 187-200.

Lazarus, Richard S. (1991). Progress on a Cognitive-Motivational-Relational Theory of Emotion. *American Psychologist, 46* (August), 819-834.

McQuarrie, Edward F. and David G. Mick (1992). On Resonance: A Critical Pluralistic Inquiry into Advertising Rhetoric. *Journal of Consumer Research, 19* (September), 180-197.

Nakanishi, Masao (1974). Decision-net Models and Human Information Processing. In G. David Hughes & Michael L. Ray (Eds.), *Buyer/Consumer Information Processing* (pp. 75-88). Chapel Hill, NC: University of North Carolina Press.

Newell, Allen and Herbert A. Simon (1972). *Human Problem Solving*. Englewood Cliffs, NJ: Prentice-Hall.

Payne, John W. (1976). Task Complexity and Contingent Processing in Decision Making: An Information Search and Protocol Analysis. *Organizational Behavior and Human Performance, 16* (August), 366-387.

Payne, John W., James R. Bettman, and Eric J. Johnson (1988). Adaptive Strategy Selection in Decision Making. *Journal of Experimental Psychology: Learning, Memory, and Cognition, 14* (July), 534-552.

Payne, John W., James R. Bettman, and Eric J. Johnson (1992). Behavioral Decision Research: A Constructive Processing Perspective. *Annual Review of Psychology, 43*, 87-131.

Payne, John W., James R. Bettman, and Eric J. Johnson (In press). *The Adaptive Decision Maker.* Cambridge, England: Cambridge University Press.

Simon, Herbert A. (1955). A Behavioral Model of Rational Choice. *Quarterly Journal of Economics, 69*, 99-118.

Simonson, Itamar (1992). The Influence of Anticipating Regret and Responsibility on Purchase Decisions. *Journal of Consumer Research, 19* (June), 105-118.

Slovic, Paul, Dale Griffin, and Amos Tversky (1990). Compatibility Effects in Judgment and Choice. In Robin M. Hogarth (Ed.), *Insights in Decision Making: A Tribute to Hillel J. Einhorn* (pp. 5-27). Chicago: University of Chicago Press.

Sujan, Mita, James R. Bettman, and Hans Baumgartner (1992). Autobiographical Memories and Consumer Judgments. Working paper, Pennsylvania State University.

Tversky, Amos, Shmuel Sattath, and Paul Slovic (1988). Contingent Weighting in Judgment and Choice. *Psychological Review, 95* (July), 371-384.

Wallendorf, Melanie and Eric J. Arnould, E. J. (1988). "My Favorite Things": A Cross-cultural Inquiry into Object Attachment, Possessiveness, and Social Linkage. *Journal of Consumer Research, 14* (March), 531-547.

Walters, Kerry S. (1989). The Law of Apparent Reality and Aesthetic Emotions. *American Psychologist, 44* (December), 1545-1546.

The ACR Match Game–1992
J. Jeffrey Inman, University of Southern California

The Problem: Assign each of over 150 papers to three of over 200 reviewers such that each reviewer receives no more than three papers and such that the paper/reviewer "fit" is maximized across 92 content areas and 46 method areas.

Such was the task for this year's ACR conference (or, for that matter, next year's conference and most other academic conferences). In the past, the solution would consist of laying out the papers and reviewers on a large table and going through the assignment process manually. This year's ACR conference organizers asked me to attempt to automate the process somewhat. The results are described in the following paragraphs in the hope that interested readers in general and prospective authors and reviewers in particular will contribute their ideas for improvements that can be designed into the 1993 ACR. Please address suggestions to me at MC-1421, Dept of Marketing, School of Business Administration, University of Southern California, Los Angeles, CA 90089-1421. Alternatively, my telephone and fax numbers are, respectively, (213) 740-5052 and 740-7828 and my BITNET is INMAN@USCVM.

So far, only the initial stage of the process is automated (i.e., calculating the numbers of matches between reviewers and papers). The actual assignment of particular papers to particular reviewers remains a manual process. Below are key aspects of the process:

Input: In the call for papers in the December 1991 ACR newsletter, each author was asked to indicate all relevant content areas from a list of 92 content areas and 46 method areas. Prospective reviewers performed a similar task regarding their own expertise in the content and method areas.

Computer Package: Lotus 1-2-3.

Entry Format: Two p x 92 and r x 92 content matrices and two p x 46 and r x 46 method matrices were constructed, where p was the number of papers (152 this year) and r was the number of prospective reviewers (over 200). Matrix cells indicated the content or method areas that were indicated by the paper's authors and the prospective reviewers. For example, a paper/content matrix cell was coded 1 if the paper's author checked that particular content area and 0 otherwise.

Matrix Manipulation: The paper and reviewer content matrices were multiplied together, resulting in an r x p matrix. A cell in this matrix indicated the *number* of content matches between each reviewer and each paper. The same was done for the method matrices.

Assigning Papers to Reviewers: The two matrices were printed and it was manually ensured that: (1) each paper was assigned to 3 reviewers, (2) that the number of matches between each reviewer and each paper was as high as possible, and (3) that no reviewer was assigned more than 3 papers. This basically amounted to looking down the column for a paper and picking off the reviewers with the most matches on that paper, with constraint (3) occasionally coming into play. Content area matches were weighted more heavily than method matches because most authors and reviewers indicated very few (none in many cases) method areas. These matches were reported back to the conference chairs, who then verified the matches and mailed out the papers to the reviewers. In addition, matches were constrained such that no paper was judged by a reviewer from the same school and such that no more than one novice reviewer was assigned to a paper.

FUTURE PLANS

Optimally, one would like for the computer to handle all of the mundane work, leaving only the portion requiring intricate tradeoffs in human hands. Below are some of the changes that I would make if asked to perform this task for next year's conference:

Input: These should be redesigned and shortened. Many input categories were scarcely used, needlessly complicating both the matrix multiplication and the matching process. In particular, the list of method areas should be drastically reduced.

Matrix Manipulation: The content and method match matrices could be summed together into a single matrix with the added condition that there must be at least one reviewer/paper match on both fronts, otherwise the cell value is zero.

Assignment: The process could be transferred to Excel to leverage its integer programming capabilities and automate the "easy" initial stage of the actual reviewer/paper assignment process. The later stages, where the constraints become active (e.g., no more than 3 papers per reviewer), will probably be best done manually.

SUMMARY

By far the most important component in the process is the quality of input provided by both authors and reviewers. With over 150 papers and nearly 200 reviewers, the process of assigning prospective papers to reviewers can improve only if the content and method areas are thoroughly selected by both authors and reviewers.

The Polish Consumer in Transition: Shopping Warsaw's Street Vendors and Open Air Markets

Terrence H. Witkowski, California State University, Long Beach[1]

ABSTRACT

Selling a broad assortment of merchandise, street vendors and open air markets have spread rapidly throughout Warsaw and other Polish cities. This paper reports an ethnographic study that investigated dealer locations, displays, wares, marketplace behavior, and consumer perspectives. The paper also discusses the rise of and outlook for street retailing in Poland and suggests a few emergent themes in post-communist consumer behavior.

INTRODUCTION

Poland's consumer culture is undergoing a difficult transition from state socialism to a free enterprise system. The economic reforms introduced on and subsequent to January 1, 1990 are encouraging privatization, competition, and capitalism (Sachs and Lipton 1990). More than at any time in its past, this Eastern European nation is opening itself to the people, products, and ideas of the West and beyond. Since these unprecedented changes are of historic proportions, they should be observed, recorded, and analyzed while they are happening.

During the 1980s, Poles had money to spend but little to buy because the communist regime produced too few consumer goods, closed off imports, and subsidized prices. Consumers coped by waiting in line, watching other people's shopping bags for information on product availability, and "cruising" shops in the hope that scarce goods possibly would arrive unexpectedly (King 1986). In 1990, after the government eliminated subsidies, dropped trade restrictions, and made the zloty a convertible currency, goods began to flood into the country and stores became well-stocked at long last (Tully 1990). The only remaining queues were those to receive shopping baskets and to pay cashiers. Prices have risen to world levels, which are often beyond the reach of the average Polish worker who earns, in late 1992, about $200 a month.

Polish consumers are experiencing new marketing arrangements, especially in the distributive trades where most wholesale and retail businesses have been privatized. One notable and sometimes controversial development has been the explosive growth in the number of street vendors and open air markets throughout the country. To investigate this phenomenon, observational, interview, and photographic data were collected at several sites in central Warsaw in November, 1990, and again in August, 1991. The following sections review some relevant literature that informed the study, describe its methodology, and present its findings. Factors that encourage and threaten informal retailing in Poland are discussed next, followed by a concluding section that offers a short list of emergent themes deserving of further research.

RELEVANT LITERATURE

There has been a reasonably active research stream on Polish marketing beginning with two articles in the *Journal of Marketing* by J. Hart Walters (1964, 1975). Observing great improvements in product availability and retail service over a period of twelve years, Walters (1975) concluded that Poland had entered its own "marketing era." More recently, the *Journal of Business Research* featured the work of seven Polish marketing scholars from the University of Lodz (Woodside and Dennis 1986). Having lived through the serious social conflicts and economic troubles of the early 1980s, the authors present a bleak view of their system. These, as well as additional descriptive (King 1983, 1986, 1989) and comparative (Dietl and Iwinska-Knop 1989) papers, have expanded knowledge of marketing in a centrally planned economy. However, given Eastern Europe's remarkable political transformation since 1989, this literature is quickly becoming obsolete.

Because of their methodological relevance and substantive contributions, several studies of non-store retailing in the U.S. (Belk, Sherry, and Wallendorf 1988; Belk, Wallendorf, and Sherry 1989; and Sherry 1990A, 1990b) have guided the present investigation. Often working in teams, consumer researchers have used qualitative methods to describe and analyze swap meets, flea markets, and other types of outdoor periodic sales. With a strong anthropological flavor, their work has pointed out the importance of "alternative conduits" for the distribution and lateral recycling of goods, the informal (underground) and festive dimensions of marketing behavior, and the strong desire for personal freedom (coupled with a tendency toward rule-breaking) exhibited by dealers. The dealer/informants in these studies generally operate from privately owned, rural and suburban venues and trade heavily in used and antique merchandise.

More comparable to their urban counterparts in Warsaw who sell mostly new goods, are the itinerant street vendors of New York City studied by Greenberg, Sherman, Topol, and Cooperman (1980). Based on direct observation and interviews at several sites, the investigators found that many peddlers are recent immigrants who work for larger-scale operators. They do not necessarily compete with fixed-location stores in terms of price. Instead, their mobility enables them to put merchandise in places convenient for customers. Street vendors take sales away from smaller stores, cause sidewalk congestion, and reduce tax revenues because of unreported income. Concluding that street peddling is parasitic because it depends upon the traffic generated by other stores, the researchers argue for the creation of designated, permanent markets separate from major retail districts.

RESEARCH METHODOLOGY

Polish marketing institutions and consumers have received press coverage (see, for example, Engelberg 1990; *The Economist* 1990a; Gajewski 1990; Tully 1990), but serious academic inquiry has not been able to keep pace with the rapidly changing environment. Thus, an interpretive approach, using naturalistic or qualitative methods, is an appropriate way of seeking knowledge (Hudson and Ozanne 1988). Because so little was known a priori, this research used an emergent design, one that builds and revises "understanding of the phenomenon as it occurs *in situ*" (Belk, Wallendorf, and Sherry 1989, p. 3). The design remained flexible in the face of unanticipated problems and opportunities the investigator encountered in the field.

From the beginning, the project emphasized four different but complementary types of data collection: observation, participant observation, unstructured interviews, and photography. The investigator observed merchandising and buyer behavior at several adjoining research sites. Shopping the street vendors showed the

---

[1] The author would like to acknowledge the financial support of the Center for International Education, California State University, Long Beach.

kinds of goods available and at what price. Visits to the open air markets provided exposure to marketing development and the penetration of foreign goods. To obtain more insight into dealer practices, the investigator purchased items in several different locations. With the help of a translator, the investigator interviewed dealers which provided insights into their knowledge of and attitudes toward the retailing process.

Data were recorded in fieldnotes and in an investigator's journal. A microcassette recorder was used at the sites and the audiotapes, along with further observations, were transcribed into fieldnotes the same evening. Taping was especially useful during the unstructured interviews when conversation flowed too quickly to be written down. The investigator aspired to the goals of comprehensiveness, accuracy, and timeliness (Belk, Sherry, and Wallendor 1988) and ultimately aimed to produce a "thick description" (Geertz 1973). The journal, a record of the investigator's personal feelings and experiences as the "research instrument," was compiled in a similar manner.

Finally, photographs were an extremely useful mnemonic device that helped the investigator cope with information overload at the research site. Photographs captured a range of phenomena from product assortments and types of displays to crowd activity. However, during the November visit, this method of data collection was hampered somewhat by cold and rainy weather and by very low light levels even at noon. Further, the sites were often very crowded with shoppers who blocked views of the vendors. One sometimes had difficulty just walking around.

RESEARCH FINDINGS

Research Sites

Warsaw, the capital of Poland, is also its largest city with a population of about 1.8 million. Largely destroyed during the Second World War, it has been rebuilt with rather drab socialist architecture. Downtown Warsaw bustles with pedestrian and vehicular traffic and appears very active commercially. During the November field research, a presidential campaign and election contributed to the feeling of urban excitement.

A great many street vendors, easily numbering in the thousands, were found throughout Warsaw's central district and in the nearby Old City, an extensive urban area consisting of carefully restored 17th-century buildings. Their numbers had grown dramatically during the previous two years. In early 1989, street retailing was limited to a few flower sellers, artists who catered to the tourist trade, and the small kiosks of convenience items operated by the SPOLEM chain (King 1989). Once the communist government fell, more and more independent fruit and vegetable peddlers began to arrive, opening the way for a veritable onslaught of vendors of all kinds.

The largest open air market in central Warsaw was situated in Defilad Square outside the Palace of Culture and Science (PCS), a "Socialist Gothic" skyscraper given by Stalin to the Polish people in the 1950s. In November 1990, the greatest number of vendors congregated on the north side. By the following summer, a second large concentration had formed on the east side near the Central Railway Station. Across Marszalkowska boulevard, vendors had taken over the sidewalks for several hundred yards on both sides of the steel and glass CENTRUM department store. In places, tables and booths were stacked three deep. However, by August 1991, city authorities had forced virtually all of them to move somewhere else. Dealers also sold outside the fashionable boutiques along Chmielna, Nowy Swiat, and Krakowskie Przedmiesce streets and from the sidewalks in front of the Marriott/LOT complex. Additional vendors worked Warsaw's Old City, a twenty minute walk to the northwest of the PCS. Still another large open air market was located in the Praga district on the opposite side of the Vistula River.

A final entrepreneurial venue could be found in the spacious pedestrian underpasses downtown. During the November visit, these sites, which also housed small, state-owned retail shops, teemed with vendors (including a number of Soviets) selling a great variety of items. At times, several musical groups, comprised of older men playing popular songs, imparted a somewhat festive atmosphere to the underpasses. These marketplaces also had a more pathetic aspect. Romanian Gypsy women and their small children begged for money. Some of the vendor assortments, not unlike those of homeless persons in New York's East Village, could be purchased in their entirety for just a few dollars. By August, 1991, far fewer vendors were working the underpasses.

Displaying Merchandise

The street vendors physically presented their wares in a multitude of ways. Many simply spread their goods over a cloth or some cardboard placed on the ground, a sidewalk, or a low cement wall, while others set up folding tables and other simple portable stands to raise their merchandise off the ground. These people typically had about 20 square feet of "display" space. Some vendors parked their cars on the sidewalks and sold through the front window (especially for cigarette sales), off the rear gate if they owned a hatchback or station wagon, or from an assortment placed on the hood. Still other vendors sold from free-standing camping tents, from tents that attached to the back of an automobile, and from small trailers towed to the site.

Hundreds of dealers had steel shelters called *szczeki* (jaws) that folded shut and stayed on site at night. When open for business, these stands were about eight feet across and consisted of a roof, a rear wall lined with shelves, and sometimes a floor made from wood slats attached to wooden rails. The person running the booth stood or sat in a chair and is generally separated from the customer by a table loaded with merchandise. A few shelters contained so many items that inventory had to be removed before shop could be closed and locked for the night.

The largest, most luxurious, and least mobile stalls were made of unpainted wood. About twelve feet on a side, they looked like little one-room cottages. Dealers sat inside behind a counter or worked the porch where extra merchandise was kept. The store could be heated (an advantage in cold weather) and illuminated to permit night sales. At closing, dealers brought everything inside and locked the door. In November, several of these structures were under construction. Although the steel shelters and wood kiosks were the most frequently encountered booths, there were many other variations. It was not uncommon for more than one person to be minding the store at the same time. Only a few of these tiny shops had exterior signs.

Kinds of Merchandise

Merchandise was quite varied, but tended toward smaller, more transportable items. Food products were available in great abundance. Some vendors dealt in fresh fruits, especially apples and bananas; others sold rich creams, cheeses, and sausages; and still others specialized in chocolates and candies. Off to one side of the open air market next to the PCS, an entire row of butchers sold chicken and beef. There was no evidence that any government health codes were being enforced.

Vendors also offered numerous assortments of packaged goods. Soaps, toothpastes, hair care products, cosmetics, and other personal hygiene items were abundant. Shoes, socks, sweaters, and jackets were the most typical lines of wearing apparel. Audio and video cassettes were popular items offered by dozens of dealers whose stock usually included a great many American artists in boxes and often printed with sexually provocative labels. Other common lines ranged from toys to housewares. A few dealers sold VCRs, but their inventory typically consisted of no more than a few units and some accessory items.

Many of the more modest dealers sold books, largely paperbacks, and most assortments had at least one title in English. One could also purchase books in German, Russian, and sometimes French. In the pedestrian underpasses a few individuals peddled small assortments of pens and pencils. A table run by three old women sold plastic tote bags like the ones given away by U.S. department stores. One very small but audacious dealer on Nowy Swiat Street sold birds, fish, brine shrimp, and other supplies within a few feet of a pet store. Although a few street vendors in the Old City sold manufactured goods, primarily audio cassettes, many more sold contemporary and folk arts and crafts. These included mediocre oil and watercolor paintings, somewhat better silver and amber jewelry, and a good selection of toys and Russian-made nesting dolls.

Aside from foods and printed material, the great majority of products sold on the streets and in the open market came from outside Poland. Germany appeared to be a common source, but a good selection of American, French, Italian, Czechoslovakian, and Soviet goods were also for sale. The investigator determined country of origin by reading the writing on the product or its package. However, one needed to use caution. A close inspection of some boxes of hair coloring printed with Cyrillic lettering revealed that they were actually produced in the former German Democratic Republic for the Soviet market.

Marketplace Behavior

During the November fieldwork, over two-thirds of the shops in the open market closed by 6 pm with the remainder locking up soon thereafter. The only shop observed keeping later hours sold sexual paraphernalia. Perhaps because of better lighting, the kiosks near the department stores and the vendors in the pedestrian underpasses kept somewhat longer hours. Very few dealers worked on Sunday except those selling souvenirs to tourists visiting the Old City.

The American dollar, virtually a second currency in Poland, was readily accepted by some dealers in the open air market. The investigator tried to haggle over price, but was not successful, perhaps because of language difficulties. Thus, the firmness of prices, as well as the extent of market pitching (Sherry 1988), is still unknown. Prices were seldom marked on packages or on products. Many dealers were able to state their prices in English as well as Polish.

One vendor, who sold toothpastes, soaps, deodorants, hair care products, and other packaged goods, said he purchased his merchandise from Polish wholesalers in Warsaw. He also was trying to buy directly from the factory in Germany. Buying toothpaste from the manufacturer cost 1.5 DM per unit; from the wholesaler it cost 3 DM. This dealer, who also owned a second booth, understood the economies of purchasing in quantity. He said he earned as much in one week at the open market as in four at his old job. He did not have any plans for future expansion.

He rented his space in the open market from the city. Some dealers questioned whether the authorities had the right to collect rents and some had stopped paying because they believed the money did not go to the city, but instead lined the pockets of officials. The rental rate had been 2000 zl a day in February 1990. Because of the high rate of inflation in early 1990, rentals increased to 5000 zl, then 10,000 zl, and, by November, the informant vendor was paying 50,000 zl a day, or a little over $5 at the then current exchange rate of 9500 zl to one US dollar. Dealers were required to pay a week in advance and some were asked for "guarantee" money ranging from 100,000 to 1,200,000 zl.

Another vendor, a tall man about 30 years of age whose booth supported he and his family, had recently worked in Toronto, but said he could make more money selling at the open market. He carried a line of colorful plastic items for the kitchen, many of which were manufactured in Czechoslovakia. He too purchased from local wholesalers some of whom were also newly established private companies (Styczek 1991). According to Normand (1990), a few dealers do buy direct from manufacturers.

In the open air market near the PCS, numerous Soviets sold merchandise ranging from small toys and handicrafts to power tools and, in one instance, a Lada automobile priced at $3000. These dealers stood outside for long periods of time in the cold, rainy November weather and in the hot August sun. Most had ten to twenty square feet of display area, frequently placing their wares on the ground, on steps, or on a low cement wall. Their merchandise got wet when it rained and dusty in the summer. Could it really be worth their while to come such a long way (one man said he was from Kiev and one car had Lithuanian tags) for what appeared to be such smallscale retailing? Powers (1991) interviewed one Latvian who claimed he could earn the equivalent of $2000 in three to four days.

Consumer Perspectives

One afternoon, an old woman in the open market grumbled "Where will this all end?" Although she seemed to be shopping herself, the enormous and rapid changes in her environment must be difficult for her to fully comprehend. After four decades of socialist marketing that purposefully limited alternatives, many Poles will have to learn the shopping arts of comparing, evaluating, and making choices. The transition from a centrally planned communist society to a free-enterprise democracy is not universally applauded in Poland. Very conservative attitudes persist in rural areas and among older people and the lower classes.

Yet, consider another informant, a nicely dressed, apparently middle-class Polish woman. She was first observed reading the English-language newspaper, *The Warsaw Voice*, something she liked to do in order to practice her English. She preferred the current situation (available goods, but high prices by Polish standards) to what it had been (few goods, low prices) because now, as she put it, people have things to see and touch and hope to acquire. Her behavior and attitudes bespoke adaptability and a future orientation. She is likely to become a skilled consumer. In their dress, hygiene, and comportment, Warsaw's women appear to be somewhat more cosmopolitan and modern than its men.

STREET RETAILING: INCENTIVES AND THREATS

Clearly, post-communist economic policies have provided strong stimuli for Warsaw's street vendors and large open air markets. A convertible currency and free trade policies mean that goods can now be more readily purchased in the West. Many private individuals are now engaging in the import trade as wholesalers (Styczek 1991) and street vending provides a makeshift channel of distribution. However, since many domestic and east bloc products are also sold, there are alternative explanations for the rapid rise of informal, non-store retailing.

First, as Greenberg, Sherman, Topol, and Cooperman (1980) observe, small, mobile retailers can quickly put their merchandise where the consumers are. In Poland, this seems especially true for food products (Engelberg 1990), but also for packaged goods. With commercials for detergents now common, one vendor claims "I watch television in the evenings to find out what powder will sell best tomorrow" (Cited in Bartyzel 1992). Hard currency stores, like the state-owned Pewex chain which carries Western and Japanese brands and denominate prices in dollars, still have limited shelf space dominatd by major brands such as Mattel and Lego for toys or Sony and Sanyo for electronic goods.

Second, street vendors can more easily operate illegally or in regulatory grey areas. For example, the people who sold cigarettes out of their cars priced very competitively because they avoided custom taxes. Cargoes of cigarette that were supposed to be shipped from Germany to the Soviet Union were diverted to the Polish market (Bartyzel 1991). Street vendors are also a major distribution channel for bootleg audio and video cassettes (*The Economist* 1990b). Although these products are not illegal in Poland, more conservative retailers may choose not to carry them.

Third, conventional Polish retailing has been plagued by a number of shortcomings. Until very recently, there have been the well-known product shortages. Other problems include run-down store interiors, unhelpful sales clerks, and cumbersome payment procedures in which the customer first gets a sales slip, then takes it to a cashier, and, in some instances, must go to a third clerk to pick up the package. Many stores keep their merchandise away from consumers by putting it in glass cases or displaying it on shelves located behind counters. This inhibits direct inspection by customers unless they are willing to wait for an available clerk and then spend more time asking to see things one by one. After years of experience in such retail settings, Polish consumers may be eager to do things differently.

Finally, since unemployment and much higher prices have accompanied economic reform, people may be turning to street retailing as an occupation simply because they need money and have no better alternatives for earning it. This would seem to be especially true for the smallest vendors in the pedestrian underpasses and for the many Soviets visiting Warsaw. Since itinerant retailing is labor intensive, street vending may mask the true level of Polish unemployment as it seems to do in other parts of the world such as Latin America (Miller and Long 1990).

Several developments cloud the future of Warsaw's street vendors. Warsaw city authorities plan to upgrade Defilad Square which many Poles describe as "a sore thumb in the center of the Central European capital" (Urbanowicz 1991, p. 7). Polish vendors will be moved to trading pavilions and foreigners will have to settle for an area on the right bank of the Vistula. Further, conventional retailers may join forces to restrict the competition on their doorsteps. Most threatening, increasingly efficient fixed-location shops could drive many vendors out of business. Small dealers lack the buying power to offer low prices, are labor intensive, and cannot provide much breadth and depth in their product lines. Perhaps the more ambitious ones will move up the retail hierarchy and establish stores of their own.

CONCLUSIONS AND EMERGENT THEMES

Collecting qualitative data in a cross-cultural context is a difficult and time consuming task. The researcher can learn from observation and participant observation, but during a relatively brief visit much of what is seen is not always comprehended. Even with the help of a professional translator, communication "noise" is prevalent and data recording suffers. Better language skills, more time in the field, and more narrowly delineated problems are strongly recommended for studies of this kind. Research teams can use more sophisticated methodologies than lone investigators and, through interaction, stimulate thinking. Having more than one translator in the field could facilitate the speed and accuracy of data collection.

The findings suggest some broad emergent themes in post-communist consumer culture that need further investigation.

(1) There will be a trend toward market segments more sharply defined by variables such as age, gender, location (rural v. urban), and social class.

(2) Accelerated cross-cultural contact will encourage continued rapid change. Polish consumer culture will be influenced by Western goods, brands, images, institutions, and travelers.

(3) Consumers will have varying ability to cope with change. For example, older consumers will experience more difficulty and disorientation in the marketplace than will younger ones.

The rapid proliferation and growth of Warsaw's open air marketing documents how quickly an alternative, private channel of distribution can take shape following the dissolution of central planning. Press reports indicate that in other countries making the transformation away from communism, informal retailing has occured on the streets, in open air markets, and even from the trains of the Trans-Siberian Railway (Kyne 1992). Being a dealer and learning how to buy and sell would seem to be good experience for adapting to a free enterprise system.

REFERENCES

Bartyzel, Dorota J. (1991), "Behind a Smoke Screen: Cigarette Import Scam," *The Warsaw Voice* (February 24), 16.

_____ (1992), "A New Experience: Advertising in Poland," *The Warsaw Voice* (June 14), A1, A3, A5.

Belk, Russell W., John F. Sherry, Jr., and Melanie Wallendorf (1988), "A Naturalistic Inquiry into Buyer and Seller Behavior at a Swap Meet," *Journal of Consumer Research* 14 (March), 449-470.

_____, Melanie Wallendorf, and John F. Sherry, Jr. (1989), "The Sacred and the Profane in Consumer Behavior: Theodicy on the Odyssey," *Journal of Consumer Research* 16 (June), 1-38.

Dietl, Jerry and Krystyna Iwinska-Knop (1989), "Trade in Poland and the Federal Republic of Germany: A Comparative Approach," *Journal of Business Research* 19 (December), 313-324.

The Economist (1990a), "Drang Nach Osten," 317 (October 13-19), 52.

_____ (1990b), "Poland's Pirate Pop," 317 (November 10-16), 81.

Engelberg, Stephen (1990), "Winning Shoppers' Hearts and Minds," *The New York Times* (August 11), 4.

Gajewski, Maciek (1990), "Poles Look West for Jobs, Products," *Advertising Age* (February 19), 42.

Geertz, Clifford (1973), *The Interpretation of Cultures*, Basic Books: New York.

Greenberg, Jerome, Elaine Sherman, Martin T. Topol, and Kenneth Cooperman (1980), "The Itinerant Street Vendor: A Form of Non-Store Retailing," *Journal of Retailing* 56 (Summer), 66-80.

Hudson, Laurel Anderson and Julie L. Ozanne (1988), "Alternative Ways of Seeking Knowledge in Consumer Research," *Journal of Consumer Research* 14 (March), 508-521.

King, Robert L. (1983), "Enterprise-Level Marketing Research Activity in Poland: The PREDOM/POLAR Experience," *Journal of the Academy of Marketing Science* 11 (Summer), 292-303.

_____ (1986), "Prices of New and Used Automobiles in the Polish Market: Centrally Administered and Free-Market Prices Under Conditions of Scarcity," *Journal of Business Research* 14 (April), 165-176.

_____ (1989), "Retail Food Distribution in a Socialist State: The Polish Experience," in *Transnational Retailing*, ed. Erdener Kaynak, Berlin: Walter de Gruyter, 239-248.

Kyne, Phelim (1992), "Department Store on Wheels," *The Warsaw Voice* (September 13), 11.

Miller, Marjorie and William R. Long (1990), "Latin Job Force Hits the Streets," *Los Angeles Times* (December 29), A1, A24, A25.

Normand, Jean-Michel (1990), "Poland Pays for a Free Market," *World Press Review* 37 (September), 59.

Powers, Charles T. (1991), "Soviets Flock West to Poland, Eager to Wheel and Deal," *Los Angeles Times* (April 13), A4

Sachs, Jeffrey and David Lipton (1990), "Poland's Economic Reform," *Foreign Affairs* 69 (Summer), 47-66.

Sherry, John F., Jr (1988), "Market Pitching and the Ethnography of Speaking," in *Advances in Consumer Research*, Vol. 15, ed. Michael J. Houston, Provo, UT: Association for Consumer Research, 543-547.

_____ (1990a), "A Sociocultural Analysis of a Midwestern American Flea Market," *Journal of Consumer Research* 17 (June), 13-30.

_____ (1990b), "Dealers and Dealing in a Periodic Market: Informal Retailing in Ethnographic Perspective," *Journal of Retailing* 66 (Summer), 174-200.

Styczek, Dariusz (1991), "Wholesale Trade: A Growing Market," *The Warsaw Voice* (August 25), 7-8.

Tully, Shawn (1990), "Poland's Gamble Begins to Pay Off," *Fortune* (August 27), 91-96.

Urbanowicz, Juliusz (1991), "Free Enterprise: Welcome to Sale City," *The Warsaw Voice* (August 18), 7.

Walters, J. Hart, Jr. (1964), "Retailing in Poland: A First-Hand Report," *Journal of Marketing* 28 (April), 16-21.

_____ (1975), "Marketing in Poland in the 1970s: Significant Progress," *Journal of Marketing* 39 (October), 47-51.

Woodside, Arch G. and Cathy S. Dennis (1986), "Research in Marketing in a Centrally Planned Economy: Poland," *Journal of Business Research* 14 (August), 281-283.

Consumers in Rapid Transition: The Polish Experience
Brian Lofman, Central Connecticut State University[1]

ABSTRACT

This paper examines how the political and economic transformation of Poland, from a socialist to a market economy, is impacting Polish consumers. Emergent themes from participant observation and interviews illustrate key aspects of the transition process. Taken together, these themes highlight the need to understand the role of prior cultural conditioning and the influence of national character on consumption activities.

CONSUMERS IN TRANSITION

On September 12, 1989, the Solidarity coalition in Poland officially took office and began to move immediately to a market economy by introducing and implementing drastic reforms. These political and economic changes served as the basis for a structural transformation that has already taken on radical dimensions (see Batt 1991). But how do changes at the macro level affect the attitudes, emotions, and behaviors of individual consumers? And how do cultural values shape consumption activities? This line of questioning was initially raised by Nicosia and Mayer (1976), who focused on what they termed "affluent" societies. These questions are directly relevant, however, for *all* types of societies. In particular, studying consumer behavior in Central and Eastern Europe at this critical juncture in time provides a unique opportunity to understand some of the most fundamental underlying aspects of consumer behavior, and perhaps to challenge certain previously accepted assumptions. This paper reviews the methods undertaken in the study, describes themes emerging from the research, and discusses some conclusions based on these themes.

METHOD

The study used methods of naturalistic inquiry (Belk, Sherry, and Wallendorf 1988) appropriate for accessing the "native point of view" (Davies and Schmidt 1991). Prior to traveling to Poland, the researcher read relevant literature and spoke with various Polish people in the United States to obtain an understanding and a historical sense for the conditions of everyday consumer life in Poland. The research *in situ* was undertaken for a period of one month in the summer of 1992. By engaging in activities similarly engaged in by many Polish people — such as shopping in various markets and using diverse modes of mass transportation, including trams, trains, and buses — the researcher thoroughly participated in the cultural milieu. The research was conducted in various cities, including Wroclaw, Krakow, Poznan, and Warsaw, and on trains taken between these cities. Most of the research was conducted in Wroclaw, a city of approximately 650,000 people situated on the Odra River in the region of Lower Silesia in southwestern Poland. Toward the end of World War II, seventy-five percent of Wroclaw was destroyed, although much of the city was later rebuilt in an effort to match its prior architectural design.

Primary research methods included participant observation and interviews with consumers and businesspeople. The methods evolved continuously to fit particular situations and to deal with unanticipated problems. Most interviews required the aid of a translator; a notebook computer was used whenever and wherever possible for immediate transcription. The computer was used primarily during interviews with marketing consultants, entrepreneurs, and business managers, and also with consumers interviewed in leisurely settings. A microcassette recorder was used to record some interviews conducted in English, but mostly to record ideas when it was inappropriate or inefficient to work on the computer. Finally, a computerized journal allowed for an ongoing record of evolving ideas grounded in the dynamic nature of the research.

In order to examine the changing aspects of consumer life, the primary research sites — a shopping pavilion and a minibrewery — were purposely chosen for their novelty. These sites have recently arisen as a result of the new demand oriented economy and are therefore symbolic of the economic transition. The sites are also of interest because consumption norms have not yet been established in these environments; it was expected that consumers would be willing to speak in great depth about their consumption experiences. Besides the primary sites, other sites included various types of shops, market squares, and busy city streets. Additionally, there was a mix of informal and formal interviews and meetings in households and businesses.

Before reviewing the results of the research, two important limitations regarding this study should be mentioned. First, research was conducted during one period of time; any comparisons made to the socialist government era are based on consumer recollections and are corroborated by various written records. Since the study is not longitudinal, it is possible that consumption activities under the planned economy were actually somewhat different from what this research suggests.

Second, the research was not intended to investigate macroeconomic issues. It can be stated, however, that given the increasing interdependencies among world nations, the nations of Central and Eastern Europe are undoubtedly developing along different paths than those followed by western industrialized nations. Poland's position in the global economy will certainly continue to reflect its unique historical and economic development.

TRANSITION THEMES

The research indicates that Polish consumers must continually make pragmatic and psychological adjustments to their everchanging environment as reflected in the increasing complexities and inconsistencies of everyday life. Several key themes emerge which, in combination, suggest a changing model of consumer behavior, specifically, one that is becoming more similar to the western model, though some important differences between consumer behavior in Poland and in western nations clearly remain. Each theme is discussed separately below, but the themes are interrelated: each theme influences and is influenced by the others.

Changes in Decision Making

To a large extent, prior to the transition, consumers were conditioned by their external environment. Scarcity of many foodstuffs, appliances, and often basic services was evident, although the extent of scarce supply clearly varied over time (Walters 1964, 1975). Under economies of shortage, consumer choices are limited; lacking freedom of choice, consumers may not be able to express real needs and preferences. Relatively speaking, consumers constrained in this way can not truly be autonomous decision makers. Purchase decisions are often simplified, though the pro-

---

[1] The author wishes to acknowledge the financial assistance provided by a USIA Grant, and the moral support of the International Business Department in the School of Business, Central Connecticut State University.

cess of purchasing tends to be complicated, and time and energy consuming (Gajewski 1992). Key decisions to be made under the socialist government were frequently questions related to process: "Who in the household will wait in line today? Should I purchase an item I don't really need in case it is not available at some future time? Should I purchase an item I don't really want, and use it to barter for a product I desire?" Conversely, for many American and Western European consumers, the purchasing process has been relatively simple, but decisions are frequently very complex due to the large number of existing brand choices and the great deal of information available about many diverse product features (Waldman 1992).

Product decision making in Poland has become particularly relevant to consumers as they have perceived there to be real choices to make in the marketplace. There are more and different types of places in which to shop, from open air markets to major department stores. Although the more expensive items are beyond the economic reach of some consumers, there are several brand choices within an expanding number of product categories, such as toothpastes, laundry detergents, and other household products. Because consumers are facing increasingly complex decisions, some have begun using heuristics to simplify decision making. For example, consumers often expressed that both product prices and quality are lowest in open markets. Furthermore, many consumers noted that open markets are appropriate for the purchase of certain products, but not for other products, due to poor or inconsistent quality. Beyond having to cope with increased complexity, consumers are facing greater risk in decision making. They must attempt to make financially prudent choices in an environment of high inflation, and where the increase in prices may be highly variable from one industry's products to another.

Changing Consumption Activities

Prior to the transition, consumers engaged in several daily ritual activities; sometimes these activities became all-consuming and took precedence over job related functions. Seeking information concerning the availability of various goods was an ongoing activity for most consumers. Unless the black market was affordable to the consumer, waiting in long queues was essential in order to gain access to the *potential* for goods purchase: consumers did not know what would necessarily be available, if anything, once they made it to the front of the line. If some products were available at the counter, then consumers might purchase whatever was available, within their budget, and sometimes up to the quantity allowed. Hoarding occurred not only due to supply inconsistency, but also due to the fact that prices were usually expected to rise in the near future. Of course, hoarding served to decrease supply and increase prices, thereby compounding an already difficult situation.

Whereas information search regarding goods availability, standing in long lines for several hours to purchase goods, and the hoarding of goods were all typical consumption activities under the planned economy, consumers are presently engaging in radically different consumption activities. Presently there is *less* competition among buyers, and *more* competition among sellers. Some consumers are involved in extensive exploratory behaviors. Comparison shopping, for instance, has become quite an adventure for many consumers, as they find that prices can vary substantially from one store to another. For some, the large variations in price can be a source of frustration. First, having to make trips from store to store to find the lowest price for an item takes considerable energy. And, second, some consumers question how such wide variations in price can even exist. In general, compared to her American or Western European counterpart, the Polish consumer appears to be more concerned with, although not necessarily more attentive to, the management of scarce resources.

Changing Expectations

Consumer expectations have changed rather dramatically over the last decade. At first, expectations were low or virtually nonexistent: many consumers were resigned to the continuation of the centrally planned economy, and had become immune to the government's largely unfulfilled promises and futile attempts at real reform, especially since such reforms had little impact on the standard of living. Beginning with the early stages of the Solidarity Movement, however, Poles were given hope that the future might bring better economic times. When the political leadership finally changed — although people were at best unsure as to how the government might be reorganized and precisely what changes would lie ahead — many were riding the crest of a wave of overly high expectations understandably related to the intense emotions experienced at that point in time.

Regardless of what the new government might achieve, even in a short period of time, it was inevitable that people would come to experience mixed emotions. The great majority of consumers interviewed indicated that they were glad the political transition occurred, and were clearly happy with certain results of the transition. For the most part, consumers are enjoying their freedom of choice, such as their increasingly greater access to a broader variety of goods and the availability of substitute brands within many product categories.

Still, many consumers are concerned about the present and the future economy in areas where previously there was minimal concern; this is apparently the case in other Eastern European countries as well, such as in Czechoslovakia (Miller 1992). Inflation has become a way of life. Full employment is no longer a priority for the government; indeed, Poles are facing increased unemployment. Although many jobs paid (and often still do pay) low wages, at least they were available and often not demanding. Universal health care has been an important part of socialized life in Poland; in the long run, the transition threatens to change the cost of as well as access to medical treatment.

The Changing Workplace

Under socialism, there was little if any incentive to be effective or efficient in the workplace. Responsibility for accomplishing goals (as opposed to tasks) was infrequently taken, and work was sometimes avoided when it conflicted with social activities or personal affairs. *Stealing time* for social networking has been a significant reason for employees not working too long or too hard at their official jobs (Clark and Wildavsky 1990, p. 130). Service workers in particular had little to no training and often held poor attitudes toward their work.

Attitudes toward the workplace appear to be related to locus of control (Goodstadt and Hjelle 1973; Rotter 1966), which "influences beliefs about who should solve problems" (Folkes 1988, p. 556). Attitudes of Polish workers have been so deeply ingrained that the employee has often sought "above all to use the resources of the company to improve his personal fortunes, whether it helps the company or not" (Clark and Wildavsky 1990, p. 143). Over the years there have been rampant problems associated with worker absenteeism and sick leave, especially since the loss of jobs in a full employment economy was virtually nonexistent (Lipton and Sachs 1990).

The extent and pace of change in workplace activities presently varies considerably depending on the size and age of the firm. Although many of the newer, small businesses are having problems just making a profit, they appear to be operating relatively efficiently and with at least somewhat of a customer service orientation. Entrepreneurs are still constrained by government regulations and policies that have outlived any usefulness they may have once had, but these businesspeople are making risky decisions and taking responsibility for the outcomes of such decisions. National companies are in the initial stages of privatization; they seem to be changing very gradually, in some cases merely changing superficial aspects of their operations. Within some of these large firms, younger people are being trained how to operate a business in a demand economy.

Generally speaking, workplace attitudes are resistant to change. Workers are still reluctant to make decisions and take responsibility for them. Poles have not been "empowered to take their lives into their own hands and experience that they can create a reality of their own choice" (Davies and Schmidt 1991, p. 27). This may represent a fairly long lasting legacy of the former socialist system, but it is also related to a strong trade union tradition. Without managerial direction, little to no initiative is taken to increase sales and to improve operations. For example, a considerable portion of floor space in shops may go unused or may be inefficiently configured, making customer self-service difficult at best, and suggesting a need for product merchandising. Also, service providers still seem to have little concept of customer service (Davies and Schmidt 1991). Employees frequently do not see the need to maintain a pleasant demeanor, nor to be outwardly helpful. Rather than greeting the customer and offering assistance, waitresses and sales clerks tend to wait for the customer to request assistance. They often seem unsure how to establish a rapport with customers, instead focusing solely on the steps required to complete the transaction at hand.

Change in Temporal Orientation

Orientation to time is an important cultural value, perhaps crucial in understanding consumption. Each culture possesses its "own unique set of temporal fingerprints. To know a people is to know the time values they live by" (Rifkin 1987, p. 1). The most critical aspect of the transition process in Poland may relate to changes required in the temporal orientation of the Polish people.

Under socialism, activities frequently tended to be procedure driven: following established procedures was often the key to consumer and worker success. At least in some ways, the Polish consumer has apparently been following the procedural-traditional model of time perception, by which activities must be done *correctly* as opposed to *on time* or *efficiently* (Graham 1981). In this model, time and money are basically disjoint concepts, essentially unrelated to one another. As opposed to active behavior, this implies very passive behavior where procedure dictates actions. Activities were often engaged in when the time was right, such as doing shopping during work hours, and buying products immediately rather than waiting for a future time when they might not be available — it thus made little sense to plan a budget. Instead of solving problems to achieve enhanced outcomes, Polish workers have tended to follow the procedures of the organization regardless of the needs of the particular customer or situation. They have seen rules as beyond their control, and thus flexibility was essentially not in the behavioral repertoire of Polish people in the workplace.

To a large extent, Poles became desensitized to concerns about the long-term future. Central planners worked assiduously on five year growth plans, prepared meticulously to meet procedural requirements as ends in themselves — yet rarely were goals achieved. Growth plans focused specifically on production objectives, but obsolete equipment has seldom been replaced (Fallenbuchl 1988). Managers have been known to pay much more attention to tactical decisions than to strategic decisions (Domanski 1986), although management historically has not had the autonomy to make even operational decisions (Walters 1964).

The transition from a command to a market economy may very well require a shift in the perception of time to allow for long-term economic growth and stability. Polish people are apparently adopting the linear-separable model of time perception. In capitalist nations, this has implied a future orientation with consumption activities indicative of means to ends, where such activities are driven by a strong connection between time and money, and where the spending of time is planned and budgeted (Graham 1981). Polish people are increasingly planning for the long-term; successful entrepreneurs are on the forefront of this trend, but consumers are also becoming keenly aware of the need to save and invest for their future consumption.

Still, orientation to time is a fundamental value orientation (McGrath and Kelly 1986), and cultural values are slow to change. The change in temporal orientation is slowed considerably by certain everyday aspects of life. Polish consumers do not have much disposable income, hence little need to consider alternative investments. Presently more than fifty percent of families do not plan expenses, instead tending to buy on impulse or relatively immediate desire (Bogucka 1992). One of the reasons for this is that prices jumped following the introduction of the demand market, and announcements concerning large increases in prices were often made only a few days in advance of such increases. Having become accustomed to rapidly increasing prices at a moment's notice, consumers have continued to buy rather quickly.

During the transition period, Polish people have had to determine the appropriate situations in which to utilize these different models of time perception; clearly, switching from one model to another is a skill in itself. It is important to gain a more precise understanding of the role that time plays in Polish consumer behavior (Bergadaa 1990; Hornik 1982), and to understand in greater depth the timestyle of Polish people, that is, the regularity in the priorities of Polish consumers as related to the limited supply of time, money, space, and personal resources (Feldman and Hornik 1981).

CONCLUSIONS

The transformation of the political and economic system of Poland is clearly impacting individual consumers, households, and businesses, and Polish people appear to be making a rapid transition in many ways. However, at least some attitudes and behaviors appear to be somewhat resistant to change. There may be many reasons for the present pace of the transition process; the emergent themes in this study suggest two plausible explanations.

First, it seems likely that several decades of socialist government have left a legacy that continues to influence Polish people in general and their consumer behavior in particular. Indeed, consumers who have lived under *any* political and economic system for an extended period of time can be expected to have been conditioned by that system, although the precise conditioning itself would likely differ from one system to another. Governments and their agencies tend to foster particular attitudes and constrain certain types of behavior. In the case of Poland and other Central and Eastern European nations, the socialist legacy reflects the cultural conditioning which occurred during the last several decades. If there exists a socialist legacy, it would be interesting to examine over what period of time the legacy continues to affect consumers, and how intense these effects prove to be over time.

The second explanation for the present pace of the transition process concerns the possibility that certain aspects of consumption in Poland, when contrasted with consumption activities throughout

Central and Eastern Europe and the rest of the world, may be unique or idiosyncratic to the Polish people. That is, in keeping with the concept of national character (Clark 1990; Gorer 1953), there may be specific features of the Polish character that differentiate Polish consumers from consumers of other nations. Perhaps national character would be relatively easy to study in Poland because of the fact that the society is relatively homogeneous. Values may be very different from one nation and one culture to another. Interestingly, although Poles are considered to be quite religious (predominately Catholic), their religious practices tend to be more ritualistic than spiritual in nature (Nowak 1981). It may be that Polish people have tended to exhibit procedure driven behavior in both their sacred life and profane existence.

Although the explanations considered were suggested by the exploratory research undertaken, it should be emphasized that these explanations have not been subjected to rigorous test. At least for the time being, cultural conditioning and national character seem to be inextricably interrelated phenomena believed to have significant impact on consumption in Poland. Perhaps the relatively permanent aspects of the Polish national character, if one can be defined, will relate to those features which remain once the new market economy has taken hold in Polish society, and after those features related to the socialist past have worn away with time.

A third explanation not provided above, and not specifically apparent from this research, should be considered in attempting to understand the seeming reluctance of Polish people to make some major changes in their way of life: many Polish consumers may simply not *want* to make such changes. They might view the structural transformation in a positive light, but they may perceive changes that impact their cultural values in a negative light. Perhaps Polish consumers are basically content with their cultural lifestyles and timestyles. This possibility implies that, beyond examining the impact that the Soviet sphere of influence has had on Polish consumer life, it is necessary to consider the increasing effects of Western European nations and the United States on Polish consumers. To what extent are these nations exporting and imposing their cultures on Polish people? Does this represent a new form of cultural conditioning? In this research, there were Polish people who expressed concern that there is too much influence from the West in terms of cultural values. For example, some Poles felt very strongly that making money has *already* become too highly valued in Polish society.

The great mix of various hopes and fears of Polish consumers demonstrate the complex nature of the transition process. The present situation regarding consumer expectations can not be represented by one single viewpoint. Many consumers are celebrating new choices, yet they are also somewhat pessimistic about their present economic position, expressing varying expectations for the long-term future. Other consumers wonder whether any political and economic system can truly make long-term changes for the betterment of society. Still others note that lifestyles can not be expected to be as flexible as government policy sometimes can be — attitudes, behaviors, and deeply held values are not easily changed (Davies and Schmidt 1991, p. 26):

> It would be a fallacy to assume that all this can easily be overcome through a short transition period and intensive training...it appears to be deeply embedded in the Polish culture.

REFERENCES

Batt, Judy (1991), *East Central Europe: From Reform to Transformation*, New York: Council on Foreign Relations Press.

Belk, Russell W., John F. Sherry, Jr., and Melanie Wallendorf (1988), "A Naturalistic Inquiry into Buyer and Seller Behavior at a Swap Meet," *Journal of Consumer Research*, 14 (March), 449-470.

Bergadaa, Michelle M. (1990), "The Role of Time in the Action of the Consumer," *Journal of Consumer Research*, 17 (December), 289-302.

Bogucka, Teresa (1992), "Temptation and Mistrust," *Gazeta Swiateczna*, 162 (July 11-12), 12-13.

Clark, John and Aaron Wildavsky (1990), *The Moral Collapse of Communism: Poland as a Cautionary Tale*, San Francisco: Institute for Contemporary Studies.

Clark, Terry (1990), "International Marketing and National Character: A Review and Proposal for an Integrative Theory," *Journal of Marketing*, 54 (4), 66-79.

Davies, Barry J. and Ruth A. Schmidt (1991), "Going Shopping in Poland: The Changing Scene of Polish Retailing," *International Journal of Retail & Distribution Management*, 19 (July/August), 20-27.

Domanski, Tomasz (1986), "Implementing a Retail Innovation by a Polish Industrial Company," *Journal of Business Research*, 18, 309-315.

Fallenbuchl, Zbigniew M. (1988), *The Polish Economy in the Year 2000: Need and Outlook for Systematic Reforms, Recovery and Growth Strategy*, Pittsburgh: University Of Pittsburgh, Center for Russian and East European Studies.

Feldman, Laurence P. and Jacob Hornik (1981), "The Use of Time: An Integrated Conceptual Model," *Journal of Consumer Research*, 7 (March), 407-419.

Folkes, Valerie S. (1988), "Recent Attribution Research in Consumer Behavior: A Review and New Directions," *Journal of Consumer Research*, 14, 548-565.

Gajewski, Stanislaw (1992), "Consumer Behavior in Economics of Shortage," *Journal of Business Research*, 24, 5-10.

Goodstadt, Barry E. and Larry A. Hjelle (1973), "Power to the Powerless: Locus of Control and the Use of Power," *Journal of Personality and Social Psychology*, 27 (2), 190-196.

Gorer, Geoffrey (1953), "The Concept of National Character," pp. 246-259 in Clyde Kluckhohn and Henry A. Murray, eds., *Personality: In Nature, Society, and Culture*, Second ed., New York: Alfred A. Knopf.

Graham, Robert J. (1981), "The Role of Perception of Time in Consumer Research," *Journal of Consumer Research*, 7 (March), 335-342.

Hornik, Jacob (1982), "Situational Effects on the Consumption of Time," *Journal of Marketing*, 46 (Fall), 44-55.

Lipton, David and Jeffrey Sachs (1990), "Creating a Market Economy in Eastern Europe: The Case of Poland," pp. 75-147 in William C. Brainard and George L. Perry, eds., *Brookings Papers on Economic Activity*, Washington, D.C.: Brookings Institution.

McGrath, Joseph E. and Janice R. Kelly (1986), *Time and Human Interaction: Toward a Social Psychology of Time*, New York: Guilford.

Miller, Cyndee (1992), "Czechoslovakia Breakup Unlikely to Cool Marketing Opportunities," *Marketing News*, October 12, 1+.

Nicosia, Francesco M. and Robert N. Mayer (1976), "Toward a Sociology of Consumption," *Journal of Consumer Research*, 3 (September), 65-75.

Nowak, Stefan (1981), "Values and Attitudes of the Polish People," *Scientific American*, 245 (July), 1, 45-53.

Rifkin, Jeremy (1987), *Time Wars: The Primary Conflict in Human History*, New York: Henry Holt.

Rotter, J. B. (1966), "Generalized Expectancies for Internal versus External Control of Reinforcement," *Psychological Monographs: General and Applied*, 80, Whole No. 609.

Waldman, Steven (1992), "The Tyranny of Choice," *New Republic*, January 27, 22-25.

Walters, J. Hart, Jr. (1964), "Retailing in Poland: A First-Hand Report," *Journal of Marketing*, 28 (April), 16-21.

_____ (1975), "Marketing in Poland in the 1970s: Significant Progress," *Journal of Marketing*, 39 (October), 47-51.

Discussant Comments
The Transition from Communism to Capitalism
Eric J. Arnould, California State University, Long Beach

Perhaps inspired by momentous political and economic change in Eastern Europe and East Asia, consumer researchers have plunged into cross- and inter-cultural research with surprising vigor. From a substantive perspective this research has focused mainly on two issues: 1) the significance of the transition from production-oriented economies to consumer-oriented economies, and 2) ascertaining the emic meanings associated with marketing mix variables and purchase behaviors. The mix of papers presented in this session raise both of these issues in varied ways.

In much of cross-cultural consumer research so far survey or content analytical methods have been employed. Much of this research seems to be concerned with developing equal measures of phenomena in two or more cultures. However, in this session only the Feick, Higie and Price paper dealing with search and decision processes related to women's cosmetics employed such techniques. In general, survey scales developed for U.S. samples are adapted for use with non-U.S. samples through back translation methods. This technique inevitably introduces systematic ethnocentric bias into the research process since back translation primarily resolves problems of denotative parallelism, rather than connotative and domain parallelism. The Feick, Higie and Price paper finesses this problem admirably by developing survey items from themes that emerged from Hungarian focus groups and participant observation in Budapest.

Consumer researchers are beginning to apply naturalistic techniques in cross-cultural contexts in an effort to understand behavior in context. Each of these studies claims to apply such methods. I applaud these authors for their recognition that naturalistic techniques are well-suited to providing a framework for translation between domains of culturally constructed experience. The most elaborate form of such research, ethnography, indeed can help us to understand others as they understand themselves. In addition, ethnography clarifies the ways culture directs the experiences of the members of a culture or sub-culture, something members may not grasp, nor articulate themselves.

But were these papers ethnographic as is claimed? A key feature distinguishing ethnography from other research traditions is the primacy given to observing human action. Ethnographic observation has the advantage of granting the researcher access to the world of everyday life. Rather than merely asking people what (they think) they usually do, what (they think) they recently did, or what (they think) they will do, ethnographic observers watch them do it. Each of these papers involved researchers in observation of behaviors occuring in Poland and Hungary, respectively. Professor Witkowski observed the development of urban open air markets in Warsaw for example, and recorded interesting details of their organization. Professor Lohman observed behaviors in a sort of new wave beer garden.

Further instead of asking respondents to form and report generalizations about their patterns of behavior as survey researchers may do, the ethnographic observer records the particular details of specific events as they are enacted. Each of the authors here reports observations like this.

In addition, ethnographers employ unstructured questioning during participant observation. Ethnographic unstructured interviews are designed to elicit material concerning shared cultural categories and meanings as behavior unfolds. Such categories and meanings provide the basis for the emergent cultural plans through which participants recall, interpret and script consumption events and give them meaning. None of the presenters in these sessions gathered data in this way, because none of them were fluent in the national languages of Hungary or Poland.

Finally, through examination of behavioral regularities across time and across many specific, detailed cases, the ethnographic researcher constructs generalizations about underlying social or cultural processes. Again, because of the short duration of their studies, a few weeks in Professor Witkowski's case, a few months in Mr. Lohman's case, and a few weeks in the case of Professors Feick, Higie, and Price, the authors could not hope to do this. In the latter case, however, the authors benefitted from a lengthy association with Hungarian marketing scholars and the frequent visits of Professor Feick to Hungary.

Although these authors did make use of at least some of the elements of ethnographic research, it cannot be said that any of them engaged in deep immersion in cultural context for any length of time. Thus, while they employed naturalistic techniques of data gathering— observation, interviews, and photography— none of them engaged in ethnography. Nor are their results ethnographies, since a well-crafted ethnography should provide a framework for understanding both convergent as well as divergent data.

In listening to these papers, I was convinved that we are witnessing a dramatic transformation of markets in eastern Europe, a transformation that is proceeding at a fantastic clip. These authors are to be applauded for their attempt to register these changes as they unfold. Indeed Professor Witkowski, speaking in a historical register, argued that description and recording of these changes should be the first order of business for academic marketing scholars since the changes underway are so far reaching and unprecedented.

Mr. Lohman and Professors Price, Higie, and Feick, however, had more ambitious aims. All sought to provide a sense of the meaning of emergent patterns in consumer beahvior. Both papers provided insight into these emergent patterns. Professors Price, Higie, and Feick providing convincing discussions of emergent heuristics consumers use in choosing cosmetics, as well as of the frustrations experienced in coping with new forms of consumer risk. Professor Lohman is also right to argue that the nature of consumer decision making has altered dramatically in Poland, requiring both more and different kinds of cognitive search and information processing than under the command economy.

As the presenters spoke, however, I couldn't help but be reminded of two critiques often made of ethnographic studies conducted by anthropologists. The first of these is the problem of drawing longitudinal inferences from cross-sectional data. A two-week or two-month study conducted in a particular neighborhood, city, or town, no matter how thorough, simply does not constitute a reliable basis for drawing conclusions about historical change. It may, however, provide a basis for discussing the very interesting questions of local perceptions of social, economic and cultural dynamics. This after all is likely to be of more interest to marketing practitioners.

A second and related problem, most evident in Mr. Lohman's paper is a tendency to impose a teleological sequence on events unfolding in real time. There can be no doubt that the command economies of Poland and Hungary are becoming market oriented economies. It may also be that consumers in these countries look to the West for models and values associated with a consumer economy. Nonetheless, this does not provide evidence that such consumers are, in fact, becoming more like "us" as Mr. Lohman appears to be arguing. Assuming "us" refers to Euro-American rather than African-, Asian-, or Latin-American consumers this would mean eastern European consumers are now beginning to share and shuttle between the Calvinist and Romantic consumption norms and values that guide Euro-American consumer behavior (Campbell 1988).

Why is the evidence untenable? First, because a small sample of consumers is unlikely to be able to report factually on emergent regularities in their behavior, particularly in an unprecedented situation, no matter how deeply felt they may be. Second, because cultures rarely change with the apparent drama evident in eastern Europe; events in the former Yugoslavia suggest continuity rather than change. And finally, there is ample evidence that the development of a market economy is not predictive of emergent cultural homogeneity (Smith 1976). For example, well-developed market economies have existed in West Africa for hundreds of years, but Islamic transnationalism rather than European secularism seems to be the emergent cultural paradigm there (Arnould 1989). And what serious scholar would argue that the Japanese are becoming Americanized in spite of their mastery of capitalism, and tremendous consumption of things occidental.

I want to close with some general comments drawn from several generations of cross-cultural work by anthropologists. These may provide some general cautions for the laudable new cross-cultural research effort by marketing scholars. Comprising cross-culturally comparable outlines of cultural materials is the ongoing project of the Human Relations Areas Files (HRAF, Murdock 1971). The journal *Ethnology* is devoted entirely to cross-cultural research. Review of these works indicates that anthropologists have developed broad general coding schemes for analyzing small group interaction (Bates and Cohen 1979); children's behavior (B. Whiting, J. Whiting and Longabaugh 1975; J. Whiting, Child and Lambert 1966); interpersonal exchange behavior (Longabaugh 1963); non-verbal behavior (Birdwhistle 1952); subsistence activities (e.g., Dufour 1983); color terminology (Berlin and Kay 1969), and kin terminologies (Fox 1967). Several of these coding schemes, notably the latter two, are the fruit of several generations of research. Conspicuous in all these efforts is the limited concern with emic meanings per se, despite cultural anthropology's general preoccupation with emic meaning. Most of the solid comparative, or ethnological, research is focused on relationships between observable elements of behavior and/or very limited domains of denotative meaning. The reasons for this are first, that getting good, comparable cross-cultural data about even simple, fundamental aspects of human behavior has proved to be extraordinarily "tough work" (Bernard 1988, p.275).

Second, developing reliable, cross-culturally valid interpretations of connotative meanings and values has proved elusive despite half a century of effort (Frazer 1950/1922; Levi-Strauss 1969). Efforts of this kind usually result in the imposition, sometimes overt, but usually subtle, of ethnocentric metaphors on alien patterns of culture. An exemplary case is Benedict's (1934) classic *Patterns of Culture* in which Native American cultural patterns were assimilated to Dionesian and Epicurian patterns derived from classical Greek models. As in the well-known experiments with perceptual closure, what the observor does not know he or she fills in, and in so doing cannot help but be guided by his or her own cultural expectations. Consequently, few contemporary anthropologists actively pursue the comparative line of inquiry (cf. Berline, Breedlove, and Raven 1973).

What cross-cultural consumer research will need is comparable rather than equivalent measures for the cultures being researched. This will often mean coming up with culturally appropriate measures that may differ in form and substance. To attain this goal, a variety of time-consuming exercises in method might be required. For example, different levels of arithmetic discrimination in two cultures might require different scales (cf. Wallendorf and Arnould 1988), or consumers tendencies to score scales in biased ways may require ipsatizing responses. Application of multiple methods rather than the same method in both cultures might be appropriate, especially the use of participant observation to develop culturally appropriate categories of purchase behaviors or household purchase roles, followed by surveys to test for variations in their distribuion. Continuous observation of behavior combined with intensive debriefing by informants of observer interpretations might be employed (Murtagh 1985) to control for the tendency to impose North American metaphors on non-North American historical experience.

REFERENCES

Arnould, Eric J. (1989), "Toward a Broadened Theory of Preference Formation and the Diffusion of Innovations: Cases from Zinder Province, Niger Republic," *Journal of Consumer Research*, 16 (September), 239-267.

Bales, Richard F. and S. P. Cohen (1979), *SYMLOG: A System for the Multiple Observation of Groups*, New York: Free Press.

Benedict, Ruth (1934), *Patterns of Culture*, Boston: Houghton Mifflin.

Berlin, Brent ad Paul Kay (1969), *Basic Color Terms: Their Universality and Evolution*, Berkeley: University of California Press.

_____ Dennis Breedlove, and Peter Raven (1973), "General Principles of Classification and Nomenclature in Folk Biology," *American Anthropologist* 75, 214-242.

Bernard, Russell (1988), *Research Methods in Cultural Anthropology*, Newbury Park, CA: Sage.

Birdwhistle, Ray L. (1952), *Introduction to Kinesics*, Louisville: University of Kentucky Press.

Cambell, Colin (1988), *The Romantic Ethic and the Sprirt of Modern Consumerism*, Cambridge: Blackwell

Dufour, Darna (1983), "Nutrition in the Northwest Amazon: Household Dietary Intake and Time-energy Expenditure," *Adaptive Responses of Native Amazonians*, New York: Academic Press.

Fox, Robin (1967), *Kinship and Marriage*, Baltimore: Penguin.

Frazer, Sir James G. (1950/1922), *The Golden Bough*, abridged edition, New York: Macmillan.

Levi-Strauss, Claude (1969), *The Raw and the Cooked*, trans. by John and Doreen Weightman, New York: Harper Torchbooks.

Longabaugh, R. (1980), "The Systematic Observation of Behavior in Naturalistic Settings," *Handbook of Cross-cultural Psychology*, vol. 2, ed. H. C. Triandis, and J. W. Berry, Boston: Allyn and Bacon.

Murdoch, George P. (1971), *Outline of Cultural Materials*, 4th revised edition, New Haven: Human Relations Area Files.

Murtagh, Michael (1985), "The Practice of Arithmetic by American Grocery Shoppers," *Anthropology and Education Quarterly* 16, 186-192.

Smith, Carol, A. ed. (1976), *Regional Analysis*, 2 vols. New York: Academic.

Wallendorf, Melanie and Eric J. Arnould (1988), "'My Favorite Things': A Cross-Cultural Inquiry into Object Attachment, Possessiveness and Social Linkage," *Journal of Consumer Research* 14 (March), 531-547.

Whiting, Beatrice W. and John W. M. Whiting with R. Longabuagh (1975), *Children of Six Cultures: A Psycho-Cultural Analysis*, Cambridge: Harvard University Press.

Whiting, John W. M., I. L. Child, and W. W. Lambert (1966), *Field Guide for a Study of Socialization*, New York: John Wiley.

A New Perspective on the Effects of Advertising Repetition: The Mediating Role of Memory Structure

Karen Finlay, University of Guelph[1]

Studies on the effects of message repetition have been dominated by wearin-wearout and mere exposure paradigms. These models argue that learning, support argumentation, and attitude valence first increase in response to message exposure, but with further repetition, wearout or overlearning sets in, counter argumentation increases, and attitude valence declines. While numerous supporting results have been reported, disparate findings have also appeared. Because work on repetition effects has been focused on the study of outcome variables alone, inconsistent findings have not been understood.

It was proposed in this session that the effects of exposure frequency can be better understood by explicitly examining the effects of message repetition on memory structure. A general hypothesis across the three papers is that repetition influences evaluations and other outcome measures via its mediating influence on aspects of information stored in memory: the extent to which memory structure becomes interconnected (links are formed among stored items); the extent to which paths to existing stored items are strengthened, rendering that information more accessible; and the extent to which items become clustered in memory when they are stored. It was argued that when the effects of repetition on memory structure are considered, a better understanding is obtained of the amount and type of information that is recalled to form the basis of reported evaluations, thereby explaining why attitude valence is not always consistent with predictions of the wearin-wearout paradigm.

All three papers examined the mediating influence of memory structure on the message repetition-outcome measure relationship. Repetition of either the entire ad or repetition of information within the ad were manipulated. By considering effects on memory structure, Prashant Malaviya (University of Illinois) was able to explain why inconsistent effects of repetition may have been found in the past. If item-specific processing does not occur to render distinctive brand properties highly accessible, attitude valence may not have been influenced. By considering memory structure, Ida Berger (University of Toronto) was able to explain why repetition and the amount of information presented influence attitude-behaviour consistency without necessarily influencing attitudes per se. Finally, by considering memory structure, Karen Finlay (University of Guelph) was able to explain why repeating incongruent information within the context of a single ad does not negatively impact brand evaluations, but increases the amount of information recalled, even above that obtained when an entire ad is repeated containing only congruent information.

The three studies begin to identify the mediating role of memory structure on the repetition-outcome variable relationship that has traditionally been studied. The session demonstrated that advertisers need to consider the mediating role of memory structure in order to maximize the effects of repetition.

---

[1] The author gratefully acknowledges the insightful comments provided by the session discussant, Rajeev Batra (University of Michigan).

The Effects Of Corporate Branding Strategies On Brand Equity
Kevin Lane Keller, Stanford University

New product development is vital to the long-term financial success of a company. A new product may vary by the extent to which it is identified with a particular company. Companies may choose to introduce a new product with the company name, a new name, or a combination of both (i.e., as a subbrand). By establishing a link with the company, existing associations for the company (due to its other products or corporate image efforts) may become linked to the brand. This special topic session considered issues related to the effect of the corporate branding strategy on brand equity by examining how consumers evaluate proposed new products depending on the branding strategy adopted and, more importantly, how the introduction of new products affected the images of the core brands.

The first paper by Kevin Lane Keller and David Aaker described the results of two laboratory experiments that examined the effects of corporate images and branding strategies on new product evaluations. Corporate images were manipulated such that the company was characterized as being innovative, environmentally concerned, involved with the community, or having high quality products. Branding strategies were manipulated such that the new product was given the company name, an individual brand name, or a subbrand name (combining the company name with an individual brand name). The results indicated that corporate images can help to establish product images if none exists and improve evaluations of a corporate brand extension. Corporate images can also enhance perceptions of a new product positioned on other image dimensions. There were no differential effects between the company and subbrand name strategies for the corporate brand extension. More favorable evaluations of a very dissimilar new product, however, were generally achieved when it was given an individual brand name. The results also indicated that advertising to position a corporate brand extension can also help to establish corporate images if none exist and enhance perceptions on image dimensions different from existing ones.

The second paper by C. W. Park, Michael McCarthy, and Sandra Milberg reported the findings of an experiment that examined two issues: (1) the extent to which brand extensions cause negative reciprocity effects on brand attitudes, and (2) how the use of an associative brand extension strategy (e.g., Syntax by Timex) might mitigate negative reciprocity effects while simultaneously allowing for favorable evaluations of the brand extensions. The results revealed that while the use of a direct brand extension strategy did tend to result in negative reciprocity effects, the use of an associative brand extension strategy tended to mitigate those effects. Furthermore, brand extension evaluations were virtually identical for the two strategies. These results indicate that marketers may be able to extend their product lines farther with an associative branding strategy than with a direct brand extension strategy, due to the possibility of avoiding negative reciprocity effects.

The third paper by Sheri Bridges and Amna Kirmani reported the findings of an experiment that considered the effects of corporate branding strategy on consumer response to extending the range of a particular product line by reducing or increasing the number of features and/or quality of the brand (i.e., "brand-line stretching"). Specifically, subjects evaluated upward and downward stretches for four brands: BMW, L.A. Gear, Pioneer, and Budweiser. In the subbrand condition, subjects were told that the new products would be called the BMW Quest, Surge by L.A. Gear, AudioPrix by Pioneer, and Steinbrau by Budweiser. In the new name alone condition, subjects were told that the new product would not bear the original brand name but would simply be called Quest, Surge, AudioPrix, and Steinbrau. Results showed a significant effect of direction of the stretch, with upward stretches being perceived as higher quality but lower value than the original brand and downward stretches being perceived as lower quality but higher value than the original brand. Branding strategy had no effect on consumer evaluations of the new product.

The concluding discussion by Susan Broniarczyk highlighted commonalities in the three papers while discussing future research areas.

The Effects of Direct and Associative Brand Extension Strategies on Consumer Response to Brand Extensions

C. Whan Park, University of Pittsburgh
Michael S. McCarthy, University of Pittsburgh
Sandra J. Milberg, Georgetown University

ABSTRACT

This study was conducted in order to examine a number of important issues related to brand extension strategies. The results revealed that while the use of a direct brand extension strategy may lead to undesirable negative reciprocity effects, the use of an associative brand extension strategy may mitigate these effects while simultaneously preserving the desired effects on the evaluation of the brand extension.

INTRODUCTION

A number of researchers (Keller and Aaker 1992; Park, Milberg, and Lawson 1991; Roedder-John and Loken 1990; Romeo 1991) have expressed concern that the use of brand extensions may also lead to brand image dilution or negative reciprocity effects. Reciprocity effects are generally defined as changes in the consumer's original brand attitude and beliefs caused by brand extensions. Although it is possible that reciprocity effects can be both positive (reinforcing the brand attitude and beliefs) or negative (diluting the brand attitude or beliefs), researchers and practitioners express the most concern for negative reciprocity effects. Since brand extensions attempt to leverage the strengths of the brand name, managers need to consider: (1) the effects of the original brand on the evaluation of the brand extension and (2) the reciprocity effects of the brand extension on the subsequent evaluation of the original brand. Unless reciprocity effects are carefully examined together with extension effects, the use of a brand extension strategy may not create the intended synergy between the original brand and the brand extension.

While previous research has primarily examined how the direct brand extension strategy facilitates evaluations of brand extensions, this study explores two other issues: (1) the extent to which negative reciprocity effects occur due to extending the original brand into new product categories, and (2) how the use of an associative brand extension strategy may facilitate favorable evaluations of brand extensions while protecting the original brand from negative reciprocity effects.

THEORY AND HYPOTHESES DEVELOPMENT

Since previous studies (Park et al. 1991; Roedder-John and Loken 1991) have shown that categorization and schema theories appear to provide a valid theoretical base for brand extension research, we base our predictions for reciprocity effects on the same theoretical ground. Specifically, we base our predictions upon theories of stereotypic belief change [see Crocker, Fiske, and Taylor (1984) for a review] which are also grounded in categorization and schema theory. While several models of the mechanisms underlying attitude and belief change have been proposed (e.g., schema + tag, bookkeeping, conversion and subtyping), they all agree that: (1) attitudes and beliefs change in response to new instances that vary in terms of the degree of congruence with the person's existing category or schema, and (2) that these changes occur via the processes of assimilation and accommodation (Crocker et al. 1984).

Assimilation occurs when the new instance is not very different from the existing schema. The relatively high degree of fit allows the instance to be integrated into the existing schema leaving it essentially unchanged by the incorporation of the new instance. Conversely, accommodation occurs when the new instance is very different from the existing schema, thereby requiring the schema to be altered to accommodate the new instance. The implications of assimilation and accommodation for brand extensions are quite straightforward. As the congruence, or fit, between the brand extension and the original brand schema increases, the degree of observed negative reciprocity effects should decrease.

While this seems to be a reasonable expectation, previous research on negative reciprocity effects (Roedder-John and Loken 1990; Romeo 1991; Keller and Aaker 1992) have not demonstrated consistent evidence of such effects. One possible explanation is that these studies manipulated the fit between the original brand and the extension along only one dimension such as typicality (Roedder-John and Loken 1990) or similarity (Romeo 1991, Keller and Aaker 1992). However, Park et al. (1991) demonstrated that different types of brand extension fit, specifically brand concept consistency and product level similarity, moderate the evaluation of extension products utilizing the direct brand extension strategy. Therefore, it is possible that different types of brand extension fit may also have different effects on the degree to which negative reciprocity effects occur. Given this premise, the present study examines how the brand concept consistency and product level similarity of a brand extension affects the extent of negative reciprocity effects caused by that extension.

In the event that brand extensions do lead to negative reciprocity effects, it would be desirable to identify an alternate branding approach which would allow marketers to realize the desirable synergistic effect of brand name leveraging, without the undesirable negative reciprocity effects. We propose the use of an associative brand strategy (hereafter referred to as associative branding), wherein a new brand name is used in combination with an existing brand name in the introduction of a new product. For example, Marriott has used associative branding twice in the introduction of two new motel chains: Courtyard by Marriott and Fairfield Inn by Marriott, offering a different level of service and accommodations than those generally associated with the Marriott hotel chain.

The use of associative branding by practitioners appears to be based upon the assumption that the combination of a new brand name with a familiar brand name allows the consumer to selectively transfer existing brand attitudes and beliefs from the existing brand memory to the associated brand. This allows the consumer to differentiate the extension from the other products associated with the brand name, thereby reducing the likelihood of negative reciprocity effects. This explanation is consistent with the schema+tag model of assimilation (Graesser, Gordon, and Sawyer 1979) which would consider the associative brand name to act as a schematic "tag", allowing the consumer to segregate the discrepancies between the brand extension and the existing brand schema.

The above discussion suggests that when brand extensions exhibit high levels of fit, there should be no difference between the direct and associative branding strategies with regards to negative reciprocity effects. However, when the level of brand extension fit is low the associative branding strategy should result in lower levels of negative reciprocity effects than the direct extension strategy.

TABLE 1
Brand Extensions Used in Experiment 1 by Brand Concept and Product Similarity

	Functional Product Concept	Prestige Product Concept
Low Product Similarity	Garage Door Opener Smoke Detector	Necktie Cologne
High Product Similarity	Batteries Calculator	Ring Bracelet

Since it is difficult to know *a priori* precisely how poor the degree of fit must be to obtain negative reciprocity effects, we define low fit as existing when either product level similarity and/or brand concept consistency is low. Based upon this definition, we hypothesize:

H1: Compared to the direct brand extension strategy, an associative branding strategy mitigates negative reciprocity effects for brand extensions exhibiting low product similarity and/or low brand concept consistency.

Although we expect the associative brand strategy to mitigate negative reciprocity effects where they occur, we can not conclude that associative branding will be preferred to direct brand extensions unless we can determine that associative branding does not also mitigate the positive effects of the brand name association on the evaluations of the brand extension. In other words, we may not be inclined to use associative branding if it were to reduce the desired extension side effects. Therefore, we must consider how the use of associative branding affects brand extension evaluations.

Prior brand extension research has proposed that, depending upon the degree of brand extension fit, existing brand attitudes and beliefs transfer from the brand to the extension. However, since we would not expect consumers to have either attitudes or beliefs toward a unfamiliar associative brand name, we would not expect any attitudes or beliefs to transfer from the associative brand to the brand extension. Therefore, under both the direct and associative branding strategies, the existing brand name should be the only source from which brand attitudes and beliefs can transfer to the brand extension. Based upon this reasoning, we expect that both the direct and associative branding strategies will lead to similar brand extension evaluations, and we advance the following hypothesis:

H2: Compared to the direct brand extension strategy, an associative branding strategy has no differential effect on the evaluations of brand extension.

METHOD

Overview

The hypotheses were tested using methods and procedures based upon Park et al. (1991). The stimuli consisted of two brands, Timex and Rolex, and eight extension products. Timex and Rolex were chosen as the parent brands for a number of reasons. First of all, Timex and Rolex respectively represent a functional and prestige brand concept. Since Park et al. (1991) showed that subjects differed in their responses to the same extension of a functional and prestige brand we wanted to explore if these types of differences would be replicated with respect to negative reciprocity effects. Moreover, these brands exhibited two additional characteristics important to the objectives of this study. First, both brands were real (not fictitious) brand names that were highly familiar to subjects, thereby increasing the external validity of our findings. Second, neither brand had been extended to other product categories at the time of data collection. This allowed us to limit our product similarity manipulations to reflect only the wristwatch product category. The eight brand extension products used in this study (see Table 1) are a subset of the twelve extensions used by Park et al., and were pretested to vary in terms of product similarity (high vs. low) and product concept dominance (functional vs. prestige).

Design and Procedure

The design is a 2 x 2 x (2 x 2) mixed design with brand name (Timex or Rolex) and brand extension naming strategy (direct vs. associative branding) as the between-subjects factors and product similarity (high or low) and brand concept consistency (high vs. low) as the two within-subjects factors. Brand concept consistency was manipulated by the combination of the brand name (Timex or Rolex) with the product concept dominance of the extension (functional vs. prestige). For example, when the brand name was Timex (Rolex), functional products such as a calculator or smoke detector were considered to be high (low) in brand concept consistency. However, products such as necktie and cologne were considered to be low (high) in brand concept consistency with Timex (Rolex).

The subjects were 96 students enrolled in the full-time MBA program at a large eastern university and participated during their regular class meeting. Subjects were randomly assigned to one of the four between-subjects conditions. In order to avoid subject fatigue, each subject evaluated only four of the eight products in Table 1, with each product representing one of the four within-subjects conditions. The eight products were randomly assigned to one of two groups: (batteries, garage door opener, ring, and necktie or calculator, smoke detector, bracelet, and cologne). Therefore, an additional between-subjects factor, serving as a replicate, was the group of products evaluated by the subject. However, since this between-subjects factor had no effect on the results, it will not be discussed further.

In order to to identify an unfamiliar brand name that could be used as an associative brand name with Timex and Rolex, a pretest was conducted with 28 part-time MBA students. Based upon the results of the pretest, the brand name of Syntax was selected because its mean familiarity rating was only 1.71 on a seven-point scale (1=not at all familiar, 7=very familiar with the brand name) while Timex and Rolex rated a 6.02 and a 6.39 familiarity rating respectively.

The procedure was as follows. Subjects were advised that they would be evaluating a number of new product ideas for Timex (or Rolex). Subjects responded by answering a series of seven-point scale items which contained the manipulation checks and the dependent measures which are described with the results. The entire procedure took 15 to 20 minutes and subjects were debriefed at a later date.

RESULTS

Manipulation Checks

Consistent with the findings of Park et al. (1991) the results indicated successful manipulations of product similarity and product concept dominance. Product similarity to a watch was measured by indicating the degree to which each product went together with a watch (1=not at all, 7=very much). As expected, products initially assigned to the high similarity condition were rated higher in similarity to a watch ($\bar{x}=4.19$) than those assigned to the low similarity condition ($\bar{x}=2.38$, $t_{(95)}=12.6$, $p=.000$).

Functional (prestige) product concept dominance was measured by indicating how important the characteristics of reliability and durability (luxury and status) were when considering the purchase of the product. As expected, the products assigned to the functional-orientation condition were judged to have higher functional importance ($\bar{x}=6.21$) than those assigned to the prestige-orientation condition ($\bar{x}=3.43$, $t_{(95)}=17.1$, $p=.000$). Likewise, the products assigned to the prestige-orientation condition were judged to have higher prestige importance ($\bar{x}=6.04$) than those assigned to the functional-orientation condition ($\bar{x}=2.76$, $t_{(95)}=22.6$, $p=.000$).

Hypothesis Testing

The tests of Hypothesis 1 were based upon the change in the subject's attitude toward the brand, which was operationalized as the difference between the pre- and post-extension measures of overall brand attitude in the following manner. First, pre- and post-extension brand attitudes were based upon measures of brand liking (1=disliked very much, 7=liked very much) and brand feelings (1=feel very bad about the brand, 7=feel very good about the brand) which were combined into a single brand attitude measure due to their high correlation (r=.782, p<.01). Then, the pre-extension brand evaluation was subtracted from the post-extension brand evaluation with negative differences indicating negative reciprocity effects. Therefore, the dependent measure for the reciprocity effect caused by a particular extension was computed by subtracting the brand evaluation prior to the consideration of any brand extensions from the brand evaluation given after the consideration of the brand extension of interest.

Hypothesis 1 was tested by comparing the significance of the negative reciprocity effects observed under the direct brand extension strategy with the the significance of the negative reciprocity effects observed under the associative branding strategy. If the difference score was significantly different from zero in the direct extension condition, then negative reciprocity effects were said to have been obtained. Evidence of mitigation of negative reciprocity effects was obtained if the difference score was not significantly different from zero in the corresponding associative branding condition.

Hypothesis 1 predicted that associative branding would mitigate negative reciprocity effects for low product similarity and/or low brand concept consistency extensions. Figure 1 presents the findings which, interestingly, supported this prediction in the Timex condition but not in the Rolex condition.

In every case, directly extending the Timex brand led to significant negative reciprocity effects on the Timex brand attitude while using an associative branding strategy did not. When the Timex extensions exhibited only low product similarity, the negative reciprocity effects were significantly different from zero under the direct strategy ($\bar{x}_{functional}=-.40$, $t_{(24)}=2.49$, $p<.01$), but not so under the associative branding strategy ($\bar{x}_{functional}=-.21$, $t_{(20)}=1.14$, p=n.s.). Likewise, when the Timex extensions exhibited only low brand concept consistency the negative reciprocity effects were significantly different from zero under the direct strategy ($\bar{x}_{prestige}=-.36$, $t_{(24)}=2.26$, $p<.05$), but not under the associative branding strategy ($\bar{x}_{prestige}=-.05$, $t_{(20)}=0.26$, p=n.s.). Finally, when the Timex extensions exhibited both low product similarity and low brand concept consistency the negative reciprocity effects were significantly different from zero under the direct strategy ($\bar{x}_{prestige}=-.88$, $t_{(24)}=4.21$, $p<.001$), but not under the associative branding strategy ($\bar{x}_{prestige}=-.45$, $t_{(20)}=1.85$, p=n.s.). These results strongly support H1 for the Timex case. In addition, when Timex extensions exhibited both high product similarity and high brand concept consistency the negative reciprocity effects were significantly different from zero under the direct strategy ($\bar{x}_{prestige}=-.32$, $t_{(24)}=2.03$, $p<.06$), but not under the associative branding strategy ($\bar{x}_{prestige}=.02$, $t_{(20)}=0.14$, p=n.s.). Although this result was unexpected, it indicates that even high-fitting extensions may lead to undesirable negative reciprocity effects which can, in turn, be mitigated by the use of an associative branding strategy.

An examination of the means for Rolex indicates that although there was directional support for the predictions of H1, there was no significant effect of associative branding for any of the Rolex brand extensions. Taken together, the results of the Timex and Rolex conditions seem to indicate that associative branding may be effective at mitigating negative reciprocity effects for functional brands, but not for prestige brands.

Hypothesis 2 predicted that there would be no differential effect of associative branding on the evaluation of brand extensions for either the product-related or prestige brands. This hypothesis was tested by using the overall evaluation of the brand extension which was computed by averaging the two measures of the attitude toward the brand extension (feel good/bad, like/dislike) which were highly correlated (r=.795, p<.01).

A 2 (Timex vs. Rolex) x 2 (direct vs. associative branding strategy) x 2 (high vs. low product similarity) x 2 (functional or prestige-orientation) mixed design ANOVA was used to test Hypothesis 2. Figure 2 presents the results of this analysis which strongly supported Hypothesis 2. First of all, none of the main or interaction effects of strategy on brand extension evaluations achieved significance at the a=.05 level. Furthermore, an additional analysis comparing the means of the direct and associative branding strategies showed that in only one case did the means of two strategies differ significantly. When Timex extensions exhibited high product similarity and low brand concept consistency, using an associative branding strategy improved the evaluation of the extension ($\bar{x}_{Direct}=2.0$, $\bar{x}_{Associative\ brand}=2.7$, $t_{(45)}=1.99$, p=.055). The combination of these findings supports the expectation that using the associative branding strategy should not adversely affect brand extension evaluations.

In addition, an analysis of subjects in the direct brand extension condition provided a replication of Park et al. (1991). Specifically, a separate 2 (Timex vs. Rolex) x 2 (high vs. low product similarity) x 2 (functional or prestige-orientation) mixed design

FIGURE 1
The Effect of Direct and Associative Branding Strategies on Negative Reciprocity Effects for Timex and Rolex

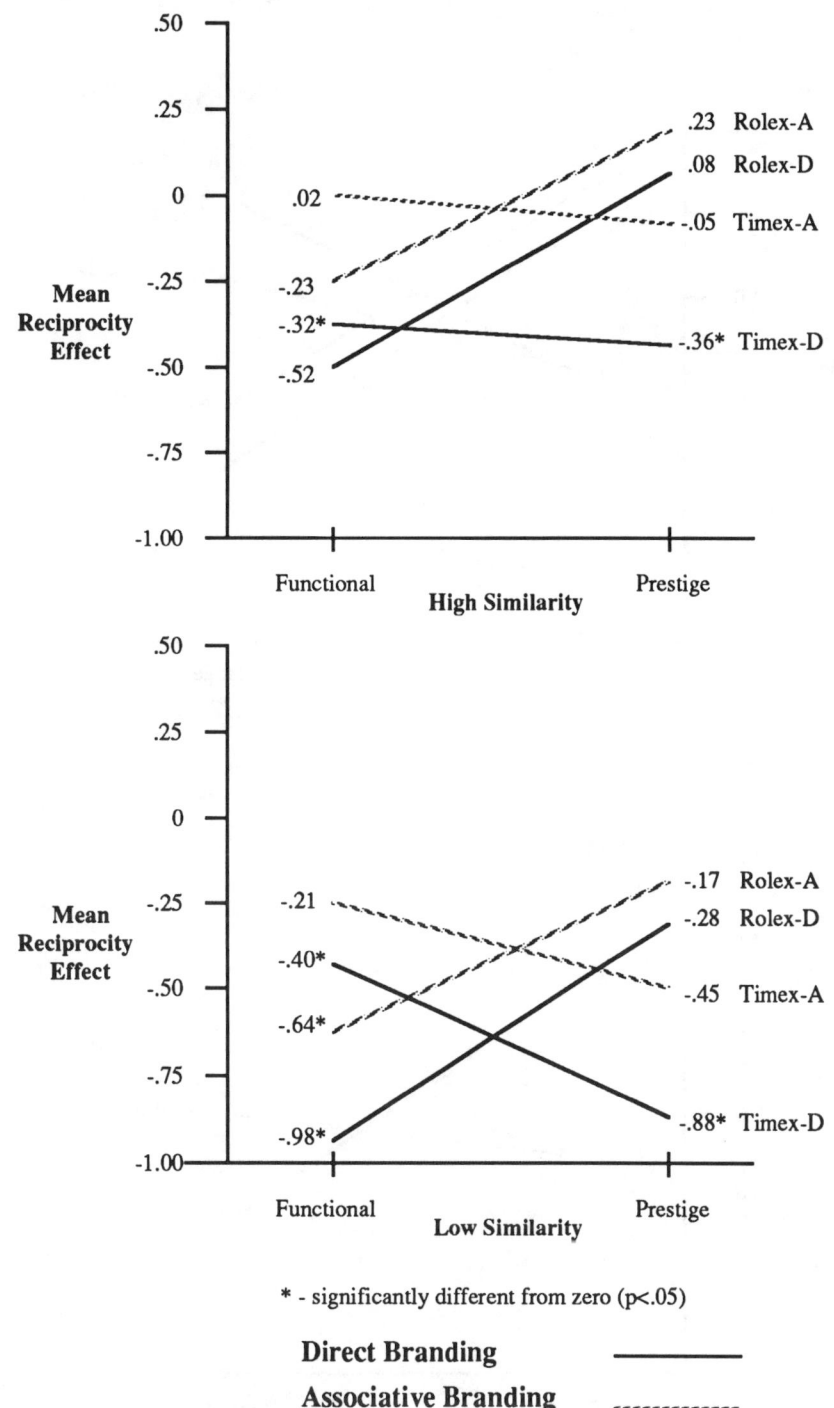

* - significantly different from zero (p<.05)

Direct Branding ─────────
Associative Branding ------------

ANOVA was performed on only the subjects in the direct branding condition. This MANOVA revealed: (1) a main effect of product similarity ($\bar{x}_{High}$=3.55, $\bar{x}_{Low}$=2.95, $F_{(1,49)}$=28.03, p=.000), (2) a brand by concept consistency interaction ($F_{(1,49)}$=99.6, p=.000), and (3) a three way interaction of brand, concept consistency, and product similarity ($F_{(1,49)}$=7.46, p=.009). The three-way interaction of brand, concept consistency, and product similarity can be seen by examining the solid lines in Figure 2. This pattern of results is virtually identical to those obtained by Park et al. (1991).

DISCUSSION

The results of the present study suggest that not only can poor fitting brand extensions cause negative reciprocity effects but that negative reciprocity effects can occur even for high fitting brand extensions. This implies that negative reciprocity effects can occur even when consumer evaluations of the brand extension are favorable. The results of this study also raise an important issue as to why the associative branding strategy effectively mitigated negative reciprocity effects for the Timex brand extensions, but not for the

FIGURE 2
The Effect of Direct Associative Branding Strategies on Brand Extension Evaluations

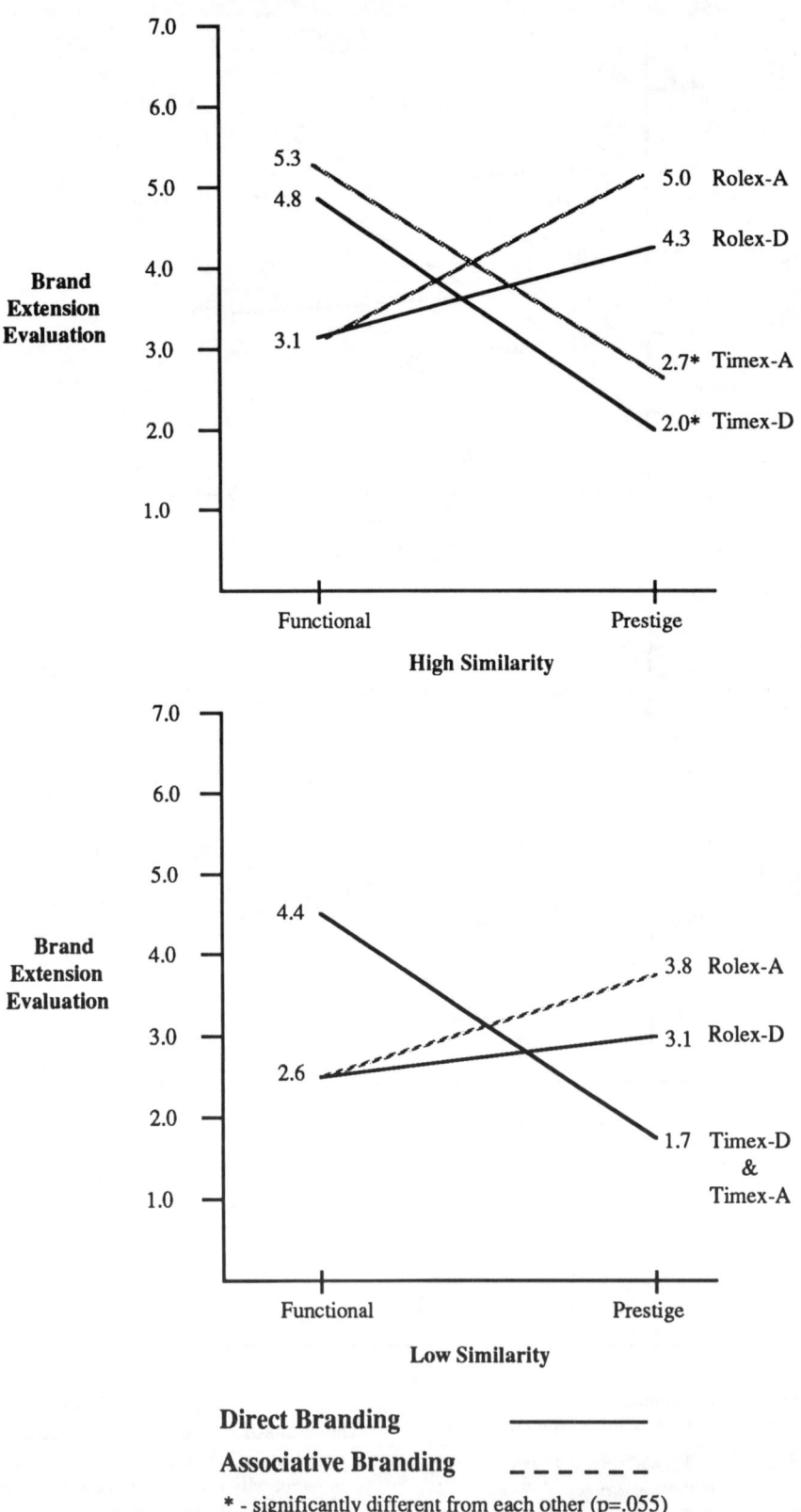

* - significantly different from each other (p=.055)

extensions of the Rolex brand. One possible explanation is the possibility of brand memory structure differences between the Timex and Rolex brands (Park, Lawson,and Milberg 1989). Assuming that Timex is primarily associated with the wristwatch product class, consumers might have difficulty assimilating non-wristwatch brand extensions into their memory structure of Timex. The associative branding strategy might facilitate this type of assimilation process by offering a basis for schema+tag processing (Graesser, Gordon, and Sawyer 1979), thereby mitigating negative reciprocity effects. However, assuming that the Rolex brand is primarily associated with the concepts of status and prestige, when the Rolex brand is extended via associative branding to products that do not share a prestige or status concept, consumers still perceive generally high levels of brand schema incongruity. Therefore, even though associative branding still appears to help to some degree, it is unable to compensate for the perceived brand category incongruity enough to reduce the negative reciprocity effects to insignificant levels. While this explanation seems plausible, more research focusing on this issue is necessary.

It should be noted that while the results of the present study offer several important findings, they also need to be understood within the study's potential limitations. Specifically, the findings of the present study are the result of within-subjects measurement of pre- and post-extension brand attitudes. Although this type of design allows us to measure the change in brand attitude due to the brand extensions, it also leaves open the possibility of demand effects. However, given the discrepancy between the Timex and Rolex results, the likelihood of demand effects seems remote since subjects should have been similarly affected by experimental demand. This explanation notwithstanding, the results of this study need to be replicated in a between-subject environment where the possibility of demand effects is much smaller. Furthermore, the limited nature of the stimuli used in this study (i.e., two brands and eight extensions) makes the generalizability of these results somewhat tenuous.

REFERENCES

Crocker, Jennifer, Susan T. Fiske, and Shelly E. Taylor (1984), "Schematic Bases of Belief Change," in *Attitudinal Judgment*, J. Richard Eiser, ed. New York, NY: Springer-Verlag, 197-226.

Graesser, Arthur C., Sallie E. Gordon, and John D. Sawyer (1979), "Recognition Memory for Typical and Atypical Actions in Scripted Activities: Tests of a Script Pointer + Tag Hypothesis," *Journal of Verbal Learning and Verbal Behavior*, 18 (June), 319-332.

Keller, Kevin Lane, and David A. Aaker (1992), "The Effects of Sequential Introduction of Brand Extensions", *Journal of Marketing Research*, 29 (February), 35-50.

Park, C. Whan, Robert Lawson, and Sandra Milberg (1989), "Memory Structure of Brand Names," in *Advances in Consumer Research*, Vol 16, ed. Thomas Srull, Provo, UT: Association for Consumer Research, 726-731.

Park, C. Whan, Sandra Milberg, and Robert Lawson, (1991), "Evaluation of Brand Extensions: The Role of Product Feature Similarity and Brand Concept Consistency," *Journal of Consumer Research*, 18 (September), 185-193.

Roedder-John, Deborah and Barbara Loken (1990), "Diluting Brand Equity: The Negative Impact of Brand Extensions", working paper, Carlson School of Management, University of Minnesota.

Romeo, Jean B. (1991), "The Effect of Negative Information on the Evaluations of Brand Extensions and the Family Brand" in *Advances in Consumer Research*, Vol. 18, Rebecca H. Holman and Michael R. Solomon, eds. Provo UT: Association for Consumer Research, 399-406.

Atmospheric Factors in the Retail Environment: Sights, Sounds and Smells
Sevgin A. Eroglu, Georgia State University
Karen A. Machleit, University of Cincinnati

Since the concept of "atmospherics" was introduced in the early 1970s, there has been a slow, but growing, interest in understanding and predicting the impact of the environment on consumer responses. The objective of this session was to showcase state-of-the-art research and practice in retail atmospherics, and to identify research opportunities in this emerging area.

The term "retail atmospherics" refers to all of the physical and nonphysical elements of a store that can be controlled in order to enhance (or restrain) the behaviors of its occupants, both customers and employees. These elements present a multitude of possibilities including ambient cues such as color, smell, music, lighting, and textures, as well as architectural and artifactual elements. This session began with a detailed overview of how some of these environmental elements are being used by professional store designers and architects to create desired retail settings. This first presentation, "Theater of Retailing: Selling Through the Senses" (Randall E. Gebhardt, Fitch Associates, Columbus, OH), included numerous examples of how retailers use sounds, scents, and visual elements of the store atmosphere to produce desired images and to increase sales. The examples included a tie store's use of leather and tobacco scents to create an atmosphere in which female gift buyers are comfortable in purchasing men's ties and a music store's use of audio engineering to create a store auditorially segmented by department.

The second presentation, "Olfaction and the Retailing Environment" (Terence A. Shimp, Pam Scholder Ellen and Paula Fitzgerald Bone), gave examples of how olfactory stimuli are being used in the retail environment, along with a discussion of the theoretical explanations for the observed effects of such stimuli. The primary response to olfactory stimuli was said to be approach/avoidance behavior. Evidence was presented that olfactory stimuli have the potential to attract attention and motivate processing, enhance mood states, and affect salesperson/customer interactions. Potential moderators and mediators of olfactory effects were also discussed.

The final presentation, "The Impact of Atmospheric Music and Retail Density on Retail Crowding Perceptions and Their Consequences: Does Song Augment the Throng?" (Karen A. Machleit, James J. Kellaris and Sevgin A. Eroglu), discussed the results of a laboratory experiment which manipulated both retail density and music loudness. The results indicated that both loudness of music and customer density increase subjects' perceptions of retail crowding; however, these independent variables did not directly affect other customer responses. Rather, outcome responses such as the feelings experienced while shopping and store satisfaction are influenced by the level of crowding experienced by the shopper.

The session discussant, Meryl P. Gardner, provided insightful comments with respect to all three presentations. Of particular note was her observation that retailers make store changes on a number of dimensions and then measure the impact on variables such as store traffic patterns and sales. To contrast, academic researchers study only one or two aspects of the environment at a time, often in artificial settings which, unfortunately, is the only realistic option available to most researchers.

In conclusion, this session intended to contribute to consumer research by identifying opportunities for research in the area of person-environment relationships in marketing contexts. Although practitioners and environmental psychologists have long been aware of the impact of environmental stimuli on human behavior, consumer research has lagged behind in this field.

Session Overview
The Feminine Imagination and Social Change: Four Feminist Approaches to Social Problems
Julie L. Ozanne, Virginia Polytechnic Institute and State University
Barbara B. Stern, Rutgers University

Feminist approaches to consumer behavior have recently emerged as a potentially fruitful research direction. In 1991, the first conference on gender and consumer behavior was held (Costa 1991), and in March, 1993, three papers based on feminist theory will be published as a special section of the *Journal of Consumer Research*. However, despite the flurry of activity in this area, most existing research has focused on presenting feminist theory and method but has stopped short of showing how such theory can be applied in consumer research. The purpose of this session is to move the theoretical contribution forward by demonstrating its usefulness in four applications of different feminist approaches.

Feminist theory's goal is to provoke social change by providing analyses and critiques of the status quo. Toward this end, feminism offers an innovative agenda for those researchers interested in social issues. While most other research approaches within the positivist and the interpretivist traditions aim at explaining or understanding society, they do not necessarily challenge the status quo (Murray and Ozanne 1991). The feminist research agenda, on the other hand, does so, for social change is an integral component.

Each paper in this session advances change as an outcome of a feminist approach to a social problem. First, Dobscha offers ecofeminism as an alternative way to study environmentally-safe consumption. She contends that ecofeminism offers a more useful research approach than earlier ones based on rational decision-making, for it emphasizes the interdependency between humans and their environment, demonstrating the value of researching environmentalism within the web of the consumer's life. Because ecofeminism rejects the nature/human dichotomy, alternative avenues of social change are possible.

Next, Bristor and Fischer use postmodern feminism to deconstruct another dichotomy, one basic to the marketing concept—the dominant (masculine) marketer versus the submissive (feminine) consumer. They demonstrate the power of feminist theory by using it to deconstruct the contradictions that pervade our discipline. Their paper points out that by challenging the overarching dichotomies, the consumer is empowered to become more socially responsible.

Hirschman's paper explores female empowerment by using semiotics to analyze feminine heroism in three films—*Aliens*, *Terminator 2* and *Thelma and Louise*. Her paper presents a rich semiotic analysis of the heroines' product consumption that reveals the image of women in American culture. This approach vivifies the feminist precept that awareness of the nature of the "other"—the gynocentric as contrasted to the androcentric *heroine—is* a necessary prerequisite for the social change process.

Last, Larsen's paper presents a sociolinguistic analysis of "feminine" and "masculine" communication styles. Because men view society as hierarchical, male conversations function as competitive opportunities to assert status. Women stress community and social interdependency and view conversations as opportunities to build trust and intimacy. His paper suggests that the "feminine" style may be a better approach within personal selling, for it helps to develop long-term customer-seller relationships. However, he suggests that we are better off being bilingual, able to switch to the best communication mode as the setting dictates.

Thus, the papers in this session contribute applications of feminist theory that offer alternative ways of gaining knowledge to post-positivist researchers and suggest new ways to study societal problems.

Women and the Environment: Applying Ecofeminism to Environmentally-Related Consumption

Susan Dobscha, Virginia Polytechnic Institute and State University

ABSTRACT

Women, as primary caretakers of families, are placed on the front line of the environmental crisis through their shopping responsibility. This paper discusses why women are playing such a major role and how ecofeminism, a branch of feminist theory, can be applied to the area of environmentally-related consumption to shed light on the connection between women and the natural environment.

INTRODUCTION

Environmentally-related consumption (hereafter, ERC) is defined as the exhibition of environmental responsibility in the marketplace by consumers through such activities as 1) choosing to buy products deemed environmentally safe, 2) choosing not to buy environmentally unsafe or unsound products, and 3) properly disposing of products (Petkus, Jr. 1991). More than 80% of consumers are labeled "generally concerned" about the environment, suggesting that ERC could become a powerful force in the marketplace (Burnside 1990).

More consumers worldwide are showing their concern for the environment in the marketplace by buying environmentally-friendly products or by responsibly disposing their waste. Interest in this consumption behavior originated in the 1970's when it became apparent that the consumption patterns of industrialized nations were creating a polluted world. Marketing research mirrored this movement in the 1970's with a plethora of research designed to determine the characteristics of the environmentally-concerned consumer and evaluate strategies that would change consumption patterns (from products deemed less safe to products deemed environmentally-safe or friendly). With the 1980's came a shift in perceptions of what were important political and social issues, and therefore, environmental issues gave way to issues such as the cold war and nuclear power. The 1990's have been marked by a return to environmental issues such as pollution, waste disposal, and ozone depletion.

Currently, there is much interest in the popular media concerning "Green Marketing" and its counterpart "Green Consumption" (Reitman 1992; Kleiner 1991; Nulty 1991). The latest trend in the environmental movement is the emphasis on reduction of waste generated at the individual household level. "Environmentally friendly" products have begun to appear on the shelves of supermarkets and consumers are purchasing them at an ever increasing rate. One poll revealed that the percentage of respondents who had chosen a product because of its environmental friendliness rose from 19% to 42% between November 1988 and May 1989 ("Cleaning Up", 1990). Another survey found that 80% of respondents could be considered at least "generally concerned" about environmental issues (Burnside 1990).

The proliferation of consumer goods targeted at the environmentally conscious has given the consumer many options. However, choosing among these options is often difficult because of a lack of, or biased information, questionable package labeling, and confusing advertising.

The purpose of this paper is to present an ecofeminist perspective on ERC. First, the research program known as ecofeminism is delineated. Next, traditional environmental research in consumer behavior is reviewed and critiqued from an feminist perspective. The paper then develops an ecofeminist agenda designed to overcome some of the problems of the traditional approaches. This agenda will take a closer look at the role women are asked to play as environmentally-concerned consumers.

WOMEN'S ROLE IN THE ENVIRONMENT

What is the connection between women and the environment in consumer research? Statistics indicate that 80% of household shopping is performed by women (Berk 1988). Therefore, environmentally-related purchase behavior is left primarily in the hands of the female consumer. She is the one who must sift through all the conflicting evidence concerning recycling of styrofoam. She must make tough decisions on whether to buy non-biodegradable plastic diapers or water-wasting reusable ones. She must be cognizant of labels that may be misleading or blatantly false.

A substantial burden has been placed on women consumers to attend to the environmental crisis. With women's role as primary caretaker still intact within most segments of society (Ferree 1987; DeVault 1987), women have had to take on an additional role: that of caretaker of the planet. Ecofeminism provides some insight into this connection between women consumers and nature.

ECOFEMINISM

Eighteen years ago, well before the current environmental movement emerged, feminist theologian Rosemary Ruether cautioned women to look with suspicion on the symbolic role that women would be asked to play in an ecological crisis as portrayed by the dominant (patriarchal) culture's perspective:

Any effort to reconcile such a male with "nature," which does not restructure the psychology and social patterns which make nature "alien," will tend to shape *women, the patriarchal symbol of "nature,"* (emphasis added) into romanticized servitude to a male-defined alienation. Women will again be asked to be the "natural" wood-nymph and earth mother and to create places of escape from the destructive patterns of the dominant culture.

Ruether's statement illustrates several elements that comprise ecofeminism. First, nature has been conceived by the dominant culture as "alien" and separate from humans. This human/nature separation is what feminists call a dualism which is when two concepts are separated and used for analysis. Feminists add the idea that when two concepts such as nature and humans are separated, hierarchy forms and one is given a higher status than another. In this case, humans dominate nature. Second, Ruether's quote suggests that women and nature have traditionally been aligned in terms of symbols and terminology. The popular media has demonstrated this by popularizing the slogan "Love your mother earth." Other examples that engender nature are "raping the land," and "virgin resources." Third, women are already very visible in local grassroots movements and other political activist groups centered on changing policy and rampant consumerism in order to save the environment. Thus, women have already begun to play that major role in the environmental movement that Ruether prophesied. One such role is that of environmentally-conscious consumer.

The primary belief of ecofeminism is that the domination of women (as studied in traditional feminism) parallels the domination of nature and that this mutual domination has led to environmental destruction by the controlling patriarchal society. Within feminism, a locus of scholars believe that a historical, symbolic, and theoretical connection exists between the domination of nature and women. This philosophy is based on four principles (Warren 1990): 1) there are vital connections between the oppression of nature and women, 2) understanding these connections is necessary to understanding the two veins of oppression, 3) feminist theory must include an ecological perspective, and 4) ecological problems must include a feminist perspective.

Ecofeminism claims that both women and nature are dominated and thus stresses the need for a more interdependent worldview. Ecofeminists believe that all living things are essential to the well being of the planet and that humans are not separate or superior. If this worldview were applied in ERC, the research agenda would be starkly different. More emphasis would be placed on the role consumers have played in environmental destruction and how basic value structures need to be changed in accordance with the concept of interdependence. This different vision is delineated in the sections that follow.

TRADITIONAL APPROACHES TO ERC

In 1971, the *Journal of Marketing* devoted an entire issue to the role of marketing in the changing social marketplace, thus marking the advent of the environmental movement as an important phenomenon to be studied by marketing scholars. Concepts such as segmentation of the market to accommodate the new consumer-citizen (Kelley 1971), application of marketing to affect social change in such areas as fund raising and health care (Mindak and Bybee 1971; Zaltman and Vertinsky 1971), and distribution of recycled wastes (Zikmund and Stanton 1971) were addressed in this issue.

The research during this period can be classified into three types. First, researchers tried to determine the characteristics of the environmentally-conscious consumer and how elements such as social class, demographics, and political ideology affected changes in consumption patterns for environmentally-friendly products (Anderson and Cunningham 1972; Kinnear, Taylor, and Ahmed 1974; Buttel and Flinn 1978a; Buttel and Flinn 1978b; Samdahl and Roberston 1989; Schahn and Holzer 1990; Vining and Ebreo 1990). Second, the impact of variables such as environmental knowledge and attitude on environmentally-related consumption was studied (Webster, Jr. 1975; Diamond and Loewy 1991; Newhouse 1990; Samuelson and Biek 1991; Williams 1991). Third, influence strategies to increase participation in environmentally-related behaviors were explored. In other words, this third research stream was driven by the desire to "fix" the damage already created by consumers by persuading them to change or eliminate certain behaviors deemed environmentally unsafe (Henion 1972; Burn 1991; Burn and Oskamp 1986; Cialdini, Reno and Kallgren 1990; Folz 1991; Folz and Haslett 1991; Hopper and Nielsen 1991; Katzev and Pardini 1987-88; Luyben and Cummings 1987-88; Simmons and Widmar 1990; Wan and Katzev 1990; Witmer and Geller 1976).

A criticism common to all three of these research streams is that nature is viewed as separate from humans, or consumers in this case. When maintained within research, this dualism leads to problems. For example, the energy crisis saw a dramatic increase in prices for resources. Most of the research done at the time focused on how to change consumption patterns and improve information dissemination to consumers on decreasing energy usage. Yet when the externalities (lower prices) were removed, consumers resumed their normal energy usage rates. No real change occurred. Also, trash disposal is another example of this separation of consumers and nature. When we place our garbage at the curb, it disappears. No real understanding of where the packaging and other waste produced from consumption goes until the local government starts to talk of a landfill in one's backyard or within smelling distance. Only then is the separation between the consequences of consumption and the nature it destroys dissolved and only then can real change occur.

As the decade came to a close, so did the environmental focus within marketing. The ERC literature that appeared during the late 1970's and early 1980's concentrated almost exclusively on energy consumption. The energy crisis of 1979 fueled consumer research in areas such as the effects of information on consumers, consumers' attitudes toward energy conservation, and consumption behavior directly related to the energy crisis (Petkus, Jr. 1991).

After 1981, which marked the year that energy conservation research proliferated marketing journals, the interest in ERC research fell off drastically. It was not until the late 1980's that ERC research began to re-emerge within marketing publications such as Marketing News and Advertising Age.

FEMINIST CRITIQUE OF ERC RESEARCH

In order to maintain a strong research and political agenda in the area of environmentally-related consumption, a new approach to research is needed. This approach will overcome the weaknesses of past research by: 1) placing less emphasis on rational plans to change behavior that will "fix" the planet, 2) placing more value on the passionate and emotional aspects of consumers' connection with the earth, 3) emphasizing the interdependency of nature and humans, and 4) allowing for a more contextual and deeper analysis of the behaviors that comprise environmentally-related consumption.

"Fix it" Ideology

The first critique is based on the "fix it" ideology. It is assumed that humans can "fix" the environment; nature is viewed as a force that can be harnessed or controlled and somehow humans are separate from nature, thereby, creating a human/nature dualism. The separation of humans and nature allows humans to do things to the environment that they would not do if they conceived of nature as being part of entire system of which humans were one part.

Ecofeminism criticizes the use of dualisms in analysis (Plumwood 1991). More formally stated, a dualism is a

> disjunctive pair [of concepts] in which the disjuncts are seen as oppositional (rather than complementary) and exclusive (rather than inclusive) and which place higher value (status, prestige) on one disjunct rather than the other (Warren 1990, p. 128).

Dualisms such as human/nature foster a value-hierarchical mode of thinking that in turns gives rise to domination. Feminist philosophy has derided the use of dualisms for categorization in all realms and ecofeminists have specifically chosen to focus on the human/nature dualism as the source of human oppression of nature. The human/nature dualism is the primary object of criticism in ecofeminism because of the manner in which humans and nature are separated and in opposition with each other. This dualism implies that humans are superior to nature and can thus dominate and control it. A recent commercial for a Time/Life Video series provides disturbing evidence for the idea that humans are superior to nature. It shows animals "in the wild" (meaning their natural habitat) "violently killing their prey" (hunting for survival). The commercial then warns the viewer that some scenes may be unsuitable for young viewers and ends with the disturbing statement: "See why we call them animals". Animals killing other animals in order to survive is a "violent" act. Yet, is it more violent than when humans kill other humans for a pair of tennis shoes?

Currently, the "just fix it" mentality prevails. Traditional ERC research reflected this principle when researchers focused on behavior modification (making the house more energy efficient, using less electricity when cooking, etc.). In tune with this behavior modification agenda, American companies are rushing to produce products that will be deemed environmentally safe or friendly by consumers. Yet, focusing on consuming differently (in terms of switching "good" products for "bad") does not solve the problem of overconsumption, which is the core problem of which buying hazardous products is a symptom. By providing products that help "fix" the environment, American firms have redirected the focus of the environmental movement away from their own wasteful manufacturing processes. As one consumer put it: "It [should] be up to the manufacturers to reduce packaging and pollution... The average person can only do so much (Reitman 1992)."

Ecofeminist research would work toward getting corporate America, the government, and consumers to share in the burden of maintaining a healthy environment. It would place much emphasis on the interdependence of humans and nature and less emphasis on the "just fix it" mentality perpetuated by the current "green marketing" trend. By placing the interdependence worldview at the forefront of environmentally-related consumption, consumers would experience a more direct link to the consequences of consumption. This direct link would consist of an understanding that all consumption has direct and dire consequences on the environmental well-being of the planet. These consequences would no longer be overlooked or minimized. There is much evidence that the government and industry have long ignored the ecological crisis as evidenced by its lack of presence in the current presidential campaign. Ecofeminist research would attempt to re-link all the major constituencies to improve the coverage of the problem and would then use agenda-setting research to change the current mindset that the environment is "not that bad off."

ERC Driven by Reason

Research that focuses on issues such as improving environmental knowledge and increasing environmental information dissemination in order to change behavior is also based on the assumption that environmentally-related consumption is reason-driven. Reason, as defined by such philosophers as Descartes and Kant, is sharply separated from emotion and has been given more legitimacy in research. This assumption is attacked on two different levels by feminists. First, the stance purports that research should be conducted without any emotion, such as passion, desire, caring, and love. Second, research should maintain an approach that focuses on rational strategies for changing behavior such as improving knowledge of environmental matters through information dispersion.

Nowhere is this ideology more prominent than in recycling research. Most recycling research studies compliance (in mandatory recycling programs) and participation (in voluntary recycling programs). Incentive-based strategies were the most prominent solutions offered to this problem. Virtually no research exists that studied the passion or emotion that often drives consumers to "think globally, act locally."

Emotion, feeling, and passion have traditionally been aligned with women and have not been given equal legitimacy within ERC (or any other) research. Unfortunately, when dealing with such a disturbing issue as global destruction stemming from flagrant consumption, the rational appeal may be the least effective and the most confusing (given all the incongruous information regarding such issues as cloth versus disposable diapers).

Feminist research into our connection with the environment would look much different. It would place passion and emotion at the center of the research and focus on the connectedness that drives consumers to perform environmentally-related behaviors. The rational style of decision making is inadequate for explaining ERC. For example, what inspires a consumer to purchase recycled computer paper when it is a lesser quality product priced higher? Utility maximization theory fails to explain fully the highly context-dependent and emotionally-driven behaviors of the environmentally-conscious consumer (see Hirschman, forthcoming). Feminist research would instead locate the female consumer and her everyday experiences at the center of the research to determine whether passion and emotion are part of the process.

Universalizing Consciousness and Behavior

Defining and quantifying the environmentally-conscious consumer in terms of demographic and socioeconomic characteristics assumes that the consciousness experienced is of a universal nature. As discussed above, ERC research had focused primarily on trying to discern those characteristics that could be used to target environmentally-conscious consumers. Universal positions based on moral abstraction and disconnection fail to capture the often context-dependent, particularistic nature of many environmental behaviors. For example, many consumers consider themselves to be positively disposed to recycling, however, there are many contexts in which it is difficult to remain true to this conviction. How many consumers are willing to carry empty aluminum cans off the airplane and to their homes just to recycle them?

The feminist research program would focus on understanding the context-dependency of such activities. Feminists stay away from totalization of any kind. Universalizing theories perpetuate the oppressive systems already in place. Feminist theory would focus more on the historical and personal experience of women as the reference point. The women's world as "problematic" (Smith 1987) would become the focal point of the research, thus eliminating the kind of universalizing theorizing viewed as controlling. Women would no longer be placed in the category of "other" and would be recognized as the primary caretakers of the family, thus, the primary consumers for household goods.

Objectivity and Detachment

Related to the concept of universal quantification is the use of detached and objective methods. ERC research is no different from any other research stream in marketing in that the subject (usually a housewife) is separated from the researcher in terms of education level and perceived power. Distancing is argued as the way to achieve objectivity. Yet, from a feminist's standpoint, distancing merely reinforces the hierarchy of domination between subject and object.

The essence of the research relationship in feminism is understanding the women's experience. The feminist researcher diverges widely from the dispassionate, uninvolved researcher in the positivist tradition by rejecting the need for separation of subject and object.

For example, feminist scholar Pauline Bart conducted research on rape survivors. She did not distance herself from the women. She cried when they cried. After conducting her study, she felt changed, different. This revelation allowed her to write an impassioned essay about rape. ERC research would take a similar approach by trying to document the amount of effort and labor needed to shop responsibly. One way is to utilize participant/observation techniques or diaries, which have been used before to measure a woman's "work" efforts in and outside of the home (DeVault 1987). The researcher would also assist the subject in making environmentally-responsible decisions by providing information and training, thus eliminating the subject/object split that has been accused of placing housewives in powerless positions (Hirschman, forthcoming) and raising consciousness.

THE ECOFEMINIST AGENDA

The female consumer has been given full responsibility for a crisis created primarily by the structure she is so oppressed by. This "servitude" is what Ruether cautioned women about 18 years ago. The responsibility has come in the form of increased (unpaid) labor in the marketplace as well as participation in local recycling co-ops and grassroots activist organizations for which, historically, women have been the foot soldiers (Lahar 1991). Studying environmentally-related consumption from an ecofeminist framework allows these discontinuities to be uncovered and thereby assists in the erosion of dominant social and political structures.

It is apparent from this historical look at ERC research that it failed to make an impression on the consumer community. Prior research emphasized the derivation of universal and quantitative measures of environmental behavior, relied on the logic of reason to evoke change in behavior, and promulgated the domination of nature by providing algorithms for change that are based on "fixing" the environment.

The unifying goal of feminist theory is to transform male-dominated society. This goal is to be achieved through research methods that work toward raising consciousness. Feminists employ consciousness-raising research to expose and change structures that are oppressive such as the current system that has left the lion's share of environmental responsibility to women consumers.

With an ecofeminist framework, ERC research would take a more emancipatory approach. The research agenda would be focused on changing corporate and public policy so that the burden for the ecological crisis would not be placed on women alone. Policy changes would include mandatory ecological labeling of all consumer goods (as is already instated in the United Kingdom and Canada) and stricter pollution regulations. Other countries such as Italy are more dedicated to the environmental movement and have already banned all non-recyclable packaging.

Education programs designed to benefit consumers would be developed in order to liberate consumers from the complexities of a marketplace that has profit as its primary motive. These educational programs would be comprised of teaching the consumer not just to consume differently, but to consume less. This redirection would aid in the development of the "green citizen" and not merely the "green consumer".

CONCLUSION

Introducing ecofeminism to consumer research provides the springboard for research into environmentally-related consumption by reshifting the focus away from the characteristics of buyers and how they may be motivated to buy environmentally friendly products to a more sociopolitical analysis that links women with nature and exposes how they have been forced into the primary role of "environmental housemaids." By exposing this connection, consumer researchers can conduct research that will benefit the female consumer in her quest to be an environmentally-responsible shopper. As Elizabeth Hirschman so elegantly stated in her Marxist-Feminist critique of consumer research:

We construct knowledge about consumers and consumer behavior. And that knowledge can be used for positive or negative purposes, can advance constructive or repressive social agendas, and can provide a fulcrum for progressive social growth or can further inhibit people's legitimate requests for greater autonomy over their own lives. Let us choose collectively to conduct our research in ways that will *benefit consumers*, rather than support the status quo which all too often manipulates, misleads, and suppresses them.

By shifting our goals to embrace Hirschman's recommendation, consumer researchers can begin to understand consumers as impassioned, emotional, and dedicated people who have extended the credo "think globally, act locally" into the marketplace.

SELECTED BIBLIOGRAPHY

Anderson Jr., Thomas W. and William H. Cunningham (1972), "The Socially Conscious Consumer," *Journal of Marketing*, 36 (July) 23-31.

Berk, Sarah Fenstermaker (1988), "Women's Unpaid Labor: Home and Community," in *Women Working: Theories and Facts in Perspective*, eds. Ann Helen Stromberg and Shirley Harkess, Mountain View, California: Mayfield Publishing Co.

Burnside, Amanda (1990), "Keen on Green," (1990), *Marketing*, (May 17), 35-36.

Buttel, F. H. and W. L. Flinn (1978b), "Social Class and Mass Environmental Beliefs: A Reconsideration," *Environment and Behavior*, 10, 433-450.

"Cleaning Up," (1990), *The Economist*, (September 8), 2-26.

DeVault, Marjorie L. (1987), "Doing Housework: Feeding and Family Life," in *Families and Work*, eds. Naomi Gerstel and Harriet Engel Gross, Philadelphia, PA: Temple University Press.

Ferree, Myra Marx (1987), "Family and Job for Working-Class Women: Gender and Class Systems Seen form Below," in *Families and Work*, eds. Naomi Gerstel and Harriet Engel Gross, Philadelphia, PA: Temple University Press.

Henion, Karl E. (1972), "The Effect of Ecologically Relevant Information on Detergent Sales," *Journal of Marketing Research*, 9 (February) 10-14.

Hirschman, Elizabeth (in press), "Ideology in Consumer Research, 1980 and 1990: A Marxist and Feminist Critique," *Journal of Consumer Research*.

Hopper, Joseph R. and Joyce McCarl Nielsen (1991), "Recycling as Altruistic Behavior: Normative and Behavioral Strategies to Expand Participation in a Community Recycling Program," *Environment and Behavior*, 23 (March) 195-220.

Katzev, R. and A. Pardini (1987-88), "The Comparative Effectiveness of Reward and Commitment in Motivating Community Recycling," *Journal of Environmental Systems*, 17, 93-113.

Kassarjian, Harold H. (1971), "Incorporation Ecology into Marketing Strategy: The Case of Air Pollution," *Journal of Marketing*, 35 (July) 61-65.

Kelley, Eugene (1971), "Marketing's Changing Social/Environmental Role," *Journal of Marketing*, (July) 1-2.

Kinnear, Thomas C., James R. Taylor and Sadrudin A. Ahmed (1974), "Ecologically Concerned Consumers: Who Are They?," *Journal of Marketing*, 38 (April) 20-24.

Kinnear, Thomas C. and James R. Taylor (1973), "The Effect of Ecological Concern on Brand Perceptions," *Journal of Marketing Research*, 10 (May) 191-197.

Kleiner, Art (1991), "What Does it Mean to Be Green?," *Harvard Business Review* (July-August) p. 38-47.

Lahar, Stephanie (1991), "Ecofeminist Theory and Grassroots Politics," *Hypatia*, 6 (Spring) 28-45.

Luyben, P. and S. Cummings (1981-82), "Motivating Beverage Container Recycling on a College Campus," *Journal of Environmental Systems*, 11, 234-245.

Newhouse, Nancy (1990), "Implications of Attitude and Behavior Research for Environmental Conservation," *Journal of Environmental Education*, 22 (Fall) 26-32.

Nulty, Peter (1991), "Finding a Payoff in Environmentalism," *Fortune*, October 21, p. 79,84.

Petkus, Jr., Ed (1991), "Implications of the Symbolic Interactionist Perspective for the Study of Environmentally-Responsible Consumption," in *Advances in Consumer Research, Vol. 19*, eds. John F. Sherry, Jr. and Brian Sternthal, Provo, UT: Association for Consumer Research, 1992.

Plumwood, Val (1991), "Nature, Self, and Gender: Feminism, Environmental Philosophy, and the Critique of Rationalism," *Hypatia* (Spring), p. 3-27.

Reitman, Valerie (1992), "'Green' Product Sales Seem to Be Wilting," *Wall Street Journal*, May 18, p. B1.

Ruether, Rosemary (1975), *New Woman/New Earth: Sexist Ideologies and Human Liberation*, New York, NY: Seabury Press.

Samdahl, Diane M. and Robert Robertson (1989), "Social Determinants of Environmental Concern: Specification and Test of the Model," *Environment and Behavior*, 21 (January) 57-81.

Samuelson, Charles D. and Michael Biek (1991), "Attitudes Toward Energy Conservation: A Confirmatory Factor Analysis," *Journal of Applied Social Psychology*, 21, 549-568.

Schahn, Joachim and Erwin Holzer (1990), "Studies of Individual Environmental Concern: The Role of Knowledge, Gender, and Background Variables," *Environment and Behavior*, 22 (November) 767-786.

Simmons, Deborah and Ron Widmar (1990), "Motivations and Barriers to Recycling: Toward a Strategy for Public Education," *Journal of Environmental Education*, 22 (Fall) 13-18.

Smith, Dorothy E. (1987), *The Everyday World as Problematic*, Boston, MA: Northeastern University Press.

Starr, Roger (1991), "Waste Disposal: A Miracle of Immaculate Consumption?" *The Public Interest*, (Fall) 17-29.

Tremblay Jr., K. R. and R. E. Dunlap (1978), "Rural-urban Residence and Concern with Environmental Quality: A Replication and Extension," *Rural Sociology*, 43, 474-491.

Vining, Joanne and Angela Ebreo (1990), "What Makes a Recycler? A Comparison of Recyclers and Nonrecyclers," *Environment and Behavior*, 22 (January) 55-73.

Warren, Karen J. (1990), "The Power and the Promise of Ecological Feminism, " *Environmental Ethics*, 12 (Summer), 125-146.

Webster Jr., Frederick E. (1975), "Determining the Characteristics of the Socially Conscious Consumer," *Journal of Consumer Research*, 2 (December) 188-196.

Williams, Elizabeth (1991), "College Students and Recycling: Their Attitudes and Behaviors," *Journal of College Student Development*, 32 (January) 86-88.

Zikmund, William G. and William J. Stanton (1971), "Recycling Solid Wastes: A Channels-of-distribution Problem," *Journal of Marketing*, 35 (July) 34-39.

Consumer Behavior Meets the Nouvelle Femme: Feminist Consumption at the Movies

Elizabeth C. Hirschman, Rutgers University

ABSTRACT

The consumer behavior of heroines in three recent motion pictures is analyzed for clues regarding women's evolving social roles. The three films, *Aliens*, *Terminator 2*, and *Thelma and Louise*, suggest that women may consume—and behave—like men more successfully in science fiction narratives than in those depicting 'real life'. Some thoughts on the messages such films send women, and men, are discussed.

INTRODUCTION

Gender roles and feminism are emerging as significant new avenues for inquiry in consumer research during the 1990's (see Bristor and Fischer 1991; Fischer and Arnold 1990; Hirschman 1991; Holbrook 1990). However, empirical studies based on popular culture materials, e.g., advertisements, television shows, have been relatively scarce thus far (for exceptions, see Stern 1991, 1989). The present study extends feminist inquiry in consumer behavior into a previously unexplored popular culture domain, that of motion pictures. Women in American films have usually portrayed traditional female roles (e.g., wife, mother, girlfriend, daughter) and conformed to traditional sex role expectations, e.g., they are nurturant, submissive, emotional, and unaggressive.

However, in the late 1970's and early 1980's a new type of female character began to appear. First noticeable in roles played by Sigourney Weaver in *Alien* (1979) and Linda Hamilton in *The Terminator* (1984), this nouvelle femme combined masculine and feminine qualities and emerged on the screen as an androgynous superwoman—resourceful, competent and courageous, while at the same time caring, sensitive and intuitive.

This new form of female heroine proved so compelling to audiences that she was reprised and given even greater depth in *Aliens* (1986) and *Terminator II* (1990). The central women characters in these two films were shown *originating* as nouvelle femmes, however. Few textual clues were offered as to how they became that way. Further, both films in which they appeared were science fiction dramas and not intended as realistic portrayals of everyday life.

And then came *Thelma and Louise* (1991), a film in which two very traditional women in very traditional roles (i.e., housewife and waitress) are transformed into resourceful, competent, courageous—an ultimately doomed—outlaws. This film taught audiences a great deal about the feminist view of male-female relations, as well as providing a forceful warning to feminists of the extraordinary costs extracted from women who strayed too far from traditional female behaviors.

The present paper closely examines the roles of 'Ripley' in *Aliens*, Sarah Conner in *Terminator II*, and Thelma and Louise in *Thelma and Louise* as *consumers*. As I shall show, their apparel, hairstyles, and product usage characteristics (especially of traditionally male goods, such as liquor, guns, tobacco, cars and machinery) is a semiotically rich avenue for understanding their meaning in current American culture.

TWO MALE DIRECTORS, FIVE FEMINIST FILMS

In the interest of providing historic context for the discussion, and because the present author is a firm believer in the *auteur* concept of filmmaking (see Wollen 1985), some background information on these three films is appropriate. *Aliens, Terminator II*, and *Thelma and Louise*, are the most recent additions to a corpus of feminist films by two male directors: Ridley Scott and James Cameron. The first contribution to this significant body of work was the film *Alien*, written and directed by Ridley Scott in 1979. This film introduced the character of Ripley, a warrant officer aboard a doomed space freighter. Ripley, portrayed by Sigourney Weaver, originated an iconic female character in American film who was strongly androgynous. Capable of functioning creatively and courageously in a barren, ultra hi-tech environment, Ripley none-the-less maintains her feminine side, mourning for dead crew members and rescuing the sole surviving representative of a human space colony—a yellow tomcat. Ripley was the first woman in film to confront a monster, technology, and violence and *survive*, through ingenuity and will. For female consumers, her appearance on the screen was an important cinematic, and cultural, milestone.

The years 1984 and 1986 saw two additional significant events in feminist films, both due to the directing and screenwriting efforts of James Cameron: A*liens (1986)* and *The Terminator (1984)*. *Aliens*, which we shall discuss in depth subsequently, reprised the character of Ripley and developed in much greater detail her iconic status as a feminine warrior. Two years earlier, Cameron's low budgeted science fiction film, *The Terminator,* had been released and originated two iconic figures: the Terminator, a robotized, completely destructive man, (played quite credibly by Arnold Schwarzenegger) and Sarah Conner, an evolved Everywoman whose task it becomes to save humankind from machines. Sarah Conner, played by Linda Hamilton, begins the narrative as a common female character—the innocent victim—who must be protected from the Terminator by a courageous male figure (Michael Biehen). However, by the end of the narrative a significant shift in her status has occurred. Her male protector has been killed and Sarah, using ingenuity and technology, kills the Terminator by herself. The narrative closes with Sarah, pregnant with the (male) future savior of humankind, driving into the desert to seek shelter from the oncoming nuclear conflagration.

In 1990, James Cameron completed his triptych of the Nouvelle Femme, with the motion picture T*erminator 2: Judgement Day*. As will be discussed in depth subsequently, the character of Sarah Conner is enlarged and enriched, making her a woman warrior remarkably similar to Ripley, but with a different mission.

A year later, Ridley Scott returned to direct his first feminist-voiced film since A*lien,* twelve years earlier. The screenplay for *Thelma and Louise* (1991) unlike those of the other four films discussed, was written by a woman, Callie Khourie. Perhaps because of this, or perhaps because it is intended as a real life narrative and not a science fiction epic, *Thelma & Louise* is both more explicitly feminist in its ideology, and also more depressingly honest about its heroines' fates. During the course of the story Thelma and Louise do "cross over the line" to become women warriors, and like Ripley and Sarah Conner they display ample ingenuity, courage and competence with technology. But unlike these other two female characters who survived their encounters with monsters and machinery, respectively, Thelma and Louise confront the more formidable foe of entrenched misogynist cultural norms and perish.

Let us now examine these women heroes more carefully and see what their behavior as consumers can instruct us about the current construction of gender.

ALIENS: A BRIEF SYNOPSIS

At the opening of the narrative, Ripley, in suspended animation in a small space craft, is discovered by a salvage team and taken to a space station hospital near earth. A corporate representative, Burke, dressed in a business suit, tells her that she was adrift in space for fifty-seven years. Ripley has recurrent nightmares of alien monsters, recalling earlier events that led to the death of her crew.

Ripley is interviewed by corporate executives who do not believe her story of alien attacks on her ship and crew and are angry she destroyed their expensive space craft. A woman in a suit and tie, smoking a cigarette, interrogates her harshly. Burke tells Ripley that seventy families have been living for twenty years on the planet Ripley claims is inhabited by aliens. Ripley's hair is short, she wears no makeup, and dresses in a tank top and pants.

A few days later, Burke comes to see Ripley, who has been working as a cargo loader on the docks, and promises to reinstate her to flight officer status. All contact has suddenly been lost with the colony and the company wants Ripley to return to the planet with Burke and a unit of marines to find out why. At first, Ripley refuses: "I'm not a soldier", because she fears returning to the planet. However, her nightmares persist and Burke assures her that the alien organisms will be killed, not brought back.

Ripley (in gray cotton underwear), the marines, and Burke fly to the planet. Their space craft is highly mechanized, metallic, and spare. Two of the marines are women, who are highly masculinized, (i.e., they are heavily muscled, have short hair, wear aviator glasses, do pull-ups, and curse). There is also an android named Bishop.

Upon their arrival, Ripley assists by working a large, mechanical loader. Ripley wears gray work overalls. The marines suit up for a search mission wearing helmets and combat gear and carrying huge rifles. They land on the planet, which is dark, barren, and wet.

They enter the colonist's station, but find no people—only signs of an intense fight. They discover some alien larvae in preserving jars. (The larvae resemble amphibians with insect-like features.). They discover a sole surviving child, a nine year old girl named "Neut". After the Marines fruitlessly attempt to interrogate her, Ripley compassionately gives Neut hot chocolate and cleans her face softly.

The marines locate a huge, slimy nest in which the colonists have been stored for use as food and incubators by the aliens. Ripley realizes that if the marines fire grenades, the station will be destroyed. The creature attacks the marines and kills several. As the lieutenant panics, Ripley drives an armored personnel carrier to their rescue. Ripley advises that they take off and "nuke" the site. But Burke, realizing the profit potential of this new species and of the site, refuses. The marines support Ripley. However, their pick-up vehicle crashes when an alien attacks the pilot.

Ripley, smoking a cigarette, calms Neut, as the men around them panic. The lieutenant is injured, and Ripley emerges as the natural leader of the group. She and the marines review their ammunition. She devises a plan to barricade their building until a rescue ship arrives. She makes intelligent, creative use of the available technology. Ripley puts Neut to bed; she is gentle and nurturant (i.e., a good mother). She gives Neut a locating device and kisses her.

Ripley, smoking cigarettes, argues with Burke, who wants to save alien specimens for profit. Ripley realizes that it was Burke who sent the colonists to investigate the aliens, causing them to be killed, after he had heard about the aliens from Ripley. Ripley tells Burke she will have him arrested when they return.

The android, Bishop, heroically patches a communication link enabling them to call in a landing ship.

Hicks, a brave marine who has been supportive and admiring of Ripley, shows her how to use the hi-tech rifle.

Neut and Ripley sleep together. Ripley awakens and realizes that Burke has put an alien larvae in their room, intending to kill them. Unable to escape, Ripley cleverly uses a lighter to turn on the sprinkler systems. This alerts the marines, who rescue her and Neut. Burke had hoped the larvae would embed itself (impregnate) in Ripley and Neut, so that their corpses could be used to bring the species back to earth. Burke would have also killed the marines to hide his crime and make profits. Ripley: "At least the (alien) species doesn't fuck each other over for a goddamned percentage".

The group barricades itself inside the operations building, but the creatures enter through the ceiling. There is a horrific firefight. Burke attempts to sabotage them, but Neut discovers an escape route through an air duct. Neut falls down a shaft and is captured by an alien creature. Hicks and Ripley search for her. Hicks is injured by an alien; Ripley helps him. The two remaining marines, Vasquez (a woman) and Gorman (the male lieutenant) die heroically fighting the creatures.

The android, Bishop, arrives with the landing craft. Ripley loads the wounded Hicks aboard and then goes back by herself to rescue Neut. She loads herself with weapons and prepares for battle. She discovers Neut alive in the creature's slimy web. Using a flame thrower, Ripley destroys the alien's eggs and larvae. The mother creature rips herself loose from her egglaying apparatus and pursues Ripley and Neut. The planet begins to self destruct. Ripley and Neut make it to the escape ship and leave the planet as it explodes. Ripley hugs and holds Neut. They arrive at the large space craft. Ripley tends to Hick's wounds and thanks Bishop, the android. Suddenly, Bishop is torn in two by the female creature, which had gotten aboard the space craft. The creature comes after Ripley and Neut. Ripley protects Neut and attracts the creature to herself. But the creature stalks Neut in revenge for Ripley's destruction of her own young. Ripley, encased within a mechanical loader, confronts the creature: "Get away from her (Neut), you bitch!"

After a fierce fight, Ripley opens the hatch causing the creature to be swept out to space. Bishop, only a top torso now, heroically saves Neut from being swept into space. Neut and Ripley embrace. At the closing of the narrative, Neut and Ripley prepare for hypersleep to return to the Earth station.

TERMINATOR 2: A BRIEF SYNOPSIS

Sarah Conner's voice narrates the opening: "Three billion people died on Judgement Day... a nuclear holocaust; the survivors had to fight an even worse terror... the machines." The world is engulfed by conflagration. The remaining humans struggle to survive against superior, self-aware computers, robots, and armored vehicles. Images of a children's playground in flames are used to convey the loss of innocent human life.

Two terminators (robot warriors) are sent back from the future to the present time. One, an early model Terminator (Arnold Schwarzenegger), is sent back to protect the young John Conner, who will grow up to become humankind's savior in the war with the machines. The other, more advanced Terminator, is sent back to destroy John Conner. The first Terminator is dressed in black "outlaw biker" leather and rides a Harley-Davidson. The second, composed of liquid, malleable metal, assumes the form of a policeman and drives a patrol car. Both go looking for John Conner who, at age eleven, is a young, smart juvenile delinquent residing with foster parents.

John's mother, Sarah (Linda Hamilton) is confined in a maximum security mental hospital after she attempted to blow-up a computer company. Sarah knows that the future (see *Terminator 1*) includes a nuclear holocaust caused by machine/computer dominance. Now in the present, she is struggling to prevent this future from occurring. In her cell, Sarah does pull-ups to strengthen her body. She wears a tank top, sweat pants and unkempt hairstyle. She wears no make-up or bra.

John and a friend ride their motor-bike to a bank machine where they use John's Atari game to steal $300. John tells his friend that his mother is a "psycho", he does not believe her wild tales of nuclear destruction and terminators.

Sarah, smoking cigarettes, tries to convince her psychiatrist that she has recovered from her "delusions" about robot warfare. The doctor does not believe her recantations. Furious, she attacks him and is put into restraints.

Both Terminators search for John at a video arcade where he is (ironically) playing computer war games. They find John and shoot at one another. John escapes on his motorbike, and is pursued by both Terminators. The "good" Terminator rescues John on his motorcycle. The "evil" Terminator kills John's foster parents.

John, realizing that the good Terminator is there to protect him, orders him not to kill humans and to help him free his mother.

Displaying substantial ingenuity and mechanical competence, Sarah uses a stolen paper clip to free herself from restraints and her locked room. She beats-up a guard with a mop handle and uses a poison-filled syringe to hold her psychiatrist hostage. John and the good Terminator rescue her. As they drive away, they are pursued by the evil Terminator. Sarah and the good Terminator both shoot at him.

Sarah reprimands John for risking his life to free her. She tells him that his life is very important to the future; further, "I didn't need your help. I can take care of myself."

They seek shelter in a closed gas station. The good Terminator stitches up Sarah's wounds; she in turn removes bullets from his back. The Terminator tells them he "is a learning computer. The more contact I have with people, the more I learn". In the morning, they drive South in a station wagon. Sarah smokes a cigarette.

They drive to a remote junkyard, where Sarah has stashed a large supply of weapons. Sarah talks in Spanish to a Mexican friend who has assisted her and gulps tequila with him from a bottle. Sarah is dressed in combat gear; her hair is tied back; she wears aviator sunglasses. She directs the good Terminator and John to prepare themselves for a battle. John: "One thing about my Mom, she always plans ahead."

Sarah loads her guns and smokes cigarettes. She watches John playing "HI-5" with the Terminator and decides that it will serve as a good father-figure for him. She dreams of a children's playground engulfed in nuclear flames. She decides to go kill the scientist, a black man named Tyson, who is destined to invent the super computer that causes nuclear war. In full combat gear, she arrives at Tyson's house. She shoots at him with a laser-scoped assault rifle, but misses when he bends down to get his son's electric toy car. She pins the family to the floor with death threats, but is unable to bring herself to kill Tyson, realizing that he is a good father and husband. Her son, John, and the good Terminator arrive. They tell Tyson of the future nuclear war. Sarah tells John she loves him. Sarah tells Tyson that it "is men like you who will lead to the destruction of the world" because they value power and technology above human love and life. Sarah smokes a cigarette. Tyson agrees to help them destroy all his files at Cyberdyne, the computer company.

The four go to Cyberdyne and destroy all the computer files. John uses his Atari game to gain entry to the site. A huge police force is sent to subdue them. They escape in a truck; Sarah covers John with bullet proof vests to protect him. The evil Terminator pursues them in a helicopter. Sarah is shot in the leg. The evil Terminator then pursues them in a huge truck carrying liquid nitrogen.

They arrive at an enormous iron foundry. The evil Terminator at first disintegrates in liquid nitrogen, but then reassembles itself and continues to pursue them. The good Terminator heroically battles it, but is crippled. Sarah sends John to safety and shoots at the evil Terminator with a rifle. However, the Terminator impales her arm. Before he can kill her, however, the good Terminator shoots him with a grenade. The evil Terminator falls into a vat of molten metal and disintegrates. The good Terminator then has Sarah lower him into the vat of molten metal to destroy his C.P.U., so that it cannot be used to create the supercomputer. John is upset by the suicide of his father figure. Before he perishes, the good Terminator hugs John and shakes Sarah's hand.

At the close of the story, Sarah says: "The unknown future rolls toward us; for the first time I face it with hope, because if a machine, a Terminator, can learn the value of human life, maybe we can too."

THELMA & LOUISE: A BRIEF SYNOPSIS

Louise Sawyer is a thirty-seven year old unmarried coffee shop waitress in Arkansas. Thelma Dickinson is a housewife in her late twenties married to a philandering car salesman, Daryl. Thelma prepares breakfast for Daryl, who treats her as a household servant. He leaves for work in his red Corvette. Louise calls Thelma and tells her to pack for their weekend fishing trip. Thelma, in hair rollers and eating a candy bar, packs for the trip; unable to ask Daryl's permission, she leaves him a note, a beer and dinner in the microwave. She gingerly packs a gun in her suitcase, does her hair and makeup, and puts on an attractive outfit.

Louise comes to pick her up in a borrowed green Thunderbird convertible. Like Thelma, Louise is also nicely dressed, made-up and coiffed. At Thelma's request, the pair stops at a Country Western bar. Thelma, who never drinks, orders a "Wild Turkey (bourbon) straight up", telling Louise: "My hair is coming down!" Louise orders a Margarita, with Cuervo on the side. An attractive man, Harlan, flirts with Thelma. She drinks and dances with him. While Louise is in the bathroom, Harlan takes Thelma, who is drunk and dizzy, to the parking lot and attempts to rape her. When she resists, he beats her. Louise arrives and puts a gun to his head: "You got a real fucked up idea of fun". Harlan: "Suck my cock!" Louise shoots and kills him. They hurriedly leave in their car. Louise looks at the gun in her hand. Thelma wants to talk to the police, but Louise insists the police will never believe them.

They stop at a coffee shop. Thelma is distraught: "This is some vacation!"; Louise smokes a cigarette as Thelma combs her hair. Thelma calls Daryl, but he is out (with another woman).

They next stop at a hotel. Thelma is still distraught; Louise calls her boyfriend, Jimmy, and asks him to send her money. He agrees to do so. Louise drinks a beer; Thelma, wearing a walkman and bikini, sunbathes by the pool. Their appearances have begun to become unkempt; their hair is disheveled, makeup gone.

The police begin a search for them. The FBI is called in. Thelma and Louise drive to Oklahoma City to pick up the money. Louise decides to run to Mexico. Thelma buys several 'airplane size' bottles of liquor.

Daryl is at home drinking beer and watching a football game. Thelma calls him; Daryl tells her to come back immediately: "Have you lost your mind?... get your butt back here now, goddamnit." Thelma: "Daryl, you're my husband, not my father.... Fuck you!"

At a gas station, Thelma sees a young cowboy; she is attracted to him. She puts on eyemakeup and lipstick, but Louise tells her they cannot take him along. Thelma swigs from a small liquor bottle. Louise tells her they cannot drive through Texas. (She had been raped there once).

They re-encounter the young cowboy; this time they pick him up. Louise stops to pick up the money and discovers that Jimmy is there, waiting for her. She spends the night with him, telling him nothing of what has happened. Jimmy gives her an engagement ring, but Louise declines: "Let's chalk it up to bad timing." Thelma spends the night with the cowboy, and becomes sexually awakened. The cowboy is a robber, and tells her how to rob stores.

The next morning, Jimmy and Louise have breakfast. He promises not to say he saw her and offers to go with her. They kiss emotionally, he leaves. Thelma walks in, happy from her night of passionate sex; her buttons are undone, her hair disheveled, Louise: "What happened to your hair...?" They discover, however, that the cowboy took all their money. Louise is crushed.

A horde of male FBI agents descend on Daryl's house in black government sedans, wearing khaki raincoats. They set up elaborate phone tapping equipment Thelma drives the car and holds up a convenience store to get money. Louise, disheveled, waits in the car, smoking a cigarette. She sees an older woman in a nearby window and, looking at her own face, throws away her lipstick. Daryl and the police view the videotape of Thelma's store holdup and are amazed. In addition to money, Thelma took several bottles of Wild Turkey. Thelma: "We needed money; now we have it!" Louise: "Oh shit, Oh shit, Oh shit!"

They now view themselves as outlaw women. Thelma sips whiskey from a big bottle and tells Louise: "I feel the call of the wild!" They throw all their trash in the back seat, so they won't create litter. They drive up behind a large truck with nude women on the mud flaps. The driver sucks his tongue at them. Louise: "That's gross; he's a fucking pig." They stop at a remote truck stop and wash up. They are very disheveled. Louise removes all her jewelry, including her engagement ring, and gives it to an old man for his cowboy hat.

Louise tells Thelma to call Daryl, to see if the police are trailing them. She calls; Daryl is so polite they realize the police are there. Louise calls and talks to a detective, Hal Slocum, of the Arkansas State police. He is trying to help them and pleads for them to give up. They decide against it, fearful they would be jailed or executed.

Thelma and Louise drive through the desert at night, it is very beautiful. Thelma: "I always wanted to travel. I just never got the opportunity." Louise: "Well, you got it now." They share a whiskey bottle, wear no makeup, and put-up their disheveled hair. The lewd truck driver comes up behind them; they pass him.

A policeman pulls them over for speeding. Thelma pulls a gun on the cop and forces him into the trunk of his car. She tells Louise to take his gun and shoot the radio. They also take his beer and extra ammunition. Thelma tells him: "My husband wasn't sweet to me and look how I turned out! They apologize to the policemen. They reload their guns; Thelma: "I think I have a knack for this shit!"

Louise calls Detective Slocum. He wants to help her, but she declines. They will be charged with murder. The FBI traces the call. Louise, drinking a beer, tells Thelma: "I think I fucked up; I think I'm going to get us killed." Thelma tells her not to worry, she would have been raped and Harlan would have gotten off, because they had been drinking and dancing together. Thelma: "Something's crossed over in me and I can't go back. I just couldn't live." Louise: "Yeah, I guess we don't want to end up on the damn Geraldo show." Thelma: "I feel awake.... I'm gonna get a job... work at Club Med."

They reencounter the trucker: "Baby, you ready for a big dick?," he asks. They stop. The trucker gets out expecting sex, but instead is reprimanded for sexually harassing women. They demand he apologize. Trucker: "Fuck You!" They blow up his truck by shooting it. Trucker: "You bitches from hell!" Thelma takes his cap and they drive off.

The police begin closing in, terming the pair "armed and extremely dangerous." Thelma and Louise have become outlaws. They wear a cowboy and trucker hat, no makeup, and are sunburned and dirty. Thelma: "No matter what happens, I'm glad I came with you." They both light up cigarettes; they tell each other they are good friends. After a wild ride in which they elude several police cars, they arrive at the edge of the Grand Canyon. Louise: "This is the first chance you've had to express yourself." Thelma: "Good driving!" Police cars and a helicopter surround them.

Realizing there is no escape, they clasp hands and speed the car forward: Thelma "Lets keep going!" The car flies over the canyon rim. A shot shows the back seat on which are their jewelry, scarves, makeup and the photograph of their former selves. The narrative ends with their car suspended over the canyon, before its inevitable plunge.

RIPLEY AND SARAH AND THELMA AND LOUISE AS CONSUMERS

We learn about the female heroines of *Aliens, Terminator 2* and *Thelma & Louise* not only by what they do in the narratives, but also by what they *consume*—and do *not* consume. The behavior of the four women—Ripley, Sarah Conner, Thelma and Louise—as consumers is consistently defined by their use of products commonly viewed as masculine and their nonuse of products commonly viewed as feminine. Thus, the four characters not only display the unexpected presence of masculine consumer behaviors, they also exhibit the absence of expected feminine consumer behaviors. My analysis will focus first on the exhibiting of masculine consumption by these four female characters.

Masculine Consumption

Perhaps the most semiotically explicit aspect of all four characters—and the factor that most vividly defines them as nouvelle femmes—is their engagement in many forms of masculine consumption. The women repeatedly do things that only men are conventionally expected to do in our culture; they curse, fight, smoke, and shoot. They master and control complex technology; they destroy property; they commit crimes. They all have "crossed over" to masculine modes of consumer behavior. Let us consider seven specific examples.

Cigarettes: In all four films, the female heroines are shown smoking cigarettes. The use of tobacco, including cigarettes, is culturally viewed as masculine behavior. When women smoke, they are seen as tougher, more worldly and less feminine. Further in these three films, the female characters do not smoke in a seductive fashion; rather they smoke as men do—casually, taking in deep drags of smoke. In a particularly telling scene at the outset of *Thelma and Louise*, Thelma, wanting to emulate Louise's more liberated image, sneaks a cigarette from her and practices smoking it in the car mirror. By the end of this film, both women, now clearly outlaws, draw reflectively on their cigarettes while discussing their probable deaths.

Liquor: There is no liquor present in *Aliens;* however, in *Terminator 2*, Sarah Conner gulps down tequila from a bottle she shares with her Mexican friend, Enrique. As a tough man would, she grips the bottle by the neck and drinks effortlessly. *Thelma & Louise* displays a brilliant progression of alcohol use that mirrors the characters' transformation from a waitress and housewife to liberated, outlaw status. At the Country Western bar, Thelma "lets her hair down" by drinking a bourbon straight. Louise reiterates by having a Margarita with a "Cuervo on the side". On the run after they have killed Harlan, Thelma buys several small bottles of bourbon at a convenience store. When she later robs a store at gunpoint, she steals two large bottles of bourbon, as well. Both women drink from the bottles continuously once they have "crossed over" into full-fledged outlaw status. When the women lock a policeman in his own car trunk, they steal not only his ammunition, but also his six-pack of beer. By the end of the film, alcohol has become a mainstay of their consumption.

Motorized Vehicles: In our culture (and virtually all others), men drive the motorized vehicles, while women ride as passengers. This pattern is purposely flouted in all three films. In *Aliens*, Ripley competently flies a space craft and an armored personnel carrier. Further, she drives them at high speed in combat situations, both of which are atypical for women. In *Terminator 2*, Sarah Conner drives cars, trucks and a motorcycle at high speeds over dangerous courses. And in *Thelma and Louise,* Louise drives their green, convertible Thunderbird over highways, back roads and desert flats, often at speeds of 110 m.p.h., and successfully eludes police pursuits on several occasions. Women are not supposed to be able to drive like this, but these women do, and their example creates new images of what women are capable of performing.

Technology/Machinery: Closely related to this is the competence exhibited by these four female characters in dealing with technology and complex machinery. Ripley in *Aliens* is perhaps the most compelling exemplar of this. Over the course of the narrative, Ripley exhibits technical skills superior to those of the male characters. She warns that the use of grenades in a certain area will destroy their building; she devises a plan to barricade the survivors of the creature's attack by sealing off entrances to the building; she develops a communication linkage with the command ship which provides a rescue craft; and in one ingenious scene, she signals danger by using her cigarette lighter to set off the fire sprinkler system. Finally, at the end of the narrative Ripley straps herself into an enormous mechanized loader and uses its mechanical might to battle the beast. Similarly, Sarah Conner, in *Terminator 2*, uses a paper clip to free herself from restraints and pick the lock on her door, and a hypodermic needle filled with drain cleaner as a weapon to escape from a mental hospital. In *Thelma and Louise,* there is less opportunity for hi-tech competency, but Thelma does have Louise shoot the police radio in the patrolman's car and does shoot two air holes in his trunk, before locking him in it.

Guns: These last two acts lead us to a fifth category of masculine consumption—guns. Guns are the most masculine of all products, because they symbolize not only the male genitalia (e.g., he banged her), but also the power and violence associated with men. Guns are associated with war-like violence in *Aliens* and *Terminator 2,* and with sexual violence in *Thelma & Louise.* The character of Ripley, verbally declining to become a warrior at the outset of *Aliens*, has become a magnificent Amazon by the narrative's end. She is instructed by the marine Hicks in the use of his large complex, rifle midway through the story. In the climactic scenes, she single-handedly rescues Neut from the monster armed with a flame thrower, grenade launcher, flares, and automatic rifle—a one-(wo)man army.

Similarly, Sarah Conner is completely comfortable with a variety of artillery. In the course of *Terminator 2*, she effectively uses an automatic pistol, police baton, hunting knife, laser-scoped automatic rifle, shotgun and grenade launcher. And Thelma and Louise, too timid to touch a 38 pistol at the outset of the film, become adept at using guns to shoot rapists, overwhelm policemen, rob convenience stores and blow-up the trucks of offensive drivers over the course of the story. This is a very powerful message conveyed by all three films: that women can shoot guns; that they can defend themselves with powerful, violent weapons. So often in films women have been depicted as helpless victims who must be protected by armed men. It is indeed a cultural transformation to see images of women taking this right, and responsibility, onto themselves.

Commit Crimes/Destroy Property: Just as these films depict women using guns in a masculine fashion, they also portray women engaging in crimes that are typically associated with male behavior. Thelma and Louise hold-up a convenience store, shoot-up a police car and evade police cars chasing them, causing several to crash. Ultimately, they drive their car off a cliff. Sarah Conner blows-up an entire computer company to prevent it from manufacturing super-computers for the Defense Department. She, her son, and the good Terminator also steal several cars, break into a service station, and destroy many police vehicles. Ripley, in an effort to prevent a human-devouring creature from returning to earth, blows up an entire planet and its (vacant) research complex.

One significant difference, however, between the property destruction engaged in by these characters and that usually exhibited by male characters in films is that these acts were undertaken generally for a "higher purpose". Thelma and Louise engage in crime only to elude police and survive; Sarah Conner is obsessed with saving the world from thermonuclear war; and Ripley acts to protect humans from a voraciously predatory species. As I shall argue in the closing portion of this paper, these female characters are distinguished from their male counterparts by their commitment to typically feminine agendas—the preservation and nurturance of life, rather than the acquisition of power or money.

Killing People/Monsters: Perhaps no act of consumption is more profound than the consuming of a life. Of course, to survive, all of us consume others' lives—for example, those of cattle, chickens, and pigs. Even vegetarians consume plant life. But people also consume lives by killing other people to gain material objectives or by displacing other species to expand their own species' habitat. In the three films discussed, several lives are consumed. In *Aliens,* Ripley—in a clear act of female-to-female species competition—destroys the creature's eggs and larvae, while protecting her own adopted offspring, Neut, and the human species, at large.

In *Terminator 2*, Sarah Conner beats a hospital guard and threatens the life of a psychiatrist (also breaking his arm), while escaping from a mental hospital. She also attempts to shoot an unarmed computer scientist, because he is the future inventor of a destructive super computer. However, she is unable to do so when he is protected by his terrified wife and son. (Sarah then realizes that it is morally wrong to kill a man for a crime he has not yet committed).

In perhaps the most morally troubling of the acts of interpersonal violence in these films, Louise shoots and kills a man who has beaten and attempted to rape her friend, Thelma. The man, Harlan, is clearly manipulative and brutal toward women, and we learn later that he has had many similar encounters. Further, we learn also that Louise was raped earlier in Texas and that her attacker was not punished. Thus, in a sense she was repaying two acts of sexual violence with a man's death. But, because it was her and Louise's self-respect which had been violated—and not life, itself—her willful killing of Harlan may be read as an overextraction of payment. As I will discuss later, this unfortunately confuses the ultimate message of T*helma and Louise*. Did the women die because they were the hapless victims of a misogynist, patriarchal society, or did they die because they had overstepped the boundaries of justified vengeance?

Feminine Nonconsumption

Traditionally in films women have not only failed to consume in masculine ways, they have also consumed in markedly feminine ways: female heroines are typically beautiful; they have attractively styled hair; they wear lovely clothing that enhances their sexual attractiveness; they wear lipstick and eye makeup. Just as they broke the rules regarding masculine consumer behavior, the heroines in A*liens*, *Terminator 2,* and *Thelma & Louise* also break the rules regarding feminine consumption: Their hair is unkempt, faces bare of makeup, clothes are disheveled or purposely utilitarian. Unlike most women in film, these characters sweat, get dirty, and function without regard to their appearance.

Make-up: Feminine consumption norms dictate that women use makeup to decorate their faces in order to make themselves more attractive to men. The heroines in the three motion pictures discussed here act counter to these norms by either never using makeup or by abandoning its use. Ripley and Sarah Conner are presented to us initially, and throughout the entire narrative, without makeup. Their faces are bare and plain; they make no coy or suggestive facial gestures toward men. Their faces are simply faces. Conversely, at the outset of *Thelma & Louise,* both the central female characters are lavishly made-up. Their faces are signboards of feminine attractiveness and availability—mascaraed lashes, rouged cheeks, painted lips, powdered skin. However, over the course of the story, their efforts at maintaining these facial facades are slowly abandoned, giving way at the end of the film to the bare-skinned, sunburned, dirt-creased honesty of their newfound status as female outlaws. In perhaps one of the most poignant scenes signalling this transformation, Louise begins to apply lipstick to her parched lips outside a convenience store. She glimpses an older, completely passive woman entrapped within her rural house wearing lipstick. She glances at her own worn, dusty face in the car mirror and in a moment of epiphanic self-recognition ("I am no longer what I once was"), tosses the lipstick out the car window.

Hairstyling: After their faces, traditionally perhaps women's most decorated feature is their hair. Women's hair, especially hair that is long, soft and flowing, is a distinctive cultural sign of their gender and communicates their availability to men. When Thelma told Louise she was "letting her hair down" by drinking straight bourbon and dancing with a handsome stranger, she metaphorically implied that she was seeking to make herself attractive to men other than her husband; that she was not going to behave as a proper wife should. Hair styles were an important semiotic device in all three films. At the outset of *Aliens,* Ripley's hair is shoulder length and somewhat feminine. But after she agrees to return to the distant planet and assist the search for the creature, her hair is cut short, signalling her coming evolution to warrior status. Sarah Conner's hair is shoulder-length and straight; she wears very long bangs which she uses to hide her eyes (and escape attention) from the psychiatrist. Preparing to kill scientist Tyson, she ties her hair back away from her face so she can better aim her rifle. And it remains this way for the rest of the film. Thelma and Louise begin their adventure with beautifully styled, curled hair worn draped over their shoulders. By the film's end, their unkempt, dirty hair is pinned-up in a utilitarian fashion to cool their necks. No longer viewing themselves as decorative objects, their hair styling has been relegated to functional status.

Clothing: Clothing is another highly significant gender marker. Women are culturally expected to wear dresses and skirts, and undergarments such as hosiery and brassieres. Once again, these four female heroines disregard social expectations. Ripley wears a white tank top and gray sweatpants at the outset of *Aliens.* Upon arriving on the creature's planet, she wears gray industrial overalls. She remains bra-less throughout the entire film. Similarly, Sarah Conner wears gray sweatpants and a white T-shirt at the mental hospital; she wears a black tank top and black work pants with combat boots after escaping, and puts on combat fatigues when she embarks on her mission to shoot the scientist. She remains in this apparel for the rest of the film. Like Ripley, Sarah Conner wears no bra.[1]

Thelma and Louise initially wear highly decorative, feminine apparel. They have on earrings, scarves, fringe and form-fitting clothing, all of which strongly signified their status as traditional, men-pleasing women. By story's end their apparel, like themselves, has become transformed to functional, utilitarian status. They are trying to survive, not decorate. They go over the cliff (and into iconic status) in torn jeans, rolled-up shirt sleeves, bandannas, sweat bands and wearing, fittingly, a trucker's cap and cowboy's hat.

THE MEANING OF THE NEW WOMAN: SOME HOPES AND SPECULATIONS

The commercial and critical success of these three films suggests that their presentation of the nouvelle femme struck a responsive chord in contemporary culture. That consumers viewed these characters as acceptable exemplars of female behavior is encouraging to those having feminist values and provides a provocative glimpse into shifting cultural beliefs regarding women's roles in society. Two of the films, A*liens* and *Terminator 2,* present women as competent, but compassionate, warriors who struggle selflessly against horrific threats to human life. The character of Ripley actually stands in opposition to two evil foes: a violent, predatory space monster that devours human life and an inhumane, profiteering corporation that is willing to sacrifice people for money. Ripley—an androgynous female figure—is depicted in the narrative as the appropriate choice to overcome both evils. She is courageous and intelligent enough to defeat the monster; she is also compassionate and sufficiently moral to resist the lures of material gain.

Similarly, the character of Sarah Conner in T*erminator 2* is pitted against a machine-monster and the corrupt, money-hungry computer company that permits machines to dominate humans. In their roles as strong, heroic mothers, Ripley and Sarah both metaphorically protect all humankind as their "offspring". The films teach us that women—because they value life more than power—are more to be trusted than men in securing humankind's survival.

While the underlying ideology of A*liens* and *Terminator 2* is implicitly feminist, that of *Thelma and Louise* is explicitly so. Embarking on a holiday away from their abusive husband and disinterested boyfriend, respectively, Thelma and Louise set forth on a journey through virtually every misogynist locale on the map of contemporary man-woman relations: the smooth pick-up-artist turned violent rapist, the unwillingness of the justice system to extend credulity to women who are sexually abused, the swiftness of the patriarchal police system to punish women who act aggressively against men and property, the smooth talking con men who ingratiate themselves and then vaporize with one's money, the macho men who see all women as eager recipients of their lustful-

---

[1] The bralessness of both Ripley and Sarah Conner is worth commenting on. In both films, their breasts are clearly outlined beneath their shirts, which would normally have sexual connotations. However, in both films these women's breasts are treated in a very matter-of-fact manner, simply as normal components of the female chest, rather than as sexually charged objects.

ness. On their road trip to oblivion, Thelma and Louise pass all these highly gendered markers of the inequality between the sexes.

Although it ends in the women's deaths, the film also shows us moments of female revelry, of true comradeship, of genuine freedom in the sense that Janis Joplin meant it: "just another name for nothing left to lose". These two women show us that by losing it all, they ultimately found themselves. Hopefully, in the not-too-distant future our society will support a film that shows the outlaw heroines riding-off happily into the sunset, just as the men do.

REFERENCES

Bristor, Julia M. and Eileen Fischer (1991), "Objectivity and Gender in Consumer Research: A Feminist Deconstructionist Critique," in J. A. Costa (ed.), *Gender and Consumer Behavior*, Salt Lake City, University of Utah Press, 115-123.

Fischer, Eileen and Stephen J. Arnold (1990), "More Than a Labor of Love: Gender Roles and Christmas Gift Shopping," *Journal of Consumer Research*, 17, (December), 333-345.

Hirschman, Elizabeth C. (1991), "A Feminist Critique of Marketing Theory: Toward Agentic-Communal Balance," in J. A. Costa (ed.), *Gender and Consumer Behavior*, Salt Lake City, University of Utah Press, 324-340.

Holbrook, Morris B. (1990), "The Role of Lyricism in Research on Consumer Emotions," in M. E. Goldberg, G. Gorn and R. W. Pollay, (eds.), *Advances in Consumer Research*, Vol. 17, Provo, UT: Association for Consumer Research, 1-18.

Stern, Barbara B. (1991), "Deja Vu: Feminism Revisited," in J. A. Costa (ed.), *Gender and Consumer Behavior*, Salt Lake City, University of Utah Press, 341-349.

Stern, Barbara B. (1989), "Literary Criticism and Consumer Research: Overview and Illustrative Analysis," *Journal of Consumer Research*, 16, (December), 322-334.

Wollen, Peter (1985), "The Auteur Theory," in G. Mast and M. Cohen, (eds.), *Film Theory and Criticism*, Oxford: Oxford University Press, 553-562.

A Sociolinguistic Approach to Gender and Personal Selling
Val Larsen, Virginia Tech

ABSTRACT

Drawing on sociolinguistic and social psychological research, this paper suggests that women typically differ from men in their speech styles and patterns of social interaction. For managers and salespeople, the responses typical of women are often more adaptive than those typical of men.

INTRODUCTION

At the core of feminism is an ideological boundary line which divides feminists into two broad camps: rationalist feminists who deny and radical feminists who affirm that women differ significantly from men (Rose). For the most part, the founding mothers of contemporary feminism (de Beaúvoir 1952; Freidan 1963; Lakoff 1975) were rationalists who asserted that there were no important differences between the sexes—a tactic that was easy to justify on practical grounds. Men have often used alleged differences between the sexes to justify the exclusion of women from positions of power and important sectors of the economy. Customs and laws that are portrayed as protections—the ban on women in combat, for instance—often function in practice as protectionist barriers to professional advancement for women. Thus, in many cases, the proper answer to Henry Higgins' question, "Why can't a woman be more like a man," has been, "because men won't let her."

While some customs and laws which have precluded full participation are beginning to change, there are still many formal and informal barriers which prevent women from receiving rewards commensurate with their merit. And like all protectionist barriers, these remaining sexist traditions exact an economic price from us all, but especially, as Gary Becker (1971) has pointed out in his analysis of the economics of discrimination, from women, the objects of the discrimination.[1] Thus, it is important that researchers not inadvertently reinforce prejudices which impoverish us all.

Though they are fully cognizant of the risk that distinctions between men and women may be misused, radical feminist researchers have recently begun to discover and celebrate certain qualities which seem to be characteristically female (Daly 1978; Gilligan 1982; Tannen 1990). This paper is part of that recent trend. Drawing upon social psychological and sociolinguistic research, it suggests that women typically differ from men in their styles of speech and patterns of social interaction. It applies this basic point in a business context by further suggesting that typical female responses are often more adaptive for managers and salespeople than typical male responses. The pattern of differences between the sexes is discussed in the first section of the paper, the applications to management and marketing in the second.

COMMUNITY VERSUS AGENCY

It has been shown by a sizeable body of research that men and women differ in their typical patterns of social and linguistic interaction. In a series of studies and a review of previous literature, Carlson (1971) encapsulated many of these differences by suggesting that men tend to be concerned with agentic, women with communal goals. The agentic goals typical of males involve an impersonal view of the world, a view in which the autonomous self is separated from its milieu while others are seen as a class of objects to be tested and investigated. Communal goals, on the other hand, are associated with a self defined by its social context, its interpersonal relatedness. Thus, women tend to see both self and others as socially oriented subjects, not as autonomous objects.

Carlson worked at a relatively high level of abstraction, but subsequent research has shown that the agentic and communal conceptions of the self have practical consequences. Thus, research by Maltz and Borker (1982), Goodwin (1990), and Tannen (1990) found that because men conceive of themselves primarily as autonomous agents in a divided and competitive world, they tend to view social interactions as public contests in which the prize is status and respect. Their concern with personal autonomy and public status leads them to favor hierarchical patterns of social organization. Beginning when they are very young and continuing through adulthood, males organize their work and play hierarchically. These hierarchies have the advantage of making it relatively clear what the score is—who is up, who down: those giving orders are on top, those taking them on the bottom. Who gives, who takes orders is negotiated in conversations that are a form of ritual combat. Concerned with their hierarchical position, interlocutors struggle to dominate each other intellectually and, thereby, establish the right to command (Ong 1981). They establish elaborate, apparently impersonal systems of rules to regulate conflict but often fight about how the rules are to be applied in particular cases (Maltz and Borker 1982).

Since women tend to see themselves primarily as members of a community, their typical patterns of social interaction are generally different from those of men. For them, personal status and security is a function of the community's status and strength. They will be strong if their community is strong. And the strength of the community depends on the intimacy of its members. Unlike hierarchical status, communal intimacy does not require that one person be down in order for the other to be up. On the contrary, "the essential element of connection is symmetry," so conversations among women tend to be "negotiations for closeness in which people try to seek and give confirmation and support, and to reach consensus" (Tannen 1990, pp. 28, 25). Women's speech patterns tend to be nonconfrontational. Thus, they use tag questions—i.e. "don't you think?"—at the end of their statements more frequently than men do. And they tend to resolve conflict through compromise or evasion rather than through the threats or appeals to rules favored by men (Sheldon 1990).

Though, in the interest of clarity, I have thus far made a sharp distinction between women and men, it is important to keep in mind that on all the dimensions which define agency and communion, the distributions of females and males overlap. So one cannot draw conclusions about individuals on the basis of these studies. Nor can one conclude that agency is bad, communion good, or visa versa. Indeed, Carlson (1971) suggests that the integration of agency and communion is an important developmental task for both women and men since mental and social health depend upon our achieving a degree of androgyny. Carlson also points out, however, that women are more likely than men to be characterized by androgyny, the desired state. Men—and psychiatric patients—are more likely to be one sided, exhibiting a purely agentic orientation.

While the evidence for a correlation between gender and agentic or communal orientation is strong, one intriguing study

---

[1] Becker focused on the economic consequences of discrimination against blacks, but his analysis is equally applicable to gender discrimination.

indicates that a person's orientation may be a function of power, not of gender. In this study of 415 black students at Howard University, no difference was found between female and male students: both genders manifested a communal orientation. White males were the only group which consistently emphasized the individual as a basis for self-esteem (Carlson and Levy 1970). It is possible, therefore, that people adopt an agentic orientation when they are in a position to attain power and make the rules which determine success or failure. The communal orientation, on the other hand, may have arisen as a way of coping with a world where one does not make the rules or have hierarchical status. It makes no sense to appeal to status or rules if your adversary has the status and gets to make and change the rules at will. Under such circumstances, you must, perforce, be flexible and rely upon a network of relationships to protect your interests. This seems to be the strategy that women have adopted.

The thesis of this paper can now be restated in an elaborated form. Though women probably developed their flexible, informal sociolinguistic style as a way of preserving some dignity and influence in a world where social arrangements rendered them formally powerless, the world has changed in ways that often make women's private, interpersonal, communal orientation more adaptive for both men and women than the public, autonomous, agentic orientation usually favored by males. One broad index of this favorable trend is changes in public discourse that have accompanied the demise of governing hierarchies: kings, nobles, and exclusively male electorates.

Public discourse has traditionally been the domain of males, private discourse of females (Kramarae 1981). And even today, men generally speak more in public, women more in private settings (Swacker 1972; Tannen 1990). But while the patterns of public and private discourse were quite distinct in the past, with speeches being much more formal and abstract than conversations, the differences have recently diminished. And virtually all the change has been made in the traditionally male domain of public discourse, for speeches have become more personal, informal, and conversational, more like women's private discourse (Tannen 1990).

AGENCY AND COMMUNION IN BUSINESS CONTEXTS

In his article on agency and communion, Carlson (1971) suggested that females should, on average, be more effective administrators than males because, being relatively androgenous, they are more likely to devote themselves to accomplishing shared goals rather than to amassing personal control and power. This is a remarkable observation given the dearth of women in administrative positions. But an earlier study of academics by Bernard (1964) both confirms Carlson's supposition and helps explain why so few women have been able to become and remain administrators. Bernard found that while female professors were more inclined than their male counterparts to devote themselves to serving students and the institution, their devotion was not rewarded, for it was not compatible with an organizational structure based on hierarchy and designed to reward the attainment of personal power and prestige. Women did not succeed to the degree one might expect, Bernard suggested, because they rejected or disregarded the agentic first principles upon which the university was founded.

Since business, like academia, has traditionally been dominated by males, it is not surprising that most corporations like most universities were created in the image and to the taste of men. Hierarchy—at Ford, a seventeen level hierarchy until a few years ago (Peters and Waterman 1982)—has been the preferred corporate order. Both internal relations between employees and external relations with suppliers and customers have been hierarchically organized. But in the business world, the market has, for some time now, been unkind to hierarchies. Stodgy and inflexible, wasteful of human resources, many hierarchically organized companies have been unable to keep pace in an increasingly dynamic and chaotic global economy. Competitors which have organized themselves along flatter, more communal lines have been winning market share. The consequent reorganization of many American corporations is a trend that is favorable for women because their habitual communication styles equip them to function well in the flatter, more communal, more team-oriented organizations which are emerging from the turmoil. Nor is the convergence between the ways in which businesses are organized and the communal style of women an accident. Business leaders no longer have the degree of power and control they once had. Companies have become too big, the global economy too integrated, competition too fierce, and the marketplace too chaotic for any one person at the pinnacle of a corporate hierarchy to control the market and make the rules. Everyone has become powerless to one degree or another.

What is striking in both management and marketing is the extent to which changes in perspective over the past sixty years have moved women's way, shifting the emphasis from agentic autonomy and power to communal cooperation. To focus first on relations inside a company, management gurus have long held that rigid, rule-bound hierarchies are dysfunctional. Drucker (1942) and Deming (1986) have argued since the 40's that it is workers at the bottom of a hierarchy who have the most intimate knowledge of production processes and that an organization's hierarchy must be flattened to take advantage of the workers' knowledge (Drucker 1992). They and successors like Peters and Waterman (1982), Naisbitt and Aburdeme (1985), Sink and Tuttle (1989) have argued that authoritarian management (the style most compatible with the male concern for status and order) must give way to networking, people-oriented management (a style compatible with the inclinations of women). They suggest that workers be organized in small, non-hierarchical teams which can be flexible and innovative as they solve problems. The teams that comprise this *adhocracy* can be kept small only if people who have an interest in the team's actions but are not on the team can be confident that their interests will be represented (Peters and Waterman 1982). And this, in turn, is possible only when team members have a communal rather than an agentic orientation.

To focus on just one sociolinguistic consequence of this trend toward flattened hierarchies and a people orientation, Crosby (1972) has suggested that male managers enhance their chances of achieving their first goal, survival, by adopting the indirect communication style of women, for an indirect proposal to stockholders or employees will not destroy the manager if it is denied or modified. Direct orders carry the risk of involving one in a battle to the death over something that is not very important.

Like management, marketing has seen over the course of this century a broad shift from an agentic to a communal orientation. Sales involved little more than haggling and pressure selling prior to the turn of the century (Bartels 1988), and in the early decades popular lecturers on sales like Paul W. Ivey (1925) emphasized the development of an agentic sales personality, an aggressive stance characterized by the ability to persuade customers to accept the salesperson's viewpoint and purchase the product. But by the 50's, the sales orientation was beginning to give way to the marketing concept with its customer orientation (Dawson 1970; Kolgraf 1980), and some have suggested that customer orientation may be succeeded by a still more communal societal orientation in which the interests of the larger society take precedence over those of the individual consumer (Robin and Reidenbach 1987).

The relevance of these shifts to the issue of gender becomes apparent in an anecdote recounted by Deborah Tannen. Tannen (1990, pp. 66-67) reports the experience of a woman who returned to a computer store for help in understanding how to operate her PC. On her first visit, a man assisted her. Clearly status conscious, he emphasized the difference between himself and the customer by using technical language and a condescending tone. He explained the proper use of the machine so quickly that the customer could not remember anything he had said or done by the time she got home. Dreading the encounter but still unable to use the product, the customer returned a week later and was helped by a woman. This salesperson sought to minimize the distance between herself and the customer, using non-technical terms where possible, carefully explaining technical terms she could not avoid. Instead of merely demonstrating procedures, she had the customer perform them herself. The customer left the second session well satisfied.

As trained marketers, we recognize that the salesman was deplorably deficient in customer orientation. His gender did not make that inevitable: not all men confuse their customers, and not all women make information easy to understand. Still, Tannen uses this anecdote to make a larger point about the communication styles typical of men and women. Because men tend to be agentically oriented, they generally frame conversations as adversarial contests for status from which they try to emerge one up. Thus, the salesman's behavior was a natural outgrowth of his agentic orientation. Because women, on the other hand, have a communal orientation, they tend to play down their own expertise and frame conversations as a cooperative, collegial endeavor just as this saleswoman did (Boyan 1989). Women are therefore more inclined than men to be customer oriented. They are less likely to need Dale Carnegie-type training, for viewed in the light of sociolinguistic research, it is evident that Carnegie (1981) sought to make salesmen more effective by training them to communicate and socialize as a woman would.

CAVEATS AND CONCESSIONS

I have focused in this paper on the advantages of a communal orientation to women and to businesses which hire women. But a communal orientation is not always advantageous. There are circumstances when it is important to display one's credentials or hold the floor in public or take an openly adversarial stance vis á vis an opponent. An agentic orientation equips one to do these things. So ideally, we should all be androgenous and bilingual, able to switch between agentic and communal modes of sociation and discourse as circumstances warrant. Men should develop a communal, women an agentic side to their character. That goal is probably worth pursuing (Heilbrun 1973), but it is not as simple as it seems—at least not for women.

Among the many asymmetries in our society which are disadvantageous to women is an asymmetrical willingness to tolerate untypical behavior. When women are not assertive in public settings, they are negatively judged to lack confidence or competence. When they are assertive, they are negatively judged to be unwomanly (Lakoff 1975; Leet-Pellegrini 1980; Tannen 1990).

Finally, I must concede a point to Lakoff (1975), Spender (1980), and Kramarae (1981), rationalist feminists who argue that differentiating the discourse of men and women may play into the oppressor's hands. Women's pattern of discourse has not developed in a vacuum but rather in a patriarchy jealous of its power and determined to force upon women styles of speech and sociation which frame them as subordinate and inferior. Where patriarchal assumptions remain entrenched, speech strategies which are intended to foster community may simply reaffirm the subordination of women or may be interpreted as doing so. It will, therefore, often be difficult to capitalize upon the strengths of women's communal orientation while at the same time avoiding further victimization.

WORKS CITED

Bartels, Robert (1988), *The History of Marketing Thought*, 3rd Edition, Columbus, OH: Publishing Horizons, Inc.

Becker, Gary S. (1971), *The Economics of Discrimination*, 2nd edition, Chicago: University of Chicago Press.

Bernard, J. (1964), *Academic Women*, University Park: Pennsylvania State University Press.

Boyan, Lee (1989), "Who's More Productive," *American Salesman*, 16 (November).

Carlson, Rae (1971), "Sex Differences in Ego Functioning: Exploratory Studies of Agency and Communion," *Journal of Consulting and Clinical Psychology*, 37 (October), 267-277.

_____ and Levy, N. (1970), "Self, Values, and Affects: Derivations from Tomkins' Polarity Theory," *Journal of Personality and Social Psychology*, 16, 338-345.

Carnegie, Dale (1981), *How To Win Friends and Influence People*, New York: Pocket Books.

Crosby, Philip B. (1972), *The Art of Getting Your Own Sweet Way*, New York: McGraw Hill.

Daly, Mary (1978), *Gyn/Ecology: The Metaethics of Radical Feminism*, Boston: Beacon.

Dawson, Leslie M. (1970), "Toward a New Concept of Sales Management," *Journal of Marketing*, 34 (April), 33-38.

de Beaúvoir, Simone (1952), *The Second Sex*, trans. H.M. Parshley, New York: Knopf.

Deming, W. Edwards (1986) *Out of the Crisis*, Cambridge, Massachusetts: MIT Press.

Drucker, Peter F. (1942), *The Future of Industrial Man*

_____ (1992) *Managing for the Future*, New York: Truman Talley Books.

Friedan, Betty (1963), *The Feminine Mystique*, New York: Norton.

Gilligan, Carol (1982), *In a Different Voice: Psychological Theory and Women's Development*, Cambridge, MA: Harvard University Press.

Goodwin, Marjorie Harness, *He-Said-She-Said*, Bloomington: Indiana University Press.

Heilbrun, Carolyn G. (1973), *Toward a Recognition of Androgyny*, New York: W. W. Norton & Company.

Ivey, Paul W. (1925), *Salesmanship Applied*, New York: A. W. Shaw Co.

Kolgraf, Ron (1980), "The New Sales Manager," *Industrial Distribution*, 70 (August) 28-30.

Kramarae, Cheris (1981), *Women and Men Speaking*, Rowley, Massachusetts: Newbury House Publishers, Inc.

Leet-Pellegrini, H. M. (1980), "Conversational Dominance as a Function of Gender and Expertise," *Language: Social Psychological Perspectives*, ed. Howard Giles, W. Peter Robinson, and Philip M. Smith, Oxford: Pergamon, 97-104.

Lakoff, Robin (1975), *Language and a Woman's Place*, New York: Harper and Row.

Naisbitt, John and Patricia Aburdeme (1985), *Reinventing the Corporation*, New York: Warner Books.

Maltz, Daniel N. and Ruth A. Borker (1982), "A Cultural Approach to Male-Female Miscommunication," *Language and Social Identity*, ed. by John J. Gumperz, Cambridge: Cambridge University Press, 196-216.

Peters, Thomas J. and Robert H. Waterman (1982), *In Search of Excellence*, New York: Harper & Row.

Ong, Walter J. (1981), *Fighting for Life: Contest, Sexuality, and Consciousness*, Ithaca: Cornell University Press.

Robin, Donald P. and Eric Reidenbach (1987), "Social Responsibility, Ethics, and Marketing Strategy: Closing the Gap Between Concept and Application," *Journal of Marketing*, 51 (January), 44-58.

Rose, Ellen Cronan (n. d.), "The Good Mother: From Gaia to Gilead," *Frontiers*, 12:1, 77-97.

Sheldon, Amy (1990), "Pickle Fights: Gendered Talk in Preschool Disputes," *Discourse Processes*, 13:1.

Sink, D. Scott and Thomas C. Tuttle (1989), *Planning and Measurement in Your Organization of the Future*, Norcross, Georgia: Industrial Engineering and Management Press.

Swacker, Marjorie (1976), "Women's Verbal Behavior at Learned and Professional Conferences," *The Sociology of the Languages of American Women*, ed. by Betty Lou Dubois and Isabel Crouch, San Antonio: Trinity University, 155-160.

Tannen, Deborah (1990), *You Just Don't Understand: Men and Women in Conversation*, New York: Ballantine Books.

An Investigation of Ethnicity and Sex-Role Attitude as Factors Influencing Household Financial Task Sharing Behavior

Chankon Kim, Concordia University
Michel Laroche, Concordia University
Lianxi Zhou, Concordia University

ABSTRACT

This study proposes and tests a structural equation model specifying the relationships among the English-French Canadian ethnicity, sex-role attitude, and the household finance related task sharing behavior. Findings show that a stronger French-Canadian ethnic identity of the wife and a more modern sex-role attitude of the husband are associated with a more egalitarian approach to task sharing by the couple.

INTRODUCTION

One of the topics that research on family decision making has been concerned with relates to the factors influencing family role structure or influence sharing (Corfman and Lehmann 1987; Rosen and Granbois 1983; Qualls 1987; Green and Cunningham 1975). Of the various factors investigated, two have recently attracted considerable attention - culture/ethnicity (Imperia, O'Guinn, and MacAdams 1985; Green and Cunningham 1980; Douglas 1979; Hempel 1974) and sex-role attitude of the spouse (Kim and Lee 1989; Qualls 1987; Rosen and Granbois 1983; Schaninger, Buss, and Grover 1982; Scanzoni 1977).

The impact of culture on attitudes and behaviors of individuals is pervasive. Individual values and norms are shaped and moulded to correspond to those of the culture in which they live. In the case of family life, cultural norms prescribe each spouse's roles and behaviors. Blood and Wolfe (1960) proposed long ago that cultural norms and expectations have a significant impact on the family decision making process and on the division of labor between the spouses. The reported research in general confirms the variation across cultures in the patterns of decision making (Hempel 1974; Douglas 1979; Green, Verhage, and Cunningham 1981).

Sex-role attitudes reflect, in essence, beliefs about the appropriate sex-based division of labor and power structure in the marriage (Brogan and Kutner 1976). Such beliefs are affected by the prevailing societal/cultural norms (Qualls 1987; Scanzoni 1977), and thus should vary across different cultures. There is a fair amount of evidence that sex-role attitudes of spouses in turn influence the household decision role structure and responsibility sharing (Mortimer, Hall, and Hill 1978; Bird, Bird, and Scruggs 1984; Kim and Lee 1989).

The research reported here investigates the relationships among three variables - ethnicity, sex-role attitude, and household task sharing. It proposes and tests a structural model that links the above variables. The tasks that are focused on in this study are family finance related decisions and activities (Green and Cunningham 1975; Rosen and Granbois 1983; Kim and Lee 1989).

LITERATURE REVIEW

Cultural/Ethnic Influences

Research investigating cultural/ethnic influences on family decision making typically compares families from two or more cultures/ethnic groups with respect to the husband-wife influence pattern for a variety of household purchase decisions. Some studies have compared Hispanic-American families with Anglo-American families. Imperia, O'Guinn, and MacAdams (1985) report a stronger pattern of husband dominance for durable purchase decisions in Mexican-American families than in Anglo-American families. Also found was that Mexican-American families engage in significantly less joint decision making than do Anglo-American families. A later study by Webster (1989) concurs that high-Hispanic identification couples tend to exhibit a stronger pattern of husband dominance than English-speaking and low-Hispanic couples in the home and automobile purchase situations.

Douglas (1979) investigated cross-cultural differences in husband/wife involvement using samples from Chicago, Glasgow/London, Paris, Brussels, and Quebec City. The author found a substantial similarity in husband/wife involvement in a number of household activities in all five samples. However, noticeable differences were reported between the French speaking and English speaking samples. A greater degree of wife's involvement was reported in the French speaking samples for the husband's clothing and care decisions. High levels of shared or husband involvement was observed for traditionally wife-specialized tasks such as going to the supermarket, vacuuming, and taking out the garbage. Further, there was greater joint involvement in the French language groups in the otherwise husband-dominated activity of saving and investment.

Two other cross-national studies (Green and Cunningham 1981; Green, Verhage, and Cunningham 1981) examined husband-wife decision making patterns in Venezuelan and Dutch families and compared them with the pattern in American families. The first study found greater husband dominance in Venezuelan families than in American families for seven of the nine decisions involving mostly durables, and greater joint decision making by American couples. The latter study also revealed significant cross-national variations in that American wives made more household purchase and finance decisions autonomously than Dutch wives, and that Dutch couples engaged in more joint decision making.

Hempel's (1974) study comparing families from Connecticut and Northwest England focused on husband-wife roles in the various stages of the home purchase decision process. The English couples reported a greater level of joint input than the Connecticut couples in the initiation stage. A high level of role sharing was reported by the families in both cultures for the information seeking stage. The author noted, however, that husband-wife differences in role perception were greater than international differences.

Green et al. (1983) in their study of husband-wife involvement in five countries (The United States, France, Holland, Gabon, and Venezuela) concluded that certain product categories are universally male or female stereotyped. For instance, grocery decisions are dominated by wives whereas automobile and insurance decisions tend to fall under husbands' influence. The authors associate the cross-national variations observed for other product categories with the stages of economic development, by inferring that husbands in less developed countries make more decisions than those in developed countries.

By and large, existing findings do demonstrate sufficient evidence of a cross-cultural/national variation in husband-wife decision influence and task sharing patterns. While some of this variation may well be explained by other factors such as the level of economic development, a critical determinant has to be the different set of cultural norms and values to which a society subscribes. As stated earlier, ethnicity as a factor influencing the household task sharing behavior is examined in the present study. Specifically, we examine French-/English-Canadian ethnic identity of the spouse as a factor influencing the pattern of household financial task sharing. The existing literature on the English and French Canadian comparisons on lifestyles, though not entirely germane to our purpose, provides some insights into this area.

The French- and English-Canadian lifestyle research conducted in the 70s suggests that French-Canadian families are more traditional than English-Canadian families in the division of household labor (Tigert 1973; Mallen 1977; Vickers and Benson 1972). These studies show that French-Canadian females are more strongly oriented toward the home, the family, the children, and the kitchen. Langelier (1982), in his discussion of Franco-American families, similarly states that "...it is fairly safe to assert that sex-specific roles are well defined, with almost no sharing of tasks between husband and wife." (p. 233)

While the general belief is that French Canadians are more traditional and conservative than English Canadians in their perceptions of male/female (husband/wife) roles and behaviors, recent studies by Kim and Laroche (1989) and Hui et al. (1993) suggest otherwise. These studies show that French Canadians believe more strongly that women should pursue a career outside the home and put less importance on family life and having children. While more investigation is certainly needed to ascertain the direction of the differences, some potential explanations for the discrepancies in the existing findings may include true changes in lifestyles of French and/or English Canadians over the last two decades or so and differences in the approaches to ethnic identification used in the latter studies.

Sex-Role Attitudes

According to Scanzoni (1975), sex-role norms and sex typed behaviors are acquired by contact with sociocultural agents. Cultural or societal norms and values are an important source of influence that shapes and conditions sex-role attitudes of individuals. Qualls (1987) elaborates that " ... sex-role preferences are indicative of culturally determined attitudes (traditionalism versus modernity) toward the role of wife/husband and mother/father in the household. Sex role preferences reflect the societal standards by which family members determine the rewards and costs associated with their behavioral actions." (pp. 265-266) Cross-cultural variations in sex-role attitudes, on the basis of such reasoning, can be easily expected.

Much research gives credence to the hypothesis that sex-role attitudes, in turn, influence household role behavior (Mortimer, Hall and Hill 1978; Bird, Bird, and Scruggs 1984). A general belief is that egalitarian sex-role attitudes foster a commitment to more equal sharing of household decision influences and family responsibilities. The areas in which past research has demonstrated the influence of sex-role attitudes include family financial management, household chores performance, and product purchase decision making.

Schaninger, Buss, and Grover (1982) report that for the financial tasks traditionally handled by the wife (e.g., handling expenses for food, beverages and clothing), sex-role modern families showed less wife but more joint and husband influence. On the other hand, for those traditionally husband dominated tasks (e.g., handling expenses for transportation, recreation, and saving plans), less husband but more joint and wife influence was observed among the sex-role modern families. Similarly, Qualls (1982) found that the sex-role modern husbands in his sample perceived to a lesser extent than sex-role traditional husbands that savings decisions should be husband dominant. The study by Kim and Lee (1989) shows that couples with more sex-role modern wives are likely to take a more egalitarian approach in deciding/handling expenses and in making savings decisions. The husband's sex-role attitude showed no significant relationship with the extent of financial task sharing.

The relationship between spouses' sex-role attitudes and the sharing of domestic chores has been the focus of investigation by some sociological studies. The study by Perrucci, Potter, and Rhoads (1978), examining the determinants of husband's participation in 12 selected household/child-care activities, found that the traditional sex-role perception was significantly associated with the husband's participation in fewer of these activities. Two other studies (Bird, Bird, and Scruggs 1984; Ross 1987) demonstrated the sex-role attitude and role behavior relationship, but only for husbands. They both found that the husband's sex-role attitude was a significant predictor of the household division of labor; modern sex-role husbands accepted more traditional household responsibilities.

With regards to product purchase decisions, Qualls (1982) reports that sex-role traditional husbands, much more so than sex-role modern husbands, perceived themselves as dominating purchase decisions regarding vacations, automobiles, housing, and insurance. His study similarly found that wives' sex-role attitudes on the contrary did not show any relationship to the perceived influence pattern. Schaninger, Buss and Grover (1982) investigated the influence of sex-role attitudes on the five aspects of the last durable purchase made by families. Their findings indicated that sex-role modern families show less husband's but more joint and wife's influence over three of the five aspects of the purchase (who decided initially to buy, when to buy, and where to buy).

HYPOTHESES

Based on the above literature review, the following hypotheses are proposed and tested in this study:

H_1: The stronger English- (French-) Canadian the husband/wife is, the more (less) modern sex-role attitude he/she holds.

H_2: The stronger English- (French-) Canadian the husband/wife is, the more (less) egalitarian is the pattern of household financial task sharing.

H_3: The more modern (traditional) sex-role attitude the husband/wife holds, the more (less) egalitarian is the pattern of household financial task sharing.

The conceptual model incorporating these hypotheses is presented in a diagram contained in Figure 1. The model also hypothesizes a correlational relationship between the husband's and wife's ethnicity and between the husband's and wife's sex-role attitude. Whereas the first relationship is easily envisaged, the latter may not be intuitive. The great deal of emotional and instrumental interdependence that exists between two people in marital relationship is expected to have a guiding force on the spouses' attitudes toward a more mutually compatible direction. This hypothesis that one spouse's sex-role attitude should covary with the other's has been empirically supported by Cronkite (1977) and Kim and Lee (1989).

FIGURE 1
A Conceptual Model Depicting the Relationships Among English-French Canadian Ethnicity, Sex-role Attitude and Couple's Task Sharing

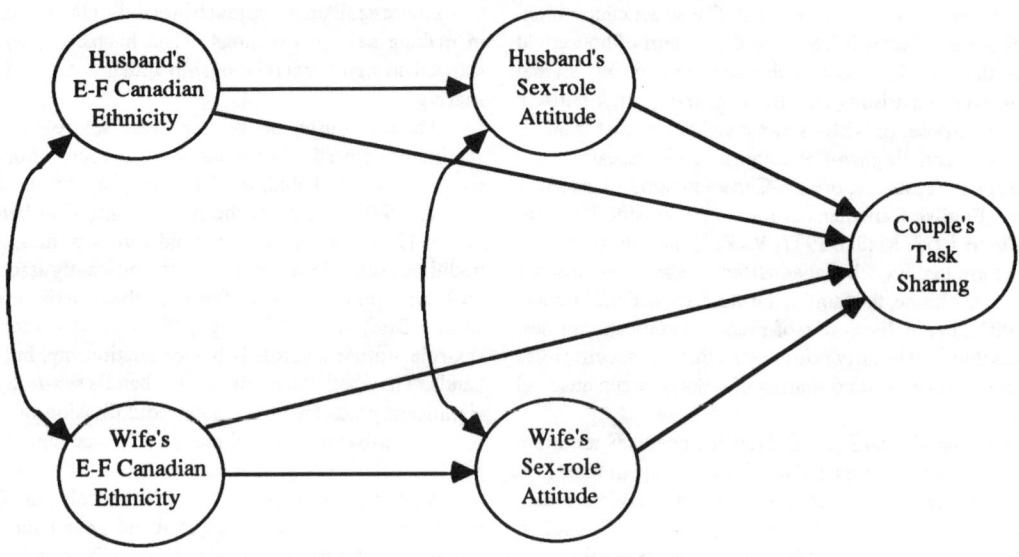

METHODOLOGY

Sample

Data used in this study came from a survey of households in four districts of the greater Montreal area. These four districts were selected in the first stage of the area sampling procedure used in this study because of their high concentrations of English- and French-Canadian populations. In the second stage, residential streets were randomly chosen, and efforts were made to contact as many households on these selected streets as possible. Interviewers contacted door to door male or female head of the household, and asked for the cooperation of those who identified themselves and their spouses as either French or English Canadians.

Two questionnaires (to be completed independently by the husband and the wife) were left with those who consented, to be either picked up by the interviewer or mailed in a self-addressed envelope. Respondents had a choice between the English and the French versions of the questionnaire. In total, 120 couples provided usable responses. The French questionnaire was used by 61 couples (51%), the English questionnaire by 52 couples (43%), and 7 couples (6%) responded to mixed questionnaires. In terms of key demographic features of the sample, the median age of the husbands was between 41 to 50 and 31 to 40 for wives, 50.8% of the husbands and 39.8% of the wives reported to have partially or fully completed university or more, and 53% (according to both the husbands' and wives' reports) had the household income of $60,000 or more. Thus, the sample consists of couples with a somewhat above average socioeconomic status.

Measurement

For the measurement of ethnic identification, each spouse was asked to indicate the extent to which he/she agrees with his/her ethnic self-identification as Anglophone and as Francophone (Items 1 and 2 below). Also used were two items (3 and 4 below) capturing his or her spouse's perception of the respondent's self-identification:

1. I consider myself to be Francophone.
2. I consider myself to be Anglophone.
3. My spouse considers himself/herself to be Francophone.
4. My spouse considers himself/herself to be Anglophone.

Seven-point Likert scales were used for these items.

Each spouse's sex-role attitude was measured with Scanzoni's (1975) 28 item sex-role attitude scale. The scale taps seven dimensions: traditional wife role; wife self-actualization; problematic husband alterations; institutionalized equality; traditional husband role; religious legitimation of mother role; and traditional mother role. These items also used seven-point Likert scales.

To measure husband-wife financial task sharing, each spouse was asked to assess his/her relative participation in 16 household finance related activities ranging from handling expenses for groceries to deciding the type of savings plan on five point scales (1=Wife always; 2=Wife more than husband; 3=wife and husband equally; 4=Husband more than wife; 5=Husband always). Since the focus of this study is on the couple's task sharing pattern rather than the pattern of role dominance, the responses on these items were recoded to reflect this: 1=Not shared at all (corresponding to 1 and 5 on the original scale); 2=Partly shared (corresponding to 2 and 4 on the original scale); 3=Shared equally (corresponding to 3 on the original scale).

ANALYSIS AND RESULTS

The hypotheses of this study depicted in the conceptual model (Figure 1) are tested using the LISREL analysis. The first stage of data analysis, however, was on the measurement items.

English-French Canadian Ethnicity

As presented, there were two sets of ethnic identification measurement items; one pertaining to self-identification and the other pertaining to the spouse's perception of the respondent's self-identification. Bipolarity of the two questions in each set was checked by examining the correlation coefficients. Correlations were very high, -.95 between the first two items (i.e., "I consider myself to be Francophone" and "I consider myself to be

Anglophone") and -.97 between the second two items (i.e., "My spouse considers... Francophone" and "My spouse considers...Anglophone"). At this point, it was decided to subtract the response on the Anglophone identification question from that on the Francophone identification question in each set. The resulting values for self-identification and the spouse's perception of the respondent's identification ranged between -6 (Strong English-Canadian identification) and +6 (Strong French-Canadian identification). These two indices as indicators of the spouse's ethnic identification correlated at .96 (Cronbach's alpha = .98) both for the husbands and wives in the sample.

Sex-Role Attitude

Reliability analysis of the 28 items contained in Scanzoni's sex-role attitude scale showed a Cronbach's alpha value of .87 for the husbands and .80 for the wives. Consequently, individual responses on the 28 item Scanzoni's sex-role attitude scale were averaged to produce an overall sex-role attitude score (1=traditional; 7=modern). The average scale scores for wives and husbands were 4.37 and 4.20 respectively, indicating that wives on the average are significantly more modern than husbands (t=2.41, p=.017). This is consistent with the past findings (Brogan and Kutner 1976; Kim and Lee 1989).

Financial Task Sharing

The sixteen financial task items were first submitted to factor analysis (principal component analysis) using the husband-wife combined sample (N=240). The solution produced three factors with eigenvalues greater than 1.0 accounting for 47.8 percent of the variance in the original 16 variables. All of the items except one (Deciding items and amounts for the monthly budget) showed clearly interpretable factor loadings (greater than .4 on their respective factors). The factor solution excluding this item produced three factors with eigenvalues greater than 1.0, this time accounting for 60.2 percent of the total variance. Factor patterns obtained from separate three-factor solutions for the husband and wife subsamples matched each other quite well. The three factors were labelled as "financial task implementation," "financial decisions," and "expenses decisions." The financial task implementation factor was represented by five items: recording deposits and withdrawals in checkbook; priority order for bill payment; reconciling bank statements; paying routine household bills; and balancing the checkbook. The financial decisions factor was represented by six items: what to do with leftover money; amount to be contributed to savings; types of savings plan; methods of financing for major appliance purchases; where to place savings and investments; and obtaining a life insurance policy. Lastly, the expenses decisions factor was represented by four items: expenses for groceries; expenses for recreation; how much to spend on clothing; and how much cash to withdraw for expenses.

In the subsequent stage, the items loading highly on each factor were averaged for the wives and husbands separately. This was done after checking the reliability of the items to be combined. For wives, Cronbach's reliability coefficients were equal to .86, .83, .69 for the measurement items of "financial task implementation," "financial decisions," and "expenses decisions," respectively. For husbands, they were equal to .87, .56, .86 for the three factors respectively. The average scores computed for husbands and wives for each group of activities were very similar: 2.19 (1=Not shared at all and 3=Shared equally) for husbands and 2.20 for wives for the financial task implementation factor, 2.49 and 2.51 for the financial decisions factor, and 2.50 and 2.45 for the expenses decisions factor for husbands and wives respectively.

The average responses of the husband and wife on the multiple items loading on the same factor are later used as two indicators of the couple's sharing of the type of financial activities denoted by the factor. Cronbach's αs for the husband's and wife's indicators were .77, .62, and .62 respectively for the factors of financial task implementation, financial decisions, and expenses decisions. For a two-indicator measure, these are all satisfactory values.

Structural Model Testing

In testing the structural relationships earlier hypothesized, the three financial task factors were incorporated into the model (Figure 1) one at a time. Figure 2 shows the LISREL model specification, and Table 1 contains the results of the LISREL analyses of the three models.

Regarding the first model incorporating the financial task implementation factor, its goodness of fit to the data is quite satisfactory; $\chi^2_{d.f.=14}=20.63$, p=.112, and GFI=.961. Significant structural coefficients (t>2.0) include β_{31} (pertaining to the influence of the husband's sex-role attitude on the couple's sharing of financial task implementation), γ_{32} (pertaining to the influence of wife's ethnicity on the couple's sharing of financial task implementation), ϕ_{21} (the covariation between husband's and wife's ethnicity), and ψ_{21} (covariation between husband's and wife's sex-role attitude).

The second model incorporating the financial decisions factor showed an excellent fit as indicated by the χ^2 value of 12.07 for 14 degrees of freedom (p=.601). The value of GFI was equal to .977. Among the structural relationships between ethnicity, sex-role attitude, and task sharing, only β_{31} (the influence of the husband's sex-role attitude on the couple's sharing of financial decision making) was significant. The estimated values and significance levels for ϕ_{21} and ψ_{21} are the same as before. The third model incorporating the expenses decisions factor also showed an excellent fit ($\chi^2_{d.f.=14}=14.31$, p=.427, and GFI=.973). The significant parameters were identical as those in the first model - β_{31}, γ_{32}, ϕ_{21}, ψ_{21}.

Thus in all three cases, only the husband's sex-role attitude has a significant impact on the couples' sharing of household finance related activities. The direction of impact is consistent; the more sex-role modern the husband is the more sharing of financial task implementation, financial decisions, and expenses decisions by couples. Regarding the influence of English-French Canadian ethnicity on the couple's task sharing, the results indicate that the stronger French-Canadian ethnicity is for the wife, the more sharing of financial task implementation and expenses decisions is done by couples. These findings are contrary to the direction hypothesized earlier (H_2). The hypothesized relationship between English-French Canadian ethnicity and sex-role attitude (H_3) was not corroborated. Finally, results did provide a confirmation for the hypothesized covariation between the husband's and wife's sex-role attitude (ψ_{21}=.543, t=5.25) as well as the husband's and wife's ethnicity (ϕ_{21}=.834, t=6.99).

DISCUSSION

Results of this study provide some tentative conclusions regarding the relationships among English-French Canadian ethnicity, sex-role attitudes of the spouses and the couple's task sharing behavior. The findings in general are encouraging, although the relationships may not be as extensive as anticipated earlier. The finding that the English-French Canadian ethnic identity of the spouse had no linkage with the spouse's sex-role attitude is contrary to the beliefs contained in the literature. We suspect that this unexpected finding may have been due to the fact

FIGURE 2
A LISREL Model Depicting The Relationship Among E-F Canadian Ethnicity, Sex-Role Attitude, and Couple's Financial Task Sharing

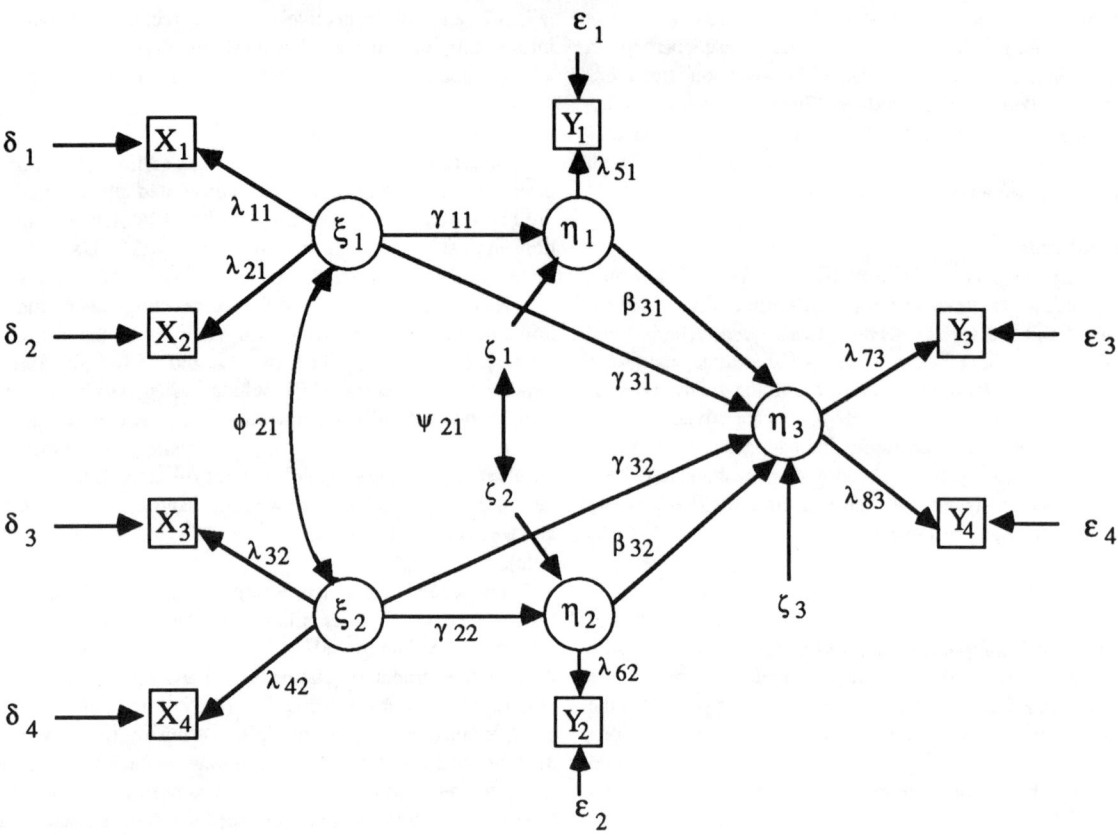

X_1 = Husband's Self-identification
X_2 = Wife's Perception of Husband's Self-identification
X_3 = Wife's Self-identification
X_4 = Husband's Perception of Wife's Self-identification
Y_1 = The Composite Measure of Husband's Sex-Role Attitude
Y_2 = The Composite Measure of Wife's Sex-Role Attitude
Y_3 = The Composite Score of Husband's Responses on a Task-Sharing Factor
Y_4 = The Composite Score of Wife's Responses on a Task-Sharing Factor

ξ_1 = Husband's E-F Canadian Ethnicity
ξ_2 = Wife's E-F Canadian Ethnicity
η_1 = Husband's Sex-Role Attitude
η_2 = Wife's Sex-Role Attitude
η_3 = Couple's Task Sharing (Financial Task Implementation in Model 1; Financial Decisions in Model 2; Expenses Decisions in Model 3)

---

that French Canadians and English Canadians in our sample come from the same region of the country. While their ancestral roots, principal languages, and self-professed ethnic affiliations differ, they coexist within the confines of the same socioeconomic environment. Thoughts and behaviors of one group are influenced greatly by the other as there are constant interpersonal and mass media contacts between them. The fact that a large proportion of the French and English Canadians in the Montreal area are bilingual facilitates the transfer of cultural norms and values.

Whereas neither spouse's sex-role attitude was significantly linked to his/her English-French Canadian ethnicity, the study did show that the couple's task sharing in two of the three areas of family financial management - financial task implementation and expenses decision making - was influenced directly by the wife's ethnic background. Regarding the insignificant relationship found between the wife's ethnicity and the couple's task sharing behavior in the area of financial decisions, one may note that these are relatively more important decisions and that they receive a high degree of joint husband-wife involvement irrespective of the couple's ethnic background. Recall that the average task sharing scores for these decisions were 2.49 and 2.51 (where 1=Not shared at all and 3=Shared equally) as computed for husbands and wives respectively. The revealed direction of the influence that stronger French-Canadian ethnicity of the wife is connected to a more egalitarian mode of task sharing is contrary to the more widely held belief that French Canadian wives are more traditional in their role perceptions than their English Canadian counterparts (Tigert 1973; Mallen 1977; Langelier 1982). On the other hand, it is in a closer agreement

TABLE 1
LISREL Results for Household Task Sharing Models[a]

Parameter	Model 1	Model 2	Model 3
λ_{11}	1.000	1.000	1.000
λ_{21}	.987 (32.12)	.986 (32.10)	.986 (32.17)
λ_{32}	1.000	1.000	1.000
λ_{42}	.974 (33.55)	.980 (33.42)	.982 (33.81)
λ_{51}	1.000	1.000	1.000
λ_{62}	1.000	1.000	1.000
λ_{73}	1.000	1.000	1.000
λ_{83}	.557 (3.01)	.947 (3.48)	.929 (3.83)
γ_{11}	-.069 (-0.77)	-.069 (-0.78)	-.069 (-0.78)
γ_{22}	.116 (1.34)	.116 (1.32)	.115 (1.31)
γ_{31}	-.095 (-0.56)	.029 (0.20)	-.172 (-1.15)
γ_{32}	.368 (2.19)	.118 (0.80)	.375 (2.44)
β_{31}	.294 (2.91)	.257 (2.73)	.337 (3.54)
β_{32}	-.036 (-0.35)	.093 (1.04)	-.047 (-0.53)
ϕ_{11}	.973 (7.45)	.974 (7.46)	.974 (7.46)
ϕ_{22}	.989 (7.57)	.984 (7.53)	.981 (7.51)
ϕ_{21}	.834 (6.99)	.833 (7.00)	.833 (7.00)
ψ_{11}	.995 (7.71)	.993 (7.71)	.993 (7.71)
ψ_{22}	.985 (7.71)	.986 (7.71)	.986 (7.71)
ψ_{33}	.980 (2.65)	.351 (2.60)	.335 (2.66)
ψ_{21}	.543 (5.25)	.543 (5.25)	.543 (5.25)
$\theta_{\delta 1}$	.027 (1.59)	.026 (1.53)	.026 (1.55)
$\theta_{\delta 2}$	.052 (3.00)	.053 (3.04)	.053 (3.05)
$\theta_{\delta 3}$	.011 (0.70)	.016 (1.02)	.019 (1.24)
$\theta_{\delta 4}$	.061 (3.63)	.056 (3.32)	.053 (3.27)
$\theta_{\epsilon 1}$	.000	.000	.000
$\theta_{\epsilon 2}$	.000	.000	.000
$\theta_{\epsilon 3}$	-.133 (-.383)	.529 (3.63)	.513 (3.78)
$\theta_{\epsilon 4}$	.648 (4.74)	.577 (4.19)	.580 (4.57)
Chi-square	20.63	12.07	14.31
d.f.	14	14	14
p	.112	.601	.427
AGFI	.900	.942	.931
RMSR	.044	.018	.024

[a]Parentheses contain t-values

with the more recent findings by Kim and Laroche (1989). One may suspect that, over the last two decades, the pattern of husband-wife task and decision influence sharing may have evolved differentially in the two cultures.

The study found consistently across the three areas of family financial management that only the husband's sex-role attitude influences the couple's task sharing behavior. Thus, the development of a more equitable pattern of couple's role structure is contingent upon the husband's attitude change regardless of the wife's. This finding corroborates earlier findings by Bird, Bird, and Scruggs (1984) and Ross (1987) that only the husband's sex-role attitude was a significant predictor of the household division of labor. However, Rosen and Granbois (1983) found that sex-role attitudes of both spouses were significant determinants of the couple's role structure regarding the financial task implementation. Further, Kim and Lee's (1989) finding showed only the wife's sex-role attitude as the significant predictor of financial task sharing. Thus, it appears that the couple's task sharing pattern is affected at least by the sex-role attitude of one spouse. Any further conclusions will require more investigation on the relationship.

Finally, the strong positive covariation found between the husband's and wife's sex-role attitude supports the view that belief systems of the spouses influence each other to become more compatible. Given the high level of interdependence between the spouses created by the intimate and relatively stable nature of marriage, this is not unexpected.

Both ethnicity/culture and sex-role attitude have recently emerged as important constructs in explaining variations in the husband-wife decision influence patterns. Past studies, however, focused on one construct at a time. This study, drawing upon the relevant literature, proposed and tested a model which integrates these two constructs in examining their effects on the couple's task sharing behavior in family financial management. A hypothesis of particular interest was the intermediary role of sex-role attitude in explaining the influence of ethnicity on the couple's financial task sharing behavior. Although no evidence was offered by this study that sex-role attitudes of spouses are affected by ethnicity, this should not discourage further investigations on their relationship using other ethnic segments in North America. Essential in the development of cross cultural marketing strategies is the understanding of different (similar) cultural norms and attitudes underlying consumer behavior. As suggested by Douglas (1979), future family studies including cross-cultural investigations should focus more strongly on the understanding of the basic forces underlying husband-wife interaction rather than simply who is involved.

REFERENCES

Bird, G.W., G.A. Bird, and M. Scruggs (1984), "Determinants of Family Task Sharing: A Study of Husbands and Wives," *Journal of Marriage and the Family*, 46 (May), 435-355.

Blood, R.O. and D.M. Wolfe (1960), *Husbands and Wives: The Dynamics of Married Living*, Glencoe, IL: The Free Press.

Brogan, D. and N.G. Kutner (1976), "Measuring Sex-Role Orientation: A Normative Approach," *Journal of Marriage and the Family*, 38 (February), 31-40.

Corfman, K.P. and D.R. Lehmann (1987), "Models of Cooperative Group Decision-Making and Relative Influence," *Journal of Consumer Research*, 14, 1-13.

Cronkite, Ruth C. (1977), "The Determinants of Spouses' Normative Preferences for Family Roles," *Journal of Marriage and the Family*, 39, 575-585.

Douglas, Susan P. (1979), "A Cross-National Exploration of Husband-Wife Involvement in Selected Household Activities," *Advances in Consumer Research*, Vol.6, 364-371.

Hempel, D.J. (1974), "Family Buying Decisions: A Cross-Cultural Perspective," *Journal of Marketing Research*, August, 295-302.

Hui, Michael, A. Joy, C. Kim, and M. Laroche (1993), "Equivalence of Lifestyle Dimensions Across Four Major Subcultures in Canada," *Journal of International Consumer Marketing*, Vol.5, No.3 (Forthcoming).

Green, R.T. and I.C.M. Cunningham (1975), "Feminine Role Perception and Family Purchasing Decisions," *Journal of Marketing Research*, 12, 325-332.

Green, R.T. and I.C.M. Cunningham (1980), "Family Purchasing Roles in Two Countries (United States and Venezuela)," *Journal of International Business Studies*, Spring/Summer, 92-97.

Green, R.T., B.J. Verhage, and I.C.M. Cunningham (1981), "Household Purchasing Decisions: How do American and Dutch Consumers Differ?," *European Journal of Marketing*, Vol.15 (1), 68-77.

Green, R.T., J.P. Leonardi, J.L. Chandon, I.C.M. Cunningham, B.J. Verhage, and A. Strazzieri (1983), "Societal Development and Family Purchasing Roles: A Cross National Study," *Journal of Consumer Research*, 9 (March), 436-442.

Imperia, Giovanna, Thomas C. O'Guinn, and Elizabeth A. MacAdams (1985), "Family Decision Making Role Perceptions Among Mexican-American and Anglo Wives: A Cross-Cultural Comparison," *Advances in Consumer Research*, Vol. 12, 71-74.

Kim, Chankon and Michel Laroche (1989), "A Communications Pattern Based Index of Ethnicity and its Relationship with Lifestyles," in *Proceedings of the Annual Conference of the European Marketing Academy*, Vol.II, 921-932.

Kim, Chankon and Hanjoon Lee (1989), "Sex Role Attitudes of Spouses and Task Sharing Behavior," *Advances in Consumer Research*, Vol.16, 671-679.

Langelier (1982), "French Canadian Families," in *Ethnicity and Family Therapy*, Monica McGoldrick, John K. Pearce and Joseph Giordano, eds., New York: The Guilford Press.

Mallen (1977), *French Canadian Consumer Behavior: Comparative Lessons From the Published Literature and Private Corporate Marketing Studies*, Montreal: Advertising and Sales Executives Club of Montreal.

Mortimer, J.T., R. Hall, and R. Hill (1978), "Husbands' Occupational Attributes as Constraints on Wives' Employment," *Sociology of Work and Occupations*, Vol.5 (August), 285-313.

Perrucci, C.C., H.R. Potter, and D.L. Rhoads (1978), "Determinants of Male Family-Role Performance," in Bryson, J.B. and R. Bryson, eds., *Dual Career Couples*, New York: Human Services Press.

Qualls, William J. (1982), "Changing Sex Roles, Its Impact Upon Family Decision Making," *Advances in Consumer Research*, Vol.9, 267-270.

Qualls, William J. (1982), "Changing Sex-Roles, Its Impact Upon Family Decision Making," *Advances in Consumer Research*, Vol.11, 270-275.

Rosen, Dennis and Donald H. Granbois (1983), "Determinants of Role Structure in Family Financial Management," *Journal of Consumer Research*, 10 (September), 253-258.

Ross, C.E. (1987), "The Division of Labor at Home," *Social Forces*, 65 (March), 816-833.

Scanzoni, John (1975), *Sex Roles, Life Styles, and Child-Bearing*, New York: The Free Press.

Scanzoni, John (1977), "Sex Roles, Economic Factors, and Marital Solidarity in Black and Write Families," *Journal of Marriage and the Family*, 39 (February), 130-144.

Schaninger, C.M., W.C. Buss, and R. Grover (1982), "The Effect of the Sex Role on Family Economic Handling and Decision Influence," *An Assessment of Marketing Thought and Practice*, ed. Walker, B., Chicago: American Marketing Association, 43-57.

Tigert (1973), "Can a Separate Marketing Strategy for French Canada Be Justified: Profiling English-French Markets Through Lifestyle Analysis," in *Canadian Marketing: Problems and Prospects*, D.N. Thompson and D.S. Leighton, eds., Toronto: Wiley, 113-147.

Vickers and Benson (1972), "Cherchez la Femme," *Marketing*, (31 January), 2.

Webster, Cynthia (1989), "The Effects of Ethnic Identification on Marital Influences in Decision Making," in *Proceedings of Southern Marketing Association*, 98-102.

A Primer for Ethnographic Research With a Focus On Social Policy Issues Involving Consumer Behavior
Ronald Paul Hill, Villanova University

ABSTRACT

The purpose of this paper is to depict the process involved in the conduct of ethnographic research as well as the problems faced by consumer behavior ethnographers. The paper opens with an introduction to the topic. Then, this qualitative method is defined and described, data collection and approaches to analysis are explicated, and recommendations for writing ethnographies are provided. Finally, troublesome issues involving objectivity, the ethnographer's presence, scientific integrity, and ethical considerations are delineated. Each facet of the ethnographic research process as well as these areas of concern are discussed within the context of research on the social issue of homelessness.

INTRODUCTION

Recent research in the consumer behavior field has utilized ethnographic methods to investigate market settings, purchase decisions, and consumption behaviors (see Belk, Sherry, and Wallendorf 1988; Belk, Wallendorf, and Sherry 1989; Heisley, McGrath, and Sherry 1991; Sherry 1990; and Wallendorf and Arnould 1991 for some excellent examples). While each of these studies makes an important methodological contribution, none has been published with the expressed intent of focussing on such issues. Therefore, the purpose of this paper is to describe the process involved in conducting ethnographic research as well as the problems faced by ethnographers in our discipline using research on homelessness as the focus (Hill 1992; 1991; Hill and Stamey 1990).

ETHNOGRAPHY DEFINED AND DESCRIBED

Historically, ethnography is interdisciplinary, arising out of the qualitative research traditions in sociology and anthropology (Adler and Adler 1987). This method is defined "by its attempt to generate participant insight into aspects of group life," and data typically is collected through "participation in settings, observations, interviews, and other discussions" with informants (Prus 1987, p. 254-255). The researcher's understanding of the phenomenon "emerges" over the course of this data collection, and moves from an item level of analysis to a search for identifiable patterns among these objects to the development of themes that show how these patterns are related to one another (Borman, LeCompte, and Goetz 1986). The final step involves an integration with existing literature and theory within the social sciences.

The following subsections discuss specific facets of ethnography and are organized according to the recommendations of Fetterman (1989).

Guiding Principles

As Fetterman (1989, p. 11) notes, "The ethnographer enters the field with an open mind, not an empty head." Thus, researchers usually take a holistic perspective that incorporates both emic and etic points-of-view. A holistic outlook attempts to gain a comprehensive picture of the group under study by framing their activities within the larger context in which they occur. For example, in my work with the hidden homeless (Hill and Stamey 1990), our investigation began with a focus on how individuals cope with a lack of consumer products from adequate shelter to health care and hygiene to food and clothing. However, data revealed that homeless persons' survival strategies are often tied to larger communities that reject the traditional welfare system as well as many of its supporting institutions. This broader context helped us understand the sources of self-esteem for the hidden homeless as well as their preferences for and avoidance of certain sources of products.

Central to this approach is the emic perspective which concentrates on natives' understandings of their world, and recognizes and accepts multiple realities among informants in a nonjudgmental fashion. For example, the hidden homeless (Hill and Stamey 1990) viewed themselves as living by their own resources, separate and apart from the welfare system while the sheltered homeless (Hill 1991) often were dependent both physically and emotionally on this same system for survival. While both subpopulations faced some of the same difficulties, they held very different views of supporting institutions. Thus, through extensive research, very distinctive realities emerged.

The etic perspective, on the other hand, represents an external, "scientific" viewpoint of this same reality. This outlook requires that the researcher make sense of the data that have been collected through scientific analysis. Occasionally, this task is performed after the ethnographer leaves the field and creates a certain amount of distance between him/herself and informants. The end result is interpretive themes that illuminate the informants' world through placement of findings within the context of theory and research in the social sciences.

Data Collection

If the emic perspective is the "heart" and the etic perspective is the "brain" of ethnographic inquiry, then field work is the "soul." Through long-term participant observation, the ethnographer is able to "internalize the basic beliefs, fears, hopes, and expectations of the people under study" (Fetterman 1989, p. 45). Using this approach, the researcher acts as a human instrument, relying on all of his or her senses for data collection.

A typical ethnographic investigation may begin using a "big net" approach where the researcher interacts with a wide variety of informants in as many different settings as possible. The ethnographer often talks with whomever is willing and able in order to gain initial access to informants' private worlds. Over time, these contacts may act as key informants, providing additional persons from their social networks for the researcher to contact. For instance, in my work with the hidden homeless (Hill and Stamey 1990), the research team visited shanty towns, abandoned buildings and cars, bridge abutments, tunnels, and wooded areas known to be inhabited by homeless persons in an attempt to understand the heterogeneity that existed within this segment of the homeless population. In each of these environments, key informants were identified and long-term relationships were established. As trust and respect developed between the research team and these homeless persons, they helped identify other individuals within their communities who faced similar struggles and provided needed introductions.

While many forms of data collection are employed by ethnographers, the interview is often the most useful. From casual conversations with implicit agendas to formal interviews with more directed purposes, researchers attempt to discover how informants think and feel compared to one another. On occasion, discussions of songs, television shows, places, or events can be used as projective techniques to explore particularly troublesome experiences. Such interactions help the researcher establish a healthy rapport, especially if informants are allowed to control the flow of the discussion much of the time. Also, the occasional use of the tape recorder captures long verbatim quotes without the disruption of note taking by the ethnographer.

My experiences at the Sisters of Mercy shelter support this position (Hill 1992; 1991). During this investigation, I had literally hundreds of conversations, discussions, and interviews during collection of the data. Such repeated exposures to and long term interactions with informants built trust and resulted in their provision of intimate details regarding their lives. Further, the tape recorder proved invaluable, particularly in my interviews with children who were delighted by the prospect of hearing their voices from the machine after the sessions were completed. Also, one peer reviewer (a social worker) suggested that I use fantasy as a projective technique to examine underlying fears among these children, and the resulting fantasies involving "rich" kids and future homes were particularly enlightening.

Data Analysis

Data analysis is probably the most misunderstood aspect of ethnography, due, in part, to the fact that there is no single form of evaluation or phase of the process where it is performed. In truth, ethnographic analyses are iterative, starting at the first stages of data collection and continuing until the final stages of writing. Further, analyses are often multiple, may take a variety of forms within a single investigation, and typically cycle through and back to different issues as distinct data sources are collected or reviewed.

Occasionally, key events that represent shared experiences among the group members under investigation are used as the focal point of analyses. The ethnographer searches through the data involving these events for underlying patterns of thought or behavior. "Crystallization" occurs when there is "a convergence of similarities that spontaneously strike the ethnographer as relevant or important to the study" (Fetterman 1989, p. 101). However, the researcher continues to seek additional sources of the same patterns (and groups of interrelated patterns often referred to as themes) as well as limiting exceptions to what appears to be important commonalities. This process, known as triangulation, is considered a test of validity, and continues until all reasonable alternative explanations have been eliminated.

My field experience with homeless women at the shelter (Hill 1991) may shed some light on this facet of ethnography. Multiple data sources were used during this investigation including field notes, audio recordings of interviews, and photographs. These data were analyzed weekly over the course of the study, and helped to revise and modify different emerging interpretations at different points in time. The key event that remained the focus of these data was their decision to seek support from the shelter. As time passed and themes crystallized, interviews with the women and conversations with the staff were directed towards negative cases in an attempt to consciously seek disconfirming evidence. After all possibilities had been explored and final analyses were conducted, the writing up phase began.

Writing Ethnographies

Writing ethnographies represents a significant challenge for researchers, particularly in a discipline such as consumer behavior that has traditionally embraced quantitative methods. Nonetheless, good ethnographic writing typically is composed of two interrelated parts: "thick" description and "thick" interpretation (see Geertz 1973). Thick description provides the context in which behaviors take place, incorporating cultural meaning into the written text. The sources of this description are the field notes recorded during and after each interaction with informants, audiotapes of all interviews as well as their transcriptions, and photographs that capture important moments, possessions, etc. Whenever possible, the voice of informants through the use of verbatim quotes should be employed to provide details regarding their thoughts and actions.

Thick interpretation provides the reader with a "road map" to help him or her understand the complex nature of the field. This part of ethnographic writing requires the explication of the patterns and themes that emerged during interpretation, embedded within existing literature in the social sciences. The end result should give the reader a gestalt of the focal environment that moves his or her understanding and consciousness of the field to a higher level.

One of the greatest difficulties faced by ethnographers during this stage is the decision involving what information to include in the final write up. Interactions with the field may uncover a wide range of data and findings, some of which may be only tangentially related to the researcher's discipline. Thus, many ethnographers choose to ignore certain data and emphasize others, or write multiple reports, each directed to a different audience.

My work with the hidden homeless (Hill and Stamey 1990) provides an example of some of the dilemmas faced by ethnographers when writing from their data. The data collection phase of this project took place over several years, resulting in a "mountain" of field notes, audio tapes, and photographs. Since the primary investigators are from different disciplines (marketing/consumer behavior and sociology), we tended to emphasize different findings and search for different meanings within the same data bases. However, because the written paper was to be submitted to the *Journal of Consumer Research*, possessions and consumption behaviors became the focus of the final report, and the social network and relationships among informants became a secondary concern.

SOME TROUBLESOME ISSUES

While there are many issues that pose significant problems for consumer researchers employing ethnography, the following four have particular relevance given the positivist orientation of the discipline and the sensitive nature of social policy matters.

Objectivity Versus Subjectivity

One of the most critical debates among ethnographers is the balance between objectivity and subjectivity which indicts the researcher's level of involvement in or detachment from the field. As Adler and Adler (1987, p. 10) note:

> Ideally, ethnographers were to get close to members, participate in some of their activities, gain their trust and confidence, and discover their subjective perspectives and interpretations. At the same time, they were to keep themselves firmly anchored in the scientific conceptual framework so that they could analyze the observations and accounts they were gathering from a detached, objective vantage.

This "balancing act" was the result of the widespread influence of positivism which recommended that ethnographers seek to improve the validity and reliability of their methods.

Existential sociologists, on the other hand, advocated that researchers get as close to the phenomenon as possible in order to gain intimacy and trust and eliminate evasive tactics by informants (see Douglas 1976). "Scientific analysis does not require objective detachment, they argue, but occurs within the theoretical self-reflection of the trained social scientist" (Adler and Adler 1987, p. 12). Thus, to gain a truly emic perspective, ethnographers must get as close to the phenomenon as possible and reflect upon their own subjective feelings and experiences with informants.

I have struggled with this issue within the context of my own ethnographic studies, particularly in my limited work with homeless children (Hill 1992). While I found no perfect position along the objective-subjective continuum, the recommendations of Borman et al. (1986) provided a reasonable guide. They suggest that ethnographers adopt a "disciplined subjectivity" that requires a rigorous search for possible biases in each interaction with informants as well as an almost psychotherapeutic introspection that demands a constant dialogue with the self. Also, periods of detachment from the field, working in teams, and seeking input from peer reviewers within and outside the discipline can broaden the researcher's perspective and supply fresh approaches to data collection and analysis.

The Ethnographer's Presence

A separate but related problem involves the physical presence of the ethnographer in the field. According to Stoddart (1986, p. 107-108), the interactional presence of researchers with the phenomenon of interest can erode "the possibility of achieving the goal that occasioned their presence in the first place." Thus, ethnographers view their attendance in the field as potentially changing its natural state, and often work to reduce the possibility of such contamination.

One potential solution to this dilemma is to "fade into the background" of the domain under investigation. The ideal ethnographer is the invisible researcher "who sees without being observed and, consequently, captures the natural field without tainting it" (Stoddart 1986, p. 108-109). However, this ideal is difficult if not impossible to attain. Instead, Stoddart (1986) suggests that ethnographers minimize their visibility through "disattending" which may involve choosing a locally appropriate style or role within the focal environment.

In my work on homelessness, this concern required attention. During the investigation of the hidden homeless (Hill and Stamey 1990), the research team was careful to avoid serious consequences of this problem by dressing informally, using informal language, and engaging in normal, communal behaviors such as eating or sharing drink. Further, in my ethnography of the shelter (Hill 1992; 1991), I assumed the role of volunteer so that I could blend into the background activities that regularly occurred. My job consisted of sweeping the floors, setting the dining room tables, preparing food, and transporting residents to and from the facility. Since the shelter employed many volunteers, my presence was a natural part of this environment.

Scientific Integrity

Serious questions regarding the scientific integrity of ethnographic research have surfaced within and outside the discipline of consumer behavior. According to Agar (1983, p. 41), "a classic criticism of ethnographic reports [is] that they present general conclusions with a few supporting anecdotes." Another criticism involves concern that multiple studies of the same or similar groups can result in very different conclusions due to dissimilarities in the cultures and backgrounds of the researchers as well as the intended audiences of publications (Agar 1982). The end result is that "there is no way to be certain that what is portrayed is anything more than a researcher's etic imposition of meanings and constructs upon a setting rather than an authentic representation of the thoughts and beliefs of the people under study" (Borman et al. 1986, p. 49).

One approach to resolving these dilemmas calls for the analysis of "strips," defined as "any bounded phenomenon against which ethnographers test their understanding of the group" such as a particular encounter or event (Agar 1982, p. 789; also see Agar 1983). These strips are then subjected to sequential analysis consisting of breakdowns, resolutions, and coherence. Breakdowns occur when the researcher's preconceived notions based on his or her background or training are violated during the evaluation of strips. Resolution of these breakdowns requires that the ethnographer "tinker" with these inferences until a new pattern emerges that incorporates this new knowledge. The result should be coherence - a clear understanding of the cause(s) of the breakdown and its integration into the researcher's view of the field.

However, this emerging perspective must be considered tentative until it has been corroborated by other sources. An active search using additional methods and informants must be employed with an emphasis on negative cases and limiting exceptions. Further, when appropriate, peer reviewers from the same and other disciplines who are concerned with the focal population or issues can provide additional insights through their own analyses of these strips.

During my investigations of the homeless, apprehension regarding the scientific integrity of ethnography began to surface in the consumer behavior discipline. Fortunately, a timely and well-conceived piece by Wallendorf and Belk (1989) was circulated among my peers and I was able to use many of their methodological suggestions to guide my work. In both of my studies (Hill and Stamey 1990; and Hill 1992; 1991), findings from and perceptions of the field were crafted into interpretations through the use of triangulation across methods and informants as well as negative cases. Further, peer reviews from professionals in the disciplines of anthropology, psychology, sociology, and social work were employed throughout the conduct of these ethnographies to broaden interpretations beyond my own training in marketing/consumer behavior.

Ethical Considerations

While ethical issues should be considered by all ethnographers, they are particularly relevant for those who investigate social policy matters. The centerpiece of long-term relationships between ethnographers and informants is trust, which places certain demands on researchers. In order to establish and maintain this trust, the ethnographer must be honest in all dealings with informants, explaining his or her purpose for entering the field in a clear and nontechnical manner. The intended uses of all forms of data, especially audio recordings and photographs, should be explained and permission must be received prior to collection.

Most importantly, the researcher should do everything possible to disguise the identity of informants during the writing up phase. This tactic is particularly relevant in situations where the ethnographer has been privy to what Fetterman (1989, p. 135) calls "guilty knowledge," described as "confidential knowledge of illegal or illicit activities." In such cases, field notes should be devoid of identifying labels, pseudonyms should be used in written reports, and the names and locations of places or organizations should be concealed. Finally, the researcher investigating social issues should play an advocacy role by disseminating findings beyond the academic world so that policy makers whose actions are currently impacting the lives of informants are made privy to results.

Clearly, my work with the homeless raised important ethical issues. In my investigation of the hidden homeless (Hill and Stamey 1990), the research team regularly came in contact with persons who illegally established living quarters in settings like abandoned buildings. Further, many persons had connected appliances to municipal electrical outlets or scavenged from buildings/containers without permission from the owners. Also, in my study of sheltered women (Hill 1991), some of my informants were concerned that if anyone knew they were living at this facility it might inhibit their ability to be reunited with their children or embarrass their families. Thus, in both situations, several steps were taken to protect the homeless including the use of pseudonyms or generic descriptions (e.g., WM 30s) to identify informants, disguising the locations of living quarters and the shelter, and only publishing photographs that did not expose persons who were vulnerable to retribution. The process of dissemination of these findings to policy makers is now underway, especially to those interested in helping homeless children or improving health care delivery systems to the homeless.

Concluding Remarks

While this paper has not addressed all of the dilemmas faced by consumer behavior ethnographers, many of the central issues have been raised and some possible solutions within a social policy context have been addressed. However, I would like to stress three additional points. First, ethnography is often very satisfying to its practitioners because it allows them to directly *experience* the world of informants and all of its variations. Living through the "highs" and the "lows" of their lives allows the researcher to know the phenomenon under investigation in a way that few other methodologies permit. Second, I have been asked by would-be ethnographers where to begin. My first reaction is to be "opportunistic." According to Reimer (1977, p. 469), this strategy recommends that researchers "rely upon their own unique biographies, life experiences, and situational familiarities in doing their research." For example, my eight years as a coach of a martial arts team took me into many lower class communities for competitions. In this environment, I learned how to mix with persons of different races and socioeconomic backgrounds which, later on, facilitated my research with the homeless. Third, as a discipline, consumer behavior is just beginning to embrace qualitative methods and must rely upon other fields for support and experience. Therefore, it is essential that we seek input from professionals in anthropology and sociology, share our findings with them, and seek long-term collaborative relationships if we are to build a coherent body of knowledge based on such explorations (see Prus 1987 for additional ways to accomplish this synergy).

In closing, the words of the writer Scott Sanders (1991; p. X) provide sage advice, especially for ethnographers:

I do not expect to arrive at the absolute center or circumference of things, at least not along a path of words. I will follow that path as far as it leads, then go on ahead in silence. The journey home is my effort to come fully awake, to understand where I actually live. If, on the way, I have discovered any secrets worth telling, they must be ones known to all of us in our clear moments. I seek a truth as common as dirt or laughter, and as rare.

REFERENCES

Adler, Patricia A. and Peter Adler (1987), "The Past and the Future of Ethnography," *Journal of Contemporary Ethnography*, 16 (April), 4-24.

Agar, Michael H. (1983), "Ethnographic Evidence," *Urban Life*, 12 (April), 32-48.

Agar, Michael H. (1982), "Toward an Ethnographic Language," *American Anthropologist*, 84, 779-795.

Belk, Russell W., John F. Sherry, Jr., and Melanie Wallendorf (1988), "A Naturalistic Inquiry into Buyer and Seller Behavior at a Swap Meet," *Journal of Consumer Research*, 14 (March), 449-470.

Belk, Russell W., Melanie Wallendorf, and John F. Sherry, Jr. (1989), "The Sacred and the Profane in Consumer Behavior: Theodicy on the Odyssey," *Journal of Consumer Research*, 16 (June), 1-38.

Borman, Kathryn M., Margaret D. LeCompte, and Judith Preissle Goetz (1986), "Ethnographic and Qualitative Research Design and Why It Doesn't Work," *American Behavioral Scientist*, 30 (September/October), 42-57.

Douglas, Jack D. (1976), *Investigative Social Research: Individual and Team Field Research*, Beverly Hills, CA: Sage Publications, Inc.

Fetterman, David M. (1989), *Ethnography Step by Step*, Newbury Park, CA: Sage.

Geertz, Clifford (1973), *The Interpretation of Culture*, New York: Basic.

Heisley, Deborah D., Mary Ann McGrath, and John F. Sherry, Jr. (1991), "'To Everything There is a Season:' A Photoessay of a Farmers' Market," in *Highways and Buyways: Naturalistic Research from the Consumer Behavior Odyssey*, Russell W. Belk, ed. Provo, UT: Association for Consumer Research, 141-166.

Hill, Ronald Paul (1991), "Homeless Women, Special Possessions, and the Meaning of 'Home': An Ethnographic Case Study," *Journal of Consumer Research*, 18 (December), 298-310.

Hill, Ronald Paul (1992) "Homeless Children: Coping with Material Losses," *Journal of Consumer Affairs*, 26 (Winter), forthcoming.

Hill, Ronald Paul and Mark Stamey (1990), "The Homeless in America: An Examination of Possessions and Consumption Behaviors," *Journal of Consumer Research*, 16 (December), 303-321.

Prus, Robert (1987), "Generic Social Processes: Maximizing Conceptual Development in Ethnographic Research," *Journal of Contemporary Ethnography*, 16 (October), 250-293.

Reimer, Jeffery W. (1977), "Varieties of Opportunistic Research," *Urban Life*, 5 (January), 467-477.

Sanders, Scott Russell (1991), *Secrets of the Universe: Scenes from the Journey Home*, Boston: Beacon Press.

Sherry, John F., Jr. (1990), "A Sociocultural Analysis of a Midwestern American Flea Market," *Journal of Consumer Research*, 17 (June), 13-30.

Stoddart, Kenneth (1986), "The Presentation of Self in Everyday Life: Some Textual Strategies for 'Adequate Ethnography,'" *Urban Life*, 15 (April), 103-121.

Wallendorf, Melanie and Russell W. Belk (1989), "Assessing Trustworthiness in Naturalistic Consumer Research," in *Interpretive Consumer Research*, ed. Elizabeth C. Hirschman, Provo, UT: Association for Consumer Research, 69-84.

Ethno: A Methodology for Studying Process Information

James H. Barnes, University of Mississippi

ABSTRACT

Using event structure modeling, we examine consumer information processing as originally developed by Bettman. Using the data reported for consumer C1 in Bettman's 1970 paper, we show how applying a formal logic to that data reveal alternative decision sequences (pathways) in that model. We found that the consumer decision structure was more sequentially structured than was shown in the original model. In addition, we introduce facilitating decisions as part of information processing structure and show how this modification refines the understanding of consumer choice as modeled by information processing.

INTRODUCTION

Consumer research has begun to focus increasingly on subjective realities. Led by qualitative researchers who make a substantial research investment to cultivate informants and attain a deep enough understanding of subjects' thinking to report the realities that the subjects cannot or will not articulate themselves, the field is approaching a greater understanding of why consumers buy. This increased emphasis on field observation and data collection may however suffer from several drawbacks. The observer may fail to correctly record the event, overlooking some critical step in the reported sequence and second, the informant may likewise fail to recall all the details of his or her actions. Some of these drawbacks have been circumvented by the introduction of new methods of qualitative analysis that offer systematic, uniform, computer-assisted procedures for data analysis. These computer-assisted procedures ask more questions than are usually put to data and demand extraordinary precision and meticulousness in descriptions of events (Corsaro and Heise 1990).

Our proposed method of analysis requires two kinds of data. First, we need experts' definitions of events and logical relations. Second, we need records of actual event sequences to aid elicitation and to define correct orderings of relevant events[though not necessarily the only permissible orderings] (Corsaro and Heise 1990, p. 5).

In this paper, we will discuss one such methodology and show how it can be used to organize consumer type data and thus result in improved collection and understanding of the process being studied.

METHODOLOGY

The method employed in the current study is derived from the theory of rational action developed in cognitive science and called the theory of production systems. The concept of these systems were introduced by Newell and Simon (1972) and have been continued and applied by psychologists (e.g. Anderson 1983), sociologists (Axten and Skvoretz 1980; Fararo and Skvoretz 1984) and computer scientists (e.g. Waterman and Hayes-Roth 1978). A PC based computer program using this theory for studying events, their logical connection, and for discovering the rules that govern specific actions has been developed by Heise (1988). The program based on the theory of production systems assumes that people's conceptions of the world are logically structured.

This approach to modeling event structures derives from action being governed by if-then rules: if a certain configuration of conditions arises *then* a certain action occurs. That is, an event cannot occur until all of its prerequisites have occurred. For example, a consumer wishing to purchase product X cannot do so until he or she has arrived at the particular retail outlet that sells the product. Such prerequisites as finding car keys, driving to the mall, parking, and walking to a certain store must all occur before purchase. In addition, this process may cause other consumption events to occur (consume gasoline, for example). Once in the shopping environment, it is not unusual to find consumers purchasing one product because they need it for an impending occasion, another because it was on sale, and a third, purchased impulsively simply because they liked the product. One must thus be able to model these different decisions.

People are, however, not very good at computing long chains of implications (Corsaro and Heise 1990). Thus, if one is questioning a consumer concerning their purchase decision process, the initial facilitating decision to drive to the mall may very well have been forgotten as a part of the process. In addition, the researcher may overlook events and fail to record them though the sequence may be video recorded or otherwise documented. That is, subtle aspects of decisions may be simply overlooked.

The idea that events are primed by if-then prerequisites is a conjunctive process. The required configuration of states for an event may be obtained in some cases through alternative prerequisite events in which case, the event is disjunctively related to its prerequisites. This results in an either-or type of condition as the priming event in a sequence. For example, in our previous example, the consumer may not go to the mall but may instead order product X through a catalog or other direct merchant in which case, other related consumptions, different from the prior example, occur.

A second assumption in production system theory is that occurrence of an event depletes the conditions that primed it. This means that the event structure does not become stuck in a loop with certain states producing the same event repeatedly (Corsaro and Heise 1990). That is, for our consumer to purchase product X again, he or she would have to come again to the retail store where the purchase was made. Events can however be repeatable if the logic of the process suggests that such is true. Our consumer could make multiple purchases of product X while in the shopping environment (one may argue that this would entail a different decision process and should be modeled differently).

A third assumption of production systems is that with exceptions, an event is not repeated until all of its consequences are used up. That is, more and more of something is not produced without being used. For our consumer, he or she would not generally continue to purchase product X without consuming it.

MODELING AND EVENT STRUCTURE

An existing program, ETHNO (Heise 1988, Heise and Lewis 1989), is used to illustrate the computerized analysis of qualitative data using the principles of event structure analysis discussed above.

The program employs a modifiable verbal framework to elicit verbally-defined elements in a desired domain and the logical relations among elements. During elicitation the program employs past answers about implications to minimize further questions (with the presumption of local logic). The program analyzes an event series for consistency with an obtained structure and then again to compute priorities. The program also allows completed models of events structures to be used for simulation (Heise 1989, p. 149).

The data used for this analysis were reported in Bettman (1970, 1979) and formed the bases for an information processing theory of consumer decision making that has gained widespread acceptance in the consumer behavior literature. Since information processing is viewed as a sequential series of activities, it represents an ideal process to subject to the rigors of a formal analytical approach.

Our analysis proceeds in the phases discussed above. Phase one consisting of entering the events and determining their logical relationship. In the present example, this logical relationship will initially be that the ETHNO model duplicates the consumer models developed by Bettman. Phase two consists of analyzing the series of decisions to make it consistent with the implicational structure or other modeling assumptions. Phase three will consist of reanalyzing the series to assess event priorities. The fourth and final phase will consist of demonstrating the revised model for simulating events.

Phase One: Building the Initial Model

The data concerned Bettman's Consumer C_1 and represents a mother of five with a husband who has recently finished medical school and currently teaches. "Her decisions were for the most part based on price, but she let the children have some of their favorites" (Bettman 1970, p. 373). The model of decision making for this consumer is shown as Figure 1 in Bettman's 1970 paper and is also discussed in his 1979 book. For purposes of data entry, we assume that the sequence of decisions reported for consumer C_1 and numbered X1 through X44 are in fact recorded in time sequence order (Later in our analysis, we find this assumption to be incorrect). To develop an event structure, one enters events in the computer program in time sequenced order. This allows the software to develop the hierarchical structure required for event analysis. Thus, the initial computer entry after defining the problem to ETHNO is event numbered X1. This is followed by event two, etc. Following each entry, the program asks, Is a specific prior event (or something similar) essential for the current event? Specifically, the program is asking the person entering data to define which prior events are prerequisites for the event being entered. Thus, the program itself does not dictate the structure but relies on the researcher to develop it based either on recorded field notes, the researcher's understanding of the process, or in the present case, another researcher attempting to examine or replicate prior findings. By asking questions, the program is forcing the researcher to examine his or her own logic and understanding of the process being modeled.

For each question and for each entered event, the answer "yes" or "no" was given such that the linkages in ETHNO represented those reported by Bettman. The ETHNO graphical model thus developed is shown as Figure 1.

The structure shown in Figure 1 is the same as reported in Bettman (1970). The key to the figure shows the definitions also reported by Bettman. ETHNO however has added a group of special relations. The special relations are shown as a "flip-flop" which is ETHNO's way of reporting commutative relations.

> The relation between some events is peculiar in that each is a prerequisite for the other, as in entering and leaving a room: after initially entering, one has to leave to enter again, and one has to enter to leave again. Such events are commutative—one or the other event happens next depending on which happened last. The events alternate or flip-flop (Heise and Lewis 1988, p. 108)

Once data are entered, we are ready to proceed to phase two of the analysis.

Phase Two: Analyzing the Model

Phase two consists of the very important step of allowing ETHNO to analyze the developed structure considering the rules for event analysis discussed earlier. In the present model, the program began to examine event one (Is this meat or produce?), proceeding to the next event determining its various consequences for other events in the system. This analysis had not proceeded very far when the program stopped and began to ask questions and suggesting ways in which a discovered structural problem in the model could be dealt with. The program suggestions for solving the problem are based on the assumptions of event structures and their relationship one to another as discussed earlier. The first problem encountered by ETHNO concerned the sequencing of X44, X41, X42, and X43 before X4. If the sequence of events had occurred as listed by Bettman in his KEY TO FIGURE 1, consumer C_1 would have practically completed her shopping before deciding if the meat or product (X42) was for a specific use. Since it appears that this decision was necessary for the meat or produce decision, our consumer could not complete her purchase choice until the prerequisite events were fulfilled and hence, the model sequence as originally formulated was unacceptable to the structure. In the case of these events, the model suggested that their sequence may have been incorrectly recorded and provided a means for a structural change to place these decisions into their proper sequence. Having no reason to suspect that the structure was indeed different from that suggested by ETHNO, we accepted the program suggestions and modified the model.

Having solved this problem, the analysis proceeded stopping at the eggs decision. At this juncture, none of the solutions offered by ETHNO seemed appropriate given the reporting by Bettman (1970). When this occurs, the program offers as its final option, the ability to add and/or delete events if necessary to make the structure consistent. At this point, the researcher is forced to reconsider the data to determine if errors in recording all events may have occurred. We considered first if the consumer had to decide if the product were meat or produce (X1) before deciding if the product were eggs (X5). Clearly, this does not appear to be a necessary step. The order in which a consumer shops is going to be a function of store layout and the products needed on any particular shopping occasion. A consumer may purchase eggs without purchasing meat or product. Based on the discussion by Bettman of consumer C_1, it does appear that independent decisions were made by the consumer. This structure suggests the need for a distinction between facilitating events and decision events. We will define facilitating events as those actions necessary to position the consumer in the correct spatial/temporal situation to make her choice. That is, one must be at the right grocery section to purchase milk and at another section to purchase produce. Varied store layouts may influence the way in which the consumer shops and the way in which he or she processes information. Although Bettman's model does not explicitly make such distinctions, some form of transition is suggested in the model in the form of questions such as X1 and X5. That is, one can assume that the consumer is in fact making her decision either in the produce, meat, or dairy section of the store. The decision to proceed from one section to the other is not recorded or is not reported in the decision structure proposed by Bettman. The shopping decision is not one continuous decision as suggested by Bettman's model but, is in fact several independent decision phases conditioned by the consumer being in the shopping environment.

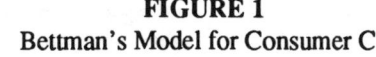

FIGURE 1
Bettman's Model for Consumer C_1

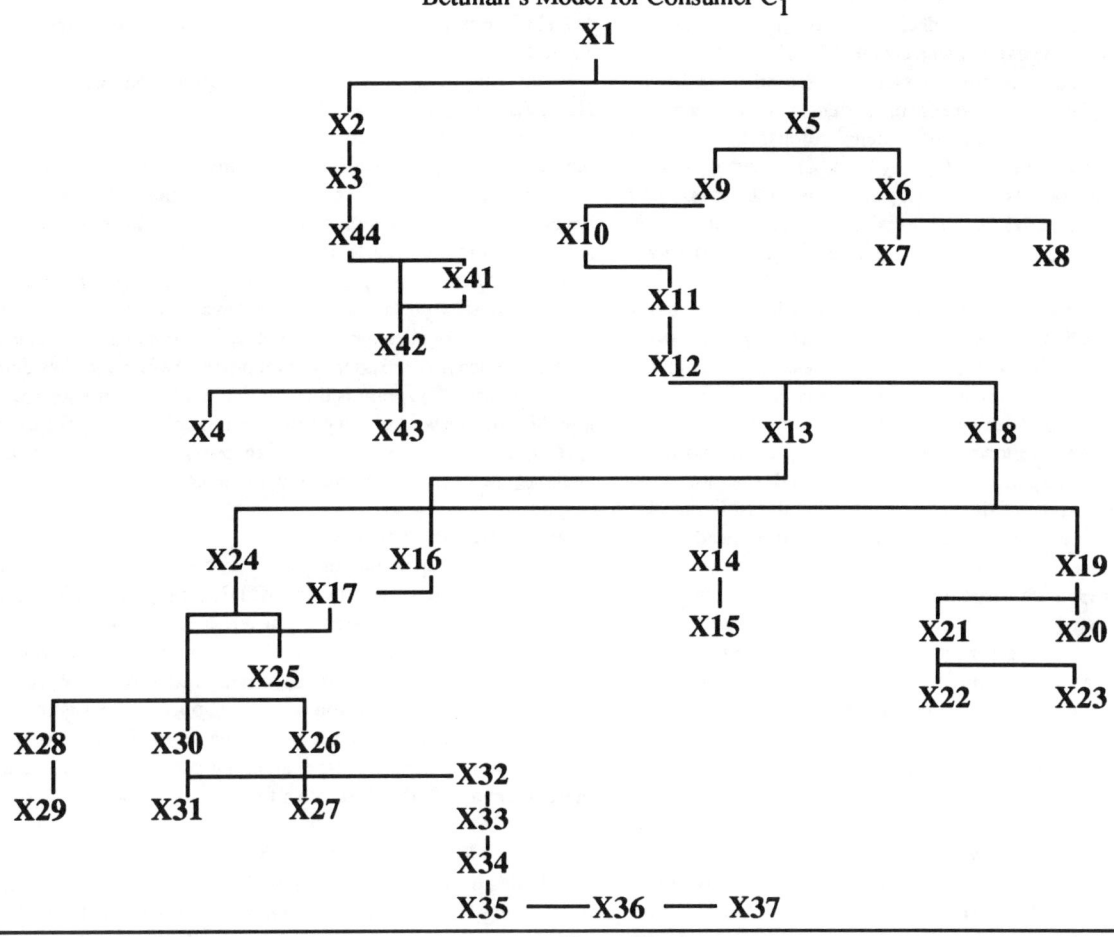

Key to Figure

X1:	Is this meat or produce?	X23:	Is this the cheapest national brand?
X2:	Is price below justified level?	X24:	Are children the main users?
X3:	Is color okay:	X25:	Did they state a preference this week?
X4:	Is this the biggest 'okay' one?	X26:	Have they used this up in the last two weeks?
X5:	Is this eggs?	X27:	Is this cheapest size?
X6:	Is the price of extra large over 5 cents more than the price of large?	X28:	Is this that one?
X7:	Is this large size?	X29:	Is this the cheapest size?
X8:	Is this extra large size?	X30:	Are several 'okay' brands cheapest (that they have in stock)?
X9:	Was this product bought last time for this product type?	x31:	Is this the cheapest (that they have in stock)?
X10:	Was experience with it okay?	X32:	Have a coupon for this one?
X11:	Is risk associated with this product (bad experience)?	X33:	Is this one biggest?
X12:	Is this product class high?	X34:	Is there a single national brand?
X13:	Do children or husband have a specific preference?	X35:	Is this it?
		X36:	Have I used it before?
X14:	Is this their preference?	X37:	Is this the closest?
X15:	Is it the cheapest size?	X41:	Does this feel okay?
X16:	Does this class have health (hygiene, diet) factors?	X42:	Is this for a specific use?
		X43:	Is this size okay for that?
X17:	Is this okay on these factors?	X44:	Is this produce?
X18:	Is this for company?		
X19:	Is the cheapest brand good enough?		
X20:	Is this the cheapest?		**SPECIAL RELATIONS**
X21:	Had a good experience with any brands in this class?		Flip-flop between X11 and X9
			Flip-flop between X42 and X44
X22:	Is this that brand?		Flip-flop between X30 and X16

To capture this conditioning process, we added those facilitating decisions such as moving from one store section to another as prerequisite events for purchase decision in each product category. It should be noted however that the events X9 to X37 may not have the correct facilitating structure. Based on a reading of the discussion offered by Bettman, we are unable to determine what and how many different products are actually being purchased. It appears from the model that consumer C_1 may have purchased as many as twelve different products on this shopping occasion. Does one infer from the Bettman model that the decision for coffee, flour, sugar, and soup are made in the same structural form? This seems unlikely.

Once the necessary structural changes have been made to the model, the analysis phase is repeated to insure that the new event sequence is compatible with the modeling rules of event analysis. The revised model of Bettman's consumer C_1 is shown in Figure 2.

In Figure 2, the decision events X_i are retained and the facilitating events are shown by a series of alpha characters made from the letters of the particular event. This revised structure allows for one to delete some of the events reported in the earlier model. For example, "X44: Is this produce?" may not be needed as a decision step since the consumer is in the produce section. However, depending on the particular store, there may be a number of non-produce items in the produce section: special bottled fruit juices, fruit/vegetable dip mixes, little cupcakes you put fresh berries on top of, etc. From the reported data, one is unable to determine if consumer C's store contained *only* produce. To be in the produce section and thus to ask if this is produce may or may not be redundant. Another advantage of the ETHNO representation of the decisions processes is that it disentangles the different decisions that the consumer makes and does not force one to represent them as a single decision of many branches.

In addition ETHNO has added additional Special relations. Along with the flip-flop situation described earlier, the term non-depletion has been added. Non-depletion indicates that the occurrence of the superordinate event does not deplete a previous occurrence of the subordinate event. As one can observe, the non-depletions occur at junctions in the decision model that allow for multiple paths through the process. These multiple paths suggest repeated operations on the part of the consumer in question.

Phase Three: Generating Priorities

In the previous section, the software used information in the event series in two different ways. The first use consisted of time ordering the sequence so some conceivable relational questions could be eliminated such as making produce decisions in the produce section and not later in the shopping event. ETHNO assumes that later events cannot be prerequisites for earlier events. The second use of information in the pattern of event series is as a cue that something may be wrong with the original structure. This second phase allows the analyst to adjust the original structure. Once the modified model is congruent with the assumptions, one can now use the event information in a third way by computing priorities.

The grammar(consumer's verbalized decision steps) of an event analysis allows a certain amount of free variation, and this free variation is examined to reveal preferences for certain events over others. The basic question elicited from the analyst and used by the software in its statistical calculations is that when several events are possible, which take priority over the others. An event is given a value of 100 if it always takes priority over alternative events 100% of the time when a choice is available. A value of 0 indicates that the event in question always happens last when nothing else is possible in the series. Other events will thus have values somewhere between these extremes. For the modified model of Bettman's consumer C_1, the priority values are shown in Table 1.

By computing the table of probabilities, one can, in some cases, gain insight into the event sequence that may not be apparent from the pictorial representation of the structure. For example in our present shopping case, it is interesting to note that decisions of an external nature such as family preference, prior experience, etc. appear later in the decision sequences and thus have lower probabilities. Another way to view these results is that our subject consumer placed less importance on the decision variables than she placed on other aspects of a more direct evaluation (color, feel, etc.) of the products in question. Alternately, one could argue that each product choice had to pass the earlier criteria before it is considered for family use. The point is that the modeling structure highlights areas that the researcher can go back to the subject and probe for the specific meaning. Without the flag provided by the computer analysis, the deeper meaning may not emerge.

Phase Four: Generate a Series

This final step in our analysis consisted of using the priorities and the model generated by the ETHNO program as an action grammar for producing a new event series. The program began by listing all events that are theoretically possible at the beginning of the data set. The events are listed from high priority to low priority. After selecting the event you want to happen, the program next offers those events that can occur after the selected event. Again as with previous analysis, several alternate pathways appeared and these were modified to produce a final revised model.

DISCUSSION

In this paper, we have attempted to demonstrate an important methodology for analyzing ethnographic data. It can help researchers systematize their findings and quantify them in interesting ways, without at the same time loosing the richness of ethnographic data. It should however be pointed out here that the data set used in the present case is less than ideal. Specifically, it is hoped that the researcher attempting to use this program would actually take it into the field so that questions of structure could be resolved with the informant. At the very least, the researcher should subject his or her data to the rigors of analysis while the collection experience is still fresh. In the present case, we were working with data that were old and even more limited by what was reported by someone else. Thus, entering the data at this time required the researcher to make a series of highly subjective judgments regarding which prior events are required for the current event to occur. These judgments may have not correctly matched the subject's perception of the world at the actual time. More specifically, one cannot determine at this later date if the problems encountered are that of omission on the part of the subject and/or faulty recording on the part of the observer. Despite these limitations, the use of a computer based analytical approach broadened the application and understanding of the previous work.

Finally, one must keep in mind that using such a program will not ease the data collection burden of the researcher but, may in fact increase his or her task by forcing a greater depth of analysis and understanding. For the research community as a whole, the use of such a tool does provide advantages in that the structure thus developed can be studied, examined, and discussed by different scholars and in different contexts.

FIGURE 2
Revised Model for Consumer C_1

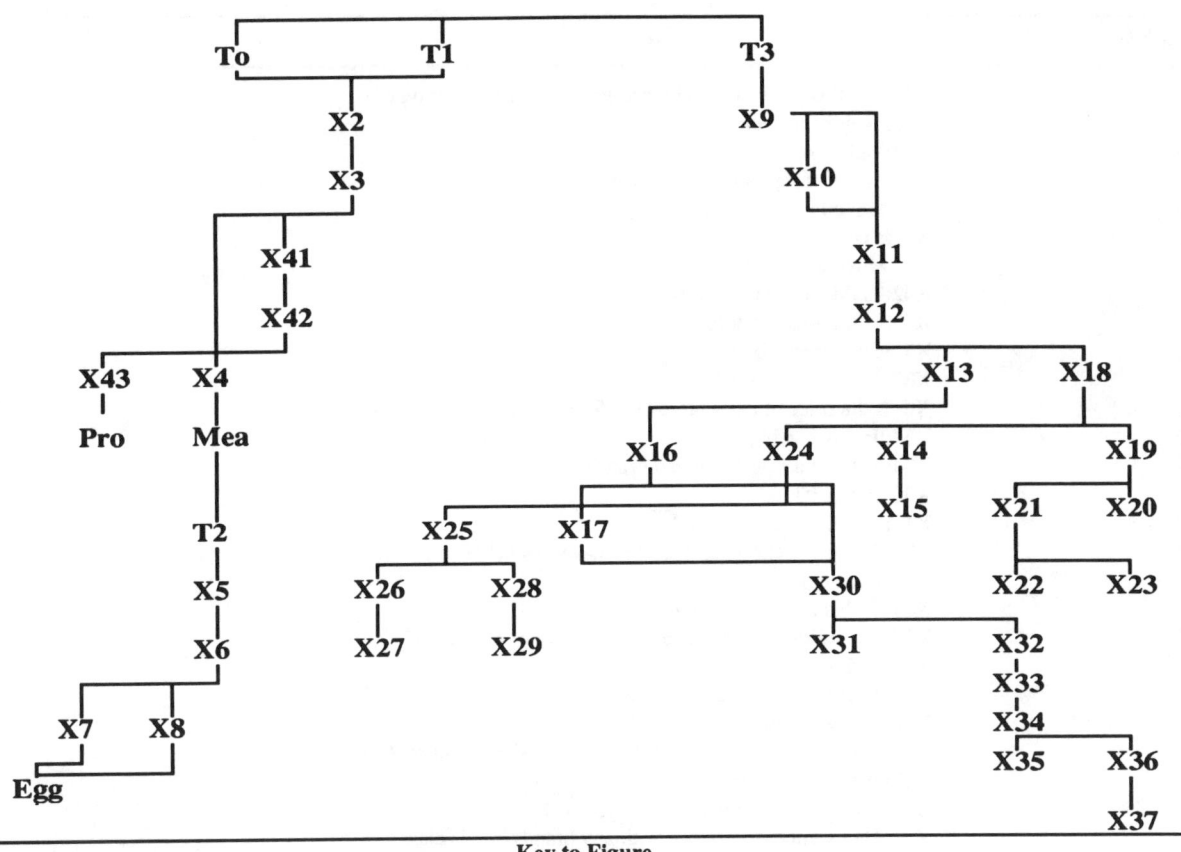

Key to Figure

T0:	Move to meat section
T1:	Move to produce section
T3:	Move to products
Egg:	Select eggs
Pro:	Select produce
Mea:	Select meat
X2:	Is price below justified level?
X3:	Is color okay:
X4:	Is this the biggest 'okay' one?
X5:	Is this eggs?
X6:	Is the price of extra large over 5 cents more than the price of large?
X7:	Is this large size?
X8:	Is this extra large size?
X9:	Was this product bought last time for this product type?
X10:	Was experience with it okay?
X11:	Is risk associated with this product (bad experience)?
X12:	Is this product class high?
X13:	Do children or husband have a specific preference?
X14:	Is this their preference?
X15:	Is it the cheapest size?
X16:	Does this class have health (hygiene, diet) factors?
X17:	Is this okay on these factors?
X18:	Is this for company?
X19:	Is the cheapest brand good enough?
X20:	Is this the cheapest?
X21:	Had a good experience with any brands in this class?
X22:	Is this that brand?
X23:	Is this the cheapest national brand?
X24:	Are children the main users?
X25:	Did they state a preference this week?
X26:	Have they used this up in the last two weeks?
X27:	Is this cheapest size?
X28:	Is this that one?
X29:	Is this the cheapest size?
X30:	Are several 'okay' brands cheapest (that they have in stock)?
x31:	Is this the cheapest (that they have in stock)?
X32:	Have a coupon for this one?
X33:	Is this one biggest?
X34:	Is there a single national brand?
X35:	Is this it?
X36:	Have I used it before?
X37:	Is this the closest?
X41:	Does this feel okay?
X42:	Is this for a specific use?
X43:	Is this size okay for that?

SPECIAL RELATIONS
Non-depletion from X7 to X6
Flip-flop between X8 and X6
Non-depletion from X10 to X9
Non-depletion from X13 to X12
Non-depletion from X14 to X13
Non-depletion from X17 to X16
Non-depletion from X18 to X12
Non-depletion from X19 to X18
Non-depletion from X20 to X19
Non-depletion from X21 to X19
Non-depletion from X22 to X21
Non-depletion from X23 to X21
Non-depletion from X24 to X18
Non-depletion from X25 to X24
Non-depletion from X26 to X25
Non-depletion from X28 to X25
Non-depletion from x31 to X30
Non-depletion from X32 to X30
Non-depletion from X35 to X34
Non-depletion from X36 to X34
Non-depletion from X11 to X9
Non-depletion from X30 to X16
Flip-flop between X42 and X44
Flip-flop between X41 and X3

TABLE 1
Probabilities for the Modified Model of Consumer C_1

Probability	Event
100	X9: Was this product bought last time for this product type?
100	X20: Is this the cheapest?
100	Mea: Select meat
100	X19: Is the cheapest brand good enough?
100	T2 : Move to dairy section
100	X3: Is color okay?
100	To : Move to meat section
100	X42: Is this for a specific use?
100	X43: Is this size okay for that?
100	X7: Is this large size?
100	X37: Is this the closest?
100	X6: Is the price of extra large over 5 cents more than the price of large?
100	X33: Is this one biggest?
100	X34: Is there a single national brand?
100	X35: Is this it?
100	X15: Is it the cheapest size?
100	X31: Is this the cheapest (that they have in stock)?
100	X5: Is this eggs?
100	X29: Is this the cheapest size?
100	X13: Do children or husband have a specific preference?
100	X27: Is this cheapest size?
100	X12: Is this product class high risk?
100	X2: Is price below justified level?
100	X11: Is risk associated with this product (bad experience)?
100	X22: Is this that brand?
100	X25: Did they state a preference this week?
94	X21: Had a good experience with any brands in this class?
94	X23: Is this the cheapest national brand?
92	X8: Is this extra large size?
74	X24: Are children the main users?
48	X30: Are several "okay" brands cheapest (that they have in stock)?
32	X16: Does this class have health (hygiene, diet) factors?
28	X36: Have I used it before?
26	X18: Is this for company?
26	X32: Have a coupon for this one?
22	X26: Have they used this up in the last two weeks?
22	X28: Is this that one?
21	X17: Is this okay on these factors?
16	X14: Is this their preference?
15	X41: Does this feel okay?
12	X10: Was experience with it okay?
8	X4: Is this the biggest "okay" one?
7	T3 : Move to products
4	T1 : Move to produce section
0	Egg: Select eggs
0	Pro: Select produce

REFERENCES

Anderson, John R. (1983), *The Architecture of Cognition*, Cambridge, MA: Harvard University press.

Axten, Nick and John Skvoretz (1980), "Roles and Role-Programs," *Quality and Quantity*, 14, 547-83.

Bettman, James R. (1970), "Information Processing Models of Consumer Behavior," *Journal of Marketing Research*, 7 (August), 370-6.

_____ (1979, *An Information Processing Theory of Consumer Choice*, Reading, MA: Addison-Wesley Publishing Company.

Corsaro, William A. and David R. Heise (1990), "Event Structure Models from Ethnographic Data," in Clifford C. Clogg, ed. *Sociological Methodology, 1990*, Oxford: Basil Blackwell.

Fararo, Thomas J. and John Skvoretz (1984), "Institutions as Production Systems," *Journal of Mathematical Sociology*, 10, 117-82.

Heise, David R. (1988), "Computer Analysis of Cultural Structures," *Social Science Computer Review* 6:1 (Spring), 183-96.

_____ (1989), "Modeling Event Structures," *Journal of Mathematical Sociology*, 14 (2-3) 139-69.

_____ and Elsa M. Lewis (1988), *Introduction to ETHNO*, Raleigh, NC: National Collegiate Software Clearinghouse.

Newell, Auther and Herbert Simon (1972), *Human Problem Solving*, Englewood Cliffs, NJ: Prentice-Hall.

Waterman, D.A. and Fredrick Hayes-Roth (1978), *Pattern-Directed Inference Systems*, New York: Academic Press.

Linking Emotions and Values in Consumption Experiences: An Exploratory Study

Debra A. Laverie, Arizona State University
Robert E. Kleine III, Arizona State University
Susan Schultz Kleine, Arizona State University

ABSTRACT

This study examines the link between emotions and values in consumption experiences. A conceptual relationship between the two constructs is developed. The proposed relationship is tested in an exploratory study that elicited subject's own consumption experiences and then measured emotions and values on a paper and pencil instrument. The data support the premise that emotions and values are related in consumption experiences. Also, the data suggest that the self is the latent variable that links emotions and values in consumption experiences.

We all spend much of our lives consuming products. How does consumption make us feel? What are the values we obtain from, or express through, our consumption? And how might these feelings and values be linked through consumption experiences? People respond to and choose activities that make them feel a certain way (Havlena and Holbrook 1986) and correspond to important values (Munson 1984). Empirically, consumption experiences are linked with both values (Beatty, Kahle, Homer, and Misra 1985) and emotions (Havlena and Holbrook 1986; Havlena, Holbrook, and Lehman 1989). However, except for Holbrook's (1986) conceptualization of consumption experience, these two constructs have not been studied jointly in association with consumption.

Do consumers associate certain emotions with certain types of value in consumption experiences? For example, the emotions one associates with the playful or fun value of a consumption experience may be very different from the emotions one associates with a consumption experience that reflects the value of being well respected. The purpose of this project is to explore empirically the connection between patterns of emotions and values as they are linked through consumption. In the next section we discuss the emotion and values constructs and their potential linkage. Then we report the results of a study which explores patterns of emotions and values associated with consumption experiences.

THE LINK BETWEEN EMOTIONS AND VALUES IN CONSUMPTION EXPERIENCES

Emotion

Empirical research demonstrates that emotions are related to consumption behavior (Havlena and Holbrook 1986). The important role that emotions play in consumer's lives suggests that emotions can explain behavior in situations where other constructs, such as attitude, do not account for all or even a significant portion of the variability in behavior. For instance, Allen, Machleit, and Schultz Kleine (1992) showed that emotions supplement attitude in predicting consumption behavior. In addition, Westbrook and Oliver (1991) demonstrated that emotions help illuminate satisfaction (attitudinal) responses to consumption.

Emotions, which are feelings linked to a specific behavior (Gardner 1984), represent a richer and more complex realm of phenomena than does the attitude construct (Allen, et al. 1992; Holbrook 1986). Emotions are either positive, negative, or mixed in valence. Complex and/or conflicting emotions are richer than attitudes. Therefore, attitude may be too simple to represent the complexity of many consumption experiences (Allen, et al. 1992).

There are several psychological frameworks that define and operationalize emotion (e.g., Izard 1977; Mehrabian and Russell 1974; Plutchik 1980). The present research uses Izard's framework which "assumes that separate and discrete emotions exist and that each has measurable, experiential, and motivational properties" (Izard 1972, p. 85). In his Differential Emotions Theory Izard (1972) conceptualizes ten fundamental emotions: joy, surprise, anger, disgust, contempt, shame, guilt, fear, interest, and sadness. Izard's typology has initiated research on emotions in a variety of consumer research contexts (e.g., Allen et al. 1988, 1992; Batra and Ray 1986; Westbrook 1987; Westbrook and Oliver 1991).

Values

Value is an abstract and complex construct that can provide underlying continuity to behavior (Pitts and Woodside 1984). Following Rokeach (1973, p. 25), we construe values as enduring beliefs that a specific mode of behavior or end-state is preferred over other alternatives. Therefore, values are a major influence on human behavior (Parsons and Shils 1951). The view that values guide behavior is evident in literature from psychology, sociology, and organizational behavior (Izard 1977; Rokeach 1973; Tolman 1951). In an interdisciplinary analysis of personal values, Clawson and Vinson (1978) suggest that:

> Values may prove to be one of the most powerful explanations of, and influences on, consumer behavior. They can perhaps equal or surpass the contributions of other major constructs including attitudes, product attributes, degrees of deliberating, product classification, and life style (p. 396).

Therefore, the consumption of a product can express or fulfill a certain value.

Consumers' preferences for certain values are likely to be expressed through consumption. For example, certain products and activities may be preferred by a person who values excitement (e.g., fast cars, mountain biking, bungee cord jumping). On the other hand, a person placing security as very important would be likely to have a different set of preferred products and activities (e.g., an airbag in their car, going for long walks in the country, attending religious services). Researchers have suggested that we need a better understanding of the links between values and behaviors, and special consideration of how values interact with situations (Beatty et al. 1985).

To study consumption related values, Kahle (1983) modified the Rokeach Value Survey (RVS) into a smaller subset of values that were person oriented and generalizable across many activities. The List of Values (LOV) includes: sense of belonging, excitement, fun and enjoyment, warm relationships with others, self fulfillment, being well respected, a sense of accomplishment, security, and self respect. The LOV approach is a parsimonious way to measure values as compared to the RVS or Values and Lifestyles (VALS) approaches. In addition the LOV contains many items that people say influence their daily lives (Kahle 1986; Beatty et al. 1985).

Values and Emotions

There are several interesting parallels between emotions and values. Psychologists (Tolman 1951; Izard 1977) and practitioners (e.g., Mowen 1988; Clawson and Vinson 1978) agree that both emotions and values play an extremely important role in behavior. Values are central beliefs expressed through specific behaviors (Rokeach 1973) and emotions are feelings linked to specific behaviors (Gardner 1985).

Values, according to Holbrook (1986), involve preference and thus are directly tied to the positive and negative affective opposition of emotions. The value expressed in a consumption experience is the result of the emotions that accompany the consumption experience. Accordingly, emotions and values are intertwined in consumption (Holbrook 1986). Thus, it makes sense that both values and emotions would be linked in consumer behaviors.

Study Objective

The objective of this research is to explore the relationship between values and emotions in consumption experiences by employing methods to represent the patterns of emotions that occur during consumption experiences that are associated with certain values. Specifically, are there discrete patterns of emotion that are linked to patterns of values in consumption experiences? Toward this end we conducted a study that examined the link between values and emotions in consumption experiences.

PRETEST

We conducted a pretest to explore the relationship between emotions and values in consumption experiences. Specifically, the pretest assessed a methodology and the measures for exploring the link between emotions and values. Using a paper and pencil instrument, subjects (n=71) were exposed to two scenarios that described consumption experiences. Each of nine scenarios expressed a particular LOV value. Subjects described a consumption experience that expressed a specific LOV value. Based on this self-reported experience subjects responded to measures of emotions and values.

Due to space limitations the empirical findings of the pretest are not reported. Results showed that seven of the ten emotions were significantly different across values (anger, contempt, and interest were not significant). However, the results appeared to be hampered by two methodological limitations. One, following Beatty et al.'s (1985) procedure, we asked subjects to rank the LOV values based on their importance to the described consumption experience. This ranking of values was difficult for the subjects because values are so closely held (Munson and McIntyre 1979) and some subjects didn't follow directions carefully. In addition, rank order data precluded the use of many types of statistical analyses. Two, the manipulation check suggested that some subjects seemed to focus on the activity depicted in the scenario more than the expressed value. Procedures were altered for the main study to overcome these methodological limitations.

AN EXPLORATORY STUDY

We conducted a study to investigate the proposed link between emotions and values in consumption experiences. Value expressive consumption experiences were elicited from subjects after which they responded to emotion and values measures. Described next are the methods and subjects used in this study. We then report the results.

Eliciting Value Expressive Consumption Experiences

A consumption experience was defined for subjects as any activity they do while using a product. Several examples of consumption experiences were provided (e.g., eating, driving a car, wearing clothes, playing volleyball, and listening to music). Subjects were then asked to recall and describe a consumption experience that was important to them because of one of the nine LOV values. For the "warm relationship with others" value, for example, subjects were asked to think of an experience when they felt warm and happy because they were with good friends and family (how each value was defined for the subjects is described in Appendix 1).

Measures

Emotions. We used Izard's (1977) DES-II to measure subject's emotions during consumption experiences. The DES-II has been an effective measure of emotions for consumer researchers (e.g., Allen et al. 1992, 1988; Westbrook and Oliver 1991). The DES-II instructions ask the subjects to consider the experience they described and to rate how often s/he experienced each emotion item during the experience. Subjects rate 30 items, 3 for each of the ten fundamental emotions. Each item is administered on a 5-point never to very often scale.

Values. Kahle's (1983) List of Values (LOV) measured the values subjects associated with the consumption experiences they described. Based on the analytical limitations of rank ordering values revealed in the pretest the LOV values were measured using Likert scales. Values assessed using Likert scales are as reliable as those measured with the ranking procedure (Munson and McIntyre 1979).

Subjects were instructed to think about the experience they described and then to use the scales to indicate the importance of each value to their experience. Each value was measured on a 5-point extremely unimportant to extremely important scale. Subjects also rank ordered the nine LOV values to afford a manipulation check.

Procedures

Subjects were 131 male and female undergraduate students from five sections of a marketing course. Each subject independently described and answered questions about two consumption experiences. Due to incomplete data one response was eliminated leaving 261 usable consumption experiences. The values described in the consumption experience elicitation instructions were randomized across subjects. The cover sheet indicated that participation in the study was voluntary, the next sheet stated the study's purpose and presented subject instructions.

Subjects read a definition of a consumption experience and then read a description of one the nine LOV values. Subjects were asked to write out a description of a consumption experience that was important to them because of the value that they were exposed to. Finally, subjects responded to Izard's DES-II emotion measures and the LOV values on Likert scales. In addition, subjects ranked the LOV values according to their importance in the experience they had described.

RESULTS

The emotion and value variables were first factor analyzed to assess the dimensionality of each construct. The variables that resulted from the factor analyses were then analyzed via canonical correlation analysis to assess the emotion-value relationship.

Structure of the Emotion Measure

The a *priori* measurement model which specified 10 factors, each consisting of three items, was analyzed via confirmatory factor analysis (SAS's Proc CALIS). The overall fit of the ten factor model, analyzing the covariance matrix, was acceptable ($\chi^2(381)=620.66$, $p>.0001$, Bentler and Bonett's Normed Index=.975, RMR=.213). All parameter estimates were reasonable

TABLE 1
Exploratory Factor Analysis of Value Items
(Varimax Rotated)

Values	Others	Self	Hedonic
Well-Respected	.778	.201	.001
Sense of Belonging	.764	-.079	.264
Warm Relationships w/ Others	.684	-.307	.356
Security	.670	.172	-.163
Sense of Accomplishment	-.065	.868	.016
Self-Fulfillment	.097	.836	.105
Self-Respect	.535	.592	-.025
Fun & Enjoyment	.127	-.043	.893
Excitement	-.009	.175	.874
Eigenvalues	2.43	2.00	1.80
Reliability	.73	.72*	.78*

Note.—These values are correlations as there were only two items.

and in the anticipated direction. The average variance extracted from the items was .59 (Bagozzi and Yi 1988). The distribution of the residuals is approximately normal. Only three residuals exceeded 2.0. Furthermore, the fit is comparable with other reported confirmatory factor analyses of Izard's measurement model (e.g., Allen, et al. 1988). Sum scales were constructed from the thirty items for the ten emotions as defined Izard (1977).

Structure of the Value Measure

The LOV values are suggested to be nine different values that are important in people's daily lives (Kahle 1983). In addition the LOV measure has demonstrated convergent and discriminant validity in past research (Beatty et al. 1985; Kahle 1983). This implies the—admittedly strong—hypothesis that if the LOV is submitted to a factor analysis nine factors will result.

An exploratory factor analysis of the scaled data on the nine LOV values using varimax rotation reveals three distinct factors (see Table 1). The first factor is defined by four highly loading values that all relate to interactions with others (e.g., a sense of belonging, warm relationships with others, security, and being well respected). Accordingly, we labeled this factor 'others'. The second factor is formed by two self related outcomes and is labeled 'self' (e.g., sense of accomplishment and self fulfillment). The value self-respect cross loads on the 'others' factor which intuitively makes sense since self respect is often governed by one's perception of what other people think about him or her. Due to the heavy cross loading this item is not used in further analyses. The third factor is labeled 'hedonic' and is made up of the values of fun/enjoyment and excitement.

These results suggest that the LOV consists of three factors in the context of consumption experiences. Kennedy, Best, and Kahle (1988) report a similar factor structure. Based on the results of the factor analysis three sum scales were constructed for the value items that loaded together on a factor. These sum scales are used in the canonical correlation analysis reported below.

Elicitation Assessment

To check the efficacy of instructions we compared the top-ranked value to the value the subjects's consumption experience was supposed to express. On average 76% of the subjects ranked the value described in their consumption experience as the most important (e.g., number one). The percentage of subjects who ranked the value described in their stimulus as number one ranged from 95% for a 'sense of accomplishment' to 57% for 'well respected'. This suggests that the nine values are well represented by subject's consumption experiences.

The Relationship Between Values and Emotions

We explored the relationship between emotions and values in consumption experiences using canonical correlation analysis. Specifically, the three values factors (e.g., others, self, and hedonic) were related to the ten emotions (e.g., joy, surprise, anger, disgust, contempt, shame, guilt, fear, interest, and sadness). Three significant canonical variates were obtained (see Table 2).

The loadings on the first canonical variate suggest that consumption experiences expressing hedonic values (e.g., fun and enjoyment and excitement) are associated with the emotions interest, surprise, and enjoyment. This variate accounts for much (37%) of the shared variance between emotions and values.

The second canonical variate suggests that interest and fear are the most salient emotions in consumption experiences that express self related values (e.g., sense of accomplishment and self fulfillment). This link accounted for 29% of the shared variance.

The third variate suggests a relationship between the others related value and the emotions of shame and decreasing surprise in consumption experiences. However, this variate accounts for only 9% of the shared variance and therefore should be interpreted with caution, despite its statistical significance (Pedhazur 1982).

Anger, sadness, disgust, contempt, and guilt, all negative emotions, did not help in explaining the linear combinations between emotions and values. The emotions related to values are typically positive. In addition, when people are asked to recall

TABLE 2
Canonical Correlation Analysis Between Values and Emotions

	Canonical Loadings		
	Variate 1	Variate 2	Variate 3
Values			
Hedonic	.896*a	-.203	-.381
Self	.477	.773*	.412
Others	.465	-.418	.771*
Emotions			
Enjoyment	.900*	-.249	.015
Surprise	.720*	.224	-.406*
Interest	.506*	.770*	.297
Shame	.188	-.280	.442*
Anger	.158	.282	-.150
Sad	.096	.244	.281
Fear	.237	.370*	-.076
Disgust	.052	.214	-.246
Contempt	.162	.105	.019
Guilt	.126	-.066	.106
Statistics			
Canonical Correlation	.609	.588	.294
$R^{2\,b}$	.37	.29	.09
F	8.39	6.45	2.85
p	.0001	.0001	.005
$R_d^{\,c}$	.169	.070	.024

a Items with an * were used to interpret the variate.
b Total R^2 for the three canonical variates=.75
c R_d shows the percentage of total variance of the emotions which is explained from linear combination of values (i.e., redundancy). Total R_d Values/Emotions=.26

something related to a value and write about it they typically pick a positive experience to discuss (Schrum, McCarty, and Loeffler 1990).

DISCUSSION

The results offer encouraging support for the proposed link between certain emotions and values in consumption experiences. These findings are a step toward a better understanding of post-purchase consumer behavior. At a minimum, these results encourage further examination of the link between values and emotions as facets of consumption experiences. In addition, the results suggest some methodological considerations that need to be addressed in future research.

The Relationship Between Values and Emotions

The results of the canonical analysis suggest that certain emotions are linked to consumption experiences that express different values. Consumption experiences that are valued because they are enjoyable are linked to positive emotions. On the other hand, experiences that are valued because of their link to the self are combined with interest and a negative emotion, fear. Values that center around others are linked to shame and decreasing surprise. It is interesting to note the parallels between this exploratory study's findings and the literature on the self.

The social-psychological literature suggests three facets of the self that can be linked to the three value variables. The 'hedonic', 'self', and 'others' values parallel the hedonic, private, and public aspects of the self (e.g., Greenwald and Breckler 1985). The 'hedonic' value relates to three emotions that all involve arousal (interest, surprise, and enjoyment). The results suggest that this variate represents a hedonic portion of the self. This aspect of the self is hedonically guided toward positive affective states (Greenwald and Breckler 1985). In addition, the hedonic self is a condition of not distinguishing sharply between self and others (Greenwald and Breckler 1985; Schlenker 1985). This state is evident in the first canonical variate. The 'others' and 'self' values load heavily and equally on this 'hedonic' variate.

The second variate labeled 'self' resembles the private self. The private self allows for self-evaluation in the absence of others (Greenwald and Breckler 1985). This condition is clear in the canonical loadings, the 'others' value loads negatively on the 'self' variate. A major task of the private self is individual achievement. The value items that load on the 'self' factor (a sense of accomplishment and self-fulfillment; see Table 1) evidence this.

The emotions related to the private self are interest and fear. Intuitively one would expect interest to be important to the private self as this aspect of the self is guided by internal standards (McClelland, Atkinson, Clark, and Lowell 1953). On the other hand, it may seem surprising that fear is an important emotion in the private self. However, the private self is developed based on the internalization of the evaluative standards of significant others (Greenwald and Breckler 1985). For example, a respondent wrote:

"I felt excited and scared going through sorority rush. I was terrified because I ... was not sure if I would fit in. ... I was scared, but I hoped that what I was wearing would make me feel comfortable and help me to fit in." Therefore, the emotion of fear may be linked to the concern of meeting the standards one has adopted for him/herself.

The third variate depicts the public self. The public self is sensitive to the evaluations of others and seeks to win the approval of those who are important to the individual (Greenwald and Breckler 1985). An important task of the public self is earning credit in exchange relationships with others. These characteristics are evident in the values that form the 'others' factor, namely 'being well-respected', a 'sense of belonging', 'warm relationships with others', and 'security'.

The emotions that are linked to the public self are shame and decreasing surprise. Although it may seem surprising that shame is an important emotion in the public self, shame is the primary *social emotion* (Goffman 1967; Lewis 1971; Scheff 1990; Rosenberg 1979). Shame is an emotion that arises from the monitoring of one's own actions by viewing one's self from the standpoint of others (Scheff 1990). Thus, it makes sense that shame is an important emotion in the public self which is concerned with what other people think of us. Likewise, the public self is adverse to the potential embarrassment of being caught by surprise in social situations. In sum, the results of the canonical correlation analysis suggest some interesting relationships between emotions and values in consumption experiences. It is encouraging that these relationships can be explained by the extensive literature on the self. Furthermore, these results lead us to speculate that the self is the underlying link between values and emotions in consumption experiences.

Limitations and Future Research

The specific findings of this study cannot be generalized without caution. As noted earlier, the research is exploratory in nature. In addition, both the values and the emotions measures are based on retrospection. Future research measuring emotions and values during the consumption experience would provide important insight into consumption experiences.

Measurement of Emotions. Most measures of emotions, such as Izard's scale used in this research, are essentially based on aided recall (Westbrook 1987). This research enhanced subjects' recollection by asking them to write a detailed description of their experience. However, alternative ways of tapping emotions may yield different information about consumption experiences. For instance, measurement directly after an experience would likely lead to richer information as compared to the emotions one can recall. As noted in the findings of this research typically just a few emotions are associated with certain values. Perhaps this is because the most important one or two emotions are all that subjects recall and they may have experienced a much larger range of emotions during the experience. Identification of the best approach for predicting consumption behavior is a task for future research.

Another question consumer researchers need to address is the appropriateness of psychological measurement schemes for consumption activities. The findings of this research suggest that the many negative emotions in Izard's scale may not be suited to value expressive consumption experiences since values are typically positive. It appears that consumer researchers should explore alternative measurement frameworks or develop a measurement procedure that is more appropriate for consumption behavior. The qualitative measurement of emotions (Smith-Lovin 1990) is one promising alternative.

Examining the Dimensions of Values. This research suggests that the dimensionality of Kahle's (1983) LOVs needs to be assessed further in the context of consumption experiences. Although designed to reflect values that consumers experience in their daily lives (Beatty et al. 1986), our findings suggest that the LOV values represent three distinct factors. This encourages further examination of the validity of this construct in the context of consumption experiences. The value factors offer a parsimonious view of values in the consumption context.

In addition, the study supports measuring values on Likert type scales. This produced better quality data and more flexibility in analysis. The Likert type approach does not force the respondent to rank order values that may be equally important and it allows for differences in the intensity with which a particular value is held (Munson 1984; Munson and McIntrye 1979; Clawson and Vinson 1973).

Emotions and Values in Consumption Experiences. Both emotions and values are rich constructs for understanding post-purchase consumer behavior. The results of this study provide evidence of a connection between patterns of emotions and values in consumption experiences. Perhaps consumers choose certain consumption experiences because of this linkage. Researchers whose interest is pre-purchase phenomena might explore how the effectiveness of promotional messages that reflect specific values and emotions differ across common segmentation variables. Furthermore, different aspects of the self may help explain the emotion-value linkage. Future research should address this role of the self in consumption experiences.

APPENDIX

The following was used to prompt a consumption experience that expresses a particular LOV value: "Think of an experience when you were using products and _____." One of the following phrases completed the sentence: 1) you were *well respected*; 2) you were *self-fulfilled*; 3) you felt a *sense of accomplishment*; 4) you felt a sense of *security*; 5) you felt a *sense of belonging*; 6) you felt *self respect*; 7) you were *excited*; 8) you felt *warm relationships with other people*; 9) you had *fun*.

REFERENCES

Allen, Chris T., Karen A. Machleit, and Susan S. Marine (1988), "Assessing the Emotionality of Advertising Via Izard's Differential Emotions Scale," in *Advances in Consumer Research*, Vol.15, ed. Michael J. Houston, Provo, UT: Association for Consumer Research, 226-231.

_____, _____, Susan Schultz Kleine (1992), "A Comparison of Attitudes and Emotions as Predictors of Behavior at Diverse Levels of Behavioral Experience," *Journal of Consumer Research*, 18 (March), 493-504.

Bagozzi, Richard P. Youjae Yi (1988), "On the Evaluation of Structural Equation Models), *Journal of the Academy of marketing Science*, 16 (1), 74-93.

Batra, Rajeev and Michael Ray (1986), "Affective Responses Mediating the Acceptance of Advertising," *Journal of Consumer Research*, 13 (September), 234-249.

Beatty, Sharon E., Lynn R. Kahle, Pamela Homer, and Shekhar Misra (1985), "Alternative Measurement Approaches to Consumer Values: The List of Values and Rokeach Value Survey," *Psychology and Marketing*, 2 (Number 3), 181-200.

Clawson, C.J. and Donald E. Vinson (1978), "Human Values: An Historical and Interdisciplinary Analysis," in *Contributions to Consumer Research V*, ed. H. Keith Hunt, Chicago: Association for Consumer Research, 396-402.

Gardner, Meryl Paula (1985), "Mood States and Consumer Behavior: A Critical Review," *Journal of Consumer Research*, 12 (December), 281-300.

Goffman, Erving (1967), *Interaction Ritual*, New York: Anchor.

Greenwald, Anthony G. and Steven J. Breckler (1985), "To Whom is the Self Presented?", in *The Self and Social Life*, ed. Barry R. Schlenker, New York: McGraw-Hill.

Havlena, William J. and Morris B. Holbrook (1986), "The Varieties of Consumption Experience: Comparing Two Typologies of Emotion in Consumer Behavior," *Journal of Consumer Research*, 13 (December), 394-404.

_____, _____ and Donald R. Lehmann (1989), "Assessing the Validity of Emotional Typologies," *Psychology and Marketing*, 6 (Summer), 97-112.

Holbrook, Morris B. (1986), "Emotion in the Consumption Experience: Toward A New Model of Consumer Behavior," in *The Role of Affect in Consumer Behavior*, eds. Robert A. Peterson, Wayne D. Hoyer, and William R. Wilson, Lexington, MA: Lexington Books, 17-52.

Izard, Carroll E. (1972), *Patterns of Emotions*, New York: Academic Press.

_____, (1977), *Human Emotions*, New York: Plenum Press.

Kahle, Lynn R. (1983), *Attitudes and Social Adaptation: A Person-Situation Interaction Approach*, London: Pergamon.

_____, Sharon E. Beatty, and Pamela Homer (1986), "Alternative Measurement Approaches to Consumer Values: The List of Values (LOV) and Values and Life Style (VALS), *Journal of Consumer Research*, 13 (December), 405-409.

Lewis, Helen B. (1971), *Shame and Guilt in Neurosis*, New York: International Universities Press.

Kennedy, Patricia F., Roger J. Best, and Lynn R. Kahle (1988), "An Alternative Method for Measuring Value-Based Segmentation and Advertisement Positioning," in *Current Issues in Research in Advertising*, Vol. 11, 139-155.

McClelland, D.C., Atkinson, J.W., Clark, R.A. and E.L. Lowell (1953), *The Achievement Motive*, New York: Appleton-Century-Croft.

Mehrabian, Albert and James Russell (1974), *An Approach to Environmental Psychology*, Cambridge, MA: MIT Press.

Mowen, John C. (1988), "Beyond Consumer Decision Making," *Journal of Consumer Marketing*, 5 (Winter), 15-25.

Munson, J. Michael (1984), "Personal Values: Considerations on Their Measurement and Application to Five Areas of Research Inquiry," in *Personal Values and Consumer Psychology*, eds. Robert E. Pitts, Jr. and Arch G. Woodside, Lexington, MA: Lexington Books, 13 33.

_____, and Shelby H. McIntrye (1979), "Developing Practical Procedures for the Measurement of Personal Values in Cross-Cultural Marketing, *Journal of Marketing Research*, 16 (February), 48-52.

Parsons, Talcott and Edward R. Shils (1951), *Toward a General Theory of Action*, Cambridge: Harvard University Press.

Pedhazur, Elazar J. (1982), *Multiple Regression in Behavioral Research*, New York: CBS College Publishing.

Pitts, Robert Jr. and Arch G. Woodside (1984), "Personal Values and Market Segmentation: Applying the Value Construct," in *Personal Values and Consumer Psychology*, eds. Robert E. Pitts, Jr. and Arch G. Woodside, Lexington, MA: Lexington Books, 55-67.

Plutchik, Robert (1980), *Emotion: A Psychoevoluntionary Synthesis*, New York: Harper and Row.

Rokeach, Milton (1973), *The Nature of Human Values*, New York: Free Press.

Rosenberg, Morris (1979), *Conceiving the Self*, New York: Basic Books.

Scheff, Thomas J., (1990) "Socialization of Emotions: Pride and Shame as Causal Agents," in *Research Agendas in the Sociology of Emotions*, ed. T. D. Kemper, Albany, New York: State University of New York Press.

Schrum, L. J., John A. McCarty, and Tamara L. Loeffler (1990), "Individual Differences in Value Stability: Are We Really Tapping True Values?," in *Association for Consumer Research*, Vol. 17, eds. Gerald J. Gorn and Richard W. Pollay, Provo, UT: Association for Consumer Research, 609-615.

Smith-Lovin, Lynn (1990), "Emotion and the Confirmation and Disconfirmation of Identity: An Affect Control Model," in *Research Agendas in the Sociology of Emotions*, ed. Theodore D. Kemper, Albany, New York: State University of New York Press, 238-270.

Tolman, Edward C. (1951), "A Psychological Model," in *Toward A General Theory of Reasoned Action*, eds. Talcott Parsons and Edward A. Shils, Cambridge: Harvard University Press, 148-163.

Westbrook, Robert A. (1987), "Product/Consumption-Based Affective Responses and Postpurchase Processes, *Journal of Marketing Research*, 24 (August), 258-270.

_____ and Richard D. Oliver (1991), The Dimensionality of Consumption Emotion Patterns and Consumer Satisfaction," *Journal of Consumer Research*, 18 (June), 84-91.

Modes of Consumer Acculturation

Sunkyu Jun, University of Nebraska-Lincoln
A. Dwayne Ball, University of Nebraska-Lincoln
James W. Gentry, University of Nebraska-Lincoln

ABSTRACT

The traditional perspective of acculturation is one of assimilation, where the immigrant/sojourner/refugee is expected to adapt to the norms of the host culture. Berry (1990) presents a model that discusses different modes of acculturation, and lists the conditions leading to their existence. We propose two distinct constructs, Cultural Identification (which is attitudinal in nature) and Level of Acculturation (which is behavioral in nature) as determinants of the mode of acculturation. We then develop an exploratory model to explain the two constructs. "Preference for residency" was related significantly to "Cultural Identification" while "Place (urban/rural) where a person was raised in the home culture" and "Amount of direct contact with the host culture" were related to "Level of acculturation." "Cultural identification" and "Level of acculturation" were marginally related to one another, lending some support to the premise that they are distinct constructs.

INTRODUCTION

As immigration is on the rise and as immigrants account for a growing portion of the United States market, understanding the acculturation process will become increasingly important for marketers. Most studies of consumer acculturation have studied African and Hispanic Americans, while relatively less attention has been paid to Asian Americans who constitute the fastest growing minority in the U.S. Andreasen (1990) points out that patterns of immigration are changing in the U.S., as the majority of current immigrants are no longer coming from cultures similar to that already here. For example, in the 1960's immigrants from Western Europe compromised 37% of all immigrants and Asians 13%. In the period of 1981 to 1986, 11% were from Western Europe and 47% from Asia. The purpose of this study is to test an exploratory model of individual acculturation of one Asian group and to suggest implications for marketing.

Traditionally, immigrants' adaptation in the U.S. has been viewed as assimilation to the new culture, but acculturating people may vary in their adaptation processes. It has been contended that acculturating groups enter into the acculturation process in different ways and to different degrees (Berry 1990). Further, every person in the acculturating group does not necessarily participate in the process to the same extent (Berry 1990).

Recent studies of acculturation have recognized that acculturation is a multidimensional concept incorporating cultural identity, language usage, religion, and social activities (Hui et al. 1992; O'Guinn and Faber 1985). Cultural identification has been treated as a sub-dimension representing an individual's subjective perception of belonging to an ethnic group (Deshpande, Hoyer, and Donthu 1986; Hui et al. 1992; O'Guinn and Faber 1985), and it may have implications which are different from those related to the extent of adopting the new culture, which is referred to here as the level of acculturation. Cultural identification may be differentiated from level of acculturation in that one's level of acculturation reflects behavioral changes and cultural identification is rather a subjective attitude towards self identification with the traditional/new culture. Factors affecting one's behavioral changes in the new cultural environment may be different from factors leading to one's attitudinal changes. The process of behavioral acculturation may not coincide with the process of attitudinal acculturation and, thus, one's consumption pattern could be close to the new cultural value while the cultural identification is close to the old culture. We propose that cultural identification and level of acculturation combine to explain the different types of acculturation. Determinants of the varying modes of consumer acculturation are suggested and their relationships with cultural identification and acculturation level are tested using Korean sojourners in the United States.

INDIVIDUAL ACCULTURATION

The classic definition of acculturation in anthropology is as follows: those phenomena which result when groups of individuals having different cultures come into continuous first-hand contact, with subsequent changes taking place in the original cultural patterns of either or both groups (Redfield, Linton, and Herskovits 1936). Under this definition, acculturation is regarded as a process which will ultimately result in changes at the population level. Berry (1990) made a distinction between acculturation at the population level and at the individual level. Under Berry's definition, psychological acculturation refers to the individual changes in psychological characteristics as a result of being in contact with other cultures and participating in the process of acculturation that one's cultural or ethnic group is undergoing. Berry's distinction between the acculturation at the population level and at the individual level is based on the different phenomena at the two levels — that is, the changes in social structure, economic base, and political organization at the population level and the changes in behavior, identity, values, and attitudes at the individual level.

Modes of Individual Acculturation

Our basic premise is that an individual who is adapting to a new culture has his/her unique mode of individual acculturation process. The categorization of the modes of acculturation suggested by Berry (1990) is as follows: (1) assimilation, which occurs when an individual does not wish to maintain what he/she has been (e.g., in terms of identity, language, and way of life) and seeks daily interaction with new culture; (2) separation, which occurs when an individual values holding his/her original culture and at the same time wishes to avoid interaction with new culture; (3) integration, which occurs when there is interest both in maintaining one's original culture and in daily interaction with new culture, and (4) marginalization, which occurs when there is little possibility or interest in cultural maintenance and little interest in the new culture.

The model of acculturation being proposed here is based on the delineation of cultural identification from the level of acculturation, unlike most presentations which have considered cultural identification to be a subdimension of acculturation level (Hui et al. 1992). While the voluntary adoption of the host culture's behavioral patterns may reflect cultural assimilation to some extent, the involuntary adoption of behavioral patterns due to structural mandates and conditions does not reflect cultural assimilation (Reilly and Wallendorf 1984). For example, the unavailability of familiar brands or the availability of vastly superior brands in the new culture may change purchasing patterns without affecting one's

FIGURE 1
Mode of Individual Acculturation

Mode of Individual Acculturation	Perception of Cultural Identification	Extent of Adoption of New Cultural Norms, Values, and Behaviors
Separation	Old Culture Oriented	Old Culture Oriented
Integration	Old Culture Oriented	New Culture Oriented
Antinomy	New Culture Oriented	Old Culture Oriented
Assimilation	New Culture Oriented	New Culture Oriented
Frustration	Not Oriented to Either Culture	Either New Culture or Old Culture Oriented

preference for the traditional culture. Alternatively, there may be social pressures that prevent the immigrant from using certain products or performing certain rituals from the culture of origin.

The norm in acculturation studies is to investigate the adaptation of individuals from collective cultures (for example, from Asia or Latin America) to more individualistic ones such as the U.S. or Canada. Triandis (1992) noted that one difference between collective and individual cultures is that collectivists can tolerate better a discrepancy between attitude and behavior. Thus, for groups such as Koreans, behavioral changes brought about by adopting the new culture do not necessarily reflect a change in one's cultural identity (Joy and Dholakia 1991; Wallendorf and Reilly 1983).

A second difference between the two dimensions (besides one being attitudinal and the other behavioral in nature) lies in their relative susceptibility to situational influence. Consistent with Weinreich, Kelly, and Maya (1989), we propose that one's cultural identity is linked to one's self-concept, which is relatively universal across situations. On the other hand, the level of acculturation describes situated identity in a specific context, as individuals may be at different levels of acculturation for different roles in the course of their daily lives. For example, an individual may behave in accord with the ethnic norms at home with the family, but the person may behave based on the cultural norms of the host society at school (O'Guinn and Faber 1985). The specific domain of interest in this study is that of personal consumption. In summary, the level of acculturation is related to "How do I behave in a situation?" while cultural identification is self definition of "Who am I?"

Our model of individual acculturation modes is shown in Figure 1, and is based on the two dimensions of cultural identification (which is attitudinal in nature) and level of acculturation (which is behavioral in nature). Under the suggested categorization, assimilation occurs when an individual is oriented to find his/her cultural identification with the new culture and has adopted more the new cultural norms, values, and behaviors while keeping less the traditional ones. Separation occurs when an individual is oriented to find his/her cultural identification with the traditional culture and maintains more the traditional cultural norms, values, and behaviors while adopting less the new ones. Integration occurs when an individual finds his/her cultural identification with the traditional culture but has adopted more the new cultural norms, values, and behaviors while keeping less the traditional ones. Antinomy occurs when an individual is oriented to find his/her cultural identification with the new culture but keeps more the traditional cultural norms, values, and behaviors. Antinomy is recognized as a premature state which can occur when an individual has not absorbed the new norms, values, and behaviors while trying to find his/her identification from the new culture. Finally, frustration occurs when an individual has lost his/her cultural identification with both of the traditional culture and the new culture.

Frustration is an unstable state which can be seen when an individual loses his/her cultural identification by self-denial and/or from exclusion from the cultural group.

Acculturation is usually assumed to be a linear-process heading toward one of the polar opposites of ethnicity or assimilation. However, the acculturation process is not necessarily a linear process toward one side but rather a non-linear trend over time (Knight et al. 1978), and an individual may be perceived as being more or less acculturated along a continuum from separation through assimilation. Thus, an acculturating person who falls in one of the modes of individual acculturation may move towards another mode over time. Further, it has been contended that an acculturating person goes through the honeymoon stage, rejection stage, tolerance stage, and the integration stage and that, as a result, the acculturation process curve resembles an inverted U shape over time (Penaloza 1989). However, the acculturation process curve is not necessarily expected to be a single curve which has one peak during one's adaptation to the new culture. An individual may experience the honeymoon stage and the rejection stage more than once, and those two stages alternate with one another until the person is ultimately melted into the host culture. Thus, the cyclical nature of the acculturation process may be repeated while one moves toward a stable stage. Moreover, the distance between the peak and the trough of the cycle may get shorter and shorter as the acculturation curve gets close to the equilibrium point.

DETERMINANTS OF THE INDIVIDUAL ACCULTURATION MODE

Determinants which influence the consumer acculturation process can be recognized at the population level and at the individual level. At the population level, the culture of the original country has an impact on the individual acculturation process such that those who come from a culture similar to the new culture tend to be more assimilation oriented, while those who have different traditional cultural backgrounds are likely to be less assimilated (Ellis et al. 1985). The individual acculturation process is also influenced by characteristics of the new society such as a high population density, settlement size, a set of social controls, and acculturation pressure (Berry 1990). Ethnic groups, native peoples, immigrants, sojourners, and refugees have different characteristics in terms of the voluntariness, movement, and permanence of residency, and members of the different groups may have different acculturation modes. Those who are voluntarily involved in the acculturation process (e.g., immigrants, sojourners, and ethnic groups) may experience less difficulty than those with little choice in the matter (e.g., refugees and native peoples). On the other hand, those only temporarily in contact and who are without permanent social supports (e.g., sojourners) may experience more difficulty than those who are more permanently settled and established (e.g., ethnic groups) (Berry 1990). The ecological setting of the community where an individual resides also influences the individual acculturation process at the population level (Knight et al. 1978). It is expected that Korean sojourners have moved into the new culture voluntarily, in that most come to the U.S. for the purpose of study, in order to provide greater economic opportunity for their families. Some Korean sojourners differ in their intent to return to Korea, though most intend to do so at some point.

At the individual level, demographic variables such as age, sex, religion, resident status, generational status, and education are associated with the individual acculturation process (Sodowsky and Plake in press; Sodowsky, Lai, and Plake 1991). Language preference and the ability to communicate through the language of the host culture have also been proposed as factors related to the individual acculturation process (Penaloza 1989). Socio-demographic factors combined with communication ability may decide how intensively a person contacts the host society. Those who spend most of the time outside the home in the host society may be directly exposed to the host culture much more than those who stay at home most of the time and, in turn, may have to rely on rather indirect experiences with the host culture. While most of the determinants are used to predict the extent to which a person can adopt the new culture, resistance to accept the new culture and willingness to maintain the home culture may be explained in part by how intensively the person was exposed to the home culture before moving into the new society. For instance, a person who was raised in rural areas of the home country may have had little chance to be exposed to foreign cultures; they may have been more dominated by the traditional culture than the person raised in an urban area. In the present paper, it will be proposed that the mode of consumer acculturation of Korean sojourners is associated with whether a person prefers to go back to Korea or not, whether the person was raised in rural areas or urban areas, and whether the person has much direct or indirect contact with the new culture.

Preference for Residency. Black and Gregersen (1991) contend that individuals start making adjustments when they first anticipate entering a new culture. Their possible anticipation of being permanent residents in a host country may also influence their adaptation to the new culture. Acculturating people may have different preferences for residency depending upon whether they have the option to live in the new culture permanently or temporarily. It is expected that the mode of individual acculturation is associated with the preference for residency. Those who prefer to go back to their home culture may keep their cultural identification more strongly than those who prefer to stay in the new culture permanently.

H1: Korean sojourners who prefer temporary residency will identify more with the Korean culture.

Rural/Urban Areas. Acculturating people within an ethnic group may have contacted the traditional culture for different periods of time, depending in part upon their ages at the time when they left the original culture. Those who left the traditional culture before much cognitive development took place may have very little significant experience with the traditional culture since pre-adolescent children are assumed not to be able to process information and deal with purchase tasks in a relatively adult manner (John and Cole 1986). The place where an individual was raised, however, may affect the intensity of contact with the traditional culture and, in turn, influence their acculturation modes. For example, tradition may be more valued and respected in rural areas than in urban areas where people have more chance to be exposed to artifacts from the imported new culture, thus diluting the influence of tradition.

It is expected that those who have had more contact with the traditional culture and those who grew up in rural areas in their home country tend to adopt less the norms, values, and behaviors of the new culture while keeping more the traditional ones.

H2: Korean sojourners who were raised in rural areas are more resistant to accept the new cultural norms, values, and behaviors than those who were raised in urban areas.

Direct/Indirect Contact with the New Culture. Acculturating people may face different social settings even though they have lived in the new culture for the same period of time because of different work demands. Some members of an ethnic group may stay at home all day without much direct contact with the new culture while others may go to work or to school where they behave in a manner acceptable to the new culture. Thus, a person may be asked to adopt the new culture if he/she works outside the home in the host culture, while a person who spends most of the time at home may find relatively little need to adopt the new culture. Lee (1989) suggests that the acculturation processes based on direct contact with the host culture are quite different from those with only indirect contact. More specifically, she speculates that the latter case would involve learning of the host culture symbolically through the mass media. Given that the reality portrayed in the mass media is not an accurate one, attempts to adopt the host culture's behavioral patterns may differ for those whose perceptions of the host culture are cultivated from mass media. Most of Korean male sojourners are studying and working in the U.S. while many female Koreans sojourners who stay with their spouses are not working outside the home, in part, due to legal restrictions.

H3: Direct contact with the new culture has a positive relationship with the extent to which the Korean sojourner adopts the new norms, values, and behaviors.

METHOD

Sample. The sample (n=53) was drawn from Korean students and their spouses at a major midwestern university. An attempt to contact all Korean students at the university was made, and approximately 50% of them responded. The sample included 26 males and 27 females. All male respondents were students, except one who worked full time; two females were students and the remainder were housewives. All of the students were graduate students and the average age of the sample was 31.3. On average, they have been in the United States for 3.8 years.

Measurement. The data were collected through a survey questionnaire which was written in English, translated into Korean, and then backtranslated. "Preference for Residency" was measured by using a seven-point Likert-type question (1=Strongly Disagree and 7=Strongly Agree), dealing with the preference of returning to Korea after the completion of studies in this country. "Rural/Urban Areas" was measured by asking the place (urban/rural) where the respondent had grown up during adolescence. "Direct/Indirect Contact with the New Culture" was measured based on whether the subject was a student, had a full time job, or was a housewife. The spouse not attending school, always the wife in the case of our data, lacks the opportunity to have much direct contact with the American culture. She is not allowed to work in the U.S. and, thus, spends much time at home. Students and those who have full-time jobs should have much direct contact with the American culture. Thus, in our sample, all male respondents had direct contact with the new culture while most of the female respondents had only indirect contact except for those attending school.

TABLE 1
Scale Items

CULTURAL IDENTIFICATION
1. I would like to be recognized as a Korean rather than an American in public.
2. I would like to have an Americanized version of my first name. (-)
3. I am proud of my Korean cultural heritage.
4. I would like to become a U.S. citizen in the future. (-)

ACCULTURATION LEVEL
1. I enjoy watching American TV programs.
2. I speak English with my Korean friends when we are together with American friends.
3. I like reading an American daily newspaper.

The responses were given on a seven-point Likert scale ranging from Strongly Disagree (1) to Strongly Agree (7).

We initially used ten items to measure "Cultural Identification" and six items to measure "Acculturation Level", and purified them by the iterative process of calculating alpha, and eliminating items with low item-to-total correlations to get the final items as measures of each construct (Churchill 1979). "Cultural Identification" was measured based on the respondent's perception on one's belonging to each culture and was scored to indicate the degree of one's cultural identification with the Korean culture, using the four items listed in Table 1. The Cronbach alpha for the four items was .55.

We used language usage and media preference as the domain for measuring "Acculturation Level." One's level of acculturation measured in terms of any one domain of social lives may not represent the person's general level of acculturation, which is believed to be multidimensional and situation specific. However, it has been found that communication in the host language is positively related to adoption of the new culture, indicating that language usage and media preference may be underlie the other domains of acculturation (O'Guinn and Faber 1985; Shah 1991). "Acculturation Level" was measured using the three items listed in Table 1. The items were scored to indicate the degree to which the respondent has adopted the American culture in terms of language usage and media usage. The Cronbach alpha for the three items was .73.

RESULTS

The model was tested using LISREL (despite the sample size limitations noted below), as well as more traditional methods of analysis. The LISREL analysis was conducted because of its ability to investigate the model being proposed here in a more comprehensive fashion. The convergence of the results from the regression analyses with those found in the LISREL analysis increase our confidence in the findings. However, we must acknowledge that this study is only an exploratory first test of the model being proposed.

The LISREL structural model in Figure 2 was developed based on previous research on acculturation, as cited in the literature review, and the hypotheses to be tested. LISREL allows for a test of each hypothesis through examination of the specific parameter estimates as well as a test of the fitness of the model suggested in the present study (Joreskog and Sorbom 1989).

The raw data were analyzed through PRELIS because the small sample size requires special care prior to using LISREL. The Weighted Least Squares method was employed because all of the scales were ordinal scales. Polychoric correlations among observed variables, which are appropriate with the Least Squares Method (Joreskog and Sorbom 1989), were used in the LISREL analysis (see Table 2).

The measures of overall fit indicate that the present model fits the data with Goodness-of-Fit index=.956 and χ^2=19.06 (d.f.=31 and p= .954). The observed variables jointly served well as measures for the two latent endogenous variables ("Cultural Identification" and "Acculturation Level"), as the Total Coefficient of Determination was .94.

"Preference for Residency" and "Cultural Identification" had a strong positive relationship (γ_{11}=.763, p< .05). Those who intend to go back to Korea after they complete study in the United States identified with the Korean culture much more than did those who intend to stay in the U.S., thus supporting the first hypothesis.

There was a marginally significant negative relationship between "Rural/Urban areas" and "Acculturation Level" (γ_{22}=-.305, p<.10), indicating that those who had been grown up in rural areas showed less adoption of the American culture in terms of language usage and media preference than those who had been grown up in urban areas. The marginal significance may result from the fact that respondents growing up in rural areas are also exposed to the American culture to some extent, as all but one of the respondents had graduated from college in Korea and they came from middle or upper-middle class backgrounds.

There was a strong positive relationship between "Direct/Indirect Contact with the New Culture" and "Acculturation Level" (γ_{23}=.755 p<.005), which supports the third hypothesis. Those who go to school or have a full-time job adopted the American culture more in terms of language usage and media preference than did the housewives staying at home.

"Cultural Identification" did not have a causal relationship with "Level of Acculturation" (β_{21}=-.103), but "Acculturation Level" had a marginally significant causal relationship with "Cultural Identification" with the Korean culture (β_{12}=-.289, p<.10). This result indicates that cultural identification is influenced by level of acculturation, but that they are independent constructs for the most part, supporting Hui et al.'s (1992) finding that identification and social behavior are separate but interdependent dimensions of acculturation. The result is consistent with past work that found that usage of mass communication in the host culture is related to a positive attitude toward the host society (Kim 1978).

Even though we have a high goodness-of-fit index, the small sample size is a problem when using LISREL. We employed two

FIGURE 2
Structural Model of Cultural Identification and Level of Acculturation

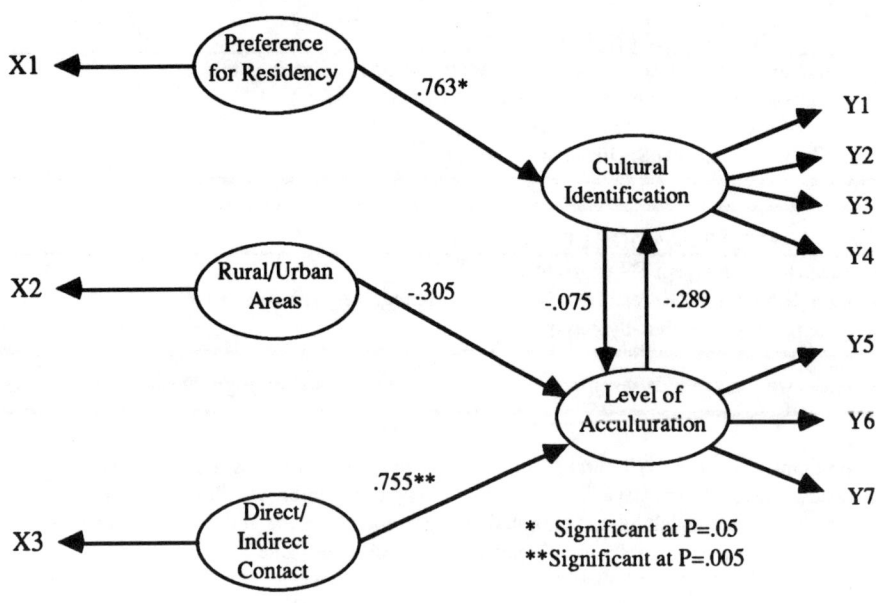

* Significant at P=.05
**Significant at P=.005

TABLE 2
Correlations Among Observed Variables

	Y1	Y2	Y3	Y4	Y5	Y6	Y7	X1	X2	X3
Y1	1.000									
Y2	0.305	1.000								
Y3	0.333	0.216	1.000							
Y4	0.266	0.535	0.101	1.000						
Y5	-0.273	-0.045	-0.191	-0.214	1.000					
Y6	-0.169	0.010	-0.041	-0.035	0.469	1.000				
Y7	-0.196	-0.083	-0.183	-0.136	0.516	0.609	1.000			
X1	0.188	0.230	0.424	0.601	0.095	0.104	0.115	1.000		
X2	0.222	0.415	0.040	0.366	-0.005	-0.388	-0.298	0.380	1.000	
X3	-0.129	0.240	0.249	0.047	0.425	0.644	0.557	0.167	0.046	1.000

Y1, Y2, Y3, and Y4: Indicators of "Cultural Identification"
Y5, Y6, and Y7: Indicators of "Level of Acculturation"
X1: Indicator of "Preference for Residency"
X2: Indicator of "Amount of Contact with the Traditional Culture"
X3: Indicator of "Amount of Contact with the New Culture"

methods to check the validity of the results. First, we proposed and tested a competing LISREL model which assumed that "Cultural Identification" and "Acculturation Level" are the same construct such that both constructs are measured by the same set of observed variables (Y1 through Y7). The solution to the model was not convergent, which indicates the possibility that the competing model is misspecified (Joreskog and Sorbom 1989). Second, we conducted multiple regression analysis to test the relationships suggested by our model. The regression result (Table 3) was convergent with the result of the LISREL model. There was a strong relationship between "Preference for Residency" and "Cultural Identification", and between "Direct/Indirect Contact with the New Culture" and "Acculturation Level". Here was a marginal relationship between "Rural/Urban Areas" and "Acculturation Level", and between "Acculturation Level" and "Cultural Identification". In addition to the relationships suggested in the LISREL model, we tested the possible relationships which were not implied by the model. "Cultural Identification" did not have a significant relationship with "Rural/Urban Areas" and "Direct/Indirect Contact with the New Culture" after removing the effect of "Preference for Residency" on "Cultural Identification". After removing the effects of "Rural/Urban Areas" and "Direct/Indirect Contact with the New Culture" on "Acculturation Level", there was not a significant relationship between "Acculturation Level" and "Preference for Residency".

One additional analysis was to relate "Cultural Identification" to the Triandis et al. (1986) measure of Individualism/Collectivism as an exploratory test of the construct's predictive validity. Indi-

TABLE 3
F-Values from Standard Multiple Regression

Variables	Cultural Identification	Acculturation Level
Preference for Residency	6.26 p<.05	N.S (a)
Rural/Urban Areas	N.S (b)	3.25 p<.10
Direct/Indirect Contact	N.S (b)	12.68 p<.001
Cultural Identification	—	3.94 p<.10

(a) Estimated after removing the effect of "Rural/Urban Areas" and "Direct/Indirect Contact" on "Acculturation Level".
(b) Estimated after removing the effect of "Preference for Residency" on "Cultural Identification".

vidualism/Collectivism is an underlying cultural dimension (Triandis 1992), which finds the U.S. at one extreme (individualistic) and Korea near the other extreme (collectivistic). As one's cultural identity moves from culture of origin (Korea) to the culture of residence (U.S.), one would be expected to become more individualistic. The correlation of "Cultural Identification" with Individualism/Collectivism was .33 (p<.05).

DISCUSSION AND IMPLICATIONS

Our study provides evidence to support the proposition that acculturation level can be distinguished from cultural identification and that both of the constructs are influenced by different factors. The validity of the variables is limited by the use of single-indicator measures for the independent variables, and by the low alpha for "Cultural Identification," which emphasizes the need to develop further measures of cultural identification. The sample of Korean students and their families from one university used in this study restricts the ability to generalize the results. Finally, the small sample size limits the power of the chi-square test used by LISREL to test the null hypothesis of model fit. While we are reasonably confident in our model because of the high goodness-of-fit measures, the better fit than that of a competing model, and the convergent results from regression analyses, it is possible that other models used with a larger data set might reveal a different structure.

In spite of the limitations mentioned above, the results support the distinction of cultural identification from acculturation level and provide insight into understanding the different modes of individual acculturation. Cultural identification is influenced by the preference for permanent residency or temporary residency while acculturation level is affected by the place (urban/rural) where a person was raised in the home culture and the amount of direct contact with the new culture. Those who want to remain in the host society tend to identify themselves with the new culture while those who want to go back to their home country keep their cultural identification with the traditional culture. Acculturating people from rural areas are more hesitant to abandon the traditional culture. Acculturating people who have more direct contact with the new culture adopt the new culture to a greater extent.

Promotional activities may benefit from the delineation of behavioral acculturation from attitudinal acculturation in that the consumption pattern of acculturating people is more determined by one's behavioral changes than one's cultural identification. If the target audience of a promotional communication has less direct contact with the new culture and, thus, is less acculturated in behavioral terms, the promotion should use ethnic media using the native language. If the target audience is those who prefer a permanent residency and have their cultural identifications toward the new culture, the symbolic cultural meaning of the product could be stressed to appeal to the target audience. The different mode of acculturation can be used as a segmenting dimension for an ethnic market in the sense that the importance evaluation of the attributes of a product may vary depending on one's acculturation mode. Consumers who maintain cultural identification with the traditional culture may seek products with inherent symbolic ethnic meanings, while consumers who want to identify with the new culture may show a conspicuous consumption pattern to help them to be recognized as members of the host society. Consumers who maintain cultural identification with the traditional culture may be strongly attached to possessions which provide cultural meaning, and consumers who have not adopted the new culture to much extent may show a traditionally ethnic consumption pattern. Marketers may reach those having troubles with adopting the new culture by providing the product information through their original language and ethnic media.

This paper is an exploratory attempt to delineate the determinants of the various modes of acculturation. Marketing efforts based on the assumption that assimilation is the only mode of acculturation may well alienate large segments of the acculturating groups. Greater sensitivity may result in such marketing efforts as providing different appeals (in content as well as in language) in the English and in the native language versions of print media aimed at a particular ethnic group. Those reading the English version may seek portrayals of brands as being "traditionally American" or "what every American family uses." On the other hand, appeals in the native language version of the medium should try to position the American brand as fitting well with the original culture.

REFERENCES

Andreasen, Alan R. (1990), "Cultural Interpenetration: A Critical Consumer Research Issue for the 1990s," *Advances in Consumer Research*, 17, 847-849.

Berry, John W. (1990), "Psychology of Acculturation," in *Cross-Cultural Perspectives*, Proceedings of the Nebraska Symposium on Motivation, 1989, John J. Berman (Ed.), 201-234.

Black, J. Stewart and Hal B. Gregersen (1991), "The Other Half of the Picture: Antecedents of Spouse Cross-Cultural Adjustment," *Journal of International Business Studies*, 22(3), 461-477.

Churchill, Jr., Gilbert A. (1979), "A Paradigm for Developing Better Measures of Marketing Constructs," *Journal of Marketing Research*, 16, 64-73.

Deshpande, Rohit, Wayne D. Hoyer, and Naveen Donthu (1986), "The Intensity of Ethnic Affiliation: A Study of the Sociology of Hispanic Consumption," *Journal of Consumer Research*, 13, 214-220.

Ellis, Seth, James McCullough, Melanie Wallendorf, and Chin Tion Tan (1985), "Cultural Values and Behavior: Chineseness Within Geographic Boundaries," *Advances in Consumer Research*, 12, 126-128.

Hui, Michael K., Annamma Joy, Chankon Kim, and Michel Laroche (1992), "Acculturation as Determinants of Consumer Behavior: Conceptual and Methodological Issues," *Proceedings*, AMA Winter Educator's Conference, San Antonio.

John, Deborah Roedder and Catherine A. Cole (1986), "Age Differences in Information Processing: Understanding Deficits in Young and Elderly Consumers," *Journal of Consumer Research*, 13, 297-315.

Joreskog, Karl G. and Dag Sorbom (1989), *LISREL7 A Guide to the Program and Applications*, Chicago: SPSS Inc.

Joy, Annamma and Ruby Roy Dholakia (1991), "Remembrances of Things Past: The Meaning of Home and Possessions of Indian Professionals in Canada," *Journal of Social Behavior and Personality*, 6(6), 385-402.

Kim, Young Y. (1978), "A Communication Approach to the Acculturation Process: A Study of Korean Immigrants in Chicago," *International Journal of Intercultural Relations*, 2,197-224.

Knight, George P, Spencer Kagan, William Nelson, and Jann Gumbiner (1978), "Acculturation of Second- and Third-Generation Mexican American Children: Field Independence, Locus of Control, Self-Esteem, and School Achievement," *Journal of Cross-Cultural Psychology*, 9(1), 87-97.

Lee, Wei-Na (1989), "The Mass-Mediated Consumption Realities of Three Cultural Groups," *Advances in Consumer Research*, 16, 771-778.

O'Guinn, Thomas and Ronald J. Faber (1985), "New Perspectives on Acculturation: The Relationship of General and Role Specific Acculturation with Hispanics' Consumer Attitudes," *Advances in Consumer Research*, 12, 113-117.

Penaloza, Lisa N. (1989), "Immigrant Consumer Acculturation," *Advances in Consumer Research*, 16, 110-118.

Redfield, R., R. Linton, and M. J. Herskovits (1936), "Memorandum on The Study of Acculturation," *American Anthropologist*, 38, 149-152.

Reilly, Michael D. and Melanie Wallendorf (1984), "A Longitudinal Study of Mexican-American Assimilation," *Advances in Consumer Behavior*, 11, 735-740.

Shah, Hemant (1991), "Communication and Cross-Cultural Adaptation Patterns Among Asian Indians," *International Journal of Intercultural Relations*, 15, 311-321.

Sodowsky, Gargi Roysircar and Barbara S. Plake (In Press), "Acculturation Options for International People and Implications for Sensitivity to Within Group Differences," *Journal of Counseling and Development*.

_____, Edward Wai Ming Lai, and Barbara S. Plake (1991), "Moderating Effects of Sociocultural Variables on Acculturation Attitudes of Hispanics and Asian Americans," *Journal of Counseling and Development*, 70, 194-204.

Triandis C. Harry (1992), "Individualism and Collectivism as Cultural Syndromes," *Presentation*, 21st Annual Meeting of Society for Cross-Cultural Research, Santa Fe.

_____, R. Bontempo, H. Betancourt, M. Bond, K. Leung, A. Brenes, J. Georgas, C. H. Hui, G. Marin, B. Setiadi, J. B. P. Sinha, J. Verma, J. Spangenberg, H. Touzard, and G. Montmollin (1986), "The Measurement of the Etic Aspect of Individualism and Collectivism across Cultures," *Australian Journal of Psychology*, 38(3), 257-269.

Wallendorf, Melanie and Michael D. Reilly (1983), "Ethnic Migration, Assimilation, and Consumption," *Journal of Consumer Research*, 10, 292-302.

Weinreich, Peter, Aidan Kelly, and Candlish Maya (1987), "Situated Identities, Conflicts in Identification and Own Group Preference: Rural and Urban Youth in South Africa", in *Growth and Progress in Cross-Cultural Psychology*, ed. Cigdem Kagitcibase, Swets & Zeitlinger B.V., Lisse.

Telling Stories: A Sociolinguistic Analysis of Language Use in a Marketplace
Elisabeth Gilster, University of Arizona

While consumer behavior researchers have illustrated the fact that certain products and consumption contexts offer consumers some sort of intangible yet very special meaning, little work has focused on the discursive interaction between sellers and consumers which serves to convey the "specialness" or the sacred qualities of the products. An analysis of the language used in a sales setting allows us to examine how the value of products and images of their producers are enhanced through the telling of stories. Sociolinguistic analysis yields findings that call for future research employing a critical theory research approach.

INTRODUCTION

Stories that are told in the sales context are elaborated by the sellers in response to their perceptions of consumer wants and needs. These stories serve to enhance the value of the products they accompany. Hence, this is an excellent example of the marketing concept. Despite long recognition as the central philosophy of business, there has been, little attention to the theoretical development of this concept (Kohli and Jaworski 1990). Other authors have pointed out that a strong marketing orientation has led to business practices that are unwise (Houston 1986) or have adverse effects on society (Murray and Ozanne 1991). This paper provides an analysis that encourages us to re-evaluate the implications of this concept.

The sociolinguistic approach used here was never intended to call for social change. Nonetheless, it does illuminate what some may consider a "dark side" of the marketing concept. Consequently, future research in this area may well benefit from the critical theory approach to research (Murray and Ozanne 1991) which extols a balance between the objective and the interpretive paradigms and a goal of effecting change.

The majority of the consumer behavior literature on language use in advertising and promotion has been restricted to the primary or formal economic sector (Sherry 1988). Much work utilizing an analysis of language and semiotics to explore consumption issues has focused on "finished" products. On the other hand, Sherry's (1988) work on market pitching, along with that of Pinch and Clark (1986), contributes to our knowledge of the dramaturgical aspects of the sellers' behavior and how consumer perceptions of value are enhanced by the discursive interaction which takes place in some market settings.

Notions of the processes of sacralization have been carefully articulated by Belk et. al. (1989). These processes occur within the context of the consumption experience with little concern for the actual purchase experience. Minimal attention has been given to the language and other persuasive techniques sellers use to convince consumers that the products they are selling will fulfill consumers' "special" and sometimes spiritual needs. Through an analysis of language use in a marketplace, this paper explores this form of persuasion in the context of the sales of specialty items which are perceived by consumers to fulfill such needs.

This research presents data collected at North American Indian arts and crafts sales settings where the interaction between sellers (who are often producers as well) and consumers is marked by the cultural differences between the producers and the consumers. The consumers are attracted to aspects of what they perceive to be the traditional culture of the producers. As the analysis shows, the language and the stories that are used in the sales context reflect the cultural stereotypes and capitalize on this attraction. The stories link the products with the Indian producers and, in doing so, enhance the value of the products.

BACKGROUND

The commercialization of Indian arts and crafts has created a multi-billion dollar industry which has improved the lives of many producers, especially those in the Southwestern U.S. This phenomenon also perpetuates many of the stereotypes of the American Indian. The data offered here illustrate how the success of this market depends on the strength of the association between the art object and the "Indianness" of its maker.

The art objects are embellished with stories and narrative descriptions which convey the sense that the objects are special, imbued with sacred characteristics, and/or traditionally made by authentic Indians. These stories are shared by producers, traders, retailers and consumers and serve to make the arts and crafts more marketable to prospective buyers. The production of the identity, that is the co-construction of the stereotypes, has been achieved through negotiation between the producers of arts and crafts and the consumers via the telling of these stories.

This construction of what it is to be "Indian" is closely interrelated with what sells to middle and upper middle class Anglo consumers. Hence, this definition is managed so that consumers are gratified, enchanted, mystified and intrigued. Many of the realities of the Native American historical experience are absent from this scenario. The presentation of self is carefully customized to appeal to the consumers. The success of Indian artists depends on their ability to present themselves in ways that are attractive to the consumers they depend on. This acceptance, then, is actualized in the consumption of their artistic output.

The identities of these American Indian individuals are defined within the acceptable standards of consumers and then articulated through stories that are told by the artists, embedded in the products they produce, reiterated by traders and retailers, and embraced and retold by the consumers who purchase the arts and crafts. Only the more financially successful artists, who represent the top five percent of producers (Parezo 1992), seem to be concerned with challenging the entrenched stereotypes. These attempts are embraced by an equally small proportion of consumers. The images that are most often rewarded are those that link the Indians and their products with spiritual power, quaint tradition, and, to a lesser extent, an affinity with nature.

METHODOLOGY

The extensive speech data presented here were collected at twenty different sales settings where Indian artists, traders and retailers sell arts and crafts. These settings include regional shows, retail shops, a large scale Swap Meet and a major juried outdoor market in the Southwest. Brochures, newspaper articles and magazines were combed for additional examples of the language used to promote these products. Such publications are intended for audiences of prospective buyers of these objects. I attended the above events in the role of participant observer, shopping, browsing, and even assisting sellers. Some natural exchanges between artist/seller and consumer were recorded; however, this was difficult because many artists and/or sellers were not comfortable with the obvious presence of a tape recorder at their selling location. Consequently, the excerpts cited below are from informal interviews conducted on location during lulls in sales activity, more formal interviews conducted after closing and the above cited print material.

In the analysis I will first consider the production of the identity of the producers, then discuss how this identity is maintained. These processes of identity production and preservation are accomplished through the interaction in the sales setting. Within these discussions, language data will be examined for linguistic components (those that are in italics) which reveal specific meanings. Finally, a brief summary of what is being done by some artists to counter the stereotypes that the stories support will be presented.

PRODUCTION OF IDENTITY

The construction of the producers' socially acceptable identities is accomplished through their interaction with the prospective buyers of their arts and crafts in a manner reminiscent of Shutz' (1967) idea of the intersubjective construction of one's identity. The "life world" of the Indian artists is constructed through the intersubjective experience they share with the Anglo consumers. Stereotypes were formed early in the history of the industry and have evolved over time. Edgar Lee Hewitt, the founder of the first Indian Market in Santa Fe in 1922, was an anthropologist and philanthropist dedicated to the preservation of the Native American culture. In a publication distributed during the 1991 Indian Market, he was quoted as calling the Indians "the most priceless possession of America" (Tarchinski 1991:17). While this is an example of Anglo sentiment in 1922 when the Indian people were seriously objectified, the quote appears in a very recent publication circulated to promote Indian products.

More recently, a Pueblo potter conveyed his impression that the stereotypes are still with us. He stated, "...people still think of Indians wearing war bonnets and feathers." (Tarchinski 1991:38) While there may be Indians from a few tribes who dress in this manner for special ceremonial occasions, it is not the everyday attire for all Indians as the stereotype suggests. Although a handful of artists are challenging these stereotypes (as will be discussed later), it is much more common for artists to either consciously or unconsciously manipulate and utilize them in the service of economic ends. The management of these stereotypes entails reshaping them to render them inoffensive to producers and consumers alike. This is partially accomplished through the incorporation of the stereotypic images into the stories that are told about the artists and their products.

According to Goffman (1963), management of the presentation of self serves many purposes, especially for members of a stigmatized group. It has recently been reiterated that there is a very lucrative market for artwork and crafts produced by "primitive societies" (Torgovnick 1990). The survival of the Indians who are stigmatized by Goffman's definition in the multi-cultural world in which they live is contingent upon their ability to manage their identities as a component of managing their livelihoods. Aware of the trend of the commercialization of the output of "primitive societies", they are cleverly taking advantage of it to enhance the marketability of their products.

Life history stories related by producers and intermediaries in the sales context provide opportunities for the management of identities. These stories offer the prospective buyers a seemingly intimate view of the artist's life. Such stories tend to elaborate on the unique "Indianness" and spirituality of the artist. These details which convey the uniqueness and sacredness of the objects are related metonymically (Lakoff and Johnson 1980) to the artists themselves. To increase the reach of the message, artists often have brochures available to customers visiting their booths.

One artist offered an extensive brochure based on an article by Mary Carroll Nelson (n.d.) in *Southwest Profile,* a regional art publication. Here the reader is given the impression that the artist is extraordinary in an almost supernatural way.

Perfectita (Baca) and Seriaco Toya had been childless for all the long years of their marriage when, in her 40s, she gave birth to their "*miracle baby*" Mary (her Tewa name is *Kal-La-Tee, meaning New Indian Basket*) on July 12, 1945 at Jemez Pueblo. The Toyas were faithful Catholics, but they raised Mary, who is a member of the *Sun Clan, to honor and practice her Indian religion,* as well as Christianity.

The label "miracle baby" implies that this artist has from birth been an extraordinary person. The inclusion of her Tewa name and its meaning also gives the reader a sense of the artist's identity. Finally, the identification of her clan and the statement that she participated in her native religion tells us that she is a full fledged Indian, not only physically but also spiritually. This is not to imply that these are false statements about this artist, but that they are emphasized to convey these specific images in relation to the products.

In addition to the identities of artists, the attributes of products are also managed through the stories that accompany them. Stories that are told include narratives about the production process, descriptions of a particular piece, and ones that promise that possession and use of a particular object will provide a blessing and/ or good luck to the consumer. The stories have common certain key images that are associated with their producers, including the spiritual, powerful, natural, and supernatural. The sellers attempt to persuade the customer that if the object is purchased, its magic, an intrinsic part of its "Indianness", will be passed on. This contagious magic is related metanymically to the producer, and is transferred to the consumer.

In the brochure provided by potter Mary Small, salient details of the production of her work were included. The following excerpt lists the sacred attributes a piece produced by this artist possesses and the benefits it will provide for the purchaser. (Nelson n.d.)

When they are finished, they are *blessed*. They have *power*. Whoever buys the pottery should have a nice home, a happy life and a sacred object, because there are a lot of prayers in my *potteries*. The *designs mean something to me*. They mean good weather, pretty raindrops. . .

Clearly, the words "blessed" and "power" signify the sacredness of the pots. The nice home and happy life are among the benefits the pot offers and perhaps also deserves. Additionally, the artist is quoted using the word "potteries". It is common in Indian-English dialects for speakers to use the plural "s" ending for words which are mass nouns (House 1986). The inclusion of this linguistic pattern gives the reader a greater sense of the authenticity of the artist and perhaps a renewed sense of intellectual superiority over the non-native English speaking Native American groups. Finally, the statement that the "designs mean something to me" assures consumers that the designs are symbols which are special and authentic to the people who produce them.

Consumers take delight in sharing stories about the products they have purchased.

it was a *heavenly stone* and as a stone it *would bring good luck* always. So, the thing to do is wear your Indian jewelry. *I'm not superstitious* but I've always worn it and I think I've always *hit the duck*!

Here, the power of the jewelry is conveyed through the words "heavenly stone" and the statement that the stone "would bring good luck." This consumer claimed to have found good fortune from wearing the jewelry through the use of the expression "hit the duck." Additionally, she attempted to give herself more credibility by inserting the phrase "I'm not superstitious". This notion that good fortune accompanies the consumption of a product is supported in relation to another type of art by another consumer who also attends to her credibility by a disclaimer about her decor.

> the only reason I bought the sand painting is because I need something *to bless my house*. And *my decor in my home is not southwestern or Indian or anything*, so I bought the sandpainting for the blessing.

MANAGEMENT OF IDENTITY

Individuals and groups are aware that it serves them well to present themselves in a socially acceptable way (Goffman 1963) and they find creative ways to do so. Bauman (1986) emphasizes that storytelling gives individuals a way to encode and present themselves to construct an image for themselves. Bauman illustrates that notions of truth and reality are negotiated through stories. American Indian artists are involved in similar processes. One of the most prominent techniques used in the co-construction and management of identity is the telling of stories.

The title of this paper, "Telling Stories", intentionally carries a double meaning. Storytelling is the most natural language form that emerges in the sales setting. Indians conserve their history and culture via the oral tradition of storytelling. Children from within the mainstream North American culture learn about Indians through stories. Hence, a romanticized vision of Indian life is closely connected to the telling of stories. The other meaning of the expression "Telling Stories" is that they are just "stories" which may or may not very closely resemble "the real truth." I propose that Indian artists and sellers, as well as Anglo traders and consumers, are involved in the telling of stories about the objects they are dealing. While some of these stories do have a basis in reality, many are fabricated to maintain the connection between the product and the stereotypical image of the producer in order to enhance the value of the arts and crafts.

Just as stories are central to the transaction for artists, sellers and traders, they are important to the consumer as well. The artist/seller below explains how he feels consumers value and use the stories they hear.

> Because people, when they collect your art you know they're more interested in the artists. You know, not only the art but the artists. And when you have your piece, they want a story with it. So when they have *the background* of the artist, *they know them and they know what he's all about, they appreciate his artwork*. They have the story and when they show the collection to their friends when they visit their homes and gardens, they can just *rattle* on. (laughter)

This artist believes that consumers prefer to have a certain amount of background information on the artist. This increased knowledge gives them additional prestige when they are entertaining friends and showing off their art. The use of the word "rattle" suggests that the artist feels that what the consumers say when they are telling their stories is lengthy and not terribly profound. Nonetheless, the stories serve to preserve the constructed identity of the Indian artist.

Anglo retailers and traders capitalize on the fact that consumers enjoy learning about the Indian through the stories that accompany the arts and crafts. The following excerpts reflect the strategies such sellers use to make the most of the stories that are connected to the products. When asked about a particular piece, one retailer gave the following explanation:

> ...that is a dream catcher. Are you familiar with the *little story on it*? The small ones they used to put over the Indian baby's bed and the *Indian baby would have good dreams* because the bad dreams get caught in the webbing and the good dreams go through the center.

The modifier, "little," denotes a story that is not big, perhaps not too important. That is, it may be a bit contrived rather than absolutely true. The benefit of the product was to give the "Indian baby good dreams" which suggests that perhaps a baby needs to be Indian for it to work. Finally, the use of the modal-verb "would have" suggests that it was something that was true some time ago and perhaps is no longer valid. As these qualifying statements are not absolute, the possibility exists that even today a non-Indian baby would benefit from a dream catcher.

Sellers' stories also support the affinity between the objects and the stereotypic view of the creators. The same retailer discussed the importance of stories for her customers. In the excerpt below, she outlines how she shares these stories.

> we have stories *on* all the kachinas because *in Indian*, everyone loves to relate to stories so everything they buy, they want a story *on*, so the burden baskets...I try and *do up* stories *on* ... Yeah here, *I put stories on them*. (points out card on burden basket)

The most salient language form here is the use of "on" to denote the relationship of the story to the object. The preposition "on" implies that the story does not emerge from within the object. It is instead something from without that is attached. The retailer also chooses to use an interesting verb form, "do up", to describe how she conveys the stories. This conjures up a sense of making something up rather than merely reporting something factual. It is interesting that the woman refers to the Native American cultures and/or languages with the generic term "in Indian." This implies that she is content to make generalizations about literally hundreds of tribes, cultures and languages.

The act of telling the story, that is, the performance, serves to express the connection between the products and the Indian image and provide consumers with the perception that they have had a role in the performance. Bauman (1986) suggests that performances have the power to rearrange the structure of social relations within the event. A Flathead Indian trader/auctioneer elaborates on this theme:

> The first thing I try to accomplish to relax the people— say something *funny* and get people in light spirits. I often tell auction *anecdotes concerning a particular artist* whose work will go on the block.. I want to put a smile on people's faces. I want them to feel we are one *big happy family*. I want them in a buying mood so that when the time comes, they'll *go a couple of bids past what they thought they really wanted to*. I keep reminding the people — it's only money. (Epstein 1991: 14)

The power of humor is used a great deal in the entertaining auction monologue. The anecdotes about the specific artists foster the buyer's illusion of knowing the artist. To accompany the bidding of a painting, the auctioneer told a story about the artist before he had achieved recognition. The phrase "one big happy family" suggests a positive relationship between the customers' sense of solidarity with the artists and the amount of the bids. Later during the same auction, the auctioneer told a story about the way things are done up at his trading post in Montana.

> We sell a lot of beadwork and rawhide items and a lot of things like were seen in *Dances with Wolves* so we have a joke. It's a joke with us it isn't really with the people I guess. Someone will come in and ask ... hanging on the wall and they say "how much is that?" Well, the clerk, who are either all my children or grandchildren and about as smart as I am which ain't too smart, but we're good at certain things and selling things is one of them. One yells across the room, "Auntie, how much is this... that they used in *Dances with Wolves*?" It don't make any difference what the price is, the guy says "I'll take it!" We got jewelry that Kevin Costner wore behind the scenes! "Auntie, how much is this turquoise bolo tie?", "Is that the one Kevin Costner wore down in Billings when they were making the movie?" "$300", "I'll take it!" We don't really do that with the jewelry, but we do it with the other things. And any of you who bought stuff from me, we ain't giving you your money back!

In addressing a supposedly sophisticated group of prospective buyers in an elegant hotel suite, the auctioneer pokes fun at less sophisticated consumers who are on the pro-Indian bandwagon which was spurred by the film *Dances With Wolves*. Here he demonstrates to the group that Indian entrepreneurs are clever enough to capitalize on this if they want to.

Sometimes the piece of art itself represents a story. Tom Nez describes a ring and bracelet set he made.

> *This is the San Xavier Mission*, the first church building in Arizona, that's Father Kino walking, there's eagle flying over his head, there a saguaro cactus, there's a road runner, this is the Monument Valley where the rocks stickin in it, there's a bird, a jackrabbit, coyotes, and these little dots represents the water table. See that thing sticking out of the ground? That's called mesquite wood. It has my name inside too Nez. *There you go*.

This artist/seller is also an actor and a singer. I was directed to him by the producer of an Indian arts and crafts show because he was an "expert" at talking about his work. What is interesting about this story is that it has a beginning and an end indicated by "This is San Xavier Mission" and "There you go" respectively, yet it does not have any plot or depth. It is merely a list of discrete objects and places that are used to stereotype the Southwest. This is created by an artist who makes a lucrative living from playing the stereotypical Indian in television shows and films, as well as in the sales setting. He is well known among the other sellers as one who exploits his Indianness. I asked a seller at the next booth if I could record some of the stories he tells about the sand paintings he sells and he adamantly refused, exclaiming "I'm no Tom Nez!" Although this seller refused to be recorded, his selling strategy was not unlike that of Nez, that is, spinning stories to increase marketability of his products.

Consumers may be mistaken if they perceive that they have learned all about an Indian artist and his or her culture. Nez illuminated other suspicions regarding the credibility of these stories.

> I don't really tell the *whole whole* story you know, especially in Navajo culture. It takes uh almost a week to just to explain something you know, what it means. In general detail, you can do it you know, just like that...Everything I say here is *just in general*, but people like it.

Nez explains that the thumb-nail sketches serve to appease consumers without requiring him to expose too much of his own culture. The reduplication of the word "whole" may emphasize the fact that the entire story is bigger than one would expect. Finally, Tom prefaces the phrase "in general" with the word "just" to minimize the importance of the detail he omits from the stories. He stresses that people do enjoy his abbreviated stories.

Another selling technique involving stories was employed at a gallery run by a jeweler who creates designs based on Aleut stories and legends passed down through her grandmother. During Indian Market week, a Yup'ik storyteller performed in the back room of the gallery. He was quoted (Podany 1991) as saying:

> What I do is because of my *grandmother*. Most of the songs I initially learned were from her. So, it's *her singing through me. We're all in this together*.

Here, we see reference to an elder, a grandparent. Stories seem to have greater power, greater authenticity, if they are passed down through the generations. The phrase "her singing through me" also indicates a special, perhaps supernatural, transference of the stories. Finally, in stating "We're all in this together", the storyteller is implying a solidarity which is shared by native peoples. In this, he suggests that it is important to retain the old traditions and he is pleased to be able to share these. What is not said is that consumers associate the power and authenticity of the stories with the products and the gallery.

Throughout this discussion of the language used to promote these products, the following metaphors have been presented:

> The Indian is a spiritual being. The Indian lives a traditional lifestyle. Indians are connected to stories that are passed on through the generations. Indians are associated with symbols that bring luck, blessings, rain, etc.

Also we have seen one example of the metaphor of the Southwest in Tom Nez' design description. As Lakoff and Johnson (1980) point out, metaphors have power to create reality as well as merely describe what exists. This is demonstrated here as the consumers who are purchasing products are also purchasing the metaphors to fulfill certain needs and desires. Indian producers are romanticized beings who cannot be purchased, but their products, which convey the metaphors do provide meaning for consumers.

CHALLENGING THE STEREOTYPES

An outcome of the use of stories to convey the meaning of these arts and crafts is the creation and maintenance of stereotypes. While some of the artists thrive on allowing themselves to be stereotyped and even collude in this stereotyping, there are some successful artists striving to reject stereotypes. One artist featured in an Indian Market publication (Kress 1991) is reportedly interested in educating Anglos with the hope of overcoming the stereotypes.

> Namingha will only reveal a gleaning of his work's meaning realizing that he must be careful with his tribe's

heritage. Still he hopes that people will intuitively grasp his work's message. With luck, he seeks to *"bridge the gap" between the Anglo world which collects his work and the Indian world, so that "they become more interested and respectful of other cultures, not only my tribe but other tribes also."*

Namingha, a Hopi, aspires to reach Anglos through art, so that they will better understand and appreciate all Indian culture. This Pan Indian sentiment is also evident in a published excerpt from an interview with Larry Yazzie, a Navajo.

There are a lot of people now *like I was,* who don't know anything about our own way. And I don't want to leave those people out. I want to *make them feel important*...A lot of my work depict the serenity in Native American people. A lot of *people need to be educated, to break the stereotypes* about Indian people. It's a *religious responsibility* for me, I believe the Creator has given me this gift to leave something for the *younger people,* and I approach my art that way. (Faunteleroy 1991)

This artist believes he has made a transformation for the better from "like I was", and he is hoping to help other Indians. His words "to make them feel important" suggest that he believes that he is now empowered to have an impact on their lives. The statement "people need to be educated" shows that Yazzie now sees himself in the position of one who has learned from experience and is prepared to transmit the information to others. He then explicitly states that stereotypes need to be broken. Yazzie also articulates the driving force behind his objectives and expresses that his mission is to teach others.

Political messages are expressed in the art forms of some of the more outspoken artists. A few have not only created art which conveys political and controversial points, but also have been involved in massive protests. Adam Fortunate Eagle, who has found fame in sculpting and pipe making, was the leader of the 1969 takeover of Alcatraz Island. He creates sculptures that communicate serious messages about the history of his people.

Death Song at Wounded Knee depicts eight faces of Indians either singing their death song or speaking of the deaths of others, When an Indian knew death was near he would sing his death song preparing himself to make the journey to the spirit world. Every person has their own death song. You prepare yourself for another journey and that's what this alabaster sculpture represents. I will have a number of bronzes, including *Prelude to the Trail of Tears* that relates to the Cherokee long walk and a small one titled *Tide of History* that tells the story of life.

The titles Fortunate Eagle has given to his art work bring to mind the injustices that the Native American people have faced. He weaves the sacred traditions of his people into the description of the pieces. His discussion of the journey to the spirit world evokes a feeling of the inevitability of death, and for the Indian, a suffering brought on by injustice. Like Yazzie, he is involved in conveying a Pan-Indian message, using historic incidents from the experience of quite dissimilar tribes from different parts of the continent.

David Bradley, a successful painter and an instructor at the Institute of American Indian Art, uses his art to attack stereotypes. The most visible piece is a take-off on the "Land O' Lakes" butter label. In this piece, the same charming and beautiful Indian maiden is depicted, but the label above her head reads "Land O Bucks." In a published interview (Tarchinski 1991: 39), he said he is "showing a mirror to the non-Indians hoping they will realize the consequences of their actions," although it is not clear whether the people to whom he shows the mirror actually see themselves in it.

While the artists discussed here have actively challenged stereotypes and have been successful, the majority of producers feel they must create products that meet the demand of the market. Numerous informants have indicated that they refrain from producing contemporary items because consumers show preferences for the more "traditional" pieces. It appears that artists will only feel confident about challenging stereotypes after they have achieved recognition and stability in the industry.

Perhaps the dedication of the challengers of the stereotypes and the consciousness raising that many of them seem prepared to do will interact with the power of the performance (Bauman 1986) and the power of the metaphor (Lakoff and Johnson 1980) to allow Native American artisans and craftspeople to attain a truly "authentic" contemporary artistic achievement. Until then, they will be constrained by the demand of mainstream Anglos for what is considered "typical" or "traditional" Indian arts and crafts and accompanying stories.

CONCLUSION

It is indeed a paradox that American Indians must continue to support and perpetuate the stereotypes of themselves in order to market their products. Until a producer receives recognition, it is very risky to attempt to thwart stereotypes and/or create very innovative and contemporary designs. This brings to mind the dilemma posed by new product development. The most successful producers are the ones who innovate. Nonetheless, the costs and risks involved in new product development tend to be discouraging. The more successful producers take these risks via the creation of market niches. For example, the above mentioned challengers of the stereotypes and the producers of the more contemporary designs are placing their work above the level of the mass marketed products. The stories they tell tend to be more descriptive and profound than those related by the sellers of the lower end products. It suggests that the consumers of these differentiated products demand more specialized and carefully constructed stories.

Other questions concerning the symbiotic relationship between the production of Indian arts and crafts and the recent development of the Anglo consumers' sense of New Age spirituality suggest a very intriguing area for future research. One issue that has been recently examined in the popular press is how "sacred" objects are sold to consumers (Romancito 1992). Public policy issues are raised concerning the authenticity of sellers' claims and of the ethical issues that are raised by the commercialization of the religions of the American Indian.

An analysis of language use in a sales setting allows us to examine the interactional skills and processes involved in selling and consumption. Many consumers agreed that the purchase experience and the product are made more meaningful through meeting the producer and hearing the stories. Hence, this research provides us with examples of deeper meanings of consumption such as the role of possessions in the definition of self and others.

REFERENCES

Bauman, R. (1986) *Story, Performance and Event*. Cambridge University Press: Cambridge.

Belk, Russell, Melanie Wallendorf, and John F. Sherry, Jr. (1989), "The Sacred and the Profane in Consumer Research: Theodicy on the Odyssey," *Journal of Consumer Research*. 16 (June), 1-38.

Epstein, Pancho (1991), "A Quintessential Quest for Identity", *Indian Market: The Santa Fe New Mexican.* Aug. 15, 14.

Faunteleroy, Gussie, "Yazzie Hopes to Speak to All with Spiritual, Evocative Art," *Indian Market: The Santa Fe New Mexican.* Aug. 15, 28.

Goffman, E. (1963) *Stigma*. Prentice Hall: Englewood Cliffs.

Hill, Richard (1991) "Disenchanted Reality," *Crosswinds.* V. III, No.VIII, (August), 12-13.

House, Deborah (1986) Personal Communication.

Houston, Franklin S. (1986) "The Marketing Concept: What It Is and What It Is Not," *Journal of Marketing.* 50 (April), 81-87.

Kohli, Ajay K. and Bernard J. Jaworski (1990) "Market Orientation: The Construct, Research Propositions, and Managerial Implications," *Journal of Marketing.* 54 (April) 1-88.

Kress, Stephen, (1991) "Namingha's Spirited Art" *Crosswinds.* V. III, No. VIII, (August), 11.

Lakoff, George and Mark Johnson (1980) *Metaphors We Live By.* The University of Chicago Press: Chicago.

Murray, Jeff B. and Julie L. Ozanne (1991) "The Critical Imagination: Emancipatory Interests in Consumer Research," *Journal of Consumer Research.* 18 (September) 129-144.

Nelson, Mary Carroll (n.d.) "Pottery With Power," *Southwest Profile.*

Parezo, Nancy J. (1992) Personal Communication.

Pinch, Trevor and Colin Clark (1986) "The Hard Sell: 'Patter Merchanting' and the Strategic (Re)Production and Local Management of Economic Reasoning in the Sales Routines of Market Pitchers," *Sociology.* 20, 2, 169-191.

Podany, Jimbo (1991) "Visions of Alaska" *Pasatiempo: The Santa Fe New Mexican.* August 16, 5.

Romancito, Rick (1992) "Is it Art? Is it Sacred?" *Indian Market Magazine.* 54-55.

Sherry, John (1988) "Market Pitching and The Ethnography of Speaking," *Advances in Consumer Research.* 543-547.

Shutz, Alfred (1967) *The Phenomenology of the Social World.* Chicago: Northwestern University Press.

Torgovinick, Marianna (1990) *Gone Primitive: Savage Intellects, Modern Lives.* University of Chicago Press: Chicago.

Tarchiniski, Pamela J. (1991) "Market Matures into World Class Event" *Indian Market '91: The Albuquerque Journal.* August 13, 17-39.

Social Control Versus Social Stability: A Conceptualization of Contradictory Goals and Hybrid Outcomes on Ethnic Relations, Consumer Satisfaction, and Entrepreneurship in the Former USSR

Oleg I. Gubin, Moscow State University, Russia
Melissa Martin Young, University of Utah
Alexander G. Osipov, University of Utah
Natasha Kostioutchenko, University of Utah

ABSTRACT

In this conceptual paper, we contend that two dimensions — *Social Control and Social Stability* — strongly influence three topics of importance to consumer researchers in the post-coup era of the Former Soviet Union [hereafter referred to as the *FSU*]: (1) ethnic relations; (2) consumer satisfaction; and (3) private entrepreneurship. Ethnic relations — an ancient source of instability between the 128 ethnic nationalities of the FSU (e.g., Lenin 1917) — are becoming ever more chaotic as the 15 nation-states of the FSU continue to disintegrate in the post-coup era (e.g., Franklin 1992; Krupnik 1991; Shevardnadze 1992). Consumer satisfaction remains an oxymoronic term, as consumer *dis*satisfaction is the norm in the FSU, not the exception, as widely-publicized throughout the Cold War era (e.g., Bonnell 1989; Heller and Nekrich 1986; Kaiser 1976) *and* the post-coup era (e.g., Antonian 1992; Khubulava 1992; Soloviev 1992). Entrepreneurship, a reform measure introduced by the Gorbachev administration, has failed to live up to both Western *and Soviet* expectations (e.g., Lewin 1991; Markov 1992; Piyacheva 1992). We investigate these three subjects — ethnic relations, consumer satisfaction, and entrepreneurship — using contemporary literature and personal observations in the FSU before, during, and after the August 1991 coup. We describe consumer and market conditions in the FSU, contradictory goals of the 15 nations-states, and possible hybrid outcomes of these goals on marketization and democratization.

SOCIAL STABILITY AND SOCIAL CONTROL

In order to provide the framework for the remainder of our paper, we begin by defining Social Stability and Social Control. We define Social Stability as "the *actual observance* of governmentally-formalized, regulated and enforced laws, rules, and norms for societal relations." This could be quantified as the ratio of the *number of actual observances* of governmentally-formalized, regulated, and enforced laws, rules and norms for social relations to the *total number* relevant to societal relations. In other words, a high-stability society is one in which a large number of governmentally-formalized, regulated, and enforced laws, rules, and norms are observed. Likewise, a less stable society is one in which a small or non-existant percentage of governmentally-formalized, regulated, and enforced laws, rules, and norms are observed.

Figure One, next page, describes the structure of FSU society in general terms. *GOV* refers to government, and governmentally-formalized, regulated, and enforced laws, rules, and norms for societal relations. *A, B, C, and D* are individuals, groups, organizations, and corporations; in essence, all of society which is not part of government. *U, V, W, X, Y, and Z* refer to the societal relations between individuals, groups, organizations, and corporations. The government is thought to influence societal relations, and vice-versa.

We define Social Control as "the *formalization and regulation of societal relations* (this includes relations between individuals, groups, and businesses), which are realized through the creation and enforcement of governmental laws, rules and norms." This could be quantified as the ratio of the *number of formalized, regulated, and enforced* governmental laws, rules, and norms concerning societal relations relative to the *total number* of societal relations. Therefore, a very controlled society is one in which the majority of social relations are formalized, regulated, and enforced through governmental laws, rules, and norms. Likewise, a relatively less-controlled society is one in which few, or no, social relations are formalized, regulated, and enforced via governmental laws, rules, and norms.

Given our preceeding framework and definitions, we now discuss ethnic relations, consumer satisfaction, and entrepreneurship in the FSU.

ETHNIC RELATIONS

We begin our discussion by noting that the FSU currently is in a state of chaotic, crisis-level disintegration — economically, politically, and ethnically (DeBardeleben 1992; Draper 1991; Prybyla 1992). Franklin (1992) comments that 20 of the 23 borders between the 15 republics of the FSU are being disputed: In fact, recent research at the Russian Academy of Sciences Institute of Geography found only 3 undisputed borders — those between Belorus and Russia, Belorus and Latvia, and Latvia and Lithuania. There were 160 border *disputes* in the *FSU* as of December 1991, and more than 90 border *changes* have occurred in the *USSR* since 1921 (Franklin 1992). Of the 128 ethnic groups in the FSU, 109 live primarily in Russia alone.

Resolution of this oft-mentioned "National Problem" (e.g., Gurevich 1991; Krupnik 1991; Lenin 1917) will be a major determinant of the future of the FSU; *and thus, the consumer and market futures of the FSU*. "Nationalism," *as defined in the USSR*, was meant to force ethnic groups to conform with one another (e.g., Arutyunov 1990; Bromley 1989; Gellner 1983). From the Tsarist era to the Stalin era, borders were forcibly altered and tribes were removed from their homelands; almost at whim. During the Soviet period, ethnic divisiveness and diversity were suppressed under Communist power. Then, during the Gorbachev period, perestroika and glasnost' led to an unexpected outcome — the unleashing of bitter national conflicts which had been fermenting for centuries. Now, following the downfall of Gorbachev, some of these long-silenced ethnic/national problems are developing into outright wars (Franklin 1992); threatening the people of the FSU, lowering production, and deterring Western businesses from venturing East.

The 128 nationalities of the FSU are spread among 15 SSRs (Soviet Socialist Republics, such as Uzbekistan), 15 ASSRs (Autonomous Soviet Socialist Republics, such as Tatarstan), 8 AOs (Autonomous Regions, like Nagorno-Karabakh), and 4 NOs (National Regions, such as Koriak); many of which want to split off from the FSU (Mackenzie and Curran 1992, see Map One). These include the Chuckchi ASSR (the ethnic group that traversed the Bering Straits via land bridge into Alaska), the Yakut ASSR (in northeastern Siberia), the Tatar ASSR (in European Russia, which

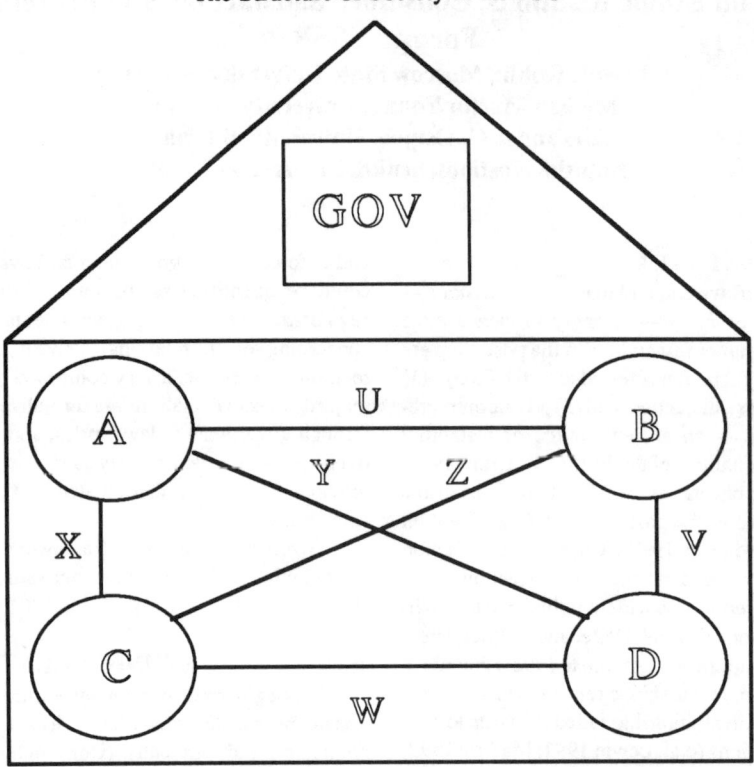

FIGURE 1
The Structure of Society in the FSU

now is the independent nation of Tatarstan), the Chuvash ASSR on the North Volga), the Buriat ASSR (of Mongolian ancestry), and many others (Sullivan 1992).

Recently, there have been at least seven explanations for the independent national movements in the FSU (Krupnik 1991): (1) Extremism; (2) Food Shortages; (3) Political Deformation; (4) Natural Disintegration of the Russian Empire; (5) Feedback Violence; (6) Violations of Guarantees of Sovereign Nationalities; and (7) Theories that Soviet Industrialization of the 20th Century is Out-Dated for the 21st Century. The first explanation for ethnic and national conflicts, *Extremism*, is reminiscent of old Communist propaganda, in that it blames current strife on radicals—corrupt mafia, enemies of perestroika, ideological enemies, Foreign Secret Service Agents, and/or bureaucrats and apparatchiks — all of whom are thought to be organizing large demonstrations to persuade the masses to panic *unnecessarily*. The second explanation, *Food Shortages*, blames national tensions on the economy's inability to meet the people's current food requirements. The third explanation, *Political Deformation*, is a political/historical explanation which blames the failure of the Union Treaty and the Commonwealth of Independent States on distortions of Stalinist suppression/oppression of ethnic groups during the 1920s to 1930s. This theory notes that if the difficulties had been resolved in the past, attempts to form a new balance between the center and the sovereign republics might succeed. The fourth explanation for nationalistic movements is based on an evolutionary theory, *"Natural" Disintegration of the Russian Empire*, which argues that the founding of the Soviet Union was a violation of the goals of the Bolshevik Revolution, in that Lenin and Stalin reinstated a single nation along the frontiers of the former Tsarist empire. This political and historical argument *is accurate*, in that both Lenin and Stalin opposed Federalism *prior* to the Revolutions of 1917, then radically reversed their positions by 1918 (Lenin 1917; Stalin 1953). The fifth explanation for ethnic unrest, *Feedback Violence*, is a contemporary sociological/cultural theory which says that the disintegration of multinational empires increases nationalistic movements because empires tend to degrade ethnic traditions, religions, and languages. This theory implies that efforts to return to a single nation (such as the CIS) will increase, rather than decrease national oppression in the FSU (Gellner 1983). *Violations of Guarantees of Sovereign Nationality*, the sixth explanation, is a psychological theory which states that past violations of national sovereignty will lead to more aggressive nationalism in order to acquire *revenge* (Gellner 1983). The seventh explanation, *Beliefs that Soviet Industrialization from the 20th-Century is Out-Dated for the 21st Century*, is a historical argument based on the former failures of all great empires (e.g., Roman, Byzantine, Ottoman, Persian). This theory claims that all multi-ethnic empires eventually must return to smaller, more manageable entities.

Figure Two, next page, illustrates our theoretical conceptualization of four potential hybrid ethnic outcomes of the balance of Social Stability and Control: (1) *Ethnic Cooperation*; (2) *Ethnic Competition*; (3) *Ethnic Warring*; and (4) *Ethnic Suppression/Exploitation*. One feature of our conceptualization which should be pointed out is that we limit our discussion to the 15 nations-states of the FSU rather than the 128 ethnic groups living in the FSU. A more complete conceptualization is beyond the scope of this paper. Another facet of our framework which must be considered is whether the 15 former republics of the USSR represent nation-states or ethnic groups. We believe they are nation-states; however, this is not a universally-shared opinion. The third, and perhaps most unsettling feature of our framework which must be noted, is our inability to place *any* nation-states in the *Ethnic Cooperation* quadrant.

Indeed, it is possible to locate all 15 nations of the FSU in the *Ethnic Warring* quadrant; particularly if minor armed conflicts and

MAP 1

interpersonal crimes are considered. We place most republics of the FSU in the third quadrant, *Ethnic Warring*, because we believe this is the *dominant mode of ethnic relations* in at least 9 nation-states. Russia, as the "police state," is involved in some ethnic conflicts by invitation—such as Tadzhikistan—but in many cases the opposite is true. In all cases, we emphasize that the FSU is passing through such rapid changes that what is accurate today may be inaccurate tomorrow (Rich 1992).

One of the worst ethnic wars is occurring between Armenia and Azerbaijan. The Armenian-Azeri conflict is as savage as the fighting between the Croats and Serbs in Yugoslavia and reminiscent of Lebanon (Mackenzie 1992). The key dispute between Christian Armenia and Islamic Azerbaijan is that Armenia wants to annex the Nagorno-Karabakh AO (an Autonomous Region within the borders of Azerbaijan), which wishes to secede to Armenia on the grounds that the population in Nagorno-Karabakh is overwhelmingly Armenian. As Armenians fight to control the Nagorno-Karabakh AO, Azerbaijan has retaliated by forcibly removing Armenians living in other Azeri regions — especially the Azeri capital, Baku (Mackenzie 1992). This ethnic warring is rooted in religious and territorial differences (e.g., Grunwald 1992; Kaplan 1991; Wilson-Smith 1990), and is unlikely to end soon. Ashot Mancharian, a young Armenian leader remarked in a speech in 1989: "For us there is no turning back." Likewise, Rufat Novrozov (1990), an Azeri economist, said: "This fight over territory has become a fight for our worth...our dignity as a people [and] as a nation" (Smith 1991).

Another major conflict in the Transcaucasus is occurring in Georgia, where Islamic Ossetians want to secede from Christian Georgians. Although the war is tied to religious ideologies, it is more than a mere religious revival (Chelyshev 1991). It is a territorial dispute involving the restoration of a whole complex of cultural values. Georgia, perhaps best known as the birthplace of Stalin, and oft-misrepresented in Russian literature as a nation of quasi-Islamic character, oriental background, and unchecked cruelty (Layton 1992), has renewed hopes for peaceful solutions now that Eduard Shevardnadze has assumed its presidency. Yet, the Moscow-imposed state of emergency (*The Salt Lake Tribune*, November 3, 1992), in combination with the recent legalization of rifles and tear-gas guns for all citizens, indicates that an all-out war with North and South Ossetia is growing ever more feasible (*The Salt Lake Tribune*, November 12, 1992).

Another key conflict is occurring in Moldavia, a small nation-state located between Ukraine and Romania (Franklin 1992). Moldavia is trying to reunite with Romania, which could lead to a flare-up of violence over Northern Bucovina, which used to be part of Romania, but which Stalin gave to Ukraine when Soviet Moldavia was formed from what used to be Bessarabia. Romania wants Moldavia back, which could fuel Romanian nationalism; and this in turn, could elevate tensions with a Hungarian minority in Transylvania, leading to increased anti-Romanian passion in Hungary proper (Franklin 1992). Ethnic escalation, like nuclear escalation, will threaten Romanian/Ukrainian/European relations and their economic recovery programs.

Ethnic warring also is occurring throughout the Asian nation-states (i.e., Kirgiziya, Tadzhikistan, Turkmenistan, Uzbekistan, and sometimes Kazakhstan, but the latter is different because nearly half of its population is Russian). The most recent fighting is

FIGURE 2
Social Control Versus Social Stability:
Hybrid Outcomes and Ethnic Relations Between the 15 Nation-States of the FSU

	Low Social Control	High Social Control
High Social Stability	**Ethnic Competition** Belorus Kazhakstan	**Ethnic Cooperation**
Low Social Stability	**Ethnic Warring** Transcaucasian Nations Kirgiziya Moldavia Russia Tadzhikistan Turkmenistan Uzbekistan	**Ethnic Suppression/Exploitation** Estonia Latvia Lithuania Ukraine

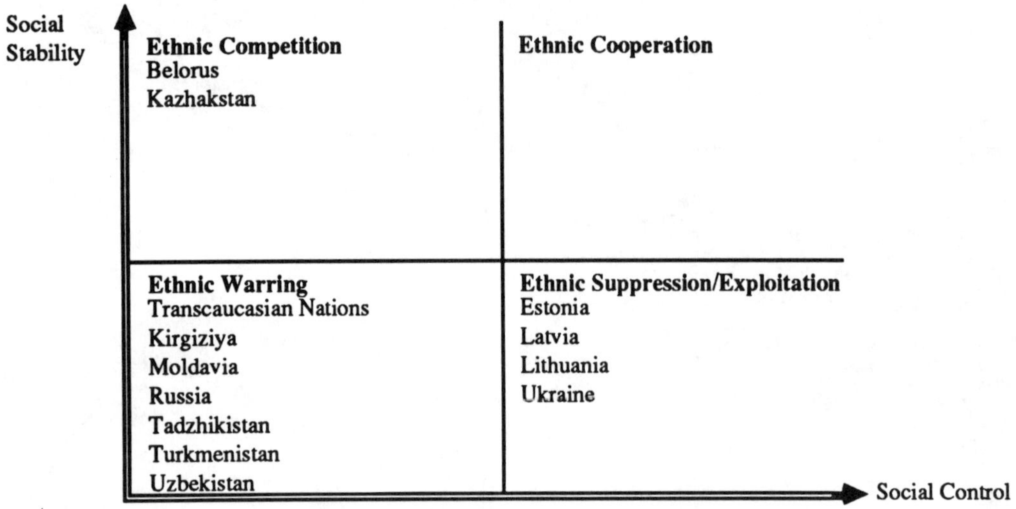

happening in Tadzhikistan, where paramilitary forces led by hardliners are attempting to overthrow a democratic government in the capital of Dushanbe (*The Salt Lake Tribune*, November 7, 1992). In spite of the lack of international media attention, estimates of the number of refugees from the Asian nation-states range well into the millions. 200,000 Tadzhiki refugees were driven from their homes during the same time period that most United States newspapers focused on 16,000 refugees in Travnik, Bosnia-Herzegovina (*The Salt Lake Tribune*, November 13, 1992). Media disinterest may imply that the Asian nations have been "written off" as market prospects (at least by Westerners).

If we limit the *Ethnic Warring* quadrant to nations which are experiencing relatively *continuous warring between opposing military forces*, then we believe Belorus and Kazakhstan should be put in the second quadrant, *Ethnic Competition*, since neither nation is engaging in any military action at present (Iwanow 1992).

In contrast, the *dominant mode of ethnic relations* in both the Baltics and Ukraine is *Ethnic Suppression/Exploitation* of Russian nationals (e.g., Karaganov 1992; Rudenshiold 1992; Uibopuu 1992). Fierce nationalism in the Baltic States and Ukraine is a threat to Russia, and it is unclear if Russia will permit these nation-states to maintain their sovereignty (e.g., Ellsberg 1992; Kozyrev 1992; Wan-Chin 1992) — particularly if Yeltsin loses his grasp on Russian leadership. However, it also is unclear if Russia is able to control these breakaway nations.

For example, given the recent announcement by Ukraine that it plans to keep (rather than destroy) its nuclear missile silos — which violates the 1991 START treaty — it is becoming increasingly obvious that Ukraine does not trust Russia, and that their relationship is deteriorating (*The Salt Lake Tribune* November 1, 1992). Russia and Ukraine are contesting ownership of not only nuclear missile silos in Ukraine, but also the Black Sea Naval Fleet and its multi-ethnic crew, as well as the Crimea (e.g., Eberle 1992; Subtelny 1988).

Such disputes over territory are a predictable part of national movements. For example, Lenin (1917) claimed that the 4 criteria of national identification are: (1) territory; (2) language; (3) culture (e.g., customs, values, beliefs); and (4) economy (e.g., the division of productive resources). As such, Ukrainian efforts to retain territory in the Crimea (Franklin 1992), restore the Ukrainian language by renaming Ukrainian cities, revitalize culture by recovering Ukrainian artifacts from Russian museums, and take control of the economy by switching from Russian rubles to Ukrainian currency represent predictable manuevers to recover national identity.

The Ukrainian situation is merely one example of a general trend among the 15 republics of the FSU. All of the ethnic groups of the FSU are — to a greater or lesser extent — establishing unique national identities. While some of these movements represent governmental push (rather than individual pull) strategies, Ukrainian independence is first and foremost an individual (grassroots) movement, and is seen in the changing value-systems, attitudes, behaviors, and possessions of individual Ukrainians.

While consumer researchers traditionally regard ethnicity and nationality only as a means of market segmentation, ethnic and national tensions in the FSU may explain much of the *economic regression* now occurring within and between the nation-states of the FSU (Alekseev 1991). It is vital to remember that "Russian Dominance" and "Neo-Russian Dominance" represent the central paradigms which have prevailed through the histories of both the Russian and Soviet empires (Mackenzie and Curran 1991). While ethnic pluralism is the purported goal of most political parties currently vying for control of the above nation-states (Frank 1992), the hard reality is that a return to a socialist/centralized/authoritarian state is possible (e.g., *Marxist-Leninist League* 1992; Smirnov 1991; Zinov'ev 1991).

CONSUMER SATISFACTION

Landy (1991, p. 17) writes: "Virtually all major Western analysts seem to agree that the [Former] Soviet Union and Eastern Europe should make a rapid leap from a disintegrating party-state command economy into one based on a free market and private property." Although this method rarely is questioned by Westerners, Landy goes on to state that Western advice does not match FSU realities. Using examples from Eastern Europe, Landy makes a compelling point that 'shock therapy' has electrocuted the 'patient.' Daniloff (1992, p. 46) gives an example of this:

FIGURE 3
Social Control Versus Social Stability
Hybrid Outcomes on Consumer Satisfaction

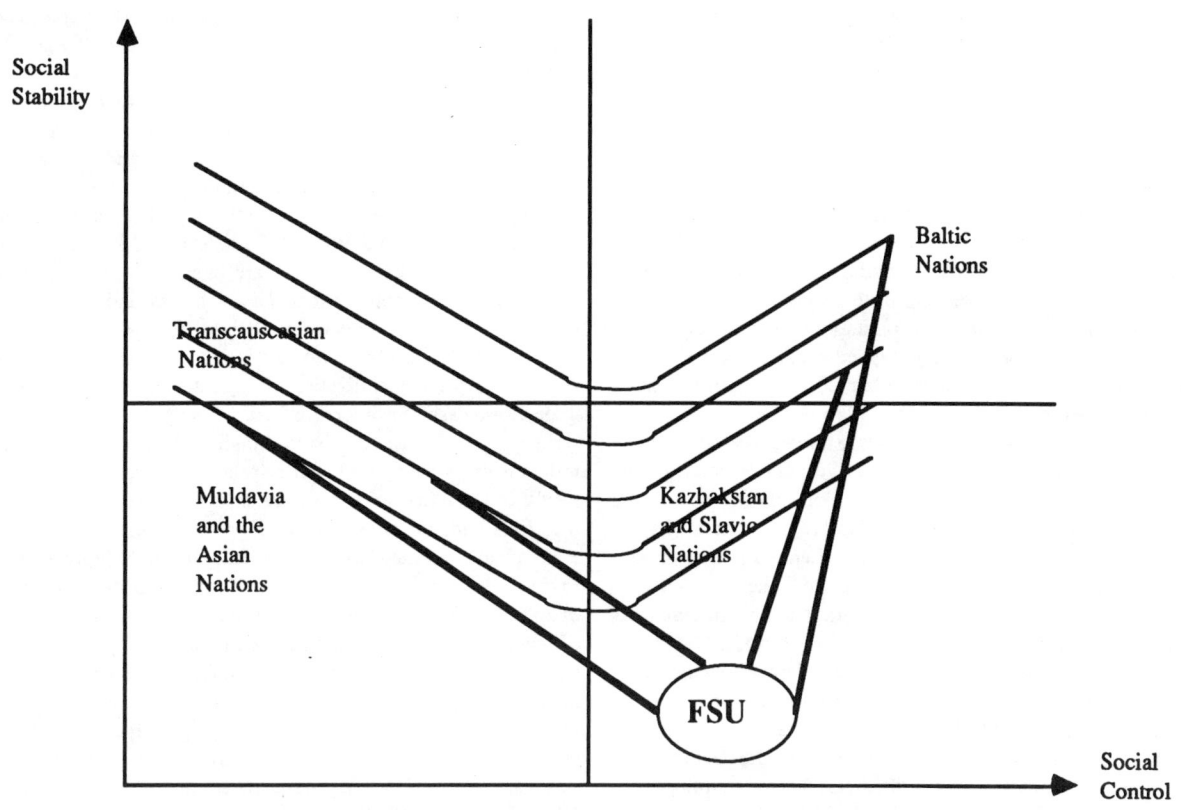

"'Speech' is cheap in Moscow these days, but food is dear. Prices of most goods have gone up 300% since April, as subsidies have been reduced. And, unless controlled, inflation overall is expected to reach 700% for 1992."

A survey of 4849 Russians in 1991 (*World Opinion Update* 1992) revealed that 44% of Russians are "Not Very Satisfied" or "Not Satisfied At All" with their Housing Conditions, 64% with Food, 68% with Personal Income, and 69% with Clothing. The survey respondents listed their three top concerns as: (1) Economic Crisis; (2) Rising Crime/Social Disorder; and (3) Danger of War. More recent surveys paint an even bleaker picture (Khubulava 1992).

Two short years ago most Soviet citizens considered themselves to live on an average level; neither poor, nor rich. Now the population may be divided into four disparate groups (Khubulava 1992). The first group consists of people with monthly incomes below 3,500 rubles (nearly half of which live below the poverty line of 1,950 rubles per month). Approximately 36% of the population falls into this category; most of whom are agricultural and industrial workers, scientists, and the so-called cultural elite, such as artists. People in this category are not too far from the homeless in America. While education and medical services are still free, their quality continues to deteriorate, and bribes are necessary to get "Western" service (Ripp 1990). The second group, still lower class, has incomes of 3,500 to 10,000 rubles per month. Remarkably, people in this category spend nearly 80% of their salaries on *food*. Approximately 34% of the population is in this group; including engineers, doctors, academics, some service workers, and some people involved in commerce. The third group, "the middle class," has incomes of 10,000 to 15,000 rubles per month, but still spend about 40% of their salaries on food. Only 19% of the population fits into this category; primarily people who are working for joint ventures, cooperatives, and private enterprises. The fourth category, "the upper class," has incomes ranging from 15,000 to 45,000 rubles or more per month; about 11% of the population. Most of these people are working for the government or engaged in black market activity or both (as the two go hand-in-hand).

Figure Three, below, diagrams our conceptualization of "relative" consumer satisfaction in the 15 nation-states of the FSU. We place the FSU in the lower right quadrant since, viewed as a whole, the FSU remains high in regard to Social Control and low in respect to Social Stability. The curves represent levels of consumer satisfaction relative to Social Control and Social Stability. The four vectors show differences between the nation-states. Interpretation of our graph shows that the Baltic nations (Estonia, Latvia, Lithuania) are the most balanced in terms of Social Control and Social Stability, and have the highest levels of consumer satisfaction. The Slavic nations (Belorus, Russia, Ukraine) have *higher* levels of Social Control, but *lower* levels of Social Stability, leading to lower levels of consumer satisfaction. (Kazhakstan, although an Asian nation, is put on this vector because it is highly-industrialized and has a Russian population of almost 50%.) A negative situation is observed in the Transcaucasian nations (Armenia, Azerbaijan, Georgia), as well as Moldavia, which have *lower* levels of Social Control, and thus, lower levels of consumer satisfaction. The worst cases in our framework are in the Asian nations (Kirgiziya, Tazhikistan, Turkmenistan, Uzbekistan), which have the *lowest* levels of Social Control and Social Stability; thus, the lowest levels of consumer satisfaction.

A disadvantage in understanding changes over time in consumer satisfaction is the lack of valid data from the Soviet period which can be used to compare and contrast with the present data. Thus, despite our realization that economic indicators reveal downward trends in real GNP and consumers are expressing ever more frustration with rising prices, it is difficult to compare and contrast the present situation with the pre-coup era (e.g., Babosov 1992; Nelson, Babaeva and Babaeva 1992).

ENTREPRENEURSHIP

The most dramatic changes during the Revolutionary era of Russia occurred in the economic sector of society. For several generations following the October Revolution of 1917, the Bolsheviks and Communists attempted to eradicate private interests in the individual and social consciences of the Soviet people, claiming that capitalism leads to worker exploitation, poverty, social conflict, and war. Therefore, the most typical manifestation of private interest–entrepreneurship–was proclaimed illegal, and existing enterpreneurs were deemed criminals (Trotsky 1932).

The elimination of private economic interest was achieved by a set of laws which had three major objectives: (1) to confiscate and nationalize all private means of production; (2) to support and enrichen government-owned property; and (3) to suppress (by any means) the rebirth of enterpreneurship. Lenin's policy of War Communism and Nationalization eliminated, literally and economically, the top-level domestic and international entrepreneurs in the Soviet Union (MacKenzie and Curran 1991).

Stalin completed the task proclaimed in the *Communist Manifesto* (Marx and Engels 1848/1968) by expropriating the expropriators. By eliminating the kulaks (well-to-do peasants) and hetmen (high-ranking military officers) and introducing the death penalty for so-called "economic crimes," Stalin eradicated traditional entrepreneurship during the Great Purge (MacKenzie and Curran 1991).

However, entrepreneurial activity did not completely disappear. Instead, it moved to criminal spheres of society, where certain strata of people inclined to violate the law used entrepreneurship as an easy means of making money (e.g., Grossman 1977; MacKenzie and Curran 1991). Surprisingly, the roots of these new forms of criminal entrepreneurship were fertilized by the Bolsheviks themselves by putting kulaks and hetmen in prisons and labor camps with hardcore criminals. These people formed a new class of underground entrepreneurs with a new version of business ethics which, in opposition to previous ethics, were based primarily on violence, murder, blackmail, racketeering, and fraud (Grossman 1977). Thus, the Bolsheviks' main achievement was to force market activities underground; *not* to eradicate capitalism.

Another important "achievement" of the Bolsheviks in their struggle against entrepreneurship was the formation of mass dependence. As the government became the sole possessor of the means of production and the sole distributor of wealth, Soviet people did not need to take care of themselves anymore. The "unofficial" goal of each individual was not to produce commodities with exchange-values and trade them with other individuals for commodities with use-values (consumption), but rather to abuse distribution channels to obtain values without any production or participation in their creation. Thus, state-imposed, forced dependence led to "distributor entrepreneurship," an illegal form of making money by siphoning goods from distribution channels.

The introduction of cost accounting by Khrushev and Brezhnev formed another type of Soviet entrepreneurship — "supply entrepreneurship." It was not legal, but neither was it criminal. Cost accountants and managers in a deficit economy, whose primary responsibilities were to demonstrate "high levels of achievement," manipulated figures to get more and more aid from the government. This form of entrepreneurship is referred to as the "unreported or unrecorded economy." Most managers who worked in the Soviet command-administrative system participated in this illegal form of entrepreneurship under Soviet power. Now these same people now lead businesses in the aftermath of the Soviet Union (Feige 1987, 1989).

During and following the Gorbachev era, a dramatic reversal from political suppression of traditional entrepreneurship to its promotion began taking place. Nation-states are shifting from total state control to accelerated privatization through the issuance of vouchers, competitive bidding, auctions, and direct sales (e.g., Filatotchev, Buck, and Wright 1992; Rumer 1992; Zamoshkin 1992). Former state enterprises are being privatized as closed corporations, open corporations, joint ventures, and other partnerships (see Filatotchev, Buck, and Wright 1992).

Originally, the objectives of privatization were rather moderate; to help price liberalization through the commercialization of trade, to increase consumer satisfaction through the development of service industries, and to develop small-scale entrepreneurship by relinquishing state control over certain enterprises. However, the results of these first attempts were unsuccessful.

Following the failure of partial privatization, Yeltsin's accelerated plan of privatization was introduced. It is forcible privatization, in much the same manner as Stalin's collectivization was forced upon people. Key features of the new plan are total "voucherization" of the population (each citizen is entitled to a supposedly equal share of the national wealth via possession of negotiable government notes — vouchers), as well as accelerated conversion of state-owned property into private, collective, and corporate ownership (however, industries that form the infrastructure remain centralized/nationalized) (e.g., Filatotchev, Buck, and Wright 1992; Rumer 1992; Zamoshkin 1992).

Yet, these are just the outward manifestations of entrepreneurship. Figure Four, next page, illustrates our vision of the four hybrid economic outcomes in the FSU based on our dimensions of Social Control and Social Stability: (1) *Mixed Economy*; (2) *Western-Style Economy*; (3) *Early-Market Economy*; and (4) *Monopolistic Economy*.

The first type of economy, *Mixed Economy*, possesses features of capitalism and socialism. When consumers are not satisfied with private entrepreneurs, they demand more control over their activities — sometimes by nationalizing specific industries. Social Stability is maintained because individual entrepreneurs and corporations still exist. The dominant interests are therefore both governmental and corporate, and the primary expressions of these interests are a combination of national income and long-term profit.

The second type of economy, what we term a *Western-Style Economy*, is best described as developed capitalism. Few or no industries are controlled by the government, although corporations still must take into account the interests of their shareholders, their employees, the government, other authorities, and the public at large. The dominant interest is the survival of the corporation, and is expressed through long-term profit.

We define the third type of economy, an *Early Market Economy*, as developing capitalism, although there is no guarantee that such an economy will develop into capitalism. It perhaps is equally likely to develop into socialism. This form of economy typically is found where there are low levels of both Social Control and Social Stability. The dominant interest in this type of economic system is the sole proprietor, and is expressed through short-term profits and minimal investment.

The last type of economic system, a *Monopolistic Economy*, is dominated by government. Its main expression is national income

FIGURE 4
Social Control Versus Social Stability: Hybrid Outcomes and Economic Systems

	Low Social Control	High Social Control
High Social Stability	**Western-Style Economy** Developed Capitalism Dominant Interest: Corporate Main Expression: Long-Term Profit	**Mixed Economy (Galbraith)** Socialism/Capitalism Dominant Interest: Government/Corporate Main Expression: National Income/Long-Term Profit
Low Social Stability	**Early Market Economy** Developed Capitalism Dominant Interest: Individual Main Expression: Short-Term Profit	**Monopolistic Economy (Lenin, Marx)** Socialism Dominant Interest: Government Main Expression: National Income

(GNP). This form of economic system is characterized by relatively high Social Control, but—as observed in efforts to enact this form of economic system in the Soviet Union–Social Stability tends to remain low.

Given this conceptualization of economic systems, we now extend Figure Four in Figure Five, next page, which depicts our vision of entrepreneurial opportunities in the 15 nation-states of the FSU. We place the FSU in the lower right quadrant since there is no doubt that the FSU, as a whole, remains centralized, with high Social Control and low Social Stability, despite numerous efforts to accelerate privatization and raise consumer satisfaction.

The four vectors depict differences between the nation-states of the FSU. We believe that the Baltic nations, the Slavic nations, and Kazhakstan have the ability to gravitate toward a *Mixed Economy* (e.g., Filatotchev, Buck, and Wright 1992; Rumer 1992; Zamoshkin 1992), whereas the Transcaucasian nations, Moldavia, and the Asian nations, all of which are involved in significant *Ethnic Warring*, are trapped in an *Early Market Economy*. The latter 8 nation-states are operating at a relatively primitive, corrupt, individualistic level; as might be expected during times of war. To escape this chaos, we contend that these nation-states must find an improved balance between Social Stability and Social Control — a fulcrum point which resolves their ethnic and economic woes.

Regardless of the relative positions of our vectors in Figure Five, it is clear that all 15 nation-states of the FSU face considerable business obstacles. Critical factors confronting new entrepreneurs include the lack of social, legal, political, educational, and other structures to support competitive, regulated, Western-style business operations.

Azrael, Brukoff, and Shkolnikov (1992, p. 324), summarizing and analyzing the *RAND Conference on Prospective Migration and Emigration from the Former USSR* (held in November 1991), comment that several "participants anticipate that the economic crisis" in the FSU "will deepen and persist...in the foreseeable future given the intractability of the command administrative economic system to reform, the almost complete absence of a market infrastructure, and the shortage of [what may be termed] entrepreneurial skills among 'Soviet' citizens."

Given the preceding assessment, we do not disagree that Figure Five might be overly optimistic. To the contrary, we question whether marketization is able to proceed in the absence of the structures needed to support free markets. Thus far in the post-coup era, it would appear that it cannot.

CONCLUSION

"We shall survive the current crisis if we forget the offenses, intrigues, and contradictions that existed formerly...if we are able to unite for the sake of saving the most sacred thing we possess."

Eduard Shevardnadze, 1992

Our goal in writing this article is to emphasize that three factors–ethnic relations, consumer satisfaction, and entrepreneurship–are of great importance to consumer researchers in the FSU and Eastern Europe. The euphoria of the fall of the Iron Curtain and Soviet Communism has subsided. The much-heralded shock therapy reforms of Yeltsin and his Eastern European brethren have led to severe ethnic divisiveness, consumer desperation, and widespread business corruption.

It may be time to step back and consider the gravity of the situation now facing the FSU as it struggles to find an ideal balance between Social Stability and Social Control. The peoples of the 15 nations and the 128 ethnic groups in the FSU — long misunderstood by "Western" and Soviet researchers alike (Tishkov 1992) — have contradictory goals. So far, these contradictory and competitive goals have led to economic and social chaos.

On November 4, 1992, the Wednesday after the 42nd president of the United States was elected, *The Salt Lake Tribune* reported that the first ethnic-related deaths occurred in Russia: "26 Killed in First Ethnic Fighting on Russian Soil." While inaccurate from historical and contemporary points-of-view, this headline, in combination with large numbers of violent deaths throughout the FSU, has led experts to conclude that a real threat to the Russian constitutional system exists; not only in Moscow, but throughout the FSU (*The Salt Lake Tribune*, November 12, 1992). We wish to emphasize that it is naive to think this is a Soviet problem. Rather,

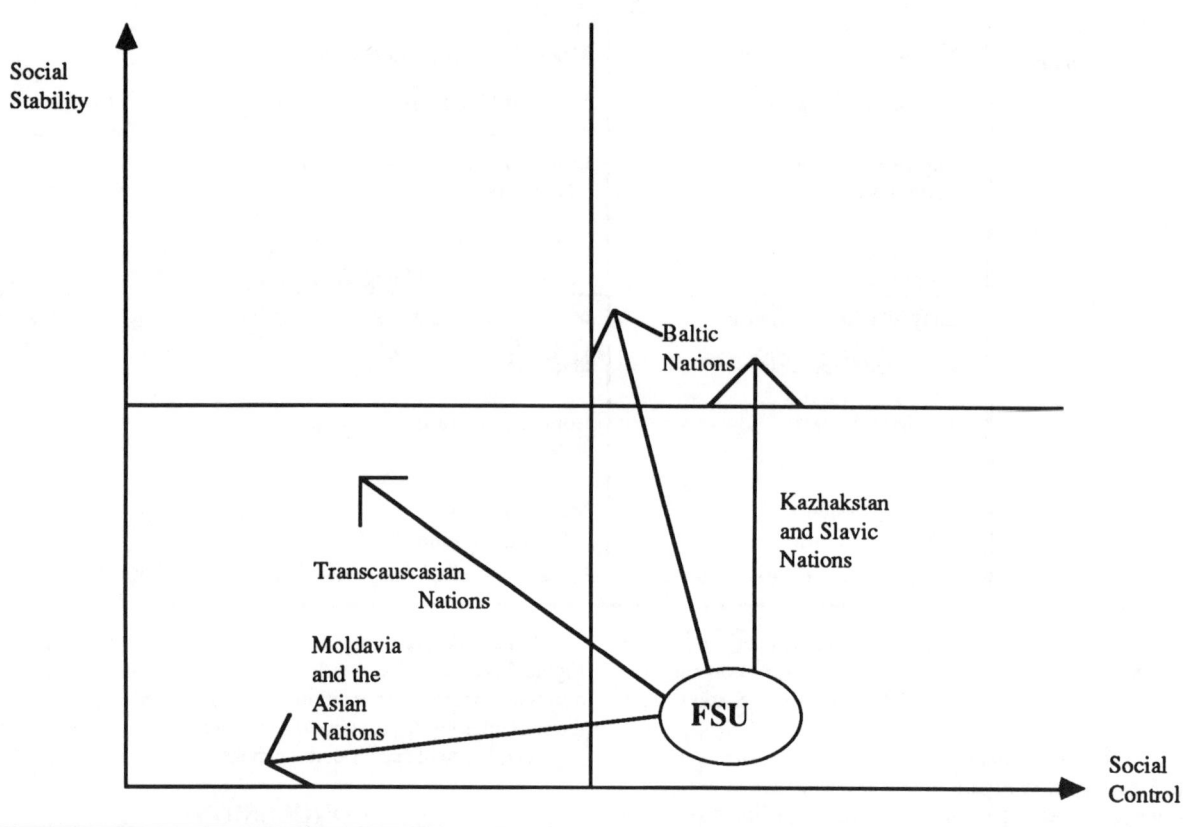

FIGURE 5
Social Control Versus Social Stability:
Hybrid Outcomes on Entrepreneurship

the transition from communism to capitalism is a global problem (Alekseev 1991).

In this article, we have presented some potential hybrid outcomes of Social Stability and Social Control, but attempted to refrain from offering predictions about the future of ethnic relations, consumer satisfaction, or entrepreneurial opportunities in the FSU. Gorbachev (1988) said: "Perestroika is not manna from heaven. Rather than waiting for it to be brought in from somewhere, it must be developed by the people themselves." Likewise, we suggest that the consumer and market dreams of the peoples of the FSU rest with the people themselves, and may be tied to overcoming one ancient characteristic of the Russian character which is truly its misfortune — namely, that Russia has never enjoyed a happy present, but instead, periodically changes its dreams of a happy future (Likhachev 1991). The future, we maintain, must be now if there is to be any future at all. *[For references, please contact Melissa Martin Young, Department of Marketing, David Eccles School of Business, University of Utah, Salt Lake City UT, 84112.]*

Complaints and Compliments about Service Encounters: A Comparison of American and Bulgarian Consumers

Lalita A. Manrai, University of Delaware
Ajay K. Manrai, University of Delaware

ABSTRACT

This paper develops a conceptual model and twelve propositions comparing the complaining and complimenting behavior of American and Bulgarian consumers. The conceptual model describes the nature of relationship between government, consumer and service provider under three scenarios, i.e., in the free-market economy of USA, in the communist party-state controlled economy of Bulgaria (under former communist rule in Bulgaria) and in the democratic party-state controlled economy of Bulgaria (under present situation in Bulgaria). The propositions integrate Weiner's (1980) three-dimensional taxonomy of attributions with this conceptual model and compare the American and Bulgarian consumers in terms of the type of attributions they make for extremely satisfying and extremely dissatisfying service encounters and their subsequent complimenting/complaining behavior.

INTRODUCTION

As East European countries move from communism to capitalism, the beliefs, attitudes and behaviors of East European consumers are changing as well. The importance of cross-cultural consumer research in international marketing has been amply acknowledged by researchers (Lee 1966; Levitt 1983). Yet the studies of cross-cultural consumer behavior have been rather limited in number and there is need for much more work in this area. Considering the dramatic changes and the rapid transition that is currently taking place in the former communist countries, this need is more pressing than ever before.

The impact of this transition should be particularly noticeable in service industries because, overall, perhaps services are the least-developed sector of the economy in East European countries. Under the former communist rule, the economy was centrally controlled and consumers had rather limited choices in terms of the service options and the extent to which they had any say in the marketing of services. It will be interesting to study how a move towards a free market economy and privatization has changed the consumer thinking. In particular, whether the consumers in these East European countries feel free to voice their complaints in case of dissatisfying service encounters and likewise whether the satisfying service encounters lead to compliments.

Attribution theory has been found to be particularly useful in explaining the complaining and complimenting behavior of consumers in developed countries like USA (Curren and Folkes 1987; Folkes 1984; Krishnan and Valle 1979; Richins 1983; Valle and Wallendorf 1979). The aim of our research is to study the applicability of these attribution-based findings in the context of a changing economy like Bulgaria. Towards this end, the research reported in this paper compares the complaining and complimenting behavior of American and Bulgarian consumers. Specifically four research issues would be addressed in our paper related to consumer responses to bad and good service experiences. These are:

1. Do American and Bulgarian consumers differ as regards the type of attributions they make for extremely dissatisfying service experiences?

2. Do American and Bulgarian consumers differ as regards the type of attributions they make for extremely satisfying service experiences?

3. Do American and Bulgarian consumers differ as regards the relationship between the type of attributions they make for extremely dissatisfying service experiences and their complaining and other post-consumption behavior?

4. Do American and Bulgarian consumers differ as regards the relationship between the type of attributions they make for extremely satisfying service experiences and their complimenting and other post-consumption behavior?

In the next section, we develop a conceptual model describing the nature of relationship between consumers and service providers and the role the government has in this relationship depending upon the type of economy. Then, we develop twelve propositions that address the four research issues discussed above. The behavior of the American consumer is predicted based on the relevant research in the areas of attribution, consumer satisfaction/dissatisfaction and services marketing. The extent to which the Bulgarian consumers will exhibit a similar or different behavior (i.e., a cross-cultural comparison) will depend upon the similarity and differences in the cultural, social, economic and political influences in these two countries' environments. Practically no published information exists on the impact of these factors on a Bulgarian consumer's behavior. On the other hand, some very useful insights were obtained by conducting depth interviews with 4 Bulgarian nationals and 5 American participant-observers, i.e., American nationals, 4 of whom had lived in Bulgaria for 3 to 8 months and one had visited Bulgaria for 2 weeks. Participant observations has been long used by ethnologists (Guthe and Mead 1945) and has been equally accepted by consumer researchers (Grunert, Grunert and Beatty 1989). We draw substantially on these participant observations and depth interviews to develop our conceptual model and propositions relating to the behavior of Bulgarian consumers.

CONCEPTUAL MODEL AND PROPOSITIONS

Type of Attributions: Comparison of American and Bulgarian Consumers

Attribution Taxonomy:

Most attribution researchers accept the three-dimensional taxonomy proposed by Weiner (1980). The three dimensions of attributions included in this taxonomy are locus of causality, controllability and stability. Locus of causality deals with internal versus external location of the cause (Weiner 1985, 1986). Thus causes such as ability, effort, patience and mood are considered as internal whereas causes such as task difficulty and luck are considered as external. The second dimension of attributions has to do with whether the outcome could have been controlled or not. Thus causes such as patience and effort are considered as controllable and causes such as ability, mood, task difficulty and luck are considered as uncontrollable. Finally, the third dimension of attributions describes whether the outcome is very likely to happen again, i.e., stable or whether the outcome is very unlikely to happen again, i.e., unstable. Thus causes such as ability, task difficulty and patience are considered to be relatively stable and causes such as luck, effort and mood are considered to be relatively unstable.

Bulgaria in Transition:

In a free market economy like that of United States, the relationship between a customer and service provider is by and large independent of the state or government, i.e., the state or the government does not exercise any direct control on the consumer in terms of which service provider to choose, it does not control the service-mix of the provider, etc. On the other hand under the former communist controlled state rule, the behavior of both consumer and (especially) the service provider was very much controlled by the communist government. Almost all service businesses, e.g., airlines and ground transportation, hotels/restaurants, utilities, banking, retailing including supermarkets and department stores were completely controlled by the communist government. The communist government even controlled the people's freedom to travel within the country. "People had to register before they took a trip" indicated one of the participant-observers. "We had to carry our passports all the time with us - even for travel within the country" said a Bulgarian national. Thus the consumers in Bulgaria felt very much controlled during the communist regime and didn't think that "they had any role to play really as consumers in the way it is in America" expressed another Bulgarian national.

What has happened now with the fall of communism in Bulgaria? A very consistent theme emerged in each and every depth interview conducted with participant-observers and Bulgarian nationals. People feel that "psychologically" they are better off now compared to the communist regime but "economically" they are much worse. What does this mean and why has this happened?

The fall of the communist government means that communist party is no more under control. It *does not* mean that the economy is not state controlled. What has happened is simply a change of control from hands of communists to the currently ruling democratic government. The economy is very much controlled by the government. Only difference is that the government is no more communist. The economy of Bulgaria is still a far cry from privatization and there are many obstacles to privatization. Some of the major problems that the Bulgarian economy is facing currently and how it has affected consumer behavior is discussed below.

Under the communist government, there was not much by way of goods and services but whatever was there was available to people. Most people were employed and had housing. Now the disparities between classes has increased with the result that many are jobless and homeless. There is a small percentage of population that has become wealthy but most of the common public is economically in a much worse situation. While some of this newly acquired wealth is due to skills, most is on account of the "connections", observed one of the interviewees. Another participant-observer said "Privatization is taking place through Communist Mafia, i.e., communists have moved into the economic system and the situation is much worse." The same participant observer told about auction of a gasoline station for over 50 million levas (equivalent of over $2.5 million) and said it was obvious who will have this kind of money. "Connections are everything," he concluded. Thus economically most of the population is much worse.

The good thing that the fall of communism has done is that "people at least feel free to talk about their problems" said a participant-observer. "People complain constantly" said another participant-observer. While most of the service businesses continue to be state controlled, there is some limited privatization that has taken place and this is mostly in small retailing businesses, i.e. small kiosks, repair shops, some small restaurants, etc. "There is a world of a difference in the service that you get in a private restaurant versus in a state controlled restaurant. Although private restaurants are much more expensive and beyond the reach of a common man," felt one of our interviewees. Nevertheless the consumers are at least able to see and feel the difference that true privatization can do and they openly talk about it.

This transition process that Bulgaria is currently going through is represented in a conceptual model (Figure-1). Diagram 1A depicts conditions in a free-market economy like USA where the relationship of consumers and service providers is very much independent of the state. Diagram 1-C depicts conditions in a communist party-state controlled economy of Bulgaria where the communist/state controlled behaviors of both the consumers and the service providers. As Bulgaria moves towards privatization, the link between the government and the consumers has somewhat loosened or become free but the state continues to control the service providers. This transition stage is depicted in diagram 1-B.

Impact of Transition in Bulgaria on Type of Attributions Bulgarian Consumers Make and Their Comparison with American Consumers:

What impact will these changes have on consumer behavior in response to extremely favorable and unfavorable service outcomes, in particular on the three types of attributions discussed earlier? We will next examine the research issues #1 and #2 and develop propositions relating to them.

Considering the state of the economy in Bulgaria where most businesses continue to be state controlled, quality of service in general continues to be poor. "Service is unknown," said a participant observer. Thus most dissatisfying or extremely negative experiences are likely to be a common thing. We define the stability of attributions as the likelihood of that service experience happening again and propose that:

P_1A: Stability of attributions for most dissatisfying or extremely negative service experiences will be higher for Bulgarian consumers than for American consumers.

As regards the controllability of attributions for these bad experiences, American consumers are more likely to feel that they could control the experience whereas Bulgarian consumers will feel that the state has the control. We define the controllability of attributions as the extent to which the consumers feel that they have the control on that service experience and propose that:

P_1B: Controllability of attributions for most dissatisfying or extremely negative service experience will be higher for American consumers than for Bulgarian consumers.

The stability and the controllability dimensions are more likely to be influenced by the control that state has over the service providers/businesses and thus are more driven by economic considerations. On the other hand, psychological considerations are more likely to influence the consumers' freedom to talk about the internal versus external causes. As discussed earlier, the direct control of the government or the state on the consumer is now much less compared to the communist regime. Thus in terms of their freedom to talk about their bad service experiences, the Bulgarian consumers are likely to be quite similar to American consumers. We define

FIGURE 1
Relationship Between Government, Consumer and Service Provider

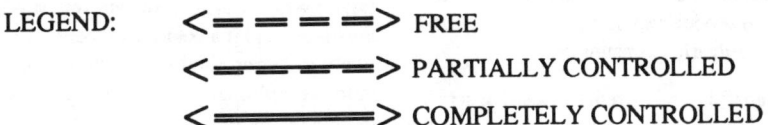

Diagram 1-A:
Free-Market Economy of USA

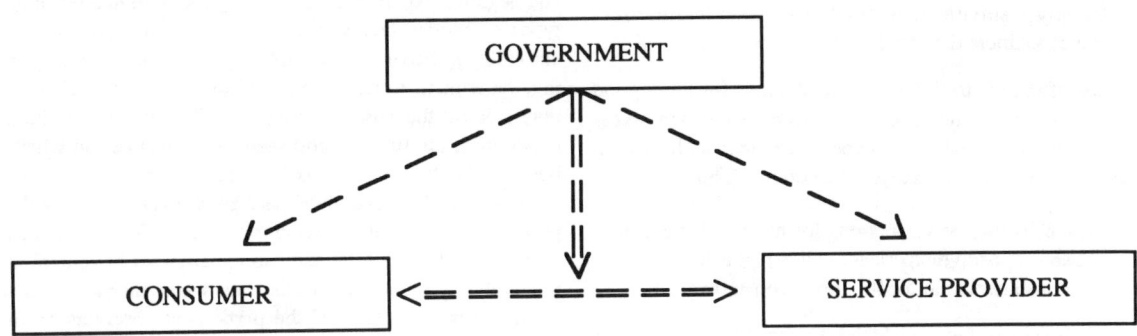

Diagram 1-B:
Democratic Party-State Controlled Economy of Bulgaria

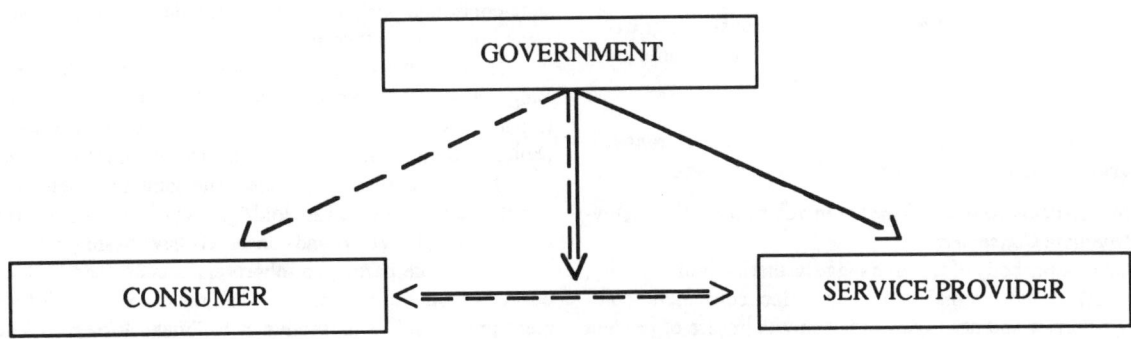

Diagram 1-C:
Communist Party-State Controlled Economy of Bulgaria

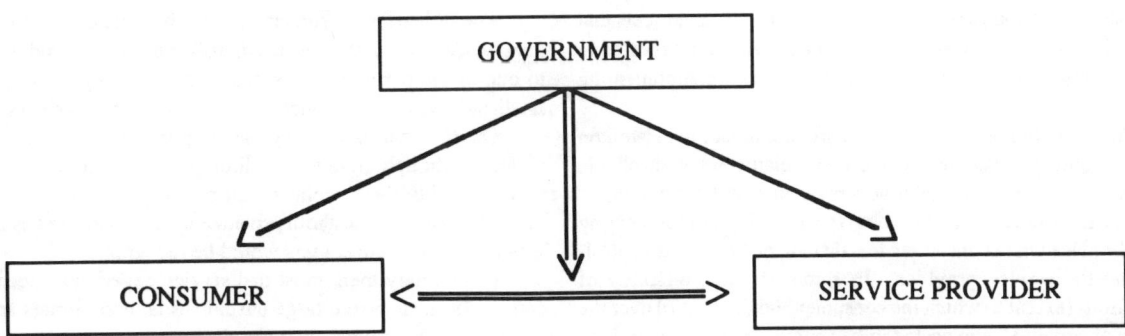

the externality of attributions as the extent to which the consumers feel that the service experience was due to the service provider and propose that:

P₁C: Externality of attributions for most dissatisfying or extremely negative service experiences will be same for American and Bulgarian consumers.

As regards the most satisfying or extremely positive service experiences, these are likely to be more frequent or common for American consumers than for Bulgarian consumers. When probed about an extremely satisfying experience, one participant-observer commented "they are rare and if at all will happen in small private businesses." Thus we propose that:

P₂A: Stability of attributions for most satisfying or extremely positive experiences will be higher for American consumers than for Bulgarian consumers.

In terms of the controllability of attributions for these good experiences, once again, the American consumers are more likely to feel that they could control the experience whereas Bulgarian consumers will feel that the state has the control. Thus:

P₂B: Controllability of attributions for most satisfying or extremely positive experience will be higher for American consumers than for Bulgarian consumers.

The psychological factors which influence the externality of attributions of Bulgarian consumers for bad experiences are also likely to influence the externality of their attributions for good experiences. Thus for good experiences also, Bulgarian consumers are likely to make similar external attributions as American consumers. Thus:

P₂C: Externality of attributions for most satisfying or extremely positive service experiences will be same for American and Bulgarian consumers.

Type of Attributions and Complaining/Complimenting: Comparison of American and Bulgarian Consumers

Type of Attributions and Complaining/Complimenting Behavior of American Consumers:
A substantial body of research suggests that locus of causality, i.e., internal versus external attributions affect consumers' complaining behavior and negative word of mouth in case of product failure (Krishnan and Valle 1979; Richins 1983; Valle and Wallendorf 1979). These researchers found that external attributions in case of product failure led to more complaining and negative word of mouth. By contrast, it could also be conjectured that in case of good experiences, external attributions would lead to more complimenting than internal attributions. In summary, the externality of attributions (extent to which the consumer feels that the service experience was due to service provider) is expected to be positively related with both complaining and complimenting behaviors.

The second dimension of attribution is controllability. Hamilton (1980) found that people receive more blame for controllable actions than for noncontrollable actions. Likewise it can be conjectured that more credit is likely to be given, i.e., more complimenting will take place when consumers feel that the outcome was controllable by the service provider. In summary, controllability of attributions (extent to which the consumer had the control over the service experience) is expected to be negatively related with both complaining and complimenting behaviors.

As regards the third dimension of attributions, i.e., stability, the work of Folkes and her colleagues (Curren and Folkes 1987; Folkes 1984) suggests that consumers were more likely to warn their friends against buying a product when they felt that product failure was due to stable causes and was likely to happen again. On the other hand if a positive outcome is expected to be stable, i.e., is likely to be repeated in the future, consumers are likely to make more compliments. In summary, stability of attributions (the likelihood of the outcome happening again) is expected to be positively related with both complaining and complimenting behaviors.

Pessimism/Optimism Towards Future of Privatization in Bulgaria:
In the United States, a free market economy, both the positive and negative experiences are equally likely to happen in different types of service businesses, i.e., a consumer can have both an extremely positive and an extremely negative experience in banking, department store, auto repair, hair styling, etc. However, this may not be the case in Bulgaria. The nature of the service experience, i.e, bad or good seems to depend upon whether that business is state run or has been privatized. Practically all the interviewees felt that they had good experiences with small, privatized businesses such as small retailing (kiosks), small restaurants, etc., whereas they had bad experiences in general with the relatively bigger, state controlled businesses such as hotels, department stores, etc. One of the participant-observers narrated an extremely positive experience in a small private gift shop where the owner replaced a broken (in transit) piece of dishware free of cost. On the other hand, the same participant-observer narrated how he was waiting along with 30 other people in line while 4 of the cashiers in a large, state-run department store simply stood in a corner and kept chit-chatting. "There are still no incentives in these state-controlled businesses and motivation is a big problem" observed one of our other interviewees.

How do the consumers react to all this? Several of the Bulgarian nationals when interviewed about their feelings related to poor service indicated that they feel awful but had hardly any choices. "Seller is the king as opposed to customer is the king," felt one of our participant-observers. The same participant-observer narrated how consumers are told "go away" and "don't bother me" by the service providers and consumers have to simply live with it.

One of the participant-observers was amused to discover a business motive which he said "contradicts all standard management practices." This motive is to "make losses." When this participant called a hotel for a room, he was told that there was no vacancy, whereas in reality 300 or more rooms were vacant. The hotel manager and staff were deliberately trying to make losses so that they could purchase the stock from the government at low prices. This kind of approach obviously deteriorates service quality in the state-run service businesses.

The Bulgarian consumers seems to be quite frustrated with the quality of service in these state controlled businesses and according to one of the participant-observers, it is creating a "deep-seated fatalism" about service quality in these state-run businesses.

On the other hand, things seem quite different in the private sector. Although there is very little privatization, the outlook on service quality there seems much better. Moreover, consumers seems to be optimistic about privatization and feel that it is the only way their role as consumers would be recognized.

In summary then, most bad service experiences seem to be coming from state-run, large businesses and consumers are quite pessimistic about what they can do as consumers. On the other hand, the limited number of good service experiences seem to be coming from private, small businesses and here consumers feel quite optimistic about their role as consumers.

Impact of Pessimism/Optimism on Relationship Between Type of Attributions and Complaining/Complimenting Behavior of Bulgarian Consumers and Their Comparison with American Consumers:

Bulgarian consumers' pessimism/optimism about their role as consumers is likely to affect the relationship between the type of attributions they make and their complaining/complimenting behavior. When consumers feel pessimistic (as in the case of a bad experience) about their role as consumers, they are likely to feel that there is no point in complaining because that is not going to make any difference to these state-run businesses. Thus their feelings of whose fault it was (internal versus external attributions), whether the bad experience was controllable by them or not (controllable versus uncontrollable attributions) and whether the bad experience will happen again (stable versus unstable attributions) are not likely to be related to their complaining behavior. On the other hand for American consumers, as discussed earlier, the externality and the stability of attributions would be positively related to complaining, whereas the controllability of attributions would be negatively related. Thus the propositions:

P3A: Externality of attributions for most dissatisfying or extremely negative service experiences would be positively related with complaining behavior for American consumers. For Bulgarian consumers, these would not be related.

P3B: Stability of attributions for most dissatisfying or extremely negative service experiences would be positively related with complaining behavior for American consumers. For Bulgarian consumers, these would not be related.

P3C: Controllability of attributions for most dissatisfying or extremely negative service experiences would be negatively related with complaining behavior for American consumers. For Bulgarian consumers, these would not be related.

However, for most satisfying or extremely positive experiences, the Bulgarian consumers are likely to have a more optimistic disposition. They are likely to feel that expressing compliments is likely to make a difference to these private-run businesses. Thus the complimenting behavior of Bulgarian consumers will be similar to that of American consumers, i.e., the externality and the stability of attributions would be positively related with complimenting behavior, whereas the controllability of attributions would be negatively related. Thus the propositions:

P4A: Externality of attributions for most satisfying or extremely positive service experiences would be positively related with complimenting behavior for both American and Bulgarian consumers.

P4B: Stability of attributions for most satisfying or extremely positive service experiences would be positively related with complimenting behavior for both American and Bulgarian consumers.

P4C: Controllability of attributions for most satisfying or extremely positive service experiences would be negatively related with complimenting behavior for both American and Bulgarian consumers.

REFERENCES

Curren, Mary T. and Valerie S. Folkes (1987), "Attributional Influences on Consumer's Desire to Communicate About Products," *Psychology & Marketing*, 4, 31-45.

Folkes, Valerie S. (1984), "Consumer Reactions to Product Failure: An Attributional Approach," *Journal of Consumer Research*, 10 (March), 398-409.

Grunert, Klaus G., Susanne C. Grunert and Sharon E. Beatty (1989), "Cross-Cultural Research on Consumer Values," *Marketing and Research Today*, February, 30-39.

Guthe, C. E. and Margaret Mead (1945), "Manual for the Study of Food Habits," Report of the Committee on Food Habits (National Academy of Science, Washington, D.C.).

Hamilton, V. L. (1980), "Intuitive Psychologist or Intuitive Lawyer," *Journal of Personality and Social Psychology*, 39, 767-772.

Krishnan, S. and Valerie A. Valle (1979), "Dissatisfaction Attributions and Consumer Complaint Behavior," in *Advances in Consumer Research*, Vol. 6, ed. William L. Wilkie, Ann Arbor, MI: Association for Consumer Research, 445-449.

Lee, James A. (1966), "Cultural Analysis in Overseas Operations," *Harvard Business Review*, 44 (March-April), 106.

Levitt, Theodore (1983), "The Globalization of Markets," *Harvard Business Review*, 83 (May-June), 92-102.

Richins, Marcia L. (1987), "A Multivariate Analysis of Response to Dissatisfaction," *Journal of the Academy of Marketing Science*, 15 (Fall), 24-31.

Valle, Valerie A. and Melanie Wallendorf (1977), "Consumers' Attributions of the Cause of their Product Satisfaction and Dissatisfaction," *Consumer Satisfaction, Dissatisfaction and Complaining Behavior*, ed. Ralph L. Day, Bloomington, IN: Indiana University School of Business.

Weiner, Bernard (1980), *Human Motivation*, New York: Holt, Rinehart & Winston.

_____ (1985), "An Attributional Theory of Achievement Motivation and Emotion," *Psychological Review*, 92 (October), 548-573.

_____ (1986), *An Attributional Theory of Motivation and Emotion*, New York: Springer-Verlag.

The Development of Consumer Desire in Marketizing and Developing Economies: The Cases of Romania and Turkey

Güliz Ger, Bilkent University
Russell W. Belk, University of Utah
Dana-Nicoleta Lascu, University of Richmond

ABSTRACT

Developing and marketizing economies in Romania and Turkey are examined in the present research in an effort to understand how consumption desires change with the rapid influx of consumer goods and services into economies of scarcity. Based on observations, interviews, and questionnaires tapping a range of consumers in both countries, we found and describe rapidly escalating consumer desires, confusions, and frustrations. A case study of cigarette consumption in Romania illustrates these developments and the unique image of Western products before and after Communism.

To contemporary Western consumers immersed in a world of excessive goods, excessive advertising, and excessive consumption it is difficult to imagine modern worlds in which scarcity, shortages, long lines, and lack of choice prevail. Yet such worlds are the dominant life experience for nearly all Romanians as they were for most Turks until recently as well. Romanians, along with other Eastern Europeans, and Turks a decade earlier, have also recently seen dramatic and sudden explosions in range and depth of available consumer goods and services. What happens to consumer desires nurtured under conditions of scarcity when this situation suddenly changes as it has with the political and economic revolutions of 1989? Slavenka Drakulić (1991) describes her experience as a recent immigrant from Yugoslavia on encountering New York's Bloomingdale's:

> I recognize...the feeling that it is just absurd to look at so many things and so many kinds of one thing, as if one is enclosed in a room with mirrored walls that endlessly reflect each other. It has to stop somewhere — you think — this multiplying, this plentitude doesn't make any sense. Coming from the world of shortages, one's idea of plenty is mainly of fruit, meat, vegetables, or shampoo, soap, or toilet paper. Here, you are murdered by variations on each of these and by the impossibility of distinguishing the differences. First you discover an immense greed, a kind of fever, a wish to buy everything — the primordial hunger of consumerism. Then you discover powerlessness — and the very essence of it, poverty. Moreover, you start to realize that Bloomingdale's for you is a museum, not a real store where you can buy real things for your real self (p. 121).

Several conflicting reactions are evident in Drakulić's account: confusion, desire, and, due to relative poverty, ultimate despair and feelings of impotence. The present study uses recent Romanian experiences to better understand this range of reactions.

Because Turkey has gone through a somewhat similar shift from scarcity to market abundance a decade earlier than Romania, the experience of Turkish consumers offers a longer term perspective on what may possibly be ahead for Eastern European consumers and perhaps too for consumers in the less economically developed world (Belk 1988). Although their cultures, religion, recent political histories, and levels of education are different, Romanian and Turkish societies have a shared history — Ottoman — and frequent current business relations. Many Romanians are now coming to Turkey for shopping or business transactions (including "suitcase trade"), and Turks are setting up businesses in Romania. In both countries there is rampant inflation which fuels consumption, or at least seems to rationalize it since currency will buy less tomorrow.

The authors are, respectively, a Turk who once spent 9 years in the United States and has recently supervised two Romanian graduate students researching Romanian consumption, an American who spent 1991-92 teaching and doing research in Romania, and a former Romanian who immigrated to the United States in 1982 and recently returned to conduct research in Romania. The present research is based on participant observation, focus groups, and several questionnaires administered in these two countries with both students and nonstudents (in several areas of each country), and depth interviews conducted in Romania. The Romanian data came from 110 survey respondents, 73 depth interviews (including 6 key informants), and 26 focus group participants. Depth interviews were conducted primarily in restaurants, coffee shops, and informants' homes, and focus groups as well as depth interviews were conducted in both urban and rural settings. The Turkish data included 357 student survey respondents from four cities and 24 focus group participants. Group discussions focused on consumer desires, attitudes toward having and spending money, and views of various consumer lifestyles. The several questionnaires focused on consumption aspirations, categorization of various products as necessities or luxuries, consumption experiences, and (not reported here) measures of materialism. And the depth interviews included these topics as well as a focus on cigarette brands among 23 of the informants in Bucharest.

BRIEF BACKGROUND

Romania spent almost 45 years under Communism before its short but bloody revolution during the 1989 Christmas season. A program of industrialization raised Romania's per capita GNP to 37th in the world by 1977 (Nelson 1990), but corruption, shoddy goods, mismanagement, and a large national debt precipitated a sharp economic downturn starting about this time. Markedly exacerbating these deteriorating economic conditions was Romanian leader Nicolae Ceausescu's drive to erase the national debt by exporting all possible industrial and consumer goods. This was in fact achieved just before the revolution, but at the expense of the Romanian people who suffered through severe shortages of such staples as food, clothing, fuel, heat, water, and electricity, with severe rationing of such goods as flour, sugar, meat, bread, and gasoline. Long lines for bread, milk, and gasoline were the rule and ubiquitous state apartments were heated and lighted at cave-like levels. Heat and water for the now predominantly urban Romanians were provided part of the day and hot water might be available a few hours per week. Although prices were controlled and inflation was virtually non-existent, the lack of goods in stores made their prices largely irrelevant. Under these conditions of shortages, clerks used their access to scarce goods to command "under the hand" extra payments from consumers who wanted such items as shoes, a good hair cut, or medical care. Shopping became a matter of connections, hours in lines, and constant vigilance to find goods that might unexpectedly turn up in stores and markets. Televisions and automobiles were luxury purchases available to the elite, and were restricted to outdated Romanian models that depended upon a few hours of daily state television programming and rationed gasoline.

Although the Ceausescu years were years of extreme political scrutiny involving close monitoring by the secret police force (securitate), it does not exaggerate to say that the revolution in Romania was based more on economic rather than political frustration. Occasional glimpses of Western consumption through travel by the privileged few, a black market in expensive foreign goods, occasional Western television and films (the series "Dallas" was shown with the intent of portraying the decadence of capitalism), and broadcasts from Radio Free Europe, the British Broadcasting Corporation, and the Voice of America, helped foster dissatisfaction (Bar-Haïm 1987). Western goods represented not only quality, abundance, and freedom, but modernity, status, and the good life. Since the revolution, many of these desired consumer goods have become available in Romania, but the income to buy them has not, with most Romanian incomes averaging $20-$40 (U.S.) per month. It is impossible to have a true consumption revolution without an accompanying economic revolution and the latter has hardly begun. Furthermore, inflation and unemployment, are now becoming rampant, even though still more contained than elsewhere in the former Communist Economic Community.

Although Turkey has always been an anti-communist country, it shares with Romania (and other Eastern European countries) the tradition of statism and isolation (even though the state control and political scrutiny were never as extreme as in Romania). Following the Ottoman Empire, Turkey had a protected economy and a closed sociocultural environment. A single-party regime reigned until 1950, followed by a multiple-party "democracy" with 3 military interruptions in 1960, 1972 and 1980, which preceded the current more open political environment. The late 1970's were characterized by economic downturn, social and political unrest, shortages, and long lines — very similar to the conditions in Romania. Since 1983, Turkey has been going through a transition from state controlled capitalism to privatized and liberalized market economy, and is increasingly opening itself to the world socioculturally as well as economically.

Turkey is one of the more developed of the developing countries. For instance, electricity reaches 99% of the homes, but only 77% have plumbing, and 8% have hot water (Yaşadiğimiz Dünya 1992). Turkey's currently high economic growth rate, mostly driven by exports, is accompanied by very high inflation, unemployment, and high levels of imports, along with a budget deficit, very unequal income distribution, huge differences between urban and rural life (60% are urban, but there is also a new, recently-urban class of the impoverished/poor), high population growth, and relatively low levels of education and health. Its world rank in quality of life (54th based on education and health) is lower than its rank with respect to economic indicators, such as GNP/capita (43rd), GNP/capita growth (33rd), and industry as % of GDP (19th) (Austin 1990). Production (often involving licensing and assembly, and more recently joint ventures and foreign investment) and importing have created an abundance of foreign and domestic brands and products. Luxury imported cars, car phones, Rolex watches, electronics, brand name clothing and athletic shoes, as well as exotic fruits, candy bars and soft drinks are widely available for those who can afford them.

Consumption has increased accordingly. Eighty-three percent of the households have refrigerators, 78% have radios, 40% have color Tvs, and 13% have cars (Yaşadiğimiz Dünya 1992). Although the product availability and consumption have increased tremendously, it is primarily for the privileged consumer (Ger 1992). Overall private consumption expenditures are still much lower than in the West and in the 22 industrialized economies among which Turkey is placed (World Economic Forum 1992).

RESULTS

Consumer Desires in Post-Revolution Romania

The consumer desire that helped precipitate the Romanian revolution showed first in a frenzy of buying. For instance oranges, unavailable in the markets for years, were liberated from the supplies intended for the nomenclatura and securitate (see Codrescu 1991). In the year following the revolution there was a rash of automobile buying. In our survey of student material desires in 1991, an automobile was the number one choice. The film "E.T." was shown on Romanian television during the revolution and there are now two hours a day of music video from Europe's Skychannel. Foreign stereos and televisions are also high on student wish lists, and in each of 22 Romanian homes visited, whether factory managers or peasants, the home had a television (often color) as a prominent possession. They are inevitably displayed in the main living/dining/bedroom and are proudly played throughout visits and dinners. Status-seeking is also evident on a smaller scale, as when foreign sunglasses are worn with the brand labels still prominently attached. Any t-shirt with foreign, especially English, brand names on it is a status symbol as well. Still, this abundance has not brought instant bliss to Romanians. One 20-year-old woman reflected on her current material lifestyle versus that of her parents, this way:

> In terms of consumption, I think I have a larger field of consumption. I have more, but I want more now. I think I have a better life, compared to my parents....I say also that my life is more complicated, stressed. It is an informational explosion I feel. And that is good; perhaps I cannot live without [these things], but this, more and more, stresses me often.

While this young woman is already overwhelmed by the choices she now has, to Americans used to overwhelming abundance, the stores of Romania are still bare and bleak. If stress and confusion are evident now, they are not likely to soon dissipate.

After an automobile, the most desired good for younger Romanians is fashionable clothes or shoes. Also very important are electronic goods and an apartment or house. Supply of dwellings has decreased since the revolution as the state building system came to a virtual halt and no general contractors existed to take its place. The cost of an apartment has skyrocketed and waiting lists are impossibly long, even for those with the money. This is the case with many other goods as well. As a focus group participant who lives in a small village summarized the current situation:

> Before we had nothing to buy from shops. Everywhere you could find the same products (if any was available in the market). Now there are so many goods there, but no money to buy them.

Another villager added, "I feel worse than before when I see so many things but there is no money to buy them." Not only do Romanians now feel their relative poverty in the world more clearly, there is a new class structure emerging in which money and goods rather than position in the Communist party are determinants. Competitive consumption is evident in one comment that "I would feel that I was the shame of the village if I wouldn't be able to keep up with the others." The more conspicuous consumers are objects of both admiration and envious hatred. They are seen as "obsessed" or taken with "consumption fever." This, plus the unaffordability of some formerly affordable goods like housing, cause many Romanians to lament that they were better off before the revolution.

Status goods are nearly inevitably foreign. This was true before the revolution, but then scarcity made such goods very hard to acquire. Now it is more a matter of their greater cost, plus their continued association with foreign lifestyles, that imparts status to their owners. Kohák (1992) notes a similar situation elsewhere in the former Soviet bloc:

> The unfortunate truth is that as the former subjects of the Soviet empire dream it, the American dream has very little to do with liberty and justice for all and a great deal to do with soap operas and the Sears catalogue. The Americans of Czech popular imagination are people who never have to deny themselves anything, who can charge anything that strikes their fancy to their credit cards without ever worrying how they will pay for it. They live in an enchanted land free of all mundane cares, a land where wishing makes it so. Most of all, they live in a land which is totally dedicated to the unlimited expansion of individual material affluence. That is approximately what most Czechs unthinkingly assume the dream of freedom to be, seldom pausing to reflect that it is a dream made up mostly of irresponsibility, unreality, and instantly gratified greed (p. 209).

Beginning at least with the "kitchen debates" between Kruschev and Nixon in the 1950s, in which the two argued about which nation had the highest consumer standard of living, it was implicit or explicit U.S. policy to try to bring down communism with images of abundance and luxurious consumption in the West. But the images that many Romanians have of U.S. lifestyles suggest that they have been seduced by a fantasy.

Nevertheless, this fantasy is so vivid and so alluring that what U.S. (as well as European and Japanese) marketers are now selling in Romania is not the product as much as the symbol of a better life. Drakulić (1991) notes that in Poland, Coke is more of a symbol than a beverage. Even though Poland produces a great deal of fruit, there are no fruit juice, while Coca Cola is everywhere. Romanians find it disgraceful and bewildering that Coke and Pepsi are deluging the market with competitive advertising, but they are quick to adapt these products as symbols of the good life. While it may foster economic imperialism, having a conspicuously consuming country of origin is the key to success for many products. Television cigarette advertising of such "American" brands as "Hollywood," "Cowboy," and "American" cigarettes employs English voiceovers and American rock music just to be certain that their supposed origin is not lost upon the audience. While imported cigarettes cost only half of what they would cost in the U.S., a Romanian of average income would have to spend it all on these cigarettes in order to buy a pack a day. With this in mind, we turn to a case study of cigarette consumption.

Kent Cigarettes in Romania

During the communist regime, Kent constituted not only the cigarette of choice for gift giving and consumption (when they could be afforded), but also the most secure and legal financial vehicle. Kent cigarettes — described by economists as commodity money — were (unlike official currency) not subject to devaluation, and (unlike hard currency) did not carry the risk of illegality (Thurow 1986). Since the revolution, competing brands have rapidly made their way to the marketplace. Cigarette ads for American and French cigarettes are now ubiquitous in shop windows, on billboards, and on television screens. American, French, and Greek imports are available at every street kiosk, in bars, restaurants, and shops. Nevertheless, Kents remain the cigarette of choice. Of 23 informants in the present case study (13 males and 10 females, ages 22 to 68), 17 indicated either that they were likely to purchase Kent cigarettes for gift giving, or that Kent was among the cigarettes considered for this purpose. In a related survey, 14 out of 46 student respondents indicated that in their opinions Kent would be the cigarette of choice for a high-status person. While during the communist regime, if you flashed a pack of Kent, you could avoid standing in line or you could buy a taxi ride, fine cuts of meat, and other hard-to-obtain products and services (Thurow 1986), nowadays Kent cigarettes still come in handy if you want preferential treatment or if you want to give someone a useful gift — perhaps to facilitate transactions and obtain favors.

The depth interviews exploring the Romanian consumer's continued preference for the Kent brand, despite the widespread availability of alternative brands, revealed that Kent's dominance in the Romanian cigarette market for two decades has created strong brand loyalty. Consumers perceive Kent to be a desirable brand with good taste, superior quality, and a positive image:

> ...I grew up with this (Kent) brand being seen as the best brand of cigarettes, so I smoked it too and got used to it. Now that it is available, I spoil myself with it.

Kent ads portraying successful chic young professionals are aired on television in the middle of the "Dallas" television series — a celebration of opulence, wealth, and greed, and a program rich in consumption imagery (c.f. Hirschman 1988, p. 345). The image created is very appealing to Romanian consumers' desires to identify with Americans and to project affluence through their consumption:

> ...I don't think that all Romanians like this (Kent) cigarette. Only the simple ones do, because they think that this is what Americans smoke.

> ...the French (cigarettes) are too strong, the English too expensive, and the others are not as good (as Kent). [How about Camels, Marlboros...?] They taste differently. Plus...I could get Camels, but that is not an elegant cigarette. And Marlboro, why would I want to smoke...the cigarette of the American peasant, the cowboy?

Romanians do not want to associate with peasants — a low status group, from whom many are only a generation or two removed.

Visitors to Romania are frequently advised to give Kent cigarettes to their hosts or acquaintances. Although many other products — liquor, perfume, and other cigarette brands — are appreciated and readily available in shops, Kents continue to have appeal:

> ...(Kent) is the cigarette that everyone got used to and likes. I have given Kents as gifts because I know they will be happily received. You always give Kent cigarettes to others. If they don't smoke, they give it away.

Despite Kent's popularity, however, the market for cigarettes is becoming increasingly segmented. Some are beginning to perceive it as a cigarette that appeals to the masses; those with more refined tastes are thought more likely to prefer the more expensive British and French brands.

...if it is a good friend or an important person who appreciates that I have spent a lot for a pack of cigarettes for him, I buy Rothmans and Dunnhills. If it is a peasant, I buy him Kent. All peasants know about Kent.

...(I give as bribes/gifts) Kent, Cartier — Kent for males and females, and Cartier for females....Because everybody likes Kent....Cartier is more sophisticated. A woman will appreciate it more than a man.

But despite the increased availability of competing brands and the fact that other brands (e.g., Marlboro) are preferred in neighboring Eastern European countries, Kent continues to reign in Romania's cigarette market. Kent is the preferred cigarette for gift giving and as a "luxury smoke" for a notable proportion of Romania's smoking population. Kent is so ingrained in Romanian tradition that popular jokes refer to it (Banc and Dundes 1986). Is Kent's reign guaranteed for the future? Being the first (and still the dominant) foreign brand in the market, it probably will still retain numerous loyal consumers. But slippage seems inevitable as exposure to a multitude of competing brands increases, and as Romanians step into a world of many differentiated symbols of the good life, rather than one or a few, and learn more subtleties of brand images:

(Kents were the only cigarettes) you used to be able to get on the black market. Now we have everything, and it depends on the purpose of the gift, if it is for influence, if it is for a friend, it depends what kind of cigarettes you buy.

The Development of Consumer Desire in Turkey

The wide availability of a variety of products, more and more attractively displayed in shops crowding the streets of Turkish cities, stimulate consumer desires. Magazines have a section devoted to new products in the West and in Turkey. Television (with 8 Turkish channels — up from one in 1985, and many European channels and CNN on cable), provides a tempting exhibit of a wide range of products appearing in the numerous American programs such as "Dallas" (late 1970's), "The Bold and the Beautiful", game shows ("Wheel of Fortune" is the current frenzy), European music videos, and similar domestic programs. Furthermore, tourists in greater numbers than ever, and "guest" workers in Germany who make return visits to their villages, become role models for consumption. Also there is a new class of nouveau riche who show off their possessions and add to the success, status and power symbolism of consumption, and hence, to its desirability. This abruptly appearing showcase exacerbates the desire for consumption and the interest in brands. Cars, in particular, are a craze; even adolescents know all the makes and recognize new models. The percent of Turks who consider a car to be necessary is found to be greater than the percent who see hot running water as a necessity. A car was, by far, the first choice of the Turkish students surveyed about material desires. Their wish lists include stereos, VCRs, CD players, dwellings, clothes/shoes, home computers, sports gear, travel and entertainment, books, and even a summer house, plane, and a boat. Interest in consumption is obvious not only in wants but also in the prominent display of, and talk about, products — especially the status brands. "People even use the shopping bags of prestigious stores to carry things to the beach or to carry things they buy from other stores." "Not buying brands implies you are a 'kro' (of rural background)", which, as in Romania, is negative. Yet, continuously buying and flashing brands, and new products are also considered 'kro' and unrefined by some.

Consumption of foreign products is highly desirable to Turks. The synonymy of progress with ever-present Westernization whets the appetite for the now-available foreign products. A detergent brand advertises that it is the one most preferred by European housewives. Status brands are mostly foreign, although a few elite Turkish brands qualify. Furthermore, the perceived low quality of the Turkish products (versus the objectively high quality of some of them), adds to this tendency, or justifies it. For example, Levi's (which, interestingly are made in Turkey, although this fact is kept quiet) are preferred over local brands. They reign due to their image — being a symbol of modern Western lifestyle and being "in". A young female student admits that "I don't even think of other brands, not even Lee's. I don't know why, may be because all my friends wear Levi's".

In a society where interpersonal relations are of prime importance, status-seeking leads to a contagion of buying certain things that are "in" with respect to status or a certain lifestyle. Two years after one man bought a plane, three of his friends also had planes. A businessman said: "In one day I applied to several banks to get credit cards from each, then bought a car phone and a remote control key for my car. When I came back to my office I asked myself why I did it. I think because everybody had these things and if I did not it would have been a prestige loss." The urbanites imitate what they perceive to be Western patterns of consumption. In turn, the rural and the newly urban inhabitants imitate the urbanites. "When my relatives [three families] moved from their village to Istanbul, they each bought a house in same neighborhood and furnished it very similarly, imitating what we had." Our survey results indicate that the only differences between the wants of small versus large city inhabitants are the absence of sports gear and travel in the lists of small city inhabitants who instead want appliances and money.

The novelty of abundance and of products fuel these consumer desires. The feeling is: "There are new products everyday. Newer products are better. So, I want new products, but lose interest after purchase." Some of this interest may wear off as the novelty wears off: McDonalds and Pizza Huts are not as crowded any more. "My parents and their neighbors used to talk about who in the building has what brand of appliance. No longer."

Since abundance is a recent phenomenon, consumers are not experienced in facing alternatives, searching for products and information about products (if it exists), or evaluating alternatives. While some take delight in the newly found opportunity to choose ("I enjoy making a decision while buying something, anything."), many count on friends' choices and brands to guide their selection: "I rely on prestige brands to avoid making a mistake and save searching time. They are a safe bet when I don't want to or cannot make a choice." Furthermore, the evolution of the cigarette demand suggests that as consumers acquire experience, brands or some magically favorite products may lose some of their initial importance. Cigarettes, as in Romania, were among the first foreign brands in the market. Interestingly, Kent was also the first foreign cigarette in Turkey. Later, Marlboro became an obsession. Even people who could not really afford them bought Marlboros. Eventually, choices became varied as other foreign brands entered the market. Recently, there is a switch back to some brands of Turkish cigarettes, partially due to their improved quality, better marketing, more attractive packaging, and lower prices, but also because consumers are learning to choose more knowledgeably.

But, the desire for consumption in this context of the sudden exposure, creates some problems. Confusion about priorities may emerge (Ger and Belk 1990) when the poorer consumers have to make major compromises. A mechanic or an office boy smokes (at least formerly) Marlboros, wears brand name jeans, and buys a VCR, but may not have adequate nutrition. Confusion, in a less drastic sense, also emerges in the absence of knowing how to judge quality, to acquire product information, and to assess alternatives:

"I feel I am being ripped off by the perfumeries, but I cannot risk buying a fake in small stores." Dissatisfaction occurs when products don't perform. For instance, people who don't want to pay the prevalent high prices venture into the spot markets that have been popping up in open-air marketplaces (where food used to be sold). Anything from Russian caviar, t-shirts, and gadgets, to electronics, (and sometimes even cars) are sold in these marketplaces. Although the products are cheaper there, there is no guarantee whether something is in working condition. Dissatisfaction also occurs when purchased products are not utilized. For example, "I regret having bought the VCR which we were 'forced' to buy because all our friends had one, but which we never use." As experience with consumption builds up, some of these confusions and dissatisfactions may dissipate. But, consumers also feel angry, frustrated, or at best helpless, when they cannot buy; and that is the case for the majority. Unless consumption is more democratized and accompanied by consumer education, confusion, dissatisfaction, frustration and anger will prevail.

CONCLUSIONS

While both Romanians and Turks have high consumption desires, there are differences in how these desires arise and in the objects on which they focus. Both national groups have wish lists that include a car, fashionable clothes and shoes, electronics, dwelling, a home computer, books and sports gear. These desires suggest common Western influences in the global village. But Romanians also want basics such as food, water, cigarettes, furniture, appliances, and grooming products. Greater deprivation and scarcity shape these desires. Turks, a notch up in affluence, want more luxurious products.

The present findings also detect common difficulties that arise from too sudden an influx of products and promotions: sudden exposure to global communications, dramatic increases in foreign products (as well as domestic goods in Turkey), abrupt opening up of society following the "defeat" of communism or statism. Such marked disruptions create lowered confidence and esteem. People in these countries feel they have missed out on something and they yearn to catch up quickly. They feel excluded from the world and want to belong. The way to close this gap is to consume as (they perceive) the more modern world does. Both the Romanians and the Turks feel they are not getting what they should and that they deserve more. They cannot rely on previous experience in the face of sudden change and have no better way of knowing what to do than to imitate the "successful" Westerners. And so they imitate what is most obvious: the things that diffuse most readily across cultures are consumption artifacts (Ger and Belk 1990; Mehta and Belk 1991).

This emulation seems to occur differently in the two countries. Driven by scarcity Romanians have a more simplistic and unrealistic view of the Western world and want everything — whatever is available. Romanians are not very discriminating in what they want and consider to be necessary — they want it all according to our survey results. Having no experience in making brand choices, they have difficulty and rely on gross brand stereotypes. Turks are starting to discriminate and evaluate choices. Prestige goods are still significant, but there is greater subtlety and more nuanced choice. These differences suggest that the development of consumer desires and the parallel emulation of the West, based on the interpretation of the images of the West symbolizing the good life, may be occurring in phases, with Romania showing only the early first stage.

While confusion and the feeling of being overwhelmed by choice may well dissipate in moving from Romania's fledgling free market in consumer goods toward Turkey's more open consumer market, feelings of frustration may not. Former social status, interpersonal connections, party position, and shrewdness matter less. Money matters more. And money is increasingly unevenly distributed in both countries. Being a have-not country in a world of apparent have countries is one thing, but going from being poor among a nation of poor to being poor in a nation with increasingly conspicuous wealthy may be quite another.

The similarities and differences in consumer desires, confusions, and frustrations, interpreted in the context of the common and unique characteristics of the two countries suggest some factors which influence the development of such desires. The consumption frenzy in the two countries seems to be manifesting itself differently, at least partially due to the recency and abruptness of the marketization and change from the previous scarcity and lack of choice in all aspects of life. The commonalities in, and phase-like appearance of the desires, despite religious, sociocultural, and political differences, point to the importance of the impact of the factors of abrupt change, relative deprivation, and globalization or Western influence. Marked disruptions in economic, political, and socio-cultural environment, relative deprivation, and global/Western commercial influences appear to be some of the factors that foster the development of consumption desires. However, many behavior patterns may remain local, and not everything will change or change in a standardized way, due to the culturally specific processes in each country. For instance, the branding, packaging, and location (home vs. restaurant) of meals may change, but the content of these meals in each country have remained much more unique and traditional than the cigarette, clothing, electronics, automobile, music, and media consumption of consumers in Romania and Turkey. It will be some time, if ever, before global consumption patterns obliterate such local differences.

REFERENCES

Austin E. James (1990) *Managing in Developing Countries: Strategic Analysis and Operating Techniques*, New York: The Free Press.

Banc, C. and Alan Dundes (1986), *First Prize: Fifteen Years!: An Annotated Collection of Romanian Political Jokes*, Cranbury, NJ: Associated University Presses.

Bar-Haïm, Gabriel (1987), "The Meaning of Western Commercial Artifacts for Eastern European Youth," *Journal of Contemporary Ethnography*, 16 (July), 205-226.

Belk, Russell W. (1988), "Third World Consumer Culture," *Marketing and Development: Toward Broader Dimensions*, A. Fuat Firat and Erdogan Kumcu, eds., Greenwich, CT: JAI Press, 103-127.

Codrescu, Andrei (1991), *The Hole in the Flag: A Romanian Exile's Story of Return and Revolution*, New York: William Morrow.

Drakulić, Slavenka (1991), *How We Survived Communism and Even Laughed*, New York: W. W. Norton.

Ger, Güliz (1992), "The Positive and Negative Effects of Marketing on Socioeconomic Development: The Turkish Case," *Journal of Consumer Policy*, 15, 229-254.

Ger, Güliz and Russell W. Belk (1990), "Measuring and Comparing Materialism Cross-Culturally," *Advances in Consumer Research*, Volume 17, Gerald Gorn, Marvin Goldberg and Richard Pollay, eds., Provo: Association for Consumer Research, 186-192.

Hirschman, Elizabeth C. (1988), "The Ideology of Consumption: A Structural-Syntactical Analysis of 'Dallas' and 'Dynasty,'," *Journal of Consumer Research*, 15 (December), 344-359.

Kohák, Erazim (1992), "Ashes, Ashes...Central Europe After Forty Years," *Daedalus*, 121 (Spring), 197-215.

Mehta, Raj and Russell W. Belk (1991), "Artifacts, Identity, and Transition: Favorite Possessions of Indians and Indian Immigrants to the United States," *Journal of Consumer Research*, 17 (March), 398-411.

Nelson, Daniel N. (1990), "The Romanian Disaster," *Research on the Soviet Union and Eastern Europe*, 1, Anthony Jones, ed., Greenwich, CT: JAI Press, 83-111.

Thurow, Roger (1986), "In Romania, Smoking a Kent Cigarette is Like Burning Money," *Wall Street Journal*, January 3.

World Economic Forum (1992), *The World Competitiveness Report 1992*.

Yaşadiğimiz Dünya (1992), *Ekonomik ve Jeopolitik Yillik* (The World We Live In 1992: Annual of Economy and Geopolitics), Istanbul: Metis Yayinlari.

"Yes, I remember it well...":
The Role of Autobiographical Memory in Consumer Information Processing

Geeta Menon, New York University
Gita Johar, Columbia University

Autobiographical memory can be defined in general terms as memory for personal experiences. The focus of interest of psychologists in this area has been on the manner in which personal and social experiences are stored in memory and later retrieved. While some researchers used themselves as subjects in an attempt to study memory for everyday events (e.g., Linton 1875, 1978, 1982; Wagenaar 1986; White 1982), other researchers had subjects maintain records of their behavior at random time intervals, and then later retrieve information about these behaviors (e.g., Brewer 1986, 1988).

This session had two broad objectives. First, most of the work on autobiographical memory has been outside the area of consumer behavior and marketing. However, this research has far-reaching implications for how consumers store product information in memory, how they retrieve information to process subsequent information to formulate judgments, and how they behave in future interactions with the product and to its advertising. Therefore, we hoped to stimulate consumer researchers' interest in this area. Second, the session investigated the similarities and differences between memory for product experiences and memory for other kinds of personal experiences within the realm of autobiographical memory.

We had two papers in this session. In the first paper, Mita Sujan, Hans Baumgartner and James Bettman extend their research published in the first issue of the *Journal of Consumer Psychology* (Baumgartner, Sujan and Bettman, 1992). In a series of two studies they demonstrate that in the product domain, increasing the accessibility of autobiographical memory leads to higher levels of emotion. In addition, brand evaluations do not differ as a function of the strength of the argument in the ad when such autobiographical memory is evoked, suggesting a reduced analysis of product information. However, the extent to which this affect is transferred over to the product judgment depends upon the extent to which the personal memory is linked to the brand in the ad.

In the second paper, Gita Johar and Geeta Menon find that unlike autobiographical memory for personal or social experiences, positive product experiences are not always more salient than negative product experiences. They then demonstrate that an evoked autobiographical memory (i.e., actual experiences) could impact brand judgments and ad processing in a different manner compared to other types of memory such as reported memory (i.e., information acquired through word-of-mouth or media).

Julie Edell was the discussant for this session. She brought her expertise in the area of affect, advertising and information processing to the area of autobiographical memory. She talked about how the degree of affect associated with an autobiographical memory could be dependent upon the specificity of the memory evoked (e.g., personal memory vs. autobiographical facts vs. generic personal memory as per Brewer's 1986 classification). This is affected by the kind of retrieval cue use: for example, Sujan et al. used a general cue as opposed to the specific one used by Johar and Menon. She also proposed that future research examine the strength of affect associated with autobiographical memory and the valence of this affect, context effects created by evoking autobiographical memory, and how the incongruity between encountered information and that retrieved from memory could be resolved. An important link was also established during audience discussion between autobiographical memory and the self-referent encoding literature (e.g. Klein and Kihlstrom 1986).

We believe that this research stream should be of interest to three groups of people: (a) academic researchers interested in the theoretical areas of memory and affect; (b) researchers in the area of product satisfaction/dissatisfaction; and, (c) advertisers who could apply the findings of the studies presented in deciding the kind of information and cues to be included in advertising.

REFERENCES

Baumgartner, Hans, Mita Sujan and James R. Bettman (1992), "Autobiographical Memories, Affect, and Consumer Information Processing", *Journal of Consumer Psychology*, 1/1, 53-82.

Brewer, William F. (1986), "What is Autobiographical Memory?", in *Autobiographical Memory*, ed., Rubin, David C., New York, NY: Cambridge University Press, 25-49.

_____ (1988), "Memory for Randomly Samples Autobiographical Events", in *Remembering Reconsidered: Ecological and Traditional Approaches to the Study of Memory*, eds., Neisser, Ulric and Eugene Winograd, New York, NY: Cambridge University Press, 21-90.

Linton, Marigold (1975), "Memory for Real-World Events," in *Explorations in Cognition*, eds., Donald A. Norman and David E. Rumelhart, San Francisco, CA: W. H. Freeman and Company, 366-404.

_____ (1978), "Real World Memory After Six Years: An In Vivo Study of Very Long Term Memory," in *Practical Aspects of Memory*, eds., Michael M. Gruneberg, Peter E. Morris and Robert N. Sykes, New York, NY: Academic Press, 77-83.

_____ (1982), "Transformations of Memory in Everyday Life," in *Memory Observed: Remembering in Natural Contexts*, ed., Ulric Neisser, San Francisco, CA: W. H. Freeman and Company, 77-92.

Klein, Stanley B. and John F. Kihlstrom (1986), "Elaboration, Organization, and the Self-Reference Effect in Memory", *Journal of Experimental Psychology: General*, 115/1, 26-38.

Wagenaar, Willem A. (1986), "My Memory: A Study of Autobiographical Memory over Six Years", *Cognitive Psychology*, 18, 225-252.

White, Richard T. (1982), "Memory for Personal Events", *Human Learning*, 1, 171-183.

Unethical Seller Practices: A Neglected Issue in Consumer Satisfaction and Dissatisfaction Research

Alan R. Andreasen, University of Connecticut

ABSTRACT

The research literature on dissatisfaction and complaining behavior has largely ignored instances of unethical behavior on the part of marketers. Three biases have led to this outcome. Research has focused on outcomes rather than processes. It has largely ignored possible ethical problems in interactions with sellers after purchase. And, economic costs have been emphasized over emotional and psychological costs. Policing systems do not appear likely to correct unethical seller behaviors and thus better monitoring is needed as is new research exploring the impact of the three sources of past bias.

INTRODUCTION

The 1980s have seen a very rapid acceleration in interest in the topic of consumer satisfaction and dissatisfaction on the part of both marketers and public policymakers. Marketers have become increasingly concerned, in part, because of their growing emphasis on quality as a key determinant of future profitability and their realization that service intangibles play an extremely important role in determining that quality. For their part, public policymakers are increasingly concerned because of a growing realization that lack of oversight has been a major contributor to the ethical excesses in business performance in the 1980's.

This rapidly growing interest has led to a significant outpouring of research. A recently review cited over 900 entries on consumer satisfaction and dissatisfaction and complaining behavior through 1990, the majority of these completed since 1982 (Perkins 1991). This literature has covered a wide range of topics including papers on the process of post-purchased evaluation, alternatives to measuring dissatisfaction and dissatisfaction, determinants of complaint behavior, characteristics of complainers, use of third party interveners, and the responses of the business community. The literature has been particularly responsive to the needs of commercial marketers. It has, however, been much less responsive to the needs of public policymakers.

Public policymakers look to such research to provide two kinds of input (Andreasen and Manning 1980). First, they expect the literature to help them *detect* problems that are in need of public intervention. Second, they need help in *priority-setting*. Given limited financial and political resources, regulators must make careful strategic judgments as to where to intervene to achieve maximum ameliorative impact. These judgments require four types of information. They need to know:

1. The frequency of market problems in need of potential intervention;
2. The seriousness of these problems, which is, in turn, a function of:
   a. The economic and social cost of each instance; and
   b. The characteristics of those who are primarily affected (e.g. whether they are in some ways disadvantaged);
3. The availability and potential costs (to all parties) of possible solutions, including seller or industry action; and
4. The likelihood that proposed solutions will have the desired impact.

Research Biases

While a certain amount of the existing published research addresses these issues, it is seriously deficient in failing to address a major concern of public policymakers, namely, the existence and impact of *unethical* marketing behavior. In my judgment, this gap is attributable to three major biases in the research literature on consumer satisfaction and dissatisfaction. The first bias is found in the almost universal tendency to focus consumer satisfaction and dissatisfaction research on the *ends* of the purchase process and not on the process itself. We study how products and services turned out in the post-purchase evaluation phase. We investigate whether prior expectations are met by the product or service and whether there is a "disconfirmation" experience. A typical research protocol asks consumers first to think about a situation in which a *purchase* turned out to be unsatisfactory and then to tell the researcher what they did about it.

The trouble with this way of framing the issue is that it tends to minimize the chance that researchers would detect consumer exposure to unethical marketer behavior. It generates comments about outcomes; i.e. was the product or service satisfactory? It does not prompt consumers to think about — or comment on — cases where there might be seller misconduct in the *process* of creating the transaction. Such misconduct could include the following:

- Misrepresentation and deception
- Excessively high pressure selling
- Unreasonable use of fear tactics
- Demeaning references to race, age, and sex

In all of these cases, these unethical practices involve the *selling process*, not the performance of the goods and services per se.

A second major bias in the research literature also minimizes the detection of cases of unethical behavior. This is the tendency to measure consumer satisfaction in terms of what I have called *initial* evaluations (Andreasen 1977). Researchers ask how the *purchase* turned out but do not investigate interactions with sellers after the purchase takes place. In our own research in the mid-70s (Andreasen and Best 1977), we found that consumers had problems with purchases about 20 percent of the time. When things went wrong, they voiced a complaint to the seller about 40 percent of the time. This means that perhaps *eight* percent of all purchases involve some kind of post-purchase interaction with the seller. These post-purchase encounters also present many opportunities for unethical marketer behavior. For example:

- Refusal to honor warranties
- Illegal use of threats to secure payment (e.g. threatening to call employers, advise neighbors, secure court orders, and so on)
- Denial of responsibility
- Disparagement of buyer and his or her judgment, integrity, truthfulness.

The third bias in the literature would make it difficult to calibrate the *impact* of unethical marketer behavior even if it were detected. This bias is the emphasis on *economic* losses. A typical measure used to assess the impact of dissatisfaction is to take the cost of the purchase or the cost of repairing some problem (sometimes including the economic cost of lost time to the consumer). The difficulty here is that the cost of unethical behavior to consumers is very often *emotional* and *psychological*. Take for example these hypothetical, but not atypical, cases:

- An elderly person is contacted by a door-to-door salesperson selling hearing aids. In order to convince the consumer he or she needs the product, the seller pretends not to hear the consumer or uses a rigged "testing device" to prove that the consumer needs help. Certainly, the consumer will have wasted money on an unneeded product. But, surely, the cost in personal self-worth may well be enormous, especially for an elderly person who felt heretofore that he or she "was not really that old."
- A poor minority household is sold a set of encyclopedias by a salesperson who shames them into believing that, without the seller's product, their children are destined to live in poverty like them. When the head of the household loses his or her job, the seller insists on other collateral and, when payments are still not made, threatens to take the buyer to court, pointing out that "people like you never win in the courts, it's a white man's institution." Again, there are certainly economic costs. But the social and psychological costs of this personally damaging and racist behavior are great and may, indeed, last a lifetime.

These biases in the CS/D literature significantly reduce the possibility of public policymakers becoming aware of the incidence and nature of the ethical problems that exist in the marketplace. Because the orientations and protocols of present research designs tend to ignore ethical problems and to neglect emotional and psychological costs, they also diminish the likelihood of finding that some groups bear inordinate impacts of unethical behavior. This was the finding in the late 60s and 70s (e.g. Caplovitz 1964; Andreasen 1975). It is undoubtedly true today. One of the frequent findings of research, including my own, is that the poor, the elderly and minority groups often report *fewer* problems and voice them about as often as non-disadvantaged groups. I suspect that this may well be attributable to the way we did the studies!

Regulatory Systems

Does it matter that we do not detect or measure unethical behavior very well? Even if such biases do exist, is it possible that the marketplace *already* addresses and resolves these problems without the need for outside intervention? If the answer to this question is in the negative, the issue then becomes one of how to develop a signalling system that does not have the biases I have just described. First, let us consider how consumer satisfaction and dissatisfaction is dealt with by the market already.

1. Self-correcting Systems: In an ideal self-correcting system, signals reporting problems experienced by consumers are sent back to sellers who take note of them and correct their own behavior (while also compensating parties already injured). A basic problem with self-correcting systems is that they cannot attempt to correct a problem if it is not detected by consumers. This can happen for one of three reasons:

a. Problems are invisible even to experts given the present state of detection technology;
b. Problems are *made* invisible by the deceptive practices of sellers;
c. Detection of problems requires a level of sophistication beyond the reach of most consumers (ölander, 1977)

If a problem is detected, the system could still fail if the consumer chooses *not* to send a signal. This can happen for a number of reasons:

a. Consumers are not "certain" the problem really exists;
b. Consumers attribute responsibility for the problem fully or partially to themselves and/or to other conditions and not to the seller;
c. Consumers believe the economic, social or psychological costs of sending the signal exceed the potential gain;
d. Consumers believe the size of the potential gain from complaining and/or the probability of obtaining it do not justify action.

It would seem highly unlikely that a system that relies on consumers to detect unethical behavior and send signals to sellers about them would be effective for a number of reasons:

1. Very often, unethical behavior is designed to insure that consumers do not notice that they are being wronged. Indeed, the definition of deception requires that the consumer be deceived.
2. Unethical practices are often directed against groups that may have more difficulty realizing that they are being subjected to such practices. These groups would include the elderly, the undereducated, and those who do not speak English.
3. Part of the unethical practice itself may be designed to make the buyer believe that, if something is wrong, it is probably the buyer's fault and should not be acted upon.
4. Consumers subjected to unethical practices may know that the seller is unethical and expect that:
  a. The seller will not respond even if the buyer did send a signal;
  b. Sending a signal may subject the consumer to *even more* psychological and emotional pain through harassment, name-calling and so on.
5. Assuming that unethical practices are more often directed against the disadvantaged, these consumers may decide that they should not jeopardize their limited access to market alternatives and credit by speaking up.

Assuming that consumers do detect the unethical behavior and do decide to send a signal, they have two options that Albert Hirschman refers to as "exiting" and "voicing" (Hirschman 1970). Exiting behavior is Adam Smith's classic "Invisible Hand." It is the action of individual consumers who simply choose to "exit" a particular buyer-seller relationship and take their patronage elsewhere. In theory, the cumulative weight of dozens of exit behaviors signals to the seller the existence of a problem which the seller then, in an ideal system, sets about correcting, sometimes after further primary research to ascertain the exact nature and cause of the problem. Exit signals are effective in a great many situations. However, they are likely to prove unsatisfactory in the case of unethical behavior, even in the unlikely case that the seller wishes to correct the problem, under one or more of the following conditions:

1. Even though buyers vow never to buy a product or service or to patronize an unethical seller, purchase cycles are sufficiently long that exit signals do not emerge until substantial economic or personal injury has been done (both to buyers and to sellers);
2. Even though buyers exit quickly and repurchase cycles are short, competition is so dynamic that exit signals are masked by the "noise" of temporary in-switching by other consumers;

3. The consumer has no real option for changing behavior (i.e. sending a market signal).

The alternative method of signalling displeasure is by voicing a complaint directly to the seller. Again ideally, the seller will take note of this signal and correct an unsatisfactory market condition. One would think that sellers would actively seek out voicing (complaints) in that it (a) provides early warning in the case of products or services with long repurchase cycles; (b) provides a signal that will be distinct from other marketplace noise; and (c) provides detail as to the exact nature of the problem, thus often obviating the need for further research.

Of course, the most serious defect in self-correcting systems is that they will not work if sellers choose not to respond *even when* a signal is detected. There are a number of cases in which a seller will not respond in the case of unethical behavior:

1. The seller is truly unethical and ignores all signals of dissatisfaction of any kind;
2. The seller believes that the costs of correcting the problem are greater than the potential lost business (the Pinto case);
3. If the signal is a voicing signal, the seller believes that there will be no lost sales because customers will not take their patronage elsewhere;
4. Those consumers who do complain are of limited interest to the seller;
5. Buyers who are ignored are unlikely to cause the seller other problems such as bad publicity;
6. The seller's business does not involve repeat purchases and so he or she does not care if customers are unhappy.

Often unethical sellers are involved in one-time scams like the classic Holland Furnace case. Further, because the victims of unethical practices may be customers disadvantaged with respect to income, age, race and/or language, sellers may have little to fear either because the buyers have few alternatives or because loss of their patronage may be of little consequence.

2. Amplified Systems: If markets are not self-correcting through the actions of *individual* consumers protecting themselves, they may still not require intervention by public regulators in one of two cases. One possibility is that *elites* will police the market for them. In such cases, sellers respond to a small number of prosperous and educated consumers because these consumers either are very vocal in their dissatisfaction or represent a significant loss to the seller if they exit. While this group *could* police unethical behavior on behalf of all consumers, they are less likely to be victims or to be aware of the victimization of the disadvantaged.

The second possibility is for buyers to *amplify* their voices by taking their dissatisfaction to others. The most common forms of amplification available to dissatisfied consumers are:

1. Engaging in negative word-of-mouth that results in other consumers exiting or voicing (Richins, 1983) or even going to the extreme of undertaking consumer boycotts (Smith 1990);
2. Creating publicity for the problem in the media (e.g. in consumer "help" columns or feature articles);
3. Enlisting the help of influential individuals such as celebrities or politicians to whom the seller and/or the media are likely to pay attention;
4. Enlisting the help of formal or informal associations such as the Consumer Federation of America, industry-specific consumer groups such as the Airline Passengers Association, or nonconsumer groups such as church clubs and labor unions to make the seller aware of the problem;
5. (Finally) Resorting to a formal or informal complaint proceeding such as an industry arbitration system, small claims or other court or a federal, state or local regulatory agency to coerce the seller into paying attention.

To the extent that these amplification mechanisms do not distort the original consumer interest, they can be very helpful. Amplifiers can command more resources and expertise to investigate and document problems, to bring them to the attention of sellers, and to press for change or individual resolution. However, if those subjected to unethical behavior are primarily disadvantaged consumers, then the literature suggests that they are unlikely to know about or have the assertiveness to use these amplification alternatives.

3. External Monitoring: If, as seems likely, the marketplace will not be self-correcting and consumers faced with unethical behavior will not be protected by either "elite policing" or amplification systems, then public policymakers such as the FTC and the FDA will need to intervene. The question still remains: how will they detect and evaluate unethical marketer behavior? There are a number of options ranging from the informal to the scientifically rigorous:

1. Reliance on direct "mailbag" complaints, assuming that faint signals of unethical behavior represent the tip of a large iceberg;
2. Reliance on the investigative "research" of amplification agencies such as Consumers Union or individuals such as Ralph Nader;
3. Requiring industries to keep specific records of complaints, as in the airline industry;
4. Funding of a systematic Dissatisfaction Tracking System.

The latter has been explored in the past by government agencies in the U.S. through the work of Day and his colleagues (e.g. Day and Bodur 1978) and through the Technical Assistance Research Program, Inc. (1979). There have been periodic studies in Canada and Great Britain and a more serious continuing effort just begun in Sweden (Fornell 1992).

Research Implications

Clearly, a major challenge facing the consumer research community is to begin a series of studies of unethical marketer behavior that overcomes the biases outlined earlier. First, consumer satisfaction and dissatisfaction research needs to be undertaken that focuses on *both* outcomes and processes that result in purchases of goods and services. Second, studies should be undertaken that identify purchase problems, ask consumers what they did about these, and, for those who did contacted sellers, ask whether this experience involved any unethical behavior on the part of the sellers. Finally, in both these types of studies, when unethical behavior is reported, researchers need to investigate both the economic and *non*economic costs incurred.

Finally, further research should be undertaken of other behaviors that may reflect responses to unethical selling practices. These include studies of consumer boycotts, use of third party complaint handling agencies, and grudgeholding (Hunt and Hunt 1990).

REFERENCES

Andreasen, Alan R. (1975), *The Disadvantaged Consumer*. New York: The Free Press.

_____ (1977) "A Taxonomy of Consumer Satisfaction/Dissatisfaction Measures," *Journal of Consumer Affairs*, 11, 2, 11-24.

_____ and Arthur Best (1977) "Consumers Complain — Does Business Respond?" *Harvard Business Review*, 55, 4 (July-August), 93-101.

_____ and Jean Manning (1980) "Information Needs for Consumer Protection Planning," *Zeitschrift fur Verbraucherpolitik/Journal of Consumer Policy*, 4, 1, 115-126.

Caplovitz, David (1967). *The Poor Pay More*. New York: The Free Press.

Day, Ralph L. and M. Bodur (1978), "Consumer Response to Dissatisfaction with Services and Intangibles," in *Advances in Consumer Research*, 3, 263-268.

Fornell, Claes (1992), "A National Customer Satisfaction Barometer: The Swedish Experience," *Journal of Marketing*, 56, 1 (January), 6-21.

Hirschman, Albert O. (1970), *Exit, Voice and Loyalty: Responses to Declines in Firms, Organizations, and States*. Cambridge, MA: Harvard University Press.

Hunt, H. David and H. Keith Hunt (1990), "Consumer Grudgeholding: Further Conceptualization and Analysis," *Journal of Consumer Satisfaction, Dissatisfaction and Complaining Behavior*, 3, 117-122.

Ölander, Folke (1977), "Consumer Satisfaction: A Skeptic's View," in H. Keith Hunt (ed), *Conceptualization and Measurement of Consumer Satisfaction and Dissatisfaction*. Cambridge, MA: Marketing Science Institute, 409-452.

Perkins, Debra S. (1991), "A Consumer Satisfaction Dissatisfaction and Complaining Behavior Bibliography: 1982-1990," *Journal of Consumer Satisfaction, Dissatisfaction and Complaining Behavior*, 4, 194-228.

Richins, Marsha L. (1983), "Negative Word-of-Mouth by Dissatisfied Consumers: A Pilot Study," *Journal of Marketing*, 47, (Winter), 58-78.

Smith, N. Craig (1990), *Morality and the Market: Consumer Pressure for Corporate Accountability*, London: Routledge.

Technical Assistance Research Program (TARP) (1979), *Consumer Complaint Handling in America: Final Report*. Washington, DC: U.S. Department of Health, Education, and Welfare.

Ethical Consumption Experiences and Ethical Space

Elizabeth Cooper-Martin, Georgetown University
Morris B. Holbrook, Columbia University

ABSTRACT

This paper describes exploratory research on ethical consumer behavior, which refers to decision making, purchases, and other consumption experiences that are affected by the consumer's ethical concerns. First, to capture the diversity of this behavior, respondents listed nearly 200 consumption experiences that involve strong ethical considerations or implications for morality. Second, based on this list, a separate set of consumers rated how good or bad it is to perform various acts of consumption. These ratings were used in multi-dimensional scaling to generate a two-dimensional map or "ethical space." The first dimension appears to represent a continuum from selfish to selfless. The former includes self-indulgent consumption experiences, whereas the latter includes products and behaviors that require self-discipline. The second dimension seems to reflect a continuum from active to passive. Active ethical consumption experiences require the consumer's overt participation or directly affect animate objects (i.e., people or animals). Passive ethical consumption experiences involve a more reactive response of pursuing good by *not* buying harmful items or affect animate objects only indirectly.

INTRODUCTION

To date, the study of marketing ethics has focused on managers, rather than consumers. For instance, a review of marketing ethics articles published in the 1980s included over 50 papers, yet none concerned consumers (Murphy and Pridgen 1991). Another review of business ethics with a focus on marketing covered over 300 papers (Tsalikis and Fritzsche 1989). But even this broader survey mentioned only two papers devoted to consumers; both discussed the ethical responsibilities of consumers, rather than ethical consumption per se (Davis 1979; Stampfl 1979).

By contrast, our interest in the present research is the influence of the consumer's own ethical concerns on decision making, purchases, and other aspects of consumption. Such concerns may be humane (e.g., eating union grapes), religious (e.g., boycotting the movie "The Last Temptation of Christ"), personal (e.g., giving money to a charity), or environmental (e.g., recycling aluminum cans). However, as noted by Smith (1990), the only significant stream of research on ethical consumer behavior (though not by this label) has focused on environmental concerns. Given this dearth of research, the goal of the present study is to gather information on two important basic questions: What products and consumption experiences involve ethical consumer behavior? What are the key dimensions that underlie such ethical products and consumption experiences?

The first question focuses on identifying the range of goods and services involved in ethical consumer behavior, from the point of view of the individual consumer. Although the results are likely to include products that have already been identified as involving ethical concerns (e.g., disposable diapers, dolphin-safe tuna, recycled paper), we hope the respondents will identify additional products that engage consumers' ethical concerns. Thus, the first goal of this study is to capture the diversity of ethical consumption experiences.

The second goal is to organize or categorize this diversity by developing an "ethical space" of consumption experiences that involve ethical considerations. Through multidimensional scaling, a visual display will be produced to group together products that are associated in the ethical judgments they elicit. Interpretation of the axes along which the products are arrayed should identify dimensions that differentiate ethical consumption experiences, such as direct effect on the consumer versus indirect effect or severe versus minimal consequences.

The second section briefly reviews the literature to date that bears on issues related to ethical consumer behavior. The third section concerns the method and results for a study that addressed the first question of this research. The fourth section covers these topics for a second study that addressed the second research question. The fifth and final section discusses the findings and offers ideas for future research.

LITERATURE REVIEW

The stream of research that is most relevant to ethical consumer behavior did not use this term, but instead was concerned with socially conscious consumption, with an emphasis on describing consumers whose concerns for the environment affected their consumer behavior. This work began with a study by Kassarjian (1971), who explored the demographic and socioeconomic characteristics of the environmentally concerned consumer. However, in common with subsequent researchers, Kassarjian did *not* find a consistent or reliable demographic profile. Psychographics were more useful; for example, Kinnear, Taylor, and Ahmed (1974) found that perceived effectiveness, openness to new ideas, and desire to know how things work were useful predictors of ecologically conscious consumption. Other researchers have used lifestyle (Belch 1979) and the influence of pro-social behavior (Tucker, Dolich, and Wilson 1981) to describe similar consumers.

Only a few studies have examined ethical consumer behavior other than environmentally concerned consumption. Smith (1990) studied consumer boycotts organized by pressure groups; he was particularly interested in how such boycotts affect corporate accountability in a free market. Boycotts are clear examples of ethical consumer behavior; consumers refuse to buy certain products due to ethical concerns (e.g., the boycott of Nestlé due to their marketing of infant formula in underdeveloped countries).

Meanwhile, Whalen, Pitts, and Wong (1991) recognized that ethical expectations and judgments are one of the purchase criteria used in consumer decisions. Their experiment showed that unethical behavior by a store manager decreased subjects' intentions to shop at the store more when the behavior affected the consumer personally than when such behavior did not directly affect the consumer.

In sum, although there is a growing understanding of consumers whose decisions and behaviors are motivated by concerns for the environment, little has been published on other types of ethical consumer behavior. Our research addresses this need for work on a wider array of ethical consumer behavior through two exploratory studies, as described below.

STUDY 1

Method

The goal of Study 1 was to identify the diversity of products and consumption experiences related to ethical consumer behavior by means of a small survey.

TABLE 1
Consumption Experiences Identified as Involving Ethical Judgments (Counts)

aerosols/CFC/hair spray (23)	liquid detergents/detergents (4)
adult store (3)	march/rally (3)
air conditioner/electricity (3)	McDonald's (2)
airline (2)	meat/other animals used as food (14)
alcohol/beer/drinking (46)	movies (9)
aluminum/aluminum cans (10)	motor oil/motor oil disposal (7)
animal (2)	music (2)
animal-tested products (6)	Nestlé products (2)
apartment (2)	newspapers (9)
athletic shoes (5)	nude/topless bar (3)
bags: plastic, paper (14)	office supplies from work (3)
bars (10)	packaging/packing materials (3)
batteries (2)	paper/office paper (14)
Ben & Jerry's ice cream (7)	paper products (5)
birth control (15)	photocopies (5)
cans (9)	plastic products (8)
cars/US vs. foreign cars (23)	Playboy/Playgirl (3)
CDs (2)	pornographic magazines (9)
chemical products (4)	prostitute (6)
church, going to (2)	Purdue chickens (2)
cigarettes/tobacco (24)	recyclable/non-recyclable products (17)
condoms (22)	retailers, ethnic (4)
Coors beer (5)	retailers, perceived as racist (6)
disposal, various goods (7)	Safeway's "Savings Club" (2)
Domino's pizza (12)	software/pirated software (6)
donations (4)	stealing/taking products (8)
drugs (13)	stock (2)
DuPont products (2)	stolen goods (3)
eating meat on Fridays during Lent (2)	styrofoam products (15)
expensive products (8)	suit (2)
Exxon gasoline (17)	tampons, type of applicator (3)
firearms/B.B. guns (10)	tickets from a scalper (6)
fake I.D. (4)	tipping (3)
fur products (17)	tires (2)
gasoline (10)	tobacco company's products (3)
glass bottles (20)	tuna/dolphin-safe tuna (20)
homeless:money to,food to (7)	U.S. vs. foreign products (14)
ivory products (5)	veal (10)
lawyers (2)	voting (8)
leather products (5)	X-rated movies or videos (8)

products through a friend who gets employee discounts (2)
products/events whose proceeds go to charity (9)
products sold by children for fundraising (9)
products of a company that has investments in South Africa (9)
products from various animal/plant species (e.g., alligator) (7)
products of countries/companies with controversial policies (13)

Subjects. The 112 subjects were a convenience sample of 79 undergraduates in a consumer behavior course and 32 MBA students in a marketing course. Subjects responded during class time.

Questionnaire. Each subject received the following instructions:

Please list ten of your consumption experiences that involved strong ethical considerations or implications for morality. A consumption experience can be information seeking, buying, refraining from buying, using, or disposing of a product. A product can be a good, service, store, event, person, or idea. Please be brief; for example, buying a hat.

Note that the survey asked respondents to identify product-related consumption experiences for which a variety of consumer behaviors, not simply purchase, included ethical judgments.

Results

In response to the survey, all respondents mentioned at least a few experiences; most listed ten, suggesting that ethical consumer behavior is not a rare experience. Responses that mentioned the same or similar consumption experiences were grouped together. Table 1 presents all 85 consumption experiences that more than one subject identified as having ethical considerations. There were 114 other consumption experiences that received a single mention.

TABLE 2
Characteristics of the Sample

Ethnic Group		Occupation	
Caucasian	72%	Professional	44%
African American	15	(lawyer, editor, professor)	
Hispanic	8	Office Worker	30%
Other	5	(receptionist, secretary)	
Religious Affiliation		Service Worker	12%
Catholic	54%	(sales clerk, restaurant)	
Protestant	36	Not Employed	10%
Other	10	(retired, homemaker, unemployed)	
		Other	4%

This study suggested the frequency, range, and diversity of ethical consumer behavior. To explore the ethical dimensions of these consumption experiences, we did a second study, as follows.

STUDY 2

Method

The goal of the second study was to explore the underlying dimensionality of ethical consumption experiences.

Subjects. Subjects in Study 2 were non-student adults, who were recruited by students in a class of the first author. In exchange for their help, students received extra credit on a test.

A total of 142 questionnaires were received by the deadline. The sample was 57% female and 43% male; mean age was 31 years. Ethnic affiliations, religions, and occupations of the sample are summarized in Table 2.

Questionnaire. The questionnaire included nearly all consumption experiences mentioned by three or more respondents in Study 1, plus six experiences that were mentioned by two respondents. Further, the authors added some products that have ethical considerations but had not been identified by the respondents in Study 1 (e.g., gambling, rap music, heavy metal, Gallo wine, a tape recording of a friend's CD, LP, or tape). Also, because most of the consumption experiences on the survey seemed more bad than good, products that seemed good were added to provide balance (e.g., exercising, haircut, milk). The final questionnaire included 104 items.

For each consumption experience, the respondent indicated the degree to which buying, using, or disposing of that product in the conventional way is good or bad. The good/bad scale was used to capture the extent of the consumer's ethical concerns when consuming each product. Subjects indicated their response by circling a number from 1 (TOTALLY GOOD) to 9 (TOTALLY BAD). The order of items on each page was determined randomly and the order of the pages in the questionnaire was rotated across questionnaires. At the end of the questionnaire, the subject answered the demographic questions.

Analysis. The good/bad responses were analyzed using multidimensional scaling (MDS). However, due to limitations of the MDS program utilized (SYSTAT), the total number of products analyzed had to be reduced. This reduction was accomplished through a principal components analysis of the ratings for all items; the ratings were first normalized within subject to have a mean of zero. The results of the principal components analysis revealed a declining difference (i.e., an "elbow") in the amount of explained variance after the second eigenvalue: 12.8, 8.2, 5.8, 4.9, 4.3, 3.7, 3.1. Therefore only the first two components were retained; they explained 20% of the total variance. Any item with a loading that had an absolute value of .40 or greater on either of the first two components was used in the MDS analysis. By this criterion for inclusion, a total of 48 items was used.

Results

Because we retained two components from the principal components analysis, we performed a two-dimensional MDS analysis of the 48 items. The resulting map attained a stress score of .145. This ethical space appears in Figure 1.

The first dimension, shown as the horizontal axis, appears to represent a continuum from selfish to selfless. On the left are *selfish* consumption experiences; they include self-gratification or self-indulgence (e.g., a topless bar, crack) as well as experiences that provide convenience or pleasure to the self but harm or possibly injure others (e.g., ivory, disposable diapers, stealing). On the right are *selfless* consumption experiences; they include products or behaviors that benefit others (e.g., dolphin-safe tuna, food to the homeless, recycling), as well as products that require self-discipline or self sacrifice (e.g., exercise, health food, school).

The second dimension, shown as the vertical axis, seems to reflect levels of activity. The consumption experiences at the top are *active* because they require a purposeful purchase to do good (e.g., buying recycled products or products whose profit goes to a good cause), demand the active participation of the consumer (e.g., passing a fake ID or recycling glass), directly affect human beings (e.g., giving food to the homeless or to beggars), or explicitly involve a lovable animal (e.g., using dolphin-safe tuna). The consumption experiences at the bottom are *passive* because they require only a more reactive response of *not* buying the item to do good (e.g., disposable diapers), affect human beings only indirectly (e.g., buying Nestlé products), or involve a lovable animal only by inference (e.g., using ivory).

As a corollary to the active-passive distinction, it is interesting to note that survey items mentioning an animate object specifically (i.e., products not tested on animals, dolphin-safe tuna, food to a homeless person, food to a beggar) appear near the top of the map. But those items that implicate other people only indirectly (i.e., products from companies investing in South Africa, Nestlé products) or animals only by inference (i.e., ivory, leather) appear near the bottom of the space.

Mean good-bad ratings were regressed on the coordinates of each item in the ethical space to obtain a goodness vector with fit of $R = .96$ (see Figure 2). This vector aligns closely with the horizontal dimension of the space, suggesting that consumption experiences toward the right (i.e., selfless) versus the left (i.e., selfish) are seen as ethically superior. The influence of the active-passive distinction on the perception of good is more complicated, as detailed in the discussion section below.

116 / *Ethical Consumption Experiences and Ethical Space*

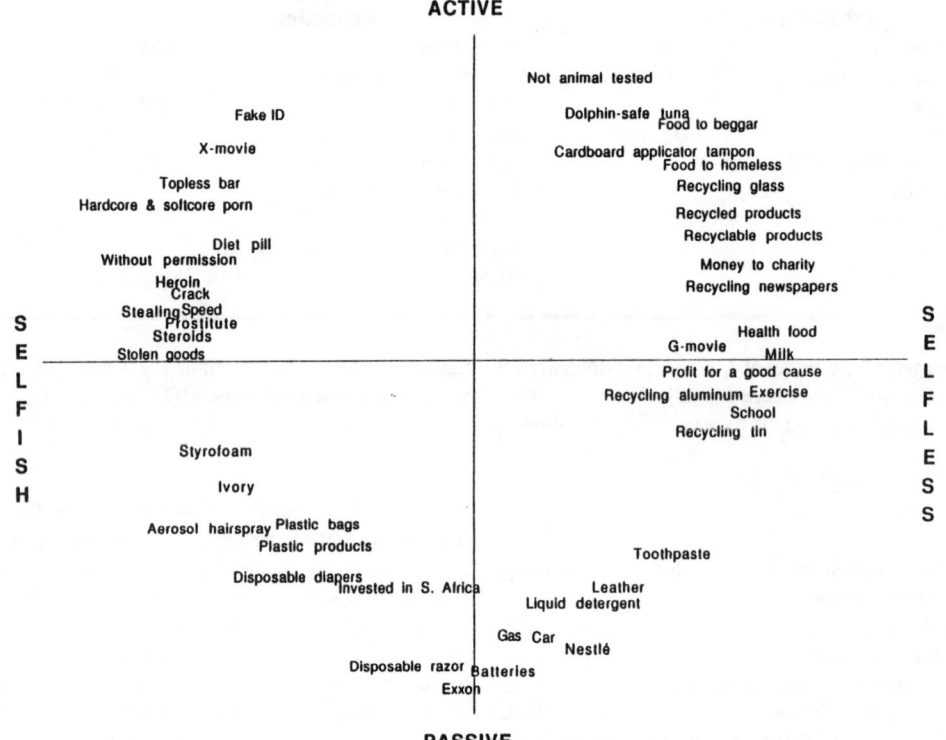

FIGURE 1
Ethical Space of Consumption Experiences

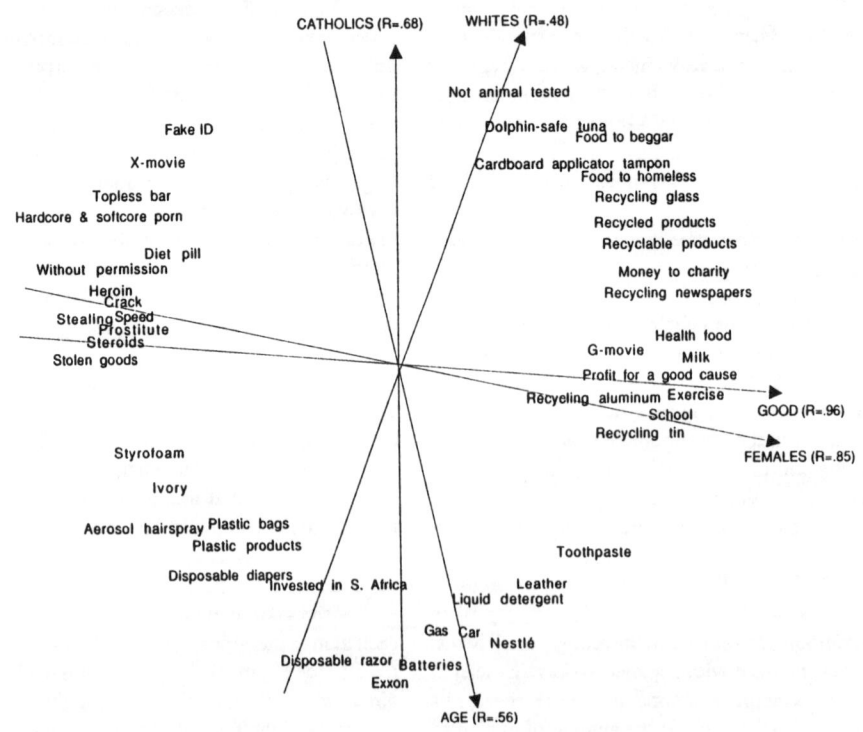

FIGURE 2
Ethical Space of Consumption Experiences with Vectors

To explore the relationship between demographics and ratings of ethical consumption experiences, we created differential ethical vectors, as follows. Dummy variables were formed for sex (female or male), ethnic group (white or non-white), and religion (Catholic or non-Catholic). Each dummy variable plus age was correlated with the good-bad ratings of the items in the ethical space. The set of correlations for each demographic variable was regressed, separately, on the coordinates of each item in the ethical space to obtain four vectors. Each vector indicates the direction in which differences between the demographic groups in their relative goodness ratings of various consumption experiences increase the fastest (see Figure 2).

The vector for sex ($R = .85$) lines up with the good versus bad vector and suggests that women show stronger relative ethical judgments than men. The vector for religion ($R = .68$) falls on the y-axis and indicates that Catholics, versus other religious groups, are more favorable toward active consumption experiences. Meanwhile, the vector for age ($R = .56$) shows that older respondents rate passive consumption experiences relatively more highly than did younger respondents. Lastly, the vector for ethnic group ($R = .48$) suggests that whites, relative to non-whites, are more favorable toward active, selfless consumption experiences.

DISCUSSION

The results of our first study suggested a wide diversity of ethical consumption experiences. The issues mentioned included religion, animal rights, discrimination, homelessness, sexuality, labor rights, patriotism, violence, and integrity. Subjects identified consumption experiences that spanned all stages of consumer behavior: information seeking (e.g., going to an expensive store to learn about a product and then buying it at a cheap store), buying (e.g., scalped tickets), not buying (e.g., firearms), using (e.g., alcohol), and disposal (e.g., getting rid of a mattress). The types of "products" mentioned included physical goods (e.g., car), services (e.g., lawyer), events (e.g., concerts for the benefit of AIDS), ideas (e.g., pro-choice), people (e.g., David Duke), organizations (e.g., McDonald's), and retail outlets (e.g., stores considered racist).

The second study suggested that ethically superior consumption experiences are selfless and active and that ethically heinous consumption is selfish and *also* active. The dimension of selfless versus selfish was very dominant in distinguishing between good and bad. Nonetheless, within the group of selfless items (i.e., those to the right of the vertical axis on the map), active ones (i.e., those near or above the horizontal axis, such as aid to needy people or recycling) appear better than passive ones (i.e., those below the horizontal axis, such as buying toothpaste or leather). But among the selfish items (i.e., those to the left of the vertical axis), active ones (i.e., those above the horizontal axis, such as hard drugs, stealing, or X-rated items) appear worse than passive ones (i.e., those below the horizontal axis, such as hairspray, diapers, or razors).

Meanwhile, the passive consumption experiences in our study tend to fall toward the middle of the good/bad vector. In particular the passive and selfless quadrant is sparse. One explanation is the lack of any items that referred to boycotting a product. The refusal to buy something considered harmful (e.g., items with excessive packaging) would seem to be a selfless, passive, ethical consumption experience.

However, conclusions from this research must be considered preliminary. The sample sizes for both studies were modest (less than 150) while the sample in the first study was exclusively students. The items on the survey in the second study were chosen partially in a subjective, and thus perhaps biased, manner; and not all of them could be included on the map. Building on this exploratory study, future research could correct some of these weaknesses so as to confirm that selfish-selfless and active-passive are the underlying dimensions for ethical consumer behavior. It would also be useful to test explicitly that consumers view selfless and active consumption experiences as ethically superior and selfish and active consumption as ethically heinous.

The two dimensions identified in this study support Holbrook and Corfman's (1985) work on value in the consumption experience. These authors defined a moral or virtuous consumption experience as other-oriented (vs. self-oriented) and active (vs. passive). Additionally, they suggested that a moral consumption experience is intrinsically motivated (vs. extrinsically motivated). Such motivation involves the appreciation of an experience for its own sake or as an end in itself (e.g., virtue is its own reward). The distinction between intrinsic and extrinsic value does not appear in the present ethical space, but may be taken as a general characteristics of *all* consumer behaviors regarded as ethical.

In a study that has come to our attention subsequent to conducting the present research, Muncy and Vitell (1992) collected consumers' perceptions of how wrong 27 consumption-related situations were. They factor analyzed these scores and interpreted the dimensions as whether the consumer was active or passive, whether the consumer was deceitful, and the degree of harm. Their discovery of an active-passive dimension further supports the validity of the vertical dimension in our ethical space. The absence in Muncy and Vitell's study of a selfish/selfless factor comparable to our horizontal dimension probably reflects the range of items in their survey. Rather than spanning a continuum from good to bad, all of the consumption experiences in Muncy and Vitell's survey could be viewed as morally wrong.

The goal of our study was to increase the knowledge of ethical consumer behavior by building on consumers' experiences and by asking consumers about ethical concerns when consuming or disposing of products, as well as when choosing or purchasing them. Although exploratory, we believe our research has met this goal. We are intrigued by these results on ethical consumer behavior and feel that this work extends not only the field of consumer behavior but that of marketing ethics as well.

REFERENCES

Belch, Michael A. (1979), "Identifying the Socially and Ecologically Concerned Segment Through Life-Style Research: Initial Findings," in *Conserver Society*, eds. Karle E. Henion II and Thomas C. Kinnear, Chicago: American Marketing Association, 69-81.

Davis, Rose M. (1979), "Comparison of Consumer Acceptance of Rights and Responsibilities," in *Ethics and the Consumer Interest: 25th Annual Conference Proceedings of the American Council on Consumer Interests*, ed. Norleen M. Ackerman, Columbia, Missouri: American Council on Consumer Interests, 68-70.

Holbrook, Morris B. and Kim P. Corfman (1985), "Quality and Value in the Consumption Experience: Phaedrus Rides Again," in *Perceived Quality: How Consumers View Stores and Merchandise*, eds. Jacob Jacoby and Jerry C. Olson, Lexington, MA: Lexington Books.

Kassarjian, Harold (1971), "Incorporating Ecology into Marketing Strategy: The Case of Air Pollution," *Journal of Marketing*, 35, 61-65.

Kinnear, Thomas C., James R. Taylor, and Sadrudin A. Ahmed (1974), "Ecologically Concerned Consumers: Who Are They?," *Journal of Marketing*, 38 (April), 20-24.

Muncy, James A. and Scott J. Vitell (1992), "Consumer Ethics: An Investigation of the Ethical Beliefs of the Final Consumer," *Journal of Business Research*, 24 (June), 297-311.

Murphy, Patrick E. and M. Dee Pridgen (1991), "Ethical and Legal Issues in Marketing," in *Advances in Marketing and Public Policy*, Vol. 2, ed. Paul Bloom, JAI Press Inc., 185-244.

Smith, N. Craig (1990), *Morality and the Market*, New York: Routledge.

Stampfl, Ronald W. (1979), "Multidisciplinary Foundations for a Consumer Code of Ethics," in *Ethics and the Consumer Interest: 25th Annual Conference Proceedings of the American Council on Consumer Interests*, ed. Norleen M. Ackerman, Columbia, Missouri: American Council on Consumer Interests, 12-20.

Tsalikis, John and David J. Fritzsche (1989), "Business Ethics: A Literature Review with a Focus on Marketing Ethics," *Journal of Business Ethics*, 8, 695-743.

Tucker, Lewis R., Ira J. Dolich, and David Wilson (1980), "Profiling Environmentally Responsible Consumer-Citizens," *Journal of the Academy of Marketing Science*, 9 (4), 326-340.

Webster, Frederick E. (1975), "Determining the Characteristics of the Socially Conscious Consumer," *Journal of Consumer Research*, 2, 285-293.

Whalen, Joel, Robert E. Pitts, and John K. Wong (1991), "Exploring the Structure of Ethical Attributions as a Component of the Consumer Decision Model: The Vicarious Versus Personal Perspective," *Journal of Business Ethics*, 10, 285-293.

The Role of Ethical Concerns in Consumer Purchase Behavior: Understanding Alternative Processes

Sandra J. Burke, Georgetown University
Sandra J. Milberg, Georgetown University
N. Craig Smith, Georgetown University[1]

ABSTRACT

This paper proposes a model that describes how consumers' ethical concerns about business practices may influence their purchase behavior. The model links ethical concern, attitudes toward the brand and the organization, and purchase intentions. It was tested in a preliminary pilot study that provides some initial support for an explanation of how a form of "ethical purchase behavior" may come about, including the role of "family" or "individual" branding strategies and whether the business practice of concern is product/brand-related or at the level of the organization.

INTRODUCTION

Ethical decision-making and purchase behavior has received relatively little attention from consumer behavior researchers. A related stream of research examined "environmentally concerned consumption" (also described as ecologically concerned/responsible or socially conscious/responsible consumption), with the objective of developing a demographic and socioeconomic profile of the environmentally concerned consumer. Prompted by the consumerism movement of the 1970's, these studies were interested in the "consumer who takes into account the public consequences of his/her private consumption or who attempts to use his/her purchasing power to bring about social change" (Webster 1975). They identified characteristics of environmentally concerned consumers for segmentation purposes.

In contrast to this earlier work on environmentally concerned consumption, our interest is in a broader array of ethical concerns that may influence purchase behavior. All purchase behavior is in some sense ethical, involving moral judgement. This paper is focused on ethical decision making involving purchase decisions where those ethical concerns are tied to business practices. For example, a consumer is concerned about the abuse of human rights in a foreign country, say South Africa. Corporate involvement in South Africa may then become a factor in the consumer's purchasing decisions. Similarly, consumers concerned about animal rights may consider whether a cosmetics product has been tested on animals. The research is intended to improve our understanding of consumer behavior. It also has significant implications for business ethics, public policy and marketing strategy.

In *Morality and the Market*, Smith suggests the market can act as an arbiter of "good" and "bad" business practice. At work is "ethical purchase behavior," defined as "an expression of the individual's moral judgement in his or her purchase behavior" (Smith 1990: 178). Smith conducted case research of consumer boycotts, a clearly identifiable form of ethical purchase behavior. He showed how consumers, in conjunction with pressure groups, can use their purchasing power to influence corporate policies and practices. For example, the consumer boycott of Barclays Bank in the United Kingdom was a major contributing factor in the bank's decision to withdraw from South Africa—it had been the largest consumer bank in that country (Smith 1990: 234-41). Key factors in boycott effectiveness and success are moral outrage of consumers and the firm or product's connection with the "grievance". Consumers have to be concerned, willing and able to act for a boycott to work. Connection with the grievance means the consumer is able to connect a purchase decision to a concern about business practices and a more fundamental ethical concern. For example, in the California grape boycott, consumers could readily connect grapes with their feelings of moral outrage over the treatment of farm workers (Smith 1990: 250-53, 261).

In this research, we are attempting to establish the conditions under which ethical concerns influence purchase behavior and, thereby, provide for social control of business. All we can say at present is that consumers may express concern about business ethics in their purchase decisions. We are uncertain as to when they will do this, the form it will take, and what mediates their behavior. The boycotts research suggests it is important to examine when there is a greater or lesser connection between the ethical issue and the purchase decision. To operationalize "connection", we are currently studying two key variables. First, whether the practice is product-based (for example, the use of environmentally harmful packaging) or whether it is organization-based (corporate involvement in South Africa). Second, whether the link between the brand product and the parent organization is known, a variable that influences whether consumers connect a product-based practice with all of an organization's products as well as whether they connect an organization-based practice with a brand product.

One rationale for the maxim "good ethics is good business" is that unethical conduct is penalized in the marketplace and ethical conduct rewarded. Yet, in many circumstances, firms may be immune to marketplace sanctions. This research examines the conditions under which firms are called to task or rewarded by consumers; i.e. as reflected in consumer attitudes toward the brand and the organization, and purchase intentions. As well as implications for business ethics, the research also has implications for public policy. When marketplace sanctions cannot operate there is a requirement for public policy interventions. These interventions may take various forms, including the promotion of consumer activism. In the Barclays boycott, pressure groups succeeded in connecting the bank, in consumers' minds, with apartheid.

From the corporate perspective, the research has implications for marketing strategy in two respects. First, it indicates how firms acquire (or lose) competitive advantage through ethical (or unethical) conduct. Second, it highlights the strengths and weaknesses of "family" and "individual" branding strategies. Despite the economic advantages of a family branding strategy, where all of an organization's products carry the same brand name (e.g. Kellogg), many firms pursue individual branding strategies. An organization often has individual brand names for its different products (e.g. Procter and Gamble). One reason for this is the fear that a problem with one product will "spillover" and harm all the organization's products. Research has found that negative evaluations of a brand product may lead to negative spillover (or "reciprocity"), i.e. less favorable attitudes toward all products under the same brand name (Romeo 1991; Park, McCarthy and Milberg 1992; Milberg 1992).

---

[1] Each author contributed equally. The authors wish to thank the anonymous reviewers of the session proposal for their helpful suggestions.

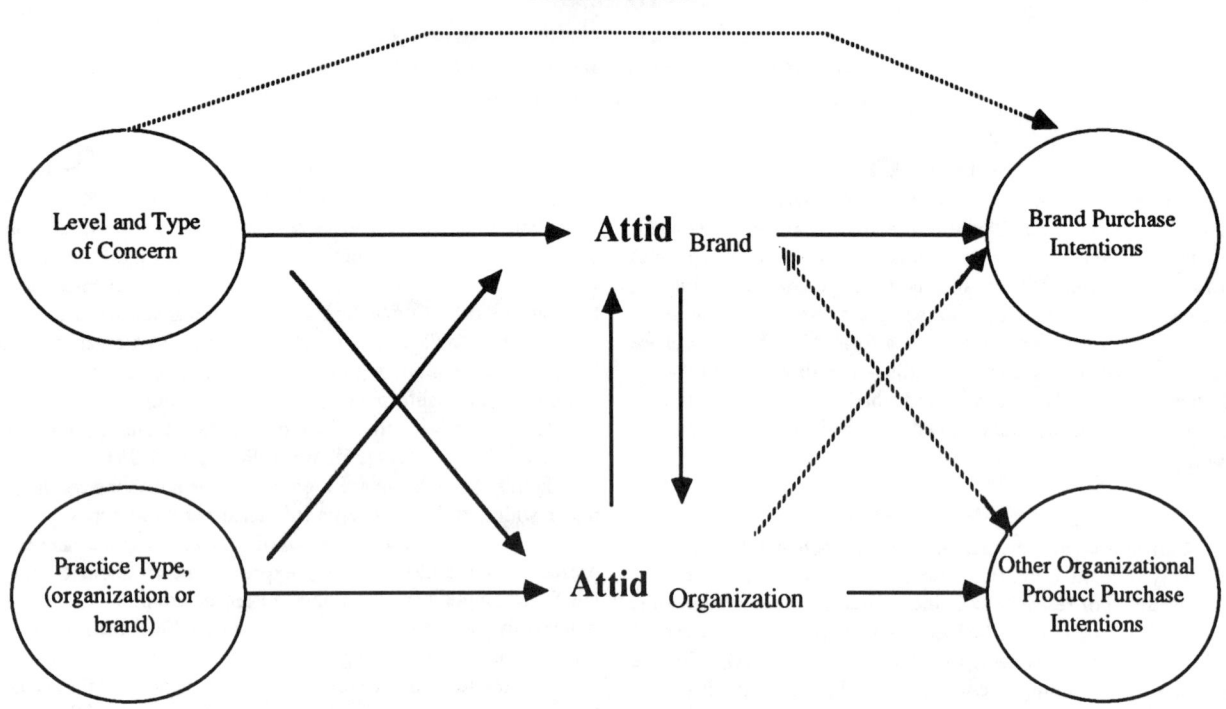

FIGURE 1
Research Model

Milberg has found positive as well as negative reciprocity effects (Milberg 1992).

In keeping with the earlier work on both consumer boycotts and reciprocity effects, we are specifically investigating the impact of level of ethical concern ("moral outrage"), branding, and whether the ethical issue ("grievance") is at the firm or the brand level. The factors found to be key in consumer boycotts have become independent variables in the research model for this study and our attempts to explain how ethical concerns related to business practices influence purchase behavior. Because we are interested in individual behavior (rather than the collective behavior found in pressure group organized consumer boycotts), we are examining attitudes, purchase intentions and the link between the two, and investigating their antecedents.

CONCEPTUAL DEVELOPMENT

A model is proposed that examines the underlying driving effects of consumers' ethical concerns about business practices on purchase intentions (see Figure 1). The model examines the interactions between attitude toward the ethically "charged" practice (shown as level and type of ethical concern), attitude toward the brand, attitude toward the organization, and purchase intentions. Within this framework, a number of alternative "causal" paths may best represent the relationship between attitudes toward the ethical issue (issue attitude) and purchase intentions. For example, issue attitude may effect purchase intentions only indirectly through attitude toward the brand. Alternatively, this link may occur through attitude toward the organization. Furthermore, direct links between issue attitude (and/or attitude toward the organization) and purchase intentions, as well as interactions among all variables may be possible process paths.

Which of these alternative paths, if any, are operating in a given situation may depend on a number of moderating variables. As discussed above, we believe a key variable is whether the concern is primarily manifest in brand practices (e.g. killing dolphins in the production of tuna) or organizational practices (e.g. discriminatory employment practices). The other key moderating variable is the strength of the link between the brand name and the parent organization. Thus, depending on the given situation, different paths are proposed to capture the underlying processes. The following hypotheses specify predicted relationships among the variables:

HYP1: Level of concern regarding ethically charged practices will significantly affect attitudes toward the brand and/or organization. Specifically,

HYP1A: In low or high link situations, level of concern will affect the attitude toward 1) the organization when the unethical practice is organization-based and 2) the brand when the unethical practice is brand-based.

HYP1B: However, in high link situations, level of concern should also impact brand attitudes if the practice is organization-based and, conversely, organizational attitudes if the practice is brand-based.

HYP2A: Ethically charged brand practices will primarily impact attitude toward the brand and ethically charged organizational practices will primarily impact the attitude toward the organization.

HYP2B: However, in high link situations brand practices should also impact attitudes toward the organization and, conversely, organizational practices should also impact attitudes toward the brand.

HYP3: Purchase intentions will be impacted by brand and/or organizational attitudes. Specifically,

HYP3A Brand attitudes will primarily impact target brand purchase intentions and organizational attitudes will primarily impact purchase intentions toward other organizational products.

HYP3B: However, in high link situations, brand and organization attitudes will impact purchase intentions for both target brand and other organizational products.

For all situations, while negatively charged ethical practices are expected to result in less favorable attitudes and purchase intentions, positively charged practices are hypothesised to result in more favorable effects.

METHODOLOGY

Overview

This research examines reciprocity effects of ethical or unethical business practices on consumers' attitudes and purchase intentions towards brands and organizations associated with these practices. To investigate the central issues of concern, this study examines the effects of three variables on brand and organizational attitudes and purchase intentions: level of concern toward various types of positive and negative, ethically charged business practices (e.g., environmental responsibility), whether the practice occurs at a brand or organizational level, and whether the link between brand and parent organization is known. Specifically, level of concern was measured via a battery of scale items. Respondents were then categorized as either high or low concern subjects. The ethical practices examined were either associated with 1) a brand practice, i.e., the killing of dolphins in the production of Star-Kist tuna; or 2) an organizational practice, i.e., Heinz engaging in discriminatory employment practices. In addition, the link between the brand and parent organization, i.e., Heinz owns Star-Kist tuna, was either explicitly provided or not provided. Thus, the overall design was a 2X2X2 between-subjects' design, with level of concern (high or low), practice (brand, organizational) and link (known, unknown) as the three independent variables.

Subjects and Procedure

Subjects were eighty undergraduate business students enrolled in a mid-size eastern university. Each subject was randomly assigned to one of the four treatments. Subjects participated in the study as part of a voluntary in-class exercise.

Each subject was given a cover story in the form of a newspaper article which focused on either a brand or organizational "unethical" practice. In addition, the article either did or did not provide information connecting the brand and the organization. Following the newspaper article, subjects completed a questionnaire assessing purchase intentions for Star-Kist and other brands, attitudes toward Star-Kist and Heinz, and overall level of ethical concern for numerous practices. Upon completion of the questionnaire, subjects were fully debriefed.

RESULTS

Using an ANOVA, partial support for hypothesis 1 was found. Specifically, concern for animal rights significantly affected ($F=5.75$, $p=.01$) attitude toward the brand (Star-Kist) when the practice was brand-based (i.e., killing dolphins to produce tuna). However, concern for unfair organizational employment practices had only a directional, but nonsignificant affect on attitude toward the organization (Heinz) when the practice was organization-based (i.e., discriminatory promotion practices toward women and minorities). Specifically, an average attitude rating of 4.5 on a 5-point scale was observed in low concern subjects versus 2.86 in high concern subjects. Additionally, no support was found for hypothesis 1b.

Regarding hypothesis 2a the results reveal that whether the unethical practice was brand-based or organization-based significantly affected brand attitudes ($F=4.73$, $p=.03$). Specifically, brand attitudes were significantly lower ($X=2.84$) when the practice was brand-based than when the practice was organization-based ($x=3.64$). However, no effect on attitude toward the organization was observed. Further, the effect of the interaction between link and practice on attitudes toward the brand or organization (HYP2B) could not be examined (a manipulation check revealed that the low link/brand practice manipulation was ineffective).

Finally, the results support hypothesis 3a. Specifically, Star-Kist brand attitudes significantly impacted purchase intentions for Star-Kist ($F=101.9$, $p=.000$) but not those for Heinz Ketchup. In addition, attitude toward the organization (Heinz) significantly affected purchase intentions for Heinz Ketchup ($F=5.2$, $p=.03$) but not purchase intentions for Star-Kist tuna, in high and low link conditions. However, hypothesis 3b could not be examined for the reason stated above.

DISCUSSION

By incorporating respondents' different levels of ethical concern, this research goes beyond a conventional attitude-purchase intention study. The antecedents of purchase intention are found to have important and separate effects, with intensity of ethical concern manifest in brand attitude and attitude toward the organization. This encourages our belief in the usefulness of research examining ethical concerns in purchase behavior.

Concern about business practices that are brand-based is manifest in brand attitudes and, in turn, purchase intentions for the target brand. More surprising perhaps, is that brand-based business practices do not appear to influence attitude toward the organization, even though the link between the brand and the organization is known. While attitude toward the organization affects purchase intention, if this attitude is unaffected by brand-based business practices, products other than the target brand will not suffer. If this preliminary finding can be confirmed, it has interesting implications for branding strategies. A rationale for individual branding is the reduced exposure to problems with one brand affecting the firm's other brands. This may not hold. Conversely, pressure groups identifying a brand-based practice of concern would have little to gain from attempting to organize boycotts of all the organization's brands.

Organization-based practices appear to have less impact than brand-based practices. Again this questions conventional wisdom on branding. Organization-based practices had much less effect on brand attitudes and no effect on attitude toward the organization. However, an alternative explanation may lie in the respondents' strongly favourable attitude toward Heinz, suggesting an alternative organization may need to be chosen in future studies. Asked for any comments on the stimulus materials, a number of respondents mentioned their loyalty to Heinz and to Heinz Ketchup:

- "My feelings for the H. J. Heinz Co. are VERY GOOD."
- "I wonder why I dislike Heinz tuna because they kill Flipper, but not Heinz Ketchup?
  I guess when I really think about it I shouldn't buy either..."
- "Before reading this article I had no idea of their business practices. Heinz is the only ketchup I eat thus making that my only conflict."
- "Although I strongly disagree with the discrimination against women and minorities in Heinz, I have already formed a certain loyalty to Heinz because I enjoy its taste (I'm talking especially about its ketchup)."

It is also possible that the organization-based practice (discrimination against women and minorities) was less salient to the respondents and may also need to be changed. A further limitation was the ineffectiveness of the brand-link manipulation. This problem did not allow investigation of the interaction between the level of practice and the link conditions. More extensive pre-testing will be conducted to improve stimulus materials and manipulation effectiveness.

In summary, the results of the study partially support the relationships between ethical concerns, brand/organizational attitudes and purchase intentions. In particular, ethical concerns as well as type of practice (brand vs. organization) were shown to have separate effects on brand and organizational attitudes. Further, these brand and organizational attitudes had subsequent influences on purchase intentions for brand and other organizational products. Thus, evidence was found in support of the overall model, suggesting the need for further, more conclusive investigation. Phase two of our research program will focus on the same variables, but in addition will investigate the underlying processes which drive the attitudinal and purchase intention outcomes derived in phase one, once completed. Phase three will compare the effects associated with "ethical" issues with those associated with other "product" issues (e.g. product quality), to determine if ethical issues effect attitudes and purchase intentions differently than other product issues.

REFERENCES

Milberg, Sandra J. (1992), "Reciprocity Effects of Brand Extensions: Dilution, Fortification, Expansion." Working Paper. School of Business Administration, Georgetown University.

Park, C. Whan, Michael S. McCarthy, and Sandra J. Milberg (1992), "An Examination of Negative Reciprocity Effects Associated with Direct and Sub-Branding Extension Strategies." Working Paper. Graduate School of Business, University of Pittsburgh.

Romeo, Jean B. (1991), "The Effect of Negative Information on the Evaluations of Brand Extensions and the Family Brand," in Rebecca H. Holman and Michael R. Soloman (ed.) *Advances in Consumer Research* (Provo, UT: Association for Consumer Research), pp. 399-406.

Smith, N. Craig (1990), *Morality and the Market: Consumer Pressure for Corporate Accountability* (London and New York: Routledge).

Webster, Frederick E., "Determining the Characteristics of the Socially Conscious Consumer," *Journal of Consumer Research*, Vol. 2 (December 1975), pp. 188-96.

Consumer Resistance: A Conceptual Overview
Lisa Penaloza, University of Colorado at Boulder
Linda L. Price, University of Colorado at Boulder

INTRODUCTION

This session was conceptualized as a consequence of a presentation last February by Mark Poster in which he addressed the idea of *consumer agency and resistance* (1992), engendering a discussion among ourselves that lasted through the weekend and for many weeks to come. What we would like to do today is depict a picture of what consumer resistance looks like in a first-world country and invite your speculations along with our own for what that means to us as consumer researchers. The picture we depict is unstable because the boundaries between consumption and resistance to consumption are porous.

In an insightful portrayal of the work of de Certeau, Poster elaborated on resistance and agency in the region of consumption. He began with a definition of resistance. Although his description seems a less encompassing definition of resist than "to withstand the force or affect of," it serves to focus our attention on the interplay between the agents of resistance and the structures withstood. Poster notes, cultural studies focused on resistance investigate "the way individuals and groups practice a strategy of appropriation in response to structures of domination" (1992, p. 1). This description implicitly represents a recursive interplay between the actions of the resisters and the structures of domination.

Much current criticism of marketing practice focuses on how consumption constitutes a structure of domination (c.f. Rudmin and Richins 1992). Certainly at the hands of the Frankfurt School, and many other post-structuralists, the region of consumption constitutes a pervasive structure of domination and is "a degraded world without hope or signification, a region so corrupted and baleful as to be virtually unintelligible." (Poster 1992, p. 14). The question remains whether there is hope for resistance within this degraded world, and, if so, what would be its nature and forms.

In the consumption domain (characterized by passivity, inertia, empty time, and waste), de Certeau recognizes moments of production, active re-creation and dispersed, tactical and makeshift resistance. Poster (1992) writes:

> Like a traveler in a strange land, the consumer, for de Certeau, is one who brings a repertoire of practices into a space that was designed for someone else .... The consumer inscribes a pattern into space that was not accounted for in its design.

Thus, in contrast to many post-structuralists who depict consumers as passive receptacles into which media images are poured, Poster's reflections, when juxtapositioned against our own research passions encouraged us to see the form, substance and consequences of consumer resistance in a new way. New manifestations of consumer resistance were evident in every corner of time and space, and the inevitable recursive interplay between consumer resistance and marketing agents and institutions appeared even more pronounced.

The Nature and Form of Consumer Resistance

Fundamental to our discussion today is, first, *there are many, many forms of consumer resistance*. Very few of these forms of resistance have caught the attention of consumer behavior researchers. Exhibit one pictures consumer resistance along four dimensions. One axis represents an organizational dimension and ranges from individual to collective action. A second axis represents a goals dimensions and ranges from reformist to radical. A third dimension represents tactics of resistance and varies from actions directed at altering the marketing mix (for example, fighting for product safety features or against ads on television), to actions directed at altering the meaning of products (for example, using products in unintended ways and incorporating novel production into purchased objects). Finally, a fourth dimension recognizes the importance of the consumer's relationship to marketing institutions and agents, acknowledging that consumer resistance may appropriate marketing institutions and agents as their tools of resistance, or may try to stand outside these institutions using non-marketing institutions and agents as instruments of change.

To date, discussions of consumer resistance have been limited and focused primarily on collective (organized) actions directed at changes in marketing mix structure and composition (c.f. Friedman 1991; Herrmann 1992). For example, consumer boycotts have been directed at affecting changes in the composition of the marketing mix and also at more radical reform of the structure of marketing practice (Friedman 1991). Note that boycotts appropriate the structural form of "a vote in the marketplace" as the weapon of resistance. Similarly, the creation of alternative providers of goods and services (e.g., consumer-controlled enterprises), appropriates the tools of marketing to withstand its institutions.

Individual acts of resistance are less commonly explored, and are rarely labelled or linked to resistance. Instead, individual actions focused on may be described and discussed as complaining behavior, negative word-of mouth, or exit (Hirschman 1970). Moreover, the range of actions viewed as resistance is fairly narrow. Consumer acts directed at altering the meanings of consumption and consumption objects are neglected. There are many simple individual acts that transform purchase into production. For example, individuals combine many purchased commodities into a meal that is "homemade", (Wallendorf and Arnould 1991), or use the refrigerator as a community bulletin board and display case. Consumers transform mass produced commodities into highly individuated possessions or experiences. For example, the purchase of a $10 mass produced poster at the end of a mountain biking vacation is described as "an adventure that I alone experienced," (Arnould, Price and Walker 1992). Each of these categories of action may be viewed as resistance against a culture of consumption and the marketing of mass-produced meanings. Other individual acts, such as anorexia and bulimia, can be viewed as failed resistance— exemplifying "the extreme isolation of the individual whose only, and overwhelmingly obsessive, relationship is to the rejected world of commodities," (Willis, p. 20).

A second theme evident in our discussion today is that *identification of consumer resistance is obfiscated by its immediate and recursive interplay with marketing agents and institutions*. We will give you many illustrations over the course of this session and our presentation. This recursive interplay between marketing and consumer resistance is visually represented in Exhibit 2.

Although the rationale behind this exhibit will become more apparent in later portions of the presentation, let me posit a couple anticipatory questions. How are we to understand a glossy media indictment of glossy media? Is it the sheep in wolves' clothing or it is the wolf? Also, how are we to understand individual acts of resistance when they are appropriated by marketing institutions and packaged for mass appeal? Consider, for example, ripped up jeans

EXHIBIT 1
Consumer Resistance
An Overview

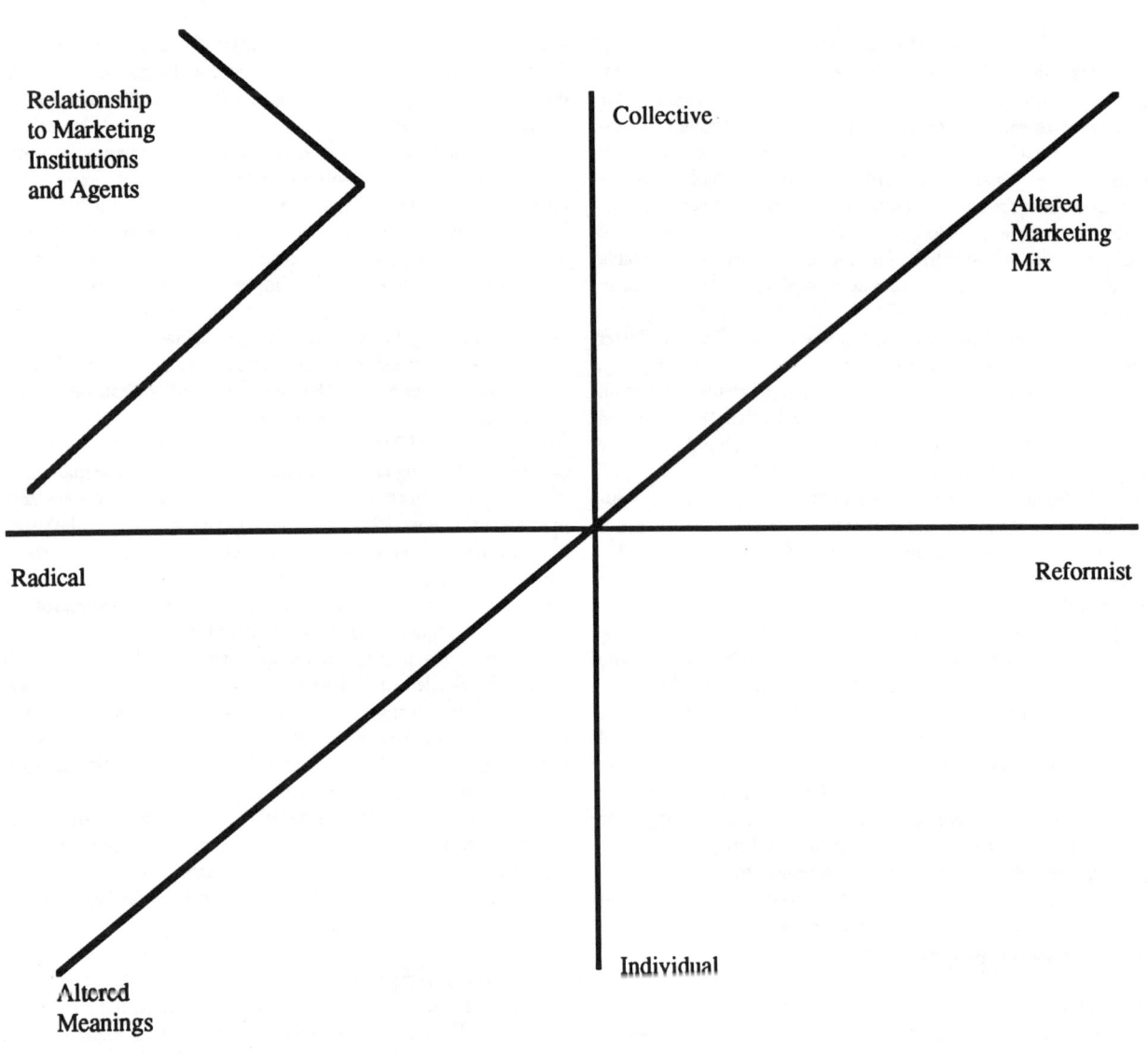

("anticonsumption") sold at premium prices. Something that starts as an individual act of resistance, emulated by rock stars (such as Samantha Fox and the lead singer of Death Leopard), becomes a "fashion statement" that identifies membership in a particular consumption group (Weiss 1992).

In the next section of the presentation we sketch a poststructuralist and postmodern view of consumer resistance as a way of expanding our research and policy parameters.

STAKING OUT THE POSTS: POSTSTRUCTURALIST AND POSTMODERN VIEWS OF CONSUMER RESISTANCE

This section outlines four issues relevant to consumer resistance that appear in sharp relief as we consider consumers within the context of their postmodern lives. Each of these focuses on aspects of the dialectic between forces that oppose consumers' agency and tactics of resistance.

The Question of The Consuming and Marketing Subject

For marketers and consumer researchers, consumer resistance represents trouble with the sudden intrusion, the unanticipated agency of a consuming subject who inexplicitly reverses the marketer's gaze and contests the place and authority of the marketing position.[1] Consumer researchers interested in resistance can benefit from applications of poststructuralist thought that examine the ways in which the consumer and the marketer are constituted *in the practice of consumer research*. *Our* challenge is to incorporate a more fully human agency and subjectivity in our research at both the individual and collective levels.

---

[1] We extrapolate this description of the problematic relation of consumers and marketers from the work of Judith Bulter (1990), who so poignantly described an analogously problematic relation, that of woman in male dominated discourse.

EXHIBIT 2
Consumer Resistance to Marketing and the Marketing of Consumer Resistance

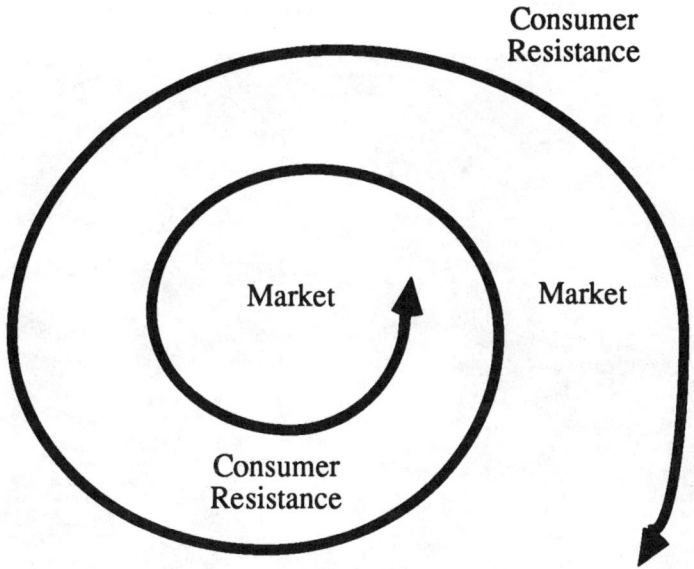

As marketers and consumer researchers continue to deny consumers' agency it is very likely that there will be ever expanding research opportunities in the area of consumer resistance. Marketing and consumer researchers deny consumers' agency by: 1) aggressive marketing strategies and consumer research, for example "hard sell" telemarketing campaigns that come at dinner time and/or are masqueraded as consumer research, 2) irresponsible/ unethical use and distribution of consumer information, for example Lotus Marketplace: Households, a joint venture of Lotus and Equifax that offered information on 80 million households on a CD rom, which was to sell for $695[2], or Circuit City's policy of collecting consumer information on all customers at time of purchase[3], 3) promotions disguised as news or programming, for example the increasingly prevalent video news releases and infomercials, respectively (Lieberman 1992), and 4) sterotypical, offensive representations of consumers.

Given the dialectical relation between marketing practice and consumer resistance it is imperative to incorporate a more comprehensive treatment of market practices in our studies of consumer behavior. In this manner we can begin to understand phenomena like product tampering billboard sabotage, and advertisement parody (see Exhibit 3).

Michel de Certeau (1984) offers a very useful approach in his distinction between strategies and tactics. For de Certeau, subversion does not lie soley in the *strategies* of people's rejection or even alteration of the policies of those who have power over them, but rather in their daily practices, *tactics* that are grounded in a signification system foreign to the system they have no choice but to accept (p. xiii). de Certeau illustrated his tactics referring to the Spanish colonization of indigenous peoples on the American continent, which is appropriate to mention today because this weekend marks the 500th anniversary of Columbus' "Discovery of America." Acts of resistance may be found in Native Americans' acts of going to Catholic Church and worshipping the sacred icons of the conquerors, because these Christian icons were imbued with the characteristics of those sacred beings they had worshipped previously. Today the Virgin Mary and the Virgin of Guadalupe retain such a juxtaposed relation.

There is a sense in which consumers' options, too are structurally limited. To limit acts of resistance to radical interventions that result in structural change is to overlook the constraints in which consumers find ourselves. For example, I can choose to ride the bus in southern California and I can choose to spend 45 minutes traveling 6 miles! We must examine consumer resistance within the context of the marketing structure that preceded it, especially given marketers uncanny ability to incorporate and appropriate consumer resistance in their marketing practices.

Market Fragmentation

Continuing with de Certeau's conceptualization of resistance as tactics (i.e., daily practices grounded in an alternative signification system), we turn next to the issue of market fragmentation. It is more than a little ironic that while some consumers' resistance has been *to get outside the marketing system,* others' resistance has been *to be included in the marketing system.*

Examples of resistance attempting to move outside the market include the Uptown cigarettes that were heavily protested by the African American community, and more recently Native Americans' resistance to the use of the name of one of their tribal leaders, Crazy Horse, on bottles of malt liquor. Other examples of resistance are from "minority" communities that have resisted their exclusion from the mainstream market, and call for their inclusion

---

[2] In January 1991 Lotus Marketplace was withdrawn from the market, after both companies received pressure from privacy advocates and computer consultants. One of the major concerns was that Equifax was using information from its consumer credit files. In July 1991 Equifax announced it would no longer use information taken from its credit files (Smith 1992).

[3] One of the authors was told she could not purchase an item without providing personal information, because that was the "policy"of the organization. She replied that it was not her "policy" to provide such information and asked to see a manager. The sales clerk quickly turned and went to the back office, only to return, saying that such information was no longer necessary.

EXHIBIT 3
An Adbusters Advertisement Parody
(courtesy of the Media Foundation, Vancouver)

in the market. Such examples include African, Hispanic and Asian Americans invisible in advertising and other marketing strategic practices and the virtual absence of African, Hispanic and Asian featured dolls. Until recently Mattel's African American Barbie, Crissy, had caucasian features that were merely colored brown, and the "skin color" crayons bore the unmistakable hue of White Americans. Today Mattel has doll with African American features and Krayola has added plural skin tones to their box of crayons.

The challenge to consumer research is to recognize and investigate consumer resistance that is both from inside out of the market as well as from the outside in.

Simulacra and Hyper-Reality

Drawing from the work of Jean Baudrillard (1988), we will next relate the condition of simulacra and hyper-reality to the topic of consumer resistance. In the arguably postmodern, postindustrial era, as Baudfillard asserts, we are caught up in a world of images that have lost their referents. This raises the question, do consumers know what is real anymore?

There is some evidence that the real is increasingly confused with its representation. Examples of simulated market offerings include the "real" life television talk shows and dramas, such as *Crime Stoppers, 911, and A Current Affair*. All of these, while in some way(s) based on truth, are not the whole story. They simulate the real. Part of their draw is the authenticity of the event, yet the simulation lies in its reproduction. Another example is Cybil Shepherd and Bruce Willis talking directly to the audience in *Moonlighting* even as they proceed to go back to the show.

Hyper-reality and simulacra create an extremely difficult arena for marketers to operate in. At least some of the resistances we have been talking about are fueled by "unreal" expectations that are the result of hyped-up images and unsubstantiated and unsubstantiable claims. Yet (even) here the real comes crashing in; it threatens at every point, peering around the corner of consumer transactions like that James Thurber cartoon character that is simultaneously built into and peering around the house.

Hyper-reality and simulacra present ready material spurring consumer resistance. It is not clear that referents are totally absent; although in many cases what is signified by signs and products increasingly relies on the associations and significance of other signs and images, many developed by marketers. But even when developed by marketers, signs are not employed without some trace to the consumer domain, for that is what enables consumers to relate to the product. What becomes convoluted in this process are not only the ways products and their "benefits" are simulated, but also the ways in which consumers may be simulated in and through the discourse of marketing and consumer research.

Against Utopia

You can never dismantle the master's house with the master's tools

Audre Lorde

We would like to close this presentation with a discussion of the postmodern challenge to the modern view of social change, the utopian impulse (Hebdige 1988). As the expression goes, you cannot fight fire with fire. Translated to the problem of consumer resistance, this means that effective strategies and tactics of resistance are limited to those stemming from outside the market.

On the other hand, consider the Adbusters parody advertisement. The media are a very powerful vehicle for marketers, their tool, if you will. Yet many consumer resisters are trying to challenge marketers' "monopolization of the airwaves," as George Gerbner (1991) of the Annenberg School of Communication and of the Cultural Environmental Movement terms it.

In another example, Tim Robbins was the guest host for Saturday Night Live recently. While the show will probably be best remembered for Sinead O'Connor's performance in which she sang to the audience to fight evil wherever they find it and ended by tearing up a photograph of Pope John Paul, at least as controversial was Robbins' opening act. He began by stating that General Electric is the parent company of NBC network, and that the company is perhaps best known as a producer of light bulbs and consumer electronics, with the slogan, We Bring Good Things to Life. What most people do not know, he continued, is that GE is also the producer of the detonators for nuclear weapons, and maybe their slogan should be, We Bring Good Things to Death. Suddenly the television went blank, as if someone at the network had "pulled the plug."

The next thing we saw was one of the executives of NBC waking from a dream/nightmare. Although somewhat buffered by the dream format, and definitely overwhelmed by O'Connor's controversial performance, Robbins' skit was at least as potentially damaging to the parent company, General Electric and all of this took place on ABC network television. Our point is to suggest that the challenge to those of us intent on examining consumer resistance is to recognize that there is no total escape, no place out there totally outside the market from which positive social change, including effective consumer resistance and freedom from market domination will emanate.

The topic of consumer resistance is rendered further complex given the convergence of consumption and production. Consumers are increasingly taking on marketing tasks (e.g., price clubs, coops and credit unions), just as marketers are taking on more of what has traditionally been in the consumers' domain (e.g., meal preparation, child care, shopping services).

While Audre Lorde makes a very compelling point, not all consumer resistance stems from a position outside of and against the market, although some surely does, for example, the recent movement favoring nationalized health care in the U.S. Consumer resistances are also found within the logic of the market. We miss an important part of consumer resistance if we just focus on structural change. As noted by de Certeau, key consumer resistances are also found in the day to day minutia of product use and signification.

REFERENCES

Arnould, Eric J., Linda L. Price and Beth Walker, "Consumer Behavior and the Crisis of Legitimation: Authenticating Acts and Authoritative Performances," working paper, University of Colorado, Boulder Colorado.

Baudrillard, Jean (1988), *Selected Writings*. Stanford, CA: Stanford University Press.

Butler, Judith 0990), *Gender Trouble: Feminism and the Subversion of Identity*, New York: Routledge.

de Certeau, Michel (1984), *The Practice of Everyday Life*, Los Angeles, CA: University of California Press.

Ewen, Smart 0988), *All Consuming Images: The Politics of Style in Contemporary Culture*, New York: Basic Books.

Freidman, Monroe (1991), "Consumer Boycotts: A Conceptual Framework and Research Agenda," *Journal of Social Issues*. 47 (1), 149-168.

Herrmann, Robert O. (1992), "The Tactics of Consumer Resistance: Group Action and Marketplace Exit," Advances in Consumer Research. Vol 20, eds, Michael Rothschild and Leigh McAlister, Provo, UT: Association for Consumer Research.

Gerbner, George (1991), "The Second American Revolution," *Adbusters*, Fall/Winter, p. 7-10.

Hebdige, Dick (1988), *Hiding in the Light*, London: Routledge.

Hirschman, Albert O. (1970), *Exit. Voice and Loyalty: Responses to Decline in Firms. Organizations and States*. Cambridge, MA: Harvard University Press.

Jameson, Fredric (1984), "Postmodernism, or The Cultural Logic of Late Capitalism," *New Left Review*, July-August, No. 146, p. 53-92.

Lieberman, David (1992), "Fake News," *TV Guide*. February 22, p. 10-16, 26.

Poster, Mark (1992), "The Question of Agency: De Certeau and the History of Consumption," *Diacritics*. Forthcoming.

Rudmin, Floyd W. and Marsha L. Richins, eds. (1992), *Meaning. Measure and Morality of Materialism*. Provo, UT: Association for Consumer Research.

Smith, Robert Ellis (1992), "Privacy's End," *Utne Reader*, January/February, p. 64-68.

Wallendorf, Melanie and Eric J. Arnould (1991), "'We Gather Together': The Consumption Rituals of Thanksgiving Day," *Journal of Consumer Research*, 18 (June), 13-31.

Willis, Susan (1991), *A Primer for Daily Life*. London: Routledge.

Weiss, Gabriel (1992), from an interview with a student at CU.

Media Resistance to Consumer Resistance: On the Stonewalling of "Adbusters" and Advocates
Richard W. Pollay, University of British Columbia

Several new institutions have recently emerged with intent to comment on and counteract the commercialization of every venue of our culture: *Adbusters* Magazine, the Center for the Study of Commercialism (CSC), the Foundation for Media Education (FME), and the Cultural Environmental Movement (CEM). This presentation emphasized the activities of more populist *Adbusters* and CSC, with briefer comment on the educational FME and the association of academics, CEM, led by Dean George Gerbner, at Pennsylvania's Annenberg School of Communications. Despite experience, expertise and appropriate financial resources, both *Adbusters* and CSC have experienced major difficulties getting their efforts carried by the media.

The Center for the Study of Commercialism is based in Washington, D.C. "to encourage a simpler lifestyle and combat Madison Avenue's advertising barrage." With experience and success (as an off-shoot of the Center for the Science in the Public Interest), CSC researches, documents, publicizes and exposes the "excessive intrusion of commercial interests." Through conferences, production of pamphlets, books and videos, lobbying efforts, pedagogical materials, it advocates measures to counter or halt certain forms on marketing, e.g. Channel One commercial TV in grade schools. Its first major study, "Dictating Content: How Advertising Pressure Can Corrupt a Free Press," was the subject of a press conference that was largely boycotted by major media. Subsequent coverage, led by NPR, focused on this boycott by commercial media.

Adbusters is a quarterly magazine with the twin goals of (1) raising consciousness of commercial excess and (2) elevating the media awareness and skills of those in the environmental movement. Distributed to 7,000 educators, environmentalists, business leaders and advertising agencies by the Media Foundation, this 72 to 96 paged medium has now completed 6 issues. It provides an "environmental strategist" column, advertising satire, and articles with provocative titles such as: The McBraining of America, American Excess, The Buy-ological Urge, The Casino Society, Guerilla Advertising, etc. It is proactive with its education of environmentalists and several on going campaigns such as a "Tubehead" PSA campaign against TV addiction and TV spots which highlight the "American Excess." The PSAs were be shown, a rare opportunity, as they have been typically boycotted by broadcasters despite willingness to pay for airtime. Sample copies of the current issue of *Adbusters* were available.

The Tactics of Consumer Resistance: Group Action and Marketplace Exit
Robert O. Herrmann, Penn State University

ABSTRACT
One of the alternatives open to discontented consumers is to exit the marketplace. Group exit actions may take the form of boycotts or the creation of alternative providers of needed goods and services. These market exit groups have sought both functional goals (changes in the marketing mix) and structural goals (broader social and economic changes). In recent years, boycotts have come into increasing use and increasingly have sought structural goals but may be losing their impact. The alternative providers considered include food buying clubs and consumer co-ops; the product information provider, Consumers Union; credit unions and the mail-order drug and insurance operations of the American Association of Retired Persons. Because of their origins these consumer-controlled organizations have faced special goal conflicts and financial problems. The organizations which have succeeded best have emphasized conventional business principles and functional goals even when this conflicted with their structural goals.

INTRODUCTION
Consumer discontent which manifests itself as consumerism and other forms of consumer resistance may grow out of concern both with particular business practices and with the broader societal impact of business behavior. A variety of responses are available to consumers concerned about lapses in business performance. Hirschman (1970) has classified these into exit (refusals to buy), voice (complaining actions) and loyalty (continued patronage in hope of change). This paper deals with two broad categories of exit responses, boycotts and the creation of alternative, consumer-controlled providers of goods and services.

Historically, consumer groups seeking change in business practices have focused both on changes which will benefit them directly and on more fundamental structural changes in the social and economic environment. Jensen (1989) has labeled efforts to change the composition of the marketing mix as *functional goals* and efforts to change the broader competitive environment as *structural goals*. This paper will focus on the pursuit of both functional and structural goals by organized groups of consumers who have exited the mainstream marketplace. The activities examined thus fall at the collective end of Penaloza and Price's (1992) organizational dimension and range along the radical-reformist continuum of their goals dimension. The focus of this paper suggests the possibility of an exit-no exit tactical dimension and perhaps also a voice-no voice dimension.

BOYCOTTS
The consumer boycott has a long history of use as a device to force changes in marketing practices and to promote broader social and political change (Friedman 1985, Garrett 1987). The tactic has come into increasing use in recent years. One recent estimate suggests that there were some 200 boycott actions in place in the early 1990s (Putnam and Muck 1991). A major proportion of these boycott activities seem to involve structural goals (Garrett 1987, Friedman 1991). This represents a change from the supermarket boycotts of the 1960s which were motivated by the functional goal of bringing down prices (Friedman 1971).

Boycotts seem to work best when the target is readily accessible. Producers of frequently-purchased consumer goods and retailers are particularly accessible and vulnerable. When the offender is less accessible, it may be necessary to target some surrogate who, it is hoped, will apply pressure on the offender (Friedman 1991).

As a protest tactic, the boycott seems to have several advantages and to have achieved increasing acceptance in recent years. In 1992 16 percent of grocery shoppers questioned said they had joined in a boycott as compared to 8 percent eight years earlier (Opinion Research Corp. 1992). Boycotts are a flexible tactic, adaptable to the resources available. Thus, a group with limited resources may choose to mount a short-term boycott to obtain media coverage for its views and embarrass the target. Friedman (1991) has labeled this tactic the *media-oriented boycott*.

Alternatively, if more resources are available, an organization may decide to mount a full-scale *marketplace boycott* aimed at the sales of the target corporation. This tactic is most appropriate when the target has been particularly resistant, but does require the commitment of substantial resources. During a survey of boycott principals, one respondent told Garrett (1987) that an organization needs to be prepared to commit the time of five people for a full year in order to mount an effecive marketplace boycott.

Another advantage of the consumer boycott is its apparent effectiveness. A 1977 survey found that business leaders considered boycotts to be more effective than other forms of consumer protest (Harris 1977). The heavy use of boycotts as a protest tactic in recent years may, however, have reduced their newsworthiness and, as a consequence, their effectiveness.

ALTERNATIVE PROVIDERS OF GOODS AND SERVICES
The creation alternative providers of goods and services is another time-honored tactic of consumer resistance. Consumer co-op leader James Warbasse (1942) suggested that there was a role for cooperatives wherever "... things are not done well, where needs are not supplied, or where profit business is failing." Warbasse's list of precipitating factors seems to apply to a wide range of consumer-controlled enterprises. All of the organizations to be examined were formed with functional goals (e.g., better prices, access to needed goods and services and provision of an alternative to unreliable ad claims) and structural goals (enhancement of the welfare of the group served and their empowerment through information and educational services and political action).

Consumers Union
The creation of a consumer-controlled organization to provide objective product information has provided a market exit device reducing dependence on business advertising. During the 1920s there was a flood of advertising for new and unfamiliar products along with new and extravagant claims for familiar ones. The result was growing confusion and uncertainty about ad claims, concern over the wasteful proliferation of brands and over money wasted when products which did not live up to their claims (Herrmann 1982). One result was growing interest in the use of laboratory testing and product standardization as ways of assuring product quality. In 1927 a new book by Stuart Chase and F.J. Schlink (1927) described an existing "Consumers' Club" which was conducting product tests and preparing product ratings using published research results and the help of local high school science teachers. Their report produced a surge of interest and resulted in the formation of a national organization, Consumers' Research Inc. (CR).

By 1932 CR had 42 thousand subscribers for its magazine and was, in addition, publishing a variety of books and pamphlets promoting functional and structural goals. The CR board soon, however, split on the allocation of resources between its political and educational activities and its testing program (Silber 1983). Tensions grew under Schlink's autocratic management, a low wage policy and a forced move to rural New Jersey. The organization split after a bitter strike in 1935 with the breakaway staff members forming Consumers Union (CU). In the first issue of its magazine (Consumers Union 1936), the new group set out to provide product test information and also committed itself to such structural goals as aiding in creating and maintaining decent living standards, working with other groups to promote consumer welfare and reporting on the working conditions under which tested products were produced.

Along with its testing program, the young organization was involved in testifying before government bodies, joining in labor movement picketing, supporting anti-fascist boycotts and conducting promotional drives among the poor (Silber 1983). Testing had to compete with these activities for attention and conflict developed as some became concerned that unsystematic and unscientific test procedures were being used. One result in 1939 was the development of new laboratory facilities and new efforts to obtain outside technical advice (Silber 1983). CU gradually moved away from the radicalism of the 1930s. In 1938 it ceased its coverage of labor conditions in firms producing rated products (Silber 1983).

Over time CU realized that most of its members were middle and upper income and that its efforts to interest low-income and blue collar people were a failure. The emphasis to be given to activistic goals was, however, a continuing source of conflict within the organization. New conflicts arose in the 1950s between the activists and those more committed to the product testing program. Board president Colston Warne pushed for more involvement in both areas (Silber 1983, Gordon 1980, Warne 1980a). One result was the creation of a Washington office to represent the consumer interest there and a variety of new public service projects.

As *Consumer Reports* became increasingly successful in the 1950s and 1960s there were continuing struggles over the appropriate allocation of expenditures. Under Internal Revenue Service pressure to justify its not-for-profit status, CU began a program of assistance to outside organizations. Major beneficiaries were the Council on Consumer Interests (now the American Council on Consumer Interests) which Consumers Union helped found in 1953, the International Organization of Consumers Unions (a worldwide federation of consumer product testing organizations and consumer interest groups) which CU helped found in 1960 and the Consumer Federation of America founded in 1968 (Warne 1980a). CU also poured substantial resources into its consumer education program promoting the use of *Consumer Reports* in the classroom.

Despite this extensive program of grants and projects, some activists felt that CU was not realizing its full potential as an engine for social change. After he joined the CU board in the late 1960s, Ralph Nader made repeated efforts to get the organization to take a more activistic stance. He had some successes, but was exasperated by his failure to win over the CU board and ultimately resigned in 1975 (Warne 1980b).

While financial strains in the late 1970s and early 1980s slowed CU's structural change activities, they were expanded as the subscriber base grew rapidly in the 1980s and 1990s (5 million at the end of 1991). The three advocacy offices were expanded, focusing on health care, banking and housing issues with special attention to the problems of low-income consumers. A new grants program for grassroots consumer organizations in the U.S. and new consumer groups abroad was begun along with a new policy research group and a revitalized consumer education program for children.

Silber (1983) has argued that the strength of CU's approach has been that its calls for structural reforms are based on objective scientific evidence of product failures and safety risks. While CU's subscribers seem to value *Consumer Reports* principally for its product reports, they also value its coverage of broader structural issues such as auto safety and health care policy (Thorelli, Becker and Engledow 1975). As a result, the promotion of functional goals remains CU's primary mission and its promotion of structural goals is dependent on the success of this primary mission.

Food Buying Clubs and Consumer Co-ops

The cooperative idea dates from 19th century Rochdale, England where a group of unemployed weavers banded together to obtain food at the lowest possible cost. Their principles of open membership, one-member one-vote, sales at market prices with the return of surplus to members on the basis of patronage and the use of a portion of surplus earnings for educational purposes continue to guide all types of co-ops. Today's consumer cooperatives continue both to seek savings for members, to foster a sense of community and to promote shared social goals (Sommer 1991). One such goal is to encourage the improvement of business offerings and to serve as a yardstick against which they can be judged. Because American retailing generally is more efficient than that in Europe, there is less need for alternative providers here and American consumer co-ops have not enjoyed the success of their European counterparts.

Interest in the simplest form of consumer co-op, the food buying club, has surged when cost-of-living pressures have mounted. The recession of the early 1980s resulted in a surge of interest as has the current recession. Contemporary food buying clubs' overriding interest has been lower prices, while access to natural foods also has been a significant motivating factor, especially in college communities. Food co-ops also have been developed in inner-city areas as a solution to the limited or high-cost retail operations there. Food politics, ecological issues, and food safety are continuing interests in many food buying clubs (Sommer 1991).

The typical food buying club has about 40 member households, although the number may range from 10 to 40. The clubs operate on a pre-order basis, with members indicating in advance what they wish to buy. Emphasis typically is on dry groceries, although some clubs move into the provision of produce and meat. Deliveries are distributed from a member's garage, a church, a community center or other non-commercial facility. Members contribute labor and management effort to help cut costs. Studies in the 1970s and 1980s found that the cost savings produced amounted to 20-40 percent of retail (Cotterill 1982).

Food buying clubs generally are not long-lived, typically lasting only a few years (Cotterill 1982). Clubs often are formed by financially-pressed young families which over time find themselves both better off and more time-pressed and less able to contribute labor to the club. Those who have watched the development of food buying clubs believe that while cost savings motivate the formation of clubs, their survival depends on commitment to cooperative ideals. Some more successful clubs move to the next stage of development, the opening of a store-front operation. This often proves to be a risky step.

Cooperative food retailers range in size from small store fronts to supermarket operations. Operations of all sizes have been dogged by fierce competition, financial problems, difficulty in getting needed capital and capable managers, and by conflicts within their boards of directors and between the board and management. Another chronic problem has been balancing the co-op commitment to a high level of service to members with the need to make a profit.

The consumer welfare and service activities of co-op supermarkets have taken a variety of forms. Co-ops have been leaders in providing unit price and product information and supporting consumer protection legislation (Sommer 1991). The Berkeley Co-op was notably active in providing testimony on consumer issues at both the state and federal level. As a part of their efforts to promote structural goals, co-ops also may support consumer boycotts or provide information on them to their members. Refusals to stock items which are judged to be over-priced, nutritionally-inferior or environmentally-injurious or which are under boycott, of course, conflict with both profitability goals and the commitment to serve members.

Two of the largest co-op supermarket operations in the country failed in the 1980s. The Greenbelt Co-op (Washington DC) closed down in 1984 (Mayer 1984) and the Berkeley Co-op, which had been a flagship operation for the entire movement, closed its last stores in 1988 (Bishop 1988). The Berkeley stores were hurt by the high wage costs of a senior labor force, the diseconomies of a limited sales volume and problems in adapting to the changing tastes and variety preferences of their customers (Pollack 1985). Another problem seems to have been the decline in group spirit and commitment due to the large size of the co-op.

Maintaining member involvement and democratic control while operating within a capitalist business system and pursuing the growth, efficiency and profitability goals essential to survival is a continuing concern of co-op leaders. Sommer (1991) also has pointed out "the paradox of size": "small idealistic cooperatives lack the resources for formal advocacy and protection programs, while the larger and economically more powerful organizations ... possess the resources but lack the idealism."

Consumer Credit: Credit Unions

By the late 1800s there was growing awareness of the problems working people experienced in getting access to credit. Banks and credit grantors did not deal with most working people leaving them to high-rate lenders and pawnshops charging 30 to 50 percent interest rates. To some, the credit unions which had grown up in Europe and in Canada seemed a solution. Member-controlled credit unions emphasizing self-help and cooperation first appeared in New England in 1909 (Moody and Fite 1971). The idea spread slowly, hampered by the lack of anyone to promote it actively. However, with the support of Boston department store owner and philanthropist Edward Filene, the concept gained momentum and by 1920 had established itself nationwide.

The credit union movement was grounded in the Rochdale principles of cooperation. To these was added the principle that members should share some common bond — a common occupation, place of employment or church, lodge or union membership (Dorfman 1984). This common bond was expected to make it easier to judge the character of prospective borrowers and to discourage default. These ideals were joined with insistence on sound business practices. There was early recognition that the growth of credit unions would depend on maintaining a solid reputation. Despite this, growth was hampered by public skepticism — the credit union idea sounded too much like another "wildcat" banking scheme.

In 1934 the growing movement banded together to form a national association charged with providing services to the member credit unions, promoting legislation favorable to credit unions and promoting the organization of new credit unions (Moody and Fite 1971). The national association has been instrumental in promoting such structural goals as the formation of new groups in less-developed countries and in promoting legislation to protect credit consumers (e.g., truth-in-lending). The credit unions have succeeded chiefly among wage and salary workers. They have had little success among the hardcore poor who lack the means to repay. Efforts to organize credit unions among the poor, most notably during the 1960s "war on poverty," typically have failed even when federal aid has been available. Credit unions are one of the notable successes among the alternative institutions discussed. Currently there are some 15,000 credit unions nationwide with some 62 million members (NCUA 1991). One indication of their roles in credit markets is the fact that in 1990 they provided over 12 percent of all consumer credit and over 16 percent of all car loans. While credit unions have not solved the problem of access to credit at reasonable rates for everyone, they have shown commercial lenders the potential for consumer credit, helped to keep interest rates down and provided access for many whose only option previously had been loan sharks.

Despite their success, credit unions are faced with a continuing problem of finding the right balance between service and the need for sound management. From the earliest days of the movement it was clear that professional management was essential to deal with the financial complexities of operation. With the resulting emphasis on business-like management has come continuing concern about preserving the original ideals of self-help, cooperation and democracy.

Services for the Elderly: AARP

From its founding in 1958, the American Association of Retired Persons (AARP) has provided products and services to its members and promoted social change which will benefit older people. One of its major benefits is its mail order drug service, whose price advantages have made it a top mail-order drug outlet. AARP also has served as a price negotiator for its members who are eligible for discounts on hotel rooms and rental cars. Another early benefit was access to health insurance coverage at a time when such coverage was not easily available to older people.

AARP's most serious internal conflicts are of a different type than those of the other consumer-controlled organizations discussed above. Funding is a problem for all consumer-controlled organizations due to the absence of corporate funding mechanisms and the reluctance of lenders. AARP dealt with this problem by obtaining funding from its insurance providers who were given exclusive access to the membership. By the mid-1970s, health insurance for the elderly had become more widely available and the policies being offered came under increasing criticism from Consumers Union and others. This lead AARP to sever its exclusive arrangements with Colonial Penn Insurance and open up its insurance business to open competition. The faith of some of AARP's members in its offerings may not be fully warranted. A 1988 review of AARP services by *Money* magazine (Time-Life 1988) suggests that while most were competitively-priced, better deals often were available elsewhere.

AARP's success in delivering on its functional goals, its modest membership fee (currently $8 a year) and its easy membership requirements (membership is open to anyone 50 or over and spouse) have attracted a huge membership. In 1992, the organization had over 32 million members and is likely to continue to grow. In 2015, when the last of the Baby Boomers reach 50, 46 percent of the adult population will be eligible for membership. Some have questioned whether the AARP discount program will still be workable when almost half the adult population is eligible for a discount (Time-Life 1988).

The membership of AARP has, in fact, become so large and diverse that it constrains the pursuit of structural goals. Partisan political activity is not feasible. AARP does, however, work to inform its members about the records of candidates and encourage voting. Despite these constraints on partisan activity, AARP has become an important voice for other structural changes of concern to older people. The expertise of the AARP policy analysis staff is recognized and appreciated on Capitol Hill (Smith 1988). This expertise coupled with AARP's sizable lobbying staff have given it unusual influence in issues affecting older people.

CONCLUSIONS

While many discontented consumers have simply voiced their concerns, others have chosen to exit the marketplace altogether. Some of this group have chosen to boycott offending sellers in hopes of forcing functional and structural change. And some have joined in developing new, consumer-controlled organizations to serve as alternative providers of goods and services.

While most boycott groups have pursued both functional and structural changes, in recent years the relative emphasis on structural goals appears to have increased. The boycott tactic appears to have come into increasing use, but may be less effective than formerly. The more intangible goals being pursued may make it harder to win adherents and the frequent use of the tactic may be causing it to lose its news and shock value.

Those exiting the conventional marketplace have organized themselves to provide a wide range of needs, including the pursuit of functional and structural goals. Conflict between these goals has been both common and frequent. The organizational forms which have proven most effective, Consumers Union, AARP and the credit unions, appear to have emphasized conventional business and scientific principles even when these principles and functional goals conflicted with some of the structural goals of the organization. The consumer food co-ops faced with continuing internal conflict and tough competition from mainstream retailers have had a harder time of it.

Organizations of this type seem to experience other types of problems which also are linked to their consumer-controlled status. Access to needed capital and capable managers has been a frequent problem. Board-management conflicts arising from board members' lack of business knowledge and their insistence on activistic and service goals which conflict with financial goals also are common. Because of their ties to labor, these organizations frequently have found it difficult to control labor costs. Efforts to recruit and to serve lower income consumers typically have been a disappointment despite the best of intentions.

The organizations of the alternative marketplace have been innovators in fulfilling unmet consumer needs. They have pioneered in providing unit price information, product test information, health insurance for seniors and consumer credit for ordinary working people. Frequently they have seen their ideas adopted by business and provided by mainstream sellers. Typically this is viewed philosophically as a way of forcing needed changes on business rather than as a threat or usurpation.

As they have grown and developed, all the organizations discussed have had increasing difficulty in maintaining member involvement and commitment. For some, such as the consumer co-ops, this deterioration in interest has been fatal. For others, committed as they are to consumer-governance, lack of member interest is simply a cause of concern and embarrassment.

REFERENCES

Bishop, Katherine (1988), "Who'll Sell Tofu Puffs After Co-ops Are Gone?" *New York Times*, June 6, 1988, A14.

Chase, Stuart and F. J. Schlink (1927), *Your Money's Worth: A Study in the Waste of the Consumer's Dollar*, New York: Macmillan.

Consumers Union (1936), "Consumers Union Reports," *Consumers Union Reports*, 1(1), 1 and 24.

Cotterill, Ronald (1982), "Marketing and Organizational Strategies for Retail Cooperatives," in *Consumer Food Cooperatives*, ed. Ronald Cotterill, Danville IL: Interstate, 77-118.

Dorfman, Mark H. (1984), *But for Service: A History of the Credit Union Movement in Pennsylvania*, Harrisburg PA: Pacul Services.

Friedman, Monroe (1985), "Consumer Boycotts in the United States, 1970-1980: Contemporary Events in Historical Perspective," *Journal of Consumer Affairs*, 19(Summer), 98-117.

Friedman, Monroe (1991), "Consumer Boycotts: A Conceptual Framework and Research Agenda," *Journal of Social Issues*, 47(1), 149-168.

Garrett, Dennis E. (1987), "The Effectiveness of Marketing Policy Boycotts: Environmental Opposition to Marketing," *Journal of Marketing*, 51(April), 46-57.

Gordon, Leland (1980), "The Development of a Consumer Economist," in *They Made a Difference: The History of Consumer Action Related by Leaders in the Consumer Movement*, ed. Erma Angevine, Washington, DC: National Consumers Committee for Education and Research, 476-492.

Harris, Louis and Associates (1977), *Consumerism at the Crossroads: A National Opinion Survey of Public, Activist, Business and Regulatory Attitudes toward the Consumer Movement*, Stevens Point WI: Sentry Insurance Company.

Herrmann, Robert O. (1982), "The Consumer Movement in Historical Perspective," in *Consumerism: The Search for the Consumer Interest*, 4th ed., David A. Aaker and George S. Day, New York NY: Free Press, 23-32.

Herrmann, Robert O. (1991), "Participation and Leadership in Consumer Movement Organizations," *Journal of Social Issues*, 47(1), 119-133.

Hirschman, Albert O. (1970), *Exit, Voice and Loyalty: Responses to Decline in Firms, Organizations and States*, Cambridge MA: Harvard University Press.

Jensen, Hans Rask (1989), "Consumer Policy in Co-op Denmark as Perceived by Member Representatives," *Journal of Consumer Policy*, 12(December), 465-483.

Mayer, Caroline F. (1984), "Cooperative to Close Food, Gas Services," *Washington Post*, January 4, 1984, C7 and 9.

Moody, J. Carroll and Gilbert C Fite (1971), *The Credit Union Movement: Origins and Development 1850-1970*, Lincoln NE: University of Nebraska Press.

National Credit Union Association (1991), *Credit Union Report: 1990*, Madison WI: National Credit Union Association.

Opinion Research Corporation (1992), *Trends 92: Consumer Attitudes and the Supermarket 1992*, Washington, DC: Food Marketing Institute.

Penaloza, Lisa and Linda L. Price (1992), "Consumer Resistance: A Conceptual Overview," in *Advances in Consumer Research*, vol. 20, eds. Michael Rothschild and Leigh McAlister, Provo, UT: Association for Consumer Research.

Pollack, Andrew (1985), "Food Co-ops In a Struggle," *New York Times*, February 23, 1985, 29,40.

Putnam, Todd and Timothy Muck (1991), "Wielding the Boycott Weapon for Social Change," *Business and Society Review*, No.78(Summer), 5-8.

Schurenberg, Eric and Lani Luciano (1988), "The Empire Called AARP," *Money*, 17(October), 128-146.

Silber, Norman Isaac (1983), *Test and Protest: The Influence of Consumers Union*, New York: Holmes & Meier.

Sommer, Robert (1991), "Consciences in the Marketplace: The Role of Cooperatives in Consumer Protection," *Journal of Social Issues*, 47(1), 135-148.

Smith, Lee (1988), "The World According to AARP," *Fortune*, 117(Feb. 29), 96-98.

Thorelli, Hans B. H. Becker and J.L. Engledow (1975), *The Information Seekers: An International Study of Consumer Information and Advertising Image*, Cambridge MA: Ballinger.

Time-Life Inc. (1988), "Should AARP Handle Your Finances?" *Money*, 17(October), 148-164.

Warbasse, James Peter (1942), *Cooperative Democracy: Through Voluntary Association of the People as Consumers*, New York: Harpers.

Warne, Colston E. (1980a), "Consumers Union's Contributions to the Consumer Movement," in *They Made a Difference: The History of Consumer Action Related by Leaders in the Consumer Movement*, ed. Erma Angevine, Washington DC: National Consumers Committee for Research and Education, 150-200.

Warne, Colston E. (1980b), "The Nader Network for Consumer Impact," in *They Made a Difference: The History of Consumer Action Related by Leaders in the Consumer Movement*, ed. Erma Angevine, Washington DC: National Consumers Committee for Research and Education, 554-568.

A Comparison of Three Behavioral Intention Models: The Case of Valentine's Day Gift-Giving

Richard G. Netemeyer, Louisiana State University
J. Craig Andrews, Marquette University
Srinivas Durvasula, Marquette University

ABSTRACT

Three models of behavioral intention, Ajzen and Fishbein's (1980) theory of reasoned action (TORA), Ajzen's (1985) theory of planned behavior (TOPB), and the Miniard and Cohen (1983) model (MCM) were compared in terms of predictive ability and their ability to effectively separate normative form personal influence. For predicting gift giving intention, TOPB performed better than did TORA and MCM. The results also suggest that MCM exhibited greater ability to separate its components than did TORA or TOPB. For predicting gift giving behavior, results indicate that intention represents the direct antecedent to behavior over that of the perceived behavioral control component of TOPB.

The theory of reasoned action (Ajzen & Fishbein, 1980) has been widely used across the social sciences. Though results support the model's predictive ability (see Farley, Lehman, & Ryan, 1981 and Sheppard, Hartwick, & Warshaw, 1988 for meta-analytic reviews), questions remain regarding one of its' boundary conditions, behavioral control, and its' ability to reflect the separate effects of attitudinal versus normative influence for explaining intentions. Recently, alternatives to the theory of reasoned action (TORA) have emerged. The theory of planned behavior (TOPB) is an extension of TORA that includes perceived behavioral control as a variable for predicting intentions and behavior (Ajzen, 1985), and the Miniard and Cohen (1983) model (MCM) assesses the separate contribution of personal and normative influence for the prediction and explanation of intentions. Though these two models show promise, TOPB has yet to be examined across a wide domain of behavior, and few published tests of MCM exist (e.g., Bearden & Rose, 1990; Miniard & Cohen, 1983). Furthermore, the three models (TORA, TOPB, and MCM) have yet to be compared across the same behavioral domain.

The primary goals of this article are to 1) compare TORA, TOPB, and MCM in terms of their ability to predict BI, and 2) compare the models with regard to their ability to separate normative from personal (attitudinal) influence for explaining BI. As a secondary goal, this study will also examine if the perceived behavioral control component of TOPB enhances behavioral prediction. As such, the study is congruent with the need to examine models where variables related to control may impact intention prediction and behavioral achievement (Ajzen & Madden, 1986; Sheppard et al., 1988), and the call to assess the contribution of normative and personal (attitudinal) influence for explaining behavioral intention across models (Miniard & Cohen, 1983). Also, since the behavioral domain of this research is gift giving, this study examines the personal vs. interpersonal motivations of gift giving. That is, it assesses the relative importance of personal attitudes and the perceived influence of relevant others (i.e., the recipient) for the prediction of gift giving - an issue receiving only limited empirical attention in the consumer behavior literature.

THREE BEHAVIORAL INTENTION MODELS

The Theory of Reasoned Action (TORA)

TORA posits that behavioral intention (BI) is the direct antecedent of behavior. BI, in turn, is determined by an individual's attitude toward performing the behavior (Aact) and the individual's perception of what relevant others think of the behavior, i.e., subjective norm (SN). The central equations of the theory are as follows:

$$\text{Behavior} \sim BI(w_1) \quad (1)$$
$$BI = Aact(w_1) + SN(w_2) \quad (2)$$

where w_is are empirically determined regression weights. BI is expected to accurately predict behavior if three boundary conditions hold: 1) the intention and behavior measures correspond in terms of specificity of target, context, action, and time frame; 2) intention does not change in the interval between BI and B assessment; and 3) the behavior in question is under the actor's volitional control, i.e., the actor can decide at will to perform or not perform the behavior (Ajzen & Fishbein, 1980; Fishbein & Ajzen, 1975). Within these boundary conditions, support for the validity of TORA to predict BI and behavior is extensive (Ajzen & Fishbein, 1980; Farley et al., 1981; Sheppard et al., 1988). However, when boundary conditions are not met, explained variance estimates in BI and B are attenuated (Ajzen & Fishbein, 1980; Sheppard et al., 1988). The present study examines one of the boundary conditions, volitional control.

Another important function of BI models involves the degree to which a model accurately reflects the separate contribution of its' components to explain intention. In this regard, TORA has been questioned, as it has often been the case that Aact and/or SN correlate significantly with BI, but receive nonsignificant regression weights (Miniard & Cohen, 1979, 1983). This has largely been attributed to the view that Aact partially taps normative influence and SN partially taps attitudinal (personal) influence, which results in a high correlation between these two components. Thus, even though SN may be posited as a determinant of BI (but less so than Aact), SN may be nonsignificant in a regression equation due to its' overlap with Aact, reducing TORA's overall level of diagnostic utility (Miniard & Cohen, 1979, 1983). This study investigates this issue by comparing the normative-personal (attitudinal) overlap of TORA and TOPB to MCM.

The Theory of Planned Behavior (TOPB)

TOPB is an extension of TORA that incorporates nonvolitional elements for predicting behavior. As in TORA, the key antecedent to behavior prediction is BI and the relationships among Aact, SN and BI are identical for the two models. By adding a control variable though, TOPB expands the boundary conditions of TORA to goal-directed behavior - behavior not completely under an actor's volition. It has been suggested that even the most mundane of behaviors are sometimes subject to the influence of factors beyond one's control (Ajzen & Madden, 1986; Sarver, 1983). From this perspective, TOPB posits that most intended behaviors are those whose attainment is subject to some degree of uncertainty, and the chance of success a person will have of performing a behavior not only relies on intention, but factors that may interfere with behavioral control (e.g., resources such as money, time, opportunity and the cooperation of others). To enhance the prediction of intention and behavior, TOPB proposes measuring perceived behavioral control (PBC) - the person's belief as to how easy or difficult performing a behavior will be (Ajzen, 1985). Support for PBC as a predictor of BI and behavior has been demonstrated (Ajzen & Madden, 1986; Schifter & Ajzen, 1985).

As with previous studies, two versions of TOPB will be tested. The first version assumes that PBC is a predictor of BI, and that BI is *the* antecedent of behavior. The central equations of the first version are as follows:

Behavior ~ BI(w_1)   (1)
BI = Aact(w1) + SN(w2) + PBC(w3)   (2)

The second version considers the possibility of a direct effect from PBC to behavior as well as an effect via BI:

Behavior ~ BI(w_1) + PBC(w_2)   (1)
BI = Aact(w1) + SN(w2) + PBC(w3)   (2)

An effect from PBC to B is expected if the behavior of study is not under the individual's complete volitional control. This study, then, explores the possibility of PBC as an additional predictor of behavior and examines the volitional property of gift-giving.

The Miniard and Cohen Model (MCM)

The Miniard and Cohen (1983) model suggests that informational influence should be reflected only in one's personal attitudes and should be unrelated to normative beliefs about behavior. Their conceptualization is based upon earlier work in social psychology (Deutsch & Gerard, 1955; Kelman, 1961) and states that the opinions of others often serve as an important source of information about one's environment. The acceptance of the information depends on the source's credibility, and behavior based upon this information is independent of its' visibility or knowledge to a referent. Conversely, the normative aspects of MCM are restricted solely to a referent's normative power. Behaviors motivated by normative reasons are directly linked to an individual's desire to attain a reward or avoid some sanction from referents to whom the behavior would be known or visible. Miniard and Cohen (1983) indicate that these two influences are conceptually and empirically distinct in their model.

In essence, MCM was developed to reflect the separate effects of normative and personal influence for explaining intention, and to predict BI. The central equations of MCM are as follows.

Behavior ~ BI(w_1)   (1)
BI = IPCPE(w1) + NPCNE(w2)   (2)

IPCPE is the global evaluation of behavior based solely on personal reasons and NPCNE is the global evaluation of behavior based solely on normative reasons. Behavior, BI and w_is are the same in MCM as they are in TORA. Tests of MCM have shown a high level of validity for BI prediction. In fact, it was shown that MCM predicted BI as well as TORA (Miniard & Cohen, 1983). Studies also demonstrated MCM's ability to register the relative influence of personal and normative variables for explaining BI (Bearden & Rose, 1990; Miniard & Cohen, 1983). These results support MCM's predictive and diagnostic validity.

The preceding review of the three models suggests that TORA and MCM should exhibit comparable validity for the *prediction* of BI. Thus, explained variance estimates for TORA and MCM should be relatively equal for BI prediction. The addition of PBC though, should result in greater predictive ability, and it is therefore expected that TOPB will explain more variance in BI than TORA or MCM for the same behavioral domain. In terms of effectively separating its' components, the preceding review suggests that MCM will more accurately register the separate effects of its components than will TORA or TOPB. Thus, the IPCPE-NPCNE correlation of MCM should be significantly lower than the Aact-SN correlation of TORA and TOPB.

BEHAVIORAL DOMAIN

Gift giving was used as the behavior of study for a number of reasons. What follows is a brief review of the gift giving literature and a rationale for using gift giving as the behavioral domain of the present study.

Gift giving has been studied from several perspectives including the functions it serves (Belk, 1979), from an interactive paradigm (Banks, 1979), and from an anthropological viewpoint (Sherry, 1983). Belk (1979) posits that gift giving serves the four functions of communication, social exchange, economic exchange and socialization, while the interactive paradigm states that gift giving is a four stage process including a purchase stage, an interaction-exchange stage, a consumption stage and a communication-feedback stage (Banks, 1979). In a thorough review, Sherry (1983) has identified three dimensions of gift giving (i.e., social, personal and economic) that encapsulate the functions identified by Belk (1979) and the stages posited by Banks (1979). These dimensions are briefly discussed below.

From a social dimension, research suggests that gift giving is a form of social obligation or political maneuvering where a gift is given because it is expected or it will yield some favorable normative result (Schieffelin, 1980). Gift giving also serves to define the closeness of a relationship (Banks, 1979; Belk, 1979), and the role expectations in a relationship (Csikszentmihalyi & Rochberg-Halton, 1981). The major premise here is that the more intimate the relationship, the greater the gift in terms of monetary and time expenditures (Banks, 1979). It is also widely felt that the intimacy of a relation moderates gift type and number (Belk, 1979), and that special occasions (Christmas, weddings, birthdays) result in the giving of more expensive gifts. From a personal perspective, gift giving has been found to be a reflection of one's self-concept (Banks, 1979). For example, research suggests that the ideal self-concept of the giver may be more strongly related to gift choice than either the giver's self-concept or the perceptions of the gift by the recipient (Belk, 1979). From an economic dimension (i.e, the conferring of material benefit on a recipient) research shows that individuals attempt to maximize the equality of gift exchange, and that gift purchasers are more likely to begin search with an a priori specified price range than those buying the same items for personal use.

The above literature has offered great insight with regard to the functions, stages and dimensions of gift giving. However, gift giving has yet to be interpreted satisfactorily by social scientists and little attempt has been made to examine its structural and motivational components (Belk, 1979; Lutz, 1979; Sherry, 1983). Many scholars have encouraged research focusing on explanatory constructs as a means of examining motivational components, and it has been suggested that expectancy value models should capture the underlying influences that determine gift giving (Lutz, 1979; Sherry, 1983). Behavioral intention models provide the structure needed for examining some of these influences. For example, personal influences toward gift giving should be captured by the Aact component of TORA and the IPCPE component of MCM. Similarly, the influence of relevant others toward the purchase of various gifts should be captured by the SN and NPCNE measures of the two models. Possible control factors affecting gift purchase, such as the availability of the gift or the cost of the gift, should be reflected in the PBC component of TOPB. In addition to capturing these influences, BI models should allow for the estimation of the importance of each influence type. From this viewpoint, gift giving represents a behavior amenable to the goals of this study in that BI models can examine the motivational influences behind gift giving.

METHOD

Elicitation procedures

Valentine's Day was chosen as the gift giving occasion of study for several reasons. First, it is viewed as an obligatory gift giving occasion (Belk, 1979) where the number and types of gifts are determined traditionally. Since it was important that a manageable number of gift types was considered, the limited types of gifts given on Valentine's Day made it suitable to the study. Second, the literature has called for a better understanding of gift giving by studying specific gift giving occasions, and Valentine's Day provides such an occasion (Sherry, 1983). Lastly, students represent a primary target of Valentine's Day gifts.

To ensure that a proper set of gift types would be considered and that possible control factors affecting the giving of each specific gift type included, elicitation procedures were conducted (Ajzen & Fishbein, 1980; Ajzen & Madden, 1986). Two female student samples were used; one for the gifts types (n=28) and one for the control factors (n=29). The gifts women most frequently and almost exclusively listed as giving their boyfriends for Valentine's day were clothing, flowers, dinner, greeting cards, and candy. After determining the relevant gift types, the elicitation procedure for control factors was conducted. Subjects frequently mentioned lack of money for clothing, dinner and flowers. Lack of time was also mentioned for clothing. The other gifts consistently elicited no response.

Subjects and Measures

Eighty-two female undergraduate students participated in the main study. Each subject was screened to determine that she was currently dating someone on a steady basis. In the first phase, one week before Valentine's day, all subjects received questionnaires identical in content with full instructions and practice questions familiarizing them with the scale format. Operational measures of the three models were completely counter-balanced within the questionnaire (across subjects) as was the order of presentation of each models' components. Scales were developed to reflect the components of each model and were all 7-point items. Subjects responded to all measures across all gifts and models.

TORA

Operationalization of TORA followed procedures set by Ajzen and Fishbein (1980). All items were scored on a -3 to +3 basis. Aact toward each gift was assessed via the average of three semantic differential items (good-bad, foolish-wise, beneficial-harmful) in response to the statement *"The purchase of _____ as a Valentine's day gift for my boyfriend would be. . ."*. Aact alpha estimates ranged from .84 to .92 across the gifts. SN was evaluated via a single item scale (approve-disapprove) in response to the statement *"If I bought _____ as a Valentine's day gift for my boyfriend, most people who are important to me would. "*. (An SN measure that was boyfriend specific was also collected. This measure produced results similar to those reported in Table 1.)

TOPB

With the exception of perceived behavioral control, TOPB was operationalized with the same measures as used for TORA. Two approaches to measure PBC were undertaken. First, for each behavioral alternative, two items were used following Ajzen and Madden's (1986) procedures. These items read *"If I wanted to, I could easily buy _____ as a Valentine's day gift for my boyfriend. . .* (likely-unlikely) and *"For me to buy _____ as a Valentine's day gift for my boyfriend is. . .* (easy-difficult). In addition, for those alternatives where the elicitation procedures produced factors that might interfere with behavioral achievement (i.e., flowers, dinner, clothing), extra statements were developed. For example, *"The lack of money might prevent me from taking my boyfriend out to dinner as a Valentine's day gift. .* (strongly agree-strongly disagree). For each gift, PBC items were scored on a -3 to +3 basis, and then averaged to form an index. PBC alpha estimates ranged from .53 to .84.

MCM

The measures and procedures of Miniard and Cohen (1983) were used to operationalize MCM. The global constructs of IPC, PE, NPC and NE were measured by the following single item scales, respectively:

Suppose you were to buy _____ as a Valentine's day gift on the *sole* basis of *personal considerations* (e.g., your own private feelings about buying _____ as a Valentine's day gift). *Given this*, how favorable or unfavorable would you then feel about buying _____ as a Valentine's day gift for your boyfriend? (extremely favorable-extremely unfavorable).

In making your decision concerning the buying of _____ as a Valentine's day gift for your boyfriend, how much importance will you place on your on *personal considerations* (e.g., your own private feelings about buying _____ as a Valentines day gift)? (absolutely no importance-the greatest importance)

Suppose you were to buy _____ as a Valentine's day gift on the *sole* basis of *interpersonal considerations* (e.g., how important others like your boyfriend might react to your purchase). *Given this*, how favorable or unfavorable would you then feel about buying _____ as a Valentine's day gift for your boyfriend? (extremely favorable-extremely unfavorable).

In making your decision concerning the buying of _____ as a Valentine's day gift for your boyfriend, how much importance will you place on *interpersonal considerations* (e.g., how others like your boyfriend might react to your purchase)? (absolutely no importance-the greatest importance)

The PE and NE measures were scored from +3 to -3 and the IPC and NPC measures were scored from 0 to 6. To obtain the overall IPCPE and NPCNE constructs, IPC was multiplied by PE, and NPC was multiplied by NE. All models used the same single item intention measure for each of the five gifts: *"I intend to buy _____ as a Valentine's day gift for my boyfriend* (likely-unlikely). Also, as with other tests of MCM, instructions explaining the differences between personal and normative influence were included for the MCM portion of the questionnaire.

In the second phase of the study, three days after Valentine's day, subjects responded to behavioral measures toward the gifts: *"Which of the following did you purchase as a Valentine's day gift for your boyfriend? Please check the appropriate space(s)."* Spaces checked were coded "1" and spaces not checked were coded "0". Twelve respondents either did not give a gift or gave a gift other than the five examined, and thus, were excluded from all analyses.

TABLE 1
BI Prediction

Model	Personal (Attitudinal) β	r	Normative b	r	PBC β	r	R	R²
Flowers								
TORA	.25*	.43**	.28*	.44**			.48	.24
TOPB	.04	.43**	.30*	.44**	.36**	.48**	.57	.32
MCM	.33**	.40**	.25*	.34**			.46	.21
Clothing								
TORA	.40**	.49**	.18	.42**			.52	.26
TOPB	.34**	.49**	.17	.42**	.16	.32**	.55	.29
MCM	.34**	.36**	.04	.12			.36	.13
Dinner								
TORA	.21**	.41**	.36**	.47**			.51	.28
TOPB	.05	.41**	.34**	.47**	.31**	.46**	.57	.32
MCM	.22*	.25*	.12	.17			.28	.08
Candy								
TORA	.42**	.58**	.24*	.51**			.61	.37
TOPB	.42**	.58**	.24*	.51**	.04	.45**	.61	.37
MCM	.21	.30*	.38**	.43**			.48	.23
Card								
TORA	.48**	.64**	.24*	.56**			.67	.45
TOPB	.43**	.64**	.23*	.56**	.09	.47**	.67	.45
MCM	.46*	.56**	.22*	.43**			.59	.35

*p < .05. **p < .01.

RESULTS

BI Prediction

Table 1 presents a comparison of the three models for BI prediction. For each gift, the correlation of each predictor variable with BI (r), the respective standardized regression coefficient (β), the multiple correlation (R), and R^2 are reported.

First, we will compare the predictive validity of TORA and TOPB. Since TOPB is an extension of TORA, the comparisons were made using hierarchical regression where Aact and SN are entered on the first step and PBC on the second step. The difference in explained variance from step one to step two serves as a comparison of the two models predictive utility (Ajzen & Madden, 1986). For BI-flowers, TORA produced an R^2 of .24, but when PBC was added to the model, the R^2 rose to .32 (F-change=8.50, p < .01). For BI-clothing, the R^2 for TORA was .26 and the R^2 for TOPB was .29, but this difference was not significant (F-change=2.26, p < .12). For BI-dinner the R^2 for TORA was .28 and the R^2 for TOPB was .32 (F-change=6.19, p < .01). Lastly, TOPB and TORA yielded identical results for the prediction of BI-candy and BI-card with R^2s of .37 and .45, respectively (F-changes=.00 and .65, respectively, ns).

Overall, it would seem that only modest support for TOPB as a better predictor of BI than TORA exists. However, since we looked at multiple dependent variables in comparing the two models, we also calculated an overall effect across the five gifts. To do this, Rosenthal and Rubin's (1986, p. 403) equation for combining nonindependent effects was applied to the data. Essentially, this equation calculates a t-test by combining statistics (such as *t*s, *z*s or *F*s) in a manner that depends upon the degree of intercorrelation among the dependent variables considered. The overall effect for comparing TOPB to TORA for predicting BI was t=5.80 (p < .01, df=66), and suggests that TOPB was better than TORA for BI prediction.

To compare the predictive validity of TORA and MCM, and TOPB and MCM, we used a procedure suggested by Tabachnick and Fidell (1983, pp. 114-115). In essence, this procedure calculates a z-test between multiple Rs and compares explained variance estimates for two sets of predictors on the same dependent variable. First, we will compare TORA to MCM. Recall that is was hypothesized that TORA and MCM should exhibit equal predictive validity. Across gifts, TORA's R was higher than MCM's R, but the differences were not statistically significant. For BI-flowers, the R for TORA was .48 and the R for MCM was .46 (z=.17, ns). For BI-clothing, the Rs for TORA and MCM were .52 and .36, respectively (z=1.33, ns). For BI-dinner, the R for TORA was .51 and the R for MCM was .28 (z=1.80, p < .10), and for BI-candy, the R for TORA was .61 and the R for MCM was .48 (z=1.69, p < .10). Lastly, TORA's R for BI-card was .67 and MCM's R for BI-card was .59 (z=1.23, ns).

To further compare TORA and MCM's predictive ability, we calculated an overall effect size again using Rosenthal and Rubin's (1986) procedure (t=2.15, p < .05, df=67). Thus, though there were no significant differences between TORA and MCM when comparing them on an individual dependent variable basis, the combined effect shows that TORA predicted BI better than did MCM.

It was also hypothesized that TOPB would exhibit greater predictive ability than MCM. For BI-flowers, the R for TOPB was .57 and the R for MCM was .46. Though directionally supported, this difference was not statistically significant (z=1.21, ns). A similar result was found for BI-card as TOPB's R of .67 was greater than MCM's R of .59, but the difference was not statistically

TABLE 2
Behavior Prediction

Predictors	BI β	PBC β	r	R	R2
Flowers					
BI	.44**			.44	.19
BI, PBC	.49**	-.09	.14	.44	.19
Clothing					
BI	.68**			.68	.46
BI, PBC	.67**	.04	.25*	.68	.46
Dinner					
BI	.36**			.36	.13
BI, PBC	.39**	-.05	.13	.37	.14
Candy					
BI	.48**			.48	.23
BI, PBC	.42**	.14	.33**	.50	.25
Card					
BI	.64**			.64	.41
BI, PBC	.61**	.07	.36**	.65	.41

*p < .05. **p < .01.

significant (z=1.22, ns). However, for the other three gifts, TOPB explained significantly more variance in BI than did MCM. For BI-clothing, BI-dinner, and BI-candy TOPB's R estimates were .55, .57, and .61. These estimates were greater than corresponding estimates produced by MCM of .36, .28, and .48 (z=1.91, 2.74, and 1.70, p < .05, respectively). Furthermore, the overall effect size was t=3.03 (p < .05, df=67). These results suggests that TOPB was superior to MCM for BI prediction, as hypothesized.

Separation of Components

It was predicted that MCM would separate its normative and attitudinal (personal) components better than TORA/TOPB. To test this prediction, we calculated a z-test for differences between correlations within the same sample (Tabachnick & Fidell, 1983). This test allows for a significance test when both criteria and predictors are different. Thus, we tested if the IPCPE-NPCNE correlation was less than the Aact-SN correlation, and across the five gifts, the IPCPE-NPCNE correlation was significantly less than the Aact-SN correlation. For flowers, the IPCPE-NPCNE correlation was .28 and this was significantly lower than the Aact-SN correlation of .65 (z=2.98, p < .01). For clothing, the IPCPE-NPCNE correlation of .22 was less than the Aact-SN correlation of .54 (z=2.30, p < .01). The correlations between IPCPE-NPCNE and Aact-SN for dinner were .24 and .52, respectively (z=1.91, p < .05), and the correlations between IPCPE-NPCNE and Aact-SN for candy were .23 and .65 (z=3.52, p < .01). The IPCPE-NPCNE correlation for card of .43 was less than the corresponding Aact-SN correlation of .64 (z=1.72, p < .05). Lastly, the overall effect was also significant (t=3.36, p < .01, df=67).

Behavioral Prediction

Table 2 presents the results pertaining to the prediction of behavior. Again, the correlation between predictor and criterion (r), the standardized regression coefficient (β), R, and R^2 are offered. Each model (TORA, TOPB and MCM) considers BI as the predictor of behavior. TOPB, however, suggests that PBC will also be a significant predictor of behavior under conditions of imperfect control. Consistent with the earlier TOPB studies (Ajzen & Madden, 1986; Schifter & Ajzen, 1985), PBC was added to the regression equation after BI in hierarchical fashion. Across gifts, BI was the only significant predictor of behavior. The overall effect, via Rosenthal and Rubin's (1986) procedure, was also not significant (t=.85, ns). Thus, though correlated with behavior for three of the five gifts, PBC did not enhance behavioral prediction beyond that of BI.

DISCUSSION

This study compared the theory of reasoned action, the theory of planned behavior, and the Miniard and Cohen model. It was predicted that TORA and MCM would show no significant differences for BI prediction, and on an individual dependent variable basis, this was the case. However, when combining the effects from all five comparisons, TORA showed an improvement in predictive validity over that of MCM. It was also hypothesized that TOPB would be a better predictor of BI than TORA and MCM. As expected, TOPB was significantly better than TORA for predicting BI for three of the five gifts, and the overall effect showed a significant improvement in BI prediction of TOPB over TORA as well. TOPB also explained more variance in BI than did MCM for three of the five gifts, and this was further emphasized by the significance of the overall effect for comparing TOPB to MCM. These results, coupled with previous tests of TOPB, TORA, and MCM (Ajzen & Madden, 1986; Bearden and Rose, 1990; Schifter & Ajzen, 1985), suggest that PBC should be considered as an additional predictor of BI in future studies involving these models.

In terms of the ability to separate normative from personal (attitudinal) influence, MCM was superior to TORA/TOPB. The differences between TORA/TOPB and MCM are due to the relationships between attitudinal (personal) and normative influences as specified by each model. MCM posits that personal and normative influences are separate from one another, while TORA and TOPB state that normative and attitudinal influences may affect each other through inferential processing (Fishbein & Ajzen, 1975; Ryan, 1982). Thus, one would expect a stronger correlation between Aact and SN, as compared to the IPCPE-NPCNE correlation, and this was the case in the present study. Consistent with Miniard and Cohen though, MCM does more accurately separate the effects of personal (attitudinal) and normative variables for explaining BI than does TORA. This result highlights MCM as a valuable research tool since one of the purposes behind the development of the model was to isolate normative from personal influence. In the design of behavioral change strategies, identifying the separate effect of normative and personal influence is often required.

For behavior prediction, BI was the only direct antecedent. PBC had no predictive efficacy for the purchase of the gifts considered beyond that of intention. This suggests that Valentine's Day gift giving is best viewed as a volitional behavior, and consistent with Ajzen (1985), PBC will only be a direct antecedent of behavior for goal-directed or nonvolitional behaviors.

Gift giving

Though the primary purpose of this study was to compare three models in terms of predictive validity and the ability to separate their normative and personal (attitudinal) components, the results offer some interesting insights into gift giving. First, since Valentine's Day is classified as an obligatory gift giving occasion (Belk, 1979; Sherry, 1983) and this study looked at subjects in a well defined relationship, one might expect normative influence (SN, NPCNE) to play the dominant role for explaining and predicting BI. Across gifts though, Aact was more highly correlated to BI than SN, and IPCPE was more strongly correlated to BI than NPCNE for four of the five gifts. This result is not inconsistent with extant research where it was found that for certain gifts (i.e., clothing, jewelry) the attitudinal variable was more strongly correlated to BI than the normative variable (Warshaw, 1980). This result is also consistent with Belk's (1979) contention that, even for a behavior like gift giving where the consideration of the receiver seems paramount, personal considerations are of great influence. However, it is possible that financial constraints, which should have been captured by the PBC construct for TOPB, may have also been reflected in subjects' responses to Aact and IPCPE, contributed to the higher Aact-BI and IPCPE-BI correlations.

A second finding of interest for gift giving pertains to its' volitional properties. Though PBC was shown to be a significant predictor of BI beyond that of Aact and SN, after accounting for the impact of BI, PBC had no effect on actual gift giving behavior. This suggests the gifts examined in this study are relatively free of control problems.

A third finding pertains to the number of each gift type actually given. Clothing was the most popular gift purchased (about 32% of the subjects gave it to their boyfriends as a gift for Valentine's day). This finding is consistent with Belk's (1979) finding where clothing was the gift most often given to others. Candy and dinner were both given by 19% of the subjects, but only about 7% of the respondents gave flowers. What at first seemed a bit surprising was the fact that a greeting card was the second most popular gift given. Approximately 22% of the subjects gave it to their boyfriends as their *only* gift. Given the intimacy of the relationship and the view that the closer the relationship the dearer the cost (Belk, 1979), one might expect that a card alone would be one of the least given gifts. Clearly, a card is the least expensive of the five gifts in monetary terms. However, a greeting card can be a token gift or the result of thoughtful hours of search and may be used to express or reconfirm some special aspect of a relationship (Sherry, 1983). In the present case then, the giving of a greeting card only may be the result of considerable time investment, and the more intimate the relationship, the more time spent in gift search (Belk, 1979; Sherry, 1983). It still must be recognized that the financial constraints endemic to college students may have contributed to the choice of gift(s) given.

Future Research Involving BI Models

Future studies may want to consider several issues. First, TORA/TOPB typically uses multiple items to operationalize their constructs. In the present study, we used single items to measure SN and BI (i.e., potentially low reliability) which may have resulted in some variability in prediction. Future studies should employ multiple items for SN and BI measurement. Along this line are concerns related to the MCM measures. MCM also uses single items where low reliability may affect predictive results. Also, it is possible that the clearer separation of components for MCM may have benefitted from the MCM instructions explaining the differences between personal and normative influence. Future studies may want to devise multiple items for MCM constructs and test if MCM instructions affect the separation of personal from normative components. Lastly, classifying a behavior as volitional or goal-directed a priori should be helpful. By doing so, PBC measures that more accurately reflect all possible factors affecting behavioral achievement can be developed, enhancing behavioral prediction.

REFERENCES

Ajzen, I. (1985). From intentions to actions: A theory of planned behavior. In J. Kuhl & J. Beckman (eds.), *Action-control: From cognition to behavior*, Hillsdale, NJ: Erlbaum, 11-39.

Ajzen, I., & Fishbein, M. (1980). *Understanding attitudes and predicting social behavior*. Englewood Cliffs, NJ: Prentice Hall.

Ajzen, I., & Madden, T.J. (1986). Prediction of goal-directed behavior: Attitudes, intentions and perceived behavioral control. *Journal of Experimental Social Psychology*, 22, 453-474.

Banks, S. (1979). Gift-giving: A review and an interactive paradigm. in *Advances in Consumer Research*, Vol. 6, W. Wilkie (ed.), Ann Arbor, MI: Association for Consumer Research, 319-324.

Bearden, W.O., & Rose, R.L. (1990). Attention to social comparison information: An individual difference factor affecting consumer conformity. *Journal of Consumer Research*, 16, 461-471.

Belk, R. (1979). Gift-Giving Behavior. *Research in Marketing*, Vol. 2, J. Sheth (ed.), Greenwich, CT: JAI Press, 95-126.

Csikszentmihalyi, M., & Rochberg-Halton, E. (1981). *The meaning of things: Domestic symbols and the self*. New York, NY: Cambridge University Press.

Deutsch, M., & Gerard, H.B. (1955). A study of normative and informational influence upon individual judgement. *Journal of Abnormal Psychology*, 51, 629-636.

Farley, J.U., Lehman, D.R., & Ryan, M.J. (1981). Generalizing from 'imperfect' replication. *Journal of Business*, 54, 597-610.

Fishbein, M., & Ajzen, I. (1975). *Belief, attitude, intention, and behavior: An introduction to theory and research*, Reading, MA: Addison-Wesley.

Kelman, H.C. (1961). Processes of opinion change. *Public Opinion Quarterly, 25,* 57-78.

Lutz, R.J. (1979). Consumer gift-giving: Opening the black box. in *Advances in Consumer Research,* Vol. 6, W. Wilkie (ed.), Ann Arbor MI: Association for Consumer Research, 329-331.

Miniard, P.W., & Cohen, J.B. (1979). Isolating attitudinal and normative influences in behavioral intention models. *Journal of Marketing Research, 16,* 102-110.

Miniard, P.W., & Cohen, J.B. (1981). An examination of the Fishbein-Ajzen behavioral intentions model's concepts and measures. *Journal of Experimental Social Psychology, 17,* 309-339.

Miniard, P.W., & Cohen, J.B. (1983). Modeling personal and normative influences on behavior. *Journal of Consumer Research, 10,* 169-180.

Ryan, M.J. (1982). Behavioral intention formation: The interdependency of attitudinal and social influence variables. *Journal of Consumer Research, 9,* 263-278.

Rosenthal, R., & Rubin, D.B. (1986). Meta-analytic procedures for combining studies with multiple effect sizes. *Psychological Bulletin, 99,* 400-406.

Sarver, V.T. (1983). Ajzen and Fishbein's "theory of reasoned action": A critical assessment. *Journal for the Theory of Social Behavior, 13,* 155-163.

Schieffelin E. (1980). Reciprocity and the construction of reality. *Man, 15,* 502-517.

Schifter, D.B., & Ajzen, I. (1985). "Intention, perceived behavioral control and weight loss: An application of the theory of planned behavior. *Journal of Personality and Social Psychology, 19,* 843-851.

Sheppard, B.H., Hartwick, J., & Warshaw, P.R. (1988). The theory of reasoned action: A meta-analysis of past research with recommendations for modifications and future research. *Journal of Consumer Research, 15,* 325-343.

Sherry, J.F. (1983). Gift giving in anthropological perspective. *Journal of Consumer Research, 10,* 157-168.

Tabachnick, B.G., & Fidell, L.S. (1983). *Using multivariate statistics.* New York, NY: Harper & Row.

Warshaw, P.R. (1980). Buying a gift: Product price moderation of social normative influences on gift purchase intention. *Personality and Social Psychology Bulletin, 6,* 143-148.

A Strategy For *A Priori* Segmentation In Conjoint Analysis

James B. Wiley, University of Alberta

ABSTRACT

The general multivariate regression (GMR) model is used as an integrating framework for conjoint analysis. An advantage of the GMR approach is that it offers extensive capabilities for formulating and testing hypotheses. Particularly appealing is the way hypotheses pertaining to interactions between group membership and attribute profiles may be formulated. Group by attribute interactions can provide the basis for segmentation strategies. Illustrations of the formulation of a variety of hypotheses are provided in the present paper using a simple prototypical conjoint task.

Conjoint analysis, introduced to marketing by Green and Rao (1971), enables marketers to determine the relative impact of product/service attribute levels on preference and other dependent variables. The term "conjoint analysis," however, does not imply a specific technique for data collection, manipulation, or estimation. Rather, there are a variety of approaches — differing in how data is collected, the amount of aggregation prior to estimation, the approach to estimation, statistical assumptions, and the like — all of which qualify as conjoint analysis.

Typically, however, estimates are based on individuals' responses to judiciously constructed attribute profiles which are characterized in terms of a common set attributes. The profiles differ in terms of the levels ("yes/no", "$1.98/2.58", "often/sometimes/never") that the attributes assume. The respondent is shown a set of profiles and is asked to evaluate each. The relative impact of each attribute level can then be determined using linear (i.e., OLS) or monotonic (Kruskal, 1965) regression, LINMAP (Srinivasan and Shocker, 1973), or other estimation procedures. Ordinary least squares (OLS) regression probably is the currently most widely used estimation tool.

In this paper it is shown how generalized multivariate regression (GMR) may be used for estimation in CA applications. As a conceptual and estimation tool, GMR offers at least three advantages over the OLS regression traditionally used:

- Different forms of *a priori* segmentation can be introduced in a natural and consistent fashion.

- The fact that individuals make repeated responses, which probably are correlated, is recognized in estimation.

- A broad variety of hypotheses–both within group and across groups–can be formulated and tested within the framework.

Hagerty (1985) and Kamakura (1988) used a structurally equivalent model to implement their respective approaches to aggregated conjoint measurement. The present approach differs from the Hagerty and Kamakura approaches in two ways.

- First, GLS (generalized least squares) estimation is used and, hence, a variety of covariance structures can be accommodated. As a result, hypothesis tests are more efficient than the OLS counterparts in the sense that more of the available information is included in the test statistics. Kamakura (1988) used OLS estimation procedures.

- Second, the emphasis with the present application is on applications where aggregation segments are defined a priori. The emphasis in the Hagerty and Kamakura papers is on *post hoc* aggregation. Since the segments are defined *a priori* group membership does not depend on the dependent variable and hypotheses regarding differences between groups on the dependent variable may be tested using traditional testing procedures. *Post hoc* procedures are widely used in marketing segmentation studies. Generally these procedures seek to maximize some measure of difference between the *post hoc* groups on the dependent variable. It is well known that under these conditions the assumptions of traditional procedures for testing the significance of differences between groups are violated. One can form groups using the procedures of Kamakura (1988), or test hypotheses using the procedures described below, but one should *not* do both.

2. TRADITIONAL OLS APPROACHES TO CA

There are three ways CA commonly is formulated as an OLS regression problem: as individual, aggregate, and grouped analyses.

- Provided each respondent evaluates a sufficient number of concepts, separate sets of partworths may be estimated for individuals. The number of observations no corresponds to the number of concept evaluations provided by each respondent and the number of parameters estimated by OLS is equal to the number of partworths np.

- At the other extreme, data from all respondents may be pooled by "stacking" individuals' vectors of observations. The resulting vector of observations will have no *times* the number of respondents ns elements. The number of parameters estimated by OLS remains equal to the number of partworths np. However, the partworths now are the average of the partworths estimated using individual analysis.

- A middle ground that retains idiosyncratic differences, at least at the segment or group level, is to cluster respondents accoMwing to some criterion or criteria, and then perform a grouped regression for each cluster. Green and Srinivasan (1978) suggest that respondents be clustered according to their partworth utilities. Alternative approaches would be to cluster on the observation vector Y, or on the basis of covariates, such as demographic, socioeconomic, or lifestyle data.

The three approaches, their advantages, and disadvantages are summarized in Figure 1.

3. THE GMR APPROACH TO CA

Aside from the problems mentioned above, each of the traditional approaches to CA suffer from a common set of conceptual shortcomings. First, the data generated by each respondent probably is best thought of a set of repeated trials in which the individual makes a series of responses to a set of profiles which have the factorial structure that typifies conjoint methodology. That is, the data of a conjoint study can more appropriately be thought of as a (ns x no) matrix of responses (i.e., ns respondents each make no responses) than as a ($ns*no$ x 1) vector as in Equation (T2, Figure 1). Second, in the typical study there is only one set of profiles

FIGURE 1
Traditional OLS Estimation Strategies

Disaggregate		Aggregate		Grouped	
\multicolumn{2}{l}{The conjoint model is represented as follows; (T1) $\;\;E(^iY)_{no \times 1} = X_{no \times np} * {}^ib_{np \times 1}$. where the i superscript identifies the ith individual and ranges from 1 to ns, ns equals the number of subject/respondents, no is the number of observations, np is the number of parameters to be estimated, Y, with element $\{y_j\}$, is a matrix of observations, X, with element $\{X_{jk}\}$, is a design matrix, and b, with element $\{b_k\}$, is a vector of parameters to be estimated.}		\multicolumn{2}{l}{Equation (1) is reformulated as; (T2) $\;\;E(Y)_{ns*no \times 1} = X_{ns*no \times np} * b_{np \times 1}$. That is, the vectors of observations are stacked and the design matrix X is repeated ns times in the data set. There is one vector of partworths which is assumed appropriate for each of the ns respondents.}		\multicolumn{2}{l}{Equation (2) is reformulated as; (T3) $\;\;E(gY)_{ng*no \times 1} = X_{ng*no \times np} * g_{b \, np \times 1}$. Here, the vectors of observations are stacked within each group and the design matrix X is repeated ng times where ng is understood to represent the number of individuals in group g.}	
Advantages	Disadvantages	Advantages	Disadvantages	Advantages	Disadvantages
It allows the maximum degree of ideosycrasticity to be captured.	It introduces the need for subjects to generate sufficient data in order to be able to estimate the model at the individual level and leave adequate degrees-of-freedom to evaluate error. It ignores the repeated measures aspect of the within subject data. It will tend to capitalize on chance and inflate the degree to which the model fits the data, since the number of parameters estimated will typically approach the number of observations.	By estimating over larger members, parameter estimates should be less biased and more stable than in the disaggregate case and error degrees-of-freedom can be accumulated for evaluating the fit of the within group models.	Disregards important structural aspects of the data, such as individual differences among subjects.	Allows idiosyncratic differences in partworths at the group level. Benefits of pooling on reliability of estimates is gained.	Post hoc clustering restricts the range that will be observed within groups on the dependent variable and hence the within group patterns of covariation upon which subsequent regression analysis will be based.

represented by the design matrix X, rather than ns (or ng) profiles which happen to be the same, which might be inferred from the multiple appearances of X in Equations (T1, T2 and T3 - Figure 1). The realities of the *aggregated* data are captured by the generalized multivariate regression (GMR) formulation of Potthoff and Roy (1964), and Khatri (1966):

(1) $_{no}Y'_{ns} = {_{no}}X_{np} * {_{np}}b_{ng} * {_{ng}}A_{ns} + {_{no}}e_{ns}$,

where Y' is the transpose of the matrix of observations, X is the common design matrix, b is a matrix of parameters, A is a known matrix associated with group membership, and e is a matrix of errors whose columns are independently distributed as a no-variate distribution with common covariance matrix $_{no}S_{no}$ and mean vector 0. The matrices X and A are assumed to be of full rank. The interpretation of the respective matrices are as follows:

3.1 The Matrix of Observations, Y

It is assumed that each on ns respondent generates a no x 1 vector of responses to no concepts. Typically, the responses take the form of ratings or rank orders. Thus, the ith respondent's data consists of the vector $y_i = {_{no}}y^1$. The matrix Y' has the structure:

$Y' = y_1, y_i, ..., y_{ns}$.

Each column of Y' contains the data of a single respondent. Each row of Y' contains the responses of ns individuals to one of the concepts. Each individual is assumed to belong to one or more of ng groups of *a priori* interest.

3.2 The Covariance Matrix, S

The covariance matrix S can be given the partitioned structure:

$$\begin{bmatrix} s_{11} & \cdots & s_{1j} & \cdots & s_{1p} \\ \vdots & \ddots & \vdots & & \vdots \\ s_{i1} & \cdots & s_{ij} & \cdots & s_{ip} \\ \vdots & & \vdots & \ddots & \vdots \\ s_{p1} & \cdots & s_{pj} & \cdots & s_{pp} \end{bmatrix}$$

where p = no, the number of concepts in the CA application. No special assumptions regarding the elements $\{s_{ij}\}$ of the covariance matrix S need to be made. For example, the variance element $\{s_{11}^2\}$ captures variation in responses to concept one due to uncertainty, position, unique combinations of attributes, or whatever; and covariance element $\{s_{12}\} = s_{11}^{-2} * s_{22}^{-2} * r_{12}$ captures the effect of heteroscedasticity and correlation between concept one and two that may result from the fact that one follows the other in the questionnaire.

3.3 The Parameter Matrix, b

The parameter matrix $_{np}b_{ng}$ contains the np partworth estimates for ng groups. As described in the next section, with "dummy" coding in the A matrix, the first column contains the estimates for group one, the second column the estimates for group two, and so forth. Interpretations of the elements of b will differ, however, with alternative codings of A. Following Morrison (1976) and Grizzle and Allen (1969), the estimator of b in Equation 1 is:

(2)   b = $(X' D^{-1} X)^{-1} X' D^{-1} Y' A' (A A')^{-1}$, where
(3)   D = $Y' Y - Y' A' (A A')^{-1} A Y$.

The matrix D is an estimate of the matrix S, the covariance matrix of e in Equation 1.[1] It should be noted that the amount of heteroscedasticity and multicollinearity in conjoint data is an unresolved empirical issue. While GLS estimates may be obtained using (3) in (2), corresponding OLS estimates may be obtained by replacing (3) with D = I, where I is the identity matrix of appropriate rank. Procedures for formulating and testing hypotheses are not effected. The interpretation of the elements of b depends on the coding scheme selected for the grouping matrix A.

3.4 The Grouping Matrix, A

Which group, or groups, the individual belongs to is indicated by the matrix A. Under various codings for A, individuals may be represented as a) belonging to a unique group, b) have a probability, or fuzzy, association with groups, or c) belong to several groups corresponding to a sample structure, such as jointly being a member of gender, lifestyle, income, or usage groups.[2] In order to simplify the exposition of the overall approach, in the present paper it is assumed that individuals belong to one of two unique groups.

"Dummy" and "effect" coding are the most common strategies for coding the grouping matrices (Kerlinger and Pedhauser, 1973.) When used to code the A matrix, the two approach result in quite different interpretations of the parameter estimates. With "dummy" coding, respondents would be coded as A_1 in Figure 2. The first row of the A matrix would contain "1's" if the respondent was in group one, zero otherwise. The second row would contain "1's" in the second row if the respondent was in group two, zeros otherwise. With this coding, the term $ng[(A A')^{-1}]ng$ of Equation 2 has the inverse of the group sizes on the diagonal and zeros off-diagonal. The term $_{no}[Y' A']ng$ is the sum of the observations in each group. The product of the two terms gives the mean response for the groups. Assuming the design matrix X is coded as below (with the first column coded as the constant) parameters b_{11} and b_{21} are the within group constants for group one and two, respectively. The parameters b_{12} b_{13} b_{14} b_{15} and b_{22} b_{23} b_{24} b_{25} are the mean partworth for the respective groups. In this respect, dummy coding provides an analysis that is equivalent to the grouped analysis summarized in Figure 1.

---

[1] It should be noted, however, that a pooled covariance is assumed to apply for all groups and hence S can at best be an approximation of the true ones of the respective groups. If the groups respond to the concepts in different orders or if they have markedly different preferences for the concepts, then the pooled covariance matrix may not be a good approximation of the true covariance matrices of the groups. Generally speaking, however, studies are conducted using printed questionnaires and concepts are presented in the same order, so the repeated measures aspects of the studies are the same across groups. Also, the attributes used to describe the concepts generally are costs or benefits for which there are monotonic relationships between levels and partworths across groups. In such cases, one would expect that a pooled covariance matrix would be a reasonable approximation across groups.

[2] The practical difference between the present paper and Kamakura (1988) is that in the present paper the elements of A are taken to be known, hence they are not conditional on Y, while Kamakura uses iterative procedures to estimate the elements of A, hence they are conditional on Y.

$$b' = \begin{vmatrix} b_{11} & b_{12} & b_{13} & b_{14} \\ b_{21} & b_{22} & b_{23} & b_{24} \end{vmatrix}$$

$$X = \begin{matrix} & \mu & \alpha_{lin.} & \alpha_{quad.} & \beta \\ & 1 & -1 & 1 & 1 \\ & 1 & 0 & -2 & 1 \\ & 1 & 1 & 1 & 1 \\ & 1 & -1 & 1 & -1 \\ & 1 & 0 & -2 & -1 \\ & 1 & 1 & 1 & -1 \end{matrix}$$

An alternative way to code respondents into mutually exclusive groups would be to "effect" code the A matrix, as A_2 of Figure 2. The first row of the A matrix would contain a vector of "1's". The second row would contain "+1's" if the respondent was in group one and "-1's" if the respondent was in group two. With this coding, the term $_{ng}[(AA')^{-1}]^{ng}$ of Equation 2 has the inverse of the sample size on the diagonal and the difference between the sample sizes of the two groups off-diagonal. The first column of $_{no}[Y'A']^{ng}$ is the sum of the observations across all groups. The second column contains the difference between the responses of group one to each concept and the responses of group two to the concept. Again assuming the first column of X is coded for the constant, parameter b_{11} is the grand mean and b_{12} b_{13} b_{14} and b_{15} are the partworths for the data pooled across groups. The parameters b_{21} b_{22} b_{23} b_{24} b_{25} capture the two-way interactions between group membership and partworths, i.e., a direct test that the within group partworths are equal. For example, if b_{21} is zero, then the mean responses for the two groups are equal to the grand mean. If b_{22} is equal to zero, the estimate of the parthworth of the first level of the first attribute based on the pooled data and be used in both groups. If not, the partworth for group one is $(b_{12} + b_{22})$ and for group two $(b_{12} - b_{22})$. If it were known that the groups differed in the partworths, A_1 would be the logical coding for the analysis. If on the other hand it were known that the groups did not differ, the A_2 coding would make the most sense.

3.5 The Design Matrix, X

The within subject matrix, X, must be the same for all individuals. The parameters associated with columns of X, however, can differ and assume the value of zero for some individuals or groups. The coding of X follows familiar conventions in CA. For example, the coding for X provided in the previous section illustrates the use of orthogonal polynomials to code quantitative variables. That is, it is assumed that two groups of respondents evaluate a set of concepts that are profiled in terms of two attributes. The first attribute, α, is assumed to be a *quantitative* attribute having three levels. Three price levels — low, medium, and high — would generate such an attribute. Given the three levels, linear and quadratic effects can be estimated. The linear effect would be expected to be negative for price; higher prices should result in lower preference. The quadratic component can be interpreted as an indication of whether there is "concavity" or "convexity" in the ratings of the quantitative variable. That is, the {1 -2 1} coding for the quadratic effect represents the difference between the *sum of the lowest and highest values* and *twice the middle value*. Alternatively, the quadratic effect with three levels is equal to $[(\alpha_{low} + \alpha_{high})/2 - \alpha_{middle}]$. Assuming the linear component indicates a significant trend, if the middle value is significantly less than the mean of the extreme values, then the partworths are increasing at an increasing rate (or decreasing at a decreasing rate). If the middle value is greater that the mean of the two extreme values, then the rate of increase is decreasing (rate of decrease is increasing). The test of significance on the component provides the appropriate test of the null hypothesis and the sign indicates the direction of change. The following section illustrates how hypotheses may be formulated within the framework of the GMR model.

The second attribute, β, is assumed to be a two level *qualitative* attribute. A study evaluating two hypothetical brands would generate this sort of attribute. A significant main effect within a group would indicate group members have relative greater preference for one of the brand names. There will be four parameters to estimate within each group (np = 4), i.e., the mean, μ, linear effect for the "price-like" attribute α, quadratic effect for α, and main effect for the "brandname-like" attribute β. The first column of X gives the coding for the mean, the second and third the coding for linear and quadratic polynomials for α, and the fourth gives main effect coding for β (Kirk, 1982, p.830).

4. HYPOTHESIS TESTING

Hypotheses of the form $H_0: FbC' = 0$ against the alternative $H_1: FbC' \neq 0$ may be formulated and tested using procedures provided in the Appendix. The matrix $_rF^{np}$ identifies the rows of b that will enter into the hypothesis test. The matrix $_tC'^{ng}$ identifies the columns of b that will be used.[3]

A variety of hypotheses formulated in terms of F and C are interpreted in Figure 3. For example, Figure 2 indicates that under A_2 the interaction terms for each of the four parameters are in the second column of b. Accordingly, in Figure 3 (set 1) there are ones in each column of F — indicating that each of the parameters is to be selected — and a one in the second column of C' — indicating that it is the second column of parameters that are to be selected. The test is that the values b_{21} *and* b_{22} *and* b_{23} *and* b_{24} *and* b_{25} *simultaneously* are equal to zero. The equivalent coding under A_1 tests the hypothesis that the parameter values are equal in the two groups, i.e., their difference is zero. As with the A_2 formulation, the F matrix is coded to select each row, but the C' matrix is coded to take the *difference* between the parameters in each row. If the difference is zero, then there is no group by attribute interaction. Figure 3 (set 2) gives the test of no group by attribute α interaction. The F matrix selects the parameters corresponding to the linear and quadratic effects. The C matrix under A_1 tests the hypothesis that the difference between the two sets simultaneously are equal to zero. The C matrix under A_2 directly tests whether the interaction parameters simultaneously are equal to zero. Figure 3 (set 3) selects

---

[3] It is evident from Equation 2 that information about the covariance structure of errors D (Eq. 3) is incorporated in the covariance structure of partworth estimates. The typical conjoint study in which individuals make repeated responses to a fixed set of concepts is the sort of setting that might generate a data set with an arbitrary covariance structure that differs from that assumed for OLS estimation. While the magnitude of the estimates may be robust to departures of D from (iid), significance levels of hypotheses defined on the estimated parameters can vary depending on the nature of the departure.

FIGURE 2
Interpretation of the Elements of b
Under Alternative Coding of A

Parameter	Interpretation under A_1	Interpretation under A_2
b_{11}	Mean for group one.	Grand mean for both groups.
b_{12}	Linear effect for attribute α for group one.	Pooled linear effect for attribute α.
b_{13}	Quadratice effect for attribute α for group one.	Pooled quadratic effect for attribute α.
b_{14}	Main effect (partworth) for attribute β for group one.	Pooled main effect of attribute β.
b_{21}	Mean for group two.	Main effect of group on mean preference, i.e., group by mean interaction.
b_{22}	Linear effect for attribute α for group two.	Interaction between group and linear effect for attribute α.
b_{23}	Quadratice effect for attribute α for group two.	Interaction between group and quadratic effect for attribute α.
b_{24}	Main effect (partworth) for attribute β for group two.	Interaction between group and main effect of attribute β.

$$A_1 = \begin{matrix} 1 & 1 & 1 & \ldots & 0 & 0 & 0 \\ 0 & 0 & 0 & \ldots & 1 & 1 & 1 \end{matrix}$$

$$A_2 = \begin{matrix} 1 & 1 & 1 & \ldots & 1 & 1 & 1 \\ 1 & 1 & 1 & \ldots & -1 & -1 & -1 \end{matrix}$$

only the quadratic component and test it for group by attribute interaction. Figure 3 (set 4) shows how to test whether the grand mean is equal to zero. Under A_1, the means of the two groups must be selected and pooled to get the grand mean, which is then tested to see whether it is equal to zero. Under A_2, the b_{11} element corresponds to the grand mean and the test is whether it is equal to zero. Taken as a whole, the set of hypotheses provides they basis for so-called "step-down" hypothesis tests on the "price-like" attribute.

Further illustration that the interpretation of the hypothesis corresponding to F and C matrices (depending on the coding of A) is provided by Figure 3 (set 5 and 6). Under A_1, set 5 tests the hypothesis that the "brand" effect in group one is zero. Under A_2, set 5 tests the hypothesis that the average "brand" effect *across groups* is zero. Set 6 provides the formulations for testing the hypothesis that the "brand" effects across the two groups are *equal*.

5. CONCLUSION

The aggregated CA problem may be formulated in terms of the generalized multivariate regression model. Using this approach, hypotheses of the form H_0 : F b C' = 0 against the alternative H_1 : F b C' $\neq$ 0 may be formulated. The matrix $_r F^{np}$ identifies the rows of b that will enter into the hypothesis test. That is, hypotheses regarding partworths, or linear combinations of partworths, are specified by F. The matrix $_t C'^{ng}$ identifies the columns of b that will be used. In other words, it specifies which groups are used in the hypothesis. A particularly appealing aspect of the approach is that hypotheses regarding interactions between group membership and partworth values may be formulated in an efficient and compact form through judicious choice of F and C. Examples are provided by hypothesis sets one through six of Figure 3. The appeal of having an efficient mechanism for screening group by attribute interactions is that significant interactions of this sort provide evidence for potential market segmentation strategies. That is, significant interactions indicate that members of the respective groups may respond differently to concept formulations.

The difference between the outlined approach and the group approach summarized in Figure 1 is that a covariance matrix that captures empirical heteroscedasticity and collinearity in responses is available. Estimation and subsequent hypothesis tests incorporate this information. Two directions for additional research are planned. First, is evident that the estimation procedure may be formulated as a within subjects design with conjoint attributes corresponding to "trials" factors and the group factor corresponding to "between group" factors. Many statistical software packages can accommodate within subjects designs. Formulating the GMR formulation as a within subjects design will make widely available estimation packages available for CA hypothesis testing. Secondly, there are numerous empirical response processes that might affect the typical conjoint study. A study in currently under way to

FIGURE 3
Matrices F and C for Testing Specified Hypotheses Under A_1 And A_2 Coding

Set	Test of Hypothesis that:	Matrices Under A_1		Matrices Under A_2	
		F	C	F	C
1	All group by attribute <u>interactions</u> = 0.	$\begin{matrix} 1 & 0 & 0 & 0 \\ 0 & 1 & 0 & 0 \\ 0 & 0 & 1 & 0 \\ 0 & 0 & 0 & 1 \end{matrix}$	$\begin{matrix} 1 \\ 1 \\ 1 \\ -1 \end{matrix}$	$\begin{matrix} 1 & 0 & 0 & 0 \\ 0 & 1 & 0 & 0 \\ 0 & 0 & 1 & 0 \\ 0 & 0 & 0 & 1 \end{matrix}$	$\begin{matrix} 0 \\ 1 \\ 1 \\ 1 \end{matrix}$
2	Group by α_{lin} <u>and</u> α_{quad} <u>interactions</u> = 0.	$\begin{matrix} 0 & 1 & 0 & 0 \\ 0 & 0 & 1 & 0 \end{matrix}$	$\begin{matrix} 1 \\ 1 \end{matrix}$ -1	$\begin{matrix} 0 & 1 & 0 & 0 \\ 0 & 0 & 1 & 0 \end{matrix}$	$\begin{matrix} 0 \\ 1 \end{matrix}$
3	Group by α_{quad} <u>interaction</u> = 0.	$\begin{matrix} 0 & 0 & 1 & 0 \end{matrix}$	$1 \; -1$	$\begin{matrix} 0 & 0 & 1 & 0 \end{matrix}$	0
4	Grand <u>mean</u> = 0.	$\begin{matrix} 1 & 0 & 0 & 0 \end{matrix}$	1	$\begin{matrix} 1 & 0 & 0 & 0 \end{matrix}$	0
5	Partworth (<u>main effect</u>) B = 0, within group 1 (under A1), pooled value (under A2).	$\begin{matrix} 0 & 0 & 0 & 1 \end{matrix}$	$1 \; 0$	$\begin{matrix} 0 & 0 & 0 & 1 \end{matrix}$	0
6	Partworth (<u>main effect</u>) $B_{group\,1} = B_{group\,2}$.	$\begin{matrix} 0 & 0 & 0 & 1 \end{matrix}$	$1 \; -1$	$\begin{matrix} 0 & 0 & 0 & 1 \end{matrix}$	0

simulate a number of the possibilities and evaluate the sensitivity of hypothesis tests to violations of the assumption of OLS which is commonly used for estimation.

6. APPENDIX

Testing hypotheses of the form $H_0 : F b C' = 0$ against the alternative $H_1 : F b C' \neq 0$ may be tested using the following likelihood ratio test. F is a ($r \times np$, $r \leq np$) specified matrix. C' is a ($t \times ng$, $t \leq ng$) specified matrix. The tests are based on the hypothesis and error matrices:

(A1) $H = F b C' (C R C')^{-1} (F b C')'$
(A2) $E = F (X D^{-1} X)^{-1} F'$, where
(A3) $R = (A' A)^{-1} + (A' A)^{-1} A' Y D^{-1} Y' A (A' A)^{-1} - b (X' D^{-1} X) b$

A test of H_0 is given by the U statistic (Srivastava and Carter, p. 184):

(A4) $U_{r,n,t} = |E| / |E + H|$,

where $n = ng_1 + ng_2 - no + np - ng$, ng_i = the number in group i, and $|\cdot|$ is the determinant of the indicated term. For large n, an asymptotical test may be based on:

(A5) $TSTAT = -[n - (r - t + 1)/2] \ln(U)$,
(A6) $P\{TSTAT \geq z\} \approx P\{\chi^2_{rt} \geq z\}$.

REFERENCES

Green, Paul E., and V. R. Rao (1971), "Conjoint Measurement for Quantifying Judgmental Data," *Journal of Marketing Research*, 8, 355-63.

Green, Paul E. and V. Srinivasan (1978), "Conjoint Analysis in Consumer Research: Issues and Outlook," *Journal of Consumer Research*, 5 (September), 103-23.

Grizzle J. E. and D. M. Allen (1969), "Analysis of Growth and Dose Response Curves," *Biometrics*, 25, 357-81.

Hagerty, M. R. (1985),"Improving the Predictive Power of Conjoint Analysis: The Use of Factor Analysis and Cluster Analysis," *Journal of Marketing Research*, (May) XXII, 168-84.

Kamakura, W. A. (1988), "A Least Squares Procedure for Benefit Segmentation with Conjoint Experiments," *Journal of Marketing Research*, (May) XXV, 157-67.

Kerlinger, F. N. and E. J. Pedhauser (1973) *Multiple Regression in Behavioral Research*, New York : Holt, Rinehart and Winston, Inc.

Khatri, C. G., (1966) "A Note on a MANOVA Model Applied to Problems in Growth Curves," *Ann. Inst. Statist. Math.*, 18, 75-86.

Kirk, R. E., (1982) *Experimental Design: Procedures for the Behavioral Sciences, 2nd ed*, Monterery, Ca: Brooks/Cole Publishing Company.

Kruskal, J.B. (1965) "Analysis of Factorial Experiments by estimating Monotone Transformations of the Data," *Journal of the Royal Statistical Society B*, 251-263.

Morrison, D.F. (1976), *Multivariate Statistical Methods*, New York: McGraw-Hill Book Company.

Potthoff, R. R. and S. N. Roy (1964) "A Generalized Multivariate Analysis of Variance Model Useful Especially for Growth Curve Problems, *Biometrika*, 51, 313-26.

Srinivasan, V. and A. D. Shocker (1973) "Linear Programming Techniques for Multidimensional Analysis of Preferences," *Psychometrika*, 38, 337-369.

Srivastava, M. C. and E. M. Carter (1983) *An Introduction to Applied Multivariate Statistics*, New York : North Holland.

A Hybrid Conjoint Model With Individual-Level Interaction Estimation

Paul E. Green, University of Pennsylvania
Abba M. Krieger, University of Pennsylvania
Catherine M. Schaffer, University of Denver

With the advent of larger-scale industry applications, there has been a corresponding need to develop conjoint modeling methods that can cope with large numbers of attributes and levels. The authors describe a hybrid model that estimates individual-level interactions and smooths parameter estimates by empirical Bayes methods.

INTRODUCTION

In their recent review, Green and Srinivasan (1990) report that one of the most active research areas in conjoint analysis involves the development of part-worth estimation methods designed to increase reliability and predictive validity. The need for such methods has become acute as conjoint applications include ever larger numbers of attributes and levels.

Hagerty (1985) has outlined several classes of part-worth estimation methods; the taxonomy of Figure 1 is partially based on his earlier remarks. The left-most branch denotes traditional full-profile-only analysis; the principal parameter estimation methods are MONANOVA (Kruskal 1965), LINMAP (Shocker and Srinivasan 1977), and, increasingly, OLS dummy variable regression.

More recently, however, researchers (Pekelman and Sen 1979; Krishnamurthi and Wittink 1989) have augmented traditional part-worth modeling with mixtures of linear, quadratic, and part-worth parameters. Gains in reliability/validity may also be obtained by constraining part-worths to respect within-attribute monotonicity (Srinivasan, Jain, and Malhotra 1983), or by various aggregation methods, such as those proposed by Hagerty (1985), Kamakura (1988), and Green, Krieger, and Zelnio (1989).

If the researcher also collects self-explicated data on individual attribute-level desirabilities and attribute importances, further improvements are possible, as illustrated by the Bayesian-like method of Cattin, Gelfand, and Danes (1983) and the parameter constrained approach of van der Lans and Heiser (1990). In both cases, considerably more data collection is entailed since each of these methods assumes that a large enough set of full profiles is obtained to estimate part-worths from either profile *or* self-explicated data.

In contrast, the hybrid models (Green, Goldberg, and Montemayor 1981; Green 1984) and the ACA model (Johnson 1987) collect a limited number of full or partial profiles which serve largely as either a "polishing" operation to refine self-explicated part-worths (ACA), or as a way to estimate additional group-level parameters (hybrid models). Given their reduced data demands, these latter approaches have received extensive commercial application.

Finally, in the right-most branch, we note that in CASEMAP (Srinivasan 1988; Srinivasan and Wyner 1989) there are no profile data at all. The entire exercise consists of self-explicated data collection.

To date, extensive empirical comparisons across classes of the models have been few. In a comparison of Hagerty's and Kamakura's models with traditional conjoint, Green and Helsen (1989) found no improvement in internal validity for the newer approaches. Traditional conjoint also appears to outperform hybrid models and ACA, at least in cases involving sufficient degrees of freedom for error estimation. Hybrid models, in turn, tend to outperform self-explicated models (Green 1984); that is, even a limited number of full profiles adds something in terms of predictive ability.

Features of The Proposed Model

The model proposed here is part of the hybrid model family. In addition, it employs features that are analogous to the Hagerty approach. In contrast to previously published methods, the proposed hybrid model:

1. Employs a convex combination technique that optimally weights self-explicated attribute importances with group-level, conjoint-derived importances, so as to maximize the correlation of the resulting composite with the individual's (holdout) sample of profile evaluations.
2. Uses empirical Bayes procedures to "smooth" individual-based parameters in accord with information obtained from the full sample.
3. Fits selected two-way interaction terms on a disaggregate basis. This is accomplished by the use of Tukey's one-degree-of-freedom procedure (Tukey 1949) in which two-way interactions are linear functions of previously computed individual main effects.
4. Contains a built-in cross-validation procedure that helps the user select an appropriate number of two-way interaction effects to fit on a stagewise basis.

THE MODEL

The proposed model collects information on respondent:

1. Self-explicated attribute level desirabilities (typically expressed on a 0-10, equal interval rating scale).
2. Self-explicated attribute importances (typically expressed in terms of a constant sum, 100 point allocation scale).
3. Likelihood-of-purchase ratings (0-100 scale) of a limited set of full profiles, drawn from a much larger master design of orthogonally constructed profiles.

These steps are similar to the procedures followed in most hybrid models (Green 1984).

Main Effects Estimation

The first phase of the analysis entails estimating main effects parameters at the individual-respondent level. First, we assume that the best estimate of the "true" attribute-level desirabilities is found in the self-explicated desirabilities. There are reasonable grounds for this assumption. Our own research (Green, Krieger, and Agarwal 1992) has found very high test/retest reliabilities for attribute-level desirabilities (on average, 0.90 in a sample of 51 subjects). In contrast, the test/retest reliability of self-explicated importances was only 0.48 for the same group of subjects.

Subjects' conjoint profile evaluations are then separately used to obtain group level attribute importances. These group level importances are optimally combined with each individual respondent's self-explicated importances to obtain a set of weighted importances that (along with the respondent's self-explicated

FIGURE 1
A Taxonomy of Part-Worth Estimation Methods

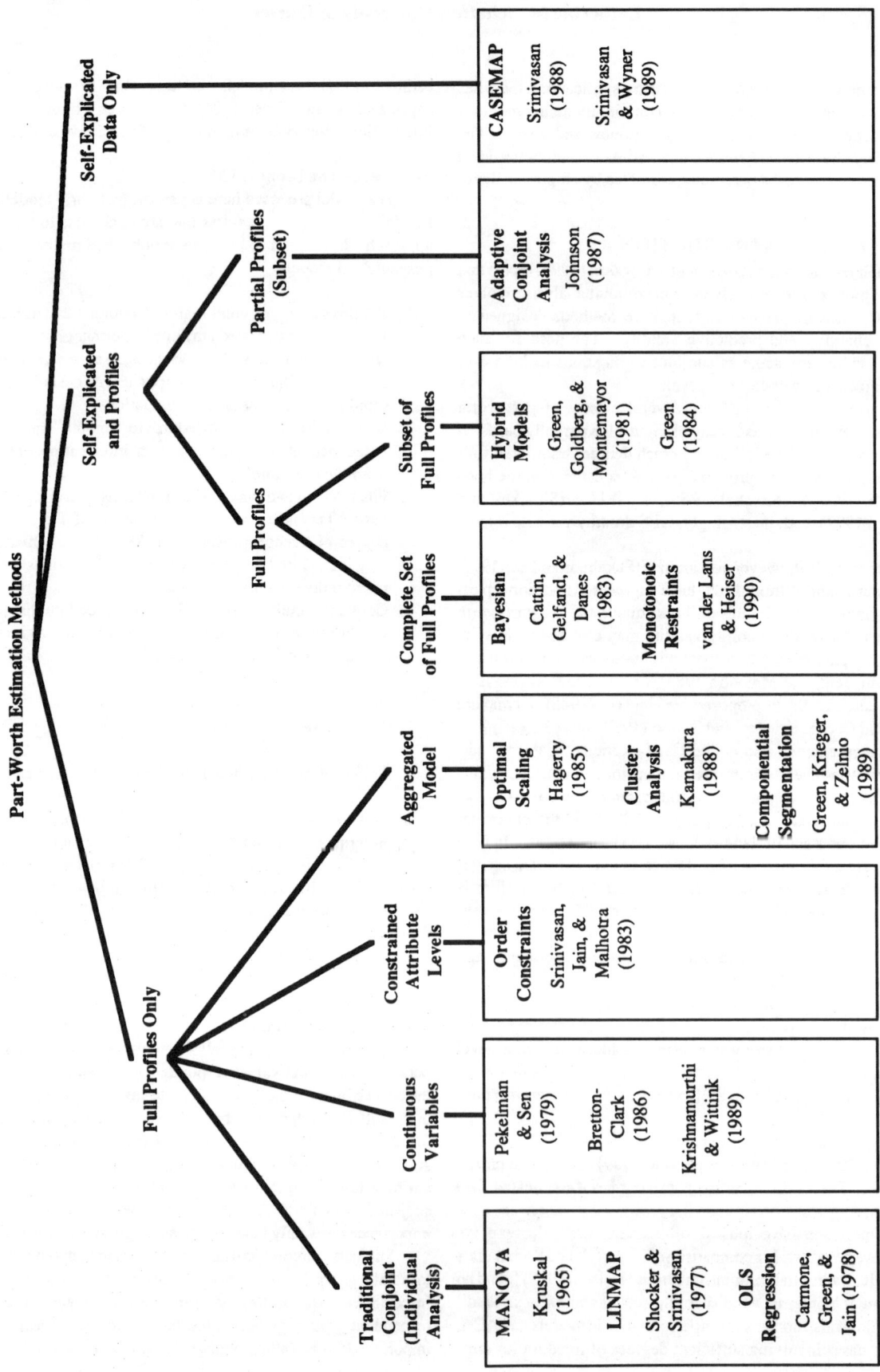

desirabilities) maximally correlate with the subject's actual conjoint profile evaluations.[1]

At this point the EMBAY procedure has estimated a main effects, part-worth model for each respondent.[2] A set of residuals are then obtained by subtracting the respondent's predicted profile evaluations from his/her actual profile evaluations. These sets of respondent residuals become dependent variables for the next phase of model fitting.

Interaction Estimation

EMBAY fits selected two-way interactions to each subject's residuals, using Tukey's one-degree-of-freedom method (Tukey 1949). The two-way interactions are selected in a stepwise manner, according to highest accounted-for variance in the residuals across all respondents.[3] All arguments continue to be the individual's main effects parameters.

The Tukey procedure estimates a single slope parameter at each stage of the two-way interaction fitting. Each time an interaction is fit, it is internally cross validated, subject by subject. The average cross-validations are used diagnostically to stop the fitting process. Several sets of descriptive statistics (including cross-validated R^2) are computed to see if it is worthwhile continuing the "extraction" of two-way interactions.

We next provide a more formal elaboration on the topics of Tukey's one-degree-of-freedom method and the empirical Bayes procedure.

Tukey's One-Degree-of-Freedom Interaction

Tukey's one-degree-of-freedom interaction model can be written as follows:

$$A_{ij} = \mu + x_i + y_j + \lambda x_i y_j + \varepsilon_{ij} \tag{1}$$

where the usual assumptions:

$$\varepsilon_{ij} = NID(0,\sigma^2); \Sigma x_i = \Sigma y_j = 0,$$

are assumed to hold. We note that the single interaction term is expressed by the slope parameter λ, where the arguments x_i and y_j are previously estimated main effects, expressed as deviations around the grand mean.

Our model computes R^2's for all two-way interactions and selects the pair of attributes with the highest R^2. A cross-validated R^2 is also fit. New residuals are computed and the program continues the approach at the user's discretion.

Empirical Bayes

The OLS estimation problem, generally framed, assumes that

$$Y_{ij} = \alpha_i + \beta_i X_{ij} + \varepsilon_{ij}, \tag{2}$$

where i varies over individuals and j over profiles. We assume that the ε_{ij} are independent and identically distributed normal random variables. This model applies at the self-explicated stage, where X_{ij} represents the predicted utility for the jth profile for individual i and Y_{ij} denotes the corresponding actual score given to this profile. The model also applies at the stage of fitting interaction terms; see equation (1). In this latter case, however, Y_{ij} denotes the residuals after the self-explicated fitting stage; X_{ij} is the product of the part-worths (after mean centering) for the two-way interaction of interest.

As noted earlier, each intercept α_i is fitted at the individual level; once we estimate β_i then $\hat{\alpha}_i = \overline{Y}_i - \beta_i \overline{X}_i$ where $\overline{X}_i$ and $\overline{Y}_i$ are the respective means for X and Y, averaged over the profiles. We estimate β_i separately for each individual; this is tantamount to running OLS for each individual. As noted above, we denote this estimate by β_i.

We can also estimate β_i by assuming that the slopes are equal across individuals. This implies that the common slope is:

$$\beta = \frac{\sum\limits_{i,j} (Y_{ij} - \overline{Y}_i)(X_{ij} - \overline{X}_i)}{\sum\limits_{i,j} (X_{ij} - \overline{X}_i)^2} \tag{3}$$

An intermediate approach is to use a Bayesian framework. We assume the β_i are generated independently from a common normal distribution with mean β_0 and variance σ_0^2. It follows from standard Bayesian analysis that the posterior distributions of the β_i are independent normals with means:

$$\lambda_i^* \beta_i + (1-\lambda_i^*) \beta_0 \tag{4}$$

and variances:

$$Var(\beta_i) \sigma_0^2 / (Var(\beta_i) + \sigma_0^2) \tag{5}$$

where $\lambda_i^* = \sigma_0^2 / (\sigma_0^2 + Var(\beta_i))$ and $Var(\beta_i)$ is the variance of the OLS regression coefficient.

We follow the approach employed by Rubin (1980); that is, we use empirical Bayes to estimate β_0 and σ_0^2 in equations (4) and (5).

We define s_i^2 to be the estimate of $Var(\beta_i)$.

We find the β_0 and σ_0^2 that maximize the likelihood, given β_i and s_i^2, after integrating over the random parameters, β_i. This likelihood cannot be maximized directly and so we use an iterative approach (also followed by Rubin) that is based on the EM algorithm of Dempster, Laird, and Rubin (1977).

PILOT STUDY

Our pilot test of the EMBAY model uses data obtained from a hybrid conjoint study involving student evaluations of apartment descriptions; details of the experiment can be found in Green and Schaffer (1991).

Table 1 shows the list of attributes and levels. The sample size is 177. Self-explicated desirabilities were rated on a 0 - 10 equal-

---

[1] Details of the weighting procedure can be obtained from the authors.

[2] The preceding method also estimates an idiosyncratic intercept term for each respondent, using that subject's own full profile evaluations.

[3] Whichever two-way interaction that is selected by the stepwise procedure is assumed to be relevant for all respondents.

TABLE 1
Attributes and Levels Used in Pilot Study

A. Walking Time to Classes
1. 10 minutes
2. 20 minutes
3. 30 minutes

B. Noise Level of Apartment House
1. Very quiet
2. Average noise level
3. Extremely noisy

C. Safety of Apartment Location
1. Very safe location
2. Average safety
3. Very unsafe location

D. Condition of Apartment
1. Newly renovated throughout
2. Renovated kitchen only
3. Poor condition

E. Size of Living/Dining Area
1. 24 by 30 feet
2. 15 by 20 feet
3. 9 by 12 feet

F. Monthly Rent (Utilities Included)
1. $540
2. $360
3. $225

---

interval scale. Attribute importances were obtained from a 100-point allocation (constant sum) procedure. In the calibration stage, each respondent received 18 full profiles, designed according to an orthogonal array. The respondent rated each profile on a 0 - 100 likelihood-of-renting scale. After some demographic data were collected, each respondent was shown 16 holdout apartment descriptions, utilizing levels 1 and 3 of the attributes shown in Table 1. These stimuli were also designed by an orthogonal array. The same 0 - 100 likelihood-of-renting scale was used for the holdout sample as well.

Testing the Model

Previous experience with the data set suggested that self-explicated models would probably fit the full profile calibration data well. Hence, we would not be surprised if the residuals from the self-explicated main effects had relatively little signal left for two-way interaction estimation.

Four different models were fit to the data:

1. A main effects, part-worth model that used only self-explicated importances (i.e., OLS derived importances were not employed).
2. The same model as above, with the addition of two interaction terms.
3. A main effects, part-worth model that employed an optimally weighted composite of self-explicated *and* the group-level, conjoint-derived importances.
4. The same model as above, with the addition of two interaction terms.

Each of the models was evaluated in terms of its cross-validation, subject by subject, with the 16 holdout profiles. Table 2 summarizes the results.

Descriptive Results

As we anticipated, fits of the two main effects models to the 18 calibration profiles were very good. Table 2 shows that the convex combination model (of self-explicated and derived importances) fits the subjects' calibration profile response somewhat better than the self-explicated importances alone. This also holds true for the calibration model that incorporates two additional interaction terms.

As it should, we note that the addition of two interaction terms increases the calibration model fits—correlations of 0.811 (versus 0.776) and 0.790 (versus 0.752). However, the increases are not dramatically large. Figure 2 suggests why this is so. This chart shows plots of the two average two-way interactions. As noted, no cross-over interaction effects are found. While the line segments are not parallel, the interaction effects do not appear to be extreme.

Cross Validation

Table 2 also summarizes the results of correlating predictions of the four calibration models with actual responses to each subject's 16 holdout profiles. We note that the main effects model cross validates better than the model that also includes interaction terms. For the convex combination model the correlation is 0.731 for main effects versus 0.696 for main effects plus interactions. Counterpart results for the self-explicated importances model are 0.712 and 0.663.

First-choice validations also show the same pattern in which the main-effects-only model out-predicts main effects plus interactions. This finding is consistent with those of Green (1984) in which hybrid models, with and without interaction terms, were also compared. Significance tests for main effects only versus main effects plus interaction indicated that one could not reject the null hypothesis of no difference (alpha level of 0.05) for the correlation results, but one could reject the null hypothesis for the first-choice predictions. Insofar as the convex combination versus the self-explicated model alone is concerned, differences in correlations and first-choice predictions are not significant at the 0.05 alpha level.

CONCLUSIONS

The pilot study provides some support for the value of the convex combination model over the use of self-explicated impor-

TABLE 2
Summary of Correlation Results for Pilot Study

Actual Versus Fitted Calibration Model	Convex Combination Model	Self-Explicated Importances Alone
Main-effects-only model	.776	.752
Main-effects plus two interactions	.811	.790
External Validations		
Main-effects-only model	.731	.712
Main-effects plus two interactions	.696	.663
First Choice External Validations (Incidence of correct predictions)		
Main-effects only model	46.0%	45.3%
Main-effects plus two interactions	37.7%	36.5%

tances alone in fitting the main effects model. The differences are not dramatic, however, in terms of either cross validation correlation or first-choice hit incidence.

Somewhat more surprising is the finding that the simpler main effects model appears to cross validate at least as well as the more general main effects plus interactions model; however, see Hagarty (1985) and Green (1984). Other data sets may exhibit a greater incidence of stable two-way interaction effects. In any case, the proposed model provides a way to measure these interactions (if they exist) and to examine how well they hold up in cross validation.

When will the empirical Bayes aspect of the model prove useful? We surmise that the empirical Bayes procedure will be most useful when the data are heterogeneous in the sense that a subset of the subjects shows highly reliable fits while another subset does not. In the first (reliable) subset, the empirical Bayes weighting parameter would give virtually its entire weight to the subject's own data (particularly if the subject differs from the rest of the sample). In the second (unreliable) subset, the group's results would receive high weight relative to the individual's and hence would "smooth" out that subject's parameter values.

The question of interaction measurement by this (or other) conjoint models is still wide open. Clearly, one would expect interactions in the case of sensory or esthetic product classes. However, little is currently known about the reliability with which interactions can be measured and, particularly, their degree of homogeneity across respondents.

REFERENCES

Cattin, Philippe, Alan E. Gelfand, and Jeffrey Danes (1983), "A Simple Bayesian Procedure for Estimation in a Conjoint Model," *Journal of Marketing Research*, 20 (February), 29-35.

Dempster, A. P., N. M. Laird, and Donald B. Rubin (1977), "Maximum Likelihood from Incomplete Data Via the EM Algorithm," *Journal of the Royal Statistical Society*, Series B, 39, 1-38.

Green, Paul E. (1984), "Hybrid Models for Conjoint Analysis: An Expository Review," *Journal of Marketing Research*, 21 (May), 155-169.

_____, Stephen M. Goldberg, and Mila Montemayor (1981), "A Hybrid Utility Estimation Model for Conjoint Analysis," *Journal of Marketing*, 45 (Winter), 33-41.

_____ and Kristiaan Helsen (1989), "Cross-Validation Assessment of Alternatives to Individual-Level Conjoint Analysis: A Case Study," *Journal of Marketing Research*, 26 (August), 346-350.

_____, Abba M. Krieger, and Manoj K. Agarwal (1992), "Man Versus Model of Man: When Do Conjoint Models Out-Predict the Decision Maker?," Working Paper, University of Pennsylvania, June.

_____, Abba M. Krieger, and Robert N. Zelnio (1989), "A Componential Segmentation Model with Optimal Design Features," *Decision Sciences*, 20 (Spring), 221-238.

_____ and Catherine M. Schaffer (1991), "Importance Weight Effects on Self-Explicated Preference Models," in R. H. Hulman and M. R. Solomon (eds.), *Advances in Consumer Research*, Provo, UT: Association for Consumer Research, 476-482.

_____ and V. Srinivasan (1990), "Conjoint Analysis in Marketing: New Developments with Implications for Research and Practice," *Journal of Marketing*, 54 (October), 3-19.

Hagerty, Michael R. (1985), "Improving the Predictive Power of Conjoint Analysis: The Use of Factor Analysis and Cluster Analysis," *Journal of Marketing Research*, 22 (May), 168-184.

Johnson, Richard M. (1987), "Adaptive Conjoint Analysis," *Sawtooth Software Conference on Perceptual Mapping, Conjoint Analysis, and Computer Interviewing*, Ketchum, ID: Sawtooth Software, 253-265.

FIGURE 2
Two-Way Interaction Effects in Pilot Study

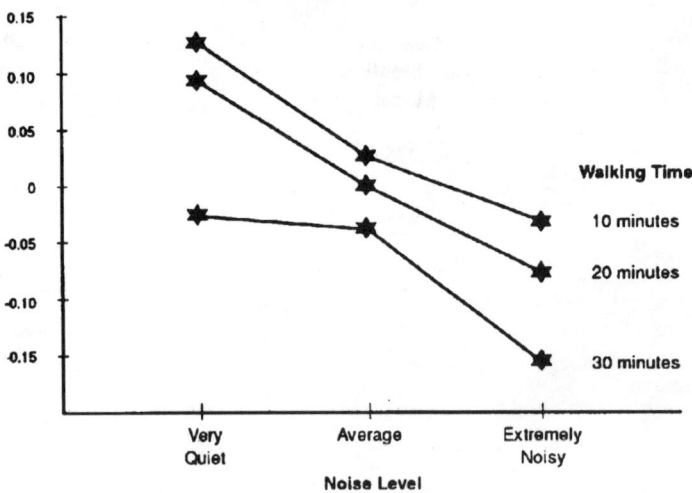

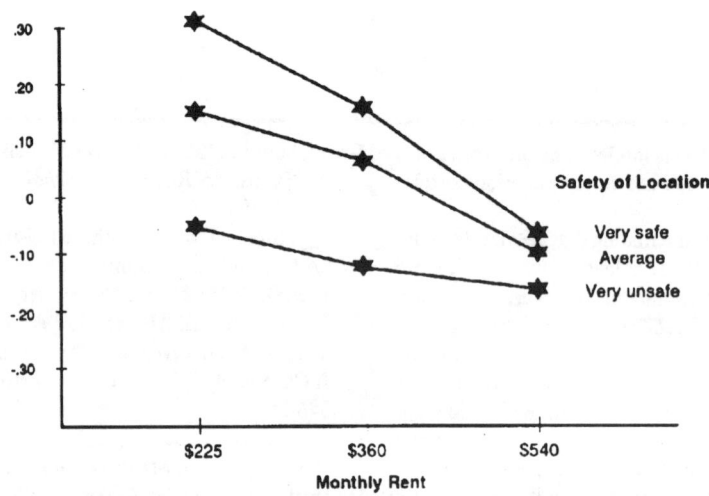

Kamakura, Wagner A. (1988), "A Least Squares Procedure for Benefit Segmentation for Conjoint Experiments," *Journal of Marketing Research*, 25 (May), 157-167.

Krishnamurthi, Lakshman and Dick R. Wittink (1989), "The Part-Worth Model and Its Applicability in Conjoint Analysis," Working Paper, College of Business Administration, University of Illinois (September).

Kruskal, Joseph B. (1965), "Analysis of Factorial Experiments by Estimating Monotone Transformations of the Data," *Journal of the Royal Statistical Society*, Series B, 27, 251-263.

Pekelman, Dov and Subrata K. Sen (1979), "Improving Prediction in Conjoint Analysis," *Journal of Marketing Research*, 16 (May), 211-220.

Rubin, Donald B. (1980), "Using Empirical Bayes Techniques in the Law School Validity Studies," *Journal of the American Statistical Association*, 75 (December), 801-816.

Shocker, Allan D. and V. Srinivasan (1977), "LINMAP (Version II): A FORTRAN IV Computer Program for Analyzing Ordinal Preference (Dominance) Judgments via Linear Programming Techniques for Conjoint Measurement," *Journal of Marketing Research*, 14, 101-103.

Srinivasan, V. (1988), "A Conjunctive-Compensatory Approach to the Self-Explication of Multiattributed Preferences," *Decision Sciences*, 19 (Spring), 295-305.

———, Arun K. Jain, and Naresh K. Malhotra (1983), "Improving Predictive Power of Conjoint Analysis by Constrained Parameter Estimation," *Journal of Marketing Research*, 20 (November) 433-438.

——— and Gordon A. Wyner (1989), "CASEMAP: Computer-Assisted Self-Explication of Multi-Attributed Preferences," in W. Henry, M. Menasco, and H. Takada (eds.), *New Product Development and Testing*, Lexington, MA: Lexington Books, 91-111.

Tukey, John W. (1949), "One Degree of Freedom for Additivity," *Biometrica*, 5 (September), 232-242.

van der Lans, Ivo A. and Willem J. Heiser (1990), "Constrained Part-Worth Estimation in Conjoint Analysis Using the Self-Explicated Utility Model," Working Paper, University of Leiden, The Netherlands.

Does Humor in Advertising Enhance Systematic Processing?
Stephen M. Smith, Ohio State University

We attempted to assess the extent to which the humorousness of an advertisement influences systematic processing of the ad copy. While it is often assumed that humor enhances systematic processing, the present prediction, based on results from research on positive moods and message processing, was that it would disrupt systematic processing. Results supported the latter hypothesis, as subjects who perceived the ad as humorous evidenced less differentiation between strong and weak advertising claims than did subjects perceiving the ad as nonhumorous.

INTRODUCTION

An important question in the field of consumer research is whether humor enhances the persuasiveness of an advertisement relative to nonhumorous advertisements. Thus, it is not surprising that a number of studies have addressed this issue (e.g., Duncan and Nelson 1985; Gelb and Zinkhan 1986). Taken as a whole, this body of research has not been conclusive in establishing the effectiveness of humorous advertisements—an effect that advertisers apparently assume to exist (cf. Madden and Weinberger 1984).

More recently, efforts have been devoted to understanding the conditions under which humorous ads might be more effective than nonhumorous ads, rather than assuming that the effect is universal. In one such study, Chattopadhyay and Basu (1990) provided evidence consistent with the idea that humorous ads are more effective than nonhumorous ads when subjects' prior brand attitudes are positive, but are less effective than nonhumorous ads when subjects' prior attitudes are negative. However, the authors' interpretation rests on the ostensibly uncontested notion that humorous ads enhance attention to the ad and hence the extent of processing, a notion that was indirectly addressed in a 1973 synthesis by Sternthal and Craig.

Sternthal and Craig (1973) forwarded the somewhat contradictory propositions that humorous messages may attract attention, but may also detrimentally affect comprehension. Subsequent research has indicated that humorous ads are indeed more attention-grabbing than nonhumorous ads (e.g., Madden and Weinberger 1982), but it is certainly conceivable that this enhanced attention would be associated with enhanced processing of advertising claims, leading to more rather than less comprehension. However, this notion has not been directly tested in an advertising paradigm—to our knowledge, argument quality has not been included as a manipulated variable in a humor and advertising experiment—and it seems at least equally plausible that humor could grab attention while disrupting processing. For example, attention could be focused on the humorous part of the ad, and deflected away from the rest of the ad. This would seem especially plausible in situations where exposure is held relatively constant—i.e., when consumers don't get to attend selectively to ads of their choosing, such as is frequently the case in laboratory studies.

Indeed, in studies concluding that humor enhances ad processing, the effects often are either evident only for subjects' amount of ad-related elaboration (Chattopadhyay and Basu 1990), or are reported for the total number of elaborations, with no distinction made between ad- and brand-related elaborations (Lammers et al. 1983). Thus, it may be that humor attracts attention to the ad, but not to the ad claims.

Another possibility is that humor in an ad acts to enhance the consumer's mood, and this mood state influences consumers' ad processing. A number of studies have examined the influence of positive moods on message processing (e.g., Batra and Stayman 1990; Kuykendall and Keating 1990; Mackie and Worth 1989). While disagreement remains as to why the effect occurs, the typical finding emerging from these studies is that positive mood states disrupt systematic message processing. Following the above authors by manipulating claim strength, we hypothesized that:

H1: Participants exposed to nonhumorous ads varying in the strength of ad claims will base their responses to the ad, at least in part, on claim strength. Thus, we anticipate more positive responses to strong versus weak ad claims on these participants':
(a) brand attitudes;
(b) ad attitudes;
(c) perceptions of claim strength;
(d) purchase intentions; and
(e) brand-related elaborations

H2: Participants exposed to humorous versions of the same ads will be less influenced by the strength of ad claims than participants exposed to the nonhumorous versions, on each of the measures (a-e) listed above.

As previous studies have found that brand evaluations can be enhanced by the presence of humor in an ad (e.g., Duncan and Nelson 1985) or by eliciting a positive mood state in the respondent (e.g., Batra and Stayman 1990), we also hypothesized that:

H3: Compared to subjects viewing the nonhumorous versions, subjects exposed to humorous versions of the ad will respond more favorably to the ad on each of the above measures (a-e).

METHOD

Subjects and Design

Sixty-seven undergraduate students enrolled in a marketing course participated for course credit. Subjects were randomly assigned to see either a humorous or nonhumorous advertisement. The copy of the ad consisted of either weak or strong claims, and subjects were randomly assigned on this factor as well. The original design was thus a 2 (Humorousness; High vs. Low) X 2 (Claim Strength: Strong vs. Weak) randomized factorial.

Procedure

Subjects participated in groups of five to twelve each. They were seated in a classroom, and were separated by at least 10' to minimize the likelihood that they would see another subject's materials. The experimenter instructed subjects that the study concerned the effects of personality factors on advertising effectiveness, and that they would be reading and evaluating two print ads, which were contained in a 6-page booklet presented to each subject. Subjects were allowed to proceed at their own pace, but no subject took longer than 20 minutes to complete all of the experimental materials.

The target ad was presented first, and was an advertisement for a fictitious life insurance company that was constructed to look quite similar to ads encountered in *Fortune* magazine. Humorousness of the ad was manipulated via a cartoon that appeared at the top of the ad. The cartoon depicted a man sitting on a cloud, presumably in heaven. For subjects in the humor condition, a caption indicated that the man was thinking, "Wish I'd brought a magazine." For subjects in the nonhumorous condition, this caption was deleted. The claim strength manipulation was carried out by varying the actual claims presented in the ad copy. Subjects in the weak claims condition read a set of five ad claims that pretest subjects had rated as predominantly weak (e.g., "we've consistently received solid B-ratings from insurance analyst A.M. Best"; "our fiscal management practices have never been questioned by the S.E.C.").[1] Subjects in the strong claims condition read a set of five ad claims that were judged relatively strong in pretesting (e.g., "we've consistently received A+ ratings from insurance analyst A.M. Best"; "our fiscal management practices exceed industry standards").[2]

The primary dependent measures were collected on the next two pages of the booklet. The first three items asked subjects to indicate their attitude toward the "Metro Group" insurance company described in the ad. Each item was presented as a 9-point scale, with the end anchors "bad-good," "not likeable-likeable," and "useless-useful." Subjects then were asked to list whatever thoughts they had in response to the ad, "including thoughts about the insurance company, thoughts about the ad itself, or even totally unrelated thoughts." Twelve lines of space were provided for the thought-listing task, which was not timed.

Next subjects were asked to indicate their attitudes toward the advertisement itself, again using 9-point scales with the end anchors "unpleasant-pleasant," "uninteresting-interesting," "not amusing-amusing" and "not funny-funny." The latter two items constituted our check on the humor manipulation.

The next page asked subjects to rate the strength of the reasons given in the ad for purchasing insurance from the Metro Group, using two 9-point scales anchored by "bad-good" and "weak-strong." Purchase intent was measured by asking subjects to respond to the statement, "If I were looking to buy life insurance right now, I would be interested in speaking to someone from the Metro Group," by completing two 9-point scales anchored by "not likely-very likely" and "impossible-very possible."

All subjects then saw a second print advertisement, for a fictitious automobile, and answered several similar questions regarding their reactions to this ad. The final page solicited demographic information about the subjects, and embedded in this last sheet was an item asking subjects to indicate their general interest in purchasing life insurance on a 9-point scale anchored by "none at all" and "very much." This data was collected with the specific intention of using it as a covariate. The last item in the booklet asked subjects to indicate what they thought was the purpose of the experiment. Inspection of responses to this item indicated that subjects were unaware of the study's purpose.

Unless otherwise noted, the results below are from ANCOVAs using subjects' ratings on the general-interest-in-purchasing-life-insurance measure as the covariate. These ratings were at least marginally related to all of the dependent measures, with p-values ranging from .01 to .18.

RESULTS

Manipulation Checks

Ratings on the 2 claim strength measures were highly correlated ($r = .87$) and hence were averaged. A 2 (Ad Humorousness) X 2 (Claim Strength) ANOVA on this index yielded a main effect for claim strength, $F = 14.14, p < .001$, indicating that the manipulation was successful. Subjects reading the set of strong claims thought the claims were stronger (M = 6.98) than did subjects reading the set of weak claims (M = 4.52).

Ratings on the 2 perceived humorousness measures were also highly correlated ($r = .89$) and hence averaged. An ANOVA on this index, however, indicated no significant effects. Thus, our manipulation of humorousness was unsuccessful. Subjects exposed to the humorous ad did not rate the ad as significantly more humorous (M = 4.31) than did subjects exposed to the nonhumorous ad (M = 3.67), $F = 1.18, p = .281$.

Since results using the manipulated levels of humorousness as an independent variable were rendered virtually meaningless, they are not reported here. We elected to perform a median split on subjects' *ratings* of the humorousness of the advertisement. While an analysis of manipulated levels of humorousness would certainly have been preferable, we believed further analysis using the self-report data might shed light on how perceptions of humor in an ad affect persuasion. Indeed, the subjective nature of humor has led some scholars to call explicitly for analyses of self-reported humor in lieu of manipulations of humor (Duncan and Nelson 1985, p.33).

The median rating of humorousness in our sample was 4.0; as this fell below the midpoint, we placed subjects with scores falling on the median in the lower ("nonhumorous") half of the split. The results reported below are based on this median split.

Brand Attitudes

Subjects' responses to the three brand attitude measures were highly intercorrelated (alpha = .93) and were thus averaged to form a single index. A 2 (Rated Ad Humorousness) X 2 (Claim Strength) ANCOVA performed on these scores indicated a main effect for perceived humorousness, $F = 13.14, p = .001$. Supporting H3a, subjects who perceived the ad as humorous liked the brand better (M = 7.25) than subjects who did not perceive the ad as humorous (M = 5.90). A significant main effect was also obtained for claim strength, $F = 12.99, p = .001$, as strong claims elicited more positive brand attitudes (M = 7.17) than did weak claims (M = 5.77).

More importantly, a marginally significant interaction between perceived ad humorousness and claim strength, $F = 3.68, p = .060$, qualified the main effects. Planned comparisons of the means within conditions (see Table 1) indicated that, as predicted in H1a and H2a, subjects low in perceived ad humorousness liked the brand better when the claims were strong than when they were weak, $F = 16.59, p < .001$, while subjects who perceived the ad as humorous did not differentiate between weak and strong claims, $F < 1$.

Ad Attitudes

Subjects' responses to the two ad attitude items were highly correlated ($r = .77$) and hence were averaged. A 2 X 2 ANCOVA

---

[1] As one reviewer noted, the weak arguments could potentially be seen as additional attempts at humor. However, no effects on perceptions of humor were observed due to claim strength, $F = 0.09$.

[2] The argument quality pretest sample consisted of 14 undergraduate subjects who saw either the weak or strong arguments, but did not see the cartoon. They reported their attitudes toward the advertised brand on scales identical to those completed by the actual participants, and also completed a thought-listing task. Those reading the strong claims reported greater liking for the advertised brand (M = 6.95) than did subjects reading the weak claims (M = 5.52), $F = 7.24, p = .02$. The weak claims also elicited a marginally greater number of counterarguments on the thought-listing task (M = 1.14) than did the strong arguments (M = 0.28), $F = 3.72, p < .08$.

TABLE 1
Cell means for primary dependent measures

	Perceived Ad Humorousness			
	Low		High	
Claim Strength:	Weak	Strong	Weak	Strong
Dependent Measure				
Brand Attitude	5.09	6.76	6.78	7.62
Ad Attitude	4.34	5.89	6.79	6.87
Claim Strength	3.64	6.97	5.84	7.00
Purchase Intent	3.47	5.88	6.00	7.17
Net Brand Elaborations	-1.39	+0.94	-0.33	+0.80
Net Ad Elaborations	-0.44	+0.18	+0.08	-0.07

on this index indicated a pattern of results similar to that found for brand attitudes. Subjects high in perceived ad humorousness rated the ad more positively (M = 6.84) than did subjects low in perceived ad humorousness (M = 5.09), $F = 18.70, p < .001$, supporting H3b, and subjects reading the strong claims rated the ad marginally more positively (M = 6.35) than subjects who read the weak claims (M = 5.32), $F = 3.70, p = .059$.

The interaction between perceived ad humorousness and claim strength was significant, $F = 5.89, p = .018$, and was again analyzed via planned comparisons. As hypothesized in H1b and H2b, subjects low in perceived ad humorousness rated the ad more positively when the claims were strong than when they were weak, $F = 10.87, p < .01$, while subjects high in perceived ad humorousness were not influenced by claim strength, $F < 1$.

Perceptions of Claim Strength

The average of subjects' responses to the 2 claim strength items were also submitted to a 2 X 2 ANCOVA. Results again indicated two main effects, as subjects high in perceived ad humorousness thought the claims were stronger (M = 6.48) than did subjects low in perceived ad humorousness (M = 5.26), $F = 8.03, p = .006$, providing support for H3c. Also, subjects reading the strong claims rated them as stronger (M = 6.98) than subjects reading the weak claims (M = 4.52), $F = 34.65, p < .001$.

Again, these effects were qualified by an interaction between perceived ad humorousness and claim strength, $F = 10.43, p = .002$ (see Table 1 for cell means). Planned comparisons indicated that subjects low in perceived ad humorousness were affected more by the claim strength manipulation, $F = 45.52, p < .001$, than were subjects high in perceived ad humorousness, $F = 1.39, p > .25$. These results provided support for H1c and H2c.

Purchase Intent

Responses on the two purchase intent measures were highly correlated ($r = .95$) and hence were averaged to form a single index. Scores on this index were analyzed in a 2 X 2 ANCOVA; results indicated significant main effects both for perceived humorousness, $F = 12.97, p = .001$, and for claim strength, $F = 11.46, p = .001$. Subjects rated their likelihood of purchase as greater when perceived ad humorousness was high (M = 6.65) than when it was low (M = 4.64), supporting H3d. Purchase likelihood was also seen as greater by subjects in the strong claims condition (M = 6.48) than those in the weak claims condition (M = 4.48).

The interaction between perceived ad humorousness and claim strength was marginal at best, $F = 2.41, p = .126$, but simple effects tests indicated that, as before, subjects low in perceived ad humorousness were influenced by the strength of the ad claims, $F = 12.23, p = .001$, while subjects high in perceived ad humorousness were not, $F < 1$. These results provided tentative support for H1d and H2d.

Number of Brand and Ad Elaborations

Subjects' responses on the thought-listing measure were classified as either brand-related, ad-related, or unrelated. Brand-related and ad-related thoughts were then disaggregated according to their valence: either positive (pro-brand or pro-ad), negative (counter-brand or counter-ad), or neutral.[3] An index of total number of brand elaborations was created by summing each subject's number of positive, negative, and neutral brand-related thoughts. A 2 X 2 ANCOVA on this measure yielded two marginal main effects: subjects low in perceived ad humorousness generated slightly more brand elaborations (M = 2.46) than subjects high in perceived ad humorousness (M = 1.85), $F = 3.64, p = .061$, and subjects reading weak ad claims generated marginally more brand elaborations (M = 2.53) than subjects reading strong ad claims (M = 1.87), $F = 3.63, p = .062$.

An index of the total number of ad elaborations was created by summing the positive, negative, and neutral ad-related thoughts generated by each subject. Analysis of this index indicated only a marginal main effect for perceived ad humorousness, $F = 2.55, p = .116$, with subjects high in perceived ad humorousness generating somewhat more ad elaborations (M = 1.00) than subjects low in perceived ad humorousness (M = 0.57).

Note that the effects of perceived ad humorousness had opposite effects on brand and ad elaborations: subjects high in perceived ad humorousness appeared to think less about the brand, and more about the ad, than did subjects low in perceived ad humorousness.

Positivity of Brand and Ad Elaborations

An index of the net positivity of subjects' brand elaborations was created by subtracting the number of negative brand elabora-

---
[3]These classifications were performed by two independent judges. The judges agreed on over 80% of the classifications, with disagreements resolved by discussion.

tions from the number of positive brand elaborations. A 2 X 2 ANCOVA on this index indicated a main effect for claim strength, $F = 20.82$, $p < .001$, as strong ad claims elicited more positively-toned brand elaborations (M = +.875) than did weak ad claims (M = -.967). Hypothesis 3e was not supported, as the main effect of perceived humorousness was not significant, $p > .25$.

The main effect for claim strength was qualified by a marginal perceived ad humorousness by claim strength interaction, $F = 3.71$, $p = .059$. As can be seen in Table 1, the net positivity of the brand elaborations of subjects low in perceived ad humorousness was strongly influenced by claim strength, simple effects $F = 23.27$, $p < .001$. The net brand elaborations of subjects high in perceived ad humorousness were, by contrast, not influenced by claim strength, $F = 1.79$, $p > .15$. These results supported H1e and H2e.

An index of the net positivity of subjects' ad elaborations was created in similar fashion, and also analyzed via 2 X 2 ANCOVA. Results indicated only a significant interaction effect, $F = 5.44$, $p = .023$ (see Table 1 for means). As was the case for net brand elaborations, subjects low in perceived ad humorousness were significantly influenced by claim strength, $F = 6.04$, $p < .025$, while the net ad elaborations of those high in perceived ad humorousness were not influenced by claim strength, $F < 1$.

DISCUSSION

The primary purpose of the present study was to determine the effects of humorous advertisements on the extent to which ad copy is processed by consumers. Contrary to the popular notion that humorous ads enhance ad processing via their impact on attention, we hypothesized that they would undermine ad processing, with ad exposure held fairly constant. Although our manipulation of ad humorousness was not effective, the results of our internal analyses provided support for our hypotheses.

Specifically, subjects scoring in the upper half on a median split on their self-reports of perceived ad humorousness (i.e., those who perceived the ad as more humorous) were less sensitive to the strength of the ad claims, as gauged by assessments of their brand attitudes, ad attitudes, perceptions of claim strength, purchase intentions, and cognitive responses to the ad, than were subjects who perceived the ad as less humorous. Indeed, the results of our simple effects tests indicated that the perception of humor in the advertisements led subjects to be relatively uninfluenced by the strength of ad claims. And while perceptions of humorousness tended to enhance both ad and brand evaluations, this enhancement only appeared in the case of weak ad claims (i.e., higher perceived ad humorousness did not enhance subjects' evaluations when claim strength was high).

While the results were consistent in supporting our experimental hypotheses, caution is advised in interpreting the present results. The present design included ads for only one product, and hence the results may be limited in their generalizability (e.g., Gardner and Scott 1990). In addition, the advertised service, life insurance, presents a context in which humor is likely to be seen as irrelevant to the claims (e.g., Weinberger and Campbell 1991). For product or service classes where humor is more relevant, it seems plausible that perceived humor may serve as a persuasive argument rather than serving to predict the extent of message processing (see Petty, Gleicher and Baker 1991 for a related discussion of the different functions mood can serve in persuasion contexts).

The life insurance ad is also likely to be low in personal relevance for the majority of our undergraduate sample, few of whom have any dependents. This implies that our effects may be limited to contexts in which the baseline level of message processing is relatively low. Put another way, our effects may be limited to situations characterized by low to moderate elaboration likelihood (see Petty and Cacioppo 1986). Given a highly involving product or service, we would expect *all* subjects to base their judgments primarily on claim strength.

Subsequent research should clarify the present results by replicating them with an effective manipulation of ad humorousness, and by indicating their generalizability to different product classes and different advertising media.

REFERENCES

Batra, Rajeev and Douglas M. Stayman (1990). "The Role of Mood in Advertising Effectiveness," *Journal of Consumer Research*, 17, 203-214.

Chattopadhyay, Amitava and Kunal Basu (1990). "Humor in Advertising: The Moderating Role of Prior Brand Evaluation," *Journal of Marketing Research*, 27, 466-76.

Duncan, Calvin P. and James E. Nelson (1985). "Effects of Humor in a Radio Advertising Experiment," *Journal of Advertising*, 14(2), 33-40.

Gardner, Meryl P. and John Scott (1990). "Product Type: A Neglected Moderator of the Effects of Mood," *Advances in Consumer Research*, 17, 585-89.

Gelb, Betsy D. and George M. Zinkhan (1986). "Humor and Advertising Effectiveness After Repeated Exposures to a Radio Commercial," *Journal of Advertising*, 15(2), 15-20.

Kuykendall, David and John P. Keating (1990). "Mood and Persuasion: Evidence for the Differential Impact of Positive and Negative States," *Psychology and Marketing*, 7(1), 1-9.

Lammers, H. Bruce, Laura Leibowitz, George E. Seymour, and Judith E. Hennessey (1983). "Humor and Cognitive Responses to Advertising Stimuli: A Trace Consolidation Approach," *Journal of Business Research*, 11, 173-85.

Mackie, Diane M. and Leila T. Worth (1989). "Processing Deficits and the Mediation of Positive Affect in Persuasion," *Journal of Personality and Social Psychology*, 57(1), 27-40.

Madden, Thomas J. and Marc C. Weinberger (1982). "The Effects of Humor on Attention in Magazine Advertising," *Journal of Advertising*, 11(3), 8-14.

_____ and _____ (1984). "Humor in Advertising: A Practitioner's View," *Journal of Advertising Research*, 24(4), 23-29.

Petty, Richard E. and John T. Cacioppo (1986). *Communication and Persuasion*. New York: Springer-Verlag.

_____, Faith Gleicher, and Sara M. Baker (1991). "Multiple Roles for Affect in Persuasion," in *Emotion and Social Judgments*, ed. Joseph P. Forgas, Elmsford, NY: Pergamon, 181-200.

Sternthal, Brian and C. Samuel Craig (1973). "Humor in Advertising," *Journal of Marketing*, 37, 12-18.

Weinberger, Marc G. and Leland Campbell (1991). "The Use and Impact of Humor in Radio Advertising," *Journal of Advertising Research*, 30(6), 44-52.

Physical Attractiveness and Personality in Advertising: More than Just a Pretty Face?
Anne M. Brumbaugh, Duke University[1]

ABSTRACT

Generally accepted in advertising is the adage that "what is beautiful is good," and the use of attractive spokespeople and models is de rigueur. Various hypotheses have been put forth to explain how attractiveness affects various measures of advertising effectiveness. Within the literature, however, it appears that for every significant result supporting attractiveness as affecting attitude towards a brand or product, another study fails to show the effect. This paper suggests that people's perception of an advertisement is affected not only by the spokesmodel's physical appearance, but also by personality inferences made by the viewer about the model.

INTRODUCTION

Advertising featuring attractive spokespersons and models fills television screens and print media, presumably because attractive people sell more products (Dion, Berscheid, and Walster 1972). Rarely is an unattractive person featured prominently in an ad, save the occasional "character" actor. However, empirical evidence is mixed in its support for the contention that physical attractiveness in a person pictured in an ad serves to increase ad effectiveness. Within the literature, it seems that for every significant result supporting physical attractiveness as affecting attitude towards a brand or product, another study fails to show the effect.

As people view an advertisement, and the person pictured in it, they form inferences about that person and his or her personality. Social psychology literature suggests that such inferences occur spontaneously and frequently as we observe others. This paper suggests that these personality inferences mediate the effect of physical attractiveness on ad effectiveness, that such personality inferences also influence directly how effective the ad will be, and that the formation and application of these inferences are affected by the gender of the observer.

The first section of this paper reviews some work on physical attractiveness in advertising. Sections two and three discuss the formation of personality inferences based on physical appearance and how advertising might be affected by such inferences. Section four proposes five hypotheses about the effects of physical attractiveness and personality inferences on attitude towards a product. Methodology and results of a study follow in sections six and seven, concluding with a discussion of the findings in the final section.

PHYSICAL ATTRACTIVENESS IN ADVERTISING

Advertisers have long accepted the idea that "beauty sells" and have utilized attractive celebrity endorsers, spokespeople, and models in their advertisements. Empirical studies bear out this phenomenon, showing that physical attractiveness of a person shown in an ad increases advertiser believability (Kamins 1990), willingness to purchase (Petroshius and Crocker 1989; Kahle and Homer 1985), direct mail response rate (Caballero and Pride 1984), attitude towards the product (Kahle and Homer 1985), and actual purchase (Caballero and Solomon 1983). Furthermore, this effect is found when both male and female models are used (Petroshius and Crocker 1989), for print advertising (Kamins 1990), for point of purchase displays (Caballero and Solomon 1984), for actual communicators in one-on-one interactions (Chaiken 1979), and for celebrity endorsements (Kamins 1990).

However, for each piece of evidence in support of the effect of physical attractiveness on attitude towards the ad or other measures of advertising effectiveness, there seem to exist several that fail to uphold the hypothesis. For example, Petroshius and Crocker (1989) show physical attractiveness to influence ratings of ad characteristics (interesting, appealing, impressive, attractive, eye-catching), but not measures of product information (believable, informative, clear) or product quality. Baker and Churchill (1977) show similar results.

While Kamins (1990) shows that the differential levels of physical attractiveness offered by celebrities Tom Selleck and Telly Savalas affect advertiser and spokesperson believability and spokesperson credibility, the difference in physical attractiveness does not affect arguably more important indicators of advertising effectiveness: attitude towards the brand, credibility of the advertisement, and purchase intention.

Caballero and Solomon (1984) find that physical attractiveness of a model pictured in a point of purchase display affects actual purchase of facial tissues, but not beer. Interestingly, the effect was not in the expected direction: the less attractive model yielded higher facial tissue sales than did the more attractive model. Their explanation for such seemingly incongruent results centered on the fact that the unattractive model may have attracted more attention to the point of purchase display than did the attractive model.

While some studies fail to show main effects of physical attractiveness on advertising effectiveness measures, some do show significant physical attractiveness by gender of subject interaction effects (Caballero and Solomon 1984; Kahle and Homer 1985). Other research specifically investigates gender differences in the impact of physical attractiveness on ad effectiveness (Debevec and Kernan 1984). In addition to the negative correlation between model attractiveness and facial tissue sales as found by Caballero and Soloman (1984), Kahle and Homer (1985) found that attractive sources were more effective with female subjects (but not male) in recognition scores for ads promoting disposable razor blades, and unattractive sources were related to lower recall scores for male subjects (but not female) for toothpaste ads.

Debevec and Kernan (1984) specifically try to assess the impact of the gender of target by gender of speaker interaction as well as model attractiveness on the effectiveness of a slide presentation soliciting support for a levy raising funds for the Cincinnati Zoo. Their results illustrate a number of gender differences in a variety of affective and behavioral measures. For example, females reacted more positively to the slide presentation picturing an attractive male model than to one showing an average male model, but were not more disposed to attending meetings or passing the levy. Conversely, male subjects' were affected on these dimensions when an attractive female model was pictured. Other results show that attractiveness affected different measures to different degrees, depending on the sex of the respondent and sex of the model featured (Debevec and Kernan 1984).

PERSONALITY AS MEDIATOR OF PHYSICAL ATTRACTIVENESS

The mixed results shown in studies of physical attractiveness of a model on attitude towards the ad, source persuasiveness,

---

[1]The author wishes to thank Debra Stephens, Ron Hill, Morris Holbrook, and Cindy Hanson for the use of their data.

attitude towards the product, purchase intent, coupled with the evidence of gender differences when the effect is shown to exist, suggest that something may be mediating the effect of physical attractiveness of the model on evaluative measures of the ad. Such a mediator might neutralize the persuasive effect of an otherwise attractive model, may enhance the effect of an average looking model, and might explain the effectiveness of less attractive models in advertising (Kamins 1990).

Physical attractiveness, or lack thereof, is a very salient, highly visible cue that observers use to form impressions of another person (Schneider, Hastorf, and Ellsworth 1979; Chaiken 1986). Based on this outward appearance, we make all sorts of inferences about the agents we observe. Among these inferences are judgments about the agent's personality (Chaiken 1979; Funder and Colvin 1988; Winter, Uleman, and Cunnif 1985; Winter and Uleman 1984; Debevec and Kernan 1984) and status (Kalick 1988). People spontaneously and unintentionally make inferences about others' personalities even after only a brief period of exposure. Even when other data about the agent are available, for example occupation, role and trait information, observers continue to rely heavily on physical appearance (Deaux and Lewis 1984). Furthermore, these inferences are surprisingly accurate. Funder and Colvin (1988) found that strangers' assessments of each other, made after only five minutes of exposure to each other, agreed with judgments made by close acquaintances as well as with self-assessments. Readily observable personality traits like extraverted, sociable, talkative, good-natured, funny, poised, status, interesting, sexually warm and responsive, and kind (Joseph 1982; Albright, Kenny, and Malloy 1988; Funder and Colvin 1988; Maddux and Rogers 1980) seem to be the most highly correlated with physical attractiveness.

Kalick (1988) had subjects match pictures of males and females of varying degrees of physical attractiveness with descriptions of different levels of ascribed (conferred through privileged background) and achieved (earned through hard work or applied talent) status. Irrespective of the status manipulation used (individual or family status, earned or inherited, rich achieved or ascribed), high status descriptions were associated with pictures of physically attractive people, and low status descriptions with less attractive photos. In assessing differences between achieved and ascribed status, he found the relationship between physical attractiveness and ascribed status to be stronger than that between attractiveness and achieved status. These assessments made solely on the basis of physical attractiveness are shown to exhibit gender differences as well. Albright et al (1988) showed that observers rated females as more conscientious when using only physical appearance as evidence of personality. Kalick (1988) found that female subjects tended to match more physically attractive photos with all status descriptions than did male subjects, and that sex of the stimulus person produced different results. When analyzing data of male stimulus persons, he found that achieved status was associated with higher physical attractiveness ratings, while for female stimulus persons achieved status was associated with lower attractiveness scores.

EFFECT OF PERSONALITY ON AD EFFECTIVENESS

That people can't help themselves from forming inferences about others on the basis of appearance seems unequivocal. Do these inferences, once formed while viewing a model in an advertisement, affect the effectiveness of the advertisement?

Advertisers frequently try to convey certain personality characteristics through their choice of actors and the traits the actors display. Trustworthiness, credibility, and expertness are all traits that seem to influence positively the scores of evaluative measures of advertisements (Ohanian 1990). Perhaps advertisers also need to be mindful of the personality inferences people make spontaneously, in addition to those personality inferences that advertisers want to induce. Presuming the existence of personality as a mediator of physical attractiveness might help explain why some studies find no main effect for physical attractiveness or otherwise unexpected results, while others offer full support for its main effects and interactions.

For example, Caballero and Solomon's (1984) finding that a less attractive model was more effective in selling facial tissues than a more attractive model might not be just because the less attractive model was more noticed. Perhaps the result might be explained in terms of personality. People viewing the less attractive model may have perceived her to be less active, less outgoing, and consequently less likely to be healthy, while they perceived the more attractive model to be extraverted and healthy. The less attractive model's perceived greater experience with illness, then, made her a much better endorser for facial tissues than the attractive, healthy model.

Results of studies in which physical attractiveness was shown to impact affective measures, but not cognitive or conative measures (Petroshius and Crocker 1989; Baker and Churchill 1977; Caballero, Lumpkin, and Madden 1989), might also be explained by personality inferences as mediators of physical attractiveness. Physical attractiveness may have elicited perceptions of extraversion and kindness, for example, which caused observers to like the ad and the spokesperson. However, kindness may not have been an appropriate trait for an endorser of computers or luxury cars (Kamins 1990), thereby reducing any positive effect due to the sheer aesthetic vision offered by the source.

Baker and Churchill's (1977) seemingly inconsistent results might also be explained by personality as a mediating variable. Male subjects' high purchase intent for perfume may have resulted from their ascribing sociable and sexual warmth traits to the attractive female model pictured, traits they might look for in a romantic partner. Conversely, their high purchase intent for coffee after viewing a less attractive model might result from their ascribing to her traits like hard-working and intelligent, perceiving her to be a knowledgeable, expert coffee drinker.

Gender differences might also be explained by the different ways men and women perceive others and utilize physical cues in making inferences. Both men and women tend to confer on men stereotypically male traits like ambitious and aggressive, while they tend to attribute to women traits like caring and frivolous (Schneider et al 1979; Deaux and Lewis 1984). This natural tendency to resort to a conventional stereotype in the absence of additional information might cause viewers to ascribe personality traits to a model pictured in an ad which, while consistent with the stereotype, are not congruent with the product. Furthermore, even if men and women perceive the same personality traits, they might subsequently interpret them differently in the context of the advertisement. For example, while both men and women rate a female model high on sociability for an ad for exercise equipment, purchase intention for the men is higher than for the women because they associate sociability with health and health with exercise, while women's intent is lower because competence, not sociability, is the trait that would make them believe that exercise equipment is a smart investment for themselves.

This paper provides an initial attempt at teasing apart the effects of personality inferences from the effects due to physical attractiveness. One advantage of this paper is the structure of the data. Most studies on appearance in advertising manipulate physical attractiveness by pretesting a number of photos or ads featuring models of different levels of attractiveness and picking as stimuli the two photos rated most and least physically attractive (or three photos including an average rating). While manipulation checks verify that physical attractiveness ratings within this type of study differ significantly in the expected direction, such a manipulation doesn't allow for individual differences in preference. In this study, each subject makes his or her own ratings of twenty models, which are then used as measures of attractiveness in this repeated measures design.

HYPOTHESES

Based on the idea that personality mediates the effect of source physical attractiveness on evaluative measures of the ad, a number of hypotheses will be examined in the following sections. First, H1 establishes that physical attractiveness of the source enhances the attitude towards the ad or, in this experiment, the "product," women's clothing.

H1: The physical attractiveness of a model pictured in an ad positively influences the attitude towards the product.

Next, it is necessary to show that attractiveness of the source is a cue that observers use to make inferences about the model's personality, particularly in the absence of other information.

H2: The physical attractiveness of a model pictured in an ad influences the formation of perceptions about the model's personality.

Once it has been established that physical attractiveness indeed influences the attitude towards the model's clothing and the personality inferences made about her, it may be hypothesized that gender of the observer plays a role in the formation of the personality perceptions as well.

H3: Gender of the subject influences the formation of perceptions about the model's personality.

It is further hypothesized that, not only does physical attractiveness affect observers' attitude towards the model's clothing, but that the personality inferences also have their impact.

H4: Perceptions about the model's personality affect the attitude towards the product.

Finally, it is hypothesized that there will be gender differences in how personality inferences affect attitude towards the product.

H5: Gender of the subject moderates the influence of personality inferences on the attitude towards the product.

METHODOLOGY

The data for this experiment were obtained from the first of two sessions to assess the impact of women's body satisfaction/dissatisfaction on their evaluation of advertisements picturing female models differing in physical attractiveness. In the first session, subjects were shown slides of 20 models and were asked to assess models' clothing, physical attractiveness, and personality. During the second session, two questionnaires measuring subjects' body dissatisfaction were administered. Only data from the first session are used in this paper.

Stimuli

Pictures of twenty models were obtained from a number of American and European fashion magazines and were selected to provide a variety of physical characteristics (hair, face, complexion, physique). Pretests with students showed that students varied in their assessment of physical attractiveness and differed in ascribing personality traits to the models based on the pictures. Tests of means on current data revealed that models differ significantly in attractiveness, with means ranging from 2.356 (unattractive) to 4.596 (attractive).

Procedures

Evaluations of models' clothing, physical attractiveness, and personalities were obtained from 90 male and 88 female undergraduate subjects. Subjects were shown 20 pictures of 20 different models three times each. During the first exposure, subjects were shown each picture for approximately 20 seconds and were then asked to rate each model's clothing. The second exposure also lasted approximately 20 seconds, after which subjects were asked to rate the models' physical attractiveness. The third and final exposure to each slide of the models lasted approximately 30 seconds, after which subjects were asked to make judgments about the models' personalities.

Measures

Models' clothing was rated using six five-position semantic differential scales: unfavorable/favorable, neat/sloppy, like/dislike, not stylish/stylish, bad/good, and tasteful/tasteless. A single measure of clothing attractiveness was obtained by averaging the five semantic differential scales. This score served as the dependent variable in the analyses.

Two sets of measurements were obtained to assess physical attractiveness of the model. In the first measurement, subjects were asked to rate the model's hair, face, complexion, and physique on a five-position scale anchored by the phrases "not at all attractive" to "very attractive." A single composite attractiveness rating was obtained by averaging these four ratings. In the second measure, subjects completed the statement "This model is more physically attractive than ___ percentage of all females I've ever seen." This measure served as a manipulation check for the mean attractiveness rating, showing it to be a reliable reflection of the model's attractiveness.

Subjects recorded their personality inferences on twenty-two five-point semantic differential scales anchored by the following pairs: active/passive, not intelligent/intelligent, hard-working/lazy, snobbish/down-to-earth, withdrawn/outgoing, happy/unhappy, feminine/unfeminine, unpopular/popular, unsuccessful/successful, healthy/unhealthy, trustworthy/not trustworthy, self-conscious/self-confident, independent/dependent, nice/mean, not sophisticated/sophisticated, weak-willed/disciplined, free spirited/traditional, fearful/brave, neat/sloppy, not likeable/likeable, boring/interesting, exciting/dull. This list of personality traits was based on inventories found in previous studies (Brenner and Hinsdale 1978, Harris, Harris and Bochner 1982, Staffieri 1972), and was modified based on students' responses to pretests of the models. The adjectives were factor analyzed with a principal components analysis with a varimax rotation to yield four factors. Factor one, labeled "sociable," includes active, outgoing, happy, popular, healthy, confident, interesting, exciting, and free spirited. Factor two, labeled "capable," includes intelligent, hardworking, independent, disciplined, and brave. Factor three, labeled "poised," includes feminine, successful, neat, and sophisticated. Finally, factor four, labeled "friendly," includes down-to-earth, trustworthy, nice, and likeable. Cronbach coefficient alphas equal .88, .76, .75, and .76, respectively.

TABLE
Manova Results

Personality Index	Model Attractiveness		Gender X Model Attractiveness	
	F	p	F	p
Sociable	2398.94	0.0001	6.04	0.0001
Capable	334.08	0.0001	4.80	0.0286
Poised	1902.44	0.0001	1.01	0.3154
Friendly	61.38	0.0001	8.89	0.0029
Overall Effect (Wilks' Lambda)	867.40	0.0001	8.62	0.0001

RESULTS

The impact of model attractiveness (MdlAttr), subject gender (Gender), and personality inferences (Sociable, Capable, Poised, Friendly) on subjects' attitude towards models' clothing (A_{cloth}) is assessed by forming a series of F_{add} calculations (Lutz 1977 p. 203). The F_{add} statistic measures the additional contribution of one or more variables to a full regression model. To test main effects of gender, attractiveness, and personality on attitude towards clothing, a full model shown in equation (1) is used, with variables being omitted in turn as appropriate to test the various hypotheses.

$$A_{cloth} = \text{Gender Subj MdlAttr Sociable Capable Poised Friendly} \quad (1)$$

To demonstrate that the formation of personality inferences is affected by subject gender and model attractiveness, a MANOVA analysis is performed using the four personality indices as dependent variables, and gender, model attractiveness, and the interaction between the two as independent variables. For further analyses of the gender main effect and interactions with personality indices, series of F_{add} statistics are calculated by omitting variables from the full model shown in equation (2).

$$A_{cloth} = \text{Gender Subj Mdlattr MdlAttr*Gender Sociable Capable Poised Friendly Sociable*Gender Capable*Gender Poised*Gender Friendly*Gender} \quad (2)$$

Interactions in a regression of equation (2) that were significant at the p=0.05 level are explored further by analyzing parameter estimates yielded by a regression of equation (3).

$$A_{cloth} = \text{MdlAttr*Gender Sociable*Gender Capable*Gender Poised*Gender Friendly*Gender} \quad (3)$$

To test hypothesis 1, physical attractiveness' influence on attitude towards clothing, a regression of equation (1) yields a significant contribution of model attractiveness on the total variance explained (F=440.93 (1, 3548), p<=0.0001). An F_{add} statistic formed by omitting model attractiveness from the full model confirms the effect of model attractiveness (F_{add}=77.31 (1, 3548), p<=.01), providing further support for hypothesis 1.

Hypotheses 2 and 3 were tested by performing a MANOVA analysis on the four personality indices, with model attractiveness, gender, and their interaction serving as independent variables. The table provides data from the MANOVA analysis which shows that model attractiveness and the interaction between gender and model attractiveness both contribute to the formation of three of the four personality indices. Gender alone does not impact the personality assessments. The third factor, poised, is not significantly influenced by the interaction between gender and model attractiveness.

To test hypothesis 4, the effect of the four personality factors on attitude towards clothing, a series of F_{add} statistics were calculated as above. First, eliminating all four personality indices from the full model in equation (1) showed significant effects of personality on attitude towards clothing (F_{add}=154.25 (4, 3548), p<=0.01). Separate F_{add} calculations for reduced models which omitted each personality index individually provided support for the personality traits of capable (F_{add}=3.70 (1, 3548), p<=.0562) and poised (F_{add}=35.62 (1, 3548), p<=.01). The effects of the personality traits of sociable (F_{add}=0.26) friendly (F_{add}=0.06) were not statistically significant.

Support for hypothesis 5 comes from tests of the interactions between gender and the personality indices. Equation (2) shows the full model for the test of subject gender as a moderator of the influence of personality on the attitude towards the models' clothing. Significant interactions included capable (F=9.74 (1, 3547), p<=.0018) and friendly (F=4.32 (1, 3547), p<=.0378). To investigate the nature of the two interactions, a regression was run on the reduced model shown in equation (3) to obtain parameter estimates of the interactions involving gender. The capable by gender interaction was significant only for female subjects (estimate=.14, t=4.10, p<=.0001), while the friendly by gender interaction was significant only for male subjects (estimate=.06, t=2.34, p<=.0192).

DISCUSSION

Support for all five hypotheses was obtained. From these results, it appears that people use both physical appearance and their spontaneous impression of the source's personality when making judgments relating to the source. Physical appearance was shown to influence attitude towards clothing directly (H1). Both physical appearance and its interaction with gender of subject influenced the formation of personality inferences about the model (H2 and H3). These inferences, in addition to the direct effect of physical appearance, affected the subjects' overall impression of the models' clothing (H4). Finally, gender differences were found in both the formation of personality inferences, as well as in their use in forming attitude towards clothing (H5). Specifically, for women, a model's apparent competence provided a positive influence on their subsequent evaluation of her clothing, while for men, their perceived friendliness of the model caused them to make more favorable evaluations of her clothing.

These results suggest that personality inferences made by viewers of an ad mediate the influence of physical attractiveness of the model on evaluative measures of the ad's effectiveness, an idea that is consistent with other theories of when and how attractive models should be utilized. Results of studies that demonstrate different effects of physical attractiveness based on level of involvement of the viewer with the product (Kahle and Homer 1985) and source expertise (Maddux and Rogers 1980) might also be explained by influence of personality traits conveyed by the source. For example, Kahle and Homer's (1985) result that an attractive source leads to higher recognition scores only for females for razor blades (the high involvement product) may be because females view razor blades as more of a beauty product, rather than a daily necessity as they might be for men, and the personality traits conveyed by the attractive source reinforced that image of the razor blades. Maddux and Rogers' (1980) manipulation of source expertise and attractiveness showed there was no significant main effect for appearance on agreement with the source message, and that expert sources produced greater agreement than nonexpert sources. A further analysis of several of their secondary analyses might explain the results. They found that expert sources were rated higher on the attribute sincere, and that experts were more effective in eliciting agreement when they were less attractive. In terms of personality, the traits of sociable, status, outgoing, sexually warm and responsive, etc., which were found to be associated with attractive sources, may have in fact detracted from the credibility of the source, while the sincere trait contributed to source credibility. Rather than attributing their findings solely to the attractiveness and expert manipulations, intervening personality attributions may have played a mediating role.

Of course, limitations exist with this study. Female models were selected from magazines as stimuli, and as one might expect, none was very unattractive. Utilizing models of both genders that span the full range of physical appearance might yield richer results. The order in which data were collected might have also influenced the results. Here, subjects were first asked about their attitude towards the product, which may have affected their subsequent perceptions of the models' attractiveness, and in turn the models' personalities. Changing the order in which questions were posed might yield different results. Finally, by forcing subjects to make inferences about the models' personalities might actually cause them to make assessments that they might not have occurred spontaneously. Using open-ended measures might have avoided this pitfall.

The contribution of this paper to consumer research is to point out that physical attractiveness of a source pictured in an ad, by itself, does not guarantee that ad's success. Rather, the impressions that viewers make about the source and their subsequent application of those inferences are also relevant. Further research is needed to determine how these inferences are made in an advertising context, whether certain personality traits are more effective for viewers of one sex or another, which ascribed traits are desirable and which are undesirable, and whether these impressions can be effectively controlled to increase ad effectiveness. Kamin's "match-up" hypothesis (1990) and the incongruent results of other studies suggest that product class might also interact with physical attractiveness and personality inferences, making the three-way interaction the variable of interest in future research.

REFERENCES

Albright, Linda, David A. Kenny, and Thomas E. Malloy (1988), "Consensus in Personality Judgements at Zero Acquaintance," *Journal of Personality and Social Psychology*, 55 (3), 387-395.

Baker, Michael J. and Gilbert. A. Churchill, Jr. (1977), "The Impact of Physically Attractive Models on Advertising Evaluations," *Journal of Marketing Research*, 14 (November), 538-55.

Brenner, David and Gary Hinsdale (1978), "Body Build Stereotypes and Self-Identification in Three Age Groups of Females," *Adolescence*, 13, 551-61.

Caballero, Marjorie J., James R. Lumpkin, and Charles S. Madden (1989), "Using Physical Attractiveness as an Advertising Tool: An Empirical Test of the Attraction Phenomenon," *Journal of Advertising Research*, August/September, 16-22.

_____ and William. M. Pride (1984), "Selected Effects of Salesperson Sex and Attractiveness in Direct Mail Advertisements," *Journal of Marketing*, 48 (January), 94-100.

_____ and Paul J. Solomon (1984), "Effects of Model Attractiveness on Sales Response," *Journal of Advertising*, 13 (1), 17-23.

Chaiken, Shelly (1979), "Communicator Physical Attractiveness and Persuasion," *Journal of Personality and Social Psychology*, 37 (August), 1387-97.

_____ (1986), "Physical Appearance and Social Influence," in *Physical Attractiveness, Stigma, and Social Behavior: The Ontario Symposium*, Vol. 3, ed. C. Peter Herman, Mark P. Zanna, and E. Tony Higgins, Hillsdale, NJ: Laurence Erlbaum, 132-77.

Deaux, Kay and Laurie L. Lewis (1984), "Structure of Gender Stereotypes: Interrelationships Among Components and Gender Label," *Journal of Personality and Social Psychology*, 46 (5), 991-1004.

Debevec, Kathleen and Jerome B. Kernan (1984), "More Evidence on the Effects of a Presenter's Physical Attractiveness: Some Cognitive, Affective, and Behavioral Consequences," in *Advances in Consumer Research*, Vol. 11, ed. Thomas C. Kinnear, Provo, UT: Association for Consumer Research, 127-132.

Dion, Karen K., Ellen Berscheid, and Elaine Walster (1972), "What is Beautiful is Good," *Journal of Personality and Social Psychology*, 24, 285-290.

Funder, David C. and C. Randall Colvin (1988), "Friends and Strangers: Acquaintanceship, Agreement, and the Accuracy of Personality Judgment," *Journal of Personality and Social Psychology*, 55 (1), 149-158.

Harris, Mary B., Richard J. Harris, and Stephen Bochner (1982), "Fat, Four-Eyed, and Female: Stereotypes of Obesity, Glasses and Gender," *Journal of Applied Social Psychology*, 12, 503-16.

Joseph, W. Benoy (1982), "The Credibility of Physically Attractive Communicators: A Review," *Journal of Advertising*, 11 (3), 15-24.

Kahle, Lynn R. and Pamela M. Homer (1985), "Physical Attractiveness of the Celebrity Endorser: A Social Adaptation Perspective," *Journal of Consumer Research*, 11 (March), 954-61.

Kalick, S. Michael (1988), "Physical Attractiveness as a Status Cue," *Journal of Experimental Social Psychology*, 24, 469-489.

Kamins, Michael A. (1990), "An Investigation into the "Match-Up" Hypothesis in Celebrity Advertising: When Beauty May Be Only Skin Deep," *Journal of Advertising*, 19 (1), 4-13.

Lutz, Richard J. (1977), "An Experimental Investigation of Causal Relations Among cognition, Affect, and Behavioral Intention," *Journal of Consumer Research*, 3 (March), 197-208.

Maddux, James E. and Ronald. W. Rogers (1980), "Effect of Source Expertness, Physical Attractiveness, and Supporting Arguments on Persuasion: A Case of Brains Over Beauty," *Journal of Personality and Social Psychology*, 39 (August), 235-44.

Ohanian, Roobina (1990), "Construction and Validation of a Scale to Measure Celebrity Endorsers' Perceived Expertise, Trustworthiness, and Attractiveness," *Journal of Advertising*, 19 (3), 39-52.

Petroshius, Susan M. and Kenneth E. Crocker (1989), "An Empirical Analysis of Spokesperson Characteristics on Advertisement and Product Evaluations," *Journal of the Academy of Marketing Science*, 17 (Summer), 217-225.

Schneider, David A., Albert H. Hastorf, and Phoebe C. Ellsworth (1979), *Person Perception*, Reading, MA: Addison-Wesley.

Staffieri, J. Robert (1972), "Body Build and Behavioral Expectancies in Young Females," *Developmental Psychology*, 6, 125-27.

Winter, Laraine and James S. Uleman (1984), "When Are Social Judgments Made? Evidence for the Spontaneousness of Trait Inference," *Journal of Personality and Social Psychology*, 49 (2), 237-252.

_____, James S. Uleman, and Cathryn Cunnif (1985), "How Automatic Are Social Judgments?" *Journal of Personality and Social Psychology*, 49 (4), 904-917.

Effects of Advertising and Experience on Brand Judgments: A Rose by Any Other Frame...

Alice A. Wright, California State University, Long Beach
Richard J. Lutz, University of Florida[1]

ABSTRACT

Consumer researchers have become increasingly interested in the effects of context on brand judgments. One contextual phenomenon receiving much attention is the effect of "framing." This research reviews the various uses of the term "framing" in the literature and summarizes the findings to date. A new form of framing is identified - the effects of trial experience on advertising response - and is contrasted with the more familiar framing effect of advertising on experience. Recommendations are proposed for research concerning the effects of experience framing advertising.

Over the past decade, consumer research has used the concept of the "frame" as a metaphor for the effects of judgment context on a variety of consumer decision phenomena. Whether under managerial control or not, important contextual variables, are seen as shaping the very nature of the decision faced by a consumer, much as a picture frame can enhance or diminish the appreciation of the artwork it surrounds. The purpose of this paper is threefold: (1) to summarize the "framing" literature in consumer research, (2) to identify a new form of framing, and (3) to describe in detail research investigating two forms of framing that entail the interaction of advertising and direct product experience.

BACKGROUND

In the consumer framing literature the term "frame" has been used in at least four distinct ways, some more closely related than others. A fifth form of framing is implied but not explicitly considered in the literature. Each of the various construals of the "frame" concept is discussed below.

Decision Frames

Kahneman and Tversky (1979) introduced the notion of *decision frame* in their influential prospect theory of decision-making under risk. In any choice situation, they argued, two stages exist: an editing stage, wherein the decision-maker structures the problem into more manageable terms, and an evaluation stage, in which alternatives are compared. A decision frame is formed at the editing stage, based on the juxtaposition of each outcome with a reference point, i.e., a "frame of reference". Armed with these framed alternatives, the decision-maker is better able to evaluate the alternatives and arrive at a choice.

Puto (1987) showed that organizational buyers were somewhat more likely to accept the riskier of two contracts when it was accompanied by a sales letter emphasizing a possible gain in cost advantage, as opposed to avoiding a possible loss. The expected values of the risky and riskless contracts were identical in both situations. Thus, a decision frame can alter judgments of the overall attractiveness of a choice alternative. In a more recent study, Maheswaran and Meyers-Levy (1990) showed a moderating effect of involvement. A positive frame was more effective in low involvement conditions and a negative frame more effective under high involvement.

Decision frames have not received a great deal of attention from consumer researchers, possibly due to the difficulty of assessing and comparing subjectively valued outcomes. As in Puto (1987), most prospect theory research has dealt with more objective outcomes and known probabilities (e.g., Thaler 1985); thus it may be better suited to more structured buying situations like organizational procurement (e.g., Qualls and Puto 1989).

Framed vs. Unframed Pictures in Print Ads

Edell and Staelin (1983) used the distinction between "framed" and "unframed" pictures in print ads to refer to ads that contain picture-related copy vs. those that do not, respectively. Essentially, in the framed case, the copy becomes a verbal label that facilitates the interpretation of the picture. When unframed, the picture is potentially a source of distraction, decreasing attentional resources devoted to processing the (unrelated) copy claims and forming a brand judgment. Edell and Staelin (1983) reported a strong effect of this form of framing, such that their subjects were deflected from using their own previously reported choice criteria when confronted with unframed pictorial ads. Indeed, they engaged in less brand evaluation than those seeing a framed pictorial ad. Marks, Kamins and Murphy (1986) and Kamins and Marks (1987) reported interactive effects of pictorial framing with audience expertise and ad sequence, respectively.

Problem Framing

P. Wright and Rip (1980) coined the term *problem framing* to describe the deliberations of a novice decision-maker in structuring the preference judgment task. Working within the dominant multiattribute preference model tradition, Wright (1977) and Wright and Barbour (1975) had earlier catalogued various strategies by which advertisers might influence, or *bias*, decision processes in their favor. For example, Wright (1977, p. 101) enumerated five distinct subproblems comprising the choice process: (a) define the number of options to be chosen; (b) define the pool of candidates; (c) define the set of choice criteria; (d) select a choice model, or combination rule; and (e) sample the relevant data and apply the appropriate model to arrive at a choice. Then, he offered (pp. 103-104) twenty explicit message strategies aimed at altering consumers' positions on these five subproblems. In a content analysis of three magazines as well as prime time television advertising, Wright and Barbour (1975, p. 257) found meager evidence that many of these strategies were being used by advertisers. Indeed, the three dominant appeals were all seen as simply advocating that a particular brand was superior concerning a particular desirable benefit. Thus, advertisers were not reaching their full potential for influencing choice processes.

Wright and Rip (1980), in their empirical work, developed "advocacy messages" specifically aimed at influencing (1) the relative importance of choice criteria and (b) the decision rule. Their results were mixed, evidencing no effect on estimated importance weights and modest effects on the use of screening strategies, as coded from free response protocols.

Subsequent studies emanating from the problem framing perspective generally have supported the proposed phenomena. MacKenzie (1986) reported attentional effects on the importance of water resistance after exposure to a print ad. He found that attention was a function of the concreteness of the ad copy, but that framing a pictorial element with copy (cf., Edell and Staelin 1983) had no

---

[1] This work was partially supported by a Scholarly and Creative Activities Grant from the California State University, Long Beach. Special thanks to John Lynch, David Mick and Alan Sawyer for comments on an earlier version.

effect on attention or attribute importance. Bettman and Sujan (1987), working with a decision-making task rather than an advertising exposure setting, showed that framing in the form of a priming manipulation affected novice consumers more than experienced consumers. Instructions to focus on either creativity or reliability in a choice between two 35mm cameras caused heightened attention (measured via cognitive responses) and increased importance ratings, particularly for novices. Finally, Keller (1991) demonstrated that placing a memory retrieval cue in the decision context can enhance recall of ad claims and heighten their importance in the brand choice process.

In general, research on problem framing has found support for the proposition that advertising messages can influence the brand preference judgments by altering key aspects of the decision process. The effects tend to be stronger for novice consumers and/or novel brands, as initially proposed by Wright and Rip (1980). The primary cognitive mechanism through which these effects occur appears to be a refocusing of the consumer's attention away from certain attributes or choice rules in favor of others. This stream of research has not considered what happens when the consumer purchases or uses the brand after having made a "framed" judgment of it.

Advertising's Framing of Product Experience

Wells (1980) and Puto and Wells (1984) developed the concept of "transformational advertising," whereby an ad literally transforms how the consumer perceives and judges subsequent brand consumption. Deighton (1988) suggested that a transformational ad exerts its influence by "framing" the experience for the consumer. Thus, unlike the problem framing literature discussed in the preceding section, advertising framing of product experience operates through both *attention* and *interpretation*. The ad causes the consumer to attend selectively to certain aspects of the consumption experience, but it also must exert some influence on how the consumer judges those aspects. This is of particular importance to the advertiser when the consumption experience is difficult to judge objectively, i.e., it is ambiguous in some respect (Hoch and Deighton 1989). This form of framing is the most powerful, in that it influences both pre- and post-consumption judgments of attributes and/or overall brand evaluations.

Advertising's transformational "frame" of product experience has no impact when taken by itself but works by modifying consumers' perceptions of product experience. This differs from the more traditional persuasive focus of advertising wherein beliefs, attitudes and intentions are modified by simple ad exposure.

Several studies have investigated the framing effect of advertising on experience and are described below. In this work, an "ad-frames-experience" paper has to include (a) actual brand experience, (b) brand experience followed by ad exposure, and (c) an experimental condition of experience only (with one exception, discussed below). The first requirement eliminates papers such as Deighton's (1984) seminal work on the advertising-evidence interaction, while the latter two requirements eliminate the consumer satisfaction literature, in which ad-plus-experience conditions are typically contrasted with ad-only (rather than experience-only) conditions.

To the extent that an ad has successfully "framed" the product experience, differences between the ad-plus-experience and experience-only conditions should be observed on such dimensions as attribute perceptions and importance weights, brand attitudes and purchase intentions.

Olson and Dover (1976, 1977, 1978). This investigation actually predated the ad-frames-experience literature but nevertheless meets the criteria for inclusion. Olson and Dover, in this series of papers, report the results of a 2-group experiment on expectancy formation and disconfirmation in which they exposed subjects to "ad-like" messages stating that a new coffee brand had no bitterness at all, but then created a very bitter brew by doubling its concentration. Their intent was to create expectancies in the form of beliefs about bitterness and then disconfirm them.

Olson and Dover reported findings as follows: (a) no framing effect on the evaluations attached to the bitterness dimension (1976, p. 172), and (b) a framing effect on the belief that the coffee was not at all bitter, such that the ad-plus-experience subjects considered it less bitter (1978, p. 33). These two results, taken together, are more indicative of an interpretation effect than an attentional effect. Though Olson and Dover did not report the attribute beliefs and evaluations for the other four attribute dimensions, they did report belief confidence ratings (Dover and Olson 1977, p. 459). Interestingly, no framing effect was apparent for bitterness (possibly due to a ceiling effect), but each of the other four belief confidence ratings was significantly higher for the ad-plus-experience group. It should be noted that none of the three ads mentioned any attribute other than bitterness, such that the ads provided no information directly pertinent to the other dimensions. This unusual, indirect effect may be attributed, at least in part, to the fact that ad-plus-experience subjects had rated the brand on all five attributes after each of the three ad exposures. Thus, the sheer repetition of their ratings may have bolstered their confidence.

Olson and Dover's framing effect was limited to the above cognitive elements, however. They found no significant differences for the overall index of cognitive structure, brand attitude or purchase intention. In sum, Olson and Dover's research demonstrated that even a deliberately deceptive ad can alter attribute perceptions and thereby "frame" product experience. However, that effect was not strong enough to carry through to brand attitudes or intentions.

Hoch and Ha (1986). Hoch and Ha conducted two experiments designed to directly investigate the impact of the ambiguity of product experience on consumers' ability to learn from that experience. In Experiment 1, six brands of polo shirts were selected as the ambiguous product, while 6 brands of paper towels represented the unambiguous product. After first rating all brands on a few attributes as well as overall quality, subjects viewed three ads in storyboard form, two of which emphasized the quality of JC Penney shirts and Bolt paper towels; experience-only subjects saw three filler ads. Then, subjects were allowed to inspect the six shirts and to use the towels to wipe up water and ketchup spills. A framing effect was observed for the JC Penney shirt, such that it was rated much more favorably after experience by the ad-plus-experience group. In contrast, Bolt was rated much more favorably by both groups after testing, as its performance was unambiguously superior. Unobtrusive observation of the subjects during the experience portion of the experiment revealed a disproportionate amount of time devoted to inspection of the JC Penney shirt compared to the other shirts, suggesting an attentional mechanism at work.

Experiment 2 attempted to replicate the findings with regard to polo shirts, using the same brands, procedures, and measures. Once again, a strong framing effect emerged for the JC Penney shirt, but somewhat inexplicably, the allocation of inspection time was unaffected. Thus, the issue of attention versus interpretation remains open. The fact that Hoch and Ha reported only overall quality ratings makes it impossible to conduct post hoc analyses on attribute ratings and importance weights that may help to unravel the nature of the cognitive dynamics underlying the effect. However, their research was instrumental in demonstrating the importance of the ambiguity of experience as a moderating factor.

Deighton and Schindler (1988). Deighton and Schindler exposed 157 students to simulated radio commercials touting the amount of "new" music played (an ambiguous but desirable attribute) by three Boston rock format radio stations. Across three levels of reported listenership a strong framing effect was found; the ad-plus-experience group rated the station higher than did the experience-only group, regardless of which particular station had been advertised.

Although Deighton and Schindler did not control the amount of experience in their research, the self-report data indicated no effect of the commercials on the amount of listening time devoted to advertised versus unadvertised stations. This finding stands in contrast to Hoch and Ha's findings with regard to inspection time (Expt.1). Thus, although the lack of experimental control leads one to discount Deighton and Schindler's data to some degree, their findings are nevertheless more supportive of an interpretation, as opposed to attentional, mechanism underlying the framing effect.

Marks and Kamins (1988). Marks and Kamins exposed students to either a slightly exaggerated or greatly exaggerated print ad on behalf of a new ballpoint pen, elicited dependent measures, had Ss use the pen for 2 minutes, and then elicited the same dependent measures again. Two other groups of subjects read the ads after having used the pen, providing measures after both the experience and the subsequent ad exposure. (A separate control group was used to rule out test-treatment interaction.) By using an internal analysis, whereby the first set of measures from the experience-plus-ad groups are used to represent experience only, a contrast with the second set of measures from the ad-plus-experience groups can yield a test of the framing effect.

Marks and Kamins did not report findings related to the five product attributes they measured on an item-by-item basis, but did report a cognitive structure index (with and without the attribute confidence ratings included), brand attitude and intention. For the slightly exaggerated ad condition, a weak positive framing effect was observed for intention only; no other measure exhibited reliable differences between the two groups. However, for the greatly exaggerated ad, a negative framing effect was obtained for attitude and intention. That is, when experience was too discrepant from the ad claims, the students in the ad-plus-experience group reacted strongly negatively, rating the pen much less favorably than did the experience-only group.

This seeming contrast effect stands in direct contradiction to Olson and Dover's (1978) finding of an assimilation effect. It is not clear that the taste of coffee is inherently more ambiguous than the performance of a pen; nor is it clear why Olson and Dover found framing effects at the individual attribute level, but not for attitude and intention. In contrast, Marks and Kamins observed effects on intention but not on cognitive structure. Presumably, some of the differences are attributable to calibration of the discrepancy between claims and actual experience, but it suggests some very real limits regarding the efficacy of an ad-frames-experience strategy. Admittedly, both Marks and Kamins and Olson and Dover set out to create deceptive ads, but there may be a fine line between "framing" and "deception."

Levin and Gaeth (1988). Levin and Gaeth, working from a prospect theory perspective, were actually the first researchers in this stream of research to articulate the position that an ad can serve as a "frame" for experience (p. 375). In their experiment they used simple "ads" consisting of the labels "75% lean ground beef" vs. "25% fat ground beef." These ads, or labels, either preceded or followed a taste test of 1.5 oz. of freshly cooked lean ground beef. In an earlier experiment Levin (1987) had employed a label-only condition, which served as the ad-only group for comparison purposes (with appropriate caveats). Subjects in both studies rated the ground beef on four dimensions, including fat/lean (the direct manipulation) and quality.

Levin and Gaeth concluded that a framing effect existed, as indicated by differences in the ratings between the positive and negative label conditions. However, they also noted that the framing effect was reduced when consumers actually sampled the product. In a sense, then, Levin and Gaeth were examining the transition from the problem framing research stream to the ad-frames-experience research stream. Levin (1987) observed a framing effect on initial product judgment, while Levin and Gaeth observed similar but smaller effects (for two of the three attributes plus overall quality) when actual experience was involved. Unlike other studies in this stream of research, Levin and Gaeth's (1988) study did not incorporate an experience-only condition. Instead, framing effects were tested by contrasting the positive and negative label conditions. Thus, their study cannot address the issue of which framing condition (if either) was closer to the subjective reality of an unframed taste test; however, it is clear that the frames affected the interpretation of the taste experience.

Experience Framing of Advertising Processing

Closer examination of Levin and Gaeth's (1988) research, which incorporates order effects (i.e., ad before experience vs. experience before ad) suggests the possibility of another interesting and potentially important framing effect: *how prior experience frames the interpretation of advertising*. It is noncontroversial that prior experience with a brand influences how the consumer responds to brand advertising. Indeed, it is often the case that advertising on behalf of a well-known brand can do little more than remind the consumer to use the brand or, perhaps, bolster the brand's salience.

What is of interest here is the case in which a consumer has direct experience with a product prior to having seen advertising for it. This occurs more frequently than one would think. Consumer promotions have been growing at a rapid pace for more than a decade, and these promotions rival media advertising expenditures in terms of the proportion of the overall promotional budget allocated to them. Product sampling campaigns aided by microsegmentation technology are commonplace. These intensified efforts by consumer package goods marketers to put the product in the hands of the consumer either directly via sampling or indirectly via deep-discount coupons have been accompanied by a rapid acceleration in the fragmentation of media exposure. It is increasingly difficult to reach a target audience through traditional media, at least with any real efficiency. As a result, it may be the case that greater numbers of consumers actually confront a new product before they confront (or at least become aware of) advertising for that product.

The question then becomes one of determining the possible "framing" impact of the experience on consumers' reactions to subsequent advertising. Note that the focus is not on evaluations of the ad per se, but rather the brand perceptions and judgments that are formed as a result of an "experience-plus-advertising" exposure sequence, standing in contrast to an "advertising-only" exposure. Prior research on attitudinal effects of direct vs. indirect experience (e.g., Fazio and Zanna 1981) suggests that experience dominates advertising in determining ultimate brand judgments. Information gleaned from one's own direct product experience is more reliable and trustworthy than that provided by advertisers, particularly when the product has many important "experience" attributes (Nelson 1974). In contrast, Nelson's "search attributes" can be veridically discovered through second-hand media (e.g., an ad describing a rug's colors, size and knots per inch). Results such as Marks and Kamins' (1988) contrast effect for greatly exaggerated advertising appeals suggest that more attention to possible experience-plus-advertising framing effects is warranted. Prior brand experience may cause consumers to be more skeptical of ad claims, leading to greater counterarguing and possible "boomerang" effects.

Only two studies (Marks and Kamins 1988; Levin & Gaeth 1988) could be located that incorporate conditions permitting examination of the "experience-frames-ad" effect. Unfortunately, Marks and Kamin's research was focused heavily on the effects of exaggerated advertising *prior* to product experience, and their article does not report the data for the ad-only condition, which is needed for the examination of experience framing.

Levin and Gaeth reported the necessary data in their Table 1 (p. 376). Comparing their "label-only" (i.e., ad-only) results with the "taste-before-labeling" results yields two tests of the experience-frames-ad phenomenon, one for the positive ("75% lean") frame and one for the negative ("25% fat") frame. Differences between the combination condition and the ad-only condition for the positive frame were -.69, -.90, -1.10, and -.82 for taste, quality, fat/lean, and greasy, respectively. Based on the significance tests reported in the article, it is reasonable to "guesstimate" that all differences were significant at $p < .05$, indicating a framing effect of experience on advertising. For the negative frame condition, the respective differences were .66, .43, .62, and .09. Again, a rough approximation suggests that all but the last difference were significant at $p < .10$. Importantly, the effect, though weaker, was in the opposite direction, indicating a positive effect of the taste experience on the interpretation of the advertising. It should be noted, however, that the ultimate brand ratings tended to be higher under the positive frame than under the negative frame, such that advertising had some effect in spite of the framing by prior experience.

In sum, Levin and Gaeth's results are indicative of a framing effect of experience on advertising, though moreso when the "ad" was positively rather than negatively worded. This pattern is consistent with the impact of exaggerated ads found by Marks and Kamins and suggests that experience will have more framing power when the ad can be more easily discounted (due to exaggerated claims) and the experience itself is unambiguous enough to lead to the formation of confidently held judgments about the product.

CONCLUSION

The present research has identified and reviewed five different kinds of "framing" in the consumer research literature. The previously unrecognized form of framing whereby initial product experience frames subsequent advertising response was explored conceptually. Despite the importance of trial experience and its effect on advertising exposure, this area is under-researched.

One issue that is open to debate is the attention vs. interpretation effects of direct experience on advertising (or the reverse). To examine a framing effect, an experiment could elicit cognitive responses and attribute level questions for one group of consumers exposed to the both trial and then advertising (or the reverse) and another group of consumers exposed to advertising alone (or direct experience). Large differences between the combination and single condition concerning the number of cognitive responses but not attribute levels might indicate a purely attentional mechanism, while the reverse might signal an interpretational influence of direct experience (or advertising) framing. Content analysis of the cognitive responses and belief levels would reveal what kinds of attributes were the attentional focus and/or most likely to be interpreted differently because of framing. Such an effort is being completed by the authors.

Future research could answer whether direct experience-frames-ad makes the consumer less sensitive to image-making advertising devices (as opposed to unambiguous product benefit description) while ad-frames-direct experience makes the consumer more sensitive to those same image-making devices. In other words, when the consumer is exposed to direct experience first, this might make the consumer more likely to ignore the exotic images that an ad attempts to associate with a product. If this is the case, the advertiser using an image-making strategy (e.g., most perfume ads) would want to make sure that all consumers were exposed to advertising before direct experience.

The attention vs. interpretation effects of framing examine the power of product exposure context. Marketing inputs like sampling programs, promotions and advertising alter the context of consumers' brand judgments and, if successful, serve to alter the enjoyment of product related activities including actual product consumption. To paraphrase Shakespeare "...a rose by any other (frame) might smell sweeter."

REFERENCES

Bettman, James R. and Mita Sujan (1987), "Effects of Framing on Evaluation of Comparable and Noncomparable Alternatives by Expert and Novice Consumers," *Journal of Consumer Research*, 14 (September), 141-54.

Deighton, John (1984), "The Interaction of Advertising and Evidence," *Journal of Consumer Research*, 11 (December), 763-70.

_____ (1988), "Two Meanings for Transformation," in *Advances in Consumer Research, Vol. 15*, M.J. Houston, ed. Provo, UT: Association for Consumer Research, 262-4.

_____ and Robert M. Schindler (1988), "Can Advertising Influence Experience?" *Psychology and Marketing*, 5 (Summer), 103-15.

Dover, Philip A. and Jerry C. Olson (1977), "Dynamic Changes in an Expectancy - Value Attitude Model as a Function of Multiple Exposures to Product Information," in *Proceedings, Summer Educators' Conference*. Chicago: American Marketing Association, 455-60.

Edell, Julie A. and Richard Staelin (1983), "The Information Processing of Pictures in Print Advertisements," *Journal of Consumer Research*, 10 (June), 45-61.

Fazio, Russell H. and Mark P. Zanna (1981), "Direct Experience and Attitude-Behavior Consistency," in *Advances in Experimental Social Psychology*, Vol. 14, Leonard Berkowitz ed. New York: Academic Press, 161-202.

Hoch, Stephen J. and John Deighton (1989), "Managing What Consumers Learn from Experience," *Journal of Marketing*, 53 (April), 1-20.

Hoch, Stephen J. and Young-Won Ha (1986), "Consumer Learning: Advertising and the Ambiguity of Product Experience," *Journal of Consumer Research*, 13 (September), 221-33.

Kahneman, Daniel and Amos Tversky (1979), "Prospect Theory: An Analysis of Decision Under Risk," *Econometrica*, 47, 263-291.

Kamins, Michael A. and Lawrence J. Marks (1987), "The Effect of Framing and Advertising Sequencing on Attitude Consistency and Behavioral Intentions," in *Advances in Consumer Research, Vol. 14*, P.F. Anderson and M. Wallendorf, eds. Provo, UT: Association for Consumer Research, 168-72.

Keller, Kevin Lane (1991), "Cue Compatibility and Framing in Advertising," *Journal of Marketing Research*, 18 (February), 42-57.

Levin, Irwin P. (1987), "Associative Effects of Information Framing," *Bulletin of the Psychonomics Society*, 25 (March), 85-6.

———— and Gary J. Gaeth (1988), "How Consumers Are Affected by the Framing of Attribute Information Before and After Consuming a Product," *Journal of Consumer Research*, 15 (December), 374-8.

MacKenzie, Scott B. (1986), "The Role of Attention in Mediating the Effect of Advertising on Attribute Importance," *Journal of Consumer Research*, 13 (September), 174-95.

Maheswaran, Durairaj and Joan Meyers-Levy (1990). "The Influence of Message Framing and Issue Involvement," *Journal of Marketing Research*, 27 (August), 361-7.

Marks, Lawrence J. and Michael A. Kamins (1988), "The Use of Product Sampling and Advertising: Effects of Sequence of Exposure and Degree of Advertising Claim Exaggeration on Consumers' Belief Strength, Belief Confidence, and Attitudes," *Journal of Marketing Research*, 25 (August), 266-81.

————, ———— and Donna Murphy (1986), "The Effects of Level of Expertise on the Processing of Framed and Unframed Pictorial Print Advertisements," in *Proceedings, Summer Educators' Conference*. Chicago: American Marketing Association, 57-61.

Nelson, Philip (1974), "Advertising as Information," *Journal of Political Economy*, 82 (July-August), 729-54.

Olson, Jerry C. and Philip Dover (1976), "Effects of Expectation Creation and Disconfirmation on Belief Elements of Cognitive Structure," in *Advances in Consumer Research, Vol. 3*, ed. B.B. Anderson. Cincinnati, OH: Association for Consumer Research, 168-75.

———— and ———— (1978), "Cognitive Effects of Deceptive Advertising," *Journal of Marketing Research*, 15 (February), 29-38.

Puto, Christopher P. (1987), "The Framing of Buying Decisions," *Journal of Consumer Research*, 14 (December), 301-15.

———— and William D. Wells (1984), "Informational and Transformational Advertising: The Differential Effects of Time," in *Advances in Consumer Research, Vol. 11*, T.C. Kinnear, ed. Provo, UT: Association for Consumer Research, 638-43.

Qualls, William and Christopher Puto (1989), "Organizational Climate and Decision Framing: An Integrated Approach to Analyzing Industrial Buying Decisions," *Journal of Marketing Research*, 26, (May), 179-92.

Thaler, Richard (1985), "Mental Accounting and Consumer Choice," *Marketing Science*, 4 (Summer) 199-214.

Wells, William D. (1980), "How Advertising Works," unpublished paper, Needham, Harper and Steers Advertising, Inc., Chicago.

Wright, Peter (1977), "Conditional Consumer Choice Processes and Advertising Strategy: An Introduction to *The Principle of Control Via Advocacy* and the *"MOD SQUAD"* for Advertising Strategists," in *Moving Ahead with Attitude Research*, Y. Wind and M.G. Greenberg, eds. Chicago: American Marketing Association, 101-6.

———— and Fredric Barbour (1975), "The Relevance of Decision Process Models in Structuring Persuasive Messages," *Communication Research*, 2 (July), 246-59.

———— and Peter D. Rip (1980), "Product Class Advertising Effects on First-Time Buyers' Decision Strategies," *Journal of Consumer Research*, 7 (September), 176-88.

Comments on "Advertising Issues"
Surendra N. Singh, University of Kansas

The three papers presented in this session address three different issues, and yet there is a common theme running through the papers — all three papers, in one way or another, relate to the advertising appeals.

Smith's paper compares the humorous and non-humorous advertising appeals; Brumbaugh looks at the effect of physical attractiveness of the models depicted in advertisements; and Wright and Lutz paper deals with the framing issues in advertising. My specific comments on each paper are given below.

The *first paper* — *"Does Humor in Advertising Enhance Systematic Processing?"* explores the thesis that humor in advertising will distract readers from paying attention to the ad copy by focusing attention on the humor instead. This idea has been present in the literature for several years but apparently it has never been tested directly. The old adage about "figure and ground" effect reflects this idea:

> "Keep the main points of the message in the foreground, do not let the background overshadow your main message".

Smith hypothesized that in non-humorous ads, claim strength would exert a greater influence on the dependent variables such as the attitude towards the ad, the attitude towards the brand, the brand related elaborations and the perception of claim strength. In contrast, in humorous ads, the claim strength would have less influence on these dependent measures. It was also predicted that humorous ads will lead to a more favorable response on various dependent variables.

These predictions are very interesting, however, the study designed to test these predictions has several methods limitations as pointed out by the author.

Since humorousness manipulation failed, a median split on the subjects' self-reported ratings of the humorousness was used to segregate the subjects into two groups: those who perceived the ad as humorous vs. those who did not.

The results obtained were mix — some effects were significant at conventional $\alpha = .05$, whereas several others were only marginally significant. Overall though, results do seem to offer tentative support for the proposed notion that subjects who perceived the ad as more humorous were less sensitive to the strength of the ad claims.

It would have been better, if we were given some additional information to interpret the results though. For instance, it would be very informative to know the effect of product relevance on the perception of humorousness? Is it possible that subjects who paid attention to the claims were those who considered purchasing life insurance very relevant and thus concentrated on the claims, compared to the subjects who had no-interest in buying insurance and thus who focused on the humor part of advertising - ignoring the claims?

The information on product relevance was collected in the study. Even though the scale used was a single item scale which asked subjects if they were interested in purchasing life insurance - and it is hard to infer the reliability of this scale - nonetheless, it would have been more informative to see the relationship between product relevance and message perception.

The thesis that humor distracts attention from ad claims seems plausible and despite methods problems, the results are encouraging and perhaps the study should be replicated to reach a more definite conclusion. Any replication effort should use ads for the product categories that are relevant to the subjects and product involvement should be measured explicitly and reliably. Also, if mood is used as an explanatory variable (as has been done in the present study which hypothesizes a direct effect of mood on Aad, A_b, etc. as well as an indirect effect via disrupting brand relevant elaborations), then strong message manipulations should be used such that the messages differ significantly not only on the humorousness dimension but also in their capacity to induce moods.

Moreover, while disruptive influence of mood is being offered as an explanation of humor's effect on ad and brand responses, there may be alternative explanations that can explain why audiences may ignore decision relevant brand information when such information is presented in emotional messages — be they humorous, romantic, or some other kind. Verbal learning literature, for example, suggests an alternative possibility.

Memory of verbal material depends on the schema chosen to govern the comprehension process and on the nature of the text. Kintsch and Young (1984, p. 112) note that:

> "Some types of texts are conventionally organized in such a way that the macrostructures i.e., (the overall interpretation of a text) that readers form are highly predictable and serve as efficient retrieval cues for the texts. This is the case with simple narratives, for which every reader brings to bear more or less the same schema, with predictable and rather satisfactory results. Other types of texts provide less efficient cues to their proper organization, and thus different readers choose somewhat different interpretations of the text. Frequently, none of these fits the text perfectly, and therefore the resulting macrostructures are not well constrained by the text. As a consequence, overall recall is low for such texts. Essays and descriptive texts are often of this type".

Whereas, in general, recall of narratives is much better than for the expository material, when a narrative contains decision relevant information, such information is recalled less well when it is presented in an expository text. This is because, when reading a narrative, people form macrostructures (the overall interpretations of the text) that contain text elements that are essential for understanding the plot, but the incidental-decision relevant information is not usually part of that macrostructure. In contrast, with the expository text, at least some people will regard the decision relevant portion of the material as macro relevant and use them to form the macrostructure leading to higher recall of decision relevant information in a descriptive text.

Perhaps something similar is happening with the emotional vs. non-emotional commercials that makes audiences pay less attention to the factual claims when such claims are presented in an emotional message format.

However, if an individual perceives the decision to be highly relevant, the schema chosen to govern the comprehension process might focus on the decision relevant information regardless of the type of message appeal. Future research should be able to verify whether this alternative explanation is valid.

The second paper —" Physical Attractiveness and Personality in Advertising: More Than Just a Pretty Face" proposes that the effects of having physically attractive models in advertising is mediated by the personality inferences which people draw spontaneously at zero acquaintances. She explains the mixed results of several past studies using this theory and the paper makes a valuable contribution in this regard.

The empirical testing part of the paper did raise some curiosities though. For example, what was the rationale for limiting the timing of the exposure and why the first two exposures were approximately 20 seconds each whereas the third exposure was 30 seconds?

Also, the dependent measure used in the study, the attitude towards the model's clothing, raises an interesting issue. The attractiveness of the model (which is an independent variable) may have been influenced by the model's clothing. Thus, the attitude towards the model's clothing is both a dependent variable, and at the same time, it is confounded with the independent variable also.

Moreover, it is reasonable to assume that the models' attractiveness should influence the attitude towards the ad directly which could in turn influence the attitude towards the brand. In the present study though, the stimuli were unframed pictures of the models only. Therefore, I suspect that it was not possible to gather information on attitude towards the ad because it was not an ad in the conventional sense to begin with.

Other than these minor points, I think it is a very nice piece of exploratory work. Some issues for future research that come to mind are:

(a) What will happen to the personality judgments inferred from the pictures with repeated exposures to the ad? Will they diminish or be enhanced or stay the same? In other words, does a model portrayed in an ad and perceived as sociable at the first exposure be perceived in the same way at later exposures?
(b) Would the verbal information provided in an ad moderate the personality inferences about an attractive model shown in the ad? How would this moderation effect vary by product class, subject involvement, message appeal type and so forth.
(c) As is pointed out in the paper, in many ads, attractive models are used simply to get attention. How could the attention value of an attractive model depicted in the ad be separately accounted for from the personality inferences?

The third paper, — *"Effect of Advertising and Experience on Brand Judgments: A Rose by Any Other Frame ...."* does a very good job of identifying various types of framing effects. It provides a nice post-hoc analysis of various studies and elaborates on different types of framing. The most important contribution of the paper is identifying a new form of framing — the effect of prior brand experience on the reactions to subsequent brand advertising.

Experience plus ad framing is opposite of transformational advertising which is described as the most important form of framing because it not only draws attention to the relevant attributes but also enhances the usage experience.

Wright and Lutz also identify a number of moderating variables affecting framing. These include, ambiguity of consumption experience, whether the consumer is a novice or an expert, and is the brand a novel brand or an existing one. The authors also propose how they intend to investigate this phenomenon in the future.

In addition to the moderator variables identified in the paper, there could be many other factors that may affect "experience plus ad framing". It would be interesting to identify these variables and develop predictions about how they could influence ad framing.

Some potential moderator variables are:

1. *The type of the consumer.*
   Is the target consumer a *loyal* user of some other brand or is (s)he likely to switch brands? Perhaps the consumer who is loyal to a brand would be less susceptible to the framing influences.

2. *The Nature of the Initial Consumption Experience.*
   Was the initial consumption experience positive or negative? If it was a satisfying experience, perhaps subsequent advertising can still have some framing effect for the later purchases — i.e., it might help reinforce the usage experience. If the initial reaction was negative, then the subsequent advertising will have much less framing power.

3. *Framing due to other variables.*
   There is bound to be some framing due to the prior experience with the other brands, the competitors' advertising in the product class, and in some product classes, there could be some framing based on the image of the retail establishment where the product was purchased from. Buying a shirt from K-mart leads to a different set of expectations than buying a shirt from the Parisians.

Finally, in real world settings, certain amount of framing for a novel brand may occur even when the subject does not see any advertising for it and her first brand experience is through sampling. These days, usually, a mail sample is preceded by a card or flyer announcing the arrival of the sample. When sample arrives, it often has an accompanying flyer and a set of coupons that too have advertising value. And then there is the packaging — all these can frame the product experience. Issues such as these need to be investigated to fully realize the potential of experience plus ad framing concept.

REFERENCE

Kintsch, Walter and Sheryl Young (1984), "Selective Recall of Decision-Relevant Information from Texts", *Memory and Cognition*, 12 (2), 112-17.

Opportunities for Consumer Researchers in Third World Food and Nutrition Development Efforts
Eric J. Arnould, California State University, Long Beach

INTRODUCTION

This presidential session stems from Alan Andreasen's campaign to prod our discipline towards a more fuller realization of its potential. His concern stems from different bases than similar calls made by many recent ACR presidents. His seem to be motivated by his active involvement in social marketing efforts over a good many years, and his desire to see more of us put our skills and expertise in the service of socially desirable outcomes. At the same time, as one of his presidential columns in the ACR Newsletter indicates, he is anxious that CB researchers avoid some of the common problems that beset academic researchers in applied, action-oriented social marketing contexts (Andreasen 1992b). These remarks are offered in the same spirit.

In remarks he made at the European ACR Conference, reprinted in the pages of the ACR Newsletter, Professor Andreasen argued that the discipline might well stretch its boundaries along five major dimensions (1992c). Three of these: increasing intellectual diversity, internationalization, and increasing interdisciplinary cross-fertilization can be met in the context of greater membership involvement in international social marketing initiatives concerning food and nutrition. These are financed by United States Agency for International Development (USAID), The World Bank, other International Development Banks, the United Nations Food and Agriculture Organization (FAO), United Nations Environmental Program (UNEP), United Nations International Children's Fund (UNICEF), and other multi and bi-lateral donor agencies. They are implemented by scores of academic research units, such as the Post-Harvest Institute at University of Idaho or the Office of Arid Lands Studies at University of Arizona; private consulting firms, such as Winrock International, International Resources Group, Development Alternatives International, Chemonics, and Abt & Associates; and, finally third sector organizations that include Private Voluntary Agencies (PVOs) and Non-Governmental Agencies (NGOs), such as CARE, Lutheran World Relief, Doctors Without Borders, Catholic Relief Services, etc.

INTERNATIONALIZATION

Work for the previously-mentioned agencies provides ample opportunities for marketing and consumer behavior researchers to gain international experience. I have personally worked for, with or in competition with, most of the organizations mentioned above over the past fifteen years. These assignments have taken me to over a dozen West African countries on natural resources and food and nutrition projects. On occasion they have also resulted in desk studies of these issues conducted at home. To give two examples, in the summer of 1990 I worked with staff of the Office of Arid Lands Studies on a report for USDA on Guidelines for Incorporating Nutrition and Food Security concerns in agriculture development projects (Arnould and Frankenburger 1990). This study focused on households consumption strategies in coping with varying levels of nutritional risk. And just this last summer, I worked with the Post-Harvest Institute on a study of Nigerien onion export marketing that took me to six countries and included a focus on consumer attitudes and behaviors (Arnould with Iddal 1992).

In arguing for greater involvement of the membership in social marketing activities, I might follow Professor Andreasen (1992a) and appeal to ACR members' desires to meet altruistic social needs. In fact, a consumer behavior perspective *is* desperately needed in many social marketing projects associated with nutrition and food security. For example, a recent New York Times editorial trumpeted Professor James Borland's "green revolution" strategy for increasing agricultural production and productivity in Africa; a strategy endorsed by former President Jimmy Carter. But green revolution strategies are akin to the familiar production orientation in consumer marketing. In response to a production orientation toward food and nutrition, consumer behavior researchers would be quick to point out that needed calories do not equal desired foods, well aware as we are that needs and wants are two different things. They might also point out the necessity of giving consideration to pre-existent product complementarity in proposing new or "improved" crops to African farmers.

Professor Borlund seems fated to repeat the mistakes of early green revolution projects in Latin America and Asia. In Latin America, these projects focused on diffusing improved yields of hybrid corn to peasant producer/consumers. In some cases, impressive yields led to rapid adoption, but then to the social marketers consternation, equally rapid rejection of the so-called "improved" seed. Why? The hybrid maizes lacked the binding enzymes that made tortillas possible. What good is food you cannot eat? Increased food crop production need not lead necessarily to improved nutrition either. As marketing oriented consumer researchers, we would also point out that at least 3 other "P"s merit consideration before jumping to such a conclusion.

Further, as Professor Andreasen pointed out in an ACR Newsletter article (1992c), consumer behavior researcher's long-standing interests in household allocation decisions could both enliven, and benefit from the ongoing debates in social marketing. This knowledge is applicable to programs designed to bring about improved household food security and achieve nutritional equity in the Third World. Given our interest in diffusion and new product adoption, consumer researchers also have something to contribute to farmers decisions to allocate scarce household resources to purchase of expensive, foreign, novel agricultural inputs as well. To take another example from early "Green Revolution" experiences in the Philippines high-yielding "miracle rice" often was not adopted by farmers. Why? As marketers pointed out, using the miracle rice required four times more inputs of supplies and twice as much labor inputs, and dramatically increased farmers' financial exposure when compared to traditional rice. Use of the rice required changes in farming household's fundamental pattern of resource use and decision-making (Felton and Sorenson 1967).

A list of consumption research questions generated in the context of another study is included in Table 1. Consumer researchers can judge to what extent they have something to offer in response to such questions, and could imagine other questions they might address.

Consumer behavior insights are also needed at the international policy level. Critiques of the activities of the World Bank over the last half-dozen years have focused in part on the impact on consumers of World Bank macro-economic "structural adjustment policies" imposed on numerous Third World governments. These policies focus on currency devaluation, relaxation of trade barriers, and ending of government agricultural subsidies. Consumer belt-tightening has been one of the primary results in many countries that have adopted the World Bank's medicine. One might well argue that had scientists with a deep understanding of both the macro and

TABLE 1
Nutritional Research Questions for Agricultural Research Projects

Most research by International Agricultural Research Centers (IARCs) and others when they have addressed nutritional issues at all have sought to "improve" nutrient quality and palatability, perhaps even processing characteristics. Alternatively, a vulnerability based strategy of research formulation might pose questions like the following:

1. In the total food system context facing major groups of vulnerable households, what is the impact of consuming different varieties of the main staple or an improved variety thereof on pregnant women?

2. Does the balance of consumption by a lactating mother, a weaned child, or other vulnerable group as between different crops or varieties of a crop, given the group's work requirements, significantly affect the at-risk group's nutrition?

3. What if any is the differential impact of crops and improved varieties on the volume, absorbability and quality of breast milk and/or weaning foods?

4. Are there nutritionally important differences among modern and traditional crop varieties in their effects on bulk, absorbability, and quality of at-risk groups total food intake?

5. As such matters are researched do they assess the impact of modern varieties total diets, intra-family food allocation and distribution procedures, food processing and cooking arrangements?

6. Do crop or varietal nutrients, and work inputs, interact for vulnerable groups, with the type and timing of infection and the building or weakening of mechanisms of immunity?

7. Do some modern crop varieties or production technologies increase the work or travel required of women, perhaps at times when they are already hard pressed to muster enough dietary energy or time for child care or other tasks?

8. Is research important that reduces preparation time and fuel costs or increases energy density of food eaten by vulnerable groups?

9. How can the caloric (rather than protein) value of modern crop varieties or minor crops be improved?

10. Where farming systems are based on cereals more than on root crops, how can more and less risking modern crop varieties be provided to provide income or output to increase dietary energy for poor, largely farming, but also wage laboring households?

11. What is the recovery rate of hulled grain from modern crop varieties as compared to traditional crop varieties using traditional milling technologies?

12. If processing and palatability characteristics are to be addressed, then ask do negative processing and palatability characteristics constrain adoption of improved yield, modern crop varieties by nutritionally vulnerable groups?

Source: Lipton and Longhurst 1989

---

micro dimensions of consumer behavior been more involved in policy formulation, some of the Bank's production and export-oriented economic policies might have been moderated in favor of consumers.

Of course all these arguments in favor of increased ACR member participation in social marketing are based on President Andreasen's suggestion that at least one of the reasons people join ACR and become consumer researchers is that participation in this community meets altruistic social needs.

INCREASING INTERDISCIPLINARY CROSS-FERTILIZATION

Professor Andreasen has pointed out in his Newsletter columns that it is unlikely that ACR members will become involved in action-oriented, applied research out of compassion and commitment, but rather out of long-term research potential (Andreasen 1991; 1992a). Sadly, I must concur with his assessment.

Even if motivated by the "doing good" agenda of the public sector social marketer, the barriers to entry into the field of social marketing can be formidable. My own experience confirms this. First of all it is expensive to develop the expertise required to work in the alien organizational cultures of the major multi- and bi-lateral donors. I well remember my own bemusement trying to make sense of the alphabet soup of acronyms casually tossed about by veterans in the business. The bureaucratic procedures and formats of donors, consulting projects and consulting project reports, can also be foreboding. The solution to this problem, however, comes with experience. It has the happy result of considerably broadening one's interdisplinary competence. The Public Administration-based language of project planning, implementation, monitoring, and evaluation soon becomes second nature to the social marketing professional.

A second barrier to entry, is the investment in specialized technical knowledge and interdisplinary collaboration involved in public sector social marketing work in nutrition and agriculture, resource management and allocation, or health care delivery. Social marketing is often team work. On any given assignment, one is apt to find oneself thrown together with unfamiliar colleagues of other scientific persuasions. Not infrequently they may harbor considerable skepticism about the merit of marketing science or consumer research. Thus, one sometimes is simultaneously trying to establish ones' intellectual turf, educate team members about one's own disciplinary perspective, and, at the same time, gather information about the problem at hand. This is quite a juggling act. But the solution to the twin problems of disciplinary bias and technical proficiency leads again to the broadening of disciplinary perspectives Professor Andreasen and other ACR presidents have advocated. After more than a decade of working with natural scientists in West Africa, for example, I have become familiar with a variety of basic concepts and relationships in geology, pedology, agronomy, climatology, ecology, and remote sensing. Unfortunately my technical expertise is limited to West Africa so I know more species of West African trees than North American, more about growing millet and sorghum than wheat or maize. More pertinently, I also know quite a lot about African marketing systems and African consumers, and this knowledge has been enriched by collaboration with colleagues from these other disciplines.

A third barrier to entry into social marketing consulting is that it typically involves work in unfamiliar cultural contexts. Second and even third language competence is often required. This too is expensive to attain and retain. Even after ten years of classroom French, I became fluent only after working in francophone bureaucratic contexts. And as for my African language ability, it is always a struggle to learn, its easily forgotten, hard to practice, and after all, useful in a limited region. Worse no one cares. On the other hand, foreign language proficiency further opens the doors to both intra- and inter-disciplinary perspectives of foreign colleagues and a broad array of surprising new consumer experiences.

A fourth barrier to entry is that work in the Third World is often uncomfortable, and although my experience with bullet dodging is fairly limited, it happens. Worse though is the mediocrity: it gets old fast staying in crummy hotels, and eating crummy food. On the other hand, the human interactions with colleagues, counterparts, and consumers are something I treasure. The scenery is nice too. This leads to a final point about increasing intellectual diversity and personal and professional outcomes.

PERSONAL/PROFESSIONAL OUTCOMES

In spite of the barriers to entry, there are good selfish reasons for ACR members to get involved in applied, action-oriented research associated with nutrition and food security, health care marketing, market system development, and management training, and other similar areas. This is because such work *can* contribute to one's own long-term research interests. This can and does happen in the two ways that Professor Andreasen (1992b) suggests. One is that social marketing research provides opportunities to apply concepts and methods already developed in new and challenging contexts that can establish their robustness. Consumption status can be threatened by a variety of factors in the agricultural system. To summarize from an earlier report (Arnould and Frankenberger 1990), food consumption deficiencies can result from:

1) inadequate production of acceptable food stuffs
2) adequate production but inadequate income levels
3) unhealthy consumption patterns or consumer pathologies
4) political constraints on consumption decisions
5) economic constraints on consumption decisions
6) social constraints on consumption decisions

Consumer researchers have worked on similar topics in other domains. Concepts developed in these domains could easily extend to nutrition and food security.

The other long term benefit of social marketing research in nutrition and food security is that social marketing research provides opportunities to extend and enrich present concepts and theories by trying to understand behavior and behavior changes processes in new and different circumstances.

To these intangibles, I might add a tangible benefit of the proposed research program. The resources available to the donors dwarf those available to organizations such as Marketing Science, and usually come with fewer strings attached than do those made available by private corporations.

As for outcomes, participation in social marketing activities has provided me with a real opportunity to test concepts in other contexts and hopefully to extend and enrich them in the process. My dissertation is a product of research conducted on an African development project concerned with resource management and marketing (Arnould 1982). The research outcomes of my recent work in social marketing is reflected in two previous *JCR* articles (Arnould 1989a, Wallendorf and Arnould 1988), and a Society for Macromarketing Conference Proceeding (Arnould 1989b). These dealt with issues related to product meaning and the diffusion of innovations. As an aside, I mention that several articles based on marketing-oriented research in food, nutrition, and resource management have appeared in development, anthropology, and Africanist journals (Arnould 1990, 1989c, 1988, 1986, 1985). These same publishing opportunities are available for others. And as we all know from Marketing 101, product line diversification spreads around the risk of single product failures! Last summers research on onion export marketing produced some interesting findings on the relationship between product quality, price, and purchase behavior that I hope will lead to future publishing possibilities.

CONCLUSIONS

Development agencies cannot rely on broad generalizations in the formulation of policy and programs designed to address nutrition and food consumption issues in agricultural development. Nor should they have to look only to specialists in agronomy, economics, rural sociology, anthropology, and health sciences for an understanding of consumer behavior. In particular contexts, development interventions should be targeted at one or more of the many linkages between production and consumption. The critical mediating steps towards improving food security, the sine qua non of economic development are formulating strategies for supporting indigenous strategies to cope with threats to consumption, and improving production/consumption linkages at the household level. With their diverse theoretical corpus and catholic methodological tool-kit their would seem to be ample opportunity for members of ACR to contribute to these aims while benefiting themselves professionally and contributing to broadening of our discipline.

BIBLIOGRAPHY

Andreasen, Alan (1991), "Notes from the President Elect," *ACR Newsletter*, December, 3.

Andreasen, Alan (1992b), "On Doing Social Marketing," *ACR Newsletter*, June, 2-4.

Andreasen, Alan (1992a), "So What's An Association Anyway," *ACR Newsletter*, March, 2-5.

Andreasen, Alan (1992c), "President's Column," *ACR Newsletter*, September, 2-4.

Arnould, Eric J. (1990) "Changing the Terms of Rural Development: Collaborative Research in Cultural Ecology in the Sahel," *Human Organization* 49(4), 339-354.

Arnould, Eric J. (1989a), "Toward a Broadened Theory of Preference Formation and the Diffusion of Innovations: Cases from Zinder Province, Niger Republic," *Journal of Consumer Research* 16 (September), 239-267.

Arnould, Eric J. (1989b) "Agricultural Development Projects in West Africa as Social Marketing: A Post-Mortem," Proceedings. Macromarketing Seminar XIV. Toledo, OH: University of Toledo.

Arnould, Eric J. (1989c), "Anthropology and West Africa Development: A Critique of Recent Debate," *Human Organization* 48(4), 135-147.

Arnould, Eric J. (1988), "Indigenous Responses to Economic Development: An Introduction," *Urban Anthropology and Studies of Cultural Systems and World Economic Development* 17(1), 1-5.

Arnould, Eric J. (1986), "Merchant Capital, Simple Reproduction, and Underdevelopment: Peasant Traders in Zinder, Niger," *Canadian Journal of African Studies* 20(3), 323-356.

Arnould, Eric J. (1985), "Evaluating Regional Economic Development: Results of a Regional Systems Analysis in Niger," *Journal of Developing Areas* 19(2), 209-244.

Arnould, Eric J. (1982), *Regional Market System Development and Changes in Relations of Production in Three Communities in Zinder Province, Niger Republic*. Unpublished Ph.D. Dissertation. Tucson: Department of Anthropology, University of Arizona.

Arnould Eric J. and Timothy Frankenberger (1990) *Guidelines for Including Food and Nutrition in Agricultural Projects*. Food and Agricultural Cooperative Agreement. DAN-5110-A-00-9095-00. Office of Nutrition, U.S. Agency for International Development. Tucson, AZ: Office of Arid Lands Studies.

Arnould, Eric J. with Sidi Mohammed Iddal (1992) *Niger Onion Marketing Study*. Post-Harvest Institute for Perishables, University of Idaho, Moscow, ID and USAID-Niger.

Felton, Edward J. Jr., and Ralph Z. Sorenson (1967), "Commentary On Seed Corporation of the Philippines," The Seminar Workshop on the Economics of Rice. Paper presented at a Conference at The International Rice Research Institute, December 8-9, 1967.

Lipton, Michael with Richard Longhurst (1989), *New Seeds and Poor People*. London: Unwin Hyman.

Wallendorf, Melanie and Eric J. Arnould (1988), "My Favorite Things": A Cross-Cultural Inquiry into Object Attachment, Possessiveness, and Social Linkage," *Journal of Consumer Research* 14(March): 531-547.

Adolescent Participation in Hazardous Activities: Identifying High Risk Groups and Implications for Intervention Policies

William J. Burns, University of Iowa

PAPERS PRESENTED

Adolescent Perception of Risk: Understanding and Preventing High Risk Behavior

Herbert H. Severson, Oregon Research Institute

Adolescent risk perceptions were examined across several studies. The findings indicate that adolescents who engage in high risk behavior perceive the risk to be smaller, better known, and more controllable, and also perceive greater benefits and more peer pressure than non-participants. Hence, risk perception may prove useful in targeting teenagers who are "at risk" of later becoming involved with dangerous activities. Such adolescents may be viable candidates for early intervention programs.

Personality→Attitude→Behavior: Models of Young Male Alcohol Consumption

John P. Murry, University of Wisconsin
John L. Lastovicka, Arizona State University
Jon R. Austin, University of Wisconsin

The goal of this modeling was to demonstrate how incorporating the motivational underpinnings of consumption beliefs enriches the cognitive insights found in traditional multiattribute research. For example, the youthful-male alcohol consumption model suggests that alcohol consumption is, in part, a function of "drinking helps socially" and "drinking impairs ability" beliefs. The "drinking impairs ability" belief is influenced by an "aggressive male" trait and the "drinking helps socially" belief is influenced by both "aggressive male" and "satisfaction with life" traits. This implies for instance that an effective strategy to change the "drinking helps socially" belief would be to demonstrate that excessive social drinking detracts from a satisfying life. Consumers often hold consumption beliefs that reflect more enduring beliefs about themselves. Uncovering the relationship between these two types of beliefs begins to address why consumption beliefs are held and suggests how these beliefs can be effectively managed.

Alcohol-Related Risk Taking Among Teenagers: An Investigation of Contributing Factors and a Discussion of How Marketing Principles Can Help

William J. Burns, University of Iowa
Sarah E. Hampson, Oregon Research Institute
Herbert H. Severson, Oregon Research Institute
Paul Slovic, Decision Research

A covariance structure analysis indicated that factors pertaining to perceptions that the benefits of using alcohol outweigh the risks, grade level, and desired independence directly affect participation in alcohol-related activities. Likewise, personality characteristics (sensation seeking, ego control, independence, and academic-orientation) appear to indirectly influence participation through their influence on adolescents' perceptions of the associated risks. These findings are integrated within a social marketing framework and offer strategies to reduce alcohol-related risk taking among adolescents. *See our paper in this volume for details.*

Adolescents Perception of Risk: Understanding and Preventing High Risk Behavior

Herbert H. Severson, Oregon Research Institute
Paul Slovic, Decision Research
Sarah Hampson, Oregon Research Institute

ABSTRACT

This paper describes a method for measuring risk perception in adolescents. The psychometric paradigm used in the work provides a rating across a wide range of activities and evaluates dimensions of an adolescent's perception of risk. Results show that adolescents who engage in high risk activities differ significantly on a wide range of perceptions from adolescents who do not engage in frequent high risk activities. When scales of risk are entered into a step-wise regression, the prediction of engagement in high risk activities is .78 ($p<.001$). The methodology of risk perception can provide a useful instrument for assessing an adolescent's view of risk taking and as a dependent measure of response to preventive interventions.

Adolescence is the only age group for which mortality rates have risen between 1960 and 1990. The three primary causes of death during adolescence are accidents, homicide and suicide, all of which are associated with preventable social, environmental, and behavioral factors (Irwin & Milstein, 1986). A diversity of theoretical development and empirical work has emerged to understand the idealogy of these high risk behaviors by adolescents. Our work is targeting, specifically, the engagement of adolescents in drug use and trying to understand and predict their involvement in this behavior. Theories have been postulated and explored which include factors such as family and peer models (Newcomb, Huba, & Bentler, 1983) tolerance of deviance or lack of conformity (Jessor & Jessor, 1977), low self-esteem (Huba, Newcomb & Bentler, 1986), and stressful events of situations (Newcomb & Harlow, 1986). Teen drug use can be viewed as a product of complex biosocial processes which involve cultural, situational, familial, peer based, and intra-individual differences. These influences may be placed on a distal proximal dimension. Toward the distal extreme, lie biological factors such as genetic pre-dispositions (e.g., alcoholism). Familial and cultural influences lie somewhere mid-range, and situational and peer influences are more proximal. Risk perceptions represent an aspect of the belief structure and cognition of an individual that enter into decisions about drug use and are among the more proximal influences to be studied.

Risk Perception

The cornerstone of our approach to understanding adolescent drug use is the construct of risk perception (e.g., Slovic, 1987). The approach to studying risk perception that we are following, has evolved over the past twenty years. During this time, researchers have been examining the opinions that people express when they are asked to evaluate hazardous activities, substances, and technologies. This research has attempted to develop techniques for assessing the complex and subtle opinions that people hold about risk. With these techniques, researchers have sought to discover what people mean when they say something is or is not "risky". The basic assumption underlining these efforts is that we need to understand the ways that people think about and respond to risk in order to promote or regulate health and safety for the population. We have applied this psychometric methodology to adolescent risk perception to better understand their engaging in high risk activities. We have conducted a number of studies involving teenagers, in grades 6-12, who were asked to make judgments about the riskiness of various activities. These activities include smoking marijuana, drinking alcohol, engaging in unprotected sex, smoking cigarettes, using smokeless tobacco, and the use of other drugs. These judgments have been related to ratings of these same activities on scales assessing other characteristics, such as perceived benefit, avoidability, and social approval for participation. This methodology has been used to analyze the differences in perception between teens who participate in high risk activities, and compare them to those that do not. Additionally, a broad strategy for studying perceived risk has been to develop a taxonomy for hazards, which can be used to understand and predict responses to risks. A taxonomic scheme might explain, for example, people's extreme aversion to some hazards, their indifference to others, and the discrepancies between the reactions and expert opinions. This psychometric paradigm or psychophysical scaling uses multi-varied analysis techniques to produce quantitative representations of risk attitudes and perceptions. Within this psychometric paradigm, people then make quantitative judgments about the current and desired riskiness of diverse hazards and the desired level of regulation of each.

Numerous studies have been carried out within this psychometric paradigm, and they have shown that perceived risk is both quantifiable and predictable. Studies have indicated that people are willing to tolerate higher risks where activities are seen as beneficial. Further studies have also shown that characteristics such as familiarity, control, catastrophic potential, equity, and level of knowledge all seem to influence the relationship between the perceived risk, perceived benefit, and the acceptance of this risk (Fishoff, Slovic, Lichtenstein, (1978); Slovic, Fishoff, & Lichtenstein, 1980). We have been conducting a series of studies which examine the perceptions of risk and benefit from activities that put young people at risk. The emphasis of these studies have been on problem behaviors which involve drugs and alcohol. Some participation in risky activities is a part of normal psychological development for a healthy adolescent. Our effort is to assess factors which may influence these perceptions of risk and benefit and use this knowledge to reduce the adolescent's participation in high risk activities. Our preliminary studies indicate that from an adolescent user's perspective, the perceived benefits of drug and alcohol far outweigh the perceived risk.

Multiple Risk Behavior

Adolescent risk taking is usually not confined to one activity, but usually involves multiple risk taking. Recent research has underscored the fact that adolescents who engage in one class of high risk activities, often engage in multiple risk activities (Metzler, Noell, & Biglan, 1992). The causes for adolescents' enthusiasm for multiple risk taking are not well understood. Some authors have postulated psychosocial variables such as peer pressure and family/environmental variables, and others have postulated for personality factors such as sensation seeking (Zuckerman, 1979). Previous research in drug use has generally concluded that peer influence is the preeminent predictor of drug use, despite accounting for only a small portion of the variance (Kandel, 1982). Moreover, prevention programs that are usually aimed at specific high risk behaviors, such as cigarette smoking or drug use, have reported only modest success rates; although, they are usually targeted on altering peer

FIGURE 1
Risk Perception Scale

Quantitative Judgements

Scales or Dimensions

Example: If you did this activity, to what extent (how much) do you believe that you would be personally at risk of getting hurt or getting sick? (Personal Risk)

Behavior	I would not be at risk							I would be very much at risk
Drinking Wine	1	2	3	4	5	6	7	
Smoking Cigarettes	1	2	3	4	5	6	7	

FIGURE 2
Predicting Participation in Risk Taking Activities

These risk perception scales and personality scales were found to be highly predictive of students' current reported participation rates. This prediction was made using all of the scales, all subjects, and all destructive activities. The multiple R was .75.

*Higher Perceived Friends' Participation

*Higher Perceived Benefits

*Higher Perceived Parental Approval

*Lower Ego Control

*Higher Perceived Peer Pressure

*Lower Perceived Personal Risk

*Lower Achievement

---

influence (Severson & Zoref, 1991). We believe that it is necessary to investigate the adolescents' perspectives on risk taking in order to gain insights into the motivation and rewards for these behaviors.

Studies on Risk Perception

We have conducted four studies of adolescents' perception or risk taking among middle school, and college students, using the same methodology. In each case, we asked them to rate a range of activities on a variety of scales. An example of the scale is shown in Figure 1. Hence, the person is asked to rate the same risk behaviors for each of the given scales. While the specific behaviors rated in these scales have varied from study to study, the results have been similar across all studies. We have found that adolescents who engage in specific high risk activities, report greater knowledge of its risks, less fear of risks, less personal risk to self and others, less serious effects, more personal control over risk, less ability to avoid the activity, and high participation in the activity by others. Adolescents who participate in high risk activities also report that they perceive greater peer influence, less desire for regulation of the activity by authorities, and greater benefits relative to the risks. A summary of these findings is shown in Figure 2. Individuals who engage in destructive behaviors such as using drugs, smoking cigarettes or drinking alcoholic beverages, also tend to obtain a higher score on scales such as sensation seeking.

A principal components factor analysis of the intercorrelations of fourteen risk scales results in two factors accounting for 68% and 15% of the variance, respectively. These factors have been identified as risk and admiration, respectively. Many of the most dangerous activities are highly admired as more socially approved forms of risk taking and this admiration may be an important motivator reinforcer for these behaviors. We have also found that adolescents that participate in high risk activities see these activities as hard to avoid doing, but also more likely to see the risks are easy to control once the activity is engaged in. This latter result is consistent with Weinstein's (1980) finding of unrealistic optimism in adolescents' reactions to negative events. The risk activities in our studies can be placed in a two dimensional factor space relative to the dimensions of risky vs. not risky and admired vs. not admired (Benthin, Slovic and Severson, in press). An example of this factor plot is shown in Figure 3.

In addition to our measurement of risk perception, we also have measured the participation of adolescents in these actual

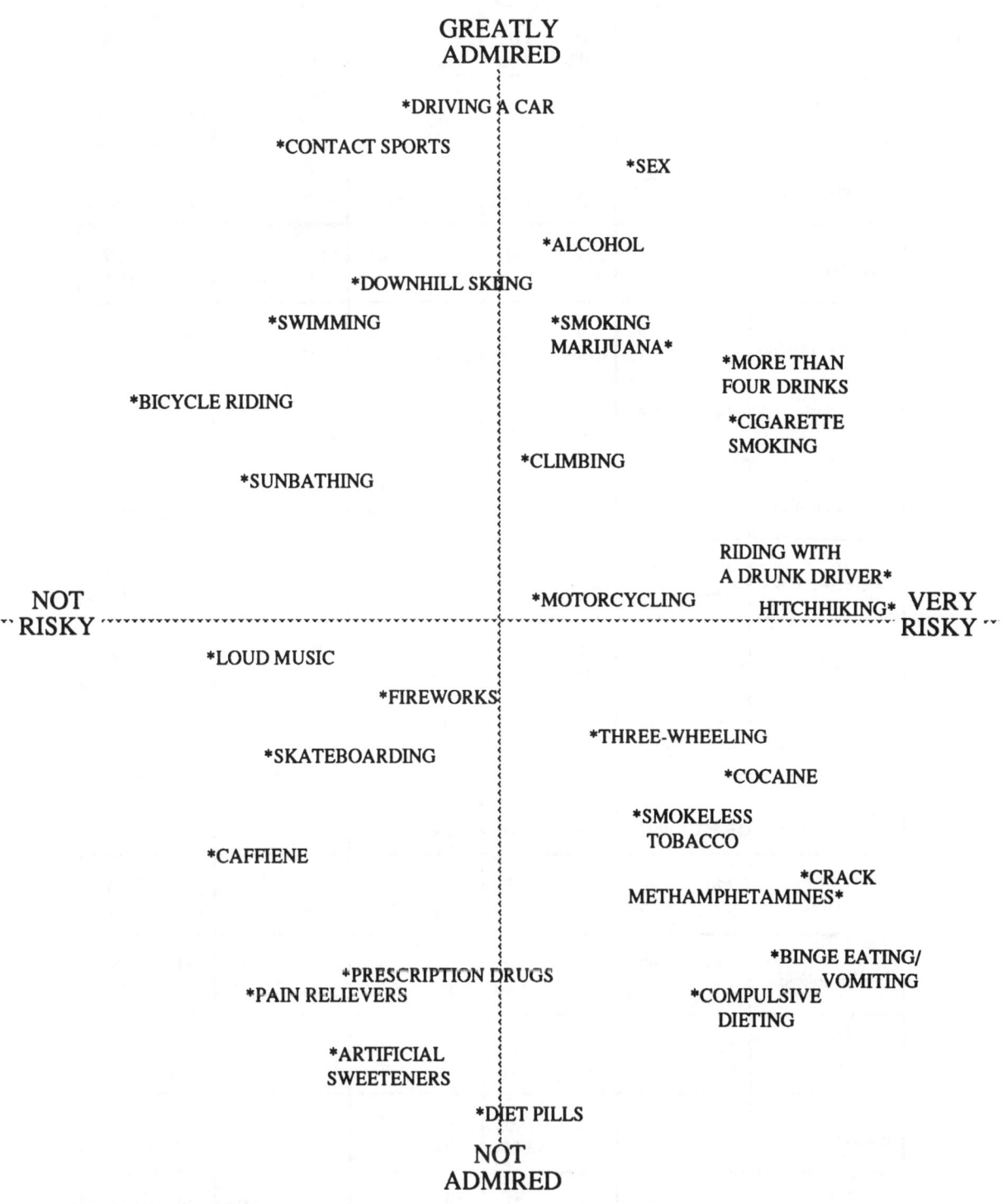

FIGURE 3
Factor Plot

Location of 30 Activities Within a Two-Factor Space Derived From the Interrelationships Among 14 Risk Characteristics

Figure taken from: Benthin, Slovic and Severson (in press)

activities. Table 1, below, shows the distribution of participation in these activities for one high school study we completed. As you can see, the use of tobacco was fairly prevalent with 33% reporting smoking at least once in the past six months and the use of smokeless tobacco, chewing tobacco or snuff is as common as cigarette use for males. Marijuana use is reported by more older students (31%), than younger ones, that is 9th and 10th grade (17%), but only a few students in either age group reported using methamphetamines over that past six months (5%). An examination by gender reveals that similar numbers of boys and girls are smoking marijuana (24% and 22%, respectively) and using methamphetamines (6% and 4%, respectively). Cigarette smoking was more

TABLE 1
Reported Frequencies of Participation by Grade

Activity	Number of Times in the Last 6 Months									
	Zero		1 to 2		3 to 5		6 to 10		11 or more	
	9th-10th	11th-12th	9th-10th	11th-12th	9th-10th	11th-12th	9th-10th	11th-12th	9th-10th	11th-12th
Drank Beer	68 38.9%	27 18.6%	38 21.7%	22 15.2%	24 13.7%	26 17.9%	18 10.3%	12 8.3%	27 15.4%	58 40.0%
Drank Wine	58 40.9%	45 21.9%	33 18.2%	31 21.9%	25 18.8%	34 17.8%	14 8.5%	21 13.7%	27 13.6%	34 25.3%
Drank Hard Liquor	94 53.7%	44 30.1%	29 16.6%	41 28.1%	19 10.9%	22 15.1%	12 6.9%	12 8.2%	21 12.0%	27 18.5%
Smoked Cigarettes	124 70.5%	99 68.3%	19 10.8%	16 11.0%	3 1.7%	10 6.9%	3 1.7%	3 2.1%	27 15.3%	17 11.7%
Marijuana	146 83.0%	100 69.4%	11 6.3%	12 8.3%	3 1.7%	8 5.6%	7 4.0%	7 4.9%	9 5.1%	17 11.8%
Drove an ATV	62 35.0%	32 22.2%	25 14.1%	42 29.2%	26 14.7%	25 17.4%	21 11.9%	8 5.6%	43 24.3%	37 25.7%
Drank 5+ Drinks	99 56.6%	57 39.3%	23 13.1%	13 9.0%	12 6.9%	20 13.8%	11 6.3%	14 9.7%	30 17.1%	41 28.3%
Used Meth	167 94.9%	137 94.5%	2 1.1%	3 2.1%	2 1.1%	2 1.4%	0 0	0 0	5 2.8%	3 2.1%
Downhill Skied	111 63.1%	80 54.8%	35 19.9%	27 18.5%	19 10.8%	17 11.6%	8 4.5%	16 11.0%	3 1.7%	6 4.1%
Drove a Car	29 16.5%	3 2.1%	28 15.9	5 3.4%	18 10.2%	5 3.4%	17 9.7%	2 1.4%	84 47.7%	130 89.7%
Rode w/ intoxicated	120 69.4%	80 55.9%	33 38.9%	35 24.5%	12 6.9%	12 8.4%	6 3.5%	8 5.6%	2 1.2%	8 5.6%
Used Smokeless	143 81.7%	97 66.4%	10 5.7%	17 11.6%	7 4.0%	8 5.5%	4 2.3%	4 2.7%	11 6.3%	20 13.7%
Bulemia	158 90.3%	142 97.3%	8 4.6%	2 1.4%	2 1.1%	0 0	2 1.1%	1 .7%	5 2.9%	1 .7%
Starvation Diet	143 81.3%	124 84.9%	14 8.0%	10 6.8%	6 3.4%	7 4.8%	7 4.0%	2 1.4%	6 3.4%	3 2.1%
Unprotected Sex	122 69.3%	69 48.3%	19 10.8%	27 18.9%	14 8.0%	12 8.4%	7 4.0%	10 7.0%	14 8.0%	25 17.5%
Drove Intoxicated	164 93.2%	105 71.9%	8 4.5%	19 13.0%	2 1.1%	14 9.6%	1 .6%	3 2.1%	1 .69%	5 3.4%

common among boys than girls (34% vs. 26%). This result is not consistent with most other surveys that find that girls smoke at a higher rate than boys for most adolescent samples. The clearest effect for gender was observed in the use of smokeless or chewing tobacco which was four times as likely to be reported by boys (41%), than for girls (10%).

In sum, the findings for the usefulness of risk perception have been replicated in four studies to date and are consistent across an age range from 12-18 and for males and females. The intercorrelation of all risk characteristics in a factor analysis has been consistently factor analyzed into two uncorrelated factors which account for approximately 83% of the variance. The factor 1 which we have identified as "risk" involves the perceived risk and the fear of consequences, while factor 2 "admiration" is the perception of admiration, knowledge, and peer influence. When these scales are entered into a stepwise multiple regression, which predicts the engagement in the high risk activities (a destructive behavior index for multiple behaviors), the correlation is .78 (p< .001).

Discussion

One message from the data using this methodology of risk perception is that the results are orderly and meaningful and lead to the general conclusion that we have developed a useful psychometric instrument to investigate how adolescents view risk. It appears that participation in risky activities is related to very distinct cognitive and social factors. From a cognitive perspective, people who engage in these activities report knowledge of the risks, less fear of the risk, more personal control and less ability to avoid the activity, and perceive higher participation in the activity by peers.

From a social perspective, participants report greater peer influence, less desire for regulation of the activity by authorities and greater benefits relative to the risk. It is also notable that results from this study point to a general problem behavior syndrome. In other words, young people who engage in one form of risk taking (e.g., excess use of alcohol) are relatively more likely to engage in other high risk activities (e.g., smoking cigarettes). These results are in line with previous research that suggest that problem behaviors during adolescence tend to be inter-related, rather than being a collection of independent activities (Biglan, Metzler, Wirt, & Ary, et al., 1990; Metzler, Noell, & Biglan, 1992).

The finding that adolescents that engage in risky activities tend to perceive this risks as well known, raises questions about the potential effectiveness of information and educational programs, which are designed to discourage young people from engaging in risk taking behaviors. If adolescents actually have adequate information with regard to the dangerousness of the activity, and are knowledgeable about the specific risks, it appears that they do not apply them to their personal behavior. Do they understand that these risks apply to them personally? And, do they know how to protect themselves from the potential harm, if they engage in this behavior? It is interesting to note that adolescents that engage in high risk activities believe that they can control the risk, but at the same time believe that they are unable to avoid participating in the risks. This personal fable of uniqueness and mortality, which is said to be a typical dimension of adolescent thinking (Seltzer, 1982), implies that this research would have direct relevance with regard to developing effective intervention programs. From a marketing perspective, one could segment the target population. That is, one could identify students whose perception make it likely that they would engage in high risk activities such that they become the target for the intervention. General preventive programs generally have had the greatest effect on students who may experiment or try engaging in risk activities, but are less likely to go for regular use. For example, in the prevention of smoking, while there has been a modest effect on deterring and reducing the onset of cigarette smoking, this effect is generally not been shown on adolescents that engage in multiple risk activities. If the perception of risk is a valuable dimension, it may be useful in designing effective interventions which can then be targeted for adolescents that are already engaging in early risk taking activities. There is evidence from an epidemiological research that adolescents that engage in high risk activities can be identified by their anti-social aggressive non-compliant behavior in early experimentation as early as their grade (Patterson, Dishion, & Bank, (1984).

The risk perception scale may also provide a valuable dependent measure to measure the effectiveness of a brief intervention. For example, if a media message or media campaign were designed and targeted for a specific high risk adolescents, one could first choose adolescents based upon their risk perception as well as participation in activities, and secondly measure the impact on these perceptions after exposure to the media message. A recent study provides support for the usefulness of the risk perception measure as a dependent variable. Virgili, Owen & Severson (1990) report that in a study of 189 Australian adolescents, a brief intervention caused a significant decrease in perceived benefit of smoking and a significant increase in perceived fear of consequences.

In sum, the implications of research on adolescent risk perceptions are:

1. Adolescents who engage in risky activities perceive the risk differently from those who do not participate.
2. Risk perceptions can be measured objectively and can predict subsequent risk taking.
3. Risk perceptions can be assessed early and they remain stable across adolescence.
4. Risk perceptions can be altered by providing information and experience.
5. Risk perceptions can be used to identify high risk youth and target media and prevention to both increase their perceptions of risk and lower the probability of their engaging in high risk behavior.

REFERENCES

Benthin, A.C., Slovic, P. and Severson, H.H. (in press). "A Psychometric Study of Adolescent Risk Perception," *Journal of Adolescence*.

Biglan, A., Metzler, C., Wirt. R., Ary, D., Noell, J., Ochs, L., French, C., & Hood, D. (1990). "Social and Behavioral Factors Associated with High Risk Sexual Behavior Among Adolescents." *Journal of Behavioral Medicine, 13*, 245-261.

Fischhoff, B., Slovic, P., Lichtenstein, S., Read, S., & Combs, B. (1978). "How Safe Is Safe Enough? A Psychometric Study of Attitudes Towards Technological Risks and Benefits." *Policy Sciences, 9,* 127-152.

Huba, G.J., Newcomb, M.D., & Bentler, P.M. (1986). "Adverse Drug Experiences and Drug Use Behaviors: A One-year Longitudinal Study of Adolescents." *Jr. of Pediatric Psych., 11,* 203-219.

Irwin, Jr., C.E., & Milstein, S.G. (1986). "Biopsychosocial Correlates of Risk-taking Behaviors During Adolescence." *Journal of Adolescent Care, 7,* 82S-96S.

Jessor, R., & Jessor, S.L. (1977). *Problem Behavior and Psychosocial Development: A Longitudinal Study of Youth.* New York: Academic Press.

Kandel, D.B. (1982). "Epidemiological and Psycho-social Perspectives on Adolescent Drug Use." *Journal of the American Academy of Child Psychiatry, 21,* 328-347.

Metzler, C.W., Noell, J., & Biglan, A. (1992). "The Valuation of a Construct of High-risk Sexual Behavior in Heterosexual Adolescents." *Journal of Adolescent Research, 7*(2), 233-249.

Newcomb, M.D., Huba, G.J., & Bentler, P.M. (1983). "Mothers' Influence on the Drug Use of Their Children: Confirmatory Tests of Direct Modeling and Mediational Theories." *Developmental Psychology, 19,* 714-726.

Patterson, G.R., Dishion, T.J., & Bank, L. (1984). "Family Interaction: A Process Model for Deviancy Training." In L. Eron (Ed.), special edition of *Aggressive Behavior, 10,* 253-267.

Selzer, V.C. (1982). *Adolescent Social Development: Dynamic Functional interaction.* Lexington, MA: D.C. Heath & Company.

Severson, H.H., & Zoref, L. (1991). "Prevention and Early Interventions for Addictive Behaviors: Health Promotion in the Schools." *Interventions for Achievement and Behavior Problems.* G. Stoner, M. Shinn, & H. Walker (Eds.) Published by the National Association of School Psychologists.

Slovic, P. (1987). "Perception of Risk." *Science, 236,* 280-285.

Slovic, P., Fischhoff, B., & Lichtenstein, S. (1980). "Facts and Fears: Understanding Perceived Risk." In R. Schwing, & W.A. Albers, Jr. (Ed.), *Societal Risk Assessment How Safe Is Safe Enough?* (pp. 181-214). New York: Plenum.

Virgili, M., Owen, N., and Severson, H. (1990). *Adolescent's Risk Perception and Smoking Behavior.* Unpublished manuscript, University of Adelaide, Australia.

Weinstein, N.D. (1980). "Unrealistic Optimism about Future Life Events." *Journal of Personality and Social Psychology, 39*(5), 806-820.

Zuckerman, M. (1978). "Sensation Seeking." In H. London and J.E. Exner, Jr. (Eds.), *Dimensions of Personality* (pp. 487-559). New York, NY: John Wiley.

Alcohol-Related Risk Taking Among Teenagers: An Investigation of Contributing Factors and a Discussion of How Marketing Principles Can Help

William J. Burns, University of Iowa
Sarah E. Hampson, Oregon Research Institute
Herbert H. Severson, Oregon Research Institute
Paul Slovic, Decision Research

ABSTRACT

The role of risk perceptions and personality in adolescents' participation in alcohol-related risk taking (including the consumption of alcohol and alcohol use in connection with driving or riding in a car) was investigated using covariance structure modeling. The modeling analysis indicated that factors pertaining to perceptions that the benefits of using alcohol outweigh the risks, grade level, and desired independence were the only variables to directly affect participation. Personality characteristics (sensation seeking, ego control, independence, and achievement-orientation) were found to indirectly influence participation through their direct influence on adolescents' perceptions of benefits and risks associated with alcohol use. This model applied equally well to boys and girls.

These findings are integrated within a social marketing framework and offer strategies to reduce alcohol-related risk taking among adolescents.

INTRODUCTION

Although alcohol use by high-school students has shown an encouraging decline in recent years, teenage alcohol consumption remains at high levels. A 1991 national survey of high school seniors (Johnston, 1992) indicated that 88% of seniors had tried drinking at least once, 54% had tried drinking in the last thirty days, and 30% report drinking 5 or more drinks at a time within the last two weeks. Particularly disturbing was the fact that almost one third did not perceive drinking four or five drinks on a nearly daily basis as a great risk. According to the U.S. Department of Education (1988) drinking and driving is common among teenagers and is the leading cause of death among people aged 16-24 years.

In this paper we begin by investigating a model of alcohol-related risk taking, in which we hypothesize that personality traits, social influences, and grade level contribute to adolescent risk taking largely through their effect on risk perceptions. We then discuss how our findings together with those of other researchers can be used to reduce alcohol-related risk taking by employing basic marketing principles.

METHOD

Subjects and Procedures

We administered our measures to an entire high school located in rural Oregon. The experimenters emphasized that the questionnaires were to be completed anonymously, and encouraged the participants to be completely honest in their responses. The experimenter remained in the classroom to answer questions and to ensure that the students worked independently. However, to protect the confidentiality of subjects' responses, experimenters did not patrol the room. Across the two days, 323 students were assessed, which is 84% of the high school's enrollment of 382 students.

Risk Perception, Social Influence, and Risk Behavior Scales

These three constructs called for ratings of 16 different activities on 12 scales. There were seven activities involving alcohol: drinking wine or wine coolers, drinking beer, drinking hard liquor, drinking five or more alcoholic beverages on a single occasion, riding in a car with an intoxicated driver, and driving a car while intoxicated. The remaining activities included other adolescent problem behaviors such as tobacco and illicit substance use, as well as more socially acceptable risk taking such as driving an all-terrain vehicle. The rating scales assessed a number of aspects of risk perception that we have examined in previous studies (e.g., Slovic, 1987) together with perceptions of social influences and reports of risky behavior: (1) *If you did this activity, to what extent do you believe that you would be personally at risk for getting hurt or sick?* (Personal Risk), (2) *If someone your age did this activity, to what extent do you believe that he/she would be at risk of getting hurt or sick?* (Risk to Others), (3) *If you did this activity, to what extent would it provide you with pleasure or other benefits?* (Benefits), (4) *If someone your age did this activity, to what extent could he or she control the risks associated with it?* (Controllability), (5) *To what extent do you feel pressure from your friends to do this activity?* (Peer Pressure), (6) *To what extent are people who do this activity admired by their friends?* (Peer Admiration), (7) *To what extent can a person your age avoid doing this activity?* (Avoidability), (8) *If you wanted to participate in this activity, how easy would it be to do so?* (Ease of Doing), (9) *Would your parents approve or disapprove of your doing this?* (Parental Approval). Scale 10 asked how often close friends did the activity (never, sometimes, often), scale 11 asked what percentage of same-age peers do this activity, and scale 12 asked for a self-reported frequency of involvement with the activity over the past six months (0=zero, 1=1 or 2 times, 2=3 to 5 times, 3=6 to 10 times, 4=11 or more times).

Personality Variables

Personality scales were administered immediately after completion of the risk-perception, social influence, and risk behavior scales. Sensation seeking, which peaks in adolescence, is associated with participation in a range of risky activities including using alcohol (Zuckerman, 1979). It was assessed by eight items from the Sensation Seeking Scale (Zuckerman, Kolin, Price, & Zoob, 1964). Two items from each of four subscales (thrill and adventure seeking, experience seeking, disinhibition, and boredom susceptibility) were used (alpha = .69). Frequent drug use is associated with poor impulse control (Shedler & Block, 1990) which was assessed by 20 items from Block's Ego Control Scale (alpha = .74). Adolescent problem behavior, including alcohol use, has been associated with low values for academic achievement and high values for independence (Jessor, 1984; Jessor and Jessor, 1977). These variables were assessed using five items each from Jessor's A and I scales (alpha = .88 and .77 respectively).

Structural Model of Alcohol-Related Risk Taking

To investigate how personality characteristics, social influence and risk perception contribute to alcohol-related risk taking we constructed the structural model shown in Figure 1 (the results from this figure are discussed in the next section). We hypothesized that Alcohol-Related Risk Taking could be explained by a combination of constructs representing risk perception, social influence, and

FIGURE 1
A Proposed Structural Model Depicting Factors That Contribute to Alcohol-Related Risk Taking[a]

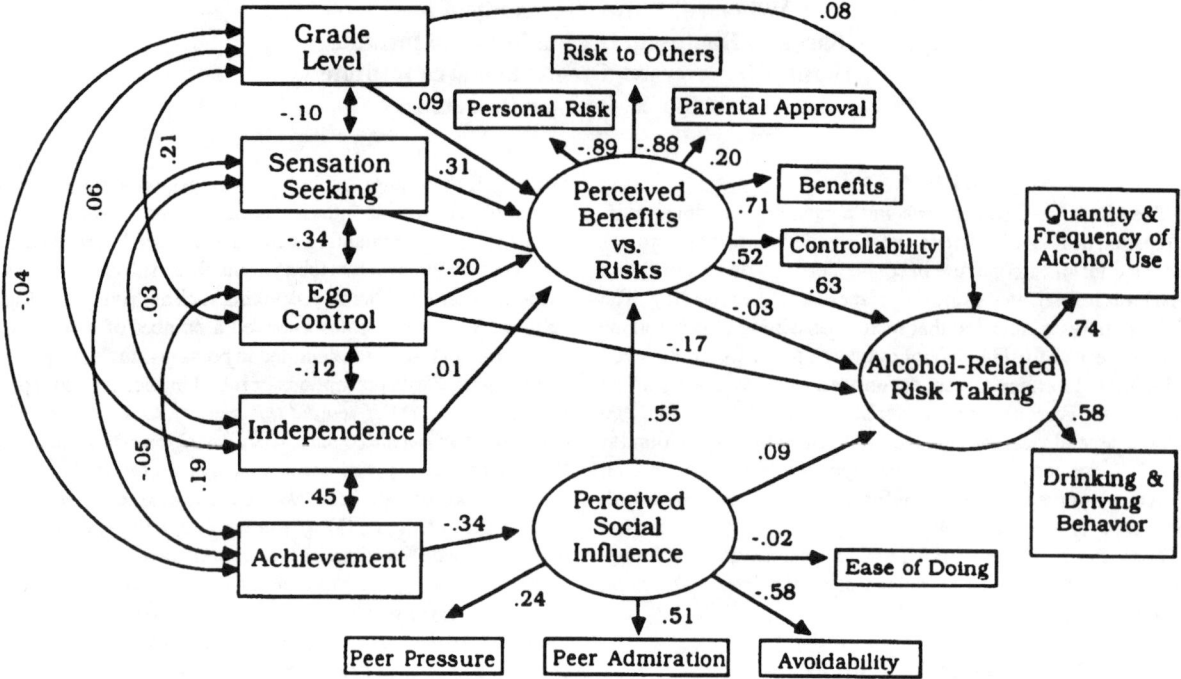

Figures 1 and 2 are taken from Hampson, Sarah, E., William J. Burns, Herbert H. Severson, and Paul Slovic (1992), "Adolescent Alcohol-Related Risk Taking: Exploring Structural Relations Among Risk Perceptions, Personality, and Risk Taking" which is currently under review at the *Journal of Studies on Alcohol*.

---

personality characteristics. Specifically, Perceived Benefits vs. Risks is thought to positively influence Alcohol-Related Risk Taking. Perceived Benefits vs. Risks was measured by perceptions of personal risk, risk to others, controllability of the risk, parental approval for the activity, and benefits. Those scoring high in terms of Perceived Benefits vs. Risks tend to believe the activity to be controllable, beneficial, and approved of by parents, and also to be of low risk to themselves and others. Thus teenagers scoring higher on this factor should be more likely engage in risky behavior. This construct represents the combination of risks and benefits that Slovic has found typical of intuitive assessments of risk (Slovic, Fischoff, & Lichtenstein, 1986). Likewise, Perceived Social Influence affects positively both Perceived Benefits vs. Risks and Alcohol-Related Risk Taking. Perceived Social Influence was measured by perceptions of peer pressure, peer admiration, avoidability, and ease of doing the activity. As such Perceived Social Influence captures the various perceived contextual factors that favor engagement in risk taking. High scorers on this construct perceive the activity to be admired by their peers, feel under pressure to engage in the activity, see it as difficult to avoid, and easy to do. Hence, adolescents perceiving greater social pressures should be more inclined to view these activities as less risky and to participate more frequently.

Four personality variables and a student's grade level are hypothesized to affect participation in alcohol-related risk taking. Grade Level, and Sensation Seeking are thought to have a direct positive effect on Alcohol-Related Risk Taking while Ego Control (low impulsiveness) is hypothesized to exert a direct negative influence on such behavior. For example, those in higher grades face more opportunities to engage in such risks, those possessing greater sensation seeking needs more often pursue such opportunities, and those exhibiting greater impulsiveness more frequently participate in risky activities without proper reflection.

Personality characteristics and grade level are also hypothesized to have indirect effects on Alcohol-Related Risk Taking. Sensation Seeking positively affects Alcohol-Related Risk Taking through its positive effect on Perceived Benefits vs. Risks. For instance, high sensation seeking needs may encourage teenagers to focus more on the benefits of risky activities than on the dangers. Ego Control affects Alcohol-Related Risk Taking negatively because of its negative influence on Perceived Benefits vs. Risks. Less impulsive individuals for example, are more apt to consider long-run consequences and thus should perceive fewer benefits (short-lived) and more long term risks. Achievement negatively affects Alcohol-Related Risk Taking through its negative influence on Perceived Social Influence. Students who place greater value on academic achievement tend to gravitate more readily toward scholastic activities and receive greater encouragement from teachers and other academically-oriented students. Hence, they should be perceive less social influence to participate in risky activities. Independence positively influences Alcohol-Related Risk Taking through its positive effect on Perceived Benefits vs. Risks. Those with higher values for Independence (i.e., independence from adult authority) are more inclined to view "adult" activities positively, and to reject warnings coming from authorities. Thus, they should perceive more benefits and less risks associated with risk taking activities. Finally, Grade Level exerts a positive influence on Alcohol-Related Risk Taking through its positive effect on Perceived Benefits vs. Risks. As mentioned, students in higher grades have greater opportunities to engage in risky activities. As a result, older students are exposed (in the short term) to more information regarding the benefits than the dangers of such activities. Thus, they should perceive more benefits than risks connected with risky activities such as alcohol use.

RESULTS

The self-reports of alcohol use indicated that 61% of the younger students (i.e., 9th and 10th grades) and 81% of the older students (i.e., 11th and 12th grades) had drunk beer on at least one occasion during the past six months. Similarly, 59% of the younger students and 78% of the older students reported drinking wine, and 46% of the younger students and 70% of the older students reported drinking hard liquor at least once. Moreover, 43% of the younger students and 61% of the older students reported at least one recent incidence of drinking five or more drinks on one occasion. These levels of alcohol involvement are comparable to levels reported in other studies. The correlations between these four alcohol-related activities were high (ranging from .73 to .82) with an alpha value of .93. Hence, these four items were summed to produce an index reflecting a students's frequency and quantity of alcohol use.

For drinking and driving, 31% of the younger students and 44% of the older students reported riding with an intoxicated driver, and 7% of the younger students and 28% of the older students reported having driven while intoxicated. The correlations between these two activities was moderately high (.69). Hence, these two items were summed to form a Drinking & Driving index reflecting the amount of drinking and driving. The two measures of Alcohol-Related Risk Taking were positively skewed because of the relatively high numbers of students reporting little or no alcohol-related risk taking. Accordingly, they were transformed to a natural log scale.

The model in Figure 1 was examined using a covariance structure modeling program called EQS (Bentler, 1989) and estimates were based on elliptical rather than normal distribution theory. The chi-square statistic (χ^2=185.98, df=89, p<.001) indicated that the model statistically did not fit very well. However, the Bentler-Bonnet Normed Fit Index (BBNFI) was .98 (.90 or higher is considered acceptable) indicating that the model performed well in accounting for covariances among model variables. The largest contribution to the poor model fit appeared to come from improper measurement of the latent constructs Perceived Benefits vs. Risks and Perceived Social Influence. Examining measurement coefficients (all path estimates represent standardized regression coefficients) indicated that only Personal Risk, Risk to Others, and Benefits were good indicators of Perceived Benefits vs. Risks. Likewise, these coefficients suggested that the variables used to measure Perceived Social Influence did not seem to share a common factor. As a result, the model proposed in Figure 1 was modified to better conform to the data but still address the original theoretical propositions.

The revised model in Figure 2 retained the construct of Perceived Benefits vs. Risk, measured now by Personal Risk, Risk to Others, and Benefits. The construct Perceived Social Influence was dropped but two of its measures, Peer Admiration and Avoidability, were retained because of their significant contribution to Perceived Benefits vs. Risks. The model shown in Figure 2 was the product of removing variables and paths that did not make a statistically significant contribution to the prediction of Perceived Benefits vs. Risks or Alcohol-Related Risk Taking. The X2 statistic (χ^2=66.22, df=40, p=.01) indicated that at best the model fit only marginally well. However, the χ^2/df ratio was 1.7 (2 or less is considered acceptable) and BBNFI was .99 indicated that the model was reasonably consistent with the data.

As anticipated, Perceived Benefits vs. Risks played a central role in explaining the behavior of Alcohol-Related Risk Taking with a direct effect of .8 (i.e., a one standard deviation change in Perceived Benefits vs. Risks produces a .8 standard deviation change in Alcohol-Related Risk Taking). As expected, Grade Level displayed a direct effect on Alcohol-Related Risk Activities. Independence was originally thought to operate on this construct only indirectly through Perceived Benefits vs. Risks but appeared to exert a direct influence as well. However, there were no other direct effects on Alcohol-Related Risk Taking. Together these three factors (Grade Level, Independence, and Perceived Benefits vs. Risks) accounted for 72% of the variance of Alcohol-Related Risk Taking. Grade Level, Sensation Seeking, Ego Control, Independence, Achievement, Peer Admiration, and Avoidability appear to indirectly affect Alcohol-Related Risk Taking through their direct influence on Perceived Benefits vs. Risks . However, these seven factors explain only a moderate portion of the variance of Perceived Benefits vs. Risks (R^2 = .46).

To determine whether the model in Figure 2 applied equally well to either sex, the sample was divided into girls (n=144) and boys (n=148) and a two-group model was estimated under the constraint that corresponding parameters were set equal to each other. Overall the two models behaved in a similar fashion.

The model has limitations that should be mentioned. First, model respecification was guided in part by considerations of fit which limits the generalizability of our findings. Replication of our findings on an independent sample is clearly needed. Second, failing to include factors representing the roles of social and parental influence probably inflated the effect of Perceived Benefits vs. Risks on Alcohol-Related Risk Taking. Lastly, a longitudinal model would better serve to capture the reciprocal relationship between perceived risks and teenage involvement with alcohol. For example, it appears reasonable that frequent involvement with alcohol may contribute to faulty perceptions of the risks that accompany this behavior.

DISCUSSION

Despite its preliminary nature, our model has several implications for interventions to reduce alcohol-related risk taking. It suggests that if we wish to decrease adolescent's involvement in such activities we need, among other things, to influence their perceptions of the risks and benefits associated with alcohol use. Our findings indicate that teaching adolescents to gain control over their impulses, encouraging their willingness to communicate with authority figures (aided by our own willingness and ability to communicate with teenagers), and heightening their motivation to do well in school may alter their perceptions of the risks and benefits of drinking. Likewise, helping teenagers to develop the social skills necessary to realize that such activities are not only avoidable but that such behavior is not admirable also may influence their perceptions of the risks and benefits. Lastly, while grade level and sensation seeking are typically not susceptible to intervention they do help indicate which adolescents are at highest risk and how we might best communicate with them.

The marketing challenge is to implement cost effective programs that influence risk attitudes towards drinking and affect behavioral change. Social marketing provides a framework in which marketing principles can be integrated with social-psychological theory and empirical findings to accomplish goals involving attitudinal or behavior change (Kotler & Roberto, 1989). What the marketing approach brings to the adoption of social change is the ability to plan in terms of the needs of specific target groups. This framework allows efforts to be trained on the needs of particular market segments and goals to be represented in terms of variables that are under our control: designing programs to encourage

FIGURE 2
A Modified Model Depicting Factors That Contribute to Alcohol-Related Risk Taking[a]

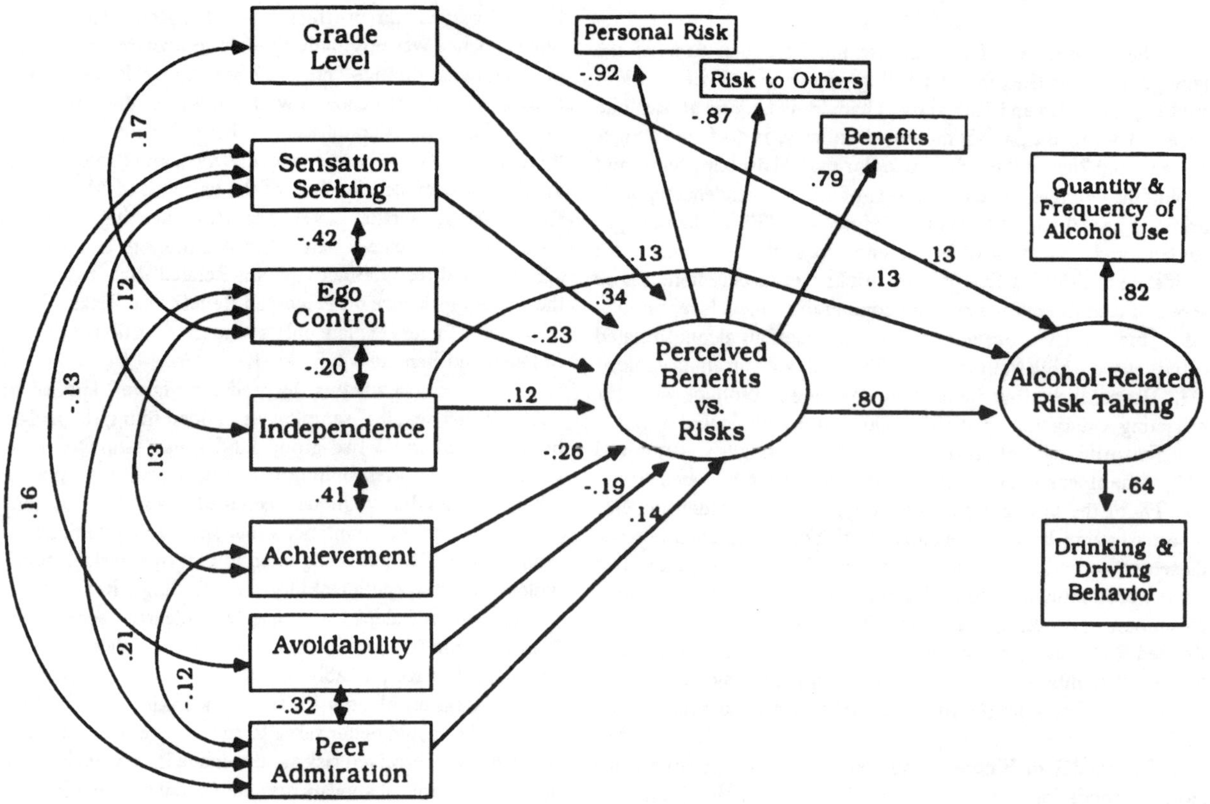

responsible alcohol consumption (Product), reducing psychological, social, economic, and convenience costs associated with the change of behavior (Price), providing accessible opportunities to learn about and behave in a responsible fashion (Place), and developing messages that communicate the benefits over the costs such as improved health and self-esteem (Promotion).

Product

Programs designed to influence alcohol-related risk taking need to be comprehensive in their scope and tailored to the needs of specific target groups. Comprehensiveness requires involving multiple publics (e.g., adolescents, parents, school and health officials) and addressing multiple behaviors (e.g., alcohol and drug use, smoking, unsafe sex, poor school performance). Tailoring programs requires recognizing that adolescents differ in their level of risk information, peer pressures, and psychological and social maturity. For example, adolescents at highest risk tend to have greater needs for thrill seeking, lower needs for academic achievement, associate with more deviate peer groups, possess less developed social skills, and often come from families with poorer parenting skills. Hence, media campaigns that focus only on the dangers of substance abuse (e.g., "This is your brain on drugs...") or social interaction (e.g., "Just say no!") ignore the fact that this group often seeks risky activities and saying no to substance abuse may spell rejection from their peer group. Likewise, educational programs that merely provide risk information without providing training and support for behavioral change are likely to produce only short lived results.

Price and Place

Programs must also make it as easy as possible to participate, being mindful of the psychological, social, and time commitments involved with such activities. This is especially true of high-risk adolescents and their parents. For example, these parents may be reluctant to participate because of time conflicts, apprehension about what to expect or failing to see the relevance to their lives. Programs designed to improve parenting skills not only require time and effort but may be psychologically threatening. Often the parents of adolescents having problems in school are not actively involved in school functions and hence may require they develop new relations with teachers and other school officials. Moreover, high-risk adolescents most likely have begun alienating themselves from teachers and associating with peers exhibiting risky behaviors. Their peer groups often condone and even encourage substance abuse. Hence, the physical, psychological, and social costs of quitting addictive behaviors is likely to be very high. Programs must seek to reduce these costs for parents and adolescents by not only facilitating behavioral change but by providing social support for the formation of new reference groups.

Promotion

Lastly, promotional efforts must convince adolescents, parents, and community members that high risk behavior presents a real danger to teenagers and a high cost to families and communities. Promotional messages must also offer definite measures to reduce such risk-related costs. These messages should be crafted to address the individual concerns of the community, parents and teenagers. To motivate adolescents it is especially important to not only present accurate information about such risks but to focus specifically on increasing their sense of personal threat. Adolescents already exhibiting risky behavior may be resistant to this message for a number of reasons. First, members of this group tend to be sensation seekers and hence they typically focus more on the benefits of risk taking than other teenagers. Second, they and their peers frequently engage in high risk activities without any apparent problems thus providing evidence that such behavior is at once exiting, not overly dangerous, and has consequences that are largely controllable. Finally, because substance abuse is physically and psychologically addicting prolonged involvement tends to promote denial of the inherent dangers connected with such activities.

Research is needed to determine effective means to counter resistant beliefs concerning the personal risk of alcohol-related risk taking. Investigators involved with AIDS intervention research have found (Kelly et al., 1991) that getting individuals to acknowledge that high risk behavior places them in genuine danger is accomplished more easily when this message comes from individuals that are highly regarded by their peer group, when they are repeatedly reminded of the value of changing their behavior, and when they have easy access to a social support system promoting behavioral change. Hence, at the national level messages concerning the dangers of substance abuse must come from highly credible sources (e.g., musicians that have used drugs and have quit), must convey personal hardship, must present a realistic way out of the problem, and must be repeated often. Likewise, at the local level peers that are in the process of changing their high risk activities can be effective role models. They can also serve to generate discussion and encouragement among their friends to seek help in changing their high risk activities.

REFERENCES

Bentler, Peter M. (1989), *EQS Structural Equations Program Manual*. Los Angeles, CA: BMDP Statistical Software.

Jessor, Richard & Shirley L. Jessor (1977), *Problem Behavior and Psychosocial Sevelopment: A Longitudinal Study of Youth*. New York, NY: Academic Press.

Jessor, Richard (1984), "Adolescent Development and Behavioral Health," in J. D. Matarazzo, S. M. Weiss, J. A. Herd, & N. E. Miller (Eds.), *Behavioral Health: A Handbook of Health Enhancement and Disease Prevention*. New York, NY: J. Wiley & Sons.

Johnston, Lloyd (1992), Report Issued by the University of Michigan's News and Information Services Regarding Teenage Substance Abuse on January 27, 1992.

Kelly, Jeffrey, Janet S. St. Lawrence, Yolanda E. Diaz, L. Yvonne Stevenson, Allan C. Hauth, Ted L. Brasfield, Seth C. Kalichman, Joseph E. Smith, & Michael E. Andrew (1991), "HIV Risk Behavior Reduction Following Intervention with Key Opinion Leaders of Population: An Experimental Analysis," American *Journal of Public Health*, 81, 2 168-171.

Kotler, Philip, & Eduardo L. Roberto (1989), *Social Marketing: Strategies for Changing Public Behavior*. New York: The Free Press.

Severson, Herbert H., Paul Slovic, Sarah E. Hampson, & Linda Schrader (1990), "Adolescent Risk Perception: A Measure to Further our Understanding of Tobacco and Drug Use." Hygie, 9, 27-29.

Slovic, Paul (1987), "Perceptions of Risk." *Science*, 236, 280-285.

Slovic, Paul, Baruch Fischoff, & Sarah Lichtenstein (1986), "The Psychometric Study of Risk Perception." In V.T. Covello, J. Menkes, & J. Mumpower (Eds.), *Risk Evaluation and Management*. New York: Plenum.

Shedler, Jonathan, & Jack Block (1990), "Adolescent Drug Use and Psychological Health: A Longitudinal Perspective." *American Psychologist*, 45, 612-629.

U. S. Department of the Health and Human Services (1990), *Seventh Special Report to the U. S. Congress on Alcohol and Health*.

Zuckerman, Marvin (1979), *Sensation Seeking: Beyond the Optimal Level of Arousal*. New York, NY: John Wiley & Sons.

Zuckerman, Marvin, Elizabeth L. Kolin, Leah Price, & Ina Zoob (1964), "Development of a Sensation-Seeking Scale." *Journal of Consulting Psychology*, 28, 477-482.

Special Topic Session Summary
Consumer Behavior Processes As Bases To Segment The 'Green' Marketplace: Applications To Solid Waste Disposal

Linda F. Alwitt, DePaul University
Ida E. Berger, University of Toronto

General opinion polls indicate that concern for the environment has become an important public issue. These polls record a growing recognition among consumers that their behaviour contributes either to environmental problems or to their solutions. This trend represents a new dimension in consumer demand offering marketers an opportunity to apply the societal marketing concept and policy makers a new vehicle to effect environmental clean-up. This trend also poses a major challenge: while many consumers say they favor a clean environment, few appear willing to change their behaviors. Marketers and policy makers want to: (1) identify consumers willing to make behavioral changes; (2) discover what changes they are willing to make; (3) find ways to influence these behaviors.

This special session brought together research on consumer behavior which examined intrinsic and extrinsic influences on how environmental concerns are related to consumer choices. The session provided both conceptual bases for understanding the inconsistencies between attitudes to the environment and behaviors, and guidance to practitioners about how to influence consumers in environmentally-differentiated segments. The researchers reached beyond socio-economic variables to consider behavioral processes as potential bases for environmental behavior segments.

Working from the assumption that motivation, knowledge and a plan of action are preconditions for consumers' behavioral intentions, Robert Pitts and Linda Alwitt (DePaul University) developed four segmentation variables in a specific product category. Based on the results of a mail survey distributed to over 1000 women they argued that in addition to general environmental attitudes 1) personal relevance of the product category, 2) awareness of the environmental problem, 3) willingness to pay to alleviate it and 4) willingness to take non-monetary action should also be considered as bases for segmenting consumers for 'green' products. They illustrated the use of these bases by successfully segmenting consumers in the disposable diaper market and showing how these variables can be used to differentially influence the segments' behavioral adaptations to the new 'green' environmental values.

George Balch (University of Illinois at Chicago) examined cognitive, behavioral, political and sociological reasons for demographic differences in the propensity to recycle solid waste in Chicago. Because his research used a heterogeneous sample (the city of Chicago) rather than the homogeneous communities studied in the past, he was able to examine recycling propensity among racial and ethnic groups. From the results of both focus groups and surveys Balch reported that recycling behavior cannot be adequately explained using simple socioeconomic variables. His study indicated that recycling can be better understood in terms of cognitive factors such as awareness, personal relevance, and the positioning of environmental problems, as well as attitudes toward the "producer" [the City]. Moreover, these cognitions can be attributed to the cultural, social, and political divisions that exist in Chicago. His results implied that marketing efforts which recognized this heterogeneity by providing a mix tailored to each segment were likely to be most effective.

Using recent research in social cognition, Linda Alwitt (DePaul University) and Ida Berger (University of Toronto) developed a new model of attitudes that explicitly recognizes the moderating role of attitude 'strength' in the process whereby attitudes influence behavior. They reported the results of a study that applied this model to predicting consumer behavioral intentions toward aseptically packaged, single servings of juice, fruit and pudding. Alwitt and Berger concluded that to fully evaluate and influence consumer behaviors toward an environmentally sensitive product, public policy makers and marketers must consider more than simply the valence of attitudes. They showed how a second aspect of attitudes, its strength, can influence the ability of an attitude to predict consumer intentions toward the product.

In commenting on these papers, Debra Scammon (University of Utah) drew attention to the different conceptual levels that existed in people's concern (ie. threats to endangered habitats vs. local air quality) and to the fact that 'green' is really a relative term. There is in fact no such thing as an 'environmentally friendly' product. What we have are products and adaptations that are perhaps "less harmful". The session concluded with a lively discussion that included a plea from a local official involved in solid waste management that researchers try to disseminate findings such as these to "those in the trenches" and to the general public.

Understanding the Link Between Environmental Attitudes and Consumer Product Usage: Measuring the Moderating Role of Attitude Strength

Linda F. Alwitt, DePaul University
Ida E. Berger, University of Toronto[1]

ABSTRACT

The ability of attitudes to predict behavior for an environmentally sensitive product can be enhanced by considering the attitude's strength as well as its valence. Attitude strength appears to be multi-dimensional. Some dimensions directly influence purchase intentions over and above the effect of attitude valence. Other attitude strength dimensions moderate the attitude-behavior relationship.

INTRODUCTION

Although about seventy per cent of consumers show high levels of concern for the environment, when it comes to consuming products and services, their actions are often inconsistent with these attitudes. One possible reason for this discrepancy between environmental attitudes and consumer behaviors may be the conflict presented by some environmentally harmful products. On the one hand, a product may offer important benefits to consumers such as convenience, performance or a good price while on the other hand, it may have severe environmental costs. For example, single-serve aseptically packaged puddings, juices and fruits provide consumers with convenience and package size control while contributing substantially to the solid waste stream.

This research proposes an approach to measuring and evaluating attitudes toward a potentially polluting product which can take into account conflicts between environmental concerns and product benefits. The research concerns a basic problem related to environmental issues in marketing: if one wants to develop marketing strategies or public policies to change consumer attitudes and thereby behaviors about environmentally polluting products, the target attitude must be reasonably predictive of behaviors. We believe that this approach can improve the ability of measured attitudes to predict consumer behavior.

CONCEPTUAL DEVELOPMENT

Research on Environmental Attitudes

Researchers have been repeatedly disappointed by the inability of measured environmental attitudes to explain environmentally responsible behaviors. For instance, this inability has been seen in the domain of energy conservation (Webster 1975; Ritchie, McDougall and Claxton 1981; Verhallen and Van Raaij 1981). Some researchers have explained these results with reference to the level of specificity with which the attitudes and behaviors were measured. Theorists suggest that for maximum attitude-behavior correspondence, attitudes and behaviors must be measured at similar levels of specificity (Ajzen and Fishbein 1977). Low correspondence between measured attitudes and subsequent behaviors has also been attributed to moderator effects. Researchers following a perspective that relaxes the assumption that attitudes always predict behavior focus on the identification of variables that systematically moderate the relationship between attitudes and behavior (a-b relationship).

Moderators of the Attitude-Behavior Relationship: The Role of Attitude Strength

Interest in moderators of the a-b relationship has been driven by the consistent finding that attitudes formed on the basis of direct experiences were more predictive of subsequent behavior than attitudes formed on the basis of indirect experiences, even though the attitudes did not differ in valence (e.g. Regan and Fazio 1977, Fazio and Zanna 1978 a and b). These a-b consistency differences were explained in terms of variables that represented non-evaluative aspects of the attitudes themselves. These included attitude certainty and attitude clarity (Fazio and Zanna 1978a); attitude confidence (Sample and Warland 1973, Fazio and Zanna 1978b); amount of information in memory (Davidson et al 1985); and attitude accessibility (Fazio et al 1982, Fazio and Williams 1986).

This body of evidence suggests that attitudes are comprised of two identifiable aspects — valence and strength (see Petty and Krosnick in press). An individual may have a positive or negative predisposition toward an object and may hold this predisposition with more or less strength. In other words, an individual may like (or dislike) a product and may hold this attitude with a varying degree of confidence, certainty, accessibility or knowledge. Furthermore, while valence signals the direction (approach vs. avoidance for example) that any behavior might take, the evidence suggests that strength influences the likelihood that these tendencies are actualized. Support for this view of attitudes can also be found in the marketing literature (Bennett and Harrell 1975; Smith and Swinyard 1983; Berger and Mitchell 1989; Berger 1992; Antil 1978; Berger and Mitchell 1989; Fazio, Powell and Williams 1989).

The Nature of Attitude Strength

From evidence such as this it is clear that a second important aspect of attitudes exists, but its exact nature is less clear. Researchers have tested a large number of variables that appear to tap this notion of strength. However, attempts to look at several different variables at one time suggest that "strength" itself may not be uni-dimensional (Raden 1985; Abelson 1988; Berger and Mitchell 1989; Alwitt 1991). Furthermore, there is mounting evidence that these unique aspects of strength have unique and identifiable influences on subsequent processes (see Berger 1992; Bargh et. al. 1992; Alwitt 1991).

In other words, the structure of the attitude strength construct and the way in which its many sub-aspects impact on behavior is still an open question. A review of the attitude literature indicates four conceptually distinct aspects of attitude strength that have particular relevance to environmentally sensitive products. These are structural consistency, attitude extremity, attitude accessibility and attitude conviction.

Four Dimensions of Strength

Multi-attribute attitude models have long argued that attitudes (overall summary evaluations) are comprised of beliefs and evaluations regarding expected outcomes (Ajzen and Fishbein 1980). In addition, some theorists have suggested that intra-component (within beliefs) and inter-component (cognitions to affect) inconsistency may be indicative of relatively weak attitudes (Ajzen 1989; Chaiken et al in press; Fazio and Zanna 1978b; Norman 1975) and thereby

---

[1] Data collection for this study was partially supported by a grant to Ida E. Berger from the Social Sciences and Humanities Research Council of Canada. Order of authorship is alphabetical.

may influence the relationship between attitudes and behavior. Notice that conflict between beliefs (such as convenience and overpackaging), or between feelings and beliefs, may not be reflected in a summary evaluation. Thus such conflicted attitudes may be relatively weaker predictors of behavior.

Related to the idea of structural consistency is the notion of judgmental extremity. Individuals with highly integrated, undifferentiated, consistent belief systems are likely to report single evaluative measures of attitudes that are relatively extreme (Tetlock 1983, 1984; Judd and Lusk 1984), representative of the overall cognitive domain (Schlegel and DiTecco 1982) and relatively predictive of behaviors (Ajzen 1989).

In a very provocative paper Abelson (1988) distinguishes between firmly held attitudes and those that are more superficial by invoking the notion of attitude "conviction". Abelson presents empirical results on a variety of attitudes that show that conviction is comprised of three unique dimensions: Emotional Commitment; Ego Preoccupation; Cognitive Elaboration. Of relevance to the environmental domain is the fact that products that have only recently been identified as potentially harmful (such as single-serve aseptic packages) may still be very important to an individual because of other sought-after benefits. Attitude conviction about such products may lead even environmentally concerned individuals to continue to purchase an environmentally harmful product.

In an extensive program of research, Fazio and his colleagues have examined the importance of attitude accessibility in the process by which attitudes guide behavior. Defined as the strength of the association between the representation of an object and its attitude in memory, and measured as latency to respond to an attitudinal inquiry, accessibility has been shown to moderate the relationship between expressed attitudes and subsequent behavior (Fazio 1986, 1989, 1990b). This moderation has been particularly evident in low involvement, time-pressured situations (Fazio, Powell and Williams 1989; Sanbonmatsu and Fazio 1990). Many environmentally sensitive products, including the product investigated here, are low involvement products that are frequently purchased during time-pressured grocery store shopping trips.

Thus structural consistency, attitude extremity, attitude conviction and attitude accessibility are all implicated in understanding environmentally related attitudes and behaviors. Furthermore, researchers have demonstrated important linkages between these aspects of attitude strength. For example, the same mechanisms that lead to evaluatively extreme attitudes (e.g., the rehearsal of an attitudinal response) also lead to attitudes that are highly accessible (Downing, Judd and Brauer 1992).

Study Purposes

The purpose of this study is to examine the structure and behavioral implications of this two-aspect model of attitude in an environmentally sensitive product domain. The study measured attitude valence and four dimensions of attitude strength with respect to a single product category, single-serve aseptic packages of juices, fruit or puddings. This category presents a potential conflict to the consumer between personal benefits and environmental costs. Survey measures of the elements of attitude were developed or adopted from research by other investigators.

METHOD

Procedure

Respondents participated in a computer-aided self-administered survey, which allowed randomization of the order in which questions were asked. In addition to responses, response times to one-second accuracy were recorded.

Measures

The computerized questionnaire measured seven sets of constructs, in the order in which they are described in this section.

Attitude toward single serve packages. Overall attitude toward single serve aseptic packages of juices fruit or puddings was measured by three seven-point bipolar scales. The scales were anchored by 'good-bad', 'harmful-beneficial', and 'like-dislike'. Attitude valence is the mean of these ratings (coefficient alpha = .79).

Beliefs and feelings about single-serve packages. Respondents indicated the level of agreement with 26 randomly ordered statements using 5-point Likert-type scales. Ten of these represented beliefs, 3 represented feelings regarding single-serve packages, and the rest were adaptations of Abelson's (1988) conviction scales.

Forced choice attitude to single-serve packages. Respondents were asked to choose between two sides of a question that explicitly raised a belief conflict followed by a question which presented a counter-argument to their response (Fletcher and Chalmers 1991). The conflict presented was that between the convenience and the environmental impact of single-serve packages. This choice was followed by a counter-arguing question which required a 'yes-no' response. Responses and response times were recorded.

Situational consistency. Respondents were asked how well suited were single-serve packages to seven different situations such as 'using while watching TV' or 'serving with dinner'. They rated the use of single-serve packages in each situation on a five-point 'not at all good-very good' bipolar scale.

Attitudes to the environment. Overall attitude to the environment was measured by agreement with three statements commonly used by the Angus Reid Polling Group (see Berger and Corbin 1992) (coefficient alpha=.75).

Purchase intent. Intention to purchase single-serve packages of juice, fruit or puddings in the next month was measured by a four-point likelihood scale.

Demographics. Data was gathered from each respondent on age, gender, marital status, living arrangements, how often food is taken from home to school or work, and income.

Attitude Strength

Fourteen variables were constructed as indicators of the four attitude strength constructs discussed above.

Structural consistency. Structural consistency was operationalised in terms of 5 variables. Three measures were developed using the responses to the 13 belief and feeling statements described above. The standard deviation of each respondent's ratings of the 13 belief and feeling statements (S1) measures cogitive consistency. A ratio of ratings of beliefs about environmental concerns for single-serve packages to ratings of beliefs about other features of these packages (S2) measures environmental conflict (see Scott 1969). Consistency of beliefs relative to feelings about the product category (S3) is the ratio of the mean rating of beliefs to the mean rating of beliefs plus feelings about single-serve packages. Consistency across situations (S4) is the standard deviation of the rated appropriateness of using single-serve packages in the seven situations. Attitudinal stability (S5), derived from the forced choice questions, is coded 1 if the respondent did not change his/her opinion when confronted with a counter-argument, and 0 if he/she did change.

Attitude Extremity. Extremity is the absolute difference between the attitude toward single serve packages, and the scale midpoint.

TABLE 1
Principle components analysis of attitude strength variables
(Varimax rotation) Factor Loadings

Variable	Factor: 1	2	3	4	5	Communality
A3 Gen. Env. Latency	.85	.01	-.05	.17	.12	.77
A4 Env. Imp. Latency	.83	-.16	-.02	-.04	-.05	.71
A5 Conv. Imp. Latency	.78	-.03	.24	.10	-.14	.70
C3 Emot. Commitment	-.15	.84	-.01	.06	.01	.74
C1 Ego Preoccupation	-.08	.84	.10	.08	-.01	.73
C2 Cog. Elaboration	.04	.71	-.16	-.05	.11	.54
S1 Cog. Consistency	.09	-.01	.86	.03	-.10	.75
S2 Envir. Conflict	.03	.08	.74	-.08	.21	.60
S4 Sit. Consistency	-.07	-.34	.52	.22	.04	.44
A1 Attitude Latency	.17	.06	.09	.81	.08	.71
A2 Forced Latency	.22	.13	-.08	.73	.11	.62
Extremity	.26	.18	-.10	-.52	.18	.41
S5 Stability	.02	.05	.21	.07	.85	.77
S3 Bel/Fel Consistency	.14	-.07	.51	.01	-.58	.62
% common variance	24.5%	23.3%	21.7%	17.2%	13.3%	

Attitude Conviction. Thirteen of the Abelson (1988) conviction items (C1-C3) were adapted to the single serve product category. Coefficient alpha for the entire scale of 13 items is .79.

Accessibility. Accessibility is an individual's response latency to several attitude and belief statements. Since individuals differ in how quickly they respond, each response time was adjusted by subtracting the individual's mean response latency to neutral items (Fazio 1990a). Accessibility of attitudes about single serve packages is measured both as the mean time to respond to the three attitude scales about single-serve packages (A1) and as the latency to the forced choice conflicted question (A2). Response times were also examined for attitudes about the environment (A3), a belief regarding the environmental impact of the product category (A4), and a belief about the convenience of the product category (A5).

Sample

Students, appropriate respondents since they are potential users of the product category under study, completed the survey. (N = 134 undergraduate students from business schools in two large urban universities.)

Analytical Methodology

Data analysis proceeded in two stages. First, the structure of attitude strength as measured by the 14 variables described above was examined using principal components analysis. Second, the way in which the two-aspect model of attitudes is related to purchase intentions was examined using moderator analysis.

RESULTS

Structure of Attitude Strength Measures

To examine the structure of attitude strength, the 14 strength variables were entered into a principle components analysis. Both an eigenvalue >1 and a scree criterion suggest that a five-factor solution is most parsimonious, and accounts for 57% of the total variance. Table 1 shows the factor loadings of each attitude strength variable on each factor following varimax rotation, as well as communalities for each variable and the common variance accounted for by each factor.

Although for the most part the variables load as conceptually expected, there are some important exceptions. *Factor 1* represents the accessibility of the *cognitions* underlying this product category. It includes response times to environmental concerns in general, environmental concerns about single serve packages and convenience of single serve packages. Notice that despite common methods variance, the other latencies do not load highly on this factor. *Factor 2* represents attitude conviction. It includes the three Abelson conviction scales. *Factor 3* represents consistency. It includes the consistency with which beliefs about single serve packages were rated, the level of environmental conflict about single serve packages and consistency of use of single serve packages across situations. Notice also that the consistency of feelings and beliefs has almost as high a loading on this factor as on Factor 5. *Factor 4* represents the accessibility of *attitudes* to single serve packages. It includes response times to attitudes about single serve packages, from both the general ratings and the forced choice questions. Interestingly, the attitude extremity item loads on this factor. *Factor 5* is best thought of as attitude stability. It represents the tendency to hold on to an opinion, despite counter argumentation.

Correlations

As a first step to understanding how these dimensions of attitude strength relate to purchase intent, the five strength factors were correlated with general attitude toward the environment, attitude valence and purchase intent (see Table 2).

As expected, a general attitude regarding the environment is not significantly related to purchase intent toward single serve packages. This result is consistent with previous findings that general attitudes about the environment are not helpful in predicting the use of environmentally sensitive products. Also as expected, the attitude toward this product category is positively related to purchase intentions. Notice that there is a significant relationship between attitude accessibility and purchase intent. Also notice that

TABLE 2
Correlations of Attitude Valence with Strength Dimensions and Purchase Intent

	Attitude Valence	Purchase Intent	General Environmental Attitude	Strength Dimensions			
				1	2	3	4
Attitude valence	1.00						
Purchase Intent	.31*	1.00					
General environmental attitude	-.16	-.03	1.00				
Strength:							
1. Cognitive accessibility	.02	-.02	-.07	1.00			
2. Conviction	-.25*	.14	.25*	-.13	1.00		
3. Consistency	.02	-.10	.06	.10	-.16	1.00	
4. Attitude accessibility	.25*	.31*	.05	.23*	.13	.00	1.00
5. Stability	-.02	.00	.00	.03	.08	.15	.13

* $p =< .05$

TABLE 3
Summary of Regression analyses of behavioral intention as a function of attitude valence and attitude strength variables

Strength Dimension	R2adj.	Attitude Valence	Beta Weights Attitude Strength	Interaction
1. Cognitive Accessibility	.09c	.31c	—	-.14d
2. Conviction	.14a	.36a	.23c	—
3. Consistency	.09b	.40b	—	—
4. Attitude Accessibility (+ extremity)	.17a	.31b	.22c	-.24c
5. Stability	.08c	.31b	—	—

a $p =< .0001$; b $p =< .001$; c $p =< .05$; d $p =< .10$

---

the correlatonal pattern supports the multi-dimensionality of attitude strength. Specifically, with one exception the attitude strength factors are uncorrelated. Only the two accessibility factors are related (r=.23, p=.008).

Attitude Strength as a Moderator

Of primary interest in this study is the way in which dimensions of attitude strength influence the nature of the relationship between attitude valence and purchase intent. The strength factors could potentially have direct influences on purchase intent and/or they could moderate the valence - intent relationship. Moderator regression analyses are used in order to evaluate these two types of influence (Evans 1990). In all regression equations purchase intent for single-serve packages serves as the dependent variable and attitude valence, the attitude strength scale and their multiplicative interaction term are the independent variables. The independent variables are centered prior to forming the interaction term in order to minimize multicollinearity (Aiken and West 1991). The results are shown in Table 3.

Of the five attitude strength dimensions, two influence purchase intent directly (conviction and attitude accessibility) and two moderate the relationship between attitude valence and purchase intent (cognitive accessibility and attitude accessibility). Because attitude extremity and attitude accessibility are conceptually distinct constructs, and because they differ in sign (that is, high latencies reflect low levels of accessibility) the attitude accessibility variable and attitude extremity were also examined in separate regressions (see Table 4).

Like conviction, attitude extremity has an important direct influence on purchase intent but does not moderate the attitude valence-purchase intent relationship. These results suggest that information regarding attitude conviction and extremity can contribute to better predictions of purchase intent. In contrast, accessibility, both cognitive and attitudinal, behaves as a moderator. A change in attitude valence is associated with a greater change in purchase intent when accessibility is high, vs. when accessibility is low.

DISCUSSION

To evaluate and influence consumer behaviors toward an environmentally sensitive product, public policy makers and marketers must consider more than simply the valence of attitudes toward that product. A second aspect of attitude, its strength, can have an impact on the ability of an attitude to predict consumer intentions toward the product. Furthermore, this research demonstrates that dimensions of attitude strength can influence consumer intentions in different ways. Consequently, these variables offer unique information to help guide public policy and marketing

TABLE 4
Summary of Regression analyses of behavioral intention as a function of attitude valence, attitude accessibility and extremity

Strength Variable	R2adj.	Beta Weights		
		Attitude valence	Attitude Strength	Interaction
A1. Attitude access.	.12b	.30b	—	-.17c
A2. Forced Choice	.11b	.30b	—	-.14c
Extremity	.11b	.29c	.19c	—

a p=< .0001; b p=< .001; c p=< .05; d p=< .10

decisions. Our results imply that several attitude strength dimensions should be included in assessments of market potential, definitions of market segments and evaluations of persuasive techniques for environmentally sensitive products.

The Conviction and Extremity dimensions of attitude strength are important because they directly influence behavioral intentions. Thus they represent another route to persuasion. To the extent that conviction reflects affective components of attitude (i.e., emotional commitment and ego involvement), it may be susceptible to affective or cognitive messages (see Millar and Millar 1990; Edwards 1990). Extremity may be susceptible to certain kinds of verbal rehearsal or repetition (see Downing, Judd and Brauer 1992).

Similarly, accessibility to beliefs and attitudes moderated the influence of attitude valence on consumer intentions toward this environmentally sensitive product. Accessibility is influenced by whether an attitude is formed on the basis of direct or indirect experience (Fazio 1986). Because consumers who use environmentally sensitive products such as single serve aseptic packages often have a lot of direct experience with them, they are likely to have positive overall attitudes which are more likely to predict their behavioral intentions toward the products. These attitudes and behaviors may be particularly difficult to change using indirect persuasion techniques (such as advertising). Rather, behavioral interventions may be called for, such as taxes to raise prices or regulation of waste disposal.

From a public policy point of view, potential rather than current users of environmentally sensitive products are better targets for indirect strategies of attitude and behavior change. This segment may require education about environmental costs, in addition to monetary or regulatory barriers that work to reduce their direct experiences with the environmentally sensitive product.

In summary, attitude strength dimensions can be used to increase the usefulness of attitude change strategies by public policy makers who want consumers to take environmentally positive actions. They can also be used by marketers to identify the scope of 'green' interest in their product category, and develop appropriate marketing strategies which will both increase profits and protect the environment.

REFERENCES

Abelson, Robert P. (1988) "Conviction". *American Psychologist*, 43, 267-275.

Abelson, Robert P., D.R. Kinder, M.D. Peters, and S.T. Fiske (1982), "Affective and Semantic Components in Political Person Perception", *Journal of Personality and Social Psychology*, 42, 619-630.

Aiken, Leona S. and Stephen G. West (1991) *Multiple Regression: Testing and Interpreting Interactions*, Newbury Park,CA: Sage.

Ajzen, Icek (1989) "Attitude Structure and Behavior". In A.R. Pratkanis, S.J. Breckler, Stephen and Anthony G. Greenwald (eds), *Attitude Structure and Function*, Hillsdale, NJ:LEA, 241-274.

Ajzen, Icek and Martin Fishbein (1977) "Attitude-behavior Relations: a Theoretical Analysis and Review of Empirical Research", *Psychological Bulletin*, 84, 888-918.

Ajzen, Icek and Martin Fishbein, (1980) *Understanding Attitudes and Predicting Social Behavior*. Englewood Cliffs, NJ:Prentice-Hall.

Alwitt, Linda F. "Attitude Strength: an Extra-content Aspect of Attitude", *Resources in Education*, ED# 326797, ERIC/CAPS Clearing House, 1991.

Antil, John H. (1978) "Uses of Response Certainty in Attitude Measurement". In R.P. Bagozzi and A.M. Tybout (eds.) *Advances in Consumer Research*, 10. Ann Arbor, MI: Association for consumer Research, 409-415.

Bargh, John A., Shelly Chaiken, Rajen Govender and Felicia Pratto (1992) "The Generality of the Automatic Attitude Activation Effect", *Journal of Personality and Social Psychology* 62(6), 893-912.

Bennett, Peter D. and Gilbert D. Harrell (1975) "The Role of Confidence in Understanding and Predicting Buyers' Attitudes and Purchase Intentions". *Journal of Consumer Research*, 2, 110-117.

Berger, Ida E. (1992) "The Nature of Attitude Accessibility and Attitude Confidence: a Triangulated Experiment", *Journal of Consumer Psychology*, 1 (2), 103-123.

Berger, Ida E. and Ruth M. Corbin (1992) "Perceived Consumer Effectiveness and Faith in Others as Moderators of Environmentally Responsible Behaviors". *Journal of Public Policy and Marketing*, 11 (2).

Berger, Ida E. and Andrew A. Mitchell (1989) "The Effect of Advertising on Attitude Accessibility, Attitude Confidence and the Attitude-behavior Relationship". *Journal of Consumer Research*, 16, 269-279.

Chaiken, Shelly, Eva M. Pomerantz and Roger Giner-Sorolla (in press) "Structural Consistency and Attitude Strength". In R.E. Petty and J.A. Krosnick (Eds.), *Attitude Strength: Antecedents and Consequences*. Hillsdale, NJ: Erlbaum.

Davidson, Andrew R., Steven Yantis, Marel Norwood, and Daniel E. Montano (1985) "Amount of Information about the Attitude Object and Attitude-behavior Consistency", *Journal of Personality and Social Psychology*, 49, 1184-1198.

Downing, James W., Charles M. Judd and M. Brauer (1992) "Effects of Repeated Expressions on Attitude Extremity". *Journal of Personality and Social Psychology*, 63(1), 17-29.

Edwards, Kari (1990) "The Interplay of Affect and Cognition in Attitude Formation and Change", *Journal of Personality and Social Psychology* 59(2), 202-216.

Evans, Martin G. (1991) "The problem of analyzing multiplicative composites", *American Psychologist*, 46(1), 6-15.

Fazio, Russell H. (1986) "How do Attitudes Guide Behavior?" In R.M. Sorrentino and E.T. Higgins (eds), *Handbook of Motivation and Cognition: Foundations of Social Behavior*, NY:Guilford: 204-223.

Fazio, Russell H. (1989) "On the Power and Functionality of Attitudes: the Role of Attitude Accessibility". In A.R. Pratkanis, S.J. Breckler and A.G. Greenwald (eds.) *Attitude Structure and Function*, Hillsdale, NJ:LEA, 153-179.

Fazio, Russell H. (1990a) "A Practical Guide to the Use of Response Latency in Social Psychological Research". *Review of Personality and Social Psychology*, 11, 74-97.

Fazio, Russell H. (1990b) "Multiple Processes by which Attitudes Guide Behavior: the MODE Model as an Integrative Framework". In M.P. Zanna (ed.) *Advances in Experimental Psychology*, 23, San Diego, CA: Academic Press, 75-109.

Fazio, Russell H., Jeaw-Mei Chen, Elizabeth McDonel and Steven J. Sherman (1982) "Attitude Accessibility, Attitude-behavior Consistency, and the Strength of the Object-evaluation Association", *Journal of Experimental Social Psychology*, 18, 339-357.

Fazio, Russell H., Martha C. Powell and Carol J. Williams (1989), "The Role of Attitude Accessibility in the Attitude-to-behavior Process. *Journal of Consumer Research*, 16, 280-288.

Fazio, Russell H. and Carol J. Williams (1986) "Attitude Accessibility as a Moderator of the Attitude-perception and Attitude Behavior Relations: an Investigation of the 1984 Presidential Election." *Journal of Personality and Social Psychology*, 51, 505-514.

Fazio, Russell H. and Mark P. Zanna (1978a) "Attitudinal Qualities Relating to Strength of the Attitude-behavior Relationship", *Journal of Experimental Social Psychology*, 14, 398-408.

Fazio, Russell H. and Mark P. Zanna (1978b) "On the Predictive Validity of Attitudes: the Roles of Direct Experience and Confidence", *Journal of Personality*, 46, 228-243.

Fishbein, Martin and Icek Ajzen (1975) *Belief, Attitude, Intention and Behavior: an Introduction to Theory and Research*. Reading, MA: Addison-Wesley.

Fletcher, John F. and M.C. Chalmers (1991) "Attitudes of Canadians toward Affirmative Action", *Political Behavior*, 13(1), 69-97.

Judd, Charles M., Roger A. Drake, James W. Downing and Jon A. Krosnick (1991) "Some Dynamic Properties of Attitude Structures: Context-induced Response Facilitation and Polarization", *Journal of Personality and Social Psychology*, 60(2), 193-202.

Judd, Charles M. and Cynthia M. Lusk (1984) "Knowledge Structures and Evaluative Judgments: Effects of Structural Variables on Judgmental Extremity". *Journal of Personality and Social Psychology*, 46, 1193-1207.

Millar, Murray G. and Karen U. Millar (1990) "Attitude Change as a Function of Attitude Type and Argument Type", *Journal of Personality and Social Psychology*, 59(2), 217-228.

Norman, Ross (1975) "Affective-cognitive Consistency, Attitudes, Conformity and Behavior". *Journal of Personality and Social Psychology*, 32, 83-91.

Petty, Richard E. and Jon A. Krosnick (in press) *Attitude Strength: Antecedents and Consequences*. Hillsdale, N.J.:LEA.

Raden, David (1985) "Strength Related Attitude Dimensions." *Social Psychology Quarterly*, 48, 312-330.

Regan, Dennis T. and Russell H. Fazio (1977) "On the Consistency between Attitudes and Behavior: Look to the Method of Attitude Formation." *Journal of Experimental Social Psychology*, 13, 38-45.

Richie, J.R. Brent, Gordon H.G. McDougall and John D. Claxton (1981), "Complexities of household energy consumption and conservation", *Journal of Consumer Research*, 8 (December), 233-242.

Sample, John and Rex Warland (1973), "Attitude and prediction of behavior". *Social Forces*, 51, 292-304.

Sanbonmatsu, D. M. and Russell H. Fazio (1990) "The role of attitudes in memory based decision making". *Journal of Personality and Social Psychology*, 59, 614-622.

Schlegel, Ronald P. and Dan DiTecco (1982) "Attitudinal structures and the attitude-behavior relation". In M.P. Zanna E.T. Higgins and C.P. Herman (eds) *Consistency in Social Behavior: The Ontario Symposium*, Vol 2, Hillsdale, NJ:LEA, 17-49.

Scott, William A. (1969) "Structure of natural cognitions", *Journal of Personality and Social Psychology*, 12(4), 261-278.

Smith, Robert E. and William R. Swinyard (1983) "Attitude-behavior consistency: the impact of product trial vs. advertising", *Journal of Marketing Research*, 20, 257-267.

Tetlock, Philip E. (1983) "Cognitive style and political ideology". *Journal of Personality and Social Psychology*, 45(1), 118-126.

Tetlock, Philip E. (1984) "Cognitive style and political belief systems in the British House of Commons". *Journal of Personality and Social Psychology*, 46(2), 365-375.

Verhallen, Theo M.M. and W. Fred van Raaij (1981) "Household behavior and the use of natural gas for home heating", *Journal of Consumer Research*, 8 (December), 253-257.

Webster, Frederick E. Jr. (1975) "Determining the characteristics of the socially conscious consumer", *Journal of Consumer Research*, 2(December), 188-196.

Behavioral Decision Research: Theory and Applications
Ravi Dhar, Yale School of Management

Since the advancement of the notion of bounded rationality by Herbert Simon, the field of descriptive decision theory has attempted to document evidence to define more precisely the bounds of human rationality and show that contrary to the assumptions of classical economic theory, consumers do not necessarily maximize utility. This viepoint of of consumers' decision making is consistent with the growing consensus among decision researchers that consumer preferences are often fuzzy, unstable, and inconsistent (Tversky, Sattah, and Slovic 1988; Payne, Bettman, and Johnson 1992). Consumers are depicted as *constructing* and expressing rankings with respect to the possibilities that they have actually considered (Dhar 1992). Such an idea makes choices sensitive to various aspects of the decision situation: the different contexts and tasks highlight different aspects of the options and suggest different considerations, often giving rise to inconsistent decisions (Tversky and Simonson 1992).

While the constructive view of individual decision making is becoming well established within consumer research, the findings have not had a similar impact on broader marketing issues. The four papers in the session differ in their degree of theoretical-applied orientation. The first paper (Hardie, Johnson, and Fader) shows how findings of loss aversion in multiattribute riskless choices observed in laboratory situations can be extended to understand its implication for market level phenomena. The authors argue that since consumers often evaluate products in relation to some reference levels, such a process may create an asymmetry in evaluation depending on whether the value is seen as a gain or a loss from the reference level. The authors analyze scanner panel data to show how a reference dependent model of consumer choice provides a better fit in estimation and forecast periods compared to a standard multinomial logit model.

The second paper (Inman and Dyer) proposes an extended paradigm of consumer satisfaction based on generalized utility theory. Building on research in decision theory, the authors propose and test a modle of satisfaction that includes the effect of foregone outcomes. The authors contend that such a description of consumer satisfaction has distinct advantages over the existing framework in: 1) resolving key ambiguities reported in the past research and 2) extending satisfaction from a post-consumption construct to a pre-consumption measure.

The third paper (Hawkins and Fischer) uses the well known contingent weighting framework in explaining how consumers make difficult choices. The authors question the normative principle of "procedure invariance" which assumes that strategically equivalent ways of assessing preferences should result in the same preference order. The authors propose two strategies that may account for the violations: scale compatibility and strategy compatibility. On testing the alternative strategies in a series of four experiments in a binary consumer choice task, they find strong support only for strategy compatibility.

The fourth paper (Dhar) examines the role of motivational based mechanisms using an information processing framework, a relatively neglected area of research. The author questions the premise that choices between relatively equally attractive alternatives create a state of indifference. The preferences among such alternatives exhibit behavior that systematically violates the theory of rational choice. The results emphasize the importance of the role of anticipated emotions and justification process in choice.

When taken as a group, the papers in the session should help to highlight some of the promising avenues that are emerging in this area of research.

How Do Consumers Acquire a New Food Consumption System When It Is Vegetarian?
Susan Schultz Kleine, Arizona State University
Amy R. Hubbert, Arizona State University

ABSTRACT
The paper describes an exploratory study of consumption pattern acquisition. Depth interviews were used to investigate how individuals unfamiliar with vegetarianism learned and negotiated *their* version of a meatfree eating pattern. The results highlight the importance of examining consumption system acquisition in light of its multidimensional social embeddedness and its relationship to personal development rather than just focusing upon product purchase and ownership behaviors.

What would you do if you wanted to take up gardening, but the products, resources, and procedures were completely unfamiliar to you? How about learning to sew? taking up birdwatching? integrating a personal computer into your work and household management procedures? How would you go about the adoption of these activity patterns if they were unfamiliar?

Each of these activity patterns and its accompanying consumption may be thought of as a consumption system (Boyd and Levy 1963). A consumption system includes a bundle of products that cohere around, and facilitate, an activity (gardening, cooking, playing softball). Taking up an unfamiliar activity and its associated product cluster (Kernan and Sommers 1967; McCracken 1988; Solomon 1988) involves more than just product acquisition. Given that most consumption is socially embedded (Kleine, Schultz Kleine, and Kernan 1992; Solomon 1983), part of *learning* an unfamiliar consumption system may involve negotiating social and developmental processes as well.

The purpose of the study reported here was to explore a case of consumption system acquisition. This food consumption system—vegetarianism—is significantly new and unfamiliar to those raised on the typical American omnivorous diet (consuming all types of foods including meat). We wished to explore how persons who had not been raised as vegetarians acquired this significantly different consumption system for themselves. *How* did they learn the new ways of meal preparation, eating, shopping; what were their sources of influence and learning; how did they cope with social situations? *How* did a person negotiate his/her own version of this consumption pattern?

The Vegetarianism Consumption System
Absence of animal flesh consumption distinguishes a vegetarian diet. Vegetarian practices vary in severity of restriction relative to mainstream American omnivorous diets. Some vegetarians adopt a diet which excludes only meat. Others also avoid dairy products and/or eggs. The most constrained completely avoid animal products in food, clothing, and other products (e.g., animal fat in soap). Changing from an omnivorous to a vegetarian diet, even in its least restrictive form, requires significant alternations in an individual's food consumption and food shopping patterns.

The literature identifies various motives for becoming vegetarian. These include ethical reasons based on concern for such issues as animal rights, environmentalism, or world hunger, and self improvement reasons involving health, religion/spirituality, or personal growth (e.g., Amato and Partridge 1989; Brown 1990). People often express multiple motives for making the transition (e.g., both animal rights and health reasons) and their motives may change or expand as they adapt to vegetarianism (e.g., starting out for health reasons, acknowledging spiritual reasons later; Amato and Partridge 1989).

Certain socio-cultural factors have influenced the greater emergence of vegetarian diet practices. The trends of environmentalism, health improvement, and an emphasis on personal growth have created a more accepting environment for vegetarianism than was once present (e.g., Amato and Partridge 1989). Growing evidence of lower protein requirements for proper nutrition, the perceived value of reduced ingestion of animal fats, and support for whole grain consumption has lent credence to vegetarian-style eating patterns. Media attention on animal rights issues combined with concern for sound environmental practices has directed attention to some reasons one might choose vegetarianism.

The marketplace has responded to these socio-cultural changes. Plenty of information is available in libraries and bookstores: materials about the health advantages and disadvantages of a meatless diet, cookbooks, magazines (e.g., *Vegetarian Times*), and other resources. Also, mainstream supermarkets and food stores carry increasingly more products that fit with a non-meat diet. In many markets natural food stores specialize in products not found in other food stores; mail order is an option. A person who wishes to learn about vegetarianism can find needed information and products.

To one who is unfamiliar with its consumption system, vegetarianism seems more than just learning how to cook and eat differently. Food consumption patterns are associated with symbolic meaning which reflect social patterns (Heisley 1992; Levy 1981). Besides significant shifts in everyday behaviors, a meatless diet would affect one's interactions with others (e.g., what will my family think? what happens when I get invited to a steak dinner? what is right for my child?). Thus, two a priori assumptions informed our methodology. First, we expected an individual's move to vegetarianism to involve changes in both the public and private aspects of his/her daily life. Second, we expected that an individual would be both helped and hindered by others in his/her attempts to change consumption patterns. These a priori assumptions influenced our data collection and analysis. Our research question, then, was: *How* does a person learn and negotiate his/her own version of a vegetarian consumption pattern?

METHOD
A semistructured depth interview method was used to explore the vegetarianism adoption process among consumers to whom vegetarianism was originally unfamiliar. Our objective was not an ethnographic portrayal; our interest was to explore initial themes about consumption system acquisition. We interviewed eight people who were referred to us through a local health food cooperative or by word of mouth. Participants ranged from those who once had practiced a strict vegetarian diet to those who ate chicken or fish occasionally (see the Table for participant profiles). Length of time and commitment to being vegetarian varied as did stage of acquisition. Three participants were early in the process; three had been at it for many years. Two participants who no longer consumed a meatless diet told us about their past "meatless" experiences. Self-perceived motives for becoming vegetarian varied as well age, occupation, gender, marital and family status. All the participants were raised in omnivorous households and thus were originally

unfamiliar with vegetarianism. Each participant lived in a location where s/he had ready access to information, products, and other resources that could guide the acquisition process.

Both authors individually conducted interviews. The backgrounds and perspectives we brought to bear on the data collection and analysis include one of us who is semi-vegetarian (eating chicken or fish occasionally) and the other who has family involvement in the cattle industry. This contrast in perspectives allowed a reliability check during data analysis.

Each interview lasted at least one hour. The interviewer first explained the interview's purpose and the nature of the questions. Then, the interviewer asked basic informational questions (e.g., what kind of vegetarian?). Next the participant was asked to explain *how* he or she became a vegetarian; *how* did s/he go about it; who and what helped or hindered the process? Three interviews were conducted by phone. An audio recorder was used for all but one of the eight interviews; tapes were transcribed for subsequent analysis.

Each interview was analyzed for themes; then themes common across interviews were identified and built into a description of the process. The results of this analysis are described next.

PROCESS OF VEGETARIAN CONSUMPTION SYSTEM ACQUISITION

A multidimensional process describes the transformation from mainstream eating habits to the adoption of vegetarianism. We chose these labels to reflect the nature of the overlapping stages and events we observed: the undercurrent, the touchstone experience, achieving a meatfree diet, and adopting vegetarianism.

The Undercurrent

The mosaic of situations and circumstances that led each informant to consider a change in eating patterns composes the undercurrent. Each experienced a unique set of situations and circumstances, yet trends emerged: interest in animal rights (Donna, Tony, Barb), spiritual reasons (Clarise), health reasons (Donna, Clarise, Barb, Nikki), political activism (Bob), environmentalism (Barb, Tony, Donna) and a distaste for meat (Carrie, Clarise, Barb, and Amanda). Behavior changed during, and as a result of, the undercurrent stage. Informants consciously began to reduce the amount of meat and/or certain meat products (e.g., hot dogs) in their diets. The duration of this period varied from just a few months (Donna, Barb and Tony) to many years (Amanda).

> First I guess it started when I read an article in *Newsweek* about Japan's diets that were mostly carbohydrates and have some fish in them. Then over the summer I was trying to diet and get into shape and I just didn't eat as much meat. (Donna)

> It's probably been a gradual process over the last year. It was just a growing concern in myself both for environmentalism and for issues, animal rights and things like that. (Barb)

> The diet change largely came out of political grounds; I got involved in [activism concerning] illegal tuna fishing practices; I did a lot of research, banning seafood from my diet kind of opened up the door. (Bob)

These circumstances interacted with interpersonal and socio-cultural influences as part of the undercurrent.

Interpersonal Influences. At least one other person who was already vegetarian significantly affected each participant's behaviors.

> I got on a kick of not eating red meat or fish...Then I ended up with a roommate who was a strict vegetarian for spiritual reasons. So then it was easy for me to transfer [to a meatless, eggless diet]. (Clarise)

> When I was 19 I went to Israel...I went off meat for 1 year...A cousin whom I was living with over there was a full vegetarian his whole life...He was really a good influence, a big influence on me...(Amanda)

> My roommate is a vegetarian...[but] I didn't really believe in being a vegetarian. Then I read another article in the Wall Street Journal about how some guy who ate mussels and something happened because of the nuclear waste in the water. And then I just picked up some of her books around the apartment...and I read about it. And decided I'm just going to try not to eat any meat. (Donna)

Socio-cultural trends and the media. Similar to Donna's reading about nuclear waste and Japanese diets, other informational influences tended to symbolize and motivate emergence of the vegetarian diet. Bob's activism-related reading resulted in a "huge file of articles about the fishing industry and its worldwide effects on the environment". Nikki read the vegetarian classic *Diet for a Small Planet*. Barb gathered information about use of animals for product testing in the cosmetic industry, in which she had been employed. Both Tony and Barb reflected upon the symbolism in a movie, as Tony explained:

> When we saw "City Slickers" where Billy Crystal said "Norman, [the calf he saved and befriended], you don't have to become lunch" we said we had made the right decision and that was just like the final kicker, but I have a feeling that if that hadn't been the final one, it would have been the first one.

The socio-cultural and interpersonal influences interacted with personal experiences to set the stage for a key behavioral change—deleting meat from one's diet.

The Touchstone Experience

Each informant encountered a touchstone experience, i.e., a specific event that served as an impetus to finally delete meat or animal products completely from their diets. Every participant could identify this specific event and credited it as their motivation for choosing a meatless diet.

> The last day I ate meat was Thanksgiving. It was pretty simple and I felt pretty good about myself and then I got this book. It's called *The Diet for a New America*. It explained and went through everything that the animals go through, basically how they are tortured and even if you don't care about the animals, all the drugs they're pumped up with, their horrible eating habits...so, I decided that when I came back from Christmas break I wasn't going to eat any dairy or eggs. (Donna)

> One of the things that really encouraged us and got us to think about [it] was when we visited Barb's uncle; he has a ranch in Colorado; he had been a beef rancher and he sold off all of his cattle except for two. We were feeding these two nice, brown gentle animals eating out of our hands. We asked about them. "Well, how come you still have these two?" and he said, "One is Rosie and the other is lunch." And when he said that it was like, Oh, that's right. You know, we were feeding our food and we just couldn't deal with that very well. And from there it just

TABLE 1

Personal Profile of Informants

Pseudonym:	Nikki	Tony	Barb	Amanda	Donna	Clarise	Bob	Carrie
Race / sex:	w/f	w/m	w/f	w/f	w/f	w/f	w/m	w/f
Age:	36	40	26	28	22	47	31	28
Marital Status:	Married	Married	Married	Married	Single	Single	Married	Single
Occupation:	Homemaker	Doctoral Student	Sales	Masters Student	College Senior	College Counselor	Advertising Executive	Program Director/ Crisis Center
Length of Time as a Vegetarian:	4 years	6 months	6 months	9 months	2 months	13 years	5 years	1 year
Type of Vegetarianism Practiced:	Lacto-ovo[a]	Semi[b]	Semi	Lacto-ovo	Vegan[c]	Lacto[d]	Lacto-ovo	Lacto-ovo
Status of Diet at the Time of the Interview:	Lacto-ovo	Semi	Semi	Omnivorous[e]	Vegan	Lacto	Lacto-ovo	Omnivorous
Primary Motives:	Health	Animal Rights	Animal Rights Environmentalism	Disgust with meat Health	Animal Rights	Spiritual	Environmental Activism	Disgust with meat
Other Household Members:	Spouse[a] Son[a]	Spouse[b] of Barb	Spouse[b] of Tony	Spouse[d]	None	None	None	None

[a] Consumes no meat products, but does eat eggs and dairy products.
[b] Only red meat products have been deleted from the diet.
[c] Consumes no meat products, eggs, or dairy products.
[d] Consumes no meat products or eggs.
[e] Consumes meat products, eggs, and dairy products.

became a conscious effort to try and avoid meat and meat products. (Tony)

I had pulled out a package of chicken breasts to prepare them and they were all bloody and I almost got sick. At that point I said I don't want to do this anymore. (Carrie)

The impact of these experiences, combined with the emerging undercurrent moved the person to drop meat from his/her diet.

Achieving A Meatfree Diet

The goal was *not* to become a vegetarian, but to achieve a meatfree diet. This was not equivalent to adopting vegetarianism or *becoming* a vegetarian. Eating a meatfree diet was something the participants *did*, but it was not something they were becoming or aspiring to.

More than making a conscious effort to become vegetarian, it was more a conscious effort to become a non-meateater; which I know sounds unusual, but it was more that you made deliberate efforts to try and cut out on the amount of meat in the meal; rather than consciously saying "I want to become a vegetarian." (Tony)

I just stopped eating meat; it wasn't difficult and I became comfortable with it really quickly; I didn't even think about it. (Carrie)

Participants simply deleted meat from the diet, typically by adapting traditional recipes to be meatless. Otherwise, the composition of the diet did not change much; new products were not incorporated.

We started out by just trying to find recipes ...in our current cookbooks to find recipes that sounded good and we found ourselves going to recipes that were similar to what we would have eaten with red meat, but just missing the meat, like a vegetable stroganoff instead of beef stroganoff. (Barb)

My meals are pretty much the same. Maybe a little bit more because vegetables aren't as filling. ...I don't really know that much. I just eat regular foods that I used to eat only I don't have [meat, dairy, or eggs] in them. (Donna)

Dropping meat from the diet was a simple and straightforward thing to do. Yet, each participant stressed the difficulty of *sustaining* a completely meatfree diet over time. Therefore, striking to us was the lack of overt information searching for guidance on achieving this challenging goal, especially given the many resources available. Participants regarded what they were doing as an act of deletion (which did not require new information), rather than an act of change or seeking new consumption behaviors (which would have required new products and new information.)

Not everyone moved beyond this stage. Informants who have not yet achieved a completely meatfree diet are still working on it (Barb, Tony). Others did practice a meatfree diet, but then returned to eating an omnivorous diet (Amanda, Carrie). However, an essential step in the process of acquiring vegetarianism required a stripping away of the old, realized with the achievement of a meatless diet. Then the informants were free to take on the new, as if putting on a mantle. Adoption of vegetarianism was the final stage in the process.

Adoption of Vegetarianism

Reaching this final stage of the process required a sustained commitment to vegetarian consumption patterns, an accumulation of knowledge via information and skills, the passage of time, and the adoption of the label "vegetarian".

Commitment. Strict adherence to the demands of a vegetarian diet revealed commitment. Interviewees with the most restrictive diets expressed a perception of a personal stake in remaining true to their decision to delete meat. These same participants credited the transformation to vegetarianism with positive changes in their nature.

This is the one area of my life that I have been disciplined [in] and I feel good about it. Quite frankly it helps with my self esteem. (Clarise)

Physically I feel like I have more energy. I feel better sticking to what I believe...I don't think I'm really losing anything [and am gaining] some self-discipline and self respect. I think I'm going to be healthier. (Donna)

These types of comments were absent from those still attempting to rid meat from their diets. Those who reverted to eating meat expressed negative changes (e.g., excessive weight loss, decline in health).

Active Information Search. After a time, the lack of variety and the feeling of being at a loss for what to cook became intolerable. The duration of this period varied. The search for information seemed driven by the need-to-know, by necessity. At this point, the participant purchased a cookbook, subscribed to a magazine (e.g. *Vegetarian Times*), and/or sought substitute food items (e.g., tofu, soy-cheese, nut-burgers).

This information search reflected developing commitment. Participants who did so sensed that they were in this for the long haul and needed to do something. Those who reverted to eating meat (Carrie and Amanda), did not get themselves over this information dearth. Amanda, for example, stated that she was not willing to make the required effort.

The process of learning and adopting appear to be iterative. By the time one is a vegetarian, s/he knows how to "do it". For example, long time vegetarians spoke of products and procedures not mentioned by recent converts or those who had quit the diet. Nikki, for example, described how she made her own soy milk, yogurt, and juice when her son was a baby. These things she learned from cookbooks or her husband. Clarise talked about cooking with tofu as a protein booster. She also attributed important learning about new foods and methods to her participation in a pro-vegetarian spiritual group. Time, learning, and experimentation resulted in the adoption of new products, as well.

Label Adoption. An important reflection of the level of commitment was the adoption (or not) of "vegetarian" as a label for one's eating patterns. Time appeared to play a role in the adoption of the label. The participants who had practiced a vegetarian diet for a long time readily classified themselves as such.

Conversely, when asked how she described her eating habits, Donna, who had only three weeks earlier deleted all animal products from her diet responded, "I guess I'd call me a vegan." She chose the label "vegan", but in a tentative way. Although she had been adhering strictly to her decision, she apparently was not comfortable in announcing "I am a vegan." Tony classified himself with a description of how he was trying to delete meat from his diet. He had not adopted a vegetarian label. Amanda completely rejected the vegetarian label, although she continued to consume very little meat.

Notably, even the more experienced participants expressed a certain discomfort with the vegetarian label for describing who they were. They readily agreed they *ate* like a vegetarian, but were reluctant to be *known* as a vegetarian. They disliked being stereotyped, as Bob described, as one of the "bug-mobile Birkenstock wearing crowd". Although they associated themselves with the label, it did not describe an identity by which they wished to be known.

Commitment and The Role of Others. Messages from others supported or challenged commitment. Family, friends, and other interpersonal interactions served as important social support systems for the maintenance of commitment to the meatless diet. Non-vegetarian parents, sisters, brothers, or friends would prepare meals or fix special foods to accommodate the vegetarian. Guests respectfully submitted to vegetarian meals served at the participant's home. Meat consuming friends agreed to go out to restaurants where the vegetarian could get something to eat. Those who adopted vegetarianism consistently reported behavioral support from those who respected the vegetarian's commitment.

Not surprisingly certain social hindrances competed with the support systems as the following comments illustrate.

Tony's brother [made it harder]...[he] insists on having meatloaf every time he comes because he love's Tony's meatloaf. So he made it tough, and he's always abusing us because we're "sticks-in-the-mud's" and won't eat meat. (Barb)

When I was pregnant with Josh, my obstetrician was very critical of the vegetarian diet...it's hard on your own against the experts. (Nikki)

My family had a difficult time understanding that I wasn't eating meat...There's not many vegetarians in Nebraska...there's a different mindset. You eat meat and potatoes and vegetarians are sissies. (Carrie)

The difficulty of finding good restaurants to go with friends or impression management concerns in professional situations (e.g., business dinners) put vegetarians in challenging situations. Discretion in revealing dietary preferences was the typical approach and participants used realistic strategies to cope. Clarise, for example, described a conference luncheon where she traded chicken for vegetables with someone at her table. And going ahead and eating some of a forbidden food was another accommodating strategy to avoid social embarrassment or hurting another's feelings. Nikki chose not to complain to her son's babysitter about feeding him the wrong foods because she felt the older woman's love for the child was more important.

The Role of Personal Resources. The relative cost of a meatless diet was not an issue for any of the participants. Several felt they were spending less in the grocery store. However, the constraint of limited *time* resources was more salient. Meal selection and preparation took more time (e.g., chopping vegetables) as did shopping (e.g., to examine ingredients lists on packages).

Consumer *knowledge* was the other personal constraint that interacted with time. Participants needed to learn what to cook, what ingredients to buy, where to shop, or how to prepare a healthy meatless meal. Surprisingly, this lack of knowledge did not always lead to information seeking, as one might expect for such a highly involving consumption pattern. The learning was more a process of experimentation and discovery than planned and organized.

Not an "Issue". All participants wished to avoid their eating habits becoming an issue with others. Each expressed the desire that their eating habits not become a barrier to personal or professional relationships. These concerns surfaced in different contexts.

When *dining out in public*, participants developed strategies to prevent uncomfortable situations: calling restaurants before selecting one, asking the waiter to request a vegetarian dish, eating before going out, or eating only "legal foods", e.g., salad, baked potatoes, french fries.

> Sometimes I'll call the restaurant ahead of time and ask if they can prepare a vegetarian meal. (Clarise)

> It is tough...I've discovered that if you do ask, they will generally provide something that's very good and often its better than what's on the menu because it's fresher. (Barb)

> It hasn't been a problem. Either I'll eat before or I'll just snack, like I'll just have french fries or something that I can eat there. (Donna)

Another strategy was to ask about the ingredients while ordering. This did not appear to be an optimal solution (mentioned by only Clarise), and she noted that if she did not feel comfortable asking, rather than draw attention to the issue, she would eat the food in question. Bob also noted the role of discretion in developing a dining out strategy that for him meant periodically eating chicken.

All expressed a desire for restaurants to feature vegetarian meals. Selecting a restaurant had become much more difficult. A decline in the frequency of eating out was a direct result of their change in eating habits.

> To this day I don't have a list of restaurants that I like to go to. Sometimes it will bother me because somebody will say well let's go out for dinner, where would you like to go? I don't know. Where will they serve a vegetarian meal? (Clarise)

> I am eating at home more than I would have been because there's not that much outside. [Before] if I was lazy I'd just go get a sandwich or a burger or something. Now, I can't, there's nothing out there. (Donna)

> I think [we are eating out] less because its difficult for us to find things, especially if its on the spur of the moment. Like if you want a pizza or something. You don't want pepperoni and you don't want sausage, so it just requires more thought, more planning. (Barb)

"Not making a scene" extended to *dining out in other people's homes* as well. A common strategy was to take their own food when invited to someone's home.

> Typically, I end up having Thanksgiving and Christmas with my family and that works out fine. Christmas I go to my brother's in Dallas and I'm responsible for taking my own chickettes [tofu chicken substitutes] and I take the makings for cheese fondue. (Clarise)

> I don't want people to go out of their way, to cook me special food or anything like that. I'll probably have to end up bringing my own things. (Donna)

Preparing meat dishes for guests in their homes and not eating it themselves was also a common occurrence.

> I can't remember the last meal I cooked for myself that involved meat. I did make a meatloaf for my brother that I felt awful about but... it was a birthday present for him, so I made it and never had any of it.... (Tony)

> This is the first year we've had guests for Thanksgiving...The thought of seeing that bird sitting there in the middle of the table sounds really pretty disgusting. We'll have a...turkey and everything...because they are guests...and we've invited them. (Barb)

Such social situations were negotiated by each participant with other's feelings and preferences in mind. It was important to minimize conspicuousness of their own dietary practices, whether the participant was a novice or experienced vegetarian. They wished to manage commitment yet avoid being stereotyped or misunderstood.

In general, the participants negotiated the social landscape through trial and error, common sense, and creativity. Mastering the "how-to's" of coping with these social situations, as well as consumer knowledge, played an important role in the emergence of the consumption pattern.

Summary. Achieving a meatless diet took a different form for each participant, yet we observed a shared multidimensional process. The *undercurrent* of personal, interpersonal, and sociocultural influences converged in participants' initial dietary meat reduction strategies. But, it took a *touchstone* experience to delete meat. All respondents *achieved a meatless diet* for a time. But not everyone *adopted vegetarianism*. The process was influenced by personal time and knowledge resources and other people's helps or hindrances. Mastering the how-to's of social situations was as important as learning to prepare a meatless meal for learning this system.

DISCUSSION

Our objective was to begin to understand how individuals learned their own way of doing the vegetarian consumption system. Several features of the process that we described deserve attention in future investigations.

Emergent vs. deliberate process. Most striking was the participants' lack of information search and planning when changing their eating patterns. There was a tendency to read about vegetarianism motives (e.g., animal rights). Yet, although participants were eventually forced into some information seeking (e.g., buying a cookbook), there was very little investigation of the vegetarian diet and its how-to's. We found this remarkable, given the resources available to each participant.

Rather than take a direct or planned approach, participants took a gradual, winding path to their goal, stopping along the way to regroup and learn more, try new things, negotiate the challenges. Acquisition of the new consumption system was more emergent than directed. Neither models of the involved, deliberate information seeker nor models of low involvement behavior explain this type of consumer learning.

Stripping away the old consumption pattern. We observed a multidimensional process that required the person to release the old consumption behaviors (become meat-*free*) before the new system could be adopted. How similar are other, less radical changes in dietary patterns? If the driving force is the desire to lose weight or achieve better health, is the process the same? Is this sort of shedding a prerequisite for taking on other new consumption patterns?

Socially embedded process. Other people were important in supporting or hindering the vegetarian learning process. Mastering the how-to's of social situations was as important as learning how to prepare a meatless meal. Participants expressed appreciation for social support, yet wished to downplay their dietary practices. Issues arising from meals shared with others were a universal concern. Thus, this process is clearly socially embedded. Future investigators of consumption system learning should investigate it as such.

What is this process? It is tempting to consider this an identity acquisition process—i.e., *becoming* a vegetarian. Such issues as label adoption, shedding old behaviors, commitment to new behaviors, or managing social interactions suggest as much. However, we are not at all certain that adopting the consumption system (eating *like* a vegetarian) is isomorphic with identity adoption (*being* a vegetarian). For example, we did not observe that a discernable identity transformation (to that of being vegetarian) was necessary for consumer behavior to change (cf. Schouten 1991). Moreover, our participants were not being brought along by initiating groups, nor did circumstances force them to change. And none of them were directing themselves toward a clearly defined goal or set of norms, beyond becoming "meatfree". Although it may involve an eventual change in the extended self (Belk 1988), the process may differ from traditionally studied transitions (e.g., becoming a physician or a sorority member) *because it is so bound to the consumer learning and marketplace available resources used to make the change.* There are many ways to eat a meatless diet; each participant developed his/her own version of doing the consumption pattern. It may be that the marketplace makes this possible.

Exploring parallels with the one-thing-leads-to-another feature of the consumption based Diderot effect (McCracken 1988) may inform future investigations. Adoption of vegetarian consumption patterns also may accompany changes in other consumption systems (e.g., attire and appearance, household energy consumption), based on a value such as voluntary simplicity (e.g., Leonard-Barton 1981).

In conclusion, becoming vegetarian is inseparable from the products that must be avoided or consumed, yet assuming this consumption pattern comprises far more than buyer behavior changes. It is clearly a socially embedded process, yet it emerges according to each person's own way of doing things. These results invite further investigation of the acquisition of vegetarianism as well as other unfamiliar (to the consumer) consumptions systems.

REFERENCES

Amato, Paul R. and Sonia A. Partridge (1989), *The New Vegetarians: Promoting Health and Protecting Life*, New York: Plenum Press.

Belk, Russell W. (1988), "Possessions and the Extended Self," *Journal of Consumer Research*, 15 (Sept.), 139-168.

Brown, Helen Hodgson (1990), *With the Grain*, New York: Carroll & Graf Publishers, Inc.

Boyd, Harper W., Jr., and Sidney J. Levy (1963), "New Dimension in Consumer Analysis," *Harvard Business Review*, (Nov./Dec.), 129-140.

Heisley, Deborah D. and Sidney J. Levy (1991), "Autodriving: A Photoelicitation Technique," *Journal of Consumer Research*, 18 (Dec.), 257-272.

Kernan, Jerome B. and Montrose S. Sommers (1967), "Meaning, Value, and the Theory of Promotion," *Journal of Communication*, 17 (June), 109-135.

Kleine, Robert E., III, Susan Schultz Kleine, and Jerome B. Kernan (1992), "Mundane Everyday Consumption and the Self: A Conceptual Orientation and Prospects for Consumer Research," *Advances in Consumer Research*, Vol. 19, eds. J. Sherry and B. Sternthal, Provo, UT: Association for Consumer Research, 411-415.

Leonard-Barton, Dorothy (1981), "Voluntary Simplicity Lifestyles and Energy Conservation," *Journal of Consumer Research*, 8 (Dec.), 243-252.

Levy, Sidney J. (1981), "Interpreting Consumer Mythology: A Structural Approach to Consumer Behavior," *Journal of Marketing*, 45 (Summer), 49-61.

McCracken, Grant (1988), *Culture and Consumption*, Bloomington, IN: Indiana University Press.

Schouten, John (1991), "Selves in Transition: Symbolic Consumption in Personal Rites of Passage and Identity Reconstruction," *Journal of Consumer Research*, 17 (March), 412-425.

Solomon, Michael (1983), "The Role of Products as Social Stimuli: A Symbolic Interactionism Perspective," *Journal of Consumer Research*, 10 (Dec.), 219-252.

_____ (1988), "Mapping Product Constellations: A Social Categorization Approach to Consumption Symbolism," *Psychology and Marketing*, 5 (Fall), 233-258.

Do Market Mavens Categorize Brands Differently?

Michael T. Elliott, University of Missouri-St. Louis
Anne E. Warfield, University of Missouri-St. Louis

ABSTRACT

A survey of 172 consumers studied the impact of market mavenism on brand categorization processes across several diverse product categories. Extending the Feick and Price (1987) seminal study, this research examines how market mavens differ from other consumers in categorizing seven brands sets based on the Brisoux and Laroche (1980) framework. Findings indicate that market mavens have (1) larger salient (unaided recall) sets, (2) larger aware (aided recall) sets, (3) larger trial sets, and (4) larger hold (undecided) sets than other consumer groups. In addition, the results were found to be generalizable over a wide range of products exhibiting varying levels of product involvement.

INTRODUCTION

The market maven, described by Feick and Price (1987) as an influencer with general marketplace expertise, represents a truly attractive target segment to advertisers and other marketers. The authors found that market mavens display higher levels of marketplace *involvement*; are engaged in extensive search activities (e.g., reading *Consumer Reports*); and demonstrate greater participation in market activities such as couponing, store browsing and reading advertisements. Furthermore, mavens appear to be an accessible market segment in that they tend to read magazines and view television more than other consumers.

Of particular note, Feick and Price reported that market mavens display an earlier awareness of new products and brands than other consumers. Since the early 1980s, there has been a proliferation of new brands within certain product categories. Food and drug manufacturers, for instance, introduced an average of 11,000 new brands during this period (For*tune*, 1985). As a result, consumer researchers have focused more attention on how individuals simplify their decision making heuristics through the process of brand categorization (Brisoux and Laroche 1980; Narayana and Marking 1975). This approach delineates brand categorization sets (i.e., awareness, salient, foggy, evoked, trial, reject, and hold) as they relate to the stages of the consumer decision making process (i.e., awareness, processing, consideration and preference).

The brand categorization paradigm offers an intriguing perspective of consumer involvement. Any given brand that the consumer knows about could move to his or her evoked set (i.e., it could become a brand that he or she considers acceptable for purchase), hold set (i.e., he or she would not have an opinion as to whether it should be accepted or rejected) or reject set (i.e., he or she would consider it unacceptable for consideration). Considering the proliferation of new product introductions and line extensions in recent years, the truly interesting question raised (and tentatively answered) by this research is: Do consumers with general marketplace expertise (i.e., market mavens) categorize their known brands differently than other consumers across a wide range of product types? If so, in what brand set categories do these differences exist?

One predicted outcome of market mavenism would be the demonstration of a greater awareness of brands across diverse product categories. Similarly, we would expect informed consumers, like market mavens, to exhibit more trial purchase behaviors. During the consideration stage (i.e., evoked, reject, and hold sets), however, we do not have an intuitively superior expectation. If we were to apply Social Judgement Theory (Sherif and Hovland 1961) without modification to answer this question, we would expect that higher levels of general marketplace involvement would cause the evoked set (analogous to latitudes of acceptance) to decrease, the hold set (analogous to latitudes of neutrality) to remain constant, and the reject set (analogous to latitudes of rejection) to increase. However, past research has not supported this view. What Brisoux and Cheron (1990) found was that, with increased product involvement, the sizes of both the evoked set and the reject set remained relatively constant while the size of the awareness and hold sets dramatically increased. This suggests that while involved consumers possess higher "top of mind" awareness, their processing of brand evaluation information is not superior to others.

In order to extend the literature on the market maven concept and provide additional empirical support for its existence, this study investigates how market mavens differ in their brand categorization processes from nonmavens. Specifically, we focus on three important questions:

1) Do market mavens categorize brands differently relative to the brand categorization process (measured in terms of brand set size)?
2) Can any differences found in brand set size among market maven groups be generalized across product categories?
3) Do differences in brand set size among market maven groups remain after taking product-specific involvement into account?

MARKET MAVENISM

The introduction of the market maven concept to marketing has precipitated a great deal of research interest (Higie and Feick 1987; Price Feick, and Higie 1987; Slama and Williams 1990). Drawn from the consumer behavior, communications and social science literatures, the market maven concept refers to "individuals who have information about many kinds of products, places to shop, and other facets of markets, and initiate discussion with consumers and respond to requests from consumers for market information" (Feick and Price, 1987, p. 85). In validating their market maven scale, Feick and Price were able to show that the tendency to be a maven, the tendency to be an opinion leader and the tendency to be early purchasers represent three related but distinct concepts.

Arguably, the most salient characteristic of market mavens is their possession of a *wide variety* of market information. That is, these consumers may possess information regarding places to shop, be aware of innovative products and more brands, or have in-depth knowledge of specific brand performance criteria through activities such as reading *Consumer Reports* (Kotler and Zaltman 1976). One other indicator of this generalized marketplace knowledge, as reported by Feick and Price (1987), is the market maven's early awareness of a large number of brands across a broad range of product categories.

These preliminary findings raise two interesting issues. First, the effects of market mavenism may well extend beyond the awareness stage of the consumer decision process. We hypothesize that the brand set sizes during the awareness, processing, consideration and preference stages differ based on degree of market mavenism. Since mavens are posited to have higher levels of marketplace knowledge and expertise, it seems plausible that they might be aware of, try, and perhaps reject more brands while at the same time consider, be unaware, and be unsure (i.e., hold and foggy) about fewer brands than other consumers. Variations in brand set sizes, if detected, would provide support for the usefulness of the brand categorization model in understanding consumer involvement and information processing activities.

Second, the theoretical underpinnings of the market maven concept depend, to a large extent, on its generalizability across a wide range of product types. Unlike the opinion leader, who exhibits mostly product-specific knowledge, the market maven's expertise is purported to exist across a wider range of product categories. Slama and Williams (1990) provided some evidence of the generalizability of the information provision tendency of the market maven by investigating twenty categories of products and services. However, the question of whether market mavenism is truly a global characteristic or whether it is simply an artifact of a more generalized form of opinion leadership manifested is still largely unresolved.

BRAND CATEGORIZATION

The manner in which consumers handle information regarding the multitude of brands that are available in many product categories has been viewed as the "psychology of simplification" in choice behavior (Narayana and Markin 1975, p. 1). Several models representing this cognitive simplification process have been proposed in the marketing literature. Topics such as category formation processes (e.g., Cohen and Basu 1987), measurement of consideration set or evoked set (Gruca 1989), as well as elements of the evoked set (Brisoux and Laroche 1980), have been addressed.

Brisoux and Laroche's (1980) brand categorization framework is an expansion of earlier models by Narayana and Markin (1975) and Howard (1977). It suggests four stages in the consumer decision process: awareness, processing, consideration and preference (see Figure). This model successfully links a consumer decision process perspective to brand set formation research.

According to their model, a consumer is either aware or unaware of all of the available brands in a given product class. The brands for which the consumer is aware can be distinguished as either processed or foggy brands. Brands presumed to be in the consumer's *foggy set* have no salient attributes by which the consumer attains comprehension of the brands. This may occur because of a lack of exposure to the brands' advertisements or a lack of experience with the product category. As an example, most consumers would likely have large foggy sets for a product such as scuba diving equipment because of a lack of experience with the product class.

Those brands possessing the salient attributes which allow for processing are further subdivided into three sets: evoked, hold and reject sets. The *evoked (consideration) set* contains those brands which the consumer has a positive attitude toward and actually considers as purchase alternatives (Howard and Sheth, 1969; Brisoux and Laroche 1980). The existence of evoked sets has been confirmed in the choice process for nondurables (grocery products - Campbell, 1969), consumer durables (cars - Gronhaug, 1974), and services (retailing - Spriggle and Sewall, 1987).

The *trial set* is viewed as a subset of the evoked set and consists of those brands that the consumer has actually purchased and consumed. Though not explicitly referred to in the Brisoux and Laroche model, it represents brands within the consideration stage possessing a higher probability of selection than other evoked brands because of prior usage experience. Trial sets also represent an indicator of the degree of brand switching and experiential behavior by the consumer.

The *hold set* consists of those brands that the consumer has perceived no advantage in purchasing. Brands exist in a consumer's hold set for various reasons. These reasons include: (1) viewing the brand as not being adequate for the buying motives or purchase situation, (2) possessing no reference group influences or (3) perceiving brands as being too high in price in relation to quality. As a result, the consumer generally has either a positive or neutral feelings toward these brands. Lastly, the *reject set* is defined as those brands that the consumer has a decidedly negative attitude toward and has completely rejected from consideration as a purchase alternative (Brisoux and Laroche 1980).

RESEARCH OBJECTIVES AND HYPOTHESES

Previous studies have demonstrated the existence of market mavens and suggest that they possess and are active providers of information about new products and brands across a wide variety of product categories (Feick and Price 1987; Slama and Williams 1990; Lichtenstein and Burton 1990). Despite this, the market maven's general awareness of brands within a wide range of product categories has not been rigorously investigated. An equally important issue concerns the disposition of those brands that the market maven has at least partially processed.

To address these empirical questions, the present study investigates differences in brand set sizes - awareness, evoked, reject, foggy, salient, trial, and hold - relative to a consumer's level of market mavenism. Several diverse product categories are used to assess the generalizability of the findings. Because of its impact on brand awareness and knowledge, the impact of product-specific involvement (Zaichkowsky 1985; Brisoux and Laroche 1990) on brand set size is adjusted for in determining the specific effects of the market maven trait. Put more generally, the purpose of this research is to assess the validity and generalizability of the purported market maven trait of general marketplace knowledge and expertise vis-a-vis the brand categorization process.

Six hypotheses pertaining to the relationship between market mavenism and brand set size are proposed. Because the conceptualization of product involvement is closely aligned with that of market mavenism, it is utilized as a covariate to better assess the impact of market mavenism separately.

H1 Consumers with a higher level of market mavenism will exhibit smaller evoked sets.

H2 Consumers with a higher level of market mavenism will exhibit larger reject sets.

Previous research has been inconclusive regarding the relationship between marketplace involvement and the evoked and reject set sizes. For instance, Jarvis and Wilcox (1973) found that individuals with greater ego-involvement in a product class (i.e., car enthusiast) have smaller evoked sets. Conversely, Brisoux and Cheron (1990) in their study of perfume purchasers, found no relationship between product involvement and either evoked or reject sets.

H3 Consumers with a higher level of market mavenism will exhibit smaller foggy sets.

This hypothesis assumes that the maven's involvement with the marketplace results in a larger number of processed brands (i.e., the converse of foggy brands). Due to the unprocessed nature of the foggy set, a larger foggy set should be associated with a lower level of market mavenism.

H4 Consumers with a higher level of market mavenism will exhibit larger salient (unaided recall) sets and larger awareness (unaided recall) sets.

FIGURE
The Brand Categorization Process

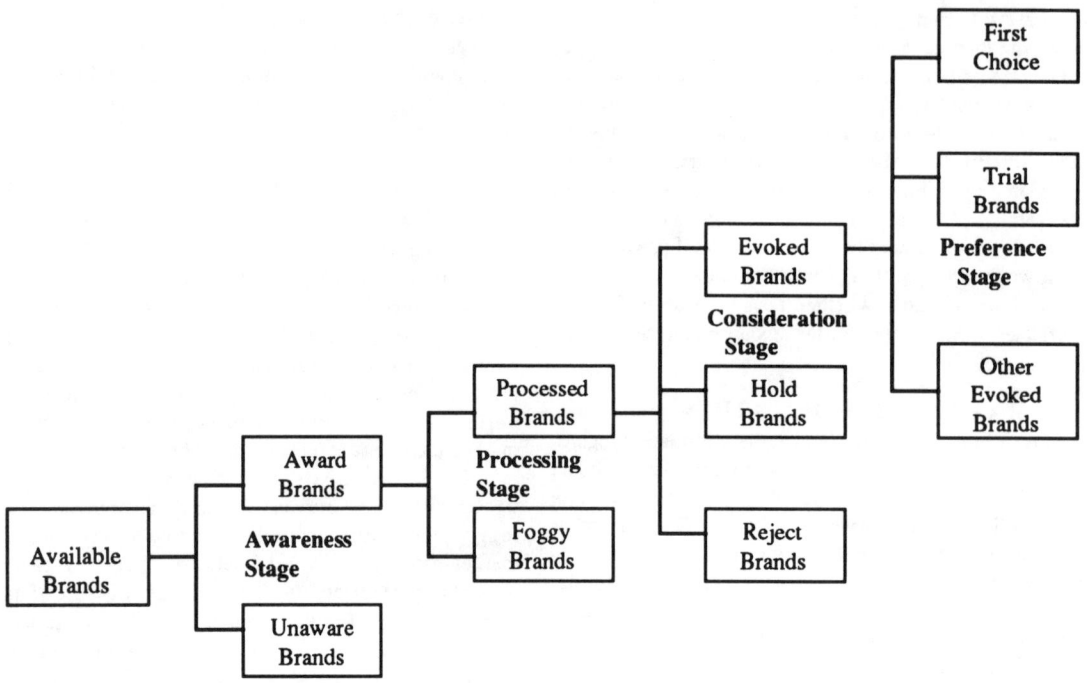

Source: Adapted from the Brisoux and Laroche (1980) framework.

H5 Consumers with a higher level of market mavenism will exhibit larger hold sets.

H6 Consumers with a higher level of market mavenism will have larger trial sets.

Hypothesis four is proposed based on the positive relationship between brand awareness and market mavenism shown by Feick and Price (1987). Similarly, the salient set (measured as unaided recall) should be larger among market mavens than other individuals. In addition, Brisoux and Laroche (1990) reported that awareness sets, trial sets, and hold sets were larger for highly involved perfume purchasers.

METHODOLOGY

Sample

A simple random sample of 1000 residents was drawn from a Midwest metropolitan statistical area (MSA) utilizing a recent voter registration list. A five-page questionnaire mailed to respondents contained an accompanying cover letter and instructions. To better ensure the validity of the brand set measures, special emphasis was place on the importance of completing each section in proper sequence. The first section of the questionnaire asked respondents to provide an unaided recall of brands within four product categories (athletic shoes, potato chips, toothpaste, and stereo receivers). Section two assessed product involvement for each product category by using a 5-item modified version of the Personal Involvement Inventory developed by Zaichkowsky (1985). In the third section, the brand set sizes (evoked, reject, trial, salient, foggy, hold, and awareness sets) for the four selected product categories were obtained by providing a current list of available brands. Respondents were asked to indicate which brands within a specified product category belonged to each brand set. In the last section the market maven measure (Feick and Price 1987) and general demographic information such as gender, age, income, education, and household size were gathered.

Of the 1000 questionnaires mailed, 182 were returned, resulting in a response rate of 18.2 percent. After removing 10 unusable responses, 172 cases were retained for analysis. The sample was primarily female (76%) and white (85%). In addition, the median age category was 40-49, the median education level was some college, and the median household income was $40,000-$55,000. Nonresponse error was assessed by comparing early respondents (i.e., first one-third) with late respondents (i.e., last one-third). Chi-square tests revealed that the two groups do not differ on any of the demographic variables or market mavenism ($p > .05$).

Product Selection

One limitation of previous brand categorization studies is that only a limited range of products have been investigated (i.e., only one or two categories) and justification for products chosen is usually not provided. The product categories selected for the present study include athletic footwear, toothpaste, stereo receivers, and potato chips.

These products were chosen because they: (1) represent both durable (stereo receivers, athletic shoes) and nondurable (toothpaste, potato chips) goods; (2) tend to be gender-neutral; (3) represent limited to extensive decision making processes (as opposed to routinized); and (4) represent a range of low to high involvement product categories. A pretest indicated a Product Involvement Inventory (see Zaichkowsky 1985) score ranging from 64 (potato chips) to 112 (toothpaste), indicative of low and high involvement products, respectively. Though an investigation of an even larger inventory of product categories would be desirable, questionnaire length was considered a methodological constraint.

Definition of Variables

The operational concepts of the brand sets (dependent variables) and of the market maven (independent variable) are defined here. The conceptualization and operationalization of the six brand sets shown in the Figure were borrowed from the previous work of Brisoux and Laroche (1980).

Salient Set: Consists of those brands of the product class that the respondent can recall without the aid of a list or other type of prompt.

Awareness Set: Expanding on the salient set, it consists of those brands that the respondent can identify from a list of brands.

Trial Set: Consists of those brands that the respondent has already bought and used for him or herself (selected from brands listed in the awareness set).

Evoked Set: Consists of those brands that the respondent would consider as a purchase alternative at that point in time (selected from brands listed in awareness set).

Reject Set: Consists of those brands that the respondent deems unacceptable for purchase at that point in time (selected from brands in the awareness set).

Foggy Set: Consists of those brands for which the respondent has not formed an opinion and will not consider buying at that point in time (selected from brands listed in the awareness set).

Hold Set: Of the remaining brands from the awareness set, those brands for which the respondent has formed an opinion but will neither consider nor reject (selected from brands listed in the awareness set).

The market maven scale, a six-item, seven-point likert scale, measures a person's tendency to be a general provider of many types of market information to others on an informal basis (Feick and Price 1987). Example items include "People ask me for information about products, places to shop, or sales," and "My friends think of me as a good source of information when it comes to new products or sales" (7=strongly agree, 1=strongly disagree). The market maven scale was shown to be reliable in this study (alpha =.89).

The definition of product involvement, taken from Zaichkowsky (1985), states: "A person's perceived relevance of the object based on inherent needs, values and interests". This definition contains the general viewpoints of several researchers (e.g., Krugman 1967; Rothchild 1984). The operational measurement of product involvement is derived from the Personal Involvement Inventory (PII) scale developed by Zaichkowsky (1985). A modified 5-item, seven point semantic differential scale (important-unimportant, of no concern for me-of concern to me, very meaningful to me-means nothing to me, interesting-not interesting, significant-insignificant) was selected after studies by Nowak (1986) and Nowak and Salmon (1987) found that shorter versions of the scale were reliable. The coefficient alpha of the PII scale in this study ranged from .83 to .92.

Data Analysis

Following the practice of several earlier studies (i.e., Feick and Price 1987; Lichtenstein and Burton 1990; Slama and Williams 1990), the respondents was divided into three categories based on their scores on the market maven scale. The top scoring one-third of respondents was designated as market mavens or the high scoring group, the next two-thirds were the medium and low scoring groups.

A series of hierarchical ANOVAs were used to test the effect of market mavenism on specific brand set sizes as specified in hypotheses one through six. This approach allows for the testing of the effect of market mavenism alone before removing the effects of the covariate, product involvement. Subsequently, multiple comparisons were examined using the Scheffe procedure, which is appropriate when samples are of different sizes and allows testing for an overall significance level of group differences.

RESULTS

Table 1 shows the average brand set sizes for the four selected product categories. The brand set size proportions appear to be both similar across product categories and are consistent with past studies. For instance, the evoked set/awareness set proportion (ranging from .23 to .46) is comparable to that reported by Crowley and Williams (1991). Also, the current study found the average evoked set size of 3.72 to be similar to the average salient set size of 4.08. This is consistent with research by Brisoux and Cheron (1986) who reported similar evoked and salient set sizes (4.70 and 4.57, respectively) for the various brands studied. The average evoked set size (3.72) in this study is also comparable to the evoked set sizes of laundry detergent and margarine (3.67 and 3.78, respectively) reported by Reilly and Parkinson (1985). Lastly, the reject set size of 1.89 is similar to the reject set size (1.98) found with Brisoux and Cheron's study of perfume purchasers.

As shown in Table 2, three groups were formed from the market maven scale using the 33rd and 67th percentiles. The low maven group included scores of 26 or below, the medium level group scored from 27 to 32 and the high level group scored above 32. Out of the 172 valid cases, the average market maven scale score was 28.36 (standard deviation = 7.19, range = 8-42). The market maven scale parameters reported here compare favorably with those originally cited by the Feick and Price (1987) study (i.e., mean = 25.6; standard deviation = 8.5; range = 6-42).

To provide evidence on the generalizability of the market maven relationships across the four product categories, a series of two-way ANOVAs were conducted in which the dependent variables were the seven brand sets and the independent variables were the four product categories and the three levels of market mavenism (low, medium, high). Of the seven ANOVAs conducted, none resulted in significant product type X market maven interaction. These results indicate that market mavenism does not have a differential effect on the brand set size for different product types. Based on these results, within-subject responses on brand set size were aggregated across product categories.

Hierarchical analysis of variance was utilized to test the equivalence of mean brand set sizes for the low, medium and high scoring market maven groups. The data shown in Table 2 displays the univariate F tests for the seven brand set sizes. The first column of F values presents the F values for a single factor design testing the effects of market mavenism alone. The second column, F_{PI}, presents conditional F values on the effect of market mavenism after removing or adjusting for the effects of product involvement. Significant differences were observed for the salient (H4), awareness (H4), hold (H5), and trial sets (H6), thereby confirming these hypotheses. After adjusting for product involvement, however, no differences were detected in the hold set (suggesting only partial support for hypothesis five). Conversely, results for the evoked set, reject sets, and foggy sets (i.e., H1-H3) indicated no difference in market maven group means. Finally, the Scheffe post-hoc contrast test, robust to non-normality and to unequal sample sizes, was conducted. Where overall differences existed, the Scheffe test indicated that the low scoring group consistently exhibited smaller

TABLE 1
Mean (Standard Deviation) of Brand Set Size by Product Category

Brand Set	Product Category				
	Athletic Shoes (n=172)	Toothpaste (n=148)	Potato Chips (n=172)	Stereo Equipment (n=172)	Total (n=658)
Salient	4.71 (1.81)	4.11 (1.62)	4.05 (1.90)	2.40 (2.24)	4.08
Awareness	9.63 (2.85)	10.86 (4.07)	13.30 (5.30)	7.47 (4.67)	11.27
Evoked	2.73 (2.33)	2.55 (2.24)	5.18 (4.11)	2.45 (2.74)	3.72
Trial	3.84 (2.53)	5.89 (3.03)	9.29 (4.41)	2.20 (2.51)	5.84
Reject	1.24 (2.23)	2.66 (3.70)	2.01 (2.64)	.88 (2.25)	1.89
Foggy	3.62 (2.64)	3.28 (3.40)	2.34 (2.37)	2.91 (3.08)	3.16
Hold	2.65 (2.90)	2.46 (3.10)	2.62 (3.61)	1.61 (2.52)	2.41

TABLE 2
ANOVA Results: Effects of Market Mavenism on Brand Set Size

Brand Sets	Mean Set Size (n=500)[a]	Low (N=193)	Medium (N=150)	High (N=157)	Contrast[b]	F	F_{PI}[c]
Salient	4.08	3.50	3.88	4.33	L < H	8.07**	4.99**
Awareness	11.27	9.48	11.52	11.74	L < M,H	15.96**	11.17**
Evoked	3.72	3.29	3.28	3.93	—	2.63	1.98
Trial	5.84	4.81	5.61	6.50	L < H	8.27**	6.79**
Reject	1.89	1.63	1.99	1.92	—	.86	.72
Foggy	3.16	3.05	3.53	3.09	—	1.58	.13
Hold	2.41	2.07	3.01	2.52	L < M	4.53*	2.14

[a] Brand set size represents aggregated within-subject responses across the four product categories. Note that total sample size is smaller than in Table 1 because of nonresponses for the toothpaste product category.
[b] Scheffe's test significant at the .05 level
[c] F ratio after effects of product involvement are removed
** $p<.01$
* $p<.05$

brand set sizes than the medium and high scoring groups. These findings lend support to the hypothesized directionality of brand set size with respect to market maven groups.

DISCUSSION

This research investigated how "market mavens" differ from other consumers (nonmavens) in categorizing the seven brand sets of the Brisoux and Laroche (1980) framework and whether these results can be generalized over diverse product categories. The findings indicate that market mavens indeed have larger salient, awareness, trial, and hold sets. The market maven processes more brands across a range of products as evidenced by his larger salient and awareness sets. Therefore, the market maven appears to have better "top of mind" awareness of more brands across different product categories. These findings support the initial Feick and Price (1987) conceptualization of the market maven. In addition, the results demonstrate that mavens have larger trial sets, indicative of their experiential buying behavior and general interest in gather marketplace information. Contrary to expectations, differences were not detected in the foggy, evoked, and reject sets.

However, an increase in overall brand awareness does not result in more acceptable (evoked) brands or unacceptable (reject) brands but in more hold brands (note that this increases the probability that any processed brand will end up in the hold set). In attempting to explain this contradiction, perhaps the maven views many product categories as being more complex and thus sees the process of categorizing any given brand as acceptable or unacceptable as more difficult. Perhaps he or she does not process as much information about any given brand and thus, though he or she is processing more brands, he or she is not processing them as deeply. Or perhaps the market maven faces information overload and thus cannot carry out the processing needed to judge brands as acceptable or unacceptable. As Munch (1990, p. 145) offers: "The limitations of our processing capabilities may cause the involved consumer to be no better informed than the uninvolved consumer." This reasoning may provide some insight into the divergent findings of the hold set as opposed that of the evoked and reject sets.

In general, what do these results suggest about the attractiveness of the market maven segment? As evidenced by their higher level of brand awareness and propensity to try more brands, market mavens appear to mirror the profile of opinion leaders and early purchasers. However, unlike the opinion leader who may serve as an influencer primarily for high involvement products, the market mavens may be an ideal target for diffusing information on low involvement products (e.g., razor blades, laundry detergent) where the communication generally concentrates on a wide array of related goods (such as in the case of supermarket advertising).

In spite of these observations, several concerns remain about targeting the market maven. First, since mavens tend to have larger hold sets and therefore are "undecided" about a greater proportion of brands than other consumers, their marketplace expertise may be either limited or narrowly defined. It is plausible that information provided by these consumers is related more to marketing mix factors such as price changes, product availability and promotional deals than with brand evaluation information. Second, the market maven, while appearing to be an active information gatherer may be a passive diffuser of new product information if he or she has not adopted a particular brand.

What are the strategic marketing implications of the market maven concept raised in this article? Clearly, a major challenge for brand managers in utilizing the word-of-mouth communication potential of the market maven in moving processed brands from less favorable brand sets (i.e., hold, foggy, reject) to more desirable categories (i.e., trial, evoked). Past research has indicated that market mavens are especially attentive to magazine, direct mail and local classified newspaper advertising (Price and Feick 1987; Higie, Feick, and Price 1987). Advertisers and other marketers might well be advised to use more informative and comparative promotional messages when using these media. Effective comparative advertising can be achieved, for example, by linking brands likely to be in consumer's evoked set (i.e., market leaders) with the advertised brand, thereby facilitating that brand's movement from the hold set.

LIMITATIONS AND FUTURE RESEARCH

It is important to note the limitations of this research in interpreting the findings. First, the sample was somewhat atypical of the sampled MSA and the U. S. population as a whole in that it was primarily female (76%), affluent (i.e., median income of $40-50,000), and older (median age of 40-49). A national sample with a demographic profile more representative of the U.S. population would have been desirable. A second concern has to do with the reliability and validity of the self-report measures of brand set size. That is, the survey method provides little control over the sequence of responses or the uniformity of time spend by each respondent. Third, it would have been desirable to investigate an even larger inventory of product or service categories. Studies of professional (e.g., legal, medical) and generic services (banks, dry cleaners) have shown that consumers exhibit very distinct search behaviors when selecting and purchasing services (e.g., Zeithmal 1981). We suspect that these differences would affect the brand (or service provider) categorization process as well.

Though this research contributes to the notion of the market maven as a knowledgeable marketplace influencer, several unanswered questions remain concerning the brand categorization process. For example:

- During the brand categorization process, do mavens require more or less time in moving brands to the evoked and trial sets?
- Can the brand categorization process be applied to services and other intangible market offerings?
- Can distinct brand categorization patterns be detected between market mavens, opinion leaders, and early purchasers?

In sum, this study of how informed consumers (market mavens) categorize brands differently both enriches our understanding of information processing and presents possible strategic opportunities to marketers. At a time when process oriented models of consumer behavior are sought, our research contributes to this end.

REFERENCES

Brisoux, Jacques E. and Michel Laroche (1980), "A Proposed Consumer Strategy of Simplification for Categorizing Brands, " in John D. Summey and R. D. Taylor Eds., *Proceedings of the Annual Meeting of the Southern Marketing Association*, Carbondale, IL: Southern Marketing Association, 112-114.

Brisoux, Jacques E., E. J. Cheron and M. Ferne (1986), "Elements de validation d'un modele de categorisation des marques," *Marketing Research, Analyzing Consumer Behavior Proceedings 13th International Research Seminar in Marketing*, I.R.E.T., LaLonde Les Maures (France), 91-112.

Brisoux, Jacques E. and Emmanuel J. Cheron (1990), "Brand Categorization and Product Involvement," *Advances in Consumer Research*, 17, Marvin Goldberg, Gerald Gorn and Richard Pollay Eds., Association for Consumer Research, 101-109.

Campbell, Brian M. (1969), "The Existence and Determinants of Evoked Set in Brand Choice Behavior," unpublished doctoral dissertation, Columbia University.

Cohen, Joel B. and Kunal Basu (1987), "Alternative Models of Categorization: Toward a Contingent Processing Framework," *Journal of Consumer Research*, 13 (March), 455-472.

Crowley, Ayn E. and John H. Williams (1991), "An Information Theoretic Approach to Understanding the Consideration Set/Awareness Set Proportion," *Advances in Consumer Research*, 19, Rebecca H. Holman and Michael R. Solomon, Eds., Association for Consumer Research, 780-787.

Feick, Lawrence F., and Linda L. Price (1987), "The Market Maven: A Diffuser of Marketplace Information," *Journal of Marketing*, 51 (January), 83-97.

Fortune, "Products of the Year," December 9, 1985, 106-112.

Gronhaug, Kjell (1974), "Some Factors Influencing the Size of the Buyer's Evoked Set," *European Journal of Marketing*, 8 (Winter), 232-41.

Gruca, Thomas S. (1989), "Determinants of Choice Set Size: An Alternative Method for Measuring Evoked Sets," *Advances in Consumer Research*, 16, Rebecca H. Holman and Michael R. Solomon, Eds., Association for Consumer Research, 515-521.

Higie, Robin A., Feick, Lawrence F. and Price, Linda L. (1987), "Types and Amount of Word-of-Mouth Communications About Retailers", *Journal of Retailing*, 63 (Fall), 260-278.

Howard, John A. (1977), *Consumer Behavior: Application of Theory*. Homewood, IL: Richard D. Irvin, Inc.

Jarvis, Lance P and Wilcox, James B. (1973), "Evoked Set Size - Some Theoretical Foundations and Empirical Evidence," *Combined Proceedings*, Thomas V. Greer, Ed., American Marketing Association, 18-37.

Kotler, Philip (1988), *Marketing Management*. Englewood Cliffs, NJ: Prentice-Hall, Inc.

Kotler, Philip and Gerald Zaltman (1976), "Targeting Prospects for a New Product," *Journal of Advertising Research*, 16 (February), 7-18.

Laroche, Michel, Jerry A Rosenblatt, Jacques E. Brisoux, and Robert Shimotakahara (1983), "Brand Categorization Strategies in RRB Situations: Some Empirical Results," *Advances in Consumer Research*, 10, Richard P. Bagozzi and Alice M. Tybout Eds., Ann Arbor, MI: Association for Consumer Research, 549-554.

Laroche, Michel, Jerry A. Rosenblatt and Ian Sinclair (1984), "Brand Categorization Strategies in an Extensive Problem Solving Situation: A Study of University Choice," *Advances in Consumer Research*, 11, Thomas C. Kinnear Ed., Ann Arbor, MI: Association for Consumer Research, 175-179.

Lichtenstein, Donald R. and Scot Burton (1990), "An Assessment of the Moderating Effects of Market Mavenism and Value Consciousness on Price-Quality Perception Accuracy," *Advances in Consumer Research*, 17, Marvin Goldberg, Gerald Gorn and Richard Pollay, Eds., Association for Consumer Research, 53-59.

Narayana, Chem L., Markin, Ron J. (1975), "Consumer Behavior and Product Performance: An Alternative Conceptualization," *Journal of Marketing*, 39, (October), 1-6.

Nowak, G. and C. Salmon (1987), "Measuring Involvement with Social Issues," Paper presented at the Association for Education in Journalism and Mass Communication, San Antonio.

Price, Linda L., Lawrence F. Feick, and Robin A. Higie (1987), "Information Sensitive Consumers and Market Information," *Journal of Consumer Affairs*, 21, No. 2, 328-341.

Reilly, Michael and Thomas L. Parkinson (1985), "Individual and Product Correlates of Evoked Set Size for Consumer Package Goods," *Advances in Consumer Research*, 12, Elizabeth C. Hirschman and Morris B. Holbrook, Eds., Association for Consumer Research, 101-109.

Sherif, Carolyn W. and Carl I. Hovland (1961), *Social Judgement: Assimilation and Contrast Effects in Communication and Attitude Change*. New Haven, CT: Yale University Press.

Slama, Mark E. and Terrell G. Williams (1990), "Generalization of the Market Maven's Information Provision Tendency Across Product Categories," *Advances in Consumer Research*, 17, Marvin Goldberg, Gerald Gorn and Richard Pollay Eds., Association for Consumer Research, 48-52.

Springle, Susan and Murphy A. Sewell (1987), "A Choice Set Model of Retail Selection," *Journal of Marketing*, 51, (April), 97-111.

Zaichkowsky, Judith Lynne (1985), "Measuring the Involvement Construct," *Journal of Marketing Research*, 12 (December), 341-352.

The Effect of Familiarity on Consumers' Choice Agendas

Judy A. Wagner, Virginia Polytechnic and State University
Noreen M. Klein, Virginia Polytechnic and State University

ABSTRACT

Consumers' choice agendas have a major impact on the information they seek and the choices they make. This paper presents empirical evidence of the top-down and bottom-up agendas described by Hauser (1986), and identifies subtypes of those agendas. Hauser's familiarity hypothesis, that bottom-up agendas will be favored at higher levels of familiarity and top-down agendas will be favored at lower levels of familiarity, may be supported for some subtypes of agendas, but not for others. In general, consumers' use of agendas, like other choice strategies, seems to be adaptive.

INTRODUCTION

"Look for the union label." "Holiday Inn. Stay with someone you know." Marketers expend considerable effort trying to change people's agendas, or the sequence of constraints they place on their decisions. Agendas are strategies of categorization and information selection that determine which attributes and alternatives are evaluated. Agendas impose a degree of organization on the buying problem, and thus make it easier for the buyer to narrow the consideration set down to the chosen alternative.

Hauser (1986) defines an agenda as a "sequence of constraints", and distinguishes between two types: top-down and bottom-up agendas. Consider his example of choosing a restaurant. The consumer may classify restaurants in terms of their cuisine - Indian, Chinese, and Italian. With a top-down agenda, the consumer constrains the choice set on the basis of that classification (e.g. deciding to eat Indian food that night), and evaluates only the restaurants that fall within a certain category. Other criteria, such as prior experience or price, may then be used to make a final selection.

A bottom-up agenda also assumes an initial categorization of alternatives. However, no single category is eliminated from consideration. Instead, a favorite is chosen from each category, and the final choice is then selected from the set of these favorites. In the example used above, the best of each of the Indian, Chinese, and Italian categories would be identified, and the final choice made from those three. Note that the alternatives in the Chinese and Italian categories have an increased probability of being chosen, compared to when a top-down agenda was used to eliminate these categories without looking at specific alternatives.

Changing the agenda structure, for instance by changing the initial constraint from cuisine to price level, may have a major impact on the final choice. In addition, the manner in which an agenda is processed (top-down versus bottom-up) alters both the probability of an alternative being evaluated and the set of alternatives to which it is directly compared. Both the structure of the agenda and the way it is processed should therefore affect choice.

From this intuitive restaurant example, one can imagine just how frequently some form of agenda is used by consumers in simplifying their purchase decisions. It is also easy to see how understanding agendas presents an opportunity for marketers. Because agendas change the choice probability of specific alternatives, the ability to influence how consumers partition and constrain their alternative sets could influence the marketplace success of a particular product or service. The advertising examples given above illustrate marketing efforts to constrain alternatives in a manner that shows the focal product to advantage.

Given the importance of agendas as a means of simplifying and influencing consumer choice, the following issues are of interest to both academicians and practitioners.

1. How closely do agendas used in consumer choices approximate the types formally modeled by Hauser (1986)?
2. What individual and situational factors lead to the use of top-down versus bottom-up agendas?
3. What is the impact of an agenda on the objective (accuracy and efficiency) and subjective (perceived difficulty and confidence) outcomes of a choice?
4. What marketing strategies most effectively influence agendas?
5. In what situations is a consumer's agenda most subject to external influence?

A series of programmatic studies is needed to answer these questions. In the current paper, we focus on two specific research objectives. These are:

1. Provide empirical evidence of bottom-up agendas, and investigate how closely natural agendas, both top-down and bottom-up, conform to the models analyzed by Hauser (1986).
2. Empirically test the familiarity hypothesis: that bottom-up agendas are favored when familiarity is high, and top-down agendas are favored when familiarity is low.

Research on Agendas

The formal models of agendas include well known choice models such as elimination-by-aspects (EBA; Tversky 1972), the Hierarchical Elimination Model (HEM; Tversky and Sattath 1979), and the Generalized Elimination Model (GEM; Hauser 1986). Hauser (1986) analyzed the effects of changes in agendas for these decision models, demonstrating how the probability of a particular choice outcome can be enhanced or reduced, depending upon the type of agenda used. Kahn, Moore, and Glazer (1987) and Glazer, Kahn, and Moore (1991) examined the effect of imposing external constraints (partitions of brands not normally used by the consumer) on top-down agendas, and found different effects on choice than those predicted by HEM. Other work shows that cutoffs that form top-down agendas are influenced by preference structures and contextual factors (Klein and Bither 1987; Huber and Klein 1991).

Both formal mathematical models and empirical investigations have focused on top-down agendas, and their use by consumers to simplify choice has been well documented. Much less is known about the frequency or form of bottom-up agendas. Given the fact that a bottom-up strategy requires the evaluation of all alternatives, it may not be frequently used. Although Hauser (1986) analyzed simple agendas which were completely top-down or bottom-up, he does acknowledge that a mixed agenda is possible. For example, a consumer might quickly eliminate all Italian restaurants in a top-down fashion and then use a bottom-up agenda to compare favorites from the remaining categories. The use of adaptive strategies, in which the consumer changes the basic choice strategy as the decision progresses, has been well documented in process-tracing studies of consumer choice (Payne, Bettman, and Johnson 1988).

What determines which type of agenda buyers use: top-down, bottom-up, or mixed? Hauser (1986) proposed that one key factor is the consumer's ability to predict the utility of particular alternatives. If one can easily evaluate how much an alternative will be liked, then the series of bottom-up comparisons will be easier and tend to yield a high quality choice. If the more intensive evaluations of a bottom-up process still leave a large degree of uncertainty about which alternative is best, then a top-down agenda is advantageous. A top-down process is less effortful, because many alternatives are quickly eliminated, and it insures that a preferred value on the partitioning attribute is achieved.

Hauser (1986) proposed that a top-down agenda is more likely to be used when one is unfamiliar with the alternatives, when the cost of search is high, or when uncertainty is high. Thus, in our restaurant example, when consumers are new in town and know little about the restaurants from which they have to choose, they will tend to simplify the choice by first selecting a preferred cuisine category. On the other hand, individuals who are very familiar with the restaurants in the choice will find it relatively easy to select a favorite restaurant for each cuisine, and compare them for a final selection. This familiarity hypothesis has never been empirically tested. The following study was designed to identify both top-down and bottom-up agendas and test the familiarity hypothesis.

METHOD

Product Selection and Sample

Selecting a context for measuring and evaluating agendas was a nontrivial problem. Several criteria were important. First, respondents had to have a wide range of familiarity with available alternatives in the product category. For both theoretical and practical reasons, the product context had to provide commonly used categories that could be easily verbalized by respondents. Respondents had to be sufficiently interested in the product, and find the choice to be of sufficient complexity, that agendas were likely to be used. After extensive pretesting, a video rental was selected as the choice context. This product was appealing because video stores arrange films by categories (e.g. drama, comedy), so that respondents are used to seeing choice alternatives within a category structure.

Undergraduate students were recruited, using extra credit and cash incentives. Although thirty students responded to the initial questionnaire in the first stage of the study, the time consuming process of creating individualized stimuli for the second stage and tracing the choice processes limited the sample in the second stage to eight respondents.

Research Design

We conducted a within-subjects laboratory experiment, in which we created three levels of familiarity (high, moderate and low). In the High Familiarity condition, the choice alternatives were relatively recent movies that the respondents had already seen. Movies in the Moderate Familiarity condition were relatively recent movies that respondents had not yet seen. Movies in the Low Familiarity condition were somewhat obscure movies from twenty to thirty years ago, which pretesting showed were not recognized by respondents. At each of the three levels of familiarity, respondents made two choices in succession from different sets of movies. This repetition of the condition allowed for adaptation and greater respondent confidence regarding the level of familiarity. In all, respondents made six choices.

The selected choice context allowed us to make a strong manipulation of familiarity. Respondents could easily make preference judgments about movies they had seen (in the High Familiarity condition), which is essential in facilitating bottom-up agendas. In contrast, they should be highly uncertain about their evaluations of the obscure movies in the Low Familiarity condition; this uncertainty should lead to greater use of the movie category information, as in a top-down agenda.

Procedure

Data collection took place in two stages. In the initial classroom questionnaire session, respondents answered questions about 140 movies. Twenty movies were listed in each of seven categories - drama, action, romance, horror, comedy, family, and science fiction. These movies were recent films which had received national distribution and promotion, and which might be generally recognized even if they had not been seen. The rated movies were clustered into categories, with the category name provided at the beginning of each cluster for easy reference. Subjects indicated on the questionnaire whether or not they had seen each of the movies. Respondents also rated their preferences for the seven movie categories on a seven-point scale. We also measured other perceptions about the movies and movie categories, but these data are not relevant to this paper.

The responses from the questionnaire were used to create individualized choice sets for the three familiarity conditions. In the second stage of the study, each respondent came to an individual session in which they were presented with six choices, two for each of the three levels of familiarity (high, moderate and low). The order of presentation of choice sets at each of the three levels of familiarity was varied across respondents. However, the two choices from a particular level of familiarity were presented in succession to allow the respondent to adapt to that level of familiarity.

Although movies in seven categories had been rated, it was not always possible to find enough titles in each category to create the familiarity conditions (e.g. someone may never have seen any of the horror films). Thus, one respondent made choices from five movie categories; all other respondents chose from six categories.

The choice materials consisted of an information board for each movie category in the choice. The front of each board was labeled with the category name, and the reverse side provided places to insert five cards, each printed with a movie title. The boards for a particular choice were placed in random order on a long table, with only the category name showing. Just as consumers in an actual video store could only be physically present in one section of the store at a time, respondents in the study were told that they could "enter one section," or turn over one information board at a time. They had to return the board to its original face-down position before proceeding to another category. Categories could be returned to as many times as the respondent wanted. Also, just as a consumer might carry one or more video boxes with them as they move about a store, respondents were told that they had the option of removing and "carrying along" any of the cards for movies that they were considering. Cards could also be "returned to the shelf" if they were no longer being considered, by placing them on top of the relevant board.

As each of the six choices was made, a concurrent protocol was tape recorded. Respondents were instructed to think aloud while making a choice of one movie to rent. Subjects were also requested to consider only their own preferences in making their decision, rather than the preferences of some other party with whom they might normally watch a movie. Before each choice, respondents were told the kind of movies from which they would be choosing (i.e. "movies that you have indicated you have seen", "recent movies you have indicated you have not seen", and "older movies that you probably haven't heard of"). This was done because pretesting had revealed a natural preference for unseen, current movies, which would actually occur in only one condition (moderate familiarity). Unless the content of the choice was made clear to respondents, they tended to execute a search for such movies and failed to evaluate the movies actually available until their search had proved fruitless. The instructions allowed them to set appropriate expectations for the level of familiarity.

Measures

Concurrent protocols were necessary to trace the choice process in sufficient detail to allow accurate identification of agenda types. Early pre-testing revealed the difficulty of determining the existence, structure, and type of agenda that respondents were using in their choices. Various formats were pretested in an effort to elicit agendas that could be clearly identified. Format proved to have a very strong effect. When alternatives were not presorted by categories (such as movie type), the use of category structure was idiosyncratic and often not spontaneously verbalized. Allowing respondents to enter only one category at a time, and allowing them to remove films from the category as one would in a video store, greatly facilitated the identification of agendas.

To clarify even further what process was being used, a log was kept to supplement the protocols. The experimenter recorded the order in which categories were entered and which titles were removed for further consideration or returned to the shelf. This information was later added to the protocol transcriptions so that it would be clear what stimuli were in front of the respondent at each point in the choice protocol.

Manipulation checks and perceptions of the choice process were measured after each choice. These included perceived knowledge of and familiarity with the alternatives in the choice, confidence and satisfaction with the choice, its difficulty and how much the respondent wanted to see the video selected.

RESULTS

Manipulation Checks

Responses to the two items measuring familiarity with and knowledge of the choice alternatives had a correlation of .86, and so were averaged to test whether familiarity was successfully manipulated. A 3 (familiarity) X 2 (repeated choice) within-subjects ANOVA showed a significant main effect for familiarity ($p<.001$, eta=.94), indicating a successful manipulation. These averaged ratings had means of 6.6, 4.8, and 1.5, for the high, moderate, and low familiarity conditions. Unexpectedly, respondents also felt more familiar and knowledgeable about the movies in the second choices made within each level of manipulated familiarity (mean=4.6) than they did with the first choices (mean=4.0, $p=.009$, eta=.80). We believe that in the process of making the first choice within each familiarity level, respondents became more comfortable with the type of movie presented in that choice set. This may have created a sense of greater familiarity.

Coding Agendas

A total of forty-eight protocols were analyzed, six protocols for each of the eight respondents. The protocols were first coded for type of agenda, with classifications of: 1) bottom-up, 2) top-down, and 3) mixed agendas. As expected, respondents used many variations of the two agenda types identified by Hauser (1986). In the initial coding, a strategy was labeled top-down if it involved the elimination of alternatives based on their category, rather than on individual merits. A strategy was coded as bottom-up if it focused on the evaluation and disposition of specific alternatives. Combinations of these two processes in one choice were labeled mixed agendas. Coding by two independent judges showed inter-rater agreement in 90 percent of the cases.

As shown in Table 1, only two agendas revealed a totally top-down strategy, while 19 (forty percent) were coded as strictly bottom-up. The majority (fifty-six percent) represented mixed agendas which combined top-down eliminations and bottom-up processing.

TABLE 1
Frequency of Agenda Types

Top-Down Agendas	2	(4%)
Bottom-Up Agendas	19	(40%)
Mixed Agendas	<u>27</u>	(56%)
	48	

Although many of the agendas were classified as bottom-up or top-down, only in the case of the two top-down agendas did the strategies exactly match the definitions offered by Hauser (1986). For every protocol coded as bottom-up, the definition had to be relaxed in some manner. For instance, some respondents selected more than one movie from a category, rather than picking only the best. Alternatively, some respondents chose favorites from only a subset of the categories, even though they examined all of them. Instead of comparing the best of each category, respondents sometimes used an ongoing elimination process in which possible choices were compared to the currently favored movie. In general, few agendas followed the elegant formulation of bottom-up strategies presented by Hauser (1986). It appears that agendas are flexible, and may be constructed as the choice evolves.

The most common pattern seen in mixed agendas was the use of a top-down elimination of one or more categories followed by some approximation of a bottom-up agenda. This finding agrees with research that describes phased strategies, with early elimination of categories of alternatives followed by more intensive evaluation of remaining alternatives (Bettman 1979).

Due to the limited sample size, few statistical tests of agenda types were conducted. However, the data were examined with respect to how often each of the two types of processing occurred at different levels of familiarity, as shown in Table 2. Note that a mixed agenda would be represented as having both types of processing. There appears to be no support for the familiarity hypothesis in these limited data. Bottom-up and top-down processing are used with similar frequency in all familiarity conditions.

TABLE 2
Frequency of Processing Type by Level of Familiarity

	Familiarity		
	High	Mod	Low
Bottom-Up	15	16	15
Top-Down	<u>10</u>	<u>8</u>	<u>11</u>
	25	24	26

Agenda Subtypes

In the course of coding protocols, it became apparent that there were certain identifiable variations on the top-down and bottom-up agendas. To gain a better understanding of these patterns, all agendas were coded with respect to subtypes. Inter-rater agreement was .94. Table 3 shows the frequency of these subtypes at the three levels of familiarity. Two forms of top-down strategies seemed distinct. A top-down agenda was coded "Favorite Category" when the respondent first made a choice about a particular *category* from which to select a movie, and then evaluated the specific movies in that category. In a top-down "Elimination" agenda, the respondent eliminated one or two less preferred categories, and then did further processing on remaining categories. The basic distinction between the two subtypes is the focus on preferred, as opposed to undesirable, categories.

TABLE 3
Frequency of Top-Down Agenda Subtypes by Familiarity Level

Top-Down	Familiarity		
	High	Mod	Low
Favorite Category	1	1	5
Elimination	9	7	8
	10	8	13

There is no significant relationship between familiarity and subtype ($X^2=2.6$, $p=.27$), the small numbers in the Favorite Category subtype are problematic. Still, it is interesting that different patterns emerge for the two subtypes across familiarity conditions, and this should be investigated in future research. According to the familiarity hypothesis, a greater number of top-down strategies should appear in low familiarity conditions. The elimination of disliked categories does not vary across familiarity levels.

This suggests that a general editing process occurs regardless of the difficulty of evaluating specific alternatives. This editing might be for simplification purposes alone. However, it is also plausible that certain categories of movies are easily identified as having sufficiently low utility that evaluation of specific alternatives is unnecessary (e.g. all horror films are disgusting). Although the specific alternatives in the high and moderate familiarity condition may be easy to judge, category information may make such judgments unnecessary. This type of opportunistic editing through a top-down agenda is unrelated to familiarity.

The data on the Favorite Category agenda follows the pattern suggested by the familiarity hypothesis, but the sample size prevents any reliance on that pattern at present. However, note that a Favorite Category agenda reduces the cost of evaluation more sharply than an Elimination agenda, because more categories are ignored. When familiarity is low, it is logical to avoid this evaluation cost because it is unlikely to pay off in a higher quality choice. Further research should explore whether decision makers seek a favorite category more often when alternatives are hard to judge.

The two subtypes of bottom-up agendas shown in Table 4 clearly had divergent relationships to familiarity ($X^2=12.6$, $p=.003$). The first subgroup is labeled Bottom-up Comparison agendas. In these strategies, one or more movies were chosen from several categories. In some cases, these favorites were evaluated against each other to reach a final choice. This agenda type was most similar to Hauser's model of bottom-up agendas. In other bottom-up comparison agendas, the respondent conducted ongoing eliminations; if a new contender was found, it was compared to the current favorite. If one seemed sufficiently less desirable, it was returned to the shelf. In some cases, respondents did both ongoing eliminations and an evaluation of a final comparison set. Table 4 shows some support for the familiarity hypothesis for this subtype; there are fewer Bottom-up Comparison agendas when familiarity is low. This follows Hauser's logic that when it is difficult to predict the utility of specific alternatives, there will be less incentive to intensively evaluate them.

TABLE 4
Frequency of Bottom-Up Agenda Subtypes by Familiarity Level

Bottom-up	Familiarity		
	High	Mod	Low
Comparison	14	13	6
Satisficing	1	4	10
	15	17	16

The second type of bottom-up strategy was labeled Bottom-Up, Satisficing. As with the other bottom-up agendas, this processing involved specific alternatives rather than categories. However, in these strategies the respondent's processing did not involve comparisons of favored alternatives but rather a search for one that was minimally acceptable. In thirteen of the fifteen instances of this subtype, respondents searched all movie categories but found only one potentially acceptable movie, or none at all. In the latter case, a new strategy, such as returning to a preferred category, was likely to be tried.

The familiarity hypothesis asserts that bottom-up agendas are most likely when consumers can easily evaluate the utility of the alternatives. Yet in Table 4 we see that many respondents tried to evaluate specific alternatives even when they had little or no way of doing so, rather than resort to a top-down category-based strategy. Respondents who took this approach often expressed great frustration at not being able to find a movie that they recognized and at not being able to evaluate the relative desirability of the low familiarity movies. It appeared that to a large extent, categories were irrelevant, and that each movie was being compared to some minimum standard for recognition.

One handicap in understanding these bottom-up agendas is the difficulty of determining how important a role the categories played in them. Many respondents who used a bottom-up, satisficing agenda focused on titles without commenting on or obviously using category information. Given that Bottom-up, Satisficing processing tended to produce no more than one viable option (if that), it is difficult to say whether a category-based agenda was operative. The fact that two different patterns emerged for the frequency of these subtypes across familiarity conditions warrants further investigation.

DISCUSSION

What conclusions can be drawn from this exploratory study of agendas? We must first acknowledge the danger of overinterpreting the results from a small sample. With that caveat, we think that these results may be useful.

Bottom-up Agendas

Our first objective was to provide some empirical evidence for the existence of bottom-up agendas. While no strategy that was observed followed the exact form of the model provided by Hauser (1986), the essential elements of the bottom-up agenda strategy were present in the 33 protocols that contained some bottom-up, comparison processing. This provides preliminary evidence of bottom-up agendas in a situation which was created to make them most apparent.

It is also quite striking that few of the protocols matched the normative models presented by Hauser (1986). Respondents seemed quite comfortable with flexible strategies. When two movies in the same category seemed attractive, both were taken for further consideration. Some respondents did pairwise comparisons for some pairs of movies they had selected from the sections, while they delayed other (more difficult?) comparisons until all categories had been searched. The finding that agendas are flexible, and that consumers appear to adapt them to the particular choice set at hand, fits in well with rapidly accumulating evidence of adaptive choice strategies (Bettman, Johnson and Payne 1991).

The difficulty of constructing a laboratory situation in which bottom-up agendas are measurable and likely to occur leads inevitably to the question of when such agendas are likely to occur naturally. Hauser (1986) suggests that bottom-up agendas will be favored when familiarity is high, uncertainty about alternatives is low, and search cost is low. However, we discovered in pretesting that unless the category structure was made very salient, with alternatives presorted, respondents did not tend to choose and compare category favorites. Products with well learned, regularly used category structures (colas versus non-colas, fast-food versus regular restaurants) seem the most likely candidates for bottom-up processing. Top-down processing, on the other hand, requires only that you distinguish preferred from less preferred levels of any attribute, making clear categories less essential. For example, you might decide not to consider cars priced higher than $12,000, even though you do not normally group cars on that basis.

Another factor that seems likely to affect the incidence of bottom-up processing is the variance in utility, both between categories and between alternatives within categories. As discussed above, even when the movies were highly familiar, a large enough variance in the expected utility of movies within different categories may be sufficient reason for a top-down agenda. If you hate horror films, there is no sense in picking your favorite. Also, when there is little variance in the utility of alternatives within a category, picking your favorite becomes more difficult and may be avoided in some categories by top-down eliminations. In contrast, when it is relatively easy to specify your favorite, and categories are similar in utility (e.g. I like both dramas and comedies), finding the best of the best in each category makes sense.

Finally, using a bottom-up agenda may be more natural when favorite alternatives for the salient categories are stored in memory. For example, when a decision is made about which restaurant to patronize, someone who is highly familiar may automatically consider only their favorite Chinese restaurant, their favorite Italian restaurant, etc. The costly alternative comparisons within categories are avoided, and bottom-up processing becomes more feasible. These remembered favorites constitute a consideration set. Of course, it could be argued that processing such a set, apart from the original within-category selections, does not constitute an agenda.

Top-down Agendas

More is known about the natural occurrence of top-down agendas. These common editing strategies are used to simplify complex choices and have been identified in many process-tracing studies. In some respects, it was surprising not to find a greater use of these agendas; 40 percent of the strategies in this study had no top-down processing of categories. One possible reason is that respondents found the task novel and entertaining, and may have searched for specific alternatives out of curiosity as to what we had chosen as alternatives. Another explanation relates to a possible weakness of our product choice. Although the categories used to sort movies were very realistic in terms of respondents' experiences in video stores, the categories were not always mutually exclusive. For example, a film can be both a drama and a romance, both a comedy and a family picture, and so on. This means that the categories may not have been very diagnostic about the desirability of specific alternatives they contained. Category information may therefore have been slighted as a basis for decision making, and more information about specific movies may have been sought.

A final explanation for the lack of top-down processing is that a respondent's natural category structure for videos may have diverged from the imposed categories. For example, if movie type is unimportant to a respondent, there is little incentive to use the category to narrow the choice set. Instead, he or she may have used their knowledge of specific alternatives to impose other top-down constraints on the choice set. These constraints may have appeared to be bottom-up processing in our analysis. However, we found no evidence in the protocols of the systematic use of other criteria.

The Familiarity Hypothesis

The second objective of this study was to provide an empirical test of the familiarity hypothesis: that bottom-up agendas are used more frequently as familiarity increases, and that top-down agendas are used more often as familiarity decreases. The results seem to depend on the manner in which agendas are defined and protocols are coded. If all bottom-up and top-down strategies are considered together, familiarity appears to have no relationship to agenda type. However, bottom-up comparison agendas did conform to the familiarity hypothesis. Further descriptive research on agendas will have to contend with definitional and classification problems.

Other Issues

Pretesting demonstrated the importance of format in decision making. During pretesting, respondents increased their report of category use (constraints) when alternatives were presented in categorized format. Additionally, respondents used the exact category names provided for them. When choices were made with no categories or alternatives suggested, the apparent use of agendas was very limited. This finding indicates the potential of marketing efforts to set agendas for customers. Explicitly guiding consumers in devising constraints on alternatives, either through advertising or a specially tailored sales approach, seems more likely to be effective in influencing choice than simply providing unstructured information. Providing the appropriate format for information could have great impact on the shaping of decisions.

Additional work on agendas is warranted. Coding and definitional issues need to be resolved, and the methodology developed for tracing the agenda process needs to be tested in a variety of contexts. There are challenging issues related to both naturally occurring and externally imposed agendas. There appears to be no simple relationship between agenda type and familiarity, perhaps because there are few simple agendas. Greater understanding of this topic will require further normative and descriptive analyses.

REFERENCES

Bettman, James R. (1979), An Information Processing Theory of Choice, Reading, MA: Addison-Wesley.

Bettman, James R., Eric J. Johnson, and John W. Payne (1991) "Consumer Decision Making", in Handbook of Consumer Behavior, eds. Thomas S. Robertson and Harold H. Kassarjian, Englewood Cliffs: Prentice-Hall, 50-84.

Glazer, Rashi, Barbara E. Kahn, and William L. Moore (1991) "The Influence of External Constraints on Brand Choice: The Lone Alternative Effect," *Journal of Consumer Research*, 18 (June), 119-127.

Hauser, John R. (1986), "Agendas and Consumer Choice," *Journal of Marketing Research*, 23 (August), 199-212.

Huber, Joel and Noreen Klein (1991), "Adapting Cutoffs to the Choice Environment: The Effects of Attribute Correlation and Reliability," *Journal of Consumer Research*, 18 (December), 346-357.

Kahn, Barbara, William L. Moore, and Rashi Glazer (1987), "Experiments in Constrained Choice," *Journal of Consumer Research*, 14 (June), 96-113.

Klein, Noreen M. and Stewart W. Bither (1987), "An Investigation of Utility-Directed Cutoff Selection," *Journal of Consumer Research*, 14 (September), 240-256.

Payne, John W., James R. Bettman, and Eric J. Johnson (1988) "Adaptive Strategy Selection in Decision Making," *Journal of Experimental Psychology: Learning, Memory, and Cognition*, 14, 534-552.

Tversky, Amos (1972) "Elimination-by-Aspects: A Theory of Choice," *Psychological Review*, 79 (July), 281-299.

Tversky, Amos and Shmuel Sattath (1979), "Preference Trees," *Psychological Review*, 84 (July), 327-352.

Consumers Reaction to Product Failure: Impact of Product Involvement and Knowledge
T. N. Somasundaram, University of San Diego

ABSTRACT

This paper investigates differences in how consumers explain why a product is a "failure" i.e. falls short of expectations. It extends the Attribution Theory framework that has been used by other researchers (e.g., Folkes, 1984 and Folkes and Kostos, 1986) by incorporating the concepts of consumers' product involvement and causal complexity stemming from product knowledge. It is suggested that consumers who are more involved are likely to be more motivated to engage in causal search following a determination of product failure. Further, consumers with higher levels of product knowledge or experience with the product class are likely to be more causally complex i.e., assign blame for the failure over a greater number of reasons and are therefore likely to be less certain as to the cause of failure. Hence, they are likely to form less extreme beliefs and attitudes about the product. These differences in how consumers explain why a product has failed are likely to impact subsequently, their choice of remedial actions.

CONSUMER SATISFACTION JUDGMENTS

The satisfaction of consumer needs lies at the very heart of the marketing concept. Satisfaction with a given brand is supposed to lead to a higher likelihood of it being repurchased, brand loyalty, positive word of mouth and higher profitability for the firm. Dissatisfaction is supposed to reduce the likelihood of attaining these goals. Further, it may generate negative word of mouth, complaints, demand for substitute goods, refunds and even litigation (Day, 1977; Richins, 1982; Bearden and Teel, 1983 and Folkes, 1984). In extreme cases, consumer dissatisfaction is likely to encourage the imposition of new legislative controls on an entire industry as was the case recently with the airline industry and its poor 'on time' performance.

Folkes (1984) proposed an Attribution theory framework for predicting consumer responses to product failure. Attribution theory pertains to the processes by which people make causal inferences from the information they receive. Within the context of consumer dissatisfaction and complaining behavior, attribution theory suggests that the perceived reason for a product's failure will influence how the consumer will respond.

Causes of product failure were classified by Folkes in terms of their underlying properties. These were 1) Stability, i.e., whether the cause is temporary or will reoccur, 2) Locus, i.e., is the cause located in the seller/ manufacturer or in the consumer? and 3) Controllability i.e., did the party responsible for the failure have any control over the outcome? Folkes suggested that the underlying causal properties influenced three types of consumer responses: (1) expectancy reactions, (2) marketplace equity reactions, and (3) anger reactions. It was shown that stable attributions lead to certainty about a product's failure and a preference for a refund rather than an exchange. When product failure is firm-related, the consumer is perceived to be owed a refund and an apology but when a failure is perceived to be consumer-related, neither a refund nor an apology is expected. When the failure is firm-related and it is perceived to have control over the reason for product failure, consumers feel angry and seek to hurt the firms business.

INTENSITY OF CAUSAL SEARCH AND PATTERNS OF CAUSAL ATTRIBUTIONS

Two issues neglected by the foregoing research relate to: 1) The intensity of causal search and 2) The patterns of causal attributions. By intensity of causal search we mean the volume of cognitive activity as measured by the number of causal thoughts evident in the subjects' thought protocols. By patterns of causal attributions we mean the locus of the attributions i.e. buyer or seller and subjects' judgments as to the controllability and stability of the factors causing failure. This paper reports preliminary results of an investigation currently in progress into these two issues by incorporating the concept of consumers' product involvement and product knowledge.

Role of Involvement

The search for the causes of product failure is a type of information processing activity undertaken following a determination that a product is unsatisfactory. The intensity of such information processing is likely to be a function of the consumers motivation to process the information. Consumers' product involvement is conceptualized as perceived personal relevance or importance the consumer assigns to the product. To the extent that a product is viewed as personally relevant in that it is perceived in some way to be instrumental in achieving their personal goals and values, the consumer is likely to be more motivated to process information about it (Mitchell, 1981 and Celsi and Olson, 1988). In the context of causal attribution search, consumers with higher involvement are more likely to ponder over the causes of a product's failure to live up to expectations. They are therefore likely to expend more cognitive effort in their causal search.

Role of Causal Complexity

There is a substantial body of research that suggests that the level of knowledge a consumer has about a product affects the amount and type of information processing (e.g. Bettman and Park, 1980; Johnson and Russo, 1981 and 1984). Sujan (1985) suggested that knowledgeable consumers were more likely to be able to discern discrepancies between a stimulus and prior expectations. Somasundaram (1989) showed that consumers with more knowledge were able to better discern when a product's performance did not match expectations for a product of that type. It is suggested in this paper that the number of plausible reasons (causes) advanced to explain product failure is likely to be a function of the consumers' knowledge or experience with a product class. For example, an avid photographer (expert) as compared to an amateur (novice) may be able to advance a wider range of reasons as to why a particular set of photographs received from a film processing facility turned out to be bad.

Further, the amount or proportion of total blame the expert as compared to the novice assigns to a given cause is likely to be different. The isolation of one or few causes is referred to as low causal complexity by Mizerski (1978) who showed that individuals who were low in causal complexity (causally simple individuals), as compared to causally complex individuals, tended to be more confident in their attributions and formed more extreme beliefs and attitudes about a stimulus.

Therefore, it is suggested here that less knowledgeable consumers are likely to be causally simple while more knowledgeable consumers are likely to be causally complex. In our photography example, more knowledgeable consumers may conclude that poor color fidelity in photograph prints received from the processing facility were the result of inherent color bias associated with that brand of film; incorrect tonal balance settings by the facility personnel; weak chemicals; or defective printing paper. Given the number of plausible causes and in the absence of further information, they may conclude that each of the causes was equally likely. Less knowledgeable consumers on the other hand might lump the majority of the blame on one or few causes. Consequently, following Mizerski (1978), it is expected that less knowledgeable consumers are likely to be more confident in their judgements as to why a product has failed and more likely to form extreme beliefs and attitudes about the product.

In addition, knowledgeable consumers and less knowledgeable consumers may differ in the locus of their attributions as well as their judgments as to the stability and controllability of the causes. Knowledge is also likely to impact the accuracy of the attributions.

HYPOTHESES

Based on the foregoing literature review, the following hypotheses are proposed:

Effect of Involvement:

Since involvement has been shown to have motivational properties,

H1: Consumers who have higher product involvement, as compared to consumers who are less involved, are more likely to engage in causal search following product "failure".

Effect of Knowledge:

Since greater knowledge translates into a greater ability to process information,

H2: Among consumers who do engage in causal search, more knowledgeable consumers (experts) as compared to less knowledgeable consumers (novices) are likely to advance a larger number of separately identified 'causes' for the failure.

Further,

H3: Since experts are likely to allocate blame for product failure to more reasons as compared to novices they are likely to be less confident about their attributions and likely to form less extreme beliefs and attitudes about the product.

PILOT EXPERIMENT

An experiment was designed to examine the differences in how consumers explain why a product has failed. The experiment involved subjects evaluation of a pair of photographs purported to have been received by them from a processing facility. Knowledge of photography and Involvement were not manipulated. Knowledge was measured using a 15 item multiple choice test designed to assess objective knowledge about photography. Involvement was measured using the Personal Involvement Inventory (PII) developed by Zaichkowsky (1984). The method of analysis was analysis of variance with involvement and knowledge as covariates.

Data was obtained from 80 male and female graduate business students at a small private university. They were presented with a pair of photographs purportedly processed at a local film processing facility. One photograph in the pair represented the "expected" photograph that they were supposed to receive while the other represented the "actual" photograph. Half the sample was assigned to the Success treatment and the other half to the Failure treatment. In the Failure treatment, the "actual" photograph suffered from several flaws: some caused by the picture taker such as poor composition and exposure selection and other flaws caused by the processing facility such as incorrect tonal balance and color proportions. In the Success treatment, both photographs in the pair were identical.

Subjects evaluated the two photographs in the pair and indicated in a thought elicitation task if and why they perceived the actual picture to be different from the expected picture. These thoughts were coded and content analyzed for distinct causal dimensions. The responses were categorized as "Causal Thoughts" and "Other Product Related Thoughts" and "Irrelevant Thoughts". The sum of "Causal thoughts and "Other Product Related Thoughts", "Total Thoughts", was taken to indicate intensity of causal search. After the open-ended responses, subjects responded to likert type statements relating to the extent the actual results matched their expectations and their level of satisfaction. They were then asked to allocate blame on a constant sum scale to the photographer, or the processing facility or to chance/ random factors. They also responded to a scale designed to determine their level of confidence in their attributions. An on-going study refines the foregoing approach and will be explained in the Modified Experiment section.

RESULTS

Manipulation Check:

Subjects responded to the statement: "How would you rate the actual picture as compared to the expected picture" on a 5-point scale anchored by "Much Worse than Expected" represented by 1 and "Much Better than Expected" represented by 5. An Analysis of Variance (ANOVA) with Success/Failure as the main factor and Involvement and knowledge as covariates revealed a significant main effect for the success/failure treatment ($F=118.35$, $p<0.000$). The cell means show that the actual picture is much worse than expected in the failure condition (mean=1.34) than in the success condition (mean=3.00). Subjects also responded to the statement measuring satisfaction with the outcome. The ANOVA results again show a significant main effect for the Success/failure treatment ($F=55.91$, $p<0.000$) with higher satisfaction scores in the success condition (mean=3.58) than in the failure condition (mean=1.82). Taken together, the results suggest that the manipulation of success and failure was successful.

Intensity of Causal Search

In H1 it was suggested that subjects motivation to engage in causal search would increase as a function of their level of involvement. Therefore the total number of thoughts generated when taken as a measure of cognitive activity would be greater as involvement increased. The ANOVA results for Total Thoughts as the dependant variable show a significant main effect for the success/failure treatment ($F=3.55$, $P<0.06$). The cell means suggest that the total number of thoughts subjects generated was greater in the failure condition (mean=5.89) as compared to the success condition (mean=4.97). The covariate involvement was not significant, thus H1 was not supported. However, the covariate Knowledge was significant ($F=5.99$, $p<0.017$) suggesting that higher levels of knowledge results in a greater ability to engage in cognitive activity.

Patterns of causal search

In H2 it was suggested that more knowledgeable subjects would have a greater ability to generate a large number of plausible causes to explain the product failure. Thus we would expect the thought protocols of these subjects should contain statements that pertain to distinct causal dimensions or Causal Thoughts. The thought protocols should also contain proportionately, fewer Other Product Related Thoughts. The ANOVA results with causal thoughts as the dependant variable showed a highly significant main effect for the success/failure treatment ($F=27.97$, $p<0.000$). The covariate for knowledge was also significant ($F=4.80$, $p<0.03$) suggesting that subjects with higher levels of product knowledge were more capable of generating a large number of plausible causes. Thus H2 was supported. The main effect for success/failure condition supports the notion that a discrepancy between expectations and actual performance in more likely to generate cognitive activity (mean=4.13 versus 1.48) than one in which expectations and performance are more congruent (Sujan, 1985; Somasundaram, 1989). The results for Other Product Related Thoughts show a main effect for the success/failure treatment ($F=12.29$, $p<0.001$). More Other Product Related Thoughts were in evidence in the success condition (means=3.48 versus 1.76) than in the failure condition. The covariate knowledge, however, was not significant.

Extremity of beliefs

In H3 it was suggested that subjects who advanced a large number of plausible causes when compared to subjects who advanced fewer causes, would be less certain that they have correctly determined the locus of blame for the failure. Our analysis for the failure condition alone, suggests that neither the number of causes advanced, nor the level of knowledge or the pattern of allocation of blame to oneself or the processing facility was significant in explaining subjects confidence in the accuracy of their blame assignment. Thus H3 was not supported.

DISCUSSION

The results that have been reported in this paper were based on a pilot experiment that has subsequently been refined and is currently being rerun. The preliminary results are encouraging in that they suggest that involvement and product knowledge are important variables that might impact the extent and pattern of causal search conducted by a consumer when a product has failed to perform as expected.

MODIFIED EXPERIMENT

Based on results obtained from the pilot study, the experiment has been made considerably more elaborate. Each subject will view two pairs of photographs where one pair will depict a prominent and well liked building that is on campus. The other pair will depict an architecturally similar off-campus building that is only moderately well known. Thus following Celsi and Olson (1988) we will be manipulating situation specific involvement.

Subjects will be put into three treatment conditions where one-third of the subjects will see two pairs of pictures both of which are successes. One-third of the subjects will be in a failure treatment where both pairs of pictures they see will represent failure. Finally, one-third of the subjects will be in an ambiguous treatment where they will see one pair of pictures that represent success and one pair that represents a failure.

Rather than have failure represented by one perfect picture labelled "Expected" paired with another flawed in a multitude of ways, labelled "Actual", failure in the modified experiment is more complex. Specifically, failure will be represented by one perfect picture paired with one that is flawed in only one of four possible dimensions. Two flaws are attributable to the photographer and two are attributable to the processing facility. Photographer attributable flaws are either controllable (poor composition) or uncontrollable (poor light owing to dusk and overcast skies). Processing facility flaws are likewise controllable (incorrect color balance) and uncontrollable (smears and blotches because the developer jammed). All failure pictures composing the failure condition are completely randomized. As before, success is represented by a pair of identical, perfect pictures.

With respect to the dependent measures, in addition to likert-type scales measuring disconfirmation of expectations and satisfaction, subjects will respond to five 7-point bipolar scales measuring the subject's locus and controllability and stability judgments as well as the accuracy and their confidence in their attributions.

The coding scheme for the thought protocols has also been considerably refined. In addition to classifying thoughts as "Causal Thoughts", "Other Product Related Thoughts" and "Irrelevant Thoughts", the "Causal Thoughts" will be subclassified into locus, controllability and stability dimensions following Folkes (1984).

Data will be collected from 144 male and female graduate and undergraduate students. Data collection is about to commence.

CONCLUSIONS

The implications of our findings for the marketer are that consumers predisposition to ponder over the outcomes of a purchase and consumption episode will be contingent on their level of involvement and knowledge of the product class. To the extent that any causal search occurs, subjects who are more knowledgeable may be better able to correctly determine the underlying causes. This suggests that firm personnel need to be in a position to assist less knowledgeable consumers in arriving at an accurate causal determination. Alternatively, a firm's marketing communication aimed at prospective purchasers needs to educate consumers to better deduce reasons underlying unsatisfactory performance. For example, a customer of a weight-loss program who has witnessed unsatisfactory results may need to know that the "failure" could have been caused by a multitude of factors. In the absence of such knowledge the customer may erroneously conclude that program was at fault or that it was inappropriate for their circumstances. Again, a firm seeking to break the loyalty of a rival brand may not be able to trigger problem recognition by consumers unless they are motivated to examine, more closely, instances when their chosen brand fails to live up to expectations. To the extent that it is difficult to heighten involvement in the field, the firm seeking to break into an established market may be better off targeting, in its introductory efforts, consumers who are already highly involved.

REFERENCES

Bearden, William O. and Jesse E. Teel (1983), "Selected Determinants of Consumer Satisfaction and Complaint Reports," *Journal of Marketing Research*, 20, 21-28.

Bettman, John and C. Whan Park (1980), "Effects of Prior Knowledge and Experience and Phase of the Choice Process on Consumer Decision Processes: A Protocol Analysis," *Journal of Consumer Research*, 7, 234-248.

Celsi, Richard L. and Jerry C. Olson (1988), "The Role of Involvement in Attention and Comprehension Processes," *Journal of Consumer Research*, 15, 210-224.

Day, Ralph L. (1977), "Toward a Process Model of Consumer Satisfaction," in H.Keith Hunt, ed., *Conceptualization and Measurement of Consumer Satisfaction and Dissatisfaction*, Cambridge, Mass.:Marketing Science Institute, 153-186.

Folkes, Valerie (1984), "Consumer Reaction to Product Failure: An Attributional Approach," *Journal of Consumer Research*, 10, 398-409.

_____ and Barbara Kostos (1986), "Buyers' and Sellers' Explanation for Product Failure: Who Done it?," *Journal of Marketing*, 50, 74-80.

Johnson, Eric and J. Edward Russo (1981), "Product Familiarity and Learning New Information," in *Advances in Consumer Research*, Kent B. Monroe ed., Ann Arbor, MI: Association for Consumer Research, 151-156.

―――― and ―――― (1984), "Product Familiarity and Learning New Information," *Journal of Consumer Research*, 11, 542-550.

Mitchell, Andrew A. (1981), "The Dimensions of Advertising Involvement," in Kent B. Monroe ed., *Advances in Consumer Research*, Ann Arbor,MI: Association for Consumer Research, 25-30.

Mizerski, Richard W. (1978), "Causal Complexity: A Measure of Consumer Causal Attribution," *Journal of Marketing Research*, 15, 220-228.

Richins, Marsha L. (1982), "An Investigation of Consumers' Attitudes Towards Complaining," Andrew Mitchell ed., *Advances in Consumer Research*, Ann Arbor,MI: Association for Consumer Research, .

Somasundaram, T.N.(1989), "An Investigation of Alternative Consumption Evaluation Processes Explaining Consumer Satisfaction Judgments," unpublished doctoral dissertation, University of Wisconsin-Milwaukee.

Sujan, Mita (1985), "Consumer Knowledge: Effects on Evaluation Strategies Mediating Consumer Judgments," *Journal of Consumer Research*, 12, 31-46.

Zaichkowsky, Judith L.(1984), "Conceptualizing and Measuring the Involvement Construct in Marketing," Unpublished doctoral dissertation, University of California, Los Angeles.

The Moderating Influence of Depth of Processing on Order of Entry Framing Effects
Karen H. Smith, University of Texas at Austin

ABSTRACT

Recent work in the pioneering literature has examined the competitive advantage created by the framing of consumer perceptions about a new product category. This paper proposes that order of entry framing effects are moderated by consumers' depth of information processing. The preference asymmetry resulting from the framing of category perceptions is posited to result from category-based, rather than attribute-based, brand comparisons. If consumers tend to or can be induced to make attribute-level brand comparisons, differentiation may be unnecessary for consumers to consider the purchase of later entering brands. Further, differentiation may fail to attract consumers who make category-level, rather than attribute-level, brand comparisons. Ten propositions that describe the moderating influence of depth of information processing on order of entry framing effects are presented. Methodological considerations in testing the propositions are also discussed.

Pioneering firms have been shown to achieve greater profitability and maintain higher market shares than their later rivals in a product category (Lieberman and Montgomery 1988; Robinson and Fornell 1985; Urban, Carter, Gaskin, and Mucha 1986). Lieberman and Montgomery (1988) review the mechanisms by which pioneering firms obtain these advantages and classify them into three groups: leadership in technology, preemption of assets, and development of tangible or intangible buyer switching costs. More recent work has focused on creating intangible switching costs via framing of consumer perceptions about a new product category. It has been proposed that a pioneer can influence the formation of consumer ideal points by defining the attributes perceived as being important (Carpenter and Nakamoto 1988, 1989). Using this mechanism, a pioneer may actually create the most attractive niche, rather than merely filling it. The essential element of a strong first-mover advantage is the creation of an asymmetry in preferences between the pioneer and later entrants which is very resistant to change.

An important factor that has not been considered in the framing literature is the depth of information processing used by consumers in making brand comparisons. Pursuit of a "me-too" strategy by later entrants has been successful in certain markets (e.g., IBM-compatible PCs, private label brands of clothing), while in other markets, differentiation has been the only successful strategy against the pioneer (Schnaars 1986; Carpenter and Nakamoto 1989, 1990). Depth of processing may account for some of the differences in the success of copy cats vs differentiated brands across product categories.

This paper contributes to the stream of research on pioneering advantage in two ways. First, it builds on the literature of pioneering advantage by further exploring the psychological basis of preference asymmetry due to framing. Drawing on additional findings from the categorization and elaboration likelihood literatures, it is proposed that the level of processing used in forming brand evaluations moderates order of entry framing effects on consumer preferences. Second, it sets forth testable propositions regarding this relationship and suggests some ways in which consumer segments likely to process the differentiated attributes of later entrants can be identified. Methodological considerations in testing the propositions are also discussed.

BACKGROUND LITERATURE AND PROPOSITIONS

Pioneering Advantage via the Framing Mechanism

Carpenter and Nakamoto (1988) suggest that rather than choosing the best position in the attribute space, a pioneer can create it by framing consumer perceptions about a new product category. These authors postulate that product categories are more similar to ad hoc or goal-derived categories as described by Barsalou (1983, 1985) than to natural categories as traditionally studied in the categorization literature (e.g., Rosch, 1978). Upon encountering an unfamiliar product category, a consumer has poorly informed expectations about brands and product attributes and develops category knowledge gradually through direct experience.

In the case of a new product, most consumer learning about the product category may occur when only one brand is available. Therefore, the initial experiences with the pioneer frame the consumer's perceptions about the category, establishing the defining features and category ideals. The order of consumer learning creates a context effect in which the pioneer is perceived as highly representative of the category and is viewed as the category prototype (Carpenter and Nakamoto 1988, 1989). Because of the goal-derived nature of the product category, representativeness is closely linked to brand preference (Loken and Ward 1990; Barsalou 1983, 1985). The prototype becomes the standard to which later entrants are compared, creating an asymmetry in preferences between the pioneer and later entrants. The result of this asymmetry is that later entering brands positioned near the pioneer are less preferred, even though they are also near the ideal point (Carpenter and Nakamoto 1989, 1990). Furthermore, these preferences will tend to be long-lived due to the persistence of category and brand expectations (Fiske 1982).

In addition to greater preference for the pioneer, Kardes and Kalyanaram (1992) have found additional framing effects due to order of entry. Sequential exposure to brand information tends to increase learning about the pioneer and decrease learning about later entrants. The authors found that recall of attributes was much lower for later entrants than for the pioneer, regardless of whether these attributes were shared with the pioneer or unique to later entrants. The authors concluded that shared attributes of later entrants are overlooked because they are considered redundant, while unique features fail to gain attention due to a truncated search process. The authors also found that preferences toward the pioneer were more extreme and held with more confidence than preferences toward other brands.

Therefore, the pioneer enjoys several advantages due to the framing of perceptions: (1) influencing the values consumers place on different attributes and the ideal attribute combination, (2) becoming the standard or prototype for the category resulting in a competitive distinctiveness, (3) influencing what attributes are learned and remembered by consumers, (4) enhancing the extremity of consumer preferences, and (5) enhancing consumers' confidence in their preferences.

However, some consumers may begin using the product only after several brands become available. Their preferences will be less likely to exhibit the asymmetry due to framing since most category learning was not focused on the pioneer alone. Kardes and

Kalyanaram (1992) found that simultaneous exposure to all brands can eliminate order of entry effects on learning and preference. Thus framing effects will be stronger for consumers who acquired most of their category knowledge when the pioneer was the only brand on the market. This leads to the first proposition:

P1: Order of entry framing effects will be stronger for consumers who began learning about the product when the pioneer was the only brand available, relative to consumers who began learning about the product when several brands were available.

Even if most category learning does occur prior to the availability of later entrants, the strength and persistence of the framing effect may vary across consumers. Therefore, the next two sections examine the categorization and elaboration likelihood literatures for suggestions regarding the types of consumers who are more likely to attend to and process information about later entrants. As a result, propositions are set forth regarding the ways in which depth of processing moderates the framing effect on consumer perceptions.

Categorization and Heuristic Processing

Categorization conserves cognitive resources by allowing one to structure information in memory, thereby increasing the amount of data that can be assimilated with a given amount of effort (Rosch 1978). Category knowledge is a pattern of expectations about the category, that is, a set of hypotheses about what attributes go together, what constitutes typical configurations of attributes and what performance levels can be expected from various attribute combinations (Sujan 1985).

Development of heuristics based on category knowledge saves cognitive effort in decision making (Alba and Hutchinson 1987; Sherman and Corty 1984). Within a product category, later entry is difficult because consumers tend to know and favor the pioneering brand. They have no reason to experiment with later entering brands, resulting in a truncation of the search process (Schmalensee 1982; Kardes and Kalyanaram 1992). This suggests that consumers may use the brand name of the pioneer as an heuristic in decision making, allowing them to make a sound choice with little cognitive effort. Thus, consumers may compare new brands to the pioneer using holistic or category-based processing, without exerting the effort necessary to process brand information at the attribute level. On the other hand, if consumers make attribute-level brand comparisons, they may know that later entrants have the same attributes as the pioneer and evaluate them similarly.

These findings suggest that preference asymmetry may be enhanced by category-based processing. If some consumers tend to (or can be induced to) process information at the attribute level, then the pioneer's competitive advantage may be weakened even without differentiation, as in the case of IBM compatible PCs. Thus:

P2: Order of entry framing effects on preference are moderated by depth of processing. The effects will be stronger for consumers who form brand evaluations about later entering brands via category-based processes, relative to consumers who form brand evaluations via attribute-based processes.

In empirical tests of recall, features of a category member that are consistent with the category are often better remembered than inconsistent features because activation of general category knowledge makes such features readily available without reference to specific knowledge about a particular member (Fiske 1982). Inconsistent features may be perceived as irrelevant and, therefore, ignored, so that they are never encoded into memory. However, if a less typical member is made salient in some way or if the individual is given sufficient time to process an incongruent feature, this inconsistency often has a favorable impact in terms of attention, evaluation, and memory (Fiske 1982).

In a product evaluation context, it has been shown that a mismatch between a brand's characteristics and category expectations can lead to greater information processing by the consumer as he attempts to assimilate or accommodate the inconsistency with prior knowledge (Sujan 1985; Sherman and Corty 1984). For some products, differentiation via an extremely discrepant attribute or via several salient attributes may be required to stimulate processing. Elaboration on inconsistent features can result in a more favorable attitude toward the product if the distinctive attributes are favorable (Fiske and Pavelchak 1986) or if the incongruity can be resolved in a way favoring the distinctive product (Mandler 1982; Meyers-Levy and Tybout 1989). While some brands resort to differentiation based on some unimportant or irrelevant attribute that fails to convince consumers of its superiority, these "meaningless" attributes have been shown to be effective in some cases (Carpenter, Glazer, and Nakamoto 1992). Thus, a differentiated later entrant may receive a more favorable evaluation than a "me-too" brand:

P3: Differentiation diminishes order of entry framing effects by inducing attribute-level processing by consumers.

However, some consumers may continue to use heuristics in decision-making even when new brands are differentiated because the unique attributes of later entrants fail to gain their attention (Kardes and Kalyanaram 1992). Use of heuristics by consumers is more likely with high time pressure, when the cognitive processing system is overloaded, or with low involvement. Novices tend to use heuristics more often than experts since they lack the necessary knowledge structures for attribute-level processing. However, experts may also use heuristics since greater knowledge about a category can induce automaticity, that is, automatic invocation of learned rules, as long as they feel that the heuristic is performing well (Sherman and Corty 1984).

Urbany, Dickson, and Wilkie (1989) distinguish between knowledge uncertainty (what information is important in making a choice) and choice uncertainty (which brand to choose). They found that some subjects were certain about which brand they would choose even though they were uncertain about what attributes were important, and this group engaged in the least amount of information search. Urbany, et. al., concluded that "high knowledge uncertainty/low choice uncertainty consumers were more likely to engage quickly a simple, satisficing choice heuristic that overrode any consideration of alternative evaluation" (Urbany, Dickson, and Wilkie 1989, p. 213). Another important finding was that the low knowledge uncertainty/low choice uncertainty group also engaged in very little information search. Thus, even knowledgeable consumers may stay with the brand they have always used.

This suggests that many consumers use simple heuristics in decision-making, where they make brand comparisons via holistic, category-based processes without considering the specific attributes of later entrants. Thus:

P4: Differentiation will be less effective in diminishing order of entry framing effects for consumers who form brand evaluations about later entering brands via category-based processes, relative to consumers who form brand evaluations via attribute-based processes.

If differentiation fails to enhance information processing, it is unlikely to be successful. Hence, consumers who process brand information at the attribute level will be more likely to try to accommodate differentiated attributes of later entering brands that are incongruent with category expectations, and they may be more likely to consider purchasing these later entering brands. The next section discusses the primary individual difference variables that have been found to influence the level of processing.

Elaboration Likelihood: Motivation, Opportunity, and Ability

MacInnis and Jaworski (1989) define level of processing as depth of understanding about a brand brought about by greater attention allocated to the brand and greater cognitive capacity allocated to brand analysis. Consumers with greater motivation, opportunity, and/or ability (MOA) to process have been found to process brand information more deeply (Petty, Cacioppo, and Schumann 1983; Alba and Hutchinson 1987; MacInnis and Jaworski 1989).

Motivation is defined as the desire to process brand information encountered. It requires goal-directed arousal, where the object of motivation is to evaluate the brand. The relevance of brand information to activated needs is the mechanism that stimulates processing (Bettman 1979; MacInnis and Jaworski 1989).

An essential component of motivation is product involvement, which has been defined as "bridging experiences" between an individual's own life and the stimulus (Krugman 1965). Involvement is a necessary, though not sufficient, element to induce arousal or desire to process brand information (MacInnis and Jaworski 1989). For example, a consumer may be highly involved in sports cars, thus attending to and processing a lot of information he encounters about the product category. However, if he is actually going to purchase one, he is more highly motivated to process information which enables him to distinguish among the brands available to meet his consumption needs:

P5: Consumers who are highly motivated to distinguish among brands in the product category will be more likely to process information about the differentiated attributes of later entrants, relative to consumers who are less motivated.

Ability is defined as skill or proficiency in interpreting brand information. Lack of ability implies that knowledge structures necessary to perform more complex operations either do not exist or cannot be accessed (MacInnis and Jaworski 1989). In choosing among competing brands, consumers may not have sufficient knowledge to determine optimal attribute levels.

Expertise has been found to influence information search and decision-making. Prior knowledge generally makes it easier to search for and assimilate information. In addition, experts tend to weight functional product information more heavily, while novices may rely on peripheral cues such as brand name or a spokesperson's traits (Alba and Hutchinson 1987). Carpenter and Nakamoto (1989) manipulated ambiguity by either providing or omitting objective information on important attributes. Giving the subjects this information is, in a way, providing them with "expertise" in the product category. Those who were given objective information showed less preference for the pioneering brand. Thus, research on level of knowledge suggests that:

P6: Consumers with greater knowledge about the product category will be more likely to process information about the differentiated attributes of later entrants, relative to consumers with less category knowledge.

In addition to motivation and ability, the consumer must have an opportunity to process. Opportunity to process is defined as "the extent to which circumstances evidenced during exposure to brand information are favorable for brand processing" (MacInnis and Jaworski 1989, p. 7). Analytic processing is inhibited by such factors as time pressure, interference from other tasks or information about other products, and information overload (Alba and Hutchinson 1987; Celsi and Olson 1988).

P7: Consumers with greater opportunity to process will be more likely to process information about the differentiated attributes of later entrants, relative to consumers with less opportunity.

Because those engaged in holistic, category-level processing will tend to rely on heuristics in decision-making, such as brand name of the pioneer, they may not attend to the distinctive attributes of later entrants. Therefore, order of entry will have a greater effect on preference for consumers processing holistically. Alternatively, consumers who are more likely to process attribute-level information about later entrants will exhibit less preference for the pioneer. Thus:

P8: The impact of differentiation on order of entry framing effects is moderated by depth of processing. Consumers with greater motivation, ability, and/or opportunity to process the differentiated attributes of later entrants will exhibit less preference for the pioneer, relative to consumers with less motivation, ability, and/or opportunity.

While studies have indicated a relationship between typicality and attitude, it is likely that those who process more deeply may not prefer the prototypical brand because of greater consideration of unique attributes of other brands. For example, some consumers may consider McDonald's to be the prototypical fast-food restaurant, yet prefer Burger King because its food is not prepared in advance. Therefore:

P9: Consumers who process the differentiated attributes of later entrants will exhibit less preference for the pioneer, even when they continue to perceive it as the prototype.

However, consumers with greater expertise and involvement often continue to rely on heuristics in choice. For these consumers, advertising cues that induce deeper processing may be required for them to re-evaluate the decision heuristic they generally use for that product category (MacInnis, Moorman, and Jaworski 1991). Such cues include providing a use context which relates product use to the consumer's self-image or arouses the curiosity of the consumer (MacInnis, Moorman, and Jaworski 1991). Since many consumers treat brand information as tentative hypotheses to be tested through experience (Hoch and Ha 1986), free samples which encourage trial of new brands may also lessen the pioneer's advantage. If the product is of a technical nature, free seminars on learning how to use it or how to enhance its usefulness may increase actual trial. Therefore:

P10: Differentiation will be more effective in diminishing order of entry framing effects when combined with advertising cues designed to increase attribute-level processing.

CONCLUSIONS AND METHODOLOGICAL CONSIDERATIONS

Some consumers may make attribute-level comparisons of new brands relative to the pioneer, rather than forming brand evaluations holistically. Consumers who process the differentiated attributes of later entrants may require a greater number of dimensions to describe the perceptual space representing their ideal point and how they perceive brands to be positioned. The greater number of dimensions in representing the relationships among brands may help break down the preference asymmetry effect by allowing consumers to compare brands along several dimensions. Thus, preference asymmetry with respect to the pioneering brand may result only for consumers who compare brands to the pioneer using a category-based process. This may explain why me-too brands have been successful in certain markets.

In the categorization literature, it has been shown that the degree of match between a brand and its product category tends to influence the level of processing (Sujan, 1985). A me-too brand may be perceived as a good match to the category, so that consumers evaluate it holistically. They may perceive it as being inferior to the pioneering brand, rejecting the claim that it has the same attributes as the pioneer. On the other hand, a differentiated brand represents a mismatch with category-based expectations. Depending on the degree of mismatch, consumers may process brand information more deeply, evaluating the distinctive attributes of a later entrant. Therefore, differentiation may be a more effective way of competing against the pioneer because it tends to foster attribute-level processing.

However, some consumers may be unable or unwilling to expend the cognitive effort necessary to critically evaluate information about distinctive attributes of new brands. They may continue to compare even differentiated brands to the pioneer in a holistic manner. The literature on elaboration likelihood suggests that consumers with higher levels of motivation, opportunity, and/or ability to process will be more likely to attend to, process, and remember brand information encountered (Petty, Cacioppo, and Schumann 1983; MacInnis and Jaworski 1989). These consumers will be more likely to consider claims made by later entrants about the superiority of their differentiated attributes. In addition, cues in advertising messages can induce deeper processing by enhancing the consumer's motivation, opportunity, and/or ability as suggested by MacInnis, Moorman, and Jaworski (1991). For differentiation to be effective, level of processing may also need to be considered.

Although lists of consumers with greater expertise and involvement are not available per se, surrogates for these variables may help target such groups. Subscribers of magazines or members of organizations focusing on the product category are often easy to obtain and may include individuals who have greater expertise and/or involvement in certain areas. Of course, if the product is totally new, this expertise/involvement may involve the more superordinate product class. For example, if the product is a new class of software, those who read *PC Magazine* may be generally very knowledgeable about using and evaluating software, even though they have no prior knowledge about the particular software being introduced.

Knowledge and involvement tend to be highly correlated, and reinforcing, constructs. It is not always feasible to separate them. In testing the propositions presented here, it may be desirable to combine the two, segregating consumers with high knowledge and involvement from those who are low on both. Although, for common, repeat-purchase products (e.g., skin care products, household items), it may possible to isolate the effects of knowledge by holding involvement at a constant, low level. Opportunity is fairly straight-forward to manipulate in an experimental setting by enforcing time constraints for making brand evaluations or by creating interference from unrelated information.

Another way to test the influence of processing would be to segregate a group of consumers who are low on both knowledge and involvement and manipulate the use of advertising cues designed to enhance processing. This procedure would allow an assessment of the effectiveness of such cues and the extent to which framing effects of the pioneer are reduced.

In summary, this paper extends previous work on pioneering by further investigating the psychological basis of order of entry framing effects and setting forth testable propositions regarding this relationship. Depth of processing may be a crucial factor in diminishing the framing effects created by a market pioneer. Differentiation by a later entrant often prompts attention and critical evaluation of attributes as consumers attempt to reconcile the incongruity with category knowledge. However, for some products a consideration of individual difference variables and/or advertising cues that enhance processing may be as important as differentiation in moderating the effects of framing.

REFERENCES

Alba, Joseph W. and J. Wesley Hutchinson (1987), "Dimensions of Consumer Expertise," *Journal of Consumer Research*, 13 (March), 411-454.

Barsalou, Lawrence W. (1983), "Ad hoc Categories," *Memory and Cognition*, 11 (3), 211-227.

_____ (1985), "Ideals, Central Tendency, and Frequency of Instantiation as Determinants of Graded Structure in Categories," *Journal of Experimental Psychology: Learning, Memory and Cognition*, 11 (October), 629-654.

Bettman, James R. (1979), *An Information Processing Theory of Consumer Choice*, Reading, MA: Addison-Wesley Publishing.

Carpenter, Gregory S., Rashi Glazer, and Kent Nakamoto (1992), "Meaningful Brands from Meaningless Differentiation: The Dependence on Irrelevant Attributes," unpublished working paper.

_____ and Kent Nakamoto (1988), "Market Pioneering, Learning, and Preference," in *Advances in Consumer Research*, Vol. 15.

_____ and _____ (1989), "Consumer Preference Formation and Pioneering Advantage," *Journal of Marketing Research*, 26 (August), 285-298.

_____ and _____ (1990), "Competitive Strategies for Late Entry into a Market with a Dominant Brand," *Management Science*, 36 (October), 1268-1278.

Celsi, Richard L. and Jerry C. Olson (1988), "The Role of Involvement in Attention and Comprehension Processes," *Journal of Consumer Research*, 15 (September), 210-224.

Fiske, Susan T. (1982), "Schema-triggered Affect: Applications to Social Perception," in *Affect and Cognition: The 17th Annual Carnegie Symposium on Cognition*, eds. Margaret S. Clarke and Susan T. Fiske, Hillsdale, N.J.: Lawrence Erlbaum, 55-78.

_____ and Mark A. Pavelchak (1986), "Category-based versus Piecemeal-based Affective Responses: Developments in Schema-Triggered Affect," in *Handbook of Motivation and Cognition*, eds. R. M. Sorrentino and E. Tory Higgins, New York: Guilford Press.

Hoch, Stephen J. and Young-Won Ha (1986), "Consumer Learning: Advertising and the Ambiguity of Product Experience," *Journal of Consumer Research*, 13 (September), 221-233.

Kardes, Frank R. and Gurumurthy Kalyanaram (1992), "Order-of-Entry Effects on Consumer Memory and Judgment: An Information Integration Perspective," *Journal of Marketing Research*, 29 (August), 343-357.

Krugman, Herbert E. (1965), "The Impact of Television Advertising: Learning without Involvement," *Public Opinion Quarterly*, 29 (Fall), 349-356.

Lieberman, Marvin B. and David B. Montgomery (1988), "First-Mover Advantages," *Strategic Management Journal*, 9, 41-58.

Loken, Barbara and James Ward (1990), "Alternative Approaches to Understanding the Determinants of Typicality," *Journal of Consumer Research*, 17 (September), 111-126.

MacInnis, Deborah J. and Bernard J. Jaworski (1989), "Information Processing from Advertisements: Toward an Integrative Framework," *Journal of Marketing*, 53 (October), 1-23.

_____, Christine Moorman, and Bernard J. Jaworski (1991), "Enhancing and Measuring Consumers' Motivation, Opportunity, and Ability to Process Brand Information from Ads," *Journal of Marketing*, 55 (October), 32-53.

Mandler, George (1982), "The Structure of Value: Accounting for Taste," in *Affect and Cognition: The 17th Annual Carnegie Symposium on Cognition*, eds. Margaret S. Clark and Susan T. Fiske, Hillsdale, NJ: Lawrence Erlbaum.

Meyers-Levy, Joan and Alice Tybout (1989), "Schema Congruity as a Basis for Product Evaluation," *Journal of Consumer Research*, 16 (June), 39-54.

Petty, Richard E., John T. Cacioppo, and David Schumann (1983), "Central and Peripheral Routes to Advertising Effectiveness: The Moderating Role of Involvement," *Journal of Consumer Research*, 10 (September), 135-146.

Robinson, William T. and Claes Fornell (1985), "Sources of Market Pioneer Advantages in Consumer Goods Industries," *Journal of Marketing Research*, 22 (August), 305-17.

Rosch, Eleanor (1978), "Principles of Categorization," in *Cognition and Categorization*, eds. Eleanor Rosch and B. Boyd, Hillsdale, NJ: Lawrence Erlbaum.

Schmalensee, Richard (1982), "Product Differentiation Advantages of Pioneering Brands," *American Economic Review*, 72 (3), 349-365.

Schnaars, Steven P. (1986), "When Entering Growth Markets, Are Pioneers Better than Poachers?" *Business Horizons*, 29 (March-April), 27-36.

Sherman, Steven J. and Eric Corty (1984), "Cognitive Heuristics," in *Handbook of Social Cognition*, vol. 1, eds. Robert S. Wyer, Jr. and Thomas K. Srull, 190-286.

Sujan, Mita (1985), "Consumer Knowledge: Effects on Evaluation Strategies Mediating Consumer Judgments," *Journal of Consumer Research*, 12 (June), 31-46.

Urban, Glen L., Theresa Carter, Steven Gaskin, and Zofia Mucha (1989), "Market Share Rewards to Pioneering Brands: An Empirical Analysis and Strategic Implications," *Management Science*, 32 (June), 645-659.

Urbany, Joel E., Peter R. Dickson, and William L. Wilkie (1989), "Buyer Uncertainty and Information Search," *Journal of Consumer Research*, 16 (September), 208-215.

Aesthetic Response and the Influence of Design Principles on Product Preferences

Robert W. Veryzer, Jr., University of Florida[1]

ABSTRACT

Although product design is increasingly being recognized by marketing practitioners and consumer researchers as an important determinant of consumer behavior, there has been relatively little investigation of the influence of *aesthetic* aspects of products on the preferences or evaluations formed by the perceivers of the products. This paper explores the systematic nature of aesthetic responses to products and proposes a conceptualization of aesthetic response that is based on design principles that operate as internal processing algorithms. A preliminary study that explores the proposed conceptualization is presented, and the theoretical implications of this preliminary investigation are discussed. The broad social implications of product aesthetics and design are also briefly discussed.

INTRODUCTION

A marketing variable that is gaining recognition as being a significant factor in the competitive marketplace is the aesthetic aspect of product design. As Bruce Nussbaum pointed out in *Business Week* (June 17, 1991, p. 62): "Recently, business has grown increasingly aware that design sells. U. S. companies, in particular, are rediscovering that good design translates into quality products, greater market share, and heftier profits." "Competitive aesthetics" as it has been called (*Time*, August 27, 1990, p. 58) is gaining recognition as a strategic activity that companies can use to gain a sustainable competitive advantage (Kotler and Rath 1984).

While consumer reaction to the aesthetic aspects of products is increasingly being recognized as an important determinant of consumer behavior (Berkowitz 1987; Wallendorf 1980) there has been relatively little investigation of how this variable affects preferences for products. Although consumer researchers have started to grapple with some of the fundamental questions in this area such as: "What is an aesthetic response?"; "How are they formed?"; and "What factors influence aesthetic responses?", progress has been greatly impeded by the lack of a conceptual framework for understanding aesthetic responses (Holbrook and Zirlin 1985; Olson 1981). Olson (1981) has discussed the need for a global conceptual framework which can be used to develop the basic issues regarding consumer aesthetics and guide the design and interpretation of empirical research. Holbrook and Zirlin (1985, p. 2) have also pointed to the lack of a "sturdy conceptual foundation" as the reason that "consumer researchers have developed little if any theory to deal explicitly with the case of esthetic behavior." The purposes of this paper are to very briefly review the nature of aesthetics and aesthetic responses, propose a design principle internal processing algorithm conceptualization of aesthetic response, and present a preliminary study that examines the proposed conceptualization of aesthetic response.

BACKGROUND AND CONCEPTUALIZATION

Aesthetics and Aesthetic Response

The word "aesthetics," which is usually used in reference to either a sensitivity to the beautiful or to the branch of philosophy that provides a theory of the beautiful and of the fine arts, is derived from the Greek word "aisthetikos" which means "pertaining to sense perception." The term was first introduced in the late 1700's by the German philosopher Alexander Baumgarten who chose it because he wished to emphasize the experience of art as a field of concrete knowledge in which content (i. e., knowledge) is communicated in sensory form as opposed to strict reasoning or logic (Berlyne 1974). His work was concerned with poetry and other arts and thus "aesthetics" was subsequently applied to the philosophical study of all the arts and manifestations of natural beauty. Throughout much of the work conducted in disciplines that have focused on aesthetics a "philosophy of art" definition has remained inseparably associated with the term "aesthetics." This view has resulted in some debate among consumer researchers concerning an appropriate definition of the aesthetic aspect of consumption. Some in the field prefer to apply aesthetic experience only to so called "artistic" or "cultural products" (Holbrook 1981; Olson 1981), while others acknowledge that virtually any product can be appreciated in an aesthetic sense (Holbrook 1981; Olson 1981). This latter view provides a more useful perspective for understanding the role of aesthetics/product design in consumer behavior. It reflects Berlyne's sentiment that " . . . aesthetics is certainly concerned with the arts, but it is not confined to the arts . . ." (Berlyne 1974, p. 1). This view is also inherent in the practice of industrial design (i. e., product design).

Although there does not appear to be any generally accepted definition of aesthetic response, there does seem to be some consensus that the concept involves the registering of affect or pleasure due to the conscious or unconscious influences of aspects (i. e., stimulus characteristics) of an object (Bamossy, Scammon, and Johnston 1983; Berlyne 1974). In a general sense, an aesthetic response refers to the reaction a person has to an object (e. g., product) based on his or her perception of the object (Berlyne 1974). The reaction is based on the qualities and configurality of the physical features (i. e., design) of the object (product). Even though the discussion to follow emphasizes visual aesthetic response, it is anticipated that the proposed conceptualization will be applicable to other forms of aesthetic experience as well.

The Systematic Nature of Visual Aesthetic Response

The difficulties inherent in understanding the highly complex phenomenon of aesthetic response has led many to think of it as being highly idiosyncratic and transcending analysis. The systematic nature of aesthetic response in the visual domain stems from the underlying common factors and principles upon which it is based. Both the construction and the perception of any object involves certain design elements (e. g., line, plane, color, etc.) and principles (e. g., unity, contrast, balance, proportion, etc.) (Lauer 1979). Design elements are the parts that make up an object. Design principles are essentially general rules of perception that involve the relationships between the parts of a visual display. For example, the design principle of unity refers to a congruity among the elements of a design such that they look as though they belong together or as though there is some visual connection beyond mere chance that has caused them to come together (Lauer 1979). Although the source (i. e., "nature" vs. "nurture") of design principles (i. e., perception principles) is still open to debate, there is evidence that these principles are present very early in life and that preferences related to these principles develop over time (e. g., Bornstein, Ferdinandsen, and Gross 1981).

---

[1] The author is indebted to J. Wesley Hutchinson, Chris Janiszewski, Richard Lutz, and S. Ratneshwar for their helpful comments on an earlier draft of this paper.

An indication of the role that design principles may play in the formation of aesthetic responses is provided by one of Lewicki's (1986) early studies that examined people's sensitivity to violations of a nonconsciously learned proportion. It was found that even though people cannot articulate even the most basic proportions of the human face, they are very sensitive to small violations of these proportions (Lewicki 1986). Lewicki suggests that in such cases people's judgments may depend directly on cognitive algorithms (i. e., internal processing algorithms) that they are unaware of and have no access to; he also suggests that these algorithms may generate preferences which are not available to introspection.

There are indications of cognitive algorithms that are sensitive to such things as the proportion and unity exhibited by objects. For example, the "golden section," which is a specific ratio of length to height (1.618 to 1) that is said to offer a visually pleasing proportion, has played a prominent role in art and architecture throughout history (Berlyne 1971). It provides an example of a design principle that may be nonconsciously acquired through exposure to the environment since people encounter "many instances of it, or approximations to it, in works of art or industrial artifacts" (Berlyne 1971, p. 230). Thus, the phenomenon of aesthetic response may involve the nonconscious development of design principle internal processing algorithms (design principle IPAs) as well as the nonconscious application of these design principle algorithms. Objects (products) that are consistent with a person's design principle IPAs would be expected to produce more positive affect than objects that violate a person's relevant design principle IPAs. This general hypothesis was studied in an experiment that is described in the next section.

A PRELIMINARY INVESTIGATION OF AESTHETIC RESPONSE

A preliminary study was designed and conducted in order to examine the Design Principle Algorithm explanation of aesthetic response. This study investigated the influence of design principles on aesthetic responses toward products.

Hypotheses

The general hypothesis that aesthetic responses are more favorable for objects that are consistent with design principle IPAs (e. g., proportion, unity) than they are for objects that are not consistent with these IPAs was discussed in the previous section. This general hypotheses suggests the following specific hypotheses for this study: (H1) Aesthetic responses are more favorable for products that exhibit ideal proportions (i. e., proportions known to be aesthetically pleasing) than they are for products that do not exhibit such proportionate relationships; and (H2) Aesthetic responses are more favorable for products that exhibit unity than they are for products that do not exhibit unity (i. e., disunity, lack of coherence). Furthermore, Gestalt psychologists hypothesize that all dimensions of a presentation (e. g., object, product) must be near an optimal level for an aesthetic response to be maximally positive (Kohler 1929). For this reason an interaction between proportion and unity was hypothesized: (H3) Good proportion and unity will interact to produce aesthetic responses that are more favorable than the sum of the proportion and unity effects. Finally, a fourth hypothesis relates to people's awareness of the rules or design principle IPAs responsible for differences in their aesthetic responses to the various versions of the product stimuli. Consistent with the findings of Lewicki (1986), it is expected that few subjects will be able to identify the cues or processes responsible for differences in their aesthetic responses to stimuli, thus: (H4) Consumers are unable to articulate the relationship between the differences in proportion and unity and their aesthetic responses to products. This hypothesis was not tested in a formal sense, however, it was explored through open-ended questions and interviews and the findings concerning it are presented.

Independent Variables

In order to examine the proposed design principle algorithm explanation of aesthetic response two fundamental design principles were selected as the factors for manipulation. Proportion, which refers to the size relation of one part to another and to the whole (i. e., ratio), was operationalized as the ratio of an object's width to height. The "ideal" proportion (e. g., golden section) for each product class was determined by two design experts and pilot testing was conducted in order to determine the minimal degree by which proportion needed to be altered in order to violate the principle of proportion. This was necessary since there were considerable differences in the configurations of the product classes that were employed. The discovery of these proportions is primarily inductive within the generic object range (Berlyne 1971). Generic object range refers to the amount of variation that is allowable in an object of a particular product category or class. The other design principle, unity, refers to the organization of parts such that they interact in a mutually supportive fashion. When parts of a design do not support each other (disunity) the resulting lack of coherence distracts or interferes with the perception of the object (product). Unity was operationalized in accordance with two Gestalt laws. The law of integration of similars and adjacents (Boring 1942) states that units similar in size, shape, and color tend to combine to make better articulated forms. The Gestalt view maintains that a "good" form is well articulated and as such tends to impress itself upon the observer. A second Gestalt law that was used to define unity was the law of "good" contour or common destiny (Katz 1950). This law maintains that parts of a figure (e. g., a line) that have a common destiny tend to form units because they seem to be continuations of each other. Objects that are consistent with a person's internal processing algorithms regarding these principles would be expected to produce more positive affect than objects that violate a person's relevant design principle algorithms.

Stimuli

The stimuli were versions of color-scanned computer images of three products (microwave oven, suntan lotion bottle, and natural sound machine[2]) drawn from different product classes. Proportion (high or low) and unity (high or low) were manipulated concurrently on the three products resulting in four versions of each product. The high or low level of each factor was achieved by adhering to or violating the operationalized principles of proportion and unity. The proportion manipulation was achieved by altering the dimensions of the computer images of the products.[3] The unity manipulation was achieved by altering products in accordance with the Gestalt laws pertaining to unity concerning lines or shapes in order to decrease unity or to maintain (or increase) unity but in a manner not typical of the product class. For example, in the case of

---

[2] A natural sound machine produces "soothing" sounds (e. g., rolling waves, rain, and waterfalls) in addition to performing the functions associated with clock radios.

[3] The proportions that were used for each product were as follows: microwave oven, 1.8 vs. 1.6; suntan lotion bottle, 1.7 vs. 2.1; and sound machine, 1.0 vs. .4 [Note: the proportion of the original image is listed first].

the microwave oven stimuli lines which exhibited "good contour" or "common destiny" were added in order to maintain or increase unity and lines that did not exhibit "good contour" or "common destiny" were added in order to decrease unity. The unity manipulation for the suntan lotion bottle stimuli was accomplished in a similar manner. Unity was manipulated for the sound machine stimuli by rounding some of the shapes found on the predominately square product; this resulted in disunity according to the Gestalt law of integration of similars and adjacents (Boring 1942).

Procedure

Twenty-four undergraduates at the University of Florida were tested singularly or in groups of two. Each subject was seated facing the computer screen that was used to present the stimuli and given a research booklet. Subjects were told that in an effort to determine the products with the best appearance they would be shown several versions of a product and asked to indicate how they felt each version looked. They were also given a brief product description for each type of product (i. e., product class) and informed that all of the versions of a product performed equally well. Subjects were simultaneously shown the four versions of each product on a computer screen. These stimuli were presented in two orders with a between-subjects instruction manipulation.[4] The subjects rated each version on a 9-point semantic differential scale anchored by "Dislike/Like." In addition, subjects were asked to indicate why they rated each product as they did in open-ended questions that followed the ratings tasks. Finally, each subject was interviewed in order to further assess the degree of awareness or conscious application of the design principles involved. Thus, the experiment employed a 2(proportion) x 2(unity) repeated measures design with a between-subjects instruction manipulation that was confounded with product order.

Results and Discussion

Standard ANOVAs were performed on each of the three products in order to assess the effects of instructions, order, proportion, unity and their possible interactions. The analyses indicated that an order effect was present for the suntan lotion bottle stimuli (F=4.71; p<.04) and a proportion by instruction effect was present for the natural sound machine stimuli (F=4.59; p<.04). The order effect on the mean evaluations of the sun-tan lotion bottle was controlled for by entering the "order" variable into the ANOVA model prior to testing for the main effects of proportion and unity.

The proportion by instruction interaction for the sound machine was as expected. The distortion of the sound machine images had masked the influence of the proportion manipulation in a pretest. Because of the image distortion problem that is present in the first order/instruction condition, only the data from subjects in the second order/instruction condition were used in subsequent analyses of the sound machine stimuli.

The means for this experiment are shown in Table 1. Proportion achieved moderate significance in the case of each of the three product types. The proportion manipulation was significant for the suntan lotion stimuli ($F(1,22)=3.04$, $p<.05$, $eta2=.12$) and marginally significant for the microwave oven stimuli ($F(1,22)=1.69$, $p=.10$, $eta2=.07$) and the natural sound machine stimuli ($F(1,11)=1.75$, $p=.10$, $eta2=.14$). These results provide some support for the proportion hypothesis (H1).

Unity reached notably higher levels of significance across the three product types. The unity manipulation was significant for the suntan lotion bottle ($F(1,22)=10.50$, $p<.01$, $eta2=.32$), the microwave oven ($F(1,22)=97.88$, $p<.0001$, $eta2=.82$), and the sound machine ($F(1,11)=2.32$, $p<.10$, $eta2=.17$). These results provide support for the unity hypothesis (H2).

Tests for interaction effects between proportion and unity were not significant for the suntan lotion bottle ($F(1,22)=0.36$) or the microwave oven $F(1,22)=0.67$), but were marginally significant for the sound machine ($F(1,11)=1.94$, $p<.10$, $eta2=.15$). This finding may be attributable to the failure to create strong manipulations for both principles on any of the three stimuli products. Given the preliminary nature of this study, the sound machine results provide at least some encouragement regarding the interaction of proportion and unity.

Subjects attributed their ratings of the different versions of products to a variety of perceived differences - very few of which reflected an awareness or conscious appreciation of the design principles involved. When discussing how they rated the different versions, subjects mentioned such things as: "styles", "packaging", "old fashioned", "modern", "sleekness", "awkwardness", "refined", "elegant", "simple", "fullness", and "deluxe-looking". Most responses (70%) were of this nature. General terms, such as "shape" and "design", were also frequently used in statements like "I liked this design" or "I didn't like the square shapes because they looked old-fashioned".

Seven subjects (30%) gave responses that seemed to reflect a conscious awareness of design principles. These responses involved references such as: "balanced look", "out of proportion", "continuity of appearance", and "pattern of line". However, subject interviews indicted that only three subjects actually seemed to have a conscious awareness of formal design principles (one of these subjects had previously been in the architecture program). The significance of results does not change even if all seven of these subjects are removed from the analysis.

The design of this experiment provided an opportunity for the subject to become aware of the design differences in the product. All four versions of each product were shown concurrently. Subjects could have easily engaged in a serial comparison of the products in order to discover their differences. Most subjects did not appear to consciously identify key differences in the products, yet were influenced by the experimental manipulations. The fact that most respondents in this study were not able to articulate the specific violations or consistencies of the design principles that the product versions exhibited should not be over-interpreted since this study was not specifically designed to address this question. In addition, it is important to recognize that the inability to describe the relationship between design principles and aesthetic responses does not necessarily mean that people were not in some way conscious of the principles. However, the finding that people are not able to articulate the relationship between proportion and unity and their aesthetic responses is consistent with findings concerning implicit and nonconscious learning (e. g., Lewicki 1986).

An issue that was considered in the design of this study but was not addressed by it is that of prototypicality. Prototype theory maintains that people most prefer a product that conforms to the familiar or prototypical product for the product class (Loken and Ward 1990). The influence of typicality on aesthetic response is a particularly complex issue since design principles and typicality may be empirically confounded in the marketplace. In this study an attempt was made to control for prototypicality by employing

---

[4] The instruction manipulation, which is confounded with product order, asked half of the subjects to ignore any slight computer distortion of the images that were displayed on the computer screen. This instruction was an attempt to solve an image distortion problem that had been encountered with the sound machine stimuli during pretests.

TABLE 1
Mean Aesthetic Responses to Stimuli

Stimulus		Proportion	
		Low	High
Suntan Lotion	Low Unity	4.92	5.88
	High Unity	6.13	6.92
Microwave Oven	Low Unity	4.37	4.46
	High Unity	7.42	7.63
Sound Machine	Low Unity	4.58	5.83
	High Unity	5.00	6.50

products that were not the category exemplar or representative of the category prototype (i. e., product versions in the high proportion/high unity cell were not more typical than any of the other product versions that were shown). Data from another preliminary study (not reported here) that investigated whether or not prototype theory provides a better explanation of aesthetic response than the design principle algorithm explanation suggests that the effect of unity goes beyond the effect of typicality. Consistency with design principles was shown to provide a better explanation of aesthetic response than prototype theory.

SUMMARY AND CONCLUSIONS

The results of this preliminary study suggest that the Design Principle Algorithm explanation appears to offer a basis for understanding how aesthetic response operates and why it can usually be described at the conscious level only as vague preferences or feelings. Aesthetic responses were shown to be influenced by the consistency of product versions with the design principles of proportion and unity. An indication of the gestalt-like nature of aesthetic response was exhibited by the marginally significant interaction of the two design principles. The general lack of conscious awareness among subjects concerning the design principles and the influence of these principles on subjects' aesthetic responses indicate that design principles operate (often nonconsciously) as internal processing algorithms and seems to suggest that the principles can be nonconsciously acquired.

The fact that significant effects of either proportion or unity or both were observed for each of the three classes of products suggests that design principles (proportion and unity) are applicable across a diverse range of products. This implies that design principle IPAs may play an important role in many, if not most, consumer purchase decisions. Differences in the results observed across the three product types are, at least in part, attributable to differences in the strengths of the proportion and unity manipulations across product types. Even so, it is likely that there is a product-specific component to consumer aesthetic response.

The implications of this preliminary investigation for consumer research are that aesthetics/product design can have a significant systematic influence on consumer behavior and that the phenomenon of aesthetic response merits the attention of consumer researchers. The conceptualization of aesthetic response that was presented here provides a concrete foundation from which theory for consumer aesthetics may be developed. This conceptualization can also guide the design and interpretation of empirical research in the area of consumer aesthetics. By moving the study of consumer aesthetics to a higher level of abstraction this work represents an important step in "the race toward aesthetic theory building" (Holbrook and Zirlin 1985, p. 2).

This exploratory investigation indicates a need for future research in several areas in addition to a more complete investigation of the Design Principle Algorithm explanation of aesthetic response. First, research is needed to assess the impact of other design principles (e. g., symmetry, contrast, etc.) on aesthetic responses. A second area that requires further study concerns the nature vs. nurture debate and the role that biological and cultural influences play in the development of design principle IPAs. A third area for future research is the influence of prototypicality on aesthetic response. Finally, a fourth area that should be researched involves determining the degree of specificity of the design principles to product categories. For example, optimal proportions may vary somewhat by product category, while unity may be a more basic principle.

Product aesthetics/design has important social implications that extend beyond the marketer's concern for a sustainable competitive advantage and increased market share. Aesthetics/design has the capacity to influence the very quality of life itself by literally shaping the products that make up so much of the "world" in which we live. The current movement of "humanity by design" is motivated to improve the lot of humankind by better harnessing technology and better expressing it in form. Through such things as "universal design", which seeks to design products that all people including people with disabilities can use easily, to the design of attractive and socially responsible products and packages that conserve resources and minimize the impact of production on the environment, aesthetics/design provides an opportunity to enhance the quality and beauty of our lives.

This research is a first step in understanding the relationships between product design and aesthetic response. The primary aims of this preliminary study were to: (1) propose an explanation of aesthetic response that is based on consistency with internal processing algorithms that relate to the relative disposition of the parts or elements of a product (e. g., design principles); and (2) demonstrate that aesthetics can systematically influence consumers' perceptions and evaluations of products. Although much more work is needed, it is hoped that this work will provide an initial framework for theorizing about the relationship among product configuration, nonconscious processes, and aesthetic responses.

REFERENCES

Bamossy, Gary, Debra L. Scammon, and Marilyn Johnston (1983), "A Preliminary Investigation of the Reliability and Validity of an Aesthetic Judgement Test," *Advances in Consumer Research*, eds. Richard P. Bagozzi and Alice M. Tybout, Ann Arbor, MI: Association for Consumer Research, Vol. 10, pp. 685-690.

Berkowitz, Marvin (1987), "The Influence of Shape on Product Preferences," *Advances in Consumer Research*, eds. Melanie Wallendorf and Paul Anderson, Provo UT: Association for Consumer Research, Vol. 14, p. 559.

Berlyne, D. E. (1971), *Aesthetics and Psychobiology*, New York: Appleton-Century-Crofts.

_____ (1974), *Studies in the New Experimental Aesthetics*, New York: John Wiley and Sons.

Boring, E. G. (1942), *Sensation and Perception in the History of Experimental Psychology*. New York: Appleton-Century-Crofts.

Bornstein, Marc H., Kay Ferdinandsen, and Charles G. Gross (1981), "Perception of Symmetry in Infancy" *Developmental Psychology*, Vol. 17, No. 1, pp. 82-86.

Business Week, "Design," June 15, 1990, pp. 170-191.

Holbrook, Morris B., (1981), "Introduction: The Esthetic Imperative in Consumer Research," in *Symbolic Consumer Behavior*, eds. Elizabeth C. Hirschman and Morris B. Holbrook, Ann Arbor, MI: Association for Consumer Research, pp. 36-37.

_____, and Robert B. Zirlin (1985), "Artistic Creation, Artworks, and Aesthetic Appreciation: Some Philosophical Contributions to Nonprofit Marketing," *Advances in Nonprofit Marketing*, Vol. 1, pp. 1-54.

Katz, David (1950), *Gestalt Psychology*, New York, The Ronald Press Company.

Köhler, Wolfgang (1929), *Gestalt Psychology: An Introduction to New Concepts in Modern Psychology*, New York: Liveright Publishing Corporation (1947).

Kotler, Philip and G. Alexander Rath (1984), "Design: A Powerful But Neglected Strategic Tool," *The Journal of Business Strategy*, Vol. 5 (Fall), pp. 16-21.

Lauer, David A. (1979), *Design Basics*, New York, Holt, Rinehart, and Winston.

Lewicki, Pawel (1986), *Nonconscious Social Information Processing*, New York: Academic Press.

Loken, Barbara and James Ward (1990), "Alternative Approaches to Understanding the Determinants of Typicality," *Journal of Consumer Research*, Vol. 17, pp. 111-126.

Olson, Jerry C. (1981), "What is an Esthetic Response?" *Symbolic Consumer Behavior*, eds. Elizabeth C. Hirschman and Morris B. Holbrook, Ann Arbor, MI: Association for Consumer Research, pp. 71-74.

Wallendorf, Melanie (1980), "The Formation of Aesthetic Criteria Through Social Structure and Social Institutions," in *Advances in Consumer Research*, ed. Jerry C. Olson, Ann Arbor, MI: Association for Consumer Research, Vol. 7, pp.3-6.

Product Perceptions, Preferences, and Knowledge: Decisions In Conducting Research
George Brooker, Central Washington University

Researchers preparing to test cause-effect relationships are confronted by an extensive number of choices and decisions. Successful completion of the research and drawing appropriate conclusions about relationships will depend on these decisions. While some choices are obvious, others are somewhat less so. The implications of many of these decisions are not always apparent; it is only after the fact that their importance can be seen.

IMPORTANCE OF THE RESEARCH

One of the decisions researchers face is whether to pursue a project at all. Simon (1969, pp. 223-226) provides several useful criteria to assess the importance of research, including: Will the study test an important theory? Are results apt to be surprising or unexpected? Does the work address contemporary arguments and open questions, or does it extend or contradict previous work?

Smith's paper provides some interesting conceptual notions on how new and later product introductions may be affected by information-processing issues. It is especially intriguing to consider in the innovation-adoption model perspective. Gatignon and Robertson (1985) present a set of propositions which range broadly across the literature on diffusion, covering most recognized topics. Smith's probing is more constrained, limited to new product entry and its immediate and subsequent effects on processing and differentiation. From the diffusion perspective, her work fits into the narrower confines of the adoption process and, implicitly, innovator characteristics.

While most of her propositions have a strong element of "common sense" and logic to them, there is some limited controversy here. Maheswaran and Sternthal (1990) suggest it is possible to motivate people to process information in detail; Smith suggests product category knowledge will dictate likelihood of processing information. These are not conflicting notions, but it will be interesting to see what the limits are for each.

It would be useful to test Smith's notions in the diffusion model; such tests could add depth to a literature which, thirty-plus years after its inception, still lacks detail in many areas. With Smith's propositions incorporating elements such as type of processing, product knowledge, and motivation, opportunity, and ability to process information from competitors, it seems they have the potential to add refinement to the innovation diffusion mural.

Veryzer gives us an interesting study looking at some elements long-neglected and only beginning to be explored by consumer researchers. The neglect is intriguing, since many products have their aesthetics consciously planned (e.g., cars, furniture, tableware, etc.), and aesthetics even may be the basis for purchase in some (e.g., telephones, silver service, paintings and other art, clothing [Holbrook 1986] and accessories, etc.). The area is one where a number of significant contributions can be made. While, in most cases, aesthetics is not the basis for the advertising appeal which is made (manufacturers seldom refer to their "attractive appliance"), it certainly could be the basis for differentiating brands in a crowded marketplace. It would be useful to explore the relationship between aesthetics and choice conceptually and empirically to define the importance of the topic.

Veryzer's hypothesis on interactive effects is an interesting application of the Gestalt principle. We should be skeptical of the test results on the natural sound machine which, apparently, had problems in the visual representation. A distortion problem in an aesthetics study seems substantial, indeed. With an improved treatment presentation, this is a notion worth reexamination.

Somasundaram's present work leaves several things unclear. As it stands, it is a simple manipulation with two covariates. The exposition left me wondering about the adequacy of some of the measures, of the dependent variable, even of the internal validity of the study. It is not clear that this experiment has tested any of the extant attribution theory models. The results of such a study are of limited value. However, the importance of this paper lies in what it may generate in the future rather than what it is here. The author intends to do a study examining the impact of involvement and product knowledge on causal attributions. Such a study would fit in the attributional bias literature (Folkes 1988).

TESTABILITY

When formulating research questions, hypotheses, or propositions, researchers must frame them in a way which will render them amenable to testing. There are at least three factors which must be considered: clear specification of relationships, maintaining a consistent perspective on concepts, and recognizing the need for operational definitions.

Unless relationships are specified clearly, there may be uncertainty regarding appropriate testing methods. If concepts are viewed inconsistently, there will be confusion regarding which perspective should be adopted in testing; ultimately, this could confound the operational definitions and operationalizations which are developed.

For example, one of Smith's major constructs is the level of processing used by potential adopters. She suggests the degree of match/mismatch or differentiation between a brand and its product category will influence level of processing, yet some of her propositions suggest level of processing is person-related. This should be clarified.

Veryzer provides a substantial amount of description of his concepts, leading to clearly understandable operationalizations. The relationships are specified clearly, and there is consistency in the use of terminology. The end result is a clear ability to test the hypotheses he presents.

Somasundaram's descriptions also meet the criteria for testability. However, some of his operationalizations need additional thought for a clear test of his hypotheses.

METHODOLOGY

In general, care and thought must be given to the research design as they are to other aspects of research. In addition to the overall design, time can be well spent reflecting about choice of manipulations, representations of concepts, choosing dependent measures, and minimizing potential for demand effects.

Veryzer's research uses a within-subjects design. He tells us few subjects appear to have a conscious awareness of design principles. Conscious awareness may not be necessary to bias a result; Janiszewzki (1991) found evidence of subconscious processing which influenced evaluations of brand names and logos. The added information available to subjects in a within-subjects design certainly has the potential to exert unusual influences. A replication using a between-subjects design would have the potential to provide a "cleaner" result.

Somasundaram's original design here was a pilot study. His presentation of the projected work raises interesting issues on some choices on methodology.

An experimenter must make decisions on the nature of the independent variable. The success-failure manipulation here seems well-defined. A decision must be made on how great the deviation of the "failure" condition must be relative to the "expected" condition to be judged a "failure." Obviously, the deviation must be substantial enough to have the intended effect, but too great a deviation may cause subjects to consider the exercise as obvious, and to treat it trivially. Pretesting of several different "failure" renderings would be desirable.

Related to this notion is the choice of photographs to study the phenomenon. I wonder if the product is important enough to raise questions about failure causes. As Folkes (1984, p. 407) states, "If the product is trivial, consumers may neglect to ask themselves why the failure has occurred." In this case, the subjects did not take the pictures, so they have no investment in them. Beyond this, poor photographs are not a tragedy. A photograph often may be retaken, and processing can be redone. The question then arises whether it is worth the effort to establish causal attributions.

The use of a comparison picture to establish an expectation raises questions about the potential for demand effects. If the "baseline" picture is seen as possible, then the "failure" picture may be perceived as an unnecessary outcome and questions may arise regarding the intent of the experiment. Since Somasundaram is using two buildings in close proximity (which may be identified in captions), perhaps a "baseline" photo is unnecessary. Then, only the "failure" photo need be presented to those in the "failure" condition, with those in the "ambiguous" condition receiving one flawed picture and one perfect picture, and those in the "success" condition receiving two perfect pictures. Again, pretesting would determine the feasibility (and need) for this approach.

Choosing buildings to manipulate situation-specific involvement assumes involvement with the architecture of the buildings. It would help to have a measure to confirm involvement differences. At minimum, manipulation checks are needed; but these are *post hoc*. Some preliminary testing might help determine, *a priori*, that the manipulations will have the intended effects. This does not obviate the need to test involvement levels; it only means the manipulations *may* work.

I have had difficulty determining what the new research design will look like. Somasundaram says 1/3 of the subjects will be put in each of the three conditions. However, each condition seems to have a different number of cells, or treatments. There is no need to balance the number of people in each of the three major conditions. In fact, this will lead to an unnecessarily large number of subjects being used.

It appears that the Success condition is a control; Failure will have four treatments (assuming within-treatment consistency of failures) representing two sources of failure (photographer and processing) and two types of controllability (controllable, uncontrollable). Within-treatment consistency of failure will reinforce the attributional ascriptions; inconsistency may confound them. The Ambiguous condition will have eight treatments (two "success" results X two failure sources X two controllability types). Thus, thirteen cells are needed. The numbers needed per cell can be estimated in pretesting.

MUNDANE REALITY

Research can have a sterile quality to it. Often, it arises from necessity. As the researcher "purifies" the design in focusing on the effects of the independent variable, and attaining a high level of internal validity, experiments can become distant from "real world" representations. In the early stages of a research program, this may be desirable to see if the research model behaves as expected. However, as the research progresses, it is desirable to see if the findings are robust. In addition, adding mundane reality to the manipulations may change perceptions.

Veryzer's study was designed to look only at two elements involved in aesthetics design - proportion and unity. In that sense, the design was quite "clean" and focused. However, products are not assessed in a vacuum; there will be other elements in the viewing field, and the buyer's schema may include, e.g., a setting in which the product will be used. The focus in this study is on the physical image of the object, in isolation from other stimuli. A manipulation including more mundane reality might change or influence aesthetic perceptions. Kleine and Kernan (1991) present evidence that context of presentation influences perceptions, affecting the meanings ascribed to ordinary objects. Certainly, future research should examine the changes which may be introduced to aesthetic response by context effects.

DEPENDENT VARIABLES AND MEASURES

The dependent variable should have soundly reasoned conceptual ties to the theory or research model being tested. There may be many different representations of the dependent variable which would be appropriate; it may be closely aligned with the manipulation, or it may be more removed (as a second-order effect); it may be behavioral or verbal. However, there is one desirable characteristic of *all* dependent variables: sensitivity appropriate to the strength of the treatment.

Somasundaram's proposed dependent measures are verbal, based on the Weiner (1986) model of attributional causes: locus, stability, and controllability. Locus and controllability will be manipulated; all three causes will be examined. I wonder if the intended dependent measures (thought listings) will be sensitive enough to show differences. Thought listings assume substantial commitment on the part of the subjects. To the extent that they do commit to the task, such an approach will be useful. However, the use of subclassifications of the thought listings may miss potentially useful experimental effects because the dependent variable fails to reveal them. The approach taken by Folkes (1984), using semantic differential scales, might prove more revealing. Certainly, Somasundaram could use his pilot test to develop sets of possible causes to be evaluated and put them in scalar form. Such an approach assumes less of the subject, with the potential to increase power to test the manipulations.

ANALYSIS

The need to plan the analysis before conducting an experiment is well known. The analysis must be appropriate for the design.

Veryzer's use of simple ANOVA leaves us in limbo regarding results. LaTour and Miniard (1983) describe the problems arising from use of between-subjects analysis in within-subjects designs. The end result of such use can be an underestimation *or* an overestimation of the alpha rate, with no way to evaluate the accuracy of the inferences. A more appropriate approach would be to use a repeated measures ANOVA or a repeated measures MANOVA. This is a correction easily made.

REFERENCES

Folkes, Valerie S. (1984), "Consumer Reactions to Product Failure: An Attributional Approach," *Journal of Consumer Research*, 10, 398-409.

_____ (1988), "Recent Attribution Research in Consumer Behavior: A Review and New Directions," *Journal of Consumer Research*, 14, 548-565.

Gatignon, Hubert, and Thomas S. Robertson (1985), "A Propositional Inventory for New Diffusion Research," *Journal of Consumer Research*, 11, 849-867.

Holbrook, Morris B. (1986), "Aims, Concepts, and Methods for the Representation of Individual Differences in Esthetic Responses to Design Features," *Journal of Consumer Research*, 11, 337-347.

Janiszewski, Chris (1990), "The Influence of Print Advertisement Organization on Affect Toward a Brand Name," *Journal of Consumer Research*, 17, 53-65.

Kleine III, Robert E., and Jerome B. Kernan (1991), "Contextual Influences on the Meanings Ascribed to Ordinary Objects," *Journal of Consumer Research*, 18, 311-324.

LaTour, Stephen A., and Paul W. Miniard (1983), "The Misuse of Repeated Measures Analysis in Marketing Research," *Journal of Marketing Research*, XX, 45-57.

Maheswaran, Durairaj, and Brian Sternthal (1990), "The Effects of Knowledge, Motivation, and Type of Message on Ad Processing and Product Judgments," *Journal of Consumer Research*, 17, 66-73.

Simon, Julian L. (1969), *Basic Research Methods in Social Science: The Art of Empirical Investigation*, New York: Random House.

Smith, Karen H. (this volume), "The Moderating Influence of Depth of Processing on Order of Entry Processing Effects."

Somasundaram, T. N. (this volume), "Consumers' Reaction to Product Failure: Impact of Product Involvement and Knowledge."

Veryzer, Robert W. (this volume), "Aesthetic Response and the Influence of Design Principles on Product Preferences."

Weiner, Bernard (1986), *An Attributional Theory of Motivation and Emotion*, New York: Springer-Verlag.

Vesting Objects and Experiences with Symbolic Meaning
Summary of a Special Session (with Discussant's Remarks)
Robert F. Kelly, University of British Columbia

INTRODUCTION
This special session was housed in the theatre-gallery of the Museum of Anthropology at the University of British Columbia.

Presentation #1
Museum as a Meaning Maker/Meaning Taker: A Study of the Reciprocal Exchange of Symbolic Properties Between the Museum, Its Objects, and Its Publics
Grant McCracken, Royal Ontario Museum

This paper considered the contemporary museum first as a "meaning maker" and then as "meaning taker." *Meaning making* occurs when the museum changes the cultural significance of its objects and publics. *Meaning taking* occurs because the museum is endowed with meanings by its publics. Publics are divided into "old wealth," "new wealth," and "the politically correct." Old wealth demonstrates the justice of its social standing; new wealth is "laundered;" and the politically correct seek to impose "a reappropriation model" so that each ethnic group may tell its own story rather than accept that offered by the museum.

Presentation #2
The Role of Nostalgia in the Appreciation of the Dear Departed Past: Update on a Program of Research
Robert M. Schindler, Rutgers University-Camden and Morris B. Holbrook, Columbia University

This paper reviewed an ongoing program of research exploring the idea that there is a component of nostalgia behind a wide array of human preferences. The method developed for this research could be called the "dated-stimulus technique." Using this technique to study a product category involves collecting a set of such dated, briefly popular stimuli that span the past sixty or more years and asking respondents of widely varying ages to rate the appeal of each stimulus in the set. A peaking of this function at an early stimulus-specific age constitutes evidence for an enduring effect of early experience on preferences. Early-experience effects have been found, thus far, in popular music, clothing and hairstyle fashions, movies, and movie stars. In the latter two studies they have evidence of "nostalgia proneness."

Presentation #3
Vesting Cultural Objects with Meaning in a Museum
Annamma Joy, Concordia University

Using an ethnographic approach this paper examines the process of negotiations through which social meaning is vested in art objects and artifacts. This process has been highly political with the artist and the public having less power than museums, the government, or other cultural institutions. Recently, however, this balance of power has shifted. The power the museum has to represent other societies and cultures has come under much scrutiny since the questions that are asked have to do with whose interests are being served. Any claim to cultural authenticity is suspect. Museum practices are to be continuously evaluated and perpetual deconstruction seems to be the most viable principle in guiding the activities of the museum. Deconstruction, however, does not merely refer to the collection of more artifacts but involves an active dialogue with the communities that they serve.

DISCUSSION: VESTING OBJECTS AND EXPERIENCES WITH SYMBOLIC MEANING
Robert F. Kelly
University of British Columbia

Purpose...
My very first inquiry involving symbolic consumption occurred here in the Museum of Anthropology well over a decade ago... what I observed exemplifies the power symbolism may exercise over the members of any society and serves as an illustration of the means by which, in any social system, objects, experiences, and settings take on meanings which may have little or nothing to do with the purposes for which they were originally created.

Asked by Director Michael Ames and Ethnology Curator Marjorie Halpin (our hosts today) to examine the nature of their visitor populations and discover motives and reactions to a visit, I began by sitting in the foyer watching parties of visitors descend from their tour buses into the museum. I charted where they went, for how long, and what their apparent reactions were based on their behaviours. Subsequently, I did pre- and post- visit interviews and observed visitor behaviours in the various spaces that comprise this museum. What I observed amazed me then and continues to amaze me today despite having observed the same phenomena in the Met and MOMA in New York, the Royal Academy and the British Museum, The Louvre, Musèe D'Orsay, The Rijksmuseum, and the National Museum of Thailand. Specifically: A significant minority of museum visitors, averaging around thirty per cent, never enter the galleries one would assume they came to visit despite travelling some distance (often from out-of-country), despite being in the museum in question for the first time, and, last but not least, despite having paid a substantial sum to be brought on a tour of this museum. To further compound the mystery, many of those interviewed did not ordinarily visit museums in their home cities.

Seeking a logical explanation for the behaviour just described introduced me to the literature of a number of related disciplines and, eventually, to the realization that I was not the first to observe this visit-the-museum-but-not-the-collection behaviour. While "wading in the shallows of other disciplines," as Doyle Weiss once characterized it, I discovered a number of possible explanations for non-collection-based visiting. All such explanations centre around the importance of *having been* to a museum rather than from having seen some item in its collection (although that too can have symbolic value). Because of time/space limitations, I am going to confine my remarks today to those who seem interested in "collecting" museums but not necessarily in viewing museum collections.

Museum visiting as pilgrimage
One possible explanation for museum collecting comes from the literature on pilgrimage. Pilgrimage provides an illuminating analog to the type of museum visiting described in the preceding section; "having been" may constitute a transformation, a rite of passage, the attainment of new, elevated status to the individual museum visitor. To carry this analogy even further, there are

liminal effects (i.e., one modifies ones behaviour once over the threshhold and into the sacred precincts), one tends to observe dress and behavioural codes consistent with the setting, there are areas of sacred visitation where the holiest of the icons are on display (e.g., the Mona Lisa at the Louvre), and sacred relics may be purchased and taken back to ones own community to signal that one has become the museum visitor equivalent of Haji.

Museum visiting as a function of peer group influence

The importance of having been to a museum may be the result of a specific statement of expectation by ones peers (i.e., "significant others") in ones home community: "You're going to Paris? You *must* go to the Musèe D'Orsay," or the Louvre, or the Rodin, or whatever. What previously constituted a discretionary leisure alternative has been transformed by ones significant others into a visit of obligation. One *might* have gone before, now one *must* go. What one does once there is of relatively little symbolic importance, but *having been* is.

The museum visit as status congruent behaviour

Alternatively, visiting world-renowned museums may have a more general symbolic importance, signalling ones sophistication, taste, and/or social *milieu*. Pierre Bourdieu argues that this constitutes a public declaration of taste and serves to establish social distance between one and the insignificant others in a society (Bourdieu 1984). Museums are accused by many as being elitist and, notwithstanding the efforts of many in the museum profession, they *are* elitist based on the demographics of museum visitors. In part, this can be attributed to the educational requirements museum exhibits place on their visitors but, also, society itself has defined museum visiting as a symbol of relatively high status. General status associations apply to a range of museum visiting experiences. Even eating and drinking in museums can have symbolic overtones. The Tate Gallery in London, MOMA in New York, and either the Louvre or the Musèe D'Orsay in Paris all attract large numbers of restaurant patrons who do not visit the museum galleries. No doubt some dine in a museum restaurant simply because they prefer the food over that available nearby; but that is hard to argue in a city like Paris where one passes renowned restaurants in approaching either of the museums named. And, finally, organizations that pay $30000 or more for the privilege of holding a cocktail party in one of the Met galleries is doing more than just hiring a hall, they are making a statement about the importance of their company and the taste and sophistication of their executive group as well.

Whether responding to peer pressure or seeking status congruent discretionary leisure activities, one need not visit a museum collection, need not accomplish any of the tasks set for one by curators and exhibit designers, but one may wish to collect something from the shop that provides unambiguous evidence of *having been* because, inevitably, one or more sight-marker associations will be placed in the publics mind where objects (i.e, reproductions of the markers) symbolize a visit (MacCannell (1976).

Finally, one need never go again to a museum once *having been* status is attained. The incremental symbolic benefits are minimal. Once a state of *having been* is attained, it is never lost. The more widely known the museum in question, the more likely it will serve as a destination for those whose museum visit is of symbolic as well as (or in lieu of) informational significance.

Museums defined as meaningful leisure alternatives

Not only do museums confer meaning on individual visitors, some individuals have the power to vest museums with meaning while themselves receiving symbolic benefits. The UBC Museum of Anthropology, for example, has been visited by many heads of state and a host of other celebrities. Several monarchs, including The Queen, have been here; so too have Jimmy Carter, Francois Mitterand, Deng Jao Peng, the leaders of all the Commonwealth Countries, and, of course, all Canadian Prime Ministers since the museum opened. Reason suggests that all, with the possible exception of woodcarver Jimmy Carter, were here for reasons beyond a simple personal wish to view the collection. I doubt that the Queen (or any other public figure) really wants another museum visit on top of the thousands she has already made. Public figures come here because MOA is a destination of obligation for all worthies who visit Vancouver; because they must be seen to be engaged in meaningful activities while here; the museum qualifies. These public figures convey special status or meaning to the institution in question as well as having their own images enhanced by the museum. The presence of public figures in a museum is made even more special by the media attention such visits attract. If the Queen thinks a museum is worth visiting, then there must be something special there for others as well.

Museum - object interactions

Just as the relationship between visitors and museums can work both ways, so too can the relationship between museums and objects. Few great world museums are perceived independent of at least some item in their collection. The Ryksmuseum is known in part because it contains the Night Watch; and The Louvre because of the Mona Lisa, for example. Everyone who knows this museum is conscious of the "Raven and the First Men" sculpture by Bill Reid that you passed on the way into this session. The object gives meaning to the museum.

The object-museum relationship can work against as well as for the museum, of course. Once one has seen the Mona Lisa, it is not really necessary to bother with the rest of the collection. This reinforces the pilgrimage analogy I discussed earlier. In pilgrimage, there is usually one object/place that, once experienced, completes a transformation; in many museums visitors behave as though their mission were complete after viewing one object (McCannell 1976). With traveling exhibits this may be engineered through promotion. When the Tut exhibit travelled through North America a few years ago, the Tutankhamen death mask was employed in all publicity as representative of the whole exhibit. For many visitors, that led to focussing almost exclusively on the death mask both in viewing and in obtaining evidence of having seen the exhibit (Wall and Knapper 1981).

How do objects get into museum collections?

The fundamental distinction between a piece of junk and an artifact is that one has been chosen and housed within the confines of a museum and the other has been discarded. Curators employ selection models acquired through formal education and passed from generation to generation. The museum itself is designated by society as the place to house both our curators and our heritage.

Considering art museums for a moment, the very fact that a painting has appeared in an art museum lends symbolic weight (and, consequently, market advantage) not only to that painting but to all other work done by the artist who created it. Until one has work in a museum, one is viewed as suspect both as an artist and as an investment.

Museums provide appropriate settings for heritage objects

Museum exhibits are installed in settings that facilitate an appropriate interpretation of the objects it contains. I'm certain most of you will agree that the UBC Museum of Anthropology provides a behavioural space that is in keeping with the objects it contains. That does not happen by accident. To illustrate how a setting conveys (or fails to convey) meaning consider a recent exhibition in Switzerland of "precious Christian objects" in a gallery made to look like the greasy interior of a small town car repair shop. That exhibition violated (intentionally) the elements of exhibit design to make a point about the static quality of museum interpretation. Its designer, Jacques Hainard, was at the centre of a great storm of controversy at a recent meeting of the International Council of Museums because he violated *the curatorial code*. (Kelly 1987a).

A trickle-down effect in museums

Since curators (or their equivalent) serve as society's arbiters and interpreters of taste and/or ethnological significance, the objects they select are seen as being "authentic," or the real thing. This authenticating process is so powerful that we immediately accept as art any object exhibited in an art museum. Even if deep down it seems like "junk," we are likely to concede that the deficiency is in ourselves rather than in the object in question. Interviewing visitors to a contemporary art museum makes that phenomenon (and the frustration and/or anger that it fosters) dramatically apparent.

We even attribute authenticity to objects sold in museum shops. We presume shop items are an extension of the museum collection or, at the very least, are "authentic museum-quality items," whatever that may mean. This sense of authenticity is strong enough to support the shops of the Metropolitan Museum of Art and the Museum of Modern Art in Rockerfeller Centre, even though neither museum is housed there. The Met has an internationally-distributed catalog and several non-New York shop locations, including five shops in Japan. If we go back to our earlier discussion about acquiring evidence of having been to a given museum, such shops, catalogues and the like enable one to collect evidence of having been *without ever having to go*. The value that tendency represents to the Met is $100 million gross this past year - and questions concerning its tax-free status.

There is a limit to the credibility of those seeking authenticity, however. Anthropologists talk about "staged authenticity" and warn that one instance of phoney or staged authenticity can lead to permanent rejection by consumers of a given institution. One famous instance of this occured when cultural tourists on a government/museum-sponsored tour discovered they were witnessing the third burial of the same corpse that day. The burial ritual which had attracted more and more tourists was robbed of its perceived authenticity and the government/museum was relieved of its powers to declare an experience as authentic.

A brief comment about those who love being in museums

What about those who visit museums because they *love being there*; who return over and over to a museum and its collection? Is there symbolism in their visiting behaviour as well? I believe so. Those for whom the objects in a museum are intellectually and/or esthetically accessible bring with them the information necessary to benefit from whatever interpretation has been given by curators/designers to the objects in an exhibition. They share with museum personnel the "curatorial code" (Bourdieu 1984; Kelly 1987b). Possession of The Code signals taste and sophistication. In Veblen's terminology, they are engaging in conspicuous display or conspicuous consumption. That is, they are demonstrating "... an instrumentally-useless style of consumption requiring many years to learn" (Veblen 1899) Whether one accepts Veblen's explanation or the "parody display" explanation John Brooks provides in *Showing off in America*, museum visiting constitutes an important symbolic statement of ones sophistication and/or level of educational attainment (Brroks 1981).

Some concluding remarks

Today, in keeping with our setting, my comments have been directed towards museum visitors and museum visiting. Most of those comments could as easily have been directed towards opera going or symphony patronage or ballet subscriptions. After years spent researching the consumption of cultural objects and cultural experiences it has become evident that, for many, the symbolic values associated with a cultural experience exceed the instrumental values it can provide. If anything, symbolic attributes enhance rather than detract from a cultural experience. For the majority of cultural consumers, the instrumental and/or educational values likely outweigh symbolic elements. But, in all cultural experiences, high or low, symbolism is a major motivating factor.

REFERENCES

Bourdieu, Pierre (Translated by R. Nice), *Distinction: A Social Critique of the Judgement of Taste*, Harvard University Press, 1984.

Brooks, John, *Showing Off in America: From Conspicuous Consumption to Parody Display*, Boston: Little, Brown, 1981.

Kelly, Robert F., "Culture as Commodity: The Marketing of Cultural Objects and Cultural Experiences," in M. Wallendorf and P. Anderson (Eds.), *Advances in Consumer Research*, Vol. XIV, 1987a.

Kelly, Robert F., "Museums as Status Symbols II: Attaining a State of Having Been," in Belk, R. (Ed.), *Advances in Nonprofit Marketing*, Vol. 2, pages 1-38, JAI Press, Inc., 1987b.

MacCannell, Dean, *The Tourist: A New Theory of the Working Class*, Schockon Books, New York, 1976.

Veblen, Thorstein, *The Theory of the Leisure Class*, (New Library Edition, 1963), 1899.

Wall, G. and C. Knapper, *Tutankhamen in Toronto*, Department of Geography Publication No. 17, University of Waterloo, 1981.

Image Theory: An Alternative to Normative Decision Theory
Lee Roy Beach, University of Arizona

ABSTRACT

Research and theory about how people make decisions has changed markedly over the years. The present article describes the course of that change, with focus on a new descriptive theory called Image Theory. The theory's basic structure is described and the research that it has motivated is discussed. Implications for consumer research are examined.

For the past forty years, research on individual decision making has been guided by normative models of choice, largely borrowed from economics. Half of that time has been spent demonstrating the failure of these models as credible descriptions of how people actually make decisions (Beach & Lipschitz, in press). In spite of the mounting evidence that normative models fail at the level of individual decision making, there has been a reticence to relinquish them.

There are, however, fresh winds blowing. Alternatives to the economic model of decision making are being developed (see Klein, Orasanu, Calderwood & Zsambok, in press). The purpose of the present paper is to present the alternative that has thus far received the greatest degree of theoretical development and the largest amount of empirical research, image theory (Beach, 1990; Beach & Mitchell, 1987, 1990; Beach, Mitchell, Paluchowski & van Zee, 1992).

IMAGE THEORY

Images

To begin, image theory assumes that decision makers use three different schematic knowledge structures to organize their thinking about decisions. These structures are called *images*, in deference to Miller, Galanter, and Pribram (1960), whose work inspired image theory. The first of the three is the *value image*, the constituents of which are the decision maker's *principles*. These are the imperatives for his or her behavior or the behavior of the organization of which he or she is a member and serve as rigid criteria for the rightness or wrongness of any particular decision about a goal or plan. Principles serve to internally generate *candidate* goals and plans for possible adoption, and they guide decisions about externally generated candidate goals and plans.

The second image is the *trajectory image*, the constituents of which are previously adopted *goals*. This image represents what the decision maker hopes he, she or the organization will become and achieve. Goals can be concrete, specific events (getting the money to buy a new Honda Accord DX) or abstract states (achieving a successful career). The goal agendum is called the trajectory image to convey the idea of extension, the decision maker's vision of the ideal future.

The third image is the *strategic image*, the constituents of which are the various *plans* that have been adopted for achieving the goals on the trajectory image. Each plan is an abstract sequence of potential activities beginning with goal adoption and ending with goal attainment. One aspect of plans, their concrete behavioral components, are *tactics*. Tactics are specific, palpable actions that are intended to facilitate implementation of an abstract plan to further progress toward a goal. The second aspect of plans is *forecasts*. A plan is inherently an anticipation of the future, a forecast about what will happen if certain classes of tactics are executed in the course of plan implementation. However, it need not be inflexible—it can change in light of information about the changing environment in which implementation is (or might be) taking place. Therefore, it serves both to guide behavior and to forecast the results of that behavior. By monitoring these forecasts in relation to the goals on the trajectory image, the decision maker can evaluate his or her progress toward realization of the ideal agendum on the trajectory image.

Two Kinds of Decisions, Two Decision Tests

There are two kinds of decisions, *adoption decisions* and *progress decisions*. These decisions are made using either or both of two kinds of decision tests, the *compatibility test* or the *profitability test*.

Adoption decisions also can be divided into two different kinds, *screening* decisions and *choice* decisions. Adoption decisions are about adoption or rejection of candidate goals or plans as constituents of the trajectory or strategic images. Screening consists of eliminating unacceptable candidates. Choice consists of selecting the most promising from among the survivors of screening.

Progress decisions consist of assaying the fit between the forecasted future if implementation of a given plan is continued (or if a particular candidate plan were to be adopted and implemented) and the ideal future as defined by the trajectory image. Incompatibility triggers rejection of the plan and adoption of a substitute (often merely a revision of the old plan that takes into consideration feedback about the environment). Failure to find a promising substitute prompts reconsideration of the plan's goal.

The compatibility test describes adoption decisions as deriving from the compatibility (or incompatibility) between the candidate and standards that are defined by the three images. Actually, the focus is upon *lack* of compatibility in that a candidate's compatibility decreases as a function of the weighted sum of the number of its violations of the standards that derive from the images, where the weights reflect the importance of the standard (Beach, Smith, Lundell & Mitchell, 1988; Beach & Strom, 1989; van Zee, Paluchowski & Beach, 1992). Violations are defined as negations, contradictions, contraventions, preventions, retardations, or any similar form of interference with the actualization of one of the images' constituents. Each violation is all-or-none (-1 or 0). The decision rule is that if the weighted sum of the violations exceeds some absolute *rejection threshold*, the candidate is rejected, otherwise it is adopted. The rejection threshold is that weighted sum above which the decision maker regards the candidate as incompatible with his, her, or the organization's principles, goals, and ongoing plans.

The formal statement of the compatibility test is:

$$I = \sum_{c=1}^{n} \sum_{s=1}^{m} W_s V_{cs}, \qquad (1)$$

where $V_{cs} = 0$ or -1, and $.00 \leq W \leq 1.0$.

That is, incompatibility, I, is zero when an option violates no principles and increases (becomes increasingly *negative*) as the number of violations increases. In the equation, c is a characteristic of an option, s is a standard, V is a violation of a standard s by characteristic c and counts as a -1, and W is the weight for each standard; W is between and including .00 and 1.00. Because violations count only as -1, incompatibility is measured as the negative sum of the importance weights of the violated standards; a particular characteristic can violate more than one standard (Beach, 1990; Beach and Mitchell, 1987; 1990).

The decision maker's tolerance of incompatibility is described theoretically as the rejection threshold. This is the critical value of I that the decision maker will tolerate before screening out an option. Because it is influenced by many factors (Beach, 1990), the critical value of I may vary from one decision to the next. Therefore, in experiments the critical value of I, the rejection threshold, must be inferred from data. Nonetheless, as we shall see, I is a theoretically viable construct, the crucial role of which in screening can be empirically demonstrated.

The compatibility test describes progress decisions as deriving from the compatibility (or incompatibility) between the trajectory and strategic images. In this case violations are of the trajectory image's constituents by the strategic image's constituents (its forecasts). The decision rule is that when the weighted sum of violations exceeds the rejection threshold, reevaluation of the plan that generated the forecast is undertaken and the faulty plan is replaced. Note that the compatibility test serves both adoption and progress decisions.

The profitability test describes choices from among the survivors of screening by the compatibility test. Unlike the compatibility test, the profitability test is not a single mechanism. Instead, it is a short-hand term for the unique repertory of choice strategies (Beach & Mitchell, 1978) that the individual decision maker possesses for adopting the potentially most profitable candidate from among a set of two or more candidates, all of which are at least minimally acceptable. The minimal acceptability of the adoption candidates from among which the choice is to be made is assured by the prior application of the compatibility test. In short, the profitability test is a 'tie breaker' when more than one adoption candidate passes the compatibility test's screening. The compatibility test describes how wholly unacceptable candidates are eliminated from further consideration and the profitability test describes how the best is chosen from among the survivors. Of course, if only one candidate survives the compatibility test there is no need to apply the profitability test—the candidate simply is adopted on the basis of compatibility. The profitability test serves adoption decisions but does not serve progress decisions.

EMPIRICAL RESEARCH ON IMAGE THEORY

Image theory draws upon a broad and varied conceptual and empirical literature (see Beach, 1990). However, because the theory is so new, the research that it has generated has necessarily been somewhat narrow in focus. Thus far the emphasis has been upon the compatibility test in screening and the profitability test in choice.

Compatibility in Screening

The study of screening had its beginning with research by Payne (1976). Based upon the way in which subjects searched for information about the characteristics of the options, Payne concluded that they began by screening out the least acceptable options using simple, noncompensatory strategies, and then switched to more complicated, compensatory strategies to choose the best option from among the survivors of screening. The most commonly accepted interpretation of these results is that subjects strive to reduce the processing demands of the task by using simple strategies to eliminate obviously flawed options, reserving their cognitive resources for the more complicated strategies by which they make choices among the survivors. In short, screening is merely preliminary to the main event, choice.

Image theory resurrects the question of screening. It proposes that decision making indeed has two steps, screening and choice, but that because screening determines the choice set from which the best will be chosen, it clearly is as central to the process as choice is. Indeed, whenever screening results in a choice set that contains only one option, a common circumstance, there is no need for choice at all and the decision is wholly determined by screening.

Image theory research on screening has followed Payne's (1976) lead in using decision options (entry level jobs, rental rooms, or condominiums) that are easily understood and evaluated by the college students who serve as research subjects. The general strategy has been to present an array of options to the subjects with instructions to examine the options' characteristics and form a 'short list' (i.e., to screen and to form a choice set). Then they are instructed to choose the best (most promising) option from the short list. Depending upon the experiment, the dependent variables are the way in which information is examined, ratings of the options' attractiveness, and subjects' selections for the short list or for the best option.

Violations. Beach and Strom (1989) asked subjects to assume the role of a newly graduated student who was looking for a job. Each subject was presented with an array of jobs; the characteristics of each job violated or did not violate the job seeker's standards. The results showed that rejection of options regularly occurred after observation of roughly four violations; this is the rejection threshold. Nonviolations played virtually no role at all in screening except to stop information search when no violations were observed (or else a perfect option never would be accepted because the search for violations would never stop). In short, the Beach and Strom (1989) study supports the hypothesis that screening relies almost exclusively upon on violations of standards. It also demonstrates the existence of a rejection threshold, and suggests that for a specific decision task the rejection threshold may remain fairly constant.

The Beach and Strom (1989) finding about the primacy of violations in screening was confirmed by Rediker, Mitchell, Beach and Beard (in press) in a different context when MBA students made decisions about various computer firms as options for acquisition by a diversifying business. A correlation of -.95 was obtained between the rated acceptability of options during screening and the number of violations by those firms of the customary practices and strategic goals (standards) of the acquiring business.

Two-step process. Van Zee, Paluchowski and Beach (1992) examined what happens to the information that has been used in screening when the time comes to choose the best from among the survivors in the choice set. In the course of the experiment, subjects made ratings of the acceptability of the options (rooms to rent) at various points in the process of screening and choosing. As expected, results showed that ratings made during screening precisely reflected the options' violations, and that violations precisely predicted which options were rejected and which were retained for the choice set. However, when ratings were made during choice, something quite unexpected was found. These ratings reflected only the information that was obtained about the surviving options *after* they had been screened. That is, the information used to screen the options did not appear to have much impact on evaluations made during choice (correlations between .02 and .07), while information received after screening had a major impact on pre-choice evaluations (correlations between .67 and .86). It was as though, as one subject remarked, the information used in screening had been 'used up' and had nothing to contribute to choice.

That the two steps, screening and choice, are quite different tasks is even more clearly shown by the results of a study by Potter and Beach (in press, b). Here some subjects were given descriptions of six options (time-share condos) and asked to screen them to create a choice set. Other subjects were given the same descriptions of the options and were asked to choose among them. The unique feature of the experiment was that in both cases each description contained information about the probability (.75 or .25) that the option would be available when the decision maker wanted it.

For the screening group, the prediction was that the availability information would be used as an absolute standard, with .25 being regarded as a violation and .75 being regarded as a nonviolation. This means that when the probability is .25 the result simply is an increase in the number of violations. In the data, this increase would be evidenced as an *additive* combination of the 'availability violation' with the other violations.

For the choice group, the prediction was that availability would be used as a probability in the manner prescribed by the expected utility choice model (Raiffa, 1968); the option's utility would be discounted by the probability, .25 or .75, that it would be available. In the data, discounting would be evidenced as a *multiplicative* combination of availability and utility.

Results were as predicted. The same information, availability, was used differently in the two tasks. The implication is that screening and choice are distinctly different tasks that rely on distinctly different information processing.

An empty choice set. Potter and Beach (in press, a) examined what happens when subjects screen and then move on to choice only to find that the options in the choice set have become unavailable. For example, suppose the job applicants on one's short list have taken other jobs, or the condos one was going to examine further and choose from among have already been taken.

In the first experiment, 35 subjects screened options (rooms to rent). Then, when they were ready to choose the best option from among the survivors they were told that none of the options in the choice set were available. They were asked whether they would prefer to search for new options or to go back and reconsider the options they had previously rejected. Thirty-one of the 35 (89%) said that they would prefer to start all over with a new set of options.

Other subjects were presented with the same task except that they were told that there were no new options to be had and they would have to rescreen the options that they had rejected and arrive at a new choice set. Two things happened. On the one hand, subjects lowered their standards a little when they rescreened. On the other hand, they also relaxed their rejection thresholds a little when they rescreened. By doing both things they were able to avoid having to make gross compromises in either the standards or in their tolerance of imperfection.

Imperfect information. Finally, Potter and Beach (1992) examined the effects on screening when only imperfect information about options (condos) was available. Each option had eight characteristics, some of which violated standards and some of which did not. Additionally, however, information about various characteristics was missing for different options. Results showed that subjects treated missing information about a characteristic as though it were a violation. The effect of doing this is to make screening increasingly conservative—the less that is known about an option, the less the decision maker is inclined to pass it on to the choice set. Then, on top of this initial conservatism is added an even greater disinclination to pass the option as its observed violations increase in number.

The Profitability Test and Choice

Research on the profitability test is older than research on the compatibility test because the former was motivated by Beach and Mitchell's earlier (1978) decision strategy selection model. As was stated above, the profitability test is a name for the decision maker's repertory of choice strategies. Image theory incorporates the Beach and Mitchell (1978) strategy selection model as the profitability test. Thus research on the profitability test, strategy selection, draws heavily from existing literature (e.g., Lussier & Olshavsky, 1979; Olshavsky, 1979; Payne, 1976; Payne, Bettman & Johnson, 1988, in press; Svenson, 1979) in addition to work done in our own laboratory (Christensen-Szalanski, 1978, 1980; Huffman, 1978; McAllister, Mitchell and Beach, 1979; Nichols-Hoppe and Beach, 1989; Smith, Mitchell and Beach, 1982; Waller and Mitchell, 1984). Because space does not permit an account of this research in the same depth as that presented above for screening, the interested reader is referred to Beach (1990) for a detailed description. Briefly, the results support the contention that decision makers possess repertories of choice strategies and that their selection of which strategy to use in a particular decision is contingent upon specific characteristics of the decision problem, the decision environment, and of the decision maker himself or herself. In the context of image theory the profitability test specifies some of these contingencies (Beach, 1990).

IMPLICATIONS FOR CONSUMER RESEARCH

For consumer research, the major implication of the results reported above is that screening and choice are very different processes. Because screening dictates what is available for choice, it is not merely preliminary to the more important and more interesting process, choice. Sometimes screening is the *only* process; when only one option is being considered or when only one option survives screening, choice is unnecessary. In fact, it is only when more than one option survives screening (meaning that from the point of view of meeting minimal standards all of the survivors are equal) that choice is required to break the tie. In the broadest sense, choice really is less interesting than screening rather than more interesting.

The second implication is that the transfer of options from the consideration set to the choice set is not based on the degree to which they comply with the decision maker's standards, as is generally assumed. Rather, retention is based on the *absence* of violations, which sounds like much the same thing, but empirically it is not. Even though decision makers prefer to know about nonviolations first, their screening decisions are almost totally determined by violations. This means that presentation of options to consumers should focus on putting the best possible light on violations (or better yet, correcting them), rather than focussing exclusively on the nonviolations.

The third implication is that decision makers apparently regard screening and choice as two separate tasks, using pre-screening information to screen options and using post-screening information to make choices. The fact that the tasks are separate and use different information suggests that appropriately timing of the presentation of information to consumers may influence their final choices.

The fourth implication is that doubts (low probability) about whether outcomes of options will in fact be forthcoming is treated as just another violation in screening (additively), but may be treated in some other way in choice, among which is discounting the attractiveness of the outcomes (multiplicatively). Similarly, missing information about options is treated as a violation during screening. Therefore, failure to present information about an option's violations will itself be treated as a violation, thereby reducing the acceptability of the option.

The fifth implication is that if the choice set is empty when it is time to make a choice, decision makers will resist having to form a new choice set from among the previously screened out options.

Empty choice sets arise when no option survives screening or when the survivors become unavailable before a choice is made. If they are forced to re-screen the rejected options, decision makers will lower their standards and readjust their rejection thresholds. This frequently is observed when consumers buy options that are in limited supply, such as houses. If the house that meets their standards has been sold by the time they are ready to buy it, prospective homeowners will select a less acceptable house by reducing the importance of some characteristics of houses and by being more tolerant of houses that previously were regarded as unacceptable.

Finally, the research on the multiplicity of strategies by which decision makers make choices has its own implications for consumer research. The research results make it abundantly clear that expected value maximization is but one class of choice strategies and that consumer research must explore the alternatives if a thorough understanding of consumer choice is to be achieved. Decision strategy selection is contingent upon the characteristics of the decision makers themselves, upon the characteristics of the decision task, and upon the characteristics of the environment in which the decision arises. The foundations for the necessary research program is provided by the citations given previously in this article and by the citations in a recent comprehensive review of the work by John Payne and his colleagues (Payne, Bettman & Johnson, in press).

REFERENCES

Beach, L. R. (1990). *Image theory: Decision making in personal and organizational contexts.* Chichester, England: Wiley.

Beach, L. R. & Lipshitz, R. (in press). Why classical decision theory is an inappropriate standard for evaluating and aiding most human decision making. In G. A. Klein, J. Orasanu, R. Calderwood & C. Zsambok (Eds.) *Decision making in action: Models and methods.* New York: Ablex.

Beach, L. R. & Mitchell, T. R. (1978). A contingency model for the selection of decision strategies. *Academy of Management Review,* 3, 439-449.

Beach, L. R. & Mitchell, T. R. (1987). Image theory: Principles goals, and plans in decision making. *Acta Psychologica,* 66, 201-220.

Beach, L. R. & Mitchell, T. R. (1990). Image theory: A behavioral theory of decisions in organizations. In B. M. Staw & L. L. Cummings (Eds.), *Research in organizational behavior* (Vol. 12). Greenwich, CT: JAI.

Beach, L. R., Mitchell, T. R., Paluchowski, T. F. & van Zee, E. H. (1992). Image theory: Decision framing and decision deliberation. In F. Heller (Ed.), *Leadership and decision making.* Cambridge, UK: Cambridge University Press.

Beach, L. R., Smith, B., Lundell, J. & Mitchell, T. R. (1988). Image theory: Descriptive sufficiency of a simple rule for the compatibility test. *Journal of Behavioral Decision Making,* 1, 17-28.

Beach, L. R. & Strom, E. (1989). A toadstool among the mushrooms: Screening decisions and Image Theory's compatibility test. *Acta Psychologica,* 72, 1-12.

Christensen-Szalanski, J. J. J. (1978). Problem-solving strategies: A selection mechanism, some implications, and some data. *Organizational Behavior and Human Performance,* 22, 307-323.

Christensen-Szalanski, J. J. J. (1980). A further examination of the selection of problem-solving strategies: The effects of deadlines and analytic aptitudes. *Organizational Behavior and Human Performance,* 25, 107-122.

Huffman, M. D. (1978). *The effect of decision task characteristics on decision behavior* (Technical Report No. 78-16). University of Washington, Department of Psychology, Seattle.

Klein, G. A., Orasanu, J., Calderwood, R. & Zsambok, C. (Eds.) (in press). *Decision making in action: Models and methods.* New York: Ablex.

Lussier, D. A. & Olshavsky, R. W. (1979). Task complexity and contingent processing in brand choice. *Journal of Consumer Research,* 6, 154-165.

McAllister, D., Mitchell, T. R. & Beach, L. R. (1979). The contingency model for selection of decision strategies: An empirical test of the effects of significance, accountability, and reversibility. *Organizational Behavior and Human Performance,* 24, 228-244.

Miller, G. A., Galanter, E. & Pribram, K. H. (1960). *Plans and the structure of behavior.* New York: Holt, Rinehart & Winston.

Nichols-Hoppe, K. T. & Beach, L. R. (1990). The effects of test anxiety and task variables on predecisional information search. *Journal of Research in Personality,* 24, 163-172.

Olshavsky, R. W. (1979). Task complexity and contingent processing in decision making: A replication and extension. *Organizational Behavior and Human Performance,* 24, 300-316.

Payne, J. W. (1976). Task complexity and contingent processing in decision making: An information search and protocol analysis. *Organizational Behavior and Human Performance,* 16, 366-387.

Payne, J. W., Bettman, J. R. & Johnson, E. J. (1988). Adaptive strategy selection in decision making. *Journal of Experimental Psychology: Learning, Memory and Cognition,* 14, 534-552.

Payne, J. W., Bettman, J. R. & Johnson, E. J. (1992). *The adaptive decision maker.* In press.

Potter, R. E. & Beach, L. R. (in press, a). Decision making when the acceptable options become unavailable. *Organizational Behavior and Human Decision Processes.*

Potter, R. E. & Beach, L. R. (in press, b). Imperfect information in pre-choice screening of options. *Organizational Behavior and Human Decision Processes.*

Raiffa, H. (1968). *Decision analysis: Introductory lectures on choices under uncertainty.* New York: Addison-Wesley.

Rediker, K. J., Mitchell, T. R., Beach, L. R. & Beard, D. W. (in press). The effects of strong belief structures on information processing evaluations and choice. *Journal of Behavioral Decision Making.*

Smith, J. F., Mitchell, T. R. & Beach, L. R. (1982). A cost-benefit mechanism for selecting problem solving strategies: Some extensions and empirical tests. *Organizational Behavior and Human Performance,* 29, 370-396.

Svenson, O. (1979). Process descriptions in decision making. *Organizational Behavior and Human Performance,* 23, 86-112.

van Zee, E. H., Paluchowski, T. F. & Beach, L. R. (1992). The effects of screening and task partitioning upon evaluations of decision options. *Journal of Behavioral Decision Making,* 5, 1-23.

Waller, W. S & Mitchell, T. R. (1984). The effects of context on the selection of decision strategies for the cost variance investigation. *Organizational Behavior and Human Performance,* 33, 397-413.

Implications of a Recognitional Decision Model for Consumer Behavior

Caroline E. Zsambok, Klein Associates Inc.

OVERVIEW

This paper presents a different approach to understanding decision making compared to the traditional decision research paradigm within the field of psychology. First, in my introductory comments, I will briefly describe those differences that have relevance for this audience. Second, I will describe Recognition-Primed Decision Making (RPD), which models how experienced people often make decisions in their operational settings. Then, I will discuss the methodology that we used to study experienced decision makers. Last, I will conclude with implications of the model and methodology for studying and influencing consumer behavior.

INTRODUCTION

Traditionally, decision researchers have used a laboratory research paradigm to study the varieties of option selection strategies that people (usually college students) use to select a single option from many. Most of these strategies require comparing options to each other in order to choose an acceptable (or the best) one. Further, while the options in the choice set often concern a domain that is familiar to the subjects (e.g., selecting a car; choosing a job), subjects are not experts with that task and cannot draw upon an experience base of decision making within that context (Zsambok, Beach, & Klein, 1992).

In contrast, we at Klein Associates Inc. have worked in operational settings with experienced people like urban firefighters, military battle managers, neo-natal intensive care unit nurses, data programmers, paramedics, and design engineers. From these studies, we have modeled a decision-making process that these experienced people use for many of the decisions they make on the job. Called the Recognition-Primed Decision Making (RPD) model (Klein, 1989), it shifts the emphasis from option selection to situation assessment. It also describes ways that decision makers evaluate options without comparing them to each other.

In settings like these, we found that the lion's share of the task involves sizing up the situation, or achieving a situation assessment. In this assessment, decision makers pay attention to critical *cues* from the environment, they watch for violations to their *expectancies* about the situation, they become aware of *goals* that are plausible for this situation, and they consider *typical actions* they have taken in the past to cope with similar situations. Therefore, the understanding of the situation suggests a reasonable option. Generally, to assess the situation is to make the option apparent.

One of the most interesting findings from our studies is that much of the time, once an option is apparent, expert decision makers do not attempt to generate more options in order to compare them and select the best one. Rather, they use mental simulation to evaluate whether the option they are currently considering will work. If they believe it will not, and if they cannot imagine how they would modify it to make it workable, they reject it and generate another one. And, after they have generated the next option, they do not compare it to the previous one to determine which is better. Thus, Recognition-Primed Decision Making involves a non-comparative option adoption process.

Why is this model of interest to people who study consumer behavior? First, if targeted consumers are not using an option-comparison strategy in order to make their purchase decisions, then marketing and advertising that intends to affect option comparison is not relevant. Rather, marketing and advertising messages should address the non-comparative option evaluation processes that we found people using, like mental simulation. Or, if the consumer base uses both comparative and non-comparative strategies, then messages should be developed that are compatible with both of them.

A second reason why this model could be of interest to the study of consumer behavior concerns the methods we used to develop the model. As I will describe below, these methods allow an interviewer to uncover the mental model that a person has of a situation or decision event. Knowing about the information contained in mental models of relevant consumers can be useful in developing marketing and advertising messages, both to retain existing customers and to attract new ones.

RECOGNITION-PRIMED DECISION MAKING

Klein (1989; Klein, Calderwood, & Clinton-Cirocco, 1986) has developed a model of Recognition-Primed Decision Making that describes how experienced people commonly make decisions in their operational settings. Based on observations from six field studies in different domains such as firefighting and tank platoon maneuvers, we found that decision makers:

1. focused more on situation assessment than on option selection
2. did not generate a number of options and then compare them to each other
3. did not look for the optimal options, but for a satisfactory one
4. evaluated options through mental simulation and selected the first satisfactory one.

As described in Klein and Klinger (1991), our initial work that led us to these conclusions began by observing fireground commanders (FGCs) and obtaining incident accounts from them. These FGCs were in charge of allocating resources and directing personnel. We studied their decisions in handling non-routine incidents during emergency events. Some examples of these types of decisions include whether to initiate search and rescue, whether to initiate an offensive attack or concentrate on defensive precautions, and where to allocate resources.

The FGCs' accounts of their decision making did not fit into a decision-tree framework, nor did it resemble an option-comparison strategy. The FGCs argued that they were not "making choices," "considering alternatives," or "assessing probabilities." They saw themselves as acting and reacting on the basis of prior experience; they were generating, monitoring, and modifying plans to meet the needs of the situations. We found no evidence for extensive option generation. Rarely were even two options concurrently evaluated. We did not see them trying to make optimal choices. The FGCs were more interested in finding an action that was "workable," "timely," and "cost effective."

Based on these and other protocol data (Klein et al., 1986), we attempted to model the way that experienced people were arriving at a workable plan, or option (see Figure 1). We found that much of their work in the decision event concerned situation assessment.

As an example, consider an experienced fire chief arriving at the scene of an unoccupied house that is on fire. He (in our studies, all chiefs were males) perceives a number of cues (features) from the environment. He sees smoke coming from under the eaves of

FIGURE 1
Recognition-Primed Decision model.

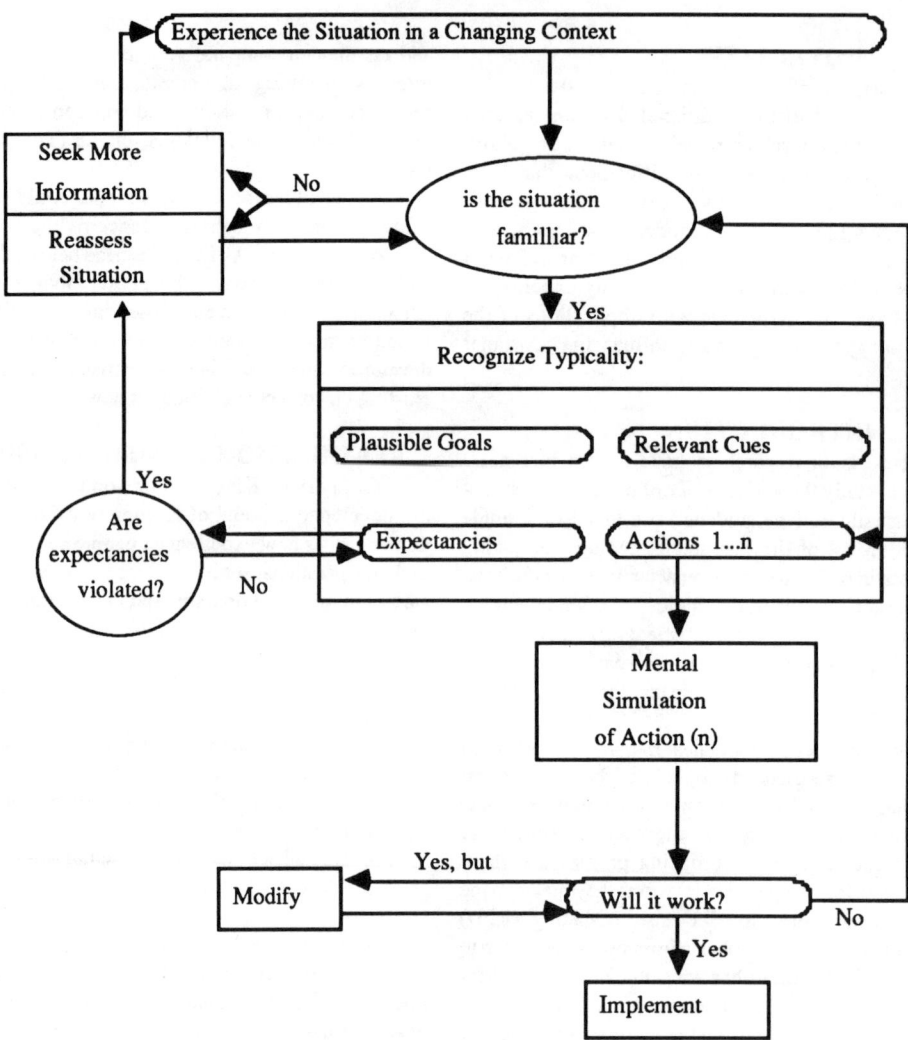

a pitched roof, a red flame shooting out the attic window, a yellowish flame forming at an adjacent second-story window. The model postulates that if the situation is familiar to the chief—if he has seen fires like this before—these features will activate his memory for other situations he has seen, or for a prototypical instance which is the amalgamation of many such situations he has seen.[1] This process corresponds to "framing" the situation, as described by Image Theory (Beach, 1990, 1992).

The initial features of the situation cue the chief's memory for past situations of this type. As a result, the chief becomes aware of additional *critical cues* to look for (wind strength and direction) besides the ones that initially drew his attention; about feasible *goals* (saving the property is not feasible, but saving the adjacent house is); about *typical actions* (three separate streams and two converging streams of water will be necessary to save the adjacent property and contain the primary fire), and about *expectancies* (you should be able to bring the red flame under control within five minutes, given these actions).

Before implementing a course of action, the chief may choose to evaluate it by mental simulation: mentally enacting or envisioning a course of action. (This process is akin to the "walk-through" process described by a number of researchers such as Gettys, 1983.[2]) That is, the chief imagines training the hoses on the designated areas using a particular angle and water pressure, for the expected amount of time. If he "sees" that the plan won't work, (he can't get the angle he needs, the plan is too vulnerable to wind shifts, the hotter of the two flames might require more of the water resource than he had planned) he modifies it, then implements. If he can't make it workable during his mental simulation and mental modification, he rejects it and retrieves other actions from memory to generate a new course of action. But, he does not compare the rejected course of action to the current one as a way to determine which is preferred.

We are not arguing that the mark of experienced people is that they use *only* a recognitional decision strategy like RPD in their

---

[1]The model does not specify the nature of stored information—examples or prototypes or both. The descriptive capability of the model remains functionally the same regardless.

[2]For a review of literature about mental simulation, see Klein and Crandall, in press.

TABLE 1
Proportion of Recognitional Decision Points in Decision Events from Five Different Operational Settings

Study Domain	Number of Decision Points	%RPD
Urban Fireground Commanders (#1)	156	80%
Urban Fireground Commanders (#2)		
Experts	48	58%
Novices	33	46%
Wildland Fireground Commanders		
Functional	79	56%
Organizational	31	39%
Tank Platoon Leaders	55	42%
Design Engineers	51	60%
Battle Managers	27	96%

operational settings. Rather, we are arguing that recognitional decisions do occur often, and that they constitute another type of decision making besides the option selection strategies that have been reported and studied under normative decision theory. And, our studies do show that the proportion of recognitional decisions increases as a function of level of expertise.

Table 1 depicts the proportion of recognitional decisions that were made by experienced people in several domains we have studied. These data were gathered in both verbal incident accounts we collected from research participants and also in observations we recorded (and later analyzed) as they were performing their jobs. First, we identified decision points within each incident. Then, we evaluated each of these decision points to determine what type of strategy was used. We looked for evidence of option comparison versus no comparison of options. To be classified as a recognitional decision, an option or course of action had to be adopted without comparing it to other options. Inter-rater reliability for each of these studies ranged from 87% to 94% (Taynor, Crandall, & Wiggins, 1987).

Notice that the lowest proportion of RPD decisions was found for three groups. First, 46% of decisions made by the novice fireground commanders (they were not inexperienced with firefighting—they were inexperienced as commanders) were recognitional, compared to 58% for experienced commanders. Second, for the tank platoon leaders, who had only five weeks experience on the job and were not considered expert, a proportion of 42% recognitional decisions was found. Third, the organizational decisions made by wildland commanders consisted of 39% recognitional decisions. These organizational decisions were made by teams, in which it was common for different members to throw out different ideas about courses of action that the team then discussed. Yet, even here 39% of the decisions were made without comparing the options. This proportion can be compared to the expected larger proportion of functional decisions that commanders made individually (56%), and with which they had considerable experience and expertise.

We believe that the reason less-experienced decision makers use an option comparison strategy more frequently than do their experienced counterparts is that they cannot assess the situation as well. Empirical support for this conclusion rests on our findings that non-experts spend less time assessing the situation than do experts, and more time comparing possible courses of action than experts do. Again, if the situation is understood, a good option often becomes apparent.

More recently, we analyzed decisions made by 31 experienced Naval officers in the Command Information Centers of AEGIS cruisers while they were at sea (Kaempf, Wolf, Thordsen, & Klein, 1992). These incidents were about situations that needed to be diagnosed as either hostile or non-hostile air threats to individual ships or whole fleets. Many of these incidents were marked with harassing acts from enemy aircraft—others contained perplexing activity from unknown aircraft. The task of the officers was to make decisions that would maintain the safety of their ship and fleet without shooting at innocent or merely harassing aircraft. Again, using protocol data from incident accounts, and applying very stringent criteria to what constituted a decision point and a non-comparative decision strategy versus any other type of decision strategy, we found that approximately 95% of the actions taken by the decision makers were based on recognitional (non-comparative) decision processes. Inter-rater reliability was 96%. The decision makers generated multiple options for purposes of comparison for only 4% of the cases. In most cases, decision makers knew what to do once they understood the situation.

The high proportion of recognitional decisions in this study and also from the battle managers mentioned in Table 1 is very likely due to the domain: many of their decisions required that they follow doctrine or standard operating procedure. In both cases, situation assessment was key. Once they understood the situation, they knew what they had to do.

There are other models of decision making that, like the RPD model, emphasize the role of situation assessment and allow for non-comparative option adoption strategies. Examples include the story model of Pennington and Hastie, Beach's Image Theory, and Rasmussen's skill/rule/knowledge-based model of cognitive control, but space does not permit a discussion of these here. For a recent review of this literature, see Klein, Orasanu, Calderwood, and Zsambok, in press; and Zsambok, Beach, and Klein, 1992.

METHODOLOGY AND THE RPD MODEL

The methods we used to develop the RPD model include an interview process called the Critical Decision method (CDM) as well as concept mapping. As described in Klein, Calderwood, and McGregor (1989), CDM is a knowledge elicitation strategy based on Flanagan's (1954) critical incident technique. Using recollection of a specific incident as its starting point, CDM employs a semi-structured interview with specific, focused probes designed to elicit particular types of information from the interviewee. Solicited information includes goals that were considered during the incident, cues that the person attended to, expectancies held about what would happen as the decision event unfolded, violations to those expectancies that they noticed, and actions they took during the course of the event.

FIGURE 2
Concept Map of Driving a Car

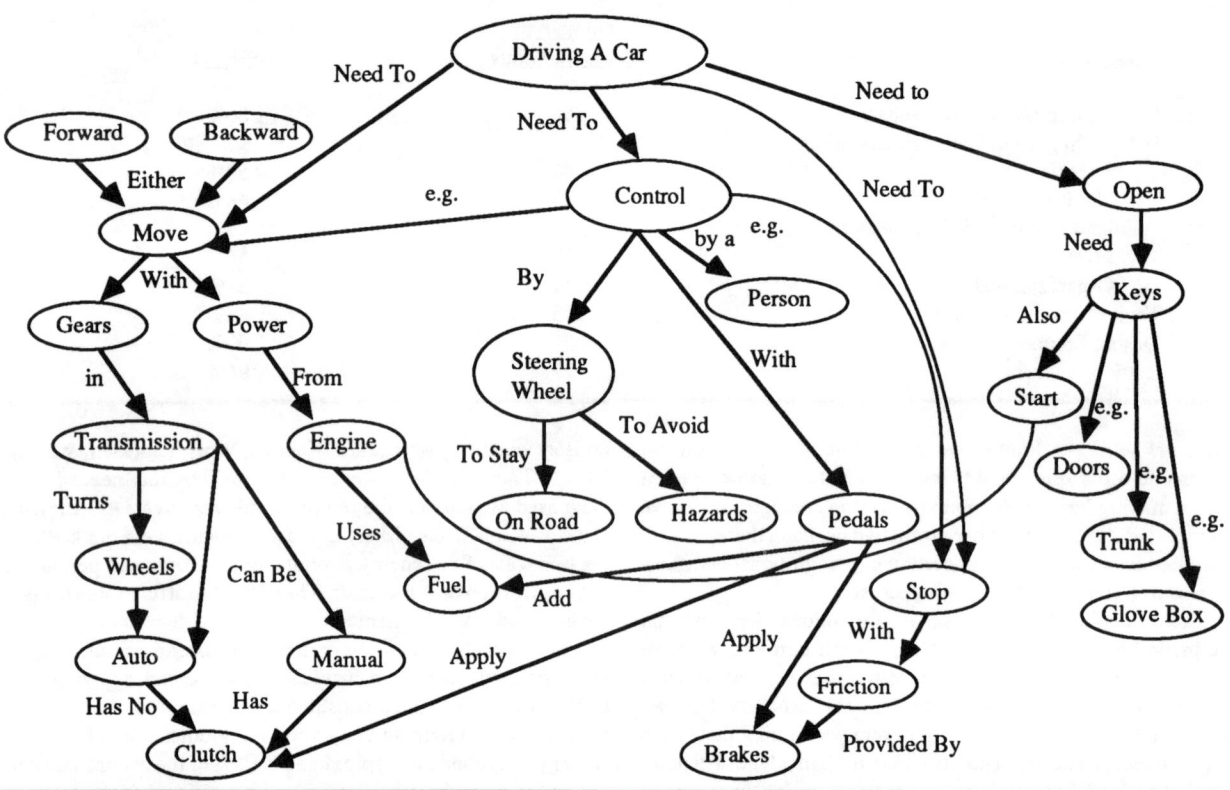

Researchers at Klein Associates developed CDM to elicit the decision strategies used by experienced people like fireground commanders and emergency rescue personnel at the scene of a fire or emergency. We found that many of these decisions relied on subtle perceptual cues and assessments of changing events that were not easily articulated by the experts. Thus, probes had to be developed that would allow experts to focus on and describe aspects of their task that are normally only tacitly understood. CDM has been demonstrated to yield information richer in variety, specificity, and quantity than is typically available in experts' verbal reports (Crandall, 1989), and we have used it successfully in over a dozen studies and in domains as varied as fireground command, battle planning, critical care nursing, corporate information management, and commercial and helicopter piloting. For a more detailed description of the CDM interview process and the work surrounding it, see Klein (1989) and Klein, Calderwood, and MacGregor (1989).

Concept mapping is a method that produces a schematic representation of the meaningful relationships among units of information, like events, objects, and states. For example, Figure 2 is a concept map about driving a car. Non-relational concepts are depicted in ellipses which in this example consist of either objects (steering wheel), actions (stop), or events (driving a car). Relational concepts are depicted by arrows and consist of linkages like "by," "need to," and "has." The most significant feature about concept maps is that the information is formatted in a non-linear fashion, and is thought by most psychologists who study memory storage and retrieval to reflect more closely the organizational structure of information in memory than a linear format would.[3] Concept maps

allow you to quickly sense the amount of inter-relationships contained in the network (an index of its complexity), and the specific nature of the system. Originally devised as an instructional and evaluation tool for use in academic settings (e.g., Gowin & Novak, 1984), concept mapping has been used more recently in applied settings. For example, Air Force operations researchers used concept mapping to identify needs of users of a decision support system, and to develop work station designs (McFarren, 1987; McNeese, Zaff, Peio, Snyder, Duncan, & McFarren, 1990).

Both CDM interview data and concept mapping provide information about a person's mental model of different types of knowledge. As described by Donald Norman (1983), a mental model is a conceptual model of a target system. A target system is the system that the person is learning or using. It could include an event (the course of a particular type of house fire, and how to put it out), or an object that is a system (a nuclear reactor). A conceptual model is invented to provide an appropriate representation of the target system, appropriate in the sense of being accurate, consistent, and complete.

According to Norman, mental models are naturally evolving models. Through interaction with a target system, people formulate mental models of that system. These models need not be technically accurate (and, he says, usually they are not), but they must be functional. A person, through interaction with the system, will continue to modify the mental model in order to get to a workable result. Mental models will be constrained by such things as the user's technical background and previous experiences with a similar system.

The important point about mental models for this discussion is that they contain information about people's understanding of how things work (or how things happen). And, we believe that knowledge of how things work can be described in terms of the informa-

---

[3] See semantic network and spreading activation research as originated by Collins and Loftus, 1975; Collins and Quillian, 1972.

tion considered during situation assessment: critical cues, plausible goals, expectancies, and actions. In fact, in research projects where we have been asked to discover what experts know about their operational domain that can be taught to intermediate-level personnel, the information that we have documented for training purposes concerns just those things: cues, goals, expectancies' and actions (Calderwood & Crandall, 1989; Crandall, Kyne, Militello, & Klein, 1992; Weitzenfeld, Klein, Riedl, Freeman, & Musa, 1991).

For example, in a study involving a neo-natal intensive care unit (NICU) at a hospital, we used the CDM method to discover what experienced nurses knew that nurses new to the unit did not know about one segment of their patient population. This segment consisted of very premature babies, called *Extremely Low Birth Weight*, or ELBW, babies who are born at 30 weeks gestational age and weigh less than three pounds. The purpose of the study was to discover how certain nurses could tell that an infant was in the beginning stages of what often becomes a fatal, systemic infection, called sepsis. This condition is common in ELBW infants because of their compromised immune system. Sometimes, if NICU staff waits until results from "hard" diagnostic tools like blood tests come back to confirm the onset of sepsis, the infant can be beyond help. The infection could have engulfed the system. But, we found that some nurses could tell when the baby was just beginning to get sick, and could alert the health care team so that early intervention could save the baby's life.

What we found (Calderwood & Crandall, 1989; Crandall & Gamblian, 1991) was that these nurses had a very different mental model, compared to new NICU nurses, of what cues to pay attention to (skin tone, alertness, muscle tone); what expectancies they should have and what the violations to these might mean (reaction to medical procedures and routine handling by nurses); what the plausible goals were ("we can't wait much longer to confirm diagnosis through tests—it's worth the risk to commence drug intervention, even with its potentially serious side effects"); and what actions they needed to take ("I'm going to stick really close to this baby—at the first sign of one more problem, I'm going to wake up the doctor to get an order for an antibiotic series").

We discovered that these nurses had learned what had not been taught to them in school. In Norman's terms, by interacting with the target system (the sick ELBW infant), they had developed a mental model that gave them a workable result: the ability to recognize and cope with the early onset of a deadly infection. In terms of the RPD model, they had refined the cue constellation that they attended to (compared to what they had been taught in school about general signs of infection), they had learned a different set of expectancies concerning the course of the illness, they had developed a set of different actions to take, and they had included new goals as plausible.

IMPLICATIONS OF THE MODEL AND THE METHODS IN CONSUMER BEHAVIOR

We have just begun using concepts derived from the RPD model and the methods we used to develop the model in order to study consumer behavior. Very recently, we completed market research projects for Procter & Gamble and Johnson & Johnson. Our approach was first, to assume that consumers might engage in situation assessment as part of their decision-making task, as opposed to generating numerous options that they would compare by weighing the pros and cons of the options' features. This meant we needed to use knowledge elicitation techniques like the CDM interview and concept mapping to uncover the mental models of consumers concerning the situation related to product use, and the manner in which the product could affect the situation.

While we cannot disclose the content of our findings, we can say that they have implications for the marketing and advertising messages that would be directed at the portion of the consumer base which uses or could be influenced to use recognitional decision making about these products. Further, we were interested in consumers who are not "expert" users of the product or diagnosers of the problem situation that the product was designed to address. These are people whose mental models do not include the most critical cues to look for in the problem situation; do not contain the most salient expectancies; do not reflect that higher goals (which the product can address) are plausible; or do not contain a full set of actions that are necessary on their part in order for the product to work as expected.

In general, the implications of our model and methods to the study of consumer behavior follow from this line of thinking:

1. The data from our studies of decision makers show that most of the work is in situation assessment (not option evaluation) and that when options are evaluated, frequently the method is mental simulation rather than comparing multiple options to each other.
2. The methods used to develop the RPD model include the CDM interview and concept mapping.
3. These methods expose knowledge about cues, goals, expectancies, and actions.
4. This information can be translated into a mental model held by an individual.
5. These methods can be useful in research about consumer behavior to
   - uncover what people believe to be true of situations that are relevant to using (buying) a particular product or service
   - uncover what people believe about the way a product or service works in those situations and what they notice in order to form these beliefs
   - develop marketing and advertising messages that reinforce, deepen, or correct these mental models as they relate to the product or service.
6. In developing these messages, our model and methods would emphasize
   - depicting how the product or service achieves its intent in ways that match consumers' mental models (for example, show how anti-lock brakes function on a car, using a visual and simplified representation to emphasize critical functions)
   - raising consumer expectations about what this type of product or service should do (and how your own product does not violate those expectations), and teaching them what cues to look for, in order to enable them to notice violations of expectancies in competitors' products or services (for example, showing how smoothly the car should stop, and what counts as less-than-perfect smoothness)
   - changing consumers' understanding of what constitutes a feasible goal (for example, slippery pavement does not mean that cars have to skid)

7. From our perspective, it would be important to know these things:
    - How much of a role does situation assessment play in the use of a particular product? (Products or services that can be cast as solving a problem, such as how to relieve a stomach ache or how to protect your home, would seem to be strong candidates for this.)
    - Are consumers likely to use an option-comparison strategy or a non-comparative strategy in selecting the product or service? (We would expect that buying items like cars and houses, which are expensive and for which consumers don't have a lot of purchasing expertise, would pull for comparative strategies. Less expensive items and those for which people have some expertise would pull for non-comparative option decisions.)

In conclusion, what we are suggesting is that marketing efforts and advertising messages can go beyond these three common current strategies and their hybrid combinations: 1) Comparing your product or service to other leading competitors in terms of how the options' features stack up to one another; 2) associating your product or service to an emotionally appealing life-style; and 3) price-point advertising. In those cases where situation assessment is likely, an additional strategy is highlighting information about the problem (situation) addressed by your product or service. This is done in such a manner that potential consumers come to refine and correct their mental model of the situation itself, as well as the effects of your product/service on the situation. Using methods like the CDM interview and concept mapping, you can pinpoint precisely *which* information is important to highlight.

REFERENCES

Beach, L. R. (1990). *Image theory: Decision making in personal and organizational contexts*. West Sussex, England: John Wiley & Sons Ltd.

Beach, L. R. (1992). Image theory: An alternative to normative decision theory. *Proceedings of the Association for Consumer Research Conference*. October, Vancouver, British Columbia.

Collins, A. M., & Loftus, E. F. (1975). A spreading-activation theory of semantic processing. *Psychological Review*, 82, 407-428.

Collins, A. M., & Quillian, M. R. (1972). Experiments on semantic memory and language comprehension. In L. W. Greg (Ed.), *Cognition in learning and memory*. NY: Wiley.

Crandall, B. (1989). A comparative study of think-aloud and critical decision knowledge elicitation. *ACM SIGART*, 108, April.

Crandall, B., & Calderwood, R. (1989). *Clinical assessment skills of experienced neonatal intensive care nurses*. Yellow Springs, OH: Klein Associates Inc. Final Report prepared for the National Center for Nursing Research, National Institutes for Health under Contract No. 1 R43 NR01911 01.

Crandall, B., & Gamblian, V. (1991). *Guide to early sepsis assessment in the NICU*. Fairborn, OH: Klein Associates Inc. Instruction manual prepared for the Ohio Department of Development under the Ohio SBIR Bridge Grant program.

Crandall, B. W., Kyne, M., Militello, L., & Klein, G. A. (1991). *Describing expertise in one-on-one instruction*. Final Report. Prepared under contract MDA903-91-C-0058 for the U.S. Army Research Institute, Alexandria, VA.

Flanagan, J. C. (1954). The critical incident technique. *Psychological Bulletin*, 51, 327-358.

Gettys, C.F. (1983). *Research and theory on predecision processes* (TR 11-30-83). Norman, OK: University of Oklahoma, Decision Processes Laboratory.

Gowin, D. B., & Novak, J. D. (1984). *Learning to learn*. NY: Cambridge University Press.

Kaempf, G. L., Wolf, S., Thordsen, M. L., & Klein, G. (1992). *Decision making in the AEGIS combat information center*. Fairborn, OH: Klein Associates Inc. Prepared under contract N66001-90-C-6023 for the Naval Ocean Command, Control and Surveillance Center, San Diego, CA.

Klein, G. A. (1989). Recognition-primed decisions. In W.B. Rouse (Ed.), *Advances in man-machine system research Vol. 5*, 47-92. Greenwich, CT: JAI Press, Inc.

Klein, G. A., Calderwood, R., & Clinton-Cirocco, A. (1986). Rapid decision making on the fire ground, *Proceedings of the 30th Annual Human Factors Society*, 1, 576-580. Dayton, OH: Human Factors Society.

Klein, G. A., Calderwood, R., & MacGregor, D. (1989). Critical decision method for eliciting knowledge. *IEEE Transactions on Systems, Man, and Cybernetics*, 19(3), 462-472.

Klein, G. A., & Crandall, B. W. (In press). The role of mental simulation in naturalistic decision making. In J. Flach, P. Hancock, J. Caird, and K. Vicente (Eds.), *The ecology of human-machine systems*. Hillsdale, NJ: Lawrence Erlbaum Associates.

Klein, G. A., & Klinger, D. W. (1991). Naturalistic decision making. *CSERIAC Gateway*, II(1), 1-4.

Klein, G. A., Orasanu, J., Calderwood, R., & Zsambok, C. E. (In press). *Decision making in action: Models and methods*. Norwood, NJ: Ablex Publishing Corporation.

McFarren, M. R. (1987). *Using concept mapping to define problems and identify key kernels during the development of a decision support system*. Master's thesis, School of Engineering, Air Force Institute of Technology, Wright-Patterson AFB, OH.

McNeese, M. D., Zapf, B. S., Peio, K. J., Snyder, D. E., Duncan, J. C., & McFarren, M. R. (1990). *An advanced knowledge and design acquisition methodology: Application for the pilot's associate*. Final Report AAMRL-TR-90-060. WPAFB, OH: Armstrong Aerospace Medical Research Laboratory.

Norman, D. (1983). Some observations on mental models. In D. Gentner and A. Stevens (Eds.), *Mental models*. Hillsdale, NJ: Erlbaum Associates.

Taynor, J., Crandall, B., & Wiggins, S. (1987). *The reliability of the critical decision method* (KATR-863(B)-87-07F). Yellow Springs, OH: Klein Associates Inc. Prepared under contract MDA903-86-C-0170 for the U.S. Army Research Institute Field Unit, Alexandria, VA.

Weitzenfeld, J. S., Klein, G. A., Riedl, T. R., Freeman, J. T., & Musa, J. (1991). Knowledge elicitation for software engineering expertise. *Proceedings of the Fifth Software Engineering Institute (SEI) Conference on Software Engineering Education*. NY: Springer-Verlag.

Zsambok, C. E., Beach, L. R., & Klein, G. (1992). *A literature review of analytical and naturalistic decisionmaking*. Fairborn, OH: Klein Associates Inc. Prepared under contract N66001-90-C-6023 for the Naval Command, Control and Ocean Surveillance Center, San Diego, CA.

The Vulnerable Consumer in the High Blood Pressure Drug Market: Bothered but Satisfied?

Dev S. Pathak, Ohio State University
Suzan Kucukarslan, Ohio State University
Deepak Sirdeshmukh, Ohio State University
Richard Segal, University of Florida

ABSTRACT

Patient satisfaction in the prescription drug industry has remained an under-researched area. Public policy concerns with access and pricing questions suggest that such research is urgently warranted. This paper reports the findings of a study that examines post-exchange phenomena in the high blood pressure prescription drug market, with regard to the elderly consumer. Since the decision making of consumers involved in exchange relationships in this market is highly restricted due to factors beyond their control, they can be classified as "vulnerable". In line with the vulnerable consumer hypothesis, the elderly in this study reported a high level of satisfaction. However, the relationship between demographic varaibles and level of satisfaction provided partial support for the vulnerable consumer hypothesis. The use of a self-reported measure such as "bothered" in place of "dissatisfied" revealed that a majority of the patients were experiencing some extent of negative post-exchange feelings. Finally, alternative influences on post-exchange behavior were examined.

INTRODUCTION

It is now generally acknowledged by consumer researchers that post-purchase feelings and actions of consumers represent an important area of examination (Westbrook 1987, Oliver and Swan 1989, Day and Landon 1977). The concept of consumer satisfaction has also gained wide acceptance in industry(Andreasen and Best 1977, Swan and Mercer 1981). While substantial research has been conducted into satisfaction and post-purchase behaviors in the areas of consumers goods, patient satisfaction remains an under-researched field. While some attention has been directed at understanding patient satisfaction in the hospital care context (Singh, 1989), research examining the post-purchase outcomes of prescription drug consumers is still needed. This paper represents an effort in that direction.

The high blood pressure market is the area being examined in this study. It represents an important area of concern for two chief reasons, namely the age group which makes up this market and the size of the market. A majority of hypertensive patients are from the elderly segment (persons over the age of 65) which represents the fastest growing segment in the U.S. The elderly are expected to make up about 20% of the population of the country by the year 2010 (Tootelian, 1991). It has also been suggested that the elderly may be open to potential exploitation by marketers since they are less likely to police the market (Deshpande and Zaltman, 1978).

The prescription drug market also represents a very large sector of the health care industry. Retail sales for high-blood pressure drugs made up 7% of a 4.3 billion dollar market for cardiac drugs in 1990 (Glaser, 1991).The U.S. pharmaceutical industry has been subject to intense federal regulations in the past designed to protect the consumer from unsafe and ineffective products. Much of the current public concern, however, is centered around the pricing and promotional practices of pharmaceutical manufacturers (Waldholz,1991). The Pryor Committee reported to the Senate that prescription prices had multiplied at three times the rate of the CPI in the 1980s (Majority Staff Report of the Special Committee on Aging, U.S. Senate, 1989,1990). As a result of the concern expressed, there have been several calls for public policy intervention to protect the prescription drug consumer from unfair practices.

Traditionally, the level of dissatisfaction in a market and the extent of complaints generated from the market l:ave been taken as signals for external intervention. Also, dissatisfied consumers have the option of self-policing the market by exiting the market or by voicing their complaints (Hirschman, 1970). However, the high-blood pressure prescription drug market has certain unique characteristics. First, the patient does not have direct control on the choice of the drug. Next, the product is technologically complex and patients do not have adequate knowledge in order to evaluate outcomes. Finally, the patient is involved in interpersonal relationships with the pharmacist and the physician and these may affect their ability to objectively evaluate the nature of their transactions. This situation suggests that the patient may be involved in transactions in a "loose monopoly" (Hirschman, 1970) where the consumer may not have recourse to exit or voice and is thus unable to police the market. In a loose monopoly situation the extent of dissatisfaction is typically under-reported by the customer and may not be an appropriate signal of market failure. Consequently, public policy intervention may be required even in the face of high reported satisfaction. Andreasen (1985) found that the physician market, with high levels of reported satisfaction, fit the description of a loose monopoly. This study examines whether the high blood pressure prescription drug market fits the description of a "loose monopoly".

Next, it has been suggested that groups who are at a disadvantage due to demographic characteristics tend to over-report their satisfaction given that they are unable to judge the performance characteristics of the service or product domain under investigation (Andreasen and Manning, 1990). These consumers are referred to as the "vulnerable consumer" and they represent a group who may need pro-active public policy initiatives in order to protect them. The post-exchange behavior of vulnerable consumers is another area that has not been adequately examined. This study examines the relationships between patient demographics such as age, income and education and reported satisfaction in the pharmaceutical drug market.

An alternative for identifying dissatisfied consumers in a "loose monopoly" who may not otherwise be identified, is explored in this study. Woodruff, Schumann, and Clemons (1990) suggest that rather than using constructs and their operationalizations derived by the researcher, it may be more appropriate to use terminology derived from the consumers themselves. Consequently, in addition to assessing "dissatisfaction," we also assessed the extent to which patients were "bothered" by specific elements of their transaction. "Bother" was a term that patients were found to use with some frequency in a focus group conducted earlier (Sirdeshmukh, Pathak, Kucukarslan, Segal, Kier, and Aversa, 1991). Further, along with global measures of overall satisfaction, consumers were asked to indicate their feelings with respect to specific attributes of the exchange process with respect to the drug manufacturer, the pharmacist, and the physician. In fact, the study deals with "post-exchange" as opposed to traditional post-purchase actions which may be a narrower conceptualization in this context. Finally, the nature of patients' post-exchange reactions including voice and behavior were examined along with reasons for such behavior. These reactions were examined using the framework suggested by Andreasen (1991).

REVIEW OF LITERATURE

The pharmaceutical market has been criticized for its promotional and pricing practices by policy makers who argue that its consumers are being exploited for commercial gains. Research has suggested that there is increasing public concern with rising drug prices and inadequate justification for such prices in the consumer's perception (Waldholz, 1991). The high-blood pressure market is particularly liable to public policy concern given that it represents a fairly large proportion of the prescription drug market and the elderly make up a large part of this market. Researchers have suggested that the elderly may be prone to exploitation by marketers and are less likely to take recourse to self policing behaviors (Deshpande and Zaltman, 1978). Further,the complex nature of high-blood pressure therapy further puts the elderly at a disadvantage. In sum, the post-exchange feelings and behavior of the elderly patient in the high-blood pressure market warrant further research.

According to traditional market theory, there would not be any concern about public policy intervention since the market would be expected to police itself. Economists maintain that consumers vote in the marketplace through the brand choices they make. A marketer not providing satisfaction would not be able to survive and eventually the market would eventually drive out the inefficient and reward those providing value. Hirschman (1970) states that when a market fails, consumers may use two mechanisms to initiate correction - voice and exit. Voice is defined as any attempt to change, rather than to escape from, an objectionable state of affairs, whether through individual or collective petition to the management directly in charge, through appeal to a higher authority with the intention of forcing a change in management, or through various types of actions and protests, including those that are directed toward mobilizing public opinion (Hirschman, 1970, p.30). Voicing is expected to occur when there is consumer recognition that voice is an option to exit and an expectation that the performance of the product/service will improve. Exit refers to the process of switching to other brand/product markets.

Hirschman (1970), however, suggests that there may be some markets which may be characterized as "loose monopolies" where a majority of the consumers may not have recourse to either exit or voice. Loose monopolies are those markets which are not true monopolies but ones where a majority of the consumers do not perceive exit as a viable option due to loyalty or high exit costs. Thus, exiting the market is no longer an avenue for market policing by consumers. Further, Andreasen (1985) suggests that a small number of "quality elites" or quality conscious consumers will exit the market. These consumers are also those who would have been most likely to voice, had they stayed in the market. The exit of the potential voicers among the quality elite and/or the lack of availability of exit as a viable option may lead to a market that is most liable to exploitation and is consequently one that could be classified as a "loose monopoly".

Andreasen (1985) tested Hirschman's industry-level evaluation of consumer satisfaction/dissatisfaction and complaining in the physician services market. He hypothesized that, based on the characteristics of the physician "industry", including the limited supply of physicians, limited consumer knowledge about alternative medical treatments, and the loyalty that patients feel toward their physicians, the physician "industry" would fit the description of a loose monopoly. He predicted that patients would be less likely to take actions when dissatisfied and providers would be less responsive to complaints. Results suggested that over a period of time, only about 17% of the patients experienced any dissatisfaction and took any action. There was very little evidence of any voicing on the part of the dissatisfied patients. On the basis of his study, Andreasen (1985) concluded that there was very little evidence of self-policing in the health-care industry.

Little research has been aimed at examining "loose monopoly" situations in the health-care industry since Andreasen's (1985) study of the physician market. As suggested above, the elderly consumer in the high blood-pressure market represents a potentially exploitable segment of the population. Further, there are reasons to believe that the prescription drug market may, as a whole, be characterized as a loose monopoly. First, the demand for pharmaceuticals is largely derived from the prescriber and not the consumer and thus the consumer has very little control over product choice. Second, prescription drugs represent a technologically sophisticated product that is difficult for the elderly patient to understand. Also, information about pharmaceuticals may not be accessible to the average consumer in a comprehensive and usable form. Finally, the process of exchange involves interpersonal relationships with the pharmacist and the physician and may be characterized by loyalty on behalf of the patient. In fact, an earlier analysis of focus group protocols revealed that "trust" and "loyalty" were frequently mentioned with respect to pharmacists and physicians and patients tended to ignore negative characteristics of the transaction in the face of strong loyalty (Sirdeshmukh et al. 1991). Thus, one important objective of this study was to examine whether based on the above characteristics, the high blood-pressure market may fit the description of a "loose monopoly".

Another concern of public policy research has been in terms of the possible exploitation of the "vulnerable" consumer. Vulnerable consumers may be defined as "those who are at a disadvantage in exchange relationships where that disadvantage is attributable to characteristics that are largely not controllable by them at the time of the transaction" (Andreasen and Manning, 1990). Andreasen and Manning (1990) further suggest that "this definition would include: children, the elderly, the uneducated, the structurally poor, the physically handicapped, ethnic and racial minorities and those with language problems". It is expected that vulnerable consumers perceive less problems, voice less complaints or take fewer actions, and it is argued that the "invisible hand" of the market may not be able to function as a form of market correction. Also, a market comprised of "vulnerable" consumers may not be able to signal market failure through voice and exit and thus pro-active public policy actions may be required and justified in such markets. This study will examine the relationship between demographic factors such as education, income, and poverty level and reported satisfaction. It is expected that demographically disadvantaged consumers will report higher levels of satisfaction, in accordance with the vulnerable consumer hypothesis.

Past research has chiefly examined consumer satisfaction using constructs developed by researchers. Woodruff et al. (1990) suggest that this practice stems from the researcher-specific definition of constructs which in turn gives rise to scale operationalizations whose meaning to the consumer may not match their intended meaning. The focus group interviews conducted for this study revealed that patients included the term "bother" frequently to describe a negative exchange experience either with the physician or pharmacist, or about the prescription product (Sirdeshmukh et al. 1991). Consequently, we hypothesized that the use of the term "bothered" in addition to "dissatisfied" may be a useful method of identifying consumers experiencing negative post-exchange feelings who may not otherwise be identified. Further, along with global measures of overall satisfaction, consumers were asked to indicate their feelings with respect to specific attributes of the exchange process.

Research has suggested that even when dissatisfied, not all consumers are likely to complain or take other action (Day and Bodur, 1978). They found that about 25% of the respondents in their study who were dissatisfied reported taking no action. Andreasen (1991) proposes that the relationship between dissatisfaction and post-exchange behavior could be explained within the framework of four "models": (1) cost/benefit; (2) personality; (3) learning; and (4) restraints. The cost/benefit model suggests that consumers objectively evaluate the extent of their dissatisfaction, the costs and benefits of complaining and the probability of success (perceived likelihood of channel member resolving the problem). The personality model suggest that a person's likelihood of engaging in some sort of post-exchange action is a function of their inherent drives and self-concept. The learning model states that complaining is a learned response to dissatisfaction. The nature of the outcome from past actions will in some way shape subsequent responses to dissatisfaction. Finally, physical constraints that may prohibit people from complaining describe the restraint model. No empirical research has been reported, to date, that compares the explanatory power of the four models. In this study, a first step has been taken toward operationalizing measures meant to tap the essential elements of each model. While we do not compare the relative explanatory power of each model, we provide a descriptive examination.

The equity-restoration model may also be used to explain the voicing behavior of dissatisfied consumers (Swan and Mercer, 1981). The process of equity is applicable to any social exchange when a focal person invests inputs in a transaction and receives outcomes. If that person feels that the relative gains (outcome minus inputs) are unequal to his exchange partner (i.e. retailer, manufacturer, etc.), inequity is said to have occurred. The result of the equity process is the feeling of fairness by the focal person if an equitable exchange has been experienced. Conversely, if the exchange between the focal person and the partner was perceived by the focal person as inequitable, a feeling of distress is expected (Oliver and Swan, 1989, Swan and Mercer, 1981). The equity-restoration model indicates that consumers who perceive inequity during the exchange process are expected to act to regain equity or their sense of fairness with the exchange by either minimizing the percieved imbalance in equity or by taking actions meant to achieve the same ends.

OBJECTIVES

The key objectives of this study were as follows:

(1) To examine the extent of reported patient satisfaction in the high blood pressure drug market.

(2) To test the "vulnerable" consumer hypothesis by examining the relationship between patient demographics and reported satisfaction.

(3) To compare the operationalization of the satisfaction construct on the basis of subjects' self-reports ("bothered") with a researcher generated construct ("dissatisfied").

(4) To examine the nature of post-exchange behaviors of prescription drug patients in response to being bothered by elements of the exchange process and to examine factors that may moderate the relationship between being bothered and taking an action in response.

METHODOLOGY

The Elderly Population

The elderly population was chosen because it purchases prescription drugs more frequently than other age groups. Although the elderly represent approximately 12 % of the total U.S. population, they accounted for approximately 34 % of the 1988 retail expenditures on prescription drugs (Drug Topics, 1990). High blood pressure (HBP) drug therapy was chosen because its treatment is chronic, and the type of prescription drug treatments vary in terms of active ingredient, dosage form, and price. Consumers of high blood pressure may be on prescription medication which may cost $10.00 per month to over $100.00 per month. Subjects were recruited from elderly resident homes in Ohio and Florida. The study was conducted in Ohio and Florida and 200 patients were surveyed in each state. Subjects were selected based on age (greater than or equal to 55 years) and current use of HBP prescription drug therapy. Each respondent was paid $10.00 for participating in the study and a total of 367 usable responses were collected.

Survey Instrument

The survey instrument consisted of a questionnaire that was developed on the basis of focus groups conducted with a sample of patients and expert opinion. Subjects were asked several questions regarding their level of overall satisfaction with the drug therapy, and satisfaction with the drug, manufacturer, physician, and pharmacist. Questions were also posed to identify issues about patients prescription drug exchange experience that bothered them and to identify actions taken in response. The perceived likelihood that some action would be taken in response to complaints about prescription prices by various channel members was also evaluated. Reasons why consumers did not complain about issues that bothered them were also identified. These reasons were included to represent the models of complaining behavior proposed by Andreasen (1991) as well as the equity-restoration model. Most items were on a seven point scale. The last section of the questionnaire consisted of background information such as gender, age, employment status, education, insurance, out-of-pocket costs for prescription drugs and health care costs, sources of income, number of persons in the household, and estimated annual income.

RESULTS AND DISCUSSION

A total of 367 persons, 55 years of age and older provided usable responses. A majority of the respondents were female (82 %), had at least a high school education (67 %), and reported an annual income of less than $11,140. A majority of the respondents had been taking their prescription drugs for high blood pressure for more than one year. Although almost 80% of the subjects had insurance for hospitalization, about half did not have insurance for prescription drugs. Therefore, one would expect price to be one of the issues of concern. Finally, a majority of the elderly purchase their prescription drugs from either a chain or independent drug store and pick up their prescription drugs themselves.

Satisfaction was measured on a 7-point scale (1=Very dissatisfied, 7=Very satisfied). Subjects were divided into satisfied, dissatisfied, and neither by collapsing across categories, as shown in Table 1. The majority of the respondents indicated that they were satisfied with all of the components of their high blood pressure

TABLE 1
Frequency Count of Respondents by Satisfaction Scores

Satisfaction with:	Total	Dissatisfied[a]		Neither[a]		Satisfied[a]	
		n	%	n	%	n	%
Drug	315	14	4.4	30	9.5	271	86.1
Pharmacist	293	6	2.0	17	5.8	270	92.2
Physician	343	8	2.3	9	2.6	326	95.1
Manufacturer	220	7	3.2	51	23.2	162	73.4
Overall	355	6	1.7	38	10.8	311	87.5

[a]Dissatisfied = 3 or less; Neither = 4; and Satisfied = 5 or more. Satisfaction was measured on a 7-point scale: 7 = Very Satisfied to 1 = Very Dissatisfied

therapy. This result may seem contradictory in the face of several reports in the lay press regarding the high concern with rising prescription prices. However, the high satisfaction reported by a the majority of the respondents is consistent with the predictions associated with the "loose monopoly" markets (Andreasen, 1985).

Next, the relationship between two demographic variables, income and education and reported satisfaction was examined. Persons with income greater than $13,400 and above the poverty level (established by the government standard combining the level of income and number of persons in a household) had significantly lower satisfaction scores (p<.05) for pharmacists (6.41 vs. 6.69), manufacturer (5.64 vs. 6.13) and overall satisfaction (6.01 vs. 6.41). Also, those with a college degree had a significantly lower overall satisfaction score (5.93 vs. 6.38, p<.05). However, there were no differences in the mean overall satisfaction scores on any of the five items reported between the three groups with income lower than $13,400 or between college graduates and non-college graduates. This data provides partial support for the hypothesis that demographically disadvantaged consumers (vulnerable consumers) tend to report higher satisfaction. Again, this would suggest that self reports of satisfaction obtained from vulnerable consumers may be an insufficient indicator of market performance.

Next, using respondent generated terminology, the term "bothered" was used to identify specific exchange issues that were negatively perceived by the respondents. Table 2 summarizes the frequency of respondents identifying issues that bothered them about their high blood pressure therapy. When compared with the number of persons dissatisfied with a particular aspect of their prescription drug therapy (2.0 to 4.4 %), the number of persons bothered by at least one attribute of the prescription drug therapy (70.2 %) is significantly greater. Figure 1 summarizes the post-exchange actions of consumers in the HBP drug market. It appears that using operationalizations with which respondents were familiar led to greater reports of negative post-exchange feelings. This finding also supports the proposition that using specific issues yields a greater number of respondents with negative exchange experiences rather than using a global exchange construct.

An analysis of the specific issues that bothered consumers revealed that greater than 20% of the respondents were bothered by four issues related to price of drugs and a fifth issue that was related to waiting time at the physician's office. The four price related issues were, cost of the drug, price variability between pharmacies, manufacturer's profit margins, and price variability between generic and brand name drugs. In sum, these results suggest that low levels of dissatisfaction with the prescription drug market discussed above, and past findings using the term "dissatisfied" may be artifacts of the measurement methodology.

Next, an analysis of the extent of behavioral action and voicing in response to being bothered was conducted. Table 3 suggests that consumers' behavioral actions in response to being bothered by the price of the drug may be classified into two categories: reduce expense or reduce consumption. The frequency of subjects reporting such actions is displayed in the table. It appears a that reduction in expense was the more common response. However, it is important to recognize that despite the small incidence of consumers reducing consumption in response to drug prices, such a response is cause for concern. Health care practitioners would be alarmed by the noncompliance of elderly patients in a market such as high blood pressure drugs. The societal cost of such noncompliance has been clearly documented in several studies (Ulmer 1987, Sullivan, Kreling, and Hazlet, 1990). Public policy makers would also be concerned about such responses from patients since ensuring access to optimal therapy has always been a concern, more so in the case of the indigent.

In terms of voicing, it was again found that price related aspects were key reasons for voicing complaints. However, even with reference to drug cost, which was bothered 40.8% of respondents, only about 21% voiced their complaints. It appears that in line with Day and Landon (1977), and Andreasen (1985), a small minority in this market seem to experience negative post-exchange feelings and complain about them. This further suggests that this market may be classified as "loose monopoly".

Next, consumers' reasons for not complaining were analyzed, according to the five models used. The data indicate that various reasons explain the non-complaining behavior of bothered consumers. These reasons may be categorized under the (1) cost-benefit model, (2) the personality model, (3) the restraint model, (4) the learning model, and (5) the equity-restoration model. Table 4 presents the results. The four key reasons for not complaining that were selected by more than 40% of the bothered patients were: "It wouldn't accomplish anything" (54.9%), "It wasn't worth the effort" (47.5%), "I did not think I could get any one to do anything about it" (51.5%) and "I didn't like the hassle of complaining' (50.0%). These reasons fall into three models: the cost-benefit model, the personality model, and the restraint model.

Taken together, they suggest that perception of apathy from channel member may be an important reason that these patients do not voice. As Hirshman (1970) suggests, the lack of adequate voicing may lead to disregard for consumer welfare on the part of the market. Also, as Fornell and Wernerfelt (1987) suggest, at a

FIGURE 1
Post-Exchange Actions of Consumers in HBP Drug Therapy Market

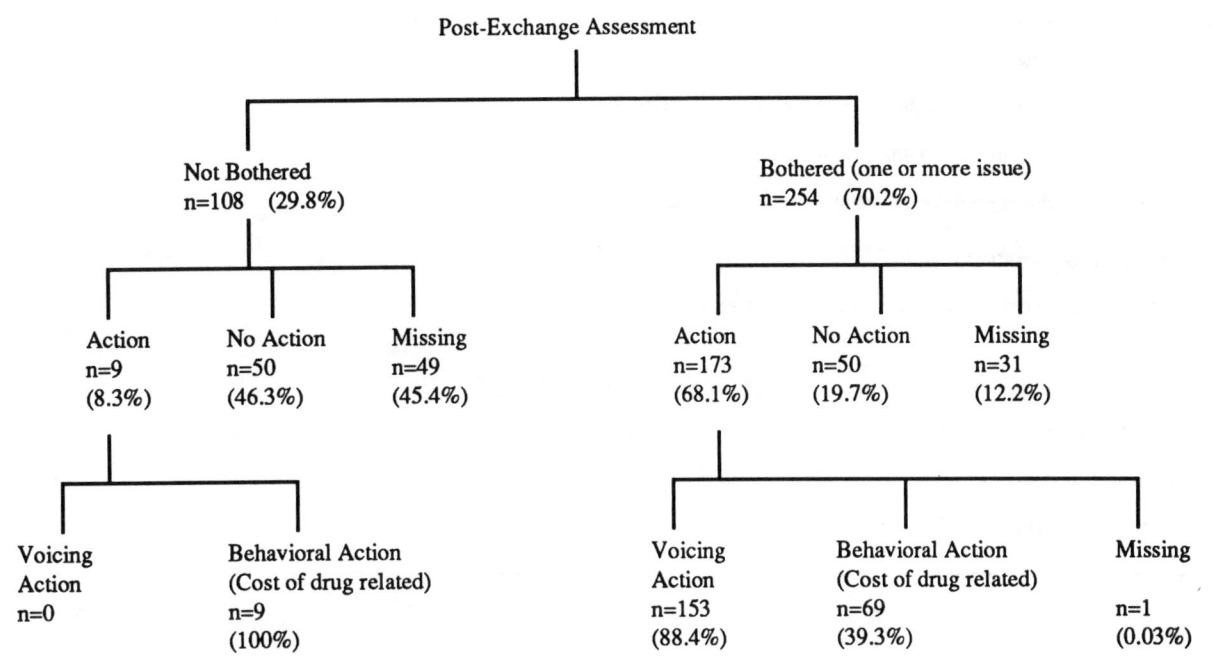

TABLE 2
Respondents Reporting One or More Bothersome Issue (n= 362)

Number of Issues	Bothersome	
	n	%
0	108	29.8
1	64	17.7
2	54	14.9
3	28	7.7
4 or more	30	29.9

time when firms are attempting to retain market share as a defensive strategy, marketers should attempt to encourage voicing from consumers. In this market it appears that perceived lack of responsiveness on the part of channel members may be leading to a reduction in voicing behaviors. Table 5 further bears out such an assertion. Patients seem to believe that consumer groups and government agencies are more likely to take action in response to their complaints, compared to the manufacturer and pharmacist. However, the mean value associated with the perceived responsiveness to complaints on the part of any channel member is dissapointingly low, with the highest mean value being only 4.43 on a seven-point scale.

CONCLUSIONS

The prescription drug market has criticized by public policy makers and citizen groups for its pricing and promotional practices. The need for regulations may be warranted if consumers are unable to police the market. This study found that a very large proportion of the patients in market indicated that they were satisfied with all components of their drug therapy. As Andreasen suggests(1985), such high reports of satisfaction in a market characterized by patient loyalty may lead to the conclusion that this market may be a "loose monopoly". This would further imply, that there may be the need for public policy intervention in order to regulate the market even in the absence of market generated signals for such intervention.

Next, it was found, in line with Andreasen and Manning's (1990) conceptualization of the vulnerable consumer that patients with lower levels of education and income seem to report higher levels of satisfaction. The vulnerable consumer, once identified may need to be educated and protected from possible exploitation. In fact, this study also suggests a methodology for identifying consumers who may be experiencing negative post-exchange feelings, but who would not be identified using traditional operationalizations of satisfaction. Using the term "bothered", it was found that in contrast to high levels of dissatisfaction reported earlier, almost 70% of the respondents were bothered by one or

TABLE 3
Behavioral Actions Taken by Consumers Bothered by Cost of HBP Drugs (n=140)

Action	Action Taken Yes	%
a. Reduction in expense		
I shopped around to find the cheapest prescription prices for this drug.	37	26.4
I reduced my expenses on other items such as food and clothing to buy my HBP drugs.	24	17.1
I asked the pharmacist to give me a cheaper alternative drug.	13	7.5
b. Reduction in consumption		
I asked the pharmacist to dispense less than the number of days supply written on the prescription.	12	8.6
I take the drug less frequently than prescribed so that my prescription drug will last longer.	7	5.0
I take it only when I feel I need it.	6	4.3
I did not get my prescription.	5	3.6
I did not buy other drugs I needed so that I can buy my HBP drug.	3	2.1

TABLE 4
Reasons Bothered Consumers Did Not Complain (n = 122)

Reason	n	%
A. The Cost-Benefit Model		
1. It wasn't worth the effort.	58	47.5
2. It wouldn't accomplish anything.	67	54.9
B. The Personality Model		
1. I am not that assertive.	32	26.2
2. I don't like the hassle of complaining.	61	50.0
3. I felt intimidated.	10	8.2
C. The Restraint Model		
1. I did not think I could get any one to do anything about it.	63	51.6
2. I did not know to whom to complain.	35	28.7
3. I did not get around to do anything about it.	22	18.0
D. The Learning Model		
1. Not much was done when I complained the last time.	20	16.4
2. I did not like the way my complaint was handled last time.	14	11.5
E. The Equity-Restoration Model		
1. It was not that important to me.	29	23.8
2. It did not bother me after a while	38	31.2

TABLE 5
Perceived Likelihood of Action in Response to Complaints Regarding Prescription Drug Prices

Channel Member	n	Likelihood of Action[a] mean[b]	SD
Consumer Groups	324	4.43	2.36
Government Agency	323	3.73	2.26
Professional Association	323	3.52	2.31
Congressmen	325	3.53	2.35
Physician	362	3.44	2.37
Pharmacist	326	3.16	2.27
Pharmaceutical Mfger	327	2.70	2.16

[a] Measured on a 7-point scale: 7=Very Likely to 1=Very Unlikely
[b] All means are significantly different from the scale mid-point (4)

more issues. This suggests that marketers may be better off developing measurement scales on the basis of language used by consumers when examining post-exchange actions. Also, the relationship between being bothered and being dissatisfied bears future examination.

Finally, it was found that a large proportion of bothered consumers did not voice their concerns. It appears that consumers in this market perceive that channel members would not act in response to their complaints and as a result they did not feel that complaining was worth the effort. Also, patients bothered by drug cost seemed to reduce their expenses or reduce consumption of the drug. The latter actions not only represent a potentially negative economic impact on manufacturers (lost sales), but suggest a compromise in the quality of therapy. Sub-optimal therapy may trigger the need for public policy to protect consumers from making such decisions.

Taken together these findings suggest that educating the public on how to express their concerns and dissatisfaction with the prescription drug market may be more valuable than implementing further regulation on an already heavily regulated industry. Hirschman (1970) proposes that the consumer's ability to articulate their complaints determines if he/she will exit the market or voice a complaint. Advertising or educational programs that provide product information to consumers may enable them to communicate their complaints or concerns to the manufacturer before they are expressed to third parties such as consumer groups or before the consumer exits the market. The role of product information on the consumer complaining process should be the subject of future research.

Also, health care practitioners, particularly physicians and pharmacists, must take a proactive position in communicating with their patients to identify issues that bother them so that complaints may be directed to the manufacturer. Future research should also include an assessment of the channel member's role in information flow from consumer to manufacturer.

REFERENCES

A Majority Staff Report of the Special Committee on Aging, United States Senate (1989), "Prescription drug prices; are we getting our money's worth?" Washington, D.C.: U.S. Government Printing Office, 1-48.

A Majority Staff Report of the Special Committee on Aging, United States Senate (1990), "Skyrocketing prescription drug prices: turning a bad deal into a fair deal," Washington, D.C.: U.S. Government Printing Office, 1-28.

Andreasen, Alan R (1977), "A Taxonomy of Consumer Satisfaction/Dissatisfaction Measures," *Journal of Consumer Affairs*, 11(2), 11-24.

Andreasen and Arthur Best (1977), "Consumers Complain- Does Business Respond?" *Harvard Business Review*, 55, 93-101.

Andreasen, Alan R. (1985), "Consumer Responses to Dissatisfaction in Loose Monopolies," *Journal of Consumer Research*, 12, 135-141.

Andreasen, Alan R. (1991), "Consumer Behavior Research and Social Policy," in *Handbook of Consumer Behavior*, eds. Thomas S. Robertson and Harold H Kassarjian, Englewood Cliffs, N.J.: Prentice-Hall Inc.

Andreasen, Alan R. and Jean Manning (1990), "The Dissatisfaction and Complaining Behavior of Vulnerable Consumers," *CS/D &CB*, 3, 12-20.

Day, Ralph L. and E. Laird Landon (1977), "Toward A Theory of Consumer Complaining Behavior," in *Foundations of Consumer and Industrial Buying Behavior*, eds. Arch Woodside, Jagdish Seth, Peter Bennett, American Elsevier.

Day, Ralph L. and Muzaffer Bodur (1978), "Consumer Response to Dissatisfaction with Services and Intangibles," in *Advances in Consumer Research*, ed. H. Keith Hunt, 5, 263-272.

Day, Ralph L (1984), "Modeling Choices Among Alternative Responses to Dissatisfaction," *Advances in Consumer Research*, 11, 496-499.

Deshpande, Rohit, and Gerald Zaltman (1978), "The Impact of Elderly Consumer Dissatisfaction and Buying Experience on Information Search," Paper Presented at the third annual conference on Consumer Satisfaction/Dissatisfaction and Complaining Behavior, Chicago, IL.

Fornell, Claes, and Birger Wernerfelt (1987), "Defensive Marketing Strategy by Customer Complaint Management: A Theoretical Analysis," *Journal of Marketing Research*, (Nov), 337-346.

Glaser, Martha (1991), "Fifty-second Annual Review: No Let Up in Prescription Drug Market Expansion," *Drug Topics*, 135(6), 53-58.

Hirschman, Albert O, (1970), *Exit, Voice, and Loyalty: Responses to Decline in Firms, Organizations, and States*, Cambridge, MA: Harvard University Press.

"Miracle Drugs or Media Drugs?" (1992) *Consumer Reports*, (March), 142-146.

Oliver Richard L. and John E. Swan (1989), "Consumer Perceptions of Interpersonal Equity and Satisfaction in Transactions: A Field Survey Approach," *Journal of Marketing*, 53 (April), 21-35.

Oliver Richard L. and John E. Swan (1989), "Equity and Disconfirmation Perceptions as Influences on Merchant and Product Satisfaction. *Journal of Consumer Research*, 16, 372-383.

"Rising Costs Affecting Drug Use by the Elderly" (1990), *Drug Topics*, (November 5) 134(21), 76, 80.

Singh, Jagdip (1989), "The Patient Satisfaction Concept: A Review and Reconceptualization," in Advances in Consumer Research, Vol. 16, ed. Thomas K. Srull, Provo, UT: Association for Consumer Research, 176-179.

Sirdeshmukh, Deepak, Dev S. Pathak, Suzan Kucukarslan, Richard Segal, Karen L. Kier, and Sheri L. Aversa (1991), "Patient Satisfaction/Dissatisfaction and Post-Exchange Actions in the High-Blood Pressure Prescription Drug Market: A Preliminary Report," *Journal of Consumer Satisfaction/Dissatisfaction and Complaining Behavior*, (4), 84-92.

Sullivan, Sean D., David H. Kreling, and Thomas K. Hazlet (1990), "Noncompliance with Medication Regimens and Subsequent Hospitalizations: A Literature Analysis and Cost of Hospitalization Estimate," *Journal of Research in Pharmaceutical Economics*, 2(2), 19-33.

Swan, John E. and Alice A. Mercer, "Consumer Satisfaction as a Function of Equity and Disconfirmation," in H.K Hunt and R.L. Day, eds, *Conceptual and Empirical Contributions to Consumer Satisfaction and Complaining Behavior*, Bloomington, IN: School of Business, Indiana University; 1981, 2-8.

Tootelian, Dennis H. (1991), "Marketing to the Mature Population, Part 1: Evaluating the Attractiveness of the Mature Population," *American Pharmacy*, NS31 (1), Jan 1991, 50-56.

Ulmer, R.A (1987), "Patient Noncompliance and Health Case Costs," *Journal of Compliance in Health Care*, (2), 3-4.

Waldholz, Michael (1991), "Drug Prices Rise 3 Times Rate of Inflation," *The Wall Street Journal*, (September 25), B4.

Westbrook, Robert A. (1987), "Product/Consumption-based Affective Responses and Postpurchase Processes," *Journal of Marketing Research*, 24 (August), 258-270.

Wolfgang AP, Perri M, Carroll NV and Kotzan JA. "Consumer Perceptions of Prescription Prices," *Journal of Pharmaceutical Marketing and Management*, 1988; 3 (1): 111-116.

Woodruff, Robert B., David W. Schumann, and Scott Clemons (1990), "Consumers' Reactions to Product Use Experienced: A Study of the Meaning of Consumer Satisfaction and Dissatisfaction," working paper, College of Business Administration, The University of Tennessee.

A Preliminary Examination of the Effects of Context-Induced Felt Ethnicity on Advertising Effectiveness

David B. Wooten, Columbia University
Tiffany Galvin, Northwestern University

ABSTRACT

Previous examinations of advertising context effects have investigated the relationship between various context-induced emotions (e.g., sadness, happiness, involvement) and advertising performance. This research considers felt ethnicity as a context-induced feeling state which may also influence various measures of advertising effectiveness. A pilot study was conducted to investigate how the advertising context can influence one's level of ethnic awareness which, in turn, can affect the performance of the embedded advertisement.

INTRODUCTION

The selection of an appropriate context for advertisements is important because ad context may affect advertising effectiveness (e.g., Yi 1990). In fact, the relationship between ad context and ad effectiveness has been listed among the top research priorities of advertisers and ad agency executives (Schultz 1979).

Previous researchers have examined the effects of advertising context on attitude toward the ad (Krugman 1983; Mattes and Cantor 1982; Soldow and Principe 1981; Yi 1990) and ad recall (Goldberg and Gorn 1987; Horn and McEwen 1977; Lambert 1980; Murphy et al. 1979; Pavelchak et al. 1988; Srull 1983), two common measures of advertising effectiveness. Findings on the relationship between ad context and advertising effectiveness have been equivocal. For example, Soldow and Principe (1981) found that interesting programs reduced advertising effectiveness. Krugman (1983), on the other hand, found that ads embedded in interesting programs were more effective than ads embedded in less interesting programs. Similar mixed results have been found to the impact of advertising context on commercial recall. For example, Mattes and Cantor (1982) found no relationship between context-induced arousal and recall, while Goldberg and Gorn (1987) found recall to be enhanced when the ad is embedded in a "happy" program. These mixed results suggest the need for additional research to increase our understanding of the effects of advertising context on commercial performance.

Meanwhile, a separate stream of research has sought to examine the influence of ethnicity on consumer behavior (e.g., Hirschman 1981; Deshpande et al. 1986; Stayman and Deshpande 1989). These studies have concluded that one's intensity of ethnic affiliation may affect how an individual behaves as a consumer. The present study seeks to merge the two separate research streams by investigating the relationships among advertising context, intensity of ethnic identification, and responsiveness to advertising. Specifically, we examine how the ad context influences felt ethnicity which, in turn, affects the recall and liking of an ethnic advertisement (Figure 1).

HYPOTHESES

Felt Ethnicity

Early examinations of the impact of ethnicity on consumer behavior have largely been criticized for two reasons. First, the studies have been "post hoc in design and descriptive in nature" (Hirschman 1981). Apparently, little effort had been devoted to developing a *priori* hypotheses regarding intergroup differences.

A second criticism of previous approaches involves the measurement of ethnic group membership with a single indicator which often considers only the researcher's perceptions of one's ethnicity (Hirschman 1981). For example, country or origin, surname, and language spoken at home have all been used individually to classify Hispanics (Stayman and Deshpande 1989). An obvious limitation of this approach is that it is inappropriate for groups (e.g., African-Americans) which are indistinguishable from Anglos on these characteristics. This approach also ignores the individual's perceptions of his own ethnicity, which may be more closely related to how he behaves as a consumer. Finally, this approach treats ethnicity as a stable sociological trait of an individual rather than as a transitory psychological state that is, at least partly, situationally determined (Stayman and Deshpande 1989).

The latter criticism has been addressed by Stayman and Deshpande (1989) who studied the effects of felt ethnicity on consumer behavior. In their model of situational ethnicity and consumption, the authors examine external influences on an individual's level of ethnic awareness. They proposed that individuals may face certain situations which influence their level of ethnic awareness. Stayman and Deshpande found support for their hypothesis that felt ethnicity is influenced by self-designated ethnicity and an antecedent state. In their study, the antecedent state was manipulated by exposing Mexican-American or Asian-American students to information about hiring biases that may or may not be relevant to their particular ethnic group.

The present study extends the results of Stayman and Deshpande by using a similar manipulation but a different ethnic group. Specifically, situational ethnicity will be manipulated by exposing African-American students to a controversial race-related article. The article represents the context in which an advertisement will be embedded. Hence, the context in which the ad appears should affect the reader's level of felt ethnicity. Thus, we hypothesize the following relationship between advertising context and felt ethnicity:

H1: African-Americans who are exposed to a race-oriented article will report a higher level of felt ethnicity than will African-Americans who are exposed to an article that does not mention race.

Advertising Context and Ad Recall

Previous examinations of the relationship between advertising context and commercial performance have attempted to relate both intensity (Goldberg and Gorn 1987; Mattes and Cantor 1982; Pavelchak et al. 1988; Srull 1983) and valence (Goldberg and Gorn 1987; Pavelchak et al. 1988; Srull 1983) of context-induced arousal to ad recall. There appears to be evidence that the intensity of context-induced arousal has an effect on the recall of embedded ads. However, the conditions under which these effects are positive (e.g., Srull 1983) or negative (e.g., Pavelchak et al. 1988) remain unclear. Mixed results have also been found for the effects of valence of context-induced arousal on ad recall.

Other studies have attempted to relate recall performance to the similarity between the ad and its context (e.g., Lambert 1980; Murphy et al. 1979). Two conflicting results have emerged from these studies. Murphy et al. (1979) found support for the contrast principle as a way to increase attention to humorous ads. They suggest that humorous ads may be more effective when embedded in non-humorous program environments. This result is similar to

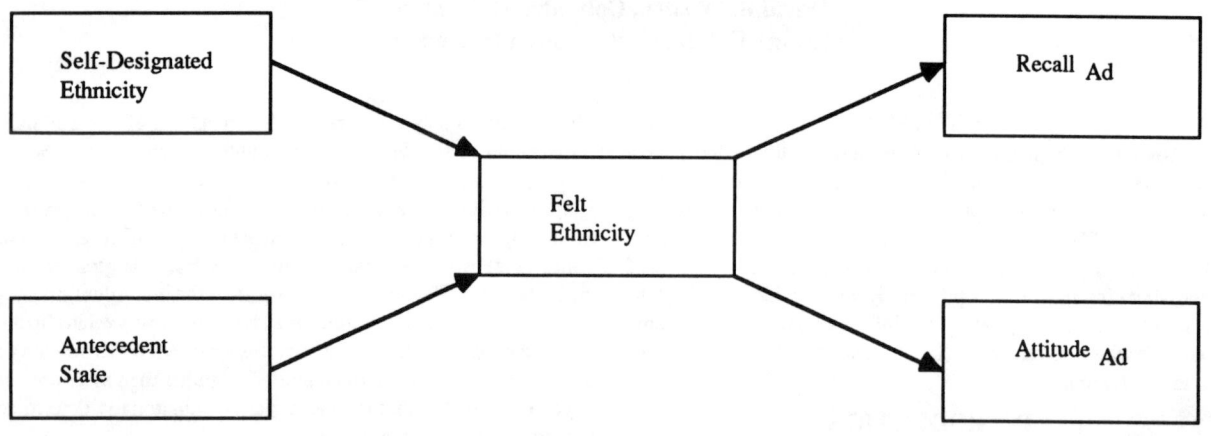

FIGURE 1
Proposed Model of Felt Ethnicity and Advertising Effectiveness

the Von Restorff effect that has been demonstrated in free-recall experiments, where distinctive items are more easily recalled when they are embedded in an otherwise homogeneous list (Baddeley 1976).

Lambert (1980) reported the opposite, that congruity between the context and the message enhances recall of embedded ads. Theoretical support for this relationship is found in the organization theory of free recall (Lambert 1980). Congruent elements are more easily organized and stored as a single "chunk" in memory and are more easily retrieved as a unit. The accessibility of the ad message is enhanced by the greater number of retrieval cues associated with this chunk of information. Essentially, congruity between the ad message and its context should facilitate the organization of material in memory and improve the recall of that material (Isen 1984).

The contrast principle and the congruity principle offer conflicting predictions concerning the influence of the similarity between the ad context and the ad message on message recall. However, following the congruity principle, we expect recall of an ethnic ad to be enhanced when the ad is embedded in an article about ethnic issues. This improved recall performance should be due to the similarity between the context-induced mood and the mood induced by the ad. Therefore, we hypothesize the following relationship between advertising context and ad memorability:

H2: A race-oriented ad embedded in an article dealing with a race-related issue will be viewed as more memorable than the same ad embedded in a non-race-related article.

Advertising Context and Attitude Toward the Ad

Despite some mixed results (e.g., Bello et al. 1983; Srull 1983) there appears to be evidence of a positive effect of context-induced arousal on attitude toward the ad (Mattes and Cantor 1982), especially for positively valenced arousal (Srull 1983). These findings have been interpreted as support for the excitation transfer process which occurs when the residual arousal from a previously arousing event is misattributed to a subsequent stimulus (Cantor et al. 1974; Singh and Churchill 1987). Thus, excitation transfer intensifies the response to the latter stimulus (Mattes and Cantor 1982).

We expect to observe an excitation transfer when an ethnic ad is embedded in editorial material on a controversial ethnic issue. The article may arouse one's felt ethnicity, with any residual arousal being transferred to the ethnic ad. If the individual is favorably predisposed to the ad in question, then we may expect the excitation transfer process to lead to an increased liking of the ad. Therefore, we hypothesize the following relationship between advertising context and attitude toward the ad:

H3: A race-oriented ad embedded in a race-related article will be viewed more favorably than the same ad embedded in a non-race-ralated article (subject to a positive portrayal of the ethnic group member in the ad).

METHOD

Stimuli

The stimuli used in the study were mock newspapers consisting of a cover page, an article, and a full-page public-service ad featuring an African-American child actor. The cover page contained only the title of the newspaper and the headline of a cover story. The article began on the second page and continued on the fourth page, with the advertisement placed between the two pages of the article. There were two versions of the mock newspaper which differed only in the content of the article. The first version contained an article which expressed strong negative opinions about affirmative action programs and their direct beneficiaries. The second article discussed trends in television programming during the 1970's without discussing race or ethnicity.

Both articles and the ad were selected by three judges who assisted with the experiment. The articles were chosen to be roughly similar in terms of length, but substantially different in the amount of race-related content. The ad was selected because the judges agreed that it conveyed a positive message.

Experimental Design and Procedures

The study used a completely randomized design with two levels (ethnic and non-ethnic) or a single factor (ad context). The subjects were 34 African-American college students enrolled in the summer session at a large midwestern university. African-American students were chosen because of the accessibility of the students and the availability of an appropriate ad. Each subject was exposed to a mock newspaper and asked to examine its contents. A different stimulus was used to create each of the two factor levels. After examining the newspaper, each subject responded to a questionnaire which measured three dependent variables: felt ethnicity, ad memorability, and attitude toward the ad.

TABLE 1
Anova Results

Variable	Mean (Ethnic)	Mean (Non-Ethnic)	F-Value	P-Value
Felt Ethnicity	5.18	2.41	26.62	.0001
Recall$_{Ad}$	5.38	4.71	2.53	.1219
Attitude$_{Ad}$	5.21	4.03	14.61	.0006

Three African-American undergraduate students were used as experimenters. The subjects and the experimenters were naive to the purpose of the study to minimize the possibility of demand artifacts.

Measures of Key Variables

Two measures were used for each dependent variable. The first measure of felt ethnicity required the subject to indicate (on a 7-point scale) the extent to which the article made one "think" about his own racial/ethnic identity. The second measure involved the extent of agreement with a statement that the article increased ones "awareness" of his racial/ethnic identity. The two measures were combined into an equally weighted scale (alpha = .870).

We examined ad memorability rather than ad recall since the ad was displayed so prominently that everyone recalled the ad. Ad memorability was measured by having subjects indicate how "memorable" the ad was and the extent to which they agreed that the ad was "not very easy to forget." These two measures were averaged to form an equally weighted scale (alpha = .837).

Finally, attitude toward the ad was assessed by having subjects respond to a question about the extent to which they "like" the ad. A second measure required subjects to indicate agreement with a statement that they "had very positive feelings" about the ad. These two measures were also averaged to form an equally weighted scale (alpha=.808).

RESULTS

Analysis of variance (ANOVA) was used to test the experimental hypotheses. The first hypothesis considers the relationship between advertising context and felt ethnicity. As expected, subjects in the "ethnic" condition reported a greater degree of felt ethnicity than did their counterparts in the "non-ethnic" condition (Table 1). The significant difference between groups ($F(1,32) = 26.62; p < .0001$) provides strong support for the hypothesis that advertising context and self-designated ethnicity combine to influence felt ethnicity.

The second hypothesis considers the relationship between context-induced felt ethnicity and the memorability of the ad. The difference in mean ad memorability ratings between the "ethnic" and the "non-ethnic" condition (5.38 vs. 4.71) was not statistically significant ($F(1,32) = 2.53; p < .1219$), but was in the anticipated direction. Therefore, the findings appear to favor the congruity principle over the contrast principle. However, the second hypothesis was not supported.

Finally, we examined the relationship between context-induced felt ethnicity and attitude toward an embedded ad. Attitude toward the ad differed significantly between the groups ($F(1,32) = 14.61; p < .0006$). African-Americans who were exposed to an African-American oriented ad embedded in a race-related article reported a significantly more favorable attitude toward the ad than did African-Americans who viewed the same ad, but in a non-race-related ad context. Therefore, our third hypothesis was supported.

DISCUSSION AND IMPLICATIONS

This study extends the work on situational ethnicity by considering the influence of ad context on felt ethnicity. More importantly, the study merges two separate research streams by relating advertising context-induced felt ethnicity to two common measures of advertising effectiveness. However, additional research is needed to examine this relationship when the ad appears in a less controversial context, since ethnic awareness may also be affected by exposure to favorable mentions of race or ethnicity. Future research should also attempt to extend these findings to other media and other ethnic groups.

The present study has a few limitations that should be discussed. First, the study used a small homogeneous sample and an artificial setting, both of which may limit the generalizability of the findings. However, the fact that statistical significance has been attained despite the small sample size is somewhat encouraging. Second, the study ignores any differences in the level of involvement associated with the two advertising contexts. Therefore, we have failed to eliminate involvement as an alternative explanation for the findings. However, despite the aforementioned limitations, this research contributes to our understanding of the relationship between ad context and advertising effectiveness by providing another instance where the advertising context enhances an individual's attitude toward the ad. Specifically, the study provides further support for the excitation transfer process by demonstrating that context-induced arousal may affect emotional responses to embedded ads. Additional research is needed to identify more contextual factors that affect advertising performance. Perhaps certain characteristics of the advertising context may enhance one measure of advertising effectiveness but inhibit another.

Finally, these findings are relevant to advertising practitioners for at least three reasons. First, this research suggests that advertisers should consider the interaction between ad content and ad context when testing advertising copy. Since the effects of ad messages vary across contexts, the context in which an ad is tested should resemble the actual ad environment (Yi 1990). Second, advertisers should be sensitive to advertising context effects especially during media scheduling. Congruity between the advertising content and the context in which the ad is embedded may enhance the memorability of the ad. Third, the present study suggests that the effectiveness of print advertisements targeting ethnic minorities may be aided by considering the interaction between the advertising message and the editorial environment. The ad message may elicit positive reactions among members of a particular ethnic group when the ad is viewed in isolation. However, attitudes toward the ad may be even more favorable when the advertisement is embedded in the appropriate ad context.

REFERENCES

Baddeley, Alan D. (1976), *The Psychology of Memory*, New York: Basic Books, Inc.

Bello, Daniel C., Robert E. Pitts, and Michael J. Etzel (1983), "The Communication Effects of Controversial Sexual Content in Television Programs and Commercials," *Journal of Advertising, 12* (3), 32-42.

Cantor, Joanne R., Jennings Bryant, and Dolf Zillman (1974), "Enhancement of Humor Appreciation by Transferred Excitation," *Journal of Personality and Social Psychology, 30* (6), 812-821.

Deshpande, Rohit, Wayne D. Hoyer, and Naveen Donthu (1986), "The Intensity of Ethnic Affiliation: A Study of the Sociology of Hispanic Consumption," *Journal of Consumer Research, 13* (September), 214-220.

Goldberg, Marvin E. and Gerald J. Gorn (1987), "Happy and Sad TV Programs: How they Affect Reactions to Commercials," *Journal of Consumer Research, 14* (December), 387-403.

Hirschman, Elizabeth C. (1981), "American Jewish Ethnicity: Its Relationship to Some Selected Aspects of Consumer Behavior," *Journal of Marketing, 45* (Summer), 102-110.

Horn, Martin I. and William J. McEwen (1977), "The Effect of Program Context on Commercial Performance," *Journal of Advertising, 6* (11), 23-27.

Isen, Alice M. (1984), "The Influence of Positive Affect on Decision-Making and Cognitive Organization," *Advances in Consumer Research, Vol. 11*, ed. Thomas C. Kinnear, Provo, UT: Association for Consumer Research, 534-537.

Krugman, Herbert E. (1983), "Television Program Interest and Commercial Interruption: Are Commercials on Interesting Programs Less Effective?" *Journal of Advertising Research, 23* (1), 21-23.

Lambert, David R. (1980), "Transactional Analysis as a Congruity Paradigm for Advertising Recall," *Journal of Advertising, 9* (2), 37-41, 44-45.

Mattes, John and Joanne Cantor (1982), "Enhancing Responses to Television Advertisements via the Transfer of Residual Arousal from Prior Programming," *Journal of Broadcasting, 26* (2), 553-566.

Murphy, John H., Isabella C. M. Cunningham, and Gary B. Wilcox (1979), "The Impact of Program Environment on Recall of Humorous Television Commercials," *Journal of Advertising, 8* (2), 17-21.

Pavelchak, Mark A., John H. Antil, and James M. Munch (1988), "The Super Bowl: An Investigation into the Relationship Among Program Context, Emotional Experience, and Ad Recall," *Journal of Consumer Research, 15* (December), 360-367.

Schultz, Don E. (1979), "Media Research Users Want," *Journal of Advertising Research, 19* (December), 13-17.

Singh, Surendra N. and Gilbert A. Churchill (1987), "Arousal and Advertising Effectiveness," *Journal of Advertising, 16* (1), 4-10.

Soldow, Gary F. and Victor Principe (1981), "Response to Commercials as a Function of Program Context," *Journal of Advertising Research, 21* (2), 59-65.

Srull, Thomas (1983), "Affect and Memory: The Impact of Affective Reactions in Advertising on the Representation of Product Information in Memory," in *Advances in Consumer Research, Vol. 10*, eds. Richard P. Bagozzi and Alice M. Tybout, Ann Arbor, MI: Association for Consumer Research, 572-576.

Stayman, Douglas M. and Rohit Deshpande (1989), "Situational Ethnicity and Consumer Behavior," *Journal of Consumer Research, 16* (December), 361-371.

Yi, Youjae (1990), "Cognitive and Affective Priming Effects of the Context for Print Advertisements," *Journal of Advertising, 19* (2), 40-48.

Age and Social Activity as Correlates of Television Orientation: A Replication and Extension
Rose L. Johnson, Temple University[1]

ABSTRACT

As individuals age, the amount of their social contact and activity decreases. Television viewing offers a substitute for social contact and an alternative means of obtaining information and entertainment. This study examines chronological age, subjective age, and indicants of social activity as correlates of television orientation and viewership. Findings suggest that age is strongly correlated with television orientation and viewership. The predictive value of social activity is less clear, but some evidence is provided that less social acitivty leads to increased television viewing and a more positive orientation toward the medium.

INTRODUCTION

Television viewing is America's predominant leisure activity, occupying seventy-five percent of our mass media time and as much as forty percent of our total leisure time. It is estimated that Americans spend more time watching television than engaging in any other activity except sleep and work (Comstock et al. 1978; Real, Anderson, and Harrington 1987).

One group of viewers for whom television may be particularly important is the elderly. Elderly viewers show greater consumption of television and other mass media than younger adults (Stephens 1981). In addition, recent recognition of the growth and economic potential of the elderly market has made it an increasingly attractive target for advertisers.

Changes in lifestyle associated with aging may be responsible for the increase in the importance of mass media in general (and television, particularly) as a source of entertainment and information (Graney 1975a; Donohew, Palmgren, and Rayburn 1987). Thus, it becomes important to consider not only chronological age but also age-related social variables. Rubin (1985) suggests that attention to life-position variables such as viewer mobility and social interaction can provide improved indicators of media use across the lifespan.

Media Use and Social Activity

As individuals age, their relationships with various social institutions undergo change. For example, individuals retire, their physical ability to engage in certain activities declines, their children grow up and leave home, and their spouses and friends die. Activity theory suggests that life satisfaction among the elderly is greatest when a socially active lifestyle is maintained (Havighurst and Albrecht 1953). To maintain an active and satisfying lifestyle, leisure activities often are sought and adopted to substitute for activities associated with those roles that are lost (Graney and Graney 1974; Havighurst and de Vries 1969). After retirement, for example, an individual may increase involvement with a church or other religious organization or may join a senior citizen's center. Another common substitution activity is use of mass media (Graney and Graney 1974).

There is some suggestion that the basic motivation for media use is a need for social contact (Finn and Gorr 1988; Nordenstreng 1970). Relationships between television viewers and television characters can resemble interpersonal relationships in many ways; we come to "know" television personalities and develop bonds of intimacy with them (Rubin and McHugh 1987). This is seen in the viewer who "coaches" players on television game shows or shares the lives of characters in a soap opera or evening drama.

Of the media available, television seems to be particularly important to the elderly consumer. Short, Williams, and Christie (1976) arrayed traditional media along a "social presence" continuum — indicating the degree to which the medium permits users to experience others as being psychologically present. They indicate that face-to-face communication is seen as having the greatest social presence, followed by audio-plus-video, audio-only, then print media. To compensate for loss of personal contacts, the elderly may turn to the medium offering the greatest social presence. Evidence exists that mass media usage is highest among those elderly with the least social interaction (Rahtz, Sirgy, and Meadow 1989; Rubin 1985).

In addition to the social value of television, audience gratifications are also derived from media content (Katz, Blumler, and Gurevitch 1974). Numerous typologies have been developed to explain the gratifications audiences derive from television. However, researchers typically are able to identify a dichotomy of entertainment-related versus information-related gratifications which seem to underly most expressed motives (Comstock 1980; Katz, Blumler, and Gurevitch 1974; c.f., Donohew, Palmgren, and Rayburn 1987).

The information value of the media may be particularly important to older viewers because of their loss of personal contacts (Graney 1975a; Graney and Graney 1974). Local news and information which at one time may have been obtained in the workplace is sought by the elderly from newspapers and television (Kubey 1980). Again, this provides a way for adults with reduced social contacts to keep in touch with society.

Despite the evidence of age-related changes in media use and orientation, chronological age has its limitations as an explanatory variable. It is not a cause of change itself, but rather, an index of biological, psyhcological, and social factors which lead to change. Especially among older adults, individuals at a given chronological age are likely to show vast differences in ability and behavior (Schonfield 1974). Examining more directly the causes of change may provide researchers with an improved understanding of consumer behavior.

PURPOSE OF THIS STUDY

Rahtz, Sirgy, and Meadow (1989) provide a picture of the elderly television viewer. They suggest that among the elderly, there is a positive relationship between age and television orientation and that television orientation also is related to social and sociopsychological variables such as unemployment, income, education, morale, concern for one's personal and financial well-being, perception of respect for the elderly, and activity level. The purpose of this study is to provide a replication and extension of that earlier work.

A first contribution of this study is an expansion of the population examined. We can learn much from studies of the elderly population. However, studying the elderly population in isolation limits our ability to generalize findings or to determine the extent to which marketing strategies developed for a wider group

---

[1] This research was funded in part by a grant from the Media Research Club of Chicago. The author gratefully acknowledges their support.

TABLE 1
Summary of Television Orientation Scale

Items	X	SD	Factor Loadings 1	2
† 1. Television provides useful information about products.	3.16	1.20	.696	.217
2. I pay close attention to television advertisements.	2.43	1.35	.681	.203
3. Television shows people the way they really are.	2.30	1.28	.677	.342
4. Television shows life as it really is.	2.30	1.24	.589	.296
5. I enjoy watching daytime television.	2.41	1.42	.506	.445
† 6. I get most of my news from television.	3.73	1.17	.451	.253
7. Television gives useful information.	3.54	1.02	.410	.382
† 8. Television is a source of companionship for me.	2.74	1.45	.225	.949
9. Television is my primary form of entertainment.	2.67	1.40	.280	.580
10. Magazines are more interesting than television. (-)	2.87	1.15	.264	.323

† new item
(-) reverse scored

---

may be appropriate or inappropriate for the elderly. This study will examine the correlates of television within the adult population overall.

A second contribution is an expansion of the evaluation of television orientation itself. While acknowledging the importance of television for both information and entertainment, Rahtz, Sirgy and Meadow (1989) examine correlates of only the entertainment dimension. The current study will provide insight into correlates of both the entertainment and information dimensions of television orientation.

This study expands on previous research by considering not only chronological age but also subjective age. Considering an individual's self-percieved age has increased appeal over chronological age since a subject's perception of his or her age is likely to be more closely related to behavioral change than is the passing of time itself (cf., Stephens 1991). For example, a senior citizen who is healthy and active is likely to have a younger perceived age than one who is limited in activity or social contact. The two individuals may also differ in the amount and content of their television viewing.

As in Rahtz, Sirgy, and Meadow (1989) a number of social activity variables are examined in this study. Loss of a spouse and having children leave home will impact social interaction in the home. Retirement, unemployment, or part-time employment will limit workplace interactions. Other social interactions may be indicated by church attendance, the number of organizations to which one belongs, and the number of personal friends.

Finally, this study utilizes measures of television viewership as well as television orientation. This will allow an examination not only of the relationship between age, social activity, and actual behavior, but also of that between television orientation and viewing.

METHODOLOGY

Subjects

Data were collected from 148 adults aged 26 to 90. The mean age within the sample was 59. Subjects were contacted through churches, senior citizens centers and retirement homes, and neighborhood and social organizations. Groups were asked to participate in a study of attitudes toward television and various types of programming; a monetary incentive was provided to encourage participation. As part of a larger study, subjects watched a video consisting of two program segments with embedded commercial material. They were then asked to complete a survey including general attitudes toward television, responses to the specific elements viewed, and lifestyle and demographic data.

Measures

Television orientation is defined by Rahtz, Sirgy and Meadow (1989) as "a disposition to use (or rely on) television for entertainment and information-gathering purposes" (p. 10). The television orientation scale used here was adapted from that earlier study. Items referring specifically to the elderly or to health issues were generalized to hold relevance for the entire population (for example, "television shows older people the way they really are" was changed to "television shows people the way they really are"). These changes were made to increase the relevance of the scale to the entire adult population and to reflect the belief that the elderly are interested in maintaining contact with the society at large rather than just the elderly segment. In addition, three items were added to the scale. Scale items are provided in Table 1.

Rahtz, Sirgy and Meadow (1989) found that the television orientation scale contained two related but distinct dimensions. A common factor analysis in this study confirmed the expected factor structure. Scale items and factor loadings are provided in Table 1. The two dimensions, information gathering (INFO) and entertainment seeking (ENTTAIN)[2], explained 46 percent of the total variance in the measures.

The Cronbach's alpha reliabilities of the INFO and ENTTAIN scales were .80 and .69 respectively. Because of the suggestion in previous research that television is more important to the elderly than to younger viewers for both its informtaion and entertainment value, both measures were used in the further analyses.

Television viewership was measured by two open-ended questions: (1) about how many hours of television do you watch in

---

[2]This labeling represents a departure from Rahtz, Sirgy, and Meadow (1989). The previous study labeled the second dimension "USAGE." The change provides greater consistency with their conceptualization of television orientation as a reliance on television for entertainment and information gathering, and also reflects changes and additions to the original scale intended to more clearly capture the entertainment value of the medium.

TABLE 2
Pearson Correlation Coefficients

	INFO	ENTTAIN	USAGE	AGE	SUBJAGE	LIVE	WORK	CLUBMEM	FRIENDS
INFO	1.0								
ENTTAIN	.615**	1.0							
USAGE	.324**	.474**	1.0						
AGE	.195*	.324**	.354**	1.0					
SUBJAGE	.204*	.326**	.373**	.902**	1.0				
LIVE	-.031	-.019	.071	-.078	-.080	1.0			
WORK	-.125	-.233**	-.298**	-.768**	-.758**	.051	1.0		
CLUBMEM	-.188*	-.223**	-.016	.041	-.043	.100	.015	1.0	
FRIENDS	-.079	-.066	.062	.051	.048	.085	-.030	.343**	1.0
CHURCH	-.028	.035	-.128	.248**	-.168	-.042	-.092	.312**	.197*

** $p < .01$
* $p < .05$

an average week, and (2) about how many hours of television did you watch yesterday. Average daily viewership was calculated as weekly viewing divided by seven. Television USAGE was calculated as the mean of average daily viewership and viewership on the preceding day. This was done to minimize noise in the measures due to likely rounding in the weekly measure and the effect of day of survey participation in the daily measure. The two items composing the USAGE scale had a correlation of .74.

Subjective age was measured via the Kastenbaum, Derbin, Sabatini, and Artt (1972) four item personal age scale. This is the same as the cognitive age scale used by Barak and Schiffman (1981) and Stephens (1991) with the exception that items are open-ended. The open ended format was preferred since it allows greater precision in responses than does a decade checklist. Also, in an earlier study in which both question formats were used, the open-ended format seemed to be less confusing for older subjects. The four items had a reliability of .93. Subjective age (SUBJAGE) was calculated as the average of the four items.

Chronological age was computed as 1991 minus response to the question "In what year were you born?"

Indicants of social interaction included: (1) LIVE — with whom the subject was currently living (spouse and children, spouse only or children only, with others, or alone); (2) WORK — employment status (fulltime, part-time, retired or unemployed); (3) CLUBMEM — the number of clubs or organizations to which the subject belonged; (4) CHURCH — frequency of church attendance; and (5) FRIENDS — the number of friends reported. Because number of friends had an extremely skewed distribution (the median response was 12; however, 9 percent of subjects reported having 99 or more friends), this variable was recoded into six categories. These items were suggested by other studies of social aging (c.f., Conner, Powers, and Bultena 1979; Graney and Graney 1975b).

ANALYSES AND RESULTS

Table 2 provides a summary correlation matrix for the variables studied. The information and entertainment components of television orientation were highly correlated (r=.615; p<.01). That is, it seems that individuals with a stronger television orientation seek both information- and entertainment-related gratifications. In addition, both components of television orientation were significantly correlated with television usage (r=.324; p<.01 and r=.474; p<.01 for INFO and ENTTAIN respectively).

As expected, age and subjective age were significantly correlated with each other (r=.902; p<.01) and with television orientation and usage. In each case, subjective age was more highly correlated with the television orientation and usage measures than was chronological age; however, the differences in correlation coefficients were very small (less than .01). Thus, contrary to expectation, the measurement of subjective age seems to hold little additional power to explain television viewing.

Overall there was some support for the suggestion that decreased social activity would lead to greater television orientation and usage. CLUBMEM was negatively related to INFO (r=-.188; p<.05) and ENTTAIN (r=-.223; p<.01), but was not significantly correlated with television usage. WORK was significantly related to both ENTTAIN and USAGE; however, this relationship may be caused by the greater availability of leisure time as well as by decreased social interaction. LIVE, FRIENDS, and CHURCH were not significantly related to television orientation or viewing behavior.

It was suspected that LIVE may not truly approximate an interval variable with respect to amount of social interaction; therefore, its relationship to television orientation and usage was also examined via analysis of variance. Once again, a significant effect failed to emerge. That is, there was no difference across LIVE categories (with spouse and children, spouse or children, others, or alone) on INFO, ENTTAIN, or USAGE.

WORK and CHURCH both showed significant correlations with age in this study. From an activity theoretic standpoint, relationships between age and the social variables are to be expected. However, the effect of the social variables which is independent of age is also of interest. To further investigate the relationship between social activity and television orientation and usage, first order partial correlations, controlling for chronological age, were examined.

After controlling for age, CLUBMEM maintained a negative relationship with INFO and ENTTAIN (r=-.229 and -.273, respectively; for both, p<.01). Further, CHURCH was negatively related to television USAGE (r=-.189; p<.05). These findings give additional support to the idea that decreased social activity will lead to increased television orientation and viewing. The full results of these analyses are contained in Table 3.

TABLE 3
Partial Correlations Controlling for Age

	INFO	ENTTAIN	USAGE
LIVE	-.038	-.057	.059
WORK	.025	.071	.009
CLUBMEM	-.229**	-.273**	-.029
FRIENDS	-.099	-.060	.010
CHURCH	.005	-.069	-.189*

** $p < .01$

* $p < .05$

DISCUSSION

The results of this study largely confirm the findings of Rahtz, Sirgy, and Meadow (1989). Strong support is provided for the importance of age, both chronological and subjective, as a predictor of television orientation. An additional step is taken in demonstrating the existence of strong relationships between age and television usage and between television orientation and television usage.

Only moderate support is provided for the existence of a relationship between social interaction and television orientation and usage. However, it is possible that different types of activity or different measures would have produced higher correlations with television orientation and usage. The low levels of correlation among the social interaction measures also signals a need for concern about their construct validity. Future research into the components of social aging is recommended.

Additional research is recommended to examine the differential importance of entertainment- versus information-motives for television viewing. While this study showed a strong correlation between information and entertainment orientations, ENTTAIN tended to have stronger correlations with age and activity measures. Rubin (1983) identified two television types: those who used the medium primarily for entertainment and those who used the medium primarily for information.

Television broadcasters provide information and entertainment services to the viewing public. In addition, they provide advertisers with a medium for reaching potential consumers. Broadcasters have a strong viewing segment in the elderly, and a group which seeks both information- and entertainment-oriented programming. An improved understanding of consumers' attitudes and television usage has great practical value, since to the extent that consumer viewing patterns and preferences are understood, both viewers and advertisers can be better served. Identifying more specific content desires of older viewers, then, may be an important media goal.

The results of this study may provide guidance not only for broadcasters, but also for public policy makers and others concerned with the information and entertainment needs of the elderly. Greater orientation toward and usage of television may have implications for how individuals respond to other aspects of their world. Shrum et al. (1991) indicate that as viewing increases, perceptions or reality may be distorted toward life as portrayed on television. Elderly viewers may be particularly susceptible to stereotyped images and portrayals of violence on television. Providers of social services to the elderly may seek to counteract these images.

The evidence seems clear that television usage and the psychological orientation toward television increases with age. As the proportion of the elderly within the population increases, so will the importance of television. Increased emphasis on the news and entertainment programming desired by older viewers will enhance the appeal of this medium to an important market segment.

REFERENCES

Barak, Benny and Leon G. Schiffman (1981), "Cognitive Age: A Nonchronological Age Variable," in Kent B. Monroe, ed., *Advances in Consumer Research*, Vol. 8, Ann Arbor: MI, Association for Consumer Research, 602-606.

Comstock, George (1980), *Television in America*, Beverly Hills, CA: Sage Publications.

_____, Steven Chaffee, Natan Katzman, Maxwell McCombs, and Donald Roberts (1978) *Television and Human Behavior*, New York: Columbia University Press.

Donohew, Lewis, Philip Palmgreen, and J. D. Rayburn, II, (1987), "Social and Psychological Origins of Media Use: A Lifestyle Analysis," *Journal of Broadcasting and Electronic Media*, 31 (Summer), 255-278.

Finn, Seth and Mary Beth Gorr (1988), "Social Isolation and Social Support as Correlates of Television Viewing Motivations," *Communication Research*, 15 (April), 135-158.

Graney, Marshall J. (1975a), "Communication Uses and the Social Activity Constant," *Communication Research*, 2 (October), 347-366.

_____ (1975b), "Happiness and Social Participation in Aging," *Journal of Gerontology*, 30 (6), 701-706

_____ and Edith E. Graney (1974), "Communications Activity Substitutions in Aging," *Journal of Communication*, 24 (Autumn), 88-96.

Havighurst, Robert J. and Ruth Albrecht (1953), *Older People*, New York: Longmans, Green, and Co.

_____ and Augusta deVries (1969), "Life Styles and Free Time Activities of Retired Men," *Human Development*, 12 (1), 34-54.

Kastenbaum, Robert, Valerie Derbin, Paul Sabatini, and Steven Artt (1972) "'The Ages of Me': Toward Personal and Interpersonal Definitions of Functional Aging," *Aging and Human Development*, 3 (2), 197-211.

Katz, Elihu, Jay G. Blumler, and Michael Gurevitch (1974), "Utilization of Mass Communication by the Individual," in Jay G. Blumler and Elihu Katz, eds., *The Uses of Mass Communications*, Beverly Hills, CA: Sage Publications, 19-32.

Kubey, Robert W. (1980), "Television and Aging: Past, Present, and Future," *The Gerontologist*, 20 (1), 16-35.

Nordenstreng, K. (1970), "Comments on 'Gratifications Research' in Broadcasting," *Public Opinion Quarterly*, 34.

Rahtz, Don R., M. Joseph Sirgy, and H. Lee Meadow (1989), "The Elderly Audience: Correlates of Television Orientation," *Journal of Advertising*, 18 (3), 9-20.

Real, Michael R., Hayes L. Anderson, and Marilyn H. Harrington (1980), "Television Access for Older Adults," *Journal of Communication*, 30 (Winter), 81-88.

Rubin, Alan M. (1983), "Television Uses and Gratifications: The Interactions of Viewing Patterns and Motivations," *Journal of Broadcasting*, 27 (Winter), 37-51.

_____ (1985), "Media Gratifications Through the Life Cycle," in Karl E. Rosengren, et al., eds., *Media Gratifications Research: Current Perspectives*, Beverly Hils: Sage Publications, 195-208.

Rubin, Rebecca B. and Michael P. McHugh (1987), "Development of Parasocial Interaction Relationships," *Journal of Broadcasting and Electronic Media*, 31 (Summer), 279-292.

Schonfield, David (1974), "Translations in Gerontology–From Lab to Life: Utilizing Information," *American Psychologist*, 29 (November), 796-801.

Short, J., E. Williams, and B. Christie (1976), *The Social Psychology of Telecommunications*, London: John Wiley.

Shrum, L. J., Thomas C. O'Guinn, Richard J. Semenik, and Ronald J. Faber (1991), "Processes and Effects in the Construction of Normative Consumer Beliefs: The Role of Television," in Rebecca Holman and Michael R. Solomon, eds., *Advances in Consumer Research*, Vol. 18, Provo, UT: Association for Consumer Research, 755-762.

Stephens, Nancy (1981), "Media Usage and Media Attitude Changes with Age and with Time," *Journal of Advertising*, 10 (1), 38-47.

_____ (1991) "Cognitive Age: A Useful Concept for Advertising?," *Journal of Advertising*, 20 (December), 37-48.

Emerging Issues in Demographic Research
Marilyn Young Jones, University of Houston - Clear Lake

INTRODUCTION

Rather than review and critique these three interesting papers individually, I will try to extract something valuable from each paper and extend that to the other papers and to consumer behavior research in general (with some emphasis on information processing issues). I think there are several general issues here and will discuss four broad points: 1) the paucity of demographic research, 2) public policy and marketing effectiveness issues, 3) the role of replication in demographic research and 4) the use of consumer-generated terminology for behavioral constructs. The attached bibliography includes all the demographic articles published in the *Journal of Consumer Research* since December, 1987.

THE PAUCITY OF DEMOGRAPHIC RESEARCH

A quick review of the last twenty issues (five years) of the *Journal of Consumer Research* reveals only ten articles that involve demographic topics directly. That constitutes approximately 4.8% (10/209) of the articles published there. Including those articles that involve demographic topics indirectly, the figure rises to 7.7% (16/209).

Three of those articles directly concerned with demographics involve children's issues. They include such topics as: children's cognitive defenses against advertising (Brucks, Armstrong and Goldberg 1988); category development among children (Roedder-John and Sujan 1990); and script development among children (Peracchio 1992). A fourth article concerns the perception of adolescent role in family decision making (Foxman, Tansuhaj and Ekstrom 1989). There are several other studies which involve either gender or sex issues: the differences in processing strategies of men and women (Meyers-Levy and Maheswaran 1991); the effects of sex roles on judgement (Meyers-Levy 1988); the effects of sex typing on judgments (Schmitt, Leclerc and Dubois-Roux 1988); and gender roles and gift giving (Fischer and Arnold 1990). Stayman and Despande (1989) introduced the notion of perceived ethnicity while others have examined adolescent shoplifting behavior (Cox, Cox and Moschis 1990). These make up the ten articles directly concerned with demographics.

Other articles address issues that are arguably similar to demographic issues: working women/dual earner households and expenditure patterns (Bryant 1988, Rubin, Riney and Molina 1990, Soberon-Ferrer and Dardis 1991), parental style and socializing children (Carlson and Grossbart 1988), and homeless issues (Hill 1990, Hill and Stanley 1990).

Historically, the treatments of demographics in the marketing literature have been descriptive (cf. Venkatesh 1980). The aim has been to describe either the search or purchase behaviors of demographic segments with less reference to the processes that account for these behaviors. Many of the aforementioned studies point to a laudable trend to integrate demographic variables with well-established theories (especially information processing theories). Several, such as those concerning children and most of those concerning sex and sex role, have sought to establish a link between an easily measured or prominent demographic variable and information processing characteristics. The studies presented today reinforce that trend. In particular, Wooten and Galvin's (1992) work on perceived ethnicity uses theories about excitation transfer and contrast and congruity effects to explain how perceived ethnicity relates to measures of advertising effectiveness. Pathak, Kucukarslan, Sirdeshmukh and Segall (1992) demonstrate that the satisfaction processing of "vulnerable" consumers differs from the satisfaction processing of non-vulnerable consumers. Johnson (1992) has related the television orientation of elderly consumers to theory about social activity.

Marketing research has been said to be a search for independent variables. Research in the past fifteen years has often focused on cognitive states (cf. Petty, Cacioppo and Schumann 1983, Johnson and Russo 1984) and affective states (cf. Murry, Lastovicka and Singh 1992)) as key independent variables. Demographic variables, however, have practical appeal because it is easy to collect information about them and they conform to existing ways of reporting media usage.

The studies presented today extend our theoretical knowledge about demographic factors. In earlier work, Stayman and Despande (1989) tested the notion that ethnicity was a perceived as well as a biological state. This introduces the idea that demographic characteristics have psychological subtleties heretofore ignored in the consumer behavior research. Johnson (1992) and Wooten and Galvin (1992) reinforce this finding for age and ethnicity respectively. Johnson (1992) and Wooten and Galvin (1992) also extend that idea to show that a subjective demographic characteristic can influence marketing responses of interest - namely media use (television viewing) and judgment. Similarly, the "vulnerable consumers" (disadvantaged racial/ethnic, age, sex, handicapped and income groups) studied in Pathak et al. (1992) may experience their demographic characteristics in a subjective as well as an objective fashion.

There seems to be a change in the way demographics are approached by researchers. The theoretical range has expanded and emerging applications go beyond simple segmentation.

DEMOGRAPHICS, MARKETING EFFECTIVENESS AND PUBLIC POLICY ISSUES

Recent advances in our understanding of the information processing and demographics suggest we are moving in the direction of greater promotion effectiveness. This raises three concerns in my mind: the application of social marketing, how to police abuses and how to enhance the effectiveness of public service campaigns.

Looking a Pollay, Lee and Carter-Whitney (1992) on targeting cigarette ads to blacks and whites, the issue of the social value of the product emerges. Better marketing techniques are praised when the product is a "good" product but damned when it is a "bad" product. Of course we can not always predict what product will prove to be "bad" product. For example, silicon breast implants were long considered a safe way for women to enhance their physical image. That viewpoint has given way in view of the recently discovered serious health risks.

A second concern is how to police abuses of particular demographic groups. The Uptown cigarette was removed from the market under pressure from black interest groups. The Dakota cigarette encountered some resistance as well. The consumer groups, for whom these brands was specifically created, were deemed unusually susceptible. These are clearly "bad" products and targeted to groups with strong lobbies. Our growing ability to understand and even influence perceptions about demographic membership (such as perceived ethnicity) and processing strikes me as harder to police than simple target marketing. While targeted cigarettes are rather easy to spot by the FTC and/or the special interest groups, media placement intended to raise perceived ethnicity and strengthen ad responses may not. It places an enormous burden on marketers to police themselves. Research firms and ad agencies, in their role as "hired guns," are not free of potential liability for "marketing malpractice."

REPLICATION AND DEMOGRAPHIC ISSUES

Johnson (1992) has presented a replication study here. Many successful replication studies have documented the changing character of demographic or cultural groups. This is in keeping with Gergen's (1976) call for replications to track changing social phenomena. Several successful studies have tracked changing behaviors of working women and changes in the practice of marketing ethics. While Johnson (1992) has not addressed how the proclivity of the elderly to use telvision as a social substitute for information and entertainment has changed, this is a characteristic that could be tracked over time. Similarly, there is a role for replication studies for many "vulnerable" consumers. Further, the stimuli that provoke different perceived ethnic states also may change over time.

THE USE OF CONSUMER GENERATED TERMINOLOGY

Popular books on management (Peters and Austin 1985) have advocated the use of consumer generated terminology as a way to better understand consumers (by being sensitive to the problems they want products to solve). One example is "itchy-scratchy eyes." This was found to be the way consumers conceive of contact lens solution problems. It stands in contrast to the chemical orientation that engineers have. I wonder about the extent to which we academic researchers are sensitive to the language used by the consumers we study. The field of cognitive linguistics addresses the notion that people's language reveals the primitive concepts held by the speakers and that this might affect the way they respond to research (Rosa 1992). The Pathak et al. (1992) study reflects this concern. They found that consumers respond differently about their level of satisfaction when the term "bothered" is used rather than the term "satisfied".

CONCLUSION

The foregoing points suggest that those with an interest in demographics have ample research opportunities in the area. There is clearly room to study the psychological aspects of demographic attributes, replicate previous findings and explore the public policy implications of marketing to vulnerable consumers.

REFERENCES

Bearden, William O. and Jesse E. Teel (1983), "Selected Determinants of Consumer Satisfaction and Complaint Reports," *Journal of Marketing Research*, 20 (February), 21-8.

Brucks, Merrie, Gary M. Armstrong and Marvin E. Goldberg (1988), "Children's Use of Cognitive Defenses Against Television Advertising: A Cognitive Response Approach," *Journal of Consumer Research*, 14 (4), 471-482.

Bryant, W. Keith (1988), "Durables and Wives' Employment Yet Again," *Journal of Consumer Research*, 15 (1), 37-47.

Carlson, Les and Sanford Grossbart (1988), "Parental Style and Consumer Socialization of Children," *Journal of Consumer Research*, 15 (1), 77-94.

Cox, Dena, Anthony D. Cox and George P. Moschis (1990), "When Consumer Behavior Goes Bad: An Investigation of Adolescent Shoplifting," *Journal of Consumer Research*, 17 (2), 149-60.

Day, Ralph and E. Laird Landon (1977), "Toward a Theory of Consumer Complaining Behavior," in *Consumer and Industrial Buying Behavior*, A.G. Woodside, J.N. Sheth and P.D. Bennett (eds.), New York: North-Holland, 425-37.

Gergen, Kenneth J. (1976), "Social Psychology, Science and History," *Personality and Social Psychology Bulletin*, 2 (Fall), 373-83.

Hill, Ronald Paul (1991), "Homeless Women, Special Possessions, and the Meaning of "Home": An Ethnographic Case Study," *Journal of Consumer Research*, 18 (3), 298-310.

Hill, Ronald Paul and Mark Stanley (1990), "The Homeless in America: An Examination of Possessions and Consumption Behaviors," *Journal of Consumer Research*, 17,(3), 303-321.

Fischer, Eileen and Stephen Arnold (1990), "More than a Labor of Love: Gender Roles and Christmas Gift Shopping," *Journal of Consumer Research*, 17 (3), 333-345.

Foxman, Ellen R., Patriya S. Tansuhaj and Karin M. Ekstrom (1989), "Family Members' Perceptions of Adolescents' Influence in Family Decision Making," *Journal of Consumer Research*, 15 (4), 482-491.

Johnson, Rose L. (1992), "Age and social Activity as Correlates of Television Orientation: A Replication and Extension, " in Leigh McAlister and Michael L. Rothchild (eds.), *Advances in Consumer Research*, Vol. XX 1993.

Meyers-Levy, Joan and Durairaj Maheswaran (1991), "Exploring Differences in Males' and Females' Processing Strategies," *Journal of Consumer Research*, 18 (1), 63-70.

Pathak, Dev S., Suzan Kucukarslan, Deepak Sirdeshmukh and Richard Segal (1992), "The Vulnerable Consumer in the High Blood Pressure Drug Market: Bothered but Satisfied," in Leigh McAlister and Michael L. Rothchild (eds.), *Advances in Consumer Research*, Vol. XX 1993.

Peracchio, Laura A. (1992), "How Do Young Children Learn to be Consumers? A Script-processing Approach," *Journal of Consumer Research*, 18 (4), 425-440.

Pollay Richard W., Jung S. Lee and David Carter-Whitney (1992), "Separate, But Not Equal: Racial Segmentation in Cigarette Advertising," *Journal of Advertising*, 21 (1), 45-57.

Roedder-John, Deborah and Mita Sujan (1990), "Age Differences in Product Categorization," *Journal of Consumer Research*, 16 (4), 452-460.

Rosa, Jose Antonio (1992), A conversation at the 1992 ACR Conference.

Rubin, Rose M., Bobye J. Riney and David J. Molina (1990), "Expenditure Pattern Differentials Between One-Earner and Dual-Earner Households: 1972-1973 and 1984," *Journal of Consumer Research*, 17 (1), 43-52.

Schmitt, Bernd H., France Lecherc and Laurette Dube'Rioux (1988), "Sex Typing and Consumer Behavior: A Test of Gender Schema Theory," *Journal of Consumer Research*, 15 (1), 122-128.

Soberon-Ferrer, Horacio and Rachel Dardis (1991), "Determinants of Household Expenditures for Services," *Journal of Consumer Research*, 17 (4), 385-397.

Stayman, Douglas and Rohit Deshpande (1989), "Situational Ethnicity and Consumer Behavior," *Journal of Consumer Research*, 16 (3), 361-371.

Westbrook, Robert A. (1987), "Product/Consumption-Based Affective Responses and Postpurchase Processes," *Journal of Marketing Research*, 24 (August), 258-70.

Wooten, David B. and Tiffany Galvin (1992), "A Preliminary Examination of the Effects of Context-Induced Felt Ethnicity on Advertising Effectiveness," in Leigh McAlister and Michael L. Rothchild (eds.), *Advances in Consumer Research*, Vol. XX 1993.

Zinkhan, George M., Marilyn Jones and Kirk Smith (1991), "The Replication Tradition in Marketing Research," working paper, College of Business Administration, University of Houston.

What Causes Youths to Start Smoking? Converging Quantitative and Qualitative Evidence on the Role of Smoking-Related Advertising

Tom Novak, Southern Methodist University
Cornelia (Connie) Pechmann, University of California at Irvine

1) DIFFUSION MODELS FOR SMOKING ONSET AND CESSATION: A SEGMENT-LEVEL HISTORICAL ANALYSIS

Thomas P. Novak, Southern Methodist University
Frank M. Bass, University of Texas at Dallas
Wagner A. Kamakura, Vanderbilt University
Clyde Dent, University of Southern California

The Bass diffusion model and Cox proportional hazard model were applied to smoking onset data from the 1990 California Tobacco Survey (CTS). The Bass model assumes that hazard for smoking onset is a linear function of cumulative onset. However, for the CTS data, this assumption is valid only until age 18. This suggests that a constant word-of-mouth parameter is appropriate only until age 18; after this point, individuals become increasingly resistant to starting smoking, and word-of-mouth effects require a time-varying coefficient.

Historical results for smoking onset for segments defined by race, education, and gender, throughout the 20th century were shown using the Cox proportional hazard model. These demographic results are highly consistent with previous research. The Cox model was also used to investigate the effect of overall tobacco industry advertising and price on smoking onset. Results suggested that higher price decreases onset hazard, particularly for those over age 18. Results for advertising were equivocal.

2) SMOKING-RELATED ADVERTISING AND ITS EFFECTS ON PRETEENS: A SOCIAL COGNITIVE PERSPECTIVE

Cornelia (Connie) Pechmann, University of California at Irvine
S. Ratneshwar, University of Florida

The age of smoking initiation is steadily decreasing as more preteens experiment with cigarettes. Why do youths continue to smoke despite the well-known health risks? The uptake of smoking is associated with beliefs or stereotypes that smokers have socially desirable attributes (for example, smokers are "cool," and are more popular, attractive, exciting, and mature than nonsmokers). The more positively youths perceive smokers, the more likely they are to take up smoking themselves.

Antismoking advocates contend that cigarette advertising, which is still permitted in print media and on billboards, helps to create or at least perpetuate such positive beliefs or stereotypes about smokers. Using a social-cognitive research approach, we investigated whether smoking-related advertising affects perceptions and judgments of smokers.

In the first phase of a controlled laboratory study involving over 300 seventh graders in Southern California, subjects were exposed to either cigarette, anti-smoking, or nonsmoking-related advertising. The ads were embedded in a professionally produced mock-up color magazine. In the second phase of the study, each subject, seated before a personal computer, was exposed to 12 comments (some positive, negative, and neutral) about a fictitious student (either a smoker or nonsmoker).

Subjects exposed to the anti-smoking (vs. control) ads tended to judge the smoker more negatively on key psychosocial attributes (e.g. attractiveness). Some subjects who saw the cigarette ads tended to have more positive thoughts about the smoker, but others were simply reminded of their negative beliefs.

The Targeting of Youths By Cigarette Marketers: Archival Evidence on Trial
Richard W. Pollay, University of British Columbia
Anne M. Lavack, University of British Columbia

ABSTRACT

Contrary to vehement industry denials, the targeting of youth is amply evidenced in corporate documents produced during the trial about Canada's cigarette advertising ban. Extensive and sophisticated research identified target segments, starting at age 15, and guided the advertising aimed at them, while recognizing addiction among adolescents. Images of independence and freedom from authority were used by competing firms to appeal to the psychological needs of young starters. Careful crafting ensured that images were not too immature, lest the brand consequently be rejected, and the activities not too aerobic, lest this precipitate cognitive counter-arguing. "Positive lifestyle imagery" was used as a matter of policy to enhance the social acceptability of smoking. The importance of images of independence to attract Canadian youths is compared to the American experience with brands like Marlboro.

INTRODUCTION

Cigarette firms "vehemently, unequivocally and unilaterally deny any youth-directed marketing efforts (*Ad. Age* 1983)." Nonetheless, in 1988 Canada passed the Tobacco Product Control Act to severely limit "inducements" to smoking, i.e. advertising and promotional activities. The constitutionality of this near ban, in intent, was challenged by Imperial Tobacco Ltd. (ITL) and R.J. Reynolds-Macdonald Inc. (RJR). These two major cigarette marketers dominate the Canadian market, sharing it only with Philip Morris (Benson & Hedges). All are affiliated with major U.S. tobacco firms. Although final adjudication of this case is still pending, large quantities of confidential documents from the marketing and advertising files of the two plaintiff cigarette firms became available for pre-trial review and many became trial evidence and entered the public domain. These documents directly contradict many of the tobacco industry's common assertions, e.g., that all cigarette advertising is aimed solely at brand switchers, not starters; or that cigarette sellers take no strategic interest in adolescents. This paper reviews these documents, focusing on the targeting of youth, providing highlights in the firms' own words.

STRATEGIC ISSUES

Tobacco marketers are well aware of the increasingly difficult conditions they face. As awareness of death risks, addiction and the perils of passive smoking have grown and smoking has become less socially acceptable, tobacco companies have made attempts to provide reassurances to smokers in a variety of ways, including the extensive use of advertising and public relations (Pollay 1990b). RJR's 1986 Tempo Qualitative Post-Launch Evaluation (AG-17[1]) points out that:

> "Many smokers are questioning their 'habit' for both health and economic reasons. The present anti-smoking climate has made smokers defensive about smoking both to themselves and to others ... These attitudes result in smokers requiring some reassurance about both the social acceptability of smoking and smoking a particular brand (p.7)."

The commitment to enhance the social acceptability of smoking was repeated often in ITL's statement of philosophies (AG-51) which prefaced most contemporary marketing documents:

> "Support the continued social acceptability of smoking through industry and/or corporate actions (e.g. product quality, positive lifestyle advertising, selective field activities and marketing public relations programs)(p.1)."

The Multiple Roles of Advertising

Cigarette marketers are acutely aware of the important roles played by their advertising. The ITL 1971 Marketing Plan states:

> "In a market with minimal product differentiation, advertising becomes a disproportionately important part of the marketing mix as compared to most other mass consumer products (p.18)."

Advertising also as not only advancing general social acceptability of smoking, and an instrument of competition preferred to price wars, but is seen as a means of influencing the attitudes, perceptions and resulting behaviors of two key consumer segments: concerned smokers (latent quitters), and young starters (new users). Advertising of maximal effectiveness for the firms and industry would (a) reinforce current smokers, inducing them to continue smoking rather than quit, and/or (b) attract starters. The dual interest in reinforcing existing smokers and recruiting new smokers is shown in many of the documents, with brand switchers of only tertiary importance. For example, RJR's 1978 Business Plan (AG-14) identified Export A has having the need to "maintain brand share of first time smokers (p.2060)." Export A's target audience for advertising was made up of "current Export A smokers," "new smokers," and lastly "full flavour switchers (p.2065)."

The Response of the Market and of Imperial Tobacco to the Smoking and Health Environment (AG-41) illustrates how product design, too, serves to retain would be quitters:

> "Smoking and Health has caused a general movement in the market down the T&N [tar and nicotine] scale.... We have evidence of virtually no quitting among smokers of those brands, and there are indications that the advent of ultra low tar cigarettes has actually retained some potential quitters in the cigarette market by offering them a viable alternative (p.2)."

The Strategic Importance of Starters

Capturing a healthy share of the starters market is particularly important in the cigarette industry, because of its phenomenally

---

[1] All corporate documents discussed were manifest in proceedings assessing the constitutionality of Canada's Tobacco Products Control Act: Imperial Tobacco Limitee & RJR-Macdonald Inc. c. Le Procureur General du Canada, Quebec Superior Court, 1990. Documents entered into evidence are cited using the trial numbers indicating who entered the documents, e.g. Attorney General (AG-###), R.J.Reynolds-MacDonald Inc. (RJR-###) or Imperial Tobacco Ltd. (ITL-###). These, and all others mentioned, were reviewed and reported to the court in Pollay (1990a) (AG-224). A condensed version of this expert opinion appears as Pollay (1992a).

high rates of brand loyalty. Because annual brand switching rates are very low, 10% or less a year in contemporary times, capturing starters builds a solid franchise base with high year to year retention. The firms that succeed in capturing starters soon dominate the industry, as best shown by Philip Morris and Marlboro. The Canadian tobacco industry has understood this for at least two decades. The 1971 Matinee Marketing Plan stated:

> "Young smokers represent the major opportunity group for the cigarette industry. We should therefore determine their attitudes to smoking and health and how this might change over time (p.11)."

More recently, the F'88 Marketing Plan of ITL notes:

> "If the last ten years have taught us anything, it is that the industry is dominated by the companies who respond most effectively to the needs of younger smokers. Our efforts on these brands will remain on maintaining their relevance to smokers in these younger groups in spite of the (poor) share performance they may develop among older smokers (p.6, emphasis in original)."

Although couched in the corporate terminology of "major opportunity group" and the desire to "respond most effectively to the needs of younger smokers," marketing documents demonstrate that the youth franchise which the primary youth-oriented brands enjoy is no accident, but instead is the result of carefully planned and executed strategies, guided throughout by extensive research.

RESEARCH

Multiple research resources and perspectives are employed for a single brand. ITL's Project Huron, for example, evaluated the feasibility of an American flavored cigarette targeted primarily at young males 15-25. It was the subject of at least 33 different market research reports, utilizing at least six external research suppliers, over the space of just four years. Market research enhances the potential impact of cigarette advertising by carefully identifying the effective appeals and executions. The techniques range from the pedestrian to the esoteric, from simple surveys and focus group discussions to elaborate and convergent analyses of multiple data bases. Most studies seek insight into the psychological dynamics of existing and potential consumers, and their perceptions, interpretations and recall of advertisements. Research documents discuss the behavior of 11, 12 and 13 year olds and the nature of the starting process. The consumer research identifies the needs, interests and concerns of target audiences so that advertising can position the product offering in terms that they will find relevant and appealing. The heterogeneity of consumers leads cigarette firms to identify segments who share similar patterns of social and political attitudes, lifestyles, product use and brand preferences.

Risks and Rationalizations

Both ITL and RJR have generated several research studies focused on starters, some of which have identified the risks and rationalizations of pre-teens and teens when beginning to smoke. Imperial Tobacco's Project 16 used focus groups of 16 and 17 year olds in the fall of 1977. It was described retrospectively in Project Plus/Minus (AG-217) as being a "memorable project" with the purpose of understanding:

> "why do young people start smoking, and how do they feel about being smokers?... The results were in depth, revealing, at times even fraught with drama in glimpses of the baring of that much investigated but still mysterious adolescent psyche (p.1)."

Project 16 (AG-216) was conducted at hotels where "closed circuit television observation facilities were in use for observers from Imperial Tobacco, McKim Advertising Limited, and Spitzer Mills and Bates [ITL's advertising agencies] (p.2)." Among the insights into starting that were revealed:

> "The adolescent seeks to display his new urge for independence with a symbol, and cigarettes are such a symbol.... Serious efforts to learn to smoke occur between ages 12 and 13 in most cases (p.i-ii)."

Project 16 also revealed that the cigarette firms know full well that many 16 and 17 year olds are already addicted to cigarettes, and are sorry they ever began to smoke:

> "However intriguing smoking was at 11, 12 or 13, by the age of 16 or 17 many regretted their use of cigarettes for health reasons and because they feel unable to stop smoking when they want to (p.vi)."

Imperial Tobacco subsequently commissioned Project Plus/Minus (AG-217), a study among young people aged 16-24 which sought additional insight into their perceptions of the pros and cons of smoking. The report concluded that:

> "Starters no longer disbelieve the dangers of smoking, but they almost universally assume these risks will not apply to themselves because they will not become addicted. Once addiction does take place, it becomes necessary for the smoker to make peace with the accepted hazards. This is done by a wide range of rationalizations ... The desire to quit seems to come earlier now than before, even prior to the end of high school. In fact, it often seems to take hold as soon as the recent starter admits to himself that he is hooked on smoking. However, the desire to quit, and actually carrying it out, are two quite different things, as the would-be quitter soon learns (p.i)."

Quebecois subjects expressed similar attitudes about being addicted. Project Plus/Minus: Young People and Smoking, Behaviors and Attitudes, 1982, Summary concluded:

> "They are sorry that they ever started smoking because it's harmful but they feel somewhat trapped. They are constantly reminded of their lack of willpower. To defend themselves they tend to put on a jaunty air. They do this to save face because they would really like to quit and not appear to be slaves to their cigarettes ... Those who have tried to give up smoking have found the experience very painful. It made them realize that, although they thought they could quit easily, they have become slaves to their cigarettes (p.12-13)."

Identifying Personality and Psychological Needs

The primary example of this focus is the Youth Target Study '87 (RJR-6), a major study with four large volumes of results. The 1,022 subjects of this research were aged fifteen (15) to twenty-four (24) years of age. Whether non-starters came from particular family and social environments was addressed by measuring adult smoking, family pressures about starting, and smoking by teenage peers. Lifestyle was measured along fifteen dimensions such as laissez-faire, workaholic, wimpishness, or dropout. Attitudes and knowledge about the association between smoking and ill health were studied in great depth. The images of smokers, quitters, and never starters were measured along seventeen dimensions. Data on the image of tobacco products was gathered on twenty five scales. Advocacy issues were tapped by measuring awareness of anti-smoking campaigns and the relative credibility of various sources of information, such as doctors, teachers, government, and manufacturers.

Perhaps the most striking component of this massive research effort, however, was the measurement of personality traits with a clinical psychometric instrument, Cattell's 16 Personality Factors. Scales of this instrument ranges from Harria (tough-minded) to Premsia (tender-minded); Alaxia (trusting) to Protension (suspicious); or Threctia (shy) to Parmia (adventuresome). Still other scales measure, in the less obscure terminology, intelligence, ego strength, submissiveness, shrewdness, imaginativeness, guilt proneness, conservatism, self-sufficiency and self-discipline.

Sample Segments

Youth Target Study '87 (RJR-6) used cluster analysis to divide the youth market into seven psychographic groups, descriptively dubbed Big City Independents, Tomorrow's Leaders, Transitional Adults, Quiet Conformers, T.G.I.F.'s, Insecure Moralists, and Small Town Traditionalists (p.8-10). The T.G.I.F. (Thank God It's Friday) segment is the largest, containing about 30% of all those aged 15-24. A whopping 62% of the T.G.I.F. group are smokers making them a primary target segment (p.39). The T.G.I.F. group is primarily comprised of underachievers who are:

> "rooted in the present. They live for the moment and tend to be self-indulgent ... Achievement and leadership is not a goal for this group compared to others. Societal issues are relative non-issues ... [and] they are the most prominent supporters of smoking ... They do read newspapers and some magazines, including *Playboy* and *Penthouse*. Heavy metal and hard rock are common music choices (p.8, 21)."

In stark contrast, Tomorrow's Leaders are described as being "gregarious and assertive, clear in their direction and oriented toward achievement and success.... They are personally active in sports and concerned about fitness. Smoking is anathema (sic)(p.13)." Small Town Traditionalists "often come from rural and small town areas and [are] imbued with the conservative values emanating therefrom (sic).... [They] are hard working, unselfish and against smoking, sexual freedom, discrimination and overt sex and violence (p.26)."

An even more elaborate effort was RJR's Family Segmentation: Segment Descriptor Study (RJR-175), which used a triangulation of three complementary approaches to segment the entire cigarette market, not just youths. The first approach used perceptual mapping on data evaluating 16 brands across a series of product/user imagery statements. This identified five brand imagery clusters: masculine, female/moderation, popular/urban, concerned, and traditional. A second segmentation approach, called "tobaccographics," also found five segments reflecting differing patterns in attitudes toward smoking: Experimenters, Quitters, Guilty Unselective Habituals, Selective Habituals, and Ostriches (the industry term for those unresponsive to health information, like the proverbial ostrich with its head buried in the sand in response to threat). The third segmentation approach defined psychographic segments based on 74 statements which reflected attitudes toward life in general. Status Seekers, Affluent Progressives, Achievers, Conservatives, Traditionalists, and Geriatrics were the identified clusters from this perspective.

HOW ADS TARGET THE YOUNG

Modelling Young People and Behaviors

Player's, an ITL starters' brand, sought the starters market in head to head competition with RJR's Export A. The F'81 Advertising: Objectives and Strategies, Creative Guidelines (AG-35) specifies that the target market will "emphasize the under 20 year old group in its imagery reflection of lifestyle (activity) tastes (p.42)." Despite the self regulatory guidelines which in Canada, like the U.S., specify that models should be and appear to be over 25, the models used in Player's advertising were intended to be particularly young looking:

> "Models in Player's advertising must be 25 years or older, but should appear to be between 18 and 25 years of age (p.52)."

RJR learned the hard way that models can be too young, however. The Tempo brand was test marketed in select cities, with most of the media budget going for out-of-home media, targeting key youth locations and meeting places close to theatres, record stores, video arcades, etc. The J. Walter Thompson creative recommendations (AG-16) targeted the young who were "extremely influenced by their peer group" using "imagery which portrays the positive social appeal of peer group acceptance ... where acceptance by the group provides a sense of belonging and security (p.4)." The creative featured notably young models, arm in arm, and wearing casual clothes seen as trendy by the young. The brand met with mixed results in the test market, in part because it was too explicitly "young" in its character. Few self respecting teenagers want an explicitly teen product, as they seek symbols of adulthood, not adolescence.

Images of Independence

The brands most successful with teenagers are those that offer adult imagery rich with connotations of independence, freedom from authority, and self-reliance. The Marlboro Man epitomizes this, as he is totally and autonomously free - usually alone and interacting with no one, and always with no parents, no older brothers, no foreman, no bullies, indeed no one at all whose authority must be respected. There is not even a sheriff in Marlboro Country.

But while the young seek independence from authority (parents, teachers, etc.), they also want peer support. Cigarettes are a visible "badge product" and the user's character is displayed every time the branded package is. How peers view your brand of cigarette is also, therefore, vitally important. The firms are aware of this delicate dialectic, and the dual role of advertising in communicating to both the potential consumer and his or her peers. ITL's 1988 Project Sting tested "overtly masculine imagery, targeted at young males ... Young males are going through a stage where they are seeking to express their independence and individuality under constant pressure of being accepted by their peers (p.1-2)."

The Export A brand had a special appeal for young adolescents, as recognized by RJR in the Export Family Strategy Document of 1982 (AG-222):

> "...very young starter smokers choose Export A because it provides them with an instant badge of masculinity, appeals

to their rebellious nature and establishes their position amongst their peers (p.7299)."

RJR carefully nurtured this image of the Export A smoker. A section titled "How We Want Consumers to View the Brand" states that:

"The Export imagery will dimensionalize (sic) the breed of men who are masculine, independent, adventurous and possess the qualities of natural leadership.... Women are attracted to these men because of their youthful virility, independence and spirit of adventure (p.7331)."

ITL's 1985 Project Stereo (AG-27) provided creative guidelines for the effective display of freedom and independence in advertising imagery for appealing to a young market. Project Stereo described how Player's and its closest rival for starting males, Export A, both imaged independence, with subtle yet very important differences. Both used ads featuring strong, masculine, hardy men, typically alone in the fresh air of the outdoors. The brand images for Player's and Export A were, however, contrasted as follows by ITL, with the far more successful Player's brand image mentioned first:

"choose to be alone vs. being a loner;
masculine/softer man vs. macho/rugged;
okay to show feelings vs. can't show feelings;
can get along with women vs. no women;
better job/steady worker vs. working class, blue collar;
adventurous/try new things vs. daredevil;
independent/strong willed vs. doesn't care about society (p.18)."

Project Stereo's Final Report (AG-27) made recommendations for designing advertisements for the Player's brand showing people "free to choose friends, music, clothes, own activities, to be alone if he wishes"; who "can manage alone" and be "close to nature" with "nobody to interfere, no boss/parents"; and self-reliant enough to experience solitude without loneliness (p. 60).

Pictures of Health

The images used in the Player's ads were carefully crafted to feature attainable activities which were appealing to youth, but which were not so 'aerobic' as to be unbelievable in the context of smoking. The Player's Filter '81, Creative Guideline (AG-222) suggests that ads feature activities which:

"should not require undue physical exertion. They should not be representative of an elitist's sport nor should they be seen as a physical conditioner. The activity shown should be one which is practiced by young people 16 to 20 years old or one that these people can reasonably aspire to in the near future. The activity should not be limited to a certain social class or inaccessible to our target group because of their modest means.... The chosen scene should ideally (sic) depict a pause or moment of relaxation before, during or after the activity.... However, the scene may show participants in action if the moment of product consumption can be assumed to be close to the scene depicted (p.1-2)."

Minimizing Counter-arguing

Although images used in cigarette advertising often portray pictures of health, these images are tested, ensuring that they elicit minimal counter-arguing from viewers. For example, in the Project Stereo Advertising Evaluation (AG-220) a windsurfing ad for ITL's Player's brand was evaluated finding that:

"The reaction to windsurfing as an activity is neutral with regard to whether or not the people who engage in it are likely to be smokers or not. However, the more physically fit and healthy-looking the protagonists, the stronger the 'no-smoking' reaction. The same person sitting on the beach—perceived by most as resting after surfing—or shown carrying a surfboard—whether getting out of the water or walking toward the ocean—evokes different reactions regarding smoking. Respondents are willing to accept the man smoking while resting but are reluctant to think of him as a smoker while his well-built body is in full view (p.6)."

DISCUSSION

The American Experience.

Cigarette manufacturers have been judged to be targeting America's young for many years. *Fortune* (1963, p.120) long ago observed that "cigarette ads often portray and seem to be pitched directly at young people." Recent analysis of the television media buying by cigarette firms in the 1960s notes that the buying patterns were significantly correlated only with the size of the teenage audience various time slots delivered (Pollay 1992b).

American advertisers, like their Canadian counterparts, have long thought that individualism, and the related notions of independence, self reliance, autonomy from authority, are important strategic concepts in ad executions, accounting for the success among starters of some of the most prominent brands, like Marlboro or Virginia Slims. One account describes the success of Philip Morris' marketing executives George Weissman and Jack Landry. Marlboro had been sold as a woman's cigarette, with devices like lipstick colored filters and a "Mild as May" slogan, since the 1920s. The first attempts at repositioning the brand as male in the 1950s featured the breathy sensual singing of Julie London and tattooed WWII veterans, paying most attention to the flip-top box packaging innovation. When Weissman assumed responsibility in the late 1950s, his research informed him that post-adolescents in search of an identity were taking up smoking as a way of declaring independence from their parents. Jack Landry, together with the Leo Burnett agency, came up "commercials that would turn rookie smokers on to Marlboro ... the right image to capture the youth market's fancy ... a perfect symbol of independence and individualistic rebellion (Meyers 1984, p.70)." The power of this image based transformational, rather than informational, style of advertising was and is still demonstrated by Marlboro's stunning success over time at capturing a significant share of starters, inevitably becoming the best selling brand.

Marlboro's success led to much imitative competition. The FTC reported that one of the popular cigarette advertising strategies of the 1960's was the use of images portraying "personality characteristics which the advertiser hopes will appeal to the audience of existing and potential cigarette smokers ... The classic example of this approach is the Marlboro cowboy — ruggedly masculine, self-sufficient ... The theme of masculine independence has been used by several other advertisers (FTC 1970, p.8)." Ads for Camel, Newport and Old Gold were named as examples, and Virginia Slims in a parallel manner appealed to feminine independence, then as now. Neither the Marlboro campaign, nor the Virginia Slims campaign, have been substantially altered in more than twenty years, a rare stability that is a sure indicator of their strategic soundness and success.

Many ad campaigns over the years have featured racers of cars, motorcycles, speedboats, etc. Many brands, like Camel, Marlboro and Winston in the U.S. and Player's and Rothmans in Canada, sponsor racing events and teams on an on-going basis. There is more to this than simply appealing to young men's interest in fast cars and other machines. A commercial study of a Viceroy campaign featuring close-ups of "a young man in auto racing garb" found that subtle visual differences, caused by the model's appearance, positioning, or other staging devices or decisions, had large effects upon consumer reactions. A test ad strongly communicated "positive personality characteristics including courageousness, independence, adventurousness and aggressiveness (Schwartz 1976, p.75)."

The sponsorship of racing car events by Marlboro may at first seem inconsistent with the cowboy character, but it is not. Philip Morris' Vice-President of Marketing Services, Ellen Merlo, explained: "We perceive Formula One and Indy car racing as adding, if you will, a modern-day dimension to the Marlboro Man. The image of Marlboro is very rugged, individualistic, heroic. And so is this style of auto racing. From an image standpoint, the fit is good (Marlboro 1989, p.5A)."

The President and CEO of Philip Morris International, Mr. R. W. Murray, discussed the Marlboro Man more generally and echoed this analysis, adding an aspect of self reliance: "The cowboy has appeal to people as a personality. There are elements of adventure, freedom, being in charge of your destiny (Trachtenberg 1987, p.109)." An ad executive who heads the account for a leading female brand, and who requested anonymity, was quoted by the Wall Street Journal: "We try to tap the emerging independence and self-fulfilment of women, to make smoking a badge to express that (Waldman 1989)."

The Importance of Images

The academic literature also recognizes that many teens believe that cigarettes enhance one's sense of maturity and reputation for autonomy (Covington and Omelich 1988). Teens may use smoking as a means of enhancing their identity (Burton, et al. 1989), or as a way of projecting an image of self (Leventhal, et al. 1991). Academic research has also suggests that cigarette advertising has predisposing as well as reinforcing effects on children's attitudes and behavior with respect to smoking (e.g. Aitken, et al. 1991). Cigarette marketers carefully craft youthful brand images which exemplify traits that the largest number of adolescents are most likely to find highly attractive - independence, freedom from authority, autonomy, self-reliance.

Positive lifestyle images are also believed by the industry to effect the continued social acceptability of smoking, as everyone is exposed to the advertising campaigns and their imagery, whether a smoker or not, whether old or young. This imagery rehearses and shapes the perceptions of smoking, both in general and for a specific brand, potentially biasing judgments about the popularity of smoking, the healthfulness of smoking, the social approval of smoking, and the independence and self-reliance characteristic of nicotine addicts. It is assumed to influence perceptions and attitudes, not only of smokers and pre-smokers, but also of their family and friends, the parents and peers of the youth target market that is the future of the industry.

CONCLUSION

Careful and extensive consumer research has been employed in all stages of the process of conceiving, developing, refining and deploying cigarette advertising strategy. The marketing research excerpts presented here sample the wealth of information and analysis which the tobacco industry has lavished on the youth starter market. This research provides the firms with considerable insight into smokers and starters, their motivations, perceptions, attitudes, interests and responses to test advertising. The research and strategic thinking identifies the psychological needs, wants and interests of the target segments, and leads to the creation of a strategic positioning of the products, presenting them in ways that promise satisfactions of their psychological needs.

For starter brands, such as America's Marlboro and Canada's Player's and Export A, images are created to address the adolescent need for adult independence, self reliance, and freedom from authority. Many ads also promote peer acceptance among targeted young people. The advertising images for brands targeting the young portray smokers as autonomous and adult, athletic and at home in nature. Test markets and copy testing has teaches cigarette advertising to craft these images carefully, avoiding models which are too young, lest the brand be rejected as immature, and avoiding activities that are too aerobic, lest the ad precipitate cognitive counter-arguing. The overall effect of these "images of independence" and "pictures of health" is intended to capture starters and promote the social acceptability of smoking.

REFERENCES

Advertising Age (1983), "Is the Youth Market Fair Game," Advertising Age, (January 31), M-16ff.

Aitken, P. P., et al. (1991), "Predisposing Effects of Cigarette Advertising on Children's Intentions to Smoke When Older," British Journal of Addiction, 86(4), 383-390.

Burton, Dee, et. al. (1989), "Image Attributions and Smoking Intentions Among Seventh Grade Students," Journal of Applied Social Psychology, 19(8, pt. 1), 656-664.

Covington, Martin V. and Carol L. Omelich (1988), "I Can Resist Anything But Temptation: Adolescent Expectations for Smoking Cigarettes," Journal of Applied Social Psychology, 18(3, Pt 1), 203-227.

(FTC 1970), "Report to Congress, Pursuant to the Public Health Smoking Act." Washington, D.C., Federal Trade Commission (Dec. 31).

(Fortune 1963), "Embattled Tobacco's New Strategy," Fortune, January, p.100ff.

Leventhal, Howard, et al. (1991), "Smoking Prevention: Towards a Process Approach," British Journal of Addiction, 86(5), 583-587.

(Marlboro 1989), "The Business of Racing," Marlboro Advertisement in New York Times Magazine, July 9, p.5A.

Meyers, William (1984), The Image-Makers: Power and Persuasion on Madison Avenue. NY: New York Times Books.

Pollay, Richard W. (1990a), "The Functions and Management of Cigarette Advertising," for Quebec Superior Court, Imperial Tobacco Limitee & RJR-Macdonald Inc. c. Le Procureur General du Canada, 38p.

Pollay, Richard W. (1990b), "Propaganda, Puffing and the Public Interest: The Scientific Smoke Screen for Cigarettes," Public Relations Review, Vol. 16 #3, 27-42.

Pollay, Richard W. (1992a), "The Functions and Management of Cigarette Advertising (Condensed)," in William Leiss, ed., Tobacco on Trial. Montreal: McGill-Queens University Press, in press.

Pollay, Richard W. (1992b), "When Advertising Ethics Went up In Smoke: Cigarettes, Self-Regulation, Teens and TV," History of Advertising Archives Working Paper, in review.

Schwartz, David A. (1976), "What Do Ads Connote for the Average Smoker?" *Advertising Age,* November 1, p.75.

Trachtenberg, Jeffrey A. (1987), "Here's One Tough Cowboy," *Forbes,* February 9, p.108-110.

Waldman, Peter (1989), "Tobacco Firms Try Soft, Feminine Sell," *Wall Street Journal,* December 19, p.B1ff.

Visual/Verbal Processing Issues in Advertising Research: Some New Topics and Perspectives
Siva K. Balasubramanian, Southern Illinois University
Susan Heckler, University of Arizona

SPECIAL SESSION OVERVIEW

The influence of visual/verbal elements in advertising information processing has evolved into a major research theme in recent years. Much of this research has examined how information presented in either or both of these formats is remembered, or how such information influences the evaluation of ads or advertised products. In contrast, the common theme of papers presented in this special session was to address unexplored, and interesting research issues in visual/verbal processing. Notwithstanding the tight focus on the visual/verbal domain, the session provided variety by covering a wide range of germane topics, and by representing several methods e.g., literature reviews, experiments, and content analyses.

SESSION SUMMARY

Balasubramanian discussed why the individual's ability to process visual/verbal information qualifies as an important variable in advertising research. His research examined inter-relationships between five ability measures of visual/verbal processing. The pattern of low correlations among these measures highlighted the need to carefully match the domain tapped by a particular ability measure with the domain most relevant to the research purpose. He then discussed ways to overcome any potentially adverse impact from visual/verbal ability factors through motivational factors; for example, will degraded visual stimuli cause individuals with low visual processing ability to pay more attention to a visually dominated message? Preliminary results supporting this hypothesis were presented.

The next paper by Thorson & Hitchon examined cross-cultural differences in the emphasis on visual/verbal channels in ads. Based upon a content analysis of a sample of British and U.S. television ads, these researchers found that (a) U.S. ads are characterized by a greater reliance on words (verbal text), (b) the visual content of American ads feature or demonstrate the brand more often than in British ads, and (c) the British visuals are more connotative and less denotative. These findings were placed in the context of (a) greater cynicism of British audiences toward the media, and (b) relatively greater use of drama (as opposed to lecture) execution style in U.K.

Edell and Keller investigated another new issue in visual/verbal processing - the coordination of advertising campaigns across media. Specifically, they examined whether exposure to a message in one medium (e.g., TV) affects visual/verbal processing of a similar message in another medium (e.g., Print). A central hypothesis of this study was that print reinforcement (seeing the TV ad first, followed by exposure to the print ad version) results in greater processing of the verbal information in the print ad than a single or repeated exposure to the print ad. Further, this greater degree of verbal information processing should result in better recall of the brand and the claims presented in the ad. Interestingly, the authors did not find support for their hypotheses. Continuing research efforts are in progress to investigate the processes underlying these unexpected findings.

Finally, Heckler and Peracchio presented a study which integrated two recent conceptual additions to the body of visual processing research: (a) the role of aesthetic ad elements (such as camera angle, close-up versus distant perspective etc.), and (b) the role of incongruency in elaborative processing. The researchers delineated ways in which aesthetic ad elements and incongruency affect the processing and evaluation of advertising information. A study was conducted which showed that when pictorial information was expected, subjects utilized a heuristic based upon camera angle to form product evaluations. Alternatively, unexpected pictorial information created more elaborative processing of the ad, and the camera angle had no effect.

Framing Dynamics: Measurement Issues and Perspectives
Donald J. Hempel, University of Connecticut
Harold Z. Daniel, University of Connecticut

ABSTRACT

Consumer researchers have historically represented decision frames as a manipulated variable within an experimental design for observing reactions to differing reference points. The typical research designs impose models that represent consumer decision frames as stable over time. A different conceptualization is presented here to focus on actual market conditions in which consumers develop and react to their own frames of reference, and operate with multiple decision frames that evolve over time. This dynamic framework provides a means of linking consumer assessments of value and risk through reference prices.

Research on consumer decision-making has drawn heavily from expected utility models with their assumption that consistent mental structures are employed in the evaluation of product alternatives. Prospect theory (Kahneman and Tversky 1979) conceptualizes evaluation as influenced by reference points in the assessment context or framework. Cognitive theorists (Rosch and Mervis 1975) also argue that reference points serve as "benchmarks" or "anchors" for comparisons. When internalized by individuals, these scales and contrasts are fundamental influences on their perceptions, information processing and judgments. Applications of prospect theory to consumer behavior suggest that product alternatives are presented (coded) relative to reference points against which they are judged as a gain or loss. Little is known about how decision frames are shaped and changed, or how these dynamics influence consumer perceptions of value (Elliot and Archibald 1989).

Issues and conceptualizations concerning the value assessment process have been summarized by Zeithaml (1988). The importance of framing in understanding relationships between value and risk is highlighted by Tversky and Kahneman (1986). Strategic marketing concerns for integrating these perspectives require more information about the evolutionary nature of framing effects (Kalwani, Yim, Rinne and Sugita 1990). The purpose of this paper is to identify some of the conceptualization and measurement issues associated with linking value and risk constructs to the evolution of decision frames we call *framing dynamics*.

THEORETICAL PERSPECTIVES

Value perception is a function of how individuals frame buying decisions (Puto 1987, Zeithaml 1988, Qualls and Puto 1989). Zeithaml (1988) suggests that the cues which signal quality and value change over time are induced by the dynamics of competition, promotional efforts, consumer tastes and available information. Such observations support our conviction that the reference points and framing context are dynamic for purchase decisions. The concept of an evolving framework of reference points stimulate concerns for both the structure of the frames imposed by decision makers as well as the dynamics of framing effects over time. Useful insights can be generated from several theoretical perspectives pertaining to the structure and evolution of decision frames and the associated effects on value-risk relationships.

Risk Perception

Theories that emphasize risk-adjusted value perception associated with decisions include Prospect Theory (Tversky and Kahneman 1986) and Venture Theory (Hogarth and Einhorn 1990). Both theories regard risk as the uncertainty in outcomes associated with a particular decision situation and postulate that an individual's evaluation of alternatives depends upon the nature of the decision frame (whether the expected outcome is viewed as a potential gain or a potential loss). Although the decision frame is regarded in both theories as the context within which a decision is made, neither theory specifically addresses the notion of evolving frame structures. The research designs typically employed draw inferences from experimental situations in which individual choices are manipulated through the frames imposed by the researcher. One could argue that such manipulations were of information rather than decision frames, leaving subjects free to formulate their own decision frames based on the manipulated information. However, these research designs are clearly not bias free. Subjects are usually placed in a problem solving situation where the artificial environment of the laboratory intensifies sensitivity to the researchers' instructions, thereby creating biased decision frames compared to the frames that subjects might form on their own. Thus, generalizations concerning framing effects derived from this research stream tend to rely on two assumptions: (1) that individuals would behave similarly when forming their own decision frames without intervention; and (2) that these decision frames are stable over time. The first assumption has been challenged (e.g., Elliott and Archibald 1989) and the latter assumption has yet to be empirically verified. Consequently, the framework derived from such studies is inadequate by itself for a complete understanding of risk-value relationships in consumer decision processes.

Value Perception

Among the theories that emphasize issues regarding value perception are Lancaster's Utility Theory (1971) and Westbrook and Reilly's Value Percept Disparity Theory (1983). While Prospect and Venture Theories regard products holistically, these theories deal with the products by their component attributes. They view products as bundles of attributes of which each possesses some intrinsic value to the consumer in terms of providing need satisfaction or personal goals and values. If personal goals and values of the individual determine the structure of decision frames, frames must evolve over time since personal values change as the individual matures.

The role of expectations in the disconfirmation paradigm of value assessment is similar to the role of reference points under Prospect and Venture theories, yielding outcomes viewed as gains or losses. For example, Thaler (1985) defines a consumer value function for differences relative to reference points rather than absolute levels. This suggests that consumer perceptions of both value and risk may be influenced by reference points in an evolving context. The dynamic role of reference points in value assessment lead to consideration of price as a framing measure (Monroe and Chapman 1987). Whereas the expectancy-disconfirmation paradigm may imply stable expectations of a product, the implications of an evolving assessment framework merit further exploration.

Reference Pricing

The notion of changing reference points is well represented in the theoretical foundations of reference price research (Winer 1988). The body of research on reference pricing is based on

Assimilation-Contrast (Sherif and Hovland 1961) and Adaption Level Theories (Helson 1964). Both theories suggest that consumers determine value on the basis of reference points, such as the prices derived from current market pricing or from past product pricing (Lichtenstein and Bearden 1989). Adaptation Level and Assimilation-Contrast theories imply that shifts in the internalized reference price or latitude of acceptance can result from changes in the overall level of market prices or by gradual changes in the price of a specific brand. It can be hypothesized from this that the decision frame represented by the reference price would also be subject to change and thereby produce dynamic framing effects.

The concept of risk in decision framing can be linked to reference pricing through studies of expectation-disconfirmation theory. Della Bitta, Monroe and McGinnis (1981) examined the impact of different-sized price discrepancies from a reference point in the form of advertised discounts from a "regular" price. They found that larger discounts increased perceived value and interest while diminishing intent to search. In this situation, the adjustment of reference prices can be interpreted as risk-reduction effects that change the value assessment context or decision frame used in the choice process.

MEASUREMENT ISSUES

A basic thesis of framing dynamics is that the sensitivity of choice tasks to context effects in major purchase decisions can be represented through the linkage of featural structure (e.g., product attributes) to value structure (e.g., reference prices and perceived risk). Prior research has outlined the conceptual issues and analytical framework involved in this linkage (Hempel and Daniel, 1992). This paper concentrates on the definition of the dimensional structure of decision frames and the effect of evolving frame structures on perceived value and risk. Belk (1975) provides relevant perspectives on similar context definition problems in his conceptualization of situational variables. He distinguishes temporal perspectives from task definition in developing a dimensional taxonomy, and highlights the significance of subjective vs. objective measurements in assessments of situational effects.

Evolving sets of multiple reference points present significant problems for representing framing effects in choice models. These problems are minimized when the relevant context is interpreted as a single decision frame, such as in experimental settings where a frame is imposed and exposure is controlled. The decision situations encountered by consumers in actual market situations may require different perceptual representations because they are separated in time. Information derived from one time-related set of reference points and its structural representation (e.g., whether alternatives are perceived as gain or loss) may be altered by temporally separated sets of subsequent reference points. For example, in housing markets pre-search encounters with media reports on overall housing sales may indicate that a loss will result from sale of the buyer's present residence, while subsequent broker communications emphasizing the reduced purchase price of an alternative property may essentially reframe the transaction as a gain. These shifting context effects may account for some of the breakdowns between geometric and algebraic representations of consumer similarity judgments noted by Glazer and Nakamoto (1991).

The structural dynamics reflected in the evolving, interactive quality of the successive sets of reference points invoked by home buyers is the main concern of this paper. Operational definitions of framing dynamics require representation of both intra-frame and inter-frame relationships. Intra-frame measures are conceptualized as structural concerns based on the measurements used in prior studies of framing effects, with extensions to include frame boundary issues. Inter-frame measures are presented as dynamic concerns that focus on the differences across measurement sets and related patterns of convergence.

Framing Structure

Measurement of framing structure requires concern for both the geometric and algebraic relationships represented in consumer similarity judgments. Glazer and Nakamoto (1991) advise that it is meaningful to think in terms of both the amount and type of structure captured by alternative representations. They caution that the structure imposed by a model operates as a constraint on the empirical relations captured. The measurement considerations outlined below focus on algebraic representations of relationships among reference prices. Concerns for the related geometric or spatial relations involved are addressed in the following discussion of zones, gradients and convergence patterns.

Reference Points are the fundamental measures used to define the dimensional structure of each decision frame. As considered earlier, the theoretical basis for this interpretation is derived from Adaptation Level Theory and Assimilation-Contrast Theory. The reference points used in this paper to define value structure are the prices of housing alternatives considered within a decision frame. Assimilation-Contrast theory postulates that these intra-frame reference points will have carry-over effects (response latencies) that influence reactions to the alternatives considered in subsequent decision frames. These inter-frame relationships are considered in the following section. The actual distribution of reference points within each frame provides the basis for defining four aspects of dimensional structure for each frame:

Density - the number of alternatives considered within a specific decision frame may range from a sparse set (e.g., only high-low reference points) to a very dense set (e.g., all the alternatives considered during search).

Range - the upper and lower values of the reference points is defined by the range of prices considered within each frame. Nwokoye (1975) presents evidence that buyers use extreme prices as anchors, i.e. the highest and lowest prices evaluated.

Stability - the relative dispersion (concentration) of reference points is represented as intra-frame variance.

Centroid - the central tendency of the reference points in a decision frame is represented as a mean or median reference price. Emery (1970) suggests that the anchor price will be an average of the prices considered by the buyer.

Decision Frames are the time-related representations of buying process stages (e.g., pre-search vs. post-search) defined in terms of the buyer's information processing and decision-making behavior. For this preliminary analysis, the sequential sets of reference points considered were limited to the six decision frames (DFs) described below. Table 1 summarizes the empirical basis for operationally defining these frame boundaries.

DF1: the set of reference points defined by the present value of the purchase price of the home purchased immediately prior to the current home, the purchase offers received for this prior home, and its selling price. If the prior residence was a rental unit, the capitalized value of the monthly rental payment is substituted as the dominant reference point.

DF2: the initial reference points invoked in the problem recognition phase of the buying process. These internalized references are derived from prior purchase experiences, pre-search media exposure, and reflective knowledge activated by initial need recognition.

DF3: the reference points invoked immediately prior to beginning active external search behavior. This pre-search frame is active at the point when a decision has been made to purchase a new home, but before any homes have been visited or any real estate agent has been contacted.

DF4: the set of reference points derived from active search behavior based on the asking prices of the entire distribution of housing alternatives visited and/or considered for purchase.

DF5: the choice or post-search reference points comprised by the set of housing alternatives the buyer seriously considered purchasing.

DF6: the reference point represented by the actual purchase price. This is both an outcome of the decision process and a decision frame for evaluating purchases of related goods (e.g., structural improvements, appliances and furniture).

Each decision frame involves a frequency distribution of reference points that can be represented by various descriptive statistics. The summary statistics used to define the structural measurements include density, range, variance and central tendency. All of these framing structure measures were standardized by dividing the reference prices reported by the final purchase price. These standardized measures reduce the magnitude of reported differences across housing price levels and thereby provide a more exact basis for comparisons across frames and cases. The defined decision frames can be interpreted as fuzzy sets with significant overlap among reference points, particularly between adjacent frames. However, the added temporal dimension derived from the time (sequence) linked decision process references serve to distinguish the frame boundaries. In fact, understanding the interdependencies among the respective frames is a focus of this research.

Framing Dynamics

Measurement of framing dynamics requires concern for the evolution of structural dimensions across stages of the buying process. In essence, the concepts of reference points and decision frames must be extended to (1) examine the relationships among successive sets of reference points; and (2) interpret the effects of evolving decision frames on the relevant context for home buying decisions. These extensions dealing with the evolution of frames are operationally defined below in terms of zones, gradients and convergence rates. Table 2 provides a summary of these inter-frame measures.

Evolving sets of interacting reference points present measurement problems that are similar to those of repeated measurement designs. These basic problems stem from concerns for the interrelationships within a series of observations, including: (1) Carry-over effects — exposure to reference points in the next decision frame occurs before the effects of the prior frame reference points have "worn off"; (2) Latency effects — exposure to reference points in the next decision frame "activate" or interact with those of the previous frame; and (3) Learning effects — exposure to reference points in successive frames "limits" or converges the selection and interpretation of reference points in future frames. These concerns are usually treated as problems or difficulties to be removed by statistical controls in repeated measurement designs. In this application, their presence is interpreted as evidence of inter-frame relationships to be highlighted as measures of framing dynamics.

In non-experimental settings, measurement of inter-frame relationships is limited by the models available for separating perceptual effects from preference effects in the evolving context. For example, the range of prices buyers actually use to evaluate alternatives are determined by perceptions and judgments within boundaries constrained by initial preferences. Subsequent preferences are influenced by the reference points emerging from alternatives to which the buyer is exposed during the buying process. The resulting pattern of framing effects must be interpreted with concern for the underlying elements of reference point continuities that extend across frames. Relevant frameworks for tracking this underlying continuity are evident in studies of the process by which internal price standards are formed, particularly those that highlight the interrelationships of prices consumers perceived market prices and latitudes of price acceptance (e.g., Lichtenstein and Bearden 1989; Della Bitta, Monroe and McGinnis 1981).

Reference point definitions focus on three related aspects of framing dynamics: the range of points judged to be relevant (zones); relations among the series of points considered (gradients); and the contrast and assimilation effects represented in the internalization of reference points (patterns). Concerns for market efficiency suggest that the rate at which these differences are reconciled or converge is an important basis for assessing performance. These measurement issues and operational definitions are summarized in Table 2. A graphical summary of the relationships among these geometric measures (zones and gradients) is presented in Figure 1.

Zones: Decision-maker uncertainty is reflected in the band or range of reference points perceived to be acceptable (Stoetzel 1970). How these internal judgment scales change across time is an essential concern in research on context effects. *Reference Zones* represent the scale of reference points linking successive decision frames defined by the high-low range of reference points in the preceding frame. *Continuity Zones* represent the consistency of references points across decision frames defined by the range of one standard deviation around the price gradient based on a global (across frames) calculation of variance.

Gradients: Measures of adaption levels have been used to represent the pooled effects of the reference points used across time (Della Bitta and Monroe 1973). Issues regarding the appropriate weighting and anchoring of these changing reference regions lead to a concern for underlying commonalities that are anchored by multivariate reference points. The *Price Gradient* is conceptualized as the "flight path" of the expected framing dynamics. It is defined by the functional relationship between the reference points in the initial (DF1) and final (DF6) decision frames. This gradient represents the evolving standard of internal judgments by which perceived value is adjusted to the quality and price relationships encountered.

TABLE 1
Operational Definitions of Framing Structure

Decision Frame & Descriptive Label	Measurement (Survey Question)
DF1: Prior Frame	"If you owned your prior residence, what was the price at which it was sold?, **or** "If you rented your prior residence, what was the monthly rental charge (excluding utilities)?"
DF2: Entry Frame	"Once you decided to buy a home, what was the maximum and minimum price you expected to pay..."
DF3: Pre-Search Frame	"..just before you visited any houses or contacted the first real estate firm ... did you know what you wanted in the price range for your house? If yes, what was the low and high prices in this range .. "
DF4: Search Frame	"During the process of looking at homes for sale, approximately how many homes in each of the following price categories did you enter for evaluation..."
DF5: Choice Frame	"During the month before you decided on buying your present home, were there any other houses you seriously considered buying..."
DF6: Purchase Price	"What price did you actually pay for the house you purchased?"

TABLE 2
Operational Definitions of Framing Dynamics

Variable Name & Label	Definition and Measurement
RZ: Reference Zone	The range of reference points invoked for the preceding decision frame.
CZ: Continuity Zone	The zone defined by one global standard deviation about the price gradient.
PG: Price Gradient	The linear function connecting the mean reference point in the two terminal decision frames (DF6 regressed on DF1).
RG: Risk Gradient	The linear function connecting the two terminal reference points defined by monthly housing payments as a percent of total household income after taxes for new vs. previous residence..."
PT: Pattern	Ratio of the coefficient of variance for the current frame (mean/range) relative to the coefficient of variance for all frames (mean/standard deviation).
PC: Price Convergence	The difference between the average (mean or median) reference point for the current frame and the midpoint [(high-low)/2] reference point of the prior frame.
RC: Risk Convergence	The predictability of the midpoint of each frame based on the range of reference points in the prior frame, measured as inter-frame entropy.

The *Risk Gradient* is a baseline reference extending across decision frames as an evolving measure of sacrifice and acceptable risk defined by the ratio of monthly housing payments to household income after taxes. This ratio is calculated to represent the change in income commitments (sacrifice) associated with the purchase decision and normalized to reflect the proportion of income spent on housing. It contrasts the level of risk (sacrifice) in the entry frame (DF1) relative to the risk level represented in the purchase frame (DF6). This measure is adjusted for first-time home buyers to consider prior rental payments as well as mortgage payments.

Pattern: The covariance of reference points across frames provides insights into the stability of internalized standards. The geometry of these changing context relationships may address measurement issues concerning the symmetry of psychological distances and their representation by algebraic measures. The *Pattern* of variance for each frame is defined relative to the variance across all frames. It is measured by a ratio of the coefficient of variance across all frames (calculated as the global mean divided by the global standard deviation), relative to the coefficient of variance for each frame (calculated as the frame mean divided by the frame range).

FIGURE 1
Framing Dynamics: Zones and Gradients

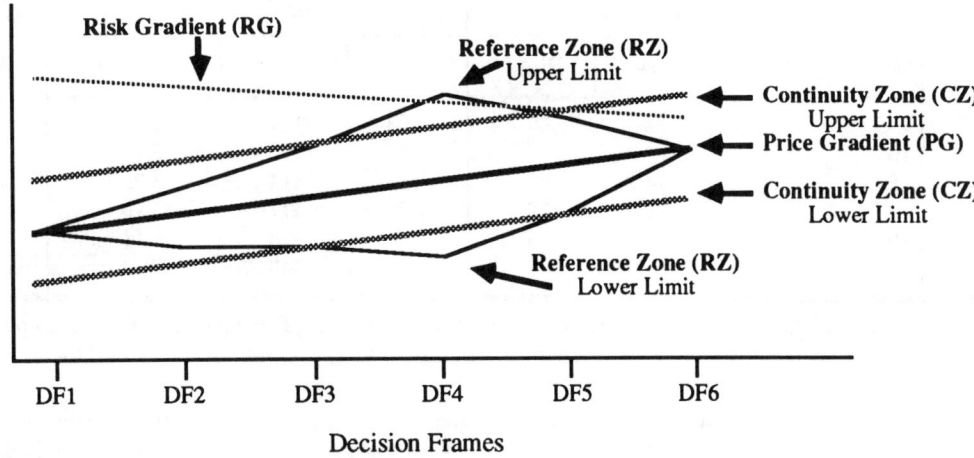

Convergence: *Price convergence* represents the trend of inter-frame reference point differences relative to the price gradient extending across decision frames. It is calculated as the difference between the average (mean or median) of the current frame and the midpoint (high minus low divided by two) of reference points in the prior frame. In effect, the midpoint of each successive frame represents the preferred reference scale while the highest and lowest reference points in the previous frame are the anchors against which it is judged (see Della Bitta and Monroe 1973 for discussion of anchoring issues). *Risk convergence* represents the trend of reference points across frames defined relative to the risk gradient. It is calculated as an entropy measure representing the information content of each frame as a predictor of the overall risk gradient defined by the housing payments ratio.

Propositions

Empirical tests are needed to confirm framing dynamics as a valid conceptualization of choice behavior. The following propositions will be tested.

Separability: In order to conclude that framing dynamics is a more appropriate representation of the consumers' decision processes than static framing, a series of evolving frames must be distinguished from a single frame conceptualization. Therefore,

P1: *The predictability of the final purchase price will be greater when both inter-frame and intra-frame variances in reference prices are represented in the predictive equation.*

Latency: If the evolving sets of reference points involved in framing dynamics are to be of value in predicting consumer behavior, the distribution of points in each decision frame should contribute to the prediction of succeeding frames. That is,

P2: *The interaction of reference points across decision frames will be reflected in a latency effect.*

Independence: In order to validate the multiple decision frame conceptualization, each decision frame must contribute significantly to the prediction of final purchase price. Although latency effects are expected in measures of the average effects over all frames, each decision frame is expected to have a unique effect beyond this latency effect.

P3: *Each decision frame will evidence a unique (contrast) effect as well as an interaction (latency) effect.*

Convergence: If learning effects drive the evolution of reference points across decision frames and enhance the effectiveness of consumer decision making, intra-frame variance should decline in successive stages of the decision process.

P4: *Intra-frame variance will decline across each succeeding decision frame.*

Price Orientation: The informational value of price is a function of the range of reference points in relation to price and risk gradients. As a result of learning effects and the internalization of pricing standards, the meaning of price evolves from a symbolic role in communicating quality to an economic role as an indicator of sacrifice. This change in roles results in an increase in the predictability of subsequent frames.

P5a: *The price gradient will be the operative orientation during the early stages of the decision process while the intra-frame variance in reference points is increasing relative to the inter-frame variance.*

P5b: *The risk gradient will be the operative orientation during the later stages of the decision process while the intra-frame variance in reference points is declining relative to the inter-frame variance.*

P5c: *The shift from a price orientation to a risk orientation will be evident in a decline of the inter-frame entropy measure.*

EMPIRICAL PERSPECTIVES: HOME BUYER BEHAVIOR

Data obtained from recent home buyers provide a basis for empirically testing these relationships in a non-experimental setting. The home buying process was selected as an empirical metaphor for purchase decision settings where framing dynamics are likely to be evident. Consumers who purchase a house have been involved in the evaluation of a durable good with significant

TABLE 3
Framing Dynamics: Frames, Gradients and Zones

Decision Frame & Price Gradient	Framing Structure (N=122)				Continuity Zones			Convergence
	Mean	SDev	Low	High	-1SD	+1SD	Coef. Var.	Price (PC*)
DF1	75	42	54	80	33	117	1.79	17
DF2	103	22	87	116	82	122	5.10	26
DF3	89	27	74	103	66	114	3.75	45
DF4	98	19	90	110	79	117	5.16	42
DF5	105	19	102	108	86	124	5.53	32
PG	105	44	NA	NA	61	149	2.39	

* Price Convergence = Percent with mean (midpoint) references prices for the decision frame greater than the final purchase price.

economic and social consequences. Housing purchases usually invoke high-involvement, extended problem solving behavior with multiple reference points and significant price effects. In this situation, propositions concerning the evolution of decision frames can be tested as observable and meaningful representations of market realities, and externally validated through macro measures. Housing choice behavior can be interpreted as an anchor point for theory development because it represents one extreme of an economic value continuum. Thus, empirical evidence of framing dynamics in this field setting provides useful benchmarks in assessing generalization of the model to other product classes.

Household level data were collected from 230 home buyers in a major regional housing market in 1988, prior to the economic slowdown in the region. The sampling frame consisted of three metropolitan areas, including 18 communities with a wide range of house prices and local market size differences. Survey methods were employed to obtain data from a systematic random sample of all households listed in deed transfers recorded during the year beginning April 1, 1988. In-depth personal interviews with household heads were conducted from June through October of 1989. Separate mail questionnaires with different questions for the male and female household heads were distributed following the in-home interviews. A series of telephone and mail follow ups were employed to achieve mail responses from approximately 70 percent of the households interviewed.

This data base provides an extensive and internally consistent empirical context for modeling framing dynamics and its effects on consumer choice behavior. It includes measures of prior home buying experiences, perceived knowledge and confidence levels, external information sources used, and the relative importance of product attributes. Subsequent analysis will consider these variables as moderators and complementary framing measures that may help to refine the definition of framing dynamics.

Generalizations about framing effects based on survey data are limited by the ability of respondents to recall their reference points and their willingness to accurately disclose them. The relatively high levels of product importance, buyer involvement and cognitive processing evident in home buying behavior help to minimize these limitations. Nonetheless, the process of eliciting subjective frames and the interpretation of how individuals independently impose frames on their choice is influenced by the data collection methodology used.

Methods and Preliminary Results

The space constraints imposed on this paper preclude the normal progression of this discussion through methodology, results and discussion sections. However, a preview of the analytical procedures and some preliminary results may facilitate assessment of the conceptualization and help to improve the research plan.

Repeated measurement designs (MANOVA) provide a framework for analyzing effects that are measured on several occasions for each respondent. These procedures incorporate allowances for dependencies that facilitate interpretation of differences across levels (or stages) of a factor. Linear combinations of differences (contrasts) can be specified to compare each level of a factor to the average of the levels that precede it. Thus, frames can be interpreted as levels or stages of a framing factor with concern for latency, carry-over and learning effects. These concerns are usually treated as problems or difficulties to be removed in repeated measurement designs. In this application, their presence is interpreted as evidence of interframe relationships to be highlighted as measures of framing dynamics.

Table 3 provides an empirical example of how the decision frame means and gradients differ across respondents. These results indicate that interpretation of all reference points as a single frame may result in significant loss of information about framing effects on choice behavior. The change in mean reference points from DF1 to DF2 and from DF4 to DF5 suggest that price may play different roles as the decision process evolves. The mean variance measured by intra-frame standard deviations was notably stable across frames, while the range changed significantly in DF3 and DF5 respectively. Relationships among frames reflected in the price and risk convergence measures indicates that exposure to market realities during the period of active search (DF4) may result in some significant restructuring of the perceptual context for home buying decisions.

CONCLUSIONS

This paper presents some measurement issues associated with linking framing dynamics to the interpretation of consumer value and risk perceptions. Our conceptualization of subjective framing effects adds several perspectives to understanding the value-risk relationship. First, decision frames are interpreted as an evolving multi-stage framework defining the perceptual domain in which value and risk are interpreted. Second, these successive frameworks are reformulated as dynamic sets of relevant reference points invoked by the consumer during the choice process. Finally, concerns for this evolutionary process extend existing paradigms of framing effects to include measures of change rates and convergence patterns.

This design differs from typical studies of perceptual effects in two critical areas. First, it examines framing effects in behavioral environments where consumers establish their own decision frames.

The concept of framing dynamics is likely to have empirical validity in realistic market environments. It may not be evident in experimental settings where the researcher's instructions control the framing process. Second, our conceptualization of framing dynamics requires measurement of reference point relationships that extend across time-linked perceptual spaces. This adaptive environment complicates the analysis by requiring measures of state change effects. It also affords the opportunity to examine the mechanisms through which perceptions of value, risk and quality are reconciled.

REFERENCES

Belk, Russell W. (1975), "Situational Variables and Consumer Behavior," *Journal of Consumer Research*, 2, 157-164.

Della Bitta, A., K. Monroe and J. McGinnis (1981), "Consumer Perceptions of Comparative Price Advertisements," *Journal of Marketing Research*, 18, 419-27.

Della Bitta, Albert J. and Kent Monroe (1974), "The Influence of Adaptation Levels on Subjective Price Perceptions," *Advances in Consumer Research*, 1, 359-69.

Elliott, Catherine S. and Robert B. Archibald (1989), "Subjective Framing and Attitudes Towards Risk," *Journal of Economic Psychology*, 10, 321-328.

Emery, Fred (1970), "Some Psychological Aspects of Price," in *Pricing Strategy*, B. Taylor and G. Wills, eds. Princeton, NJ: Brandon System Press, 98-111.

Glazer, Rashi and Kent Nakamoto (1991) "Cognitive Geometry: An Analysis of Structure Underlying Representations of Similarity," *Marketing Science*, 10, 3, 205-228.

Helson, H. (1964) *Adaptation-Level Theory*, New York: Harper and Rowe.

Hempel, Donald J. and Harold Z. Daniel (1992), "Framing Dynamics: Linking Risk and Value," in *European Marketing Academy Proceedings*, K. Grunert and D. Fuglede, eds., 599-617.

Hogarth, Robin M. and Hillel J. Einhorn (1990), "Venture Theory: A Model of Decision Weights," *Management Science*, 36, 7, 780-803.

Kahneman, Daniel and Amos Tversky (1979), "Prospect Theory: An Analysis of Decision Under Risk," *Econometrica* 47, 263-291.

Kalwani, Manohar, Chi Yim, Heikki Rinne and Yoshi Sugita (1990), "A Price Expectations Model of Customer Brand Choice," *Journal of Marketing Research*, 27, 251-62.

Lancaster, K. J., 1971. *Consumer Demand: A New Approach*, Columbia University Press, New York.

Lichtenstein, Donald R. and William O. Bearden (1989), "Contextual Influences on Perceptions of Merchant-Supplied Reference Prices," *Journal of Consumer Research*, 16, 55-66.

Monroe, Kent B. and Joseph D. Chapman, 1987. Framing Effects on Buyers' Subjective Product Evaluations. *Advances in Consumer Research*. 14, 193-197.

Nwokoye, Nonyelu G. (1975), "Subjective Judgements of Price: The Effects of Price Parameters on Adaptation Levels," *Proceedings of Fall Conference*. Chicago: American Marketing Association.

Qualls, William J. and Christopher Puto (1989), "Organizational Climate and Decision Framing: An Integrated Approach to Analyzing Industrial Buying Decisions," *Journal of Marketing Research*, 26, 179-92.

Puto, Christopher P. (1987), "The Framing of Buying Decisions," *Journal of Consumer Research*, 14, 301-314.

Rosch, Eleanor and Carolyn B. Mervis (1975), "Family Resemblances: Studies in the Internal Structure of Categories," *Cognitive Psychology*, 7, 573-605.

Sherif, M. and C. Hovland (1961), *Social Judgement*, New Haven, Connecticut: Yale University Press.

Stoetzel, J. (1970), "Psychological/Sociological Aspects of Price," in *Pricing Strategy*, B. Taylor and G. Wills, eds. Princeton, NJ: Brandon System Press, 70-74.

Thaler, R. (1985), "Mental Accounting and Consumer Choice," *Marketing Science*, 4, 199-214.

Tversky, Amos and Daniel Kahneman (1986), "Rational Choice and the Framing of Decisions," *Journal of Business*, 59, 4, 2, S251-S278.

Urbany, Joel E., William O. Bearden and Dan C. Weilbaker (1988), "The Effect of Plausible and Exaggerated Reference Prices on Consumer Perceptions and Price Search," *Journal of Consumer Research*, 15, 95-110.

Westbrook, Robert A. and Michael D. Reilly (1983), "Value-Percept Disparity: An Alternative to the Disconfirmation of Expectations Theory of Consumer Satisfaction," *Advances in Consumer Research*, 10, 256-261.

Winer, Russell S. (1988), "Behavioral Perspectives on Pricing: Buyer's Subjective Perceptions of Price Revisited," In: Timothy M DeVinney (ed.), *Issues in Pricing Theory and Research*, 35-57. Lexington, Mass: Lexington Books.

Winer, Russell S. (1986), "A Reference Price Model of Brand Choice for Frequently Purchased Products," *Journal of Consumer Research*, 13, 250-256.

Zeithaml, Valerie (1988), "Consumer Perceptions of Price, Quality, and Value: A Means-End Model and Synthesis of Evidence," *Journal of Marketing*, 52, 2-22.

Effects of Multiple Measurement Operations on Consumer Judgment: Measurement Reliability or Reactivity?

Frank R. Kardes, University of Cincinnati
Chris T. Allen, University of Cincinnati
Manuel J. Pontes, University of Florida

ABSTRACT

An experiment was conducted to investigate the effects of multiple measurement operations on judgment. Although multiple measures are needed to assess measurement reliability, the results indicate that the use of multiple measures can also change the nature of the construct undergoing assessment. Implications of the results for managing the reliability/reactivity tradeoff are discussed.

Few measurement procedures have achieved such widespread acceptance as has the use of multiple measurement operations. The use of multiple scales has become a standard practice that is rarely, if ever, questioned. The reason for this is clear: multiple scales must be used to assess measurement reliability (Churchill 1979; Cook and Campbell 1979; Peter 1979). However, recent work suggests that exposure to measurement scales can induce respondents to form judgments that would not have been generated had no measurement instruments been administered (Feldman and Lynch 1988).

How can measurement influence judgment? Consider the processes involved in responding to measurement instruments. When a consumer is asked to express a judgment about a product or service, this person is likely to (a) search the environment and memory for relevant information, (b) construe the judgmental implications of this information, (c) integrate the information to arrive at a single overall value, and (d) communicate this judgment in a manner assumed to be meaningful to the researcher (Feldman and Lynch 1988; Wyer and Srull 1989). These search, construal, integration, and communication processes increase the consumer's focus on a specific judgment.

We suggest that this increased focus can influence both the strength as well as the content of a judgment. The content of a judgment refers to its position along a subjective continuum. This position is mapped onto a set of ordered categories presented by the researcher (e.g., a seven-point scale with end-points labeled "Extremely bad" and "Extremely good"). The strength of a judgment refers to its accessibility from memory (Fazio 1989). Although several studies have examined measurement effects on judgment content (for reviews, see Feldman and Lynch 1988; Fischhoff 1991), few studies have examined measurement effects on judgment strength.

The distinction between content and strength is critical because though prior research on evaluative judgments (i.e., attitudes) centers primarily on attitude valence (for reviews, see Cohen and Chakravarti 1990; Tesser and Shaffer 1990), recent empirical evidence suggests that "strength is more important than simple favorability in determining whether attitudes are successful predictor variables" (Raden 1985). Weak attitudes are poor predictors of overt behavior, whereas strong attitudes are good predictors (Abelson 1988; Berger and Mitchell 1989; Fazio 1989; Fazio, Powell, and Williams 1989; Raden 1985). Thus, the strength of an attitude is an important moderator of the relationship between attitudes and behavior.

Related to the finding that attitudes vary in strength is the distinction between attitudes and nonattitudes (Converse 1970). This distinction stems from the observation that an individual will often respond to an item embedded in a survey even when the individual has no prior attitude toward this topic (Converse 1970; Feldman and Lynch 1988; Schuman and Presser 1981). Moreover, survey respondents are willing to express opinions toward fictitious issues, for which no prior attitudes can exist (Bishop, Tuchfarber, and Oldendick 1986). Thus, individuals may appear to have attitudes that do not actually exist in any a priori fashion.

How are responses generated when prior attitudes are unavailable from memory? Converse (1970) maintains that these responses reflect random error. However, Feldman and Lynch (1988) review evidence implying that these responses are generated systematically. The accessibility-diagnosticity model (Feldman and Lynch 1988; Lynch, Marmorstein, & Weigold 1988) suggests that if an answer cannot be retrieved directly from memory, the answer is computed on the basis of other information available from memory. Feldman and Lynch (1988) use the term "self-generated validity" to describe this process because if an answer is unavailable from memory, the answer can be constructed - on the spot - following exposure to the survey question. Thus, measurement instruments can prompt individuals to form judgments that would not have been formed otherwise.

This problem is likely to be compounded when individuals are exposed to multiple measurement instruments. Exposure to a single scale can induce respondents to generate a judgment that would not have been generated otherwise. However, repeated exposure to a measurement instrument can prompt respondents to form a new judgment and activate it repeatedly. Prior research has shown that repeated activation (retrieval) increases the strength of a judgment (Fazio, Sanbonmatsu, Powell, and Kardes 1986; Powell and Fazio 1984).

In these studies, attitude strength was operationalized in terms of attitude accessibility, or the speed with which an attitude can be retrieved from memory in response to an attitudinal inquiry. Justification for this procedure is provided by extensive empirical evidence indicating that manipulations of the strength of the association between an object and an evaluation result in a corresponding change in response latency: as attitude strength increases, faster response latencies are obtained (for a review, see Fazio 1989). Similarly, as the number of attitude scales provided increases, the number of times the focal attitude is expressed increases. To express an attitude one must access the attitude from memory, and repeated expression requires repeated attitude activation. Repeated activation results in faster response latencies to subsequent attitudinal inquiries (Fazio et al. 1986; Powell and Fazio 1984). Hence, exposure to repeated measures induces respondents to activate their attitudes repeatedly, and repeated activation increases attitude accessibility.

The purpose of the present study was to examine repeated measurement effects involving product-related stimuli (i.e., brand names such as Coke, Pepsi, Crest, Colgate, etc.) as opposed to everyday objects (e.g., gift, music, cake, guns, crime, Republicans, Democrats; see Fazio et al. 1986) or political issues (e.g., abortion, equal rights, gun control, nuclear power; see Powell and Fazio 1984). More importantly, the present study was designed to test the

TABLE 1
Evaluation Latencies as a Function of Brand Loyalty and Repeated Measurement

	One exposure	Two exposures	Three exposures
Loyal consumers	1060	860	830
Nonloyal consumers	1460	1140	1040

hypothesis that repeated measurement effects on attitude strength are moderated by attitude crystallization. Crystallized attitudes are well-defined attitudes that exist prior to measurement (Schuman and Presser 1981).

Uncrystallized attitudes are poorly-articulated and poorly-defined (Chaiken and Baldwin 1981), less stable over time (Davidson and Jaccard 1979; Schwartz 1978), and are less resistant to persuasion (Krosnick 1988; Wu and Shaffer 1987). Because uncrystallized (versus crystallized) attitudes are relatively malleable, they should also be more susceptible to repeated measurement effects.

METHOD

Overview

Subjects performed a computer-administered brand evaluation task with respect to a list of 56 different brands belonging to one of seven different product categories (e.g., soft drinks, candy bars, shampoos). Evaluation latencies toward each of these products were assessed in each of three consecutive experimental sessions. Following these sessions, subjects were asked to estimate the frequency with which they purchased each of the 56 products. Because attitudes based on direct behavioral experience (i.e., trial) are less ambiguous than attitudes based on indirect experience (e.g., advertising, word-of-mouth communications; see Fazio and Zanna 1981; Smith and Swinyard 1983), purchase frequency ratings provide a useful measure of prior attitude crystallization. On the basis of these ratings, brands to which subjects were loyal and brands to which subjects were nonloyal were identified separately for each subject (Jacoby and Kyner 1973). Hence, a 2 (Loyalty) X 3 (Measurement exposure level) repeated measures design was employed (both factors were within-subjects factors). It was predicted that mean evaluation latencies should decrease as exposure level increases, and that this repeated measurement effect should be more pronounced in nonloyal than in loyal conditions.

Subjects and Stimuli

Subjects were 31 undergraduates who received $5 for participating. Subjects were asked to judge 56 different target products. These products were members of seven different product classes (soft drinks, beer, soaps, shampoos, deodorants, candy bars, and toothpastes). Each product class was comprised of 7 to 13 different brands. For each product category, a wide variety of brands were selected to maximize the likelihood of including brands to which subjects were likely to be loyal (e.g., Coke, Pepsi, Michelob, Miller, Snickers, Three Musketeers, Crest, Colgate, Ivory, Dial) and nonloyal (e.g., Tab, Mountain Dew, Samuel Adams Lager, Bass Ale, Heath Bar, Mr. Goodbar, Aquafresh, Aim, Safeguard, Shield).

Procedure

The Response Latency Task. Upon arrival, subjects were told that they would be asked to participate in a computer-administered survey regarding their personal opinions toward several different products. Subjects were told that a single brand name would appear on the monitor and their task was to press a key labeled "good" or a key labeled "bad" as quickly as possible to indicate their judgment of the product (key order was counterbalanced across subjects). Subjects were instructed to maximize both the speed and the accuracy of their responses. The presentation was controlled by an IBM personal computer. The order in which the products were presented was randomized for each subject. Each brand name remained visible on the screen until the subject responded, and a 3-second interval separated each trial. The subject's response and latency of response (from brand name onset to response) were recorded automatically to the nearest centisecond.

This task was preceded by a set of practice trials designed to familiarize subjects with the procedure. The brand names employed in the practice trials pertained to product classes other than those used in the experiment. In the experiment, subjects judged 56 different brand names (Session 1). Each subject received a different random order of presentation of the 56 brand names; most subjects completed this task in 15 to 20 minutes. Immediately after completing this task, subjects judged the same 56 brand names, presented in a different random order (Session 2). This task was repeated again in Session 3. Order of presentation of brand names was randomized across subjects and across sessions. Most subjects completed all three sessions in less than 45 minutes.

Purchase Frequency Estimates. Following the response latency task, a paper-and-pencil questionnaire containing purchase frequency scales was administered. Subjects were asked to indicate how frequently or infrequently they purchased each brand during the past year. To ensure that these estimates would be comparable across product classes, they were asked to indicate how frequently they purchased each brand, when they purchased an item from a given product category. An eleven-point scale from "0" (never — 0%) to "10" (always — 100%) was provided for each brand. A key with a verbal label for each of the eleven scale points was provided (adapted from Juster 1966).

On the basis of these purchase frequency estimates, brands to which subjects were loyal versus nonloyal were identified. Specifically, for each subject and for each product class, the brand with the highest purchase frequency rating was assigned to the loyal category (provided that the rating was equal to or greater than the scale mid-point). Brands that were never purchased (i.e., brands that received a purchase frequency rating of 0) and brands that were rarely purchased (i.e., brands that received a purchase frequency rating of 1) were assigned to the nonloyal category. A one-way analysis of variance performed on these ratings indicated that purchase frequency ratings were greater in loyal than in nonloyal conditions (Ms=7.92 vs. 0.79), $F(1, 60)$=2194.06, $p<.0001$. Hence, the procedure used to assign brands to loyal versus nonloyal conditions was very effective.

RESULTS

Evaluation latencies (measured in centiseconds, reported in milliseconds) as a function of brand loyalty and repeated measurement are presented in Table 1. An analysis of variance performed on evaluation latencies yielded significant main effects for Loyalty, $F(1, 30)$=32.50, $p<.001$, and for Exposure level, $F(2, 60)$=16.72,

$p<.001$. Loyal consumers possess more accessible attitudes than nonloyal consumers. Attitude accessibility also increases with repeated measurement. Most importantly, these effects were qualified by a significant Loyalty X Exposure level interaction, $F(2, 60)=88.08$, $p<.001$.

Follow-up tests of the Loyalty X Repeated measurement interaction revealed that the simple main effect for Repeated measurement was more pronounced in nonloyal, $F(2, 60)=46.94$, $p<.001$, than in loyal conditions, $F(2, 60)=16.33$, $p<.001$. In loyal conditions, evaluation latencies were faster after two (versus one) exposures to measurement, $F(1, 60)=20.67$, $p<.001$, but not after three (versus two) exposures ($F<1$). In contrast, in nonloyal conditions, evaluation latencies decreased following two (versus one) exposures, $F(1, 60)=53.52$, $p<.001$, and following three (versus two) exposures, $F(1, 60)=4.67$, $p<.05$. Hence, evaluation latencies decreased with repeated measurement, and this effect was more pronounced for nonloyal consumers.

DISCUSSION

When a consumer is exposed to a response scale, the relevant judgment is activated from memory. When multiple responses are called for, the judgment is activated repeatedly. Repeated activation increases the subsequent accessibility of the judgment from memory. However, this effect is more pronounced for nonloyal consumers because their initial judgments tend to be uncrystallized. Consequently, their initial judgments are particularly susceptible to repeated measurement effects. The judgments of loyal consumers, however, tend to be better-defined, more stable, and less malleable; consequently, their judgments are less susceptible to repeated measurement effects.

Prior research on measurement effects has focused on effects due to social desirability concerns, evaluation apprehension, sensitization to experimental manipulations (Cook and Campbell 1979), self-generated validity (Feldman and Lynch 1988), and question wording (Krosnick and Schuman 1988; Schuman and Presser 1981). Essentially, these studies centered on the effects of measurement on judgment valence. We focused on the effects of measurement on judgment strength or accessibility. Exposing subjects to multiple measures artificially enhances the readiness with which the judgment can subsequently be accessed from memory. This enhancement is artificial because it would not have occurred in the absence of repeated measurement.

The present set of results is especially impressive given that a "minimal" manipulation (Prentice and Miller 1992) of repeated measurement was employed. Subjects were merely asked to categorize each brand as "good" or "bad." Relatively little cognitive effort, on the part of the respondent, is required to perform this simple cognitive task. Nevertheless, strong effects of repeated measurement were observed. It could be argued that even stronger effects may be observed if respondents are asked to perform a more complex cognitive task (Prentice and Miller 1992). For example, completing the same seven-point scales repeatedly should require greater cognitive effort than completing the same dichotomous scales repeatedly. Moreover, completing different but converging seven-point scales repeatedly should require greater cognitive effort than completing the same seven-point scales repeatedly. Because accessibility increases with cognitive effort (Tyler, Hertel, McCallum, and Ellis 1979), the effects of repeated measurement on accessibility should increase with the complexity of the measurement instrument.

One implication of this research is that if multi-item scales are required to operationalize attitudes adequately (see, e.g., Bagozzi, Tybout, Craig, and Sternthal 1979), and if exposure to multi-item scales enhances the strength of attitudes, then it is difficult to separate the effects of improved measurement versus inflated strength on attitude-behavior correspondence. We suggest that both factors are important. That is, the ability to predict overt behavior from attitude increases when multi-item (versus single-item) scales are employed because (a) the attitude is better conceptualized and operationalized, and (b) attitude accessibility is enhanced artificially due to the effects of repeated measurement.

We suggest that marketing researchers should use enough scale items to operationalize a construct adequately, but not so many scales that the construct undergoing assessment is likely to be altered dramatically. The optimal number of scales is likely to vary from constuct to construct (depending on the complexity of the construct) and from sample to sample (depending on the prior knowledge and experience of the respondent). Complex multidimensional constructs require multidimensional measures. However, exposure to multidimensional measures may induce respondents to form judgments that would not have been formed otherwise or may lead to the strengthening of pre-existing judgments. Respondents with relatively uncrystallized judgments are particularly susceptible to construction and repeated measurement effects. Finally, we suggest that a "more is better" philosophy of measurement may seriously compromise the reliability and validity of a measurement instrument by inducing respondents to construct new judgments or by increasing the strength of pre-existing judgments.

REFERENCES

Abelson, Robert P. (1988), "Conviction, *American Psychologist*, 43 (April), 267-275.

Bagozzi, Richard P., Alice M. Tybout, C. Samuel Craig, and Brian Sternthal (1979), "The Construct Validity of the Tripartite Classification of Attitudes," *Journal of Marketing Research*, 16 (February), 88-95.

Berger, Ida E. and Andrew A. Mitchell (1989), "The Effect of Advertising on Attitude Accessibility, Attitude Confidence, and the Attitude-Behavior Relationship," *Journal of Consumer Research*, 16 (December), 269-279.

Bishop, George F., Alfred J. Tuchfarber, and Robert W. Oldendick (1986), "Opinions on fictitious issues: The pressure to answer survey questions," *Public Opinion Quarterly*, 50, 240-250.

Chaiken, Shelly and Mark W. Baldwin (1981), "Affective-Cognitive Consistency and the Effect of Salient Behavioral Information on the Self-Perception of Attitudes. *Journal of Personality and Social Psychology*, 41 (July), 1-12.

Churchill, Gilbert A. (1979), "A Paradigm for Developing Better Measures of Marketing Constructs," *Journal of Marketing Research*, 16 (February), 64-73.

Cohen, Joel B. and Dipanker Chakravarti (1990), "Consumer Psychology," *Annual Review of Psychology*, 41, 243-288.

Converse, Philip E. (1970), "Attitudes and Non-Attitudes: Continuation of a Dialogue," in *The Quantitative Analysis of Social Problems*, ed. Edward R. Tufte, Reading, MA: Addison-Wesley, 168-189.

Cook, Thomas D. and Donald T. Campbell (1979), *Quasi-Experimentation: Design and Analysis Issues for Field Settings*. Boston: Houghton Mifflin.

Davidson, Andrew R. and James J. Jaccard (1979), "Variables that Moderate the Attitude-Behavior Relation: Results of a Longitudinal Survey," *Journal of Personality and Social Psychology*, 37, 1364-1376.

Fazio, Russell H. (1989). On the Power and Functionality of Attitudes: The Role of Attitude Accessibility," in *Attitude Structure and Function*, eds. Anthony R. Pratkanis, Steven J. Breckler, Anthony G. Greenwald, Hillsdale, NJ: Lawrence Erlbaum Associates, 153-179.

_____, Martha C. Powell, and Carol J. Williams (1989), "The Role of Attitude Accessibility in the Attitude-to-Behavior Process," *Journal of Consumer Research*, 16 (December), 280-288.

_____, David M. Sanbonmatsu, Martha C. Powell, and Frank R. Kardes, (1986), "On the Automatic Activation of Attitudes," *Journal of Personality and Social Psychology*, 50 (February), 229-238.

_____, and Mark P. Zanna (1981), "Direct Experience and Attitude-Behavior Consistency," in *Advances in Experimental Social Psychology*, Vol. 14, ed. Leonard Berkowitz, New York: Academic Press, 161-202.

Feldman, Jack M. and John G. Lynch (1988), "Self-Generated Validity and Other Effects of Measurement on Belief, Attitude, Intention, and Behavior," *Journal of Applied Psychology*, 73 (August), 421-435.

Fischhoff, Baruch (1991), "Value Elicitation: Is There Anything in There? *American Psychologist*, 46 (August), 835-847.

Jacoby, Jacob and David B. Kyner (1973), "Brand Loyalty Vs. Repeat Purchasing Behavior," *Journal of Marketing Research*, 10 (February), 1-9.

Juster, F. T. (1966), "Consumer Buying Intentions and Purchase Probability: An experiment in Survey Design," *Journal of the American Statistical Association*, 61, 658-696.

Krosnick, Jon A. (1988). "Attitude Importance and Attitude Change," *Journal of Experimental Social Psychology*, 24 (May), 240-255.

Krosnick, Jon A. and Howard Schuman (1988), "Attitude Intensity, Importance, and Certainty and Susceptibility to Response Effects," *Journal of Personality and Social Psychology*, 54 (June), 940-952.

Lynch, John G., Howard Marmorstein, and Michael F. Weigold, M. F. (1988), "Choices from Sets Including Remembered Brands: Use of Recalled Attributes and Prior Overall Evaluations," *Journal of Consumer Research*, 15 (September), 169-184.

Peter, J. Paul (1979), "Reliability: A Review of Psychometric Basics and Recent Marketing Practices," *Journal of Marketing Research*, 16 (February), 6-17.

Powell, Martha C. and Russell H. Fazio (1984), "Attitude Accessibility as a Function of Repeated Attitudinal Expression," *Personality and Social Psychology Bulletin*, 10 (March), 139-148.

Prentice, Deborah A. and Dale T. Miller (1992), "When Small Effects Are Impressive," *Psychological Bulletin*, 112 (July), 160-164.

Raden, David (1985), "Strength-Related Attitude Dimensions," *Social Psychology Quarterly*, 48 (December), 312-330.

Schuman, Howard and Stanley Presser (1981), *Questions and Answers in Attitude Surveys: Experiments on Question Form, Wording, and Context*, New York: Acaedmic Press.

Schwartz, Shalom H. (1978), "Temporal Instability as a Moderator of the Attitude-Behavior Relationship," *Journal of Personality and Social Psychology*, 36 (July), 715-24.

Smith, Robert E. and William R. Swinyard (1983), "Attitude-Behavior Consistency: The Impact of Product Trial Versus Advertising," *Journal of Marketing Research*, 20 (August), 257-67.

Sudman, Seymour and Norman M. Bradburn (1974), *Response Effects in Surveys: A Review and Synthesis*, Chicago: Aldine.

Tesser, Abraham and David R. Shaffer (1990), "Attitudes and Attitude Change," *Annual Review of Psychology*, 41, 479-523.

Tyler, Sherman W., Paula T. Hertel, Marvin C. McCallum, and Henry C. Ellis, (1979), "Cognitive Effort and Memory," *Journal of Experimental Psychology: Human Learning and Memory*, 5 (November), 607-617.

Wu, Chenghuan and David R. Shaffer (1987), "Susceptibility to Persuasive Appeals as a Function of Source Credibility and Prior Experience With the Attitude Object," *Journal of Personality and Social Psychology*, 52 (April), 677-688.

Wyer, Robert S. and Thomas K. Srull (1989), *Memory and Cognition in its Social Context*, Hillsdale, NJ: Lawrence Erlbaum Associates.

The Impact of Direction-of-Comparison on the Formation of Preference

Gita V. Johar, Columbia University
Elizabeth H. Creyer, New York University

ABSTRACT

Two studies explore the direction-of-comparison effect, the tendency of people to neglect features that are unique to the referent of comparison and to highlight features that are unique to the subject of comparison. The present research finds boundary conditions for these effects. In the first study, we manipulated subjects' processing goal at the time of processing information about two brands of cereal. Further, we studied the direction-of-comparison effect in a stimulus-based judgment context rather than the conventional memory-based judgment context. Results show that the direction-of-comparison effect does not occur under impression formation conditions and is attenuated even under memorization conditions. This result could be due to the stimulus-based judgment context where subjects are free to re-evaluate information at the time of preference formation. In study 2, the subject and the referent of comparison had unique positive as well as negative features. Results reveal that the direction-of-comparison effect does not extend to these situations and that the processing goal does not affect preference. Implications for marketing are discussed.

Understanding the process of comparison is necessary in order to explain many different types of judgments and choices. We often compare, people, places, products, and a variety of other things with other known items. In fact, as Houston, Sherman, and Baker (1989) note, before we can categorize or evaluate a new item, we must judge its similarity and difference to more familiar items. In particular, comparison processes are an important element of the consumer decision making process. However, prior research in the realm of consumer decision making has tended to neglect the process of comparison between pairs of options.

Contrary to common sense, the process of comparison is not a straightforward matter in which the features of one item are simply compared with the features of the other item (Sanbonmatsu, Kardes, and Gibson, 1991). Tversky (1977) has proposed a feature matching model of the comparison process. According to his model, during the comparison process one object serves as the subject of comparison while the other object serves as the target, or referent, of comparison. Asymmetries in judgments of similarities will occur, depending on the direction-of-comparison. That is, differences in judgments of similarity may result depending on which object serves as the subject of comparison.

For example, consider the following example. You have been very happy with your computer at work. In fact, you would like to by the same computer for your home but the price is very high. During the search process, your office computer will serve as the subject of comparison. The new computer you consider purchasing, called the referent, will then be reviewed and evaluated in reference to your office computer. Consequently, the unique features of your office computer will be highlighted while the unique features of the referent computer are not likely to be noticed during the comparison process.

Hence, the object which serves as the subject of comparison can significantly influence the formation of preference. Numerous studies (e.g., Payne, 1982; Slovic & Lichtenstein, 1983) suggest that consumers rarely have well-articulated preferences. Rather, research suggests that preferences are often not simply recalled from memory but are instead, contingent on the decision context (Payne, 1976, 1982; Fischhoff, Slovic, & Lichtenstein, 1980). Consequently, it is especially important for consumer behavior researchers to understand the circumstances to which the direction-of-comparison effect will generalize. Is the direction-of-comparison effect likely to occur in the aisles of supermarkets? If so, under what processing circumstances is the effect more likely to occur?

Hence, the purpose of the research is to provide insight into the generalizability of the direction-of-comparison effect. First, we review the research which has examined this phenomenon. Then, two experiments which extend prior research are described and their results discussed. Finally, the implications of this research are identified and directions for future research are presented.

THEORETICAL BACKGROUND

Interest in the process of comparison, the manner in which the similarities and differences between two objects are identified, has recently increased (Dhar and Simonson 1992; Houston, Sherman, and Baker 1989; Sanbonmatsu, Kardes, and Gibson 1991). An understanding of comparison processes is necessary to fully explain many judgment and choice behaviors. For example, comparison is an essential element of the categorization process. Marketers spend a substantial amount of time and money on product positioning which, at its most basic level, involves a consumer's judgment of a product's category membership (Cohen and Basu 1987). As Cohen and Basu (1987) note, the outcome of the categorization process "is not only a particular identification of a product, but the increased salience of information relevant to that category (and the corresponding suppression of information relevant to other categories) together with the category-based inferences that result (p.455)." Consumers may compare a target brand to an exemplar of the product category during the initial categorization process that precedes more detailed processing of the brand (Fiske and Pavelchak 1986). According to the direction-of-comparison effect, the result of the categorization process could well depend on whether the target brand is the subject or the referent of comparison.

Comparison processes also play a fundamental role in the formation of preference. Tversky (1977) has characterized an object as a set of concrete and abstract features. For example, a consumer's total base of knowledge about a specific brand of peanut butter may include the following features: high quality, creamy, tasty, comes in a jar with a blue label, high calories, and no cholesterol. However, depending on the choice context, only a limited "working" list of features may be recalled. The list of features which are recalled may be significantly influenced by the features of the object of comparison.

Sanbonmatsu, Kardes, and Gibson (1991) note that during the comparison process, the object which serves as the subject of comparison, rather than as the referent of comparison, is critically important because people are attuned to the subjects' features (p. 132). This is because people often neglect features which are unique to referent, instead comparing only features which are present in the subject of comparison. On the other hand, features which are unique to the subject tend to be highlighted by the comparison process (Sanbonmatsu, Kardes, and Gibson 1991). This phenomenon is known as the direction-of-comparison effect. Consequently, preference for a given object is not determined solely by the bundle of attributes that define that object; preference is relative to the object to which it is compared.

Houston, Sherman, and Baker (1989) conducted a series of studies which explored this phenomenon. Respondents were presented with two different objects within a variety of categories.

After reading descriptions of the different objects, respondents indicated which item they most preferred. Note that this preference measure was based on recall of the features - the actual features used to described the pair of objects was not available. Houston and his colleagues correctly assumed that the object which was most recently observed, and therefore better remembered, was the subject of comparison. They found that the subject is preferred when it possessed unique positive features. However, when the subject possessed unique negative features, the referent is preferred, even when the referent possessed an equal number of negative features.

Sanbonmatsu and his colleagues (1991) extended this research by examining whether the availability of an overall evaluation of the objects diminished the direction-of-comparison effect. They presented respondents with booklets describing two set of pens and two sets of automobiles. In one set of conditions, the objects shared positive features but had unique negative features. In another set of conditions, the objects shared negative features but had unique positive features, After either memorizing or forming an impression of each of the objects, the booklets were removed. A surprise preference measure was then administered. As expected, the direction-of-comparison effect was diminished when an overall evaluation, or impression, of the objects was formed. The availability of overall evaluations for each pair of objects reduced the need to perform a feature-based comparison and consequently, the unique features of the subject were not highlighted. The results also show that preference for the subject of comparison was significantly greater when it possessed unique positive features than when it possessed unique negative features. Thus, the notion that the features of the subject of comparison, compared to the features of the referent of comparison, has a stronger impact on the formation of preference is supported.

As discussed above, there is strong empirical evidence that the preference formation process can be influenced by determining which object is the subject of comparison and which object is the referent of comparison. However, two key questions for consumer researchers remain unanswered. The first question is — will the direction-of-comparison effect still occur when the judgment is stimulus-based, rather than memory-based? Many choice decisions occur in a context in which information about the objects is available. For example, consumers can compare the ingredients and other nutritional information of two competing brands by simply reading the package labels. While this scenario has been recently examined by Dhar and Simonson (1992), these researchers did not explicitly compare the condition where information was present at the time of making judgments and the condition where the information was not present.

A related issue is whether differences in processing goal (i.e., impression formation vs. memorization; see Sanbonmatsu et al 1991) will matter when the information used to describe the objects of comparison is available at the time of choice. Prior research suggests that consumers under high levels of involvement have an evaluation goal in place and hence process information in greater detail (Mitchell, 1983). This processing goal results in the formation of an overall evaluation based on a consideration of all product attributes, which may then be available at the time of choice (Carlston, 1980; Kardes, 1986; Lingle & Ostrom, 1979). In other words, if a consumer's goal is to form an impression of the object, then an evaluation is made at the time of processing. When these consumers later choose a brand, this overall evaluation influences the choice rather than the individual brand attributes. However, will this evaluation be used when product features are readily available?

Past research has focused on situations where (a) only unique features of both the subject and the referent of comparison are presented (cf. Dhar and Simonson 1992); or (b)the subject and the referent share features of the same valence and have unique features that are differently valenced (cf. Sanbonmatsu et al 1991). Hence, another issue that needs to be addressed is whether the features of the subject of comparison have a greater impact on preference formation when both objects have both unique positive and negative features. That is, for many product categories, different brands have different strengths and weaknesses. For example, one brand of computer may come equipped with an internal modem while lack a high speed processor while another brand of computer may have a high resolution monitor but lack a math co-processor.

In the following two studies, we examine the boundaries of the direction-of-comparison effect. In the first experiment, we determine whether processing goal, that is whether the subjects memorize the product attributes or form an overall impression of the objects, will results in differences in the strength of the direction-of-comparison effect when the features used to define the objects are available at the time of choice. In the second experiment we explore the comparison process when the objects of comparison have both unique positive and unique negative features.

EXPERIMENT 1

Method

Subjects. Forty eight students enrolled in the introductory marketing course at private, northeastern university, whose participation partially fulfilled a course requirement, served as subjects. Subjects were run in two groups of approximately equal size.

Stimuli. Descriptions of two equivalent breakfast cereals, each described by eight features were developed. Four negative features and four positive features described each brand. The cereals shared the four negative features; the four positive features were unique to each brand. These descriptions are presented below.

Brand Fir:
75 milligrams of sodium (low)
0 protein (low)
160 calories (high)
1 gram of fat (low)
8 grams of complex carbohydrates (low)
5000 I.U. Vitamin A (high)
18 milligrams of iron (high)
1 gram of dietary fiber (low)

Brand Sec:
0 milligrams of cholesterol (low)
0 protein (low)
160 calories (high)
3 grams of sugar (low)
8 grams of complex carbohydrates (low)
60 milligrams Vitamin C (high)
400 I.U. magnesium (high)
1 gram of dietary fiber (low)

Pretesting established that the four unique positive features of one brand were equal in desirability to the four unique features of the other brand.

Procedure. The experiment was described as a problem to learn more about consumer behavior. Booklets containing the instructions and stimuli were distributed to the subjects. In the impression formation condition, subjects were asked to form an overall evaluation of each of the brands. In the memorization condition, subjects were simply asked to memorize the brand's features. Subjects were given 1 minute to either form an impression or memorize the features of the first brand. After 1 minute, subjects were told to turn the page and repeat this task for the second brand. Then after another minute, a surprise preference measure was administered.

Preference was assessed on a 12 point scale anchored by "I strongly prefer (referent brand)" (1), and "I strongly prefer (subject brand)". The higher the value, the greater the preference for the most recently presented brand which was assumed to be the subject of the comparison (i.e., the focal option). Designating the second brand as the subject of comparison follows the procedure used by both Agostinelli, Sherman, Fazio, and Hearst (1986) and Houston, et al. (1989). Since, subjects are unaware of the purpose of the study, they are likely to be focused on the most recent item of the pair during the judgment process. The descriptions of both brands of cereals were provided subjects below this measure. The order of presentation of the brands was counterbalanced across conditions.

Results

As hypothesized, results reveal that the direction of comparison effect is attenuated when subjects have an impression formation goal compared to a memorization goal, at the time of processing information about the brand ($F(1,46) = 3.12$, $p < .10$). However, the means reveal that under both conditions, the subject of the comparison (i.e., the second brand presented), is not preferred much greater than the scale midpoint (6.5) that would be suggested by indifference between the two brands (memorization mean preference = 6.89; impression formation preference = 5.60).

These findings imply that the direction of comparison effect holds only when the judgment is memory based and that the effect does not carry over to stimulus based judgments. Thus, the advantage of the subject of the comparison diminishes when both brands can be re-evaluated at the time of forming preferences. The second experiment was designed to test the boundaries of the direction-of-comparison effect when the subject and the referent of comparison have unique positive as well as negative features, in memory-based judgment situations.

EXPERIMENT 2

Method

Subjects. Forty six students enrolled in the introductory marketing course at private, northeastern university, whose participation partially fulfilled a course requirement, served as subjects. Subjects were run in two groups approximately the same size.

Stimuli. Descriptions of two breakfast cereals, each described by eight features were developed. Four negative features and four positive features described each brand. However, unlike study 1, the cereals shared two positive and two negative features. Of the four features unique to each brand, two were positive and two were negative. Thus, unlike Sanbonmatsu et al (1991), the two brands shared both positive and negative features and had unique features that were positive and negative. Pretesting established that the unique features of one brand were equal in desirability to the unique features of the other brand.

Procedure. The procedure used in experiment 1 was repeated in experiment 2. Booklets containing the instructions and stimuli were distributed to the subjects. In the impression formation condition, subjects were asked to form an overall evaluation of each of the brands whereas in the memorization condition, subjects were simply asked to memorize the brand's features. After either forming impression of the brands or memorizing their features, subjects responded to a surprise preference measure. Unlike experiment 1, the descriptions of the objects were not available at the time of judgment. The order of presentation of the brands was counterbalanced across subjects.

Results

Results show that the direction-of-comparison effect does not extend to situations where the unique features of the subject brand are both positive and negative. In both the impression formation and the memorization conditions the mean preference was close to the scale midpoint (impression formation mean = 6.94; memorization mean = 6.10). Further, the processing goal did not significantly affect preference ($F(1,44) = 0.91$, p N.S.).

DISCUSSION

The findings of the two experiments reported here extend past research on the direction-of-comparison effect. Specifically, the results of Study 1 suggest that this effect does not extend to situations where the brand information is present at the time of judgment, regardless of the processing goal at the time of information processing. An impression formation goal further attenuates the effect. However, it should be noted that we have no way of knowing for sure whether subjects actually used the information which was available at the time of judgment. Perhaps, judgments were based on initial impressions of the brands. Study 2 suggests that this effect will occur mainly when the unique information from the subject of comparison is sufficiently diagnostic. When the subject of comparison has both positive as well as negative unique features, consumers will tend to turn to the unique features of the referent brand for resolution. Hence it appears that the direction-of-comparison effect is not robust to stimulus-based judgments or to situations where the subject of comparison has both positive and negative unique features.

These boundary conditions of the direction-of-comparison effect have implications for marketing. These findings suggest that manipulating the subject of comparison through advertising would work only when consumers do not have access to information about competing brands at the time of making the decision. Hence, the direction-of-comparison effect can be most fruitfully applied in the case of experience goods and credence goods where one-on-one comparison of features is not possible at the time of purchase. However, in the case of search goods, manipulating the focal option may not work to its advantage. For example, consumers may compare the nutritional value of two types of cereal at the time of purchase, regardless of a brand (e.g., Kellogs) making itself the focal option through point-of-purchase material or by comparative advertising against another brand (e.g., Total).

Second, although brands advertise only their unique *positive* features, most brands in today's market do not have the luxury of having unique features that are only positive. Hence the types of stimuli used in Study 2 add ecological validity to this area of research. It appears that the direction-of-comparison effect can be used by practitioners only when the unique features of the subject brand are positive and hence diagnostic. The findings in this research are limited in that the failure to support the direction-of-comparison effect (that is failure to reject the null hypothesis), does not imply that it does not exist. Future research is required in order to validate these findings.

REFERENCES

Agostinelli, G. Sherman, S.J., Fazio, R.H. and E.S. Hearst (1986), "Detecting and Identifying Change: Additions versus deletions," *Journal of Experimental Psychology: Human Perception and Performance*, 12, 445-454.

Carlston, D. E. (1980), "The Recall and Use of Observed Behavioral Episodes and Inferred Traits in Social Inference Processes," *Journal of Experimental Social Psychology*, 16, 779-804.

Cohen, J.B. and K. Basu (1987), "Alternative Models of Categorization: Toward a Contingent Processing Framework," *Journal of Consumer Research*, 13, 455-472.

Dhar, R. and I. Simonson (1992), "The Effect of the Direction of Alternative Comparison on Consumer Preferences," *Journal of Marketing Research*, in press.

Fischoff, B., P. Slovic, and S. Lichtenstein (1980), "Knowing What You Want: Measuring Labile Values," in *Cognitive Processes in Choice and Human Behavior*, ed. T. Wallstein, Hillsdale, NJ: Erlbaum.

Fiske, S. and M.A. Pavelchak (1986), "Category-based versus Piecemeal-based Affective Responses: Developments in Schema-triggered Affect," in *The Handbook of Motivation and Cognition: Foundations of Social Behavior*, eds. R.M. Sorrentino and E.T. Higgins, New York: Guilford.

Houston, D.A., S. Sherman, and S.M. Baker (1989), "The Influence of Unique Features and Direction of Comparison on Preferences," *Journal of Experimental Social Psychology*, 25, 121-141.

Kardes, F.R. (1986), "Effects of Initial Product Judgments on Subsequent Memory-Based Judgments," *Journal of Consumer Research*, 13, 1-11.

Lingle, J. H. and T.M. Ostrom (1979), "Retrieval Selectivity in Memory-based Impression Judgments," *Journal of Personality and Social Psychology*, 36, 180-194.

Mitchell, A.A. (1983), "Cognitive Processes Initiated by Exposure to Advertising," in *Information Processing Research in Advertising*, ed. R. Harris, Hillsdale, NJ: Erlbaum.

Payne, J.W. (1976), "Task Complexity and Contingent Processing in Decision Making: An Information Search and Protocol Abalysis," *Organizational Behavior and Human Performance*, 16, 366-387.

_____ (1982), "Contingent Decision Behavior," *Psychological Bulletin*, 92, 382-402.

Sanbonmatsu, D.M., F.R. Kardes, and B.D. Gibson (1991), "The Role of Attribute Knowledge and Overall Evaluations in Comparative Judgment," *Organizational Behavior and Human Decision Processes*, 48, 131-146.

Slovic, P. and S. Lichtenstein (1983), "Preference Reversals: A Broader Perspective," *American Economic Review*, 73, 596-605.

Tversky, A. (1977), "Features of Similarity," *Psychological Review*, 84, 327-352.

Consumer Judgments, Decisions and Framing Dynamics: An Informational Viewpoint
Narasimhan Srinivasan, University of Connecticut

The use of knowledge can be categorized along several dimensions:

(A) Composition of the decision making unit
  (a) Individual, or (b) Joint decision making;
(B) Product Category
  (a) Durables, or (b) Non-durables;
(C) Context or situation
  (a) Memory based, or (b) Stimulus based; and
(D) Type of decision
  (a) Judgment, or (b) Choice.

Conceptually, this embraces the well known person/product/context dimensions and considers the complex nature of decision making. In addition, it is also meant to include possible additional interactions. The three papers to be discussed form a subset of the various possibilities that one may construct using just the four dimensions mentioned, which provides the overarching framework. (For example, the design for Paper 1 may be denoted as $A_bB_aC_aD_b$). Brief discussions of the three papers follow:

FRAMING DYNAMICS: MEASUREMENT ISSUES AND PERSPECTIVES

This paper is rich in conceptualizing framing dynamics. Puto (1987) detailed a behavioral model of the buying decision framing process using a hypothetical buying scenario using 372 professional buyers. This study of 230 home buyers, representing a non-professional group of buyers, is a good extension.

The explicit recognition of process dynamism in purchase decisions is a highlight of this paper. Since a considerable time period passes between the onset of the "problem recognition" stage and the "final" purchase, the consumer goes through an intensive cognitive effort for important purchases (such as houses), and the presence of several environmental cues contributes toward a complex purchasing situation informationally.

It appears that the field work involved interviewing both the male and female heads of the household. Joint decision making is a very complex and exciting area of work to apply decision frames and I wish more attention to this issue is forthcoming in the future.

The authors point out that carry over effects, latency effect and learning effects present measurement problems in process data. Unfortunately, these problems have neither been measured nor addressed in the empirical part of the paper.

Six dynamic frames have been proposed, with the first five mentioning "reference prices" (plural emphasized). Maybe, the operationalization is not complete in Table 1. Table 1 does not detail how multiple figures (reference prices) were obtained for the decision frames. DF1 measures the "price at which the (previous) house was sold" or "monthly rental charge." Similarly, DF5 asks about "any other house(s) you seriously considered buying..." What if the response is "0" or "1?" A clearer demonstration of the correspondence between the conceptualization and operationalization would be helpful.

Some other specific issues that may be clarified in future work include:

- Usefulness of a global measure of variance: Are the home buyers homogenous in any meaningful respect? (particularly when the authors report a "wide range of house prices and local market size differences.")
- Segmentation of the market and different framing mechanisms for each segment might prove beneficial.
- The measure of "pattern" (Table 2) talks about the coefficient of variance as mean/range for the current frame. Shouldn't range be manipulated to use it as a measure of standard deviation?
- Propositions are not really tested at all. Rigorous testing of the propositions with clear demarcation of the decision frames would be a contribution to the literature.
- The supply side of framing is captured. What about the demand side perspective? Eagerness and willingness to expose oneself to more and more information and the real estate agent trying to "close the sale?"

THE IMPACT OF DIRECTION-OF-COMPARISON ON THE FORMATION OF PREFERENCES

This is a very interesting paper exploring the intricacies of a seemingly easy comparison of a pair of alternatives. The positive aspects of the paper include (1) the search for the boundary conditions for the direction-of-comparison effects and (2) testing under two contexts: stimulus-based judgment and memory-based judgment.

It appears that this study is a pre-cursor to a more elaborate design having three factors at two levels each: positive features (unique/shared) X negative features (unique/shared) and context (memory based and stimulus based).

A methodological concern I have is how many attributes, whether positive or negative does one include in a study. Perhaps the debate on the information overload about a decade earlier can provide some guidance. Providing just a single minute to memorize eight attributes for a brand seems to be a difficult and unrealistic task, particularly for a product like breakfast cereal. What is the motivation to assimilate all the available information? Did subjects use only part of the information provided to them? In the supermarket, consumers may take just a few seconds but don't register a lot of information in memory at least, according to Dickson and Sawyer (1990).

I am intrigued by the authors' statement that pretesting established that unique features of one brand were equal in desirability to the unique features of the other brand. I wish more details were made available. Even when brands share most all the significant technical specifications (e.g. Coke and Pepsi?), preference need not be based on that which is shared. How can unique features be taken to be equivalent, when they are different? Wouldn't it be useful to distinguish between attributes which are salient and those which are determinant?. Is desirability taken to be synonymous with both? When there is a partial sharing of attributes, there can be additional complications which are worth looking at.

It is easy to visualize someone replacing an existing brand either with the same brand (loyal) or a different brand (non-loyal). In such cases, the existing brand is the subject of comparison and the new brand is the referent of comparison. In the present set-up, how do you account for primacy and recency effects? Moreover, aren't such effects moderated by the level of involvement and the time between the arguments, according to the persuasion literature? What is the motivation to process more or less information?

FIGURE
Some Dimensions of Information

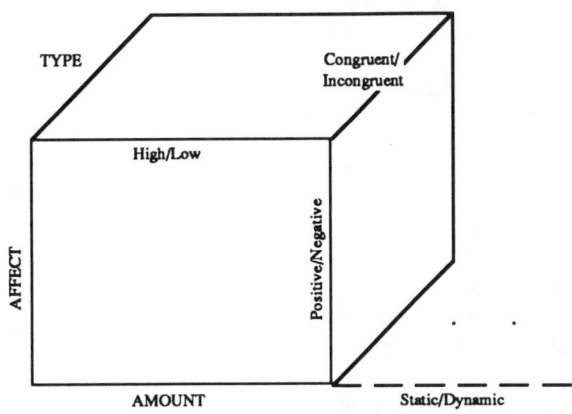

If I may abstract the preference ratings roughly:

	Memory	Impression
Experiment 1	6.89	5.60
Experiment 2	6.10	6.94

Clearly, there appears to be a reversal between the two contexts. Is this caused by the sharing of the features? It appears to be worthy of some follow-up work. Taking pair-wise contrasts and drawing some more inferences appears worthwhile. Which of them are really different from the mid-point, which is no preference, indicative of low involvement? What is the power of the tests?

Some additional points to ponder about:

- We have been talking about judgment, not choice. What happens if subjects are asked to choose?
- Though only a pair of alternatives have been compared, what happens when the evoked set contains more than 2 brands?

EFFECT OF MULTIPLE MEASUREMENT OPERATIONS ON CONSUMER JUDGMENT: MEASUREMENT RELIABILITY OR REACTIVITY?

I enjoyed reading this paper on the assessment of measurement effects on judgment strength. However, I think the title is misleading: it ought to have said "Repeated Measures," instead of "Multiple Measures."

There are several positive features in this study. As any good study does, this paper raises a lot of interesting questions:

- Is judgment distinguishable from attitude? Generalized feeling, comparison alternative, indication of purchase intent, etc.?
- 56 brands are flashed on the screen three times successively. Why is it surprising that people get quicker in pressing buttons, though fatigue might also have set in?
- How is learning accounted for? History effects? Experimentation effects?
- How about expert judgment? Automaticity of responses? (Alba and Hutchinson 1987)
* Judgments may exist when not measured, or constructed. Which judgments will be effected and to what degree by multiple measurements?
* Attitudes may reach a plateau beyond which measurement effect is not a problem, perhaps. When will this point be reached?

Purchase frequency estimates are used to identify the "non-loyal" group. Why is it not possible that one hates some brand and hence never buys this brand; according to your computation, this person will have non-crystallized attitudes because of the non-loyal categorization, though this is clearly wrong. Attitude crystallization should not be confused with valence.

I am curious about what happened to the huge number of brands which are between your "loyal" and "non loyal" groups? Wouldn't it be interesting to know what happens when opinions are not polarized?

Though both the "loyal" and "non loyal" groups show declining response times, the latency for the non-loyal group reaches 104 centiseconds in the third exposure, which is not very different from the 106 centiseconds for the first exposure for loyals. Wonder if there is a merging? What does it imply for the strength of judgment? Are we really measuring for uncrystallized attitudes and their malleability?

I think the discussion section talking about multiple-item scales is a misplaced generalization. This study is about quick and repeated measures using a button pushing technique. Maybe if the subjects were given a paper and pencil exercise, you might not have uncovered any significant differences at all, using a simple dichotomy: "good" and "bad" classifications of some brands.

Some additional questions to ponder are:

- What is the effect of any accompanying information?
- What is the effect of availability and necessity for deliberation time?
- What is the effect of involvement on response time?
- What is the applicability for multiple exposure research in advertising?

DISCUSSION

Primarily, these three papers and similar research may be seen as something on-going in the area of understanding the effect of the various dimensions of information. If we assume that we are dealing with information which is relevant (salient and deterministic), accessible (either stimulus or memory based) and diagnostic, we can conceptualize several important dimensions of information. One such attempt is depicted in the Figure.

Whether we use a low/high degree of information, congruent/incongruent type of information, or positive/negative information it will have an impact on the evoked set, which affects both judgment and final choice. However, an additional dimension which we have not successfully integrated in much of consumer research is the complexity introduced by the time dimension i.e. static versus dynamic process of information use.

The dynamism introduced by the time dimension impacts what information is presented when and in what manner for maximizing persuasibility either in advertising and in other sales contexts. For example, consumers may be "educated" to upgrade their purchase when they are shopping for houses or cars or most other durables by being presented information which is positive/negative and congruent/incongruent and try to stay within the range of the low/high continuum without causing any dysfunctionality due to information overload.

A related aspect important to policy makers is the regulation which may be required to force information disclosure to try to benefit consumers. How is prior information base assessed? To what degree can one reasonably hope to "educate" consumers, given a limited budget and a limited time frame? How much to "simplify" complex information? What information needs to be disclosed, how will it impact industry and what contributes to increasing consumer welfare are questions which need to be looked at in the context of "educating" consumers in social marketing contexts (Andreasen 1992).

REFERENCES

Alba, Joseph W. and J. Wesley Hutchinson (1987), "Dimensions of Consumer Expertise," *Journal of Consumer Research*, Vol. 13, 4 (March), 411-454.

Andreasen, Alan R. (1992), "A Social Marketing Consumer Research Agenda for the 1990s", Presidential Address delivered at the 1992 Vancouver ACR meeting.

Dickson, Peter R. and Alan G. Sawyer (1990), "The Price Knowledge and Search of Supermarket Shoppers," *Journal of Marketing*, Vol. 54, 3 (July), 42-53.

Puto, Christopher P. (1987), "The Framing of Buying Decisions," *Journal of Consumer Research*, Vol. 14, 3 (December) 301-314.

Presidential Session Overview
Designing Interventions to Prevent HIV/AIDS: Applications of Consumer Research Theory and Methods
Susan E. Middlestadt, Academy for Educational Development

The HIV/AIDS epidemic is a major problem in the country and in the world today. Not only is HIV disease a health issue, but it constitutes a significant barrier to the continued economic and social development of nations and communities. At our current state of medical knowledge, prevention and behavior change represent our most important means of controlling the epidemic. Thus, the medical and public health professionals have been turning to behavioral scientists to an unprecedented extent for assistance in designing programs. The theories and methods of consumer research represent major tools for those designing interventions. At the same time, it is clear that changing the behaviors that place people at risk of HIV infection poses a significant challenge to consumer researchers. Studies around the world show that people are, by and large, aware of AIDS, know the modes of transmission and understand what to do to prevent exposure to the virus. However, many people, everywhere, continue to engage in behaviors that place them at risk. HIV/AIDS prevention interventions must go beyond changing people's beliefs about health consequences to influencing nonhealth consequences, social norms, perceived and actual skill, perceived risk and other behavioral determinants identified by consumer research. Each of the presentations in this session will describe the application of consumer research to the development and/or evaluation of HIV prevention interventions showing both the oppportunities and challenges to behavioral scientists working to understand and change HIV/AIDS behaviors.

Social Norms for Condom Use: Implications for HIV Prevention Interventions of a KABP Survey with Heterosexuals in the Eastern Caribbean

Martin Fishbein, University of Illinois, Champaign-Urbana
Susan E. Middlestadt, Academy for Educational Development
David Trafimow, Virginia Polytechnic Institute

ABSTRACT

In the fall of 1990, a Knowledge, Attitude, Belief & Practices (KABP) survey was administered to a representative sample of residents of St. Lucia. The KABP questionnaire contained a large number of questions that could reasonably be expected to be related to whether or not people use condoms. To a certain extent each of these questions can be viewed as an attempt to assess one of the variables identified by one or more theories of behavior and behavior change. More specifically, questions on the KABP were identified as possible indicants of: AIDS Knowledge, Cues to Action, Perceived Susceptibility, Perceived Severity, Perceived (Locus of) Control, Normative Pressure and Condom Use Outcome Expectancies. Statistical analyses indicated that to some extent, each of these variables was related to condom use. However, the analyses also indicated that perceived normative pressure to use condoms was, by far, the single most important determinant of condom use behaviors on St. Lucia. The implications of this finding for designing mass media campaigns to increase condom use is discussed, and a normative campaign is strongly recommended.

INTRODUCTION

In the fall of 1990, a Knowledge, Attitude, Belief & Practices (KABP) survey was administered to a representative sample of residents of St. Lucia. St. Lucia is a small island country of located in the Eastern Caribbean. The survey was designed, developed and implemented as a collaborative project among the AIDS Technical Support: Public Health Communication Component (AIDSCOM), the Caribbean Epidemiology Centre (CAREC), the Ministry of Health of St. Lucia, Family Health International, Inc. and Caribbean Market Research Ltd. Funding was provided by the Offices of Education, Health and Population, Bureau for Research and Development, United States Agency for International Development, Project No. 936-5972, Contract No. DPE-5972-Z-00-7070-00.

The KABP questionnaire contained a large number of questions that could reasonably be expected to be related to whether or not people use condoms. Among other things, the questionnaire assessed people's knowledge about AIDS, including their understanding of how AIDS is transmitted and how it can be avoided. It also assessed the respondents' perceptions that they are personally at risk for AIDS, as well as their propensity to engage in a number of risky behaviors such as unprotected anal and vaginal sex with one or more sexual partners. In addition, the questionnaire assessed the extent to which respondents believed that they had control over their lives in general, control over their health, and, control over the likelihood that they could avoid AIDS. Further, it assessed their knowledge of condoms, their beliefs about the ease or difficulty they would experience in obtaining condoms, and their beliefs that condom use would increase or decrease their sexual pleasure. Finally, the questionnaire asked if they had discussed condoms with their friends and it asked them about their friends' use of condoms.

Many national AIDS control programs conduct basic surveys to assess the level of knowledge, attitudes, beliefs and practices (KABP) of their populations. These surveys are typically used for descriptive purposes and to provide baseline data. However, in this paper we will argue that these surveys provide valuable data for testing theoretical hypotheses and for guiding the development of behavior change interventions. To a certain extent, each of the items assessed in typical KABP survey taps variables that have been identified by different theories of behavior and behavior change. For example, surveys typically include measures of knowledge and perceived risk that are central variables in the health belief model (see, e.g., Becker, 1990; Janz & Becker, 1984). Self efficacy or one's belief in his or her ability to avoid AIDS is a central aspect of social learning theory (see, e.g., Bandura, 1977a, 1977b), and beliefs about condom use and perceived norms are central constructs in the theory of reasoned action (see, e.g., Fishbein, 1980; Ajzen & Fishbein, 1980). The present paper attempts to show how questions in the KABP survey can be used to tap these theoretical constructs and the determine which, if any, of these variables are related to condom use (i.e., to determine which of these variables discriminated between sexually experienced respondents who had Ever or Never used a condom). More specifically, 49 questions on the KABP were identified as possible indicants of seven theoretical variables: AIDS Knowledge, Cues to Action, Perceived Susceptibility, Perceived Severity, Perceived (Locus of) Control, Condom Use Outcome Expectancies and Perceived Normative Pressure.

METHOD

A complete description of the methodology of the study is available in Fishbein, Trafimow, Francis, Helquist, Esutace, Ooms and Middlestadt (in press). Briefly, respondents were 591 residents of St. Lucia between the ages of 15 and 60. They were interviewed in their homes by trained interviewers. The data presented here are weighted for age and sex to make them projectable to residents of the country within this age group. In addition, the present report is restricted to those respondents who are sexually experienced (i.e., to those who report they have had sexual intercourse). These respondents were further asked whether they had ever used condoms. Responses to this question allowed us to classify sexually experienced residents of St. Lucia into two groups: those who had *Ever* used a condom versus those who report that they had *Never* used a condom.

RESULTS

In order to better understand condom use behavior in St. Lucia, we first examined the extent to which each item (or cluster of items) was related to whether one had ever or never used a condom.

Knowledge

It has often been assumed that the more one knows about a disease and how it is transmitted, the more likely one is to engage in health protective behaviors. In order to test this notion, we considered several different indicants of knowledge:

Transmission Knowledge. Respondents were asked to describe how "people can get infected with the virus that causes AIDS". Respondents were given a score of +1 for each correct mode of transmission they identified, and a score of -1 for each incorrect transmission mode. The sum of the scores served as a measure of transmission knowledge. Generally speaking, whether people were well or poorly informed based on this index of transmission knowledge seemed to have little relationship to their condom usage. Contrary to expectations, knowledge about AIDS transmission was not significantly related to condom use (r=.07, n.s.).

Disease Knowledge. Respondents were asked three "Yes/No" questions that were focused upon the disease itself. More specifically, these questions addressed the difference between having AIDS and being HIV positive, and tested knowledge about the implications of this distinction for being able to identify people who are infected with the virus. For each question, a respondent received a +1 for a correct response, a -1 for an incorrect response, and a score of 0 when he or she was uncertain or didn't know. The sum of the scores served as a measure of disease knowledge.

In contrast to knowledge about transmission, knowing that there is a difference between being HIV positive and having AIDS and knowing the implications of this distinction is related to one's condom use behavior. The more one knows about this aspect of the disease, the more likely is one to have used a condom (r=.20, p<.01). For example, among those respondents who know there is a difference between having AIDS and being HIV positive, almost 75% have used a condom. In contrast, among respondents who believe there is NO difference between being seropositive and having AIDS, only 58% have used a condom. This difference is statistically significant (x^2=12.21, p<.001).

General Knowledge. Finally, the KABP also contained three "Agree/Disagree" questions that addressed both knowledge of the disease (e.g., People can generally sense if their sexual partner is an AIDS carrier) and more general knowledge about transmission (e.g., Little is known about how AIDS is spread). Responses to each item were scored from 1 to 5 (with 5 indicating the correct response). The sum of the scores served as a measure of general knowledge.

Consistent with expectations, this measure of general knowledge was also related to condom use behavior; the more general knowledge one had, the more likely was one to have used a condom (r=.17, p<.01).

Cues to Action

According to the health belief model and other models of behavioral change (e.g., Kanfer, 1970), one is unlikley to adopt health protective behaviors unless something happens to make the individual consider changing his or her behavior. These "cues to action" may be either internal (e.g., symptoms) or "external" (e.g., knowing someone with AIDS, being exposed to a mass media AIDS message). It follows that those exposed to one or more AIDS cues should be more likely to have used a condom than should those who have not been exposed.

Two such cues were assessed in the KABP. First, respondents were asked if they had seen a play or movie about AIDS. Second, they were asked if they personally knew someone who was HIV positive and/or who had AIDS. Consistent with expectations, those who have seen a play or movie about AIDS are significantly more likely to have used condoms than those who have not been exposed to such materials (x^2=9.75, p<.01). Similarly, those who know someone who is HIV positive and/or who has AIDS, are somewhat more likely to have used condoms than are those without such personal experiences with AIDS (x^2=3.54, p<.10).

Perceived Susceptibility and Severity

According to the health belief model, people are unlikely to engage in health protective behaviors unless (1) they believe they are personally susceptible to (i.e., at risk from) a given illness and (2) they believe that getting the illness will have severe, serious consequences on their lives. In order to test this notion we considered a number of different items.

Perceived Susceptibility. Respondents were asked if they thought they were personally at risk for AIDS. In contrast to expectations, this relatively direct assessment of perceived susceptibility was unrelated to condom use (x^2<1, r=-.03).

A number of other indicants of perceived susceptibility, however, were related to condom use. For example, respondents were asked what they thought was *the most serious health problem* on St. Lucia. Consistent with expectations, those spontaneously mentioning AIDS were significantly more likely to have used condoms than were those who did not mention AIDS (x^2=4.40, p<.05; r=.10, p<.05).

A somewhat different indicant of susceptiblity was based on four "agree/disagree" questions directed at respondent's beliefs about the degree to which one should be concerned about AIDS in St. Lucia. For example, respondents were asked whether they believed that AIDS was a serious problem on St. Lucia, whether there were more important things to worry about, and whether AIDS was a U.S. or foreign disease. Responses to these items were summed to provide an overall index of *AIDS Concern*. Consistent with expectations, the more one was concerned about AIDS in St. Lucia, the more likely was one to have used a condom (r=.15, p<.01).

One other indicator of personal susceptibility was considered. Specifically, it seems reasonable to assume that those with *multiple partners* will see themselves as more susceptible to AIDS than those who are monogamous or who have abstained from sex. If this is the case, those with multiple partners should be more likely to take health protective measures. Consistent with this, the correlation between number of partners and condom use was statistically significant (r=.10, p<.05).

Perceived Severity. Respondents were asked whether they believed that AIDS causes great suffering to those who get it. In contrast to expectations, this relatively direct measure of severity was unrelated to condom use (x^2<1, r=.04). Respondents were also asked whether they believed that there was a cure for AIDS. It seems reasonable to assume that a life threatening disease without a cure will be perceived as more severe than one with a cure and thus, those believing there is no cure should be more likely to take health protective measures. Consistent with this, those believing there is no cure for AIDS were significantly more likley to have used a condom than were those believing there is a cure (or who were uncertain), That is, among those believing there is no cure for AIDS, 67% have used a condom; among those believing there is a cure for AIDS, only 54% have used a condom (x^2=7.84, p<.01; r=.13, p<.01).

Perceived (Locus of) Control

According to almost all social learning theories (e.g., Bandura, 1977b; Kanfer, 1970; Rotter, 1954) people should be more likely to perform health protective behaviors if they believe that what happens to them is due to their own actions rather than to chance or fate. As Bandura (1977a) has pointed out however, general attributions of control may be less important than specific ones. For example, although one may feel that one has little control over one's life (in general), one may nevertheless believe that one has control over one's health (i.e., that one's health is more related to internal than to external factors). Similarly, even though one may not believe that one has control over one's health (in general), one may believe that whether or not one is exposed to AIDS is under one's control. Thus, measures of perceived (locus of) control have moved from general measures to more specific ones, and it is generally assumed that the more specific the measure the stronger its association with behavior.

Since the KABP contained items designed to measure General Locus of Control, Health Locus of Control, and AIDS Locus of Control, it was possible to explore this hypothesis. Consistent with expectations, the more one attributes outcomes to internal rather than external factors, the more likely is one to have used a condom. However, as expected, this relationship varied with item specificity. That is, the correlation between condom use and general locus of control was not significant ($r=.08$, n.s.), that between condom use and Health locus of control was significant ($r=.10$, $p<.05$), and that between condom use and AIDS locus of control was also significant ($r=.13$, $p<.01$).

In addition to these measures of locus of control, respondents were asked if they believed that it was possible to do something to protect oneself against AIDS. Consistent with expectations, those saying "Yes" were significantly more likely to have used condoms than were those saying "No" ($x^2=9.11$, $p<.01$; $r=.11$, $p<.05$).

Beliefs about Condom Use (Outcome Expectancies)

According to almost all behavior theories, the more one believes that performance of a given behavior will lead to more positive than negative outcomes, the more likely one is to perform that behavior. Several questions on the KABP appeared to address this issue. For example, people who said that one could do something to protect oneself from AIDS, were asked what could be done. Consistent with expectations, those who spontaneously said one way to protect oneself was to "always use a condom" were significantly more likely to have a used a condom than were those not mentioning this method of protection ($x^2=7.78$, $p<.01$; $r=.13$, $p<.01$).

Second, respondents were asked whether they believed that using a condom would increase, decrease or have no effect on sexual pleasure. It seems reasonable to assume that the more one believes that condom use will decrease sexual pleasure, the less likely one is to use a condom. In contrast to expectations however, exactly the opposite was true; those who believe that condom use decreases pleasure are significantly MORE likely to have used a condom than are those who believe condom use increases or does not effect sexual pleasure. Specifically, among those who believe condom use decreases pleasure, fully 76% have used a condom. In contrast, among those believing that condom use increases, or does not affect, sexual pleasure, 58% have used a condom ($x^2=15.11$, $p<.01$; $r=-.08$, n.s.).

Although initially suprising, these findings make considerable sense. That is, although beliefs about outcomes may influence future performance, they are also expected to reflect past experience. Viewed from this perspective, it is not unreasonable to have found that, in comparison to those who have never used a condom, those who have actually used condoms are more likely to believe that their use decreases sexual pleasure.

Finally, we assumed that embarrassment surrounding the purchase of condoms would be related to condom use. That is, it seems reasonable to assume that people who are embarassed to buy a condom will be less likely to purchase (and thus use) condoms than those who are not embarrassed. Consistent with expectations, this belief was positively related to condom use; those who reported they would be embarrassed to buy a condom were significantly less likely to have used one than those who reported they would not be embarrassed ($x^2=11.54$, $p<.01$; $r=.16$, $p<.01$).

Normative Pressure

According to the theory of reasoned action as well as Triandis's (1980) theory of subjective culture, perceived norms are important determinants of behavior. The more one perceives social pressure to perform a behavior, the more likely one is to actually perform that behavior. The KABP contained three questions that assess social pressure.

First, respondents were asked whether they talked to their friends about using condoms. Consistent with expectations, those who had talked to friends were significantly more likely to have used condoms than those who had not talked to their friends ($x2=101.1$, $p<.001$; $r=.44$, $p<.001$).

Second, respondents were asked whether they thought their friends used condoms. As expected, those who believed their friends used condoms were significanlty more likely to have used condoms themselves than were those who were unsure of their friends' behavior or who believed that their friends did not use condoms ($x^2=69.83$; $p<.001$; $r=.39$, $p<.001$).

Finally, respondents were asked if a sexual partner had ever suggested using condoms. Consistent with expectations, those whose partners had suggested condom use were more likely to have used condoms than were those who had not had partners who had suggested condom use ($x^2=149.88$, $p<.001$; $r=.54$, $p<.001$).

Testing the Relative Importance of the Theoretical Variables

The above analyses indicate that, to a certain extent, each of the theoretical variables is related to condom use. Thus for example, at least in St. Lucia, some types of AIDS knowledge (i.e., disease knowledge and general knowledge) are related to condom use, while other types of knowledge (i.e., transmission knowledge) are not. Similarly, some measures of susceptibility and severity are related to condom use, while others are not. In order to provide a more rigorous test of the relationships between each of these theoretical variables and condom use, individual items were combined to develop indices to assess each variable. That is, all the knowledge questions were combined to form a single knowledge index; the higher the score, the more knowledge one has about AIDS. Similarly, based upon the health belief model, a single index of perceived threat was constructed. More specifically, according to the health belief model (see Becker, 1990), Cues to Action, Perceived Susceptibility and Perceived Severity act jointly to influence one's perception of the degree to which one is personally threatened by a given illness. The greater the threat, the more likely one should be to take preventive action. Three other indices were developed: (1) a single measure of locus of control that combined the general, health, and AIDS specific items; (2) an outcome expectancy score; and (3) a measure of normative pressure.

Table 1 presents the mean standardized scores for each of the above five variables (as well as the means for the subscales or items comprising those scores) for those who have *Ever* or *Never* used a condom. In addition, the Table shows the correlation between each of the scores and condom use.

Consistent with our previous discussion, it can be seen in Table 1 that all five theoretical variables are significantly related to condom use. In contrast to those who have never used a condom, people who have used a condom: (1) have more knowledge about AIDS ($r=.21$, $p<.01$); (2) are more threatened by AIDS ($r=.24$, $p<.01$); (3) are more likely to attribute a variety of outcomes to internal rather than to external causes ($r=.13$, $p<.01$); (4) are more likely to hold behavioral beliefs supporting condom use ($r=.19$,

TABLE 1

St. Lucia: Relationships between Condom Use and Selected Theoretical Variables

	Used a Condom		
Variable	Never	Ever	r
Knowledge	-0.54	0.33 **	.21 **
Transmission	1.90	2.18	.07
Disease (Yes/No)	1.79	2.11 **	.20 **
General (Agree/Disagree)	9.66	10.73 **	.17 **
AIDS Threat	-0.47	0.32 **	.24 **
Perceived Risk	-0.41	-0.46	-.03
Most Serious Problem	0.64	0.73 *	.10 *
Perceived Concern	13.17	15.54 **	.15 **
Severity I - Suffer	4.69	4.76	.06
Severity II - No Cure	0.66	0.77 **	.13 **
Number of Partners	1.12	1.29 *	.10 *
Know AIDS/HIV	-0.85	-0.70 *	.11 *
Saw Play/Movie	0.34	0.49 **	.14 **
Perceived (Locus of) Control	1.48	2.28 **	.13 **
AIDS Locus	0.94	1.26 **	.13 **
Health Locus	0.40	0.68 *	.10 *
General Locus	0.11	0.32	.08
Outcome Expectancies	-0.35	0.24 **	.19 **
Response efficacy	0.55	0.68 **	.13 **
Embarrassed to buy	0.38	0.65 **	.16 **
[Expected Pleasure]	[-0.19	-0.29]	[-.08]
Normative Pressure	-1.77	1.04 **	.58 **
Talk to Friends	0.36	0.80 **	.44 **
Friends Use	0.07	0.64 **	.39 **
Partner Ask	0.11	0.67 **	.54 **

* p < .05
** p < .01

p<.01); and (5) are more likely to experience normative pressure to use a condom (r=.58, p<.01).

IMPLICATIONS FOR DEVELOPING MASS MEDIA INTERVENTIONS

Note that, by far, the strongest influence on condom use is perceived normative pressure. This suggests that attempts to increase condom use in St. Lucia should focus upon social norms. For example, a mass media campaign might suggest that people talk to their friends about condom use; or it might provide information about the frequency with which condoms are used on St. Lucia. That is, the message might point out that the majority of St. Lucians use condoms. Another strategy might be to suggest that one should talk to one's partner about condom use and/or suggest that one should ask one's partner to use a condom.

In order to determine whether it would also be useful to focus interventions upon one or more of the other variables, a series of statistical analyses were conducted to determine whether a consideration of any of the variables would add to our ability to explain condom use behavior. For example, as we noted above, perceived normative pressure correlates .58 with condom use. To determine whether a given variable, such as knowledge, contributes to our understanding of condom use behavior over and above perceived pressure, one tests to see if a consideration of knowlege in addition to perceived norms significantly increases the size of the correlation. That is, will the simultaneous consideration of knowledge and perceived normative pressure lead to better prediction of condom use behavior than that obtained from a consideration of only perceived normative pressure? These analyses indicated that none of the four remaining variables (whether considered individually or in combination) increased the size of the correlation. Thus, it would appear that if one conducts a normative campaign, little will be gained by directing interventions at any of the remaining four variables (e.g., Knowledge, Perceived Threat, Perceived (Locus of) Control, or Behavioral Beliefs).

SUMMARY & CONCLUSIONS

In this paper we have tried to show how KABP surveys can be used to test hypotheses derived from different theories of behavior. More important, we have tried to show that these tests can provide valuable insights into the relative importance of a number of theoretical variables as determinants of health protective behaviors. Specifically, we have seen that central variables from the Health Belief Model (e.g., Perceived Knowledge, Perceived Threat, Beliefs about Condom Use), Social Learning Theory (Locus of Control, Beliefs about Condom Use), and the Theory of Reasoned

Action (Perceived Norms, Beliefs about Condom Use) all contribute to an understanding of condom use behavior. However, the data clearly indicate that, at least in St. Lucia, the most important determinant of condom use behavior is perceived normative pressure.

This finding clearly suggests that attempts to increase condom use behaviors in St. Lucia should focus primarily upon increasing perceived normative pressure to use condoms. From a theoretical perspective, this type of campaign has the greatest potential for successfully influencing condom use behaviors.

REFERENCES

Ajzen, I. & Fishbein, M. (1980). *Understanding Attitudes and Predicting Social Behavior.* Englewood Cliffs, N.J.: Prentice Hall.

Bandura, A. (1977a). Self-efficacy. Toward a unifying theory of behavioral change. *Psychological Review, 84,* 191-215.

Bandura, A. (1977b). *Social Learning Theory.* Englewood Cliffs, N.J.: Prentice Hall.

Becker, M. H. (1990). Theoretical models of adherence and strategies for improving adherence. In S.A. Schumaker, E.B. Schron & J.K. Ockene (Eds.), *The Handbook of Health Behavior Change.* New York: Springer, pp. 5-43.

Fishbein, M. (1980). A theory of reasoned action: Some applications and implications. In H.E. Howe and M.M. Page (Eds.), *1979 Nebraska Symposium on Motivation.* Lincoln, Neb: Univ. of Nebraska Press, pp 195-259.

Fishbein, M., Trafimow, D., Francis, C., Helquist, M., Eustace, M.A., Ooms, M., & Middlestadt, S.E. (in press). AIDS knowledge, attitudes, beliefs and practices in two Caribbean countries: A compararive analysis. *Journal of Applied Social Psychology.*

Janz, N. K. & Becker, M. H. (1984). The health belief model: A decade later. *Health Education Quarterly, 11,* 1-47.

Kanfer, F. M. (1970). Self-monitoring: Methodolgical limitations and clinical applications. *Journal of Consulting and Clinical Psychology, 35,* 148-152.

Rotter, J.B. (1954). *Social Learning and Clinical Psychology.* N.Y.: Prentice Hall.

Triandis, H. C. (1980). Values, attitudes and interpersonal behavior. In H.E. Howe and M.M. Page (Eds.), *1979 Nebraska Symposium on Motivation.* Lincoln, Neb: Univ. of Nebraska Press, pp 195-259.

Encouraging Discussion with Partners and Building Negotiation Skills: HIV Prevention Strategies for Women in Relationships in Brazil, Tanzania and Indonesia

Susan E. Middlestadt, Academy for Educational Development

ABSTRACT

This presentation will discuss results from a research and intervention project being conducted in Brazil, Tanzania and Indonesia. The participants in each country are women in relationships. The goal is to increase their discussions with their partners about sex, health and ways to protect themselves from AIDS. Women are at risk of HIV disease, not only because of their own behavior but also, and often primarily, because of the behavior of their partners. For a woman, condom use is not a behavior. She must ask and then convince her partner to use a condom. A woman who has decided to limit herself to one sexual partner must also convince her partner to be monogamous. Thus, talking, discussing and negotiating represent important behaviors to analyse, understand and influence. Results show that many women recognize the benefits of such discussion in protecting themselves from AIDS, in bringing them closer to their partners and in helping him change his behavior. However, they also see negative consequences in making him angry, causing him to leave and making him suspicious. Women who talked with their partners differed significantly from those who don't in their perceptions of what significant others, such as closest friends, doctors, church members, thought they should do. Strategies for increasing dialog will be discussed. Special attention will be given to the challenges of applying consumer research tools in developing countries.

INTRODUCTION

Around the world, HIV infection is increasing and it is increasing most rapidly among women. The World Health Organization estimates that as of 1992 from 10 to 12 million adults have been infected by HIV and expects this number to reach 30 to 40 million by the year 2000. Further, the male-female ratio is soon expected to reach unity. There has not, however, been a corresponding increase in the number of successful HIV prevention programs for women. While there are many programs for women in the commercial sex industry, there are few for women in relationships. Furthermore, as yet, there are no effective methods of risk reduction that are completely under the woman's control. Abstinence and condom use require the cooperation if not the initiation of the partner. The "female" condom not only will be a long time in becoming widely available but will require the partner's knowledge and consent. Monogamy is successful for a woman only if her partner was, is and remains monogamous. In sum, women are at risk of HIV disease, not only because of their own behavior but also, and often primarily, because of the behavior of their partners. And, interventions are needed that help women influence the behavior of their partners. At the same time, it is clear that to be effective, programs for women must be developed in the context of her social, economic and/or emotional dependence on her partner. Briefly, the potential negative responses of the partner are often feared consequences of discussing AIDS, often more feared than AIDS itself.

The goal of this project is to understand the communication and negotiation behaviors of a woman with her partner and, based on this understanding, to design interventions that reduce constraints, communicate benefits and build skills around discussion with partners. In describing this project, this paper will illustrate a research process that is very different from the type of research process practiced in either academic institutions or commercial market research agencies. In essence, the research is conducted in an applied, social marketing context. Furthermore, it is collaborative one, not only between countries but between researchers, program designers and the people served by the project, its constituents.

RESEARCH CONTEXT

The Women in Development project is one activity of a larger project, the AIDS Technical Support: Public Health Communication Component (AIDSCOM). AIDSCOM is funded by the Offices of Education, Health and Population, Bureau for Research and Development, United States Agency for International Development (Project No. 936-5972, Contract No. DPE-5972-Z-00-7070-00). The AIDSCOM project is conducted by a team of five organizations, the Academy for Educational Development, Porter/Novelli, the Johns Hopkins University, the Annenberg School of Communication at the University of Pennsylvania and Prism/Day. This staff of this team provides technical assistance in the design, implementation, and evaluation of HIV/AIDS prevention programs in developing countries. The programmatic activity of the AIDSCOM project has a common set of objectives around using communications for behavior change to help prevent and control HIV disease. Similarly, the research is guided by a centralized research agenda. Within this common framework, specific projects and country programs are adjusted to the needs of the country and are conducted by local governmental and nongovernmental programmatic and research agencies.

The Women's project is being conducted in three sites: Rio de Janeiro, Brazil; Dar es Salaam, Tanzania; and Jakarta, Indonesia. Not only are these three sites from different regions of the world, but they represent different phases in the course of the epidemic. In Brazil and in Tanzania, HIV/AIDS has been recognized a problem for many years; there has been much attention in the media; and most everyone has heard of AIDS and knows the basics of sexual transmission. However, Brazil and Tanzania differ in the status of the epidemic among women. In Brazil, early cases were primarily male and it is only now that women are accounting for a significant proportion of the cases. In Tanzania, women have accounted for about half of the cases from the beginning. In contrast to both Brazil and Tanzania, HIV/AIDS is a relatively new issue in Indonesia. Infection seems to be entering through the international drug and commercial sex industries. As yet, there are few reported cases and the general population is not fully aware of how their sexual behavior places them at risk.

As a multi-site project, we have a particularly long list of collaborating agencies and individuals. Kathryn Carovano and Lorraine Lathan-Parker are coordinating the project with me in Washington. In Brazil, we are working with women attending family planning clinics through BEMFAM, a family planning organization. Our constituents are adult, sexually active women who are formally married, in consensual union with a companion or in steady relationships. Carmen Guimaraes, Elisabeth Verraz and Vera Vital Brasil are our in-country colleagues. In Tanzania, we are working with women insurance workers through OTTU, the women's department of a labor union and BIMA, an organization of insurance agencies. These women have jobs and are more educated than rural women in Tanzania; about half are married and half are not yet married. Again, all are sexually active. Lizbeth Loughran, Maudline Castico and Siham Ahmed are directing the project in Tanzania. In Indonesia, we are working with women attending a University of Indonesia clinic through LPT, an applied research unit of the Universty. The women attending the clinic are urban and moderately educated. Because of the culture, we are working with only married women in Indonesia. Bernadette Setaidi and Ninuk Widyantoro are our associates in Indonesia.

METHOD

The project consists of four phases: qualitative research; quantitative research; intervention; and evaluation. During Phase I, a qualitative study using face-to-face interviews is conducted with 40 women from each of the populations. The open-ended questions were designed to elicit salient outcomes, salient referents and effective strategies for two behaviors, "discussing with my partner the things we both need to do to protect ourselves from AIDS" and "asking my partner to use a condom everytime." Data from open-ended questions are then used to design the questionnaire for Phase II, a quantitative survey with about 200 women at each site. In addition, to demographics, knowledge about AIDS and practice of general health communication behaviors, the survey tapped constructs from three major theories of behavior, the theory of reasoned action, social cognitive theory and the health belief model.

An analysis of the Phase II survey is being used to provide input as to the content of Phase III, the intervention with about 100 women. In each country, the logic and form of the intervention is the same. It consists of weekly sessions with groups of women. The weekly meetings provide the women with a source of social support for behavior change. A facilitator using a structured guide will help the women who have successfully negotiated share their experiences and strategies with the women who have not. Through role playing and other interactive activities, the women can practice and improve their skills. In each case, the goal of the intervention is the same, to encourage communication and negotiation with partners. However, the degree of negotiation and the specific strategies to be used will evolve from the women, based on the data from the quantitative survey and the discussion groups. Phase IV is an evaluation with both qualitative and quantitative aspects.

Thus, the methodology of the project, both in its research and in the intervention aspects, is oriented toward the constituents or in the language of social marketing, the consumers. This consumer approach helps ensure that the research and the intervention are effective, appropriate and sensitive to the particular social and cultural context of each group of women. In addition to research findings, a final product will be a revised facilitator's guide that is appropriate for the constituents who helped in its development.

RESULTS

The project is still underway. But I would like to take the opportunity to illustrate this particular type of consumer research process by discussing some early findings. This paper will discuss qualitative findings on the specific communication and negotiation behavior chosen for study and for intervention, the consequences of communication and negotiation elicited from the open-ended questions of advantages and disadvantages, the referents given by the women as approving or disapproving, and the strategies recommended by the women as potentially useful.

Target behavior

A major decision in designing behavior change interventions is the selection and definition of the target behavior. The behavioral researcher plays a major role in this decision process. All too often, program design focuses on providing information and educating people. Attention is paid to selecting the target consumer, deciding what they need to know and choosing an appropriate channel to reach that consumer. In many social marketing domains, particularly health domains, the assumption is made that making people aware of the disease or condition and knowledgeable that they are at risk and that they can take certain steps to reduce that risk is sufficient to motivate behavior change. Thus, many HIV control programs begin by making people aware of the epidemic, teaching them about modes of transmission and recommending safer sex practices. In our work on HIV disease, we have found that this approach does not work for very many, if any, people. Instead, it is necessary to take a behavioral approach, that is, to define the target behavior and its determinants and to work back from that behavior. An important job of the behavioral researcher is to help the team define "what we want to encourage the women to do."

A key conclusion of the AIDSCOM Women in Development project is that the primary negotiation behavior to be addressed by the intervention needs to be different for the three different groups of women. While, after the fact, this is not surprising given the vast differences in the cultural context of the three groups of women we are working with, a discussion of the definition issues usefully illustrates the consumer research process necessary for AIDS prevention work. We began the project planning to study two behaviors, "talking with my husband or steady partner about the sex, health and AIDS prevention strategies" and "always using condom with my husband or steady partner" and hoping to intervene on one, the talking behavior. Based on pilot research with each group of women, the behavior eventually studied in detail and targeted by the intervention differed in terms of the *topic* of the discussion, the description and definition of the *partner* with whom the discussion was to occur and the specific communication or negotiation *action* recommended.

In terms of the *topic*, we knew we didn't want to encourage the discussion of "AIDS" or even "AIDS prevention". One can discuss AIDS without discussing changes in one's own sexual behavior. Discussing AIDS can mean discussing someone else's problem (e.g., foreigners, promiscuous people, gay men, prostitutes) and AIDS prevention can mean avoiding people with AIDS or taking steps to restrict the activity of people with AIDS or groups perceived to be at higher risk. The risk reduction strategy to be discussed would need to differ by country, by population and by individual. Thus, we didn't just want the couple to talk about condoms, either inside or outside the relationship. Condom use might be appropriate for some couples, but other changes in sexual behavior might also be effective strategies to discuss. In the pilot work to Phase I, we tried "sex, health and AIDS prevention strategies." We felt these three terms combined things women could easily talk about (health), with those that were more difficult (sex) and with a reason to combine them (AIDS prevention) without designating a particular risk reduction strategy. In Indonesia, using this topic, we found that the women felt we were talking about three completely different topics that had no relationship to one another. The term "strategies" was too abstract. More important, it seemed that the women in Indonesia, not being highly exposed to communications on AIDS and AIDS prevention, were not yet fully aware that their sexual behavior was connected to AIDS prevention. In Tanzania and in Brazil, we opened with a paragraph listing a variety of risk reduction strategies (all of which were familiar to the women) and noted that they all required talking with their husband or steady partner. In Tanzania, the paragraph ended with the need to talk about the "things we both need to do to protect ourselves from AIDS." In Brazil, the talk was to be about "AIDS, the risk of infection, and about how both of you can prevent and take care of yourselves." Notice the emphasis on both members of the couple. This approach was more successful, perhaps because of the increased familiarity of the urban women in Brazil and Tanzania with HIV and AIDS.

Naturally given that partnership patterns are a major source of differences between and within cultures, the *partner* with whom the discussion was to occur differed for the different groups of women. We wanted to designate a sexual partner with whom the women had a longer-term and committed relationship. Difficulties with communication and negotiation are the greatest in longer term relationships. In Indonesia, all the women were married, so the husband was the appropriate choice. In Brazil, the term husband or steady partner seemed to communicate about one partner to women in formal marriages as well as to those in consensual unions and to those in steady relationships. In Tanzania, we began with the term "husband or steady partner". For some marrried women, this phrase implied two different men. We therefore explicitly asked the women in Tanzania to think of one man: for married women, their husband and for unmarried women, their fiance or special boyfriend.

The specific *action* to be studied and targeted for change by the intervention also differed. It became clear in our pilot work, that there were a variety of possible communication and negotiation behaviors and that the appropriate one to encourage would depend on the particular context and culture of each group of women. For this project, we felt that an appropriate action to choose would be one that *some* but *not all* women in our constituent group were already practicing. If no women were yet practicing it, we would run the risk of encouraging a communication behavior that would put our constituents at risk of harm. If all the women were practicing it, there would be no room for change. In Brazil, in consultation with our colleagues, we began with "conversa", talking. On the basis of responses to behavior, intention and attitudinal questions, we verified that about half of the women were positively predisposed toward talking and about half were not. Thus, we seemed to have identified an action that was possible in that some women were already practicing the behavior, yet around which there was still room for change.

In contrast, we found in our qualitative research in urban Tanzania that the women were already talking to their partners. They found it easy to talk, almost 100% had ever talked and many had asked their partners to use a condom. This is not surprising given the length of time AIDS has been an issue, particularly for our constituents in Tanzania, relatively highly educated, urban and employed women. Thus, it was necessary and possible to go beyond the behavior of talking to more difficult and potentially more effective negotiation behaviors.

TABLE 1
Communication and Negotiation Terms in Tanzania

kuzungumzana	to talk with him
kujadiliana	to discuss with him
kushauriana	to advise each other
kumuomba	to ask him (to use a condom)
kumsisitiza	to insist/urge him (to use a condom)
kumshawishi	to convince/persuade him (to use a condom)
kumlazimisha	to force him (to use a condom)
kukataa	to refuse (to have sex if he won't use a condom)
kutumia na yeye	to use (a condom) with him

Table 1 presents a list of negotiation and communication terms that we considered and discussed with our colleagues and constituents in Tanzania. Notice they range from easy ones like talking, to more difficult ones like refusing to have sex if he won't use a condom. We decided that on the basis of the qualitative data alone, we could not select a single behavior to study in detail in Tanzania. Thus, the Phase II questionnaire used in Tanzania contained four sections, one each on four behaviors representing different points of difficulty: discussing with him, forcing him to use a condom, refusing to have sex if he wouldn't use and using a condom. And, analyses of the Phase II data would help decide the behavior to target as well as to identify potential determinants.

More generally, this list of negotiation behaviors illustrates another key conclusion of the project, that communication or negotiation represents not one behavior and not even a set of behaviors. Communication and negotiation represent a sequence, series or continuum of connected behaviors. A woman in deciding whether or how to try to negotiate with her partner, a behavioral scientist trying to understand and a program designer deciding where to intervene all must recognize that the behaviors are linked. And further, the goal of the behaviors is an outcome, to produce a change in the behavior of another.

Consequences of negotiating

Most theories of behavior recognize the role of the positive and negative consequences of a behavior in influencing the practice of that behavior. Thus, in the qualitative research phase of this project, the women were asked to indicate the advantages and disadvantages of talking with their partner. Before examining these responses, it is useful to consider their complexity. Table 2 presents a particularly informative quotation from a 28 year old, single woman with no children who participated in the qualitative phase in Tanzania.

TABLE 2

28 year old, single Tanzanian woman with no children

"Mambo mabaya ambayo yanaweza yakatokea kwa mfano tumeongelea kuhusu bila uaminifu na yeye amekwenda kinyume matokeo yake ndio hivyo bila janga litatupata namatokeo yake tutakufa na ni cha sisi wenyewe ninaweza kuenea kwa taifa zina kwasababu anaweza kutembea na kila mtu na matokeo yake hili tatizo mali taifa na huu ugonjwa ilaendelea kutumaliza."

"the bad things that may happen will (be) caused by the disloyalty of my partner. Because when we agree with each other, he pretends to appreciate the action we have taken, then on the other hand, he goes with other women without a condom. Now comes the consequences, he will carry AIDS, I will also get it, both of us will die, then this problem will affect the whole nation."

This quotation describes a chain of consequences, similar to the sequence of behaviors discussed above. The initiation of a discussion may or may not lead to asking him to use a condom outside the relationship, which may or may not lead to him agreeing to use a condom, which may or may not lead to him using a condom, which may or may not lead to infection and death for the man, which may or may not lead to infection and death for the woman, which may or may not lead to social and economic consequences for the nation. As described above, in deciding whether or not to engage in a particular negotiation behavior, one must consider as one of the consequences of that behavior that another behavior might occur carrying its own set of consequences. Clearly, it is difficult both to decide and to study these behaviors as single behaviors in isolation.

Table 3 gives the consequences elicited from the qualitative studies conducted in the three sites. Notice that this list includes multiple versions of a number of consequences. The list represents more of a universe of consequences than the salient or top of mind consequences.

TABLE 3
Consequences of Negotiating Safer Sex with Partner

Advantages
   protect from AIDS
   protect from other sexually transmitted diseases
   protect from pregnancy
   help him change his behavior
   lead him to look for more information
   help me convince him to have only one partner
   help me convince him to use condoms
   make us closer together
   strengthen our relationship
   help us lead a long and happy life

Disadvantages
   protect from pregnancy
   make him angry
   cause him to walk out on me
   break our relationship
   make him have sex with others
   make him think I go with other men
   make him think I am unfaithful
   make him think I am suspicious of him
   make me think I am safe when I am not
   make him complain of less sexual satisfaction
   get jammed inside
   be expensive

Notice that these consequences are consequences of each of the negotiation behaviors, of asking, of persuading, of refusing to have sex and of using a condom and that many refer directly or indirectly to the outcomes resulting from the performance of these behaviors. This table illustrates a key point about consequences evident in this and many other studies on health behaviors, including HIV disease: the importance of NONhealth consequences as behavioral determinants. Clearly, some of the consequences are health consequences. The women are concerned that negotiation may or may not effectively protect them from AIDS, from other sexually transmitted disease and from pregnancy. And, indirectly, they perceive the discussion may or may not help him change his sexual behavior. However, most of the consequences on this list are NONhealth ones. The women are concerned about the positive and negative effects of negotiation on their relationship. These consequences must be addressed to help encourage women to initiate discussions with their partners.

The list of consequences was remarkably similar for the three different sites and is in fact similar for a variety of other target audiences. There are differences, however, between the groups in the association that these consequences have with behavior, both within and between the three sites.

Social referents for negotiating

There is substantial evidence that normative factors are important determinants of a variety of behaviors in the domain of HIV disease. On the one hand, this is obvious in that many of the behaviors are sexual behaviors that occur in interaction with another person. Less obviously, it is becoming increasingly clear that sustained changes in sexual behavior are often based on changes in social norms. Open-ended questions on people who would approve and disapprove were asked to identify the potential reference groups.

TABLE 4
Social Referents for Negotiating Safer Sex with Partner

husband
partner
close women friends
parents
other relatives
   brother
   auntie
   same generation (saudara)
doctors and health workers
religious leaders
co-worker and neighbors
his family and friends

Table 4 gives the referents elicited from the three studies. There are few surprises in this list. As you can see, many of the referents are the same as for all behaviors, spouse, close friends, parents and other relatives. The three sites differed as to which specific other relatives were mentioned. Brothers were more frequently mentioned in Brazil; aunties, being traditionally responsible for education in sexual matters, were elicited in Tanzania; and in Indonesia, saudara or relatives of the same generation, were mentioned. Health professionals are frequently mentioned when considering a variety of health domains and religious leaders come up given the sexual behaviors that are at issue. A unique reference group was elicited in these studies, the friends and relatives of the husband. The woman's friends and relatives were most often mentioned as approving relatives; whereas, the man's relatives and friends were often listed as disapproving. Clearly, the concern for the reactions of the male partner extended to a concern for the social pressure being exerted on him by the others in his social environment.

Strategies for negotiating

It is also important to identify ways to facilitate effective negotiation. Open-ended questions were asked about the best time to talk, the best place to talk, topics that were easy to bring up, topics that were difficult to bring up and factors that would help discussion. Table 5 presents some of these results.

TABLE 5
Potential Strategies for Successful Negotiation

Passing information indirectly (through children)
Talking straight in a direct way
Mention news item to begin discussions
Mentioning names of friends and relatives who have died
Creating a relaxed setting
Referring to talk at work or visit to clinic
Having session with men

Notice that some of the women felt that discussion should occur indirectly, e.g., a discussion to the children with the husband listening or placing a pamphlet or a condom in the partner's suitcase when he is going away. Others felt that it was possible and more effective to approach the issue directly, in a straight way. Notice that many of the women felt it would be useful to have an external stimulus to initiate the discussion. A news article or a visit to the clinic could be a technique of giving a immediate reason for the discussion, outside of one's own behavior or suspicion about the other's behavior. Finally, a universal and immediate request at all three sites was to have a session with the men. In fact, this session was worked into the project as an additional optional session in Tanzania.

Perceived and actual skills in negotiating

Along with strategies for communication and negotiation comes skills at performing these behaviors. The women clearly felt a need to develop their skills in initiating discussions and in negotiating. Table 6 presents a quotation that effectively describes this need to know how to discuss.

TABLE 6
24 year old housewife from Brazil

"As pessoas dizem que tem medo de falar sobre isso, mas se eu tivesse um fundamento para falar a coisa certa, eu falaria."

"People say they are afraid to talk about this, but had I the knowledge to talk about it properly, I would talk about it."

CONCLUSIONS

One specific purpose of this presentation was to describe a particular research and intervention project, a project designed to develop strategies to help women in relationships protect themselves from HIV disease. The preliminary results from the research on this project have shown that one way to help women in relationships protect themselves from HIV disease is to help them communicate and negotiate with their partners. The research has identified potential intervention points in the form of consequences, social referents, strategies and skills. Upon completion, the project should result in specific, culturally sensitive and appropriate recommendations for interventions for women that address these points in the three sites of the project.

A second, more general purpose was to describe a particular research context, an applied collaborative social marketing research process. I hope from this presentation, I have provided some insight into how collaborative, applied research occurs and illustrated a number of advantages of this research process. Basically, in addition to the rewards of working with bright, motivated colleagues around the world and of making a social contribution, a collaborative research process highlights our methodological assumptions, encourages the use and integration of qualitative and quantitative methods, forces a focus on the consumer and challenges our theoretical definitions and conceptualizations. I hope I have inspired some consumer researchers to join me and my colleagues here and around the world in this collaborative work.

Media Magic: The Use of Media Monitoring Methodology to Develop AIDS Education Interventions

Carol Schechter, Academy for Educational Development
Susan E. Middlestadt, Academy for Educational Development
Lynne D. Doner, Porter/Novelli

INTRODUCTION

Press coverage of health issues often presents a mixed blessing for social marketers, particularly when the topic is AIDS. On one hand, the issue is always in the news. On the other, the messages conveyed by the news media rarely match the messages a program manager would like to communicate to his/her target audiences.

The influence of the media in shaping peoples' perceptions about AIDS is a factor that needs to be considered in the design of AIDS information or communication programs. The AIDS Communication Support Project, a technical assistance project funded by the Centers for Disease Control, attempted to construct a media monitoring system to help program planners include an assessment of the AIDS media environment in the development of their prevention and education programs. In my presentation today, I want to review with you some of the methodological issues we faced in developing the system, and demonstrate through three program examples how media monitoring can be used as a tool in the development of AIDS education programs.

Before discussing the methods and examples, however, I'd like to give you some background about the program and organization I work for, and the agency that funds our work, to give you some context for our media monitoring task. Along with Susan Middlestadt and Bill Smith on this panel, I work at the Academy for Educational Development, based in Washington DC. The Academy, along with two other organizations - Porter Novelli and the Johns Hopkins University - was privileged to be awarded a 5 year, $13 million contract with the Centers for Disease Control to assist their AIDS prevention programs.

The Centers for Disease Control (CDC) is a U.S. federal public health agency, headquartered in Atlanta, Georgia. The business of CDC is basically the prevention and control of disease. CDC refers to itself as the "Prevention Agency" and works largely in areas that are considered traditional public health - epidemiology, surveillance, and infectious disease control. They work primarily with and through state and local health departments. The emergence of AIDS as a serious health issue in the last decade has had a tremendous impact on how CDC does business, and approximately forty percent of CDC's current budget is now AIDS funding. Since a main focus of CDC is prevention, a large portion of this AIDS budget is devoted to developing and supporting HIV prevention programs at the national, state and local level.

The purpose of our project - The AIDS Communication Support Project - is to provide marketing and communications technical support to CDC, state and local health departments, and community organizations to improve their HIV/AIDS prevention programs. As part of our work, we began to look at developing a system to monitor AIDS messages in the media to assess how the media messages supported or competed with the educational messages we were trying to deliver through our various programs.

Content analysis is used for both theoretical and applied studies of mass communication. Content analysis of media coverage in an applied setting, however, is frequently not as formal or rigorous as in theoretical studies. It is used most often in applied settings as a process evaluation tool to assess the performance of a public relations tactic, such as a press kit or media event. Here the objective would be to capture the reach and accuracy of media coverage.

For example, a press conference sponsored by the National Cancer Institute on the 5-A-Day for Better Health program (encouraging Americans to eat five or more servings of fruits and vegetables each day) generated a very successful total of 700 newspaper stories and 41 million gross impressions in July 1992. Analysis of the media coverage indicated that NCI's nutritional messages for adults and children were reported fairly accurately.

In our project, however, we wanted to take content analysis one step further, to use it as a formative evaluation tool for designing programs. Our objectives were to identify and learn about AIDS messages disseminated in the media, and to assess their prevalence. Basically, we wanted to view the world through the eyes of our target audiences to explore the "reality" the average person is likely to construct based on his/her exposure to the mass media.

METHODOLOGY

At first glance, content analysis methodology appears relatively simple: obtain all the media coverage on a particular topic, read it and code it for key messages, then analyze and summarize the results. However, in our attempt to analyze media coverage of AIDS, we had to address three inter-related methodological issues:

- scope of the topic,
- taxonomy, and
- sampling frame.

All became issues because of the extensive and complex nature of media coverage of AIDS. During a one month period in November, 1991, for example, a sampling of the 15 top media markets produced over 1000 stories on AIDS compared with 93 stories on AZT and 10 stories following a publicity campaign on National Breast Cancer Awareness month. The large number of stories on AIDS pointed out how naive our original assumption was that we would just collect all the stories, code and analyze them. With such a large number of articles, we had to decide whether to collect all mentions of the AIDS coverage or only substantial mentions; and whether to focus on specific sub-topics or all AIDS coverage.

Sampling also became an issue given time and budget constraints and the extensive coverage. Decisions to be made included selection of print and/or broadcast-channels, time intervals and media markets.

The third area - and most challenging - was the construction of a taxonomy. The taxonomy is the coding system employed to capture the different issues and subjects addressed by the media. With a topic such as AIDS, sheer volume of coverage introduces interesting complexities of scale. The original taxonomy we developed contained over 400 categories. Figure 1 lists the broad (superordinate) categories we developed and Figure 2 presents detail under one category.

After working on the taxonomy for some time, it became apparent that we could not construct a meaningful taxonomy for all HIV/AIDS coverage. We would have to zero in on specific topics, focusing only on issues relevant to programmatic decisions. Let me

FIGURE 1

TAXONOMY

Primary Message Levels

1. HIV Virology and Immunology
2. Epidemiology
3. HIV Transmission
4. HIV Disease
5. Drug and Medical HIV Therapies
6. Services for PW/HIV/AIDS
7. Prevention/Control
8. Testing/Screening
9. Policy Developments/Debates
10. Psycho/Social Responses
11. Specific People/Groups Targeted or Affected
12. Agencies/Individuals Cited
13. Placement
14. International Developments

---

move to the discussion of specific program examples to illustrate what I'm talking about.

PROGRAM APPLICATIONS

The three examples I'm going to present all use stories related to Magic Johnson's dramatic announcement of his HIV status last November. Magic's announcement had a major impact on the amount of press coverage, the placement of stories and the messages addressed by the news media. HIV/AIDS stories began appearing in all sections of newspapers, including sports, style, as well as news sections. Analyzing coverage before and after this event presented an ideal opportunity to test issues in media monitoring methodology. Figure 3 shows a comparison of the number of stories in the top 15 media markets during three 4-week time intervals: 1 month before Magic's announcement, immediately following, and approximately 8 months following. Not surprisingly, the number of mentions of HIV/AIDS more than doubled in the month immediately following the announcement and has now almost returned to original level. The following three examples show how this coverage can be analyzed in more detail and used to provide input into program decisions.

CDC's National AIDS Hotline

The first example relates to coverage of CDC's National AIDS Hotline. The hotline operates a 24-hour toll free number (1-800-342-AIDS). Before Magic's announcement, call attempts to the hotline averaged 7000/day with occasional spikes depending on media coverage of issues. Call attempts skyrocketed to over 150,000/day immediately following Magic's announcement.

The increase in calls led CDC to conduct varied analyses around the public's use and perceptions of the hotline. One question raised was whether the public associated CDC with sponsorship of the hotline, and media coverage was one source of information used to answer this question. Figure 4 shows CDC hotline mentions before and after Magic's announcement relative to mentions of other state and local hotlines during the same time periods. From these data, it is clear that mentions of hotlines, both CDC's and other hotlines increased significantly. Figure 5 shows how CDC's hotline was referred to in various stories. Notice that the high frequency of mentioning CDC in referring to the National hotline. As a result of these and other analyses, CDC changed the official hotline name from the National AIDS Hotline to CDC's National AIDS Hotline to improve recall and recognition of sponsorship.

Homosexuality versus Heterosexuality

The second example looks at coverage of homosexual versus heterosexual transmission of AIDS. Part of the challenge of AIDS education is to make people aware that HIV does not only occur in gay/homosexual populations. Certain sexual behaviors put people at risk for HIV, and disease transmission occurs among straight and bisexual people as well as gay men. After Magic Johnson's announcement, it seemed likely that HIV/AIDS press coverage would focus more on heterosexual transmission and/or women affected by the disease, compared to prior coverage centering on men and/or homosexual transmission. To test this hypothesis, HIV/AIDS media coverage in the top 15 U.S. media markets was further analyzed for type of transmission discussed. The right side of Figure 6 shows the proportion of HIV/AIDS coverage mentioning women and/or heterosexuality in conjunction with HIV/AIDS for the three time periods. Before the announcement, 25% of the stories mentioning women and/or heterosexual transmission; immediately after, this increased to 37%. Clearly, Magic Johnson's announcement influenced the discussion of heterosexual transmission factors in the media.

From a program planning standpoint, knowing that coverage shifted from focusing on HIV/AIDS as a "gay disease" affecting mostly gay or bisexual men to focusing on women and heterosexual transmission is important. A first step in a public education program is to raise awareness. Monitoring what the media are covering can help us gauge when the public is likely to be aware of a particular issue. Knowing that Magic's announcement and the resulting media coverage raised awareness of heterosexual transmission allows program planners to take advantage of this and further promote this message.

A next step in this particular program example would be to analyze the types of messages contained in the women/heterosexual stories and assess whether they are accurate and if they reflect program strategies. It would also be important to assess the

FIGURE 2

TAXONOMY

HIV Transmission

1. Unprotected sexual intercourse
    1. receptive anal
    2. receptive vaginal
    3. insertive anal/vaginal
    4. active-penile
    5. active-vaginal
    6. active-anal

2. Sharing Contaminated injection-drug works
    1. sharing syringe works
    2. sharing other paraphernalia

3. Perinatal (mother to fetus/newborn)
    1. in-utero
    2. during birthing
    3. breast-feeding

4. Transfusion/treatments with infected products
    1. blood transfusions
    2. organ/tissue transplants
    3. hemophilia treatments

5. Health care accidents
    1. needle sticks/other blood exposures from patients to health care worker, researcher, care-giver
    2. blood exposures from workers/instruments to patients

6. Co-factors for infection (in host)
    1. other STDs
    2. alcohol
    3. other chronic disease (e.g., allergies, diabetes)
    4. poorly managed stress
    5. pregnancy
    6. poor nutrition
    7. poor general health maintenance
    8. genetic vulnerability
    9. other

7. Other circumstances affecting transmission
    1. frequency of exposures
    2. violence/roughness
    3. infector's stage of HIV disease

8. Transmission myths
    1. social/workplace (non-sexual) contact
    2. contact with intermediate surfaces (e.g., eating ware)
    3. insect intermediaries

Level-four options for all of the above include (with multiple choices possible):
1. precise clarification of risk factors/their efficiency
2. general clarification of transmission "modes" (e.g., "sex" or "sexual intercourse") or "non-modes" (e.g., "can't get it from touching") without reference to specifics
3. objectively reporting an alleged transmission case

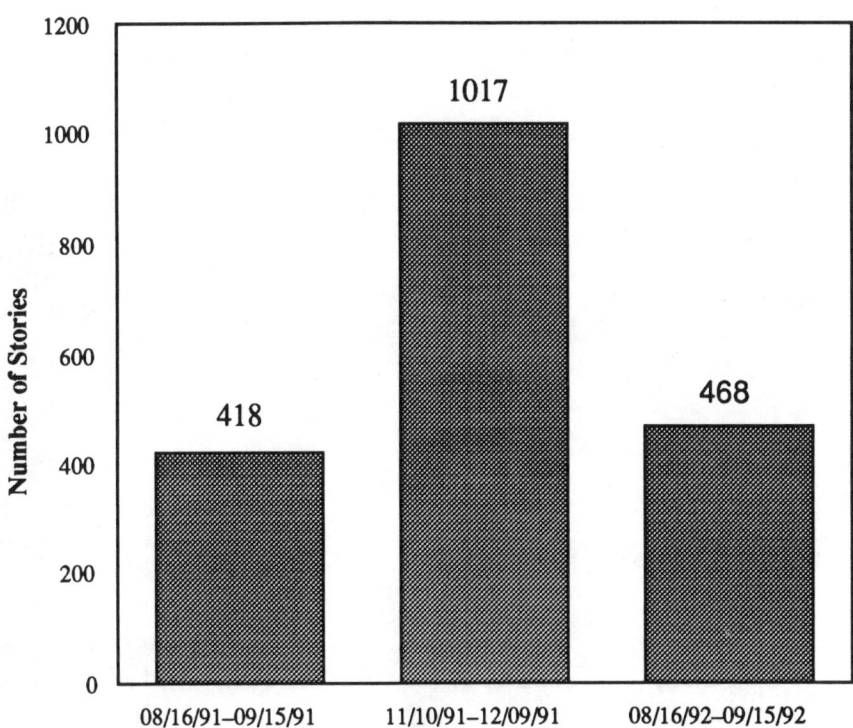

FIGURE 3
Total HIV/AIDS Stories: Top 15 Media Markets

Magic Johnson's Announcement: 11/07/91

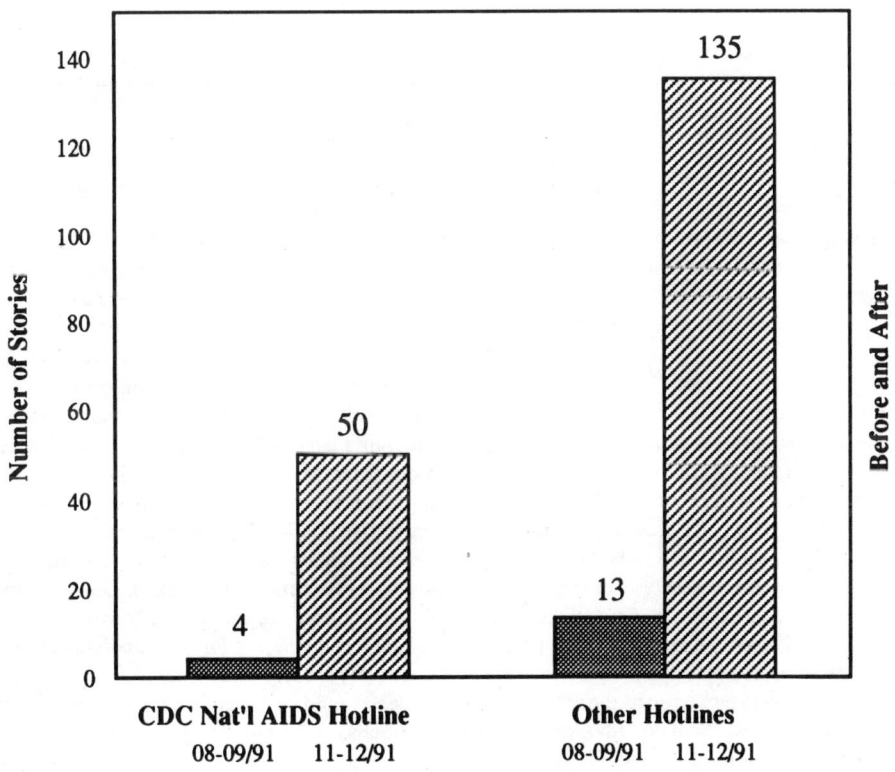

FIGURE 4
Stories Mentioning Specific Hotlines

FIGURE 5
Mentions of CDC's National AIDS Hotline by Wording of Reference

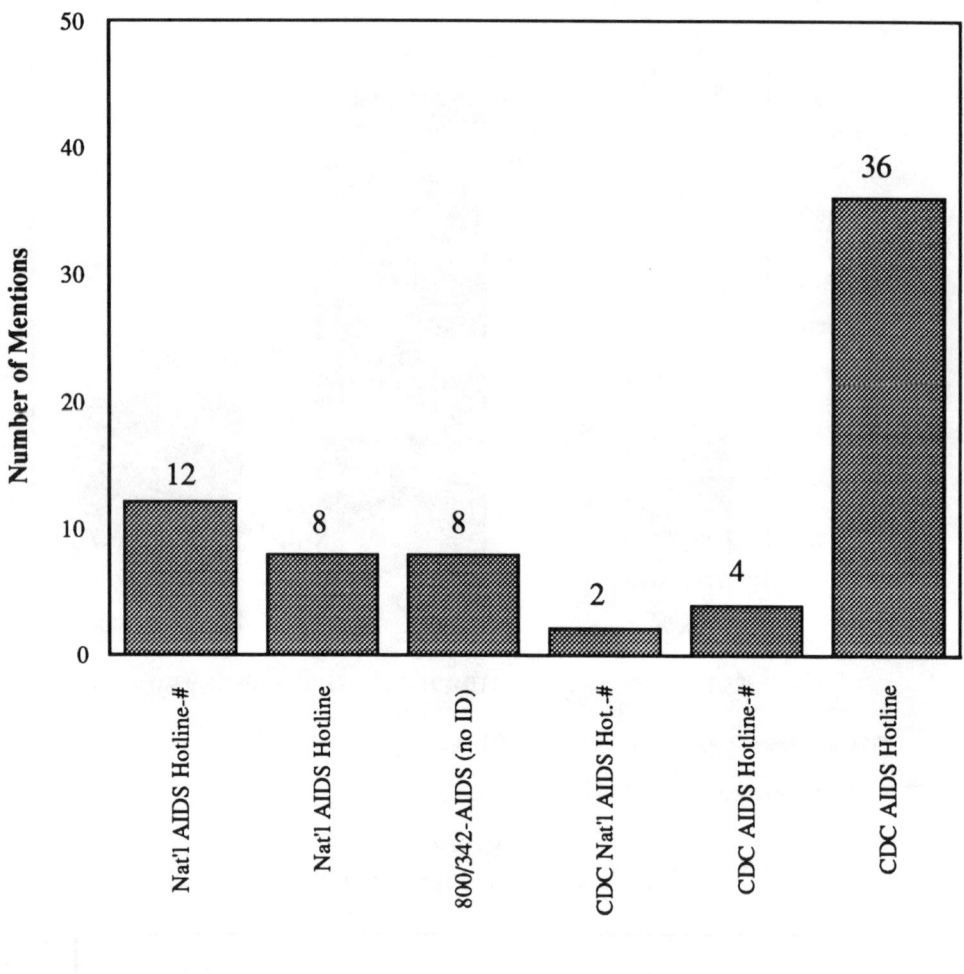

prevalence of other messages carried by the media. Some of these messages may be harmful because they are incomplete or inaccurate. Others may alert program planners to emerging issues, allowing them to determine if their communications should address such issues.

Coverage of condoms in schools

The third example looks at media coverage of condom distribution in schools. School condom distribution is a controversial proposal that has been introduced in a few urban centers. Figure 7 shows coverage of this topic, before and after Magic Johnson's announcement, nationally in 15 markets and in Washington D.C. where such a proposal was introduced. Analysis of this coverage could be very helpful to school districts and municipalities considering such an initiative. The media coverage would alert program planners to the salient issues raised by opponents in other geographic areas and which issues were picked up by the press. Based on this assessment, program planners could do "advance work" in their communities around these issues with community gatekeepers in the schools, churches, media and other key segments of the community. Under this scenario, media analysis could be used to construct a case study of a controversial topic.

SUMMARY

Content analysis in the form of media monitoring is a consumer research tool that has a number of practical applications for program planners. The three examples that have been presented today demonstrate its use in assessing sponsorship recall, determining when a message strategy shift may be warranted, and illustrating its use in providing case studies. The methodology, however, can be complex and imprecise, and careful design and planning is necessary to ensure its usefulness. Our recommendations based on this experience are that media monitoring *is* a valuable tool for program planning, but for it to be cost effective, researchers should work very closely with program planners, and the scope of the project should be carefully delineated to answer specific program questions.

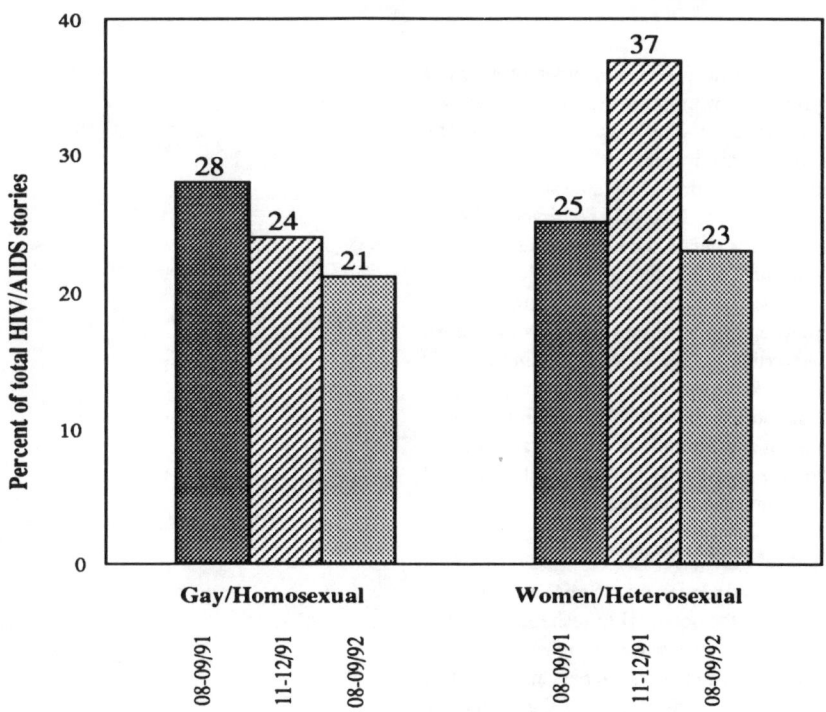

FIGURE 6
HIV/AIDS Coverage: Homosexual v. Heterosexual Mentions

Magic Johnson's HIV Announcement: 11/07/91

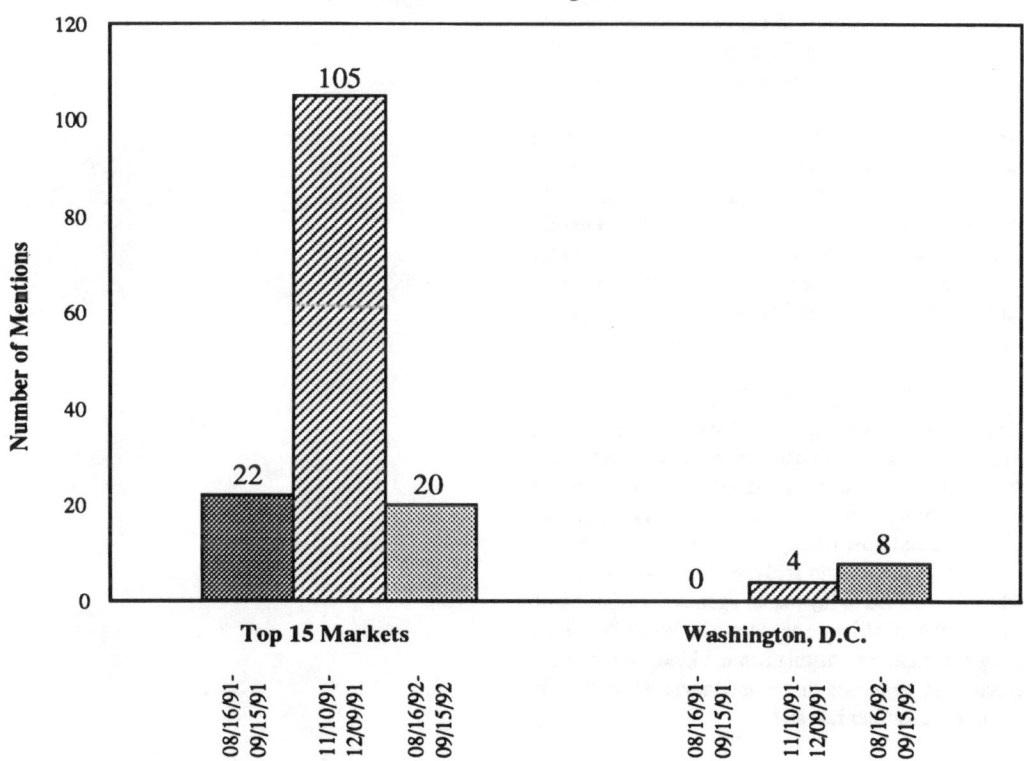

FIGURE 7
Trends in HIV/AIDS Coverage Related to Condoms in Schools
National v. Washington, D.C.

Magic Johnson's Announcement: 11/07/91

Special Topic Session: The New Advertising Rhetoric
Edward F. McQuarrie, Santa Clara University

The new advertising rhetoric offers consumer researchers fresh insights into the symbolic consumption that occurs whenever a consumer reads an advertisement. The old advertising rhetoric was scarcely visible in our discipline. It was fragmented, marginalized and infrequent, consisting of isolated studies of individual rhetorical figures, and lacking historical continuity with the rich literature on rhetoric that extends back thousands of years. Today the paradigmatic ferment within the discipline, consequent to the emergence of postmodern perspectives, has created a receptive climate for rhetoric to emerge as a unifying perspective for consumer research on advertising. The new advertising rhetoric will build on the contributions of aesthetics, hermeneutics, literary theory, and, above all, semiotics. The new advertising rhetoric dreads being dismissed as an arid formalism, despises subjectivity and obscurantism, and drives relentlessly toward an integration of form and function, device and impact, text and reader.

SESSION OBJECTIVE

The objective of this special session was to raise awareness of rhetoric as a discipline having the potential to reshape consumer research on advertising. The session was proposed out of a conviction that rhetoric offers consumer researchers an integrative view of how advertising works — an integration that cannot be found outside of rhetoric. The guiding assumption was that advertising is primarily a rhetorical phenomenon: it is communication with an ulterior motive, communication that seeks to use any available device for the achievement of its ends.

The distinctive excellence of rhetoric is the way that it links form to function. Rhetoric both illuminates the formal devices used in advertising, *and* explicates how and why these devices affect consumers. Rhetoric teaches how to construct a form so as to achieve a desired effect. Aristotle defined rhetoric as "the faculty of discovering all the available means of persuasion in any given situation." Implicit in this definition is the idea that there exists a limited number of formal devices capable of achieving certain effects, and that in any given situation some of these devices will be applicable and others not. Rhetoric seeks to understand *what works* in the area of persuasive communication. What makes rhetoric noteworthy in the context of contemporary debates in consumer research is that it expects to find the answer to "what works" in a limited and structurally differentiated set of formal and stylistic devices.

PAPERS PRESENTED

The McQuarrie and Mick paper, published in this volume, adapted ideas from Classical Rhetoric to examine the incidence and nature of rhetorical figures in magazine advertising. Scott's paper introduced reader response theory—a contemporary rhetorical approach— and discussed how its key concepts could illuminate ads that were otherwise difficult to analyze. McCracken's paper drew on Elizabethan rhetoric to lay out an agenda for what a true advertising rhetoric should strive to accomplish. Wells discussed the session using a metaphor to distinguish the kinds of moderate and radical changes in emphasis that a new advertising rhetoric might bring about in consumer research.

Reflections on Classical Rhetoric and the Incidence of Figures of Speech in Contemporary Magazine Advertisements

Edward F. McQuarrie, Santa Clara University
David Glen Mick, University of Florida

ABSTRACT

A key concept in Classical Rhetoric is the *rhetorical figure* (figure of speech), defined as an artful arrangement of words or meanings designed to produce a specific effect on an audience (e.g., metaphor, alliteration). We discuss the relevance of Classical Rhetoric to consumer advertising research, and develop propositions about the incidence and function of rhetorical figures. A preliminary study of *People* suggests that rhetorical figures occur frequently. We conclude with suggestions for how future research on rhetorical figures might proceed.

The purpose of this paper is to argue for and begin to develop the importance of ideas from Classical Rhetoric in understanding how advertising achieves its effects. Although there have been a few studies of individual rhetorical figures (Deighton 1985; Hitchon 1991; Ward and Gaidis 1990), and of specific devices used in ad headlines (Howard and Barry 1988; Swasy and Munch 1985), rhetorical analysis per se has not yet found its place in the toolkit of consumer researchers. Early efforts have typically lacked historical continuity with the rich literature on rhetoric that extends back thousands of years (Corbett 1990; Vickers 1988). Only recently have consumer researchers begun to offer explicitly rhetorical analyses of advertising (McQuarrie and Mick 1992; Scott 1990; Stern 1990). Even today, most ACR members would not define rhetoric as a discipline. What has been lost sight of is that advertising, as persuasive discourse, is a form of rhetoric; and that for many centuries Rhetoric enjoyed a more positive reputation as that body of knowledge that explained how to construct an effective persuasive message. We believe that present-day consumer researchers can profit by reviewing this ancient discipline for fresh ideas about the specific devices used in advertisements and their likely effects on the consumer. In particular, we would suggest that rhetoric can function as a way to focus the broader insights offered by semiotics into the formal structure of texts (see also McQuarrie and Mick 1992; Mick 1986, 1987).

Rhetoric is about constructing a form so as to achieve a desired effect. Aristotle defined rhetoric as "the faculty of discovering all the available means of persuasion in any given situation" (Corbett 1990, p. 3). Implicit in this definition is the idea that there exists a finite set of formal devices capable of achieving certain effects, and that in any given situation some of these devices will be applicable and others not. Historically, rhetoric has been a practical discipline. It seeks to understand *what works* in the area of persuasive communication. What makes rhetoric noteworthy in the context of contemporary debates in consumer research is that it expects to find the answer to "what works" in a limited and structurally differentiated set of formal and stylistic devices.

The Rhetorical Figure

Classical Rhetoric refers to a body of ideas on how to persuade, move or delight an audience. These ideas were first codified in Athens during the 5th century B.C., subsequently flourished for nearly a thousand years, and then went into decline with the fall of Rome. During that period rhetoric evolved from a limited set of ideas applicable primarily to judicial oratory, into a more general discipline for successfully moving any audience, on any topic, using either oral or written means. After an interruption lasting centuries, Classical Rhetoric was revived during the Renaissance and once again became the centerpiece of the liberal arts curriculum and a leading concern of humanities scholarship. However, with the rise of modern science in the seventeenth century, rhetoric went into a long-term decline, until by the beginning of the 20th century rhetoric had almost completely disappeared as a scholarly discipline.

Today rhetoric is in the midst of a robust revival across a wide variety of humanities disciplines. Such well-known American literary critics as Booth, Bryant, Burke, and Frye have all drawn heavily from the rhetorical tradition. The reliance on rhetorical ideas is even heavier on the Continent. Such prominent structuralist and poststructuralist writers as Barthes, Derrida, Eco, Genette, and Todorov, among others, have all given extensive attention to one of the central preoccupations of Classical Rhetoric: the rhetorical figure.

In a definition that dates back to the Roman orator Quintilian, a rhetorical figure can be defined as "an artful deviation from normal usage." The best known example of a rhetorical figure, and the only one widely recognized among consumer researchers, is *metaphor* (Hitchon 1991; Ward and Gaidis 1990). It is safe to say that many advertisements make use of metaphors in their verbal and visual texts. It is also commonplace to remark on the presence of *rhetorical questions*, *puns*, and *hyperbole* in advertisements. Not at all commonplace is to point out the use of *metonymy*[1] and *litotes*[2] in advertising. *All* of these are instances of rhetorical figures. All the figures just listed have been catalogued, differentiated and interrelated for over two thousand years. And, as discussed below, all of these figures can be found in contemporary magazine advertisements.

Rhetorical analysis also facilitates an examination of the underlying principles that differentiate and unite subsets of figures. An example is the pioneering work of Durand (1987), who generates a matrix of 20 rhetorical figures by means of distinguishing four operations and five types of relations among the elements within each figure. Thus, within Durand's scheme, a metaphor can be defined as the operation of substitution performed using two elements that are similar, while a metonym can be defined as the same operation of substitution, now performed using two elements that are different. Durand's schema is one example of how rhetoric uncovers patterns and rules within the set of formal devices available to advertisers.

Humanities scholars have argued that contemporary advertising is rife with rhetorical figures. As Corbett (1989) remarks: "I have on a number of public occasions declared that the Madison Avenue ad writers are among the most skillful practitioners of Aristotelian rhetoric in our times." However, to our knowledge there have been no prior attempts to catalogue the rhetorical figures found in contemporary advertising. Hence, we formulated the

---

[1] Metonymy (me-TON-y-my) uses an associated feature of an object to stand for the object as a whole: "by order of the Crown," as opposed to "by order of the King."

[2] Litotes (LIT-ot-es) refers to the deliberate use of understatement in order to accentuate the impressiveness of a claim.

following proposition to serve as a guidepost for the exploratory investigation reported in this paper.

Proposition 1. Rhetorical figures are widespread in the headlines of contemporary magazine advertising in the United States.

By widespread we mean that such figures can be found across a variety of audiences, magazines, product categories, and message strategies. Assuming Proposition 1 can be supported, why does advertising go beyond what is required by models of attitude structure and information integration? More broadly, if it can be shown that contemporary advertising makes heavy use of exactly the same verbal manipulations that were catalogued and used over 2500 years ago in a far different cultural context and another language, this would suggest that a study of rhetorical figures might reveal something rather basic about human communication.

To demonstrate that rhetorical figures are widespread in contemporary advertisements would require an extensive content analysis of a large and carefully constructed sample of ads drawn from a diverse set of magazines. Moreover, the subtlety with which rhetorical figures are defined, and the large number of these figures, would probably require the use of specialists in rhetoric and not just the graduate student judges routinely used in academic content analyses. Identifying whether a headline makes use of metaphor or litotes is a going to be a more challenging endeavor than, for example, determining whether or not a headline takes the form of a question (e.g., Howard and Barry 1988).

In light of the complete absence of any research on the incidence of rhetoric, and in view of the daunting challenges posed by a rigorous content analysis, we saw an opportunity to conduct a preliminary and exploratory analysis that would provide some insights regarding the pronouncements of scholars such as Corbett and also lay a foundation for more extensive analyses. Hence, we selected one of the most widely read magazines in the United States and inventoried the contents of several issues spread over a year's time, applying our personal understanding of the domain of rhetorical figures. What follows, then, should be thought of as a tabulated text analysis and not a formal content analysis.

METHOD

Sample and Procedure

People was selected as the magazine vehicle. During the first nine months of 1991 *People* had the highest advertising revenue of any magazine, and the fourth highest number of ad pages sold. It is widely read across age, gender and education levels. Three issues were randomly selected for examination: February 4th, August 5th, and December 9th. All full-page ads were removed, numbered and catalogued. The authors examined each ad for the presence of rhetorical figures inventoried in Corbett (1990) and described below. The analysis and findings are open to public scrutiny in the form of an Appendix, a copy of which can be obtained by writing the authors, which lists the headlines and the rhetorical devices identified therein. This Appendix provides a check on any tendency to exaggerate the number of rhetorical devices, but does not foreclose the possibility that the authors have underestimated the number of certain figures. However, here too a check is possible, in that any reader may obtain the three magazine issues mentioned and conduct an independent audit.

Inventory of Rhetorical Devices

A modified version of the inventory in Corbett (1990, pp. 427-460), containing a total of 30 devices, was developed.[3] While this is by no means a complete inventory of devices that might be found in advertising (Renaissance scholars typically identified between 100 and 200), it has the advantage of being both wide ranging and manageable. In discussing these figures, we follow the convention used by Corbett and others, and divide the overall category of rhetorical figure into two subcategories termed *schemes* and *tropes*. Whereas a figure is any artful deviation from normal usage, a scheme is further differentiated as an artful deviation in the arrangement or selection of the words themselves (e.g., alliteration), while a trope is an artful deviation in sense or meaning (e.g., metaphor). A list of the schemes and tropes along with definitions is included as Appendix A.

The examination of each ad concentrated on the headline, defined as text in a large typeface positioned so as to be the first thing read. In those cases where the headline did not contain any figure, we also examined sub-heads and taglines—i.e., text in large type occupying subordinate positions within the ad. However, the examination did not include body copy and also ignored the visual components, unless these interacted with a headline.

RESULTS

A total of 154 full-page ads[4] were found in the three issues of *People*. Of these, 120 (78%) contained one or more figures in the headline. Of the 34 ads that did not, 12 did have a figure in a subhead, yielding a total of 132 ads (86%) containing figurative headlines or subheads (hereafter, "heads"). This finding provides preliminary support for the idea that rhetorical figures may be ubiquitous in contemporary magazine ads.

The 22 ads that did not contain a recognizable figure in the heads seem to fall into 5 distinct groups. In 2 cases there was no headline or subhead at all. In 5 cases, the headline simply named the product ("Superslims from Virginia Slims"). In 3 cases, the headline took the form of an announcement of something new ("Now a national weekly entertainment magazine"). In 7 cases the headline ascribed some property to the product ("For colds and flu, doctors recommend Tylenol 6 times more often than aspirin.") Five cases were not readily classifiable.

Headlines that name, announce, or ascribe properties will be familiar to readers of advertising textbooks. Naming serves an awareness-building function; announcements harness the attention-getting power of news; and ascriptions are consistent with multiattribute judgment models in which one of the goals of advertising is to inform the consumer that the product possesses some attractive feature. The rarity with which such formulations appear in *People*, unaccompanied by any rhetorical figure, suggests that contemporary accounts that do not incorporate a rhetorical perspective may be neglecting an important characteristic of advertisements.

Turning now to the figurative ads (again, a complete listing may be obtained by writing the authors), there were 22 ads that

---

[3]Six schemes were omitted because of some doubt whether they constitute "artful deviations" from normal speech, in view of their frequent use in ordinary discourse (e.g., apposition, parenthetical remarks). Also, two tropes (synecdoche and metonymy) were combined into one, since a number of scholars have argued that the two are not readily distinguishable. Lastly, we differentiated some puns as instances of resonance, along lines described in McQuarrie and Mick (1992).

[4]Included in this tabulation are ads that occupy more than one page, ads that occupy the bottom halves of two neighboring pages, and the like.

APPENDIX A
Inventory of Figures from Classical Rhetoric With Definitions

SCHEMES

Figures of Repetition

Alliteration	Repetition of consonants (not necessarily at the beginning of words)[1]
Assonance	Repetition of vowel sounds[2]
Anaphora	Repetition of words at the beginning of successive clauses[3]
Epistrophe	Repetition of words at the end of successive clauses
Anadiplosis	Repetition of a word at the end of one clause and the beginning of the next
Epanalepsis	Repetition of a word at the beginning and end of a clause

Other schemes

Parison	Parallel structure
Antithesis	The use of words opposite in meaning
Antimetabole	Repetition of words, in successive clauses, in reverse order

TROPES

Figures of Wordplay

Pun	Use of a word so that it can be interpreted in two different senses
Pun (resonance)	A pun that interacts with a visual representation
Antanaclasis	Repeating a word but giving it a different sense the second time
Syllepsis	Using a word so that it is understood differently in relation to two or more words that it moderates or governs

Figures of Indirection

Rhetorical question	An assertion in the guise of a question
Irony	A statement that means the opposite of its literal meaning
Hyperbole	An exaggerated claim
Litotes	An understated claim
Periphrasis	A roundabout way of naming something

Figures of substitution

Metaphor	Implied comparison
Metonym	Substitution of an attribute or part for the thing itself
Simile	An explicit comparison
Personification	Investing an abstraction or thing with human qualities

Other tropes

Anthimeria	Substituting one part of speech for another; deliberate misuse of words
Oxymoron	Linking two words that ordinarily contradict one another
Paradox	An apparently impossible statement that nonetheless contains some truth

NOTE. These definitions are based on, and in some cases drawn verbatim from, Corbett (1990, pp. 427-460), which should be consulted for additional explanation and numerous illustrations.

[1] We required three or more repetitions, although there are some doubles that might be judged alliteration by Classics scholars.
[2] In most cases we used the same rule of three repetitions for assonance. The exception was an obvious rhyme.
[3] The idea of a clause has to be interpreted somewhat flexibly in advertising as compared to lines of verse; we considered any prose unit, a phrase in length or longer, to be a clause.

---

contained only schemes, 79 that contained only tropes, and 28 that contained both. It is striking to note the broad range of figures uncovered in this small sample. With the exception of *onomatopoeia*, all of the tropes drawn from Corbett's (1990) inventory were present. Similarly, only 4 of the 13 schemes drawn from Corbett were missing (*asyndeton, polysyndeton, anastrophe and polyptoton*). In all we found 77 occurrences of 9 different schemes, and 123 occurrences of 16 distinct tropes. On average, there were about 1.5 figures (200/132) per figurative ad. Note that this total can be thought of as a lower bound; it does not include purely visual figures or figures in subheads and body copy that were not examined.

In terms of specific tropes, by far the most common is the pun and related categories (53 instances). In contrast to the trend in scholarly discussions, metonyms (11 instances) are almost as common as metaphors (17). In terms of schemes, all the figures of repetition are present. Alliteration is the most common scheme (24), with anaphora (12) and parison (15) also common.

DISCUSSION

The results from this small sample of ads support the idea that contemporary advertisements are highly figurative and amenable to an analysis in terms of Classical Rhetoric. It is apparent that these ads do not simply present information; rather, they carefully arrange words and meanings into recognizable patterns that have been named and discussed for thousands of years. Future research may build on this insight to clarify both the extent and function of figuration in advertising. Our review of the *People* ads together with a corpus of other ads we have subsequently collected and examined suggest three additional propositions for research, and these are presented following a reminder of the limitations that characterize the present study.

Limitations

First, *People* may be an unusual magazine as regards the incidence of rhetoric. It is easy to identify other magazines whose editorial content and audience are very different (e.g., *Business Week, GQ, Cosmopolitan, Architectural Digest*), and which may similarly reveal different incidences and selections of rhetorical figures. Second, shortcomings in our understanding of rhetoric may have led us to overlook or misclassify individual rhetorical figures present in the ads. Third, because our analysis of an individual ad stopped once a figure was detected in the headline, the tabulation of figures has to be regarded as partial. In particular, the relative frequency with which individual figures appeared should be treated with great caution. A figure that is suitable for use in subheads or taglines, but not headlines, would be under-counted in our analysis. More generally, figures that mostly appear in body copy or in a purely visual representation would not be captured. Lastly, our analysis focused exclusively on the rhetorical figure. There is much more to the discipline of rhetoric than a catalogue of rhetorical figures (see Corbett 1990).

Future Research

We believe that rhetorical figures may be less common in the verbal text of advertisements for fashion clothing than the analysis of *People* magazine reported here would suggest. An analysis of vehicles such as *Vogue* and *GQ* would probably yield a rather different inventory. A large part of the reason is that in many such ads, the only verbal element present is the name of the product and advertiser (it would be interesting to see whether such ads are similarly bare of visual rhetoric). Along related lines, cigarette advertising does not initially appear to make intensive use of verbal rhetoric, again in part because of a minimal use of words (however, the same caveat about visual rhetoric applies). More generally, we may infer that figurative language is more appropriate in the context of certain message strategies, and less appropriate in the context of others (Wells 1988).

Proposition 2. The relative frequency of rhetorical figures in magazine advertising is contingent upon product category.

Another area where rhetorical figures appear to be less common is direct response magazine ads, in which the reader is asked to either buy the product or write away for information. These would include ads for mutual funds appearing in *Money*, mail order ads for knick knacks appearing in *Family Circle* or *Good Housekeeping*, ads for record and book clubs, and the like. Perhaps this is why so much of the advice on how to write advertising emphasizes plain talk, the direct approach, and the avoidance of ornamentation. Much of the received wisdom in the area of copy writing was forged in the direct mail arena, where experimental manipulations have been both possible and diligently pursued for over 60 years. If rhetorical figures are, for whatever reason, less useful in the context of direct response advertising, then this would go some way towards explaining why conventional wisdom has so neglected rhetorical figures.

Proposition 3. The relative frequency of rhetorical figures is lower in the case of appeals for a direct response.

An important counterargument to our thesis would point out that just because rhetorical figures are common does not mean they are important. Some might argue that these figures are really no more than a "sugar coating," and of no great moment. That is, just as ads use bright colors, attractive people, diagonal elements, sharp visual angles, and dozens of other minor devices in an attempt to smooth the path of persuasion, so also ads are decked out in rhetorical figures—these figures are simply one more source of ornament. However, most studies of rhetoric reject the view that figurative language is simply an attractive ornament that can be added as an afterthought to a basic message that does the real work of communication (cf. Eco 1976). Rather, the preferred view has been that a rhetorical figure both communicates *differently*, and communicates *more*, than a straightforward delivery of the message would have (see Scott 1990 on this point). We think figures are ubiquitous in magazine advertising because of a recognition among practitioners that persuasion goes beyond rational arguments to include irrational and symbolic components.

Another way to put this is that advertisements in an expensive and widely circulated magazine such as *People* reflect the collective wisdom of the advertising community on how best to employ tens of thousands of dollars in media expenditure (a full-page ad in *People* costs about $100,000). Thus, for example, without anyone consciously deciding on this as a policy, headlines with alliteration tended to be selected over alternative headlines that lacked alliteration. Headlines that repeated key words, headlines that made use of wordplay, and so forth, also tended be chosen over headlines that did not, as advertisers continually asked themselves, Which of these candidate executions is most likely to achieve my purpose?

It is the task of scientific inquiry to elucidate exactly what the work is that figures do. But this requires an acknowledgement that figures are widespread in advertising, and that they are put there to perform some work. And that requires that we break free of the myth that the enterprise of advertising is best compared to logical argumentation and the transmission of facts, with a little affect transfer tossed in to sweeten the pill.

Proposition 4. Rhetorical figures enhance the effectiveness of magazine advertising in a direct, primary way.

Strategies for Future Research

One strategy would be to conduct an authoritative content analysis to investigate Propositions 1-3. The criteria to be met by this content analysis would include: 1) a coherent sampling strategy; 2) a cogent analysis of the components of a magazine ad that are to be examined for the presence of rhetoric; 3) an inventory of the rhetorical devices whose presence or absence is to be detected; and 4) a reliable and valid procedure for detecting whether a rhetorical device is present. The sampling strategy should incorporate a sufficient number of magazines to reflect the wide variety in what is published. At a minimum, places to look for rhetorical devices would include the verbal elements, the visual elements, and the interaction between verbal and visual elements. A variety of inventories have been compiled over the centuries. However, the relative abstraction with which rhetorical devices must be specified, and the variety of ad components where they might be found, together with the sheer number of devices that will be catalogued, make content analysis a daunting task. Hence, it may be necessary to use specially qualified analysts (i.e., instructors of rhetoric) in order to meet the fourth criterion.

Aside from such content analyses, the second avenue future research might take is to follow up on Proposition 4. Here it will be necessary to work at the level of individual figures and formulate and test their contribution to persuasion. Ultimately this inquiry should rest on an analytic grouping similar to that of Durand (1987), with propositions adumbrated for each analytic category of figures. Here we simply want to point to a few categories of figures to suggest how this work might proceed. A framework for experimental inquiry into advertising rhetoric can be found in McQuarrie and Mick (1992), who provide evidence for the effectiveness of the rhetorical figure they termed "resonance."

For example, *figures of repetition* may facilitate both comprehension and recall. Figures of repetition include *anaphora* (repetition of words at the beginning of successive clauses), *epistrophe* (repetition of words at the end of successive clauses), *epanalepsis* (repetition of a word at the beginning and end of a clause), and *anadiplosis* (repetition at the end of one clause and the beginning of the next). Such figures may facilitate comprehension by indicating to the reader that the repeated term is a key word around which the message is organized. Similarly, repetition of stimuli is a key factor in learning and memory, hence, the probable value of a scheme that repeats a key term in a prominent way. As a second example, *figures of indirection* may facilitate persuasion through provoking a self-generated inference from the reader. Figures of indirection would include *irony* (the statement means something other than what it says), *hyperbole* (the statement presents an extreme claim), *litotes* (the statement says less than is meant), *rhetorical questions* (an assertion in the guise of a question), and *periphrasis* (a roundabout way of describing something). In his analysis of several of these figures, Fogelin (1988) suggests that they be analyzed as indirect speech acts. These figures require the reader to correct what is said in order to infer what is really meant. This in turn can be mapped onto Kardes' (1988) work on self-generated inferences (see also Swasy and Munch 1985). We might say that these are figures that seduce or invite the reader into co-constructing the advertiser's message.

We hope to have opened the reader's eyes to the rich resources offered by the discipline of rhetoric. Once consumer researchers acknowledge the profusion of figures in contemporary advertising, theory building and testing can advance.

REFERENCES

Corbett, Edward P. J. (1990), *Classical Rhetoric for the Modern Student*. New York: Oxford University Press.

Deighton, John (1985), "Rhetorical Strategies in Advertising," in *Advances in Consumer Research*, Vol. 12, Morris Holbrook and Elizabeth Hirschman, eds. Ann Arbor, MI: Association for Consumer Research, 432-436.

Durand, Jacques (1987), "Rhetorical Figures in the Advertising Image," in *Marketing and Semiotics: New Directions in the Study of Signs for Sale*, Jean Umiker-Sebeok, ed. New York: Mouton de Gruyter, 295-318.

Eco, Umberto (1976), *A Theory of Semiotics*, Bloomington, IN: Indiana University Press.

Fogelin, Robert J. (1988), *Figuratively Speaking*. New Haven: Yale University Press.

Hitchon, Jacqueline (1991), "Effects of Metaphorical vs. Literal Headlines on Advertising Persuasion," *Advances in Consumer Research*, Vol 18, Rebecca H. Holman and Michael Solomon, eds. Provo, UT: Association for Consumer Research, pp. 752-753.

Howard, Daniel J. and Thomas E. Barry (1988), "The Prevalence of Question Use in Print Advertising: Headline Strategies," *Journal of Advertising Research*, 24(August/September), 18-25.

Kardes, Frank R. (1988), "Spontaneous Inference Processes in Advertising: The Effects of Conclusion Omission and Involvement on Persuasion," *Journal of Consumer Research*, 15 (September), 225-233.

McQuarrie, Edward F. and David Glen Mick (1992), "On Resonance: A Critical Pluralistic Inquiry into Advertising Rhetoric," *Journal of Consumer Research*, 19(September), 180-197.

Mick, David Glen (1986), "Consumer Research and Semiotics: Exploring the Morphology of Signs, Symbols and Significance," *Journal of Consumer Research*, 13 (September), 196-214.

_____ (1987), "Toward a Semiotic of Advertising Story Grammars," in *Marketing and Semiotics: New Directions in the Study of Signs for Sale*, Jean Umiker-Sebeok, ed. New York: Mouton de Gruyter, 249-278.

Scott, Linda M. (1990), "Understanding Jingles and Needledrop: A Rhetorical Approach to Music in Advertising," *Journal of Consumer Research*, 17 (September), 223-236.

Stern, Barbara (1990), "Pleasure and Persuasion in Advertising: Rhetorical Irony as a Humor Technique," *Current Issues & Research in Advertising*, 12, 25-42.

Swasy, John L. and James M. Munch (1985), "Examining the Target of Receiver Elaborations: Rhetorical Question Effects on Source Processing and Persuasion," *Journal of Consumer Research*, 11(March), 877-886.

Vickers, Brian (1988), *In Defence of Rhetoric*. Oxford: Clarendon.

Ward, James and William Gaidis (1990), "Metaphor in Promotional Communication: A Review of Research on Metaphor Comprehension and Quality," in *Advances in Consumer Research*, Vol. 17, M. Goldberg, G. Gorn and R. Pollay, eds., Provo, UT: Association for Consumer Research, 636-642.

Wells, William D. (1988), "Lectures and Dramas," in *Cognitive and Affective Responses to Advertising*, Pat Cafferata and Alice Tybout, eds., Lexington, MA: D. C. Heath.

Putting More Emotion into Consumer Research: Integrating Emotional/Hedonic Experience with Traditional Attitude Models

Chris T. Allen, University of Cincinnati

Outside of advertising studies, consumer researchers' response to Holbrook and Hirschman's (1982) call for more explicit consideration of emotional phenomena has been limited. Indeed, as Cohen and Areni (1991) note, "the ability of purchase settings, consumption experiences, and want satisfaction episodes to elicit affectively-charged states is just beginning to come under systematic study" (p. 204). The goal of this special session was to examine one concrete direction for accelerating the integration of emotive phenomena into consumer research. This direction entails an attempted merger of feeling and emotive constructs with traditional attitude models. All presenters used a model proposed by Zanna and Rempel (1988) as a common point of reference.

Geoffrey Haddock presented empirical work which applied the Zanna/Rempel model in the domain of prejudicial attitudes. This research also explored the possibility that there are individual differences in the tendency to use emotive versus cognitive information as the bases for one's attitudes. This person trait was gauged with a new scale referred to as the Feeling-Belief measure. The Zanna/Rempel model received empirical support in the sense that reported emotions did account for variance in subjects' evaluative judgements beyond that accounted for by their beliefs. In addition, the relative importance of emotion versus cognition in predicting prejudicial attitudes was moderated by subjects' scores on the Feeling-Belief measure.

Chris Allen depicted the Zanna/Rempel framework as a direct extension of the Fishbein/Ajzen attitude model. Tests of hypotheses derived from this merger of theoretical frameworks were presented. Following Zanna and Rempel, the data supported the hypothesis that individuals' recollections about emotive experiences will provide substantive prediction of attitude beyond that which is furnished by traditional cognitive considerations. Additionally, in an extension of the Zanna/Rempel theorizing, results showed that emotive reports can provide prediction of actual behavior that is not mediated by attitude. It was concluded that individuals have access to information about their emotive episodes that is underrepresented by traditional constructs in the Fishbein/Ajzen model.

The third presentation was made by Rajeev Batra. He briefly reviewed several empirical studies as a basis for critiquing the Zanna/Rempel model. His primary themes involved concern about the appropriateness of treating attitude as a unidimensional, evaluative judgment, and a concern about the lack of a motivational, conative component in the Zanna/Rempel model. An alternative model was suggested which included beliefs regarding utilitarian versus hedonic attributes, emotive experience, and degree of action tendency, as four possible antecedents of behavioral intention. As was true for all the presentations, Batra suggested a variety of research questions that represent concrete opportunities for accelerating the integration of emotional considerations into consumer research.

REFERENCES

Cohen, Joel B. and Charles S. Areni (1991), "Affect and Consumer Behavior," in *Handbook of Consumer Behavior*, eds. Thomas S. Robertson and Harold H. Kassarjian, Englewood Cliffs, NJ: Prentice-Hall, 188-240.

Holbrook, Morris B. and Elizabeth C. Hirschman (1982), "The Experiential Aspects of Consumption: Consumer Fantasies, Feelings, and Fun," *Journal of Consumer Research*, 9 (September), 132-140.

Zanna, Mark P. and John K. Rempel (1988), "Attitudes: A New Look at an Old Concept," in *The Social Psychology of Knowledge*, eds. Daniel Bar-Tal and Arie Kruglanski, New York: Cambridge University Press, 315-334.

Predicting Prejudicial Attitudes: The Importance of Affect, Cognition, and the Feeling-Belief Dimension
Geoffrey Haddock, University of Waterloo
Mark P. Zanna, University of Waterloo

ABSTRACT

Zanna and Rempel (1988) have suggested that an attitude be viewed as an overall evaluation of a stimulus object which is based on affective, cognitive, and behavioral information. The present study applied this formulation of the attitude concept to the domain of intergroup attitudes, in order to discover the relative importance of affect and cognition in predicting prejudice. In addition, the study also served as a preliminary test of the hypothesis that there are individual differences in the tendency to use affective and cognitive information in guiding attitudes. Subjects completed measures of attitudes, affect, stereotypic beliefs, and symbolic beliefs toward five groups. As well, they completed a preliminary version of the Feeling-Belief Measure (FBM), a scale intended to assess individual differences in the extent to which an individual's attitudes are guided by their feelings and thoughts. The results revealed that the relative importance of affect and cognition in predicting prejudice was a function of not only the target group, but also the subject's score on the FBM. The implications of the results are discussed.

One of the most important areas of investigation in the field of social psychology is the study of attitudes. The attitude concept is clearly an important one, because attitudes, under some circumstances, guide behavior (Fazio, 1990; Fazio & Zanna, 1981). For years, researchers have sought to discover the sources of information that are most influential in predicting attitudes. Until recently, the source of information that has been most frequently examined in terms of its relation to attitude is what is typically referred to as the cognitive component (Abelson, Kinder, Peters, & Fiske, 1982; Zajonc, 1980). Indeed, many popular attitude models have reflected this preoccupation with cognition by suggesting that attitudes are based on evaluations of the characteristics associated with the attitude object (e.g., Ajzen & Fishbein, 1980). Although this focus on cognition has led to many important findings concerning the role of cognitive information in guiding attitudes, it has come at the expense of studying other sources of information (e.g., affective and behavioral information) that also serve as important antecedents of attitudes (Zanna & Rempel, 1988). In line with this multicomponent perspective of the attitude concept, researchers studying a wide range of phenomena have started to venture "beyond the cognitive," to discover the extent to which affective and behavioral information serve as important sources of information in guiding individuals' attitudes (and behaviors) (e.g., Abelson et al., 1982; Allen, Machleit, & Kleine, 1992; Breckler & Wiggins, 1989; Cohen, 1990; Edwards, 1990).

The research presented in the present paper was performed to serve as a replication and extension of previous research in which we (Esses, Haddock, & Zanna, in press) found that *both* affective and cognitive information serve as important correlates of intergroup attitudes (i.e., prejudice).[1] In addition, the present study also served as a preliminary investigation of the validity of the Feeling-Belief Measure (FBM), a scale constructed by the authors and designed to assess individual differences in the tendency to base attitudes upon affective and cognitive information. In introducing this measure, we were interested in examining whether some individuals rely primarily upon affective information in determining their intergroup attitudes, whereas others typically base their prejudice on cognitive information.

The Zanna and Rempel (1988) Formulation of the Attitude Concept

The framework from which our research is derived comes from theorizing by Zanna and Rempel (1988). They have suggested that an attitude be viewed as an overall categorization of a stimulus object along an evaluative dimension. The process of evaluation is viewed as being based upon three general sources of information: (i) cognitive information (e.g., beliefs about the attitude object), (ii) affective information (e.g., feelings about the attitude object), and (iii) information concerning past behaviors or behavioral intentions. In addition, they have stated that consistency across the different sources is not necessary (implying that they are to some extent independent), and that an individual may have more than one attitude toward a stimulus object (if, over different occasions, the evaluative judgment is based on different sources of information).

How does the Zanna and Rempel (1988) formulation of the attitude concept lend itself to the study of intergroup attitudes? With regards to the cognitive component, we (Esses et al., in press) have postulated that two separate types of beliefs are relevant. One type of cognitive information is stereotypic beliefs, that is, the characteristics attributed to typical members of a target group. For instance, an individual may believe that typical members of a group are unfriendly and/or intelligent. A second type of cognitive information involves more general, abstract beliefs, including what we refer to as symbolic beliefs. Adapted from the concept of symbolic racism (Sears, 1988), these are beliefs that social groups violate or promote the attainment of cherished values, customs, and traditions. For example, an individual might believe that members of a certain group violate the expression of freedom and/or promote the attainment of peace.

In contrast, the affective component of intergroup attitudes focuses on the emotions that are elicited by target groups. For instance, typical members of a social group may evoke feelings of fear and/or admiration within an individual. Although not entirely independent of the cognitive component of prejudice, our past research has revealed that assessing the emotions elicited by typical group members provides information that increases our ability to predict individuals' attitudes (Esses et al., in press; Haddock, Zanna, & Esses, 1992).

In our initial study, we assessed the relative importance of affect, stereotypes, and symbolic beliefs in predicting attitudes toward five groups (English Canadians, French Canadians, Homosexuals, Native Indians, and Pakistanis). In this study, we asked 71 subjects to indicate their attitude toward each of the five groups. In addition, they were asked to complete, independently for each target group, three open-ended measures. To assess affect, they were asked to indicate the emotions they experience when they see,

---

[1] In the research presented in this paper, information concerning past behaviors was not assessed. However, we have recently begun to study the role played by past experiences in predicting prejudice (see, for example, Haddock, Zanna, & Esses, 1992).

feel, or think about members of the target group. They were then asked to rate *each* of these affective responses on the extent to which it is positive or negative (i.e., a valence rating), and, finally, to indicate the percentage of group members that produce each emotion (i.e., a percentage rating). An affect score was then created for each target group by multiplying *each* valence rating by its corresponding percentage rating, summing these products, and dividing by the number of characteristics listed (Esses et al., in press).

Stereotypes were assessed by asking individuals to list the characteristics they would use to describe typical members of each group. Having completed this task, they were asked to rate each characteristic on the extent to which it is positive or negative. They were then asked to indicate the percentage of group members who possess each characteristic. A stereotype score was calculated in the same manner as for the measure of affect.

To assess symbolic beliefs, subjects were asked to list the values, customs, and traditions that they believe are blocked or facilitated by typical group members. Upon the completion of this task, they were asked to rate the extent to which each value, custom, or tradition is blocked or facilitated by typical group members, and then to indicate the percentage of group members whom they believed block or facilitate each value. A symbolic belief score was calculated in the same manner as for the measure of affect.

Regression analyses, performed separately for each target group, revealed that *both* affective and cognitive information serve as important sources of information in predicting attitudes. Further, the interplay of affect and cognition was found to be dependent upon a variety of factors. For instance, attitudes toward those outgroups that were evaluated particularly negatively were based primarily upon symbolic beliefs. In contrast, attitudes toward outgroups that were evaluated more favorably were best predicted by affective information. Interestingly, stereotypes, upon the consideration of affect and symbolic beliefs, were not uniquely predictive of attitudes toward any of the five groups. This was somewhat surprising, because stereotypes have been persistently studied in regards to their relation with prejudice. Thus, we decided to replicate these results, in order to further examine the relative importance of affective and cognitive information in predicting prejudice. In addition, we also became interested in assessing whether there are *individual differences* in the tendency to use affect and cognition in predicting intergroup attitudes. Specifically, we wondered whether some individuals tended to use mainly affective information in this domain, while others tended to rely more upon their beliefs (either stereotypic and/or symbolic) in guiding their intergroup attitudes.

Are There Individual Differences in the Tendency to Use Affect and Cognition as Sources of Evaluative Information?

In light of our finding that both affect and cognition predict prejudice, we became interested in determining whether there are stable individual differences in the tendency to use these sources of information in predicting attitudes. Unfortunately, there is, to our knowledge, no psychological instrument that directly assesses individual differences in the tendency to use affective and cognitive information in forming attitudes.[2] Thus, we have decided to create our own measure. In developing potential items for this questionnaire, we have included items that ask about a wide range of attitudinal domains, such as political and consumer attitudes. In that way, we hope to develop a measure that might be useful to researchers studying a wide range of attitudinal phenomena. In the present study, we wanted to examine whether a preliminary version of such of a scale might be helpful in differentiating individuals who base their intergroup attitudes primarily upon either affective or cognitive information.

OVERVIEW OF THE PRESENT STUDY

In this study, we had 65 undergraduates at the University of Waterloo complete the attitude, affect, stereotype, and symbolic belief measures for the five groups described earlier. In addition, they were asked to complete a preliminary version of the Feeling-Belief Measure (FBM), a scale intended to assess individual differences in the tendency to use affect and cognition as sources of information in forming attitudes. The scale used in this study consisted of 28 Likert-style items, in which subjects were asked to indicate the extent of their agreement/disagreement with items such as "I often buy products for how they make me feel rather than how useful they are" and "An individual's preference of a political party should be based upon the party's policies, rather than the image the leader conveys." The items were keyed so that low scores on the scale were representative of individuals whose attitudes tend to be based upon affect.

RESULTS

The Prediction of Prejudice

To determine the relative importance of affective and cognitive information in predicting prejudice, regression analyses were performed in which the affect, stereotype, and symbolic belief scores were entered simultaneously as predictor variables, with the attitude measure serving as the criterion variable. As in our first study, a separate analysis was performed for each of the five target groups. As can be seen in Table 1, the results of these analyses revealed that, as in our earlier study, both affective and cognitive information served as important determinants of attitudes, but that their relative importance was a function of the target group under examination. For instance, affective information was uniquely predictive of attitudes toward English Canadians, French Canadians, and Pakistanis. Symbolic beliefs were found to be uniquely predictive of attitudes toward French Canadians, Homosexuals, Native Indians, and Pakistanis. Once again, stereotypes, upon the consideration of affective information and symbolic beliefs, were not predictive of attitudes. Thus, this second study replicated our first study by showing that: (i) both affective information and symbolic beliefs serve as important sources of information in predicting intergroup attitudes, and (ii) stereotypes are not uniquely predictive of prejudice.

The Prediction of Prejudice as a Function of Individual Differences on the Feeling-Belief Measure

To what extent were scores on the FBM associated with the tendency to use affective and cognitive information in the predic-

---

[2]There are, however, some existing measures that are related to what we wanted to investigate. For example, Cacioppo and Petty's (1982) construct of need for cognition, which measures individuals' tendency to engage in and enjoy cognitive activities, might be similar to our proposed construct, in that individuals high on this dimension may be more likely to base their attitudes on cognitive information. Similarly, Leary et al. (1986) have constructed a scale measuring individual differences in "objectivism," the tendency to base one's beliefs on empirical information and logical considerations. Highly objective individuals might be expected to base their attitudes on cognitive information. In contrast, individuals scoring high in affect intensity (Larsen & Diener, 1987), might be expected to base their attitudes more on affective information, because of their heightened emotional reactivity. Unfortunately, none of the scales were constructed to assess the underlying affective/cognitive structure of individuals' attitudes.

TABLE 1
Regression Analyses Using Stereotypes, Symbolic Beliefs, and Affect to Predict Attitudes Toward Five Social Groups

Target Group	Variable	Standardized regression coefficient
English Canadians (M=80.15)	Stereotypes	-.17
	Symbolic Beliefs	.20
	Affect	.32*
French Canadians (M=68.17)	Stereotypes	.10
	Symbolic Beliefs	.29*
	Affect	.40*
Homosexuals (M=38.15)	Stereotypes	.08
	Symbolic Beliefs	.43*
	Affect	.17
Native Indians (M=62.35)	Stereotypes	.08
	Symbolic Beliefs	.26*
	Affect	.18
Pakistanis (M=57.37)	Stereotypes	-.14
	Symbolic Beliefs	.36*
	Affect	.55*

Note. (i) N=65 *p<.05
(ii) In parentheses are the mean attitudes toward each group

tion of intergroup attitudes? In order to assess the association between scores on the FBM and the affective/cognitive structure of individuals' attitudes, we needed to create an index that would allow us to quantify the consistency between individuals' attitudes, affective responses, and cognitive responses.[3] Following the work of Chaiken and her colleagues (Chaiken, Pomerantz, & Giner-Sorolla, in press), we computed a score that represented the extent to which individuals' affect and cognition scores were consistent with their attitudes. Such an index was created which examined the consistency between affective responses, symbolic beliefs, and attitudes (i.e., an "affect/symbolic belief" index).[4]

The affect/symbolic belief index was created by first standardizing, independently for each target group, subjects' scores on the attitude, affect, and symbolic belief measures. Second, we calculated, separately for each target group, the absolute difference between the standardized attitude and affect scores ("A/A" scores) and the standardized attitude and symbolic belief scores ("A/SB" scores). These A/A and A/SB scores were then summed across the five target groups. Finally, the summed A/SB score was subtracted from the summed A/A score. Thus, a negative score on this index would represent a smaller discrepancy between individuals' attitudes and affective responses, implying greater consistency between their affective responses and their attitudes.

Scores on the FBM were indeed significantly related to scores on the affect/symbolic belief index, $r=.26, p<.05$. Individuals who scored low on the FBM (i.e., those subjects whose evaluations tended to be affect-based) had attitudes that were more consistent with their affective responses than with their symbolic beliefs, thus providing some preliminary evidence that there are individuals differences in the tendency to use affect and cognition in guiding attitudes, and that the FBM might be sensitive to assessing such differences.

DISCUSSION AND CONCLUSION

For years, researchers studying the structure of attitudes have focused on the cognitive component of evaluation (e.g., Ajzen & Fishbein, 1980). However, more recent models of the attitude concept, such as that proposed by Zanna and Rempel (1988), have led researchers to reaffirm the role of affective information in guiding attitudes and behavior. In our research, we have sought to determine the importance of affective information in predicting prejudicial attitudes. In a series of studies, such as the one presented in this paper, we have discovered that the emotions individuals experience when they see, meet, or think about typical members of a target group serve as an important source of information in guiding their attitudes.

In light of our findings concerning the role of affective information in predicting intergroup attitudes, we became interested in determining whether there are individual differences in the tendency to use affect and cognition in guiding evaluations. In the present study, we obtained some preliminary evidence suggesting that there might be individual differences in the tendency to use affect and cognition, although it is obvious that much more work is required before the FBM can be used by researchers interested in studying its effects. If, as we believe, there are stable individual differences in the propensity to use affect and cognition in guiding attitudes, it would then be necessary to determine the effects of such differences. For instance, Edwards (1990) has found that affect-

---

[3] Due to our small sample size, it would not have been appropriate to perform a median split on FBM scores and run separate regression analyses for the split sample.

[4] Because stereotypes were not uniquely predictive of attitudes, an affect/stereotype index was not computed.

based attitudes exhibit greater change as a result of affective rather than cognitive means of persuasion. Thus, in the domain of intergroup attitudes, reducing prejudice by changing negative beliefs might be ineffective for individuals whose attitudes are primarily affective. Similarly, individuals whose attitudes are affective in nature might be especially influenced by advertisements that focus on the positive emotions elicited by a consumer product. Thus, the FBM, upon a rigorous investigation of its psychometric properties, could serve as an effective instrument in helping researchers determine the persuasive technique(s) most likely to be effective for a given individual.

Overall, it is an exciting time to be studying the structure of attitudes. For too long, researchers paid particular attention to cognitive information, relegating affect to a secondary role (cf. Zajonc, 1980). However, it is now clear that our emotions serve as an important source of information in the evaluative process. Future research should continue this trend, in order to better understand when, and for whom, affective responses play the primary role in guiding our attitudes and behavior.

REFERENCES

Abelson, R. P., Kinder, D. R., Peters, M. D., & Fiske, S. T. (1982). Affective and semantic components of political person perception. *Journal of Personality and Social Psychology, 42,* 619-630.

Ajzen, I., & Fishbein, M. (1980). *Understanding attitudes and predicting social behavior.* Englewood Cliffs: Prentice-Hall.

Allen, C. T., Machleit, K. A., & Kleine, S. S. (1992). A comparison of attitudes and emotions as predictors of behavior at diverse levels of behavioral experience. *Journal of Marketing Research, 18,* 493-504.

Breckler, S. J., & Wiggins, E. C. (1989). Affect versus evaluation in the structure of attitudes. *Journal of Experimental Social Psychology, 25,* 253-271.

Cacioppo, J. T., & Petty, R. C. (1982). The need for cognition. *Journal of Personality and Social Psychology, 42,* 116-131.

Chaiken, S., Pomerantz, E. M., & Giner-Sorolla, R. (in press). Structural consistency and attitude strength. In R. E. Petty and J. A. Krosnick (Eds.) *Attitude strength: Antecedents and consequences.* Hillsdale, NJ: Erlbaum.

Cohen, J. B. (1990). Attitude, affect, and social behavior. In B. S. Moore and A. M. Isen (Eds.), *Affect and social behavior* (pp.152-206). Cambridge, MA: Cambridge University Press.

Edwards, K. L. (1990). The interplay of affect and cognition in attitude formation and change. *Journal of Personality and Social Psychology, 59,* 202-216.

Esses, V. M., Haddock, G., & Zanna, M. P. (in press). Values, stereotypes, and emotions as determinants of intergroup attitudes. In D. M. Mackie & D. L. Hamilton (Eds.), *Affect, cognition, and stereotyping: Interactive processes in group perception.* New York: Academic Press.

Fazio, R. H. (1990). Multiple processes by which attitudes guide behavior: The MODE model as an integrative framework. In M. P. Zanna (Ed.), *Advances in experimental social psychology* (Vol. 23, pp. 75-109). San Diego: Academic Press.

Fazio, R. H., & Zanna, M. P. (1981). Direct experience and attitude-behavior consistency. In L. Berkowitz (Ed.), *Advances in experimental social psychology* (Vol. 14, pp.161-202). New York: Academic Press.

Haddock, G., Zanna, M. P., & Esses, V. M. (1992). *The (limited) role of stereotypes in predicting attitudes toward Native Indians.* Manuscript submitted for publication.

Larsen, R. J., & Diener, E. (1987). Affect intensity as an individual difference characteristic: A review. *Journal of Research in Personality, 21,* 1-39.

Leary, M. R., Shepperd, J. A., McNeil, M. S., Jenkins, T. B., & Barnes, B. D. (1986). Objectivism in information utilization: Theory and measurement. *Journal of Personality Assessment, 50,* 32-43.

Sears, D. O. (1988). Symbolic racism. In P. A. Katz & D. A. Taylor (Eds.), *Eliminating racism* (pp.53-84). New York: Plenum Press.

Zajonc, R. B. (1980). Feeling and thinking: Preferences need no inferences. *American Psychologist, 35,* 151-175.

Zanna, M. P., & Rempel, J. K. (1988). Attitudes: A new look at an old concept. In D. Bar-Tal & A. W. Kruglanski (Eds.), *The social psychology of knowledge* (pp.315-334). Cambridge, England: Cambridge University Press.

Women, Consumption, and the Management of Rites of Passage
Special Session Summary
Cele Otnes, The University of Illinois

This session explored women's roles in managing rites of passage in American culture. Specifically, the rites of birth, marriage and death were explored in the three papers.

Margaret Rucker (The University of California, Davis) chaired the session. Eileen Fischer and Brenda Gainer (York University) co-authored the first paper, titled "Baby Showers: A Rite of Passage in Transition." This presentation focused upon understanding the thematic elements that emerged in baby showers for first-time mothers. These themes included: a women's initiation into her new role as a mother, the emphasis upon female bonding at these events and the tension felt by the mother-to-be as she experiences a loss of self-individuation. Furthermore, ritual practices — such as gift exchange and the creation of a bonnet made of the ribbons and bows — were discussed, as well as "alternative" forms of showers (e.g., the work shower, the group shower and the feminist baby shower).

The second paper presented was "'Til Debt Do Us Part': The Selection and Meaning of Artifacts in the American Wedding," by Cele Otnes (University of Illinois) and Tina M. Lowrey (Rider College). This paper examined how brides distinguished between sacred and profane artifacts, when selecting goods and services for use in their weddings. This paper supported the analysis of sacred items described in Belk, Sherry and Wallendorf (1989). For example, brides clearly experience a sense of hierophany when selecting their wedding dresses. Furthermore, many sacred items helped the bride realize her identity and fulfill her fantasy wedding. In contrast, profane items could not or would not be elevated beyond the world of ordinary goods, or actually de-sacralized the wedding ritual.

The final paper was "An Examination of Gift Exchange at Funerals," by Kina Mallard (Union University). Mallard interviewed women who had recently planned funerals, with respect to the types of gifts they appreciated and retained. Not surprisingly, flowers and cards were retained most often. Furthermore, they were often incorporated into the lives of the bereaved (e.g., through the creation of wreaths). Mallard also offered two metaphors that appear to be salient for the funeral planner — the "funeral as drama" and the "funeral as party."

The discussant for this session was Elizabeth Hirschman (Rutgers University), who offered many insightful comments to the presenters, with respect to ways to expand their research. She noted that one can examine what values are being imparted through particular baby gifts, that it would be valuable to study the meaning of artifacts at nontraditional weddings and that one should examine why particular types of gifts are so prevalent at funerals. A spirited question and answer/discussion period followed.

In summary, modern rites of passage have tended to be neglected by social scientists. This session represents one attempt to correct that oversight, by focusing upon women's roles in the creation and management of these rites of passage.

Baby Showers: A Rite of Passage in Transition

Eileen Fischer, York University
Brenda Gainer, York University

ABSTRACT

Baby showers are consumption venues distinguished both by their "feminine nature" and their seeming role as a modern-day rite of passage. This paper, based on participant observation in baby showers and long interviews with women recently honoured by such showers, explores the transitions occurring in this rite of passage as the roles women play and societal notions about those roles evolve.

The consumer behavior literature has only recently begun to attend to the gendered nature of many consumer behaviors (e.g. Belk and Coon 1991, Bristor and Fischer 1993, Firat 1991, Firat and Lewis 1985, Fischer and Arnold 1990; Fischer and Bristor 1991; Heisley 1991; Hirschman 1991; Venkatesh 1991) and to the unique forms of consumption associated with women (e.g. Benson 1986; Fischer and Gainer 1991; Gainer and Fischer 1991). At the same time, our field has devoted increasing attention to rites of passage as personal and social experiences which are partially constructed through the use of material objects and therefore offer unique opportunities for research into and understanding of the culture of consumption in which we live (e.g. Schouten 1991). This paper focuses on baby showers as a form of consumption that has largely been a uniquely female domain and that appears to have served — and to continue to serve — as a rite of passage for women.

RITES OF PASSAGE

Van Gennep's (1960) conceptualization of the rites of passage that accompany major role transitions as individuals move from birth to death remains the standard interpretation in the field. He argued that rites of passage consist of three stages: (1) separation, in which an individual may be physically "removed" from his or her old life, but which at least carries the notion of disengagement from a former role within a society, (2) transition, a liminal state, in which one passes from one role or state into another one, and (3) reintegration, in which an individual is reunited into an existing group or integrated into a new group, and which is accompanied by the establishment of a new social role or position. Although Van Gennep's work was based on an examination of many societies which were radically different from contemporary European or North American societies, he argued that the same components characterize the rites of passage that accompany major role transitions across societies. Turner (1969, 1974), however, observed that in contemporary societies, individuals dealing with the ambiguities of the liminal state in many role transitions have few supportive rites. The rites of passage associated with childbirth would appear to be among those most robust in the face of modern trends toward social isolation. Baby showers are arguably among these rites of passage associated with childbirth.

Baby Showers as Rites of Passage (?)

Parties held in honour of women who are about to become mothers accompany one of the major role transitions that most women undergo during their lives. As we began our study with an examination of Van Gennep's conceptualization of rites of passage, we encountered some difficulty in mapping it onto the present-day North American baby shower.

If applied literally, the model appears to fit rather badly. The three phases of separation, transition and reintegration cannot be mapped even imperfectly onto the ritual behaviors that occur during a baby shower. For example, although baby showers are usually held near the end of a pregnancy when women *could* possibly retreat from society, in contemporary North American society they rarely do so and thus the separation phase is rarely observed. When it does occur, it is rarely coterminous with a baby shower. Even in a figurative sense, modern North American women rarely leave their old roles behind when they have a baby; instead they seem to add a *new* role to those they are already fulfilling.

The liminal state characteristic of the transitional phase could aptly describe the whole ninth months of pregnancy; baby showers may, at most, contribute in a limited sense to this particular phase of the rite of passage which marks the acquisition of the new role of motherhood. Of course, physical transition to motherhood does not occur during showers (at least not if the mother can avoid it), but it may be that baby showers provide a concrete opportunity for the formulation of "possible selves" which are said to characterize the transition phase of a rite of passage (Markus and Nurius 1986; Schouten 1991). At a baby shower a mother-to-be is provided both with a community of other mothers and potential mothers, and with objects she will use to fulfil her new role. Thus it seems possible that baby showers contribute to the transitional phase of a classic rite of passage by providing an opportunity for a woman to "try out" both the new equipment she will need to care for her baby, as well as to "try out" her role as a mother. By playing this (albeit limited) part in the transitional phase of the rite, baby showers seem to contribute to the eventual reintegration of the new and old selves. Full reintegration, however, occurs only after the baby's birth.

METHOD

Our study was undertaken with the objects of exploring some *a priori* themes we identified as being characteristic of baby showers, and of discerning and analyzing new themes which we anticipated would emerge from the research. We chose to use methods which would allow us to capture the complexities of our informants' thoughts and behaviors, as well as the rich details of the social context in which those occurred. Thus our study was based on participant observation in eight baby showers to which we were invited or which were held for us over the past three years. Additionally, we undertook extensive interviews with five recent recipients of baby showers.

Our informants were recruited using our personal networks. We attempted to include women who possessed a range of professional, socio-economic and ideological characteristics. We used a semi-structured interview format based on a standard list of questions we developed. The interview protocol served to prompt general conversations on the subject of baby showers with our informants, and provided "probes" to elicit more specific information on the themes we had identified and which began to emerge during the interview process. In order to test our emerging analysis as we proceeded, we supplemented the information provided by our own observations and by our main informants with short discussions with many more women who had attended baby showers or been the recipient of them.

A PRIORI THEMES

Before we began our research, we identified three *a priori* themes which we expected to observe in our study of baby showers. All three themes relate to the purposes which the showers serve.

Female Solidarity and Community

Recent studies of gift giving rituals (e.g. Cheal 1988; Fischer and Arnold 1990) indicate that part of the social function that they serve is to create and reinforce the personal relationships which form the bonds of community in which we live. Given that traditional baby showers are exclusively female, we expected they would, like other forms of collective female rituals such as Tupperware parties, foster bonds of sorority in particular (Gainer and Fischer 1991).

Loss of Independence/Recovery of Innocence

Standard notions of mother/child relationships include the idea of dependency of the child upon its mother; by logical extension these notions also include the idea that mothers become less independent as they adopt new responsibilities for the welfare of another human being. This loss of autonomy is particularly pronounced in the case of the birth of a first child.

We theorized that this loss of personal autonomy is accompanied by an increased dependence on family and friends, particularly other mothers, who are represented by the guests attending the traditional baby shower. The need for external support as one becomes a mother is not only moral, but financial, as exemplified through the giving of the necessary equipment for raising a child at a shower.

At the same time as a woman loses some of her independence by becoming a mother (and perhaps partially as a result of loss of independence) we expected that — in the eyes of others — she would experience a recovery of innocence. The cultural icon of a mother is of a woman who is devoted, loyal and above all, pure. Despite the fact that the act which creates a child is sexual, the production of a child leads the mother into a role associated with purity and even virginity. This notion was fully supported by the centrality of child-like rituals at traditional showers.

The Expertise of Motherhood

A third theme which we expected to find characterized traditional baby showers was the passing on of knowledge deemed essential for the tasks of mothering. We expected that we would find that much conversation centred on advice to the mother-to-be, as well as on the exchange of information about children among the guests. The choice of gifts, too, was thought to play a part in instructing the new mother in the correct method of caring for and socializing a baby.

Early in our research we discovered that baby showers, to the extent that they constitute rites of passage into the role of mother, are very much in transition. As traditional female and male roles undergo enormous changes, the social rituals which traditionally helped to mark the shedding of old roles and the acquisition of new ones change too. Although we found evidence that "traditional" forms of baby showers continue to take place in the 1990's in much the same form as they did in the 1950's, we also identified three new forms of baby showers that seem to be emerging in contemporary North America. In the traditional baby showers we found strong support for our *a priori* themes. In the emergent forms, we found considerable variation in not only the characteristics of the shower, but in the purposes which the shower served.

THE TRADITIONAL BABY SHOWER

Traditional baby showers are characterized by exclusively female guests lists. Usually the recipient's mother is included, as well as her sisters and possibly some aunts, nieces or female cousins. Typically friends are present, particularly friends who have had babies. While mothers of all ages are therefore included, unmarried girls (sisters, cousins, or nieces) are likely included only if they have reached adolescence. This helps to consolidate the atmosphere which is suggestive of an initiation into the mysteries of motherhood. The atmosphere of initiation and mystery is further heightened because traditional showers are always held prior to the birth of the first baby, unless nature accidentally intervenes. One respondent described as "too bad" a shower held for a friend after a premature birth.

The atmosphere is also characteristic of a child's party. Decorations usually include balloons, and often folding paper items such as umbrellas or perambulators. Childish games which involve simple guessing or luck are played. (While the games may be reminiscent of a child's party, they often have an adult twist, such as a case we discovered of a version of pin-the-tail-on-the-donkey which involved pinning a decorated penis on a cardboard man). "Childish" food and drink are also served; the drinks are usually fruit punch and/or other non-alcoholic beverages, and sweets comprise a large portion of the food provided.

A special bonnet is prepared for the mother-to-be by attaching the ribbons and bows from the gifts she receives to a paper plate or similar object. After the bonnet is completed, she is expected to don it and often the hostess has prepared special ribbons or tassels with which to attach it to her head. While the bonnet seemed to be the one unvarying feature of the traditional baby shower, the purpose it served or the meaning it conveyed to the participants was elusive. One informant, when pressed, commented that "oh, it's just to be silly together," and then further, "it's just to make her look ridiculous."

In addition to the bonnet, a special decorated chair, referred to by many respondents as a "throne," is often prepared for the shower recipient to sit in as she opens her gifts. The guests all sit in a circle to watch while the gifts are opened ceremonially and then passed around the circle for viewing. An assistant, often a younger sister or niece, usually orders and hands the gifts to the mother-to-be and is responsible for recording who gave what.

At a traditional shower the gifts are from individuals or from groups, and cover an enormous range of values, often at the same shower. For example, one informant told us of receiving a stroller and a crib from her mother-in-law at the same shower at which she received smaller items such as hand-knit booties or vaseline from others. Regardless of the price, however, gifts at the traditional shower are "necessities" for the baby such as baby clothes, toys, blankets, or equipment.

One central purpose which the traditional baby shower serves, then, is to equip the new mother with the clothes, toys, and furnishings she is going to need for the new baby. The gifts serve an economic purpose but at the same time serve to reinforce the new mother's dependence on a community of other women. And this dependence is not only based on financial and even emotional support, but also on the "insider knowledge" which is communicated as each gift is opened.

Thus the shower serves to indoctrinate the woman into the special behaviors associated with her new role in society. It is paradoxical, however, that at the same time as a baby shower seems to mark the transition to full female adulthood/motherhood, it also seems to mark the return to the innocence and purity associated with childhood. While the childish games and the beribboned bonnet infantilize the woman and seem to symbolize this return to innocence, the decorated throne may even more clearly represent a symbolic return to the virginal state associated with Mother Mary, Queen of the World.

Our findings seem to offer support to the themes regarding the woman's transition to a more dependent, but pure, state, and regarding her acquisition of the knowledge necessary to act in a manner consistent with that state. We also found evidence that baby showers have benefits for women other than the guest of honor. The women who act as hostesses, as well as the other guests, also seem to enjoy the re-enforcement of female bonds of kinship and friendship which appear to be a particularly important aspect of a traditional shower. Several of our informants mentioned that a special effort had been made to invite people whom the new mother had not seen for a long time. Two of our informants also described showers that included the women from both the mother's and the father's family, even though it appeared that the two families did not have regular contact apart from the great life passages of marriage, birth and death. One of our informants summed up the importance of this community aspect of baby showers by saying that "it's just a hen party; it's just an excuse to get together with a bunch of women."

EMERGENT FORMS OF SHOWERS

The Workplace Shower

The workplace shower is held outside the home, usually on the work premises. Like a traditional shower, it is held prior to the birth of the baby, but the timing is chosen to mark the occasion of the woman stopping work for her maternity leave more than to mark the approaching birth. The guests at a workplace shower may include men; this seems to depend on the level within the organization of the woman having the baby. If the mother-to-be occupies a clerical or secretarial position, the shower is usually attended by other female clerks and secretaries, but if the woman occupies a higher managerial position, her male co-workers or occasionally her male boss may attend, even if only for a few minutes. Despite the fact that guests may be male or female, the organizers of the workplace shower seem to be exclusively female.

Like the traditional shower, the workplace shower often has thematic decorations, and a decorated "throne" is prepared for the mother-to-be. The gifts are opened ceremonially and passed around if there are several, but at workplace showers gifts usually tend to be presented on behalf of a group of givers and tend to be major items such as a stroller, a high chair, or a car-seat. Occasionally smaller group or individual gifts of clothing or toys may be given, although these gifts seem to be more characteristic of an all-female shower (for instance of office support staff) where the guests tend to be closer friends. The games and the bonnet seem to be characteristic of these "all-female" workplace showers as well.

The workplace shower is the only type we identified which seems to mark the "separation" phase of a classic rite of passage. The pregnant woman does disappear from her workplace after the shower, and reappears later once she made the transition to motherhood and has achieved the integration of her new role as mother and old role as worker. The workplace shower serves to mark the status of the woman in the workplace; it seems to celebrate her transition to motherhood in a perfunctory way while emphasizing much more clearly her responsibilities within the work community. The workplace shower thus marks the blurred boundary between a woman's public and private lives, roles and communities.

The mix of public and private lives in the workplace shower seems often to lead to tension, however. One of our informants described the self-consciousness she felt at being singled out for this reason in the context of her work. Another informant described a workplace shower as being relatively meaningless, since "it was very formal, and [she] didn't know anyone very well." Another workplace shower in which one of us participated was characterized by a vague sense of embarrassment on the part of non-parents as tiny clothes for vulnerable babies were opened and displayed.

Thus, while the workplace shower may serve as an attempt to merge professional work roles and intimate family roles, it may achieve a rather uneasy alliance of the two.

The Mixed-Sex Shower

This type of shower, like the others, is held before the birth of the baby. Both male and female guests attend a mixed shower, but, unlike a workplace shower where a pregnant woman is honoured before departing on her maternity leave, both the mother and father-to-be are the guests of honour. The guests are usually couples, and typically friends or work acquaintances attend. Relatives are usually not invited to mixed showers. The parties are typically organized by another couple, often fairly close friends of the parents-to-be, and are held at a friend's home, usually in the evening.

The atmosphere at a mixed shower differs radically from that at a traditional shower. Alcoholic beverages replace the sweet punch and soda drinks, and the food is more typical of other adult parties, being less dominated by sweet items. The child-like games, decorated "throne," and beribboned bonnet are not part of the mixed shower. Gifts are, however, opened ceremonially and (if there are multiple gifts) passed around for inspection. Gifts range in value from shower to shower, but seem to be of more uniform value within the same shower than is the case in a traditional shower (possibly because of the absence of kin, who are often the donors of the very expensive items at a traditional shower).

One of the purposes the mixed shower serves is to signal the transition to parenthood of *both* parents. It thus reflects modern gender role attitudes about fathers having a role to play in caring for children, as well as the realization that a man's life is profoundly affected by having a child too. The shower not only reflects these attitudes, but serves as a showcase for demonstrating them by making it clear that "hen" parties, not to mention the activities that characterize them, are for those with old-fashioned values.

In addition to extending the transition phase of the classic rite of passage to men as well as women, the mixed shower also serves to reinforce the bonds creating the social world in which the couple, as opposed to the woman only, live. A specialized form of the mixed shower often includes guests from work, and may be a substitute for a workplace shower. Occasionally it is even held at the man's workplace. This suggests that for those with modern gender role attitudes, the mixed shower may be the male equivalent of the workplace shower for women. "Male" showers in this sense are still based on couples, however, since women continue to organize them and buy the gifts which are presented by the work group.

The Feminist Shower

The feminist baby shower is, perhaps ironically, the one closest in form to the traditional baby shower. It is held by a close female friend or by a sister, and is attended by relatively close female friends only. Female relatives close to the same age may be invited if they are close to the guest of honour, both emotionally and in terms of sex role attitudes. While the organizer tends to be a friend who is a mother herself, feminist showers are sometime organized by a childless friend or relative.

Although the guest list of such showers resembles that of traditional baby showers, other aspects of the feminist baby shower are quite different. The paper decorations and balloons are not used, and the women attending do not play child-like games. The mother-to-be is not presented with either a decorated throne or a bonnet. Alcoholic beverages are usually served, and the food often tends to be quite sophisticated.

The gifts are opened ceremonially, although not usually passed around the circle of guests. The gifts at feminist baby showers tend to be relatively small, or if they are group gifts (which are quite common), to require modest dollar contributions. The nature of the gifts sharply differentiates the feminist shower from the traditional shower, for they are rarely for the baby and usually tend to be a personal, sensual gift for the mother. Common gifts are soaps and toiletries, massage certificates, or in the case of one shower we attended, a day at a spa.

The gifts at a feminist baby shower may serve to reaffirm the woman in her former role as an independent, professional adult. We suspect that the restricted range of gifts reflects the deep tensions about the transition to motherhood felt by many liberal feminist women. The choice of gifts seems to reflect the participants' desire to deny that becoming a mother will change a woman substantially, and certainly to deny that she will abandon her role as an adult and a sexual being. Moreover, as one woman said, the gifts also seem to serve as a signal that the birth itself "would be a messy and physically undermining ordeal."

We found other signs of the tension liberal feminist women feel about engaging in activities associated with more traditional feminine gender role attitudes. A feminist baby shower seems to be held in spite of concern about the image of attending a "hen party." For example, guests were invited to one shower we attended in a humorous office memo which explicitly described it as a "feminist baby shower," and then queried whether such a notion was oxymoronic. In another case the hostess of a shower for a feminist friend apologized for the invitation and added "I hope you don't mind, but I thought we should have *some* kind of a celebration."

The fact that these showers are held despite concern about the image of traditional baby showers indicates that they reflect a more contemporary version of feminism (and gender role attitudes) than the mixed shower, for example. Whereas mixed showers attempt to de-emphasize the differences between men and women, feminist baby showers attempt to celebrate them. In fact the word "celebration" surfaced often among our interviews with the recipients of such showers. As in the traditional shower and the mixed shower, joint participation in a social ritual served to reaffirm the bonds which integrate the woman into her small world.

THEMES EMERGING IN THIS RITE OF PASSAGE IN TRANSITION

One theme which emerged in our study of the new forms of baby showers which are evolving is the tension between public and private lives. In a traditional baby shower this tension is missing, because the traditional view assumes that a woman does not have a public life, or at least, does not play a public role that is significantly different from the one that she will play after becoming a mother. At a traditional shower, the emphasis is very much on community support for a personal, private transition from wife to mother.

The new forms of baby showers, however, all suggest somewhat more modern gender role attitudes on the part of the participants. While each new form of shower signals recognition that a woman is about to become a mother, the structure of each also reminds participants of the woman's other, potentially conflicting, roles. The workplace shower is the one where this tension is most noticeable. As the mother-to-be becomes more and more visibly pregnant at work, her normally invisible domestic and sexual lives become increasingly difficult to bracket. At the shower, these aspects of her life — and their conflicting demands upon her — must be acknowledged. At a mixed shower the relationship between public and private lives is addressed by bringing the celebration of a woman's transition to motherhood out of the traditionally private world of women into a "public" world where men participate. Although a feminist baby shower retreats again to the "private" world of women, participants are clearly uneasy about their apparent support for a traditional ritual associated with the relegation of women to the private sphere. The gifts at these showers seemed to be chosen to demonstrate that the visible effects of this physically ruinous venture can be erased when the woman returns to her public role.

This tension between the public and the private leads to a second theme we have identified in the new forms of showers, which is an emphasis on "professionalization" in the lives of women. The workplace showers are explicitly informed by the woman's professional role in that her status within the organization determines who will attend and give gifts. At some level, these showers even serve as a signal to the woman that she is expected to return to her professional role after her maternity leave. At workplace, mixed sex and feminist showers, much of the conversation focused on how long a woman planned to be away on maternity leave, and what childcare arrangements she proposed to make when she returned to work. One of our informants said these questions were so frequently asked that she wished she had had a t-shirt printed up with the answers.

Even when a woman has decided to abandon her professional career temporarily in order to raise children, participants in the new forms of showers seem to recognize this as a career choice—that is, that she has changed careers in order to become a professional mother. Gifts choices in such a case reflect the professionalization of motherhood. For example, at a mixed shower one of our informants received the necessary "manuals" for her new work, Dr. Spock and a book on children's sleeping habits. At another shower held by professional women who had all given up their careers for motherhood, the conversation as each gift was opened seemed to indicate that the participants were vying with each other through their choice of gifts to demonstrate their professional competence and skills as mothers.

As women struggle with their public roles and their professional roles, a third theme emerges which is tension over exactly what constitutes the transition in this rite—the passage to motherhood, or the passage to parenthood? Women who do not hold traditional gender role attitudes clearly are experiencing conflict about the new role they will be expected to play as they become a mother, and whether they will be expected to play it alone. As men in couples with non-traditional attitudes begin to perform some of the household tasks associated with the role of "wife," there is an expectation that they will also take on some of the tasks and behaviors associated with the role of "mother" when parenthood occurs. The emerging forms of showers we have identified demonstrate that there is not agreement over the meaning and nature of the father's role transition, however.

At a mixed shower a father's transition to parenthood is made most explicit, and by honouring both mother and father in similar ways there seems to be an insistence at these showers that the joys, the work, and the changes associated with having a baby affect both sexes equally. These showers could be said to be based on a liberal view of sexual equality which seeks to deny that there is any meaningful difference between men and women. Feminist baby showers are a more recent phenomenon and seem to have evolved as some contemporary women who believe in equality of the sexes incorporate that notion with a belief that the experiences and roles of women and men are profoundly different. Thus the feminist shower reverts to the traditional all-female format and celebrates motherhood as a state quite distinct from parenthood.

This is not to suggest that we found evidence at feminist showers that the women attending were fully comfortable with the reappropriation of motherhood. Most seemed deeply ambivalent about whether this should be a female or a joint role transition; the guests at one such shower, for example, swapped stories about their partners' perennial inability to do the laundry properly or remember to cook vegetables for dinner.

This ambiguity about whether men acquire new roles as they become parents was linked to a fourth theme which emerged from our research, which is the ambivalence that characterizes the inescapable role transition from non-mother to mother for many contemporary women. We found that baby showers seemed to mark both an acceptance of the acquisition of a new role and a denial that anything fundamental would change. The idea of celebration and honour (for either a woman alone, or else a couple) surfaces in all the new forms of showers we identified and examined. At the same time, however, we found that the emerging forms of showers served as a reminder that women are no longer expected or able to separate from their old roles as they engage in the transition to a new one. The workplace shower served to remind a woman of her professional responsibilities and obligations which will not be left behind as she adds motherhood to her role repertoire. The mixed shower served to reinforce the bonds of the adult community in which a couple is expected to continue to play a part. The feminist shower appeared to act almost as a warning that a woman needed to beware of the "dangers" that are perceived to be associated with the traditional transition to motherhood, namely infantilization and a return to a pure and non-sexual state. Thus all the emerging forms of showers seemed to demonstrate in different ways the ambiguity of the contemporary transition to motherhood in which women no longer engage in the traditional separation from an old role as they acquire a new one, but rather seek to add an additional role to their repertoire.

REFERENCES

Belk, Russell and Gregory Coon (1991), "Men and Women on Dating and Gift-Giving: Same Planet, Different Worlds," *Gender and Consumer Behavior*, Janeen Costa, ed. Salt Lake City, Utah: University of Utah Printing Service, 94-103.

Benson, Susan Porter (1986), *Counter Cultures: Saleswomen, Managers and Customers in American Department Stores*, Urbana: University of Illinois Press.

Bristor, Julia and Eileen Fischer (1993), "Feminism: Implications for Consumer Research," *Journal of Consumer Research*, forthcoming.

Cheal, David (1988), *The Gift Economy*, London: Routledge.

Firat, A. Fuat (1991), "Consumption and Gender: A Common History," *Gender and Consumer Behavior*, Janeen Costa, ed. Salt Lake City, Utah: University of Utah Printing Service, 378-386.

_____ and Linda Lewis (1985), "A Critique of the Orientations in Studies of Women's Consumption Culture," *Historical Perspective in Consumer Research: National and International Perspectives*, Chin Tiong Tan and Jagdish Sheth, Eds. Singapore: Association for Consumer Research, 225-229.

Fischer, Eileen and Stephen Arnold (1990), "More Than a Labor of Love: Gender Roles and Christmas Gift Shopping," *Journal of Consumer Research*, 17 (December), 333-345.

_____ and Julia Bristor (1991), "The Gender of the Consumer: A Feminist Perspective on the Marketing Concept," paper presented at the Gender and Consumer Behavior Conference.

_____ and Brenda Gainer (1991), "I Shop Therefore I Am: The Role of Shopping in the Social Construction of Women's Identities," *Gender and Consumer Behavior*, Janeen Costa, ed. Salt Lake City, Utah: University of Utah Printing Service, 350-357.

Gainer, Brenda and Eileen Fischer (1991), "To Buy or Not to Buy? That is Not the Question: Female Ritual in Home Shopping Parties," in *Advances in Consumer Research*, Vol. 18, ed. Rebecca Holman and Michael Solomon, Provo UT: Association for Consumer Research, 597-602.

Heisley, Deborah (1991), "Gender Symbolism and Usage Expectations in Food," paper presented at the Gender and Consumer Behavior Conference, Salt Lake City, Utah.

Hirschman, Elizabeth (1991), "A Feminist Critique of Marketing Theory: Toward Agentic-Communal Balance," *Gender and Consumer Behavior*, Janeen Costa, ed. Salt Lake City, Utah: University of Utah Printing Service, 324-340.

Markus, Hazel and Paula Nurius (1986), "Possible Selves," *American Psychologist*, 41 (9), 954-969.

Schouten, John (1991) "Selves in Transition: Symbolic Consumption in Personal Rites of Passage and Identity Reconstruction," *Journal of Consumer Research*, 17 (March), 412-425.

Turner, Victor (1969), *The Ritual Process: Structure and Anti-structure*, Chicago: Aldine.

_____ (1974), "Liminal to Liminoid in Play, Flow and Ritual: An Essay in Comparative Symbology," *Rice University Studies*, 60 (3), 53-92.

van Gennep, Arnold (1960), *The Rites of Passage*, trans. M.B. Vizedom and G.L. Caffee, Chicago, University of Chicago Press.

Venkatesh, Alladi (1991), "Feminist Science and Consumer Research," paper presented at The Conference on Gender and Consumer Behavior, Salt Lake City, Utah.

'Til Debt Do Us Part: The Selection and Meaning of Artifacts in the American Wedding

Cele Otnes, University of Illinois at Urbana-Champaign
Tina M. Lowrey, Rider College[1]

ABSTRACT

Belk, Sherry and Wallendorf (1989) observe that the consumption occurring within the context of ritualized occasions is often viewed as "sacred" by consumers. This paper argues that even within these contexts, some artifacts may be viewed as sacred, while still others retain a profane quality. Specifically, this paper compares the "sacred" items that brides include in planning their weddings and receptions with those they regard as profane.

INTRODUCTION

Since Rook's (1985) study of the ritual dimension of consumer behavior, many researchers have examined ritualized elements of consumption. Often, these examinations have focused upon occasions that are pervasive in American culture, such as Christmas and Thanksgiving (c.f.; Belk 1989; Sherry and McGrath 1989; Wallendorf and Arnould 1991). Such occasions are notable because of their periodicity, and because they often feature a wide variety of ritualized events — such as feasting — within each occasion.

While most consumers do not participate in weddings on an annual basis, there is little doubt that these occasions are significant consumption rituals within American culture. Indeed, in industrialized societies, weddings remain one of the few ceremonial rites of passage, where an individual moves from "one age to another and from one occupation to another" (van Gennep, 1960 translation, p. 2). And Cheal (1988) notes that while rites of passage are generally thought to be of little importance in industrialized societies, "the major exception here is the complex of rites associated with marriage, which shows few signs of decline" (p. 87).

The above statements are supported by the fact that the average cost of the American wedding is now $16,000, and wedding-related goods and services account for $30 billion in annual retail sales (Abbott, 1991). Few studies have actually examined facets of the modern wedding ceremony. Ironically, more studies have examined a relatively small wedding-related event — the bridal shower — than have examined the wedding ceremony itself (Casparis 1979; Cheal 1988).

However, Barker (1978) did interview more than fifty couples and attended nearly one hundred weddings over a four-year period. She observed that the continuing popularity of the "proper wedding" — which features the church setting and the white dress — is due to the fact that it "is thought more thorough because people believe that God can help in achieving the ideal — a bonding, life-long pervasive holy union" (p. 74).

Our study attempts to provide further understanding of the wedding as a consumption-oriented rite of passage in American culture. We began by exploring which artifacts brides regard as "sacred" when planning their ceremonies and receptions. We employed Belk, Wallendorf and Sherry's definition of sacred consumption as "that which is regarded as more significant, powerful and extraordinary than the self" (1989, p. 13). Likewise, we define artifacts as items that are either purchased, used or dictated (e.g., gifts bought via a registry) by the bride.

However, during data collection we noticed that while brides regarded some items as sacred, still others remained in the realm of the profane, and were thus "ordinary and lack[ing] the ability to induce ecstatic, self-transcending, extraordinary experiences" (Belk, Wallendorf and Sherry 1989, p. 13).

Given that weddings are highly ritualized, significant and expensive occasions, we found our brides' distinction between sacred and secular items worth pursuing. Thus, we explored the following research questions:

1. Which artifacts used in the wedding and reception do brides regard as sacred?
2. How and why do these items acquire sacred status?
3. Which items used during these events do brides regard as profane?
4. How and why do these items acquire profane status?

METHOD

During the summer of 1991, focus groups were conducted in a Midwestern city (population approximately 100,000). Nineteen brides participated. Part of these focus groups was devoted to examining the ritual artifacts that brides deemed most important when planning their weddings.

In addition, nine brides were recruited from these groups for participation in a more in-depth study of the wedding as consumption ritual. These brides ranged in age from 21-35. Appendix A describes these informants.

Brides were paid $40 for participating in two in-depth interviews and allowing the researcher to accompany them on two wedding-related shopping trips. This research design had been used successfully in the study of other rituals, notably Christmas shopping (Otnes, Kim and Lowrey 1992; Otnes, Lowrey and Kim 1992).

The data were collected by three female undergraduate students, who were trained participants in a summer research program at a large university in the Midwest. Interviews were structured to examine the four aspects of the wedding ritual: artifacts, ritual scripts, performance roles and the ritual audience (Rook, 1985). Interviews included scripted questions and carefully scheduled prompts (McCracken, 1988), and typically lasted from 30-45 minutes.

Informants chose the sites for all shopping trips. These included: bridal shops, florists, caterers, fabric stores and other specialty shops. Researchers typically spent 1-1 1/2 hours with informants on each trip. Researchers created detailed field notes immediately after each shopping trip. Using interviews and shopping trips allowed us to create a "thick description" of our informants' experiences (Geertz 1973).

Transcriptions of the focus groups and in-depth interactions yielded over 500 pages of text. We addressed the trustworthiness of data (Wallendorf and Belk 1989) by triangulating methods, establishing rapport with informants, assuring anonymity when reporting results and using techniques recommended by skilled interviewers (c.f.; Bogdan and Taylor 1984; Lincoln and Guba 1985). We created our final interpretation by a process of negotiation, arriving at an agreed-upon understanding of our individual interpretations.

---

[1] The authors wish to thank Elaina Joyce, Tracey Lee and Catherine McDonald for their help in data collection. References are available upon request.

APPENDIX A
Informant Characteristics

Becky: is a professor in her mid-thirties. She and her fiance are spending approximately $5,000 for their wedding, and are inviting 200 guests. Theirs is a church wedding and sit-down reception.

Elaine: is a graduate student in her early twenties. Her parents are paying the $5,000 for her wedding. The wedding will take place at Christmastime in a church; 250 guests are expected to attend. The reception will be a buffet at the Elks' Club.

Jenny: is 30 and works as a bookkeeper. She and her fiance, who has children, live together. This is the second marriage for both. They are spending $1,500 for a church wedding with 100 guests. The reception will be held in the church rec room and they will serve sandwiches.

Jody: 35, is a TV journalist. Her parents are helping with the $5,000 in wedding costs. Over 300 guests are invited to a church wedding, with the reception in a hall near a park. The food is "elegant country," mainly sandwiches and salads.

June: is a graduate student in her early twenties. Her parents are spending nearly $2,500 on her church wedding. The reception is a formal sit-down dinner in a school dining hall.

Kate: 21, is an undergraduate. Both sets of parents are contributing to the $8,000 wedding. Three hundred guests are invited. The wedding is in a church, and the reception at a hotel.

Lynn: is a retail store manager in her early thirties. Her parents are helping with the $4,000 in wedding costs. Two hundred guests are expected; both the wedding and reception are being held at the Civic Center.

Sue: 25, is a graduate student. Her wedding will cost approximately $6,000. One hundred guests are invited to the church wedding, and there will be a sit-down lunch and a pot-luck buffet afterwards.

Val: is a writer/editor in her late twenties. She and her fiance are paying for their wedding. They are inviting 200 guests. Both their wedding and reception will be at their home in the country.

Sacred Wedding Artifacts

Interestingly, artifacts perceived as sacred by our informants were all related to the wedding and not to the reception (see Table 1). Given the symbolic nature and import of the ceremony, this finding is not surprising. In addition, our informants characterized their receptions as parties designed mainly to "reward" the guests for attending the wedding. In fact, the vows exchanged and the presence of loved ones, although not artifacts per se, were two of the most universally mentioned sacred aspects of our brides' weddings. However, this paper focuses on why *artifacts* do or do not acquire sacred status.

Reasons for Sacred Status

The wedding dress was the most often mentioned sacred artifact, but music, decorations, wedding rings, photographs, the church, and the minister were also perceived as sacred. These artifacts acquired sacred status for different reasons — and often for more than one reason — as articulated below.

1. Sacred Items Are Hierophanous. According to Belk, Sherry and Wallendorf (1989), hierophany involves both the revelation of a sacred item to an individual and the removal of such an item from common, everyday use. By far the most prevalent items granted sacred status by our informants, the bridal gown and related accessories, acquired sacredness for these reasons. For most of our brides, the selection of the wedding dress was an intense, hierophanous experience, during which the perfect selection seemed to be magically revealed to them. Jenny described her experience:

> When I found that dress, I mean I put it on...I started crying, 'cause I was like, "Lisa, this is my dress!"...and the whole thing seemed so much more real; that we were really getting married, and that this was going to happen, and it just, it just was a really overwhelming, I guess, type of feeling.

Likewise, Becky remarked:

> So I spent a little bit of time looking, but knew I wasn't going to buy anything. And I just, it just happened I went into the right store, looked at this dress, it was the first one I saw. I tried it on, with a couple of others, but that was my dress. I knew it.

Other bridal accessories elicited similar responses. Lynn described shopping for her veil:

> My maid of honor went with me when we went to look for it, and she still hasn't even seen the dress or anything, but when I tried veils and things on, you know, she cried, and I knew that was the one I needed to get.

In addition to these revelatory experiences, these artifacts are neither ordinary nor mundane. Rather, they are created solely for use in one of the most significant rituals in modern society.

2. Sacred Items Help Fulfill the Bride's Fantasy. The wedding gown is a powerful symbol of the purity, modesty, radiance and spirituality of the bride (Barker, 1978). In addition, the dress reflects the tastes and values of the bride and is thus tied to her identity. Many of our informants expressed how they had grown up with a particular fantasy image of their wedding day, particularly Elaine:

> I always imagined myself, ever since I was little, in, you know, the perfect huge white gown. And I just, you know, it's not something that I could settle for, it had to be the one you know...but you just kind of wait until you put that one on, and everyone stops and says, "This is the dress." You know, you shop until you find it.

This aspect of one's wedding fulfilling a fantasy was summarized eloquently by Jody, who said, "This is a once in a lifetime moment...it's your one day where you feel like a princess."

Other artifacts that helped fulfill the bride's fantasy were the decorations. Lynn stated, "I think that is going to be the most important part, as far as building the atmosphere, of the whole ceremony."

Similarly, Elaine explained:

TABLE 1
Sacred and Secular Items Mentioned by Brides

Sacred Items	N		Secular Items	N
Dress	8		Cake	5
Minister	5a		Invitations	5
Music	4		Unity Candle	4
Church	3		Registry	3
Decorations	3		Reception Flowers	3
Photographs	2		Ringbearer pillow	2
Rings	1		Shoes	2
			Tuxedos	2
			Attendant attire	2
			Napkins	2
			Program Cover	2
			Party Favors/Food/Basket/ Champagne glasses/Utensils/Car/ DJ/Candles/Chairs/ Hotel Rooms	1

a= Three ministers were specified by name; two were unspecified.

I want the flowers, you know, with the candlelight. I want that to be really nice, because I think my church is pretty small and it's not real elaborate, you know, it's just a small town church. And I want it to look, you know, as Christmas-y and as festive as it can.

Thus, this concern with the ambiance of the ritual — and the subsequent emphasis upon the decorations — ties in to the creation of each bride's fantasy wedding.

3. Sacred Items Are Imbued With Tradition. Several informants were incorporating clothing or other accessories into their weddings, that had been used either by their mothers or other relatives in their own ceremonies. For example, Kate was going to wear her aunt's veil and carry a handkerchief made for her by her late great-grandmother. In addition, she was considering using the flower girl's basket that she had carried in her aunt's wedding. Similarly, Jody explained:

I'm carrying my grandmother's prayer book that she carried when she was married. That was, you know, no question of whether I wouldn't or would...that she carried in 1908 and all of her sisters, my mom's sisters have carried, and that all of their kids have carried.

These items held particular significance for these informants because of the family bonds these items represented on one of the most important days of their lives.

4. Sacred Items Have Communicative Power. Several artifacts acquired sacred status due to their ability to communicate the meanings inherent in the wedding ritual. Music seemed to be of particular importance, especially to Lynn:

We're having a lot of slow songs, and we want, I would like to have people really pay close attention to the wording of the songs, and you know, the timing of them...like when we're lighting the Unity candle, we're having "You Light Up My Life" you know, that type of relation to what we're doing ...I want people to remember...the song that was sung when we lit the candles.

Interestingly, music not only communicated powerfully to the audience, but also to the bride herself, as Kate explained:

I want someone singing before and during the wedding. And then, I want music to be sung when we're lighting the candle. And then, I want the Lord's Prayer to be sung... so, I, the music really means a lot to me...because I love music and I think that it'll probably mean a lot to me when I'm standing there. I hope I don't start crying.

Our interpretation of why music was so significant is that it is one part of a scripted ritual that can be personalized to communicate the values of the bride and groom. In addition, as Lynn explained, carefully chosen songs can emphasize and enhance the specific activities being performed.

Two other artifacts, wedding rings and photographs, were considered sacred for their power to communicate long after the wedding was over. Jody commented, "The rings are important to me...that's something I'm going to have on my finger for the rest of my life." And Lynn felt that her wedding photographs were, as she explained:

...the thing that we'll have the longest. I mean that's the thing that we'll always be looking at. The dress will go in a box and I'll forget what the church looked like, but I'll have the pictures.

5. Sacred Items Are "Contaminated," and Thus "Contaminate" the Wedding. As Belk, Sherry and Wallendorf (1989) explain, particular places and individuals are contaminated with positive sacredness. In particular, places of worship and religious authorities were viewed by many of our brides as important elements of their wedding rituals. Several informants expressed a desire for a church wedding. Although they felt such a wedding was not necessary for everyone, most who expressed this desire felt that having their wedding in a church legitimized the marriage. Sue articulated this feeling:

To me it's important to have it in church because it feels more like it's blessed...It just doesn't seem married unless it's in the church...If I was just up at the courthouse, you know, it would be like, like, I don't know...like it wasn't really happening, like it was practice or pretend...Yeah, just like when you're little kids, that kind of thing.

Our interpretation of this finding is that the church has the power to positively contaminate the marriage with sacredness. For others, having the wedding in a *church* was not an essential element, but having a religious ceremony was seen as necessary.

Most of our informants viewed a wedding as a religious event. For a few, this belief meant that it was important to have a particular minister preside over the ceremony. Kelly wished to include her hometown Lutheran pastor in her wedding, even though she was converting to Catholicism and would be having a Catholic wedding. And Jody had to compromise on where to have her wedding so she could ensure that her childhood priest could perform the ceremony:

> I wanted this priest who I had known from childhood to do it ...you decide what's negotiable and what's not. And the place was negotiable at that point. He wasn't negotiable. I wanted him, so that's the way that worked out.

Even those informants who had no particular individual in mind still wanted a minister to preside over the ceremony, rather than a justice of the peace.

In summary, most of the sacred artifacts mentioned by our brides were connected to the wedding ceremony itself. Furthermore, our data lends credence to Belk, Sherry and Wallendorf's (1989) discussion of the ways in which sacredness is expressed via consumption artifacts.

Profane Wedding Artifacts

We classified artifacts as profane either because brides stated that they simply did not care about these items, or because they made other remarks that indicated these items were relatively unimportant to them. For example, Elaine remarked: "You know, the ring bearer's pillow...I'll pick up the pillow, I'll throw it in the [shopping] cart, and we're gone." Likewise, one focus group participant noted:

> Somehow my mom and my mother-in-law got it in their heads that we had to give away party favors...I just don't see why people needed something else to take home with them, but my mom went out and bought 150 little sachets that were supposed to go to everybody. And they are sitting in my room at home...and I just don't care, I just don't.

Our interpretation yielded 21 different artifacts that one or more brides regarded as profane (Table 1). One-half of these items were used for the reception, only six were used during the actual wedding ceremony and the remainder could be described as facilitating either event (e.g., wedding invitations).

In comparing the sacred and profane artifacts identified, we noticed three interesting tendencies. First, the variety of secular artifacts is much greater than the variety of sacred ones. This finding suggests that most, if not all brides may regard only an "evoked set" of artifacts as capable of embodying sacredness. It is highly possible that the items in these sets are the result of socialization. Furthermore, brides' classification of other items as sacred appears to be more of an individual choice. Second, only one profane item was actually part of the bridal costume — namely, the shoes worn during the wedding. Moreover, brides only classified their shoes as such if they had decided to use them after the wedding. However, *most* sacred items were actually worn by the bride. Thus, it appears that items comprising the bride's ritual garb are consistently considered to be imbued with sacredness more than other types of items.

Third, we were intrigued to discover that some items were considered sacred by some brides and profane by others. We could not fully explore why this was the case; however, this topic is certainly worthy of future research.

Reasons for Profane Status

Our interpretation of the text yielded six distinct reasons why brides regarded some artifacts as profane.

1. Profane Items Are Common in Everyday Life. Brides characterized some items as profane simply because they *were* ordinary, everyday items. For example, Jenny said of the utensils for her reception, "they're just plates and forks." Likewise, Val noted, "the chairs are pretty cut and dried. It wasn't like, well I want them to be colonial designed. Just give me some chairs."

Interestingly, some brides seemed ambivalent about elevating typically ordinary items to sacred status. This finding was especially evident in brides' description of the wedding cake. While many brides remarked that it was "just a cake," others — like Jody — recognized that this item could acquire elevated status:

> [The cook] is just going to make us a cute little double-decker...And the rest are going to be sheet cakes. And, who cares? I mean, people eat them, and you know, maybe it's pretty. And yes, I would like to go to a wedding and see the pretty cake, probably. I mean, I wouldn't want everyone to be like me.

Thus, it appeared that some items were so deeply entrenched in ordinary, everyday existence that no amount of contamination within the context of a ritualized occasion could elevate them beyond the ordinary. Yet brides also seemed to recognize that "ordinary" items could be elevated to a higher status, if they themselves chose to regard these items as sacred.

2. Profane Items Are Consumed or Discarded. Our emic and etic interpretation revealed that a large number of artifacts were described as secular because they simply had no permanence beyond the actual wedding or reception. A variety of artifacts was described in this manner. For example, one focus group participant noted: "This little party favor [is] just going to ride around in people's cars for a couple of weeks and then they throw them out." Kate remarked that she hated invitations, then explained: "I've received so many that I look at and think 'Oh, this is pretty.' And then ten minutes after I write it on my calendar it's in the garbage." Elaine noted:

> I worked at a flower shop last summer...so I knew how much people spent, and how much each [flower] arrangement costs for a table...it's like "Why are they doing this?" They're just going to go in the garbage.

Thus, some brides appeared to share Becky's aversion to what she called "throwaways" — or items that would literally be discarded after the wedding.

3. Profane Items Can "De-Sacralize" the Wedding Ritual. Sherry (1983) and Belk, Sherry and Wallendorf (1989) discuss how gifts can serve as conduits of sacred meaning. Yet one artifact of the wedding ritual that was deliberately excluded by three brides — the *list* of gifts created via the bridal registry — was viewed as interfering with the sacred nature of the wedding. June said "I just don't like the idea of telling people, 'I want this. Buy me this or don't buy me anything.'" Jody echoed this sentiment, noting:

I think it's stupid. To go with lists of things that you want to have. I think it's really dumb. Yuck. It's so cold...To go write down that you want this clock at $34.99 and this at $62.99, that takes a lot of the spontaneity out of giving a gift.

We interpret this finding to mean that for some brides, investing an item with "giftness" (Sherry and McGrath 1989) occurs when givers themselves select something they believe the bride and groom would like, rather than when an item is selected from a preconceived list.

4. Profane Items Do Not Impinge Upon the Bride's Identity. Our interpretation revealed that some items described as unimportant were used by other members of the wedding party. Jenny noted:

[Her fiance] didn't want to wear a tux at first. And I said, that was fine, I didn't really care if he wanted to wear jeans and a T-shirt...whatever he was comfortable in.

Likewise, when discussing her bridesmaid's dresses, Jody noted: "I don't really care what they wear."

Interestingly, both of these brides were among our older informants. Thus, older brides may not feel that artifacts used by other wedding participants add to the sacralization of the ritual. Rather, they appear more concerned that these participants are comfortable in their roles. Indeed, Jenny's opinion about her fiance's tuxedo can be contrasted to that of June, one of our younger brides:

June said that she wanted a smoky grey tux for everyone on the groom's end...However, Elaine reminded June at that moment, that she allowed Mike [June's fiance] to pick out his own color. Reluctantly, June agreed.

5. Profane Items are "Parity Products." Brides regarded some artifacts as profane because few variations of these items existed. One artifact described most commonly in this manner was the Unity Candle. Kate noted, "there was only two [in the store], and we picked it together...that didn't take five minutes." Likewise, June noted that she "just walked into the candle store and bought a candle."

Some brides also viewed cakes as parity products. One focus group participant commented: "I really couldn't care less what the cake looks like...I look through the magazine and they all start looking the same."

Our interpretation of this finding is that because brides perceive little difference between some items, they cannot imbue an item with aspects of their own identity.

6. Profane Items Viewed as Unimportant to the Audience. Our text was rich with brides' descriptions of how they sought to meet the expectations of their "ritual audience" (Rook, 1985), or the guests attending the wedding festivities. Thus, it was not surprising that one reason brides downplayed the importance of some items was because they perceived these items to be meaningless to their wedding guests. With respect to the candles for her reception tables, Kate remarked: "People aren't going to remember, ten years from now, 'Oh gosh, the candles on the tables.'" Likewise, Jenny noted that having a traditional cake made "just seemed silly...people don't care for wedding cake."

Thus, our brides appeared cognizant of the fact that not only did they regard some items as more or less sacred, but their guests did as well.

SUMMARY

This paper contributes to our understanding of consumers' distinction between sacred and secular artifacts in that it: 1) illustrates that even within a "sacred" occasion such as a wedding, orchestrators of the event themselves distinguish between sacred and secular items; 2) reveals that more items were profane than sacred, indicating that consumers planning ritualized occasions may only view an "evoked set" of artifacts as sacred; 3) reveals that sacred items are those that the bride can contaminate with meaning from either the ritualized occasion itself of from her own identity and 4) interprets secular items to be those that are ordinary or disposable, and which cannot or will not be imbued with sacred meaning by brides.

In conclusion, this paper applies the sacred and secular distinction to a highly pervasive and visible consumer ritual, the American wedding. We believe that applying this distinction to other types of rituals in American culture would likewise prove to be a fruitful endeavor.

The Effects of Ambiguity on Consumer Information Processing: What, When, Why, and How
Summary of Papers Presented at Session 5.5
S. Ratneshwar, University of Florida

Consumers often have to cope with ambiguous information environments, and in recent years this issue has become a topic of considerable interest to consumer researchers. *What* are the effects of ambiguity on consumer judgments in different domains? *When* might these effects be observed: Are they moderated by a specific set of variables? *Why* might these effects be predicted in terms of theoretical rationale? And finally, *how* might these effects be explainable in terms of mediating processes?

The purpose of the special session was to stimulate discussion and future research that might profitably address the preceding questions. Three papers were presented; all were aimed at advancing theoretical knowledge of the issue, but in addition presented empirical work. Also, all three had their theoretical foundations in recent research in the area of social cognition. A brief overview of the papers is provided below.

The paper presented by Kardes examined ambiguity in the form of *incomplete information* on product attributes. The fact that critical information is missing often may not be salient to consumers. Consequently, they may often form more extreme and more confident judgments than are warranted. Nonetheless, such effects are also likely to be moderated by factors that impact on the likelihood that consumers detect the omissions. Two experiments were presented in which the effects of missing information on product evaluative judgments were investigated under varying conditions of prior knowledge, environmental cues to the omissions, and the memorability of the original attribute information.

Chaiken and Maheswaran's paper addressed the processing of *persuasive messages* such as advertisements when the *arguments* in the message are ambiguous in terms of their evaluative implications for the advertised product. Their research built on the theoretical framework provided by Chaiken's (1980) heuristic-systematic information processing model. Specifically, it tested the proposition that the two modes of processing can act concurrently to impact on each other rather than operating in a mutually-exclusive fashion. The results suggest that heuristic cues such as source credibility can bias systematic processing when message arguments are ambiguous; however, this effect is further moderated by task importance.

Pechmann and Ratneshwar investigated the accuracy of consumers' *covariation judgments* when the *attribute information represented in memory* is relatively unambiguous (i.e., high in diagnosticity) versus when it is relatively ambiguous. They presented a set of experiments wherein subjects made price-quality covariation judgments on the basis of taste tests of products. The results show that prior beliefs or "theories" about the covariation can bias judgments when diagnosticity is low (versus high). Two follow-up studies suggest that subjects' prior beliefs did not induce *encoding* biases in taste perceptions. Instead, low diagnosticity subjects likely made heuristic use of their priors as additional inputs in forming their covariation judgments.

How Many Shopping Days Until Christmas? A Preliminary Investigation of Time Pressures, Deadlines, and Planning Levels on Holiday Gift Purchases

Anthony D. Miyazaki, University of South Carolina[1]

ABSTRACT

An investigation into the effects of purchase planning levels and deadlines on Christmas gift-purchasing behavior found that consumers' feelings of time pressure increase as Christmas approaches, and are more extreme for those with self-imposed deadlines. The extent to which consumers plan their purchases was also found to be related to their sense of felt time pressure. The study supported the assumption that the environment surrounding holiday gift purchasing serves as an excellent context in which to study time pressures and purchase planning in consumer research.

TIME

The scarce nature of time plays a unique role in the environment surrounding consumer decisions and actions. All consumer activities have an element of time, and consequently, time and time-related constructs are often used to further understand consumer behavior. From a perspective of planning and choice, consumers are often "forced" to choose between alternatives because of time constraints or "deadlines." These choices may be as simple as deciding which of two television programs to watch when both are to be shown at the same time (without the aid of the "time saving" VCR), or may be more complex, for example, choosing between investment strategies while constrained by investment or tax deadlines.

The importance of the various perceptions and uses of time has already been established in the consumer behavior literature (e.g., Feldman and Hornik 1981; Hirschman 1987; Holbrook and Lehmann 1981; Jacoby, Szybillo, and Berning 1976). In a recent paper exploring the role of time in consumer actions, Bergadaà (1990) advocates further research into the underlying reasons and the manifestations of differing temporal orientations, as well as other time-related activities such as consumer planning and decision-making. The extent to which consumers plan has been found to be related to temporal variables in certain consumption environments (see Holbrook and Lehmann 1981; Park, Iyer, and Smith 1989). In addition, societal norms implying the "appropriate" use of time (Schroeder 1989), as well as self-imposed time restrictions (cf. Rizkalla 1989), may impact consumer planning strategies and subsequent behavior.

Gift purchasing in relation to the Christmas holiday season offers a particularly unique opportunity to study the intricacies of time pressures, deadlines, and time perceptions on general consumer behavior, in that a large number of people have a societal deadline by which they "must" purchase (and prepare) Christmas gifts. In addition to the societal deadline (being Christmas Day or Christmas Eve), many consumers form self-imposed deadlines by which they intend to complete their Christmas shopping. Preliminary interviews with consumers revealed various reasons for these deadlines (e.g., "I like to get [my Christmas shopping] done early to avoid the rush" and "we're going to visit my in-laws and we leave on the 21st").

This study examines the impact of time pressures and personal deadlines, (both psychological representations of time), as well as the actual passage of time (in relation to a set "societal" deadline), on planning levels and other aspects of gift-purchasing situations.

GIFT PURCHASING

In its own right, the study of gift-giving behavior has been well researched by a number of scholars (e.g., Belk 1976; Caplow 1982, 1984; Sherry 1983), who have alerted the academic world of the importance of gift-giving behavior and its role in consumer research. The majority of the studies seem to focus on gift giving in general, with fewer studies narrowing the scope to direct more emphasis on the activities directly surrounding the actual purchase of gifts.

In Sherry's (1983) process model of gift-giving behavior, the purchase (or creation) of a gift is the final step in the "gestation stage" of this process. The purchase transaction is the step that would seem to be most salient to retailers in their positions as sellers, and is one of the two main physical transactions (or exchanges) in the gift-giving process (the other being the actual "giving" of the gift). This, coupled with the economic impact of gift purchases, particularly during the Christmas season (cf. Cutler 1989), emphasizes the importance of studying this phenomenon and its accompanying characteristics.

Belk (1982) reported that gift selection strategies differ depending on the recipient, but found mixed results regarding the proposed level of involvement and the consumer's self-justification of spending more time and effort on the selection. A recent study by Fischer and Arnold (1990) that considers gender differences in Christmas gift shopping found that women start shopping earlier in the year than men, spend more hours shopping (per gift), and give more gifts.

Although much research has investigated the impact and relevance of time with respect to consumer acquisition of frequently purchased items (e.g., Iyer 1989; Park et al. 1989; Umesh, Pettit, and Bozman 1989), time pressures and deadlines for gift purchasing have not been covered as thoroughly. Although the purchasing of gifts may occur regularly, the purchase of each new gift is a unique experience and carries with it new meaning depending on the situation surrounding the purchase, such as the occasion, the recipient, etc. (Belk 1982; Sherry 1983; Wagner, Ettenson, and Verrier 1990). It is important to note that the types of decisions and planning strategies that are affiliated with gift purchases are not necessarily the same as those for other consumer goods (Belk 1982; Caplow 1984; Sherry 1983).

PURCHASE PLANNING LEVELS

Several studies have focused on the relations between time pressures and the planning levels of shoppers (e.g., Park et al. 1989; Wright 1974). The current study differs from former studies in two ways:

(1) While the majority of the previous studies have dealt with supermarket shopping or other personal buying, this study investigates the purchase aspect of gift-giving behavior (previously mentioned as involving a different set of selection and purchase strategies).

---

[1] The author gratefully acknowledges the constructive comments of the anonymous reviewers. In addition, thanks are due to Joe Urbany, Colette Rushton Miyazaki, Carol Fiske, and Lisa Luebbehusen for helpful comments and for assistance in data collection.

(2) Many previous studies have used time pressure measurements dealing with more immediate time units (i.e., minutes), while this study furthers the investigation into deadlines and time pressure from a more distant perspective (measured in days and weeks).

The purpose of this study is to test preliminary hypotheses concerning temporal aspects (both physical and psychological) of gift-purchasing behavior. The study has been designed as a tool to explore various relationships dealing with gift-purchasing behavior that may serve to distinguish this phenomenon from other consumer activities, or conversely, to illustrate its similarities. Our goal is to present useful ideas and empirical support that may serve to further the understanding of time and its impact on consumer behavior, as well as add to the understanding of gift-giving behavior and planning strategies.

RESEARCH QUESTIONS AND HYPOTHESES

Deadlines and Time Pressure

The context of this study differs from the majority of the others that have investigated planning levels and time pressures. Nevertheless, based on preliminary interviews with shoppers, several previously suggested hypotheses (cf. Iyer 1989; Park et al. 1989) were presumed to be appropriate.

The first hypotheses concern the time pressure felt by consumers in regard to two temporal aspects, an actual (societal) deadline and self-imposed deadlines.

H1: As Christmas nears, gift shoppers will have less time to make purchases (time measured in days and weeks), and will therefore experience a greater sense of time pressure in relation to the task of purchasing gifts.

H2: Consumers who set self-imposed deadlines for completion of their holiday shopping will feel more time pressure than those who do not.

In a study on grocery shopping behavior, Iyer (1989) found supporting evidence that shoppers in that context made fewer unplanned purchases when under time pressure. For the current study, we propose that consumers who experience a higher level of felt time pressure in reference to completing their Christmas gift shopping will have less time for "browsing" and will thus plan purchases to a greater extent. Thus, the following hypothesis concerns the relation between perceptions of time pressure and the degree of purchase planning.

H3: Consumers making "planned" purchases will report higher Christmas shopping time pressure scores than those making "unplanned" purchases.

The rationale behind H3 is that a completely unplanned shopping approach necessitates having enough time to explore the selection of gifts available. A consumer who feels pressed for time may not take this more leisurely approach, and will instead plan purchases to some extent. This hypothesis suggests that the purchasing of gifts and of other consumer goods is similar in respect to the effects of time pressure on the level of planning.

Price Concerns

Berry (1979) suggests that as time becomes scarce, consumers are more likely to trade other resources to save time (see also Becker 1965). This potential trade-off between time and money leads us to our next hypothesis.

H4: The more time pressure a consumer feels, the less concern he or she will have in regard to the price of the gift, thus more will be spent on the gift item.

Several informal hypotheses and considerations concerning time pressures and planning levels were also tested. These are discussed in the analysis section of this paper.

Data Collection

The study was conducted during the four Saturdays preceding Christmas 1991 in a large city (regional population>500,000) in the United States. In order to contact consumers when felt time pressure was salient, a mall intercept technique was employed in which three trained interviewers were placed inside the mall by the main entrance (a high traffic area).

Data were collected with a paper-and-pencil instrument, with some initial guidance by the interviewers. The interviewers asked consumers to fill out the surveys only if the consumer had already purchased a gift that day. This was necessary since many of the questions dealt with respondent feelings on the day of the purchase, and it was assumed that these feelings would be more accessible if they were solicited on that day. Each respondent was initially asked to identify his or her most recent gift purchase, and then to answer several questions (described later) concerning the level of planning that went into that purchase. The remainder of the questionnaire was completed without the aid of the interviewer, and consisted of a series of Likert-type items, frequency reports, and demographic items.

Response rates were spread evenly across weeks and across interviewers, averaging 73% for the study as a whole, and resulting in 230 usable surveys (four were not usable). A pretest (n=20) had been conducted several weeks earlier to refine the wording of the items. Any differences in item responses due to interviewers were not statistically significant.

Sample demographics were compared with demographics for the metropolitan area. Per capita income was not significantly different; the median age of the sample was slightly higher than that of the area; and certain minority groups were underrepresented. Although the sample was approximately 74% female, it has been reported that women buy more gifts and are much more active as Christmas shoppers (Fischer and Arnold 1990). Considering that the scope of this paper is to explore purchase behaviors of Christmas gift shoppers, and not necessarily to generalize findings across all types of purchasing, we feel that the sample is adequate for the study.

Measures[2]

A number of measures of time and time-related constructs were used in the study (cf. Hornik 1984). Those pertinent to this particular paper are described below:

Actual time: (in weeks) leading up to Christmas.

Deadline: whether the respondent had a self-imposed deadline to finish his or her Christmas shopping.

Time left until deadline: how many days left until the deadline (or how many days after it had passed).

Felt time pressure for Christmas shopping: a subjective (psychological) measure of feeling rushed to complete the Christmas shopping task.

---

[2]The data collection instrument is available upon request.

Felt time pressure for normal shopping: the same scale as above, but applied to normal, everyday shopping.

Month started: when the respondent started his or her holiday shopping.

Single-item measures were appropriate for the majority of the time-related constructs. The responses to three 7-point Likert-type items relating to feeling rushed to complete one's shopping were summed to produce the Christmas shopping time pressure scale, as well as three others for the normal shopping time pressure scale (standardized alphas were .729 and .585, respectively).

Concern for price also consisted of the sum of three 7-point Likert-type items (standardized $\alpha=.645$). The reader is reminded that this study is preliminary and that more rigorous scales would be suggested for future research (although similar coefficient alphas have been reported in related research [e.g., Umesh et al. 1989]). Also included was Rizkalla's (1989) attitude toward shopping scale (standardized $\alpha=.778$).

A principal components analysis revealed that all items loaded highly on the first factor for each scale (with the exception of one item in the shopping scale). The scale used to measure the concern about the price of the current gift purchase was found to be negatively correlated with the price of the item ($r=-.1856$; $p \leq .01$), contributing to confidence in the measure.

Initial analysis showed that across time, respondents did not differ in their attitude toward shopping nor in the extent of their purchase planning levels. Demographic variables were also found to be similar across data collection periods, suggesting that there were no biases due to which week the data were collected.

The levels of purchase planning were delineated in a manner similar to Kollat and Willett (1967), with the modification of two of their five levels. Kollat and Willett's "general need recognized" and "general need not recognized" were changed to "purchase generally planned" and "no purchase planned," consistent with Piron (1989). ("Purchase generally planned" refers to a situation when a consumer desires to make a purchase, but has not planned on buying in a specific product class or category.)

There are two reasons underlying this change. First, considering that the formation of a need is presumably a complex and often continuous event, we found it difficult to formulate an appropriate measure of "general need" recognition, while "purchase generally planned" appears to be a more direct stage in the planning process (and in this instance refers to the consumer planning to purchase at least some item). We also found it difficult to make an appropriate distinction between when a need was only generally recognized versus when that need (or desire) was converted to an intention to purchase in the product class. Preliminary interviews with shoppers revealed this to be a difficulty for consumers as well.

Unlike Piron (1989), Kollat and Willett's (1967) terminology is retained for the other three planning levels. The series of items used to determine the level of purchase planning is listed below (cf. Piron 1989; Kollat and Willett 1967):

As you entered the mall and started shopping today,
a) ...had you expected or intended to buy at least something?   Yes   No (1)
b) ...had you planned to purchase [class] _____?   Yes   No (2)
c) ...had you planned to purchase [category] _____?   Yes   No (3)
d) ...had you planned to purchase the brand that you purchased?   Yes (5)   No (4)

Corresponding planning levels:
1. No purchase planned
2. Purchase generally planned
3. Product class only (e.g., clothing)
4. Product class and category (e.g., pants)
5. Product class, category, and brand (e.g., Levi's)

It should be noted that this study investigated the levels of planned and unplanned purchases, but did not inquire into the complexities of "impulse" purchasing behavior (e.g., Rook 1987).

RESULTS

Deadlines and time pressure

To test H1, an analysis of variance was performed on the shopping time pressure score over the four weeks of data. The assumption that consumers feel more holiday shopping time pressure as Christmas nears was supported ($F=10.29$; $p<.001$). Scheffé multiple comparison tests revealed differences at $\alpha=.05$ among the following groups (in this case, weeks): 1&3, 1&4, and 2&4 (with week 4 being the closest to Christmas).

The data also support the hypothesis (H2) that shoppers with self-imposed deadlines felt more time pressure on average than those without these deadlines ($F=17.31$; $p<.001$).

In order to evaluate the effectiveness of the measure, the holiday shopping time pressure score was compared with the "normal" shopping time pressure score. The holiday time pressure was statistically higher for weeks 2 ($p<.05$), and weeks 3 and 4 ($p<.001$). Figure 1 illustrates these comparisons. Additionally, the amount of time left until the deadline was found to be negatively correlated with the amount of felt time pressure for Christmas shopping ($r=-.4067$, $p\leq.01$).

To test H3, the levels of planning were categorized into "planned" and "unplanned" purchases in the following manner. "Unplanned" purchases were considered to be those for which the consumer did not plan to purchase the product class, category, or brand, even if a general desire to purchase *something* was present (i.e., "browsing"). In other words, a consumer that reported being in the mall to make a "general purchase," but had *not* planned to buy in the class purchased, would be classified as having made an "unplanned" purchase. In reference to the planning scale mentioned previously, unplanned purchases are designated as levels 1 and 2, while planned purchases are levels 3, 4, and 5.

An analysis of variance for the reported holiday shopping time pressure for planned and unplanned purchases across time periods supported H3 ($F=6.37$; $p=.012$). The average holiday shopping time pressure score for planned purchases (11.23) was higher than that of the unplanned purchases (9.41), supporting the assertion that less time pressure is associated with a greater tendency to "shop around." As pointed out by one reviewer, if it is posited that time pressure affects the likelihood of planning purchases, the use of ANOVA may be of concern. Thus, a chi-square was also performed using a median-split of the time pressure variable. It was statistically significant in the hypothesized direction ($\chi^2=8.98$, $p=.003$).

An analysis across all five planning levels was also statistically significant ($F=2.58$, $p=.039$; or $\chi^2=13.14$, $p=.011$). The time pressure scores tended to peak at the class and category planning levels, falling at the brand planning level. (The difference in time pressure scores for class and brand planning levels is statistically significant at $\alpha=.10$). As suggested by a reviewer, the same tests were also conducted for only those people without self-imposed deadlines in order to alleviate concern of a confound between deadlines and time pressure. The results were the same.

FIGURE 1
Christmas Shopping Time Pressure

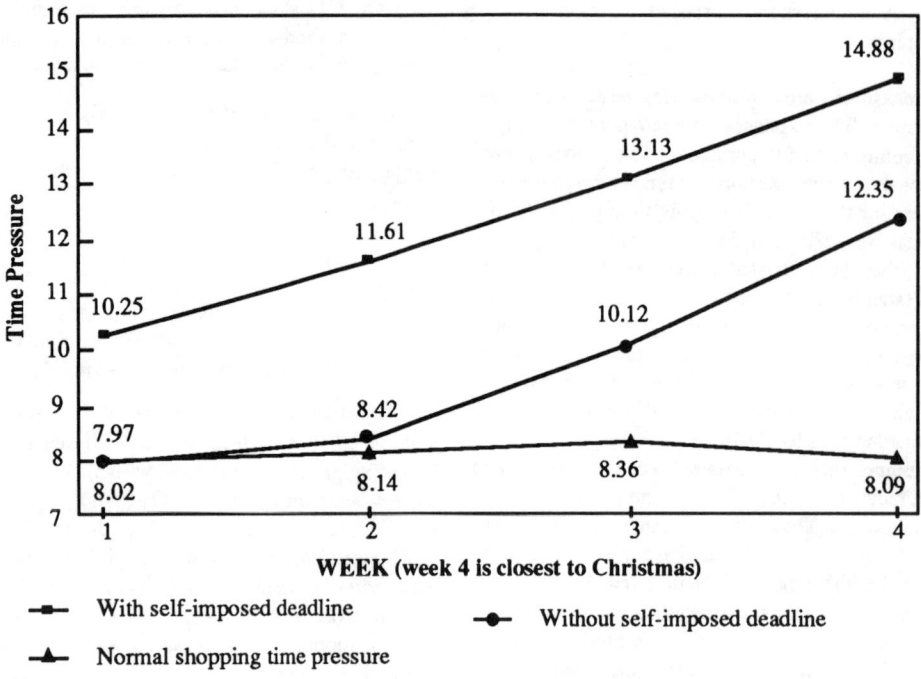

- ■ With self-imposed deadline
- ● Without self-imposed deadline
- ▲ Normal shopping time pressure

Although the initial hypothesis did not specify the degree of planning that would take place, this condition may warrant further investigation. It could be argued that the actual time saved by planning purchases at the brand level may truly be lower than at the category and class levels, thus the higher sense of time pressure. In other words, planning the exact brand may not save time (and thus, alleviate time pressure) if the consumer must search several stores to find the exact item without being able to make a substitution (i.e., another brand). (An alternate explanation suggested by one of the reviewers is that once the purchaser plans the gift to the brand level, the pressure of making the decision is lessened, and perhaps felt time pressure is reduced.)

Price Concerns

No evidence could be found to suggest that additional time pressure would elicit a decrease in concern for price or an increase in item price; thus, H4 was not supported. (Increased time pressure was, however, correlated with regret about the price paid: $r=.26$, $p \leq .01$.) It appears that consumers in this context were not willing to exchange money for time, as suggested by Berry (1979). Yet the purchase planning analyses suggest that time may more likely be exchanged with a forfeiture of choice (i.e., no browsing or shopping around), since time pressured shoppers were more likely to choose a higher planning level than to enjoy the luxury of the more relaxed, browsing strategy.

Additional Findings

Considering the diversity of the findings reported in the planning and impulse purchasing literature regarding what percentage of purchases are unplanned (see Cobb and Hoyer 1986 for a review), we report the following data on purchase planning levels for holiday gift purchases.

Percent of total (n=230)	Planning Level
9.7	1 (no purchase planned)
21.7	2 (purchase generally planned)
15.2	3 (product class planned, e.g., clothing)
31.7	4 (product category planned, e.g., pants)
21.7	5 (product brand planned, e.g., Levi's)

The relationship between the price of the item and the planning level was also investigated. The mean item price for planned purchases ($36.57) was found to be higher than that of the unplanned purchases ($24.41) ($p = .0124$). It makes intuitive sense that the purchase of more expensive items would be better planned than inexpensive items.

Although the concern over price for gift items did not change over the planning levels, analysis of the data showed that the consumers in this sample reported more concern over price for normal gift purchases than for holiday gift purchases (p<.001). One possible explanation is that Christmas gift shopping may carry with it additional meaning because of the nature of the holiday festivities that surround it (cf. Caplow 1984), thereby decreasing other concerns. Another explanation might be that the Christmas gift shopping experience was more salient at this time than gift shopping done at other times in the year. Investigation of this same comparison could be made at a time other than Christmas to test any differences of these perceptions due to the immediacy of the event.

Shoppers were also asked how long they had been planning to purchase the gift item for the recipient. This was done to evaluate the time aspect of planning, in contrast to the measure assessing the extent of planning (i.e., to what level). Analysis of the data suggested that gift purchases planned at higher levels (e.g., brand) were planned further in advance than those at lower levels of planning (e.g., class) (p<.05).

No relationships between temporal variables and demographic variables (such as age, income, education, marital status, or size of household) were statistically significant, with one exception. Women were found to begin shopping earlier in the year than men, supporting the previous findings of Fischer and Arnold (1990).

DISCUSSION

The purpose of this study was to test several preliminary hypotheses concerning the effects and relationships of time (both physical and perceived) on Christmas gift-purchasing behavior, particularly the degree of planning. Data analysis suggests that felt time pressure increases as Christmas approaches, and even more for consumers with self-imposed deadlines. Comparable to the findings of Park et al. (1989) and Iyer (1989), increased time pressure was found to be more associated with planned purchases than with unplanned purchases (although the context in which the current findings are based is quite dissimilar).

Although no apparent economic trade-off was made between time and price, an argument for a trade-off between time and freedom of choice may be reasonable. Further investigation in this direction is encouraged. Pricing implications, such as the effects of holiday sales on shoppers' strategies for planning purchases, as well as their substitution behavior, are other areas that need study.

Interesting factors to be considered in future research include investigation into the consequences of changes in purchase planning levels due to a consumer's inability to locate a previously selected item. Further study on the effects of time and temporal variables on this process may lead to a better understanding of consumer decision processes. Other promising research could be conducted to examine the differences in planning levels across persons of differing temporal orientations (e.g., those described in Bergadaà 1990).

The success of this investigation also suggests that the environment surrounding holiday gift purchasing serves as an excellent context in which to study time pressures and purchase planning in consumer research.

REFERENCES

Becker, Gary (1965), "A Theory of the Allocation of Time," *The Economic Journal*, 75 (September), 493-517.

Belk, Russell W. (1976), "It's the Thought that Counts: A Signed Digraph Analysis of Gift-Giving," *Journal of Consumer Research*, 3 (December), 155-162.

_____ (1982), "Effects of Gift-giving Involvement on Gift-Giving Strategies," in *Advances in Consumer Research*, Vol. 9, ed. Andrew Mitchell, Ann Arbor, MI: Association for Consumer Research, 408-412.

Bergadaà, Michelle M. (1990), "The Role of Time in the Action of the Consumer," *Journal of Consumer Research*, 17 (December), 289-302.

Berry, L.L. (1979), "The Time Buying Consumer," *Journal of Retailing*, 55 (4), 58-69.

Caplow, Theodore (1982), "Christmas Gifts and Kin Networks," *American Sociological Review*, 47 (June), 383-392.

_____ (1984), "Rule Enforcement without Visible Means: Christmas Gift Giving in Middletown," *American Journal of Sociology*, 89 (May), 1306-1323.

Cobb, Cathy J. and Wayne D. Hoyer (1986), "Planned Versus Impulse Purchase Behavior," *Journal of Retailing*, 62 (Winter), 384-409.

Cutler, Blayne (1989), "Here Comes Santa Claus (Again)," *American Demographics*, 11 (December), 30-33, 52-53.

Feldman, Laurence P. and Jacob Hornik (1981), "The Use of Time: An Integrated Conceptual Model," *Journal of Consumer Research*, 7 (March), 407-419.

Fischer, Eileen and Stephen J. Arnold (1990), "More than a Labor of Love: Gender Roles and Christmas Gift Shopping," *Journal of Consumer Research*, 17 (December), 333-345.

Hirschman, Elizabeth C. (1987), "Theoretical Perspectives of Time Use: Implications for Consumer Behavior Research," in *Research in Consumer Behavior*, Vol. 2, Jagdish N. Sheth and Elizabeth C. Hirschman, eds., JAI Press, New York, 55-81.

Holbrook, Morris B. and Donald R. Lehmann (1981), "Allocating Discretionary Time: Complementarity Among Activities," *Journal of Consumer Research*, 7 (March), 395-406.

Hornik, Jacob (1984), "Subjective vs. Objective Time Measures: A Note on the Perception of Time in Consumer Behavior," *Journal of Consumer Research*, 11 (June), 615-618.

Iyer, Easwar S. (1989), "Unplanned Purchasing: Knowledge of Shopping Environment and Time Pressure," *Journal of Retailing*, 65 (Spring), 40-57.

Jacoby, Jacob, George J. Szybillo, and Carol K. Berning (1976), "Time and Consumer Behavior: An Interdisciplinary Overview," *Journal of Consumer Research*, 2 (March), 320-339.

Kollat, David T. and Ronald P. Willett (1967), "Customer Impulse Purchasing Behavior," *Journal of Marketing Research*, 4 (February), 21-31.

Park, C. Whan, Easwar S. Iyer, and Daniel C. Smith (1989), "The Effects of Situational Factors on In-Store Grocery Shopping Behavior: The Role of Store Environment and Time Available for Shopping," *Journal of Consumer Research*, 15 (March), 422-433.

Piron, Francis (1989), "A Definition and Empirical Investigation of Impulse Purchasing," unpublished dissertation, University of South Carolina, Columbia, SC.

Rizkalla, Aida N. (1989), "Sense of Time Urgency and Consumer Well-Being: Testing Alternative Causal Models," *Advances in Consumer Research*, Vol. 16, ed. T. Srull, Provo, UT: Association for Consumer Research, 180-188.

Rook, Dennis W. (1987), "The Buying Impulse," *Journal of Consumer Research*, 14 (September), 189-199.

Schroeder, Jonathan E. (1989), "What Time Means to Others: Expectations of Behavior Based on Time Use Information," *Advances in Consumer Research*, Vol. 16, ed. T. Srull, Provo, UT: Association for Consumer Research, 354-358.

Sherry, John (1983), "Gift Giving in Anthropological Perspective," *Journal of Consumer Research*, 10 (September), 157-168.

Umesh, U. N., Kathy L. Pettit, and Carl S. Bozman (1989), "Shopping Model of the Time-Sensitive Consumer," *Decision Sciences*, 20 (Fall), 715-729.

Wagner, Janet, Richard Ettenson, and Sherri Verrier (1990), "The Effect of Donor-Recipient Involvement on Consumer Gift Decisions," in *Advances in Consumer Research*, Vol. 17, eds. Gerald Gorn and Richard Pollay, Ann Arbor, MI: Association for Consumer Research, 683-689.

Wright, Peter (1974), "The Harassed Decision Maker: Time Pressures, Distractions, and the Use of Evidence," *Journal of Applied Psychology*, 59, 555-561.

The Influence of Background Music on Shopping Behavior: Classical Versus Top-Forty Music in a Wine Store

Charles S. Areni, Texas Tech University
David Kim, Texas Tech University

As part of a field experiment in a large U.S. city, the background music (classical versus Top-Forty) in a centrally located wine store was varied over a two month period. The results of an ANOVA indicated that the classical music influenced shoppers to spend more money. Additional findings suggest that, rather than increasing the *amount* of wine purchased, customers selected *more expensive* merchandise when classical music was played in the background. MacInnis and Park's (1991) notion that music is more persuasive when it "fits" the persuasion context is employed to account for these results.

INTRODUCTION

Kotler (1973-1974) coined the term *atmospherics* to describe various *visual* (color, brightness, size, shape), *aural* (volume, pitch), *olfactory* (scent, freshness), and *tactile* (softness, smoothness, temperature) dimensions of a store that can influence the purchase probabilities of consumers. Although Kotler requested that further research be conducted regarding the impact of these in-store factors on behavior, the academic literature on this topic remains rather sparse. The research that *has* appeared tends to be limited to a rather narrow range of consumer reactions. Specifically, researchers have focused on overt *quantitative indicators* (i.e. dollar amount spent, time spent, etc.) or perceptions of various dimensions of *store image* (see Bellizzi, Crowley and Hasty, 1983), while largely ignoring other aspects of shopping behavior (Eroglu, Ellen, and Machleit, 1991).

Moreover, due to the difficulties of conducting atmospheric research in the field, much of the emergent research has relied on verbal (i.e. Gardner and Siomkos, 1986) or visual (i.e. Eroglu and Machleit, 1990) simulations of retail environments. While these laboratory simulation techniques offer the advantages of methodological expediency and experimental control, their ability to realistically capture the desired store atmosphere is suspect. The literature on atmospherics would, therefore, be enhanced by research examining the impact of atmospheric variables on a *wider range of consumer behavior* in an *actual retail setting*. Consistent with this objective, this study entailed the observation of: (1) the *number* of shelf items examined, handled, and purchased, (2) the *shelf location* of the items examined, handled, and purchased, (3) the *total dollar amount* of the merchandise purchased, (4) the *total amount of time spent* shopping, and (5) the frequency with which patrons consumed merchandise on site, under two background music conditions (Top-Forty versus classical) in a downtown wine store.

THE LITERATURE ON THE EFFECTS OF MUSIC[1]

The number of investigations addressing the influence of music on consumer behavior is still rather small. Although researchers have examined the effects of music *volume* (Smith and Curnow, 1966) and *tempo* (Milliman, 1982, 1986) on certain aspects of shopping behavior, Bruner (1990) suggests that the *genre* of the background music is likely to produce stronger effects on perceptions and preferences. Further, since preferences for musical genres are strongly influenced by individual differences (see Cupchik, Rickert, and Mendelson, 1982), varying the genre of a store's background music is more likely to produce differential effects across customer groups.

Yalch and Spangenberg (1990) examined this possibility by comparing the effects of easy-listening versus Top-Forty music on shoppers' estimates of the amount of time they spent shopping. They found that younger customers (under 25) reported spending more time shopping when exposed to easy-listening music, whereas older customers (25 and over) thought they were in the store longer when exposed to Top-Forty music. Yalch and Spangenberg speculated that shoppers who encounter non-typical environmental factors (i.e., younger shoppers exposed to easy listening music) perceive intervals of time being longer than they actually are.

The Yalch and Spangenberg study raises the possibility that the given musical genres can produce highly specific perceptions by consumers. In the context of the present study, the objective was to identify the background music that would create a setting appropriate for the purchase and consumption of wine. MacInnis and Park (1991) have formalized this notion by defining the "fit" of music as "consumers' subjective perceptions of the music's relevance or appropriateness" to the persuasion context (p. 162). Although MacInnis and Park were concerned with the persuasive impact of music in an advertising setting, their notion of "fit" seems applicable to the impact of atmospheric variables as well. The task then was to identify the music that best fits the context of examining, purchasing, and tasting wine.

WINE TASTING, CLASSICAL MUSIC AND SOPHISTICATION

Arlott (1984) presents the work of several authors that imply that wine tasting is associated with a certain degree of foreignness, sophistication, and even snob appeal. In discussing the undertaking of his book on wine, Kramer (1989), for example, notes that:

> At the time I knew nothing of wine and had no intention of crossing its path. Wine seemed forbidding, snobbish, and, above all, daunting in its complication. I was suspicious of its trappings and cowed by its air of sophistication (p. 8).

Empirical evidence supports this intuition. Lesch, Luk, and Leonard (1991) found that among women who consumed alcoholic beverages, wine drinkers in comparison to beer and spirits consumers, were generally younger, better educated, and earned higher incomes. Wine drinkers also had a higher appreciation for art and lower regard for traditional female roles.

This suggests that wine purchasing, tasting and consumption are associated with higher socio-economic status, prestige, sophistication, and complexity. What kind of music would "fit" such a context? Farnworth (1969) offers the following insight:

> But the diametrically opposed view, and quite possibly the more common one is [that]...the musically elite—the critics, the genius composers, and the musicologists—have discovered or on their way to discovering what constitutes 'good taste.' One's jazz loving friends have a taste of low order; a

---

[1] See Bruner (1990) for a more detailed discussion of the various effects of music on moods, preferences, and general behavior.

higher order of taste is possessed by the man who loves the music of Mendelssohn but not that of Beethoven or Bach; and a still higher status has been reached by those who are more attracted to the works of Beethoven and Bach than to those of Mendelssohn (p. 98, insert ours).

Likewise, DiMaggio (1986) has developed a model describing the patronage behavior of performing arts audiences. He recommends that firms emphasizing highly artistic/cultural (as opposed to highly extravagant/popular) performances should charge a higher admittance price to the select, well-to-do audiences having more refined tastes. Stone (1983) provides a more detailed discussion of the association of classical music with maturity, formality, and higher socio-economic status. Overall, the implication is that, if wine tasting and consumption are sophisticated, prestigious, complicated, and even snobbish behaviors, then the classical genre of music appears to be well suited for complimenting these activities.

PROPOSITIONS

Although this study was conducted on a largely exploratory basis, the general proposition suggested by the aforementioned works is that playing classical music in the background will increase the amount of merchandise: (1) examined, (2) handled, and (3) purchased, and (4) the amount of time patrons spend in the store relative to playing other genres of music in the background.

METHOD

The study was conducted in a downtown restaurant in a large southeastern city. The restaurant featured a wine cellar, clearly visible through a glass section of the floor, that was open to patrons who wished to just visit, sample some wines, or purchase some bottles of wine. This unique setting afforded the opportunity to examine the impact of background music on shopping, purchase, and consumption behavior.

Data Collection

All observations were recorded between 6 p.m. and 11 p.m. on successive Fridays and Saturdays beginning May 4, 1990 and ending July 28, 1990. Each of the two experimental conditions (i.e., classical versus Top-Forty music) was counterbalanced with respect to the day of the week via random assignment of the latter to the former. Further, no data were collected on dates where the researchers were able to identify exogenous factors (i.e., holidays, special events, etc.) likely to influence demand.

The data were collected via direct observation. Each consumer was observed as s/he entered the wine cellar. The observer, who was naive to the research hypotheses, stood behind a counter labeled 'Employees Only' and posed as an inventory keeper. From that position he was easily able to observe each consumer as s/he perused the merchandise in the cellar. Since the wine cellar averaged eleven customers per evening, there was rarely more than one customer in the store at any time, making observation of search and purchase behavior a relatively easy task.

Independent Variables

Manipulated Variables: Prior to the study, musical selections from several genres of music, including classical and Top-Forty, were randomly played on a given evening according to the whims and preferences of the manager. *Classical versus Top-Forty background music* was manipulated by repeatedly playing only selections from one of the two genres on a given night. The music played in the classical condition consisted of: The Mozart Collection, Mendelssohn Piano Concerto #2, My Favorite Chopin, Vivaldi - The Four Seasons. These recordings were selected because they were similar to the classical selections played in the wine cellar before the study began. In the Top-Forty music condition, the following sections were played: The Traveling Wilburys: Volume 1, Fleetwood Mac: Behind the Mask, Robert Plant: Manic Nirvana, Rush: Presto. In order to qualify as being "Top-Forty," the recordings had to be one of *Billboard Magazine*'s top forty albums (tapes) and have a single (song) in *Billboard*'s top twenty singles list in the six months prior to the study. The volume of the music was held constant across the two conditions.

Measured Variables: *Customer type* was measured by classifying patrons as being either single male, single female, a male/female couple, or a group of people not consisting of male/female couples. Patrons were also classified into the following *customer age* categories: 20 to 29, 30 to 39, 40 to 49, 50 to 59, 60 and up. If a couple or group of consumers were judged to consist of members belonging to more than one age category, this variable was coded as missing data.

Dependent Variables

Information Search: Similar to Hoyer (1984), information search was measured by observing subjects' inspection of the merchandise on the shelves. Four variables were recorded. The observer counted the *number of items examined*. This was defined as the sum of all items (i.e. wines) for which the customer: (1) stopped to read the shelf label for more than three seconds, (2) pointed to the bottle on the shelve, and/or (3) touched the bottle on the shelve. The observer also counted the *number of items handled*. In order to qualify as being handled, an item must have been pulled from the shelf by a customer. Since the wine bottles were stored at three distinct shelf levels, with the middle level corresponding to the "eye level" of an adult of average height, the observer was able to record the *shelf location of items examined* and the *shelf location of items handled*.

Purchase Behavior: Both observational and objective measures of purchase behavior were employed in the present study. The observer recorded the *number of items purchased*, the *shelf location of the items purchased*, and, since he had access to the register, the *total dollar amount* of each customer's purchase.

Consumption Behavior: Since the wine store contained a dining area for wine tasting and/or general consumption, the observer noted *whether any wine was consumed in the wine cellar*.

Additional Measures: Due to some of the relationships and effects implied in the literature review, the observer recorded the *amount of time each customer spent in the cellar* by noting the exact time at which the customer(s) entered and exited the wine cellar.

Data Analysis

Because this study was conducted in the field rather than the laboratory, individual subjects were not randomly assigned to each music condition. Rather, the researchers employed a counterbalanced experimental design wherein the successive Fridays and Saturdays of the sixteen week period of the study were randomly assigned to experimental conditions. Thus, background music (classical versus Top-Forty) and day of the week (Friday versus Saturday) were completely crossed experimental factors with individual shoppers nested within day of the week. Consistent with the recommendations of Keppel (1982), individual *night* rather than individual *shopper* is the appropriate unit of analysis for an ANOVA.

However, since subjects were "assigned" to experimental units conditions on the basis of having happened to enter the wine store on a particular Friday or Saturday for whatever reason, the observed variation between nights in each condition could be due to differences that existed between the groups quite independent of the music manipulation (i.e. selection bias).

TABLE 1
Means and Standard Deviations by Music Condition

	Classical	Top-Forty
Number of Items Examined[a]	3.93 (0.81)	3.85 (1.67)
Number of Items Handled	1.36 (0.96)	0.97 (0.62)
Number of Items Purchased	0.12 (0.13)	0.07 (0.09)
Total Sale (in U.S. Dollars)	7.43 (5.51)	2.18 (2.64)[b]
Time Spent (in Minutes)	11.01 (8.67)	8.97 (6.65)

[a]To be read: average of 3.93 shelf items were examined when classical music was played versus 3.85 items when Top-Forty music was played.

[b] $p < .05$

In order to check for preexisting differences between groups, chi-square analyses were performed on cross-tabulations of background music condition with each of the two primary sample descriptors, customer *age* and customer *type*. Although neither of the two analyses reached traditional levels of significance, both approached significance (chi-square < .11 for type and chi-square < .12 for age). Thus, the influence of music on each dependent variable is reported after the variance shared with customer age and type has been removed from the latter.

A second major threat to internal validity of the study concerns exogenous events (i.e. a professional basketball game at a nearby arena) that might have influenced store traffic on a given night. In order to remove variance in each dependent variable due to differences in levels of store traffic, *average* behaviors rather than *total* behaviors constituted the observations for a given night. Thus, there were sixteen observations for all dependent variables, each representing an average for the store on a given night, included in the ANOVAs reported below.

RESULTS

Table 1 presents the means and standard deviations for each dependent variable by music condition. There was little or no impact of background music on the number of shelf items examined ($F = 0.02$, $p < .90$), the number of items handled ($F = 0.93$, $p < .35$), the number of items purchased ($F = 0.65$, $p < .43$), the frequency with which patrons sampled wine on site, (Chi-square = 0.49, $p < .49$), or the amount of time spent in the store ($F = 0.34$, $p < .57$).[2] Background music did, however, influence the amount of money shoppers spent ($F = 6.01$, $p < .02$) with classical music producing a higher level of sales than Top-Forty music. When the variance shared with customer age and customer type was removed from sales, the influence of music remained significant ($F = 4.74$, $p < .032$).[3]

The findings regarding the impact of background music on total sales and the number of items purchased suggests that rather than influencing patrons to purchase *greater quantities* of merchandise, the classical music led them to buy *more expensive* items. The implications of this result are discussed below.

DISCUSSION

The result that shoppers purchased more expensive merchandise when classical music was played in the background is consistent, if not overwhelmingly supportive, of MacInnis and Park's (1991) contention that music must fit the persuasion context in order to produce the desired outcome. If consumers associate wine consumption with prestige and sophistication, then Top-Forty music may provide an incompatible cue, communicating, as Konecni (1982) suggests, a more common, less refined environment. This explanation suggests that retailers should devote considerable attention to the symbolic meaning underlying each purchase experience. If consumers are seeking sophistication, then in-store cues must suggest, and even facilitate that experience. The same holds for other sought shopping experiences like excitement, relaxation, etc.

It is also possible, however, that consumers had very little experience purchasing wines, and thus had only vague expectations and intentions upon entering the cellar. Many customers, in fact, commented that they had never visited a wine cellar. If this was the case, then the background music may have operated independently of the expected purchase experience. At least two explanations for the results are suggested under this scenario.

One possibility, suggested by the work of Markin, Lillis, and Narayana (1976), and an anonymous reviewer, is that, given the unfamiliar setting of the wine cellar, consumers, consciously or unconsciously, sought external cues as to appropriate behavior. The classical music may have communicated a sophisticated, upper class, atmosphere, suggesting that only expensive merchandise should be considered. Customers may even have felt pressure to conform to the setting implied by the music by purchasing expensive wine.

A second possibility is that the background music communicated to shoppers the price and quality of the merchandise in the store. Yalch and Spangenberg (1990) suggest that any retailer wishing to convey a high prestige, high price image should consider classical background music. The results of the present study support this contention. It is possible that shoppers, being somewhat unfamiliar with wine cellars and wines in general, used the classical music as a cue and inferred that the cellar contained mostly high priced merchandise. As noted by a second anonymous reviewer, a "no music" control condition would have been helpful for discriminating the former explanation, which implies that Top-Forty music inhibited sales, from the latter two, which suggest that classical music enhanced sales.

---

[2]Interestingly, shoppers examined, handled and purchased significantly more items from shelf level two, lending credence to the emphasis that salespersons place on obtaining "eye level" shelf space.

[3]Given the exploratory nature of the five implied hypotheses, a family-wise correction was applied to all analyses (see Keppel, 1982, pp. 145-46). The reported effect of background music on sales is significant at a family-wise error rate of 0.15.

It is interesting that the number of items examined, handled, and purchased, the total amount of time spent in the store, and the decision to taste wines on site were unaffected by the background music. A potential explanation for these null results, suggested by an anonymous reviewer, is that various aspects of musical selections affect perceptions and behaviors differently. Most of the null results were obtained for actual behaviors. Perhaps musical *tempo*, rather than *genre*, produces a stronger influence on these variables (see Milliman, 1982, 1986). However, musical genre may be more integral to affecting (conscious) perceptions regarding appropriate behaviors, merchandise quality, etc (see Bruner, 1990).

LIMITATIONS

As with any field experiment, this study is limited by two distinct but related shortcomings affecting internal validity. The first concerns a selection bias. Since subjects were "assigned" to experimental conditions on the basis of having happened to enter the wine store on a particular day for any given reason, it is possible that mean differences in information search behavior, purchase intentions, etc. existed among the experimental groups quite independent of the actual treatments. We attempted to assess selection bias by examining the distributions of customer age and customer type within each lighting condition. However, numerous other differences may have existed between the two groups, thus biasing our interpretation of the observed variation in total sales by music condition. The second threat to internal validity concerns the inability to control for exogenous factors that might have influenced the amount of store traffic on a given night. Since the dependent variables of the study were *average* rather than *total* behaviors, external influences on *store traffic* need not have influenced the results directly. However, the literature suggests that an *individual* shopper's behavior depends on the number of other customers present in the store. Further, this research implies that the presence of other shoppers may produce either beneficial (Kotler, 1973-74) or detrimental (Harrell, Hutt, and Anderson, 1980; Eroglu and Harrell, 1986; Eroglu and Machleit, 1990) effects for the retailer. Although the wine cellar rarely contained more than two customers, the interpretation of the results should be tempered somewhat due to the failure to control for these social environmental variables.

A second shortcoming of this research concerns the inability to assess the reliability of the observational measures due to reliance on a single judge. Although single observers have been employed in previous research on atmospherics (see Milliman, 1982), the behaviors to be recorded were simple in nature (i.e. time spent in a specified area) ensuring a reasonable degree of reliability (see Carlsmith, Ellsworth, and Aronson, 1976). The observational measures of information processing activity in the present study were somewhat more complex. Hoyer (1984), however, relied on a single observer to measure the information search and choice processes of supermarket shoppers. Like Hoyer, the authors of the present research attempted to minimize measurement error by developing: (1) highly specific descriptions of the behaviors to be observed, and (2) a coding scheme that was easy to implement. It was hoped that these precautions, combined with the low number of customers on a per hour basis, would produce an acceptable level of accuracy.

A third limitation of this research concerns the manipulation of classical versus Top-Forty music. First, as discussed above, since the experimental design did not include a "no music" control condition, it is difficult to determine whether classical music facilitated the selection of expensive wine, or whether Top-Forty music inhibited such selections. In addition, although the popular selections were randomly chosen from a population of cassettes determined to be the most popular by various music publications, no such procedure was employed in determining the classical selections. It is, therefore, difficult to say whether the latter music condition adequately represented the classical music genre. Moreover, the manipulation may have been confounded with several other dimensions of music (i.e. tempo, pitch, familiarity) known to influence perceptions and behavior (see Bruner, 1990).

Finally, this research failed to directly assess the "fit" of the music to the persuasion context (see MacInnis and Park, 1991), but rather inferred fit on the basis of second-hand sources. Although the present study was largely exploratory in nature, a more direct indicant of fit would have been desirable. Similarly, the work of Mehrabian (1976) and Donovan and Rossiter (1982) has focused on the dimensions of subjective experience that mediate the impact of atmospheric variables on behavior (see also Owens, 1992). However, the reluctance of store management to employ intrusive measures prevented the assessment of subjective reactions, thus leaving their status as mediators untested. Of course, the pretesting of various musical selections would have allowed for the manipulation of music conditions along subjective dimensions (see, for example, Stratton and Zalanowski, 1984). However, the implicit assumption underlying such a pretesting procedure, that individuals have relatively homogeneous reactions to the musical selections regarding the dimensions of interest, is somewhat suspect (see Cupchik et al, 1982).

CONCLUSION

This research found that patrons spent more money in a wine store when classical rather than Top-Forty music was played in the background, though the number of shelf items examined, handled, and purchased, and the amount of time spent did not vary by music condition. The findings regarding the impact of background music on total sales and the number of items purchased suggest that, rather than influencing patrons to purchase *greater quantities* of wine, the classical music induced them to purchase *more expensive* wines. Though it did not directly test formal hypotheses, this result offers support for MacInnis and Parks' (1991) notion that music must be appropriate for the context in which it is employed in order to enhance persuasion, and for Yalch and Spangenberg's (1990) suggestion that classical music evokes perceptions of higher priced store merchandise.

REFERENCES

Arlott, John (1984). *Wine*, New York, NY: The Oxford University Press.

Bellizzi, Joseph A., Ayn E. Crowley, and Ronald W. Hasty (1983), "The Effects of Color in Store Design," *Journal of Retailing*, 59 (Spring), 21-44.

Bruner II, Gordon C. (1990), "Music, Mood, and Marketing," *Journal of Marketing*, (October), 94-104.

Carlsmith, J. Merrill, Phoebe C. Ellsworth, and Elliot Aronson (1976), *Methods of Research in Social Psychology*, New York: Random House.

Cupchik, Gerald C., Martin Rickert, and Julie Mendelson (1982), "Similarity and Preference Judgments of Musical Stimuli," *Scandinavian Journal of Psychology*, 23, 273-282.

Dimaggio, Paul J. (1986). *Nonprofit Enterprise in the Arts*, New York, NY: The Oxford University Press.

Donovan, Robert J. and John R. Rossiter (1982), "Store Atmosphere: An Environmental Psychology Approach," *Journal of Retailing*, 58 (Spring), 34-57.

Eroglu, Sevgin and Gilbert D. Harrell (1986). "An Empirical Study of Retail Crowding," *Journal of Retailing*, 66, 201-221.

_____, and Karen A. Machliet (1990), "An Empirical Study of Retail Crowding: Antecedents and Consequences," *Journal of Retailing*, 66, 201-221.

_____, Pam Scholder Ellen, and Karen A. Machleit (1992), "Environmental Cues in Retailing: Suggestions For a Research Agenda," *Proceedings of the 1991 Symposium on Patronage Behavior and Retail Strategy: Cutting Edge II*, 51-60.

Farnsworth, Paul, R. (1969). *The Social Psychology of Music*, Iowa City, Iowa: The University of Iowa Press.

Gardner, Meryl P. and George J. Siomkos (1986), Toward a Methodology for Assessing Effects of In-store Atmosphere," *Advances in Consumer Research*, 13, 27-31.

Harrell, Gilbert D., Michael D. Hutt, and James C. Anderson (1980). "Path Analysis of Buyer Behavior Under Conditions of Crowding," *Journal of Marketing Research*, 17, 45-51.

Hoyer, Wayne D. (1984), "An Examination of Consumer Decision Making for a Common Repeat Purchase Product," *Journal of Consumer Research*, 11 (December), 822-829.

Inglefield, Howard G. (1968), "Musical Preferences," dissertation, The Ohio State University.

Keppel, Geoffrey (1982). *Design & Analysis: A Researcher's Handbook*, Englewood Cliffs, NJ: Prentice-Hall.

Konecni, Vladimir J. (1982), "Social Interaction and Musical Preference," in *The Psychology of Music*, Diana Deustch, ed. New York: Academic Press, Inc., 497-516.

Kotler, Phillip (1973-1974), "Atmospherics as a Marketing Tool," *Journal of Retailing*, 49 (Winter), 48-61.

Kramer, Matt (1989). *Making Sense of Wine*, New York, NY: William Morrow and Company.

Lamphier, Gary (1990). "Lobbyists Against Noise Pollution Pick Up Some Unexpected Allies," *Wall St. Journal, June 1, B1*.

Lesch, William C., Siu Hung Luk, and Thomas L. Leonard (1991), *International Journal of Advertising*, 10, 59-78.

MacInnis, Deborah J. and C. Whan Park (1991). "The Differential Role of Characteristics of Music on High- and Low-Involvement Consumers' Processing of Ads," *Journal of Consumer Research*, 18, 161-173.

Markin, Rom J., Charles M. Lillis, and Chem L. Narayana (1976), "Social-Psychological Significance of Store Space," *Journal of Retailing*, 52, 43-54.

Mehrabian, Albert (1976), *Public Places and Private Spaces*, New York, Basic Books.

Milliman, Ronald E. (1982), "Using Background Music to Affect Behavior of Supermarket Shoppers," *Journal of Marketing*, 46 (Summer), 86-91.

_____ (1986), "The Influence of Background Music on the Behavior of Restaurant Patrons," *Journal of Consumer Research*, 13 (September), 286-9.

Owens, Jan P. (1991), "Store Atmosphere: An Environmental Psychology Approach Revisited," *Proceedings of the 1991 Symposium on Patronage Behavior and Retail Strategic Planning: Cutting Edge II*, 37-50.

Smith, Patricia Cain and Ross Curnow (1966). "'Arousal Hypothesis' and the Effects of Music on Purchase Behavior," *Journal of Applied Psychology*, 50, 255-256.

Stone, Michael (1983). "Some Antecedents of Music Appreciation," *Psychology of Music*, 11, 26-31.

Stratton, Valerie N. and Annette Zalanowski (1984), "The Effect of Background Music on Verbal Interaction in Groups," *Journal of Music Therapy*, 21, 16-26.

Yalch, Richard and Eric Spangenberg (1990), "Effects of Store Music on Shopping Behavior," *The Journal of Services Marketing*, 4 (Winter), 31-39.

A Comparison of Emotional Reactions Experienced by Planned, Unplanned and Impulse Purchasers

Francis Piron, University of Alaska Anchorage

Purchasing behaviors, and more specifically purchasing outcomes are important aspects of consumer research. Recently, efforts have been made to better understand impulse purchasing (Piron 1990; Rook 1987; Rook and Hoch 1985), unplanned purchasing (Iyer 1989), and unrealized purchasing (i.e., Iyer and Ahlawat's 1986 shortfalls). In response to this renewal of interest, and following the adoption of an existing definition of unplanned purchasing and the formulation of a definition of planned and of impulse purchasing, a study was undertaken 1) to measure emotional reactions experienced by consumers who made a planned, unplanned or impulse purchase, and 2) to compare these emotional reactions among the three types of purchases.

DEFINITIONS

Unplanned Purchasing

Earlier definitions of unplanned purchasing offered in the consumer research literature simply define the phenomenon as a purchase made unexpectedly (Clover 1950; DuPont Studies 1945, 1949, 1959, 1965; West 1951). Other and somewhat more recent conceptualizations such as Engel, Kollat and Blackwell's (1978) enrich the earlier core definition and "situate" unplanned purchasing with respect to a problem (i.e., the purchase was not made "in response to a previously recognized problem") or to the location where the purchasing decision was made (i.e., the purchase was made with "no buying intentions formed prior to entering the store").

Engel et al.'s (1978) widely recognized definition of unplanned purchasing prevails in most consumer behavior textbooks and is the one to be used in this study. Specifically, Engel et al. (1978) define unplanned purchasing as:

> a buying action undertaken without a problem having been previously recognized or a buying intention formed prior to entering the store (p.483).

Planned Purchasing

An exhaustive search through the commonly available consumer behavior textbooks failed to uncover an existing definition of planned purchasing. It is interesting to note that such a pervasive phenomenon apparently remains undefined. Given the above definition and the fact that planned purchasing is the exact contrary of unplanned purchasing, planned purchasing is then conceptualized as:

> a buying action undertaken with a problem having been previously recognized or a buying intention formed prior to entering the store.

The ease of defining planned purchasing as the inverse of unplanned purchasing is complemented by the fact that the set of definitions exhaust all purchasing situations along the planned/unplanned dichotomy without overlap.

Impulse Purchasing

For over forty years, marketing and consumer researchers have strived to capture an apparently pervasive phenomenon referred to as "impulse purchasing." Unfortunately most earlier definitions suffered from "definitional myopia" and simply equated impulse to unplanned purchasing without further considerations (Clover 1951; DuPont Studies 1945, 1949, 1959, 1965; West 1951). More recently (Rook 1987; Rook and Hoch 1985), conceptualizations of impulse purchasing rested almost exclusively on the consumer's psychological and emotional reactions. Lately, Piron (1990) reviewed the existing definitions and proposed that impulse purchases be defined as unplanned purchases, caused by an exposure to a stimulus, and decided on-the-spot. In sum, while impulse purchases differ are unplanned purchases, unplanned purchases are not all made on impulse. The difference between unplanned and impulse purchases is that the latter are decided on-the-spot, where the consumer first sees the product, while the former are decided at a later time and possibly away from the product stimulus.

Finally, Piron (1990) proposed that all purchases, be they planned, unplanned or made on impulse can be experiential (i.e., accompanied by emotional and/or cognitive reactions) or non-experiential. In fact, it is not uncommon for a car buyer to experience a lot of excitement as s/he goes to the dealership to finalize, with a purchase order, lengthy and involved negotiations. Also, many unplanned purchases, while made after elaboration and/or hesitations are accompanied by joy or nagging doubts.

The next section offers an outline of the methodology used to develop a set of statements intended to tap the emotional reactions that accompany experiential purchases. Following a description of the data collection method, the paper will then focus on a comparison of the intensity with which the tapped emotions were experienced by the three groups of shoppers.

Items Relevant to the Emotion Dimension

Rook (1987) and Rook and Hoch (1985) provided a new thrust in the study of impulse purchasing with a focus on the emotional and cognitive reactions that may accompany such a purchase. The understanding that consumer researchers have of the emotional elements of impulse purchasing is primarily limited to these two studies. A careful review of these two articles helped identify the following traits within the emotion dimension: (1) a sudden and imperative desire to purchase, (2) a feeling of helplessness, (3) feeling good or bad, (4) purchasing in response to moods, and (5) feeling guilty. Items measuring the five emotion-based traits identified in Rook (1987), and Rook and Hoch (1985), were generated from personal descriptions given by their subjects. The items are either under the form of direct quotes such as "I know I went out of control" or as paraphrases of expressed feelings such as "I can say that I purchased it to change my moods." One of the items relevant to mood states was formulated from a statement given by one of the undergraduate respondents who had been asked to define impulse purchasing in their own terms. In his description, the subject specifically mentioned that the purchase had been made "to fight the blues."

Originally, a pool of 52 statements had been compiled. These 52 statements were intended to tap the dimensions identified by Rook (1987) and Rook and Hoch (1985). The statements had been selected from two sources: from Rook (1987) and Rook and Hoch's (1985) respondents, and from the undergraduate and graduate students who had been asked to define impulse purchasing in their own terms. Specifically, 29 statements tapped the emotion dimension of an experiential purchase. One question investigated whether the respondent had felt any emotion while purchasing, 7 statements

TABLE 1
List of Items According to Stages in the Purchase Decision Making Process

Predecision Stage
　　As I was deciding to purchase the product,
1) I experienced a sudden desire to purchase it (Emo1A)
2) I felt like I had to purchase it from the first time I saw it (Emo1B)
3) I felt like I could not do anything but buy the product (Emo2A)
4) the urge to purchase it overcame me (Emo2B)

Post-Purchase Stage
　　Now that I have purchased the product,
5) I personally feel good that I have bought it (Emo3A)
6) I am pleased that I have bought it (Emo3B)
7) I can say that I purchased it to change my mood (Emo4A)
8) I can say that I bought it to "fight the blues" (Emo4B)
9) I feel guilty that I purchased it (Emo5A)

---

were intended to tap the strength and urgency of the purchasing desire, while 4 considered the feeling of helplessness, 8 focused on "feeling good, bad," and 3 were chosen to represent the "feeling guilty"-trait and 6 statements referred to purchases caused by mood states.

All of the statements were then given to five experts (3 doctoral students and 2 faculty members) whose task was to assign each statement to one of the five categories mentioned above. In the first round of evaluation, any item miscategorized by one of the three doctoral students was discarded. The pool of "surviving" items was then presented to the 2 faculty members who eventually settled on a final set of 9 items. Each of the traits is measured by two items but for guilt feeling, where only one item could be generated due to the uniqueness of the trait. Finally, the 9 emotion statements were organized in two sections reflecting two stages of the purchase decision process: (1) a pre-decisional stage, and (2) a post-purchase stage (see Table 1).

DATA COLLECTION

Shoppers at two malls in the Southeastern United States were asked whether they had purchased clothing items, and if so were asked to participate in a survey. Interviewers had been trained to administer the preliminary section of the questionnaire and the nature of the purchase (i.e., planned, unplanned or impulse) was determined according to the respondents' answer concerning the length of time separating the first exposure to the product and the purchasing decision. The researchers had decided that a span of 5 seconds or less between the first exposure to the product and the decision to purchase the product would qualify the purchasing decision as having been made on the pot, while a period longer than 5 seconds would disqualify such purchasing decision as having been made on the spot. The second part of the survey was self-administered as it was felt that consumers would express themselves more freely. Three hundred and sixty one questionnaires were collected, indicating a total of 163 planned purchase, 53 unplanned purchases, and 145 impulse purchases.

DATA ANALYSIS

The principal objective of this research is to explore differences in the experience of emotional reactions between planned, unplanned and impulse purchasers. Through canonical discriminant analysis, the set of predictor variables (i.e., emotional reactions) was to be tested for its ability to significantly differentiate between respondents making planned, unplanned and impulse purchase decisions. Canonical discriminant analysis is appropriate because when, as in this study:

> [g]iven two or more groups of observations with measurements on several quantitative variables, canonical discriminant analysis derives a linear combination of the variables that has the highest possible multiple correlation with the groups. (SAS Institute, 1985, p.156).

In sum, a canonical discriminant analysis provides the results necessary to respond to the objective of this research: can planned, unplanned, and impulse purchases be differentiated along the emotional reactions experienced by consumers?

Emotional Reactions

Five dimensions make up the emotion reactions that have been identified as differentiating impulse purchasing from other types of purchasing (Rook 1987; Rook and Hoch 1985): a "Sudden and Imperative Desire to Purchase," a "Feeling of Helplessness", "Feeling Good", purchasing "In Response to Moods," and "Feeling Guilty". As indicated earlier, in all dimensions but one (i.e., feeling guilty), two items were created for each dimension.

As illustrated in Table 2, impulse purchasers' responses on paired items correlate better than planned and unplanned shoppers' responses, but for one exception: unplanned purchasers' responses to the pair of items measuring whether the purchasing was done "in response to mood," correlates better (r=.67) than other shoppers' responses.

It is not totally clear why impulse purchasers' responses on paired items correlated better than planned or unplanned purchasers' responses. However, the following argument, while speculative, may account for this finding. For instance, a "sudden and imperative desire to purchase" is an emotion that is assumed to be experienced only by impulse purchasers. Planned and unplanned purchasers' intra-pair inter-item coefficients of correlation on this dimension are respectively .37 and .47. This possibly indicates that consumers who make planned or unplanned purchases may fail to see the relevance of, or may even perceive as non-sensical, statements inquiring whether their purchase was due to a "sudden and imperative desire to purchase."

Similarly, statements inquiring whether the purchase was made "in response to moods" generated responses that correlated far less (r=.33) for consumers who made planned purchases than for

TABLE 2
Correlations between Paired Items

Variables	Type of Purchasing			
	Planned (N=163)	Unplanned (N=53)	Impulse (N=145)	Overall (N=367)
Emo1A/B	.37	.47	.65	.50
Emo2A/B	.40	.18	.43	.40
Emo3A/B	.58	.44	.64	.59
Emo4A/B	.34	.67	.53	.48

Note: Emo1A/B : Sudden and Imperative Desire to Purchase   Emo3A/B : Feeling Good
Emo2A/B : Feeling of Helplessness   Emo4A/B : In Response to Moods

TABLE 3
Mean Scores and Scheffe's Test of Significance

Variables	Mean Scores			Univariate F-test	Scheffe's test of signif. diff. between		
	P	U	I		P-U	P-I	U-I
Emo1A	3.89*	4.36*	5.36	21.34	X	X	
Emo1B	3.95*	3.09	4.70	12.43	X	X	X
Emo2A	3.35	2.53	3.87*	8.50	X	X	
Emo2B	3.69	4.13*	5.20	22.63		X	X
Emo3A	6.15	5.51	6.03	5.50	X		X
Emo3B	6.41	5.86	6.30	4.68	X		
Emo4A	3.11	3.17	3.45	1.07**			
Emo4B	1.83	2.41	2.36	4.78		X	
Emo5A	1.65	2.26	1.83	4.45	X		

Note:
P = Planned purchasing   * indicates mean value is not significantly different from 4.00 (Neither
U = Unplanned purchasing   Agree nor Disagree)
I = Impulse purchasing   ** indicates that the variable is not significant at $\alpha = .05$

consumers who made unplanned (r=.67) or impulse purchases (r=.53). Again, while there is no evidence, it is merely suggested that shoppers who are not expected to experience a particular emotion may give unrelated answers to a pair of items measuring the same dimension.

Significant Differences between Planned, Unplanned and Impulse Purchasing

Nine items make up the "Emotional Reactions Model," and account for five separate dimensions. Both canonical function are highly significant (F= 5.56, p,.01; F= 3.93, p<.0002). As a total, the nine items differentiate significantly (Wilk's Lambda=.769, p<.01) between planned, unplanned and impulse purchasing.

Differences between Planned and Unplanned Purchasing. Shoppers who planned their purchases differ significantly from shoppers who made unplanned purchases on several emotional reactions (see Table 3). Compared to shoppers who made unplanned purchases, planned purchasers agreed less that they felt a "sudden desire to purchase" (Emo1A), and "guilty" (Emo5A) about their purchase. These findings are not surprising. Since the purchasing decision had been made prior to entering the mall, planned purchasers can be expected to agree less than unplanned purchasers when asked whether they experienced the emotional reactions mentioned above.

Planned purchasers further differed from unplanned purchasers on Emo2A ("I could not do anything but buy [the product]"), and Emo1B ("imperative desire to purchase"). However, planned purchasers' mean response to item Emo1B (X=3.95, see Table 3) is not significantly different from 4.00 ("Neither Agree nor Disagree", see Table 3), while unplanned purchasers' mean response points toward a slight disagreement with the statement (X=3.09). In general, it should be noted that planned purchasers may not know how to respond to such a question, possibly finding it non-sensical, since their purchasing decision has already been made. Finally, planned purchasers differed, tending to agree more, from unplanned purchasers in their "feeling pleased" (Emo3A) and "feeling good" (Emo3B) about having purchased the product.

In summary, the results from this study indicate that some emotional reactions are experienced differently by planned and unplanned purchasers. Most of the differences may be due to the fact that, as opposed to unplanned purchasers, planned purchasers's decisions to buy are made prior to being at the point-of-purchase. It follows that the emotional reactions experienced during the decision making process by unplanned purchasers may have been experienced earlier by planned purchasers, but are not expected to recur. However, post-purchase emotional reactions such as feeling good or pleased may be experienced by either planned or unplanned purchasers.

Differences between Planned and Impulse Purchasing. Consumers who made planned purchases differed significantly from consumers who made impulse purchases on only on five of the nine emotional reactions investigated in this study (see Table 3). Rook (1987), and Rook and Hoch (1985) propose that a "sudden and imperative desire to purchase" (Emo1A and Emo1B), and a "feeling of helplessness" (Emo2A and Emo2B) characterize impulse purchasing. The analysis of the respondents' answers indicates a significant difference ($\alpha=.05$) on Emo1A and Emo1B, and on Emo2A and Emo2B where impulse purchasers agreed more that they experienced these four emotional reactions than planned purchasers (see Table 3). In other words, the results from this study point out that a "sudden and imperative desire to purchase," and a "feeling of helplessness" are emotional reactions that separate impulse from planned purchasers.

The difference between planned and impulse purchasers is further illustrated as impulse purchasers agreed more that they bought the product to "fight the blues" (Emo3B, see Table 3). In other words, impulse purchasers tend to differ from planned purchasers as they apparently attempt to assign the responsibility for the purchase to sources which are not really a part of themselves (i.e., to *"fight the blues,"*). In summary, as suggested by Rook (1987) and Rook and Hoch (1985), impulse purchasing is characterized by a "sudden and imperative desire to purchase," accompanied with a "feeling of helplessness." Experiencing these two reactions may lead impulse purchasers to try and blame sources besides themselves.

Differences between Unplanned and Impulse Purchasing. Few emotional reactions significantly discriminate ($\alpha=.05$) unplanned from impulse purchasing (see Table 3). In fact, only three emotional reactions (Emo1B, Emo2B, and Emo3A, see Table 3) are experienced differently by the two groups where impulse purchasers' agreement with experiencing the reactions was higher than for unplanned purchasers (see Table 3). A somewhat speculative explanation for the difference in "feeling good" (Emo3A) experienced by impulse and unplanned purchasers may be attributed to the unplanned purchasers's experiencing of an "imperative desire to purchase" (Emo1B) and an "overwhelming purchasing urge" (Emo2A) less strongly than impulse purchasers. It may be that the additional time and amount of deliberations accompanying the decision to make an unplanned purchase may take away from what Rook (1987) refers to as the "extraordinary and exciting" (p.191) elements of an impulse purchase, leaving unplanned purchasers with a less positive feeling than impulse purchasers.

SUMMARY

As indicated in Table 3, and with respect to the emotional reactions investigated in this study, more significant differences were found between planned and unplanned purchasing (N=10) than between planned and impulse purchasing (N=8), and than between unplanned and impulse purchasing (N=4). In only one instance (Emo1B, "[a]s I was deciding to purchase the product, I felt like I had to have it from the first time I saw it") did planned, unplanned and impulse purchasing differ significantly. These results bring some support to earlier contentions (Rook 1987); Rook and Hoch 1985) that shoppers who make impulsive purchases can be differentiated from shoppers who make planned and unplanned purchases on the basis of their experiencing emotional reactions.

BIBLIOGRAPHY

Bellenger, Danny, D.H. Robertson, and Elizabeth Hirschman (1978), "Impulse Buying Varies by Product," *Journal of Advertising Research*, 18 (December), 15-18.

Clover, Vernon T. (1950), "Relative Importance of Impulse Buying in Retail Stores," *Journal of Marketing*, 25 (July), 66-70.

Consumer Buying Habits Studies, E.I. DuPont de Nemours and Co., 1945, 1949, 1959, 1965.

Engel, James F., David T. Kollat, and Roger D. Blackwell (1978), *"Consumer Behavior,"* Hinsdale, IL: Dryden Press.

Iyer Easwar S. and Sucheta S. Ahlawat (1987), "Deviations from a Shopping Plan: When and Why Do Consumers Not Buy as Planned," in *Advances in Consumer Research*, Vol. 15, ed. Michael J. Houston, Provo, UT.: Association for Consumer Research, 246-249.

Kollat, David T. and R.P. Willett (1967), "Consumer Impulse Purchasing Behavior," *Journal of Marketing Research*, 4 (February), 21-31.

Piron, Francis (1990), "Defining Impulse Purchasing," in *Advances in Consumer Research*, Vol. 18, eds. Rebecca H. Holman and Michael R. Solomon, Provo, UT.: Association for Consumer Research, 509-514.

"POPAI/DuPont Consumer Buying Habits Study," (1978), The Point-of-Purchase Advertising Institute, New Jersey.

Rook, Dennis W. (1987), "The Buying Impulse," *Journal of Consumer Research*, 14 (September), 189-199.

Rook, Dennis W. and Stephen J. Hoch (1985), "Consuming Impulses," in *Advances in Consumer Research*, Vol. 12, eds. Morris B. Holbrook and Elizabeth C. Hirschman, Provo, UT: Association for Consumer Research, 23-27.

SAS User's Guide: Statistics, Version 5 Edition (1985), SAS Institute Inc., Cary, NC, USA.

West, John C. (1951),"Results of Two Years of Study into Impulse Buying," *Journal of Marketing*, 15 (January), 362-363.

Beauty and the Beast (of Advertising)

Barry Vacker, Southern Methodist University

ABSTRACT

This paper discusses the representations of beauty in advertising and consumer aesthetics from the context of traditional theories of beauty in aesthetic philosophy. The paper shows that the criticisms of beauty in advertising arise from the traditional subjective theory of beauty and that beauty in advertising may best be understood from the perspective of an objective theory of beauty. The paper offers a philosophical basis for understanding the production and consumption of beauty in advertising and consumer aesthetics.

INTRODUCTION

At a recent symposium entitled "Whatever Happened to Beauty?: Aesthetics in a Culture of Signs" (College of Fine Arts at the University of Texas 1992), philosophers and artists discussed the well-documented disappearance of beauty from the twentieth century aesthetic scene (Tatarkiewicz 1972), a disappearance often forgotten amid the increasing concentration by artists on expressing explicit political and social messages requiring semiotic, rather than aesthetic, interpretation. Philosopher Arthur Danto perhaps summarized the general attitude of contemporary aesthetic philosophy toward beauty and the general conclusion of symposium participants when he concluded that beauty may be in for a lengthy "exile." As a theorist in consumer aesthetics, I was a bit bemused at the nearly cavalier attitude with which beauty was being dismissed, yet I could not help but wonder about the many representations of beauty in film, architecture, and, of course, advertising and consumer aesthetics. There seems no doubt that advertising, like film and architecture, produces aesthetic representations, often the aesthetic representation is intended to be understood as "beauty." And, it is for the representation of beauty, particularly female beauty, that advertising has received the strongest of social criticism (Lakoff and Scherr 1984, Wolf 1991). In fact, one could viably conclude from Wolf's thesis that the concept of contemporary beauty is an illusory and impossible concept created by the beast of advertising (Wolf, pp. 108-119, pp. 276-279).

Beauty as a social issue raises some very intriguing questions for researchers in advertising and consumer aesthetics. While contemporary aesthetic philosophers and artists see little evidence or use of beauty in contemporary art, something intended to be understood as "beauty" is being represented by advertisers in the media. Something called "beauty" is being produced by advertisers and consumed by society in large quantities via the mass media, most predominantly in television and magazines. For example, upon the covers and in the pages of women's and fashion magazines are faces and individuals intended to be understood as possessing beauty, in some manner. Are these representations really "beauty" or are they Platonic ideals impossible to attain? Are these representations called "beauty" objective[1] in any sense or are they merely subjective[2] preferences utilized to market consumer products? Well reasoned answers to such questions can be very important to consumer research, especially when quantitative consumer research (Kamins 1990, Richins 1991) is premised on certain answers to such philosophical questions. For example, Richins (1991) bases her research methodology and effort on the assumption that the answers to the above questions are, citing Lakoff and Scherr, that the idealized beauty represented in advertising is an impossible ideal utilized to subjectively market products, resulting in self-alienation in consumers. The point of this discussion is not to engage in any market critique polemics, but simply to examine the concept of "beauty" in light of aesthetic philosophy in order to ensure that our foundation for understanding beauty and consumer aesthetics is solid and secure. If I am successful in this preliminary endeavor, then consumer research into beauty will be better founded and we may better understand the phenomenon of beauty, so much in exodus in contemporary art and so abundant in the contemporary beast of advertising.

AESTHETIC PHILOSOPHY AND BEAUTY

Perhaps the best place to begin the inquiry is not at the beginning of philosophic thought on beauty, but with the contemporary social critiques of beauty in advertising and consumer aesthetics. After distilling the essence of the contemporary critiques, we will then examine the various philosophies of beauty in order to see where the contemporary critiques fit and to see which philosophy, if any, may help us understand the concept of beauty.

The contemporary understanding of beauty seems to hold it as axiomatic that beauty is subjective or that any standard of beauty must be relative. We have all heard the phrases "beauty is in the eye of the beholder" or "what is beautiful for you may not be beautiful for me" invoked to explain differences between views on objects held to be beautiful or not. It would seem that nearly all contemporary theorists and artists hold this seemingly truthful and unassailable axiom that beauty is subjective. [An exception would be Kovach (1974), who holds that aesthetic judgments can be objective in a fundamental sense.] It is upon this axiom of beauty as subjective that Lakoff and Scherr and Wolf build their critiques of beauty aesthetics in advertising.

Beauty, for Lakoff and Scherr, is transitory, indefinable, best understood in terms of emotion, and is ultimately subjective.

"Judgments about beauty, being subjective rather than objective, differ from person to person and one person's judgment cannot be 'proved' right or wrong." (p. 67).

From this premise, they argue that the beauty represented in the media and by models in advertising is illusory and artificial. "(H)owever 'natural' the beauty may look, artificiality is at the core of the experience...beauty is pure illusion made to look invitingly common and millions nourished by this fantasy are...trying to create themselves in its image" (pp. 112-114). They conclude that this can only generate dissatisfaction and schizophrenia among

---

[1] Briefly, objective beauty means beauty is a universal aesthetic ideal derived from reality external to the mind and validated by the mind via reason. Objective beauty means the ideal was derived from the *external* reality and the beautiful object exists as an aspect of reality independently of the mind's validation of beauty. Objective beauty need not involve collective assent nor disinterest.

[2] Briefly, subjective beauty means beauty is a subjective ideal derived not from reality but from the subject's mind. Subjective means the ideal is found in the contents of mind and not in the external reality and the beautiful exists as a subjective preference based emotions, feelings, politics, or anything conceivable.

women. Wolf adopts the same premises and explicitly takes the conclusions a step further. That beauty could be objective or universal is a myth because

> "'Beauty' is a currency system like the gold standard. Like any economy, it is determined by politics." (p. 12)

Further, since "there is nothing 'objective' about beauty" (p. 36), representations implying such beauty and perfection in advertising must necessarily be untrue and, therefore, coercive. Thus, for Wolf, ultimately, the portrayal of beauty is coercion[3].

Now it seems to this author that both Lakoff and Scherr and Wolf have made some rather bold statements about consumer behavior and the power of beauty in advertising. Implicit in their conclusions is the acceptance of the position of philosophic determinism via advertising. It is not necessary here to provide the refutations of philosophic determinism (Branden 1969, Locke 1966, 1969), nor specifically advertising determinism (Kirkpatrick 1986). However, what is key here is to explore the concept of beauty to determine if it is indeed wholly subjective and illusory or if it has any objective qualities which may be misunderstood. As we shall see, Lakoff and Scherr and Wolf are not really saying anything original about the nature or understanding of beauty. In fact, the notion of beauty as coercive or corrupting has been utilized by philosophers since Plato to explain things from hedonism to the rise of totalitarianism (Kallen 1942).

As Tatarkiewicz (1972) shows, the "great theory of beauty" has virtually disappeared from twentieth century aesthetics, in both theory and practice. Perhaps facilitating this disappearance of beauty has been the "dogmatic skepticism" of aestheticians on the possibility or value of defining beauty (Osbourne 1970, p. 252). While there is no doubt that certain difficulties arise in the process of developing a definition of beauty and building theories on such definitions (Jessup 1932), this should not prevent us from assessing definitions and theories of beauty in order to improve the precision of our own thinking about beauty and possibly move us toward a clearly reasoned theory of beauty in advertising and consumer aesthetics.

Classifications of Theories of Beauty

In the history of aesthetic philosophy, theories of beauty have been loosely classified in several categories (Exhibit 1). Carritt (1914) places the various theories of beauty into five categories: Hedonistic-Moral, Realist-Typical, Intellectualist, Emotionalist, and Expressionist. The Hedonistic-Moral category is exemplified by Plato's view of beauty, wherein beauty possesses potential for moral edification, but is a mere imitation of an imitation of the Ideal Form making beauty a seductress of the hedonistic pleasure derived from worldly things. The Realist-Typical category is best exemplified by Aristotle's view that art imitates natural things as they could be or should be based on their essence (truth). Thus, beauty was represented by symmetry, order, and definiteness. The Intellectualist category is best exemplified by Kant's view of beauty as involving no quality or ideal or concept of the aesthetic object but only the harmony of mental and perceptual faculties. The Emotionalist theories are typified by Schopenhauer's conception of beauty as contemplation and Nietzsche's association of beauty, not with reason, but with Dionysian desire and spirit. The Expressionist category is exemplified by Croce's view that beauty is the passionate expression of aesthetic intuition. Moore (1942) classifies the theories of beauty into the categories of subjective and objective. The subjective theory encompasses empiricism and hedonism typified by Hume and Plato and the objective theory includes Aristotelian formalism.

Osbourne (1970), among his various classifications of general aesthetic theories, identifies three specific theories of beauty. Two of the theories he classifies as idealist, one "perfectionist" and one "metaphysical." The perfectionist idealist theory, popular with the Greeks and during the Renaissance, holds that beauty is represented by the improvement or "perfection" of natural things by eliminating any individual imperfections and focussing on universals. This Aristotelian approach is contrasted with metaphysical idealism, grounded in Plato, which conceives of representing an ideal beauty not found in nature or in the sensible world. Osbourne also identified a "functionalist" theory of beauty, a theory also founded in Greek and Aristotelian thought, which holds that there is no fundamental distinction between the fine and the utilitarian arts. From this, the functional theory holds that "adaptation to purpose" is part of the meaning of *kalos* ("beautiful") and is a necessary condition of beauty but not a sufficient condition. Thus, an aesthetic object could be beautiful if its formal design was adapted to its purpose and was visibly so.

So far, we have only briefly discussed some key elements in the classification of theories of beauty. The purpose of this discussion, while having been necessarily very brief, has been to show, in a very simple manner, how aestheticians have classified beauty, in order that we may better see where the critiques of beauty in advertising may belong. From there, we will proceed to a more substantive exploration of the essence of the concepts of beauty. To that end, the author has taken the liberty to loosely group the various categories under two headings, the "Possible" and the "Impossible," which summarize the essence of various categories of theories. The "Possible" theory of beauty is primarily of an Aristotelian nature and it sees "beauty" as potentially objective and the result of the purposeful improvement and perfection of natural things (including humans) via both form and idea. The "Impossible" theory of beauty is primarily of Platonic-Kantian origin and sees beauty as residing in some ineffable realm, either beyond the sensible world or entirely in the realm of subjective consciousness, experienced or expressed through subjective emotions or feelings or pleasures. Thus, in the 'Impossible" theory, beauty is impossible to objectively define or represent and is, ultimately, impossible to know with any certainty. It seems rather obvious that the fundamental premises of Lakoff and Scherr, Wolf, and Richins, and the critique of beauty in advertising lie within the "Impossible" theory of beauty. The key questions now arise for understanding the production and consumption of a thing understood as "beauty" in advertising (and perhaps for a better understanding of consumer aesthetics). To explore the questions of objective vs. subjective beauty and possible vs. impossible beauty, we must turn to the fundamental aesthetic ideas of Plato, Kant and Aristotle. For in these thinkers lies the essential foundation for contemporary discussions of beauty in advertising and consumer aesthetics.

Plato's Theory of Beauty

It is in Plato's theory of beauty that we find the philosophic foundation of modern theories of beauty, most specifically, the theories of Kant (1790), who laid the foundation of twentieth century thought on beauty (Osbourne 1970). For Plato, the world known via the senses was not real in any true sense, but only a reflection or imitation of the world of forms. Art (and beauty) were

---

[3]By the same logic, the portrayal of the ugly must be liberation.

EXHIBIT 1
Classifications of Theories of Beauty*

	[Possible]	[Impossible]
Value of Beauty	• Beauty as Objective • primarily Aristotle	• Beauty as Subjective • primarily Plato & Kant
Carritt (1914)	• Realist (Aristotle)	• Hedonist-Moral (Plato) • Intellectualist (Kant, Hegel) • Emotionalist (Nietzsche, Scopenhauer) • Expressionist (Croce)
Moore (1942)	• Formalist/Idealist (Aristotle)	• Empirical, Subjective, Hedonist (Plato, Kant)
Osbourne (1970)	• Perfectionist & Functional (Aristotle)	• Metaphysical Idealism (Plato)
Wolf (1991), Lakoff and Scherr (1984)		• Beauty in Consumer Aesthetics
Vacker (1993)	• Beauty as an objective Universal • Beauty in Consumer Aesthetics	

*This classification is by no means meant to be exhaustive of all possible classifications. There is no doubt that some theorists and theories overlap or incorporate elements from other classes of theories. The purpose of this exhibit is merely to show the typical classifications, in what I think is an accurate manner based on the essence of the theories, for the purposes of this paper.

only imitations of imitations of the true world of forms (Republic 600e5). While Plato thought that art could provide some moral edification, he still held that art was frivolous (Republic 602b) and potentially dangerous, warranting control by the state. Regarding beauty specifically, Plato held an other-world view best summarized by the following quotation. For Plato, the essence of beauty is:

> "...that life above all others which man should live, in the contemplation of beauty absolute; a beauty which if you once beheld, you would see not to be after the measure of gold, and garments, and fair boys and youths, whose presence now entrances you;...but what if man had eyes to see the true beauty—the divine beauty, I mean, pure and clear and unalloyed, not clogged with the pollutions of mortality and all the vanities of human life—thither looking, and holding converse with the true beauty simple and divine. Remember how in that communion only, beholding beauty with the eye of the mind, he will be enabled to bring forth, not images of beauty, but realities (for he has hold not of an image but a reality), and bringing forth true virtue to...be immortal, if any mortal man may. Would that be an ignoble life?" (Symposium 211-212)

Consistent with his general view of art, Plato places the "true" and "real" beauty beyond the senses and the sensible world of mortals and in a realm of pure contemplation of the divine. This contemplation of the divine is a source of true virtue, unspoiled by the mortal world. Thus, worldly beauty is ultimately not true nor real nor virtuous. This is the first philosophical source for the critique of beauty in advertising and the source of the views of Wolf and Lakoff and Scherr.

Aristotle's Theory of Beauty

In contrast to Plato, Aristotle's theory of beauty places beauty (and the perfect) in the realm of nature or the natural sensible world and not in any mystical, ineffable, or supernatural realm. Nature or the natural world, in Aristotle's meaning, is all the elements and particulars of this world, including all living things such as trees, animals and man. And, importantly, the productive and creative works of man are also natural, to man. For Aristotle, beauty is found in nature and is known through man's reason via the senses. This conception of beauty is complex and has important ramifications.

"Beauty" and "the good" were synonymous for Aristotle in a fundamental sense (Marshall 1953). The beautiful and the good are in nature and are at the beginning of knowledge and movement of many things (Metaphysics 1072b31). Thus, beauty has an ontological and teleological status, not just an aesthetic status, both of which are fundamental to its aesthetic status. The source of beauty is nature (including the works of man), and, nature can often cause perfect beauty, even in animals and man (Parts of Animals 645a16-25). Because beauty is an ontological concept, Aristotle held that the sciences and mathematics can demonstrate the definition or prove the attributes of the beautiful (Metaphysics 1078a31-35). The attributes or content of beauty would include order, symmetry and definiteness (Metaphysics 1078b1); number and magnitude (Politics 1326a33); a unity and perceivable wholeness (Poetics 1450b35-38); and an absence of the haphazard and a purposefulness of all parts to an end (Parts of Animals 645a16-25). Since beauty is natural and possible for both woman and man (Rhetoric 1361a8), beauty would entail a good-sized, or appropriate (Marshall 1953) body, and the attributes of beauty would vary over one's life as one aged (Rhetoric 1361b5-15). Since beauty is natural and its attributes are demonstrable or quantifiable, it is of value to woman and man. Not only is beauty synonymous with the good, it also goes together with the "best" (Metaphysics 1072a32-35), it is a constituent of happiness and *eudaimonia* (the full life of thought and action) (Rhetoric 1360b22), and beauty is a good thing which is pleasant and sometimes desirable in and for itself (Rhetoric 1362b8). For Aristotle, beauty is real, natural, has a measurable content, and is a value to woman and man.

With regard to Aristotle's conception of beauty in aesthetics, one must grasp the concept of teleology and purposiveness in art. Aristotle considered the teleological movement of organic nature, including man and his art, toward the "better" or "best" (Butcher 1896). For man and art, the "best" is identified with one's purpose, end, or design. While "purposiveness" and "best" are fundamental to nature and art, nature can sometimes not fulfill or reach its purpose and its best (due to chance or accident). Thus man and art, by discovering the universals of nature through reason, will assist nature in reaching its end by eliminating the accidentals and imperfections and stressing the essential in order to improve the object in nature (Physics II8). Therefore, art is concerned with coming-to-be and perfecting nature. With regard to beauty, the artist creates beauty by discovering and following the essence of beauty in nature. "Thus, it is possible for the artist to create works of beauty...what must be achieved in art is the production of beauty which is like the beauty of nature; and this is not slavish imitation." (Marshall p. 230).

This view of beauty was very influential during the Renaissance, wherein artists such as Michaelangelo and Da Vinci believed in some form of "objective" criteria for producing beauty in art. However, the "objective" theory of art became more of an "intrinsic" theory of art with the seventeenth century Formalists' dogmatic advocacy of certain rules. Eventually both gave way to Humean empiricism and Kantian subjectivism. With regard to beauty in advertising, it has been held that "aristotelian aesthetic" is fundamental to advertising aesthetic (Vacker 1992). It also seems obvious that the critiques of Lakoff and Scherr and Wolf are not consistent with Aristotle's conception of beauty.

Kant's Theory of Beauty

Kant's (1790) theory of beauty is perhaps the singularly most influential treatise on beauty in history. It has certainly laid the foundation, or posed the problems, for all subsequent aesthetic thought, including that of the twentieth century, which has yet to emerge from the spectre of Kant (Osbourne Ch. 7). Like Aristotle's thoughts on beauty, Kant's are extremely complex and unlike Aristotle's scattered sentences about beauty, Kant's thoughts are contained in a systematic treatise. Kant's theory is a complex modern form of Platonism and he comes to nearly the exact opposite conclusions of Aristotle.

Kant held that our knowledge of the natural world, or reality, is formally structured by our sensory perceptions and categories of comprehension. He theorized that a "transcendental aesthetic" mediated between the sensible world of appearance and the supersensible world of ultimate reality and comprehension (White 1979). Since our sensory perceptions structured our knowledge of the sensible or natural world, we were aware only of a subjective appearance of the natural world, not the world in any objective sense. The aesthetic evaluation of these mediating perceptions were to be under the auspices of "judgment" (Kant, pp. 1-40). In contrast to Aristotle, Kant held that we do not directly know reality but only the "appearance" of reality and that "taste" was the faculty of estimating the beautiful of "appearance." Thus, Kant's theory is concerned with the subjective forms of beauty.

Kant posited four "moments" of aesthetic judgment of beauty. In the first moment, the moment of "quality," a judgment of beauty refers not to an object in the natural world, but only to imagination, and is non-cognitive, non-logical and, necessarily subjective (pp. 41-50). In the second moment, called "quantity," beauty must be disinterested, subjective, non-conceptual, and "free" from the liking of an object (pp. 50-60). The third moment, the "relation" of ends, "beauty" is *a priora* and independent of "perfection." (pp. 60-68). Thus, the "average" is the "stature of the beautiful man" (p. 78). However, beauty "involves no thought whatsoever of the object" (p. 70). For beauty to be "free" it must be independent of a purpose or end and cannot be perfection. "Dependent" beauty is ascribed to an object with a purpose or end or utility. Further, since purposes or ends entail a good, to combine good with beauty mars beauty (p. 73). The fourth moment of "modality" involves, somehow, the universally subjective becoming objective. While Kant's four moments are complex (see Johnson 1979, Petock 1973, and Zimmerman 1963), some conclusions can be drawn for the purpose of this paper.

Kant sees beauty as the judgment of subjective feelings of appearances (of reality) formally structured in our sensory perceptions (for an enlightening critique of Kant's theory of perception, see Kelley 1986). Thus beauty is non-objective, non-conceptual, and non-logical wherein such judgments are apart from objects, reason and purpose. In contrast to Aristotle, beauty does not entail the good or perfection. A thing cannot be proved to be beautiful on the ground that it belongs to a certain class or has certain characteristics or has utility because a judgment of beauty is non-cognitive and is the pure feeling of the observer (Osbourne pp. 174-175). Therefore, for Kant, it is "impossible" to identify any universal principles or properties of beauty. Further, for a beauty to be "free" it must not have a concept of object, perfection (the "best"), or a relationship with purpose or utility value (Osbourne p. 177). A free beauty entails no notion of how a thing, or person, "should be;" or, for that matter, what a thing "is." Unlike Aristotle, who held that beauty was a perfection of nature and man or woman, Kant held that beauty involves not the best, but the average in nature and man or woman. Ultimately, as with Plato, beauty is found in "contemplation" apart from reality.

Kant's theory of beauty has influenced all subsequent thought on beauty (for example, see Schiller 1795, Santayana 1896, Gadamer 1986) and was very influential in the decline of beauty in aesthetics (Tatarkiewicz 1972). Kantian thought directly influenced Schiller and Marx (Morawski 1970), and the critique of commodity aesthetics first started by Marx and Engels (1947) and furthered recently by Haug (1986).

BEAUTY IN ADVERTISING

Thus far we have been discussing the general categories of theories of beauty and the three preeminent theories of beauty in order to ascertain the fit of the critiques of beauty in advertising. Primarily, the task has been descriptive, not evaluative, of the theories and critiques. This has been to briefly show the philosophical traditions which embody the theories and where beauty in consumer aesthetics may belong. Now the task must move to an evaluative effort so that we can see which theories may best support sound research into the production and consumption of beauty in advertising. The task here will not be to develop a full theory (a task well beyond the scope and length of this paper) but only to critique the theories and to offer a modest speculation on the theory of beauty in advertising and consumer aesthetics.

The "Impossible" Theory of Beauty

Earlier in the paper, I loosely categorized the theories of beauty into the "Impossible" and the "Possible" beauty. For the purposes of this paper, I think this categorization accurately describes the essence of the existing theories. The "Impossible" theory of beauty holds that, ultimately, it is impossible to know with certainty the attributes, characteristics, qualities, or definition of beauty which is ascribed to an object in the real world. This theory is best exemplified by Plato and Kant and is commonly held to be a subjectivist theory. This is the view held in the critiques of beauty aesthetics in advertising. However, this subjectivist view which is prevalent today, is highly problematic, especially when applied to criticize other conceptions of beauty.

Aristotle disagreed with the Platonic-Mystical conception of beauty (Metaphysics 1078a31-35) and recently others have seen the difficulty of making Kant's subjectivism intelligible in understanding beauty (Petock 1973, Johnson 1979). At root, the subjectivist theory seems to leave us with no possible conception of beauty, beyond arbitrary assertions. And, especially with beauty in advertising, if representations of beauty are subjective, then there are no valid grounds to criticize any representation, even those in advertising—because, after all, beauty is subjective. Fundamentally, the subjectivist criticism of beauty in advertising denies the premises upon which a criticism should rest. If we are to criticize a representation of beauty in advertising then it seems we should have some form of objective and logical ground to rest such criticisms. Plato's mysticism and Kant's subjectivism, both variants of "impossible" beauty, simply do not leave us with valid grounds for criticisms of beauty.

The critiques of beauty by Lakoff and Scherr and Wolf are of explicit Kantian origin, particularly in Kant's aesthetic "moments." The criticism that beauty in advertising is subjective and falsely attributes beauty to individuals and commodities (Haug 1986) or objects is rooted in Kant's first moment. The idea that beauty is non-logical results in beauty in advertising being criticized as emotional coercion via "images" of beauty. The criticism of representations of beauty in advertising as being false and only in the advertiser's or media's interest is rooted in Kant's second moment where true beauty is found in disinterested contemplation. The criticism that the beauty in advertising is "perfection," impossible to almost all people, is rooted in Kant's third moment where true beauty must be independent of "perfection." The criticism that beauty in advertising is coercion (Wolf) is also founded in the third moment where "free" beauty must be independent of perfection, liking an object (commodity), and purpose or end. For beauty to be "free" it must be independent of objects, individuals, and purposes, all of which are manifest in advertising. Because of Kant's problematic view of the "form" of sensory perception (Kelley 1986), he denies the possible objectivity of aesthetic judgment, purpose, and object and leads him to separate perfection, beauty, and freedom from the natural sensible world. Thus, anything beautiful cannot be beautiful, perfect, or free because it exists and is. Such are the inherent problems of the "impossible" theory of beauty, which is explicit in the critiques of beauty in advertising.

The Possible Theory of Beauty

At first thought, one might assume that if the beautiful is not in some mystical realm or in a subjective consciousness, then it must be *in* the objects in reality, such as in paintings or buildings or statues or individuals and objects in advertising. However, this is not the case, because if it were, then beauty would be "intrinsic" to the object (Santayana, p.21). The intrinsic theory of beauty is tautologous because in it the object is beautiful because it is; or it is beautiful in and of itself, apart from anything of which it may be beautiful to or for. Therefore, this is just another variation on the subjectivist theory of beauty. The questions then arise: Where and what is "beauty?"

Fundamental to discovering where and what beauty *is* is understanding Aristotelian teleology and its relationship to beauty. Aristotelian teleology holds that universal values can be derived from facts by understanding natural ends or functions (Gotthelf 1976). "Goodness is neither an intrinsic feature of things or actions, nor is it simply a subjective phenomenon of consciousness. Rather, goodness is an aspect of reality in relation to the needs or ends of living things" (Rasmussen and Den Uyl p. 57). Thus,

> "There are no intrinsically beautiful or good or right things, only things that are good, right, or beautiful in relation to living entities *for* which things can be good, right, or beautiful in terms of purposes or goals" (Tibor Machan quoted in Rasmussen and Den Uyl, p. 57).

This complex theory of where beauty is may be better grasped by understanding what beauty is. Beauty exists as a universal in reality, a universal founded in the relation between things and human purposes. Beauty is a broad universal because it is ideal. Beauty as a universal ideal arises in the complex relation between things and humans purposively living their lives.[4] Thus, beauty requires a metaphysical dimension and an epistemological structure and beauty exists in the relation between the dimension (the thing) and the structure (the universal ideal). Beauty is universal in that its structure can accommodate an open-ended range of particular things on its dimension. Ideals arise from the necessity of choice in human living (see footnote 4), and since choice requires potentials, beauty is the actualization of a potential or a universal ideal. As a potential actualized, beauty is realized when its dimension (a thing) quantifiably satisfies its structure; thus, beauty may be said to be the contextual quantification of an aesthetic ideal according to purpose. This quantification of dimension according to structure is, for beauty, the relation between things and human purposes for which things can be beautiful. For our purposes, this conception of beauty has three important implications. First, since beauty is the actualization of potentiality, beauty exists in the unison of the *is* and the *ought* (or should be) and this gives rise to the broad normative implications of beauty. Thus, the beautiful is synonymous with the moral or the good. However, it could be that because beauty is an actualized potential ideal and exists in the unison of is and ought, beauty could be more fundamental than the moral and this may explain why the beautiful or the aesthetic can be more moving than just the moral. Second, since beauty exists as the actualization of a potential, then beauty is clearly possible and real. As a universal ideal, beauty (and perfection) can exist as the best possible for a purpose within a context, a context found in the nature of things and their ends. That real things can be beautiful would seem to indicate an objective status for beauty and that principles of beauty can be derived from the actualized beauty, principles that offer wide latitude due to the variety of things and human purposes. Further, the actualization of potential beauty would also indicate a purposive or functional element in the structure of beauty, an element which provides both structural and dimensional utility and requires interest, not disinterest as most theories hold. Third, this theory of beauty sees beauty not as an "appearance" nor as "skin deep" but as the actualization of potentiality requiring the unity of inner and outer or function and form or the moral and the beautiful. If this theory of beauty is correct, then the beauty in advertising is not an "appearance" or "image" but is the representation of potential actualized and is possible not impossible.

From this Aristotelian context, we can postulate a modest theory of how beauty is produced and consumed in advertising and consumer aesthetics. The production of beauty begins with things or objects in reality (dimension) and is guided by principles or ideals (structure) based on purposes and context. The production of beauty involves the process of aesthetic abstraction, an epistemological process of moving from the particular to the universal. Aesthetic abstraction involves the selection of universals and omission of non-universal of things in reality, and the measurement, quantification and contextualization of such universals according to purpose. For example, the production of a beautiful woman in an ad involves the selection of a model based on her universal features (the dimension) which satisfy the principles or ideals (the structure) derived from the context and purpose of the ad. The measurement, quantification, and contextualization processes involve the selection, photography, lighting, make-up, set design, apparel selection, and airbrushing. Thus, the selected model is a particular thing in reality, chosen among many, through which the universal is conveyed via the process of aesthetic abstraction. A universal "should be" is represented by a particular "is." The dimension and structure of beauty require beauty to exist in the unison of is and ought and this is no less true for beauty portrayed in advertising and consumer aesthetics, be it a woman, man, product, package, location or any conceivable thing of beauty. Aristotelian aesthetics involve the representation of things as they "could be" or "should be" based on the universal of the thing represented and are held to be fundamental to advertising (Vacker 1992). Beauty as a "should be" is conveyed as a universal through its representation as an "is".

The consumer of beauty, in an Aristotelian interpretation, consumes not *the* particular representation of beauty in the particular ad, but, *through* the particular representation, consumes the universal of beauty. Thus, what is consumed is not the actual object of beauty, but the universal or essence of beauty. What is consumed is the "should be." The consumer consumes the universal of beauty by applying the universal of beauty to the particulars, context, and purposes of their own life. The universal of beauty is then measured or quantified for utility in one's own life. In this context, every female does not necessarily want to be exactly like (top model) Uma Thurman; they may only want to be the "best" they can be in terms of universal beauty represented by Thurman. It is this production and consumption of beauty according to freely chosen purposes (of course, not all purposes are "objective") that provides beauty with a catallactic function and which may partially explain why "beauty" is demanded and produced in such large quantities in the media and consumer aesthetics.

Beauty is produced and consumed in a complex manner, the full extent of which is beyond the scope of this paper. However, it is important to realize in this context that an evaluative standard is operating in both producers and consumers of beauty. For example, if the consumer evaluating the beauty in the ad holds an "impossible" ideal of beauty, then these possibilities may seem impossible. Thus, this consumer may at first be attracted to such beauty, but because of the belief in the impossibility of such beauty the consumer would feel frustration in any attempt to emulate such impossible beauty. This is the philosophical source for consumer alienation with respect to beauty. There is no doubt that such "alienation" exists among some consumers (Richins 1991), for if one accepts the impossible theory then alienation will inevitably result from the sight of beauty. Such alienation results not from beauty or the use of beauty per se but from the philosophy of the consumer. Consumers subscribing to a "possible" theory may be more likely to find inspiration, not alienation, in such beauty and would be more adept in applying the universal to their own lives. Additionally, it is the implicit acceptance of the impossible theory of beauty on the part of advertisers that results in the aesthetic representation of negative stereotypes of female beauty in some advertising. For example, in a beer commercial, the aesthetic representation of a mostly disrobed curvaceous young female as beauty object or sexual ornamentation and the portrayal of appreciative (pseudo-masculine) "average males" clearly reflects the "impossible" theory. The "beauty" represented is a beauty of superficiality, wherein the advertiser portrays the average male as a being to whom the mind of a female would be of no importance because beauty is found only in the immediately (Kantian) sensate world of appearances and physical gratification. The "beauty" of the female portrayal represents the same principle; she is portrayed as approving of being seen as a beauty object whose physical appearance is more important than an intelligent mind. The emphasis of the sensate to the exclusion of the mental can only result in beauty representations designed for the lowest common denominator. No doubt such males exist and though the advertiser may think he/she is representing "reality" as it is, in reality, the advertiser is trying to represent beauty and sexuality without substance or context. For in reality, beauty and sexuality can only exist in a being of integrated mind and body, not in only a purely physical representation. These mindless representations are merely mannequins and not "beautiful" humans. And, it is for these mannequins that advertising deserves the strongest condemnation.

---

[4]In the process of living life, the human being is faced with many choices, some given and some self-created, and must volitionally choose from among them. From this context, the necessity of choosing from many alternatives or possibilities to sustain one's life, one's ideals naturally arise. For the normal adult, ideals arise as the end product of numerous choices made over time in answer to the question of what is best for one's life. Choices are potentialities and they are real. If one seeks to further one's life, one chooses the best among the available potentialities known to one in a given context. From having to choose throughout one's life the best among the potentialities, one develops a conception of the best or the "ideal" potentiality for one's life which serves as a standard for choosing what is best to actualize in living one's life. Thus, the ideal as a cognitive abstraction identifies what *is* best for one's life and the ideal becomes a normative abstraction when it identifies what *ought* to be best for one's life. These cognitive and normative abstractions are not physical entities, they are mental existents of mind in reality. Thus, the need to "see" or "show" these ideals in a perceptual form naturally arises. Aesthetic ideals are abstractions which identify what ought to be the best among possibilities in reality, possibilities which can become actualities if one chooses and follows the proper course. Beauty is the actualization of a potential, a potential in the form of an aesthetic ideal.

Such condemnations are best supported by the "possible" theory of beauty.

CONCLUSION

This paper has examined the "beauty" in advertising and consumer aesthetics in light of traditional theories of beauty. It seems that not all theories of beauty are compatible with understanding beauty in advertising. This paper has termed the "possible" theory of beauty as offering the best understanding of the production and consumption of beauty, wherein beauty is seen as real and potentially objective. Grasping these fundamental ideas should insure that our thought and research about beauty in advertising and consumer aesthetics is securely grounded.

REFERENCES

Aristotle (1941) *The Basic Works of Aristotle*, New York: Random House.

Branden, Nathaniel (1969) "Free Will, Moral Responsibility and the Law," 42 *S. California Law Review* 264.

Butcher, S. H. (1896) *Aristotle's Theory of Poetry and Fine Arts*, New York: Dover (1951).

Carritt, E. F. (1914) *The Theory of Beauty*, London: Methuen & Co.

Gadamer, Hans-Georg (1986) *The Relevance of the Beautiful*, Cambridge: Cambridge University Press.

Gotthelf, Allan (1976) "Aristotle's Conception of Final Causality" in *The Review of Metaphysics*, December, pp. 226-254.

Haug, W. F. (1986) *Critique of Commodity Aesthetics*, Minneapolis: University of Minnesota Press.

Jessup, T. E. (1932) "The Definition of Beauty" in *Proceedings of the Aristotelian Society, Vol. XXXIII*.

Johnson, Mark L. (1979) "Kant's Unified Theory of Beauty" in the *Journal of Aesthetics and Art Criticism*, Vol. XXXVIII, No. 2, pp. 167-178.

Kallen, Horace (1942) *Art and Freedom*, New York: Greenwood Press.

Kamins, Michael A. (1990) "An Investigation into the 'Match-Up' Hypothesis in Celebrity Advertising: When Beauty May Be Only Skin Deep" in the *Journal of Advertising*, Vol. 19, No. 1, pp. 4-13.

Kant, Immanuel (1790) *Critique of Judgment*, Oxford: Clarendon Press (1928).

Kirkpatrick, Jerry (1986) "A Philosophic Defense of Advertising" in the *Journal of Advertising*, Vol. 15, No. 2, pp. 42-49.

Kelley, David (1986) *The Evidence of the Senses*, Baton Rouge: Louisiana State University Press.

Kovach, Francis J. (1974) *Philosophy of Beauty*, Norman, OK: University of Oklahoma Press.

Lakoff, Robin Tolmach and Raquel L. Scherr (1984) *Face Value: The Politics of Beauty*, Boston: Routledge & Kegan Paul.

Locke, Edwin A. (1966) "The Contradiction of Epiphenomenalism" in *British Journal of Psychology*, pp. 203-204.

Locke, Edwin A. (1969) "Purpose Without Consciousness: A Contradiction," *Psychological Reports*, Vol. 25, pp. 991-1009.

Marshall, John S. (1953) 'Art and Aesthetic in Aristotle" in the *Journal of Aesthetics and Art Criticism*, Vol. XII, No. 2, pp. 228-231.

Marx, Karl and Frederick Engels (1947) *Literature and Art*, New York: International Publishers.

Moore, Jared S. (1942) "Beauty as Harmony" in the *Journal of Aesthetics and Art Criticism*, No. 1, pp. 40-50.

Moraski, Stefan (1970) "The Aesthetic Views of Marx and Engels" in *Journal of Aesthetics and Art Criticism*, Vol. XXVIII, No. 3, pp. 301-314.

Osbourne, Harold (1970) *Aesthetics and Art Theory*, New York: E. P. Dutton & Co., Inc.

Petock, Stuart Jay (1973) "Kant, Beauty and the Object of Taste" in the *Journal of Aesthetics and Art Criticism*, Vol. XXXII, No. 2, pp. 183-186.

Plato, *Symposium*.

Rasmussen, Douglas B. and Douglas J. Den Uyl (1992) *Liberty and Nature*, LasSalle, Illinois: Open Court.

Richins, Marsha L. (1991) "Social Comparison and the Idealized Images of Advertising" in *Journal of Consumer Research*, Vol. 18 (June), pp. 71-83.

Santayana, George (1896) *The Sense of Beauty*, Cambridge: MIT Press (1988)

Schiller, Friedrich (1795) *On The Aesthetic Education of Man*, New York: Continuum (1990).

Tatarkiewicz, Wladyslaw (1972) "The Great Theory of Beauty and its Decline" in the *Journal of Aesthetics and Art Criticism*, Vol. XXXI, No. 2, pp. 165-180.

Vacker, Barry (1992) "The Marlboro Man as a Twentieth Century David: A Philosophical Inquiry into the Aristotelian Aesthetic of Advertising" in *Advances in Consumer Research*, Vol. 19.

White, David A. (1979) "On Bridging the Gulf Between Nature and Morality in the Critique of Judgment" in *Journal of Aesthetics and Art Criticism*, Vol. XXXVIII, No. 2, pp. 179-188.

Wolf, Naomi (1991) *The Beauty Myth*, New York: William Morrow and Company, Inc.

Zimmerman, Robert L. (1963) "Kant: The Aesthetic Judgment" in the *Journal of Aesthetics and Art Criticism*, Vol. XXI, pp. 333-344.

"An Emerald Green Jaguar, A House on Nantucket, and an African Safari:" Wish Lists and Consumption Dreams in Materialist Society

Susan Fournier, University of Florida
Michael Guiry, University of Florida

ABSTRACT

This paper explores a new area of consumer behavior: pre-purchase dreaming. Toward the goal of providing a foundational understanding of pre-consumption dreaming episodes and behaviors, a review of descriptive information on conscious fantasy behavior is first provided. The results of an exploratory survey which investigates general consumption dreaming, planful/ anticipatory versus pure daydreaming styles of activity, and the manifestation of consumption dreams in the form of consumer "wish lists," are then presented. Implications of the findings for the study of materialism are discussed, and ideas for future investigations are offered.

INTRODUCTION

In the last decade, the scope of consumer research has been expanded beyond choice and decision-making to include the experience of consumption, the meanings of possessions, and processes of product disposition. Some have suggested broadening this range yet further to include important *pre*-acquisition phenomena such as materialistic aspirations (Fournier and Richins 1991), wish lists (Belk and Zhou 1987), anticipatory consumption experiences (MacInnis and Price 1990), consumption fantasies (Hirschman and Holbrook 1982), and vicarious consumption experiences (MacInnis and Price 1987). Most discussions of consumer states of pre-purchase fantasy remain at the macro-theoretical level; the extent to which consumers dream about products or experiences they have yet to acquire, and the consequences of such activity have only rarely been considered for empirical investigation (MacInnis and Price 1990). The present paper supports the expanded "pre-acquisition" view of consumer behavior, providing descriptive survey data on pre-purchase dreaming activities, especially as they are manifest in consumer "wish lists."

PRE-PURCHASE DREAMING ACTIVITIES IN MATERIALIST CULTURE

There is reason to believe that pre-purchase dreaming activities flourish in materialistic cultures. The preoccupation with consumption that characterizes these societies encourages cultivation of purchase goals, on-going entertainment of consumption dreams, and eternal search for suitable consumption prospects (Leiss et al. 1986)—activities that occur largely in the imagination. It has been suggested that "longing," the simple act of contemplating possible consumption opportunities, is filled so much with enjoyable states of fantasy that the simple *anticipation* of consumption comes to serve as a desired end-state in and of itself (Campbell 1987). It has been argued that imaginary consumption activities enjoy superordinate status above actual purchase and usage experiences (Campbell 1987). In fact, the contemplation of future acquisitions has been identified as one of life's fourteen "simple pleasures" in recognition of this positive experience-value (Bentham 1789/1987).

Cultural critics argue that marketing and advertising institutions encourage the imaginative "desiring mode" by actively supporting the dream quality of consumption and purchase (Leiss et al. 1986). This is reflected in popular terms chosen to describe media and marketplace functions: the "dream industry" of advertising, the "dream world" of shopping malls, catalogue "wish books." These institutions, by allowing the consumer to entertain thoughts of ownership without making a commitment to purchase, encourage a pattern of anticipation in consumption. The consumer credit industry further reinforces the dream-like quality of consumption by allowing ownership without payment.

Cultural attitudes and practices are highly supportive of pre-consumption dreaming activities. Surveys consistently reveal highly positive opinions toward and frequent engagement of consumption-related daydreams (Caughey 1984; MacInnis and Price 1990; Singer 1966). "Wish list" activity is overtly encouraged among cultural members, and examples of situations which demand the generation and availability of wish lists abound. The cultural practice of gift-giving and the commoditization of the Christmas holiday virtually guarantee preparation of wish lists. Wish lists also commonly guide self-gift reward behavior (Mick and DeMoss 1990). Similarly, the tradition of bridal registration at department stores, in which detailed lists of purchase desires are complied, requires wish list formulation. Lastly, the question of lottery winning disbursement commonly entertained in day-to-day fantasy activities (Caughey 1984; Singer and McCraven 1961) cultivates wish list generation. Considering that training in wish list construction begins at an early age with the compilation of lists for Santa, one enters an environment wherein pre-acquisition dreaming is not only accepted, but highly encouraged as well.

PURPOSE AND OBJECTIVES

The present study proceeds along the assumption that entertaining *ideas* about consumption, as expressed through a variety of pre-purchase dreaming activities, is a very real form of consumer behavior. The study explores the status of pre-purchase dreaming activities *as acts of consumption*, investigating their popularity, content and structure, underlying motivations, and process dynamics. The purpose of the research is to provide a descriptive, sociological account of a variety of pre-purchase consumption dreaming activities including wish list construction, anticipatory consumption planning, and fantastical entertainment of consumption possibilities. The impact of consumer well-being and materialist orientation upon the incidence and form of pre-purchase dreaming activities is investigated in detail.

Two contributions are offered. First, the study broadens the scope of research on fantasy-related consumer behaviors. Rather than focussing on *post*-acquisition fantasies sparked by the consumption of hedonic products or fantasy-reflective goods and experiences (Holbrook et al. 1984; Rook 1985), the study concerns the neglected *pre*-acquisition phase of consumption fantasy. In this sense, the study contributes to our understanding of consumption-related fantasy behaviors in particular, and to the operation of materialist culture in general. Second, the study moves beyond the conceptual comments that have largely characterized interest in this area to date, providing much-needed foundational data on the extent and patterning of pre-consumption dreaming activities. The study thus helps to establish a base of factual information that can support the development of theory related to consumption fantasy.

BACKGROUND LITERATURE

This section presents a selective review of the literature on daydreaming and conscious fantasy behavior, focussing on descriptive information that can illuminate the current research goals. In light of current objectives, the unconscious aspects of the fantasy experience are not considered.

Forms and Functions of Daydreaming and Fantasy

Fantasy has been defined as "an imagined sequence of events or mental images that serves to express unconscious conflicts, to gratify unconscious wishes, or to prepare for anticipated future events" (APA 1975, p.55). It is recognized that a continuum of the realistic to the fantastical exists such that two basic forms of fantasy behavior can be discussed. On one extreme are "creative fantasies," planful forms of daydreaming grounded in future experiences (Singer and Antrobus 1963). Planful fantasies include the anticipation of probable future actions (MacInnis and Price 1990), as well as the entertainment of alternative possibilities for likely future actions (Singer and McCraven 1961). Planful fantasy activities serve preparatory and exploratory functions. On the other extreme are "pure daydreaming" fantasies in which highly improbable events or fanciful wishes are entertained. Such activities are undertaken for purposes of vicarious consumption (MacInnis and Price 1987), or for the positively-reinforcing experience the fantasy offers (Klinger 1971; Singer 1966). With both planful and pure daydreaming fantasies, the gratification and stimulation can be so positive that the fantasy serves as a surrogate experience (Singer 1966), allowing the delay of gratification where situational contingencies block goals, or motivating future behaviors where no barriers exist (MacInnis and Price 1987).

The Content and Character of Daydreams and Fantasies

Psychologists have generally argued for the idiosyncratic character of fantasies in recognition of their service of selfish wishes and private desires. Singer and McCraven (1961) measured the frequency of daydreams in 93 specific categories including passion, death, personal/career aspiration, aggression, consumption experience, monetary wealth, and material possession, and found the specific content of dreams to be highly individualistic.

Those with an anthropological perspective regard fantasy as a cultural phenomena that reflects individual desires, but only as they have been shaped and structured by societal forces (Caughey 1984). Through his ethnographic interviews, Caughey discovered strikingly similar patterns in the thematic content of American fantasies, identifying three basic components in what he termed the "American fantasy set." The set reflects access to, living of, and having "The Good Life," and includes dreams of career success, imaginings of exotic experiences, and the acquisition of great wealth or possessions. In a similar vein, Riesman and Roseborough's (1964) concept of the "standard package of aspirational goods" suggests homogenization of possessions and experiences entertained in the imagination. Even in developing consumer societies, wish lists have been found to exhibit marked similarity across cultural members (Belk and Zhou 1987), evidence for the standardization of imaginary consumption desires toward the American ideal.

Fantasy Behaviors, Consequences, and Correlates

Investigations have shown that daydreaming and fantasy behaviors are remarkably widespread. Over 96% of U.S. adults report some form of conscious daydreaming daily (Singer and McCraven 1961), with fantasy behaviors serving anticipatory or planning functions especially prevalent (MacInnis and Price 1990). In general, fantasy behaviors are met with positive public opinion; they are openly embraced for the enjoyment and stimulation they offer, and often serve positive, adaptive functions such as motivation, exploration, compensation, delay of gratification, and escape (Caughey 1984; MacInnis and Price 1990; Singer and McCraven 1961). Some potential negative consequences of fantasizing about the unattainable have been identified, however, including the development of anger, frustration, and negative self-regard (Rhue 1987).

Certain demographic factors have been associated with the propensity to engage in dreaming activities. Upwardly-mobile socio-economic groups have been shown to demonstrate a tendency toward increased fantasy activity, perhaps for the imaginary exploration it affords (Singer and McCraven 1961). It has also been suggested that groups experiencing some form of relative deprivation rely on fantasy behaviors for the compensatory, adaptive functions they provide (Singer 1966). Persons plagued by compulsion or anxiety are also prone to increased fantasy activity for the escape it offers (O'Guinn and Faber 1989; Rhue 1987). As could be expected, the tendency to daydream or fantasize declines with age. The narrowing of possibilities typically associated with maturity suggests a lessened need for planful fantasy behaviors (Singer and McCraven 1961). Alternatively, this pattern could be tied to more general trends in materialistic values. As detailed in the introduction, much of the positive reception to consumption daydreaming is driven by materialist beliefs. As materialist values decline with age, engagement in consumption fantasies may likewise decline.

This selective research review has highlighted issues that bear upon the design and analysis of the present research. The discussion now turns to the methodological details of the study.

THE STUDY

Methodology

In line with stated objectives of this preliminary investigation, the survey method has been chosen. Prior work (MacInnis and Price 1990; Singer 1966) has proven questionnaire data both illuminating and relatively free of social desirability bias, supporting the utility of the method in studies of fantasy behavior:

> "It seems reasonable to conclude that a fairly direct approach by questionnaire can be fruitful. The range of responses suggests that people responding to a questionnaire will reveal considerable material concerning their private daydreams and admit to some thoughts that one might expect only a clinical relationship could elicit." (Singer and McCraven 1961, p.162)

Pre-Purchase Dreaming Activity Measures

Four classes of pre-purchase dreaming activity were explored in the present study. First, the frequency of general consumption-related dreaming activities was included as a dependent variable of interest. Respondents indicated "how often they dream about things that they do not have" on a 5-point scale from (5) very often to (1) never. Singer (1966) and MacInnis and Price (1990) report the use of similar dream frequency measures.

The planful versus pure daydreaming functions of fantasy referenced earlier were also measured. A review of the literature suggested seven attitudinal statements to tap this range of possible pre-consumptive fantasy activities [See Table 1]. A factor analysis with varimax rotation of the seven items confirmed the two dreaming forms. Regression analyses sought to identify variables associated with each type of dreaming.

TABLE 1
Factor Analysis Results

	Means*	Factor Loadings Planful Dreaming	Factor Loadings Pure Day-Dream
I always have something in mind that I look forward to buying.	3.42	.82	.00
Ads for expensive new products and fun-filled experiences give me ideas for things to put on my "wish list" of things to own or do.	3.57	.73	.23
I Often think how great it would be to actually own and do the things shown in ads.	3.67	.57	.47
When I go shopping, I like to try on clothes/play with products even if I have no intention of buying them.	2.40	-.22	.80
It's fun to think about all the different things my money can buy.	3.50	.34	.59
When I look at ads that show people who are well-off, I like to pretend I'm living the lives the people in the ads are living.	2.58	.34	.57
I like to look through catalogs and just imagine owning some of the merchandise.	3.41	.26	.53
Variance Explained		38%	26%
Cronbach's Alpha		.68	.59

* 5-point scale from (5) strongly agree to (1) strongly disagree

A 7-item semantic differential scale reflecting overall attitudes toward pre-consumption dreaming (α=.84) was also administered. The scale included dimensions of productivity, health, encouragement, enjoyment, motivation, and normality in addition to overall goodness/badness.

The final class of measures concerned one particular manifestation of pre-purchase consumption dreaming activities: consumer "wish lists." For purposes of the present study, the wish list was defined as a hierarchical set of yet unacquired products or experiences that reflect materialistic desires, consumption dreams, and life aspirations and that serve as objects of contemplation in pre-acquisitive consumption dreaming activities. The wish list serves an organizing function for its user, prioritizing the options available in the consumption universe upon which "extra money" could be spent or against which gift solicitations could be applied. The wish list thus serves as a broad "consideration set," a restricted list of alternatives that have satisfied some criterion of desirability. Whether these items are actually intended for future purchase is open to question; the list includes products of both planful consumption dreams and pure daydreams.

In line with previously discussed cultural evidence for the validity of consumer wish lists, the construct was measured with a direct open-ended question: "What is on your list of things that you would like to own or do someday?" Responses were content-coded in terms of number of wishes, type of wish (i.e., material possessions versus consumption experiences versus ideals versus money), vividness or detail of item description, and shared, cultural character. Additional diagnostic categories suggested by the literature or inspired by the data included complementarity among individual wish list items, reference to status, reflection of trade-up in consumption level, reflection of "basic" and "complete" consumption packages, and indication of consumption excess. Two judges coded the data; all disagreements were resolved through discussion. Regression analyses focussed on the scope (i.e., total number of wish list ideas) and character (i.e., distribution of possessions versus experiences versus ideals) of the lists. Other content categories were explored for their descriptive value.

To tap the fanciful character of lists, respondents also provided estimates of the "percentage of items they believed they would realistically attain someday." Regression analyses identified factors associated with more and less realism.

Independent Variables and Correlates

Informed by the literature, eight potential correlates of consumption dreaming activities were investigated. *Life satisfaction* was measured with a 5-item scale (α=.81) that tapped overall happiness, general life satisfaction, and satisfaction with specific life domains. A scale of (1) people who are really poor to (6) people who have really made it was used to measure both *aspirational group* and *relative standard of living*, with the latter reflecting the gap between ratings of current living standard and the perception of the average American level of living. *Materialistic value orientation* (Richins and Dawson 1990) was measured with a 15-item scale (α=.78). *Sex, age, income,* and *education* were also measured.

Sample and Data Collection

One hundred twenty respondents completed the survey. Data were collected using a three-step purposive strategy. First, 47 business and non-business undergrads at a major university completed the questionnaire in exchange for extra course credit. The

TABLE 2
Wish List Content

Item Category	Number of Items	% of Total Items	% of Items in Category	Average Mention	% of Total Sample
Total Ideas	616	100		5.3	
Possessions	267	43	100	2.2	80
House	108	17	40		71
Car	53	9	20		44
Luxuries	44	7	16		29
Electronic	31	5	12		12
Misc	31	5	12		18
Experiences	162	26	100	1.4	74
Travel	93	15	57		59
Other Consumption	69	11	43		32
Ideals	161	26	100	1.3	69
Career	78	13	48		48
Family	45	7	28		26
Health/Happiness	29	5	18		16
Charity	9	1	6		6
Money	26	4	100	0.4	22

students provided a sample of consumers with presumably unmet consumption desires. Older, more full-fledged members of consumer culture were the targets of the next two data collection phases. A total of 83 surveys were distributed by the authors at an outlet mall. Thirty-three surveys from predominantly upper middle/ middle class respondents representing 5 different southeastern states were returned. In the third wave, 51 surveys were mailed (40 returned) to selected contacts, including a working-class Boston bar and secretarial offices in ID, NY, and PA. The sample included a range of age, education, income, and social class groups.

RESULTS

Content analysis of the wish list question is presented in Table 2. Table 3 contains regression results for the four groups of dependent measures.

Wish List Content

An average of 5.3 ideas were listed in response to the open-ended wish list generation question (SD=2.9, range 1 to 12). There was strong agreement among respondents in the type of items put on their lists. Generally speaking, lists were dominated by desires for material possessions. Over three-quarters (80%) of the sample listed at least one possession on their wish lists; 43% of total items listed were consumer products. The most popular wish item (17% of total items, mentioned by 71% of sample) was the desire for a new, bigger, or more beautifully-situated home. Almost half the sample (44%) also mentioned desires for new cars. Over one in four (29%) listed luxury items such as yachts, antiques, jewelry, and designer clothes.

Travel and consumption experiences were also popular among consumption dreamers. Three-in-four respondents (74%) put some form of experience on their wish lists, with experiences representing 26% of total items listed. A majority (59%) expressed a desire for travel throughout the US or Europe, or for vacations to exotic places. A third (32%) added other forms of consumption experience to their list of desires, including cultural experiences such as learning a foreign language or attending sporting/art events, and more particularistic adventures (e.g., rafting and safaris).

Interestingly, 69% of the respondents listed at least one idealistic goal in their wish list. The number of ideals listed (26% of total items) matches total experiential ambitions. Four types of ideals were identified (i.e., career, family/society, health/happiness, and charity), with career goals most commonly (48%) mentioned. A fifth (22%) of the sample covered all consumption possibilities by stating a wish for unlimited funds.

Wish lists also varied in terms of specificity and uniqueness. Three-quarters of respondents embellished at least one item with specific details; 42% of all items were vividly described. Individuality was expressed through dream-like stories in which the particulars of a "fairy-tale" life were recounted. This level of detail and elaboration could reflect that consumers have "perfect things" in mind when they formulate wish lists.

There was also evidence of a culturally-motivated, shared quality in wish lists. One-quarter (24%) of respondents elicited items in the "American fantasy set" (Caughey 1984), and 23% recounted a "basic package" of consumption items (i.e., a car, house, and travel). Desires for the same quintessential wish list items (e.g., the emerald green Jaguar) and luxury goods (e.g., Lear jet, estate home, yacht) were also reflected.

Lists also varied along a dimension of complementarity. While the majority (62%) of registers took the form of simple itemized shopping lists, others (38%) included possessions, experiences, and ideals intertwined in a meaningful pattern and reflective of respondents' proposed life paths.

Some interesting findings related to the materialist character of lists also emerged. The theme of consumption excess was reflected (30% want at least two houses, cars or vacations), as was consumption escalation and trade-up (22% state wishes for newer/ bigger/better possessions and experiences).

TABLE 3
Regression Results

Standardized Beta Coefficients
(Significance Levels)

Independent Variables

Dependent Variables	Age	Sex	Income	Educ	Life Sat	Rel Std	Asp Group	Mat	R^2
Total Ideas	ns	ns	.29 (.01)	.18 (.05)	-.32 (.005)	ns	ns	ns	.20 (.003)
Anticipated Attainment	-.49 (.0001)	ns	ns	ns	ns	ns	ns	ns	.25 (.0005)
Possessions	ns	ns	ns	.17 (.08)	-.24 (.04)	ns	ns	ns	.19 (.006)
Relative Proportion of Experiences	.31 (.003)	ns	ns	ns	ns	ns	ns	-.26 (.01)	.20 (.004)
Dream Frequency	-.27 (.003)	ns	ns	ns	ns	ns	ns	.30 (.001)	.34 (.0001)
Planful Dreams	ns	ns	ns	-.19 (.02)	ns	ns	.17 (.06)	.51 (.0001)	.41 (.0001)
Pure Daydreams	ns	.18 (.05)	ns	-.29 (.002)	ns	ns	ns	.18 (.07)	.25 (.0001)
Dream Attitude	-.30 (.003)	ns	-.21 (.06)	-.18 (.05)	ns	.20 (.09)	ns	ns	.29 (.0001)

Educ = Education Level
Life Sat = Life Satisfaction [5-item scale, α=.81]
Rel Std = Relative Standing
Asp Group = Aspirational Group
Mat = Materialism [Richins and Dawson (1990) 15-item scale, α=.78]

Factors Influencing the Scope and Content of Wish Lists

Certain socio-demographic factors were associated with the total number of wish list items generated as well as distribution of those items across classes. Life satisfaction was negatively related to the total number of ideas generated (β=-.32, p=.005) and to the number of possessions listed (β=-.24, p=.04). That dissatisfaction is associated with increased, possession-focussed dreaming may reflect a hope that the road to happiness is paved with currently-unrealized consumption desires, or a tendency to revert to fantasy for escape. Consumers with greater levels of satisfaction may have garnered many of their desires, become more selective in constructing their lists, or learned the negative effects of wishing for unattainable goals. Reflecting the ability to fulfill wishes, the number of ideas generated was positively related to income (β=.29, p=.01) and education (β=.18, p=.05). Interestingly, age was not significant (β=-.15, p=.14). Two factors were associated with the tendency to cite experiential consumption items over possessions or ideals. Materialism was negatively correlated with the dominance of experience items (β=-.26, p=.01) reflecting a preference for tangible possessions over fleeting experiences. Age was positively related to the tendency to cite invigorating consumption experiences over possessions or ideals (β=.31, p=.003). The number of ideals listed was fairly constant across demographic groups, as reflected in a non-significant regression model.

Issues of Wish List Attainment

Respondents felt they would attain most of the goals stated in their lists; the average anticipated attainment was 68%. Surprisingly, over half the respondents (56%) believed that they would fulfill at least 75% of their wishes, and one in three (29%) stated that they would realize a full 90% or more of their consumption goals. The high level of anticipated attainment suggests that for a number of consumers, "wish lists" are more appropriately regarded as "want lists" or prioritized plans for likely future consumption.

Attainment expectations were negatively associated with age (β=-.49, p=.0001). It appears that consumers become more realistic in their consumption goals over time; fledgling consumers on the verge of promising careers foresee no obstacles to proposed consumption paths. Another factor affecting attainment estimates was item specificity. More specific lists were associated with lower levels of expected attainment (β=-.24, p=.009), a reflection that more specifically-identified items are often harder to realize.

Consumption Dreaming Activity

The discussion now turns from the content of consumption dreaming to the extent of consumer engagement in such activity. Survey results suggest that consumption dreaming is an essential part of consumer culture. Three-quarters (76%) of the sample report at least occasionally dreaming about things they do not own;

27% admit to doing so very often. As dreaming increases in frequency, the number of wishes generated goes up ($\beta=.74$, $p=.01$). Interestingly, dreaming frequency is not related to estimates of attainment, suggesting that frequent dreamers engage in both planful dreaming targeted towards realistic consumption aspirations and pure daydreaming without intention to buy.

Materialism was positively related to dream frequency ($\beta=.30$, $p=.0001$), suggesting that pre-acquisitive imagination is an important materialistic hobby. Age was negatively related to consumption dream frequency ($\beta=-.27$, $p=.003$). As consumers move through life and acquire consumption packages, the range of possibilities remaining open becomes limited, which reduces the need for consumption dreaming. Moreover, older consumers are not as future-oriented as their counterparts, a trait that by definition lessens the role played by dreaming. Lastly, age is negatively related to materialism ($r=-.41$, $p<.05$), an orientation that encourages dreaming.

While not significant in the regression model, both aspirational group and relative standing were positively correlated with increased dream frequency ($r=.20$ and $r=.21$, respectively; $p<.05$). Thus, Singer's (1966) idea that consumers aspiring to move up the social ladder dream about the symbols of their target groups, and his hypothesis that those who feel disadvantaged dream about unfulfilled acquisitions as a means of escape receive only partial support in the data. In a similar vein, life satisfaction was not significantly related to dream frequency, although it was negatively correlated with the dependent measure ($r=-.23$, $p<.05$).

Planful Dreaming and Pure Daydreaming

The strongest regression results were obtained for the prediction of planful dreaming [$R2=.41$, $p=.0001$]. Engagement in planful dreaming was positively related to the magnitude of respondents' group aspirations ($\beta=.17$, $p=.06$), an indication that the path of upward mobility is associated with the formulation of specific acquisition goals. Planful activity was also negatively associated with current education levels ($\beta=-.19$, $p=.02$), perhaps a reflection of this same phenomenon. Planful dreaming was positively associated with the trait of materialism ($\beta=.51$, $p=.0001$), mirroring the central role that future acquisitions play in the materialists' life.

The relationship between materialism and consumption dreaming was not restricted to that of planful dreaming, however. Materialism was also positively associated with the engagement in more fanciful consumption dreaming ($\beta=.18$, $p=.07$). In addition, females were more likely to participate in playful daydreaming than males ($\beta=.18$, $p=.05$). Lastly, lower levels of education were associated with increased levels of playful dreaming ($\beta=-.29$, $p=.002$), perhaps reflecting the escape functions of this activity form.

Attitudes Toward Consumption Dreaming

Survey results indicate that dreaming about things not owned is considered a normal endeavor that is motivating, encouraging, healthy, and enjoyable. Age, education, and income were negatively related to favorable attitudes; the magnitude of group aspirations was positively related to favorable attitudes. As might be expected, consumers' attitudes towards dreaming are positively associated with dreaming frequency ($\beta=.42$, $p=.0001$). Attitudes are not related to attainment estimates, however. This suggests that realistic and fanciful dreams are regarded as equally beneficial and stimulating.

DISCUSSION

The research reported herein gives important insight into a popular yet neglected cultural phenomenon—pre-acquisition dreaming. The data suggest that pre-acquisitive dreaming plays a viable role in consumer culture. Consumers entertain dreams of yet unacquired products and experiences for purposes of anticipatory consumption and purchase prioritization, as well as for speculation and intrinsic enjoyment of the experience. Several implications for the study of imaginary consumption and the conceptualization of materialism are suggested in the present findings.

The data suggest the existence of two different forms and functions of consumer wish lists. The high level of anticipated attainment attached to some lists suggests that they are reflective of anticipated purchase goals, while others are manifestations of consumption dreams in the purest sense. Lists therefore range from "want lists" of true consumption priorities to "wish lists" of fanciful desires. The differential effects of these list types on well-being should be investigated. It is important also to consider consumers' estimates of attainment for individual items in future research.

A broadening of perspective on the materialistic ethos is also suggested. While possessions dominated consumer wish lists, a significant experiential component was also in evidence. The popularity of experiences may signify their place as new symbols of status for the 1990s, a move away from the conspicuous product consumption of the 1980s. In a mass-produced world where everyone can buy almost everything, exotic travel and consumption experiences seem more privileged, thus replacing possessions as wish list targets. Wish lists also had an equally-strong idealistic flavor; they did not take the form of simple, self-centered shopping lists. The inclusion of ideals suggests value in broadening the boundaries of materialistic consumption yet further to include the enhancement of self, family, and society in addition to the consumption of products and experiences.

The most significant predictor of consumption dreaming activities to emerge from the study was that of materialism. Materialist values were strongly related to frequency of consumption dreaming, both in general and for specific planful and entertainment-driven forms of dreaming as well. This finding supports the reconceptualization of materialism proposed by Fournier and Richins (1991) in which the materialist's domain is expanded beyond the acquisition of possessions to include pre-acquisition states of fantasy in support of future purchase. However, the present data suggest an even broader view of the materialist's experience, one that includes the inherent enjoyment and satisfaction of product-related thought. It suggests a renewed definition of materialism that is organized by the simple enjoyment of products, in action and in thought, whether accompanied by future purchase intentions or not. This is in sharp contrast to popular existing definitions that focus on acquired possessions as sources of satisfaction.

AREAS FOR FUTURE RESEARCH

By design, this preliminary investigation has provided only foundational background material on pre-acquisition fantasy behaviors, leaving open several avenues for future research. Several methodological refinements are suggested to more fully explore the range of pre-acquisition fantasy behaviors. Within the survey context, refinement of scale measures and development of multi-item indicators for dream activity will greatly improve reliability. The use of reaction time measures to assess spontaneity of response to questions regarding fantasy behaviors could also prove helpful. The posing of a general question for wish list elicitation has also been limiting. This tactic implies that the wish list itself is collective when in fact, wish lists may be situation-specific (e.g. self-gift reward lists). This possibility also deserves investigation. Lastly, the restrictions of the operational definition of the wish list employed herein are also noted. Requirements for verbalization in the survey context demand that the wish list reflect only those items in the conscious register of consumption dreams. The possibility that subconscious desires lie at the heart of pre-acquisition fantasies suggests promise in applying psychoanalytic approaches to study (e.g., TAT).

Future research should also be directed toward understanding the positive and negative effects of pre-consumption dreaming. While fantasy activity may be so pleasurable that a great variety of improbable thoughts are tolerated without consequence to well-being, others may be caught in the cycle of anticipatory consumption dreaming (Campbell 1987). The very act of engaging in fantasy can create systematic biases in expectations. Imagining an event positively biases the perceived likelihood of attaining that event (Carroll 1978). In fantasy, the person also envisions positively biased outcomes (MacInnis and Price 1987), imagining a world characterized by perfection, quintessence, and the absence of negatives (Caughey 1984). Since reality rarely unfolds as conceived in the imagination, disappointment and frustration in connection with anticipatory fantasy behaviors are expected (MacInnis and Price 1987). However, research has shown that the experience of anticipatory fantasy can actually enhance feelings of satisfaction, regardless of whether expectations are met or not (MacInnis and Price 1990). The potential moderating influence of aspirational levels, life satisfaction, item specificity, and estimates of attainment on the consequences of fantasy behavior should be considered. Carefully designed research can delineate situations in which dreaming leads to frustration, and those in which the experience is positive and motivating.

REFERENCES

American Psychiatric Association (1975), *A Psychiatric Glossary*, Washington: American Psychiatric Association, 55.

Belk, Russell and Non Zhou (1987), "Learning to Want Things," *Advances in Consumer Research*, Volume 14, eds. M. Wallendorf and P. Anderson, Provo, UT: Association for Consumer Research, 478-481.

Bentham, Jeremy (1789/1987), "An Introduction to the Principles of Morals and Legislation," in *Utilitarianism and Other Essays: J.S. Mill and Jeremy Bentham*, ed. A. Ryan, London: Penguin Books.

Campbell, Colin (1987), *The Romantic Ethic and the Spirit of Modern Consumerism*, Oxford: Basil Blackwell.

Carroll, John (1978), "The Effect of Imagining an Event on Expectations for the Event: An Interpretation in Terms of the Availability Heuristic," *Journal of Experimental Social Psychology*, 14, 88-96.

Caughey, John L. (1984), *Imaginary Social Worlds: A Cultural Approach*, Lincoln: University of Nebraska Press.

Fournier, Susan M. and Marsha L. Richins (1991), "Some Theoretical and Popular Notions Concerning Materialism," *Journal of Social Behavior and Personality*, 6(6), 403-414.

Hirschman, Elizabeth C. and Morris B. Holbrook (1982), "Hedonic Consumption: Emerging Concepts, Methods and Propositions," *Journal of Marketing*, 46 (Summer), 92-101.

Holbrook, Morris B., R. W. Chestnut, T. A. Oliva and E. A. Greenleaf (1984), "Play as a Consumption Experience: The Role of Emotions, Performance, and Personality in the Enjoyment of Games," *Journal of Consumer Research*, 11 (September), 728-739.

Klinger, Eric (1971), *Structures and Functions of Fantasy*, New York: John Wiley and Sons.

Leiss, William, S. Kline, and S. Jhally (1986), *Social Communication in Advertising: Persons, Products, and Images of Well-Being*, Toronto: Methuen.

MacInnis, Deborah J. and Linda L. Price (1990), "An Exploratory Study of the Effects of Imagery Processing and Consumer Experience on Expectations and Satisfaction," *Advances in Consumer Research*, Volume 17, eds. M. Goldberg et al., Provo, UT: Association for Consumer Research, 41-47.

_____ and Linda L. Price (1987), "The Role of Imagery in Information Processing: Review and Extensions," *Journal of Consumer Research*, 13 (March), 473-491.

Mick, David Glen and Michelle DeMoss (1990), "Self-Gifts: Phenomenological Insights from Four Contexts," *Journal of Consumer Research*, 17 (December), 322-333.

O'Guinn, Thomas C. and Ronald J. Faber (1989), "Compulsive Buying: A Phenomenological Exploration," *Journal of Consumer Research*, 16, (September), 147-157.

Rhue, Judith W. (1987), "Fantasy Proneness and Psychopathology," *Journal of Personality and Social Psychology*, 53(2), 327-335.

Riesman, David and Howard Roseborough (1964), "Careers and Consumer Behavior," in *Abundance for What?*, ed. David Riesman, New York: Doubleday, 113-137.

Rook, Dennis W. (1985), "The Ritual Dimension of Consumer Behavior," *Journal of Consumer Research*, 12 (December), 251-264.

Singer, Jerome L. (1966), *Daydreaming: An Introduction to the Experimental Study of Inner Experience*, New York: Random House.

_____ and J.S. Antrobus (1963), "A Factor-Analytic Study of Daydreaming and Conceptually-Related Cognitive and Personality Variables," *Perceptual and Motor Skills*, Supplement, 3-V17.

_____ and Vivian G. McCraven (1961), "Some Characteristics of Adult Daydreaming," *The Journal of Psychology*, 51, 151-164.

Self-Gifts and the Manifestation of Material Values
Kim K.R. McKeage, University of Massachusetts, Amherst
Marsha L. Richins, University of Missouri
Kathleen Debevec, University of Massachusetts, Amherst

ABSTRACT

Self-gifts have recently emerged as a mode of purchasing for the self that may be linked to both cultural and personal values. This study examines the link between self-gifts and materialism as a personal value. In general, materialists seem to have a greater propensity to give self-gifts than non-materialists. This is especially true for occasions relating to mood management, indicating that self-gift behavior may be particularly linked to the materialistic belief that purchasing and consumption are appropriate and perhaps necessary activities in the pursuit of happiness.

"I bought a diamond ring for myself. It made me feel worthwhile, loved, secure. My husband doesn't believe in giving diamond rings, so I had to accept the fact that I had to buy one for myself if I wanted to get all those good feelings.

It *was* expensive. I did something expensive for me and I did it because I truly feel that I'm worth it. It was always associated with a selfish feeling if I did something for myself rather than doing for other people. So this was a milestone for me to recognize that I could buy myself presents, and *expensive* presents.

Also, I've nurtured this marriage for ten years, and there are ten diamonds in the ring. There is all this symbolism that makes me feel really good, and successful, like I've succeeded in something and this is a symbol of that success, and I can pat myself on the back for it." — Female, 39

INTRODUCTION

Self-Gifts

In consumer behavior, we're often concerned with people's purchases for themselves. As indicated in the above account of a jewelry purchase, some purchases for the self are also special, out-of-the-ordinary gifts to the self. While the idea that people give gifts "from me to me" is not new (see Schwartz 1967), researchers have only recently begun to explore the phenomena and its significance. According to Mick and DeMoss (1990b) self-gifts can be considered symbolic communications from one aspect of the self to another aspect of the self. They define self-gifts as "personally symbolic self-communication through special indulgences that tend to be premeditated and highly context bound" (Mick and DeMoss 1990a, p. 328). Self-gifts arise from a variety of motivations and contexts, such as mood management, rewards or inducements, celebrations, and simply to be nice to oneself. The gift itself can be a product, service, or experience, or even the special meaning attributed to something above and beyond what is normally purchased, such as ordering dessert at lunch (Mick and DeMoss 1990a, 1990b).

The giving of self-gifts is encouraged in our culture with avertising and promotion using self-gift themes, such as "the perfect little thank me," (Andes mints), "the perfect recess," (Parliament Lights cigarettes), "sometimes you just have to stop and smell the leather," (the Lexus automobile), and "I just did something nice for myself" (Keepsake Diamond Jewelry). These themes are thought to be effective because they incorporate the values of our consumer culture (Mick, 1991). The relationship between one of these cultural values, materialism, and self-gifts is explored and empirically tested in this research.

Materialism

Materialism can be considered a value that guides behavior (Richins and Dawson 1992). Ward and Wackman (1971) defined materialism as the belief that possessions and money are important for personal happiness and social progress. It has been characterized as a pursuit of the "good life" rich in material possessions (Belk and Pollay 1985), where success and gratification can be had "with a minimum of effort" (Lasch, 1984, p. 191).

Materialism and self-gifts may be linked in three ways. First, materialism involves some degree of self-centeredness (Fromm 1976; Heilbroner 1956) which includes qualities such as alienation and indifference, narcissism, and lack of concern for others (Fournier and Richins 1991). Several writers have noted materialists' detachment from personal relationships (Beatty, Kahle, and Homer 1991; Mukerji 1983).[1] Materialistic people, upon unexpectedly receiving a sum of money, are more likely to spend it on themselves than others (Richins and Dawson 1992). People high in envy, nongenerosity, and possessiveness, traits associated with materialism, tend to celebrate or do something for themselves when feeling good; those low in these traits tend to share, do things for others, or act joyful in a similar circumstance (Belk 1985). This greater focus on the self by materialists suggests that they would be more likely to give self-gifts than non-materialists.

Second, materialists tend to define themselves through their possessions. They have a general tendency to define success as the adequacy of one's possessions in terms of amount and quality (Richins and Dawson 1992). Mick and DeMoss (1990b) have noted that self-gifts are also self-defining. In addition, both materialism and self-gifts decline with age (Richins and Dawson 1992; Mick and DeMoss 1992) paralleling a shift from active self-definition to contemplation of relationships as people grow older (Rochberg-Halton 1984, 1986).

Third, materialism is characterized by the belief that purchase and consumption lead to happiness. At a societal level, the pursuit of hedonic fulfillment is part of what Lasch (1978) has called the "therapeutic sensibility," the desire for fleeting and sometimes illusory feelings of health, well-being and psychic comfort. At the personal level, the law of hedonic contrast may require ever-increasing levels of consumption in the pursuit of pleasure (Scitovsky, 1992). Mick and DeMoss (1990b) found that self-gifts tend to result in intense, positive feelings. Therefore, materialists might be particularly prone to engage in this type of consumption as part of their search for pleasure and happiness. Therapeutic self-gifts (those designed to cheer oneself up from depression and boredom), and those designed to maintain a good mood, are linked

---

[1] But note that Csikzentmihalyi and Rochberg-Halton (1981) found that cherished objects were generally associated with relationships with people, and that people who disavowed being materialists also tended not to have strong or extensive relationships with other people.

with management of affect. Excessive consumption of these types of self-gifts has been proposed as a symptom of belief in the link between consumption and happiness (Mick, DeMoss and Faber 1992).

While the general obsession of materialists with mundane consumption might not be expected to affect their propensity to indulge in special purchases such as self-gifts, their pursuit of consumption that will bring happiness and satisfaction should make them more prone to be involved with such purchases. Materialists tend to experience greater negative affect from their purchases, and self-gifts may be one area within which materialists can avoid negative feelings while cultivating happiness and satisfaction.

This suggests that materialists would be more likely to buy self-gifts than non-materialists. It is also possible that materialists might be inclined to give themselves gifts in different contexts or situations than non-materialists. Mick et al. (1992) suggest that materialists might be more likely than non-materialists to buy self-gifts to cheer themselves up. Belk's (1985) finding that persons high in nongenerosity were more likely than people low in this trait to buy things for themselves when they were feeling particularly good or bad supports this point.

McKeage (1992) examined the connection between materialism and context in an exploratory study of materialism and self-gifts. Given a series of hypothetical scenarios similar to the self-gift situations described in Mick and DeMoss (1990a, 1992), respondents described what they would do in a variety of situations. Materialists had a greater propensity to give self-gifts than non-materialists on their birthday, to cheer themselves up, to be nice to themselves, and because they hadn't bought themselves anything in a while. However, the use of specific scenarios in that study precluded generalizing about self-gift behavior in different situations within a particular context (such as to cheer oneself up).

Finally, materialism might influence the type of self-gifts chosen. Materialists value possessions and often attempt to make experiences tangible through acquisitions such as souvenirs and mementos (Ger and Belk 1990). This preference for the tangible may lead materialists to choose self-gifts they can have rather than those they can experience.

This study explores the links between self-gifts and materialism by examining the following research questions:

1. Do materialists have a greater propensity to give themselves gifts than non-materialists? Because materialists are expected to give primarily tangible self-gifts, the analysis for this research question was restricted to objects purchased as self-gifts.

2. Do materialists give themselves gifts in different situations than non-materialists?

3. Do materialists give themselves different items as self-gifts than non-materialists?

METHOD

Overview and Sample

Data were collected using a self-administered survey. Respondents were 51 females and 46 males from various classes at a large public university and a small private college in the northeast. Most participants were single (93%) undergraduates (94%) ranging in age from 19 to 55 (mean = 21.9). They came from 35 majors representing 8 colleges within the university and received extra credit or were entered into a research lottery for their participation. The questionnaire was administered in a laboratory setting during a two week period.

Measurement

Self-Gifts. Type and context of self-gifts were measured by open-ended questions about an actual self-gift episode. Respondents described the nature of the gift, what prompted the gift, the amount of time spent on the self-gift event, and the monetary cost of the self-gift. The questions were designed to encourage participants to discuss experiences as well as tangible objects as self-gifts. The introductory paragraph emphasized that self-gifts were something you "do" or "buy" for yourself, and this was emphasized twice. The opening question asked "What did you do or buy for yourself." Pretesting indicated that respondents understood that a discussion of either tangible or intangible self-gifts was appropriate.

Propensity to give self-gifts was measured by adapting a scale used by Mick and DeMoss (1992). The focus of the measure was on the contexts or motives for self-gifts, and it was useful for determining the situations in which respondents were most likely to give themselves gifts. However, it cannot assess how frequently respondents give themselves gifts.[2]

Mick (1991; also Mick and DeMoss 1990a) noted that the propensity to give self-gifts could be measured by eliciting subjective estimates of past behavior, and that approach was used here. After the open-ended questions, respondents were asked "How often do you *buy* something special for yourself" followed by 11 previously identified self-gift situations (Mick and DeMoss, 1990a; 1992). The nine-point response scale ranged from never (1) to very often (9).[3] The aggregate response to these items was taken as a measure of the overall propensity to give self-gifts, while each individual context was examined for differences in self-gifts across three levels of materialism.

Reliability analysis revealed that a self-gift "because it was something you needed" had a low item-total correlation (.30). While Mick and DeMoss (1990a) included this item, it is not consistent with the scale in this study. One possible reason for this inconsistency is that the item wording calls attention to its lesser degree of "specialness" in comparison with the other items, causing respondents to consider it differently from the others. Since the intent in this study was to aggregate these items to indicate overall propensity to give self-gifts, and not to distinguish between self-gifts and more mundane purchases for the self, this item was dropped from further analysis. Reliability for the remaining items was .83 (mean = 49.2, standard deviation = 14.2).

Materialism. After describing their self-gifts and responding to the propensity scale, participants completed Richins and Dawson's (1992) material values scale. This scale assesses three aspects of materialism often discussed in the literature: centrality of acquisition in one's life, the role of acquisition in the pursuit of happiness,

---

[2] Wording for the Mick and DeMoss (1992) measure is as follows: "In the past, when you have acquired products, services, or experiences for yourself, how often have you felt you acquired them..." followed by a list of 8 contexts or motives they had identified in prior research as leading to self-gifts.

[3] Because materialists are expected to give more material, but not necessarily more experiential, self-gifts, this measure was restricted to purchased items to provide a valid test of research question 1.

TABLE 1
Contexts for Giving Self-Gifts Cited by Low and High Materialism Respondents

Context	Frequencies Materialism Low (n = 31)	High (n = 31)	Total*
To reward yourself	5	1	10
To cheer yourself up	2	2	5
To relieve stress	–	1	5
Because you have extra money to spend	2	2	5
Because you haven't bought for yourself in a while	2	–	3
Because you're feeling good	–	1	1
Because it's your birthday	1	–	2
Novelty	4	7	15
Because you wanted it	4	3	12
Because it was something needed	2	6	12
Because it was a good deal	2	1	4
To go with something else	2	1	3
Other	3	4	14

Note. — Columns do not add to Total column because total refers to entire sample, including middle tercile taken out of analysis of high/low materialists. Total number of contexts cited adds to 91 because 6 respondents did not cite a context for their self-gift.

and the role of possessions in defining success. It has been shown to possess adequate reliability and validity when used with adult respondents, but has not been used previously with college students. A principal components analysis was performed to assess its suitability for this population. The analysis yielded a factor structure similar to that reported in Richins and Dawson (1992).[4] Coefficient alpha was .89, similar to that obtained on adult samples. The scale mean was 58.0, higher than that reported by Richins and Dawson (1992) for adults.

RESULTS

Demographic Correlates and Propensity to Give Self-Gifts

Prior to addressing the research questions, the association between the propensity to give self-gifts and demographic characteristics was assessed in an attempt to replicate earlier findings. Consistent with prior research, the propensity to give self-gifts was negatively related to age ($r = -.20$, $p < .05$). In addition, females showed a significantly greater propensity to give self-gifts (mean = 53.6) than did males (mean = 44.2; $t=3.42$, $df = 11.7$, $p < .001$). The other demographic items showed no significant relationship to the propensity to give self-gifts.

The first research question asked whether materialists have a greater propensity to give tangible self-gifts than non-materialists. The correlation between the summated propensity scale and materialism was .30 ($p < .01$), indicating that more materialistic students had a greater propensity to give themselves tangible gifts.

Self-Gift Contexts

The second research question concerns the situations or contexts in which people give themselves gifts. Given that materialists are more likely to give themselves gifts than are others, does this tendency apply to some or to all self-gift contexts? Information from two sources—the open-ended questions and the propensity scale—were used to address this issue.

The open-ended questions asked respondents to describe a specific episode, including what prompted the self-gift. Respondents were divided into terciles based on materialism scores. The motives for self-gifts reported by respondents in the high and low terciles are given in Table 1.

The most frequent responses involve wanting or needing as a primary motivation. Forty-three percent of the sample purchased the item because they wanted novelty, wanted that specific item, or believed it was needed. Other frequently-mentioned motives are rewarding oneself for an accomplishment and cheering oneself up. The self-administered format could not discern whether respondents gave self-gifts solely out of necessity or desire, or whether there was some other precipitating condition, such as an opportunity to reward or cheer themselves.

While the sample size precluded statistical comparisons of high and low materialists' responses to the open-ended questions, the propensity scale items allow for such comparisons. Respondents indicated how often they buy something special for themselves in each context. Table 2 shows the responses of the three groups on these items.

The mean frequency of giving self-gifts was greater among high materialists in every context, and significantly different in six contexts. The difference between the two groups was most striking for the context "have extra money to spend;" there were also large differences for the contexts of "cheer yourself up" and "feeling good" and "just to be nice to yourself." These findings are consistent with McKeage's (1992) analysis of materialism and self-gift contexts with two notable differences. She found materialism and self-gift propensity to be related in only three (rather than six) contexts. Also, the birthday context was significant in that study, but not here. The inconsistencies may be attributed to the different types of measures used. McKeage (1992) asked respondents to indicate the likelihood of giving themselves a gift in specific

---

[4] Factor scores are not reported here but are available from the authors upon request.

TABLE 2
Materialism and the Propensity to Give Self-Gifts

Context	Materialism			Correlation between Materialism, Propensity
	Low (n = 31)	Medium (n = 35)	High (n = 31)	
Reward for accomplishing something	4.68	4.34c	5.29c	.16
Cheer yourself up	5.00a	5.49	6.23a	.32***
Because it's a holiday	3.39	3.63	4.06	.14
To relieve stress	4.52	5.06	5.13	.19*
Have extra money to spend	5.74a	5.77b	7.45a,b	.32***
Haven't bought for yourself in a while	4.90c	4.94d	5.90c,d	.17*
Feeling good	5.06a	5.17b	6.19a,b	.26**
Incentive to reach a goal	3.23c	4.03	4.23c	.14
Because it's your birthday	4.35	4.37	4.52	-.01
Just to be nice to yourself	4.74c	4.54a	5.77a,c	.23**

-Note— Degrees of freedom for all tests are 60.
*   p < .10
**   p < .05
***   p < .005

a,b denote groups that are different from one another at p < .05.
c,d denote groups that are different from one another at p < .10.

scenarios, while the present study attempted to capture more general behavior given a precipitating context or motivation (e.g., having extra money to spend).

While the results show that materialism is related to an overall propensity to give self-gifts, this result is not consistent across all of the self-gift contexts. Different reasons may exist for this inconsistency. In the context of birthdays or holidays, the propensity to give self-gifts was low for all groups, possibly indicating that the expectation of gifts from others moderates the inclination to give self-gifts stemming from materialism. For rewards or stress relief, cultural habits of affect management may lead to fewer individual differences in values. Untangling the effects of social expectations and personal motivations would require further research.

Types of Self-Gifts

The third research question concerns the relationship between materialism and the type of self-gifts. The open-ended question at the beginning of the survey solicited respondents' descriptions of a single self-gift. The question was worded to include both material self-gifts and activities that are a self-gift. Table 3 lists the types of items mentioned. Consistent with earlier studies (Mick and DeMoss 1992), clothing and other adornments were frequently mentioned. Musical media were also popular self-gifts.

Because materialists are possession oriented and tend to tangibilize their experiences, it was suggested that they would be more likely than others to choose material self-gifts and less likely to choose activities or experiences. However, only four respondents chose to discuss explicit experiences as self-gifts. In addition, while materialistic respondents were more likely to mention trips (which are activity-related) as a self-gift, many of them discussed the purchase of the tickets or consumption-related activities of the trip, such as shopping and dining out at their destination. Also, trips are experiences that can be readily tangibilized through photographs and souvenirs. However, the relationship of materialism to experiential consumption awaits further study. This study provides only preliminary evidence for speculation on the relative propensities of materialists and non-materialists to consume intangible self-gifts.

The monetary cost and time involved for the self-gifts of those low and high in materialism were also examined. While respondents high in materialism spent more time planning and carrying out their self-gifts and more money ($493 versus $169) than low materialism respondents, neither of these relationships was significant. With respect to the latter finding, it is possible that the generally restricted income of the college student sample limited the amount of money available for self-gifts. A test of the relationship between materialism and the cost of self-gifts would be more valid in a population with more discretionary income.

Conclusions

The results lend preliminary support to our expectations regarding the relationship between materialism and the propensity to give self-gifts. In particular, materialism was related to a

TABLE 3
Self-Gifts Described by Low and High Materialism Respondents

	Frequencies		
	Materialism		
Category of Item	Low	High	Total [a]
Clothing and Personal Adornments[b]	12	16	42
Records/Tapes/CDs	4	4	11
Electronics	3	–	5
Trips[c]	1	4	8
Automobiles/Motorcycles	–	3	5
Food and beverages[d]	4	–	7
Other	4	3	12

[a] Columns do not add to total as it represents the entire sample, including those scoring in the middle tercile on materialism.
  In addition, total number of gifts mentioned adds to 90 due to 3 respondents not discussing a self-gift. Four other respondents, not included in the analysis, mentioned engaging in an activity as their self-gift.
[b] Includes accessories, jewelry, perfume, cosmetics, and personal care items.
[c] Respondents discussed buying trips (e.g. tickets, package deals) rather than actually going on the trips.
[d] Includes alcoholic beverages and one respondent who mentioned drugs.

propensity to buy self-gifts when one has some money to spend, is feeling good, or wishes to cheer oneself up. The latter relationship confirms Mick et al.'s (1992) speculation that materialists use self-gifts to generate positive feelings. It is also consistent with the notion that materialists perceive consumption as a means to increase happiness and other positive feelings.

The study is limited in using a college student population. Future research using more diverse populations would be useful for generalization. The scale used to measure the propensity to give self-gifts is also exploratory in nature. It is a self-reported, retrospective measure and does not tap attitudes about giving self-gifts. Further conceptual and methodological refinements are needed. For example, propensity to give self-gifts could be conceptualized as a behavioral intention preceded by attitudes towards gifts to the self, and an appropriate scale may be developed. Such a task, however, was beyond the scope of the present study.

Future research might also explore the impact of self-gifts on consumers' affective responses. While materialists believe that possessions bring happiness, Richins, McKeage and Najjar (1992) found that materialists experience a variety of negative emotions about their purchases. Comparisons could be made between the affective responses of those high and low in materialism, both in terms of the nature of those responses and their duration. Also, since materialists tend to be self-focused, future research might examine affective responses to self-gifts versus gifts given to others.

The implications for materialism in experiential consumption also need to be explored, including self-gifts consisting of activities and experiences that are intangible, such as services. Materialists' participation in shopping as a leisure activity could also be investigated. Historically, materialism has been conceptualized as involving consumption of tangible objects, but as the United States increasingly moves towards a service economy, experiential aspects of materialism in the pursuit of "the good life" deserve investigation.

BIBLIOGRAPHY

Beatty, Sharon E., Lynn R. Kahle and Pamela Homer (1991), "Per-sonal Values and Gift-Giving Behaviors: A Study Across Cultures," *Journal of Business Research*, 22 (March), 149-157.

Belk, Russell W. (1985), "Materialism: Trait Aspects of Living in the Material World," *Journal of Consumer Research*, 12 (December), 265-280.

_____ and Richard W. Pollay (1985), "Images of Ourselves: The Good Life in Twentieth Century Advertising," *Journal of Consumer Research*, 11 (March), 887-897.

Csikzentmihalyi, Mihaly and Eugene Rochberg-Halton (1981), "Object Lessons," *Psychology Today*, (December), 79-85.

Fournier, Susan and Marsha L. Richins (1991), "Some Theoretical and Popular Notions Concerning Materialism," *Journal of Social Behavior and Personality*, 6, 403-414.

Fromm, E., (1976), *To Have or To Be?*, New York: Harper and Row.

Ger, Guliz and Russell W. Belk (1990), "Measuring and Comparing Materialism Cross-Culturally," in *Advances in Consumer Research*, Vol. 17, eds. Marvin E. Goldberg, Gerald Gorn, and Richard W. Pollay, Provo, UT: Association for Consumer Research, pp. 186-192.

Heilbroner, R. L., (1956), *The Quest for Wealth: A Study of Acquisitive Man*, New York: Simon and Schuster.

Lasch, Christopher (1978), *The Culture of Narcissism*, New York: W.W. Norton & Co., Inc.

_____ (1984), *The Minimal Self*, New York: W.W. Norton & Co., Inc.

McKeage, Kim K.R. (1992), "An Exploratory Investigation of the Role of Materialism in Self-Gifts," in *Meaning, Measure, and Morality of Materialism*, eds. Floyd Rudmin and Marsha Richins, Provo, UT: Association for Consumer Research, pp. 140-148.

Mick, David Glen (1991), "Giving Gifts to Ourselves: A Greimassian Analysis Leading to Testable Propositions," in *Marketing and Semiotics: The Copenhagen Symposium*, eds. Hanne Hartvig Larsen, David Glen Mick, and Christian Alsted, Copenhagen: Handelshoskolen Forlag, pp. 142-159.

_____ and Michelle DeMoss (1990a), "To Me from Me: A Descriptive Phenomenology of Self-Gifts," in *Advances in Consumer Research*, Vol. 17, eds. Marvin E. Goldberg, Gerald Gorn, and Richard W. Pollay, Provo, UT: Association for Consumer Research, pp. 677-682.

_____ and Michelle DeMoss (1990b), "Self-Gifts: Phenomenological Insights from Four Contexts," *Journal of Consumer Research*, 17 (December), 322-332.

_____ and Michelle DeMoss (1992), "Further Findings on Self-Gifts: Products, Qualities, and Socioeconomic Correlates," forthcoming in *Advances in Consumer Research*, Vol. 19, eds. John F. Sherry, Jr. and Brian Sternthal, Provo, UT: Association for Consumer Research.

_____, Michelle DeMoss and Ronald J. Faber (1992), "A Projective Study of Motivations and Meanings of Self-Gifts: Implications for Retail Management," forthcoming in *Journal of Retailing*.

Mukerji, Chandra (1983), *From Graven Images: Patterns of Modern Materialism*, New York: Columbia University Press.

Richins, Marsha and Scott Dawson (1992), "A Consumer Values Orientation for Materialism and Its Measurement: Scale Development and Validation," forthcoming in *Journal of Consumer Research*.

_____, Kim K.R. McKeage and Debbie Najjar (1992), "An Exploration of Materialism and Consumption-Related Affect," forthcoming in *Advances in Consumer Research*, Vol. 19, eds. John F. Sherry, Jr. and Brian Sternthal, Provo, UT: Association for Consumer Research.

Rochberg-Halton, Eugene (1984), "Object Relations, Role Models, and Cultivation of the Self," *Environment and Behavior*, 16 (May), 335-368.

_____ (1986), *Meaning and Modernity*, Chicago: The University of Chicago Press.

Schwartz, Barry (1967), "The Social Psychology of the Gift," *The American Journal of Sociology*, 73 (July), 1-11.

Scitovsky, Tibor (1992), *The Joyless Economy: The Psychology of Human Satisfaction*, New York: Oxford University Press.

Ward, Scott and Daniel Wackman (1971), "Family and Media Influences on Adolescent Learning," *American Behavioral Scientist*, 14 (January-February), 415-427.

Persuading Women to Have Mammograms: Practical and Theoretical Perspectives
Paul N. Bloom, University of North Carolina at Chapel Hill

This Presidential Session was organized to accomplish the goal of improving the dialogue between practitioners of social marketing and more theoretically-oriented ACR researchers. Four papers were presented. The first two papers were written by people who have been involved with real-world programs that seek to persuade women to have regular mammograms. The second two papers were written by academic researchers who have been testing theories that would appear to have considerable relevance for persuading women to have regular mammograms. The discussants (Christopher Puto, University of Arizona, and George Balch, University of Illinois, Chicago) commented on the papers from both practitioner and academic perspectives.

The first paper was by Cathy Coyne (AMC Cancer Research Center), Diane Bloom (School of Public Health, University of North Carolina), and Julie Andresen (freelance consultant) and was titled "Using Qualitative Research to Develop Strategies to Reach Women with Cancer Screening Messages." The presentation summarized the findings of a series of focus groups that were done with Colorado women on their feelings about mammograms and pap smears. These findings have been used to guide communications programs of the AMC Cancer Research Center and other institutions. This paper can be found in this proceedings.

The second paper was by Cynthia Currence (American Cancer Society) and was titled "Tailoring Mammography Communications Using Compass Analysis." The presentation described a PC-based target marketing software system that the American Cancer Society has acquired and used to guide it in designing communications. The system enables the Society to obtain a richer profile of target audiences. By drawing on secondary data sources (primarily Census data), it is possible to profile dominant traits of people living in certain areas. The dominant demographic characteristics, buying habits, transportation habits, and media behaviors can all be identified.

The third paper was by Radhika Puri and Joan Meyers-Levy (both of the University of Chicago) and was titled "The Power of Numbers." The presentation reported on an experimental study that tested the persuasiveness of alternative means of presenting statistical information. Their results showed that two forms of numeric representation — incidence rates and percentages — are equally persuasive unless the percentages are illustrated with pie charts, in which case the message is less persuasive.

The final paper was by Lauren Goldberg Block (New York University) and Punam Anand (Columbia University) and was titled "When to Accentuate the Negative: The Effects of Perceived Efficacy and Message Framing on Intentions to Perform a Health Related Behavior." The presentation reported on an experimental study that found (1) negatively framed messages produced greater behavioral intentions when subjects were uncertain about the efficacy of the preventive behavior and (2) positively framed messages produced greater intentions when subjects saw the preventive behavior as having high efficacy.

Using Qualitative Research to Develop Strategies to Reach Women with Cancer Screening Messages[1]

Cathy A. Coyne, AMC Cancer Research Center
Diane Bloom, Bloom Research
Julie Andresen, Bloom Research

INTRODUCTION

Traditionally, cancer control activities have focused on the "general public," and have not been specifically targeted to any ethnic or socioeconomic population group. Programs and materials have, therefore, been designed with the "majority" in mind, that being the middle income white population. In a review of the literature conducted in 1991, few studies were identified which focused on the needs of populations not adequately reached with breast and cervical cancer screening messages (Coyne et. al., 1992). Fewer than 6% of the 318 studies reviewed were devoted to the identification of breast and cervical screening barriers among low income black women. No studies were identified which addressed factors related to the low prevalence of screening of Native American women, among whom the rates of cervical cancer incidence and mortality are elevated.

Several organizations have been concentrating significant efforts on reaching culturally diverse populations with cancer control messages. The American Cancer Society (ACS) has made reaching the socioeconomically disadvantaged a major initiative throughout all their program efforts and has identified breast cancer detection as a unit core activity. In addition, the National Cancer Institute has funded several research projects that are seeking to identify methods to effect behavior change among "special populations." The passage of the Breast and Cervical Cancer Mortality Prevention Act, signed into law August, 1990, has also helped to stimulate research and application activities in this area. This law established a program of grants, administered through the U.S. Centers for Disease Control (CDC), to fund state health departments to increase the number of women screened for breast and cervical cancer. One component of the comprehensive programs funded by the CDC is public education. The intent of this component is twofold: to educate the public regarding the importance of early detection in the control of breast and cervical cancer, and to motivate women to be screened. The law specifically states that priority must be given to low income and Native American women in the provision of screening services.

To support the efforts of the state health departments, the CDC awarded a cooperative agreement to the AMC Cancer Research Center (AMC) to provide technical assistance in the area of public education. This technical assistance includes qualitative research to obtain insights into the beliefs, attitudes, and behaviors of the target audiences. Two series of focus groups were conducted with women living in the Denver, Colorado, area as part of this qualitative research. The purpose of these groups was to provide state health departments with information to use in the conceptualization and development of their public education programs and collateral material. The focus group discussion guides were designed to explore the barriers that inhibit women from being screened, and to elicit suggestions regarding messages and channels to use to increase the numbers of women receiving mammograms and Pap tests.

Prior to designing the discussion guide, published literature on the barriers to breast and cervical screening was reviewed. Barriers to screening were found to be very similar among different populations of women. Lack of physician referral, lack of perceived risk, and cost were identified as common barriers to screening mammography. With regard to obtaining Pap tests, lack of knowledge, embarrassment, and fear of finding cancer were suggested as barriers. The relative saliency of these barriers among the different population groups was not well addressed in any of the studies examined. There were few studies that addressed the needs of culturally diverse populations.

The literature review provided researchers with information on which to base the discussion guide and, also provided an understanding of the research gaps. Accordingly, an attempt was made in the first series of focus groups to identify the most inhibitory barriers in order to address the issue of saliency. The second series of groups was designed to explore the influence of culture on screening behavior, and to gain insight into appropriate message framing and delivery.

RATIONALE FOR USING FOCUS GROUPS

Qualitative research is well suited to developing strategies to reach identified populations with health care messages. It addresses the "why," rather than the "how much." When used alone, or in conjunction with quantitative studies, qualitative research offers insights into attitudes, beliefs, motives, and behaviors essential to developing health care intervention strategies. Qualitative research does not seek the hard and fast answers, rather the subjective and intuitive elements, which give a clearer picture of the decision process. For these studies, focus groups, instead of in-depth interview, were chosen as the most productive method for identifying barriers and developing appropriate strategies.

This methodology was chosen because it lends itself to brainstorming, eliciting a rich exchange of thoughts and ideas that build upon each other. Focus groups offer a natural environment for probing the emotional and contextual aspects of human response. In this qualitative research study, the group format may have provided a more comfortable setting in which to discuss attitudes and feelings about potentially sensitive issues related to the body.

Focus groups supply valuable qualitative research data. The appropriate use of qualitative data can enable the researcher to tie together clusters of behavior and identify relationships helpful for determining the barriers to desirable health behaviors. Focus groups were appropriately used in this project to develop hypotheses and gain insights for formulating interventions to promote the use of cancer screening tests. However, focus groups can be used inappropriately. The small number of respondents and the absence of random sampling techniques make drawing statistical conclusions impossible. No attempt should be made to draw firm conclusions or to generalize results to the population at large.

Group Participants and Topics

The eligibility criteria for participants in the two series of focus groups that comprise the qualitative study being discussed in this paper are presented in Table 1. In the first series, primary source of health care was selected as a proxy for income. It was postulated that a major issue for low income individuals is access to health care and, therefore, the inclusion of women who use public health clinics

---

[1] This research was funded under U.S. Centers for Disease Control Cooperative Agreement #U50/CCU806186.

TABLE 1
Focus Group Eligibility Criteria

Criteria	First Series	Second Series
Income	—	≤ 133% poverty
Age	≥ 50 years	≥ 50 years
Mammography use	adherers/nonadherers	Never had or ≥ 5 years ago
Residence	urban/rural	urban
Race/ethnicity	black/white	black/Latina/Native American
Primary source of health care	public/private	—

may reveal barriers in this regard. A proxy was selected to avoid possible participant refusal based upon unwillingness to reveal income. It was also posited that differences would exist in the perception of barriers between women who adhere to the ACS mammography screening guidelines (adherers) and women who do not adhere (non-adherers). The ACS's screening guidelines recommend that asymptomatic women between the ages of 40-50 years obtain screening mammograms every one to two years; for women 50 years of age and older, mammograms should be obtained annually. Differences in residence, whether urban or rural, were also explored to determine whether any barriers exist which may be related to difficulties in transportation, cultural variances, or other issues of urbanization. Examination of the behavioral influence of culture based upon race was also sought.

The second series of focus groups involved women of lower incomes and different ethnic backgrounds as compared to those involved in the first series. Although the women using public health clinics, as recruited in the first series of groups, were assumed to be of low income, they did not appear to the researchers as being at the lowest end of the income scale. The researchers, therefore, decided to study the needs of women at or below 133% of the federal poverty level in the second series of groups, using income as a screening criteria. Since previous research has not adequately addressed the needs of women from different minority populations, specifically Latinas and Native American women, composition of the focus groups in this second series included women from these populations.

Similar topics were explored in both series of groups. However, in the second series, the researchers also explored characteristics of print materials that might make brochures more appropriate for different population groups. The women participating in these latter groups were asked to review sample print materials on breast and cervical screening. Additionally, the latter groups devoted more attention to the influences of family and religion on decision-making.

RESULTS AND DISCUSSION

Results from first series of groups

Several barriers to obtaining mammograms and Pap tests were identified in the first series of 12 focus groups. Themes and patterns emerging from these barriers are as follows:

Dissatisfaction with health care providers. Dislike and distrust of doctors surfaced primarily in the groups of white women. This distrust was most evident in the urban, white groups. Even the women who said that doctors were most capable of influencing personal health care behavior later vented hostility toward their physicians, whom some perceived as callous and greedy. Stories were shared about physicians whom the women perceived did not spend enough time with them, did not really listen, and were too quick to prescribe surgery or medication. They believed that doctors sometimes ordered tests not because they were necessary, but because it would help them "rake in the bucks."

Misconceptions about Pap tests. Women in all groups were asked questions about the Pap test and cervical cancer. Misconceptions about the purpose of this test were widespread among all the groups. Many women perceived the Pap test as being able to detect everything from cervical cancer, uterine cancer, and ovarian cancer, to hormone levels, venereal disease, AIDS, yeast infections, and cysts. Most respondents thought a woman should get a Pap test every year, yet they were uncertain regarding the age at which cervical screening should be initiated. There was also confusion about whether or not women needed Pap tests after menopause or after a hysterectomy.

Role of positive attitudes. The very strong importance women placed on "a positive mental attitude" was a theme that came out in all groups. A positive outlook was thought to be a deciding factor in staying healthy and also in surviving cancer and coping with other serious diseases. Some women said that because they had a positive attitude, they would not get cancer and, therefore, did not need mammograms. Many felt that cancer resides in most people, but, with a healthy perspective on life, one can control the cells and keep cancer from emerging.

Role of lack of knowledge and denial. More African American women saw themselves at risk for breast cancer as compared with the women in the white groups. Women in all groups were aware of some of the factors that would put a woman at risk for breast cancer; however, many held misconceptions, believing that factors such as trauma to the breast and large breast size influence risk. Age was not mentioned as a major risk factor by women in the groups. It was common for women to say that they would not get breast cancer because neither their mother or sister had ever been diagnosed with the disease. Often, the non-adherers used the absence of these risk factors as evidence that they personally were not susceptible to breast cancer. This was an excuse for them to choose not to have mammograms.

Cost of having cancer. It was interesting to note that many women in the uninsured groups intentionally did not get mammograms. One point that came up repeatedly in the public non-adherer groups was that women who had no money or health insurance made a rational choice not to seek health treatment. As one woman said, "I can't get sick — we can't afford it." Even if they could afford the mammogram, they could not afford to have breast cancer. Thus, having a mammogram to learn that they were going to suffer and die did not make sense to them.

Fear as a barrier. When women in all of the groups mentioned fear as a reason for not having a mammogram, they were referring to several components of concern. Of greatest concern was the fear of finding cancer. Subsequent fears expressed were those of surgery, treatment, suffering, death, losing a breast, and losing a male partner.

Mammograms causing cancer. A pattern that emerged throughout the session with the group of urban private non-adherers was the feeling that a "bad mammogram," defined by the women as one in which a woman receives an overdose of radiation or one in which the technician bruises her breasts, would leave them worse off than if they never had a mammogram. They were afraid that the radiation or trauma to the breast could actually trigger cancer.

Rural, urban differences. Some variations were noted between the urban and rural participants which could suggest differences in attitude. For example, the majority of participants in the urban groups were distrustful of the medical community and sought out alternatives to going to medical doctors — such as self-education, prayer, osteopaths, or chiropractors. Those who sought medical care, asserted themselves by requesting information from their providers to help them make decisions regarding personal health care. Women in the rural adherer's group, though more trusting of physicians, were not as comfortable asking questions of their doctors. They mentioned seeking the advice of pharmacists who were able to spend more time answering their questions. Women in the non-adhering, rural groups expressed a feeling of being victimized by a heartless health care system. One strongly voiced concern in the non-adhering rural group was the indifference and lack of opportunity for good health care for the middle-aged woman without insurance.

Adherer, non-adherer differences. Many adherers, who regularly received mammograms, did so on the recommendation of their doctors or because they had detected a lump. Many of the non-adherers had not seen doctors in several years. In the urban groups, the women seemed to find reasons other than cost to be important in deciding whether to visit a physician. Denial, reliance on the power of positive thinking in cancer control, and distrust of medical tests and doctors were the primary reasons these women did not have mammograms. In the rural areas, cost was a more important consideration because members of these groups did not seem to distrust the medical community. In the urban, public groups, cost was also more of a factor than in the private groups.

Black, white differences. No major differences were noted between the two racial groups with regard to their attitudes and beliefs about breast and cervical cancer. A greater percentage of the African American women saw themselves at risk for breast cancer as compared with the white women. More of the African American women also mentioned that they would listen to the advice of their pastor or minister regarding health, and that the church was an appropriate location to conduct educational health programs on breast cancer. This religious influence was not evident among women in the white groups.

Group support. One interesting phenomena was observed in all of the groups. After experiencing an intense discussion during the focus groups about topics such as cancer, suffering, pain, and death, the women became cohesive and mutually supportive. This supportive environment was noted as being a factor in motivating women to be screened.

Strategies for promotion of mammography. The women in all groups were asked to assume the role of committee members assigned the task of devising a plan to encourage every woman over 40 in their community to have a mammogram. A common theme that came up in many of the groups was, "Take care of yourself." They felt that women tend to put their husbands, children, and jobs first and often have no time left over for themselves. The themes, "Do it for you," and "You're worth it," came out repeatedly. Another theme that came up in the groups was, "Do it for peace of mind." A mammogram connoted reassurance for them. Another possible theme that came up frequently was, "Early detection can save your life and your breast." Participants also suggested using a flyer or brochure with a simple explanation of a mammogram. Other information for the brochure would include: the place and time of testing, how long it will take, assurances that the equipment is safe and that the technician is well-trained and experienced, and when and how they will be informed of the results.

Saliency of Barriers. An attempt was made during the focus groups to ascertain which of the barriers mentioned were the most salient. The women were asked to rank the barriers in order of their ability to absolutely inhibit women from obtaining a Pap test or mammogram. Although this process helped women to eliminate the least important barriers, they were not able to come to consensus regarding the most salient barrier.

Results from second series of groups

It is beyond the scope of this paper to discuss the results of the second series of focus groups in great detail. Therefore, only major findings relevant to health education program design and implementation are presented. Many similarities across the three ethnic groups were evident with regard to beliefs, knowledge, sources of health information, and perception of risk. Similarities to the responses provided by the women in the first series of focus groups were also evident. Differences among the various groups will be highlighted and discussed.

The discussions that were part of the second series of focus groups provided health education program planners with insights into the educational needs of women who are not being adequately screened. Women were, in general, knowledgeable about mammography (i.e., what it is and its efficacy in detecting cancer early) and were aware of the benefits to early detection. Many, however, could not precisely describe the procedure. As in the earlier groups, several misconceptions were voiced by the women, which may have influenced their perception of risk and dissuaded them from being screened. The women, who were all over the age of 50, did not view age as a risk factor for breast cancer and, therefore, did not see themselves at risk. Trauma to the breast was seen as a causal factor for breast cancer. Other risk factors identified by the participants, including family history, also served to reduce the women's perception of susceptibility. If applying the Health Belief Model, perceived susceptibility is one variable that influences an individual's behavior (Rosenstock 1991). Other variables of the Health Belief Model, including perceived severity and perceived benefit did not appear, in this case, to be influential in the screening behavior of the focus group respondents. A majority of the women participating in the groups viewed cancer as a very serious disease, frequently with a fatal outcome. Yet, even though they recognized the severity of the illness and saw benefits to early detection methods such mammography and the Pap test, the women were not willing to adopt screening behavior. Thus, their lack of perceived susceptibility had greater influence over their behavior.

Embarrassment was viewed as a barrier to screening, especially for cervical cancer, by many of the participants. Embarrassment, if experienced by a woman upon initial screening, may dissuade her from returning for subsequent tests.

Fear of finding cancer was mentioned by many participants as one reason women may not choose to be screened. Value expectancy theories (Carter 1991) of health behavior are useful in predicting individuals' behaviors when expected outcomes are known. Women who fear the outcome of being diagnosed with cancer are more hesitant to have a mammogram or Pap test. Although the focus group participants did understand that early detection of cancer resulted in better outcomes, their fear of cancer as an outcome overshadowed any rational understanding of early detection.

Other barriers that were mentioned include cost, transportation, and other issues related to the provision of screening services (e.g., child care). Cost did not seem to be the most salient barrier among these women, as anticipated by the researchers. There was greater discussion regarding cost among the women in the first series than among the women in these groups.

When asked whether their church or religious beliefs would have any influence over their behavior to be screened, the majority of the women, regardless of ethnicity, responded that they would not. The Native American women did state that, although religious beliefs may not directly influence their behavior, those beliefs would most likely encourage screening as a means of keeping themselves healthy.

None of the women, in any of the groups, felt that their families would discourage them from being screened. Although some of the women responded that it would not be something they would talk about with their husbands, and in some cases their children, they did feel that their families would be supportive.

The participants also shared their perspectives on how the message should be delivered and by whom. Participants in all of the groups, regardless of ethnicity, mentioned that they rely on family and friends for health information. Many women mentioned that they would listen to the advice of their daughters, or that of a friend or relative who had either undergone the procedure or had the disease. Other information sources included lay medical books and health pamphlets. Some of the women mentioned that they would rely on their physicians for health information. As expressed by women from one of the groups in the first series, participants in one of the African American groups expressed tremendous distrust of the health care system and stated that they were very skeptical of physicians' motives in providing health care. Unlike the earlier group, women in this particular discussion based much of their skepticism on feelings of discrimination based on racism. White physicians were believed to be especially untrustworthy. This feeling of victimization was voiced very strongly by women in this group of very low income African American women. In the other group of African American women, this feeling was expressed, though not with such fervor. The reason for this belief being so strongly held by one group and not the others has not yet been explained. A possible explanation is that one participant in the group felt very strongly about this issue and voiced her opinion adamantly. This may have given the other women in the group "permission" to express themselves candidly on this topic.

Identification of appropriate, as well as inappropriate, spokespersons to deliver the health education message is an extremely important consideration when designing a health education program. The most well conceived message, if communicated by someone considered to be untrustworthy or unbelievable, will not be received. Therefore, use of a white physician as the spokesperson to encourage women to be screened would not be effective in reaching some African American women in Denver. Many of the focus group participants, regardless of ethnicity, stated that they felt a message would be more believable and relevant if they were able to identify with the person who was delivering the message.

Being able to identify with the message or the spokesperson was also a factor in the design of educational print material. When asked to look at six brochures and choose the one they would most likely pick up and read, a majority of the women in all groups selected a brochure that they felt was specifically targeting them. A brochure with an Indian design on the cover was chosen by the Native American women because they felt the content of this brochure must be addressing the needs of Native women. A majority of the African American women selected a factsheet entitled, "Facts About Breast Cancer, Mammography, and Black American Women." The women also identified with brochures that contained phrases like "for every woman," "advice for women 40 and over," and drawings of women they could identify with.

The layout and typeface are also important considerations when designing an educational brochure. Participants in each of the groups stated that brochures with large print size and generous amounts of white space would be easier to read, and, therefore, more likely to be read. There was not a consistent opinion regarding colors used in the brochures. All groups stated that the color was not a deciding factor when picking up and reading a brochure. For some women, the size of the brochure did influence whether or not they would pick it up. This was especially the case among the Native American women who preferred smaller brochures that would fit into their pocketbooks. They would not want others to see the brochures they were reading, particularly if they contain illustrations of female anatomy, as many mammography and Pap test brochures do. The Native American women also preferred that any visuals of the female anatomy be placed inside the brochure, rather than on the front cover. The other ethnic groups were not as sensitive to the type of visuals used in the brochures, although some of the Hispanic women stated that they would have to hide a pamphlet showing a woman having a mammogram because it was embarrassing.

The preferences regarding the form and content of the educational print material expressed by the women in the focus groups made it clear that when designing health education materials, the planners must have a tremendous understanding of their intended audience. Use of focus group methodology can be very effective in this regard.

Participants were also asked for suggestions regarding appropriate locations to conduct educational programs on breast and cervical cancer. Women in the African American and Hispanic groups suggested churches as good sites, as these are generally central locations that many women frequent. Use of a mobile mammography van to perform breast cancer screening was also suggested as a means of getting more women from the community to be screened. The participants agreed, however, that the church or a mobile unit was not an appropriate site to perform Pap tests, which they feel should be administered in clinics or physicians' offices.

HOW INFORMATION DERIVED FROM THE GROUPS HAS BEEN USED

The information and insights derived from the focus groups are being used by state health departments in the design of the public education components of their breast and cervical cancer programs. One state health department, in particular, has used the information obtained from the first series to develop messages that will be used in educational programs intended to reach inadequately screened women. These messages are to be delivered by women from the community who are being trained as lay health educators. Hence, the intended audience and recipients of the messages should be able to identify with the spokespersons, as they will be "women like them," from the community. The program planners from the state health department also found that identification of the information needs of the women was helpful in narrowing the content of the program. They were able to tailor the message so as to address misconceptions and beliefs that may have potentially served as barriers to screening. The participants' input into the design of educational brochures has also encouraged health educators to consider those characteristics which are important to the intended audience.

In addition, the focus groups provided program planners with an awareness of how much the skill and demeanor of the mammographic technician influences whether a woman will choose to return for a mammogram according to screening guidelines. This insight persuaded program planners to include in the professional education component of their programs, a focus on establishing rapport and maintaining the woman's dignity during the examination. Awareness of the importance of appropriate logistical arrangements for the screening programs was also heightened by the responses of the women in the groups.

DISCUSSION: WHERE DO WE GO FROM HERE?

As noted, qualitative research can provide insights into the development of effective strategies to deliver health messages and motivate behavior change. The information from the focus groups discussed in this paper has assisted planners in the design of breast and cervical cancer screening programs that will reach women with messages motivating them to have mammograms and Pap tests. However, there are still several research gaps that need to be explored. One issue that must be addressed if program planners are to tailor their messages to the specific needs of their intended audiences is that of which barriers—as identified by the women— are the most salient. Focus groups may not be the best method to use in prioritizing barriers, as it is most effective in generating ideas through brainstorming. The use of quantitative methodologies should be explored as a means of identifying the most salient barriers effecting women's behavior, as these methods enable the researcher to quantify that which is generated through qualitative research. Larger numbers of women may need to be recruited to explore the issue of saliency, as women tend to be at various stages of behavior change and the barriers may be related to these stages.

There is a paucity of research that focuses on the specific needs of culturally diverse populations. As revealed through a review of the literature, few studies have addressed the needs of these population groups. More research must be directed toward populations that have been traditionally underserved by cancer control efforts. Greater emphasis should also be placed on developing effective research methodologies that provide a better understanding of how to reach very low income populations with health messages. Traditional strategies of recruitment and focus group facilitation are not effective in reaching individuals from low income communities. An emerging area of research is the development of strategies to deliver health education messages that do not rely on the printed word. Brochures and pamphlets are not effective tools to reach all segments of the population with health information, particularly individuals with limited or no reading skills, and those persons who traditionally rely on oral communication.

Qualitative research has contributed tremendously to health education program planning. These efforts should continue and expand to include populations not adequately reached by previous health education programs.

REFERENCES

Coyne, Cathy A., Karin Hohman, and Arnold Levinson (1992), "Reaching Special Populations with Breast and Cervical Cancer Public Education," Journal of Cancer Education, 7(4), 293-303.

Rosenstock, Irwin M. (1991), "The Health Belief Model: Explaining Health Behavior Through Expectancies," in *Health Behavior and Health Education*, eds. Karen Glanz et. al., San Francisco: Jossey-Bass, 39-62.

Carter, William B. (1991), "Health Behavior as a Rational Process: Theory of Reasoned Action and Multiattribute Utility Theory," in *Health Behavior and Health Education*, eds. Karen Glanz et. al., San Francisco: Jossey-Bass, 63-91.

Demographic and Lifestyle Data–A Practical Application To Stimulating Compliance With Mammography Guidelines Among Poor Women

Cynthia Curence, American Cancer Society

BACKGROUND

In the 1930s, the data were available to enable organizations and individuals to predict human behavior and responses based on analysis of basic demographic characteristics, lifestyle habits and dominant media behavior. At that time, however, the technology was not available to perform the analysis. Today, several companies have blended the power of the computer with available demographic, lifestyle and media data to offer a dynamic marketing tool to progressive businesses.

The American Cancer Society (ACS) purchased such a tool two years ago from Claritas. The product, called Compass, crunches census data, consumer buyer behavior data, and media behavior data to divide residents of the United States into one of 40 types of people. Members of each type or cluster have similar characteristics and tend to behave in similar ways. The ACS has been using Compass effectively to save lives from cancer through targeted efforts to educate people about their risk of cancer, to focus delivery of services to cancer patients and their families, and to tailor fundraising activities to specific types of people.

In the area of breast cancer, ACS staff and volunteers knew through experience and other behavioral research, that they were not reaching the poor woman as effectively as they were the middle-class woman. This was validated in recent research commissioned by ACS (Jacobs Institute, 1992), which showed that over a two year period, while a 10% increase was measured among middle-class women having mammograms, no increase was detected among poor women. The ACS determined that the product of mammography screening needed to be made more relevant for poor women. Through Compass, ACS generated secondary data that (along with primary qualitative research on attitudes and barriers to mammography among poor women) enabled a dramatic adaptation of the product to the poor market.

It should be noted that Compass is just one tool used to understand the market and suggest product adaptations. Qualitative and quantitative research regarding attitudes, perceptions, barriers and benefits are critical to overall strategy development.

STATEMENT OF PROBLEM

To increase the percentage of older poor women (over age 50 and making less than $20,000 annually) in Atlanta's inner city who follow the ACS mammography guidelines.

ANALYSIS

Reports and mapping capabilities available through the Compass target marketing system shows the specific census tract areas in Atlanta where an investigator is twice as likely to find the target audience (women over age 50 making less than $20,000 per year). Some of the key demographic descriptors of the five types of poor that dominate this area are:

Characteristic	Index
• African-American	415 *
• Households w/o cars	272
• Households w/ single parents	213
• Population unemployed	173
• Population in service jobs	162
• Less than high school education	160

* An index of 100 is average.

These data suggest that to reach this target audience, it is likely that issues of transportation, day care, employment and literacy (or low reading levels) will have to be addressed.

Some key consumer buyer characteristics of this group are that they:

Characteristic	Index
• Listen to soul/black music	170
• Listen to gospel/sacred music	158
• Saw 4+ movies in the past 90 days	123
• Travel by bus	119
• Consume cola drinks regularly	118

Although not as dramatic as the demographic characteristics, these data reinforce transportation-related issues. They also point to a type of radio that may be favored, low-cost entertainment that might be a good communication vehicle, and a possible sponsor for activities reaching this group.

Some key media behavior characteristics follow:

Characteristic	Index
• Batch black entertainment TV	318
• Top 20% day time TV viewing	184
• Urban/contemporary radio	292

Although television viewership is high, since nonprofits do not have control over the placement or frequency of free TV commercials and most nonprofits do not have budgets for paid advertising, television is not the best place to advertise. Further, even though radio ranks very high, because of the importance of transportation and employment issues, it is likely that a significant portion of the target group may be watching TV or riding the bus during drive-time radio periods.

The system can graphically map the highest concentration of low-level service jobs and the location of hospitals in the area.

Qualitative and quantitative research shows that the greatest barriers to this market seeking mammograms are the lack of physician referrals, cost, fear, and a realistic attitude about access to follow-up health care. Even if a program could satisfy concerns relating to transportation, cost, day care, and referral, the market still might not respond because of limited access to further care. In other words, if a woman finds out that she has cancer, she would have limited treatment alternatives. Therefore, some would prefer not to know and would choose not be to screened.

RECOMMENDATIONS

1. Work with the six hospitals in the heart of the Atlanta market's residence and day time population.
2. In cooperation with the hospitals, develop a program that addresses day care and transportation needs, cost, treatment alternatives, and low level reading capabilities of the target market.
3. Create/make available low reading level literature and increase one-to-one contact with the market to address fear and concerns about access to care.
4. Work with area clinics to inform doctors about the availability of low-cost/free screening and the availability, if

possible, of treatment support to encourage them to refer poor women to the hospitals for screening.
5. Use such nontraditional media as bus shelter posters, bus cards, billboards, and theater trailers to promote the availability of mammography for the poor.

Children as Consumers: Are They "Marketing" Literate?
Deborah Roedder John, University of Minnesota
Laura Peracchio, University of Wisconsin-Milwaukee

In our society, children become avid consumers long before they learn the basic skills of reading, writing, and arithmetic. As children's roles as consumers have increased, so have concerns over children's abilities to evaluate advertising and promotion for these products and their abilities to make informed judgments as consumers. The purpose of this session was to bring together researchers interested in the children's area to focus on the topic of consumer literacy and learning in children.

The first presentation, *"Effects of Channel One: Adolescent Knowledge of and Attitudes Toward Advertising" by Marian Friestad and David M. Boush*, investigated how knowledgeable adolescent consumers are in terms of interpreting advertising tactics, such as the use of celebrity endorsers and humor. These knowledge structures were then related, along with other individual difference factors such as self-esteem and media habits, to adolescent attitudes toward advertising. Data from students from three middle schools were used to explore differences across three grade levels (grades 6-8). In addition, the authors explored how adolescent knowledge and attitudes might be affected by the recent introduction of Whittle Communication's Channel One programming.

The second presentation, *"Young Children's Understanding of Visual and Aural Televised Messages" by Laura Peracchio*, continued the theme of what children learn from advertising by examining the role that message modality plays in the learning process. Though young children tend to favor information that is presented in an audio-visual format, much important advertising information is conveyed aurally. This paper examined why aural presentations usually tend to be inferior to audio-visual ones and identified methods to increase young children's comprehension of aurally presented information. Findings from two experiments suggest that modality differences are due to differences in the degree of memory elaboration provided by audio-visual messages. More importantly, the results indicate that young children's acquisition of aural information can be enhanced by encouraging further elaboration of these messages.

The third presentation, *"How Capable are Children as Decision Makers? An Exploratory Study of Information Search Behavior" by Jennifer Gregan-Paxton and Deborah Roedder John*, investigated children's predecisional search behavior. Although children are called upon to make numerous consumer decisions at early ages, we know very little about how "skillful" they are in making decisions and in acquiring information to make informed decisions. This paper examined how young children (4 to 7 years of age) search for information in a consumer choice task, given different costs and benefits of obtaining information. Findings from an experimental study indicated that younger children in the sample had more difficulty making cost-benefit tradeoffs, whereas older children were more able to perform the same type of tradeoffs.

Temporal Dimensions of Decision-Making: How Long, and When, to Decide
Deborah J. Mitchell, Temple University

There are at least two temporal dimensions underlying consumer decision-making. One dimension is *the amount of time spent deciding;* it includes time spent by the consumer on various predecisional activities such as problem framing, information search, and evaluation of alternatives. A second dimension is *purchase timing,* or the point in time at which an exchange occurs, usually based at least in part on predecisional activities. These two dimensions are clearly related, since one component often underlying the decision to delay or accelerate a purchase is the individual's perception of whether they need more or less time in order to make a high-quality choice. This special topic seminar addressed each of these questions, by (1) presenting current research dealing with both temporal dimensions of decision-making, time spent deciding and purchase timing, and (2) discussing how these dimensions may interact.

Recently researchers have shown a strong renewed interest in questions relating to both of these dimensions of decision time. One area of work has focused on whether the amount of time available to a consumer actually affects the nature or quality of the decision-making process. In general, findings support the notion that time pressure, or the lack of time, changes the decision-making process and may result in sub-optimal decisions (e.g., Wright 1974). However, there is evidence that eventually individuals may adapt and perform quite well, given the time constraints (Payne, Bettman, and Johnson, 1988).

Purchase timing has also been the focus of recent research: when (and perhaps in what order) will consumers buy? Purchase timing has received considerable attention for frequently-purchased consumer packaged goods, and numerous models have been developed to predict when a consumer will buy. Other work has focused on the planning of purchases and the timing of durable goods acquisition. In addition, the timing of consumers' purchases has been an underlying issue for work on impulse buying and time-inconsistent preferences.

However, in examining these two temporal dimensions of consumer decision-making, both separately and in terms of how they may interact, many issues remain unresolved. First, consider time spent on decision-making. A strong intuitive belief that most consumers, researchers, and even clinicians share is that although people can 'get by' under pressure, more time usually helps decision-making (within realistic limits). However, are there particular contexts in which increasing the amount of time spent deciding might result in a lower quality decision? One way to spend more time on decision-making is to introspect about one's tastes and preferences. Does spending more time on introspection improve decision-making? Most consumers would say yes; Deborah Mitchell presented data to suggest otherwise, however.

In addition, should we as researchers and consumers be more concerned with the effect of time pressure on decision quality than previous research would suggest? Past research suggests that in the face of time pressure decision-makers pay attention to the most important product information. But what if they do not have the knowledge to discern the most critical information? In such situations decision-makers may focus even more intently on irrelevant or misleading information than they would if there was no pressure. France Leclerc presented data consistent with this hypothesis.

Next, consider the timing of consumers' purchases. What factors trigger consumers to end the decision-making process and actually act, thus causing acceleration or delay? Some clinicians seek to identify these factors in order to aid individuals who have a problem with impulsive behavior; they wish to delay or "turn off" the potential purchase act. However, both managers and social policy makers wish to understand how to accelerate or "turn on" consumer purchasing in the face of sluggish demand. The reasons consumers delay were presented by Eric Greenleaf and Don Lehmann.

Finally, how well do consumers predict their own future purchases? This question is important if managers and policy makers wish to use these intentions to help determine as quickly as possible the need to stimulate consumer demand, rather than waiting for actual purchasing to decline. Vicki Morwitz addressed this issue in her presentation.

REFERENCES
Payne, John W., James R. Bettman, & Eric J. Johnson, E. J. (1988), "Adaptive strategy selection in decision making," *Journal of Experimental Psychology: Learning, Memory and Cognition*, 14, 534-552.

Wright, Peter. L. (1974), "The harassed decision-maker: Time pressures, distractions, and the use of evidence," *Journal of Applied Psychology*, 59, 555-561.

Session Overview
Context Effects on Consumer Goals, Brand Awareness, and Decision Making
Cynthia Huffman, University of Pennsylvania

Organizer: Allan D. Shocker, University of Minnesota
Chair: Cynthia Huffman, University of Pennsylvania
Discussant: C. Whan Park, University of Pittsburgh

Papers:

The Role of Usage Context in Consumer Choice: A Problem Solving Perspective
  Luk Warlop, University of Florida
  S. Ratneshwar, University of Florida

Understanding Brand Awareness: Let Me Give You a C(l)ue!
  Stephen J. Holden, ESSEC, France

On the Transferability of Feature/Level Preferences Across Competing Products Serving the Same Purpose
  Milos D. Graonic, University of Minnesota
  Allan D. Shocker, University of Minnesota

This special session is the second in a continuing annual series that revolves around situational and contextual effects on consumers' goals, the resulting multidimensionality of consumption experiences, the situationally- and contextually-based knowledge that develops from these experiences, and the effects of flexible, contextually-based goal-oriented knowledge structures on our consideration sets and the evaluative criteria we use in decision making.

There are three main themes behind this stream of research. First, the work is firmly based on the recognition that much of consumer behavior is purposive. Second, the research revolves around the notion that consumers experience objects in different contexts and usage situations, with different goals, and that these contextual and goal aspects are incorporated into the knowledge structures that develop from these experiences. Further, it is recognized that the situations and goals that organize our knowledge affect future decision making through cued selectivity in the use of evaluation criteria and in the formation of consideration sets.

This overview and the Figure serve to relate the papers from this session to each other and to other recent papers in this area (note that it is not meant as a flow chart of what might occur in a particular choice experience). The first link in the figure, in which situational context is shown to be a powerful influence on a consumer's goals (the benefits that are desired), is represented by Graonic and Shocker (1993) and by Warlop and Ratneshwar (1993). Graonic and Shocker demonstrate that at least in some cases (they looked at noncomparable product choice sets such as bicycles versus in-line skates), situational context is a better determinant of goals and desired benefits than are the product characteristics themselves (which in noncomparable situations differ among the product alternatives). Warlop and Ratneshwar, on the other hand, provide a descriptive account of how aspects of a consumption situation trigger goals and benefits relevant to the choice. One example they use is finding a snack before a Saturday evening date; the relevant goals triggered include a snack that is not messy, is easy and quick to eat, and does not make one's breath smell. Note that we recognize also that while adaptation to situational context is important, current goals are also impacted by the individual's more enduring values (Link 2, see Gutman 1982).

The third link in the figure (Huffman and Houston 1992) represents the notion that a consumer with goals in mind will tend to exhibit a goal-oriented approach to information acquisition and choice. Information from these experiences will eventually form categorical knowledge structures in which brands and features are organized in terms of the goal(s) that motivated the consumption experiences. Because the situational context helps to determine the goals around which knowledge is organized, the situational context is also a means by which feature and brand knowledge can be accessed and used.

The process by which consideration sets are formed and choice criteria are determined is represented by the fourth link. This link represents the idea that the access and use of knowledge is strongly impacted by situational factors and current goals through their role in cueing information residing in memory. Ratneshwar and Shocker (1991) and Pechmann, Ratneshwar and Shocker (1991) have previously demonstrated that recall of product alternatives and ultimate choice differ depending on the usage situation. For example, the usage situation for snack foods, i.e. a snack to eat before a Saturday evening date, helps to determine which of the many snack food options are appropriate for consumption. Holden (1993) and Warlop and Ratneshwar (1993) take other approaches to examining the influence of usage situation on the formation of consideration sets by distilling and describing several possible processes by which individuals might recall or construct consideration sets in familiar and unfamiliar usage situations, respectively. They argue that one process by which this occurs is that the situation helps to determine consumption goals and those goals then activate alternative (brand) and feature information that in the past was learned to be appropriate for and relevant to those goals. This of course recognizes that on many occasions the situational context and a consumer's goals operate in a top-down manner to provide constraints to the problem solving situation (Park and Smith 1989). Presumably, the more numerous and specific the situational cues, the more constraints exist in the problem solving.

Finally, the fifth link (Warlop and Ratneshwar 1993) represents the direct impact episodic memory (memory for particular consumption experiences as opposed to categorical knowledge) has on both the formation of consideration sets from memory and on solution recognition in stimulus-based choice. This is presented as an alternative process by which one may arrive at solutions to a consumption situation, one in which categorical knowledge per se is not necessarily accessed.

Taken collectively, the papers show that situational cues, working directly through episodic knowledge of consumption experiences and indirectly through goal-specification and the organization of knowledge structures, have great impact on both consumer learning and consumer decision making. The formation of consideration sets and the evaluative criteria employed in choice (i.e. feature importance ratings) have been specifically shown to be determined by the intended usage situation. The work that is continuing in this area is attempting to uncover the processes underlying these effects.

REFERENCES

Gutman, Jonathan (1982), "A Means-End Chain Model Based on Consumer Categorization Processes," *Journal of Marketing*, 46 (Spring), 60-72.

Huffman, Cynthia and Michael J. Houston (1992), "Goal-Oriented Experiences and the Development of Knowledge," Working Paper, University of Pennsylvania.

FIGURE

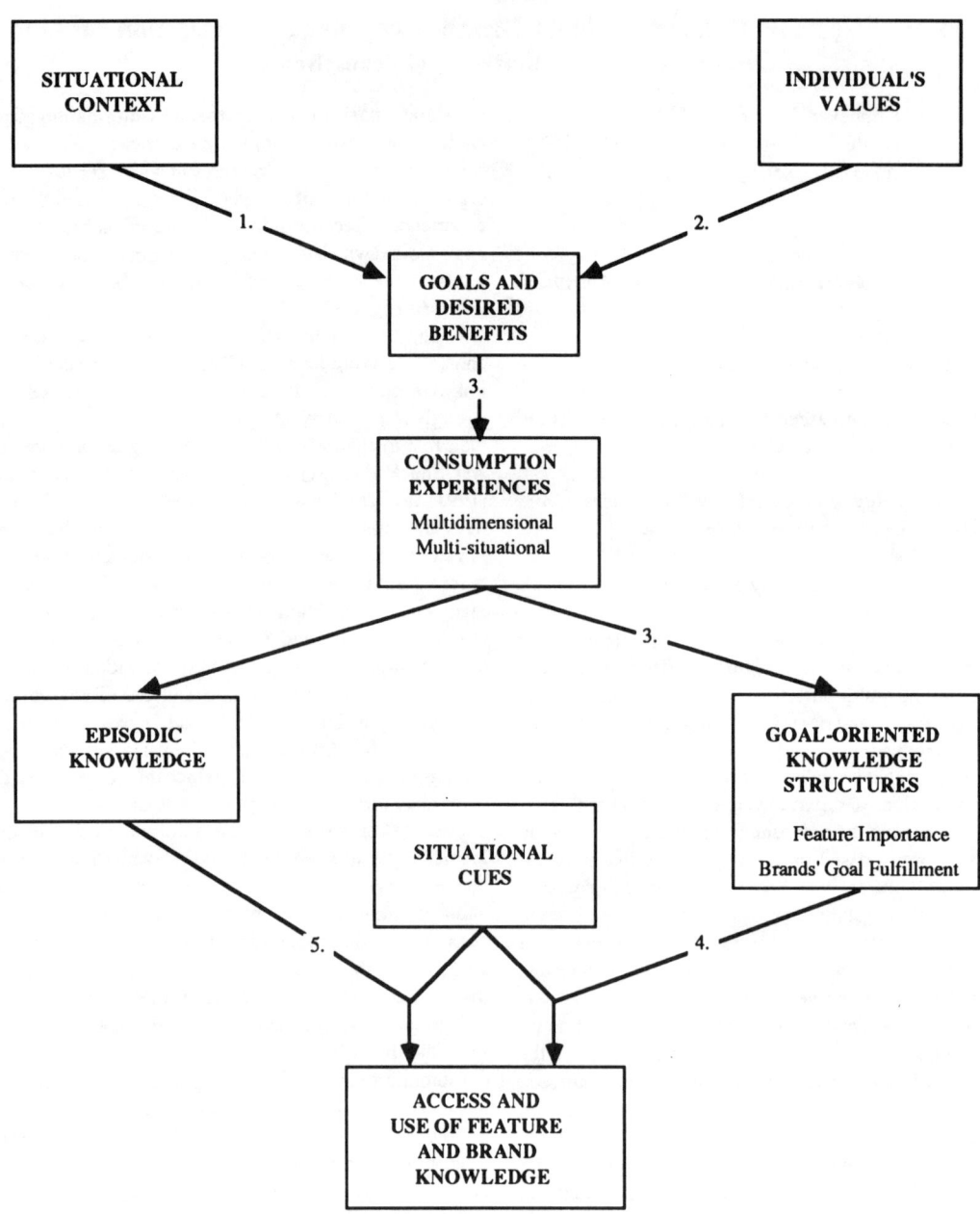

1. Graonic and Shocker 1993, Warlop and Ratneshwar 1993
2. Gutman 1982
3. Huffman and Houston 1992
4. Holden 1993, Park and Smith 1989, Pechmann, Ratneshwar and Shocker 1991, Ratneshwar and Shocker 1991
5. Warlop and Ratneshwar 1993

Park, C. W. and Daniel Smith (1989), "Product-level Choice: a Bottom-up or a Top-down Process?" *Journal of Consumer Research*, 16 (December), 289-299.

Pechmann, Cornelia, S. Ratneshwar, and Allan D. Shocker (1991), "Goal-Derived Product Categories: Situational and Individual Determinants," Paper presented at the 1991 Annual Meeting of the Association for Consumer Research, Chicago.

Ratneshwar, S. and Allan D. Shocker (1991), "Substitution-in-Use and the Cognitive Structure of Product Categories," *Journal of Marketing Research*, 28 (August), 281-295.

The Role of Usage Context in Consumer Choice: A Problem Solving Perspective
Luk Warlop, University of Florida
S. Ratneshwar, University of Florida[1]

A considerable amount of prior research has documented that usage situations or contexts play a major explanatory role in consumer preference/choice (eg., Stefflre 1971; Belk 1975; Dickson 1982; Miller & Ginter 1979; Srivastava, Alpert, & Shocker 1984). Much of this literature has tended to take a "black box" approach with respect to situational effects. There is little understanding at this point of the role of usage context in the cognitive processes that are involved in consumer decisions (Ratneshwar & Shocker, 1991). The present research seeks to contribute to this area by examining usage context in terms of its role in consumer problem solving.

We start from the premise that the usage context of a product is an ecological factor that can aid consumer decision-making by imposing, in cognitive terms, constraints on the problem-solving process and therefore also on the possible solutions (Bransford & McCarrell, 1974; Ratneshwar & Shocker 1991). Based on this premise, we suggest that usage context can have two kinds of effects on the choice process. First, it may directly facilitate remembering of "known solutions" to the choice problem by directing retrieval processes toward context-appropriate product alternatives. We shall later offer a more fine-grained description of this process. Second, situational problem definition might frame the construction of a problem representation in terms of the product benefits that should be sought in the usage context and the constraints the situation imposes on a solution set.

Both of these processes may well go on in parallel in many situations. But it is probably reasonable to assume that the constructive process becomes prominent only when on account of lack of familiarity with the situation there are no "known solutions" available in memory. This process may also be invoked when none of the physically available alternatives match the retrieved set. The present paper focuses on the cognitive processes that are involved in both of these routes to finding solutions to contextually-situated choice problems, and how these processes might be moderated by situational familiarity. We report two exploratory studies. The first one utilizes verbal protocols to investigate the influence of usage context on memory-based processes in the formation of consideration sets. The second one examines how usage context might affect solution recognition in stimulus-based choice.

STUDY 1

Our efforts in study 1 were mainly directed at arriving at a better understanding of the role of usage context in the problem-solving process with regard to the generation of potential solutions from memory. Our approach to this was a discovery-oriented, verbal protocol analysis study. 13 undergraduate student subjects were each presented with different product usage situations printed on cards and asked to come up with acceptable alternatives in those situations, while verbalizing their thought process as it led to such a set of alternatives. Situations were manipulated to be either relatively familiar to the subjects (eg., "A beverage that you might drink while relaxing at a swimming pool with friends during summer vacation") or relatively unfamiliar (eg., "A beverage that you might carry in your backpack and drink while hiking all day on a steep trail in the Grand Canyon"). The target product categories were beverages and snacks; they were selected on the basis of prior research that has demonstrated usage situation influences in these categories (see Belk 1975). There were four possible situations for each category, two familiar and two unfamiliar. The subjects saw one situation in each product category, and saw either all familiar or all unfamiliar situations, to reduce the likelihood of demand awareness. The target situations were separated by filler situations, that were not included in the analysis.

The use of protocol analysis to study decision processes is based on the assumption that during decision making the information available for use, which is the output of lower order retrieval and recognition processes, is present in working memory. We conducted the study in accordance with Ericsson & Simon's (1984) guidelines to maximize the reliability of the protocols. The study was introduced as one in which we were interested in "how people like yourself relate to different consumption situations." Each individual's session commenced with a training/familiarization phase with three trial situations during which the experimenter first emphasized the need to verbalize everything that "passes through your head while you think about this situation" and then provided corrective feedback. Sessions were audio taped and later transcribed for analysis.

Considering the limited number of subjects involved in the study, we regard this as an exploratory investigation. We used the protocol analysis in an inductive manner; the examples given should be regarded as mere illustrations, and the ideas we develop remain to be tested in a more systematic study. Our discussion of study 1 is organized so as to highlight our distinction between the direct retrieval of known solutions (when the usage context is familiar) and the more constructive processes used to generate potential solutions (when the usage context is unfamiliar).

Familiar Situations and the Direct Retrieval of Known Solutions

In accordance with our initial expectations, the protocols obtained from subjects presented with familiar situations were characterized by little or no evidence of constructive thought processes: virtually no mention of product attributes or benefits, and hardly any mention of the goals and constraints implied by the situation. Instead, these protocols suggested three qualitatively different processes by which consumers might directly retrieve known solutions when the usage context is familiar: (1) Retrieval based on contextually-organized product category structures, (2) Retrieval based on event scripts cued by the situation, and (3) Retrieval based on episodic memory of similar situations.

(1) Although subjects were encouraged throughout the training period to verbalize everything that came to mind, in many cases the resulting protocol was hardly more than a list of context-appropriate alternatives. Consider, for example, this subject's response when given the situation "A snack that you might eat when you are at a movie theater with a friend":

(M. M.): "Popcorn, M & M's, raisin, raisin nuts, raisin nut things, a chocolate candy bar, on of them sour tart candy type deals, I want to pick up a soda pop or a drink, something like that, licorice, that's about it."

The same subject produced the following when presented with the "swimming pool" situation described earlier:

---

[1]The authors thank Cynthia Huffman for helpful comments on an earlier draft of this paper.

(M.M.): "Beer..some kind of beer, light beer, soda or ice water it doesn't matter and that's about it, that is all I would drink, ice water, soda or beer, light beer."

These protocols suggest that the subject is directly accessing instances of categories organized around familiar usage contexts. Research on the graded structure of usage context-defined categories (Ratneshwar & Shocker, 1991) has shown that differential accessibility of brands and products in a given usage situation, as measured by the order of recall, is positively (and strongly) associated with typicality judgements of the same products in that situation. These results suggest that for familiar (i.e., well-established) usage contexts, the structure and organization of the stored knowledge base of potential solutions may come to resemble the graded structure of a taxonomic category (see also Barsalou 1991). The mental representation of the encountered usage situation could then serve as a retrieval cue that selectively accesses this contextually-defined, categorical knowledge base. Consequently, it cues retrieval of appropriate solutions in the order of their accessibility in the relevant category.

(2) In some other cases, the retrieval processes resembled the mental running-off of an *event script*. Such script recalls are characterized by (a) frequent use of verbs (e.g. "go", "get", "do") denoting activities that are typical of the event script, and (b) mentioning of "irrelevant" objects that are thematically related to the script. For example, the movie-going protocol discussed earlier mentioned "pick up a soda pop" with the list of snacks. But in the next example the evocation of an event script comes through much more clearly. The situation was a "A snack that you might eat between classes on a busy weekday when you don't have time for a regular lunch."

(H. U.): "... I just like to go to the vending machine and I get a peanut butter cracker and a cup of coffee, that is what I do... When I am in this area, like the business buildings here, I may just go across the street and go to Burger King and just get a cheese burger or whatever..."

This subject appeared to rely on an abstract or "scripted" memory of a familiar life event rather than a *specific* past occurrence of a similar event. Research by Nelson and her colleagues has documented the importance of scripts in the development of a conceptual knowledge base (see, e.g., Nelson 1988). Nelson suggested a close relationship between a child's comprehension of the functional role of objects in different life events and the individual's formation of category concepts. A child's repeated experiences with similar events (eg., different occasions of "breakfast") lead to a generalized event representation or script in which different objects become slot fillers. For example, both "pancakes" and "cereal" become slot fillers for the slot "what I eat" in the breakfast script. Other developmental psychologists also suggest that situational or "thematic" categorization forms the basic organizational principle of young children's knowledge (Markman & Callanan, 1984).

(3) Both of the processes described earlier involved the use of *abstract* knowledge representations based on past experience to access known solutions. However, our protocols revealed that direct—that is, not mediated by controlled search activity—retrieval of alternatives could also be based on *specific* episodes of similar situations in an individual's past. For example, given the situation "A snack that you might eat between classes on a busy weekday when you don't have time for a regular lunch":

(D. A.): "I am starting to envision the little stands that go through campus, the guy that parks over here in the business quad. Running over to the library to grab a banana from him, especially when I have a hard time staying awake...I am grabbing a banana from him and a diet Mountain Dew from the soda machines right next door and then run back to class..."

Unfamiliar Situations and the Construction of Potential Solutions

In the previous section we discussed different cognitive processes by which consumers, when given a familiar situation, might directly retrieve solutions appropriate to the problem defined by the usage context. When the situation is unfamiliar, however, the decision-maker may have to rely on more strategic processes to construct possible solutions to the choice problem. Barsalou (1991) proposes that the construction of ad hoc and goal-derived categories proceeds through an active, top-down, and relatively effortful process in which existing knowledge about object attributes is manipulated in working memory—a process he refers to as conceptual combination. Many choices among products in relatively unfamiliar usage situations can be construed as mediated by the formation of an ad hoc category. When faced with a situation such as "a beverage to carry on a hiking trip on a steep trail in the Grand Canyon during summer", people are very unlikely to have stored in memory a well-established category with potential solutions that corresponds to the situation. Neither are they likely to have individualized (i.e., episodic) or scripted event memories for that particular event. On the other hand, none of the elements of the situation nor any of the beverages that might be potential candidates are as such unfamiliar. Most people should be able, based on their general "world knowledge", to derive the benefits a beverage in those circumstances should provide (eg., fluid replenishment and energy) and the constraints that are imposed on the solution by the usage context (eg., shouldn't spoil easily in the heat, a light-weight and sturdy container.) Based on the benefits and constraints that are relevant to the situation, the product attributes and attribute values that are most desirable in the particular situation (cf. Barsalou's 1991, "ideals"; also see Bransford & McCarrell 1974) can be derived, and the resulting ideal representation compared to the available alternatives.

We tentatively propose that the retrieval of alternatives in unfamiliar usage situations occurs in three stages. First, the consumer forms a reduced cognitive representation of the "total" consumption situation. This is followed by a recognition of benefits and constraints involved in the elements of that representation. Then, by a process of association, attributes and alternatives are retrieved that fit these benefits and constraints. The more of the diagnostic situational information that is implicated in the generation process, the less likely it is that non-appropriate alternatives are retrieved.

We coded the idea units in the protocols as either referring to goals (constraints or benefits), lower-level attributes, alternatives, or exclusions (an alternative or class explicitly excluded). Compared to the familiar situations, where hardly any goals were mentioned, they were abundant for the unfamiliar situations, and mostly they preceded the mentioning of alternatives. Also, often subjects point out which class of alternatives they would definitely not consider, before mentioning the alternatives they find appropriate. The following protocol was typical:

Situation: "A snack that you might eat at home shortly before going out on a Saturday evening date."

(M. S.): "I want something that is real quick, and that won't give you bad breadth or anything. You don't want to eat a sandwich or something to that effect. A piece of fruit or something, something to tide me over till dinner. It will not bother your stomach or anything like that. And nothing that is messy, in case you are all dressed up. You wouldn't want to spill on your clothes ... I'd like an apple or something, or some grapes, or some crackers, and you wash it down with something like water. That's about it."

This subject clearly constructed a solution to the problem, based on the constraints and goals that are relevant to the situation. The appropriate alternatives were found through a process of conceptual combination and were clearly not accessible immediately. In this example the retrieval of situation-relevant information and the generation of alternatives were more or less separated, and problem-solving proceeds in a straightforward, linear fashion. In other cases, subjects went back and forth between goals and related alternatives, ultimately to come back to a few alternatives that seem to satisfy all criteria. In other words, subjects seemed to gradually "zoom in" on a solution. For example:

Situation: "A snack that you might eat in the evening shortly after a workout or an aerobics class when you know you will be meeting some friends for dinner in a couple of hours"

(A. F.): "Something like TCBY yoghurt, because it is not that heavy. Fruit, ... it is like an appetizer ... like a watermelon, an orange or something like that, and I would stay away from meats, because they seem to stay on you, but fruit definitely, or some yoghurt. Nothing fattening, like ice cream, or anything like that, because it tends to stay with you and spoil your appetite. Something that can carry me over, even a Snickers bar, something that will hold me over, you know, Snickers satisfies the hunger in you..., something with less preparation, that I can go buy quick. No burritos or sandwiches, maybe some crackers and cheese, something not as solid, not a solid substance, that is easily digestible and that is quick. Maybe fruit, because that has that quick energy and it gets you OK. Something with a lot of potassium or carotene, even a few slices of bread or something."

An interesting observation was that some of the problem solving behavior was reminiscent of the reliance on surface characteristics by novices in technological domains. For example, when reacting to the situation "A snack that you might eat shortly after a workout or an aerobics class when you know you will be meeting some friends for dinner in a couple of hours", quite a number of subjects emphasized that the snack should be "healthy", "no fastfood" or provide "quick energy". They seemed to rely more on the "workout" element and its health-related associations than on the (normatively) more diagnostic cue that they would have to eat dinner in a couple of hours. Admittedly, the examples we have discussed are the clearest and the most demonstrative in the whole set. Many protocols were less clear cut. For example, for some undoubtedly unfamiliar situations some subjects came up with alternatives immediately. Speculatively, what seems to have happened there is that subjects disregarded much of the situational information and concentrated on a few elements that were most salient, actively reducing the situational representation to something that is familiar.

In summary, one basic pattern clearly emerged from the study 1 data. In familiar usage contexts, subjects in almost all cases evoked a series of (situationally appropriate) alternatives without, or before, mentioning any attribute or goal-related information. In unfamiliar situations the subjects' behavior was more variable. Subjects occasionally seemed to be able to come up with alternatives directly when they were able to reduce the complexity of the situation by ignoring detail; otherwise, they relied on constructive problem solving.

STUDY 2

Our discussion so far has focused on the cognitive processes by which usage context impacts on the alternatives evoked from memory. This issue is of considerable significance since it affects the manner in which consideration sets are formed by consumers. But equally important to consumer problem-solving are the processes by which usage context affects *solution recognition*: the ability to "pick out" (discriminate) among currently available choice alternatives.

Consistent with our previous suggestions, situational familiarity is likely to play an important role in governing the processes by which the consumer discriminates among available alternatives. Consider, first, the case where the situation is highly familiar, as indexed by the number of previous encounters with "similar" situations. As we discussed, "known solutions" to the choice problem (in the form of context-appropriate product alternatives) should be retrieved from long-term memory in a more or less automatic fashion. The consumer is then likely to compare this set of alternatives retrieved into working memory with the alternatives currently available in order to detect "acceptable" solutions.

In contrast, when the features of the usage context are relatively unfamiliar, the consumer might perceive this unfamiliarity and not bother to search long-term memory for an appropriate analogue (category, script, or episode) to the current situation. Alternatively, the search might take place but fail to reveal "known solutions." In such novel situations, the goals and constraints imposed by context might still facilitate discrimination, but by a qualitatively different process. These problem-defining goals and constraints might have an *orienting effect* (William James's "point of view") wherein the consumer's attention is attuned to a small number of contextually-relevant product attributes on the basis of which the available choice alternatives might be evaluated. Thus, context might shape the attentional gate which regulates the information that is processed with regard to the alternatives in the environment. But to reiterate the point made earlier, this process may come to the fore only when the novelty of the situation prevents the spontaneous retrieval of known solutions, or when none of the retrieved solutions are available to the consumer.

In the preceding paragraphs we have suggested that usage context plays a key role in consumer problem-solving by impacting the discriminability of choice alternatives and that the implicated processes might vary with situational familiarity. Since higher levels of discriminability between alternatives generally should result in faster decisions, an important consequence for consumers might be in terms of *decision-making time*. Consumers make numerous "low involvement" decisions during the course of a day, and often these decisions are made from potentially very large numbers of options open to them. To the extent that many of these decisions take place in well-defined situations or contexts, contextual goals and constraints might help the consumer to discriminate acceptable alternatives from a much larger available set. Consequently, consumers might be able to able to make these constrained decisions quickly and with relatively low cognitive effort. For example, consider a usage context wherein a consumer has to make a choice among beverages upon returning home from a work-out on a hot summer day. The context might facilitate swift solution-recognition in terms of suitable alternatives such as Gatorade and also facilitate "disconfirmation" of contextually inappropriate options such as coffee. Even when the situation is relatively less familiar or "scripted" and the decision-maker has to take a more constructive approach to evaluating the alternatives, our earlier discussion suggests that situational constraints might still facilitate discrimination (and quick decisions) by focusing the consumer's attention on context-relevant product features.

We investigated some of the aforementioned speculations in an exploratory study in the category *snack foods* for which normative data on product preferences in various usage contexts were available through prior research (see Ratneshwar & Shocker 1991). The experimental task required our undergraduate subjects (n = 50) to make choices from pairs of product alternatives whose names were displayed on a PC screen while the computer recorded decision-making time (DMT). All subjects made choices from 12 different choice pairs on 12 different "trials." But on each trial the display of the stimulus choice pair on the screen was preceded by a description of the choice condition for that trial: either a specific usage context or merely the category name (the latter was the control condition). Note that the time taken to read this description was not included in DMT. Six usage contexts that varied in familiarity were selected and the design was balanced so that the twelve choices made by a subject were equally divided between category-level and context-level choices. Further, the stimuli were designed so that the usage context either enhanced discriminability (ED) for the particular choice pair or it did not (ND). For the ED choice pairs, the prior data on preferences revealed that *one* of the two products was appropriate for the particular usage context (mean = 84%), while the other was inappropriate (mean appropriateness = 21% of subjects). For the ND choice pairs, *both* products had been judged appropriate (mean = 73%), with little difference in contextual appropriateness between the products in a pair (mean difference = 5.5%). In order to familiarize them with the task, subjects were first guided through six practice trials where choices were made in categories unrelated to snack foods. Subjects then made choices on 36 trials out of which every third trial related to snack foods, while the remaining filler trials dealt with unrelated categories and situations. After completing the choice task on the computer, subjects filled out questionnaires with measures designed to check the experimental manipulations and also to assess the familiarity of the usage contexts.

We report here some of the key results. The grand mean DMT was 2.53 seconds, and it ranged from 0.75 to 9.29 seconds. Across the 50 x 12 = 600 observations, as expected, a significant negative correlation (r=-.21, p .01) was found between DMT and stimulus discriminability as indexed by the absolute value of the difference in preference scores for the two alternatives. An ANOVA was conducted on DMT after carrying out a logarithmic transformation in order to stabilize variance. The predicted interaction between choice pair type (ED vs. ND) and choice condition (usage context vs. category) was significant, $F(1,576)=10.03$, $p<0.01$. However, this was qualified by a significant three-way interaction of usage context block x choice pair type x choice condition ($p<0.01$) suggesting that the hypothesized interaction was not obtained uniformly across all usage contexts.

As anticipated, subjects made significantly faster choices at the usage context level (vs. category level) for ED choice pairs (2.37 vs. 2.77 seconds, $p<0.05$). The opposite was true of ND pairs: Subjects were significantly slower in their choices when provided with the usage context than at the category level (2.64 vs. 2.32 seconds, $p<0.05$). Thus, for example, when provided with a snack usage context that depicted "a Friday evening party while drinking beer or other beverages," subjects made faster choices (2.58 vs. 3.55 seconds at the category level) between the ED pair "mixed nuts" and "oatmeal soft cookie"; not surprisingly, they also displayed more consistency in their choice, with 92% picking the former alternative at the context level vs. 44% at the category level. In contrast, with the same usage context, subjects made slower choices between the ND pair "crackers" and "hot dog," presumably because the context did not enhance their discriminability (2.91 vs. 2.21 seconds at the category level).

Interestingly, and consistent with the earlier theorizing, the study revealed evidence of faster decisions even in unfamiliar usage contexts. For example, DMT was lower for the ED pair "grapes" and "cereal" when subjects were provided with the usage context of a snack "you might eat while waiting for your Saturday evening date to show up." This context had the lowest familiarity rating of the six that we used, yet subjects were significantly quicker at picking the preferred alternative (grapes) given the contextual description (2.49 vs. 3.65 seconds at the category level). However, when provided the same usage context with the ND pair "raisins" and "potato chips," subjects were significantly slower in their decisions (3.29 vs. 1.77 seconds at the category level).

While this study was only exploratory and more research is needed before any definitive conclusions can be reached, the results were encouraging in terms of the present perspective. The cognitive constraints resulting from usage situation or context can play a problem-definition role such that consumers discriminate effectively and efficiently among available alternatives. Further, discrimination may be facilitated even in relatively unfamiliar situations, which we attribute to the attentional constraints imposed by usage context.

DISCUSSION

Problem-solving research in consumer behavior has been closely modeled after issues in the general problem-solving literature where processing differences due to differential domain expertise have often been the central issue (e.g., Sujan, 1985). We deal with a conceptually different issue: one wherein consumers are likely to possess the "technical" knowledge of a product category (e.g., beverages or snack foods) necessary to solve the problem (the choice of a product), but where the "problem" essentially resides in the use of that knowledge base to arrive at appropriate solutions in the context of familiar and less familiar usage situations.

At its current stage our research has necessarilly been exploratory in nature; but the findings of the two studies, one dealing with the retrieval of alternatives from memory and the other with stimulus-based choice, suggest some tentative conclusions. First, we found support for the idea that the role of usage context in consumer choice is one of constraining the problem-solving process, and, as a consequence, one of guiding the search for, and evaluation of, potential solutions. Second, we found some tentative support for the hypothesis that the actual processes by which solutions are found are qualitatively different in familiar and nonfamiliar situations.

In familiar situations, the cognitive representation of the situation seems to cue a set of potential solutions directly, that is, not mediated by a controlled search of memory. The protocol data from study 1 suggest that such direct retrieval may be based on category structures and/or event scripts that are well-established in memory as well as specific past episodes that are analagous to the current situation. The retrieved set is then likely to be compared to the the alternatives available in the environment to detect "acceptable" or satisfactory solutions.

When the situation is relatively unfamiliar, alternatives (potential solutions) are retrieved from memory through more constructive processes that involve cognitively mapping the situation on to contextually-relevant goals and constraints in terms of the benefits desired of the product, and then retrieving products that are associated with those benefits. Further, such contextual attunement likely guides the decision-maker's attention to relevant product attributes in order to discriminate between the available alternatives. In general, the particular features that get the decision-maker's attention are likely to be those that have relevance for the *goal* context of the ongoing situation and/or those that have high diagnostic value for the *local* context of alternatives (see Garner 1974; Tversky 1977). For example, in an unfamiliar situation such as "A snack that you might eat while waiting for your Saturday evening date to show up", discrimination between the two alternatives, potato chips and "Doritos" tortilla chips (a garlic-flavored product), might be enhanced by focusing on whether a product affords "good breath". Suppose the choice set had also included a third alternative, grapes. It is possible that doing so might enhace the contrast value of the garlic-flavor feature and thus further expedite the rejection of Doritos as an acceptable option.

The problem-solving perspective we employ is related to the means-end chain tradition (see, e.g., Guttman 1982; Olson 1988), but in line with the more traditional expectancy-value approaches to consumer motivation (see Cohen & Warlop 1992), we limit the scope of the means-end chain to goals and benefits consumers take into account when thinking about products, rather than to the terminal "values" from which they (in part) may have arisen. Aditionally, our emphasis on the role of usage context in solution recognition contrasts with the context-free approach that seems to be taken by most means-end applications (but see Olson 1988).

Our exploratory studies served to discover some interesting questions and speculations rather than decisive answers. For example, recent research by Hutchinson, Mantrala, and Raman (1992) suggested that consumers are able to screen out exemplars of nontarget taxonomic categories during retrieval from memory, but that typical category brands not in the situation-specific subcategory could not be screened out. Our results on the other hand indicate that situation-based selectivity (e.g., on the basis of event scripts) during retrieval is possible. When, and how, consumers are able to selectively access situationally appropriate alternatives are important issues, because to the extent that they fail to do so, it may be possible for marketers to influence consideration sets by creating top-of-mind awareness through advertising (see also Ratneshwar and Shocker 1991).

A second interesting research question is to identify the conditions under which the proposed attentional gating mechanism fails. Our framework assumes that consumers faced with a product choice "in-context" form a mental representation of the situation. In forming such a problem representation of a less familiar usage situation, however, consumers may be subject to "functional fixedness" (Duncker 1945), ignoring diagnostic situational detail, and relying on a superficially similar, but familiar analog. In that case they might bypass the solution construction process, and retrieve potentially nonoptimal "known solutions".

In conclusion, it might be remarked that the present contribution is part of an emerging stream of research that seeks to emphasize the role of context and goals in consumers' learning, their representation and organization of knowledge, and their use of that knowledge in decision-making (see, e.g., Huffman & Houston 1993; Park & Smith 1989; Ratneshwar & Shocker 1991). Traditional information-processing research in consumer choice behavior has typically contented itself with stimulus and subject task manipulations (see, e.g., Bettman, Payne, & Johnson 1991). The "new look" (cf. Bruner 1957), however, is firmly based on the notion that all consumer behavior ultimately is purposive, and to understand in cognitive terms such behavior, it is important to understand the ongoing context in which it is grounded.

REFERENCES

Barsalou, L. W. (1991), "Deriving Categories to Achieve Goals," in *The Psychology of Learning and Motivation, Vol. 27*, ed. G. H. Bower, pp 1 - 64.

Belk, R. W. (1975), "Situational Variables and Consumer Behavior," *Journal of Consumer Research*, 2 (December), 157-164.

Bettman, J. R., J. W. Payne, and E. J. Johnson (1991), "Consumer Decision Making," in *Handbook of Consumer Behavior*, ed. T. S. Robertson and H. H. Kassarjian, Englewood Cliffs, NJ: Prentice Hall, 50 - 84.

Bransford, J. D. and N. S. McCarrell (1974), "A Sketch of a Cognitive Approach to Comprehension: Some Thoughts about Understanding what it Means to Comprehend," in *Cognition and the Symbolic Processes*, eds. W. Weimer and D. S. Palermo, Hillsdale, NJ.: Erlbaum, 189 - 229.

Bruner, J. S. (1957, "On Perceptual Readiness," *Psychological Review*, 64, 123-157.

Cohen, J. B. and L. Warlop (1992), "Motivational and Cognitive Perspectives on Means-End Chains," Working Paper, University of Florida.

Dickson, P. R. (1982), "Person-Situation: Segmentation's Missing Link", *Journal of Marketing*, 46 (Fall), 56-64.

Duncker, K. (1945),"On Problem Solving," *Psychological Monographs*, 58 (No. 270).

Ericsson, K. A. and H. A. Simon (1984), *Protocol Analysis: Verbal Reports as Data*, Cambridge MA, MIT Press.

Garner, W. R. (1974), *The Processing of Information and Structure*, Potomac, MD: Erlbaum.

Gutman, J. (1982), "A Means-End Chain Model Based on Consumer Categorization Processes," *Journal of Marketing*, 46 (Spring), 60-72.

Huffman, C. and M. J. Houston (1993), "Goal-Oriented Experiences and the Development of Knowledge," *Journal of Consumer Research*, forthcoming.

Hutchinson, J. W., M. K. Mantrala, and K. Raman (1992), "Finding Choice Alternatives in Memory: A Markov Model of Brand Name Recall," Working Paper, University of Florida.

Markman, E. M. and M. A. Callanan (1984), "An Analysis of Hierarchical Classification," in *Advances in the Psychology of Human Intelligence*, ed. R. J. Sternberg, 325 - 366.

Miller, K. E. and J. L. Ginter (1979), "An Investigation of Situational Variation on Brand Choice Behavior and Attitude," *Journal of Marketing Research*, 16 (February), 111-123.

Nelson, K. (1988), "Where Do Taxonomic Categories Come From ?," *Human Development*, 31, 3-10.

Olson, J. C. (1988), "Theoretical Foundations of Means-end Chains," Working Paper, Penn State University.

Park, C. W., and D. C. Smith (1989), "Product-level Choice: a Bottom-up or a Top-down Process?," *Journal of Consumer Research*, 16 (December), 289 - 299.

Ratneshwar, S. and A. D. Shocker (1991), "Substitution in Use and the Role of Usage Context in Product Category Structures," *Journal of Marketing Research*, 28 (August), 281 - 295.

Srivastava, R. K., M. I. Alpert, and A. D. Shocker (1984), "A Consumer-Oriented Approach for Determining Market Structures," *Journal of Marketing*, 48 (Spring), 32-45.

Stefflre, V. (1971), *New Products and Enterprises: A Report of an Experiment in Applied Social Science*, Irvine, CA: Unversity of California, Irvine

Sujan, M. (1985), "Consumer Knowledge: Effects of Evaluation Strategies Mediating Consumer Judgements," *Journal of Consumer Research*, 12 (June), 31 - 46.

Tversky, A. (1977), "Features of Similarity," *Psychological Review*, 84, 327 - 352.

Understanding Brand Awareness: Let Me Give You a C(l)ue!
Stephen J.S. Holden, Ecole Superieure des Sciences Economiques et Commerciales (ESSEC)

ABSTRACT

Despite the importance of brand awareness to brand choice, consumer researchers have given little attention to developing an understanding of awareness as a construct. Focusing on brand awareness in memory-based situations (i.e., where the brands must be brought to mind), this paper reports on a qualitative research project that explores how brands come to mind in a variety of choice situations. A subsequent quantitative study shows that associates identified in the qualitative research act as cues, and that brand awareness varies significantly depending on the cues that are salient.

INTRODUCTION

Brand awareness is a much neglected construct and deserves considerably more attention due to its central importance in brand choice. From an empirical point of view, numerous researchers have shown that brand awareness measures are powerful predictors of consumer choice behavior (e.g., Axelrod 1968; Haley and Case 1979; Nedungadi and Hutchinson 1985). Furthermore, from a conceptual or theoretical point of view, brand awareness has been recognized as preceding and necessary to brand evaluation (Howard and Sheth 1969; Holden and Lutz 1992; Nedungadi 1990). That is, evaluation is a process of selection from the set of alternatives which are evoked.

This paper outlines some concepts for understanding brand awareness, reports research which explores and tests notions arising from that framework and concludes by noting some of the theoretical and practical implications of this expanded understanding of brand awareness.

BRAND AWARENESS AS CUED MEMORY

Brand awareness is typically measured by recall or recognition (Rossiter and Percy 1987). When talking of situations where the brands are not present (the focus of this paper), the appropriate measure is recall measured by presenting a product category and asking respondents to recall brands from that category. For situations where the brands are present, researchers typically take a recognition measure in which they present the brand name and ask respondents whether they know of the brand.

Rossiter and Percy (1987) make an important observation that measures of recognition of the brand name may not necessarily reflect the recognition process that takes place in the choice situation. They note that in the choice context, brand awareness may be mediated by recognition of one or more of a number of elements of the product, for example, the package, the colors, the brand logo, etc. Furthermore, measures of ease of recognition (Alba and Hutchinson 1987) may be more appropriate.

Similarly, one may ask the question of whether measures of brand recall by product category are reflecting the process of brand evocation in the choice process. Such measures assume that consumers' memory is organized by category, and perhaps more importantly, that choice is a process that utilizes these categories. Accordingly, researchers have viewed the category production task in which subjects generate exemplars in response to a category cue as the most relevant experimental paradigm for understanding product recall (Alba, Hutchinson and Lynch 1991). However, advances in categorization research and renewed attention to the way in which consumers actually make choices suggest that there is a need to replace (or at least modify) this paradigm.

First, the role of situation in influencing brand evocation is important. Generally, the influence of situation on choice has been considered to be mediated by an influence on the weighting of attributes in the multi-attribute model (e.g., Miller and Ginter 1979). However, research from the categorization literature (Roth and Shoben 1983) has suggested that contextual factors can change the graded structure of a category. Given the relationship between graded structure (typicality) and recall (Nedungadi and Hutchinson 1985), it might be hypothesized that contextual factors would also affect recall. Ratneshwar and Shocker (1991) have shown that situations influence the recall of products (or product variants) in the overall category of snack foods.

In addition and somewhat belatedly, consumer researchers have begun to recognize the importance of motives in consumer choice. Rossiter and Percy (1987) noted that ads should link brands to the category need in order to be effective. In a similar vein, Warshaw (1980) noted that brand attitudes are better able to predict behavior if intentions towards the product category are known.

More generally, a person's motives may be satisfied by products from different categories. Studies on categorization have distinguished between taxonomic categories (e.g., product categories) and goal-derived categories such as "things to take on a camping trip" (Barsalou 1985). One of the features of a goal-derived category is that elements may be drawn from a range of taxonomic categories. The notion that decisions may be made between alternatives which are noncomparable alternatives (e.g., Johnson 1988) implies evoked sets which comprise brands drawn from different product categories. In addition to being noncomparable, brands in an evoked set which is goal-derived may be complementary, or at least not competitive, as in "things to take on a camping trip." The evaluation task is therefore one of selecting one or more of the items depending on other constraints (e.g., financial).

Both the influences of context (or situation) and motives are captured by a model (Holden and Lutz 1992) that suggests that brand awareness is a function of the cues that are salient in the retrieval situation. The model proposes that the brand be considered to be a central node in memory with links to it from various other nodes representing situations, benefits, attributes, product category and other brands (see Holden and Lutz 1992, p. 105). Any of these nodes is posited to have the potential to act as a cue to the brand, the success of the cuing being dependent on the associative strength between the cue and the brand.

It is further posited that the links to the brand may be direct or indirect. For instance, a situation may directly evoke a particular brand while other situations may lead to thought of some benefit which in turn leads (directly) to the evocation of a brand.

Research Objectives

The research reported in this paper is a preliminary examination of some of the principles that arise from this model.

1) Examine nature of associates salient at choice
   - categories or types of cues
   - direct and indirect cues
2) Examine nature of evoked sets
   - evidence for goal-derived categories
   - basic level of recall (Rosch 1975)
3) Test influence of associates on brand awareness
   - variation in evoked set formation by cue

A qualitative project focuses on the first two objectives and subobjectives while a quantitative study focuses on the third objective.

QUALITATIVE STUDY — NATURE OF CUES AND EVOKED SETS

An exploratory qualitative project was undertaken to examine the nature of brand associates salient at choice and the nature of evoked sets. The qualitatitive approach is in line with the call from a number of researchers for "discovery-oriented" studies (e.g., Lutz 1991; McGuire 1983).

Based on the theory of spreading activation (Collins and Loftus 1975), the method utilized presumes that increased activation of some node in response to a cue will be reflected in an association task or a generation task. That is, subjects asked to list thoughts in response to a given cue word will list those words corresponding to nodes which are relatively strongly associated with the cue word.

Method

Subjects saw one of four situations for each of three product-types. The three product-types (and four products for each product-type) were drinks (weekend party, in class, breakfast, studying); snacks (missed breakfast, watching TV, road-trip, after a workout) and restaurants (late night, weekday lunch, dinner and Sunday brunch). Interviewed on a one-on-one basis, subjects considered all three product-types in a random order. They were provided with one, randomly selected situation cue for each of the three product-types. A total of 15 University of Florida students from the undergraduate marketing fundamentals course were interviewed. The sample comprised eleven females and four males. All subjects considered one of four situations for each of the three product-types. The interview was recorded to ensure "top-of-mind" responses were captured.

In each interview, situation associates were measured first. Subjects were exposed to three situations and were asked to list whatever thoughts came to mind to each. A second measure, similar to benefit laddering (Reynolds and Gutman 1988) provided evocation cues. After generating situation associates, subjects were asked to reconsider each situation in turn and to generate products coming to mind within the target product-type. Following evocation for all three product-types, subjects were asked to consider the evoked sets they had generated for each situation and were questioned in more depth about why the *group* of brands was evoked. The subsequent probes aimed at exploring the ladder of what was presumed to be cues were similar to probes used in benefit laddering (see Reynolds and Guttman 1988).

Results and Discussion

This section is organized along the lines of the formulation of the research questions rather than the dependent measures. As the data are qualitative, verbatims from the qualitative data are used to support observations made and conclusions drawn.

Associates Salient at Choice. An illustration of the situation associates and the evocation cues generated by four people in response to one situation is provided in the Table 1. More general conclusions are made in the following remarks. It will be noted in Table 1 that brand associates (i.e., situation associates and evocation cues) have been classified into four different types: situations, benefits, attributes and products (including category labels and brands). This is the categorization suggested by Holden and Lutz (1992). It should be noted that the classification of some responses was difficult suggesting a need for further research and specification of cue types.

Overall, the data gave strong evidence for the existence of direct and indirect cues. Provision of the situation cue alone (i.e., without any product-type prompts) led to numerous mentions of brands and products. For example "breakfast" elicited mentions of brands and/or products from a number of subjects: "Carnation Instant Breakfast," "Special K and bananas," "toast or Pop-Tarts, or dishing out money for Krystals," and "coffee, newspaper." Similarly, "weekend party" elicited numerous mentions of "beer." All situations describing a meal such as breakfast, dinner and lunch tended to be more likely to directly elicit brands of restaurants and drinks (e.g., Coke).

As might be expected given the notion of a direct cue, closer examination of situations as direct cues revealed that subjects seemed to be unable to articulate the links between the situation and the products or brands brought to mind. For instance, one subject who was asked to imagine after a workout responded that the first thing that came to her mind was "food—I wanna eat." When probed on why that was the case, she responded "I don't know. I think it's just a mental thing," and later suggested that she ate after working out "because [of] habit."

Evidence for situations acting as indirect cues came from two sources. First, some responses represented "ladders" of associates from the situation cue to benefits to brands: "After working out? Like lots of—rest. Eating the right foods, with the right vitamins, right nourishment and stuff. Always have like some protein—meat like chicken or beef, with rice for starch, and always take some fruit afterwards. And I would always take Amino 1000s which is just lots of protein." This subject appears to be progressing from the situation cue, through a number of benefit associates (e.g., healthy) and attribute associates (e.g., vitamins, protein and starch) to finally reach specific products (e.g., chicken, beef or rice).

A second, perhaps more compelling form of evidence for indirect cuing from situation cues is the way in which many subjects were able to clearly take the situation cue, and through the provision of self-generated subcues, provide different evoked sets for sets of subcues which could be considered more direct cues. For instance, one subject's response after being asked what snacks came to mind in a situation after a workout responded as follows: "If I am in a healthy mood, I'll have a yoghurt, or fruit or something. If I'm in a bad mood, chocolate. Chocolate and Coke." In this case, the motive or benefit sought appears to be something healthy and something uplifting respectively.

A somewhat surprising observation was that some cues tended to directly evoke brands or products even though those products or brands were not preferred or even liked. The result is surprising as it runs counter to the generally accepted notion that more preferred brands are recalled earlier (e.g., Nedungadi and Hutchinson 1985). One subject asked to list what drinks came to mind when she thought of weekend parties mentioned a brand she liked, and then, in the same response, evoked a product at the same time as she indicated she did not like the product: "Bartles and James. At this point, I don't like beer." Another subject cued with weekday lunch (and no product-type) responded "Cafeteria food. Yuck." It seems in both cases, that these are alternatives that are very closely associated with the situation even though the products themselves are negatively evaluated.

Nature of Evoked Sets. It was clear that the evoked sets generated had a number of characteristics of goal-derived categories. For example, one subject asked for products that came to mind when thinking about studying volunteered "Colored pens. I always used colored pens a lot to try and keep me awake.... Other things that I think of is A+ notes.... I think of sitting down with diet Coke and pretzels." This list might be designated as those things neces-

TABLE 1
Situation Associates and Brand Cues–After a Workout

Situations	Benefits	Attributes	Products
Situation Cues			
Sitting down	Sore muscles	Vitamins	Glass of water
Sleeping	pain	Protein	Food
Studying	Tired/rest	Starch	Beef/chicken
Listening to	Relaxing	Rice	
the radio	Want to eat	Fruit	
	Want a shower	Amino 1000s	
	Wake up		
	Energy		
	Feel good		
	about myself/		
	satisfaction		
	Nourishment		
Evocation Cues			
Watch TV	Snack meal	Light/not	Chips
Late night studying	Boost/energy	heavy	Ham/PB sandwich
Trips	Habit/what I	Calcium	Little Debbie
Late at night	always do	Caffeine	cakes
Morning	Easy prep/	Low calorie	Lays
	no effort	Snackpack	Cheese/cheddar
	Reward/treat	size	Bordens
	Something	Caffeine free	Chocolate/Kit Kat
	healthy		Yoghurt
	Something bad		Fruit
	/nothing to		Coke
	lose		Water
	Can eat a lot		Salad
	Not too		Toast
	filling		Grilled chicken
	Anxious/stress		Tuna
	Replace fluids		Crackers
	/salts		Peanut butter
	Avoid gaining		Broccoli/carrots
	weight		French fries
	Wake up		Iced tea
	Like the taste		Juice
			Health shake
			Ice cream

sary to study. In terms of the more direct cue, the colored pens, diet Coke and pretzels were all identified by the subject (without prompting) as assisting in the objective of "staying awake."

In addition, it may be noted in the above example, and in other responses provided by subjects, that they were comfortable mixing mentions of brands and products. Another subject listing what came to mind when she thought of breakfast mentioned "Raisin Bran, bananas, toast, hash browns and chocolate milk."

This mixing of the mentions of brands and products reflects Rosch's (1975) notion of "basic levels" of categorization. However, it also represents the limit of categorization for some subjects. At least some subjects made the comment that "I don't know the brands of things." It seems plausible that this lack of brand knowledge may reflect that subcategorization and branding is not particularly important to consumers—that is, a banana is adequate whether it is Chiquita or some unknown brand. On the other hand, brands like Coke enjoyed very high recall being mentioned virtually whenever drinks were under discussion.

It was noted that subjects did not always use the category labels that might be given to a category by a marketer. One example was that some subjects mentioned Coke; however, their subsequent comments and responses indicated that they were referring to the category of sodas. A similar example was the mention of Pop-Tarts which sometimes referred to the Kellogg's brand, and sometimes to the category of toaster pastries.

When discussing snacks, many mentioned the category of "junk food." The attributes of the category were not altogether clear. Despite this, subjects did not generally appear to feel a need to articulate the nature of the category implying that there was a shared understanding about the nature of junk food. Similarly, many restaurants were grouped as fast-food, which in the words of one subject, is where "you can go through a drive-through."

TABLE 2
Chi-Squared Analysis of Evocation by Cue

Drinks: Overall chi-squared - 222.4*

	Socializing	Thirst Quenching	Breakfast	Party
Relaxing	36.1*	46.5*	39.7*	36.0*
Socializing		95.1*	69.8*	8.7
Thirst Quenching		70.7*	59.1*	
Breakfast			50.0*	

Snacks: Overall chi-squared: 152.6*

	Limited time	Watching Nutritious	Mid-TV	Afternoon
Filling	26.5*	58.0*	35.1*	12.8
Limited time		57.9*	30.3*	15.1
Nutritious			54.0*	26.0*
Watching TV				30.5*

Restaurants: Overall chi-squared - 218.7*

	Romantic	Sunday Different	With Lunch	Family
Romantic	73.1*	58.2*	51.8*	44.7*
Different		40.7*	60.3*	33.7*
Sunday Lunch			34.2*	30.2*
With Family				28.0

* Chi-squared significant at p < 0.05

Finally, some subjects indicated that they were not sure what to call some categories of products. One subject recalling brands of potato chips said "Planters for their kind of things, but not for potato chips." Perhaps if forced on the issue he could have given a label to the category of "their kind of things," but clearly it was not a label that was readily accessible.

QUANTITATIVE STUDY — CUING INFLUENCES ON BRAND AWARENESS

The quantitative study tested the hypothesized cuing influence of salient associates on brand evocation. The method and results are summarized here; some of the elements of the design and method that are not relevant to this paper have been omitted (see Holden 1992 for more complete details).

Method

Utilizing a small selection of the cues found in the qualitative pretest, the brand evocation study examined the hypothesis proposing that evoked sets vary as a function of the associates provided at retrieval. Subjects were asked to list brands coming to mind for one of five cues for each of the three product-types (drinks, snacks and restaurants). The five cues, nested in product-type, were three benefit cues and two situation cues identified in the qualitative pretest: drinks - breakfast, party, relaxing, thirst quenching, socializing; snacks - watching TV, mid-afternoon, filling, limited time, nutritious; restaurants - Sunday lunch, with family, different, healthy, romantic.

The brand evocation measure was a questionnaire requiring subjects to generate three evoked sets. Subjects generated an evoked set for one of the five cues associated with each of the three product-types. The order of the product-types in each questionnaire was randomized. Subjects were assigned to cues on a random basis with the constraint that the cues for each product-type were of the same type. That is, if one of the cues for one of the product-types was a situation cue, then the other two cues selected for the other two product-types were also situation cues.

The brand evocation measure was administered to four large groups (classes) of undergraduate students in marketing to give a total sample of 116 students. Subjects were allowed 20 seconds to generate each evoked set, and were then required to move on to generate the next. The brand evocation measure also included a measure of indirect recall: after generating an evoked set for each cue ("direct recall"), subjects were instructed to return to each cue and to list up to three brands for each mention of a product or product category rather than a brand ("indirect recall"). There was no time limit imposed on subjects for completion of the indirect recall task.

Results and Discussion

All brands and products evoked were coded and entered as data into the analysis. As was expected, there was a mixture of products and brands in subjects' recall, and this was preserved in the coding of the data. That is, evocation at the "basic level" (Rosch 1975) forms the level at which analysis was conducted.

In an analysis similar to that conducted by Ratneshwar and Shocker (1991), a chi-squared analysis of the frequency of recall of the five most frequently recalled brands (products) for each of the five cues for each product-type was conducted. The analysis revealed that there was a significant difference in evocation by cue for all three product-types (see Table 2).

In addition to the overall analysis, a comparison of each cue with each other cue within each product-type revealed that there were significant differences in recall between every pair of cues except three (see Table 2). The recall of drinks in response to "socializing" was not significantly different from recall cued by "party." The recall of snacks in response to "filling" and "limited time" were significantly different from each other, but neither of the evoked sets generated for these two cues was significantly different from recall to the cue, "mid-afternoon."

The lack of differences in recall in the three cases described are perhaps not surprising. Given the student population from which the sample was drawn, the benefit of socializing and the situation of party are likely to be very closely related. Indeed, it implies that at a party, a major benefit sought is socializing. Perhaps the result seen in snacks can be explained in a similar manner. The situation of wanting a snack in the middle of the afternoon is perhaps associated with limited time and/or a desire for something filling, and hence, recall of brands to the cue, mid-afternoon, is not significantly different from the recall cued with filling or limited time even though the two latter cues lead to significantly different recall.

Clearly, the recall data support the findings of Ratneshwar and Shocker (1991) and extends their finding by showing that recall varies by situation cue across a range of product-types. In addition, the data provide clear support for the notion that evoked sets vary by the cuing benefit. Interestingly, the only non-significant differences in recall appeared in the comparison of situation cues with benefit cues. One interpretation of these cases is that the situation cues are operating indirectly via the benefit cues; evocation would not be expected to be significantly different between benefit cues and situation cues which evoke those same benefits. That is, the situation operates as an indirect cue and the benefit operates as a more direct cue.

Given the basic result showing support for the model of brand awareness being a function of the cues present at brand retrieval, it might be possible to extend the present research to alternative measures of brand awareness. As the basic construct in the model is one of associative strength, the model would predict that measures of brand accessibility based on response time (see Fazio 1990) should be related to brand accessibility. Preliminary results (Holden 1992) supporting this contention are reported briefly in the following.

Subjects in a response time experiment were asked to state whether each word appearing on a computer screen was a real word or a nonsense word (i.e., a lexical decision task). The major manipulation was the word-prime (cue) that immediately preceded the presentation of the target brands with the hypothesis being that stronger associative strength between the cue and the brand being reflected in faster response times for identification of the brand. The cues were a selected from the set used and reported here in the brand evocation measure. Comparing the average response times for brand identification with the frequency of brand evocation in response to the same cue, a strong correlation was found. The relationship between the two measures supports the notion of brand awareness as a function of the accessibility of the brand in response to the cue.

CONCLUSIONS AND IMPLICATIONS

The qualitative research found brand associates of various types that appeared to be operating as cues to brand retrieval. It was possible to classify cues as suggested by Holden and Lutz (1992), but some borderline cases suggested a need for clarifying and perhaps exploring further the types of brand associates that might operate as cues at brand retrieval.

Evidence for direct and indirect cuing was found in the qualitative research. However, when an indirect measure of cuing was incorporated into the brand evocation measure, it did not increase the relationship between brand evocation and brand verification. An improvement in the relationship would be expected given that the verification measure implicitly measures both direct and indirect cuing.

Both the qualitative research and the brand evocation measure found evidence to support the notion that evoked sets are best described as goal-derived categories where the basic level of recall might be a brand and/or a product category. The elements within the sets were often from different product (taxonomic) categories, and in the qualitative research at least, it was clear that the items included were often complements rather than substitutes.

The analysis of brand evocation clearly showed an influence of cues on evoked set formation. In addition, the probability of evocation was found to be highly correlated with the average response time for identification of the brand when presented after the corresponding cue.

The results have a number of interesting implications for marketers. First, the measurement of brand recall in response to a product category cue tends to ignore the significant differences in evocation across situations and across benefits. Marketers targeting a particular usage segment (Srivistava 1980) or benefit segment would get a more appropriate measure of their "awareness" relative to others by measuring evocation in response to the appropriate situational or benefit cues.

Second, the consideration of brands (and product categories) appears to be potentially manipulable if communication strategies take into account the cues that facilitate retrieval of the marketer's brand. By placing cues known to facilitate retrieval in the choice situation, the probability of brand evocation is increased, and thereby increases the probability of choice of the brand—without evocation, the probability of choice is zero.

Finally, and more subtly, a marketer could identify cues that are salient in the choice situations in order to link the brand to those cues in marketing communications. To the extent that the marketer is successful in modifying the consumer's memory, salience of the cues in the choice situation will lead to the marketer's brand coming to mind. As this is a memory effect, it seems likely that it will be at least somewhat enduring. Hence, given that the probability of brand choice is likely to increase as a function of the increase in the probability of evocation (Nedungadi 1990), this notion suggests a perspective on brand equity that derives from brand awareness.

REFERENCES

Alba, Joseph W. and J. Wesley Hutchinson (1987), "Dimensions of Consumer Expertise," Journal of Consumer Research, 13 (Mar), 411-454.

Alba, Joseph W., J. Wesley Hutchinson and John G. Lynch, Jr.(1991), "Memory and Decision Making," in Handbook of Consumer Theory and Research, eds. H.H. Kassarjian and T.S. Robertson, Englewood Cliffs, NJ: Prentice Hall, 1-49.

Barsalou, Lawrence W. (1985), "Ideals, Central Tendency and Frequency of Instantiation as Determinants of Graded Structure in Categories," Journal of Experimental Psychology: Learning, Memory and Cognition, 11 (4), 629-653.

Fazio, Russell H. (1990),"A Practical Guide to the Use of Response Latency In Social Psychological Research," Research Methods in Personality and Social Pscyhology, 11, 74-97.

Haley, Russell I. and Peter B Case (1979), "Testing Thirteen Attitude Scales for Agreeement and Brand Discrimination," Journal of Marketing, 43 (Fall), 20-32.

Holden, Stephen J.S. and Richard J. Lutz (1992), "Ask Not What the Brand Can Evoke; Ask What Can Evoke the Brand," *Advances in Consumer Research*, 19, 101-107.

Holden, Stephen J.S. (1992), "Brand Equity Through Brand Awareness: Measuring and Managing Brand Retrieval," Doctoral dissertation, University of Florida.

Howard, John A. and Jagdish N. Sheth (1969), *The Theory of Buyer Behavior*, New York, NY: John Wiley and Sons.

Johnson, Michael D. (1988), "Comparability and Hierarchical Processing in Multialternative Choice," *Journal of Consumer Research*, 15 (Dec), 303-314.

Lutz, Richard J. (1991), "Editorial," *Journal of Consumer Research*, 17, March.

McGuire, William J. (1983), "A Contextualist Theory of Knowledge: Its Implications for Innovation and Reform in Psychological Research," *Advances in Experimental Social Psychology*, 16, 1-47.

Miller, Kenneth E. and James L. Ginter (1979), "An Investigation of Situational Variation in Brand Choice Behavior," *Journal of Marketing Research*, 16, February, 111-123.

Nedungadi, Prakash (1990), "Recall and Consideration Sets: Influencing Choice Without Altering Brand Evaluations," *Journal of Consumer Research*, 17 (Dec), 263-276.

Nedungadi, Prakash and J. Wesley Hutchinson (1985), "The Prototypicality of Brands: Relationships with Brand Awareness, Preference and Usage," *Advances in Consumer Research*, 12, 498-503.

Ratneshwar, S. and Allan D. Shocker (1991), "Substitution in Use and the Role of Usage Context in Product Category Structures," *Journal of Marketing Research*, 28 (Aug), 281-295.

Reynolds, Thomas J. and Jonathan Gutman (1988), "Laddering Theory, Method, Analysis, and Interpretation," *Journal of Advertising Research*, 28 (Feb), 11-31.

Rosch, Eleanor (1975), "Cognitive Prepresentations of Semantic Categories," *Journal of Experimental Psychology*, 104, 192-233.

Rossiter, John R. and Larry Percy (1987), *Advertising and Promotion Management*, New York, NY: McGraw Hill.

Srivistava, Rajendra K. 1980), "Usage-Situational Influences on Perceptions of Product Markets: Response Homogeneity and its Implications for Consumer Research," *Advances in Consumer Research*, 7, 644-649.

Warshaw, Paul R. (1980), "Predicting Purchase and Other Behaviors from General and Contextually Specific Intentions," *Journal of Marketing Research*, 17 (Feb), 26-33.

On the Transferability of Feature/Level Preferences Across Competing Products Serving the Same Purposes

Milos D. Graonic, University of Minnesota
Allan D. Shocker, University of Minnesota

ABSTRACT

This paper explores implications of a change in context or goal on product evaluations. Common consumption goals can lead to quite different products being grouped together in a consumer's consideration set. Previous research had demonstrated this, but did not provide an explanation for the mechanism behind it. Using categorization research and research on importance of goals and contextual determinants of human knowledge, this paper suggests that goal-derived categories and the process of their evaluation might be at the heart of the transferability of preferences across competing products serving the same purpose.

INTRODUCTION

A number of recent studies have indicated the importance of taking into account consideration set influences on consumer decision-making and choice (Srivastava et al. 1984; Nedungadi 1990; Ratneshwar and Shocker 1991). This research has demonstrated that prior to choice, a consumer can sometimes consider a set of products from different nominal product categories (termed "non-comparables" by Johnson [1984]). These studies do not suggest a mechanism behind the phenomenon. A reasonable speculation regarding such a mechanism is that all the products in the consideration set may offer the same benefits in the given context and could therefore compete. An especially interesting issue for research arises from the logical conclusion that preferences for (i.e., judgments about) at least some attributes or characteristics of such alternative products may be transferable from one product to another, since competing products would be evaluated on their ability to serve the same purpose(s).

This study is exploratory and is the first in a series of studies aimed at explaining the mechanism behind the formation of consideration sets containing noncomparables, and how preferences for different products serving the same purpose could be transferable from one product category to another. A potential explanation and theoretical foundation are suggested by recent research on the role of goals and context in people's decision making and categorization research.

PREVIOUS RESEARCH AND THEORETICAL FOUNDATION

Research in Consumer Behavior

There has been much literature which directly or indirectly addresses issues of concern in this research. As we have already mentioned, consideration set research (for an overview see Shocker, Ben-Akiva, Boccara, and Nedungadi [1991]) and Johnson's (1984) research on noncomparables are two important streams of such research. Two findings from consideration set research are central for the present study. First, this research indicates that people often recall from memory a set of products to serve as a basis for eventual choice. Second, it seems that the process of choice is characterized by the movement of a *product set* (the composition of which could be modified), not simply an individual product, through different stages of thought before the decision is made. Johnson's (1984) research indicated that comparison of different product categories necessitates a certain level of abstraction to compare physically different products.

The Role of Goals and Context in Consumer Decision-Making

It has been demonstrated in many different areas of social sciences that human knowledge is structured and organized in different ways and by various means. For purposes of our inquiry we are interested in the role of context (situation) and goals in human knowledge and, therefore, consumer decision making. We argue that context and goals impose important constraints on human knowledge and therefore must be included in the study of consumer choice process and choices.

First, consider the role of context. It has always been easy to criticize knowledge-related experiments from the standpoint that testing people's skills at performing a particular task is not valid if the task is not relevant to the "real world" (Lynch 1983). In other words, laboratory experiments should desirably be relevant to the real world to serve the purpose of explaining and predicting real world behavior and determining a level of skill (Dreyfus and Dreyfus 1986). It might seem as though people make inconsistent decisions in experiments, but often they are consistent with respect to the criterion they are using, if it was properly understood by the experimenter. Human understanding is organized by perspective; a simple rewording of a question on a choice task can change the choice.

Thinking is intrinsically interwoven with the context of the problem to be solved. Context includes a problem's physical structure, it's conceptual structure, the purpose of the activity, and a social milieu (Rogoff 1984). This implies that even an experimental setting, which is intended to be "neutral" and context free, provides a particular context. Thinking, as a practical activity, is adjusted to meet demands of the situation. Therefore, logical problem-solving in one environment may not be logical problem-solving in another (e.g., see the results of research on the Wason selection task in Cosmides [1989]).

A very good example for the contextual dependency of skills in consumer behavior is presented by Lave, Murtaugh, and Rocha (1984). The authors studied grocery shopping as an example of everyday activity in context. They compared results on an identical arithmetic task (selection of the least expensive alternative based on comparisons of price and quantity) during an actual shopping process and in a laboratory situation. Supermarket calculations were much more accurate than laboratory calculations (98% error free compared to 59% error free). Not only were the shoppers more precise, but they also carried out many more calculations (2.5 calculations on average) for each grocery item. The authors hypothesized that this happened because the supermarket situation juxtaposes problem, solution, and checking activities, i.e., a realistic setting for a problem creates better solutions.

A very broad picture of the role of goals in consumer behavior was presented by Gutman (1982) who used means-end analysis to explain how a product or service selection facilitates the achievement of a desired end state. His model assumes that people are aware of product benefits and their consequences, and their goal is to choose the product whose benefits can satisfy values the consumer cherishes. Indeed, other experimental research has also demonstrated that consumer goals are drivers in the choice process (Park and Smith 1989; Bettman and Sujan 1987; Huffman and Houston 1992).

The cognitive psychology literature has also indicated a role for goals as a basis for categorization (Barsalou 1983). In the course of engaging in goal-directed behavior people often create specialized concepts called goal-derived categories. For example, a goal to lose weight can create the category of "foods not to eat on a diet." Since human behavior is believed to be largely goal-driven, this suggests that goal-derived categories might prove useful in the explanation of preferences and choices.

Theories about Concepts and Goal-based Categorization

The dominant approaches to human categorization (i.e., prototypicality and exemplar) have been criticized in the cognitive psychology literature and appear unsatisfactory for understanding substitution among products. They do not adequately deal with the question of how categories initially are formed, but rather they accept a category as given and seek to describe its composition and membership. A promising new approach is offered by Medin and his associates (for a more complete conceptualization, see Medin 1989). They claim that the complexity of human categorization could be explained by a "theory-driven" approach.

Our concepts are often embedded in "theories" about the way the world functions. We often find a deeper essence and use that to provide meaning when other information is not available. That is, our "theories" help us to construct meaning which can take us beyond the explicit information given. Those "theories" are very often of causal (cause-effect) relationships and are of an explanatory nature. A goal-derived category involves "knowing" a set of dynamic causal relations. Therefore concepts are dependent upon a network of relations in which they are embedded.

It is possible to find numerous examples of people using some kinds of personal theory when categorizing by looking at published experimental work. For example, when asked to list the attributes of a particular category, respondents would most often list particularly salient attributes. In addition, respondents would also list some non-salient attributes, but ones which are diagnostic in people's background knowledge (Murphy and Medin 1985). As another example, assumed correlations between the attributes in a concept have been shown not to be random ideas, but the result of thought processes caused by very different stimuli at different times (Malt and Smith 1984). Even more, people often see illusory correlations which can not be based on facts, but only upon their "theories" (Medin and Shoben 1988).

There are already two proposals for prospective theories of product categorization in the literature of consumer behavior. First, Boush and Loken (1991) proposed categorization based on brand. All products that have the same brand could be considered as one category regardless of their parallel membership in different product classes. Second, Bettman and Sujan (1987) and Park and Smith (1989) demonstrated that Barsalou's idea (1983) of goal-related categories could very usefully be applied to group products by their ability to satisfy the same goal. This last idea represents the approach we use in the present research. Since goal-derived categories are not already given common taxonomic categorization, for example as fruit or animals, to be able to consider different nominal products as members of the same category, a reasonable conjecture is that consumers theorize how the different products could fulfill the same goal. Creating a category using members from different product classes thus becomes an example of a theory-driven approach to categorization. Only personal cause-effect theories could help people understand how a set of quite different attributes embedded in different products could offer the same benefit(s).

RESEARCH FRAMEWORK AND HYPOTHESIS

The research framework encompasses several elements, as shown in Figure 1. Context is a general representation of the situation in which a consumer might be involved or expect to be and which is presumed to impose constraints upon his or her decision. A context could have several dimensions as, for example, social (there might be other participants), temporal (particular time of day or night), spatial (at home, at work, in a mall), *etc.* See Belk (1975) for such a concept of the situational context.

A context relevant for decision-making could suggest particular goals to the decision-maker or the decision-maker seeking a particular goal might choose a particular context. Let's say, if somebody is in McDonald's only a limited number of goals would be plausible - for example, to eat fast food oneself, to accompany friends or family who came to eat fast food, etc. Choice of goals is delimited by the particular context. In the present research we do not distinguish between goals and context and specify both together as part of our instructions to respondents. Context is, of course, a broader construct than a goal. It can encompass several goals (and the same goal could be relevant to several different contexts). But, there is frequently a strong and plausible relationship between context and goal so that specification of one may suggest the other.

Given a goal there may be a set of products which can satisfy and fulfill the goal to an acceptable degree. For example, if a student lives only a few miles from school and wants to ride there on a pleasant sunny day, s/he could use a bicycle, in-line skates, car, bus, *etc.* for this purpose (assuming the availability of all these alternatives and the skill to use each). Although all these products could satisfy the goal of "getting to school" they don't have identical physical characteristics. So, the different products could represent members of a goal-derived category. In spite of their different physical characteristics, all products could offer the benefits needed to achieve the goal. The benefits or choice criteria could be, for example, "amount of comfort", "length of time to get to school", "enjoyment level of the physical activity", *etc.* Therefore, instead of comparing products on physical characteristics, consumers may compare "non-comparables" on the benefits required for the particular goal.

Trade-offs among benefits and costs can be thought to be a natural outcome of goal-driven decision-making - whether comparables or non-comparables are involved as choice objects (see the substantial literature on conjoint analysis and other multi-attribute models of decision-making for support for this contention). Consumption purpose (goal) proscribes criteria (benefits) which the alternatives considered (*e.g.*, products/services) must meet.

An obvious practical problem lies in the definition of what are benefits and what are attributes. There may be no precise line which would separate benefits (which are generally more abstract) from attributes (generally more concrete). The abstractness-concreteness dimension (Johnson and Fornell [1987]) is not always unambiguous in distinguishing benefits from attributes (e.g., low cost may be regarded as a benefit, yet may be quite concrete).

In considering how attributes may relate to benefits, it is important to recognize that there may be more than one way to create a given benefit. For example, if the goal and context is to "get to school rapidly (goal) on a pleasant sunny day (context)" and if the products considered are a bicycle and in-line skates, it is possible that a benefit such as "comfort" could be generated for both products in two very different ways:

FIGURE 1
Framework For Product Evaluations in Context

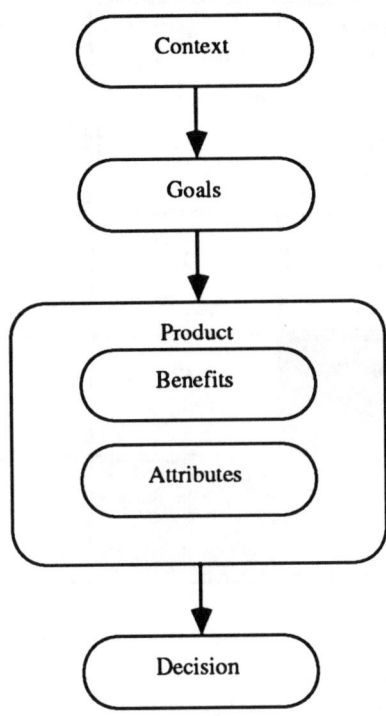

Bicycle:
Seat cushioning
Size of frame
Type of bicycle
Curvature of handle bar
Pedal type/style

In-line skates:
Weight
Lacing/Closure
Design of shoe
Fit of boots
Padding in shoe

Attributes unique to each given product category can plausibly give rise to a similar benefit. Thus, a product can be represented in our framework by both its attributes (possibly unique) and the levels of benefits it provides. In the same product category, attributes are likely to be encoded into benefits similarly; while in the case of "non-comparables," alternatives may be comparable only in terms of their benefits. After considering the levels of benefits and/or attributes provided by each alternative, consumers make their choice; therefore the final element in our framework is the decision.

If different products serve the same goal, there must be a way to relate and maybe transfer preferences between these different products. A first step in pursuing this idea would be to see whether preferences for the same products change with a change in goal. Since the present study is first in a series, our first hypothesis for the project is the one that is empirically investigated here:

Hypothesis 1: The importance of features in customer preferences for the same product will change with a change in goal or purpose.

METHOD

Overview

In order to investigate whether preferences for different and identical products change as goals change, we conducted an exploratory study. It was of particular importance to construct "natural" situations with goals and products that the particular subject population might be involved with in their everyday lives (Snyder 1981). Since we planned to sample from an undergraduate student population, we focused on products and related goals which were relevant to that population.

Through a series of (3) focus groups (each involving 2 - 6 students, who were paid for their participation) and a pretest (involving some 37 undergraduate marketing students in a large midwestern university who were given class credit for participating) we identified two product sets and two distinct goals for each which appeared to enable a test of the hypothesis. Each set consisted of two products. The sets were constructed in a way which would enable investigation of the phenomena. Two products in one set are distinctly different, while two products in the other set are similar, but "different." The first consisted of a bicycle and in-line skates and the two goals were "To travel a few miles to school on pleasant, sunny days" and "To exercise on pleasant, sunny days". These products are "non-comparables" since they don't have most or all physical attributes in common. Another set of products selected were a backpack and shoulder bag. These were considered by the students as different products, but were similar enough so that they could be represented by similar attributes, with the main differences being in styling and appearance (e.g., backpacks have two shoulder straps while a shoulder bag has one). The goals were "To carry books, notes, pencils, *etc.* to school" and "To carry things on an airplane trip".

In the focus groups, we had asked participants to take a given product and to suggest alternative usages for that product and other products they would consider for those same usages. The benefits suggested by the students were determined from the usages suggested and the general discussion surrounding conditions of use.

TABLE 1
Rank Order Correlations of Attribute Importances Given Context–Shoulder Bag and Backpack

PRODUCT - CONTEXT	Back pack - Context 1	Back pack - Context 2	Shoulder bag - Context 1	Shoulder bag - Context 2
Back pack - Context 1	1.0	.72*	.95**	.63
Back pack - Context 2	.72*	1.0	.69*	.84**
Shoulder bag - Context 1	.95**	.69*	1.0	.72*
Shoulder bag - Context 2	.63	.84**	.72*	1.0

One tail significance *: .01 and **: .001

From all the potential benefits that both products can offer, we selected those common to both goals, i.e., which were suggested in *both* contexts of use for the products.

Self-administered questionnaires were completed by 74 undergraduate marketing students who participated in the research to receive course credit. Manipulation of the goals was conducted "between subjects" so that different subjects were randomly assigned to one of two different goals. Each questionnaire contained both product sets (i.e., bicycle - in-line skates and backpack - shoulder bag) and only one particular goal for each product set. We could potentially get a confound when participants evaluated more than one product for each specific context but, given the small number of respondents available and the duration of the task, that possibility seemed necessary.

Participants were asked to indicate the importance of each in a list of pre-specified benefits and then the importance of the prespecified attributes for both products, *given the specified goal*. Next participants indicated to which degree a particular product offers benefits. Thus there were three predictor variables: judged importances of each benefit, judged importances of each attribute, and degree to which a product offers a benefit. All three variables were measured using 5-point scales: the responses for importance questions ranged from "Not at all important" to "Extremely important" and the responses for the degree to which products offer benefits ranged from "Not at all" to "Extremely high". Finally we collected data on ownership, involvement, and individual characteristics of participants.

ANALYSIS AND RESULTS

To test the hypothesis we conducted two related sets of analyses. First, we used aggregate rank order correlations to determine whether and how rankings of importances of attributes and benefits differed between the two contexts. Second, logistic regression was applied to determine whether attribute and benefit importances differed between two contexts and, if they do, which attributes and benefits in an overall regression model could be used to predict the goal participants had in mind (the dependent variable) when evaluating attribute and benefit importances.

As shown in Tables 1 and 2, rank order correlations of attribute importances changed from one context to another. In other words, the importances of attributes (physical characteristics of the products) change as context/goal changes, although the product itself is not changed. In the case of the backpack and shoulder bag (the two products which had the same set of attributes) rank order correlations were higher for two "different" products evaluated within the same context than for two "identical" products evaluated in two different contexts (although the latter correlation was computed "between subjects," thereby confounding the interpretation). This outcome is repeated for all four situations (2 products x 2 contexts) as shown in Table 1.

As noted in Table 2, since bicycles and in-line skates don't share attributes, rank order correlations of attribute importances could not be compared. But, again in the case of bicycles importances of attributes changed between the two contexts (the rank order correlation is .79). In the case of in-line skates, attribute importances did not change between the two contexts - an unexpected result. Three explanations occur to us. First, our manipulation of context/goal may not have been sufficiently different in the case of this product (subjects may have not seen going to school and recreation as sufficiently different in terms of what they would expect from the product). Second, in-line skates, being a relatively new product (on the market only a few years), it is possible that consumers still don't have as sophisticated an opinion about the product and its potential usages as they have for the other products used in the research (e.g., the incidence of ownership of in-line skates was markedly lower than for bicycles in our sample). Finally, it is possible that expertise could play a role here. We were able to test this final possibility (using self-reported measures of product knowledge) and found no expertise effect.

Rank order correlations of benefits were expected to change even more between two contexts than were the rank order correlations of attributes. As shown in Table 3, rank order correlation of benefits in the case of shoulder bags and backpacks reveals a change in importances between two contexts. But, rank order correlation in the case of bicycles and in-line skates reveals extreme change from one context to another. In other words, the importance of

TABLE 2
Rank Order Correlations of Attribute Importances Given Two Different Contexts

Bicycle	In-line skates
.79**	1.0**

One tail significance *:.01 and **: .001

TABLE 3
Rank Order Correlations of Benefit Importances Given Two Different Context

Bicycle and In-line skates	Backpack and Shoulder bag
-0.15	.8*

One tail significance *:.01

TABLE 4
Percentage change in importance of attributes and benefits between two contexts

PRODUCT	% of attributes	% of benefits
Bicycle	7 (1/15)	30 (4/10)
In-line skates	8 (1/13)	30 (4/10)
Shoulder Bag	23 (3/13)	44 (4/9)
Back pack	23 (3/13)	44 (4/9)

Note that numbers in parenthesis are the number of attributes/benefits that changed over total number of attributes/benefits

benefits almost changes completely from one context to another, in the case of bicycle and in-line skates.

A complementary analysis made use of logistic regression. Again, we used data on attribute and benefit importances as independent variables and context/goal as the dependent variable. The objective was to determine, from a regression model, which attributes and benefits differ between the two contexts. In other words, which attributes or benefits could better be used to account for the context.

The summary results from the logistic regressions are shown in Table 4. As we can see, in the case of all the products, the importances of attributes and benefits is different between the two contexts. It is worth noting that the importances of benefits change much more than the importances of attributes. This suggests that it may not be enough to test for differences in attribute importances between two contexts; rather it may be more important to test for differences in benefit importances.

DISCUSSION AND FUTURE RESEARCH

This exploratory research was conducted to see whether differences in product evaluations occur with a change in context/goal. Our preliminary analyses provide several interesting results. First, context changes judgments of attribute and benefit importances. Second, the data suggest the possibility that different products could be more similarly evaluated within a given context than the same product would within two different contexts. Finally, the importances of benefits appear to change more than the importances of attributes between the two different contexts.

The results could have important marketing implications. First, they demonstrate that for different purposes (goals) consumers could use different criteria when evaluating the same products. Therefore, assuring constancy of purpose (*i.e.*, controlling for goals or usage) may be very important for modeling consumer decision-making (*e.g.*, through conjoint analysis, discrete choice modeling, *etc.*). These implications could be felt not only in product design, but also in promotion (different features might be emphasized when different contexts are emphasized), pricing (the product could possess monopoly power in some contexts), display (complementary products with differential packaging emphasized), *etc*. Second, the idea that purpose changes evaluations could be strategically used to help a manager better understand the nature of competitive threat and more precisely define and segment "customers" (*i.e.*, all consumers who encounter relevant purposes could be regarded as potential customers, even if they have not purchased in the category before).

Evidence is growing that goals play an important role in human decision-making. We have speculated about that role and provided limited evidence for our speculations in this exploratory research. One of the advantages of conducting such work is the opportunity to learn from these experiences. Future research in this arena must contend with several problems and issues. For example, we hope to analyze future work at the individual-level and not just at an aggregate level, as was done in the present study. Individual level analysis is in accord with the theory and eliminates aggregation bias (possibly at expense of greater demand effects). We expect to use multiple measurement techniques, possibly conjoint analysis and direct measurement (*e.g.*, Fishbein attitude measurement or self-explicated measures). Next, it seems necessary to investigate in future research the "ease" with which subsets of product attributes or characteristics of different products can be related to the functional benefits and costs used in the study. One of the implications of the theoretical perspective we have adopted is enhanced recognition for the fact that different subsets of product characteristics may provide similar benefits (or the same characteristics are functional in different ways in different product applications). We anticipate using subjective judgments of "experts" to provide evidence in support of hypothesized attribute - benefit relationships. Finally, the theoretical basis we have posed for the research while plausible, has not been tested previously. Our first concern in this sequence of studies is to investigate support for the hypothesized effects and relationships; a second is to investigate alternative theoretical explanations for the findings.

REFERENCES

Barsalou, L.W. (1983). Ad hoc categories. *Memory & Cognition*. 11 (3), 211-227.

Belk, Russel W. (1975), Situational Variables and Consumer Behavior, *Journal of Consumer Research*, Vol. 2, December, 157-236.

Bettman, James R. and Mita Sujan (1987), Effects of framing on Evaluation of Comparable and Noncomparable Alternatives by Expert and Novice Consumers, *Journal of Consumer Research*, Vol. 14, September, 141-154.

Boush, David M. and Barbara Loken (1991), A Process-Tracing Study of Brand Extension Evaluation, *Journal of Marketing Research*, 28 (February), 16-28.

Cosmides, Leda (1989), The logic of social exchange: Has natural selection shaped how humans reason? Studies with the Wason selection task, *Cognition*, 31, 187-276.

Dreyfus, Hubert L. and Stuart E. Dreyfus (1986), *Mind Over Machine - The Power of human Intuition and Expertise in the era of Computer*, New York: The Free Press.

Gutman, Jonathan (1982), A Means-End Chain Model Based on Consumer Categorization Processes, *Journal of Marketing*, 46 (Spring), 60-72.

Huffman, Cynthia and Michael J. Houston (1992), "Goal-Oriented Experiences and the Development of Knowledge", *Working paper*, University of Pennsylvania.

Johnson, Michael D. (1984), Consumer Choice Strategies for Comparing Noncomparable Alternatives, *Journal of Consumer Research*, Vol. 11, December, 741-753.

Johnson, Michael D. and Claes Fornell (1987), The Nature and Methodological Implications of the Cognitive Representations of Products, *Journal of Consumer Research*, Vol. 14, 214-228.

Lave, Jean, Michael Murtaugh, and Olivia de la Rocha (1984), In Barbara Rogoff and J. Lave (Eds.), *Everyday Cognition: Its Development in Social Context*, Harvard University Press, 67-94.

Lynch, John G. (1983), The role of External Validity in Theoretical Research, *Journal of Consumer Research*, Vol. 10, 109-111.

Nedungadi, Prakash (1990), Recall and Consumer Consideration Sets: Influencing Choice Without Altering Brand Evaluations, *Journal of Consumer Research*, 17 (December), 263-76.

Medin, D. (1989). Concepts and Conceptual Structure. *American Psychologist*, 44, 1469-1481.

Murphy, G.L and D.L. Medin (1985), The Role of Theories in Conceptual Coherence, *Psychological Review*, 92, 289-316.

Park, C. Whan and Daniel C. Smith (1989), Product-Level Choice: A Top-Down or Bottom-Up Process?, *Journal of Consumer Research*, Vol. 16, December, 289-299.

Ratneshwar, S. and Allan D. Shocker (1991), Substitution in Use and the Role of Usage Context in Product Category Structures, *Journal of Marketing Research*, 28 (August), 281-95.

Rogoff, Barbara (1984), Introduction: Thinking and learning in social context, In Barbara Rogoff and J. Lave (Eds.), *Everyday Cognition: Its Development in Social Context*, Harvard University Press, 1-8.

Shocker, Allan D., Moshe Ben-Akiva, Bruno Boccara, and Prakash Nedungadi (1991), Consideration Set Influences on Consumer Decision Making and Choice: Issues, Models, and Suggestions, *Marketing Letters*, 2:3, 181-197.

Snyder, Mark (1981), "On the Influence of Individuals on Situations," *In N.Cantor and J.F. Kihlstrom (eds.), Personality, Cognition, and Social Interaction*, Hillsdale, N.J.: L. Erlbaum, 309-329.

Srivastava, Rajendra K., Mark I. Alpert, and Allan D. Shocker (1984), "A customer oriented approach for determining market structures," *Journal of Marketing*, 48, 32-45.

Context Effects on Consumer Choice, Brand Awareness and Decision Making
C. Whan Park, University of Pittsburgh

Several important themes underscore recent research into the effects of goals and context on consumer choice, including the observations that choice is goal-dependent, goals are context-specific, and both benefits and usage situations can perform as important cues which influence the make-up of consumers' consideration sets. It is important that work continue in this area in order to better specify the roles of goals and context in the various stages of consumer choice - particularly the consideration set formation stage - and to better identify the general implications of this line of research for both researchers and managers. Since Huffman discussed each of the three papers (Warlop and Ratneshwar, Holden, and Granoic and Shocker), I will primarily highlight the implications of current research in this area as well as specify a potential future research agenda.

There appears to be some ambivalence and/or confusion as to the proper relationships among consumption goals, benefits, and usage situations. In many cases consumption goals seem to be thought of independent of usage situations. They are more or less equated with consumption benefits. However, given the premise that product/brand choice is consumption goal-driven, it seems clear that usage situations must be explicitly incorporated into the definition of goals. Without considering usage situations as an integral part of the consumer's consumption goal, it is difficult to conceive of product/brand choice as goal-driven. Therefore, I propose that goals are a function of two key elements: benefits and usage situations. A consumer's goal can be most accurately defined and described in terms of the specific benefits sought in light of the specific usage context. For example, consider a consumer's need to quench his or her thirst. Without any additional information to define the usage context or the specific benefits sought, the consumer's consumption goal lacks specificity and product choice is not likely to occur, given this lack of specificity. However, if the usage situation finds the consumer at a baseball game on a blistering, hot day, and the consumer desires a product solution (set of benefits) that is flavorful, refreshing, and low-calorie, then product/brand choice is more likely to occur - in all likelihood from a consideration set which includes diet soft or fruit drinks, and/or low-calorie beers. On the other hand, a thirsty consumer at a football game on a cold, windy day is more likely to consider alternatives such as coffee or hot chocolate. Note that the specific benefits sought and the specific usage situation can help specify the consumer's consumption goal and have a resulting impact on consideration set formation and choice. The point is not usage situations or benefits by themselves are ineffective predictors of choice. Rather, both usage situations and benefits constitute the consumer's consumption goal - and it is these goals that may be the most influential factors affecting consideration set formation and choice.

Defining consumption goals as consisting of both benefits and usage situations is important. Because many versatile products provide a range of benefits that are applicable across various usage situations, this conceptualization of goals means that alternatives in consideration sets need not be members of the same product category - suggesting opportunities for certain brands to pursue sales growth by proactively competing with brands from other product categories.

This view of consumer goals also prescribes that the most effective cues for influencing the storage and retrieval of consideration sets from memory may be those that are explicitly "goal-related." Therefore, the goal itself may be a critical encoding and retrieval cue which facilitates the inclusion of certain products in consumers' consideration sets. In particular, consumption goals as effective encoding cues for potential product-level consideration sets may be of principal importance because effective retrieval is unlikely to occur without effective encoding in the first place.

However, in order to understand this encoding process, it is necessary to examine the actual process of goal specification. Consumption goals are not always initially formulated in a specific form or at a relatively concrete level of representation. As such, consumers can often be expected to engage in a "goal-editing" process which changes the composition of their consumption goals from being relatively abstract to being more concrete or specific prior to making a product or brand choice.

Benefits and usage situations, as the key components of goals, underlie this process. As shown in Figure 1, the relative specificity or abstractness of benefits and usage situations combine to determine the overall specificity of the consumer's consumption goal. The examples provided by Figure 2 illustrate the varying levels of goal specificity.

When usage situations and benefits are abstract, consumers may modify and edit their consumption goals, making them more choice relevant. This editing may involve benefits and usage situations, as demonstrated in Figure 2. The manner in which consumers refine both benefits and usage situations to make the abstract goal concrete may, in turn, offer important implications for developing effective encoding strategies that increase consideration set membership for the brand. The challenge of researchers is, thus, to determine how to best utilize goals, consisting of benefits and usage situations, as effective encoding cues which facilitate consideration set formation, and successful product level competition. Research strategies that manipulate the relevance between a brand and certain consumption goals, and measure the resulting impact on consideration set membership, should be a part of future research efforts.

The papers in this issue are useful in the continuing exploration of the effects of goals and context on consumer choice. They constitute the beginning of a serious research agenda that must focus further attention on the processes and implications of goals and context in consumer decision making.

FIGURE 1
Components of a Goal

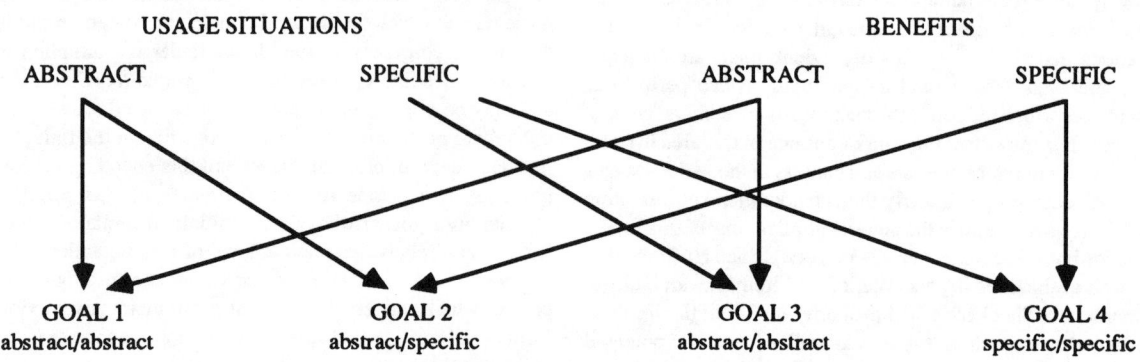

(=> specificity of consumer's goal representation =>)

FIGURE 2
Goal Specificity

Level of Specificity	Benefit		Usage Situation
Abstract			
A	. . .	snack you may eat	. . .
A	. . .	snack you may eat	at home
A	nutritious	snack you may eat	at home
A	nutritious	snack you may eat	at home before going out on a Saturday evening date
A	nutritious and mouth refreshing	snack you may eat	at home before going out on a Saturday evening date
A	nutritious and mouth refreshing	snack you may eat	at home before going out on a Saturday evening date at an all-you-can-eat Mexican restaurant
Concrete			

Progress and Limitations of Social Marketing: A Review of Empirical Literature on the Consumption of Social Ideas.

Katryna Malafarina, University of Minnesota
Barbara Loken, University of Minnesota

Social marketers have suggested limitations on the application of the marketing concept to the consumption of social issues. Several of these concerns were explored through a content analysis of empirical literature over the past decade. In general, findings suggest that although some criticisms were substantiated in the literature, others were not supported. Constraints that did occur in social marketing included negatively predisposed target segments and complex cost considerations. Concerns over lack of good secondary data, and unreliable or invalid measures; difficulties in identifying consumer behavior determinants, in identifying target segments, in defining effectiveness of measures and in evaluating programs; and the need to use personal, in-depth forms of communication were not substantiated. Study implications and limitations are discussed.

INTRODUCTION

Social marketing, defined by Kotler and Zaltman (1971) as "the design, implementation, and control of programs calculated to influence the acceptability of social ideas and involving considerations of product planning, pricing, communications and marketing research" (p. 5), encompasses a broad range of consumer behavior topics from smoking cessation to AIDS prevention to environmental awareness. Because of the social nature of these topics, consumer and marketing researchers have raised important questions about whether the marketing of social ideas is compatible with the general marketing concept. In contrast to earlier conceptual work in social marketing, the present paper attempts to analyze the extent to which *empirical* articles on the consumption of social issues support prior claims made about the limitations of applying the marketing concept to social issues. It is our contention, which the data appear to support, that some of the assumed limitations of conducting social marketing programs and research occur for some, but certainly not most, social marketing programs and research.

The particular issues that we address in this paper, which are by no means comprehensive, can be divided into two general types of problems faced by social marketers that previous authors have discussed: (a) issues relating to the manner in which social marketing research and evaluation are conducted and interpreted, and (b) issues relating to the use of social marketing program elements such as pricing and communications.

Research and Evaluation Issues

With regard to the research and evaluation problems, several authors have argued that obtaining high quality data is more difficult to achieve in social marketing than in product marketing. Limitations on data quality result primarily from fewer financial resources available to social marketers but also can occur due to less continuity between social marketing research studies on a particular topic. Among the specific data quality concerns are (a) an absence of good secondary data available to social marketers, (b) lower reliability and validity of measures, (c) difficulty in identifying the determinants of the social consumer's behavior, and (d) difficulty in identifying through marketing research particular segments to target. Each of these concerns is elucidated below. See also Table 1.

First, good secondary data are often unavailable, since social marketers have limited syndicated services or panels that provide data on social marketing issues. Academic journals may be consulted, but these sources often may contain narrowly focussed research which is harder to generalize to another realm of social marketing (Bloom and Novelli 1981, Fox and Kotler 1980).

Second, problems with reliability and validity of primary data collected is assumed to frequently occur for social marketing studies, since people give more socially desired responses to sensitive issues such as smoking, charitable donations or sex (Bloom and Novelli 1981, Fox and Kotler 1980).

Third, researchers have argued that social marketing issues are more complex than non-social marketing issues, making it difficult for social marketers to isolate factors that affect an individual's behavior (Barach 1984, Bloom and Novelli 1981, Fox and Kotler 1980). Therefore, the determinants of the social consumer's behavior are more difficult to identify.

Fourth, attitudinal and behavioral data used to identify target segments are assumed to be less accurate when the issue pertains to social marketing. For example, it may be difficult to identify "users" and "nonusers", and differentiate groups from one another. Self-report measures may be misleading when measuring attitudes and behaviors pertaining to breast self-examination or contraceptive usage, and it may be impossible to use other behavioral measures such as observation in these circumstances (Bloom and Novelli 1981, Fox and Kotler 1980, Kotler and Zaltman 1971, Sheth and Frazier 1982).

Finally, it has been suggested that social marketers have difficulty evaluating their programs effectively. Determining the nature of the effectiveness variables may be difficult. Is the social marketing program designed to create awareness of an issue, alter consumers' knowledge or attitudes toward a social issue, change people's behavior, or save lives (e.g. Barach 1984, Bloom and Novelli 1981, Bloom and Ford 1979, Fox and Kotler 1980)? Further, the contribution of the marketing program in accomplishing certain objectives may be difficult to estimate (Barach 1984, Fox and Kotler 1980, Bloom and Novelli 1981, Bloom and Ford 1979). Part of the reasoning behind this latter train of thought is the assumption that social marketers have a limited ability to implement randomized experiments or quasi experiments. Often they are forced to use after only or before and after with no control group studies (Bloom and Novelli 1981, Fox and Kotler 1980).

Program Implementation Issues

In addition to the research and evaluation issues noted above, questions concerning implementation of program components have been raised (see also Table 1). For example, researchers have argued that key target segments in a social marketing program may be negatively predisposed to the offering, which, of course, results in the added difficulty of reaching these target segments (Barach 1984, Bloom and Novelli 1981). For example, a program that tries to promote safe sex through use of condoms will often have trouble reaching an audience of teenagers who may be embarrassed or unwilling to address the issue. Bloom and Novelli (1981) have suggested that this difficulty results from target markets who are frequently highly involved with their negative feelings, making them much more resistant to changing their views.

A second program implementation concern is that pricing strategies in social marketing often involve more than monetary

TABLE 1
Scoring Procedure for Coding of Social Marketing Articles

Research and Evaluation Issues	Code*	Decision Rule
1. Are good secondary data unavailable to the authors? (Has previous research been conducted on this issue? Are syndicated services or panels available?)	Yes.....	Article mentions that there is an absence of good secondary data.
	No......	Article cites secondary data sources or refers to established data bases in conducting research.
2. Are researchers able to obtain valid or reliable measures of salient variables? (Is the issue sensitive, will individuals be likely to give socially desirable responses?)	Yes.....	Article made a point that it was difficult to obtain valid or reliable measures, possibly due to the sensitivity of the issue.
	No......	Article reports that measures used were reliable or valid.
3. Is there difficulty identifying the determinants of behavior? (Can factors influencing behavior be isolated by the researcher?)	Yes.....	Article reported that factors affecting behavior could not be identified on the basis of their data.
	No......	Article identified factors that significantly affect behavior.
4. Do researchers not have accurate attitudinal or behavioral data to use in identifying segments? (Who are users and nonusers?)	Yes.....	Article identified no significant differences between target or user groups.
	No......	Article identified significant differences between target or user groups.
5. Are there difficulties in trying to define effectiveness measures for a study? (What should the study measure — attitude, behavior, or something else?)	Yes.....	Determining effectiveness measures was difficult or empirical results were very weak.
	No......	Article identified study elements that could be changed.
6. Is it difficult to estimate contribution of program toward achievement of certain objectives? (Could researchers determine if goal had been obtained?)	Yes.....	Results do not indicate whether or not program element contributed to overall program.
	No......	Authors were able to determine whether program element contributed to the overall program goals successfully or unsuccessfully.
Program Implementation Issues		
1. Are one or more key target segments negatively predisposed to offering?	Yes.....	Article mentioned one or more segments of consumers that have a negative predisposition or are difficult to reach.
	No......	Article stated that consumers tested positive or neutral in their predisposition.
2. Does pricing involve more than monetary costs? (Are psychic, energy or time costs incurred by consumers when engaging in the desired social behavior?)	Yes.....	Issue and/or research examined more than monetary costs.
	No......	Issue and/or research examined only monetary costs.
3. Are personal, in-depth forms of communication needed? (Is direct mail or mass media used, or is more direct contact needed to communicate desired response?)	Yes.....	In-depth interviews or direct contact with respondents were used to communicate message.
	No......	Mass media, direct mail, or written forms of communication were used.

* When neither of the decision rules was met, the article was not included in the analysis.

costs; psychic, energy, and time costs are also involved (Andreasen 1984, Bloom and Novelli 1981). Because of this, social marketers may have less control over consumer costs (Barach 1984, Bloom and Novelli 1981, Fox and Kotler 1980, Kotler and Zaltman 1971, Rothschild 1979).

Finally, communications strategies may cause problems for social marketers. For example, the information to be communicated may be complex. Social marketers may need to educate consumers about certain types of behaviors and may also need to describe benefits of the behavior and recommendations for change

(Bloom and Novelli 1981, Fox and Kotler 1980, Rothschild 1979). Due to the complexity of the social marketing issue, more personal forms of communication such as using health care professionals or other intermediaries may be necessary. Several articles in the literature have proposed suggestions on successfully implementing communications strategies (Kotler and Zaltman 1971, Fox and Kotler 1980, Sheth and Frazier 1982, Barach 1984, Andreasen 1984, Rothschild 1979).

Objectives of the Study

As indicated by the above discussion, concerns have been raised about the implementation, research, and evaluation of social marketing programs. The objective of the present research was to determine if the relevance of these issues is borne out in recent literature. Much anecdotal evidence exists on these issues, but no one has performed a content analysis to determine the extent to which these problems exist. In this paper, we attempt to remedy this omission and present the results of a content analysis of social marketing studies that have appeared in major marketing journals in recent years.

METHODOLOGY

Empirical articles that have appeared in marketing journals since 1980 were included in the analysis. In particular, articles that appeared in *Journal of Consumer Research* (1980-1991), *Journal of Marketing Research* (1980-1991), *Journal of Marketing* (1980-1991), *Advances in Consumer Research* (1981-1991), and *Journal of Public Policy and Marketing* (1982-1991), were evaluated and selected on the basis of the article's title and abstract. Conceptual articles and empirical articles designed to test only theoretical issues (e.g. studying categorization theory in the context of a health care issue) were excluded from our sample. Further, Fox and Kotler's (1980) interpretation of the scope of social marketing was used to determine the nature of the issues to be included: "Social marketing should be distinguished from 'societal marketing' on the one hand and 'nonprofit organization marketing' on the other" (p. 25). Societal marketing refers to marketing's social responsibility and its impact on society. Nonprofit organization marketing includes the marketing of issues that are not relevant to social causes (e.g. marketing of political candidates or urban police departments). We used this definition in order to eliminate some of the multitude of articles that we encountered. Thus, articles pertaining to cause-related marketing and many nonprofit issues (e.g. political marketing) were excluded from our sample. Finally, since the number of articles pertaining to energy conservation and environmental issues was proportionally so much greater than other social issues, only 51.1% of the former articles were sampled for inclusion in analyses.[1] The final sample included 76 articles, shown in Table 2.

Two judges evaluated 35% of the articles, based on content relating to the nine research, evaluation, and program implementation issues discussed previously and the scoring procedure shown in Table 1. Each article was scored as either (a) supporting the proposition, (b) providing negative support for the proposition, or (c) not addressing the issue. Analysis of these scores resulted in an inter-rater reliability of .844. While this reliability index is somewhat lower than standard levels, it is consistent with other reliability indices found for content of research articles in social marketing (cf. Ford et al 1990). The remaining articles were each evaluated by only one of the two judges.

RESULTS

Results, shown in Table 3, are reported by percentage of articles supporting each issue. In addition, results are presented as a function of specific content areas, including energy conservation and other environment issues, nutrition, smoking, alcohol and drug use, and, finally, other miscellaneous issues (including organ and the charitable donations, elderly social issues, shoplifting, gambling, homeless, patriotism and the performing arts).

Research and Evaluation Issues

The first issue addressed was whether empirical studies on social marketing had secondary data sources available that were relevant to hypothesis generation and/or interpretation of results (see Table 1). The vast majority of articles (89%) were able to cite sources of data (generally, previously published results of studies) that were relevant to the study at hand. Availability of secondary data was particularly evident for studies pertaining to smoking cessation, alcohol and drug use, nutrition, and energy and the environment, where, especially recently, an abundance of research findings has been accumulating. Not surprisingly, secondary sources of data were less prevalent for "miscellaneous" issues for which few studies have been published (e.g. compulsive behaviors like gambling, shoplifting, and studies of the homeless).

The second issue addressed whether, although people may be willing to be interviewed, they may give biased or socially desirable responses, resulting in lower reliability and validity of measures. While this issue was difficult to evaluate based solely on stated reports of issue sensitivity, many authors nevertheless provided indices of reliability and/or validity of measures or discussions of measure appropriateness. Results indicated that, in most cases (61% of the articles), authors reported measures of acceptable reliability and/or validity of their measures, or specifically mentioned the use of questions or measures that did not rely on socially desirable responses. For example, in some cases, self-report measures (e.g. of energy conservation) were verified through other data sources. Analyses of specific content domains suggest that, perhaps not surprisingly, articles pertaining to the sensitive issues of smoking, alcohol and drug use (41%), and other miscellaneous issues (38%, but especially AIDS prevention and use of contraceptive devices) yielded the lowest rates of reported reliability of measures.

The third issue tested was whether empirical studies supported the proposition that social marketing studies have difficulty in ascertaining the determinants of behavior due to the greater complexity of the issues. In examining whether each research article was able to identify specific determinants of the cognitive and behavioral criteria examined, we found overwhelming evidence against this proposition. In fact, *all* of the articles that investigated variables relevant to this issue were able to identify significant determinants of social attitudes and behavior. For example, age and cognitive style were found to be determinants of the processing of nutrition information (Cole and Gaeth 1990). It might be argued, of course, that had significant determinants of attitudes and behavior *not* been found, these studies may have gone unpublished. This question will be addressed later. Similarly, in examining the question of whether it was possible to differentiate user or preference groups by means of self-reports, observational data, or by whatever other method was used in the article, again, all of the studies that reported subgroup analyses reported significant differ-

---

[1] The analyses were conducted with and without the total number of energy conservation/environmental articles as well as the 51.1% reported. Interestingly, results were not changed substantively by omitting 48.9% of the articles.

TABLE 2
Empirical Articles Reviewed

Social Marketing Topic & Articles	Specific Issue Investigated
I. Energy Conservation/Environment	
Aaker and Bagozzi (1981)*	Air pollution
Allen (1982)	Energy conservation
Allen, Calantone and Schewe (1982)	Energy conservation
Anderson and Claxton (1980)	Energy conservation
Awad et al (1983)	Energy conservation
Burns and DeVere (1982)	Gasoline conservation
Crosby and Gill (1981)	Bottle recycling
Crosby, Gill and Taylor (1981)	Container recycling
Frey and LaBay (1983)	Energy conservation
Fritzsche (1981)	Energy conservation
Granzin and Olsen (1991)	Newspaper recycling
Heslop (1986)	Energy conservation
Henion, Gregory, and Clee (1981)	Ecological product purchases
Hutton and Ahtola (1991)	Air pollution
Hutton and McNeil (1981)	Energy conservation
Jensen (1986)	Energy conservation
Leonard and Barton (1981)	Energy conservation
Longstreth, Coveney and Bowers (1984)	Energy conservation
Rudelius, Weijo and Dodge (1984)	Energy conservation
Seligman, Hall and Finegan (1983)	Energy conservation
Sexton, Johnson and Konakayama (1987)	Energy conservation
Tripple and Makela (1986)	Energy conservation
Walker (1980)	Energy conservation
II. Nutrition	
Brucks, Mitchell and Staelin (1984)	Nutritional information in advertising
Cole and Gaeth (1990)	Utilization of nutrition information
Feick (1983)	Search for nutrition information
Hackleman (1981)	Food labeling
Heimbach (1981)	Food labeling
Levy et al (1985)	Utilization of nutrition information
Moorman (1990)	Utilization of nutrition information
Muller (1985)	Point of purchase nutrition displays
Prabhaker and Sauer (1988)	Utilization of nutrition information
Rudell (1984)	Nutrition information format and impact
Russo et al (1986)	Point of purchase nutrition displays
Saegert and Young (1982)	Nutrition knowledge
Stewart (1981)	Food labeling
Vandenberg (1981)	Food labeling
Venkatesan et al (1986)	Nutrition information in advertising
III. Smoking, Alcohol and Drug Abuse	
Andrews et al (1990)	Alcohol warning labels
Andrews and Franke (1991)	Determinants of cigarette consumption.
Atkin and Block (1984)	Alcohol advertising
Bhalla and Lastovicka (1984)	Cigarette warning label
Bloom and Franzak (1982)	State alcohol regulations
Bozinoff, Roth and May (1989)	Anti-drug and anti-alcohol campaigns
Darley and Lim (1991)	Drinking and driving
Ford, Ringold and Rogers (1990)	Cigarette advertising
Hornik (1989)	Determinants of cigarette consumption
Lastovicka et al (1987)	Drinking and driving
Levy and Sheflin (1985)	Alcohol demand and price elasticity

TABLE 2 (CONT'D)
Empirical Articles Reviewed

Social Marketing Topic & Articles	Specific Issue Investigated
Mayer, Smith and Scammon (1991)	Alcohol warning labels
Ornstein and Hanssens (1985)	State alcohol regulations
Popper and Murray (1989)	In-ad warning formats and impact
Ringold (1987)	Cigarette advertising
Ringold and Calfee (1990)	Cigarette advertising
Smith (1990)	Alcohol warning labels

IV. Other/Miscellaneous

Alexander and McCullough (1981)	Cervical cancer screening program
Allen (1985)	Health care cost containment policies
Andreasen and Belk (1980)	Performing arts
Barnett et al (1987)	Organ donation
Burns et al (1990)	Lottery playing and gambling addiction
Bush and Davies (1989)	Government and the AIDS crisis
Cox, Cox, and Moschis (1990)	Adolescent shoplifting.
Daser and Meric (1987)	Patriotism and purchase behavior
Friedman and Churchill (1987)	Dimensions of health care behavior
Hill (1991)	Homeless consumers
Hill and Stamey (1990)	Homeless consumers
Hornik and Sclinger (1981)	Dimensions of health care behavior
Hoyer and Jacoby (1983)	Contraceptive decision making
Marquis, Davies and Ware (1985)	Choosing health care providers
McIntyre et al (1987)	Organ donation
Moschis et al (1987)	Adolescent shoplifting
Rosenblatt et al (1986)	Charitable donations
Ross (1982)	Public policy and the elderly
Smead and Burnett (1981)	Blood donors
Stewart et al (1985)	Choosing health care providers
Wilm et al (1987)	Organ donation

*Due to the large amount of literature reviewed, we selectively entered references. Anyone who wants to see the full set of references may contact the authors.

ences between target groups. Again, these results suggest that the problem of obtaining useful data for identifying target segments may be overrated, or, alternatively, has been remedied in recent years.

Finally, with only two exceptions, results indicated most studies (97%) did not have the expected difficulty in defining effectiveness measures. Such measures ranged from memory for information on nutrition labels, to increased knowledge of AIDS-prevention measures, to decreased sales of alcoholic beverages over time. With regard to the contribution of findings to a social marketing program, most articles (68%) did not discuss results in the context of a particular social marketing program. For example, articles on nutrition and smoking often measured the effectiveness of warning labels, and included experimental designs that examined factors that were hypothesized to enhance warning effectiveness. However, of the articles that *did* report results of a social marketing program, most (92%) were able to determine whether the program element contributed significantly (whether successfully or unsuccessfully) to the program goals.

Program Implementation Issues

With regard to program implementation, we first examined, where relevant, whether any of the segmented targets was negatively predisposed to the program offerings. This proposition was also supported if the article specifically mentioned difficulty in reaching a particular segment that was "high risk" for the social issue in question. Of the articles for which this issue was relevant, the majority (64%) did report or imply that potential problems exist in reaching at least one high-risk segment that is negatively predisposed to the social marketing issue. The content areas in which these concerns were most dramatic pertained to smoking, alcohol and drug use. However, all content areas appeared to be affected by this problem to some extent.

The second program implementation issue examined was whether costs of changing the social consumer's behavior involved more than monetary costs. In over 90% of the articles, and across all content areas, non-monetary constraints on behavior (including psychic, energy, and/or time costs) were considered in the studies, thus supporting this proposition.

Finally, we examined whether, for studies that included a marketing communications component, more personal forms of communication (e.g. home visits, physician appointments) were used (and/or required) rather than mass media or direct mail, to convey information. We found that almost all (96%) of the articles that included a marketing communication component reported the use of mass media or direct mail, rather than a more personal form

TABLE 3
Number and Percent of Articles Confirming the Social Marketing Problem Examined

Social Marketing Topic

		Energy Consv./ Environment	Nutrition	Smoking, Alcohol and Drug Abuse	Other/ Misc.	Total
I. Research and Evaluation Issues						
1. Are good secondary data unavailable?	# Yes	0	1	0	7	8
	% Yes	0%	6.7%	0%	33.3%	10.5%
	# of articles*	(23)	(15)	(17)	(21)	(76)
2. Measures are not reliable or valid.	# Yes	6	0	10	13	29
	% Yes	27.3%	0%	58.8%	61.9%	38.7%
	# of articles	(22)	(15)	(17)	(21)	(75)
3. Difficulty identifying consumer behavior determinants.	# Yes	0	0	0	0	0
	% Yes	0%	0%	0%	0%	0%
	# of articles	(23)	(14)	(14)	(21)	(72)
4. Difficulty identifying target segments through research.	# Yes	0	0	0	0	0
	% Yes	0%	0%	0%	0%	0%
	# of articles	(20)	(14)	(13)	(20)	(67)
5. Difficulty in defining effectiveness measures.	# Yes	1	0	0	1	2
	% Yes	4.4%	0%	0%	5.9%	3.0%
	# of articles	(23)	(15)	(12)	(17)	(67)
6. Program contribution can not be evaluated.	# Yes	0	1	0	1	2
	% Yes	0%	20%	0%	20.0%	8.3%
	# of articles	(6)	(5)	(8)	(5)	(24)
II. Program Implementation Issues						
1. Segment exists with a negative predisposition.	# Yes	11	3	8	8	30
	% Yes	52.4%	42.9%	100%	72.7%	63.8%
	# of articles	(21)	(7)	(8)	(11)	(47)
2. Pricing involves more than monetary costs.	# Yes	20	13	15	21	69
	% Yes	86.9%	100%	93.8%	100.0%	94.5%
	# of articles	(23)	(13)	(6)	(21)	(73)
3. Personal, in-depth forms of communication used.	# Yes	0	0	0	2	2
	% Yes	0%	0%	0%	33.3%	4.0%
	# of articles	(22)	(15)	(7)	(6)	(50)
Total Number of Articles Considered		23	15	17	21	76

*Number of articles included in each analysis was determined by the number of articles for which a "yes" or "no" code could be determined (see Table 1) as supporting or not supporting the contended issue. Articles for which the particular issue could not be addressed, or was not addressed, were omitted from analysis.

---

of communication to convey information. Furthermore, the information conveyed (whether about the amount of sugar content in food or a plea to reduce one's thermostat) was often in the form of a simplified, rather than a complex, message.

DISCUSSION

Research and Evaluation Issues

The results of our study suggest that although some assumed limitations do occur in social marketing programs, many of these limitations occur for relatively few of the social marketing issues addressed in empirical research. Most of the research and evaluation issues examined in the present analysis were not problematic for most social marketing research studies. While studies of newly researched social marketing topics (e.g. AIDS, the homeless) yielded a paucity of secondary data sources, studies of most topics (smoking cessation, alcohol use, nutrition, energy conservation) did not indicate these concerns. Furthermore, concerns about identifying determinants of attitude and behavior, or identifying differences between preference or user groups, were not supported by the literature. Similarly, authors of research articles were able to successfully define their effectiveness measures (whether awareness, attitudes, behavior, etc.) and, where relevant, determine whether research results could be interpreted as successfully or unsuccessfully contributing to the social marketing program.

Even with regard to the reliability and validity of measures, problems were not encountered as frequently as expected. In most cases, researchers sought creative solutions to problems of reliability or self-report measures that were anticipated for the issues examined. For example, measuring a respondent's self-reported views on energy conservation could be verified through electricity costs (Fritzsche 1981).

Given that the research and evaluation problems anticipated in the social marketing literature were not supported by the present literature, the question remains as to how the discrepancies between the conceptual and empirical literatures can be resolved. One possibility is that, while research problems exist for social marketers, researchers have striven to overcome these obstacles in their research efforts. A contributing factor for these discrepancies may be that most criticisms levied on social marketing were made in the early 1980's. Since then, and included in the present review, the lion's share of the research on social marketing has been reported in the literature. Thus, the earlier problems anticipated for social marketers were not borne out to the degree anticipated. On the other hand, a possible limitation to the present results is that only published empirical studies were examined or that information relevant to our analysis was not included in the article. One might argue that numerous unpublished findings would reveal a different set of conclusions. Published data may show greater reliability of measures, greater ability to identify target segments, and greater ability to evaluate program effectiveness. Furthermore, the criteria for determining support or nonsupport for a proposition tested in the present research may have been unduly restrictive, although, as noted earlier, the present analysis was not meant to be exhaustive in addressing all potential problems faced by social marketers.

Finally, a possible explanation for the discrepancy between earlier conceptual articles and the empirical data reported here is that problems for social marketers exist for only a subset of social marketing issues. In particular, novelty of the issue, the size of the program, or the nature of the resources (financial, expertise, etc.) available to the program, may be moderating variables that affect whether research problems exist. Clearly, novelty of the issue (e.g. AIDS, the homeless) may affect the extent to which secondary data are available to the social marketer. Size of the program, and financial and expert resources available, may affect whether the appropriate amount and level of research data are collected, and the resulting reliability and validity of data findings. Although these moderating variables may create problems for social marketers, such problems are *not* specific to the marketing of social ideas. Future research might address the role of such moderating variables in creating limitations for social marketing research and program evaluation.

Program Implementation Issues

In contrast to the research and evaluation issues, concerns examined about program implementation were often supported by the empirical literature. For most social marketing topics, empirical articles suggested that a key market segment exists that is negatively predisposed to messages directed toward them or toward changing their behavior. These concerns were particularly important for smoking, alcohol and drug use studies, as well as miscellaneous other health issues. For example, alcohol abuse programs target chronic alcoholics who are so highly involved with drinking that changing their behavior would require a drastic change in their lifestyles. Unlike marketing of products, where marketers target those consumers most interested in the product, social marketing often requires targeting messages to segments that are initially unfavorable toward the message.

Both monetary and nonmonetary costs were found to be examined in social marketing research, consistent with prior conceptual arguments about the complexity of social marketing issues. Thus, for example, in addition to considering the price of cigarettes, the consumer is also likely to consider the social, health, and other psychological costs in his or her decision to quit smoking (or to continue smoking). However, it is important to note that nonmonetary costs are also important for virtually *all* marketing decisions, and are not unique to social marketing. For example, purchasing an automobile involves consideration of a complex array of factors, and, in fact, may be a more complex decision than deciding whether to turn down the thermostat in one's home an additional two degrees during the winter months. Moderating factors such as novelty of the decision or social marketing issue, the consumer's felt involvement in the decision, or, more generally, the extensiveness of information processing required for the decision, may be greater determinants of the complexity of the decision than whether the marketing decision is social or non-social (e.g. relating to a product). Future research might address the effects of such moderating influences.

The need for personal, educational, or in-depth, forms of communication in social marketing was not supported by the empirical literature. Generally, messages about social marketing issues (nutrition, smoking, energy conservation) were designed to be simple and easily conveyed to a wide audience and through mass media or direct mail. For example, hazards associated with smoking are presented on package labels (Bhalla and Lastovicka 1984). Hearts printed next to heart healthy items on restaurant menus, or colored tags next to items in grocery stores, have been used to convey to the consumer that these items are low-fat selections. Such simple messages were often quite effective. In fact, the extent to which a complex, "educational", message is required may be determined by the same moderating factors as noted previously. That is, the greater the novelty or innovativeness of the social marketing topic, or the greater the consumer involvement in the topic (cf. Rothschild 1979), the greater the need for high informational messages. In this sense, social marketing may yield more similarities than differences with non-social (e.g. product) marketing, where these moderating factors are likewise influential.

Implications and Conclusions for Research on Social Issues

The findings reported here have implications for future social research programs. First, social marketing is a progressing field that has perhaps overcome many of its early research difficulties, through enhanced database sources and improvements in the quality of research. Second, the issues involved in social marketing may be susceptible to the same concerns as found in product marketing. Both social and product marketers need to research and evaluate more carefully complex offerings. Third, there is a tendency for important high-risk target segments to be negatively predisposed to social marketing offerings, and these segments cannot be ignored in many programs. Social marketers need to be aware of this problem, and tailor their programs to attempt to alleviate discomfort or difficulties that consumers face in relation to an offering. Fourth, social marketers should continue to emphasize the importance of research and evaluation procedures to program organizers.

By making the effort to obtain high quality data at all stages of the program, social marketers can more effectively target communications and segments of the population in need of the offering.

Finally, social marketers need to continue to adopt techniques that facilitate behavior change. For example, energy conservation may be facilitated by thermostat monitors that automatically reduce temperatures during the night. Consumers concerned about AIDS may be more likely to seek information if an anonymous source, such as a counselor obtained through a toll-free number, is available for this sensitive issue. Examples in the literature abound (e.g. Hutton and Ahtola 1991, Levy et al 1985, Alexander and McCullough 1981) in which social marketing programs completed their goals by facilitating the social consumer's behavior change. As consumer researchers expand their work in these areas, we can probably expect continued success at impacting social change. Such findings should also continue to have significant political ramifications to enhance positive social change.

REFERENCES

Alexander, Katherine and James McCullough (1981), "Cultural Differences in Preventative Health Care Choice: A Study of Participation in a Cervical Cancer Screening Program Among Mexican-Americans," *Advances in Consumer Research*, 8, 617-632.

Andreasen, Alan R. (1984), "A Power Potential Approach to Middlemen: Strategies in Social Marketing," *European Journal of Marketing*, 18 (4), 56-71.

Barach, Jeffrey A. (1984), "Applying Marketing Principles to Social Causes," *Business Horizons*, (July-August) 65-69.

Bhalla, Gaurav and John L. Lastovicka (1984), "The Impact of Changing Cigarette Warning Message Content and Format," *Advances in Consumer Research*, 11, 305-310.

Bloom, Paul N. and Gary T. Ford (1979), "Evaluation of Consumer Education Programs," *Journal of Consumer Research*, 6 (December), 270-279.

Bloom, Paul N. and William D. Novelli (1981), "Problems and Challenges in Social Marketing," *Journal of Marketing*, 45 (Spring), 79-88.

Cole, Catherine A. and Gary J. Gaeth (1990), "Cognitive and Age-related Differences in the Ability to Use Nutritional Information in a Complex Environment," *Journal of Marketing Research*, 17, 175-184.

Ford, Gary T., Debra J. Ringold, and Martha Rogers (1990), "Cigarettes in the Popular Press, 1930-1960: Preliminary Research," *Advances in Consumer Research*, 17, 467-473.

Fox, Karen F.A. and Philip Kotler (1980), "The Marketing of Social Causes: The First 10 Years," *Journal of Marketing*, 44 (Fall), 24-33.

Fritzsche, David J. (1981), "An Analysis of Energy Consumption Patterns by Stage of Family Life Cycle," *Journal of Marketing Research*, 18, 227-232.

Hutton, R. Bruce and Olli T. Ahtola (1991), "Consumer Response to a Five-Year Campaign to Combat Air Pollution," *Journal of Public Policy and Marketing*, 10 (1), 242-256.

Kotler, Philip and Gerald Zaltman (1971), "Social Marketing: An Approach to Planned Social Change," *Journal of Marketing*, 35 (July), 3-12.

Levy, Alan S., Odonna Mathews, Marily Stephenson, Janet E. Tenney, and Raymond E. Schucker (1985), "The Impact of a Nutrition Information Program on Food Purchases," *Journal of Public Policy and Marketing*, 4, 1-13.

Rothschild, Michael (1979), "Marketing Communications in Nonbusiness Situations or Why it's so Hard to Sell Brotherhood Like Soap," *Journal of Marketing*, 43 (Spring), 11-20.

Sheth, Jagdish N. and Gary L. Frazier (1982), "A Model of Strategy Mix Choice for Planned Social Change," *Journal of Marketing*, 46 (Winter), 15-26.

A Longitudinal Examination of Addictive Consumption: Its Behavioral and Psychological Pattern and Consequences

Keiko I. Powers, University of California, Los Angeles

ABSTRACT

Research on deviant or abnormal behavior has been rare in the field of consumer behavior. The present paper provides empirical data on deviant consumer behavior, focusing on the case of narcotics addiction. Retrospective self-report data on addiction histories were collected from over 300 male addicts. Three sets of analyses were conducted: (1) comparisons of various behaviors between the addiction and non-addiction periods, (2) time-series analysis of relationships between narcotics use and economic behavior, and (3) examinations of perceived health/emotion status and family relationships. Results clearly indicated negative effects of prolonged drug addiction on their behaviors and perceived physical and psychological status.

INTRODUCTION

Investigations of "abnormal" or "deviant" behavior have been quite rare in the consumer behavior field (Krych, 1989; Moschis, 1989). Although more researchers have started focusing on the issues recently, related topics have been limited to compulsive spending (Faber and O'Guinn, 1989; O'Guinn and Faber, 1989) or impulsive buying (Rook, 1987), credit card abuse (Faber and O'Guinn, 1988), shoplifting (Cox et al, 1990), and consumption patterns among homeless people (Hill and Stamey, 1990).

As Moschis and Cox (1989) stated, full understanding of consumer behavior requires examinations of the undesirable as well as desirable patterns and consequences of the behavior. Deviant consumer behavior can be more common than we might expect. For example, sudden unemployment due to layoffs could cause many people to adjust their consumption behaviors to a deviant pattern until they find a new job with comparable compensation. Need for long-term health care might be another case of deviant consumer behavior. A family member may need expensive health care to the point that the related cost destroys the balanced consumption pattern of the household.

Still, another example of deviant consumer behavior is the case of drug addiction. To many individuals in the United States today, addictive consumption of drugs is one of the most serious personal as well as social problems. It is often the case that consumer behavior of these drug dependent individuals is heavily affected by a physical and psychological need for the drug. The purpose of the present study is to illustrate how addictive consumption of drugs influences an individual's life patterns. More specifically, the paper examines effects of prolonged narcotics addiction on various behaviors (e.g., crime involvement, marital/family status, or employment) and psychological/health status. In conclusion, the paper discusses common features of the present findings compared to other literature on abnormal consumer behavior (i.e., compulsive spending or homeless people).

METHODS

Sample

The sample consists of 354 male narcotics addicts selected from admissions to the California Civil Addict Program (CAP) in 1962-64[1]. These subjects were interviewed twice in follow-up studies conducted in 1974/75 and 1985/86. A more detailed description of the sampling procedure can be found in Anglin and McGlothlin (1984). Background characteristics of the sample are presented in Table 1. The ethnic make-up is 28 blacks, 204 Chicano, and 122 whites. Most were from middle- or working-class families and had semiskilled or unskilled occupations. The majority were legally married at some time point of their life and had children. The mean ages at which narcotics use and legal system contact occurred indicate that the subjects were involved in criminal activities and started using narcotics in their late teens.

Interview Procedure

The interview procedure was adapted in part from one developed by Nurco and colleagues (Nurco, Bonito, Lerner, and Balter, 1975) and has been described in detail in an earlier paper (McGlothlin, Anglin, and Wilson, 1977). Briefly, a schematic time chart was prepared before the interview, showing all official records of arrests, intervals of incarceration, legal status, and treatment. The interviewer established the date of first narcotic use on the time chart, then augmented the time chart with respondents' self-report of other important life events (e.g., births, moves, or employment) suitable to assist in recall. Starting from the time of first narcotics use, the interviewer recorded all time points when narcotics use changed from less than daily use to daily use (or vice versa), or when the respondent's legal supervision or treatment status changed. These time points were used to divide the respondent's addiction history into several intervals, which were uniform in terms of narcotics use, legal status, and drug treatment enrollment. Self-reported data were then collected for each of these intervals on narcotics, alcohol, and other drug use; employment; drug dealing; criminal behavior; and certain other variables. In this way, the entire addiction history was recorded, from the time of first narcotics use to the time of interview.[2]

Variables and Planned Analyses

The present longitudinal data cover over 30 years of their addiction histories, including various behavioral (e.g., drug addiction, dealing, crime), social-function (e.g., marriage, employment), and intervention (e.g., legal supervision, treatment) time-series measures. In addition, several measures on self-perceptions of physical and psychological status are provided.

Three sets of analyses are based on these time-series and perception measures to explore the patterns and effects of addictive consumption: (1) comparisons of various behavioral involvements

---

[1] The California Civil Addict Program (CAP), initiated in 1961 and administered by the California Department of Corrections, had two phases over a seven-year commitment period: incarceration and then parole, or monitored release into the community. The CAP program was the only compulsory program in California for the treatment and control of narcotic addiction, which provided nonpunitive legal treatment.

[2] The interview was conducted by trained professionals under the face-to-face setting to maximize the information accuracy. Hser, Anglin, and Chou (in press) examined the test-retest reliabilities of the data. The reliabilities of the variables used in the present study ranged from moderate to high (.43 - .73).

TABLE 1.
Background Characteristics

	N	% or Mean
Gender (%)		
Male	354	100.0
Ethnicity (%)		
Black	28	7.9
Chicano	204	57.6
White	122	34.5
Socioeconomic status of family (%)		
Poor		13.9
Working class		36.1
Middle		36.4
Upper-middle		13.6
Mean highest grade completed		10.1
Family drug problem (%)		19.1
Family alcohol problem (%)		38.4
Main occupation (%)		
Skilled		39.8
Semiskilled		44.4
Unskilled		14.7
Never worked		1.1
Mean age at		
First arrest		18.0
First narcotics use (FNU)		18.3
First daily use		20.1
First legal supervision		22.5
CAP admission		25.0
CAP discharge		31.2
First interview		36.5
Second interview		47.7
Incarcerated >30 days prior to FNU (%)		50.8
Married at least once (%)		83.6
Had children (%)		86.4

Note: the values are based on the information obtained at the time of second interview.

between the period of daily narcotics use and that of either non-daily-use or abstinence status, (2) time series analysis of economic behavior[3], which examines the relationship between narcotics use and changes in monetary activities (i.e., employment, welfare, dealing, and property crime) over time, and (3) an examination of effects of narcotics use on self-perceptions of their physical, psychological, and family status.

These analyses were conducted for the pre-CAP (Civil Addict Program) and post-CAP periods separately to examine consistencies and differences between the two periods[4]. The second analysis was based on group-aggregate time-series measures. To obtain the aggregate time series, first, time series on activity involvement (e.g., daily narcotics use or employment) for each subject was provided separately, using bimonthly periods as time intervals. (To accommodate to the part-time factor, if the activity involvement was less than two months for any given interval, the value was weighed accordingly.) Next, for each of the bimonthly periods, the mean across all the subjects was calculated. The obtained values represent the percentage of subjects involved in the activity for a given bimonthly period. The same method was used for all the variables. These time series variables were used to develop two multivariate time-series models, one for the pre-CAP period and the other for the post-CAP period[5].

---

[3] According to van Raaij (1991), economic behavior is defined as "the behavior of consumers/citizens that involves economic decisions, and the determinants and consequences of economic decisions" (p. 383).

[4] During years 1964 through 1969, the majority of the subjects were under the CAP in-house treatment and were "off street." Therefore, an assessment of their addiction-related behavioral patterns was irrelevant for this period. Furthermore, it was expected that their addiction life style was quite different between the pre-CAP and post-CAP periods. The present study compared the two periods whenever appropriate.

[5] Time-series models based on these group-aggregate measures focus on group dynamics over time. The models do not allow us to discuss individual differences; however, these models are useful for understanding the relationships between narcotics use and various behaviors as the global social phenomenon.

TABLE 2
Comparisons of Various Activity Involvement between Daily-Use and Non-Daily-Use Periods

	Pre-CAP period (1954-1964)		Post-CAP period (1970-1986)	
	Daily-Use Period	Non-Daily-Use Period	Daily-Use Period	Non-Daily-Use Period
(Mean no. of month)	(34)	(43)	(51)	(122)
Activity[a]				
Dealing	55	22	58	19
Property crime	49	25	40	7
Employment	46	61	36	76
Welfare	0	1	9	11
Treatment	0	0	6	19
Married[b]	—	—	28	49
Common-law[b]	—	—	32	18
Alcohol use	19	50	26	42
Daily marijuana use	11	29	6	11
Other drug use	5	9	7	4

[a] The values represent the mean activity involvement across all the subjects (N=354). For example, the subjects were employed 46 percent of the pre-CAP daily-use period and 61 percent of the pre-CAP non-daily-use period. When the subject was incarcerated, that time period was excluded from the computation.
[b] missing information for the pre-CAP period.

RESULTS AND DISCUSSION

Comparisons between Daily-Use and Non-Daily-Use Periods

Table 2 presents the means of various behavioral measures across the 354 subjects for the four periods, i.e., (1) the pre-CAP daily-use (i.e., using narcotics daily), (2) the pre-CAP non-daily-use (i.e., using less than daily or being abstinent), (3) the post-CAP daily-use and the (4) post-CAP non-daily-use periods. As a group, the mean number of months for the four periods was 34, 43, 51, and 122, respectively (see the top column in Table 2). These values excluded the time the subject was incarcerated. The mean activity values indicate the changes in behavioral involvements among the four periods. For example, the subjects were, on average, employed 46 percent of the pre-CAP daily-use period (i.e., approximately 26 months out of the 34-month period) but 61 percent of the pre-CAP non-daily-use period.

These values clearly indicate the effect of narcotics addiction on various behaviors. Compared to the non-addiction period, the addiction period shows more dealing, and more property crime, but less employment and welfare, and less marijuana use. The patterns are consistent between the pre- and post-CAP periods. Methadone treatment (i.e., medical treatment for narcotics addicts), marital status, and common-law relationship during the post-CAP period also show clear effects of narcotics use. Although most of the values are similar between the pre- and post-CAP periods, methadone treatment and welfare show a substantial increase during the post-CAP period compared to the pre-CAP period.

Relationships between Narcotics Use and Economic Behavior

In order to better understand how the addicts' dependency on different income sources changed over time and whether or not the pattern differed between the pre- and post-CAP periods, two time-series models for each period were developed for the four monetary measures in Table 2. Two narcotics use measures, daily use and no use (abstinence from narcotics), were also included to examine their relationships to these monetary measures. Figures 1 and 2 plot the six time-series variables for the pre-CAP and the post-CAP period, respectively.

Figure 1 illustrates changes of narcotics use and economic behavior between 1954 and 1964, before CAP admission, at the group-aggregate level. The period covers the average age of late teens to early twenties. The time-series plots clearly show a steady increase in the percentage of subjects using narcotics daily (Daily Use) over time and a corresponding decrease of abstinence status (No Use). Both Dealing and Crime are fairly stable over time; however, Employment displays a sharp decline right before CAP admission. Dependency on welfare is very low (almost zero on the plot) during the entire pre-CAP period.

Figure 2 covers years 1970 through 1986, the period after CAP discharge. The subjects are in their thirties and forties on the average during this period, and narcotics use and economic behavior seem to reflect the age factor. The time-series plots show a steady increase in abstinence status (No Use) and a progressive decrease of Daily Use. Employment and Welfare also show increasing trends over time. Although Dealing and Crime are stable over time, their overall levels are lower compared to the pre-CAP period.

Multivariate time-series models were developed on narcotics use and economic behavior, using a new time series technique called "cointegration and error-correction modeling" (Engle and Granger, 1987). The approach allows a differential assessment of long-term, short-term, and contemporaneous relationships. Briefly, long-term relationships depict how time-series stochastic trends relate to each other, whereas short-term relationships describe how temporary fluctuations from the trends of one variable are related to those of other variables. The former relationship focuses on "equilibrium," or closely tied relationships over time. On the other hand, the latter represents how the changes of one variable from one

FIGURE 1
Time Series Data for the Pre-CAP Period (1954-1964)

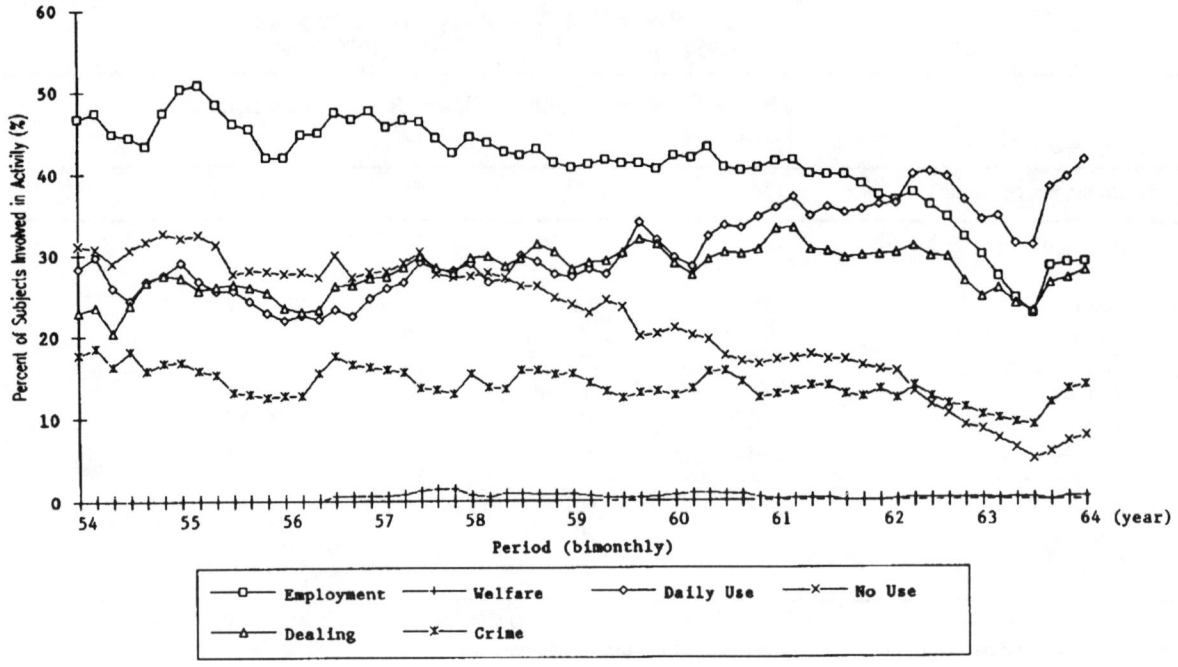

FIGURE 2
Time Series Data for the Post-CAP Period (1970-1986)

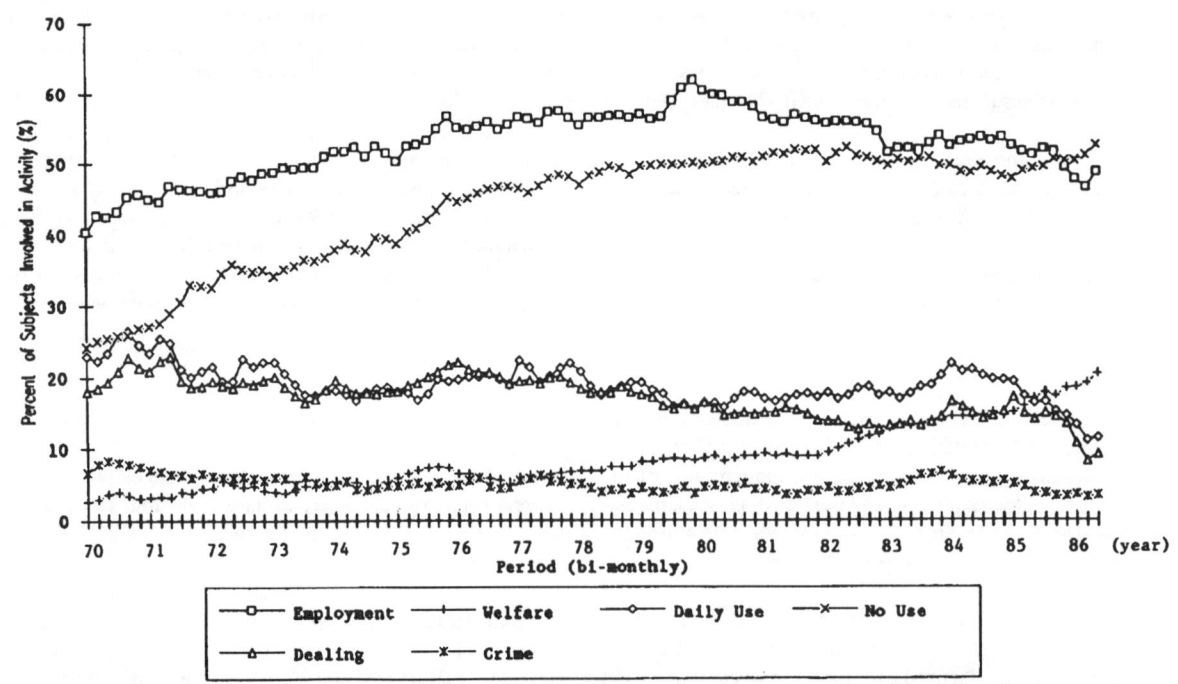

TABLE 3
Long-Term and Contemporaneous Relationships between Economic Behavior and Narcotics Use

(1) Long-Term Relationships

	Employment	Welfare	Dealing	Crime	No Use	Daily Use
Employment						
Welfare	2−					
Dealing	1+ 2+	1+				
Crime	1+		1− 2−			
No Use	1+ 2+					
Daily Use			1+ 2+	1+ 2+		

(2) Contemporaneous Relationships

	Employment	Welfare	Dealing	Crime	No Use	Daily Use
Employment						
Welfare						
Dealing	1+ 2+					
Crime	1+		1+			
No Use	1+ 2+		1+	1+		
Daily Use	1+		1+ 2+	1+ 2+	2−	

Note: For each cell, the numbers indicate that the relationship between the column and the row variables is statistically significant. The numbers "1" and "2" are for the pre-CAP and for the post-CAP period, respectively. The symbol '+' represents the positive association, and '−' represents the negative association.

Short-term relationships were virtually nonexistent, and therefore a summary table was not provided here. The only significant short-term relationships were (1) a negative association between No Use and the lagged Welfare (i.e., welfare status at the previous time period) for the pre-CAP period and (2) a positive association between Daily Use and the lagged Daily Use for the post-CAP period.

---

time period to the next are related to those of other variables. Contemporaneous relationships are similar to the regular correlational relationship, but with this approach, this last type of relationship is controlled for the long-term and short-term relationships (see Powers et al., 1991, for more detailed discussion).

Table 3 gives a summary of the multivariate time-series models for the pre- and post-CAP periods[6]. Each cell in Table 3 represents the relationship between the column and the row variables. An empty cell means there is no statistically significant relationship. The numbers "1" and "2" indicate the existence of a relationship for the pre-CAP and the post-CAP period, respectively. The symbol "+" after the number represents a positive association, and "−" represents a negative association.

[6] The parameter estimates of the time-series models can be obtained from the author upon request.

Overall, the system dynamics are characterized by long-term and contemporaneous relationships for both pre- and post-CAP periods. Virtually, no short-term relationships are observed; the only significant short-term relationships are a negative association between No Use and the lagged Welfare (i.e., welfare status at the previous time period) for the pre-CAP period and a positive association between Daily Use and its own previous status for the post-CAP period. The following section further discusses the relationships found with the time series models, focusing on the relationships of narcotics use with legal (i.e., employment and welfare) and illegal (i.e., dealing and crime) economic behavior.

Narcotics Use and Legal Economic Behavior. A consistent pattern between the pre- and post-CAP periods is the positive association between Employment and No Use. The positive relationship implies that these addicts were more likely to behave as a more productive citizen, holding legitimate jobs, when they could maintain abstinence from narcotics. On the other hand, no clear relationship is observed between Welfare and the drug use variables; the only significant relationship is the negative short-term relationship between No Use and the previous Welfare status during the pre-CAP period. This negative relationship could be a reflection of their misuse of welfare income to support their narcotics habit, but further investigation is needed to cross-validate the relationship.

Narcotics Use and Illegal Economic Behavior. The close links between narcotics use behavior and crime/dealing are clearly seen in Table 3. For both pre- and post-CAP periods, the time-series models indicate the positive associations between Daily Use and Dealing and between Daily Use and Crime. The addicts tended to get involved in dealing and property crime more when they were using narcotics daily. Rather surprising is, however, the positive relationships of No Use with both Dealing and Crime for the pre-CAP period. The pattern seems to reflect the addicts' heavy criminal involvement during their young ages, even at the time when they were maintaining their abstinence status.

Legal and Illegal Economic Behavior. When relationships among the four income-generating behaviors are examined, a consistent pattern observed is the positive relationship between Dealing and Employment. For both pre- and post-CAP periods, as dealing increased, employment tended to increase, and visa versa. Other significant relationships are the negative long-term and positive contemporaneous relationships between Dealing and Crime, and the relationships involving welfare status (i.e., the positive relationship with Dealing for the pre-CAP period and the negative relationship with Employment for the post-CAP period).

The above relationships represent how these addicts allocated their efforts among different income-generating activities over time. Particularly interesting are the positive long-term association between Dealing and Employment and the negative long-term association between Dealing and Crime. Though further analyses would be needed to determine the causal direction of these relationships, the observed relationships suggest that these addicts tended to hold a legitimate job and deal drugs at the same time but tended not to commit property crime when dealing drugs. Some possible explanations are that the addicts acted businesslike, being engaged in multiple income-generating activities to financially support themselves. However, they might have considered the legal activity (i.e., employment) different from the illegal activities. As a result, when they are heavily involved in dealing, for example, they spent less time in committing property crime while they maintained their employment status.

Overall, the multivariate models provided data to support various relationships, such as the positive relationships between daily use and dealing/crime and the positive relationship between no use and employment. Some relationships, however, were unexpected, such as the positive associations between Employment and Crime and between Employment and Daily Use during the pre-CAP period. A possible explanation is that the relationships reflect these addicts' "out-of-control" status (i.e., heavy narcotics use and associated pattern of economic behavior) before the CAP admission.

Self-Perceptions of Physical/Psychological/Family Status

Table 4 summarizes the addicts' perception of family relationships during their past and that of their physical and psychological status at the second interview conducted in 1985/86. For the physical and psychological status, the total sample was divided into two groups, those who were using narcotics (Active) and those who were not (Inactive) at the time of interview, in order to examine if the drug-use status affected their self-perception.

The frequency distributions clearly illustrate negative consequences of narcotics addiction on all the measures. More subjects stated that they were happier and spent more time with family when not using narcotics during the past. Comparisons between the Active and Inactive groups indicated that the latter tended to feel more positive about their health and emotional status and tended to be happier at the time of interview. Furthermore, many expressed their concern about AIDS infection, especially the active addicts.

Two of these perception measures (the remaining measures were not available) were examined for the first interview to compare and contrast the perception changes. The first interview was conducted approximately 10 years prior to the second interview. While the same pattern was obtained for "opinion of life now," the measure "physical health now" indicated a much more positive viewpoint at the first interview. More than 30% of them reported "excellent," and approximately 15% reported "poor" or "fair." Furthermore, the narcotics use status at the time of interview did not show any effect on their perception of physical health. The results imply the negative long-term impacts of narcotics use on the perception of their physical condition.

GENERAL DISCUSSION

Behavioral/Psychological Pattern of Narcotics Addiction

The purpose of the present study has been to illustrate the longitudinal pattern of consumer behavior affected by narcotics addiction and the consequences of such a consumption pattern on physical and psychological status. The majority of the sample was those who had been heavily involved in criminal activities with numerous arrest records. Despite their criminal activities, however, most of them held employment, particularly when they were not using narcotics daily. Over 80% of these subjects married at least once, and about the same proportion of them had fathered children.

Effects of narcotics abuse on various parts of their lives were evident in all the data provided in the present study. For both the pre-CAP (approximately 10 years) and the post-CAP (about 16.5 years) periods, daily narcotics use was associated with more illegal activities and with less socially desirable activities. Time series analysis was conducted to examine the longitudinal pattern of economic behavior and narcotics use. The models demonstrated the effects of narcotics use on their monetary activities. Particularly important were the positive relationship of daily narcotics use with dealing and property crime and the positive relationship of abstinence from narcotics with employment status. The relationships illustrated the consistent and persistent pattern of how these individuals allocated their time for earning money, which was mainly used to support their narcotics use habit. The pattern seems to highlight these addicts' "locked-in" status where their economic behavior was virtually dictated by their needs for narcotics consumption.

Finally, effects of drug involvement were observed on perceptions of family relationships, life fulfillment, health concern, and psychological status. In particular, comparisons between the Inactive and Active subjects indicated negative views by more individuals of the Active group on most of the measures. The negative long-term effect of narcotics use on perception of physical condition was supported by the observed difference between the first and the second interview.

Narcotics Addiction and Deviant Consumer Behavior

Krych (1989) listed problems associated with addictive behavior: family problems, monetary problems, health and emotional problems, and legal, job, and social problems. The present study illustrated that addictive drug consumption is closely tied to all these problems. Anglin and Powers (in press) found that though medical treatments and legal interventions are effective in control-

TABLE 4
Self-Perceived Physical/Psychological States and Family Relationships Reported at the Second Interview

(I) Narcotics use and family relationships

	%
Spend time w/ family when using daily	
Never/rarely	46.0
Sometimes	36.6
Often/always	17.4
Spend time w/ family when not using	
Never/rarely	13.0
Sometimes	29.6
Often/always	57.4
Happier (during the past)	
When using	20.1
Not using	66.6
Can't say	13.3

(II) Comparisons of physical/psychological states between Active and Inactive groups

	Active[a] (N=209)	Inactive[a] (N=145)
	%	%
Physical health now +[b]		
Poor	9.6	6.9
Fair	23.9	23.5
Good	56.6	49.7
Excellent	10.0	20.0
Concerned about health now		
Not at all/very little	18.5	14.9
Moderate	19.4	31.2
Much/very much	62.1	53.9
Concerned about AIDS now **		
Not at all/very little	62.3	83.3
Moderate	12.1	6.3
Much/very much	25.6	10.4
Emotional state now **		
Poor	8.1	5.5
Fair	31.6	21.4
Good	40.7	37.9
Very good/excellent	19.6	35.2
Opinion of life now ***		
Unhappy	31.9	12.4
Mixed	27.1	25.5
Satisfied	41.1	62.1

[a] Active Group and Inactive Group were defined as those who were using narcotics daily at the time of second interview and those who were not, respectively.

[b] The comparisons were based on chi-square statistics (+ = $p<.10$ * = $p<.05$ ** = $p<.01$ *** = $p<.001$)

ling illegal activities and promoting more socially desirable behaviors among drug-dependent individuals, these individuals are not receiving sufficient interventions. Direct and indirect social costs due to drug addiction are astonishingly high (estimated over $60 billion in 1985 (Rice et al., 1990)). The intensity of this serious social problem suggests the importance of a better understanding of drug addiction to provide more effective social interventions.

In the consumer behavior context, future research efforts that compare and contrast or integrate various forms of deviant behavior may be fruitful. For example, behavioral/psychological patterns associated with drug addiction share several common features with other forms of deviant behavior. Hill and Stamey (1990) reported that homeless people become totally focused on obtaining food and shelter. Likewise, lives of narcotics addicts are centered upon consumption of drugs. These two cases share the common feature that the consumer pattern is affected by some uncontrollable (or out-of-control) external factor. Furthermore, the strong urge to use drugs, or its psychological status, resembles the drive to buy, which is observed in compulsive buying (O'Guinn and Faber, 1989). Both homelessness and compulsive buying are very likely associated with family or monetary problems, as with the case of drug addiction. The possibility of subsequent health/emotional or other related problems (e.g. job loss) are also not negligible for all these cases. The comparisons clearly indicate the underlying commonalties among these different forms of deviant consumer behavior.

The existence of the commonalties suggest that these various forms of obsessive-compulsive problems can possibly be studied by applying the same underlying theories and principles. In fact, Mule (1981) emphasized the importance of understanding commonalties among various excessive behaviors for better treatment or prevention. Furthermore, from the perspective of consumer behavior, research efforts on these related topics are a valuable step toward the notion of "the intersection of consumer behavior and social policy" advocated by Andreasen (1991). Exploring how "normal" consumption goes wrong can help us better understand both normal and abnormal consumer behavior (O'Guinn and Faber, 1989). These factors underscore the worth of integrating various forms of deviant problems. The idea of abnormal or deviant consumer behavior is still new. More research efforts are called for which further explore this important topic.

REFERENCES

Andreasen, Alan R. (1991), "Consumer Behavior Research and Social Policy," in Thomas S. Robertson and Harold H. Kassarjian (Eds.), *Handbook of Consumer Behavior*, Englewood Cliffs, New Jersey: Prentice Hall.

Anglin, M. Douglas, and William H. McGlothlin (1984), "Outcome of Narcotic Addict Treatment in California," in F. Tims and J. Ludford (Eds.), *Drug Abuse Treatment Evaluation: Strategies, Progress, and Prospects, NIDA Research Monograph 51, DHHS Publication No. (ADM) 84-1349*. Rockville, MD: NIDA.

Anglin, M. Douglas, and Keiko I. Powers (in press), "Methadone Treatment and Legal Supervision: Individual and Joint Effects on the Behavior of Narcotics Addicts," *Journal of Applied Behavior Science*.

Cox, Dena, Anthony D. Cox, and George P. Moschis (1990), "When Consumer Behavior Goes Bad: An Investigation of Adolescent Shoplifting," *Journal of Consumer Research*, 17, 149-159.

Engle, Robert F. and Clive W.J. Granger (1987), "Co-Integration and Error Correction: Representation, Estimation, and Testing," *Econometrica*, 55, 251-276.

Faber, Ronald J., and Thoman C. O'Guinn (1988), "Compulsive Consumption and Credit Abuse," *Journal of Consumer Policy*, 11, 109-121.

Faber, Ronald J., and Thoman C. O'Guinn (1989), "Classifying Compulsive Consumers: Advances in the Development of a Diagnostic Tool" in Thomas K. Srull (Ed.), *Advances in Consumer Research*, Vol. 16, 738-744.

Hill, Ronald P., and Mark Stamey (1990), "The Homeless in America: An Examination of Possessions and Consumption Behaviors," *Journal of Consumer Research*, 17, 303-321.

Hser, Yih-Ing, M. Douglas Anglin, and Chih-Ping Chou (in press), "Reliability of Retrospective Self-Report by Narcotics Addicts," *Psychological Assessment: Journal of Consulting and Clinical Psychology*.

Krych, Raymond (1989), "Abnormal Consumer Behavior: A Model of Addictive Behaviors," in Thomas K. Srull (Ed.), *Advances in Consumer Research*, Vol. XVI, 745-748.

McGlothlin, William H., M. Douglas Anglin, and Bruce D. Wilson (1977), "A Follow-Up of Admissions to the California Civil Addict Program," *American Journal of Drug and Alcohol Abuse*, 4, 179-199.

Moschis, George P., and Dena Cox (1989), "Deviant Consumer Behavior," in Thomas K. Srull (Ed.), *Advances in Consumer Research*, Vol. XVI, 732-737.

Mule, S. Joseph (1981), *Behavior in Excess: An Examination of the Volitional Disorders*, New York: the Free Press.

Nurco, D.N., and A.J. Bonito, M. Lerner, and M.B. Balter (1975), "Studying Addicts over Time: Methodology and Preliminary Findings," *American Journal of Drug and Alcohol Abuse*, 2, 183-196.

O'Guinn Thoman C., and Ronald J. Faber (1989), "Compulsive Buying: A Phenomenological Exploration," *Journal of Consumer Research*, 16, 147-157.

Powers, Keiko I., Dominique M. Hanssens, Yih-Ing Hser, and M. Douglas Anglin (1991), "Measuring the Long-Term Effects of Public Policy: The Case of Narcotics Use and Property Crime," *Management Science*, 37, 627-644.

van Raaij, W. Fred (1991), "Economic Psychology," in Harold H. Kassarjian and Thomas S. Robertson (Eds.), *Perspectives in Consumer Behavior*, Englewood Cliffs, New Jersey: Prentice Hall.

Rice, Dorothy P., S. Kelman, L. Miller, and S. Dunmeyer, (1990), *The Economic Costs of Alcohol, Drug Abuse, and Mental Illness — 1985*, Institute for Health and Aging, University of California, San Francisco.

Rook, Dennis W. (1987), "The Buying Impulse," *Journal of Consumer Research*, 14, 189-199.

Social Marketing and Consumer Behavior: Influencing the Decision To Reduce Alcohol Consumption

Jean C. Darian, Rider College

ABSTRACT

The purpose of this study was to use a marketing approach to deal with the problem of alcohol abuse on a college campus. A survey collected data pertaining to the process students would go through in the decision to reduce their alcohol intake. We segmented the students on the basis of their drinking and abuse levels, and used the results to formulate product, pricing, promotion and distribution strategies. We conclude that there are challenges to be overcome when applying a marketing approach, particularly in the area of product development.

INTRODUCTION

There has been some dispute about the concept of social marketing since Kotler and Zaltman (1971) introduced the idea two decades ago, including a questioning of the appropriateness of broadening the marketing discipline to include social marketing (Luck 1974). Whyte (1985) however, holds that "once the idea of intangible products and non-monetary prices is accepted, then the marketing paradigm is valid for the whole domain of marketing". This paper discusses the results of a survey conducted in 1990 to help choose effective marketing strategies to reduce alcohol abuse at a northeastern college, a case where the product is intangible and the price is primarily non-monetary. We will discuss the advantages of a marketing approach as well as some difficulties encountered in applying this approach.

According to Kotler and Roberto (1989), included among the goals of social marketing is bringing about a change from an adverse behavior. This is the goal of the college administration in the area of the alcohol-related behavior of students. The overall objective of the college administration is to eliminate alcohol abuse and its undesirable consequences, while maintaining responsible drinking. This objective recognizes some of the broader objectives of the college as a whole, which include providing a conducive learning environment for students, and projecting a positive image to students, their parents, and the public at large. Any strategies employed to reduce alcohol abuse should aim to do this without threatening the college's overall objective. For example, effectively eliminating alcohol abuse on campus but shifting it to off-campus locations would harm the college's image.

In investigating strategies for reducing alcohol abuse at the college, we considered the following areas. 1. Segmentation of the student population on the basis of alcohol related behaviors. 2. Product substitutes. Our exploration of this was limited as we did not know prior to conducting the survey what combination of wants alcohol consumption was satisfying for abusive drinkers. We chose several nonalcoholic recreational activities as direct substitutes, and reduced stress and personal problem resolution as indirect substitutes. 3. The "price" of abusive drinking and of substitutes. As previous scholars have noted (Bloom 1980, Kotler and Roberto 1989), the price of a behavior includes psychic, energy, and time costs as well as monetary. Our survey has investigated costs and benefits of drinking and of reducing drinking as perceived by the students. We view stricter college alcohol policies as increasing the price (cost) of abusive drinking. 4. Promotion, including what type of information and education would be effective in persuading abusive drinkers to change their behavior. 5. Distribution, where we place alcohol counseling and peer counseling because they provide access to product substitutes, and so are analagous to service retailers.

These marketing strategies can affect students at various stages of the consumer decision-making process, and as DePaulo et. al. (1986) noted, they may have different effects at each stage.

METHODOLOGY

The sample

The survey instrument involves a questionnaire with 142 structured questions and one open-ended question. The questionnaire was pretested and revised twice before being administered to the final sample. We used a systematic, stratified cluster sample, with a dormitory room as the sampling unit. The drop-off method was used to distribute 841 questionnaires, and 459 were completed and returned, a response rate of 54.6%. The remaining questionnaires were either not received (not-at-homes, outright refusals, or prolonged delays), or filled out incorrectly. The final, usable, number of responses was 388, about 20% of the college resident population. 60% of the sample are females, indicating a higher female response rate, but the sample is representative of class standing. 61 percent are under 21 years.

Analysis

We analyze the total sample at various stages of the consumer decision-making process using frequency distributions of responses. In addition, we have segmented the respondents on the basis of their drinking behavior and its negative consequences. Students were asked how many drinks they typically had on each day of the week, how many times they had drunk alone, with a group, and at specified locations. They were also asked how many times in the past three months they had (specified) negative or undesirable experiences as a result of drinking. The sample was segmented on the basis of these behavioral variables using principal components and cluster analysis (average linkage between groups). Principal components analysis was used to reduce the 25 behavioral variables to a few linear combinations. With a minimum eigenvalue of 2.0, this analysis yielded two factors. The first factor reflected the quantity of drinking, and the second the amount of abuse, i.e. the number and frequency of negative consequences resulting from drinking. Respondents were clustered on the component scores of the two factors. After aggregating clusters with very small populations, the drinking population formed four segments (four cases were unclassified due to incomplete information). The nondrinkers form a fifth segment. A description of the segments is given below:

N	Segment Name	Description
40	Nondrinkers	Never drink alcohol
139	Responsible drinkers	Light drinkers, low abuse
140	Teflon drinkers	Heavy drinkers, low abuse
52	Hazardous drinkers	Heavy drinkers, high abuse
13	Troubled drinkers	Light drinkers, high abuse

All segment names have been coined by the author. The four drinking segments have a similar range of scores on the drinking factor, but the hazardous segment has a wider range on the abuse factor than the other three groups. Although the troubled drinkers'

FIGURE 1

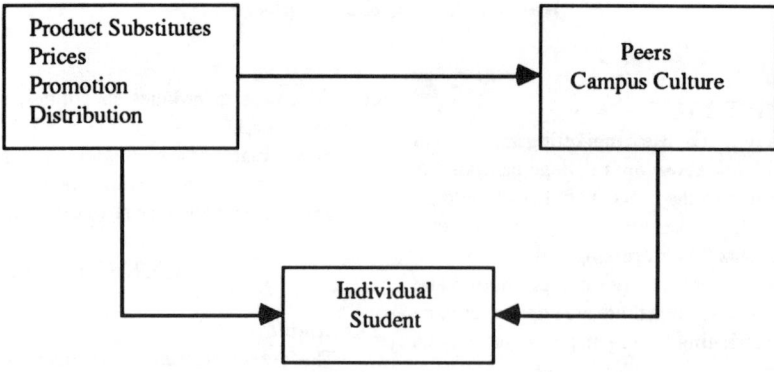

segment is very small, it is included in the analysis as it exhibits some intriguing patterns.

The college has no desire to change the behavior of the nondrinkers and responsible drinkers, but would clearly like to affect the behavior of the hazardous and troubled drinkers. The position of the teflon drinkers is less clear. A survey conducted at another college by Matross (1982) found that students do not view this type of drinker as a problem drinkers. In addition, their low abuse level suggests they are not an immediate problem for the administration. However, their high level of alcohol consumption clearly puts them at risk.

For variables using rating scales, we used analysis of variance to test for the significance of differences between segments. The least squares difference test was used to test for significant differences between each pair of segments. For nominally-scaled variables, we used chi-square analysis. Throughout the paper, any differences between segments that are mentioned in the text are significant at the .05% level.

CONSUMER BACKGROUND VARIABLES

Our sample is drawn from a specialized segment of the total United States drinking population; resident undergraduate students in a small college. Hence the respondents differ from the general U.S. drinking population in demographic and lifestyle characteristics, and in their social environment. As we will discuss, this leads to a distinctive drinking environment which suggests different strategies from the general population.

Drinking Behavior and Consequences

Drinking at the college is widespread. Over half (52 percent) of students who drink said they typically had five or more servings at least one day per week. This high drinking level is consistent with that found in other studies of campus drinking (Harford et.al. 1983, Kraft, 1985; Smith, 1989; U.S. Department of Health and Human Services, 1989). There are no significant differences in drinking levels by age, in spite of the fact that drinking on campus is illegal for students under 21. There are large variations in drinking levels by day of the week, with a concentration of drinking on Thursdays, Fridays and Saturdays.

The percent of drinking respondents who reported experiencing the following negative consequences of drinking at least once during the past three months are as follows:

80%	Getting drunk
42%	Cutting classes or poor performance on examinations
32%	Conflict with a close friend or a girl/boy friend
23%	Thinking should cut down on or stop drinking
27%	Having a fight with someone
25%	Driving a car after having several drinks
19%	Having sex without birth control
12%	Damaging property or pulling a fire alarm
9%	Having trouble with the school administration

Social Environment at the College

Studies of drinking on campus have found that the social environment at colleges is a major contributor to drinking problems, especially when drinking becomes a primary social activity (Gonzalez, 1988; Kraft, 1985). Our research is consistent with other studies (Harford, 1983) in showing that drinking at the college is mainly a social activity. Only 5% of respondents had drunk alone three or more times in the previous month. However, only 14 percent of respondents said peer pressure was an important reason for their drinking, and only 24 percent that drinking because their friends drink is important. Also, 92% indicated that it was okay to turn down an alcoholic drink at the college. Peer pressure implies resistance. These responses suggest that respondents happily comply with social influences.

The social nature of drinking on the campus presents both opportunities and threats to the administration. On the negative side, a campus culture conducive to widespread social drinking encourages a lot of drinking with the concomitant risk of abuse, and provides an umbrella for highly abusive drinkers to function inconspicuously. On the positive side, there is a potential to change the drinking behavior of the most abusive or potentially abusive students by altering the campus culture.

A change in the campus culture could be brought about through substitute activities, stricter policies, provision of services, and effective information and promotion. Each of these will be discussed later in the paper. Before doing this, however, we will address the issue of intervention more generally. Kraft (1985) pointed out that intervention can take place at least three levels: 1. at the level of the individual student and his/her knowledge, attitudes and behavior, 2. among primary affiliative groups of students and their norms and behavior, 3. at the institutional level. We should note that institutional controls are more effective if they stimulate or reinforce informal social controls (Moskowitz 1989). Therefore an appropriate strategy for reducing abuse is to improve informal controls by changing the campus culture. The diagram in Figure 1 indicates that proposed programs and policies should be evaluated not only on the basis of their direct impact on the individual student, but also on the indirect effect, via an impact on the social environment.

With the above approach the college can develop a long run strategy aimed at nonabusers as well as abusers. This approach has the advantage of mitigating two problems encountered in social marketing that were noted by Bloom (1980). First, Bloom pointed out that, in contrast to the usual situation in commercial marketing, target segments in social marketing must often consist of those consumers who are the most negatively predisposed to the marketers offerings. Secondly, he noted that agencies often have difficulty implementing long-term positioning strategies.

ATTITUDES, BELIEFS AND KNOWLEDGE

Attitudes and Beliefs

The general picture that emerges is that students hold an accepting attitude toward drunkenness. As shown below:

Percent Saying That Is Is Okay To Get Drunk If It Doesn't Interfere With Responsibilities

Nondrinkers	33%
Responsible drinkers	49%
Teflon drinkers	80%
Hazardous drinkers	68%
Troubled drinkers	31%
Total sample	61%

The most accepting attitude is held by the teflon drinkers. In general, students' perceptions of their own drinking vastly understate their actual drinking. Only 7% say they get drunk and yet, in response to a later question, 20% admit to getting drunk six or more times during the last three months. This disparity appears to reflect the phenomenon of denial. However, this denial is not complete, since the hazardous drinkers are more likely than others to say they frequently get drunk (32 percent, compared to less than 7 percent for each of the other segments).

Knowledge

Surveys on other college campuses found that knowledge of alcohol facts is not enough to deter students from abusing alcohol (Gonzales, 1988; Kraft, 1985; Moskowitz, 1989). However, although information, per se, is not enough, Moskowitz (1989) suggests that information and education are probably valuable as reinforcers of other methods, e.g., policies, and of existing positive attitudes. Responses to the question shown below point to the need for clear presentation of relevant information.

Consumption Of Grain Alcohol Is More Likely To Lead To Alcohol Abuse Than Beer Or Wine

	Yes	No	Don't Know
Nondrinkers	40%	30%	30%
Responsible drinkers	31%	41%	29%
Teflon drinkers	30%	42%	27%
Hazardous drinkers	28%	40%	32%
Troubled drinkers	36%	64%	0%
Total	31%	41%	28%

Just one week before this survey was conducted, all students received a memorandum from the Alcohol Abuse Task Force, which clearly stated that grain alcohol in all forms would be prohibited because it is more likely to lead to abuse than wine or beer. Student responses to this survey question suggest that the majority had not carefully read this memorandum. Survey results do show that students are aware of the policies that are strictly enforced on campus. For example, they know that drinking is not permitted in the resident hallways. However, 82% did not know that under current policy alcohol cannot be consumed in the dorm rooms by students under 21 years old. For policies to be effective, students must be fully aware of them. We should also note that, in order to communicate policies clearly to students, alcohol policymakers must have a very clear idea of how close surveillance will be, and how strictly policies will be enforced.

STIMULUS

What stimuli might move the student to the problem recognition stage in the decision to reduce alcohol consumption ? We should note that most students have probably considered reducing their alcohol consumption many times. We did, however, ask questions that are relevant to this stage in the decision-making process. Results (for all drinkers) are shown below.

Percent Agreeing That The Following Event Might Make Them Consider Drinking Less

- 61% A friend of mine has serious problems with alcohol
- 47% A student at my college is killed in an auto accident when driving under the influence of alcohol
- 42% I have a bad hangover
- 31% A mass media news story that a student at a U.S. college died from heavy drinking at a fraternity party
- 21% I receive information about the negative consequences of drinking from a fraternity/sorority educational program

These results show that a mass media story of a student alcohol-related death has less impact than a bad hangover. The most important influence is personal involvement with a friend who has a serious alcohol problem. These results suggest it is necessary to emphasize personal susceptibility, although this could be for a friend, not necessarily oneself. With the exception of the hangover, hazardous drinkers were the least likely to be influencing by any of these stimuli.

PROBLEM RECOGNITION

Responses to questions asking for the reasons why students were already controlling their drinking are as follows:

Percent Saying The Following Reasons For Controlling Their Intake Of Alcohol Are Important

- 77% Could hurt my academic performance
- 74% I prefer other activities
- 73% Could be bad for my health in the long run
- 72% Makes me ill
- 63% Could get into trouble with the police
- 62% Can't afford it
- 62% Could have negative social/work consequences in the long run
- 51% Could get into trouble with the college administration
- 33% Friends disapprove

With the exception of a preference for other activities, the factors that have led to problem recognition for students fall under the rubric of price (including nonmonetary). The three most important of these relate to academic performance and health effects. These negative consequences of drinking could be emphasized in campus-wide promotions. The majority of students mention financial costs as a constraint. Stricter policies or stricter enforcement would also seem to be a promising approach, but some problems with this will addressed later. The least important factor is disapproval of friends, reflecting the current social environment of the campus. In general, the teflon, hazardous, and troubled drinkers consider these factors less important than do the other two segments. In particular, they are less likely to say that preferring other activities is an important reason for controlling their alcohol intake.

INFORMATION SEARCH

Preferences for different sources are shown below:

Percent Who Would Use The Following Sources If They Wanted To Reduce Their Drinking

59%	Friends or other students
34%	The college counselor
30%	Counselor off-campus
27%	Don't know what would do
26%	Hall coordinator, resident advisor, or house manager
23%	Library

The most popular source is peers. This suggests that peer counselors and a change in the campus culture would be effective strategies. More effective promotion of counseling services might increase the number considering counseling and reduce the number who don't know what they would do. The small percentage choosing resident personnel may be due to the dual role of these employees, i.e. informal counselor and policy enforcer.

EVALUATION OF ALTERNATIVES

Evaluative Criteria

The costs and benefits of drinking as perceived by students provide an indication of the evaluative criteria they will use when considering alternatives. We have already discussed costs when looking at problem recognition. The figures below show some benefits that are important to students.

Percent Saying The Following Were Important Reasons For Drinking

89%	To celebrate special occasions
54%	To help me relax
50%	To add excitement to my life
41%	To cheer me up when I'm in a bad mood
38%	To escape the pressures of life
38%	To get high
34%	To overcome shyness
30%	Because there is nothing else better to do
24%	Because people I know drink
19%	So that I won't feel left out
14%	Because it makes sex more pleasurable
14%	Because of pressure from others

The troubled drinkers were the most likely to drink so they wouldn't feel left out, but less likely than the hazardous drinkers to drink because they were in a bad mood or for excitement. The hazardous and troubled drinkers were more likely than the other segments to drink for all the other reasons. Wiggins (1987) has noted that problem drinkers are most likely to drink for mood-altering reasons such as to relax or escape the pressures of life. The hazardous drinkers clearly fall into this category, but the troubled drinkers are somewhat mixed. The teflon drinkers are more likely than the responsible drinkers to drink for excitement, to get high, to cheer up and because there is nothing better to do. However, they are not more likely to drink to relax, to overcome shyness or to escape pressure.

Substitute Activities

Substitute social activities on the campus could potentially provide most of these benefits. We asked whether students would go to non-alcoholic events that we believed would be close substitutes for drinking, e.g., dance nights, major sports events nights. The interest expressed was fairly high overall; five of the six activities had a level of preference over 70%. However, 58 percent of the respondents said they would still drink on the evening of the non-alcoholic event, and a higher proportion of hazardous drinkers reported this than other drinkers. One would hope that the level of drinking would be lower, as the emphasis on drinking would decrease.

Counseling

Counseling can potentially provide some of the benefits sought by students through drinking, either directly, e.g., by helping students to relax, or indirectly, e.g., by reducing the need to get high. We investigated student preference for specific forms of counseling they would like if they wanted to reduce the amount of their drinking. Results are shown below.

Percent Agreeing That They Would Like The Following Types Of Help To Reduce Their Drinking

60%	Specific suggestions on how to consume less alcohol at social occasions
41%	Counseling to help deal with personal problems
38%	Stress management training
28%	Training in refusal skills

The highest levels of interest were shown by the responsible and troubled drinkers. Teflon and hazardous drinkers showed less interest in general. However, the teflon drinkers were as interested as others in specifice suggestions, and the hazardous drinkers were just as interested in personal counseling. Most students said they would prefer one-on-one counseling with someone who has had a prior alcohol problem, either a peer or a professional. Students' general perception is that people benefit from counseling only if they go voluntarily.

In response to these needs and interests, the college could provide skill-related programs and promote the benefits of counseling more effectively. Time and place convenience could be provided by having college counselors come to the dormitories to speak about what they do, what services are offered at the Counseling Center, and how these services help students. In this setting, the counselor would have the opportunity to make contact with students who would not go to the counseling center on their own. In addition, if forced counseling remains in place, the counselor should provide convincing evidence that students who have been forced to get alcohol counseling have benefitted. Finally, to increase source credibility, informal advisors with prior alcohol problems should be available to meet with students.

We also see several advantages to using peers for giving support to students with alcohol problems. Students know the relevant issues surrounding alcohol among their peers, the abuse potential of planned activities, and understand the stresses experienced by their peers. In addition, students are aware of peers with problems, many of which are shut off to staff and faculty. Finally, a peer program would create greater student involvement and awareness, and would help to alter the social environment. Survey responses indicate that there is adequate interest on the campus for peer support programs, although females are far more interested than males. The majority of interested students said they could be available 2-4 hours per week, and only 15 percent said they would need financial support. As students have a preference for peers as information sources, peer volunteers could prove to be very effective intermediaries.

College Alcohol Policies

Finally, we examined the role of college alcohol policies as a way of increasing the cost of alcohol abuse. Students reacted negatively when asked questions about changes in their drinking behavior if stricter policies were implemented. 74% of those aged 21+ indicated that they would drink more off campus if stricter policies were implemented. Only 21% of all respondents indicated they would drink less under a stricter policy, and 41% of all respondents said that students would vent their problems in ways other than drinking given a stricter policy. These responses suggest that if policies are too strict, not only might this be bad for student-administration relationships but also students may drink more off campus. On the other hand, if policies are too lenient, this could permit more abuse which would be bad for the college's image and aggravating to responsible/non drinking students. Probably the best course of action for the college would be to monitor the policies of other colleges, and plan a carefully sequenced phasing in of progressively stricter policies.

SUMMARY AND CONCLUSIONS

Our analysis has outlined some ways in which marketing strategies can be used at various stages of the decision-making process to influence the decision to consume less alcohol. On the basis of our findings, we suggest a two-pronged targeting approach. First, students who abuse alcohol need to be targeted directly. Both the troubled and hazardous groups are more likely than others to say they need help to control their drinking, indicating they are at least at the problem recognition stage of the decision-making process leading to reduced alcohol consumption. In addition, both abusing segments are more likely to have social difficulties and to experience interpersonal conflict as a result of their drinking. The troubled drinkers are the least happy of all segments with their current drinking behavior. They are more likely than either the hazardous or teflon drinkers to say they would like help with refusal skills, and to favor stricter college alcohol policies. Interestingly, the troubled drinkers reported having the strictest parents with respect to their drinking of all the segments, and none of the troubled drinkers reported that either parent drank frequently. This family background may partly account for the troubled drinkers feeling of dissonance about their drinking behavior. By contrast, the hazardous drinkers reported having parents who drank more frequently than those of other segments, and who were the most lenient about their child's drinking. This segment has the highest frequency of drunken driving and, together with the teflon drinkers, is most likely to be against stricter alcohol policies. This segment contains the highest proportion of males, and exhibits some "macho" attitudes, e.g., a low interest in learning refusal skills. Lastovicka et. al.(1987) suggest that promotion targeted at this group should focus on such appeals as "a "real man's" control of himself is threatened by drinking".

The second thrust of targeting would aim at the entire campus with the goal of producing a social environment that is less conducive to drinking. Our findings suggest that initially the responsible drinkers would be most responsive to alternative social activities. However, the campus is small, and different segments frequently mix together socially because of shared residence and academic majors. In addition, a peer counseling program, and better communication between counselors and students would also promote a change in the social environment. One area where marketing can potentially make an important contribution to reducing adverse social behaviors is that of product development. The marketing approach involves substituting a product of greater perceived value to the targeted consumer than their current product. This approach has an advantage over the more traditional way of dealing with social problems which focuses chiefly on eliminating or reducing the undesirable behavior. This is an area that should be investigated further in future surveys. Unfortunately, this is not an easy undertaking as many of the substitutes are either extremely intangible, e.g., higher self esteem, or provide only long-term benefits.

Our survey results indicate that monetary prices are one evaluative criterion influencing students' drinking levels. Alternate activities should be provided at a lower cost than an evening's drinking, and skills training and counseling should be provided free of charge. Nonmonetary costs of abusive drinking can be increased by having stricter policy rules and enforcement, and by having a social environment where peers show less tolerance of abuse. The nonmonetary costs of counseling can be reduced through more effective distribution, e.g., by having the counselors visit the students' residences.

More generally, the distribution function should be to have nonalcoholic social activities, skills training session and counseling available at convenient and appropriate times and places. The best nights to hold the social activities would be on the heavy drinking days of Thursday, Friday and Saturday, and during times of the year when the frequency of alcohol abuse is high (e.g. at the beginning of the semester).

Finally, promotion must include much more than alcohol facts. Promotion of the costs of abuse should emphasize personal susceptibility. Promotion of substitutes must clearly communicate benefits. Active involvement of student peers in the promotion effort will greatly increase its reach and credibility.

BIBLIOGRAPHY

Bloom, Paul N. and William D. Novelli (1981), "Problems and Challenges in Social Marketing," *Journal of Marketing*, 45 (Spring), 79-88.

De Paulo, Peter J., Mary Rubin and Brenton Milner (1986), "Stages of Involvement with Alcohol and Heroin: Analysis of the Effects of Marketing on Addiction," *Advances in Consumer Research*, 14, 521-525.

Gonzalez, Geraldo M. (1988), "Should Alcohol and Drug Education be a Part of Comprehensive Prevention Policy? The Evidence From the College Campus," *Journal of Drug Issues*, 18 (3), 355-365.

Harford, Thomas C., Henry Wechsler, and Mary Rohman (1983),"The Structural Content of College Drinking," *Journal of Studies of Alcohol*, 44 (4), 722-731

Kotler, Philip and Eduardo L. Roberto (1989). *Social Marketing*. New York: The Free Press.

———, and Gerald Zaltman (1971), "Social Marketing: An Approach to Planned Social Change," *Journal of Marketing*, 35 (July), 3-12.

Kraft, David P. (1985), "The Prevention and Treatment of Alcohol Problems on a College Campus," Tenth Anniversary Symposium, Interdisciplinary Alcohol/Drug Studies Center, Jackson State University (March)

Lastovicka, John L., John P. Murray Jr., Erich A. Joachimsthaler, Gaurav Bhalla, Jim Scheurich (1987), "A Lifestyle Typology to Model Young Male Drinking and Driving," *The Journal of Consumer Research*, 14, No. 2, 257-263.

Luck, David J. (1974), "Social Marketing: Confusion Compounded," *Journal of Marketing*, 38 (October), 70-72.

Matross, Ronald and Max Hines (1982), "Behavioral Definitions of Problem Drinking among College Students," *Journal of Studies on Alcohol*, 43 (7), 702-712

Moskowitz, Joel M. (1989), "The Primary Prevention of Alcohol Problems: A Critical Review of the Research Literature," *Journal of Studies on Alcohol*, 50 (1), 54-88

Smith, Michael C. (1989), "Students, Suds, and Summonses: Strategies forCoping with Campus Alcohol Abuse," *Journal of College Student Development*, 30 (March), 118-122

Thomas, Micheal J. (1983), "Social Marketing, Social Cause Marketing, and the Pitfalls Beyond," *The Quarterly Review of Marketing*, 9 (Autumn), 1-5.

U.S.Department of Health and Human Services (1989), "Drug Use, Drinking, and Smoking: National Survey Results from High School, College, and Young Adult Populations 1975-1988," Washington D.C.: U.S. Government Printing Office.

Whyte, J., (1985), "Organization, Person and Idea Marketing as Exchanges," *The Quarterly Review of Marketing*, (Winter), 25-30.

Wiggins, James A. and Beverly B. Wiggins (1987), "Drinking at a Southern University: Its Description and Correlates," *Journal of Studies on Alcohol*, 48 (4), 319-324.

Assessing Self-Concept Discrepancy in Consumer Behavior: The Joint Effect of Private Self-Consciousness and Self-Monitoring

Stephen J. Gould, Fairleigh Dickinson University

ABSTRACT

The measurement of self-concept in consumer behavior and marketing contexts has traditionally been plagued by problems in self-disclosure and self-awareness. This paper demonstrates how procedural aspects of self-concept, i.e. private self-consciousness and self-monitoring, affect the self-report of the contents of self-concept and related lifestyle items. As hypothesized, individuals, high in private self-consciousness and low in self-monitoring, report larger discrepancies between actual and ideal self-concepts than do others. Similar results are found when demographics are included as covariates. Finally, implications are drawn for consumer research.

The measurement and assessment of self-concept is a central issue in consumer research, especially when considered in terms of the self-congruity between products and oneself and also in terms of the various components of one's multiple self, such as the ideal and actual self-concept (Sirgy 1982; Sirgy et al. 1991). How one sees oneself will be mirrored in what one buys (Malhotra 1988; Sirgy et al. 1991) and how one makes self-report responses in consumer and market research surveys (Sirgy 1982). Individual differences are likely to play a role in self-concept research as evidenced by Malhotra's (1988) study in which he found that cognitively complex individuals produced a better match between preference for houses and congruence with their self-concepts than did what he called cognitively simple individuals. Moreover, individual differences with respect to one's self-reported self-concept likely exist because of self-disclosure issues, which cause some consumers to be more troubled about revealing intimate generalizations concerning the self than others (Sirgy 1982). Thus, according to self-awareness (also sometimes referred to as self-focus) theory, which is concerned with the degree of focus on the self and which Sirgy mentioned as being in implicated in self-disclosure issues, some individuals may also feel uncomfortable confronting such topics concerning the self internally and may wish to avoid them or seek distractions (Duval and Wicklund 1972; Fenigstein, Scheier, and Buss 1975). Other individuals may not have clear ideas concerning their self or various aspects of it and/or may have difficulty in accessing them (Carver and Scheier 1981a).

In order to further investigate the relationship between self-reporting and self-concept, this paper will apply a theoretical approach which makes use of self-awareness theory and which has previously been applied in attitude-behavior consistency and expectancy research. This approach involves the self-relevant traits of private self-consciousness and self-monitoring, both of which are thought to affect attitude-behavior consistency (Miller and Grush 1986, 88). The rationale for using both these traits is that they allow us to account for the joint influence of both one's self-awareness of oneself and one's attunement to social norms on the self-reporting of one's self-concept.

Private self-consciousness, which is the trait equivalent of state self-awareness or self-focus, concerns the degree to which an individual tends to focus on his own inner thoughts or feelings (Fenigstein, Scheier, and Buss 1975). It is thought to affect attitude-behavior consistency in reflecting the degree that a person is able to access and know his/her own attitudes - a person higher in private self-consciousness being more likely to exhibit such consistency than others (Carver and Scheier 1981b; Miller and Grush 1986). In addition, when experimental inductions of self-awareness, such as facing a mirror, are applied to subjects, they have been found to provide more veridical self-reports than non-self-aware controls (Carver and Scheier 1981b). Similarly, Scheier (1980) reported that individuals, high in private self-consciousness, tended to display stronger relationships between privately held beliefs and publicly stated attitudes than did others.

Another possible factor influencing one's self-reported self-concept is self-monitoring which assesses the degree to which an individual tends to guide his self-presentation in response to social cues (Snyder 1974). Low self-monitors have been found to exhibit greater attitude-behavior consistency than have high self-monitors (Miller and Grush 1986). According to Miller and Grush (1986), low rather than high self-monitors will exhibit greater attitude-behavior consistency because they act more in accord with their own attitudes rather than with social norms. But high self-monitors would tend to show higher norm-behavior consistency.

Using both private self-consciousness and self-monitoring, Miller and Grush (1986) conducted a study of attitude-behavior consistency within the theory of reasoned action context (Ajzen and Fishbein 1980). They operationalized their joint use by creating median splits of the measures of each construct and combined them to form four cells: HH, HL, LH, and LL. As hypothesized, individuals high in private self-consciousness and low in self-monitoring (HL) exhibited more attitude-behavior consistency than did the other three groups in relation to an academic study task. However, the other three exhibited greater norm-behavior consistency than did the HLs.

SELF-CONCEPT, PRIVATE SELF-CONSCIOUSNESS AND SELF-MONITORING

Both private self-consciousness and self-monitoring have been conceived and studied with respect to self-report and self-disclosure. They both may viewed as procedural elements or schema of the self-concept which trigger or determine the contents of self-concept (e.g. "I am a person who possesses good self-control") that an individual will perceive, recall, and self-report (Ingram et al. 1988; Nasby and Kihlstrom 1986). Private self-consciousness reflects the degree to which one possesses the tendency to focus on one's own inner self. In related self-awareness research, high self-focus individuals have been found to report larger perceived discrepancies between the actual and ideal self-concept (Duval and Wicklund 1972). These discrepancies, themselves, are thought to be indicants of more self-knowledge and to lead to more accurate self-report and also to greater self-report/self-concept consistency. Larger discrepancies also produce discomfort which is predicted by both the self-focus (awareness) and self-concept discrepancy theories (Wicklund and Hormuth 1981; Higgins, Klein, and Strauman 1985). Self-monitoring in contrast to private self-consciousness reflects response to social cues and norms. Individuals who are high self-monitors will monitor the self-presentation of others in order to find cues for their own self-presentation (Snyder, 1974). According to Snyder, such individuals are more likely to give socially desirable responses than low self-monitors because they possess the skills to find out what others expect of them.

Consistent with the research of Miller and Grush (1986) and also with the concept of a network of procedural and content elements of self-concept, it is likely that individuals will display differences in their assessment of their self-concepts with the high private self-conscious and low self-monitoring individual reporting the largest discrepancy. These individuals will tend more often to be able to access discrepancies and also to find larger ones than will others, while at the same time, not being as responsive or subject to external social cues, cues which often will dictate the suppression of discrepancy reporting.[1] On the other hand, those low in private self-consciousness but high in self-monitoring will be just the opposite. Their responses will tend mainly to be guided by their monitoring of external cues. The other two groups of individuals, high private and high self-monitoring individuals, and low private and low self-monitoring individuals will fall somewhere in between. The former when faced with a self-report situation will confront self-relevant information which tends to conflict (i.e. internally focused self-consciousness cues versus externally-oriented self-monitoring cues). In their responses, they will tend to suppress extreme responses so as to conform with what they perceive as expected social norms. The latter group also tend to not give extreme responses. Being low in self-consciousness, they do not see much discrepancy on the one hand, but as low self-monitors, they also have less reason to change, repress, or hide what they do perceive on the other. Another way of describing this process is that individuals in this group tend to elaborate self-relevant information less than others, at least with respect to the internal and social interaction cues represented by self-consciousness and self-monitoring. Therefore, it is hypothesized that:

H1: High privately self-conscious and low self-monitoring consumers (HL) will display greater self-concept discrepancy than others while low privately self-conscious and high self-monitoring consumers (LH) will display the least self-concept discrepancy. The remaining two groups (HH and LL) will fall in between the first two.

METHOD

Sample and Procedure

The sample consisted of 337 adults in the Northeastern U.S. who returned questionnaires out of a potential quota of 340. The questionnaire was administered on a drop-off and pick-up basis by business school students for classroom credit. Each student was required to fulfill a quota of four adults: a male and female from 25 to 39 years of age and a male and female forty or older. Since some students did not fulfill their quota exactly, the final sample consisted of 51.3% females and 50.4% were 40 or older. Along with the completed questionnaires, the students handed in a separate list of respondents and their telephone numbers for validation. Approximately 20% of the respondents were telephoned for this purpose and asked whether they had answered the questionnaire and what they remembered from it. They all remembered something about the survey.

Measures

The measures assessed in this study and described in the following sections, include the two trait measures of private self-consciousness and self-monitoring, self-concept discrepancy measures, and demographic measures.

Private Self-Consciousness. This trait concerns the degree to which individuals focus on their own thoughts and feelings. It was assessed as part of the Self-Consciousness Scale and is represented by ten items (Fenigstein, Scheier and Buss 1975). A sample item is "I reflect about myself a lot."

Self-Monitoring. Self-monitoring is a trait, reflecting the degree to which a person monitors his or her self-presentation in accord with social cues. It was assessed using Snyder's (1974) scale in its refined and condensed eighteen item form (Snyder and Gangestad 1986). A sample item is "I would probably make a good actor."

Self-Concept Discrepancy Measures. The self-concept discrepancy measures consisted of thirty items which assessed how close or how far a person felt s/he was from his or her ideal state with respect to a variety of self-characteristics. The items were selected on an exploratory basis so as not only to reflect the inner psychological self-perceptions usually assessed in self-concept research (e.g. self-confidence) but also to reflect a broader range of self-relevant psychographic data, reflective of consumer lifestyles, from perceived physical well-being (e.g. health) to perceived socio-economic status (e.g. wealth) - see Table 1. This broader sample of self-concept items will provide more information in demonstrating how the proposed theoretical framework operates across various aspects of self-concept than would be the case were they excluded. At the same time, given this exploratory perspective, they do not represent so much a formal scale as much as a first attempt to construct one, and to serve the purpose of testing the hypothesized joint effect of private self-consciousness and self-monitoring over as wide a range of self-relevant material as possible. The items were measured on a 10 point scale with a "1" indicating that an individual felt his/her actual states to be "Very Close" to ideal (a small discrepancy) and a "10" indicating that s/he felt his/her actual states to be "Very Far" from ideal (a large discrepancy).

Demographics. Sex (0=female, 1=male), age, education (0 = "grade school or less" to 7 = "graduate degree") and income (0 = "less than $15,000" to 7 = "over 74,999") were also assessed.

RESULTS

Factor Analysis of the Self-Concept Measures

The thirty self-concept discrepancy items were reduced to eight factors, using varimax-rotated principal components analysis, and only including items which had loadings of .5 or better, as shown in Table 1. The items "strong character" and "masculinity if you are a man or femininity if you are a woman" and "intellectual stimulation" did not load on any factor and were dropped from further analysis. The resulting factors include: (1) "Physical Shape," (2) "Self-Efficacy," (3) "Age and Love," (4) "Wealth and Work," (5) "Excitement," (6) "Good Quality," (7) "Private Self," and (8) "Other." The items for each factor were added together using equal weights of 1 for each item which had a factor loading of .5 or greater and the resulting scores were used in further analysis. The data was handled in this way to reduce it to manageable proportions and the resulting factors are not meant to represent any more than exploratory scales as noted above. Nonetheless, all

---

[1] A reviewer made the interesting observation that discrepancies may either be larger for high private self-conscious and low self-monitoring individuals than others or that they may be just less likely to be suppressed in self-report. This is a question not covered by this study, but I suspect that aspects of both may be at play, depending on the individuals (i.e. some individuals actually perceive larger discrepancies within themselves than others, but other individuals, given equally large discrepancies when compared to others, are less responsive to social norms, which are negative concerning the self-report of discrepancies, and thus, report larger discrepancies).

TABLE 1
Factor Analysis of the Self-Concept Discrepancy Measures

Variable	1	2	3	4	5	6	7	8
Health	.69							
Appearance	.61							
Weight	.82							
Height								.59
Income				.88				
Job Satisfaction				.58				
Good Friendship								
Amount of Stress								-.53
Self-Control		.63						
Achievement				.54				
Power to Control My Own Life		.54						
Good Body Shape and Muscle Tone	.78							
Self-Confidence		.59						
Privacy							.64	
A Fair Shake in the Tax System								
Attractiveness			.85					
Age			.90					
Love			.84					
Good Medical Care					.59			
Masculinity if You Are a Man or Femininity if You Are a Woman								
Positive Attitudes about Your Life		.61						
Ability to Deal with and Understand All the Changes in Modern Life		.65						
Good Relationships						.71		
Intellectual Stimulation								
Variety and Novelty in My Life					.81			
Enough Time to Myself							.71	
Excitement in My Life					.81			
Decent Housing						.54		
Wealth				.84				
Strong Character								
Variance Explained	3.12	3.06	2.80	2.73	2.62	1.89	1.72	1.26

(Note: The loadings for "Masculinity if You Are a Man or Femininity if You Are a Woman," "Intellectual Stimulation" and "Strong Character" did not load on any factor — a minimum loading of .5 was required).

factors had coefficient alphas exceeding .5, the minimal level for exploratory reliability (Nunnally 1967), except for factor 8 which was dropped from further analysis — it also lacked face validity in combining height and amount of stress as a factor (see Table 1). The first three factors had alphas of .81, the fourth factor had an alpha of .80, the fifth, .60, the sixth, .56, and the seventh, .51.

Multivariate Analysis of Variance Results

A four-group variable, PSCSM, was created by dividing Private Self-Consciousness (Md = 1.5) and Self-Monitoring (Md = 8.5) at their respective medians and merging the two as described by Miller and Grush (1986, 88). The two scores were also independent and uncorrelated (r = .04). The self-monitoring scale had a coefficient alpha of .69. For private self-consciousness, the short version reported by Gould (1986) and designated by him as "private reflective self-consciousness" was more reliable (coefficient alpha = .71) than the full version of the scale (coefficient alpha = .60), so it was used in all subsequent analyses. The following describes the four groups: (1) individuals low in self-consciousness and high in self-monitoring (LH), (2) those low on both variables (LL), (3) those high on both (HH), and (4) those high on private self-consciousness and low on self-monitoring (HL).

The overall multivariate (MANOVA) effect of PSCSM for the seven factors was significant, $F(21, 893) = 2.07$, $p<.0033$. There were significant univariate effects for all but the last factor, $p<.05$, as shown in Table 2. In addition, planned comparisons revealed that the HLs exceeded LHs in the size of their discrepancy for all but the last factor, $p<.05$. Furthermore, for all factors, the other two groups fell in between though not necessarily at levels of statistical significance. For the psychological self-concept measures of Self-Efficacy and Excitement, the planned comparisons revealed that the HLs exceeded all three other groups. This result strongly supports the idea that individuals, high in private self-consciousness and low in self-monitoring, are more likely to perceive discrepancies between their actual and ideal selves than others, particularly those low in private self-consciousness and high in self-monitoring. Thus overall, the hypothesis proposed for this study is supported.[2]

TABLE 2
Means, Standard Deviations and Univariate F Tests For the Self-Concept Discrepancy Variables

(Note: A higher score indicates a larger discrepancy; the standard deviations are in parentheses)

Variable	Group				F	Prob.
	LH	LL	HH	HL		
Physical Shape	15.79	18.90	17.76	19.64	3.80	.0106
	(7.12)	(7.66)	(7.41)	(7.40)		
Self-Efficacy	14.76	18.01	16.45	20.33	7.99	.0001
	(5.69)	(7.60)	(5.51)	(9.20)		
Age and Love	9.97	12.13	11.67	14.86	4.71	.0031
	(4.15)	(5.37)	(5.06)	(4.85)		
Wealth and Work	15.19	17.06	17.58	19.28	4.55	.0039
	(5.73)	(6.73)	(6.12)	(8.23)		
Excitement	7.61	8.83	8.07	10.39	5.97	.0006
	(4.40)	(4.31)	(4.05)	(4.56)		
Good Quality	7.17	8.26	9.20	9.44	5.18	.0017
	(3.23)	(3.72)	(3.83)	(4.28)		
Private Self	7.71	8.13	8.43	9.25	2.04	.1080
	(4.02)	(4.09)	(3.39)	(4.30)		
N	70	88	72	79		

(Note: N does not add to sample size because of missing values)

Groups
LH - Low private self-consciousness/high self-monitoring
LL - Low private self-consciousness/low self-monitoring
HH - High private self-consciousness/high self-monitoring
HL - High private self-consciousness/low self-monitoring

When sex, age, income, and education were included as covariates in a MANOCOVA analysis, the results changed slightly. In this case, the overall MANOVA effect of PSCSM was also significant, $F(21,791) = 1.67$, $p < .0301$. There were also significant univariate effects for all the lifestyle factors, $p < .05$. The significant covariates included sex on Physical Shape, $p < .0005$; sex and education on Self-Efficacy, $p < .0022$ and .0070, respectively; sex, age and income on Age and Love, $p < .0409$, .0001 and .0008, respectively; education and income on Wealth and Work, $p < .0143$ and .0042, respectively; sex on Excitement, $p < .0015$; income on Good Quality, $p < .0001$; and education on Private Self, $p < .0301$. Finally, zero order Pearson correlations, matching the independent variables with each other and with the dependent self-concept variables, reveal that some demographic variables may be markers for private self-consciousness and self-monitoring, as well as being related to and explaining some of the variance in the self-concept variables, themselves. Age especially is correlated (negatively) with both private self-consciousness and self-monitoring. As an example of a demographic-self-concept discrepancy relationship, a higher income is associated with a smaller discrepancy in both Wealth and Work and Good Quality.

---

[2] An alternative MANOVA was also run with separate significant main effects for private self-consciousness, $p < .0279$, and self-monitoring, $p < .0017$, while the interaction was not significant, $p < .6613$. This result indicates that each construct had its own separate additive effect, thus supporting the Miller and Grush method which is based on their cumulative, joint effects.

DISCUSSION

The results of this study support the hypothesized relationship between self-concept actual-ideal contents, on the one hand, and private self-consciousness and self-monitoring, as the procedural elements of the self-concept network, on the other. Thus, they also support the approach of Miller and Grush (1986, 88). Specifically, it was found that the differences were clearly most pronounced for HLs (people high in private self-consciousness and low in self-monitoring) and LHs (people low in private self-consciousness but high self-monitoring) in that HLs consistently reported greater self-concept discrepancies than did LHs. Also as predicted, the two other groups, HHs and LLs generally tended to fall in between. Moreover, when the demographics were included in a MANOCOVA analysis, a self-consciousness/self-monitoring effect remained over and above them. In order to assess these results, a number of limitations and implications need to be discussed.

Limitations

Threats to validity exist because of the some of the procedures employed in this study. Since the sample was not random but rather a convenience, quota sample, it is possible that biases existed in the self-selection of respondents. It is also possible that some students administering questionnaires were delinquent in some way in this procedure although great effort was made to control and verify this study. However, even with these limitations, it was thought better to conduct this exploratory study on a broader, more inclusive demographic base than merely to use students as is often done in such studies. This enhances the external validity although the sample is still limited in terms of representativeness and randomness. Nonetheless, the results remain intriguing because they

TABLE 3
Pearson Correlations for the Independent Variables in the Study with the Self-Concept Discrepancy Variables and with Each Other

(Note: Physical Shape through Private Self are assessed as discrepancies which range from smaller to larger)

Variable	PSC	SM	Sex	Age	Education	Income
Private Self-Consciousness (PSC)	1.00	.04	-.05	-.23**	.04	-.13*
	(324)	(293)	(324)	(324)	(319)	(294)
Self-Monitoring (SM)	.04	1.00	-.19**	-.22**	.01	-.13*
	(293)	(298)	(298)	(298)	(293)	(294)
Physical Shape	.05	-.16	-.22**	.12*	-.13*	.01
	(321)	(295)	(332)	(332)	(327)	(300)
Self-Efficacy	.18**	-.21**	-.26**	.13*	-.26**	-.06
	(319)	(203)	(329)	(329)	(324)	(299)
Age and Love	.06	-.12	-.13**	.16**	-.15**	-.19**
	(316)	(291)	(327)	(327)	(322)	(295)
Wealth and Work	.13*	-.09	-.09	-.08	-.20**	-.26**
	(316)	(291)	(328)	(328)	(323)	(297)
Excitement	.10	-.18**	-.24**	.10	-.14*	-.06
	(324)	(297)	(336)	(336)	(331)	(304)
Good Quality	.12*	-.06	-.08	-.05	-.13*	-.29**
	(319)	(294)	(332)	(332)	(327)	(301)
Private Self	.06	-.10	-.10	.00	-.13*	.01
	(320)	(296)	(333)	(333)	(328)	(302)

** p < .01
* p < .05

represent additional support for a theory which has previously been shown to be predictive and because they extend the theory into the area of self-concept and self-report consistency. Another limitation applies to what was considered in the study. Other measures could have been included which either assess other aspects or measures of self-concept, product image and self-concept or other related attitudinal or behavioral measures. These remain for future research.

Interpretation and Implications of the Study

Private Self-Consciousness/Self-Monitoring and Self-Concept. The interpretation of these results revolve around questions of what the self-concept and discrepancies in it mean to different consumers. One question to be asked concerns whether personality types, based on the combined private self-consciousness/self-monitoring variable, vary in the size of their perceived self-concept discrepancy because their gaps between actual and ideal are really different, or because their degrees of self-monitoring cause them to report them differentially, even though in effect, their gaps are the same. In other words, does a large gap for HLs in some way mean the same thing in its cognitive structure or behavioral consequences as a smaller does one for LHs? If so it would mean that some sort of adjustment has to be made in our analysis of the self-concept discrepancy, which requires us to consider the four separate private self-consciousness/self-monitoring groups, and to look for changes or deviations in each group's self-concept when manipulating it experimentally or assessing it in a survey. On the other hand, it seems more likely, in conformity with self-monitoring and self-consciousness theory, that LHs felt it was socially desirable to report a smaller self-concept discrepancy, as well as finding a smaller discrepancy to begin with. Likewise, HLs would act in accord with their self-consciousness and monitoring traits and find a larger discrepancy. They would also find less reason in terms of social norms to obfuscate and reduce that discrepancy in the process of survey self-report. Finally, whatever the case for the meaning of self-concept and its discrepancies to various consumers, researchers need to consider that these differences exist and relate them to other dimensions of personality and a wide-range of attitudinal measures (cf. Miller and Grush 1986).

Self-Concept Scales. The self-concept items used in this study represent an attempt to move in the direction of broadening the range of items included in self-concept measures. More work is indicated in continuing in this direction, testing other dimensions not included here, and relating them to prior self-concept research.

Product Use. Beyond the potential improvement in assessing self-concept, it is possible (although not addressed here) that the combined private self-consciousness/self-monitoring assessment can aid in predicting the use of various types of products and services, themselves. HLs may actually seek out products or services that make them more self-aware or cause them to focus on themselves. For example, Fenigstein, Scheier, and Buss (1975) had originally related higher self-consciousness to the individual's tendency to participate in such activities as transactional analysis, encounter groups, sensitivity training, and meditation. LHs, on the other hand, may be especially sensitive to image-related advertising appeals and image-related products (Snyder and Debono 1985).

Demographic Relationships. Further research seems indicated for demographics in relation to private self-consciousness, self-monitoring, and self-concept. While the results found here should be interpreted with great caution because they were not predicted a priori, they nonetheless suggest that demographic differences may exist for various aspects of one's self-concept and also for self-consciousness and self-monitoring, which serve as processual aspects of the perceiving and schematizing of it. Consumer researchers should conduct field studies grounded in the theory of each of those demographics to verify and possibly extend these results, both between and within specific categories.

CONCLUSION

This paper has assessed the utility of Miller and Grush's (1986; 88) combining of self-monitoring and private self-consciousness as an independent variable in predicting self-concept discrepancy. Whether or not the demographic covariates were included, the results supported the basic hypothesis that HLs (LHs) will generally display greater (less) self-concept discrepancy than others, and demonstrated that the responses on self-reported self-concept measures are subject to individual differences based on the merger of these two variables. These results could be very important in interpreting the larger network of procedural and content elements of consumers' self-concepts. They are also suggestive of how psychological trait theories, often tested in laboratory experiments with students, apply to field research settings, where individual differences, based both on traits and demographics, may be found.

REFERENCES

Ajzen, Icek and Martin Fishbein (1980), *Understanding Attitudes and Predicting Social Behavior*, Englewood Cliffs, NJ: Prentice-Hall.

Carver, Charles S. and Michael F. Scheier (1981a), *Attention and Self-regulation: A Control Theory Approach to Human Behavior*. New York: Springer-Verlag.

_____ (1981b). "Self-consciousness and Reactance," *Journal of Research in Personality*, 15 (March), 16-29.

Duval, Shelley and Robert A. Wicklund (1972), *A Theory of Objective Self-awareness*. New York: Academic Press.

Fenigstein, Allan, Michael F. Scheier and Arnold H. Buss (1975), "Public and Private Self-consciousness: Assessment and Theory," *Journal of Consulting and Clinical Psychology*, 43 (August), 522-527.

Gould, Stephen (1986), "The Self-consciousness Scale: A Confirmatory Analysis," *Psychological Reports*, 59 (October), 809-810.

Higgins, E. Tory, Ruth Klein and Timothy Strauman (1985), "Self-concept Discrepancy Theory: A Psychological Model for Distinguishing among Different Aspects of Depression and Anxiety," *Social Cognition*, 3 (Spring), 51-76.

Ingram, Rick E., Debra Cruet, Brenda R. Johnson and Kathleen S. Wisnicki (1988), "Self-focused Attention, Gender, Gender Role, and Vulnerability to Negative Affect," *Journal of Personality and Social Psychology*, 55 (December), 967-978.

Malhotra, Naresh K. (1988), "Self Concept and Product Choice: An Integrated Perspective," *Journal of Economic Psychology*, 9 (March), 1-28.

Miller, Lynn. E. and Joseph Grush (1986), "Individual Differences in Attitudinal Versus Normative Determination of Behavior," *Journal of Experimental Social Psychology*, 22 (May), 190-202.

_____ (1988), "Improving Predictions in Expectancy Theory Research: Effects of Personality, Expectancies, and Norms," *Academy of Management Journal*, 31 (March), 107-122.

Nashby, W., and John F. Kihlstrom (1986), "Cognitive Assessment of Personality and Psychopathology," in R. E. Ingram (ed.), *Information processing approaches to clinical psychology*. Orlando, FL: Academic Press, 217-239.

Nunnally, Jum C. (1967), *Psychometric Theory*, New York: McGraw-Hill.

Scheier, Michael F. (1980), "Effects of Public and Private Self-Consciousness on the Public Expression of Personal Beliefs," *Journal of Personality and Social Psychology*, 44 (September), 627-644.

Sirgy, M. J. (1982), "Self-concept in Consumer Behavior: A Critical Review," *Journal of Consumer Research*, 9 (December), 287-300.

_____, J. S. Johar, A. C. Samli and C. B. Claiborne (1991), "Self-Congruity Versus Functional Predictors of Consumer Behavior," *Journal of the Academy of Marketing Science*, 19 (Fall), 363-375.

Snyder, Mark (1974), "Self-monitoring of Expressive Behavior," *Journal of Personality and Social Psychology*, 30 (October), 526-537.

_____ and Kenneth Debono (1985), "Appeals to Image and Claims about Quality: Understanding the Psychology of Advertising," *Journal of Personality and Social Psychology*, 49 (September), 586-597.

_____ and Steve Gangestad (1986), "On the Nature of Self-monitoring: Matters of Assessment, Matters of Validity," *Journal of Personality and Social Psychology*, 51 (July), 125-139.

Wicklund, Robert A. and Stefan Hormuth (1981), "On the Functions of the Self: A Reply to Hull and Levy," *Journal of Personality and Social Psychology*, 40 (June), 1029-1037.

Dispossession and Perceptions of Self in Late Stage HIV Infection
Teresa Pavia, University of Utah

This research explores the relationship between perceptions of self and the dispossession experiences of people with HIV (human immunodeficiency virus) infection. Depth interviews were conducted with 10 individuals in the late stages of HIV infection. Informants described the impact that this disease on their ownership of material goods and on their daily lives. The themes that emerged from these interview suggest that losses associated with the ability to do things, such as job loss or social ostracization, more strongly influence self perception than the loss of any material goods.

An individual's relationship to his or her possessions, where possessions are broadly defined to include one's body, attitudes, and personal relationships, as well as material goods, is closely tied to the individual's perception of self (Belk 1988). It follows that dispossession — the loss of ownership of a possession–may challenge one's self perception or may be associated with a change in self perception. This notion has received substantial empirical support (e.g., Andreasen 1984, Belk 1988, Young 1990). Serious, life threatening illness may be viewed as a complex array of dispossessional events since it represents the loss of one's health, the potential loss of one's job, material goods, social network, lifestyle, and ultimately the loss of one's life. For the terminally ill, a chain of involuntary dispossessions begins with their diagnosis (e.g., a loss of their status as "healthy"). Then, their diagnosis may stimulate a chain of voluntary dispossessions (e.g., quitting an unrewarding job, or dispossessing belongings).

The focus of this work is on the relationship between perceptions of self and the dispossession experiences of people infected with the human immunodeficiency virus (HIV). HIV reduces the body's ability to fight off infections and leads, in its final stage, to Acquired Immune Deficiency Syndrome (AIDS), a diagnosis that most regard as terminal. One would expect HIV infection to profoundly challenge a person's sense of self; this work aims to understand changes in self perception through an exploration of the dispossessional experiences of infected persons.

HIV infected persons were selected for this study for a variety of reasons. First, the number of people infected with HIV in the U.S. is estimated at between one and one and a half million (CDC 1990). This group, while large and growing, has received limited attention from consumer researchers. Second, most HIV infected persons are relatively young and are facing significant dispossession events in contrast to other consumers of the same age who are acquiring heavily. Third, because many HIV infected persons are not involved in traditional, legally recognized relationships, dispossession decisions that may be straightforward for other terminally ill young people (e.g., leave it all to your spouse) may not be available. Fourth, the time between HIV infection and death is uncertain, making dispossession decisions difficult. Fifth, beyond their own physical condition, many of these individuals face negative reactions to the their diagnosis from co-workers, friends and family. This may force premature endings to relationships, increase uncertainty and reduce the number of potential beneficiaries for their belongings.

HIV INFECTION

The U.S. Public Health Service estimates that between 1 and 1.5 million Americans are infected with the human immunodeficiency virus (HIV) (CDC 1990). Individuals infected with HIV will be afflicted by a variety of illnesses as their immune systems become progressively weakened. The course of HIV infection can be roughly divided into four stages: (1) the weeks or months immediately following infection in which the individual may have flu-like symptoms; (2) an asymptomatic period which may last for years; (3) a period of time in which the individual may develop an increasing variety of problems such as swollen lymph glands, night sweats, weight loss, herpes zoster or oral candidiasis; and finally (4) the stage in which the individual contracts one of the diseases that define AIDS, such as Kaposi's sarcoma (Lifson 1988). This final stage is often referred to as "full blown AIDS." While the rate of progression varies greatly from person to person, the median time from infection until the onset of AIDS is 10 years; the median survival after developing AIDS is about 2 years (Lifson 1988).

One of the most notable aspects of HIV infection is that it progressively assaults the individual, wearing down his or her immune system, but the progress of the disease is not predictable. The types of diseases one may develop are very different and the time from infection until a serious, debilitating illness is not predictable. Furthermore, current medical therapies are evolving, and "anxiety over when and how they will die has become a major component of living with AIDS, especially as medical therapies become more effective" (Wadland and Gleeson 1991).

Fiske and Taylor (1984) demonstrated that stress associated with one's knowledge that something bad is going to happen is increased when the individual anticipates the negative event but does not know when it is likely to occur. This phenomenon is apparent in many individuals infected with HIV, as Chuang et al. (1989) notes:

Although the endpoint of AIDS may force an individual to deal with such issues as death, dying and the resolution of unfinished business, earlier stages may introduce equally - if not more - threatening stressors, such as uncertainties about the progression of the illness, fears of pain and suffering, social isolation and rejection and more general fears of the unknown.

METHODOLOGY

To explore dispossession in late stage HIV disease, depth interviews were conducted with 10 individuals in stages three and four of HIV infection during the Fall of 1991. All ten informants were volunteers at, or beneficiaries of, a food bank operated by a statewide AIDS organization in a western state. This state has an incidence of HIV infection close to the median rate for the U.S. (CDC 1991). Most interviews lasted 45 minutes to an hour and were conducted at the AIDS organization on days that the food bank distributed food. The interviews were tape recorded and transcribed. Informants received a $10 honorarium for their participation.

The informants represented a mix of backgrounds: some had previously held well-paying, steady jobs (e.g., interior decorator, nurse, secretary); others had previously worked in low paying, episodic jobs (e.g., construction worker, waiter); and some had only worked in underground jobs (e.g., drug dealer). Three women and seven men were interviewed. Six were homosexual or bisexual, three were IV drug users and one informant was infected through heterosexual contact. To preserve confidentiality, informants were identified only by age and gender. Consequently, all the names used in the discussion below are fictitious, and any similarity with actual persons living or dead with the same name is coincidental.

Unstructured, in-depth interviews were selected as the preferred methodology for this research because they allowed a detailed exploration of dispossession among HIV positive individuals (Glaser and Strauss 1967, Miles and Huberman 1984). Interviews were open ended discussions stimulated by the question "Has you attitude toward possessions changed since your diagnosis of HIV infection, and if so how?" The informants were allowed great leeway in taking the interview in various directions and most exercised this option extensively. The ideas discussed below were identified by exploring the ten transcripts for relevant themes that arose frequently and/or consistently.

DISPOSSESSION AND PERCEPTIONS OF SELF

The most fundamental loss facing someone who has just been informed of a terminal illness is the loss of life itself. Several informants recalled this moment; their comments reflect the impact that knowledge of this upcoming involuntary loss had:

Angela [Female, 41]: All my life I've been trying to kill myself, ever since I can remember. And then one day they told me I was going to die and it was like, "I don't want to die, I want to live."

William [Male, 44]: I started dying that day on the phone [when I found out my diagnosis]. I don't mean it to sound that way, I'm very much alive, but that day I found out I was going to die, I started playing [and working less].

As time passed and as informants watched their health progressively and uncontrollably worsen, some implied that they started to hope they will die sooner rather than later. This desire was still presented as an involuntary loss. None of the informants expressed immediate suicidal ideation, although several expressed their intention to commit suicide when they became severely ill.

Ivan [Male, 25] I am prepared to leave [die] at any moment ... I have been told that there is going to be a cure for AIDS, and I don't want it. I am already prepared [for death], and I am ready. There's too much damage done to this body, I would not want to make it live any longer than it has to.

Samantha [Female,33]: Sometimes I wish I would go sooner because I am tired of this lingering. I'm tired of taking all the pills I have to take, I'm tired of going to the doctor every two weeks, I'm tired of getting stuck and jabbed and poked and prodded like a piece of beef ...

Closely related to a loss of life is a loss of health and an associated loss of energy. This type of loss affects the informant's day to day plans and their ability to engage in activities that had previously been an important part of their lives.

William [Male, 44]: You don't feel well enough to create ... You have days like now when you feel fabulous, where you go out and do what you want to do. But, these are the days that kill me because tomorrow I'll pay for it — I'll be burned ... Now what I have to do is really pace myself.

The challenge of coping with HIV is exacerbated by cyclical ups and downs experienced as patients fluctuated between periods of severe illness and periods of relative good health. These problems notwithstanding, most informants felt that they have at least some control over their health (see also Gould 1990). As Zack [Male, 32] said, "I am torn between [death] and living. I have a belief that a cure is going to happen so I am going to do the best [I can] to take care of myself in the meantime so I have the opportunity to live."

For many informants, especially those in the gay community, watching their friends get sick and die has made them acutely aware of the process of losing their own health:

Arnold [Male, 28]: My friends were all dead. First, it was John who died, and he died right after I found out about me. Then it was the guy who gave it to me who died. Now, I'm hearing about it, you know, people are dying all around me. Then I woke up one day and I was feeling kind of depressed over something normal in my life — not AIDS — and I couldn't find anybody to talk to. They were all dead.

Likewise, many informants indicate that their friends and family have become worried about losing them. This usually has intensified the informants' own concerns about their health:

Arnold [Male, 28]: [My mother is like] "What am I going to do without you? My son is dying." My mother thinks that she is the one who is going through all the hardship because I am dying; because I have this disease; because she is going through all this hardship, and she doesn't pay mind to what I am going through. I am the one who is dealing with this and she doesn't even recognize it. I am just one of her possessions.

While losses of life and health are set in the future, upon diagnosis, the patient is frequently subject to an immediate loss of control over the information concerning his or her health status. Almost all of the informants voiced anger when others broadcasted the news of their infection and anger and/or irritation over the friends and family that rejected them after finding out they were infected. Several of the informants described feelings of contamination of self and personhood, typically instigated by the negative reactions of others to their illness:

Ivan [Male, 25]: I moved home for just a little while and [my father] just flipped out. He got really irate over [me] using the toothpaste.

Jean [Female, 26]: ... A lot of my friends, when they found out I was sick and started to be in hospitals and started not to do well, left.

Samantha [Female, 33]: ... so I lost my job, I had to move, and my friends abandoned me .. I locked myself away for several months. I moved so no one would know me. It took me over a year before I could face anybody ... Then I came back and started a new life with different friends ... I did not tell anybody. I still kept it a secret because everyone I told turned their back. So I just learned to keep my mouth shut.

In fact, although Samantha's family lived in another state, they began to receive death threats when the knowledge of her infection became widespread in their town. To relieve this source of tension, they decided to have her obituary printed in the local newspaper *before* she died. According to Samantha [Female, 33], "They finally printed my obituary in 1987 saying that I had died of AIDS at St. Mary's Hospital ... It was easier for the family to do that than to be scared." Given her experiences of rejection due to HIV infection, Samantha understood her family's behavior and held no grudge against them for this action.

The presence of a stigmatizing illness may also "contaminate" the individual's possessions making dispossession more difficult.

Jean has no children but she was concerned that the options for placement of her dog may be limited because of contamination. She described manifestation of the problem in which neighborhood children were forbidden to play with her dog because Jean was infected.

On the other hand, a stigmatizing illness and its "contamination" factor may facilitate some dispossessions such as loss of home, loss of friends and family, or job loss. Everyone that had held a steady job talked about that loss with sadness:

> Arnold [Male, 28]: I was moving up the secretarial ladder very quickly and then I found out that I couldn't even work. My whole attitude has changed. It was like, I don't personally feel this way, but maybe subconsciously I may [say] "Why bother?" And since then I haven't been able to hold down a job because I'm too tired to work. It's starting to affect my physical self and things have changed a lot. I'm now poor, I mean completely poor. I live on disability and all of those young childhood dreams have just disappeared ... My drive came from my pride in what I was doing and I just lost it all.

> Jean [Female, 26]: That was my idea of who I was. So to have to find inside who I was, was really difficult. I had to introduce myself as "... this is what I do." and then all of the sudden it was, "Well, I stay at home. I am an ex-nurse."

Informants began a series of involuntary losses as their financial resources declined. No one liked having less money, although some freely admitted squandering what little money they did have. Toby [Male, 28] received a lump sum Social Security payment of $10,000 and spent it all on drugs, alcohol and luxury items. Although he expressed regret for his actions he explained his reasoning at the time by saying, "It's kind of like, this is the end of my time so why shouldn't I enjoy this last bulk and flash out on it." And Arnold [Male, 28] who heretofore had an excellent credit record recounts, "I did not pay may rent, I just didn't do it ... I can only afford to live, exist, or afford to have fun. Well, I am dying, so I am going to have fun."

Rather than indiscriminately spending their remaining assets, other informants were more purposefully dispossessing in order to qualify for disability payments. Although these dispossessions were somewhat voluntary, they reflected a more encompassing need to conform to government standards in order to qualify for Social Security or Aid to Families with Dependent Children. Informants discussed either spending down their assets to qualify for government aid or shifting the title of their assets to someone else. The two items that the individuals specifically discussed retitling were homes and cars. Zack [Male, 32]: "I took the house out of my name.... I have to secure myself for opening up the only means I will have for taking care of me...the state ... Financially, you have to play the game." When asked if her retitled car was still hers, Jean said "My car is mine [because] I'm the only one who drives it." However, from a larger perspective Jean says, "it makes me feel like I'm not a person, because I can't have anything [and still qualify for Social Security]."

Although in the above quote Jean expressed a close link between material goods and a sense of self, most informants described a belief that material goods were less important to them now than relationships, experiences and their independence.

> Jean [Female, 26] Things aren't as important now as they were. I don't care about the car or the house.

> Kingston [Male, 28] What the heck, you can't take it with you.

> Arnold [Male, 28] I told my parents and my sisters, and everybody in my life right now, "Don't get me anything for Christmas because I don't want anything; I don't need anything."

> Ivan [Male, 25] I had an entire house worth of goods and I just left it all ... I just left [my roommates] everything and started over.

> Angela [Female, 41] The house was the first thing to go and everything in the house, and some of the stuff that was really good, got put in the dumpster. I threw it all away.

While the informants placed less emphasis on material goods, many retained a subset of material goods which continued to be very important. Included in this set were pets, family photographs, family heirlooms, special collections of artwork, insurance policies, and Dungeon and Dragon gaming supplies. Informants were concerned about finding appropriate beneficiaries for these possessions.

Reflecting a changed perspective on the importance of their various material goods relative to each other and relative to relationships, experiences and independence, most informants cited attempts to improve relations with friends and family:

> Zack [Male, 32] I have grasped [HIV] as an opportunity and life looks different now. My family is really important to me now, whereas I used to take it for granted ... I think it has brought us closer. I think that anytime you see a family member that is this young in life and who has this kind of a diagnosis, it is pretty devastating at first, and I know that [my family] was devastated. Through all of that my dad has come to accept my sexuality. He is trying to bring our relationship closer than it ever was. In his own awkward way, he is trying to do that...I have put a lot into perspective... I am more or less living day to day. It takes practice and I don't do it well yet, but I am working on it and [I am] better than I was.

> Ivan [Male, 25]: I have made amends with all my friends and anybody I have ever argued with.

> Kingston [Male, 28]: You want to see people, you want to have a clean slate so to speak.

> Samantha [Female, 33]: My husband and I were going through a custody battle at the time this happened. I called him to work one day and I said, "We must talk. I think it's best that you do keep the children." He was real shocked.

> Angela [Female, 41] Now I do all these homemaking things with the kids, we make cookies and we clean and it's more of a family life than we have ever had.

DISCUSSION

These informants associated the greatest loss of self with the loss of jobs, energy and motivation rather than with the loss of material goods. Notions that "we are what we own" (Belk 1988) rest on an implicit assumption that we are able to acquire what we own. Someone who identifies closely with an art collection does not say, "I am an art collection," instead he or she says, "I am an art collector," which implies that "I have the means to acquire art" (e.g., money, appropriate knowledge, the right connections, etc.). This person may lose the art collection, and suffer a loss of self, but still retain the means to collect (e.g., a theft of the collection); or the person may lose the collection as well as the means to collect, and suffer an extraordinary deep loss of self. This deep loss of self is the type of loss experienced by the informants and may describe why the loss of their material goods was described as relatively less important than their other losses.

The informants were also inclined to describe greater distress associated with a loss of control over what they did, rather than a loss of control over the material goods that they owned. For example, in dispossessing to qualify for government assistance, the dispossession of material goods was described as a visible sign of the loss of control over personal actions. Similarly, a loss of control over personal health information was devastating not because privacy was lost, but because the loss generally resulted in limitations on the individual's actions and ability to socialize. Finally, one of the problems which frustrated every one of the informants was the loss of energy associated with the infection and the diminution of their ability to do the things that were integral to their perception of self.

Although the informants described a variety of losses, most retained a few material goods which they valued highly. Further, some felt that they were happier now than they had been before and that their lives were more centered:

Zack [Male, 32]: If it is God's way that they find a cure, if that happens, I think I'll be better off for it. This has changed my life significantly and I hope I can hang on and grasp the good things that I've got, because I don't know if I would have ever learned those things otherwise.

Angela [Female, 41]: It's really strange, but I don't think I've ever been this together in my life.

While some aspects of dispossession and changes in self perception may be common among a range of terminally ill people, the informants suggest that HIV infection casts a unique light on the process. Dispossession of items that have been in close physical contact with the infected person may be more difficult because of fears of contamination. In contrast, possessions without physical contact, such as jobs, may be dispossessed more easily due to contamination. Reestablishing or mending family ties may be complicated by lifestyles associated with HIV infection, such as a long history of drug use or an admission of a sexual orientation unacceptable to the family. And, unlike other diseases, it is also likely that an infected person will know many others that have contracted and died from the same disease, leading to losses of friendship and support.

With regard to the permanent nature of the infection, long symptom free periods from other terminal illnesses may signal a remission or even a possible cure; long symptom free phases in an HIV patient are generally viewed as periods between illness with the understanding that symptoms will return, probably in a more unpleasant form. One may argue that it is relatively easy for the person who finds out about his or her infection to relinquish material goods that were intimately linked with a previous vision of self because HIV infection changes one's self perception so much. An alternative explanation for willingly relinquishing a substantial fraction of one's material goods is that the knowledge that one's life may end prematurely stimulates a belief that material goods are not as important as some other aspects of life. Either of these lines of reasoning may partially explain why many of the informants left everything and moved to another location when learning of their infection. As discussed above, these decisions were driven in part by the reactions of friends, family and coworkers to the infection, but it is notable that none of the informants described these losses with deep regret.

In summary, while some of the dispossession decisions and changes in self perception described here may be found in other terminally ill individuals, HIV infection provides a singular set of features that influence the process. The disease challenges self perception in a very basic way and this challenge is reflected in the dispossession events described by the informants. Many acts of dispossession were seen as symbolic of an increasing inability to behave in a manner consistent with the informant's pre-infected self perception. All informants had reduced their number of material goods since becoming informed of their infection. None liked their reduced financial resources, but few spoke of their material losses with deep regret. Deep regret and sadness were reserved for losses in the control of, and ability to, engage in basic activities which were central to their self perception. The loss of one's job, home, health, or relationships were particularly painful because the informants believed that, due to their illness, these things could *never* be replaced. Nonetheless, the informants described attempting to establish control and reaffirm their sense of self by focusing on things such as family relationships, wellness, and making a new life with new, supportive friends.

REFERENCES

Andreasen, Alan R. (1984), "Life Status Changes and Changes in Consumer Preferences and Satisfaction," *Journal of Consumer Research*, 11 (December) 784 - 794.

Belk, Russell W. (1988), "Possessions and the Extended Self," *Journal of Consumer Research* 15 (September), 139-168.

CDC (1990), "HIV Prevalence Estimates and AIDS Case Projections for the United States: Report Based Upon a Workshop," *MMWR* 39 (RR-16), 1-31.

CDC (1991), "HIV/AIDS Surveillance Report," (August), 1-18.

Chuang, Henry, Gerald Devins, John Hunsley and M. John Gill (1989), "Psychosocial Distress and Well-Being Among Gay and Bisexual Men with Human Immunodeficiency Virus Infection," *American Journal of Psychiatry* 146 (7), 876-880.

Fiske, Susan and Shelley Taylor (1984), *Social Cognition*, Reading: MA, Addison-Wesley.

Glaser, Barney G. and Anselm L. Strauss (1967), *The Discovery of Grounded Theory: Strategies for Qualitative Research*, Chicago: Aldine.

Gould, Stephen, Ed. (1990). "Applying a Cultural Framework of Health and Healing in the AIDS Context: The Study of a Group of Treatment Shopping Consumers," *Research in Consumer Behavior*, Vol 4, ed. Russell Belk, 85-114, JAI Press.

Lifson, Alan, George Rutherford and Harold Jaffe (1988), "The Natural History of Human Immunodeficiency Virus Infection," *The Journal of Infectious Diseases* 158 (6), 1360-1367.

Miles, Matthew B. and A. Michael Huberman (1984), *Qualitative Data Analysis: A Sourcebook of New Methods*, Beverley Hills: Sage Publications.

Wadland, William and Cathleen Gleeson (1991), "A Model for Psychosocial Issues in HIV Disease," *The Journal of Family Practice* 33 (1), 82-86.

Young, Melissa Martin, (1990), "Disposition of Possessions During Role Transitions," *Advances in Consumer Research*, Vol 18, eds. Michael Solomon and Rebecca Holman, Provo: Association for Consumer Research, 33-39.

The Evolving Self in Consumer Behavior: Exploring Possible Selves
Amy J. Morgan, Memphis State University

ABSTRACT

This paper proposes the incorporation of an explicitly future-oriented dimension into the study of the self-concept in consumer behavior. The first sections of the paper briefly discuss the progress of self-concept studies in the consumer literature, as well as the limitations of this earlier work. Next, some of the more recent perspectives on the self which have emerged in the field will be explored. Finally, the possible self concept will be introduced through discussion of its theoretical foundation, definition and functions, specific propositions and testing issues and implications for the study of consumer behavior.

INTRODUCTION

The self-concept has been of interest to consumer behavior researchers for a period of nearly forty years. Drawing on earlier works proposing a symbolic importance of products (e.g., Goffman 1951, Hall and Trager 1953), Levy (1959) argued that consumer behavior may be less influenced by a product's functional properties than by the images perceived to be associated with the product and, most significantly, by the interaction of this product image with the consumers' self-image. This assertion by Levy is credited as being the first influence to "...sensitize consumer behavior researchers to the potential influence of consumers' self-concept on consumption behavior" (Sirgy 1982a, p. 289).

In the decades following its introduction to the study of consumer behavior, the self-concept has been addressed from a diverse variety of perspectives, some psychologically-oriented and others drawing from the field of sociology. Consistent with the discipline's shift toward a broadened perspective of the consumer, has been a change in direction aimed at examining the relationship between the ways in which consumers view themselves and the consumption activities undertaken. Treatment of the self-concept has moved toward a more holistic interpretation of the construct than may be found in earlier research endeavors.

The purpose of this paper is to further the broadening perspective on the self-concept in consumer behavior by proposing an additional dimension, in the form of possible selves. This dimension, grounded in self-schema theory, represents an all-encompassing perspective on the self-concept, recognizing that the individual's working self-concept spans past, present and future (Markus and Nurius 1986). Incorporation of this future-oriented dimension would well serve efforts to arrive at a holistic definition of the self-concept, through the recognition that each person's view of self is not solely informed by an image of the present self, but rather an image influenced by that individual's recollections of the past and visions of the future as well.

The contribution of possible selves to the study of consumer behavior may best be viewed in the context of the progress of self-concept studies found in the extant literature. The first sections of this paper trace the evolution of self-concept research as it has been incorporated at various stages of the discipline's growth. Initially, the early self-concept literature will be briefly addressed, followed by a discussion of limitations identified in this body of research. Next, more recent paradigmatic perspectives, including Belk's (1988) extended self, will be explored. Finally, the theoretical foundations and definition of the possible self will be elaborated, as will specific propositions and empirical considerations and the benefits which may be gained from incorporating this perspective into the study of consumer behavior.

CONSUMER SELF-CONCEPT

Early Treatments of the Self-Concept

On the basis of Levy's (1959) work discussed above and Rogers' (1951) theory of individual self-enhancement, Grubb and Grathwohl (1967) developed the first formal model of the self-concept in consumer behavior, depicting a reciprocal relationship between product image and consumers' self-image. Several empirical studies subsequently appeared exploring the nature of this relationship. An excellent discussion of the first twenty-five years of self-concept study in consumer behavior is provided in M.J. Sirgy's (1982a) critical analysis.

Sirgy's (1982a) review classifies early consumer self-concept studies on the basis of five emergent research themes. Additionally, the studies are grouped according to the definition of the construct being investigated. Three broad definitional categories may be observed as encompassing a majority of the studies: [1] one-dimensional definitions (e.g., Birdwell 1968, Green et al 1969, Grubb and Hupp 1968, Allison et al 1980); [2] two-dimensional definitions (e.g., Delozier and Tillman 1972, Dolich 1969, Landon 1971); and [3] multi-dimensional definitions (e.g., Munson and Spivey 1980, Sirgy 1980). Beyond these categories, however, any clear consensus of definition is lacking. Within each of these categories, an overwhelming array of terms may be found (e.g., actual self, real self, now self, ideal self, desired self, looking glass self, social self, ideal social self, expressive self, product expressive self, etc.), many of them apparently addressing the same construct under a different name. Clearly, a serious limitation of this early research is the lack of a clearly articulated or commonly accepted definition of the self-concept construct. As noted by Sirgy (1982a) "...ambiguity and confusion on the precise conceptualization of self-concept in the consumer behavior literature" (p. 288) seriously detracts from the potential usefulness of this body of research.

Two early research treatments of the self-concept are notably unique in their divergence from the more traditional treatment of self-concept as an innately static entity. These works by Schenk and Holman (1980) and Burnkrant and Page (1982) acknowledge the self-concept as a dynamic entity, changing as a result of different situational influences. While these studies did not entirely avoid the ambiguity of definition in other self-concept literature, they are to be commended for introducing new direction to the study of self in consumer behavior with the recognition of the impact of situational factors.

Another limitation of this early consumer self-concept literature is the lack of development of a theoretical base on which research could be continued. The majority of studies in the area focused on repeated empirical testing of largely atheoretical models and constructs. While many of the studies reported significant findings, a different treatment by another researcher was often able to negate the significance of previous conclusions.

Noting the dearth of theoretical grounding and lack of consensus emerging from the body of self-concept literature, Bettman et al (1978) observed that the study of self-concept in consumer behavior had reached the decline stage of its life cycle. Few examples of the early research treatments may be found in the literature following Sirgy's (1982a) review. Rather, recent works have focused on "self" in a more implicit and less managerially-oriented way. New research focuses on exploring the meaning of consumption activities and the relationship between this meaning and the consumers' self-concept.

A BROADENING PERSPECTIVE OF SELF

The shift in approach to studies of consumers' self-concept closely paralleled the discipline's growing acceptance of an alternative view to the information-processing paradigm. Belk (1987) described this change in direction as a move away from the consumer-as-computer model to a recognition of the consumer as human being. Consistent with this shift in paradigmatic perspective, the study of consumers' self moved away from seeking to describe, explain, and predict buyer behavior based on congruence between self-image and product-image, toward a more encompassing view of self as a dynamic construct impacting on all manner of consumption activities.

The Extended Self

Emerging from the body of work recognizing the reciprocal relationship between possessions and the consumers' view of self, Belk's (1988) advancement of the extended self, offered a new perspective on the study of self in consumer behavior. Based on a diverse collection of literature from a variety of disciplines including "...psychology, consumer research, psychoanalytic theory, material and popular culture studies, feminist studies, history, medicine, anthropology, and sociology" (p. 145), Belk contended that "(a) key to understanding what possessions mean is recognizing that, knowingly or unknowingly, intentionally or unintentionally, we regard our possessions as parts of ourselves" (p. 139). The extended self was defined as being comprised of the "body, internal processes, ideas and experiences, and those persons, places and things to which one feels attached" (p. 141). While the extended self has provided a valuable impetus in the "acknowledgement of the need to extend our view of consumer behavior well beyond the traditional confines of the individual as a mechanistic buyer of goods" (Solomon 1990, p. 68), the extended self conceptualization has not been able to surmount all of the limitations which plagued earlier treatment of the self-concept in consumer behavior, particularly in terms of ambiguity inherent in its definition (e.g., Cohen 1989, Solomon 1990).

Despite these limitations, a variety of articles have subsequently appeared based on Belk's extended conceptualization of self. Drawing on observations made during the 1986 Consumer Behavior Odyssey, Belk et al (1988) examined the relationship between collections and the extended self. Hill and Stamey (1990) addressed the extended self-concept in their examination of the possessions and consumption behaviors of the American homeless. Three papers published in the 1990 Association of Consumer Research Proceedings addressed specific domains of the extended self (Belk 1990, Mick and DeMoss 1990, Sanders 1990). Belk's (1990) paper argued for a broadened temporal definition of self and concluded with the statement that "...self extends not only to the present material environment, but extends forward and backward in time" (p. 674). This statement provides a point of departure to examine a key issue found to be lacking in recent treatments of the self-concept in consumer behavior.

Future Extensions of Self

As described by Belk (1990), the self spans past, present and future. While treatments of past and present "self" exist in the recent literature, a tripartite view of self, comprised of past, present and future dimensions, has not been fully developed. A notable exception, Schouten's (1991) discussion of identity enhancement and rites of passage offers the only explicit discussion of a future dimension of self to date. It is the contention of the current paper that recognizing and more fully exploring a future dimension of the self-concept, in the form of possible selves, will enhance the current status of consumer self-concept research.

POSSIBLE SELVES

Theoretical Foundation and Definition

Recent attention to possible selves in the field of developmental psychology (e.g., Cross and Markus 1991, Inglehart, Markus and Brown 1989, Markus and Nurius 1986, Markus and Ruvolo 1989, Oyserman and Markus 1990 a,b) has grown out of earlier work in that field which developed a formulation of the self-concept as an integrated system of self-schemas (Markus and Ruvolo 1989). Under this schematic representation of the self-concept, the individual selectively creates a different self-schema for each of the variety of domains (e.g., attributes, abilities or talents, or roles) deemed to be of critical personal importance. These self-schemas, in some instances (Cross and Markus 1991) referred to as the working self-concept, organize self-relevant information in each given domain, integrating memories of past actions, generalizations about current activities and the responsibility for future actions (Markus 1977).

As a component of these schema, possible selves may be viewed as "...the elements of the self-schema that give structure and meaning to the future in the individual's domains of investment and concern" (Markus and Ruvolo, p. 213). In other words, possible selves represent "...what we could become, what we would like to become and, most importantly, what we are afraid of becoming" (Markus and Nurius, p. 954). An important point to reiterate is that possible selves are not only "future" selves per se. Rather, as part of the working self-concept, they draw from representations of self and experiences encountered by the individual in the past and the activities of the current self, combining these with imagined representations of the self in the future.

Consistent with the distinctiveness postulate addressed by McGuire et al (1978), which argues that many of our conceptions of self are derived from interactions in the social domain, Markus and Nurius (1986) contend that while possible selves are obviously a personalized formulation, they are also distinctly social in nature. A significant social impact may be seen to influence the development of various possible selves. Acknowledging that the individual may create a wide variety of possible selves, they also propose that "(t)he pool of possible selves derives from the categories made salient by the individual's particular sociocultural and historical context and from the models, images and symbols provided by the media and by the individual's immediate social experiences" (p. 954).

The Role of Possible Selves

As incentives toward future behaviors, representing the individual's significant hopes, fears, aspiration and fantasies (Cross and Markus 1991), possible selves may be seen as acting in the role of a powerful motivational force. "As individuals choose among tasks or actions,...they are often guided by a sense, an image, or a conception of what is possible for them" (Cross and Markus, p. 232). The development of these possible selves permits the individual to imagine him/herself in a potential role or situation. As noted by Neisser (1985), the ability to clearly imagine a future role or situation is a significant factor in guiding behavior toward or away from that envisioned role or situation, as well as in devising plans of action aimed at accomplishing or avoiding the envisioned future self.

Possible selves may be either positive (e.g., the educated self, the successful self, or the healthy self) or negative (e.g., the indebted self, the out-of-shape self or the alcoholic self). Thus, the motivating function of possible selves is to encourage approach or avoidance behaviors perceived as relevant to the possible self. The recognition of a negative possible self may be a motivator for the individual to undertake certain behaviors, such as the purchase of exercise equipment or a health club membership or enrollment in an academic program; or to eliminate certain behaviors, such as excessive alcohol consumption or smoking, as a means of avoiding realization of the negative possible self. Conversely, a positive possible self may encourage the individual to avoid behaviors detrimental to the achievement of the possible self, or to undertake certain activities which would enhance the potential for realizing this positive possible self.

Examining Consumers' Possible Selves

Exploratory studies aimed at assessing the viability of the possible self concept (Markus and Nurius 1986) indicate that individuals are indeed able to reflect on and articulate their possible selves. Additionally, it was determined that descriptions of possible selves may be recognized as distinctively different from descriptions of current or past selves. Supplementary studies by Markus and Nurius (1986) were also able to corroborate the ability of respondents to distinguish an independent dimension within the working self-concept related to their hopes and fears. Successful corroboration of several possible self hypotheses (Cross and Markus 1991, Markus and Nurius 1986) indicates that the construct is indeed definable and measurable and, if incorporated into the current conceptualization of consumers' extended self, may serve to allay some of the concerns regarding the operationalization of the extended self. However, the possible self construct cannot simply be transferred into the study of consumer behavior. Clearly, a considerable research background would need to be developed to further support an incorporation of possible selves into the extended self concept. Specific research propositions aimed at drawing possible selves into consumer research would include:

RP1: Individuals are able to identify and articulate a distinct possible self dimension.
RP2a: Individuals are able to attribute certain consumption behaviors to the approach of envisioned positive possible selves.
RP2b: Individuals are able to attribute certain consumption behaviors to the avoidance of envisioned negative possible selves.

Several initial research questions would need to be addressed concerning the ability of consumers to recognize and articulate possible selves in the motivation of consumption behaviors. For instance, to what extent (if any) are possible selves seen as being primary motivators for consumption behaviors. Comparison of the motivational properties of positive and negative possible selves to explore any differences in terms of impact on consumption behaviors is of interest as well.

Future research questions may also address the social and situational factors which contribute to the motivating capacity of possible selves needs further exploration in a consumer context. Also of interest is the assessment of different levels of possible self influence on activities involving various product and service categories.

Routes to testing consumers' possible selves may make use of similar methods to those used in the existing body of research into possible selves (Markus and Nurius 1984, 1986, Cross and Markus 1991). These studies have combined the use of an objective survey instrument with a series of open-ended interview questions to prompt respondents to more fully articulate their experience with the phenomenon. A similar approach would be appropriate for exploratory studies explicitly addressing consumers as well.

Implications for Consumer Behavior Research

On several levels, the exploration of a possible self dimension operating on consumption behavior bears merit and future research attention. Several authors writing in the area of personality now espouse the view that those goals a person is striving to attain, or the imagined person that the individual is in the process of becoming are strong functional motivators. These future oriented images are *at least* as important in influencing behavior as the person's conception of who they currently are (Cross and Markus, 1991).

It seems reasonable to assert that as possible selves play a significant motivational function in guiding individual's behavior, a majority of these activities will involve some type of acquisition, consumption or disposition behavior of interest to consumer researchers. Explicitly addressing a future dimension appears to be the next logical step in the development of a holistic definition of the self-concept in consumer behavior. The incorporation of a possible self factor may prove a valuable tool in uncovering a variety of motivations which are not addressed in any of the current conceptions of self recognized in consumer behavior.

Consistent with the proposed extended self, possible selves would allow for a wholly encompassing construct to integrate past, present and future selves. By extending the view of self to incorporate what the consumer is afraid or in hopes of becoming, consumer behavior researchers may be more adequately able to address some of the more experiential aspects of consumption. An incorporation of possible selves into research questions aimed at discovering why consumers behave as they do is consistent with the current broadened perspective of the self-concept. A recognition that images of what the future may hold, past actions and experiences and all manner of situational and environmental factors impact the individual's view of self offers an all-encompassing definition of the construct.

Discovery of common possible selves among various consumer segments may serve as better indicators of the motivations underlying consumption behaviors for those segments than inquiry aimed at current perceptions of self. The J. Peterman Company of Kentucky has embraced the future orientation of its target consumers as a part of its mission. This specialty catalog retailer operates on the philosophy that "(c)learly, people want things that make their lives the way they wish they were" (The J. Peterman Company, *Owner's Manual No. 14*, 1991).

Many product or service categories purchases are essentially aimed with an eye toward assisting the consumer in achieving a positive or avoiding a negative possible self. Further examination of the ways in which these selves are recognized and the actual impact that they are able to create is warranted. Similarly, certain disposition behaviors, such as environmentally-friendly activities, may be motivated by a desire to avoid or approach possible selves, rather than being motivated by perceptions of the current self.

REFERENCES

Allison, Neil K., Linda L. Golden, Gary M. Mullet, and Donna Coogan (1980), "Sex-Typed Product Images: The Effects of Sex, Sex-Role Self-Concept and Measurement Implications," in *Advances in Consumer Research* Vol. 7, Jerry C. Olson, ed., Ann Arbor, MI: Association for Consumer Research, 604-609.

Belk, Russell W. (1990), "The Role of Possessions in Constructing and Maintaining a Sense of Past," in *Advances in Consumer Research* Vol. 17, Marvin E. Goldberg, Gerald Gorn, and Michael W. Pollay, eds., Provo, UT: Association for Consumer Research, 669-676.

_____ (1988), "Possessions and the Extended Self," *Journal of Consumer Research*, 15 (September), 139-168.

_____ and Melanie Wallendorf, John Sherry, Morris Holbrook, and Scott Roberts (1988), "Collectors and Collecting," in *Advances in Consumer Research* Vol. 15, Michael Houston, ed., Provo, UT: Association for Consumer Research, 548-553.

Bettman, James R., Harold H. Kassarjian and Richard J. Lutz (1978), "Consumer Behavior," in *Review of Marketing 1978*, Chicago: American Marketing Association, 194-239.

Birdwell, Al E. (1968), "A Study of Influence of Image Congruence on Consumer Choice," *Journal of Business*, 41 (January), 76-88.

Burnkrant, Robert E. and Thomas J. Page Jr. (1982), "On the Management of Self Images in Social Situations: The Role of Public Self Consciousness," in *Advances in Consumer Research* Vol. 9, Andrew Mitchell, ed., Ann Arbor, MI: Association for Consumer Research, 452-455.

Cohen, Joel B. (1989), "An Over-Extended Self?" *Journal of Consumer Research*, 16 (June), 125-128.

Cross, Susan and Hazel Markus (1991), "Possible Selves across the Life Span," *Human Development*, 34, 230-255.

Delozier, Maynard W. and Rollie Tillman (1972), "Self Image Concepts — Can They Be Used to Design Marketing Programs?" *Southern Journal of Business*, 7(1), 9-15.

Dolich, Ira J. (1969), "Congruence Relationship Between Self-Image and Product Brands," *Journal of Marketing Research*, 6 (February), 80-84.

Gardner, Burleigh B. and Sidney J. Levy (1955), "The Product and the Brand," *Harvard Business Review*, 33 (April), 33-39.

Green, Paul E., Arun Maheshwari, and Vithala R. Rao (1969), "Self-Concept and Brand Preference: An Empirical Application of Multidimensional Scaling," *Journal of the Market Research Society*, 11(4), 343-360.

Goffman, Erving (1951) "Symbols of Class Status," *British Journal of Sociology*, 2 (December), 294-304.

Grubb Edward L. and Harrison L. Grathwohl (1967), "Consumer Self Concept, Symbolism and Market Behavior: A Theoretical Approach," *Journal of Marketing*, 31 (October), 22-27.

_____ and Gregg Hupp (1968), "Perception of Self, Generalized Stereotypes and Brand Selection," *Journal of Marketing Research*, 5 (February), 58-63.

Hall, Edward T. and George L. Trager (1953), *The Analysis of Culture*, Washington DC: American Council of Learned Societies.

Ingelhart, Marita Rosch, Hazel Markus, and Donald R. Brown (1989),"The Effects of Possible Selves on Academic Achievement - A Panel Study," in *Recent Advances in Social Psychology: An International Perspective*, J.P. Forgas and J.M. Innes, eds., North Holland: Elsevier Science Publishers B.V., 469-477.

Landon, E. Laird Jr. (1974), "Self Concept, Ideal Self Concept and Consumer Purchase Intentions," *Journal of Consumer Research*, 1 (September), 44-51.

Levy, Sidney J. (1959), "Symbols for Sale," *Harvard Business Review*, 37(4), 117-124.

Markus, Hazel and Ann Ruovo (1989), "Possible Selves: Personalized Representations of Goals," in *Goal Concepts in Personality Research*, L.A. Pervin, ed., Hillsdale, NJ: Lawrence Erlbaum Associates, 211-241.

Markus, Hazel and Paula Nurius (1986), "Possible Selves," *America Psychologist*, 41 (9), 954-969.

McGuire, William C., Pamela Child, and Terry Fujiota, (1978), "Saliency of Ethnicity in the Spontaneous Self-Concept as a Function of One's Ethnic Distinctiveness in the Social Environment," *Journal of Personality and Social Psychology*, 36 (5), 511-520.

Mick, David Glen and Michelle DeMoss (1990), "To Me From Me: A Descriptive Phenomenology of Self-Gifts," in *Advances in Consumer Research* Vol. 17, Marvin E. Goldberg, Gerald Gorn, and Michael W. Pollay, eds., Provo, UT: Association for Consumer Research, 677-682.

Munson, J. Michael and W. Austin Spivey (1980), "Assessing Self-Concept," in *Advances in Consumer Research* Vol. 7, Jerry C. Olson, ed., Ann Arbor, MI: Association for Consumer Research, 598-603.

Neisser, U. (1985), "The Role of Invariant Structures in the Control of Movement," in *Goal Directed Behavior: The Concept of Action in Psychology*, M. Frese and J. Sabini eds., Hillsdale, NJ: Lawrence Erlbaum Associates, 97-109.

Owner's Manual No.14, (1991) Lexington, KY: The J. Peterman Company.

Oyserman, Daphna and Hazel Rose Markus (1990a), "Possible Selves and Delinquency," *Journal of Personality and Social Psychology*, 59 (1), 112-125.

Oyserman, Daphna and Hazel Markus (1990b), "Possible Selves in Balance: Implications for Delinquency," *Journal of Social Issues*, 46(2), 141-157.

Rogers, Carl (1951), *Client-Centered Therapy: Its Current Practices, Implications and Theory*, Boston: Houghton Mifflin.

Sanders, Clinton R. (1990), "The Animal 'Other': Self Definition, Social Identity and Companion Animals," in *Advances in Consumer Research* Vol. 17, Marvin E. Goldberg, Gerald Gorn, and Michael W. Pollay, eds., Provo, UT: Association for Consumer Research, 662-668.

Schenk, Carolyn Turner and Rebecca H. Holman (1980), "A Sociological Approach to Brand Choice: The Concept of Situational Self Image," in *Advances in Consumer Research* Vol. 7, Jerry C. Olson, ed., Ann Arbor, MI: Association for Consumer Research, 610-614.

Schouten, John W. (1991), "Personalized Rites of Passage and the Reconstruction of Self," in *Advances in Consumer Research* Vol. 18, Michael R. Solomon and Rebecca H. Holman, eds., Provo, UT: Association for Consumer Research, 49-51.

Schouten, John W. (1991), "Selves in Transition: Symbolic Consumption in Personal Rites of Passage and Identity Reconstruction," *Journal of Consumer Research*, 17 (March), 412-425.

Sirgy, M. Joseph (1982a), "Self-Concept in Consumer Behavior: A Critical Review," *Journal of Consumer Research*, 9 (December), 287-300.

_____ (1982b), "Self-Image/Product-Image Congruity and Advertising Strategy," in *Advances in Consumer Research* Vol. 9, Andrew Mitchell, ed., Ann Arbor, MI: Association for Consumer Research, 129-133.

_____ (1981), "The Self-Concept in Relation to Product Preference and Purchase Intention," in *Advances in Consumer Research* Vol. 8, Kent B. Monroe, ed., Ann Arbor, MI: Association for Consumer Research, 350-354.

Solomon, Michael R. (1990), "The Imperial Self," in *Advances in Consumer Research* Vol. 17, Marvin E. Goldberg, Gerald Gorn, and Michael W. Pollay, eds., Provo, UT: Association for Consumer Research, 68-70.

Perceptions of Self: The Effects of Self-concept Discrepancy, Possible Selves and Dispossession

J. Michael Munson, Santa Clara University

Three recent studies on self-concept and various aspects of consumer behavior (Gould 1993; Morgan 1993; Pavia 1993) all reflect a sense of frustration with its conventional conceptualization and measurement. Noting inadequacies in the traditional ways of assessing self, Gould contends that a better measure is one which also includes psychographic and demographic characteristics, in addition to the more usual traits. Morgan suggests that "Possible Selves" may hold more promise. Pavia is less concerned with how to conceptualize self-concept per se, and does not offer a clear definition of the construct; rather her focus is more on how dispossession affects self-concept. Key ideas, contributions, and limitations of each of these studies will be discussed below.

Gould's primary goal is to assess how the "procedural aspects of self-concept — private self-consciousness (SC) and self-monitoring (SM) — affect the self-report of the contents of self-concept and related life-style items." While it is unclear how these two apparent "traits" of self-concept are "procedural," the study does help clarify our understanding of the conceptual and operational distinctions between SC and SM. A major contribution of Gould is combining SC and SM within the same study to assess their individual and possible interactive effects. Moreover, he notes the strong possibility that subscales in the Self Consciousness Scales (SCS) developed previously may be related to the instruments measuring Self Monitoring (SM), especially the two SCS dimensions of Public Self Consciousness and Social Anxiety. Therefore he minimizes potential confounding by using only one dimension of the SCS (Private Self-Consciousness).

The study, however, raises both conceptual and methodological questions. There remain ambiguities regarding the expected behaviors of individuals characterized by various levels of high vs. low SC or SM. For example, the definition of private self-consciousness seems problematic: "...the trait equivalent of state self-awareness or self-focus (Fenigstein et al 1975)... It [SC] is thought to affect attitude-behavior consistency in reflecting the degree that a person is able to access and know his/her own attitudes—a person higher in private SC being more likely to exhibit such consistency than others" (Carver and Scheier 1981; Miller and Grush 1986). It remains unclear from this definition why a high SC individual would exhibit more "behavioral consistency." Contending so would seem to assume the absence of social or environmental influences.

Regarding methodological issues, the quota sampling procedures used raise some caveats, and we gain only sketchy insight into the sample's demographic characteristics, limiting external validity. Questions also arise regarding the instrument used to assess self-concept discrepancy and the specific task instructions for its completion. A rather unconventional 30-item inventory was used, containing a variety of disparate items, ranging from traditional self-attributes (masculine/feminine, achievement) to much less traditional items (decent housing, taxes, height). Rather than a measure of self-concept, this instrument is perhaps more appropriately described as a melange of items, some indexing aspects of self, others life-style and demography. Key psychometric properties of the self-concept measure are also unknown or unreported.

Regarding task instructions, one would like to know more about this rather unique way of assessing self-concept discrepancy (i.e., a 10 point scale with a "1" indicating the person felt his/her actual states to be "very close" to ideal (a small discrepancy) and a "10" indicating actual states to be "very far" from ideal (a large discrepancy). Would the self-reported discrepancies be similar if actual and ideal images were each respectively assessed first, and then the researcher (not the respondent) computed the total discrepancy score between the two self components? The factor analysis also raises some questions; the rationale for using principal components with varimax rotation, rather than oblique, is not articulated. Although this yielded 8 factors the eighth factor was dropped and the remaining seven were interpreted. A more appropriate procedure, given the decision to drop this factor, would have been to rerun the analysis, constraining results to a 7-factor solution. This might yield a different set of final factors, loadings, and interpretations.

These limitations notwithstanding, this study improves our understanding of the possible ways in which SC and SM individually and jointly affect self-concept and self-report measures. The results are encouraging in that the effects of SC and SM remained even after controlling for specific demographics. Future studies should strive to incorporate fuller, more conventional measures of self-concept and investigate other types of task instructions.

Morgan (1993) identifies three main goals: (1) to review the evolution of self-concept research in consumer behavior and its limitations; (2) to explore Belk's (1988) extended self paradigm; and (3) to elaborate theoretical definitions of Possible Selves (PSs), as well as specific propositions and empirical considerations and benefits from incorporating this perspective into consumer behavior. Regarding the first goal, one must disagree with her contention that much of the prior research "... lack[s] of development of a theoretical base..." Such criticism, while applicable to some studies, is too sweeping for at least three reasons. Many earlier studies were: (1) built upon the notions of symbolic communication and the theoretic propositions that some objects (products, brands,) and/or actions may be imbued with "surplus meaning" or badge value and therefore useful to the consumer for communicating desired aspects of self to others; (2) grounded in congruity theory, with it's attendant notions of matching products (brands) to one's self-concept (actual, ideal, etc.) and assuming that the closer the match, the greater the likelihood of preference, usage, ownership, etc.; (3) built upon the conceptual notion that the discrepancies between components of self (ex., actual, ideal) can motivate behavior to reduce the gap via approach or avoidance of some product or brand.

Regarding the second major goal, the study does little to explore Belk's (1988) paradigm of extended self per se, or how the construct of PSs is theoreticially linked to, or different from extended self. Citing his contention that "...self extends not only to the present material environment, but extends forward and backward in time" (Belk 1988, p. 674), Morgan implicitly suggests that this is the conceptual link between extended self and PSs. She further suggests that "... if [the possible self] is incorporated into the current conceptualization of consumers' extended self, [it] may serve to allay some of the concerns regarding the operationalization of the extended self." However, this assertion remains untested and perhaps overly optimistic, for it's truthfulness requires a much more thorough discussion of how extant notions of possible selves are similar and dissimilar to those of extended self. Without such explication it will remain unclear to many why both conceptualizations of self (possible and extended) are needed, or for what types of research situations or consumption problems each conceptualization may prove more useful.

Regarding the third major goal, the study does make consumer researchers more aware of the construct of PSs. Morgan's discussion of the theoretic bases of PSs and the recent work in psychology provide useful background on the construct, as do her two specific propositions aimed at drawing PSs into consumer research: (1) individuals are able to identify and articulate a distinct PS dimension; (2) individuals are able to attribute certain consumption behaviors to the approach (avoidance) of envisioned positive (negative) PSs. Given the theoretic as opposed to empirical orientation of this study, these propositions are perhaps the study's biggest contribution. In effect, they define the starting point for those interested in PSs and their relevance to consumer behavior.

Beyond these propositions, however, four other important questions relevant to the possible utility of the PS construct in consumer behavior not identified by Morgan are also suggested. First, can we conceptually and empirically distinguish among the major, conventional measures of self-concepts — actual, ideal, social, looking glass, extended, and possible selves? A good empirical study, using multitrait-multimethod procedures, would help to answer whether PSs had a viable future in consumer behavior. Second, does the number, content, and intensity of various PSs vary as a function of such factors as the individual's involvement, and personality traits (ex., cognitive complexity, self-consciousness)? Third, with how many "possible selves" must consumer behavior researchers be concerned? The discipline must guard against becoming seduced by the potential unboundedness seemingly implied by this construct (as well as by extended self). Without extreme vigilance researchers could find themselves invoking a multitude of ambiguously conceptualized PSs for defining and explaining consumer behavior. This concern is all the more valid in light of Markus and Nurius' (1986) contention that all but the most routine human actions will implicate a PS, thereby implying the necessity to identify and operationalize each relevant PS across a multitude of possible marketing situations. Fourth, does the content of various PSs self-schema include identical dimensions (attributes, contents, traits), with each being assessed under dissimilar situations, or are the contents (dimensions, etc.) of each PS totally unique?

Pavia (1993) uses depth interviews to explore the relationships between self-perceptions and the dispossession experiences of people with HIV infection. She argues that one would expect HIV infection "...to profoundly challenge a person's sense of self..." and that the aim of her research is "... to understand changes in self-perception through an exploration of the dispossessional experiences of infected persons." Unfortunately, due to various methodological and conceptual limitations, these goals are not fully realized. The small sample size (n=10) constrains external validity. More importantly, questions of internal validity arise because no precise operational measures are suggested for the two most important variables under study (self-concept and dispossession behavior); hence it's not possible to quantitatively assess their relationship. Dispossession seems to be loosely defined and to cover many different things, including reduced income, decisions about who to leave things to, getting away or escaping from existing, unsatisfactory relationships, as well as activities required to qualify for state health benefits.

Also the reasons given for targeting AIDS suffers, while all relevant, are not necessarily unique to AIDS-infected individuals. With the exception of the final reason (i.e., "Many [AIDS sufferers] face negative reactions to their diagnoses from co-workers, friends and family"), these reasons don't preclude looking at other populations to study dispossession and its relation to self, including for example, terminal cancer patients or those undergoing chemotherapy.

Going beyond Pavia's (1993) study, many researchers would be interested in learning more about how specific dimensions of self-concept, or specific self-images (eg., actual, ideal, or various PSs) "change" as a consequence of two things: the progression of the individual through the four stages of HIV infection, and as a consequence of the individual's dispossession behavior. Does knowing one has the HIV virus differentially affect various PSs (current, expected and hoped-for)? One might conjecture that the self-concept may involve a variety or PSs: the denying self, progressing to the angry, enraged, or bitter self, transitioning to the depressed, perhaps despondent self; and moving ultimately to a more contented, or integrated self in the final stage. Admittedly, while these notions are speculative, the measurement of such potential changes in self-concept as the individual transitions through the various stages of HIV infecton would seemingly offer invaluable information for those involved in treating and administering services to this group.

The "conclusion" that material goods are not seen as valuable as personal relationships by HIV-infected individuals is probably applicable, again, to many situations where imminent death is the ultimate prospect— not just among people with AIDS. That HIV-infected individuals have a greater sense of loss at losing control over what they formally did or could do, compared to loss of control over "What they owned" is not surprising. As the man named Arnold in Pavia's study said: "I am what I do." His sentiments and those of other respondents are consistent with previous research suggesting that self defining activities and behaviors, those actions implicating our abilities to socialize and our interpersonal relationships, are generally more important and valued aspects of self-definition and identify than are objects.

If dispossession and its possible relationship to self-concept is to become an important consumer behavior research topic, then more elaborate conceptualization and operationalization of these two key constructs is required. Nonetheless, Pavia's study does make several useful contributions: (1) it gives us insight into the "human condition" of AIDS victims and the catastrophic effect it has on their lives, including the social stigma and the loss of job, friends, and family; (2) it promotes understanding of the tragic sense of personal loss which AIDS victims feel, and that a large component of this loss is in their sense of self; (3) it increases our understanding of the types of objects which are dispossessed and the associated pain; (4) it gives us some glint into the gross inadequacies of the social, economic, and political systems which fail to provide for the needs of AIDS victims. Studies in this vein are highly consistent with the recent appeal of Alan Andreasen, the Association for Consumer Research president, for more research addressing relevant social marketing issues. Such research has important implications for both the medical and service communities which treat HIV-infected individuals.

REFERENCES

Belk, Russell W. (1988), "Possessions and the Extended Self," *Journal of Consumer Research*, 15 (September), 139-168.

Carver, Charles S. and Michael F. Scheier (1981), "Self-Consciousness and Reactance," *Journal of Research in Personality*, 15 (March), 16-29.

Fenigstein, Allan, Michael F. Scheier and Arnold H. Buss (1975), "Public and Private Self-consciousness: Assessment and Theory," *Journal of Consulting and Clinical Psychology*, 43 (August), 522-527.

Gould, Stephen J. (1993), "Assessing Self-concept Discrepancy in Consumer Behavior: The Joint Effects of Private Self-Consciousness and Self Monitoring," in Leigh McAlister and Michael L. Rothschild (eds.), *Advances in Consumer Research*, Vol. XX. Provo, UT: Association for Consumer Research.

Markus, Hazel and Paula Nurius (1986), "Possible Selves," *American Psychologist*, 41 (9), 954-969.

Miller, Lynn E. and Joseph Grush (1986), "Individual Differences in Attitudinal Versus Normative Determination of Behavior," *Journal of Experimental Social Psychology*, 22 (May), 190-202.

Morgan, Amy J. (1993), "The Evolving Self in Consumer Behavior: Exploring Possible Selves in Leigh McAlister and Michael L. Rothschild (eds.), *Advances in Consumer Research*, Vol. XX. Provo, UT: Association for Consumer Research.

Pavia, Teresa (1993), "Dispossession and Perceptions of Self in Late Stage HIV Infection," in Leigh McAlister and Michael L. Rothschild (eds.), *Advances in Consumer Research*, Vol. XX. Provo, UT: Association for Consumer Research.

Consumer Research Priorities for the MSI Research Competition on "Using Marketing to Serve Society"

Paul N. Bloom, University of North Carolina at Chapel Hill

This paper provides an overview of the special topic session with the title listed above. The session was designed to communicate information to ACR members about a Marketing Science Institute research competition on the topic of "Using Marketing to Serve Society." The competition was organized to support research in public policy toward marketing and social marketing. The hope of the session was to encourage ACR members to submit proposals to the competition, which was approaching its submission deadline of December 18, 1992. By the time this paper appears in print, the winners of this competition will have been announced. Plans were to award as many as four awards for up to $9,000 of research expenses. The top three proposals were to receive prizes of $5,000, $2,500, and $1,500.

The competition was co-founded by the Marketing Science Institute and the Kenan-Flagler Business School of the University of North Carolina at Chapel Hill. Paul Bloom served as the competition chair. Ten companies provided financial support, with Anheuser-Busch and Quaker Oats serving as sponsors, and BurroughsWellcome, Kellogg, Leo Burnett, Miller Brewing, Polaroid, Porter/Novelli, Glaxo, and R.J. Reynolds Tobacco serving as affiliates. An Advisory Board consisting of representatives from the supporting companies, leading academics, and MSI management guided the development of research priorities for the competition and the selection of winning proposals.

The session during the ACR Conference had short presentations made by Paul Bloom, Richard Staelin, William Wilkie, and Michael Mazis. All were members of the competition's Advisory Board. Bloom went first and described the history of the competition. He covered how the idea for the program originated and how the fundraising and priority-setting were completed. He stressed that he hoped the competition would serve as a first step toward establishing a more permanent funding source for research on public policy toward marketing and social marketing. Staelin then discussed the Marketing Science Institute's role in the competition. He talked about how this competition fits with other MSI competitions and programs.

Wilkie provided some historical perspectives on research in public policy toward marketing and social marketing. He offered the opinion that there was considerable room for making valuable research contributions in these areas. Next, Mazis reviewed the specific research priorities of the competition under the heading of public policy toward marketing. He pointed to topics and questions that might be particularly appropriate for ACR members to address. The presentations concluded with Bloom discussing specific research priorities in social marketing. Following the short presentations, a question-and-answer period took place in which audience members made inquiries about a variety of aspects of the competition.

Readers interested in further information can contact MSI at 617-491-2060 or Paul Bloom at 919-962-3222.

Understanding Donation Behavior: Strategic Implications from Consumer Research

James W. Peltier University of Wisconsin Whitewater
April Atwood, University of Washington
Lynora Bayless, United Way of Southern Nevada
Tracy Bier, Puget Sound Blood Center
William Carter, School of Business, University of Washington
Catherine Cole, University of Iowa
Mary Huneke, University of Iowa
Patrick Murphy, University of Notre Dame
Dee Myer, Puget Sound Blood Center
John A. Schibrowsky, University of Nevada-Las Vegas
Sandra Tausend, Puget Sound Blood Center

INTRODUCTION

Donations are the life-blood of altruistic cause organizations like the United Way, the American Cancer Society, and the American Red Cross. Unfortunately, numerous barriers exist that make it difficult for charitable organizations to motivate and understand gift-giving behavior. Specifically, recent economic downturns, perceived funds mismanagement and abuse, AIDS and other health effects have become major concerns for potential monetary and blood donors.

It is clear that consumer research can provide meaningful guidance to better understand the nature and scope of the altruism process. The session addressed three key topics that are important to the development of successful charitable campaigns. These topics included: 1) understanding the donation process; 2) researching key experimental manipulations; and 3) turning research into action.

Understanding The Donation Process

The findings from two unpublished studies designed to identify the key factors underlying the donation process were presented. In the Peltier and Schibrowsky study, a comprehensive model containing various dimensions that proportedly influence the decision to donate money was constructed and tested. In their presentation, special attention was given to the discussion of the psychological, attitudinal, sociological, economical, demographical, and behavioral dimensions that differentiate donors from nondonors, and high donors from low donors. The Atwood et. al. study used a different approach to attempt to identify the key dimensions underlying the donation process. Here, a behavioral decision model for predicting the nature and extent of repeat blood donations was developed and tested.

Researching Key Experimental Manipulations

The Cole et. al. presentation examined the effect of emotional and informational direct mail appeals on cognitive responses, attitudes toward the ad, and intentions to donate blood. They drew upon research on emotional advertising to predict whether donors and nondonors differ in their responsiveness to appeal types.

Turning Research Into Action

Lynora Bayless, Senior Vice-President of Market Research and Donor Services at the United Way of Las Vegas served as the discussant. She discussed the transition from studying the donation process, and testing experimental manipulation, to developing marketing strategies based on these findings. She discussed how the United Way of Las Vegas has taken a research perspective, and how this orientation has contributed to their success as one of the top United Way agencies. She concluded with a discussion of how important it is for academics to become involved in helping their local charitable organizations with their research needs.

The Two Sides of the Accessibility Coin: Factors that Enhance and Impede Information Accessibility
Prakash Nedungadi, Indiana University

Recent discussions of consumer decision making and choice processes emphasize the importance of information accessibility. For instance, during brand choice, the ability to retrieve information is important when the consumer is bringing a consideration set of brands to mind and when information is being used to select from among the considered brands. Analogously, the effectiveness of advertising will depend critically on the consumer's ability to access information relayed by the ad at choice. Factors acting at information encoding (e.g., frequency and recency of ad exposure) as well as retrieval (e.g., ad retrieval cues) have been shown to increase information recall and use. The three papers presented in this session explored conditions under which the factors that usually enhance information accessibility could, in fact, *suppress* information leading to contrary effects on brand recall, evaluation and choice.

The first paper by Kevin Keller examined these effects in terms of advertising retrieval cues. Based on the theoretical notions of "retrieval effort", this study hypothesized that although memory retrieval cues may facilitate recall initially, they could result in lower effort and thus more substantial declines in recall at a later point in time. To test this hypothesis, the study used a 2 X 2 design where the presence or absence of ad retrieval cues at time 1 (ten minutes after ad exposure) is crossed with presence or absence of the same cues at time 2 (one week later). Keller found that, consistent with prior research, recall of ad claims was enhanced in the presence of ad retrieval cues (at time 1). Moreover, recall of ad claims was also higher at time 2 for those subjects who had not been cued at time 1, when the ad cue was present at time 2, as compared to when it was not. As hypothesized, recall declined for subjects who had been cued during time 1 but were not cued at time 2. An interesting finding was that the decline in recall of ad claims was also observed *for subjects who were cued at time 1 and cued again at time 2*. Importantly, the effects of retrieval effort on ad claim recall also extended, selectively, to brand attitudes and purchase intent.

The second paper by Manoj Hastak and Anusree Mitra explored the boundary conditions under which the provision of brand/subcategory cues may lead to facilitiation or inhibition of brand recall. For instance, the provision of a single brand cue has been shown to facilitate recall of certain brands, while the provision of multiple cues inhibits recall. They examined the effect of providing brand and subcategory cues on retrieval. In their paper they directly compared conditions under which brand cues facilitate recall to those in which inhibition may occur. They also explored some of the conditions under which cues may have neither facilitatory nor inhibitory effects on recall. Finally, they examined implications of their findings for brand consideration and choice.

The third paper, by Amitava Chattopadhyay and Prakash Nedungadi extends an earlier study in which they showed that a highly likeable ad which captures attention at encoding could reduce accessibility of brand information at retrieval, particularly under conditions of low attention. In this paper, they examined whether repetition of the ad would attenuate this effect, that is, whether by increasing the relative accessibility of brand information, ad repetition could reduce the likelihood of "interference" from an affective ad. In a 2 X 2 X 2 between-subjects design they varied a) ad liking, b) delay and c) ad repetition. They replicated the finding that (due to interference) a likeable ad leads to fewer brand cognitions and lower attitudes at a delay. Further, as expected, ad repetition did prevent decay of brand and ad cognitions and attitudes. Interestingly however, ad repetition did not result in greater elaboration of the brand claims at exposure rather, subjects appeared to be rehearsing existing thoughts and attitudes. As a result, ad repetition could not counteract the interfering effects of an affective ad on accessibility of cognitions and thus on attitudes, at a delay.

Discussant, Wes Hutchinson noted that the ad/delay manipulations of the first and third papers and the brand/subcategory cue manipulation of the second paper were conceptually similar in that they inhibited recall by increasing interference. He also noted that many of the results observed in the three studies were consistent with the idea that recall is enhanced by both the strength of a retrieval cue and the extent to which that cue matches information that is present at encoding.

A Critique Of Critical Theory: Response To Murray And Ozanne's "The Critical Imagination"

Val Larsen, Virginia Polytechnic Institute and State University
Newell D. Wright, Virginia Polytechnic Institute and State University

ABSTRACT

This paper critiques an article (Murray and Ozanne 1991) which introduces critical theory into consumer research. It makes explicit the neo-Marxist roots of critical theory and shows that important assumptions of the theory are untenable. It calls into question the normative foundation proposed by Murray and Ozanne, and it argues that in their paper, critical theory fails the test of praxis. This comment ultimately claims that critical theory is unworkable in consumer research because of its flaws.

INTRODUCTION

Most marketing academics now regard social marketing as an integral part of their discipline (Hunt 1976). Perhaps because they see it as part of the larger enterprise, there has been little effort to build for it an independent theory base. One exception is a recent JCR article, "The Critical Imagination: Emancipatory Interests in Consumer Research," in which Murray and Ozanne (1991; hereafter M&O) attempt to root social marketing and socially conscious consumer research in the neo-Marxist analytic called *critical theory*. As an explication of critical theory, the M&O article is a great success, for it succinctly and lucidly lays out the assumptions, history, and methods of this complex research tradition. But these virtues notwithstanding, the article does not provide a reliable program for consumer and marketing research because it never explains how the basic weaknesses of critical theory can be overcome. In this response, we argue that the weaknesses cannot be transcended and, consequently, that critical theory cannot provide an adequate theoretical foundation for socially conscious marketing research.

M&O acknowledge but do not make sufficiently clear the Marxist roots of critical theory, which was designed to reconstruct an intellectually credible Marxism in the light of historical developments following Marx's death, developments which meant there would be no dictatorship of the proletariat, no withering of the state, no natural evolution into a classless society (Habermas 1973, pp. 196-198). Critical theorists of the first generation (Horkheimer, Adorno, Marcuse, Fromm, among others) undertook the reconstruction, unified by two value judgements—"human life is worth living," "human life can be improved"—and by a shared terminal goal, their desire to create "a form of social organization that makes possible freedom, justice, and reason" (Marcuse 1964; M&O, p. 134). Though M&O mention this first generation, they focus on Jürgen Habermas, the most prominent critical theorist of the second generation. Habermas sought to address two basic questions which had been raised in the work of earlier theorists: a) how can critical theory be connected to political practice, i.e. who or what will be the agent of social change, and b) how can a theory which arises within history provide a basis for an ahistorical, universal critique? Critical theorists must confront these two questions, for if they are not answered, the value judgments and terminal goal of critical theory become mere platitudes, abstract ideals subscribed to by most everyone, not guides to responsible and effective social action. Unfortunately, as we argue below, neither Habermas nor M&O adequately answer these questions.

We discuss the failure to answer Habermas' first question in the section on agents of change, the failure to answer the second question in the section on normative foundations. In the third section of our paper, we go on to critique M&O's examples, suggesting that they do not pass the important test of praxis.

AGENTS OF CHANGE

Critical theorists do have an answer, albeit an unsatisfactory one, for Habermas' first question, which answer M&O espouse. Since the proletariat, Marx's agent of change, did not act as predicted, effecting a radical restructuring of society, critical theorists propose that they themselves and other like-minded intellectuals serve as the agents of change (Habermas 1973, pp. 1-7; Horkheimer 1974). This answer is unsatisfactory partly because it leads directly to Habermas' second question, which has no answer, partly because it casts critical practitioners in a paternalistic role that seems inconsistent with genuine emancipation. The paternalism is evident in M&O's suggestion that critical researchers must

> move beyond mere observation of subjects or participation in the informants' social reality and attempt through dialogue to reveal constraints, thereby motivating informants to engage in conscious political action (praxis). Simply put, the purpose of the critical research is to make life better for the social actor. ... Metaphorically, the critical theorist is a "liberator" seeking through dialogue to make social actors aware of oppressive structures, a first step on the road to social change. (M&O, p. 136)

M&O imply that critical practitioners should intervene in the lives of others, acting as liberators, because they perceive the condition and interests of their informants better than the informants themselves and are thus positioned to stimulate them to discover or create just and reasonable solutions for their practical problems. This amounts to a claim on the part of the critical practitioner of *special insight into social ethics*. But, to take M&O's own example, on the issue of minivan safety, why should the ethical views of a critical researcher be any more valid than those of others who are intimately involved with this issue: UAW members and officers, Chrysler managers, National Highway Traffic Safety Administration bureaucrats, Consumer Union automotive specialists, politicians, consumers, the groups and individuals who presently work out a solution to the problem in the public arena? While consumer researchers have their own domain of expertise and can certainly contribute to the debate on this and other issues, they cannot claim the central role unless their moral understanding transcends that of other human beings. This is all the more true because consumer researchers are not empowered by an explicit constituency as are politicians, managers, union officials, and even employees of the Consumer Union. While democratic values or crude utilitarianism—the greatest good for the greatest number—might have justified Marx's proletariat had it taken up the agent-of-change role, the intellectual elite of critical theory can assume this role only if their actions are firmly grounded in superior moral understanding. This brings us to Habermas' second, more fundamental question: is it possible for critical theory to arise within history and yet provide superior moral understanding and the basis for a universal social critique?

NORMATIVE FOUNDATIONS

While reviewing weaknesses of critical theory at the conclusion of their article, M&O concede that the theory is undermined by a fundamental contradiction, a problem

> rooted in the critical theorists' claim that all knowledge is historical. If that is so, how can a researcher step out of this historicity and offer a critique of society by a transcendent rational standard? It is difficult to defend the existence of historical knowledge while at the same time suggesting that an ahistorical basis for critique exists.... Although we recognize the problem, we choose to align with Habermas and his notion of an ideal speech situation. (M&O, p. 141)

This is a remarkable passage, for in it, M&O describe very clearly a fundamental flaw of critical theory, and yet they "choose" to overlook the flaw. Given their practice of making much hay of contradictions discovered in the thought or behavior of others, it ill behooves critical theorists to accept so easily a basic contradiction in their own thought. In this section, we show that the contradiction cannot be passed over, for it undermines the entire critical theoretic endeavor, transforming it from an objective moral science into an exercise in personal politics. We focus first on the *ideal speech situation*, a relatively concrete foundation for social norms, then discuss the critical theoretic view of *reason*, *tradition*, and *science*, concepts which provide the larger context in which critical theorists make normative claims.

Ideal Speech Situation

As mentioned above, the abstract ideals and terminal goals of critical theory—freedom, justice, and reason—are mere platitudes unless they are concretized in a comprehensive analysis of social relations. In M&O's article, Habermas' ideal speech situation provides the requisite concretization, for their discussion of the ideal speech situation is the one place where they spell out their normative social vision. Nor is this just one foundation among many that are available to critical theorists. As Fay (1987, p. 184), a scholar sympathetic to critical theory, points out, "This is by far the most sophisticated and powerful argument advanced in support of [the ideal of collective autonomy] from within the tradition of critical social science." If this foundation proves inadequate, there is in the tradition no other to supplant it.

M&O effectively encapsulate Habermas' position. An ideal speech situation is "a condition of symmetrical free speech,"

> in which all people have an equal opportunity to engage in discourse unconstrained by authority, tradition, or dogma.... All participants must have the same chance to employ constantive, regulative, and representative speech acts. This requirement ensures that no assertion will be exempt from critique, no single participant will gain privilege, and the participants will be truthful so that their inner natures will become transparent to others. (p. 134)

What one finds here in a new, sociolinguistic frame is Marx's utopian classless society, the commune devoid of hierarchy and social tension, which Marx held to be the *terminus ad quem* of history (Marx 1977, pp. 169, 190-91). The utopian terminus and standard of truth for Habermas is "rational consensus," allegedly the natural result of a speech situation in which everyone fully understands everyone else. This consensus discloses an underlying truth, thereby providing a foundation for social criticism (Fay 1987, p. 187-190; Habermas 1983; 1987, pp. 27, 71-72).

The limitations of this analysis become apparent when M&O attempt to apply it. As an approximate example of the ideal speech situation, they offer the Calvert Social Investment Fund (CSIF), a mutual fund which specializes in socially responsible investing. The CSIF advisory board includes representatives of various progressive social movements, environmentalists, educators, health care professionals, labor unionists, etc. The board invests in a company when the various advisors come to a rational consensus on the wisdom of doing so, all having participated openly, honestly, and with equal power in a discussion of the company's merits.

Though admirable in some respects, this speech situation is hardly ideal, for while the advisory board might achieve consensus on occasion, it does so by being ideologically homogeneous to begin with. The board includes no representatives of the political right, i.e. Eagle Forum, the NRA, groups supported by millions of Americans. Consequently, a certain viewpoint is privileged before the discussion even begins. And given the exclusion of the right, a whole range of assertions will probably be exempt from criticism. Were the right included, on the other hand, the advisory council might never reach consensus, a failure which would again call the entire concept of an ideal speech situation into question.

It is worth noting that while M&O say the ideal speech situation should "serve as a guide or as a critical standard from which actual discourse can be evaluated" (p. 134), they do not conform their own research program to this standard. Thus, in their minivan example, they do not suggest that a researcher bring company management, union officers, government regulators, and consumer groups together in order that they may forge a rational consensus—perhaps for the very good reasons that these groups would not assemble at the bidding of a consumer researcher and would not achieve consensus if they did assemble. Instead, they propose that the researcher, having talked with the various groups, act unilaterally to publicize the contradiction between the manufacturer's safety claims and the van's actual lack of safety, an act which the manufacturer surely and the unions probably would have vetoed if consensus were required as the basis for action. *Given that a consensus is not sought or achieved, the consumer researcher has no foundation except personal politics, insights, and values when she or he acts unilaterally to bring about social change.* It is appropriate to act upon such insights and values, but they are not a foundation for the kind of ahistorical, universal social critique critical theory claims to offer. One might add that Habermas' analysis is at odds with the most powerful contemporary emancipatory force, the multicultural movement, which has sought to empower minorities and broaden participation in social and economic institutions by arguing that the perspectives of minorities are unique, that no universalizing consensus can capture those perspectives (Hooks 1989).

Reason, Tradition, and Science

Reason and Tradition. It is no accident that *rational* consensus is the alleged product of an ideal speech situation. Critical theory takes for granted the existence of an autonomous rationality which is capable of discovering and disclosing objective truths that have been hidden by ideology and false consciousness (Fay 1987; Habermas 1983). It poses a problem—people are oppressed but do not perceive the oppression—and proposes a solution, a rational critique of the oppression which will make people aware of their true circumstances and, thereby, motivate them to change the social order making it more just and reasonable. (See steps 4 and 5 in M&O's methodological approach to critical research). This critique is possible, in the critical theoretic view, only when reason is uncontaminated by the corrupting influence of an inherited intellectual and social tradition, for only then are valid, i.e. rational, social norms revealed (Habermas 1973, pp. 32-37; 1984, 61-66).

Fundamental though it is to critical theory, the concept of autonomous rationality cannot be sustained. The notion that reason is autonomous and tradition corrupt derives, Ricoeur (1981) argues, from the Enlightenment. Fay (1987, pp. 161-2) traces it further back in the Age of Reason to Descartes who tried to doubt away everything that was dubitable and then to reconstruct the world upon a rationally certain foundation. But it is unrealistic, Fay says, for "those enthralled by the Enlightenment spirit which animates critical social science ... to insist that no part of a tradition be sacrosanct, exempt from scrutiny and assessment."

> To bracket or question everything about oneself is to condemn oneself to silence. Without accepting some of the contents of one's tradition, there can be no questions and no answers; indeed, there can be no person to ask or answer them. This is why the notion of scrutinizing any and all of one's inheritance is literally nonsense. (Fay 1987, pp. 161-2)

Thus, reason, the abstraction which the ideal speech situation makes concrete, is no more adequate as a foundation for ahistorical critique than the speech situation itself, for reason is bound up with inherited assumptions, as Ozanne herself has very clearly shown (Hudson and Ozanne 1988).

M&O acknowledge the difficulty of actually attaining rational autonomy, but they nevertheless adopt it as a regulative ideal in their research program. They express the usual critical theoretic antipathy for tradition, which is held to distort discourse, and for established institutions, which are held to embody injustice. Thus, they refer to tradition as one of the "constraints" that lead to "distorted communication" (p. 135), meaning communication that produces belief systems which "could not be validated if subjected to rational discourse" (p. 142). Like the philosophers of the Enlightenment, they suggest that it is possible to subject any and all traditions to a critical examination, then, if contradictions arise, to imagine a better social order and replace the old with the new. But even dramatic revolutions like those in France and Russia have been unable to expunge the cultural continuities which memory and habit preserve (Johnson 1979; Koenker, Rosenberg, and Suny 1989). And a number of consumer researchers, Ozanne among them, have shown that cultural traditions endow products with meaning (e.g., Belk 1991; Claiborne and Ozanne 1990; McCracken 1988; Ozanne 1992; Ozanne, Hill and Wright 1992). While these culturally grounded meanings are not always rational, they are the indispensable substance of our lives. Moreover, as Fay has indicated, researchers must be grounded in some intellectual tradition, for traditions make insight possible (Chalmers 1982; Hudson and Ozanne 1988). Without a tradition to build upon, there can be no progressive deepening of understanding (Gadamer 1975).

Science. In their use and discussion of the term *science*, M&O display a kind of conceptual schizophrenia. On the one hand they use the prestige and credibility of the word (Chalmers 1982) to buttress the claim that critical theorists have special insight into the nature of a properly rational social order. Thus, they repeatedly refer to critical theory as a science and claim that "*genuine* knowledge (products of science)" is the critical theorist's "most effective instrument for the emancipation of humans" (p. 131, italics added), as if science were a kind of fixed Archimedean point with which one could get rational leverage on the world. (For an extended critique of this conception of science, see Anderson 1983, 1986; Latour 1987; and Rorty 1979). In using the term this way, they try to lay a foundation for the critical theorist's ahistorical social critique (Ricoeur 1981). On the other hand, they also claim that all knowledge is socially constructed, that "researchers cannot produce neutral knowledge" (p. 138), that "knowledge is inescapably tied to interests. The issue," they say, is "not whether one can be apolitical in research, but rather what political stance one takes" (p. 130). Here, they hold that knowledge is a function of political preferences. If this view of science is applied to critical theory itself, then the critical theorist's social vision, like that of others, becomes a function of personal political preferences, not of ahistorical and objective rational analysis.

The same conceptual schizophrenia is apparent in their distinction between subjective and objective reality. This dichotomy smuggles into the analysis another implicit claim that critical theory is built on a foundation of rational certainty, for it suggests that critical theorists have access to objective reality, to things as they really are, whereas others perceive realities that are merely subjective. From these assumptions, it follows that critical theorists can transform the consciousness of others by helping them to see the contradictions between their subjective perceptions and the objective truth, i.e. by helping them to see the world as a critical theorist does. However, if M&O are correct about the social construction of reality, then their distinction between subjective and objective realities becomes untenable, for all realities become subjective, including the reality of the critical theorists themselves. And if this is so, then constituents merely exchange one subjective view for another when they adopt the viewpoint of a critical theorist.

The emphasis in the article on grasping the "historical totality" is, implicitly, another foundationalist claim. As McInnes (1967, p. 175) has pointed out, "With this notion of totality the [neo-Marxist] relativists have brought back the Absolute that they first threw out in favor of the historically relative." The notion that human beings can grasp the historical totality is rooted in nineteenth-century science and historiography (Carr 1961, pp. 3-15) and in one of the weaker claims of Marx's mentor Hegel (Hegel 1977, pp. 479-493; cf. Copleston pp. 216-218 for criticisms of the idea). The notion is inconsistent with the "epistemological limits" which circumscribe the range of possible human experiences (Fay 1987, pp. 144-5), for it ignores human finitude and the inherent opacity of human life. In the case of the minivan, for example, no individual or team could ever engage the social and historical totality imbricated with it, the demographic, lifestyle, strategic, design, engineering, and marketing considerations to name just a few of the relevant social and historical factors. So though M&O deny it, what they call "the problem of implementation" (p. 141) is a basic flaw in critical theory. This is all the more true because their totalization objective is inconsistent with their rational consensus objective. Nearly impossible to achieve even in relatively small groups, rational consensus is unimaginable among all the people involved with a mass market product like the minivan.

EXAMPLES AND THE TEST OF PRAXIS

The weaknesses of critical theory as an analytic framework become most apparent when M&O try to apply it to particular marketing phenomena. *When they turn to concrete instances, both negative and positive, their major theoretical points are generally not applicable and are not applied.* Thus, in their examples, they do not analyze the specific business situation and managers' consequent motivations, showing how perverted social arrangements induce managers to behave corruptly. And apart from the original exemplification of the idea, they never use the ideal speech situation to establish norms, i.e. to explain how a business should act in a given situation. As a result, managers in the negative examples seem malevolently conspiratorial when their behavior does not serve the public interest, and those in positive examples seem inexplicably benevolent when it does.

The hint of conspiracy is apparent in a negative example which suggests that manufacturers mass produce even though doing so does not serve the interests of their customers.

> Many consumers in the United States believe a democratic ideology exists that allows free speech, individualism, and pluralism. As a consequence, they believe they exercise free will in their consumption choices. However, the people who control mass production benefit by producing homogeneous products, so the production technology constrains choices. The interpretive understanding of the subject (that we freely consume) is contradicted by the concrete social reality (mass consumption). (M&O, p. 133)

But have owners and managers really conspired, as M&O hint, to limit consumers' choices to mass-produced products? It seems more plausible to suggest, as Marx (1977, pp. 226, 307ff) did, that the limits imposed by available production technologies constrain producers just as much as consumers. And, indeed, as opportunity has arisen, producers have shown a willingness to provide consumers with a broader range of choices. Using new technologies that have recently made shorter production runs economical, they have increasingly taken up niche marketing and product customization (DiMingo 1988; McKenna 1988; Smith 1956). In any case, there seems to be no necessary contradiction between freedom and mass consumption. Even when other options are available (i.e. customized or hand-made goods), consumers may freely choose the price/performance mix made possible by mass production efficiencies and economies of scale.

Other examples of socially irresponsible business practices—the sale of sugared cereals and the export of goods not approved for sale in the United States—suffer from a similar failure to analyze the motives of the business people and consumers involved. M&O assert that "the manufacturers of sugared foods have created a social production process that serves their interests but not the interests of parents and children" (p. 134). They never ask, however, what motivates manufacturers to advertise sugared rather than unsugared cereals on programs targeted at children. Why are these companies anxious to sell one kind of cereal rather than another? Do they own sugar plantations or sugar factories? Are they simply malevolent? A conventional analysis grounded in the marketing concept (Kholi and Jaworski 1990) would probably suggest that the companies are motivated by the eating pleasure of their customers, the children, i.e. by the children's self-defined interests. Anxious to move as much product as possible, they capitalize on children's natural taste for sweets (Conner and Booth 1988), advertising and selling the kind of cereal that their customers will consume most avidly. And many parents at least acquiesce in these purchases, casting their dollar votes for sugared rather than unsugared cereal. While a nutritionist might disagree with the choices made by these children and their parents, the logic of the marketing concept makes it at least arguable that the cereal companies *should* be attuned to the desires of their customers, letting them make their own choices.

M&O associate their positive examples with critical theory no more convincingly than their negative examples, for they show no necessary connection between the examples and their critical theoretic program of research. They cite as positive examples Starkist's marketing of dolphin safe tuna, the Council on Economic Priorities' pamphlet called "Shopping for a Better World," and The Body Shop's manufacture and marketing of cosmetics without pollution, animal testing, or unreasonable product claims. While each of these organizations do engage in social marketing, there is no evidence that they were motivated to do so by a critical theoretic study. Nor is there any reason to assume that a laborious critical analysis would be required to induce companies to adopt such socially responsible policies. These examples may well reflect two rather basic marketing principles. First, owners and managers express their values in their business decisions just as consumers express theirs when they make a purchase. Second, if businesses can embody a value in a product, then they can use that value attribute to differentiate the product, making it more attractive to consumers who hold that value (Kahle 1983). These principles are applicable even if, as we have argued, ahistorical critique and rational consensus are illusions and the critical theoretic research program is unworkable. And since this kind of social marketing occurs in the absence of a critical study, these examples cannot be held to show the usefulness of critical theory.

We offer this extended critique of M&O's examples because practical applications are especially important for critical theory. P*raxis*, a theoretically grounded program of action, is the final step in the critical theoretic research method (M&O, p. 138). If, as we have argued, the analysis of the practical examples is flawed or there is no clear connection between theory and practice, then critical theory fails by its own ultimate criterion.

CONCLUSION

Like Marx and Freud, the two figures who most influenced them, critical theorists see the surfaces of experience as a disguise which masks an underlying reality (Ricoeur 1974, pp. 21-22; 1981). This insight reflects the experience of discovering that one's prior beliefs, especially social beliefs, have been systematically distorted. Though we accept this basic insight as sometimes valid, we differ with critical theorists on the status of the new reality against which the old ideas are measured and found wanting. With "a proud gesture of defiance," critical theory purports to measure old ideas and social structures against a monistic and ahistorical ideal standard. Much more defensible is the pluralism of the conceptual and moral marketplace in which ideas must compete to become the temporary standard of thought and value. This liberal pluralism is embodied in the "humble" gesture of hermeneutics, the approach we prefer because it makes conceptual and social progress possible without denying "the historical conditions to which all human understanding is subsumed in the reign of finitude" (Ricoeur 1981, p. 87).

REFERENCES

Anderson, Paul F. (1983), "Marketing, Scientific Progress, and Scientific Method," *Journal of Marketing*, 47 (Fall), 18-31.

_____ (1986), "On Method in Consumer Research: A Critical Relativist Perspective," *Journal of Consumer Research*, 13 (September), 155-173.

Belk, Russell W. (1991), *Highways and Buyways: Naturalistic Research from the Consumer Behavior Odyssey*, ed., Provo, UT: Association for Consumer Research.

Chalmers, A.F. (1982), *What is This Thing Called Science?* St. Lucia, Queensland: University of Queensland Press.

Claiborne, C.B. and Julie L. Ozanne (1990), "The Meaning of Custom Made Homes: Home as a Metaphor for Living," in *Advances in Consumer Research*, eds. Marvin E. Goldberg, Gerald Gorn, and Richard W. Pollay, Provo, UT: Association for Consumer Research, 367-374.

Conner, M.T. and David L. Booth (1988), "Preferred Sweetness of a Lime Drink and Preference for Sweet over Non-sweet Foods, Related to Sex and Reported Age and Body Weight," *Appetite*, 10 (February), 25-35.

Copleston, Frederick (1965), *Modern Philosophy: Ficte to Hegel*, New York: Image Books.

DiMingo, Edward (1988), "The Fine Art of Positioning," *The Journal of Business Strategy*, 9 (March/April), 34-38.

Fay, Brian (1987), *Critical Social Science*, Ithaca, NY: Cornell University Press.

Gadamer, Hans-Georg (1975), *Truth and Method*, New York: Seabury Press.

Habermas, Jürgen (1973), *Theory and Practice*, trans John Viertel, Boston: Beacon.

_____ (1984), *Reason and the Rationalization of Society*, Vol. 1 of *The Theory of Communicative Action*, trans. T. McCarthy, Boston: Beacon.

_____ (1987), *Lifeworld and System: A Critique of Functionalist Reason*, Vol. 2 of *The Theory of Communicative Action*, trans. T. McCarthy, Boston: Beacon.

Hegel, G.W.F. (1977), *Phenomenology of Spirit*, Oxford: Oxford University Press.

Hooks, Bell (1989), *Talking Back: Thinking Feminist, Thinking Black*, Boston: South End Press.

Horkheimer, Max (1974), *Critique of Instrumental Reason*, New York: Seabury Press.

Hudson, Laurel Anderson and Julie L. Ozanne (1988), "Alternative Ways of Seeking Knowledge in Consumer Research," *Journal of Consumer Research*, 14 (March), 508-521.

Hunt, Shelby D. (1976), "The Nature and Scope of Marketing," *Journal of Marketing*, 40 (July), 17-28.

Johnson, Douglas (1979), "French History and Society from the Revolution to the Fifth Republic," in *France: A Companion to French Studies*, ed. D.G. Charlton, London: Methuen.

Kahle, Lynn R. (1983), *Social Values and Social Change: Adaptation to Life in America*, New York: Praeger.

Koenker, Diane P., William G. Rosenberg, and Ronald Grigor Suny, eds. *Party, State, and Society in the Russian Civil War*, Bloomington: Indiana University Press.

Kohli, Ajay K. and Bernard J. Jaworski (1990), "Market Orientation: The Construct, Research Propositions, and Managerial Implications," *Journal of Marketing* 54 (April), 1-18.

Latour, Bruno (1987), *Science in Action*, Cambridge, MA: Harvard University Press.

Marcuse, Herbert (1964), *One-dimensional Man*, Boston: Beacon.

Marx, Karl (1977), *Karl Marx: Selected Writings*, ed. David McLellan, Oxford: Oxford University Press.

McCracken, Grant (1988), *Culture and Consumption: New Approaches to the Symbolic Character of Consumer Goods and Activities*, Bloomington, IN: Indiana University Press.

McInnes, Neil (1967), "Marxist Philosophy," *Encyclopedia of Philosophy*, New York: Macmillan.

McKenna, Regis (1988), "Marketing in an Age of Diversity," *Harvard Business Review*, 66 (September/October), 88-95.

Murray, Jeff B. and Julie L. Ozanne, (1991), "The Critical Imagination: Emancipatory Interests in Consumer Research," *Journal of Consumer Research*, 18 (September), 129-144.

Ozanne, Julie L. (1992), "Secular Consumption in a Spiritual World: Coming of Age in the Mormon Faith," in *Advances in Consumer Research*, eds. John F. Sherry, Jr. and Brian Sternthal, Provo, UT: Association for Consumer Research 397-399.

_____, Ronald Paul Hill, and Newell D. Wright (1992), "Adolescent Challenges and Consumer Behavior: A View from Two Contrasting Worlds," unpublished working paper, Marketing Department, Virginia Polytechnic Institute and State University, Blacksburg, VA 24061.

Ricoeur, Paul (1974), *The Conflict of Interpretations*, Evanston: Northwestern University Press.

_____ (1981), *Hermeneutics and the Human Sciences*, Cambridge: Cambridge University Press.

Rorty, Richard (1979), *Philosophy and the Mirror of Nature*, Princeton: Princeton University Press.

Smith, Wendell R. (1956), "Product Differentiation and Market Segmentation As Alternative Marketing Strategies," *Journal of Marketing*, 20, 3-8.

Using Qualitative Techniques to Explore Consumer Attitudes: Insights From Group Process Theories

Terry Bristol, Oklahoma State University
Edward F. Fern, Virginia Polytechnic Institute and State University

ABSTRACT

Consumer researchers often use qualitative techniques (e.g., focus groups) to examine consumer attitudes. Yet, our knowledge of the adequacy of these techniques is lacking. This paper examines several theoretical explanations of group phenomena and hypothesizes that group thought eliciting techniques cause attitude polarization. The attitudinal output from these qualitative methods may reflect group attitude formation processes rather than the individual's attitudes.

INTRODUCTION

The use of qualitative research methods is prevalent in both basic and applied consumer research. For example, the use of focus groups for consumer research has been described as a small and growing industry (McQuarrie and McIntyre 1988). The total expenditure on focus group interviews in the U.S has been estimated to be $312 million (Goldman and McDonald 1987) and is growing. Nevertheless, group interviewing is not enthusiastically embraced by everyone. Clancy and Shulman (1991), the chairman and CEO of Yankelovich Clancy Shulman, claim that focus group interviews are neither serious nor helpful marketing research tools. Moveover, they question whether this qualitative technique is a wise basis for marketing decision making. According to Clancy and Shulman, focus group research is not as accurate or useful as survey research. Nevertheless, their survey of corporate CEO's revealed that 41.2% agreed with the statement "More often than not, the information produced by focus group research is as accurate and useful as the results of survey research at less than half the cost (Clancy and Shulman 1991)." The Clancy and Shulman position may be extreme. Nevertheless, we thought it was important to question whether focus groups, and more generally qualitative research methods provide accurate and useful information about consumers' attitudes.

Two assumptions have motivated this manuscript. First, consumer attitude research is important and is a frequent goal of group qualitative research techniques. Second, since attitude formation is an individual affective and cognitive activity, it is best theorized and studied at the individual respondent level. When the research interest is in group effects on individual attitude formation (e.g., household attitude formation) groups may be appropriate. Because of the inherent conflict between the above two assumptions, this paper will review theories that may explain the extent to which group influences affect individual attitude formation across four different qualitative research techniques.

QUALITATIVE RESEARCH

Qualitative methods are defined in terms of the information gained from their use—subjective, in-depth understandings of the consumer, and the nature or structure of the consumers' attitudes, feelings, and motivations (Calder 1977; Goldman and McDonald 1987). Qualitative research methods attempt to uncover what people think or how they feel, achieving greater depth and detail of responses, and resulting in close-up descriptions that better realize the subjective nature of the phenomenon studied (Bellenger, Bernhardt, and Goldstrucker 1976; Van Maanen, Dabbs, and Faulkner 1982).

Although, there has been some empirical research on qualitative methods (e.g., Bouchard and Hare 1970; Claxton, Ritchie, and Zaichkowsky 1980; Fern 1982b; Nelson and Frontczak 1988; Reynolds and Johnson 1978), there is a lack of research on what informational output is gained from these methods and how different types of qualitative techniques affect this output.

One type of output frequently sought from the various qualitative techniques is consumer's thoughts, e.g., attitudes, beliefs, opinions, and purchase intentions. For example, these techniques have been used to gain insights into the brand attitudes of women (Kanner 1990), attitudes towards packaging aesthetics (Shapiro 1990), and attitudes towards financial services (Trachtenberg 1987). However, none of the extant research has examined the adequacy of qualitative techniques for exploring attitudes.

There is reason to be concerned about the appropriateness of several of these qualitative techniques for attitude research. In discussing the future of qualitative marketing research, Calder (1977) warned about extending the use of this research approach to all constructs (e.g., attitudes, values, traits, roles, norms, etc.), without regard to their amenability to existing scientific methods. Axelrod (1975) specifically warned against the use of focus groups to determine consumers' preferences: "This kind of 'voting' for preferences is more often than not just an intellectual exercise (p.6)." Dietz (1975) represents the most extreme position on the appropriateness of focus groups for attitude research. Dietz claimed that focus groups are sold at inflated prices "because they are sold under the pretense of providing insight into consumer concepts, perceptions, opinions, and attitudes. It is a pretense that in many instances has deceived the research supplier more than the receiver (p. 6)."

To illustrate the nature of the problem, consider the following. One authority on focus groups cited a case where a respondent declared that he would not buy a prestige car because it was ostentatious. After one hour and thirty minutes of focus group discussion, the same respondent declared the he was fickle and that he would buy a prestige car and show it off to his friends. Presumably, this revelation provides insights into the respondent's "true" attitude about prestige cars. However, it may also indicate that people change their attitudes during group discussion. At best, professional judgment by the moderator is necessary to make these types of determinations.

In summary, our theoretical and empirical knowledge about qualitative techniques is lacking. As a first step in filling this void, we reviewed the group process literature to uncover theoretical explanations for differences in the effectiveness of qualitative techniques for measuring consumer attitudes. The implications of this review for the conduct of attitude research will be discussed. First, however, we will review the types of qualitative techniques used for examining and assessing consumer attitudes.

Qualitative Research Techniques

Consumer researchers have reported the use of four types of qualitative research techniques to investigate consumer attitudes: open-ended surveys, individual interviews, focus group interviews, and nominal group interviews. These techniques vary in the exact procedures and settings used to collect the information, and in their assumptions of the quality of the output gained.

Open-ended surveys (or self-administered questionnaires) provide respondents with written instructions and questions, yet do not provide structured responses. Researchers often use surveys to measure consumer attitudes. Surveys are easily and economically administered on a mass basis to a sample of individuals. Additionally, researchers often use unstructured, open-ended response formats to preclude constraining and/or biasing individual's responses (Schuman and Presser 1981).

Individual interviews involve relatively open-ended, but interviewer guided, discussions of specific topics. Interviews allow the researcher as interviewer to probe responses and redirect questions towards the respondent. Thus, individual interviews can be more adaptive and less structured than surveys. However, the former are costly when a large number of respondents are desired.

Like individual interviews, focus group interviews also involve a moderator guided open-ended discussion of specific topics. However, focus groups are interactive as the topics are simultaneously discussed by a small group of individuals. Researchers often use focus groups to gain insight into consumer attitudes because of the convenience in interviewing several respondents simultaneously, and because consumers are more likely to respond in a group interview setting (Fern 1982a). Thus, focus groups can provide data quicker and more economically than individual interviews (Stewart and Shamdasani 1990).

Nominal group techniques are highly structured group interviews that restrict spontaneous interaction (Claxton, Ritchie, and Zaichkowsky 1980; Stewart and Shamdasani 1990). Nominal groups differ from focus groups in the added structure to the interview. For example, participant's responses are often written and shared with the group on a cumulative basis rather than spontaneously and openly discussed as found in focus groups. Additionally, vocal evaluation of the output is prohibited—the moderator collects written evaluations by each individual. Like focus groups, the nominal group technique purportedly results in higher involvement and response rates compared to non-group techniques (Claxton, Ritchie, and Zaichkowsky 1980).

Thus, the users of each technique have assumed that they are valid and useful methods for examining consumer attitudes. Current theories in social psychology can clarify the presumed attitudinal output of each of these techniques.

THEORETICAL INSIGHTS

Although the effects of using qualitative techniques on the quality of attitudinal output has not been empirically examined, some work has proceeded in social psychology that applies to this problem. Many studies have found that initial tendencies of individual group members intensify or sometimes change with group discussion (Kaplan 1987; Whitney and Smith 1983). Several theories have been suggested to explain this phenomenon, several of which apply to the use of qualitative techniques to measure consumer attitudes. Reviewed below are theories of social facilitation, social impact, social comparison, and persuasive-arguments.

Social Facilitation and Social Impact

Social facilitation is perhaps the simplest theory from which predictions can be posited about measuring attitudes across social and nonsocial settings. This theory suggests that the mere presence of others is a sufficient explanation of behavior in groups (Allport 1924). The presence of observers or coactors has been found to result in greater individual effort and performance (Markus 1978; Zajonc 1980). However, we are interested in the effect of others on individual attitudes. Ideas from self-awareness theory (Duval and Wicklund 1972) apply here. The presence of others leads individuals to focus attention on themselves and increases self-awareness and thought about one's own attitudes and feelings (Carver 1979). Increased self-awareness has been found to lead to polarized attitudes and evaluations (Ickes, Wicklund, and Ferris 1973; Scheier and Carver 1977). Attitude polarization refers to individuals adopting more extreme attitudinal positions than those previously held—it is a shift or change in degree but not in direction (Allison and Messick 1987). Thus, the mere presence of others leads to increased self-awareness that increases thought about one's own attitudes, resulting in attitude polarization.

Focus group and nominal group interviews contain 5 to 12 participants, whose presence may lead to increased self-awareness and attitude polarization by each individual. The interviewer is present in an individual interview and thus, this technique also may lead to polarization. However, no other individual need be present for an individual to respond to an open-ended survey.

In summary, we expect individuals' attitudes to become more polarized when others are present during the thought eliciting procedure. Therefore, we expect that the interviewer-directed thought eliciting methods (i.e., focus groups, nominal groups, and individual interviews) will produce more polarized attitudes than using open-ended, self-administered questionnaires.

Any polarization in the individual's attitudes that is detected in the thought eliciting procedure should endure only while the individual is subject to the self-awareness and increased thinking about her or his position that results from the presence of others. When others are not present, individuals will fall back on their pre-existing attitude state. The polarized beliefs will not be salient or persist beyond the interview setting. The polarization of attitudes that is due to self-awareness has been found to dissipate over time (Ickes, Wicklund, and Ferris 1973). Therefore, we have concluded that any attitude polarization that results from the presence of others will be temporary and will not endure beyond the interview situation.

Social impact theory goes beyond the mere presence of others in its predictions. This theory predicts that the impact of others on individuals' beliefs, cognitions, values, and emotions is some power function of the number of other people present (Latané and Nida 1980). Latané and Nida (1980) provide evidence from the conformity literature in support of their notions. According to social impact theory the effects of social facilitation should increase with the presence of more individuals. Thus, the greater the number of other people present, the greater self-awareness and the more polarized the attitudes. Latané and Nida would also predict that the status of group members would impact on attitude polarization—higher status individuals would cause greater attitude shift than lower status individuals.

Alternate predictions of attitude polarization due to mere presence result from applying social impact theory. Attitude shifts should occur in the group techniques and these shifts should be greater than in individual interviews in which an interviewer is present with the respondent (i.e., a group of two). Moreover, any attitude shift in individual interviews should be greater than shifts in open-ended surveys and could be attributed to the mere presence of the interviewer. Again, attitude polarization due to the impact of the social situation should endure only as long as the individual remains in the presence of others.

In summary, individual attitude polarization should increase as the number of others present increases such that polarization in focus and nominal groups will be greater than that in individual interviews, which will be greater than that in surveys. Additionally, as the number of individuals within the each group increases the positive effect on attitude polarization should increase. Finally, the shift effect should be transitory. Attitude polarization resulting from the presence of others is temporary and it should not endure beyond the interview situation.

Normative Influence Through Social Comparison

Social comparison theory was originally formulated by Festinger (1954) to explain the effects of social communication on opinion change in groups. One derivation of the theory has been used to go beyond mere presence theories to explain the polarization of group member attitudes that result from group discussion. Simply, group members' desires to be favorably evaluated leads them to adopt an attitude that is more extreme than the group norm, to the extent that they are aware of this normative position (Goethals and Zanna 1979).

There are three necessary conditions for social comparisons to cause attitude polarization: (1) participants must desire to be favorably evaluated, (2) the setting must provide a standard of comparison, and (3) the setting must allow for the evaluations of others. Thus, in settings where others provide a standard of comparison, a desire to be favorably evaluated may motivate individuals to adopt/express more extreme attitudes (Allison and Messick 1987; Harkins and Szymanski 1987). The standard of comparison in group interviews is a normative position on an issue that is explicitly stated by the interviewer/researcher or implicitly derived from the statements provided by group members during the discussion. Additionally, to be evaluated (favorably or unfavorably), the individual's views must be expressed and identified to others (Harkins and Szymanski 1987).

The desire to be favorably evaluated by others is pervasive. This desire is a source of evaluation apprehension—an individual's anticipation of positive or negative outcomes when around others serves as an incentive function (Cottrell 1972). Similarly, the impression management literature has assumed that a primary goal of self-presentation is the attainment of social approval (Arkin 1981). According to social impact theory, we might expect this desire for favorable evaluation to be greater when other group members are acquaintances rather than strangers (i.e., people they will never see again) and higher status individuals rather than lower status individuals.

Standards of comparison can be personal, objective, or social (Harkins and Szymanski 1987). It is this latter social standard that is produced in a setting in which others' views are shared. Individuals have been found to compare themselves with similar others in these settings (Zanna, Goethals, and Hill 1975). Both objective and social standards have been found to affect various types of responses (Harkins and Szymanski 1987).

Applied to the context at hand, the three necessary conditions for social comparisons to cause attitude polarization are only present when focus group interviews are used. Standards for comparison can develop in both focus groups and nominal groups, but are less likely to develop in individual interviews. In focus groups each individual's attitudes are expressed and can become the focal point of discussion during the group exchange. However, in nominal groups the attitudes of individuals may be elicited but no conscious effort is made to discuss or otherwise scrutinize individuals' contributions. Since the ideas expressed within nominal groups are not openly discussed, the individual participant is less likely to be apprehensive about being evaluated by the other group members. With less emphasis on the evaluation of others, standards of comparison are less likely to affect attitude formation and change in nominal groups. The result should be less shifting in attitudes compared to focus group interviews.

In individual interviews and open-ended surveys, other members are not available for evaluation, consequently no standard of comparison exists, assuming the interviewer or questionnaire does not offer cues to such a standard. Thus, attitudes expressed by participants in individual interviews and open-ended surveys should not polarize or shift from what the individual believed prior to the interview or questionnaire, compared to focus group interviews.

In summary, individual attitude polarization should increase under normative pressures. Polarization should be greater among focus group than nominal group participants. As previously noted, group attitude polarization should be more pronounced than polarization in individual interviews and open-ended surveys.

Any change in the individual's attitudes that is detected in the interview will endure only as long as normative pressures are acting on the individual. When the norms are no longer governing individuals' behaviors, they will fall back on their pre-existing attitude structures.

Informational Influence Through Persuasive Arguments

An alternate explanation of attitude polarization or change in groups is information influence or persuasive-arguments theory (Kaplan 1987; Vinokur and Burnstein 1974). This theory posits that the exchange of information in groups can lead members to consider facts that they had not previously considered when initially forming their attitudes (Allison and Messick 1987). This new information could not only lead to attitude polarization, but to attitude change or depolarization (Vinokur and Burnstein 1978). Weakly held attitudes may be more easily changed because the individual is more influenced given contradictory information provided by others. Evidence for both polarization and depolarization given group discussion has been reported (Vinokur and Burnstein 1978; Whitney and Smith 1983).

Information is shared in both focus groups and nominal groups but is not provided to respondents in individual interviews and open-ended surveys. In focus groups each individual contributes information about her or his feelings. This information is often the focal point of group discussion. Although not interactively discussed in the group, information about the attitude object is also expressed in nominal group interviews. The individual participant is the only source of information in individual interviews and open-ended surveys, assuming the interviewer or questionnaire produce no demand artifacts. Therefore, attitude polarization should be greater in group interviews because more beliefs, opinions, and feelings are shared and discussed among participants.

As opposed to the other theories presented, information influence should result in an enduring change in the individual's attitudes. Attitudes that change because of new or additional information should remain stable outside the interview setting. The new information or beliefs should be salient and persist beyond the interview.

To summarize, individual attitude change or polarization, resulting from shared information, will be greater for group interview techniques than individual interviews or open-ended surveys. Moreover, the attitude change or polarization resulting from information influence is relatively permanent and will endure beyond the interview situation.

IMPLICATIONS

The Table summarizes the relationships between the techniques and degree of attitude shift predicted by the theories. If attitudes are influenced by the group's or interviewer's presence,

TABLE
Theoretical Predictions of Attitude Shift

Theory	Qualitative techniques			
	Focus group	Nominal group	Individual interview	Survey
Temporary shift				
Social facilitation	Polarization*	Polarization	Polarization	No shift
Social impact	Polarization	Polarization	Less polarization	No shift
Social comparison	Polarization	No shift	No shift	No shift
Enduring shift				
Persuasive-arguments	Polarization or change	Polarization or change	No shift	No shift

*Predicted effect of qualitative technique on attitude shift.

then the interview technique itself may unintentionally produce polarization. Similarly, if attitudes are influenced by group norms, or information shared in the group, then group qualitative methods for collecting attitudinal information may inadvertently polarize or change individual members' attitudes. Regardless, it is not known whether these attitude shifts are transitory or enduring. Individuals may express attitudes during a discussion that differ from their previous attitudes. After the discussion is completed, individuals may either revert to their original attitudes or permanently adopt the polarized attitudes. In either case, the output may result from group attitude formation processes rather than individual attitude processes. Consequently, managerial prescriptions and theoretical descriptions based on group attitude research procedures may be problematic. If the attitudes are transitory, prescriptions will be based on attitudes that no longer exist. If the new attitudes are enduring, the prescriptions will only apply to those experiencing comparable group phenomena.

CONCLUSION

Several theories were reviewed which may add to our understanding of the use of qualitative techniques. Other theories of group processes can be applied to this context. For example, coalition formation (Goldman and McDonald 1987) and social identity theory (Tajfel and Turner 1986; Mackie 1986) have been used to explain the polarization of attitudes within groups. However, these offer no further insight into the problem because predictions derived from these theories duplicate those posited above.

We hope that this paper will prompt empirical exploration of the efficacy of using qualitative techniques to examine consumer attitudes. While much has been written about qualitative research, most of what is known about these techniques is based on experiential reports by moderators and interviewers. This information may be useful but it tends to be idiosyncratic to the researcher and her or his firm. Therefore, empirical validation is necessary to discover whether the output from group qualitative techniques represents group attitude formation processes or individual attitudes. If no attitude shift is found, we can assume that the output represents individual attitudes and not the effects of group interaction. Additionally, we need to show empirically the utility of these qualitative techniques for exploring consumer attitudes.

Empirical testing of these notions will enable prescriptions about collecting attitude information without the unintended effects of group interaction. If we find that attitudes do not change or polarize in the group techniques, then prescriptions for choosing among techniques can be based on factors such as cost and convenience, rather than on quality of the output. Considering the frequency of use and the amount of money spent on qualitative research, the results of further empirical studies should be highly relevant to both academicians and practitioners.

REFERENCES

Allison, Scott T. and David M. Messick (1987), "From Individual Inputs to Group Outputs, and Back Again: Group Processes and Inferences About Members," in *Group Processes*, ed. Clyde Hendrick, Newbury Park, CA: Sage Publications, 111-143.

Allport, Floyd Henry (1924), *Social Psychology*, Boston, MA: Houghton Mifflin.

Arkin, Robert M. (1981), "Self-presentation Styles," in *Impression Management: Theory and Social Psychological Research*, ed. James T. Tedeschi, New York: Academic Press, 311-333.

Axelrod, M. D. (1975), "Marketers Get an Eyeful When Focus Groups Expose Products, Ideas, Images, Ad Copy, Etc. to Consumers," *Marketing News*, 9 (February 28), 6-7.

Bellenger, Danny N., Kenneth L. Bernhardt, and Jac L. Goldstrucker (1976), *Qualitative Research in Marketing*, Chicago, IL: American Marketing Association.

Bouchard, Thomas J., Jr., and Melanie Hare (1970), "Size, Performance, and Potential in Brainstorming Groups," *Journal of Applied Psychology*, 54 (February), 51-55.

Calder, Bobby J. (1977), "Focus Groups and the Nature of Qualitative Marketing Research," *Journal of Marketing Research*, 14 (August), 353-364.

Carver, Charles S. (1979), "A Cybernetic Model of Self-Attention Processes," *Journal of Personality and Social Psychology*, 37 (August), 1251-1281.

Clancy, Kevin J. and Robert S. Shulman (1991), *The Marketing Revolution*, New York: Harper Business.

Claxton, John D., J. R. Brent Ritchie, and Judy Zaichkowsky (1976), "The Nominal Group Technique: Its Potential for Consumer Research," *Journal of Consumer Research*, 7 (December), 308-313.

Cottrell, Nickolas B. (1972), "Social Facilitation," in *Experimental Social Psychology*, ed. C. G. McClintock, New York: Holt, Rinehart, and Winston, 185-236.

Dietz, Leonhard (1975), "Can Focus Group Interviews Survive?" *Marketing News*, 9 (October 10), 6-7.

Duval, Shelley and Robert A. Wicklund (1972), *A Theory of Objective Self-Awareness*, New York: Academic Press.

Fern, Edward F. (1982a), "Why Do Focus Groups Work: A Review and Integration of Small Group Process Theories," in *Advances in Consumer Research*, Vol. 9, ed. Andrew Mitchell, Ann Arbor, MI: Association for Consumer Research, 444-451.

_____ (1982b), "The Use of Focus Groups for Idea Generation: The Effects of Group Size, Acquaintanceship, and Moderator on Response Quantity and Quality," *Journal of Marketing Research*, 19 (February), 1-13.

Festinger, Leon (1954), "A Theory of Social Comparison Processes," *Human Relations*, 7 (May), 117-140.

Goethals, George R. and Mark P. Zanna (1979), "The Role of Social Comparison in Choice Shifts," *Journal of Personality and Social Psychology*, 37 (September), 1469-1476.

Goldman, Alfred E. and Susan Schwartz McDonald (1987), *The Group Depth Interview: Principles and Practice*, Englewood Cliffs, NJ: Prentice Hall, Inc.

Harkins, Stephan G. and Kate Szymanski (1987), "Social Loafing and Social Facilitation: New Wine in Old Bottles," in *Group Processes and Intergroup Relations*, ed. Clyde Hendrick, Newbury Park, CA: Sage Publications, 167-188.

Ickes, William John, Robert A. Wicklund, and C. Brian Ferris (1973), "Objective Self-Awareness and Self-Esteem," *Journal of Experimental Social Psychology*, 9 (May), 202-219.

Kanner, Bernice (1990), "The Secret Life of the Female Consumer," *Working Woman*, 15 (December), 68-71.

Kaplan, Martin F. (1987), "The Influencing Process in Group Decision Making," in *Group Processes*, ed. Clyde Hendrick, Newbury Park, CA: Sage Publications, 189-212.

Latané, Bibb and Steve Nida (1980), "Social Impact Theory and Group Influence: A Social Engineering Perspective," in *Psychology of Group Influence*, ed. Paul B. Paulus, Hillsdale, NJ: Lawrence Erlbaum, 3-34.

Mackie, Diane M. (1986), "Social Identification Effects in Group Polarization," *Journal of Personality and Social Psychology*, 50 (April), 720-728.

Markus, Hazel (1978), "The Effect of Mere Presence on Social Facilitation: An Unobtrusive Test," *Journal of Experimental Social Psychology*, 14 (July), 389-397.

McQuarrie, Edward F. and Shelby H. McIntyre (1988), "Conceptual Underpinnings for the Use of Group Interviews in Consumer Research," in *Advances in Consumer Research*, Vol. 15, ed. Michael J. Houston, Provo, UT: Association for Consumer Research, 580-586.

Nelson, James E. and Nancy T. Frontczak (1988), "How Acquaintanceship and Analyst Can Influence Focus Group Results," *Journal of Advertising*, 17 (1), 41-48.

Reynolds, Fred D. and Deborah K. Johnson (1978), "Validity of Focus Group Findings," *Journal of Advertising Research*, 18 (June), 21-24.

Scheier, Michael F. and Charles S. Carver (1977), "Self-Focused Attention and the Experience of Emotion: Attraction, Repulsion, Elation, and Depression," *Journal of Personality and Social Psychology*, 35 (September), 625-636.

Schuman, Howard and Stanley Presser (1981), *Questions and Answers in Attitude Surveys*, San Diego, CA: Academic Press.

Shapiro, Sid (1990), "Focus Groups: The First Step in Package Design," *Marketing News*, 24 (September 3), 15-17.

Stewart, David W. and Prem N. Shamdasani (1990), *Focus Groups: Theory and Practice*, Newbury Park, CA: Sage Publications.

Tajfel, Henri and J. C. Turner (1986), "An Integrative Theory of Intergroup Relations," in *The Psychology of Intergroup Relations*, eds. Stephen Worchel and William G. Austin, Chicago, IL: Nelson Hall, 7-24.

Trachtenberg, Jeffrey A. (1987), "Listening, the Old-Fashioned Way," *Forbes*, 140 (October 5), 202-204.

Van Maanen, John, James M. Dabbs, Jr., and Robert R. Faulkner (1982), *Varieties of Qualitative Research*, Beverly Hills, CA: Sage Publications.

Vinokur, Amiram and Eugene Burnstein (1974), "Effects of Partially Shared Persuasive Arguments on Group-Induced Shifts: A Group-Problem-Solving Approach," *Journal of Personality and Social Psychology*, 29 (March), 305-315.

_____ and _____ (1978), "Depolarization of Attitudes in Groups," *Journal of Personality and Social Psychology*, 36 (August), 872-885.

Whitney, John C. and Ruth A. Smith (1983), "Effects of Group Cohesiveness on Attitude Polarization and the Acquisition of Knowledge in a Strategic Planning Context," *Journal of Marketing Research*, 20 (May), 167-176.

Wicklund, Robert A. (1975), "Objective Self-Awareness," in *Advances in Experimental Social Psychology*, Vol. 8, ed. Leonard Berkowitz, New York: Academic Press, 233-276.

Zajonc, Robert B. (1980), "Compresence," in *Psychology of Group Influence*, ed. Paul B. Paulus, Hillsdale, NJ: Lawrence Erlbaum, 35-60.

Zanna, Mark P., George R. Goethals, and Janice F. Hill (1975), "Evaluating a Sex-related Ability: Social Comparison with Similar Others and Standard Setters," *Journal of Experimental Social Psychology*, 11 (January), 86-93.

Action Identification Theory: An Examination of Consumers' Behavioral Representations
George W. Hunt, University of Texas at Austin
Wayne D. Hoyer, University of Texas, Austin

The principles of the theory of action identification (Vallacher and Wegner 1985) are introduced with respect to their applicability to consumer research and behavioral change mechanisms. The theory provides insight into the ways in which people conceptualize their actions and how this affects the maintenance of action as well as the emergence of new behavior. It appears that action identification could be utilized for the influence of behavior and attitudes, as well as providing another dimension on which consumer experience can be described. The results of a preliminary study of consumer identifications of the act of using various products and services are discussed for illustrative purposes.

If we were to interrupt 100 shoppers in the midst of the act of exchanging money for a pair of jeans and ask them, "What are you doing?", the responses would be likely to vary considerably, ranging from "taking money out of my wallet" to "buying pants" to "trying to stay in fashion" to "answering a silly question". In other words, while the mechanical details of their actions may be nearly identical at the moment of the query, the cognitive representation or identification of their actions may differ remarkably. We may encounter an even wider array of such identifications with respect to more complex consumption behaviors such as buying a house, dining at an elegant restaurant, or driving a car. Yet consumer researchers rarely measure behavior in terms of how it is conceptualized by the consumer; rather, it is assumed that, like objects, actions are real and that the researcher's identification of the action is "correct". In doing this, important information may be lost because the consumer's identification of his or her action has implications for the maintenance of the action and for the possible emergence of new behaviors (Vallacher and Wegner 1985; Wegner et al. 1984).

The theory of Action Identification (Vallacher and Wegner 1985) treats actions as *reifications*, mental constructs that impose a presumed reality on experience. In order to access the subjective dimensions of action as perceived by individuals, Vallacher and Wegner (1985) have developed a method of eliciting inventories of potential identifications of an action and subsequently measuring individual tendencies to endorse these identifications. Action identification differs from other theories of action cognition in that it focuses on the *level* of detail or abstraction at which an individual conceptualizes a given action. As we will discuss in more detail subsequently, these conceptual representations guide the performance of action and often may provide cues that lead to the emergence of alternate behaviors. To consumer researchers this information may be useful in providing insight into possible ways of influencing consumer attitudes, satisfaction judgments, and behaviors, as well as possibly adding insight into how consumers currently perceive the consumption behavior in question.

The aim of this paper is to lay the groundwork for the incorporation of action identification principles into consumer behavior and marketing research. We begin with an abbreviated introduction to action identification theory, particularly with respect to consumption-related actions. We then enumerate several areas in consumer research where we believe the theory may provide insights, followed by an explanation of the methodology and results of a recently completed study of consumer identifications of the act of consuming each of 15 different products and services.

ACTION IDENTIFICATION THEORY

When we observe behavior, we seldom question the accuracy of our label of the behavior. Utilizing cues from memory and from the behavioral context, we are easily able to construct an identification of the action being performed. For example, upon seeing a person sitting at the wheel of a moving automobile, we are able to say that s/he is "driving a car". However, the driver may hold other identifications of his or her act, such as "looking for a place to eat," "trying to get through traffic," "listening to music," or "sitting and holding a steering wheel."

Often in consumer research we claim to be measuring behavior that we assume has been correctly labelled. Fortunately, there is an increasing awareness of the danger in this practice as evidenced by developments in both the experimental or empirical and naturalistic/humanistic/interpretive, or N-H-I (Hunt 1989) research traditions. In experimental empirical research, for example, the problem of "demand artifacts" (Sawyer 1975; Shimp, et. al. 1991) implicitly draws attention to the fact that we may not be measuring what we think we're measuring. What appears to be "purchasing the product" may in fact be "trying to impress the nice researcher." While action identification theory cannot provide the rich description of subjective consumption experience that is found in the N-H-I research, it nevertheless does attempt to gain insight from at least one dimension of individual representations of action, i.e., the level of identification.

Action Identification theory (Vallacher and Wegner 1985; Wegner and Vallacher 1986) holds that the performance of an action is accompanied by an identification of that action, and that this identification has significant implications for the performance, maintenance and control of the action. The theory proposes that a person who is asked "What are you doing?" will always have a response that is most accessible to him or her at that moment. This label for his or her action is termed the p*repotent identity*. If asked to consider other explanations of what s/he is doing, s/he could come up with further identifications of both the mechanical details, or *low level* identities, and other *high level* identities pertaining to the possible consequences, side effects, and meanings of the action. These identifications together comprise the *act identity structure*.

The relational term *by* links together the identity statements in an act identity structure. Thus, for example, one may "escape from stressful thoughts and feelings" *by* "enjoying a scenic trip through the countryside," *by* "driving a car," *by* "sitting and holding a steering wheel," and so forth. With a little imagination, we could link each of these identity statements with countless alternatives, leading to a vast network of act identities. The activation of a particular subset of these identities may be guided by processes similar to the activation of ad hoc categories (Barsalou 1983) or associative networks (Collins and Loftus 1975).

Principles of the Theory

Vallacher and Wegner (1985) have proposed three principles governing the relationship between action and corresponding identification levels. Underpinning these principles are two forces that may compete or work together: the desirability of understanding one's actions in the most comprehensive and meaningful way possible, and the need to be able to perform actions to their satisfactory completion.

The first principle states that action is maintained with respect to its prepotent identity. People have in mind an idea of what they are doing and this prepotent identity serves as a guide for the maintenance and stability of action. Just as identities exist at different levels, actions are similarly maintained. One person may sustain the act of reroofing a house by attending to the action of "hitting nails through shingles", while the next person may identify the act as "finishing a job so I can go play golf". According to the first principle, people will only consciously entertain the prepotent identity of their action at any point in time and will maintain the action in accordance with it.

The identity that becomes prepotent is the subject of the other two principles. According to the second principle, there is a tendency for higher level identities to become prepotent. In other words, we find it more interesting and useful to think in terms of goals, consequences, and meanings of behavior. An action identification such as "moving my arm" conveys little in the way of meaningful description; one performs this movement as a component of literally millions of actions. The action is better understood if identified in higher level terms, such as "throwing a football", "eating", "raking leaves", or "typing a research paper". Even these identifications may be less meaningful than, say, "trying to score a touchdown" or "sharing a meal with my family".

The tendency to move to higher levels of identification is somewhat constrained by reality. As the third principle points out: when an action cannot be maintained in terms of its prepotent identity, there is a tendency for a lower level identity to become prepotent. For example, most of us can remember learning to use a stick shift. At first, our attention was focused on the low level details of the act. But there was probably a tendency to want to think in terms of racing along an open road, or impressing a friend with our newly acquired skill. Just about the time we found our thoughts turning to these higher level identities however, we lurched up onto a curb or into the bushes.

Thus, an action for which we do not have adequate skill is more successfully performed with respect to details of the action (i.e, a lower level identity). As we gain experience and become familiar with an action, there is less need for conscious attention to its fundamental components and well-learned behaviors may be carried out with no conscious attention at all (Langer 1978). But a "pleasant drive in the country" can quickly become "trying to stay on the road by holding onto the wheel" in the event of a sudden burst of wind, and a professional baseball player who is accustomed to thinking about "lining it up the middle" may need to revert to minding the mechanics of his swing in order to break out of a slump. Thus, while high level identities are most appealing in terms of comprehensive understanding, they will be abandoned in favor of lower level identities if they prove to be ineffective guides to action control. (Some pathological behaviors such as alcoholism and compulsive shopping, however, may be perpetuated by the unwillingness or inability of individuals to abandon inappropriate high level identification of their actions.)

Action Emergence: A Mechanism for Behavior Change

There is experimental evidence that an act normally identified at a high level can be disrupted such that the identification is brought down to a lower level. Subjects in one experiment (Wegner, et al 1984) were shown to lower their identification level of the act of eating Cheetos when they were instructed to pick them up using chopsticks. In another experiment (Wegner, et al 1984), subjects were given coffee in either normal or unwieldy mugs. Subjects in the latter condition (the "low level" condition) showed significantly greater susceptibility to suggestions of new high level meanings of their action, and subsequently displayed behavior more in keeping with these suggested meanings than did those in the control group.

The latter result, along with several other findings (see Wegner and Vallacher 1986 for a summary) reveal what Wegner and Vallacher (1986) call *action emergence*. The complexity of links between identities in an act identity structure is partly a function of the fact that a given low level identity (e.g., "walking") may have links to many different higher level identities (e.g,. "getting exercise" and "going to the neighborhood bar"). Any force, such as a disruption, that interferes with the maintenance of an action at a high level of identification will tend to lower the identification level. Once at a lower level, people tend to be more susceptible to any cues that might indicate a new high level meaning, as action details are often congruent with several alternative high level identifications. By this process, new actions may emerge. This is the central mechanism by which action identification can result in behavior change (Wegner et al, 1984; Wegner et al 1986).

Measurement of Identification Levels

The method developed by Vallacher and Wegner (1985) for revealing the action identification levels of research participants begins with a pilot study designed to generate a general inventory of possible identities for a specified action. Survey respondents are asked to think about the various ways an action can be identified and are encouraged to include all possible levels of perceiving the action. They are then asked to write down as many one-sentence descriptions of the action as they can think of in 15 or 20 minutes.

The lists of identities are then compiled into a single inventory that includes those items most frequently mentioned, usually resulting in a total of anywhere from 20 to 50 identifications. A second study is then conducted in which respondents are asked to consider the action and to state the degree to which each statement is a good description of the action by circling a number from 1 to 7, anchored by the end points "describes very poorly" and "describes very well." The results of this survey are then correlated across subjects, factor analyzed by principal components, and rotated to a varimax solution. The factors thus obtained generally have interesting interpretations with respect to the ways in which different individuals identify actions. One pattern that consistently appears in studies of act identity structures is the manner in which identity statements load onto factors. Typically a single low level factor is found, often explaining the greatest amount of variance, along with several distinct higher level factors with interpretable meanings.

APPLICATIONS IN CONSUMER AND MARKETING RESEARCH

Attitude and Behavior Influence

The following is a sample of the many potential applications of action identification theory to issues in attitude and behavior research:

Warning labels and product safety: Often a potentially hazardous product can be used without requiring much conscious attention. Insecticides, for instance, are very easy to use in aerosol form. Other products like liquid propane gas are generally used by people who have a great deal of experience with them. In both instances, the consumer is likely to identify the usage of the product at a high level (e.g., "killing cockroaches"), and thus will be less susceptible to an alternative high level identification associated with the danger involved (e.g., "inhaling toxic fumes because there is inadequate ventilation"). Drawing attention to warnings and instructions, and persuading consumers to act accordingly, may require incorporating a devise that lowers identification levels by disrupting the normal flow of procedures involved in product usage, followed by drawing attention to messages that convey the appropriate new high level identification.

Cuing and reinforcing desirable high level identifications: When a consumer is at a low level of identification for the act of consuming a product or service, s/he is apt to be susceptible to cues that suggest higher level identifications. Marketers may be able to take advantage of this tendency by, for instance, designing advertising campaigns that are congruent with positive outcomes of consumption, thus cuing and reinforcing stable high level identifications. This might work in the following way: when a new product design is tested on a sample market, act identity structures for its use may be measured, along with other variables pertaining to consumer satisfaction with the product. The interpretation of one or more positively valenced high level identification factors might serve as a guide to appropriate messages that could be communicated through advertising and through the design and packaging of the product. For example, if the act identity structure for the use of a new kitchen appliance yields dimensions such as "being a sophisticated cook" and "having convenience", advertising can be designed to convey these concepts. The consistency between expectations and postpurchase experience that should result would increase consumer satisfaction (Oliver 1980) and reach the most appropriate target market as compared with advertising messages that are discrepant from postpurchase processes.

In many instances where new products are being introduced, or where an existing product or service is being promoted in a new manner, high level identifications may already be present in the minds of most consumers. Most users of financial investment services have a high level conceptualization of the act of using these services, so that a new entry into this market faces preconceived notions about its products. It may be possible to structure advertising in a way that disrupts these high level identifications, by introducing incongruencies and unexpected images that force the target audience to engage in processing novel information. A number of experiments (Wegner and Vallacher 1986) have shown that disruptions of action result in movement to lower levels of identification; perhaps disruption of the information environment would have a similar effect. Hoch and Deighton (1989) have suggested that ambiguity of the information environment provides marketers with increased influence over consumer learning. It may be that lower action identification levels are involved in this situation, allowing for greater susceptibility to new high level identifications that may be cued from memory or from the environment.

Retail settings and other service environments (Bitner 1990; 1992) can also be designed to provide high level cues. This appears to be implicitly understood, as most service environments are carefully or inadvertently reflective of the image that the firm wishes to convey. High fashion clothing outlets are designed to give an impression of quality, taste, and luxury, while discount stores often convey images of thrift such as high stock levels that imply volume purchasing and cost savings.

Managing customer perceptions of service quality: Service encounters (Bitner 1990; Solomon et al. 1985; Zeithaml et al. 1988) provide opportunities for trained staff to provide cues during the performance of the service. Bitner et al. (1990) found that nearly one-fourth of freely recalled satisfactory critical incidents in service encounters were directly related to service *failures*. The authors remarked that "the fact that such incidents can be remembered as very satisfactory is somewhat surprising" (p. 81). Action identification theory would predict such a result, as the service failure would constitute a disruption leading to lower levels of identification and, consequently, greater susceptibility to cues provided by the service provider and/or the environment. This implies that the service firm's greatest opportunity to influence customer evaluations of service quality may well lie in the moments immediately following a service disruption. Solomon et al. (1985) argued a similar point from the perspective of role theory. They proposed that any significant deviation from a well-learned "service script" could bring about the need for active cognitive processing; in this activated state, the service encounter would take on an affective valence, leading to greater extremes (both positive and negative) in evaluations. Action identification offers an explanation of a possible mechanism by which this may occur.

Product meaning and symbolism: The majority of the studies of "meaning" in consumer behavior have come out of the N-H-I research stream. Underpinning much of this research is the belief that a complete understanding of consumer behavior is not possible without considering the meaning of phenomena from the perspective of the consumer (Holbrook and O'Shaughnessy 1988; Ozanne and Hudson 1989). Meaning-based constructs discussed in the N-H-I literature include symbolic consumption as it pertains to self-concept (Belk 1988; Belk, Bahn and Meyer 1982; Schouten 1991; Solomon 1983), symbolic consumption as communication (Belk, Bahn and Meyer 1982; Holman 1980), the sacred/secular dimension of consumption (Belk, et al, 1989; Hirschman and LaBarbera 1989; O'Guinn and Belk 1989), cultural meaning transmitted through possessions (McCracken 1986), and "homeyness" (McCracken 1989). Other studies have applied quantitative methods to consumer meaning constructs, such as the dimensions of emotion patterns (Westbrook and Oliver 1991), the influence of context on meaning (Kleine and Kernan 1991), means-end chain analysis (Gutman 1982) and value segmentation (Kamakura and Mazzon 1991). While the research method in action identification is empirical in nature, it may be useful in identifying meaning-based dimensions of product usage and symbolism, as well as potential consumer segments, through the identification and interpretation of the act identity factors.

Implications for research methodology: Wegner et al. (1986) found that subjects who identified the act of participating in an experiment at low levels were more likely to agree with suggestions that they were "being helpful" or "being selfish." Individuals who identify experiments at low levels may show more demand effects. In general, experimental conditions provide novel stimuli to subjects, which is likely to promote lower levels of action identification (Vallacher and Wegner 1987). From this lower level, subjects may be more susceptible to cues provided by the experimental context. Such a problem would cast doubt on the external validity of many behavioral experiments.

A PRELIMINARY STUDY

Our central purpose in carrying out this study was to determine if consumers do, as expected, identify consumption behavior and experience in measurable, interpretable ways, and if the factors corresponding to dimensions of consumption experience correspond to what the theory would predict. There is little reason to suspect that action identification principles would not apply to the broad class of actions related to consumption. If the theory holds, we should expect to find similar results in studies of actions involving the consumption of goods and services as are found in the studies conducted by Vallacher and Wegner. Specifically we expect to find a low level identity factor (as described above) along with factors that might reflect knowledge of the practical purposes commonly associated with the product or service (e.g., Alba and Hutchinson 1987), and other factors reflecting more subjective meanings or dimensions of affective consumption experience (Belk 1988; Havlena and Holbrook 1986; Hirschman and Holbrook 1982; Westbrook and Oliver 1991). Such factors and the degree to which consumers vary in their endorsement of them may provide marketers with a better understanding of how their products are perceived and how they fit into the lives of the individuals who use them. Negatively viewed dimensions of consumption experience may be revealed as well, possibly giving insight into problem areas that can be addressed at the levels of design and production and/or perception.

In addition, because an action that is well-learned and familiar tends to be identified at higher levels, we expect to find that knowledge of and familiarity with a given product or service will correlate negatively with individuals' scores on low level factors. To the extent that consumers who are less knowledgeable are found to be at lower identification levels, we expect them to be more susceptible to cues suggesting high level meanings of products and services. This may partially account for why "novices" tend to generate more simple evaluative thoughts and be more extreme in their evaluations than "expert" consumers (Sujan 1985). In other words, novices may have been exposed to advertising and other suggestive cues to higher level product meaning that they readily adopted. Thus, we may also find positive correlations between certain high level factors that are image-oriented and low levels of product or service class knowledgeability. Sujan's (1985) work would also indicate that knowledgeable consumers will be more likely to endorse action identification statements that reflect pragmatic attribute-oriented aspects of product/service use.

METHOD

A pilot study was conducted using 85 undergraduate business students at a large southwestern university. Each student received a list of three products and/or services, drawn randomly from a total of 15 that were included in the study. These 15 items were selected with the objective of representing the dimensions of complexity, hedonic vs. utilitarian consumption (Hirschman and Holbrook 1982), and products vs. services. Respondents were asked to generate as many one sentence descriptions as they could think of for the act of using each product/service in a total of 20 minutes. Thus, each product/service had lists generated by 17 different respondents. The identities most commonly listed were compiled into act identity inventories, with the number of statements in each inventory ranging from 24 to 35.

In the second stage, 171 students participated in rating each of the statements in three different randomly ordered inventories according to how well they fit the acts of consumption in question. Participants were instructed to rate how well each statement described the act of using the particular product or service by circling a number from 1 to 7 corresponding to "describes very poorly" to "describes very well," respectively. At least 34 respondents rated inventories for each of the 15 consumption objects in this process. Participants were also asked to rate their knowledgeability and familiarity with respect to each of the three product/service classes they rated (Brucks 1985).

The ratings compiled from stage two were intercorrelated across subjects and then factor analyzed by principal components and rotated to a varimax solution. This analysis resulted in between five and nine factors with eigenvalues greater than one for each of the 15 consumption items. In some cases, reduction of the number of factors to five or six gave solutions with the most meaningful interpretations, without sacrificing a significant amount of explained variance.

RESULTS AND INTERPRETATION

In each factor analysis, one low level factor emerged, along with 4 to 7 other factors with eigenvalues greater than 1.0. In general, factors were easily interpreted, especially for generally higher involvement products. To illustrate, Table 1 contrasts the identity factors for 2 of the consumption objects: a higher involvement service (elegant restaurants) and a higher involvement product (personal computers). In each case, the low level factor explains less variance than two higher level factors, which contradicts the normal factor structure found in the studies by Vallacher and Wegner. This may be due to the relatively high levels of familiarity that respondents reported with respect to the items in the survey, combined with the prevalence of messages about consumption objects that consumers are exposed to, which may tend to drive identifications into various high level factors. It is also possible that respondents accessed their own scripts (Abelson 1981) for the process of engaging in the consumption behavior without adequately imagining themselves performing the act. Ideally, action identification levels would be measured immediately following the action.

An interesting trend was found with respect to the knowledge and familiarity scale. A pattern of positive correlations between certain high level factors and familiarity appeared, although caution is necessary in interpreting this result because the knowledge and familiarity scale violated normality assumptions and sample sizes were too small to compensate. In table 1, factor 2 for elegant restaurants ("feeling pretty special") showed a strong positive correlation with familiarity. This is intuitively appealing, as the elements of this factor indicate actual experience with the consumption object. Four factors in the personal computer category showed significant correlations with familiarity: factors 3 ("low level") and 4 ("frustration") correlate negatively, while 2 ("being more productive") and 5 ("doing work") show positive correlation. This also confirms expectations; the low level factor is more likely among those with less knowledge, while factors indicating experience with and appreciation for the results computers can achieve correspond to persons with greater knowledge. Additionally, the "frustrating" factor's negative correlation with familiarity may apply to other categories where negative affect could be generated by a limited amount of exposure to a product or service that requires significant learning in order to obtain its benefits.

We emphasize that these are preliminary results and that more extensive testing needs to be done with larger and more heterogeneous samples. However, the initial findings appear to be promising.

SUMMARY

Action identification theory addresses a number of issues of interest to consumer researchers. It explicitly takes into account the importance of an individual's subjective interpretation of his/her behavior, while providing an empirical technique for capturing some of that interpretation in identity "factors". The possibility that action identification levels with respect to the purchase and use of goods and services are subject to influence suggests a new means of influencing behavior. From the results we have obtained in our preliminary study, it appears that action identification may provide marketers with a tool for gaining additional insight into the dimensions of consumption experience and consumer scripts for the use of products and services. In addition, research into possible applications of the theory in attitude and behavioral influence seems warranted.

TABLE 1
A Comparison of Identity Factors for Elegant Restaurants and Personal Computers

PC factors and Loadings		Restaurant Factors and Loadings	
1. "Using the Computer"		1. "Wine, dine, and romance"	
Using a keyboard	.88	Drinking wine	.86
Using menus for help	.84	Looking at the wine list	.81
Putting disk in drive	.82	Eating a 5 course meal	.80
Entering data	.80	Valet parking	.68
Saving on a disk	.80	Being romantic	.66
Printing	.75	Small amount of food	.55
Using as typewriter	.65	2. "Feeling pretty special"	
Storing information	.62	Feeling classy	.86
Turning it on	.59	Dressing up nice	.84
		Feeling special	.81
2. "Being more productive"		Listening to quiet music	.70
Saving time	.87		
Being productive	.86	3. "Low level"	
Having convenience	.81	Deciding what to eat	.87
Organizing work	.72	Looking at the menu	.86
Being efficient	.61	Driving there	.85
Using graphics	.55	Putting a napkin in lap	.54
		Hearing utensils clinking	.49
3. "Low level"			
Sitting in a chair	.75	4. "Not worth the trouble"	
Looking at the screen	.65	Spending alot of money	.78
Following instructions	.62	Remembering etiquette	.69
Hearing beeping noises	.58	Having to get reservation	.67
		Having linen napkins	.58
4. "Frustration"			
Feeling frustrated	.73	5. "Atmospherics"	
Straining eyes	.72	Being in nice atmosphere	.82
Investing a lot of money	.67	Being seated by maitre d'	.73
Getting a headache	.52	Being in dim lighting	.60
Playing	.64		
		6. "Dates aren't relaxing"	
5. "Doing work"		Eating good food	.64
Using for homework	.77	Relaxing	.57
Generating documents/reports	.66	Being on a hot date	-.62
Organizing thoughts	.50		

REFERENCES

Abelson, Robert P. (1981), "The Psychological Status of the Script Concept," *American Psychologist*, 36, 715-729.

Alba, J.W. and Hutchinson, J.W. (1987), "The Dimensions of Consumer Expertise," *Journal of Consumer Research*, 13(March), 411-454.

Barsalou, Lawrence W. (1983), "Ad Hoc Categories," *Memory and Cognition*, 11(3), 211-227.

Belk, Russell W. (1988), "Possessions and the Extended Self," *Journal of Consumer Research*, 15(September), 139-168.

_____, Kenneth D. Bahn, and Robert N. Mayer (1982) "Developmental Recognition of Consumption Symbolism," *Journal of Consumer Research* 9(June), 4-17.

_____, Melanie Wallendorf, and John F. Sherry, Jr. (1989), "The Sacred and the Profane in Consumer Behavior: Theodicy on the Odyssey," *Journal of Consumer Research*, 16(June), 1-38.

Bitner, Mary Jo (1990), "Evaluating Service Encounters: The Effects of Physical Surroundings and Employee Responses," *Journal of Marketing*, 54(April), 69-82.

_____, (1992), "Servicescapes: The Impact of Physical Surroundings on Customers and Employees," *Journal of Marketing*, 56(April), 57-71.

_____, Bernard H. Booms, and Mary Stanfield Tetreault (1990), "The Service Encounter: Diagnosing Favorable and Unfavorable Incidents," *Journal of Marketing*, 54(Jan.), 71-84.

Brucks, Merrie (1985), "The Effects of Product Class Knowledge on Information Search Behavior," *Journal of Consumer Research*, 12(June), 1-16.

Collins, Alan M., and Elizabeth F. Loftus (1975), "A Spreading Activation Theory of Semantic Processing," *Psychological Review*, 56: 54-59.

Gutman, Jonathan (1982), "A Means-End Chain Model Based on Consumer Categorization Processes," *Journal of Marketing*, 46(Spring), 60-72.

Havlena, William J. and Morris B. Holbrook (1986), "The Varieties of Consumption Experience: Comparing Two Typologies of Emotion in Consumer Behavior," *Journal of Consumer Research*, 13(December), 394-404.

Hirschman, Elizabeth C., and Morris B. Holbrook (1982), "Hedonic Consumption: Emerging Concepts, Methods, and Propositions," *Journal of Marketing*, 46(Summer), 92-101.

_____, and Priscilla A. LaBarbera (1989), "The Meaning of Christmas," in *Interpretive Consumer Research*, ed. E. Hirschman,

Hoch, Stephen J. and John Deighton (1989), "Managing What Consumers Learn from Experience," *Journal of Marketing*, 53(April), 1-20.

Holbrook, Morris B. and John O'Shaughnessy (1988), "On the Scientific Status of Consumer Research and the Need for an Interpretive Approach to Studying Consumer Behavior," *Journal of Consumer Research*, 16(December), 398-204.

Holman, Rebecca H. (1980), "Clothing as Communication: An Empirical Investigation," *in Advances in Consumer Research* vol. 7, ed. Jerry C. Olson, Ann Arbor, MI: Association for Consumer Research, 372-377.

Hunt, Shelby D. (1989), "Naturalistic, Humanistic, and Interpretive Inquiry: Challenges and Ultimate Potential," in *Interpretive Consumer Research*, ed. Elizabeth C. Hirschman, Provo, UT: Association for Consumer Research, 185-198.

Kamakura, Wagner A. and Jose Afonso Mazzon (1991), "Value Segmentation: A Model for the Measurement of Values and Value Systems," *Journal of Consumer Research*, 18(September), 208-218.

Kleine, Robert E.III and Jerome B. Kernan (1991), "Contextual Influences on the Meanings Ascribed to Ordinary Consumption Objects," *Journal of Consumer Research*, 18(December), 311-324.

Langer, Ellen J. (1978), "Rethinking the Role of Thought in Social Interaction," in N*ew Directions in Attribution Research* vol. 2, ed. J. H. Harvey et al., Hillsdale, NJ: Erlbaum, 35-58.

McCracken, Grant (1986), "Culture and Consumption: A Theoretical Account of the Structure and Movement of the Cultural Meaning of Goods," *Journal of Consumer Research*, 13(June), 71-

_____ (1989), " 'Homeyness': A Cultural Account of One Constellation of Consumer Goods and Meanings," in *Interpretive Consumer Research*, ed. Elizabeth C. Hirschman, Provo, UT: Association for Consumer Research, 168-183.

O'Guinn, Thomas C. and Russell W. Belk (1989), "Heaven on Earth: Consumption at Heritage Village, USA," *Journal of Consumer Research*, 16(September), 227-237.

Oliver, Richard L.(1980),"A Cognitive Model of the Antecedents and Consequences of Satisfaction Decisions," *Journal of Marketing Research*, 17(November), 460-469.

Ozanne, Julie L. and Laurel Anderson Hudson (1989), "Exploring Diversity in Consumer Research," in I*nterpretive Consumer Research*, ed. Elizabeth C. Hirschman, Provo, UT: Association for Consumer Research, 1-9.

Sawyer, Alan G. (1975), "Demand Artifacts in Laboratory Experiments in Consumer Research," *Journal of Consumer Research* 1(March), 20-30.

Schouten, John W. (1991), "Selves in Transition: Symbolic Consumption in Personal Rites of Passage and Identity Reconstruction," *Journal of Consumer Research* 17(March), 412-422.

Shimp, Terence A., Eva M. Hyatt, and David J. Snyder (1991), "A Critical Appraisal of Demand Artifacts in Consumer Research," J*ournal of Consumer Research* 18(December), 273-283.

Solomon, Michael R. (1983), "The Role of Products as Social Stimuli: A Symbolic Interaction Perspective," *Journal of Consumer Research* 10(December), 319-329.

_____, Carol Surprenant, John A. Czepiel, and Evelyn Gutman (1985), "A Role Theory Perspective on Dyadic Interactions: The Service Encounter," *Journal of Marketing* 49(1), 99-111.

Sujan, Mita (1989), "Consumer Knowledge: Effects on Evaluation Strategies Mediating Consumer Judgements," *Journal of Consumer Research* 12(June), 31-46.

Vallacher, Robin R. and Daniel M. Wegner (1985), A *Theory of Action Identification*, Hillsdale, NJ: Erlbaum.

_____, and _____, (1987), "What Do People Think They're Doing? Action Identification and Human Behavior," *Psychological Review* 94(1), 3-15.

_____, and _____, and Maria P. Somoza (1989), "That's Easy for You to Say: Action Identification and Speech Fluency," *Journal of Personal and Social Psychology* 56(2), 199-208.

Wegner, Daniel M. and Robin R. Vallacher (1986), "Action Identification," in H*andbook of Motivation and Cognition*, ed. R.M. Sorrentino and E.T. Higgins, New York: Guilford, 550-582.

_____, _____, G. Macomber, R. Wood, and K. Arps (1984), "The Emergence of Action," *Journal of Personality and Social Psychology* 46(Feb.), 269-279.

_____, _____, George W. Kiersted, and Denise Dizadji (1986), "Action Identification in the Emergence of Social Behavior," *Social Cognition* 4(1), 18-38.

Westbrook, Robert A. and Richard L. Oliver (1991), "The Dimensionality of Consumption Emotion Patterns and Consumer Satisfaction," *Journal Of Consumer Research* 18(June), 84-91.

Zeithaml, Valerie A., Leonard L. Berry, and A. Parasuraman (1988), "Communication and Control Processes in the Delivery of Service Quality," *Journal of Marketing* 52(April), 35-48.

Interpretation Strikes Again, Again, and Again: A Postpositivist Reflection on Papers by Bristol and Fern, Hunt and Hoyer, and Larsen and Wright

Craig J. Thompson, University of Wisconsin-Madison

The differences among these papers initially seemed more prominent than their similarities. Hunt and Hoyer employ a hypothetico-deductive, experimental methodology to measure the effects a hypothesized psychological process may have on consumer attitudes and behavior. Bristol and Fern draw on group process theory to assess potential biases posed by the interpersonal dynamics of focus groups. A more dramatic contrast is offered by Larsen and Wright who adopt a postpositivist orientation (i.e. hermeneutics) to critique recent proposals regarding the use of critical theory in consumer research (Murray and Ozanne 1991). Upon further reflection, I realized that they could be interpreted in a way that highlights a series of parallels and mutual implications.

My interpretive synthesis is that each of these papers address the role of interpretation in consumer research: Hunt and Hoyer address how consumers interpret their actions; Bristol and Fern address how consumer researchers should interpret the interpretations consumers express in focus group settings; Larsen and Wright address how consumer researchers should conceptualize the nature of their own interpretations (and critiques) regarding the actions of marketing firms. This common focus is not immediately apparent for two reasons; 1) different aspects of interpretation are being considered; and 2) the differing philosophical world-views that underlie the papers motivate contrasting stands on the question whether the interpretive circle is "vicious" or productive. As a useful starting point for comparing these papers, I would like to give a brief consideration to these differences in worldview.

TALKING ABOUT AN INTERPRETIVE REVOLUTION

The question of interpretation has been most explicitly pursued by researchers who ascribe to a postpositivist worldview (Hudson and Ozanne 1988). A central theme of postpositivist research is that the interpretative circle is a necessary and productive dimension of all forms of human understanding, including that resulting from the scientific research process. Rather than seeking to make understandings more objective by reducing sources of "subjective bias," the postpositivist agenda is to explore how interpretive presuppositions necessarily shape understanding. This goal applies to the understandings of research participants and, in a more self-reflexive sense, to the understandings of the researchers themselves (Joy 1991). This reflexive implication is the one that Larsen and Wright most explicitly address. Their primary critique is that advocates of critical theory claim that their analyses reveal the "objective conditions" of social life. This claim implicitly assumes that critical theory provides an evaluative framework that stands outside of the interpretive circle and, as such, critical theorists do not recognize the interpretive presuppositions manifested in their own analyses. By deconstructing Murray and Ozanne's (1991) recent proposals for critical theory, the Larsen and Wright paper engages in the prototypic postpositivist tasks of demonstrating that all understandings, including those of critical theorists, are interpretations "all the way down."

While postpositivists seek to highlight the interpretive circle, researchers ascribing to a more positivistic worldview generally prefer to discount this dimension of understanding because it conflicts with preferred conceptions of objective knowledge. The interpretive circle implies that understandings always and necessarily evoke historically bound of presuppositions. As such, the presumed objectivity of scientific research methods and knowledge claims would become subject to more relativistic conceptions (Anderson 1986). Second, the explicit recognition that human understanding is interpretive also conflicts with positivistic assumptions regarding the stability of social phenomena (Hudson and Ozanne 1988). To say that consumer understandings emerge from an interpretive process is also to accept that these expressed understandings can change in reflection of different contextual circumstances. These two implications pose numerous complexities (and anomalies) for the methodological and theoretical orientations that derive from a positivistic world-view (see Hudson and Ozanne 1988).

Despite this differential emphasis on the issue of interpretation, it would be misinterpretation to conclude that only postpositivist researchers are active participants in the "interpretive turn" transpiring in all branches of the social sciences. This "turn" is one that has impacted the general zeitgeist (or general philosophical context) in which social science is conducted (Hekman 1986). Regardless of methodological world-view, social science researchers are recognizing the interpretative dimension of human understanding in some form. Perhaps the most common recognition is that "meaning" is not objectively determined by the characteristics of a situation but rather it emerges from the interplay between the person and the situation-as-interpreted; as such, different individuals can ascribe very different meanings to the "same" situation, event, or object (Thompson, Locander, and Pollio 1989). This particular issue is the one that Bristol and Fern and Hunt and Hoyer pursue while still remaining within a more positivistic framework.

REFLECTIONS ON HUNT AND HOYER

A major thesis of this paper is that situational characteristics are best understood in relation to the perspective of the actor. Hunt and Hoyer offer Action Identification Theory as way to explain the interpretive dimensions of consumer understanding in terms of psychological processes that are beyond the subjective control of the actor. In this regard, the Hunt and Hoyer paper follows in a long tradition of psychological research approaches seeks to provide an objective explanation of subjective differences in perceptions on the basis of objective processes. That is, the subjective is reduced to the outcome of psychological processes that are stable, not contingent on personal perceptions, and they generate reliable and predictable effects. In accord with the explanatory axiology of the positivistic tradition, the variability in perceived meanings that emerges from this interpretive encounter between person and situation is treated as a controllable phenomenon having important managerial implications.

From my postpositivist perspective, one major contribution of this paper is that it highlights the often overlooked fact that consumption is not just a concept. Hunt and Hoyer suggests a need to more systematically explore the meanings and understandings that emerge through a person's embodied interactions with products. A large array of context specific understandings may be focal when using products but may not be evoked when a person considers the "meaning of things" in a more abstract fashion.

COMMENTS ON BRISTOL AND FERN

This paper explores the question of how situations interpreted by consumers and, more specifically, what effects do social processes have on these interpretations. A key assumption is that these social processes exert an unreflected or unconscious influence on understanding. That is, the actors participating in this group process are not explicitly aware of the processes motivating their shift in attitudes. A corresponding assumption is that informed researchers can understand the individuals better than they understand themselves and ascertain that processes that impact their interpretations. This logic bears a strong similarity to that found in critical theory; namely, that consumers are often immersed in a state of "false consciousness" in which they adhere to an ideology of consumption values and beliefs that conflict with the objective conditions of their everyday experiences (Murray and Ozanne 1991). In light of this similarity, the logic of the Larsen and Wright deconstruction of critical theory can also be applied to the Bristol and Fern paper. That is, the "objective" assessment of the biases ensuing from group processes is contingent on a series of strong assumptions.

The basic assumption of the Bristol and Fern paper is that "real" attitudes are formed through an individuated, cognitive activity. Although this assumption is commonplace, it is not a self-evident fact but rather it is a theoretically (and culturally) based presuppositions. For example, cultural anthropology (Geertz 1973), Skinnerian behaviorism (1972), sociological phenomenology (Berger and Luckmann 1967) are but a few of the research programs that indicate personal understandings are fundamentally intertwined with broader societal forces and processes. This socio-cultural orientation would reverse the entire logic of the Bristol and Fern paper. That is, focus groups and other methods that document consumer meanings as they emerge in a social context would be become the implicit standard of "reality" whereas the validity of methods and measures that isolate consumers from social interactions would become more suspect. As such, the implicit standard of methodological rigor is contingent on the researchers interpretive frame of reference.

This paper also demonstrates the role of researcher interpretations in another important way. That is, it shows that focus groups simply cannot be expected to produce "self-evident" facts. Focus group data is no more inherently meaningful at face value than is quantitative data. Rather it must be interpreted in order to be meaningful and the quality of focus group research is no better or worse than the quality of the interpretations that derive from it. In light of Bristol and Fern's analysis, interpreters of focus group research should be aware that these consumer meanings were formed and expressed in a particular social context and, that in another context, the panel members could have derived different meanings. This caveat, however, is one that is an inevitable consequence of the interpretive dimension of consumer understanding and, therefore, would apply to any research situation.

COMMENTS ON LARSEN AND WRIGHT

In global terms, this article focuses on the issue of whether interpretations can somehow get outside of the interpretive circle. The paper's deconstructive logic evokes many of the issues raised in the much noted debates between the seminal critical theorists Jurgen Habermas and the seminal hermeneutic theorists H.G. Gadamer (see Hekman 1986). At the core of this debate is the question of whether critiques of socio-cultural practices can be verified or justified by appeal to an ahistoric framework of rational discourse. An inverse way of stating this question is whether such an ahistoric framework is a necessary condition for effectively critiquing contemporary social practices? Gadamer endorses the hermeneutic thesis that all understanding derives from culturally bound interpretations. As such, there is no presuppositionless framework or form of discourse from which to issue an "objective" critique of socio-cultural practices. Rather, such critiques would always be relative to a particular culture bound point-of-view. In contrast, Habermas (1972) portrays this hermeneutic position as one that "bangs helplessly from within the walls of tradition" and, instead, contends that effective critiques require a framework of rational analysis that transcends the culturally constructed meanings being considered. The Larsen and Wright paper does a very thorough job in evaluating these issues from a perspective that favors the Gadamerian position. In terms of this interpretation, the project of critical theory, as advocated by Habermas, simply represents another unattainable quest for an omnipotent view of "how things really are."

When commentators discuss the Gademer-Habermas debate, there is a tendency to render their positions as being more polemical than the actual texts of the debates might otherwise indicate. Perhaps the group processes noted by Bristol and Fern operate at a more macro level in regard to scholarly interpretations of scholarly debates. In any case, it should be noted that the Gadamer-Habermas debate also was dialogue between two intellectuals who were, in many respects, each others most learned students (Bernstein 1986). Through their ongoing dialogues, Gadamer and Habermas became more responsive to the criticisms issued by the other and their positions evolved in a mutually informed direction (Ricoeur 1986). This dialogical transformation is often ignored or discounted by those who report on the debate itself. "Habermasian" critics of Gadamer often leave the impression that his hermeneutic position would render social actors as unreflective slaves to tradition and authority. Gadamer, however, became increasingly aware that tradition and authority need to be challenged and that distinctions can be made between justifiable and unjustifiable "prejudgments." As with critical theory, Gadamer's hermeneutics manifests a suspicion of the "technocratic interest:" that is, an alignment of science and technology in which the ability to use techniques for social control becomes the standard of knowledge. In his latter works, Gadamer (1986) asserts that hermeneutic reflection is means to offer an historical (culturally) based evaluation of the technocratic interests and overcome this alienation. As such, hermeneutic reflection is offered in the service of the emancipatory interest discussed by critical theorists.

In a similar vien, hermeneutic critics often portray Habermas as remaining hopelessly enamored with the ideal of an omnipotent perspective that stands outside of all history and meaning. Another reading of Habermas, however, is that his agenda has attempted to take into account the many compelling critiques that have been issued against this form of Cartesian rationalism (see Held 1980). In terms of this reading, Habermas is seeking to identify a social context and mode of reasoning that enable fully historical and situated social actors to critically reflect upon the society in which they live. For example, Habermas notes that the ability to attain a rational consensus is contingent on the development of "ideal speech situations" that are free from the distorting influence of power and, accordingly, in which all participants in the discourse are equals. Although the concept of an ideal speech situation is often critiqued as being Utopian, it does demonstrate that the rationalism advocated by Habermas is quite different from that of the classic Cartesian-Kantian genre.

If we suspend the polarizing issue of the "ahistoric framework" and the litany of critiques and counter critiques that follow from it, it can be recognized that Gadamer and Habermas (and by implication hermeneutics and critical theory) can both meaningfully speak to the question of how socially constructed knowledge is related to cultural practices. Murray and Ozanne employed critical theory as a vehicle for encouraging consumer researchers to give more consideration to the cultural implications and ramifications that derive from marketing knowledge and practices. This same call, however, could have been framed and justified in hermeneutic terms. In sum, the theoretical and practical efficacy of critical theory and hermeneutics has been, and will continue to be, enhanced through their critical dialogues. As interpreters of these dialogues, however, we should remain aware that common meanings and interests are often expressed in different theoretical languages.

Due to space limitations references have been omitted. For a list of references, please contact the author.

Kinship Exchange Networks and Family Consumption

Ritha Fellerman, University of Massachusetts
Kathleen Debevec, University of Massachusetts[1]

ABSTRACT

The effect of kinship exchange behavior upon household consumption is examined through a consideration of the family as a social unit embedded within the extended family network. A series of propositions are offered to explicate: 1) the influence of kinship structure and socioeconomic conditions on the extent to which families rely upon each other, 2) the relationship between kinship exchange behavior and family consumption, and 3) the conditions under which the kinship network may be the appropriate unit of analysis for the study of family consumption behavior. Specific examples are presented to illustrate the various aspects of kinship exchange during periods of crisis and life transition. Fundamental questions are raised concerning the generalizability of the nuclear family model in consumer research.

INTRODUCTION

The majority of research on consumer households has been based on the assumption that the most relevant unit of analysis is the nuclear family. While this approach may apply to some upper- and middle-class Caucasian families, the relevant unit of analysis for a number of subgroups, including the rural poor, urban Blacks, and ethnic families, may be the extended family network. Regardless of socioeconomic status, nuclear family structures may quickly become extended when families turn to their kin for help during periods of crisis, such as divorce, unemployment, and illness. Even when conditions are not difficult, it would be unwise to dismiss the influence of deep emotional bonds between extended family members as a powerful force affecting consumer behavior.

KINSHIP NETWORKS AS CHANNELS OF RESOURCE FLOWS

A kinship network is like a spider web—a family transition in one part of the network can affect family members throughout the network. By providing *resources* and *constraints* which influence the behavior of individual family units, extended family ties can lead to *consumption interdependence*, or a situation in which families are linked by the communal distribution of resources within a kinship network. The effect of exchanges between kin upon household consumption behavior may be direct, such as when one family decreases consumption in order to assist another within the network, or indirect, such as when a family changes consumption behavior in order to cope with role overload.

Hirschman (1985) maintains that an important outcome of exchange networks may be that "the group, rather than the self, comes to be viewed as the provider of food, apparel, and other of life's necessities." Family networks may operate as forces unto themselves, with distinct patterns of reciprocal exchange which aggregate to form "underground" economies, and thereby mitigate the extent to which consumers rely upon the formal market for their needs. For example, cohesive family networks and the collective distribution of resources are characteristics of the Amish, Mennonites, and Mormons, whose self-sufficient consumption behaviors have remained relatively unaffected by many marketing trends (e.g. Schaefer 1984, pp. 157-163).

Exchanges between households within a kinship network can be characterized by *two distinct and independent forms of utility*: an instrumental utility and a utility derived from the social capital built up between the exchange partners (e.g. Frensen and Davis 1990). Determining the value of the social capital in exchanges, such as emotional support and the confidence associated with "belonging," is difficult. For example an elderly parent may value their childrens' assistance with household tasks, such as home repairs or lawnwork, because it is difficult for them to do it on their own (instrumental utility), or because of the emotional security of being loved and cared for (social capital utility). Gouldner (1960, pp. 174-175) maintains that individuals in a social dyad may never be certain that they have fully repaid what they owe, and thus may make multiple repayments on their perceived obligations; consequently, the process of reciprocity may be partially driven by the difficulty in placing a value on social capital.

Research which takes as its base the kinship network may provide important insights into the relationship between family consumption behavior and variables such as the duration, frequency, and stability of interactions between family members *as the family structure evolves* and children grow up and establish families of their own. Interhousehold influence may be affected by variables such as changes in family structures (i.e. birth, divorce, illness, aging, death) or changes in the environment (i.e. economic fluctuations, migration, technological developments). These variables can change the relative access of kin to resources in the formal economy, foster dependence upon other households in the kinship network for consumption needs, and thus affect the direction of exchange flows between households.

One of the most intriguing aspects of kinship exchange is the exchange of goods and services between relatives. An important aspect of these exchange networks may be the tendency towards *multiple modes of exchange*, such as barter, gift-giving, borrowing, recycling, and sharing, *which involves the migration of products past the point of purchase*. Intangible services play an important role in exchanges based on social affiliations (Williams 1988); the *household* appears to be the site of production for many of these services (Benson 1990).

A quote by Stack (1974, pp. 33-34) illustrates the extent to which kinship groups can function as lively exchange markets, where the "value" of what is exchanged is determined by its ability to tie the exchange partner into future transactions:

> "Those engaged in reciprocal gift giving are recruited primarily from relatives and from those friends who become defined as kin...They trade food stamps, rent money, a TV, hats, dice, a car, a nickel here, a cigarette there, food, milk, grits, and children...When people in The Flats swap goods, a value is placed upon the goods given away, but the value is not determined by the price or market value of the object...The value of an object given away is based upon its retaining power over the receiver; that is, how much and over how long a time the giver can expect returns on the gift."

A striking implication of Stack's research is that the *utility of a bundle of goods may be stretched by increasing the exchange velocity of goods within a network*. For example, a lawnmower is only "useful" periodically, that is, when the lawn needs mowing; on the other hand, if it is purchased and shared by multiple families, its shared utility may more than offset its decrease in useful life. Similarly, the cost of products whose capacity tends to exceed their period of usefulness, such baby clothing, children's furniture, and maternity clothes, may be reduced by recycling behavior.

This section leads to the following propositions:

P1) Kinship networks structure collective reciprocal exchange behaviors into informal underground economic systems. Reciprocal exchanges of goods and services between kin: 1) decrease the dependence of households upon formal markets by providing access to resources produced outside of the paid economy, and 2) increase consumption interdependences among related households by creating obligations and responsibilities which constrain atomistic market behavior.

P2) Kinship exchange networks are characterized by multiple modes of exchange, such as barter, gift-giving, borrowing, and recycling, which involve the migration of products past the point of purchase. Thus, a given level of resources within a kinship network may be stretched to serve more people by increasing the velocity with which resources circulate within the network.

P3) Kinship exchange is positively associated with the transference of consumption values, attitudes, and behavior among related households. The direction of consumer influence within a kinship network shifts with changes in the relative access of related households to resources in the formal economy and their dependence upon extended family resources for their consumption needs.

STRUCTURAL CHARACTERISTICS OF KINSHIP NETWORKS

An analysis of the structural characteristics of kinship networks is vital to understanding the underlying forces which shape and direct resource flows between families, and thus affect the extent of consumption interdependencies among families within a network. *Depth* is defined in terms of the number of generations "up" or "down" within a particular relationship in the network. Parents, aunts, and uncles are one generation up, children are one generation down, and siblings are equivalent in depth. The *range* of a kinship tie refers to the number of links between individuals; near kin are distinguished from distant kin by the number of links which connect them. Network *density* is the extent to which kin know and interact with each other.

In North America, kinship ties usually become non-salient beyond three of four links in depth and range (Rossi and Rossi 1990); however, research indicates that not only the saliency of ties, but also the extent to which families rely upon each other, may vary substantially. Studies throughout the 1960's and 1970's have found that the working class relies heavily on extended family networks for camaraderie, job opportunities, advice on purchases, and help during crises (e.g. Coleman 1983). Among the poor, research indicates that extended kinship networks may serve two functions: 1) as privatized welfare systems, picking up the slack where welfare fails to provide sufficient resources, or providing sole support for families who do not qualify for public assistance, and 2) as a coping mechanism for the stress associated with persistent poverty (Kelly 1985).

Extended family networks have been documented within most of the major ethnic populations, including Chinese, Southeast Asians, Chicanos, Puerto Ricans, Cubans, and Afro-Americans (Barrow 1988; Benson 1990; Godsheider and Godsheider 1989; Schaefer 1984; Stack 1974). The importance of the family in preserving the ethnic consumption behaviors among these groups has been noted (Hirschman 1985). In some rural areas, such as Alaskan native communities, intermarriage between relatives results in communities where nearly everyone is related; in Appalachian communities, lineage is an important factor affecting the flow of not only goods and services, but also family land (Bryant 1981). The overlap of these diverse segments of the population into multiple categories (i.e. poor rural Black families) prevents the use of census data to determine the size of each group. However, the number of groups which have been documented to rely upon extended family networks indicates that the focus of consumer research upon the nuclear family may have failed to capture significant variables affecting consumer behavior among a sizable portion of the population.

Close geographic proximity may be the most important factor in explaining the high level of extendedness, interaction, and exchange which takes place among many kinship networks. As access to economic resources declines, the most important function of extended family ties may be the frequent exchange of mutual aid, requiring dense network structures and high levels of physical proximity between kin (Stack 1974). While only a small percentage of the middle and upper class live close to their kin, 45 percent of the working class and 55 percent of the lower-class live within one linear mile (Coleman 1983). However, the poor don't just live near each other, they often live *with* each other (Angel and Tienda 1982). Furthermore, family constellations tend to be in perpetual transition as members move between households (Beck and Beck 1989), leading some researchers to state that the *primary* unit of analysis for this group should be the kinship exchange network (Kelly 1985).

There are two approaches to studying exchange networks: one focuses on the dyad and the other on the effect of network structure on social linkages (Uehara 1990). Research in consumer behavior has tended to focus on the variables which affect the former; however, there may be pitfalls in conceptualizing groups as if they were a collection of dyadic relationships. Social exchange networks, such as kinship networks, can involve both generalized and restricted forms of exchange (Ekeh 1974). Restricted exchange is dyadic (A gives to B), while generalized exchange links several network participants (A gives to B who gives to C who gives to A). Consequently, studies which focus on dyadic relationships may only capture a portion of the exchange process, and miss the synergies of group cohesion created by generalized exchange.

This section leads to the following proposition:

P4) Research studying the consumption interdependence among related households should measure and account for: 1) the depth, range, and density of the kinship structure, 2) the geographic proximity of members, and 3) the direction, frequency, and duration of network exchange behaviors. Analysis should not be limited to dyadic exchanges, but should include all network participants who may be involved in more generalized forms of exchange.

INTERPERSONAL RELATIONSHIPS IN KINSHIP NETWORKS

The effects of exchange behaviors upon family consumption depends upon the nature and strength of relationships between kin. The *intensity* of a relationship is measured by the degree of perceived obligations between kin, while *encapsulation* refers to the extent to which family members are more "intensely" linked to each other than to those outside of the network. High levels of density, intensity, and encapsulation have been associated with generalized exchange behaviors and group cohesion (Uehara 1990), and may account for some of the structural barriers which impede consumer assimilation among ethnic groups.

Within the family network, the highest level of intensity is felt toward spouse and children (Robins and Tomanec 1966). Kinship ties to members of the family of origin—parents and siblings—tend to be stronger than other extended kinship ties—grandparents, aunt, uncles, cousins (Sussman and Burchinal 1966). Higher obligations are expressed to descendants than to ascendants, and to females than to males (Rossi and Rossi 1990). Variables such as age, marital status, and financial status can affect perceptions of obligation to kin (Aldous 1987; Stoller 1983). For example, the very young and the very old cannot be expected to participate in reciprocal relationships, implying that the direction of consumer influence between kin may change directions over an individual's life cycle.

Since an individual's role complexity within the kinship network tends to increase with age, the rising longevity of the population has resulted in an increasing number of individuals who are "sandwiched" between generations. Research on role function within kinship networks consistently indicates that the overwhelming majority of kinkeeping activities is carried out by middle-aged women, who do most of the visiting, telephoning, and letter writing, orchestrate family gatherings, and assume primary responsibility for the physical care of kin (e.g. Rosenthal 1985). When multiple family members require simultaneous assistance, the multiple roles held by these women (mother, daughter, wife, sister) increases the number of individuals whose behavior is in turn affected. This indicates that middle-aged women may function as critical links in the path of resource flows between extended family members. Since exchanges often involve services, such as physical care for the very young or the very old, indirect effects upon consumption behavior may be considerable, and include changes in household task allocation, shopping patterns, eating habits, and other activities which reduce the role overload of the caregiver.

The preceding section leads to the following propositions:

P5) The level of perceived obligations between kin positively affect consumption interdependencies among extended family members. Thus, family consumption behavior will be more affected by exchanges with family members from the family of origin than by exchanges with more distant family members.

P6) Resources within a kinship network will tend to flow between links in which at least one female is present and will affect more individuals as role complexity increases; therefore, consumption interdependencies will be greater among households related by a family tie involving at least one mature female linkage.

KINSHIP SUPPORT STRUCTURES AND FAMILIES IN CRISIS

Two trends in American society illustrate how a crisis in one family can affect the resources and consumption behavior of other families within kinship structure: 1) the increasing number of single parent families and 2) the aging population.

About two-thirds of all divorces involve children (McLanahan and Garfinkle 1989). The majority of mothers retain custody of their children; however, only 60 percent of divorced mothers receive a child support award (Teachman 1990), while only approximately 44 percent of these receive the agreed-upon amount (U.S. Bureau of the Census 1991). Because of the way the welfare system works, some mothers, particularly in black urban areas where male employment opportunities are limited, may avoid marriage all together (Stack 1974). Consequently, 36 percent of households headed by single parents live at or below the poverty level (U.S. Bureau of the Census 1991).

Many single mothers turn to their kin, whose consumption is in turn affected in a variety of ways as they rally to help. Crossman and Edmondson (1985) found that 77 percent of divorced respondents reported receiving some form of assistance from parents, siblings, extended kin, and children following marital dissolution. Gerstel (1988) found that approximately two-thirds of divorced respondents reported borrowing money from at least one relative, and that divorced mothers tended to rely upon kin for help with household chores. Divorce has also been linked to the return of young adults, such as single mothers, to the parental home (Clemens and Axelson 1985). These multigenerational households experience blurred stages of the family life cycle which affect consumption behavior, such as when grandparents help with childcare or act as surrogate parents. In families where the grandmothers are still working, research indicates that adults juggle schedules so that both mother and daughter may work (Pressler 1989). In their study, however, Crossman and Edmondson (1985) note that—in every instance—divorced mothers received nothing from the father's kin, implying that one of the effects of divorce is to destabilize and truncate the kinship structure, usually on the father's side.

Another family crisis which activates kinship networks is the long-term care for the elderly. Approximately 80 percent of care for the elderly is provided by relatives (Benjamin 1984). It is well documented that women (wives and daughters) do most of the work (e.g. Finley 1989). In most cases they do so without the benefit of public or private support; Medicare and Medicaid do not pay for most home healthcare services, private services are almost nonexistent, and entry into three-quarters of all nursing homes is clogged by long waiting lists (Archbold 1983; Vladeck 1980).

Providing care for an elderly parent can be an enormous psychological and physical burden. Its impact upon family consumption behavior can be substantial, and it can affect multiple families. It usually occurs when the caregiver is in middle age or early old age (Archbold 1983). Unlike childbirth, it cannot be planned for. Unlike childcare, it does not get easier. And it lasts a long time—a British study cited by Abel (1986) found that about one-half of caregivers had provided care for at least five years, while almost one-quarter had provided care for *more than ten years*. In addition to the substantial drain on family resources, the duration of care can lead to severe role overload and chronic stress, which may lead to significant changes in family consumption behavior— or even the breakup of the family.

Kinship assistance to single parents and the aged are merely two examples of why life status changes cannot be studied from the sole perspective of the nuclear family. Critical life status events such as birth, the establishment of an independent household, marriage, unemployment, illness, and death tend to activate kinship exchange behavior among extended family members, affecting both families receiving assistance *and* families providing it.

IMPLICATIONS FOR FUTURE RESEARCH

Research on kinship family structures offers three important contributions to consumer research which are overlooked by traditional approaches to family consumption behavior. First, the family is viewed as a social unit embedded within the context of the kinship structure rather than as an isolated entity, thus reintegrating the family with its significant social setting. Second, kinship research examines the socioeconomic forces which create the broad demographic categories such as family life cycle or social class, thus decreasing the reliance of consumer research upon static taxonomies. Third, kinship research offers significant implications regarding the direct and indirect effects of kinship exchange behavior upon family consumption. By broadening the perspective of family consumption behavior to include the impact of social exchange networks, kinship research expands the definition of "consumption" to include non-market forms of exchange based upon reciprocity rather than profit relationships. The implementation of such a shift in perspective may increase our understanding of consumption behavior after the point of purchase, such as the "migration" of products through sharing, bartering, and borrowing.

Kinship research illustrates the critical importance of the fundamental structural assumptions which define the family and the unit of analysis used to measure it. Not all family models fit all segments of the population; social and economic factors can radically alter the extent to which families depend upon each other for support. A basic component in understanding many of the conditions which affect family consumption behavior is *also* the understanding of how conditions in one family affect other families within the network. At some economic levels, the exchange activities of kin may be so interrelated that measurements of consumption behavior must be aggregated. Current social and economic issues such as single parent families (zero-parent families in many inner-city areas), health care for the elderly and chronically ill, and high unemployment rates indicate that kinship support structures may be a particularly timely topic for consumer researchers. Such subgroups represent sizable segments of the population, whose consumption behavior is largely unaccounted for by traditional family consumption models.

BIBLIOGRAPHY

Abel, Emily (1986), "Adult Daughters and Care for the Elderly," *Feminist Studies*, 12(Fall), 479-497.

Aldous, Joan (1987), "New Views on the Family Life of the Elderly and the Near Elderly," *Journal of Marriage and the Family*, 49(May), 227-234.

Angel, Ronald and Marta Tienda (1982), "Determinants of Extended Household Structure: Cultural Pattern or Economic Need?" *American Journal of Sociology*, 87 (March), 1360-1383.

Archbold, Patricia G. (1983), "Impact of Parent-Caring on Women," *Family Relations*, 32(January), 39-45.

Barrow, Anita (1988), "Generations of Persistence: Kinship Amidst Urban Poverty in Sao Paulo and New York," *Urban Anthropology*, 17(Summer/Fall), 193-228.

Beck, Ruby W. and Scott Beck (1989), "The Incidence of Extended Households Among Middle-Aged Black and White Women," *Journal of Family Issues*, 19(June), 147-168.

Benjamin, Jr., A.E. (1985), "Aging and Family Resources: Availability and Proximity of Kin," in *Long-Term Care for the Elderly: Public Policy Issues*, ed C. Harrington, Beverly Hills, CA: Sage, 206-216.

Benson, Janet E. (1990), "Households, Migration, and Community Context," *Urban Anthropology*, 19(Spring/Summer), 9-29.

Bryant. F. Carlene (1981), *We're All Kin*, Knoxville, TN: University of Tennessee Press.

Clemens, Audrey W. and Leland J. Axelson (1985), "The Not-So-Empty Nest: The Return of the Fledgling Adult," *Family Relations*, 33(April), 613-621.

Coleman, Richard P. (1983), "The Continuing Significance of Social Class to Marketing," *Journal of Consumer Research*, 10(Dec), 265-280.

Crossman, Sharon M. and Jean E. Edmondson (1985), "Personal and Family Resources Supportive of Displaced Homemakers' Financial Adjustment," *Family Relations*, 34(Oct), 465-474.

Ekeh, Peter P. (1974), *Social Exchange Theory: The Two Traditions*, Cambridge, MA: Harvard University Press.

Finley, Nancy J. (1989), "Theories of Family Labor As Applied to Gender Differences in Caregiving for Elderly Parents," *Journal of Marriage and the Family*, 51(Feb), 79-86.

Frenzen, Johnathan K. and Harry L. Davis (1990), "Purchasing Behavior in Embedded Markets," *Journal of Consumer Research*, 17(June), 1-11.

Gerstel, Naomi (1988), "Divorce and Kin Ties: The Importance of Gender," *Journal of Marriage and the Family*, 50(Feb), 209-218.

Godsheider, Frances K. and Calvin Goldsheider (1989), *Ethnicity and the New Family Economy*, Boulder, CO: Westview Press.

Gouldner, A.W. (1960), "The Norm of Reciprocity: A Preliminary Statement," *American Sociological Review*, 25(Fall), 161-178. *Organizational Behavior and Human Performance*, vol. 23.

Hirschman, Elizabeth (1985), "Primitive Aspects of Consumption in Modern American Society," *Journal of Consumer Research*, 12(Sept), 142-154.

Kelly, Robert F. (1985), "The Family and the Urban Underclass: An Integrative Framework," *Journal of Family Issues*, 6(June), 159-184.

McLanahan, Sara S. and Irwin Garfinkel (1989), "Single-Mothers, the Underclass, and Social Policy," *Annals of the American Academy of Political and Social Sciences*, Vol. 501, 92-102.

Pressler, Harriet B. (1989), "Some Economic Complexities of Child Care Provided by Grandmothers," *Journal of Marriage and the Family*, 51, 583-591.

Robins, Lee N. and Miroda Tomanec (1966), "Closeness to Blood Relatives Outside the Immediate Family," in *Kinship and Family Organization*, ed. B. Farber, New York: Wiley and Sons, Inc, 1134-141.

Rosenthal, Carolyn (1985), "Kinkeeping in the Familial Division of Labor," *Journal of Marriage and the Family*, November, 965-974.

Rossi and Rossi (1990), *Of Human Bonding*, New York: Walter de Gruyter, Inc.

Schaeffer, Richard T. (1984), *Racial and Ethnic Groups*, Boston, MA: Little, Brown, and Company.

Stack, Carol B. (1974), *All Our Kin: Strategies for Survival in a Black Community*, New York: Harper and Row.

Stoller, Eleanor P. (1983), "Parental Caregiving by Adult Children," *Journal of Marriage and the Family*, 45(Apr), 851-858.

Sussman, Marvin B. and Lee G. Burchinal (1966), "Kin Family Network: Unheralded Structure in Current Conceptualizations of Family Functioning," in *Kinship and Family Organization*, ed. B. Farber, New York: Wiley and Sons, Inc, 123-133.

Teachman, Jay D. (1990), "Socioeconomic Resources of Parents and Award of Child Support in the United States: Some Exploratory Models," *Journal of Marriage and the Family*, 52(Aug), 689-699.

Uehara, Edwina (1990), "Dual Exchange Theory, Social Networks, and Informal Social Support," *American Journal of Sociology*, 96(Nov), 521-557.

U. S. Bureau of the Census (1991), "The Economics of Family Disruption, *Statistical Brief*, U.S. Department of Commerce, SB/91-10, March.

Vladeck, Bruce C. (1980), *Unloving Care: The Nursing Home Tragedy*, New York: Basic Books.

Williams, Flora L. (1988), "Value Provided by Interfamily Exchange of Goods and Services in Two Cultures," *Lifestyles: Family and Economic Issues*, 9(Fall), 221-239.

Children's Susceptibility to Peer Group Purchase Influence: An Exploratory Investigation

Gwen Rae Bachmann, University of Minnesota
Deborah Roedder John, University of Minnesota
Akshay R. Rao, University of Minnesota

ABSTRACT

The purpose of this paper is to examine how children of different ages factor peer group influence into their purchase decisions. In contrast to the prevailing view that peer influence becomes greater as children progress through early childhood into adolescence, our findings indicate that peer influence operates in a more subtle fashion. As children grow older, they begin to recognize that peer influence is important in some product situations, such as those involving publicly consumed items, but not in others, such as those involving privately consumed items. These results are discussed in terms of their importance for understanding the development of peer group influence in children's purchase decisions and for designing consumer education programs for increasing the awareness of such influence in children of all ages.

INTRODUCTION

Questions surrounding the role of media, specifically television advertising, in influencing aspects of children's consumer behavior have been the focus of much academic research and public policy debate. Starting with the Federal Trade Commission's proposal in the late 1970's to ban television advertising to young children, academic researchers have focused much of their attention on the influence of advertising on children's product preferences (Goldberg 1990; Goldberg, Gorn, and Gibson 1978), purchase requests to parents (Galst & White 1976; Robertson and Rossiter 1976), and actual product choices (Goldberg and Gorn 1982; Roedder, Sternthal, and Calder 1983). This body of research clearly documents the impact of television advertising on young children.

Less clear, however, is the role other influence agents play in children's product preferences and purchase decisions. In particular, there has been a surprising lack of research on the topic of peer influence as it impacts children's consumer behavior and decision making. Anecdotal evidence would suggest that peer influence becomes very important as children enter their teenage years and that peer influence exerts more impact for some products (e.g., athletic shoes) than others (e.g., gloves). And, some evidence from studies of general consumer socialization patterns would support these age trends in susceptibility to peer influence (e.g., Churchill and Moschis 1979). Apart from these preliminary indications, however, little research evidence exists on how peer groups influence children of different ages.

Accordingly, the purpose of this paper is to examine the emergence of peer group influence in children's purchase decisions. While there are many different sources and types of influence, this study focuses on the *normative* component of peer influence.[1] Specifically, we investigate the degree to which children of different ages factor peer group opinions into their product decisions, depending on the nature of the product class involved in the decision. Evidence to this effect is important not only for a more complete understanding of children's consumer behavior, but also as a basis for consumer education programs that seek to develop children's critical thinking skills about the purchase decisions they make.

CONCEPTUAL OVERVIEW

While our focus is *peer* influence on children's decision making, an existing body of research, reference group influence, is used to frame our question and draw theoretical arguments. Reference group influence is discussed next.

Reference Group Influence Defined

A reference group can be defined as "...a group of people that significantly influences an individual's behavior" (Bearden and Etzel 1982, p. 184). In consumer behavior contexts, reference groups are typically comprised of significant others from the individuals' social network, including family members, co-workers, peers and friends as well as inspirational figures such as sports heroes, movie stars, and fictional characters. For children, family members and peers are undoubtedly the most dominant reference groups, followed by more distant figures such as sports heroes and movie stars (Shaffer 1988).

The influence that reference groups exert on the types of products and brands an individual purchases is diverse, with referents exercising three forms of influence on decision making: information, utilitarian, and value-expressive (Deutsch and Gerard 1955; Kelman 1961). Seeking out information from a referent, feeling that a purchase would enhance one's image with a reference group, and allowing one's liking of the reference group to influence one's decision to purchase a product would be examples of information, utilitarian, and value-expressive components of reference group influence, respectively. Empirically and conceptually, the utilitarian and value-expressive component are difficult to distinguish and are often combined, into a "normative" component of influence (Bearden, Netemeyer & Teel, 1989). It is this normative component of peer influence that we address.

Age Differences in Reference Group Influence

In order for reference groups, such as peer groups, to exert influence on children's product decisions, children must have developed certain social sensitivities and cognitive skills. First, a child must be able to take another person's perspective and realize that another person's preferences may be different from one's own preferences. Second, a child must understand and/or believe that people draw inferences about each other based on product choices and possessions. And, third, other people's opinions must be important to the child in forming his or her own self concept. Without one of these "building blocks," reference group influence of any kind may be weak if not altogether absent.

These three building blocks can provide a basis for predicting and explaining when peer influence might emerge and how it might develop as children mature. Several frameworks from child psychology that discuss the emergence of these key aspects of social-cognitive development may be applicable when examining peer influence at different ages. These frameworks are diagrammed in Table 1.

---

[1] Normative influences are based on an individual's need to identify with group norms, standards and values.

TABLE 1
Comparison of Age Differences in Stage Theories

Age (in years)	Selman Role-taking Abilities	Barenboim Impression Formation	Erikson Psychosocial Development
0-1			Trust/Mistrust
1-2			Autonomy vs. Shame/Doubt
2-3			Autonomy vs. Shame/Doubt
3-4	Ego-Centric		Initiative vs. Guilt
4-5	Ego-Centric		Initiative vs. Guilt
5-6	Ego-Centric		Initiative vs. Guilt
6-7	Social Information Role-taking	Behavioral Comparisons	Industry vs. Inferiority
7-8	Social Information Role-taking	Behavioral Comparisons	Industry vs. Inferiority
8-9	Self-Reflective Role-taking	Psychological Constructs	Industry vs. Inferiority
9-10	Self-Reflective Role-taking	Psychological Constructs	Industry vs. Inferiority
10-11	Mutual Role-taking	Psychological Constructs	Industry vs. Inferiority
11-12	Mutual Role-taking	Psychological Comparisons	Industry vs. Inferiority
12-20	Social and Conventional Role-taking	Psychological Comparisons	Identity
20-40	Social and Conventional Role-taking	Psychological Comparisons	Intimacy
40-65	Social and Conventional Role-taking	Psychological Comparisons	Generativity
65+	Social and Conventional Role-taking	Psychological Comparisons	Ego Integrity

Selman (1980) suggests that, in order to role play a child must be able to take on another person's perspective, understand their thoughts and feelings, and anticipate the other person's reactions versus their own. In the first stage, ego-centric role-taking, young children are unaware of any perspective other than their own. By the second stage, social-informational role-taking, a child may realize that others may have different perspectives but has difficulty anticipating what they might be. In the third stage, the self-reflective stage, a child can anticipate and consider another's person's viewpoint but is unable to simultaneously consider his/her own perspective and that of another. The final stage, social and conventional system role-taking, involves not only mutual role taking but a consideration of the situation or context.

A second framework of impression formation, Barenboim (1981), is a three-step developmental sequence describing the changes in children's impressions of others during the grade school years. In the first stage, the behavioral comparisons phase, children's impressions involve comparisons in concrete behavioral terms (e.g., "He's the best climber"). In the second stage, the psychological constructs stage, children begin to base their impressions on regularities in other's behavior and describe others in terms of abstract psychological attributes (e.g., "She's stubborn"). In the final stage, the psychological comparisons phase, children begin to compare others on important psychological dimensions (e.g., "Sara is more generous than Mary").

Erikson's (1972) theory of psychosocial development is based on the belief that humans are adaptive beings who go through eight social-conflict stages in a lifetime. The eight stages or crises are based on the development of trust, autonomy, initiative, industry, identity, intimacy, generativity (productivity in work and family responsibilities), and ego integrity. The key feature of these stages for our purpose is the fact that the primary social agents involved in resolving each stage's social conflicts differ by stage. In the first three stages, parents and family are the primary social agents. For children in the fourth stage, teachers and peers are the primary social agents. In the fifth stage, peers once again are the primary social agents. Spouses and lovers are added to the list in the sixth stage. In the seventh stage, primary social agents are spouses, children, and cultural norms. In the final stage, social agents have not been specified.

Since these three frameworks address different social-cognitive skills, the number of stages and the specific ages at which they occur varies between frameworks. However, these frameworks are remarkably similar in identifying major breaks in children's development across domains: ages 5 and under, ages 6 to 8, ages 9 to 11, ages 11/12 and older. Because each of these frameworks was selected to provide evidence of the prerequisites necessary for peer influence, such as perspective (role) taking and social impression formation, these major age breaks appear to indicate relevant differences between age groups in their use of peer influence.

Specifically, based upon the developmental theories just reviewed, children 5 years of age and under would seem to be the least susceptible to referent group influence. Because children of this age have greater difficulty in acknowledging and taking another person's perspective, they most likely view other's preferences to be similar to their own, leaving little room for external influences. Children between the ages of 6 and 8 are more likely to be influenced by their peers. Yet, their impression formation skills are such that they are not prone to the type of sophisticated inferences involved in recognizing that other people not only have their own preferences but also that these preferences are used as a basis of comparison in judging other people. Children 9 to 11 years of age would appear to be even more susceptible to reference group influence than their younger counterparts by virtue of the fact that they can anticipate others' reactions to their opinions and behavior, can consider their own preferences in conjunction with others' opinions, and have rather well-developed person impression skills. In short, they are beginning to understand external influences and are open to influences from their peers. Finally, children 12 years of age and older are probably the ultimate purveyors and receivers of reference group influence. Not only do they now recognize the intricacies of social interactions with others, but are also painfully aware of the tendency for psychological impressions to be formed on the basis of consumption preferences and choices.

This characterization of age differences is quite consistent with the prevailing notion that reference group influence, particularly peer group influence, increases as children progress through childhood to adolescence. But, the increasing sophistication in impression formation skills also suggests that reference group influence probably varies by the product context and situation as children become more socially adept. An important factor in this regard, suggested by studies of reference group influence with adult consumers, is the type of product involved in the purchase decision. It is to this topic that we now turn.

Product Class Differences in Reference Group Influence

Recent investigations into reference group influence in consumer decision making have identified the need to consider the conspicuousness of the product or brand of interest. Product conspicuousness is a function of two dimensions (see Bearden and Etzel 1982). First, the extent to which the product is not owned by everybody makes it exclusive, and thus, conspicuous. Thus, *luxuries*, which are more exclusive than *necessities*, tend to be relatively more conspicuous. The second dimension refers to the degree to which product usage is performed in public versus in private. *Publicly consumed* items are, of course, more conspicuous than *privately consumed* products. Four types of products emerge from these two dimensions: publicly consumed luxuries, publicly consumed necessities, privately consumed luxuries, and privately consumed necessities.

Extant research indicates that the degree of reference group influence varies by product conspicuousness. For peer group influence, both Bearden and Etzel (1982) and Childers and Rao (1992) find that public luxuries and private necessities make up the ends of the conspicuousness continuum, with public luxuries being subject to significantly more influence than private necessities. In addition, there is a tendency for public products of all types, regardless of whether they are luxuries or necessities, to be subject to more reference group influence than private products of all types.

In light of these findings, peer influence in children's decision making should also be linked to product conspicuousness, at least for some age groups. Recall though, that this study is only addressing the normative component of peer influence, not all types of reference group influence. Specifically, it would seem that peer influence should vary by product type for children with the requisite social-cognitive skills to understand the consequences of ignoring others' opinions for products that are conspicuously displayed and used versus those that are not. It is, in fact, a fairly sophisticated view of social interaction that would need to be held in order to understand that other people's opinions matter *only* for those products that are in public view or are exclusive.

Following this line of reasoning, the ability to make distinctions between product types in terms of how much peer influence should be considered should develop with age. Older children, with a more sophisticated view that allows them to view peer influence in different situational contexts, will be more likely to factor peer opinions into some types of product decisions (e.g., those involving publicly consumed items) but not others (e.g., those involving privately consumed items). Younger children will be more likely to either dismiss peer influence altogether, or simply believe that their friends' opinions are somewhat important no matter what type of product is being considered. Therefore, consistent with the age groups identified earlier, and their corresponding levels of social-cognitive skills, the following hypotheses are advanced:

H1: Differences in peer influence as a function of product conspicuous will be larger for older than younger children.

H1a: Product conspicuousness will make no difference in the degree of peer influence for children in the early elementary school years (ages 6-8).

H1b: Product conspicuousness will make a small to moderate difference in the degree of peer influence for children in the middle elementary school years (ages 9-11). If a difference emerges, it will be a distinction between the most extreme ends of the product conspicuous continuum, public luxuries versus private necessities.

H1c: Product conspicuousness will make a moderate to large difference in the degree of peer influence for children in the later elementary school years (ages 12-14). Distinctions are likely to be made not only at the extreme ends of the product conspicuous continuum, but also for public versus private products and for luxuries versus necessities.

METHOD

Sample

One hundred forty one children from an elementary school in a major metropolitan area were recruited for the study. In order to obtain subjects in the appropriate age groups, consent forms were sent home to children in the first, second, fourth, fifth, seventh, and eighth grades. Of those returning consent forms and participating in the study, 54 children were 6-8 years of age, 49 children were 9-11 years of age, and 38 children were 12-14 years of age. In return for their participation, children received a small prize and the school received a small donation for their cooperation.

Design

The study employed a 3 (Age) x 4 (Product Conspicuousness) x 3 (Version) factorial design. The age of the child (AGE) was a between subject factor, whereas product conspicuousness (CONSPIC) was varied on a within-subject basis to represent the four product types of interest (public luxuries, public necessities, private luxuries, private necessities). In order to provide multiple operationalizations of the four product types, three versions of the questionnaire (VERSION) were compiled, with each version containing a different operationalization of each product type. Different versions of the questionnaire were administered to different groups of subjects; therefore version was a third (between subject) factor. The statistical model employed to test the various hypotheses considered the appropriate mean squared error terms in light of the one repeated factor.

Independent Variables

Based on the developmental research reviewed earlier, and the hypotheses of interest, three age groups were included in the study: 6-8 year olds, 9-11 year olds, and 12-14 years olds. Children under 6 were excluded from the study due to problems that surfaced in a pilot study with regard to understanding the instructions and measurement scales. Children over 14 were excluded from the study due to potential problems in identifying products representative of each product category for a large age range.

For the *product conspicuousness* factor, pretests were conducted to identify a set of products representing the four product types: public luxury, public necessity, private luxury, and private necessity. A large list of possible products that were gender-neutral and familiar to children of all ages was generated. Children were presented with the list of products and asked to classify each product as either public or private and as a necessity or a luxury. Before responding to the list of products, children were provided with a concrete definition of each term and were given two "practice" products as a training task. To record their answers, older subjects simply circled the appropriate term (e.g., "public" or "private"), whereas younger children circled a picture that portrayed the concept of "public" (many children watching the owner), "private" (owner by himself/herself), "luxury" (very few owners), and "necessity" (many owners).[2] The results were analyzed by age group to identify a set of 12 products, three for each product type, that were classified correctly by the large majority of children (at least 60%) in each of the three age groups. Most of the products, in fact, were classified correctly by at least 75% of the children across age groups.

These twelve products were then used to create three *versions* of the questionnaire. Each version included a public luxury, a public necessity, a private luxury, and a private necessity, resulting in the following sets: (1) snow skis, winter coat, TV for own room, pajamas; (2) ice skates, pants, home computer, hair brush; (3) 10-speed bike, shoes, stereo for own room, toothbrush.

Dependent Variable

The measure of peer group influence was developed from similar scales used in previous studies of reference group influence in adults (Bearden and Etzel 1982; Bearden, Netemeyer and Teel 1989; Childers and Rao 1992; Park and Lessig 1977). In modifying these scales for use with children, the number of items was kept at a reasonable number to avoid fatigue, and the scale points were kept at a minimum to make it easier for younger children to respond. The final scale, adapted from the one developed by Bearden et al. (1989), included seven items that children indicated their agreement or disagreement with on a four-point YES-No scale ("YES" "yes" "no" "NO"). Children's responses to the items were summed, based on results indicating that the scale was unidimensional with a more than acceptable degree of inter-item reliability (alpha = .94)[3].

Procedure

Questionnaires were administered to children in their classrooms during the school day. After receiving general instructions about the study, and specific instructions about the YES-NO scale, subjects were given a training task to ensure that they understood the rating scale. For this purpose, children were asked to respond to a series of test items, such as "I like cookies" and "I like icky medicine", using the YES-NO scale. After the training phase, subjects were given the major task, involving their responses to the YES-NO purchase influence scale for each of four products. The order in which products appeared was randomized to minimize possible order effects. In addition, a distractor task was presented in the middle of the task, to minimize possible fatigue or boredom with the rating task. As a manipulation check, subjects completed some final questions regarding the conspicuousness category of each product. Children were then thanked, given a prize, and dismissed.

RESULTS

Children's responses to the peer purchase influence scale were first analyzed using a 3 (age) x 4 (product conspicuousness) x 3 (version) repeated measures MANOVA. The results indicate general support for our hypothesis that the degree of peer group influence would vary as a function of age and product conspicuousness, with a significant AGE x CONSPIC interaction emerging from the analysis ($F(6,396)=8.66$, $p<.01$). Also of interest, though not predicted, a significant main effect for conspicuousness was observed ($F(3,396)=35.04$, $p<.001$). Of less direct interest, there were two significant effects involving the VERSION factor, specifically the main effect for VERSION ($F(2,132)=5.86$, $p<.005$) and the VERSION x CONSPIC interaction ($F(6,396)=5.92$, $p<.001$). These results indicate, as might be expected, that different operationalizations of the four product types were not always equivalent in terms of how much peer influence was exerted, thus confirming the importance of our inclusion of multiple operationalizations for the conspicuousness factor. The use of multiple operationalizations and the finding of significant version effects are common in this literature (Bearden & Etzel, 1982; Childers & Rao, 1992). Note, however, the important finding that the VERSION x AGE interaction was not significant, indicating that the pattern of results for each of the products was consistent across age groups. Consequently, the remainder of our analysis examined data collapsed across the three versions. Means and standard deviations for the experimental conditions are presented in Table 2.

Further analyses were conducted to examine the predictions regarding differences between product types within each age group. Specifically, contrasts between means for the four product types

---

[2] Interested readers may contact the authors for complete pretest instructions and pictures used to represent conspicuousness dimensions.

[3] Interested readers may contact the authors for complete influence scale.

TABLE 2
Means and Standard Deviations Categorized by Age and Product Type

Age	Product Type			
	Public Luxury	Public Necessity	Private Luxury	Private Necessity
6-8 Years	2.18 (0.93)	2.14 (0.88)	2.10 (0.83)	2.12 (0.91)
9-11 Years	2.09 (0.76)	2.15 (0.78)	1.88 (0.62)	1.76 (0.57)
12-14 Years	2.46 (0.72)	2.50 (0.66)	1.94 (0.64)	1.65 (0.63)
All Ages	2.22 (0.83)	2.24 (0.80)	1.98 (0.71)	1.87 (0.76)

NOTE: S.D. in parentheses. Higher numbers indicate greater susceptibility to peer influence.

were conducted within each age group using a Newman-Keuls' procedure. The appropriate error term based on the repeated measures analysis was used. The results, shown in Table 3, indicate general support for our hypotheses by age group. For the *youngest age group*, none of the contrasts between product types was significant, as predicted. The data suggest that children in this age group view the degree of peer group influence as rather constant across product types. It appears that these children have not yet developed an understanding of the social significance of using products in different contexts. Distinctions with regard to peer influence are not made between publicly consumed and privately consumed goods, nor between luxuries and necessities. Even differences at the ends of the conspicuousness continuum, public luxuries versus private necessities, are not recognized.

Consistent with our predictions, children in the *middle age group* reacted differently to peer group influence depending on product conspicuousness, distinguishing between products at the extremes of the conspicuousness continuum (public luxuries versus private necessities). But, interestingly, these children also showed an understanding of the social implications of the public versus private dichotomy. An examination of the results indicates that only the (1) public luxury versus public necessity, and (2) private luxury versus private necessity contrasts were not significant. It would appear that the significance of the luxury versus necessity distinction emerges later in children, probably intertwined with an understanding of economic concepts such as relative price (a principal determinant of luxury prices) and relative scarcity.

Finally, as predicted, children in the *oldest age group* demonstrated the most sophisticated sensitivity to peer group influence. These children exhibited differences in peer group influence for almost every product type tested, with the only nonsignificant contrast being the one between public luxuries and public necessities. Further, when the influence scores for both luxury items were combined and contrasted with the influence scores for both necessity items, a paired T-test of the luxury/necessity comparison was significant for this age group, whereas it was not significant for the two younger age groups. The remaining contrasts, all significant, indicate an ability to adapt to different social contexts, with a full consideration of the public versus private dichotomy and a partial understanding of the luxury versus necessity distinction. In point of fact, it is quite likely that these older children may have exhibited a much more definitive appreciation of the luxury-necessity dichotomy even for publicly consumed items had the price differences between the luxury and necessity products in the public category (e.g., ice skates and pants) been as great as the ones evident in the private category (e.g., computer versus hairbrush).

DISCUSSION

Our findings indicate that peer group purchase influence emerges slowly as children progress through their elementary school years. In contrast to prevailing wisdom, however, peer group influence does not accelerate with increasing age for a wide range of products. With advancing age, children become more susceptible to peer group influence *only* for those products that are more conspicuous in nature, such as public luxuries. Older children are more susceptible to influence for some products, such as public luxuries, but are less susceptible to influence for other products, such as private necessities. Distinctions such as these are no doubt fueled by the increasingly sophisticated view of social interaction and impression formation possessed by older children.

These findings suggest that peer group influence, and probably other types of reference group influence as well, is a far more complex phenomenon than previous anecdotal evidence would suggest. As children progress from early childhood to adolescence, what develops is an awareness that peer groups are an important influence in some types of product decisions, but are irrelevant in others. As this "contingency view" develops, children will no doubt begin to incorporate opinions from their peers for some types of decisions but incorporate opinions from different referents for other types of decisions.

Due to the concern over television advertising as a major influence on children, most of the current consumer education efforts have focused on helping children understand the persuasive intent of ads and on providing skills to detect possible puffery or deception. Considering the findings presented here, it would appear to be important to consider peer group influence in these consumer education efforts. Increasing children's awareness of the role that peer influence plays in their purchase decisions, and discussing the positive and negative aspects of this type of influence, would seem to be important in improving the critical thinking skills of young and developing consumers.

TABLE 3
Contrasts Between Product Types Within Age Groups

Contrast	6-8 years	Age Group 9-11 years	12-14 years
Public Luxuries vs. Public Necessities	=	=	=
Public Luxuries vs. Private Luxuries	=	>	>
Public Luxuries vs. Private Necessities	=	>	>
Public Necessities vs. Private Luxuries	=	>	>
Public Necessities vs. Private Necessities	=	>	>
Private Luxuries vs. Private Necessities	=	=	>

= Not Statistically Significant at p<.05; > Statistically Significant at p<.05

Additional research is warranted to provide a more complete view of peer group influence than the preliminary one offered here. Several avenues for extension should be considered. First, future research should examine the impact of peer group influence on children's brand-level decisions in addition to the product-level decisions explored in our study. It is quite possible that peer influence may be more pervasive, but may develop later, for brand decisions than for product decisions (see Bearden and Etzel 1982). In pursuing this line of research, investigators will need to be particularly cautious, however, in selecting brands that are familiar to children across a wide range of age groups.

A second direction for future research would involve a more detailed examination of the different components of peer or referent groups influence identified in research with adults. The information component and the normative component may yield different effects (Bearden and Etzel 1982; Bearden et al. 1989). Finally, different methodologies should be pursued in future research to provide convergent evidence of the age differences observed here. Validation of our findings in an experimental setting, in which peer group opinions are manipulated and purchase influence directly measured, would be beneficial in increasing our confidence that the self-report methodology used in this study did indeed capture the nature of the peer influence phenomenon for children of all ages.

An experimental methodology might also be useful in assessing the usefulness of consumer education efforts aimed at developing critical thinking skills about peer group influence. Considering the interest among parents and educators in promoting decision making skills in children, research in this area would serve to further the goal of making children more informed and more knowledgeable consumers. With children exerting more direct and indirect influence in a wide range of individual and household purchase decisions, such research could not be more timely nor more important.

REFERENCES

Barenboim, Carl (1981), "The Development of Person Perception in Childhood and Adolescence: From Behavioral Comparisons to Psychological Constructs to Psychological Comparisons," *Child Development*, 52, 129-244.

Bearden, William O. and Michael J. Etzel (1982), "Reference Group Influence on Product and Brand Purchase Decisions," *Journal of Consumer Research*, 9 (September), 183-94.

_____, Richard G. Netemeyer, and Jesse E. Teel (1989), "Measurement of Consumer Susceptibility to Interpersonal Influence," *Journal of Consumer Research*, 15 (March), 473-481.

Childers, Terry L. and Akshay R. Rao (1992), "The Influence of Familial and Peer-Based Reference Groups on Consumer Decisions," *Journal of Consumer Research*, (September), 198-211.

Churchill, Gilbert A., Jr. and George P. Moschis (1979), "Television and Interpersonal Influences on Adolescent Consumer Learning," *Journal of Consumer Research*, 6 (June), 23-35.

Deutsch, M. and Harold B. Gerard (1955), "A Study of Normative and Informational Social Influences Upon Individual Judgment," *Journal of Abnormal and Social Psychology*, 51, 624-636.

Erickson, Erik H. (1972), "Eight Stages of Man," in C.S. Lavatelli and F. Stendler (eds.), *Readings in Child Behavior and Child Development*, San Diego, CA: Harcourt Brace Jovanovich.

Galst, Joann Paley and Mary Alice White (1976), "The Unhealthy Persuader: The Reinforcing Value of Television and Children's Purchase-influencing Attempts at the Supermarket," *Child Development*, 17, 1089-1096.

Goldberg, Marvin E. (1990), "A Quasi-Experiment Assessing the Effectiveness of TV Advertising to Children," *Journal of Marketing Research*, 27 (November), 445-54.

_____ and Gerald J. Gorn (1982), "Behavioral Evidence of the Effects of Televised Food Messages on Children," *Journal of Consumer Research*, 9 (September), 200-205.

_____, _____, and Wendy Gibson (1978), "TV Messages for Snack and Breakfast Foods: Do They Influence Children's Preferences?" *Journal of Consumer Research*, 5 (September), 73-81.

Kelman, Herbert C. (1961), "Processes of Opinion Change," *Public Opinion Quarterly*, 25, 57-78.

Robertson, Thomas S. and John R. Rossiter (1976), "Short-Run Advertising Effects on Children: A Field Study," *Journal of Marketing Research*, 13 (February), 68-70.

Roedder, Deborah L., Brian Sternthal, and Bobby J. Calder (1983), "Attitude-Behavior Consistency in Children's Responses to Television Advertising," *Journal of Marketing Research*, 20 (November), 337-49.

Selman, Robert L. (1980), *The Growth of Interpersonal Understanding*, Orlando, FL: Academic Press.

Shaffer, David R. (1988), *Social and Personality Development*, Pacific Grove, CA: Brooks/Cole Publishing Company.

Female-Headed Single Parent Families: An Exploratory Study of Children's Influence in Family Decision Making

Roshan "Bob" D. Ahuja, Xavier University
Kandi M. Stinson, Xavier University

ABSTRACT

This study examines the relationships among selected characteristics of female-headed single parent families, and the influence the children have in the family decision making process. The characteristics of interest are, the mother's age, education, income, sex role orientation, employment status, and the number of years since the mother's separation, divorce, or widowhood, the household size, the age and sex of the oldest child. The results indicate that children's influence in this family type varies according to demographic characteristics of the family, according to the mother's sex role orientation, according to the type of product investigated, and according to the stage in the decision making process.

INTRODUCTION

Consumer behavior researchers have been encouraged to study the family, especially with respect to decision making (Sheth 1982; Davis 1976). Too much consumer behavior theory and research has been focused on the individual consumer and too little attention has been given to the decision making processes involving group behavior, such as those processes of the household (Sheth 1982). Davis (1976) proposed that a theory of household decision making will not emerge by concentrating on decision outcomes, such as who decided or who won. Rather, theoretical progress will be made when more is known about the processes that families use to make decisions.

The most comprehensive existing theoretical marketing model on family decision making (Sheth 1974) assumes the children are growing up in an intact or two parent family structure. The Engel, Kollat, and Blackwell (Engel, Blackwell, and Miniard 1986) model of consumer behavior is oriented around the "normal" (page 270) family structure, i.e., a married couple with children. Ekstrom, Tansuhaj, and Foxman (1987) proposed that a child's influence varies according to family structure. Much empirical information already exists in the marketing literature regarding the child's level of influence in married family households (Atkin 1978; Belch, Belch, and Ceresino 1985; Berey and Pollay 1968; Foxman, Tansuhaj, and Ekstrom 1989; Jenkens 1979; Mehrotra and Torges 1977; Nelson 1979; Szybillo, Sosanie, and Tennenbein 1977; Szybillo and Sosanie 1977; Ward, Wackman, and Wartella 1975; Ward and Wackman 1972); however, very little is known in this area about the female-headed single parent family. The two parent family structure, while still considered the "traditional" or the "normal" family structure by most researchers, is not the typical or modal family structure in the United States in the 1990's.

Marketing academicians and researchers must devote greater attention to the decision making process within the fastest growing family type in the United States, the female-headed single parent family. Too much marketing research has concentrated on the two parent family structure, and too little on the single parent family form, especially the female-headed household. Since 88 percent of all single parent families are headed by women (Statistical Abstract 1989 t67), the study of female-headed single parent families is particularly needed. Since the family is the basic purchase and consumption unit, marketers need to continuously study changes in family structure as they relate to changes in market behaviors.

The specific research objective for this exploratory study is to examine the relationships among selected characteristics of single mother's families, and the influence the children have in the family decision making process. The nine characteristics of interest are, 1) the age of the mother, 2) the education of the mother, 3) the mother's income, 4) the mother's sex role orientation, 5) the mother's employment status, 6) the number of years since the mother's separation, divorce, or widowhood, 7) the household size, 8) the age of the oldest child, 9) and the sex of the oldest child. These objectives were carried out in a national probability sample of female-headed single parent households.

LITERATURE REVIEW

It has been estimated that the 1990 census will show that there are 94 million households in the United States, with 67 million or 71 percent considered family households and 27 million or 29 percent considered nonfamily households (Waldrop and Exter 1990). Of the 67 million family households, approximately 12 percent will be females heading families alone, compared to 5 percent in 1970. Female-headed single parent families represent the fastest growing family type, up 36 percent since 1980 (Waldrop and Exter 1990).

A review of the marketing literature revealed only five studies that, in addition to other issues addressed, also measured the type of family structure and used this measure to investigate the effect that family structure has on selected marketing related variables. With only five studies, it would seem unlikely that similarities exist in the topics studied, but this is not the case.

Similarities do exist along several dimensions. For instance, four studies measured parental perception of the child's influence in the family decision making process (Darley and Lim 1986; Taylor, Moore, and Glynn 1986; Taylor, Glynn, and Taylor 1985; Kourilsky and Murray 1981). One dealt with grocery shopping behaviors specifically (Sinkula 1984) while two had measures for the child's grocery shopping autonomy (Taylor, Moore, and Glynn 1986; Taylor, Glynn, and Taylor 1985). Two studies considered child age as relevant (Darley and Lim 1986; Taylor, Moore, Glynn 1986) while two considered the age of the adult (Taylor, Moore, and Glynn 1986; Taylor, Glynn, and Taylor 1985).

Darley and Lim (1986) investigated parental perception of the child's influence for leisure-time activities and concluded that in the timing of aspects in the decision process, single parents perceive greater child influence. Taylor, Moore, and Glynn (1986) found children from single parent families are much more likely to purchase food products on their own and influence brand choices more than children from the other family structures. Taylor, Glynn, and Taylor (1985) found children in single parent homes had the greatest influence when their parents were younger, had higher income levels or higher educational levels.

Kourilsky and Murray (1981) studied the use of an economic reasoning model in family budgetary decision making and concluded that children in a single parent family may be treated more like adults, may be more likely to be consulted about expenditures, and may be better informed about the limitations of family resources. Sinkula (1984) included only single parents in his population and attempted to differentiate between female and male headed single parent families using four life style constructs. He found that, compared to male single parents, female single parents are more organized and use coupons more. He also found there is an inverse relationship between usage of frozen foods and food shopping preplanning efforts in both types of single parent families.

HYPOTHESES

This exploratory research starts with the proposition that child influence in mother-only single parent households is not homogeneous within this family type. Rather, differences in child influence among female-headed single parent families may be found relative to differences in the nine variables under investigation.

It is hypothesized that child influence in the decision making process increases in an inverse relation to the mother's age, and in direct relation to the mother's education and income (Taylor, Glynn, and Taylor 1985; Taylor, Glynn, and Marlow 1984).

According to Buss and Schaninger (1984), a woman's sex role orientation affects her household task allocation behavior, finance handling, and influence in the family decision making process. Green and Cunningham (1975) found that, in married families, a wife's sex role orientation affects the family's decision making process and purchasing behavior. It is hypothesized that the more liberal a single mother's sex role orientation, the more influence the children will have in family decision making.

Colletta (1983) found divorced mothers working full time lack the option of leaving their children home, and often take them along on shopping trips. These mothers reported shopping took more time, caused more tension, and often involved buying the children things the mother felt she could not afford. It is hypothesized that children will have more influence in single parent families in which the mother is employed compared to the households in which the mother does not work.

In single parent families formed by divorce, the mothers often lose power. Taylor, Glynn, and Taylor (1984) point out that the influence of children expands with the passage of time in the single parent family. Therefore, it is hypothesized that the greater the number of years since the mother's separation, divorce, or widowhood, the greater the children's influence.

It is hypothesized that older children in the mother-only household will have more influence in family decision making than younger children (Burden 1986; Devall, Stoneman, and Brody 1986; Dornbusch et al. 1985; Taylor, Glynn, and Marlow 1984; Weiss 1979).

Peters (1985) found that differences existed in the way single mothers assign household tasks to their male and female children. She reported that single mothers tend to overwork their daughters and underwork their sons. Devall, Stoneman, and Brody (1986) also found gender effects regarding household task allocation in mother-only households. Therefore, it is hypothesized that girls will have more influence than boys.

While measures for the number of children in the household have largely been ignored in marketing studies, there is support in the sociology literature that the number of children affects the process and outcomes of a family's division of labor decisions regarding household chores (Brody 1986; Gonga 1982; McLanahan 1983; Weiss 1979). It is hypothesized that the larger the household size the greater the influence of the children.

METHODOLOGY

Grocery Products Chosen

Grocery shopping is a task every household must perform on a regular basis and children have been shown to exert discernible levels of influence for these types of products. Eleven products were chosen to represent the grocery product domain 1) breakfast cereal, 2) snack foods, 3) candy, 4) soft drinks, 5) hot dogs, 6) luncheon meats, 7) cheese, 8) soups, 9) laundry detergent, 10) housecleaning products, and 11) children's personal grooming aids.

All of theses products have been used in previous marketing research on parent-child interactions in family decision making. For example breakfast cereal was used by Ward and Wackman (1972), Belch, Belch, Ceresino (1985), Taylor, Moore, and Glynn (1986), Berey and Pollay (1968), Atkin (1978); snack foods by Ward and Wackman (1972), Adler (1980), Mehrotra and Torges (1977), Ward, Wackman, Wartella (1975), Taylor, Moore, and Glynn (1986); candy by Ward and Wackman (1972) Ward, Wackman, Wartella (1975), Mehrotra and Torges (1977), Adler (1980); soft drinks by Ward and Wackman (1972), Mehrotra and Torges (1977), Taylor, Moore, and Glynn (1986), Adler (1980); hot dogs by Mehrotra and Torges (1977); luncheon meats by Mehrotra and Torges (1977); cheese by Mehrotra and Torges (1977); soups by Ward, Wackman, Wartella (1975); housecleaning products by Ward and Wackman (1972); laundry detergent by Ward and Wackman (1972); and children's personal grooming aids by Taylor, Moore, and Glynn (1986), Ward and Wackman (1972).

Survey Development and Sampling

An ex post facto research design with cross-sectional survey data was used for data gathering purposes. Revisions were made to the questionnaire following a pretest of the instrument.

The sampling frame consisted of single mother households taken from the national membership list of the Market Facts, Incorporated's Consumer Mail Panel (CMP). The CMP is representative of the geographical divisions in the United States with respect to the characteristics of U.S. households such as age of the panel member, household size, and household income.

A random sample was taken from a population consisting of female-headed single parent families formed by divorce, separation, or widowhood, with at least one child 18 years old or younger living with the mother. A total of 378 surveys were mailed out to mothers heading families alone. A total of 210 surveys were returned, resulting in a 56 percent response rate.

Dependent Variables: Child Influence Measures

The mother's perceptions of her children's level of influence were measured for each of the five decision making stages considered individually, using all eleven products as the dependent variables. The five decision stages were: (1) the initiation stage, (2) the search for information stage, (3) the evaluation of alternatives stage, (4) the final decision stage, and (5) the purchase stage. Child influence was measured through the use of a 100 point constant sum scale. Mothers were asked to allocate 100 points between themselves, their oldest child, and their other children. The children's influence scores were summed into one measure.

Previous research has indicated that child influence varies by product type, therefore a preliminary analysis of the children's influence scores for the eleven products (within each stage) was performed using a principal-component factor analysis with varimax rotation. With the exception of minor differences between stages, an analysis of the factor loadings indicated that certain products clustered into three groups. The specific products in each group paralleled the findings of Mehrotra and Torges (1977).

Table 1 presents the results of the reliability analysis (using Cronbach's Alpha) for each factor within each stage. Factors in Group A included breakfast cereal, hot dogs, luncheon meats, cheese, soups, and the children's personal grooming products; Factors in Group B included laundry detergent and housecleaning products; Factors in Group C contained snack foods, candy, and soft

TABLE 1
Reliability Scores for the Three Factors
(Cronbach's Alpha)

	Decision Stages				
Factors	Initiation	Search	Evaluation	Final Decision	Purchase
Group A	.72	.80	.81	.79	.95
Group B	.88	.91	.94	.87	.98
Group C	.65	.83	.85	.86	.85

drinks. It was concluded that, given the results of this factor analysis, given the high reliability scores for the three factors, and given the existence of previous research with similar groupings, each of these factors and product groupings represent adequate unidimensionality to be treated as separate dimensions of child influence. Therefore, three separate dependent variables were used for each stage, representing a summed child influence score for each of the three product groupings presented in Table 1.

Independent Variables

Some of the independent variables, e.g., age of the mother, education of the mother, household size, the age of the oldest child, and the sex of the oldest child, were part of the data base provided by Market Facts. Sex of the oldest child was coded as a dummy variable. The education of the mother was provided by Market Facts as categorical data. This variable was recoded to approximate a metric measure. The mid-points for the categorical data were used as an estimate of the mother's educational level.

The remaining variables were collected on the self-report survey instrument completed by the mothers. The mothers provided a dollar figure indicating the amount of income earned by their employment. The mother's were asked if they worked outside the home; this response was recoded as a dummy variable. Mothers also provided the number of years since separation, divorce, or widowhood.

The mother's sex role orientation was measured metrically using Arnott's (1972) feminism autonomy scale. Arnott's scale is a typical scale used in consumer research (Engel and Blackwell 1982). It has been used in studies by Green and Cunningham (1975) and Venkatesh (1980). The mothers were asked to rate their level of agreement on ten items using a Likert-type seven-point scale. The higher the woman's score on all ten items, the more positive her attitude towards women's autonomy. While other scales are available and have been used in marketing research to measure sex role orientation (Gentry and Haley 1984; Qualls 1987; Rosen and Granbois 1983; Spiro 1983; Schaninger, Buss, and Grover 1982), Arnott's has proven to be a reliable, valid, and compact measure in previous empirical research (Venkatesh 1980).

RESULTS

Results of the stepwise regression analyses are presented in Table 2. There are 15 separate regression equations, three for each of the five decision stages. In each stage the eleven products are in one of three product groups, Group A includes breakfast cereal, hot dogs, luncheon meats, cheese, soup, and children's grooming aids, Group B represents laundry detergents and housecleaning products, and Group C contains snack food, candy and soft drinks.

For the Initiation (stage 1), the three product groupings resulted in different levels children's influence. Age of the oldest child positively effects children's influence in group A; while age of the oldest child has a positive influence and the mother's education has a negative influence on the children's influence for products in group B. In Group C, household size has a positive effect on children's influence.

In the Information Search Stage, the age of the oldest child has a positive effect and the mother's education a negative effect on the level of the children's influence for products in Group A. For products in Group B, both the mother's sex role autonomy score and her education have negative effects on children's influence. In Group C, the age of the oldest has a positive effect on children's influence for these products.

In the Alternative Evaluation stage the age of the oldest child has a positive influence and the mother's education a negative influence on children's influence for products in Group A. For products in Group B, the mother's income has a positive effect while her education and sex role autonomy have negative effects on children's influence. There were no variables significant for products in Group C for this stage.

In the Final Decision stage, there were no variables significant for products in Group A. For products in Group B, as the mother's education increases and her sex role autonomy increases, her children's influence decreases. As the age of the oldest child increases, the children's influence increases for those products listed in group C.

In the Purchase stage, as the mother's education increases and her sex role autonomy increases, her children's influence decreases for products in Group A and Group B. For products in Group C, the older the first born, the higher the children's influence, while as the sex role autonomy of the mother increases, the children's influence decreases.

CONCLUSIONS

Not all female-headed single parent families are alike with respect to the children's level of influence in decision making. Children's influence in this family type varies according to the type of product investigated, according to the mother's sex role orientation, according to demographic characteristics of the family, and according to the stage in the decision making process. Most of the findings in this study are consistent with previous research on parent-child interactions in decision making; similarities and differences were found and are discussed next.

We found that the children's influence is product-specific, consistent with the findings of other researchers investigating single parents (Darley and Lim 1986; Taylor, Moore, and Glynn 1986; Taylor, Glynn, and Taylor 1985) and consistent with the findings of researchers investigating married families (Belch, Belch, and Ceresino 1985; Mehrotra and Torges 1977; Szybillo, Sosanie, and Tennenbein 1977; Szybillo and Sosanie 1977, Ward, Wackman, and Wartella 1975; Ward and Wackman 1972).

Two demographic predictor variables, the mother's income, and household size, had positive effects on children's influence. In this study the mother's income had an effect only on the children's

TABLE 2
Regression of Products and Decision Stages on 9 Predictor Variables
(statistically significant findings reported)

Dependent Variables		Sex Role Orientation	Sex of 1st Born	Household Size	Mother's Age	Employment Status	Years Since Divorce	Mother's Education	Income	Age of 1st Born	Adjusted R^2
Stage 1:											
Group A	B									6.038	
	b									.2171	
	t									2.466 b	.04
Group B	B							-4.319		1.101	
	b							-.394		.177	.18
	t							-4.860 c		2.186 b	
Group C	B			18.133							
	b			.212							.04
	t			2.409 b							
Stage 2:											
Group A	B							-11.418		6.715	
	b							-.228		.231	.09
	t							-2.644 c		2.676 c	
Group B	B							-4.143			
	b							-.349			.16
	t							-4.068 c			
Group C	B	-.596								5.658	
	b	-.175								.282	.07
	t	-2.062 b								3.238 c	
Stage 3:											
Group A	B							-12.429		5.368	
	b							-.249		.189	.09
	t							-2.871 c		2.189 b	
Group B	B	-.712						-4.834	9.5(-04)		
	b	-.192						-.369	.343		.19
	t	-2.292 b						-4.279 c	3.974 c		
Group C	B										
	b										
	t										

TABLE 2 (CONTINUED)

Dependent Variables		Sex Role Orientation	Sex of 1st Born	Household Size	Mother's Age	Employment Status	Years Since Divorce	Mother's Education	Income	Age of 1st Born	Adjusted R2
Stage 4:											
Group A	B										
	b	-.601									
	t	-.204									.14
Group B	B	-2.386 b						-3.033			
	b							-.292			
	t							-3.417 c			.06
Group C	B									5.261	
	b									.259	
	t									2.961 c	
Stage 5:											
Group A	B	-2.113						-9.837			
	b	-.228						-.301			
	t	-2.698 c						-3.568 c			.16
Group B	B	-.793						-2.690			
	b	-.270						-.261			
	t	-3.214 c						-3.098 c			.16
Group C	B	-1.356								4.099	
	b	-.177								.269	
	t	-2.066 c								3.130 c	.10

a $p < .10$ b $p < .05$ c $p < .01$

influence for cleaning products (detergent and housecleaning), and only in the alternative evaluation stage of decision making. Ward and Wackman (1972), studying married families and the only previous parent-child interaction study to consider these two products, did not find statistically significant levels of child influence. Since children in single parent families spend more time on household tasks (such as cleaning), and are held more accountable for the performance of the work (Peters 1985; Weiss 1979), it is possible that the higher income single parent may be financially able to let the child have more influence in the choice of cleaning products used by the family.

As mentioned earlier, household size has rarely been included in marketing studies. We found that children's influence increased as household size increased; however, only in the Initiation stage and only for snack products (snacks, candy, and soft drinks). The effect of household size for single parent families may be different compared to its effect on married households. In single parent families the loss of the additional adult (father or mother) means the transfer of influence to the children. This transfer may be more pronounced as the number of children increases. Since single parents tend to shop with their children, it may be that the initial suggestion for these products occurs prior to or during the shopping trip.

Three predictor variables, age of the oldest child, the mother's educational level, and the mother's sex role autonomy resulted in consistent effects on children's influence across the individual stages. As the age of the oldest child increased, children's influence in family decision making increased. As the mother's educational level increased and her sex role autonomy increased, children's influence decreased. While the effect with respect to age of the oldest child was expected and is consistent with previous marketing and sociological studies on the single parent family, what was not expected was the inverse relationship between the mother's education, the mother's sex role autonomy, and the children's influence.

It may be that time constrained single mothers are less able to engage the children directly in discussions about products and purchase decisions. The better educated, more sex role autonomous single mothers, more confident (than the less well educated, less autonomous single mothers) in their ability to make the best decisions for their family, and facing constant time pressures, may seek less direct input from the children. Instead, these mothers are taking the interests and preferences of their children into account, therefore attributing more of the influence to themselves. The result is that the children become less involved in the decision process.

A similar idea was originally proposed by two of the earliest sociologists writing on single parent families, Glasser and Navarre (1965). They noted that, given the single parent's need to accomplish household tasks in an efficient manner in terms of time and energy expended, children may become less involved in some tasks. Colletta (1983) found support for this proposition and reported that there was a trend for children in moderate income single parent families to help themselves the least. The lack of self-help was related to the constant time pressures single mothers were under. Mothers reported it was easier for them to do things for the child rather than expect the child to accomplish the tasks on their own.

A similar conclusion may be reached for this study. Grocery shopping is a household task all family structures must accomplish. Better educated, more autonomous single mothers are placing more of the burden for family decision making (for grocery products) on themselves, and attributing less influence to their children, a tactic that may be easier for the mother in terms of time and energy expended.

REFERENCES
(partial list provided, others available upon request)

Arnott, Catherine C. (1972), "Husband's Attitude and Wives' Commitment to Employment," *Journal of Marriage and Family* 34, No. 4, (November), 673-684.

Colletta, Nancy D. (1983), "Stressful Lives: The Situation of Divorced Mothers and Their Children," *Journal of Divorce* 6, (Spring), 19-31.

Darley, William K. and Jeen-Su Lim (1986), "Family Decision Making in Leisure-Time Activities: An Exploratory Investigation of The Impact of Locus of Control, Child Age Influence Factor and Parental Type on Perceived Child Influence," *Advances in Consumer Research* 13, Richard J. Lutz, ed., Provo, UT: Association for Consumer Research, 370-374.

Davis, H. L. (1976), "Decision Making Within the Household," *Journal of Consumer Research* 2 (March), 241-260.

Foxman, Ellen R., Patriya S. Tansuhaj, and Karin M. Ekstrom (1989), "Family Members' Perceptions of Adolescents' Influence in Family Decision Making," *Journal of Consumer Research* 15 (March), 482-491.

Glasser, Paul H. and Elizabeth Navarre (1965), "Structural Problems of the One-Parent Family," *Journal of Social Issues*, 21 (June), 98-109.

Kourilsky, Marilyn and Trudy Murray (1981), "The Use of Economic Reasoning to Increase Satisfaction with Family Decision Making," *Journal of Consumer Research* 8 (September), 183-188.

Mehrotra, Sunil and Sandra Torges (1977), "Determinants of Children's Influence on Mother's Buying Behavior," *Advances in Consumer Research*, William Perreault Jr. ed., Atlanta: Association for Consumer Research, 56-60.

Sinkula, James M. (1984), "A Look At Some Shopping Orientations in Single Parent Households," *American Marketing Association Educator's Proceedings*, Series 50, Russell W. Belk et al., eds., Chicago, IL: American Marketing Association, 22-25.

Statistical Abstract of the United States (1989), U.S. Government Printing Office, Washington, D.C.

Szybillo, George J. and Arlene K. Sosanie (1977), "Family Decision Making: Husband, Wife and Children," *Advances in Consumer Research* IV, William D. Perrault, ed., Atlanta, GA: Association for Consumer Research, 46-49.

Taylor, Ronald D., Karen Glynn and Nancy Marlowe (1984),"Family Buying Patterns: A Comparison of Dual-Career and Traditional Families," *Marketing in a Dynamic Environment*, Atlantic Marketing Association, 145-151.

Taylor, Ronald D., Karen Glynn and Jan C. Taylor (1985), "The Influence of Children in the Purchasing Process Used by Families: An Analysis Comparing Children from Three Different Family Structures," *Proceedings of Atlantic Marketing Association*.

Waldrop, Judith and Thomas Exter (1990), "What the 1990 Census Will Show," *American Demographics*, 12, Number 1, (January), 20-29.

Ward, Scott and Daniel Wackman (1972), "Children's Purchasing Influence Attempts and Parental Yielding," *Journal of Marketing Research* 9 (August), 316-319.

Weiss, Robert S. (1979), *Going It Along: The Family Life and Social Situation of the Single Parent*, New York, NY: Basic Books, Inc.

Attraction and Compromise Effects in Choice: Moderating Influences and Differential Loss Aversion to Quality and Nonquality Attributes

Timothy B. Heath, University of Pittsburgh
Subimal Chatterjee, University of Pittsburgh

Two studies in this session assessed the importance of the type of comparisons made when making decisions. Sen and Johnson found that experimentally created reference brands were chosen more often than non-reference brands. More importantly, referent designation caused systematic variations in search patterns. Comparisons involving a particular brand were more common when it was the referent, especially when losses were involved. Simonson, Nowlis, and Lemon manipulated type of potential comparisons in two different ways across three experiments. In one case, comparisons were manipulated by having some consumers engage in pairwise comparisons ({A,B}, {B,C}, and {A,C}) prior to choosing from the set of all three brands ({A,B,C}). Pairwise comparisons increased the market share of the least expensive brand. Similar effects were found from variations in the ways in which alternatives were displayed.

Kahn, Huber, and Holbrook presented a number of experiments in this session demonstrating an unexpected effect of time pressure. Consumers were initially given well-known brand names within a product category and asked to indicate their preferences. They were later given a choice involving these brands where (1) information on price and quality was present, and (2) their favorite brand was highest on both attributes. It was expected that consumers would simplify time-pressured decisions by choosing the brand that they had previously indicated as their favorite. However, the opposite pattern held. Time pressure decreased the tendency to choose the previously favored brand. The results stimulated a vigorous discussion of potential mechanisms, although no clear-cut explanation emerged.

The session also included Chatterjee and Heath's meta-analysis of research reporting that asymmetrically dominated entrants can increase the share of existing brands (the *attraction effect*; Huber, Payne, and Puto 1982). Such entrants were found to consistently increase the share of higher quality brands, but to rarely increase the share of lower quality brands. Attraction to lower quality brands occurred only when, relative to the entrant, the target brand was superior on the quality dimension and at the same level on the non-quality dimension.

The studies reported here illustrate the importance of anchoring and adjustment processes in multiattribute decisions and are therefore consistent with theories of referent-dependent choice (Tversky and Kahneman 1991). They further support the principle of loss aversion in general, and more specifically the growing body of evidence indicating that loss aversion to quality dimensions is more severe than loss aversion to nonquality dimensions (e.g., Hardie, Johnson, and Fader 1991). Differential loss aversion despite initial choices of lower quality alternatives suggests the possibility that relative attribute weights shift following choice.

Finally, the effects of paired-alternative presentations and display formats support theories of extremeness aversion (Simonson and Tversky 1992). They suggest (1) that using paired-comparisons in conjoint measurement may inflate estimates of price's importance relative to estimates based on rankings or ratings of the entire choice set, and (2) ways through which marketers can influence consumer decisions.

REFERENCES

Hardie, Bruce G. S., Eric J. Johnson, and Peter S. Fader (1991), "Modeling Loss Aversion and Reference Dependence Effects on Brand Choice," Working Paper #91-025, Wharton Marketing Department, University of Pennsylvania, Philadelphia, PA 19104-6371.

Huber, Joel, John W. Payne, and Christopher Puto (1982), "Adding Asymmetrically Dominated Alternatives: Violations of Regularity and the Similarity Hypothesis," *Journal of Consumer Research*, 9 (June), 90-98.

Simonson, Itamar and Amos Tversky (1992), "Choice in Context: Tradeoff Contrast and Extremeness Aversion," *Journal of Marketing Research*, 29 (August), 281-295.

Tversky, Amos and Daniel Kahneman (1991), "Loss Aversion in Riskless Choice: A Reference Dependent Model," *The*

Imagery in Marketing Communications: Beyond Pictures and Visual Processing
Gayathri Mani, University of Arizona

Recent interest in consumer research has centered on the effects of mental imagery on memory and persuasion. However, while the imaginal properties of pictures have received widespread attention, less attention has been focused on imagery generated through other means (e.g., concrete words, imagery instructions). The significance of the use of concrete words and imagery instructions is that they highlight the imagery evoking properties of verbal information. Relatedly, unlike pictures (which are restricted to visual media), these techniques can be used to explore imagery processes generated by auditory stimuli as well. Finally, research in consumer behavior has focused almost exclusively on visual imagery. Extending the study of consumer imagery to other modalities is important because consumers' everyday experiences with products often encompass multiple modalities. The papers selected for the session (i) highlight the use of concrete words and imagery instructions and (ii) introduce the study of consumers' sensory and imaginal experiences in multiple modalities.

The paper by Anand and Goldberg-Block examines the differing effects of imagery and referencing on elaboration and persuasiveness of a fear vs. a nonfear appeal. The ads in the experiment either did vs. did not include mention of fearful consequences and were either directed at the subject or at others. Subjects were instructed to either use their imagination or be analytical while viewing the ad. The results showed that self-referencing and imagery increased elaboration and persuasion for nonfear appeals but not for fear appeals.

Unnava and Agarwal hypothesize that reading engages the same resources in memory as visual imagery and will thus interfere with the ability to generate visual images to a greater extent than listening to the same information. Their study used ads with high vs. low imagery information presented either as print ads or through a cassette player. The results showed lower recall in the visual condition than in the auditory condition for high imagery ads but no differences across conditions in the recall of low imagery information.

Chakravarti, MacInnis and Mani explore the memory effects arising from sensory and imaginal processing in the visual and olfactory modalities. Subjects in the study were either exposed to pictures or smells of products and were asked to imagine either the smell or the picture of each product. The results suggest that identification of olfactory stimuli is poorer than that of visual stimuli, leading to more impoverished images for olfactory stimuli. Further, visual imagery was uniformly rated as more vivid than olfactory imagery. Finally, olfactory processing led to less accessible but more durable memory traces than visual processing.

Concluding remarks were provided by Debbie MacInnis who described a framework integrating the three papers and discussed avenues for future research.

Societal and Public Policy Issues with Retail Pricing
Dhruv Grewal, University of Miami
Ronald C. Goodstein, UCLA

Given the competitive nature of today's marketplace, retail pricing strategies are often used by consumers as a signal of quality, information, and service. Retailers have reflected these changes in the pricing policies they have adopted, such as the use of price premiums as an indicant to consumers of a product's or service's quality. The language used to signal promotions has also become more complex, sometimes offering comparative information (e.g., "Our Price"/"Their Price") and other times providing more vague information ("Special Price"). Finally, pricing systems such as UPC scanners have become more popular with retailers and may indicate to consumers better in-store service by those outlets adopting them.

Many other important areas of pricing have received attention in the consumer literature, such as reservation price effects, discounting, couponing, and reference prices. Notwithstanding the importance of these topics, issues involving premiums, promotions, and pricing systems cover a wide spectrum of issues that constitute a retailer's pricing policies. However, societal and public policy issues relating to these issues have been an under-researched area.

From a societal and public policy perspective, many of the heuristics (rules-of-thumb) that consumers use to simplify the marketplace are relevant and important to understand. The fact that pricing policies (e.g., premiums, promotions, and systems) are often used as cues of quality, therefore, becomes an issue worthy of further scrutiny by researchers. When these rules are accurate and are respected by both retailers and consumers, then the marketplace becomes more efficient. However, if these rules are violated either because consumers cannot understand the relationships or because retailers take advantage of consumers' reliance upon them, then societal and public policy concerns arise.

The first presentation in this session examines pricing accuracy in stores employing UPC scanner systems (Goodstein, Escalas, and Kassarjian). Consumerists believe that since item prices are eliminated as scanners are adopted, pricing accuracy cannot be easily assessed by shoppers. This study indicates that pricing accuracy has not been improved by the adoption of scanner systems. The second presentation examines consumers' use of price-quality heuristics as a defensive buying strategy (Rao, Monroe, and Bergen). This paper suggests that consumers may pay premium prices to avoid losses of product quality. The research also suggests that consumers may be able to successfully search for quality information and monitor the product quality provided by the retailer or seller. The third presentation examines consumers' interpretation of the semantic cues retailers provide to signal a promotion (Grewal and Compeau). The paper suggests that semantic cues used to communicate price information have the potential to be either informative or deceptive. The session coordinators would like to recognize and thank Michael Mazis for his service as the discussant for this session.

Public policy, such as regulation, directly relates to each of these three presentations. In the case of scanning errors, regulation assuring more accurate pricing would benefit consumers shopping in scanner stores. In terms of price "gouging," regulation of prices could harm the consumer in situations where product quality is not easily assessed. Premiums, in this case, are an economic incentive used to assure price/quality tradeoffs. Finally, regulation might be used to encourage retailers to define different semantic cues so that meaning is made clear to consumers. In this way consumers could better evaluate the true value of a "promotional" price.

UPC Scanner Pricing Systems: Is the Consumer Really Better Off?
Ronald C. Goodstein, UCLA
Jennifer Edson Escalas, Duke University
Harold H. Kassarjian, UCLA

Today, 93% of mass merchandisers and 94% of supermarkets employ scanner systems (*Chain Store Age Executive* 1990). As promised by manufacturers in the early 1970's, scanners have numerous advantages: retailers enjoy both cost savings and improved inventory management; consumers spend less time in retail checkout lines; and academics examine marketing phenomena with rich data bases. The question remains, however, as to whether or not scanner systems "allow retailers to take unfair advantage of their customers" (Pommer, Berkowitz, and Walton 1980). Retail promotions (e.g., advertised price reductions and end-aisle displays) have a significant positive influence on consumer sales (Guadagni and Little 1983; Inman, McAlister and Hoyer 1990), yet consumers have very poor recall of the prices charged at the point of purchase (Dickson and Sawyer 1990; Zeithaml 1982). Based on this evidence, consumerists conclude that retail promotions are a ripe area for deception in stores employing scanner systems. Retail trade associations (e.g., National Association of Food Chains) assure customers that such abuses do not take place, but consumer distrust remains. In this study we empirically test and disturbingly, support consumers' concerns of retail deception.

Data were collected from three large chains of retail stores within one of California's large counties. Two of the firms are very large supermarket retailers, and the third firm is a leading discount department store. Five stores from each chain were randomly selected for inclusion in the study. Within each store, 30 items were purchased following a methodology based on random selection of ten advertised specials, ten items on end-aisle displays, and ten regularly-price, non-featured items. Purchases were made in each store on three dates: 1) the first day of the sale week as advertised in the local newspaper; 2) the middle of the sale week; and 3) on the last day of the sale week.

Based on the limitation that the study was based on examining 15 stores in one California county, the results indicate that scanner systems have resulted in significant numbers of overrings and underrings. Planned contrasts indicate that underring rates significantly exceed industry estimates. Further, the rate of overrings significantly exceeds the rate of underrings for advertised and end-aisle promotions. This fact indicates that error is not purely random, and is higher and in the retailers' favor for promotional items. Arguments that the correct charges are entered later in the sale week were not supported, the date of purchase had no effect on the number of misrings.

If this data base is representative of other retailers throughout the country, then several implications seem appropriate. For public policy makers, the implication of this study is that consumer deception is occurring at an alarming rate in stores employing scanner systems. This may explain the recent upsurge in legal proceedings against major grocers across the country (Bartholomew 1992). For retailers, lack of consumer trust and discounting of discounts (cf. Gupta and Cooper, 1993) may be well-deserved and policy changes could be examined to overcome these problems. For academics, the findings suggest that scanner-based research examining promotions must be re-examined, especially where results rely on dollar market shares. Our study indicates that reliance on dollar shares may bias promotional effects in an upward manner, and that unit shares may provide a more reliable estimate of promotional effects.

REFERENCES

Bartholomew, Doug (1992), "The Price Is Wrong," in *INFORMATIONWEEK*, September 14, 26-30.

Dickson, Peter R. and Alan G. Sawyer (1990). "The Price Knowledge and Search of Supermarket Shoppers," *Journal of Marketing*, 54 (July), 42-53.

"Electronic Retailing a Thing of the Past," *Chain Store Age Executive*, July 1990.

Guadagni, Peter M. and John D.C. Little (1983), "A Logit Model of Brand Choice Calibrated on Scanner Data," *Marketing Science*, 2 (Summer), 203-238.

Gupta, Sunil and Lee G. Cooper (1993), "The Discounting of Discounts," *Journal of Consumer Research*, 19 (December), 401-411.

Inman, J. Jeffrey, Leigh McAlister, and Wayne D. Hoyer (1990), "Promotion Signal: Proxy for a Price Cut?" *Journal of Consumer Research*, 17 (June), 74-81.

Pommer, Michael D., Eric N. Berkowitz, and John R. Walton (1980), "UPC Scanning: An Assessment of Shopper Response to Technological Change," *Journal of Retailing*, 56 (Summer), 25-44.

Zeithaml, Valerie A. (1982), "Consumer Response to In-Store Price Information Environments," *Journal of Consumer Research*, 8 (March), 357-369.

Interpretations of Semantic Phrases in Comparative Price Advertisements: Some Preliminary Evidence on a Public Policy Issue

Dhruv Grewal, University of Miami
Larry Compeau, Clarkson University

ABSTRACT

The informative and deceptive potential of *semantic price phrases* depends on the *meaning interpreted by the consumer* and the *meaning intended by the retailer*. The purpose of semantic phrases is to communicate information about prices to the consumer. The more vague the semantic phrase, the greater the likelihood of differing interpretations and the chance that the meaning will not be shared. Consequently, there is a greater potential for deception. This utilization of vague semantic phrases is contrary to the Federal Trade Commission's objective of enhancing factual comparisons (Grewal and Compeau 1992).

A semantic phrase can enhance the believability and perceived value of the price-promotional offer by providing more information (e.g., an ad: "was $24.99, now $17.99" provides more information than an ad: "Sale Price, $17.99") (Barnes 1975). The use of different semantic phrases to denote the same amount of saving in the price-promotion (e.g., "was $2.00, now $1.00" versus product advertised for "$1.00., 1/2 off regular price") affects consumers' purchase and search behaviors (Lichtenstein, Burton and Karson 1991). Consequently, how advertisers and retailers word their price claims can influence consumers' perceptions and their behavioral responses (Compeau and Grewal 1990).

A number of different semantic labels for the reference price are used by advertisers in their price advertisements (e.g., "Regular", "Original", and "Compare at"). These semantic phrases may be informative or deceptive depending on whether both the consumer and the advertiser share the same interpretation for the semantic phrase. If they do share the same interpretation of the semantic phrase, then the potential for deception is small. However, if they do not share an interpretation of the semantic phrase, then the potential for deception is great. For example, retailers frequently label an actual selling price as a "Special". A consumer may interpret an item labelled "special" as unusual merchandise, or an attempt to reduce inventory, or a limited time offer.

A semantic phrase that is vague or imprecise is open to multiple interpretations and has a greater likelihood to be deceptive. Richards (1990, p. 30) has pointed out that, "courts have determined that if a statement in an ad lends itself to more than one interpretation by the ordinary recipient of the ad, and *one* of those interpretations is deceptive, the representation will be construed to be deceptive, *in toto*." Public policy makers can develop shared meaning by legally defining the common semantic phrases used in comparative price advertisements and then educating retailers and the public as to these definitions. Furthermore, it is critical that they then enforce their appropriate use by advertisers. Such labelling practices have been used to label different levels of cut and fat in ground meat (e.g., ground round, ground chuck, ground beef). Thus, the semantic phrase informative content must be weighed against its potential for deception.

The meanings consumers assign to commonly used semantic phrases need to be researched (Grewal and Compeau 1992). How do consumers interpret the various semantic phrases "Regular Price/Sale Price" or "Compare At" or "Special" or "Their Price/Our Price"? The research to date has not looked at the everyday meanings of commonly used semantic phrases from the a consumer's perspective. Therefore, the primary objective of this research is to examine the consumer meanings or interpretations of these commonly used semantic phrases.

This study is part of a larger on-going examination of the everyday meaning of semantic cues from a consumer's perspective. The results presented were based on five in-depth qualitative interviews conducted during the summer of 1992 (additional interviews have been conducted since that time). The participants, all women, are primary shoppers for their families. Two are married with no children, two are married with two and five children respectively, and one is a single parent with two children. The participants ages range from twenty-seven to fifty-two. Three participants are employed in full-time positions, one has gone back to graduate school, and one is a full-time housewife (with five children).

Each interview was conducted by both of the principal researchers in the participants' homes or at a convenient meeting place during their lunch hour. The interviews lasted anywhere from 45 to 90 minutes. The interviews were conducted based on an existential-phenomenological approach (Giorgi 1975; Kvale 1983; Thompson, Locander, and Pollio 1989, 1990). This approach was adopted as a means of focusing on the everyday meaning of semantic phrases through an interpretive analysis of the participants' lived-experiences. However, it was also recognized that due to the rather specific nature of the topic, the unstructured existential-phenomenological approach would need to be augmented with a more structured component where participants could provide meanings in their own words for specific semantic phrases. Thus, each interview started with a broad open-ended question asking the participant to recall a recent experience when they purchased an item and felt that they got a good deal or where they saw an advertisement that they thought offered a good deal. The goal was to capture the experiences of the participant related to dealing with price offers.

Typically, a participant related several experiences before indicating that she could not remember any other experiences and could not recall any other advertisements. The conduct of the interview then shifted to a more structured approach requesting participants to respond to semantic phrases presented on a series of 8.5" by 11" cards. The cards contained semantic phrases, in a simple print format by themselves, or embedded in an actual print media advertisement. The phrases selected were based on a detailed review of advertisements from newspapers and circulars from three large eastern cities and several smaller towns over three months. The phrases represent those phrases which appeared most often in the comparative price advertisements.

Each interview was tape recorded and transcribed verbatim. The verbatim transcripts served as the data from which themes were identified. Careful readings of the transcripts, many times over, lead to an understanding of each participant's experiences. In a hermeneutical fashion, the interpretation progressed via an iterative process of relating part of the text to the whole (Bleicher 1980; Ricoeur 1976).

A second stage of analysis was performed after the themes were identified. All responses to the semantic phrase cards presented to the participants were categorized by phrase. The responses were analyzed, giving special attention to definitional types of responses in order to arrive at interpretations regarding the everyday meaning of the semantic phrases to consumers.

The results of the study suggest that the use of semantic phrases can be informative or deceptive. To be informative, the phrase must provide the consumer with accurate information that the consumer does not already have available. To be deceptive, the semantic phrase must simply provide for one confusing or misleading interpretation. Thus, it is inherently much easier for a semantic phrase to be deceptive than informative. The results of this study suggest that for all but regular price and sale price, currently popular semantic phrases are confusing and more likely to be deceptive than informative. In order to make the phrases more informative, significant attention to detail is required.

This study is limited by the small sample size and future efforts are underway to include other participants. Moreover, future research may want to consider a survey methodology to tap a much broader spectrum of consumers. Identifying meanings is always difficult since we are inherently limited by the words which are at our disposal. Thus, the use of semeiotics may be a fruitful avenue to explore the meanings of semantic phrases.

REFERENCES

Barnes, James G. (1975), "Factors Influencing Consumer Reaction to Retail Newspaper 'Sale' Advertising", *Proceedings*, Vol. 37, ed. Edward M. Mazze, Fall Educators' Conference, Chicago, IL: American Marketing Association, 471-477.

Bleicher, Josef (1980), *Contemporary Hermeneutics*, London: Routledge & Kegan Paul.

Compeau, Larry D. and Dhruv Grewal (1990), "Comparative Price Advertising: A Methodological Review and Critique," in *AMA Educators' Proceedings*, Vol. 56, Chicago, IL: American Marketing Association, p. 56.

Giorgi, Amadeo (1975), An Application of Phenomenological Method in Psychology, in *Duquesne Studies in Phenomenological Psychology*, Vol.2, eds. A Giorgi, C. Fischer, and E. Murray, Pittsburgh, PA: Duquesne University Press.

Grewal, Dhruv and Larry D. Compeau (1992), "Comparative Price Advertising: Informative or Deceptive?" *Journal of Public Policy and Marketing*, 11 (Spring), 52-62.

Kvale, Steinar (1983), "The Qualitative Research Interview: A Phenomenological and a Hermeneutical Mode of Understanding," *Journal of Phenomenological Psychology*, 14 (Fall), 171-196.

Lichtenstein, Donald R., Scot Burton and Eric J. Karson (1991), "The Effects of Semantic Cues on Consumer Perceptions of Reference Price Ads," *Journal of Consumer Research*, 18 (December), 380-391.

Richards, Jef I. (1990), *Deceptive Advertising: Behavioral Study of a Legal Concept*, Hillsdale, NJ: Lawrence Erlbaum Associates.

Ricoeur, Paul (1976), *Interpretation Theory*, Fort Worth, TX: Texas Christian University Press.

Thompson, Craig J., William B. Locander, and Howard R. Pollio (1989), "Putting Consumer Experience Back Into Consumer Research: The Philosophy and Method of Existential-Phenomenology," *Journal of Consumer Research*, 16(September), 133-116.

Thompson, Craig J., William B. Locander, and Howard R. Pollio (1990), "The Lived Meaning of Free Choice: An Existential-Phenomenological Description of Everyday Consumer Experiences of Contemporary Married Women," *Journal of Consumer Research*, 17 (December), 346-361.

An Investigation of Determinants of Recycling Consumer Behavior

Anita L. Jackson, Louisiana State University
Janeen E. Olsen, Louisiana State University
Kent L. Granzin, University of Utah
Alvin C. Burns, Louisiana State University

ABSTRACT

Previous research on recycling consumer behavior (RCB) has been largely descriptive. The authors posit a conceptual model wherein RCB is determined by its importance as judged by benefits-to-costs deliberations. These, in turn, are hypothesized to be impacted by social influence, personal values, felt norms, and external cues. A preliminary empirical study reveals that RCB is affected by all these factors although in various ways. The authors note possible improvements in subsequent research and claim that their results suggest environmentally protective consumer behaviors define an arena of fruitful research.

INTRODUCTION

Over the past several decades, consumers have become aware of the environmental problems facing the planet. This growing concern has led many people to alter their lifestyles in a manner they see as more ecologically friendly. Nevertheless, our environmental problems are far from being solved. In fact, experts warn that environmental conditions have become worse over the years. Solid waste has increased as potential landfills become scare. Toxic waste has led to soil and groundwater contamination (Rice 1988). Carbon emissions are being blamed for depletion of the ozone layer that protects the Earth (Williams 1989). It is clear that even with growing numbers of people supporting the environmental movement, still more consumers must be encouraged to consider the environmental consequences of their consumption decisions.

Recycling programs are a voluntary environmental protection activity in which consumers are often encouraged to participate. For many years recycling efforts were hampered due to lack of reverse distribution channels, markets for collected items and inconvenient methods of collection (Barnes 1982). Many of these difficulties have been addressed recently as recycling centers and collection programs have become more popular. More and more, consumers are finding recycling a feasible alternative for the disposition of containers, packaging, spent products, and trash in general.

As noted above and elaborated on below, while some descriptive research has been applied to Recycling Consumer Behavior (RCB), little has been done in the way of explanatory investigation. Given that: (1) recycling is recognized as a means of alleviating environmental damage, (2) institutional structures such as recycling centers exist for the disposition of unwanted glass, aluminum, paper and other recyclable materials, and (3) RCB is voluntary product/packaging disposition behavior, it seems worthwhile to attempt research to better understand its dynamics. Accordingly, this paper presents an initial conceptual model of possible influences and determinants of RCB. It reports an exploratory empirical test of this model, and its discusses implications of the findings.

LITERATURE REVIEW

Academic interest in environmental issues is not new. It can be traced to the time the environmental movement itself began to gain momentum (Kotler and Zaltman 1971; Kassarjian 1971; Anderson and Cunningham 1972; Fisk 1973; Kinnear and Taylor 1973). The broad range of environmental issues that has been investigated reflects the variety of environmental problems facing consumers, including the needs for pollution control, energy conservation, and recycling (Zikmund and Stanton, 1971; Barnes 1982).

Over the years, many of the empirical studies that have been conducted have followed the format of segmentation research. The primary objective of this approach has been to identify environmentally concerned individuals and/or participants of pro-environmental behaviors (Anderson and Cunningham 1972). In keeping with the segmentation orientation, studies have found demographic variables to be useful predictors of environmental concern. For example, with regard to recycling, higher education levels are often associated with recycling activities, and age has also been useful in identifying people who participate in recycling activities (Mohai and Twight 1987; Vining and Ebreo 1990). Income was also found to be a significant predictor for recycling (Jacobs, Bailey and Crews 1984; Vivivg and Ebreo 1990). However, while previous research has demonstrated that demographics can be useful variables for segmentation studies, the specific findings themselves may quickly become obsolete. Furthermore, recent studies suggest that demographics are only modest or ineffective predictors of environmental concern (Manzo and Weinstein 1987; Samdahl and Robertson 1989; Granzin and Olsen 1991). Also, environmental concern can spread to new segments of the population quite rapidly, effectively diluting demographic correlates.

Thus, one could argue that a fruitful strategy may be to investigate internal predispositions in consumers. Accordingly, depictions of environmentally concerned citizens have also relied on psychological and personality variables (Brooker 1976; De Young 1986; Balderjahn 1988) and personal values (Dunlap, Grieneeks and Rokeach 1983; Rankin 1983; Neuman 1986). As in the case of demographics, the studies investigating psychological and personality variables have emphasized how the environmentally concerned consumers differ from those that are not, and moderate success has been the result (Granzin and Olsen 1991).

In summary, prior research has experienced modest success using demographics and/or internal predispositions hypothesized to relate to an individual's desire to participate in recycling programs. The next logical step is to develop and test more comprehensive models that may better explain environmental protection behavior such as recycling.

CONCEPTUALIZATION OF DETERMINANTS OF RCB

To identify salient components of RCB, we searched for a similar consumer behavior phenomenon which has been addressed both conceptually and empirically. We concluded that RCB can be compared to preventive health care behavior in that all three of the conditions noted earlier are present. That is, preventive behavior is a means of avoiding harm which may occur in the future; there are endorsed regimens and institutionalized programs for prevention, and the behavior is voluntary. Thus, we scrutinized the preventive health care literature for a theoretical structure as a beginning point in our modeling of RCB. The Health Belief Model (HBM) has received much conceptual and empirical attention (see for example,

FIGURE 1
A Priori Model

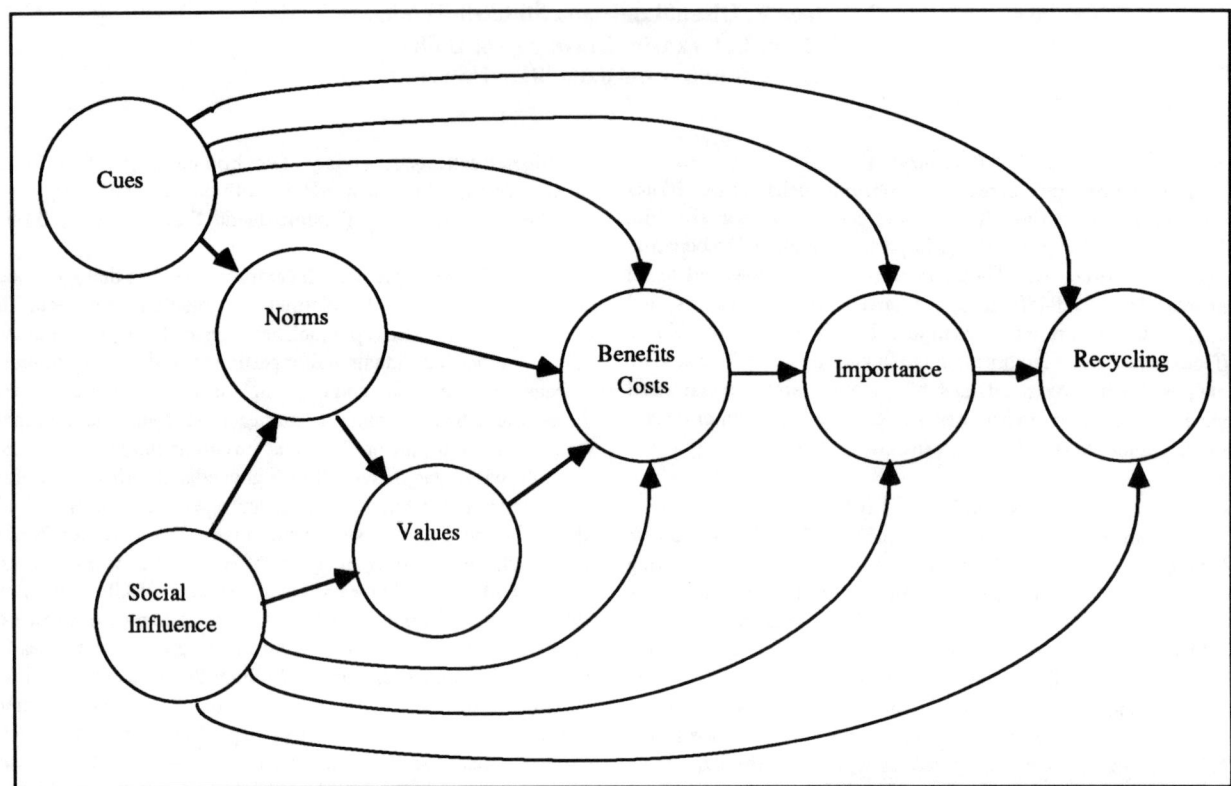

Becker 1985; Becker, Drachman, and Kirscht 1974a, 1974b; Becker et al 1977). Consequently, we adapted its components in developing an initial conceptual model of RCB. The HBM posits that behavior results from a benefits-to-costs deliberation on the part of the individual. The likelihood of preventive health care behavior is a function of this benefits-costs comparison. If benefits outweigh costs, then health care actions are likely, while if costs (e.g. inconvenience, side effects, etc.) are perceived to exceed benefits, health care actions are unlikely. At the same time, the behavior is influenced by three other factors. One is the perceived threat of whatever disease or illness is being contemplated, while another is cues in the forms of impersonal (i.e. media) warnings, and the third is social pressures. High perceived susceptibility and severity combine to determine perceived threat, and high threat can directly impact the likelihood of taking recommended action. Cues and social interaction also serve to influence the amount of perceived threat. In our judgement, perceived severity, susceptibility and threat are not reasonable as constructs underlying RCB; however, the other factors in the HBM are relevant, namely cues and social pressures. Admittedly, our justification for the use of the HBM as a conceptual framework here is not as compelling as one might wish, but it is a cohesive model with a research tradition which might afford insights into RCB.

The HBM has been compared to Fishbein's (1967) behavioral intentions model by Oliver and Berger (1979) as well as Rosenblatt, Cusson and McGown (1984). In both instances, the authors concluded that a combining of key constructs in the two models is advantageous; consequently, normative compliance (behavioral norm) was drawn from this model. Felt norms appear to be a logical construct for possible explanation of voluntary RCB. Since no formal rewards accompany RCB, nor does any penalty ensue for individuals who fail to practice RCB, felt norms may well be an important determinant. In addition, personal values were incorporated as they have been found to be associated with environmental protection actions on the parts of consumers (see Granzin and Olsen 1991).

The a priori model adopted for this study appears in Figure 1. As can be seen, it posits RCB as a function of a blend of decision-making, internal predispositions, and external influence factors. RCB is modeled as the direct result of the considered importance of RCB. We have opted to use importance rather than intention for two reasons. First, intention may be preempted by situational factors such as lack of knowledge, storage constraints, transportation difficulties or other obstacles. Also, Rosenblatt, Cusson and McGown (1984) found importance to be a construct through which other factors influenced donation and personal health care behavior.

Consequently, we have opted to rely on importance as an mediating factor translating conscious decision making into a precursor for action. If consumers do not view recycling as important to themselves or society as a whole, we cannot expect them to exhibit sustained RCB.

Importance, in turn, is largely affected by three separate influences. First, it is postulated to be the result of a conscious weighing of the benefits and costs associated with the practices. Benefits are for instance, protection of the environment, energy conservation or less litter, while costs include storage of recyclables, necessary washing and bundling, and hauling. In other words, RCB is assumed to depend on a deliberation process on the part of the individual consumer where these benefits and costs are subjectively compared.

Further, we postulate these deliberations to be influenced by both internal factors and external influences. With regard to internal factors, both values and norms are assumed to be reflected

TABLE 1
Estimated Parameters for the Measurement Model

Structural Construct and Cronbach Alpha	Indicant	Lisrel Estimate
Endogenous Constructs:		
	*Paraphrased Item**	
Values (α=.70)	We must work for common good.	.759
	Help others when they need it.	.785
	Important to live in beautiful world.	.767
Benefits -Costs (α=.72)	It takes too much effort.	.440
	It takes too much time.	.375
	I am responsible for one small part.	.592
	It makes me feel good.	.747
	People think better of me if I help.	.418
	It will save me money in the long run.	.488
Importance (α=.83)	Importance of newspaper recycling	.808
	Importance of bottle recycling	.855
	Importance of alum. can recycling	.795
RCB (α=.83)	Participation in newspaper recycling	.710
	Participation in bottle recycling	.800
	Participation in alum. can recycling	.730
Exogenous Constructs:		
Cues (α=.65)	Weekly reading of magazines	.575
	Weekly reading of newspapers	.709
Social Influence (α=.82)	Influence of others	.812
	Influence of friends	.943
	Influence of family	.592
Norms (α=.61)	Not my responsibility...	.738
	Individuals should not worry about...	.672
	Government and industry should...	.396

*Items are paraphrased to conserve space; all negatively worded items were reverse scored.
Note: all parameter estimates are significant judged by t values above 2.5

in the decision making process. If a consumer values conservation, beauty, and preservation of the environment, for example, we would anticipate these values to enter into the deliberation process. Similarly, if a consumer nurtures a belief that recycling is expected of him/her, we anticipate this felt norm will also influence the deliberation outcome. As can also be seen, one would expect a high degree of comparability between the values harbored by a consumer and his/her subscription to certain behavioral norms. Similarly, social pressures mold normative compliance and affect one's value system. External forces exist both in the form of social pressures such as the urging or prompting of peers, family or significant others as well as informational cues garnered from nonpersonal sources. In our view, cues to RCB are a likely external influence as recycling has received and continues to receive attention in the forms of newspaper articles, televisions specials, and news broadcasts.

To summarize our thinking, we have cast a person's voluntary recycling behavior as largely determined by how important that person considers recycling to his and/or society's well being. This importance level is a result of a conscious comparison of the benefits and costs (both personal and societal) associated with recycling. The deliberation outcome is, in turn, a reflection of the person's values and internalized norms of appropriate behavior. At the same time, external parties are issuing information and persuasion to encourage recycling. These cues are primarily mass media-based, and they may impact the benefits-costs deliberation ("It is easy to recycle"), the attribution of importance ("Recycling saves trees and energy"), or recycling behavior itself ("Put newspapers in a paper grocery bag for easy storage"). Similarly, social pressures can encourage any of these three pivotal factors as well. Social approval of RCB (a benefit), realization of widespread recycling (importance), or neighborhood drives (participation), for instance, all have credence as possible determinants of RCB. Finally, social influences are assumed to have a role in creating and reinforcing behavioral norms and the individual's values with respect to RCB.

TABLE 2
Test Statistics for the Models Tested

Null Model
Chi Sq.   2895.4   df 253   p=.000
GFI   .446
AGFI   .396
RMR   .227

A Priori Recycling Consumer Behavior Model
Chi SQ.   531.56   df 216   p=.000
GFI   .882
AGFI   .849
RMR   .059

Refined (Trimmed) Recycling Consumer Behavior Model
Chi SQ.   534.43   df 221   p=.000
GFI   .882
AGFI   .852
RMR   .060

Fit Statistic based on Comparison of Null to Refined Model
Bentler and Bonnet Index   .815
Tucker Lewis Index   .864
Bentler's CFI   .883

METHOD

We opted to test the model with an exploratory empirical study. A questionnaire was designed to measure the constructs represented in the model. An attempt was made to measure the several constructs identified in the model with multiple indicators. Because no known scales have been developed to measure these constructs as they pertain to RCB, it was necessary to generate a number of items for each and to scrutinize them for reliability. Cronbach's alpha was used, and items were deleted based on low item-to-total correlations. In all cases a 7-point agree-disagree scale was used as the response scale. The final operationalizations of the constructs were as follows with number of items and alpha indicated: RCB (3; .83), importance (3; .83), benefits-costs (6; .72), values (3; .70), norms (3; .61), social influence (3; .82), and cues (2; .65). See Table 1.

The data was gathered using a quota sampling of 348 adults from a large metropolitan area in the western United States. The sample was designed to represent the general population with respect to age, sex, and socioeconomic characteristics of the most recent census for the area. Respondents completed the self-administered questionnaire in the presence of interviewers knowledgeable about the purpose of the study. The interviewers served as motivators, helped interpret the instructions when necessary, and monitored for compliance with instructions.

FINDINGS

The objective of our study was to develop and test a causal model of RCB. Table 1 gives the standardized parameter estimates for the measurement model and Table 2 shows the goodness of fit indices for the refined model. The model was formulated as a structural equation model and estimated with Lisrel VII (Joreskog and Sorbom 1989). The final model shown in Figure 2 is a refinement of Figure 1 after nonsignificant paths were deleted in order to obtain a more parsimonious model.

Evaluation of the maximum likelihood solution includes a chi square goodness-of-fit test, two goodness-of-fit indexes, and the root mean squared residual. Overall fit statistics based upon analysis of the correlation matrix show that the trimmed model fits the data with a GFI of .882, an AGFI of .852 and a RMR of .060. The other fit indices are high. The size of the standardized parameters of the structural and the measurement models, along with large t values for these parameters indicate which of the proposed relationships are significant. Table 3 gives the total effects of each of the constructs on the endogenous constructs of the model. Total effects sizes suggest that the underlying model is sound.

The results of the measurement model show that the factor loadings are high and consistent in sign with the theoretical constructs of the structural model (see Table 1). The t values of the measurement model parameters ranged from a low of 6.275 to 17.168 indicating that they are highly significant. The total coefficient of determination for the x variables it is .987, and for the y variables, it is .989. In addition, Cronbach alphas indicate that the reliabilities of the measures of the theoretical constructs are acceptable for exploratory research.

The trimmed structural equation model is shown in Figure 2 along with parameter estimates. The model explains a considerable amount of the variance in the relationships and is parsimonious and theoretically reasonable. Similarly, the size of the parameter estimates and their t values indicate that the relationships are strong. However, a few of the original hypothesized relationships are not significant. After dropping these paths the model was run again. The Chi Square, GFI, AGFI, and RMR were not changed significantly by the exclusion of these relationships. We feel that the resulting model is more parsimonious and still theoretically reasonable given the circumstances and constraints of our study.

DISCUSSION

Figure 2 and Table 3 afford interesting verification and possible refinement of the original conceptual model of recycling consumer behavior. In particular, RCB is a function of a myriad of influences as was initially hypothesized. Our results reveal that benefits-costs deliberations and importance are key translation

FIGURE 2
Final Trimmed Model

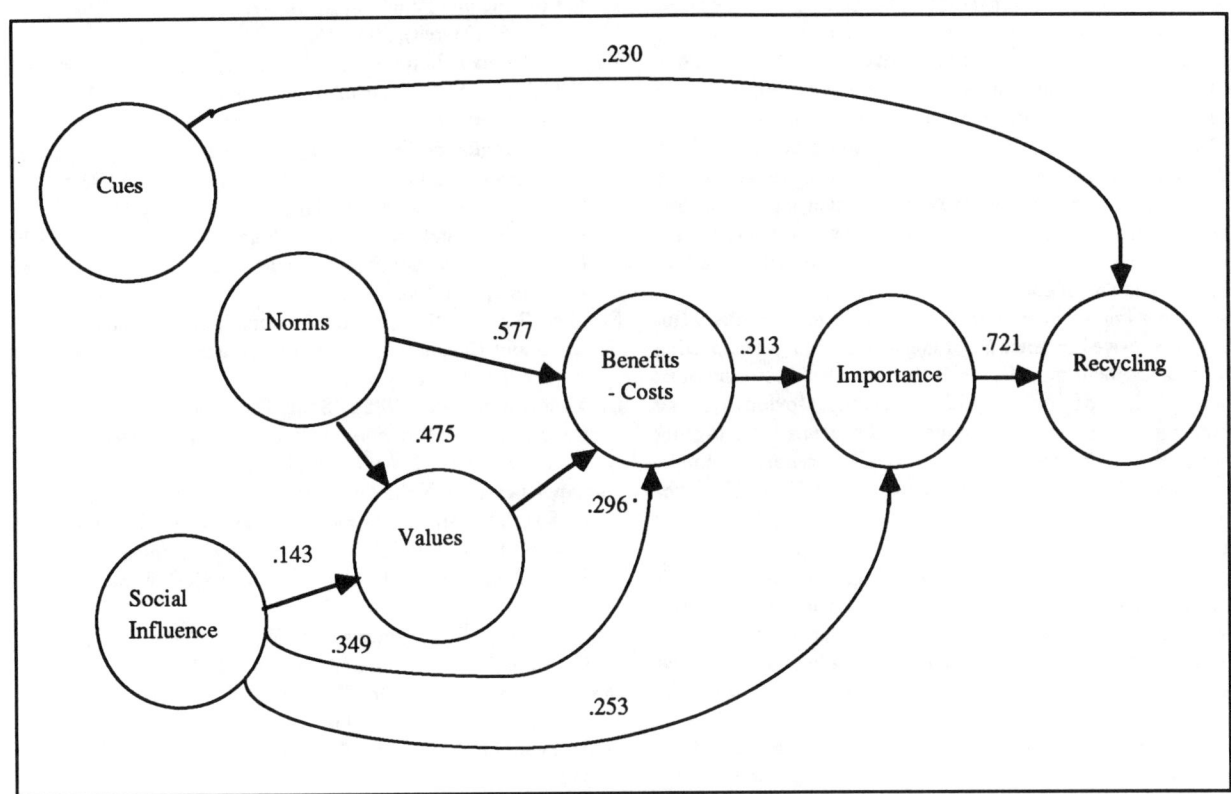

TABLE 3
Total Effects of Latent Constructs on Endogenous Constructs*

Construct	Values	Benefits -Costs	Import-ance	Cues	Social Infl'nc	Norms
Values	.000	.000	.000	.000	.109	.364
Benefits-Costs	.228	.000	.000	.000	.232	.425
Importance	.097	.426	.000	.000	.303	.181
Recycling Consumer Behavior	.062	.270	.634	.163	.192	.115

*Column variables are effectors; row items are consequences

constructs for personal and social forces affecting RCB. Further, an external influence on recycling behavior is media exposure. One can claim that cues and social influence act as stimulators of recycling behavior, and the findings suggest they operate through different modes. Social influences work through the individual's value system, plus they have a bearing on deliberations of the pros and cons of recycling, and they sway the individual's assessment of the importance of recycling. Cues, on the other hand, appear to have direct and unmodified effects on RCB. Finally, as suspected initially, the individual's felt norms and values enter into the cognitive decision process associated with evaluating the importance of RCB. In sum, we consider these preliminary results as encouragement for future work utilizing these constructs modeled according to our logic and/or findings.

There are obvious improvements which we can point out at this time. One which immediately comes to mind is the cues construct. The cues used in this study were assumed to be the every day reporting of environmental issues in the media. Their significance in the model indicates the potential for including explicit promotions of recycling. Our findings reveal that nonspecific cues have a direct effect on recycling behavior, but no indirect effects. However, this result may reflect the type of cues we measured in this study. Our cues measure is an indicant of general knowledge rather than a measure of promotions targeted to convince the public to participate in recycling. By the same token, other cues to action could be included in future studies; for example the appearance of a rubbish pile in a residential neighborhood (i.e., illegal dumping) could be a cue that prompts recycling concern or behavior. In short, information or persuasion that signals a need for recycling or a danger to the environment could be a cue to action, and the fact that our general measure of cues proved significant as a determinant implies success for more specific, personally-relevant operationalizations of cues.

Another improvement concerns social factors. Social influence is a pervasive influence according to our findings. Inspection of the measurement model reveals that friends exerted the most influence, followed by others and then by family. Obviously, social dynamics are important in promoting and encouraging recycling behavior. However, precisely how social influences are communicated to the individual is unknown at this time. Possible improvements in future research include addressing how, when, and the circumstances of various social forces as they are perceived by the individual with respect to adopting recycling behavior.

Next, the operation of norms on recycling behavior bears close examination. We noted that a distinguishing aspect of recycling is its voluntary nature. As such, felt norms are a logical theoretical determinant, and this premise was verified in our exploratory study. Nonetheless, the origins of these norms and the forces working to mold them remain unclear. Better measurement of either or both constructs may resolve this relationship in future research. Finally, the decision making process must be examined further. What exactly goes into the decision to recycle or not recycle? Benefits-to-costs deliberations include the underlying items that go into the evaluation of recycling, but hidden at this time is the way a person subjectively weighs advantages and disadvantages of the complete recycling activity. A reasonable course for future research is to apply qualitative techniques such as focus groups, protocol analysis, or open-ended questions to attempt to map the deliberation process and its dimensions. This investigation may well alert researchers to a host of cognitive process constructs which operate in this area just as it should uncover the mechanisms by which consumers judge their product/packaging disposition behavior options.

In conclusion, we certainly do not view our research as definitive. Instead, we consider it only a first step in developing an understanding of why consumers do or do not engage in recycling which, in itself, is but one facet of environmentally protective consumer behavior. Clearly, the potential for much fruitful research exists in this arena.

REFERENCES

Anderson, W. Thomas, Jr., and William H. Cunningham (1972), "The Socially Conscious Consumer," *Journal of Marketing*, 36 (July), 23-31.

Balderjahn, Ingo (1988), "Personality Variables and Environmental Attitudes as Predictors," *Journal of Business Research*, 17 (August), 52-

Barnes, James H., Jr. (1982), "Recycling: A Problem in Reverse Logistics," *Journal of Macromarketing*, 2 (Fall), 31-37.

Becker, Marshall H. (1985), "Patient Adherence to Prescribed Therapies," *Medical Care*, 23 (May), 539-555.

Becker, Marshall H., Robert H. Drachman, and John P. Kirscht (1974a), "A New Approach to Explaining Sick-role Behavior in Low-Income Populations," *American Journal of Public Health*, 64 (March), 205-216.

Becker, Marshall H., Robert H. Drachman, and John P. Kirscht (1974b), "A Field Experiment to Evaluate Various Outcomes of Continuity of Physician Care," *American Journal of Public Health*, 64 (November), 1062-1070.

Becker, Marshal H., Louis A Maiman, John P. Kirscht, Don P. Haefner and Robert H. Drachman, (1977), "The Health Belief Model and Prediction of Dietary Compliance: A Field Experiment, *Journal of Health and Social Behavior*, Vol. 18, December, 348-366.

Brooker, George (1976), "The Self-Actualizing Socially Conscious Consumer," *Journal of Consumer Research*, 3 (september) 107-112.

De Young, Raymond (1986), "Some Psychological Aspects of Recycling: The Structure of Conservation Satisfactions," *Environment and Behavior*, (July), 435-449.

Dunlap, Riley E., J. Keith Grieneeks and Milton Rokeach (1983), "Human Values and Pro-Environmental Behavior," *Energy and Material Resources: Attitudes, Values, and Public Policy*, ed. W.D. Coon, Boulder, CO: Westview Press, 145-168.

Fisk, George (1973), "Criteria For a Theory of Responsible Consumption," *Journal of Marketing*, 37 (April), 24-31.

Granzin, Kent L. and Janeen E. Olsen (1991), "Characterizing Participants in Activities Protecting the Environment," *Journal of Public Policy & Marketing*, Vol 10, No 2 (Fall), 1-27.

Joreskog, Karl G. and Dag Sorbom (1989), *Lisrel 7 A Guide to the Program and Applications*, SPSS Inc., Chicago, Ill.

Kassarjian, Harold H., (1971), Incorporating Ecology into Marketing Strategy: The Case of Air Pollution," *Journal of Marketing*, 35 (July), 61-65.

Kinnear, Thomas C. and James R. Taylor (1973), "The Effect of Ecological Concern on Brand Perceptions," *Journal of Marketing Research*, 10 (May), 191-197.

Kotler, Philip and Gerald Zaltman (1971), "Social Marketing: An Approach to Planned Social Change," *Journal of Marketing*, 35 (April), 3-12.

Manzo, Lynne C. and Neil D. Weinstein (1987), "Behavioral Commitment to Environmental Protection: A Study of Active and Nonactive Members of the Sierra Club," *Environment and Behavior*, 19 (November), 673-694.

Mohai, Paul and Ben W. Twight (1987), "Age and Environmentalism: An Elaboration of the Buttel Model Using National Survey Evidence," *Social Science Quarterly*, 68 (December), 798-815.

Neuman, Keith (1986), "Personal Values and Commitment to Energy Conservation," *Environment and Behavior*, 18 (January), 53-74.

Oliver, Richard L. and Philip K Berger (1979), "A Path Analysis of Preventive Health Care Decision Models," *Journal of Consumer Research*, Vol. 6, September, 113-122.

Rankin, William (1983), "The Influence of Human Values on Conservation and Energy Shortage Beliefs," in *Energy and Material Resources: Attitudes, Values, and Public Policy*, ed. W. David Conn, Boulder CO: Westview Press.

Rice, Faye (1990), "Where Will We Put All That Garbage?" *Fortune*, (April) 96-100.

Rosenblatt, Jerry A., Alain J. Cusson, and Lee McGown (1984), "A Model to Explain Charitable Donation-Health Care Behavior," *Advances in Consumer Research*, Volume XIII, Richard J. Lutz (ed.), Association for Consumer Research, 235-239.

Samdahl, Diane M., and Robert Robertson (1989), "Social Determinants of Environmental Concern: Specification and Test of the Model," *Environment and Behavior*, 21 (January), 57-81.

Vining, Joanne, and Angela Ebreo (1990), "What Makes a Recycler?: A Comparison of Recyclers and Nonrecyclers," *Environment and Behavior*, (January), 55-73.

Williams, Maurice (1989), "Sustainable Development: A SID Perspective," *Development, 2 (No.3)*, 7-9.

Zikmund, William G. and William J. Stanton (1971), "Recycling Solid Wastes: A Channels-of-Distribution Problem," *Journal of Marketing*, 35 (July), 34-39.

Exploring Green Consumers In An Oriental Culture: Role Of Personal And Marketing Mix Factors

Prem Shamdasani, National University of Singapore
Gloria Ong Chon-Lin, National University of Singapore
Daleen Richmond, National University of Singapore

ABSTRACT

Although still in its infancy, the green movement has started to make its impact on the consumption decisions and behaviors of Singaporean consumers. This exploratory study examined differences among ecologically-concerned and non-ecologically-concerned consumers with respect to their personal and social characteristics, and their perceptions of the marketing of green products. Significant differences were found in terms of attitudes and personality traits among green and non-green consumers. Additionally, while there was a perceived lack of marketing effort for green products and services, green consumers were more aware of green alternatives and were willing to pay higher prices and expend more time and effort to adopt environmentally-friendly consumption behaviors.

INTRODUCTION

While the concern for the environment and ecology has been receiving a great deal of attention in the developed countries in the last two decades, it has only recently surfaced in the rapidly industrializing South-East Asian countries. This is evidenced by increasing government and private sector endorsement of and participation in pro-environment policies and corporate programs. The green movement has finally arrived in this part of the world through the concerted efforts of local and international publics as well as state and private organizations.

Singapore has taken the leadership in the greening of South-East Asia by actively promoting environmental awareness in Singapore and aggressively pursuing its vision to become a model "Environment City". Singapore aspires to be a regional base for environmentally friendly products and services as well as to help transfer green technology from developed countries to this region (*Business Times* 1992).

The timing is therefore right for consumer research that examines factors that motivate and hinder the adoption of green behaviors and products in an Asian context. This research has been further motivated by ACR's call for papers on social issues of which the "green" issue and its implications for consumer behavior will no doubt be a major preoccupation for both academics and practitioners in the 1990s and beyond.

This paper seeks to answer basic questions about Asian consumers' personal and social characteristics that influence environmentally-friendly consumption decisions and the role of external agents, such as government agencies and private firms, in facilitating the adoption of green products and services. Since the green movement in Singapore is still in its infancy stage, this is one of the first research attempts to provide a descriptive profile of the environmentally-concerned consumer and assess the relative influence of the fledgling green marketing movement in encouraging environmentally-friendly consumption behavior among Asian consumers.

The green consumer is generally defined as one who adopts environmentally-friendly behaviors and/or who purchases green products over the standard alternatives. In this study, the terms 'green', 'environmentally-friendly' and 'ecologically-conscious' are used interchangeably. Green or environmentally-friendly products are broadly defined as products "that will not pollute the earth or deplete natural resources, and can be recycled or conserved" (*D&B Reports* 1990). The green products of interest in this study are consumer household products, personal care products, and recycled paper and stationery since they are most affected by environmental concerns and are sold in retail outlets in Singapore. The study also includes non-purchase related behaviors such as recycling paper for other uses, avoidance of styrofoam containers for food, recycling of drink cans or bottles and sorting of trash from recyclable materials when disposing of wastes.

The basic objective of this paper is therefore to explore differences between "green" and "non-green" Singaporean consumers on personal, social and marketing mix dimensions. We first review past research on the ecologically concerned consumer and factors that influence the adoption of green products. This is followed by a discussion of the methodology and validation of the constructs. Finally, the differences between green and non-green consumers are analyzed and implications of the findings discussed.

LITERATURE REVIEW

Personal Characteristics

Consumer attitudes have been used in past studies to predict energy conservation, recycling and ecologically-conscious purchase and use of products. Kassarjian (1971) studied consumers' reaction toward a gasoline that reduced air pollution and found that there was a positive correlation between concern for air pollution and willingness to pay higher prices for it. Attitude toward air pollution (expressed by concern) was the most important variable in determining consumers' behavior toward the product. Kinnear and Taylor (1973) investigated attitudinal and behavioral dimensions of ecological concern and found them to have marked effects on brand perceptions for laundry products. In a study conducted in West Germany, Balderjahn (1988) found that a positive attitude toward ecologically-conscious living resulted in ecologically-responsible buying and using of products, including the use of automobiles. It also prompted consumers to publicly show environmental concern by signing ecologically relevant petitions and supporting or joing an antipollution organization.

Past research has shown that socially- or ecologically- concerned consumers do possess certain personality traits that consumers low in social or ecological concern do not possess. Anderson and Cunningham (1972) found that social consciousness tended to vary inversely with dogmatism and conservatism. Personal competence (a feeling of mastery of one's personal life and environment) was slightly less effective as a discriminator, tending to vary inversely with social consciousness. Kinnear, Taylor and Ahmed (1974) explored the relationship between socioeconomic and personality characteristics of consumers and the amount of ecological concern. They found that the ecologically concerned consumer tended to perceive strongly that individuals could be effective in pollution abatement; was more open to or tolerant of new ideas; desired to understand the workings of things and scored moderately with respect to harm avoidance.

Crosby, Gill and Taylor (1981) studied the concept of alienation as a personality variable to determine the ecological behavior of voting for the deposit law. Alienation, which was defined as powerlessness or meaninglessness and not isolation, was found to be very significant in predicting the behavior of voting for the deposit law. In other words, perceived consumer effectiveness and ecological behavior were strongly related. Balderjahn (1988) also studied the relationship between ecological concern and personalitiy variables: alienation, emotional expression and ideological control. The concept of ideology control was similar to the perceived consumer effectiveness dimension identified by Kinnear et al. 1974. He found that ideology control was more significant in predicting ecologically-responsible consumption patterns than alienation or emotional expressiveness. Consumers who were internally controlled saved more energy and displayed ecologically responsible buying and consumption patterns. Anderson and Cunningham (1972) discovered that cosmopolitanism was more effective than alienation in discriminating between high and low social consciousness, and that the socially-conscious consumer was more cosmopolitan and less alienated (that is, more socially involved or integrated).

While demographics have been used by various researchers in determining ecologically conscious behavior, the results have not been consistent. Studies that have found significant relationships between ecological consciousness and demographics (e.g., Anderson and Cunningham 1972; Kinnear et al. 1974; Anderson, Henion and Cox 1975; Murphy 1978; Belch 1980; Van Liere and Dunlap 1980; Roper Organization 1990) generally suggest that environmentally-conscious consumers tend to be younger; are more highly educated; come from households with higher incomes; and have higher occupational status. Other researchers (e.g., Granzin and Olsen 1991; Crosby et al. 1981; Balderjahn 1988) found that demographics had little or no effect on environmental behavior. Although Webster's (1975) socially concerned consumer was a nonconformist member of the upper middle class with a high family income, he concluded that demographics were not as good predictors as personality and attitude measures.

Marketing Mix Variables

Past research has largely focused on personal charateristics as correlates of ecological behavior. Very little has been done to examine the impact of green marketing efforts on the adoption of green products and services. In a study on the American consumers' environmental behaviors and attitudes, the Roper Organization Inc. (1990) found some of the following marketing mix related reasons for not behaving in an environmentally-friendly manner:

(1) the green alternatives were not functionally superior;
(2) the green alternatives were too expensive;
(3) the labels claiming that the product was environmentally-safe were not believable; and
(4) the green alternatives were too difficult to find.

The perceived relative advantage (e.g., quality and functional performance) of green products over standard alternatives is likely to influence their rate of adoption (Rogers 1983). The relative advantage of green alternatives would have to be weighed against their prices. The analysis of this cost-benefit relationship is complicated by the fact that prices of green products reflect other costs in addition to money costs. These include opportunity costs, energy costs and psychic costs. If the major benefits of green products, compared to the major costs are higher, then consumers will be motivated to purchase these products even if they are priced somewhat higher than non-green substitutes (Kotler and Zaltman 1971).

The Roper Organization's (1990) survey found that consumers in general were not ready to bear the cost of improving the environment, in the form of higher prices for green products. Even the most environmentally committed group in the survey appeared to be highly price-sensitive, willing to pay only 7.4% more for green products and a fifth of them would pay nothing more. From focus group interviews of American consumers, Progressive Grocer (1990) reported that consumers were either not willing to pay more for green products or were willing to do so only if they liked the product or if the product was of comparable quality to the regular brand. In a study of Australian consumers, Suchard and Polonsky (1991) found that 61.5% of the respondents would pay more for environmentally safe products while 22.2% were unsure if they would pay more for green products. On the average, those respondents who indicated that they would pay more for green products were willing to pay between 15% and 20% more.

The promotion and distribution of green products contribute to consumers' awareness of the selection and availability of green alternatives. This awareness, however, does not always lead to ecologically-friendly consumption decisions. A recent survey of Singapore consumers by the Business Times (1991) showed that almost all of the respondents interviewed indicated that they would like to know where to buy environmentally friendly products. But, they were not willing to pay a higher price for green products if they were priced higher than conventional products. In another instance, where green alternatives were known to be available in stores and sold side by side, standard brands outsold their green substitutes by as much as 30 to 1, even though the green substitutes were competitively priced.

METHODOLOGY

Sample and Procedure

The data were collected through self-administered questionnaires that were distributed by hand. Judgement was used in distributing the questionnaires to various respondents in shopping malls, restaurants, clinics, theaters, exhibitions, colleges, and residential neighborhoods. Respondents were selected based on their involvement in or ability to influence actual purchase decisions, and being capable of voluntarily adopting environmentally-friendly behaviors.

Of the 300 questionnaires that were distributed, 207 or 69 percent were returned and usable for analysis. The final sample of respondents comprised of Singaporean consumers who came from a cross-section of backgrounds including professionals and executives, clerical and administrative staff, production and technical staff, students, homemakers, secretaries, security and military personnel, and retirees. In terms of age, respondents ranged from fifteen to fifty-five years. Based on chi-square analysis, differences among respondent groups on age, education and household income categories were not significant at alpha = .10.

Classification of Green Consumers

Respondents were classified as green or non-green consumers based on their composite scores on a 12-item index which was adapted from The Roper Organization's (1990) study of American consumers' public attitudes and individual behavior with regard to the environment. The scale measured respondents' frequency with which they performed each of the twelve environmentally-friendly purchase (e.g., buy products made from recycled materials) and non-purchase related behaviors (e.g., return containers for recycling). A respondent was operationally classified as an environmentally-concerned or green consumer when his or her cumulative frequency score on the scale was greater than 31 (the mean cutoff score). Those respondents whose score was 31 or less were classified as non-environmentally-concerned or non-green consumers.

APPENDIX A
Predictor Variables: Reliabilities And Sample Items

Variable (sample item)	Number of Items	Cronbach Alpha
I. Personal Characteristics		
Attitude (Comfort) (e.g., I would sacrifice personal if this could help improve the environment.)	4	.65
Attitude (Environmental Risks) (e.g., I'm not bothered about the possible dangers posed by environmental problems.)	3	.63
Attitude (Environmentalism) (e.g., Everyone should adopt environmentally-friendly behaviors.)	3	.38
Locus of Control (e.g., The individual consumer can't do anything about preserving the earth.)	3	.69
Dogmatism (e.g., I do not hesitate to try new products.)	2	.57
Social Integration (e.g., I like attending parties or social get-togethers.)	4	.60
Cosmopolitanism (e.g., I don't foresee any adjustment problems if I work overseas.)	4	.59
II. Marketing Mix		
Product (e.g., Recyclable packaging is not as convenient as disposable ones.)	2	.68
Price (e.g., It is not worth paying higher prices for green products.)	4	.66
Promotion (e.g., There should be special displays for green products.)	4	.65
Placement (e.g., I don't use green products because they are not readily available)	5	.47

Based on this criterion, the final sample consisted of 97 environmentally-concerned consumers and 110 non-environmentally-concerned consumers.

It should be noted that ecological-consciousness is a continuum consisting of consumers who are more or less ecologically-conscious. The classification of consumers who are more ecologically-conscious as "green" and those who are less-ecologically-conscious as "non-green" was done for two purposes: (1) to develop an exploratory, descriptive profile of a "green" Singaporean consumer; and (2) to enable broad comparisons between green and non-green consumers to be made. Future research needs to examine in greater detail the correlates of ecological-consciousness as a continuous dimension.

Validation of Measures

The first stage of the validation exercise involved performing factor analyses on 72 items measuring personal characteristics and marketing mix variables that were hypothesized to influence environmentally friendly consumption behavior. Since this research is at an early stage, exploratory factor analysis was performed to reduce a large number of measures to a more manageable, statistically independent and reliable set of constructs. Principal components was used for extraction of factors and rotation was performed using the Varimax method. Four marketing mix variables (factors) and seven factors corresponding to personal characteristics were extracted. The percentages of variation explained by personal characteristics and marketing mix variables were 55.2% and 49.4% respectively. Only items with loadings greater than .4 were considered for interpretation.

The second stage of the validation exercise involved subjecting the 11 factors identified to reliability testing. Cronbach's alpha was the measure of reliability used. Since this research is in its early stage, modest reliability in the range of 0.5 to 0.6 is recommended (Nunnally 1967). The Cronbach's alphas for the marketing mix and personal characteristic factors were in the range of .38 to .65 and are reported in Appendix A.

TABLE 1
Predictors of Ecological Consciousness: Means and Significance

Variables	Green Consumers*	Non-Green Consumers*
I. Personal Characteristics		
Attitude (Comfort)[a]	15.16 (2.73)	13.77 (2.99)
Attitude (Environmental Risks)[a]	12.67 (2.47)	11.78 (2.58)
Attitude (Environmentalism)[a]	13.06 (1.69)	12.35 (2.17)
Locus of Control[b]	12.54 (2.61)	11.81 (2.87)
Dogmatism[b]	7.87 (1.31)	7.44 (1.70)
Social Integration[b]	14.11 (2.77)	13.31 (3.00)
Cosmopolitanism[b]	14.70 (2.95)	13.77 (3.06)
II. Marketing Mix		
Product[a]	9.39 (2.37)	8.63 (1.79)
Price[a]	14.30 (2.92)	13.62 (3.02)
Promotion[b]	17.44 (2.22)	16.95 (2.53)
Placement[a]	10.73 (3.48)	9.23 (2.81)

*Composite means with standard deviations in parantheses. Items measured on a 5-point "strongly disagree/strongly agree" scale.
[a] $p < .01$; [b] $p < .05$

ANALYSIS AND FINDINGS

The first stage of the analysis involved exploratory testing of individual-level differences between green and non-green consumers on personal characteristics and marketing mix variables using t-tests. This was followed by the development and testing of a predictive model that discriminates between green and non-green consumer using discriminant analysis.

Personal Characteristics

The t-test results of the differences between ecologically-concerned and non-ecologically-concerned consumers are presented in Table 1 (I). Green consumers possess more favorable attitudes toward the environment than non-green consumers. They are more willing to scarifice personal comfort and adopt environmentally-friendly behaviors for environmental gains. They are more likely believe that the environmental crisis is real and legitimate, and are more concerned and aware of risks posed by environmental threats.

Green consumers are more internally-controlled as they believe that an individual consumer can be effective in environmental protection. Thus, they feel that the job of environmental protection should not be left to the government, business, environmentalists and scientists only; they as consumers can also play a part. They are also less dogmatic and more open-minded or tolerant toward new products and ideas. Their open-mindedness helps them to accept green products and behaviors, which are new ways of doing things, more readily.

Socially, green consumers are more cosmopolitan and socially integrated. Being more cosmopolitan, exposes them to environmental problems and solutions in other countries which in turn makes them more knowledgeable and environmentally proactive. However, no differences were found between green and non-green products in terms of the perceived influence of the government ($t=1.22$, $p>.10$) and satisfied users of green products ($t=1.06$, $p>.10$) in encouraging the adoption of green products.

No demographic differences between ecologically-concerned consumers and non-ecologically-concerned consumers were found. Using chi-square analysis, there were no significant differences between the groups at alpha = .10 with regard to age ($X^2=7.17$), education ($X^2=5.65$), household income ($X^2=7.52$), and occupation ($X^2=.73$). These findings are consistent with previous studies (Webster 1975; Crosby et. al. 1981; Balderjahn 1988) which revealed that demographics are weak predictors of ecological behavior.

Marketing Mix

Results of the tests of differences between green and non-green consumers on their perceptions of the marketing mix of green products and services are reported in Table 1 (II).

These results indicate that there are significant differences between green and non-green consumers on perceptions of product, price, and placement of green products. Green consumers do not perceive environmentally-safe products as less superior to non-green alternatives and they are less deterred from adopting green products by the lack of product variety ($t=2.64$, $p<.01$).

Green consumers are also more willing to pay higher prices for environmentally-safe products than non-green consumers ($t=2.62$, $p<.01$), as they perceive green products as being able to provide value for money and it is worth paying a higher price for them, especially if the green products possess the level of quality in a regular brand.

There were significant differences in behaviors and attitudes concerning the distribution and accessibility of green products ($t=3.44$, $p<.01$) between green and non-green consumers. Green consumers are willing to expend effort to search for green alternatives, are aware of where green products are sold and are more willing to frequent stores that sell green products. On the other hand, non-green consumers find the narrow distribution of green products inconvenient.

Although green consumers differed from non-green consumers on their perceptions of the promotion of green products ($t=1.44$, $p<.10$), both groups of consumers could be equally deterred from adopting green products by the lack of promotion. Green as well as non-green consumers perceive a need for more promotion of green products, through special displays, dissemination of information and a distinctive labelling scheme.

TABLE 2
Discriminant Function Coefficients For Significant Predictors

Predictor Variable	Coefficients Unstandardized	Standardized	Rank
Attitude (Comfort)	.08	.24	4
Attitude (Environmental Risks)	.16	.41	2
Attitude (Environmentalism)	.15	.28	3
Dogmatism	.11	.17	5
Product	.03	.06	6
Price	-.01	.03	7
Placement	.22	.71	1
Constant	-8.25		

Mean Discriminant Score: Green Consumers = .39
Non-green Consumers = -.38

Wilks' Lamda	Chi-square	d.f.	Significance
.87	18.72	7	.009

Predicting Green Consumers

A predictive model comprising selected personal, social and marketing mix factors was developed and tested using discriminant analysis. Two-thirds (i.e., 139) of the respondents formed the analysis subgroup, while the remaining one-third (i.e., 68) of the respondents formed the holdout sample for testing the predictive validity of the model. Using the Wilk's lamda criterion, the model that significantly differentiates between green and non-green consumers is presented in Table 2. The final discriminant model comprised 7 variables and was significant at p<.01. The classification results for both the analysis and holdout samples are about 65% and 66% respectively.

Despite the modest predictive efficacy of the discriminant model, it provides some preliminary insights into the relative importance of factors that influenced adoption of green products and behaviors. In this model, the distribution and accessibility of green products was found to be the most important factor, followed by attitudinal variables, namely, attitude toward risks, attitude toward environmentally-friendly behavior and attitude toward comfort. Other variables that were found significant included the relative dogmatism of the consumer and the perceptions of price and product attributes of green products.

DISCUSSION AND CONCLUSION

This exploratory study examined the differences among green and non-green consumers with respect to their personal and social characteristics and their perceptions of the marketing of green products. Given the encouraging results, it was thus possible to develop a preliminary profile of the ecologically-conscious consumer in Singapore.

In general, the green consumer when compared to the non-green consumer, has more favorable attitudes toward the environment, is more internally controlled and open-minded, more socially-integrated and cosmopolitan. In terms of demographics, however, ecologically-concerned consumers were not different from their non-ecologically-concerned counterparts. It is also interesting to note, that green consumers do not significantly differ from non-green consumers with regard to two sources of influence - the government and other satisfied users of green products. However, it does not mean that these two sources of "green" influence are not important in shaping environmentally friendly attitudes and behaviors. Due to their limited treatment in this study, additional research incorporating a more elaborate explication of these influence constructs is needed in order to enable us to better understand and appreciate the nature and extent of their impact on green behavior.

The results also suggest that the current marketing of green products, or the lack of it, forms a barrier to the acceptance of green products, and that non-green consumers are more likely to be deterred from adopting environmentally-friendly products than green consumers. It was acknowledged by both groups that there was a general lack of green promotion. However, the higher prices, unavailability and narrow distribution of green alternatives in Singapore did not deter existing green consumers. They are more likely to expend a greater amount of time and energy than non-green consumers in locating and purchasing green products and services.

The findings seem to suggest that Singaporeans' decision to adopt environmentally-friendly consumption decisions is largely driven by personal factors (e.g., personality and attitudes) rather than by the government. This conclusion is at best tentative and future research needs to more precisely delineate the relative influence of various change agents such as the government. External influence attempts from government agencies through green campaigns, for example, may help shape positive attitudes toward green products and services, but not necessarily behavior. For example, the Singapore Government had to subsidize unleaded gasoline to encourage motorists to switch from leaded to unleaded gasoline. The resulting lower prices of unleaded gasoline have been slowly, but surely, encouraging motorists to switch away from leaded gasoline.

However, given the growing and immediate concerns of the government about environmental issues, pro-environmental legislation in the future will probably be more pervasive and used more effectively to encourage environmentally-friendly consumption behaviors in Singapore. This does not, however, preclude the need for greater public education as well as economic incentives to reinforce consumers' green attitudes and behaviors.

Future research should examine in greater depth the attitude-behavior inconsistencies arising from conflicts between internal (e.g., personal beliefs or lifestyle) and external (e.g., social conformity) pressures. Also, the effectiveness of various public and private environmental programs should be compared especially between those that involve moral suasion and financial incentives/disincentives.

REFERENCES

Anderson, Thomas W. and William H. Cunningham (1972), "The Socially Conscious Consumer," *Journal of Marketing*, 36 (July), 23-31.

_____, Karl E. Henion, and Eli P. Cox (1975), "Socially vs Ecologically Responsible Consumers," in *1974 Combined Proceedings*, ed. Ronald C. Curhan, Chicago: American Marketing Association, 304-311.

Balderjahn, Ingo (1988), "Personality Variables and Environmental Attitudes as Predictors of Ecologically Responsible Consumption Patterns," *Journal of Business Research, 17*, 51-56.

Business Times (1992), "Resolution on Environment and Development Adopted-Fifth Asean Meeting on the Environment," (February 19), Singapore.

_____ (1991), "The Changing Attitudes of Singaporeans to the Environment," (May 25), Singapore.

Crosby, Lawrence A., James D. Gill, and James R. Taylor (1981), "Consumer/Voter Behavior In The Passage of The Michigan Container Law," *Journal of Marketing*, 45 (Spring), 19-31.

Granzin, Kent L. and Janeen E. Olsen (1991), "An Investigation of the Characteristics of Participants in Conservation and Environmental Protection: An Emphasis on Helping Behavior," in *1991 AMA Educators' Proceedings*, eds. Mary G. Gilly et al., (Summer), Chicago: American Marketing Association, 177-186.

Kassarjian, Harold H. (1971), "Incorporating Ecology Into Marketing Strategy: The Case of Air Pollution," *Journal of Marketing*, 35 (July), 61-65.

Kinnear, Thomas C. and James R. Taylor (1973), "The Effect of Ecological Concern On Brand Perception," *Journal of Marketing Research*, 10 (May), 191-197..pa

_____, James C. Taylor, and Sahrudin A. Ahmed (1974), "Ecologically Concerned Consumers: Who Are They?" *Journal of Marketing*, 38 (April), 20-24.

D & B Reports (1990), "The Selling of the Green," (September/October), 38 (5), 30-31/35.

Kotler, Philip and Gerald Zaltman (1971), "Social Marketing: An Approach To Planned Social Change," *Journal of Marketing*, 25 (July), 3-12.

Murphy, Patrick E. (1978), "Environmentally Concerned Consumers," in *Proceedings of the 1978 Educator's Conference*, ed. Subash Jain, Chicago: American Marketing Association, 316-320.

Nunnally, Jum C. (1967), *Psychometric Theory*, New York: McGraw-Hill Book Company.

Progressive Grocer (1990), "Consumers Speak Out on the Environment," (November), 16-22.

Rogers, Everett (1983), *Diffusion of Innovation*, New York: The Free Press.

The Roper Organization, Inc. (1990), "The Environment: Public Attitudes and Individual Behavior," July.

Suchard, Hazel T. and Michael J. Polonsky (1991), "A Theory of Environmental Buyer Behavior and Its Validity: The Environmental Action-Behavior Model," in *1991 AMA Educators' Proceedings*, eds. Mary C. Gilly et al., (Summer), Chicago: American Marketing Association, 187-201.

Van Liere, Kent D. and Riley E. Dunlap (1980), "The Social Bases of Environmental Concern: A Review of Hypotheses, Explanations And Empirical Evidence," *Public Opinion Quarterly*, 44 (Summer), 181-197.

Webster, Fredrick. E. (1985), "Determining the Characteristics of the Socially Conscious Consumer," *Journal of Consumer Research*, 2 (December), 188-196.

Anatomy of Green Advertising

Easwar Iyer, University of Massachusetts
Bobby Banerjee, University of Massachusetts

ABSTRACT

Much work has been published, both in scholarly journals and the popular press, about the greening of the American consumer. Most of the past work, if not all, deal with consumer profiles; none deal with "green" advertising. This work is the first attempt to analyze "green" print advertisements. In this study we first provide a framework for analyzing green ads and then use that very framework to analyze a sample of print ads.

INTRODUCTION

Green is in, no question about it. The term "green", as we intend it, implies an underlying concern for preservation of the evnironment and a noninvasive lifestyle. Generally targets for concerns are the preservation of the planet earth, personal health, and animal life. Moreover, the goal of preservation is generally accompanied with a belief that noninvasive methods have to be employed in achieving those goals. Thus, activities causing the least damage to the planet earth, its environment, human and animal life are preferred.

Concern along these target dimensions have been rising steadily over the past few decades (Bremner, 1989) and is having a major impact on consumer purchasing behaviors (Roper, 1990). According to the Roper Organization study (1990) 11% of all Americans are True-Blue Greens and yet another 11% are Greenback Greens (See Table 1). These segments are identified by their environmental attitudes and behaviors and represent the two greenest segments in the 5-way classification scheme used in the Roper study. Together, they represent a little under one-quarter of all consumers — a very significant market segment especially when one compares it to the market shares of very successful national brands. For example, many heavily advertised and promoted cigarettes turn in a handsome profit with market shares varying between 1% and 3%. Many lesser known brands of household products such as soap and toothpaste survive on market shares as low as 5% or less (Simmons Market Research Bureau, 1990). The point is that the green segment is big enough to accommodate quite a few brands. Further, the two greenest segments, i.e., True-Blue Greens and Greenback Greens comprise of the most lucrative and desirable consumers — affluent and college educated. While the national median income is $27,100, the median income of these two segments is $31,850 (Schwartz and Miller, 1991). Likewise, only 19% of all Americans have a college degree; over 27% of these two segments have graduated from college (American Demographics, February 1991).

Many factors have contributed to the growth of the green movement, but none could be more important than the emerging perception that the world is a more polluted place than it was 20 years ago (New York Times/CBS News Poll, April 1990). According to this poll, not only did 75% of the respondents feel that the air was more polluted and 80% feel that the water was more polluted, but that 41% feel that both air and water would be more polluted 20 years hence unless something is done right now. Such pessimistic perceptions have sent a message to political and business leaders who are scrambling to create platforms and programs that placate the environmentally conscious segment. For example, corporations have responded to this shift in the consumer attitudes and the resultant emergence of a new market by launching new products with a green appeal at an ever growing rate. In 1984, 54 new green products were launched; in 1988 178 new green products were introduced (Hinds, 1989). This represents a 230% growth in that 4-year span.

WHO IS GREEN

Consumer researchers have done an excellent job in identifying the green consumer. One of the most detailed studies was carried out by the Roper Organization in which many behaviors deemed environmentally friendly, i.c., using biodegradable/recycled products, and recycling bottles, cans and newspapers, were reported. The list also included behaviors indicative of environmental concern such as reading packaging labels, contributing to environmental groups and lobbying politicians. Cluster analysis was used to identify five distinct segments: True-Blue Greens (11%), Greenback Greens (11%), Sprouts (26%), Grousers (24%), and Basic Browns (28%). This study also confirmed that green consumers tend to be better educated, earn higher incomes, and hold professional/white collar jobs. (See Table 2 for details), making them a very desirable target market.

Yet, others prefer to classify green consumers in terms of their motivation (Ottman, 1991). Based on a careful analysis of the different type of activist groups and causes, Ottman (1991) postulates three distinct consumer motives: preservation of the planet, preservation of personal health, and preservation of animal life. The first group, "planet passionates", are likely to belong to "Keep America Beautiful" and engage in recycling bottles, cans, and newspapers; whereas the second group, "health fanatics", are likely to belong to "Americans for Safe Food" and buy organic produce only. Lastly, the third group, "animal lovers", are most likely members of the "Humane Society" and buy "cruelty-free" cosmetics and boycott fur coats. (See Table 3 for details.) Such a classification scheme is very useful in terms of understanding the primary motives that drive a green consumer. It is also helpful in creating new product positions.

GREEN ADVERTISING

Although much is known about the green consumer, very little is known about green advertising. There are three very compelling reasons why it is timely and important to study and analyze green advertising. First, the new media has picked up on the green theme and is reporting very extensively on the subject. For instance, the *Tyndall Report* found that there was an increase of 76% from 1988 to 1989 in the number of minutes devoted by network television to environmental issues. Second, and a closely allied factor, most consumers get information on environmental issues from the mass media (TV, newspapers, magazines, and radio) far more so than either environmental newsletters or government publications (Scott Paper Company study, March 1990). Third, despite the high dependence on mass media for information, consumers do not find that information believable or reliable. In fact, from a survey done by Abt Associates (March 1990) it was reported that the most credible source of information was an environmentally active organization and the least credible was an advertisement place by a major company.

Given the growing attention placed on environmental issues and the heavy reliance of the consuming public on mass media, the dire lack of credibility in green advertising is a shocking state. We

TABLE 1
Green Consumers

Five Segments

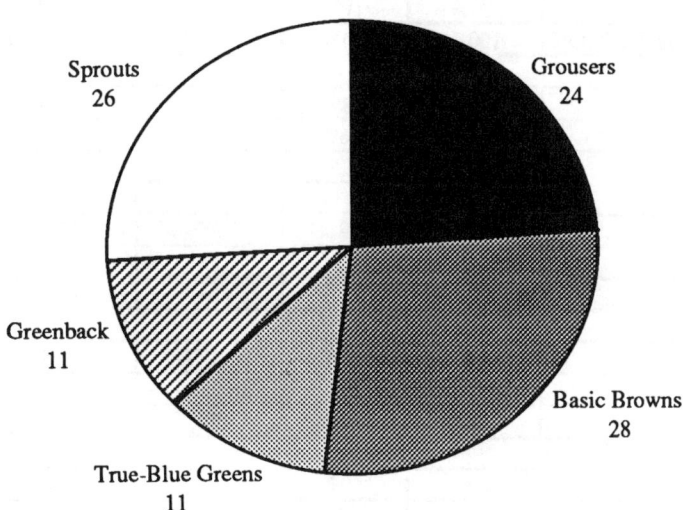

Source: The Roper Organization (1990)

---

believe this to be a strong signal calling for an analysis of green ads. Thus, our paper is about the anatomy of green advertising. At first we present a framework to categorize green ads. Next, we use this framework to analyze our sample of print ads. The results, we believe, will help us understand some of the trends in green advertising.

METHODOLOGY

Being the first attempt at classifying green advertising, there was no categorizing scheme to fall back upon, although there were quite a few studies categorizing advertisements in general. For example, Shimp, Urbany and Camlin (1988) have categorized print ads for mass-marketing products in the U.S.A., while Tse, Belk, and Zhou (1989) have used content analysis to compare three "similar" societies. Yet others (Pollay, 1985) have employed content analysis to develop and describe a history of print advertising in the USA. Thus, even though there is a tradition of employing content analysis in the literature, there were no ready-made categories for our purposes. Therefore, we had to adapt available categories and create some new ones as we went along.

Among a host of critical issues on methodology, two stood out. First, we had to identify ads that would be included in our study and second, we had to develop a set of relevant categories to classify the ads. These two steps are loosely the equivalent of data gathering and scale development.

CHOICE OF ADS

We decided to focus on print ads for a variety of reasons. The print medium has a broader base than television. This is manifest in two separate ways. First, print medium accounts for more volume of advertising than any other medium, and second, it has a larger array of advertisers, including small businesses and local businesses, participating. The first factor, i.e., volume of advertising, is important in that we could generate a large sample of ads for our analysis. The second factor, i.e., array of advertisers, is important in that it represents a larger spectrum of participants thereby ensuring that our sample ads was adequately representative of the advertising community.

Over and above those were practical considerations. We were given access to a personal library that was the store house of thousands of ads, articles and reports that addressed the issues of environment, health, and animal life preservation. We selected the ads for our study from this vast pool, using three cardinal principles. First of all, it had to be an ad; we rejected all articles and reports from this collection. Second, we included an ad in our study only if it addressed any one of the three issues, i.e., preservation of the planet, personal health or animal life. Third, and finally, multiple occurrences of the same ad were eliminated by including each ad only once. It is important to note here that we did include multiple ads for the same product/brand/company as long as they were not identical. The result was a collection of 173 ads that were used in the study. Although this procedure was dictated by a matter of convenience, it is not entirely flawed. The original collection was a large assortment of ads, articles and reports compiled over five years or more. Thus, we believe that the specific ads selected for our study represents a fair cross-section of green ads in general.

MAIN TAXONOMY AND SUB-CATEGORIES

The main taxonomy used in this study was derived from past literature as well as our interest in the subject matter. There were four broad items in the main taxonomy: AD TARGET, AD OBJECTIVE, ECONOMIC CHAIN, and AD APPEAL.

The first item, AD TARGET, was used to identify the target of the ad. Based upon past literature (Ottman, 1991) we identified three targets. These three sub-categories are:

TABLE 2
Segmentations by Environmental Attitudes and Behaviors

	Total Adults	True-Blue Greens	Green-back Greens	Sprouts	Grousers	Basic Browns
TOTAL	100%	100%	100%	100%	100%	100%
SHARE OF ADULT POPULATION	100%	11%	11%	26%	24%	20%
SEX						
Male	47%	34%	42%	48%	46%	55%
Female	53%	66%	58%	52%	54%	45%
EDUCATION						
Less than High school	21%	11%	11%	15%	26%	30%
High school graduate	38	39	35	33	43	39
Some college	22	22	28	25	19	20
College grad. or more	19	28	26	28	12	11
OCCUPATION						
Executive/Professional	16%	25%	17%	22%	13%	11%
White collar	18	18	28	19	18	15
Blue collar	28	19	24	22	31	36
MARITAL STATUS						
Married	62%	69%	62%	71%	55%	59%
Single	37	30	38	29	44	41
POLITICAL/SOCIAL IDEOLOGY						
Conservative	39%	43%	37%	41%	40%	36%
Middle of the road	37	26	33	35	39	41
Liberal	20	28	29	21	18	16
REGION						
Northeast	22%	31%	24%	25%	23%	17%
Midwest	26	27	26	29	26	22
South	33	18	28	28	30	48
West	19	24	23	18	21	13
RACE						
White	85%	82%	92%	91%	80%	82%
Black	10%	11	3	6	13	13
Other	4%	3	4	4	6	3
WITH CHILDREN UNDER AGE 13	34%	34%	43%	33%	33%	32%
MEDIAN AGE (in years)	41	44	34	42	39	42
MEDIAN INCOME (in thousands)	$27.1	$32.1	$31.6	$32.0	$24.9	$21.2

Source: The Roper Organization, New York, NY.

PLANET PRESERVATION
ANIMAL LIFE PRESERVATION
PERSONAL HEALTH PRESERVATION

The second item in the taxonomy was AD OBJECTIVE. This was used to identify whether the ad promoted a CORPORATE IMAGE or the PRODUCT/SERVICE itself; these constituted the two sub-categories were identified. Inputs, the first minor category, was defined when the ad highlighted the raw material or production processes used. The second minor category, packaging, was defined when the product's packaging was emphasized in some manner. Finally the overall product/service itself was defined as a minor category when the product/service was promoted in general. Following is a summary of the sub-categories and minor categories.

CORPORATE IMAGE

PRODUCT/SERVICE CHARACTERISTIC
  Inputs
  Packaging
  Overall Product/Service

The third item in the main taxonomy was ECONOMIC CHAIN. This was used to identify the different activities involved in the closed loop of an economic system. Our identifying this item in the taxonomy is in response to the call to expand the focus of marketing from that of a purely selling institution (Kotler and Levy, 1969). Nicosia and Mayer (1976, p. 69) used the terms buying, using, and disposing in their theory on the sociology of consumption. We have adapted that trilogy for our purpose and the sub-categories we use are PRODUCTION, CONSUMPTION, and DISPOSITION. Essentially we have changed the emphasis from buying to production, while retaining the other two categories. This is because motivating a consumer to buy is the implicit goal of all advertising, and hence that sub-category may not be very useful. However, ads that emphasize production would be worthy of being identified as a separate sub-category. We wish to point out that there is a logical sequence to these sub-categories in that production typically precedes consumption and both of them precede disposition[1]. Thus, the three sub-categories are:

PRODUCTION
  Raw Materials
  Process

CONSUMPTION

DISPOSITION

Only in the case of PRODUCTION, we identified two minor categories, i.e., Raw Materials and Process. Ads that emphasized the inputs to a production process would be classified under the first minor category, whereas those that emphasized the actual process itself would be classified in the second minor category.

The fourth and final item in the main taxonomy was AD APPEAL. This was used to categorize the type of appeal employed in the ad. Based on the literature (Russell and Lane, 1991; Ottoman, 1991) and our own analysis of the ads, we identified five sub-categories, with each sub-category encompassing a few minor categories. Those that could not be easily classified were coded under a catch-all category. The sub-categories and the minor categories are as follows:

ZEITGEIST
  Mere Statement
  Bandwagon

EMOTIONAL
  Fear
  Guilt
  You Make a Difference

FINANCIAL
  Money-Off
  Cause Subsidy

EUPHORIA
  Health
  Natural

MANAGEMENT
  Control
  Social Responsibility

OTHERS
  Comparison
  Exemplar
  Celebrity Endorsement

---

[1] Actually "buying" (or purchasing) will be in between these two activities, but has been omitted for reasons already specified.

ZEITGEIST is defined as the general climate prevailing at a time. Thus, any ad that merely tried to ride on the current wave of the green movement was classified in this category. An ad was placed in the first minor category if there was nothing more than a bland statement, e.g., Brand X is environmentally friendly. It was placed in the second minor category if there was an obvious attempt to hitch the company to the green movement, e.g. In response to the growing demand for an environmentally friendly product, we are proud to offer Brand X. All ads that heavily relied on an emotional appeal to stimulate a consumer were classified in the second sub-category, i.e., EMOTIONAL. Those using the emotions of fear or guilt were placed in the respective minor categories. Ads that made the consumer the focal point were placed in yet another minor category. The next sub-category, FINANCIAL, was used to identify all of those ads that emphasized the financial aspects either directly through money-off coupons (first minor category) or through subsidizing certain causes (second minor category). The theme in the next sub-category, EUPHORIA, was intended to capture all the ads emphasizing a sense of well-being. Typically a sense of euphoria was invoked either by emphasizing the health aspects or the use of natural ingredients; these determined placement of an ad in the appropriate minor category. The last sub-category, MANAGEMENT, was used to identify ads implying that the corporate entity was, in some sense, proactively involved in the green movement. If the message ascribed a fair degree of management control through a conscious programmatic effort, then the ad was placed in the first minor category, i.e., control. However, an ad was placed in the second minor category, i.e. social responsibility, if the message generally emphasized that characteristic of the corporate sponsor.

CODING

The two researchers themselves acted as the two coders in this study. This does not pose any particular problem of a bias since there were no *à priori* hypotheses to be tested. Rather, this study is in the tradition of grounded theory (Glaser and Strauss, 1967) wherein the data are analyzed, not with any preconceived hypothesis to support, but with the intent of seeing a pattern emerge. Both the coders simultaneously coded the ads, and any discrepancies were discussed till there was agreement. This one-step procedure was possible because the coding scheme was quite simple. Moreover, being a preliminary attempt at analyzing green ads, we felt that our coding method was satisfactory and adequate.

RESULTS

Given the nature of the data and the exploratory ground-up orientation of this study, (Glaser and Strauss, 1967) analysis of frequencies and cross-tabulation were thought to be the most appropriate techniques. The overall analysis of frequencies is presented in Table 4 and the cross-tabulation in Table 5.

From the analysis of AD TARGET, it is evident that planet preservation is the most extensively used target. This is consistent with the general perception that the green movement grew from environmental concerns. Witness, for instance, the description of the most visible green event, i.e., Earth Day, in the popular press (Begley, Hager, and Wright, *Newsweek,* March 26, 1990). The entire report speaks of the movement wherein corporations can be seen as "friends of the Earth" and corporations have set up "Save The Planet Departments" (ibid. p.60). The green movement, in order to sustain momentum and growth, will have to expand its target to include other concerns as well.

Advertisers appear to emphasize corporate image slightly more often than product/service itself, but the difference is rela-

TABLE 3
Segmentation by Consumer Motives

PLANET PASSIONATES	HEALTH FANATICS	ANIMAL LOVERS
Likely to belong to:	**Likely to belong to:**	**Likely to belong to:**
Sierra Club	Americans for Safe Food	Greenpeace
Natural Resources Defense Council	Mothers and Others Against Pesticides	World Wildlife Fund
American Rivers	National Coalition Against the Misuse of Pesticides	National Audubon Society
Rainforest Alliance		Earthwatch
Friends of the Earth		Humane Society
Keep America Beautiful		The Nature Conservancy
		People for the Ethical Treatment of Animals
Likely environmental behavior:	**Likely environmental behavior:**	**Likely environmental behavior:**
Conserve energy, water	Buy organic foods and bottled water	Boycott tuna, ivory
Recycle bottles, cans	Use sunscreens	Buy "cruelty-free" cosmetics
Buy recycled paper	Buy unbleached coffee filters	Avoid fur
Avoid excessive packaging	Read *Organic Gardening*	Boycott Exxon
Buy cloth diapers	Read *Prevention*	Read *Animal Agenda*
Read *Garbage* magazine		

Source: J. Ottman Consulting

---

tively small. We are not exactly sure about the implication of this finding; we can merely offer a speculative view. Stern and Resnik (1991) replicated an earlier study by Resnik and Stern (1977) and found that other than institutional advertising, information content in advertising had generally increased. In the case of institutional advertising, the reduction in the number of information cues was dramatic (Stern and Resnik, 1991, p. 41, Table 2). since we found more than one-half of the green ads emphasizing corporate image, we can speculate that green advertising may suffer from low information content, thereby leading to its low credibility (Ottman, 1991) and it being perceived as deceptive exploitation (*Newsweek*, March 26, 1990, p.60).

Based upon our analysis of ECOCHAIN, one striking conclusion was that the three-way categorization was not applicable to over one-half of the ads. For those ads that could be categorized using this scheme, most emphasis was placed on the production phase of the chain.

Within this category, advertising copy typically emphasized the use of ecologically friendly raw materials most often. It is clear that advertisers view the production emphasis as a key one in wooing the green consumer. Disposition was emphasized less frequently than production, although it was moderately frequent in and of itself. With the increasing awareness on subjects like landfill wastes and ever growing laws that regulate disposal behavior (e.g., bottle redemption) it is hardly surprising that disposition is emphasized in over one-third of the green ads.

The concept of locus of control can be gainfully used to shed additional light on the distribution of the ecochain categories. Emphasis on production, whether it be raw materials or process, clearly places the locus of control with the corporate sponsor. That message suggests that the corporate entity is behaving responsibly and being sensitive to the green issues. On the other hand, an ad emphasizing disposition, suggests that the locus of control is shared by the corporate entity and the consumer, although the onus of responsibility lies with the consumer. The implication is that the consumer must behave in a responsible manner and contribute her/his mite by regulating her/his disposal behavior. This approach has the advantage of bringing a consumer into the green movement thereby benefitting the corporate sponsor as well.

We felt that AD APPEAL was the most important variable. Hence, we decided to crosstabulate the frequency distributions of AD OBJECTIVE and ECOCHAIN, respectively, with AD APPEAL. These results are presented in Table 5; both the results were significant ($p<0.001$). Rather than describe all aspects of these results, in this portion of the discussion, we will selectively highlight aspects worthy of discussion.

The financial appeal, for example, was skewed more toward corporate image advertising. A further breakdown of the financial appeal into its two subcomponents, i.e., cause subsidy and money-off, was very striking. All those that were categorized as "cause-subsidy" (7) were used to promote a corporate image exclusively, whereas "money-off" ads (4) were exclusively used in the case of product/service promotions. Clearly corporate image is better promoted by associating the corporate name with visible and/or major causes (Ross, Patterson, and Sutts; 1992). The other distribution of interest was that of Euphoria; it was mostly used for promoting product/services rather than a corporate image. The one exception was a case when an attempt to build a corporate image was made by emphasizing the use of only natural ingredients.

The crosstabulation of AD APPEAL and ECOCHAIN resulted in many sparse cells since a large number of ads could not be classified under this scheme. In light of this, emphasis on statistical significance must be softened. Nonetheless, there were interesting patterns worthy of discussion. For instance, consumption was rarely used in many of the appeals. However, production and disposition were more extensively used. The use of financial

TABLE 4
Analysis of Frequencies

		# OF ADS	%	% NOT INCL. N/A
I. AD TARGET				
Planet Preservation		135	78.0%	
Animal Life Preservation		26	15.0	
Personal Health Preservation		12	7.0	
TOTAL		173	100.0%	
II. AD OBJECTIVE				
Corporate Image		96	55.5%	
Product/Service Characteristic		77	45.5	
Inputs	28 (36.4%)			
Packaging	26 (33.8%)			
Overall	17 (22.0%)			
Others	6 (7.0%)			
TOTAL		173	100.0%	
III. ECOCHAIN				
Production		49	28.3%	59.0%
Raw Materials	37 (75.5%)			
Process	12 (24.5%)			
Consumption		6	3.5	7.3
Disposition		28	16.2	33.7
Not Applicable		90	52.0	—
TOTAL		173	100.0%	100.0%
IV. AD APPEAL				
Zeitgeist		55	31.8%	
Mere Statement	29 (52.7%)			
Bandwagon	26 (47.3%)			
Emotional		36	20.8	
Fear	9 (25.0%)			
Guilt	10 (27.7%)			
You	17 (47.3%)			
Financial		14	8.1	
Money-off	7 (50.0%)			
Cause Subsidy	7 (50.0%)			
Euphoria		15	8.7	
Health	6 (40.0%)			
Natural	9 (60.0%)			
Management		38	22.0	
Control	19 (50.0%)			
Social Resp.	19 (50.0%)			
Others		15	8.7	
Comparison	4 (26.6%)			
Exemplar	10 (66.7%)			
Celebrity	1 (6.7%)			
TOTAL		173	100.0%	

TABLE 5
Crosstabulation of Frequencies

I. AD APPEAL X AD OBJECTIVE

AD OBJECTIVE	AD APPEAL						TOTAL
	Zeitgeist	Emotional	Financial	Euphoria	Management	Others	
Corporate	29	20	10	1	23	13	96
Prod./Serv.	26	16	4	14	15	2	77
TOTAL	55	36	14	15	38	15	173

II. AD APPEAL X ECOCHAIN

ECOCHAIN	AD APPEAL						TOTAL
	Zeitgeist	Emotional	Financial	Euphoria	Management	Others	
Production	10	7	0	13	14	5	49
Consumption	1	4	0	1	0	0	6
Disposition	14	4	3	0	5	2	28
TOTAL	25	15	3	14	19	7	83*

*This crosstabulation was not applicable to 90 of the 173 ads, and hence the smaller grand total.

appeals (3) was exclusively related to disposition; even more interesting was that all these appeals were of the "money-off" type. Euphoria was almost exclusively used (13) with production. Clearly advertises found it easy to associate health and naturalness with their production capabilities.

CONCLUSION

This was an exploratory attempt in categorizing green ads; nonetheless we cautiously advance three broad recommendations to green advertisers and leaders of the green movement. We found that green ads were most often associated with planet preservation and other environmental issues. The implied target of the green movement is much broader in scope; however, our results show that the target of green advertising is very limited in their scope. Thus, our first recommendation would be that other targets will have to be addressed more directly and more frequently by the advertising community. In fact, that may be the only way to sustain a continued expansion of the green movement.

We also found that corporate image ads were more frequent than product oriented ads. As we have stated earlier in the paper, this alone does not account for the low credibility of green ads. Nonetheless green ads are plagued by low credibility (Economist, 1990) thereby leading to many governmental probes (Lawrence and Freeman, 1990). Our second recommendation would be for the advertising community to be proactive and create a standard lexicon for many over used word such as "environmentally friendly", "recyclable", "safe", and "natural". In fact, government regulators have already initiated work in this regard. The advertising community can go a long way in assuaging consumers' feelings and ward off potential backlash by adopting a proactive and cooperative stance.

Lastly, we found that consumption was rarely emphasized in green ads; the predominant emphasis was on production. This is almost like a throwback to the pre-marketing era from which we have emerged. Our third and final recommendation would be that green advertisers adopt the fundamental marketing maxim, i.e., emphasize the consumer and consumption, not the producer and production.

REFERENCES

Abt Associates, Inc. (1990), *Environmental Consumerism in the U.S.*

Begley, Sharon, Mary Hager, and Lynda Wright (1990), "The Selling of Earth Day", *Newsweek*, (March 26), 60-61.

Bremner, Brian (1989), "The New Sales Pitch: The Environment", *Business Week*, (July 24), 50.

The Economist (1990), "Marketing Greenery. Friendly to Whom?" (April 7), 83.

Glaser, B.J. and A.L. Strauss (1967), *The Discovery of Grounded Theory*, Chicago: Aldine.

Hinds, Michael de Courcy (1989), "In Sorting Trash, Householders Get Little Help From Industry", *New York Times*, (July 29).

Kotler, Philip and Sidney J. Levy (1969), "Broadening the Concept of Marketing", *Journal of Marketing*, 33, (January), 10-15.

Lawrence, Jennifer and Laurie Freeman (1990), Marketers Study State Guidelines", *Advertising Age*, Vol. 61 (47), (November 12), 74.

New York Times/CBS News Poll (1990), (April).

Nicosia, Francesco M. and Robert N. Mayer (1976), "Toward a Sociology of Consumption", *Journal of Consumer Research*, 3, (September), 65-75.

Ottman, J. (1991), *Environmental Consumerism: What Every Marketer Needs to Know*, J. Ottman Consulting, Inc.: New York:

Pollay, Richard W. (1985), "The Subsiding Sizzle: A Descriptive History of Print Advertising, 1900-1980," *Journal of Marketing*, 49, 24-37.

Resnick, Alan J. and Bruce L. Stern (1977), "An Analysis of Information Content in Television Advertising", *Journal of Marketing*, 41 (1), 50-53.

The Roper Organization (1990), *The Environment: Public Attitudes and Individual Behavior*, commissioned by S. C. Johnson and Son.

Ross, John K., Larry T. Patterson, and Mary Ann Stutts (1992), "Consumer Perceptions of Organizations that use Cause-Related Marketing", *Journal of the Academy of the Marketing Science*, (Winter), Vol. 20 (1), 93-97.

Russell, Thomas J. and Ronald Lane (1991), *Kleppner's Advertising Procedure*, Englewood Cliffs, N.J.: Prentice Hall.

Schwartz, Joe and Thomas Miller (1991), "The Earth's Best Friends", *American Demographics*, (February), 26-35.

Scott Paper Company Study (1990), (March) cited in Ottman (1991).

Shimp, Terence A., Joel E. Urbany, and Sarah E. Camlin (1988), "The Use of Framing and Characterization for Magazine Advertising of Mass-Marketed Products", *Journal of Advertising*, Vol. 17 (1), 23-30.

Simmons Market Research Bureau, Inc. (1990).

Stern, Bruce L. and Alan J. Resnick (1991), "Information Content in Television Advertising: A Republication and Extension", *Journal of Advertising Research*, (June/July), 36-46.

The Tyndull Report, cited in Ottman (1991).

Tse, David K., Russel W. Belk, and Nan Zhou (1989), "Becoming a Consumer Society: A Longitudinal and Cross Cultural Analysis of Print Ads from Hong Kong, The Peoples Republic of China and Taiwan", *Journal of Consumer Research*, 15, (4) (March), 457-472.

The Determinants of Consumer Satisfaction: The Moderating Role of Ambiguity
Youjae Yi, University of Michigan[1]

ABSTRACT

This study has investigated the moderating role of ambiguity in the process of consumer satisfaction formation. It is found that product ambiguity moderates the way that expectation, performance, and disconfirmation determine consumer satisfaction. When the product is ambiguous, consumer expectations have direct effects on consumer satisfaction as well as indirect effects through disconfirmation. On the other hand, when the product is unambiguous or easy to evaluate, product performance has direct effects on consumer satisfaction as well as indirect effects via disconfirmation. The theoretical and practical implications of these findings are discussed as well.

Consumer satisfaction (CS) is a central concept in modern marketing thought and practice. The marketing concept emphasizes delivering satisfaction to consumers and obtaining profits in return. As a result, overall quality of life is expected to be enhanced. Thus, consumer satisfaction is crucial to meeting various needs of consumers, business, and society. The realization of this importance has led to a proliferation of research on consumer satisfaction over the past two decades. Attempts to make significant contributions toward understanding this important area have been made, including numerous studies and annual conferences on consumer satisfaction/dissatisfaction and complaining behavior (e.g., Hunt and Day 1982, 1985; Oliver 1980). See Yi (1990) for a recent review.

Out of this empirical research has come the confirmation/disconfirmation paradigm whereby consumer satisfaction is hypothesized to result from a process of comparison. Theoretical support for this model comes from the adaptation level theory positing that one perceives stimuli only in relation to an adapted standard (Helson 1964). The standard is a function of perceptions of the stimulus, the context, and the organism. Once created, the adaptation level serves to guide subsequent evaluations in that positive and negative deviations will remain in the general vicinity of one's original position. Oliver (1980) applied this theory to the study of consumer satisfaction by arguing that expectations about product performance can be seen as an adaptation level. He suggested that expectations create a frame of reference for comparative judgments.

According to the model, consumers judge satisfaction with a product in comparison with their expectations about the product performance. If the performance is above the expectations, an increase in satisfaction is expected. If the performance is below expectations, a decrease in satisfaction is expected. Disconfirmation is thus expected to affect consumer satisfaction. Oliver (1980) found that disconfirmation was positively related to consumer satisfaction. Positive disconfirmation (perceived performance above the expectation) increased consumer satisfaction, while negative disconfirmation (perceived performance below the expectation) decreased consumer satisfaction. Thus, consumer satisfaction is hypothesized primarily as a function of disconfirmation.

Although many studies accept this paradigm, the exact nature of CS processes is not so straightforward. For example, one might ask a question: What is the role of perceived performance in the CS model? One might view perceived performance merely as a standard for comparison to assess the confirmation or disconfirmation. In this view, all influences of perceived performance on CS are expected to be captured by disconfirmation. Another view is that perceived performance has its own influence on CS as another predictor. That is, perceived performance is expected to have a direct effect on CS, in addition to the indirect effect through disconfirmation.

The findings as to this issue are mixed. Some studies have found the direct effect of perceived performance on CS (e.g., Churchill and Surprenant 1982; Oliver and DeSarbo 1988; Tse and Wilton 1988). Oliver and DeSarbo (1988), for example, have found that perceived performance has its own effect on CS; in fact, the importance of perceived performance was second only to that of disconfirmation. Tse and Wilton (1988) also examined the role of perceived performance in consumer satisfaction formation with a tape recorder. The model with perceived performance outperformed other single predictor models with expectations or disconfirmation, and two-variable models with expectations and disconfirmation. In addition, perceived performance had indirect effects on consumer satisfaction through its influence on perceived disconfirmation. Thus, perceived performance seemed to have both direct and indirect effects (through its effect on disconfirmation) on satisfaction. Consumer satisfaction could be increased not only by minimizing disconfirmation, but also by increasing performance. On the other hand, the direct effect of perceived performance has not been examined or significant in other studies (e.g., Cadotte, Woodruff, and Jenkins 1987; Oliver 1980).

Another question might arise: What is the role of expectation in the CS model? That is, does it influence CS indirectly only through disconfirmation? Or does it affect CS directly as well? The findings are again mixed. On the one hand, some studies have found the direct effect of expectations on CS, in addition to the indirect effect mediated by disconfirmation (Bearden and Teel 1983; Churchill and Surprenant 1982, plant; Oliver and Linda 1981; Swan and Trawick 1981; Tse and Wilton 1988; Westbrook and Reilly 1983). On the other hand, the direct path from expectation to CS was not examined or significant in other studies (e.g., Cadotte, Woodruff and Jenkins 1987; Churchill and Surprenant 1982, video disc player; Oliver and Bearden 1983). For example, Oliver and Bearden (1983) found that expectations did not have any significant effects on consumer satisfaction, although the effect of disconfirmation was found.

In summary, there are mixed findings as to the antecedents of consumer satisfaction. Consumer satisfaction was found to be directly affected by expectations in some studies. On the other hand, some studies showed that expectation had little effect on consumer satisfaction, while perceived performance had a significant effect on consumer satisfaction. See Figure 1 for an overview.

These findings suggest that the effects of expectation and performance on consumer satisfaction may be more complex than hypothesized by the original expectation-disconfirmation model. How can we resolve the issue? The present study attempts to shed new light on this issue by taking a different perspective. Rather than asking whether or not there is a direct effect of a certain variable (e.g., expectation) on satisfaction, one can ask the following question: When does a certain variable have a direct effect on satisfaction? In other words, a shift is proposed from the "Is" question to

---

[1]This research is in part supported by the Sanford R. Robertson Assistant Professorship at the Michigan Business School. I wish to thank Kent Nassen for his assistance in this research project.

FIGURE 1
Expectation Disconfirmation Model of CS

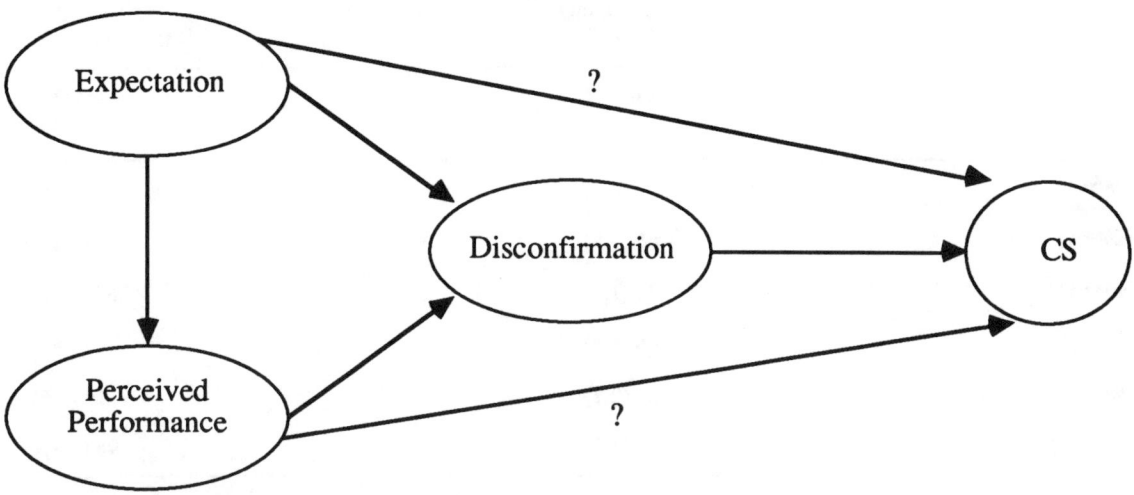

the "When" question. The purpose of this study is therefore to identify conditions under which the effects of expectations, disconfirmation, and performance on satisfaction would be strong or weak. Specifically, product ambiguity is proposed as a moderator of the CS formation process.

THE ROLE OF AMBIGUITY IN CS PROCESSES

The above review suggests that the views vary across studies as to how expectation, disconfirmation, and product performance influence CS. One factor in particular that has been overlooked is the degree to which ambiguity associated evaluation of the product affects CS. In other words, how does product ambiguity moderates the formation of CS?

Product experience can often be ambiguous, such as when the quality of a product is difficult to evaluate. The difficulty may arise when a product (e.g., clothes or insurance) cannot be judged based on objective criteria, or when a product (e.g., diamond) may have many credence qualities or subjective attributes (Darby and Karni 1973; Holbrook 1978). Alternatively, there might be a potential for multiple interpretations of product quality (e.g., Hoch and Deighton 1989). Sometimes it is difficult to determine what is acceptable, desired, or valued from the product. If product experience is difficult to evaluate or ambiguous, consumers are likely to lack confidence about their performance ratings.

The concept of ambiguity can be illustrated by looking at compact disc players. When compact disc players first came on the market, many consumers did not know how to judge what made a good compact disc player. Even after a number of years on the market, it is still difficult to evaluate compact disc players as they offer many different features, come in different sizes and power capacities, produce very different sound reproduction levels, and vary greatly in price. This example suggests that product evaluations can often be ambiguous.

It is proposed in this study that ambiguity will affect the relative importance of predictor variables on satisfaction. Human judgements in general pose a contest between expectations and evidence, prior expectations and situational information, or theory and data (Alloy and Tabachnik 1984; Bobrow and Norman 1975). In the context of consumer satisfaction, expectations are consumers' a priori theories about the product, whereas product performance represent the influence of the data or evidence provided in a given situation. When products are ambiguous, consumers' satisfaction is hypothesized to be determined largely by their prior expectations. If there is no objective way of judging a product, consumers may subjectively judge the product based on prior expectations. That is, consumers use a top-down, theory-driven process to judge satisfaction. Such an assimilative processing has been found when the evidence is ambiguous (Herr, Sherman and Fazio 1982; Hoch and Deighton 1989). Ambiguous information is easy to assimilate because consumers believe that ambiguous evidence is not actually ambiguous (Hoch and Ha 1986). Self-perception theory also suggests that consumers will reply on internal cues such as prior expectations when confronted with ambiguous information.

When products are unambiguous or easy to evaluate, on the other hand, consumers are likely to follow a bottom-up, data-driven process to evaluate a consumption experience. Unambiguous evidence is difficult to assimilate, because the evidence is relatively obvious and clear to the consumers. In such cases, perceptions of product performance are formed with conviction and they should be highly diagnostic in the formation of CS. That is, for products which can be objectively judged, consumers are certain of the performance levels of the products. Thus, when products are unambiguous, consumers' satisfaction judgements would be determined primarily by product performance.

Based on the above arguments, the following hypotheses are proposed.

H1. When product experience is ambiguous, consumer expectation is highly likely to have direct effects on CS.
H2. When product experience is unambiguous, product performance is highly likely to have direct effects on CS.

METHOD

A pretest was conducted to determine which products are easy or difficult to evaluate. Forty one students at the University of Michigan participated in the pretest. They rated the difficulty of evaluating product quality for twenty categories on a ten-point

TABLE 1
Summary of Results

Path	Lo ambiguity (cereal) estimate (t-value)	Hi ambiguity (laundry detergent) estimate (t-value)
E → P	.43 (4.9)	.69 (8.6)
E → D	−.66 (9.5)	−.40 (3.2)
E → CS	.32 (1.3)	.67 (3.0)
P → D	.66 (8.8)	.50 (3.6)
P → CS	.67 (2.7)	.19 (.74)
D → CS	.60 (1.8)	.98 (2.9)
Fit	$\chi^2(14)=27.71$ p = .02 GFI = .95	$\chi^2(14)=34.39$ p = .002 GFI = .93

Note: E = expectation, D = disconfirmation, P = performance, CS = consumer satisfaction

scale. From these twenty products two were to be selected and used in the main study. Ten of the products were low-involvement, frequently purchased products, whereas the other ten products were high-involvement, infrequently purchased products. These products were considered familiar to the potential subjects of the study. Comparison of these products were also made with regard to the following: the amount of information seeking done before the purchase decision and the relative importance of the product.

Laundry detergent, insurance, aspirin, camera, microwave oven, and computer were rated among the difficult to evaluate, whereas soft drinks, cereal, jeans, and ball-point pen were rated as easy to evaluate. Cereal and laundry detergent were selected as low and high ambiguity products, respectively, based on the mean ratings on difficulty of evaluation (Ms=2.75 vs. 6.27, p<.001). These products were relatively similar in other aspects such as information seeking and importance.

A main study was then conducted to compare the CS processes across low and high ambiguity products. Subjects consisted of 117 business students at the University of Michigan who were asked to respond to a consumer satisfaction survey. They were first asked to state the brand of laundry detergent that they had most recently purchased. The most recently purchased brand was chosen because the preferred brand may not have been purchased most recently, and the image brought forth by the preferred brand may present biases in consumers' judgments of the products. They were then asked to evaluate the most recently purchased brand. Next, they were asked similar questions about the cereal. Thus, each subjected responded to the surveys for both laundry detergent and cereal.

Multiple measures were used to assess key constructs. For example, two measures of perceived performance were taken. One measure consisted of the following question: "How do you evaluate the quality of of the detergent (cereal) after having experience with it?" A 7-point scale was used to record responses (1=very low, 7=very high). Another measure was obtained by asking how good each respondent found the detergent (cereal) to be. Similarly, each of the other key constructs (expectation, disconfirmation, and consumer satisfaction) were measured with two indicators.

Three measures were obtained to ascertain that product ambiguity indeed varied between the two products as expected. First, the absolute difficulty of evaluation was assessed by asking respondents "Overall, how difficult was it to evaluate this product?" The responses were given on the 7-point scale (1=very easy, 7=very difficult). The mean ratings showed that there were expected variations in ambiguity (Ms=4.72 vs. 6.07, p<.01). Second, the relative measure of evaluation difficulty was obtained with a question "How difficult was it to evaluate this product, compared to an ink pen?" The responses ranged from "much easier" (1) to "much more difficult." The results indicated that cereal was considered easier than laundry detergent (Ms=3.28 vs. 5.14, p<.01). Third, subjects' confidence in evaluation was measured by asking them how confident they were in their judgments of the product quality. As expected, subjects had less confidence in the evaluation of laundry detergent than that of cereal (Ms=4.20 vs. 5.83, p<.01). These manipulation checks showed that the two products were indeed different in ambiguity.

In addition, the importance of the product was also measured and compared. The results showed that there was no significant difference in the importance of the product to respondents. This check gave a rough indication that there was no confounding of ambiguity and involvement in the study.

RESULTS

The model in Figure 1 was estimated for the laundry detergent (high ambiguity) and cereal (low ambiguity) products, respectively. Since multiple measures were available for all constructs, the data were analyzed via LISREL. Table 1 provides a summary of results.

When the model was fit to the cereal data, it gave the following results: χ^2 (14)=27.71, p=.02, GFI=.95. The direct path from performance to CS was .67, which is statistically significant at the 0.5 level. On the other hand, the direct effect of expectation on CS was .32, which is not significant. These results supported the hypothesis that product performance is likely to have direct effects for low ambiguity products.

FIGURE 2
CS Processes Under Low and High Ambiguity

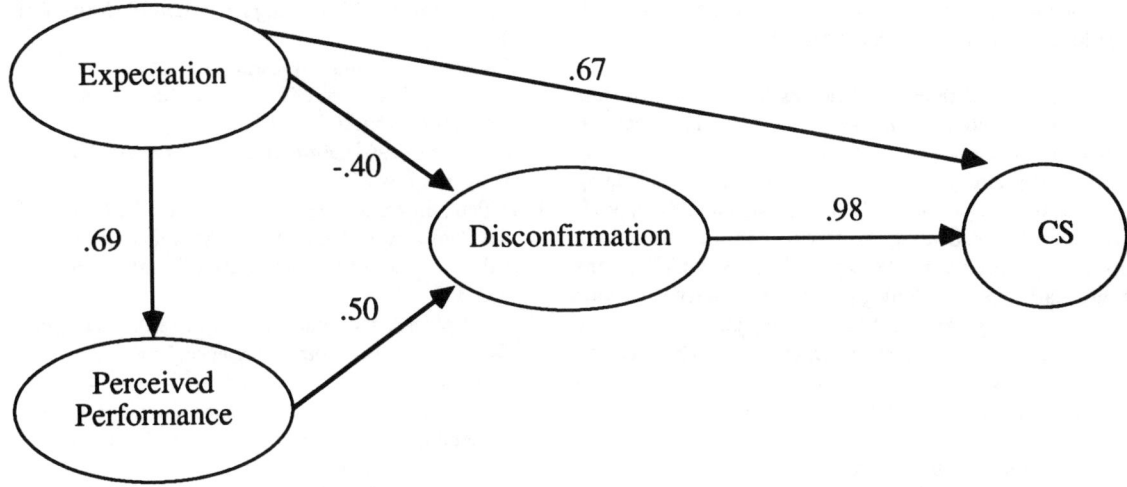

CS Process for High Ambiguity (Laundry Detergent)

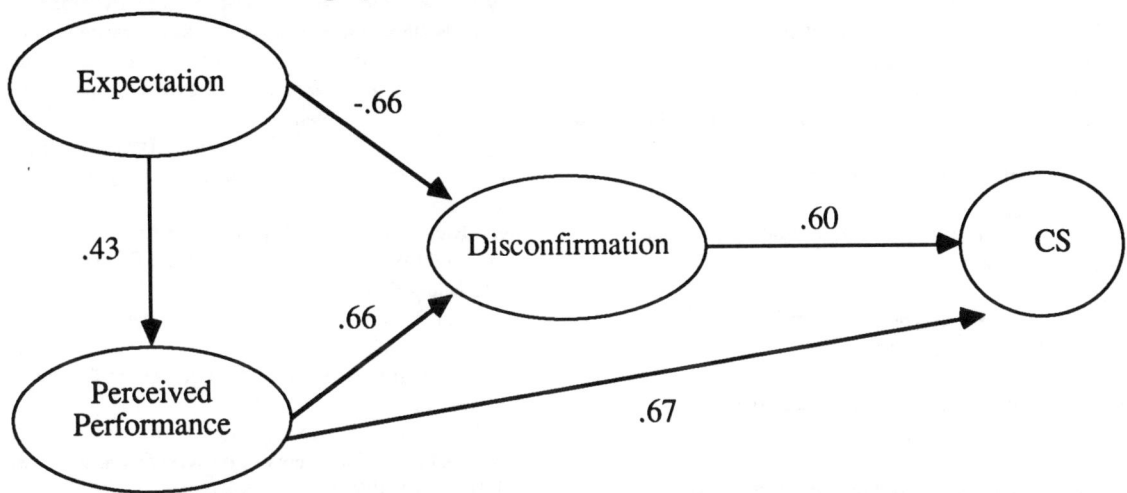

CS Process Under Low Ambiguity (Cereal)

The model was also fit to the laundry detergent data, and the following results were obtained: $\chi^2(14)=34.39$, p=.002, GFI=.93. The direct effect of performance on CS was not significant (.19 with the t-value of .74), whereas the direct effect of expectation on CS was significant (.67 with the t-value of 3.0). These results supported the hypothesis that expectation is likely to have direct effects on CS for high ambiguity products.

Figure 2 provides a summary of key results in the model. Only significant paths are included in this figure to gain a better understanding of the CS processes. We can note several findings that are common to low and high ambiguity products. First, expectation and performance had significant effects on disconfirmation, which in turn had significant effects on CS. That is, expectation and performance had indirect effects on CS through disconfirmation for both products. Second, perceived performance was influenced by expectation under low and high ambiguity.

We can also note some interesting differences between low and high ambiguity products. First, the direct effect of expectation was significant under high product ambiguity, but not under low product ambiguity. Second, the direct effect of performance was significant under low product ambiguity, but not under high ambiguity. Third, the impact of expectation on performance was greater under high ambiguity than under low ambiguity. Fourth, the model fit was better under low ambiguity than under high ambiguity.

DISCUSSION

The findings of the present study have several implications. First, it suggests that the nature of CS process varies across product categories. This result challenges the implicit assumption of the conventional model that CS formation processes are the same across product categories. Specifically, when products are ambiguous, the direct effect of expectation increases and the direct effect of performance is reduced. When products are unambiguous, the direct effect of expectation decreases and the direct effect of performance increases. Thus, a marketer needs to know how ambiguous the product is for a better understanding of the CS process.

This study has implications for advertising as well. If a marketer has discovered that he or she has an ambiguous product, then the marketer might wish to create high expectations. The marketer can make claims that can neither be proved nor disproved. Emotional, rather than rational, appeals could be used in the promotion campaign to build up consumer expectations. When products are ambiguous and the performance cannot be directly observed or tested, consumer expectations are likely to influence product evaluations and satisfaction judgments. On the other hand, when products are unambiguous, the role of expectations will be reduced.

The finding has different implications for topdog marketers (market leaders) and underdog marketers (new or existing companies with market share below topdogs). The marketers of topdog products would benefit by increasing subjective criteria for judging their products, because consumers' expectations would color product evaluations. Provided that consumer expectations about topdog products are high, their evaluations would be favorable. On the other hand, marketers of underdog products should try to educate consumers on how products can be objectively judged, especially if the underdog product is in fact comparable to or better than the topdog product. Having a comparable or superior product may not lead to higher CS, if the product is viewed ambiguous by consumers.

Some limitations of the present study should be noted. We have measured product ambiguity in a survey, rather than manipulating it in an experiment. One may need to manipulate ambiguity in a controlled experiment. This would ensure that one is in fact testing the effects of ambiguity and not some other confounding factors. Also, the current operationalization of ambiguity is rather limited, and one should find a better way to measure or determine the level of ambiguity associated with a product. The following are additional questions that may help one to determine the degree of ambiguity associated with a product.

Do you think that everyone would evaluate this product on the same attributes?

How many attributes do you think people use to evaluate this product? List as many as you can.

How easy or difficult is it for you to choose criteria with which to judge this product?

List characteristics which you feel make this product easy or difficult to evaluate.

Which of the following words (phrases) best describes the process of evaluating this product: easy-difficult, quick-slow, consistent-inconsistent, etc.?

REFERENCES

Alloy, Lauren B. and Naomi Tabachnik (1984), "Assessment of Covariation by Humans and Animals: The Joint Influence of Prior Expectations and Current Situational Information," *Psychological Review*, 91 (January), 112-149.

Bearden, William O. and Jesse E. Teel (1983), "Selected Determinants of Consumer Satisfaction and Complaint Reports," *Journal of Marketing Research*, 20 (February), 21-28.

Bobrow, Daniel G. and Donald A. Norman (1975), "Some Principles of Memory Schemata," in *Representation and Understanding: Studies in Cognitive Science*, eds. D. G. Bobrow and A. Collins, New York: McGraw-Hill.

Cadotte, Ernest R., R. B. Woodruff, R. L. Jenkins (1987), "Expectations and Norms in Models of Consumer Satisfaction," *Journal of Marketing Research*, 24 (August), 305-314.

Churchill, Gilbert A., Jr. and C. Surprenant (1982), "An Investigation into the Determinants of Customer Satisfaction," *Journal of Marketing Research*, 19 (November), 491-504.

Darby, Michael R. and Edi Karni (1973), "Free Competition and the Optimal Amount of Fraud," *Journal of Law and Economics*, 16 (April), 67-88.

Helson, Harry (1964), *Adaptation-level Theory*, New York: Harper & Row.

Herr, Paul, Steven J. Sherman, and Russell H. Fazio (1982), "On the Consequences of Priming: Assimilation and Contrast Effects," *Journal of Experimental Social Psychology*, 19, 323-340.

Hoch, Stephen J. and John Deighton (1989), "Managing What Consumers Learn from Experience," *Journal of Marketing*, 53 (April), 1-20.

_____ and Y. Ha (1986), "Consumer Learning: Advertising and the Ambiguity of Product Experience," *Journal of Consumer Research*, 13 (September), 221-233.

Holbrook, Morris B. (1978), "Beyond Attribute Structure: Toward the Informational Determinants of Attitude," *Journal of Marketing Research*, 15 (November), 545-556.

Hunt, H. Keith and Ralph L. Day (1982), *Conceptual and Empirical Contributions to Consumer Satisfaction and Complaining Behavior*, Bloomington, IN: Indiana University.

_____ and _____ (1985), *Consumer Satisfaction, Dissatisfaction and Complaining Behavior*, Bloomington, IN: Indiana University.

Oliver, Richard L. (1980), "A Cognitive Model of the Antecedents and Consequences of Satisfaction Decisions," *Journal of Marketing Research*, 17 (September), 46-49.

_____ and William O. Bearden (1983), "The Role of Involvement in Satisfaction Processes," in *Advances in Consumer Research*, Ann Arbor, MI: Association for Consumer Research.

_____ and Wayne S. DeSarbo (1988), "Response Determinants in Satisfaction Judgments," *Journal of Consumer Research*, 14 (March), 495-507.

_____ and G. Linda (1981), "Effects of Satisfaction and Its Antecedents on Consumer Preference and Intention," in *Advances in Consumer Research*, Kent B. Monroe, ed. Ann Arbor, MI: Association for Consumer Research, 88-93.

Swan, John. E. and I. Frederick Trawick (1981), "Disconfirmation of Expectations and Satisfaction with a Retail Service," *Journal of Retailing*, 57 (Fall), 49-67.

Tse, David K. and Peter C. Wilton (1988), "Models of Consumer Satisfaction: An Extension," *Journal of Marketing Research*, 25 (May), 204-12.

Westbrook, Robert and Michael D. Reilly (1983), "Value-Percept Disparity: An Alternative to the Disconfirmation of Expectations Theory of Consumer Satisfaction," in *Advances in Consumer Research*, Richard P. Bagozzi and Alice M. Tybout, eds. Ann Arbor, MI: Association for Consumer Research.

Yi, Youjae (1990), "A Critical Review of Consumer Satisfaction," in *Review of Marketing 1990*, ed. Valarie A. Zeithaml, Chicago; American Marketing Association, 68-123.

Expectations Versus Desires: A Direct Test of Two Comparison Standards Assessing Consumer Satisfaction

Richard A. Spreng, Michigan State University
Scott B. MacKenzie, Indiana University
Richard W. Olshavsky, Indiana University

While the disconfirmation of expectations model has dominated research on consumer satisfaction, recently this model has been challenged on both conceptual and empirical grounds. A number of comparison standards other than expectations have been suggested. This paper suggests that the consumer's desires should be utilized as the appropriate standard, and defines desires within means-end theory (Gutman 1982). The study reports the preliminary results of a study that allows a direct comparison between the disconfirmation of expectations and desires congruency (how closely performance matches desires). Results indicated that the effect of desires congruency on satisfaction is very strong, while disconfirmation has little or no effect. The results of the relative effect of desires congruency and disconfirmation should induce businesses to adopt desires rather than expectations as the standard for both measuring satisfaction as well as the goal toward which the organization strives. Other implications are discussed.

Hey You, Can Ya Spare Some Change? The Case of Empathy and Personal Distress As Reactions to Charitable Appeals

Mitch Griffin, Bradley University
Barry J. Babin, University of Southern Mississippi
Jill S. Attaway, Illinois State University
William R. Darden, Louisiana State University

One aspect of consumer behavior relevant to the nonprofit-sector is that of charitable giving. Compared to some other areas of nonprofit marketing, such as cause-related marketing (e.g., Varadarajan and Menon 1988; Ross, Patterson, and Stutts 1992), little academic research has investigated consumer responses to charitable appeals on behalf of individuals in need (c.f., Burnett and Wood 1988; Allen, Kent, and Barr 1992). On close inspection, this is somewhat surprising considering a growing interest in antecedents and consequences of consumer emotion (see Cohen and Areni 1991 and Babin, Darden, and Griffin 1992 for a review) and heightened levels of emotional involvement among consumers contemplating a decision to give or not to give to a charitable appeal (Mullen and Johnson 1990).

Recent studies have demonstrated the impact of emotion on consumer behavior in a number of different contexts. For example, emotions evoked by advertisements have been shown to affect consumer attitudes toward both the advertisement and the related brand (Burke and Edell 1989; Holbrook and Batra 1987), influence shopping behavior (Donovan and Rossiter 1982), and relate to consumer product evaluations (Westbrook and Oliver 1991). In addition, consumer emotions have been hypothesized as a major mediating variable in a comprehensive model of consumption experiences (Holbrook 1986). However, the role of consumer emotions associated with decisions to give to a charity has not been specifically addressed. The purpose of this study is to explore the effects of two specific and distinct emotions likely to be evoked by charitable appeals - true empathy (altruism) and personal distress - on the decision to give.

EMOTIONS AND HELPING BEHAVIOR

As revealed by a recent mega-analysis (Cialdini and Fultz 1990), a substantial number of studies appearing in the psychology literature have found a positive relationship between negative feelings and various types of helping behavior. However, the precise size and nature of this effect across different contexts remains a subject of debate (Carlson and Miller 1987). While a significant number of these studies focus on the general tone of emotional states (i.e., positive or negative) at the time one is presented with the opportunity to help, others concentrate on the specific emotions elicited by the exposure to the suffering of another person (e.g., Coke, Batson, and McDavis 1978). Two emotions, *personal distress* and *empathy*, have been shown to be common "emotional responses to seeing another person suffer" (Batson et al. 1983, p. 706). Although these emotions can both be evoked by the same situation (such as an encounter with a person in need), they have been shown to result in a unique reaction.

Empathy

Empathy can be defined "as an other-oriented emotional response congruent with the perceived welfare of another person [which] can evoke motivation to help that person" (Batson et al. 1988, p. 52). Further, empathy evokes motivations to act in a manner which directly benefits the suffering person rather than toward some direct form of self-benefit. Thus, empathy is based on the premise that some motivations are truly altruistic rather than egoistic in nature. Despite an element of debate (Cialdini et al. 1987), the majority of evidence appears to support an empathy-altruism hypothesis which implies that people do not always act in an egoistic manner (see Dovidio, Allen, and Schroeder 1990 or Batson et al. 1988 for reviews).

Although few personal variables have been found to consistently relate to empathy (Batson, Bolen, Cross, and Neuringer 1986), its presence appears to consistently lead to higher levels of helping behavior. For example, subjects reporting relatively high levels of empathy, when exposed to a compatriot participating ostensively in an "experiment" in which he/she receives electric shocks for incorrect responses, are more likely to volunteer to take his/her place than are other subjects (Batson and Coke 1981; Batson et al. 1986). High levels of empathy have also been associated with an increased willingness to associate with lonely people (Fultz et al. 1986) and a greater likelihood of participating in an experiment without any additional incentive over and above helping a researcher (Dovidio et al. 1990). In a more consumer-oriented study, increased empathy has been related to consumers' verdict awards in products liability suits (Darden et al. 1991). Given these effects, it is likely that increased empathy will influence consumer responses to a charitable appeal.

Personal Distress

In contrast to empathy, personal distress is an inner-oriented emotion that creates a concern more for one's own welfare or comfort than for that of the suffering person who elicited this negative feeling state (Batson and Coke 1981). Thus, personal distress motivates one toward actions that will alleviate personal discomfort which could often take the form of escaping the victim (Batson et al. 1983). To illustrate the distinction between distress and empathy, consider the following situation. Upon encountering a blind beggar on a downtown street, you could either feel true empathy or personal distress or some level of both. If empathy is the dominant emotion, an approach response is likely to be evoked that would involve a donation. If personal distress is operant, you may consider walking on the other side of the street to minimize contact with the beggar.

Personal distress has also been found to mediate behavior between a situation and a subsequent response. For example, in the shock experiments described above, subjects experiencing personal distress are highly unlikely to agree to take any shocks for the victim so long as it is easy to simply avoid the situation (Batson et al. 1983; Fultz et al. 1990). These same experiments, however, show that when a subject is presented with a situation that is not easy to escape, personal distress can also lead to helping behavior. In this case, such actions are taken in an effort to minimize personal discomfort rather than out of a desire to help the person in need. Ease of escape is generally manipulated by either telling a subject that he/she no longer has to watch a victim should he/she decide not to help, or that he/she must continue watching regardless of his/her decision. Alternatively, empathy/distress has been influenced by altering instructions to subjects with respect to elaborating the material presented (Batson et al. 1988). Thus, only under certain conditions, such as when difficulty to escape is high, will empathy and personal distress evoke similar responses.

HYPOTHESES

Empathy and personal distress appear highly relevant emotions to examine in an effort to understand consumers' decisions to make (or not to make) a charitable contribution and, if so, how much to give. We propose these two emotions are likely to mediate consumer behavior in a typical situation involving an opportunity to make a contribution. To explore this possibility, a number of hypotheses are introduced below. While the focus of the study is clearly on the effects of empathy and distress, two antecedent variables based on prior evidence are considered as well. Figure 1 helps to illustrate the relationships hypothesized in this study.

Gender Effect

While few individual difference characteristics have been found to reliably relate to situational levels of distress and empathy (Batson et al. 1986), some evidence suggests that females are likely to express higher levels of empathy and lower levels of distress than are their male counterparts (Batson and Coke 1981; Fultz et al. 1990). Therefore, men and women are expected to react differently in terms of their emotions upon encountering a charitable appeal. Thus, the following hypotheses are offered:

H1: A charitable appeal will evoke greater levels of empathy among women than among men.

H2: A charitable appeal will evoke greater levels of personal distress among men than among women.

In addition, an earlier study of donating behavior revealed a direct relationship between gender of respondents and intentions to give (Pessemier, Bemmaor, and Hanssens 1977). Pessemier et al. (1977) found that women are more likely to respond favorably to an appeal to donate body parts than are men. Thus, the following hypothesis is offered:

H3: Women will have greater intentions to give to a charitable appeal than will men.

Attributions

People naturally seek to find causes for events occurring in their environment (Kelley 1967). Weiner (1985) discusses how the dimensions of causality, in turn, affect subsequent emotional responses and behavior. For example, attributions can determine whether internally or externally-oriented emotions are evoked.

In a charitable giving situation, consumers are likely to ponder the potential causes of the object of sympathy's plight. Some consumers are likely to perceive the victim to be the primary cause of his/her plight while others will view external factors as having greater causal influence. If consumers view the victim as having little (great) control of his/her plight an empathetic response is more likely (unlikely) (Weiner 1985; Hoffman 1982). The differences among consumer responses can be illustrated by considering appeals designed to help alcoholics, the homeless, or AIDs victims. Some consumers are likely to see victims of these situations as primarily responsible for their own plight, while others will perceive the victim as helpless when compared to potential causal agents such as liquor manufacturers, childhood upbringing, or society at large. We suggest that assignment of causality is likely to affect emotional responses of consumers exposed to a sympathetic appeal. Thus, the following hypothesis is offered:

H4: Causal attributions assigned to the victim (other sources) will lead to greater (lower) levels of empathy.

While the effect of attributions on personal distress are less clear, some insights can be offered. Consumers perceiving an object of sympathy to have been relatively helpless, especially if they can easily see themselves in a similar situation, are likely to express greater levels of personal distress (Darden et al. 1991). Further, since empathy and personal distress are expected to have common antecedents (Batson et al. 1983), attributions can be expected to have the same or similar effects on each. Thus, the following hypothesis is offered:

H5: Causal attributions assigned to the victim (other sources) will lead to greater (lower) levels of personal distress.

Although we have depicted empathy and personal distress as intervening between causal attributions and helping behavior, it is not likely that these emotions totally mediate the relationship. In fact, we propose that assignment of blame will directly influence behavior in sympathy evoking situations as well. From a cognitive standpoint, consumers may be less likely to see the need to make a donation if the victim has some control over his/her condition. For example, in the case of careless use of a product, consumers were found to be less willing to indicate that compensation for the injured party was due (Darden et al. 1991). Thus, the following hypothesis is offered.

H6: Causal attributions assigned to the victim will directly relate to intentions to give to a charitable appeal.

Empathy and Distress

Considering that consumers encounter the majority of charitable appeals in situations where escape is relatively easy (such as the cash register of a convenience store, a can passed in a darkened movie theater, or a television commercial), different effects due to empathy and distress can be expected. While both empathy and distress can lead to helping behavior, empathy is more likely to be operant in these situations. Thus, the following hypotheses are offered.

H7a: A positive relationship exists between empathy and intentions to give.

H7b: The relationship between empathy and intentions to give is greater than the relationship between personal distress and intentions to give.

STUDY APPROACH

To investigate the issues presented above, respondents were presented with a written charitable appeal imbedded within other stories in a newsletter type format. The appeal described a man who had lost his vision while using a "weed-eater" to trim grass in his yard without the aid of protective goggles. He is described as being unable to work, without insurance, and unable to pay the accumulated $250,000 in medical bills. These conditions were structured in a manner that would allow variance among respondents in assigning responsibility for the victim's condition. The appeal asks for assistance to help with medical bills and future living expenses of day-to-day life. Respondents were told they would be evaluating the content of the materials they were instructed to peruse. Following exposure to the stimulus, respondents were presented a survey

FIGURE 1
Hypothesized Predictors of Intentions to Give

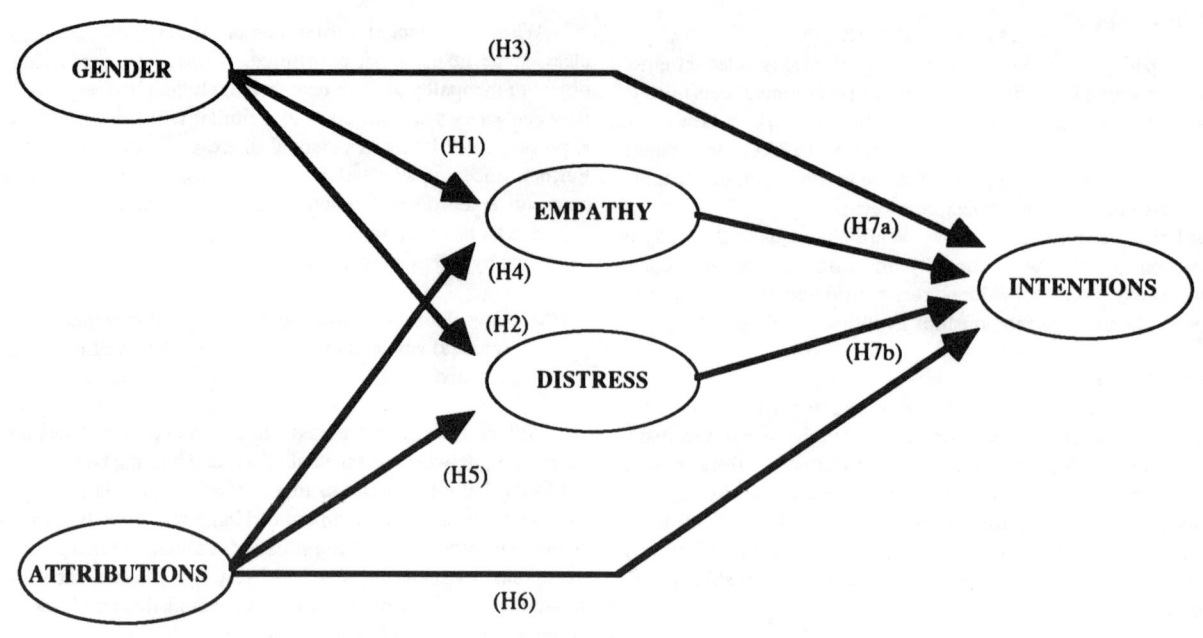

TABLE 1
Measures of Personal Distress and Empathy

Scale Item	Factor Loading 1	Factor Loading 2	Reliability
Distress			.8822
Alarmed	.6877	.2387	
Grieved	.7819	.2730	
Upset	.7705	.2335	
Worried	.7015	.1725	
Disturbed	.8045	.2339	
Perturbed	.6692	.1310	
Distressed	.7845	.2994	
Empathy			.9170
Troubled	.2388	.6801	
Sympathetic	.1730	.7569	
Moved	.2340	.7462	
Compassionate	.1976	.8317	
Tender	.2368	.8200	
Warm	.2144	.7772	
Softhearted	.2031	.7981	

instrument which included measures assessing their responses to the appeal for assistance.

To assess emotional responses to the appeal, scales developed and administered frequently to assess two pervasive emotional responses to another's suffering (empathy and personal distress) were administered (Coke et al. 1978; Batson and Coke 1981; Batson et al. 1983). Respondents were asked to record their responses to these items based on the charitable appeal on a 7-point scale ranging from "DID NOT FEEL" to "FELT VERY STRONGLY". Factor analysis of these items, the results of which are shown in Table 1, proved consistent with previous applications. Considering these results and the high coefficient α for each dimension, items for each scale were summed creating separate empathy and personal distress scales. Empathy and distress were simply measured rather than manipulated because previous studies have demonstrated similar results across both approaches (Batson et al. 1988).

Four items designed to assess causal attributions for the victim's plight were also included. Coefficient α for these items is .92 and thus they were summed to form one measure. High scores

TABLE 2
Results of Tests of Research Hypotheses

Hypothesis	Predictor Variable	→	Dependent Measure	Regression Equation	β	Level of Significance
H1	Gender	→	Empathy	1	.10	.0500
H2	Gender	→	Distress	2	.08	.1570
H3	Gender	→	Intentions	3	-.02	.9615
H4	Attrib.	→	Empathy	1	.32	.0001
H5	Attrib.	→	Distress	2	.20	.0010
H6	Attrib.	→	Intentions	3	.55	.0001
H7a	Empathy	→	Intentions	3	.15	.0100
H7b	Distress	→	Intentions	3	-.02	.7020

on the scale are indicative of a high amount of responsibility for the victim's own actions and low scores are indicative of causal attributions of blame to less controllable factors. Similarly, a four item scale was devised to assess intentions to give. The items express the likelihood that respondents would (would not) give as well as the amount that they would be likely to give. These items also achieved high reliability (a = .86) and were summed to form a single measure.

The data collection procedure followed the approach suggested by Abramson and Mosher (1975; Abramson, Goldberg, Abromson, and Gottesdiener 1975) and utilized by Feild (1978). Abramson and Mosher (1975) suggest using a large number of interviewers with varied demographic and personality traits in the data collection process in an effort to eliminate any interviewer bias. Following their suggested procedure, students enrolled in marketing research courses at a large midwestern university were thoroughly familiarized with the survey instrument, and received training in its administration. Each student completed interviews with four members of the urban community, excluding students and university personnel, in exchange for course credit. Telephone surveys were conducted with a subsample of the respondents to control the quality of the survey. In total, 468 research questionnaires were distributed and 384 questionnaires returned in usable form (response rate of 82.1%). The distribution of the sample closely matches that of the population across several demographic characteristics.

RESULTS

Three multiple regression analyses was conducted to test the hypotheses presented above. Table 2 shows the path coefficients obtained by estimating the multi-equation system. In terms of overall fit, each equation explained a significant portion of the variance in the dependent measure (p≤.001) providing justification for interpretation of the path estimates (Neter, Wasserman, and Kutner 1985).

The Effect of Gender

Hypotheses one, two, and three deal with effects of gender on empathy, distress, and intentions to give respectively. Of these, only H1 receives statistical support as indicated by estimating the path between gender (coded 1 = female) and consumer empathy. Female respondents reported modestly higher levels of empathy due to the appeal for a donation compared to male respondents (ß = .10, p≤.05).

The Effect of Attributions

Hypotheses four, five, and six represented relationships between consumer causal attributions of control or responsibility for the injury. Each of these hypothesized relationships is supported as indicated by its corresponding path estimate. Consistent with H4, respondents expressing a belief that the victim was responsible for his own condition expressed lower levels of empathy than did other respondents (ß = .32; p≤.0001). Likewise, H5 is supported by a significant and negative relationship between attributions of responsibility and feelings of distress expressed by respondents (ß = .20; p≤.001). Finally, H6, represented by the path between attributions and intentions to give, is also supported (ß= .55; p≤.0001). Respondents assigning high levels of responsibility for the injury to the victim expressed correspondingly lower intentions to give compared to others.

The Impact of Emotions

The last hypothesis posits two paths representing the direct impact of empathy and personal distress on intentions to give. As can be seen in Figure 2, a positive and significant relationship exists between levels of empathy expressed by respondents and intentions to give (ß = .15; p≤.01), supporting H7a. Further, support is found for H7b which suggested a stronger relationship between empathy and intentions to give (ß = .15) than would be found between distress and intentions to give (ß = -.02; p≥.6). That is, feelings of empathy appear more instrumental in creating intentions to make a charitable donation than are feelings of personal distress.

Finally, conceptual models of the role of emotion in consumer decision processes have posited emotions as a mediating variable (e.g., Holbrook 1986). In the context of this study, the emotions of empathy and personal distress were hypothesized to mediate relationships between intentions to give and cognitive antecedents such as causal attributions. However, since personal distress was not a significant predictor of intentions it could not be a mediator variable (see Baron and Kenny 1986). To examine the possibility of empathy as a mediator, a regression was run using only gender and attributions of responsibility to directly predict intentions to give; in other words, the model was retested using only direct effects due to gender and attributions (Baron and Kenny 1986). The estimate

FIGURE 2
The Effect of Predictor Variables on Intentions to Give

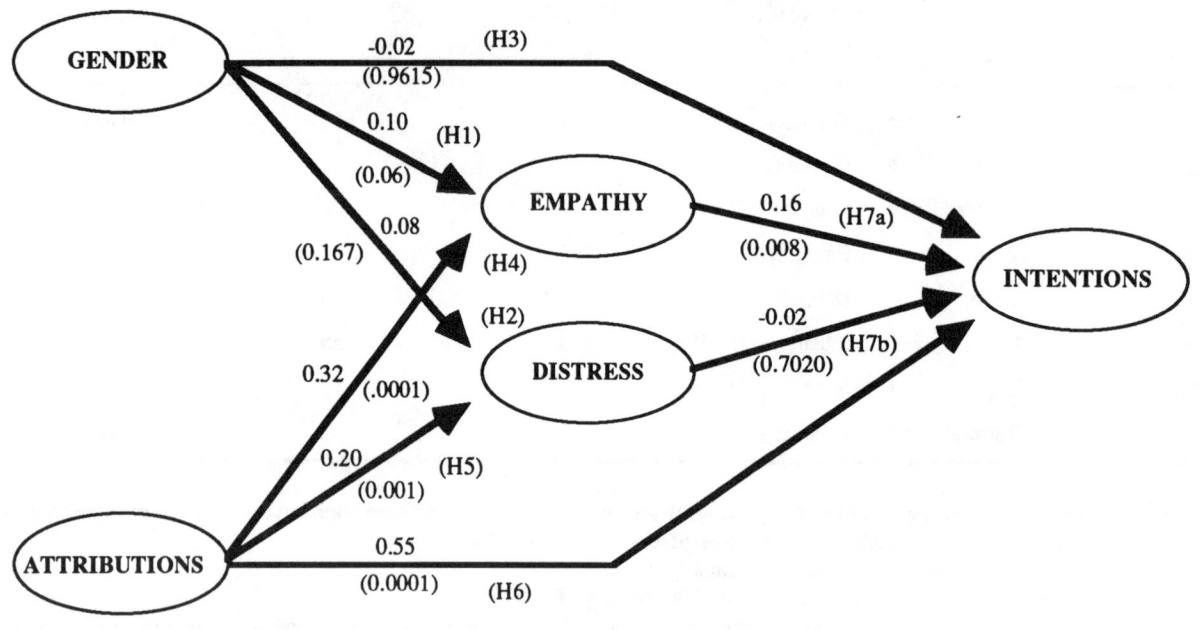

of the relationship between attributions and intentions to give (H6) obtained testing this model ($\beta = .75$; $p \leq .0001$) exceeds that obtained in a model including empathy as a mediating variable as shown above. This analysis illustrates that inclusion of empathy in the model of intentions to give to a charitable appeal attenuates the relationship between a cognitively oriented variable - attributions - and intentions to give. Thus, consistent with the role of emotions hypothesized by Holbrook (1986), evidence is presented that some degree of emotional mediation takes place when modeling consumption experiences involving charitable appeals similar to the one studied here.

The hypothesized relationships and the results of the statistical tests of these hypotheses are presented in Figure 2. The figures inside the (parentheses) are the level of significance, those without parentheses are ß coefficients.

DISCUSSION

This study examined the effects of select variables on intentions to give to a charitable appeal. In particular, the study shows that under conditions similar to those in which a charitable appeal is commonly encountered, feelings of empathy relate more strongly to, and lead to, greater intentions to give than do feelings of personal distress. The findings also empirically demonstrate that causal attributions have both a direct and indirect effect (through empathy) on intentions to give providing further support for a mediating role of consumer emotions in models of consumption experiences. This study also extends previous work into the effects of consumer emotions by demonstrating their relevance to understanding consumer intentions to give to a charitable appeal.

The results have significant and direct implications for charitable and non-profit organizations. To function effectively as a non-profit, organizations must receive help in the form of donor support and volunteer effort. Most of the appeals by charitable organizations stress the need for monetary contributions to cover administration costs, costs of educational and instructional materials, fund research efforts, and to provide service to the needy. As demonstrated by the results of this study, an empathy-evoking appeal will result in higher levels of charitable giving.

Charitable and non-profit organizations must also receive contributions in the form of volunteer time to accomplish their public education and fundraising goals and to provide personal service to the needy. For example, transportation to treatment centers for cancer patients and assisting AIDS victims are a common service provided by charitable organizations. While donations of time were not examined directly in this study, empathy-evoking pleas are likely to lead to higher levels of helping behavior in the form of volunteerism as well.

In both cases, however, the critical point is the distinction between appeals that evoke empathy and those giving rise to personal distress. Certainly making an emotional appeal is no secret to charitable organizations, but most of these organizations appear to take a "the more, the better" approach. Organizations must realize that appeals that are too powerful and explicit may be inducing personal distress and thus fail to motivate potential donors. For instance, the graphic depictions used by those opposing abortion could very well fail to generate financial or political support for their position. In these cases, an opportunity to gain support for the sponsor's position or elicit a donation may be lost. The measures described within this study could prove useful in pretesting appeals being contemplated by these groups.

Limitations and Future Research

Several characteristics of the study design limit interpretations of the findings and provide avenues for future research. First, the conditions in which the study was conducted created an environment where escape from the emotion-inducing stimulus was rather easy. Respondents were asked to peruse the materials but were not given specific instructions as to the degree of elaboration or an amount of time to spend processing each piece of information. While this created the advantage of allowing for naturally occurring variations in emotions among respondents (Batson et al. 1988), it does not represent other possible environment in which a charitable appeal could be presented. Thus, the results seem quite applicable to charitable appeals encountered in newsletters from local civic and religious organizations, at the counter of a convenience store, in advertisements in magazines and on late night television, all conditions where escape is easily accomplished by turning a page or "clicking" the channel. Different emotional consequences might be expected in other types of environments. Indeed the environment in which the appeal takes place might "manipulate" ease of escape and effect its emotional consequences on consumers and subsequently, their level of giving. An advertisement presented on the subway, in the workplace, at the front door, or other conditions where escape is more difficult, may lead consumers experiencing distress instead of empathy no choice but to make some contribution to relieve the negative affective state.

Further, the effects of gender may be attenuated in this study due to a potential confound. The emotion-inducing stimulus described the individual in need as a man. Thus, the degree of identification with the victim may have been higher among male respondents. This may account for a failure to replicate previous findings indicating higher intentions to give among female respondents (Pessemier et al. 1978). Left for further study is the effect of gender and degree of personal identification on emotions and giving behavior. Put more broadly, additional variables are necessary to more fully explain the dependent variables employed here.

Another interesting aspect left for future study is the effect of giving on emotions. Considering the strong motivational forces at work in creating consumers' emotional responses and behavior when encountering an appeal on behalf of one in need, an extension of this model to other consequence variables could prove enlightening. Not unlike models of satisfaction in the profit-sector literature (Westbrook and Oliver 1991), how do consumers evaluate their response to a charitable appeal? What kind of personal emotional state is created by a person experiencing altruism and giving compared to others? For example, behaviors associated with altruism may be efforts to achieve positive emotional states (e.g., caring, compassion, etc.) whereas behaviors motivated by distress might be designed to avoid negative emotional states (e.g., shame, guilt). These resulting emotional states may enable prediction of which types of consumers and conditions could lead to "loyalty" among donors.

Conclusions

This paper describes an initial attempt at explaining emotional reactions and intentions to give to a charitable appeal. It provides evidence that consumers will react differently based on the relative levels of empathy and distress evoked by a charitable appeal. Under conditions where an audience is not captive, appeals should be designed to evoke maximum levels of empathy and minimum levels of distress to maximize consumer intentions to give. Further, the study provides evidence that giving is increased when causal attributions of a victim's plight are placed on factors outside of his/her control. This has direct implications for the type of appeal used by nonprofit organizations soliciting appeals for victims of behavioral afflictions such as AIDS or alcoholism. In addition, the findings stimulate a host of future research topics into factors which may explain charitable giving.

REFERENCES

Abramson, Paul R. and Donald L. Mosher (1975), "Development of a Measure of Negative Attitudes Toward Masturbation," *Journal of Consulting and Clinical Psychology*, 43, 485-490.

Abramson, P., P. Goldberg, D. Mosher, L. Abramson, and M. Gottesdiener (1975), "Experimenter Effects on Responses to Explicitly Erotic Stimuli," *Journal of Research in Personality*, 9, 136-146.

Allen, Chris T., Robert J. Kent, and Terri F. Barr (1992), "A Field Test of Influence Strategies for Sustaining Blood Donation: Emotional Arousal versus Self-Concept Enhancement," in *Advances in Consumer Research*, Vol. 19, in press.

Babbin, Barry J., William R. Darden and Mitch Griffin (1992), "Some Comments on the Role of Emotions in Consumer Behavior," in *Enhancing Knowledge Development in Marketing*, Robert P. Leone and V. Kumar, eds., 1992 AMA Educator's Proceedings, Chicago: American Marketing Association, 130-139.

Baron, Reuben M. and David A. Kenny (1986), "The Moderator-Mediator Distinction in Social Psychological Research: Conceptual, Strategic, and Statistical Considerations," *Journal of Personality and Social Psychology*, 51 (6), 1173-1182.

Batson, C. Daniel, Janine L. Dyck, J. Randall Brandt, Judy G. Batson, Anne L. Powell, M. Rosalie McMaster, and Cari Griffitt (1988), "Five Studies Testing Two New Egoistic Alternatives to the Empathy-Altruism Hypothesis," *Journal of Personality and Social Psychology*, 55 (July), 52-77.

Batson, C. Daniel, Karen O'Quinn, Jim Fultz, Mary Vanderplas, and Alice M. Isen (1983), "Influence of Self-Reported Distress and Empathy on Egoistic Versus Altruistic Motivation to Help," *Journal of Personality and Social Psychology*, 45 (September), 706-718.

Batson, C. Daniel, Michelle H. Bolen, Julie A. Cross, and Helen E. Neuringer-Benefiel (1986), "Where is the Altruistic Personality?" *Journal of Personality and Social Psychology*, 50 (January), 212-220.

Batson, Daniel C. and J. S. Coke (1981), "Empathy: A Source of Altruistic Motivation for Helping," in *Altruism and Helping Behavior*, J.P. Rushton and R.M. Sorrentino eds., Hillsdale, NJ: Erlbaum.

Burke, Mariam Chapman and Julie A. Edell (1989), "The Impact of Feelings on Ad-Based Affect and Cognition," *Journal of Marketing Research*, 26 (February), 69-83.

Burnett, John J. and Van R. Wood (1988), "A Proposed Model of the Donation Decision Process," in *Research in Consumer Behavior*, Elizabeth Hirschman and Jagdish Sheth, eds., Greenwich, CT: JAI Press. 1-47.

Carlson, M. and N. Miller (1987), "Explanation of the Relation Between Negative Mood and Helping," *Psychological Bulletin*, 102, 91-118.

Cialdini, Robert B. and Jim Fultz (1990), "Interpreting the Negative Mood-Helping Literature via "Mega"-Analysis: A Contrary View," *Psychological Bulletin*, 107 (February), 210-214.

Cialdini, Robert B., M. Schaller, D. Houlihan, K. Arps, Jim Fultz, and A.L. Beaman (1987), "Empathy-Based Helping: Is it Selflessly or Selfishly Motivated?" *Journal of Personality and Social Psychology*, 52 (March), 749-758.

Cohen, Joel B. and Charles S. Areni (1991), "Affect and Consumer Behavior," in *Handbook of Consumer Theory and Research*, Thomas S. Robertson and Harold H. Kassarjian, eds., Englewood Cliffs, NJ: Prentice-Hall, 188-240.

Coke, J. S., C. Daniel Batson, and K. McDavis (1978), "Empathetic Mediation of Helping: A Two-Stage Model," *Journal of Personality and Social Psychology*, 36, 752-766.

Darden, William R., James DeConinck, Barry J. Babin, and Mitch Griffin (1991), "The Role of Consumer Sympathy in Product Liability Suits," *Journal of Business Research*, 22 (January), 65-89.

Donovan, Robert J. and John R. Rossiter (1982), "Store Atmospherics: An Environmental Psychology Approach," *Journal of Retailing*, 58 (Spring), 34-57.

Dovidio, John F., Judith L. Allen, and David A. Schroeder (1990), "Specificity of Empathy-Induced Helping: Evidence for Altruistic Motivation," *Journal of Personality and Social Psychology*, 59 (2), 249-260.

Feild, Hubert S. (1978), "Attitudes Toward Rape: A Comparative Analysis of Police, Rapists, Crisis Counselors, and Citizens," *Journal of Personality and Social Psychology*, 36 (February), 156-179.

Fultz, Jim, C. Daniel Batson, Victoria A. Fortenbach, Patricia M. McCarthy, and Laurel L. Varney (1986), "Social Evaluation and the Empathy-Altruism Hypothesis," *Journal of Personality and Social Psychology*, 50 (April), 761-769.

Griffin, Mitch, Barry J. Babin, and William R. Darden (1992), "Consumer Assessments of Responsibility for Product Related Injuries: The Impact of Regulations, Warnings, and Promotional Policies," in *Advances in Consumer Research*, Vol. 19, John F. Sherry, Jr. and Brian Sternthal, eds., 870-878.

Hoffman, M. L. (1982), "Development of Prosocial Motivation: Empathy and Guilt," in *Development of Prosocial Behavior*, N. Eisenberg-Borg, ed., New York: Academic Press, 281-313.

Holbrook, Morris B. and Rajeev Batra (1987), "Assessing the Role of Emotions as Mediators of Consumer Responses to Advertising," *Journal of Consumer Research*, 14 (December), 404-420.

Holbrook, Morris B. (1986), "Emotion in the Consumption Experience: Toward a New Model of the Human Consumer," in *The Role of Affect in Consumer Behavior*, Robert A. Peterson, Wayne D. Hoyer, and Wiliam R. Wilson, eds., Lexington Books: Lexington, Mass. 17-52.

Kelley, Harold H. (1973), "The Process of Causal Attribution," *American Psychologists*, 28 (February), 107-128.

Mullen, Brian and Craig Johnson (1990), *The Psychology of Consumer Behavior*, Hillsdale, NJ: Lawrence Erlbaum Associates.

Neter, John, William Wasserman, and Michael H. Kutner (1985), *Applied Linear Statistical Models: Regression, Analysis of Variance, and Experimental Design*, Homewood, IL: Irwin.

Pessemier, Edgar A., Albert C. Bemmaor, and Dominique M. Hanseens (1977), "Willingness to Supply Human Body Parts: Some Empirical Results," *Journal of Consumer Research*, 4 (December), 131-140.

Ross, John K., larry T. Patterson, and Mary Ann Stutts (1992), "Consumer Perceptions of Organizations That Use Cause-Related Marketing," *Journal of the Academy of Marketing Science*, 20 (Winter), 93-97.

Varadarajan, P. Rajan and Anil Menon (1988), "Cause-Related Marketing: A Coalignment of Marketing Strategy and Corporate Philanthropy," *Journal of Marketing*, 52 (July), 58-74.

Weiner, Bernard (1985), "An Attributional Theory of Achievement Motivation and Emotion," *Psychological Review*, 92 (October), 548-573.

Westbrook, Robert A. and Richard L. Oliver (1991), "The Dimensionality of Consumption Emotion Patterns and Consumer Satisfaction," *Journal of Consumer Research*, 18 (June), 84-91.

Extrahousehold Giving in Popular Gift Categories: A Socioeconomic and Demographic Analysis

Janet Wagner, University of Maryland
Thesia Garner, Bureau of Labor Statistics

The purpose of this research was to analyze the effect of the socioeconomic and demographic characteristics of households on the probability of expenditures for extrahousehold gifts, including clothing, toys, plants and flowers, china and dinnerware, and small appliances. Data were from the 4,139 households in the 1984-85 Consumer Expenditure Survey. The results of probit regression analyses demonstrated that income, family size, stage in the family life cycle, and ethnicity are related to the probability of expenditures in all categories. The number of female adults is related to the probability of expenditures in all categories except plants and flowers and small appliances. The results for education, urbanization and region were mixed.

Gift-giving is a topic of growing interest in consumer behavior. Much of this interest has been inspired by the Sherry (1983) model, in which consumer gift-giving is explored from an anthropological perspective. In the holistic tradition of that discipline, the gift-giving model integrates concepts from sociology and psychology. The economic dimensions of gift-giving are acknowledged but not well-developed, reflecting the ambivalence of anthropologists toward economic theory and the indifference of economists toward some types of nonmarket exchange. Although gift-giving involves nonmarket exchange, most gifts are purchased in the market, suggesting that economic theory and methods may have much to contribute to development of the gift-giving model. Exploring the economic aspects of consumer gift-giving is an important research endeavor, because gift expenditures may account for as much as ten percent of the typical household budget (Belshaw 1965). Extrahousehold gifts—gifts given to individuals, households and organizations outside the consumer unit—are estimated to account for at least one-third of that amount (Belk 1979; Garner and Wagner 1991).

Previous research on economic aspects of extrahousehold giving has focused on total annual gift expenditures (e.g., Garner and Wagner 1991) and expenditures for charitable contributions (e.g., Reece and Zieschang 1985). The purpose of our study was to extend that research by exploring expenditures for purchased gifts. As such, we analyzed the effect of income, in conjunction with a set of other socioeconomic and demographic variables, on the probability of households reporting expenditures for extrahousehold gifts in popular gift categories including clothing, toys, plants and flowers, china and dinnerware, and small kitchen appliances. Data were from the internal files of the Bureau of Labor Statistics' (BLS) Quarterly Interview Component of the 1984-85 Consumer Expenditure Survey (CEX) (U.S. Department of Labor 1984-85), the largest and most comprehensive source of information on the expenditures of U.S. households, classified by socioeconomic and demographic variables. The results should be of interest to scholars, in developing economic aspects of the Sherry (1983) model, and to marketing practitioners, in segmenting the market for gifts.

ECONOMIC THEORY AND EXTRAHOUSEHOLD GIVING

According to Sherry (1983), gift-giving has three major components—a gift, an exchange relationship between a donor and a recipient, and a situational context. Because gift-giving involves social, rather than economic exchange, anthropologists (Burling 1962; Cancian 1966; Douglas and Isherwood 1979; Herskovits 1952) and economists (Arrow 1975; Becker 1974; 1976) have debated the appropriateness of applying economic theory and methods to gift-giving. The focus of this argument has been whether or not utility maximization, the principle assumption of the economic theory of consumer behavior, can be applied to gift-giving. Under utility maximization, it is assumed that consumers allocate income among commodities—goods and services needed or wanted for personal consumption—subject to a budget constraint. The objective of such decisions is to maximize personal satisfaction. The objective of giving, on the other hand, is purportedly to maximize the satisfaction of others. Becker (1974;76) suggested resolving this argument by extending the concept of a commodity to include social needs, such as love, status, or distinction, which are met by giving. In purchasing and giving gifts, consumers produce "social commodities" by combining market goods and services, household resources (such as income and education), environmental factors (such as the norm of reciprocity), and the characteristics and satisfaction of recipients. Social commodities produced by giving enter the household utility function. Thus, in giving, consumers maximize both their own satisfaction and that of others.

Consumers differ in the utility engendered by giving. Although most choose to give, some do not. Those choosing to give must also make decisions about what goods and services to give. According to Lutz (1979), the choice of a gift is one of the most important decisions in the study of consumer gift-giving.

The social norm motivating gift-giving is reciprocity, the obligation to give, receive and return gifts (Mauss 1967). Reciprocity is related to the extent of social interaction between donor and recipient. While most gift-giving occurs within the family, giving is also extended to unrelated individuals, households and organizations with whom family members have frequent contact (Becker 1974; Belk 1979).

Research on the social dimensions of giving shows that extrahousehold gifts create and maintain "networks of love", cross-household ties with family, kin and friends (Belk 1979; Caplow 1982; Cheal 1987). Social networks differ with respect to their range and their composition. According to Douglas and Isherwood (1979), the range of a household's social network increases with income (the central concept in an expenditure analysis). This suggests that, as income increases, households have more opportunities to give gifts. Therefore, we expected to find that in every gift category the probability of extrahousehold gift expenditures would increase with income. Social networks tend to be homophilous—that is, they tend to be composed of households of similar socioeconomic and demographic status. This suggests that within a socioeconomic or demographic group, households may have similar tastes and preferences for gifts. By extension, we expected to find that socioeconomic and demographic groups would differ in the types of gifts given.

The "best" gifts—those most likely to maximize the satisfaction of both donor and recipient—are personalized by age, sex and taste, and can be conspicuously consumed (Caplow 1982). Thus, the most popular gift is clothing. Other popular gifts include toys, plants and flowers, jewelry, china and dinnerware, small appliances and sporting equipment (Belk 1979; Caplow 1982; Jolibert and

Fernandez-Moreno 1983). In this research, we used a probit qualitative choice model (Maddala 1984) to analyze the effect of income and other socioeconomic and demographic variables on the probability of households having expenditures for extrahousehold gifts in selected product categories. The categories chosen were those shown by a frequency analysis to be the most important, including clothing, toys, plants and flowers, china and dinnerware, and small kitchen appliances.

METHOD

Data were from the Quarterly Interview Component of the 1984-85 U.S. Continuing Consumer Expenditure Survey (CEX). This survey is based on a rotating panel, the composition of which is determined by a national probability sample. The sample size is targeted at 5,000 interviews per quarter, with 20 percent of the consumer units rotating out and being replaced each quarter. In this survey, a consumer unit is defined as "... 1) all members of a housing unit related by blood, marriage or adoption, 2) two or more persons who pool their incomes to make joint expenditures, or 3) a single consumer who is financially independent." (U.S. Department of Labor 1989). The 4,146 consumer units in the sample were those from which four consecutive quarters of expenditure data were available. Seven consumer units reporting extreme values for either total annual expenditures or gift expenditures were eliminated, leaving a subsample of 4,139 consumer units.

Our research was based on a probit qualitative choice model (Maddala 1984). Details of the model are provided in Appendix 1 of Garner and Wagner (1991). The probability of expenditures for extrahousehold gifts in each category—women's clothing, men's clothing, infants' clothing, plants and flowers, china and dinnerware, toys and small kitchen appliances—was modeled separately.

In the CEX, expenditure data are collected by product category. For each category, respondents are asked, "Since the 1st of (month, 3 months ago), have you or any members of your CU purchased or rented any of the following items for your CU or as a gift to someone outside your CU?" Respondents who answer "Yes" are asked to indicate which items were purchased for own use and which were purchased to be given as gifts. In our research, gift purchases were coded 1; purchases and rentals for own use were coded 0.

The independent variables included total annual expenditures (a proxy for income),[1] family size, number of female adults in the household, stage in the family life cycle, ethnicity, education, degree of urbanization and region. Total annual expenditures, family size and number of female adults were treated as continuous variables. The remaining variables were treated as sets of dummy variables. Definitions of the independent variables appear in Garner and Wagner (1991).

RESULTS AND DISCUSSION

Absolute and relative frequencies for households reporting extrahousehold gifts in each category are presented in Table 1.

These frequencies are consistent with the results of previous research on the social dimensions of giving by Belk (1979), Caplow (1982), and Jolibert and Fernandez-Moreno (1983) in showing clothing, plants and flowers, toys, china and dinnerware, and small appliances to be the most frequently given gifts. The highest relative frequency was in women's clothing; 36 percent of the respondents reported expenditures in that category. Women's clothing was followed by plants and flowers (34 percent), toys (28 percent), china and dinnerware (19 percent) and small appliances (19 percent).

Descriptive statistics and the results of the probit analysis are presented in Table 2. Total annual expenditures, the proxy for income, was positively related to the probability of expenditures in all of the extrahousehold gift categories. This result is consistent with economic theory and lends support to the results of previous research (Garner and Wagner 1991) showing that as total annual expenditures increase, the probability of extrahousehold gift expenditures increases.

Family size was negatively related to the probability of having an expenditure in all of the extrahousehold gift categories. That is, as family size increased, the probability of expenditures for extrahousehold gifts decreased. For most households, the primary social relationships are within the family. Consequently, the larger the family, the greater the demand for gifts to be given within the household, and the less likely it is that there will be extrahousehold giving. Camerer (1988) suggests that consumers derive more utility from giving to family members than from giving to others; because family members are familiar with each others' tastes and preferences, there is less risk involved.

The number of female adults in a household was positively related to the probability of extrahousehold gift expenditures in all categories except plants and flowers and small appliances. This finding lends support to the notion that women are responsible for the maintenance of the social networks of their households (DiLeonardo 1987) and corroborates the results of previous research showing that women are involved in most gift-giving decisions (Belk 1979; Caplow 1982; Fischer and Arnold 1990). The number of female adults had no effect on the probability of extrahousehold gift expenditures for either plants and flowers or small appliances, however.

As suggested by Sherry (1983), stage in the family life cycle affected extrahousehold expenditures in all of the gift categories. Its effect was most extensive, however, in infants' clothing. Young married adults (YMA) were more likely than YSA to give gifts of infants' clothing. Douglas and Isherwood (1979) suggest that rituals of reciprocity are likely to be similar among households in a given life cycle stage. The concept of homophily suggests that YMA's and MMA's are likely to include other households of childbearing age, so baby showers are likely to be commonly shared gift-giving rituals. A popular gift for such events is often clothing. In fact, gifts are the primary source of infants' clothing for many households (Britton 1969).

Older single (OS) and older married (OM) adults were less likely than YSA to give gifts of either men's or women's clothing. Because it is personalized, a gift of clothing implies a degree of intimacy. The social networks of older adults, reduced by retirement and death, may include fewer close relationships, with correspondingly fewer opportunities to give clothing.

The probability of expenditures for gifts of toys was greater among mature married parents with children five years of age or younger (MMARPI) than among YSA. Birthday parties are shared rituals among households in this stage and toys are likely to be preferred gifts (Caron and Ward 1975). In contrast, mature married

---

[1] The use of total consumption expenditures as a proxy for income is consistent with the permanent income hypothesis (Friedman 1957), which posits that in the short run, households have more control over expenditures than income. While there may be bias resulting from the use of this proxy, because expenditures for gifts in each category are one component of total annual expenditures, this bias should be minimal, because extrahousehold gifts are, on the average, a relatively small part of total annual expenditures (see Garner and Wagner 1991).

TABLE 1

Gift Category	Absolute Frequency	Relative Frequency
Women's Clothing	1,489	0.36
Men's Clothing	1,396	0.34
Infants' Clothing	1,354	0.33
Men's Clothing	1,263	0.31
Toys	1,161	0.25
China and Dinnerware	800	0.19
Small Appliances	781	0.19

TABLE 2
Descriptive Statistics and Results of the Probit Analysis of Expenditures in Most Popular Gift Categories

		Gift Category						
		Clothing						
Variable		Men's	Women's	Infants'	Toys	Plants	China	Appl.
	Means							
LTOTEXP	21,720	0.470**	0.505**	0.435**	-0.398**	0.511**	0.454**	0.800**
FAMSIZE	2.74	-0.177**	-0.146**	-0.091**	-0.972**	-0.122**	0.122**	-0.680**
FEMADULT	1.16	0.160**	0.281**	0.329**	0.165**	0.078	0.195**	0.075
	Frequencies							
SPAR	195	-0.140	-0.140	0.116	-0.109	-0.234	-0.042	-0.169
YMA	125	-0.056	-0.178	0.373**	0.187	-0.511**	0.002	0.139
YMPARI	235	-0.168	-0.088	0.552**	0.011	-0.121	0.214	-0.003
YMPARII	177	-0.224	-0.082	0.444**	-0.174	-0.185	0.030	-0.052
MSA	447	-0.202	-0.102	0.125	-0.157	-0.155	-0.004	0.115
MMA	620	0.081	0.115	0.336**	0.031	0.007	0.261*	0.066
MMPARI	198	-0.026	0.000	0.539**	0.279*	0.056	0.290	-0.049
MMPARII	277	-0.151	-0.309*	0.376**	-0.046	-0.025	0.054	-0.208
MMPARIII	327	-0.026	-0.112	0.259**	-0.290**	-0.191	0.145	-0.023
OS	427	-0.405**	-0.377**	-0.149	-0.141	-0.062	-0.077	-0.350**
OM	432	-0.221**	-0.241**	0.150	-0.071	-0.116	0.153	-0.020
OTHER	400	-0.305**	-0.365*	0.069	-0.10	-0.173	0.013	-0.094
(YSA)	(279)							
AFRO	403	-0.389**	-0.428**	-0.222**	-0.756**	-0.451**	-0.589**	-0.494**
HISP	219	-0.096	-0.262**	-0.012	0.073	-0.379**	-0.170	-0.135
ANGLO	1,134	0.002	0.049	0.058	-0.105	0.055	-0.031	0.060
OTHEUR	428	-0.008	0.006	0.030	-0.059	0.029	-0.073	0.095
ASIAN	104	-0.022	-0.269	-0.037	-0.006	-0.299*	-0.558**	-0.412**
(OTHER)	(1,851)							
ELEM	597	-0.225**	-0.196**	-0.119	-0.115	0.044	-0.120	-0.132
LTHS	566	-0.171*	-0.141**	-0.062	-0.002	0.034	-0.033	0.064
LTCOLL	844	-0.043	-0.013	-0.039	-0.029	0.128*	0.081	0.045
COLL	468	-0.069	-0.086	-0.146*	-0.116	0.040	0.171*	0.075
POSTGRAD	434	-0.137	-0.091	-0.287**	-0.069	0.053	0.162*	-0.076
(HS)	(1,230)							

parents with children between the ages of 12 and 18 (MMPARIII) were less likely than YSA to report expenditures for toys, reflecting the preference of children of this age for other gifts.

Young married adults (YMA) were less likely than YSA to purchase extrahousehold gifts of plants and flowers, reflecting, perhaps, differences in living situations. While YMA may give plants and flowers to spouses in the same consumer unit, YSA may give plants and flowers to lovers in other consumer units. According to Belk (1979), consumers may be absolved from giving by situational factors. Since YMA often incur expenses associated with new household formation, households in this stage may be absolved from giving gifts for all but the most obligatory occasions.

Older single adults were less likely than YSA to give extrahousehold gifts of small kitchen appliances. This may reflect the fact that older consumers often show less interest than younger consumers in new technology (Douglas and Isherwood 1979).

TABLE 2 (CONTINUED)
Descriptive Statistics and Results of the Probit Analysis of Expenditures in Most Popular Gift Categories

Variable		Gift Category						
		Clothing						
		Men's	Women's	Infants'	Toys	Plants	China	Appl.
SOUTH	1,203	-0.169**	-0.773	-0.078	-0.036	-0.124*	-0.071	-0.161*
NE	891	-0.130**	-0.085	-0.041	-0.091	0.092	-0.211**	-0.150*
WEST	865	-0.099	-0.028	0.068	-0.079	0.101	-0.011	-0.091
(MWEST)	(1,180)							
CITY	1,433	-0.121*	-0.086	-0.148**	0.035	-0.052	-0.075	-0.076
RURAL	1,096	-0.020	-0.097	-0.131*	-0.068	0.094	-0.094	-0.003*
(SUBURB)	(1,610)							
Chi-square (d.f.=30)		432.51	532.23	437.38	389.73	398.24	362.41	303.98
Rho-squared		0.084	0.098	0.085	0.080	0.089	0.089	0.075

n=4,139
[a] $p \le .05$
[b] $p \le .01$

Mature married adults were more likely than YSA to purchase extrahousehold gifts of china and dinnerware, a result consistent with those of gift industry surveys identifying "Mature Moderns" as major purchasers of china and dinnerware ("Gift Retailing..." 1987).

Ethnicity affected the probability of expenditures in all of the extrahousehold gift categories. The effect of Afro-American ethnicity was negative in all categories. Hispanic ethnicity was negatively related to expenditures for plants and flowers, and Asian ethnicity was negatively related to expenditures for china and dinnerware as well as small appliances. The pervasiveness of the effect of Afro-American ethnicity is consistent with the results of Garner and Wagner (1991), who found Afro-Americans less likely than consumers of European extraction to report expenditures for extrahousehold giving. Garner and Wagner found no effect, however, for either Hispanic or Asian ethnicity. Our results suggest that ethnic groups may have different perceptions of what constitutes an appropriate gift. In the case of Afro-Americans, previous research by Stack (1974) suggests that gifts of time and services may be exchanged in lieu of newly purchased goods.

The most obvious effects for education were in men's, women's and infants' clothing, as well as in china and dinnerware. Less educated households (elementary school or less than high school education) were less likely than other households to report expenditures for gifts of either men's or women's clothing. According to Young and Willmott (1973), the social networks of less educated consumers are often confined to family and close friends. This implies than less educated consumers have little need for conspicuous consumption in their wardrobes and may not view clothing as a desirable gift. Well-educated households (college or postgraduate education) were less likely than others to report gifts of infants' clothing, reflecting, perhaps, the low fertility rate (Fuchs 1983) among the well-educated. On the other hand, well-educated consumers reported more gifts of china and dinnerware. According to Douglas and Isherwood (1979), china is a "pure marker"—a good conveying information about the status of a household. As such, china and dinnerware may be gifts understood and appreciated primarily by the well-educated.

Both urban and rural households were less likely than suburban households to have expenditures for gifts of infants' clothing. In urban areas, social networks are often diffuse. In rural areas, social networks may lack scope. In either case, opportunities for shared rituals surrounding the birth of a child may be limited. Rural households were less likely than suburban households to have expenditures for gift of small appliances. This result lends support to the work of Ryans (1977), who reported that rural residents were less likely than urban residents to purchase gifts of appliances, and may reflect limited access to shopping. Region is a variable usually included in expenditure analyses to capture regional differences in tastes, preferences and prices. Our results show that households in the South and the Northeast were less likely than households in the Midwest to report expenditures for gifts of either men's clothing or small appliances. Households in the South were less likely to report expenditures for plants and flowers.

The chi-square values in Table 2 show the models were significant in explaining the probability of expenditures in all seven of the extrahousehold gift categories. The rho-squared value of the models ranged from 0.075 for plants and flowers and small appliances to 0.098 for women's clothing. According to Domencich and McFadden (1985), these values are comparable to R-squared values ranging from 0.20 to 0.24.

Our results must be interpreted in light of limitations inherent in the CEX data. First, while the data on expenditures and characteristics of donors are extensive, there are no data on recipients. Second, there is no information on gifts-in-kind. This may be particularly important in product categories like infants' clothing, in which gifts of hand-me-downs are common (Britton 1969), and plants and flowers, in which gifts of cuttings are frequently given (Schnudson 1986). Finally, the CEX data are limited to expenditures for extrahousehold gifts. Information on expenditures for gifts given within the household would enhance our understanding of the gift-giving process.

CONCLUSIONS AND IMPLICATIONS

Our results are consistent with economic theory in demonstrating that total annual expenditures, a proxy for income, is positively related to the probability of extrahousehold gift expenditures in seven of the most popular gift categories. When the effect of total consumption expenditures is controlled, family size, stage in the family life cycle and ethnicity are related to the probability of expenditures for gifts in all seven categories. The effects of other socioeconomic and demographic variables, including the number of female adults, education, urbanization and region, appear to vary by gift category.

Our results also have implications for the Sherry (1983) model. We show that socioeconomic and demographic characteristics of donor households, particularly total consumption expenditures, family size, ethnicity, and stage in the family life cycle, are related to the probability of expenditures in the most popular extrahousehold gift categories; we submit that the economic dimensions of the Sherry model would be enhanced by their inclusion. Given the scope of the CEX data, we recommend extending this research to other popular gift categories, such as jewelry and cosmetics. An intriguing possibility is a longitudinal study of the involvement of women in gift-giving to determine if, as sex roles, change, men begin to assume more responsibility for giving. For researchers interested in ethnography, we suggest investigating reasons for the differences we observed in categories of gifts chosen by Hispanic and Asian consumers.

REFERENCES

Arrow, Kenneth (1975), "Gifts and Exchanges," in *Altruism, Morality and Economic Theory*, ed. Edmund Phelps, New York: Russell Sage, 13-28.

Becker, Gary (1974), "A Theory of Social Interaction," *Journal of Political Economy*, 82 (November/December), 1063-1093.

_____ (1976), *The Economic Approach to Human Behavior*, Chicago: The University of Chicago Press.

Belk, Russell (1979), "Gift-Giving Behavior," in *Research in Marketing*, ed. Jagdish Sheth, Greenwich, Connecticut: JAI Press, 95-126.

Belshaw, Cyril (1965), *Traditional Exchange and Modern Markets*, Englewood Cliffs, New Jersey: Prentice-Hall, Inc.

Britton, Virginia (1969), "Gifts and Handed-down Clothing Important in Family Budgets," *Family Economics Review* (September), 10-12.

Burling, Robin (1962), "Maximization Theories and the Study of Economic Anthropology," *American Anthropologist*, 64, 802-821.

Camerer, Colin (1988), "Gifts as Economic Signals and Social Symbols," *American Journal of Sociology*, 94, S180-S214.

Cancian, Frank (1966), "Maximization as Norm, Strategy and Theory," *American Anthropologist*, 68, 465-470.

Caplow, T. (1982), "Christmas Gifts and Kin Networks," *American Sociological Review*, 47 (June), 383-392.

Caron, Andre and Scott Ward (1975), "Gift Decisions by Kids and Parents," *Journal of Advertising Research*, 15 (4), 15-20.

Cheal, David (1987), "Showing Them You Love Them: Gift Giving and the Dialectic of Intimacy," *Sociological Review*, 35 (1), 150-169.

Douglas, Mary and Baron Isherwood (1979), *The World of Goods*, New York, Basic Books, Inc.

DiLeonardo, Micaela (1987), "The Female World of Cards and Holidays: Women, Families, and the Work of Kinship," *Signs*, 12 (Spring), 440-453.

Domencich, T.A. and D. McFadden (1985), *Urban Travel: A Behavioral Analysis*, Amsterdam: North Holland.

Fischer, Eileen and Stephen J. Arnold (1990), "More Than A Labor of Love: Gender Roles and Christmas Gift Shopping," *Journal of Consumer Research*, 17 (December), 333-345.

Friedman, Milton (1957), *A Theory of the Consumption Function*, Princeton: Princeton University Press.

Fuchs, Victor R. (1983), *How We Live*, Harvard University Press, Cambridge, Massachusetts.

Garner, Thesia and Janet Wagner (1991), "Economic Dimensions of Household Gift-Giving," *Journal of Consumer Research*, 17 (December).

"Gift Retailing: Here Comes the Nineties," *Gifts and Decorative Accessories*, December 1987, 185-186.

Herskovits, Melville J. (1952), *Economic Anthropology*, New York: Alfred A. Knopf.

Jolibert, J.P. and Carlos Fernandez-Moreno (1983), "A Comparison of French and Mexican Gift-Giving Practices," in *Advances in Consumer Research*, 10, eds. Richard P. Bagozzi and Alice M. Tybout, Ann Arbor: Association for Consumer Research, 191-196.

Lutz, Richard (1979), "Consumer Gift-Giving: Opening the Black Box," in *Advances in Consumer Research*, 6, ed. William L. Wilkie, Ann Arbor: Association for Consumer Research, 329-331.

Maddala, G.S. (1977), *Econometrics*, New York: McGraw-Hill Book Company.

Mauss, Marcel (1967), *The Gift*, New York: W.W. Norton & Company, Inc.

Reece, William S. and Kimberly D. Zieschang (1985), "Consistent Estimation of the Impact of Tax Deductibility on the Level of Charitable Contributions," *Econometrica*, 53 (March), 271-293.

Ryans, Adrian B. (1977), "Consumer Gift Buying Behavior: An Exploratory Analysis," in *Contemporary Marketing Thought*, Series No. 44, eds. O. Bellinger and B. Greenberg, Chicago: American Marketing Association, 99-104.

Schnudson, Michael (1986), "The Giving of Gifts," *Psychology Today* (December), 26-29.

Sherry, John (1983), "Gift-Giving in Anthropological Perspective," *Journal of Consumer Research*, 10 (September), 157-168.

Stack, Carol (1974), *All Our Kin*, New York: Harper & Row.

U.S. Department of Labor, Bureau of Labor Statistics (1984-85), Quarterly Interview Component of the Consumer Expenditure Survey, internal files for 1984-85, Washington, D.C.

_____ (1989), *Consumer Expenditure Survey: Quarterly Interview Survey*, Report 778, Washington, D.C.: U.S. Government Printing Office.

Young, Michael and Peter Willmott (1973), *The Symmetrical Family*, London: Routledge & Kegan Paul.

Three Motivations for Interpersonal Gift Giving: Experiental, Obligated and Practical Motivations

Mary Finley Wolfinbarger, California State University, Long Beach
Laura J. Yale, Fort Lewis College

ABSTRACT

While consumer researchers and other social scientists have investigated gift giving behavior, there has been a tendency to infer motivations from behavior, rather than to allow receivers to express their self-perceived motivations. This research is an effort to develop three distinct constructs — experiential/positive, obligated, and practical motivations towards giving — and to develop items which measure these motivations.

INTRODUCTION

Gift giving has been a field of study in consumer behavior, at least since the mid '70s (cf. Belk 1976, 1979; Sherry 1983). However, the topic has recently received increased attention from consumer researchers. In the last two years, three papers on the topic have appeared in the *Journal of Consumer Research* (Fischer and Arnold 1990; Garner and Wagner 1991; Mick and Demoss 1990), and scores of articles have appeared in conference proceedings, especially those sponsored by the Association of Consumer Research. Various gift-giving topics have concerned consumer behavior scholars, including satisfaction from giving, the projection of self-concept and concept of the receiver in giving, attributes sought or avoided in gifts, search time and effort of givers, self-gifts, the impact of various demographics on amount spent for a gift, gift giving as a signal in dating situations, and gender orientation and its subsequent impact on gift giving effort (for instance, time spent and amount spent) at Christmas. Moreover, since gift giving is an involving consumer behavior, it is often used as a manipulation in consumer behavioral experiments (cf. Belk 1982; Clarke and Belk 1978).

Rarely, however, have consumer scholars empirically broached the question of *why* people give, and constructs and measurement items have not been developed to measure givers' self-perceived motivations. Sherry (1983) pointed out that gift giving motivations needed to be better understood, and that naturalistic study was required in order to dig underneath the various dependent and independent variables in consumer research studies which did not seem to address *why* questions. He and McGrath (1989) spent 6 weeks *in situ* at two gift shops, and talked to givers about their gift choices. They concluded:

> Gift choices by customers are often emotional and intuitive, with prospects — most notably females — often needing to "fall in love" with an object prior to purchase...The object, which is "loved" by at least one of the exchange partners, will form a link between the two individuals (p. 160).

While Sherry (1983), Sherry and McGrath (1989), Wolfinbarger (1990) and Fischer and Arnold (1990) all uncover motivations for giving in their studies, none of these studies was directed at developing and measuring such motivations. Such an effort is warranted as these general motivations are likely to differ between individuals, interact with situational variables of interest, such as occasion and closeness of the receiver, and impact dependent variables such as gift-giving effort expended, the type of gifts bought, and the expressiveness of symbolism likely to be encoded in gifts.

Furthermore, it is unlikely that such motivations are unidimensional. Several sensitive authors have noted the ambivalence often present in the act of giving (Schwartz 1967; Sherry and McGrath 1989; Tournier 1963). It is our expectation that these motivations are multifaceted, and thus the act of giving may reflect several conflicting desires. Based on gift-giving literature (reviewed briefly below) three individual difference variables are suggested as important in gift choice: an experiential/positive attitude towards giving (giving for the enjoyment of giving), an obligated attitude (giving to reciprocate or because of social norms) and a practical attitude (giving to supply practical assistance to the receiver). This paper is an attempt to develop measures to assess these three motivations for giving. Following is a discussion of the literature utilized in developing these measures, a description of the study, and a discussion of the results.

MOTIVATIONS FOR GIVING: EXPERIENTIAL, OBLIGATED AND PRACTICAL ATTITUDES

Motivation is "an internal factor that arouses, directs and integrates a person's behavior" in a given set of circumstances in order to achieve some goal (Murray 1964, p. 7). Motives are often divided into utilitarian and hedonic motives. Utilitarian motives constitute desires to achieve functional benefits while hedonic motives are those that are based on emotional, experiential, subjective rewards (Solomon 1992). We believe that motivations can be more successfully measured and related to consumer behavior when they are developed for a particular consumer behavioral context, and thus have developed motivational constructs specific to gift-giving behavior.

Sherry (1983) has written that gift-giving motivations may range from altruistic (maximize satisfaction of receiver) to agonistic (maximize personal satisfaction). Not coincidentally, the existence of these two motivations for giving (altruistic vs. agonistic) have been posited and debated in academic discussions of gift giving, with giving out of obligation or to obligate others generally being believed to be the motive for giving (cf. Bourdieu 1977, 1979; Caplow 1982, 1984; Cheal 1988; Levi-Strauss 1965; Mauss 1954). However, a unidimensional "spectrum" view, with positive motivations on one end, and obligated, self-interested motivations on the other end, may be misleading, as Sherry and McGrath (1989) noted that gift shoppers often express ambivalence about choosing gifts. Therefore, the two factors (an obligated and an experiential/positive attitude) are posited to represent two distinct motivations, rather than opposite ends of a spectrum. An experiential/positive attitude towards giving, or giving to show love, is primarily a hedonic motive, while giving out of obligation can reflect both hedonic (giving to avoid guilt) and utilitarian motives (giving to obligate someone else).

A third conceptually distinct motivation considered is the orientation towards giving practical gifts. Functional gifts are given in order to provide the receiver with practical assistance, and thus the motivation is primarily utilitarian. While such gifts predominate for rites of passage such as weddings (Devere, Scott and Shulby 1983), there are some types of givers who tend to give such gifts, regardless of the receiver or occasion (Belk 1979). Following is a more complete discussion of each of these motivations.

AN EXPERIENTIAL/POSITIVE ORIENTATION TOWARDS GIVING

An experiential/positive orientation toward giving is reflected in the fact that these givers (1) give a great deal of thought and effort to gift selection, (2) enjoy choosing gifts and (3) feel that gifts are a way of showing love and friendship to receivers. The popular press generally offers articles every gift-giving season on choosing gifts, and generally focuses on expressing positive attitudes. For instance, Barbara Bertocci, writing for the *Reader's Digest*, offers the following advice: (1) Be sure the gift has special meaning to the recipient, and ask yourself what is important to the recipient (2) be alert for a gift the recipient may want without realizing it (3) offer your time and talent (4) don't wait for a special occasion because it shows people you really care (1991).

Barnett (1954) writes of the "carol philosophy" expressed in the novel *A Christmas Carol* (Dickens 1843), pointing out that the book's continued popularity is in part due to the enduring appeal of the book's theme that individual selfishness leads to misery, while brotherhood, kindness and generosity are rewarded. The same theme is apparent in O'Henry's "Gift of the Maji," in which Dell sells her long hair to buy a chain for her husband Jim's heirloom watch, while Jim sells his watch to buy tortoiseshell combs for her hair. Nevertheless, social scientists have been less quick than novelists and journalists to focus on this theme in giving. Recently, however, Cheal (1988) has offered a softer interpretation of gift giving than most other scholars. He separates interpersonal giving (between 2 people) from intergroup giving (between representatives of groups) and uses this as a basis for pointing out the former giving relationship belongs to the sphere of our domestic private lives, where caretaking activities are a focus (the "moral economy"), while the latter belongs to the marketplace (the "political economy"). One of the manifestations of this moral economy is the desire to give to others as an expression of love for them (Cheal 1988).

Giving to others in some sense allows us to include those others in our extended selves (Belk 1988). In support of this idea, Beatty et al. (1991) discovered that across both Oriental and American students, those who reported warm relationships with others as their most important value were more likely to perceive that they exerted more effort than did others in gift giving. These "warm" givers most likely perceive a link between themselves and the giver, and between themselves and the object given. Appadurai (1986) argues that economic exchange of commodities tends to dissolve links between persons and things; gift giving behavior, it can be argued, restores and creates these links. Similarly, Sahlins (1972) writes that the material flow of gifts "underwrites and initiates social relations" (p. 140).

OBLIGATED ATTITUDES TOWARDS GIVING

Giving because one feels obligated is behavior which is motivated by compliance with the social norm of giving. Obligated givers (1) experience guilt if they don't give, (2) give because of others' expectations and, (3) feel they must reciprocate when they have received a gift. In fact, manipulative, self-interested giving is possible insofar as receivers feel they must conform with the social norm of reciprocation.

In general, social scientists have tended to assume motivations for giving, and more often than not, this motivation is assumed to be the creation of obligation for the receiver to reciprocate with gifts, or be permanently indebted. The creation of obligation was central to Mauss' (1954) study of gift giving in primitive societies. Similarly, Barnett (1954), in his analysis of Christmas gift giving from the 1800s to the 1950s in the United States, comments on a similar phenomenon, calling it "pseudo-giving" and a "polite form of bribery." Levi-Strauss (1965, 1969), Bourdieu (1977), Firth (1983), Gregory (1982) and Moschetti (1979) all emphasize the theme that the voluntary appearance of gift giving is in reality an illusion. Recently, consumer behavior scholars Garner and Wagner (1991) have joined the cynics, concluding from the finding that gifts are a "luxury good," that gifts are used to "buy" social interaction.

PRACTICALITY OF THE GIFT GIVER

A practical gift-giving motivation is reflected in the giver's perception that especially useful gifts that receivers need are the best kind to buy. For practical gift givers, the primary motivation for giving is to provide practical assistance to receivers. This rationale can be understood as partially motivating the use of various rites of passage as gift-giving events as these gifts are often given largely to support the creation and regeneration of households. In fact, in Canada, many brides and grooms indicate in their invitations that "presentations" will be accepted. This notation means that money (perhaps the most practical of gifts) is preferred to presents; during the wedding reception, guests line up and hand the couple envelopes with money as they go through and congratulate the couple (Cheal 1988). In Japan, weddings in particular, but other gift giving events as well, are likely to draw money from most givers (Johnson 1974). This money is given to defray the cost of the wedding reception and is scaled to the perceived expense of the reception.

Sherry and McGrath's (1989) study of 2 upscale gift shops shows that the shops' strategy was to sell gifts that *are not* practical, with one promotional brochure reading "everything you don't need, can't afford, but can't live without." Popular literature on gift giving often offers advice *against* giving particularly practical gifts, with the prototypical bad practical gift being a man giving his wife a kitchen appliance (Browning 1990). Moreover, Sherry and McGrath (1989) believe that we invest expressive gifts with greater symbolic value than utilitarian gifts. Nevertheless, practical gifts such as Cross Pens for retirees, blenders and toasters for brides, and dictionaries for graduates are a prominent feature of gift occasions.

STUDY 1

Forty one attitudinal items were investigated in order to develop these constructs. These items were based on several sources: (1) extant gift-giving literature (2) three prior gift-giving questionnaires which included attitudinal items (3) open ended responses of respondents in a role playing experiment when asked why they would choose a particular gift item (4) an earlier questionnaire constructed by Beatty (1990). A special effort was made to include items which it was felt would be representative of the three constructs. Moreover, many reverse scored items were included, but do not appear in the final scales, as their semantic content was not judged by respondents to have equal but opposite meanings to their counterparts. Items appeared on a seven point semantic differential scale from strongly disagree to strongly agree. Respondents were 159 undergraduate marketing students at a major Southern California University. Results of the analysis must be interpreted somewhat cautiously, as Hair, Anderson and Tatham (1991) suggest 4 to 5 as many observations as scale items as a conservative rule for factor analysis; the ratio in this study is 3.9:1.

ANALYSIS OF ITEMS

The original 41 items were pared to 15. Items were dropped from analysis based on the following criteria: (1) An item did not load on any factor which, as indicated by the scree plot, should be retained for analysis; (2) An item loaded strongly on multiple factors, and thus failed to adequately discriminate one construct

TABLE 1
Study 1, Factor Analysis of Items, Varimax Rotation

	Experiential	Obligated	Practical
CAREFUL	.74970	-.05260	.03222
UNIQUE	.74664	-.01344	.10861
CREATE	.74059	-.13853	-.02151
FUN	.56517	.03968	-.05438
MESSAGE	.54348	-.11427	.10314
GOODJOB	.53813	-.18665	-.03855
LOVE	.49910	-.12708	.20169
OBLIGE	.03380	.80757	.08148
GUILTY	-.08217	.76089	.16668
EXPECT	-.14127	.60416	-.12769
OBLIGATE	-.01246	.48794	.07507
WAIT	-.11231	.44651	.02156
USEFUL	-.01365	.00965	.77072
NEED	.12755	.04082	.64650
LAST	.14432	.04629	.51781

from another; (3) A tabulation of responses for the item indicated that the results were heavily skewed to one end of the scale, indicating that the item did not discriminate between constructs; (4) A cutoff of .30 was used in deciding which items to retain (Hair et al. 1991).

Because the purpose was the identification of constructs rather than data reduction, principle axis factoring (common factor analysis) was utilized as the method of factor analysis (Hair et al. 1991). The rotated solution (Varimax rotation) appears in Table 1. The questionnaire items utilized appear in Table 2. Both the scree plot and eigenvalues indicate that a three factor solution is appropriate. Forty-eight percent of the variance is explained by the three factor solution.

A further check of the solution is provided by reliability analysis. Cronbach's alpha was calculated for each of the constructs. For the seven items making up experiential/positive motivations, the alpha was a strong .82. Reliability for the five items making up the obligation scale also had a strong alpha of .75. For the last item, practicality, the alpha was .68, indicating further need of development. Table 3 portrays correlations between factors. Only experiential and obligated attitudes were related, but the correlation, though significant, was low (r=-.20, p<.01). The three constructs, it can be concluded, represent different factors.

STUDY TWO

The fifteen items suggested by the analysis of study one were retained. Because the scale representing practicality had reliability of only .68 in the previous study, one item was added to the analysis, making a total of 16 items. As before, items appeared on a seven point semantic differential scale from strongly disagree to strongly agree. Respondents were 225 staff at a major Southern California University. The group was fairly diverse: ages ranged from 22 to 78 with 41 being average, and 40 being the median; 1.4% had household incomes under 19,999, 25% had incomes between 20,000 and 34,999, almost 20% had incomes between 35,000-49,000, 35% had incomes between 50,000 and 75,000, and 20% had incomes of 75,000 or more. Education ranged from high school graduate or less (5%), to some college (34%) to college graduate (35%) to graduate degree (25%). Fully 73% of respondents were female.

ANALYSIS OF ITEMS

Again, principle axis factoring was utilized with Varimax rotation. The loadings for factors appear in Table 4. All 16 items loaded as expected. Forty five percent of the variance was explained by the three factor solution. Looking at the scree plot, explained variance drops off sharply after the third factor.

A further check of the solution is provided by reliability analysis. For the seven items making up experiential motivations, the Cronbach's alpha was .78. For the 5 items making up the obligation scale the alpha was .79. The four items making up the practical scale had a reliability of .83.

Discriminant validity between factors is shown in Table 3. There are no significant correlations between positive and obligated or between practical and positive attitudes. However, there was an unexpected moderate and significant positive relationship between practical and obligated attitudes (r=.29, p<.001). Nevertheless, the correlation is low enough to consider the two motivations to be different constructs. Also, this correlation did not appear in sample 1, suggesting either differences between the two samples, or the fact that this correlation may be coincidental.

NOMOLOGICAL VALIDITY

The following are results predicted by gift-giving researchers with respect to the three variables. Women are disproportionately involved in the "moral" domestic economy and are thus more likely to have an experiential

motivation for giving. This expectation was borne out (M_f=37.5; M_m=34.7, p=.001.)

Older women, in their roles of keepers and teachers of tradition, are more likely to give out of social obligation. However, sex was not related to the feeling that one was obligated, while age was actually inversely related to the feeling of giving out of obligation (older respondents expressed *less* of a feeling of obligation) (r=-.19, p=.001). Perhaps the norm of giving is stronger among these older respondents, and they are less likely to experience giving as an obligation, but rather as a socially appropriate and desirable event.

With respect to practical gifts, popular literature has suggested that men are more likely to give practical gifts, while Caplow's findings (1982) are consistent with the notion that men give more practical gifts. Tannen (1990) notes that men tend to play the role

TABLE 2
Items Used in Studies

Experiential/Positive Motivations For Giving

Carefully selecting a gift is important to me.
It is important to me to choose a unique gift.
Choosing gifts brings out my creative side.
I especially like to give gifts that are fun.
I try to choose gifts that convey a personal message to the receiver.
I think I do a better job choosing gifts than do most people.
Gifts are an important way of communicating love and friendship to others.

Obligated Motivations For Giving

I often feel obliged to give gifts.
I often give gifts because I would feel guilty if I didn't.
I often give gifts because I am expected to give them.
When I receive a gift, I feel that I am obligated to reciprocate at that time or at some time in the future.
I often wait until the last minute to purchase a gift.

Practical Motivations For Giving

I feel it is especially important to give gifts that are useful to the receiver.
It's important to choose gifts that everybody needs, but don't yet own.
I think it is important to give gifts that last a long time.
*I like to buy practical gifts.

*Item appeared only in Study 2.

TABLE 3
Correlation Matrices

Study One:

	Obligated	Practical	Experiential
Obligated	1.00	.08	-.20*
Practical		1.00	.15
Experiential			1.00

Study Two:

	Obligated	Practical	Experiential
Obligated	1.00	.29**	-.14
Practical		1.00	.04
Experiential			1.00

* $p<.01$
** $p<.001$

of problem solver with respect to interpersonal relationships, while women tend simply to provide emotional support, a notion consistent with the idea that men are more likely to buy practical gifts. However, men were only slightly more likely than women to express a preference for giving such gifts ($M_f=17.3$, $M_m=18.6$, $p=.09$).

Based on Cheal's (1988) case analyses, and on the common sense notion that those with less money would focus more on utilitarian rather than symbolic giving, it was expected that lower income givers would be more likely to express practical giving motivations; however, no relationship was found between income level and practical motivations. However, another element of socioeconomic status, education, was found to be related to practicality of giving, with college graduates and post-graduates less likely to report a preference for giving practical gifts, as compared to those with less education ($M_g=17.1$, $M_{ng}=18.6$, $p=.04$). Predictive validity at this point is moderate, and is hampered by the fact that there have been few theoretical and empirical findings concerning gift-giving motivations.

POTENTIAL USEFULNESS OF THE SCALES

This study represents the culmination of a series of studies aimed at the development of measures which would reliably and validly measure these three gift-giving constructs of interest. The three constructs of interest, experiential, obligated and practical motivations have been shown to be three relatively distinct attitudes which are measurable utilizing the 16 items extracted in these studies. This research effort buttresses the notion that more positive, experiential attitudes and more (negative) obligated attitudes are not necessarily at opposite ends of an attitudinal spectrum,

TABLE 4
Study 2, Factor Analysis of Items, Varimax Rotation

	Experiential	Obligated	Practical
MESSAGE	.74266	-.04900	.02027
UNIQUE	.70406	.07567	-.04256
CREATE	.69263	-.10523	-.04461
CAREFUL	.54507	-.09736	.02795
GOODJOB	.44003	-.13908	.04226
FUN	.37835	-.01238	-.02378
LOVE	.36815	.00701	.16903
GUILTY	-.00536	.84947	.14293
OBLIGED	.00983	.82975	.20292
EXPECT	-.10524	.74105	-.00868
OBLIGATE	.00400	.54968	.18418
WAIT	-.18830	.32009	.08690
USEFUL	.01428	.15093	.84077
PRACTICAL	-.05087	.18087	.72026
NEED	-.05973	.19469	.71337
LAST	.07845	.01129	.65609

which supports Sherry and McGrath's (1989) and Tournier's (1963) observations about the existence of ambivalence in gift-giving attitudes.

A further contribution of this effort is a concession of sorts to givers in allowing them to express their perceived feelings and motivations about giving, rather than to have these motivations deduced or (perhaps) imposed by scholars. Motivations for interpersonal gift-giving are complex, and, not surprisingly, are not monolithic in the sense that they are not driven completely by self-interest, or completely by other-interest. Hopefully, this effort represents one small step in demystifying *why* people give, as the givers have been allowed to express their own self-perceived motivations.

These concepts and items may serve well as predictors and covariates in gift-giving studies. For example, motivations for giving are probably the causal link between gender orientation of givers and gift giving effort discovered by Fisher and Arnold (1990), as it would be expected that more feminine givers are more likely to express experiential, positive attitudes towards giving. If such relationships were found, nomological validity for these scale items would begin to be established.

Moreover, it is likely that these individual difference variables impact symbols chosen. In an exploratory study wherein subjects were asked to identify a recent gift-giving experience and then asked to answer a series of open-ended questions regarding why the gift was given, what communication was intended, and what was expected in return, Goodwin et al. (1990) found support for the notion that, when giving was perceived as obligatory, gifts were less likely to express recipient or donor identities (to be symbolic of the giver and receiver), and less likely to communicate feelings (to be emotionally significant). In addition, givers with more obligated attitudes would be expected to choose more conventional gifts, as such gifts are generally easier to select and buy than other types of gifts. Moreover, those givers with more practical orientations would perhaps be likely to choose less emotionally significant and individualized gifts, and more conventional gifts. On the other hand, givers with more experiential motivations would be expected to select more emotionally significant and individualized gifts for receivers.

Also, in addition to expending less effort in symbolic enhancement of gifts, those whose motivation for giving is obligation may spend less money on gifts. This prediction is consistent with the finding that givers spent more on flower purchases perceived as voluntary as opposed to those perceived to be obligatory (Scammon, Shaw and Bamossy 1982).

The few gift-giving studies undertaken in cross-cultural contexts indicate differences in giving attitudes (Green and Alden 1988; Jolibert and Fernandez-Moreno 1983). For instance, Japanese givers seem to feel more obligated and less positive about giving than do American givers (Witkowski and Yamamoto 1991). The development of these attitudinal scales and applications in other cultures should allow a deeper understanding into the differences between cultures in gift-giving attitudes and behavior.

An understanding of these variables could lead to segmentation strategies for gift marketers, especially if such attitudes are reliably related to demographic variables such as sex and income. For instance, the Sherry and McGrath (1989) study seems to indicate that among upper middle class women, there are positive attitudes towards giving, and a desire to buy emotionally significant and individualized gifts, and to avoid buying practical gifts. Knowing the attitudes of the target market can lead to more effectively choosing products and advertising copy for different segments.

LIMITATIONS OF SCALE DEVELOPMENT EFFORT

Further validation of these scales is required. With respect to nomological validity, we have speculated that these motivations will be useful in predicting several kinds of outcomes, but we have only offered limited empirical support. Further research utilizing these scales is necessary in order to establish their predictive power.

Moreover, content validity would be enhanced if judges were employed to rate consistency of items with definition of the constructs. Also, members of a sample could be asked open ended questions as to why they give, and these responses could be coded and correlated to responses on scale items. Test-retest reliability should be employed to determine reliability across time. Criterion-related validity would be determined by comparing scores on dimensions with more direct measures. For instance, positive givers would be expected to give more gifts than others. Practical gift givers should report a higher percentage of practical gifts actually given than do other givers.

Importantly, discriminant reliability is limited as none of the constructs were compared to existing constructs that may measure similar motivations. An experiential/positive attitude toward giving may be related to possessiveness and generosity (Belk 1985). This dimension may also be related to Tellegen's scales concerning positive (agentive and communal) emotionality (1985). Giving because of perceived obligation may be related to Noller et al.'s social conformity scale (1987). Giving practical gifts may be related to Hogan's prudence scale (1986). In short, future scale development must focus more concertedly on content, predictive, and discriminant validity.

CONCLUSION

We have argued and presented evidence that motivations for giving are multifaceted. Furthermore, although there are likely to be situational variables such as occasion and closeness to the receiver which would impact these motivations, we have posited that givers also have general orientations towards giving and that these general orientations may differ between givers. Moreover, we have developed scale items in order to measure these motivations in giving. Such development should facilitate gift-giving research by enabling researchers to allow givers to express their self-perceived motivations for giving. This development is especially useful if these self-perceived motivations are shown to have power in predicting gift-giving behavior.

REFERENCES

Appadurai, Arjun (1986), *The Social Life of Things: Commodities in Culturual Perspective*, Cambridge: Cambridge University Press.

Barnett, James (1984), *The American Christmas: A Study in National Culture*, Salem, New Hampshire: Ayer Company.

Bartocci, Barbara (1991), "Real Ways to Say You Care," *Reader's Digest*, November, 47-52.

Beatty, Sharon E., Lynn R. Kahle, and Pamela Homer (1990), "Personal Values and Gift-Giving Behaviors: A Study Across Cultures," *Journal of Business Research*.

Beatty, Sharon, (1990), Personal Communication.

Belk, Russell, "Possessions and the Extended Self," *Journal of Consumer Research*, 15 (September), 139-168.

Belk, Russell, "Trait Aspects of Living in the Material World," *Journal of Consumer Research*, 12 (December), 265-280.

(1982), "Effects of Gift-Giving Involvement on Gift-Giving Strategies," in *Advances in Consumer Research*, Vol. 9, ed. Andrew A. Mitchell, Ann Arbor, MI: Association for Consumer Research, 531-536.

(1979), "Gift-Giving Behavior," *Research in Marketing*, Vol. 2, ed. Jagdish Sheth, Greenwich, CT: JAI Press, 95-126.

(1976), "It's the Thought that Counts: A Signed Digraph Analysis of Gift-Giving," *Journal of Consumer Research*, 3 (December), 155-162.

Bordieu, Pierre (1979), *Algeria 1960*, Cambridge: Cambridge University Press.

(1977), *Outline of a Theory of Practice*, Cambridge: Cambridge University Press.

Browning, Graeme (1990), "What's Hot and What's 'No Way' When It's Time to Give a Gift," *Los Angeles Times (Orange County Edition)*, December 21, E2.

Caplow, Theodore (1984), "Rule Enforcement Without Visible Means: Christmas Gift-Giving in Middletown," *American Journal of Sociology*, 89 (6), 1306-1323.

(1982), "Christmas Gifts and Kin Networks," *American Sociological Review*, 47(3), 383-392.

Cheal, David (1988), *The Gift Economy*, New York: Routledge.

Clarke, Keith and Russell Belk (1978), "The Effects of Product Involvement and Task Definition on Anticipated Consumer Effort", *Advances in Consumer Research*, ed. William Wilkie, Chicago, Illionois: Association for Consumer Research, 313-318.

Devere, Stephen P., Clifford D. Scott, and William L. Shulby (1983), "Consumer Perceptions of Gift-Giving Occasions: Attribute Saliency and Structure," in *Advances in Consumer Research*, eds. Richard P. Bagozzi and Alice M. Tybout, Ann Arbor, MI: Association for Consumer Research, 185-190.

Fischer, Eileen and Stephen J. Arnold (1990), "More Than A Labor of Love: Gender Roles and Christmas Gift Shopping," *Journal of Consumer Research*, Volume 17, No. 3, December, 333-345.

Firth, Raymond (1983), "Magnitudes and Values in Kula Exchange," in *The Kula: New Perspectives on Massim Exchange*, eds. J. W. Leach and E. Leach, Cambridge: Cambridge University Press.

Garner, Thesia I. and Janet Wagner (1991), "Economic Dimensions of Household Gift Giving," *Journal of Consumer Research*, Volume 18 (3), December, 368-379.

Goodwin, Cathy et al. (1990), "Gift giving: Consumer Motivation and the Gift Purchase Process" in *Advances in Consumer Research*, Vol. 17, eds. Richard Pollay and Gerald Gorn, Provo, UT: Association for Consumer Research, 690-698.

Green, Robert T. and Dana L. Alden (1988), "Functional Equivalence in Cross-Cultural Consumer Behavior: Gift Giving in Japan and the United States," *Psychology and Marketing*, Volume 5 (2), Summer, 155-168.

Gregory, Christopher A. (1982), *Gifts and Commodities*, London: Academic Press.

Hair, Joseph, Ralph E. Anderson and Ronald L. Tatham (1991), *Multivariate Statistical Analysis*, 3rd ed., New York: Macmillan Publishing Company.

Hogan, R. (1986), *Hogan Personality Inventory Manual*, Minneapolis: National Computer Systems.

Johnson, Colleen L. (1974), "Gift giving and Reciprocity among the Japanese Americans in Honolulu," *American Ethnologist*, I (2), 295-308.

Jolibert, Alain J. P. and Carlos Fernandez-Moreno (1983), "A Comparison of French and Mexican Gift-Giving Practices," in *Advances in Consumer Research*, Vol. 10, ed. Richard P. Bagozzi and Alice M. Tybout, Ann Arbor, MI: Association for Consumer Research, 191-196.

Levi-Strauss, Claude (1965), "The Principle of Reciprocity," in *Sociological Theory*, eds. L. A. Coser and B. Rosenberg, New York: McMillan.

Mauss, Marcel (1954), *The Gift*, London: Cohen and West.

Maslow, Abraham H. (1970), *Motivation and Personality*. New York: Harper and Row Publishers, Inc.

Murray, Edward J. (1964), *Motivation and Emotion*. Englewood Cliffs, N. J.: Prentice-Hall, Inc.

Mick, David Glen and Michelle DeMoss (1990), "Self-Gifts: Phenomenological Insights from Four Contexts," *Journal of Consumer Research*, 17 (3), December, 322-332.

Moschetti, Gregory J. (1979), "The Christmas Potlatch: A Refinement on the Sociological Interpretation of Exchange," *Sociological Focus*, 12, 1-7.

Noller, P., H. Law, and A. L. Comrey (1987), Cattell, Comrey and Eysenck Personality Factors Compared: More evidence for the five robust factors? *Journal of Personality and Social Psychology*, 53, 775-782.

Sahlins, Marshall (1972), *Stone Age Economics*. Chicago: Aldine.

Scammon, Debra, Roy Shaw and Gary Bamossy (1982), "Is a Gift Always a Gift? An Investigation of Flower Purchasing Behavior Across Situations," in *Advances in Consumer Research*, Vol. 9, ed. Andrew Mitchell, Provo, UT: Association for Consumer Research, 408-411.

Sherry, John and Mary Ann McGrath (1989), "Unpacking the Holiday Presence: A Comparative Ethnography of the Gift Store," in *Interpretive Consumer Research*, ed. Elizabeth Hirschman, Provo, UT: Association for Consumer Research, 148-167.

(1983), "Gift Giving in Anthropological Perspective," *Journal of Consumer Research*, 10 (September), 157-167.

Solomon, Michael R. (1992) *Consumer Behavior: Having, Being and Buying*. Boston, MA: Allyn and Bacon.

Tellegen, A. (1985), "Structures of Mood and Personality and their Relevance to Assessing Anxiety, with an Emphasis on Self-Report. In A. H. Tuman and J. D. Maser (Eds), *Anxiety and Anxiety Disorders*, Hillsdale, N.J.: Erlbaum, pp. 681-716.

Tannen, Deborah (1990), *You Just Don't Understand: Women and Men in Conversation*, New York: William Morrow and Company, Inc.

Tournier, Paul (1963), *The Meaning of Gifts*, Richmond: John Knox Press.

Witkowski, Terry and Yoshito Yamamoto (1991), "*Omiyage* Gift Purchasing by Japanese Travelers in the US," in *Advances in Consumer Research*, Vol. 18, eds. Rebecca Holman and Michael Solomon, Provo, UT: Association for Consumer Research, 123-128.

Wolfinbarger, Mary (1990), "Motivations and Symbolism in Gift-Giving Behavior," in *Advances in Consumer Research*, Vol. 17, eds. Richard Pollay and Gerald Gorn, Provo, UT: Association for Consumer Research, 699-706.

Measuring Cohort Role On Husband-Wife Differences In Temporal Behavior

Jacob Hornik, University of Chicago and Tel-Aviv University

ABSTRACT

Recent studies demonstrated inconsistencies in husbands and wives responses to various social issues. This paper presents a measurement procedure for comparing the responses of husbands and wives while also considering one of the groups cohort. The procedure was employed in a study concerning consumers' temporal orientation. The method is based on D^2 distances. In addition to constructing the differences between the groups, the paper compares the statistical procedures for assessing significant differences among the measured distances. Formal statistical tests are employed, as well as graphical methods for presenting results. The suggested approach seems useful in a variety of consumer research areas over and beyond the area of husband-wife differences.

INTRODUCTION

The literature in the social sciences and particularly in consumer behavior contains a growing number of studies concerned with similarities and differences between husbands and their wives with respect to their attitudes, preferences and decision-making processes.[1] Notable examples are the studies on sex-role orientation and its influence on the household decision process (e.g. Qualls 1987); differences in product evaluation (Sung-Tai and Toner 1989); inconsistencies in contraceptive use responses and sexual behavior (Koening, Simmons and Misra 1984); differences in general life-style determinants (Roberts and Wortzel 1979); media usage (Hornik and Schlinger 1981); and, more recently, differences between husbands and wives in their perception of time (Umesh, Weeks and Golden 1988) their time use, time orientation and preferences (e.g. Hornik 1985).

These findings led many researchers to challenge the use of the household as a unit of analysis and to call for more methodological studies as well as measurement procedures to compare husbands and their wives on various behavioral domains (Blau and Ferber 1986).

The present paper was part of a more comprehensive project investigating individuals' time allocation, perception and orientation. The primary objective of this paper is to offer a general statistical framework based on Mahalanobis distances (Kshirsager and Arseren 1975; Morrison 1988) to compare husbands with their wives with regard to their time orientation, while considering cohort influences, too. This paper is, therefore, more concerned with the methodological than the comparison issue.

Time Orientation

The many facets of time as a concept central to household behavior have been much discussed by economists, psychologists, and consumer behavior researchers. These investigations are primarily concerned with three aspects of household time: time allocation/behavior, time perception, and time orientation. Time orientation (or perspective) refers to the relative dominance of past, present, or future in a person's thoughts and its perceived pace (Reichler and Brickman 1989). If people make daily decisions on the basis of their expectations concerning the present, and the future, their time perspective is obviously important. Individual differences in time orientation was used, for example, to explain decision differences in adopting new products (Lee and Ferber 1977) and in conducting negotiations (Qualls 1987). Recently Bergadaa (1990) found that those with present time orientations selected vacations with an emphasis on relaxation, while those with a future time orientation were more likely to select a vacation by considering the enrichment dimension. Complete individual orientation to and preference for the past, present or future do not necessarily reflect a stable inner state (Rakowski 1986). They are, rather personal judgments which, like other judgments, are subject to a variety of influences, including those of the family, age cohort and other social groups (Holahan and Gilbert 1979). The evolving status of women, fuelled by their increasing education and occupational attainment coupled with the feminist movement has been regarded in the literature as a major force underlying cohort influence on married women's temporal attitudes and preferences. Some investigators (e.g. Holahan and Gilbert 1979) have argued that recent social trends made wives closer to their cohort than to their husbands on some dimensions of their life style and time orientation. Therefore, reported temporal inconsistencies between individual members are suggested to be coused, primarily, by cohort influences, especially on wives. Indeed, recent studies beg the question of whether wives were closer to their husbands or their cohort with respect to their time orientation (e.g. Reichler and Brickman 1989). However, previous research on these issues has been hampered by a variety of methodological problems, including data limitations (Settle, Alreck and Glasheen 1977), lack of statistical rigor, and possible bias in parameter estimation (Feldman and Hornik 1981). Kiker and Ling Chu Ng (1990) as well as Reichler and Brickman (1989) called, independently, for the development of analytical methods to compare spouses on their temporal behavior while controlling for possible social influences.

METHODS

As noted before, the data for this study came from two recent experiments that were part of a larger study on consumers' intertemporal choices and preferences. A full description of data and procedure is provided in a companion paper (Hornik and Meir 1992). For brevity, we will not repeat all details of the data collection methodology employed. To review very briefly, participants were married females attending a child development session in a University extension program. Subjects were asked to respond to a two-page form containing a time-orientation task.

For this investigation a cohort group was obtained using Glenns (1976) "cohort table". Specifically, from the women who participated in the two experiments, in this study were included 397 married women who were born between 1953 and 1960. Also, a group of husbands (n=73), selected randomly from the interviewed women, was also included. This group was smaller than the women's group for practical reasons. Husbands followed the same procedure and completed the same questionnaire (without the presence of their wives). The comparison of each wife with her husband, regarding time perspective, was obviously performed on the data relating to the couples only. However, it should be emphasized that the larger data set, which was available for the entire group of wives, was also utilized in the study. This extra information was incorporated in the construction of the statistical distances.

Instrument: Of the time-orientation instruments suggested by researchers, the Time Reference Inventory (TRI) was used in the

---

[1] For a recent comprehensive review see Menasco and Currey (1989).

present study. The TRI was developed by Roos and Albers (1965) and further modified by others (e.g., Fitzpatrick, Donovan and Johnson 1980). The modified TRI is a 32-item paper and pencil instrument. Items refer to different life events and their perceived speed of movement. It is based on four subscales: future orientation (FO), present orientation (PO), past orientation (ST), and pace perception (PP). The TRI is intuitively appealing and scored.[2]

ANALYTICAL FRAMEWORK

Consider any population, and let x_i denote the k-dimensional vector of the values of the random variable X for the ith subject in the population. Let Σ be the covariance matrix of X. The Mahalanobis squared distance (D^2) between subjects i and j is defined as:

$$D^2(x_i, x_j) = (x_i - x_j)' \Sigma^{-1} (x_i - x_j) \quad [1]$$

where x_i, x_j are the respective X values for subjects i and j. Unlike the Euclidean distance, D^2 takes into account the correlations and variances of the components of X. In this study, the components of X are the time perspective items, and they take any integer value between 1 and 5. We need to define three distances: between the husband and his wife, between the wife and her cohort (other wives), and between the husband and his wife's cohort.

For constructing the distance between any two wives, there is no question of which Σ to use in D^2 because both belong to the same population. However, for the distance between a husband and his wife we could use for Σ either the covariance matrix of the husbands, or that of the wives, or a pooled estimate. In the present case, it seemed more appropriate to use the wives' covariance matrix because we were interested in distances with respect to the wife population. Thus, all the Mahalanobis distances that were constructed were expressed in terms of the covariance matrix of the wife population. For estimating this matrix we took advantage of the large sample of wives (N=397).

Algebraic Formulation

Let $\hat{\Sigma}$ denote the estimated covariance matrix based on the N observations. $\hat{\Sigma}$ is usually a consistent estimate of Σ.[3] Denote each paired observation of (wife, husband) by (x_i, x_j), $i = 1,...,n$. The squared distance between the wife and her husband, denoted by $D^2(x_i, y_i)$, is defined according to equation 1 by the following:

$$D^2(x_i, y_i) = (x_i - y_i)' \Sigma^{-1} (x_i - y_i) \quad [2]$$

where Σ is the sample covariance matrix of X, based on the X values of the N wives.

We now define the distance between wife i (i = 1,...,n) and her cohort, denoting it by $D^2(x_i, X)$. Again, we take advantage of the N available observations. According to equation 1 the squared distance between any two wives is $D^2(x_i, x_j)$, j = 1,...,N; j ≠ i. Thus we can define as $D^2(x_i, X)$ the average:

---

[2] An early analysis of the TRI instrument showed the following internal consistency reliabilities (Chronbach's alpha) for the four time-orientation subscales: past .85; present .91; future .87; and pace .84.

[3] For large N (as N = 397), the estimated $\hat{\Sigma}$ can be considered as being practically equal to Σ.

$$D^2(x_i, X) = \frac{1}{N-1} \sum_{\substack{j=1 \\ i \neq j}}^{N} D^2(x_i, x_j) \quad [3]$$

Similarly, we define the squared distance between the ith husband and his wife's cohort as:

$$D^2(y_i, X) = \frac{1}{N} \sum_{j=1}^{N} D^2(y_i, x_j) \quad [4]$$

The question of whether wives are closer to their husbands or to their cohort is answered by comparing the paired data values of ($D^2[x_i, y_i]$, $D^2[x_i, X]$). Our analysis on the wife-husband relationship is based on the three distances defined by equations 2-4.

Note that another distance should be considered - between an individual (husband or wife) and the wife population. As the squared distance -between wife i and her cohort we could consider $D^2(x_i, \bar{x})$, namely, the squared distance of wife i from the centroid of the wives population. $\bar{x}$ is defined as the average:

$$\bar{x} = \frac{1}{N} \sum_{i=1}^{N} x_i \quad [5]$$

Given that $D^2(x_i, x_j)$ (and $D^2[x_i, y_i]$) are squared distances between individuals, that is, between two random observations, whereas $D^2(x_i, \bar{x})$ is the squared distance between an individual and a mean, these distances should not be compared without a correcting factor. The expected value of $D^2(x_i, x_j)$ is:

$$E(D^2[x_i, x_j]) = 2k$$

Therefore, the average $D^2(x_i, X)$, defined by equation 3, also has an expected value of 2k. Similarly, under the null hypothesis that there is no correlation between x_i and y_i and that there is no difference between husbands and wives, y_i is a random observation from the X population and

$$E(D^2[y_i, x_i]) = 2k \quad [6]$$

On the other hand,

$$E(D^2[y_i, \bar{x}_i]) = k \quad [7]$$

Indeed, one may expect a much larger distance between two observations drawn at random from a population than between a random observation and the sample mean. Therefore, to answer whether wives are closer in their time perspective to their husbands or their cohort, we could have considered comparing the three statistics: $2D^2(x_i, x)$, $2D^2(y_i, x)$, and $D^2(x_i, y_i)$. Our choice of comparing instead the three measures, $D^2(x_i, X)$, $D^2(y_i, X)$, and $D^2(x_i, y_i)$, was arbitrary.

One should also note the relationship between the two possible measures under discussion: {$2D^2(x_i, x)$} and $D^2(x_i, X)$. Their averages over the N wives are essentially equal because

$$\frac{1}{N-1} \sum_{i=1}^{N} \{2D^2(x_i, \bar{x})\} = \frac{1}{N} \sum_{i=1}^{N} D^2(x_i, X) \quad [8]$$

This formula is analogous to the well-known relationship for univariate data: $X_i,...,X_N$ (Anderson 1958):

$$s_x^2 = \frac{1}{N-1} \sum_{i=1}^{N} (x_i, \bar{x})^2 = \frac{1}{N(N-1)} \sum_{i \neq 1} (x_i, x_j)^2 \qquad [9]$$

The Empirical Model

For each of the n paired observations (x_i, y_i), three distances were constructed. Our main purpose was to compare $D(x_i, y_i)$ with $D(x_i, X)$, though we can also learn about the husband-wife relationships by investigating $D(y_i, X)$.

The first part of comparing $D(x_i, y_i)$ with $D(x_i, X)$ is a location comparison for paired observations. The Wilcoxon signed rank test is suitable for the comparison.

A graphical summary of the three distances can be performed by drawing a triangle whose edges are proportional to the three "typical" distances. For each of the subscales one can draw a triangle whose edges are proportional to the average of the square root of the Mahalanobis distances formally presented:

$$\frac{1}{n} \sum_{i=1}^{n} D(x_i, X); \frac{1}{n} \sum_{i=1}^{n} D(y_i, X); \frac{1}{n} \sum_{i=1}^{n} D(x_i, y_i) \qquad [10]$$

The triangle was drawn in this case such that its base was proportional to the first of the three averages in formula 10, namely,

$$\bar{D} = \frac{1}{n} \sum_{i=1}^{n} D(x_i, X)$$

Because

$$E(D^2[x_i, X]) = 2k$$

the value of $\bar{D}$ should be approximately equal to $\sqrt{2k}$. Given that

$$2k = ED^2 \geq (ED)^2$$

one should expect

$$\bar{D} \leq \sqrt{2k}$$

Indeed, as shown by the data obtained, the bases of the triangles were less than $\sqrt{2 \times 8} = \sqrt{16}$. Figure 1 displays the triangles of two subscales.

The size of the triangle gives a picture of the magnitude of the distances; its shape shows the relationships between these distances. The null hypothesis is that for each wife, the husband is neither closer nor further than any other individual from the population. Under this hypothesis the triangle should be equilateral. If husbands were closer to their wives, we would find that the edge corresponding to $D(x_i, y_i)$ will be smaller than the others. A visual comparison can be made between the subscales on the basis of their triangles.

Graphical Display of Ranking

Another graphical representation of the distances is based on principles similar to the biplot (Gabriel 1971) and as presented by Cohen and Mallows (1980). The method enables one to display data matrices graphically by using their singular decomposition. For our particular problem, the data matrix will be of rank $r = 2$.[4]

For each of the n pairs we rank the three respective distances: $D(x_i, X)$, $D(x_i, y_i)$ and $D(y_i, X)$. Thus if (1,2,3) is the ranking obtained for the eighth pair, then $D(x_i, X) < D(x_i, y_i) < D(y_i, X)$. Under the null hypothesis, all $3! = 6$ possible permutations are equally probable. The data of the rankings for the n pairs are summarized by an n x 3 matrix whose rows are permutations of the integers 1,2, and 3. Denote this matrix by P. The sum of each row in P is a constant, so that its rank is not larger than 2. Thus, it can be fully described in a two-dimensional space.

For displaying P in the plane, we consider a matrix Q of dimension 6 x 3 whose rows are the six possible permutations of (1,2,3). We express Q by the spectral decomposition:

$$Q = \sum_{i=1}^{2} \lambda_i U_i V_i' \qquad [11]$$

where $\lambda_i (i=1,2)$ are eigenvalues of Q (and of Q'Q), $U_i (i=1,2)$ are the respective normalized eigenvectors of QQ', and $V_i (i=1,2,)$ are the respective normalized eigenvectors of Q'Q. The normalization is such that the length of each vector is 1. Let U_{ij} denote the ith element of $U_j (i=1,...,6; j=1,2)$ and let V_{ij} denote the eighth element of $V_j (i=1,2,3; j=1,2)$. We plot the six vectors $g_i' = \sqrt{\lambda_1} U_{i1}, \sqrt{\lambda_2} U_{i2}$ as points in the plane, as well as the three vectors $f_i' = \sqrt{\lambda_1} V_{i1}, \sqrt{\lambda_2} V_{i2}$. The six points corresponding to g_i form the vertices of a symmetric hexagon, while the three points corresponding to f_i form the vertices of an equilateral triangle. The graph provides an exact representation of Q: the (i,j)'th element of Q is the scalar product $g_i' f_j$.

A geometric model of rank correlation has been introduced by Schulman (1979). When k objects are ranked, his model yields an equilateral polyhedron with k! vertices. We consider here the particular case of k=3. It has been shown by Schulman (1979) that the distance between any two vertices in the hexagon obtained for k=3 is a function of the rank correlation between the permutations corresponding to the two vertices.

The technique of displaying data matrices by using the singular decomposition is the basis of various methods: principal components, biplot, correspondence analyses. In general, the matrix is of rank $r > 2$ and the singular decomposition consists of r terms. For the graphical display, the terms of the decomposition are ignored so that the display is only an approximation of the data matrix. For our problem, the n x 3 ranking matrix P is of rank r = 2, so that it can be displayed exactly. Each of the rows in P is one of the six possible permutations of (1,2,3). Because n = 73 (>> 6), several subgroups of rows in P must be equal. Actually, P consists of the same rows as in Q, except that the frequency of each permutation (row) in P is not necessarily 1. The important information for our study is the frequency $(n_i, i=1,...,6)$ of each of the six

---

[4] Cohen and Mallows (1980) discuss this particular case in detail, but they also generalize the graphical method for data matrices with $r > 2$.

FIGURE 1
Graphical Presentation of Groups Differences for Two Subscales

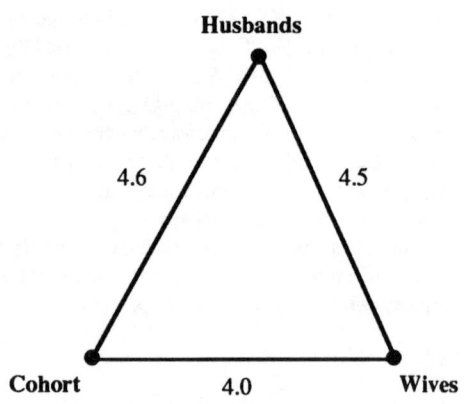

(a) PACE PERCEPTION (PP)

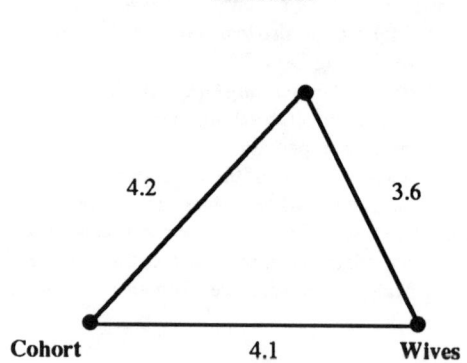

(B) PRESENT ORIENTATION (PO)

permutations in P. This information can be displayed as follows. First, we draw the hexagon and triangle that describe the matrix Q. Recall that each permutation corresponds to a vertex of hexagon. Then, around each vertex (i=1,...,6) we draw a circle the area of which is proportional to n_i. Having the area proportional to the variable of interest seems to provide the proper visual impact (Cleveland et al. 1980). If all rankings were equally probable, we would obtain six circles with approximately equal areas. The graphical display shows which rankings are more frequent or, in other words, which distances tend to be smaller than others.

ANALYTICAL COMPARISONS

The purpose of this section is to compare our method, which is based on the distances, with classical procedures that could be applied for the comparison of wives and their husbands. First, we consider the method based on the Hotelling T^2 test. As before we denote by $x_i, y_i (i=1,...,n)$ the time perspective of the eighth wife and her husband, respectively. Let

$$d_i = x_i - y_i$$

$$\bar{d} = \frac{1}{n} \sum_{i=1}^{n} d_i$$

$$s^2 = \frac{1}{n-1} \sum_{i=1}^{n} (d_i - \bar{d})^2$$

We can test the null hypothesis of no differences in means between wives and their husbands by using the Hotelling T^2 statistic (e.g., Morrison 1988):

$$T^2 = n(\bar{d}' S^{-1} \bar{d})$$

Under the null hypothesis,

$$\frac{T^2}{n-1} \cdot \frac{n-k}{k} \sim F_{k, n-k} \qquad [12]$$

The question that is answered by using T^2 is whether wives differ from their husbands in their mean time perspective. However, this does not entirely answer the question raised by the present research, of whether wives are closer to their husbands or their cohort. The question as posed in the present research involves not only means. We shall illustrate this point in the following example. For simplicity, our example will be concerned with k=1. Suppose that for half of the sample the husband's time perspective is y=4 while his wife's perspective is x=2. For the other half of the sample x=4, y=2. In other words, there is a strong negative correlation between x and y. In this case, there will be no difference in means between husbands and wives, though wives are further removed from their husbands than from their cohort. Our method of comparing distances would indeed show the cases where wives are closer to their age-group than to their husbands with respect of some of the subscales.

The T^2 test is based on the assumption that the data are multivariate normal whereas our method is nonparametric. Normally, this would imply that if the data were indeed normal and if wives differed from their husbands in their mean time perspective, then the T^2 test should be more powerful than our test. It is not clear that for our particular study we could draw such a conclusion. Recall that our data have an unusual structure: there are values for n pairs of wives and their husbands, but there are also temporal reports for a large number of wives whose husbands were not interviewed. Unlike the T^2 tests, our method takes advantage of this added information and increases the power of our test.

Other classical multivariate methods could be considered by rewriting the data in a MANOVA framework (Anterson 1958), but our above arguments would still apply.

ILLUSTRATIVE ANALYSIS

The following analysis consists of the correlation scores between wives and husbands on each scale item as well as the mean differences between them. Given that the intent of this paper was

FIGURE 2
Graphical Display of the Rankings for Pace-Perception

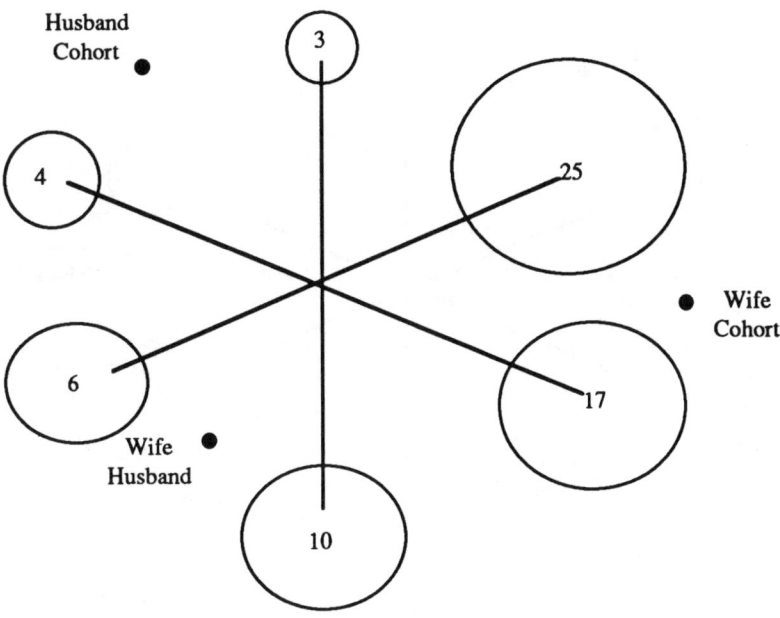

to present the measurement procedures, in this section we shall only present the results in a brief form and for only two subscales: Pace perception (PP), and present orientation (PO). These two subscales were selected because the results are different and illustrative.

Pace perception and present orientation were each measured with k=8. In both subscales none of the husband-wife correlations were statistically significant. The overall F statistics for PP and PO were 5.12 and 3.23, respectively. Both were highly significant (P < .001). Thus the classical method shows that there are significant differences in the mean results, for the two subscales, between wives and their husbands. However, there are notable differences between the two subscales.

Comparing the two triangles in Figure 1 we can see the average distances of $D(X_i, y_i)$, $D(x_i, X)$, $D(y_i, X)$. The PP triangle is not equilateral and its edges are larger than the base. This indicates that wives tend to be closer to their cohort than to their husbands. The husbands are almost close to their wives as they are to the entire age group of their wives. The Wilcoxon signed-rank test indicates (with $\alpha<.001$) that the distance between the wife and her cohort is smaller than the distance between the wife and her husband.

The triangle for PO is also not equilateral, but it differs in shape from the one corresponding to PP. Here, the small edge corresponds to the distance between the husband and his wife. Also, the area of the triangle for PO is smaller than the area of the triangle corresponding to PP. This shows that the distances for PO tend to be smaller than for PP. The Wilcoxon signed rank test indicates that the distances between wives and their husbands tend to be smaller ($\alpha<.001$) than between the wives and their age-group.

Figures 2 and 3 present the matrix ranking (P) for the subscales. The asymmetric structure indicates that the six permutations are not equally likely. For definiteness, in the center of each circle (corresponding to a permutation), we also provided their frequency (n_i) in P. The two largest circles in Figure 2 correspond to rankings for which the distances between the wife and her cohort were smaller than the other distances. The smallest circles correspond to permutations where the smallest distance among the three was between the husband and his wife's cohort. The ranking plot for PO (Figure 3) differs from the one shown for PP. In the case of the present-orientation subscale the large circles are placed where distances are smaller between the husband and wife.

SUMMARY

It is generally recognized that the "family" rather than the "individual" should be the basic unit of analysis in the study of individual time behavior and preferences. Studying family decision making and response is difficult, however, in as much as it entails the synthesis of the goals, preferences, and perceptions of all family members, who also belong to broader social groups. Important differences characterize family members, and important changes occur (especially in wives) as a result of their interaction with their work and age cohort.

The major intent of this paper was to introduce a statistical procedure for comparing husbands and wives, considering also the wives' cohort. The methodology was utilized in a study concerning individuals' temporal orientation. The data provided the opportunity to demonstrate the procedure's applications and significance. The findings are of both theoretical and practical value. Theoretically, they provide further empirical support to the notion that the information provided by different family members might be incongruent. Separate responses by husbands and wives should be obtained therefore, if one is attempting to investigate "family" temporal preferences. Furthermore, studying the time orientation of both spouses can be used to better understand their attitudes towards work and household production (Robinson 1987); shopping time preferences (Hornik 1985; 1992); the timing of childbirth (Happel, Hill and Low 1984); and to predict the future activities that

FIGURE 3
Graphical Display of the Ranking for Present Orientation

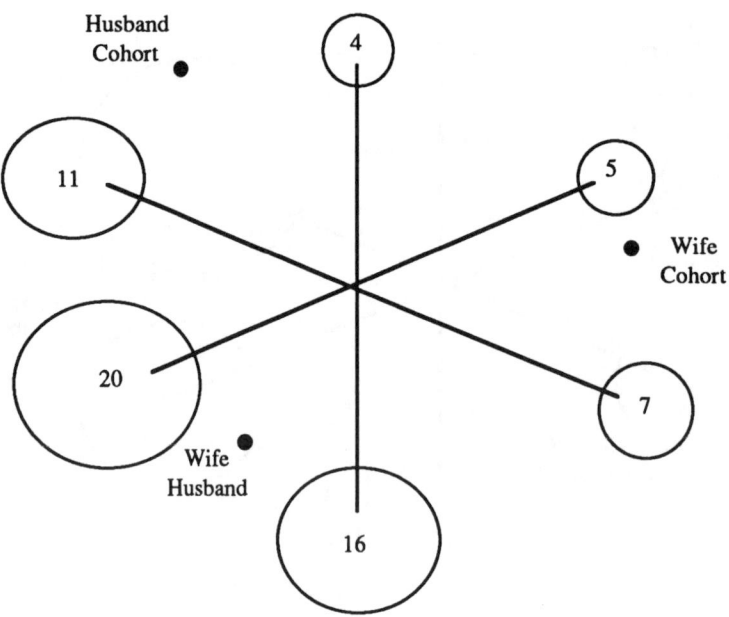

will be performed jointly or separately by husbands and their wives.

The statistical procedure introduced in the present study can be easily applied to other husband-wife comparisons such as predicting spousal preferences (Davis, Hoch and Ragsdale 1986). It may also be used in other group comparisons, such as, investigating whether adolescents are more influenced by their parents or peers (Shah and Zalnik 1981).[5]

REFERENCES

Bergadaa, Michelle, M. (1990), "The Role of Perception of Time in Consumer Research", *Journal of Consumer Research* 17, 277-288.

Blau, Francine and Marianne A. Ferber (1986). *The Economics of Women, Men and Work*, Englewood Clifs, NJ: Prentice-Hall.

Cleveland, W. S., C. S. Harris and R. McGill (1980), "Circle Sizes for Thematic Maps", The Harvard Library of Computer Graphics Mapping Collection, Vol. II.

Cohen, A. and C.L. Mallows (1980), "Analysis of Ranking Data", Bell Laboratories Technical Memorandum.

Davis, Harry L., Stephen J. Hoch and E.K. Easton Ragdale (1986), "An Anchoring and Adjustment Model of Spousal Predictions", *Journal of Consumer Research*, 13, 25-37.

Feldman, Laurence P. and Jacob Hornik (1981), "The Use of Time: An Integrated Conceptual Model", *Journal of Consumer Research*, 7, 407-419.

Gabriel, K.R. (1971), "The Biplot Graphic Display of Matrices with Applications to Principal Component Analysis", *Biometrika*, 58, 453-467.

Glenn, Norval D. (1976), *Cohort Analysis*, Beverly Hills: Sage Publication.

Happel, S.K., Hill, J.K. and Low, S.A. (1984), "An Economic Analysis of the Timing of Childbirth", *Population Studies*, 38, 299-311.

Holahan, Carole A. and Lucia A. Gilbert (1979), "Conflict Between Major Life Roles: Women and Men in Dual Career Couples", *Human Relations*, 32, 451-67.

Hornik, Jacob (1985), "A Household Production Approach to Consumer Shopping Time Behavior", *Advances in Consumer Research*, 11, 200-204.

Hornik, Jacob and Mary. J. Schlinger (1981), "Allocation of Time to the Mass Media", *Journal of Consumer Research*, 7, 343-356.

Hornik, Jacob and N. Meir (1992), "Affect Role in Consumers' Temporal Judgments", *Psychology and Marketing*, 9 (in print).

Hornik, Jacob (1992), "Effects of Physical Contact on Customers' Shopping Time and Behavior, *Marketing Letters*, 3, 49-55.

Kiker, B.F and Ying Chu Ng (1990), "A Simultaneous Equation Model of Spousal Time Allocation", *Social Science Research*, 19, 132-152.

Koening, M.A., G.B. Simmons and B.D. Misra (1984), "Husband-Wife Inconsistencies in Contraceptive Use Response", *Population Studies*, 38, 281-98.

Kshirsagar, A.M. And E. Arseven (1975), "A Note on the Equivalency of Two Discrimination Procedures", *The American Statistician*, 129, 38-39.

Lee, Lucy C. and Robert Ferber (1977), "Use of Time as a Determinant of Family Market Behavior", *Journal of Business Research*, 5, 75-91.

---

[5] Another important aspect to consider is the effect of measurement errors on the method. To obtain an Appendix on this issue please write to the author.

Menasco, Michael B. and David J. Currey (1989), "Utility and Choice: An Empirical Study of Wife-Husband Decision Making", *Journal of Consumer Research*, 16, 87-97.

Morrison, Donald F. (1988), *Multivariate Statistical Methods*, New York: McGraw-Hill.

Qualls, William J. (1987), "Household Decision Behavior: The Impact of Husbands' and Wives' Sex Role Orientation", *Journal of Consumer Research*, 14, 264-79.

Rakowski, William (1986), "Future Time Perspective: Application to Health Context of Later Adulthood", *American Behavioral Scientist*, 29, 730-740.

Rao, R.C. (1965), *Linear Statistical Inference and its Applications*. New York: John Wiley.

Reichler, Arne and Clifford Brickman (1989), "Time Orientation: Past, Present and Future Perceptions", *Psychological Reports*, 64, 1199-1205.

Roberts, M.I. and C.H. Wortzel (1979), "New Life-Style Determinants of Women's Food Shopping Behavior", *Journal of Marketing*, Summer, 28-29.

Robinson, W.C. (1987), "The Time Cost of Children and Other Household Production", *Population Studies*, 38, 299-311.

Roos, Philip and Robert Albers (1965), "Performance of Alcoholics and Normals on a Measure of Temporal Orientation", *Journal of Clinical Psychology*, 21, 34-36.

Schulman, R.S. (1979), "A Geometric Model of Rank Correlation", *American Statistician*, 33, 77-80.

Settle, Robert, Pamala Alreck and John W. Glasheen (1977), "Individual Time Orientation and Consumer Lifestyle", in *Advances in Consumer Research*, 5, 315-319.

Shah, F. and M. Zelnik (1981), "Parent and Peer Influence on Sexual Behavior: Contraceptive Use and Pregnancy Experience of Young Women", *Journal of Marriage and The Family*, 43, 339-348.

Sung-Tai, Hong and Julie F. Toner (1989), "Are There Genders Differences in the Use of Country-of-Origin Information in the Evaluation of Products?", *Advances in Consumer Research*, 16, 468-72.

Umesh, U.N., William A. Weeks and Linda L. Golden (1988), "Individual and Dyadic Consumption of Time: Proposition on the Perception of Complementarity and Substitutability of Activities", *Advances in Consumer Research*, 15, 426-29.

Gender Differences in the Perception of Leisure: A Conceptual Model

Suzana de M. Fontenelle, University of Houston
George M. Zinkhan, University of Houston

ABSTRACT

The purpose of this paper is to develop a conceptual model to study gender differences in the perception of leisure. The model attempts to explain how leisure is differently perceived by men and women, given the diversity of roles they play in contemporary society. After outlining various approaches for defining leisure, it is suggested that gender differences studied in a social context can better explain differences in the perception of leisure than biological sex alone. Propositions of how gender differences may affect the perception of leisure are presented.

INTRODUCTION

Leisure is important, because people need freedom to become and to express themselves (Kelly 1982). However, no consensus exists of what leisure really is. Researchers have continuously struggled with definitions of leisure (Iso-Ahola 1980, Neulinger 1974), but no dominant model of leisure has emerged.

Past research has generally defined leisure as time off work; and, consequently, the study of leisure has focused on behavior during non-work time and non-work activities. In more recent years, research attention shifted to the psychological attributes associated with leisure, as research efforts concentrate on the subjective dimensions of leisure and the meanings attached to it. The more recent research focus on the subjective dimensions and meanings of leisure draws attention to the task of defining what leisure is (Samdahl 1991).

It has become evident in recent leisure scholarship that differences do exist in the way females and males address leisure. However, there are some limitations associated with research efforts to date. First, research on males and females has generally investigated sex differences, rather than looking at gender with its social construction of roles based upon biological sex. Secondly, extant research has emphasized proving the existence of gender differences and has used gender differences as explanatory variables of leisure behavior, rather than considering these differences as the starting point of research. By considering gender differences as the starting point of research, it is possible to identify where these differences actually exist and why. Without this focus, research remains merely descriptive (Henderson 1990).

If gender differences are to be treated as the basis for research, the theoretical conceptualization of leisure needs to be re-evaluated. What is considered to be leisure may depend on how men and women were socialized and the extent to which they subscribe to the roles assigned for them in society. The effects of gender differences in leisure behavior cannot be entirely understood without examining how these differences influence what is considered to be leisure in the first place.

Consumer researchers have been aware of the importance of leisure not only because the leisure experience is associated with the acquisition of products and services, but also because leisure is generally recognized as an important component in life satisfaction (Andrews and Withey 1976; Robinson 1977; Unger and Kernan 1983). Besides the interest in the contribution of leisure to life satisfaction, consumer researchers have been increasingly interested in the analysis of hedonic experiences (including leisure) and the way that consumer behavior may be pursued for the subjective and emotional benefits it provides (Havlena and Holbrook 1986; Hirschman and Holbrook 1982a; Hirschman and Holbrook 1982b; Holbrook et al. 1984). The investigation of gender differences in the perception of leisure may provide a fruitful ground for the analysis of hedonic experiences, leisure being an example of such experiences.

Hedonic experiences deserve special attention from consumer researchers, particularly when: (a) individuals are placing self-fulfillment, self-enhancement, travelling, hobbies and other leisure experiences, as their top priorities for the future (Hymowitz 1991); (b) the redefinition of traditional gender roles and changes in what society considers to be accepted behavior for men and women affect how men and women experience leisure. When trying to balance their lives between work, family and friends, men and women start to feel time pressures with little opportunity to experience leisure in a way to promote self-enhancement or a sense of fulfillment. This state of affairs suggests important questions for consumer behavior researchers: what do men and women perceive to be leisure, given their roles in society? What aspects of the leisure experience are perceived to be the most important? Are these aspects perceived to be equally important for men and women?

The purpose of this paper is to present a conceptual model to study gender differences in the perception of leisure. The proposed model offers an exploratory framework for investigating consumers' leisure experiences. The model attempts to integrate:

(a) A conceptualization of gender differences in a social and cultural context.
(b) A conceptualization of leisure that accounts for individual differences in goals, experiences, and attitudes towards work or life.

The paper is organized as follows. First, definitions of leisure are reviewed, and the social nature of leisure is highlighted. Second, a conceptualization of gender differences is presented and its contribution to the study of leisure perceptions is discussed. Third, a conceptual model of gender differences in leisure perceptions is briefly described. Fourth, some implications for research in consumer behavior are outlined and suggestions for future research are made.

The following section presents an overview of conceptualizations of leisure and emphasizes the definition of leisure as an experience. It is argued that this definition of leisure best retains the social nature of leisure.

LITERATURE REVIEW

The conceptualization of leisure

Consumer behavior researchers have studied leisure in a variety of ways. Research on time usage identifies leisure time as being qualitatively different from the time consumers allocate to other pursuits (Jacoby, Szybillo and Berning 1976; Holbrook and Lehmann 1981). For example, Jacoby and his colleagues noted that time has value and that consumers seek to reduce time spent for mandated activities to more desirable free-time activities. More recent studies about time usage have concentrated on the subjective notions of time and focused on the meanings and satisfactions derived from what was experienced during a particular time frame.

These studies moved from a more utilitarian perspective of time to a more subjective notion of experiential time (Hirschman 1987, Hornik 1984). Bergadaà (1990) offers insights into distinct perceptions of time different individuals and cultures have and how these perceptions influence their choices. The conceptualization of time as polychronic time was discussed by Hall (1976) and has recently been approached in the consumer behavior literature (Kaufman, Lane, and Lindquist 1991), which might prove helpful to the consideration of leisure within the context of role overload and leisure as a cultural and social phenomenon.

Quality-of-life studies have investigated the extent to which leisure can promote a feeling of well-being and a general feeling of satisfaction towards life (Andrews and Withey 1976). These studies of life quality found that satisfaction with "how much fun you are having" was the strongest contributor to a general sense of well-being, among twelve selected predictors.

Leisure has also been discussed in the literature in terms of its hedonic aspects as a consumption experience (Hirschman and Holbrook 1982a; Hirschman and Holbrook 1982b; Holbrook et al. 1984, Ahtola 1985). Distinct levels of product involvement and product enthusiasm have also been studied as characterizing consumer experiences linked to leisure pursuits (Bloch and Bruce 1985, Bloch 1986). Leisure viewed as "experiential consumption" provides a way to consider the subjective aspects of consumption experiences, rather than exclusively focusing on consumers as rational, economic entities.

Definitional problem

What is leisure? There is no clear answer to this question (or no "correct" answer). The objective of this section is, first, to address several issues that are pertinent to the definition of leisure, rather than advocating one definition as optimal. Second, the conceptualization of leisure as a social experience is presented.

Samdahl (1988) calls attention to the necessity of explicitly identifying the definition of leisure being used within each study so that: (a) the compatibility/incompatibility of distinct lines of research become apparent; (b) the uniqueness of the phenomenon being studied is established; and (c) a linkage between leisure and non-leisure phenomena is provided. These issues discussed by Samdahl serve as guidelines for the way leisure is defined in this paper.

Traditional definitions of leisure

Leisure has traditionally been defined as free-time or non-work time. Leisure is equated to free time by Robinson (1977), who defined free time as the time left after paid work and all activities related to the maintenance of the family, the household and personal care. Another traditional definition of leisure is in terms of participation in particular types of activities (Neulinger 1974), or as activities that individuals choose to pursue in their free time.

The definition of leisure in terms of time and activity presents advantages to researchers to the extent that it enables quantification and comparison. One advantage, for example, is that this definition of leisure enables quantifiable statements about leisure such as: X has twice as much leisure as Y (Wearing and Wearing 1988). However, certain limitations of these definitions deserve consideration.

First, the conceptualization of leisure as free time or as activity does not promote investigation into the meaning of leisure, or into more qualitative aspects of the leisure experience, such as: why does the choice of certain leisure activities prevail over others? What makes these experiences more or less enjoyable? Traditional conceptualizations offer only a descriptive analysis of leisure behavior.

Second, the conceptualization of leisure as free time may not always be appropriate. Many women, for example, feel that they do not have any free time; and women with small children and who also work outside the home do not feel that they have the right to dispose of free time "freely" for themselves (Wearing and Wearing 1988). Furthermore, the lives of women who combine work outside the home and family responsibilities are characterized by role conflict and overload which frequently result in fatigue, emotional depletion and in some cases maternal guilt (Shank 1986).

A third consideration relates to the definition of leisure as an activity. This definition can create theoretical problems according to Kelly (1982), since almost anything may be an obligation under some conditions. One activity can be performed under several different circumstances and be categorized under leisure or not; for example, reading can be for leisure, for work, or for school. Cooking can be for leisure or out of necessity.

As a result of their descriptive nature, the definitions of leisure as free time or as an activity do not provide a framework for studying how leisure experiences may contribute to a better life or to the achievement of self-fulfillment. These definitions are also limited in their capacity to explain potential gender differences in the perception of leisure, given the diverse roles that men and women play in contemporary society.

Leisure as an experience

For the purposes of this paper, leisure is conceptualized as an experience. This definition of leisure takes into account the individual's choice, motivation and perception of the activity and its experience. Leisure conceptualized as an experience can lead to the analysis of the quality of leisure, uncovering anticipated benefits associated with leisure such as self-expression, self-enhancement, enjoyment of the development of social relationships, and/or the joy of integrating mind and body in the activity itself (Neulinger 1974; Kelly 1982). Given the large domain of leisure experiences, in order to fully comprehend the various meanings attached to these experiences, it may be helpful to analyze these experiences in light of their social and cultural context.

The social nature of leisure experiences

Leisure takes place in the social world. It is a product of a particular time and culture, reflecting economic and social structures (Kelly 1982). Given the social nature of leisure experiences, it may be assumed that the meaning of such experiences will also be shaped by social and cultural contexts. As time passes, cultural, economic and social contexts change, and consumers' leisure experiences adapt accordingly. The investigation of gender differences in the perception of leisure needs to account for the social context in which men and women live and interact with each other. Given the dynamic nature of the social context and of male/female interactions, leisure is then a dynamic concept rather than a static one. The conceptualization of leisure as a social experience is adopted in this paper. The next section presents and discusses the concepts of gender identity and gender role attitudes as a way to investigate gender differences in leisure perceptions.

Gender identity and gender role attitudes

Individuals are born male or female but learn to become masculine and feminine through the socialization they receive (Spence and Helmreich 1978). However, people vary in the degree to which they identify with feminine or masculine traits.

The degree to which individuals accept the traits and attributes that are associated with their biological sex is called gender identity. A person who primarily identifies with feminine traits is "feminine", while those identifying with masculine traits are "masculine". Those who identify themselves with both masculine and feminine traits are "androgynous" (Bem 1974; Spence and Helmreich 1978). Inventories such as the Bem Sex Role Inventory (Bem 1974) and the Personal Attributes Questionnaire (Spence and Helmreich 1978) are the tests most widely used to measure gender identity (Beere 1990). Individuals are asked to rate themselves on a five-point Likert-type scale in regard to socially desirable traits for men and women. Depending on the scores obtained from these tests, individuals of both sexes may be classified as "Masculine", "Feminine", or "Androgynous" with respect to gender identity.

The concept of gender roles refers to behavior patterns which are differently displayed by the sexes. These patterns are also established through socialization and determine attitudes and life styles for men and women (Colley 1987).

When one's sense of maleness and femaleness (gender identity) is being developed, this emerging sense of gender identity tends to stimulate the adoption of stereotypical gender-roles. However, once gender identity is established, a myriad of variables tend to influence the individual's attitude towards the roles that are typically assigned for the sexes. These variables have to do with several situational factors such as: one's position in the life cycle, sanctions/rewards for exhibiting a particular type of behavior, abilities, interests, and the relationship of the individual to significant others (Spence and Helmreich 1980). The level of agreement towards roles stereotypically assigned to men and women (gender-role attitudes) can be measured with items developed by Scanzoni (Scanzoni and Szinovacz 1980). These items assess attitudes toward traditional roles for wives and husbands, alterations in husbands' roles etc. Responses are indicated on five-point Likert-type scales.

The influence of gender roles in leisure behavior has also been a topic of research interest. Hirschman (1984) investigated the relationship between gender roles and motives for pursuing leisure activities and found that gender roles consistently explained more variance in leisure activity motives than biological sex. The value of gender roles as predictors of leisure behavior was presented by Colley (1984), who indicated how situational antecedents of leisure (e.g., personal capacities, interest, social acceptance) may be affected by gender roles, and also how gender role expectations may determine the level of satisfaction derived from leisure. However, Colley does not describe the dynamics involved in the process.

A conceptual model of gender differences in the perception of leisure

The leisure literature offers no consensual model of leisure and its underlying dimensions. However, there are certain dimensions of the leisure experience which are more prominent in the literature (Iso-Ahola 1980, Kelly 1982, Neulinger 1974). These leisure dimensions are: perceived freedom, self-expression, social evaluation, and enjoyment.

The first dimension of leisure, perceived freedom, is defined by Neulinger (1974) as a state in which the person feels that what s/he is doing is being carried out freely, without constraint or compulsion, in order to be considered leisure. The second dimension of the leisure experience is self-expression. This dimension relates to the ability of expressing one's true self while at leisure, and to allow for the opportunity to explore one's possibilities. Kelly (1983) alluded to self-expression by presenting leisure as a social space in which we develop expressivity, where individuals do more than respond to norms, where people are able to be and become themselves. The third dimension of leisure, social evaluation, relates to the conscious monitoring of one's self in regard to social standards and expectations (Samdahl 1991). The social evaluation dimension is related to the self-expression dimension given that self evaluation constitutes a barrier to self-expression. Kelly (1983) refers to the social evaluation aspect of leisure when he indicates that, when an individual engages in leisure, there is a degree of approval seeking, acceptance and respect as ways to validate one's selfhood. Enjoyment is the fourth dimension of leisure and it relates to the fact that leisure promotes pleasure and fun (Shaw 1985). It is suggested here that leisure will be experienced in its pure sense when individuals perceive their freedom level as high, are able to express themselves truly, feel that social evaluation is absent, and feel the experience is enjoyable.

The importance of the four constituent elements of leisure (freedom, self-expression, social evaluation, and enjoyment) may be differently perceived by masculine, feminine, or androgynous individuals. An analysis of these differences is the focus of this paper. Figure 1 presents a model for the investigation of gender differences in the perception of leisure. It is proposed in the model that people are born either male or female but acquire masculine, feminine or androgynous gender identities through socialization. According to their gender identities, individuals tend to develop gender role beliefs. These beliefs are constantly under the influence of a series of situational variables which challenge or confirm such beliefs. According to the specific situation people are in, they develop gender role attitudes which may agree/disagree with what is traditionally considered to be acceptable behavior for each sex (traditional/non-traditional gender role attitudes). It is the contention of this paper that:

(a) Individuals with traditional gender role attitudes present a strong sense of gender identity *either* feminine or masculine and tend to subscribe to the gender roles that are typically assigned to each sex.

(b) Individuals with non-traditional gender role attitudes do not present a strong sense of gender identity either masculine or feminine but identify themselves with *both* masculine and feminine traits. These individuals tend to subscribe to gender roles that are typically assigned to *both* sexes indiscriminately.

The focus here is on which leisure dimension will be more important to consumers, as a function of their gender role attitudes. Certain relationships are of particular interest to the study of leisure at a time when men and women are looking for a better balance between work, family, and when self-fulfillment ranks high on their priorities for the future. A detailed representation of the relationships proposed in the model is depicted in Table 1. The research propositions are also presented in the Table and subsequently discussed in the text.

Relationships are predicted between feminine, masculine, androgynous individuals and their perception of leisure (as a function of the freedom dimension, for example). Feminine individuals are assumed to have a higher level of agreement with the roles that are traditionally allocated to women, such as the roles of homemaker and caregivers. Several studies have indicated that the adoption of such roles presents limitations in the ability to freely experience leisure (Colley 1984; Henderson 1991; Shank 1986). These limitations may assume different forms; for example, to the extent that feminine individuals accept traditional female roles, they are bound to regard their leisure as being closely tied to the leisure of their partners and children (Woodward and Green 1988). Leisure for them might be inherently associated with the leisure, needs and demands of others (Deem 1986). The adoption of female roles implies that family and spouse duties are to be given priority,

FIGURE 1
Proposed Model of Gender Differences in the Perception of Leisure

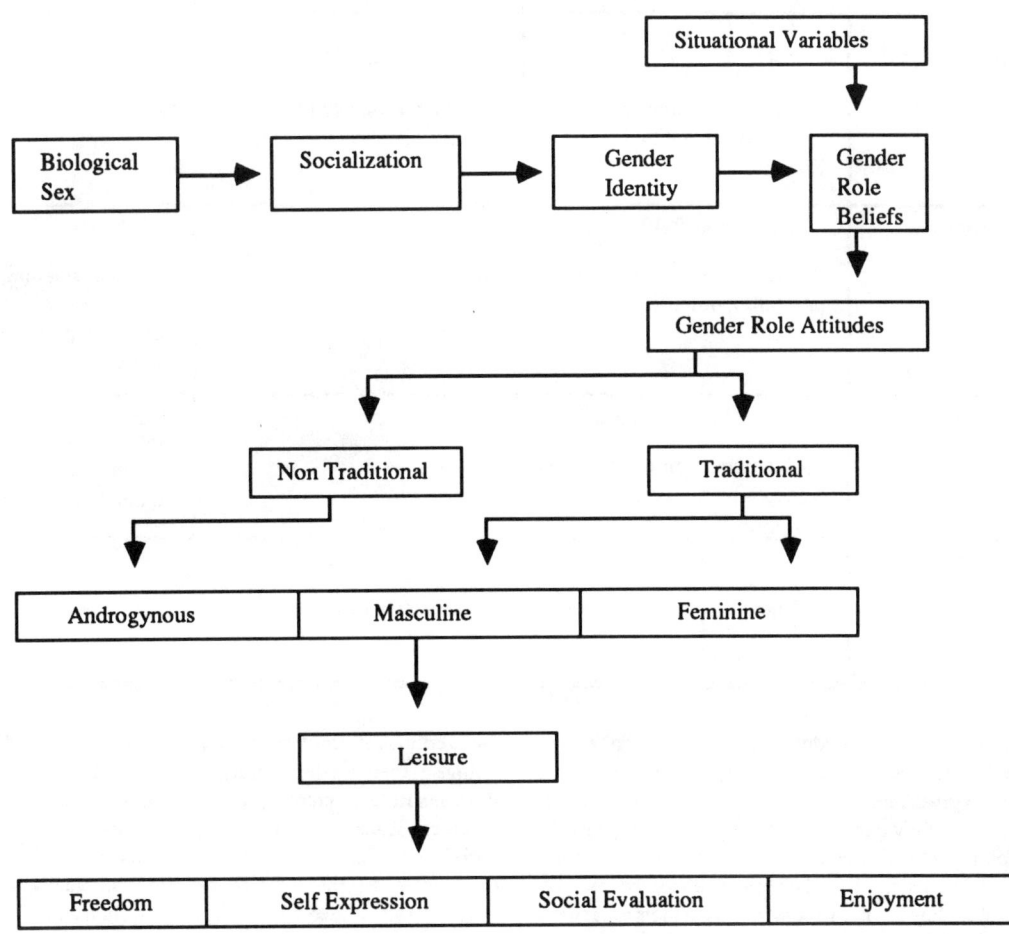

and personal leisure is not viewed as a viable option if it represents putting family and spouse in second place. The adoption of feminine roles may also result in the accumulation of work inside the home as well as outside the home, resulting in less opportunities to choose freely time, place, or leisure companions. Therefore, the freedom dimension is not expected to be closely associated with leisure perceptions for feminine individuals (P1 in Table 1). Here, leisure is not expected to be experienced, free from social obligation or responsibility.

Given that masculine individuals are assumed to accept the roles typically assigned to men, it is predicted that these individuals will have fewer constraints with regard to their ability to experience leisure. The adoption of male roles decreases the degree of responsibility towards housework and child care, for instance, and increases the degree of independence these individuals can enjoy. For masculine individuals, leisure is experienced with relative freedom to choose leisure locations, companions, and activities; leisure may be experienced independently from the needs and demands of others. It is predicted that, for masculine individuals, the perception of leisure is more closely tied to its freedom component (P2A).

Androgynous individuals do not subscribe to any particular set of roles exclusively, and are able to conform to roles that can best fit their lifestyles and conveniences. They are free to choose leisure partners, activities and so forth. Therefore, it is also predicted that androgynous individuals will perceive leisure to be closely associated with their ability to independently choose leisure activities and companions (P2B).

Another set of relationships is hypothesized for the social evaluation component of leisure. Both masculine and feminine individuals tend to adopt traditional gender role attitudes and, consequently, conform to the roles that are assigned to the sexes. Deviations from these traditional roles may cause the feeling of not adopting the "correct" behavior or, not doing the "right" thing. These individuals are expected to be apprehensive in regard to the judgments of others and are expected to be concerned about making a good impression on others. Consequently, social evaluation plays an important role in the way they experience leisure (P3A and P3B). In contrast, androgynous individuals tend to adopt non-traditional gender role attitudes and do not subscribe to those roles which are traditionally assigned to the members of each sex. Routinely, they tend to adopt a myriad of roles; and social evaluation is expected to be absent from their leisure experience (P4).

Masculine and feminine individuals tend to accept what is traditionally expected of men and women in society; and, consequently, they may have limited opportunities to express themselves, given their adherence to more traditional roles. As a result of the way that social evaluation permeates the leisure experience

TABLE 1
Relationships Proposed in the Model

	Feminine	Masculine	Androgynous
Freedom	P1: Freedom is not closely related to perception of leisure.	P2A and P2B: Freedom is closely related to perception of leisure.	
Social Evaluation	P3A and P3B: Social evaluation is closely related to perception of leisure.		P4: Social evaluation is not closely related to perception of leisure.
Self Expression	P5A and P5B: Social expression is closely related to perception of leisure.		P6: Self expression is not closely related to perception of leisure.
Enjoyment	P7: Enjoyment is closely related to the perception of leisure.		

of masculine and feminine individuals, these consumers are expected to define leisure as a function of self-expression. Given their limited ability to express themselves, something will be perceived to be leisure the more they can express themselves and ignore the social evaluation aspect (P5 A and 5B). The same does not apply to androgynous individuals. Given their lower adherence to stereotypical gender roles, they are not so constrained in their capacity to express themselves. Therefore, their perception of leisure is not as dependent on the self-expression dimension, as it may be for feminine and masculine individuals (P6).

Leisure perceptions are not expected to vary for the enjoyment dimension. Although the association between leisure and enjoyment has not been investigated thoroughly (Samdahl 1991), it is presumed here that people universally perceive leisure to be a function of the enjoyment they derive from it (P7).

MEASUREMENT ISSUES

When trying to measure the impact of gender differences on leisure perceptions, measurement is a crucial issue. For example, the social context of gender differences in leisure experiences cannot be fully understood without trying to comprehend how consumers experience leisure in their daily lives. This type of understanding may best be achieved through the utilization of qualitative methodologies which promote an unobtrusive observation of the leisure experience in its natural context.

Advantages of qualitative methodologies have been discussed by leisure researchers and have centered around the argument that such techniques have the potential to provide better descriptions of phenomena being studied, since situational and contextual circumstances are present. Furthermore, the variety of contexts and social systems in which consumers are involved may become more apparent.

Survey methodology may also prove fruitful. For example, the seven propositions presented in Table 1 could be tested through the administration of surveys in which: (a) individuals provide ratings of their gender identity (Personal Attributes Questionnaire/ Bem Sex Role Inventory); (b) individuals indicate their gender-role attitudes (Scanzoni Scales); and (c) dimensions of leisure (freedom, social evaluation, and enjoyment) are operationalized. It may also be useful to determine which specific leisure activities (or experiences) are associated with each leisure dimension. Of course, there may be important gender differences in these ratings.

DISCUSSION

Implications for Consumer Behavior Research

The preceding sections of this paper examined issues related to the perception of leisure which may be beneficial to consumer research. First, the investigation of leisure was linked to a broader research topic in consumer behavior, the study of hedonic consumption and experiential aspects of consumption. Attempts were made to show how the investigation of leisure perceptions may contribute to our understanding of how consumers attach meanings to hedonic consumptions (e.g., purchase of leisure goods, travelling, attending the opera or the ballet).

Second, leisure perceptions were investigated in light of more contemporary concepts of gender differences (which have already appeared in the consumer behavior literature but not specifically in consumer studies of leisure). The consideration of gender differences in a social context reveals interesting aspects concerning the distinctions between men and women and how these differences may affect perceptions of leisure experiences. The proposed model also attempts to present a more comprehensive view of how gender related variables may moderate the way leisure is perceived and, therefore, how gender influences leisure behavior.

Third, in this paper, leisure perceptions were examined as part of a broader social context where an individual's perception of what is considered to be leisure is based upon one's interpretation of the social context and one's interaction with the social environment. For example, it may be that consumers view certain leisure activities as related clusters, and experience with one activity from within a cluster may influence perceived satisfaction with other activities within that cluster (Zinkhan and Wallendorf 1985).

Practical Implications

Marketing managers may want to consider other means for segmenting the markets for leisure goods and services beyond biological sex. The consideration of leisure activities and preferences typically assigned to males and females may have to be re-evaluated. Also, marketing managers may want to consider the complexity of the social relations embedded in people's perceptions of leisure. Promotional themes may be expanded to address the social aspects involving leisure and to place leisure goods and services in contexts that make sense to people, given their social realities.

Assumptions about time, place and companionship for leisure may also have to be reconsidered. For instance, women's changing roles in society may provide them with a wider latitude for choice of time, place and companions for leisure. More women may be willing to go to a bar with only female friends; more men may be willing to spend more time with their children. Thus, there may be implications for consumer behavior researchers who are interested in studying consumers' allocation of time.

There are, of course, important segments within the broader male/female population which should be studied. For example, professional female managers possess certain personality traits which allow them to climb the corporate ladder; but these same traits may put them at odds with traditional assumptions about feminity. Since corporations need their research and strategy skills, female executives often experience rapid upward job mobility. However, such women may be accused by some of their male peers as emotionally cold and unfeminine, since they do not conform to traditional social roles of women as extroverted, caring and overtly compassionate persons (Kroeger and Thulsen 1992). In our analysis, we have largely assumed that males or females would follow traditional sex-role patterns; and this might not always be the case. And this, in turn, raises important concerns about the work place (and, consequently, concerns about leisure patterns) in the twenty-first century.

Directions for Future Research

The model proposed here could serve as basis for future research. Beyond the issue of empirically testing the proposed relationships (Table 1), it would be interesting to assess the relationship between perceptions of leisure and subsequent leisure behavior. Also, it is important to substantiate the dimensions of leisure used in the model.

The proposed model assumes dimensions of leisure which may be relevant to the way Americans, and members of other western societies, experience leisure. However, leisure dimensions may vary cross-culturally given that leisure experiences are considered to be socially and culturally determined. The consideration of what constitutes masculinity, femininity and androgyny is also culturally determined. Future research is needed to expand the relationships being proposed here to other cultures and societies.

As discussed in the measurement issues section, it may be fruitful to operationalize leisure through a variety of observational and survey methods. Qualitative methodologies may contribute with valuable insights of what cultural and social elements make up for potential variations in what constitutes leisure for men and women in environments different than our own. It is important to realize that the traditional survey methodologies available, such as the Bem Sex Role Inventory, translate cultural definitions of femininity and masculinity typical of the American Society (Payne 1985). Although the BSRI has been used in cross-cultural studies (Beere 1990), its results need to be considered in the light of American standards of femininity and masculinity. The investigation of gender differences in leisure perceptions may contribute to the development of knowledge in consumer behavior research. Changing times require novel ways of looking at old ideas; this paper may serve to stimulate a new stream of leisure research.

REFERENCES

Ahtola, Olli T. (1985), "Hedonic and Utilitarian Aspects of Consumer Behavior: An Attitudinal Perspective," *Advances in Consumer Research*, Vol. 12, ed. Elizabeth C. Hirschman and Morris B. Holbrook, Provo, UT: Association of Consumer Research, 7-10.

Andrews, Frank M. and Stephen B. Withey (1976), *Social Indicators of Well-Being*, New York: Plenum.

Beere, Carole A. (1990), *Gender Roles: A Handbook of Tests and Measures*, Greenwood Press.

Bem, Sandra L. (1974), "The Measurement of Psychological Androgyny," *Journal of Consulting and Clinical Psychology*, 42, 155-162.

Bergadaà, Michelle M.(1990), "The Role of Time in the Action of the Consumer," *Journal of Consumer Research*, 17 (December), 289-302.

Bloch, Peter H. (1984), "Product Involvement as Leisure Behavior," *Advances in Consumer Research*, Vol. 11, ed. Thomas C. Kinnear, Provo, UT: Association of Consumer Research, 197-202.

_____ (1986), "Product Enthusiasm: Many Questions, a Few Answers," *Advances in Consumer Research*, Vol. 13, ed. Richard Lutz, Provo, UT: Association of Consumer Research, 539-543.

_____ and Grady D. Bruce (1984), "The Leisure Experience and Consumer Products: An Investigation of Underlying Satisfactions," *Journal of Leisure Research*, 16 (1), 74-88.

Colley, Ann (1987), "Sex Roles in Leisure and Sport," in *The Psychology of Sex Roles*, David J. Hargreaves and Ann M. Colley, eds. New York: Hemisphere Publishing Company, pp.233-249.

Colley, Ann (1984),"Sex Roles and Explanations of Leisure Behavior," *Leisure Studies*, 3 (3), 335-341.

Deem, Rosemary (1986), *All Work and No Play? A Study of Women and Leisure*, Milton Keynes, England: Open University Press.

Hall, Edward T.(1976), *Beyond Culture*, Doubleday, New York: Anchor Press.

Havlena, William J. and Morris B. Holbrook (1986), "The Varieties of Consumption Experience: Comparing Two Typologies of Emotion in Consumer Behavior," *Journal of Consumer Research*, 13 (December), 394-404.

Henderson, Karla (1991), "The Contribution of Feminism to an Understanding of Leisure Constraints," *Journal of Leisure Research*, 23 (4), 363-37

_____, (1990), "Anatomy is Not Destiny: A Feminist Approach of the Scholarship on Women's Leisure," *Leisure Sciences*, 12, 229-239.

Hirschman, Elizabeth C. (1984), "Leisure Motives and Sex Roles," *Journal of Leisure Research*, 16 (3), 209-223.

Hirschman, Elizabeth C. and Morris B. Holbrook (1982a), "The Experiential Aspects of Consumption: Consumer Fantasies, Feelings, and Fun," *Journal of Consumer Research*, 9 (September), 132-140.

Hirschman, Elizabeth C. and Morris B. Holbrook (1982b), "Hedonic Consumption: Emerging Concepts, Methods and Propositions," *Journal of Marketing*, 46 (Summer), 92-101.

Holbrook, Morris B., Robert Chestnut, Terence A. Oliva, and Eric A. Greenleaf (1984), "Play as a Consumption Experience: The Roles of Emotions, Performance, and Personality in the Enjoyment of Games," *Journal of Consumer Research*, 11 (September), 728-739.

Holbrook, Morris B. and Donald R. Lehmann (1981), "Allocating Discretionary Time: Complementarity Among Activities," *Journal of Consumer Research*, 7 (March), 395-405.

Hornik, Jacob (1984), "Subjective vs. Objective Time Measures: A Note on the Perception of Time in Consumer Behavior," *Journal of Consumer Research*, 11 (June), 615-618.

Hymowitz, Carol (1991), "Trading Fat Paychecks for free time," *The Wall Street Journal*, August 5, B1.

Iso-Ahola, E. Seppo (1980), "Basic Dimensions of Definitions of Leisure," *Journal of Leisure Research*, 11 (1), 28-39.

Jacoby, Jacob, George J. Szybillo, and Carol Kohn Berning (1976), "Time and Consumer Behavior: An Interdisciplinary Overview," *Journal of Consumer Research*, 2 (March), 320-329.

Kaufman, Carol Felker, Palul M. Lane and Jay D. Lindquist (1991), 'Exploring More than 24 Hours a Day: A Preliminary Investigation of Polychronic Time Use," *Journal of Consumer Research*, 18 (December), 392-401.

Kelly, John R. (1983), *Leisure Identities and Interactions*, London: George Allen & Unwin, Publisher.

_____ (1982), *Leisure*, Englewood Cliffs: Prentice Hall.

Kroeger, Otto and Janet M. Thulsen (1992), *Type Talk at Work: How the 16 Personality Types Determine Your Success on the Job*, New York: Delacorte Press.

Neulinger, John (1974), *The Psychology of Leisure*, Springfield, IL: Charles C.Thomas.

Payne, Frank D.(1985), *The Ninth Mental Measurements Yearbook*, Vol.1, ed. James V. Mitchell Jr., Buros Institute of Mental Measurements, NE: Lincoln, 178-179.

Robinson, John P. (1977), *How Americans Use Time: A Social-Psychological Analysis of Everyday Behavior*, New York: Praeger.

Samdahl, Diane (1991), "Issues in the Measurement of Leisure: A Comparison of Theoretical and Connotative Meanings," *Leisure Sciences*, (13), 33-49.

_____ , (1988), "Symbolic Interactionist Model of Leisure: Theory and Empirical Support," *Leisure Sciences*, 10, 27-39.

Shank, John W. (1986), "An Exploration of Leisure in the Lives of Dual Career Women," *Journal of Leisure Research*, 18 (4), 300-319.

Shaw, Susan M. (1985), "The Meaning of Leisure in Everyday Life," *Leisure Sciences*, 7 (1), 11-24.

Spence, Janet T. and Robert L. Helmreich (1980), "Masculine Instrumentality and Feminine Expressiveness: Their Relationships with Sex Role Attitudes and Behavior," *Psychology of Women Quarterly*, 5 (2), 147-163.

_____ and _____ (1978), *Masculinity & Femininity: Their Psychological Dimensions, Correlates and Antecedents*, Austin: University of Texas Press.

Unger, Lynette S. and Jerome B. Kernan (1983), "On the Meaning of Leisure: an Investigation of Some Determinants of the Subjective Experience," *Journal of Consumer Research*, 9 (March), 381-392.

Wearing, Betsy and Stephen Wearing (1988), "All in a Day's Leisure: Gender and the Concept of Leisure," *Leisure Studies*, 7 (May), 111-123.

Woodward, Diana and Eileen Green (1988), "Not Tonight, Dear! The Social Control of Women's Leisure," in *Relative Freedoms*, Erica Wimbush and Margaret Talbot, eds. Milton Keynes, England: Open University Press, 131-146.

Zinkhan, George M. and Melanie Wallendorf (1985), "Service Set Similarities in Patterns of Consumer Satisfaction/Dissatisfaction," *International Journal of Research in Marketing*, 2 (4), 227-235.

What's Mine is Mine and What's Yours is Ours: Challenging the Income Pooling Assumption

Judith J. Marshall, Carleton University
Frances Woolley, Carleton University[1]

ABSTRACT

Social policy makers, economic analysts, marketing and business strategists have regarded income which accrues to an individual family or household member as family income. However, there is a growing body of evidence calling this presumption into question. In this paper, the authors challenge the validity of the pooling assumption, then draw and discuss the major implications following from this challenge for social policy makers and marketing strategists. The challenge is based on a review of the literature in the fields of anthropology, social policy and consumer behaviour, as well as on research conducted by the authors.

INTRODUCTION

"...and all my worldly goods with thee I share..."
– Husband's traditional vow in Anglican Church of Canada wedding ceremony, Book of Common Prayer, 1959.

Social policy makers, economic analysts, marketing and business strategists have regarded income which accrues to an individual family or household member as family income (i.e., Eichler 1988; MacIntyre 1990). For example, in the U.S. tax, liabilities are based on family income. When calculating eligibility for social assistance in Canada, the husband's and wife's incomes are added together to find family income. Similarly, total family or household income is widely used as a market segmentation or market descriptor variable. The ubiquitous use of total family income in social policy, economic and business analysis is based on the presumption that all household income enters a common pool to which both husband and wife have equal and unfettered access.

However, there is a growing body of evidence that the pooling of income in families may not be as pervasive as generally believed (Edwards 1981; Morris 1984; Pahl 1989). Moreover, there is reason to believe that the financial roles of wives and husbands in the family have been changing, because of women's increased money income, shifting family values, economic stresses such as increased unemployment, and because of changes in money management technology associated with the increased use of automated teller machines, debit and credit cards, automatic pay cheque bank deposits and deductions and so on (Asser and Bobinski 1991; Granbois, Rosen, and Acito 1986; Jamison 1991; Kim and Lee 1989; Marshall and Heslop 1988; Pahl 1983; 1989; Rosen and Granbois 1983; Schaninger, Buss and Grover 1982).

The purpose of this paper is twofold. First, the authors challenge the validity of the pooling assumption, then draw and discuss the major implications following from this challenge for social policy makers, marketing strategists and consumer researchers in 3 areas: (1) taxation policy, (2) the measurement of poverty and affluence and (3) definitions of household. The challenge is based on a review of the literature in the fields of anthropology, social policy and consumer behaviour, as well as on research conducted by the authors. The second purpose of the paper is to argue the need for a program of future research to investigate the actual financial arrangements used by different families and links (if any) between financial arrangements adopted in the family and predictor variables (such as sex-role attitudes, sources of income) as well as outcome variables (such as spending patterns, consumer decision making patterns, quality of life).

CHALLENGING THE POOLING ASSUMPTION

Family financial arrangements including the study of household budgets, flows of resources, marital roles in family financial behaviour and decisions about how to allocate and consume financial resources are usually relegated to a "black box" by consumer researchers. There are, however, a number of notable exceptions, such as Asser and Bobinski 1991; Ferber and Lee 1974; Granbois, Rosen and Acito 1986; Rosen and Granbois 1983; Schaninger, Buss and Grover 1982. Moreover, outside the consumer behaviour research stream, the subject of family financial allocation practices has begun to attract a little attention (Pahl 1989; Wilk 1989). Existing literature will be reviewed briefly below in an attempt to assess the validity of the pooling assumption.

Anthropological Research

A number of different models describing household resource allocation in a variety of cultures and subcultures have been outlined in the anthropological literature - see, for example, Guyer 1986; McMillan 1986; Wilk 1989). The work of anthropologists demonstrates the variety of financial allocation systems that have been adopted by families in different cultures. In an overview of anthropological work on household resource management flows, Wilk (1989:38) concludes:

"It may appear that we are dealing here with two basic types of households; one ... which has no household pool or fund, and one like the Euro-American single-account household. But most of the world's households actually lie in between, with some communal or conjugal funds, and other funds that are individually managed."

Social Policy Research

The study of family financial allocation systems has also been tackled by social policy researchers working primarily in Britain. One of the leading writers and researchers studying family financial allocation systems, Jan Pahl (1983; 1989) argues that in societies in which money is a source of power, it is likely that the balance of power between husband and wife will be reflected in their control over economic resources. She focuses work on couples living together in married or marriage-like states.

A major contribution of Pahl's (1983) work has been the development of a typology consisting of four different types of family financial management systems: (1) whole wage system, (2) allowance system, (3) shared management system, (4) independent management system. Each of these systems is summarized below:

---

[1] The authors would like to acknowledge and thank the Winnipeg Area Study, Department of Sociology, University of Manitoba, Winnipeg, Manitoba, R3T 2N2 for supplying empirical data used in this paper, and the support of a Carleton University research grant.

Whole Wage System. In households using this system, one partner, usually the wife, is responsible for managing all finances of the household and is also responsible for all expenditures except for the personal spending money of the other partner. In this system, both partners have access to the money coming into the household, but the wife is responsible for management.

Allowance System. In households using this system, the husband gives the wife a set amount of money every week or month to which she adds her own earnings if there are any. The woman is responsible for paying for specific items while the remainder of the money stays under the control of the husband and he pays for other items. The husband has access to the main source of income, the wife has access to only that part of it which he chooses to give her. There can be many variations in this system because of varying patterns of responsibility for different items. For example, if the wife's domain of financial responsibility is large, she has access to a larger portion of the income coming into the household.

Pooling/Shared Management. The key characteristic of this system of financial allocation is the philosophy (held by both partners) that "its not my money, its not his/her money, its our money". Families using this system utilize a joint account or common kitty into which all income is paid and from which both can draw. Both husband and wife have access to all income and responsibility for expenses is shared more or less equally.

Independent Management System. This system may be used when both partners have an income and neither has access to all household funds. Each maintains separate control over his/her own income and each partner is responsible for specific items of expenditure.

Of direct relevance to the thesis of this paper are the studies that have researched empirically the frequency of use of these or similar systems. These studies have been summarized in Table 1. A review of Table 1 shows:

(1) Strong evidence for challenging the pooling assumption. Pooling/Shared Management was used by just over one-half of the families in Pahl's (1989) study but was used much less by families (from 2%-29%) in all other studies. In the majority of the research, use of pooling was found in fewer than half the families. A careful reading of this research leaves many unanswered questions about the pooling system. The ideology behind this system is clearly one of equal access to a couple's resources and sharing of management tasks. However, the extent of sharing can vary enormously. Who checks account statements, pays major bills and so on? Does spending have to be justified to the other partner? Pahl (1989) reported that pooling couples have a greater degree of jointness than couples using other systems - more joint bank accounts and so on. In spite of this jointness, she also found that wives tended to be more accountable to husbands for spending than did husbands to wives.

(2) There have been a number of studies utilizing the Pahl (1983) typology of financial allocation systems which facilitates comparisons. However, the studies have been small scale and concentrated in the U.K. (three), with one in each of Australia, India and Scotland. Given the small scale of the studies and methodological differences in financial system measurement, it is not surprising that there is a wide variation in the reported frequencies of each management system.

(3) Little is known about North American families (either Canadian or American). Given the differences in culture, the emergence of different family forms and the demise of the traditional family - this is a significant gap.

Consumer Research

Much consumer research has been devoted to studying families in the context of North American culture. Research on husband/wife roles in family economic behaviour has tended to focus on who does what tasks in the family rather than tracing the financial allocation systems used. In their seminal study of 230 newlywed couples in the United States during their first year of marriage and one year later, Ferber and Lee (1974) identified the family financial officer (FFO) as the individual (could be couple) who carried the main responsibility for family finances. Ferber and Lee (1974) reported that most often the couple did this, but that the incidence of joint action decreased over time (49% in Wave 1 and 37% in Wave 2). The husband was the FFO in a little over one-quarter of couples (26%-Wave 1 and 27%-Wave 2) and the wife's role appeared to increase over time (Wave 1-25%, Wave 2-37%). This work does not provide information to allow the reader to determine the extent of pooling of income earned by partners or the extent to which each partner has access to the income earned by the other partner.

Similarly, Rosen and Granbois (1983) conducted highly structured joint husband-wife interviews with 82 couples covering:

(1) implementation - who handled bookkeeping, balanced checkbooks, reconciled checkbooks, corrected checkbook errors, reconciled savings statements and paid bills, and

(2) decision-making activities including who decided on method of saving, amounts to be contributed to savings, number and ownership of checking accounts, items and amounts for monthly budget, what to do with leftover money, the system of budgeting and/or spending from income, the method of financing purchases, the priority for paying bills, and amounts to pay on three different kinds of credit card bills. Jamison (1991) compared two LIMRA studies examining the roles of husbands and wives in family financial behaviour. He found that in 1965, men played less of a role in running family finances than many suspected. Duties such as keeping a budget, tracking expenses and signing checks tended to be either shared or done by wives. By 1990, husbands reported that the husband played a larger role - the husband is more apt to keep the budget and keep track of bills. Wives reported roles similar to those in 1965.

A CANADIAN STUDY OF FAMILY FINANCIAL ALLOCATION

Additional empirical evidence regarding the extent of pooling/shared management was gathered by analyzing data gathered from a large study (conducted in a major mid-western Canadian city) designed to describe financial decision making and gift giving patterns in Canadian households. Key features of this research are described below.

Data used in this study were collected as part of the 1988 Winnipeg Area Study. A systematic random sample of 753 addresses was selected for personal interviewing from a computerized list of addresses. The household was the primary sampling unit. After pretesting in 65 households, the questionnaire was

TABLE 1
Frequency Of Use Of Family Financial Allocation Systems

Study	Sample Size/ (Households)	Whole Wage	Allowance	Pooling/ Shared Management	Independent Management	Other
Edwards (Australia) 1981	50	50%	14%	14%	22%	—
Gray (Scotland) 1979	86	52%	45%	2%	—	—
McRae (United Kingdom) 1987	30 (*Cross Class)	43.4% Female Control 3.3% Male Control	10%	3.3%	33.3%	6.6%
Morris (United Kingdom)	40 (Male Laid Off)	52.5% Female Control 12.5% Male Control	17.5%	17.5%	—	—
Pahl (United Kingdom) 1989	102	14% Female Control	22%	56%	9%	—
Sharma (India) 1980	28	14%	54%	29%	—	3%

*Cross Class Households - woman earns as much or more than the male.

finalized and interviewing was conducted by trained, experienced interviewers. All potential respondents were mailed a letter explaining the survey and asking their cooperation in advance of the first interviewer contact. The mean length of the interview was 48 minutes. Interviews were completed in 528 residences for a completion rate of 72.1% of eligible households, or 70.1 percent of the original sample. Analysis (see Currie (1988) for a detailed analysis of these issues) reveals that the neighbourhood distribution, household size and home ownership, as well as sex and age of the respondents are consistent with the 1986 census data on the Winnipeg population.

Sample Description

A total of 314 husband/wife households (married or common-law) were included in the sample. In 154 of these households, the male was the household respondent, while females were interviewed in the other 150 households. The average age of household respondents was 41 years and median family income was $40,000-$44,999.

The sample consisted of (1) 37.8% dual income families where both the husband and wife worked full-time, (2) 14.3% of families where the husband worked full-time and the wife part-time, (3) 19.7% of families where the husband worked full-time and the wife did not work, (4) 9.2% of families where the wife worked full-time and the husband did not, (5) 19.0% of families where neither worked full-time (this category consisted of a combination of students, retirees and so on).

Results

Respondents were asked whether the income in their family goes into a common fund where each member can draw on it or whether it is handled by the male, female or divided between the partners. Table 2 shows that over half of the households reported that the main income does not go into a common fund accessed by both the husband and wife. In about 41% of families the income does go into a common fund where each member draws on it. In about 1/4 of families, the male handles the main income and the female handles it in another quarter. Relatively few respondents (4.4%) reported that income was divided among the family members.

There is a significant difference between the way male and female respondents report the way the main income is handled in their families ($\chi^2=10.0$, p<.05). Women are more likely to report that income is put into a common fund (46.3% of female respon-

TABLE 2
How Main Income Is Handled

	% Of Households
Main Income Goes Into Common Fund Where Each Member Draws On It	41.2
Male Handles Most of It	26.8
Female Handles Most of It	24.0
Income is Divided	4.4
Other	3.6
Total	100.0

dents and 36.2% of male respondents report that the main income goes into a common fund) or that they handle it (26.8% of female respondents report that they handle it themselves while 21.3% of male respondents said that their female partners handled it). Men are more likely to report that they handle the money (32.2% of male respondents say they handle it, 21.1% of female respondents say that their male spouse handles it).

Overall, study participants did not believe that the person whose money pays the bills should have the most say in subsequent decision making. However, female respondents were significantly more likely to disagree with this view of family power ($\chi^2=12.3$, p<.01). 84.4% of females disagreed, 1.3% were neutral, and 14.4% agreed with this view of power, while 74.6% of the male respondents disagreed, 6.5% were neutral, and 18.8% agreed.

CONCLUSIONS AND IMPLICATIONS FOR SOCIAL POLICY MAKERS AND CONSUMER BEHAVIOUR

This brief analysis of control and management of family financial resources all but shatters the pooling assumption which has characterized thinking about family financial arrangements in North American families. The research shows that equal and unfettered access to all household income appears to be a minority approach to family financial arrangements. A number of implications resulting from these conclusions are outlined below.

Taxation Policy

First, implications for taxation policy follow a rejection or modification of the pooling assumption. American couples are taxed on the basis of their combined incomes, while the Canadian tax system is for the most part based on individual earnings. Advocates of joint taxation often defend their position by arguing that couples pool their income. For example, MacIntyre (1990) advocates making married couples tax units because "an overwhelming majority of husbands and wives claim they receive approximately equal consumption benefits from their aggregate marital income" (p. 155).

Our research indicates that the structure of family finances is complex. While 91 percent of respondents to the Winnipeg study consider their earnings to belong to the family, one third of females and 44 percent of males have separate bank accounts. Only 41 percent report that the main income goes into a common fund where each member draws on it. Much household income is shared. But not all household income is. And makers of taxation policy must be aware of the separation as well as the sharing within households.

Measurement of Poverty and Affluence

Second, rejecting or at least questioning the common pooling/ equal sharing assumption points to the need for questioning what is the appropriate income to be used by social policy makers in determining eligibility for social security programmes. What is the appropriate income unit for marketing strategists and consumer researchers to utilize in the measurement and analyses of purchasing power - household income or individual income? The fundamental issue is how should *poverty and affluence* be measured? Most consumer researchers, social policy makers and business strategists take it for granted that all members of any one family household have the same standard of living (level of poverty or affluence) and that they all receive equal or equitable shares of money coming into the family. If two individuals sharing a household are of the same sex or of different generations, the assumption of pooling and sharing is less likely. Given the emergence of large numbers of different family forms, it is becoming increasingly essential to investigate financial arrangements in alternate household forms. The evidence reviewed in this paper suggests that for the purpose of analyzing purchasing behaviour, the family is not a homogeneous unit; rather it is a collection of individuals whose social relationships affect substantially their claim on family resources. This leads to the inescapable conclusion that hardship or affluence may be concealed by the assumption that the household is an economic unit within which resources are shared equitably.

Definition of Household

The third implication resulting from this review of family financial management and control relates to both our definition and analysis of household formation and dissolution. The term household in North America typically refers to people who live at the same address, having meals prepared together and with common housekeeping. However, as most consumer behaviour theorists recognize, there are many different dimensions to the formation of households. Individuals in the same household may share accommodation, eat meals together, pool money for housekeeping expenses, enter a sexual relationship, spend leisure time together, help other household members with domestic work and so on or they may not. When the idea of a household is used it is often assumed that either a person is in a household or out. Yet data from the Winnipeg study shows that, at least with respect to income sharing, household boundaries can be hard to draw. Some households pool all their income, others do not. Moreover, individuals in households share their income with others outside the household: 12.5 percent of our total sample supported at least one person who did not live with them, most commonly a son, daughter, or ex-partner, and 10.5 percent received financial support, most often from their mother or ex-partner.

We do not know the social processes involved in forming or dissolving a household - is there a typical sequence of events in which people form a household along one dimension of their life before amalgamating along another dimension? Do the income transfers between separated individuals facilitate other links, such as joint custody of children? Given the number of different household forms in North American society, can we characterize households differently depending on the aspects of life which are amalgamated? We need to improve our understanding of relationships between patterns of allocation of money and other elements which combine together in our definition of household.

THE NEED FOR FUTURE RESEARCH

In conclusion, research on financial allocation arrangements in a variety of household types needs to be done. Our understanding of consumers' financial behaviour is lagging far behind our knowledge of most other aspects of consumer behaviour. Evidence reveals that families have organized their money in a variety of ways. The research question that needs attention is: What are the patterns of control and financial management systems used by households in late twentieth century North America? The first task of consumer researchers is to describe patterns of control and financial management in different household forms. The second task is to identify and test relationships among predictors and outcomes and patterns of control and management of family finances. The extant literature does provide some tentative ideas about patterns we might observe in varying household types. For example, the literature suggests that independent control and management of incomes is more likely to occur in dual career families. As well, since research suggests that time brings better understanding by one partner of another's preferences, we hypothesize that the use of joint or shared management systems is likely to be lower in families further on in the family life cycle. Focusing on outcome variables, we expect there to be a relationship between family financial management and quality of life. The existing literature (Pahl 1989) suggests that joint control of family finances and joint or independent management are positively related to marital satisfaction, financial well-being and satisfaction with financial management. Lastly, we hypothesize that the degree of control exercised over the process of resource allocation and the financial management system will be reflected in husband/wife product decision making patterns. For example, joint control of finances is likely to be associated with joint patterns of husband/wife consumer decision making.

A mix of quantitative and qualitative approaches is necessary to advance knowledge in the field. An ideal study would incorporate a fairly quantitative survey in conjunction with detailed depth interviews of a smaller subsample. There are a number of other issues which must be tackled - it is necessary to study financial practices in different household forms - ones where there are grown children or perhaps an aging parent in the household, ones composed of same sex individuals in roommate situations as well as more permanent ones, blended families and so on. The role of children (both adult and dependent) in family financial management and the fate of the money they bring to the household has also been under-researched.

REFERENCES

Asser, Amardeep, and G.S. Bobinski, Jr. (1991) "Financial Decision Making of Babyboomer Couples," in *Advances in Consumer Research*, Vol.18, Holman, R.D and M.R. Solomon (Eds), Provo, UT: Association for Consumer Research, 657-665.

R.F. Currie (1988) *Selected Findings From the Winnipeg Area Study*, Winnipeg Area Study Research Reports, Research Report No.24, Department of Sociology, The University of Manitoba, Winnipeg, Manitoba, R3T 2N2, 19 pages.

M. Eichler (1988) *Families in Canada Today*, Toronto: Gage Educational Publishing Company.

M. Edwards (1981) "Financial Arrangements Within Families", *Social Security Journal*, 1-16.

Ferber, Robert, and L.C. Lee (1974) "Husband-Wife Influence in Family Purchasing Behavior", *Journal of Consumer Research*, 1 (June), 43-50.

Yolanda, K. Grift (1988) "The Excess Burden of the Tax and Social Premium System for Dutch Married Women", *De Economist*. 136 (2), 185-204.

Granbois, D.H., Rosen, D.L. and F. Acito (1986) "A Developmental Study of Family Financial Management Practices", *Advances in Consumer Research*, 13, Richard Lutz (ed.), Provo, UT: Association for Consumer Research, 170-174.

A. Gray (1979) "The Working Class Family as an Economic Unit", in *The Sociology of the Family*, C. Harris (Ed.), Keele Sociological Review Monograph.

J.I. Guyer (1981) "Intra-Household Processes and Farming Systems Research: Perspectives from Anthropology", in J. Moock (ed.), *Understanding Africa's Rural Households and Farming Systems*, Boulder: Westview Press, 92-105.

Kent S. Jamison (1991) "The Family Financial Officer Then and Now", *Household Conference: Consumption and Production Perspectives*, University of California, Irvine.

Kim, C. and H. Lee (1989) "Sex Role Attitudes of Spouses and Task Sharing Behavior", in *Advances in Consumer Research*, Vol 16, T.K. Srull (ed.), Provo, UT: Association for Consumer Research, 671-679.

D. McMillan (1986) "Distribution of Resources and Products in Mossi Households", in A. Hanson and D. McMillan (eds.), *Food in Sub-saharan Africa*, Boulder: Lynne Rienner.

Marshall, Judith, J. and Heslop, Louise A. (1988) "Technology Acceptance in Canadian Retail Banking: A Study of Consumer Motivations and Use of ATMs", *International Journal of Bank Marketing*, 6 (3) 31-41.

S. McRae (1987) "The Allocation of Money in Cross-Class Families", *Sociological Review*, 35, 97-122.

Michael J. McIntyre (1990) "Implications of Family Sharing for the Design of an Ideal Personal Tax System." *The Personal Income Tax: Phoenix from the Ashes?* S. Cnossen and R.M. Bird eds. Amsterdam: North Holland.

Lydia, D. Morris (1984) "Redundancy and Patterns of Household Finance", *Sociological Review*, 32, 492-523.

Jan Pahl (1983) "The Allocation of Money and the Structuring of Inequality Within Marriage", *Sociological Review*, 13(2), 237-262.

Jan Pahl (1989) *Money and Marriage*, London: Macmillan Education Limited.

Rosen, D.L. and D.H. Granbois (1983) "Determinants of Role Structure in Family Financial Management", *Journal of Consumer Research*, 10 (Sept.), 253-258.

Schaninger, C.M., Buss, W.C. and R. Grover (1982) "The Effect of the Sex Roles on Family Economic Handling and Decision Influence", in *An Assessment of Marketing Thought and Practice*, B. Walker (ed.), Chicago: American Marketing Association, 43-57.

U. Sharma (1980) *Women, Work and Property in North-West India*, London: Tavistock.

Richard R. Wilk (1989) "Decision Making and Resource Flows Within the Household: Beyond the Black Box", in *The Household Economy*, Richard R. Wilk (ed.), San Francisco: Westview Press, 23-51.

Summary of Special Session
Self-Gifts: An Emerging Category of Consumer Behavior from Multiple Perspectives
David Mick, University of Florida

This special session was organized by David Mick and chaired by Ed Petkus. It was attended by approximately 30 persons. The purpose of this session was to extend self-gift research and knowledge development by bringing together several researchers who would look upon the topic from multiple viewpoints.

The first paper by McGrath, Sherry, and Levy emanated from a cultural-anthropological and motivational-research perspective. Using sentence completion tasks and a story-telling technique, these researchers found that magic, mystery, ambivalence, and indulgence are associated with self-gifts, just as they are with interpersonal gifts. Guilt emerged as a potential consequence, more so than in prior research, whereas themes of self-esteem, specialness, and perfect choices were also discerned, corroborating prior findings by Mick and DeMoss.

The second paper by Olshavsky and Lee offered an information-processing explanation of self-gifts based on meta-cognition—**awareness** of one's own cognitive processes—which implies the dimension of self-communication in self-gifts. The authors argue that if a person is aware of his/her cognitive state, then that person can influence the cognitive/emotional integrity of his/her information processing system through self-gift behavior. They conclude that, while a new theory to explain self-gifts is unnecessary, the major contribution of self-gift research has been the recognition of a new consumer motivation that cannot be readily traced to Maslow's hierarchy of needs.

The third paper by Faure and Mick reviewed prior self-gift research and Weiner's attribution theory of motivation and emotion to derive several predictions about self-gift likelihood following achievement task outcomes. For example, they proposed that certain emotions (e.g., pride, guilt) and a sense of deservingness will mediate the influence of achievement outcomes (success/failure) and causal attributions (locus, controllability) on self-gift likelihood. They also discuss different methodological options for testing their hypotheses.

The fourth paper by Shapiro reported survey results that indicated that individuals with an internal (external) locus of control engage in more (less) therapeutic self-gift behavior. He explained this finding in terms of Deci's self-determination theory, i.e., internals may be more inclined to take action to repair their emotional states with therapeutic self-gifts.

The discussant for this special session, Dennis Rook, raised several important questions about the concept and research of self-gifts. For example, he asked "If you manage to get someone else to buy you a gift that you really want, is it a self-gift?" The possibility of compulsive therapeutic self-gifts was also raised in discussion, and Mick argued that this notion is oxymoronic, i.e., any gifting activity that is out of control is probably not perceived by the gift recipient as authentic gift giving. Rook concluded by calling for more grounded theory and naturalistic research on self-gifts.

Self-Gifts: A Metacognition Perspective

Richard W. Olshavsky, Indiana University
Dong Hwan Lee, State University of New York at Albany

ABSTRACT

Metacognition is the key to the development of an information processing theory of self-gift giving. We argue that if a person can be aware of his/her cognitive state, then a person can also be aware of the necessity of maintaining or enhancing the cognitive/emotional integrity of his/her information processing system in order to achieve important goals in the life goal. We conclude that a major contribution of research on self-gifts is that it has led to the identification of a previously unrecognized and important type of consumer motivation.

INTRODUCTION

On the basis of past research (Levy 1982; Mick 1986; Mick and DeMoss 1990a, 1990b), we agree that self-gift giving is a unique and important type of consumer behavior, that self-gift giving may commonly occur, and that the study of self-gift giving may lead to a more refined understanding of consumer behavior. What appears to be lacking is a systematic explanation of self-gift giving. The purpose of this paper is to argue that information processing theory, in conjunction with the concept of metacognition, can parsimoniously explain most, if not all, of the behaviors that have been classified as self-gift giving. If our proposed explanation holds up under future scrutiny by others, then further research and theory development on self-gifts can be integrated into the mainstream of research on consumer behavior.

METACOGNITION

"Metacognition is the knowledge of and awareness about our own cognitive processes." (Matlin 1989, p. 237) Specific examples of metacognition that have received empirical research pertains to attention (Reisberg and McLean 1985), memory (Brown and McNeill 1966; Hart 1965; Leonesio and Nelson 1990; Lovelace 1984; Reber 1989), comprehension (Maki and Berry 1984) and problem solving (Metcalfe 1986). Also see Feick and Park (1991). For example, in the context of "metamemory" it has been found that students can predict with some accuracy which general-information questions they can answer correctly. High ability students can predict how well they will do on tests. And, students can predict which words they will be able to recall on a list-learning task (Matlin 1989).

Metacognition can be viewed as the basis for self-consciousness or self-concept. Philosophers have considered reflection the essence of human self-consciousness. Haugeland (1985, p. 220) argues that "reflective self-awareness is certainly a critical element in much that we regard as particularly mature, sophisticated, profound, insightful, and the like. ... no system incapable of metacognition could reflect." Symbolic interactionists conceptualize the self-concept as an organization of various identities developed out of an individual's own reflexive positional designations, which creates internalized expectations with regard to their own behavior (Lee 1990).

Having cognitions about one's own cognitions implies "self-dialogue" (Haugeland 1986; Laird, Newell, Rosenbloom 1987). Self-dialogues can focus on issues external to the self (e.g., the weather, sports) or, importantly, self-dialogues can focus on various aspects of the self (e.g., self esteem, self concept, ideal self, real self). Self-dialogue is mostly a continuous and automatic process, but sometimes it is under an individual's control.

Although there has been some controversy concerning the extent to which people have access to their cognitive processes (Nisbett and Wilson 1977) there is general agreement that under certain conditions access is possible (Ericsson and Simon 1984; Fiske and Taylor 1991; Wright and Rip 1981).

Given that metacognition can be handled within an information processing framework (Haugeland 1986; Laird, Newell, Rosenbloom 1987), it is the key to the development of an information processing theory of self-gift giving as will be described below.[1]

CONSUMER BEHAVIOR FROM AN INFORMATION PROCESSING PERSPECTIVE

Information processing theory has been widely accepted in cognitive psychology (Matlin 1989) and more recently in social psychology (Fiske and Taylor 1991). See Laird, Newell, and Rosenbloom (1985) for a description of a powerful architecture of cognition developed within information processing theory. Information processing theory has also been widely applied to consumer behavior; indeed, some have characterized it as the dominant theory (Holbrook and Hirschman 1982). There are however many different versions of IPT (see e.g., Bettman 1979; Sternthal and Craig 1982). What follows is a brief description of how our version (Olshavsky 1975; 1985) of information processing theory explains consumer behavior.

Types of Consumer Behavior

Consumer behavior is defined here as those behaviors relating to the formation of goals involving goods, the acquisition of goods, the consumption of goods, and the disposition of goods. A *good* is defined as a product or service and all associated services. In addition, consumer behavior encompasses all behaviors *with respect to information* that originate within each of the four types of consumer behavior *with respect to goods*.

Each of these four types of consumer behavior with respect to goods consists of one or more subtypes. Goal formation encompasses four subtypes: desire formation, priority formation, preference formation, and intention formation. Desire formation encompasses those behaviors relating to the formation of desires for goods including the type of good, timing, amount, and intensity of desire. Priority formation refers to those behaviors that establish the relative importance of desires. Preference formation pertains to the selection of the most desired brand and store. Intentions formation pertains to the allocation of limited resources (money and time) to all desired goods to form plans to purchase specific goods within a particular time period. Acquisition encompasses three subtypes: travel to the store, purchase of the good, and transport of the good. Consumption encompasses three subtypes: storage, preparation, and use. Disposition refers to the disassociation of the good from the consumer (e.g., selling a car).

---

[1] Information processing theory has the important virtue of avoiding the homuncular "infinite regress" problem that characterizes many other attempts to explain intelligence and specifically self-dialogues about the self (Haugeland 1986, pp. 113-4).

Explaining Preference Formation

The most frequently studied type of consumer behavior has been preference formation (i.e., brand and store choice). Most types of preference formation can be explained in terms of the attempt by the consumer to apply his/her evaluative criteria to the alternatives within the consideration set, given a particular image of each of the alternatives, using a particular choice rule (e.g., conjunctive). The outcome (and the process) of the execution attempt depends upon the interaction that occurs over time between the characteristics of the consumer and the characteristics of the environment (Olshavsky 1985).

Explaining Desire Formation

To explain desire formation it is first necessary to describe some basic assumptions concerning the nature of desires within an individual's life goal. If an individual's life goal is graphically represented as an inverted "tree," then "happiness" can be viewed as the highest goal within an individual's life goal. Five branches emerge from happiness representing the five basic needs identified by Maslow; i.e., physiological needs, safety, love, status, and self-actualization. Other desires in a person's life goal can be represented as additional branches (subgoals) that emerge from each of Maslow's needs. Each of these subgoals (consequences or benefits), in turn, can branch to additional subgoals, until the level of highly specific desires in the form of evaluative criteria (Gutman 1982; Peter and Olson 1987) is reached. At all levels within the tree (needs, consequences, attributes), desires may have hedonic as well as utilitarian aspects (e.g., most foods are desired for their good taste as well as for their nutritional content). Differences among individuals in the specific goals desired (i.e., what will make a particular individual happy) begin to appear at the level of Maslow's needs and continue to unfold until the level of attributes is reached. Thus, each individual's life goal is unique.

Desire formation occurs prior to preference formation and refers to the process by which desires in the life goal are added, deleted or modified. At the concrete level, desire formation pertains to those behaviors that establish the evaluative criteria, the consideration set, the image of alternatives within the consideration set, and the choice rule to be used during preference formation with respect to goods. But desire formation also encompasses behaviors relating to the formation of desires at the highest levels of abstraction (e.g., determining the types of subgoals relating to status).

Desires within the life goal are determined biologically, sociologically, psychologically or by some combination of these determinants. For example, the desire for goods relating to Maslow's physiological needs are largely biologically determined (e.g., food is innately linked to hunger). The desire for specific types of foods (e.g., a steak) and the way these foods are prepared (e.g., grilled) is largely sociologically determined. Idiosyncratic desires for foods are formed largely by psychological processes.

It is important to note that information processing theory has always been (Newell and Simon 1972) restricted to the "cognitive" or psychological level of explanation; it does not attempt to explain behaviors determined by either biological or sociological processes.

One very important type of psychological desire formation process begins with a comparison of the individual's desired state to his/her perceived actual state. If a discrepancy is noticed and if this discrepancy is greater than the relevant threshold then a subgoal is established to "solve this problem" (Engel, Blackwell and Miniard 1990). The process selected to solve this problem may take one of several forms (Newell and Simon 1972). For example, the consumer may use the "generate-test" process; here alternative solutions are generated and then tested, in sequence, until an acceptable solution is found. The solution to the problem then takes on drive or motivational properties. As with preference formation, the outcome (and the process) of this desire formation process is determined by the nature of the interaction that occurs over time between characteristics of the consumer and characteristics of the task environment.

Explaining Priority Formation

Priority formation can be explained in a similar manner. In this instance, the goal is to rank all goods currently desired on the basis of the relative intensity of desire. For example, a pairwise comparison process would produce the required priorities.

Explaining Intentions Formation

Intentions formation can be explained in terms of the application of some type of budgeting strategy (Hauser and Urban 1986). For example, a consumer may allocate available financial and temporal resources by first planning to purchase "necessities" and then planning to purchase "luxuries" in a sequence determined by that consumer's priorities, up to the current financial and temporal limits.

Explaining Acquisition, Consumption, and Disposition

These behaviors also entail the execution of a desired strategy. For example the "preparation" of certain foods may be guided by the directions provided on the package, by recipes provided in a cookbook, or by procedures stored in long term memory.

GIFT GIVING FROM AN INFORMATION PROCESSING PERSPECTIVE

Explaining Interpersonal Gift Giving

Typically goods are consumed by the individual who acquires the good. But one very important *use* of a good (particularly goods such as flowers, candy, perfume, toys, and jewelry) is to give it to another person for their use. Why do consumers give gifts to others? Or, more to the point, why do consumers *desire* to give gifts to others? In our view, interpersonal gift giving is largely determined by socialization processes (Belk 1979; Sherry 1983); hence, these behaviors are beyond the present scope of information processing theory. That is, individuals are explicitly taught, directly or indirectly, to whom gifts are to be given, when gifts are to be given, what kinds of gifts to give, and even why gifts are given. Interpersonal gift giving that is not explained by socialization processes can be explained in terms of psychological processes in the same way that desire formation for goods was explained above. That is, a comparison of the individual's desired state to his/her perceived actual state is made. If a discrepancy is noticed and if the discrepancy is greater than the relevant threshold, then a subgoal is established to solve this problem. A specific problem solving strategy is selected and executed and the outcome may take the form of a desire to give a good to someone. (But we find it difficult to think of a good example of interpersonal gift giving that cannot readily be explained in sociological terms.)

Explaining Self-Gifts

How is self-gift giving explained? We argue that if a person can be aware of his/her cognitive state, that person can also be aware of the necessity of maintaining or enhancing the cognitive/emotional integrity of his/her information processing system in order to be able to achieve the goals contained within the life goal. More specifically, a comparison is postulated between the desired state (e.g., the desired motivational level) and the perceived actual state (e.g., the perceived motivational level). If the discrepancy is larger than the relevant threshold and if the problem solving effort is successful, a drive is formed for the solution. The solution may take many forms such as the purchasing of a good (e.g., clothing), using a good (e.g., watching TV), or engaging in an activity that does not explicitly involve the purchase or use of a particular good (e.g., taking a walk in a park). Self-gift giving, therefore, can be conceptualized as a special case of desire formation. (Note that even this psychological process may be heavily influenced by sociological factors. For example, a child may have learned to control his/her own motivational states with self-gifts by observing his/her parents engage in similar behaviors.)

What remains to be explained is why some behaviors relating to system maintenance and enhancement sometimes take on gift-like dimensions. According to Mick and DeMoss a purchase for oneself takes on gift giving characteristics when it shares three dimensions that characterize interpersonal gift giving: symbolic communication, exchange, and specialness. Self-gifts are defined as "... (1) personally symbolic self-communication through (2) special indulgences that tend to be (3) premeditated and (4) highly context bound." (Mick and DeMoss 1990b, p. 328) Why then do certain desires take on the dimensions of symbolic communication, exchange, and specialness? And, it remains to address two additional defining characteristics of self-gifts: premeditativeness and context-boundedness. Six "themes" characterizing self-gifts (Mick and DeMoss 1990b) will also be addressed: self-esteem, identity, deserving, perfect thing, escape, and discovery.

The Personal Symbolic Communication Dimension. "In general, the communication dimension in interpersonal gift giving involves the participants' expression of feelings and thoughts, including the imposition of identities." (Mick and DeMoss, 1990b, p. 325) According to Mick, DeMoss, and Farber (1991, p. 1), "... celebration, congratulations, and consolation are among the most typical of self directed messages."

The comparison that takes place between the desired state of one's own system and the perceived actual state of one's own system can be viewed as a self-dialogue focused on the self. An individual's desired state constitutes an integral part of the "self." Here constructs such as "ideal self" or "desired self" are relevant. And, an integral component of every individual's perceived actual state is the perceived self. Thus constructs such as "self-esteem," "self-concept," "real self," and "identity" are relevant. In effect, feelings and thoughts are exchanged between the desired state of self and the perceived actual state of self during the comparison process. It is important to note that in this case "system maintenance and enhancement" is nearly synonymous with "self maintenance and enhancement." This is because the definition of self can be very broad, encompassing one's physical attributes as well as one's mental capabilities and can even include one's possessions (Belk 1988).

Of the many types of self-dialogues focusing on the self, some take on a special significance because of the unique, personal, and important nature of the desired state or the perceived actual state. For example, if a person's "ideal self" includes a desire to have "strong willpower" and that person's perception of his/her actual willpower is very high on a particular occasion (such as the successful completion of a weight reduction program) then a drive may be formed (through subgoaling) for a good that will symbolically communicate to that individual his/her willpower capability long after the occasion has passed. In this particular case, metacognition relates both to an awareness of the fluctuations that occur in one's perception of one's willpower over time (i.e., from very high to very low) and to an awareness of the fallibility of one's own long term memory. The individual purchases a good for oneself (i.e., a self-gift) to symbolically communicate, in the form of a reminder, the message that he/she has strong willpower.

This explanation can be generalized to other self-directed messages arising from perceived discrepancies in other motivational or emotional states of the self such as those relating to celebration, congratulations, and consolation.

The Exchange Dimension. "Interpersonal gift giving has also been characterized as a continuing cycle of reciprocity in which people are obligated to give, receive, and repay (Belk 1979; Mauss 1954). This contractual aspect of gift giving predicates and even optimizes human behavior (Sherry 1983). Thus, as exchange, gift giving establishes, perpetrates, and clarifies interpersonal relationships (Belk 1979)." (Mick and DeMoss 1990b, p. 326)

Self-dialogues focusing on the self can address a variety of issues (willpower, appearance, competence, depression, etc.). One very important issue is motivation. A comparison (by the individual) of the desired state of motivation and the perceived actual state of motivation can result in a discrepancy that is large enough to result in a desire for a good or non good to correct the motivational problem. For example, a student who detects that his/her current level of motivation to complete school is too low may attempt to raise the actual motivational level by promising himself/herself a particularly attractive good (e.g., an automobile) as an incentive. Metacognition is crucial to this explanation because the consumer must be able to monitor the motivational aspects of both the desired and the actual states to establish the preconditions for this type of self-contractual arrangement. "Deserving" is an important theme here because it relates directly to societally inculcated ideas of "fair" contracts (e.g., the Protestant ethic) for interpersonal relations as well as for intrapersonal relations.

The Specialness Dimension. "Sincere interpersonal gifts are special, even sacred, binding individuals through a ritual communion of cultural values and deeply felt emotions (Belk, Wallendorf, and Sherry 1989)." (Mick and DeMoss 1990b, p. 326)

Goods that are classified as "high involvement" typically are those that are related to the self (Krugman 1965). The specialness dimension of self-gifts can be attributed to the centrality of the self in all activities undertaken by the individual. The individual must be properly motivated and emotionally adjusted in order to pursue the many goals in the life goal. Hence, a good purchased for oneself that is critically linked to the integrity of the self takes on the gift characteristic of specialness. Metacognition plays a critical role here in as much as the preconditions for such subgoaling involve recognition of one's own cognitive/emotional states. This explanation can easily be generalized to a variety of other self-related issues such as motivation, competency, identity, and worth.

The "perfect thing" theme is important here because of the uncertainty and complexity that so frequently characterize our desires. Typically it is very difficult for the average consumer to specify with any degree of precision the criteria to be used for the selection of a good (e.g., a car, life insurance, food). Therefore, if a consumer does happen to know exactly which good would serve as an incentive or as therapy this would have an element of specialness to it. Here, metacognition pertains to knowing what it takes to maintain or to enhance our selves.

Certain activities or goods may enable an individual to "escape" the continuing self-dialogue focused on the self by focusing the self-dialogue on some external stimulus. By buying time away from the issue (i.e., putting it aside for a while), some individuals may be better able to cope with the specific motivational or emotional problem at hand. Metacognition speaks to the issue of how the individual knows whether an escape strategy works for him/her and knowing which specific activities (e.g., watching TV) are capable of distracting one's self. "Discovery" is an important theme because discovery involves novel stimuli which could have the desired distracting effect.

Premeditatedness. The relative importance of desired goods is an important input to the intentions formation process, the process that determines which of all desired goods will be purchased in a particular future time period. Because the motivational and emotional states related to the self are so crucial to the successful performance of the individual, goods related to the self can be viewed as being of great relative importance. Thus, it follows that intentions for the purchase of a self-gift will on occasion be formed prior to their purchase (i.e., they would be premeditated). An example of this would be the self-gift that was promised (perhaps years earlier) as a reward for the successful completion of a task (e.g., a car on graduation).

Context Boundedness. Mick and DeMoss (1992, p. 4) report "... of the 392 reports, 134 were rewards, 145 were therapeutic, 39 concerned birthdays, and 74 concerned extra money to spend." Self-gifts arise in these contexts because contexts involving rewards and therapy, by definition, involve important changes in either the desired state or the perceived actual state. In the case of therapy, for example, failing an exam forces a negative change in one's perceived actual state. In the case of reward, for example, the ability to complete a weight reduction program leads to a positive change in the perceived actual state. Holidays serve as a context for self-gift giving because the timing and the nature of the desired state has been predetermined by society. Birthdays are particularly important because the individual is *supposed to receive* special attention and gifts on this day. Having extra money to spend relaxes the income constraint and enables the purchase of the next good on the priority list or it may stimulate desire formation to occur.

DISCUSSION

We believe that self-gift giving is parsimoniously explained by information processing theory if a person's metacognition capabilities are addressed. We believe we have explained why reward and therapy are the dominant contexts in which self-gift giving arises, why birthdays and having extra money to spend also serve as important contexts for self-gifts, why self esteem, identity, deserving, perfect thing, escape, and discovery are dominant themes, why self-gifts take such a wide diversity of forms, why the timing of a purchase and the amount of a good purchased can serve as a self-gift, why simply using a good can serve as a self-gift, and why self-gifts are premeditated.

As previously stated, in order to achieve goals within the life goal, the individual must maintain and perhaps enhance the information processing system or self that actually performs the various goal-oriented behaviors. From this perspective, a major contribution of research on self-gifts is that it has led to the identification of a previously unrecognized and important type of consumer behavior, one that has its own unique source of motivation. Given that the relevant subgoal underlying self-gifts is to maintain or to enhance the capabilities of one's own information processing system, it is difficult to "trace" these desires directly back to Maslow's needs (or to other basic value systems). We use the word trace in the sense of "laddering," a depth interviewing procedure described by Gutman (1982). This is perhaps what Mick and DeMoss (1990b, p. 328) mean by their statement that "... the consumer is seeking to consummate a desire that goes beyond intrinsic human needs."

The Moderating Role of Interpersonal Gift Giving on Self-Gift Giving

Even if the individual desires the gift and has the necessary resources to acquire the gift, self-gift giving may not occur. First, the context or occasion (e.g., need for a reward, need for therapy, or birthday) that gives rise to the desire for a self-gift by Person A may be observed by Person B and an appropriate gift may be purchased by Person B for Person A. There are, of course, many reasons why this type of interpersonal gift-giving may not occur. For example, Person B may be unaware of the Person A's circumstance. Or, if Person B is aware of Person A's circumstance, Person B may be unwilling or unable to provide the gift. Still, if such "unsolicited" interpersonal gift-giving does occur, it reduces the likelihood of occurrence of self-gift giving.

Second, Person A may be able to induce Person B to give the gift that is desired by Person A. There are, of course, several reasons why such an influence attempt may fail. For example, Person B may not agree that Person A needs the gift. Or, Person B may be unwilling to buy the gift desired by Person A at the time the gift is desired. Or, Person B may disagree as to the affordability of the gift. Or, Person A may find it too difficult to communicate to Person B exactly what is desired. Still, if such "solicited" interpersonal gift giving does occur, it reduces the likelihood of occurrence of self-gift giving.

At a minimum, the possibility that gifts to oneself can be obtained from others with or without solicitation threatens the conceptual clarity of the term "self-gifts." Of course, this problem can be side stepped by classifying these two types of gifts as instances of interpersonal gift giving. However, in empirical research, this distinction must be made clear to the respondents to avoid misunderstandings and to avoid overestimating the frequency of occurrence of true self-gift giving.

There are at least two additional types of interpersonal gift giving that confuse the distinction between interpersonal and self-gift giving. The first occurs when pairs of individuals mutually agree not to exchange gifts but rather to purchase their own gift in each other's name. For example, after many years of interpersonal gift giving, a married couple may agree that it is more efficient and effective to buy their own gifts on all subsequent gift-giving occasions. The second occurs when a "gift certificate" or "cash" is given; in effect the gift-giver instructs the gift-receiver to engage in the selection of the gift. For example, when relationships are characterized by physical separation (e.g., a grandmother and grandchild living in geographically distant locations) this may spur the giving of cash or gift certificates because the gift giver does not know the recipient's desires well enough. Interpersonal relations involving a person who is "difficult to please" is yet another circumstance in which interpersonal gift giving may be abandoned for some type of self-gift giving or selection.

This problem too can be avoided by classifying such gift giving as special cases of interpersonal gift giving. But, in empirical research this distinction should be made clear to the respondents to avoid misunderstandings and to avoid overestimating the frequency of occurrence of self-gift giving.

Directions for Research

Given this explanation, it is possible to propose a few directions for research. First, we should expect large individual differences in the ability to recognize the need to maintain and to enhance one's own system. Further, even given this recognition we should expect that individuals will differ in response to this need. For example, beliefs about the appropriateness of self-therapy and the form it should take are likely to differ greatly among individuals within a culture. Some individuals believe that vacations are necessary for increased and continued job productivity; others do not. One particularly interesting research area pertains to children; children are known to be less aware of their own cognitions and cognitive states (Matlin 1989). Therefore we should expect that self-gifts will occur less frequently among children. Another area pertains to introversion/extroversion; an introverted person may be more aware of his/her cognitive state and the necessity of maintaining or enhancing the self. Gender is another interesting variable to explore.

Second, we expect that an awareness of oneself may be greatly moderated by the cultural milieu. For example, within certain Asian countries that are heavily influenced by Confucian collectivist culture, an individual tends to think more in terms of the group or the family rather than the self (Hofstede 1980). Even if members of these cultures do think of themselves, it may be socially inappropriate to act on this individualistic desire (i.e. to buy gifts for oneself).

Third, we agree with Mick and DeMoss (1990b) that an individual's attribution for a particular motivational or emotional state is very likely to impact on the occurrence of self-gift giving in the manner they suggest.

Finally, the fact that self-gifts can be solicited or unsolicited in the form of interpersonal gifts can reduce the occurrence of self-gift giving. The impact of such interpersonal gifts on the likelihood of occurrence of self-gifts is likely to be highly context bound. For example, a serious illness may result in unsolicited gifts from many friends and relatives. Further, an individual's *expectations about the occurrence* of interpersonal gift giving may also play a significant role in the occurrence of self-gift. That is, if an individual expects that another person (e.g., a spouse) will recognize his/her need for a reward, then self-gift giving may be less likely to occur. Also, an individual's *expectations about the appropriateness* of the gift to be received from another person may influence the likelihood of occurrence of self-gift giving. That is, if an individual expects to receive a gift that is not strongly desired (e.g., a tie for Christmas), then self-gift giving is more likely to occur.

REFERENCES

Belk, Russell W. (1979), "Gift-giving Behavior," in *Research in Marketing*, Vol. 2, ed. Jagdish Sheth, Greenwich, CT: JAI, 95-126.

_____ (1988), "Possessions and the Extended Self," *Journal of Consumer Research*, 15(2), 139-168.

Bettman, James R. (1979), *An Information Processing Theory of Choice*, Reading, MA: Addison-Wesley Publishing Co.

Brown, R. and D. McNeill (1966), "The 'Tip of the Tongue' Phenomenon," *Journal of Verbal Learning and Verbal Behavior*, 5, 325-377.

Engel, James F., Roger D. Blackwell, and Paul W. Miniard (1990), *Consumer Behavior*, Chicago, IL: The Dryden Press.

Ericsson, K. Anders. and Simon, Herbert A. (1984), *Protocol Analysis–Verbal Reports as Data*, Cambridge, MA: The MIT Press.

Feick, Lawrence F. and C. W. Park (1991), "Knowledge and Knowledge of Knowledge: What We Know, Why We Think We Know, and Why the Difference Makes a Difference," Special Session 3.4, *Association for Consumer Research*, Annual Conference, Chicago.

Fiske, Susan T. and Shelley E. Taylor (1991), *Social Cognition*, New York, NY: McGraw-Hill, Inc.

Gutman, Jonathan (1982), "A Means-End Chain Model Based on Consumer Categorization Processes," *Journal of Marketing*, 46 (Spring), 60-72.

Hart, J.T. (1965), "Memory and the Feeling-of-Knowing Experience," *Journal of Educational Psychology*, 56, 208-216.

Haugeland, John (1985), *Artificial Intelligence: The Very Idea*, Cambridge, MA: The MIT Press.

Hauser, John R. and Glen L. Urban (1986), "The Value Priority Hypothesis for Consumer Budget Plans," *Journal of Consumer Research*, 12 (March), 446-462.

Hofstede, Geert (1980), *Culture's Consequences: International Differences in Work-Related Values*, Beverly Hills, CA: Sage.

Holbrook, Morris B. and Elizabeth C. Hirschman (1982), "The Experiential Aspects of Consumer Behavior: Consumer Fantasies, Feelings, and Fun," *Journal of Consumer Research*, 9 (September), 132-140.

Krugman, Herbert (1965), "The Impact of Television Advertising: Learning without Involvement," *Public Opinion Quarterly*, 29 (Fall), 349-356.

Laird, John E., Allen Newell, and Paul S. Rosenbloom (1987), "SOAR: An Architecture for General Intelligence," *Artificial Intelligence*, 33, 1-64.

Lee, Dong Hwan (1990), "Symbolic Interactionism: Some Implications for Consumer Self-Concept and Product Symbolism Research," in *Advances in Consumer Research*, Vol. 17, pp. 386-393 (eds.) Goldberg, Marvin E., Gerald Gorn, and Richard W. Pollay.

Leonesio, R.J. and T.O. Nelson (1990), "Do Different Metamemory Judgments Tap the Same Underlying Aspects of Memory," *Journal of Experimental Psychology: Learning, Memory, and Cognition*, 16(3), 464-470.

Levy, Sidney (1982), "Symbols, Selves, and Others," in *Advances in Consumer Research*, Vol. 9, ed. Andrew Mitchell, Ann Arbor, MI: Association for Consumer Research, 542-543.

Lovelace, E.A. (1984), "Metamemory: Monitoring Future Recallability During Study," *Journal of Experimental Psychology: Learning, Memory, and Cognition*, 10, 756-766.

Maki, R.H. and S.L. Berry (1984), "Metacomprehension of Text Material," *Journal of Experimental Psychology: Learning, Memory, and Cognition*, 10, 663-679.

Matlin, Margaret W. (1989), *Cognition*, 2nd Edition, New York, NY: Holt, Rinehart and Winston, Inc.

Metcalfe, J. (1986), "Feeling of Knowing in Memory and Problem Solving," *Journal of Experimental Psychology: Learning, Memory, and Cognition*," 12, 623-634.

Mick, David Glen (1986), "Consumer Research and Semiotics: Exploring the Morphology of Signs, Symbols, and Significance," *Journal of Consumer Research*, 13 (2), 196-213.

_____ and Michelle Demoss (1990a), "To Me from Me: A Descriptive Phenomenology of Self-Gifts," in *Advances in Consumer Research*, Vol. 17, ed. Pollay, Richard et al., Provo, UT: Association for Consumer Research, 677-682. (1990b),

_____ and _____ (1990b) Self-Gifts: Phenomenological Insights from Four Contexts," *Journal of Consumer Research*, Vol. 17, (December), 322-332.

_____, _____, and Ronald J. Faber (1991), "A Projective Study of Motivations and Meanings of Self-Gifts: Implications for Retail Management," *Journal of Retailing*, forthcoming.

Nisbett, R.E. and T.D. Wilson (1977), "Telling More Than We Can Know: Verbal Reports on Mental Processes," *Psychological Review*, 84, 231-259.

Newell, Allen and Herbert A. Simon (1972), *Human Problem Solving*, Englewood Cliffs, N.J.: Prentice-Hall, Inc.

Olshavsky, Richard W. (1975), "Implications of an Information Processing Theory of Consumer Behavior," in *Combined Proceedings, Marketing in Turbulent Times and Marketing: The Challenge and the Opportunities*, American Marketing Association, Edward M. Mazze (ed.), 151-155.

_____ (1985), "Toward a More Comprehensive Theory of Choice," *Advances in Consumer Behavior*, Elizabeth C. Hirschman and Morris Holbrook (eds.), Vol. 12, 465-470.

Peter, J. Paul and Jerry C. Olson (1987), *Consumer Behavior*, Homewood, IL: Irwin.

Reber, A. S. (1989), "Implicit Learning and Tacit Knowledge," *Journal of Experimental Psychology: General*, 118 (3), 219-235.

Reisberg, D. and J. McLean (1985), "Meta-attention: Do We Know When We Are Being Distracted?," *Journal of General Psychology*, 112, 291-306.

Sherry, John F., Jr. (1983), "Gift Giving in Anthropological Perspective," *Journal of Consumer Research*, Vol. 10 (September), 157-168.

Sternthal, Brian and C. Samuel Craig (1982), *Consumer Behavior — An Information Processing Perspective*, Englewood Cliffs, NJ: Prentice-Hall, Inc..

Wright, P. and P.D. Rip (1981), "Retrospective Reports on the Causes of Decisions," *Journal of Personality and Social Psychology*, 40, 601-614.

Self-Gifts Through the Lens of Attribution Theory
Corinne Faure, University of Florida
David Glen Mick, University of Florida

ABSTRACT

This paper examines some of the antecedents of self-gift likelihood. Specifically, we explore how the three dimensions of causal attributions developed by Weiner (1986)—locus, controllability, and stability—can serve to predict self-gift likelihood in achievement contexts. Using previous research on emotions and on deservingness, we propose that causal attributions can lead to self-gift behavior through two routes, one affective and the other cognitive. Nine hypotheses are developed. We conclude by examining some ways by which our hypotheses can be tested through correlational and causal approaches.

INTRODUCTION

In the consumer behavior literature, there has been new and increasing research attention to the concept of self-gifts. Empirical work focused on self-gifts has so far been mostly exploratory (e.g., Mick and DeMoss 1990a) or descriptive (e.g., Mick and DeMoss 1990b, Mick, DeMoss and Faber 1992), which is not surprising during the earliest theory-building stages of a novel construct. We believe it is time for some self-gift research to shift to a hypothetico-deductive arena wherein past insights from self-gifts research are combined with significant theoretical developments in the social sciences to produce empirically testable claims about self-gift behavior (see also Mick 1991). The main purpose of this paper is to identify certain systematic factors that increase the likelihood that consumers will give gifts to themselves and to generate hypotheses about these factors for future investigation.

According to Mick and DeMoss (1990b), two of the most prevalent contexts of self-gifts (and thereby two types of self-gifts) are rewards for accomplishments and therapeutics for disappointments, associated with positive and negative life situations respectively. This insight points to achievement tasks and outcomes as possible triggers for giving gifts to oneself.

Not only may self-gifts originate from achievement situations, but more importantly from the interpretations consumers make about the outcomes. Relative to this point, Mick and DeMoss (1990b) intimated that attribution theory might be useful in understanding self-gifts. Attribution theories concern the way by which individuals try to make sense of the world in which they live and of the actions of the people around them, including themselves. Therefore, just as people make causal attributions about the behavior of others, they also make similar attributions for their own actions. In achievement situations they will infer different causes for the outcomes of the tasks they engage in. In this paper, we review Weiner's (1986) attribution theory of motivation and emotion, and we suggest ways by which achievement task outcomes, causal attribution dimensions, deservingness, and emotions influence the likelihood of a self-gift. On the basis of these insights, we generate specific hypotheses for future research and discuss potential methodological approaches to test these hypotheses.

CONCEPTUAL BACKGROUND AND HYPOTHESES

Gift-giving and Self-Gifts

One of the characteristics of gifts in general, and of self-gifts in particular, is that they are typically highly motivated and, thereby, perceived as justifiable. For example, gifts are offered on culturally normative occasions determined by calendar (e.g., Christmas, birthdays) or determined by emergent life situations (e.g., to celebrate a job promotion, to cheer up someone who is ill). Whatever the occasion, it is a common trait of gifts that they are offered under some pretext, and that this pretext helps to make the gift acceptable to the receiver (Tournier 1963). The fact that individuals readily identify some self-directed purchases as self-gifts and distinguish them from other self-directed purchases (see Mick and DeMoss 1990a) points to the existence of normative criteria for distinguishing between these different types of purchases. This fact also suggests the existence of a partial rationalization process for self-gifts, similar to those identified for gifts to others. Indeed, Mick and DeMoss (1990a) found that personal accomplishments, disappointments, and holidays were the three prevalent circumstances under which people give gifts to themselves. In further research, Mick and DeMoss (1990b) identified three essential aspects of self-gifts. First, self-gifts are a means to communicate with one's self, and in particular to influence one's self-definition and self-esteem. This function of *communication* appears especially relevant to self-gifts following accomplishments or disappointments. Second, self-gifts are a special type of *exchange*, acting as a kind of self-contract. Mick and DeMoss (1990b) pointed out that this notion of exchange is particularly linked to reward self-gifts and illustrated by the theme of deservingness. As we will discuss, deservingness and exchange can also be associated with therapeutic self-gifts. Third, there is an aspect of *specialness* that refers to the idea that self-gifts often have special meanings for consumers as compared to common, everyday, self-directed purchases. This aspect also accrues from the highly context-bound character of self-gifts. In sum, the insights gained from prior self-gift research point to the potential importance of achievement contexts as common precursors of self-gift behavior.

Bernard Weiner's (1986) attributional theory of motivation and emotion seems particularly well-suited for elucidating certain self-gifts. This theory focuses on achievement contexts and identifies different dimensions along which people make causal ascriptions and the consequences different ascriptions have on specific emotions. Moreover, this theory offers two main characteristics that make it particularly attractive for understanding self-gift behavior. First, Weiner (1986) is explicitly concerned with issues concerning the self. Second, the theory is based on laws, rather than individual differences, and stresses the situational specificity of behavior. Given the highly context-bound character of the situations in which people indulge in self-gifts identified in previous research, Weiner's theory seems appropriate for self-gift research.

Achievement Outcomes

According to Weiner (1986), achievement outcomes first generate attribution-independent emotions. Failure produces a general feeling of sadness, while success leads to happiness, both feelings being independent of the specific cause ascribed to the success or failure. Moreover, to the extent that the outcome is either particularly important or unexpected, individuals will engage in a process of causal ascriptions in order to explain the outcome.

Previous research in social psychology has addressed the effects of success and failure on concepts such as self-gratification (e.g., Mischel, Coates and Raskoff 1968) and deservingness (e.g., Feather 1992), which are closely linked to self-gift issues. Mischel et al. (1968) found that children who experienced success in an achievement task were more likely to indulge in self-gratification than non-successful children. This finding might also apply to Western adults and self-gift behavior by virtue of the Protestant work ethic and its underlying achievement values (McClelland 1961). That is, as Mick (1991) has discussed, success in everyday Western life often leads to an "I earned it" attitude that translates into consumption indulgences. This is not to say, however, that self-gifts do not follow from failed achievement contexts. Further research by Underwood, Moore, and Rosenhan (1972) refined Mischel et al's (1968) finding by showing that while children tend to be more generous toward others and themselves after a success, they still indulge in self-gratification after a failure, but share less with others. In general though, we posit:

HI: In achievement contexts, successes will lead to greater self-gift likelihood than failures.

Causal Attributions and Emotions

Weiner (1986) proposes three major dimensions that underly causal inferences: locus (internal/external), controllability (low to high volitional control), and stability (low to high). According to his theory, these dimensions are orthogonal and they generate different attribution-dependent emotions. The first dimension, locus, refers to the perceived origin of the cause for the outcome. This dimension appears as a continuum from internal (outcome due to something within the individual him/herself) to external (outcome due to something outside or beyond the individual). The second dimension, controllability, concerns the degree of volitional control ascribed to the cause. This dimension is orthogonal to the first in the sense that control can be exercised by oneself (internally) or by someone else (externally). For instance, success on an exam can be attributed to an internal controllable cause (hard work), an internal uncontrollable one (a general positive mood), an external controllable one (the teacher likes you), or an external uncontrollable one (luck). Finally, the last dimension identified by Weiner (1986), stability, refers to the perceived persistence of the cause. Ability, for instance, is perceived as a more stable cause of success than effort.

On the basis of these causal dimensions, Weiner (1986) suggests a number of attribution-dependent emotions. For successful outcomes, attributions to internal controllable causes (e.g., strong effort) tend to generate high self-esteem (a feeling of pride). As pointed out by Weiner (1986), attributions for success are also characterized by a self-serving bias, which means that people will tend to attribute most of their successes to internal controllable causes. An external controllable success generates feelings of gratitude toward the external agent, while in general uncontrollable successes (both internal and external) tend to elicit more general feelings of luckiness and happiness. Compared to successful outcomes, failures result in a greater variety of outcome-related affect (Weiner 1986). For example, a failure attributed to an internal controlled cause (e.g., weak effort) elicits guilt, whereas a failure attributed to an external controlled cause (e.g., a devious person) elicits anger. Feelings of shame are likely to be experienced for failures attributed to an internal uncontrolled cause (e.g., low intelligence), whereas an individual failing because of an external uncontrolled cause (e.g., bad luck) is likely to feel victimized while also experiencing feelings of self-pity and helplessness. These various emotions and the intensities with which they are experienced may have different implications for self-gift likelihood. Thus, Weiner's (1986) focus on the emotions generated by causal attributions suggests the existence of an affective route to self-gift behavior.

A complementary cognitive route to self-gift behavior is implicated in Feather's (1992) work. Feather (1992) has explored the effects of success and failure attributions on perceptions of outcome deservingness. His results show that an outcome itself (success or failure) is perceived as deserved when the actor is responsible for it, and when there is a fit between the value of the action and the value of the outcome. For instance, someone who passes a test because of hard work will deserve this outcome more than someone who passes it through cheating; conversely, the cheater will be perceived as deserving to fail the test, while the hard worker will not. It is important to note that Feather (1992) manipulates the controllability of the cause and keeps locus constant (internal). Also of interest is the fact that his dependent variable is outcome deservingness, that is to say, the extent to which the outcome obtained is perceived as deserved. This should not be confused with self-gift deservingness as identified by Mick and DeMoss (1990b). Indeed, while one can expect a match between these two types of deservingness for success situations (the individual who deserves to win also deserves a reward), a mismatch can be expected for failure situations (the individual who deserves to fail is not entitled to get a gift, whereas the one who does not deserve the failure might deserve a gift as a compensation for an unfair outcome). Nonetheless, Feather's (1992) research provides additional credence to Mick and DeMoss's (1990b) theme of deservingness as an important cognitive antecedent of self-gift behavior based on achievement outcomes and attributions.

To recapitulate, the preceding discussions on Weiner (1986) and Feather (1992) suggest two possible routes for the effects of causal attributions on self-gift likelihood. That is, there appears to be two parallel mediating routes for self-gift likelihood, an affective route (emotions experienced) and a cognitive route (sense of deservingness).

Specific hypotheses on the effects of the causal dimensions on self-gift likelihood can also be delineated. Self-efficacy theory (Bandura 1982) suggests that people monitor their own behavior as a consequence of the attributions they make for their own actions and outcomes. Specifically, Bandura (1982) posits that people motivate themselves in achievement contexts by making reward-incentives contingent on the attainment of certain performance goals. Then, people give themselves rewards when they attain their goals and are proud of it. On the other hand, they engage in self-criticism when they fail to attain goals, especially if they feel responsible for failing the goals. Previous research suggests that, following a successful achievement outcome, people feel particularly proud of their success when they can attribute it to an internal controllable cause such as effort (Bandura 1982). The effect of locus has been well-documented in the attribution literature, and there is some evidence that internal attributions after successful outcomes lead to higher self-esteem than external ones (Bandura 1982, Weiner 1986). Thus, one can expect self-gift likelihood to be highest following success when causal attributions are internal rather than external. The effects of controllability are less straightforward, but there is nevertheless a tendency to consider outcomes due to controllable causes as more valuable than those due to uncontrollable ones. Indeed, as Weiner (1986) points out, successes attributed to external controllable causes (e.g., a friend's help) tend to generate higher self-esteem than successes attributed to external uncontrollable causes (e.g., luck), because people tend to believe that the help from the external controllable cause was triggered by their own likable nature. Hence, self-gift likelihood following success should be greater when the cause is considered controllable rather than uncontrollable.

In failure situations, a reverse pattern is expected. Research on excuse-giving (Weiner, Amirkhan, Folkes and Verette 1987) has shown that people tend to avoid attributing their failures to internal controllable causes when making an excuse. This is due to the fact that this type of attribution generates guilt (Weiner 1986) and the negative outcome is perceived as deserved (Feather 1992). Bandura (1982) stresses that in this type of situation people do not engage in self-reward because that behavior would not be socially acceptable. By contrast, failures due to external causes generate emotions such as anger or self-pity, and generally minimize the degree to which the individual feels that he/she deserves the outcome realized. Similarly, failures due to uncontrollable causes also minimize the feeling that the outcome was deserved. Given the specific types of negative feelings experienced in those situations (mentioned earlier), the likelihood that consumers will engage in self-gift behavior to cheer themselves up should be elevated. That is, following a failed achievement outcome, self-gift likelihood should be higher when the cause is considered external rather than internal, and when it is considered uncontrollable rather than controllable.

The third dimension identified by Weiner (1986), stability, may come into play in a different manner. Weiner (1986) notes that stability affects expectancy of performance on future tasks. When the individual has reason to think that the causes for a successful outcome are internal and stable (e.g., giving a good speech as a result of intrinsic personality qualities), he/she should anticipate similar results in the future. To this extent, a successful achievement on any particular speech-giving occasion may not be sufficiently special to trigger a self-gift. On the other hand, an attribution to an internal unstable cause for the same outcome (e.g., giving a good speech as a result of a detailed research effort regarding the specific topic) should make the outcome more special since it was not as predictable or expected due to the instability of the cause. Indeed, an attribution to an unstable internal cause as opposed to a stable internal cause should heighten the specialness of the situation, which then should increase the likelihood of a reward self-gift. Similarly, in a failed achievement context, an attribution to an unstable external cause (e.g., doing poorly in an annual race due to bad weather) should also be perceived as more special than an attribution to a stable external cause (e.g., doing poorly in an annual race due to the hilly nature of the course which doesn't suit your abilities). The instability of the cause lends more specialness to the situation, thereby potentially increasing the likelihood of a therapeutic self-gift.

In summary, the preceding discussion has articulated these formalized hypotheses.

H2: Following successful achievement outcomes, attributions to internal causes lead to greater self-gift likelihood than attributions to external causes.

H3: Following successful achievement outcomes, attributions to controllable causes lead to greater self-gift likelihood than attributions to uncontrollable causes.

H4: Following failed achievement outcomes, attributions to external causes lead to greater self-gift likelihood than attributions to internal causes.

H5: Following failed achievement outcomes, attributions to uncontrollable causes lead to greater self-gift likelihood than attributions to controllable causes.

H6a: Following successful achievement outcomes, attributions to internal unstable causes lead to greater self-gift likelihood than attributions to internal stable causes.

H6b: Following failed achievement outcomes, attributions to external unstable causes lead to greater self-gift likelihood than attributions to external stable causes.

H7: Following an achievement outcome, the effects of causal attributions on self-gift likelihood are mediated by emotional responses (affective route).

H8: Following an achievement outcome, the effects of causal attributions on self-gift likelihood are mediated by the extent to which the gift is perceived as deserved (cognitive route).

METHODOLOGICAL SUGGESTIONS

We now turn to a brief discussion on how the preceding hypotheses may be tested. One possible correlational approach would require that the subjects themselves classify causes of achievement outcomes. For instance, using the method of critical incident, as used by Mick and DeMoss (1990b), one could ask subjects to describe achievement occasions where they gave themselves a gift after a failure or a success. Then, using a causal attribution instrument developed by Russell (1982), subjects could be asked to rate the perceived causes for these outcomes in the described circumstances. Russell's scale enables the classification of causes along Weiner's causal dimensions, which would then facilitate insights about the most common dimensions of causal attributions preceding self-gift behavior. The main problem with this approach is that subjects self-select the situations, and most likely would describe situations where, according to our hypotheses, self-gift propensity is highest (internal, controlled attributions for successes and external, uncontrolled attributions for failures). Such a selection would not enable a full test of our hypotheses.

A more promising causal approach would involve manipulating the dimensions experimentally. One variation of this approach would be to create situations where subjects are actually asked to perform a task, and then receive feedback on how they performed and the reasons for their performance. Another variation would be to use imagined achievement scenarios. While the use of direct manipulations appears more appealing, the problems of credibility encompassed in dealing with feedback are quite big. Indeed, as noted by Weiner (1983), there are some difficulties in manipulating causes experimentally. Weiner (1983) identifies three sources of possible discrepancies between the instructions and feedback given to the subjects: the objective characteristics of the task, the life experience of the subject, and the experience of the subject during the experiment. Thus, in an experimental setting, one has to worry whether the subjects will really perceive the causes and their dimensions as they were intended to be manipulated. Manipulating the dimensions by imagined scenarios has risks as well, since it would require from the subjects that they project themselves into the situations, which presents the disadvantage of lower involvement and less concreteness than real-life situations. On the other hand, attribution dimensions can be manipulated with more control, and this approach has been used in the past by other attribution researchers (e.g., Feather 1992). Thus, experimental research with the use of scenarios would enable researchers to manipulate the achievement outcomes and to manipulate the dimensions of causal attributions. In particular, based on Weiner's (1986) theory, it appears quite possible to manipulate orthogonally the dimensions of locus and controllability in an unstable context. A 2 by 2 by 2 experimental design (outcome - success/failure, locus - internal/external, controllability - controlled/uncontrolled) appears to be a reasonable way to test most of the hypotheses developed here.

The third dimension identified by Weiner, stability, appears more difficult to manipulate. Indeed, it may be impossible to have experimental subjects really believe that they are always bad or good at a particular achievement task (e.g., tests, sports). Thus, while it appears possible to manipulate experimentally some unstable causes, stable causes appear much more difficult given the contrived setting of an experiment. One option, however, would be to measure beforehand the stable attributions individuals typically make of their achievements in certain contexts. On the basis of these measures individuals could then be assigned to experimental groups where the attributions would be manipulated in an unstable way. Thus, stable attributions would be used as a blocking factor. It should be the case that when stable and unstable attributions are congruent, individuals tend to react less than when they are at odds with one another. Imagine for instance the case of a subject who tends to perform poorly in a specific sport and thinks that he/she does not have the abilities required to be a good performer at this sport. Now, put him/her in a situation where he/she wins a tough competition because of hard training. The likelihood that he/she will give himself/herself a gift as a reward for his/her performance should be higher than for another student who tends to perform well at this sport and believes that he/she has the required abilities to do so. Assigning subjects to experimental groups on the basis of the most important dimension of causal attributions (locus) seems quite promising.

CONCLUSION

The objectives of this paper were to develop theoretically-derived hypotheses about the antecedents of self-gift likelihood and to propose ways to test these hypotheses. Through the effects that causal dimensions have on both cognitive and affective processes—as described or implicated in Weiner's (1986) attribution theory—we believe it is possible to identify specific achievement situations in which people give themselves gifts, thus extending our understanding of self-gift behavior beyond a description of the phenomenon. We believe that this approach offers two important contributions. First, it expands our view of the substantive topic of self-gifts, which appears to be a fairly common and important phenomenon in Western consumer behavior. Second, it also extends the usefulness of attribution theories as they have been used so far in the consumer behavior literature.

Although researchers have long ago perceived the potential of attribution theories for explaining consumer behavior (e.g., Folkes 1984, 1988), attribution theories have not been used to their full potential. These theories have been used to predict the reaction of individuals toward causal agents (e.g., consumer reaction toward the company who is considered responsible for a product failure, Folkes 1988) or to study the motivational effect that attributions have on future behavior in the same activity (e.g., the tendency to exert more or less effort at work depending on the attributions made about one's prior performance, Sujan 1985). By contrast, this paper considers attribution theories for the consequences attributions have on consumer buying behavior, particularly self-gifts. Hence, this paper extends the application of attribution theories in consumer research.

Finally, as discussed in the beginning of this paper, Mick and DeMoss (1990b) identified an exchange dimension relevant to self-gift behavior. Research on resource exchange theory (Brinberg and Wood 1983) and on mental accounting (Thaler 1985) suggests that people give special meanings to the things they exchange or buy, and tend to match what they buy with the reasons why they engage in buying or exchanging in the first place. Thus, of interest in the framework we have developed is to test whether there are any differences between the types of self-gifts one buys after a success or after a failure (e.g., purchasing a new sweater vs. going to an expensive restaurant), and whether one can identify a mental match between the type of self-gift, the achievement outcome (success or failure), and the causal attributional dimensions. Such insights would extend our framework further and yield a more complete understanding of the self-gift phenomenon.

REFERENCES

Bandura, Albert (1982), "The Self and Mechanisms of Agency", in *Psychological Perspectives on the Self*, Vol. 1, ed. Jerry Suls, Hillsdale, NJ: Erlbaum.

Brinberg, David and Ronald Wood (1983), "A Resource Exchange Theory Analysis of Consumer Behavior", *Journal of Consumer Research*, 10 (December), 330-338.

Feather, N. T. (1992), "An Attributional and Value Analysis of Deservingness in Success and Failure Situations", *British Journal of Social Psychology*, 31 (2), 125-145.

Folkes, Valerie S. (1984), "Consumer Reactions to Product Failure: An Attributional Approach", *Journal of Consumer Research*, 10 (March), 398-409.

Folkes, Valerie S. (1988), "Recent Attribution Research in Consumer Behavior: A Review and New Directions", *Journal of Consumer Research*, 14 (March), 548-565.

McClelland, David C. (1961), *The Achieving Society*, Princeton, NJ: Van Nostrand.

Mick, David Glen (1991), "Giving Gifts to Ourselves: A Greimassian Analysis Leading to Testable Propositions", in *Marketing and Semiotics: Selected Papers from the Copenhagen Symposium*, eds. Hanne Hartvig Larsen, David Glen Mick, and Christian Alsted, Copenhagen: Handelshojskolens Forlag, 142-159.

Mick, David Glen and Michelle DeMoss (1990a), "To Me From Me: A Descriptive Phenomenology of Self-Gifts", Vol. 17, *Advances in Consumer Research*, eds. Marvin E. Goldberg, Gerald Gorn and Richard W. Pollay, Provo, UT: Association for Consumer Research, 677-682.

Mick, David Glen and Michelle DeMoss (1990b), "Self-Gifts: Phenomenological Insights from Four Contexts", *Journal of Consumer Research*, 17 (December), 322-332.

Mick, David Glen, Michelle DeMoss and Ronald J. Faber (1992), "A Projective Study of Motivation and Meanings of Self-Gifts: Implications for Retail Management", *Journal of Retailing*, 68 (2), 122-144.

Mischel, Walter, Brian Coates and Antonette Raskoff (1968), "Effects of Success and Failure on Self-Gratification", *Journal of Personality and Social Psychology*, 10 (4), 381-390.

Russell, Dan (1982), "The Causal Dimension Scale: A Measure of How Individuals Perceive Causes", *Journal of Personality and Social Psychology*, 42 (6), 1137-1145.

Sujan, Harish (1986), "Smarter Versus Harder: An Exploratory Attributional Analysis of Salespeople's Motivation", *Journal of Marketing Research*, 23 (February), 41-49.

Thaler, Richard (1985), "Mental Accounting and Consumer Choice", *Marketing Science*, 4 (3), 199-214.

Tournier, Paul (1963), *The Meaning of Gifts*, Richmond, Virginia: John Knox Press.

Underwood, Bill, Bert S. Moore and D.L. Rosenhan (1973), "Affect and Self-Gratification", *Experimental Psychology*, 8 (2), 209-214.

Weiner, Bernard (1983), "Some Methodological Pitfalls in Attributional Research", *Journal of Educational Psychology*, 75 (4), 530-543.

Weiner, Bernard (1986), *An Attributional Theory of Motivation and Emotion*, New York: Springer-Verlag.

Weiner, Bernard, James Amirkhan, Valerie S. Folkes and Julie A. Verette (1987), "An Attributional Analysis of Excuse Giving: Studies of a Naive Theory of Emotion", *Journal of Personality and Social Psychology*, 52 (2), 316-324.

Compulsive Buying and Self-Gifts: A Motivational Perspective
Jon M. Shapiro, Virginia Polytechnic Institute and State University

Giving gifts are a positive experience for most consumers since they help enhance one's self-concept and affective state (Mick and DeMoss 1990). However, the desire to buy self-gifts may become a compulsion for some consumers. This study reviews the gift-giving, self-gift giving and compulsive buying literature and explains the link between self-gift giving and compulsive buying.

The relationship between locus-of-control, loneliness, and compulsive therapeutic self-gift giving was examined in a survey. It was found that consumers with an internal locus-of-control (Rotter 1966), who tend to attribute reinforcements to personal behavior, are more likely to be frequent, compulsive buyers of therapeutic self-gifts. Deci's (1980) theory of intrinsic motivation provides an explanation for this relationship. Due to their belief in a strong link between effort and reinforcement, people with an internal locus-of-control respond more readily to intrinsic and extrinsic cues. They are motivated to buy because they believe their efforts will lead to a desired result.

Lonely consumers were found to be less likely to engage in this form of compulsive consumption. Apparently, their overall lack of motivation keeps them from participating in the buying environment. Further study of the relationship between locus-of-control and compulsive self-gift giving may offer consumer researchers and clinical psychologists new means of aiding compulsive buyers.

REFERENCES

Deci Edward L. (1980), *The Psychology of Self-Determination*, Lexington, Massachusetts: Lexington Books.

Hancock, Barry W. (1986), Loneliness: Symptoms and Social Causes", New York, University Press of America.

Mick, David Glen and Michelle DeMoss (1990), "Self-Gifts: Phenomenological Insights from Four Contexts," *Journal of Consumer Research*, 17 (3), 322-332.

Rotter, J.B. (1966), "Generalized Expectancies for Internal Versus External Control of Reinforcement," *Psychological Monographs*, 80, 1-28.

Solano, Cecilia H (1989), "Loneliness and Perceptions of Control" in "Loneliness: Theory, Research, and Applications" ed. Mohammadreza Hojat and Rick Crandall, London, Sage.

Special Session: Music in Ads, Stores and Homes
M. Elizabeth Blair, Ohio University
James Kellaris, University of Cincinnati

The objective of this special session was to examine a variety of perspectives on the uses of music in marketing.

Randy Rose discussed his work with Terry Shimp on the use of music as a background stimulus in retail environments. They wanted to see if they could reproduce the large effect sizes that were reported by Milliman, when he varied the tempo of background music in a grocery and a restaurant. They varied both the tempo and the style of music. In one study, conducted at the factory outlet stores, the presence of music, either soft rock or contemporary background, was found to have no significant effect on sales. In a zoo gift shop, music treatments did produce greater sales than the non-music treatments, with slow music producing higher sales than fast music. The mood of the employees as a result of the music was thought to influence sales. At the zoo, for instance, the employees preferred music to no music. Randy concluded that several other variables including store location, clientele, and day of week were found to moderate the effects of background music on shopping behavior.

Bob Kent presented his work with James Kellaris on how the objective properties of music, such as pitch and tempo, influence consumers' affective responses. Their conceptual model has four components: objective stimulus properties, moderators, mediators and outcomes. Objective properties of music include time related variables (e.g. tempo, meter, duration, rhythm), pitch related variables (e.g. mode, melody, harmony) and texture related variables (e.g. timbre, loudness). Listener characteristics, such as gender, age, extent of musical training, musical tastes and cultural conditioning constitute the moderating variables. Subjective properties of music (e.g. pleasantness, arousingness, novelty, complexity) are the proposed mediators. Outcomes include affective, cognitive and behavioral responses. Through experimentation, they found that time and pitch attributes influence listeners' feelings but they appear to operate through different mechanisms.

Linda Scott's work emphasizes the fact that a musical piece should not be separated from its' cultural context. She discussed how changes in technology and a marketing emphasis within the music industry have led to the unprecedented importance of "popular" music. The ability to record music has led to a great deal of cross-cultural sharing, not only from country to country but from marginalized groups to mainstream society. Linda discussed the use of music to represent social subgroups in a dialogic form within narrative, a concept known as heteroglossia. An example of this occurs in a Pepsi commercial featuring rap-dance star Hammer, in which someone inadvertently hands him a Coke. He stops rapping and starts to sing "Feelings" in "lounge lizard" style. Finally, someone hands him a Pepsi and he goes back to dancing and rapping, much to the audience's relief. In this commercial, music is used to represent a social "in-group" (youthful rappers) and a social "out-group" (older, white, unhip culture) specifically by reproducing the sounds they make.

The Visible Hand In Marriage: An Exploratory Assessment Of The Marriage Promotion Campaign in Singapore

Siew Meng Leong, National University of Singapore
Swee Hoon Ang, National University of Singapore[1]

ABSTRACT

Using the campaign to increase the marriage rate among graduates as the research focus, two studies are conducted to ascertain the effectiveness of social advertising in Singapore. Study 1 compares the effectiveness of the Marriage Promotion Campaign versus the Courtesy Campaign on the factors of persuasiveness and sensitivity. Study 2 furnishes a more specific assessment of one ad in the campaign by comparing it against another execution using more attractive models on attitude and perception dependent variables. Implications of the findings are discussed and suggestions for future research furnished.

INTRODUCTION

There has been a dramatic growth in the use of social marketing to a wide range of international social problems. Kotler and Andreason (1991) note that millions of dollars have been spent annually on marketing programs affecting family planning, child survival, and AIDS in developing countries. Such efforts have proven effective in reducing losses due to forest fires, recruiting of blood donors, reducing infant mortality, encouraging non-smoking, and making family-planning products and services more accessible in many countries worldwide. Indeed, these scholars remark that international social marketing is "an idea whose time has clearly come" (Kotler and Andreason 1991, p. 8).

Singapore is no stranger to social marketing. In particular, public campaigns are launched regularly and run repeatedly over time. Themes for such campaigns include "Another Satisfied Customer" (a productivity drive), "Courtesy Begins With You," "Speak More Mandarin and Less Dialect," "Don't Litter," "Don't Spit," "Flush The Toilet After Use," "Save Precious Water," "Save Electricity," "Eat More Wheat," "Eat Frozen Meat," "Go Metric," "Stop Drug Abuse," and "Keep Singapore Clean, Green, and Beautiful". Unlike the United States where corporations play a central role in some cause-related marketing efforts (cf. Varadarajan and Menon 1988), it is the government which initiates and organizes such campaigns in Singapore. These campaigns are promoted particularly through advertising in mass media that are largely government owned. The reach of such media as television and radio is impressive, given their very high ownership levels in the island republic. Indeed, the government typically has one of the largest budgets of all advertisers in Singapore.

As Kotler and Roberto (1989) note, these campaigns are intended to persuade the target adopters to accept, modify or abandon certain ideas, attitudes, practices, and behavior. Given that its citizens are familiar with developmental programs of this nature, Singapore offers an ideal context for studies involving public campaigns. An added benefit obtained is that the target audience in Singapore is relatively isolated and clearly defined, thus facilitating the examination of any effects these campaigns have on consumer attitudes and behavior.

In this paper, we focus on assessing the impact of a recent campaign which has stirred domestic and international interest — the so-called "Marriage Promotion Campaign." Two studies were conducted in this connection. Study 1 evaluates the persuasiveness and sensitivity of the campaign relative to the Courtesy Campaign, a well-known campaign introduced in the mid-70s to inculcate the habit and value of courtesy among Singaporeans. In Study 2, we focus on an ad from the Marriage Promotion Campaign and compare its effectiveness on various attitude and perception variables with another execution using more attractive models.

In the remainder of this paper, we first provide the background to the Marriage Promotion Campaign in Singapore. We then furnish the rationale for Study 1, our broad assessment of the campaign, followed by a description of the method used in the study. The results and discussion arising therefrom are next presented. The same is done for Study 2, our more focused ad-related study. We conclude with some suggestions for future work in social marketing from the insights gained in our research.

BACKGROUND

Former Prime (now Senior) Minister Kuan Yew Lee fired the opening salvo in what has locally become known as "The Great Marriage Debate" in the early 1980s when he singled out the segment of female graduates who (1) were too career-minded and did not view marriage as a priority option, and (2) preferred to remain single rather than marry "downwards," i.e., to men with lower educational qualifications. Lee (1987) also noted that Singaporean men did not marry "upwards," but chose to wed women of lower or with similar educational backgrounds:

"The choice of a spouse is an intensely personal matter. Advice on matrimony has been the prerogative of parents, priests, doctors, and relatives. But when the statistics show that more than 40 percent of each year's graduate women will never get married because graduate men cannot shake off their cultural conditioning, then something must be done."

As a consequence of "cultural bias, structural segmentation, or an attitudinal problem" (Social Development Unit 1991), Singapore's 1980 census showed there were too many unmarried women with a tertiary education and too many unmarried men with a primary education. Singapore's current Prime Minister Chok Tong Goh (1986) further noted that with as many females in the university as males, the problem of unmarried graduate women will worsen in future. Aside from social consequences, this problem also has dire economic ramifications. As Singapore has no natural resources, its people are its most precious assets. Hence, economic success will be a function of the size and quality of its population. At present rates, the population is not growing fast enough to replace itself in the long term. Essentially, too many Singaporeans, particularly the well qualified, remain unmarried, and those who do marry tend to marry later and have fewer children (Government of Singapore 1991).

---

[1]The authors thank Susan Chan of the Social Development Unit and staff of the Family Life Education Coordinating Unit for their insights. The research assistance of Aik Hwa Ang, Chieu Yuen Boh, Gerald Bartholomew, Kevin Chua, and Lynn Heng is also appreciated. This research was funded by a grant from the National University of Singapore to the first author.

The government's highly successful "Stop At Two" (children) campaign in the 1970s may have contributed to the present situation. The current campaign has shifted to "Have Three Or More (children) If You Can Afford It". Another development has been the increasing rate of divorce in Singapore which has reached 12 per day recently. Single motherhood, while on the rise, is rare. The government restricts artificial insemination to married couples at its National Sperm Bank and six in-vitro fertilization clinics. However, this procedure is available overseas and is offered by the private sector as well. The government is also very selective in approving applications for adoption of babies by single women — only 105 cases were approved in the past three years (*Straits Times* 1992).

Intervention came in the form of the Social Development Unit (SDU) established in 1984 under the Ministry of Finance. Its objectives are to: (1) increase single graduates' awareness of the importance of marriage, (2) provide opportunities for them to meet, (3) change their attitude in the choice of a spouse, and (4) direct the policies and coordinate the activities of ministries, statutory boards, government-owned companies, and affiliated private companies through social development committees set up within each organization (Social Development Unit 1991, p. 11). Among its activities are computer matchmaking, personal effectiveness workshops held locally and overseas, weekend stays at hotels, chalets, or campsites, outdoor games (e.g., relay races, treasure hunts, car rallies, etc.), hobby courses (e.g., social dancing, interior design, etc.), sports (e.g., horse riding, ice-skating, etc.), tours to Malaysia, Indonesia, Thailand, and other places of interest, and social gatherings (e.g., tea dances, theme parties, karaoke sessions, etc.). While such activities were fully subsidized initially, participants now pay the direct cost for joining them. However, participants still obtain the benefit of fully-paid, unrecorded leave of absence from work.

Initial public reaction was predictably hostile (the SDU acronym was defined by some to mean Single, Desparate, and Ugly). Charges of social engineering were also heard. However, the SDU has reported a consistently increasing number of marriages among its members, from 91 in 1985 to 315 in 1991. Some 1,432 marriages during that period in Singapore were between SDU members. Similarly, the number of members has also escalated from 1,320 in 1985 to 12,177 in 1991. More females (about 55 percent of members annually) than males join the SDU. Prospective members who joined free before 1990 now have to pay a one-time entry fee of S$10 (S$1.62 = US$1). Indeed, there has been two more such units established under the People's Association, a statutory board of the Ministry of Community Development — the Social Development Section (to serve non-graduates) and the Social Promotion Section (to serve those with less than secondary education). Members of each unit are not allowed to participate in activities organized for those of the other units.

Despite the presence of these and other organizations, the SDU has received the bulk of public and media attention locally and overseas. Interestingly, such coverage has been obtained with an advertising budget of less than S$30,000 per year. Most of the advertising has been by another government body — the Ministry of Health's Family Life Education Coordinating Unit (FLECU). However, these ads have often been mistaken as being disseminated by the SDU. The ad of interest in Study 2 is one such instance. The SDU itself runs no television commercials but uses more focused periodicals read by local graduates and undergraduates. It also publishes a quarterly magazine, *Link*, for its members.

STUDY 1

Despite the interest generated by the Marriage Promotion Campaign, no empirical study has been reported regarding its effectiveness. Study 1 attempts to do so by assessing the persuasiveness of the campaign relative to another well-known campaign in Singapore focusing on courtesy. We also attempt to compare the relative degree of sensitivity of the two campaigns.

While both marriage and courtesy are richly cherished in the Asian culture, getting married may not be (to the target adopters of the campaign at least) the favored practice or a strong priority. Marriage may in fact have been more greatly influenced by liberal western values and modern social and economic developments in recent years than courtesy. The Marriage Promotion Campaign is also likely to be more sensitive than the Courtesy Campaign. It deals with a highly personal issue and may be viewed as intrusive. Thus, it would be expected that the Marriage Promotion Campaign would be evaluated as being more sensitive and less persuasive than the Courtesy Campaign.

Method

Respondents evaluated descriptions of two social campaigns held in Singapore — the Marriage Promotion Campaign and the Courtesy Campaign (CC). The more popularly used Get Married Campaign (GMC) was employed in place of its more formal coinage for ease of respondent identification. The descriptions shown to respondents were as follows:

The Get Married Campaign: The Get Married Campaign is aimed at getting single Singaporeans of marriageable age to find a life partner and to encourage them to settle down as soon as possible. This is because of the declining number of people marrying thus leading us to a situation where we are unable to replace ourselves.

The Courtesy Campaign: The Courtesy Campaign is aimed at encouraging Singaporeans to be more polite and courteous to fellow Singaporeans. This is because of the declining level of courtesy amongst Singaporeans. Singaporeans are thus asked to give up their seats in public transportation to the elderly and the handicapped, to say 'Thank you' and 'Please', to extend a smile, and the like.

After reading each description, respondents indicated on five-point agree (5)/disagree (1) scales their reactions to 12 statements, with six items designed to each measure persuasiveness and sensitivity. A sample item for the persuasiveness scale used was 'The stand taken in the Get Married/Courtesy Campaign is a reasonable one'. That for the sensitivity construct would be 'I feel that the Get Married/Courtesy Campaign is an invasion of my privacy'. The items were randomly ordered. Finally, demographic data were obtained.

Respondents. Respondents were 109 undergraduate students at the National University of Singapore, 38 of whom were male. Given that NUS produces the bulk of graduates in Singapore targeted by the SDU, the sample appeared appropriate.

Results

Preliminary tests. Principal components analyses of the 12 items generated two factors for both campaigns. The items loaded cleanly onto either the persuasiveness or sensitivity factors. The two factors accounted for 59.3% and 59% of the total variance for the GMC and CC items respectively. In addition, reliability tests for the GMC indicated high alphas of 0.86 and 0.81 for persuasiveness and sensitivity respectively. The item-to-total correlations were likewise high, ranging from 0.44 to 0.74. For the CC, the alphas were 0.83 and 0.84 for persuasiveness and sensitivity respectively. The item-to-total correlations ranged from 0.37 to 0.82. Collec-

TABLE 1
Means on Persuasiveness and Sensitivity for Campaigns

	Courtesy		Marriage Promotion	
	Male	Female	Male	Female
Persuasiveness	4.19	4.08	3.45	3.32
Sensitivity	2.03	2.15	3.01	3.25

tively, the evidence suggests that the scales developed had convergent validity and were internally consistent. As such, mean scores for persuasiveness and sensitivity were computed and used in subsequent analyses.

Courtesy versus Marriage Promotion. The CC was rated at 4.11 on persuasiveness, while the GMC scored 3.37 ($t=11.69$, $p<0.01$), thus indicating that respondents did not think the GMC was as persuasive as the CC. However, respondents thought that the GMC dealt with an issue that was more sensitive (x=3.16) compared to the CC (x=2.11; $t=15.86$, $p<0.01$).

Males versus Females. Table 1 provides the mean values for persuasiveness and sensitivity among male and female respondents for the two campaigns. Males and females were no different in their ratings towards the GMC's persuasiveness ($t=0.98$, $p>0.10$), though marginally, females thought that the campaign dealt with a more sensitive issue (x=3.25 versus 3.01; $t=1.73$, $p<0.10$). In contrast, no differences were obtained for the CC on both persuasiveness and sensitivity between males and females (t's=1.07 and 0.92 respectively, p's>0.10).

Discussion

The results suggest that at least two distinct bases can be used to evaluate social campaigns — persuasiveness and sensitivity. Whereas most research efforts would likely focus on the persuasiveness dimension, our findings indicate that it may be useful to measure sensitivity for added insights into the effectiveness of such campaigns. Indeed, our evidence suggests that assessments of the criteria may not covary. Gender differences did not appear to be evident in assessments along the two dimensions for both campaigns.

However, since the current results only speak to the effectiveness of the Marriage Promotion Campaign relative to the Courtesy Campaign, other more meaningful yardsticks could be employed to gauge its persuasiveness and sensitivity. Such baselines as using a group not being exposed to the campaign as well as measurements before and after exposure to the campaign may be useful. Finally, better measures of the sensitivity construct involving both positively and negatively phrased items may be developed in future research. Such a scale may be employed to explicitly test the relationship between the sensitivity of public campaigns and their persuasiveness as the present set of items appear to be attitude statements phrased in a negative fashion.

STUDY 2

While Study 1 dealt with a broad evaluation of the Marriage Promotion Campaign, Study 2 focuses on an ad from the campaign to evaluate its effectiveness at a more micro-level. Clearly, a single ad does not a campaign make. Indeed, Rothschild (1979) argues that personal selling would be preferable to advertising in circumstances where response involvement is extremely high and complex for "closing the sale". Advertising aids in attracting attention, creating awareness, and increasing knowledge, with little direct impact on behavior. Marriage certainly contains a complex bundle of intangible attributes (e.g., personal growth, excitement, and the opportunity to assure Singapore's continued economic well-being) as well as having a complex price (e.g., changing lifestyle and giving up the right to make many independent decisions). Hence, it would be reasonable to assess only more immediate measures of advertising effectiveness such attitudes toward the ad, rather than changes in actual behavior or behavioral intent.

More specifically, a print ad that involved stressing the positive aspects of intervention was selected for analysis. The ad used three models, with one playing the role of introducer to the other two. The ad was selected because pre-testing had revealed that the models involved did not appear physically attractive. Since communicator attractiveness has been found to affect message effectiveness (Berscheid and Walster 1974, Chaiken 1979), the notion of using better looking models for the ad was explored. Specifically, research has demonstrated that an attractive model has greater persuasion than an unattractive model because of the identification process where consumers are likely to adopt the attitudes, behaviors, interests, and preferences of the attractive model (Kahle and Homer 1985). Clearly, it may be expected that the ad using the more attractive models would be more positively evaluated in terms of attitudes toward the ad and SDU as well as on subjects' perceptions of people joining the SDU vis-a-vis that with the less attractive models.

Method

Design and Stimulus Ad. A two-level one-factor between-subjects design was used. The models in the stimulus ad were either attractive or unattractive. The stimulus print ads showed a night beach scene where a young woman and a young man were introduced by a second woman. The layout and copy was the same in both ads. The headline read: "It's just an introduction. The rest is up to you," with the following body copy:

> "We all need introductions to help us get along in life.
> In business. To get better service. Even to get a good
>   mechanic — an introduction is always useful.
> So why not an introduction to someone who might be able
>   to make life better for you?
> It doesn't necessarily mean anything. But it could be the
>   start of a happy lifetime partnership. If you want it to."

The stimulus used in the unattractive condition was an actual ad from the Marriage Promotion Campaign, while a more attractive couple in a similar pose was used in the other condition. Professional models were employed in both conditions. Four six-point items were used as manipulation checks for model attractiveness (unattractive/attractive; uninteresting/interesting; old fashioned/cool; and boring/fun).

Subjects. Subjects were 40 undergraduates at the National University of Singapore, equally divided between the sexes.

TABLE 2
Means on Attitudes and Perceptions for Experimental Groups

	Attractive-Model Ad	Unattractive-Model Ad
Attitude towards Ad:		
• Appealing	4.10	2.75
• Fun	3.65	2.55
• Interesting	3.90	2.85
• Cool	3.50	2.75
Attitude towards Message:		
• Appealing	4.00	3.45
• Fun	3.50	2.75
• Interesting	3.85	3.10
• Cool	3.50	2.90
Attitude towards SDU:		
• Appealing	4.15	2.90
• Fun	4.10	2.75
• Interesting	4.10	2.70
• Cool	3.85	2.60
Perception of People who join SDU:		
• Innovative	3.80	3.15
• Realistic	3.75	3.65
• Homely	3.30	3.70
• Oriental	3.55	3.70
• Cautious	3.25	3.40
• Imaginative	3.20	2.85
• Compliant	3.15	3.80
• Restless	3.45	3.20

Dependent Variables. Four items each measured subjects' attitudes toward the ad, the ad message, and SDU; and perception of the people who join SDU. They were unappealing/appealing, boring/fun, uninteresting/interesting, and old fashioned/cool. The order in which the items were asked varied for each of the three attitude types. All items were measured on six-point scales. Perception of the people who took part in SDU activities were obtained on eight characteristics (e.g., conservative/innovative, idealistic/realistic). Again, six-point scales were used.

Experimental Procedure. Subjects were informed that they were taking part in a consumer behavior project. They were shown a 8" x 10" color poster of the attractive/unattractive model ad. Because the unattractive-model ad is a real ad introduced in 1989, subjects may be more aware of it relative to the attractive-model ad which they would see for the first time. While this poses methodological problems, it does provide (1) insights into how the original execution was perceived and whether it can be improved upon using more attractive models, and (2) a stronger test of the hypothesis since the mere exposure effect would predict that familiarity with the original ad may lead to more positive attitudes (Obermiller 1985). Following the viewing, subjects were asked to indicate their attitudes and perceptions on the dependent measures used. Finally, the manipulation checks for model attractiveness and subjects' demographic data were obtained.

Results

Manipulation Check. At $p<0.001$, subjects rated the models in the attractive condition to be more attractive (x=4.40 versus 2.70; t=5.33), more interesting (x=4.20 versus 2.70; t=4.33), more fun (x=4.15 versus 2.6; t=5.07), and more cool (x=4.25 versus 2.55; t=6.25) than models in the unattractive condition. Hence, the values on each item were equally apart from the scale midpoint of 3.5, suggesting that the manipulation was successful.

Attitude towards Ad. The means for the dependent variables in the experimental groups are furnished in Table 2. Consistent with expectations, the attractive model ad was found to be more appealing, fun, interesting, and cool than the unattractive model ad (t's>2.43, $p<0.05$).

Attitude towards Message. The influence of attractive models on the advertising message was also evident, though less strong. No significant difference was found in terms of how appealing the message was (x=4.00 versus 3.45; t=1.35, $p>0.10$). However, subjects in the attractive condition rated the message to be marginally more interesting and cool (x=3.85 versus 3.10, t=1.97; and x=3.50 versus 2.90, t=1.79 respectively; p's<0.10). The message was also rated to be significantly more fun in the attractive compared to the unattractive condition (x=3.50 versus 2.75; t=2.14, $p<0.05$).

Attitude towards SDU. Again, consistent with expectations, attitude towards SDU was found to be more favorable when attractive models were used (p's<0.001). SDU was rated to be more fun (x=4.10 versus 2.75; t=3.98), more interesting (x=4.10 versus 2.70; t=3.83), more cool (x=3.85 versus 2.60; t=3.74), and more appealing (x=4.15 versus 2.90; t=3.49) for the attractive-model ad.

Perception of People who join SDU. Contrary to expectations, perceptions of people who joined the SDU were generally no different across levels of attractiveness. Subjects in the attractive-model ad condition rated people who joined SDU to be marginally more innovative than those who saw the unattractive-model ad version (x=3.80 versus 3.25; t=1.70, $p<0.10$). Directionally, attractive- relative to unattractive-model ad subjects perceived such people to be more realistic, more imaginative, more restless, less homely, less oriental, less cautious, and less compliant.

Discussion

The consistent influence of model attractiveness on attitudes toward the ad, the message, and SDU suggests that it may be a prime factor in influencing public acceptance of the campaign. Consistent with Kelman's (1961) argument that attractiveness of a source results in consumers identifying with the source, this study found that the ad with attractive models induced a subject to accept the message because the models formed a part of his/her self-image. Forming favorable first impression is also important especially since there is ad clutter. To achieve this, ads should employ attractive models because they are more likely to be favorably evaluated. This is particularly more evident at the first exposure when there is less opportunity to process information substantively. Our findings may be particularly noteworthy since we employed an actual ad for comparison. Using the original ad could have led to a mere exposure effect working against our hypothesis (i.e., familiarity generates liking). However, this mere exposure effect did not seem to be a critical influence given the advantage found for the new ad.

There is also the argument that using models similar to the audience is advantageous because the audience identifies with them. This study shows otherwise. Using models that appear to be less attractive, and hence, more typical of the population, seems less viable than employing those with looks that the audience can aspire to. Perhaps the most potent combination, but one which is untested here, may be using SDU's best-looking members as models to maximize source credibility perceptions and subsequent attitude change.

Interestingly, it was found that perceptions of people who joined SDU did not differ significantly regardless of the models used. A likely conceptual reason for this may be that personal experience with an attitude object has a greater impact on such perceptions than indirect experience through an ad (Fazio and Zanna 1981). Moreover, it may be that the ad was not directed towards enhancing the image of the SDU or its members. Rather, its message was to encourage key SDU member referents (friends, colleagues, and family members) to introduce mutual single friends to each other and to urge singles to accept such introductions. Last, inspection of the means shows that perceptions about SDU members were more neutral than either favorable or unfavorable.

Despite the more favorable responses obtained for the ad with more attractive models, its effectiveness in actually getting singles to get married was not measured. To the extent that attitudes are generally considered as predictors of behavior (Fishbein and Ajzen 1975), we may expect it to be more effective in accomplishing the behavioral objective of the Marriage Promotion Campaign than that with the less attractive models.

CONCLUSION

Research into the effectiveness of social campaigns have generally focused on issues emanating from and samples in North America, despite their implementation worldwide. As Capon and Cooper-Martin (1990) note, the ethnocentricity in this area needs to be overcome. The two empirical studies here augment extant literature by using an Asian setting and dealing with a campaign not conducted elsewhere thus far. The research context also offers the added advantages of a geographically small location and an audience eminently reachable by traditional mass media vehicles and who have been exposed repeatedly to such campaigns.

Clearly, Singapore may be a useful laboratory in which natural experiments may be conducted from a social marketing perspective. Specifically, the research here may be extended by using larger samples or covering different campaigns. Such issues as understanding the socialization of graduates in Singapore, their media habits, attitudes toward matchmaking and marriage in general, and their perceptions of the SDU may be investigated. Empirical research that is more theoretically driven is also possible. For example, more dimensions and levels of source credibility may be considered in determining advertising effectiveness. Moderating factors affecting consumers' ability and motivation to process social marketing information (Petty and Cacioppo 1981) may be included as well. The relative role of personal selling efforts in this connection also merits research attention (cf. Carroll et al. 1985). The insights garnered may then be tested elsewhere for enhanced generality. Moreover, the boundary conditions of consumer research findings in the public or nonprofit sector may likewise be assessed in Singapore. Collectively, these avenues offer fruitful directions for future research in international social marketing.

REFERENCES

Berschied, E. and E. Walster (1974), 'Physical Attractiveness,' in *Advances in Experimental Social Psychology*, Vol. 7, L. Berkowitz, ed., New York, NY: Academic Press.

Capon, Noel and Elizabeth Cooper-Martin (1990), 'Public and Nonprofit Marketing: A Review and Directions for Future Research,' in *Review of Marketing*, Vol. 4, Valarie A. Zeithaml, ed., Chicago, IL: American Marketing Association, 481-536.

Carroll, Vincent P., Ambar G. Rao, Hau L. Lee, Arthur Shapiro, and Barry L. Bayus (1985), 'The Navy Enlistment Marketing Experiment,' *Marketing Science*, 4 (Fall), 352-374.

Chaiken, Shelly (1979), 'Communicator Physical Attractiveness and Persuasion,' *Journal of Personality and Social Psychology*, 3, 1387-1397.

Fazio, Russell H. and Mark P. Zanna (1981), 'Direct Experience and Attitude-Behavior Consistency,' in *Advances in Experimental Social Psychology*, Vol. 14, ed. L. Berkowitz, New York: Academic Press.

Fishbein, Martin and Izek Ajzen (1975), *Beliefs, Attitude, Intention, and Behavior: An Introduction to Theory and Research*, Reading, MA: Addison-Wesley.

Goh, Chok Tong (1986), 'The Singles Problem — A Nation's Concern,' *Petir*, June, 3.

Kahle, Lynn R. and Pamela M. Homer (1985), 'Physical Attractiveness of the Celebrity Endorser: A Social Adaptation Perspective,' *Journal of Consumer Research*, 11 (March), 954-961.

Kelman, H. C. (1961), 'Processes of Opinion Change,' *Public Opinion Quarterly*, 25, 57-78.

Government of Singapore (1991), *Singapore: The Next Lap*, Singapore: Times Editions Pte Ltd.

Kotler, Philip and Alan Andreasen (1991), *Strategic Marketing for Nonprofit Organizations*, 4th ed., Englewood Cliffs, NJ: Prentice Hall.

_____ and Eduardo L. Roberto (1989), *Social Marketing: Strategies for Changing Public Behavior*, New York, NY: Free Press.

Lee, Kuan Yew (1987) as quoted in Social Development Unit (1991).

Obermiller, Carl (1985), 'Varieties of Mere Exposure: The Effects of Processing Style and Repetition on Affective Response,' *Journal of Consumer Research*, 12 (June), 17-30.

Petty, Richard E. and John T. Cacioppo (1981), *Attitudes and Persuasion: Classic and Contemporary Perspectives*, Dubuque, IO: Wm. C. Brown.

Social Development Unit (1991), *The Need for Social Development in Singapore*, Singapore: Social Development Unit.

Straits Times (1992), 'Single Mums: A "Threat to Marriage and Society",' March 17, 24.

Rothschild, Michael L. (1979), 'Marketing Communications in Nonbusiness Situations or Why It's Harder to Sell Brotherhood Like Soap,' *Journal of Marketing*, 43 (Spring), 11-20.

Varadarajan, P. Rajan and Anil Menon (1988), 'Cause-Related Marketing: A Coalignment of Marketing Strategy and Corporate Philanthropy,' *Journal of Marketing*, 52 (July), 58-74.

Segmenting Prostitutes' Need for Information about AIDS: A Field Study

Per Østergaard, Odense University, Denmark[1]

ABSTRACT

This paper presents results of a field study on prostitutes' knowledge concerning HIV/AIDS. Ethnographic methods are used to reveal the prostitutes' attitudes toward HIV/AIDS. The prostitutes are divided into three segments: the drug abusive prostitute, the "sociable" prostitute and the professional prostitute. It is shown how these segments display a different attitude toward AIDS, and how the segments therefore require a differentiated campaign effort in a future information strategy.

INTRODUCTION

Since 1985 a comprehensive campaign drive has been conducted in most European countries and in North America with the intention of informing about the risk of being infected with HIV, and thereby the risk of developing AIDS (Misztal and Moss 1990). In Denmark, the campaigns have been very comprehensive, and just about every possibility and opportunity to inform people have been explored. With the exception of the special campaign efforts aimed at the two traditional high-risk groups, gays and bleeders, it has been characteristic of the information campaigns not to attempt to categorize the recipients of information according to their needs.

The research leading to the results presented was motivated by considerations concerning the fact that there are actually other high-risk groups apart from gays and bleeders. Female prostitutes constitute one of these groups. The health authorities had no information concerning the effect of existing campaigns on female prostitutes, whereas a number of field studies had been completed concerning the general population's knowledge of HIV/AIDS, and possible effects of the campaign.

In order to be able to establish the extent to which female prostitutes had been affected by these previous general information campaigns, a field study was initiated with financial support from the Danish Ministry of Health.

It has not only been the intention with this study to establish how previous information campaigns have affected female prostitutes, but also to attempt to uncover how it would be possible to inform this target group in a more effective way, should it turn out to be necessary.

When studying literature in consumer research it soon becomes apparent that, with a few exceptions (e.g. Gould 1989, 1990), the question of HIV/AIDS is an untouched subject in consumer research. The issue of HIV/AIDS has been subject to growing attention among sociologists (e.g. Muir 1991; Huber and Schneider 1992) during the last five years. Especially, attention is payed to the possibilities of applying experiences from marketing and consumer research to campaign actions concerning HIV/AIDS (Muir 1991). Plant (1990) being an exception, it has not been possible to find much information regarding the issue concerning female prostitutes and their knowledge of HIV/AIDS. Therefore this field study practically started from scratch.

THE PROSTITUTION MARKET

The field study has taken place in a medium-sized Danish city (200,000 inhabitants) in the time between May and September 1990. It is difficult to state the exact number of prostitutes in any Danish city although prostitution takes place quite openly and the authorities do not interfere directly, even though prostitution is not legal.

The prostitution market can be divided into four categories representing a status hierarchy: 1) Escort-prostitution; 2) Bar and hotel prostitution; 3) Massage prostitution; 4) Street prostitution. In this study, massage and street prostitution have primarily been the centre of focus because these forms are most commonly seen in this city. Escort prostitution and bar and hotel prostitution do exist, but only as a limited proportion of the total market. One possible estimate of the total number of prostitutes could be a maximum of 100, but the figure is probably closer to 50 if only "full-time" prostitutes are considered.

On a prostitution market like the one described, there is furthermore great mobility between the different prostitution categories. Within a year it is quite possible for a prostitute to have worked within all four categories. Taking this into consideration, we chose to focus our field study on street prostitution making a few "detours" into massage prostitution. Hereby, we could gain contact to all types of prostitutes in this city.

APPROACH

Prostitutes can be regarded as producers of sexual services. In this paper though, they are not seen in this perspective. Instead, the prostitutes are regarded as consumers of information concerning HIV/AIDS. When we divide the prostitutes into segments later on, it is not due to their differing services, but according to differences in the way they perceive information. This perception process is determined by a number of relations. It has been crucial to move beyond traditional variables such as social background, media consumption and specific knowledge of HIV/AIDS. These aspects have of course been taken into account, but focus has been put on e.g. the prostitute's perception of the future, of herself as a prostitute and of social authorities. These relations are to be regarded as ideal type constructions. According to Weber (1972), the concept of ideal type has been developed regarding social action. In other words, it is a theoretical construction which should increase the understanding of why different groups act and perceive differently in their life-world.

When it is important to illustrate the prostitute's perception of the future, of herself and of the authorities, it is because a thorough description of these concepts in the interviews can provide us with information concerning the prostitutes' life-world. In relation to a future campaign strategy, knowledge of their life-world will be essential. This is because the possibilities of affecting the prostitutes through information depend on their perception of the future, of themselves as prostitutes, of the authorities and of the importance and significance of HIV/AIDS (Uexküll 1986; Treichler 1987). It has not been the intention with this field study to deliver final results for a future campaign strategy. For this purpose the topic is too new and unexplored.

METHOD

Since no significant research on the topic was available beforehand, we had to practically start from scratch. This implied that we had to work up a theory on the topic. In our opinion, the best way of doing this was to use "Grounded Theory" by Glaser and Strauss (1967), in spite of the various objections which can be made against this theory (e.g. Brown 1973). Our primary reason for using

---

[1] The author is indebted to Hanne Manata and Morten Elbaek Petersen regarding several ideas in this paper.

"Grounded Theory" was that, when the methodological perspective had to be determined, two male-researchers were working on the project, and men could not conduct these field studies within the prostitution environment. At least not if reliable data were supposed to be the outcome. We therefore planned to hire a woman to conduct the field work. In the initial planning phase we did not know whom we were eventually going to hire and therefore wanted to ensure that our method was understandable to a non-academic person.

From the beginning we were aware of the necessity of establishing a platform in the environment in order to be able to enter this very closed circle. Our plan was to establish a free coffee bar in the street were most prostitutes hang out. We had many worries though, concerning how to establish this coffee bar. We did not want to establish a place to conduct our research, and then simply close down the place when the work had been completed. This would be too cynical. Luckily, we discovered that the Y.W.C.A. was planning to open up a permanent coffee bar in the area. We allied ourselves with the Y.W.C.A. and we were able to sponsor them with a relatively large amount. After the establishment of the coffee bar as the base from which the research was to be conducted, we hired a woman (with an academic background) as our field worker.

The research was supposed to be completed within a time span of 6 months during which the field worker worked part time in the coffee bar. We had decided not to withhold the identity and reason for employment of our field worker. The plan was that the first two months were to be spent on participant observation and on collecting secondary data, as well as interviews with key informants outside the prostitution environment but with thorough knowledge of the environment.

During the first two months when interviews were not carried out within the environment, the time was used for gaining thorough knowledge of life in the street and in the coffee bar. This thorough knowledge of the everyday life of the prostitutes would be of great help to us later, in relation to questions of validity. In these situations it would be easier for us to judge the reliability of the different statements made by respondents. This introductory period was furthermore used for selecting subjects for the personal interviews and for establishing confidence in the field worker who was going to conduct the interviews.

After two months the semi-structured personal interviews were begun. They were conducted with the aid from an interview guide which was structured in a way which both enabled us to collect information of a factual character (social background, media habits, specific knowledge concerning HIV/AIDS) as well as information of a more metaphysical kind (conception of the future, self conception, the importance and significance of HIV/AIDS). We conducted 13 interviews lasting approximately 1 to 2 hours each. They were all taped and transcribed word for word. The prostitutes were payed a sum equal to 100 $ per interview as compensation for lost earnings. In most cases, this payment of the prostitutes was unnecessary, as they were eager to participate in a project of this kind. However, the payment gave us the opportunity of interviewing a number of prostitutes who would not otherwise have participated in such a project. These prostitutes who did it for the money, so to say, provided us with a lot of information which we would otherwise never have had access to.

RESULTS

Supported by the collected data, the prostitutes' knowledge of HIV/AIDS was initially considered. After this, we started working up our theoretical constructions which were supposed to contribute to understanding differences in the ways in which the prostitutes had perceived the information concerning HIV/AIDS. This was motivated by a wish to provide prostitutes with more effective information in the future.

While working with the data, two obvious segments soon became apparent: the drug-abusive prostitute and the professional prostitute. The drug-abusive prostitute is a woman who is addicted to different kinds of drugs and/or alcohol. The professional prostitute is a woman who is involved in what was earlier defined as massage prostitution. This means that she runs her own independent business where she sells her services more or less legally. These two ideal types reflect different frames of perception or universes of meaning in relation to the perception of information about AIDS. It was more difficult to identify further ideal types from the data. This is not to say that no other types existed, but rather that other types just did not stand out as clearly and well-defined as the two former ones.

After further analysis of the data we identified a third ideal type called the "sociable" prostitute. This type of prostitute is characterized by the fact that she is neither addicted to drugs or alcohol, and that it is not possible specifically to explain why she has become a prostitute. This prostitute cannot be restricted to certain environments, but is found both on a street level, in massage prostitution and maybe especially among escort, bar and hotel prostitution. This prostitute type can be characterized as a woman to whom prostitution has become a "lifestyle".

It is an important condition for understanding these ideal types that one is aware of the fact that these ideal types cannot necessarily be found in a complete form, as real people. They are theoretical constructions made from the collected data. It might seem a bit confusing that two of the ideal types, the drug-abusive and the professional prostitute, seem to be easily identified empirically. This though, should not lead to the conclusion that the ideal types are simply synonymous with people who can be observed in real life. In the further practical and theoretical work with a future campaign strategy, the ideal types can be of great help.

THE DRUG-ABUSIVE PROSTITUTE

This type represents a significant proportion of the prostitution market. She is a woman who is addicted to different kinds of drugs. In most cases she is addicted to heroin, but often she uses various other kinds of narcotics and alcohol because of a lack of money. For this type, prostitution is necessary in order to provide money for narcotics (often 400$ a day is required).

Concerning social background it is not possible to draw up a clear picture of this type of prostitute. It is, however, possible to provide clear guidelines to the present social situation of this type of prostitute. Most often this is a woman who lives alone or temporarily with a boyfriend. If she has any children, they have been removed from her and put into public care. This type normally has no obligations except from providing money for drugs every day. She is a person who rarely feels motivated by anything other than getting money for the next day's drugs.

This type only prostituted because of the need for a large amount of money for drugs. Mostly, she dislikes the whole idea of being a prostitute, and she expresses this feeling frequently. She only does it for the money. A statement about this could be:

"I only stay here until I have the money I need for my shit every day, but I come here every day, summer and winter (...) Now I haven't been here for a few days, because I have worked in a clinique and have made enough money to last for a couple of days (...) I never talk to my customers. It's none of their business, my private life. If they become too personal, I shut up. That isn't what they pay me for–they pay to get layed."

In comparison, we can now observe what a "sociable" prostitute stated about the same topic:

"I like my work, and I'm proud of what I do. I think many are. Actually I think all real hookers are (...) It's not just a job that has to be done. It is people who come to you and want to buy you. And what you give them cannot be translated into money. We can feel the personal warmth, and they say: 'We need a hug today', and then they get a hug and maybe a bit more."

Later on these differences will be discussed more thoroughly.

The drug-abusive prostitute has sufficient knowledge of HIV/AIDS, and she knows that she must use a condom and have her own needles for narcotics. We are dealing with a type of prostitute whose life is split up into working to provide money for drugs, and sleeping as much as possible. The more sleep, the less narcotics she needs.

This type often has a very negative view on information stemming from the public system, and this is why she is very difficult to reach through information campaigns. It is also doubtful whether the information has any effect. Because even though the drug-abusive prostitute constantly swears that she always uses condoms, the accuracy of her statement is questionable. It is a well-known fact within the environment that the drug-abusive prostitute is willing to sell sex without the use of a condom when she needs money, and she often does. Thus it is very difficult to handle this type of prostitute.

THE "SOCIABLE" PROSTITUTE

Here we are dealing with a prostitute who is neither addicted to drugs nor alcohol. It is not possible to give specific reasons for her choice of profession. When we call her a "sociable" prostitute, we are not indicating that she only does it for the company, but we are pointing to the fact that, at the moment, it would be hard for her to live without the social life linked to prostitution. As one prostitute expressed this:

"Maybe it started out as a tragedy, but it ended up being a lifestyle."

A common background for this kind of prostitute is some kind of feeling of having been let down in the past. This could have happened in different ways. All from the parents' divorce or other problems to the prostitute's own divorce are common reasons. Situations when her trust in other people has been broken down. This ideal type has been able to rebuild that lack of self-confidence through prostitution. As a street prostitute expresses it:

"Why I'm a prostitute? Well, first of all it is for the money, and that is 100%. Another thing is probably the environment. With time, I have gotten to know so many people down here. I can just sit and talk and talk, but I think some of the girls are a bit mad at me. They are on drugs, whereas I don't need the sort of money they do."

As another one expresses it:

"I was 37 years old when I started, I was alone with two grown up kids with problems in school. But I thought my kids were smart enough to be able to graduate with some kind of diploma. So I sent them to a private boarding school where they had to stay for 3 years, and that was expensive. And I couldn't get any subsidies because it wasn't the school psychologist who had sent them. At first I took an overdraft in order to pay the school fees, but shit man, I ran out of money. That alone cost 1500$ a month plus clothes and pocket money. Therefore I started as a prostitute. I had never heard about it before, otherwise I would have started earlier."

Here we are dealing with a woman who, at least on the surface, is fairly well-balanced socially. In a way, she has rebuilt a personal integrity through life as a prostitute which has allowed her to become economically independent and to practice a social life. One prostitute says:

"Shit, I have to admit that I wouldn't miss this. Now I haven't been able to work for some time, well, I really have to admit that I was bored shitless at home."

These women are very open and interested, both in general social problems, and in living conditions among prostitutes. Therefore the AIDS issue also occupies them very much. It is characteristic of these women that they have obtained knowledge of AIDS on their own initiative, and they often have a very thorough knowledge of the subject. Since these women furthermore have a very varied media usage, it ought to be easy to inform these prostitutes. Very often their knowledge of HIV/AIDS is satisfactory, but there is often a gap between their knowledge and their behavior, because the "sociable" prostitute has many regular customers whom she has known for a very long time (often several years). In such cases, it can be difficult to use a condom. As one "sociable" prostitute notes:

"But this one I've been to bed with at least 500 times through many years. He only has me and his wife, so there's no risk."

The customers become friends because this kind of prostitute seldom has any social contacts apart from the other prostitutes and her customers. On the whole though, one must say that this type of prostitute is easier to inform about HIV/AIDS than the drug-abusive prostitute. The "sociable" prostitute fears AIDS and sees it as a threat to her life which is completely centred around being a prostitute. A certain lack of a sense of reality can be characteristic of this type of prostitute, especially concerning future plans where the dreams often seem completely unrealistic. It is not as easy as it might seem to inform this type of prostitute in a way which will also make her change her behavior.

THE PROFESSIONAL PROSTITUTE

This type of prostitute is a well-known phenomenon in Denmark, and every day a great number (often more than 100) of ads specifying their services can be found in one of the biggest newspapers in the country. This type of prostitute runs her own small business where she offers different kinds of massage. Often there are more than one owner of each clinique, or other prostitutes can be employed there.

When it comes to social background and upbringing, these women do not differ from the two other groups. The professional prostitute is never a drug addict, but sometimes she has a drinking or a hash problem. What characterizes the professional prostitute in comparison with the two other groups is that she wishes to be open about her profession. She would like her business to be recognized just like any other business. One of them expresses it like this:

> "There was a time when I used to say to myself, but only because of other people's opinions, you know - 'I can't go on doing this, I have to earn some money so that I can get started on something else'. I like my job today, and personally I feel good about it. My surroundings don't mind my job either. Neither my family, my sportsclub nor my neighbours."

Because of the need for openness concerning her profession, this type of prostitute is very interested in information on HIV/AIDS. She sees AIDS as a threat to her livelihood and to the profession as a whole. That this type of prostitute actually perceives herself as an ordinary business woman is illustrated by this statement:

> "I have a massive income. I run faster and faster, and I've never worked as hard as I do now to pay my taxes. That's the reason why you get sick of your job. But unfortunately, that goes for all small business people. It's not only me, it's not only to aim specifically at prostitution. Our tax system is constructed like that, it gets the small ones."

This great need for recognition of the profession also leads to demands that the public authorities introduce some kind of health guarantee for prostitutes. This would imply that the professional prostitutes could be guaranteed HIV/AIDS-free. Their openness concerning their own profession (many are registered companies) could provide them with a competitive advantage over the two other groups. One professional prostitute says:

> "I think we need an adviser on the cliniques for a face to face discussion about HIV/AIDS. They must look at our remedies, and consider what can be done to help us. Bring along a thermometer and take the temperature of the water. What I'm trying to say is that if this had been a bakers shop, they would have been here a long time ago to take the temperature of the water. But just because this is a massage parlour everything, so to say, is permitted concerning hygiene. They don't show the least interest in this."

The professional prostitute is very active in her search for information. Since she perceives her own body as a means of production which must function in the most optimal way, she is also very careful concerning having her regular medical check-ups and being tested for venereal diseases.

It is not difficult to inform these women about the risk of HIV/AIDS. The difficult part about the information campaign is whether it is possible to provide her with sufficient information, and in a serious manner. One of the most common complaints from this type of prostitute is that the hospital is unable to answer her questions concerning the risk connected with different kinds of uncommon sexual behavior. If the intention is to keep in touch with these women in the future, it is essential that they have access to such specific information.

IMPLICATIONS FOR FUTURE INFORMATION CAMPAIGNS

The general level of knowledge concerning the risk of HIV/AIDS was found to be satisfactory among the prostitutes who participated in the field study, since it is our belief that their knowledge is at least comparable to the rest of the Danish population. The field study also shows though that the prostitutes have a need for much more detailed information concerning the risk of HIV/AIDS. In their work, the prostitutes in some cases participate in sexual behavior which most of the population cannot even imagine. Therefore prostitutes often confront doctors with questions which they can only answer very hesitatingly and conditionally because medical science simply has no certain answers to the, often highly unusual, questions.

It is very difficult to supply the drug-abusive prostitute with further information on the topic because, in many ways, she is annoyed by the fact that the social authorities interfere with her life. Secondly, her work as a prostitute is a repressed part of her identity. Her most urgent worry is not being infected with HIV/AIDS, but to obtain money for drugs every day. As one of the drug-abusive prostitutes replies when asked about her fear of AIDS:

> "You can't walk around thinking about that all the time. I don't walk around thinking of cancer either (...) I take one day at a time, that's all. No, I don't think about the future at all. Only about today."

Here we are dealing with a type of prostitute who's behavior it is very difficult to change because her risky behavior is so closely linked to her life as a drug addict. The only solution to her problem would be to wean her off or to supply her with free drugs.

The "sociable" prostitute and the professional prostitute have a number of common traits which make it possible to treat them as one in relation to considerations concerning the need for further information. Both types of prostitutes are very interested in receiving information concerning the risk of being infected by HIV/AIDS. Both groups require that future campaign efforts must be delivered in a sober and serious fashion, and the sort of information needed goes far beyond the general information needs of the population. It is also important to keep in mind that these women do not need to overcome any mental barriers when it comes to talking freely about sex, as previous campaigns directed at the whole population have tried taking into account. Instead, specialists are required to supply these groups with information in future campaign efforts. This could be practised in different ways. One option is to hire specially trained doctors for the campaign in the prostitutes environment. Another option is to train some of the most qualified prostitutes, and thereby enable them to participate in the campaign work of informing other prostitutes of HIV/AIDS.

In this connection, especially the "sociable" prostitute could prove qualified because of her natural sociable attitude. As a "sociable" prostitute expresses it herself:

> "Yes, instead of hiring useless schoolteachers and social workers as AIDS-instructors, I would like to be offered a course as an instructor. Because so many ask me for advice. And they are the users, God damn it."

The solution in relation to future information campaigns aimed at the three groups mentioned here would be to employ specially trained people to work within the environment. In such a case it would be crucial that this staff had a professional attitude, and were able to talk with the prostitute on her own terms. Furthermore it would be unwise to take on the traditional role of a social worker who annoy the prostitutes and therefore would be unlikely to take advice from. A combination of both specially trained doctors and prostitutes would presumably result in the most effective spread of information.

LIMITS TO ENLIGHTENMENT: A CONCLUSION

If one regards the prostitute as a producer of sexual services, the other part of the transaction, namely the customer, has not been discussed. This is not because the customer is not interesting, but rather that we in our research have chosen to perceive the prostitute as a consumer of information, and therefore the customer aspect has been neglected. In relation to the discussion of the gap between specific knowledge of HIV/AIDS and the actual behavior of the prostitute, her customers play an important part. In spite of the fact that the prostitute in some cases has comprehensive knowledge of HIV/AIDS, the customer still exercises a great influence concerning whether this knowledge is translated into proper behavioral patterns.

Irrational behavior on the customer's part creates some limitations as to how much the prostitute can be expected to change her behavior in relation to safe sex. The prostitutes are not necessarily the hardest group to convince of the virtues of safe sex. As a "sociable" prostitute explains it:

"Yes, they still ask for sex without a condom, and how I cried, really, after AIDS had practically been printed into the minds of the Danes, and still 8 cars in a row stopped to ask for sex without a condom."

It is difficult to say whether these numerous requests for sex without a condom are what they seem. It has turned out to be a way for some customers to avoid the most risky groups of prostitutes. If the prostitute agrees to having sex without a condom, the customer will refuse and start the search for another prostitute.

One thing is certain though. When dealing with information campaigns about "unsafe sex", both among prostitutes and among other people, some very complex issues arise. As Georges Bataille (1987) expresses it, sex is marked by a number of mythological, ritual and imaginary forces which very often go beyond our rational and moral defense mechanisms.

These limits to enlightenment concerning information about the risk of being infected by HIV/AIDS though, should not make us give up further campaign efforts and attempts to make the campaigns more effective. We just have to be conscious of and prepared for the limitations we are confronted with in our work.

REFERENCES

Baggaley, J.P. (1988), "Perceived Effectiveness of International AIDS Campaigns," *Health Education Research*, 3 (1), 7-17.

Bataille, Georges (1987), *Erotism*, London: Marion Boyars.

Brown, George W. (1973), "Some Thoughts on Grounded Theory," *Sociology*, Vol. 7, 1-16.

Glaser, Barney and Anselm Strauss (1967), *The Discovery of Grounded Theory*, Chicago: Aldine.

Gould, Stephen J. (1989), "The AIDS Consumer Movement and the FDA: A Potential Paradigm Shift in Health Care Policy," *Journal of Public Policy and Marketing*, 8, 40-52.

Gould, Stephen J. (1990), "Applying Cultural Framework of Health and Healing in the AIDS Context: The Study of a Group of Treatment Shopping Consumers," in *Research in Consumer Behavior*, Vol. 4., ed. Elizabeth Hirschman, Greenwich, Conn.: Jai Press Inc., 85-114.

Huber, Joan and Beth E. Scheider, eds. (1992), *The Social Context of AIDS*, London: Sage Publications.

Mitztal, Barbara A. and David Moss, eds. (1990), *Action on AIDS: National Policies in Comparative Perspective*, New York: Greenwood Press.

Muir, Marie A. (1991), *The Environmental Context of AIDS*, New York: Praeger.

Plant, Martin, ed. (1990), *AIDS, drugs and prostitution*, London: Routledge.

Treichler, Paula A. (1987), "AIDS, Homophobia and Biological Discourse: An Epidemic of Signification," *Cultural Studies*, 1 (3), 263-305.

Uexküll, Thure von (1986), "Medicine and Semiotics," *Semiotica*, 61 (3/4), 201-217.

Weber, Max (1972), *Wirtschaft und Gesellschaft*, 5. rev. Auflage, J.C.B. Mohr: Tübingen (original 1922).

Choosing to Misbehave: a Structural Model of Aberrant Consumer Behavior
Ronald A. Fullerton, Providence College
Girish Punj, University of Connecticut

ABSTRACT

Aberrant consumer behavior violates the generally accepted norms of consumer behavior in exchange settings. It has financial, psychological, and social costs for both consumers and marketers. Much such behavior appears to result from the interaction of individual traits and predispositions with marketplace influences rather than either in isolation. Drawing upon a sizeable literature in the sociology of deviance, criminology, and psychology, this paper presents a preliminary structural (i.e., input/output) model whose interaction framework characterizes the consumer decision to misbehave or not.

INTRODUCTION

Aberrant consumer behavior (hereafter ACB) may be defined as behavior in exchange settings which violates the generally accepted norms of conduct in such situations and which is therefore held in disrepute by marketers and by most consumers. The three major outcomes of ACB are: 1) destruction of marketer property—vandalism; 2) abuse, intimidation, and physical and psychological victimization of other consumers and marketer personnel; and 3) material loss through various forms of theft including insurance, credit card, and check fraud, and shoplifting. ACB includes both individual and group acts. It can result in serious financial, physical, and/or psychological harm to marketing institutions and their employees, and to other consumers. Recent news accounts put annual total losses for automobile insurance fraud at $10 billion, shoplifting at $30 billion, and phone service fraud at $1 billion (e.g., Keller 1992; Kerr 1992). These costs are ultimately born by consumers. The psychological costs to those victimized by misbehaving consumers have not been measured, but clearly include discomforting levels of stress, anxiety, and even fear.

ACB also has social costs arising from its potential to make the marketplace an arena of disillusionment rather than of fulfillment for both marketers and consumers. ACB can cast a pall over the aspirations of a highly developed consumer society.

Despite its clear impact upon consumer costs, indeed upon the entire consumer experience, ACB has been a neglected topic among consumer and marketing researchers. Authors have acknowledged the possibilities of misbehavior by marketers, but have slighted those by consumers. The topic is ignored in marketing, consumer behavior, and business ethics texts, and aside from a few studies of shoplifting little has appeared in the marketing and consumer journal literature during the past dozen years. In current practitioner-oriented literature, on the other hand, ACB receives a great deal of attention, suggesting that many marketing practitioners consider it to be a significant problem (e.g., Bernstein 1985, Caggiano 1987).

Studies in other disciplines such as the sociology of deviance, criminology, and abnormal psychology, however, provide a starting point for enquiry by consumer researchers. Well-developed research traditions in these disciplines have produced a rich array of theoretical works and case-based studies which can illuminate ACB. Drawing upon this body of work, the present paper provides a preliminary structural (i.e., input/output) model to characterize the consumer decision to misbehave or not. Hopefully the model will encourage consumer researchers to investigate this important but neglected phenomenon.

BUILDING THE MODEL: ISSUES AND ASSUMPTIONS

Available research indicates that ACB is *pervasive* among consumers (Johnson 1987). At the minimum, occasional misbehavior appears to be widespread. Two thirds of the general population studied by Ray (1983) admitted to having shoplifted at least once. The perpetrators of most acts of deviant consumer behavior, moreover, are ordinary-seeming people who cannot be differentiated from other consumers on sexual, genetic, socioeconomic, racial, educational, or lifestyle grounds. In fact, much of the time, those consumers who have misbehaved, do not necessarily do so again, at least not in a consistent manner (See Sutherland 1937). Misbehavers are *representative* of consumers overall, not a group apart. The challenge for researchers is to identify those factors or interactions of factors which are likely to lead some consumers to misbehave some of the time.

Several factors have been used to explain ACB. These have been drawn from two broad categories: 1) consumer traits and predispositions (e.g., Cox, Cox, Moschis 1990); and 2) characteristics of marketing institutions and exchange settings (e.g., Smigel 1956). Typical of this type of an approach is the finding that a particular factor may lead to a particular form of ACB, for example, that thrill seeking may lead to vandalism (Levy-Leboyer 1984). Concentrating upon these singular (direct) explanations of ACB, however, is likely to limit our understanding of the phenomenon. While some incidents of ACB can be adequately explained in this manner, there is growing evidence that most misbehavior by consumers results from interplay among several individual and marketer influences (Moore 1984; Steiner, Hadden, & Herkomer 1976; Zimbardo 1977). In order to study these *interactive* influences, an interaction framework of the type proposed by Endler and Magnusson (1976) is needed.

By using an interaction framework to study ACB it eventually becomes possible to identify both the direct and indirect effects of any and all singular influences on ACB. Further, the framework will provide a basis for assessing the relative impact of the various influences either separately or in interaction with one another. Overall understanding of ACB will thereby be enhanced.

At this point the prediction of specific acts of ACB is not our objective. This would be as elusive a goal as predicting particular acts of acceptable consumer behavior. It is more reasonable for now to focus on delineating the scope of aberrant consumer behavior, seeking to distinguish it from acceptable consumer behavior, and focussing on the various influences that can lead to both. In so doing we are also likely to better understand the boundaries between the two, i.e., how and why certain influences lead to unacceptable behavior on some occasions and acceptable on others. The model presented in the next section is an attempt to gain such an understanding. It is a necessary step before attempting to understand and predict specific forms and types of ACB.

A STRUCTURAL MODEL OF THE ACB/CB INTERFACE

As mentioned above, the model is drawn from two sets of factors and the interactions between and within them: 1) consumer traits and predispositions and 2) the characteristics of the exchange setting and marketing institutions. Within each set of factors there

FIGURE
A Structural Model of the ACB/CB Interface

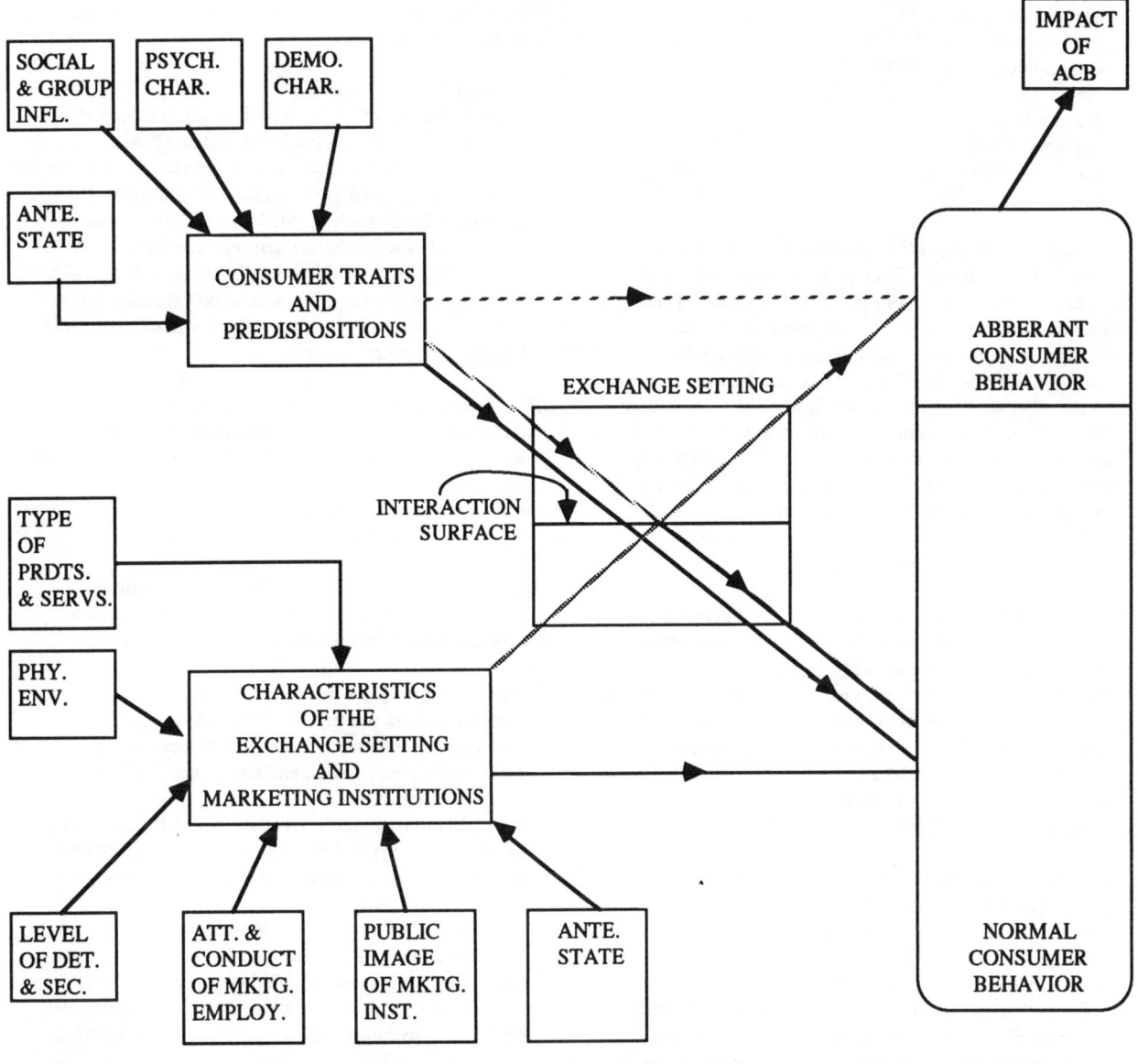

are subsets. These factors, subfactors, and their interactions are presented below. The overall model, which is shown thematically in the figure, attempts to explain behavioral propensities to misbehave or not.

I. The Consumer

A. Demographic Characteristics

Age: all age groups are represented, but not equally for all forms of ACB. There is more shoplifting, vandalism, and rowdyism by adolescents, who are generally more prone to violent and overtly daring conduct than are adults; more insurance and credit card fraud by adults, who are more likely than adolescents to have the savvy and opportunity to perpetrate such misbehavior (See Hirschi & Gottfredson 1983).

Sex: Both sexes participate fully but, again, the forms of ACB tend to vary, e.g., males are more likely to vandalize (Levy-Leboyer 1984).

Economic status: perpetrators of ACB come from all income levels, but their motivations may be different (greed vs. need).

Education/occupation: as with other demographic characteristics, this 1)cuts across all levels, but 2)forms of ACB tend to differ, e.g., price tag switching, credit card, and check frauds are usually committed by better educated people (Steiner, Haden, Herkomer 1976). Increased education may enhance consumer ability to carry out sophisticated frauds.

B. Psychological Characteristics

Personality traits. Much of the relevant literature on ACB in other disciplines identifies relationships between personality traits and forms of misbehavior. The traits are used here to predict general tendencies towards misbehavior. Several personality trait schemes are available. We chose that presented in Ward & Robertson 1973 (pp. 181ff) because it provides a specific personality measurement instrument for each trait; these are given in parentheses:

- need for affiliation (EPPS)[1]
- need for aggression (EPPS)
- need for compliance (EPPS)
- need for dominance (EPPS)
- emotional stability (GPP)
- impulsive (TTS)
- need for order (EPPS)
- responsibility (GPP)

These traits are related to tendencies towards and against consumer misbehavior. Therefore it is difficult to predict the precise effect of any one of them *in isolation*. However, we would expect traits such as responsibility and the need for order to work towards restraining consumers from aberrant behavior. A trait such as the need for aggression, on the other hand, would likely heighten the possibility of violent forms of consumer misbehavior such as physical and verbal abusiveness and vandalism. Traits such as the need for affiliation and for compliance could lead either towards or away from misbehavior, depending upon the dominant behavioral norms in the group with which compliance or affiliation is being sought.

Level of moral development. Moral constraints are checks against conduct perceived to be wrong. Their presence and strength appears to play a large role in differentiating misbehaving from other consumers, since both are exposed to the same stimuli in an exchange setting. To the misbehaver, acts of ACB are simply not perceived as immoral; a common variant of this idea is the belief that an act may be immoral in general, but is not really wrong in the perpetrator's case (Moore 1984; Kallis & Vanier 1985).

Unfulfilled aspirations (Merton's "Strain" Theory): The sociologist Merton's well-known "Strain" theory attributes deviant conduct to the discrepancy between widely held material aspirations and the availability of legitimate means to realize them (Merton 1968; Messner 1988). Merton believes that marketing activities have overstimulated and thus magnified consumers' desires to the point where misbehavior in order to realize them has become a common phenomenon.

Propensity for thrill-seeking: The sociologist Lofland (1969) theorizes that the quest for thrills is a basic motivation for misconduct. Some shoplifters and vandals, for example, experience a powerful, sexual-like, sensation of release when they have been successful (Katz 1988). There is also evidence that some consumers engage in misbehavior to enliven otherwise drab lives (Moore 1984).

Psychological problems: Some aberrant consumer behavior clearly reflects deeply disturbed, abnormal, psyches (Pfohl 1984, pp. 96-100).

---

[1]The full names of these instruments are: EPPS - Edwards Personal Preference Schedule. GPP - Gordon Personal Profile. TTS - Thurston Temperament Schedule.

Attitude towards big businesses: Consumers tend to be more willing to victimize large rather than small businesses (Smigel 1956; Moore 1984). Explanations for this deal with consumer perceptions of impersonality, size, and social distance.

C. Social/Group Influences

Differential association: Based on the sociological theories of Sutherland (1947) and Cohen (1966), differential association is the idea that misbehavior is learned in and engaged in, by small groups, whose norms are antithetical to those of larger society. Misbehavior helps promote group identity and cohesiveness, and can serve as an initiation ritual. Consumers can be socialized into misbehavior through differential association (Moschis & Cox 1988). This can also be true of some misbehavior which is learned in a group but performed on an individual basis.

D. Consumer's Frame of Mind

Antecedent state: A consumer's mood state or high anxiety level can sometimes increase proneness to misbehave, through weakened self control. When this happens, consumers are likely to attribute their actions to influences beyond their volition, including supernatural ones.

II. The Exchange Setting & Marketing Institution

Conditions here can influence the consumer's motivation towards, and sense of opportunity regarding, ACB.

Type(s) of products/services offered: The key elements here are the mix of merchandise or services offered and how they are presented, extended services such as access to credit and return policies, and the extent of self service.

Physical environment: location, size, lighting, layout, noise, aromas, type of display (open vs. closed counter), colors and materials employed (e.g., concrete vs. wood).

Type and level of deterrence/security: Security and deterrence can be active and visible, or passive; in some cases it is hardly existent. Marketer willingness to aggressively prosecute misbehavers - and to signal such willingness to consumers - can influence misbehavior.

Attitudes and conduct of marketing employees: The degree to which marketer employees are helpful, alert, informed, and polite, can also either exacerbate or diminish consumers' propensities towards misbehavior.

Public's image of marketing institution: This refers to a firm's image as, for example, a good or bad corporate citizen, and the extent to which it is perceived as friendly or intimidating. Mills (1979) reported that department stores which projected an image of intimidating power were more likely to be victimized by consumers.

Antecedent state: This refers to conditions in the exchange environment which are known to be related to ACB and which vary across time - the extent of crowding, changes in store hours, times associated with above normal stresses and/or aggressiveness among consumers (Friday evenings, weekends, the Christmas season, full moon).

III. Interaction Effects

Many of the above factors form components of interactions that affect misbehavior. In some instances the interaction effects are subordinate to the main influences discussed above. In many other situations, however, the interaction effect is the dominant influence. In some such situations we can expect the components of an interaction to offset one another, thereby precluding misbehavior. A consumer's strong moral inhibitions or need for order could checkmate the lure of open, alluring, unguarded displays in a retail store. In other instances, however, the components can be synergistic with one another, intensifying the likelihood that misbehavior will occur. The precise nature of each interaction is, however, a subject for further research.

Both the main (i.e., direct) and the interaction effects are manifest in the exchange setting. The exchange setting is thus the flash point for ACB.

The interactive effects on ACB have not been explicitly recognized. Several of the reasons advanced for ACB in the literature are actually components in interactions which may or may not lead to misbehavior. It is the purpose of this model to help us isolate those components which play a major role in interactions leading to ACB. Some illustrative examples are:

Hedonic deviance: Deviant hedonic impulses interact with the type and level of perceived deterrence. The more deterrence, the greater the risk and hence the greater the thrill for the misbehaving consumer. Thus this influence is highly situational as argued by Dotter and Roebuck (1988).

Perceived size and impersonality of business: The larger and more impersonal a business is perceived to be, the greater the propensity to misbehave by consumers. The propensity would be more likely realized, however, when it interacts with such components as a low level of moral development and a personality trait such as the need for aggression.

Calculating opportunism: Involves rational assessment of the risks and rewards of acts of misbehavior. "Good" opportunities are then acted upon. Calculating opportunism is considered by many practitioners and theorists to be biggest single cause of aberrant behavior (Becker 1968; French, Crask, & Mader 1984). The sense of opportunity is known to be enhanced by such exchange setting characteristics as open displays, liberal return policies, easily-switchable price tags, difficult-to-monitor nooks, seeming indifference towards losses from ACB (e.g., by insurance firms), and perceived weak deterrence. Whether acts of ACB are then realized, depends upon such consumer characteristics as the level of moral development, the frame of mind, differential association, and age and sex.

Consumer's personal disaffection with marketer: In some cases consumers do not stop with conventional complaining behavior when dissatisfied, but rather become vindictive and attempt to achieve revenge through such acts of misbehavior as verbal or physical abuse of marketing employees or vandalism (Curtis 1971, pp. 55-56). The consumer's dissatisfaction may be intensified by such antecedent conditions such as long queues and crowding.

Provocative situational and temporal factors: Crowding, unsettling amounts of heat and noise, unguarded enticing displays, and some music. Any or all of these, when experienced by a consumer whose psychological problems have made him/her highly volatile, or by one with high impulsiveness and need for aggression, could trigger acts of ACB, especially those directed against other consumers or marketer employees.

CONCLUDING REMARKS

The model has scientific as well as managerial uses and implications. It can help make scientifically respectable use of the voluminous anecdotal material which exists on ACB in journalistic accounts and practitioners' heuristics. Interactions are implicit in much of the anecdotal material. Anecdotes are not replicable, of course. If, however, one decomposes an anecdote into its components, i.e., those comprising the interaction, these *can* be replicated and hence made subject to scientific inquiry. A extensive study of the interactions in the above manner could help us define the sometimes elusive boundary between acceptable and aberrant consumer behavior. Using an interaction model enhances the potential for measuring the relative individual influences on ACB. Where prior research has focussed on description, we have proposed a framework which is amenable to measurement.

The model has managerial implications. It can help managers to distinguish between those interactions leading to ACB which can be dealt with, and those which cannot. As an example, it would give guidance as to whether to use visible or passive deterrence to prevent thrill-seeking by teenage packs. Each managerial situation is much like the instance just mentioned, i.e., it is unique. To base ACB policy upon the generalized experience of other marketers as presented in anecdotes, is problematic. Each manager needs to decide what his/her own interactive situation is. Does for example more ACB come from thrill-seekers than coolly calculating opportunists, or are angry and revenge-prone customers the biggest problem? Then the manager can design a realistic policy for dealing with misbehavers, using the components presented in the model.

Future research.

ACB clearly merits more attention from consumer researchers. The model presented here is an effort to encourage such attention. To expand the work here, future research should proceed along three lines. The first is to refine the conceptualization of ACB, in particular dealing with the question of who shall decide precisely what it is (e.g., marketers, lawmakers, law enforcement personnel, consumers themselves). Second, the typology of consumer misbehaviors should be expanded to take into account the ever-growing variety of ACB, whose ever-new manifestations indicate rapid seizing of social and technological opportunities (e.g., widespread CATV theft). Third, new factors and interactions, going beyond those shown here, need to be identified and analyzed.

REFERENCES

Becker, Gary S. (1968), "Crime and Punishment: An Economic Approach," *The Journal of Political Economy*, 76 No. 2, 169-217.

Bernstein, Paul (1985), "Cheating - The New National Pastime?" *Business*, (Oct-Dec), 24-33.

Caggiano, S. (1987), "The New Improved EAS," *Security Management*, 31 (October), 83-7.

Cohen, Albert J. (1966), *Deviance and Control*, Englewood Cliffs: Prentice-Hall.

Cox, Dena, Cox, Anthony, & Moschis, George P. (1990), "When Consumer Behavior Goes Bad: An Investigation of Adolescent Shoplifting," *Journal of Consumer Research* 17, No. 2 (September), 149-159.

Curtis, Bob (1971), *Security Control: External Theft*, New York: Chain Store Age Books.

Dotter, Daniel L., & Julian B. Roebuck (1988), "The Labeling Approach Re-examined," *Deviant Behavior*, 9 No. 1, 19-32.

Endler, Norman S., and David Magnusson (1976), "Personality and Person by Situation Interactions," in *Interactional Psychology and Personality*, eds. Norman S. Endler and David Magnusson, Washington, D.C.: Hemisphere.

French, Warren A., Melvin R. Crask, and Fred H. Mader (1984), "Retailer's Assessment of the Shoplifting Problem," *Journal of Retailing*, 60 (Winter), 108-15.

Hirschi, Travis, & Michael Gottfredson (1983), "Age and the Explanation of Crime," *American Journal of Sociology*, 89 No. 3, 552-584.

Johnson, Elmer H. (1987), "Prevention in Business and Industry," in Elmer H. Johnson (ed.), *Handbook on Crime and Delinquency Prevention*, Westport, CT: Greenwood, 279-301.

Kallis, M. J. and D. J. Vanier (1985), "Consumer Shoplifting: Orientations and Deterrents," *Journal of Criminal Justice*, 13(5), 459-73.

Katz, Jack (1988), *Seductions of Crime,* New York: Basic Books.

Keller, John J. (1992), "'Call-Sell' Rings Steal Cellular Service," *Wall Street Journal* (March 13).

Kerr, Peter (1992), "A Heavy Toll is Being Paid for Auto Fraud," *Providence Journal Bulletin* (February 13).

Kraut, Robert E. (1976), "Deterrent and Definitional Influences on Shoplifting," *Social Problems*, 23, 358-368.

Levy-Leboyer, Claude, ed. (1984), *Vandalism: Behavior and Motivations*, Amsterdam, New York, Oxford: North Holland.

Lofland, John (1969), *Deviance and Identity*, Englewood Cliffs: Prentice-Hall.

Merton, Robert K. (1968), *Social Theory and Social Structure*, New York: Free Press.

Messner, Steven F. (1988), "Merton's `Social Structure and Anomie'," *Deviant Behavior*, 9 No. 1, 32-53.

Mills, Michael K. (1979), "A Power-Contextual Analysis of Deviant Consumer Behavior in Retail Stores," unpublished Ph.D. dissertation, University of Pittsburgh.

Moore, Richard H. (1984), "Shoplifting in Middle America,"*International Journal of Offender Therapy and Comparative Criminology*, 28, 53-64.

Moschis, George, & Dena Cox (1988), "Deviant Consumer Behavior," presented at the 1988 ACR Conference.

Pfohl, Stephen J. (1985), *Images of Deviance and Social Control*, New York: McGraw-Hill.

Ray, Joann Emmler (1983), "The Twelfth Shopper: A Description and Gender Comparison of Shoplifting in Spokane, Washington," Ph.D. diss., University of Washington, *Dissertation Abstracts*.

Smigel, Erwin O. (1956), "Public Attitudes Toward Stealing as Related to the Size of the Victim Organization," *American Sociological Review*, 21, 320-327.

Steiner, John M., Stuart C. Hadden, & Len Herkomer (1976), "Price Tag Switching," *International Journal of Criminology and Penology*, 4, 129-143.

Sutherland, Edwin H. (1937), *The Professional Thief*, Chicago: University of Chicago Press.

_____ (1947), *Principles of Criminology*, 4th ed., Lippincott: Philadelphia.

Wilson, James Q., & Richard J. Herrnstein (1985), *Crime and Human Nature*, New York: Simon and Schuster.

Zimbardo, Philip G. (1977), "The Psychology of Evil," in Lester Krames et.al, eds., *Aggression, Dominance, and Individual Spacing*, New York & London: Plenum Press, 155-169.

Brand Loyalty and Lineage: Exploring New Dimensions for Research
Barbara Olsen, State University of New York–Old Westbury

ABSTRACT

Research on the transfer of brand loyalties has had a long gestation. Much of the focus has been on how children learn and process consumer values. This paper represents a conceptual exploration of the transfer of branded goods and consumer practices from a qualitative investigation with several families; including grandparents, parents and children. Intergenerational patterns of product use emerge through life history interviews. This study suggests a departure for intergenerational research to probe deeper into the functional and dysfunctional reasons why we adopt or reject family patterns. The conclusion situates socialization to brand loyalty within the domain of current marketplace practices.

INTRODUCTION

Consumer socialization occurs primarily within family settings where branded goods become imbued with meaning from the social contexts in which they are used. Research on learning consumer behavior has involved the socialization process and increasingly considers the quality of the interpersonal communication through which it takes place (Carlson et al. 1990; Moore and Moschis 1981; Moschis 1985; Moschis and Moore 1979).

For many of us advertising is our first introduction to a brand, while other brands have been in our families for generations. Until the early 1980s advertising's primary emphasis for heavily competitive products was on the differentiation of features and quality among an increasing glut of parity goods. Consumers came to distrust these messages and knew essentially that most products were the same. Advertising followed with lifestyle messages that were more subtle in the bonding practice (Jhally 1990; Leiss et al. 1990). Advertising continues to employ an emotional bond between goods and human needs by emphasizing loyalty earned from earlier generations to attract their children and grandchildren (Brooks Brothers, Fieldcrest Mills, Romano Bread, Vicks VapoRub).

One area of consumer research is concerned with the contextual meaning of goods (Kleine III and Kernan 1991); their connection to our early socialization (Bahn 1986; Carlson et al. 1990; Foxman et al. 1989; McNeal 1987; Moschis and Churchill 1978; Moschis and Moore 1983; Ward et al. 1977); how we learn to project our evolving social roles through brand/product constellations (Solomon and Assael 1987); and how we match branded products with our emotional needs as adults (McCracken 1990). The growing trend to understand these relationships utilizes qualitative research obtained from life histories and depth interviews (McCracken 1988; Rothberg 1989).

This exploratory study seeks to gain a further understanding of family influence on brand loyalty and consumer behavior among several generations of individual families. How and why does a pattern of brand preference or consumer behavior recur in the next generation for brands that have been in existence for two or three generations?

LITERATURE REVIEW

Early research on intergenerational consumption patterns ranged from behavior (Miller 1975), product choice in financial planning (Hill 1970) and auto insurance between fathers and sons (Woodson et al. 1976), to brand preference prediction and shopping strategy congruence between mothers and daughters (Moore-Shay and Lutz 1988). Guest's longitudinal study covering twenty years recognized the lifetime dimension of brand loyalty learned during childhood (1964, 1955). These studies demonstrate that preference was repeated generationally but do not address why. Similar research connects product preference to early family socialization and shows that parental influence wanes with age and fluctuations in income (Moschis and Moore 1983).

Consumer socialization research focuses on how adult consumer habits are formulated during childhood (Carlson et al. 1990) and during adolescence (Bahn 1986; Foxman et al. 1989; Moschis and Churchill 1978; Moschis and Moore 1979, 1983; Moschis, Moore and Smith 1984). This research has traditionally taken two routes and is often a combination of both. The first focuses on the importance of social agents; environmental and media factors in the social learning model (Moore and Stephens 1975; Moschis and Churchill 1978; Ward et al. 1977) and the second centers on children's developing psychology to process consumer information in the cognitive development approach (Alba and Hutchinson 1987; Bahn 1986; Bettman 1979; Foxman et al. 1989; Hoch and Deighton 1989; McNeal 1987). Bahn suggests that a family's religious orientation may influence early adoption of certain brands of beverages (1986: 392). Other socialization research emphasizes family patterns of communication. The concept orientation encourages children's consumer involvement while the socio-orientation stresses children's deference to parental decisions (Carlson et al. 1990; Moore and Moschis 1981; Moschis 1985; Moschis and Moore 1979). Foxman et al. (1989) found that adolescents and mothers share more of an influence on each other than fathers. Ward et al. also demonstrate the mother's role in socialization, however, they found mothers are often not conscious of attempting to "teach" consumer behavior (1977: 116). Further research is needed to ascertain how socialization affects particular patterns of consumer behavior. In the present exploratory work several cases clearly indicate a correlation between a dysfunctional socialization and rejection of parental behavior, while others correlate warm family ties with patterns of loyalty. Brands used since childhood can become "friends" with whom relationships are fashioned early in our social lives (Aaker 1991: 34, 40-41).

Studies have shown certain goods attract a loyal following. One survey revealed product categories with personal loyalties of over fifty percent: cigarettes, mayonnaise, toothpaste, coffee, headache remedy, film, bath soap and ketchup. Reasons varied from flavor and taste - ketchup and cigarettes; to image - beer, cigarettes and perfume (Centennial Survey 1989: B1,1).

Douglas and Isherwood have written that "Goods are neutral, their uses are social; they can be used as fences or bridges" (1979: 12). Thus, intergenerational transfer often represents the "bridge" of an emotional bond with the personal relationship. Conversely, alternative behavior or product rejection represents a "fence," signifying rebellion against a social relationship.

As part of the consumption process we engage in possession, grooming and divestment rituals (McCracken 1990: 85-88) during which we employ an "object-code" encoding/decoding process when social values are "made material" in goods that become loaded with cultural meaning. Sometimes we invest this meaning with a transcendent quality that positions a good within the sacred dimension (Belk et al. 1989). We also use goods to impress our roles within cultural categories (age, gender, occupation, class, space, time) that are contoured by cultural principles - the values of our society (Douglas and Isherwood 1979, McCracken 1990, Sahlins 1976). We learn to choose brands that constitute "product constellations" and speak a psychographic message (Solomon and Assael 1987). Thus, shared social values often find expression by members of an "'image tribe'" (Image..." 1989: 8). Members identify with each other through "charismatic brands" (Aaker 1991: 210) that possess a mystical quality called "quintessence" through which individuals relate in "a cult of 'true believers'" (Belk et al. 1989: 16).

METHODOLOGY

The current work seeks a deeper understanding of intergenerational transfer. It represents a conceptual production and suggests areas to be probed in further research. Marketing students at a college in the north-east were asked to participate as "junior collaborators" (Wallendorf and Arnould 1991) using self-as-instrument (McCracken 1988: 32) in a class project. Although controversial, the methodology does allow for a wider sampling than could be obtained by a sole researcher and was useful for an exploratory penetration of familial product use to be followed-up in more rigorous research. Students conducted ethnographies of product use within their own families during four semesters from 1989 to 1991. Twenty five students participated each semester. From 100 students, half were able to interview parents and grandparents thereby contributing usable responses. The citations in the current work are examples from the sample and represent occurrences of lineage influence.

To obtain an initial reading for more systematic, rigorous follow-up research, "junior collaborators" conducted their own interviews using the ethnographic approach: participant observation and life history depth interviews with grandparents, parents and siblings. Broad product categories were suggested to help situate branded products within family consumption patterns. Topics revolved around the purchasing habits of consumables and durables over time with emphasis on the importance of price, quality, value, advertising, peer pressure, word-of-mouth, brand loyalty or other influence on behavior. In this initial study, the objective was to determine product occurrence. Generational transfer was not a consideration to prevent bias.

As consumer behavior is learned during the socialization process and related to family communication patterns, consciously learned or unconsciously observed, the expectation is that there will be a pattern of congruence communicating brand preference and behavior from one generation to the next. Research has shown that mothers are the primary socialization agents within families (Carlson et al. 1990; Foxman et al. 1989; Ward et al. 1977), therefore, we expect to find a pattern of preference between mothers and children of both genders. Fathers are also expected to influence particular product categories.

CASE HISTORIES / GENERATIONAL BRIDGING

Product identification with a member of the older generation acts as a "bridge" reinforcing a bond of affection and respect. This is true for a student speaking of what he/she will do upon establishing one's own household after graduation.

(*Early Twenties, Italian-American male*) "My mother still buys almost every brand that her mother did. She is scared to try anything else, for it will not meet the standards, and (she) would feel bad not buying something that has been with her so long" (sisters also use the same brands).

(*Hispanic-American female*) "I believe that one of the reasons that my mother and her mother still buy some of the same products ... (is) that they go shopping together every week."

(*West Indian-American female*) "I find it hard to break away from the things I've been using since I was little; like Vaseline products, Ivory soap, Lipton tea, and corn flakes. I live on campus so I have to do my own shopping, and when I do I see a lot of my mother in myself. I buy things I'm accustomed to using, ... products my mother buys for the house."

(*27 year old, Russian-Jewish-American male*) "All of us have used Crest toothpaste, Breakstone butter, Hellmann's mayonnaise, and Bumble Bee tuna. All these products have been passed on and we all have remained incredibly loyal. Brand loyalty is almost mystical. It transcends time. We all use these products today."

The transcendental quality in brand loyalty is similar to the sacred described by Belk et al. (1989). This informant stressed the importance of being "faithful to our religion." The link of religion to brand loyalty has been noted by Bahn (1986). Lately, his food choices changed to healthier versions of these brands.

(*Early twenties, German-American male - repairing car with father*) "I happened to notice that we were working on a Dodge and that all our cars were Dodges. I also noticed that he was using Craftsman tools, drinking Schaeffer beer, and smoking Camel cigarettes. I asked him about these products and he said he got them from his father, all except the Camels which he started with his friends ... I'm very influenced by my father in terms of cars, auto parts, the tools that I use and my newspaper."

(*Mid-twenties, Irish-American male*) "My sister, 21 years old and married is a carbon copy of my mother. She controls the money and decides when things will be purchased just like the other women in the family tree ... the males are extremely brand loyal with price having no effect on their decisions. One noticeable difference happens on the female side. My grandmother was very brand loyal, but my mother and sister are not due to ... the coupon ... Every time I purchase a product, I hear the voices of my father and grandfather in the back of my head."

There were many cases of loyalty to a brand because an elder had worked for the company. A similar sense of loyalty is communicated by parent generations for buying American cars.

REBELLION

There also exist opposite behavior patterns in rituals of rebellion. Rejecting products, behaviors, and relationships in defense of one's own loyalties are echoed by the daughter whose mother bought only bargains and in bulk: "I hope never to become a manic-crazy coupon cutter when I become a mother." More severe rejections represent a "fence" constructed during the socio-oriented socialization process demanding obedience to parental consumer choice. Asserting independence through rejection can be silent statement about one's socialization process.

(*25 year old, Italian-American male*) "... my mother felt forced as a child to use her parents' products, so (she) wanted to break free and have her own identity and buy her own products ... her tastes and needs were totally different from her mother's. She swore to change to her own when possible. The only soap, for example, that was used in her house as a child was Ivory; now today my mother won't buy it."

(*Mid-twenties, Anglo-American female*) "My mother was comfortable with ... brands that she grew up with (Del Monte sauce, Betty Crocker baking goods, Campbell's soup, Lipton iced tea, Pledge, Windex, Boar's Head cold cuts, Woolite), and ... for over fifteen years she probably hardly ever used these brands because ... my father did all of the shopping and only bought what was the cheapest brand that week. When she did begin to shop (after divorce), she chose ... brands that she was loyal to from her past."

(*Early twenties, German-American female*) "My ... father revealed that when he entered college he bought many brands used at home plus new ones based on status ... When he married, ... he chose the durables while Mom chose all consumables. After the divorce, ... he reverted to the same products he bought when he entered college. He said he was '48 going on 22.'"

(*28 year old, Italian-American female*) "My mother completely mandated all product usage in our household. If any of us brought home a product other than the usual ones, she would pass derogatory remarks about the product. Reading between the lines, she was telling us that if she did not approve the product, it was no good. As a result of this rebellion my sister (age 42) and I turned to different types of products altogether. My mother uses frozen vegetables, we use canned. My mother drinks cola, we drink the 'uncola.' My mom buys Campbell's (canned) Soup, we use Lipton (packaged). And the list goes on: Lipton - Tetley tea; Colgate - Close-Up toothpaste; Robitussin - NyQuil cough syrup; French's - Gulden's mustard; Ivory - Palmolive dish detergent; All powder - Era liquid detergent; Downey liquid - Bounce sheets fabric softener; American - Japanese car."

A follow-up interview with this woman revealed the sisters were raised with three brothers (two are married in their thirties, one lives home with parents). The sons were "treated like royalty." Mother was "too protective of them" and "cared too much by doing everything for her boys." Mother was emotionally abusive to both daughters. Her sister left home at 19 when the informant was 5. The informant revealed she was sexually abused by her father until age 13. She cannot yet recall the onset of abuse. Mother was never an ally, nor is she close with her sister. "Now, when we see each other we fight." By analyzing consumption habits and personal histories we strip away the materials in which social relations are constituted and reveal the relationships they cover (Alderson 1957: 186-87). Perhaps we may discover why rejection of consumer socialization can also be a statement about family relationships.

Insights from anthropology focus a powerful lens upon ourselves. In the ethnographic context certain animals are good to "think" - reserved for totem status and tabooed for food. They are better to contemplate within the clan structure of the "social idiom" rather than to be eaten and thus acquire a different cultural meaning (Levi-Strauss 1963). So too, goods enter a sacred domain in which they come to represent our totems and our taboos (Belk et al. 1989). In analyzing the cultural consumption of goods, we should also research the irrational component, beyond functional utility, where consumption fulfills emotional needs. Brands become good to "think" for statements we make about ourselves and our social relationships. We should consider the dysfunctional quality of socialization and our reactions played out in consumer behavior that help maintain our homeostasis (Alderson 1957: 172, Sherry 1991). We know from observing children in the marketplace that there is a powerful satisfaction obtained in controlling brand preference.

RESULTS

We pattern our consumption behavior after role models. The study revealed that certain product categories were transferred between generations more than others. For instance, toothpaste was cited in ten families and transferred between sixteen generations; ten times between mother-daughter, five times between mother-son, and once between grandmother-grandson. Mayonnaise, cited in eight families, was transferred between twelve generations; six times between mother-daughter and six between mother-son. Bath soap, cited in seven families, was transferred between eight generations; seven times between mother-daughter and once between father-son. Ketchup, cited in six families, was transferred between seven generations; four times between mother-daughter and three times between mother-son. Automobiles were cited in seven families and transferred between ten generations; once between mother-daughter and nine times between father-son.

Why do some brands become friends? Over time a product acquires a significant investment in brand equity (Aaker 1991). For the average person a branded good is a "bundle of satisfactions" including memories and meanings that get wrapped around its advertised use value to solve problems with various benefits. These memories and meanings include individuals and contexts associated with its use.

Goods also represent a way of declaring one's own identity as shown in the cases of rebelling against a parent's preferences or establishing a sense of self after divorce. One follow-up interview revealed the scar of abuse in a dysfunctional home. A mother after divorce renewed her esteem by returning to brands she grew up with. A father rebuilt his life after divorce by returning to brands used in college. Further research could uncover the relationship between product choice and self-esteem.

MARKETING IMPLICATIONS

It has been a little over a hundred years since brand names have differentiated one product from another. Branding simplified the purchasing process by enabling individual portions to be sold in pre-packaged units displaying the trademark. This was a revolutionary departure from selling in bulk from bins and carried away in nondescript bags.

There is an enduring quality to the notion of brand equity. While marketers always look for ways to attract new customers, they realize it can cost "up to 15 times the amount to attract a new customer than to keep existing clients (Marketing Review Panel 1990: 18), while "'The probability of converting a non-user to your brand is about three in 1,000...'" (Centennial 1989: 10). Aaker says "there usually is an enormous payoff in retaining existing customers, ... A customer base is like a leaky bucket: Increasing the input may be more wasteful than patching the leaks" (1991: 52-53). To encourage intergenerational linking we are seeing more ads geared to keeping the brand in the family:

"Recent Clinical Studies Prove Your Grandmother Was Right" (Vicks VapoRub). "We've put fiber in Roman Meal for 75 years because people need fiber from day one - So do something your kids will appreciate for the rest of their lives. Start them on fiber-rich Roman Meal breads today" (Romano Bread). "The man in the Brooks Brothers Suit - Who says charm isn't hereditary? We've been helping it along for 172 years. And while change is inevitable, a tradition of quality is our legacy. And yours" (Brooks Brothers). "Why six generations of Americans have turned to St. Marys for warmth and comfort" (Fieldcrest Mills).

This ad style is also evident in television commercials. A Kellogg's Corn Flakes commercial in which two individuals recall the cereal of their childhood ends with the slogan, "Kellogg's Corn Flakes: Taste them again for the first time." Despite eroding brand loyalty from couponing, one report suggests that certain goods (canned soups, cereal, dairy products, salad dressing) maintain sales despite higher prices due to a "strong emotional attachment in tough times" ("Brand Loyalty..." 1991: 1). Considering the importance of family in this copy style, intergenerational ads are best targeted to the new traditionalist and those for whom nostalgia is a powerful sentiment.

On the other hand, marketers are rushing to become the main socialization agents by cultivating early brand loyalty to their goods and services. Many corporations are encouraging this loyalty by advertising on school materials. AT&T, IBM, Dun & Bradstreet (Donnelley Marketing), Mars (Milky Way), Scholastic, Nike, Reebok, Coca-Cola (Minute Maid), Pepsi Cola and Whittle Communications are winning support to supply schools with badly needed educational programs, supplies and services in return for displaying logos, trademarks and advertisements in strategic locations ("Cola..." 1991: 18; Deveny 1990).

CONCLUSION

It is clear from the interviews that brands are an important component in generational bridging. McCracken reflects that each family now has a limited role connecting generations. Goods we purchase are often replacements for what we no longer inherit and their meaning changes to suit the moment (1990: 52). What we now pass on to those generations, demonstrated by this study, is the brand itself. The product becomes a symbol of the socialization process and can function as a "bridge" or "fence" as individuals interpret their own identity.

Early adoption of a brand into the construction of our commodity oriented social universe is very important to marketers as they come to appreciate the truly emotional content in the meaning of the good. "Charismatic brands" help identify social roles; Nike neighborhoods, Ann Taylor lifestyle, PAM people, Pepsi generation, Bud drinkers, Ford family. These themes are incorporated in the communication message of the ads we see. They are the subtle reminders that our cultural categories are circumscribed by commodities. When we replenish our supplies with brand named goods we also renew the relationship we have with those products and with the people who introduced us to them.

FUTURE RESEARCH

Several instances in the present work present new dimensions for further research. What is the connection between the mother and grandmother who shop together every week and buy the same brands? Why is one mother "scared" to depart from brands her mother used? Why does another informant find it "hard to break away" from brands used since childhood. The question for future research is: What is going on in the "bridge" that links the lineages? What particular roles do the models play?

A fertile area for future research resides in the "fence" built for protection from a dysfunctional social experience. Emotional and physical abuse, the most extreme forms reported in this work, as well as divorce, exemplify the layers of experience we can begin to peel away. These layers reveal the interconnection between our personal selves, our social selves and our perpetual reinterpretation of "self" through the commodities we buy. Continuing ethnographic research involves life history analysis working with incest survivors and adult children of alcoholics to investigate the relationship between dysfunctional socialization experiences and consumption. One on-going project considers the differences in consumption between recently divorced men and women. Another study explores the role of ethnicity and brand loyalty.

Future research on the contextual meaning of our goods will reveal the roles they play in the rituals of our lives. A brand may signal different meanings for each generation even though it is transferred between several. McCracken (1990) mourns with Mrs. Lois Roget that none of her children wish to inherit the heirlooms that have descended for seven generations. He claims that in our consumer culture each family can now reconstruct itself without the encumbrances of past generations by buying new. In the reconstruction process, perhaps what we now "inherit" are brands!

REFERENCES

(This paper contains a select subset of the total references. For a complete set contact the author).

Aaker, David A. (1991), *Managing Brand Equity*, NY: Free Press.

Alderson, Wroe (1957/1978), *Marketing Behavior and Executive Action*, IL: Irwin / NY: Arno Press.

Bahn, Kenneth (1986), "How and When Do Brand Perceptions and Preferences First Form? A Cognitive Developmental Investigation," *Journal of Consumer Research*, Vol. 12 (December), 382-393.

Belk, Russell W., Mellanie Wallendorf and John F. Sherry, Jr. (1989), "The Sacred and the Profane in Consumer Behavior: Theodicy on the Odyssey," *Journal of Consumer Research*, Vol. 16 (June), 1-38.

"Brand Loyalty Undermined By Steep Discount Sales/Coupons" (1991), *Modern Grocer*, November 22, 1991: 1, 14.

Carlson, Les, Sanford Grossbart and Ann Walsh (1990), "Mothers' Communication Orientation and Consumer-Socialization Tendencies," *Journal of Advertising*, 19 (3), 27-38.

Centennial Survey (1989), "Brand Loyalty is Rarely Blind Loyalty: Use in Coupons, Choices Blamed for '80s Erosion," The American Way of Buying/Series, *Wall Street Journal*, (October 19), B 2, 10.

"Cola Companies Vie for School Vending Machines, Young Buyers," (1991), *Marketing News*, (February 4), 25 (3), 18.

Deveny, Kathleen (1990), "Consumer-Products Firms Hit the Books, Trying to Teach Brand Loyalty in School," *Wall Street Journal*, (July 17, 1990).

Douglas, Mary and Baron Isherwood (1979), *The World of Goods*, New York: Basic Books.

Guest, Lester (1955), "Brand Loyalty-Twelve Years Later," *Journal of Applied Psychology*, 39 (6), 405-408.

_____ (1964), "Brand Loyalty Revisited: A Twenty-Year Report," *Journal of Applied Psychology*, 48 (2) 93-97.

Hill, Reuben (1970), *Family Development in Three Generations*, MA: Schenkman.

"Image Gains Importance As Consumers Form Tribes" (1989), *Marketing News*, (November 11), 8.

Jhally, Sut (1990/1987), *The Codes of Advertising*, NY: Routledge.

Kleine III, Robert E. and Jerome B. Kernan (1991), "Contextual Influences on the Meanings Ascribed to Ordinary Consumption Objects," *Journal of Consumer Research*, 18 (3): 311-324.

Levi-Strauss, Claude (1963), *Totemism*, Boston, MA: Beacon Press.

Marketing Review Panel (1990), "The Challenges of Measuring Consumer Satisfaction," *Marketing Review*, 46 (2), 18.

McCracken, Grant (1990), *Culture and Consumption*, Bloomington: Indiana University Press.

McNeal, James V. (1987), *Children as Consumers*, MA: D.C. Heath.

Miller, B. (1975), "Intergenerational Patterns of Consumer Behavior," *Proceedings*, Association for Consumer Research, pp 93-101.

Moore, Roy L. and George P. Moschis (1981), "The Effects of Family Communication and Mass Media Use on Adolescent Consumer Learning," *Journal of Communication*, 31 (Fall), pp 42-51.

Moore-Shay, Elizabeth S. and Richard J. Lutz (1989), "Intergenerational Influences in the Formation of Consumer Attitudes and Beliefs About the Marketplace: Mothers and Daughters," *Advances in Consumer Research*, 15, 461-467.

Moschis, George P. (1985), "The Role of Family Communication in Consumer Socialization of Children and Adolescents," *Journal of Consumer Research*, 11 (March), 898-913.

_____ and Roy L. Moore, and Ruth B. Smith (1984), "The Impact of Family Communication on Adolescent Consumer Socialization," *Advances in Consumer Research*, Vol 11, Thomas C. Kinnear, ed., Chicago, IL: Association for Consumer Research, 314-319.

Rothberg, Randall (1989), "Ad Research Shifts From Products to People," *The New York Times*, (April 6), D1, 10.

Sahlins, Marshall (1976), *Culture and Practical Reason*, Chicago, IL: University of Chicago Press.

Sherry, John F., Jr. (1991), "Post Modern Alternatives: The Interpretive Turn in Consumer Research," in *Handbook of Consumer Behavior*, Thomas S. Robertson and Harold H. Kassarjian, eds., NJ: Prentice-Hall, 548-591.

Solomon, Michael R. and Henry Assael (1987), "The Forest or the Trees?: A Gestalt Approach to Symbolic Consumption," in *Marketing and Semiotics: New Directions in the Study of Signs for Sale*, Jean Umiker-Sebeok, ed., Berlin: Mouton de Gruyter, 189-217.

Ward, Scott, Daniel B. Wackman and Ellen Wartella (1977), *How Children Learn to Buy*, Beverly Hills, CA: Sage.

Woodson, Larry G., Terry Childers and Paul R. Winn (1976), "Intergenerational Influences in the Purchase of Auto Insurance," in *Marketing Looking Outward*, Business Proceedings, Series #38, William Locander, ed., American Marketing Association, 43-49.

Testing for Perceptual Underestimation of 9-Ending Prices

Robert M. Schindler, Rutgers University-Camden
Thomas Kibarian, Innovation and Information Consultants, Inc.

ABSTRACT

Although perceptual underestimation of 9-ending prices is one of the most common explanations for the tendency of price setters to choose retail prices which end in the digit 9, two studies using an immediate recall task fail to provide evidence for the existence of any substantial perceptual underestimation. However, the pattern of recall errors found in these studies does suggest that the rightmost digits of a price receive less consumer attention than the leftmost digits. These results direct further research toward more sophisticated conceptions of price perception and how it may be affected by the price setter's choice of rightmost digits.

INTRODUCTION

Retail price setters show a marked tendency to set prices just below round numbers (Friedman 1967; Kreul 1982) and in particular to choose prices which end in the digit 9 (Twedt 1965). This pricing technique has often been termed "psychological pricing," apparently because of the belief that 9-ending prices act on the consumer via "special psychological effects" (Mason and Mayer 1990, p. 442).

Although a number of such special psychological effects of 9-ending prices have been hypothesized, the one which is probably the most common and persistent is that a 9-ending leads consumers to perceptually underestimate the level of a price (e.g., Georgoff 1972, pp. 4-6; Lambert 1975; Schindler and Warren 1988; Simon 1989, p. 183). This will be termed the *underestimation hypothesis*. This view maintains that consumers' tendency to minimize effort often leads to the use of truncation rather than rounding when perceiving prices. Thus, a consumer would perceive a price such as $29.99 by dropping off the rightmost 9's and thinking of it as "around $20" or "twenty and some dollars" rather than rounding it up to $30.

The underestimation hypothesis is certainly not the only plausible psychological mechanism for an effect of 9-ending prices. It is possible that 9-endings carry a symbolic meaning to the consumer (Schindler 1991) or that consumers use round numbers as cognitive reference points and thus perceive a 9-ending price as one where the price setter has knocked off a penny (Kreul 1982). However, the commonness and persistence of the underestimation hypothesis suggests that it deserves some careful examination.

The difficulty of measuring perception directly has often led memory measures to be used as surrogates of perception in advertising research (e.g., Ostlund 1978). A similar approach might be useful for testing the underestimation hypothesis. At this early stage of research, a recall measure would be more appropriate than a recognition test since it would not require specifying ahead of time expectations as to the exact underestimated price each consumer will perceive.

The presumption of the use of a recall measure is that when consumers recall a price which they have seen, they will recall it as they perceived it. If the consumer's perceptual processes fail to encode one or more of the rightmost digits of a price and instead represent them with a default value such as zero or some other low number, then the perception of a 9-ending price would be an underestimate of the true price. That underestimate is then what the consumer would be expected to recall. Thus, if the underestimation hypothesis is true, the average recalled price for a 9-ending price should be considerably more than one cent lower than the average recalled price for the equivalent (i.e., one-cent higher) 0-ending price.

Schindler and Wiman (1989) have conducted such a recall test and have found that at least some types of 9-ending prices will tend to be underestimated when they are recalled. However, this result is unconvincing as evidence for the underestimation hypothesis because Schindler and Wiman tested the subjects' price recall a full two days after they were exposed to the price. This delay*ed* recall procedure raises the possibility that the subjects may have perceived the 9-ending prices accurately, but then dropped off the rightmost digits over the two-day period before the recall test.

More convincing evidence for the underestimation hypothesis would be the demonstration that 9-ending prices are underestimated relative to the equivalent 0-ending prices even when a price is recalled within a few minutes of having been seen. This *immediate* recall procedure does not remove the possibility that rightmost digits are being dropped during the period following the perception of the price. But reducing the post-perception period to minutes versus days would be expected to sharply reduce the degree to which this would occur. Demonstration that the underestimation of 9-ending prices persists under immediate recall conditions would provide much stronger evidence that this underestimation occurs at the time of perception rather than at some later time.

STUDY 1

This study was an attempt to replicate the Schindler and Wiman finding but using an immediate recall measure rather than delayed recall. Three pairs of advertisements were prepared so that one member of the pair displayed a 0-ending price while the other member of the pair was identical except that it displayed the 9-ending price one cent lower than the 0-ending price. Each subject was shown one of these six advertisements and, within three minutes, was asked to recall the price which was contained in that ad. The underestimation hypothesis would predict that the mean recalled price for the 9-ending prices would be substantially lower than the mean recalled price for the 0-ending prices.

Method

Design. Each subject saw one of three different advertisements in either its 9- or 0-ending form. Thus, the three-level between-subjects variable, Advertisement, was crossed with the two-level between-subjects variable, Price Ending. Recalled price was the dependent variable.

Although the purpose of the experiment was to determine whether 9-ending prices are underestimated, the 0-ending condition was included in order to control for the possibility of a *general* tendency to underestimate prices.

Subjects. The participants in this study were women recruited from church groups and PTAs in middle-income suburban neighborhoods. Data were collected from 145 individuals, but four subjects failed to follow instructions and their data were discarded. Thus, the results reported here are based on 141 subjects.

Materials. Each subject received a packet consisting of two booklets attached by a paper clip. The first booklet consisted of two pages. The first page was a cover sheet with introductory instructions. The second page showed a reproduction of a newspaper advertisement. Below the ad was a question which asked whether the price in the ad was "in line with what stores in this area would charge for this item." The subjects responded by checking one of

TABLE 1
Mean Recalled Prices in Each Condition of Study 1

Advertisement	9-Ending Prices	0-Ending Prices
Dress		
Actual Price	49.99	50.00
Mean Recalled Price	49.81	50.04
Difference (Recalled-Actual)	-.18	.04
Sports Coat		
Actual Price	119.99	120.00
Mean Recalled Price	123.10	122.09
Difference (Recalled-Actual)	3.11	2.09
Patio Furniture		
Actual Price	299.99	300.00
Mean Recalled Price	299.63	297.08
Difference (Recalled-Actual)	-.36	-2.92

three possible responses. The sole purpose of this question was to insure that the subjects look at the price in the advertisements.

Each of the three ads used featured only one product and showed only one price. The ads were selected from among real newspaper ads which featured a product of some relevance to middle-class women and which prominently displayed a price. An attempt was made to choose a set of advertised products which represented the diversity of items likely to be of interest to the subjects. One of the three ads selected featured a dress, another featured a sports coat, and the third featured patio furniture. To reduce the possibility that subjects might happen to know the advertised price before seeing the ad, the ads were selected from out-of-town newspapers and were chosen so that both the stores and (if identified) the brands advertised lacked national reputations.

Each ad was altered to produce two versions: one with a 0-ending price, and one with the corresponding 9-ending price (one cent less than the even price). For example, in one version of the patio furniture ad, the price was $300.00. In the other version, otherwise identical to the first, the price was $299.99. In order to prevent the possibility that the price in one version might look more realistic than the other ad's price, the price was redrawn in b0*th* versions of the ad.

Since there were two versions of each of three ads, there was a total of six ads: the dress at $49.99, the dress at $50.00, the sports coat at $119.99, the sports coat at $120.00, the patio furniture at $299.99, and the patio furniture at $300.00. Since only one of these ads appeared on the second page of the first booklet, there were six versions of the first booklet.

The second booklet contained one of the three advertisements that had been used in the first booklet. However, for this booklet, these ads were altered so that the price was replaced by a blank line. Each subject's second booklet contained the same advertisement that her first booklet contained. For example, if a subject's first booklet had the advertisement for the dress at either $49.99 or $50.00, her second booklet had the same advertisement for the dress, but without the price. The subjects were asked to write, on the blank line, the exact price they had seen in the first booklet.

This second booklet included a cover sheet and was sealed to prevent the subjects from seeing its contents while they were viewing the first booklet. Also, no one was allowed to begin the second booklet until everyone completed the first booklet and it had been collected. This prevented subjects from looking back at the first booklet as they were responding to the second one.

Procedure. The subjects were run in groups ranging in size between twenty and fifty. The six different packet types were distributed randomly to the subjects in each group, so as to insure random assignment to the experimental conditions. Each group was told that the study concerned "how a store which is entering a new area should advertise." Subjects were told that they would see an advertisement for a store which they were probably not familiar with and should "look at this ad as you would if you saw it in your local newspaper," and answer the question below the ad. The subjects were given no indication that they would later be asked to recall anything concerning the ad they were about to see.

All subjects in a group began the first booklet at the same time. After everyone completed the first booklet, it was collected. The subjects were then told about the contents of the second booklet and were instructed to write, on the blank line, the "exact price" they had seen in the first booklet's ad. In all groups, the time between having seen the ad containing the price in the first booklet and writing the recalled price into the second booklet was less than three minutes.

Results

The mean recalled prices in each of the six experimental conditions can be seen in Table 1. A two-way, between-subjects analysis of variance indicated that there was a highly significant main effect of Advertisement $F[2,135] = 10876.0$, $p < .001$), no significant main effect of Price Ending ($F[1,135] < 1$), and no significant interaction between Price Ending and Advertisement ($F[2,135] < 1$). Replicating this analysis with both the actual and percent recalled-actual price differences also yields no significant Price Ending effect or Price Ending by Advertisement interaction (all F's < 1). Clearly, there is no substantial underestimation of the 9-ending prices in this immediate recall task.

However, while an analysis of the recalled prices indicates that there was no substantial underestimation of the 9-ending prices, examination of the recall errors reveals evidence for a considerable tendency to drop off the cents digits of the 9-ending prices (see Table 2). Of the 71 subjects who saw the 0-ending prices, 2.8% recalled a price which was an underestimate of the price they had seen. By contrast, of the 70 subjects who saw the 9-ending prices, far more (55.7%) recalled an underestimate of the actual price ($X^2[1] = 47.8$, $p<.001$). Further, almost all of the underestimates produced by the 9-ending subjects involved the cents digits of the price. Twenty-eight percent of the 9-ending subjects dropped four cents from the correct price (e.g., recalling $49.99 as $49.95), 16%

TABLE 2
Distribution of Recalled Prices for 9- and 0-Ending Prices

Category of recalled price	Percentage of recalled prices in each category	
	9-ending prices (n = 70)	0-ending prices (n = 71)
Overestimate by $1.00 or more	1.4	4.2
Overestimate by $.01 - $.99	0.0	1.4
Exactly correct	42.9	91.5
Underestimate by $.01 - $.99	54.3	0.0
Underestimate by $1.00 or more	1.4	2.8

dropped 99 cents from the correct price (e.g., recalling $49.99 as $49.00), and 10% dropped either one to three cents or 5-49 cents from the correct price. Interestingly, not one of the 70 subjects who saw a 9-ending price recalled the even price which was one penny higher.

Although the majority of the 9-ending subjects underestimated the cents digits of the price, the mean extent of this underestimation was only 35 cents. It is easy to see how this small difference would be overwhelmed by the small number of larger recall errors which were made and thus fail to substantially affect the mean recalled prices.

Analysis of the overestimation errors must remain very limited, since only five such errors were made. Four of these five overestimation errors occurred to the $119.99/$120.00 prices. Two subjects recalled $120.00 as $129.00, one subject recalled $120.00 as $150.00, and one subject recalled $119.99 as $199.00. The fifth overestimation error consisted of $50.00 being recalled as $50.98. Note that the extreme leftmost digit was recalled correctly in each case, and that it appears that the digit 9 occurs more often than chance would predict in the recall errors for the rightmost digits.

Discussion

This study failed to support the prediction of the underestimation hypothesis that there would be substantially greater underestimation of 9-ending prices than there would be for the equivalent 0-ending prices. However, the pattern of errors, overestimation errors as well as underestimation errors, does offer a bit of support for the underestimation hypothesis. This pattern of errors indicates that the leftmost digits of the prices were recalled more accurately than the rightmost digits. This is consistent with the possibility that consumer perceptual processes give more attention to the leftmost digits of a price.

STUDY 2

The results of Study 1 may have been influenced by the artificiality of the experimental situation. The subjects were not actually shopping for the items pictured in the ads, and were aware that they were participating in a consumer behavior study as they examined the advertisements.

Study 2 was an attempt to remedy these problems by investigating immediate recall of prices in a field setting. As has been done with past research (e.g., Conover 1986; Dickson and Sawyer 1990), a grocery shopping situation was found to be an appropriate and convenient setting. Supermarket shoppers were stopped as they were leaving the store and asked the prices of some of the items they had just purchased. The underestimation hypothesis would predict greater underestimation of those items whose prices ended in the digit 9 than those items whose prices did not end in the digit 9.

Method

Design and materials. The study focused on the recall of prices in twelve categories of grocery products (coffee, milk, eggs, flour, canned tuna, margarine, sugar, jelly, apple juice, trash bags, toilet paper, and dish detergent). The twelve categories selected were commonly purchased and contained a mix of 9-ending and non-9-ending prices at the time of the study (since very few supermarket prices ended in the digit 0, all prices ending in the digits 0-8 were grouped together to form the alternative to 9-ending pricing). Several large signs listing each of these twelve product categories were prepared.

Sample. The respondents were shoppers of a major supermarket chain in a large metropolitan area. They were selected at random from shoppers leaving the store. Shoppers were sampled at eight different outlets of the chain on seventeen separate occasions. These occasions included daytime, evening, and weekend time periods.

A total of 1511 recalled prices were obtained. The vast majority of the respondents provided data on only three or fewer items. However, due to an error, the number of prices recalled per respondent was not systematically recorded. Thus, for the purposes of statistical analysis, it was necessary to assume that the 1511 recalled prices approximated independent observations. It was judged that such an approximation would not interact meaningfully with the hypotheses of the study.

Procedure. The interviewer approached shoppers leaving the store and asked if they had purchased any of the products listed on the sign. If so, they were asked if they would be willing to answer a few brief questions about these purchases. Approximately two-thirds of the eligible shoppers who were approached agreed to participate.

Each respondent was asked to recall the exact price of the items which he or she had purchased which were among the product categories listed on the sign. When the recalled prices had been recorded by the interviewer, the respondent was asked to find the actual item purchased in the shopping bag so that the brand and size could be recorded by the interviewer and so the actual price of the item could be determined.

The respondents were first exposed to the prices of the grocery items by the shelf tags. They were again exposed to the prices when they appeared on the checkout screen as the items were scanned. Most interviews occurred within four minutes of this second exposure.

Results

The mean actual and recalled prices for the 9-ending prices and the non-9-ending prices can be seen in Table 3. T-tests showed no significant difference in recall between the 9- and non-9-ending

TABLE 3
Mean Actual and Recalled Prices in Study 2

	9-ending prices	Non-9-ending prices
Mean Actual Price	1.45	1.09
Mean Recalled Price	1.46	1.09
Difference (Recalled-Actual)	.01	.00

TABLE 4
Distribution of Recalled Prices for 9- and Non-9-Ending Prices

Category of recalled price	Percentage of recalled prices in each category	
	9-ending prices (n = 921)	Non-9-ending prices (n = 590)
Overestimate by $1.00 or more	0.9	0.0
Overestimate by $.01 - $.99	14.1	28.5
Exactly correct	66.6	53.6
Underestimate by $.01 - $.99	18.0	17.5
Underestimate by $1.00 or more	0.4	0.5

prices whether recalled-actual differences (t[1509] < 1) or percent recalled-actual differences (t[1509] < 1) were used.

The pattern of recall errors of the 9- and non-9-ending prices can be seen in Table 4. There was no significantly greater tendency to produce an underestimate for 9- than for non-9-ending prices ($X^2[1] < 1$) in this immediate recall task. The percentage of recall underestimates for the 9-ending prices (18.4%) *was* higher than the percentage of recall underestimates for the forty-seven 0-ending prices which occurred in the data (12.8%). However, because of the small number of 0-ending prices, this difference was not statistically significant ($X^2[1] < 1$).

Although there were no significant differences between the likelihood of underestimating 9- and non-9-ending prices, there was a greater likelihood of producing an *over*estimate in the recall of non-9-ending prices than in the recall of 9-ending prices ($X^2[1] = 40.5, p < .001$). Further examination of this difference showed it to be due entirely to a greater likelihood of overestimates of 9 cents or less (2.3% of all 9-ending recalls vs. 19.2% of all non-9-ending recalls). In fact, most (74%) of these incremental overestimations were due to the subjects recalling the extreme rightmost digit of the non-9-ending prices as the digit 9 rather than as one of the digits 0 through 8. It is the small average size of these incremental overestimations (4.3 cents) which led them to be overwhelmed by the small number of much larger errors and thus fail to substantially affect the mean recalled price.

Discussion

The results of Study 2 agree with those of Study 1 in that they provide no evidence that 9-ending prices are substantially underestimated in an immediate recall task. These results also agree with those of Study 1 in the finding of a nonrandom pattern of recall errors. However, the nature of the nonrandom pattern of errors differs between the two studies. In Study 1, the differences between 9- and 0-ending prices concerned the proportion of underestimates. In Study 2, the differences between 9- and non-9-ending prices concerned the proportion of overestimates.

There are numerous differences between the two studies which may have contributed to these differences in the distribution of recall errors. It is likely that the small proportion of 0-ending prices in the Study 2 data and the nonexistence of prices ending in the digits 1 through 8 in Study 1 strongly influenced the overall error distribution. It is also possible that the greater length of the prices in Study 1 than in Study 2 (4-5 digits vs. 2-3 digits) may have played a role in the large proportion of recall underestimates to the 9-ending prices of Study 1. The longer prices may have increased the subjects' motivation to minimize effort and give less consideration to the rightmost digits.

The use of a natural situation in Study 2 may also have affected the results. Unlike the participants in an artificial experimental situation, the respondents of Study 2 were able to draw on general knowledge that most prices of supermarket items do in fact end in the digit 9. This knowledge creates an expectation of 9-ending prices which is capable of serving as a source of bias in the recall task (Helgeson and Beatty 1987).

Although the pattern of recall errors differed between the two studies, in both studies the vast majority of errors involved only the rightmost two digits. In this respect, the results of both studies are consistent with the presumption of the underestimation hypothesis that the rightmost digits receive less consumer attention.

GENERAL DISCUSSION

Both of the two studies reported here failed to show any substantial underestimation of 9-ending prices in an immediate recall task. Although a study employing a much larger sample size than that used in the present studies would certainly be more sensitive to very small differences in mean recall level, there is no reason to believe that such a larger study would find differences larger in extent than those, insignificant from a practical standpoint, found in the present studies.

This result contradicts at least a simple form of the underestimation hypothesis, that price perception invariably involves perceiving rightmost 9's as 0's or other low-value digits. It also suggests that the recall underestimation found in Schindler and Wiman's (1989) delayed recall task may have been due more to processes of memory than perception. For example, the consumer's memory trace of the rightmost digits of a price may tend to fade more rapidly than the memory trace of a price's leftmost digits.

It is interesting that, in both studies, the overestimation errors provided evidence for a bias toward recalling the digit 9 for the rightmost digits. This bias was most apparent in Study 2, where the presence of a meaningful context was able to clearly guide consumer expectations. Although such a bias may affect only how the consumer generates a response for an unrecallable digit during the retrieval process (Bettman 1979), it also raises the possibility that the perceptual default value of an unencoded digit may not always be 0 or some other low number. In other words, under some circumstances, prices which do not end in the digit 9 may be perceived as if they did, and thus be overestimated. In either event, the apparent sensitivity of recall to the context of the price information highlights the importance of taking contextual variables into account in research on price-ending effects.

Even though these two studies were consistent in their failure to find substantial underestimation of 9-ending prices, there is an important reason why they should not be used as grounds for a general rejection of the underestimation hypothesis. Both studies provided evidence that consumers give less attention to the rightmost digits of a price. The preponderance of small underestimates of 9-ending prices in Study 1 and the large number of small overestimates of non-9-ending prices in Study 2 both indicate this. These errors derive from biases in the processes used to estimate values of the rightmost digits. But note that it is these digits which are usually the ones which need to be estimated. The leftmost digits are usually recalled correctly.

Conclusions and Directions for Future Research

Although these studies both failed to show any substantial difference between 9-ending prices and non-9-ending prices in level of recalled price, they both do provide evidence for the mechanism which is thought to be behind the hypothesized underestimation effect. This suggests that future research on the underestimation hypothesis should focus on this mechanism, the tendency to give less attention to the rightmost digits of a price.

One approach to further study of this attentional mechanism would be to conduct studies under conditions where this effect would be expected to be greatest. In both of the studies reported here, consumers were tested under conditions where they were likely to have given the price at hand their full attention. In Study 1, they knew they were in an experiment, and in Study 2, they had just selected and purchased the items which were being tested. It is possible that the conditions of these studies allowed the subjects to devote so much attention to the prices that the effects of the tendency to give less attention to the rightmost digits were largely swamped by the generous amount of attention available. Perhaps a substantial underestimation effect would be found only under conditions where the total amount of attention the consumer expends on a price is very limited. Although several studies of price ending effects have attempted to create such limited attention situations (Lambert 1975; Alpert et al. 1981; Schindler and Warren 1988), only the Schindler and Warren study produced consistent evidence for a price-ending effect under these conditions.

Another approach to the study of this mechanism would be to apply new methods to measure the effects of differences in the amount of attention consumers give to the digits of a price. For example, it may be the case that the consumer's perception of a price may not occur instantaneously, but rather may develop in stages over a brief, but measurable time period (e.g., Posner and Mitchell 1967). The earliest stages of this perceptual process may provide a preliminary impression of the price in which the rightmost digits are ignored. While this fleeting impression may usually be elaborated and corrected by the later stages of perception, it may exert an enduring "first-impression effect" on the consumer's evaluation of the price.

The results of the two immediate recall studies reported here do constitute evidence against a simple form of the underestimation hypothesis. But they also provide some support for the mechanism thought to underlie the hypothesis. Thus, these results should not be used to reject the underestimation hypothesis. Rather they should serve to direct further research toward the formulation and investigation of more sophisticated versions of this plausible and interesting mechanism which may lie behind the effects of "psychological pricing."

REFERENCES

Alpert, Mark I., John E. McGrath, and Judy I. Alpert (1984), "Magic Prices: An Extension," in *Proceedings and Abstracts of the Thirteenth Annual Meeting of the Western Regional Conference*, American Institute for Decision Sciences.

Bettman, James R. (1979), "Memory Factors in Consumer Choice: A Review," *Journal of Marketing*, 43 (Spring), 37-53.

Conover, Jerry N. (1986), "The Accuracy of Price Knowledge: Issues in Research Methodology," in *Advances in Consumer Research*, Vol. 13, ed. Richard J. Lutz, Ann Arbor, MI: Association for Consumer Research, 589-93.

Dickson, Peter R., and Alan G. Sawyer (1990), "The Price Knowledge and Search of Supermarket Shoppers," *Journal of Marketing*, 54 (July), 42-53.

Friedman, Lawrence (1967), "Psychological Pricing in the Food Industry," in *Prices: Issues in Theory, Practice, and Public Policy*, eds. Almarin Phillips and Oliver E. Williamson, Philadelphia: University of Pennsylvania Press, 187-201.

Georgoff, David M. (1972), *Odd-Even Retail Price Endings*, East Lansing, MI: Michigan State University.

Helgeson, James G. and Sharon E. Beatty (1987), "Price Expectations and Price Recall Error: An Empirical Study," *Journal of Consumer Research*, 14 (December), 379-386.

Kreul, Lee M. (1982), "Magic Numbers: Psychological Aspects of Menu Pricing," *The Cornell Hotel and Restaurant Administration Quarterly*, 23, (August), 70-75.

Lambert, Zarrel V. (1975), "Perceived Prices as Related to Odd and Even Price Endings," *Journal of Retailing*, 51 (Fall), 13-22, 78.

Mason, J. Barry and Morris L. Mayer (1990), *Modern Retailing: Theory and Practice*, 5th edition, Homewood, IL: BPI/Irwin.

Ostlund, Lyman E. (1978), "Advertising Copy Testing: A Review of Current Practices, Problems and Prospects," *Current Issues and Research in Advertising*, 87-105.

Posner, Michael I. and R. F. Mitchell (1967), "A Chronometric Analysis of Classification," *Psychological Review*, 74, 392-409.

Schindler, Robert M. (1991), "Symbolic Meanings of a Price Ending," in *Advances in Consumer Research*, Vol. 18, eds. Rebecca H. Holman and Michael R. Solomon, Provo UT: Association for Consumer Research, 794-801.

_____ and Lori S. Warren (1988), "Effect of Odd Pricing on Choice of Items from a Menu," in *Advances in Consumer Research*, Vol. 15, ed. Michael J. Houston, Provo, UT: Association for Consumer Research, 348-353.

_____ and Alan R. Wiman (1989), "Effect of Odd Pricing on Price Recall," *Journal of Business Research*, 19 (November), 165-177.

Simon, Hermann (1989), *Price Management*, Amsterdam, The Netherlands: Elsevier Science Publishers.

Twedt, Dik W. (1965), "Does the '9 Fixation' in Retail Pricing Really Promote Sales?," *Journal of Marketing*, 29 (October), 54-55.

Effects of Prior Belief on Feature-Based Price Estimates

Tridib Mazumdar, Syracuse University
Cheoul Ryon Kim, Syracuse University

ABSTRACT

When advertising models in a product line, sellers sometimes describe the model features but do not provide the specific price of each model. This article examines how buyers, in such situations, estimate the price of an *individual* model based on the features it offers. We find that price estimates depend on the features offered as well as on buyer characteristics. Specifically, we find that buyers who strongly believe that quality and price are positively related in the product category, provide higher price estimates of the models than those who are less encumbered by this belief. The study also finds that the difficulty in assessing the importance of the features lowers the price estimates. Implications of these findings are discussed.

INTRODUCTION

Stores sometimes advertise the attributes or features of several models of a product line but do not provide specific price information for each model. For example, consumer electronics stores may advertise several models of VCR with different features and indicate that prices range from $200 to $500. Real-estate firms may advertise "Homes from $150,000" and then provide descriptions (or pictures) of the models (e.g., number of bedrooms, wooded lot, cul-de-sac etc.). While these types of price ads are being used by retailers, it is unclear whether these practices are more effective than providing buyers with specific price information.

When specific price of a model (e.g., a preferred model) is unknown, buyers may either initiate external search for the price information or they may try to estimate its price *based on the feature descriptions* provided in the ad. These estimates may have important consequences for buyers' subsequent store patronage as well as their choice decisions. For example, if the price estimate of an otherwise preferred model exceeds the acceptable price limit, buyers may exclude the brand from their consideration set and decide not to visit the store at all. Also, if buyers decide to actually visit the store, the initial price estimate may serve as a reference point for judging the actual purchase price. Clearly, the price judgment and choice decision of the buyer will depend upon whether the actual price compares favorably or unfavorably with their original estimate (Winer 1986).

The objective of this article is to report the results of an *exploratory study* that examines how feature-based price estimates are influenced by: (1) the degree to which buyers believe that there is a positive association between quality and price in the product category (hereafter referred to as either "prior belief" or simply "belief") and (2) the difficulty experienced by buyers in assessing the importance (or usefulness) of the features offered by different models. Conceptual arguments leading to specific hypotheses are presented next. We then discuss the procedures and results to test the hypotheses. Finally, we discuss the managerial implications of the findings and highlight the limitations of the study.

CONCEPTUAL BACKGROUND

Prior Belief

Buyers, through a variety of direct or indirect experiences, detect relationships among marketing phenomena. When reinforced, these associations develop into beliefs such as, Japanese cars are more reliable than domestic cars, convenience stores are more expensive than supermarkets, specialty outlets carry better quality products than discounters, higher-priced brands are of better quality than lower-priced brands. Beliefs such as these are considered efficient ways for consumers to organize past experiences in memory (Crocker 1981; Alloy and Tabachnik 1984) and use them for subsequent evaluation and categorization of stores and merchandise (Peterson and Wilson 1985; Zeithaml 1988). However, strongly held beliefs, once formed, are often resistant to changes even in the face of conflicting evidence, resulting in biased consumer judgments (Bettman, John, and Scott 1986) and search behavior (John, Scott, and Bettman 1986).

In this paper we focus on one such belief that involves a positive association between product price and quality. Considerable research has been done to examine the validity of a positive price-perceived quality relationship (Monroe and Krishnan 1985; Zeithaml 1988; Rao and Monroe 1989). From a normative standpoint, this relationship is considered natural because products with superior performance may require deployment of greater resources and therefore, firms should receive higher prices to recover additional costs (Scitovsky 1945; Lancaster 1966; Ratchford 1975). However, several studies have shown that product prices are not always ordered according to their "objective" (e.g., *Consumer Reports*) qualities, causing the price-"objective" quality relationship to vary in its strength as well as direction across product class (Oxenfeldt 1950; Morris and Bronson 1969; Riesz 1978; 1979; Geistfeld 1982; Gerstner 1985; Tellis and Wernerfelt 1987; Kamakura, Ratchford, and Agrawal 1988). Evidence also suggests that buyers' reliance on price for judging product quality depends on whether or not there is a positive relationship between price and "objective" quality (Lichtenstein and Burton 1989). In summary, buyers may be "aschematic" or "schematic" (Peterson and Wilson 1985 p. 263), depending upon whether the quality-price schema in buyers' memory is weak or strong respectively in a given evaluative context.

That the strength of belief about a positive quality-price relationship varies implies that the price estimate of a given model based on the features it offers may also vary as a result[1]. That is, when estimating price of the model, buyers not only take into account the feature information, but their prior belief also plays an important role in the estimation process (Chapman and Chapman 1967; Jennings, Amabile, and Ross 1980). Researchers have shown that buyers who strongly believe that price and product quality is positively related have a higher level of acceptable prices than those who do not believe that such a relationship exists (Lichtenstein,

---

[1] Product quality is a multidimensional construct (Zeithaml 1988). Buyers may define quality on abstract dimension such as durability, reliability, trouble-free performance, or superior workmanship. However, in many product categories, the basic or the core product is the same across models or brands, but additional features discriminate higher quality models from lower quality ones. In this paper, we examine the latter situation where buyers equate product quality with intrinsic attributes or features offered by a given model or brand. These types of situation have been identified in past research (e.g. Alba and Marmorstein 1987; Zeithaml 1988).

Bloch, and Black 1988). Extending this finding to the current context suggests that when a model contains a number of features, a strong belief may lead buyers to infer that the model should also cost more. In contrast, buyers who are relatively unencumbered by this belief may consider only the objective feature information and weigh these features according to their relative importance weights to arrive at a price estimate. Thus, given a set of feature descriptions of several models, a strong belief about a positive quality-price association may serve to raise the price estimates of the models. The following hypothesis is therefore proposed:

H1: Given a set of feature descriptions of several models, the stronger the belief about a positive quality-price association in the product category, the higher will be the price estimates for the models.

Difficulty in Assessing Feature Usefulness

When advertising models of a product, retailers often provide a rather long list of features each model contains, and buyers may experience difficulty in assessing the usefulness of these features. Researchers have noted that buyers experience uncertainty not only about the existence of certain features in a given brand, but also about the importance of these features (Urbany, Dickson, and Wilkie 1989). Inability to assess the importance of features may be caused by buyers' lack of familiarity with the product class or because they do not possess the necessary knowledge to determine what functions the features perform (Brucks 1985; Alba and Hutchinson 1987). Even in instances where buyers are capable of comprehending the functional property of a feature, they may still experience uncertainty about its importance because they are unable to forecast accurately when and how frequently they will use these features (Kahn and Meyer 1991).

Kahn and Meyer (1991) show that buyers perceive greater value for an extra feature offered in a product when there is less uncertainty surrounding the importance weight they should assign to the feature. In light of this evidence, we may argue that buyers who can predict the usefulness of the features offered in a model may estimate a higher price for the features than buyers who experience difficulty in assessing the utilities of the features. We propose the following hypothesis:

H2: The more difficulty buyers experience in predicting the usefulness of the features contained in a model, the lower will be the estimated price of the model, *ceteris paribus*.

Interactive Effects

The relative difficulty experienced by buyers in predicting the usefulness of the features may also mediate the effect of buyers' prior belief about a quality-price relationship on their price estimates (proposed in H1). Buyers who can not discriminate the important features from the unimportant ones may assign equal weights to each feature (Park 1976) and simply count the number of features to make an assessment of the overall value of a product (Brucks 1985; Alba and Marmorstein 1987). Less knowledgeable buyers may also rely on extrinsic cues (i.e., cues not related to the physical product itself) such as, brand name or product price to evaluate product quality (Park and Lessig 1981; Rao and Monroe 1988). Similarly, when buyers try to estimate prices of different models based on the features these models offer but are relatively uncertain about the potential usefulness of the features, they are more likely to invoke their belief about the quality-price relationship than buyers who are more able to assess the importance of the features.

H3: The greater the difficulty in assessing the usefulness of the features offered by a model, the stronger will be the positive effect of prior belief on buyers' price estimates (proposed in H1).

RESEARCH METHOD

Stimulus

As noted earlier, buyers may evaluate a model from the physical features as well as on dimensions such as durability, reliability, and workmanship, which are not readily observable. Since the effects of unobservable dimensions on price estimates of study participants are difficult to control and assess, we decided to use a product class where product quality could be judged on the basis of the presence or absence of features (see also footnote).

The product chosen was "electric iron." Informal discussions with salespersons of several appliance stores revealed that all models of electric irons perform the same basic functions, but the quality and price levels of the models vary because of the additional features each model offers. From the catalog of a local merchandiser, we picked eleven models and described them on six features using a matrix format. The number of features in each model ranged from one to six (see Table 1). To eliminate the brand name effect, the real brand names were concealed and the models were placed in the rows in random order (with identifications A through K). The six features namely, temperature light (TEMP), auto shut-off (AUTO), self-clean (CLEAN), extra steam spray (STEAM), non-stick coating (NOSTICK), and water window (WW), were presented in the column, again in random order. The cells provided the feature values (present or absent). Many store catalogs use this format to present feature information of different brands or models, thus making our stimulus presentation format ecologically valid.

Study Participants

Eighty undergraduate students (40 males and 40 females) enrolled in two sections of introductory marketing management course were selected for the study. The participants were told that the study was aimed at assisting a local appliance store in setting prices of different models of irons.

Measures of Independent Variables

Quality-Price Belief. Following the procedure used by previous researchers (e.g., Bettman et. al. 1986; John et. al. 1986), participants' belief concerning a positive quality-price relationship was measured rather than manipulated. On a seven point scale, participants responded to what extent they agreed that "the better the quality of an electric iron, the higher will be its price".

Difficulty in Assessing Feature Usefulness. Participants were told that the models of electric irons available in the local store may contain one or more of the six features described earlier. They were then asked to rate on a seven point scale the difficulty they would experience in predicting the usefulness of these features, relative to that experienced by the average student population (significantly lower - significantly greater). This type of self-perceived relative knowledge measure has also been used in past research (e.g., Brucks 1985).

Quality Ratings and Price Estimation Tasks

The participants then received the stimulus information and were asked to provide quality ratings for each model using a 0-10 point ["substantially below average quality(0) - substantially above average quality (10)"] scale. They were free to use any criteria for making quality judgments. This quality measure was needed to

TABLE 1
Mean Quality Ratings and Estimated Prices[a]

Model ID[b]	Features[c]	Quality Ratings	Estimated Prices($)[d]
J	TEMP	1.85 (1.29)	13.10 (2.75)
I	CLEAN	2.43 (1.42)	14.85 (3.98)
K	AUTO, WW	3.86 (1.42)	18.41 (4.22)
F	AUTO, STEAM	4.24 (1.62)	18.91 (4.61)
D	CLEAN, WW	3.79 (1.37)	19.21 (5.52)
E	TEMP, WW, NOSTICK	4.95 (1.46)	21.73 (4.91)
H	TEMP, WW, CLEAN	5.31 (1.23)	23.18 (5.55)
A	AUTO, CLEAN, NOSTICK, WW	7.36 (1.48)	28.81 (5.73)
B	TEMP, AUTO, STEAM, WW	7.09 (1.60)	29.00 (5.04)
G	TEMP, AUTO, CLEAN, STEAM, NOSTICK	8.78 (0.83)	34.14 (4.56)
C	TEMP, AUTO, CLEAN, STEAM, NOSTICK, WW	9.79 (0.63)	38.28 (4.34)

a Figures in parentheses are respective standard deviations.
b Models are presented in ascending order of estimated prices.
c TEMP=temperature light, AUTO=auto shut-off, CLEAN=self clean, STEAM=extra steam spray, NOSTICK=nonstick coating, WW=water window.
d The correlation between the number of features and mean estimated price is 0.86 (p<0.0001).

ascertain if the participants indeed perceived the brands with many features as better quality models than those with fewer features.

After rating the qualities, the participants were told that prices of the eleven models range from $13 to $39 in the local store but the prices of individual models are unknown. The participants were then asked to provide an estimate of the actual price that they would be expected to pay in the store for each of the models. They were then asked to conjecture what the true purpose of the study was. None related the price estimation with quality-price belief or perceived feature usefulness issues. They were then debriefed and thanked for their participation.

ANALYSIS AND RESULTS

The number and types of features offered by each of the eleven models and the respective mean quality ratings and the price estimates are presented in Table 1. Model J and I, each with one feature, obtained the lowest quality ratings. At the high end, Model C contained all the features and Model G had five features. These two models were judged the best and the second best quality models. A high correlation of 0.86 (p<0.0001) between the number of features and the overall quality rating ensured that as intended, the participants did use the provided feature information to infer the quality of respective models.

Tests of Hypotheses

The belief about a positive quality-price association (H1) and the difficulty in assessing the usefulness of the features (H2) were respectively hypothesized to be positively and negatively related with buyers' price estimates based on feature information. It was also postulated (H3) that greater difficulty in assessing the feature usefulness would enhance the effect of quality-price belief on buyers' price estimates. Thus, a positive interaction effect between difficulty in assess feature usefulness and prior belief is expected. To test these hypotheses, the following regression model was tested:

$$PRICE_j = f(BELIEF, DIFF, BELIEF \times DIFF, \sum_{j=1}^{11} DUM_j) \quad (1)$$

$PRICE_j$ = the estimated price for model j, j=1,2,..... 11;
BELIEF = respondents' self-reported belief scores (1-7),
DIFF = respondents' self-reported relative difficulty in assessing feature usefulness (1-7),
DUM_j = model-specific dummies taking values of 1 if model=j and 0 otherwise.

Note that the structure of the model is similar to that of Analysis of Covariance, where the dummies represent the discrete levels. The coefficients of the dummies reflect the effects of the *feature combinations* contained in the models on the price estimates. The coefficients associated with BELIEF, DIFF, and the interaction term will capture the incremental effects of the respective variables and the interaction term on the price estimates for all the eleven models combined.

The parameter estimates and the corresponding t-statistics are reported in Table 2. Since the model dummies are ordered according to increasing price estimates, all dummy coefficients are posi-

TABLE 2
Regression Results

Variable	Coefficient	t^b
Intercept[a]	8.36	4.56***
DUM1 (Model I)	1.75	2.36**
DUM2 (Model K)	5.31	7.16***
DUM3 (Model F)	5.81	7.83***
DUM4 (Model D)	6.11	8.23***
DUM5 (Model E)	8.62	11.62***
DUM6 (Model H)	10.07	13.57***
DUM7 (Model A)	15.71	21.16***
DUM8 (Model B)	15.90	21.42***
DUM9 (Model G)	21.05	28.26***
DUM10 (Model C)	25.19	33.82***
BELIEF	**1.01**	**2.68***
DIFF	**-0.71**	**-1.66***
BELIEF x DIFF	**0.15**	**1.58**

NOTE.- Dependent variable is estimated price.
[a] Base for dummy variables is Model J.
[b] Error d.f.= 864 (there were 2 missing observations).
*** $p<.01$
** $p<.05$
* $p<.10$

tive. An adjusted R^2 of 0.73 indicates a good overall fit of the model. In addition, the coefficient for the BELIEF variable is positive and significant, supporting H1. The DIFF coefficient is in the hypothesized direction (i.e., negative) but is significant only at $p<0.10$, providing a moderate support for H2. Finally, as predicted we have a positive BELIEF x DIFF interaction, but the effect is not significant at the conventional level.

SUMMARY AND DISCUSSION

Buyers' price estimates of a model are found to be a function of the features it offers, weighted by the perceived importance of the features[2]. The price estimates are also found to be influenced by two characteristics of the buyers, namely (1) their belief concerning a positive quality-price relationship in the product category and, (2) the relative difficulty they experience in assessing the usefulness of different features.

First, the study finds that a strongly held belief about a positive quality-price relationship serves to increase buyers' price estimates of a given model. This finding has important implications in managerial decisions involving whether to provide potential buyers a price range or specific prices for models being advertised. Past research indicate that the belief about a positive quality-price relationship vary across product classes (e.g., durable versus nondurables) (Zeithaml 1988; Lichtenstein and Burton 1989). In product categories where the belief is strong, our result suggests that buyers' price estimates of a model based on its feature may be biased upwards. Since these estimates may serve as reference points for buyers' future price judgments, firms may capitalize on this bias by advertising models in these product categories by presenting feature descriptions and a price range rather than specific prices. However, it may be important to note that based on a strong quality-price belief, buyers may estimate prices of certain models that exceed their upper thresholds of acceptable prices. Buyers, in such situations, may judge the brands as "too expensive" and decide not to visit the store (Monroe and Petroshius 1981).

The second finding of our study is that buyers' price estimate of a model based on its feature(s) is negatively related to the difficulty in assessing the usefulness of these features. This finding implies that in instances where the advertised brands or models belong to a new product class and where the benefits of the features are unclear and ambiguous to potential buyers, the price estimates based on feature descriptions are likely to be biased downwards. In such cases, firms may wish to advertise specific prices of each model, which will eliminate the need for estimating prices of models based on feature information. Alternatively, firms could try to provide clear explanations about the benefits of the features and help potential buyers visualize the occasions and frequency of using these features.

Limitations and Future Research Directions

As noted in the beginning of this article, the research reported here was carried out as an exploratory research. There are several

---

[2] To assess the importance weights of the respective features, an analysis of variance was performed with price estimate only as a function of the features, each with two levels (present or absent). The t-values for each feature are statistically significant ($p<0.0001$). The respective t-values in increasing order are: STEAM=8.29, AUTO=8.73, NOSTICK=9.46, TEMP=9.70, WW=11.83, CLEAN=16.24.

ways the research can be improved. From a theoretical standpoint, since the price estimation is used as a judgment task, the research needs to incorporate the preference reversal and anchoring and adjustment literature to provide a stronger theoretical foundation and propose additional hypotheses. From a methodological perspective, there is a clear need for using multiple and reliable measures of quality-price belief and difficulty in assessing feature importance so that the study results can be unambiguously interpreted. We also did not rotate the orders across subjects when presenting the model descriptions. This may have resulted in anchoring and adjustment biases in subjects' price estimates. Finally, we realize in retrospect that the product class used here (i.e., iron) may not have been relevant for student subjects. To improve the generalizability of the findings, the study must be replicated using other product categories.

REFERENCE

Alba, Joseph W. and J. Wesley Hutchinson (1987), "Dimensions of Consumer Expertise," *Journal of Consumer Research*, 13, 411-454.

_____ and Howard Marmorstein (1987), "The Effects of Frequency Knowledge on Consumer Decision Making," *Journal of Consumer Research*, 5, 14 (June).

Alloy, Lauren B. and Naomi Tabachnik (1984), "Assessment of Covariation by Humans and Animals: The Joint Influence of Prior Expectations and Current Situational Information," *Psychological Review*, 91(January), 112-149.

Bettman, James R., Deborah Roedder John, and Carol A. Scott (1986), "Covariation Assessment by Consumers," *Journal of Consumer Research*, 13 (December), 316-326.

Brucks, Merrie (1985), "The Effects of Product Class Knowledge on Information Search Behavior," *Journal of Consumer Research*, 12, 1-16.

Chapman, Loren J. and Jean P. Chapman (1967), "Genesis of Popular but Erroneous Psychodiagnostic Predictions," *Journal of Abnormal Psychology*, 72(3), 193-204.

Crocker, Jennifer (1981), "Judgment of Covariation by Social Perceivers," *Psychological Bulletin*, 90 (September), 272-292.

Geistfeld, Loren V. (1982), "The Price-Quality Relationship - Revisited," *Journal of Consumer Affairs*, 16(Winter), 334-335.

Gerstner, Eitan (1985), "Do Higher Prices Signal Higher Quality?," *Journal of Marketing Research*, 22, 209-215.

Jennings, Dennis L., Teresa M. Amabile, and Lee Ross (1980), "Informal Covariation Assessment: Data-based versus Theory-based Judgments," in *Judgment Under Uncertainty: Heuristics and Biases*, eds. Daniel Kahneman, Paul Slovic, and Amos Tversky, Cambridge, England: Cambridge University Press, 211-230.

John, Deborah Roedder, Carol A. Scott, and James R. Bettman (1986), "Sampling Data for Covariation Assessment: The Effect of Prior Beliefs on Search Patterns," *Journal of Consumer Research*, 13 (June), 38-47.

Kamakura, Wagner A., Brian T. Ratchford, and Jagdish Agrawal (1988), "Measuring Market Efficiency and Welfare Loss," *Journal of Consumer Research*, 15 (December), 289-302.

Kahn, Barbara E. and Robert J. Meyer (1991), "Consumer Multiattribute Judgments under Attribute-Weight Uncertainty, *Journal of Consumer Research*, 17 (March), 508-522.

Lancaster, Kelvin J. (1966), "A New Approach to Consumer Theory," *Journal of Political Economy*, 74(April), 132-157.

Lichtenstein, Donald R. and Scot Burton (1989), "The Relationship Between Perceived and Objective Price-Quality," *Journal of Marketing Research*, 26, 429-443.

_____, Bloch, Peter H., and William C. Black (1988), "Correlates of Price Acceptability," *Journal of Consumer Research*, 15, 2(September), 243-252.

Monroe, Kent B. and R. Krishnan (1985), "The Effect of Price on Subjective Product Evaluations," in *Perceived Quality*, J. Jacoby and J. Olson, eds. Lexington, MA: Lexington Books, 209-232.

_____ and S. Petroshius (1981), "Buyers' Perceptions of Prices: An Update of the Evidence," in T. Robertson and H. Kassarjian (eds.), *Perspectives in Consumer Behavior*, 3rd ed. Glenview, Il.: Scott Foresman, 23-42.

Morris, Ruby T. and Claire S. Bronson (1969), "The Chaos in Competition Indicated by Consumer Reports," *Journal of Marketing*, 34, 103-112.

Oxenfeldt, Alfred N.R. (1950), "Consumer Knowledge: Its Measurement and Extent," *Review of Economics and Statistics*, 32, 300-314.

Park, C. Whan (1976), "The Effect of Individual and Situation Related Factors on Consumer Selection of Judgment Methods," *Journal of Marketing Research*, 13 (May), 144-151.

_____ and V. Parker Lessig (1981), "Familiarity and Its Impact on Consumer Biases and Heuristics," *Journal of Consumer Research*, 8 (September), 223-230.

Peterson, Robert A. and William R. Wilson (1985), "Perceived Risk and Price-Reliance Schema and Price-Perceived-Quality Mediators," in *Perceived Quality*, J. Jacoby and J. Olson, eds. Lexington, MA: Lexington Books, 247-268.

Rao, Akshay R. and Kent B. Monroe (1988), "The Moderating Effect of Prior Knowledge on Cue Utilization in Product Evaluations," *Journal of Consumer Research*, 15(2), 253-264.

_____ and _____ (1989), "The Effect of Price, Brand Name, and Store Name on Buyers' Perceptions of Product Quality: An Integrative Review," *Journal of Marketing Research*, 26 (August), 351-357.

Ratchford, Brian T. (1975), "The New Economic Theory of Consumer Behavior: An Interpretive Essay," *Journal of Consumer Research*, 2, 65-75.

Riesz, Peter C. (1978), "Price Versus Quality in the Marketplace, 1961-1975," *Journal of Retailing*, 54(Winter), 15-28.

_____ (1979), "Price-Quality Correlations for Packaged Food Products," *Journal of Consumer Affairs*, 13(Winter), 236-247.

Scitovsky, T. (1945), "Some Consequences of the Habit of Judging Quality by Price," *Review of Economic Studies*, 12, 100-105.

Tellis, Gerard J. and Birger Wernerfelt (1987), "Competitive Price and Quality under Asymmetric Information," *Marketing Science*, 6 (Summer), 240-253.

Urbany, Joel E., Peter R. Dickson, and William L. Wilkie (1989), "Buyer Uncertainty and Information Search," *Journal of Consumer Research*, 16 (September), 208-215.

Winer, Russell (1986), "A Reference Price Model of Brand Choice for Frequently Purchased Products," *Journal of Consumer Research*, 13, 250-256.

Zeithaml, Valarie A. (1988), "Consumer Perceptions of Price, Quality, and Value: A Means-End Model and Synthesis of Evidence," *Journal of Marketing*, 52, 2-22.

Some Brand Loyalty and Pricing Issues in Consumer Research
Ved Prakash, Baltimore, Maryland

INTRODUCTION

The purpose of this paper is to discuss the issues raised by the three papers accepted by the Association for Consumer Research for presentation at the session 9:4 on "Brand Loyalty and Pricing Issues". The title of this session deals with two separate topics of brand loyalty and pricing. The two papers on pricing deal with two diverse issues, one dealing with the underestimation of 9-ending prices and the other dealing with the effects of prior beliefs on feature-based price estimates. This makes the task of developing a coherent discussion of the issues involved that much more difficult. However, the specific papers under discussion are as follows:

1) Barbara Olsen, "Brand Loyalty and Lineage: Exploring New Dimensions for Research".

2) Robert M. Schindler and Thomas Kibarian, "Testing for Perceptual Underestimation of 9-Ending Prices".

3) Tridib Mazumdar and Cheoul Ryon Kim, "Effects of Prior Belief on Feature-Based Price Estimates".

These three papers are discussed in the order of their presentation at the session.

OLSEN'S PAPER AND BRAND LOYALTY ISSUES

The purpose of Olsen's paper seems to be a study of brand loyalty through the process of intergenerational transference. The main feature of this paper is the methodology of ethnographic investigation, i.e., life history interviews with families including grandparents, parents and children. The main rationale provided for this methodology is that consumer socialization occurs primarily within family settings where brand names begin to achieve social significance. The author does a good job of drawing conceptual foundations from the consumer behavior literature (Bahn 1986; Belk, Wallendorf and Sherry 1989; McCracken 1990; Moschis 1985; Moschis, Moore and Smith 1984). These studies suggest the influence of family, environmental and religious forces on the process of family socialization and learning. This in turn influences knowledge about brands in early childhood that are subsequently repeated in adulthood. The author opines that brands learned in the family become either "bridges" in the intergenerational process (as products are carried forward from one generation to the next), or these brands become "fences" signifying rebellion against a social relationship.

The study was undertaken with the help of a class project where some 50 students provided usable ethnographies of product usage within their own families. The students interviewed their own parents and grandparents. The author presents a verbatim account of responses provided by families from various ethnic and nationality backgrounds in the United States. Some results from this qualitative ethnographic approach are quantified. For instance, toothpaste was cited in ten families and transferred from sixteen generations, i.e., ten times between mother-daughter, five times between mother-son, and once between grandmother-grandson. Some other products that emerged as "bridges" to indicate the existence of intergenerational transfer of brand loyalty were mayonnaise, bath soap, ketchup and automobiles. The main reason given for brand loyalty was the level of product satisfaction over a period of time. Some examples of advertisements emphasizing the intergenerational process provided by the author were: Vicks Vaporub, Roman Meal bread and Brooks Brothers men's clothiers.

While Olsen's paper has made a useful contribution in drawing our attention to the ethnographic approach in understanding brand loyalty, it has raised more issues than it has answered. I would like to make the following suggestions in an attempt at a better understanding of brand loyalty. First, it is very important to get a better grasp of brand loyalty from conceptual (definitional) and operational (measurement) points of view which have been completely ignored in Olsen's paper. Jacoby and Chestnut (1978) did a thorough job of exploring the various meanings of the construct of brand loyalty. Equally difficult is the measurement of brand loyalty from operational point of view. There is a lack of consensus in the literature on what precisely constitutes a brand loyal consumer. As cited in Jacoby and Chestnut (1978) some consumer researchers think that a consumer who purchases a specific brand 50% of the times or more within a certain given time span is brand loyal, some others think that this incidence of purchase should be 75% or more. The sequence of purchases of a given brand is also a pertinent consideration in determining brand loyalty. In the absence of a clearly laid out criteria of brand loyalty, ethnographic approach is not likely to shed any reliable information. Incidentally, Olsen has not provided any estimates of reliability and validity of ethnographic approach as applied to the data in this case.

Further, it would have been better for Olsen to provide a more detailed discussion of the ethnographic approach found in the literature. It would have been better to quantify the results provided on pages 12-13 of the paper. This is a fundamental problem encountered in the application of qualitative techniques to consumer research, i.e., in the absence of quantitative results the conclusions do not seem convincing.

The next issue concerns the intergenerational transfer of values. It is very important to study this model in the *overall* context of transmission of cultural values. In Olsen's paper there is no conceptual framework of the intergenerational transfer of values and its linkage with transfer of brands. It may be possible to establish this linkage with the help of such values as terminal and instrumental values suggested by Rokeach (1973). The model of family communication and effects on consumer socialization suggested by Moschis, Moore and Smith (1984) could also be a good framework for testing the transfer of brand loyalty from one generation to the next.

Some other issues raised by Olsen's paper are: a) whether brand loyalty is due to the level of satisfaction attained with product attributes or whether it is due to classical conditioning learning process of transference. There seems to be an inherent contradiction in these two explanations which future researchers may investigate; b) any satisfactory study of intergenerational transfer of brands would have to be a longitudinal one where a fixed group of consumers would have to be studied over several years during the various stages of the family life cycle somewhat on the lines of recent films on social class by Michael Apted titled, 7 and up, 14 and up, 21 and up, 28 and up and 35 and up (the latest film). This is going to be an enormously difficult task for consumer researchers to undertake.

PRICING ISSUES

Schindler and Kibarian's Paper

Schindler has previously published several papers on the subject of price endings (Schindler 1984, Schindler 1989, Schlindler 1991, Schindler and Warren 1988, Schindler and Wiman 1989). In Schindler (1991), he looked at the psychological meanings of various price endings and the causes of these meanings. In the present paper, Schindler and Kibarian propose to test whether 9-ending prices tend to be underestimated as compared to zero-ending prices. This is termed as the "underestimation hypothesis". This hypothesis was first tested in Study 1 with the help of an experimental design. This study was done with the help of 141 subjects who were exposed to several advertisements (ads) indicating prices with various endings, and then requiring the subjects to recall those prices. The products involved in the ads were: a dress, sports coat and patio furniture. The results of the study did not support the underestimation hypothesis.

Subsequently, these authors undertook a field study in Study 2. This involved recall of prices in 12 categories of grocery products (coffee, milk, eggs, flour, canned tuna, margarine, sugar, jelly, apple juice, trash bags, toilet paper, and dish detergent). Shoppers were sampled at eight different locations of a supermarket chain on seventeen separate occasions. A total of 1511 prices were obtained. The vast majority of respondents provided prices data on three or fewer items. Respondents were asked to recall prices displayed in the store. Once again, the results of the study showed that the 9-ending prices were not substantially underestimated as compared to non 9-ending prices. Schindler and Kibarian speculated that perhaps substantial underestimation would only occur in circumstances where a consumer expends limited amount of time on price. The authors recommend further improvisation of the hypothesis underlying psychological pricing and studying the plausible mechanism behind underestimation.

This study by Schindler and Kibarian seems to have been well conducted in most respects: literature review, testing, analysis of the results and recommendations for further research. I can only offer some speculative explanations about the lack of support for the underestimation hypothesis. It is possible that results were due to the artifact of testing. Subjects were asked to *recall* prices. Perhaps the technique of verbal protocols might have yielded different results. Dickson and Sawyer (1990) suggested that supermarket shoppers tend to spend only a short time in making the selection and consequently do not carefully check the prices of the items selected. In their study, more than half the subjects could not correctly name the prices of items just placed in the cart and more than half the consumers were unaware that prices had been reduced. Therefore Dickson and Sawyer recommended that reduced prices be prominently displayed in the store so that consumers become aware of these prices at the point of purchase. Consequently, in the Schindler and Kibarian study the technique of recall of prices might have been problematic in obtaining results in the predicted direction. A second explanation for the lack of support for the underestimation hypothesis might have been the low level of price sensitivity of the consumers especially with respect to the grocery products. Thirdly, it is possible that from the conceptual point of view consumers pay more attention to the leftmost prices (or to the dollar amounts) rather than to the rightmost prices (or the cent amounts). Therefore, even if the rightmost digits are 9-ending consumers do not perceive that to be substantially lower than zero-ending prices. Consequently, expectation of rightmost 9-ending prices being underestimated is an unrealistic one and underestimates the intelligence of the consumers. Perhaps, future research can be done on the comparison of 9-ending prices in the dollar amounts (or leftmost prices), with the 9-ending prices on the rightmost (or cents prices).

Two more related issues also need to be looked into by future researchers. If there is no empirical evidence for underestimation of rightmost 9-ending prices by consumers, why do marketers continue to practice them as a part of psychological pricing? Perhaps a survey of business executives on this matter may be useful. Secondly, it may be fruitful to do a comparative study of several psychological pricing tactics used by marketers (Nagle 1987).

Mazumdar and Kim's Paper

I found the subject matter of this paper to be rather challenging. This paper deals with some very interesting issues raised in Lichtenstein, Bloch and Black (1988), Rao and Monroe (1988), Rao and Sieben (1992), and Zeithaml (1988). The basic issue is the perceived price-quality relationship and its effect on price estimation by consumers. The allied pertinent issue is how the consumer response is influenced by moderating variables such as consumer beliefs, knowledge and familiarity. Zeithaml (1988) has introduced an interesting dichotomy of product attributes or cues. Intrinsic attributes relate to product features, but extrinsic attributes deal with price and brand name of the product. Rao and Monroe (1988) have suggested that consumers with low familiarity are guided by extrinsic cues of the product, moderately familiar consumers are guided by intrinsic cues and highly familiar consumers know when to be guided by extrinsic cues in addition to being basically guided by intrinsic cues. Rao and Sieben (1992) have shown that acceptable price range was found to be the lowest for the low-knowledge subjects; moderately knowledgeable subjects made least use of the information on prices and extrinsic cues; this study basically reinforced the findings of the earlier Rao and Monroe (1988) study.

Mazumdar and Kim's is a limited experimental exploratory study. It tests two main hypotheses: 1) consumers who have positive association between price and quality based on features of the product will have higher estimate of the price; 2) consumers who have difficulty assessing the usefulness of the product features will have lower estimates of the price. (It seems that the construct of feature based attributes is similar to the concept of 'intrinsic attributes' suggested by Zeithaml (1988)). The two hypotheses were tested in the framework of a regression model where price estimate was the dependent variable and prior feature based beliefs, difficulty of assessing the usefulness of the feature, and the interaction of beliefs and difficulty of assessing usefulness of features, were the independent variables. The overall fit of the model seemed to be good with an adjusted R^2 of 0.73. Hypothesis 1 was supported, suggesting the significant role of the prior beliefs of the price-quality relationship. Hypothesis 2 (the inverse relationship between difficulty of assessing usefulness of features and price estimates), was marginally supported. The interaction effect was not significant.

While Mazumdar and Kim have made useful contribution on the role of prior beliefs, I feel that the hypotheses are too simplistic. The literature review could have been more in depth, thus providing more solid foundation for the hypotheses. I think it is very important to bring in the intervening variables of knowledge, familiarity, reference price, acceptability range and other antecedents of the consumers in studying their perceptions of price. The distinction between intrinsic and extrinsic cues as suggested by Zeithaml (1988), Rao and Monroe (1988), Rao and Sieben (1992) is an important one while studying the role of antecedent (or moderating) variables. The conceptual model presented by Rao and Sieben (1992, P. 261, Figure 1) could be a useful framework for future research.

Some other areas of pricing research that deserve future research are the role of choice difficulty or uncertainty in making decisions about the prices (Urbany, Dickson and Wilkie 1989) and the role of regret experienced after the purchase. Also, I have been fascinated by the psychological explanations provided by theories such as prospect theory developed by Kahneman and Tversky (1979, 1984). More research needs to be published on this theory's application to pricing perceptions. Finally, the role of reference prices in the context of the theories of assimilation and contrast deserves further exploration (Urbany, Bearden and Weilbaker 1988).

CONCLUSION

The three papers discussed above have made useful contributions to consumer research in the areas of brand loyalty and pricing strategy. Some very interesting issues have been raised by these authors. I have attempted to discuss some of the issues in these areas and pointed out directions for future research.

REFERENCES

Bahn, Kenneth (1986), "How and When Do Brand Perceptions and Preferences First Form? A Cognitive Developmental Investigation", *Journal of Consumer Research*, Vol. 12, No. 3 (December), 382-393.

Belk, Russell W., Mellanie Wallendorf and John F. Sherry, Jr. (1989) "The Sacred and the Profane in Consumer Behavior: Theodicy on the Odyssey", *Journal of Consumer Research*, Vol. 16, No. 1 (June), 1-38.

Dickson, Peter R. and Alan G. Sawyer (1990), "The Price Knowledge and Search of Supermarket Shoppers", *Journal of Marketing*, 54 (July), 42-53.

Jacoby, Jacob and Robert W. Chestnut (1978), *Brand Loyalty: Measurement and Management*, New York: John Wiley & Sons, Inc.

Kahneman, Daniel and Amos Tversky (1979), "Prospect Theory, An Analysis of Decision Under Risk", in *Econometrica*, 47 (March 1979), 263-91.

Kahneman, Daniel and Amos Tversky (1984), "Choices, Values and Frames", *American Psychologist*, 39, No. 4 (April), 341-350.

Lichtenstein, Donald R., Peter H. Bloch and William C. Black (1988), "Correlates of Price Acceptability", *Journal of Consumer Research*, 15, 2 (September), 243-252.

McCracken, Grant (1990), *Culture and Consumption*, Bloomington: Indiana University Press

Moschis, George P. (1985), "The Role of Family Communication in Consumer Socialization of Children and Adolescents", *Journal of Consumer Research*, 11, No. 4 (March), 898-913.

Moschis, George, P., Roy L. Moore and Ruth B. Smith (1984), "The Impact of Family Communication on Adolescent Consumer Socialization", *Advances in Consumer Research*, Vol. 11, Thomas C. Kinnear, (ed.), Provo, UT: Association for Consumer Research.

Nagle, Thomas T. (1987), *The Strategy and Tactics of Pricing*, Englewood Cliffs, N.J.: Prentice Hall.

Rao, Akshay R. and Kent B. Monroe (1988), "The Moderating Effect of Prior Knowledge on Cue Utilization in Product Evaluations", *Journal of Consumer Research*, 15, No. 2 (September), 253-264.

Rao, Akshay R. and Wanda S. Sieben (1992), "The Effect of Prior Knowledge on Price Acceptability and Type of Information Examined", Vol. 19, No. 2 (September), 256-270.

Rokeach, Milton (1973), *The Nature of Human Values*, New York:The Free Press.

Schindler, Robert M. (1984), "Consumer Recognition of Increases in Odd and Even Prices", in *Advances in Consumer Research*, Vol. 11, Thomas C. Kinnear (ed.), Provo, UT: Association for Consumer Research.

Schindler, Robert M. (1989), "A Field Test of the Effects of Price Ending On Sales", Working Paper, School of Business, Rutgers University-Camden, Camden, NJ.

_____ (1991), "Symbolic Meanings of a Price Ending" in *Advances in Consumer Research*, Vol. 18, Rebecca H. Holman and Michael R. Solomon, (eds.), Provo, UT: Association for Consumer Research, 794-801.

_____ and Lori S. Warren (1988), "Effect of Odd Pricing on Choice of Items from a Menu", in *Advances in Consumer Research*, Vol 15, Michael J. Houston (ed.), Provo, UT: Association for Consumer Research, 348-353.

_____ and Alan R. Wiman (1989), "Effect of Odd Pricing on Price Recall", *Journal of Business Research*, 19 (November), 165-177.

Urbany, Joel E., William O. Bearden and Dan C. Weilbaker (1988), "The Effect of Plausible and Exaggerated Reference Prices on Consumer Perceptions and Price Search", *Journal of Consumer Research*, Vol. 15, No. 1 (June), 95-110.

Urbany, Joel E., Peter R. Dickson and William L. Wilkie (1989), "Buyer Uncertainty and Information Search", Vol. 16, No. 2 (September), 208-215

Zeithaml, Valerie A. (1988), "Consumer Perceptions of Price, Quality, and Value: A Means-End Model and Synthesis of Evidence", *Journal of Marketing*, 52, July, 2-22.

The Effects of Adding Products to a Brand on Consumers' Evaluations of New Brand Extensions

Peter A. Dacin, University of Wisconsin–Madison
Daniel C. Smith, University of Pittsburgh

ABSTRACT

In this study, we examine whether increasing the number of products associated with a brand decreases or increases that brand's strength. We develop and test hypotheses related to both positions. The main conclusion of our study is that when products affiliated with a brand have relatively little variance in terms of their perceived attribute performance, consumers' confidence in using the brand to evaluate a new extension (i.e., brand strength) seems to increase as the number of products affiliated with the brand increases. This finding holds even when the products affiliated with the brand are not perceived to be similar to each other.

INTRODUCTION

One of the more valuable resources a company has is the reputation of its brands. An increasing number of companies are attempting to leverage this asset by extending their brand names into new product areas (e.g. Gerber day care centers, McDonald's children's' clothing). While this strategy facilitates new product acceptance with less marketing investment than the introduction of a new brand (Smith and Park 1992) these benefits also come with an increased potential for negative side effects.

A common view of the effects of adding products to a brand holds that as the number of products introduced under a brand name increases, the meaning of the brand becomes diluted—the brand is no longer associated with any single product. It is generally believed that this disassociation results in less favorable judgments of future brand extensions (see, for example Farquhar 1990, Ries and Trout 1983, Tauber 1981). Although this is a widely held position, there may also be conditions under which favorability of judgments of extensions does not automatically decrease as the number of products affiliated with the brand increases (Park, MacInnis and Jaworski 1986).

The purpose of this study is to empirically investigate these opposite effects. To accomplish this, for each perspective, we outline its theoretical justifications and formulate propositions about the effects of increasing the number of products affiliated with a brand on: a) the favorability of consumer judgments of subsequent extensions, and b) how confident consumers feel about these judgments. Then we design and report the results of an experiment that tests these propositions.

THEORY AND HYPOTHESES

The Negative Effects of Multiple Products

As noted, it is widely believed that adding products to a brand weakens it. This position follows from the reasoning that, as products are added to a brand, consumers no longer associate the brand with a particular product or highly related class of products. Consider the following statement that is reflective of this perspective:

"In an over-communicated society you are lucky if your brand can mean one thing. Almost never can it mean two or three things." (a statement offered by Al Ries in an interview with the *Economist*, February, 1990, p.78)

The theoretical justification for this perspective relies on categorization theory to describe how consumers form judgments about extensions based on their knowledge of other products affiliated with the brand (Aaker and Keller 1990, Bridges 1989, Farquhar, Herr and Fazio 1990). When categorizing a brand extension, consumers try to construct a relationship between the extension and the set of existing products affiliated with the brand based on perceived similarity. Successfully constructing this relationship, in turn, alters the meaning of the brand.

For example, until recently many consumers associated the brand name of Honda with motorcycles and automobiles. Based on these highly related products, consumers may have thought of Honda as being synonymous with "motorized transportation vehicles." However, when Honda introduced a line of lawn and garden equipment, some consumers may have related these new products to other Honda products based on their primary component parts (i.e., gasoline engines, etc.). In so doing, these consumers may have altered the meaning of Honda to "products that use gasoline engines."

Following from this logic, once the meaning of the brand changes, so does its strength—the brand no longer provides a sound basis for making inferences about future extensions. Specifically, when categorizing an extension to other products affiliated with the brand, consumers are assumed to transfer their existing beliefs and feelings about the brand to the extension. The extent to which this occurs depends on the similarity or category fit between the extension and other products affiliated with the brand (Aaker and Keller 1990, Farquhar, Herr and Fazio 1990, Bridges 1989, MacInnis and Nakamoto 1990, Park, Lawson and Milberg 1991, The Minnesota Consumer Behavior Seminar 1987). As the number of dissimilar products affiliated with a brand increases, the meaning of the brand changes and becomes less distinct in the minds of consumers. As a result, it becomes difficult for consumers to use the brand in categorizing subsequent extensions, thus, reducing the likelihood of transferring brand affect to the extension.

However, when a brand is affiliated with a portfolio of highly related products, the meaning of the brand will change less than when it is affiliated with highly dissimilar products. That is, the meaning of the brand remains relatively distinct in the minds of consumers. Consequently, conditions of high similarity among products affiliated with the brand should facilitate the use of the brand as a basis for categorizing subsequent extensions, reducing the negative effect of having multiple products affiliated with the brand.

This discussion leads to the following propositions:

H1: As the number of products affiliated with the brand increases, the favorability of the judgments about an extension of the brand decreases.

H2: The negative effects of having multiple products affiliated with a brand on the judgments of an extension will decrease as the similarity of products affiliated with the brand increases.

The Favorable Effects Multiple Products

The theory outlined above assumes that in categorizing a new extension, consumers attempt to interpret the extension in terms of the entire set of other products affiliated with the brand. Indeed, what may be more critical is that consumers are able to identify at least one other product that is somehow related to the extension. For example, the Yamaha brand is associated with electronics, motorcycles, and musical instruments. Following the reasoning described earlier, one would conclude that the Yamaha name is highly diluted and should not have a favorable effect on consumer inferences of a new extension, say, watches. However, consumers may perceive the skills needed to manufacture watches as being similar to those needed to produce electronic devices and thus, successfully relate watches to the brand even though watches, on the surface, appear to be quite dissimilar to other products affiliated with the brand.

In addition, while the logic of the potential hazards of using a single brand to represent multiple products is intuitively appealing, there exists an opposing perspective. Many firms intentionally follow a strategy of brand extensions focusing on a particular abstract dimension rather than specific product characteristics (e.g., AMF's "We Make Weekends", Johnson and Johnson's "We Know Babies"). In essence, consumers can equate the abstract dimension with the brand in much the same way as they equate a specific product with a brand at its inception. So, while the meaning of brand associations may become abstracted as the number of products affiliated with the brand increases, it does not necessarily follow that this will negatively affect the favorability of judgments about subsequent extensions.

Given this, from a consumer decision making perspective, it is easy to argue that adding products to a brand can strengthen the brand. In this perspective, consumers rely on a brand name as a decision heuristic (Johnson and Russo 1984), and as a vehicle for managing perceived risk (Cox 1967). Therefore, whether a brand is harmed or helped by being affiliated with multiple products is found in the extent to which consumers rely on it as a basis for making inferences about a new extension. Reliance on a brand in evaluating a new extension, in turn, is expected to be a function of the extent to which consumers believe that their knowledge of other products affiliated with the brand is an accurate predictor of the experience they will have with the new product.

Given this conceptualization, we can see how adding products to a brand can strengthen it. The products affiliated with a brand essentially represent a "data base" from which consumers draw information in forming judgments about the experiences they can expect from an extension. As the number of products increases, the breadth of data increases—consumers have knowledge of the brand in multiple product contexts. Consequently, consumers' confidence in a brand is expected to depend not only on the breadth of data, but also on the degree of variability or consistency in the data.

For instance, consumers might find the quality of Izod jackets and slacks substantially above that of its suits and socks, but well below that of its polo shirts. In contrast, the quality of the product offerings associated with another brand, say Ralph Lauren, may be more consistent. The overall level of quality associated with Ralph Lauren products, then, may not be as high as the quality associated with some Izod products. However, because of the consistency in outcomes associated with the brand, we expect consumers to feel more confident in their judgments of a subsequent Ralph Lauren extension than an Izod extension.

Therefore:

H3a: Under conditions of *high consistency* in past outcomes, consumer confidence in judgments about brand extensions will increase as the number of products affiliated with the brand increases.

H3b: Under conditions of *low consistency* in past outcomes, consumer confidence in judgments about brand extensions will decrease as the number of products affiliated with the brand increases.

The consistency of past outcomes associated with the brand should also account for some of the variation in consumer evaluations of brand extensions. Low consistency in past outcomes will tend to create conditions of uncertainty in consumers' expectations about the brand that should lead to reluctance on the part of consumers to use any specific past outcomes to generalize to brand extensions. Therefore, conditions of low consistency in past outcomes are expected to give rise to less favorable evaluations of subsequent brand extensions than conditions of high consistency in past outcomes.

H4: In general, judgments of brand extensions will be more favorable under conditions of high consistency in past outcomes associated with the brand than conditions of low consistency of past outcomes.

Finally, we expect the effect of the number of products affiliated with a brand on favorability of extension evaluations to be moderated by the degree of consistency in past outcomes. Following from the same logic used to develop H3a and H3b we hypothesize that:

H5a: Under conditions of *high consistency* in past outcomes, favorability of judgments about brand extensions will increase as the number of products affiliated with the brand increases.

H5b: Under conditions of *low consistency* in past outcomes, favorability of judgments about brand extensions will decrease as the number of products affiliated with the brand increases.

METHOD

The above hypotheses were tested using a 2 X 2 X 2 between subjects factorial design with two levels of similarity of extension to the products associated with the brand (similar and dissimilar), two levels of consistency of outcomes of other products associated with the brand (consistent and inconsistent), and two levels of the number of products affiliated with the brand (three and seven).

Stimuli

We incorporated all three manipulations in a brand ratings table typical of those found in magazines such as *Consumer Reports* or *Consumer Guide*. We manipulated the consistency of outcomes of other products associated with the brand by altering the pattern of ratings found in the table. Furthermore, to ensure that subjects' perceptions of consistency did not affect their overall feelings towards the brand we also included a summary evaluation of the brand in the table.

We manipulated similarity and the number of products affiliated with the brand by altering the products listed in the ratings table. Products listed in the "similar" conditions were chosen to be either similar or dissimilar to each other and to the brand extension (electric clothes irons). The three-product similar manipulation consisted of: small kitchen appliances, electric razors, and hair dryers/curling irons. The three-product, dissimilar manipulation consisted of: kitchen appliances, 10 speed bicycles and, sports watches. For the seven-product manipulation, we added four products to each table. In the similar case, we included small electric power tools, electric garage door openers, hand held vacuum cleaners and electric pencil sharpeners. In the dissimilar case, lawn and garden tools, electric garage door openers, camping equipment (tents, backpacks), and wooden patio furniture were added. Manipulation checks revealed that these manipulations were successful.

We selected the hypothetical brand name "Jasil" for two reasons. First, pretests revealed that subjects were unaware of this name, therefore, previous experience could not interfere with the manipulations. Second, pretests also demonstrated that associating Jasil with a variety of unbranded products did not alter the evaluation or cognitive associations of these products. This was important since the experiment required that we manipulate both the beliefs subjects had for the brand (i.e., consistency) and the number of products they affiliated with the brand. This would have been difficult to achieve with well established brands.

Subjects and Procedures

One hundred twenty undergraduate students were recruited from undergraduate business classes. For their participation, subjects were offered extra credit. The subjects were randomly assigned to the eight cells so that each cell contained 15 subjects.

An experimenter handed subjects a booklet as they entered the laboratory. The first page of the booklet contained a paragraph orienting subjects to the task. It told them that they would see a table consisting of a number of products being offered under the Jasil brand name and that following this table, they would be responding to several questions about the products. Subjects were given two minutes to read these instructions and then were told to turn the page.

The second page of the booklet presented the brand ratings table containing the manipulations. Instructions informed subjects that this table was from *Consumer Reporter,* a publication that, as a service to its readers, reviews consumer products in terms of their performance on a number of important attributes. Each product was rated on six attributes obtained from pretests. These were: durability, customer satisfaction, value for the money, goodness of warranty, style/design and, reliability/engineering. Subjects studied the table for four minutes to study the table and then turned the page and continued through the booklet, responding to all the questions on the remaining pages.

After questions about the products in the table, we gave subjects a scenario that stated that the same manufacturer decided to introduce a line of electric clothes irons under the Jasil brand name. Following this, subjects responded to questions about this brand extension.

In order to determine whether subjects identified the purpose of the study, randomly selected subjects were asked extensive debriefing questions after the experiment. The subjects' responses to these questions indicated that none had guessed the purpose.

Measures

Subjects' Perceived Consistency of Outcomes. This measure was composed of two seven-point items. The first item asked subjects to indicate the extent to which they felt that the attribute ratings varied between products in the table (varies a lot - does not vary at all). The second item asked how consistent subjects felt the products were in terms of their attribute ratings (very consistent - very inconsistent). The correlation between these two items was .87. An average of these two items was used as a perceived consistency score.

Subjects' Perceived Similarity of Products Affiliated With the Brand and Similarity of the Extension to Other Products Affiliated with the Brand. Following from previous research, (see for example, Aaker and Keller 1990, MacInnis and Nakamoto 1990), subjects were asked to indicate how similar they felt the products affiliated with the brand were in terms of: (1) the types of needs the products satisfy, (2) situations in which the products are used, and (3) physical features. Each item used a 7-point scale anchored by very similar - very dissimilar. Coefficient alpha for the three-item scale was 0.74. The three items were averaged to represent consumer perceptions of similarity.

The above dimensions were also used to measure the perceived similarity of the brand extension (electric clothes irons) to the other products affiliated with the brand. Coefficient alpha for this scale was 0.77.

Overall Evaluation of the Jasil Brand Name and Overall Evaluation of the Jasil Clothes Iron. We measured subjects' evaluations of the Jasil brand name and the Jasil electric clothes iron using 7-point scales. One scale asked subjects how they felt about the Jasil brand name and the other scale asked subjects how they felt about the Jasil electric clothes iron. Each scale was anchored by very favorable - very unfavorable.

Expectations for Various Attributes for Any Future Products Affiliated with Jasil and the Confidence in These Expectations. For this measure, subjects were presented with a list of the six attributes that appeared in the ratings table. Beside each attribute was a 7-point scale anchored by far above average - far below average on which the subjects were to indicate their expectation for that attribute for any future product associated with the Jasil brand name. Coefficient alpha for this scale was 0.97. An average of these items was used to indicate subjects' expectations.

In addition, a second 7-point scale was associated with each attribute. This scale, anchored by very confident - not confident at all was used to obtain the subjects' rating of their confidence in their expectation for that attribute. Coefficient alpha for this scale was 0.76. Again, an average of these items was used.

Expectations for Various Attributes for the Jasil Clothes Iron and Confidence in These Expectations. Identical measures to those just described were used to obtain subjects' expectations and confidence in their expectations for the Jasil electric clothes iron brand extension. Coefficient alpha for the extension expectation scale was 0.96 and for the confidence scale 0.74.

Knowledge of clothes irons. A measure of knowledge was taken because it was felt that knowledge might affect subjects' judgments of the product. However, in all analyses, knowledge had no effect as a covariate.

RESULTS

As a preliminary test of the hypotheses concerning the role of similarity on the effects of having multiple products affiliated with a brand (H2), and the effects of consistency and number of products affiliated with the brand on the favorability of judgments (H4, H5a, H5b), we ran a 3-way analysis of variance. In this analysis, we used consumers' evaluations of the brand extension as the dependent variable and the manipulated similarity, consistency of past outcomes and number of products affiliated with the brand as independent variables.

The results of this analysis appear in Table 1. In this table, a higher number represents more favorable evaluations. None of the interactions were significant (three way interaction [$F(1,112)=0.03$, p=n.s.]; similarity x number of products [$F(1,112)=0.05$, p=n.s.]; similarity x consistency [$F(1,112)=0.24$, p=n.s.]; consistency x number of products [$F(1,112)=0.08$, p=n.s.]). There were significant main effects for both the similarity and consistency manipula-

TABLE 1
Means and (Standard Deviations) for Evaluations of the Jasil Electric Iron Brand Extension

	High Similarity		Low Similarity	
	Three Products	Seven Products	Three Products	Seven Products
High Consistency	3.58 (0.79)	3.77 (0.83)	3.27 (0.79)	3.60 (0.84)
Low Consistency	3.31 (0.95)	3.17 (0.94)	2.90 (0.74)	2.75 (1.07)

TABLE 2
Means and (Standard Deviations) for Confidence for Jasil Brand Associations

	High Similarity		Low Similarity	
	Three Products	Seven Products	Three Products	Seven Products
High Consistency	3.47 (0.98)	3.99 (0.74)	3.36 (0.54)	3.38 (0.81)
Low Consistency	3.57 (0.62)	3.32 (1.05)	3.13 (0.58)	2.97 (0.48)

tions (similarity [$F(1,112)=4.21$, $p<0.05$]; consistency [$F(1,112)=8.39$, $p<0.05$]). These results suggested initial support for the role of the similarity of a brand extension to current products affiliated with the brand (H2) and of the consistency of outcomes associated with the brand (H4). Furthermore, the mean evaluation in these conditions indicated that; a) under conditions of low consistency, evaluation decreased as the number of products affiliated with the brand increased and, b) under conditions of high consistency, evaluation increased as the number of products affiliated with the brand increased. Although these contrasts were not statistically significant, the directions were consistent with the predictions of H5a and H5b. Finally, the evaluation of the extension was not affected by the number of products affiliated with the brand (H1) [$F(1,112)=0.85$, $p=n.s.$].

In order to further test the hypothesis concerned with the role of similarity on the effects of having multiple products affiliated with a brand (H2) and to test the effect of consistency of past outcomes on consumer confidence in their judgments (H3), the 3-way analysis of variance was run on the dependent variable of confidence in outcomes associated with the brand. The results appear in Table 2. In this table, a higher number represents greater confidence. Of all the interactions, only the consistency x number of products interaction was significant [$F(1,112)=5.13$, $p\leq0.05$]. Two main effects, similarity [$F(1,112)=3.01$, $p\leq0.05$] and consistency [$F(1,112)=7.11$, $p\leq0.05$], were also significant. The main effect for consistency was interpretable since the significant interaction in which it appears was ordinal. Furthermore, although none of the contrasts were statistically significant, under conditions of low consistency, confidence decreased as the number of products affiliated with the brand increased while, under conditions of high consistency, confidence increased as the number of products affiliated with the brand increased. The direction of these findings were consistent with the predictions of H3a and H3b.

Regression analysis was used as an additional test of the effects of consistency and similarity on subjects' judgments of the brand extension. In this analysis, we used the continuous measures of similarity and consistency to test for the relative contributions of each variable on the judgments of favorability for the electric iron brand extension. Tests for multicollinearity revealed that it was not a problem.

The incremental F test in the hierarchical regression for the consistency x similarity interaction was not significant [$DR^2=0.01$ [$F=1.53$, $p=n.s.$]. In the main effects model, the standardized betas for the variables were 0.174 for similarity [$t=1.66$, $p\leq0.10$] and 0.355 for consistency [$t=5.104$, $p\leq0.05$]. The model explained approximately 16% of the variance in the dependent variable. These results suggested that the perceived consistency of past outcomes had a much more important role on subjects' judgments about the brand extension than did subjects' perceived similarity of the brand extension to other products affiliated with the brand. This supported the role of consistency and partially supported the role of similarity in judgments of favorability.

In summary, the results of these analyses suggested that both the favorability of consumers' inferences about an extension and the confidence in these inferences increased with the consistency of past outcomes. Similarity, on the other hand, had no effect on confidence and, compared to consistency, had a relatively small effect on the favorability of judgments about the extension.

DISCUSSION

This study investigates the effects of the number of products affiliated with a brand. While there is a commonly held belief that detrimental effects increase as the number of products affiliated with the brand increases (Farquhar 1990, The Economist 1990, Tauber 1981), no strong evidence for this emerges from this study. In general, the number of products affiliated with a brand does not affect subjects' judgments of a brand extension.

Another belief found in extant literature is that extensions should be as similar as possible to existing products affiliated with the brand (Aaker and Keller 1990, Farquhar, Herr and Fazio 1990,

Bridges 1989, MacInnis and Nakamoto 1990, Park, Lawson and Milberg 1991, The Minnesota Consumer Behavior Seminar 1987). While our study finds some support for this relationship, similarity provides only a partial explanation for consumers' judgments of brand extensions.

A major contribution of this study is that we extend the thinking about the effects of adding products to a brand by focusing attention on the degree of consumers' reliance on a brand in decision making. This differs considerably from current thought which focuses primarily on the extent to which a brand's meaning changes. Adding a product to a brand need not result in unfavorable judgments of that extension. Indeed, our findings support this. Furthermore, we find that the number of products affiliated with the brand moderates the relationship between consistency and confidence. Under high consistency, there tends to be a positive relationship between the number of products affiliated with the brand and confidence. Under low consistency the opposite is true.

We recognize that there are limitations with our study. One of the study's major limitations emerges from our use of a single exposure to a *Consumer Reporter* table to manipulate the consistency of the outcomes of products associated with the brand, which we hypothesize to affect confidence. In a natural setting, a consumers' confidence in using information about a brand to make judgments about an extension will, no doubt, develop over multiple exposures and experiences. However, the purpose of this study is to examine a number of theory based predictions. Therefore, we require tight controls over a variety of cognitive phenomena. To accomplish this we consciously sacrifice some external validity. While we have no doubt that the confidence we create in the minds of the subjects may be relatively short lived and unstable compared to confidence built over multiple exposures and experiences with the brand, the results we obtain in the context of our study are very encouraging.

Our results demonstrate the importance of accounting for consistency in future research concerned with the effects of brand extensions. Furthermore, a number of managerial implications emerge from the role of consistency and confidence on brand dilution. The first group of implications are concerned with the strategies necessary to manage favorable judgments of brand extensions. Since the key determinant of brand dilution is the consistency in previous outcomes with products affiliated with the brand, the task of marketers is to monitor the outcomes consumers attach to the products affiliated with the brand. Consumers will only use the brand to make judgments about future extensions when they have built some confidence in the brand as a result of associating it with consistent outcomes.

The second group of implications deals with the way in which managers should evaluate the importance of a brand in brand extensions. Contrary to current thinking, a brand does not necessarily suffer as more products are added to it. While the meanings associated with a brand change as products are added, consumers are still able to rely on the new meanings to make inferences about subsequent extensions. Indeed, the results of this study suggest that it is more important to consider the consistency of outcomes that consumers associate with the brand than simply the sheer number of products affiliated with the brand or the similarity of an extension to the current products associated with the brand.

REFERENCES

Aaker, David A. and Kevin L. Keller (1990), "Consumer Responses to Brand Extensions," *Journal of Marketing*, 54 (January), 27-41.

Bettman, James A. and C. Whan Park (1980), "Effects of Prior Knowledge and Experience and Phase of Choice Process on Consumer Decision Making Processes," *Journal of Consumer Research*, 7 (December), 234-248.

Bridges, Sheri (1990), "A Schema Unification Model of Brand Extensions," Working Paper, Stanford University.

Cox, Donald F. (1967), *Risk Taking and Information Handling in Consumer Behavior*. Cambridge, MA: Harvard Business School.

Farquhar, Peter H. (1990), "Managing Brand Equity," *Marketing Research*, (September), 24-33.

Farquhar, Peter H., Paul Herr, Russell H. Fazio (1989), "Extending Brand Equity to New Product Categories," Working Paper, Center for Product Research, Carnegie Mellon University.

Johnson, Eric and J. Edward Russo (1981), "Product Familiarity and Learning New Information," *Journal of Consumer Research*, 13 (June), 38-47.

MacInnis, Deborah J., and Kent Nakamoto (1990), "Cognitive Associations and Product Category Comparisons: The Role of Knowledge and Context," Working Paper, School of Business, University of Arizona.

Minnesota Consumer Behavior Seminar (1987), "Affect Generalization to Similar and Dissimilar Brand Extensions," *Psychology and Marketing*, 4 (3), 225-237.

Park, C. Whan, Robert Lawson, Sandra Milberg (1991), "Bases of Categorization Judgments for Brand Extensions," *Journal of Consumer Research*, 18 (September) 185-193.

Park, C. Whan, Deborah J. MacInnis, Bernard Jaworski (1986), "Strategic Brand Concept Management," *Journal of Marketing*, 50 (October), 135-145.

Smith, Daniel C. and C. Whan Park (1992), "The Effect of Brand Extensions on Market Share and Advertising Efficiency," *Journal of Marketing Research*, 29 (August), 296-313.

Sujan, Mita (1985), "Consumer Knowledge: Effects on Evaluation Strategies Mediating Consumer *Judgments*," *Journal of Consumer Research*, 12 (June), 31-46.

Tauber, Edward (1981), "Brand Franchise Extensions: New Products Benefit From Existing Brand Names," *Business Horizons*, (March/April), 36-41.

Line extensions: A Categorization and an Information Processing Perspective

Kalpesh Kaushik Desai, The University of Texas at Austin
Wayne D. Hoyer, The University of Texas at Austin

ABSTRACT

This paper addresses the theoretical principles involved in the processing and evaluation of line extensions by the consumers. We propose a theoretical model of processing of line extensions and identify some moderating factors influencing the evaluation of line extensions. We also develop a classificatory framework and discuss the implications of the theoretical concepts for the framework.

INTRODUCTION

With the cost of launching new products greatly on the rise and with an ever increasing failure rate for new products, companies have started paying closer attention to the importance and value of existing brand names. Clear evidence of this fact is that companies have launched many new variants of brand which are called line extensions. Line extensions are using the same brand name to launch new variants in the same product category. Of the 10,000 new products launched in the packaged goods industry in 1988, about 90 % were line extensions (Marketing and Media Decisions 1989). Take any product category and you will find that there is hardly any brand which has not extended its line, be it toothpastes, automobiles, music systems, etc. In the toothpaste product category, for example, a consumer can purchase Crest Fluoride, Crest Tartar control (regular flavor and cool mint flavor), and Crest Sparkle.

In light of ever increasing launches of line extensions, managerial guidelines regarding which brands should extend into what variants is badly needed. Despite its importance, however, it is surprising to find that this area has hardly been studied by marketing and consumer researchers. It is the opinion of the authors that theory and research on categorization and consumer information processing have much to offer marketers in developing managerial guidelines. Thus the objectives of this paper are : (1) To discuss the theoretical concepts involved in the introduction of line extensions, (2) To propose a model of processing of line extensions, (3) To highlight the factors moderating the evaluation of line extensions, (4) To put forth a framework to classify line extensions.

LINE EXTENSIONS VS BRAND EXTENSIONS

In relation to present interests, an evaluation of line extensions involves the task of trying to judge the similarities between two instances of the same product category. For example, line extensions involve the task of judging the similarities between "Crest tartar toothpaste" and "Crest fluoride toothpastes". This is in contrast to brand extensions where the consumers judge the similarities between two instances bearing the same brand name but which are in two different product categories ("Crest toothpastes" and "Crest chewing gum"). As a result, Barsalou (1989) concludes that intraconcept similarity (line extensions) should generally be higher (and hence more acceptable to consumers) than interconcept similarity of two related concepts (brand extensions). A second difference between the two concepts is that with brand extensions, the company is trying to exploit the potential of the brand in different product categories. Therefore, the brand is trying to woo the same group of consumers who are currently using the parent brand. Alternatively with line extensions, the company is trying to exploit the potential of the brand within a product category. Thus, the brand usually is trying to woo new users (in most of the cases) and extend the usage of brand by making the current users use the different variants. Most of the research in this area has focused on brand extensions. The present paper represents an attempt to extend previous work in four important ways. First, none of the previous studies has examined issues related to line extensions, the focus of the present paper. Second, this paper attempts to go beyond previous efforts by introducing new variables from the categorization theory — "concept conjunction"; "dominant concept"; "concept confusability"; and "concept incompatibility" to explain the evaluation of line extension. A third contribution is the identification of moderating factors which influences the acceptance of line extensions and finally, this paper develops a classificatory framework which will help us classify the different types of line extensions so that meaningful strategies for each of the types could be developed.

THEORETICAL CONCEPTS

Before presenting a theoretical model of line extensions, it is necessary to define a few key concepts. These are: brand concepts; concept conjunction; and dominance concept.

Brand Concepts

"Concept" is one of the important variables in the categorization literature (Barsalou 1987; Brooks 1978). Barsalou (1987) defines the "concept" as the particular information used to represent a category (or an exemplar) on a particular occasion. According to Barsalou (1987), the concept has two parts, one which is context independent information (cii), which is the information used to represent the category in most of the contexts. For example, whenever a person thinks of Honda s/he immediately thinks of "reliability" and "good quality" or for Macintosh the ciis might be "user friendliness." Because the ciis are so accessible, they may be automatically incorporated into all the concepts constructed for it. This would result in their being "cores" for the concepts. Such cores provide the consumers with expectations that are useful for interacting with a category in most contexts. According to Barsalou (1980), properties high in diagnosticity (useful in distinguishing instances of one concept from other concept instances) and properties relevant to how people typically interact with instances of respective concept would become the ciis. We also posit that since context independent information form the core of the brand concept, unique brand associations, important associations common to all the variants of the brand and some evaluative attributes like "reliability", "quality" etc would also form part of the ciis. However, it is not essential that the ciis be same for different consumers (or group of consumers), therefore there can be more than one ciis for the same stimuli or brand.

The other part of "concept" is the context dependent information (cdi) or the information used to represent the category in that context. For example, the concept of "power" and "excitement" would be felt by a person driving a Honda motorbike (but not a Honda car) and similarly for Macintosh, it could be the "good graphics facility when one is using graphics. Properties of a concept not typically found for familiar referents may become cdis through *disuse* (Barsalou 1980). We also posit that context dependent information would consist of context specific attributes and specific functional attributes of the brand. Just as in case of ciis, different consumers (or group of consumers) might hold different cdis for the brand. Therefore the brand concept (against which the

FIGURE 1
A Model of Evaluation of Line Extensions

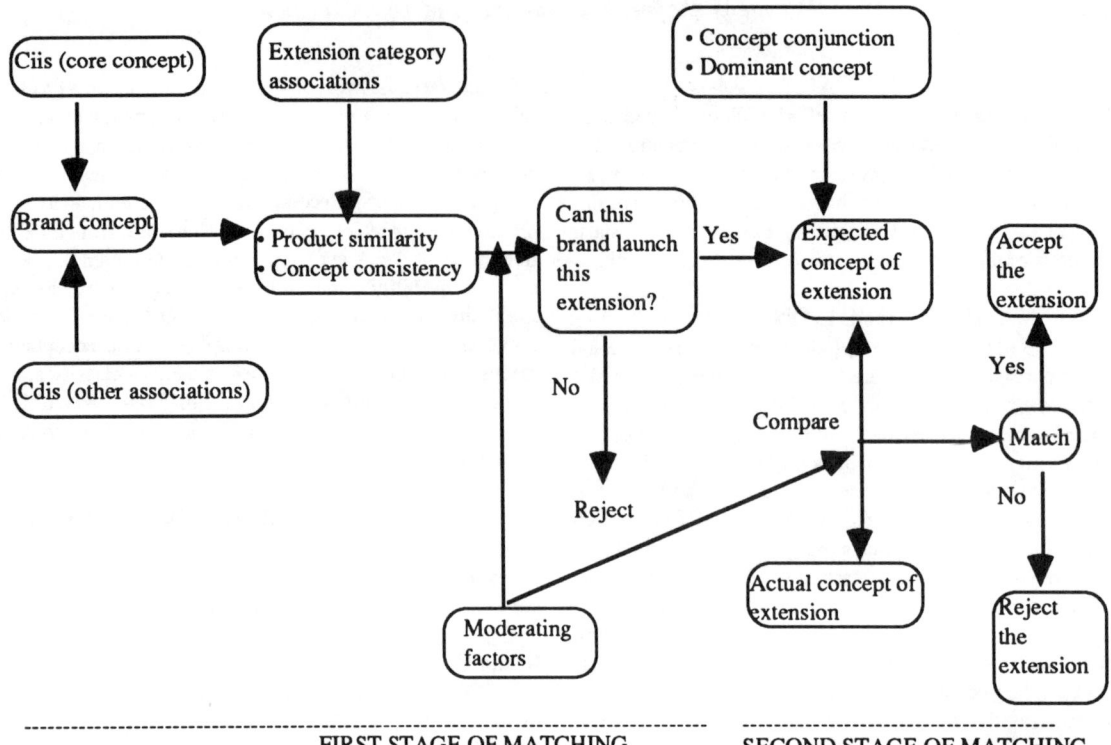

FIRST STAGE OF MATCHING —— SECOND STAGE OF MATCHING

new line extension will be compared) will differ from one consumer to another.

Concept Conjunction

Hampton (1987) proposed a model of concept conjunction to explain the nature of the resulting concept which arises when the two concepts are combined. The principle of concept conjunction will explain as to which attributes of the two concepts (to be combined) will be important for the new line extension as perceived by the consumers. Thus, his model would help us know what the new concept of "Head & Shoulders natural shampoo" be, when the two concepts of "Head & Shoulders shampoo" and "Natural shampoo" are combined. The model proposes that the attributes of the new concept— Head & Shoulders -Natural shampoo are formed by the union of the attribute sets of the two existing concepts, namely those of "Head & Shoulders shampoo" and "Natural shampoo". According to this model, (1) attributes that are necessary for either of the two concepts will also be important for the new concept and (2) attributes that are impossible for either of the concepts will also be impossible for the new concept. For example, good quality engine is necessary for Honda concept, therefore this attribute of "engine quality" will also be important for Honda's extension into sports car, but the attribute of "more leg space" is impossible for a sports car and therefore "more leg space" is not going to be important for the new extension of Honda into sports car. However, if one of the attribute is necessary for one of the concept and impossible for the other concept, then we posit that this attribute would not pass on to the conjunction because the conjunction can't be formed with an impossible attribute. The relative importance (relative to other important attributes) of an attribute will depend on the importance of that attribute for both the concepts. The attribute which is important for both the concepts will be more important for the new line extension than the attribute which is important for only one of the concepts. For example, "fuel economy" is more important for Honda concept than it is for "sports car" concept, whereas the attribute of "durability" is important for both the concepts, therefore the latter attribute will be more important than the former for Honda's extension in sports car. In this way, the "important" attributes of the new extension concept reflects consumers' expectations of the nature of the new extension concept. Now, how would the ciis and cdis influence the formation of concept conjunction ? We hypothesize that since the ciis form the core of the brand concept, they would pass over to the conjunction whereas, the transfer of cdis would differ from one line extension to another.

Dominant concept

The dominant concept is related to the previous principle of concept conjunction. This principle tries to explain which of the existing two concepts involved in a line extension context will be dominant in determining the concept of the new line extension. The basic principle is that if one of the concepts has a greater number of salient and important attributes (for the new line extension) than the other concept, the new concept (line extension) will bear greater similarity to the former concept. Thus, the former concept would be the dominant concept. For example, if Rolls Royce were to extend into a sports car segment, then the dominant concept will determine whether this new car would be (consumer expectations) more similar to the "Rolls Royce" concept or the "sports car" concept. Therefore the dominant concept would by definition include only the important attributes of the constituent concept.

A MODEL OF EVALUATION OF LINE EXTENSIONS

Having introduced the theoretical concepts in the previous section, we now propose a model of evaluation of line extensions (fig 1.). The purpose of this model is to trace the process underlying the acceptance or rejection of the new line extension.

As shown in the figure, the starting point in the process of evaluating line extensions are the ciis and the cdis which together form the brand concept. For example, the ciis for Rolls Royce car could be "good engineering'" and a "luxury" car, whereas the cdis could be "good after sales service", and "excellent interior decor" of the car. Once the consumer becomes aware of the launch of the new line extension, s/he will decide whether the brand could launch this new extension. This is the first stage of "matching". The input to the first stage of matching is the brand concept and the extension product category associations. These two determine "product similarity" and "brand concept consistency" which are involved in the first stage of matching. The actual matching involves using "product similarity" and "brand concept consistency" to compare the new extension concept and the current brand concept (Murphy and Medin 1985; Park et al 1991).This is an overall evaluation i.e., without comparing attribute by attribute. Product similarity in case of line extension is not very important as the extension is in the same product category. The brand concept consistency would involve asking whether there is any inconsistency in the brand launching a particular extension. For example, can a conservative luxury car like Rolls Royce launch a sports car? A negative answer will lead to the rejection of the new extension whereas, a positive answer would lead to the next stage of matching. In the second stage, using the principles of concept conjunction and dominant concept, the consumers try to visualize what the concept of new line extension should be (i.e which attributes of the original two concepts should be incorporated in the new extension). This concept is defined as the "expected" concept of the new extension. Let us assume that in our case, after using the principles of "concept conjunction" and "dominant concept" the consumers expect that the new Rolls Royce sports car should have the following features of the "Rolls Royce" concept : "excellent engineering"; "smooth ride"; "good interior decor"; and "high price" and it should also incorporate the following features of the "sports car" concept : "quick acceleration"; "good styling of the car"; and "one door." Looking at the desired features of the two concepts (Rolls Royce and sports car), the new line extension in this case will be more similar to the concept of "Rolls Royce car" than that of "sports car", since the number of features or attributes of the "Rolls Royce" concept desired in the extension is greater than those desired of the "sports car concept". Therefore the concept of "Rolls Royce car" will be the dominant concept in this case. This means that the consumers expect the new extension to be more similar to Rolls Royce car than to sports car. However for some consumers, the product concept might be dominant (for e.g., those who are indifferent to the different variants, those who are "variety seekers"). This expected concept is then compared to the "actual concept" of the new extension. This is the second process of "matching". Since the concept conjunction and dominant concept reflect consumer's *expectations* about the new extension concept, a mismatch between the expected and the actual concept would lead to a negative evaluation and possible rejection of the new line extension —— Satisfaction literature (Oliver and Desabro 1988). However, if the new concept is as per their expected concept, the line extension will be accepted. So for example, for those consumers, whose dominant concept is Rolls Royce car, if the actual concept of Rolls Royce sports car is tilting more toward the sports car concept than the Rolls Royce concept, the new extension will be rejected. For example in its attempt to be a good sports car, the new extension compromised on the ciis of the "Rolls Royce concept" like "good engineering" and "smooth driving", the consumers might not perceive the new extension to be a "Rolls Royce" car and might reject the new extension.

How would the ciis and cdis influence brand evaluation? As we discussed above, since the ciis would always be passed over to the concept conjunction and the passing of cdis would vary from one case to another, the chances of rejection of a line extension are much greater if there is a mismatch on the ciis than if they are on the cdis.

A related issue is how would the dominant concept impact evaluation of a line extension ? We posit that since dominant concept receives a greater weight in the formation of a conjunction, the chances of rejection of a line extension are greater if there is a mismatch on the dominant concept than if there was a mismatch on the nondominant concept.

The proposed model of line extensions is different from the current models of brand extensions in the following ways:

(1) The current models of brand extensions consider only the first stage of matching (i.e between the existing brand concept and the new concept of the extension) whereas, our model takes one more matching process into account and that is between the expected new concept and the actual concept of the extension. This second stage is important because, even if there is a consistency between the extension concept and the old brand concept, if the actual performance of the extension (as determined by the "actual concept" of extension) is not as per the consumers' expectations (as reflected in the "expected concept" of the extension), the extension would be rejected.

(2) The model identifies various factors (discussed below) that could moderate the two processes of matching. The moderating factors could either increase or decrease the importance of the two matching processes described above. For example, an expert consumer will give more weight to these matching processes than a novice consumer because an expert would like to maintain the coherence of her / his product knowledge, whereas the novice might not be even able to define the concept (expected concept) of the new extension.

(3) This model also takes into account the difference in individual brand concepts positing that it might not be possible for all brands to launch a particular line extension. For example, it would be difficult for Rolls Royce to launch a sports car because of its conservative, exclusive, luxury brand concept, however, it would be relatively less difficult for Lexus to launch a sports car because of its modern, and liberal luxury car brand concept.

However, as our model deals with categorization constructs like brand concept, context independent information, context dependent information, category differentiation etc, and since the theory of categorization is equally applicable for brand extensions, this model would also be applicable to brand extensions.

MODERATING FACTORS

After discussing the process of "matching" between the line extension concept and the old brand concept, let us now look at some of the factors which could moderate these matching processes. These factors could be divided into two broad categories —— individually related and product related.

Individually Related Factors

(1) *Expertise*: Experts, with their detailed and complex knowledge structure of the target product category, should be able to see the relationships between different attributes more clearly

than the novices (Alba and Hutchinson 1987). Hence, in the line extension context, experts are more likely to detect any inconsistency between the brand concept and the new line extension concept (whose knowledge of the category is not very deep and who normally process information via the peripheral route— Sujan 1985; Alba and Hutchinson 1987). Since our model posits that the extensions will be rejected if the consumers detect any inconsistency between the old brand concept and the new extension concept, experts would accept lesser number of line extensions than novices.

(2) *Model of Categorization Used*: Smith and Medin (1981) divided the models of categorization into three basic types. *The classical theory* holds that all instances of a category share common properties that are necessary and sufficient conditions for defining the category. For example, according to this rule all brands of toothpastes should be white in color, have sweet taste, should freshen breath and should be in paste form. Any brand which does not satisfy any of the above mentioned criteria (a very stringent restriction) would not be categorized as toothpaste. The *exemplar view* says that a category may be represented by their individual exemplars and assignment of a new instance to a category is determined by whether the instance is sufficiently more similar to one or more of the category's known exemplars. For example, an individual might have two exemplars in the toothpaste product category, Crest and Colgate. To determine whether a new product s/he encounters is a toothpaste or not, s/he will compare the new product with either Colgate or Crest. If it is perceived to be quite similar to either of these brands, the new product would be categorized as toothpaste. The *probabilistic or prototypical view* says that there are no necessary and defining properties, rather categories or concepts are represented in terms of properties that are only characteristic or probable of class membership. Thus, membership in a category is graded such that "better" members have more properties than the "poorer" ones i.e the membership in a product category is evaluated on a continuum (rather than a yes or no condition) of how good or bad the new instance is of the brand concept (a more flexible restriction compared to the classical model). Hence, it is clear that the chances of a new instance being accepted as a member of the base category would be highest in individuals following the prototype model and lowest for the individuals following the classical model.

(3) *In Group / Out Group Members*: According to the theory of in-group vs out-group members (Park and Rothbart, 1982), in group members judge their own group members as more dissimilar to one another than they judge the out group members. This results mainly from the more extensive interpersonal contact which occurs between the in group members in relation to the contact between out group members. This contact aids the in group members in observing more detailed information about the in group members. Therefore, in the line extension context, brand users (in group members) would see more dissimilarities in the variants of their own brand than they would in the variants of the other brands. Thus, the line extensions of other brands would be perceived as more similar to the parent brand concept and, hence, accepted as legitimate line extensions of those brands. For their own brands, however, since they see more differentiation between the various variants, the chances of their accepting the line extensions of their own brands is relatively less.

(4) *Affect Toward the Parent Brand*: Isen (1984) have shown that people store not only cognitive information about a product category in their memory but, also, the affect or feelings associated with that cognitive information. This means that consumers will have not only stored the product information about the brand but also the affect (positive or negative feelings) associated with that information. Research on the effects of affect on categorization (Isen 1984, 1987) has shown that people who are feeling more happy (positive affect) sort objects into more inclusive or broader categories. Therefore, in case of line extensions, consumers with a more positive affect toward the parent brand might get into a positive affect state on seeing or hearing the brand name and might see more extensions similar to the parent brand, leading to the acceptance of a greater number of extensions as compared to consumers with lesser positive affect towards the parent brand.

Product Related Factors.

(1) *Degree of Product Differentiation*: Product differentiation refers to the variation in the different types of brands available in a product category (Mervis and Crisafi 1982). As discussed previously, objects within a category are more similar compared to objects between two categories. As a result, distinguishing between different types of objects within the same product category becomes more difficult. For example, tartar control toothpastes and fluoride toothpastes are the two different subcategories of the toothpaste category. Not only are the different members of tartar control toothpaste category quite similar, but, in general, they are quite similar to fluoride toothpastes. Because of this high "within category" similarity and "between category" similarity at the subcategory level, the differentiation at this level is low. Therefore, it is relatively difficult to discover the differentiating features between the tartar control and fluoride toothpastes. However, the subcategory level differentiation might vary from one product category to another. For example, in the "automobiles" category there are many types of cars : "sports cars"; "luxury cars"; "compacts"; "subcompacts"; "sedans"; "convertibles", etc and each of this type has further subtypes. Thus, it would be easier to discover the differentiating features among the various types in automobiles category than in the toothpaste category. Furthermore, the easier it is to discover the differentiating features, the more difficult it is to see the two variants of a brand as similar. Also, the more difficult it is to see the two variants as similar (and hence the degree of perceived fit between the old brand concept and the new line extension concept), more difficult it is to get the new extension accepted.

(2) *The Position of the "Extension" Attribute in the Product Hierarchy*: In the field of consumer behavior, the use of hierarchies to organize products and attributes has been proposed for some time. Howard (1977) views consumers as systematically grouping and distinguishing products into hierarchies on the basis of similarity. He posits that consumers make choices at different levels of these hierarchies or at different levels of abstraction. Category level choices occur at the most abstract level of a hierarchy, while the brand level choices occur at the more concrete level. His model also posits that consumers form hierarchies of attributes from the abstract to the concrete levels that correspond to their product hierarchies. For example, the product hierarchy for Crest toothpastes might look as shown in figure 2.

The horizontal extension (Crest Fluoride to Crest Tartar) involves a change in the concept of the brand, since according to our discussion on concept conjunction, the new line extension concept will be a conjunction of the two concepts— Crest (till now only a fluoride toothpaste) and tartar control toothpastes. In the vertical extension—Crest Fluoride—regular flavor launching a 4.6 oz and 6.4 oz pack sizes, the dominant concept is still that of a tartar toothpastes since the flavors are included in the higher concept of tartar. The acceptance of horizontal extension will therefore be relatively difficult compared to the vertical line extensions which

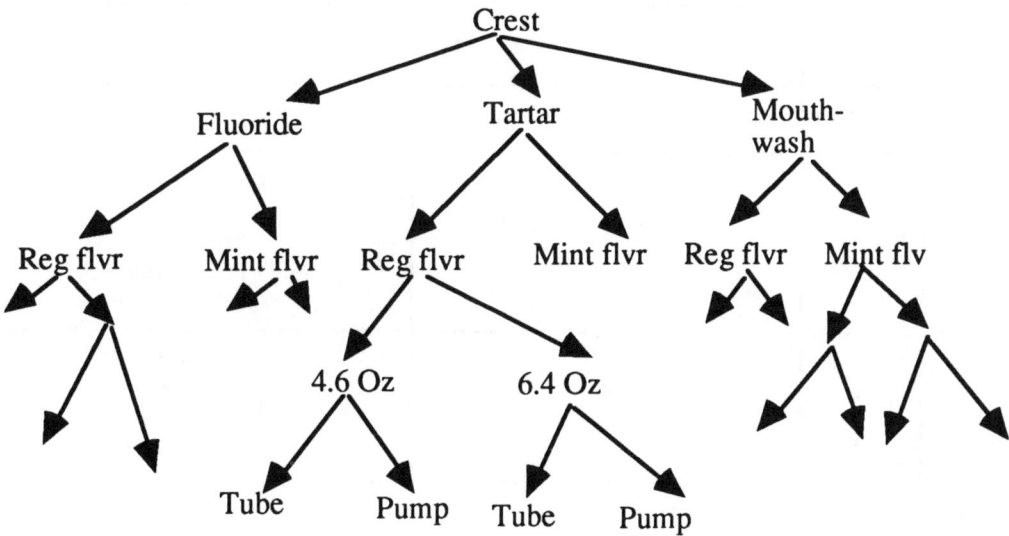

FIGURE 2
A Product Hierarchy of Crest Toothpaste

does not involve any concept modification (since the brand is still a tartar toothpaste).

(3) *Abstractness of the Current Positioning*: According to Johnson (1984; 1987), choice among non-comparable alternatives (i.e among different product categories) occurs by comparing these product categories on some abstract attributes (more general aspects of a brand) which these product categories share. Therefore, as the choice moves from comparable to the non-comparable alternatives (i.e from "within category" to "between categories"), not only does the choice process involves comparing a greater number of product categories, but the comparison among those product categories is made in terms of more abstract attributes. This is in contrast to the more concrete attributes (which directly describe some specific aspects of a brand) used to compare alternatives in the same product category. Therefore, a given abstract attribute will encompass a greater number of product categories than a concrete attribute would. Extending this principle a step further, current positioning of a brand could center on a concrete attribute as in case of "fluoride" toothpaste, or it could be an abstract positioning as in the case of "a total dental care" toothpaste. Because of the specificity of the positioning in the concrete case, the chances of an extension being perceived as incompatible to the existing concept is much higher in the concrete case than in the abstract case, where the overall global positioning of "good toothpaste" can subsume almost all of the new attributes used by the new line extensions.

(4) *Pervasiveness of the New Line Extension*: The chances of acceptance of a line extension which is already being introduced by competitors will be much higher than that of a line extension which is being introduced for the first time in the market. This would occur because a more common extension would be perceived as more of a prototype (i.e as having feature shared by majority of the brands in the market) than a new line extension which is introduced for the first time in the market.

Having looked at the theoretical aspects, what are some of the problems associated with line extensions ? As competition in different product categories intensify, companies are resorting to indiscriminate launches of line extensions, to protect their flanks from ever growing competition.

This has led to the problems of brand concept confusability (when the brand tries to be everything to everyone), and cannibalization (where the extension takes share from existing variants rather than from competition.

CLASSIFICATION OF LINE EXTENSIONS.

To make some sense out of the myriad of line extensions available in the market, a framework classifying the different types of line extensions is proposed (Table 1).

One way of classifying line extensions would be to see : (1) Which attributes (new vs old) are used to extend the brand and (2) To whom is the new line extension targeted (new vs old segment). This is related to brand objectives of increasing the market share either among the current users or nonusers of the brand. In doing this a 2X2 matrix is developed. The principle of concept conjunction will be used to hypothesize the nature of the new line extension and the implications of concept confusability; concept incompatibility; and cannibalization would be discussed for each type of extensions.

Cell 1–Same Attribute Same Segment

The first cell refers to those cases where the parent brand uses the same attribute to target the new line extension to the current users of the brand. The different types of line extensions which are possible in this cell are as follows:

- *Pack sizes* : This would refer to any variant/s of the current brand extending in new pack sizes. For example, Crest Fluoride could launch a new pack size of 10 Oz. Assuming that the concept of "new pack size" is not important in most cases, the existing concept of "Crest Fluoride" would be the dominant concept and hence the question of incompatibility does not arise. The new extension might cannibalize an existing variant if its per unit price is lower than those of other variants. Too many pack sizes for each variant might make the consumers spend more time and effort (and hence irritate) in his / her choice decision.

- *Pack types* : This would refer to any variant/s of the current brand extending itself in a new packaging. For example, Crest Sparkle launching a pump version of its toothpaste. For the same reasons as mentioned above for "pack size," Crest Sparkle would be the dominant concept

TABLE 1
A Classificatory Framework of Line Extensions

		Users	
		Current	New
Attribute	Same	• Pack sizes • Pack types • Flavors	• Flavors • Pack sizes • Pack types • Price variant • Age variant
	New	• Improvements • Combination of attributes	• Horizontal • Improvements • Combination of attributes

and hence there is no question of any incompatibility between the two concepts. The arguments for "cannibalization" and "consumer irritability" would be the same as mentioned for "pack types."

• *Flavors* : One way to extend the usage of the brand among current consumers is to launch different flavors, provided each flavor is positioned as a different concept. For example, in category of fruit juices, orange juice could be positioned as a breakfast drink whereas, apple juice could be positioned as a "lunch" drink. The same arguments for concept dominance as in case of pack sizes and pack types would be applicable here. However, there could be an incompatibility if the new flavor is not compatible with the existing taste of the product (more sour when the general taste of the brand is sweet). Cannibalization and Consumer irritability might not arise if the new extension is not positioned distinctively.

Cell 2–Same Attribute New Segment

The second cell refers to those cases where the brand uses the same attribute to target it to the new users. The different types of line extensions which are possible in this cell are as follows:

• *Pack sizes and Pack types and Flavors*: (As in cell one) could also be used to target the new segment/s. Same arguments as those made for Cell 1 would be applicable here. However, since the new extension is targeted to new users, the problem of cannibalization does not arise.

• *Price variants:* This would refer to any variant/s of the brand extending to a different price level within the same attribute positioning. For example., Rolls Royce launching a cheaper version of its current brand to broaden its target market base. The dominant concept in this case would be that of old Rolls Royce (for a not very well known brand name like Pontiac, the market concept of "economy" cars might be the dominant concept). There could be incompatibility in terms of "image" of Rolls Royce (status symbol vs an "economy car"). Whereas, incompatibility in terms of "capability" might arise in case of an "economy" brand like Honda launching a "luxury car," and this could be one of

the reason why Honda used a different brand name (Accura) to launch its luxury car. Since the new extension is targeted to new users, the question of cannibalization does not arise. Brand confusability might arise if the brand "positioned" at one end of a price continuum launches an extension at the other end of the continuum (e.g., a "premium" car launching an "economy" extension).

• *Age variant*: In this case, the brand uses the same attribute. For example, Johnson and Johnson used the attribute of "softness" to extend its baby shampoo to adults. The dominant concept in this case could be either the concept of "J & J " shampoo (since the "adult" consumers might strongly desire the presence of "J & J " shampoo attributes in their new shampoo) or it could be the concept of "adult shampoo," if the consumers are not sure about the performance capability of a baby shampoo for adults. To the extent that "J & J " is no longer exclusively associated with children products, there would be brand concept confusability.

Cell 3–New Attribute Same Segment

The third cell refers to those case where a new attribute is used by the parent brand to target the extension to the current consumers.

• *Improvements* : In this case, the brand improves one of its variants to target the current users. For example, Tide liquid launching Tide with bleach. The dominant concept in this case would be that of old Tide because the improvement in performance would be with respect to the old Tide and the consumers would not be able to form expectations of "laundry detergent with bleach" as the improvement would be launched for the first time. The problem of incompatibility might arise if the new extension does not perform as well as the parent brand on some important attributes. The chances of cannibalization are high unless the per unit price differential between the two is high. As the new variant replaces the old (in most extensions of such types), there is not much scope of concept confusability. However, consumer irritability might increase if this improvement is launched in all the different pack sizes and pack types of the brand currently available.

• *Combination of Benefits*: Here one or more new benefits are combined with one of the existing benefits (currently offered by the brand) to launch a new line extension. For example, Tylenol launched a new line extension Tylenol cold and flu, after combining the benefit of "flu" with the existing variant of Tylenol cold. Depending upon individual preferences, the dominant concept in this case could be either, Tylenol cold or flu remedies. There might be an incompatibility problem if the new attribute added is inconsistent with the old brand concept (very rare). There could be some cannibalization if the per unit price difference between the two variants is not very high. Confusability of such extensions is high because the brand is now no longer associated with one attribute.

Cell 4–New Attribute New Segment

The fourth cell refers to those cases where the brand uses a new attribute to target the extension to new users. The change in the brand concept (relative to other three cells) is maximum. The different types of line extensions which are possible in this cell are "improvements," "combinations," of the third cell. A horizontal line extension would also be classified in this category. Referring to the figure 2 above, the extension of Crest from fluoride to tartar control would be an example of a horizontal extension. The dominant concept in this case could either be the "core" Crest or it could be the tartar prototype, depending upon such factors as "is the consumer a "brand user" or a "segment user"? [if a user is a brand user (i.e., if s/he does not mind using any variant of Crest), then the concept of "Crest Fluoride" might be the dominant concept; and if the user is a "segment" user (the user prefers to use "tartar" toothpastes, but does not mind which tartar brand is s/he using), then the dominant concept will be that of "tartar" toothpaste]. Incompatibility could arise in few instances as in the case of a "tough on dirt" detergent extending into a detergent which is "soft on clothes". Confusion will arise since the core of the brand is getting diffused.

Our framework is superior to Kotler's (1991) framework (product line stretching) because whereas Kotler's framework could apply for line extensions and multibrand strategies (with different brand names), our framework is more specific in terms of it being relevant for line extensions only. Also Kotler's (1991) framework could account for only two (price and improvements) out of the eight types of line extensions as classified by our framework. Since our framework is more detailed, we expect it would be more useful to the practitioners.

Therefore, depending upon the brand objectives (increasing market share among new users vs current users), and other factors like brand concept confusability, incompatibility, consumer irritability, and cannibalization, product managers could use the above framework in deciding which variant/s should a brand extend into.

MANAGERIAL RECOMMENDATIONS

Having discussed the various issues involved in the introduction of line extensions, we now propose some managerial recommendations.

(1) The concepts of "concept conjunction" and "dominant concept" have implications for advertising strategy and product development. Both should emphasize "brand" features (brand name and brand attributes respectively) if brand concept is the dominant concept. Whereas, the "extension category" features should be emphasized if the market concept is the dominant concept. This could be done by advertising the new extension as how good a member the new extension is of the extension product category and by incorporating more features of the extension product category than those of the brand.

(2) The problem of confusability could be reduced if the manufacturers make the new extensions distinctive from the current brand concept — satisfying a distinct need. The example of a laundry detergent for "colored" clothes given above would be relevant here. The packaging could be made more distinctive in tune with the modified concept of the brand.

(3) To attract the nonusers, the brand should try to rectify its "negative image" among them.

(4) The managers should take advantage of moderating factors (wherever possible), to get a favorable response from the consumers. For example, by positioning the parent brand on an "abstract attribute," by keeping the advertising of the extension simple so as to attract the novices.

REFERENCES

Alba, Joseph W and J Wesley. Hutchinson (1987), "Dimensions of Consumer Expertise," *Journal of Consumer Research*, vol 13 (Mar), 411-454.

Barsalou, Lawrence W and G H. Bower (1980), "A Priori Determinants of Concepts' Highly Accessible Information," Paper presented at the Annual Meeting of the American Psychologists Association, Montreal

_____ (1987), "The Instability of Graded Structure : Implications for Nature of Concepts" in *Concepts and Conceptual Development*, ed. Ulric Neisser. Cambridge : Cambridge University Press

Brooks L (1978), "Nonanalytic Concept Formation and Memory for Instances" in *Cognition and Categorization*, eds E. H Rosch and B. B Lloyd, Hillsdale, NJ : Lawrence Erlbaum Associates.

Bullmore, J (1984), "The Brand and its Image Revisited," *International Journal of Advertising*, 3, 235-38.

Fannin, Rebecca (1989), "Where are the New Brands," *Marketing and Media Decisions*, 24 : 7, 20-7.

Hampton, James, (1987), "Inheritance of Attributes in Natural Concept Conjunctions," *Memory and Cognition*, 15 : 1, 55-71.

Howard, John A (1977), *Consumer Behavior : Applications of Theory*, New York : Mcgraw-Hill.

Isen, A. M and Kimberly A Daubman (1984), "The Influence of Affect on Categorization," *Journal of Personality and Social Psychology*, 47: 6, 1206-17.

_____ , K A. Daubman and G P. Nowicki (1987), "Positive Affect Facilitates Creative Problem Solving," *Journal of Personality and Social Psychology*, 52 :6, 1122-31.

Johnson, Michael D (1984), "Consumer Choice Strategies for Comparing Non-Comparable Alternatives," *Journal of Consumer Research*, 11 (Dec), 741-53.

Kotler Philip (1991), *Marketing Management— Analysis, Planning, Implementation and Control* Englewoods, NJ : Prentice Hall Inc.

Mervis , C. B and Maria A. Crisafi (1982), "Order of Acquistion of Subordinate, Basic, and Superordinate Level Categories, " *Child Development*, 53, 258-66.

Murphy, Gregory L and Douglas L. Medin (1985), "The Role of Theories in Conceptual Coherence," *Psychological Review*, 92 (July), 298-316.

Murray, Noel, H. Sujan, E. R Hirt, and M. Sujan (1990), "The Influence of Mood on Categorization : A Cognitive Flexibility Interpretation," *Journal of Personality and Social Psychology*, 59 (Sept), 298-316.

Newman, J W (1957), "New Insights, New Progress for Marketing," *Harvard Business Review*, Nov-Dec, 95-102.

Oliver, Richard L and Wayne S. DeSabro (1988), "Response Determinants in Satisfaction Judgements," *Journal of Consumer Research*, 14 (March), 495-507.

Park, B and M Rothbart (1982), "Perception of Out-group Homogeneity and Levels of Social Categorization : Memory for the Subordinate Attribute of In-group and Out-group Members," *Journal of Personality and Social Psychology*, 42, 1051-68.

Smith, E. E and D. L Medin (1981), *Category and Concepts*. Cambridge, MA : Harvard University Press.

An Examination of the Effects of Multiple Brand Extensions on the Brand Concept[1]
Sandy D. Jap, University of Florida[2]

ABSTRACT

This study examines the effects of multiple extensions on two types of brand equity: equity of the original parent brand or anchor product, and a global "family brand" image. Unlike most previous work stressing equity as brand affect, equity is construed in terms of its impact on brand concept accessibility, evaluations and accessibility of brand specific beliefs. The results indicate that consistent extensions lead to higher brand concept accuracy and accessibility. Independent extensions are associated with higher accuracy and do not appear to detrimentally affect family brand equity, but can lead to decreased accessibility of brand beliefs.

INTRODUCTION

Brand extensions have been defined as the use of a brand to introduce products in different categories outside of the parent brand category as a means of achieving higher sales growth rates, higher ROI, and advertising and promotion efficiencies (Baldinger 1990). More recent research has examined the effects of multiple brand extensions on perceptions and evaluations of the proposed extension as well as the original core brand (Keller & Aaker 1992). The present research takes an additional step toward better understanding the effects of multiple extensions with respect to the original core brand and its anchor product.

The purpose of this study is to examine how multiple extensions might affect the brand at the level of the original parent product and at a more global, family level. More specifically, it is hypothesized that extensions can enhance and reinforce the parent brand concept, when they are made in a manner consistent with brand-specific associations. However, when extensions are made in a manner independent of the brand specific associations, the brand's global, family concept may be detrimentally affected.

THE BRAND CONCEPT

The brand extension literature has found that consumers tend to search for a common "link" or degree of similarity that explains the extension in relation to the brand (See Keller 1991 for a review). Although similarity is often defined as similarity of product categories, the fit or consistency of a brand extension to the parent brand in the present research is defined as a function of the brand concept resulting from *brand-specific* features or associations (Broniarczyk 1992).

The brand concept consists of the primary brand-specific association, either at the attribute or product image level, including abstract meanings (e.g. "durability," "quality," "status") or concrete attributes (e.g. "pure ingredients," "dandruff control"). Although brands often have multiple associations, this study assumes that a dominant association can be identified that is able to explain or link the original product and all its extensions as a group. Brand concepts serve to position the product within its category, often referring to the distinguishing feature that differentiates the brand from its competitors. According to this conceptualization, similarity is a search for a meaningful commonality among what might otherwise be a dissimilar product grouping under a common brand name.

FAMILY BRAND AND PARENT BRAND EQUITY

Just as "Smith" refers to a family name, and "Tom Smith" refers to a specific member, brand concepts can exist at two levels: the family level and the parent product level. When brand names such as Kelloggs, and Kodak are associated with multiple products, the family brand concept (e.g. "breakfast foods," "photography") encompasses the entire product line. The parent brand concept is almost always the same as the family brand concept, since the parent product is the brand's anchor product. However, this does not preclude the possibility that the brand concept may be one that is independent of the family brand concept[3]. Brand equity should be strengthened at the family or parent level when a concept is strongly associated to a particular brand, and diluted[4] when the concept is weakly associated with the brand.

Consistent Extensions

Brand concepts can act as explanations or theories, that simplify reality, making a category of knowledge increasingly informative, useful and efficient (cf. Murphy & Medin 1985). When multiple extensions are made on a basis consistent with the family brand concept, each extension emphasizes the same brand concept as the original product, making the family brand concept increasingly coherent. Consequently, when consumers are exposed to the family brand name or any of its products, the family brand concept should be quickly and accurately recalled.

Consistent extensions increase the opportunity for cognitive elaboration (relative to a control group) as exposure to the family's products strengthens the family concept and causes consumers to make the association between the original brand concept and the new product. As the family and product level brand concepts are repeatedly strengthened, beliefs concerning its nature should be enhanced. This reduction in uncertainty can lead to positive affect (Nuttin & Greenwald 1968; Obermiller 1985). Changes in evaluation are unlikely to be dramatic, such as positive evaluations becoming negative; however, preexisting positive evaluations may become more positive.

Given the prior discussion, if the original family brand concept is maintained over an increasing number of product categories, the brand concept becomes increasingly accessible because extensions are made in accordance with the consumer's prior knowledge/ expectations of the brand and are continually fortifying the brand's original family concept. Constant repetition of the brand concept through multiple extensions should also strengthen existing beliefs about the nature of the brand concept and increase liking for the

---

[1] This is a condensed version of the originally submitted manuscript. A longer, more readable version is available from the author; her address is: University of Florida, Dept. of Marketing, 212 Bryan Hall, Gainesville, FL 32611.

[2] This manuscript has benefitted greatly from the insightful advice and comments of Joe Alba, Rich Lutz, and especially John Lynch.

[3] In other instances, firms may introduce independent brand concepts by creating independent brand names in conjunction with the family name (e.g. Black & Decker Dust Buster, Nabisco Cheez-its). The use of "double" brand names is an interesting direction for future research in brand equity, but is beyond the scope of the present study.

[4] Brand dilution is defined as a decrease in the strength of beliefs about the parent brand (Roedder John & Loken 1990).

brand via reduced uncertainty. Additionally, there is no reason to believe that this might differentially affect the parent brand at the family or parent brand level.

> H1: Consistent extensions lead to increased family and product brand concept accessibility, increased belief strength, and more positive evaluations of the original product and the family brand name.

This hypothesis further assumes that the brand concept is positively valued and ceiling effects on brand concept accessibility, belief strength, and evaluations are nonexistent.

Independent Extensions

Brand dilution research is sometimes examined as the result of inconsistent extensions, where an inconsistent extension basis represents the opposite end of the brand concept continuum (i.e., gentle—harsh, high quality—low quality). This is a convenient assumption, and one that lends itself well to hypotheses similar to those found in the stereotype and schema revision literature. In reality, few firms would introduce brand extensions that blatantly contradict the original brand concept. Firms that want to broaden their customer base to include new segments are likely to use an independent brand name with an association that does not conflict with their current brand concept. Therefore, this study is based on the premise that firms are more likely to introduce brand extensions on bases *independent* of the family brand concept, as opposed to extension bases directly opposed to the parent brand concept. An independent brand extension does not necessarily imply that the extension basis is irrelevant in the product class; rather, it means that the extension association is made on a dimension that has no necessary implication for the parent brand association, or an association that is subjectively uncorrelated with the parent brand concept. If Neutrogena's family brand concept is "pure ingredients," independent extensions may emphasize other associations such as "deep cleaning," "invigorating scent," or "pricey."

Family Level. Independent extensions are more likely to result in equity dilution at the family level than at the parent brand level because as the association set size linked to a brand name increases, the strength of a "link" or "retrieval path" is weakened (Anderson 1976; Raaijmakers & Shiffrin 1981), and competing associations inhibit and interfere with retrieval (Anderson 1976; Meyers-Levy 1989; Sujan & Bettman 1989). Over time, the brand may lose its definitive meaning or association. Additionally, the presence of new independent associations may lead to decreases in the strength or accessibility of the consumer's beliefs about the family brand concept.

Decreases in brand concept accessibility and brand beliefs are likely to impact evaluation of the parent brand, as evaluations are subject to change as an individual learns more about a stimulus. If a consumer is unable to integrate the independent associations into a coherent brand concept, uncertainty and aversive tension may arise leading to decreased affect (i.e., Biehal & Chakravarti 1986; Johnson & Levin 1985; Obermiller 1985; Meyer 1981; Simmons & Lynch 1991). Thus, it is expected that brand evaluations will also be lower at the family level than at the parent brand level.

Parent Brand Level. Independent extensions are likely to lead to minimal dilution effects of the original parent brand, because these associations are the most well-learned over time, and because the category context in which the information was originally encoded may trigger encoding specificities (Tulving & Thomson 1973) that enhance recall when the category is cued. Therefore, it is hypothesized that independent extensions differentially dilute brand equity at the family and original product level. This occurs because independent associations in various product categories make it increasingly difficult to cognitively process all the information into a coherent family brand concept. Encoding specificities that occur at the time of learning, in conjunction with the presence of a category cue, may account for the apparent lack of dilution, and changes in brand beliefs and evaluation that are observed with respect to the original parent product.

> H2: Independent extensions have little effect on parent brand concept accessibility, brand beliefs, or brand evaluation at the product level. However, independent extensions reduce brand concept coherence, brand beliefs, and brand evaluation at the family level.

Recent research on brand equity dilution has reported seemingly conflicting findings. Roedder John and Loken (1990) examined conditions that lead to dilution at the brand's global image level; they found that dilution occurred when moderately similar brand extensions were made. In contrast, Keller and Aaker (1992) reported that unsuccessful extensions in dissimilar product categories do not adversely impact the parent brand. This apparent difference might be explained by better understanding the procedures that were used. Roedder John and Loken (1990) cued subjects by the parent brand name and reported their beliefs and associations about the parent brand at the family brand level.

However, in the Keller and Aaker (1992) study, subjects were presented with the original parent brand *product* and then the dependent parent brand measures were taken. Encoding specificities with regard to the original product could likely have been triggered as a result of exposure to the product, inhibiting the occurrence of dilution. The difference in the results of the two studies might thus be attributed to whether or not a specific product category was cued. It could be that merely asking, "does Brand A mean gentleness?" leads to qualitatively different results than when the same question is posed in the presence of a specific product category cue (i.e. "does Brand A *product* mean gentleness?"). This study will account for both of these situations by using category cues when dependent measures are taken at the parent brand level, and taking family level dependent measures in the absence of product cues.

METHOD

Procedure

Subjects were students enrolled in an introductory marketing class at a major university in the Southeast United States. Forty subjects were shown sixteen health and beauty aid advertisements. The group was given five minutes to study an ad book and product display, and were told that although the ads were relatively standardized, there was enough information to form some opinions about each product. The ad for the focal parent brand, Coast soap, was always the third ad in the booklet. Following this ad were ads for extensions of Coast soap. Ten subjects saw shampoo, anti-perspirant, and sunblock extensions that made a consistent "clean scent" claim. Ten subjects saw extension ads that made independent claims ("body building" shampoo, "dry" anti-perspirant, and "maximum sun protection" sunblock). Twenty subjects saw no extension advertisements. Subjects were allocated in such a manner so as to provide a stable baseline estimate for the control condition, since many of the focal contrasts would be made with respect to this group. All other filler brands were randomized within the book. Each condition had four randomized versions of the ad books. The product display contained the high and low market share brands and high and low quality brands (arranged by product category) used to anchor the affect ratings administered later in the procedure.

A five-minute filler task was administered, and then subjects were given an additional five minutes to review the ads and product display a second time to insure sufficient opportunity to elaborate upon the product associations and form opinions. This was followed by another five-minute filler task after which subjects were given sheets of paper with brand names. They were asked to take into consideration all that they knew about the brand and then list five associations (e.g. product qualities, images, characteristics and features) that came to mind whenever they saw the brand name.

Subjects were then seated at computers and presented with ten true/false statements in random order. Each subject's response time and accuracy were unobtrusively recorded by the computer. Subjects then responded to sixteen randomly ordered brand belief questions; they were told to take into account all that they knew about the brands. The final portion of the computerized questionnaire asked for evaluative ratings. Subjects were first presented with the brand names displayed on the product table, in order to "anchor" their rating scales equivalently across conditions before making their evaluations of the treatment brands. At this point, subjects completed a 30-minute filler task, the free association measures, and the computerized measures at the other level of measurement (family or parent brand). A post-experimental questionnaire was administered at the conclusion of the experiment.

Design

A 2x3x2 factorial design was used, with measurement level (family level; parent brand level) as a within subject variable, and extension type (consistent, independent, control) as a between subject variable. An order variable of measurement level (parent brand first—family second, family-first—parent brand second) was also introduced, to test for order effects; this variable was not significant, reducing the overall design to a 2x3 factorial.

Pretesting of Stimuli. In order to avoid any possible effects that might result from category expertise, three health and beauty aid product categories were chosen; differences in knowledge were expected to be minimal. Each product category was pretested to insure that product familiarity did not differ significantly by gender and all brands used were moderately familiar. This was done to avoid ceiling effects and dependent measure ratings that might be biased upward.

The extension positionings were pretested to insure that they were similarly perceived across individuals and were relevant to their product categories. In order to reduce demand artifacts and hypothesis guessing, the extensions were not emphasized as extensions of the original product category; they were merely seen as products with the same brand name in the ad book.

Dependent variables. The dependent measures emphasized the brand's primary image positioning in the advertisement and were comprised of four tasks. Brand concept accessibility was measured by its effects on recall order in free association listings and response times for association verification. Accessible brand concepts should be one of the first associations recalled upon exposure to the brand name. This measure did not yield significant findings in any condition and subsequently will not be addressed further. The association verification task at the family level required the subject to answer true/false to ten statements such as, "Coast means clean scent." At the parent brand level, subjects saw a product category name before responding to the true/false statements.

Brand beliefs were measured by questions such as, "To what degree do you believe that Coast actually possesses a clean scent?" At the parent brand level, the question was phrased, "To what degree do you believe that Coast soap actually possesses a clean scent?" Responses were indicated on a 7-point Likert scale (1=I don't believe the brand has it; 7=I do believe the brand has it).

Brand evaluation was measured by presenting the subject with a brand name and asking the subject to indicate the extent to which he/she felt the brand represented an inferior/superior product. Individuals in the parent brand level condition were given the product category before making their responses. Responses were indicated on a 7-point Likert scale (1=inferior product; 7=superior product).

RESULTS

Only two subjects indicated an awareness of Coast as the treatment brand in the post-experimental questionnaire. Analysis of the data without their responses indicated no significant differences, so their responses were retained in the analysis. The questionnaire further indicated that demand effects were not a threat. The results are displayed in Table 1.

Consistent Extensions vs. Controls

Consistent extensions were not expected to differentially affect family and product level equity. As predicted, there were no significant interactions of extension type (consistent vs. control) and level on any of the dependent variables. Response times to the verification statement in the consistent extension condition (m=1528) were significantly lower ($F_{1,31}=7.22$; $p<.05$) than response times for the controls (m=2310). Subjects in the consistent condition also displayed a significantly higher accuracy rate (m=1.0) than the control group (m=.78), ($F_{1,31}=8.24$; $p<.01$).

Brand beliefs were higher following consistent extensions (m=6.5) then following no extensions (m=5.9), although this was not significant ($F_{1,31}=2.51$). The accessibility of these beliefs in the consistent condition (m=3958) did not differ significantly from the controls (m=4167), ($F_{1,31}=.035$). Additionally, subjects' evaluations in the consistent condition (m=6.0) became more positive than the controls (m=5.5) although the difference was not significant ($F_{1,31}=1.74$).

In sum, there is partial support for hypothesis 1, consistent extensions appear to lead to more accessible brand concepts and higher accuracy. The results for the brand beliefs and evaluation prediction are directionally correct, but did not reach significance. These results might be due to the fact that some of the contrasts were underpowered. The power was .56 ($w^2=.049$) for the brand belief contrast, and .50 ($w^2=.042$) for the evaluation contrast. With larger cell sizes, these differences may approach statistical significance.

Independent Extensions vs. Controls

The predicted interaction of measurement level and extension type on the response times of the verification task was not significant ($F_{1,31}=.035$), although reaction times in the independent condition at the family level (m=2172) were higher than at the product level (m=1929). Response times in the independent condition did not differ significantly from the controls at the family level ($F_{1,31}=.796$). As predicted, for parent brand response times, the difference between control subjects and those exposed to independent extensions was not significant ($F_{1,31}=.21$).

The interaction of measurement level and extension type on accuracy was not significant ($F_{1,31}=1.7$). However, a main effect of extension type on accuracy was significant ($F_{1,31}=4.9$, $p<.05$); accuracy in the independent condition (m=.95) was higher than the control group (m=.78). This was an unexpected finding; it could be

TABLE 1
Dependent Measures

	Consistent n = 10	Independent n = 10	Control n = 20
Family Brand Level			
Brand concept accessibility*	1515	2172	2407
Brand concept accuracy	1.0	1.0	.70
Brand beliefs	6.5	6.3	5.9
Brand beliefs accessibility*	3119	4884	3974
Evaluation	5.8	5.8	5.6
Parent Brand Level			
Brand concept accessibility*	1541	1929	2212
Brand concept accuracy	1.0	.90	.85
Brand beliefs	6.4	6.4	6.0
Brand beliefs accessibility*	4798	6447	4360
Evaluation	6.2	5.5	5.5
Total Means			
Brand concept accessibility*	1528	2050	2310
Brand concept accuracy	1.0	.95	.78
Brand beliefs	6.5	6.4	5.9
Brand beliefs accessibility*	3958	5666	4167
Evaluation	6.0	5.7	5.5

* measured in msec.

that exposure to the treatment brand "reminds" the subjects of the original parent brand concept such that accuracy is maintained, even in the presence of newly learned, independent associations.

The hypothesized interaction of measurement level and extension type on brand beliefs was also not significant ($F_{1,31}=0$). At the product level, the brand belief difference between the independent (m=6.4) and control group (m=6.0) was not significant, as predicted ($F_{1,31}=.629$).

The interaction of measurement level and extension type on response times to the brand belief statements was not significant ($F_{1,31}=.74$). However, there was a significant main effect of extension type on response time ($F_{1,31}=7.25$; p<.05); brand belief accessibility in the control condition (m=4167) was higher than the independent group (m=5666). Additionally, the independent condition response time was significantly higher ($F_{1,31}=9.40$; p<.01) than the consistent condition (m=3959).

The interaction of measurement level and extension type on evaluation was not significant ($F_{1,31}=1.07$). Contrary to expectations, independent extensions increased family brand evaluations (m=5.8) while having no effect on parent brand evaluations (m=5.5); however, this difference was not significant.

Taken together, these data partially support hypothesis two in that no significant differences were found at the parent brand level. The results suggest that learning new independent associations inhibits brand belief accessibility without affecting brand concept accuracy.

DISCUSSION

Limitations

There are several modifications that can improve the study. First, larger sample sizes in the consistent and independent conditions should improve statistical power for key contrasts. Second, multiple measures of brand evaluation would strengthen confidence in the reliability of the measures. Finally, the theory might be better tested with dependent measures that are less "noisy" so that effects are easily detected. Response times are characterized by a high error component resulting in the need for large sample sizes in order to bring the power of the study to a satisfactory level.

CONCLUSIONS

One purpose of this study was to show that brand extensions can enhance and reinforce the original parent brand concept when extensions are made in a manner consistent with the family brand's primary brand-specific associations. The results seem to lend partial support to hypothesis 1. Consistent extensions lead to significant increases in brand concept accuracy and accessibility. Although consistent extensions did not lead to significant increases in brand beliefs, they did become higher, suggesting that future research may be worthwhile to better understand the process by which this occurs.

There was mixed support found for hypothesis 2; parent brand equity in the independent condition did not differ significantly from the controls. However, independent extensions improved brand concept accuracy at both the family and product level. A plausible explanation for this result might be that exposure to the treatment brand reminds subjects about the original brand concept, enabling them to maintain a high degree of accuracy. Although subjects were exposed to independent associations, family equity appeared resistant to dilution effects; there were virtually no significant decreases in category accessibility, brand beliefs and evaluations at the family level.

The limitations of a laboratory study may account for why dilution effects were not observed. First, in the real world, it is likely that dilution effects occur over *time*, and so the half-hour filler task delay was not long enough for memory deficits to occur. Second, brands often have several strong associations as opposed to a single, dominant brand concept. It could be that new extensions that emphasize only one of a family brand's multiple associations may result in dilution of the non-emphasized associations. Finally, since independent associations did not introduce information that disconfirmed or contradicted the original brand concept, there may have been no reason to modify original beliefs that "Coast possesses a clean scent."

Independent associations had a detrimental effect on brand belief accessibility, holding serious implications for brand equity. If the product and brand concept association is not accessible, then the product is less likely to enter the consumer's evoked set in a memory based choice situation. Even if the brand were to enter the consumer's evoked set, an inaccessible brand concept might result in the brand being evaluated on its competitors' strengths instead of its own strengths.

Nevertheless, the decomposition of brand equity at the family and product level is conceptually useful, holding strategic implications for brand management. Certain types of extensions may be instrumental in strengthening the global brand meaning in the consumer's mind. Alternatively, management might deliberately use extensions to weaken a brand's family image, perhaps with the goal of providing a broader platform for launching future new products.

Future Research

Future avenues of research that have been highlighted by this study include further examination of the consequences of accessibility of the brand concept and beliefs. Inaccessible beliefs can prevent a brand from being evoked and considered, as well as prevent the brand from being evaluated on its dimensions of strength.

Additional research is also needed that examines the role of uncertainty in the development of beliefs and evaluations toward the parent brand or any of its products. Uncertainty was not explicitly manipulated or measured in this study, but a better understanding of its effects would contribute to our knowledge of brand equity.

There is still much to be learned about how brand extensions might be used to effectively implement long term corporate strategy goals. This study attempted to take a step in this direction by better understanding how consistent and independent extension types might affect consumer perceptions of the corporate family brand and parent brand.

REFERENCES

Anderson, John R. (1976), *Language, Memory, and Thought*, Hillsdale, NJ: Lawrence Erlbaum Associates.

Baldinger, Allan L. (1990), "Defining and Applying the Brand Equity Concept: Why the Researcher Should Care," *Journal of Advertising Research*, 30, RC2-RC5.

Biehal, Gabriel, Dipankar Chakravarti (1986), "Consumers' Use of Memory and External Information in Choice: Macro and Micro Perspectives," *Journal of Consumer Research*, 12, (March), 382-405.

Broniarczyck, Susan M. (1992), unpublished dissertation, Department of Marketing, University of Florida.

Johnson, Richard D., Irwin P. Levin (1985), "More than Meets the Eye: The Effect of Missing Information on Purchase Evaluations", *Journal of Consumer Research*, 12, (September), 169-177.

Keller, Kevin Lane (1991), "Conceptualizing, Measuring, and Managing Customer-Based Brand Equity," Working paper, Stanford University.

_____, David A. Aaker (1992), "The Effects of Sequential Introduction of Brand Extensions," *Journal of Marketing Research*, 29, (February), 35-50.

Loken, Barbara, James Ward (1990), "Alternative Approaches to Understanding the Determinants of Typicality," *Journal of Consumer Research*, 17, (September), 111-26.

Meyer, Robert J. (1981), "A Model of Multiattribute Judgments Under Attribute Uncertainty and Informational Constraint," *Journal of Marketing Research*, 18, (November), 428-441.

Meyers-Levy, Joan (1989), "The Influence of a Brand Name's Association Set Size and Word Frequency on Brand Memory," *Journal of Consumer Research*, 16, (September), 197-207.

Murphy, Gregory L., Douglas L. Medin (1985), "The Role of Theories in Conceptual Coherence," *Psychological Review*, 92, (3), July, 289-316.

Nuttin, Joseph and Anthony G. Greenwald (1968), *Reward and Punishment in Human Learning*, New York: Academic Press.

Obermiller, Carl (1985), "Varieties of Mere Exposure: The Effects of Processing Style and Repetition on Affective Response," *Journal of Consumer Research*, 12, (June), 17-29.

Raaijmakers, Jeroen G. W., Richard M. Shiffrin (1981), "Search of Associative Memory," *Psychological Review*, 88, (March), 93-134.

Roedder John, Deborah, Barbara Loken (1990), "Diluting Brand Equity: The Negative Impact of Brand Extensions," University of Minnesota, working paper.

Simmons, Carolyn J., John G. Lynch, Jr. (1991), "Inference Effects without Inference Making? Effects of Missing Information on Discounting and Use of Presented Information," *Journal of Consumer Research*, 17, (March), 477-491.

Sujan, Mita, James R. Bettman (1989), "The Effects of Brand Positioning Strategies on Consumer's Brand and Category: Some Insights from Schema Research," *Journal of Marketing Research*, 26, (November), 454-467.

Tulving, Endel and Donald M. Thomson (1973), "Encoding Specificity and Retrieval Processes in Episodic Memory," *Psychological Review*, 80, (September), 352-373.

Candidates as Engendered Products: Prototypes in Political Person Perception

Basil G. Englis, Rutgers University
Greta Eleen Pennell, Rutgers University

ABSTRACT

Current models of voting behavior consider voting as partly based on an evaluation of the candidate as a person. Such candidate-centered approaches to voting direct our attention voting as a social judgment. Thus, voters' prototypes of the "ideal" politician become important in considering how individual candidates will be judged and how votes will be cast. Moreover, a better understanding of voters' perceptions of the "ideal" politician can be useful strategic input for the positioning of political candidates. Previous studies of the prototypes associated with ideal candidates have not provided a sufficiently detailed examination of the content of voter prototypes (content domains) nor have they considered potential differences in prototypes as a function of level of office or candidate gender. The findings of the present research emphasize the difference between the prototypes of ideal candidates when gender is left unspecified, as compared with the prototypes for ideal political candidates whose gender is specified as either male or female. The discussion considers the implications of the results for the positioning of *female* politicians.

The growing dominance of electronic media in the marketing of political candidates has dramatically affected the manner in which voters are exposed to politicians. One hundred, or even fifty, years ago voters generally only read the speeches of politicians as printed in pamphlets and in newspapers, or they read articles written about their issue positions and speeches. Only in the realm of local politics did voters have any form of more "direct" contact with politicians. Even then politicians were usually seen in a crowded setting — a smoke-filled auditorium or waving from the back of a departing train. And, at the national level of politics only a small fraction of the electorate ever *actually* heard or saw politicians. The advent and proliferation of radio acted to "humanize" political information, transforming politicians into people and enabling voters to make inferences about candidates as *people*. For example, when a politician increased the volume or cadence of his or her speech a listener might infer that the speaker was determined, whereas hesitations and stutters might convey a lack of certainty (cf. Englis 1992).

Today, television dominates voter "contact" with politicians (e.g., Graber 1984; Swerdlow 1988). In bringing politicians into the intimacy of America's homes, television directs voters' attention to the personal characteristics and qualities of politicians. It allows viewers to examine subtle changes in facial expression and posture. Television also provides "behind the scenes" (although often staged) views of politicians at home with their families, on vacation, or at social gatherings. As a result, personal attributes (i.e., personality, physical appearance) become inescapable aspects of politicians as people. Although these media bites "humanize" political leaders, the access provided to voters also highlights the need for marketers to "manage" mass-mediated voter impressions. The recent case of President Bush's gastric disturbance in Japan highlights the risks of "uncontrolled" television coverage.

This emphasis on politicians as "people" has in part arisen from the properties of broadcast media, and in part by a shift in the nature of political campaigns. Increasingly, "style becomes substance" (McGinniss 1969, p. 30) as "modern politicians are created and marketed [for public consumption] much like a bar of soap" (Solomon 1992, p. 29). In much the same way as personal advertisements promote people as products (Hirschman, 1987), politicians are commodified and voters are lured by presumably desirable constellations of personal characteristics. Today it is people, more than ideologies or issues, that are the products of politics. The basis for voters' evaluations, attitudes, and eventual voting behavior has shifted from the traditional arena of parties and issues to that of social judgment. This paper examines the personal characteristics that voters associate with "ideal" politicians and considers the importance of these perceptions in the positioning and marketing of political candidates.

Models of Voting Behavior

Since the 1940s, three general models of voting behavior have dominated political science: these emphasize either the party (party-centered), policies (policy-centered), or the person (candidate-centered) (e.g., Campbell, Converse, and Miller 1960; Kirkpatrick, Lyons, and Fitzgerald 1975; Popkin et al. 1976). Party-centered models dominated from the 1940s through the 1960s and conceptualized voting as a choice between parties that was dictated by long-standing party loyalties. Thus, party label acted like a brand name by representing both a mark of affiliation with one group over another, and a general set of expectancies regarding future policies. As long as important differences do not exist between the product offered (platform) and the consumer's own needs, party is assumed to be the basis of voter decision-making. However, historical analyses (e.g., Stokes and Miller 1962) reveal that party membership data alone have rarely been sufficient to predict voting behavior in national elections.

Policy-centered models gained prominence during the 1960's and 1970's when specific issues (i.e., the Vietnam War, Watergate) polarized the electorate along other than traditional party lines. These models conceptualize voting as the result of a voter's evaluations of each candidate's positions on important issues, and how well the candidates' positions match the voter's own views (e.g., Fiorina, 1981). Policy-centered models assume that voters are in a high-involvement choice situation and that actual differences between the issue positions of the candidates are of central importance in determining voting behavior.

However, unless issues loom large for the voter either because of their personal relevance or the nature of the election, there is little incentive to make the complex judgments often required in differentiating between candidates' issue positions and policies (cf. Popkin et al. 1976). Candidate-centered voting models conceive of voting as a choice between candidates as people, rather than as a choice between policies or parties. It is assumed that voters either have little reason for incurring the cost of analyzing true policy differences, or that the differences are so small as to be virtually nonexistent, or finally, that issue involvement is so low that choice is based on candidate attributes rather than issue position. Several early studies suggest that voter choice has become progressively more candidate centered (e.g., Kirkpatrick, Lyons, and Fitzgerald, 1975; Popkin et al, 1975). Thus, voters are in the position of appraising candidates' personal qualities in judging their ability to carry out the demands of office, and the personal characteristics that candidates convey to voters become important factors in the social judgment assumed to underlie voting.

Prototype Theory and Voting as Social Judgments

The contexts, processes, and consequences of social judgments have been widely studied under the rubric of social cognition. Much of this research has focused on the ways in which information about people is selectively gathered, organized and used in social life. Cantor and Mischel (1977) argue that much social information is coded "in terms of . . . a few simple cognitive categories" (p. 6) which are organized into prototypes. Such social prototyping acts as a kind of "personnel file," providing ". . . a convenient *precis* of the one with whom we wish to deal" (Klapp 1972, p. 4). Social prototypes act as "*cognitive reference points*" forming the basis for inferences and other forms of reasoning (Rosch 1975; 1981).

As noted by Lakoff (1987), the content of prototypes can be non-stereotypical, and can include rare, abstract, ideal cases that are then used in categorization and decision making. Thus, people can readily describe their ideal home, mate, or boss even though the ideal case has never been encountered in reality. The use of prototypes has been examined in several judgment areas relevant to the present study. For example, occupational prototypes have been shown to be organized around the traits and abilities needed for their enactment (Ostrom and Lingle 1977). Recent consumer research has applied a prototype framework to understanding how consumers use product attributes to represent product categories (Sujan 1985), and how consumers use patterns of consumption activities to represent lifestyle groups (Englis and Solomon 1992a,b).

To the extent that voting has become more candidate centered, a prototype framework should be useful for examining the cognitive organization of voters' perceptions of ideal politicians. Indeed, in the early 1980s systematic research was undertaken to identify candidate characteristics that might be related to voter's choices (e.g., Abelson et al. 1982 Kinder and Abelson, 1981; Sullivan et al. 1984). For example, in 1980 the pre-presidential National Election Survey protocol was modified to include structured questions concerning the traits and emotions voters associated with the candidates. Analyses showed that 60% of the variance in preference for Carter or Reagan was accounted for by trait and emotion measures alone (Kinder and Abelson 1981; also Abelson, Kinder and Fiske 1982). As Kinder and Abelson (1981) note:

> "Trait judgments and affective reactions are not merely rationalization for party allegiance. ... the substantial autonomy of traits and affects from party attachments contributes to our general case. The choice of a president is very much a choice between two people — in particular, the traits they convey and the feelings they elicit." (p. 23)

Clearly, perceptions of candidates as people contribute to voting behavior independently of more "traditional" factors such as party identification or the candidate's stand on the issues of the day. Although these findings strongly suggest that social judgment is an important component of voters' decision making, they do not shed much light on voters' conceptions of what attributes define the "ideal politician."

One group of researchers (Kinder et al. 1980) used an open-ended protocol to assess the characteristics voters associated with ideal and "anti-ideal" presidents, and measured personality traits (e.g., honesty, recklessness) and areas of performance (e.g., provides strong leadership, breaks the law). The results showed that association of positive and negative characteristics with different candidates was related to voter support. However, other content domains (e.g., physical appearance) are important in social judgment, and there is empirical evidence to suggest that voter perceptions of politician attributes are partly dependent on level of office.

One study (Adams 1974) showed that a national office (such as president) is seen as a more symbolic role than is a local office (where voters may expect a concrete outcome). And, attributes associated with groups under-represented in politics (i.e., women or people of color) were found to be liabilities for candidates in national but not local elections. In the present study we examine differences in politician prototypes as a function of level of office, and we expand the range of content domains.

Gender[1] has long been considered an important factor in social judgment. Gender has been shown to influence the overall evaluation of female candidates (e.g., Mend, Bell and Bath 1976), and physical attractiveness acts as a liability for female but not for male candidates (e.g., Bowman 1984; Sigelman et al. 1986). However, little attention has been paid to the question of how the characteristics associated with female politicians compare with those associated with males, and how each compares with voter prototypes when gender is unspecified.

Since the great majority of office holders have been male, voter prototypes of ideal politicians should over-represent "male" characteristics. Phenomena which co-occur frequently become tightly linked in people's minds (Tversky and Kahneman 1974). Taken to the extreme, one well-understood or easy-to-perceive aspect of a category may come to stand for the entire category (Lakoff 1987). In the case of political prototypes the high level of covariation between being a politician and being male may have "masculinized" the role of politician. The "engendering" of social roles is found in research on highly sex-segregated occupations. Such jobs take on the "... gendered attributes associated with the sex of their workforce" (Williams 1989, p. 2). For example, secretaries (99% women) and are expected to be emotionally sensitive and nurturing whereas airplane pilots (99% men) are assumed to be emotionally reserved and detached (Williams, 1989). The extent to which the prototypes of the ideal and ideal *male* politician overlap with one another and differ from ideal female prototypes provides one indication of how each level of office is engendered. Comparison of the prototypes for female politicians with those for males, as well as to the prototype for an ideal politician when gender is unspecified can provide strategic input to how female candidates may best be positioned for election into particular offices.

Research Overview and Hypotheses

One of the primary limitations of previous research concerning political prototypes has been the treatment of politicians as a relatively homogeneous group, with little consideration of the effect of politician gender or level of office on the content and elaboration of prototypes. This study was designed to test four hypotheses concerning the effects of politician gender and level of office on political person prototypes.

H1: Since there is a strong historic association between males and political office, the prototypes for the ideal when gender is unspecified and for the ideal male politician will be similar in content and will differ from those associated with ideal female politicians. A corollary to this hypothesis is that we do not expect to find differences between the prototypes of the ideal and male political figures.

---

[1]Whereas "sex" is typically used to denote the biological factors that differentiate mean and women, "gender" is used to indicate that male and female represent socially constructed categories.

H2: Since voters have less exposure to and experience with female politicians, there should be a narrower range of characteristics (i.e., less elaboration and greater sterotypy) associated with female prototypes than for either the gender-unspecified ideal or male politicians.

H3: Since there is more media attention paid to the presidency than other levels of office, presidential prototypes should be more elaborated than either the gubernatorial or legislative prototypes. Moreover, we do not expect a significant difference in the degree of elaboration of the latter two prototypes.

H4: Greater familiarity with and exposure to the presidency should result in a prototype that displays the greatest level of variation of content (less stereotypy). Since gubernatorial office and the presidency are both executive roles, the prototypes for these offices should be similar and distinct from the prototype of the ideal legislator (irrespective of gender).

METHOD

Sample. One hundred seventy nine undergraduates (average age 21 yr.) enrolled in an introductory marketing course received class credit for their participation in the study. Five respondents were dropped from all analyses due to incomplete questionnaires or extreme levels of response (>3 standard deviations above the sample mean; see Mosteller and Tukey 1977, pp. 16-25 on contaminated distributions). The final sample (N = 174) was comprised of 59 males and 115 females. Eighty percent of the sample was registered to vote and 50% had voted in the last election. Seventy-six percent described themselves as moderate on most political issues and nearly half of the registered voters in the sample (48.8%) were registered Republicans. The sample was generally a suburban, upper middle class group (average family income $71,500) with 66.6% having fathers with a managerial or professional occupation).[2]

Procedure. Respondents were told that the study was concerned with the characteristics, qualifications, abilities, and behaviors voters associate with ideal political figures. They were given an open-ended questionnaire concerned with ideal political figures and encouraged to write whatever came to mind for each question, and to feel free to use their own words and phrases in their descriptions. Recent work in social cognition and gender stereotypes has led researchers to conclude that these belief systems are composed of more than personality traits (Ashmore and Del Boca 1981), and that the multiple descriptive domains are only loosely interconnected (cf. Ashmore and Del Boca 1986; Deaux 1985). Thus, we included traits, physical appearance, abilities, and emotions as content domains in our assessment of political person prototypes. The questions were designed to encourage respondents to imagine or picture their ideal politician and were worded as follows: "Please try to imagine the ideal president [or legislator or governor]. When you think of this person what are the traits or personality characteristics that come to mind? List and/or describe these characteristics and traits in the space below." A similar format was used for the physical appearance, ability, and emotion content domains. Thus, the design was a between-subjects factorial manipulation of candidate gender (male, female, or unspecified) and level of office (president, governor, or state legislator/representative); respondents were assigned to *one* of the resulting nine conditions.

Prototype elaboration was measured by a simple count of the number of items mentioned in response to each question. Prototype content was coded with a data-driven scheme designed to stay as close as possible to the idiographic data. Initial content coding yielded 187 trait categories, 172 physical appearance categories, 155 abilities and 92 emotions. A strong decision rule was used to collapse categories on the basis of semantic similarity (thesaurus lists of synonyms). Items similar in meaning to the others in the group and representative of the larger category were combined. Then, using a "scree slope" approach within each content domain, the point of discontinuity in the frequency of category use was identified as a cut-off point. On this basis, the number of categories was reduced to 28 traits, 26 physical appearance attributes, 17 abilities, and 14 emotions.

RESULTS

Prototype Elaboration

Separate analyses were conducted for the elaboration scores within each prototype content domain. A 3 (politician gender) x 3 (level of office) x 2 (sex of voter) x 2 (voter/non-voter) between-subjects ANOVA was the full model for each analysis. The strongest effects were obtained for the emotion component of the prototypes. There was a significant effect of politician gender [$F(2, 141) = 5.113, p < .007$], where prototypes were more elaborated for the gender-unspecified ideal ($M = 3.07$) and *male* politicians ($M = 3.35$) than for the female politician ($M = 2.63, p < .003$). There was also a significant main effect for sex of respondent [$F(1, 141) = 8.658, p < .02$]. Females provided more descriptors of how their ideal political figure would make them feel ($M = 3.20$) than did males ($M = 2.66$). The ANOVA also revealed a significant interaction involving sex of respondent and voting behavior [$F(1, 141) = 6.640, p < .048$]. In this interaction males and females who did not vote in the last election had equally well-elaborated prototypes ($M = 2.7$ and 3.0, respectively). However, male voters, generated fewer responses to this question ($M = 2.6$) than did female voters ($M = 3.45, p < .005$).

Analyses of the physical appearance characteristics revealed a significant level of office by sex of voter interaction ($F(2,142) = 13.35, p < .05$). This interaction was carried primarily by the greater elaboration of the physical appearance prototype for the ideal president by female voters ($M = 6.08$) than by male voters ($M = 4.0, p < .0003$). Males provided significantly fewer descriptors of their ideal president's physical appearance ($M = 4.0, p < .05$) than they did for their ideal legislators ($M = 5.46$) or governors ($M = 4.78$). Females, on the other hand, listed more physical appearance attributes for an ideal president ($M = 6.08, p < .05$) than for an ideal legislator ($M = 5.03$) or governor ($M = 5.1$).

There were no significant main effects or interactions in prototype elaboration for traits or abilities. However, one planned comparison for level of office showed that a greater number of traits was used to describe the ideal president ($M = 6.186, p < .04$) than for either legislator ($M = 5.245$) or governor ($M = 5.417$).

Prototype Content

Quantitative as well as qualitative approaches were used to examine the *content* of politician prototypes. Contingency tables were constructed to examine whether or not content category use (e.g., the specific patterns of traits mentioned) differed as a function the independent variables in the design (level of office, politician gender, and so on). Category use was contingent upon politician

---

[2] Owing to the higher than average SES of our sample, the findings may not generalize to all Americans and may be limited to the prototypes held by college-educated, upper-middle class voters—a considerable block of voters.

gender (TraitsX2(54) = 96.66, p < .0003; Physical Appearance X2(50) = 130.88, p < .0001; Abilities X2 (32)= 47.84, p < .034; Emotions X2 (26)= 45.43, p < .011). In addition, the descriptors used across the three levels of office differed significantly in content in all of areas except physical appearance (Traits X2 (54)= 79.76, p < .013; Abilities X2 (32)= 51.53, p < .016; Emotions X2 (26) = 39.03, p < .049). There were no effects of sex of voter and voting experience. Although category usage was contingent *overall* upon level of office and politician gender, there were also several commonalities in politician prototypes. In order to provide a sense of general prototype content, the following summarizes the most commonly used descriptors overall.

In general, ideal political figures are seen as possessing the traits of honesty, warmth and charm, and being knowledgeable and open-minded. They are also intelligent, strong, and confident. The prototypic appearance is of someone in their 40's or 50's, who is well-dressed, tall (over six feet), and attractive but not too attractive. Many respondents were quite specific in terms of what constitutes appropriate attire, including not just "suits" but "Brooks Brothers" or "navy business suit" in their descriptions. Hair color and style, along with facial features (e.g., eye color, smiles, wrinkles) were also frequently mentioned. The most prominent ability area related to communication skills — public speaking, writing well, and giving clear answers; related abilities included being good at working with a wide range of personalities, being a skilled manager and negotiator, and keeping in touch with and trying to meet the needs of the people. In addition, the ideal politician is seen as persuasive, organized, good at listening, and able to make decisions. Another ability area included having a broad understanding and knowledge of the issues in general and within specific areas such as defense, budget, and social problems. The emotions associated with an ideal politician included general feelings of happiness and security — feeling safe (protected and secure), trusting, comfortable (at ease, relaxed) and self-confident. Others involved belief or faith in the politician, a feeling of being "in good hands," and the feeling that an ideal politician is someone to look up to who elicits feelings of pride.

Analyses of content within the gender of politician and level of office conditions also revealed many subtle differences in the traits, physical appearance, abilities and emotions used to describe ideal political figures. The following highlights a few of these differences, especially as they vary as a function of gender and level of office. Tables 1 through 4 provide a detailed listing of the content of each prototype. The percentages included in these tables were computed on the basis of the *total* number of responses generated by all subjects within each cell of each table.

Politician Gender

As predicted, the content of the female politician prototypes differed in important ways from male or gender-unspecified prototypes. Although being intelligent and knowledgeable were frequently associated with gender-unspecified and male prototypes, these traits were not part of the female prototype.[3] It is interesting to note, that although intelligence was not part of the female legislator or governor prototype, being well-educated was part of both. It appears that although intelligence may be sufficient in most cases, that general trait requires some type of credential in women to be validated. A similar pattern was found for the trait "confident." The prototypical female political figure is seen as conservatively dressed, as are all presidential prototypes. Voters were more likely to mention facial features when asked about an ideal female politician. Keeping in touch with the needs of the public, organization, and being able to get the job done and accomplish goals were abilities commonly found in all prototypes except those for female politicians. Although persuasive abilities were scattered across the prototypes, all female targets included this ability. Finally, the emotions respondents anticipated experiencing in relation to their ideal female political person were more likely to involve respect and a sense that the person was a role-model or someone to look up to.

Level of Office. Responses to the question regarding the abilities of the various political figures provided the clearest distinction between the three levels of office. Presidents and governors were described as being good at negotiations and at decision making. Despite the different branches of government represented by governors and legislators, these two offices shared many features including people skills and keeping in touch with the needs of the public. A possible explanation for this is that both represent a more "local" level of office.

DISCUSSION

In this study we examined the elaboration and content of nine political person prototypes. The most striking pattern in the present results is that degree of elaboration of politician prototypes is generally constant across level of office and politician gender, but that the content of these prototypes is dependent upon *both* variables. Prototypes were more well-elaborated among female respondents and among those with prior voting experience (i.e., more highly involved respondents), than for males and non-voters. This result may be partly due to women's greater verbal fluency. And, those with prior voting experience have most likely given more thought to the qualities they seek in a politician as part of their decision making when they vote. This higher level of involvement may be reflected in the more extensive prototypes among voters. Despite the differential elaboration of prototypes by men and women and by voters and non-voters, these groups did not differ significantly in the content used to describe their ideal political figures.

Our examination of prototype content provided strong support for our hypotheses that the category of political persons is not homogeneous and that female political figures are perceived very differently from either the gender-unspecified ideal or male politician. This result supports our assumption that prior treatment of political candidates as a homogeneous group is too simplistic for understanding how political candidates are perceived by voters. The findings clearly indicate that the prototype of an president is different from that of an ideal legislator or governor. This study represents a preliminary foray into differentiating the larger category of "politician" into meaningful subordinate categories. Future research should consider how those differences arise as a function of different responsibilities of office (e.g., legislative vs. executive) and as a function of the perceived closeness of the office to the respondent. For example, governors and legislators may be seen as being in direct contact with the average citizen whereas the president is relatively isolated from such contact. Research is also needed which examines the effects of media exposure on the shaping of political prototypes.

Important differences between ideal female politicians and the gender unspecified and male ideal politicians were also evident. Of particular note was the *omission* of numerous traits, abilities, and emotions that were pervasive in descriptions of the gender-unspecified and male ideals. These omissions *may not* indicate that people

---

[3] An exception was the case of the female president which included intelligent but not knowledgeable.

TABLE 1
The six most frequently occurring traits in each political person prototype.

Politician Gender	Level of Office		
	President	Governor	Legislator
Ideal [a]	Warm (11.3)[b]	Warm (12.1)	Honest (15.5)
	Leader (9.6)	Honest (8.8)	Knowledgeable (12.6)
	Intelligent (8.7)	Intelligent (8.8)	Warm (7.8)
	Knowledgeable (7.8)	Communicative (6.6)	Intelligent (6.8)
	Strong (6.1)	Genuine (5.5)	Communicative (4.9)
	Honest (6.1)	Represents All (5.5)	Strong (4.9)
Male	Knowledgeable (9.5)	Warm (10.6)	Honest (11.0)
	Strong (7.1)	Honest (8.7)	Knowledgeable (9.8)
	Charm (7.1)	Intelligent (6.7)	Communicative (7.8)
	Intelligent (7.1)	Communicative (6.1)	Trustworthy (8.5)
	Leader (6.4)	Friendly (5.8)	Intelligent (7.3)
	Communicative (5.6)	Knowledgeable (5.8)	Warm (7.3)
Female	Strong (13.0)	Strong (8.2)	Strong (12.4)
	Intelligent (6.0)	Warm (7.2)	Honest (8.6)
	Warm (5.0)	Leader (6.1)	Open-Minded (7.4)
	Communicative (5.0)	Confident (6.1)	Warm (7.4)
	Leader (5.0)	Open-Minded (6.1)	Confident (7.4)
	Confident (4.0)	Intelligent (6.1)	Educated (6.2)

[a] Gender was not specified in this condition.
[b] Numbers in parentheses represent the percentage of the total number of items mentioned within that cell of the table.

TABLE 2
The six most frequently occurring physical appearance attributes in each political person prototype.

Politician Gender	Level of Office		
	President	Governor	Legislator
Ideal [a]	Age - 50's (13.2)[b]	Age - 50's (11.3)	Age - 40's (9.0)
	Well-Dressed (7.0)	Age - 40's (10.4)	Wears Suits (8.0)
	Average Build (6.1)	Wears Suits (7.6)	Well-Dressed (6.0)
	Conservative Dress (6.1)	Hair (5.7)	Age - 30's (6.0)
	Tall (5.3)	Well-Dressed (5.7)	Male or Female (5.0)
	Masculine (5.3)	Tall (5.7)	Average Build (5.0)
Male	Well-Dressed (9.6)	Age - 40's (11.6)	Wears Suits (11.3)
	Wears Suits (8.0)	Well-Dressed (8.5)	Tall (7.2)
	Tall (7.2)	Tall (7.8)	Age - 40's (7.2)
	Age - 50's (6.4)	Age - 50's (6.2)	Age - 50's (6.2)
	Average Build (5.6)	Average Looks (5.4)	All American Look (6.2)
	Conservative Dress (4.8)	Wears Suits (5.4)	Face (6.2)
Female	Hair (10.0)	Age - 40's (9.1)	Age - 40's (12.0)
	Conservative Dress (10.0)	Well-Dressed (8.2)	Well-Dressed (9.0)
	Wears Suits (9.0)	Feminine (7.3)	Hair (8.0)
	Age - 40's (8.0)	Wears Suits (6.4)	Average Looks (8.0)
	Age - 50's (7.0)	Age - 30's (6.4)	Conservative Dress (6.0)
	Face (6.0)	Age - 50's (6.4)	Face (6.0)

[a] Gender was not specified in this condition.
[b] Numbers in parentheses represent the percentage of the total number of items mentioned within that cell of the table.

TABLE 3
The six most frequently occurring abilities in each political person prototype.

Politician Gender	Level of Office		
	President	Governor	Legislator
Ideal [a]	Commun. Skills (15.7)[b]	Commun. Skills (28.6)	Commun. Skills (25.0)
	Deals w/ Issues (6.0)	Persuasive (8.6)	Organizational Skills (6.9)
	Persuasive (4.8)	Deals w/ issues (6.9)	Gets Job Done (6.9)
	Negotiation (4.8)	Listening Skills (7.1)	Deals w/ Issues (5.6)
	Resp. to Publ. Need (4.8)	Resp. to Publ. Need (5.7)	Resp. to Publ. Need (5.6)
	Leadership (4.8)	Decision Making Skills (2.9)	Leadership (5.6)
Male	Commun. Skills (17.3)	Commun. Skills (21.5)	Commun. Skills (13.9)
	Deals w/ Issues (8.0)	People Skills (6.3)	Resp. to Publ. Need (9.7)
	Organizational Skills (6.7)	Gets Job Done (6.3)	Deals w/ Issues (6.9)
	Diplomacy (5.3)	Organizational Skills (5.1)	Gets Job Done (6.9)
	Negotiation (5.3)	Decision Making (3.8)	People Skills (6.9)
	Decision Making Skills (2.7)	Negotiation (3.8)	Persuasive (5.6)
Female	Deals w/ Issues (14.5)	Commun. Skills (16.4)	Commun. Skills (15.3)
	Commun. Skills (8.1)	Listening Skills (8.2)	Deals w/ Issues (15.3)
	Negotiation (8.1)	Intellectual Skills (4.9)	Keeps Camp. Prom. (5.1)
	Persuasive (6.5)	Deals w/ Issues (4.9)	Leadership (3.4)
	Listening Skills (6.5)	Decision Making (3.3)	Not a Pushover (3.4)
	Diplomacy (4.8)	Persuasive (3.3)	Persuasive (3.4)

[a] Gender was not specified in this condition.
[b] Numbers in parentheses represent the percentage of the total number of items mentioned within that cell of the table.

TABLE 4
The five[a] most frequent emotions associated with each political person prototype.

Politician Gender	Level of Office		
	President	Governor	Legislator
Ideal [b]	Proud (15.2)[c]	Safe (16.7)	Safe (19.0)
	Safe (12.1)	Self-Confident (11.1)	Believe in Him/Her (10.3)
	Self-Confident (7.6)	Proud (9.3)	Proud (8.6)
	Patriotic (7.6)	Trusting (5.6)	Self-Confident (8.6)
	Trusting (6.1)	Respect (5.6)	Trusting (5.2)
Male	Safe (15.9)	Safe (10.8)	Safe (14.8)
	Proud (11.6)	Happy (10.8)	Proud (9.3)
	Self-Confident (11.6)	Proud (9.2)	Believe in Him/Her (9.3)
	Happy (8.7)	Self-Confident (9.2)	Self-Confident (7.4)
	Trusting (7.2)	Look Up To Him (4.6)	Happy (5.6)
Female	Proud (11.4)	Proud (16.7)	Good (14.0)
	Trusting (6.8)	Look Up To Her (8.3)	Safe (11.6)
	Look Up To Her (4.5)	Safe (8.3)	Look Up To Her (7.0)
	Respect (4.5)	Happy (6.3)	Proud (4.7)
	Good (4.5)	Respect (6.3)	Interested (4.7)

[a] Since the prototypes for emotions were smaller than the other content domains, only the top five emotions are reported here.
[b] Gender was not specified in this condition.
[c] Numbers in parentheses represent the percentage of the total number of items mentioned within that cell of the table.

adjust what they believe to be ideal when they think of female politicians. These omissions, especially when compared to the more abstract ideal, may instead reflect the salience of particular features in characterizing a particular social category. For example, we do not think that because knowledgeable was excluded from the ideal female president prototype that people do not feel a female president needs to be informed or that knowledgeable is somehow less important for a female president than a male or the ideal president. We are suggesting that when people think about their ideal female president, for example, being knowledgeable simply does not occur to them.

Such selective misperception may result in a disadvantage for female candidates, who may as a consequence be perceived as being further from the ideal. Conversely, there are instances in which the female prototype is closer to the gender-unspecified ideal than the male prototype. Highlighting this proximity is potentially an important factor in enhancing candidate success. Exploring the multiplicity of ways in which the female prototype differs from and is similar to the ideal is a first step in understanding how female candidates can be positioned within the constellation of traits, appearance, abilities, and emotions associated with ideal political leaders.

REFERENCES

Abelson, Robert P., Kinder, Donald R., Peters, Mark D., Fiske, Susan T. (1982), "Affective and Semantic Components in Political Person Perception." *Journal of Personality and Social Psychology*, 42, 619-630.

Adams, William C. (1974), "Candidate Characteristics, Office of Election, and Voter Responses," Paper presented at the 1974 annual spring meeting of the National Capital Area Political Science Association, Washington, D.C.

Ashmore, Richard D., and Del Boca, Francis K. (1981), "Conceptual Approaches to Stereotypes and Stereotyping," in *Cognitive Processes in Stereotyping and Intergroup Behavior*, D. L. Hamilton ed., Hillsdale, NJ: Lawrence Erlbaum.

_____ (1986), "Gender Stereotypes," in *The Social Psychology of Female-Male Relations: A Critical Analysis of Central Concepts*, Richard D. Ashmore and Francis K. Del Boca eds., New York: Academic Press.

Bowman, Ann. (1985), "Physical Attractiveness and Electability: Looks and Votes," *Women and Politics*, 4, 55-65.

Campbell, Angus, Converse, Philip E., Miller, W. E., and D. E. Stokes (1960). *The American Voter*. NY: Wiley & Sons.

Cantor, Nancy and Walter Mischel (1979), "Prototypes in Person Perception," *Advances in Experimental Social Psychology*, Vol. 12, in Leonard Berkowitz,ed., New York: Academic Press, 4-52.

Deaux, Kay (1984), "From Individual Differences to Social Categories: Analysis of a Decade's Research on Gender," *American Psychologist*, 39, 105-116.

Englis, Basil G. (1992). "The Role of Affect in Political Advertising: Voter Emotional Responses to the Nonverbal Behavior of Politicians," in *Advertising and Consumer Psychology*, Eddie Clark, Timothy Brock and David Stewart eds., Hillsdale, NJ: Lawrence Erlbaum.

Englis, Basil G. and Michael R. Solomon (1992). "Consumption Constellations: Implications for Advertising Strategy." *Proceedings of the Society for Consumer Psychology*, 23-30.

Englis, Basil G. and Michael R. Solomon (1992b), "To Be *and* Not to Be?: Reference Group Stereotyping and *The Clustering of America*," Rutgers University, unpublished manuscript.

Fiorina, M. D. (1981). *Retrospective Voting in American National Elections*. New Haven, CT: Yale University Press.

Graber, Doris A. (1984). *Mass Media and American Politics*, 2nd ed. Washington, DC: Congressional Quarterly Press.

Hirschman, Elizabeth C. (1987), "People as Products: Analysis of a Complex Marketing Exchange," *Journal of Marketing*, 51 (January), 98-108.

Kinder, Donald R. and Robert P. Abelson (1981), *Appraising presidential candidates: Personality and affect in the 1980 campaign*. Paper presented at the 1981 annual meeting of the American Political Science Association.

Kinder, Donald R., Mark D. Peters, Robert P. Abelson, and Susan T. Fiske (1980), "Presidential Prototypes," *Political Behavior*, 2, 315-337.

Kirkpatrick, S. A., W. Lyons, and M. R. Fitzgerald (1975), "Candidates, Parties, and Issues in the American Electorate." *American Politics Quarterly*, 3, 247-283.

Klapp, Orrin E. (1972), *Heroes, Villians, and Fools: Reflections of the American Character*, San Diego: Aegis.

Lakoff, George (1987), *Women, Fire, and Dangerous Things: What Categories Reveal About the Mind*, Chicago: University of Chicago Press.

McGinniss, Joe (1969), *The Selling of the President 1968*, New York: Trident.

Mend, Michael R., Tony Bell and Lawrence Bath (1976), "Dynamics of Attitude Formation Regarding Women in Politics," *Experimental Study of Politics*, 5, 25-39.

Ostrom, Thomas M., and J. H. Lingle (1977), *Thematic Constructions in Person Impressions*. Paper presented in a symposium titled "New Directions in the Analysis of Impression Formation," American Psychological Association Convention.

Popkin, S., J. W. Gorman, C. Phillips, and J. A. Smith(1976). "What have you done for me lately? Toward an investment theory of voting," *The American Political Science Review*, 70, 779-805.

Rosch, Eleanor (Eleanor Heider) (1975) "Cognitive Reference Points." *Cognitive Psychology*, 7, 532-547.

_____ (1981) "Prototype Classification and Logical Classification: The Two Systems" in *New Trends in Cognitive Representation: Challenges to Piaget's Theory*, E. Scholnick ed., Hillsdale, NJ: Lawrence Erlbaum, pp. 73-86.

Sigelman, Carol K., Dan B. Thomas, Lee Sigelman, and Frederick D. Ribich (1986). "Gender, Physical Attractiveness, and Electability: An Experimental Investigation of Voter Biases." *Journal of Applied Social Psychology*, 13, 229-258.

Solomon, Michael R. (1992), "Celebritization and Commodification in the Interpersonal Marketplace," Rutgers University, unpublished manuscript.

Stokes, D. E. and W. E. Miller (1962), "Party Government and the Saliency of Congress." *Public Opinion Quarterly*, 26, 531-546.

Sujan, Mita (1985), "Consumer Knowledge: Effects on Evaluation Strategies Mediating Consumer Judgments," *Journal of Consumer Research*, 12 (June), 31-46.

Sullivan, Denis G., Roger D. Masters, John T. Lanzetta, Basil G. Englis, and Gregory J. McHugo (1984). *The Effect of President Reagan's Facial Displays on Observers' Attitudes, Impressions, and Feelings About Him*. Paper presented at the 1984 annual meeting of the American Political Science Association, Washington, DC.

Swerdlow, Joel L. (ed.) (1988), *Media Technology and the Vote*, Boulder, CO: Westview Press.

Tversky, Amos & Kahneman, Daniel, (1974) "Judgment under Uncertainty: Heuristics and Biases." *Cognitive Psychology*, 5, 207-232.

Williams, Christine, L. (1989), *Gender Differences at Work: Women and Men in Nontraditional Occupations*, Berkeley: University of California Press.

A Framework for Explaining Multiple Request Effectiveness: The Role of Attitude Towards the Request

Rohini Ahluwalia, The Ohio State University
Robert E. Burnkrant, The Ohio State University

ABSTRACT

This article proposes a conceptual framework, based on the availability valence hypothesis, for explaining multiple request effectiveness (foot-in-the-door and door-in-the-face). We hypothesize that an important factor determining compliance to the target request is the attitude towards the request (AR). Its position on the Attitude-Nonattitude continuum, would determine whether AR would have a main effect or interact with other variables in this framework (i.e. request behavior and own behavior) in influencing compliance. We propose that the two techniques are influenced differentially by the AR because their underlying processes are different.

INTRODUCTION

How can you induce a person to comply with reasonable requests? This is a question of great importance for non-profit organizations, requiring donations to maintain their operations, for market research companies desiring to increase questionnaire response rates, and for salespersons wanting to induce compliance to their requests without coercion. Indeed it is an important question for marketers in general.

Freedman and Fraser (1966) published two articles that demonstrated strong support for a compliance technique they labeled, the "foot-in-the-door" (FITD) phenomenon. Their data indicated that once a person has complied with a small request, he or she will be more likely to comply with a subsequent larger request. Thus, the FITD technique starts with a small request, which has a high probability of acceptance, and is followed by a larger request which by itself would induce little compliance.

A second technique that has been found to enhance compliance–the "door-in-the-face" (DITF) was introduced by Cialdini et al. (1975). An extreme request is first made, which is almost certain to be rejected, and this is followed by a more moderate second request, the one which was actually desired.

While reviews by DeJong (1979), Beaman et al. (1983), and Dillard, Hunter and Burgoon (1984) have shown FITD and DITF to be reliable, controversy exists with regard to their underlying processes. Self-perception theory (Bem, 1972) has been employed to explain the FITD phenomenon. Numerous explanations have been put forth to account for DITF: the reciprocal concessions model (Cialdini et al., 1975); the perceptual contrast explanation (Miller et al., 1976); and the worthy person hypothesis (Foehl and Goldman, 1983). Finally, Tybout, Sternthal and Calder (1983) offered and tested a single explanation for both the FITD and DITF: an availability explanation.

The purpose of this paper is to extend the framework provided by Tybout et al. (1983) to account for some of the findings in this literature, that have not been dealt with in previous work. We also attempt to explain more thoroughly the processes underlying the two multiple request techniques and highlight the differences between them. The purpose of this review is to offer a conceptual framework for future research and to propose some testable postulates.

AVAILABILITY VALENCE HYPOTHESIS

According to the Tybout, Sternthal and Calder (TSC) framework, which is based on the availability valence hypothesis, information about one's "own behavior" (OB) and information about the behavior of the requestor or "request behavior" (RB) determine compliance in multiple request situations. Compliance is enhanced when favorable information about either one's own behavior or the request behavior is available: compliance is undermined when unfavorable information about either own behavior or request behavior is available. Further, there should be no systematic effect when favorable information of one type is as available as unfavorable information of the other type.

In both multiple request strategies there are two requests, and the second one is the "critical" one i.e. the one which is actually desired. In the case of FITD, the first request is small and has a high likelihood of acceptance, thus OB is favorable (due to acceptance of the first request). However, in the case of DITF the first request is very large and has a high likelihood of being refused, implying that OB is unfavorable.

The second request in FITD represents an escalation in the request size (i.e. unfavorable RB) whereas in the case of DITF it represents a concession (i.e. favorable RB). Thus, if RB is more available, the subject's response to the second request would be negative for the FITD and positive for the DITF. However, if "own behavior" (OB) to the first request is more available, then the subject's response to the target request would be favorable for FITD and unfavorable in the case of DITF.

Fern, Monroe and Avila (1986) in their integrative review of the multiple request phenomena present seven theoretical predictions derived from the TSC framework, and provide a synthesis of previous multiple request research results in terms of these predictions. Fern et al. (1986) found some evidence in favor of the TSC framework. Three of the seven hypotheses were supported by the data at p<.10, and there was some directional support for three of the other theoretical predictions.

The TSC framework not only provides a parsimonious explanation for both the multiple request phenomena, but is also able to accommodate a number of the contradictory explanations proposed in this literature. For instance, self-perception theory (Bem 1972) and the concessions explanation (Cialdini et al. 1975) are inconsistent with each other. Self-perception theory would anticipate a lower level of compliance with the DITF technique, and the concessions explanation would predict that FITD will be totally ineffective (Dillard et al. 1984). The TSC framework resolves this inconsistency by stating that, depending on what is available, both the explanations can be supported. In the studies where favorable OB information is available many of the self-perception predictions are met. In studies where favorable request behavior is available many of the concession and the contrast model predictions are supported.

However, the TSC framework is not able to explain some of the findings reported in this literature. For instance, it is frequently found that FITD works in business or non-charity contexts (Goldman et al. 1981; Katzev and Johnson 1984; Patch 1986; Reingen and Kernan 1979), whereas DITF is effective with pro-social requests (Dillard et al. 1984; Foehl and Goldman 1983; Goldman et al. 1981; Mowen and Cialdini 1980). According to Tybout et al. (1983) both the multiple request techniques are more likely to be effective in contexts where requests pertain to favorable issues. They do not anticipate FITD to perform better than DITF in commercial settings, and don't explain why and how the processes underlying the two techniques are different.

Further, some research has shown that even when the issue is favorable and request is pro-social, and thus favorable information is available, multiple request techniques may still not be effective (see Goldman et al. 1984; Kilbourne 1988; Mowen and Cialdini 1980). The TSC framework does not deal with this possibility as well.

The TSC framework proposes that the favorability of the information available would influence the compliance behavior. However, it does not specify very completely what is available and is not able to account for some of the results obtained in this literature.

We need to consider what other information, in addition to RB and OB, may be available and may have an influence on the compliance outcome. The role of the attitudes related to the request i.e. towards the source of the request, the issue in the request and the task being requested has not been considered by the literature in this area. We argue that these are important determinants of the compliance outcome and the TSC framework should be extended to include them.

Attitude towards the source would be the respondent's evaluation of the person or the organization making the request. The source of a request could be a public oriented citizens' organization, or a profit oriented private company or a friend of the respondent etc. The attitude towards the issue deals with how the respondent evaluates the issue in the request which could be traffic safety or electricity conservation, or the effect of television on children etc. The attitude towards the task deals with the task being requested e.g. a 15 minute interview, or donation of money or escorting teenagers to the zoo etc.

In this paper we will refer to the combined effect of these three attitudes relevant to the request as Attitude towards the Request (AR). If one or more of these attitudes relevant to the request is very accessible then AR would be highly accessible. If at least one of these attitudes is moderately accessible then AR would be termed as moderately accessible, and only when all of these are low in accessibility will AR be considered as falling on the nonattitude end of the attitude-nonattitude continuum discussed in the following section.

The Attitude-Nonattitude continuum:

We could view the attitude towards the request (AR) in terms of an attitude-nonattitude continuum — one that focuses on the accessibility of the attitude from memory (Fazio 1986, 1989). At the lower end of the continuum is the nonattitude which implies that no a priori evaluation of the attitude object exists in memory. As we move along the continuum, an evaluation does exist and the strength of the association between that evaluation and the object and, hence, the chronic accessibility of the attitude, increases. In the case of a weak association, the attitude can be retrieved via an effortful, reflective process but is not capable of automatic activation. At the upper end of the continuum is a well-learned, strong association that is likely to be activated automatically upon mere observation or mention of the attitude object.

The effectiveness of persuasion strategies may be limited to attitudes that occupy a relatively low position along the attitude-nonattitude continuum (Fazio 1989; Wood, Kallgren, & Priesler 1985). More accessible attitudes are more likely to be activated upon mere mention or observation of the attitude object. These attitudes are apt to serve as a filter through which the available information is viewed, and hence are more likely to influence behavior (Fazio, 1986). If the relevant association is too weak to be activated, then behavior will follow from a definition of the event that is not attitudinally based. The behavior may be determined by whatever features of the situation and the attitude object are sufficiently salient to influence the individual's immediate perceptions. Therefore, persuasion strategies are more likely to be effective in the latter scenario.

We propose that both the availability and valence of AR will influence a person's compliance to the target request. But, the nature of this influence will depend on where the AR is located on the attitude-nonattitude continuum.

Scenario 1: High Accessibility of Attitude towards the Request

When the attitude towards the request is located at the higher end of the attitude-nonattitude continuum, then it is very likely that the AR will guide the compliance behavior, and leave very little or no scope for the multiple request techniques to work. The high accessibility of AR will automatically activate it upon mention of the request. This highly accessible AR, would then, instead of RB and OB, be more likely to guide the subject's response to the target request. In the case where the AR is positive and very accessible, it is very likely that the target request will be accepted, with or without the multiple request techniques being used. However, if the AR is negative and highly accessible, then it is likely that this attitude will influence behavior and result in the rejection of the critical request. This would also hold for scenarios in which the AR is not chronically accessible, but is made accessible due to some situational manipulations. Therefore, our first postulate is as follows:

Postulate 1: The multiple request techniques will not be effective in inducing compliance when the attitude of the respondent towards the request is highly accessible. The AR will, in this case, guide the compliance behavior.

Several of the FITD and DITF studies have failed to find any significant effects (see Beaman et al. 1983; and Fern et al. 1986). One reason for this could be the high accessibility of the AR which would dominate the RB and OB. A positive and highly accessible AR would be very likely to guide the compliance behavior and push up the compliance level to its ceiling. We will discuss below some published studies from the literature that lend support to our hypothesis.

Kilbourne (1988) anticipating that social norms of friendship may result in atypical FITD effects (without hypothesizing the direction of these effects), used two different types of sources for the same FITD requests: friends and strangers. According to our framework, the respondent's attitude towards a friend is expected to be positive and accessible and hence guide the compliance behavior, whereas towards a stranger it would tend to lie closer to the non-attitude part of the continuum. Therefore, we would not expect a FITD effect in the condition where a friend was making the request, because the control group compliance would be pushed up to a ceiling level. But in the case where the requestor was a stranger, a FITD effect would be expected. Kilbourne's results confirm our hypothesis — when the FITD experimental and control conditions comprised of friends as requestors, there was no FITD effect since the control group compliance was very high, but a reliable effect was obtained in the stranger-requestor condition.

Mowen and Cialdini (1980) tested several ways of increasing target request compliance in the DITF context. One of their manipulations comprised emphasizing to the subjects, how much their compliance with the request would "help out" the company. The authors anticipated this manipulation would enhance the legitimacy of the request and hence the compliance with DITF. However, our framework would predict results in the opposite direction. In this study (survey about home and dorm safety), the AR is likely to be positive. The "help" emphasis or the stress on the altruistic aspects of the request in this manipulation may increase the accessibility of the positive AR which may now guide the compliance levels. This would render the DITF manipulation ineffective. The results of this study are consistent with our expectations. The data indicate that when help was emphasized, control group compliance reached a ceiling level, wiping out the DITF effect.

Scenario 2: Moderate Accessibility of Attitude towards the Request

In this situation, the attitude towards the request is not highly accessible, and therefore it is not automatically activated upon presentation of the request. It appears reasonable to assume that a moderately accessible attitude is not very likely to have an extreme valence, since a number of researchers have reported a significant relationship between attitude accessibility and attitude extremity (Berger and Mitchell 1989; Fazio and Williams 1986; Powell and Fazio 1984). The compliance with the target request will then be determined by an interaction between the AR and the situational variables (i.e. RB and OB) and their relative accessibility and diagnosticity. Much of the published research in the multiple request techniques corresponds to this scenario. For instance a request for information by a new radio station would be considered as falling in this scenario.

Foot-In-the-Door: When the respondent is confronted with the second request, the OB from past acceptance of the first request is expected to be positive and the RB, since it is an escalation, is expected to be negative. The subject would have consented to the first request mainly due to it's small size.

As we have already discussed in the previous section, when one of the three components of the model (i.e. AR, OB or RB) is very accessible it will dominate the other components and determine the compliance outcome. In the FITD scenario, past compliance with the initial request is likely to make OB accessible. This is because OB deals with own behavior and reactions which are related to the self, a highly accessible schema (Rogers, Kuiper and Kirker 1977). This would be more so when the respondent not only agreed to the request but performed it, since direct experience (Fazio and Zanna 1981) and elaboration (Petty and Cacioppo 1986) are expected to increase the accessibility of the response information. Thus, in this case, the accessibility of the OB will dominate the AR, which is only moderately accessible. So, FITD may even be effective with requests in which the AR is neutrally or negatively valenced, since there is a low likelihood of it being retrieved and considered while responding to the target request. This leads us to our next postulate:

Postulate 2: When the accessibility of Attitude towards the Request (AR) is moderate then FITD is not likely to be very sensitive to the valence of AR.

Door-In-the-Face: In this case the first request is rejected due to its large size. Subsequently, a concession is made on the size dimension. The respondent then reconsiders the request which now seems more reasonable in size due to it's contrast with the previous request. Here OB is not likely to dominate the short-term memory since a behavior was not performed in response to the first request, and hence unlike the FITD scenario the OB information is not highly accessible. Since the respondent does not have a past experience of compliance easily accessible, and needs some relevant information to make a decision, he/she is likely to use the AR, which is relatively more accessible than the OB. Pressure from the concessionary RB would lead the subject to comply, given that the valence of the AR is positive or neutral. However, if the AR is negatively valenced, the respondent is likely to refuse the request.

Postulate 3: When the accessibility of Attitude towards the Request (AR) is moderate then DITF is likely to be sensitive to the valence of AR.

Thus, in the DITF condition, the AR is considered when making a compliance decision, because OB is not accessible. However in the FITD condition, AR will most likely not come into the picture, due to the dominance of the positive OB. This difference in the relative availability of OB in the two techniques, leads to their differential sensitivity to the valence of the AR. The need for the source and issue to be positive is more crucial for the success of the DITF than the FITD. This reasoning implies that in a business context, there would be a greater likelihood for the FITD to work than DITF.

The literature in this area lends support to our proposed postulates. FITD has been shown to work in cases where the AR was not positive and the compliance of the control group was quite low (Dillard et al. 1984; Katzev and Johnson 1984), and it is expected to be successful across a broader spectrum of requests than the DITF (Fern et al. 1986). But DITF appears to be successful mainly in pro-social contexts. Foehl and Goldman (1983) proposed and found evidence for the Worthy Person Hypothesis. According to it, DITF is likely to be effective only when the source is positive or "worthy" and/or the issue in the request is a pro-social or worthy one. For instance, a charity organization, or a cause benefiting the public.

Patch (1986) hypothesized that since FITD promotes pressure toward internal consistency and DITF puts normative pressure on the respondent, source legitimacy would be more likely to influence the success of the latter than the former. He tested the FITD and the DITF under conditions of low and high source legitimacy. In the critical request subjects were asked to respond to a survey about television viewing preferences. The source of the request was manipulated as either a public interest group — Parents for Good Television Programming (a source which is likely to be rated as positive by the subjects but not likely to be very highly accessible for most of the respondents), or a private consulting firm (a profit oriented organization, towards which the attitude of the respondents is not likely to be positive or accessible). For each condition, the source was constant across the requests. We would predict that FITD would be successful with both the sources because the valence of AR is not likely to be important for its success. This is because with FITD, OB should dominate this relatively inaccessible AR. But the DITF would only be likely to be effective when the AR is positive. Patch's results are consistent with these predictions — only FITD was effective when the source of the request was the private consulting firm, whereas both the techniques were effective when the organization conducting the survey was the public interest group.

Goldman, Gier and Smith (1981) randomly selected people from a telephone directory and asked them to answer questions for a new radio station — a profit oriented request towards which the attitude of the respondents is not likely to be positive. They found that only FITD worked in this context, and even when they manipulated the difficulty level of the requests, the DITF technique failed to enhance compliance with the target request.

Scenario 3: Low Accessibility of the Attitude towards the Request

Finally, as we move towards the lower end of the continuum, we come to a situation in which either the respondent does not have an attitude towards the request (a non-attitude) or has a very weak attitude which is not easily accessible. In this case, the AR would not be expected to play a role in compliance behavior due to it's extremely low accessibility and somewhat neutral valence. Both the FITD and DITF would be expected to work, provided the other conditions necessary for their success, as proposed by the TSC framework, were satisfied. So, FITD would enhance compliance as long as the "own behavior" was very accessible and "request behavior" was not accessible. DITF would work, when the "request behavior" was more accessible than the "own behavior". This is the scenario in which the basic framework with RB and OB, would guide the compliance behavior without any input from AR. Our final postulate about multiple request effectiveness is as follows:

Postulate 4: When the AR is located closer to the nonattitude side of the continuum, then the relative availability of RB and OB will guide the compliance behavior.

DISCUSSION

This manuscript argues that when the attitude towards the request is highly accessible or located towards the attitude end of the attitude-nonattitude continuum, AR will guide compliance, and the situational variables in the multiple request techniques i.e. OB and RB will have little role to play.

The second case, where the AR is moderately accessible, is the most interesting one, and perhaps the one that is most often observed in the literature. The relative accessibility and valence of OB, RB and AR determines compliance. In the case of FITD the positive and accessible OB dominates the moderately accessible AR, and therefore this technique is not very sensitive to the valence of the AR. However, in the DITF technique OB is not dominant and AR considered in the decision making situation, making it more sensitive the valence of AR.

The AR does not have any role to play in the last scenario. Thus, as we keep moving towards the nonattitude part of the continuum, AR's role keeps on decreasing and towards the non-attitude end of the continuum, it does not play any role in the compliance process. At this point in the AR continuum, only RB and OB are needed to explain the multiple request effectiveness.

Based on our review, we can make some suggestions about the suitability of these multiple request techniques. When the AR is highly accessible, it may not be very effective to use the multiple request techniques. If the AR is positive, but not very accessible, instead of using two requests, it may be more efficient to increase the accessibility of the AR, and use just one request i.e. if it is possible to increase its accessibility (e.g. Mowen and Cialdini 1980). FITD would be the best technique to pick for a business and/or a non-humanitarian request when the AR of the respondents is likely to be moderately accessible. But, DITF would only be suitable if the respondents are likely to have a positive or neutral attitude towards the request.

Although we have reviewed the results of previous studies and found them to be consistent with the predictions of our framework, these results have not been empirically verified. Further evidence would be provided in support of this framework by demonstrating that the valence and accessibility of the requests in these studies confirms to our assumptions. A stronger test of this framework would be provided by actually manipulating attitude valence and accessibility and examining the effects of these manipulations on compliance using FITD and DITF techniques. It would also be important to measure the accessibility and valence of RB and OB, in order to provide support for the entire framework.

REFERENCES

Beaman, Arthur L., C. Maureen Cole, Marilyn Preston, Bonnel Klentz and Nancy M. Steblay (1983), "Fifteen Years of the-Foot-in-the-Door Research — A Meta-Analysis", *Personality and Social Psychology Bulletin*, 9 (2), 181-196.

_____, Nancy M. Steblay, Marilyn Preston and Bonnel Klentz (1988), "Compliance as a Function of Elapsed Time Between First and Second Requests", Journal of Social Psychology, 128(2), 233-243.

Bem, Daryl J. (1972), "Self-Perception Theory", in *Advances in Experimental Social Psychology*, ed. L. Berkowitz, New York: Academic Press, 1-62.

Berger, Ida E. and Andrew Mitchell (1989), "The effect of advertising on attitude accessibility, attitude confidence, and the attitude-behavior relationship", *Journal of Consumer Research*, 16, December, 269-279.

Cantrill, James G. and David R. Seibold (1986), "The Perceptual Contrast Explanation of Sequential Request Strategy Effectiveness", *Human Communication Research*, 13 (2), Winter, 253-267.

Cialdini, Robert B., J. E. Vincent, S. K. Lewis, J. Catalan, D. Wheeler and B. L. Darby (1975), "A Reciprocal concessions Procedure for Inducing Compliance", *Journal of Personality and Social Psychology*, 31, 206-15.

DeJong, William (1979), "An Examination of Self-Perception Mediation of the Foot-in-the-Door Effect", *Journal of Personality and Social Psychology*, 37 (12), 2221-2239.

Dillard, James P., John E. Hunter and Michael Burgoon (1984), "Sequential Request persuasive Strategies— Meta-Analysis of Foot-in-the-Door and Door-in-the-Face", *Human Communication Research*, 10 (4), Summer, 461-488.

Fazio, Russel (1989), "On the power and functionality of attitudes: The role of attitude accessibility", in *Attitude Structure and Function*, Eds. Pratkanis, Breckler and Greenwald, Hillsdale, NJ: Earlbaum, 153-179.

_____ (1986), "How do attitudes guide behavior?", in *The Handbook of Motivation and Cognition: Foundations of Social Behavior*, Eds. Sorrentino & Higgins, New York: Guilford Press, 204-243.

_____ and Carol Williams (1986), "Attitude accessibility as a moderator of the attitude-perception and attitude-behavior relations: An investigation of the 1984 presidential election", *Journal of Personality and Social Psychology*, 51, 505-514.

_____ and Mark P. Zanna (1981), "Direct experience and attitude-behavior consistency", *Advances in Experimental Social Psychology*, 14, 161-202.

Fern, Edward F., Kent B. Monroe and Ramon Avila (1986), "Effectiveness of Multiple Request Strategies: A Synthesis of Research Results", *Journal of Marketing Research*, XXIII, 144-52.

Foehl, J. C. and Morton Goldman (1983), "Increasing Altruistic Behavior by using compliance techniques", *Journal of Social Psychology*, 119, 21-29.

Freedman J. L. and S. C. Fraser (1966), "Compliance Without Pressure: The Foot-in-the-Door Technique", *Journal of Personality and Social Psychology*, 4, 195-202.

Goldman, Morton, Joseph Gier, and D. E. Smith (1981), "Compliance as Affected by Task Difficulty and Order of Tasks", *Journal of Social Psychology*, 114, 75-83.

Goldman, Morton, James F. McVeigh and J. L. Richterkessing (1984), "Door-in-the-Face Procedure: Reciprocal Concession, Perceptual Contrast, or Worthy Person", *Journal of Social Psychology*, 123 (2), August, 245-251.

Katzev, Richard D. and Theodore Johnson (1984), "Comparing the effects of monetary incentives and foot-in-the-door strategies in promoting residential electricity consumption", *Journal of Applied Social Psychology*, 14(1), 12-27.

Kilbourne, Brock K. (1988), "A New Application of the Foot-in-the-Door Technique: Friend or Stranger?", *Psychological Reports*, 62, 31-36.

Miller, Richard, Clive Seligman and Malcolm Bush (1976), "Perceptual contrast versus Reciprocal Concession as Mediators of Induce Compliance", *Canadian Journal of Behavioral Science*, 8, 401-409.

Mowen, John C. and Robert B. Cialdini (1980), "On Implementing the Door-in-the-Face Compliance Technique in a Business Context", *Journal of Marketing Research*, XVII, 253-58.

Patch, Michael (1988), "Differential perception of source legitimacy in sequential request strategies", Journal of Social Psychology, 128 (6), 817-823.

_____ (1986), "The role of source legitimacy in sequential request strategies of compliance", *Personality and Social Psychology Bulletin*, 12 (2), 199-205.

Petty, Richard and John Caccioppo (1986), "Communication and persuasion — central and peripheral routes to attitude change", NY: Springer-Verlag.

Powell, Martha and Russell Fazio (1984), "Attitude accessibility as a function of repeated attitudinal expression", *Personality and Social Psychology Bulletin*, 10, 139-148.

Reingen, Peter H. and Jerome B. Kernan (1979), "More evidence on interpersonal yielding", *Journal of Marketing Research*, 26(November), 365-69.

Rogers, T. B., N. A. Kuiper and W. S. Kirker (1977), "Self-reference and the encoding of personal information", *Journal of Personality and Social Psychology*, 35(9), 677-688.

Tybout, Alice M., Brian Sternthal and Bobby J. Calder (1983), "Information Availability as a Determinant of Multiple Request Effectiveness", *Journal of Marketing Research*, XX, (August), 280-90.

Wood, Wendy, Carl A. Kallgren, R. M. Preisler (1985), "Access to attitude-relevant information in memory as a determinant of persuasion: The role of message attributes", *Journal of Experimental Social Psychology*, 21, 73-85.

Attitudes Toward "Buy America First" and Preferences for American and Japanese Cars: A Different Role for Country-of-Origin Information

Irwin P. Levin, University of Iowa
J. D. Jasper, University of Iowa
John D. Mittelstaedt, University of Iowa
Gary J. Gaeth, University of Iowa[1]

ABSTRACT

Subjects rank-ordered their likelihood of purchasing an automobile from each of six companies described by country of origin (America or Japan) and percentage of American and Japanese workers. Additional questions measured perceived differences in quality between American and Japanese cars and workers, and reactions to "Buy America First." Subjects tended to assign more favorable characteristics to Japanese cars and workers, but most endorsed "Buy America First" and gave preferential rankings to American companies and companies that employed mostly American workers. Country-of-origin appears to invoke both feelings of nationalism and perceptions of quality, with nationalistic biases predominating in pre-purchase considerations.

The slumping American economy is nowhere more evident than in the automobile industry where imports, particularly those from Japan, have cut deeply into American auto sales. The rallying cry from American labor leaders and politicians has been "Buy America First." Closer inspection, however, reveals that for the consumer the issue is not as simple as one might suspect (Ettenson & Gaeth, 1991). Today, any one car company (including American firms) may have various parts manufactured and/or assembled in several different countries. In fact, some companies may establish entire manufacturing operations or "transplant" facilities on foreign soil. Thus, for example, a "Japanese" car company may have permanent facilities located in America and employ many American workers.

The underlying issue, that has long interested researchers in this area, is what role the perceived country-of-origin plays in terms of consumer attitudes, intentions, and purchase behavior. Much of the research on country-of-origin effects centers on perceptions of quality (e.g., Dickerson 1981; Wall & Heslop 1986). As suggested above, however, current concerns for the American economy and the American worker may lead to another role of country-of-origin information: evoking nationalistic or patriotic feelings that may be independent of perceptions of quality.

These two components of country-of-origin may, in some instances, conflict with each other. The goals of this exploratory study are to separate out these component reactions to country-of-origin and to examine the trade-offs consumers make when specification of country-of-origin leads to nationalistic feelings and quality perceptions which conflict with each other. For example, if it can be shown that American consumers prefer American products *in spite of* perceptions of inferior quality, then this would support the hypothesis that nationalistic biases are a dominant reaction to country-of-origin information.

In order to pursue these goals, the present study uses a controlled experimental task which includes attitudinal measures designed to reveal meaningful patterns of individual differences. An information integration task is used to reveal the preferences of subjects for American or Japanese companies and American or Japanese workers. Individual differences are then assessed through questions that involve listing the distinguishing features of American and Japanese cars and workers and expressing the degree of agreement or disagreement with the statement, "Buy America First." These measures of individual difference are then used to discriminate between those respondents with different patterns of revealed preferences in an attempt to better understand the attitudes and perceptions underlying the preference for American or Japanese cars.

METHOD

The study was conducted in March, 1992. Seventy-one undergraduate students (46F, 25M) completed a two-part survey. Instructions for the rank-ordering task of Part 1 were as follows:

As you know, there is currently some controversy over the relative merits of buying an American or a Japanese car. Complicating matters is the fact that Japanese auto manufacturers often have some of their parts made or assembled in the United States by U.S. workers, while U.S. auto manufacturers often have some of their work done in other countries such as Japan. In this study we want you to rank-order the likelihood that you would buy a car of a given model with each of the characteristics described below. Each car will be described by whether the car is made by an American or a Japanese company and the percentage of workers on that car from the U.S. and Japan.

Subjects were then given six types of cars, identified by the letters A through F, where three of the cars were labeled as manufactured by an American company and three were labeled as manufactured by a Japanese company. Within each type of company, the composition of workers was identified as being either 80% American - 20% Japanese, 50% American - 50% Japanese, or 20% American - 80% Japanese. This 2 x 3 stimulus design is summarized in Table 1. A random order was used in assigning types of car to consecutive letters of the alphabet.

The subjects' task was to rank-order these six types of cars using the numbers 1-6. Each number was to be used exactly once, where "1" was assigned to the type of car they would want to buy most, and "6" to the type of car they would want to buy least. Ties were not permitted.

In Part 2 subjects were asked a series of questions. The first question asked them to list the most important distinguishing characteristics of American and Japanese cars. The second question asked them to list the most important distinguishing characteristics of American and Japanese workers. Two independent raters scored these questions. For each classification (American or Japanese) within each question, they arrived at a score for each subject by counting +1 for each favorable statement (implying high quality), -1 for each unfavorable statement (implying low quality), and 0 for each statement not implying a judgment of good or poor

---

[1] This project was funded by the National Science Foundation, Grant No. SES-9010243 awarded to Irwin P. Levin and Gary J. Gaeth.

TABLE 1
Weighted median rankings, all subjects combined ($N = 71$).

	% American/Japanese Workers		
	80-20	50-50	20-80
American Companies	1.21	2.50	4.65
Japanese Companies	3.04	4.30	5.81

quality of the product or workmanship (e.g., "Japanese work for less money"). These values were then combined to provide a single algebraic attitude score for each subject in each classification for each of the two questions. An American-Japanese difference score was then computed for each of the two questions. For example, a given subject may have scored -1 for American workers and +1 for Japanese workers, resulting in an American-Japanese difference score of -2. The inter-rater correlations for difference scores were .85 for cars, and .76 for workers. For purposes of statistical analysis a single difference score was later agreed upon in each situation by the two independent raters. In only two cases did the raters disagree about the direction of a difference score; a neutral score (zero difference) was then given. The last question asked subjects how much they agreed or disagreed with the statement, "Buy America First." Response categories were "strongly agree", "slightly agree", "neither agree nor disagree", "slightly disagree", and "strongly disagree".

RESULTS

Table 1 gives the weighted median ranking of each type of car in Part 1, averaged over all 71 subjects. Statistical significance was determined by applying a Friedman two-way analysis of variance by rank. Rankings were significantly more favorable (lower ranking) for American companies than for Japanese companies. Furthermore, rankings were significantly more favorable the higher the percentage of American workers employed.

Responses to the questions in Part 2 were used to classify subjects. Most revealing were responses to the statement "Buy America First." The majority of subjects agreed with that statement. Twenty-one subjects (30%) strongly agreed with the statement; 27 subjects (38%) slightly agreed; 12 subjects (18%) neither agreed nor disagreed; nine subjects (13%) slightly disagreed; and one subject (1%) strongly disagreed.

Part 1 rankings were then compared across the resulting subject classifications. Table 2 gives the weighted median rankings separately for subjects who agreed (strongly or slightly), disagreed (strongly or slightly), and neither agreed nor disagreed with the statement "Buy America First." Considerable differences can be observed across these subgroups. The pattern seen in Table 1 of preference for American companies and preference for American workers is especially strong for the largest subgroup, subjects who agreed with "Buy America First". For these subjects the weighted median rank was close to 1.00 for the combination of an American company and the highest percentage of American workers, and it was close to 6.00 for the combination of a Japanese company and the lowest percentage of American workers. By contrast, subjects who disagreed with "Buy America First" showed the strongest preference for Japanese companies over American companies and no preference for companies with mostly American workers.

For subjects who agreed with "Buy America First", rankings were significantly more favorable for American companies than for Japanese companies, and rankings were significantly more favorable for companies employing higher percentages of American workers. For subjects who disagreed with "Buy America First", rankings were significantly more favorable for Japanese companies than for American companies and there was no significant difference as a function of worker composition.

Table 3 gives the frequency distribution of attitude scores towards American and Japanese cars and American and Japanese workers. It can be seen that mean scores were on the favorable side in each case but that they were more favorable for Japanese than for American cars and more favorable for Japanese than for American workers. Each of these mean scores was significantly greater than zero (neutral) and in each case the mean score for Japanese was significantly higher than the mean score for American.

For the purpose of categorizing subjects on each of these two questions, each subject was given a difference score between American and Japanese and was classified on the basis of the direction of that difference score. The correlation between these two sets of difference scores was .37. The correlation between these difference scores and responses to "Buy America First" was .52 and .30, respectively, for perceptions of American and Japanese cars and perceptions of American and Japanese workers. For each question the comparison of interest was between those who favored American and those who favored Japanese workers. (Subjects with a difference score of zero were not included.) Table 4 compares Part 1 rankings for subjects who favor American cars and subjects who favor Japanese cars. Table 5 compares Part 1 rankings for subjects who favor American workers and subjects who favor Japanese workers.

Table 4 shows that subjects who favor American cars over Japanese cars in their description of distinguishing characteristics do, in fact, show a large preference for American companies in the rank-order task, and they also show a large preference for companies that employ a large percentage of American workers. Subjects whose description of distinguishing characteristics favor Japanese cars over American cars also show a preference for American companies and American workers in the rank-order task; this preference is somewhat reduced compared to subjects who favor American cars. A similar pattern can be observed in Table 5 where subjects are classified on the basis of their descriptions of American and Japanese workers, although one must be cautious in interpreting these results because the subgroup of subjects who favor American workers is composed of only 8 subjects. In each subgroup of Tables 4 and 5 the rankings were significantly more favorable for companies employing a high percentage of American workers. The observed preference for American companies over Japanese companies failed to reach statistical significance ($p > .05$) *only* for those subjects who favored Japanese cars (top half of Table 4). Clearly, however, these subjects did not give more favorable rankings to Japanese companies.

DISCUSSION

Revealed preferences uncovered in the rank-order task showed that subjects in this study tend to prefer cars made by American companies over cars made by Japanese companies and they tend to

TABLE 2
Weighted median rankings as a function of response to "Buy America First."

Subjects who agreed with "Buy America First" (N = 48).

	% American/Japanese Workers		
	80-20	50-50	20-80
American Companies	1.06	2.30	4.70
Japanese Companies	3.03	4.33	5.95

Subjects who neither agreed nor disagreed with "Buy America First" (N = 13).

	% American/Japanese Workers		
	80-20	50-50	20-80
American Companies	3.83	3.50	4.75
Japanese Companies	3.30	2.21	4.50

Subjects who disagreed with "Buy America First" (N = 10).

	% American/Japanese Workers		
	80-20	50-50	20-80
American Companies	5.75	3.67	4.38
Japanese Companies	3.00	2.38	3.00

TABLE 3
Distribution of attitude scores towards American and Japanese cars and American and Japanese workers.

Characteristics of American and Japanese cars

Score	frequencies	
	American	Japanese
+4	4	5
+3	10	10
+2	13	17
+1	11	18
0	17	17
-1	9	4
-2	5	0
-3	2	0
mean:	+.82	+1.38
variance:	3.09	1.78

Characteristics of American and Japanese workers

Score	frequencies	
	American	Japanese
+3	0	2
+2	5	12
+1	20	27
0	33	30
-1	11	0
-2	2	0
mean:	+.21	+.80
variance:	.80	.67

prefer companies that employ mostly American workers. The latter tendency was especially strong. Responses to the questions in Part 2 helped explain these preferences as well as reveal individual differences in reaction to country-of-origin information.

The observed preferences for American companies and companies which employ mostly American workers were tied to endorsement of the statement, "Buy America First." Over two-thirds of the subjects agreed with this statement. These subjects showed a strong preference for cars made by American companies over cars made by Japanese companies, and an even stronger preference for companies which employ mostly American workers. The relatively small number of subjects who disagreed with "Buy America First" showed a preference for cars made by Japanese companies over cars made by American companies and no clear preference for a particular worker composition.

Responses to the other two questions were not so closely tied to the preference rankings. For many subjects the listing of distinguishing characteristics of American and Japanese cars and American and Japanese workers favored Japanese. Even for these subjects, however, preference rankings tended to favor American companies and workers. For example, one subject indicated that Japanese cars are of higher quality than American cars and that American workers "don't give so much attention to quality." Yet, that same subject strongly agreed with the statement "Buy America First" and his preference rankings clearly favored American companies and companies that employed mostly American workers.

Taken together, attitudes tapped by responses to "Buy America First" appear to represent a form of nationalism separate from perceptions of quality and seem to be an overriding factor in preference rankings, especially for worker composition. A repre-

TABLE 4
Weighted median rankings as a function of response to distinguishing characteristics of American and Japanese cars.

Subjects who favor Japanese cars (N = 28).

	% American/Japanese Workers		
	80-20	50-50	20-80
American Companies	2.00	2.94	4.61
Japanese Companies	3.11	3.64	5.75

Subjects who favor American cars (N = 20).

	% American/Japanese Workers		
	80-20	50-50	20-80
American Companies	1.12	2.29	4.67
Japanese Companies	3.29	4.44	5.94

TABLE 5
Weighted median rankings as a function of response to distinguishing characteristics of American and Japanese workers.

Subjects who favor Japanese workers (N = 31).

	% American/Japanese Workers		
	80-20	50-50	20-80
American Companies	1.44	2.96	4.58
Japanese Companies	2.93	3.92	5.71

Subjects who favor American workers (N = 8).

	% American/Japanese Workers		
	80-20	50-50	20-80
American Companies	1.40	2.00	5.25
Japanese Companies	3.33	4.00	5.63

sentation of our conceptualization of this process is given in Figure 1, which is an adaptation of Shocker, Ben-Akiva, Boccara and Nedungadi's (1991) conceptualization of the mediating roles of context, awareness, and consideration on choice. Whereas previous research has focused on Country-of-Origin as a cue to quality, the conceptualization in Figure 1 allows for country-of-origin to impact purchase intentions in other ways as well, such as nationalistic biases in the formation of consideration sets. In fact, there is evidence that perceptions of quality, provided by country-of-origin cues, may not have a preeminent role in a compensatory choice process involving other price and quality cues (Ettenson, Wagoner & Gaeth, 1988; Johansson, Douglas, & Nonaka, 1985; Wall, Liefeld, & Heslop, 1991).

Nationalistic feelings may serve to make potential car buyers *aware* of the importance of country-of-origin and employment of American workers when forming their consideration sets based on pre-purchase intentions. Laurent and Lapersonne (1990) argue that individuals consider alternatives that others want them to consider, even when the individuals would not ordinarily consider these alternatives themselves. Nationalism (as represented by "Buy America First") appears to be a vehicle through which societal wishes influence individual choice, separate from purchase intentions based on individual perceptions of quality.

We view this study as an early attempt to support the usefulness of the model depicted in Figure 1 which assigns multiple roles to country-of-origin information. One unique cue affecting pre-purchase intentions may be nationalistic feelings which, as we have seen, may dominate other perceptions based on country-of-origin.

Future research can study this process more microscopically by including finer-grained analyses of these nationalistic feelings through a multi-item scale of nationalism. A separate research strategy would be to include varying numbers of additional product attributes to be combined with country-of-origin and examine the relative weight of country-of-origin information at different phases of the purchase decision (e.g., by asking consumers to generate consideration sets, later asking them to narrow their consideration set to a fixed number, and ultimately asking for their final choice). Of particular interest would be studying at each phase the trade-offs among the conflicting cues evoked by country-of-origin. It would be interesting, for example, to show that while the nationalistic role of country-of-origin predominated during the early stages, the quality role predominated during the later stages of the purchase decision.

REFERENCES

Dickerson, K. G. (1982), "Imported Versus U.S.-Produced Apparel: Consumer Views and Buying Patterns," *Home Economics Research Journal*, 10 (March), 241-252.

Ettenson, R. and G. Gaeth (1991), "Consumer Perceptions of Hybrid (Bi-National) Products," *Journal of Consumer Marketing*, 8 (Fall), 13-18.

Ettenson, R., J. Wagner, and G. Gaeth (1988), "Evaluating the Effect of Country of Origin and the 'Made in the USA' Campaign: A Conjoint Approach," *Journal of Retailing*, 64 (Spring), 85-100.

FIGURE 1
A conceptualization of choice as impacted by country-of-origin
(Adapted from Shocker, et al., 1991 model of the role of consideration sets)

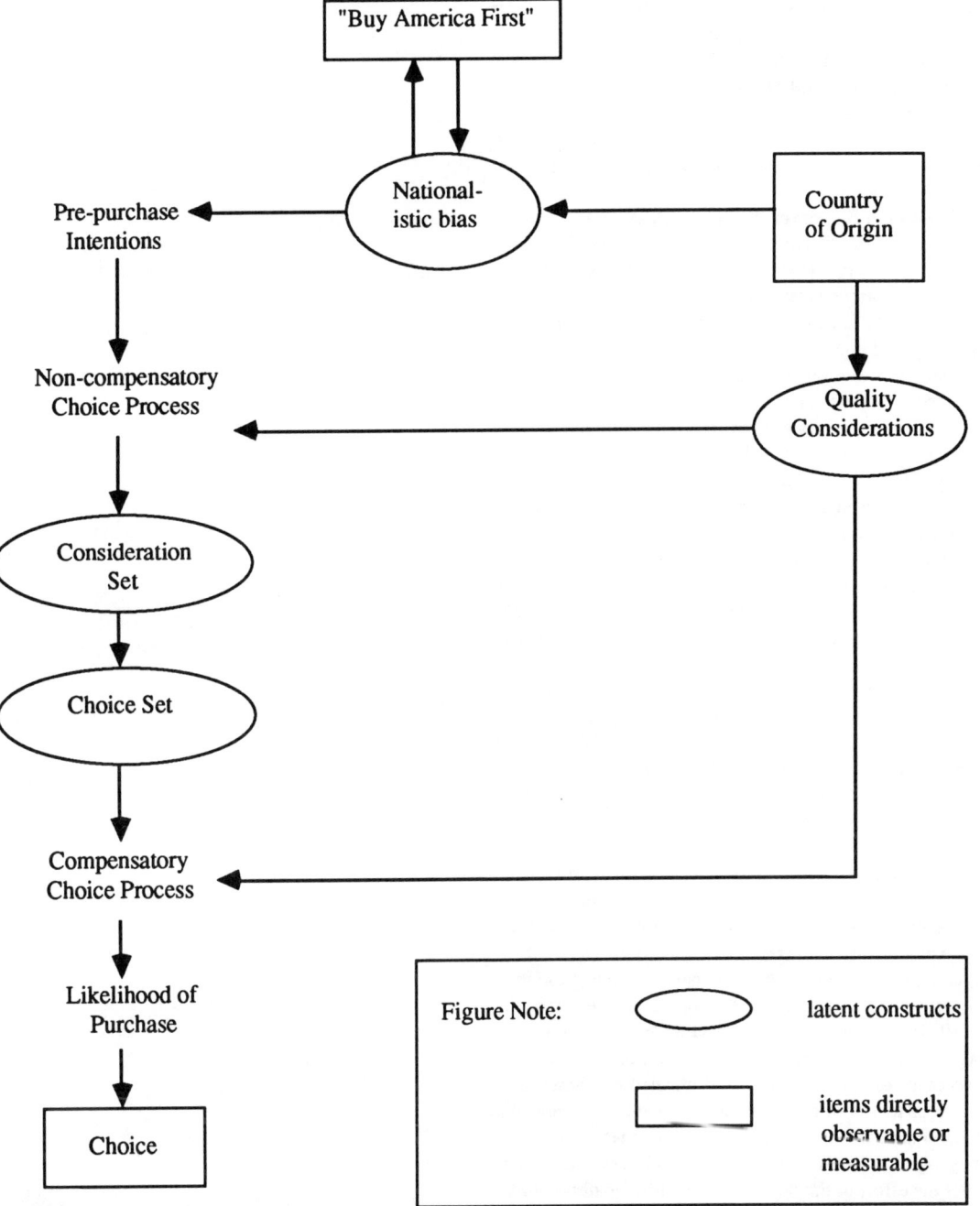

Johansson, J. K., S. P. Douglas, and I. Nonaka (1985), "Assessing the Impact of Country of Origin on Product Evaluations: A New Methodological Perspective," *Journal of Marketing Research*, 22 (November), 388-396.

Laurent, G. and E. Lapersonne (1990), "Consideration Sets of Size One?" Working Paper. Jouy-en-Josas, France: Ecole Des Hautes Etudes Commerciales, Centre HEC-ISA.

Shocker, A. D., M. Ben-Akiva, B. Boccara, and P. Nedungadi (1991), "Consideration Set Influences on Consumer Decision-Making and Choice: Issues, Models, and Suggestions," *Marketing Letters*, 2 (August), 181-187.

Wall, M. and L. A. Heslop (1986), "Consumer Attitudes Toward Canadian-Made Versus Imported Products," *Journal of the Academy of Marketing Science*, 14 (Summer), 27-36.

Wall, M., J. Liefeld, and L. A. Heslop (1991), "Impact of Country-of-Origin Cues on Consumer Judgments in Multi-Cue Situations: A Covariance Analysis," *Journal of the Academy of Marketing Science*, 19 (Spring), 105-113.

The Influence of Environmental Factors on Consumer Behavior: A Decade Later
Richard F. Yalch, University of Washington

In their 1982 Journal of Retailing paper, Donovan and Rossiter suggested that consumer behavior in a retail store was primarily an emotional response to the factors making up the retail environment. Using a Stimulus-Organism-Response (S-O-R) paradigm, they adapted measures developed by Albert Mehrabian and James Russell (1974) to model the relationship between environmental factors and consumer behavior. This session acknowledged the importance of their effort and summarized continuing efforts to validate their approach.

In the session's first paper, Donovan, Rossiter and Nesdale reviewed Donovan and Rossiter's seminal piece and discussed a follow-up study. In it, urban shoppers in Australia stated the amount of time and money they intended to spend prior to entering two discount variety stores. After several minutes in the store, shoppers completed the Mehrabian-Russell emotional response scales (Pleasure and Arousal only). On leaving the store, interviewers intercepted shoppers for a third time and asked about their purchases. The interviewers also recorded shopping times.

The results were that both unplanned spending (the difference between intended and reported spending) and extra shopping time (the difference between intended and observed shopping times) were related to the reported level of pleasure while shopping. Consistent with the 1982 study, "arousal" was not related to extra time, but approached significance for unplanned spending. An insignificant interaction between arousal and pleasure was attributed to few shoppers considering the stores to be unpleasant environments.

In the session's second paper, Ruth Belk Smith and Elaine Sherman also presented a follow-up to a previously published paper based on Donovan and Rossiter's methodology (Sherman and Smith 1987). Their study analyzed nine hundred exit interviews in two cities. The questionnaire included mood (PAD) measures, store image measures, and self-reported shopping behavior.

Statistical analysis using LISREL revealed a good fit of the data. There was a significant positive influence of store image on mood. Also, moods positively influenced the behavioral response variables. With mood as an intervening variable, the influence of store image on outcomes was positive and highly significant.

Together, these two studies show that store image can influence a buyer's mood. Further, this atmosphere-induced mood may enhance affiliate behavior within the store; e.g., spending more time and money than planned. Whereas cognitive factors may largely account for store selection and planned purchases, emotional reactions to a store's environment may encourage spending extra time shopping and motivate unplanned purchases. Discussant T. J. Olney urged continued in-store research with revised measures to consider the effect of the dominance-submissive dimension.

REFERENCES

Donovan, Robert J. and John R. Rossiter (1982), "Store Atmosphere: An Environmental Psychology Approach," *Journal of Retailing*, 58 (Spring), 34-57.

Mehrabian, Albert and James Russell, (1974), *An Approach to Environmental Psychology*, Cambridge, Mass.: MIT Press.

Sherman, Elaine and Smith, Ruth Belk (1987), "Mood States of Shoppers and Store Image: Promising Interactions and Possible Behavioral Effects, in *Advances in Consumer Research*, Vol. 14, eds. M. Wallendorf and J. Anderson, Provo, UT: Association for Consumer Research. 251-254.

Effects Of Store Image And Mood On Consumer Behavior: A Theoretical And Empirical Analysis

Ruth Belk Smith, University of Baltimore
Elaine Sherman, Hofstra University

ABSTRACT

Although considerable research has focused upon the traditional information processing paradigm to explain or predict consumer behavior, only a minimal effort has been concerned with affective factors' influence on cognition, attitudes, and behavior of the consumer. In addition, most basic research in cognitive psychology has been conducted within the confines of the laboratory using carefully delineated tasks and techniques. These have resulted in advancing the study of cognition and, although useful for isolating intellectual processes of interest, such tasks and the conditions under which they are administered are not representative of the whole of human thought. They need to be supplemented by more broadly based investigations, because in natural life situations, reasoning and remembering are carried out in social contexts and are influenced by affective as well as cognitive factors.

In response to this, some researchers in marketing have recently turned their attention to the consumer's mood. Mood as a concept has been studied quite seriously and for much longer by psychologists, and much of what we know is due to these efforts. Again, however, most of the studies of the influence of mood on human behavior in general and consumer behavior in particular, have been confined to laboratory type experiments. Examples include how an induced positive mood (receiving a small gift) influences helping behavior and the influence of advertising on moods or vice versa. These types of studies lack external validity and practically speaking, may not be of much use to the retailer who seeks to understand what should be done to induce positive consumer moods. It is known that positive mood is related to affiliative behavior, thus a retailer seeks methods to enhance consumer mood in order to induce "approach" (rather than "avoidance") behavior, such as spending more time and money in the store, enjoying the shopping experience, and wishing to return.

The store image is a concept including a variety of factors such as merchandise, service, convenience, promotional activities, prices, and "atmospherics". The term "atmospherics" refers to the managerial effort to design buying environments to produce specific emotional states in the buyer that enhance the probability of purchase. Managers can manipulate the design of the building, the interior space, aisle layout, carpet and wall textures, scents, colors, shapes, and sounds experienced by the customers. Thus store image is a result of many variables which can be manipulated by the retailer to influence consumer mood and, subsequently, the buyer's behavior. Since the store image can in this way be considered a stimulus and the consumer's mood an organismic variable, the study is cast into the S-O-R framework. The path of influence is shown in table 1.

Data were collected from 907 respondents at the point of purchase. Moods are transient, and collecting field data in a natural setting offers a solution to the problem of retroactivity measuring them. In addition, actual behavior has just occurred and is easily remembered. Scales developed in previous research were used to measure store image, mood, and behavior.

Analysis of the data using LISREL revealed a good fit of the data to both the measurement and structural model. There is a significant positive influence of store image on mood, and a significant positive influence of moods on the response variables. With mood as an intervening variable, the influence of store image on the outcomes is negative and insignificant. Without it, the effect of store image on the outcome is positive and highly significant. The goodness of fit indices are χ^2=252.15, 27 df; GFI=.944; AGFI=.89; RMSR=.064; Bentler and Bonett index=.91.

These findings imply that store image, as a manipulative variable, can influence a buyer's mood, and that this atmosphere-induced mood may enhance affiliative behaviors within the store; e.g., spending more time and money than planned, intention to revisit. Whereas cognitive factors may largely account for store selection and for most planned purchases within the store, emotional reaction to the store's environment may influence unplanned purchasing, extra spending, and time spent inside the store. Thus, retailers have the opportunity to enhance such affiliative behavior by manipulating a controllable variable: the atmosphere of the store and its resulting image to the consumer.

TABLE 1

STIMULUS	ORGANISM	RESPONSE
Store Image Components e.g.,	Emotional Response Components	Approach/Avoidance Behavior e.g.,
a. layout	a. pleasure/displeasure	a. time spent in store
b. sounds, smells, color	b. arousal/nonarousal	b. money spent
c. building design	c. dominance	c. number of items brought prices
		d. intention to revisit store

Using Store Music for Retail Zoning: A Field Experiment
Richard F. Yalch, University of Washington
Eric Spangenberg, Washington State University[1]

ABSTRACT

Zoning, playing different types of music in different parts of a store to appeal to specific consumers, is common in retailing. However, the effects of store music on shopper behavior have been studied on a store by store basis not by departments within a store. To address this issue, an experiment was conducted in a national apparel chain store located in the northwestern part of the United States. Three types of music were played in two departments differing in their appeal to consumers based on age and sex in ninety-minute segments over a two-week time period. During the segments, business school students observed and interviewed shoppers in the store to determine their mood, how much time and money they spent, and their evaluation of the store and its merchandise.

The results showed that playing the appropriate music for a specific department enhanced the environment resulting in more shoppers making purchases and spending more money. Additional analyses suggest that store music interacts with age but not gender. Middle-aged (25-49) shoppers spent more and shopped longer when foreground music was played, whereas older shoppers (over age 50) shopped longer and purchased more when background music was playing. Other factors such as shopping alone or with someone, shopping for a specific item or browsing, and shopping during the week or on a weekend or holiday, did not substantially alter how shoppers reacted to the different music conditions. Moods did not explain the music effects but store perceptions partially did. This supports the view that music may influence shopping by stimulating cognitive associations rather than altering emotional states.

INTRODUCTION

Music is one of several environmental or atmospheric factors available to differentiate a retail store from competing stores. Music is a particularly attractive atmospheric variable because it is relatively inexpensive to provide, is easily changed, and is thought to have predictable appeals to individuals based on their ages and life styles. For example, teenagers usually listen to rock music, older professional adults may prefer classical music, and middle-aged, blue collar adults may prefer country and western. These preferences are expected to result in shoppers spending more time and money in stores playing liked music and less time and money in stores playing disliked music. Larger stores often differentiate areas by varying the music played in one or more departments, a practice referred to as zoning by the environmental music industry. Managers expect store music to be more effective when tailored to the listening preferences of the demographic segment shopping in a particular department compared to when the same type of music is played in all departments.

A review of published and some unpublished research reveals relatively few studies of the effects of music in a retail environment and virtually no studies evaluating the effects of zoning. One exception is a study that considered the interaction between shopper demographics and store music. Yalch and Spangenberg (1990) exposed younger (under 25) and older (25 and over) clothing store shoppers either to background (environmental) or foreground (contemporary) music. Contrary to expectations, shoppers self-reported spending more time than expected in the store when exposed to the music that was different from their preference (i.e., foreground for older shoppers and background for younger shoppers) compared to when they were exposed to their preferred music (i.e., background for older shoppers and foreground for younger shoppers). Unfortunately, there was no observation of the actual amount of time spent shopping so it could not be determined if the effect was behavioral (actually spent more time), perceptual (spent the same amount of time but perceived it to be longer) or a combination of the two.

Other music research suggests a relationship between store music and shopping times. For example, Milliman (1982) reported that supermarket shoppers shopped longer, moved slower, and purchased more when slow tempo music was played compared to fast tempo music. Smith and Curnow (1966) reported that shoppers shopped for a shorter period of time when loud music was played compared to soft music. However, neither study addressed the possibility that demographics might alter these effects. Further, neither study considered music preferences.

Preference is potentially an important variable because it is well-established that environments affect behavior through a combination of at least two factors. Mehrabian and Russell's (1974) Pleasure-Arousal-Dominance (PAD) model is probably the most frequently used perspective in environmental psychology. This model postulates that the environment affects individuals' moods or emotions by altering their state of pleasure, arousal and dominance. Figure 1 provides an overview of the theorized process. For a more complete discussion of this model than is possible in a conference paper, please see Yalch & Spangenberg (1992).

The previously mentioned effects of music on shopping times can easily be explained using this model. For example, fast music should be arousing, causing individuals to move more quickly through their environment (store). Similarly, loud music should also be arousing and similarly cause faster shopping.

The effects of the pleasure dimension in the context of retail shopping are less clear. In an advertising context, listening to liked music was found to enhance brand preference relative to listening to disliked music (Gorn 1982). However, altering brand preferences is not the same as motivating a purchase. In fact, if purchases are based on perceived needs instead of moods, there should be no change in behavior. On the other hand, if shoppers are enjoying the shopping experience, they may shop longer and be exposed to more merchandise. Also, they may misattribute good feelings stimulated by the music to the merchandise. These factors would increase the likelihood of shoppers purchasing something.

In their seminal atmospheric study, Donovan and Rossiter (1982) tested the effects of arousal and pleasure on shopping behavior using the PAD model. Subjects were instructed to visit various retail stores. While in the stores, they completed a survey indicating their mood and likely shopping behavior. The results revealed positive correlations between pleasure and favorable shopping intentions such as purchasing and spending more time in the store. Interestingly, in pleasant environments, shoppers reported that they would spend more time in the store if their arousal level was high compared to if it was low. This contradicts experimental findings of negative correlations between arousing music (fast or loud) and observed shopping times (cf. Milliman 1982; Smith and Curnow 1966).

---
[1] Special thanks to Ellen Goldblatt of MUZAK for assisting in planning and executing this study.

FIGURE 1
The Role of Moods in Mediating Atmospheric Effects on Shopping Behavior

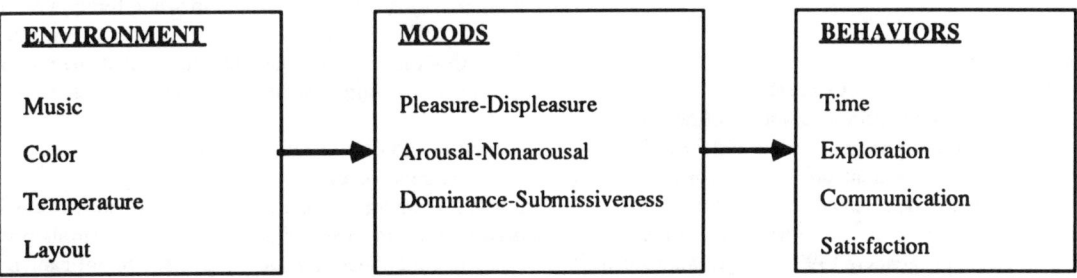

In a study using a procedure similar to Donovan and Rossiter's, Sherman and Smith (1987) interviewed eighty-nine shoppers who had just made a purchase. After combining the PAD measures into an overall mood measure, they found a positive correlation between mood and the amount of unplanned purchases but no association with actual or excess time spent in the store. Thus, these findings only partially supported Donovan and Rossiter's results.

Our review of music experiments and in-store mood surveys shows inconsistent findings regarding the role of mood as a mediating factor in the atmosphere-shopping behavior relationship. One problem is that shoppers' moods reflect their experiences prior to entering a store as well as what happens in the store. Factors such as the time of day and weather may create moods not easily altered by in-store factors. Further, there are many factors besides music that can influence a shopper such as the lighting, merchandise layout, temperatures, and colors. Also, the behavior of other shoppers and the sales clerks may be more critical than atmospheric factors. Individuals who are in a store to purchase a specific item or shopping with other persons are less likely to be influenced by music compared to those who are browsing or shopping alone. Fifth, atmospheric factors may have opposite effects on different shoppers. Arousing music may energize some shoppers resulting in their quickly completing their shopping. However, other shoppers might find the arousing music stimulating, decide to explore more of the store, and end up spending more time shopping. Further, what constitutes pleasant music varies across shoppers. A desire to assess the variation due to store and customer characteristics motivated the research presented in this paper.

THE FIELD STUDY

The research presented in this paper looks at the effects of music by considering the possibility of different effects on consumers shopping in different departments. It was conducted in a large apparel store to ensure an adequate range of consumers and music. It also compares the mediating role of mood using on-line measures with cognitive factors such as store and merchandise perceptions. Finally, actual as well as reported behavior was used to assess the effects of music.

Design

A true experimental design was used with one manipulated factor, two context factors, and four self-reported factors. The manipulated factor was the type of music played over the store system for periods ranging from ninety minutes to two hours. Four music conditions (two types of background, one type of foreground, and a period with no music) were rotated. Interviews and observations occurred in two different departments (men's sportswear on the lower level and women's coats and dresses on the upper level of the store). The other context factor was created by conducting the study over a two-week period with approximately the same amount of interviews on weekdays (Monday through Friday) and weekends and holidays (Saturdays, Sundays and Veteran's Day). Two of the four self-reported factors involved asking shoppers to indicate their shopping purpose (browsing or buying a specific item), and whether they were shopping alone or with a companion. The other two were the shopper's self-reported age and gender.

Procedure

Three male and two female undergraduate students from the University of Washington were stationed at various times in the two different departments. Unobtrusively, they recorded the exact time when individuals entered the department and when they appeared to complete their shopping. As the individuals were about to depart, they were intercepted and asked to complete a one-page survey in return for receiving a dollar. The survey determined how much money the shoppers spent, their mood, the amount of time they thought they had spent in the department, and their opinion of the store and its merchandise. In addition, the survey included questions about why they were shopping, whether they were shopping with someone, and their evaluation of the store music.

At predetermined intervals, the store music was switched between the different sources. The transition involved a brief period of no music. Interviewing was delayed until the new music had been playing for 15 minutes to ensure that all customers surveyed had been exposed to only one type of music. The music was varied between the current background system (instrumentals represented by MUZAK's environmental channel, ENV1), updated background (faster tempo instrumentals represented by MUZAK's New Age channel), and foreground music (slow tempo music with vocals represented by MUZAK's FM1 channel). The environmental channel was taken as received by the store's music system. The other two types of music were provided on a specially installed tape player. During some periods, no music was played.

An equal number of interviews was scheduled to be conducted across types of music, departments, and time of the week. Unfortunately, there was a variation from the desired distribution. The New Age music was inadvertently not played on a weekend. Because of this, some effects occurring during the New Age may be due to shopping day differences rather than the type of music. Most of the analysis compares only the regular background and foreground periods.

Other Independent Variables

In addition to music, department and time of week, five shopper characteristics were selected for study. These included the shopper's exact age (later classified as under 25, 25-49, and 50 or over), gender, whether the shopper was browsing or seriously intending to buy something before entering the department, whether or not the shopper had a partner, and the shopper's musical preference.

Dependent Variables

The major dependent variables were shoppers' mood, perceptions of the store and its merchandise, amount of time spent in the department (both observed and self-reported) and the self-reported amount of money spent. Given the difficulty of conducting intercept interviews, mood was determined using a shortened version of the Mehrabian-Russell scale similar to that used in previous research (cf., Yalch and Spangenberg 1990). The pleasure dimension consisted of responses to four scales (happy-unhappy, bored-relaxed, satisfied-unsatisfied, and annoyed-pleased). The arousal dimension included responses to four scales (calm-excited, sluggish-frenzied, sleepy-wide awake and dull-jittery). Store perceptions were assessed using five point scales with endpoints labeled modern-old fashioned, friendly-unfriendly, cramped-spacious, sophisticated-down-to-earth, and noisy-quiet. Merchandise evaluations were assessed with three five-point scales (inexpensive-expensive, good value-bad value, and high quality-low quality). Responses were recoded to ensure that favorable responses were indicated by higher numbers.

RESULTS

The results are presented first in terms of the effects of music with all other characteristics ignored. Next, the effects of music are analyzed by departments to evaluate zoning. Then, the potential moderating role of the customer characteristics of gender and age are assessed. Although it was originally intended to look at multiple combinations of contextual factors, the limited sample size make these result too tentative to report.

Measures Assessing Music Effectiveness

The effect of type of store music alone was analyzed using a one-way analysis of variance of the responses to the in-store survey. Table 1 provides the mean scores and one-way analysis of variance for the different measures as a function of the type of store music being played. Although most differences were statistically insignificant, some are noteworthy. Looking first at the evaluations of the music, the surveyed shoppers rated all above the midpoint of the scale and reported that the foreground music was more similar to the type of music that they usually listened to than the background or New Age music. Despite the fact that respondents thought that the foreground music was most similar to their usual music, there was little difference in the moods created by the three music conditions or in the moods with or without music.

Next the results were analyzed to determine if music affected the shoppers' behavior in terms of how much time and money they spent in the department. Shoppers spent the most time in the department when the New Age music was being played. However, the New Age music was only played during the week and shoppers did shop significantly longer during the week than on the weekend. Thus, it appears that some of the longer shopping times during the New Age music may be attributed to weekday shoppers spending more time in the store.

When music was played, about 55% of the shoppers made a purchase compared to 47% when no music was played. However, this difference is not statistically significant. Further, it did not affect total expenditures because the average amount spent per person making a purchase (as opposed to the number of shoppers) was highest in the no music condition ($51.70 compared to $43.29 when music was being played).

Lastly, the type of music had little effect on the shoppers' opinion of the store and its merchandise. The two exceptions were that shoppers saw the store as having the least expensive merchandise and being most down-to-earth when foreground music was played. Unfortunately, the survey did not include questions about the desirability of these characteristics so that one must infer from the purchase results that these were desirable qualities.

Effects of Music as a Zoning Device

The relative effectiveness of background and foreground music for zoning was analyzed using interviews occurring in two departments, one oriented toward younger, male shoppers and the other toward older, female shoppers. Significant interactions between music and department were found for the percent of shoppers who made a purchase and for the amount spent. When background music was played in the Women's Department compared to foreground music, shoppers were more likely to make a purchase (57% versus 26%, t(54) = 4.4, p < .05) and spent more money ($22.22 vs. $8.91, t(54) = 1.75, p < .1). On the other hand, shoppers in the Men's Department were more likely to make a purchase (76% versus 57%, t(44) = 2.2, ns) and spent more when foreground music was played compared to background music ($34.18 vs. $18.13, t(44) = 81, p < 1).

Efforts to explain these differences using mood measures, store and merchandise perceptions revealed a few interesting differences. In the Men's Department, shoppers perceived the store as more inexpensive (3.75 vs. 3.29, t (52) =2.01, p < .05) and more spacious (3.8 vs. 4.2, t (52) = 1.7, p < .1) when foreground music was played relative to when background music was used. For the Women's Department, perceptual effects also corresponded to the music effects.. The store was perceived as friendlier when background music was played compared to foreground music (4.4 versus 3.8, t(46) = 1.86, p < .07). Also, it was perceived as more sophisticated and less down-to-earth with background music playing (3.5 versus 2.9, t(46) = -2.07, p < .07). Interestingly, the effects in the Women's Department could not be attributed to a greater liking of background music relative to foreground music. The Women's Department shoppers reported liking the foreground music more than the background music (4.0 versus 3.3, t(42) = 1.67, p < .1) and that it was more similar to the type of music they usually listened to (3.7 versus 2.4, t(41) = 3.28, p < .002). These findings further support a cognitive as opposed to mood explanation for the behavioral effects.

Effects of Music by Age and Sex

As mentioned, the two departments differed in their appeal to shoppers based on the shoppers' age and gender. Therefore, to help explain the zoning effects, interactions of the music with demographics were analyzed using the 33 male and 72 female persons shopping during the background and foreground music times. The analyses of the interaction between music and gender revealed only one significant difference. Female shoppers perceived the store to be more mature when background music was playing whereas male shoppers perceived it as being more mature when foreground music was playing. However, there were no behavioral differences (shopping times and purchases).

Previous research has established that music's effects depend on the age of the shopper (Yalch & Spangenberg 1990). Our final sample included 21 persons aged 18-24, 49 aged 25-49, and 36 over age 50 who were exposed either to the background or foreground music. Age differences in music preference were verified (see Table 2). Younger shoppers (under age 50) preferred the foreground music and indicated that it was more similar to their usual music than the background music. On the other hand, older

TABLE 1
Effects of Music on Dependent Measures

	Background	Foreground	None	New Age	F	p
Music						
Liking of	3.5	3.8		3.5		
Listen to	2.5[a]	3.3[b]		2.6[a]	4.1	.02
Mood						
Pleasant	16.1	15.7	16.1	16.6		
Active	12.2	11.8	11.7	12.4		
Behavior						
Actual Time	11.7[a]	11.0[a]	10.9[a]	14.7[b]	3.1	.3
Perceived Time	15.3	18.6	17.8	20.4		
Money Spent	$20.2	$23.6	$24.3	$27.5		
% Purchasing	56.5%	55.4%	46.9%	52.2%		
Merchandise						
Good Value	4.3	4.3	4.2	4.1		
Inexpensive	3.3	3.7	3.3	3.3	2.0	.11
High Quality	3.6	3.8	3.7	3.6		
Store						
Friendly	4.2	4.1	4.4	4.2		
Spacious	3.7	3.8	3.8	3.8		
Down-to-Earth	3.1[ab]	3.5[a]	3.2[ab]	2.9[b]	3.1	.03
Modern	4.0	3.8	4.0	3.8		
Mature	3.2	3.1	3.0	3.3		
Quiet	4.0	4.0	3.9	3.9		

Note. Means with different superscripts are significantly different from each other (Student Newman-Keals range test).

shoppers (50 and over) preferred the background music but indicated that they were no more likely to listen to it than the foreground music.

Despite the relatively small differences in music preferences across the three age groups, the interaction of music with age is consistent with the department effects. For example, the oldest shoppers spent more money ($20.5) and time (12.3 minutes) when listening to background music compared to foreground music ($13 and 10.4 minutes). On the other hand, middle-aged shoppers spent more money ($33) and time (12.2 minutes) when listening to foreground music compared to background music ($25 and 11.3 minutes). Interestingly, the youngest shoppers (under 25 years) spent more time shopping when background music was playing (12 minutes versus 9 minutes) but spent more when foreground music was playing $19.60 versus $6.10). With the exception of the unexpected difference in shopping times for the youngest shoppers, these findings support playing different types of music in departments clearly catering to different aged customers.

CONCLUSION

These results support the proposition that the effects of store music may be altered by departmental and customer characteristics. Although the overall effects of the type of store music being played were negligible, they varied substantially by the type of shopper and department. In a department catering primarily to younger male shoppers, playing foreground music resulted in more purchases. On the other hand, in a department catering more to older women, background music was associated with more purchases than the foreground music.

Although it was proposed that moods induced by the music would account for the shopping differences, there were few reported differences in moods. This may be attributed to difficulty in assessing moods using a brief survey in a field setting. On the other hand, the behavioral effects were associated with perceptual differences. Shoppers perceived the departments to have more desirable characteristics when certain types of music were played. They also purchased more. However, causality must be inferred because it is possible that the act of purchasing an item may have enhanced the store evaluations.

Efforts to identify other factors that might moderate the music-shopping behavior relationship were unsuccessful. Our sample size did not provide sufficient power to test many possible relationships. Previous published research has yielded inconsistent findings making it difficult to predict which factors may affect consumers' responses to store music. Further, in a field setting, there are many factors that may influence shopping behavior and the influence of any single factor is likely to be small. Also, there are likely to be many higher order interactions among these factors. It appears that designing store atmospheres may remain an art rather than a science for many more years.

REFERENCES

Donovan, Robert and John Rossiter (1982), "Store Atmosphere: An Environmental Psychology Approach," *Journal of Retailing*, 58 (Spring), 34-57.

Gorn, Gerald J. (1982), "The Effects of Music in Advertising on Choice Behavior: A Classical Conditioning Approach," *Journal of Marketing*, 46 (Winter), 94-101.

TABLE 2
Effects of Music and Age on Behavior

	Background Music	Foreground Music
Liking of Music		
under 25	2.6	3.2
25-49	3.6	4.3
50 and over	4.1	3.5
Listen to Music		
under 25	1.4	2.5
25-49	2.5	3.5
50 and over	3.3	3.5
Actual Time		
under 25	12.0	9.3
25-49	11.3	12.2
50 and over	12.3	10.4
Perceived Time		
under 25	17.8	10.4
25-49	15.2	16.9
50 and over	13.9	25.2
Money Spent		
under 25	$6.1	$19.6
25-49	$25.5	$33.0
50 and over	$20.5	$13.2

Mehrabian, A. and J. Russell (1974), *An Approach to Environmental Psychology*, Cambridge, Mass.: MIT Press.

Milliman, Ronald E. (1982), "Using Background Music to Affect the Behavior of Supermarket Shoppers," *Journal of Marketing*, 46 (Summer), 86-91.

Sherman, Elaine and Ruth Belk Smith (1987), "Mood States of Shoppers and Store Image: Promising Interactions and Possible Behavioral Effects, in *Advances in Consumer Research*, Vol. 14, eds. M. Wallendorf and J. Anderson, Provo, UT: Association for Consumer Research. 251-254.

Smith, Patricia Cane and Ross Curnow (1966), "Arousal Hypotheses and The Effects of Music on Purchasing Behavior," *Journal of Applied Psychology*, 50 (no. 3), 255-256.

Yalch, Richard and Eric Spangenberg (1990), "Effects of Store Music on Shopping Behavior," *Journal of Services Marketing*, 4 (Winter), 31-39.

Yalch, Richard and Eric Spangenberg (1992), "The Effects of Music in a Retail Setting on Real and Perceived Shopping Times," working paper, University of Washington.

Using Moderator Variables in Structural Equation Models
Paul L. Sauer, Canisius College
Alan Dick, University at Buffalo (SUNY)

ABSTRACT

This article provides a brief tutorial on extending the concept of moderator variables to structural equation model systems. Procedures and theoretical rationale for application of the moderator concept to structural equation systems are described. Appropriate tests of discrete and continuous moderator variables are discussed. Tests of discrete (categorical) moderator variable effects can be performed by utilizing the moderator to divide the sample into groups and performing a Chi-square test of the significance of the difference between designated structural parameters across groups. Tests of continuous moderator variable effects can be performed by specifying interaction effects within the structural equation model context.

INTRODUCTION

There is increasing concern among researchers for distinguishing between moderator and mediator effects of variables in tests of alternative theories in marketing (e.g., Batra and Stayman 1990; Chattopadhyay and Basu 1990; Olney, Holbrook and Batra 1991). Furthermore, the use of structural equation models to statistically specify and test causal processes in marketing contexts has strong theoretical appeal from a comprehensive theory testing perspective (Anderson and Gerbing 1988; Bagozzi 1984). The application of structural equation methodologies is becoming more widespread and prevalent (e.g., Bagozzi 1990; Bagozzi and Yi 1991; Mittal 1990; Wind, Rao, and Green 1991). This is in part because application of structural equation techniques is made simpler with the incorporation of structural equation algorithms in standard PC and mainframe based statistical packages (e.g., LISREL (Jöreskog and Sörbom 1989) in SPSS and EQS (Bentler 1985) in BMDP). Structural equation techniques are also becoming applicable to a wider variety of theory and measurement configurations through such methodological improvements as generalizations and adaptations in statistical procedures (Bentler 1986; Bentler and Dijkstra 1985; Browne 1984), incorporation of discrete rather than continuous measures (Müthen 1984) and accommodation of higher-order factor structures (Jöreskog 1971b; Weeks 1980). The purpose of this work is to describe a methodological approach for incorporating tests of moderator variable effects in the context of structural equation models.

Though Baron and Kenny (1986) suggest that multi-group analysis be used in LISREL to model moderator variable effects in a structural model context, the procedure is not described. This article builds on this suggestion by describing a procedure for incorporating moderator variable effects on relationships between constructs into a structural equation model and statistically testing these effects using multi-group analysis (Jöreskog 1971a; Jöreskog and Sörbom 1989).

Moderator and Mediator Variables

A literature base has developed regarding differentiation between mediator and moderator variables, primarily in the psychology literature (e.g., Abrahams and Alf 1972; Baron and Kenny 1986; James and Brett 1984; Judd and Kenny 1981). A brief review of terms and concepts is provided here to set the stage for the description of application to structural equations systems which follows. The interested reader is referred to Baron and Kenny (1986) and James and Brett (1984) for a more thorough development of the distinction between moderator and mediator variables.

Baron and Kenny define a mediator as any variable which "accounts for the relation between the predictor and the criterion" (1986 p. 1176). That is, if $Y=f(X)$ and $Z=f(Y)$, but $Z \neq f(X)$, then variable Y is a mediator of the effect of variable X on variable Z (James and Brett 1984). Baron and Kenny define a moderator as "a qualitative or quantitative variable that affects the direction and/or strength of the relation between an independent and dependent or criterion variable" (1986, p. 1174). If $Z=f(X)$ and W is a moderator variable, then for different values of W, the form and/or strength and/or sign of the $Z=f(X)$ relationship may vary depending upon the value of W (James and Brett 1984; Sharma, Durand and Gur-Arie 1981). It is also possible that a variable may be a hybrid in which a it acts as both a mediator and a moderator. If the moderator effect of W on the effect of X on Z is mediated by the variable Y, this effect is called "Mediated Moderation" (Baron and Kenny 1986). If the moderator variable W interacts with the mediator variable Y to effect Z and the variable Y has a mediation effect on the relationship between X and Z, the interaction effect is termed "Moderated Mediation" (James and Brett 1984).

In addition to these categories of mediator/moderator variables, Sharma et al. (1981) define a typology of moderator variables which distinguishes between moderator variables which affect the strength of the relationship between predictor and criterion, and moderator variables which affect the form of the relationship. Moderator variables which affect the form of the relationship can be either quasi moderator variables or pure moderator variables. If a moderator variable both interacts with the predictor variable and is directly related to the criterion variable it is a quasi moderator. If a moderator variable only interacts with the predictor variable it is a pure moderator (Sharma et al. 1981). Sharma et al. (1981) contended that quasi moderators were not considered moderator variables in the psychometric literature. That restriction appears to have been relaxed, as Baron and Kenny note that "there may also be significant main effects for the predictor and the moderator, but these are not directly relevant conceptually to testing the moderator hypothesis" (1986, p. 1174). While it is possible to statistically evaluate whether a variable is functioning as a mediator, a moderator, or a hybrid, the overriding concern should be whether the theory being tested supports a moderator or mediator role for the variable in question (James and Brett 1984; Sharma et al. 1981). That is, *theory* should be used to define the functional form of the model (James and Brett 1984).

Theoretical and Methodological Considerations

The ability of structural equation models to address the theoretical testing needs of marketing science will depend upon the robustness and flexibility of structural equation methodologies in addressing both measurement and structural form varieties encountered in theory development. The realms of structural equation model applications are expanded by the ability to include alternative functional forms containing both moderator and mediator variables within a global model (cf., Baron and Kenny 1986). This expansion addresses both the metatheoretical issues relevant to evaluative tests of competing theories and the metamethodological issues relevant to competing statistical approaches to modeling alternative functional forms (cf., Leong 1985). The ability of structural equation systems to model a variety of functional forms, ranging from simple regression forms to complex latent variable regression forms (Jöreskog and Sörbom 1989) is the primary reason that such systems appear to offer metamethodological promise for metatheoretical investigations into the superiority of competing theories of marketing phenomena. The greater the variety of functional forms which can be included in a single system, the greater the variety of theories which can be statistically tested. The inclusion of variables as moderators rather than antecedents or mediators when such form would be more theoretically appealing affords an expansion of the metamethodological as well as metatheoretical role which structural equations can have in tests of competing theories.

A methodology which has the ability to embrace within itself a set of other methodologies offers the metamethodological framework which enables the metatheoretical evaluation of competing theories, specifying perhaps competing measurement and/or structural functional forms, within the umbrella of a single, global methodology. This is perhaps why Bagozzi (1984) argued for structural equation modeling as the dominant form of methodological testing in marketing. To this end, structural equation techniques are increasingly being generalized to offer the metamethodological advantages over other statistical methodologies. Flexibilities such as non-continuous variable indicators (Müthen 1984), reflective and formative indicators (Fornell and Bookstein 1982; Jöreskog and Wold 1982), two-step model testing (Anderson and Gerbing 1988); higher-order factor structures (Jöreskog 1971b; Weeks 1980) and the moderator variable approaches discussed in this article are examples of improvements in methodological flexibility afforded by structural equation techniques such as LISREL which facilitate more global testing of competing theories.

LISREL provides the ability to model latent variable constructs and to estimate the parameters for both the observed variable - latent variable relationships and the structural relationships simultaneously using the full information contained in the observed variance-covariance matrix.

When using a more restrictive methodology such as regression, the tendency has been to add or average multiple items in a formative manner to yield a single composite value. This may not always be appropriate as latent constructs such as attitude, for example, theoretically lend themselves to a representation in which the latent variable is reflected by observed indicator variables. The distinction is exemplified by comparing the reflective approach to modeling of LISREL and EQS to the formative approach used in multiple regression. Theoretical considerations should prevail over measurement issues in determining the functional form of the model.

Though such a decision should be made a priori using a well-developed theoretical rationale, a problem that may arise is that theoretical rationales may differ depending upon the philosophical approach to theory development taken by the researcher. Philosophical approaches to theory development and testing range from the logical positivist / empiricist approach on one extreme to the relativist / constructionist approach on the other extreme (See, for example, Leong 1985 and the special issue on Marketing Theory in *The Journal of Marketing*, Fall 1983). While it is beyond the scope of this article to deal with all the issues surrounding these and other philosophical approaches, it is important to note that the role of theory and methodology in determining the status of a variable as either a mediator or moderator is dependent upon the adopted philosophy.

If one were to prefer to base the model specification on methodology, techniques capable of capturing both roles and providing a test of the competing merits of each would be required (cf., Baron and Kenny 1986). Techniques should be employed which provide capabilities for capturing both the moderator and mediator roles of a variable. To this end statistical methodologies which provide the most global approach to embracing alternative functional forms would be more appealing (Leong 1985). Because linear models such as ANOVA, MANOVA and regression are special cases of the more general structural equation models, structural equation models offer a metamethodologically superior tool for testing marketing theory.

Moderator Variables in Structural Equation Models

In this paper structural equation models refer to causal models containing reflective measured variables as indicators of constructs which are structurally linked to one another. These models are frequently tested using full information likelihood techniques such as LISREL (Jöreskog and Sörbom 1989) or EQS (Bentler 1985).

Assuming the moderator variable is defined based on a priori theory, moderator variables may affect relationships between observed and/or latent variables in a variety of ways as previously discussed. We do not consider quasi moderators which are equivalent to hybrid types of moderated-mediator or mediated-moderator variable effects, but rather focus on the evaluation of what Sharma et al. (1981) label pure moderator effects.

Discrete Moderator Variables

Many variables which have potential for use as moderators in marketing are by their very nature discrete (e.g., nominally scaled demographic variables such as gender or occupation). Moderator variables which are at least ordinally scaled could be made discrete by using theoretically appealing cutpoints (Baron and Kenny 1986, James and Brett 1984). In such cases multi-group analysis is the recommended approach (Baron and Kenny 1986).

Statistical programs such as LISREL estimate the parameters of a structural equation model by minimizing a fitting function which compares the observed sample covariance matrix of the measured indicator variables with the covariance matrix from the parameters estimated for the entire model. In the application of LISREL to discrete moderator variable effects, the covariance matrices or any set or subset of parameters may be constrained to be equal in a multi-group analysis (Jöreskog 1971a; Jöreskog and Sörbom 1989). The test for a pure moderator effect can be performed using a multi-group specification of the structural equation model in which the structural and/or measurement parameters (linking the observed indicators to the latent constructs) are constrained equal across groups. In this presentation of the pure moderator effect we limit constraints to the structural parameters, although it is simple to constrain any or all parameters, whether measurement or structural, to be equal. The discrete moderator variable is used to form theoretically homogeneous groups of observations from the overall sample.

Two runs of the data are required. In the first run the appropriate structural parameters (linking the latent constructs) are constrained to be equal across groups (see Jöreskog and Sörbom 1989 for a description of how to set up the LISREL commands). This generates an estimated covariance matrix for each group and an overall Chi-Square value (χ^2_H) for the sets of submodels as part of a single structural system.

In the second LISREL run the structural parameter constraints are removed, resulting in a Chi-Square (χ^2_N) with additional degrees of freedom. It is important to note that this is not a LISREL run using aggregate data with no groups. Rather, groups (e.g. male, female) are specified with all parameters free to be unique to each group. The moderator effect is then statistically tested by taking the difference in the two Chi-Square values (i.e., $\chi^2_N - \chi^2_H$) which is itself a Chi-Square value with degrees of freedom equal to the difference in degrees of freedom of the (χ^2_H) and (χ^2_N) values. This difference is distributed as χ^2, therefore, the test of the null hypothesis proceeds according to classical test theory.

Though all structural parameters may be constrained to be equal simultaneously, it may be more desirable to constrain only one of these parameter to be equal during each LISREL run. Though this will depend upon the theory being tested, the primary reason is the interpretability of the Chi-square test results with respect to the parameters which were constrained equal.

In conventional tests of structural equations models one typically tries to accept rather than reject the null hypothesis (i.e., the model matches the data). This approach creates some statistical problems with the use of χ^2, therefore, alternative measures of fit such as the goodness of fit index (Bentler and Bonett 1980) and the root mean square of the residual are recommended. The χ^2 difference test, however, eliminates the need to compute alternative measures of fit since it relies on classical test theory. The comparison of the effect size of the constrained versus unconstrained structural models can then be made across groups using the estimated standardized coefficients values. The significance of these coefficients can in turn be tested using the standard error of each coefficient which is provided in the LISREL output.

Continuous Moderator Variables

Though a moderator variable may be either discrete or continuous, James and Brett (1984) suggest that if a moderator variable is continuous it be rescaled as discrete. Bagozzi, Baumgartner, and Yi (1992), however, argue that when variables are measured as continuous it is preferable to model moderated variable effects as multiplicative interactions to retain the full information contained in continuous variables. Specifically they contend that modeled interactions are favored over multi-group analysis because: 1. multi-group analysis may have lower statistical power and may confound group variance differences with true moderator effects while moderated regression maintains original scores on a moderator variable and avoids loss of information resulting from transformation of a continuous variable to a qualitative (discrete) one; 2. a median split into groups may create groups which do not exist at least for the present sample; and, 3. observed relationships can sometimes be very sensitive to cutoff points used to form groups, especially when there is no natural cutoff point.

If moderator variables are continuous, it is possible to model their effect using interaction terms (Bollen 1989; Hayduk 1987) in a manner similar to that used in multiple regression (Baron and Kenny 1986). If the moderator variable is simply an observed variable, one approach to modeling involves forming a new variable which is the product of two variables, one of which is the moderator variable. The reader is referred to texts such as Hayduk (1987) and Bollen (1989) for a detailed discussion of how interaction effects in the structural component may be modeled using structural equation techniques such as LISREL. The primary caution with modeling interaction effects is that the observed variables which interact must themselves be multinormally distributed (Bollen 1989).

Assuming one of the models is nested in the other, two LISREL runs would be necessary, one in which the formed interaction variable is present as an indicator, the other in which it is absent. The difference in Chi-square values may then be computed and the test using the Chi-square difference would proceed as with the case for discrete moderator variables previously described. Structural parameters may similarly be compared across models.

If moderation is a function of a latent construct rather than a measured variable, the structural positioning of the latent construct determines its function as either a mediator or moderator variable. Essentially the alternative forms presented by James and Brett (1984) for linear regression models can be extended to the forms for the relationships between structural parameters. One approach would involve adding a link in which the moderating latent variable serves as a mediator while the direct link between the exogenous and endogenous latent constructs is retained. If the mediational role of the latent construct is non-significant, but the value of the direct link is significantly altered, the latent variable is functioning as a pure moderator variable. On the other hand, if the direct link is rendered insignificant, the latent construct is actually not moderating the relationship, but rather is functioning as a mediator variable. If both the direct link and the mediated link are significant and the parameter value of the direct link is significantly different than when the moderating latent construct is present, a type of hybrid moderator variable effect is occurring (Baron and Kenny 1986; James and Brett 1984). Assuming one of the models is nested in the other it is possible to again perform a Chi-square difference test by making two LISREL runs, one of which constrains the direct link between exogenous and endogenous variable to be zero.

Conclusion

This paper has presented a brief tutorial overview of potential procedures for treating moderator variable effects in structural equation models. While in this brief tutorial it was not possible to provide the detail required for a complete understanding of these techniques, it is hoped that the reader will pursue references noted here in constructing tests and will also include hybrid modeling efforts such as moderated-mediation and mediated-moderation in designing future structural equation analyses in empirical research.

REFERENCES

Abrahams, N.M. and E. Alf Jr. (1972), "Pratfalls in Moderator Research," *Journal of Applied Psychology*, 56, 245-251.

Anderson, James C. and David W. Gerbing (1988), "Structural Equation Modeling in Practice: A review and Recommended Two-Step Approach," *Psychological Bulletin*, 103 (3), 411-423.

Bagozzi, Richard P. (1984) "A Prospectus for Theory Construction in Marketing", *Journal of Marketing*, 48 (Winter), 11-29.

_____ (1990), "Structural Equation Models in Marketing Research," in *Advanced Research Techniques Forum Proceedings First Annual*, ed. W.D. Neal, Chicago American Marketing Association.

_____, Hans Baumgartner and Youjae Yi (1992), "State versus Action Orientation and the Theory of Reasoned Action: An Application to Coupon Usage," *Journal of Consumer Research*, 18 (March) 505-518.

_____ and Youjae Yi (1991), "Multitrait-Multimethod Matrices in Consumer Research," *Journal of Consumer Research*, 17 (March), 426-439.

Baron, Reuben M. and David A. Kenny (1986), "The Moderator-Mediator Variable Distinction in Social Psychological Research: Conceptual, Strategic, and Statistical Considerations," *Journal of Personality and Social Psychology*, 51 (6), 1173-1182.

Batra, Rajev and Douglas M. Stayman (1990), "The Role of Mood in Advertising Effectiveness," *Journal of Consumer Research*, 17 (September), 203-214.

Bentler, Peter M. (1985), *Theory and Implementation of EQS: A Structural Equations Program*, Los Angeles: BMDP Statistical Software.

_____ (1986) *Lagrange Multiplier and Wald Tests for EQS and EQS/PC.*, Los Angeles: BMDP Statistical Software.

_____ and Bonett (1980), "Significance Tests and Goodness-of-fit in the Analysis of Covariance Structures," *Psychological Bulletin*, 88, 588-606.

_____ and T. Dijkstra, (1985), Efficient Estimation via Linearization in Structural Models," in P. Krishnaiah, ed. *Multivariate Analysis - IV*, Amsterdam: Elsevier, 9-42.

Bollen, Kenneth A. (1989) *Structural Equations with Latent Variables*, New York: John Wiley and Sons

Browne, Michael (1984), "Asymptotically Distribution-free Methods for the Analysis of Covariance Structures," *British Journal of Mathematical and Statistical Psychology*, 37, 62-83.

Chattopadhyay, Amitava and Kural Basu (1990), "Humor in Advertising: The Moderating Role of Prior Brand Evaluation," *Journal of Marketing Research*, XXVII (November), 466-476.

Fornell, Claas and Fred L. Bookstein (1982) "Two Structural Equation Models: LISREL and PLS Applied to Consumer Exit-voice Theory," *Journal of Marketing Research*, 19, (November), 440-452.

Hayduk, Leslie A. (1987), *Structural Equation Modeling with LISREL*, Baltimore: John Hopkins University

James, Lawrence R. and Jeanne M. Brett (1984), "Mediators, Moderators, and Tests for Mediation," *Journal of Applied Psychology*, 69 (2), 307-321.

Jöreskog, Karl G. (1971a), "Simultaneous Factor Analysis in Several Populations," *Psychometrika* 36 (December), 409-426.

_____ (1971b), "Statistical Analysis of Sets of Congeneric Tests," *Psychometrika*, 36, 109-133.

_____ and Dag Sörbom (1989), *LISREL 7 User's Reference Guide*, Mooresville, IN: Scientific Software.

_____ and Herman Wold (1982), "The ML and PLS Techniques for Modeling with Latent Variables: Historical and Comparative Aspects," in K. Jöreskog & H. Wold, eds., *Systems Under Indirect Observation: Causality, Structure, Prediction. Part I*, Amsterdam: North-Holland, 263-270.

Judd, C.M. and David A. Kenny (1981), *Estimating the Effects of Social Intervention*, New York: Cambridge University Press.

Leong, Siew Meng (1985), "Metatheory and Metamethodology in Marketing: A Lakatosian Reconstruction," *Journal of Marketing*, 49 (Fall), 23-40.

Mittal, Banwari (1990), "The Relative Roles of Brand Beliefs and Attitude Toward the Ad as Mediators of Brand Attitude: A Second Look," *Journal of Marketing Research*, 27 (May), 209-219.

Müthen, B. (1984), "A General Structural Equation Model with Dichotomous, Ordered Categorical, and Continuous Latent Variable Indicators," *Psychometrika*, 49, 115-132.

Olney, Thomas, Morris B. Holbrook and Rajev Batra (1991), "Consumer Responses to Advertising; The Effects of Ad Content, Emotions, and Attitude toward the Ad on Viewing Time," *Journal of Consumer Research*, 17 (March) ,440-453.

Sharma, Subhash, Richard M. Durand, and Oded Gur-Arie (1981), "Identification and Analysis of Moderator Variables," *Journal of Marketing Research* 18 (August), 291-300.

Weeks, David G. (1980), "A Second-order Longitudinal Model of Ability Structure," *Multivariate Behavioral Research*, 15, 353-365.

Wind Jerry, Vithala R. Rao and Paul E. Green (1991), "Behavioral Methods" in *Handbook of Consumer Behavior*, eds. T.S. Robertson and H.H. Kassarjian, Englewood Cliffs, NJ: Prentice-Hall, Ch. 14, 507-532.

A Structural Equation Analysis of the Relationships of Personal Values, Attitudes and Beliefs About Recycling, and the Recycling of Solid Waste Products

John A. McCarty, University of Illinois at Urbana-Champaign
L. J. Shrum, Rutgers University - New Brunswick

ABSTRACT

Although there has been a fair amount of research on the role of personal values in consumer behavior, few studies have addressed the nature of the links between values, attitudes and beliefs, and behavior. This study explores the relationships between personal values, attitudes and beliefs about the recycling of solid waste products, and recycling behaviors, using a causal modeling framework. Consistent with previous structural modeling work by Homer and Kahle (1988) on values and health food purchases, this study shows that attitudes and beliefs provide a mediating role between the abstract values and specific behaviors. Theoretical issues and practical implications are discussed.

INTRODUCTION

Social scientists have been concerned with the importance of values to human behavior for a number of decades (e.g., Kluckhohn 1951; Rokeach 1973; Spates 1983). In recent years, investigators in the area of consumer behavior have likewise turned their attention to the study of personal values. Research has demonstrated relationships between values and a variety of consumer variables including the importance of product attributes, the purchase of a variety of products, and the extent to which individuals engage in socially conscious behaviors such as organ donation (see Homer and Kahle 1988 for a discussion). In general, these studies have shown modest relationships between values and the constructs of interest in particular studies.

One issue is particularly noteworthy concerning most studies relating personal values to consumer behaviors. As Homer and Kahle (1988) point out, studies have tended to focus on the relationship of single values to behavior and have failed to consider value dimensions within a larger theoretical framework. Homer and Kahle further discuss that the nature of the relationships of values to behavior has not been investigated in the context of potential mediating variables such as attitudes. Many studies have simply searched for correlations between values and behavior without considering the complexity of the relationships. The 1988 study by Homer and Kahle is a notable exception in that it examined personal values, attitudes about health foods, and the purchase of health foods within a causal modeling analysis. They discovered an indirect influence of values on behavior, with attitudes providing a mediating role.

Most of the studies relating consumer behaviors to personal values have found relationships in instances where the behaviors are ones that would be expected to be driven by principles. Behaviors such as cigarette consumption, donating organs, and use of health foods would be expected to be related to values. The use of health foods and the consumption of cigarettes presumably relate to one's feelings about health, which would be expected to be value driven. The donation of organs might relate to one's concern for others. In contrast to these types of behaviors, it is not surprising that few, if any, studies have shown strong relationships between values and low involvement consumer behaviors.

Clearly, traditional wisdom would suggest that the extent to which individuals engage in such socially conscious behaviors as donating time and money to charity, giving blood, and buying environmentally safer products would be influenced by their values. The current study selected one such behavior for consideration: the recycling of solid waste items.

Recycling of waste products was selected for two reasons. First, little is currently known about the reasons individuals choose whether to recycle waste items, although there is a growing concern about environmental issues among consumers, marketers, and academic researchers. More research on the antecedents of these behaviors is clearly needed. Secondly, such prosocial behaviors should show stronger relationships with values than less involved consumer activities and, therefore, studying such behaviors should provide a better opportunity to understand the role of personal values in influencing behavior.

The Recycling of Solid Wastes

There is a small but growing literature relating to the antecedents of recycling behavior and other environmentally conscious behaviors. Shama and Wisenblit (1984) examined the relationships of general value orientations and the interest in a number of behaviors including recycling, finding positive relationships between general orientations and specific behaviors. Cialdini, Reno and Kallgren (1990) investigated the complex relationship of cultural and situational norms on littering, showing that the focus of the individual on specific norms is critical to the adherence to norms. Williams (1979) provided a descriptive study on the attitudes and behaviors of college students concerning recycling. Vining and Ebreo (1990) found that knowledge about recycling and perceived inconvenience were related to the extent to which individuals recycled. De Young (1986) investigated the importance of intrinsic motives to recycling. These and similar studies provide pieces to the puzzle regarding recycling, yet none have examined the complex relationships among antecedents.

Although we have stated that values may well be antecedents to socially conscious behaviors such as recycling, it is important to stress that one's basic values likely operate through intervening variables and other situational factors that may also influence such behaviors. A characteristic of many socially conscious behaviors such as recycling is that there are trade-offs between long run societal gains and short run individual needs. Individuals may feel that recycling is important in the long run for society, but they may also feel that it is inconvenient. Therefore, there may be positive and negative attitudes and beliefs about such socially conscious behaviors, both of which may be influenced by a person's personal values.

Overview and Hypotheses of the Study

The intent of this study was to understand the values - attitudes/beliefs - behavior hierarchy in the context of the socially conscious behavior of recycling solid wastes. A specific interest was to understand if and how personal values relate to these behaviors. Nine personal values that relate to different primary motivations in individuals were measured in the study. Attitudes and beliefs that relate to the *importance* of recycling for society and the *inconvenience* of recycling for the individual were also measured. It was felt that societal importance and personal inconvenience represented two areas that individuals likely consider when deciding whether to recycle. The behaviors of interest in the study were the recycling of cans and bottles/jars, and the frequencies of these behaviors were provided via self-report.

Similar to Homer and Kahle, it was expected that values would influence the extent to which individuals recycle solid wastes. However, it was expected that the influence of values would work through attitudes and beliefs regarding recycling. This was expected since values are abstract, while attitudes and beliefs should play a more proximal role to behavior. It was expected that both the importance of recycling and its inconvenience would influence the extent to which individuals engage in the recycling behaviors. The importance of recycling should have a positive influence on recycling while inconvenience should show a negative relationship with the behaviors.

METHOD

Sample and Procedure

The data for the study were collected from undergraduate students at a large state university; participation in the study fulfilled a course requirement. The sample consisted of 89 respondents. The measures for the study were all contained within a questionnaire booklet that respondents completed in a group situation. Respondents were allowed to work at their own pace after being provided with a set of general verbal instructions.

Measures

The Kahle (1983) List of Values (LOV) was used as the instrument to measure personal values. The scale consists of nine values that are believed to relate to general motivations people have in everyday life (Beatty et al. 1985). The scale is similar to the terminal scale of the Rokeach Value Survey (Rokeach 1973) in that it measures desired end states in life, but is shorter and easier to administer. The written instructions indicated that the respondents should rate each of the values with respect to importance, using a 1 to 10 scale from "very unimportant" to "very important."

The measures of attitudes and beliefs about recycling were imbedded in a portion of the questionnaire that included questions on a variety of personal and societal issues. Three statements related to the importance of recycling for the environment and three related to the inconvenience recycling may pose for the individual. The belief and attitude statements were measured on 5-point Likert type scales.

The behavior items were included in a part of the questionnaire that asked the extent to which respondents engaged in a number of behaviors. The recycling questions asked how frequently the respondents recycled cans and how frequently they recycled jars and bottles. The behaviors were measured on 5-point scales from "Very Seldom or Never" to "Very Frequently."

ANALYSIS AND RESULTS

Analysis

The primary statistical tool in this study was structural equation analysis using LISREL 7 (Jöreskog and Sörbom 1988). LISREL is useful when the researcher desires to explore the causal relationships among a set of variables.[1] In the present study, the LISREL analysis employed both a measurement model and a causal equation model simultaneously. That is, the full LISREL model evaluated: 1) the extent to which the observed variables (individual values, attitudes and beliefs, and behaviors) were indicators of the hypothesized underlying constructs, and 2) the strength of the relationships among the latent variables as specified by the paths. Prior to the structural analysis, however, exploratory factor analyses were conducted on the set of nine values and the set of attitudes and beliefs relating to recycling behaviors. These analyses were conducted to get a general sense of the underlying dimensions of the values and to determine if the a priori expectation that the attitudes and beliefs comprise two factors, inconvenience and importance, was tenable.

Results

The exploratory factor analysis of the nine values of the LOV scale indicated that a three factor solution was a reasonable fit for the value scales and these were used in the LISREL analysis that followed.[2] The factors are shown in Table 1. The first factor related primarily to internal personal motives focusing on *respect/achievement*. The second factor related to *enjoyment*, while the third factor dealt with *security*. Kahle (1983) has made the distinction between internal and external value dimensions and these three factors are consistent with this distinction. The first two dimensions are internal, with one relating to a desire for respect and the other to enjoyment. The third factor is clearly more external than the first two in that it relates to what we need from other individuals. The exploratory analysis of the beliefs and attitudes indicated that a two factor solution was indeed appropriate for the attitudes and beliefs relating to recycling and these are shown in Table 1. Table 1 also presents the standardized factor loadings and *t* values for the measurement part of the LISREL analysis. As is apparent from the table, all of the variables loaded significantly on the hypothesized factors.

It was expected that the attitudes and beliefs about recycling would provide a mediating role between personal values and recycling behaviors. This was tested in a model that specified three exogenous variables (the three value factors) and three endogenous variables (the two attitude/belief factors and the recycling behavior factor). It was anticipated that values would show significant relationships with the attitude factors and the two attitude factors would in turn have significant relationships with the recycling behaviors. It was expected that the exogenous value factors would *not* have direct effects on recycling behaviors. Thus, the paths between the value factors and behavior should not be significant.

Figure 1 presents the full model that was tested and Table 2 provides the standardized path coefficients and the *t* values of the model. The paths between latent constructs that are significant are indicated by heavy lines.

As is shown in the figure and reported in Table 2, the first value factor (respect/achievement) was negatively related to the inconvenience attitude factor. Thus, the more a person values achievement, self-respect, respect from others, and self-fulfillment, the less he or

---

[1] The use of structural equation modeling using LISREL generally requires a sound theoretical development and a large sample size. The sample size in this study was somewhat small, although it approaches the recommendation of Bagozzi (1981) that samples where the number of respondents minus the number of estimated parameters is fifty or greater are acceptable. The authors felt that structural equation modeling was the best approach to understanding the relationships between the constructs. However, given the small sample size and the early stages of theoretical development, the results should be considered with some degree of caution. Given these cautions, parameters that were significant at the $p < .10$ level are reported as significant.

[2] Space limitations prevent a detailed presentation of the results of the exploratory factor analyses.

TABLE 1
Measurement Model Results

Construct	Standardized Factor Loading	t
ξ_1 *Value Factor 1: Respect/Achievement*		
Self-Fulfillment	.659	4.799
Being Well-Respected	.542	a
Self-Respect	.911	5.682
Sense of Accomplishment	.805	5.367
ξ_2 *Value Factor 2: Enjoyment*		
Excitement	.522	a
Fun and Enjoyment	.860	4.752
ξ_3 *Value Factor 3: Security*		
Sense of Belonging	.528	a
Warm Relationships	.915	4.812
Security	.437	3.736
η_1 *Recycling Attitudes: Inconvenience*		
Recycling is inconvenient	.547	a
I hate to wash out bottles	.628	3.905
Recycling is too much trouble	.624	4.341
η_2 *Recycling Attitudes: Importance*		
Recycling will save land that would be used as dumpsites	.653	a
Recycling will reduce pollution	.302	2.040
Recycling is important to save resources	.414	2.431
η_3 *Recycling Behaviors*		
Recycle Cans	.604	a
Recycle Bottles/Jars	.853	4.420

a - fixed during analysis, no *t* values given
All loadings are significant at .05

she is likely to believe that recycling is inconvenient. The enjoyment value factor was positively related to beliefs about the importance of recycling. Therefore, those who value enjoyment and fun tend to believe that recycling is important. The third factor, which represents security and affiliation, was negatively related to the importance of recycling, suggesting that individuals who are security-oriented are less inclined to feel recycling is important compared with those who are less security conscious. Therefore, as expected, values do have influences on the attitudes and beliefs related to the recycling of solid waste. Also as expected, the values did not show direct relationships with recycling behaviors.

It is apparent from the endogenous path coefficients (those between the attitude factors and recycling behaviors) that the convenience of recycling has a much stronger relationship with whether one engages in recycling than does the feeling of importance of recycling. As would be expected, the more inconvenient people feel recycling is, the less frequently they report engaging in such behaviors. The relationship between beliefs about the importance of recycling and recycling behaviors was in the expected direction but far from significant.

The measures of overall goodness of fit for the entire model were acceptable, given the sample size and number of parameters estimated. As Table 2 shows, a nonsignificant chi square was obtained, suggesting the observed covariance matrix was a good estimate of the hypothesized matrix. The goodness of fit index was slightly below the .90 heuristic of Bentler and Bonett (1980), indicating that the fit of the model could be improved. We tested an alternative model where the direct paths between the value factors and recycling behavior were constrained to be zero. This model would allow the value factors to affect behavior only indirectly through attitudes. The alternative model did not differ significantly from the full model ($\chi^2 = 91.17, \Delta df = 108; \chi^2 = 2.61, \Delta df = 3$), indicating that this more parsimonious alternative model is a preferred model.

DISCUSSION

The study reported here provides both a theoretical and practical contribution to understanding the determinants of recycling behavior. From a theoretical perspective, the results of the study conceptually replicate Kahle and Homer (1988) in terms of the relationships between values, attitudes and beliefs, and behaviors. That is, attitudes and beliefs were shown to have a mediating role between behaviors and the abstract values. Values did not show any significant direct relationships with behaviors.

The observed value-attitude relationships make sense from an internal/external value perspective. The external value dimension, which included values that involve other people, was related to attitudes about the importance of recycling to society. However, the direction of the relationship was negative. In other words, the more one valued security, a sense of belonging, and warm relationships with others, the less one thought recycling was important. The reasons for this negative relationship are less than clear. From a

TABLE 2
Causal Model Results

Paths	Standardized Path Coefficients	t
Exogenous		
γ_{11}	-.562	-1.662*
γ_{12}	-.212	-.789
γ_{13}	.396	1.344
γ_{21}	.243	.649
γ_{22}	.683	2.021**
γ_{23}	-.668	-1.853*
γ_{31}	.088	.302
γ_{32}	-.456	-1.305
γ_{33}	.137	.444
Endogenous		
β_{31}	-.658	-2.813**
β_{32}	.188	.835

χ^2	88.56	* $p < .10$
df	105	** $p < .05$
p	.876	
GFI	.882	

social adaptation viewpoint, it could be that recycling is not viewed as a means of fulfilling these end states. On the other hand, the value dimension that included excitement and fun and enjoyment was positively related to the importance of recycling. Although this value dimension is not necessarily external, it does in some ways involve other *things*, if not other people. Thus, if those who value fun and enjoyment in life see a fulfillment of this end state through interaction with the environment, then this positive relationship is intuitive. Finally, the clearly internal value dimension, which included values such as self-respect and self-fulfillment, was negatively related to attitudes about the inconvenience of recycling. In other words, the more individuals valued respect, fulfillment, and achievement, the less they were inclined to feel that recycling was inconvenient.

The link between the respect/achievement value dimension and inconvenience is important because inconvenience was the only attitude/belief factor to show any relationship with recycling behaviors. As expected, the more one viewed recycling as inconvenient, the less one tended to recycle. Conversely, the beliefs about the importance of recycling showed no significant relationship with behavior, suggesting that the less self-involved and less concrete aspects of recycling (i.e., attitudes regarding the importance of recycling to the environment) tend not to translate into behavioral actions. Therefore, the short term concerns for the individual appear to be more influential to recycling behavior than the importance of recycling to society.

These results have important implications for strategies toward attitudinal and behavioral change. For this particular sample, two avenues are apparent. One is to address perceptions of the inconvenience of recycling, which has a direct influence on recycling behavior. If individuals can be persuaded that recycling is really not all that difficult or inconvenient, then perhaps a behavioral change can be obtained. It could very well be that these attitudes about inconvenience are merely perceptions, and not based on experience. On the other hand, it is clear that making recycling more convenient, at least for this sample, would be a useful strategy.

A second avenue towards behavioral change, and a less direct one, is to focus on the importance of recycling. As stated previously, this attitude/belief factor did not significantly influence recycling behavior. However, this is one area where values research, and understanding the underlying dimensions of attitudes, may be important. The results of this study suggest that the more one values excitement and enjoyment, the more one thinks that recycling is important. Yet, this link does not translate into recycling behavior. As stated before, this result suggests that individuals in this sample may view recycling (or more generally the environment) as a means or facilitator of fulfilling these end states of fun and excitement. If this is indeed the case, then one strategy might be to make this link more salient, and impress upon the target that individual participation in recycling may have very direct and immediate impact on fulfilling one's values or desired end states.

Limitations

Although the results presented are consistent with our theoretical reasoning, they should clearly be interpreted with caution. There are some obvious limitations to this study that bear on the reliability and generalizability of the observed effects. First, the study used a convenience sample of college students. This poses two problems. One, the importance or centrality of certain values to these college students may differ markedly from the general population. Further, the particular links between values and attitudes/beliefs, and attitudes/beliefs and behavior may differ from the general population as well. The behavior of recycling may be quite different in terms of motivation, convenience or availability for college students. Consequently, with respect to generalizability, one should interpret the findings of this study only in terms of their

FIGURE 1
Structural Equation Model

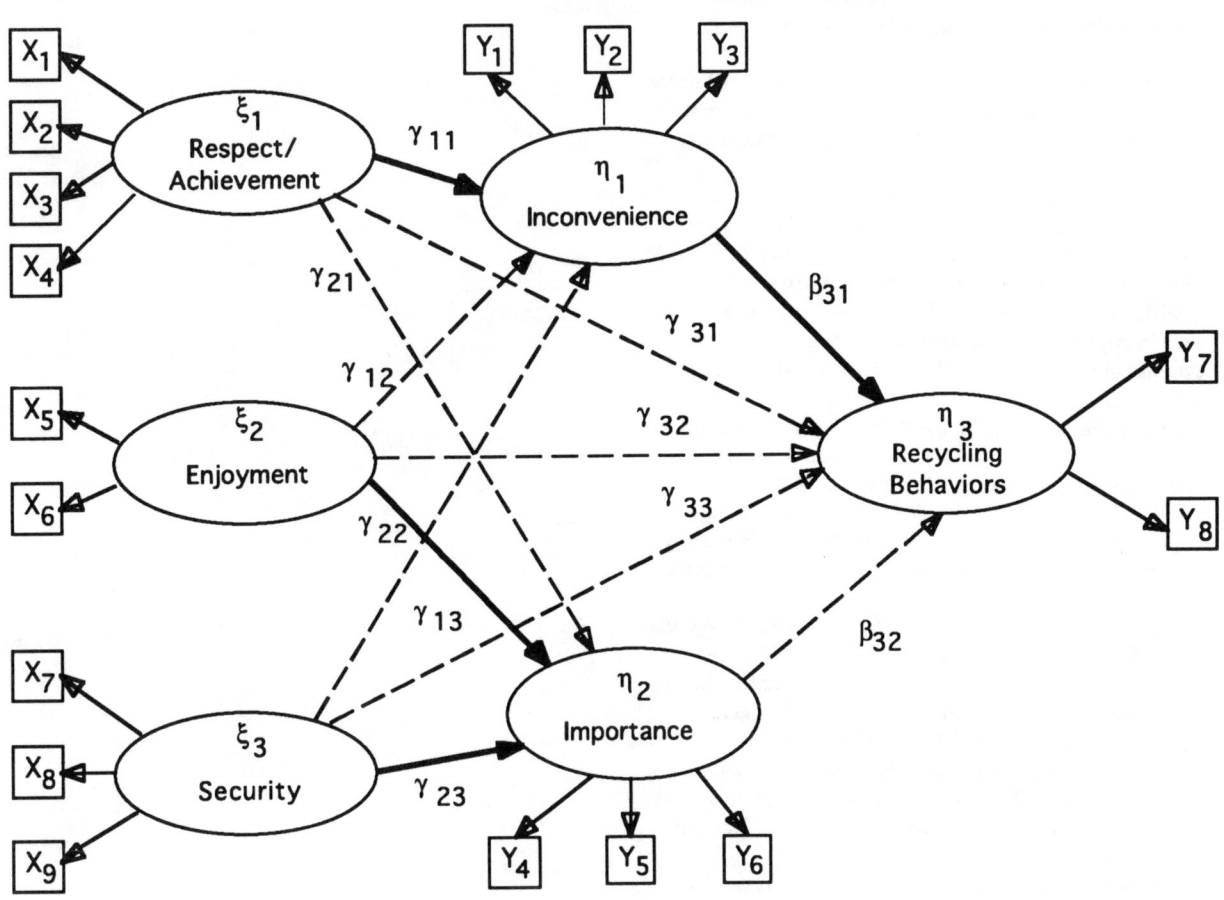

Structural Equation Model. ξ_1, ξ_2, ξ_3 are the value factors; η_1 = inconvenience of recycling; η_2 = importance of recycling; η_3 = recycling behaviors; x_1 = self-fulfillment; x_2 = being well respected; x_3 = self-respect; x_4 = a sense of accomplishment; x_5 = excitement; x_6 = fun and enjoyment; x_7 = a sense of belonging; x_8 = warm relationships with others; x_9 = security; y_1 = recycling is inconvenient; y_2 = I hate to wash out bottles; y_3 = recycling is too much trouble; y_4 = recycling will save land that would be used as dump sites; y_5 = recycling will reduce pollution; y_6 = recycling is important to save natural resources; y_7 = recycle cans; y_8 = recycle bottles/jars; γ_i = relationships among value factors and attitude and behavior factors; β_i = relationships between attitude and behavior factors. Paths that are significant are represented by heavy lines. For simplicity, the loadings among observed variables (λ_i) and measurement errors (δ_i, ε_i) are not indicated in the table.

meaning for the particular sample involved. A second limitation of the study, as previous mentioned, is the sample size. Stability of the parameter estimates would increase with sample size and, if these findings are obtained with a larger sample, we can have more confidence in the relationships between the variables.

CONCLUSIONS

In spite of the limitations discussed above, this study makes some tentative but important contributions to both values research and research on prosocial behavior. This study conceptually replicates the work by Homer and Kahle (1988) in that it demonstrates a link between values and attitudes/beliefs, and attitudes/beliefs and behavior. This is very important because it suggests that values may be very crucial to understanding behavior, but their importance may not be apparent in instances when critical mediating constructs are not explored. Most of the earlier work on personal values only addressed the value-behavior link or the value-attitude link, and the results tended to demonstrate consistent effects, but only weak to moderate in strength. By studying values in the context of beliefs and attitudes as well as behaviors, future values research will move toward a greater understanding of the role of values in behavior.

This study adds to our understanding of the antecedents of recycling. It is apparent that personal values may relate to beliefs and attitudes toward the behavior, but this does not always translate into action. Values showed strong relationships to beliefs about the importance of recycling, but the importance of recycling had a negligible influence on action. Clearly, further research on recycling is dictated. This study suggests that future work should continue to explore the complex relationships among antecedents of recycling.

REFERENCES

Bagozzi, Richard P. (1981), "Evaluating Structural Equation Models with Unobservable Variables and Measurement Error: A Comment," *Journal of Marketing Research*, 18(August), 375-381.

Beatty, Sharon E., Lynn R. Kahle, Pamela Homer and Shekhar Misra (1985), "Alternative Measurement Approaches to Consumer Values: The List of Values and the Rokeach Value Survey," *Psychology and Marketing*, 2(Fall), 181-200.

Bentler, P. M. and Douglas G. Bonett (1980), "Significance Tests and Goodness of Fit in the Analysis of Covariance Structures, *Psychological Bulletin*, 88(November), 588-606.

Cialdini, Robert B., Raymond R. Reno and Carl A. Kallgren (1990), "A Focus Theory of Normative Conduct: Recycling the Concept of Norms to Reduce Littering in Public Places," *Journal of Personality and Social Psychology*, 58(June), 1015-1026.

De Young, Robert (1986), "Some Psychological Aspects of Recycling: The Structure of Conservation Satisfactions," *Environment and Behavior*, 18(July), 435-449.

Homer, Pamela and Lynn R. Kahle (1988), "A Structural Equation Test of the Values-Attitude-Behavior Hierarchy," *Journal of Personality and Social Psychology*, 54(April), 638-646.

Jöreskog, Karl G. and Dag Sörbom (1988), *LISREL 7: A Guide to the Program and Applications*, Chicago: SPSS Inc.

Kahle, Lynn R., ed. (1983), *Social Values and Social Change: Adaptation to Life in America*, New York: Praeger.

Kluckhohn, Clyde (1951), "Values and Value Orientations in the Theory of Action: An Exploration in Definition and Classification," in *Toward a General Theory of Action*, eds. Talcott Parsons and Edward Shils, Cambridge: Harvard University Press, 388-433.

Rokeach, Milton (1973), *The Nature of Human Values*, New York: The Free Press.

Spates, James L. (1983), "The Sociology of Values," in *Annual Review of Sociology, Vol. 9*, eds. Ralph H. Turner and J. F. Short, Palo Alto: Annual Reviews, Inc., 27-49.

Shama, Avraham and Joseph Wisenblit (1984), "Values of Voluntary Simplicity: Lifestyle and Motivation," *Psychological Reports*, 55(August), 231-240.

Vining, Joanne and Angela Ebreo (1990), "What Makes a Recycler? A Comparison of Recyclers and Nonrecyclers," *Environment and Behavior*, 22(January), 55-73.

Williams, Elizabeth (1991), "College Students and Recycling: Their Attitudes and Behaviors," *Journal of College Student Development*, 32(January), 86-88.

Testing Consumer Behavior Theories: LISREL Is Not A Panacea
Banwari Mittal, Northern Kentucky University

ABSTRACT

In the consumer research literature, LISREL (a procedure to estimate structural equations with latent or manifest variables) has been frequently used to estimate causal models. It is argued here that LISREL cannot distinguish between a correlational link between two given variables and a causal link between those variables. Although LISREL has some desirable features over the more conventional multi-variate techniques such as regression analyses, when it comes to resolving questions of causality, it is shown that LISREL is just as unhelpful as the conventional procedures are.

INTRODUCTION

The use of causal modeling for testing theoretical relationships is increasing in consumer research. Since the publication of Bagozzi's seminal book on causal modeling (Bagozzi 1980), marketing and consumer researchers have increasingly cast their theories as networks of variables interconnected by causal paths. LISREL (Joreskog and Sorbom 1984) has been a popular procedure to estimate such network models. Increasingly one sees use of LISREL modeling even for uncomplicated regression models (for example those involving 1 criterion and 2 or 3 predictor variables). Furthermore, use of LISREL modeling is increasing to test *alternative* causal models. Some of these alternative models test the alternative causal direction between two variables (i.e., a→b versus b→a). An assumption is unwittingly made that LISREL modeling can settle the issue of which direction of causality is the right one. This assumption and model testing strategy are both wrong. The purpose of this paper is to illuminate some of the issues concerning LISREL's ability to test causality in correlational data.

Background

The practice of marketing rests crucially on assumptions of cause and effect. Marketing managers assume that certain salesperson compensation schemes will improve sales productivity, certain price deals will lure brand-switchers, certain product claim messages will induce favorable brand pre-dispositions, and certain combination of after-sale service attributes will yield high customer satisfaction. Correspondingly, marketing theories in the academic literature are increasingly being cast in causal terms. Causal Models have been advanced and tested for such diverse marketing phenomena as salesman satisfaction with pay (Churchill and Pecotich 1982), customer satisfaction (Churchill and Suprenant 1982), intra-channel reward and power relations (Gaski 1986), Hierarchy of Communication Effects (Zinkhan and Fornell 1989), Theory of Reasoned Action (Burnkrant and Page 1982; Bagozzi 1982; Shimp and Kavas 1984), and brand- and ad-attitude relationship (e.g., Mackenzie, Lutz, and Belch 1986).

Bagozzi (1980) enumerates some benefits of casting one's theories in causal terms. These include: (a) explicit documentation of assumptions, variables, and hypothesized relationships; (b) precision in the specification of operationalizations and functional relationships; and (c) better representation of complex social and psychological processes. The overall benefit is that "the causal model provides a framework for constructing and testing the internal consistency of one's theories and measurements as well as the degree of correspondence between theory and observation" (Bagozzi 1980, p. 75). These benefits legitimize the use of causal modeling for testing the hypothesized causal paths, i.e., for testing the significance of paths which are a priori posited to play a causal role. What the causal modeling does not do, however, is to confirm that the variable assumed to be a cause is indeed a cause rather than an effect or rather than a mere correlate. We illustrate this point below by an empirical analysis.

We define as cause an event which necessitates a subsequent event. This is the second type of cause in Aristotle (1930), as described in Bagozzi (1980, p. 2). In Bollen's (1989) terms, this concept of causality entails the three conditions of isolation, association, and temporal priority. Given this definition, causality can be *empirically* tested by (i) experimental manipulation of the causal variable and subsequent observation of the ensuing effect, and (ii) by time-separated measures of the causal and consequent variables. A majority of the causal models in the consumer research literature are however tested on correlational data. Because the models are depicted as causal diagrams and because LISREL is employed to estimate the path coefficients, LISREL-unfamiliar readers run the risk of inadvertently assuming that somehow causality is being tested. The empirical example below is designed to illuminate the fallacy of this assumption.

METHOD

Data

We use a research setting where consumers are exposed to an advertisement for an unfamiliar brand. Post exposure measures assess consumer ratings on brand attitudes, attitude toward the advertisement, utilitarian brand beliefs, and image brand beliefs. Brand attitudes are hypothesized to be caused by attitude toward the advertisement, and by brand beliefs (both utilitarian and image beliefs). This research setting and the hypothesis is described in Mittal (1990). The research hypothesis is intended to show that inclusion of image beliefs as predictors reduces the independent contribution of attitude toward the advertisement. Four regression equations needed to test this hypothesis are presented in Table 1. In Mittal (1990), these four regression equations are represented as Models 1, 2, 3, and 4. We use this research paradigm here to explore as to what happens when certain variables are connected by a correlational linkage versus when they are connected by a causal path. Using the same shampoo ad as in Mittal (1990), we obtained post-exposure ratings from a group of 80 students. These data are utilized to estimate the four regression equations of Table 1 via LISREL, and then subsequently explore alternative models.

Analysis

The solutions to the four regression equations (estimated via LISREL) are presented here as Models 'A', 'B', 'C', and 'D' in Figure 1. In Model 'A', utilitarian beliefs, image beliefs, and ad-attitude are shown as antecedents to brand-attitude. In all the models discussed in this paper, ad-attitude and brand-attitude are measured with multiple indicators (three indicators for each), while for image beliefs, and likewise for utilitarian beliefs, an index is computed by a weighted summation of individual beliefs as in multi-attribute models. For simplicity in presentation, the measurement model for the ad-attitude and brand-attitude is not shown in figures. In Model 'B', ad-attitude is omitted as a predictor; in model 'C', image beliefs are omitted; and in Model 'D' both image beliefs and ad-attitude are omitted as predictors. In all four models, only

TABLE 1

Brand Attitude = $a_1 + a_2 * (UB) + a_3 * (IB) + a_4 * (AAD) + e_1$ —————— Eq. 1

Brand Attitude = $b_1 + b_2 * (UB) + b_3 * (IB) + e_2$ —————— Eq. 2

Brand Attitude = $c_1 + c_2 * (UB) + c_4 * (AAD) + e_3$ —————— Eq. 3

Brand Attitude = $d_1 + d_2 * (UB) + e_4$ —————— Eq. 4

Legend: UB: Utilitarian Brand Beliefs
IB: Image Brand Beliefs
AAD: Attitude Toward the Ad

---

correlational linkages are modeled among the 3 antecedents. Both models 'B' and 'C' fit better than model 'D', based on a chi-square difference test (for one degree of freedom difference, the chi-square difference exceeds the critical value of 3.84, at p<.05). The R-Squared is also substantially more for models 'B' and 'C' than in model 'D'. On similar grounds, model 'A' is superior to all 3 models. This establishes the non-redundant contributions of all 3 antecedents.

A regression procedure would yield similar findings. When all 3 predictors are in the regression, the total explained variance would be exactly the same as in Model 'A'. The beta coefficients of the three predictors would also be exactly the same as in the LISREL solution. This identity of results between the LISREL and regression solutions is observed for the other 3 models as well. Furthermore, nested models comparison test for two hierarchical regression models (such as between models 'A' and 'B') will yield the same conclusion (as do the LISREL models) about the significance of the incremental or non-redundant contribution of any of the predictors.

The Effect of Causal Relations Among the Predictors

Figure 2 shows Models 'A1' and 'A2' which are modifications of Model 'A'. The modification is that among the three antecedents to brand-attitude, causal rather than correlational paths are modeled. Note that (a) the overall model fit (i.e., chi-square statistic), (b) the R-squared value for brand-attitude, and (c) the causal coefficients of the 3 antecedents are exactly the same as they were in Model 'A'. The only difference is that some of the estimates of the paths among the three predictors themselves are different between models 'A', 'A1', and 'A2'. We shall return to this finding shortly. The important result for now is that prediction of brand-attitude is not affected at all. Recall that this prediction was also the same as in the regression models. Thus, just because LISREL simultaneously allows modeling of causal linkages among the predictors of a criterion variable, it is no reason to expect that LISREL modeling (with or without such causal paths among predictors) will yield additional insight about the regression-estimatable predictor-criterion relationships themselves. This is not an isolated finding. The modification of model 'B' into Model 'B1' and Model 'B2' also yields similar findings (see Figure 3). (Note that in Model 'B2' we incorporate mutual causation between two of the antecedents of brand-attitude.) These results are not mere coincidence. The fact is that as long as the same predictors remain connected to a criterion or endogenous construct, and as long as each antecedent or predictor remains either connected or unconnected with any other antecedents in any two models being compared, the overall model fit and criterion-predictor coefficient estimates will remain unaltered.

WHEN ARE CAUSAL PATHS DIFFERENT FROM CORRELATIONAL PATHS?

Let us return to Models 'A', 'A1' and 'A2' (Figure 2)— this time to examine the estimates of the paths among the 3 predictors themselves. For convenience, we shall abbreviate utilitarian beliefs as UB, image beliefs as IB, and ad-attitude as AAD. In Model 'A1' (compared to Model 'A'), only the path between UB and IB remains unaltered (0.19). In Model 'A2' (compared to model 'A'), only the path between UB and AAD remains unaltered (0.27). What happens is this. In Model 'A1', IB is the only construct with single path *terminating* into it. That is, it has only one antecedent. Since it has only one antecedent, its linkage with that antecedent is same whether we make that linkage a causal or a correlational one. Since AAD has two paths terminating in it, each of these paths will be lower than their value in the correlational model (unless of course if the two antecedents to AAD in Model 'A1' were totally uncorrelated, in which case the causal and correlational paths would have been identical). This explains why UB→AAD path in Model 'A2' is same as the correlational path between UB and AAD in model 'A'. Since the overall fits of the models 'A', 'A1', and 'A2' are the same, this sort of model fitting will not enable us to resolve the choice between correlational and causal linkages. Indeed, if we rerun Model 'A' as a four-factorial model (with all 4 constructs mutually correlated among one another), its overall chi-square fit statistic will still be 32.94 (with same degrees of freedom). The fact is that LISREL modeling cannot distinguish between causal and a correlational linkage.

Can Direction of Causality be Tested?

Models 'A3' and 'A4' are further modifications of Model 'A' (see Figure 4). These two models are identical except that the direction of causality between IB and AAd has been reversed. Again, every parameter estimate in Models 'A3' and 'A4' is identical. Furthermore, the estimate for the IB-AAD link in Models 'A3' and 'A4' (which is 0.56 in magnitude) is the same as that of the same link in the correlational model 'A'. The point is that the zero order correlation between IB and AAD is 0.56 (see Model 'A'), and this magnitude of relationship cannot change no matter how we link these two variables.

They cannot change, that is, as long as in the causal model the linkage is an exclusive one. Add another linkage terminating in either of the variables, and the picture would of necessity change. This is what happens in Models 'A1' versus 'A2' (see Figure 2).

FIGURE 1
Four Nested LISREL Models

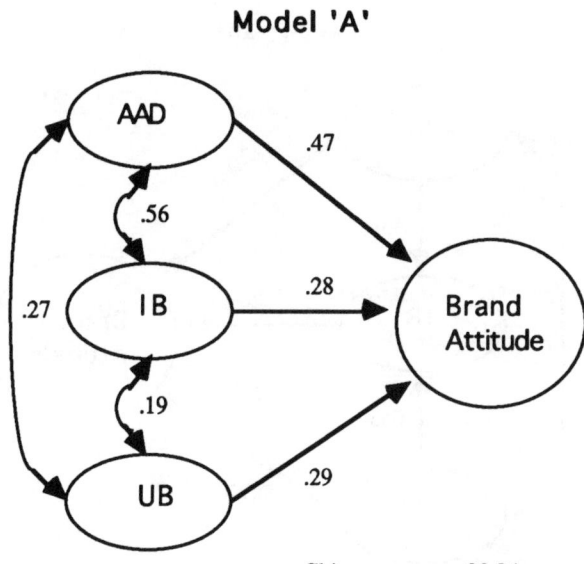
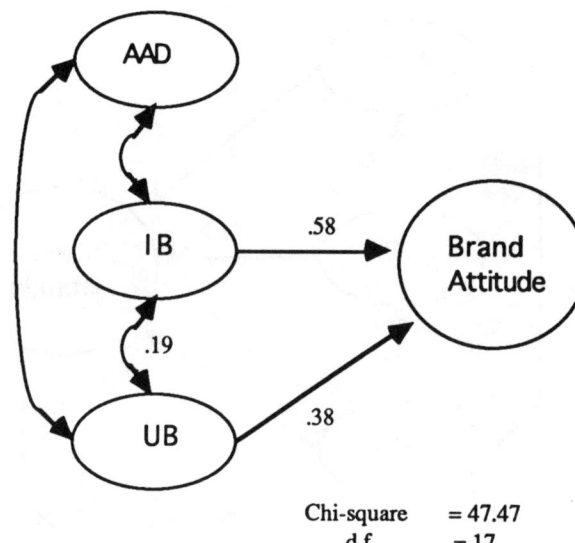
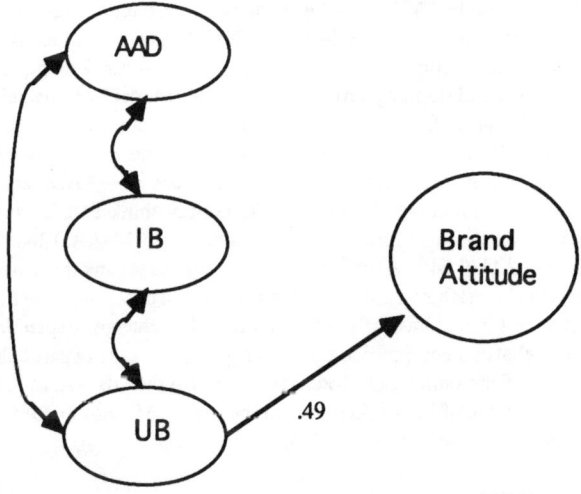

Exogenous Constructs:
AAD -- Attitude-toward the ad
IB -- Image Brand beliefs
UB -- Utilitarian brand beliefs

FIGURE 2
Two LISREL Models: Correlational Paths Among the 3 Exogenous Constructs in Model "A" Replaced Here by Alternative Causal Paths

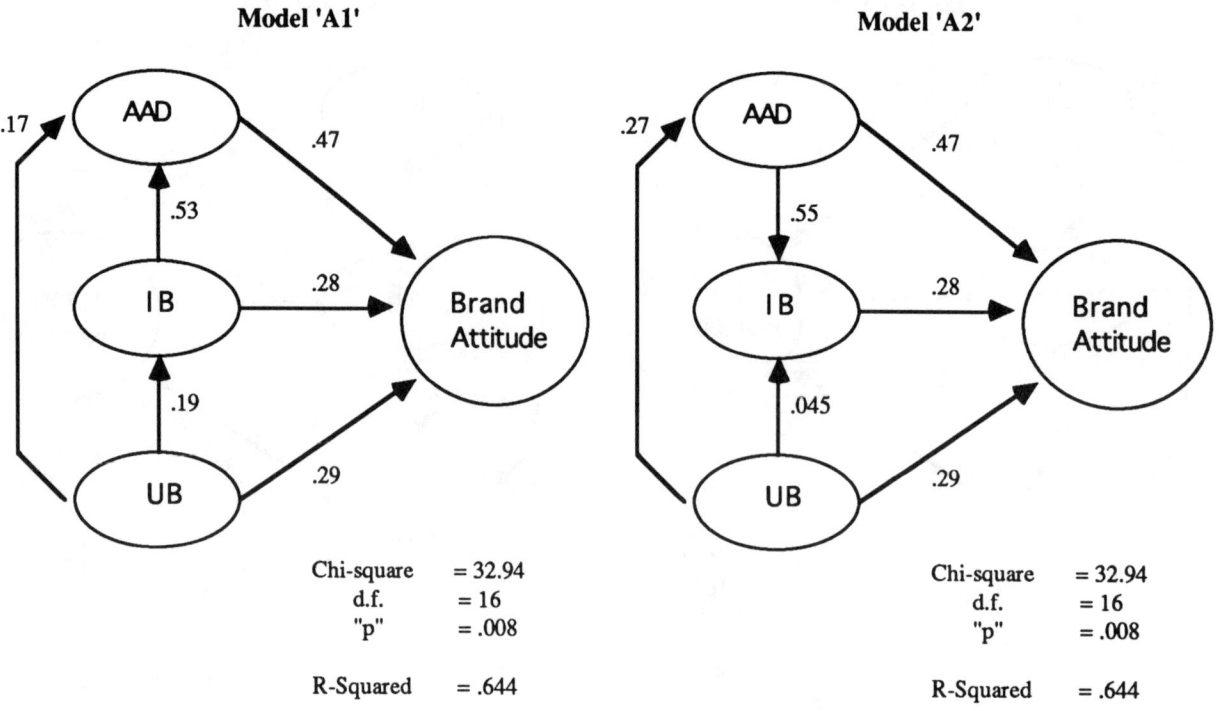

There, in Model 'A1', IB→AAD link is 0.528, but in Model 'A2', the reverse link, AAD→IB, is 0.549. This is because in Model 'A1', another path terminates in AAD (namely, UB→AAD path), and likewise, an additional path terminates in IB in Model 'A2' (namely, UB→IB path). Because all constructs are interconnected in both models 'A1' and 'A2', the overall model fit is same, and this overall model fit cannot serve us in choosing between IB→AAD versus AAD→IB direction of causality. One may think that because AAD→IB link in Model 'A2' is greater than IB→AAD link in Model 'A1' (0.549 versus 0.528), the former causal link is stronger than the latter; this inference will in our opinion be wrong. The link between them is basically 0.56, and its value changes depending upon what other co-predictor the link happens to have in a particular model. For example, in Model 'A1', remove the UB→AAd link, and the value of IB→AAD link will become 0.56 (thus exceeding its present value in Model 'A2').

Discussion

LISREL is an efficient technique for testing causal models, but it cannot establish causality. The question of causality can be addressed only by (i) experimental manipulation of causal variables, (ii) time-separated measures of variables (as in multi-wave data), (iii) by open-ended protocols in qualitative studies, and (iv) by a priori theoretical reasoning (this last one, Bollen 1989 views as a sort of "mental experiment" to assess temporal priority).

Both LISREL and conventional regression procedures can alike estimate causal models. However if the data are merely correlational (and one can fit causal models on correlational data), neither Regression nor indeed LISREL procedures provide evidence of causality. In this respect, contrary to what may be inadvertently assumed, LISREL modeling offers no advantage over the regression modeling. The advantages of LISREL modeling reside elsewhere, and they are these: (1) LISREL modeling allows incorporation of measurement errors, and (2) It allows modeling of causal rather than merely correlational paths among the predictors themselves. The latter feature can raise two false hopes. First, it may be thought that somehow the predictor-criterion coefficients will change (and be more valid) if inter-predictor linkages are properly modeled; of course they cannot. Second, one may think that this would establish causality between any two constructs against the rival correlational hypothesis. This hope too is misfounded.

The ability to model measurement errors is and should be a major motivation for use of LISREL modeling. And, *efficiency* in estimating a complex network of simultaneous equations (which can also be estimated via several separate regression analyses) is of great value. LISREL is useful for certain other applications as well; for example: (i) Confirmatory factor analysis (e.g., Anderson 1987), (ii) testing a scale for its claimed unidimensionality (Gerbing and Anderson 1988), and, more generally, testing the dimensionality underlying a scale (see Shimp and Sharma 1983, for an application), (iii) for construct validation (e.g., see Peter 1981, for concept discussion, and Hunter, Gerbing, and Boster 1982, for an application), and (iv) second order factor model fitting (Kumar and Dillon 1990, Hunter and Gerbing 1982). These advantages and applications (and other features, such as simultaneous estimation of models for multiple groups) should deservedly make LISREL the preferred method in many research applications. At the same time,

FIGURE 3
Two LISREL Models: Correlational Paths Among the 3 Exogenous Constructs in Model 'B' Replaced Here by Alternative Causal Paths

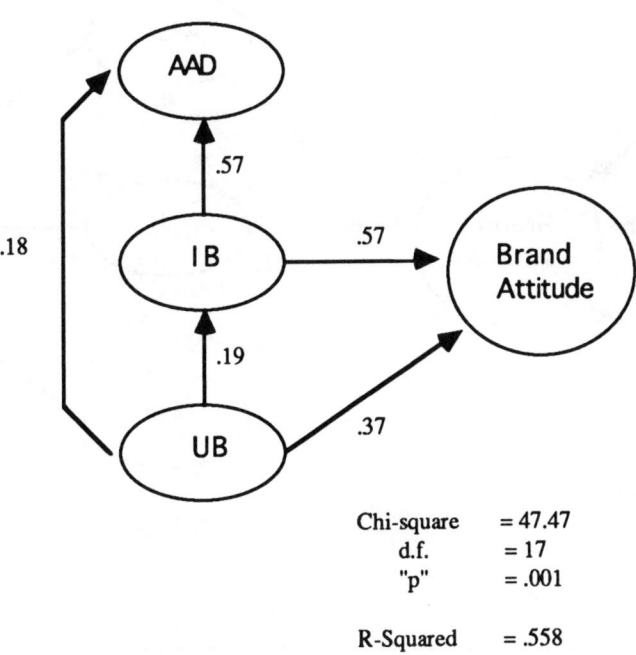

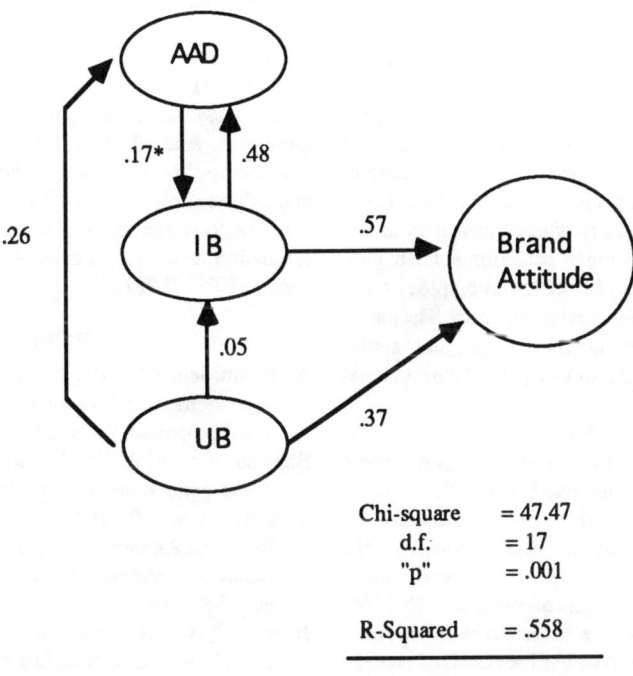

* Not significant

FIGURE 4
Two LISREL Models With Direction of Causality Reversed

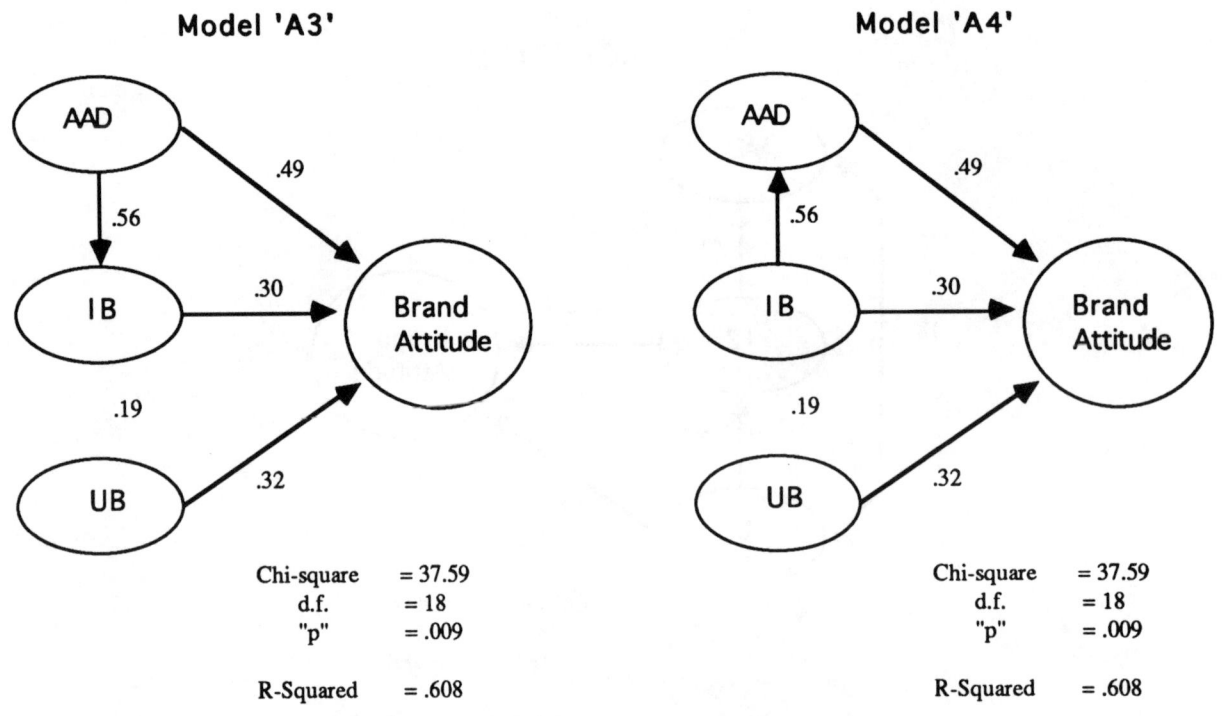

when LISREL is used to estimate causal models, researchers should be careful in implying any "proof" of causality, just because the estimation procedure was LISREL.

We do *not* believe that in the consumer behavior literature, researchers have used LISREL wrongly to estimate causal models. These researchers have first grounded their causal models in a priori theory, and *then* employed LISREL to *estimate* the parameters of what on *a priori* grounds is a "causal" model. (See, for example, Churchill and Suprenant 1982; Mackenzie and Lutz 1989). There is some danger, however, that readers whose interest is in the substantive aspects of these consumer behavior studies may unsuspectingly assume that because LISREL was employed, the causality has been established in the correlational data. The use of LISREL should not distract one's attention from rigorously applying a priori logic as the only acid test of causality in correlational data.

When the data are experimental (with truly independent variables), the acid test of causality is still a priori logic (since some other unmeasured variable could intervene between the manipulated variable and the measured effect); but here additionally we would have empirical basis to support the causal hypothesis if the "effect" estimate is significant. This "effect" may be estimated either via the more conventional Analysis of Variance (ANOVA) procedure or via LISREL. If LISREL is chosen to be employed, it is simply because it is more efficient and/or because it can handle latent constructs (and multiple indicators of these latent constructs are available). The LISREL procedure in and of itself does nothing, even in the experimental data, to reinforce or dispute the hypothesized causality. LISREL is simply a technique to *estimate* the value of the theory-driven causal path, and not to further any claims about the *causal nature* of the estimated effect.

Conclusion

LISREL cannot establish causality. It is perfectly legitimate to use LISREL to test causal models which are theoretically grounded. And when LISREL supports them, it is legitimate to assert empirical validity for those causal models. It is to be understood, however, that the grounds for claims of causality continue to reside in a priori reasoning, and *not* in the empirical estimation technique; it does not matter that the moniker on that technique is *LISREL*.

REFERENCES

Anderson, James C. (1987), "An Approach for Confirmatory Measurement and Structural Equation Modeling of Organizational properties," *Management Science*, 33 (April), 525-541.

Bagozzi, Richard B. (1980), *Causal Models in Marketing*. New York: John Wiley & Sons, Inc.

Bagozzi, Richard P. (1982), "A Field Investigation of Causal Relations Among Cognitions, Affect, Intentions, and Behavior," *Journal of Marketing Research*, XIX (November), 562-584.

Burnkrant, Robert E. and Thomas J. Page (1982), "An Examination of the Convergent, Discriminant, and Predictive Validity of Fishbein's Behavioral Intention Model," *Journal of Marketing Research*, XIX (November), 550-561.

Bollen, Kenneth A. (1989), *Structural Equations with Latent Variables*, New York, NY: John Wiley & Sons.

Churchill, Gilbert A. and Anthony Pecotich (1982), "A Structural Equation Investigation of the Pay Satisfaction Valence Relationship Among Salespeople," *Journal of Marketing*, Vol. 46, No. 4, 114-124.

Churchill, Gilbert A. and Carol Suprenant (1982), "An Investigation into the Determinants of Customer Satisfaction", *Journal of Marketing Research*, XIX (November), 491-504.

Gaski, John F. (1986), "Interrelationships Among a Channel Entity's Power Sources: Impact of the Exercise of Reward and Coercion on Expert, Referent, and Legitimate Power Sources," *Journal of Marketing Research*, XXII (February), 62-78.

Gerbing, David W. and James C. Anderson (1988), "An Updated Paradigm for Scale Development Incorporating Unidimensionality and Its Assessment" *Journal of Marketing Research*, (Citation to be completed)

Hunter, John E., David W. Gerbing (1982), "Unidimensional Measurement, Second Order Factor Analysis, and Causal Models," in B. M. Staw and L. L. Cummings (eds.) *Research in Organizational Behavior*, Vol. 4, 267-299.

_____, _____, and Frank J. Boster (1982), "Machiavellian Beliefs and Personality: The Construct Invalidity of the Machiavellian Dimension," *Journal of Personality and Social Psychology*, 43 (December), 1293-1305.

Joreskog, Karl and Dag Sorbom (1984), *LISREL VI:Analysis of Linear Structural Relationships by the Method of Maximum Likelihood*. Chicago: National Educational Resources, Inc.

Kumar, Ajit and William R. Dillon (1990), "On the Use of Confirmatory Measurement Models in the Analysis of Multiple-Informant Reports," *Journal of Marketing Research*, XXVII (February), 102-11.

MacKenzie, Scott B., Richard J. Lutz, and George E. Belch (1986), "The Role of Attitude Toward the Ad as a Mediator of Advertising Effectiveness: A Test of Competing Explanations," *Journal of Marketing Research*, XXIII (May), 130-143.

Mittal, Banwari (1990), "The Relative Roles of Attitude-Toward-The Advertisement and Brand Beliefs in Explaining Brand Attitudes: A Second Look," *Journal of Marketing Research*, XXVII (May), 209-219.

Peter, Paul J. (1981) "Construct Validity: A Review of Basic Issues and Marketing Practices," *Journal of Marketing Research*, 18 (May), 133-145.

Shimp, Terence A. and Subash Sharma (1983), "The Dimensionality of Involvement: A Test of the Automobile Involvement Scale," in *Research Methods and Causal Modeling in Marketing*, eds. W. R. Darden, K. B. Monroe, and W. R. Dillon. Chicago: American Marketing Association, 58-61.

Shimp, Terence A. and Alican Kavas (1984), "The Theory of Reasoned Action Applied to Coupon Usage," *Journal of Consumer Research*, Vol. 11, No. 3, 795-809.

Zinkhan, George M. and Claes Fornell (1989), "A Test of the Learning Hierarchy in High- and Low-Involvement Situations," in Thomas K. Srull (ed.), *Advances in Consumer Research*, Provo, UT: Association for Consumer Research, 152-159

Discussant Comments on "Issues in Structural Models"
Tom Page, Michigan State University

The comments presented here serve to highlight the contribution of the papers presented in this session, as well as to point out some concerns that readers should be aware of. The only common thread among the three papers is the use of LISREL. The paper by Sauer and Dick is a very good tutorial on the use of moderator variables in structural equations. The paper by Mittal is a cautionary note on what LISREL can and cannot tell us, and the paper by McCarty and Shrum is an application of structural equations to the issue of recycling. The papers will be discussed in the order in which they were presented.

SAUER AND DICK

The objective of this paper is to provide the reader with a tutorial on moderator variables in structural equations. The authors first provide a useful discussion of the distinction between mediators and moderators, and even discuss mediated moderators and moderated mediators. This is a distinction that is often confused, and the authors' explanation of exactly what constitutes mediation and moderation is both clear and succinct.

The main contribution of the paper is the discussion of moderator variables in structural equations. Two types of moderators are discussed, discrete and continuous. For discrete moderators, such as nominal variables like gender, the authors advocate using multiple group analysis with the categories serving to identify the groups. Then, in one analysis, the relevant paths are constrained to be equal, and in the other analysis they are unconstrained. Then, the chi-square difference and the path coefficients are examined to determine the nature of the mediating relationship.

This is one area of the paper that should be expanded. In other words, exactly how does one tell if s/he has a moderator relationship or not? If the chi-square difference is significant, it means that the path coefficients are not equal across the groups. However, how big should the difference be before a moderating relationship is supported?

In the continuous case, the authors examine the case of both observed and latent moderator variables. For the observed case, they advocate forming an interaction term and refer to several sources for a description of the procedure. The test for moderation, however, is not clear in this case. If two analyses are performed as described, one of which contains the interaction term and one which does not, the chi-square difference test, suggested by the authors, is not appropriate since the models are not nested. That is, the two analyses are not based on the same set of variables. This point needs to be clarified. In the continuous latent moderator case, the authors do a good job of explaining what to look for in examining path coefficients.

The discrete case is one that every structural equation user should be especially aware of since it is also applicable to experimental design. Too often researchers attempt to analyze experimental data by modeling the manipulation as an exogenous variable and combining all of the groups into one analysis. Not only does this violate some of the assumptions of LISREL, but it also precludes a clear interpretation of the path coefficients. The preferred method of analyzing such data should be the technique described by Sauer and Dick for discrete moderators.

MCCARTY AND SHRUM

This paper explores the links among personal values, attitudes, and behavior concerning recycling. The objective is to determine whether personal values about recycling directly affect behavior or their effect is mediated by attitudes about the behavior. The authors make a good case for examining the effects of values in predicting behavior. Their results basically show that values are related to attitudes, but not directly related to behavior.

There are several suggestions that perhaps should be considered in future research in the area. First, it might be useful to include the construct of intention to perform recycling behavior as a mediator between attitudes and behavior. Most research has shown that the link between attitudes and intentions, and intentions and behavior is stronger than the direct link between attitudes and behavior. This may account for the lack of a significant effect of one of the attitude constructs on behavior.

Second, instead of using the frequency of recycling behavior as the final endogenous construct, it might be useful to measure percentages of items recycled. For individuals that do not have convenient methods of recycling (i.e., curbside pickup), frequency may not be a very relevant measure of recycling. For example, I recycle 100% of my bottles and newspapers, but I only go to a recycling center about three times a year.

A final minor point concerns the scale used to rate the values on the LOV instrument. This scale ranges from very unimportant to very important. While this response format is often employed, it is not clear how something can be "very unimportant." In other words, once something becomes unimportant, how can it be any less important. Something can have degrees of importance but not unimportance. Furthermore, it is questionable to expect respondents to be able to reliably interpret ten degrees of importance regardless of the endpoints.

MITTAL

The purpose of this paper is to illuminate some of the issues concerning LISREL's ability to test for causality in correlational data. The author proceeds to analyze various combinations of paths in a model examining the relationships among attitude toward the brand, attitude toward the ad, image beliefs, and utilitarian beliefs.

The paper makes two very important points concerning the use of LISREL. First, LISREL does not provide "proof" of causality. Second, a priori theory is the only true test of causality in correlational data. These are both useful caveats to remember when interpreting structural equation models. While the technique can be used in an exploratory sense, this should be done with caution, and should always be based on a priori theory. Just because a modification produces a better fit statistic or significant path coefficient does not, in and of itself, constitute the establishment of a causal link.

The only minor concern with the paper has to do with Figure 3. Both model B1 and B2 have the same degrees of freedom (17), but model B2 has one more parameter being estimated (one of the simultaneous paths between Aad and IB) so it must have one less degree of freedom. This needs to be clarified.

SUMMARY

All three of the papers are well worth reading, and the reader can certainly benefit from them. The authors are to be commended for their work.

Brand Name Memory Following Ad Exposure: Inhibition, Interference and Attenuation Processes as Revealed by Direct and Indirect Tests of Memory

Shanker Krishnan, Indiana University
Carol Pluzinski, New York University

The goal of this session was to point to new directions for measuring and interpreting attenuated memory for ad content. Especially highlighted were: (1) *factors* that might lead to poor memory such as the competitive environment and inherent brand name characteristics, (2) *processes* of inhibition and interference, (3) *testing* for such effects. The causes underlying poor brand memory may depend on several factors, each implying differences in the nature of information processing induced by ad exposure, for example, inhibition vs. interference (Wallace and Hasher). Since recall and recognition (direct tests) do not always capture the full extent of consumer memory, the papers provided a blend of direct and less traditional indirect tests in assessing ad memory. Indirect tests reveal memory by a demonstrated facilitation in task performance, and can provide access to memories that cannot be retrieved by direct tests. These papers have operationalized indirect tests as reaction times (Pluzinski and Johar), stem completions and preference judgments (Shapiro and Krishnan).

The first paper by Pluzinski and Johar specifically investigated the relationship between subjective and objective familiarity and their effects on brand processing and memory. The findings from their study suggest that the manner in which an ad is encoded has an effect on whether the brand name is recalled, but even if the brand name is NOT recalled, encoding affects the accessibility of the brand name as revealed through indirect measures of memory (i.e., reaction times). When an ad is processed superficially, the level of subjective familiarity with the brand as revealed by consumers' feelings-of-knowing the brand name plays a role in the accessibility of brand names. Brand names appeared to be more accessible to consumers who feel that they know the brand even though they did not encode the ad deeply and cannot recall the brand name.

In the second paper, Wallace and Hasher used frequency judgments as a test of memory and found that competing brand ads clearly impact the encoding and/or retrieval of target ads. Frequency judgments reliably discriminate actual frequency even when a) consumers are tested in a natural viewing context, b) multiple brands within a category are advertised, and c) consumers are tested 24 hours after watching the program. However, on immediate tests, competitive ads appear to inhibit frequency judgments of target ads. Generally, factors that would be expected to increase recall do not appear to affect frequency judgments. Wallace also raised several theoretical issues regarding inhibition research, and cautioned that complex ad stimuli and differing test characteristics posed special problems.

The third paper by Shapiro and Krishnan showed that memory for some brand names is attenuated due to their inherent characteristics such as word-frequency. Their results suggest that these effects are not pervasive across all memory tests, and depend on whether a direct (recall and recognition) or indirect (stem-completion and preference) test was administered. Finally, they test the efficacy of different encoding manipulations in reducing this inhibitory effect caused by frequency. Their findings indicate that ad repetition is more effective on an indirect test, whereas semantic elaboration causes increments in performance on the direct test.

As session discussant, Dipankar Chakravarti brought his expertise in consumer memory processes and task effects to understand brand memory issues. He lauded the use of the various indirect measures of ad effects, particularly since these may be indicators of choice and brand equity. He cautioned that research in this area needs to distinguish between tracing methods and trace types. He proposed that future research should focus on using patterns across several tests to understand how information is processed.

Leaving It All Behind: Service Loyalties in Transition

Robin A. Higie, University of Connecticut
Linda L. Price, University of Colorado at Boulder
Julie Fitzmaurice, University of Connecticut

ABSTRACT

This paper reports on the disengagement process that occurs when people who are moving discontinue service provider relationships. We examined the reasons 115 individuals who recently moved gave for their last visit to fifteen commonly used service providers (classified using Lovelock's Tangible/Intangible and Person/Thing dimensions). The results indicate that consumers' reasons for scheduling last visits vary by service characteristics. In particular, for Tangible-Person services (eg., hair stylist and doctor), consumers' last visit was tied to their personal relationship with the service provider and/or the quality of service. For Thing services (eg., auto repair and banking), consumers were concerned with actions related to closing accounts and preparing for the move. Finally, for Tangible services (eg., hair stylist and auto repair), inventorying was important, whereas for Intangible-Thing services (eg., banking and legal services), closing out business was important.

INTRODUCTION

Each year millions of Americans pick up stakes and move their place of residence (U.S. Department of Commerce, Bureau of the Census, 1989). A substantial amount of literature related to moving has focused on the post-move stage, and how individuals adapt to new surroundings and situations, learn about and access new retail outlets and service providers and become familiar with products available in the new area (Andreasen 1984; Andreasen and Durkson 1968; Andreasen and Ratchford 1976; Hyman 1987). Like disposition and disengagement research, generally, people's pre-move, disengagement behaviors have received scant attention (Belk 1988; Holbrook 1987; Jacoby 1978).

People in the midst of relocation face many changes (Sell and DeJong 1983) from saying good-bye to friends to closing out bank accounts. They often find themselves being separated from their former identity, roles, acquaintances, possessions and service providers (Belk 1988; Belk, Wallendorf and Sherry 1989; Schouten 1991a). This paper is an exploratory investigation that examines the process by which consumers disengage from their service providers prior to moving. The research involved post-move interviews, in which we elicited consumers' reasons for scheduling their last visit with service providers. This paper discusses consumers' reasons for scheduling their last visit at fifteen commonly used service providers, and offers some directions for future research in this domain.

BACKGROUND

Transitions and the Disengagement Process

Research in marketing and other disciplines has investigated the transitions associated with numerous major life events (Andreasen 1984), including moving (Andreasen and Durkson 1968; Andreasen and Ratchford 1976), divorce (Berman 1988; McAlexander 1991), job loss (Roberts 1991) and children leaving home (Lowenthal 1972). These and other related studies indicate that during life status changes, disposition of possessions and disengagement from relationships can be very emotional and stressful (Andreasen 1984; Belk 1988; Dohrenwend and Dohrenwend 1974; McAlexander 1991). Moreover, the disengagement process may entail separation from a role, relationship, or other critical part of the extended self (Mehta and Belk 1991; Schouten 1991a, 1991b; Young 1991).

Service Providers and Their Roles in Consumers' Lives

Marketers have directed a significant amount of attention to services marketing and understanding the service encounter and consumer choice among service providers (Lovelock 1983; Murray 1991; Solomon et al 1985). This literature indicates that consumers perceive choices among service providers as risky decisions (Brown and Fern 1981; Davis, Guiltinan and Jones 1979; Murray and Schlacter 1990), and that consumers take great care in the selection of their service providers, relying heavily on personal sources for information (Murray 1991). Once consumers develop trust in the service provider and satisfaction with the service, consumers' continual interaction with their service providers gives rise to long-term commitments (Lovelock 1983). Through these service loyalties, consumers reduce their transaction costs and ensure themselves of quality service over time (Schlenker, Helm and Tedeschi 1973).

An important component of the service encounter is personal interaction (Solomon et al 1985; Surprenant and Solomon 1987). The person-to-person encounter that frequently occurs with service providers often leads consumers to develop strong relationships with service providers (Parasuraman, Zeithaml, and Berry 1985; Shostack 1985; Surprenant and Solomon 1987; Solomon et al 1985). Crosby, Evans and Cowles (1990) note that relationship quality; that is, trust in the service provider and the quality of service, reinforces the consumers' personal investment in the relationship. Given that the importance of personalized service provider relationships is well-documented, it is likely that consumers would be reluctant to discontinue relationships with qualified and trusted service providers.

Service Classification Schemes

In recent years, services and services marketing have received increased attention (Bitner, Booms and Tetreault 1990; Murray 1991; Zeithaml, Parasuraman and Berry 1985), and numerous researchers have attempted to develop schemes to classify services (Grove and Fisk 1983; Lovelock 1983; Price, Feick and Higie 1989). One of Lovelock's (1983) schemes classifies commonly used services on two dimensions: 1) what is the nature of the service act (i.e., Tangible/Intangible: are the actions tangible or intangible) and 2) who or what is the direct recipient of the service (i.e., Person/Thing: is the service directed at the person or directed at goods and other physical possessions). Figure 1 illustrates the exemplars that have been classified as Tangible-Person, Tangible-Thing, Intangible-Person and Intangible-Thing services. Because Lovelock's scheme and stated exemplars capture a broad array of customer services that people frequently use, we adopted this particular scheme for our investigation.

THE PRESENT STUDY

In conversations with people who recently moved, we found that consumers believed that disengaging from service providers was a difficult and often unpleasant experience. Some people recounted having to close-out accounts and prepare to make the

FIGURE 1
Lovelock's Service Classification Scheme

Nature of Act	Direct Recipient of Service: Person	Direct Recipient of Service: Thing
Tangible Actions	o Doctor o Beauty Salons o Restaurants o Dentist o Eye Doctor	o Auto Repair o Dry Cleaning o Veterinary Care o Shoe Repair o Tailor
Intangible Actions	o Education o Broadcasting o Info Services o Theaters o Museums	o Banking o Legal Services o Accounting o Securities o Insurance

transition to their new surroundings. Others who had developed special personal relationships with their service providers or who respected the service delivered by their hairdressers, doctors and attorneys, for example, were reluctant to sever ties. In many cases, this reluctance to disengage from service providers translated into scheduling appointments with these service providers even after consumers had moved.

The present study reports on an exploratory investigation designed to examine how consumers view disengagement from their service providers. This descriptive study reports on data collected from people who recently moved, examines their separation from fifteen service providers, and identifies relationships between categories of services and disengagement behaviors.

METHOD

Procedure and Sample

Personal interviews, using a structured questionnaire, were conducted with a convenience sample of 115 people who had moved between 100 and 7,000 miles. The average move was 1,385 miles. Data were collected in two university towns, one in New England and one in the Western U.S. Respondents were identified either by key informants or by new faculty and staff listings at the two universities.

The average age of the respondents was 32 years; over half (57.4%) were married, and nearly a third (30.4%) were single. Approximately 56% were female and the number of people per household averaged 2.6.

Investigated Services

This research examined 15 services, five services in each of three of the four categories identified by Lovelock (1983). The three categories include: Tangible-Person Services, Tangible-Thing Services and Intangible-Thing Services. During preliminary investigations, no instances of Intangible-Person Services (eg., information and broadcasting services) were noted; therefore, we did not include any services from this category in the present investigation.

Service Disengagement Coding Scheme

During the interview, respondents indicated whether or not they had visited each of the 15 services (see Table 1) prior to moving. Interviewers probed respondents regarding their reasons for scheduling the last visit to each service provider and respondents averaged 1.22 reasons per visit. To develop a comprehensive coding scheme, we selected one instance of a service encounter from each of 45 respondents (three encounters for each service). Three independent judges examined the responses and agreed on seven response categories: Prepare, Closeout, Inventory, Relationship Quality, Personal Relationship, Getting Together and Regular Visit.

Prepare involves completing needed work for the move, and examples of this are: going to the auto mechanic to "get the car a tune-up and set for a long distance trip", visiting the bank "to get cash in traveler's checks to pay for moving expenses" and scheduling with doctors "to get recommendations for a doctor" at the new location.

Closeout of business with service providers involves final transactions, for example with banks ("I closed my account and withdrew money since I did not plan to return") and the dentist ("completed dental bridge work that was already in progress").

Respondents also obtained service prior to moving to avoid the need to immediately engage a new service provider after moving; we refer to this as *Inventory*. Examples of *Inventory* include seeing a dentist "to get my teeth cleaned in case it took a while to find a new doctor", using the dry cleaning services because he didn't "want to worry right after the move" and scheduling an appointment at the hair salon prior to moving because he did "not want a hair cut to be a service I have to look for while other more important things are on my mind".

Respondents who had developed strong customer relationships based upon trust and quality service, that is *Relationship Quality*, reported visiting a dentist because "I don't trust others, I trust him," and a veterinarian because of "faith in the vet".

Respondents also scheduled last visits because of *Personal Relationships* that they had developed with service providers. Customers visited a doctor because of "a personal relationship", a hair stylist because "I had a close relationship with the lady who cut my hair" and a restaurant "for sentimental reasons".

Finally, *Getting Together* with friends before leaving was a commonly cited reason for restaurant patrons making a final visit to a favorite restaurant.

Some visits were not an acknowledged part of the disengagement process, but rather just a continuation of the service relation-

TABLE 1
Service Encounters and Reasons for Last Visit

Service	Number of Visits Made[a]	Reasons for Last Visit[b]						
		Prepare	Close-Out	Inventory	Relationship Quality	Personal Relationship	Together	Regular
Tangible-Person								
Hair Salon	50	7	—	20	15	18	—	7
Dentist	46	8	9	22	11	7	—	7
Doctor	46	13	10	20	6	14	—	5
Restaurant	42	—	—	1	23	4	18	2
Eye Doctor	12	1	1	4	2	4	—	3
Sub-total	**196**	**29**	**20**	**67**	**57**	**47**	**18**	**24**
Tangible-Thing								
Auto Repair	47	39	1	6	6	1	—	2
Dry Cleaner	29	13	—	16	4	—	—	1
Veterinarian	14	10	2	1	4	2	—	1
Shoe Repair	10	4	2	2	1	1	—	—
Tailor	8	1	1	3	3	—	—	3
Sub-Total	**108**	**70**	**6**	**28**	**18**	**4**	**0**	**7**
Intangible-Thing								
Banker	89	38	56	2	1	1	—	1
Insurance	53	31	20	1	1	1	—	—
Accountant	22	10	5	2	5	2	—	3
Attorney	21	10	9	2	2	1	1	—
Stock Broker	6	4	1	1	—	—	—	—
Sub-Total	**191**	**93**	**91**	**8**	**6**	**5**	**1**	**4**
Total	**495**	**192**	**117**	**103**	**81**	**56**	**19**	**35**

[a] The 115 respondents indicated which services they visited prior to moving, eg., 50 respondents scheduled visits to a hair salon.
[b] Some respondents gave more than one reason for visiting a service provider; hence the number of reasons exceeds the number of visits.

ship. Hence, a seventh code, *Regular*, was used when respondents identified their last visit to doctors, dentists, eye doctors, or hair stylists, as a "regular visit".

Three independent judges coded each response. A modal scoring convention was used (MacKenzie, Lutz, and Belch 1986). If at least two of three judges agreed on the code for the response, it was assigned to the category. This coding procedure resulted in 586 of 603 (97.2%) of the responses being successfully coded. A fourth judge resolved the 17 discrepant cases.

RESULTS

Before moving, the 115 respondents made 495 visits to the 15 services under investigation in this study, an average of 4.3 services per person. Table 1 shows the number of respondents who visited each service. Banks were the most commonly visited service provider prior to a move (77.4% of respondents visited a banker), whereas stock brokers and tailors were the least used services (less than 10 percent of the respondents). Respondents made 196 visits (39.6%) to Tangible-Person services, 108 (21.8%) to Tangible-Thing services and 191 (38.6%) to Intangible-Thing services.

Table 1 also reports the distribution of respondents' reasons for scheduling a last visit with service providers. The most common reasons that a last visit was scheduled were 1) to prepare to get to the new location (31.8%), 2) to close out business (19.4%), and/or 3) to inventory the service so as to not have to obtain the service immediately after the move (17.1%). Approximately 13.4% of the responses were concerned with relationship quality, 9.3% with personal relationship, and 3.2% with getting together with friends. Approximately 5.8% of the reasons were "regular" visit.

The results indicate that consumers' reasons for scheduling their last visits vary by service characteristics (See Table 1). The primary reasons given for visiting the Tangible-Person services (eg., dentist, doctor, hair stylist) include inventorying services, seeing a trusted/quality service provider and saying good-bye to service providers. On the other hand, the primary reasons for visiting Tangible-Thing services (eg., auto repair, dry cleaner, shoe repair) were inventorying services and preparing for departure, and the primary reasons for visiting Intangible-Thing services (eg., banker, accountant, insurance) were closing out of accounts and preparing for the post-move situation. Together and Regular were not primary reasons for making a last visit to a service provider prior to moving.

DISCUSSION

Our preliminary research on consumers' disengagement with service providers offers interesting and some surprising results. Our research indicates that reasons for making a last visit to a service provider vary by service characteristics. As illustrated in Figure 2, consumers made last visits to Tangible-Person service providers mainly to inventory services, for the relationship quality,

FIGURE 2
Service Characteristics and Reasons For Making a Last Visit to a Service Provider

Direct Recipient of Service

	Person	Thing
Nature of Act **Tangible Actions**	o Inventory o Relationship Quality o Personal Relationship	o Prepare o Inventory o Relationship Quality
Intangible Actions		o Prepare o Close-Out

or due to the personal relationship established. Last visits were made to Tangible-Thing service providers usually to prepare for the move, inventory services, or obtain service from someone whose relationship was valued. Consumers visited Intangible-Thing providers mainly to prepare for the move or close-out business prior to moving.

Patterns of reasons given for making the last visit emerged for Person versus Thing services and for Tangible versus Intangible services. First, for Person services, consumers appear to value quality, personalization and friendliness of the service provider so much so that they have developed personal relationships with for example, hair stylists and doctors. Thus, the disengagement process from service providers is not unlike the disengagement from one's possessions, roles and friends. For example, consumers noted that they "had a personal relationship" with their hair stylist or that they scheduled a last visit to see their doctor, in part, "to say good-bye." In other instances, consumers reported visiting a restaurant "for sentimental reasons" or because it was "a favorite place."

In contrast to the Person services, consumers use their last visits for Thing services to prepare for the move and to bridge pre-move to post-move life. For example, some respondents scheduled last visits with dentists and doctors and noted their reason for doing so was to "get a recommendation for new a doctor." Similarly, some respondents scheduled visits with their insurance agent or accountant in order "to check if the policy is good in new area" or "to get tax records and financial statements before moving."

Finally, inventorying of services appears to be more important for Tangible services than for Intangible services. Our interviews indicate that consumers "stock-up" on some services prior to moving in an attempt to reduce the pressure to learn about the new marketplace immediately after moving. Several consumers scheduled a last trip to the hair salon because they "needed a good cut and didn't know where they could get one in their new location" or because they were "not sure that they would be able to find a good beauty salon right away." Also, some consumers went to the dry cleaners or shoe repair to get service because they "thought it may be difficult to find one at new location." In contrast, for Intangible-Thing services, compared to Tangible services, closing out banking and insurance policies to formally conclude business were the impetus for many final visits.

Some research has suggested that consumers may experience a stressful time when disengaging from a role, relationship or other critical part of the extended self (Fellerman and Debevec 1992; McAlexander, Schouten, and Roberts 1992; Mehta and Belk 1991). Carver, Scheier, and Weintraub (1989) identified two coping strategies commonly used for coping with stressful life episodes: problem-focused coping (i.e., actively attempting to change the source of the stress by managing the situation) and emotional-focused coping (i.e., relying on emotional support of friends, etc.). Using these definitions of alternative coping strategies, it seems that Relationship Quality, Personal Relationship, and Together are emotional-focused strategies, whereas Prepare, Close-Out and Inventory are problem-focused strategies.

Our research suggests that consumers use both problem-focused and emotional-focused strategies for coping with breaking service provider ties, and that these strategies may vary with service characteristics. It appears that reasons for visiting Intangible-Thing services are mainly characterized as problem-focused coping strategies (i.e, Prepare and Close-Out). In contrast, Tangible services were linked to both emotional- and problem-focused coping strategies. Tangible-Person services were mainly visited for reasons associated with emotional-coping strategies and Tangible-Thing services were mainly visited for reasons associated with problem-focused coping strategies.

FUTURE RESEARCH

This exploratory investigation offers several directions for future research. First, research on pre-move attitudes and behaviors might be investigated prior to moving, as compared to this study which involved retrospective accounts of pre-move behavior. Additionally, research might take a closer look at movers' disengagement from Intangible-Person services, such as churches, museums and theaters. A more systematic examination of reasons given for last visits to service providers may provide guidelines for the development of a taxonomy of move-related disengagement behaviors, or disengagement behaviors more generally.

The marketing literature on services discusses service providers' inability to inventory services (Zeithaml, Parasuraman and Berry 1985). This exploratory research provides some insights about *customers* stockpiling services. Our research indicates the people who are going to move inventory services from hair stylists, dentists, doctors and dry cleaners. Consumers reported that they scheduled these visits in order to reduce the need to find such service providers immediately after moving. More investigation might look specifically at stockpiling, people's resistance to disengagements from service providers, and the effects of a person's coping style to both the disengagement from and the re-establishment of a relationship with a service provider.

A related area of research might focus on the emotional responses to disengagement, given that moving is one of life's more stressful and disruptive events (Andreasen 1984; Dohrenwend and Dohrenwend 1974). Research might investigate the relationship between move-related stress and the disengagement process. A longitudinal study could focus on pre-move coping and disengagement strategies and post-move adaptation and market learning.

Finally, the study of disengagement and disposal processes continues to be a neglected research domain. While this study examined the disengagement with service providers, other research might be expanded to consider disengagement behaviors related to retail outlets and products and brands that may not be accessible after the move. Also, some of the relationships identified in this research might be examined in a more rigorous and systematic fashion by using an experimental design.

REFERENCES

Andreasen, Alan R. (1984), "Life Status Changes and Changes in Consumer Preferences and Satisfaction," *Journal of Consumer Research*, 11 (December), 784-794.

_____, and Peter G. Durkson (1968), "Market Learning of New Residents," *Journal of Marketing Research*, 5 (May), 166-176.

_____, and Brian T. Ratchford (1976) "Factors Affecting Consumers' Use of Information Sources," *Journal of Business Research*, 4 (August), 197-212.

Belk, Russell W. (1988), "Possessions and the Extended Self," *Journal of Consumer Research*, 15 (September), 139-168.

_____, Melanie Wallendorf, and John F. Sherry, Jr. (1989), "The Sacred and the Profane in Consumer Behavior: Theodicy in the Odyssey," *Journal of Consumer Research*, 16 (June), 1-38.

Berman, William H. (1988), "The Role of Attachment in the Post-Divorce Experience," *Journal of Personality and Social Psychology*, 54 (3), 496-503.

Bitner, Mary Jo, Bernard Booms, and Mary Stanfield Tetreault (1990), "The Service Encounter: Diagnosing Favorable and Unfavorable Incidents", *Journal of Marketing*, 54 (January), 71-84.

Brown, James R. and Edward F. Fern (1981), "Goods vs. Services Marketing: A Divergent Perspective." In O.C. Ferrell, S.W. Brown, and C.W. Lamb, Jr. (eds.), *Conceptual and Theoretical Developments in Marketing*, Chicago: American Marketing Association, 205-207.

Carver, Charles S., Michael F. Scheier, and Jagdish Kumari Weintraub (1989), "Assessing Coping Strategies: A Theoretically Based Approach," *Journal of Personality and Social Psychology*, 56 (2), 267-283.

Crosby, Lawrence A., Kenneth R. Evans, and Deborah Cowles (1990), "Relationship Quality in Services Selling: An Interpersonal Influence Perspective," *Journal of Marketing*, 54 (July), 68-81.

Davis, Duane L., Joseph P. Guiltinan, and Wesley H. Jones (1979), "Service Characteristics, Consumer Search, and the Classification of Retail Services, " *Journal of Retailing*, 3 (Fall), 3-23.

Dohrenwend, Barbara Snell and Bruce P. Dohrenwend (1974), *Stressful Life Events: Their Nature and Effects*. New York: John Wiley.

Fellerman, Ritha and Kathleen Debevec (1992), "Till Death Do We Part: Family Dissolution, Transition and Consumer Behavior." In John F. Sherry and Brian Sternthal (eds.), *Advances in Consumer Research*, Vol. 19. Provo, UT: Association for Consumer Research. 514-521.

Grove, Stephen J. and Raymond P. Fisk (1983), "The Dramaturgy of Services Exchange: An Analytical Framework for Services Marketing," in *Emerging Perspectives in Services Marketing*, eds. L.L. Berry, G.L. Shostack and G.D. Upah, Chicago, IL: American Marketing Association.

Holbrook, Morris B. (1987), "What is Consumer Research?" *Journal of Consumer Research*, Vol. 14 (June), 128-132.

Hyman, Michael R. (1987), "Long-Distance Geographic Mobility and Retailing Attitudes and Behaviors: An Update," *Journal of Retailing*, 63 (Summer), 180-204.

Jacoby, Jacob (1978), "Consumer Research: A State of the Art Review," *Journal of Marketing*, Vol. 43 No. 2 (June). 87-96.

Lowenthal, Marjorie Fiske (1972), "Transition to the Empty Nest," *Archives of General Psychiatry*, 26 (January), 8-14.

Lovelock, Christopher H. (1983), "Classifying Services to Gain Strategic Marketing Insights," *Journal of Marketing*, 47 (Summer), 9-20.

MacKenzie, Scott B., Richard J. Lutz, and George E. Belch (1986), "The Role of Attitude Toward the Ad as a Mediator of Advertising Effectiveness: A Test of Competing Explanations," *Journal of Marketing Research*, 23 (May), 130-143.

McAlexander, James H. (1991), "Divorce, the Disposition of the Relationship, and Everything." In Rebecca H. Holman and Michael R. Solomon (eds.), *Advances in Consumer Research*, Vol. 18. Provo, UT: Association for Consumer Research. 43-48.

_____, John W. Schouten, and Scott D. Roberts (1992), "Consumer Behavior in Coping Strategies for Divorce." In John F. Sherry and Brian Sternthal (eds.), *Advances in Consumer Research*, Vol. 19. Provo, UT: Association for Consumer Research. 555-556.

Mehta, Raj and Russell W. Belk. (1991), "Artifacts, Identity and Transition: Favorite Possessions of Indians and Indian Immigrants to the United States," *Journal of Consumer Research*, 17 (March), 398-411.

Murray, Keith B. (1991), "A Test of Services Marketing Theory: Consumer Information Acquisition Activities," *Journal of Marketing*, 55 (January), 10-25.

_____, and John L. Schlacter (1990), "The Impact of Services Versus Goods on Consumers' Assessment of Perceived Risk and Variability," *Journal of the Academy of Marketing Science*, 18 (1), 51-65.

Parasuraman, A., Valarie A. Zeithaml, and Leonard L. Berry (1985), "A Conceptual Model of Service Quality and its Implications for Future Research," *Journal of Marketing*, 49 (Fall), 41-50.

Price, Linda L., Lawrence F. Feick and Robin A. Higie (1989), "Preference Heterogeneity and Coorientation as Determinants of Perceived Informational Influence", *Journal of Business Research*, 19 (November), 227-242.

Roberts, Scott D. (1991), "Consumption Response to Involuntary Job Loss." In Rebecca H. Holman and Michael R. Solomon (eds.), *Advances in Consumer Research*, Vol. 18. Provo, UT: Association for Consumer Research. 40-42.

Schouten, John W. (1991a), "Personal Rites of Passage and the Reconstruction of Self." In Rebecca H. Holman and Michael R. Solomon (eds.), *Advances in Consumer Research*, Vol. 18. Provo, UT: Association for Consumer Research. 49-51.

_____ (1991b), "Selves in Transition: Symbolic Consumption in Personal Rites of Passage and Identity Reconstruction," *Journal of Consumer Research*, 17 (March), 412-425.

Schlenker, B. R., B. Helm, and J. T. Tedeschi (1973), "The Effects of Personality and Situational Variables on Behavioral Trust," *Journal of Personality and Social Psychology*, 25 (3), 419-427.

Sell, R. and DeJong, C.F. (1983), "Deciding Whether to Move: Mobility, Wishful Thinking and Adjustment," *Sociology and Social Research*, 67 (2), 146-165.

Shostack, G. Lynn (1985), "Planning the Service Encounter," In *The Service Encounter*, John A. Czepiel, Michael R. Solomon, and Carol F. Surprenant (eds.), New York: Lexington Books, 243-254.

Solomon, Michael R., Carol Surprenant, John A. Czepiel, and Evelyn G. Gutman (1985), "A Role Theory Perspective on Dyadic Interactions: The Service Encounter," *Journal of Marketing*, 49 (Winter), 99-111.

Surprenant, Carol F. and Michael R. Solomon (1987), "Prediction and Personalization in the Service Encounter," *Journal of Marketing*, 51 (April), 86-96.

U.S. Department of Commerce, Bureau of the Census (1989), "Geographic Mobility: March 1986-March 1987," *Current Population Reports*, Series P-20, No.430.

Young, Melissa Martin (1991), "Disposition of Possessions During Role Transition." In Rebecca H. Holman and Michael R. Solomon (eds.), *Advances in Consumer Research*, Vol. 18. Provo, UT: Association for Consumer Research. 33-39.

Zeithaml, Valarie A. A. Parasuraman, and Leonard L. Berry (1985), "Problems and Strategies in Services Marketing," *Journal of Marketing*, 49 (Spring), 33-46.

Attitudes, Advertising, and Automobiles: A Functional Approach
Richard Ennis, University of Waterloo
Mark P. Zanna, University of Waterloo

ABSTRACT

Two studies explore a methodology for identifying the psychological functions of attitudes toward a multifunctional consumer product: the automobile. We hypothesize that the needs met by consumer products will better be reflected in the beliefs that underlie attitude rather than in overall attitudinal evaluations. The results are discussed in terms of a functional approach in attitudinal research and some implications for consumer research.

The investigation of the psychological importance of attitudes has been collectively described as the functional approach. Although work within this approach was initiated some thirty years ago (Smith, Bruner and White 1956; Katz 1960), it disappeared from the mainstream of psychological research due to the lack of an adequate methodology. Fortunately, there has been a renewed interest in this perspective and researchers have begun examining the needs met by various attitude objects such as personal possessions (e.g., Abelson 1986; Belk 1988) and the role of attitude function in advertising and persuasion (e.g., DeBono 1989; Shavitt 1989; Shavitt and Fazio 1987).

Although various functional taxonomies have been proposed (e.g., Herek 1986; Katz 1960; Shavitt 1989; Smith, Bruner and White 1956), all agree on a broad distinction between instrumental and symbolic functions. Instrumental attitudes focus on the features and attributes of the target object and their utility in providing better functioning in the environment. Symbolic attitudes represent events, relationships, thoughts or feelings that are important or meaningful to an individual; or provide a means of self-expression. Belk (1988) described the instrumental function as "a capability for doing;" we would be unable to do the same things without the attitude object. He distinguishes the symbolic function as "a capability for being;" we would not be the same person without the target item.

Consumer products such as the automobile can, therefore, be differentiated by the needs that they might serve. Furthermore, the functional capacity of a particular model will be reflected in the attitudes and opinions that one holds. This has led researchers to hypothesize that functionally consistent advertisements will be more persuasive than inconsistent appeals. Recent empirical evidence has supported such a position. For example, Shavitt and her colleagues (e.g., Shavitt and Fazio 1987) have shown that subjects primed by instrumental products will subsequently rate information-based appeals more highly than image-based appeals, while symbolically-primed subjects find image-based ads more convincing.

This apparent propensity for functional consistency has several implications for consumer psychology. If one can identify the psychological functions of a product as reflected in consumer attitudes this would greatly enhance product development, market segmentation, and advertising strategies. An ability to match persuasive appeals with the needs of a market would improve brand name identification and expand targeted audiences. This is especially true for multifunctional products such as the automobile.

We believe, however, that the potential for functional measurement and manipulation is not at the level of attitudes but at the level of beliefs which underlie those attitudes. Overall evaluations provide little, if any, evidence of the needs that a product might meet. Attitudinal dispositions are a summative expression of the salient thoughts, feelings, and behaviours associated with the target item (Ajzen and Fishbein 1980; Zanna and Rempel 1988). It has been demonstrated that the beliefs associated with an object (i.e., the beliefs comprising an attitude) can be readily identified (Ajzen and Fishbein 1980; Cacioppo and Petty 1981) and coded according to psychological function (Herek 1986; Shavitt 1989). We believe that the constellation of functional beliefs associated with a product will indicate the needs that the product is currently satisfying and the needs that it can potentially satisfy. Furthermore, we believe that the functional capacities of a product can be influenced by advertising appeals designed to manipulate the belief structure underlying consumer attitudes toward that product.

To explore these hypotheses, we conducted two experiments. We began by selecting four models of automobiles which we felt, a priori, would serve different patterns of needs. We assumed that subcompact and family models would meet predominantly utilitarian purposes while, in contrast, sport and luxury models would demonstrate a greater multifunctional capacity by meeting both instrumental and symbolic needs. In Study One, we tested our a priori assumptions about the functional distinctions amongst the car models and we looked for evidence that these distinctions are reflected in the attitudinal beliefs associated with each model. In Study Two, we tested the impact of advertising slogans on the functional perceptions of an unknown, hypothetical car.

STUDY ONE

We began by eliciting the attitudinal beliefs associated with each of the four car models using the method suggested by Fishbein and Ajzen (1980) which has received general acceptance in the literature. In a between-subject design, two different belief elicitation instructions were used to explicitly pull for either instrumental or symbolic thoughts. We sensed that the traditional procedures are biased for utilitarian attributes, therefore might not capture the full richness of the symbolic needs served by an automobile. Using the two sets of instructions as an independent variable, we hypothesized that the symbolic instructions would generate not only more symbolic beliefs, but would also provide empirical evidence of the relative importance of these beliefs.

Having accomplished the elicitation of attitudinal beliefs, we then constructed a manual for coding each idea according to the psychological need that it addresses. We relied on Shavitt's (1989) coding procedures which she has successfully applied to consumer products such as air conditioners, coffee, perfume, and soft drinks. We hypothesized that automobiles, in general, are a multifunctional product. Therefore, we should find that each of the four models generates a substantial number of attitudinal beliefs associated with both instrumental and symbolic functioning. We also assumed that vehicle models differ in their ability to serve expressive needs. We have hypothesized that luxury and sport cars are more multifunctional (i.e., better able to serve symbolic needs) relative to subcompact and family models. By coding each belief according to the function it serves, we can test these assumptions empirically.

Method

Subjects in this study were sixty (34 females and 26 males) introductory psychology students who participated as part of a course requirement. For half the subjects, the initial instructions explained the instrumental function served by automobiles which

TABLE 1
Mean Ratings of Functions Served by Each Car Model

	Function	
Models	Instrumental	Symbolic
Subcompact	3.97	2.97
Family	4.05	2.90
Luxury	3.18	3.88
Sport	2.98	4.14

Notes: N = 60. Scale 1-5, with higher numbers indicating greater contribution to attitude.

read, in part: "we continually assess how 'useful' objects are; and how certain features or attributes of each item contribute to, or detract from, that usefulness. Attitudes toward everyday objects are based, in part, on our analysis of the good and bad characteristics of the object."

The remaining subjects received an explanation about the symbolic functions that might be served by automobiles which read, in part: "we can learn something about a person by the items and objects that he/she uses and owns. They provide us with a means of identifying what kind of person he or she is — what might be good or bad; likeable or dislikeable about someone who owns or uses a particular item. Attitudes toward everyday objects are based, in part, on our analysis of the good and bad characteristics expressed by the object."

Subjects then described their beliefs about each type of vehicle on separate thought-listing sheets (Cacioppo and Petty 1981) with the order of responding counterbalanced in a latin-square design. Next, subjects' attitudes toward each model were assessed on two 7-point bipolar scales with endpoints labelled "extremely good"/"extremely bad" and "extremely like"/"extremely dislike." Responses on these two evaluative scales were summed.

Finally, subjects completed a direct measure of the functions served by each car model. This form was adapted from a similar measure used successfully by Shavitt (1989). Subjects were asked to rate on a 5-point unipolar scale, with endpoints of "does not contribute at all to my attitude" to "contributes a great deal to my attitude," the contribution of instrumental and symbolic factors to their attitudes toward each model. For each type of vehicle, the instrumental function was described as "my past experiences with the object: how useful I found the item"; the symbolic function was described as "my social identity: what the item tells others about me" and "my values: what the item means to me."

Results

The direct measure of function confirmed our a priori assumptions about the different models of cars. Recall that subcompact and family models were assumed to serve greater utilitarian and less symbolic needs than luxury and sports models. The results presented in Table 1 provide a pattern consistent with this functional ordering. The planned contrasts reveal that the utilitarian factor contributed more toward subcompact and family vehicles than luxury and sport models, $t(59)=5.79$, $p<.001$; while the symbolic factor contributed more to luxury and sport vehicles, $t(59)=9.43$, $p<.001$. A between-group (instrumental vs. symbolic instructions) analysis revealed no significant differences in these measures suggesting that subjects' perceptions of the functions served by the known vehicles were not influenced by the instructions.

We then created a manual which would allow us to code the individual beliefs according to their relevance to specific psychological needs. The responses provided by the first 30 subjects were classified as either instrumental or symbolic based on the conceptual definitions presented earlier. The resultant themes were used as examplars for the coding manual. Two judges then used the coding manual to independently code the belief statements provided by the remaining 30 subjects. The agreement rate for the 743 beliefs was 90.2% which was superior to that reported as acceptable by Shavitt (1989).

In total, the 60 subjects provided 1,256 beliefs which could be coded for the four models of cars. There were no between-group differences in the number of beliefs elicited suggesting that our instruction manipulation did not adversely affect subjects' ability to generate attitudinal beliefs. Table 2 shows, however, that subjects provided with instrumentally-oriented instructions (those traditionally used in thought-elicitation procedures) generated more beliefs relevant to utilitarian functions and fewer associated with symbolic functions than did subjects receiving symbolically-oriented instructions, $t(59)=2.79$, $p<.01$ and $t(59)=2.91$, $p<.01$, respectively. Although not shown in Table 2, we repeated these analyses for each of the four cars and found that the differing rates of elicitation were statistically significant for all but the sports model, and these results demonstrated a pattern consistent with the other models.

By tailoring instructions to effectively pull for specific types of beliefs we were able to obtain a more complete picture of the multifunctional nature of automobiles in general, and these four models in particular. This technique allows us to discriminate amongst these similar attitudinal objects in terms of their capacity to fulfill certain needs. Based on our exploration to this point, it would appear that subcompacts, followed closely by family models, are the most unifunctional of these cars, serving predominantly instrumental requirements. The luxury and sport models appear more multifunctional as they possess a greater capacity to serve symbolic, as well as utilitarian, needs.

This first study has provided a repertoire of beliefs associated with automobiles and it appears that the psychological needs met by this product are reflected in the attitudinal belief set. Taken on its own, these findings seem rather obvious: we successfully generated data consistent with instructional demands. However, when we examined the measures of overall attitude toward the four cars, we discovered there were no between-group differences (*means*: 2.10 vs 1.87 for subcompacts; 1.93 vs 1.20 for family; 2.10 vs 2.00 for luxury; and 2.77 vs 2.97 for sports). Despite being measured following the manipulation, attitudes do not reflect the functional distinctions that are evident amongst the attitudinal beliefs. This offers some tentative support for our contention that advancement in the functional approach will benefit by measurement techniques that focus on the attitudinal beliefs. If our methodology is to have any practical significance, however, it is essential that we establish

TABLE 2
Mean Number of Functional Beliefs Elicited by Instructional Group

	Instructional Group	
Belief Function	Instrumental	Symbolic
Instrumental	16.47	12.03
Symbolic	5.20	8.17

Notes: N = 60; n=30. Mean number of beliefs based on total beliefs per subject for all 4 car models.

---

that an attitude toward a product does indeed serve the needs suggested by the associated beliefs despite this obfuscation. Study Two explores the functional consistency between attitudes, attitudinal beliefs, and psychological needs.

STUDY TWO

We have theorized that the psychological needs that a product satisfies are reflected in the structure of the attitude rather than the attitude toward that product. In this study we examine this notion by experimentally manipulating the function of the belief set. We hypothesize that such a manipulation will affect the functions met by the attitude but will not be evident in overall attitude.

In order to conduct this experiment, we needed an automobile model that was not familiar to subjects. Study One demonstrated that known cars are perceived as serving distinct patterns of needs so we created a model that would not permit subjects to enter the experiment with set perceptions about its functional capacity. The fictitious car was identified as the "DL-22" which was "still in the design stages." No additional information was provided.

In order to manipulate the belief set associated with this unknown car we adopted a priming procedure similar to that used by Shavitt and Fazio (1987) and DeBono (1989). Our intent was to prime subjects with either instrumental or symbolic beliefs about an automobile then compare the function of their attitudes toward the car. For our priming task we generated two sets of advertising slogans appealing to instrumental or symbolic psychological needs. Each slogan was a brief statement that was worded identically except for a word or brief phrase chosen from Study One to reflect the different needs. We predicted that, in the absence of previous knowledge of the fictitious model of car, subjects would perceive it as meeting the need consistent with the priming slogans. Specifically, subjects given the instrumental version of the beliefs would rate the DL-22 as relatively unifunctional and similar to our subcompact and family models (i.e., predominantly instrumental) while those given the symbolic version would rate the DL-22 as similar to the more multifunctional luxury and sports models.

Method

The subjects were 40 (20 female and 20 male) introductory psychology students who participated for course credit. They were brought into the lab individually and were told that the study was designed to test advertising slogans for a new car which would reach the market in the near future and their task would be to assess a variety of written slogans which might be used in future advertising for the DL-22. Subjects were then provided with 20 slogans, each printed on a separate 3" x 5" card, that were written in one of two functional versions: instrumental or symbolic (see Figure 1 for examples). This manipulation constituted the independent variable.

In order to prime the predominant function featured in the slogan cards, subjects were given a filler task which involved sorting the cards according to how appealing and, then, how convincing each was. Subjects then rated the DL-22 on two evaluative dimensions: good/bad and like/dislike. A 7 point bipolar scale was used for each and the responses were summed to form a measure of overall attitude toward the fictitious vehicle. Finally we obtained a direct measure of attitude function for the DL-22 and the four familiar car models using the same procedure from the previous study.

Results

As in the previous study, we first examined the direct ratings of function for the known models of cars (subcompact, family, luxury and sports) and for the hypothetical DL-22. For the familiar car models, the results were consistent with the data from Study One in that planned comparisons revealed that the subcompact and family models differed significantly from the luxury and sports models for each function measured; $t(39)=7.54$, $p<.001$ for instrumental function and $t(39)=6.40$, $p<.001$ for symbolic function.

The priming manipulation was, however, effective in producing different functional perceptions of the unknown and unfamiliar DL-22. As can be seen in Table 3, subjects rated the hypothetical vehicle as serving a pattern of needs consistent with our hypothesis regarding the priming impact. A repeated measures ANOVA revealed a significant interaction between priming condition and function, $F(1,38)=17.85$, $p<.001$. Generally, the symbolic primes resulted in lower instrumental and higher symbolic ratings of the DL-22 than did the instrumental prime. Furthermore, the priming effect was limited to the DL-22; there were no significant between-group differences for the four known types of automobiles. It would appear that our manipulation had an impact on the functional nature of a novel belief structure without affecting existing attitudinal structures.

We included the four common car models in this study to serve as comparative data for the functional measures of the DL-22. Looking first at the group primed with instrumental beliefs (the first two columns of data in Table 3), we found that these subjects provided function ratings of the DL-22 that were statistically similar to the unifunctional subcompact and family cars. In other words, the DL-22 was significantly different from the luxury model, $t(38)=2.70$, $p<.05$ for instrumental and $t(38)=3.32$, $p<.01$ for symbolic ratings. The same was true for the sports model, $t(38)=5.77$, $p<.001$ for instrumental and $t(38)=6.24$, $p<.001$ for symbolic ratings. The DL-22 did not differ significantly from the subcompact and family models.

The opposite was true for subjects primed with expressive ideas (the last two columns of data in Table 3). In this instance the function ratings of the DL-22 did not differ significantly from the luxury and sports models but did differ from the unifunctional cars. These differences were at least marginally significant for the subcompact, $t(38)=2.03$, $p<.10$ for instrumental and $t(38)=2.78$,

FIGURE 1
Examples of Slogans Used in Priming Conditions
(instrumental/symbolic)

The DL-22 is a lot of (*car/prestige*) for the money.
Protect your (*investment/image*) with the DL-22.
The DL-22 (*mileage/reputation*) is impressive.
The DL-22 is the new shape of (*competence/independence*).
The DL-22 is a unique blend of value and (*satisfaction/fashion*).

TABLE 3
Mean Ratings of Functions Served by Hypothetical and Known Cars By Priming Condition

	Function Ratings			
	Instrumental Prime		Symbolic Prime	
Models	Ins.	Sym.	Ins.	Sym.
DL-22	4.75	3.55	4.15	4.10
Subcompact	4.55	3.50	4.55	3.35
Family	4.90	3.40	4.95	3.30
Luxury	4.25	4.20	3.75	4.75
Sports	3.65	4.65	3.55	4.45

Notes: N = 40, n=20. Scale 1-5, with higher numbers indicating greater contribution to attitude.

$p<.05$ for symbolic ratings. The comparisons with the family car were significant, $t(38)=4.66, p<.001$ for instrumental and $t(38)=2.32, p<.05$ for symbolic ratings.

We then examined the measure of attitude toward the DL-22 and found there were no between-group differences in mean attitude (2.05 for instrumental group and 2.00 for value-expressive group). This was also true for the four familiar car models. As hypothesized, the functional variability of the DL-22 appears to take place at the level of beliefs without being evident at the more general level of overall evaluative attitudes.

DISCUSSION

This research used the automobile as a consumer product that is capable of meeting and satisfying a variety of psychological needs. In Study Two, subjects provided with the instrumental beliefs in the form of advertising slogans came to perceive the DL-22 as being predominantly a unifunctional product. Those primed with symbolic ideas came to perceive the fictional car as being more multifunctional. As support for our thesis, recall that these distinct profiles were created by introducing function-relevant beliefs identified in Study One. Recall further that these distinct perceptions of the DL-22 were not reflected in the attitudes toward the car.

In terms of method, the belief elicitation and coding employed in Study One appears to be both efficient and valid. Once a coding manual is composed it becomes possible to empirically describe and measure the range or capacity of a product to meet consumer needs. Our ability to differentiate between car models suggests these procedures may also allow brand distinctions within broader product categories. By permitting the identification and functional classification of beliefs associated with a target item, this methodology may allow researchers to better understand and, perhaps control, the needs being served by various consumer products.

In Study Two we have evidence that attitudinal belief sets of new products may be especially susceptible to persuasive communications that might influence consumers' functional expectations. In many cases, an advertiser may simply want to know the predominant function of a product and design appeals consistent with it. There are, however, other intriguing possibilities for multifunctional products such as the automobile. If one knows the full functional profile of a product, one can then design persuasive appeals to change or enhance attitudes toward the product that would reflect the variety of needs that might be satisfied. Changing attitude function may suggest new uses for a product; generate new markets; improve brand name loyalty; or increase involvement with the product.

There are two ways that persuasive communications might accomplish this task. First, an advertiser might introduce new functional beliefs not previously associated with the product in the hopes of creating a new potential demand. For example, an economy car may be advertised as showing the owner "conserves energy" or "cares about our planet." These new expressive ideas would suggest that the economy car can serve more than the utilitarian needs such as fuel efficiency and transportation.

The second tactic available to the advertiser is manipulating beliefs already associated with the product by improving the strength, importance, or salience of certain ideas within the existing belief structure. The targeted beliefs could be chosen on the basis of their functional affiliation thus enhancing the scope of psychological needs that the product might serve. For example, the safety features of a family car might be promoted in expressive rather than instrumental terms as "caring for your loved one" or "being a parent first and a chauffeur second." Similarly, the instrumental nature of a luxury car can be suggested by "allowing you to arrive well-rested and ready for business."

Both advertising tactics require the mapping of attitudinal beliefs and their functional associations that our methodology may provide. This mapping might also permit an ongoing evaluation of advertising and marketing programs by tracking changes in the functional profile of a product over time. Analysts would be able to empirically measure the success of programs designed to change particular thoughts or ideas within the set.

Given the early stage of our exploratory research, we must emphasize that these applications are speculative. Obviously, the studies presented here are only suggestive of the applied potential of the functional approach. Currently, we are examining the compatibility of our functional approach within the more traditional and popular notions of attitude structure as represented by the work of Ajzen and Fishbein (1980). We also plan to use persuasion techniques with familiar consumer products to directly test some of the applied possibilities suggested in this paper.

REFERENCES

Abelson, R. P. (1986). Beliefs are like possessions. *Journal for the Theory of Social Behaviour*, 16, 223-250.

Ajzen, I., and Fishbein, M. (1980). *Understanding attitudes and predicting social behavior*. Englewood Cliffs, NJ: Prentice-Hall.

Belk, R. W. (1988). Possessions and the extended self. *Journal of Consumer Research*, 15, 139-168.

Cacioppo, J. T., and Petty, R. E. (1981). Social psychological procedures for cognitive response assessment: The thought-listing technique. In T. V. Merluzzi, C. R. Glass and M. Genest (Eds.), *Cognitive assessment*. New York: Guilford Press.

DeBono, K. G. (1989). On the processing of functionally-relevant consumer information: Another look at source factors. *Advances in Consumer Research*, 16, 312-317.

Herek, G. M. (1986). The instrumentality of attitudes: Toward a neofunctional theory. *Journal of Social Issues*, 42, 99-114.

Katz, D. (1960). The functional approach to the study of attitudes. *Public Opinion Quarterly*, 24, 163-204.

Shavitt, S. (1989). Operationalizing functional theories of attitude. In A. R. Pratkanis, S. J. Breckler and A. G. Greenwald (Eds.), *Attitude structure and function* (pp. 311-338). Hillsdale, NJ: Erlbaum.

Shavitt, S., and Fazio, R. H. (1987, May). *Attitude functions in the attitude-behavior relationship*. Paper presented at the annual meeting of the Midwestern Psychological Association, Chicago, IL.

Smith, M. B., Bruner, J. S., and White, R. W. (1956). *Opinions and personality*. New York: Wiley.

Zanna, M. P., and Rempel, J. K. (1988). Attitudes: A new look at an old concept. In D. Bar-Tal and A. Kruglanski (Eds.), *The social psychology of knowledge*. New York: Cambridge University Press.

Valenced Emotions in Satisfaction: A Look at Affect in Shopping
Mai Neo, University of Pittsburgh
Audrey J. Murrell, University of Pittsburgh

ABSTRACT

Emotion and satisfaction were studied in the context of shopping for oneself and for another person. Four clusters were identified for each situation: (1) positive/happy, (2) unemotional, (3) negative/sad and (4) positive/efficacy. Three core emotions were also identified, (1) efficacy, (2) negative and (3) positive while shopping for oneself, and (1) efficacy and (2) negative while shopping for others. The results showed that people have positive/happy emotions while shopping for themselves and positive/efficacious emotions while shopping for others. This positive/happy cluster exhibited higher satisfaction while shopping for oneself, whereas the positive/efficacy cluster exhibited higher satisfaction while shopping for other people.

BACKGROUND

Emotion can be thought of as a specific instance of affect states. Emotions are an intense and stimulus-specific affect state (Clark and Isen 1982; Gardner 1985) that demand more attention to a stimulus and can disrupt ongoing goal-directed activity (Clark and Isen 1982). To the extent that emotions appear in marketing research, they tend to be conceptualized in a very global context, where the individual components are aggregated to form a single positive-negative emotion continuum (Schwartz and Shaver 1987; Shaver, Schwartz, Kirson and O'Connor 1987; Westbrook 1987).

In marketing, emotion is extensively studied in the advertising and media contexts in terms of positive or negative feelings toward the ad (i.e., prepurchase situations). It has been noted by researchers that exploring the antecedents of attitudes, such as emotions, is important because they are responsible for the consumer's liking or disliking of the ad (Murry, Lastovicka and Singh 1992), act as intervening variables that mediate the relationship between ad content and viewing time (Olney, Holbrook and Batra 1991) and have strong effects on attitude toward the ad (Holbrook and Batra 1987; MacInnis and Park 1991). Consumers frequently generate more than one emotion after exposures to stimuli (Polivy 1981). For example, Aaker, Stayman and Vezina (1988) provided an inventory of 31 feeling clusters, 16 positive and 15 negative that were elicited by advertising (e.g., "delighted", ""warm/tender", and "sad"). However, these prepurchase situations are not the only context where emotions play an important role. Other researchers have explored the impact of affect in postpurchase contexts. Research in this area of marketing has looked at the impact on consumer satisfaction and product consumption (Westbrook 1980; Westbrook 1987; Westbrook and Oliver 1991). This research asserts that satisfaction is not solely a cognitive phenomenon. Rather, it is also comprised of affect or feeling, in that consumers feel subjectively good (satisfaction), or subjectively bad (dissatisfaction) concerning shopping decisions. Westbrook (1980) demonstrated that affect is linked to high levels of consumer satisfaction. While this research assumes that multiple sources of affect produce an effect on product satisfaction, limited evidence exists that specifies a taxonomy for these multiple affect sources.

Recently, Westbrook and Oliver (1991) investigated the interrelationship between consumption emotion and satisfaction by way of taxonomic and dimensional analyses to identify patterns of emotional response to product experiences. Consumption emotion refers to emotional responses elicited during product usage or consumption experiences. These emotions can be can be assessed as distinctive categories (e.g., joy, anger, and fear) or they can be analyzed in terms of structural dimensions underlying these emotional categories, such as pleasantness/unpleasantness, relaxation/action, or calmness/excitement (Russell 1979).

To develop this taxonomy, Westbrook and Oliver (1991) conducted a field study on a sample of owners of newly purchased cars. A convenience sample of 125 respondents were surveyed on their "feelings and attitudes" toward their most recent car purchase. To measure consumption emotion, Izard's (1977) DES-II scale was used. Positive emotions examined were interest and joy. Negative emotions surveyed were anger, contempt, disgust, shame, guilt, sadness, and fear. Surprise, as a neutral emotion, was also examined along with an overall consumer satisfaction scale.

Using a k-means cluster analysis, a five-cluster solution was revealed. The *happy/content* cluster contained people who reported frequent interest and joy but infrequent surprise and negative emotions. Those in the *pleasant/surprise* cluster were people who were high on joy and surprise but low on all negative emotions. The *unemotional* cluster contained subjects whose scores fell below all measures of consumption emotion, especially joy and surprise. Subjects in the *unpleasant/surprise* cluster were high on surprise and most negative emotions (especially sadness) yet low on joy. The *angry/upset* cluster contained subjects who reported frequent negative emotions, especially disgust and contempt, and somewhat frequently surprise and interest emotions. These emotion clusters were then related to an overall satisfaction measure for the product. Results showed that the two most satisfied groups were the happy/content and the pleasant/surprise clusters. The happy/content cluster appeared slightly less satisfied than the pleasant/surprise group. Next in the level of satisfaction were the dissatisfied groups, which included the unemotional, unpleasant/surprise, and the angry/upset groups (in descending order).

As noted by Westbrook and Oliver (1991), their own work has three limitations that are addressed in the current research. First, their exploration of consumption-emotion patterns is limited to the categories of basic emotions developed in Izard's (1977) typology. Other typologies may yield different patterns of emotional response as well as different relationships to satisfaction. Second, the product category they used was automobiles. Other product categories may yield different patterns of emotional responses as well or a more generalized affect state can be realized. Lastly, the dimensionality of consumption-emotions and its relationship to satisfaction should be studied across multiple consumption contexts. Individuals may have different emotional responses depending on the nature of consumption behavior; that is, when consumption is for self or for other people.

PROPOSED RESEARCH

Our study extends the Westbrook and Oliver (1991) research by addressing these three limitations. Specifically, we examine the impact of emotions other than those provided by the Izard (1977) typology. The taxonomy provided by Izard (1977) and used by Westbrook and Oliver (1991) utilized a limited number of affect terms that included 7 negative emotions, 2 positive emotions and 1 neutral emotion. We include a larger number of positive emotions to provide a more diverse index of emotions.

Second, we examine consumer shopping behavior in general, instead of for a specific purchase. There is some evidence for a general affect state associated with consumer response to advertising (Aaker, Stayman and Hagerty 1986) and consumer satisfaction (Westbrook and Oliver 1991). Thus, by examining a diverse set of emotions, we may be able to isolate a core set of emotions experienced during shopping.

Third, we examine the emotions experienced while shopping for oneself and while shopping for others. Shopping affect may depend on the product being purchased as well as on the recipient. Dawson, Bloch and Ridgway (1990) posits that strong shopping motives are associated with positive emotional responses that occur in the marketplace. In addition, these emotional responses are particular to a specific context or situation. Thus, by exploring a shopper's satisfaction in terms of the recipient of the action (i.e., shopping for self or shopping for another), we hope to find differences in the affect experienced by these two shopping activities.

METHOD

Subjects

Two hundred forty-six undergraduate students participated in this study. One hundred twenty-seven students were recruited from introductory and social psychology courses at the University of Pittsburgh. The remaining one hundred nineteen participants were enrolled in a study skills course at Fisk University. The sample was composed of seventy-three (29.7%) males and one hundred seventy-three females (70.3%). One hundred twenty-six (51.2%) were black, one hundred thirteen (45.9%) were white, and 7 (2.8%) came from other minority groups. Our sample had an average age of 19.6 years old and 91.4% of subjects were between 17 and 22 years old.

Procedure

All participants completed a questionnaire that asked about themselves and various aspects of their shopping experiences. Students were asked to provide some descriptive data about themselves, including information about their education, future plans, and family background. Next, students were questioned about their shopping behavior.

An affect measure was employed in order to determine the kinds of emotions these shoppers experience during and after shopping. Specifically, participants were asked to rate the extent to which they experience each of eleven states while shopping for themselves and for others separately. Ratings were reported on a 1 (not at all) to 5 (very much) frequency scale. Students also completed the Westbrook and Black (1985) shopping motivation measure which involves considering how much satisfaction they derive from seventeen different types of shopping experiences, settings and outcomes. These items were rated on a 1 (none at all) to 7 (a great deal) magnitude scale. After completing all measures, students were debriefed and thanked for their participation.

MEASURES

Affect States

The affect scale created in order to assess the types of emotions shoppers are likely to feel while shopping for themselves and for someone else was taken directly from Murrell, Frieze, Schmidt, Neo and Federouch (under review). The eleven emotions included were: happy, independent, silly, attractive, depressed, sad, guilty, confident, competent, helpful, and loving. These affect descriptors were adapted from Westbrook and Oliver (1991) with two changes. Several positive adjectives were added to include a range of affect experiences during shopping. And second, to be more applicable to general shopping activities, adjectives were selected that described general affect states. Participants used the affect scale to rate how they felt in two situations: while shopping for themselves and while shopping for others.

Shopping Motivation

Westbrook and Black's (1985) measure of shopping satisfaction consists of seven shopping motivation subscales. Anticipated utility, the first subscale, described the expectations of benefits or pleasure that the shopper hopes to receive by purchasing a product. Role enactment is a motivation which occurs when the consumer shops in order to fulfill a particular role which is related to shopping activity, such as being a housewife. Negotiation is shopping in order to bargain with salespeople over the price of the product. The fourth shopping motivation, choice optimization, involves searching for exactly the right product in the least amount of time. Shopping with the purpose of interacting with other individuals, either shoppers or salespeople, is called affiliation. The power and authority subscales refer to controlling or enjoying a position of higher status over someone else, usually a salesperson. Finally, stimulation motivation is at work when a shopper wants to see new and interesting surroundings. Westbrook and Black's reliability coefficient for these subscales were .64, .69, .54, .73, .67, .57, and .79 respectively. Most of the reliability coefficients from the present sample were higher than those reported than in the Westbrook and Black (1985) study, improving substantially for the anticipated utility and negotiation subscales, but decreasing slightly for power and authority subscale: .74, .73, .81, .73, .60, .72, .81. These differences could be explained by the sample differences in that college students typically have limited financial resources and would be more concerned about the utility and price merchandise and less over the use of power and authority, relative new dimensions for these individuals. The reliability coefficient for the overall shopping motivation measure was .84 for the present sample.

RESULTS

A k-means cluster similar to that used in Westbrook and Oliver (1991) was performed on the individual emotion ratings. The k-means clustering algorithm used indicated that a four-cluster solution of consumers produced both the most efficient results and interpretable solution. Five cluster solutions were examined to replicate that of Westbrook and Oliver (1990), with the four cluster solution being preferred, as it yielded the largest proportionate reduction in the trace of the within-clusters matrix, a measure of within-group homogeneity. These analyses were conducted separately for emotion states experienced while shopping for oneself and while shopping for others. In terms of emotions states experienced while shopping for oneself, four clusters were revealed. These clusters differed significantly across all emotion states (Wilk's Lambda = .067, F = 29.53, p<.0001 for self; Wilk's Lambda = .064, F = 29.56, p<.0001 for other).

We labeled Cluster 1 the *positive/happy* shoppers (n=20) were subjects who reported frequently on happy, independent, silly, attractive, confident, competent, helpful and loving emotions and infrequently on negative emotions. Cluster 2 was labeled the *unemotional* shoppers (n=31) reported infrequent experiences on all emotion states. Cluster 3 was labeled the *negative/sad* shoppers (n=60) and were subject to the highest frequency of depressed, sad, and guilty emotion states. Cluster 4 was labeled *positive/efficacy* (n=135) and was moderately high on positive emotions such as happy, independent, attractive and also high on instrumental emotions such as competent, confident, helpful and loving (see Figure 1).

For emotions experienced while shopping for others, we labeled cluster 1 (n=46) the *negative/sad* shoppers which was

FIGURE 1
While Shopping for Self

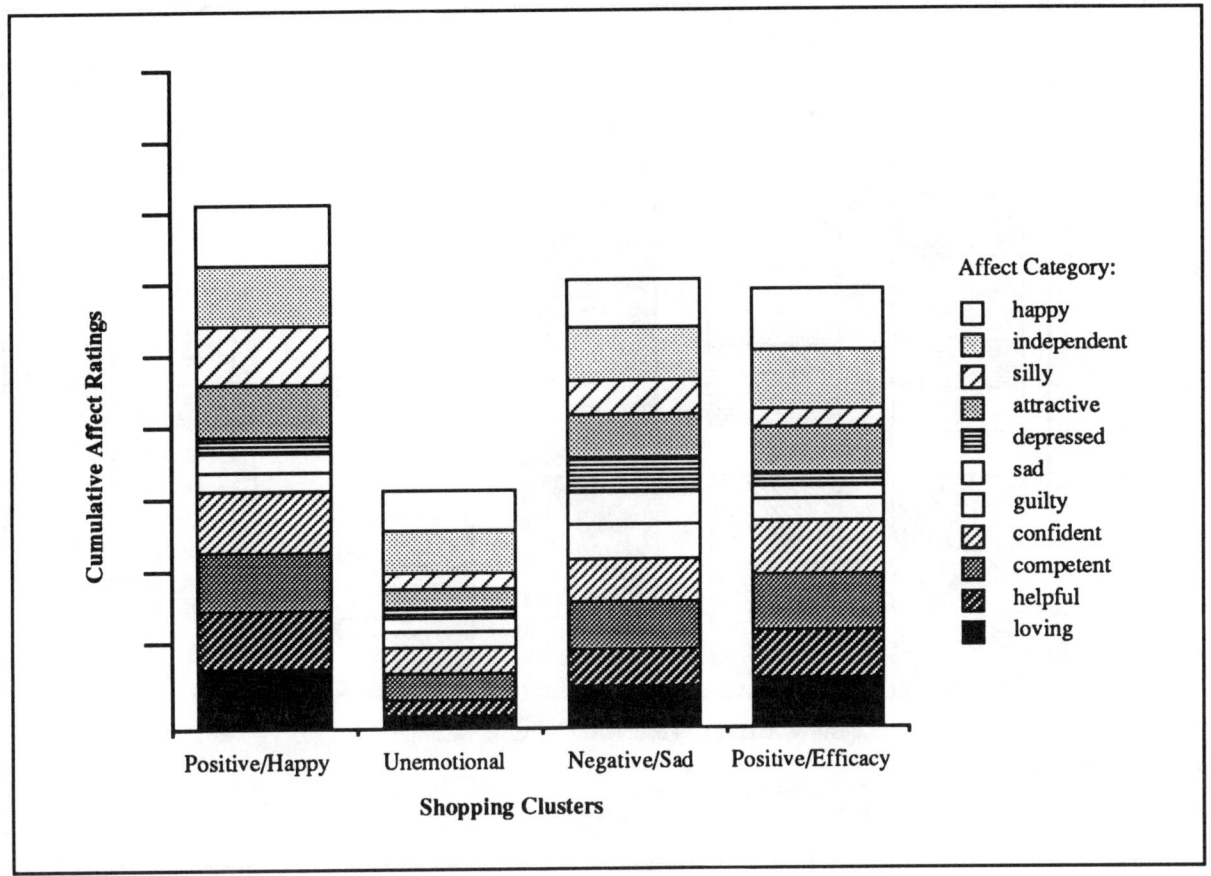

highest on the silly, depressed, sad, and guilty emotion states. Cluster 2 (n=82) was labeled the *positive/average* shoppers and was low across all emotion states. Cluster 3 (n=100) was labeled the *positive/efficacy* shoppers and was high on positive dimensions such as happy, independent, and attractive, and also on instrumental emotion dimensions such as confident, competent, helpful, and loving. Cluster 4 (n=18) represents the smallest cluster group and consistent of the *unemotional* shoppers. These individuals were the lowest across all emotion states (see Figure 2).

Several similarities and a few differences emerged between the emotions clusters when shopping for oneself and when shopping for another person. In both cases the largest cluster group was the positive/efficacy group or those individuals who experienced both positive emotions (e.g., happy) and instrumental emotions (e.g., competent) when shopping for oneself or others. The second largest cluster group when shopping for oneself however, was the negative/sad affect cluster. These individuals experienced primarily negative emotions when shopping for themselves (e.g., sad). While this cluster was present for affect experienced when shopping for others, this group was small in number and also experienced feelings, labeled as "silly" as part of this negative affect. Interestingly, feeling silly when shopping for oneself was contained in the positive/happy cluster, suggesting that feeling silly represents a fun and frivolous type of emotion when shopping for oneself, but a foolish or nonsensical feeling when shopping for others.

To examine the relationship between patterns of consumer emotions and satisfaction, the mean satisfaction ratings were compared for each of the Westbrook and Black (1987) dimensions (utility, negotiation, power, affiliation, choice optimizing and stimulation) across the four cluster groups, examining self and other ratings separately. For emotions experienced while shopping for oneself, the cluster groups differed significantly across the utility dimension (F (3,242) = 3.79, p<.01), the negotiation dimension (F (3,241) = 5.86, p<.001), the affiliation dimension (F (3,242) = 5.42, p<.001) and the stimulation dimension (F (3,242) = 4.59, p<.004) of shopping satisfaction scale. The four clusters differed only marginally across the role dimension (F (3,239) = 2.19, p<.10) and were not significantly different for the choice optimizing dimension of shopping satisfaction. Post-hoc comparison (Tukey HSD tests) indicated that the positive/happy cluster was significantly higher in satisfaction on the utility, negotiation, affiliation, power and stimulation dimensions than the negative/sad cluster. In addition, the positive/happy cluster was significantly higher in satisfaction derived from the utility, affiliation, power and stimulation dimensions compared to the positive/efficacy cluster. This cluster was significantly higher than the unemotional cluster group on the utility and affiliation dimensions of consumer satisfaction (in all cases, p<.05). Thus, similar to the findings of Westbrook and Oliver (1991), the positive/happy cluster appears to have the highest level of satisfaction across the various satisfaction dimensions (see Table 1).

For emotions experienced while shopping for others, the four cluster groups differed significantly across the utility (F (3,242) = 4.80, p<.003), negotiation (F (3,242) = 2.74, p<.004), affiliation (F (3,242) = 3.95, p<.009), power (F (3,242) = 6.58, p<.001), and stimulation (F (3,242) = 4.04, p<.008) dimensions of consumer satisfaction. The four cluster groups did not differ across the role or choice optimizing dimensions of satisfaction. Post-hoc compari-

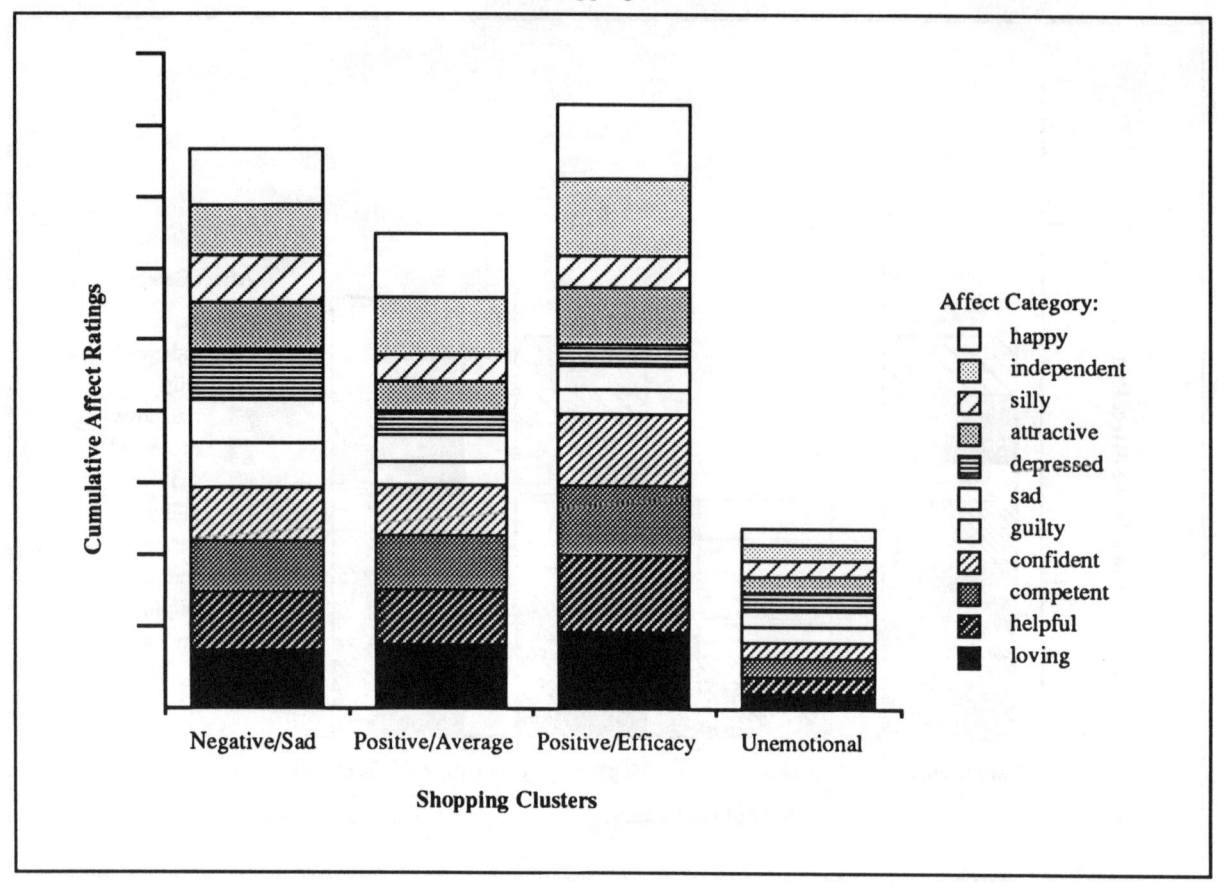

FIGURE 2
While Shopping for Others

TABLE 1
Means for Satisfaction Experienced While Shopping for Self
Emotion Clusters

Satisfaction dimensions	Happy	Sad	Unemotional	Efficacious
Utility	5.7	4.5	5.0	5.3
Role	5.2	4.3	5.0	5.1
Negotiation	5.7	3.8	4.2	4.7
Choice	5.5	5.0	5.4	5.5
Affiliation	5.3	3.9	4.0	4.3
Power	5.0	3.5	3.9	4.6
Stimulation	5.0	3.3	4.2	4.2

sons (Tukey HSD tests) revealed that the positive/efficacy cluster was significantly higher in satisfaction derived from the utility, negotiation, affiliation, power and stimulation dimensions than the unemotional cluster group. In addition, the positive/efficacy cluster was significantly higher in satisfaction derived from the utility dimension than the average cluster group and was higher in satisfaction derived from affiliation than the negative/sad cluster group (see Table 2).

To determine the nature of the "core" emotion states experienced during shopping, subjects' responses to the eleven emotional states were factor analyzed using an oblique rotation for self and others' ratings, separately. Results revealed that when shopping for self, three factors emerged and accounted for 61% of the total variance. Factor 1, *Efficacy* (Eigenvalue=3.53) was composed of helpful, loving, confident, competent and attractive emotions. Factor 2, *Negative* (Eigenvalue=2.01), was composed of depressed, sad and guilty emotions. Factor 3, *Positive* (Eigenvalue=1.12), was composed of happy and independent emotions (see Table 3).

In terms of emotions experienced while shopping for others, two factors emerged and accounted for 61% of the total variance. Factor 1, *Efficacy* (Eigenvalue=4.16), contained confident, competent, independent, loving, happy, helpful and attractive emotion states. Factor 2, *Negative* (Eigenvalue=2.54), contained depressed, sad, guilty and silly emotion states (see Table 4).

TABLE 2
Means for Satisfaction Experienced While Shopping for Others
Emotion Clusters

Satisfaction dimensions	Happy	Sad	Efficacious	Unemotional
Utility	5.0	4.9	5.5	4.4
Role	4.9	4.9	5.2	4.5
Negotiation	4.6	4.2	4.9	4.0
Choice	5.4	5.5	5.5	4.8
Affiliation	3.9	4.1	4.6	3.9
Power	4.3	3.9	4.8	3.4
Stimulation	4.1	4.2	4.4	2.9

TABLE 3
Factor Analysis (Shopping for Self)

Factor	Loadings
Efficacy	
Helpful	.819
Loving	.749
Confident	.655
Competent	.664
Attractive	.594
Negative	
Depressed	.869
Sad	.850
Guilty	.646
Positive	
Happy	.817
Independent	.690

DISCUSSION

The results of the present study showed that people tend to exhibit primarily positive/happy emotions (happy, independent, silly, attractive, confident, helpful and loving) while shopping for themselves and positive/efficacious emotions (happy, independent, attractive, confident, competent, helpful and loving) when shopping for other people. These results are consistent with the results of the Westbrook and Oliver (1991) study which showed that a large percentage of consumers experience positive emotions during consumption (e.g., 21% in the "happy/content" cluster and 23% in the pleasant-surprise cluster).

In addition, we found the positive/happy cluster was significantly higher on many of the satisfaction dimensions compared to other clusters when shopping for oneself. The positive/efficacy cluster was higher on many of the satisfaction dimensions than the other clusters while shopping for other people. These results show that people generate positive emotions when shopping, although they tend to be more goal-directed in their emotions while shopping for others than when they shop for themselves. Again, these results are consistent with that of Westbrook and Oliver (1991) who found that significantly higher levels of satisfaction among the happiness/contentment and pleasant-surprise patterns across all clusters. An implication of this finding is that emotion and satisfaction is contingent upon the context in which the activity takes place. One direction for future research is investigate whether contexts drive affect or whether context colors a consumer's affect judgments.

The core emotions identified in this research while shopping for oneself were efficacy, negative and positive. Efficacy and negative were the core emotions identified while shopping for others. These results showed that primarily positive emotions were exhibited while people shopped for themselves. When they shopped for others, the efficacious and positive emotions merged under one core emotion which we labeled efficacy. One implication of this finding is that when people shop for themselves, they may do so because of the pleasure of shopping, whereas when they shop for others, they tend to be goal-directed, a characteristic not unusual in the marketplace.

Another implication of this finding of core emotions is that it goes beyond simply being product-specific. Westbrook and Oliver (1991) had only looked at consumption of automobiles, a focus too narrow to capture the full effect of consumer evaluations. As stated by Westbrook (1980), being product-specific may not be particularly important to all consumers. Therefore, by looking a behavioral context such as shopping, core emotions yielded may be more generalizable to other consumer contexts.

Overall, satisfaction in shopping for self is higher than for other. This suggests that high levels of satisfaction and positive affect was higher for self because of an exposure effect. In other

TABLE 4
Factor Analysis (Shopping for Others)

Factor	Loadings
Efficacy	
Confident	.854
Competent	.793
Independent	.783
Loving	.757
Happy	.750
Helpful	.744
Attractive	.629
Negative	
Depressed	.903
Sad	.867
Guilty	.792
Silly	.566

words, subjects shopped more frequently for self than other due to familiarity and exposure to the activity, thus increasing the affect and satisfaction experienced. A closer examination of emotions demonstrated by this study will help marketers better understand the role of emotions in consumer behavior.

A contribution of this paper is that it looks at satisfaction and emotional responses within a behavioral context, and not solely in a product-specific context. Our research has found that consumers tend to generate a more positive range of emotions when they shop, than previously observed in the literature. We have also shown that positive emotions have more dimensions than merely joy and interest as noted by Westbrook and Oliver (1991). We have incorporated the various dimensionalities of satisfaction and consumption emotions to provide a better understanding of the two constructs, and examined core emotions that are generated by consumers when they shop. One limitation of this research is the use of self-reporting rating scales to tap into the affective dimensions. However, we feel that these findings are nonetheless important because the link between emotion and satisfaction has implications for product evaluations, preferences, and choice.

REFERENCES

Aaker, D.A., Stayman, D.M. and Vezina R. (1988), "Identifying Feelings Elicited by Advertising," *Psychology and Marketing*, 5 (Spring), 1-16.

_____ and Hagerty, M.R. (1986), "Warmth in Advertising: Measurement, Impact, and Sequence Effects," *Journal of Consumer Research*, 12 (March), 365-381.

Clark, M. and Isen, A. M. (1982), "Toward Understanding the Relationship Between Feelings States and Social Behavior," in *Cognitive Social Psychology*, eds. Albert Hastoff and Alice Isen, New York: Elsevier/North-Holland, 73-108.

Dawson, S., Bloch P.H., and Ridgway, N.M. (1990), "Shopping Motives, Emotional States, and Retail Outcomes," *Journal of Retailing*, 66 (Winter), 408-427.

Gardner, M. P. (1985), "Mood States and Consumer Behavior: A Critical Review," *Journal of Consumer Research*, 12 (December), 281-300.

Holbrook, M. B. and Batra, R. (1987), "Assessing the Role of Emotions as Mediators of Consumer Responses to Advertising," *Journal of Consumer Research*, 14 (December), 404-420.

Izard, C. E. (1977), *Human Emotions*, New York: Plenum.

MacInnis, D.J. and Park, C.W. (1991), "The Differential Role of Characteristics of Music on High-and Low-Involvement Consumers' Processing of Ads," *Journal of Consumer Research*, 18 (September), 161-173.

Murrell, A.J., Frieze, I.H., Schmidt, L.C., Neo, M., and Federouch, A.G. (under review), "The Impact of Shopping Motivation on Consumer Behavior and Affect: A look at Young Adult Shoppers," *Journal of Retailing*.

Murry, J.P. Jr., Lastovicka, J.L., and Singh, S.N. (1992), "Feeling and Liking Responses to Television Programs," *Journal of Consumer Research*, 18 (March), 441-451.

Olney, T.J., Holbrook, M.B., and Batra, R. (1991), "Consumer Responses to Advertising: The Effects of Ad Content, Emotions, and Attitude toward the Ad on Viewing Time," *Journal of Consumer Research*, 17 (March), 440-453.

Polivy, J. (1981), "On the Induction of Emotion in the Laboratory: Discrete Moods or Multiple Affect States?" *Journal of Personality and Social Psychology*, 41, 803-817.

Russell, J. A. (1979), "Affective Space Is Bipolar," *Journal of Personality and Social Psychology*, 37 (September), 345-356.

Schwartz, J. C. and Shaver, P. (1987), "Emotions and Emotion Knowledge in Interpersonal Relations," *Advances in Personal Relationships*, 1, 197-241.

Shaver, P., Schwartz, J., Kirson, D. and O'Connor, C. (1987), "Emotion Knowledge: Further Exploration of a Prototype Approach," *Journal of Personality and Social Psychology*, 52 (June), 1061-1086.

Westbrook, R. A. (1980), "Intrapersonal Affective Influences upon Consumer Satisfaction with Products," *Journal of Consumer Research*, 7 (June), 49-54.

_____ and Black, W. C. (1985), "A Motivation-Based Shopper Typology," *Journal of Retailing*, 61, 78-103.

_____ (1987), "Product/Consumption-Based Affective Responses and Postpurchase Processes," *Journal of Marketing Research*, 24 (August), 258-270.

_____ and Oliver, R. L. (1991), "Dimensionality of Consumption Emotion Patterns and Consumer Satisfaction," *Journal of Consumer Research*, 18 (June), 84-91.

An Exploratory Investigation of Holistic and Analytic Modes of Product Perception
Hans Baumgartner, Pennsylvania State University

ABSTRACT

A methodology for studying holistic and analytic product perception is described, and some conditions under which products are perceived holistically (i.e., as unitary entities) or analytically (i.e., as composites of individual components) are specified. The results of a study in which subjects have to classify triads of sweaters shows that the proposed procedure is useful for studying holistic versus analytic product perception and that consumers' classification behavior is systematically related to their motivational task set (spontaneous versus meticulous impression formation) and two individual difference variables (need for cognition, style of processing).

INTRODUCTION

When a consumer perceives a product, his or her perceptual experience may consist in a holistic apprehension of the stimulus as a unitary entity, in an analytic registration of various product attributes, or a mixture of both. Later on I will define the terms holistic and analytic perception operationally, but for now it suffices to say that when consumers look at products holistically, they form a global impression of the product as a unitary whole, whereas when consumers look at products analytically, they view the product as a composite of individual components.

How sensory input is encoded (i.e., in a holistic or analytic fashion) depends on aspects of the stimulus (e.g., whether an object is described verbally or presented visually; cf. Holbrook and Moore 1981), on characteristics of the person perceiving the stimulus (both temporary individual differences such as a person's mood state and chronic individual differences such as a consumer's general tendency to structure the environment in a global or differentiated fashion; cf. Murray et al. 1990; Witkin et al. 1962), on the kind of task a person is engaged in (e.g., whether two or more products are considered simultaneously or sequentially; cf. Holbrook and Moore 1981), and on the context in which the task is to be accomplished (e.g., whether or not there is time pressure; cf. Smith and Kemler Nelson 1984).

This paper reports an exploratory investigation of the phenomenon of holistic versus analytic perception of stimuli in the context of product categorization. My objectives are twofold. The primary goal is to explore the applicability of a methodology used successfully by researchers in psychology (e.g., Garner 1974; Smith and Kemler Nelson 1984; Ward 1980, 1983) to distinguish between holistic and analytic modes of product perception. Traditionally, this problem (if addressed at all in consumer research) has been approached by use of regression analysis with interaction effects (e.g., Holbrook and Moore 1981). Because of the robustness of the linear model, this may not be the most effective procedure. On the other hand, existing research in psychology has used rather artificial stimuli (e.g., squares varying in size and brightness), and it is not obvious that the methodology is applicable to more 'real' product stimuli.

A secondary goal is to look at several variables that are expected to influence whether product stimuli are processed holistically or analytically. Evidence for differences in mode of processing as a function of these variables would attest to the usefulness of the proposed methodology and also point to the need for increased attention to whether consumers perceive product stimuli in a holistic or analytic fashion.

PRIOR RESEARCH

Most research on product perception in consumer behavior has explicitly or implicitly espoused an analytical view of the world. Products are often regarded as bundles of attributes, and models of attitudes (Wilkie and Pessemier 1973) and judgment and decision making (Bettman 1979) - the two dominant research streams in the field - are built on this fundamental assumption. Thus, attitudes toward products are assumed to derive from evaluations of product attributes, and product choices are thought to be based on comparing alternative products on their various attributes.

Only recently have researchers begun to look at alternative conceptualizations. For example, in the area of categorization several researchers have discussed holistic forms of comparisons (based on overall similarity between objects) of a stimulus to category prototypes or exemplars (see Cohen and Basu 1987 for a review). This interest in holistic approaches to categorization has spilled over to the attitude area, where researchers have proposed affect generation mechanisms in which a product is endowed with an evaluation of a product category to which it is similar (cf. Sujan 1985; Wright 1975). In a related vein, in the study of judgment and decision-making, researchers have examined the notion of configural judgments, the basic idea being that overall evaluations of products are more than just the sum of individual attribute evaluations (see, for example, Holbrook and Moore 1981). On balance, however, holistic approaches to product perception have not figured prominently in consumer research.

Despite the dearth of empirical work on the topic, the issue of when consumers process product information holistically or analytically is clearly important. Product perceptions form the basis for subsequent higher-order cognitive processes such as attitude formation and judgment and decision making. As indicated, most models in these areas of research explicitly or implicitly assume that product perceptions are analytic. The present study will provide evidence that analytic processing is restricted to certain situations and that, in the future, consumer researchers will have to concern themselves more with cases in which product perceptions are actually holistic.

Research shows that holistic processing occurs frequently under conditions in which cognitive resources are limited (e.g., when people are not able, not motivated, or do not have the opportunity to engage in analytic processing; see Alba and Hutchinson, 1987, and Cohen and Basu, 1987, for reviews). Many consumer situations are exactly of this type (Alba and Hutchinson 1987). The research described in this paper makes an important first step in outlining an approach to studying holistic and analytic product perception and in delineating some conditions under which each process is most likely to occur.

THEORETICAL DEVELOPMENT

The impetus for the proposed research comes from work in perceptual and cognitive psychology on integral and separable attribute combinations (cf. Garner 1974, Lecture 5). Attributes are called integral if they combine to form an entity that is ordinarily processed in a holistic fashion. Attributes are called separable if they produce an entity that is generally processed analytically. Instances of integral attribute combinations are difficult to come by, the premier example being brightness and saturation (two of the three psychological attributes of colors). Instances of separable attribute combinations are more common, form and size being a frequently cited example.

Research has shown that judgements of similarity are based on overall similarity in the case of integral stimuli and are derived from shared components for separable stimuli. There is also evidence that children treat as integral attribute combinations that are perceived as separable by adults (e.g., Ward 1980). Furthermore, it has been found that under certain conditions - when there is a time constraint, when attention is diverted by a concurrent task, or when people are instructed to respond impressionistically (cf. Smith and Kemler Nelson 1984; Ward 1983) - even adults treat separable stimuli as integral.

In the study described below I will investigate the effects of a consumer's motivational task set (spontaneous versus meticulous impression formation) and two individual difference variables (need for cognition, style of processing) on mode of product perception for product stimuli that are separable. As pointed out by Mervis and Rosch (1975), aspects of stimuli that are normally called attributes are mostly separable, and integral attributes are at a lower level of abstraction that is probably not very relevant to marketing (e.g., brightness and saturation as dimensions of color). Furthermore, if stimuli that are in principle separable are processed as unitary entities under certain circumstances, this would provide fairly strong evidence that products composed of attributes at a level of abstraction useful to marketers are not always perceived analytically and that consumer researchers will have to deal more explicitly with situations in which products are perceived holistically.

The experimental paradigm used to distinguish holistic and analytic processing is based on restricted classifications of triads of stimuli (cf. Garner 1974, Lecture 5). Subjects are presented with sets of three objects and asked to select the two that "go the most together" (cf. Smith and Kemler Nelson 1984). In the simplest case the stimuli are constructed from two underlying dimensions. One pair of objects in a triad is identical on one dimension but substantially different on the other. A second pair is slightly different on both dimensions, but overall the two objects are quite similar. Classifications on the basis of overall similarity are reflective of holistic processing, whereas classifications based on identical values on one dimension are indicative of analytic processing. The third possible classification is considered haphazard.

Using this procedure, the effects of the following variables on mode of perception are investigated. First, the way in which consumers form an impression of the product stimuli should be related to classification behavior. Specifically, it is expected that subjects who are told to classify without much thinking and to rely on first impressions (spontaneous motivational task set) will provide more holistic (less analytic) classifications than subjects who are told to be careful and to take all the time needed (meticulous motivational task set). This prediction follows from the work of Smith and Kemler Nelson (1984, Experiment 5) and Ward (1983).

In addition, some subjects will not be given instructions as to how to classify the stimuli (control group). For these subjects (and possibly for subjects in one of the other two conditions whose task set resembles the one for control subjects), it is hypothesized that need for cognition (a person's preference for engaging in and enjoying thinking; cf. Cacioppo and Petty 1982) and style of processing (a person's preference for engaging in visual versus verbal processing of information; cf. Childers, Houston, and Heckler 1985) will be related to mode of classification. Specifically, it is expected that need for cognition will be positively correlated with the extent to which classifications are analytic, and it is also hypothesized that being a visualizer (verbalizer) will encourage more holistic (analytic) classification behavior. The rationale for the former hypothesis comes from the fact that need for cognition assesses enjoyment of "effortful *analytic* activity" (Petty and Cacioppo 1986, p. 151, emphasis added) and that, as discussed by Cacioppo and Petty (1982), need for cognition is related to field independence/dependence (the tendency of a person to structure the environment in a differentiated or global fashion, cf. Witkin et al. 1962), an individual difference variable which has been found to determine preference for analytic and holistic processing. The rationale for the latter hypothesis is that preference for engaging in visual processing of information involves imagery, which is holistic (MacInnis and Price 1987), and that imagery processing should lead to more holistic classifications than verbal processing (Holbrook and Moore 1981).

METHOD

Subjects

A total of 48 undergraduate students (25 females, 23 males) in two sections of a consumer behavior class participated in the study during class time. Subjects were assigned randomly to one of three treatment conditions: spontaneous motivational task set, meticulous motivational task set, and control group. Sixteen subjects participated in each of the three conditions.

Stimuli

Pictorial sweater designs similar to those used by Holbrook and Moore (1981) were developed which varied two attributes on four levels: size of the sweater (size) and density of the dot pattern (pattern). Convenience samples of students were used to calibrate the spacing of the four attribute levels.

Triads of sweaters were constructed such that two of the sweaters in each triad were identical on one dimension but were maximally different on the other dimension, whereas another pair of sweaters within each triad differed by only one scale step on both dimensions so that overall the two sweaters were quite similar although the two sweaters differed on both dimensions. With four levels on each of two attributes, this procedure yields 24 triads of sweaters; in 12 of these, two sweaters were identical on the size dimension, and in the other 12 there was an identity on the pattern dimension.

Stimulus booklets were then constructed which contained the 24 triads of sweaters, each on a separate page, with size and pattern identities in alternate order. The arrangement of the three sweaters in each triad was such that holistic, analytic, and haphazard classifications involved the left and middle, left and right, and middle and right sweaters equally often.

Procedure

Subjects received a booklet that contained all experimental tasks. They were told that they would be shown three objects at a time side by side (arranged in the order 1-2-3) and that they had to decide which two of the three objects went the most together. They were to indicate their decision by putting down 12, 13, or 23, depending on whether they thought the left and middle, left and right, or middle and right sweaters went the most together. It was stressed that there were no right or wrong answers, and subjects were also told that at the beginning and at the end of the classification task they would be required to mark down the time (to the nearest minute) from a big clock placed on a table in front of the classroom.

Immediately before subjects started the classification task, their motivational task set was manipulated. In the spontaneous motivational task set condition, subjects were told, "When grouping the three objects, make your classification without thinking about it. Just give your first impression, just let whatever happens happen." In the meticulous motivational task set condition, subjects were told, "When grouping the three objects, carefully decide which two objects should go together. Be meticulous and careful, taking all the time you need." In the control condition, no instructions were given to subjects.

Subjects then put down the time to the nearest minute and classified the 24 sweaters. When they were done, they again put down the time to the nearest minute, and they indicated how important they thought the dimensions of size and pattern had been in their classifications of the sweaters (11-point scale from -5 to +5, with endpoints of 'size much more important' and 'pattern much more important').

Finally, subjects completed the 34-item need for cognition scale (Cacioppo and Petty 1982) and the 22-item style of processing scale (Childers, Houston, and Heckler 1985). Higher scores on the two instruments are indicative of greater need for cognition and a preference for visual rather than verbal processing of information.

RESULTS

Manipulation check

The time taken to perform the classification task was used to check whether the manipulation of motivational task set had the intended effect. Statistical tests of mean differences among conditions were performed using dummy variable regression (with levels of significance referring to one-sided tests because of the directional nature of all the tests).

The overall regression was significant ($F(2,44)=5.99$, $p<0.01$), and as expected, subjects who were told to classify spontaneously completed the task significantly faster than subjects who were asked to be meticulous (means of 4.56 min and 6.73 min, respectively, $t_{44}=3.36$, $p<0.01$). Subjects in the control condition (mean of 6.06 min) also took significantly longer than spontaneous subjects ($t_{44}=2.36$, $p<0.05$), and their classification time did not differ significantly from that of meticulous subjects ($t_{44}=1.04$, n.s.). In the context of this experiment, the 'natural' classification strategy adopted by subjects in terms of time taken was thus to be meticulous.

Effect of motivational task set on mode of classification

In classifying a given triad of sweaters, there are three possible outcomes: holistic, analytic, or haphazard. Before looking at the hypotheses of substantive interest, it is necessary to check that (1) the incidence of haphazard classifications is low and that (2) a spontaneous motivational task set does *not* primarily lead to more haphazard classifications.

Overall, the mean number of haphazard responses was 2.67 out of 24 (11 percent), which is low. Furthermore, there were no significant differences in the mean number of haphazard responses by condition (means of 2.50, 2.75, and 2.75 for spontaneous, meticulous, and control subjects, respectively).

An index reflecting mode of classification for each subject was constructed as the ratio of number of analytic classifications to holistic plus analytic classifications (summed over all 24 triads of sweaters and excluding haphazard responses). The resulting index ranges from 0 to 1, with 0 indicating entirely holistic processing and 1 indicating entirely analytic processing. Across all subjects, the mean on the classification index was 0.36, with a range from 0 to .96. Thus, on average 36 percent (64 percent) of the classifications were analytic (holistic). Since the stimuli were presented in visual form in all conditions, this may have resulted in relatively holistic classifications (Holbrook and Moore 1981). However, it is not the overall classification behavior across conditions that is of interest here, but the relative proportion of holistic and analytic classifications by condition.

Since control subjects took just as long to classify the sweaters as meticulous subjects, regression analysis with contrast coding was used to test the following two hypotheses (which involve orthogonal contrasts): control and meticulous subjects will be equally holistic/analytic in their classifications, and control and meticulous subjects combined will provide significantly more analytic (less holistic) classifications than spontaneous subjects.

Although the overall regression was not significant, the specific effects tended to confirm this prediction. Control and meticulous subjects did not differ significantly in their classification behavior (means of .40 and .38, respectively, $t_{45}=.23$, n.s.), and control and meticulous subjects classified in a more analytic/less holistic fashion than spontaneous subjects (means of .39 for control/meticulous condition and .29 for spontaneous condition, $t_{45}=1.53$, $p<0.10$). It was also checked whether pattern or size identities led to more analytic classifications, but there were no differences.

The pattern of the means is clear-cut, although the statistical significance of the result is admittedly not very strong. In part this is probably due to the small sample size. Another reason may be that the manipulation of motivational task set was too weak.

Effect of classification time on mode of classification

To get further insights into subjects' classification behavior, an internal analysis was conducted on the relationship between classification time and mode of classification. The correlation between the two variables was .25 ($t_{45}=1.73$, $p<0.05$), indicating that the longer a person took to classify the sweaters, the more analytic/less holistic his or her responses tended to be. There were no differences in the strength of this relationship by condition.

The effects of need for cognition and style of processing on mode of classification

Regressions of the mode of classification index on the dummy-variable (or contrast) coded manipulations, need for cognition (or style of processing) and their interactions were conducted to test whether the two individual difference variables have an effect on classification behavior and whether the strength of the relationship differs by condition.

Overall, the correlation between proportion of holistic/analytic classifications and need for cognition was .24 ($t_{46}=1.71$, $p<.05$). Furthermore, the correlations by condition showed an interesting pattern: $r=-.04$ for spontaneous condition ($t_{14}=-.17$, n.s.), $r=.30$ for meticulous condition ($t_{14}=1.18$, n.s.), and $r=.73$ for control condition ($t_{14}=3.95$, $p<0.01$). Based on the results of an overall regression analysis ($F(5,42)=2.45$, $p<0.05$), the difference in the magnitude of the correlations between meticulous and control groups was of borderline significance ($t_{42}=1.51$, $p<0.10$), while the difference between control and spontaneous groups was clearly significant ($t_{42}=2.36$, $p<0.05$). The relationship between classification behavior and need for cognition in the combined meticulous and control groups ($r=.44$) was significantly higher than the correlation for the spontaneous group ($t_{42}=2.18$, $p<0.05$).

The relationship between proportion of holistic/analytic classifications and style of processing for the entire sample was not significant ($r=-.14$), but by condition there was again an interesting pattern: $r=.38$ ($t_{13}=1.47$, $p<.10$) for spontaneous condition, $r=-.28$ for meticulous condition ($t_{13}=-1.11$, n.s.), and $r=-.44$ for control condition ($t_{13}=-1.78$, $p<0.05$). Based on the results of an overall regression analysis (F(5,40)=1.63, n.s.), the strength of the relationship between classification behavior and style of processing was not significantly different for meticulous and control subjects (t_{40}=-.07, n.s.). However, the correlation of -.35 for both groups combined indicates that visualizers were more holistic in their classifications than verbalizers (t_{29}=-2.03, p<.05). Subjects in the combined meticulous and control groups differed significantly from subjects in the spontaneous group (t_{40}=2.27, p<0.05).

Mode of classification and dimensional importance

Subjects were asked to indicate how important they thought the dimensions of size and pattern had been in their classification behavior, relative to each other. It was expected that subjects who indicated that they had relied strongly on one of the two dimensions in their classifications would show more analytic responses. Since the importance scale had endpoints of 'size much more important' and 'pattern much more important,' the hypothesis implies a U-shaped relationship between classification behavior and self-ratings of importance.

The predicted result was obtained. In a regression of proportion of holistic/analytic responses on self-rated importance (F(2,45)=4.53, p<0.05), both the linear term (t_{45}=-2.35, p<0.05) and the quadratic term (t_{45}=2.07, p<0.05) were significant in the expected direction. The minimum of the function was at 1.38 on a -5 to +5 scale. The hypothesis can also be tested by correlating the absolute value of the importance scale with classification behavior; the correlation was significant (r=.30, t_{46}=2.16, p<0.05).

DISCUSSION AND CONCLUSION

The substantive findings of this study can be summarized as follows. First, subjects who were instructed to classify without much thinking and to rely on first impressions categorized product stimuli in a more holistic (less analytic) fashion than subjects who were told to be careful and to take all the time they needed. Subjects who were not given any instructions provided responses similar to meticulous subjects. In addition, an internal analysis of the data showed that the time spent on classifying the stimuli was positively related to the extent to which classifications were analytic. These findings suggest that, as hypothesized by Alba and Hutchinson (1987) and Cohen and Basu (1987) on the basis of research in psychology, product perceptions will be less analytic in situations in which cognitive resources are limited (i.e., when consumers are not able, not willing, or do not have the opportunity to expend the time and effort necessary to form a thorough impression of a stimulus).

Second, two individual difference variables — need for cognition and style of processing — were found to have an effect on how product stimuli were perceived. Specifically, consumers high in need for cognition and verbalizers tended to view products more analytically (less holistically) than consumers low in need for cognition and visualizers. These relationships existed most clearly when subjects were allowed to follow their natural inclinations in classifying the stimuli (control group) or when subjects were told to be meticulous (which tended to be the natural tendency in the context of this study, in the sense that the classification behavior of control subjects, whose motivational task set was not manipulated, was similar to that of meticulous subjects). When subjects were instructed to rely on first impressions, need for cognition and style of processing had no effects on mode of product perception.

In addition to these substantive findings, the present study indicates that the triad classification task is a useful methodology for distinguishing between holistic and analytic modes of product perception and thus for investigating which factors influence whether consumers perceive products holistically or analytically. With the help of this procedure, researchers should be able to examine a variety of other factors that are expected to have a bearing on whether products are perceived holistically or analytically.

The basic argument of this research is that whether products are perceived holistically or analytically depends on a variety of factors, and the study reported in this paper makes an important step in delineating some conditions under which the two forms of processing are likely to occur. Some authors have suggested that the conditions that favor holistic processing occur frequently in everyday consumer behavior (e.g., Alba and Hutchinson 1987). The implications for marketing are clear: In the future, researchers will have to concern themselves more with the case in which product perceptions are holistic and develop models of attitude formation and judgment and decision making that are applicable in this situation.

As always, certain limitations of the study should be kept in mind when interpreting the findings. First, the difference in classification behavior between spontaneous and meticulous subjects was not particularly strong. One possible reason for this result is that the manipulation of motivational task set was not strong enough. Although subjects in the two conditions differed significantly in terms of the time taken to classify the stimuli, the absolute magnitude of these differences was not very large. Another reason for the borderline significance of the statistical test is that the sample size was too small. Second, the research was conducted in a classroom setting, and it would be desirable to replicate the study in a more controlled experimental environment. Third, the research should be extended using other stimuli and other subject populations. Despite these shortcomings, the results thus far look encouraging and the implications of the difference between holistic and analytic perception for attitude formation and judgment and decision making are profound so that further investigations of the topic seem warranted.

REFERENCES

Alba, Joseph W. and J. Wesley Hutchinson (1987), "Dimensions of Consumer Expertise," *Journal of Consumer Research*, 13 (March), 411-454.

Bettman, James R. (1979), *An Information Processing Theory of Consumer Choice*. Reading, MA: Addison-Wesley.

Cacioppo, John T. and Richard E. Petty (1982), "The Need for Cognition," *Journal of Personality and Social Psychology*, 42 (January), 116-131.

Childers, Terry L., Michael J. Houston, and Susan E. Heckler (1985), "Measurement of Individual Differences in Visual Versus Verbal Information Processing," *Journal of Consumer Research*, 12 (September), 125-134.

Cohen, Joel B. and Kunal Basu (1987), "Alternative Models of Categorization: Toward a Contingent Processing Framework," *Journal of Consumer Research*, 13 (March), 455-472.

Garner, Wendell R. (1974), *The Processing of Information and Structure*. Potomac, MD: Erlbaum.

Holbrook, Morris B. and William L. Moore (1981), "Feature Interactions in Consumer Judgments of Verbal Versus Pictorial Presentations," *Journal of Consumer Research*, 8 (June), 103-113.

MacInnis, Deborah J. and Linda L Price (1987), "The Role of Imagery in Information Processing: Review and Extensions," *Journal of Consumer Research*, 13 (March), 473-491.

Mervis, Carolyn B. and Eleanor Rosch (1981), "Categorization of Natural Objects," *Annual Review of Psychology*, 32, 89-115.

Murray, Noel, Harish Sujan, Edward R. Hirt and Mita Sujan (1990), "The Effects of Mood on Categorization: A Cognitive Flexibility Hypothesis," *Journal of Personality and Social Psychology*, 58 (September), 411-425.

Petty, Richard E. and John T. Cacioppo (1986), "The Elaboration Likelihood Model of Persuasion," *Advances in Experimental Social Psychology*, 19, 123-205.

Smith J. David and Deborah G. Kemler Nelson (1984), "Overall Similarity in Adults' Classification: The Child in All of Us," *Journal of Experimental Psychology: General*, 113 (January), 137-159.

Sujan, Mita (1985), "Consumer Knowledge: Effects on Evaluation Strategies Mediating Consumer Judgments," *Journal of Consumer Research*, 12 (June), 31-46.

Ward, Thomas B. (1980), "Separable and Integral Responding by Children and Adults to the Dimensions of Length and Density," *Child Development*, 51, 676-684.

_____ (1983), "Response Tempo and Separable-Integral Responding: Evidence for an Integral-to-Separable Processing Sequence in Visual Perception," *Journal of Experimental Psychology: Human Perception and Performance*, 9 (1), 103-112.

Wilkie, William L. and Edgar A. Pessemier (1973), "Issues in Marketing's Use of Multiple-Attribute Attitude Models," *Journal of Marketing Research*, 10 (November), 428-441.

Witkin, H.A., R.B. Dyk, H.F. Faterson, D.R. Goodenough and S.A. Karp (1962), *Psychological Differentiation: Studies of Development*, New York: Wiley.

Wright, Peter L. (1975), "Consumer Choice Strategies: Simplifying Versus Optimizing," *Journal of Marketing Research*, 11 (February), 60-67.

Country-of-Origin, Perceived Risk and Evaluation Strategy

Dana L. Alden, University of Hawaii
Wayne D. Hoyer, University of Texas
Ayn E. Crowley, Washington State University

ABSTRACT

This study finds that consumers evaluate a new offering from a frequently purchased, non-durable product category in fundamentally different ways depending on whether the product is manufactured in a country perceived as high or low on product quality risk. When consumers associate low risk with the product's country-of-origin (CO) attribute, they evaluate the good based primarily on product category-level generalizations. A high risk CO results in significantly greater use of attribute information associated with the actual product. Based on this research, firms planning to manufacture convenience goods in foreign countries perceived as risky should consider modifying promotional materials to better match consumer evaluation strategies.

INTRODUCTION

Developments such as the impending free trade agreement between Mexico and the United States are likely to increase *foreign* production of lower involvement, consumer convenience goods (Business Week 1991). However, research investigating the effects of country-of-origin (CO) on evaluation strategies and outcomes has focused primarily on higher involvement, durable products such as cars and VCRs (Ozsomer and Cavusgil 1991). Thus while marketing managers have information on the ways that CO can affect evaluation strategies for high involvement goods (cf. Hong and Wyer 1989), far less is known about possible CO effects on evaluation of routinely purchased convenience items such as toothpaste, cereal and film.

Unlike high involvement goods, low involvement goods are rarely evaluated rigorously prior to purchase (Hoyer 1984). For most low involvement purchases, consumers tend to rely on a few salient, surface features (e.g., brand name) that activate generalizations from memory about the product category and brand reputation (Petty and Cacioppo 1986). These evaluation strategies differ from the more deliberate, multiattribute approaches associated with high involvement products (cf. Fishbein and Ajzen 1975; Petty and Cacioppo 1986).

Research in psychology and consumer behavior suggests that certain factors associated with a low involvement product's country-of-origin may cause consumers to shift from relatively passive evaluation strategies to more active strategies associated with higher involvement products. However, this possibility remains untested. Thus, the following study tests for ways that high perceived risk associated with a product's country-of-origin can affect evaluation strategies for a new low involvement brand within a mature product category.

COUNTRY-OF-ORIGIN AND EVALUATION STRATEGY

Research concerning country-of-origin (CO) effects on evaluation strategy has focused on several issues (for a general review, see Ozsomer and Cavusgil 1991). First, researchers have employed multiattribute models to examine interactions between overall evaluation, attribute evaluation and CO (cf., Johansson, Douglas and Nonaka 1985; Han 1989). Second, relationships between product category familiarity, CO and evaluation strategy have been studied (cf., Heimbach, Johansson and MacLachlan 1989). Third, researchers have tested alternative processing models that help explain CO effects. For example, Hong and Wyer (1989) find that CO effects on cognitive processes that mediate evaluation are most consistent with the elaboration likelihood model (Petty and Cacioppo 1986). Having established an elaboration effect, Hong and Wyer (1989, p.185) call for research that will answer "the question of why a product's country of origin stimulates interest in other product information." We now review literature that may help answer this question.

THE CATEGORIZATION PERSPECTIVE

People often attempt to match newly encountered persons with existing stereotypes based on one or two salient features (Fiske and Pavelchak 1986). For example, seeing a middle-aged male wearing a gray suit in an office elevator may activate the category stereotype, "typical businessman." If the man in the suit matches the perceiver's stereotype for a typical businessman, "category-based" evaluation is hypothesized (Fiske and Pavelchak 1986). Under category-based evaluation, the evaluator remains relatively uninvolved and bases his or her impression on thoughts and feelings stored in memory about businessmen in general. Actual information about the individual (e.g., type of watch worn) is less likely to be included in the evaluation.

However, certain factors may cause observers to shift from reliance on summary information from memory to closer analysis of individual attributes associated with the person or object. For example, if the observer notices something unexpected about the businessman (e.g., he or she is carrying a red rose) a shift to "attribute-based" evaluation may occur (Fiske and Pavelchak 1986; Sujan 1985). In addition, Neuberg and Fiske (1987) found that subjects shifted to from category-based to attribute-based evaluation of a new person when they had to depend on the person to achieve an important goal. However, when they weren't dependent on the new person to achieve an important goal, subjects continued to used category-based evaluation. This result was obtained regardless of whether information about the new person was consistent or inconsistent with a category label (e.g., "schizophrenic") provided by the researchers describing that person.

The present study applies findings from the categorization literature to the issue of country-of-origin effects on evaluation strategy. It does so by testing whether a third factor, perceived risk associated with a product's country-of-origin, can also cause a shift from category-based to attribute-based evaluation.

APPLICATION OF CATEGORIZATION THEORY TO CO EFFECTS ON EVALUATION STRATEGY

The categorization perspective may be applied to understanding how a product's CO can impact product evaluation strategy for low involvement consumer goods. Based on that stream, category-based evaluation would be predicted when the product's CO does not strongly deviate from general expectations.

The prediction of category-based evaluation for a low involvement good given a CO that does not deviate strongly from expectations appears to run counter to Hong and Wyer (1989) who concluded that the CO attribute's "inherent interestingness" can produce elaboration. However, Hong and Wyer (1989) used two highly involving products (vcr's and pc's). As a result, motivation to process is likely to have been relatively high. Under these conditions, elaboration may have been more easily triggered by a CO cue, particularly if the CO was seen as providing information relevant to the product category (Heimbach, et al. 1989). On the other hand, an expected, low risk CO attribute (e.g., "Made in the USA" for toothpaste) seems unlikely to motivate elaboration when product category involvement is low, experience is high and other attributes match expectations. Thus, for many frequently purchased non-durables, regardless of CO, consumers seem likely to favor category-based over attribute-based evaluation strategies.

However, there may be times when a CO causes a shift to attribute-based evaluation, even when product involvement is relatively low. As noted, certain CO labels (e.g., developing nations) are associated with increased perceptions of risk and negative evaluations (Bilkey and Ness 1982). Higher risk in turn has been found to increase task involvement (cf. Lichtenstein, Bloch and Black 1988). Under conditions of higher task involvement, related research suggests that individuals are likely to become motivated to form more accurate judgements of attribute information (cf., Neuberg and Fiske 1987; Kruglanski and Freund 1983). As a result, they are likely to rely more on attribute-level information and less on category-level generalities cued from memory. Thus, it appears reasonable to predict a greater use of attribute-based evaluation as opposed to category-based evaluation when a high versus a low risk CO is perceived.

While there may be instances in which the CO label simply won't be noticed for low involvement products, it seems likely that as American convenience goods manufacturers shift production to Mexican factories to take advantage of lower labor costs and less stringent environmental regulations (Business Week 1991) the salience of the CO attribute will increase, causing more consumers to more actively search-out or at least notice that attribute. In the longer term, the U.S. Congress could require more prominent display of CO as pressure from labor groups is levied, further increasing the likelihood that the attribute will be noticed.

Finally, based on Bilkey and Ness (1982), it is also likely that consumers will have relatively more negative attitudes towards a high risk versus a low risk CO. If so, given that a shift from category-based to attribute-based evaluation occurs, relatively less favorable attitudes toward the brand with the high versus the low risk CO would be expected (Fiske and Pavelchak 1986; Sujan 1985). These propositions are now tested.

METHOD

Subjects

Subjects from a large American university were used in this study because young adults are regular purchasers of consumer non-durables (Peter and Olson 1990). In addition, the study applies an experimental approach recommended in causal research (Cook and Campbell 1979). As such, one's ability to generalize must be weighed against threats to statistical conclusion validity (Cook and Campbell 1979). Thus, while use of a fairly homogeneous subject pool may limit external validity, chances of finding actual effects are increased.

Pretests

Based on an initial pretest with 40 subjects, a regularly purchased product category (toothpaste) rated as low on enduring involvement was selected for the main study. Attributes typically associated with the category were elicited using an open ended approach from 31 new subjects (cf., Sujan 1985). The four attributes listed most frequently (freshens breath, fights cavities, great taste and available in gel or regular) were selected for further pretesting.

Next, two new groups of 15 subjects were randomly exposed to descriptions of a "new toothpaste product being considered for introduction nationally." The description included the four attributes discussed above (plus brief descriptions following Sujan 1985) and one of two CO attributes, "Made in USA" or "Made in Mexico." Mexico was selected based on pretests indicating that it was seen as significantly riskier than the US for toothpaste ($p<.001$), but similar to other developing countries (e.g., Bangladesh and India) and because of its growing importance as an offshore production site for American consumer goods (Business Week 1991). The CO label was listed as the first attribute below the "Toothpaste" heading, although Hong and Wyer (1989) indicate that CO order effects may be minimal. As expected, the description with the Mexico CO (Mean=3.64) was rated as significantly higher on risk (8="very risky"; 1="not at all risky") than the description with the US CO (Mean=2.20; $t[27]=2.76$, $p<.005$).

The same two groups of pretest subjects were also asked to rate the extent to which either description was similar to "toothpastes already on the market." As noted, previous research indicates that a strongly unexpected or strongly atypical CO attribute may produce elaboration effects on processing that are similar to those predicted to result from a high risk CO (cf., Fiske and Pavelchak 1986). Thus, establishing that a product description with a Mexico CO is perceived as highly risky but not strongly unexpected would strengthen confidence that any observed elaboration effects were due primarily to risk and not pleasant surprise or risk-free curiosity. To this end, the same subjects rated the Mexico and US CO descriptions on two 8-point scales designed to tap perceptions of typicality and similarity to existing products in the U.S. (e.g., 8=very typical;1=not at all typical). The Mexico CO description (Mean=6.86) and US CO description (Mean= 6.13) were rated as equally typical of ($t[27]= 1.19$, $p>.25$) *and* equally similar to (Mexico Mean=7.1; US Mean=7.2; $t[27]=0.39$, $p>.70$) other toothpastes already on the U.S. market.

Based on these pretests, within a product description context, the Mexico CO seems far less likely to produce amused surprise or curious interest and far more likely to increase perceived risk, probably due to uncertainty concerning developing country production standards (Bilkey and Ness 1982). However, even if the Mexico CO is viewed as somewhat "atypical," this perception could exert an elaboration effect *indirectly* by increasing perceptions of risk. That is, because a central cause of perceived risk is "uncertainty" (Dowling 1986), an unexpected CO that also heightens uncertainty (rather than simply producing pleasant surprise) should also heighten perceived risk. For these reasons, only the possibility of a direct effect from pleasant, risk-free surprise would appear to constitute a genuine threat to the study's internal validity. This possibility will be examined further in the main study.

A final pretest was conducted to determine whether or not presence of a well-known American brand name would counter higher levels of perceived risk associated with the Mexico CO. Two groups of 20 new subjects were exposed to one of two descriptions that were verbally introduced as a Proctor and Gamble product that would be marketed under the brand name "Crest." In addition, above the description of the new product was the statement, "This product, which will be sold as a CREST brand, has the following features." Below this statement was either the Mexico or the US CO and the same four attributes pretested previously. Despite the leading American manufacturer's brand name, the product description with the Mexico CO (Mean = 2.85) was judged to be significantly higher on a 7-point purchase risk scale than the description with the US CO (Mean = 1.80, $t[38]=2.45$, $p<.02$). And, once again, ratings of typicality did not vary by CO. Thus, the presence of a well-known brand name does not appear to negate the perception of higher risk associated with the Mexico CO, nor does it appear to affect the perceived typicality of the two descriptions.

Procedures for the Main Study

Forty-four subjects participated in the main study. Two subjects were dropped from the sample, one whose age exceeded the mean sample age by more than three standard deviations and another who had lived in the U.S. for two months. All remaining subjects were raised in the U.S. except for two who had lived in the country for three and ten years respectively. There were no significant differences between treatment groups in terms of age or sex. Subjects were run individually by a trained experimenter blind to the study's hypotheses.

Subjects first read an introductory passage explaining that a company considering introduction of a new toothpaste was sponsoring the study and that the firm's name was confidential. After completing a demographic questionnaire, the experimenter asked them to "form an impression of the new product based on this description" (i.e., the same description used in the pretest). When finished, subjects were asked by the experimenter to verbalize thoughts they had while forming their impression (Wright 1980). Evaluation times and thoughts were recorded using a small camcorder unobtrusively positioned out of the subject's view. Finally, subjects were asked to respond to several scale items which measured attitude toward the brand, purchase intention, perceived risk and product description typicality.

Manipulation Checks

Manipulation check items were collected after the thought listings. Risk perceived for the new toothpaste product was operationalized in terms of purchase risk (7-point scale with 1="not at all risky" and 7="very risky") and in terms of perceived product quality (7-point semantic differential scale with "high" and "poor quality"). On the purchase risk scale, the product description with the Mexico CO (Mean=3.38) was judged as significantly riskier than the description with the US CO (Mean=1.86; $F[1,40]=12.9$, $p<.001$). On the product quality scale, the description with the Mexico CO (Mean=3.71) was judged as significantly lower on quality than the US CO description (Mean=5.29; $F[1,40]=12.26$, $p<.001$).

The mean difference in typicality ratings for the two descriptions was significant (Mexico CO Mean=5.24 and US CO Mean=6.05; $F[1,40]=4.003$; $p<.05$). However, this difference was less than one scale point. In addition, multiple classification analysis revealed that the perceived risk effect of the CO manipulation was substantially stronger ($R^2=.24$) than the atypicality effect ($R^2=.09$). Finally, analysis of thought listing data indicated that while 60% of the subjects reported thinking about product risk for the description with the Mexico CO, fewer than 10% (2 subjects) expressed surprise without also mentioning risk. Differences in the reported thoughts of the two groups are clearly reflected in Figures A and B. These results, coupled with pretest data, indicated that the Mexico CO enhanced perceived risk relative to the US CO for the overwhelming majority of subjects as intended.

Finally, analysis of thought listings indicated no evidence of hypothesis guessing or other demand effects.

Analysis Overview

Multivariate analysis of variance with CO (U.S. vs. Mexico) as a two-level independent factor, four dependent process measures (described below) and a covariate was used to test the proposition that a high risk CO can cause a shift in evaluation strategy for low involvement, frequently purchased goods.

Dependent Measures

Response Time: In conjunction with other dependent measures, it is assumed that the longer one takes to form an impression, the greater the likelihood of attribute rather than category-based evaluation (Sujan 1985; Neuberg and Fiske 1987). This is because memory-based category evaluation is relatively rapid while evaluation based on actual product attributes is thought to take longer (cf. Sujan 1985). Response time, based on eye contact with the description, was measured post-hoc from videotapes of the session by an experimenter blind to treatment conditions. Time taken to read the introductory passage served as a baseline reading speed measure.

Thought Listings: Verbal responses were collected immediately following exposure to the description (Sujan 1985). Subjects described all thoughts they remembered having while looking at the description. Verbal responses were later coded by two assistants (blind to the study hypothesis) as: category thoughts, attribute evaluation thoughts or other thoughts. Interjudge agreement, based on coder agreement on classification of thoughts across all three categories, was 81% which is acceptable for studies using this approach (Wright 1980). Disagreements were resolved through discussion with a tie-breaking vote by the experimenter needed in only four cases. Three measures of evaluation strategy were used: number of category thoughts, number of attribute evaluation thoughts and number of total thoughts (category, attribute evaluation and all other thoughts). Subjects engaged in category-based evaluation were expected to have more category evaluation thoughts, fewer attribute evaluation thoughts and fewer total thoughts while the opposite was expected for those engaged in attribute-based evaluation (Fiske, Neuberg, Beattie and Milberg 1987).

Attitude Toward the Brand

In addition to the MANCOVA analysis described above, attitude towards the brand was also measured. A four item semantic differential affect scale (like-dislike, good-bad, appealing-unappealing, and desirable-undesirable) was found to exhibit high internal reliability with Cronbach's alpha equal to .95. As a result the scale items were summed to form a single measure of attitude toward the brand.

RESULTS

Analyzing the MANCOVA model first, an initial plot of evaluation response time and the reading speed covariate indicated non-linearity. Optimal fit was achieved with a log transform of the dependent measure (r-squared=.24, $p<.001$). In the full model, reading speed was significantly related to the log transform of evaluation time ($F[1,39]=14.04$, $p<.001$) but not to the other dependent measures (all Fs<1). In addition, the homogeneity of regression assumption for covariance analysis was satisfied (F<1).

The multivariate model provides evidence for concluding that subjects exposed to the high risk CO relied significantly less on stereotypes from memory and more on actual product description attributes than those seeing the low risk CO (Hotelling's T-square $[4,36]=4.21$, $p<.007$). Thus, higher levels of CO risk appear to cause shifts in evaluation strategy away from category-based approaches to attribute-based approaches.

Univariate analyses were consistent with this conclusion (see Table for sample means). As expected, high risk subjects (Adjusted Mean = 41.14) took marginally longer to evaluate the product description than low risk subjects (Adjusted Mean = 36.42; $F[1,39]=3.13$, $p<.08$). Furthermore, as predicted, high risk subjects had: 1) significantly more total thoughts than low risk subjects (7.57 versus 4.71; $F[1,40]=9.28$, $p<.004$); 2) marginally fewer category thoughts (0.76 versus 1.33; $F[1,40]=3.43$, $p<.06$); and 3)

TABLE
Cell Means for Dependent Measures

	USA Country of Origin	Mexico Country of Origin
Dependent Measures		
Processing Speed (seconds)	36.42	41.14
Category Thoughts	1.33	0.76
Attribute Evaluation Thoughts	0.95	2.86
Total Thoughts	4.71	7.57
Covariate		
Reading Speed (seconds)	43.35	42.59
Cell Sizes	21	21

significantly more attribute evaluation thoughts (2.86 versus 0.95; $F[1,40]= 15.95, p<.001$). In addition, the difference on the attribute evaluation measure remained significant even when all thoughts referring to the CO attribute were removed (1.76 versus 0.81; $F[1,40]= 4.82, p<.034$). This result suggests that the shift in processing strategy due to high risk produced significantly more elaboration regarding all product attributes and not just the CO attribute.

Finally, as hypothesized, attitude towards the brand with the Mexico CO (Mean=17.1) was significantly lower than for the brand with the US CO (Mean= 21.62; $F[1,40]= 8.04, p<.007$). Overall, these results provide convergent evidence that subjects exposed to the Mexico CO relied more on attribute-based evaluation and less on category-based evaluation compared to those exposed to the US CO. Furthermore, pretests and manipulation checks suggest that these observed effects were due primarily to perceived risk.

DISCUSSION

This study demonstrates that country-of-origin (CO) can have a significant impact on the evaluation strategy used by consumers for a new product from a routinely purchased product category. Subjects exposed to the high risk CO for a new toothpaste product took longer to form an impression, had more total and attribute evaluation thoughts, had fewer category thoughts and had more negative attitudes toward the brand. These results provide strong convergent evidence of a shift from category-based to attribute-based evaluation due to the presence of the Mexico CO label (Sujan 1985).

In terms of theory development, our findings extend the current consumer behavior literature by demonstrating that perceived risk, possibly in combination with some degree of unexpectedness, can cause a shift in consumer evaluation strategies from category-based to attribute-based evaluation. Prior to this study, only incongruity with expectations (given ability) had been shown to produce such a shift in the consumer behavior field (Sujan 1985). Hence, risk as well as ability and unexpectedness appear to be related to consumers' relative reliance on category-based or attribute-based evaluation.

Second, this study extends the country-of-origin stream by demonstrating a specific type of elaboration response that can occur when consumers encounter a high risk CO. Although Hong and Wyer (1989) note that a CO's "interestingness" may enhance elaboration, they do not test for a shift from category-based to attribute-based evaluation. Neither do they examine low involvement product categories. Thus, these results indicate that Fiske and Pavelchak's (1986) model of alternative evaluation strategies accurately predicts one consumer processing response to perception of high CO risk for a new, low involvement good.

On this note, one might argue that the effects of a high risk CO observed in this study were due not to a shift from category-based to attribute-based evaluation but rather resulted from a shift to another category schema (cf. Meyers-Levy and Tybout 1989). For example, subjects may have taken longer to process the product description with the Mexico CO not because they shifted to attribute-based processing but because they shifted to a general schema for "products from Mexico" which could have then guided their evaluation.

However, two of the study's findings provide evidence for strongly questioning this alternative explanation. First, after removing attribute evaluations that referred to CO, the total number of such evaluations was still significantly higher for the Mexico CO description. This result indicates that subjects increased elaboration of actual description attributes rather than cuing a second schema from memory. Second, the fact that subjects exposed to the Mexico CO expressed significantly fewer category thoughts than subjects who saw the US CO suggests that the former group indeed shifted to attribute-based evaluation rather than remaining at the category level. In sum, while there may be times when consumers continue to use category-level evaluation upon encountering a risky CO, this does not appear to have happened here. At the same time, conditions under such alternative evaluation responses may occur deserve additional attention.

From a managerial perspective, the study suggests the importance of a match between CO, consumer evaluation strategy and the depth and breadth of information provided in promotional materials. For example, an established U.S. consumer goods manufacturer may decide to move production of a new line of toothpastes to a Mexican "maquiladora" to take advantage of lower labor costs and the impending free trade agreement. In light of this study, the firm should consider providing more detailed package information than it would for a domestically manufactured toothpaste brand, e.g., additional information on ingredient quality, a money back guarantee and a toll free number. Should consumers shift to attribute-based evaluation, positive attribute affect should be combined with feelings about toothpastes in general and negative affect for the Mexico CO. Thus, inclusion of such additional positive information should enhance evaluation relative to a standardized, domestic packaging strategy which assumes that a few salient cues are sufficient regardless of CO.

FIGURE A
Examples of Typical Thoughts Expressed After Review of Product Description*
United States Country-of-Origin

Category Thoughts

* I thought the product sounds just like any other toothpaste practically.
* I thought it sounds like every other toothpaste on the market.
* It basically sounded kind of ordinary from what I read.
* I thought the toothpaste reflected the toothpastes that are on the market.
* It said the same thing that all the other toothpastes talk about.

Attribute Evaluation Thoughts

* I thought it was really good because it helps fight cavities.
* Made in the United States...I thought that was good.
* I like the toothpaste because it seems to take care of cavities.
* I like the fact that you don't have to use mouthwash after you brush your teeth.
* I feel the product is good because it freshens your breath

*Each example is from a different subject.

FIGURE B
Examples of Typical Thoughts Expressed After Review of Product Description*
Mexico Country-of-Origin

Category Thoughts

* Basically similar to what's on the market right now.
* It sounded like a really general toothpaste.
* I thought it sounds just like every other toothpaste.

Attribute Evaluation Thoughts

* "Made in Mexico" gives it a more negative feeling than positive because of their standards of food, drug and safety.
* Green would make it look yucky ... blue makes it look cool and fresh.
* The thing that stuck in my mind was that it was "Made in Mexico" - I'm sure that's why it had a negative connotation to it.
* Minty taste - I don't care for it.
* When you think of Mexico it's kind of "iffy" because you're not sure if they follow the same standards.
* I like that you don't have to use a mouthwash.
* I like the minty taste it says it has.

*Each example is from a different subject.

Limitations

Limitations to this study point to potential avenues for future research. First, use of the experimental method which is crucial to ruling-out alternative explanations nonetheless introduces elements of artificiality that may not be operative in the real world. For example, given increased salience of America's ongoing trade problems and the growing numbers of consumer goods produced overseas (e.g., "Made for Hartz in Thailand"), recognition of the CO attribute seems likely to grow for many convenience goods. Even so, for many products, consumers may not notice the "Made-In" label. Thus, having found a strong risk effect in a controlled environment, future researchers should investigate ways in which these findings are affected by factors that may be operative in non-experimental settings such as supermarkets.

Second, one product (toothpaste), one country (Mexico) and one consumer segment (students) were used in the study. Incorporation of additional product categories, countries and consumer segments would increase generalizability. For example, CO effects on evaluation strategy are likely to interact with other important marketing factors such as brand name (e.g., Crest), warranty and store reputation (Thorelli, Lim and Ye 1988). Such potential mediating factors need to be investigated.

Finally, future researchers may want to attempt to include high risk, expected countries in their design so that the specific effects of risk and unexpectedness can be better discerned experimentally. While pretest and experimental data demonstrated that the Mexico CO was first and foremost a manipulation of risk, CO atypicality probably exerted some indirect effect (i.e., by heightening uncertainty and therefore risk) and possibly a mild direct effect (e.g., pleasant surprise or curiosity). However, it may not be possible to remove all unexpectedness from a high risk CO manipulation. If so, future researchers should present evidence (as in this study) of a strongly predominant manipulation effect to demonstrate construct validity.

CONCLUSION

In sum, this study indicates that the riskier the CO, the more likely it is that consumers will use attribute-based evaluation rather than simple cues and category-level images from memory. Managers may find that increasing the depth and breadth of attribute information on the package, in point-of-purchase displays and/or in advertising is a beneficial response. Consumers might then form more positive evaluations than they would in response to standard promotional material as enhanced attribute benefits would be available to compensate for the high risk CO.

REFERENCES

Bilkey, Warren J. and E. Ness (1982), "Country-Of-Origin Effects on Product Evaluations," *Journal of International Business Studies* 35 (Spring), 89-99.

Business Week (1991), "Assembly Lines Start Migrating from Asia to Mexico," (July 1), New York, NY: Mc-Graw Hill, 43.

Cook, Thomas D. and Donald T. Campbell (1979), *Quasi-Experimentation: Design and Analysis Issues for Field Settings*, Boston, MA: Houghton-Mifflin Co.

Fishbein, Martin and Icek Ajzen (1975), *Belief, Attitude, Intention and Behavior: An Introduction to Theory and Research*, Reading, MA: Addison-Wesley.

Fiske, Susan T., Steven L. Neuberg, Ann E. Beattie, and Sandra J. Milberg (1987), "Category-Based and Attribute-Based Reactions to Others: Some Informational Conditions of Stereotyping and Individuating Processes," *Journal of Experimental Psychology* 23, 399-427.

_____ and Mark A. Pavelchak (1986), "Category-Based versus Piecemeal-Based Affective Responses: Developments in Schema-Triggered Affect," in *Handbook of Motivation and Cognition*, R.M. Sorrentino and T.E. Higgins (eds.), New York: The Guilford, 167-203.

Han, C-M (1989), "Country Image - Halo or Summary Construct?," *Journal of Marketing Research* 26(2), 222-229.

Heimbach, Arthur E., Johny K. Johansson, Douglas L. MacLachlan (1989), "Product Familiarity, Information Processing and Country-of-Origin Cues," in *Advances in Consumer Research* 16, Thomas K. Srull (ed.), Provo, Utah: Association for Consumer Research, 460-67.

Hong, Sung-Tai and Robert S. Wyer, Jr. (1989), "Effects of Country-of-Origin and Product Attribute Information on Product Evaluation: An Information Processing Perspective," *Journal of Consumer Research*, 16 (2), 175-80.

Johansson, Johny K., Susan P. Douglas, and Ikujiro Nonaka (1985), "Assessing the Impact of Country-of-Origin on Product Evaluations: A New Methodological Perspective," *Journal of Marketing Research*, 22 (November), 388-396.

Kruglanski, D. and Freund, T. (1983), "The Freezing and Unfreezing Lay-Inferences: Effects of Impressional Primacy, Ethnic Stereotyping, and Numerical Anchoring," *Journal of Experimental Social Psychology*, 19, 448-468.

Lichtenstein, Donald R., Peter H. Bloch and William C. Black (1988), "Correlates of Price Acceptability," *Journal of Consumer Research*, 15 (2), 43-52.

Meyers-Levy, Joan and Alice Tybout (1989), "Schema Congruity as a Basis for Product Evaluation," *Journal of Consumer Research*, 16(1), 39-54.

Neuberg, S.L. and S.T. Fiske (1987), "Motivational Influences on Impression Formation: Outcome Dependency, Accuracy-Driven Attention and Individuating Processes," *Journal of Personality and Social Psychology*, 53 (3),431-44.

Ozsomer, Aysegul and S. Tamer Cavusgil (1991), "Country-of-Origin Effects on Product Evaluations: A Sequel to Bilkey and Ness Review," in *1991 AMA Educators' Proceedings* 2, Mary Gilly, et al. (eds.), Chicago, IL: American Marketing Association, 269-277

Peter, J. Paul and Jerry C. Olson (1990), *Consumer Behavior and Marketing Strategy*, 2nd Edition, Homewood, IL: Irwin.

Petty, Richard E. and John T. Cacioppo (1986), *Communication and Persuasion: Central and Peripheral Routes to Attitude Change*, New York: Springer-Verlag.

Sujan, Mita (1985), "Consumer Knowledge: Effects on Evaluation Strategies Mediating Consumer Judgements," *Journal of Consumer Research* 12 (June), 31-46.

Thorelli, Hans B., Jeen-Su Lim, and Jongsuk Lee (1988), "Relative Importance of Country of Origin, Warranty and Retail Store Image on Product Evaluations," *International Marketing Review*, 6 (1), 35-46.

Wright, Peter (1980), "Message-Evoked Thoughts: Persuasion Research Using Thought Verbalizations," *Journal of Consumer Research*, 7 (September), 151-175.

The Roles of Country Of Origin Information on Buyers' Product Evaluations: Signal or Attribute?

Wai-kwan Li, University of Illinois
Kwok Leung, Chinese University of Hong Kong
Robert S. Wyer, Jr., University of Illinois

ABSTRACT

Although recent studies have suggested that country of origin information can be used to infer product quality, (a signalling role), or as a product attribute that can provide benefits, (an attribute role), it is unclear under what conditions each of these roles may occur, and whether one may dominate the other. This study found that the occurrence of these two roles are contingent on two factors: Amount of product information, and motivation. It was found that country of origin information signalled the style, but not the functional performance, of a product. Moreover, the signalling role has dominated the attribute role.

The blooming of international business has brought about important changes in manufacturing locations and marketing of products. Given these changes, marketing managers need to consider whether buyers' evaluations of a product are influenced by knowledge of the country in which it is made. Although previous research has provided evidence of country-of-origin *(COO)* effects on product evaluations, not much is known about *how* country of origin affects buyers' product evaluations (Bilkey and Nes 1982; Ozsomer and Cavusgil 1991).

In an in-depth interview, Li and Monroe (1992) reported that, when the products considered were of high technology, informants used COO information to infer product quality, that is, COO information played a signalling role. On the other hand, when the products considered were handicrafts, COO functioned as a product attribute that can provide benefits to consumers, that is, it played an attribute role. However, an issue remaining to be explored is what role(s) COO may play if the manufacturing process of a product, such as watches, involves both technical and handicraft skills. Does one role dominate the other, or does COO play both signalling and attribute roles simultaneously?

Another interesting issue is what conditions may facilitate or inhibit the use of COO in these capacities. In other words, what are the boundary conditions of these two roles?

To investigate these two issues, we manipulated two factors, information amount and motivation, in such a way that the combinations of the factors might (1) facilitate only the signalling role, (2) facilitate only the attribute role, (3) facilitate both roles, or (4) inhibit both roles.

COO AS A SIGNAL OF PRODUCT QUALITY

Johansson (1989, p.55) argued that COO may function as a "summary cue" that produces a cognitive inference effect: "the cue might be used by the customer to guess the attributes of a product". Supporting Johansson's "summary cue" proposition, Han (1989) found that COO may function as a "halo", from which buyers can infer beliefs. Parallel to them, Havlena and DeSarbo (1991) found that COO functioned as an "indicator" of perceived risk.

Although the terminology used by these authors were slightly different, they suggested similar effects: COO may *signal* [2] perceived quality in product evaluations. This tentative conclusion is consistent with the findings in the pricing literature indicating that price (also an extrinsic attribute) may serve as a signal of perceived quality (Rao and Monroe 1989; Steenkamp 1989; Zeithaml 1988).

What does COO Signal?

Although researchers have offered convincing arguments that COO can play a signalling role in evaluating product quality, *what* it signals has not been specified. For example, while Johansson (1989) postulated that COO may be used by customers to infer product quality, it is unclear whether he referred to the overall product quality, or the quality of some product attributes. Similarly, Han (1989) proposed that COO can be used to infer the beliefs about a product, but the particular beliefs to be inferred was not specified. If COO influences only some beliefs, then the question is: What are these beliefs?

To investigate this issue, the present study asked subjects to evaluate a product with respect to a comprehensive set of product attributes. By factorizing the set of product attributes, different domains for evaluating a product were identified. Then, the significance of COO effects on these domains were assessed, and we could determine whether COO signals beliefs on some domains of product quality, or on the overall product quality.

Effect of Information Amount on the Signalling Role

Under what conditions do consumers use an extrinsic cue to signal product quality? Scitovszky (1945) postulated that when consumers were not able to assess product quality directly, they might use surrogate measures, such as company size, market success and price to infer product quality. Consumers may be unable to assess product quality in at least two situations. First, when consumers are asked to evaluate a product for which they do not have sufficient knowledge to understand the intrinsic attribute information, they may use the product's extrinsic attributes as indicators of product quality (Rao and Monroe 1988). Second, when consumers are asked to evaluate a product for which only limited product information is available, they may also employ the product's extrinsic cues, such as COO, to infer product quality, and lead to COO effects on product evaluations.

On the other hand, when consumers are confronted with sufficient amount of comprehensible product information, they should be able to evaluate the quality of the product based on the

---

[1]The authors would like to thank Kent B. Monroe and Marielza Martins for their thoughtful comments on the earlier drafts of the article.
This article is based on the master's thesis of the first author, submitted to the Department of Psychology, Chinese University of Hong Kong, under the supervision of the second author. This study was supported by the Hong Kong and China Gas Postgraduate Research Scholarship granted to the first author.

[2]It should be clarified that the signalling process is different from the heuristic process. By signalling, consumers use a piece of information to infer product quality, when information is not available, or difficult to comprehend (Scitovsky 1945). By heuristic, consumers only use a subset of available information to infer the product quality, in order to save their mental effort (Chaiken, Liberman & Eagly 1989).

TABLE 1
Predicted Effects of COO on Product Evaluations as a Function of Information Amount and Motivation

	Low Information Amount		High Information Amount	
	Low Motivation	High Motivation	Low Motivation	High Motivation
Signalling hypothesis	Strong COO effect	Strong COO effect	No COO effect	No COO effect
Attribute hypothesis	No COO effect	Strong COO effect	No COO effect	Strong COO effect

information provided, and therefore have little reason to make any inferences from extrinsic cues. Hence, if COO plays the signalling role, then:

H1: The effect of COO is more likely to occur when a limited amount of product information is available, than when large amount of product information is available. (See Table 1)

COO AS A PRODUCT ATTRIBUTE

Three experimental studies have reported that COO, similar to other intrinsic product attributes, was considered as a product attribute in product evaluations (Hong and Wyer 1989, 1990; Li and Wyer 1991). However, COO usually appears as a "made in" label on a product, it is interesting to investigate what benefits COO (as a product attribute) can provide to consumers. Li and Monroe (1992) identified five kinds of benefits: authenticity, exoticness, patriotism, personalization, and enhanced social standing. For example, Americans may prefer Chinese china to American china, because it is authentic and/or exotic; Americans may prefer American automobiles to Japanese automobiles for patriotic reasons.

Effect of Motivation on the Attribute Role

Literature on motivation and information search suggests that in high motivation situations, consumers have been shown to exert extensive effort in information search (Celsi and Olson 1988; Harris 1987; Zaichkowsky 1986), and attend to both salient and non-salient information (Borgida and Howard-Pitney 1983). On the other hand, in low motivation situations, consumers tend to make quick and effortless decisions, suggesting that only limited information processing would take place (Hoyer 1984), and only salient information was considered (Borgida and Howard-Pitney 1983).

Based on this logic, consumers with high motivation will consider more product attribute information than consumers with low motivation. Hence, if COO is considered as one of the many product attributes, highly motivated consumers are more likely to include COO in the product evaluation process, whereas unmotivated consumers will have a lower probability of including it. Therefore, COO is more likely to play the attribute role in product evaluations, and therefore lead to COO effect, when consumers are of high motivation, rather than when they are of low motivation. Hence, if COO plays an attribute role, then:

H2: The effect of COO on product evaluations is likely to be greater when the motivation of consumers is high, than when it is low. (See Table 1)

CAN SIGNALLING AND ATTRIBUTE ROLES OCCUR SIMULTANEOUSLY?

As discussed above, low information amount will enhance COO to play the signalling role on product evaluations, whereas high motivation will enhance COO to function as a product attribute. Integrating these two factors together, an interesting question arises. Which role(s) may COO play if consumers are highly motivated and only a limited amount of information is available? Will both roles co-exist, or one will dominate the other? Since no data have been reported that one role will dominate over the other, we expect that both roles will co-exist. The predicted effects of country of origin based on signalling and attribute hypotheses are summarized in Table 1.

METHOD

Subjects and Design

Subjects in the main study were 256 undergraduates (128 men and 128 women) at the Chinese University of Hong Kong who participated to fulfill a course requirement. Sixteen subjects (8 of each gender) were randomly assigned to each cell of a 4-factor design involving COO (favorable vs. unfavorable), information amount (high vs. low), motivation to make a correct judgment (high vs. low) and information presentation order[3] (COO first vs. COO later in the information sequence).

Selection of Stimulus Materials

Product. Watches were chosen as the product to be evaluated for two reasons. First, since virtually every student owned a watch, product information should therefore be comprehensible to all subjects. Second, manufacturing a watch may involve both technical skills, such as to increase the accuracy, and handcrafting skills, such as workmanship in hand-made watches.

COO. Two countries were selected that had substantially different reputations in manufacturing watches but evoked similar amounts of prior knowledge concerning these products. To make these selections, two sets of pilot data were collected. First, 24 undergraduates who did not perform in the main experiment evaluated the quality of watches made in each of 20 countries along a scale from 1 (extremely poor) to 9 (extremely good), with 0 indicating no impression at all. Ten countries were screened out because more than 10% of the subjects reported that they had no

---

[3] It should be noted that the purpose of including the last factor in the present design is for counterbalancing any plausible unexpected effect caused by the order of information presented.

impression about watches made in those countries. The two countries with the highest ratings were Switzerland ($X=8.71$) and Japan ($X=8.04$). The two countries with lowest ratings were Mainland China ($X=3.42$) and Taiwan ($X=5.83$).

A different group of 48 subjects was asked to write down product information about the watches made in each of the four countries noted above. The number of attributes mentioned was greatest for watches made in Japan ($X=9.25$), followed by Switzerland and China (in each case, $X=7.67$) and Taiwan ($X=4.08$). These differences were assumed to reflect the differences in the amount of information (about watch-making) that could be signified by these country names. Based on these differences, Switzerland and China were chosen as the countries of origin to be used in the main experiment. These two countries, therefore, differed extremely in reputation, whereas the number of inferences subjects could make was the same.

Attribute information. A total of 45 different attribute dimensions were mentioned by the pilot subjects described in the previous paragraph. The 32 attribute dimensions that were mentioned most frequently were selected for use as product information. The eight dimensions that were mentioned most frequently by pilot subjects were assumed to be the most commonly considered bases for judging watches. Attributes along these dimensions, which included price, style, durability and accuracy, were used as product information in all conditions. Of these, four conveyed the favorable pole of the dimension in question, and four conveyed the unfavorable pole of the dimension[4]. Attributes along the other 24 dimensions, which were mentioned less frequently by pilot subjects, were used as product information in high-information-load conditions only.

Procedure

Subjects participated in the experiment in groups of four. They were introduced to the study with instructions that they would be asked to view some slides containing information about a watch, and that after receiving this information, they would decide whether or not they would like to purchase the product. They were told that if they made a correct decision, they would receive a monetary reward of either HK$10 (*high-motivation* conditions) or HK$1 (*low-motivation* conditions). The criterion for "correctness" was ostensibly based on objective criteria they would be told about later.

Subjects were exposed to each stimulus slide for 5 seconds. (Pretesting determined that this duration was sufficient to read and comprehend the information conveyed.) The first, warm-up slide indicated that the experiment was sponsored by the "Hong Kong and China Gas Company Ltd." This procedure was expected to increase the plausibility of the motivation manipulation, suggesting indirectly that subjects would actually receive the monetary reward indicated. The slides that followed each contained a different piece of information.

In *low-information-amount* conditions, subjects received descriptions of the COO and eight attributes, with the COO information conveyed either first or seventh in the series. In *high-information-amount* conditions, subjects first received the 24 additional attributes, followed by the eight attributes, with the COO information presented either first or twenty-fifth in the series. (The eight attributes were presented after the 24 additional attributes in order to control for the time interval between subjects' receipt of the important attribute information and the judgments they were asked to make.)

Assessment of Dependent Variables

After viewing the stimulus slides, subjects completed a product-evaluation questionnaire. First, they evaluated the watch with respect to each of the 32 attributes, regardless of whether they had received information about the attribute. These ratings were made along semantic differential scales from -4 (e.g. ugly, inaccurate) to +4 (e.g. beautiful, accurate). Then, they estimated (a) the overall quality of the watch along a scale from -4 (very bad) to +4 (very good), and (b) how well they liked the watch along a scale from -4 (dislike very much) to +4 (like very much).

Three manipulation checks were obtained. First, subjects were asked to recall the product's COO and then to evaluate the general quality of the watches made in that country along a scale from -4 (very poor) to +4 (very good). Then, they rated the reward they were given for correct judgments along a scale from -4 (too little) to +4 (very reasonable), and the amount of product information they had received along a scale from -4 (insufficient) to +4 (too much).

Upon completing the questionnaire, subjects were debriefed about the nature of the experiment. They were asked not to disclose any information about the experiment to any person. Subjects were then paid according to what they were told, and dismissed.

RESULTS

The evaluations of the 32 product attributes were first reduced to two factors. Then, to verify if the data resemble the pattern suggested by the signalling and/or attribute hypotheses, the effect of COO was initially examined via three 4-way ANOVAs, with COO (Switzerland vs. China), information amount (high vs. low), motivation (high vs low) and information presentation order (COO presented first vs. near the end of the stimulus series) as independent variables; the two factors (from the solution of factor analysis) and overall product evaluation as dependent variables. Information presentation order had no significant effects, and so it will not be discussed further. (The results reported below are based on analyses that are pooled over this factor.)

Manipulation Checks

The manipulations were successful. Subjects believed that watches made in Switzerland were generally of better quality than those made in China ($X=2.13$ vs. $X=-1.56$), $F(1,254)=365.10$, $p<.01$. Subjects felt the incentive was more reasonable if they had been promised HK$10 than if they had been promised HK$1 ($X=.98$ vs. $X=-.20$), $F(1,254)=22.10$, $p<.01$. Finally, subjects who had seen 32 pieces of information felt they had received more information than those who had seen only eight pieces ($X=1.27$ vs. $X=-2.15$), $F(1,254)=195.50$, $p<.01$.

Identifying domains of Specific Product Evaluations

Factor analysis, with oblique rotation, was performed to identify the domains of specific product evaluations. The scree test suggested that a two-factor solution was appropriate. Three attributes were deleted due to double loadings on both factors. The remaining 29 attributes were then reanalyzed and condensed to two factors, which explained 41% of variance. The alpha coefficients were .88 and .87 for factor 1 and 2, respectively. All factor loadings were above .43 and .32 for factor 1 and 2, and no double loadings occurred in the final solution.

Examples of attributes that fell into factor 1 were decoration, style, and color matching. This factor can be conceptualized as

---

[4] English translation of these and other attributes used in the study may be obtained from the first author.

TABLE 2
Effects of COO on Product Evaluations as a Function of Information Amount and Motivation

	Evaluations of Style Attributes	Evaluations of Function Attributes	Overall Evaluations
Low Information Amount, Low Motivation			
Switzerland	.60	-.36	-1.39
China	-.06	-.74	-1.78
difference	.66*	.38	.39
Low Information Amount, High Motivation			
Switzerland	.78	-.37	-1.19
China	.20	-.33	-1.11
difference	.58*	-.04	-.08
High Information Amount, Low Motivation			
Switzerland	-1.29	1.23	-1.98
China	-1.64	1.29	-1.98
difference	.35	-.06	.00
High Information Amount, High Motivation			
Switzerland	-1.02	1.88	-0.80
China	-1.40	1.69	-2.09
difference	.38	.38	1.29*

*Difference is significant at $p<.01$.

"style". Examples of attributes that loaded on factor 2 were water resistance, durability, and shocking resistance. This factor can be labelled as "function". The correlation between these two factors was -.04 (n.s.) which suggests these two factors represented two different domains of watch evaluation, namely, style and function.

Specific and Overall Product Evaluations

Specific product evaluations. The evaluations of the two specific factors, style and function, are shown in Table 2 as a function of information amount, motivation, and COO. The effect of COO on style evaluations was significant in the low information amount conditions, but not in high information amount conditions. However, its effect on function evaluations was not significant in any conditions.

This pattern of results is consistent with the signalling hypothesis and therefore implies that COO played a signalling role, but not an attribute role, on the evaluation of the style of a watch. However, in evaluating the function of the watch, COO did not have a significant role. This finding is consistent with our intuition that evaluation of style is more subjective, and therefore more likely to be affected by our inferences.

Overall Product Evaluations. Subjects' estimates of the quality of the product were correlated .76 with their liking estimates. The two ratings were therefore averaged to provide a single index of overall product evaluations. These evaluations are shown in Table 2. The effect of COO was significant only when both information amount and motivation were high.

This pattern of results lends partial support to the attribute hypothesis, and does not support the signalling hypothesis. Hierarchical regression analyses were therefore conducted on overall product evaluations, to verify if COO really played an attribute role in the high-information-amount and high-motivation condition.

If COO was considered as a product attribute which can provide benefits that are unique and different from other attributes, its effect on overall product evaluations should be over and above the effects of the other attributes. Hence, evaluations of style and function were entered first into the regression equation, followed by COO. The adjusted R^2 for style and function together was .20 ($p<.01$), whereas the change of R^2 was .08 ($p<.01$) when COO was entered into the equation.

Realizing that the two factors might not be a good representation of all 32 attributes, a hierarchical regression analysis was again performed with the 32 attributes entered first, followed by COO. The adjusted R^2 for the 32 attributes was .42 ($p<.01$), whereas the change of R^2 was .05 ($p<.05$) when COO was entered into the equation[5]. The results of regression analyses, therefore, confirmed that COO was considered as a product attribute in the overall product evaluation of a watch when both information amount and motivation were high.

---

[5] It should be emphasized that the COO effect on overall product evaluation is over and above the effect of the other 32 attributes, and therefore a change of .05 in R^2 should be appreciable. In fact, when country of origin was entered first into the regression equation, it explained 37.2% of variance on overall product evaluation.

DISCUSSION

We have considered two plausible roles that COO may play on product evaluations. Results indicated that COO can play both the signalling and attribute roles on product evaluations. This finding is consistent with the integrative framework proposed by Johansson (1989), as well as the verbal protocols reported by Li and Monroe (1992). In addition, the present study identified the conditions for the occurrence of the signalling and attribute roles. Furthermore, the data also suggest that the signalling role dominated the attribute role under the conditions in which both roles were facilitated.

The Signalling Role

The results reported above provide support for Hypothesis 1. Specifically, subjects used COO as a signal for the style, but not for the functional performance, of a watch. Therefore, we conclude that COO may only signal a certain domain, but not every domain, of product quality. Moreover, COO did not directly signal the overall product quality. The indirect effect of COO on overall product evaluation suggests that whether there is a COO effect or not depends on the relative importance of the "affected" and "unaffected" domains in making overall product evaluations. As in the two conditions in which the signalling role was supported, the regression coefficients of style on overall product evaluations were .22 and .32, respectively. However, the regression coefficients of function on overall product evaluations were .47 and .54, respectively, heavier than that of style on overall product evaluations. Since COO effect was only significant in the less important domain (style), but not significant in a more important domain (function), therefore, COO effect on overall product evaluations was not significant.

The finding that COO only signalled a certain domain of product quality when limited information was presented, but not when sufficient amount of information was presented, can be explained in the light of the economics of information. Stigler (1961) argued that consumers would employ cost and benefit analysis in order to decide whether to conduct information search or not. Obviously, the net benefits of conducting an internal information search are higher when subjects only have limited product information. Therefore, the signalling process occurred in low information amount conditions, but not in high information amount conditions.

The Attribute Role

The results also suggest that subjects regarded COO as a product attribute that can provide benefits to them. This occurred when both motivation and information amount were high. This finding provides partial support to hypothesis 2. However, in the high-motivation and low-information-amount condition, in which both signalling and attribute roles were expected to occur, only a signalling effect was observed. This finding suggest that the signalling role dominated the attribute role.

The dominance of the signalling role over the attribute role can also be explained by economics of information. If we assume consumers do not use a piece of information twice to prevent any "double counting", then the benefits of using COO to infer several different attributes are obviously higher than using it as a single piece of information. Therefore, using COO as a signal was preferred to using it as a product attribute when limited information was available.

On the other hand, when information amount is sufficient, highly motivated subjects were more likely to process and use all of the available information, whereas subjects with little motivation selectively attended to and used only part of the available information in the overall product evaluation process.

Conclusion and Direction for Future Research

The findings reported above revealed that COO can play two different roles in making product evaluations, a signalling role and an attribute role. While the signalling role is more likely to occur when information amount is low, the attribute role is more likely to occur when motivation is high. However, when the condition favors both roles to occur (low information amount and high motivation), the signalling role will dominate the attribute role, and therefore they will not occur simultaneously. Nevertheless, this is only the first study to report the dual roles did not occur simultaneously. There may be some situations in which both roles can occur at the same time. Further replications are necessary to validate the present findings.

It is important to note that COO signalled only the subjective aspect (style) of the product but not the objective aspect (function) of the product. Therefore, we speculate that COO may have stronger effect on "affective" products, such as perfume or earrings, but weak effect on "functional" products, such as paper and pencil. However, we definitely need more studies to verify this speculation.

It should be noted that the product we used may limit the external validity of the present finding. As Li and Monroe (1992) indicated, the type of product considered can affect the role that COO may play. Therefore, future studies should try to incorporate products of different technological level to extend the external validity of the present findings.

It is also important to understand whether other extrinsic cues, such as price and brand names, can also play these two roles. Future studies can incorporate these extrinsic cues to examine if their underlying processes are the same as those we identified in the present research. These studies might stimulate the development of a more general theory of extrinsic cues on product evaluations.

REFERENCES

Bilkey, Warren J. and Erik Nes (1982), "Country-Of-Origin Effects on Product Evaluations," *Journal of International Business Studies*, 13(Spring/Summer), 89-99.

Borgida, E., and Howard-Pitney, B. (1983), "Personal Involvement and the Robustness of Perceptual Salience Effects," *Journal of Personality and Social Psychology*, 45(March), 560-570.

Celsi, Richard L. and Jerry C. Olson (1988), "The Role of Involvement in Attention and Comprehension Processes," *Journal of Consumer Research*, 15(September), 210-224.

Chaiken, Shelly, Akiva Liberman and Alice H. Eagly (1989), "Heuristic and Systematic Information Processing within and beyond the Persuasion Context," in *Unintended Thought*, eds. James S. Uleman and John A. Bargh, NY: Guilford Press, p.212-253

Han, C. Min (1989), "Country Image: Halo or Summary Construct?" *Journal of Marketing Research*, 26(May), 222-229.

Harris, Greg (1987), "The Implications of Low-Involvement Theory for Advertising Effectiveness," *International Journal of Advertising*, 6(3), 207-221.

Havlena, William J. and Wayne S. Desarbo (1991), "On the Measurement of Perceived Consumer Risk," *Decision Sciences*, 22, 927-939.

Hong, Sung-tai and Robert S. Wyer (1989), "Effects of Country-of-Origin and Product-Attribute Information on Product Evaluation: An Information Processing Perspective." *Journal of Consumer Research*, 16(September), 175-187.

Hong, Sung-tai and Robert S. Wyer (1990), "Determinants of Product Evaluation: Effects of the Time Interval Between Knowledge of a Product's CO and Information about its Country of Origin Specific Attributes," *Journal of Consumer Research*, 17(December), 277-288.

Hoyer, W. D. (1984), "An Examination of Consumer Decision Making for a Common Repeat Purchase Product," *Journal of Consumer Research*, 11, 822-829.

Johansson, Johny K. (1989), "Determinants and Effects of the Use of 'Made in' Labels," *International Marketing Review*, 6(January), 47-58.

Li, Wai-Kwan, and Kent B. Monroe (1992), "The Role of Country of Origin Information on Buyers' Product Evaluations: An In-depth Interview Approach," in *AMA Educators' Proceedings: Enhancing Knowledge Development in Marketing*, in press.

Li, Wai-Kwan and Robert S. Wyer, Jr. (1991), "Country-Of-Origin Effects on Product Evaluations: The Role of Information Load, Decision Importance, and Product Familiarity," Working paper, University of Illinois at Urbana-Champaign.

Ozsomer, Aysegul and S. Tamer Cavusgil (1991), "Country-Of-Origin Effects on Product Evaluations: A Sequel to Bilkey and Nes Review," in *AMA Educators' Proceedings: Enhancing Knowledge Development in Marketing*, Volume 2, eds. Gilly et al., Chicago, 269-277.

Rao, Akshay R. and Kent B. Monroe (1988), "The Moderating Effect of Prior Knowledge on Cue Utilization in Product Evaluations," *Journal of Consumer Research*, 15(September), 253-64.

Rao, Akshay R. and Kent B. Monroe (1989), "The Effect of Price, Brand Name, and Store Name on Buyers' Perceptions of Product Quality: An Integrative Review," *Journal of Marketing Research*, 26(August), 351-7.

Scitovszky, Tibor (1945), "Some Consequences of the Habit of Judging Quality by Price," *Review of Economic Studies*, 12(Winter), 100-105.

Steenkamp, Jan-Benedict E.M. (1989), "A Model of the Quality Perception Process,: from *Product Quality*, Assen/Maastricht, The Netherlands: Van Gorcum, 99-129.

Stigler, G. (1961), "The Economics of Information," *Journal of Political Economy*, 69(June), 213-225.

Zaichkowsky, Judith L. (1986), "Conceptualizing involvement," *Journal of Advertising*, 15(2), 4-14.

Zeithaml, Valarie A. (1988), "Consumer Perceptions of Price, Quality, and Value: A Means-End Model and Synthesis of Evidence," *Journal of Marketing*, 52(July), 2-22.

Comments of Evolving Country of Origin Research
Carl Obermiller, Seattle University

THE ROLES OF COUNTRY OF ORIGIN INFORMATION ON BUYER'S PRODUCT EVALUATIONS: SIGNAL OR ATTRIBUTE?
(Li, Leung, and Wyer)

By the time I reached the results section of this paper, I had several critical comments. First, why examine two processes with two manipulations and consider only the main effects of one manipulation on one process and the other manipulation on the second process, as if this were two studies conducted on the same subjects. Both information load and motivation are apt to influence both the roles of CO as signal and as attribute; yet, no hypotheses are presented for half the outcomes of the design. Second, the logic of the second, and more interesting, hypothesis is not compelling. The hypothesis assumes that the attribute value of CO is less salient than other attribute information. No justification for such an assumption is given, and several counter-examples come quickly to mind—French champagne, Russian caviar, German automobiles, American politicians. For American consumers of any of these products, CO labels confer authenticity, social standing, or patriotism directly and immediately; for some products, at least, CO is a highly salient cue. An alternative interpretation of H2 logic is that CO is but one of many cues that might be processed; and, higher motivation leads to more cues' being processed. This interpretation assumes that increasing motivation has no effect on the relative salience of the cues. One might argue that increasing motivation shifts salience away from such peripheral cues as CO labels. In which case, higher motivation might lead to a reduced attribute effect. Thus, although H2 was an interesting conjecture, I felt it lacked sufficient a priori justification for an hypothesis.

My third criticism of Li, et al, (up to the point at which they presented results) was the confounding of information level with time of presentation. The high information condition was about 300% longer duration. Although in both conditions the important eight attributes immediately preceded the dependent measures in both conditions, one could expect that attention to those eight attributes waned in the high information condition. Thus, any lack of effect of signalling might be due to a design artifact. An alternative procedure might have been presenting the information simultaneously, as in a print format; which would allow the viewer to scan and focus attention on important bits of information.

My more serious questions of Li, et al arise with the presentation and interpretation of the results. At the heart of the problem is the lack of a measure of the effect of attribute processing. Recall that the dependent measures were 32 attribute scales and several scales of global quality. It is surprising that, having done prior research demonstrating the attribute effect, no measures specific to it were included. In fact, the only evidence presented for the hypothesized attribute process effect is the result of step-wise regressions in which the attribute ratings are entered first, followed by the CO labels. The significant change in adjusted R^2 is attributed to the attribute process. While it is clear from such an analysis that the attribute ratings do not explain all the variance captured by the CO labels; it is also true that we cannot simply assume that the additional explained variance is due to the CO-as-attribute processing. Something else is contained in the CO labels, but this study cannot claim to have ruled out all but two possible effects of country-of-origin labels. The lack of a direct measure of the attribute effect is a serious flaw.

Equally distressing and even more confusing is the introduction of another variable in the results section. The 32 attributes are factor-analyzed into two categories, interpreted as style and function. Most of the ensuing discussion of the results focuses on the different outcomes for style and function evaluations, with considerable effort to present these differences as support for the original hypotheses. The discussion is so dedicated to style and function that one might wonder if the second half of this paper were not mismatched with the first. It is unclear if the style/function dichotomy ought to have been anticipated in the hypotheses. I think the problem reflects the failure to design the research with adequate dependent measures. The hypotheses of the study do not warrant measures of 32 specific attributes (but do warrant measures of the attribute effect). The style/function split is sensible; but the different effects of these two dependent measures, combined with the indirect assessment of attribute effects, results in a confusing presentation of the studies results and a tenuous interpretation.

Included in the interpretation are three points that raised questions. First, the limited effect of information on signalling (for style but not function) was explained in terms of information economics. Why is this theoretical base introduced in the discussion section rather than as justification for the hypothesis? Second, the dominance of the signalling role over the attribute role (an arguable conclusion) is suggested as explainable if we assume that consumers do not use any piece of information more than once. This assumption is supported by the argument that CO would be used as a signalling cue rather than an attribute. The justification is that a signalling cue can be used to infer "several different attributes." Why should we assume that consumers can use a cue to infer multiple attributes but not to infer an attribute and a value? Moreover, we have substantial evidence to suggest that consumers show no such limitation in their interpretation of price cues, which are used both to infer other attribute values and to imply economic sacrifice and to impute social standing and to estimate future prices, etc, etc. Finally, the stress of inadequate dependent variables leads to the speculation that CO labels have stronger effects on "affective" products than on "functional" products. While some marginal difference may exist, and the question may lead to fruitful investigations, both the premise and the implication appear erroneous. The premise is that product type differences dominate other factors. I think it unlikely that a such a gross dichotomy as affective/functional product type will be as fruitful as psychological variables. Not only are few products likely to be purely one or the other, there may be no products for whom there is consensus of perception—what is affective for one person is functional for another. The implication, that one should expect a main effect across products, runs contrary to most of the CO research that has been done, which has examined a long list of primarily functional products—including, automobiles, computers, cameras, camping stoves, and stereo systems.

COUNTRY-OF-ORIGIN, PERCEIVED RISK AND EVALUATION STRATEGY
(Alden, Hoyer, and Crowley)

I found the Alden, et al study a sophisticated research design; my two questions address its flanks, the ramparts of its middle being well fortified. First, the question of applying the results: The authors cite the impending free trade agreement as a reason to study the Mexico label and as a reason to expect CO to become more relevant as product information. No evidence is offered, however, to indicate the extent to which consumers outside the lab attend to CO labels. In fact, I would use the study's own pretest results to argue that consumers may gloss over the CO label. I can offer no other explanation for the finding that "Made in Mexico" as part of a description of toothpaste did not differ in typicality from "Made in the U.S." I should require a great deal of persuasion to be convinced that consumers equally expect their toothpastes to be produced in these two countries. On the other hand, I can easily accept that consumers pay little heed to where their toothpastes are made. Low involvement products are low involvement products, after all; and, before we extend our findings too far from the lab, we should determine the extent to which CO cues are processed under low involvement. ("Low" involvement outside the lab is likely to be considerably lower than inside.)

The second question is both more and less important. Less important because the results stand regardless of the naming of the constructs; more important because the results may be misunderstood as conceptualized. This question involves the three constructs—involvement, perceived risk, and typicality. Alden, et al argue that higher perceived risk, as indicated by CO, triggers a shift in involvement; independent of the typicality of the CO cue. My question is, how can the risk associated with the CO cue be interpreted unless involvement is high. As I reason above, for low involvement products, consumers are not apt to examine peripheral cues in order to make evaluative inferences. In short, consumers will not recognize any implications of the CO cue unless the country is atypical. An unexpected bit of information (atypical CO) would increase motivation to process, shifting evaluation from category- to attribute-based, and lead to a negative effect of higher perceived risk. Given the study that was done, the confusion of constructs is difficult to sort out, since Mexico is arguably both less typical and higher in perceived risk. A test of the differences might be conducted with CO's of equal perceived risk but different levels of typicality and different implications for evaluation. For example, Italy and U.S. may be equally risky CO's for dress shoes; Mexico, again, more risky. Italy may signal the highest quality, U.S. middle quality, and Mexico low quality. If this is so, the Alden, et al logic would suggest equal evaluations for U.S. and Italy, lower for Mexico, based on the perceived risks. I would suggest both the Italy and Mexico labels would seem atypical and would shift consumers to further analysis, with the results positive for Italy and negative for Mexico, relative to the U.S.

AN EXPLORATORY INVESTIGATION OF HOLISTIC AND ANALYTIC MODES OF PRODUCT PERCEPTION
(Baumgartner)

This paper does not deal with CO, although I see its significance to that research stream. Like the other authors, Baumgartner examines alternative processing modes. He discusses holistic and analytic perception, presents a methodology for examining them, and tests the methodology in a product perception study. The dichotomy Baumgartner addresses is quite similar to the category/attribute distinction considered by Alden, et al. As is typical in consumer behavior's borrowing of theory from psychology, some of the limitations have been loosened. Consumer behaviorists who have examined category-based processing do not limit processing to integral attributes as holistic processing is characterized in psychology. (Integral attributes are characteristics of an object that cannot be considered separately from the object, e.g. brightness.) In general, Baumgartner applies holistic processing to product perception much as Alden, et al do category-based processing—perception based on little motivation, little elaboration. Baumgartner focuses on perception; but, his logic is consistent with the subsequent differences in evaluation that are the primary concern of Alden, et al.

Baumgartner's study is an adequate introduction to a new methodology and a potentially fruitful theory; but, several aspects are troublesome. The first is his appeal to low statistical power in defense of marginal significance levels. On the one hand, he suggests power *may* be low; he should compute the power and answer his own conjecture. On the other hand, he ought to have considered power beforehand and designed the study with adequate statistical conclusion validity. (Too few of us consider power until it's too late; Mea culpa.) A second problem is the reversal of endpoints for the classification index (in the revised draft; I do not know if this error persisted to the final copy). Holistic processors may skip over the mistake; analytic processors are apt to be confused and dubious. My final disagreement is with Baumgartner's conclusion that the finding that decision time was related to classification process implies that consumers' time budgets will influence their decision processes. Although I agree with him, I think the conclusion should be tempered; the results are consistent with the conjecture, but not suggestive. The manipulation of decision process caused a change in decision time. One cannot logically conclude that a change in decision time would, therefore, cause a change in decision process.

CONCLUSION

None of the papers focused on the description or meaning of specific cues. Early research on country-of-origin accomplished little beyond identifying which countries supplied positive, which negative effects on product evaluations. Much of the motivation of the research stream came from disagreements about whether CO cues did or did not have significant effects; but, of course the discrepancies came, in part, from using different countries, different subjects, different products, and different processing situations. The current papers show a marked advance in our level of analysis. They share a strong grounding in theory. The two papers that address CO could as easily have dealt with other bits of product information—price, brand name, store name, or product category. Specific country effects on product evaluation can, as a result, be expected to differ as conditions change their typicality, perceived risk, or their value as attributes. Moreover, the nature by which consumers process CO cues depends on basic forces such as motivation, time, ability, and expectations. Different findings for specific country effects may be explainable as differences in the underlying theoretical framework for product evaluations.

An important next step, if CO research is to remain vibrant, is to address the question of relevance. More work should be done on the way consumers use CO information in mundane situations. How salient is CO? Does CO salience differ by product involvement? Outside the laboratory, what determines the extent to which consumers process categorically/holistically versus by attribute/analytically? And, how does CO influence the process of evaluation, and how is it treated in each? To answer these questions, we need to do more field research, surveys, observations, intercept questionnaires, etc. And, we need to design laboratory studies that simulate the relevant dimensions of natural environments—lack of focused attention, realistic levels of involvement, perhaps even controlled levels of distraction such as might be encountered in stores or in advertising viewing environments. Although I have raised questions about many of the details of the research in these papers, I commend the authors for their grounding of the work in theoretical frameworks that can be generalized. Now, I think we can turn some attention to expanding those theories, making them robust enough to survive outside the lab.

An Extended Perspective on the Role of Emotion in Advertising Processing

Hyongoh Cho, University of Texas at Austin
Patricia A. Stout, University of Texas at Austin

ABSTRACT

The emotion construct in advertising processing continues to capture the attention of advertising researchers. This paper extends the perspective of the role of emotion in advertising processing in two ways: by integrating consumption characteristics or value-expressive beliefs into the role of emotional responses in the advertising context and by relating the emotional responses to a multidimensional construct of Aad. Three TV commercials representing a range of transformational and informational appeals are tested. Results indicate that certain emotional responses tend to exert greater influence on the affective dimension of Aad than the cognitive dimension of Aad. The relative impact of emotional responses on the value-expressive and utilitarian beliefs is contingent upon ad type. The impact of emotional responses on brand attitude is completely mediated by the multidimensional measures of Aad and Cb. Overall, the relative strength of the causal linkage between emotional responses and the multidimensional constructs of the mediating parameters depends on specific emotional characteristics as well as the type of ad execution.

Since the early 80s, many advertising researchers have extended their attention from the cognitive structures of advertising (e.g., product beliefs, comprehension of ad message, source-related cognitive responses) to the role of the affective properties in advertising processing (e.g., emotional responses, Aad, mood, music). It is suggested that affect and cognition are separate and partially independent systems and that although they ordinarily function conjointly, affect may not require the mediation of cognitive processes as a necessary element in the generation of emotional states (Zajonc 1980). Attitude is not only mediated by salient beliefs about the product attributes, but also by mere association with the affective stimuli in the ad (Mitchell and Olson 1981).

Although the unique role of emotional responses in the consumer behavior has been widely investigated, it is our feeling that current knowledge about the emotion construct is still narrowly focused and discloses a wide gap between the emotional processing in the advertising context and the emotional characteristics in the consumption experience. This paper intends to integrate the consumption characteristics into the role of emotional responses in the advertising context. More specifically, we examine the impact of the emotional responses on attitude toward the ad (Aad), brand cognition (Cb), and brand attitude (Ab) and attempt to relate various consumption experiences and motives to these relationships.

THE ROLE OF EMOTIONAL RESPONSE IN ADVERTISING PROCESSING

The relationship between emotional response and Aad

Extensive research has investigated the causal linkage between a variety of emotional properties and Aad. For instance, Aad can be influenced by various emotional properties such as PAD (or Pleasure, Arousal, and Dominance) dimensions (Holbrook and Batra 1987), discriminant negative and positive feelings (Edell and Burke 1987), various depth of emotional associations with oneself (Stout and Leckenby 1986), emotional intensity (Stephens and Russo 1987) and warmth (Stayman and Aaker 1988). Despite some conceptual ambiguity between emotional responses (ERs) and other types of affective constructs, it appears that ERs are not only distinct from Aad and other types of affect but play a discriminant role in the formation of Aad.

However, previous research tended to oversimplify the Aad construct by conceptualizing it as a unidimensional construct and measuring it as the overall evaluation of the ad stimuli. Many studies have evidenced the multidimensional Aad construct consisting of cognitive and affective components (Burton and Lichtenstein 1988; Madden et al. 1988; Miniard et al. 1990; Olney et al. 1991). The multidimensional construct is not only superior to the unidimensional approach in predicting Ab, but provides in-depth information on the dynamic relationship between the Aad and other competing parameters.

While few studies investigated how ERs relate to the multidimensional construct of Aad, the incorporation of ERs into the multidimensional Aad construct is expected to enrich our understanding about the characteristics of the affective properties in ad processing. A dual processing perspective for the formation of Aad may provide an useful framework underlying this relationship. Several studies propose that Aad can be formed via central and peripheral processing (MacKenzie and Lutz 1989; Miniard et al. 1990). Although ERs have not been directly incorporated in their models, ERs have been characterized as an affective construct and are likely to represent the affective dimension of the Aad. Based on the multidimensional perspective of the formation of Aad and dual processing perspectives, we hypothesize that:

H1: ERs exert significant influence on the formation of Aad. The impact of ERs on the affective dimension of Aad is greater than their impact on the cognitive dimension of Aad.

The relationship between emotional response and brand cognition

While many studies postulated ERs as an antecedent of Aad and Ab, few studies have studied the causal linkage between ERs and Cb (Burke and Edell 1989; Edell and Burke 1987). Even those studies which found a significant relationship between ERs and Cb did not provide an adequate explanation about the underlying mechanism for the transfer of ERs to Cb. The insufficient theoretical support for this relationship in the stream of Aad research may be partly attributed to the widespread perception that ERs are likely to represent and facilitate heuristic (Chaiken 1980) or peripheral processing (Petty and Cacioppo 1981). ERs can occur even in the absence of minimal cognitive processing and tend to be automatic or involuntary (Zajonc 1980).

Contrary to the previous emotion studies, we suggest that ERs can influence the evaluation of the product attributes for three reasons. First, the affective and cognitive elements of the persuasion process may be highly intertwined and have a synergistic effect on consumers' information processing. ERs not only affect the amount of cognitive processing, but also increase the accessibility of certain types of product attributes congruent with their emotional state (Forgas and Bower 1987). ERs also have a direct and an indirect impact on brand beliefs via ad judgment (Burke and Edell 1989; Edell and Burke 1988). Thus, it appears that various types of ERs can enhance or decrease the evaluation of product information, creating discriminant impacts on Cb. Secondly, previous emotion and Aad studies tended to narrowly define the boundary of Cb.

Most studies have focused on only functional, tangible or utilitarian characteristics of product attributes in the measure of Cb or the development of test ads. Considering that many researchers have distinguished between utilitarian and value-expressive functions of a product (Hirschman and Holbrook 1982; Howard and Sheth 1969), it is rather surprising that the value-expressive characteristics of product attributes have been largely ignored in advertising processing. The incorporation of image benefits or value-expressive attributes to the multiattribute measure of brand beliefs demonstrated significant incremental contribution of Cb to Ab (Mittal 1990). Finally, the extension of the consumer research from buying decision to consumption experience has enriched our understanding about the importance of value-expressiveness or imagery in the consumption process. The value-expressiveness of product consumption has been reflected in the studies of hedonic consumption (Hirschman and Holbrook 1982), meaning of the possession (Prentice 1987), consumption motives (McGuire 1976), symbolism in the product (Belk 1982), and self-concept (Sirgy 1982).

The value-expressive and utilitarian attributes can be characterized by the tangibility of the product attributes, type of benefits, and drives underlying the consumption. Value-expressive attributes are directed at abstract, subjective or intangible aspects of a product whereas the utilitarian attributes derive from the concrete, objective or tangible characteristics of a product (Fin 1985). Value-expressive attributes are targeted at the aesthetic or symbolic benefits as a means to express valued personal traits, whereas utilitarian attributes contribute to the instrumental or functional benefits as a means to affect and control the physical environment (Prentice 1987; Swan and Combs 1976). Finally, the product attributes can be characterized by either hedonically driven consumption motives or economic, utilitarian motives to manage the surrounding environment (Hirschman and Holbrook 1982; McGuire 1976).

Overall, the emotional components in the consumption experience are inseparable from self-expressiveness of oneself, and when consumers look for emotional experience in the product, they are likely to become more receptive to the value expressive attributes in the product as opposed to utilitarian attributes of the product. Therefore, it is our contention that the ERs created by ad exposure will stimulate and facilitate the processing of value-expressive and imagery characteristics of product attributes. We hypothesize that:

H2: ERs are a significant predictor of brand cognition. The effect of the ERs on the value-expressive responses is greater than their effect on the utilitarian responses.

The direct impact of ERs on Ab beyond the mediation of Aad and Cb

Previous studies demonstrate somewhat conflicting findings regarding the direct impact of ERs on Ab beyond the mediation of Aad. Many studies find that the impact of ERs on Ab becomes insignificant when Aad is incorporated in the equation, suggesting the path between ERs and Ab as being completely mediated by Aad (Batra and Ray 1986; Edell and Burke 1987; Holbrook and Batra 1987). In contrast, Stayman and Aaker (1988) found that some of the feeling responses were not completely mediated by Aad, indicating the direct impact of the feeling responses on Ab. They explain that "the single exposure typically used in previous studies may have been insufficient to obtain either the necessary variation in feeling response or the the association between the response and attitudes" (p. 371). More conclusive evidence for the direct impact of ERs on Ab beyond Cb and Aad is provided by Burke and Edell (1989). While each dimension of feeling responses had direct and indirect impact on Aad and Cb via ad judgment response, upbeat and negative feelings had a direct impact on Ab beyond the mediation by either Aad or Cb. Therefore, it is likely that a wide range of ERs is a necessary condition for its direct impact on Ab beyond Aad.

Considering that these findings are based on unidimensional constructs of Aad and Cb, it is unclear whether the direct effect of ERs on Ab would be still significant after multidimensional measures of Aad and Cb are introduced. Since the global evaluation of Aad would explain less variance of Ab than the multidimensional measures of Aad, it is likely that the direct impact of ERs on Ab decreases when Aad is operationalized as a multidimensional construct. Also, some variance of Ab directly explained by ERs may be captured by the multidimensional measures of Cb. We hypothesize the following:

H3: The direct impact of the ERs on Ab with unidimensional measures of Aad and Cb becomes insignificant when both Aad and Cb are measured as a multidimensional construct.

METHOD

Subjects: Fifty five student subjects were recruited from undergraduate communication courses at a large southwestern university and given course credit for participation.

Stimuli: The test ads include three 30-second TV commercials that have not been aired previously in the area and are for brands not available in the area to avoid the confounding effect of prior Ab with the ad-generated responses. The three products include beer, toilet tissue, and insect repellent, typically used by the target subjects.

Since we intend to test the causal linkage between ERs and other types of cognitive and affective parameters (i.e., value-expressive vs. utilitarian brand beliefs, affective vs. cognitive dimensions of Aad), it is important to extend the opportunity to generate a wide range of cognitive and affective responses to ad. We employed the informational/transformational scales of Puto and Wells (1984) to select the ads representing both emotional and informational appeals. Based on a pretest of eighteen ads, three 30-second commercials were selected. The test ads include 1 primarily transformational ad (t value= 3.63, p <.01), 1 primarily informational ad (t value= -8.75, p <.001), and 1 equally transformational/informational ad (t value= .20, p= .844).

Procedures: Subjects were instructed to view each of the three videotaped commercials. The sequence of the commercials was equally randomized to minimize any order effect. After the subjects viewed each videotaped commercial three times, they were asked to indicate their ERs, Aad, Cb, and Ab for each of the test commercials.

Measures

ERs: The emotion checklist consisting of 50 adjective items was developed on the basis of the analysis of the previous emotion measures (Edell and Burke 1987; Holbrook and Batra 1987; Westbrook and Oliver 1991). Holbrook and Batra's (1987) 7-point check-mark scales are employed to measure the emotion scales with instructions on "*how the experience of watching the ad affected you emotionally, not how you describe the ad.*"

Aad: Sixteen 7-point semantic items were extracted from the previous Aad studies which successfully captured both affective and cognitive components of Aad in the measures (Burton and Lichtenstein 1988; Madden et al. 1988; Olney et al. 1990).

Cb: Subjects were asked to write down any thoughts, feelings or images toward the brand that went through their mind while watching the commercial. In addition, they were instructed to indicate the intensity of the valence for each thought by putting a number ranging from +3 to -3 with +3 representing a very positive thought and -3 a very negative thought. It is believed that the intensity of the valence may vary across different thoughts and by allowing unequal weight for each thought we may be able to measure the subjects' Cb more accurately. Two expert judges were employed to encode the subjects' free thoughts into the utilitarian and value-expressive responses toward the brand and commercial-related thoughts. Brand-related responses which may not be interpretable as either utilitarian or value-expressive responses are treated as general responses to the brand.

Ab: Ab was operationalized by three 7-point semantic differential scales. The scales of Ab include like/dislike, favorable/unfavorable, good/bad.

DATA ANALYSIS AND DISCUSSION

First, the emotion scales and the Aad scales were factor analyzed. In the emotion scales, 7 principle components with an eigenvalue greater than 1 emerged, far too many to use in the present analysis. A further examination of the scree test indicates that three factors are clearly distinguished from the rest. Accordingly, we extracted three principal components, all with eigenvalues greater than 4, accounting for 61.5 percent of the variance in the emotion scores. Due to the page limitation, loadings on the resulting dimensions using varimax-rotation are not reported here. Forty of 50, or 80 percent, of the emotion scales have correlated loadings greater than 0.50 on the three factors.

The structure of the emotional dimensions strongly supports the feeling scales identified in the studies of Edell and Burke (1987; Burke and Edell 1989). We refer to these three dimensions of feeling scales as upbeat, warm, and irritated feeling responses. In fact, these dimensions are not totally in conflict of the traditional PAD model. The Arousal dimension is well reflected in the upbeat scales, whereas the Pleasure dimension may not be a unidimensional construct, but rather consists of two distinct dimensions; that is, warm feelings and irritated feelings. Previous studies show that the positive and negative emotional responses can occur simultaneously and do not necessarily share a unidimensional structure (Burke and Edell 1989; Edell and Burke 1987). The absence of the dominance dimension may be attributed to the limited set of the test commercials. Alternatively, it may be argued that dominance dimension is not an important aspect of the consumers' ERs to TV commercials in general. The coefficient alpha for each scale is .97 for warm, .95 for upbeat, and .92 for irritated feelings.

The principal component analysis for the Aad measures strongly supports two distinct dimensions with eigenvalue greater than 1, accounting for 68.2 percent of the variance. Fourteen of 16 items have high loadings greater than .5 on these two dimensions. The structure of these two dimensions are virtually identical to the affective and cognitive dimensions developed in previous research. While the third dimension may be interpreted as "interestingness", as suggested by Olney et al. (1990), it is not included in our study due to the small amount of the variance explained by this dimension and the inadequate theoretical explanation for the dimension. The scalar items highly loaded on the affective dimension include affectionate/not affectionate, coldhearted/warmhearted, depressing/uplifting, fun to watch/not fun to watch, pleasant/unpleasant, soothing/not soothing, tasteful/tasteless and unattractive/attractive. The adjectives indicating the cognitive dimension are believable/unbelievable, convincing/not convincing, helpful/not helpful, ineffective/effective, informative/uninformative and persuasive/nonpersuasive. The coefficient alpha for each scale is .95 for the affective dimension, and .90 for the cognitive dimension. Three emotion scales and two Aad scales were formed by summing the ratings for those items that loaded greater than 0.5 on a factor, reverse scoring where necessary.

After coding the open-ended question for Cb, the interjudge reliability for the value-expressive and utilitarian measures of Cb was 83 percent. Overall, 86 percent of brand-related responses were either "utilitarian" or "value-expressive" responses, leaving the remaining 14 percent under a "general response" category. For the subsequent analysis, the scores of the utilitarian and value-expressive responses are computed by counting the number of value-expressive and utilitarian thoughts and multiplying them by the intensity of the valence for each thought. In the other dependent measures, the coefficient alphas for global Aad and Ab are .96 and .96 respectively.

A separate analysis for each commercial is conducted to examine the relationship between the ERs and the subsequent parameters because averaging the scores across three commercials may confound the idiosyncratic effect of the ad executions with the impact of emotional responses on the other explanatory variables. LISREL modeling (Joreskog and Sorbom 1986) is employed to test the causal linkage among ERs, Aad, Cb and Ab. In the model testing, ERs are postulated as having direct and indirect impact on Ab via multidimensional Aad and two components of Cb. Each of the multidimensional components of Aad and Cb is also hypothesized to have a direct effect on Ab (see Figure 1).

To conserve space, no further discussion on the latent measurement statistics is reported. In a sense, the proposed model does not exclude any alternative models; rather it mainly tests the relationship between ERs and the other explanatory variables of the interest. The proposed model fits the data fairly well for all three commercials in terms of chi-square and Joreskog and Sorbom's (1986) goodness-of-fit index. While chi-square may not be a reliable measure for a small sample size, the satisfactory GFI indicates a relatively good fit in the proposed model. Table 1 contains the path coefficients resulting from Generalized Least Square estimation of the model parameters.

Relationship between ERs on Multidimensional Aad

It is hypothesized that the impact of ERs on the affective dimension of Aad is greater than their impact on the cognitive dimension of Aad. The standardized path coefficients of the equation show that warm feelings have a significant effect only on the affective dimension of Aad across all three commercials, whereas upbeat and irritated feelings tend to exert significant influence on both affective and cognitive dimensions of Aad depending on the type of ad execution. More specifically, upbeat feelings demonstrate a strong impact on the affective Aad in the trans/informational ad, whereas the relationship becomes significant only through the cognitive dimension of Aad in the transformational ad. No impact of upbeat feelings on the multidimensional Aad is found for the informational ad type. On the other hand, irritated feelings become a salient indicator of the affective Aad in the trans/information and transformational ads. For the informational ad, irritated feelings influence both affective and cognitive components of Aad. Although the mechanism underlying the transfer of the upbeat and irritated feelings to the cognitive dimension of Aad is not known, our findings support the study of Burke and Edell (1989) in that upbeat and negative feelings demonstrate strong influence on the evaluation judgment which can be interpreted as the cognitive dimension of the Aad.

Overall, H1 is strongly supported for warm feelings and partially supported for irritated feelings. However, the relationship between ERs and multidimensional Aad appears to be far more

FIGURE 1
Proposed Model on the Role of Emotion in Advertising Processing

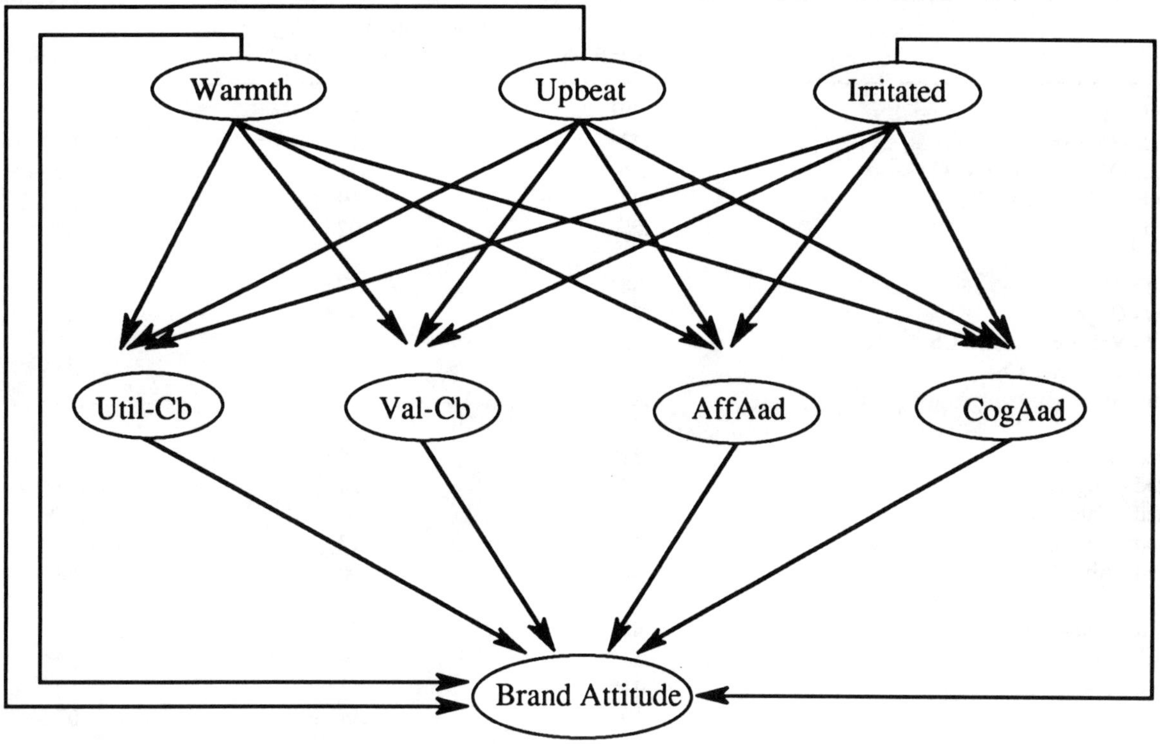

complex than hypothesized, indicating that the relative strength of the causal linkage between the ERs and the multidimensional measures of Aad may be contingent upon specific emotional characteristics as well as the executional types.

Effects of ERs on Multicomponents of Cb

As predicted in H2, ERs are found to be an important indicator of multidimensional Cb. As a further step, the impact of ERs on Cb is hypothesized to become salient via the effect on the value-expressive Cb. This hypothesis is partially supported for the trans/informational ad in that only value-expressive component of Cb is significantly influenced by upbeat and irritated feelings. For the informational ad, upbeat feelings have a substantial impact on value-expressive Cb (p=.10) whereas irritated feelings become a significant determinant of both value-expressive and utilitarian Cb. On the contrary, no direct relationship between ERs and multidimensional Cb for either individual or jointed ERs is observed in the transformational ad. It appears that ERs generated by a transformational appeal tend to activate the salience of the executional features in the ad without influencing brand-related responses. Similarly, warm feelings do not have any significant impact on either value-expressive or utilitarian Cb across various types of ad execution, indicating that warm feelings represent solely execution-based peripheral processing.

In sum, the effect of warm feelings on Ab is completely mediated by the Aad construct. On the other hand, upbeat feelings are likely to interfere with the value-expressive attribute processing, whereas irritated feelings tend to exert influence on both value-expressive and utilitarian Cb depending on ad type. It may be argued that the same type of emotional responses leads to various communication outcomes depending on the executional elements which characterize the emotional reaction. The complexity of the relationship between ERs and multidimensional Cb across various types of the ad exceeds the initial expectation and requires more discrete analysis in the future. Nevertheless, considering that little effort has been given to the relationship between ERs and the multidimensional construct of Cb, this preliminary conceptualization may be considered as an initial step toward a comprehensive framework for the ad processing involving multidimensional constructs of the mediating parameters.

Direct Effects of ERs on Ab

H3 predicts a significant decrease in the direct impact of the ERs on Ab when both Aad and Cb are measured as a multidimensional construct. None of the individual ERs or their joint effects are significant across the three commercials. The result indicates that the impact of the ERs on Ab is completely mediated by the multidimensional measures of Aad and Cb. In order to examine whether it holds true for the unidimensional constructs of Aad and Cb, a separate analysis with a unidimensional design was conducted. The result from the reduced unidimensional model shows that upbeat feelings have a direct impact on Ab (path coefficient= .48, p<.05) in the transformational ad whereas the direct path ERs-Ab is not significant for either the individual ERs or their joint effects in the other types of the ads. The direct effect of upbeat feelings on Ab beyond the global measures of Aad and Cb is consistent with previous findings (Burke and Edell 1989). Thus, this result supports H3 for the transformational ad in that certain ERs which directly influence Ab become insignificant after multidimensional measures of Aad and Cb are introduced.

A further look at the multidimensional constructs shows that the effect of warm feelings on Ab is mainly mediated by affective dimension of Aad regardless of various types of ad execution. Upbeat feelings tend to influence Ab through its impact on the

TABLE 1
Parameter Estimates for the Causal Linkage

	Standardized Path Coefficients		
	Trans/Inform	Transform	Inform
warmth - AffAad	.39*	.63*	.67*
warmth - CogAad	.23	.15	-.05
warmth - Value-expressive Cb	-.06	.37	-.19
warmth - Utilitarian Cb	.28	.49	.39
warmth - Ab	.00	-.02	.06
upbeat - AffAad	.38*	.07	.04
upbeat - CogAad	.29	.59*	.24
upbeat - Value-expressive Cb	.42*	-.24	.50
upbeat - Utilitarian Cb	.08	-.42	-.04
upbeat - Ab	.29	.10	-.25
irritated - AffAad	-.52*	-.29*	-.43*
irritated - CogAad	-.23	-.24	-.82*
irritated - Value-expressive Cb	-.47*	.03	-.47*
irritated - Utilitarian Cb	-.19	-.13	-.52*
irritated - Ab	-.06	.00	.38
Affective Aad - Ab	-.46	-.21	.11
Cognitive Aad - Ab	.58*	.59*	.89*
Value-expressive Cb - Ab	.41*	.53*	.42*
Utilitarian Cb - Ab	.10	.17	.07
chi-square score	29.05	20.68	26.01
d.f	20	20	20
GFI	.89	.92	.90
p =	.09	.42	.17

total subjects (N=55)
* indicates significance level of less than .05 (two-tailed test)

multicomponents of Aad and value-expressive Cb. On the other hand, the impact of irritated feelings on Ab appears to be mediated by both affective/cognitive Aad and value-expressive/utilitarian components of Cb depending on the type of ad execution. Therefore, warm feelings appear to activate mainly a peripheral processing route by influencing the affective dimension of Aad, whereas upbeat and negative feelings are likely to facilitate both central and peripheral processing by affecting both multidimensional components of Aad and Cb.

This study attempted to extend the role of emotion in the ad processing by incorporating ERs and multidimensional constructs of Aad and Cb. In an attempt to elaborate on the causality among these extended constructs, three specific hypotheses were presented. Overall, the extended model reveals rich diagnostic information about how ERs interact with the mediating variables toward the formation of brand attitude. Yet this study is not without limitations. Due to the small sample size, the explanatory power of this study is certainly limited. Although we attempted to include different types of appeals, the limited set of TV commercials may not have captured an adequate range of emotional responses, limiting our ability to test certain relationships in the model. While different ad processing mechanisms may exist across various types of ad appeals, we failed to find any consistent pattern in this regard. A more discrete approach is likely to enrich our understanding about the role of ERs in ad processing since the relative impact of ERs on the subsequent parameters may be contingent upon specific emotional factors as well as ad characteristics.

REFERENCES

Batra, Rajeev, and Michael L. Ray (1986), "Affective Responses Mediating Acceptance of Advertising," *Journal of Consumer Research*, 13 (September), 234-249.

Belk, Russell (1982), "Developmental Recognition of Consumption Symbolism," *Journal of Consumer Research*, Vol.9 (June), 4-17.

Burke, Marian C., and Julie A. Edell (1989), "The Impact of Feelings on Ad-Based Affect and Cognition," *Journal of Marketing Research*, 26 (February), 69-83.

Burton, Scot and Donald R. Lichtenstein (1988), "The Effect of Ad Claims and Ad Context on Attitude Toward the Advertisement," *Journal of Advertising*, 17 (1), 3-11.

Chaiken, Shelly (1980), "Heuristic Versus Systematic Information Processing and the Use of Source Versus Message Cues in Persuasion," *Journal of Personality and Social Psychology*, Vol. 39, No. 5, 752-766.

Edell, Julie A. and Marian C. Burke (1987), "The Power of Feelings in Understanding Advertising Effects," *Journal of Consumer Research*, 14 (December), 421-433.

Fin, Adam (1985), "A Theory of the Consumer Evaluation Process For New Product Concepts," in Jagdish N. Sheth, eds., *Research in Consumer Behavior*, Vol. 1, Greenwich, CT: JAI Press, 35-65.

Forgas, Joseph P. and Gordon H. Bower (1987), "Mood Effects on Person-Perception Judgments," *Journal of Personality and Social Psychology*, Vol. 53, No. 1, 53-60.

Hirschman, Elizabeth and Morris B. Holbrook (1982), "Hedonic Consumption: Emerging Concepts, Methods and Propositions," *Journal of Marketing*, 46 (Summer), 92-101.

Holbrook, Morris B., and Rajeev Batra (1987), "Assessing the Role of Emotions as Mediators of Consumer Responses to Advertising," *Journal of Consumer Research*, 14 (December), 404-420.

Howard, John A. and Jagdish N. Sheth (1969), *The Theory of Buyer Behavior*. New York: Wiley.

Joreskog, Karl G. and Dag Sorbom (1986), *LISREL VI: Analysis of Linear Structural Relationships by the Method of Maximum Likelihood*. Mooresville, IN: Scientific Software, Inc.

MacKenzie, Scott B. and Richard J. Lutz (1989), "An Empirical Examination of the Structural Antecedents of Attitude Toward the Ad in an Advertising Pretesting Context," *Journal of Marketing*, 53 (April), 48-65.

Madden, Thomas J., Chris T. Allen and Jacquelyn L. Twible (1988), "Attitude Toward the Ad: An Assessment of Diverse Measurement Indices Under Different Processing "Sets"," *Journal of Marketing Research*, 25 (August), 242-252.

McGuire, William J. (1976), "Some Internal Psychological Factors Influencing Brand Choice," *Journal of Consumer Research*, 2 (March), 302-319.

Miniard, Paul W., Sunil Bhatla and Randall L. Rose (1990), "On the Formation and Relationship of Ad and Brand Attitudes: An Experimental and Causal Analysis," *Journal of Marketing Research*, 27 (August), 290-303.

Mitchell, Andrew A. and Jerry C. Olson (1981), "Are Product Attribute Beliefs the Only Mediator of Advertising Effects on Brand Attitude?," *Journal of Marketing Research*, 18, 318-332.

Mittal, Banwari (1990), "The Relative Roles of Brand Beliefs and Attitude Toward the Ad as Mediators of Brand Attitude: A Second Look," *Journal of Marketing Research*, 27, 209-219.

Olney, Thomas J., Morris B. Holbrook and Rajeev Batra (1991), "Consumer Responses to Advertising: The Effects of Ad Content, Emotions, and Attitude toward the Ad on Viewing Time," *Journal of Consumer Research*, 17 (March), 440-453.

Petty, Richard E. and John T. Cacioppo (1981), *Attitudes and Persuasions: Classic and Contemporary Approaches*, Dubuque, IA: William C. Brown.

Prentice, D. (1987), "Psychological Correspondence of Possessions, Attitudes and Values," *Journal of Personality and Social Psychology*, 53 (6), 993-1003.

Puto, Christopher P. and William D. Wells (1984), "Informational and Transformational Advertising: The Differential Effects of Time," in *Advances in Consumer Research*, 11, ed. Thomas C. Kinnear, Provo, UT: Association for Consumer Research, 572-576.

Sirgy, M. Joseph (1982), "Self-Concept in Consumer Behavior: A Critical Review," *Journal of Consumer Research*, 9, 287-300.

Stayman, Douglas M. and David A. Aaker (1988), "Are All the Effects of Feelings Mediated by Aad?," *Journal of Consumer Research*, 15 (December), 368-373.

Stephens, Debra L. and J. Edward Russo (1987), "Predicting Post-Advertising Attitudes," working paper, University of Maryland.

Stout, Patricia A., and John D. Leckenby (1986), "Measuring Emotional Response to Advertising," *Journal of Advertising*, 15, (4), 35-42.

Swan, John E. and Linda J. Combs (1976), "Product Performance and Consumer Satisfaction: A New Concept," *Journal of Marketing*, 40, (April), 25-33.

Westbrook, Robert A. and Richard L. Oliver (1991), "The Dimensionality of Consumption Emotion Patterns and Consumer Satisfaction," *Journal of Consumer Research*, Vol. 18, 84-91.

Zajonc, Robert B. (1980), "Feeling and Thinking: Preferences Need No Inferences," *American Psychologist*, 35 (February), 151-175.

Poisoning the Well: Do Environmental Claims Strain Consumer Credulity?
Robert N. Mayer, University of Utah
Debra L. Scammon, University of Utah
Cathleen D. Zick, University of Utah

ABSTRACT

Current proposals for the regulation of environmental claims in advertising and on labels are aimed at protecting consumers, the market for environmental products, and ultimately the environment. At issue is whether environmental claims are currently accurate and well understood. The degree to which environmental claims are seen as credible may affect consumers' search for, belief in, and reaction to such claims. We explore the relationship between exposure to and perceived credibility of environmental claims with data from a survey with 403 adults who are the primary shopper in their household.

INTRODUCTION

Public policy makers in the United States and abroad are currently considering whether and how to regulate environmental claims made in advertising and on product labels. A key assumption on the part of those favoring immediate action is that *vague or misleading claims will confuse and disillusion consumers. As a result, an important opportunity to harness environmental concern on the part of consumers will have been wasted*. This assumption can be found in numerous documents. In its Green Report (1990), a Task Force of U.S. Attorneys General wrote:

> The Task Force feared that if consumers began to feel that their genuine interest in the environment was being exploited, consumers would no longer seek out or demand products that are less damaging to the environment. If this were to occur, the environmental improvements that could be achieved by consumers purchasing more environmentally benign products would be lost (p.6).

In a notice of federal rule making (Federal Register 1991), the Environmental Protection Agency asserted:

> If national consensus over the use of these terms is not reached in the near future, we face the danger of losing a valuable tool for educating the public and influencing the production and use of more environmentally oriented products. Consumers may come to distrust or ignore all environmental claims (p.10).

In written testimony to the Federal Trade Commission, Walter Coddington (1991), representing Persuasion Environmental Marketing, Inc., claimed that "consumers' distrust of environmental labelling is already high. If this distrust continues, a substantial opportunity to improve the environment could be missed" (p.9). And as a final example, Dr. Brenda Cude (1991) of the University of Illinois, in testimony to the U.S. Environmental Protection Agency, cautioned that "without guidelines, some consumers have come to mistrust many claims; at best they discount potentially useful information and at worst they ignore it entirely" (p.1).

The common theme in these statements is that there is a real risk that vague or deceptive environmental claims may create distrust, cynicism, and alienation among consumers, with the result that a genuine opportunity will have been lost to harness consumer concern about the environment. Put differently, vague and deceptive environmental claims hinder the effectiveness of legitimate environmental claims, thereby poisoning the well of green marketing.

Is there evidence for the assertion that vague and misleading environmental claims are in fact creating consumer cynicism about green buying and green products? The research reported here constitutes an exploratory effort to examine this question. Data from a statewide representative sample of adults is used to examine the relationship between consumer exposure to environmental claims and belief in their credibility.

RESEARCH QUESTIONS AND LITERATURE REVIEW

Consumer researchers have devoted a great deal of attention to identifying the characteristics of environmentally concerned consumers and examining the relationship between environmental attitudes and behavior. A meta analysis by Schwepker and Cornwell (1991) portrays environmentally concerned consumers as younger, politically liberal, better educated and with higher income, occupational status and socioeconomic status than their environmentally less concerned counterparts. If environmental claims are lacking in credibility, then these consumers are likely to have the political skills and purchasing power to communicate their displeasure to government agencies and firms. (The profile of environmentally concerned consumers shares several characteristics with that of the "information elite," making it even more likely that these people will complain about environmental claims that are vague or misleading.)

Environmental claims could strain consumer credulity for at least two reasons. First, claims could be lacking in specificity or accuracy (e.g., that a product is "environmentally friendly" without suggesting the relevant environmental benefit). Alternatively, environmental claims might be specific and accurate but raise complex scientific issues that confuse consumers (e.g., that a product is photodegradable leaving unanswered questions about exposure to sunlight and time required to degrade). There is evidence for both mechanisms.

Kangun, Carlson, and Grove (1991) performed a content analysis of environmental claims in advertising. They reported that 68% of the ads were judged by non-expert judges (i.e., university faculty and staff without any specific training in environmental fields) to be misleading or deceptive, most often because of their vagueness of ambiguity. Thus, there is at least some systematic evidence that "companies display a propensity to make environmental claims that are misleading" (Kangun et al. 1991, p.54).

The inherent complexity of environmental impacts may also contribute to consumer confusion about and disbelief of environmental claims. A national study of consumer knowledge about the issues raised by environmental claims (Roper Organization 1991) suggests that consumers may not be well informed about the complex scientific issues involved with assessing the environmental impact of products. Especially with regard to environmental priorities (e.g., solid waste management vs. atmospheric pollution) and lifecycle impacts (e.g., impacts during production, consumption, and disposal), consumers are likely not to have complete, relevant information available to help them decode—and place into proper context—environmental claims.

Recently, research probing the ways in which consumers interpret environmental claims has found a good deal of confusion about the issues raised in these claims. Consumers appear to have difficulty understanding both vague (e.g., "environmentally friendly") and technical (e.g., "photodegradable") terminology (Cude 1991; Environmental Research Associates 1991; Mayer, Scammon, and Zick 1992). Lack of comprehension of environmental claims on the part of consumers may decrease the likelihood of consumers placing much credence in such claims.

A handful of studies has begun to examine the credibility of environmental claims. One study, sponsored by the Good Housekeeping Institute in 1990, focused exclusively on women. Of those women who said they had seen or heard environmental claims in advertising, 43% believed that most of these claims were accurate (cited in Coddington 1991). A second study conducted by the J.W. Thompson agency found that 62% of Americans who recall environmental advertising believe the message (cited in Coddington 1991). Whereas these two studies focus on environmental claims in advertising, a study by Gerstman and Meyers, Inc. (1991) asked 318 women in six U.S. cities about environmental claims found on packages; 22% of respondents said that these claims are not believable, with an additional 63% describing them as only somewhat believable.

Taken together, the results of these three studies suggest that the credibility of environmental claims is relatively low. This conclusion is strengthened by the fact that the three studies differ with regard to (1) the nature of their respondents (e.g., females only or all adults), (2) whether they focus on claims made in advertising or on labels, and (3) whether they ask about the perceived accuracy or believability of the claims. None of these three studies correlates exposure to environmental claims with perceptions of the credibility of these claims. Indeed, two of these studies only ask the credibility question of those respondents who indicate having been exposed to environmental claims. The purpose of the study reported here is to examine more closely the relationship between consumer exposure to environmental claims and the credibility of these claims.

The relationship between exposure and credibility is potentially quite complex. Given the relative newness of environmental claims, we view exposure as preceding judgments of credibility although, over time, credibility is likely to influence the consumer's likelihood of exposure or attention to environmental claims. Although this study does not investigate the effects of claim credibility, there is at least one study that suggests that vague or misleading environmental claims may undercut consumer motivation to buy green products. A national study conducted by the Roper Organization (1990) for S.C. Johnson & Son, Inc. asked a nationally representative sample of adults about eight factors that might account for "why you don't personally do more about the environment." In response to the statement "I don't believe that a lot of the products which are labeled 'environmentally safe' are any better for the environment than other products," 14% of the sample said this was a major reason and 38% something of a reason why they didn't do more. The finding that a lack of credibility in environmental claims contributes to consumer inaction provides a possible explanation when environmental concern does not translate into environmental action.[1]

Of course, environmental claims represent only one type of claims about which consumers may be interested when making purchase decisions. But, if the same factors influence the degree to which the credibility of the *content* of claims is important to consumers as influence the degree to which the credibility of the *source* of information is important to consumers, one might expect that the credibility of environmental claims would be highly relevant to consumers. Research on source credibility suggests that the source of information is especially important to consumers when they are making decisions in the face of uncertainty (due to complexity of the decision or lack of information) and about products that are important to them (e.g., socially conspicuous, expensive, or durable products). Since environmental claims deal with complex issues about which consumers have limited information but that are important to them both directly and indirectly, the credibility of those claims is likely to be particularly important to consumers.

METHODS

Research Design and Data Collection

The data used to investigate consumer exposure to and perceived credibility of environmental claims come from a statewide (intermountain west) telephone survey of 403 adults 18 years of age or older. The interviews were conducted during September 1991. Unlike statewide surveys that sample randomly among the adults living in a given household, this survey asked for the "person in the household who does most of the shopping for food and household items." (The results can be generalized to the statewide population, however, by weighting the sample.) The survey cooperation rate was 80%, and the interviews took an average of 12 minutes.

Measures

The survey contained a variety of measures relevant to consumer perception of environmental claims. The results for some of these measures (e.g., consumer interpretation of recyclability and photodegradability claims) are reported elsewhere (Mayer, Scammon, and Zick 1992). Attention in this paper is directed at measures of consumer exposure to environmental claims and the perceived credibility of these claims.

There are two ways in which consumers may acquire information about the credibility of environmental claims. One of these ways is through encountering environmental claims and judging them on the basis of personal experience and beliefs. We call this personal evaluation. The other way is through reading and hearing about the judgments of others regarding the credibility of environmental claims. For example, a person might read an article in a newspaper about a federal agency's complaint about the truthfulness of a firm's environmental claims. We call this means of acquiring information third-party evaluation.

Some information sources provide both personal and third-party information while others provide one or the other type. For instance, newspapers and television carry both advertisements containing environmental claims as well as news reports about the truthfulness of these claims. A product label would contain only information that could be used by consumers in making their own assessments of credibility, while an article in *Consumer Reports*

---

[1] Alternative explanations include an attitude that environmental protection should be the responsibility of firms that contribute to environmental problems and a feeling that one's own behavior will have little impact in the greater scheme of things. In fact, in the Roper study, the most commonly cited reason for inaction was: "I feel that it's basically large companies which are causing our environmental problems and I think it's these companies—not people like me—who should solve the problem." Research has found a positive relationship between perceived self-efficacy and participation in some environmentally conscious behaviors (see for example, Ellen, Weiner, and Cobb-Walgren 1991).

would contain only judgments of the credibility of environmental claims. In this exploratory study we have included measures of exposure to both personal and third-party information, but we have not tried to distinguish the amount of each type of information to which our respondents have been exposed in each medium.

If one accepts the notion that information affects consumer decision making after having undergone some extent of cognitive processing, there are several stages in this process that are of interest. One might focus on consumers' opportunity to encounter a particular message, actual exposure to the message, or even consumers' reliance upon the message in decision making. In this study, exposure to environmental information is assessed in several ways. First, the opportunity for exposure to environmental information in the general environment is assessed by measuring the amount of television typically watched per day and whether the household subscribes to a newspaper. Second, actual exposure to environmental claims is assessed by the respondent's recall of exposure to environmental claims (either in mass media or on product labels) and the respondent's deliberate reading of environmental information on labels when shopping for household items.

Our respondents watch an average of 2.4 hours of television per day and almost 60% subscribe to a newspaper. As these two media are widely used by advertisers making environmental claims, there appears to be ample opportunity for our respondents to have been exposed to these claims as well as to third-party judgments of them.

When respondents were asked if they recalled seeing any environmental claims on labels or in advertisements, 73.1% answered that they did. (Note that the sample consisted of primary shoppers in a household, so these figures might be higher than they would be for a representative sample of all adults.) It is interesting to note that 42.7% of all respondents claimed that they "read labels specifically to see which brands are better for the natural environment." Of these respondents, 53.8% claim to do this "on a regular basis," while the remaining 46.2% claim to read labels for environmental information "from time to time." Taken together, our data suggest that respondents not only have an opportunity to be exposed to environmental claims, but they report recalling such exposure and actively seeking such information.

Although credibility of environmental claims is probably a function of credibility of marketing messages generally as well as credibility of environmental claims specifically, we chose to focus exclusively on environmental claims and did not include a measure of the credibility of seller claims in general. Our measure of the credibility of environmental claims was a modified version of an item used by the Roper Organization (1990). Respondents were asked the extent to which they agreed or disagreed with the statement that:

> A lot of the brands that claim to be better for the environment are *no better* for the environment than brands that do not make such claims.

A slight majority of our respondents agreed with this statement: 6.4% strongly agreed; 48.9% agreed; 40.5% disagreed; and 4.3% strongly disagreed. Only eleven respondents said they were unable to answer the question. Because of the wording of the statement, *agreement* implies a perceived *lack of credibility* for environmental claims.

In addition to the measures of exposure to and perceived credibility of environmental claims, the survey included information on basic sociodemographic characteristics, such as respondent sex, age, education, political orientation, household size, and area of residence.

The average respondent was a female (79.0%) about 40 years of age, who had some college education. Typically, there were three people living in the household and their total family income during the past 12 months was about $30,000.

MODEL SPECIFICATION AND RESULTS

A longitudinal data set in which the same respondents are re-interviewed over time would provide a strong basis for determining whether exposure to environmental claims influences the credibility of these claims in the eyes of consumers. In a cross-sectional data set, however, one can only examine the association between exposure and credibility, controlling for sociodemographic characteristics. Because these sociodemographic variables could conceivably influence both exposure and credibility, one approach to analysis would involve deriving predicted values for the four measures of exposure to environmental claims and then using these values, along with sociodemographic variables, to predict perceived credibility. This approach was deemed overly complex, especially in light of limited knowledge of how to predict exposure to environmental claims. A reduced form approach was adopted in which the credibility of environmental claims was modeled as a function of all four measures of exposure and six sociodemographic variables (i.e., respondent age, respondent sex, respondent education, rural vs. urban residence, political orientation, and household size).

In using four approaches to assessing respondents' exposure to environmental claims, there is the potential problem of multicollinearity. The correlations among our exposure measures show, however, that the items are not highly correlated and likely measure different aspects of exposure to environmental claims. (In fact, only one of 10 correlations was statistically significant at the .05 level.)

Given the small percentage of respondents either agreeing or disagreeing *strongly* with the credibility question, these extreme responses were combined with the more moderate agree or disagree responses and the dependent measure was simply coded either agree (1) or disagree (0). (Remember that because of the wording of the statement, those agreeing with the statement did *not* find environmental claims credible.) Accordingly, a logit analysis was conducted in which the estimated coefficients are cast so that a one-unit change in an independent variable produces a percentage change in the natural log of the odds ratio, holding all other factors constant. (Marginal effects are sometimes calculated to enhance interpretation of the data.) Table 1 provides descriptive statistics, including an explanation of how variables were coded.

The hypothesis being tested is that individuals who are more likely to be exposed to environmental claims (whether by virtue of their general media patterns or their reported exposure to environmental claims) find environmental claims less credible than individuals without such exposure. If exposure is positively related to a lack of credibility, then the concerns about missing an opportunity to direct consumer action toward environmental protection may be correct and there may be a need for immediate regulation. If there is no such relationship, then a more deliberate approach to the regulation of environmental claims may be justified.

The data presented in Table 2 show that only two of the modeled variables are related to whether respondents find environmental claims credible: the age and education of the respondent. Younger respondents and less well educated respondents find environmental claims less credible than their older and better educated counterparts. Credibility is not related to the three other sociodemographic variables. More important, none of the four

TABLE 1
Descriptive Statistics

Variable	Mean	Std. Dev.
Claim Credibility (1=not credible; 0=credible)	.55	.50
Television Viewing (hours per week)	2.39	1.69
Newspaper Subscription (1=yes; 0=no)	.57	.50
Recall a Claim (1=yes; 0=no)	.73	.44
Read Labels Regularly[a] (1=yes; 0=otherwise)	.23	.42
Read Labels Occasionally[a] (1=yes; 0=otherwise)	.20	.40
Age (in years)	42.54	15.78
Education (years of schooling)	13.64	2.32
Sex (1=female; 0=male)	.79	.41
Household Size (number of members)	3.44	1.88
Rural (1=rural; 0=otherwise)	.09	.28
Democrat[b] (1=Democrat; 0=otherwise)	.21	.41
Independent[b] (1=Independent; 0=otherwise)	.37	.37

[a] The omitted category in this sequence of dummy variables is composed of those respondents who do not read product labels for environmental information.

[b] The omitted category in this sequence of dummy variables is composed of those respondents who described themselves as Republicans.

measures of exposure to environmental claims is related to the credibility of environmental claims.

DISCUSSION AND CONCLUSION

The absence of a relationship between exposure to and perceived credibility of environmental claims must be interpreted with care. There were multiple measures of exposure to environmental claims but only a single measure of their credibility. Thus, any deficiencies in this measure could affect the results. It is possible, for example, that the measure of credibility taps the credibility of all advertising rather than environmental claims in particular. This could explain why sociodemographic characteristics predict credibility while the exposure measures do not.

To the extent that credibility potentially influences exposure, the model is mis-specified. (This is far more probable for the two measures of actual exposure than the measures of potential exposure — television viewership and newspaper subscribership.) Perhaps a model in which influences can be multi-directional would be a more accurate representation of the relationship between exposure and credibility.

Despite the absence of a relationship between exposure to and perceived credibility of environmental claims, the sociodemographic correlates of credibility remain important. Other research has found that younger age and higher education are consistently related to measures of concern about the natural environment, participation in the environmental movement, support for public policies designed to protect the natural environment, and environmentally conscious purchasing. In this study, younger and *less* educated respondents are most likely to be skeptical of environmental claims. Thus, credibility of environmental claims does not appear to be a simple function of support for environmentalism.

More educated consumers are more likely than less educated ones to seek information about environmental issues generally and the differential impact of various brands on the environment in

TABLE 2
Parameter Estimates of the Logit Analysis for the Probability of Finding Environmental Claims Lacking in Credibility

Variable	Logit Coefficient
Constant	-2.11
	(.96*)[1]
Television Viewing	-.01
	(.07)
Newspaper Subscription	.25
	(.24)
Recall a Claim	.03
	(.26)
Read Labels Regularly	-.37
	(.28)
Read Labels Occasionally	.31
	(.28)
Age	.03
	(.01**)
Education	.11
	(.05*)
Sex	-.28
	(.29)
Household Size	-.09
	(.06)
Rural	.25
	(.39)
Democrat	.08
	(.29)
Independent	.46
	(.25)

[1] Standard errors are reported in parentheses.
Note. -N = 385. Model X2 = 29.41, p<.01.
* t-value statistically significant at the .05 level.
** t-value statistically significant at the .01 level.

---

particular. In so doing, they are more likely to use a variety of information sources, including specialized magazines, lectures and presentations by environmental activists, and informal discussions with friends. Less educated consumers are likely to rely most heavily on the mass media as a source of environmental information. If these generalizations about the behavior of more and less educated consumers are correct, enhancing the credibility of environmental claims, particularly those made in the mass media, becomes crucial if environmentally conscious buying is to spread to all segments of the buying public.

Our finding that younger respondents are less likely to find environmental claims credible also highlights the importance of ensuring that such claims are truthful and relevant. These younger consumers are the most likely to have idealistic motivations to do their share for the environment. If they do not find environmental claims to be credible they are likely to disregard a widely available source of information for identifying the brands least detrimental to the environment.

A general lack of credibility in environmental claims may contribute to some more specific attitudes towards brands promoted on the basis of their environmental superiority. For example, if consumers do not put a lot of credence in claims that a brand is better for the environment, they may assume that the advertiser is making that claim in order to be able to charge more for the brand. Consumers thus might assume that brands accompanied by environmental claims are more expensive (though really no better than) brands that do not make such claims. Similarly, consumers may feel that to make brands superior with regard to their impact on the environment marketers must "take something else away." Consumers may thus conclude that brands advertised as the correct environmental choice may in fact taste worse, be harder to use, or otherwise somehow be of less value than brands that do not make environmental claims.

Further research investigating the relationships between the constellation of beliefs consumers harbor about the environmental attributes of products is warranted. The bases for these beliefs, the sources of information influencing these beliefs, and the behaviors that are ultimately affected by these beliefs are all of concern to marketers and public policy makers. This study suggests that there may be several reasons to believe that credibility of environmental claims is in question and efforts by advertisers and policy makers to bolster this credibility may be warranted.

REFERENCES

Coddington, Walter (1991), Comments prepared for the U.S. Federal Trade Commission's hearings on environmental claims in product labeling and advertising, Washington, D.C. (July 17).

Cude, Brenda J. (1991), Comments prepared for the U.S. Environmental Protection Agency hearings on the use of the terms recycled and recyclable and the recycling emblem in environmental marketing claims, Washington, D.C. (November 13).

Ellen, Pam Scholder, Joshua Lyle Wiener, and Cathy Cobb-Walgren (1991), "The Role of Perceived Consumer Effectiveness in Motivating Environmentally Conscious Behaviors," *Journal of Public Policy & Marketing*, 10 (2), 102-117.

Environmental Protection Agency (1991), "Guidance for the Use of the Terms "Recycled" and "Recyclable" and the Recycling Emblem in Environmental Marketing Claims; Notice of Public Meeting," *Federal Register*, 56, No. 191 (October 2), 49992-50000.

Environmental Research Associates (1991), *The Environmental Report*, a study sponsored by the Council on Plastics and Packaging in the Environment, Washington, D.C. (July).

Gertsman and Meyers, Inc. (1991), *Consumer Solid Waste: Awareness, Attitude, and Behavior Study III* (July).

Granzin, Kent L. and Janeen E. Olsen (1991), "Characterizing Participants in Activities Protecting the Environment: A Focus on Donating, Recycling, and Conservation Behaviors," *Journal of Public Policy & Marketing*, 10 (2), 1-27.

The Green Report: Findings and Preliminary Recommendations for Responsible Environmental Advertising (1990), a report by the attorney general of California, Florida, Massachusetts, Minnesota, Missouri, New York, Texas, Utah, Washington, and Wisconsin (November).

Kangun, Norman, Les Carlson, and Stephen J. Grove (1991), "Environmental Advertising Claims: A Preliminary Investigation," *Journal of Public Policy & Marketing*, 10 (2), 47-58.

Mayer, Robert N., Debra L. Scammon, and Cathleen D. Zick (1992), "Turning the Competition Green: The Regulation of Environmental Claims," Proceedings of the 1992 Marketing and Public Policy Conference, eds. Paul N. Bloom and Richard G. Starr, Jr., Washington, D.C. (May 16) 152-165.

Roper Organization (1991), *America's Environmental GPA*, a study commissioned by S.C. Johnson & Son, Inc. (November).Roper Organization (1990), *The Environment: Public Attitudes and Individual Behavior*, a study commissioned by S.C. Johnson & Son, Inc. (July).

Schwepker, Charles H., Jr. and T. Bettina Cornwell (1991), "An Examination of Ecologically Concerned Consumers and Their Intention to Purchase Ecologically Packaged Products," *Journal of Public Policy & Marketing*, 10 (2), 77-101.

Spokesperson Effects in High Involvement Markets
Timothy B. Heath, University of Pittsburgh
David L. Mothersbaugh, University of Pittsburgh
Michael S. McCarthy, University of Pittsburgh[1]

Existing theory and research suggest that persuasive cues such as spokesperson fame are ineffective when consumers engage in issue-relevant thinking. However, these studies examined behavior in noncompetitive, between-subjects settings. Experiment 1 replicates the procedures of past research, whereas Experiment 2 mimics marketplace competition by varying spokesperson fame within subjects. Spokesperson fame had significant effects on brand attitudes and choice only in Experiment 2's competitive setting. The data suggest that (1) existing theory be extended with the concept of cue neutralization, (2) attitude research use within-subjects designs to capture marketplace persuasion processes, and (3) persuasive cues such as spokesperson fame are increasingly important as markets mature and competitive parity increases.

Spokesperson effects have been studied by social psychologists and consumer researchers (Hovland and Weiss 1951; Kahle and Homer 1985). Existing research shows that spokespeople influence consumers primarily when consumers are unable to base their evaluations on issue-relevant thinking (Batra and Ray 1986; Chaiken 1980; Petty and Cacioppo 1981, 1986; Greenwald and Leavitt 1984). However, practitioners often use spokespeople to promote products, even those products commanding considerable pre-purchase deliberation such as automobiles. The current study proposes and tests competitive effects that partially explain this discrepancy.

Unlike the environments studied in traditional attitude research, those faced by practitioners are often competitive. Consumers see multiple ads and brands within each product class. Whether competition influences the effectiveness of spokesperson fame is investigated here. As in past research, Experiment 1 tests spokesperson effects in noncompetitive settings. Experiment 2 then tests the moderating role of competition by replicating Experiment 1's stimuli and procedures in a competitive setting.

THEORY AND RESEARCH

Traditional attitude research has documented many variables affecting attitude change including personality (Hovland and Janis 1959), classical conditioning (Staats and Staats 1958), cognitive dissonance (Festinger 1957), self perception (Bem 1972), and cognitive responses (Greenwald 1968). Many of these effects have been subsumed under broader theories recognizing the wide array of processes through which attitudes are formed and changed.

Primary among the multi-process theories are Chaiken's (1980) Systematic/Heuristic Model and Petty and Cacioppo's (1981, 1986) Elaboration Likelihood Model (see also Greenwald and Leavitt 1984). These models distinguish between attitude change based on product features and attitude change based on less substantive stimuli such as spokesperson fame. The processes underlying these two are referred to respectively as *systematic* and *heuristic processes* by Chaiken, and as *central* and *peripheral routes to persuasion* by Petty and Cacioppo.

Multi-process theories of attitude change maintain that peripheral cues are relatively ineffective when consumers engage in issue-relevant thinking. This is consistent with earlier research on communication effects (Krugman 1965; Ray et al. 1973; Robertson 1976) and has received considerable empirical support (for reviews see Greenwald and Leavitt 1984; Petty and Cacioppo 1986). For example, famous spokespeople have been found to improve brand attitudes in low but not high involvement (e.g., Petty et al. 1983).

Evidence of limited peripheral-cue effects in high involvement is confined primarily to experimental designs where peripheral cues are manipulated between subjects. Subjects typically see one ad for one brand within a given product class, where the ad contains either a weak or a strong peripheral-cue (e.g., nonfamous or famous spokesperson). Each subject then evaluates that brand (e.g., Petty et al. 1983). In contrast, however, peripheral cues vary within subjects in the marketplace. Each consumer sees multiple brands with corresponding ads and cues. In such competitive situations, a persuasive ad is of little use if competitors' ads are even more persuasive. In the marketplace, therefore, persuasion relative to that of the competition is more important than absolute persuasion.

Choice research inherently addresses relative persuasion. Regardless of whether the process is compensatory or noncompensatory, choice implies cross-alternative comparisons. Whereas absolute persuasion is effected little by the distribution of attribute levels across alternatives, relative persuasion is. The less variation in attributes across alternatives, the less influence each has on relative persuasion, especially when measured with choice (Tversky 1972). The tendency for consumers to ignore attributes held constant across alternatives has been referred to as *cancellation* in the study of risky decisions (Kahneman and Tversky 1979).

Similar processes may exist in multi-attribute product contexts. We propose that *cue neutralization* often occurs in the marketplace. For example, if three television brands have identical levels of picture resolution and warranty, the persuasiveness of Brand A's warranty is neutralized by the warranties of the other brands. If all central cues are neutralized, then peripheral cues may play a critical role in the decision since there are no other features on which the brands can be differentiated. As central cues become increasingly neutralized, peripheral cues are hypothesized to become more important *ceteris paribus*, regardless of the level of issue-relevant thinking.

Homogenous product features reflect the simplest type of cue neutralization; namely *within-attribute cue neutralization*: Television A's picture resolution is neutralized by Television B's picture resolution. However, *cross-attribute cue neutralization* is also possible, and distinguishes neutralization from Kahneman and Tversky's (1979) cancellation. For example, Television A might have superior picture resolution, while Television B has superior sound quality. If the televisions are liked comparably, then Television B's superior sound quality is said to neutralize the persuasiveness of Television A's superior picture resolution. Consumer preferences across brands are homogenous despite product heterogeneity (cf. Slovic 1975). As with within-attribute cue neutralization, as cross-attribute neutralization of central cues increases, the power of peripheral cues is expected to increase regardless of the level of issue-relevant thinking.

The present study examines the effects of spokespeople in between-subjects (Experiment 1) and within-subject environments

---

[1] This research was partially supported by a research grant from the Katz Graduate School of Business.

(Experiment 2). Experiment 2 assesses spokesperson effects in the face of within-attribute cue neutralization. This is important for both theory and practice. For theory, peripheral-cue effects in the face of issue-relevant thinking would suggest extending multi-process theories with the concept of cue neutralization. For practice, existing evidence suggests that U.S. markets are increasingly characterized by competitive parity and homogenous products (Wall Street Journal, October 19, 1989, Page B1). If spokesperson effects occur in such settings, peripheral cues may become more important in the marketplace as markets mature regardless of involvement.

STUDY OVERVIEW AND HYPOTHESES

Two experiments assess the power of spokespeople in a high-involvement competitive environment where central cues are neutralized within attributes. These experiments test spokesperson effects on brand attitudes using both between-subjects (Experiment 1) and within-subjects manipulations (Experiment 2). The within-subjects manipulation of Experiment 2 further assesses the effects of spokesperson fame on brand choice.

The between-subjects manipulation of Experiment 1 replicates the procedures of traditional attitude research reporting a lack peripheral-cue effects in high involvement. It therefore examines the following null hypothesis:

H1: Spokesperson fame will not influence attitudes when manipulated between subjects and when there is issue-relevant thinking.

Experiment 2 uses a within-subjects replication of Experiment 1 to mimic marketplace competition. Between-subjects manipulations have been the primary source of empirical support for existing multi-process attitude theories. Whether the predictions of these theories hold in environments more akin to the marketplace remains to be tested. Therefore, Experiment 2 tests the following hypothesis:

H2: Spokesperson fame will influence brand attitudes when manipulated within subjects as long as central cues are neutralized, even when there is issue-relevant thinking.

Experiment 2 further tests the effects of spokespeople on choice:

H3: Spokesperson fame will influence choice probabilities as long as central cues are neutralized, even when there is issue-relevant thinking.

EXPERIMENT 1

Method

Pretests. Twenty-five student subjects at a large eastern university rated the fame of six potential spokespeople on a 9-point ratings scale ranging from 1 (not famous) to 9 (famous). Two of the spokespeople were considered famous a priori (Michael J. Fox and Jay Leno), whereas the others were fictitious (Alex Tyler, Darrell Spencer, Tom Hite, and John Meyers). As expected, Michael J. Fox and Jay Leno were rated as more famous than the others. Therefore, Michael J. Fox and Alex Tyler were selected for use in the experiments (M's = 7.6 and 2.7, respectively; $t_{(24)}$ = 10.97).[2]

Subjects and Design. Experiment 1 varied spokesperson fame (nonfamous vs. famous) between subjects. Twenty-one subjects enrolled at a large eastern university were randomly assigned to each of the two conditions. When spokesperson fame was manipulated, two similar versions of ad copy were counterbalanced. The counterbalancing of similar ad copies was needed to reduce demand in Experiment 2's within-subject's manipulation, and was included in Experiment 1 to make the two experiments comparable. The second version of the ad copy for the spokesperson conditions was created by making minor wording changes to the first.

Procedure. The first section of the booklet consisted of an introductory cover story to provide a rationale for the study and heighten involvement. Students were told that cruises were becoming increasingly popular, and that their responses would be instrumental in the development of the products or services they evaluated.

Following the cover story, subjects read an advertisement for the brand they were to evaluate. The ad was in the form of a radio script. Using radio scripts helped eliminate confounding effects of elements typically found in print ads (photos, layout, typeface, etc.) and broadcast ads (music, editing, camera angles, etc.). The ad used a disguised brand name (Cruise L) to avoid the effects of brand name familiarity or liking on product evaluations. The scripts identified the announcer (spokesperson) as Michael J. Fox or Alex Tyler.

After reading the radio script, subjects examined a table containing attribute information about the cruises. The information addressed eight cruise attributes (price, overall quality, number of days, number of islands, night club, Olympic pool, athletic activities, casino). As in prior research, attribute information was held constant across nonfamous and nonfamous spokesperson conditions.

After reviewing the ad and the attribute table, subjects evaluated the cruise on 9-point bad/good, unsatisfactory/satisfactory, and unfavorable/favorable scales ranging from -4 to +4 (cf. Petty et al. 1983). They then responded to a check on the manipulation of spokesperson fame, a measure of issue-relevant thinking discussed later, and experimental demand.

Results

Demand Check. The demand check asked subjects if they felt there was an alternative purpose to the study. If they answered *yes*, they were then asked to describe the alternative purpose. None of the subjects mentioned an alternative purpose that was remotely related to the manipulation of spokesperson fame.

Manipulation Checks. The manipulation of spokesperson fame was checked with the same 9-point scale used in the pretest. As in the pretest, Michael J. Fox was rated as more famous than Alex Tyler (M's = 7.6 and 2.4, respectively; $t_{(19)}$ = 8.2).[3] Thus, the manipulation of spokesperson fame was successful.

To test the study's hypotheses, it was critical that consumers engage in issue-relevant thinking. Issue-relevant thinking was checked with two items. The first measured how carefully subjects evaluated the brand compared to the care used in evaluating household products such as paper towels, laundry detergents, and cleansers. The second measured how carefully subjects evaluated

---

[2] All inferential statistics are evaluated with respect to α = .05.

[3] Throughout the analyses, the data are collapsed across the counterbalanced variables. There were no main effects of the counterbalanced variables, and interactions with them (1) did not alter the interpretations of spokesperson effects, (2) were small, and (3) were uninterpretable.

the brand compared to the care used in evaluating consumer electronics such as televisions, stereo equipment, and microwave ovens. These two sets of product classes were considered representative of relatively low and high involvement products, respectively.

The two thinking scales ranged from -8 (much less carefully) to 0 (about as carefully) to +8 (much more carefully), and indicated that subjects engaged in issue-relevant thinking. Subjects evaluated cruises more carefully than household products, although the difference did not achieve statistical significance ($M = 1.0$; $t_{(20)} = 1.3$). Likewise, subjects evaluated cruises less carefully than consumer electronics products, although again the difference was not statistically significant ($M = -1.5$; $t_{(20)} = -1.75$).

Spokesperson Effects. Consistent with the predictions of multi-process theories, Hypothesis 1 predicted that spokespeople would not influence brand attitudes under high involvement. The three items used to measure brand attitudes were combined due to high reliability (Cronbach's $\alpha = .97$). As expected, there was no effect of spokesperson fame on brand attitudes. Brand attitudes were virtually unaffected by peripheral cues varied between-subjects ($M_{Nonfamous} = 2.6$ and $M_{Famous} = 2.5$).[4]

Discussion

Although impossible to prove a null hypothesis, Experiment 1 suggests that spokesperson fame does not affect attitudes when (1) it is manipulated between subjects, (2) product features are held constant across conditions, and (3) consumers engage in issue-relevant thinking. This is consistent with many prior between-subjects assessments reporting that peripheral cues are ineffective in high involvement (e.g., Petty et al. 1983).

Since brand attributes were easy to understand and since subjects were given unlimited time to examine them, subjects should have possessed sufficient ability and opportunity to process brand information. Given this, the ineffectiveness of spokesperson fame supports our contention that it is, in fact, a peripheral cue. Whether such a peripheral cue is ineffective in competitive environments is assessed in Experiment 2.

EXPERIMENT 2

Experiment 1 replicated past research and offered further support for the following principle of multi-process theories: Peripheral cues such as spokesperson fame are relatively ineffective in high involvement. However, Experiment 1 and prior studies supporting this principle do so in noncompetitive environments and thereby assess absolute persuasion. They do not allow for competitive processes such as cue neutralization to further moderate the effects of peripheral cues. To test such effects, Experiment 2 used the same peripheral and central cues as Experiment 1, held central cues constant as in Experiment 1, and varied spokesperson fame within subjects.

Experiment 2 tested Hypotheses 2 and 3. They predict that spokespeople will influence attitudes and choices in the face of considerable issue-relevant thinking if central cues are neutralized. Cue neutralization was affected in Experiment 2 by configuring two of the four competing brands to be equally liked and liked more than the others.

Method

Subjects and Design. Experiment 2 varied spokesperson fame (nonfamous vs. famous) within subjects. Subjects saw four brands, two of which had comparable product features (target brands) and were superior to the other two (nontarget brands). Two counterbalanced variables were manipulated between subjects: (1) task order (attitude then choice vs. choice then attitude), and (2) the target brand receiving the stronger peripheral cue (Brand L vs. Brand N). Fifty-nine students enrolled at a large eastern university were randomly assigned to the four conditions resulting from the counterbalancing.

Relative to a between-subjects manipulation, a within-subjects manipulation provides many benefits including increased statistical power and assessments of competitive effects. However, it also increases the transparency of the manipulation and thereby increases the potential for experimental demand. Two procedures were used to reduce demand artifacts (Shimp, Hyatt, and Snyder 1991). First, subjects indicating any sense of the experiment's intent were dropped. Second, and based on the pretests, nontarget brands and ads were configured to disguise the experiment's intent. Spokesperson fame varied across target brands (Michael J. Fox vs. Alex Tyler) *and* nontarget brands (Jay Leno vs. Tom Hite). Moreover, the copy varied across the four ads. Two similar versions were counterbalanced across the two target brands. Thus, subjects saw four ads that differed in copy and spokesperson. Two used a famous spokesperson while two used a nonfamous spokesperson.

Stimuli and Procedure

To compare the results from Experiment 1 with those from Experiment 2, the stimuli and procedures used in the two experiments had to be as similar as possible. Therefore, Experiment 2 used the spokespeople and ad copies of Experiment 1 to manipulate spokesperson fame and counterbalance ad copy. Experiment 2 also used the same radio-ad format and the same levels of product features for the two target brands.

Subjects first examined ads for each brand. In order to avoid any effects of brand name liking or familiarity, the brands were labeled Cruise J, L, N, and P. Immediately following the four ads was a table containing the attribute values for each of the four advertised products (central cues).

The tables were constructed subject to various constraints. The two target brands were superior to the two nontarget brands. Further, to facilitate cross-experiment comparisons, the product features of the target brands were identical to those used in Experiment 1. Thus, features did not vary across target brands. This increased the comparability of Experiment 2's within-subjects cue manipulation with the between-subjects cue manipulation of Experiment 1 and prior research supporting multi-process theories. However, unlike between-subjects designs where consumers never see comparable products, exposure to comparable products in Experiment 2 was expected to neutralize central-cue effects and thereby increase the power of peripheral cues.

After reviewing the ads and brand information, subjects (1) chose the brand they would buy if they were in the market today and (2) reported their attitudes toward each of the four brands. To control for carryover from one measure to the next, task order was counterbalanced. Half of the subjects reported attitudes before making their choices, while the other half chose first. Brand attitude measures, the demand check, and manipulation checks were the same as those in Experiment 1.

---

[4]One concern is that the relatively small n's rendered insufficient statistical power. Two factors mitigate against this concern: (1) the small samples had sufficient power to verify the spokesperson manipulation, and (2) brand-attitude means were directionally inconsistent with the manipulation checks and Hypothesis 2.

Results

Demand Check. Nine of the fifty-nine subjects mentioned an alternative purpose of the study that was at least remotely akin to the manipulation of spokesperson fame. These subjects were dropped from subsequent analyses although this had no effect on the conclusions.

Manipulation Checks. The manipulation of spokesperson fame was checked with the same 9-point scale used in the pretests and Experiment 1. Michael J. Fox was rated as more famous than Alex Tyler (M_{Famous} = 7.7 vs. $M_{Nonfamous}$ = 2.0; $t(48)$ = 16.2).

Issue-relevant thinking was checked with the same measures used in Experiment 1. Subjects evaluated the cruises more carefully than household products (M = 3.3; $t(49)$ = 5.4) and about as carefully as high-involvement consumer electronics products (M_{Cruise} = -.48; $t(49)$ = -.85). Thus, subjects did in fact engage in issue-relevant thinking.

Spokesperson Effects on Attitudes. Hypothesis 2 proposed that peripheral cues would influence brand attitudes in high involvement if central cues were neutralized. This was tested by analyzing a composite brand attitude measure consisting of the average of the three brand attitude items (Cronbach's α = .93). Consistent with Hypothesis 2, spokesperson fame increased brand attitudes ($M_{Nonfamous}$ = 2.9 and M_{Famous} = 3.3; $t(46)$ = 3.02).

Spokesperson Effects on Choice. In extending multi-process persuasion theories to a within-subjects environment with central-cue neutralization, we hypothesized that spokesperson fame would increase choice probabilities (Hypothesis 3). The effects of spokesperson fame on choice were assessed with a LOGIT model. Consistent with Hypothesis 3, spokesperson fame increased the likelihood of brand choice ($\chi^2_{(1)}$ = 16.9). Brands with the famous spokesperson were chosen 82% of the time.

GENERAL DISCUSSION

Summary

Experiment 1 replicated prior null effects of spokesperson fame in noncompetitive, between-subjects settings. When there is no competition but issue-relevant thinking exists, peripheral cues have little effect on brand evaluations. Experiment 2 examined spokesperson fame in a competitive environment where fame was manipulated within subjects such that each consumer saw various levels of spokesperson fame across competing brands. As in Experiment 1, central cues were held constant across the two target brands which, in a competitive within-subjects environment, was expected to affect central-cue neutralization. As hypothesized, the same peripheral cues that were ineffective in Experiment 1 were, in fact, persuasive in Experiment 2. They improved brand attitudes and increased market share despite considerable issue-relevant thinking.

Evidence of peripheral-cue effects in high involvement markets is important for three reasons. First, the effects of competition require modifications to existing multi-process theories of attitude change. Popular principles regarding the persuasiveness of peripheral cues in high involvement must be tempered by the level of central cue neutralization in the marketplace. Second, the results suggest that if attitude research is to generalize to the marketplace, within-subjects manipulations are required. Third, the results suggest a growing importance of peripheral cues since U.S. markets evidence increasingly high levels of product homogeneity. As markets continue to mature and central cues become more neutralized, peripheral cues should become more powerful regardless of involvement.

Limitations and Future Research

The current study suffers from the use of a single peripheral cue and product class. The generalizability of the findings must therefore be expanded in future research by using a wider range of stimuli. Furthermore, the current study assessed spokesperson effects when central cues were neutralized through the use of homogenous brands. Future research must assess whether peripheral-cue effects exist in the face of issue-relevant thinking and heterogenous brands. Since negative correlations across attributes make decisions particularly difficult (e.g., Johnson, Meyer, and Ghose 1989), it is likely that such effects will prevail. Finally, future research is needed to assess other potential causes of Experiment 2's peripheral-cue effects. For example, within-subjects manipulations may introduce perceptual contrast and thereby increase the perceived difference between peripheral-cue levels (Lynch, Chakravarti, and Mitra 1991).

REFERENCES

Batra, Rajeev and Michael L. Ray (1986), "Situational Effects of Advertising Repetition: The Moderating Influence of Motivation, Ability, and Opportunity to Respond," *Journal of Consumer Research*, 12 (March), 432-445.

Bem, Daryl J. (1972), "Self-Perception Theory," in *Advances in Experimental Social Psychology*, Vol. 6, ed. Leonard Berkowitz, New York: Academic Press, 2-57.

Chaiken, Shelly (1980), "Heuristic Versus Systematic Information Processing and the Use of Source Versus Message Cues in Persuasion," *Journal of Personality and Social Psychology*, 42 (January), 116-131.

Festinger, L. (1957), *A Theory of Cognitive Dissonance*, Stanford, CA: Stanford University Press.

Greenwald, Anthony G. (1968), "Cognitive Learning, Cognitive Response to Persuasion, and Attitude Change," in *Psychological Foundations of Attitudes*, eds. Anthony G. Greenwald, Timothy C. Brock, and Thomas Ostrom, New York: Academic Press, 147-170.

Greenwald, Anthony G. and Clark Leavitt (1984), "Audience Involvement in Advertising: Four Levels," *Journal of Consumer Research*, 11 (June), 581-592.

Hovland, Carl I. and Irvin L. Janis, eds. (1959), *Personality and Persuasability*, New Haven: Yale University Press.

Hovland, Carl I. and W. Weiss (1951), "The Influence of Source Credibility on Communication Effectiveness," *Public Opinion Quarterly*, 15, 635-650.

Johnson, Eric J., Robert J. Meyer, and Sanjoy Ghose (1989), "When Choice Models Fail: Compensatory Models in Negatively Correlated Environments," *Journal of Marketing Research*, 26 (August), 255-270.

Kahle, Lynn R. and Pamela M. Homer (1985), "Physical Attractiveness of the Celebrity Endorsers: A Social Adaptation Perspective," *Journal of Consumer Research*, 11 (March), 954-961.

Kahneman, Daniel and Amos Tversky (1979), "Prospect Theory: An Analysis of Decision Under Risk," *Econometrica*, 47 (March), 263-291.

Krugman, Herbert E. (1965), "The Impact of Television Advertising: Learning without Involvement," *Public Opinion Quarterly*, 29 (Fall), 349-356.

Lynch, John G. Jr., Dipankar Chakravarti, and Anusree Mitra (1991), "Contrast Effects in Consumer Judgments: Changes in Representations or in the Anchoring of Rating Scales," *Journal of Consumer Research*, 18 (December), 284-297.

Petty, Richard E. and John T. Cacioppo (1981), *Attitudes and Persuasion: Classic and Contemporary Approaches*, Dubuque, IA: William C. Brown.

Petty, Richard E. and John T. Cacioppo (1986), *Communication and Persuasion: Central and Peripheral Routes to Attitude Change*, New York, Springer.

Petty, Richard E., John T. Cacioppo, and David Schumann (1983), "Central and Peripheral Routes to Advertising Effectiveness: The Moderating Role of Involvement," *Journal of Consumer Research*, 10 (September), 135-146.

Ray, Michael L., Alan G. Sawyer, Michael L. Rothschild, Roger M. Heeler, Edward C. Strong, and Jerome B. Reed (1973), "Marketing Communication and the Hierarchy of Effects," in *New Models for Mass Communication Research*, Vol. 2, ed. Peter Clarke, Beverly Hills, CA: Sage Publications, 147-176.

Robertson, Thomas S. (1976), "Low-Commitment Consumer Behavior," *Journal of Advertising Research*, 16 (April), 19-24.

Shimp, Terence A., Eva M. Hyatt, and David J. Snyder (1991), "A Critical Appraisal of Demand Artifacts in Consumer Research," *Journal of Consumer Research*, 18 (December), 273-283.

Slovic, Paul (1975), "Choice between Equally Valued Alternatives," *Journal of Experimental Psychology: Human Perception and Performance*, 1, 280-287.

Staats, A. W. and C. K. Staats (1958), "Attitudes Established by Classical Conditioning," *Journal of Abnormal and Social Psychology*, 57, 37-40.

Tversky, Amos (1972), "Elimination by Aspects: A Theory of Choice," *Psychological Review*, 79, 281-299.

The Consumption of Insignificant Rituals: A Look at Debutante Balls
Jennifer Edson Escalas, Duke University

ABSTRACT

This project examines the vitality and significance of a traditional American ritual, the debutante ball, using qualitative data gathered through participant observation and in-depth interviews. The debutante ball is a rite of passage with marked social status symbolism. This ritual is high in vitality, due to the strong presence of tangible components of ritual behavior. However, the lack of lasting behavioral change and rejection of social implications cause the debutante ball to lose significance for the participants. Thus, the modern celebration of this ritual creates dissonance for the debutantes, which they reduce by emphasizing positive motivations for participation.

INTRODUCTION

During the decade of the 1980's, participation in traditional activities that had been on the decline throughout the late 1960's and 1970's experienced a strong resurgence. A primary example of this was the sharp rise in Sorority and Fraternity membership on college campuses. Another example, and the one that will be examined in this study, is the revival of debutante balls. A variety of reasons for this cyclical participation pattern have been proposed. The increased materialism and return to conservative values in the '80's, contrasted with the rejection of social conformity popular in the '60's, have been posited as reasons for the increased participation in these traditional events.

This study was undertaken with the principle research objective of understanding the motivation to engage in and benefits received from participation in a debutante ball. The primary goal is to gain insight into the phenomenological experiences of a few young women relating to their personal involvement in the debutante events.

THE DEBUTANTE BALL

Both the history of the debutante ball and its modern form provide insight into the significance of this event.

Historical Evolution

Many societies have rituals to signal youths' transition to adulthood. Often, a woman's coming of age is associated with her reaching puberty and becoming able to bear children (Turner 1966). Presenting young women as debutantes is one of the few remaining Western ceremonies that formalizes coming of age and the entrance of a young woman into the matrimonial market.

The word debutante was adopted into English from French during the reign of Queen Elizabeth I in England in the second half of the 16th century, when she began the custom of formally presenting eligible young women at court. Three centuries later, Queen Victoria gave the ceremony its present form with girls dressed in white and the official bow called a "curtsey." In Victorian days, young girls were kept closely guarded at home until about age 18. Their presentation to society meant that they were now formally allowed to be seen in public with a man and begin courtship.

When America began to prosper in the late 19th century, the custom of debutante presentations crossed the Atlantic. The ritual symbolized family wealth, but another dimension emerged in the impoverished post-civil war South: an emphasis on who had been well-born before the war. So in addition to ritual aspects of coming of age and entering the matrimonial market, family wealth, social status, and lineage are entrenched symbols in the debutante ball.

The Modern Ball

As part of the research for this study, I attended two debutante balls hosted by the Assistance League of Long Beach (California). I videotaped both events and wrote field notes as well. The balls I attended were in July of 1989 and 1990. The following is a description of some of what occurred at the 1990 ball.

At 6:30 p.m. hors d'oeuvres are served in the foyer outside the Hotel Ballroom. Approximately 300 guests, consisting of the debutantes' families, other members of the Assistance League accompanied by spouses, and past debutantes, are in attendance. The dress is formal, with men in tuxedos with black ties and women in dresses of sequins, silk, and taffeta. At 8:00 p.m. the guests move into the Ballroom and the formal presentation of the debutantes begins. The Presenter, Gloria Deukmejian, First Lady of California and Long Beach Assistance League member, gives a 5 minute speech, praising the Assistance League's service to the community. Ms. Deukmejian is the first women Presenter in the 30 year history of this debutante ball. She introduces the mothers and then the young men invited to be escorts and stags.

Finally, the debutantes are presented, in descending order of height. There are seven "debs" this year. Each girl is presented by her full name and title. She curtsies under a gazebo arch set up center stage. Her father is introduced, also by his full, formal name and title, and together they walk around the ballroom floor. He twirls her under his arm, then she hugs her mother sitting at a table adjacent to the dance floor. They continue walking around, she twirls again, and her father returns her to the stage. Her name is read again, she again curtsies, and then walks over to one side of the stage where she waits as all the other girls are presented and go through the same routine, each taking approximately two minutes. The dinner crowd applauds after the girl's name is read, both times. Finally all line up on stage and curtsey, while the crowd applauds for them all.

The ever important father-daughter waltz comes next. The escorts are asked to cut in after about 5 minutes by the Presenter. They dance and then return to their seats for dinner, which is served at 8:45 p.m. By 10:00 p.m. dessert is served and the Orchestra begins to play. Guests begin dancing ballroom style. The music switches into more modern Rock 'n' Roll with a Disc Jockey for the younger guests at 11:00 p.m. The dancing continues until about 1 a.m. when the music stops and the last guests depart.

RITUALISM

As can be seen from both the historical development of the debutante ball and the events occurring at the modern ball environment, the debutante experience is highly ritualistic. Rook (1985) defines a ritual as:

> ...a type of expressive, symbolic activity constructed of multiple behaviors that occur in a fixed, episodic sequence, and that tend to be repeated over time. Ritual behavior is dramatically scripted and acted out and is performed with formality, seriousness, and inner intensity. (p. 252)

Rituals can be classified in terms of their behavioral origins. Levy (1978) elaborates a typology of rituals by identifying five sources of behavior and meaning: human biology, individual aims and emotions, group learning, cultural values, and cosmological beliefs. Debutante balls fall into what anthropologists label rites of passage (van Gennep 1960), whose meaning emanates from the fourth source: cultural values. The focus of rites of passage is the social observance of events which symbolically mark a social status change for the individual. The debutante ball is a symbolic mechanism to reflect the permanent change from adolescence to adulthood for young women.

Rook (1985) also specifies four tangible components to ritual experiences: ritual artifacts, a ritual script, ritual performance roles, and a ritual audience. The debutante ball possesses all four components. The main ritual artifact for the debutante ball is the long, white (or sometimes pastel) gown worn by the young women. Similar to the wedding dress, the deb gown symbolizes her purity as she enters the adult world and interaction with the opposite sex for the first time. The above description of the events that took place at the ball in Long Beach, California is remarkably similar to those that occur at debutante balls and presentations across the country, indicating the presence of a strong ritual script. The introduction of the girls by name, white dresses, and curtsey all originated in Victorian England and are still an integral part of the modern ceremony.

In terms of ritual performance roles, the debutantes' behavior at the ceremony is highly scripted. They enter, curtsey, promenade around the dance floor, and waltz with their fathers year after year, city after city across the country. The debutantes perform the role of protected young women being introduced to society for the first time. The audience of the debutante ball is twofold. The immediate audience consists of the people watching the ceremony, the debutante's family and friends, and the members of the sponsoring organization. But on a greater scale, the audience is society itself, for now the debutante has come of age and is entering the adult social world.

In assessing a ritual's vitality and significance, it can be seen that although the debutante experience contains all four ritual elements very extensively, it has lost significance in modern society. Erikson (1977, 1982) has developed a theory that connects large scale, public ritual expressions with the individual's development of everyday ritualized behaviors. In a rite of passage ceremony, the change in everyday rituals occurring after the event should reinforce the new social status that has been obtained. Because this is not the case for debutante balls, the ritual significance is being lost.

The debutante ball takes place during late adolescence/early young adulthood when personal issues of identity and intimacy are most critical (Erikson 1977, 1982). Historically, the ball initiated a series of new behaviors, such as courtship and marriage. A women's identity as an adult and her relationships with men changed dramatically after the ball. In modern times, however, a young women's daily, ritualized experiences do not change after being presented to society. She has already experienced dating and her escort may in fact be a boyfriend or fiancé. Additionally, she considers herself a young women, not a child. There exist other symbols of passage for young women, including driving at the age of 16 or legally drinking at the age of 18 or 21, depending on the state.

Given this loss of ritual significance, one would expect participation in such events to stagnate. However, the number of debutantes in the 1980's actually rose quite dramatically. The purpose of this research project is to a) talk with debutantes to discover if there is still some symbolic meaning found in their experience and b) uncover some of the individual level reasons, including motivations and perceived benefits, for this upswing in participation.

A PRIORI THEMES

In order to approach this investigation, the following a priori themes were developed. These four explanations of participation in debutante balls were formulated before interviewing informants in order to guide the initial data gathering process. The a priori themes are built on my past exposure to debutante balls, where I had seen lavish displays of conspicuous consumption. My notion of the event was that only the social elite and/or those wishing to elevate their social status participated in debutante balls. It was based on these impressions that I myself rejected an offer to be formally presented while in High School.

Theme #1: Young women may be motivated to participate in debutante balls in order to receive both emotional and material attention from their parents.

Theme #2: Young women may be motivated to participate in debutante balls in order to gain social status and/or acceptance.

The first two a priori themes point to the fact that the debutante ball is a social experience that influences the young women participants' self concepts through their formal presentation to society. Social psychological theory has demonstrated that people use many strategies to create favorable images of themselves (Lippa 1990). These self presentation strategies have the goal of gaining rewards and power while avoiding negative occurrences in social relationships.

These a priori themes are also based on the idea that young women participate in debutante balls in order to conform to their parents and society. Conformity has been well documented in social psychology (Lippa 1990). People often conform to the opinions of others in order to manage impressions of similarity and likableness (Schlenker 1980). Meta-analyses also show support for the hypothesis that women conform more than men on average (Lippa 1990).

Theme #3: Young women may be motivated to participate in debutante balls in order to attend a fun party.

Theme #4: From a historical perspective, young women were motivated to participate in order to meet eligible men, leading to marriage.

Consumer behavior until recently has ignored many phenomena that are important aspects of consumption. Such phenomena include leisure activities, hedonic responses, variety seeking, sensory pleasure, emotional responses, and play, to name just some (Holbrook & Hirschman 1982). An important determinant in making a decision to participate in a particular activity is the amount of enjoyment one will receive.

METHOD

Because participation experiences are highly sensitive to social contexts, this study required a research method capable of in-depth phenomenological inquiry into the thoughts, feelings, and behaviors of informants, accounting for the situational contexts of those phenomena (Heisley & Levy 1991). Therefore, ethnographic interviews were conducted, using both the photoelicitation technique of autodriving and in-depth, conversational interviewing techniques.

Five initial interviews were conducted with the young women shown in the following table (Table 1). The informants were recruited by networking through family, friends, and the graduate students at a large, state run graduate school of management on the West Coast. Each informant had participated in a debutante ball in

TABLE 1

Pseudonym	Age/Marital Status	Race	Age as Debutante	Hometown	Occupation
Julie	20/S	White	18	Long Beach, CA	College Student
Leslie	28/M	White	17	Long Beach, CA	Housewife
Sue	34/S	Black	16/17	Charleston, SC	Graduate Student
Meg	25/S	White	17	Sacramento, CA	Graduate Student
Kim	19/S	White	17	San Diego, CA	College Student

her late teens. The initial interviews lasted about an hour. In the majority of cases, strong rapport was established between the interviewer and informant, evidenced by their willingness to share personal and intimate thoughts, feelings, and memories, enriching the qualitative data for the research project. I took notes of the interview and used them to produce more complete field notes immediately afterward. As themes were supported and emerged over the course of the study, follow up questions were directed at some of the five participants to gain both feedback on the relevance of the themes and additional experiential information.

Autodriving

Autodriving is a projective interviewing technique where informants are given external stimuli drawn directly from their experience, such as photos of their families or audio recordings of themselves, that drive the interview process. The use of projective techniques is based on the logic that people's behavior is invariably meaningful and expressive of personality and cultural values (Heisley and Levy 1991). In terms of photoelicitation techniques, how a person tells a story about a picture reflects how s/he "structures and interprets life situations and reacts to them" (Levy 1963a). As a part of their debutante activities, Julie and Leslie (the first two informants interviewed) had made scrap books of their entire experience. At this exploratory stage of the research process, autodriving was especially useful. In both interviews, the photographs elicited strong memories and prompted in-depth follow-up questions.

In-depth Interviews

The interview has been referred to as the most powerful means for attaining an in-depth understanding of another person's experiences (Thompson et. al. 1989). Descriptive questions are utilized, flowing from the conversation rather than a predetermined path. As with autodriving, this loosely structured format allows the informants to discuss those aspects of their debutante experience that they felt were most important and relevant. The final three interviews utilized this conversational technique. Beginning with broad, phenomenological questions, I opened dialogues with Sue, Meg, and Kim about their debutante experiences. As the interview progressed I probed more deeply on those issues that appeared most important to the informant as well as those issues that had emerged as critical to the previous debutantes.

Analysis and Interpretation

After transcribing each interview, I began to interpret the qualitative data. As new interviews were conducted, the additional data were analyzed in the context of the previously examined information, with an emphasis on common patterns, or themes, that transcended individual experiences, as well as on those aspects that varied from one informant to another (Schouten forthcoming). The analysis procedure was an iterative system of coding, categorizing, and abstracting the data (McCracken 1988). The final analysis attempted to integrate the a priori themes supported by the interviews with the additional emergent themes into a model which provides insight into the debutante experience. I also gained valuable assistance through the help of two colleagues to whom I submitted my interview analyses for review.

A PRIORI THEMES SUPPORTED AND ENRICHED BY EMERGENT FACTORS

This study gave support to the a priori themes generated above. Furthermore, additional detailed elaboration emerged from the interview and analysis process.

Theme #1: Young women may be motivated to participate in debutante balls in order to receive both emotional and material attention from their parents.

Both emotional and material aspects of this theme were touched upon by all the informants. In terms of attention, the audience included one's parents, friends, and other ball guests. As Leslie describes, being center stage was very important:

L: We had it at the Grand Ballroom of the Disneyland Hotel. It was good because it had a lowered dance floor that highlighted the girls as they walked around and did the father-daughter waltz.

Julie enjoyed the attention she received from her entire family, including her older sister who helped her with her makeup. She also describes the attention she received at a tea prior to the actual ball:

J: This is the Medallion Tea. This was a mother/daughter thing... Sisters and grandmothers went too, and all the Assistance League members. There were about 50 people there. They called our names in alphabetical order and showed slides of when we were babies. They talked about our hobbies and interests. We sat center stage.

Family friends also lavished attention on the debutantes. As Julie recounts, "People sent cards and flowers... to say congratulations on being a deb."

Particularly important was the opportunity to participate in an activity with one's father. Julie, when asked what the debutante ball meant to her, replied "something you do with your father." The father-daughter waltz and father's feelings of pride were highlighted by Leslie:

L: It was weird, but the fathers really got into it and were proud... I figure we all do more things with our mothers and so its neat to spend time with your dad. Some girls weren't as close to their dads and they had problems talking to them, so it was really nice for them.

The debutante experience was also perceived as an opportunity to receive material gifts from parents. Objects such as bouquets, clothing for the pre-ball events, a gold medallion necklace, and of course, the long dress were mentioned by many informants. For example, Meg talked about the expense of the experience:

M: My dad paid the symphony fee. My mom paid for the dress. They split the cost of the preparty [which she hosted]... For every preparty you had to buy a new outfit. You wanted to look nice. So it was indirectly expensive along the way.

An additional aspect to the theme of parental attention emerged from the interviews. The girls desired to please and obey their parents, to make them happy. The only reason that Sue participated in the debutante experience at all was at her mother's insistence: "Oh, there was no decision. My mother wanted me to do it so I did it. The only decision I ever made at that age was the clothes I wore on my back!" Kim, whose relationship with her parents was strained during the time of the debutante ball, vehemently denied any desire to act out their wishes: "I wasn't pushed into it by my parents [in contrast to Assisteens, which her mother forced her to join]. I don't do things for them. I do them because I want to."

Theme #2: Young women may be motivated to participate in debutante balls in order to gain social status and/or acceptance.

Two aspects of this theme emerged from the interviews. The ball represented an opportunity to both gain social status and/or acceptance into society and be honored by the community for individual achievements.

The main aspect of attention from society was found in the inclusion of the debutante activities in local newspapers. As Leslie describes a tea prior to the ball, "It also presented us to the press for the first time. There were a lot of media people there. There was lots of publicity, with our pictures in the paper and magazines." One article she had saved was very unbecoming in its portrayal of the debutantes and their parents. It criticizes the event for its conspicuous consumption and celebration of social status:

... The event, meant to celebrate their daughters' emergence into society, doubled as a chance for the parents to recelebrate their own roles as upstanding members of that society. (Tim Grobaty, staff writer for the *Long Beach Press Telegram*, July 1980).

Thus the debutante ball is perceived to be a status symbol through which material wealth is expressed. As social mobility theory explains, in stratified societies, members aspire to move to higher social strata (Goffman 1959). Along these lines, many debutantes mentioned the important people who attended the event. For example, at the Assistance League of Long Beach events, the Governor & First Lady, a City Councilwoman, a Supreme Court Justice, and a U.S. Assemblyman (now State Attorney General) all attended the debutante ball.

An important contrast arose in some of the interviews. Although none of the debutantes I interviewed discussed their own participation in terms of gaining social status, the motivation emerges as the informants project this motivation onto others. As Meg explains:

M: But other people thought it was a formal presentation to society... Those are more the old Sacramento family types with lots of money. Some girls' parents were hung up on the community's perception of them. They were into their social image. Very status conscious.

Furthermore, some girls indirectly referenced the social status aspect of their participation. For example, Kim stated that part of her attraction to the deb ball was that "I thought that a lot of people wouldn't get to do this. People aren't wealthy enough to put on debutante balls of their own [hence they put them on through organizations such as the Assistance League]." Thus elements of conspicuous consumption, where social status is obtained through a product that is visible and exclusive, are associated with the "product" of the debutante ball. Leslie also admitted that "Sometimes I do say 'I was a deb' in a snobby sense, but that is silly."

The debutante ball gave parents the opportunity to instruct their daughters in formal social behavior. This socialization was found throughout the debutantes' descriptions of the events. They were taught how to waltz and curtsey. The social gatherings had finger sandwiches, and most balls had full course, formal meals, and the young women were expected to eat politely. Thank you cards were required to be sent after each party to the hostesses and parents as well. Thus the debutantes were being prepared for their future roles as sorority members, hostesses, and wives.

Finally, the ball attended by the black informant, Sue, honored the debutantes for their individual achievements. This exception highlights the role of blacks in our society, where a lineage-based model of prestige fails due to multiple generation suppression and exploitation. Thus a debutante is honored based on individual merit, rather than celebrating family heritage. Sue was chosen by a women's sorority, Alpha Kappa Alpha, to be honored by the community:

S: [After the debutantes were introduced and had curtseyed...] they listed our achievements, those things that warranted our being a debutante... I was in the National Honor Society and in a Math Honor Society. I received lots of academic awards.

Thus it appears that while for white participants the ball was preparation for their adult social lives, for the black debutante the ball was an honor and achievement in and of itself.

Theme #3: Young women may be motivated to participate in debutante balls in order to attend a fun party.

Fun was the most significant memory of the debutante ball to emerge from the five interviews. The word was used 27 times in reference to the pre-ball and ball events. When asked about their recollections about being a debutante, four of the five mentioned fun as a primary factor. The debutantes considered the following things to be fun:

- Dressing up in formal clothing
- Attending the thematic preparties
- Receiving attention/being honored
- Dancing

- Meeting young people, girls and guys
- Being with existing friends
- Participating in activities: bowling, boating, playing cards, swimming, etc.
- Having a large ratio of men to women present

Meg's descriptions of the fun at the ball are full of energy:

M: The dancing at the ball was really fun. We were on the dance floor having a blast dancing and everything... It was like celebrating the end of six months of parties with all your new friends.

On the other hand, Sue, the black debutante who, although she was honored by her ball, was compelled to participate by her mother, had the least fun. Some of the things that her debutante event lacked in comparison with the other girls include dancing after the formal waltz, developing friendships with other girls, a full course meal, a familiar date, more young men than young women, and an overall party atmosphere.

Theme #4: From a historical perspective, young women were motivated to participate in order to meet eligible men, leading to marriage.

The opportunity to meet young men was cited in many of the interviews as contributing to the appeal of the debutante experience. In many of the balls, men were invited to be stags in addition to the official escorts for the debutantes. Usually the girls got to choose the young men invited as stags in addition to choosing their escorts. As Leslie recalls:

L: There were 5 guys for each girl. What great odds!... I figured with so many guys there it would be really fun.

Some dating outside the debutante activities with these young men did occur over the course of the preparties and ball. Julie explains her personal experience:

J: I got to be friends with my escort at this party. I never dated him outside the deb activities — he had a girlfriend. I dated another stag and another girl's escort, but she didn't care.

For those for whom meeting guys was less important, the debutante ball was less enjoyable. One girl who had a fiancé was considered by an informant to be "less social." Kim explains her dilemma:

K: My escort was, hmmm, interesting... He was a math major so he saw everything in terms of fractions. He didn't dance with me that much. He liked another debutante and so went chasing after her... [but that] was no problem. It's not like I had any strings over him. There's no implied relationship with your escort.

PURELY EMERGENT THEMES

The following themes emerged from the iterative interview and analysis process.

The Opportunity to Make Girlfriends

The need for socialization was important. Young women were drawn to the ball by the opportunity to make friends with other young women. There were three ways this emerged in the data. First, the debutantes displayed an interest in developing new friendships with previously unknown individuals, particularly those girls who attended different high schools or were not close in high school. Second, the girls also desired to be with existing friends. And third, several informants mention snobbery and cliquishness among the girls, particularly at the more informal activities. The young men participated in this cliquishness as well.

All the informants mentioned the idea of making new friends. This was considered part of the fun offered by the debutante experience. For example, meeting new people was a strong motivating factor for Meg:

M: I met a lot of people. Socially it was great. I made lots of new friends. I'd say that was really fun, meeting people outside of the groups you usually associate with in your high school.

On the other hand, the inability to make new friends detracted from Sue's experience:

S: I didn't feel like I was friends with the other girls. That would have been a nice by-product of the whole thing. This may have been my fault... I probably just kept to myself.

The informants were also motivated by the opportunity to have fun with existing friends. Two of the informants, Kim and Julie, had participated in philanthropic activity groups in high school that were precursors to becoming a debutante. Therefore they had developed strong friendships with the other girls slated to become debs. Meg mentioned she was friends with girls from her public high school. Furthermore, a convincing factor in her decision to participate came when her best friend decided to join in the debutante activities. For Sue, again, the lack of existing friends among the debutantes detracted from her debut.

Although the idea of snobbery was touched on by all the informants, some discounted the problem. In response to the derogatory newspaper article quoted above, which also accused the young people of being cliquey, Leslie claimed, "It's natural with 18 year olds, you talk to the people you know." For two informants, Julie and Meg, however, the problem could not be minimized as easily as it could for others. For example, Julie felt left out by the girls who had become good friends in Assisteens, the precursor philanthropic organization for high school girls. For Meg, the snobbery problem almost led to her not participating as a debutante. She worried about the girls who might fit the "stereotypical rich, snobby, social role associated with debutantes." Meg found that there were some girls who did, while others did not:

M: The private catholic school girls had the more status conscious moms and families... [I] felt a barrier with these girls. I couldn't get too close, even though we were friends of a sort. I guess you'd call them shallow friendships, all on the surface... The girls from the public high schools were more eager to meet other people.

Support of a Good Cause

For some, but not all of the debutantes, the fact that the ball raised money for a charitable purpose was mentioned as important. The sponsoring organizations of the debutante balls attended by the informants were either a symphony or a philanthropic organization such as the Assistance League or a Sorority. Meg spoke out the most about the good cause being an important motivation for participation: "The ball raised money for the Symphony... I liked the fact that it was a good cause. That was one of the main reasons why I did it." Kim, on the other hand, actually denied the fact that the charitable aspect of the ball had anything to do with her decision:

K: ... the debutante thing was just a fun party and a place to meet people. There were no personal fund raising efforts. The party raised money for the League, but that didn't really have anything to do with my being a debutante.

The charitable aspect was mentioned by the other informants as a positive influence despite the fact that not much was known about the Assistance League of Long Beach or Alpha Kappa Alpha Sorority and their sponsorship of the events. For example, Julie described the Assistance League as "a group of women who have luncheons and fashion shows." Perhaps the charitable angle is the social salve for what would otherwise be a purely hedonic event.

The Ritual Dimension

The vitality and tangible ritualistic elements of the debutante ball were acknowledged by all the informants. The young women's recounting of the event included ritual artifacts, performance roles, audience, and script. The long ball gown is the primary ritual artifact for the debutantes. As such, it was treated with respect and considered a very positive aspect of the debutante experience by all five young women. Four of the five wore a white dress. In many cultures, white's flawless and unspoiled aspects are associated with virgins and deities. The western culture of wearing a white wedding dress has classical origins: virgins in Rome wore white to symbolize their innocence, wisdom and purity (Osman 1973).

Sue, the one black debutante I interviewed, was the only person who didn't wear a white dress. Nevertheless, some symbolic significance of dress color remained: "My dress was a pastel color. But it was a long gown. We had to wear soft pastel colors. You couldn't come dressed in red or black." An interpretation may be that in black society, the color symbolism of white=purity and black=sin found in Western cultures is less pervasive.

In the realm of white debutantes, the purity of the young women as they are presented to society is symbolically represented by the long, white gown. Every sponsoring organization had strict guidelines about the dress, as Meg illustrates:

M: Everyone's had to be white... They preferred tasteful dresses, no strapless, no cleavage hanging out... I think the white dress represents a purity kind of thing.

All the white debutantes associated their gown with weddings. Julie actually wore her sister's wedding dress. Leslie compared the entire evening to a wedding: "A wedding without a groom. You get all the attention, you get to wear a long white dress and dance, and then you go home and you're not married." Meg said, "I felt like a princess. You're in a dress you only wear once. The only other time you do that is when you get married."

The ritual performance roles and audience were also identified and treated with dignity. Most of the informants mentioned being nervous about receiving the attention of so many people. Another reason for their anxiety may come from participating in an unfamiliar, yet involving ritual (Rook 1985). Julie stated that what she remembered most was "Being nervous about being on stage and having to follow instructions." Meg also worried about her actions:

M: I was nervous. I mean, you are introduced and there are 300 to 400 people there. All the eyes are on you. It was exciting and intimidating... I thought I was going to fall and mess up or trip! ... I wore flat shoes to be safer.

Furthermore, traditions and formalized rules that make up the ritual script were often referred to by the interviewees. Particularly interesting was the fact that many of the debutante ball activities referred to by the informants were identical over a ten year time span and across the country. All five referred to the formality of the occasion. Sue stated that the ball was "very traditional. Ritualistic even." The curtsey was a particularly vital scripted behavior. As Leslie explains:

L: Then we curtsied. I still remember, an 8 count curtsey. Down on 2, wait 2, head bowed for 2, then up on 2. We all had to do it the same way.

Finally, Kim actually referred to her tightly scripted behavior at the ball as a "performance." The debutante ball fits Goffman's (1959) theoretical description of an institutionalized social front, with its expected abstract stereotyped interpretation of meaning by the audience.

Nevertheless, despite all the ritual vitality present in the debutante experience, the significance of the ritual was disturbing to the informants. The girls did not like the stereotypical snobbery, social status implications of the debutante ball, although they referred to others who did, as mentioned in the discussion of a priori theme #2 above. As Meg put it "Only some people said things like 'I'm from X family and you aren't.'"

All argued that the "coming out" aspect of the debutante ball had been lost. Many referenced the fact that times had changed. As Meg explained:

M: It used to be a coming of age, I guess. I think of Scarlet O'Hara in *Gone with the Wind*. You are supposed to meet eligible young men and courting can begin afterwards. But that's a negative stereotype of women. Times have changed. Women go to college now. I was at Berkeley at the time.

Nonetheless, Meg did admit that part of the reason she was chosen to be a debutante was the fact that "We come from an old Sacramento family." Kim explained that although "the ball symbolizes coming out into society... It really doesn't mean that much today." Julie felt the deb ball was more tied into celebrating one's high school graduation. Leslie also explained why the debutante ball was "not one of the most important events in my life" by stating that:

L: I suppose if it was what it really is supposed to be, if we had to wait to go out in public with men until after the party, then it would be important. But we're too old to be "coming out;" society has changed. To us it was a fun party.

Some felt disappointed that there were no long term changes resulting from the event. This supports the claim of Erikson that rituals are significant only when they result in changes in the subsequent everyday behavior of the participants. Sue felt the most strongly about this point: "There were no consequences, though. Nothing came as a result of this whole event. I didn't belong to the sorority afterwards or anything."

There is an undercurrent of conflict in terms of the ritual element of the debutante ball. While the young women recognize the historical significance of the event, and refer quite readily to the artifacts and scripts associated with the ritual, they are unwilling to accept either the coming of age or social status significance of the debutante ball.

DISCUSSION

The informants' memories of their debutante experience were for the most part positive. Their principle motivations for participating in the events were to meet people and make friends, receive attention, please their parents, and have fun. The traditional and ritual elements of the debutante ball were well-recognized and treated with respect and dignity. The significance of the experience, however, was almost completely ignored or denied. Neither the rite of passage symbolism nor the attainment of social status significance of the ball were accepted as motivations for participation.

Of particular interest is the fact that the informants realized the implications of their involvement in this event but were unwilling to accept them. The debutantes referred to other people as being interested in the social status aspects of the ball, but would not confess to any similar motivation. The young women were unwilling to subscribe to the traditional importance of family, wealth, and society. They were willing to participate, but convinced themselves that this negatively perceived element of the ritual did not apply to them.

There are various theoretical research explanations for this conflict. The first comes from sociological theory regarding conflicting self conceptions. Sociologists distinguish between two opposite ways in which people come to have status. The first is via ascription, where a person is assigned a role by others on the basis of biological considerations or birth into a particular family. Other roles are achieved and are thus voluntary or dependent on the attainment of a specific set of qualifications (Hewitt 1976). The contrast between ascription and achievement is important because it emphasizes the fact that a person's choice of identity in a specific situation is not entirely free.

Often the roles associated with the achieved self concept are in conflict with those of the ascribed self concept. In the case of the debutantes, their achieved self concepts are a function of such things as their success or failure in school and their social relationships. Their ascribed self concepts relate to their family and their sex. The social status symbolism of the debutante ball falls under the roles associated with ascribed self concepts. By rejecting the ball's ritual significance, they are withdrawing the recognition of others who would be more inclined to judge them on the basis of their ascribed selves. In this way they are asserting their independence and giving increased importance to their achieved self concepts, over which they have more control.

People arrange their presentations of self in various situations so as to manifest the qualities and characteristics they value. Goffman (1959) proposes that there needs to be coherence between what he defines as one's appearance, which provides the cues to social status, and manner, which confers interaction role expectations. By downplaying the status significance of the ball, the debutantes separate themselves from the appearance derived from their participation in order to better reflect their own concept of their manner. Goffman (1959) mentions this dilemma of participating in an unsuitable social front:

> ... a performer tends to conceal or underplay those activities, facts, and motives which are incompatible with an idealized version of himself... (p. 48)

Thus the informants experience tension between the symbolic interpretation of their roles as debutantes and their own idealized self concept.

An additional theoretical explanation proceeds from social psychology. Consistency theory asserts that people find inconsistency unpleasant and are motivated to reduce this negative arousal state by attempting to restore consistence. Leon Festinger's cognitive dissonance theory proposes that two elements (for example, beliefs, cognitions, or behavior) are inconsistent or dissonant when knowledge of one suggests the opposite of the other (Petty and Cacioppo 1981). This dissonance can be resolved by modifying attitudes and beliefs to fit behavior, or vice versa.

In this study, the debutantes showed a great deal of dissonance between their knowledge of the ritual significance of the debutante ball, particularly the social status implications, and their personal attitudes and beliefs. Evidence of this can be found by the informants' continual discussion of the ball being for a good cause while little was actually known about the sponsoring organizations and their activities. Furthermore, in order to create consistency between their participation in the event and their disdain for the ritual significance, they developed elaborate explanations for why their motivations to participate in the event were not related to gaining social status. Part of these explanations included contrasting themselves with other people whose social ambitions were a stronger motivation.

The other aspect of the ritual significance of the debutante ball was the rite of passage into adulthood. This too created inconsistency for the debutantes because their daily rituals did not change after the debutante ball occurred. Thus the crossing from childhood to womanhood was not cemented by the event. Again, the informants dealt with this dissonance by downplaying the importance of this ritual significance and emphasizing other, more positive aspects of the ball, such as having fun and making friends.

Finally, this conflict does enable one to understand some of the cyclical fluctuation in the participation levels of debutante balls. As Meg succinctly explained: "Maybe it's due to rebellion against social grouping." During those eras where social consciousness is relatively high, young women are unable to reconcile their desire to receive attention, make friends, and have fun with their disdain for the symbolic social significance of the debutante ritual.

CONCLUSION

In conclusion, this paper has taken an in-depth look at the modern ritual of the debutante ball from the perspective of five young women participants. The research has revealed the motivations for and conflicts resulting from being involved in the debutante experience. The analysis has pointed to some of the reasons for the fluctuating popularity of this ritual event. While the conclusions drawn from this study appear credible within the context of the informants' experiences, their broad applicability to other persons or other contexts should not be presumed. The goal of this research project was to arrive at a better understanding of the symbolic consumption of the debutante ritual.

Future directions for research arising from this study include examination of other rites of passage present in modern society (e.g. Bar and Bat Mitzvahs, Quinzeañeras, "Sweet 16" parties, high school proms) which may have also experienced evolutions in symbolic significance. Additional research directions might include a historical content analysis directed at studying contrasting attitudes from periods of strong participation in traditional activities with those of lower levels, and an in-depth study of the socialization aspect of modern rituals by looking at the present societal roles of past participants. Finally, many goods today are socially frowned-upon, such as cigarettes and gas-guzzling automobiles. An extension of this study of debutante balls, which also receive mixed reviews from various societal groups, would be to examine how consumers deal with dissonance created from their consumption of socially unacceptable products.

REFERENCES

Goffman, Erving (1959), *The Presentation of Self in Everyday Life*, Garden City, NY: Doubleday & Company, Inc.

Heisley, Deborah and Sidney J. Levy (1991), "Autodriving: A Photoelicitation Technique," *Journal of Consumer Research*, v.18, pp. 257-272.

Hewitt, John P. (1976), *Self and Society: A Symbolic Interactionist Social Psychology*, Boston, MA: Allyn and Bacon, Inc.

Holbrook, Morris and Elizabeth Hirschman (1982), "The Experiential Aspects of Consumption: Consumer Fantasies, Feelings and Fun," *Journal of Consumer Research*, v. 9, September, pp. 132-140.

Lippa, Richard A. (1990), *Introduction to Social Psychology*, Belmont, CA: Wadsworth Publishing Company.

McCracken, Grant (1986), "Culture and Consumption: A Theoretical Account of the Structure and Movement of the Cultural Meaning of Consumer Goods," *Journal of Consumer Research*, v. 1, June, pp. 71-84.

Osman, Randolph E. (1973), *Iconocom: Cross Cultural Iconography for the Community*, The Santa Barbara Museum of Art, Santa Barbara, CA: Triple-R-Press.

Petty, Richard E. and John T. Cacioppo (1981), *Attitudes and Persuasion: Classic and Contemporary Approaches*, Dubuque, Iowa: Wm. C. Brown Company.

Rook, Dennis W. (1985), "The Ritual Dimension of Consumer Behavior," *Journal of Consumer Research*, v. 3, December, pp. 251-264.

Schlenker, Barry R. (1980), *Impression Management: The Self-Concept, Social Identity, and Interpersonal Relations*, Monterey, CA: Brooks/Cole Publishing Company.

Schouten, John W. (forthcoming), "Selves in Transition: The Consumption of Aesthetic Plastic Surgery," *Journal of Consumer Research*.

Thompson, Craig J., William B. Locander, Howard R. Pollio (1989), "Putting Consumer Experience Back into Consumer Research: The Philosophy and Method of Existential-Phenomenology," *Journal of Consumer Research*, v. 16, September, pp. 133-146.

Turner, Victor (1966), *The Ritual Process: Structure and Anti-Structure*, Ithaca, NY: Cornell University Press.

AUTHOR INDEX

Aaker, David A. 27
Ahluwalia, Rohini 620
Ahuja, Roshan D. 469
Alden, Dana L. 678
Allen, Chris T. 280, 314
Alwitt, Linda F. 188, 189
Andreasen, Alan R. 1, 109
Andresen, Julie M. 366
Andrews, J. Craig 135
Ang, Swee Hoon 559
Areni, Charles S. 336
Arnould, Eric J. 23, 172
Attaway, Jill S. 508
Atwood, April 437
Babin, Barry J. 508
Bachman, Gwen Rae 463
Balasubramanian, Siva K. 272
Ball, A. Dwayne 76
Banerjee, Bobby 494
Barnes, James H. 63
Baumgartner, Hans 673
Bayless, Lynora 437
Beach, Lee Roy 235
Belk, Russell W. 102
Berger, Ida E. 188, 189
Bettman, James R. 7
Bier, Tracy 437
Blair, Liz 558
Bloom, Diane L. 366
Bloom, Paul N. 365, 436
Bristol, Terry 444
Brooker, George 229
Brumbaugh, Anne M. 159
Burke, Sandra J. 119
Burnkrant, Robert E. 620
Burns, Alvin C. 481
Burns, William J. 176, 183
Carter, William 437
Chatterjee, Subimal 475
Cho, Hyongoh 692
Chon-Lin, Gloria Ong 488
Cole, Catherine 437
Compeau, Larry 479
Cooper-Martin, Elizabeth 113
Coyne, Cathy 366
Creyer, Elizabeth H. 284
Crowley, Ayn E. 678
Currence, Cynthia 371
Dacin, Peter A. 594
Daniel, Harold 273
Darden, William R. 508
Darian, Jean C. 413
Debevec, Kathleen 359, 458
Desai, Kalpesh Kaushik 599
Dhar, Ravi 195
Dick, Alan 637
Dobscha, Susan 36
Doner, Lynne D. 302
Durvasula, Srinivas 135
Elliott, Michael T. 202
Englis, Basil G. 612

Ennis, Richard 662
Eroglu, Sevgin A. 34
Escalas, Jennifer Edson 478, 709
Faure, Corinne 553
Fellerman, Ritha 458
Fern, Edward F. 444
Finlay, Karen 26
Fischer, Eileen 320
Fishbein, Martin 292
Fitzmaurice, Julie 656
Fontenelle, Suzana de M. 534
Fournier, Susan 352
Fullerton, Ronald A. 570
Gaeth, Gary J. 625
Gainer, Brenda 320
Galvin, Tiffany 253
Garner, Thesia I. 515
Gentry, James W. 76
Ger, Guliz 102
Gilster, Elisabeth 83
Goodstein, Ronald C. 477, 478
Gould, Stephen J. 419
Granzin, Kent L. 481
Graonic, Milos D. 389
Green, Paul E. 149
Grewal, Dhruv 477, 479
Griffin, Mitch 508
Gubin, Oleg I. 89
Guiry, Michael 352
Haddock, Geoffrey 315
Hampson, Sarah E. 177, 183
Heath, Timothy B. 475, 704
Heckler, Susan 272
Hempel, Donald J. 273
Herrmann, Robert O. 130
Higie, Robin A. 656
Hill, Ronald Paul 59
Hirschman, Elizabeth C. 41
Holbrook, Morris 113
Holden, Stephen J. 383
Hornik, Jacob 527
Hoyer, Wayne D. 449, 599, 678
Hubbert, Amy R. 196
Huffman, Cynthia 375
Huneke, Mary 437
Hunt, George W. 449
Inman, J. Jeffrey 12
Iyer, Easwar 494
Jackson, Anita L. 481
Jap, Sandy D. 607
Jasper, J. D. 625
Johar, Gita V. 108, 284
John, Deborah Roedder 373, 463
Johnson, Rose L. 257
Jones, Marilyn Young 262
Jun, Sunkyu 76
Kardes, Frank R. 280
Kassarjian, Harold H. 6, 478
Kellaris, James 558
Keller, Kevin Lane 27
Kelly, Robert F. 232

Kibarian, Thomas	580
Kim, Chankon	52
Kim, Cheoul Ryon	586
Kim, David	336
Klein, Noreen M.	209
Kleine III, Robert E.	70
Kleine, Susan Schultz	70, 196
Kostioutchenko, Natasha	89
Krieger, Abba M.	149
Krishnan, Shankar	655
Kucukarsalan, Suzan	245
Laroche, Michel	52
Larsen, William Val	48, 439
Lascu, Dana-Nicoleta	102
Lavack, Anne	266
Laverie, Debra A.	70
Lee, Dong Hwan	547
Leong, Siew Meng	559
Leung, Kwok	684
Levin, Irwin P.	625
Li, Wai-kwan	684
Lofman, Brian	18
Loken, Barbara	397
Lowrey, Tina M.	325
Lutz, Richard J.	165
Machleit, Karen A.	34
MacKenzie, Scott B.	507
Malafarina, Katryna	397
Mani, Gayathri	476
Manrai, Ajay K.	97
Manrai, Lalita A.	97
Marshall, Judith J.	541
Mayer, Robert N.	698
Mazumdar, Tridib	586
McCarthy, Michael S.	28, 704
McCarty, John A.	641
McKeage, Kim K. R.	359
McQuarrie, Edward F.	308, 309
Menon, Geeta	108
Mick, David Glen	309, 546, 553
Middlestadt, Susan E.	291, 292, 297, 302
Milberg, Sandra J.	28, 119
Mitchell, Deborah	374
Mittal, Banwari	647
Mittelstaedt, John D.	625
Miyazaki, Anthony D.	331
Morgan, Amy J.	429
Mothersbaugh, David L.	704
Munson, J. Michael	433
Murphy, Patrick	437
Murrell, Audrey J.	667
Myer, Dee	437
Nedungadi, Prakash	438
Neo, Mai	667
Netemeyer, Richard G.	135
Novak, Tom	265
Obermiller, Carl	690
Olsen, Barbara	575
Olsen, Janeen E.	481
Olshavsky, Richard W.	507, 547
Osipov, Alexander G.	89
Østergaard, Per	565
Otnes, Cele	319, 325
Ozanne, Julie L.	35
Page, Thomas J.	654
Park, C. Whan	28, 395
Pathak, Dev S.	245
Pavia, Teresa	425
Pechmann, Connie	265
Peltier, James W.	437
Penaloza, Lisa	123
Pennell, Greta	612
Peracchio, Laura	373
Piron, Francis	341
Pluzinski, Carol	655
Pollay, Richard W.	129, 266
Pontes, Manuel J.	280
Powers, Keiko I.	405
Prakash, Ved	591
Price, Linda L.	123, 656
Punj, Girish N.	570
Rao, Akshay R.	463
Ratneshwar, S.	330, 377
Richins, Marsha L.	359
Richmond, Daleen	488
Sauer, Paul L.	637
Scammon, Debra L.	698
Schaffer, Catherine M.	149
Schechter, Carol	302
Schibrowsky, John A.	437
Schindler, Robert M.	580
Segal, Richard	245
Severson, Herbert H.	177, 183
Shamdasani, Prem	488
Shapiro, Jon M.	557
Sherman, Elaine	631
Shocker, Allan D.	389
Shrum, L. J.	641
Singh, Surendra N.	170
Sirdeshmukh, Deepak	245
Slovic, Paul	177, 183
Smith, Daniel C.	594
Smith, Karen H.	219
Smith, N. Craig	119
Smith, Ruth Belk	631
Smith, Stephen M.	155
Somasundaram, T. N.	215
Spangenberg, Eric	632
Spreng, Richard A.	507
Srinivasan, Narasimhan	288
Stern, Barbara B.	35
Stinson, Kandi M.	469
Stout, Patricia A.	692
Tausend, Sandra	437
Thompson, Craig J.	455
Trafimow, David	292
Vacker, Barry	345
Veryzer, Jr., Robert W.	224
Wagner, Janet	515
Wagner, Judy A.	209
Warfield, Anne E.	202
Warlop, Luk	377
Wiley, James B.	142
Witkowski, Terrence H.	13
Wolfinbarger, Mary Finley	520
Woolley, Frances	541

Wooten, David B.	253
Wright, Alice A.	165
Wright, Newell D.	439
Wyer, Jr., Robert S.	684
Yalch, Richard F.	630, 632
Yale, Laura J.	520
Yi, Youjae	502
Young, Melissa Martin	89
Zanna, Mark P.	315, 662
Zhou, Lianxi	52
Zick, Cathleen D.	698
Zinkhan, George M.	534
Zsambok, Caroline E.	239